VETERINARY OBSTETRICS AND GENITAL DISEASES (THERIOGENOLOGY)*

Stephen J. Roberts D.V.M., M.S.
Professor of Veterinary Medicine and Obstetrics in the
New York State Veterinary College at Cornell University

SECOND EDITION

CBS Publishers & Distributors Pvt. Ltd.
New Delhi • Bengaluru • Chennai • Kochi • Kolkata • Mumbai
Hyderabad • Nagpur • Patna • Pune • Vijayawada

***(Term proposed by D. Bartlett and others to indicate all aspects of *veterinary* obstetrics, genital diseases and animal reproduction; "therio" = animal or beast and "gen" = coming into being from Greek medical terminology.)**

ISBN: 81-239-0922-5

First Edition: 1956
Second Edition: 1971
Indian Reprint: 1982
Reprint: 1998, 1999, 2002, 2004 2021

Published by **Satish Kumar Jain** and produced by **Varun Jain** for
CBS Publishers & Distributors Pvt. Ltd.,
4819/XI Prahlad Street, 24 Ansari Road, Daryaganj, New Delhi - 110002
delhi@cbspd.com, cbspubs@airtelmail.in • www.cbspd.com
Ph.: 23289259, 23266861, 23266867 • Fax: 011-23243014

Corporate Office: 204 FIE, Industrial Area, Patparganj, Delhi - 110 092
Ph: 49344934 • Fax: 011-49344935
E-mail: publishing@cbspd.com • publicity@cbspd.com

Branches:
- ***Bengaluru:*** 2975, 17th Cross, K.R. Road, Bansankari 2nd Stage, Bengaluru - 70 • Ph: +91-80-26771678/79 • Fax: +91-80-26771680 E-mail: cbsbng@gmail.com, bangalore@cbspd.com
- ***Chennai:*** No. 7, Subbaraya Street, Shenoy Nagar, Chennai - 600030 Ph: +91-44-26681266, 26680620 • Fax: +91-44-42032115 E-mail: chennai@cbspd.com
- ***Kochi:*** Ashana House, 39/1904, A.M. Thomas Road, Valanjambalam, Ernakulum, Kochi • Ph: +91-484-4059061-65 Fax: +91-484-4059065 • E-mail: cochin@cbspd.com
- ***Kolkata:*** 6-B, Ground Floor, Rameshwar Shaw Road, Kolkata - 700014 Ph: +91-33-22891126/7/8 • E-mail: kolkata@cbspd.com
- ***Mumbai:*** 83-C, Dr. E. Moses Road, Worli, Mumbai - 400018 Ph: +91-9833017933, 022-24902340/41 • E-mail: mumbai@cbspd.com

Representatives:

• Bhubaneswar	0-9911037372	• Hyderabad	0-9885175004	• Jharkhand	0-9811541605
• Nagpur	0-9021734563	• Patna	0-9334159340	• Pune	0-9623451994
• Uttarakhand	0-9716462459	• Dhaka (Bangladesh)	01912-003485		

Printed at: Chaman Enterprises,Delhi

VETERINARY OBSTETRICS AND GENITAL DISEASES

CONTENTS

PART I—OBSTETRICS

CONTENTS

PART II—GENITAL DISEASES

TABLES

FIGURES

FIGURES

Number | Page

FIGURES

Number Page

FIGURES

PREFACE

It was with some serious misgivings, that have since been fully justified, that the author undertook the task of attempting to organize material, write and then extensively revise a textbook on the subject of veterinary obstetrics and genital diseases. The classical texts of the late Dr. W. L. Williams will remain for many years as outstanding contributions to our knowledge in this field. Other outstanding authors in this field to whom this author is deeply indebted because of their extensive and scholarly texts are R. Zemjanis, G. H. Arthur, F. Benesch, and J. Richter and R. Gotze.

In recent years, advances in the fields of endocrinology, surgery, physiology, bacteriology, virology, and therapeutics have rapidly increased our knowledge of the diseases of the genital organs. With the amazing growth of artificial insemination in dairy cattle, interest in bovine reproductive physiology and pathology has markedly increased. The past twenty years have seen a great increase in research in human reproductive physiology and diseases with great emphasis based on pharmacology and endocrinology in efforts to control population growth and to prevent teratologic defects that occur during the gestation period. Many human investigators have used animals or animal models in their studies which has had many implications and provided much new knowledge in the veterinary field. Research on these problems is at present in progress at nearly all the medical, agricultural and veterinary centers in the country. Similar research is also proceeding in other countries. Such rapid progress and developments in the many facets of our knowledge make a textbook out of date the day it is published.

Improvements in surgery, surgical techniques, supportive treatments, and antibiotic therapy have wrought a great change in our methods and techniques of relieving dystocia. Some obstetrical operations described by Williams are seldom if ever used at the present time. Cesarean section in all animals, even the mare, is commonly performed by many practitioners with a high degree of success. Many infections of the genital tract that were previously difficult to cure or resulted in a high mortality rate can now be promptly controlled by antibiotic therapy.

During the twenty years preceding the first edition of this text much of our knowledge concerning veterinary obstetrics and genital diseases was available to students and practitioners only in periodicals. The assembling and organizing of this material into a textbook was greatly needed. The author sincerely hoped that someone eminently better qualified than he would have performed this task. The advances in our knowledge in the past fifteen years have required the author to greatly enlarge the sections of the text on reproductive physiology, genetics, teratology, diseases of the male and abortions. In regard to the latter, diagnosis will undoubtedly remain a difficult problem because of the autolytic changes occurring in the fetus between the time of its death and its expulsion.

The author planned a text limited only to obstetrics and genital diseases in cattle. He was induced by practitioners and by the need of students for source material to include the horse and then the dog in his material. As into Noah's Ark, the other animals soon followed, not because of outside requests but because of the author's interest aroused by his comparative studies of the various domestic animals. Many comparative conditions exist and provide a fertile source of study for those who have the interest and curiosity. For this reason rather extensive and pertinent bibliographies concerning each section are included. The domestic animals considered in this text include the cow, horse, sheep, goat, pig, dog and cat.

The author has purposely not tried to simplify, eliminate controversial material, or omit any phase of the subject that concerns itself with veterinary obstetrics or genital diseases of domestic animals. This book was written for veterinary undergraduates and those practitioners who are still students. The layman was not considered, as to do so would make the text less satisfactory for its intended readers. The author has stressed diagnosis and physiology throughout the text because he feels these phases of the problem are of greatest concern for veterinarians. An accurate diagnosis often requires an extensive knowledge of the field and of all the possible conditions that may be responsible for certain symptoms. As Bertillon, the famous French detective said, "One can only see what one observes, and one observes only things which are already in the mind."

In any such work as this, the author is bound by man's imperfection and ignorance to make many errors and omissions. He has knowingly sacrificed literary style on the altar of time so as to include additional factual information and references and for this decision he hopes he will be excused. He earnestly hopes for and humbly requests readers' criticisms and suggestions so that as future material is presented it will be more correct, complete and useful.

As in any undertaking of this type the efforts of many persons other than the author have made this text possible. Without them this task could never have been performed. To them the author expresses his sincere and grateful appreciation. He especially wishes to acknowledge the advice and assistance of Drs. M. G. Fincher, W. D. Sack, R. Kahrs, R. Foote and William Hansel. Dr. K. McEntee besides supporting and encouraging this second edition of this text was most helpful and generous in providing many of the illustrations from his extensive collection. He greatly appreciated the granting of a leave of absence and a sabbatic leave in which a major portion of this work was done. Recognition is due his associates in the Department of Large Animal Medicine, Obstetrics and Surgery, who were helpful and considerate and took over extra duties in order to further this endeavor. The author's associates in the basic studies of anatomy, physiology, pathology, endocrinology, nutrition, and artificial breeding in the New York State Veterinary College and the New York State College of Agriculture gave freely of their time and knowledge. The care and diligence of the medical artist, Miss Marion Newson, was greatly appreciated. Lastly, the author wishes to express his appreciation for the understanding and forgiveness of his wife and children for the many times he was **in absentia** and other times he might better have been.

Ithaca, New York S. J. Roberts
June 1970

Part I

INTRODUCTION

Veterinary obstetrics has in the past been defined as that branch of surgery dealing with the oversight of the female animal during pregnancy and parturition. However, with our increased knowledge of genital diseases of female and male animals, the study of veterinary obstetrics has expanded to include that highly important field. The livestock industry depends upon reproduction. Any disease or pathological condition causing sterility or infertility in our domestic animals, whether it be a sporadic or enzootic condition, must be the concern of veterinary practitioners. The recent introduction and rapid growth of artificial insemination, and its inherent problems, require the modern veterinarian, especially in cattle practice, to be well acquainted with this field of obstetrics. The fields of reproductive physiology, endocrinology, nutrition, genetics, embryology, teratology, anatomy, virology, bacteriology, pathology, surgery, and medicine, all supply important necessary links in our chain of obstetrical knowledge. In the broad field of veterinary obstetrics and genital diseases, as in any clinical field of study, the advances made in the basic sciences must be studied, considered, and applied.

For the veterinarian entering practice the importance of this field of obstetrical and genital disease cannot be overestimated. The figures from the large New York State Veterinary College Ambulatory Clinic, in which 85 to 90 percent of the animals treated are dairy cattle, show that about 25 to 30 percent of the cases treated were obstetrical or dealt with the reproductive system. These include such common conditions as dystocia, retained placenta, pregnancy examination, sterility examination and treatment, abortion, metritis, blood testing, vaccinating for brucellosis and other abortion diseases and the treatment of many other genital conditions. From a purely business viewpoint, the volume of obstetrical work in a large animal or small animal practice is considerable. One must realize that the average layman or farmer places an undue amount of importance and significance on the successful handling of obstetrical cases and breeding problems. The young or inexperienced veterinarian may make or ruin his chances for success with a certain farmer or in a certain territory by the way in which he handles a single obstetrical case.

Chapter I

FEMALE GENITAL ANATOMY AND EMBRYOLOGY

The bony and ligamentous structures comprising the pelvis are of particular interest in obstetrics. The bony pelvis is composed of the **sacrum,** the first to third **coccygeal vertebrae,** and the two **os coxae,** each formed by the ilium, ischium and pubis.

The **sacrum** is composed of five fused vertebrae in the cow. It is somewhat triangular in form with the base articulating cranially with the last lumbar vertebra and caudally with the first coccygeal vertebra. The ventral face of the sacrum is smooth and concave. The dorsal surface exhibits the sacral spine. The wing of the sacrum articulates or fuses with the ilium laterally. In older animals the first coccygeal vertebra may fuse with the sacrum in the horse, cow and pig.

The **ilium** is irregularly triangular in shape. The broad, flat, dorsal part of the ilium is called the wing. The medial portion of the wing is called the tuber sacrale and its ventral medial aspect articulates with the sacrum. The external portion of the wing of the ilium is called the tuber coxae, hip bone, or "hook" bone. Dorsally the wing of the ilium in the horse, cow, sheep and pig is concave, providing attachment for the gluteal and back muscles. Ventrally the wing is convex. In the dog and cat the wing of the ilium is rotated laterally so it lies nearly parallel to spinal column. The narrow, ventral part of the ilium is called the body or shaft and resembles the long bones of the body. This bone fuses ventrally with the ischium and pubis at the acetabulum. Its medial or pelvic surface is smooth and is grooved for the obturator vessels and nerve.

The **ischium** forms the caudal part of the ventral floor of the pelvis. Its dorsal surface is smooth and rather concave. The caudal border of the ischium slopes inward and forward to join with the opposite ischium to form the ischiatic arch. The caudal lateral portion of these bones are called the tuber ischii or "pin" bones. The tuber ischii in the pig are largely cartilaginous in nature and the symphysis does not undergo complete ankylosis until 6 or 7 years of age. The cranial border of the ischium forms the caudal margin of the obturator foramen. Dorsally the ischium bears the ischiatic spine, cranial and caudal to which are the greater and lesser sciatic notches respectively. These notches become foramina when the sacrosciatic ligament completes their boundaries. The ischiatic spines are prominent in the sow and cow. Medially the ischial and pubic bones fuse to form the pelvic symphysis. In the cow and ewe the portion of the pelvic floor formed by the two ischia is deeply concave from side to side.

The **pubis** is the smallest of the three bones of the os coxae and forms the cranial portion of the pelvic floor. The dorsal or pelvic surface is smooth and usually concave in females, while in males it may be convex. Occasionally in the young cow a sharp tuberosity projecting into the pelvic canal is present on the cranial portion of the pubic symphysis. This prominence may rarely cause contusion or even laceration of the birth canal during a difficult birth. The cranial medial border of the pubic bone provides attachment for the prepubic tendon. The caudal border forms the cranial border of the obturator foramen.

The **acetabulum** is formed by the fusing of the ilium, ischium, and pubis. These bones form a cotyloid cavity lodging the head of the femur. The acetabulum consists of articular and non-articular portions. The acetabular notch is made into a foramen by the transverse ligament and transmits the accessory ligament to the head of the femur in the horse. The round ligament is a short, strong band between the head of the femur and the acetabulum.

There are three, single or paired, **pelvic ligaments** that maintain the relationship of the pelvis to the spinal column. (1) **The dorsal and lateral sacroiliac ligaments,** which are attached to the medial wing of the ilium and the lateral portion of the sacrum and the summits of the sacral spines. This articulation is very firm and rigid and is further maintained and supported by the sacrosciatic ligament and the prepubic tendon. (2) The **sacrosciatic ligament** is an extensive quadrilateral ligamentous sheet that completes the lateral wall of the pelvic cavity. The ligament extends from the lateral border of the sacrum and the transverse processes of the first two coccygeal vertebrae to the ischiatic spine and tuber ischii. It furnishes attachment for the large gluteal muscles and the vulva. In the dog this ligament, called the sacrotuberous ligament, is a narrow strong band extending from the caudal part of the lateral margin of the sacrum to the tuber ischii. (3) The **prepubic tendon** is essentially the tendon of insertion of the recti abdominis muscles and others except the transversus abdominis muscle. It is attached strongly to the cranial border of the pubic bones. It is of importance in fixing the sacroiliac articulation and maintaining the bony pelvis in its proper position.

The pelvic cavity is somewhat cone-shaped, with the base of the cone located cranially. This base is formed by the bony pelvis. The pelvic inlet is roughly oval in shape in all species, with the largest diameter being sacro-pubic. The size of the pelvic inlet varies greatly within a species due to breed, age and size. The sow and cow have the most elliptical pelvic inlets; while the mare and some dogs have nearly round inlets. (See Figure 1) The approximate diameters of pelvices of domestic animals are given in Table 1.

Table 1. Approximate Diameters of the Female Bony Pelvis

Species	Sacro-pubic		Bisiliac	
	cm	inches	cm	inches
Mare	20.3-25.4	8.0 -10.0	19.0-24.1	7.5 -9.5
Cow	19.0-24.1	7.5 - 9.5	14.6-19.0	5.75-7.5
Sheep	7.6-10.8	3.0 - 4.25	5.7- 8.9	2.5 -3.5
Sow	9.5-15.2	3.75- 6.0	6.3-10.2	2.5 -4.0
Bitch	3.3- 6.3	1.3 - 2.5	2.8- 5.7	1.1 -2.25

In our larger domestic animals the cross section of the fetal chest or hips may be greater in diameter than the maternal pelvic inlet but birth is possible by the displacement and realigning of the fetal parts at the time of parturition. The caudal portion of the pelvic cavity is smaller than the cranial portion formed by the bony pelvis but the caudal portion at the time of parturition dilates markedly to allow the passage of the fetus. This ability to dilate is brought about by the relaxation of the pelvic ligaments, especially the sacrosciatic ligament. This relaxation in the cow is an obvious indication of approaching parturition.

The pelvis of the male domestic animal differs from the female in a number of definite points. The diameter of the pelvic inlet is smaller in the male and the ischiatic arch is usually narrower. The pelvic cavity is smaller and less roomy than in the female. The obturator foramen is smaller in the male. The cranial floor of the pelvis is more apt to be convex in the male while it is usually concave in the female. The bones of the pelvis are thicker and heavier in the male. The pelvis of the male castrated at an early age resembles that of the female. These differences are most noticeable in the larger domestic animals.

The comparative differences, other than size, between the pelvis of the various animals should be noted. In the mare the transverse or bis-iliac and sacro-pubic diameters are nearly alike, making the pelvic inlet almost spherical. The coxal tuberosities are large and prominent and the wings of the ilia are nearly perpendicular to the long axis of the body. In the cow the ischial tuberosities are prominent and high. The ilia and coxal tuberosities are smaller than in the mare. The pelvic inlet is more elliptical than in the mare. The pelvis of the ewe is similar to the cow in the shape of the inlet but the wings of the ilia are more nearly parallel to each other and the tuber ischii are relatively much smaller. In the sow the pelvic inlet is long and narrow. The wings of the ilia are not prominent and large, as in the cow and horse. The symphysis pubis in the sow is thicker and does not undergo complete ankylosis. The tuber ischii are not completely ossified. In the dog the wings of the ilia are small and nearly parallel with the median plane. The ischium has a twisted appearance, since the caudal part is nearly horizontal. The pelvis of the cat is similar to that of the dog but has a relatively larger obturator foramen.

The **coxo-femoral** articulation is a ball-and-socket joint with the head of the femur fitting into the acetabular fossa made deeper by the cotyloid ligament. This is a fibrous band circling the acetabular fossa. The transverse ligament is that portion of the cotyloid ligament which crosses the acetabular notch. The round ligament extends from the subpubic groove in the acetabulum to the head of the femur and is intra-articular. In occasional cases this ligament may be small or absent.

The increased frequency of hip joint or coxo-femoral dislocation in the cow is due to the shallowness of the acetabulum, lack of bulky muscle around the joint, the small, or occasionally absent, round ligament, absence of an accessory ligament as in the horse, the awkward gait, excessive relaxation of the pelvic ligaments in advanced pregnancy and with cystic ovaries, and the large size and weight of the abdomen in advanced pregnancy, twin pregnancy and hydrops of the fetal membranes.

The Ovaries and Female Genital Tract

The generative organs of the female consist of the ovaries, and the tubular portion of the reproductive tract including the oviducts, uterus, cervix and the cranial portion of the vagina arising from the primitive Mullerian or paramesonephric ducts. The vulva, vestibule and the caudal portion of the vagina develop from the urogenital sinus.

The **ovaries** consist of a stroma or network of connec-

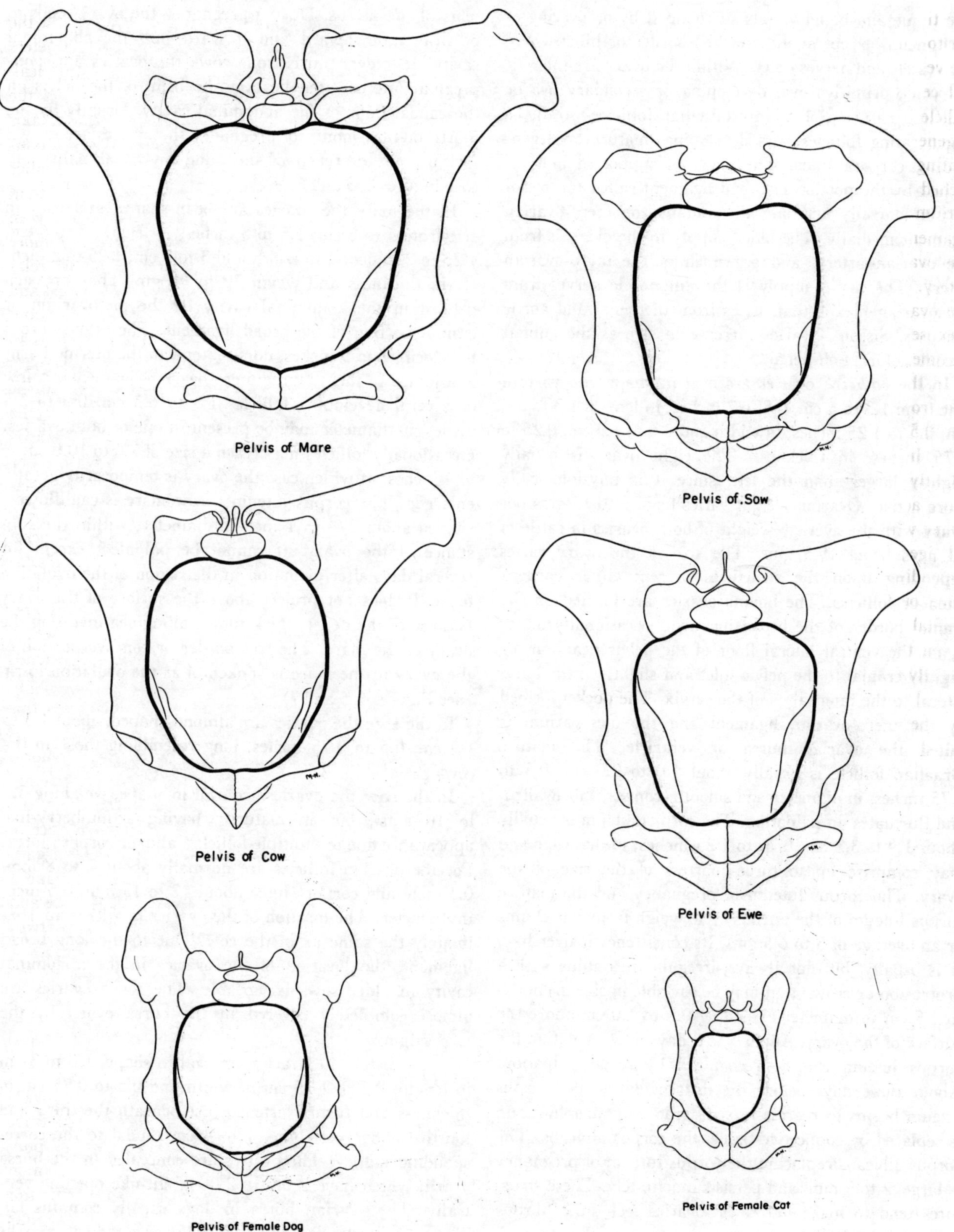

Figure 1. Pelvices of the domestic animals.

tive tissue and blood vessels surrounded by a covering of peritoneum except at the attached border or hilus where the vessels and nerves enter. Within the ovary are interstitial cells, primitive ova, developing or secondary ova or follicles, maturing or mature Graafian follicles, atretic or degenerating follicles, and developing, mature or degenerating corpora lutea. The ovary is supported and attached by the portion of broad ligament called the mesovarium dorsally and laterally and by the utero-ovarian ligament medially. The blood supply to the ovary is from the ovarian artery, and a branch of the utero-ovarian artery. The nerve supply is the autonomic nerves from the ovarian plexus that arises from the renal and aortic plexuses, Sisson. Ovaries increase in size as the animal becomes older, Foley et al..

In the **cow** the ovaries are oval in shape and vary in size from 1.3 to 5 cm, 0.5 to 2 inches, in length, 1.3 to 3.2 cm, 0.5 to 1.25 inches, in width and 0.6 to 1.9 cm, 0.25 to 0.75 inches, in thickness. The right ovary is usually slightly larger than the left, since it is physiologically more active. Ovarian weight varies from 5 to 15 gms per ovary with the average weight of both ovaries in cattle of all ages being 19.5 gms. The size of the ovary varies depending upon the structures present either corpora lutea or follicles. The bovine ovaries are located on the cranial border of the broad ligament, occasionally under it, on the ventral lateral floor of the pelvis near, on, or slightly cranial to the pelvic inlet and slightly cranial and lateral to the internal os of the cervix. The pocket formed by the utero-ovarian ligament and the mesovarium is called the ovarian bursa or ventricle. The mature Graafian follicle is usually about 1.0 to 2.0 cm, 0.5 to 0.75 inches, in diameter and smooth, convex, thin-walled, and fluctuates on palpation. The corpus luteum is usually about 1.9 to 3.2 cm, 0.75 to 1.25 inches, in diameter and may comprise up to three-quarters of the size of the ovary. The corpus luteum of pregnancy and the mature corpus luteum of the estrous cycle weigh from 3 to 9 gms or an average of 5 to 6.5 gms. Its consistency is liver-like. It is usually, but not always, irregular in outline with a protrusion or crown that may be variable in size, from 0.5 to 1.5 cm in diameter extending 0.5 to 1.0 cm above the surface of the ovary. About 3 to 5 days after ovulation the corpus luteum can be recognized by rectal palpation. About three days before the next ovulation the corpus luteum begins to regress in size, gradually atrophies and is replaced by connective tissue, the corpus albicans. The corpus albicans replacing the corpus luteum of pregnancy is large, 2 to 5 mm, and persists indefinitely. These structures tend to make old cows' ovaries feel quite fibrous and roughened. The position of the ovary in the cow varies with the stage of pregnancy or with the size and contents of the uterus. During pregnancy the ovary tends to be drawn downward and forward into the abdominal cavity. In older, pluriparous cows the ovaries and nonpregnant uterus often lie over the brim of the pelvis on the caudal floor of the abdominal cavity. Usually by the fourth or fifth month of pregnancy the ovaries are drawn forward out of reach of the hand on rectal palpation. (See Figures 2, 3 and 6)

In the mare the ovaries are bean-shaped and vary in size from 4 to 8 cm, 1.5 to 3 inches, in length, 3 to 6 cm, 1.25 to 2.5 inches, in width and 3 to 5 cm, 1.25 to 2 inches, in thickness and weigh 30 to 90 gm. They are suspended in the abdominal cavity by the mesovarium or cranial portion of the broad ligament. The ovaries are 5 to 7.5 cm, 2 to 3 inches, dorso-lateral to the uterine horns and joined to them by the utero-ovarian ligaments. A few or several developing follicles 1.3 to 6.3 cm, 0.5 to 2.5 inches, in diameter may be present in one or both ovaries. Occasionally follicles may reach a size of 7.5 to 10.0 cm, 3 to 4 inches, in which case the ovary is temporarily greatly enlarged. The corpus luteum in the mare is cauliflower-shaped about 3/4 to 1 inch in diameter, within the substance of the ovary. It cannot be palpated, except for several days after ovulation in the region of the ovulation fossa. It does not project above the surface of the ovary because of the dense, thick tunica albuginea investing the ovary of the mare. The free border or concave portion of the ovary in the mare is spoken of as the ovulation fossa (See Figures 4, 5 and 7)

In the **ewe** the ovaries are almond-shaped, about 1.3 to 1.9 cm, 0.5 to 0.75 inches, long resembling those in the cow.

In the **sow** the ovaries are oval in shape, weighing 3.5 to 10 gms., but in maturity having a mulberry-like appearance due to multiple follicles, and/or corpora lutea. Porcine ovarian follicles are normally about 7 to 8 mm, 0.3 inch, and corpora lutea about 12 to 15 mm, 0.5 inch, in diameter. The location of the ovaries in gilts is approximately the same as in the cow. Due to the long broad ligament, the location of the ovaries in the abdominal cavity in older sows is variable. The sow's ovaries are almost completely covered in the bursa ovarii by the mesosalpinx.

In the **bitch** the ovaries are oval in shape, 1.0 to 3 cm in length, 0.7 to 1.25 cm in width and 0.5 to 0.75 cm in thickness and firmly fastened just beneath the third and fourth lumbar vertebrae, 1 to 4 cm caudal to the corresponding kidney. The ovaries are concealed in the bursa ovarii, which have a 0.6 to 2.0 cm slit-like opening ventrally. The ovarian bursa in dogs usually contains fat. The ovary in the dog, like that of the sow and cat, may be mulberry-like in appearance due to multiple follicles or

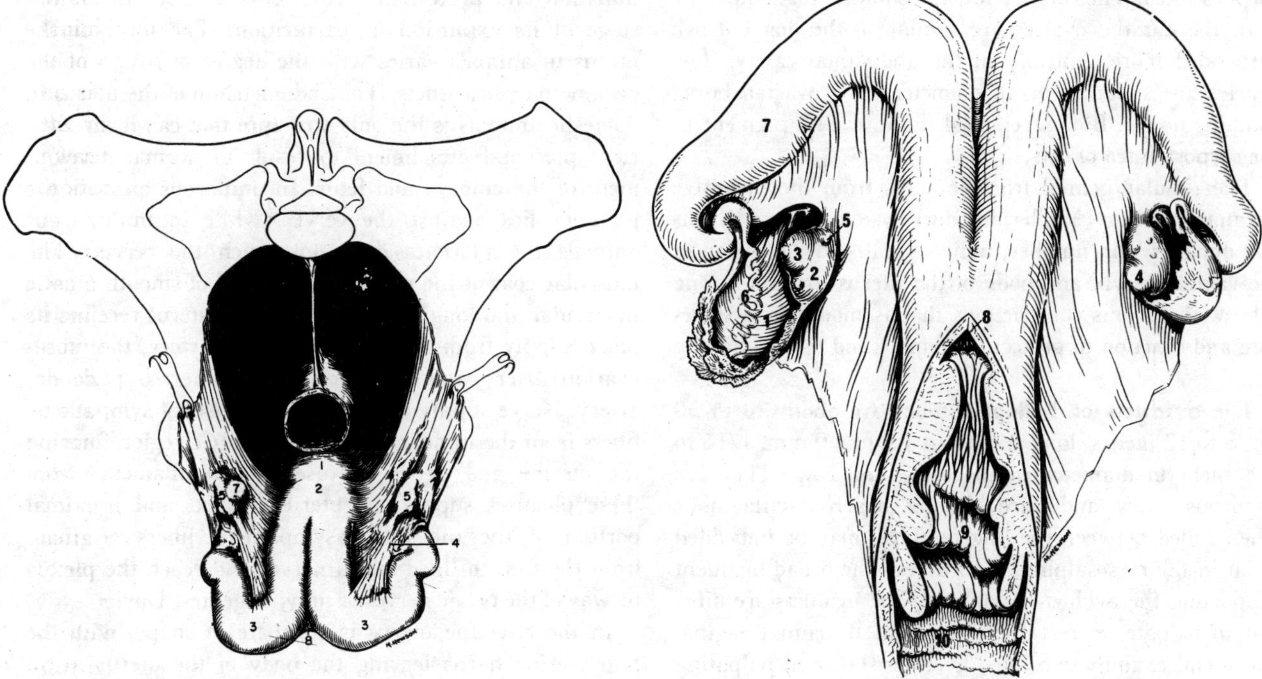

Figure 2. Nonpregnant uterus of the cow, cranial aspect. 1. Cervix, 2. Body of uterus, 3. Horn of uterus, 4. Oviduct, 5. Ovaries, 6. Ovarian ventricle, 7. Corpus luteum, 8. Intercornual ligament, 9. Rectum.

Figure 3. Uterus of cow, dorsai aspect. 1. Ovarian bursa, 2. Ovary, 3. Corpus luteum, 4. Follicle, 5. Corpus albicans, 6. Oviduct, 7. Uterine horn, 8. Uterine body, 9. Cervix, 10. Vagina.

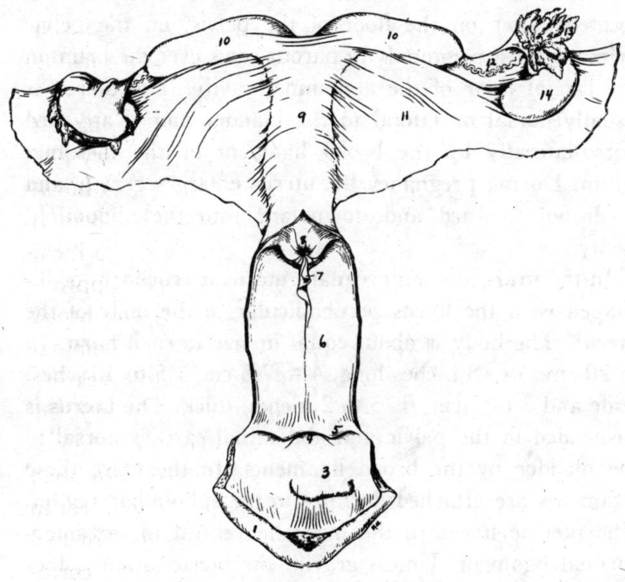

Figure 4. Genital tract of the mare. 1. Vulvar lips, 2. Clitoris, 3. Vestibule, 4. Urethral orifice, 5. Vulvovaginal fold, 6. Vagina, 7. Frenulum, 8. Cervix, 9. Body of uterus, 10. Horns of uterus, 11. Mesometrium, 12. Oviduct in mesosalpinx, 13, Fimbria of oviduct, 14. Ovary.

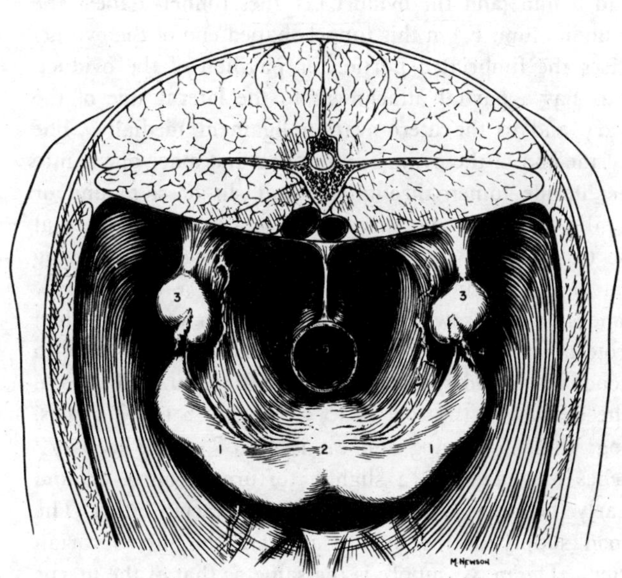

Figure 5. Nonpregnant uterus in the mare. 1. Uterine horns, 2. Uterine body, 3. Ovaries, 4. Oviduct, 5. Rectum.

corpora lutea. The corpora lutea contain no pigment.

In the **cat** the ovaries are similar to the dog but are suspended more ventrally in the abdominal cavity. The ovaries are about 1 cm. in diameter. The ovarian bursa contains no fat. Bloom reported there was no pigment in the corpora lutea of cats.

The tubular genital tract develops from the primitive paramesonephric (Mullerian) duct system. These primitive ducts, two in number, unite caudally in the region of the vagina, cervix and body of the uterus to form a long tube with various constrictions that is modified in structure and function to protect the female and the developing fetus.

The **oviducts** or Fallopian tubes are about 20 to 30 cm, 8 to 12 inches, long and about 1.5 to 3.0 mm, 1/16 to 1/8 inch, in diameter in the mare and cow. They are torturous, wiry and hard, feeling nearly cartilaginous when rolled between the fingers. They may be imbedded in fat in the mesosalpinx, a portion of the broad ligament supporting the oviduct or salpinx. The oviducts are difficult to palpate on rectal examination. Bimanual vaginal and rectal examination often is of assistance in palpating the oviduct. Another technique in the cow is to slip several fingers into the ovarian bursa or ventricle and palpate the oviduct between them and the thumb. The distal or caudal, short segment, 1 to 3 cm in length, attached to the tip of the uterine horn is called the isthmus; while the major portion of the oviduct from the isthmus to the infundibulum is called the ampulla. The diameter of the oviduct at the ovarian end becomes larger, 4 to 8 mm, and the oviduct becomes funnel-shaped, the infundibulum. From this funnel-shaped end of the oviduct arises the fimbriated portion or pavilion of the oviduct. This has a partial attachment to the lateral side of the ovary and to the utero-ovarian ligament medially. The uterine end of the oviduct in the dog and mare opens into the uterine lumen through a small slit on a mound or papilla. In cattle and sheep there is a marked flexure at the transition of the isthmus with the elongated curving end of the uterine horn. The latter has a very narrow lumen. In the sow and dog the mucosa of the oviduct projects into the uterine lumen as folds well-supplied with blood, Hook and Hafez, Hafez and Blandau, and Bloom. The oviduct of the sow is 15 to 30 cm, 6 to 12 inches, long; that of the dog and cat is 4 to 7 cm, 2 to 3-1/2 inches long and has a slightly torturous course around nearly the entire circumference of the ovarian bursa. The blood supply of the oviduct is from the utero-ovarian artery. The nerve supply is the same as that of the uterus and ovary.

The **uterus** is a muscular membranous structure designed for the reception of the fertilized ovum, for the nutrition and protection of the fetus, and for the initial stage of its expulsion at parturition. The form of the uterus in animals varies with the degree of fusion of the paramesonephric ducts. The endometrium of the uterus in domestic animals is the only structure that can form sufficient placental attachment to result in normal development of the embryo and fetus. In uniparous animals the placenta lies against the cervix, while in multiparous animals the placenta does not touch the cervix. The muscular coat of the uterus is composed of smooth muscle in circular and longitudinal layers. The uterus receives its blood supply from the (middle) uterine artery, the utero-ovarian artery and a branch of the internal pudendal artery. Nerve supply to the uterus consists of sympathetic fibers from the lumbar and lower thoracic region forming the uterine and pelvic plexuses. Nerve filaments from these plexuses supply the uterus, cervix, and proximal portion of the tubes. Parasympathetic fibers originate from the first to third sacral nerves and reach the plexus by way of the pelvic nerves or nervi erigentes; Doyle.

In the **cow** the uterus is cornuate in shape, with the two uterine horns leaving the body of the uterus at an acute angle and lying nearly parallel to each other. The body is about 2.5 to 4 cm, 1 to 1-1/2 inches, long. Depending on the age and breed of the cow the horns are 20 to 40 cm, 8 to 15 inches, long and from 1.25 to 5 cm, 0.5 to 2 inches, in diameter in the nonpregnant state. The horns are joined by the dorsal and ventral intercornual ligaments for about one-half their length. The uterus is located either on the floor of the pelvis, on the pelvic brim, or most commonly in parous cows over the brim on the caudal floor of the abdominal cavity. The uterus is usually dorsal or lateral to the bladder and is attached dorso-laterally by the broad ligament or the mesometrium. During pregnancy the uterus enlarges greatly and is drawn forward and downward into the abdominal cavity.

In the **mare** the nonpregnant uterus is cruciform or T-shaped with the horns perpendicular to the body of the uterus. The body is about equal in size to each horn, 15 to 20 cm, 6 to 8 inches long, 4 to 7.5 cm, 1.5 to 3 inches, wide and 2 to 5 cm, 0.75 to 2 inches, thick. The uterus is suspended in the pelvic and abdominal cavities dorsal to the bladder by the broad ligaments. In the mare these ligaments are attached dorsally to the sublumbar region. The uterine horns in the mare lie ventral to the intercornual ligament. Unless gravid, the uterus usually does not lie on the floor of the pelvic or abdominal cavities.

In the **ewe** the uterus is shaped like that of the cow and located similarly. Each horn is 10 to 12 cm, 4 to 5 inches, long.

In the **sow** the uterine body is about 5 cm, 2 inches,

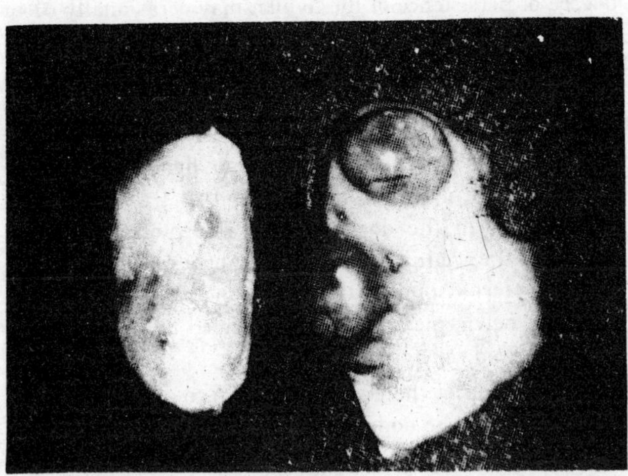

Figure 6. Bovine Ovaries – The right ovary contains 2 corpora lutea and an atretic follicle. Left ovary is small since a double ovulation occurred in the right ovary about 6 days ago.

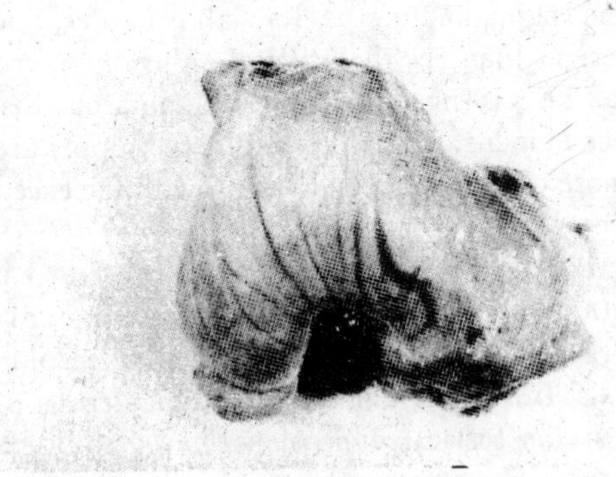

Figure 7. Equine Ovary–The corpus luteum is protruding into the ovulation fossa. Note depression over CL due to loss of follicular fluid at the time of ovulation about 48 hours ago.

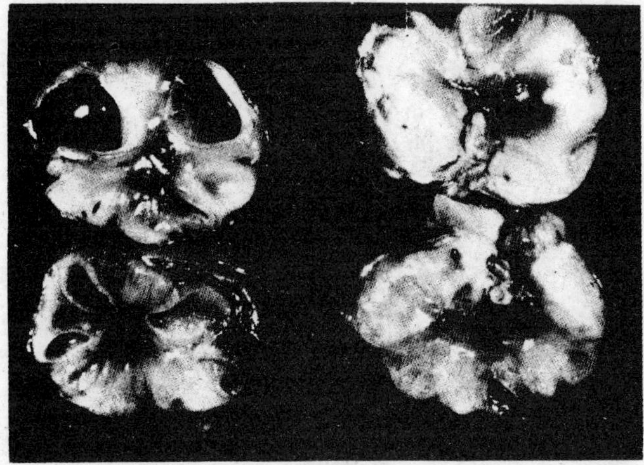

Figure 8. Ovaries of mare bisected – Note pear-shaped follicles with narrow portion toward the ovulation fossa.

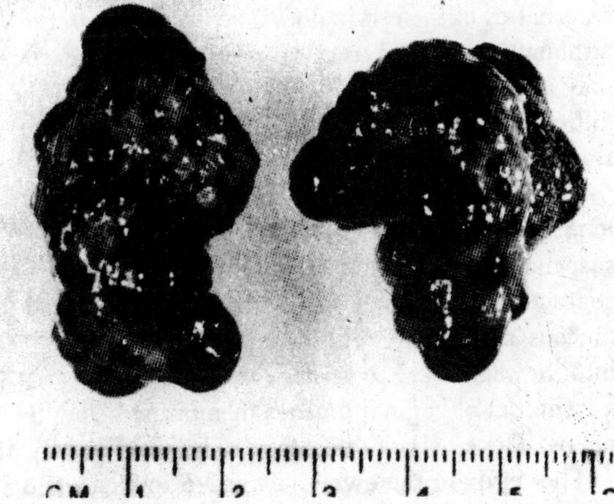

Figure 9. Ovaries of sow – Note mature corpora lutea and small follicles.

long with long torturous horns that are freely movable because of the long broad ligaments. In pregnant animals the horns may be 1.2 to 1.8 m, 4 to 6 feet, long.

In the nulliparous medium-sized **bitch** the uterus has a short body, 2.5 cm, 1 inch, long with straight horns 12 to 15 cm, 5 to 6 inches, long and 0.5 to 1.0 cm, 0.2 to 0.4 inches, in diameter that diverge at an acute angle toward the poles of each kidney. Suspended from the sublumbar region by the broad ligaments, the uterus lies entirely within the abdominal cavity.

The **cervix** is a powerful tubular sphincter muscle between the vagina and uterus. Its wall is harder, thicker, and more rigid than are the walls of either the uterus or the vagina. This is more noticeable in uniparous than in multiparous animals. The blood and nerve supply are the same as those of the uterus and vagina with the exception of the utero-ovarian artery.

The cervix in the **cow** is about 5 to 10 cm, 2 to 4 inches, in length by 1.5 to 7 cm, 0.75 to 2.75 inches, in diameter, the larger of the measurements occurring in pluriparous animals. In some Brahman or Brahman-cross, pluriparous cows the cervical dimensions may greatly exceed these averages. The cervix is located caudal to the uterus either in the pelvic cavity, on the pelvic brim, or in the abdominal cavity. During pregnancy the cervix is drawn forward into the abdominal cavity. The cervix of the cow is composed of 3 to 5 muscular fibrous transverse annular folds that have an almost cartilaginous consistency. The external os of the cervix does not protrude into the vagina, although prolapsed cervical rings in pluriparous cows may present such an appearance. The cervix of the cow is difficult if not impossible to dilate manually. It dilates slightly during estrum.

The cervix of the **mare** is 5 to 7.5 cm, 2 to 3 inches, long and 2.5 to 5 cm, 1 to 2 inches, in diameter. It is suspended in the pelvic cavity caudal to the uterus and is characterized by numerous small low longitudinal folds of mucous membrane. The caudal os of the cervix extends into the vagina 2.5 to 5 cm, 1 to 2 inches, carrying with it a frenulum of vaginal mucous membrane below the external os. The cervix of the mare can be rather easily dilated.

The cervix of the **ewe** is about 2.5 to 5 cm, 1 to 2 inches, long and is similar to that of the cow. Its external os is located in the cranial ventral portion of the vagina and is partially covered by a projecting "hood" of mucosa.

The cervix of the **sow** and **dog** as of other multiparous animals, is poorly defined, being characterized by a thickened wall with transverse folds. The sow's cervix is about 10 to 20 cm, 4 to 8 inches, long and is directly continuous with the vagina (See Figure 6). The cervix or neck of the uterus in the dog is very short, 0.5 to 1 cm in length and externally the cervix projects into the vagina.

The **vagina** is a muscular membranous structure lying in the pelvic cavity dorsal to the bladder that acts as a copulatory organ and as a passage for the fetus at the time of parturition. The vagina is capable of great dilation. Its caudal extremity is just cranial to the urethral opening in the region of the hymen. The hymen is a slight, circular constriction between the vagina and the vulva. A varying degree of persistence of the hymen may occasionally occur in all species, from a thin vertical central band to a completely imperforate structure. Perkins, Olds, and Seath reported that 14.1 per cent of the heifers they examined had hymenal remnants. These usually disappear after copulation or parturition. Prominent hymenal folds are present in the mare. Bloom reported that a true hymen was lacking in the dog and cat. The blood and nerve supply of the vagina arises from branches of the urogenital and internal pudendal arteries and autonomic nerves from the pelvic plexus. It is surrounded by loose connective tissue and varying amounts of fat.

The **vagina** of the **cow** is about 25 to 30 cm, 10 to 12 inches, long in the nonpregnant animal. The recto-genital

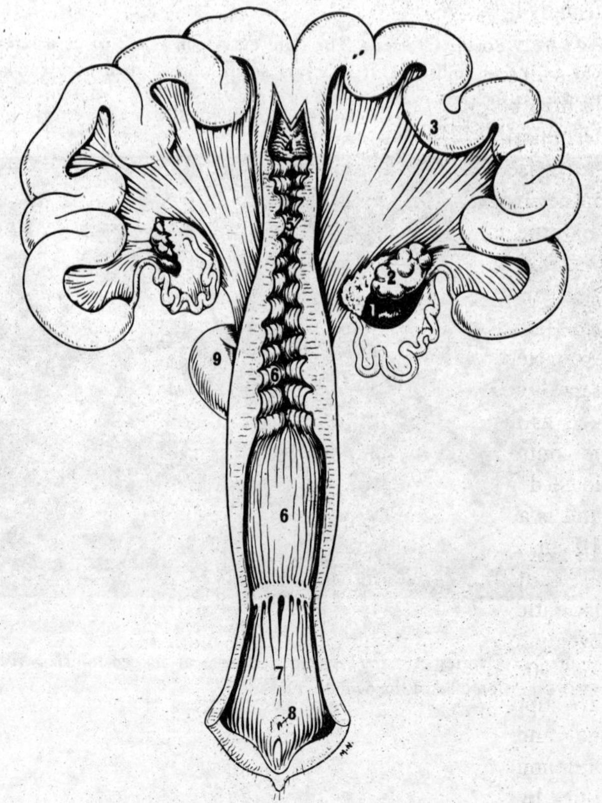

Figure 10. Genital organs of the sow 1. Ovarian Bursa, 2. Ovary, 3. Uterine horn, 4. Uterine body, 5. Cervix, 6. Vagina, 7. Vestibule, 8. Clitoris.

pouch of peritoneum extends backward about 12 cm, 5 inches, on the dorsal cranial surface and 5 cm, 2 inches, on the ventral cranial serous surface of the vagina. On the ventral floor of the vagina, beneath the mucosa and running the length of the vagina, the two Gartner's ducts, one-tenth inch diameter, remnants of the primitive mesonephric or Wolffian ducts, are frequently present. Cysts of these structures may occasionally be observed.

The vagina of the **mare** is about 18 to 23 cm, 7 to 9 inches, long and 10 to 13 cm, 4 to 5 inches, in diameter when dilated. Most of the vagina, except a small dorsal cranial portion, is retroperitoneal. Mesonephric ducts are only occasionally present.

The vagina of the **ewe** is 7.5 to 10 cm, 3 to 4 inches, long and similar to the cow's.

The vagina of the **sow** is 7.5 to 11.5 cm, 3 to 4.5 inches, long. It is small in diameter, with a thick muscular coat. Mesonephric ducts are occasionally present.

The vagina in the **bitch** is long, 10 to 14 cm, and narrow, 1.5 cm. The muscular coat is thick, and mesonephric ducts are usually absent. In the cat the vestibule and vagina are the same length, and mesonephric ducts are usually lacking.

The **vulva,** comprised of the two labia, the dorsal and ventral commissures and the clitoris, and the **vestibule** located between the vulva and the vagina form the caudal termination of the genital tract. These two structures do not arise from the primitive paramesonephric ducts but rather from the entoderm of the primitive urogenital sinus and the ectoderm. The urethra opens into the cranial ventral portion of the vestibule. The vestibule has several circular or sphincter-like muscles that close the genital canal to the outside. These muscles are attached to the sphincter muscle of the anus and the coccygeal and last sacral vertebrae. Thus during parturition the vestibule acts as the point of attachment for the entire genital tract to contract upon when expelling the fetus. The clitoris is located in the caudal portion of the ventral commissure and is a homologue of the penis. The clitoris is about 5 to 10 cm, 2 to 4 inches, long in most animals, but practically all of it is hidden in tissues between the vulva and the ischiatic arch. The vulvar lips normally come together evenly, do not gape, and the vulvar opening normally lies at a 90° angle to the pelvic floor. The vestibule and vulva are supplied with blood from the urogenital and the external and internal pudendal arteries and have the same autonomic innervation as the vagina. They are well-supplied by the sensory nerve fibers of the pudendal and genital nerves. The vulva and vestibule are the only reproductive organs of the female well-innervated by sensory nerve fibers.

The vestibule of the **cow** is about 10 to 12.5 cm, 4 to 5 inches, long on the ventral floor and 7.5 to 10 cm, 3 to 4 inches, long on the dorsal wall. Beneath the urethral orifice is the suburethral diverticulum, which is about 2.5 to 4 cm, 1 to 1.5 inches, long. The external visible portion of the clitoris in the cow is small in size. The vestibular or Bartholin's glands, are two in number, one on each side, located in the constrictor muscles of the vestibule. They are about 1.5 to 3 cm in diameter. This gland in the cow opens by a single duct in the lateral wall of the vestibule about 2.5 cm caudal to the vagina.

The vestibule of the **mare** is similar in size to that of the cow. Eight or 10 ducts from each vestibular gland open through its dorso-lateral wall. The external visible portion of the glans of the clitoris of the mare is large and prominent, 2.5 to 5 cm, 1 to 2 inches, long and 2 to 2.5 cm, 0.75 to 1 inch wide. It is composed of erectile tissue similar to the penis. Contractions of the vestibular and vulvar sphincter muscles elevates the clitoris and protrudes it between the vulvar lips. This is called "winking."

The vestibule and vulva in the **ewe** are similar to that of the cow, but the suburethral diverticulum is very small. The vestibule is about 2.5 to 3 cm long. Vestibular glands are frequently absent. The clitoris is short, with the glans concealed in a fossa.

The vestibule in the **sow** is fairly long, about 8.9 cm, 3.5 inches. The labia are thick. The vestibular glands are small and variable in number. The clitoris is located about 2 cm cranial to the ventral commissure. On either side of the cranial portion of the floor of the vestibule there is a cul-de-sac.

The vulva in the **bitch** and **cat** has thick labia. The vestibule is 2.5 to 5 cm long. The urethral orifice opens on the urethral tubercle, which is elevated above the floor of the vestibule. There are small depressions on either side of the urethral orifice. Vestibular glands are absent in the dog but present in the cat. The clitoris in the dog and cat has a small, 0.6 cm long by 0.2 cm diameter, pointed glans and lies in a fossa. The dorsal commissure of the vulva is 8 to 9 cm below the anus.

The anatomy of the perineal region of the cow and mare has been well-described by Habel.

References

Anonymous (1958/1959) Postmortem Examination of the Genital Tract of the Sow. Dept Prod. Div. Milk Marketing Board, Thames Ditton, Surrey, England, 103.

Benesch, F. (1952) Lehrenbuch Der Tierarztlichen Geburtshilfe and Gynakologie. Urban and Schwarzenberg, Wien-Innsbruck, Austria.

Bloom, F. (1954) Pathology of the Dog and Cat, American Veterinary Publication Inc., Evanston, Ill.

Doyle, J. B. (1954) Ovulation and Effects of Selective Utero-tubal Denervation, Fert. and Steril., **5**, 2, 105.

Dukes, H. H. (1947) The Physiology of Domestic Animals, 6th Ed., Comstock Publishing Co., Ithaca, N.Y.

Foley, R. C., Black, D. L., Black, W. G., Damon, R. A., Howe, G. R. (1964) Ovarian and Luteal Tissue Weights in Relation to Age, Breed and Live Weight in Nonpregnant and Pregnant Heifers and Cows with Normal Reproductive Histories, J. An. Sci., **23**, 3 752.

Habel, R. E. (1966) The Topographic Anatomy of the Muscles, Nerves and Arteries of the Bovine Female Perineum, Amer. J. Anat. **119**, 1, 79.

Hafez, E. S. E. and Blandau, R. J. (1969) The Mammalian Oviduct, Univ. of Chicago Press, Chicago, Ill.

Hook, S. J. and Hafez, E. S. E. (1968) A Comparative Study of the Mammalian Uterotubal Junction, J. Morphol. **125**, 2, 159.

Miller, M. E. (1964) Anatomy of the Dog, W. B. Saunders Co., Phila, London.

Reutner, T. F. and Morgan, B. B. (1948) A Study of the Bovine Vestibular Gland, Anat. Rec., **101**, 2, 193.

Sisson, S. and Grossman, J. D. (1953) The Anatomy of the Domestic Animals, 4th Ed. Revised, W. B. Saunders Co., Philadelphia, Pa.

St. Clair, L. E. (1958) Anatomy in *Diseases of Swine* edited by H. W. Dunne, Iowa State College Press, Ames. Iowa, 3.

Williams, W. L. (1943) Veterinary Obstetrics, 4th Ed., Miss Louella Williams, Upland Rd., Ithaca, N.Y.

EMBRYOLOGY OF THE FEMALE REPRODUCTIVE TRACT

The urogenital system is formed mainly from mesodermal tissue that in the early embryonic period forms the nephric and genital regions. The ovaries develop from the undifferentiated gonads that form late in the embryonic period in the genital or gonadal ridge located between the dorsal mesentery and the mesonephros. The primordial germ cells from the wall of the yolk sac in the region of the hind gut have migrated into the gonad by the early fetal period. The surface epithelium of the female gonad gives rise to cortical cords that contain primitive germ cells, later called oogonia. The surrounding epithelial cells from the surface epithelium form the follicular cells. Thus secondary cortical cords are characteristic of the early female gonad. The ovaries remain in the abdominal cavity suspended by the mesovarial portion of the broad ligaments.

In both the male and female during the embryonic period, two pairs of genital ducts are formed that enter the cloaca, the mesonephric or Wolffian tubules and ducts and the paramesonephric or Mullerian ducts. The mesonephric duct development is described in the section on embryology of the male reproductive tract. The paramesonephric ducts arise as longitudinal invaginations of the coelomic epithelium in the same region as the mesonephric tubules and ducts. The cranial portion of the paramesonephric ducts differentiate in the female to form the oviducts while the caudal portions of the ducts unite or fuse to form the uterus, cervix and the cranial two-thirds or more of the vagina. The septum initially present between the two ducts in the caudal region disappears early in the fetal period. The caudal one-third or less of the vagina is formed by evaginations from the wall of the urogenital sinus. The hymen is formed by the epithelial

Table 2. Undifferentiated Genital Structures in the Embryo and Their Adult Male and Female Counterparts

Embryological Structure	Adult Female	Adult Male
Gonad	Ovary	Testis
Mesentery	Mesovarium	Mesorchium
Gubernaculum	Round ligament of the uterus and proper ligament of the ovary	Ligamentum testis
Paramesonephric duct (Mullerian duct)	Oviducts Uterus Cervix Vagina (cranial portion)	Appendix testis Uterus masculinus
Mesonephric tubules and duct (Wolffian duct and body)	Epoophoron Paroophoron (Parovarian or mesonephric duct cysts) Gartner's ducts	Efferent ducts Epididymis Ductus (vas) deferens (ductuli aberrantes, appendix epididymis, paradidymis)
Genital tubercle	Clitoris	Penis (phallus)
Genital folds	Vestibule	Penile urethra
Genital swellings	Vulvar lips	Scrotum

linings of the vaginal canal, the urogenital sinus and a thin intermediate layer of mesoderm. In the male the paramesonephric ducts degenerate but portions may persist as remnants, as the appendix testis near the head of the epididymis, and the uterus masculinus between the ampullae and near the prostate gland. Portions of the mesonephric tubules and ducts may persist as remnants in the female forming the epoophoron on the cranial pole of the ovary, the paroophoron or parovarian cysts, and Gartner's ducts in the vaginal floor. (See Table 2)

Early in the fetal period the external undifferentiated genitalia become modified so the genital tubercle forms the clitoris, the genital folds failing to unite as in the male become the vestibule and the genital swellings enlarge to form the vulvar lips.

Arey, L. B. (1954) Developmental Anatomy, 6th Ed., W. B. Saunders Co., Philadelphia.

Langman, J. (1963) Medical Embryology, Williams and Wilkins Co., Baltimore

Miller, M. E. (1964) Anatomy of the Dog, W. B. Saunders Co., Philadelphia

Patten, B. M. (1948) Embryology of the Pig, 3rd Ed., The Blakiston Co., Philadelphia.

Chapter II

EXAMINATIONS FOR PREGNANCY

An accurate, early diagnosis of pregnancy, cyesiognosis, in the cow and mare is essential to a successful breeding program. The ability to make an accurate, early diagnosis is required of most successful large animal practitioners. This ability is the base upon which successful programs for the management of infertility in cattle and horses is built. The development of this ability requires much study, and especially practice. In addition to the ability to diagnose pregnancy, the duration of pregnancy should be able to be indicated with accuracy to within several days to a week or two depending upon the stage of pregnancy. Pregnancy should be able to be differentiated from other conditions such as pyometra, mummification of the fetus, mucometra, fetal maceration, tumors, and metritis.

The average student or young veterinarian is prone to make two mistakes that can be very embarrassing and should be avoided. The first is one of commission, when he states a cow is pregnant when, because of his inexperience, he does not know or is not sure, but the history indicates that the animal is probably pregnant. In this instance he is giving the owner a false sense of security. If the examiner is not sure of a pregnancy diagnosis he should state the fact, indicate the cow as possibly or probably pregnant, and reexamine the animal after several weeks or a month, at which time the diagnosis is more easily and accurately made. The only alibi for a mistake of this sort is that the cow aborted unseen. Although in some cases it may be true, especially where a skilled examiner has made a positive diagnosis of a bovine pregnancy at 30 to 40 days or an equine pregnancy at 20 to 35 days, the explanation is reluctantly accepted by the client.

The second mistake is one of omission. In this instance the veterinarian has been informed by his client that a certain animal fails to come into estrum. Without carefully examining the uterus, including the palpation of each horn to its apex, the veterinarian removes the corpus luteum, gives a large slowly-absorbed dose of estrogen or douches the uterus of a pregnant animal, and abortion ensues several days later. The client, although he has given misleading information, is rightfully indignant.

Pregnancy Diagnosis in the Cow

External indications of pregnancy include service by a bull or by artificial insemination. Occasionally this information is not known, either through error, lack of records, or accidental breeding. Cessation of estrum or heat periods, is fairly accurate if the herdsman observes animals closely for estrum, but is not infallible as the herdsman may not observe signs of estrum or the animal may not exhibit signs of estrum. Early embryonic deaths or abortions may occur. Zemjanis and Belling reported that 15 per cent or more of cattle not observed in estrus after service were not pregnant when examined 60 days or so after service. Pathologic changes may occur in the uterus, such as pyometra or in the ovaries, such as cysts, resulting in failure of estrum. Some cows may exhibit signs of estrum during pregnancy. Williams stated that 1 to 2 per cent of pregnant cows showed heat. Arthur cited Knapp and coworkers as reporting an incidence of 4.5 per cent. Donald, Rahlmann and Mead, and Erb and Morrison reported the incidence of estrum during pregnancy as 3.5, 5, and 5.6 per cent respectively. The latter reported that 55 per cent of cows showed estrus within 35 days after conception. Many cows exhibiting post-conception estrus had a history of cystic ovaries. According to Donoho and Rickard about 6 per cent of 1454 cows had one or more heat periods after conception. Most of the cows showed estrum for only a few times. Estrum was observed most frequently the first trimester of pregnancy. This estrum is usually associated with follicular growth but ovulation and corpus luteum formation during pregnancy rarely occurs in cattle.

Postestrous bleeding, "menstruation", or the passage of blood and mucus, 24 to 48 hours after service is cited by some as an indication that conception did not occur. Reports indicated that about 50 to 60 per cent of cows and 75 to 85 per cent of heifers showed some bleeding at the vulva after estrum. Where careful studies have been made there was found to be no relationship between postestrous bleeding and conception, Trimberger, and Steere.

In advanced pregnancy, the abdomen, of cattle tends to increase in size but this is not as reliable an indication of pregnancy in uniparous animals as it is in the multiparous species. The udders of heifers at 4 to 5 months of pregnancy begin to increase in size and development. In older pluriparous cows the enlargement and edema of the udder is often not evident until the final 1 to 4 weeks of pregnancy. Cows become quieter and move more slowly and carefully as pregnancy advances, especially the last few weeks. There is a tendency for an increase in body weight. The pelvic ligaments begin a progressive relaxation, and in thin animals a marked sinking of the croup occurs. Edema and relaxation of the vulva is noticeable the last few weeks of pregnancy.

The fetus usually may be ballotted or its movements observed through the abdominal wall after the sixth month of pregnancy. Occasionally in some thin animals where the fetus lies close to the wall, this may be done as early as the fifth month of gestation. In fat animals this may not be possible until the eighth or ninth month of pregnancy. Depending upon the size of the fetus, the condition of the cow and the size and degree of fullness of the abdomen, the fetus can be ballotted in 5 per cent or less of pregnant dairy cows at 5 months of gestation, 10 to 50 per cent at 6 months, 70 to 80 per cent at 7 months, 80 to 90 per cent at 8 months and over 90 per cent at 9 months. Abdominal ballottement of the fetus is easy in the cow because of the relaxed, flaccid abdominal walls. The fist is pushed in an intermittent manner in a dorsal medial direction deeply into the lower right abdominal wall. If the fetus is ballotted, it is felt as a large hard solid object suspended or floating in the softer structures of the abdomen, such as the uterus, uterine contents and the abdominal viscera. The more advanced the pregnancy or the larger the fetus, the more dorsal in the right flank region the fetus may be ballotted.

The fetal heart may be auscultated in the right flank region from the sixth to seventh month of pregnancy to term only with great difficulty due to the thick abdominal walls and viscera and the difficulty of obtaining a sufficiently quiet location. By comparison with other techniques, this technique is not practical in the cow as there is too much chance for error. Fetal electrocardiography has been used to study the fetal heart and as an aid in the diagnosis of twin pregnancy and fetal mummification after the fifth month of pregnancy in cattle, Larks et al. and Too and Kanagawa et al.

Internal indications of pregnancy in the cow:

The rectal examination of the uterus, ovaries, and uterine vessels is the most practical and accurate, as well as the earliest means of diagnosing pregnancy in the cow.

Prior to the actual rectal examination, the breeding history of the cow should be studied, including the date of the last calving, the dates and number of services, and information on any pathologic or disease condition previously affecting the reproductive organs. Complete breeding and reproductive records are very helpful to an accurate and rapid pregnancy or sterility examination of a cow or herd. Unfortunately many herds, especially range beef herds, do not have this information, Koger.

If a herd is to be examined it is helpful if someone is available to record notes on the results of the examination. The operator should wear proper protective clothing, consisting of rubber boots, a pair of clean, short-sleeved coveralls, or rubber pants, and a short-sleeved cloth jacket, and a thin rubber surgical glove and obstetrical sleeve. Presently many practitioners are using disposable plastic gloves and sleeves because they are sanitary and cheap. Their principal drawbacks are their lack of durability and their sharp sealed edges that irritate and lacerate the rectal mucosa. The glove and sleeve is essential to protect the examiner's arm from chafing, infection, dirt, filth, and odor. It also protects the cow's rectum from irritation due to the examiner's hair and fingernails. No rings, especially rings with settings, should be worn on the examining hand. The fingernails should be short. Either hand may be used for the examination, but if many examinations are to be made it is usually desirable to use the stronger arm. Many prefer to do examinations with the left hand, so that the right is free for writing and for the manipulation of instruments such as cervical forceps and uterine catheters. The cow should be fastened or held securely to prevent forward or lateral motion. If many cows are to be examined it is helpful for an assistant to hold up the tail away from the examiner's arm. Caution should be exercised when examining cows near posts or other obstructions that might cause the examiner injury if the cow moved her rear parts suddenly. Cows seldom kick when being examined rectally but the excitable dairy cow or beef cow may occasionally kick backwards and injure the operator. This kick usually occurs prior to or as the hand enters the anus. When beef cows are in a chute a bar should be placed behind the cow above the hocks. Applying a nose lead or forcing the cow's tail dorsally and cranially in a firm manner may be necessary to restrain certain cows that kick.

The arm should be well-lubricated with a non-iritating soap or liquid soap. The fingers and the hand are inserted into the rectum in the form of a cone. They are advanced into the rectum beyond the organ or structure to be palpated. Do not introduce the hand and arm a short distance into the rectum and push the rectum forward, thus stretching and irritating the rectal wall. With the arm well-inserted, bring back a portion of the rectum as a fold upon the hand and arm, thereby giving more freedom to the hand and producing greater relaxation of the rectum. It is usually necessary to remove most of the fecal material from the rectum before a thorough examination can be made. This can be done by raking the feces from the rectum with the hand or by stimulating peristaltic contractions and defecation by massaging the rectal wall just anterior to the anus and by allowing some air to enter the rectum to dilate it. In the older, larger dairy cows one can leave the arm and hand, the latter in the shape of a cone, in the rectum when a peristaltic wave is passed backward. However, in heifers and small beef cattle such a practice occasionally results in a tearing of the mucosa or even the rectal wall. In some cases, particularly where cattle have been on lush pasture and the feces are thin and loose, the rectal mucosa is easily irritated and the cow will suck air into the rectum, making examination nearly impossible through the dilated, tense rectal walls. Stimulating peristalsis, as mentioned above, will result in evacuation of the air. This may be aided and hastened by hooking the fingers cranially into a peristaltic contraction ring and pulling it gently caudally. The cow's back should not be pinched down, since this tends to fill the rectum with air. Examinations of cows under epidural anethesia usually result in a ballooning of the rectum that cannot be overcome until the anesthesia wears off. All rectal examinations should be done with care, gentleness, and patience to avoid traumatizing the mucosa or rupturing the rectum. If mucosal damage results in bleeding, the examination should cease.

The presence of free blood, or a fresh blood clot, in amounts of 1/2 to 1 ounce or more, not mixed with the feces, is highly indicative of a rupture. If a rupture of the rectum occurs in the cow, examinations should cease immediately. Supportive treatment with penicillin and streptomycin, tetracyclines or sulfonamides and atropine are indicated. If the cow is not valuable, or at the first sign of diffuse peritonitis characterized by a marked increase in pulse rate or temperature, anorexia, and stiffness, immediate slaughter may be indicated. If recovery follows rectal trauma with perforation, adhesions of the rectum to the genital tract, occasionally associated with abscesses, may occur.

A regular routine for examining the female genital tract should be developed and followed at each examination so no structure or portion of the tract will be overlooked. In making a rectal examination the hand is introduced to the pelvic inlet or bony pelvis and is passed or swept from one side downward, across, and up the other side. If no structure is palpated the uterus is in the pelvic cavity. Usually the cervix or uterus is palpated on the brim of the pelvis in older cows. The hard, firm cervix is relatively easily located on the floor of the pelvis or cranial to it. The uterine body, cornua, and intercornual ligaments can be palpated in nonpregnant cows or cows in early pregnancy. The ovaries may be palpated lateral and slightly cranial to the cervix. As pregnancy develops they are drawn forward, especially the ovary corresponding to the horn containing the fetus, until by the fourth to sixth month of pregnancy they are out of reach. The uterus may be located laterally in the pelvic cavity if held there by a full bladder or a short broad ligament. The normal nonpregnant uterus in the heifer and cow vary greatly in size from 1.25 to 2 cm, 0.5 to 0.75 inches, and 2.5 to 6.5 cm, 1 to 2.5 inches, in diameter and 15 to 20 cm, 6 to 8 inches, and 20 to 30 cm, 8 to 12 inches, in length, respectively. The uterus is normally soft, pliable and relaxed with a slight amount of tonicity in early pregnancy. A completely flaccid atonic uterus is characteristic of true anestrus and chronic cystic ovarian disease. At the time of estrus or following vigorous massage the uterus may become quite erect and turgid. In late estrum and early postestrum, 1 to 2 days after ovulation, the uterus may be thick-walled and edematous. Often about 20, 40 or 60 days post-conception the uterus may be quite erect and tonic together with some follicular activity in the ovaries but a normal corpus luteum is present.

Zemjanis and others have described the important technique for manual retraction of the nonpregnant or one- to three- month pregnant bovine uterus into the pelvic cavity from the abdominal cavity to facilitate its examination. This involves caudal traction on the cervix, then further caudal traction on the ventral intercornual ligament. The cranial border of the broad ligament medial to the ovary may also be retracted. In particularly difficult cases the application of Knowles cervical forceps to the external cervical os is helpful in retracting the uterus. This causes little trauma. The ovary may be grasped and slid between the middle and third fingers and held there while it is carefully palpated by the thumb and index finger.

Taking into consideration a number of factors including the age of the cow, rectal examination to diagnose pregnancy can be made quite accurately from about 35 days after conception. It is easier to detect early pregnancy in heifers than in cows. After 45 to 55 days of gestation, pregnancy diagnosis is usually easy for the experienced veterinarian. Hawk and coworkers reported a high figure of 10 per cent of normal pregnancies diagnosed per rectum at 35 to 41 days of gestation that were lost before 150 days. They cited Fosgate and Smith as reporting that 3.6 per cent of pregnancies diagnosed at 34 to 50 days were lost before 150 days. Belling reported an average abortion rate of 8 per cent at 60 days post-conception in cows diagnosed pregnant earlier. These reports and other work indicates that the earlier in gestation a diagnosis of pregnancy is made the greater the chances of early embryonic or fetal death occurring. This is especially true for the 30 to 45 day diagnoses. According to Barrett, Casida and

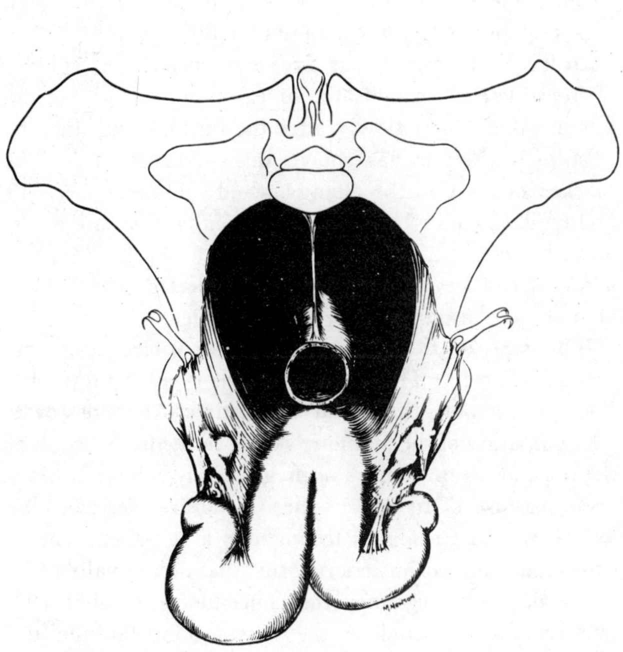

Figure 11. Uterus of a cow. 60 to 70 days pregnant.

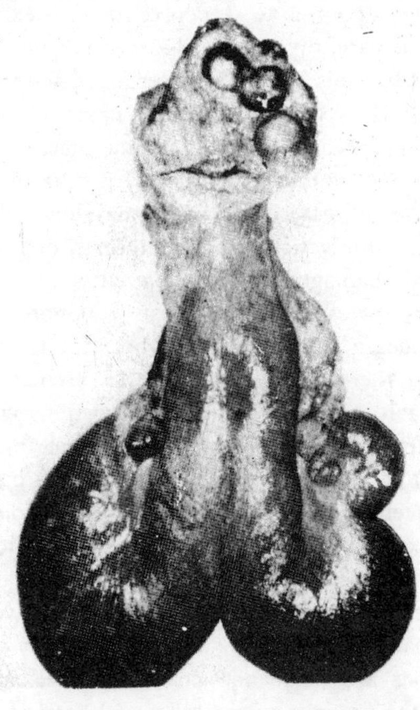

Figure 12. Twin, bicornual bovine pregnancy, 60 days pregnant. Note CL in each ovary and lymphocytomas in the vagina. (Courtesy K. McEntee)

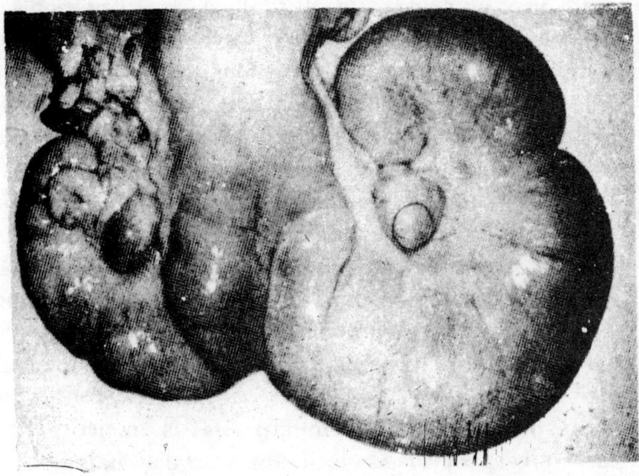

Figure 13. Uterus of cow 60 to 70 days pregnant. Note CL in the left ovary and large follicle in the right ovary.

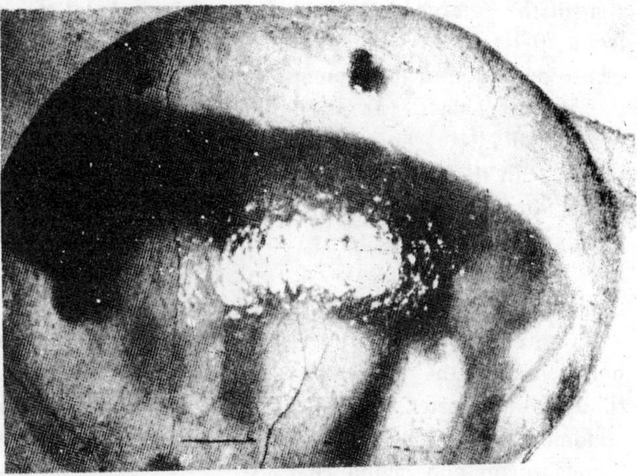

Figure 14. Sixty-day-old bovine fetus in the amniotic sac within the chorioallantoic membranes. Note beginning development of the cotele-dons. (Courtesy K. McEntee)

Lloyd the incidence of fetal death from 60 days to term is much lower, about 2 to 3 per cent. The examination itself, if done carefully and gently, may not be a factor in these losses but this cannot be ascertained with accuracy. The author is certain that several examinations of an early, 30– to 45– day, pregnant bovine uterus by inexperienced student examiners frequently results in abortion. Ball and Carroll, Steere and Stoll have shown the 30– to 45– day amniotic vesicle may be ruptured or the embryo can be easily damaged by rectal palpation, manipulation and excess pressure. The most common cause of embryonic death is rupture of the heart or the vessels at the base of the heart resulting in hemorrhage into the amniotic cavity. Prompt or delayed abortions will follow within a few days or weeks. The greatest incidence of abortion or fetal death not related to trauma occurs during organogenesis and attachment of the fetal membranes the first six weeks of pregnancy in the cow. This "natural" fetal death rate may be augmented by early pregnancy diagnosis per rectum. Thus it behooves veterinarians to be particularly gentle and careful if early diagnostic examinations are made and possibly to reexamine and reconfirm the pregnancy after 55 to 60 days of gestation or to avoid early routine pregnancy examinations if only one examination is to be made.

The definite or certain signs of pregnancy in the cow as determined by a rectal examination are: (1) The palpation of the enlarged horn containing the placental fluids from 30 to 90 days of gestation. (2) The careful, very gentle palpation of the amniotic vesicle in early pregnancy, 30 to 50 days. (3) The slipping of the fetal membranes, allantois chorion, upon gentle pinching of the uterus with the thumb and forefinger in early pregnancy, 40 to 90 days. (4) The palpation or ballottement of the fetus in the enlarged uterus containing fetal membranes and placental fluids. (5) The palpation of the placentomes. (6) The palpation of the enlarged, thin-walled, "whirring" uterine arteries. Less definite signs of pregnancy include the increase in size of the uterus and a thinning and distension of its walls, its location in the abdominal cavity, the location, size and persistence of the corpus luteum and vaginal changes.

Uterine changes during pregnancy: During early pregnancy, the uterine horns, especially the horn containing the fetus increase in size due to the distention of the horn by the amniotic vesicle, placental fluids, the membranes, and the fetus. This increase in the diameter of the uterine horns is characterized by a thinning of the uterine wall and a fluid, watery "alive" feeling of the uterine horn. The uterine horns have a fair amount of tone due to their tenseness and distention. From 40 to 90 days of pregnancy, the uterus feels somewhat like a thick rubber balloon nearly filled with water. The approximate size of the horn containing the fetus during the first 5 months of pregnancy is given in Table 3.

Since the size of the fetus is small during the early stages of pregnancy the amount of fluid in the uterine horn largely determines its size or diameter. The volume of fluid increases rapidly the first 5 months of pregnancy but increases more slowly after the fifth or sixth month. (Table 3). Arthur has shown that in cattle there is a marked increase in the allantoic fluid volume between 40 and 65 days and 6-1/2 and 7-1/2 months of gestation and a marked rise in amniotic fluid volume between 3-1/2 and 4 months of gestation that is not reflected in the total volumes of placental fluids given in Table 3.

The size of the amniotic vesicle varies in size as noted in Table 3. The amniotic vesicle is spherical in outline up to about 40 days, at which time it becomes oval. The palpation of the amniotic vesicle in the free portion of the horn at 30 to 45 days of pregnancy is helpful in diagnosis because of its tense spherical nature, described by Wisnicky and Casida as feeling like a soft-shelled hen's egg. Hawk and coworkers reported that occasionally at 35 to 41 days of pregnancy the chorionic or trophoblastic membranes and fluid in the gravid horn but not the amniotic vesicle may be felt. If the latter is not palpable the embryo may have died and is macerating. If the operator is experienced, skillful and gentle early embryonic death may be detected at 30 to 40 days of gestation by palpation of the amniotic vesicle. Studer reported that in 1,130 early pregnancy examinations that 45 or 3.9 per cent were abnormal. This was based on finding too small or collapsed amniotic vesicles. These embryos were resorbed Palpation of the amniotic vesicle should be performed very carefully and gently to avoid rupturing it or to avoid placing direct pressure on the embryo and its exposed organs. The fingers and thumb gently palpate the gravid horn; as they are moved slowly back and forth the vesicle can be felt to slip between them. If such an examination cannot be done skillfully and gently it is best to omit it.

Slipping of the fetal membranes is another aid to early pregnancy diagnosis in the cow that is best performed from 35 to 90 days of gestation, although the membranes may be slipped at nearly any stage of gestation. The technique as described by Fincher consists of gently picking up and pinching or compressing either horn of the uterus and feeling the fetal membranes, the allantois chorion, slip between the thumb and the fingers before the uterine wall escapes from between the fingers. In early pregnancy the fetal membranes are very thin and may be difficult to palpate. Zemjanis recommended grasping the entire horn and letting it slip

Table 3. Size and Characteristics of the Bovine Fetus and Uterus during Pregnancy*

Days of Gestation	Diameter of the Horn Containing the Fetus	Amount of Fetal Fluid	Diameter of the Amniotic Vesicle	Length of the Fetus (C-R)	Weight of the Fetus	Diameter of the Placentomes	Diameter of the Uterine Artery	Fetal and Placental Characteristics
30	2-4 cm (7/8-1 1/2")	30-60 ml	1.0 cm (2/5") (pea size)	.8-1 cm (1/3-2/5")	.3-.5 gm			Head and limb buds recognizable, placenta not attached.
40	3-6 cm (1 1/4-2 1/2")	75-100 ml	2.5-3.0 cm (1-1 1/4") (size of plum)	1.75-2.5 cm (2/3-1")	1-1.5 gm			
50	5-7 cm (2-2 3/4")	90-200 ml	3.5-5.0 cm (1 1/2-2")	3.5-5.5 cm (1 1/2-2 1/4")	3-6 gms			
60	6-9 cm (2 1/2-3 1/2")	200-450 ml	6-7.5 cm (2 1/2-3")	6-8 cm (2 1/2-3 1/4") (mouse size)	8-30 gms (1/4-1 oz.)			Claw buds and small scrotum recognizable, palate and sternum closed, placenta attached and lens-sized cotyledons present.
70	7-10 cm (2 3/4-4")	350-650 ml		7-10 cm (2 3/4-4")	25-100 gm (1-3 1/2 oz.)	0.5-0.75 cm (1/5-1/3")		
80	9-12 cm (3 1/2-4 3/4")	500-800 ml		8-13 cm (3 1/4-5 1/4")	120-200 gms (4-6 1/2 oz.)	0.5-1.0 cm (1/5-2/5")		
90	10-13 cm (4-5")	750-1400 ml		13-17 cm (5-6 1/2") (rat size)	*200-400 gm (6-13 oz.)	1-1.5 cm (2/5-3/5") (size of dime)	0.3-0.5 cm (1/8-1/5")	Hair on lips, chin and eyelids, scrotum present.
120	12.5-18 cm (5-7")	2000-3500 ml		22-32 cm (8 1/2-12 1/2") (small cat size)	1000-2000 gm (2-4 lbs.)	1.5-2.5 cm (3/5-1") (size of quarter)	0.5-0.8 cm (1/5-1/3")	Fine hair on eyebrows, claws developed and yellow-colored, epithelial plaques present on amnion, horn pits present.
150	18-23 cm (7-9")	4000-5000 ml		30-45 cm (12-17 1/2") (large cat size)	3000-4000 gm (6 1/2-10 lbs.)	2.5-4 cm (1-1 1/2") (size of 1/2 dollar)	0.6-1.0 cm (1/4-2/5")	Hair on eyebrows and lips, testes in the scrotum, teats developing.
180		4000-7500 ml		40-60 cm (15 1/2-24")	5-10 Kg. (11-22 lbs.)	4-5 cm (1 1/2-2")	0.9-1.25 cm (3/8-1/2")	Hair on inside of ear and around the horn pits, tip of tail and muzzle.
210		6300-10,000 ml		55-75 cm (22-30")	8-18 Kg. (17.5-40 lbs.)	5-7.5 cm (2-3")	1.25-1.5 cm (1/2-3/5")	Hair on metatarsal, metacarpal and phalangeal region of extremities and beginning on the back, long hair on tip of tail.
240		8000-12,000 ml		60-85 cm (24-34")	15-25 Kg. (33-55 lbs.)	6-9 cm (2 1/2-3 1/2")	1.25-1.7 cm (1/2-2/3")	Fine short hair all over the body. Incisor teeth not erupted.
270		12,000-20,000 ml		70-100 cm (28-40")	20-50 Kg. (44-110 lbs.)	8-12 cm (3 1/4-4 3/4")	1.5-1.9 cm (3/5-3/4")	Hair coat complete and long, fetus large, incisor teeth erupted.

*Richter & Goetze, Vitums, Swett, Matthews and Fohrman, Gier and Marion, Zemjanis, Arthur, Winters, Green and Comstock. These are all approximate figures as there is much individual variation especially between heifers and cows.

through the fingers so that the connective tissue band and allantoic vessels on the lesser curvature of the uterus which are three to four times thicker than the chorio-allantoic membrane could be palpated. Excessive or rough pinching of the uterus particularly over the amniotic vesicle is to be avoided, to prevent damage to the embryo or fetus. This technique of slipping the membranes is especially valuable in the differential diagnosis of pregnancy from uterine diseases characterized by fluids causing uterine distention, such as pyometra or mucometra.

Location of the pregnant uterus The uterus in heifers usually is located in the pelvic cavity until the third to fourth month of pregnancy. In older cows, since the uterus in the nonpregnant state lies on or over the brim of the pelvis, the pregnant uterus is found in the abdominal cavity as early as at the time of conception to the second to third month of pregnancy. In all ages of cattle the uterus lies on the floor of the abdominal cavity after the fourth month of pregnancy. In uteri that hang forward in the abdominal cavity the allantoic fluid tends to gravitate to the apices or pendant portions of the uterus frequently out of reach of the operator unless he retracts the uterus into or towards the pelvic cavity. In heifers or young cows 2 to 3 months pregnant, the uterus often lies in the pelvic cavity and the horn containing the fetus exhibits a typical dorsal bulging or terracing because of its location. By the fifth to sixth month of pregnancy the uterus is drawn well-forward and downward in the abdominal cavity so that in some cases only the cervix and uterine vessels can be palpated per rectum. By the sixth to seventh month the fetus becomes large enough so that it can again be palpated on rectal examination in nearly all cows: and by the eighth or ninth month the fetus may, in a few cows, actually extend caudally so that the nose and feet are resting in the pelvic cavity. As the uterus drops forward into the abdominal cavity during pregnancy the mesometrium stretches and thickens and the ovaries are also drawn ventrally and cranially. The ovaries can usually be palpated through the fourth month of gestation and occasionally during the fifth month. During the latter month the ovary on the side of the uterine horn containing the fetus is usually drawn out of reach of the hand in the rectum.

Fetal size and characteristics at various stages of pregnancy:

The statistics of bovine fetal, length, and weight have been recorded by Winters, Green and Comstock, Arthur, Swett et al., Nichols, Gilmore, and Richter and Gotze. The average figures and records given by these workers are noted in Table 3. The author estimates that the fetus may be palpated per rectum in over 95 per cent of cows at 3 to 4 months of gestation, about 40 to 70 per cent of cows at 5 and 6 months of gestation, about 80 per cent of cows at 7 months and about 95 per cent or more of the cows at 8 to 9 months of gestation. Palpation of the fetus before 60 to 70 days of gestation is not possible because of the tense, distended amniotic vesicle and the small size of the fetus. The larger and deeper the abdomen of the cow and the longer the mesometrium the greater the difficulty in palpating the fetus per rectum during midgestation. Thus in heifers the fetus can often be palpated per rectum the entire gestation period. If the fetus cannot be felt, pregnancy diagnosis is based on the position of the uterus, the size of the uterine arteries, the palpation of the placentomes and the slipping of the fetal membranes. After the sixth month of pregnancy one can elicit or cause fetal movements by pinching the claws, grasping and pulling a fetal leg, pinching the eyballs, or grasping the nose of the fetus either through the rectal or vaginal wall. The latter is possible only during the last month or so of pregnancy. If the bovine fetus can be secured and measured an approximation of its age, especially up to 6 months of age, since thereafter there is too much variation in breeds, may be obtained by doubling the crown-rump length in inches and taking the square root of the result which is equal to the months of gestation, Ball.

The fetal electrocardiogram is an accurate means of diagnosing pregnancy, even twins, the last trimester of gestation in the cow. The fetal heart rate at 6 months of gestation is 150, at 7 months is 140, and at 9 months is 120 beats per minute, Lindahl et al..

Palpation of placentomes Although the placentomes are forming by 60 to 70 days of pregnancy, they seldom can be palpated as definite structures until 75 to 80 days. At this time they can be palpated in the uterine wall at the level of the intercornual ligaments of the horn containing the fetus as ovoid thickened areas. They increase in size as the fetus develops. (See Table 3). In general the placentomes in the middle of the horn containing the fetus and nearest the attachment of the middle uterine artery are larger than those placentomes in the cervical or apical end of the horn or in the opposite horn. Thus the largest placentomes from the fifth month of pregnancy to term are usually out of reach of the rectal hand.

The development of the middle uterine artery is closely associated with the development of the fetus and the duration of pregnancy. As gestation advances, the blood supply to the uterus increases. The artery supplying the largest amount of blood to the uterus is the middle uterine artery. Palpation of changes that occur in the size of this artery and the character of its pulse are of diagnostic value. The middle uterine artery arises from the internal iliac artery close to its origin at the aorta. In the nonpregnant cow it curves caudally in the broad ligament over the dorsal part of the shaft of the ilium into the pelvic cavity and then downward and forward over the pelvic brim to enter the concave aspect of the uterine horn near its center. As pregnancy progresses the artery is pulled more cranially as the uterus drops forward in the abdominal cavity until in the latter half of pregnancy it may be located 5 to 10 cm, 2 to 4 inches, cranial to the shaft of the ileum. One should not confuse the internal iliac artery which is securely fastened by fascia to the shaft of the ileum with the middle uterine artery in the broad ligament which is movable for a distance of 10 to 15 cm, 4 to 6 inches. In heifers a change in the size of this artery to the horn containing the fetus may be noted as early as 60 to 75 days of pregnancy, when it may be 0.15 to 0.3 cm, 1/16 to 1/8 inch, in diameter. In older cows the change in size of the middle uterine artery to the horn containing the fetus can be noted at 90 days, when the artery is about 0.3 to 0.45 cm, 1/8 to 3/16 inch, in diameter. The approximate size of the artery at different stages of gestation are noted in Table 1. The middle uterine artery to the horn not containing the fetus also enlarges but the changes are not so great as those in the artery to the other horn and they occur later. With this change in size of the artery the arterial wall becomes thinner, so that instead of feeling a pulsation in the artery a characteristic "whirr," "thrill" or fremitus is felt. This is first recognized at about 80 to 120 days of pregnancy, but the time may be variable. By the fourth to fifth month of pregnancy it is always palpable. If the uterine artery is pressed too tightly this fremitus may stop, so that only a pulsation is felt. In advanced pregnancy this artery, when palpated lightly, feels much like a stream of water surging intermittently through a thin rubber hose. Aneurysms producing localized fremitus of the uterine artery in the cow are rare. This change in size and character of the pulse in the middle uterine artery especially to the horn containing the fetus is helpful in diagnosing pregnancy about the fifth and sixth months, when the uterus is forward in the abdominal cavity and the fetus cannot be palpated. It is of value and aid in determining the stage of pregnancy. If both uterine arteries are equally enlarged, twin bicornual pregnancy should be suspected. The characteristic fremitus of the pulse is often of value in determining whether or not a normal pregnancy with a viable fetus is present. In advanced pregnancy an increase in the size of other uterine arteries, such as the posterior uterine, occurs.

The horn of the pregnant bovine uterus not containing the fetus may vary greatly in size. In most bovine pregnancies a portion or usually all of the nongravid horn takes part in the placental attachments. There is a progressive enlargement of the nongravid horn, the uterine artery, and placentomes but they never reach the size of the gravid horn. In possibly 10 to 20 per cent of cows, some or most of the caruncles and cotyledons in the nongravid horn fail to develop normally or may be absent, in which case this horn is smaller than normal or is nonfunctional. As a result an excessive burden maybe placed on the gravid horn, with an hypertrophy of the placentomes causing them to become 15 cm, 6 inches, in diameter in some cases.

Examination of the ovaries. Zemjanis and Carroll recommend grasping the ovary gently between the first and second fingers and palpating the unattached surface with the thumb. The ovary following ovulation develops a corpus luteum in the ruptured follicle. If fertilization and development of the ovum and embryo proceed normally this corpus luteum persists throughout pregnancy in the cow. The corpus luteum of pregnancy or corpus luteum verum is slightly larger 2.46 cm in diameter and 6.5 gms in weight than the corpus luteum of the estrual cycle 2.3 cm and 5.7 gms, respectively. These small differences are of no diagnostic value, Edwards. However, as pregnancy progresses the corpus luteum tends to develop a darker golden-brown color and its projection above the surface of the ovary is less prominent due to a heavy layer of epithelium and stroma that covers it. It remains essentially the same size until near parturition.

Records on large numbers of cows indicate that the right ovary is more active than the left. Asdell, Neilsen, Erdheim and others have reported that 60 per cent of the ovulations were on the right ovary and 60 per cent of the fetuses were in the right horn in dairy cattle. Erdheim reported that in pregnant beef cows the number of fetuses occupying each horn was nearly equal. The reason for this difference between dairy and beef cows has not been explained.

With few exceptions the corpus luteum of pregnancy is on the ovary corresponding with the horn of the uterus containing the fetus. According to Perkins, Olds and Seath, less than 2 per cent of the corpora lutea of pregnancy were in the ovary opposite the horn containing the fetus. Erdheim reported only one such case in 3,824 pregnant cattle. Arthur reported such an occurrence in 1 out of 100 cases. Belling reported an incidence of 0.52 per cent. The author and Settergren have observed this condition in about 1 in 3000 to 4000 pregnant cows, 0.03 percent. Woelffer recorded 9 cows in early pregnancy where the corpus luteum was on the opposite ovary and four of these aborted prior to midgestation. Abortions in this condition may be due to the local effect of the luteolytic substance from the endometrium of the nongravid horn on the adjacent corpus luteum resulting in its involution. Thus more than 99 per cent of cows have the corpus luteum of pregnancy on the ovary corresponding to the horn containing the fetus. The possible reasons for the presence of the corpus luteum being on the ovary opposite the horn containing the fetus might include: (1) External migration of the ovum across the peritoneal cavity. This is highly unlikely. (2) Internal or transuterine migration of the early embryo through the uterine body. (3) Regression of the corpus luteum of pregnancy and the development of another corpus luteum on the opposite ovary. This was observed in one case by Morrow and the author in the first trimester of pregnancy. (4) Bilateral double ovulation with death of one ovum and regression of the opposite corpus luteum; or (5) Possibly a single ovulation with development of identical bicornual twins and the subsequent death of one twin.

If a rectal examination of a cow 18 to 24 days after service reveals a normal corpus luteum on one ovary and no signs of estrum, the examiner can be reasonably sure that conception has taken place. Ludwick and Rader noted that ovaries and corpora lutea of pregnant cows remained similar and constant in size upon examination at 8 to 18 days and 23 to 30 days after service. These early diagnoses are about 80 to 90 per cent accurate. This can be confirmed on re-examination at 40 to 50 days by the presence of the corpus luteum in the site on the same ovary with typical changes occurring in the gravid uterine horn. The removal of the bovine corpus luteum of pregnancy the first 5 months of gestation will invariably result in abortion.

Vaginal changes during pregnancy as determined by examination with a speculum and light or manually may be of some diagnostic value but are of only secondary importance to the uterine changes. During pregnancy the vagina usually develops a pale, dry, sticky mucous membrane similar to that observed in diestrum. The external os of the cervix is closed and pale. In about 60 to 70 per cent of the cows the cervical seal which forms after conception increases in size until it protrudes or covers the external os and is visible and palpable between 40 to 120 days of pregnancy. In the rest of the cattle it is present in the cervical canal but does not become visible. The seal is a translucent, whitish mucus that is very tough, adhesive, and tenacious. This seal may remain after the fetus has died in such diseases as mummification of the fetus and trichomoniasis with fetal maceration. Occasionally there may be a normal pregnancy with a cervicitis of the external os and a purulent vaginitis. In such an instance, the cervical canal and internal os have a normal cervical seal present. There is in rare cases a condition characterized by a cervical seal of large proportions called mucocervix. This is characterized by a cervix with a diameter of 7.5 to 10 cm, 3 to 4 inches, filled with a tenacious mucus and accompanied by a persistent corpus luteum or cyst and failure of estrum. Just prior to parturition and abortion the cervical seal breaks down and is discharged in strings. The vaginal mucous membrane becomes more moist and hyperemic, and the cervix relaxes and dilates. Thus a vaginal examination is of value in diagnosing impending abortion or parturition. Passing a catheter or insemination pipette through the sealed cervix in a pregnant cow may introduce infection into the uterus and cause the death of the fetus and subsequent abortion. In advanced pregnancy a manual examination of the vagina frequently reveals the presence of a portion of the uterus and fetus in the pelvic cavity dorsal or lateral to the vagina. The cervix is pulled forward by the weight of the gravid uterus, causing a lengthening of the vaginal cavity.

Biologic and chemical tests for the diagnosis of pregnancy in the cow have been reported but are not as accurate as the rectal diagnosis of pregnancy by a competent veterinarian. Because of the very low levels of hormones, such as progesterone, estrogens and gonadotropes, produced during pregnancy in the cow no practical, diagnostic, biologic, hormonal test for pregnancy has been reported. Scott-Blair and Glover reported that by testing the consistency or flow elasticity of cervical mucus with a "consistometer," pregnancy diagnosis was 80 to 90 per cent accurate from 5 to 6 weeks to term. Pathology of the external os of the cervix interfered with the test. Smears of cervical mucus during estrum when dried produce long fern-like crystals due to the sodium chloride present in the cervical mucus in this estrogenic stage of the estrous cycle. This crystalline pattern is lacking in cervical mucus smears made during the luteal phase of the cycle or during pregnancy. A direct test for the presence of sodium chloride in cervical mucus has also been described, McSweeney and Sbarra. Tavenner and Green described a possible diagnostic test for pregnancy by placing a balloon filled with air into the bovine vagina and administering oxytocin intravenously. In pregnant cows, cows in estrum, and cows with cystic ovaries, the vaginal walls contracted on the balloon and this could be recorded by a manometer. Nonpregnant cows showed little or no pressure changes. By using these tests singly or in combination an 80 to 90 per cent accuracy in diagnosing bovine pregnancy could be obtained, Ghannam and Sorensen. Thus these tests lacked the accuracy and ease of application of the manual rectal method of pregnancy diagnosis.

Differential Diagnosis in Pregnancy Examinations

Anatomically there is no reason for confusing a pregnant uterus with such structures as the **bladder,** the pendulous **left kidney** or the **rumen.** Careful rectal examination, consideration of the anatomical structure and relationships of these organs and their consistency, will prevent erroneous diagnoses.

Tumors may be confused with pregnancy in the cow if a careful examination is not performed. The tumors most commonly confused with pregnancy are lymphocytoma, granulosa cell tumor of the ovary, and fat necrosis in the mesentery, Ribelin and Deeds. Other tumors of the uterus or genital tract of the cow such as leiomyomas and fibromas that might be confused with pregnancy are rare.

Mummification of the bovine fetus characterized by the death of the fetus from 3 to 8 months of gestation, failure of abortion, absence of estrum or parturition, absorption of the fetal and placental fluids, contraction and thickening of the uterine walls, resorbtion of the placentomes, and the presence of the hard, firm fetus in the closely applied uterine horn lying deep in the abdominal cavity may be confused with pregnancy. The history of apparent conception but failure of udder development, failure of increase in the size of abdomen or fetus, and failure of parturition should cause the examiner to suspect the presence of this condition. On rectal examination the uterus is usually drawn forward into the abdominal cavity and may require caudal traction on the cervix or lifting of the abdominal wall to bring it within reach of the rectal hand. In mummification of the fetus there are no placentomes or fetal fluids. A thick uterine wall is tightly contracted around a hard, firm fetus, with an absence of the typical "whirring" or fremitus in the uterine artery. If palpable the ovary on the horn containing the fetus has a corpus luteum of pregnancy.

Pyometra or accumulation of pus, from 200 to 20,000 ml in amount, in the uterus is characterized by failure of estrum and may be confused with pregnancy. Pyometra may occur either postpartum or post-service. In most cases pyometra follows a retained placenta and postpartum metritis, in which case there is frequently an intermittent discharge of pus from the vagina. In trichomoniasis or other infections early pregnancy may occur and the fetus may be destroyed by the organisms. The fetus and fetal membranes then macerate with pyometra resulting. In these cases the cervical seal may remain in the cervix for long periods. In pyometra the uterine walls are usually thick and heavy and lack tone. The fluid in the uterus may be watery, syrup-like or viscous. The uterine horns are usually unequal in size as in pregnancy. The pus tends to gravitate and collect in the pendant portion of the horns and there is no dorsal bulging of the horn as is often palpated during early pregnancy. The fetus or placentomes cannot be palpated and the fetal membranes cannot be slipped. The uterine arteries are usually contracted and do not "whirr." If the diagnosis is uncertain, reexamination in one to two months is indicated. In normal pregnancy progressive development of the fetus and uterus occurs, whereas in pyometra the condition remains essentially the same. As in mummification of the fetus the corpus luteum remains in the ovary.

Maceration of the fetus exhibits symptoms similar to those of pyometra with the exception that death of the fetus after the fourth month of pregnancy results in the presence of fetal bones in the uterus causing crepitation when palpated.

Mucometra or hydrometra may occur secondarily to an imperforate hymen, in the defective horn of a cow with uterus unicornis, in other anomalies of the development of uterus, cervix, or vagina, segmental aplasia, and in long-standing cases of cystic ovaries causing a cystic degeneration of the uterine wall. This condition is variable in its manifestation. Anomalies of the development of the paramesonephric or Mullerian duct system may not be characterized by failure of estrum, whereas in cystic ovaries failure of estrum is common. The mucus varies in consistency from a thin, watery secretion seen in cystic degeneration of the uterine wall, to a heavy mucus secretion in heifers with imperforate hymens, to a gummy and inspissated type of mucus that might be confused with a mummified fetus in certain defects including segmental aplasia of the uterine horn. The uterine wall in most of these conditions is fairly thin but in cystic degeneration of the uterine wall it may be so extremely thin that it is difficult to palpate. These conditions differ from pregnancy based on the history; and on rectal examination by a failure to "slip" or feel fetal membranes, by the absence of the fetus and placentomes, lack of fremitus or "whirring" or increase in size of the uterine artery, and a failure of the progressive development of the uterus as in a normal pregnancy.

Embryonic or early fetal death with abortion or possible absorption. Death of the embryo or fetus prior to 70 to 90 days of gestation may be followed by immediate abortion or not uncommonly delayed abortion as described by Ball and Carroll, Zemjanis and others. In early pregnancy the fetal membranes may continue to grow and develop for several weeks after fetal death before showing degenerative changes. Thus a positive diagnosis of fetal death and absorption can only be made late in the absorbtive process when the signs of pregnancy do not correspond with the breeding history, a diminished amount of fetal fluids are in the uterus, the membranes feel collapsed and wrinkled upon slipping between the fingers and thumb, the amniotic vesicle may be atonic and flaccid or be absent, and the uterine wall is thick and somewhat contracted. These cases when detected or suspected should be brought to the attention of the owner sc that he can watch the cow closely for a recurrence of the estrous cycle or if this is not observed the cow can be reexamined two to four weeks later. Probably in most of these cases, expulsion or abortion of the degenerated partially macerated embryo and its membranes occurs and is unobserved.

Careful rectal examination may reveal abnormalities or pathology of the pregnant uterus and fetus in such conditions as hydrops amnii and allantois, fetal monsters, twins, torsion of the uterus, adhesions of the pregnant uterus to other abdominal structures, rupture of the uterus with an extra-uterine fetus, metritis characterized by lack of tone of the uterus and gaseous crepitation within the uterus that occasionally precedes bacterial abortion.

The diagnosis of twins may be based on the findings of equal enlargement of both uterine horns or uterine arteries, the presence of two amniotic vesicles, or the presence of two fetuses—usually one in each horn, but occasionally two in one horn. In most cases there are two corpora lutea, usually one on each ovary, as bicornual twins are by far more common than unicornual twins. Dizygotic bovine twins are much more common than monozygotic twins.

There is ample evidence to indicate that in the cow the right ovary is more active than the left, as shown by reports of Fincher, Erdheim, Arthur, Belling and others on the incidence of right- and left-horn pregnancies in cattle, Garm and the author's observations on the incidence of cysts in cystic ovaries, and Moberg's work on the incidence of disease of the oviduct. These reports indicate that about 60 per cent of pregnancies occur in the right horn and 40 per cent in the left horn. Erdheim pointed out that in beef cattle these percentages are more nearly equal.

If pregnancy examinations are done carefully and gently no harmful results such as abortions should occur. The dangers of early pregnancy diagnosis from 28 to 45 days of gestation have been previously discussed. Excessive manipulation or pressure on the ovary is not necessary and may be dangerous, as some corpora lutea enucleate rather easily. Some persons indicate or believe that even careful pregnancy examination by an experienced operator may result in abortion or mummification of the fetus. There is no foundation for these beliefs or statements, as the incidence of abortion following properly conducted rectal examinations should be and is no higher than in cattle not examined, Belling and others. Mummification of the fetus is not caused by examination of the genital organs. It has been the experience of the author and other professors that 30 or more inexperienced students can examine cows from 55 to 60 days of pregnancy to term two to three times a week for several months without abortions resulting.

Pregnancy Diagnosis in the Mare

The external indications of pregnancy in the mare are similar to those in the cow. Following service the mare should be teased regularly by a stallion or an aggressive, or testosterone-primed gelding every one to two days to determine the end of estrum, and especially about 21 and 42 days later to determine if conception has failed to occur. It is not unusual for the pregnant mare to exhibit some or all the symptoms of estrum, especially the first several months of gestation, Caslick, Van Niekerk. The latter reported that under certain circumstances, such as pasturing mares on legume pastures, estrum could occur in over ten percent of pregnant mares. These symptoms usually last for only one or two days. Other mares may show no signs of estrum after breeding and yet have failed to conceive. Since the breeding season for most mares is short, early and accurate pregnancy diagnosis is essential in a good breeding program. Post-estrual bleeding as seen in cattle after estrum does not occur in the mare. Diagnosis of pregnancy in the mare based on an increase in the size of the abdomen is hazardous even though most mares in advanced pregnancy show a marked increase in the size and a characteristic shape of the abdomen. The pregnant mare's abdomen after the fifth to sixth month of pregnancy is usually pear-shaped with the greatest width in the ventral third. In fat mares or mares fed large amounts of roughage the abdomen is large but round with the greatest width in the middle third. The last month of pregnancy the mammary glands begin to enlarge. Distention of the teats with colostrum occurs the last 3 to 4 days of gestation and in most mares "waxing" of the teats due to the expression of colostrum occurs 4 to 48 hours before foaling. This may be absent or in a few mares occur up to ten days before foaling. Edema of the abdomen just anterior to the udder may occur in advanced pregnancy. Relaxation of the pelvic ligaments late in gestation occurs but is not as evident in the mare as in the dairy cow.

Ballottement of the fetus in the mare in advanced pregnancy is difficult due to the thick abdominal wall and because the mare will tense the abdomen. Ballottement in the mare, however, is occasionally possible on either or both sides of the abdomen. Fetal movements may be observed through the abdominal wall the last months of pregnancy especially after the mare has ingested cold water. Prior to parturition the vulva becomes enlarged, flaccid, and edematous. Larks et al. and Kanagawa et al. have reported on the use of the fetal electrocardiogram for the diagnosis of pregnancy in mares from 5 to 6 months of pregnancy to term.

Internal examination for pregnancy in the mare. Before the internal examination for pregnancy in the mare is performed, a good clinical breeding history should be obtained if possible. The foaling and breeding dates, dates of estrum, the frequency and efficiency of teasing before and after breeding, and knowledge of the regularity of the mare in her estrual cycles and past foalings are helpful.

The rectal diagnosis of pregnancy in the mare by an experienced veterinarian is the earliest and most accurate method available. In making a rectal examination in a mare the same equipment, dress, and mode of procedure is used as for examination of the cow, with the following exceptions. Restraint is more essential in mares. Many mares require the application of a nose twitch to control and make them stand quietly and prevent them from kicking the operator. Some veterinarians have the mare's tail forced firmly dorsally and cranially over the sacrum as a form of restraint. Certain excitable mares that object to restraint must be handled gently and quietly if a rectal is to be performed. Often these mares may be examined by having only a foreleg elevated. In rare cases tranquilization or even sedation may be required. If breeding hobbles are used to restrain a mare, kicking is prevented but the hocks may be raised suddenly and injure the operator if he is standing too close to the rear quarters. A mare can be examined in stocks, around a stall partition, or by being backed up to a manger or several bales of hay or straw. If a mare is in stocks, the rear rope or board should be low so that if the mare drops her hind quarters suddenly the examiner's arm will not be injured. It is best to bandage the mare's tail and have it held upward and to one side by an assistant so the long tail hair does not irritate the anus and rectum at the time the arm is inserted and the tail does not become soiled. A bland, nonirritating lubricant should be used on the arm. The rectum of the mare is drier than that of the cow and the operator's arm requires frequent liberal lubrication. The author favors a bucket of soapy water made with a bland soap and applied to the arm with a sponge. **DIAL** (Armour's) liquid soap can be applied frequently to the arm and anus during the rectal examination without causing irritation of the rectum. The peristaltic waves in the mare are stronger than in a cow. The hand and arm should be withdrawn from the rectum when a peristaltic contraction occurs. Trauma to the rectum is more easily produced than in the cow and has more serious and sometimes fatal results because of the mare's increased susceptibility to peritonitis. Rectal examinations should therefore be made with quiet restraint, care, and gentleness. Withholding feed, especially roughage, for 12 to 24 hours definitely aids the examination.

After entering the rectum of the mare and locating the bony pelvis, it is easier to locate one of the ovaries, until with more experience the uterus can be readily found. The distinct fibrous bean-shaped ovary, 4 to 8 cm. long by 3 to 5 cm, in thickness is located about 10 to 20 cm. cranial to the shaft of the ilium and about 5 to 10 cm. below the lumbar vertebrae in the nonpregnant mare or mare in early pregnancy. The operator who uses his right hand can more readily locate the left ovary of the mare and vice versa. After locating one ovary the hand is passed down the utero-ovarian ligament to the uterus. The uterus is cupped in the hand between the fingers and thumb and palpation of the cranial border, ventral, and dorsal portions of the nonpregnant or early pregnant uterine horns, the opposite ligament and the opposite ovary is performed. The nonpregnant completely-involuted uterus is pliable, soft, flat, and rather flaccid, 4 to 7 cm. wide and 2 to 5 cm, thick. In the maiden or young mare the nonpregnant uterus is suspended above the floor of the pelvis and abdomen. In older mares, especially the first month after foaling, the uterus may have dropped more ventrally and be hanging cranial to the pelvis in the abdominal cavity. Dimock advised operators that in circumstances where the uterus was located well-forward and downward in the abdominal cavity, traction on the broad ligament, or bimanual examination, with the other hand in the vagina grasping and exerting traction on the cervix, could be helpful.

Uterine changes during pregnancy. In most mares rectal palpation of the uterus to diagnose pregnancy can be performed by an experienced operator with great accuracy from 30 to 40 days of gestation. Diagnosis usually is easier for the less experienced veterinarian from 40 to 50 days of pregnancy. Pregnancy diagnosis is easier in maiden mares or primigravidae, and barren, nonfoaling mares than in mares conceiving on foal estrum when the uterus has not completely involuted. Highly skilled veterinarians may diagnose pregnancy as early as 17 to 30 days of gestation but great care must be used not to injure the embryo, and the chorionic or blastodermic vesicle, Zemjanis, Van Niekerk, Garbers and others. It is often desirable to reexamine the mare once to twice to make certain embryonic death and resorption did not occur. In the mare as in the cow early embryonic deaths are not uncommon with an incidence of 2 to 10 per cent or greater between early pregnancy diagnosis and 110 days of gestation, Zemjanis, Patterson, Sager, and Britton. Following a survey of 100 equine practetioners, Jackson reported that 5 to 6 per cent of mares abort after having been diagnosed pregnant early in gestation. Van Niekerk reported early embryonic deaths with absorptions or probably abortions from 25 to 30 days of gestation in mares on a low plane of nutrition. "Spurious" conceptions may follow a normal service in a healthy cycling mare in which further estrous cycles, if present, are not exhibited on regular teasing, and on rectal examination at a later date the mare is not pregnant. Some of these are undoubtedly due to early embryonic death and unobserved abortion. Although embryos may die and be aborted promptly, some embryonic sacs or structures may survive the death of the embryo, or the dead structures may lie in the uterus where their fluids are slowly absorbed. It is probable that nearly all of these dead embryos are aborted early or late and not observed because of their small size and very thin membranes that can resemble mucus. In a few instances and most commonly where one of a pair of twin embryos in unipara or several embryos in multipara, die early, the dead embryo and its membranes may under go maceration and absorption without abortion and the normal embryos survive to term.

The thickness of the uterine wall increases slightly in both pregnant and nonpregnant mares from days 10 to 16 after the onset of the estrum. From day 16 to 21 there is a 3-fold increase in thickness in the uterine wall in pregnant mares while in nonpregnant mares the thickness of the uterine wall declines to a low point at the onset of the next estrum. The tone of the uterine wall follows the same pattern, with a definite increase in the tone of the uterine wall of both the pregnant and nonpregnant mares to day 16 followed by a decline in tone in nonpregnant mares to a soft flaccid state about one day before the next estrum. In pregnant mares the uterine tone continues to increase after day 16 with the uterine horn becoming round and tubular about 5 days later, Van Niekerk, and Bain.

Palpation of the chorionic or blastodermic vesicle During pregnancy the uterine horns enlarge. (See Table 4). The earliest this can ordinarily be detected is 20 to 30 days. This enlargement is characterized by a circumscribed **ventral** bulge or distention of the uterine horn just to the right or left of the center or bifurcation of the horns. A dorsal bulging of the horn is not observed until after 40 days of gestation and then is not marked. Rarely the embryo and its membranes may develop more laterally in either horn or in the body of the uterus. The spherical bulge or swelling is caused by the chorionic or blastodermic vesicle in early gestation and later by the oval chorioallantoic vesicle containing the enclosed amniotic sac and embryo, the vitelline or yolk sac and the allantoic sac. From 3 to 6 weeks the vitelline or yolk sac is large and the amniotic cavity around the embryo is small. The allantoic cavity grows rapidly from 5 to 7 weeks of gestation when it contains much fluid, Ewart. This chorionic veiscle at first is slightly oval and then as it enlarges it assumes a more ovoid, tubular or sausage-shaped outline and extends into the body of the uterus about 60 to 90 days of gestation. The uterine wall during this early stage of pregnancy is more tubular in shape, has a more tonic feel to it, and is thinner, especially over the ventral bulge. As in the cow these changes are primarily due to filling of the uterine horn and body with fetal membranes and fluid, imparting the feeling of heavy, water-filled rubber balloon.

By 60 to 70 days the chorioallantoic vesicle is so large it is difficult to delineate its extent and the early tonus is less evident. Although Arthur reported that fetal membranes may be slipped at this time in the mare, it is seldom done because the discrete, localized oval area of the uterus occupied by the conceptus in early pregnancy readily differentiates pregnancy from pyometra or mucometra and the thicker, more tonic, equine rectal wall makes this technique hazardous.

Palpation of the changes in the size of the horn and body containing the fetus has been outlined in Table 4. Since the size of the round and later oval chorionic and chorioallantoic vesicle is closely correlated with the size of the uterine horn, the diagnosis and duration of early pregnancy may be ascertained.

The pregnant uterus in the mare is usually suspended above or on the level of the floor of the pelvis until the third to fourth month of gestation, when it drops enough to rest on the abdominal floor and the ventral surface of

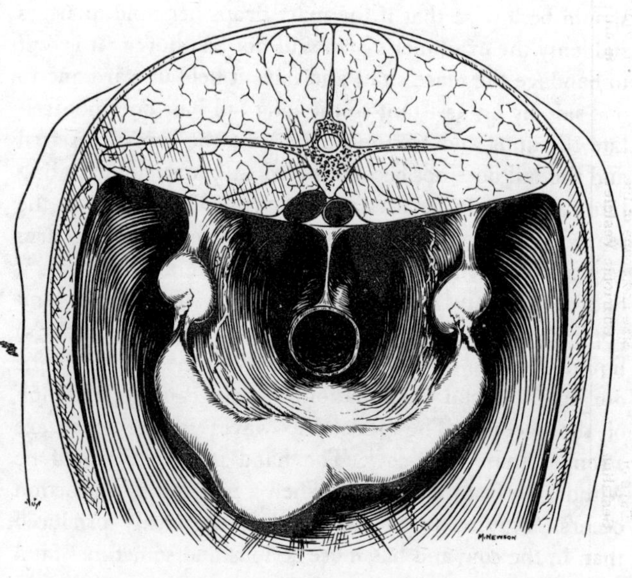

Figure 15. Uterus of a mare, 60 days pregnant.

Table 4. Size and Characteristics of the Equine Fetus and Uterus During Pregnancy*

Days of Gestation	Size and Shape of the Chorionic Vesicle	Amount of Fetal Fluids in ml.	Diameter of the Horn Containing the Fetus	Weight of the Fetus	Length of the Fetus (C-R)	Fetal and Placental Characteristics
16	1.8-2.2 cm (3/4-4/5") Pigeon's egg (round)				0.32 cm	
20	2.6-3.2 cm (1-1 1/4") Bantam's egg (slightly oval)				0.66 cm	
25	3.0-3.8 cm (1 1/4-1 1/2") Pullet's egg (slightly oval)	30-40			0.6-0.85 cm	
30	4.2-4.5 cm (1 1/2-1 3/4") Small hen's egg (oval)	40-50	4 1/2-5 cm (1 3/4-2")	0.2 gm	0.9-1.0 cm	Eye, mouth and limb buds visible, chorionic vesicle present only in the uterine horn.
35	4.4-5.9 cm (1 3/4-2 1/4") Large hen's egg (oval)	60-90	4.5-6.5 cm (2-2 1/2")		1.5 cm	
40	5.7-6.9 cm (2 1/4-2 3/4") Turkey's egg (oval)	100-150	7-8.5 cm (2 3/4-3 1/3")		1.8-2.2 cm	Eyelids and pinnae have appeared.
45	7.6 x 5 cm (3 x 2") Goose's egg	150-200	7.5-9 cm (3-3 1/2")		2.0-3.0 cm	
50	8.9 x 6.3 cm (3 1/2 x 2 1/2") Orange (oval)	200-350	8.3-9.5 cm (3 1/3-3 3/4")		3.0-3.5 cm	
60	13.3 x 8.9 cm (5 1/4 x 3 1/2") Small melon (oval)	300-500	8.9-10 cm (3 1/2-4")	10-20 gms	4-7.5 cm (1 3/4-3")	Lips, nostrils, and beginning development of feet observed, eyelid partially closed. Placenta not attached but beginning to go into the body of uterus.
90	23 x 14 cm (9 x 5 1/2") Small football (oval)	1200-3000	12.5-15 cm (5-6")	100-180 gms (3-6 oz.)	10-14 cm (4-5 3/4")	Villi of placenta present but without firm attachment, mammary nipples and hoofs visible, body and horn of uterus both involved and enlarged.
120		3000-4000		700-1000 gms (1 1/2-2 lbs.)	15-20 cm (6-8")	External genitalia formed but scrotum is empty, placenta attached, ergots and orbital areas prominent.
150		5000-8000		1500-3000 gms (3-6 lbs.)	25-37 cm (10-14 1/2")	May or may not have fine hair on orbital arch and tip of tail, prepuce not yet developed.
180		6000-10,000		3-5 Kg (6.5-12.5 lbs.)	35-60 cm (14-24")	Hair on lips, orbital arch, nose, eyelashes and fine hair on mane.
210		6000-10,000		7-10 Kg (15.4-22 lbs.)	55-70 cm (22-28")	Hair on lips, nose, eyebrow, eyelids, edge of ear, tip of tail, back and mane.
240		6000-12,000		12-18 Kg (26.4-39 lbs.)	60-80 cm (24-32")	Hair on mane and tail, back and distal portion of extremities.
270		8000-12,000		20-27 Kg (44-59.4 lbs.)	80-90 cm (32-36")	Short fine hair over entire body.
300		10,000-20,000		25-40 Kg (55-88 lbs.)	70-130 cm (36-52")	Body completely covered with short hair, prepuce developed, hair in mane and tail increased.
330		10,000-20,000		30-50 Kg (66-125 lbs.)	100-150 cm (40-60")	Complete hair coat and hair coat gets its final color, testes descend.

*Richter and Gotze, Benesch, Arthur, Day, Dimock, Zemjanis, Vitums, Zietzschmann and Krolling, Bergin, Van Niekerk, Cole and Cupps.

the uterus can't be palpated. In older mares it may rest there by the third month. When the uterus lies deep in the abdominal cavity it can be drawn caudally by retraction on the cranial border of the broad ligament. If the mare is more than 3 months pregnant it will be difficult or impossible to pull the uterus back, due to its weight; whereas if the mare is not pregnant the uterus can be drawn back and palpated. By the fifth to sixth month of pregnancy the uterus is well-forward in the abdominal cavity and the broad ligament is under definite tension. The ovary may be 20 to 25 cm., 8 to 10 inches, below the lumbar vertabrae and is moved with difficulty because of the stretching of the mesovarium.

Palpation of the fetus through the rectal wall can usually be performed from 90 to 120 days of gestation when the fetus feels like a small, heavy, submerged but floating object as the hand contacts it. It is usually possible in most mares to palpate the fetus per rectum from the third month throughout the rest of the gestation period. The size and weight of the equine fetus during the various stages of pregnancy are noted in Table 4. In a few deep-bodied mares palpation of the fetus may be difficult from the fifth to seventh month of gestation. In these mares the location of the uterus, the position of the ovaries, and the palpation of the enlarged, whirring uterine artery will aid or confirm a diagnosis of pregnancy. Fetal electrocardiograms may be employed to diagnose pregnancy in mares the last trimester of gestation, Holmes and Darke.

The ovaries of the mare during early pregnancy, differing from the cow, are of no value in determining the uterine horn containing the fetus. A portion of the corpus luteum is only palpable for a few days after ovulation in the region of the ovulation fossa before it is covered by the dense fibrous ovarian tunic. Furthermore although ovulation occurs more commonly, 52 to 63 per cent, in the left ovary, about 60 per cent or more of the fetuses develop in the right horn, Amoroso and Rowlands, Hancock, and Arthur (1946). Apparently the fertilized embryo can undergo intrauterine migration in both directions, Arthur citing Day.

Cole, Howell, and Hart have reported some interesting findings concerning the ovaries of mares during pregnancy. They divided the gestation period into four periods in relation to the changes that occur in the ovaries. The first period, from ovulation to 40 days, was characterized by the presence of a single corpus luteum of pregnancy and a number of various-sized follicles on both ovaries. Van Niekerk and Bain reported great follicular activity between 17 and 30 days after conception and before the secretion of gonadotropin by the endometrial cups. The second period, from 40 to 150 days, was characterized by marked ovarian activity with as many as 10 to 15 follicles over 1 cm. in diameter and the formation of corpora lutea. It was believed that ovulation did occur during this period and Amoroso and Rowlands confirmed this by recovering ova from the oviduct. Usually 3 to 5 or more accessory corpora lutea are present in each ovary. This ovarian activity with follicle and corpora lutea formation is probably produced by the high level of gonadotropic hormones secreted by the uterine endometrium from 40 to 120 days of gestation. The third period, from 150 to 210 days, was characterized by a regression of the corpora lutea, and large follicles were absent. The fourth period, from 210 days to foaling, no corpora lutea or follicles were present. During these latter two periods gestation is maintained by steroid hormones produced in the placenta, Short.

The vaginal examination as an aid in pregnancy diagnosis may be helpful but it is not as accurate as the rectal examination of the uterus. By 30 days of pregnancy the normal equine vagina and cervix, on examination with a speculum, are very white and pale. They are more white and pale than at any time during the estrual cycle and resembles a mare's vagina in anestrus during the winter months. The mucous membrane is very dry, sticky, and gummy. There is less tendency for the vagina to balloon when the speculum is inserted than during the estrual cycle. More of this gummy mucus is present on the mucous membrane of the vagina during pregnancy than during the anestrous period. About 75 per cent of pregnant mares show these characteristic vaginal changes, Dimock. The other pregnant mares may show a more hyperemic or congested mucous membrane with less mucus. In rare cases a vaginitis with a mucopurulent exudate may be seen. The cervix in pregnant mares is usually tightly closed and small with a puckered external os. It is usually pulled downward and to one side. The external os of the cervix usually becomes covered with gummy, sticky mucus. In advanced pregnancy it may be easier to palpate the fetus through the vagina than through the rectum, as the mare objects less to the vaginal examination.

Differential diagnosis in pregnancy examinations should be considered by the inexperienced examiner. From 70 to 110 days a distended bladder may be confused with pregnancy. Pneumovagina or a uterus filled with air might be mistaken for pregnancy. From 90 to 120 days an enlarged or distended right colon or pelvic flexure of the colon might rarely be confused with a pregnant uterus. Pyometra and mucometra associated with focal cystic degeneration of the endometrium are occasionally found in the mare. The uterine wall may be thick and heavy and the fluid contents of the uterus sluggish. Tumors are rare in the mare. Mummification of a single fetus has not been observed in the mare. Fetal maceration is uncommon.

Double ovulation occurs in 18 to 20 per cent of mares and twin pregnancies are quite commonly diagnosed. But the incidence of twin births is low, 1.0 to 1.5 per cent, due to embryonic or fetal death and abortion of possible of one, or more often, both fetuses, Arthur, Osborne. Twin embryos may be detected early by the palpation of two chorioallantoic vesicles or ventral bulges, often with one in each horn. Later, twin fetuses might be palpated and both uterine arteries might be enlarged. Embryonic deaths in mares may be diagnosed at 30 to 45 days by a loss of fluid and tone in the chorioallantoic vesicle. The uterine wall, however, may remain tonic and thick for a considerable period, even though the size of the ventral bulge regresses. Niekerk and others have observed that these affected mares may not return to estrum for 40 to 80 days; possibly because of the absorbing embryo and membranes. Douching the uterus with 500 ml of warm saline, if performed before 45 or 50 days of gestation, usually results in a return to estrus within a few days in these mares. If early embryonic death is suspected, repeated examinations per rectum may be needed to confirm it. Although Wohanka and Bain reported that frequent examination of the pregnant uterus per rectum from 20 to 80 days of gestation in the mare was of minor importance in causing abortion, it behooves veterinarians to perform rectal examinations for pregnancy in a gentle careful manner to prevent injury to the fragile embryo and fetal membranes.

The Biologic Tests for Pregnancy in the Mare

These tests are practical and nearly as accurate as pregnancy diagnosis per rectum. They are indicated in highly nervous or vicious mares and small ponies. Veterinarians not experienced in the techniques of pregnancy diagnosis per rectum frequently employ these tests. The two hormones present at high levels during the equine gestation period that may be used for these biologic tests are gonadotropins and estrogens.

The test most commonly used for detecting the presence of gonadotropic hormones in mare serum is the Ascheim-Zondek, A.Z., or rat test. The immunological test, the Friedman modification of the A.Z. test or rabbit test, the frog or toad test and others are used less commonly. The gonadotropic hormone from the endometrial cups is first found in mare serum from 40 to 42 days of gestation, reaches its maximum between 50 and 80 days and gradually declines and is absent after 150 days. Ten to 20 ml of blood should be drawn from the mare's jugular vein into a sterile tube. After clotting and separation of the serum at room temperature, the serum should be removed and refrigerated. Overheating of the sample should be avoided. This test may be conducted with a good degree of accuracy from 42 to 50 days of pregnancy, a high degree of accuracy from 50 to 80 days, and a good degree of accuracy from 80 to about 100 to 120 days. Tests before 40 days and after 120 days of gestation in the mare may be inaccurate due to a low level of circulating gonadotropins in the blood. This test if conducted properly is usually considered to be about 95 per cent accurate, Cole and Cupps, Santamarina and Joven, and Cowie.

The Ascheim Zondek test requires one or preferable two to three immature female rats about 22 days of age. Two ml of whole fresh blood or serum from the mare to be tested are injected intraperitoneally in the immature rats; 5 ml of serum can be injected subcutaneously, or 0.5 ml of serum can be injected subcutaneously daily for 2 to 4 days. The rats are killed 72 hours later when injected intraperitoneally, and 96 or 120 hours later when injected subcutaneously. A positive test is indicated by finding hemorrhagic spots or corpora hemorrhagica on the ovaries and an edema of the uterine horns causing them to be 2 to 4 times normal size. Vaginal swabs of these rats show many cornified epithelial cells. A negative test is characterized by no definite change in the ovaries or uterus.

A strain of mouse that had proven to be a reliable in this test, could also be used at an age of 22 days but only 0.5 ml of serum was given subcutaneously, Santamarina and Joven. After 48 hours positive mice showed ovarian stimulation and uterine congestion, hyperemia and distention. The Friedman modification of the A.Z. test described by Cowie and Roberts is not commonly performed because of the cost of a rabbit. The basic procedures in this test are similar to the rat test, but the age of the rabbit, the dose of serum injected and the hours postinjection that the rabbit's ovaries are examined will vary.

Many diagnostic laboratories, particularly in the southern U.S. and in Central America, use a wide variety of male frogs and toads, for example: **Bufo valliceps** or **woodhousi, Rana pipiens** or **esculenta,** and etc. to test for the presence of gonadotropes, Cowie, Neto, Creutzberg and others. If a toad or frog is used immediately after capture the cloaca should be aspirated with a pipette containing a little saline and examined for the presence of spermatozoa. If the test animals have been in isolation or with other males for some time this is not necessary. One ml of serum from a mare is injected with a pipette into the dorsal lymph sac of preferredly two male frogs or toads at one hour intervals for three injections. The cloaca is examined for spermatozoa, indicative of a positive test, 1 to 6 or more hours after the last injection. The basis of this test is that sperm cells are emitted only when stimulated by amplexus with a female or by a gonadotropic hormone.

Other recently developed immunologic tests for gonadotropic hormones such as the direct latex agglutination test used for the diagnosis of human pregnancy or the hemagglutination inhibition test are highly accurate and reliable, over 90 per cent, and can be applied to mares, Fink and Frei, Short, Solomon and Hoff,Graham and Kalish, Chak and Bruss, and Jeffcott et al.. The hemagglutination inhibition test utilizes the principle that PMS gonadotropins inhibit the agglutination of horse erythrocytes coated with PMS gonadotropin in the presence of PMS gonadotropin antiserum. This test is sold commerically in the U.S. by the Denver Mfg. Co., Stanford, Conn. for use by veterinarians on mares 40 to 120 days after breeding. Richards, and Wormstrand have described a highly accurate immunological pregnancy test in mares utilizing the gel diffusion method.

The tests for gonadotropic hormone in pregnant mare serum are based on the development of endometrial cups in the region of the junction of the horn containing the embryo and the body of the uterus at about 30 to 40 days of gestation. These endometrial outgrowths are closely invested by the chorioallantois. The endometrial cups enlarge and fill with a mucoprotein secretion very rich in gonadotropic hormone the amount of which parallels levels in the blood, Cole and Cupps and Clegg et al.. At 40, 80 and 150 days of gestation the total gonadotropic activity in the cups and their secretion and in the serum of the mare were 21,000 I.U. and 0.1 to 6.0 I.U./ml, 73,000 I.U. and 6 to 296 I.U./ml, and 42,000 I.U. and less than 0.5 to 106 I.U./ml, respectively. The endometrial cup secretion tends to accumulate in chorioallantoic sacs that become pedunculated. Although most workers believe that the equine gonadotropin is produced by the endometrial cells it is possible that it might be produced by the apocrine glandlike cells of the chorion. The endometrial cups and their associated structures begin to involute at 120 days of gestation and have largely disappeared by 180 days.

Clegg and coworkers (1962) reported that when a mare is carrying a mule fetus the equine gonadotropin concentration of her serum is about one-tenth that associated with a horse fetus, 1 to 20 I.U./ml vs 43 to 211 I.U./ml from 50 to 80 days of gestation. Cole stated that ponies have as much as 8 times the concentration of gonadotropin as the draft breeds. This might be a breed difference or due to a dilution factor. Rowlands showed that mares with twin pregnancy of 52 to 72 days duration usually had over 200 I.U./ml of gonadotropin in their serum compared to over 100 I.U./ml in mares carrying single fetuses. This difference was apparently due to a double set of endometrial cups in mares carrying twins. Ovarian activity was not closely correlated to gonadotrophin levels in the blood. Gonadotropins are not found in the urine of pregnant mares as they are in women.

If the tests for equine gonadotropin are performed by experienced technicians in a good laboratory following a proven technique the results are highly accurate. False negative reactions in test animals may occur due to taking serum from mares at 30 to possibly 45 days and from 100 to 130 days of gestation when the level of serum gonadotropin may be low or absent in some mares. False negative reactions may also be due to overheating of the serum or storage for too long a period at room temperature. If mare serum is to be stored before testing, it should be kept in a refrigerator to 40 C.. False positive reactions in mares may be due to early embryonic deaths and abortion or possible absorption.

Loy, Fallon and the author have observed about 10 or more mares that were diagnosed pregnant at 40 to 45 days of gestation on an examination per rectum but at 55 to 70 days of gestation these mares were nonpregnant based on another rectal examination. However, these mares had a positive A-Z test that lasted for up to 120 to 150 days after conception. Repeated douching of the uterus of these mares, experiencing embryonic or fetal death after 45 to 60 or more days of gestation, in contrast to early embryonic deaths at 20 to 35 days, failed to promote estrus in nearly all cases. Evidence tends to indicate that either the equine gonadotropin is continued to be secreted by the endometrial cups of these aborting mares or mares that resorb their fetuses, or the secretion of these cups is stored in the chorioallantoic pouches or sacs and released slowly, or gonadotropin has a prolonged life in the mare's blood stream. In any case a period of apparent "pseudopregnancy" occurs. Because of these occasional false results when testing for equine gonadotropin most owners rely on rectal examination by a skilled veterinary examiner, if he is available, for the most accurate determination of pregnancy in mares.

The tests used for detecting the presence of estrogenic hormone in the urine of pregnant mares are highly accurate when applied from 120 to 150 days of pregnancy, or preferably from 150 to 290 days of pregnancy, but not accurate when applied from 75 to 120 days of pregnancy. After 250 to 290 days the amount of estrogens in the urine of mares falls as the end of the gestation period approaches, Asdell and Nalbandov. The estrogen is produced by the fetal placenta. By 120 to 150 days of gestation even the inexperienced operator should be able to diagnose pregnancy by rectal examination.

Therefore, these tests for urinary estrogens are not very practical. The urine is collected during micturition or by a catheter.

A chemical test that is fairly simple and requires a minimum of laboratory equipment is the Cuboni test. To 15 ml of urine is added 3 ml of concentrated hydrochloric acid. This is heated in a boiling water bath for 10 minutes and cooled under a tap. Following the addition of 18 ml of benzene the tube is shaken vigorously for at least half a minute and the supernatant solution, mainly benzene, is poured off. To this supernatant fluid is added 3 to 10 ml of concentrated sulfuric acid and this mixture is heated in a water bath at 80° C. for 5 minutes and shaken at intervals during this time. The mixture is then cooled. In pregnant animals, whose urine contains large amounts of estrogen, a dark, oily, green fluorescent color is present in the lower sulfuric acid layer. A negative result is characterized by the absence of this fluorescent color and the sulfuric acid layer is brownish in color. Lyngset has used with accuracy a simple chemical method described by Lunaas for the detection of urinary estrogens that is a refinement of the Cuboni test. This consisted of adding 1 ml of urine to 10 ml of distilled water in a 100 ml flask. Then 15 ml of concentrated sulfuric acid was added. After 3 to 5 minutes the flask was cooled. A strong narrow, 3 to 5 mm flashlight beam was placed close to the flask in a dark room. A positive test was indicated by the presence of a light green fluorescence.

Other tests for the presence of estrogen in the urine of mares are the vaginal cornification, mouse or rat test using ovariectomized female rats or mice, and the phenolsulfonic acid test devised by Mayer. These tests were described by Arthur. This latter author also described the mucin test employing vaginal mucus, which according to Miller and Day was 77 per cent accurate from 20 to 40 days and 94.8 per cent accurate from 70 days to the end of gestation.

Pregnancy Diagnosis in the Ewe

Pregnancy diagnosis in the ewe is based primarily on post-conception clinical observations of changes in the animal similar to those occurring in the cow and mare, such as: service by a male, cessation of estrum, and in advanced pregnancy, increase in size of the abdomen and udder. Williams et al. and Lamond have reported that during gestation up to 20 to 30 per cent of pregnant ewes exhibit an estrous period of about 18 hours' duration one or more times. These periods were most common during early pregnancy but also occurred even in the late stages of gestation. Ovulation apparently does not occur. Lamond stated that 94 per cent of ewes failing to return to estrus by 21 days after service were pregnant but matings must be closely supervised and observations recorded. In the ewe one can occasionally observe fetal movements in advanced pregnancy and ballot the fetus on the right side from 3-1/2 to 4 months of pregnancy to term. Ford and coworkers reported that a radiographic diagnosis of pregnancy can be made in 90 per cent of large ewes from 90 days of gestation to term and in a higher per cent in small ewes from 70 days of gestation to term.

The use of the fetal electrocardiogram as described by Larks and coworkers in horses and cattle has not proven practical for pregnancy diagnosis in sheep. Lindahl and Harper, Lindahl, and Hulet reported that the use of an ultrasonic Doppler instrument by rectal insertion was over 90 per cent accurate in the detection of pregnancy in ewes and goats from 75 to 135 days of gestation. This Doppler instrument detects movements of the fetus and the blood in the heart and large vessels of the fetus. Lamond described a direct method of palpation of the uterus with the fingers through a small abdominal incision in the inguinal region between 5 to 8 weeks of gestation. With proper equipment and assistance this was a practical procedure and had an accuracy of 97 per cent.

About 10 to 20 per cent of the embryos in sheep, especially with double ovulation, will undergo transuterine migration from one horn to the other. Sixty-two per cent of single ovulations in ewes and 56 per cent of multiple ovulation occurred on the right ovary, Casida et al.. According to Zietzschmann and Krolling and Vitums, ovine fetal crown-rump length at various stages of gestation are as follows: 30 days, 1.5 cm.; 60 days, 5.0 cm; 90 days, 15 cm; 120 days, 27 cm; and 150 days, 50 cm.

Pregnancy Diagnosis in the Sow

Clinical observations may be used to diagnose pregnancy in swine as in sheep, cattle and horses. Nalbandov cited Warnick as reporting that 55 per cent of ovulations in sows occurred on the left ovary but due to transuterine migration the numbers of fetuses in each horn were equal. Dhindsa and Dzuik showed that embryonic migration in sows started at 8 days and was completed by 13 days of gestation. As a means of diagnosing pregnancy Huchzermeyer and Plonait described a method of palpation of the enlarged, thin-walled middle uterine artery per rectum the third month of pregnancy in large sows weighing over 325 lbs.. Lunaas, and Cupps et. al. confirmed earlier workers' observations that the pregnant sow excretes high urinary levels of estrone at 4 to 5 weeks, 26 to 30 days, of gestation and at a second peak about 11 to 12 weeks, 75 to 90 days, of gestation. Pregnant sows excreted an average of 25.6 mg. of estrone per 100 ml. of urine, range 5.7 to 73.5, at 26 to 30 days of gestation while nonpregnant sows excreted an average of 1.6 mg./100 ml., range 0.5 to 4.3. Based on farrowings this test was 90.3 per cent accurate.

In recent years a vaginal biopsy from 31 to 90 days of gestation has proven about 94 per cent accurate in pregnancy diagnosis, Busch, Herman, and Walker. A biopsy specimen is taken from the anterior vagina of the sow without restraint at the time of feeding and placed in 10 per cent formalin solution. After sectioning and staining with hematoxylin and eosin the epithelium is examined. Pregnancy is characterized by a thin epithelial layer of up to 2 to 4 rows of cells totalling about 12 to 15 microns in thickness. Sows in diestrum have epithelium of up to 4 to 5 rows of cells thick, and 20 to 24 microns in thickness. Sows in estrum have a greatly thickened vaginal epithelium. This technique could be practical in large well-managed herds.

The fetal crown-rump length of swine fetuses at various stages of gestation is: 30 days, 1.8 to 2.5 cm.; 60 days, 8 to 11 cm.; 90 days, 17 to 23 cm. and at farrowing, 23 to 29 cm., Zietzschmann and Krolling, Vitums, and Ullrey et al..

Pregnancy Diagnosis in the Bitch and Cat

During pregnancy in the bitch there is usually a marked progressive increase in abdominal size from 35 days to term due to the deposition of fat and the increase in size and weight of the uterus. The teats between 35 to 45 days of gestation become enlarged and turgid. After 45 days they soften and become still larger. The mammary glands become enlarged and edematous from 50 to 55 days of pregnancy. Since these changes are even present, but usually less apparent, in nonpregnant bitches following estrum due to the pseudopregnant state, one must be careful in diagnosing pregnancy on the basis of the above signs. Pseudopregnancy in the bitch extends for approximately the same period of time as gestation and is frequently followed by lactation if suckling is allowed. In dogs abdominal distention may also result from ascites, splenic enlargement, abdominal tumors, pyometra, or other causes.

Palpation of the uterus through the abdominal wall is one of the best methods of diagnosing early pregnancy in the bitch. The ease with which this is done will depend on a number of factors such as: the temperament of the dog, size of the dog, the period of gestation, the number of fetuses in the uterus, and the degree of obesity, Arthur. At 18 to 21 days the embryos and their chorioallantoic vesicles produce a series of round swellings about 1.25 cm., 1/2 inch, in diameter in the uterine horns which frequently may be difficult to palpate at this time through the abdominal wall. From 24 to 32 days of pregnancy these round ping-pong ball-like swellings in the uterus are about 2.5 to 4.0 cm., 1 to 1-3/4 inches, in diameter and are usually readily palpable. From 35 to 45 days the swellings increase in size, elongate, lose their tenseness and come to rest on the abdominal floor and in some cases abdominal enlargement is noticeable. At 40 days of gestation these uterine swellings are 5.4 × 8.1 cm. in pregnant Beagle bitches, Evans.

It is easier to palpate the caudal portions of the uterus. Fecal material in the colon should not be confused with pregnancy. From 45 to 55 days of pregnancy the size of the uterine horns and fetuses increase rapidly. The caudal fetuses are about 7.5 cm., 3 inches, long in medium-sized dogs and may be palpated. The horn, since it is greatly distended and elongated, is usually bent in the middle at the liver. The apical portion of the horn is bent caudal and lies lateral and dorsal to the cervical portion of the horn. From 55 to 63 days the size of the fetuses are such that they can readily be detected. Rectal palpation with the finger with the forequarters elevated often is successful if abdominal palpation is difficult. The crown-rump length of the canine fetus at various stages of gestation are: 21 days, 1.0 cm.; 30 days, 1.0–3.0 cm.; 40 days, 5–8 cm.; 50 days, 12–14 cm. and 60 days, 16 to 21 cm, Zietzschmann and Krolling, Vitums. Similar techniques of abdominal palpation may be used in the cat but with greater ease, due to the thin abdominal wall. Biologic tests are not available in the bitch and cat.

Radiography may be a helpful diagnostic aid in the bitch especially late in pregnancy since fetal bones calcify during the last 15 days of gestation. With careful technique and experience the introduction of air, 200 to 800 ml., depending on the size of the dog, into the abdominal cavity producing pneumoperitoneum, may delineate the swellings in the uterus as early as 30 to 35 days of pregnancy. The ultrasonic Doppler instrument has been shown to be useful in dogs to diagnose pregnancy from 32 to 35 days of pregnancy to term, Helper.

General References

Arthur, G. H. (1964) Wright's Veterinary Obstetrics, 3rd Ed. Williams and Wilkins Co., Baltimore.

Fraser, A. F. (1968) Tables of Data on Livestock Reproduction, Edinburgh Univ. Press, Edinburgh.

Richter, J. and Gotze, R. (1960) Tiergeburtshilfe, 2nd Ed. Paul Parey, Berlin and Hamburg, W. Germany.

Williams, W. L. (1943) Diseases of the Genital Organs of Domestic Animals, 3rd Ed., Louella Williams, Upland Rd., Ithaca, N.Y.

Zemjanis, R: (1962) Diagnostic and Therapeutic Techniques in Animal Reproduction, Williams and Wilkins Comp., Baltimore.

Pregnancy Diagnosis in Cattle

Arthur, G. H. (1951) Pregnancy in the Cow with the Corpus Luteum in the Contralateral Ovary, Vet. Rec., **63,** 581.

Arthur, G. H. (1957) Some Notes on the Quantities of Fetal Fluids in Ruminants, Brit. Vet. J. **113,** 17.

Asdell, S. A. (1964) Patterns of Mammalian Reproduction, 2nd Ed., Cornell Univ. Press, Ithaca, N.Y.

Ball, L. (1967) Personal Communication.

Ball, L. and Carroll, E. J. (1963) Induction of Fetal Death in Cattle by Manual Rupture of the Amniotic Vesicle, J.A.V.M.A. **142,** 373.

Barrett, G. R., Casida, L. E. and Lloyd, C. A. (1948) Measuring Breeding Efficiency by Pregnancy Examinations and by Nonreturns, J. Dairy Sci. **31,** 682.

Belling, T. H Jr. (1964) Dairy Herd Reproductive Health Program: Part IV Discussion of Clinical Observations and Treatment, Vet. Med. **59,** 5, 177.

Donald, H. P. (1943) Heat During Pregnancy in Dairy Cows, Vet. Rec. **55,** 297.

Donoho, H. R. and Rickard, H. E. (1955) The Occurrence of Estrus During Pregnancy in Several Holstein Herds, J. Dairy Sci. **38,** 6, 602.

Edwards, M. J. (1962) Weights of Cyclic and Pregnancy Corpora Lutea of Dairy Cows, J. of Reprod. and Fert. **4,** 93.

Erb, R. E. and Morrison, R. A. (1958) Estrus after Conception in a Herd of Holstein Friesian Cattle, J. Dairy Sci. **41,** 2, 267.

Erdheim, M. (1942) The Incidence of Right and Left Horn Pregnancies in Dairy and Beef Cattle, J.A.V.M.A. **100,** 781, 343.

Fincher, M. J. (1942) Methods of Increasing Fertility in Domestic Animals, Transact. of the Amer. Soc. for the Study of Sterility, 1.

Ghannan, S. A. M., and Sorensen, A. M. Jr. (1967) Early Pregnancy Diagnosis in the Bovine, J. Dairy Sci. **50,** 4, 562.

Gier, H. T. and Marion, G. B. (1960) Prenatal Growth Measurements of the Bovine, J. Dairy Sci. **43,** 6, 865.

Gilmore, L. O. (1952) Dairy Cattle Breeding, F. B. Lippincott Co., N.Y.C.

Hawk, H. W., Tyler, W. J. and Casida, L. E. (1955) Effect of Sire and System of Mating on Estimated Embryonic Death Loss, J. Dairy Sci. **38,** 4, 420.

Kanagawa, H., Too, K. and Kawata, K. (1965) Fetal Electrocardiogram in Dairy Cattle. II Diagnosis for Twin Pregnancy, Jap. J. of Vet. Res. **13.** 4, 111.

Kanagawa, H., Too, K., Kawata, K. (1966) Fetal Electrocardiogram in Dairy Cattle. IV Diagnostic Application for Fetal Mummification, Jap. J. Vet. Res. **14,** 3 and 4, 114.

Koger, L. M. (1960) Routine Pregnancy Examination in Beef Cattle Practice, J.A.V.M.A. **136,** 3, 130.

Larks, S. D., Holm, L. W. and Parker, H. R. (1960) A New Technique for the Demonstration of the Fetal Electrocardiogram in the Large Domestic Animal (Cattle, Sheep, Horse), Cor. Vet. **50, 4,** 1959.

Lindahl, I. L., Reynolds, P. J. and Allman, K. E. (1968) Fetal Electrocardiograms in Dairy Cattle, J. An. Sci. **27,** 5, 1412.

Ludwick, T. M. and Rader, E. R. (1958) Diagnosis of Early Pregnancy in Cattle by Ovarian Analysis, J. Dairy Sci. **51,** 1, 74.

McSweeney, K. J. and Sbarra, A. J. (1967) Pregnancy Testing Using Cervical Mucus, Fert. and Steril. **18,** 6, 866.

Morrow, D. (1967) Personal Communication.

Nichols, C. W. (1944) The Embryology of the Calf, Am. J. Vet. Res. **5,** 15, 135.

Nielsen, F. (1949) Sterility in Cattle, Proc. 14th Internat. Vet. Congress, Vol III Section 4 (c), 105.

Perkins, J. R., Olds, D. and Seath, D. M. (1954) A Study of 1000 Bovine Genitalia, J. Dairy Sci. **37,** 10, 1158.

Rahlmann, D. F. and Mead, S. W. (1958) False Heat During Pregnancy, Hoard's Dairyman, Sept. 883.

Ribelin, W. E. and Deeds, F. (1960) Fat Necrosis in Man and Animals, J.A.V.M.A. **136,** 3, 135.

Scott-Blair, G. W. and Glover, F. A. (1957) More Early Pregnancy Tests from Studies of Bovine Cervical Mucus Brit. Vet. Jour. **113,** 417.

Settergren, I. (1970) Personal Communication.

Steere, J. H. (1959) Bovine Gynecology in Denmark, Mod. Vet. Pract. **40,** 22, 32.

Stoll, I. V. (1959) A Practitioner's Approach to Breeding Problems in Cattle, N.A. Vet. **38,** 289.

Swett, N. W., Matthews, C. A. and Fohrman, M. H. (1948) Development of the Fetus in the Dairy Cow, U.S.D.A. Tech. Bull. 964, Washington, D.C.

Studer, E. (1969) Early Pregnancy Diagnosis and Fetal Death, Vet. Med., **64,** 7, 613

Tavenner, H. W. and Green, W. W. (1959) Diagnosis of Bovine Pregnancy by Measuring Vaginal Response to Oxytocin, J. An. Sci. **18,** 3, 865.

Too, K., Kanagawa, H., and Kawata, K. (1965) Fetal Electrocardiogram in Dairy Cattle, I Fundamental Studies, Jap. J. Vet. Res. **13,** 3, 71.

Trimberger, G. W. (1941) Menstruation Frequency and Its Relation to Conception in Dairy Cattle, J. Dairy Sci. **24,** 819

Winters, L. M., Green, W. W. and Comstock, R. E. (1942) The Prenatal Development of the Bovine, Tech. Bull. 151 Agr. Exp. Stat. Univ. of Minn., St. Paul, Minn.

Vitums, A. (1960) Personal Communication.

Wisnicky, W. and Casida, L. E. (1948) A Manual Method for the Diagnosis of Pregnancy in Cattle, J.A.V.M.A. **113,** 451.

Woelffer, E. (1966) Personal Communication

Pregnancy Diagnosis in Mares

Amoroso, E. C. and Rowlands, I. W. (1948) Ovarian Activity in the Pregnant Mare, Nature **161,** 355.

Arthur, G. H. (1958) An Analysis of the Reproductive Function of Mares Based on Postmortem Examination, Vet. Rec. **70,** 682.

Bain, A. M. (1967) The Ovaries of the Mare During Early Pregnancy, Vet. Rec. **80,** 6, 229.

Bain, A. M. (1967) The Manual Diagnosis of Pregnancy in the Thoroughbred Mare, N. Z. Vet. Jour. **15,** 12, 227.

Benesch, F. (1952) Lehrbuch der Tierarztlichen Geburtshilfe and Gynakologie, Urban and Schwarzenberg, Wien-Innsbruck, Austria.

Bergin, W. C., Gier, H. T., Frey, R. A. and Marion, G. B. (1967) Developmental Horizons and Measurements Useful for Age Determination of Equine Embryos and Fetuses, Proc. Amer. Assoc. Equine Pract., New Orleans, La., 179.

Britton, J. W. (1947) Clinical Studies on Early Equine Abortion, Cor. Vet. **37,** 1, 14.

Caslick, E. A. (1937) The Sexual Cycle and Its Relation to Ovulation with Breeding Records of the Thoroughbred Mare, Cor. Vet. **27,** 2, 187.

Chak, R. and Bruss, M. (1968) The M.I.P. Test for the Diagnosis of Pregnancy in Mares, Proc. 14th Ann. Conv. A.A.E.P., Phila., 53.

Clegg, M. T., Boda, J. M., Cole, H. H. (1954) The Endometrial Cups and Allantochorionic Pouches in the Mare with Emphasis on the Source of Equine Gonadotrophin, Endocrin. **54,** 448.

Clegg, M. T., Cole, H. H., Howard, C. B. and Pigon, H. (1962) The Influence of Fetal Genotype on Equine Gonadotrophin Secretion, J. of Endocrin, **25,** 245.

Cole, H. H. (1938) High Gonadotropic Hormone Concentration in Pregnant Ponies, Proc. Soc. Exp. Biol., N.Y., **38,** 193.

Cupps, P. T. (1959) Reproduction in Domestic Animals, Vol I, Academic Press, N.Y.C. and London.

Cowie, A. T. (1948) Pregnancy Diagnosis Tests, A Review, Commonwealth Agricult. Bureaux, Edinburgh.

Creutzberg, F. (1955) Drachigheids—Onderzoek Van Merries Met Behulp Van De Galli-Mainini Test en De Aschheim-Zondek Reactie, Tijdschr v. Diergeneesk. **80,** 20, 1045.

Dimock, W. W. (1947) Early Clinical Examination of Mares for Pregnancy, Ken. Agr. Exp. Stat., Univ. of Ken. Circular 61.

Ewart, J. C. (1897) Critical Period in the Development of the Horse, Adam and Charles Black, London.

Fallon, Edw. (1967) Personal Communication.

Fink, H. and Frie, A. (1966) A Rapid Direct Reading Latex Agglutination Pregnancy Test, Obst. and Gynec. **28,** 5, 660.

Garbers, G. (1967) Personal Communication.

Graham, M. A. and Kalish, P. E. (1966) A Comparison of a New Latex Agglutination Pregnancy Test with an Established Latex Agglutination-Inhibition Test, Tech. Bull of Registry of Med. Techn. **36,** 12, 306.

Hancock, J. L. (1948) Notes on Oestrus, Ovulation and Pregnancy in the Mare, Vet. Rec. **60,** 679.

Holmes, J. R. and Darke, P. G. G. (1968) Fetal Electrocardiography in the Mare, Vet. Rec. **82,** 651.

Jackson, R. S. (1968) Preliminary Report on Survey of Causes of Equine Infertility, A.A.E.P. Newsletter, **2,** 29.

Jeffcott, L. B., Atherton, J. G. and Mingay, J. (1969) Equine Pregnancy Diagnosis, A Comparison of Two Methods for the Detection of Gonadotropin in Serum, Vet. Rec. **84,** 80.

Kanagawa, H., Too, K., Kawata, K., Ogaraski, Y., Sano, S. (1967) Fetal Electrocardiogram at Late Gestational Stages in Horses, Jap. Jour. Vet. Res. **15,** 1, 15.

Larks, S. D., Holm, L. W. and Parkes, H. R. (1960) A New Technique for the Demonstration of the Fetal Electrocardiogram in the Large Domestic Animal, Cor. Vet. **50,** 4, 459.

Lyngset, O. (1965) Pregnancy Diagnosis in the Mare: A Comparison Between the Chemical Methods of Cuboni and Lunaas, Vet. Rec. **77,** 218.

Loy, Robt. (1967) Personal Communication.

Nalbandov, A. V. (1964) Reproductive Physiology, 2nd Ed., W. H. Freeman Co. San Fransisco and London.

Neto, J. F. T. (1949) The Reaction of the Male Toad to Pregnant Mare's Serum and Its Comparative Study with the Cole-Hart Test, Am. J. Vet. Res. **10,** 34, 74.

Osborne, V. E. (1966) An Analysis of the Pattern of Ovulation as it Occurs in the Annual Reproductive Cycle of the Mare in Australia, Austral. Vet. Jour. **42,** 149.

Patterson, A. W. Jr. (1965) Personal Communication.

Richards, C. B. (1967) Simple Immunological Method for the Diagnosis of Pregnancy in Mares, Nature (Longon), **215,** 1280.

Rowlands, I. W. (1949) Serum Gonadotrophin and Ovarian Activity in the Mare, J. of Endocrin. **6,** 184.

Roberts, S. J. (1959) Veterinary Obstetrics and Gential Diseases, 1st Ed. Distributed by Edwards Bros. Inc., Ann Arbor, Mich.

Sager, Floyd (1963) Personal Communication.

Santamarina, E. and Joven, L. L. (1959) Evaluation of the Reliability of a Diagnostic Test for Pregnancy in Mares Based on the Presence of Gonadotrophic Hormones, J.A.V.M.A. **135,** 7, 383.

Santamarina, E. and Joven, L. L. (1960) Factors Influencing the Accuracy of a Gonadotrophin Test for Pregnancy in Mares, J.A.V.M.A. **137,** 9, 522.

Short, R. V. (1965) Recent Advances in Equine Reproductive Physiology, Proc. Brit. Eq. Vet. Assoc.

Solomon, W. J. and Hoff, G. (1969) An Immunologic Pregnancy Test for Mares, J.A.V.M.A. **155,** 1, 42.

VanNiekerk, C. H. (1965) Early Clinical Diagnosis of Pregnancy in Mares, J. S. Afr. Vet. Med. Assoc. **36,** 1, 53.

Van Niekerk, C. H. (1965) Early Embryonic Resorption in Mares, J. S. Afr. Vet. Med. Assoc. **36,** 1, 61.

VanNiekerk, C. H. (1965) The Early Diagnosis of Pregnancy, the

Development of the Fetal Membranes and Nidation in the Mare, J. S. Afr. Vet. Med. Assoc. **36,** 4, 483.

Vitums, Arturs (1960) Personal Communication.

Vitums, A. (1969) Development and Transformation of Aortic Arches in Equine Embryos, Z. Anat. Entwickl.-Gesch. **128,** 243.

Wohanka, K. (1961) Untersuchungen Der Ursachen Des Verfohlens, 4th Internat. Vet. Congr. on An. Reproduction, the Hague.

Wormstrand, A. (1969) Immunological Pregnancy Diagnosis in the Mare, Acta Vet. Scand. **10,** 299.

Zietzschmann, O. and Krolling, O. (1955) Lehrbuch Der Entwicklungs-Geschichte Der Haustiere, Paul Parey, Berlin and Hamburg, Germany.

Zemjanis, R. (1961) Pregnancy Diagnosis in the Mare, J.A.V.M.A. **139,** 5, 543.

Pregnancy Diagnosis in Ewes

Casida, L. E., Woody, C. O. and Pope, A. L. (1966) Inequality in Function of the Right and Left Ovaries and Uterine Horns of the Ewe, J. An. Sci. **25,** 4, 1169.

Ford, E. J. H., Clark, J. W. and Gallup, A. L. (1963) Detection of Fetal Numbers in Sheep by Means of X-rays, Vet. Rec. **75,** 958.

Hulet, C. V. (1969) Pregnancy Diagnosis in the Ewe Using An Ultrasound Doppler Instrument, J. An. Sci. **28,** 1, 44.

Lamond, D. R. (1963) Diagnosis of Early Pregnancy in the Ewe, Austral. Vet. Jour. **38,** 192.

Lindahl, I. L. and Harper, D. (1966) A Pregnancy Tester for Ewes, Farm Jour. October 56 H.

Lindahl, I. L. (1969) Pregnancy Diagnosis in Dairy Goats Using Ultrasonic Doppler Instruments, J. Dairy Sci. **52,** 4, 529.

Williams, S. M., Garrigus, U. S., Norton, H. W. and Nalbandov, A. V. (1959) The Occurrence of Estrus in Pregnant Ewes, J. An. Sci. **15,** 978.

Zeitzschmann, O. and Krolling, O. (See above).

Vitums, A. (See above)

Pregnancy Diagnosis in Sows

Busch, W. (1963) Beitrag Zur Histologischen Diagnose der Trachtigkeit beim Schwein Durch Vaginal Biopsie, Monatshefte fur Veterinarmed.**18,** 813.

Cupps, P. T., Briggs, J. R., Hintz, H. F. and Heitman, H. Jr. (1966) Pregnancy Diagnosis in the Sow, J. An. Sci. **25,** 3, 646.

Dhindsa, D. S. and Dzuik, P. H. (1965) Time of Embryonal Migration in Pigs with One Ovary, J. An. Sci. **24,** 3, 916.

Herman, J. (1966) Pregnancy Diagnosis in Sows by Means of Vaginal Biopsy, Vlaams. Diergeneesk. Tijdschr. **35,** 2, 81.

Huchzermeyer, F. and Plonait, H. (1960) Pregnancy Diagnosis in Swine by Rectal Examination, Tierarztl. Umschau **15,** 399.

Lunaas, T. (1963) The Estrogens of the Sow in Early Pregnancy: Accumulation of Estrone in the Allantoic Fluid, J. of Endocrinol. **26,** 401.

Nalbandov, A. V. (1958) Reproductive Physiology, 1st Ed., W. H. Freeman Co., San Fransisco.

Ullrey, D. E., Sprague, J. I., Becker, D. E., and Miller, E. R. (1965) Growth of the Swine Fetus, J. An. Sci. **24,** 3, 711.

Vitums, Arturs (1960) Personal Communication.

Walker, D. (1967) Diagnosis of Pregnancy in Pigs by Examination of Vaginal Mucosae, Vet. Rec. **81,** 25, 648.

Zietzschmann, O. and Krolling, Oh. (1955) See Above.

Pregnancy Diagnosis in the Bitch

Evans, H. E. (1967) Personal Communication.

Evans, H. E. (1956) A Dog Comes into Being, Gaines Dog Research Progress, Fall 1956, 2.

Vitums, Arturs (1960) Personal Communication.

Zietzschmann, O. and Krolling, O. (1955) (See above).

Helper, L. C. (1970) Diagnosis of Pregnancy in the Bitch with an Ultrasonic Doppler Instrument, J.A.V.M.A. **156,** 1, 60.

Chapter III

GESTATION PERIOD—EMBRYOLOGY, FETAL MEMBRANES AND PLACENTA—TERATOLOGY

The gestation or pregnancy period is the period from fertilization or conception, to parturition or the birth of the young. During this period single cells divide and develop into highly organized individuals. This antenatal period is the least understood and probably one of the most important periods of life. There is a separate and distinct physiology of the fetus and placenta that is beginning to be intensively studied. The mortality rate of the ovum, embryo, or fetus during this period is much gre ter than for any other period of equal length after birth. Because they are usually unrecognized, early deaths of the fertilized ovum, or the small embryo, with resulting resorption or abortion are often considered as sterility or infertility. The expulsion of a dead embryo or fetus that has reached recognizable size is called an abortion. The expulsion of a live fetus is called a birth. Until birth has occurred the viable bovine or equine fetus should not be called a calf or foal. The antenatal bovine individual or fetus, not a "calf," is present in the uterus and may be ballotted through the abdominal or rectal wall. Dead fetuses, not "calves," may be aborted, or expelled at term. Calves are only born alive and the term "born dead" is improper. Through common usage the fetuses expelled dead at parturition in swine are called stillbirths. Those born before the end of the normal gestation period are spoken of as premature calves, foals, pups and etc..

The gestation period can roughly be divided into three parts, based on the size of the individual and the development of its tissues and organs. According to Winters, Green and Comstock these three periods in the gestation period of the cow are: **The period of the ovum or blastula**—This period of about 10 to 12 days in the cow extends from the time of fertilization, that usually occurs within a few hours after ovulation, to the development of the zygote's primitive fetal membranes in the uterus. The size of the ovum in domestic animals, not including the zona pellucida or granulosa cells, is about 120 to 180 microns at the time of fertilization and the shedding of the second polar body. During the period of the ovum, division or cleavage of the fertilized ovum progresses in the region of the ampullary—isthmic junction of the oviduct to the morula stage characterized by the inner and outer cell masses totalling about 16 to 32 cells. The morula enters the uterus on the 3rd day in the sow and 4th to 5th days in the other domestic animals. By 6 to 10 days after fertilization the zona pellucida has fragmented and a blastocyst has formed composed of the embryoblast or inner cell mass and trophoblast or outer cell mass and fluid, probably absorbed from the uterine cavity. By 11 days in the ewe and 12 days in the cow the blastocyst is about 1 and 1.5 mm in diameter, respectively, and elongation of the blastocyst has not occurred. During this period defective ova die and are absorbed. The corpus luteum is developing and producing progesterone, a hormone necessary for the growth and preparation of the endometrium, so a favorable environment for the ovum and embryo will be present in the uterus.

Period of the embryo and organogenesis—This period extends from 12 to 15 days to about 45 days of gestation in the cow, 11 to about 34 days in the ewe and probably about 12 to 55 to 60 days in the horse. During this period the major tissues, organs and systems of the body are formed and changes in body shape occur so that by the end of this period the species of the embryo is readily recognizable. This usually coincides with the development of the eyelids, Sack. Starting at 12 days of gestation in the ewe and 14 days in the cow the trophoblast elongates very rapidly so by 14 days in the ewe and 17 days in the cow it is 10 cm to 30 cm in length, respectively. By 18 to 19 days of gestation in the cow the trophoblast may extend into the opposite horn, Rowson and Moor, Greenstein and Foley, and Marion and Gier. In the sow during this same period, 13 to 17 days, the lengthening of the trophoblast and the migrating and positioning of embryos in the uterus occurs, Dzuik et al.. By 24 days of gestation the trophoblasts in the sow are about 24 cm long, Arthur. In the horse, dog and cat the trophoblast or blastodermic vesicle does not elongate but remains oval during this period causing a localized enlargement in the uterus helpful in early pregnancy diagnosis. In the cow the amnion is completely formed and closed and somites are forming by 20 days of gestation, by 22 days the heart is crudely formed and beating, by 25 days the neural tube is closed and 25 somites are present, the allantois is well developed, anterior limb buds are formed and eye and brain development are well advanced.

In the cow, as in other animals, attachment of the fetal membranes is a gradual process that begins with the formation of the first villi about 30 days of gestation and progresses to a primitive attachment of the chorioallantois to the endometrium in the caruncular areas about 33 to 36 days of gestation, Greenstein and Foley. In the sheep attachment begins at about 17 to 20 days and is well-developed by about 28 to 30 days, Davies and Wimsatt. While in the horse, attachment is delayed until 70 to 90 days when villi develop on the chorion and project into crypts in the endometrium, Bergin et al.. In domestic animals the term attachment is preferred to the term implantation or nidation. Implantation refers to the process in humans and rodents where the zygote erodes, penetrates and implants itself within the endometrium. Up until the time of the well-developed attachment of the chorion to the endometrium the nourishment of the ovum and embryo is provided by the secretion of the uterine glands called "uterine milk," a yellowish or whitish, thick, opaque secretion grossly resembling and occasionally mistaken for a purpulent exudate.

During this period nearly all of the more severe teratologic defects or anomalies of development occur. Also during this period the embryo may die, be expelled unnoticed at the next estrum, or become macerated and absorbed without external signs.

The period of the fetus and fetal growth. This period extends from about 34 days of gestation in the sheep and dog, 45 days in cattle and 55 days in the horse, to parturition. During this period minor details in the differentiation of organs, tissues, and systems occur along with the growth and maturation of the antenatal individual. Changes in the bovine fetus from 70 days to parturition are not radical. During this period caruncles and cotyledons develop and enlarge to supply nutrition to the fetus in the cow and ewe. Bratton and Foote, Bergin et al. and others illustrated the fact that the increase in size of the fetus is a geometric-like curve, with the weight of the bovine and equine fetus increasing very rapidly the last two to three months of gestation. From 210 to 270 days the increase in weight of the bovine fetus is equal to three times the increase from the time of fertilization to 210 days.

The prenatal development of the ovine fetus has been carefully reported by Cloete, and Green and Winters and the bovine fetus by Winters et al. and Swett et al.. Patten has reported extensively on the embryology of swine. Bergin et al. and Evans have provided recent valuable information on embryology in horses and dogs, respectively.

Embryology

Embryology is the study of the physiological development and growth of the antenatal individual. **Teratology** is the division of embryology and pathology dealing with abnormal development and malformations of the antenatal individual. Teratologic studies are of value because they constitute important available records of injury and arrested or pathologic development of the embryo or fetus. These studies explain the nature of some of the teratologic abnormalities in the fetus that frequently result in dystocia as well as other defects of the reproductive and other body systems. The embryology of importance in obstetrics, excluding that relating to the male and female reproductive systems which are discussed in detail elsewhere, is as follows:

The nervous system. The hypophysis or pituitary gland is an important endocrine gland. It is composed of the anterior, intermediate, and posterior lobes. The former and latter are of greatest significance. The posterior lobe arises embryologically as a downward extension of the floor of the diencephalon, a portion of the primitive brain. The deep portion of Rathke's pocket loses its original connection with the stomodeal ectoderm and becomes closely applied to the infundibulum and forms the anterior lobe. Thus the posterior lobe of the hypophysis arises from neural tissue and the anterior lobe from ectodermal tissue. Teratologic defects or arrests in development of the nervous system may result in such conditions as: ankyloses, hydrocephalus, hypoplasia of the cerebellum, cerebral hernia, cyclopia, lack of optic tissue, and persistence of the anterior neuropore with failure of facial bones to fuse or **Schistocephalus bifidus,** Williams.

The digestive system. This system is of little importance in obstetrical studies in animals. Arrested development at the terminal portion of the digestive system may result in atresia ani, or the lack of a rectum, seen usually in the male. Occasionally a common cloaca is observed in the female or atresia ani is made less acute by the rectum emptying its contents into the vulva. Anomalous development of the gut may result in atresia coli. In the mouth region arrested development may result in a cleft palate or persistence of epithelial linings of the pharyngeal pouches, as seen by pharyngeal cysts in dogs.

The circulatory system. The heart, arising from the fusion of the primitive endocardial tubes, develops initially in the neck region caudal to the gill clefts or pharyngeal arches and then descends into and is enclosed by the chest around the fifth to sixth week of gestation in the bovine embryo. If this fails to occur the condition of ectopia cordis results. When the heart descends, the aortic arches descend also and carry with them the laryngeal nerves. The left aortic arch persists and the right aortic arch disappears. In dogs and cattle and rarely in other animals, the right aortic arch persists and the left disappears. In these instances, if the left ductus arteriosus is present, a chronic stenosis of the esophagus occurs as it passes over the base of the heart. It is compressed between the trachea, the aorta, the ligamentum or ductus arteriosus, and the base of the heart.

The fetal venous circulation of blood consists largely of "arterial" blood rich in oxygen and nutrients coming from the placenta into the umbilical vein of the fetus. This vein passes through the umbilicus into the liver of the fetus where it anastomoses with the portal vein. In the liver in most animals including the dog, cow, and sheep there is a direct shunt, called the ductus venosus, from the umbilical vein to the posterior vena cava. The blood that enters the portal veins goes through the liver tissue and into the posterior vena cava by means of hepatic veins. From the posterior vena cava, the blood then enters the right atrium where about 50 per cent of it, according to Dawes, is immediately shunted through foramen ovale into the left atrium. The remainder passes into the right ventricle and is pumped into the pulmonary artery, where again a large portion of the blood is shunted through the short ductus arteriosus into the aorta. A small amount goes through the pulmonary artery into the lungs as only a small blood supply is needed since the lungs are not functional in the fetus. Blood from the lungs is returned to the left atrium by the pulmonary veins. Blood that comes through the foramen ovale is mixed in the left atrium with blood from the pulmonary veins, passes to the left ventricle, and is pumped into the aorta and thence through the arteries to the various organs and tissues of the body. The aorta carries blood caudally to the rear quarters and in the region of the last lumbar vertebrae the two large umbilical arteries arise that carry largely "venous" blood down on either side of the bladder through the umbilicus to the placenta where waste products and carbon dioxide can be exchanged for nutrients and oxygen. More than 50 per cent of the fetal cardiac output goes to the placenta, Dawes. Assali reported that in the fetal lamb at 130 days of gestation 48 per cent of the blood volume was in the placenta; at near term about 26 per cent of the blood volume was in the placenta. The effects of allowing the cord to remain intact for a short time after birth to increase the blood volume in the newborn remains to be scientifically assessed. Hemoglobin values and red blood cell numbers in the fetus are much higher than in the adult. These values rapidly drop to normal after birth. Fetal hemoglobin apparently has a greater affinity for oxygen and releases it more slowly than does hemoglobin in the adult. The fetus has a high heart rate, about twice that of a young animal, greatly promoting a high cardiac output per unit of body weight necessary to compensate for the low oxygen content of the fetal blood, Assali.

According to Franklin et al. and Dawes, marked changes occur in the fetal circulatory system at the time of

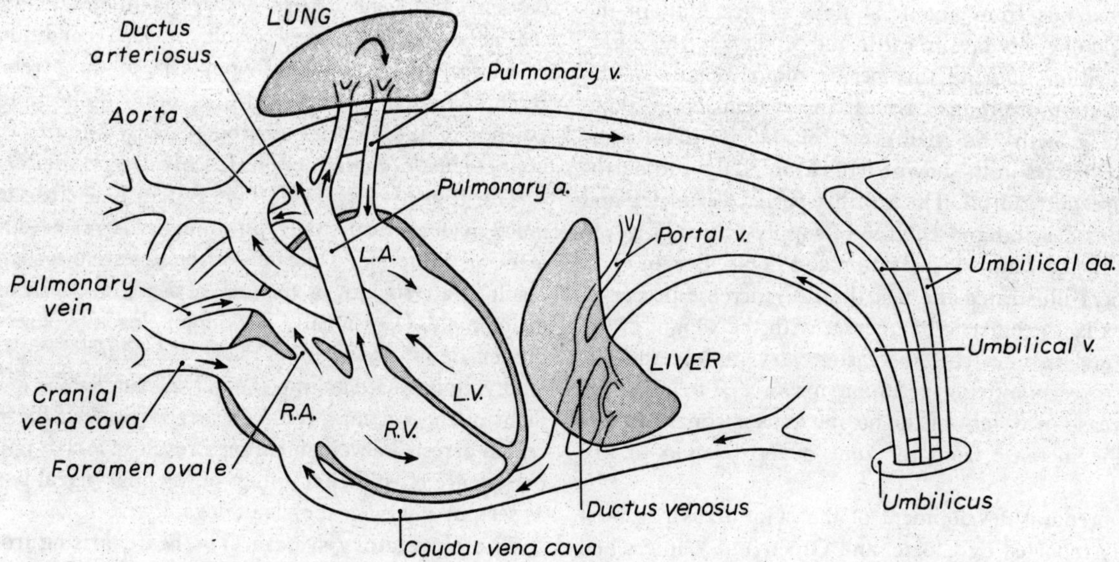

Figure 16. Diagram of fetal blood circulation (arrows indicate the direction of the blood flow).

birth. The umbilical cord ruptures. The umbilical vein present in the umbilical stump apparently closes due to a smooth muscle effect. The remnant of this vessel from the umbilicus to the liver becomes in later life the round ligament of the liver. The ductus venosus is apparently closed by a smooth muscle sphincter within 5 to 30 minutes after separation of the umbilical cord. In later life it becomes the ligamentum venosus in the substance of the liver. The liver then has the entire volume of portal blood going through its lobules instead of about one-third the volume. The foramen ovale closes mechanically within 5 to 20 minutes after birth by the closing of its lumen with the thin fold of tissue lying in close apposition to the foramen. This thin membrane or valve is maintained by an increase in blood pressure in the left atrium over the right. Finally after a year or more a complete septum is formed. The ductus arteriosus is closed by smooth muscle within 4 to 5 minutes after birth. This closure is apparently associated with an increased supply of oxygen in the blood of the newborn. The ductus arteriosus atrophies and eventually becomes the ligamentum arteriosum. The umbilical arteries are stretched at the time the cord is broken and they contract into the abdominal cavity and are closed by smooth muscle contraction. These are similarly affected by an increased oxygen level in the blood. The umbilical arteries later become the round or lateral ligaments of the bladder. Concomitant with these changes after separation of the fetus from the placenta at birth is a marked rise in arterial blood pressure, Assali. Defects in cardiac development are occasionally seen in animals, especially calves, dogs and pigs, where they may be associated with weakness, signs of circulatory failure, and death soon after birth.

The urinary system. This system is formed mainly from mesodermal tissue. The earliest or most primitive urinary or excretory organ in the embryo is the pronephros with two pronephric ducts, one on each side in the body wall dorsal to the peritoneum. This organ soon degenerates, to be succeeded by the mesonephros or Wolffian body. This structure, using the earlier pronephric ducts now called mesonephric or Wolffian ducts opens into the common cloaca. Later in the development of domestic animals the mesonephros, or Wolffian body, degenerates and the metanephros or true kidney develops more caudally as an outpocketing of the mesonephric ducts. These ducts become the ureters, which open into the bladder. This latter structure opens caudally by the urethra into the amniotic cavity and cranially by the urachus into the allantoic cavity. During most of the late development of the fetus, urinary wastes are discharged principally into the allantoic cavity and little passes through the urethra into the amniotic cavity. Occasionally in domestic animals anomalies of the urinary system are observed, with polycystic kidneys or dilations or stenoses of the ureter. In rare cases a horse-shoe kidney, ren arcuatus, in which both kidneys are joined, is observed. This condition is noted more frequently in fetal monsters. The embryology of the genital system of the male and female animals are discussed separately in chapters relating to the anatomy of the genital tract.

The physiology of the fetus is a fascinating study. It has been shown that contractions of the heart and circulation of the blood through the vessels occurs early in the embryonic period. During this period respiratory movements are present, and although they may occur intermittently at first, they become more frequent and occur continually during the period of the fetus. Huggett reported the principal carbohydrate circulating in the ovine, caprine, equine, porcine and bovine fetuses was fructose produced by the placental tissues while in the canine and feline fetuses it was glucose. Fructose did not pass through the placenta into the dam's circulation. The fetus starts swallowing late in the embryonic or early in the fetal period. Undoubtedly large amounts of amniotic fluid are swallowed and absorbed, some of the waste products being stored in the rectum and colon as part of the meconium. This swallowing reflex on the part of the fetus may be associated with maintaining the proper amounts of amniotic fluid. In fetal monsters, where defects of the cranial portion of the fetus or alimentary canal are present, hydrops amnii often occurs. Fetal movements begin early and are more or less continuous in the form of paddling movements of the limbs and moving of the head and neck. If these movements do not occur or are markedly restricted, ankyloses with such abnormalities as wry neck may result.

The Fetal Membranes and Placenta

The fetal or extra-embryonic membranes serve as protection, a means of getting nutrients from the dam to the fetus, in caring for fetal waste products and synthesis of enzymes and hormones. The latter are necessary for the maintenance of pregnancy in most domestic animals. The fetal membranes are discarded at the time of parturition. The fetal membranes consist of the primitive yolk sac, the amnion, the allantois and the trophoblast or chorion which when combined with the allantois forms the chorioallantois. The trophoblast is the most important single tissue of the fetal membranes and placenta as it has functions of absorbing transmitting and handling nutritive and waste products. It has an erosive action on the endometrium mediating the attachment of the blastocyst; and it has a regulating function by being the site of the synthesis of enzymes and hormones. The needs of the embryo and fetus are supplied and cared for as follows: water, oxygen, and nutrients are taken from the maternal structures as the uterus and, after placental attachment has occurred, the maternal blood and carried to the developing embryo and fetus by the yolk sac, the amniotic chorion and the chorioallantois. The first two structures develop early in the life of the embryo of domestic animals and only function a short period of several weeks until the chorioallantois develops. Waste products from the embryo and fetus such as carbon dioxide and urea are eliminated by the same structures. The allantoic cavity stores much waste material from the fetal kidneys. The large intestine and rectum of the fetus store waste products from the digestive tract as meconium. The amnionic cavity may play an early role in the care of some waste products. The fetal fluids permit the growth and movement of the fetus by distending the uterine lumen. Protection of the embryo and fetus is performed principally by the amnion, although the allantois, uterus, and maternal body assist in this function. Heat and immunity to early diseases of the newborn are supplied by the mother's body. These immune bodies in domestic animals are mainly supplied by the colostrum. The fetal membranes and placentae are well-described by Amoroso, Wimsatt, Villee, and Bjorkman.

The **yolk sac** is a primitive structure developing early in the embryonic period from the entoderm and disappearing after a short period of time in ruminants and swine but persisting for 4 to 6 weeks in the horse, Bjorkman, before becoming a remnant in the fetal membranes. Prior to the formation of the amnion, the blastocyst or blastodermic vesicle and then the yolk or vitelline sac perform limited placental functions of providing nutrients and care of waste for the early embryo. The endometrial or uterine glands, under the influence of progesterone from the corpus luteum, produce a secretion called "uterine milk." This contains protein, fat globules, organic and inorganic solids, and possibly other nutrients, Parkes and Amoroso. This uterine secretion is absorbed by the blastocyst and yolk sac for the nutrition of the early embryo and later by the chorioallantois for the early fetus. Its role in middle or late gestation is probably not important.

The **amnion** forms about 13 to 16 days after conception in the sheep and cow, probably about the same time in the horse, and slightly earlier in the pig, dog, and cat. The amnion is an ectodermic vesicle that arises from an outfolding of the chorion, or from a space in the inner cell mass of the blastocyst, as a double-walled sac that completely surrounds the fetus except at the umbilical ring. When this sac is completed it is filled with amniotic fluid suspending the embryo and thus is a mechanical protection to the fetus. Habel indicated there is a thin sheet of smooth muscle in the amnion that contracts producing a tense amniotic vesicle. Amniotic fluid also prevents adhesions between the soft developing tissues of the embryo and the surrounding membranes which might cause malformations. The inner layer of this double-walled sac is the "true amnion" and the outer layer is the "false amnion," amniotic chorion, or portion of the trophoblast or serosa over the true amnion. Until the allantois is formed and the external portion of it fuses with the chorion, the amnionic chorion acts for a very short period, as did the yolk sac, in providing for the transfer of nutrients and for the care of wastes for the embryo.

The amnion during the fetal stage of development is a rather transparent tough membrane. It provides the outer covering of the amniotic portion of the umbilical cord. On the inner surface of the bovine amnion are small, 1/16 to 1/2 inch, irregular-shaped, flat, white, elevated epithelial thickenings, called amniotic plaques. They are most noticeable during the third to seventh months of gestation. The portion of the amnion covering the cord of the bovine fetus is also covered with these amniotic plaques but at this site they are coarse, elongated villi or papillary elevations. They vary widely in number and consist of edematous epithelial cells that sometimes are keratinized. These amniotic proliferations are also found to a lesser degree in horses, sheep and goats but not in swine and carnivores. The etiology or significance of these amniotic plaques is not known. They apparently are not due to infectious agents, either bacterial or viral. There are no inflammatory lesions associated with these plaques, Millar.

The amniotic fluid is clear, colorless, and mucoid in nature. According to Parkes and Amoroso, Arthur, Williams and Wislocki, this fluid is present toward the end of gestation in amounts of 2000 to 8000 ml. with an average of 5000 to 6000 ml. in the cow, 3000 to 7000 ml. in the mare, 400 to 1200 ml. in the goat, 350 to 700 ml. in the ewe, 40 to 200 ml. in the sow, and 8 to 30 ml. in the dog and cat. According to Merkle, amniotic fluid contains the following substances: pepsin, a diastatic ferment, a lipolytic ferment, protein, fructose, fat, and salts. It is bactericidal and prevents adhesions. He recommended concentrated bovine amniotic fluid for the prevention of peritoneal adhesions following abdominal operations in humans.

The source of the amniotic fluid in early to midgestation is probably from the amniotic epithelium and from the fetal urine as the fluid is quite watery. As gestation advances the allantoic fluid increases in volume while the amniotic fluid volume remains fairly static but becomes viscid and glairy because the bladder sphincter prevents the further release of urine into the amniotic cavity. The probable source of the mucoid amniotic fluid is then the saliva and secretions of the nasopharynx of the fetus. The volume of amniotic fluid is probably regulated by swallowing by the fetus, Arthur, Villee, Assali. The normal fetus does not inhale amniotic fluid into the lungs. The amniotic fluid aids parturition because its slippery, mucoid consistency lubricates the fetus and birth canal.

Pathologically, especially in fetal monsters or certain types of fetuses carried overtime, the amounts of amniotic fluids may be greatly increased up to 8 to 10 times. This condition is called hydrops amnii. Another abnormal finding in the cow and sheep is the presence of meconium in the amniotic fluid, causing staining and smearing of the fetus. Davis indicated that this was probably caused by perinatal asphyxia or hypoxia. In rare instances hairballs may be found in the amniotic fluid, especially in prolonged gestations associated with fetal giantism.

The **allantois** arises the second and third week of gestation in bovine fetuses as an outpocketing of the hind gut almost as soon as the hind gut is formed. The allantois consists of entoderm covered by a vascular layer of splanchnopleuric mesoderm. The outer layer of the allantois is eventually richly supplied with blood vessels connected to the aorta of the fetus by the umbilical arteries and to the liver and posterior vena cava by the umbilical vein. As the allantois grows and enlarges it extends between the true and false amnion. The outer layer of the allantois fuses with the trophoblast, false amnion, or serosa to form the chorioallantois. The inner layer, largely devoid of blood vessels, lies against the amnion and invests the allantoic portion of the umbilical cord. The allantoic sac or cavity is filled with allantoic fluid. The allantois is completely formed in the larger domestic animals by 24 to 28 days after conception and extends the entire length of the fetal membranes except the undilated apices of the chorionic or blastodermic vesicle in the sheep, pig, and cow. Because they are not supplied with blood vessels, these undilated apices atrophy and become necrotic and are called the necrotic tips of the chorioallantois. The small amount of allantoic fluid present before the fetal kidneys are active probably comes from the allantoic epithelium or by absorption from the uterine lumen. A precipitation of calcium in the allantois chorion causing white streaks or mottling is commonly observed from 60 to 90 days of gestation in the cow after which time it is removed and disappears as it is deposited in the fetal bones. A similar calcium storage in the allantois chorion has been reported in pigs between 20 and 46 days of gestation, McCance and Widdowson.

The allantoic cavity stores the waste products of the fetal kidneys, which pass to it from the bladder through the umbilical cord by means of the urachus. This fluid is clear, watery, and amber in color and contains albumen, fructose, and urea. In a number of animals such as the sow and sheep the amount of allantoic fluid rises sharply during early pregnancy, rises more slowly around midpregnancy and then rises sharply toward the end of gestation. Wislocki reported that the allantoic fluid in the sow may decline the latter half of gestation. In all animals the amounts of amniotic and allantoic fluids are variable, Wislocki, Arthur, Parkes and Amoros, Richter and Gotze and others. Toward the end of gestation the volume of allantoic fluid varies from 4000 to 15000 ml. averaging about 9500 ml. in the cow, from 8000 to 18,000 ml. in the mare, 500 to 1500 ml. in the sheep and goat, 100 to 200 ml. in the sow, 10 to 50 ml. in the dog, and 3 to 15 ml. in the cat.

Occasionally excessive amounts of allantoic fluid, 40,000 to 160,000 ml. or more, may accumulate in the allantoic cavity. This condition is called hydrops allantois. This excessive fluid has the specific gravity and characteristics of a transudate. The cause is most commonly due to a vascular disturbance in the allantois. There is some evidence that gonadal hormones may influence the amounts of allantoic fluid, Alexander and Williams.

Amorphus, semisolid, amber-colored, soft, pliable, rubber-like, irregular-shaped masses or bodies, thinner at the edges and thicker in the center, 2.5 to 15 cm., 1 to 6 inches, in diameter and from 0.3 to 3.8 cm, 1/8 to 1-1/2 inches, in thickness are commonly found in the allantoic cavity floating in the allantoic fluid of the cow, horse, sheep, goat and pig. These bodies are called hippomanes. In a few cases these masses, resembling fibrin in appearance, have been observed fastened to a fold of the allantois. King and Dickerson et al. described hippomanes as allantoic "calculi" consisting of a central nucleus of desquamated cell debrii upon which were deposited in a concentric manner a denatured mucoprotein complex and minerals, mainly calcium phosphate. This allantoic "calculi" has a higher specific gravity than allantoic fluid and if free-floating will sink to the bottom of the allantoic cavity. Occasionally the allantois will become pathologically thickened and edematous, edema of the allantois chorion.

The **chorioallantois** or **allantois chorion** is formed by the fusion of the outer layer of the vascular allantois and the trophoblast, chorion, or serosa. This structure, richly supplied with blood vessels communicating with the fetus and in intimate contact with the endometrium, is designed to carry on the metabolic interchanges of gases, nutrients, and wastes between the fetal and maternal circulations. It actively begins this function with its formation and grows and develops as required by the needs of the fetus. The allantois chorion is the fetal placenta. Although liquids and gasses may pass through the chorion to the maternal and fetal circulations, solids and most bacteria ordinarily cannot pass unless disease of the chorion allows their penetration. Certain bacteria, viruses and parasitic larvae can pass through the intact placental barrier.

In the cow, pig, and sheep the allantois is attached to the amnion at various points. This divides the allantois into a number of compartments. In the dog, cat, and horse the amnion containing the fetus floats free in the allantoic cavity attached only by the umbilical stalk. In these latter animals the young are more apt to be born covered by the amnion or a portion of it. Unless it is promptly removed, they will smother if it lies over the nostrils and mouth. This rarely happens in the cow, pig, and sheep. The necrotic tips of the chorion, found at the apices of the chorioallantois, are observed in the sheep, cow, and pig, and are usually about 1 to 2.5 cm, 1/2 to 1 inch, long and about 0.3 cm, 1/8 inch, in diameter. In the mare an irregular bare spot in the diffuse placenta of the chorion is found over the internal os of the cervix and is called the "cervical star." Since the allantois chorion and endometrium are in intimate contact for most of the gestation period, disease or abnormalities of either is mirrored on the other. A careful examination of the fetal placenta after parturition will given an accurate index of the health of the uterine endometrium.

The Placenta

The placenta is composed of two parts: the fetal placenta, or allantois chorion, and the maternal placenta or endometrium. For a few weeks in the early embryonic period the yolk sac and amniotic chorion act as primitive placentae. During the first month or more of gestation, the blastocyst becomes attached to the endometrium, and the fetal membranes, including the allantois chorion, develop. At this time the villiform projections of the chorion and the maternal crypts in the endometrium, into which they extend, are rudimentary, small, and friable. During this early period in domestic animals much of the nutrients still are absorbed from the uterine secretions. Not until the end of the first third of gestation do the anatomical attachments of the maternal and fetal placentae become sufficiently intimate and complex to prevent the very easy separation of these two structures. Until this time the fetal membranes and embryo are held in place in the uterus by the accumulation of fluid within the membranes.

That a pregnant animal does not reject her placenta is an apparent biological paradox. With half of the genetic make-up of the fetus and placenta contributed by the sire there should be sufficient tissue incompatability to induce an immune reaction in the dam and subsequent rejection of the conceptus. Wynn postulated that the greater the trophoblastic invasiveness, as in man and rodents, the greater the necrosis of both chorionic and endometrial tissue. This resulted in the development and deposition of a mechanical acellular barrier of acid mucopolysaccharide in those animals such as man and rats having a hemochorial placenta. In the epitheliochorial placentas of the mare, cow, sow, and sheep where the interdigitating microvilli of the chorion or trophoblast and endometrial epithelium are closely apposed, no extensive degeneration or deposition of fibrinoid is present. Therefore in the former an acellular mechanical barrier and in the latter the absence of trophoblastic antigenicity offer reasonable explanations for retention of the placental homograft. The inability of immunologically active maternal cells to penetrate into the fetal circulation may also be important.

Anatomically the placenta of animals may be divided into 4 general types based on their shape; the diffuse, the cotyledonary, the zonary, and the discoidal.

The diffuse type. In the horse and pig the entire surface of the allantois chorion is covered with villi and microvilli that project into crypts or pockets in the endometrium. The entire endometrium and chorion take part in the placentation except over the openings of the uterine glands where the glandular secretion causes a separation of the two structures. These whitish structures are large and abundant in the pig placenta and are called areolae. In the mare the region of the internal os of the cervix is devoid of villi as are occasional bare areas elsewhere due to placental folding. In the sow the apices or paraplacental zone of the placentas that abutt against the adjacent zone of the next placenta are free of villi and as pregnancy progresses the trophblast and allantois in this area disappear and these areas fuse. The placental bed of each porcine fetus enlarges until nearly all of the endometrium is utilized, Ashdown and Marrable.

The cotyledonary or multiplex type. In ruminants, including the cow, sheep and goat, only a portion of the maternal placenta, or the endometrial caruncles, and portions of the allantois chorion, or cotyledons, which closely appose each other to form the placentome, take part in the placental functions. In these structures the villi, secondary villi and microvilli of the cotyledon fit together closely with the maternal crypts and microvilli in a more complex arrangement than in the diffuse type of placenta. In the ruminant uterus the caruncles are arranged in 4 rows, 2 ventral and 2 dorsal, the length of each uterine horn. There are between 75 and 120 placentomes in the preg-

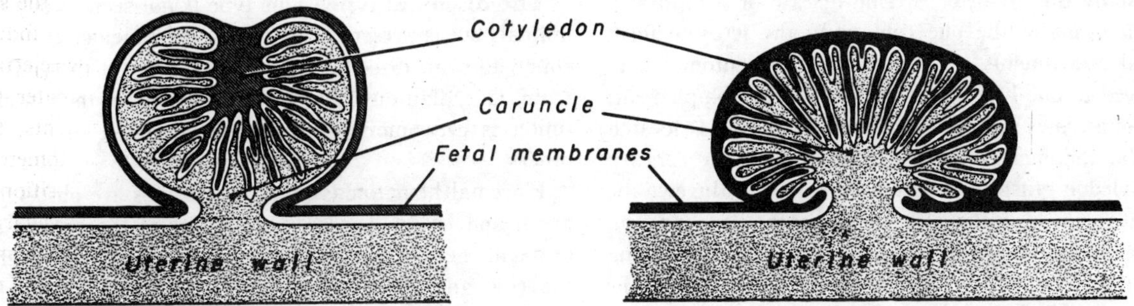

Figure 17. Placentome of the ewe.

Figure 18. Placentome of the cow.

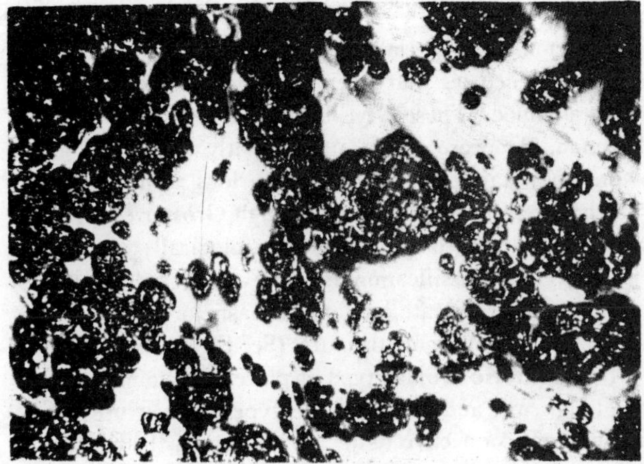

Figure 19. Normal placenta of a cow. Weight, 12 lbs., passed 4 hours after birth of calf, 52 cotyledons in gravid horn and 50 in nongravid horn. Note those in nongravid horn are smaller.

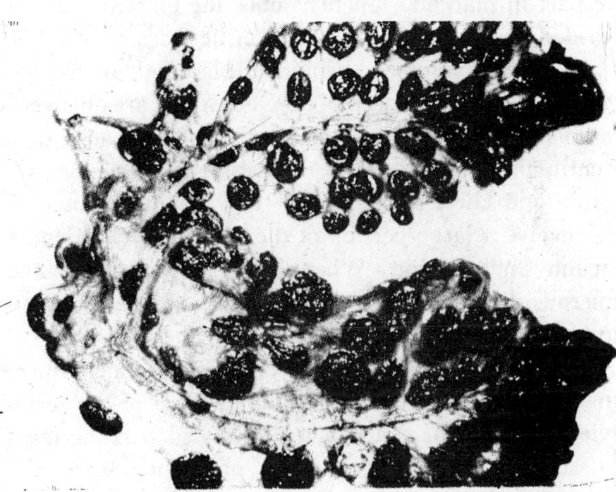

Figure 20. Adventitious placentae in a cow. (Courtesy of K. McEntee)

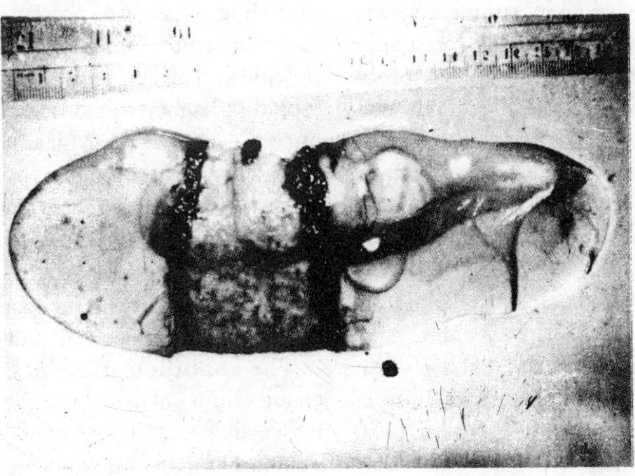

Figure 21. Zonary canine placenta.

nant uterus of the cow, and about 80 to 90 in the ewe. Occasionally due to prior uterine disease or a failure of the horn opposite the one containing the fetus to form placental attachments, the numbers of placentomes may be reduced to one-half or less of the normal complement. In pregnant cows the convex uterine caruncle is elevated above the endometrium like a button, with the concave fetal cotyledon grasping it (See Figure 18). In the ewe the maternal caruncle is also elevated above the endometrium but it is concave in shape, with the fetal cotyledon fitting into it (See Figure 17). The endometrium between the caruncles is called the intercaruncular endometrium and the fetal placenta between the cotyledons is called the intercotyledonary placenta. This area normally does not take part in placental functions once the placentomes are formed. Occasionally because of uterine disease or due to a lack of placentomes, primitive placental structures, simulating a diffuse placenta, develop in this area between allantois chorion and the endometrium. These are called adventitious placentae, or "accessory placentomes," Marion and Gier. These may be few in number or they may involve a large portion of the intercaruncular endometrium and chorion. When these are extensive and numerous the pregnancy is usually insecure and the possibility of subsequent normal pregnancies questionable.

A confusion in nomenclature existed in the older American veterinary literature regarding the use of the term, cotyledon. Williams stated that the cotyledon is the mass of tissue which develops during pregnancy upon the summits of the caruncles. Recent veterinary authorities including Amoroso and Bjorkman stated that the cotyledon was the fetal placenta that produced villi which projected into the crypts of the maternal caruncle that had become greatly enlarged. These two structures, the maternal caruncle, and the fetal cotyledon in ruminants was termed a placentome. American veterinarians commonly speak of the enlarged caruncle developed during pregnancy as a cotyledon, as proposed by Williams. They also speak of the combined maternal and fetal placental structure palpated through the uterine wall of a pregnant uterus during a rectal examination as a cotyledon. The nomenclature used by Amoroso and Bjorkman is preferred by the author.

The zonary type. In the dog and cat the placenta forms a zonary band or girdle about 2.5 to 7.5 cm., 1 to 3 inches, in width around the circumference of the uterine lumen in the middle of the oval chorionic sac. It is a highly complex structure. In carnivores the placenta is of a labyrinthine, rather than a villous, type that interlocks more intricately than does the maternal and fetal placentae in the larger domestic animals. The rest of the chorion is bare and devoid of villi and does not take part in placental functions during most of the gestation period.

The discoidal type. This type is not seen in domestic animals but is present in primates and rodents. There is a round to oval, disc-shaped placental area of the endometrium and allantois chorion. In these species the placental union is even more intricate and intimate than in the others.

Placental hematomas or extravasations are observed as green and brown borders or margins of the zonary placenta in the dog and cat, respectively. These are seen in the cow and sheep as multiple hematomas within the placentome at the base of the chorionic villi. They are considered to play an important role in the nutrition of the fetus because this stagnant maternal blood breaks down providing a source of iron that is utilized by the fetus, Wimsatt.

Another method of classifying placental types is by the tissues or structures that intervene between the maternal and fetal blood. These have been described by Grosser, Mossman, Amoroso, Wimsatt. Recently Bjorkman and Wynn have examined placentae of various animal species with the electron microscope. Although Grosser originally classified the types of placentae physiologically and anatomically, this classification is used at the present time only as an approximate anatomical basis for the study of placental morphology or structure. (See Figure 22).

The epitheliochorial type of placenta is found in the horse, pig, cow, and sheep. In this type six structures: the endothelium, connective tissue, epithelium of the endometrium and the trophoblast or chorion, mesenchyme and endothelium of the fetal tissue separate the maternal and fetal blood.

The syndesmochorial type was formerly considered present in ruminants. In this type all the tissues of the preceding type are present with the exception of the maternal epithelium. The loss of uterine epithelium was previously considered to occur in the placentomes in this type by phagocytosis and cytolysis by the cells of the trophoblast, Amoroso, Marion and Gier. and others. Syndesmochorial relationships are found in ruminant placentae when infections or other pathological disturbances have destroyed the maternal epithelium. At present Bjorkman would prefer to drop the term syndesmochorial, because of the great structural and functional similarity of the placentae between the horse, pig, cow and sheep.

The endotheliochorial type in the dog and cat has the endothelium of the uterine vessels and the chorion, mesenchyme, and endothelium of the fetal tissues or 4 structures separating the maternal and fetal blood.

The hemochorial type present in man and rodents has only the fetal tissues of the chorion, mesenchyme, and endothelium that lie or bathe in a "lake" of ma-

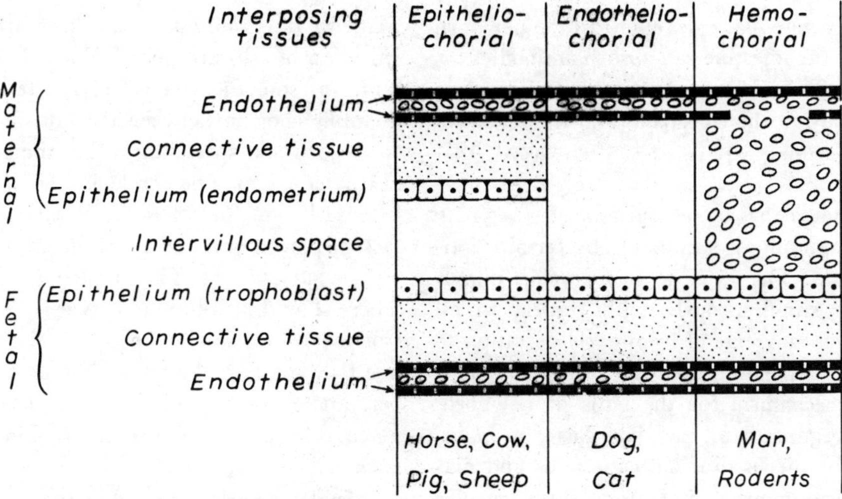

Figure 22. Diagramatic modification of Grosser's classification of the placentae of domestic animals. (after Bjorkman)

ternal blood since all maternal tissues have been eliminated. Bjorkman reported considerable difference in the structure of the hemochorial placenta in the different species. He also reported that extensions of Grosser's classification to include endothelioendothial and hemoendothelial types of placenta have been suggested where the trophoblast appeared to be lacking; but when the electron microscope has been used to examine these proposed types, a trophoblast was always present.

It was previously believed that the thickness of the placental membranes determined the efficiency of the barrier. But the various cell layers described in Grosser's model are not so regularly arranged. Amoroso has shown for example that in the epitheliochorial placenta that capillaries migrate into intra-epithelial locations so fetal and maternal blood streams may at certain points be quite closely apposed. In the placenta there probably are definite transport mechanisms for most substances rather than a passive diffusion type of transport. Furthermore the inference that the epitheliochorial placenta is less efficient or more primitive than the endotheliochorial or hemochorial is not supported by the growth rates of fetuses in the various species and the type of placentation found in both primitive and advanced species, Bjorkman, Amoroso and Wimsatt.

A third more general classification is made of the placental types of domestic animals into the **deciduate** or conjoined, and **indeciduate** or apposed. The deciduate type, or placenta vera, is that seen in man and rodents and in a slightly modified form in the dog and cat. In this type, the decidua composed of portions of the maternal epithelium or endothelium, submucosa, decidual cells and the fetal placenta are shed at parturition leaving a portion of the endometrium denuded. The **indeciduate** or **adeciduate** type of placenta is seen in larger domestic animals such as swine, horses, and also ruminants, Bjorkman. In this type the fetal membranes and placenta are expelled at the time of parturition, leaving the endometrium intact except in ruminants in which only the surfaces of the caruncles are devoid of epithelium after the caruncle sloughs about 6 to 10 days following parturition.

The placenta is not only an organ for exchange. It can synthesize substances required by the fetus, produce enzymes necessary for the attachment of the trophoblast and intracellular digestion, and produce the hormones, estrogen and progesterone, to maintain pregnancy. It can store and catabolize other compounds. Because of the varied functions of the placenta it has some of the biochemical and even structural resemblances to adult organs such as liver, lung, kidney, small intestine and endocrine glands.

The passive transfer of immunity is necessary for the protection and survival of the newborn. To provide young mammals with a passive immunity against disease for a considerable time after birth, antibodies are transferred from the dam **in utero** or by the colostrum after birth or both. According to Brambell, the cow, sheep, goat, pig, and horse transfer this immunity only by the colostrum. The human, guinea pig, and rabbit transfer immune bodies to the fetus only in the uterus through the placenta, or in the case of the rabbit through the yolk sac early in gestation by absorption from the uterine secretion. Dogs, cats, rats, and mice receive small amounts of antibody through the placenta but the major portion comes from the early mammary secretion. In the newborn of domestic animals the intestine can absorb antibodies for only approximately 24 to 36 hours after birth. The concentration of antibody in the colostrum and the serum of the 3 to 7 day-old neonate equals and often exceeds that in the dam's serum.

Silverstein has shown that ovine and other fetuses may develop an active immunity if stimulated by certain antigens during gestation. The fetus doesn't develop immunologic competence simultaneously with respect to all antigens. This period may extend from early gestation to sometime after birth depending upon the antigen. This is a further defense mechanism for the fetus or newborn. Antibodies in the pregnant dam, may be a factor in maintaining asepsis of the uterus to protect the fetus and placenta from infectious organisms. This study of the transfer of immunity is of great importance in treating hemolytic diseases of the newborn.

As is obvious in this discussion of placental types and the means of placental transfer of immunity, the number of layers of tissue between the maternal blood and fetal blood have no relation to the manner in which the passive immunity is accomplished, Brambell.

The procedures used in the examination of the placentae of the cow and mare are described because of the importance of this examination in valuable animals in providing an accurate picture of the health of the endometrium of the uterus at the time of parturition. The placenta should be examined as soon as possible after expulsion. If it is retained an excessively long period it will not be suitable for examination because of autolytic and putrefactive changes. If it cannot be examined at once it should be refrigerated. If possible the quantity, color, and nature of the fetal fluids should be noted. The membranes should be spread out to see if they are complete. Occasionally in the mare or cow the tip or apex of the fetal placenta may be torn off and left within the uterus where it may act as a focus of infection. In the mare the apices or tips of the placental horns are often edematous and if this edematous tip is incarcerated by the contraction of the uterine horn just distal to the apex, tearing or retention of the placenta may occur, Prickett. The external surface of the placenta is examined for the presence of abnormal exudate or blood. The blood may be old, dark, clotted, dried, or fresh. It may rarely be in the form of dry, amber-colored, inspissated granules, called "uterine sand." Edema or necrotic leathery areas and rarely calcified portions of the allantois chorion should be noted as to their severity or extent. With the aid of a stream of water, dirt or loose material may be cleaned from the uterine surface of the allantois chorion and the size, nature, and uniformity of the cotyledonary villi may be observed. Evidence of clumping of villi, bare areas, necrosis, or calcification of villi are noted. Normal cotyledonary villi are uniform, smooth, and velvety. After incising the bovine allantois chorion between the dorsal and ventral rows of cotyledons and spreading it flat, the uniformity of the size of cotyledons may be checked. The presence of giant cotyledons, 15 cm, 6 inches, in diameter, usually indicates a lack of placentomes or a lack of placental areas or caruncles for attachment. The number in each horn is counted. There should be a total of between 75 and 120 cotyledons. Cotyledons are smaller in size in the horn opposite to the one that contains the fetus. The presence, location, number, and extent of adventitious placentae in the cow is noted. The size of the necrotic tips in the bovine placenta is observed.

Rectal examinations and slaughter-house examinations of uteri of dairy cattle from the third to eighth month of gestation frequently reveal the horn not containing the fetus to be much smaller than is normal. On examination of the uteri, fetal membranes, and placenta, there is found a slight to complete lack of development of fetal membranes and placentae in this horn, often with a varying amount of necrosis of the membranes. The horn containing the fetus, the placenta, and the fetal membranes will appear normal. No studies have been made in the cow to determine the cause for this rather common failure for normal development of the placenta in the horn opposite to the one containing the fetus.

Evidence of thrombosis or disease of placental blood vessels is rarely observed. In placentae expelled after twin births in cattle the blood vessels should be examined for evidence of anastomosis. The amnion should be examined for evidence of disease and edema.

The fetal membranes should be weighed. Jennings found that in Thoroughbred mares the normal healthy placenta weighs about 10 to 14 lbs. He stated that in mares having fetal membranes weighing more than 14 lbs. there was often definite evidence of uterine disease. According to Williams, the fetal membranes of cows should weigh between 9 and 18 lbs. Udall reported that a large number of fetal membranes from Guernsey cattle examined by him weighed between 6 and 18 lbs., with an average of 7 to 9 lbs. The weight of the foal and calf is about 6 to 10 per cent of the postpartum weight of the dam. The weight of the afterbirth, or fetal membranes, is about 11 per cent of the foal's weight and about 14 per cent of the calf's weight. The total weight of the newborn young in the ewe and sow is about 5 to 10 per cent of the dam's postpartum weight.

Tumors or anomalies of the placenta are very rare in animals. Benesch and Folger described and illustrated cystic or hydatid, villous, and fibrous moles or tumorous placental growths and several other types that resembled hemagiomas or sarcomas. Olafson has observed a few of these tumors or hyperplastic tissue growths involving the placenta of cattle. In animals they are usually benign and are shed with the fetal membranes after parturition. Bloom reported that in dogs hydatiform mole of the placenta was not a true tumor. The condition was due to cystic changes in the villi. They were very rare. Chorioepithelioma is rare and maligant and usually occurs after parturition. Bloom reported only three cases and all were in dogs.

The umbilical cord connects the fetus and the placenta. In uniparous animals it is directed from the fetus toward the lesser curvature of the uterus and toward the middle uterine artery. Evans reported that in dogs and cats the umbilical stalk is attached to the zonary placenta on the opposite side of the uterus from the mesometrial attachment. It is composed of the allantoic and amniotic portions. According to Williams, the umbilical cord in the equine fetus is strong and averaged 48 cm or 19 inches in length, although others stated the cord may occasionally be as long as 90 to 100 cm, 36 to 40 inches. The umbilical cord of the bovine fetus is 30 to 40 cm, 12 to 16 inches, in length. In the porcine fetus the cord is relatively long, about 25 cm or 10 inches. In the dog and cat it is quite strong and short with a length of only 4 to 5 inches. In cattle, sheep, and usually swine, the cord is ruptured as the fetus passes through the birth canal. In the dog, cat, and mare the cord usually ruptures by the actions of the dam after the fetus has been born or of the newborn itself. In domestic animals it is safer from the standpoint of possible hemorrhage or infection to allow the cord to break naturally by traction than to ligate and cut it as is done in humans. The point of rupture in the foal and calf is about 2.5 to 5 cm, 1 to 2 inches, from the umbilicus at a constriction of the cord between the cord proper and the umbilical base or cutaneous navel. After rupture, the arteries retract into the body, the vein collapses, and the urachus shrinks and ceases to function. Possibly, due to the long umbilical cord and the fact that the fetus and amnion float free in the allantoic cavity, the umbilical cord in the mare is usually twisted spirally left to right or clockwise. Twisting of the cord in the mare may occasionally be severe and result in torsion of the umbilical vessels, followed by the death of the fetus due to obstruction of the blood supply from the placenta. The umbilical cords of the other domestic animals are seldom twisted. Occasionally during pregnancy the umbilical cord may become looped around the head, neck, body, or limbs of the fetus.

During the early stages of development the intestines of the fetus rest partly in the umbilical cord because of their early rapid growth. Later the body walls enclose this area and the umbilical ring contracts, forcing the intestines back into the abdominal cavity. If this does not occur, an umbilical hernia results. A cross section of the umbilical cord in the amniotic portion reveals the amnion as the investing membrane. Fine granular villous elevations of the amnion occur over the umbilical cord in cattle and to a lesser degree in horses, sheep, and goats. Inside the investing amnion are two umbilical arteries and two umbilical veins which fuse in the amniotic portion of the cord near the fetus to form a single vein. The urachus, the vestige of the yolk sac which can be seen only on histologic section, and Wharton's jelly which surrounds the above structures are also present within the amniotic membrane. The allantoic portion of the cord consists of a mass of branching vessels. The urachus expands just beyond the amniotic portion of the cord to open into the allantoic cavity.

General References

Arthur, G. H. (1964) Wright's Veterinary Obstetrics, 3rd Ed., The Williams and Wilkins Co., Baltimore, Md.

Hafez, E. S. E. (1968) Reproduction in Farm Animals, 2nd Ed., Lea and Febiger, Philadelphia, Pa.

Langman, J. (1963) Medical Embryology, The Williams and Wilkins Co., Baltimore, Md.

Nalbandov, A. V. (1964) Reproductive Physiology, 2nd Ed., W. H. Freeman and Co., San Francisco and London.

Parkes, A. S. (Edit.) 1952. Marshall's Physiology of Reproduction Vol. II, 3rd. Ed., Longmans, Green and Co., New York City and London.

Patten, B. M. (1948) Embryology of the Pig, 2nd Ed., The Blakiston Co., Philadelphia, Pa.

Williams, W. L. (1943) Veterinary Obstetrics, 4th Ed., Miss Louella Williams, Upland Rd., Ithaca, N Y.

Specific References

Alexander, G. and Williams, D. (1968) Hormonal Control of Amniotic and Allantoic Fluid Volume in Ovariectomized Sheep, J. of Endocrinol. **41,** 477.

Amoroso, E. C. (1952) Mammalian Placentation, in Marshall's Physiology of Reproduction Vol. II, 3rd Ed., Edited by Parkes, A. S., Longmans, Green and Co., N.Y.C., London.

Amoroso, E. C. (1961) Histology of the Placenta, Foetal and Neonatal Physiology, Brit. Med. Bull. **17,** 2.

Arthur, G. H. (1957) Some Notes on the Quantities of Fetal Fluids in Ruminants, Brit. Vet. Jour. **113,** 17.

Arthur, G. H. (1965) Further Observations on the Fetal Fluids of Cattle, Vet. Rec. **77,** 623.

Arthur, G. H. (1969) Fetal Fluids of Domestic Animals, J. Reprod. Fert., Suppl. 9, 45.

Ashdown, R. R. and Marrable, A. W. (1967) Adherence and Fusion Between Extremities of Adjacent Embryonic Sacs in the Pig., J. Anat. **101,** 2, 269.

Assali, N. S. (1967) Some Aspects of Fetal Life in Utero and Changes at Birth, Amer. J. of Obstet. and Gynec **97,** 3, 324.

Assali, N. S. (1968) Biology of Gestation, The Fetus and the Neonate, Vol. II, Academic Press, N.Y.C.

Benesch, F. (1952) Lehrbuch der Tierartzlichen Geburtshilfe and Gynakologie, Urban and Schwarzenberg, Wien-Innsbruck, Austria.

Bergin, W. C., Gier, H. T., Frey, R. A. and Marion, G. B. (1967) Developmental Horizens and Measurements Useful for Age Determination of Equine Embryos and Fetuses, Proc. Amer. Assoc. Eq. Pract., New Orleans, La., 179.

Bloom, F. (1954) Pathology of the Dog and Cat, Amer. Vet. Public, Inc., Evanston, Ill.

Bjorkman, N. (1965) The Fine Morphology of the Area of Foetal-Maternal Apposition in the Equine Placenta, Z. Zellforsch, **65,** 285.

Bjorkman, N. (1965) The Fine Structure of the Ovine Placentome, J. Anat. **99,** 283.

Bjorkman, N. (1965) On the Fine Structure of the Porcine Placental Barrier, Acta Anat. **62,** 342.

Bjorkman, N., (1967) Placentation—Mimeographed material.

Bjorkman, N. and Bloom, G. (1957) On the Fine Structure of the Foetal-Maternal Junction in the Bovine Placentome, Z. Zellforsch, **45,** 649.

Brambell, F. W. R. (1958) Prenatal Transference of Antibodies, Vet. Rec. **70,** 1060.

Brambell, F. W. R., (1958) The Passive Immunity of the Young Mammal, Biological Reviews, November.

Cloete, J. H. L. (1939) Prenatal Growth in the Merino Sheep, Onderst. J. Vet. Sci. and An. Ind. **13,** 2, 417.

Davies, J. and Wimsatt, W. A., (1966) Observations on the Fine Structure of the Sheep Placenta, Acta Anat. **65,** 1–3, 182.

Davis, J. A. (1961) Practical Problems of Neonatal Pediatrics Considered in Relation to Animal Physiology, Foetal and Neonatal Physiology, Brit. Med. Bull. **17,** 2.

Dawes, G. S. (1961) Changes in Circulation at Birth, Foetal and Neonatal Physiology, Brit. Med. Bull. **17,** 2.

Dickerson, T. W. T., Southgate, D. A. T., and King, J. M. (1967) The Chemical Composition of Fetal Fluids and Hippomanes, J. Anat. **101,** 2, 285.

Dzuik, P. J., Polge, C. and Rowson, L. E. (1964) Intrauterine Migration and Mixing of Embryos in Swine Following Egg Transfer, J. An. Sci. **23,** 1, 37.

Evans, E. (1956) A Dog Comes Into Being, Gaines Dog Research Progress, Fall, 2.

Evans, E. (1956) Personal Communication.

Folger, A. F. (1934) On Hydatiform Mole in Cattle, Acta. Path. et Microbiol. Scand. Suppl. 18, 104.

Franklin, R. J., Barclay, A. E. and Pritchard, M. M. L. (1946) The Circulation in the Fetus, Blackwell Scientif. Public Ltd., Oxford, England.

Green, W. W. and Winters, L. M. (1945) Prenatal Development of the Sheep, Univ. of Minn., Agr. Exp. Stat., Tech. Bull. 169.

Greenstein, J. S. and Foley, R. C. (1958) The Early Embryology of the Cow with Notes on Comparable Human Development, Internat. J. of Fert. **3,** 1, 67.

Greenstein, J. S. and Foley, R. C. (1958) Early Embryology of the Cow, J. Dairy Sci. **41,** 3, 409.

Grosser, O. (1909) Vegleichende Anatomie and Entwicklungsgeschichte des Eihaute and der Placenta mit Besonderer Berucksichtigung des Menschen, W. Braumiller, Vienna and Leipzig, Germany.

Habel, R. (1964) Personal Communication.

Huggett, St. G. (1961) Carbohydrate Metabolism in the Placenta and the Fetus, Foetal and Neonatal Physiology, Brit. Med. Bull. **17,** 2.

Jennings, W. (1941) Some Common Problems in Horse Breeding, Cor. Vet. **31,** 2, 197.

King, J. M. (1967) The Origin and Development of Hippomanes in the Horse and Zebra, The Location, Morphology and Histology of the Hippomanes, J. Anat. **101,** 2, 277.

Lanman, J. (1967) Personal Communication.

Marion, G. B. and Gier, H. T. (1958) The Process of Placentation in the Bovine, J. An. Sci. **17,** 4, 1216.

Marion, G. B. and Gier, H. T. (1956) Histological and Cytological Changes in the Bovine Uterine Epithelium, Ann. Meeting Amer. Soc. of An. Production, Chicago, Ill.

Marion, G. B., Gier, H. T. and Haldiman, J. T. (1957) Time of Placentation in the Bovine, Ann. Meeting Amer. Soc. An. Prod., Chicago, Ill.

McCance, R. A. and Widdowson, E. M. (1961) Mineral Metabolism in the Fetus and Newborn, Foetal and Neonatal Physiology, Brit. Med. Bull. **17,** 2.

Milton, A. A., Berry, R. O. and Butler, O. D. (1951) The Interval Between the Time of Ovulation and the Attachment of the Bovine Embryo, J. An. Sci. **10,** 4, 993.

Merkle, H. J. (1944) A New Technique In Instilling Amniotic Fluid Concentrate Intraabdominally at the Close of Operations, Amer. J. of Surg. **NS65,** 2, 210.

Millar, P. G. (1955) Plague-like Placental Lesions in Cattle, Brit. Vet. J. **111,** 6, 258.

Mossman, H W. (1926) The Rabbit Placenta and the Problem of Placental Transmission, Amer. J. Anat. **37,** 433.

Naaktgeboren, C. and Zwillenberg, H. H. L. (1960) Untersuchungen Leber Die Auswuchse Amnion und an der Nebelschur bei Wallen and Huftieren, Mit Besonderer Berucksichigung Des Europoischen Hausrinder, Acta Morph. Neberlando-Scand. **4,** 1, 31.

Prickett, M. E. (1967) The Pathology of the Equine Placenta and Its Effects on the Fetus, 13th Ann. Meeting A.A.E.P., New Orleans, 201.

Olafson, P. (1954) Personal Communication.

Rowson, L. E. A. and Moore, R. M. (1966) Development of the Sheep

Conceptus During the First Fourteen Days, J. Anat. **100,** 4, 777

Richter, J. and Gotze, R. (1960) Tiergeburtshilfe, 2nd Ed., Paul Parey, Berlin and Hamburg.

Sack, W. (1967) Personal Communication.

Silverstein, A. M. (1964) Ontogeny of the Immune Reponse, Science **144,** 1423.

Swett, N. W., Matthews, C. A. and Fohrman, M. H. (1948) Development of the Fetus in the Dairy Cow, U.S.D.A. Tech. Bull. No. 964.

Udall, D. H. (1952) Personal Communication.

Villee, C. A. (1960) The Placenta and Fetal Membranes, Williams and Wilkins Co., Baltimore, Md.

Wimsatt, W. A. (1962) Some Aspects of the Comparative Anatomy of the Mammalian Placenta, Amer. J. Obstet. **84,** 11, Part 2, 1568.

Winters, L. M., Green, W. W. and Comstock, R. E. (1942) The Prenatal Development of the Bovine, Tech. Bull. 151, Agr. Exper. Stat., Univ. of Minn., St. Paul, Minn.

Wislocki, G. B. (1935) On the Volume of the Fetal Fluids in the Sow and Cat, Anat. Rec. **63,** 183.

Wynn, R. M. (1967) Comparative Electron Microscopy of the Placental Junctional Zone, Obst. and Gynec. **29,** 5, 644.

Teratology

Teratology is the division of embryology and pathology dealing with the abnormal development and malformations of the antenatal individual. Teratologic, abnormal development or arrests in development of the ovum, embryo or fetus may result in death or malformations of the antenatal individual. In recent years amazing developments and break-throughs have occurred in the fields of genetics, embryology, pathology, virology and biochemistry resulting in the new and rapidly expanding fields of molecular and cellular biology and cytogenetics. Cytogenetics is the branch of genetics devoted to the study of the cellular constituents, chromosomes and genes, which are concerned in heredity. Since a new mammalian zygote originates by the combining of an ovum and a spermatozoa to form a single cell, all of the genetic information needed to form a new enormously complex animal is present in that cell. As stated by a recent popular press article, all these instructions, if written out in English, would require several 24 volume sets of encyclopedias. Yet they are packaged into two ten-trillionths of an ounce of DNA in the nucleus of the single-celled zygote.

Molecules of DNA, deoxyribonucleic acid, a nucleoprotein which are composed of nucleotides containing four bases, adenine, guanine, thymine and cytosine in an enormous variety of sequences arranged in ladder-like, double rows in a coiled, spiral helix, form genes which direct and control the chemical processes of each cell along certain lines by means of messenger and transfer RNA, ribonucleic acid, another nucleoprotein. These complex protein units of DNA or genes are carried on structures called chromosomes. These are best seen in anaphase, or that stage of cell division in which the chromosomes have separated and are diverging toward opposite poles of the cell. About 100,000 loci or gene locations are present on each chromosome except the Y chromosome which has less. The usual procedure followed in the study of chromosomes is to culture leucocytes, skin, tissue of other organs, or cells from the amnion obtained by amniocentesis for a few days so mitoses develop and then add colchicine to arrest mitosis. After a few hours hypotonic salt solution is added to the cells to swell them. They are then prepared, fixed, stained and examined under a microscope, Pakes and Griesemer. Chromosomes consist of a pair of chromatids held together by a centromere the location of which together with the size of the chromosome aids in the identification of the chromosomes. Their systematized arrangement in pairs and groups is called a karyotype or idiogram. The latter is a diagramatic or formalized karyotype. Each normal cell contains two sex chromosomes and the rest of the chromosomes are called autosomes. A metacentric chromosome is one with a median centromere (X). A submetacentric chromosome is one nearly the same as the former with a submedian

Table 5. The Diploid Chromosome Number of Domestic Animals*

Species	Chromosome Number	Chromosome Characteristics
Cattle	60	58 acrocentrics, 2 submetacentric sex chromosomes
Horse	64	38 acrocentrics, 26 metacentrics
Donkey	62	
Pig	38	12 acrocentrics, 26 metacentrics
Sheep	54	47 acrocentrics, 7 metacentrics
Dog	78	76 acrocentrics, 2 metacentric sex chromosomes
Cat	38	5 acrocentrics, 33 metacentrics
Man	46	11 acrocentrics, 35 metacentrics

*Hsu and Benirschke.

centromere. A telocentric chromosome is one with a terminal centromere (Λ). An acrocentric chromosome is one nearly the same as the former with a subterminal centromere. These very short arms are hard to distinguish. Chromosome analyses in mammals have been used to provide increased understanding of possible species differences and their evolutionary relationships. Since chromosomes can now be examined and studied, cytogenetics is providing further insights into chromosomal or genetic aberrations as they are related to teratologic defects. (See Table 5).

The genetic make-up of cells may be altered at the time of meiosis in a number of ways. The normal process of segregation of chromosomes may fail to occur producing **nondisjunction** resulting in an extra chromosome, trisomy, or a lack of a chromosome, monosomy, in the new zygote. Excellent examples of nondisjunction with an extra chromosome is mongolism or Down's syndrome in humans characterized by trisomy of chromosome 21 resulting in a total of 47 chromosomes in the individual and Turner's syndrome due to a missing Y chromosome, monosomy, of the sex chromosomes resulting in a total of 45 chromosomes. Parts of two nonhomologous chromosomes of a germ cell at meiosis may break off and be relocated on other chromosomes resulting in **translocation.** When a portion of a chromosome breaks off and is lost **deletion** results. All of these abnormal processes affecting one or more chromosomes during division may also occur during mitosis in an early zygote leading to abnormalities in certain tissues or organs but not in others. Fechheimer has presented an excellent discussion of chromosomal aberrations. It is of interest to note that cells in a variety of tumors including bovine lymphocytoma and canine transmissible tumors have irregular numbers and abnormal appearing chromosomes, Noronha.

The occurrence in an individual of two or more cell populations or tissues each with a different chromosome complement derived from a single zygote is called **mosaicism.** If a similar condition is present but the cell populations arise from different zygotes, as in twins with placental anastomoses, the condition is called **chimerism.**

If nondisjunction, translocation, or deletion of chromosomes is moderate to severe the zygote usually succumbs early in gestation during the period of the ovum or embryo. Some survive longer as fetal monsters, parasites on the placenta of the normal twin, or defective individuals. Defects of the sex chromosomes, since they usually do not have much influence on organ and body development, are found most frequently. Most of the genetic defects of animals are related to one or several genes on a chromosome and at our present state of knowledge these cannot be identified and studied.

The mode of inheritance of genetic causes for a disease or abnormality varies greatly. It is usually due to a natural mutation that is recessive in character but may be dominant. In many diseases inherited as autosomal recessive defects neither the sire nor dam is usually affected but the disease comes from both. Dominant genes causing disease would cause defects in half of the offspring of a defective parent. Dominant defective characters are rare in animals. Dominance may be incomplete. The effect of certain genes may be influenced by modifiers or other modifying genes or by incomplete penetrance of the character as in hypoplasia of the gonads in Swedish Highland cattle due to a recessive autosomal gene with incomplete penetrance. In this condition only 50 per cent of the homozygous cattle are able to be clinically diagnosed. Individuals affected with a single gene defect may exhibit a great difference in the expressivity or degree to which it is manifested. Certain genes exhibit multiple or pleiotropic effects probably due to some abnormality of cellular physiology. If penetrance is fairly high, dominant factors are largely self-limiting. If there are no desirable pleiotropic effects in heterozygotes, the frequency of simple recessive factors can be kept low if a constant survey of the population is implemented, Fechheimer. The female (X) sex chromosome carries genes other than those that determine sex while the male (Y) sex chromosome does not carry genes other than those that determine sex. So genes on the X chromosome produce characteristics that are **sex-linked.** Recessive sex-linked defects are uncommon in animals. Characteristics found only in one sex such as cryptorchidism, milk or egg production, and "white heifer" disease are **sex-limited** in character. Certain quanitative characters such as body size, milk and butterfat production and fertility are caused by many genes, **polygenes,** or multiple factors. There is a close relationship between environmental factors and certain genetic factors as they influence the expression of disease. For example, skin lesions in hematoporphyrinuria in a cow with white skin will not be observed if the cow is kept from direct sunlight. Mutant defective or lethal genes are carried by nearly every animal but the heterozygosity of the animal populations usually prevent their frequent expression except under unusual circumstances of inbreeding or selection.

The Inherited or Genetic Anomalies or Malformations in Domestic Animals

These have been well-described by Hutt, Stormont, Young, Johansson, Lerner, Gilmore, Innes and Saunders, Koch and coworkers, Fechheimer and others. Lauvergne has recently compiled an extensive bibliography of genetic anomalies in cattle.

The inherited lethal and semilethal characters in cattle are:

Achondroplasia, or dwarf, "comprest" or "bull dog" calves. These are seen in all breeds but most commonly in the Hereford, Ayrshire, Angus and Dexter breeds. The most common type is the brachycephalic "snorter" dwarf in Herefords with a short, broad head, bulging forehead, malocclusion of the jaw, prognathism of the mandible, pot-belly, low viability and great susceptibility to bloat and dystocia. This type was generally considered to be due to a simple autosomal recessive defect with some modifiers, Marlow, Blood and Henderson and Hutt. (See Figure 23) The use of the profilometer in evaluation of the head shape or radiography have not proven to be highly satisfactory in the detection of carrier animals, Dinkel and Gregory. Julian et al. and Gregory et al. in extensive studies on brachycephalic, dolichocephalic or long-headed, intermediate, Dexter-type, and comprest dwarfs indicated that achondroplasia was inherited in a complex manner both in a dominant and recessive form, mainly the latter, and with modifiers. Dev and Lasley have shown that dwarfs, carriers, and normal cattle had the same levels of growth hormone in the blood plasma. Thus dwarfism is probably due to the failure of target organs to respond to the hormone. Mead and coworkers have reported a proportionate dwarfism in Jersey cattle not recognizable until one year of age when the small size is evident. Koger et al. have described "midget" Brahmans and "stumpy" Shorthorns caused by recessive genes as well as small guinea cattle in crossbreeds native to Florida in which the causative gene may be dominant or incompletely dominant, Fechheimer. The "comprest" Hereford is the result of incomplete dominance. In Ayrshire, Dexter and other cattle, extreme "bulldog" calves are usually aborted about the fifth to eighth month of gestation. (See Figure 31) Hydramnios occurs in pregnant Dexter cattle carrying a "bulldog" calf. Normal Dexter cattle are heterozygotes.

A type of Aberdeen Angus dwarf characterized by inferior brachygnathism, bulging eyes, narrow nose, death occurring during parturition or soon after, and moderate hydrops amnii has been observed as an apparent recessive character in several purebred Angus herds by Thomsen and the author. Affected calves have brittle, easily broken bones that upon examination are solid and devoid of marrow cavities. If the calf lives a few hours central nervous signs of opisthotonus and nystagmus are present.

Epitheliogenesis imperfecta is a condition where skin fails to form. It occurs most commonly on the legs below the knees and hocks and on the muzzle, ears, tongue and mucous membranes. It has been described in Holsteins, Ayrshires, Jerseys, Brown Swiss and Shorthorns, Stormont.

Hypotrichosis congenita or alopecia is a recessive defect characterized by degrees of hairlessness in Holsteins, Blood and Henderson, Polled Herefords, Craft and Blizzard, and Durhams. It was also described in Swedish Friesian cattle, Nordlund, and Holsteins, Holmes and Young; in Jerseys having other defects such as a short lower jaw, short ears and anophthalmia, Wipprecht and Horlacher. Streaked hairlessness was reported as a sex-linked lethal in Holsteins, Eldridge and Atkeson.

Ichthyosis congenita is characterized by a lack of hair and a thick scaly, horny epidermis with raw fissured skin around the body orifices. It is due to single autosomal recessive genes in Brown Swiss and Red Polled Cattle, Julian.

Acroteriasis congenita or amelia and hemimelia is seen in Holsteins and Brown Swiss and other breeds, Stormont, Fechheimer. This is characterized by missing, shortened, deformed, or "amputated" limbs.

Ankylosis, hydrops, death and mummification of the fetus in the last month of gestation was reported in Red Danish cattle, Stormont and Thompson et al., due to a pair of single autosomal recessive genes.

Cerebellar hypoplasia and degeneration is seen in Herefords, Guernseys and Holsteins and is probably autosomal recessive in nature, Innes and Saunders, Blood and Henderson, Stormont. This conclusion may be erroneous as BVD-MD virus can produce this defect in fetuses. (See nongenetic defects or anomalies in animals)

Sex-linked lethals (Holsteins and other breeds)

Ataxia with leucodysplasia seen in Angus, Shorthorns, Jerseys, Herefords and possibly in Holsteins and Hariana cattle at 2 or more weeks of age is due to a recessive condition, Innes and Saunders, Young.

"Doddlers" in Herefords was described by High et al. as due to a pair of autosomal recessive genes and possibly causing cerebellar or other brain stem lesions, Innes and Saunders.

Cerebral pseudolipidosis, ataxia and tremors was reported in Angus cattle in Australia, Innes and Saunders.

Paralyzed hind quarters have been reported in Red Danish calves at birth due to a pair of autosomal recessive genes, Stormont, Christensen and Christensen. Innes and Saunders reported a similar condition in Norwegian Red Poll cattle that also developed a keratitis.

Curved limbs with both rear and forelimbs curved anteriorly, have been observed in Guernseys as an autosomal recessive trait. Calves were usually stillborn or died promtply, Freeman.

Muscle contractures and ankyloses, or arthrogryposis has been reported as a recessive in Dole cattle in Norway by Nes; and a dominant with incomplete penetrance in England by Johnston and Young. It has also been described in Shorthorns in Canada by Dale and Moxely, in Holsteins by Blood and Henderson, in Herefords by Shupe et al. and in other cattle by Fechheimer.

Hydrocephalus in Herefords, Ayrshires, Holsteins and other breeds have been reported by Baker et al., Belling and Holland, Huston et al., Urman and Grace, Gilman, Fechheimer and others. It is characterized by the birth of "dummy" or "bawler" calves that are unable to nurse properly and die in several days. The heads may be enlarged or normal in size but section of the head and brain reveals distended ventricles. The disease may be associated occasionally with hydramnios, dwarfism and high copper levels in the liver, Nuss and coworkers. This is due in an uncomplicated form to a simple autosomal recessive gene. It is possible that some of these cases of hydrocephalus might be associated with BVD-MD or blue tongue viruses infecting the bovine fetus.

Congenital dropsy due an autosomal recessive gene has occurred in Ayrshires and Swedish Lowland cattle, Donald et al. and Herrick and Eldridge. It may be characterized by the abortion of a "bulldog" anasarcous fetus often with cysts on the tip of the ears or the birth of calves with severe persistent edema of the limbs or head. (See Figures 27 and 28)

Brachygnathism or underdevelopment of the mandible has been reported in nearly all breeds of cattle includ-

Figure 23. Brachycephalic Hereford dwarfs, yearling "snorter" dwarfs.

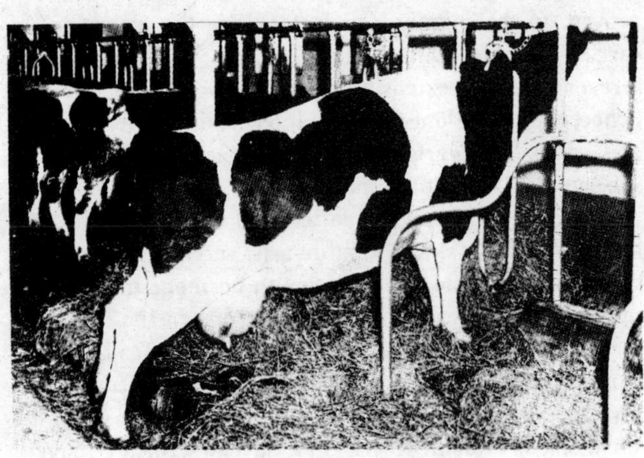

Figure 24. Spastic syndrome, "stretches," in a grade 9-year-old Holstein cow.

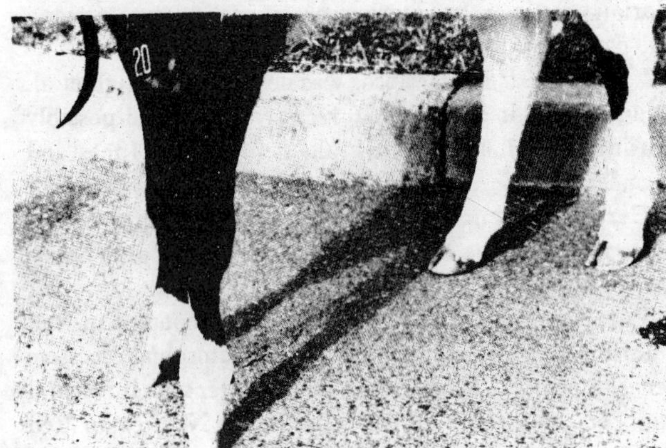

Figure 25. Syndactyly of the forelimbs of a Holstein calf.

Figure 26. Spastic paresis in a Holstein calf, note the rigidly extended left hind leg.

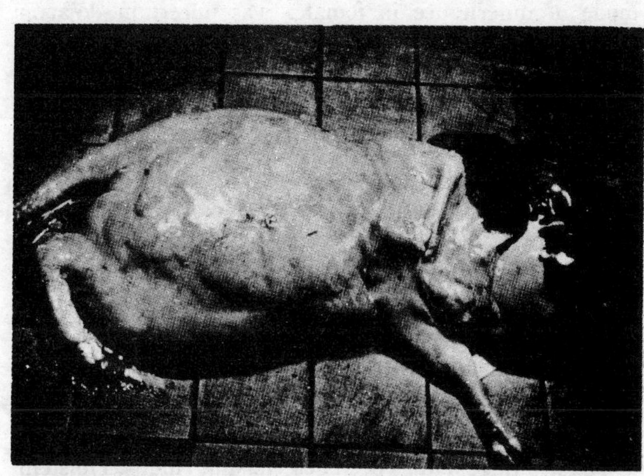

Figure 27. Congenital dropsy and anasarca in an aborted Ayrshire fetus. (Courtesy K. McEntee)

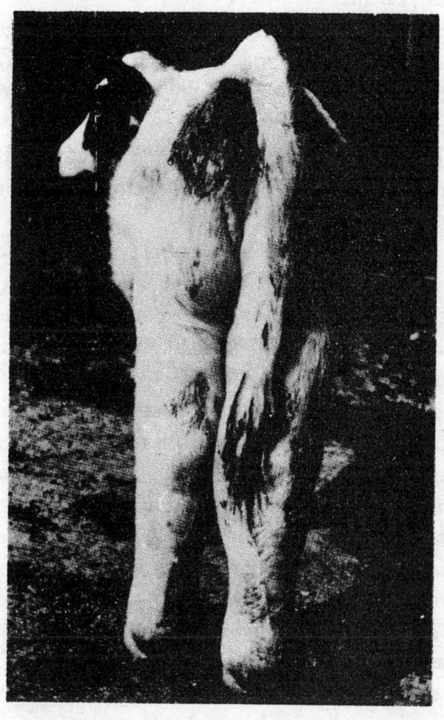

Figure 28. Congenital dropsy or edema in an Ayrshire calf. (Courtesy M. G. Fincher)

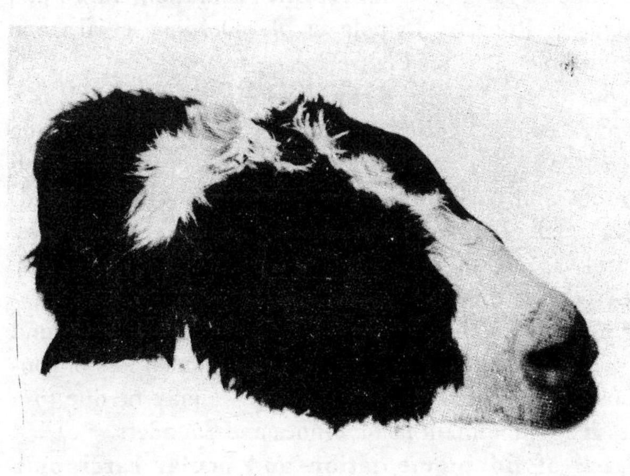

Figure 29. Cerebral hernia in an overtime Holstein fetus.

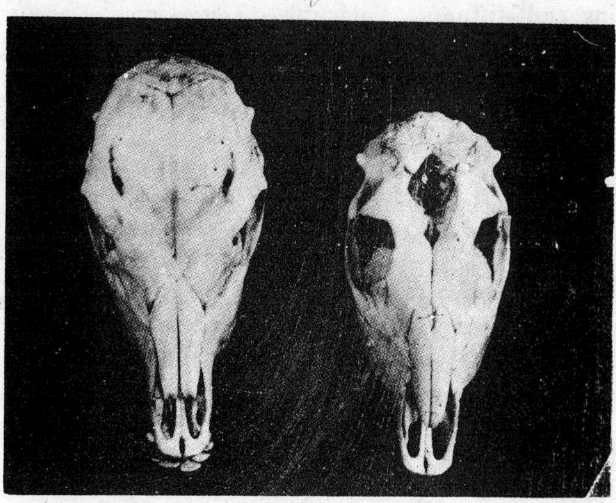

Figure 30. Skulls of a normal calf (left) and a calf with a cerebral hernia (right).

ing Shorthorns, Jerseys and Herefords. Inheritance is more than just a simple recessive but it is not complex, Smith et al., Grant.

Malocclusion, probably due to a recessive gene, is observed in Herefords and characterized by shortened long bones and a misshapen mandible, Gregory and coworkers.

Cleft lip and palate have been reported in Jerseys, Shorthorns and other breeds as a genetic defect, Shupe et al., and Wheat.

Atresia of the colon and ileum were reported as possible genetic defects in Swedish Highland cattle and Holsteins, Nihleen and Erikson, Osborne and Legates.

Atresia ani has been reported in Holsteins, and possibly Angus and Guernseys, Gilmore, Lerner.

Cerebral hernia or "Catlin mark" is an opening in the frontal and parietal bones associated with severe central nervous system defects, prolonged gestation and dystocia in Holsteins. (See Figures 29 and 30)

Cardiac defects of patent ductus arteriousus, persistent foramen ovale and septal defects have been described in Herefords and Jerseys and are probably due to genetic causes, Ternan et al., Regan et al., and Belling.

Chediak-Higashi Syndrome is an autosomal recessive defect characterized in Hereford cattle, and mink, by white animals or those with a ghost pattern in normally pigmented areas, hypopigmentation of iris and photophobia and reduced viability, Padgett and coworkers.

Partial alopecia, failure of horn growth, slobbering and stiffness ("Baldy calves") developing at about two months of age in calves and terminating in death by 6 to 12 months has been described in Holsteins by Blood and Henderson. The evidence indicated that it was probably an hereditary condition.

Laminitis is a possible autosomal recessive character in Jersey cattle 1 to 6 months of age, Merritt and Riser.

Other inherited but generally nonlethal defects of cattle cited by Lerner, Gilmore, Hutt, Koch et al., Lauvergne, and Fechheimer include:

Polydactylism in Holsteins and Herefords, Roberts and Lauvergne, is possibly an autosomal dominant character with incomplete penetrance.

Syndactylism or "mule-foot" affecting one or both front feet or all four feet has been reported in Jerseys, Hariana cattle and Holsteins and has a single autosomal recessive mode of inheritance, Eldridge et al.. Affected Holsteins were unable to withstand stress due to high ambient temperatures and became hyperthermic, Liepold et al.. The front feet of the Holstein calves were much more frequently affected with syndactyly than the rear feet. (See Figure 25)

Muscular hypertrophy, or "double" muscling is characterized by reduced fat deposits, light bone, thin skin, and large muscles. It is seen in many breeds of cattle including Herefords, Holstein, Angus, Charolais and Piedmont. In the latter it may be inherited as an incomplete dominant while in the former breeds it may be a recessive with incomplete penetrance and variable expression, Mason and MacKellar. When fetuses are affected dystocia often occurs.

Umbilical hernia was described as being a probable sex-limited dominant character in male Holsteins but the mode of inheritance in females was uncertain, Warren and Atkeson. Gilman and Stringham reported that umbilical hernia in Holsteins was caused by one or more pairs of autosomal recessive genes of low frequency. The condition was seen more often in females but was probably not sex-linked.

Osteoarthritis and hip dysplasia in Holsteins, Jerseys and Herefords have been described by Sittman and Kendrick, and Carnahan et al.. In dairy breeds the lesions were noted in the stifle joint at 5 to 13 years of age and were possibly due to a single autosomal recessive gene. In yearling Herefords the lesions were in the hip joint and it was possibly due to an incompletely penetrant dominant character.

Spastic paresis has been described in Angus, Holstein, Charolais, Shorthorn, Ayrshire, Simmental and rarely Jersey calves usually 2 to 8 months of age with straight rear legs and a contracted gastrocnemicus muscle causing the rear leg to be held off the ground and swung rigidly. It is due to an autosomal recessive condition, Innes and Saunders, Roberts, Leipold et al., DeMoor et al., and Denniston et al.. (See Figure 26)

Spastic syndrome, Krampfigkeit, "Stretches" is a latent recessive condition developing at 2 to 7 years of age and characterized by spastic contractions of the rear limb or limbs and back that occur intermittently in the standing animal. The condition affects Holsteins, Guernseys, Charolais, Ayrshires, and occasionally other breeds, Roberts. (See Figure 24)

Epilepsy has been reported in Swedish Red cattle and Brown Swiss cattle characterized by a sudden loss of consciousness preceded by a convulsion. It may be due to a recessive or dominant factor, Innes and Saunders.

Lack of lid pigmentation and ocular carcinoma is seen mainly in Herefords but also Holsteins and Ayrshires exposed for long periods to sunlight. Pigmentation of the eyelid is strongly heritable so selection for pigmented eyelids can reduce the incidence of carcinomas, Anderson.

Heterochromia irides and albinism in Herefords was described due to a dominant mode of inheritance. These cases were more like color dilution rather than true

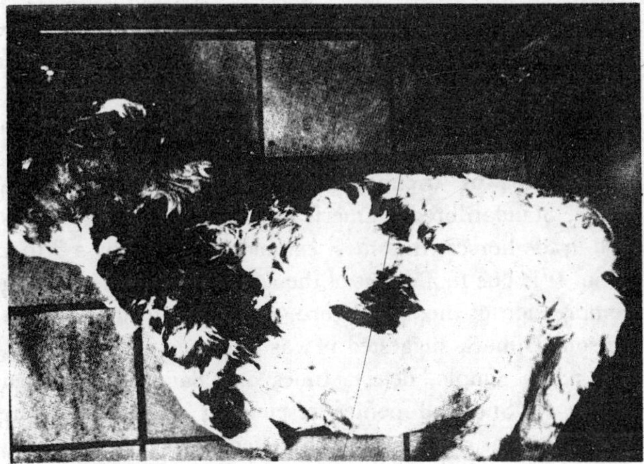

Figure 31. "Bulldog" achrondroplastic fullterm Ayrshire fetus.

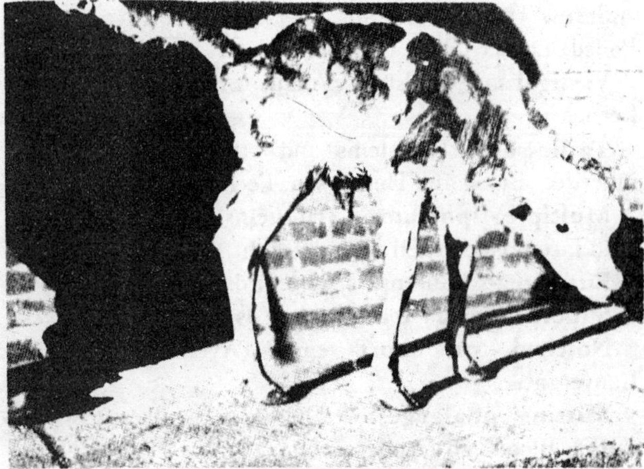

Figure 32. Hypotrichosis congenita or hairlessness in a Guernsey calf.

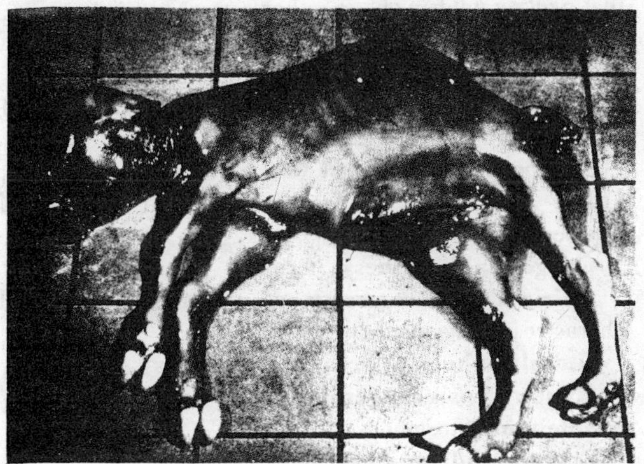

Figure 33. Guernsey fetus with adenopypophysial hypoplasia causing a prolonged, 338 day gestation. (Courtesy of K. McEntee)

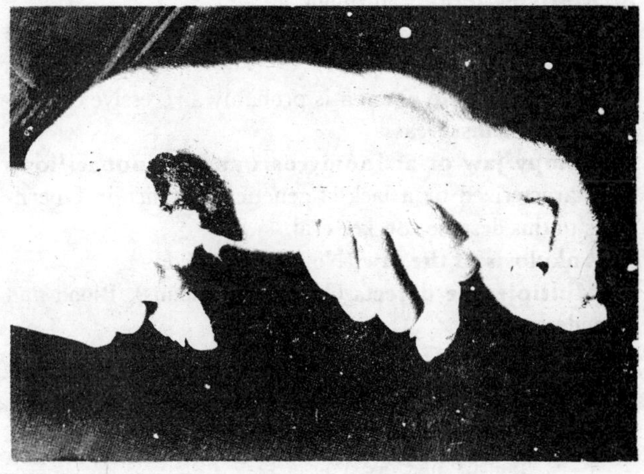

Figure 34. Epitheliogenesis imperfecta in a Yorkshire pig.

albinism. Some affected cattle had blood dyscrasias, Leipold and Huston, and Ament and O'Mary.

Congenital cataract and blindness (Jerseys and Holsteins) Gilmore, Lerner, Carter.

Strabismus and exophthalmos "cross-eyed" or "pop-eyed" (Shorthorn, Guernsey and Jersey) are inherited as recessive characters, Blood and Henderson, Regan et al., Fechheimer.

Hypotrichosis congenita, hairlessness has been described as a nonlethal character in Guernseys by Hutt and Saunders and Becker et. al.. (See Figure 32)

Red factor is a simple recessive defect in Holstein and Angus cattle where red substitutes for the normal black color of the hair.

Congenital porphyria, or pink tooth has been observed in Holsteins, Shorthorns and Jamaican Red cattle as a simple autosomal recessive condition resulting in photosensitivity and dermatitis of white or even pigmented skin, pink to brown teeth and bones that fluoresce with ultraviolet light, Wass and Hoyt, Jorgensen and Nestel.

Polycythemia in one- to two-month-old Jersey calves characterized by congested mucous membranes, lethargy, dyspnea and reduced growth rate was due to a single autosomal recessive gene, Tennant et al..

Curly coat (Ayrshires and Swedish cattle), Hutt.

Deformed limbs or flexed pasterns (Jerseys), Hutt, Lauvergne.

Wry tail (all breeds) Lerner, Hutt, Gilmore.

Wry muzzle (Jerseys) Lerner, Hutt, Gilmore.

Screw tail (Holsteins, Jerseys, Shorthorns, Red Polled) Lerner, Hutt, Gilmore.

Vestigal tail (Holsteins, Angus, Shorthorns) Gilmore, Lerner.

Taillessness (Holsteins and other breeds) possibly inherited, Blood and Henderson, Fechheimer.

Multiple lipomatosis (Holsteins), a dominant trait with incomplete penetrance, Albright.

Fused teats (Guernseys, Herefords), Lauvergne.

Supernumerary teats (all breeds).

Notched or short ears (Ayrshires, Jerseys), Lauvergne.

Missing phalanges or "Creeper" calves (Swedish cattle), Blood and Henderson.

Impacted premolars and "parrot-mouth" (Shorthorns)

Short spine (Norwegian cattle)

Ljutikow lethal, Stormont.

Agnathia or absence of a lower jaw (Jerseys and other breeds)

Opacity of the cornea is probably a recessive character in Holsteins, Deas.

Lumpy jaw or actinomycosis and actinobacillosis is characterized by a lack of genetic resistance in Guernseys to this desease, Becker et al..

Ankylosis of the jaw (Norwegian cattle)

Multiple eye defects (Jerseys, Holsteins), Blood and Henderson.

Prognathism (Herefords and others).

Dermoid cysts on cornea, (Herefords and Guernseys), Herrick.

Smooth tongue (Holsteins and Brown Swiss), Huston et al.

Genetic diseases or conditions related to cattle reproduction and the reproductive organs such as; prolonged gestation in Holsteins and Guernseys, segmental aplasia of the mesonephric and paramesonephric ducts, imperforate hymen or white heifer disease, gonadal hypoplasia, cystic ovaries, hermaphroditism, cryptorchidism, seminal defects, failure of the median wall of the paramesonephric ducts to fuse, impotentia coeundi, penile defects, inguinal hernia, and others will be described and discussed later, Johansson.

The inherited lethal or semilethal characters in horses are:

Atresia coli in Percherons is often associated with brain defects, Stormont.

Hemophilia, Hutchins and coworkers, Sanger et al.

Fredericksborg lethal, related to sterility in inbred white horses, Stormont.

Epitheliogenesis imperfecta, affects lower limbs, Stormont.

Sex-linked lethal, ratio of 2 females to 1 male, Stormont.

Hereditary ataxia, Oldenberg breed, Stormont.

Wobbles or incoordination is seen in Thoroughbreds, Standardbreds, American Saddle and other breeds and grade horses. It is most common in males by a 3 to 1 ratio. It is due to a defect of the cervical vertebrae causing compression of the spinal cord, Dimock, Blood and Henderson. Dimock suggested it was inherited as a recessive, but not a simple, defect. Innes and Saunders reported ataxia in Shetland ponies resembling wobbles but the condition was associated with degeneration of the spinal nerve roots. The condition might be genetic in nature. Prickett has described wobbles due to three distinct types of pathological lesions and listed 6 other disease entities that may resemble wobbles in horses.

Cerebellar hypoplasia is possibly a genetic defect in Arabians, Sponseller.

Absence of a retina is a recessive character, Blood and Henderson.

Hydrocephalus, Koch et al.

Other Inherited, Generally Nonlethal Defects of Horses are:

Congenital blindness, Stormont.

Aniridia with cataracts was a dominant autosomal character in Belgians, Eriksson.

Umbilical hernia, Koch et al., Williams.

Hypotrichosis congenita

Sidebone, Stormont.

Cryptorchidism, Blood and Henderson.

Brachygnathism of the mandible, Koch et al.

Subluxation of patella, ponies and others, Koch et al.

Multiple exostosis is possibly hereditary in Quarter horses, Morgan et al..

Heaves, pulmonary emphysema (?), Koch et al.

Roaring, laryngeal hemiplegia (?), Koch et al., Quinlan and Morton, Crewe and Buchanan.

Dysplasia of the hip, (Dole horses), Blood and Henderson.

"Bleeders," epistaxis (?), Crewe and Buchanan.

Some of the above conditions and others sometimes referred to as genetic diseases such as: splints, ringbone, spavin, scrotal hernia, muscle contractures or arthrogryposis and others may or may not be genetic in horses as few actual breeding trials have been conducted. Severely defective animals are usually immediately destroyed. The long interval between births makes test matings very costly. Rollins and Searle have presented excellent summaries of the inheritance of coat color in horses and also other animals.

The inherited lethal or semilethal characters in swine are:

Cerebral hernia, "Catlin" mark, Stormont, Gilman.

Hydrocephalus is reported in Duroc Jerseys due to recessive genes, Stormont, Hutt.

Paralysis of hind limbs due to spinal cord lesions, Stormont, Birge, Thurley et al. and Innes and Saunders. This is a recessive semilethal character.

Atresia ani, Stormont, Young.

Thickened forelimbs, Stormont, Blood and Henderson.

Acroteriasis congenita, "amputated" is caused by a single autosomal recessive gene, Gilmore, Stormont, Hutt.

Cleft palate is seen occasionally with harelip in the Large White breed and transmitted as a single autosomal recessive, Stormont, and Nes.

Other Inherited Generally Nonlethal Defects of Swine are:

Epitheliogenesis imperfecta in Berkshires and Yorkshires. (See Figure 34)

Wattles, or tassels, Stormont, Hutt (1946).

Testicular hypoplasia, Young citing Holst.

Screw or kinky tail, Stormont, Donald.

Umbilical hernia, Lerner, Hutt, Gilmore.

Inguinal or scrotal hernia, Stormont; sex-limited and may affect male pseudohermaphrodites, Gregory.

Hypotrichosis congenita, Lerner, Hutt, Gilmore.

Congenital bent legs, Stormont.

Split ears, deformed rear quarters and occasionally cleft palates in Tamworths, Stormont.

Diverticulosis, chronic ileitis in Berkshires, Stormont.

Congenital porphyria, a dominant character, Stormont, Jorgensen.

Cryptorchidism, Stormont, Blood and Henderson.

Eye defects, micropthalmia, anopthalmia, Stormont.

Syndactyly and polydactyly, Stormont.

Sexual impotency, Koch et al.

Hermaphroditism, Koch et al. and Pond et al.

Inverted teats, Koch et al., Young.

Hypertrophy of muscle, Pietrain pig in Belgium, Hutt.

Subaortic stenosis in Denmark, King.

Dermatosis vegetans, Dove et al., and Blood and Henderson, is a semilethal autosomal recessive condition of the Danish Landrace breed and associated with a giant cell pneumonitis, dyspnea and efflorescent skin lesions.

The inherited lethal or semilethal characters in sheep and goats are:

Muscle contracture, ankylosis, arthrogryposis or flexed limbs and wry neck. These are expelled dead and are due to simple recessive genes, Stormont and Rae.

Paralysis of hind limbs is seen in Corriedales as a simple recessive, Stormont, Rae.

Rigid fetlocks is characterized by a deformed body, short wool and hernias, Stormont, Rae.

Acroteriasis congenita or amputated limbs, Stormont, Rae.

Lethal gray is seen in gray Karakul lambs with obstruction of the gut and possibly nerve damage, Innes and Saunders, Stormont, Rae.

Lethal myodystrophia, inheritance is questionable, Stormont.

Dwarfism or achondroplasia is seen in Ancon sheep due to simple autosomal recessive genes, Stormont, Hutt, Rae.

Agnathia is observed in a variety of forms, Stormont, Rae.

Cerebellar hypoplasia or "daft" lambs, is a simple autosomal recessive character in Corriedales, Hutt, Stormont.

Photosensitization with blindness in Southdown sheep is due to a simple recessive, Blood and Henderson, Cornelius and Gronwall.

Prolonged gestation, Karakuls and others.

Other Hereditary Generally Nonlethal Defects in Sheep:

Malocclusion, brachygnathism or prognathism, Lerner, Hutt, Gilmore.

Hypotrichosis congenita, Lerner, Hutt, Gilmore.

Hermaphroditism is common in polled goats, especially Saanen.

Cryptorchidism is a recessive character in goats and sheep, Rae.

Yellow fat is a simple recessive character, Hutt, Rae.

Acaudate, "no tail" sheep, Hutt.

Hairy Wool in Romney sheep is caused by an incomplete dominant gene, Hutt.

Myotonia congenita or "fainting" goats, Hutt, Blood and Henderson, Innes and Saunders.

Entropion has probably a complex polygenic inheritance, Littlejohn, Koch et al., Rae, and Crowley and McGloughlin.

Wattles in sheep and goats is due to a single dominant gene, Koch et al., Rae.

Hydrocephalus, Koch et al.

Atresia ani, Koch et al.

Sperm granuloma is seen secondary to anomalies of the mesonephric duct in male goats, Koch et al..

Blindness may be due to a simple autosomal recessive gene, Rae, Zwiep.

Fleshy outgrowth on the top of the ear in Karakuls is inherited as a simple autosomal recessive character, Rae.

The inherited lethal and semilethal characters in dogs are:

Abnormal stenotic larynx in Skye Terriers, Stormont.

Failure of the closure of the fontanelles in Cocker Spaniels, Stormont.

Cleft palate in brachycephalic breeds, Stormont.

Otocephaly in Beagles with a lack of a lower jaw and ears uniting beneath the head, hydrocephalus and other defects, Fox.

Cranioschisis in Cocker Spaniels is possibly recessive, Fox.

Esophageal achalasia or megaesophagus is seen in Wirehaired Fox Terriers, German Shepherd Dogs and other breeds. It is probably inherited as an autosomal dominant, Osborne et al., Burns and Fraser.

Lymphedema of limbs and trunk is inherited as an autosomal dominant condition in Labradors, Cairn Terriers and others, Patterson.

Hemophilias, type A or deficiency of factor VIII, and type B or deficiency of Factor IX (Christmas disease) are seen in Collies, German Shepherd Dogs, Beagles, Labradors, Cairn Terriers, Irish Setters, Greyhounds, Aberdeen Terriers, Scotch Terriers and others. Both are due to sex-linked recessive genes on the sex (X) chromosome and characterized by joint and subcutaneous hemorrhages in male dogs, Stormont, Patterson.

Deficiency of blood factor VII, a mild condition resulting in hemorrhage at the time of surgery in Beagles is due to an autosomal recessive gene, Patterson.

Hemolytic anemia in a chronic form in young Basenji dogs is due to a corpuscular defect causing a shortened red blood cell life span and is probably genetic, Ewing, Tasker et al..

Cardiac malformations or anomalies, probably due to a polygenic mode of inheritance, has been reported in Keeshonden, Patterson. Detweiler reported on 9 German Shepherd Dogs and 10 Boxers out of 22 dogs observed with an aortic stenosis and indicated a possible hereditary influence in these breeds. He also reported on two chromosomal abnormalities in dogs with defective hearts.

Patent ductus arteriosis was the most common congenital cardiac defect in dogs. It is a heritable defect seen most often in female Poodles, Collies and Pomeranians, Patterson.

Subaortic stenosis was the cause of 15 per cent of congenital heart disease in dogs and was possibly genetic in nature as it was seen mainly in German Shepherd Dogs, Boxers and Newfoundlands, Patterson and Flickinger.

Spontaneous hyperparathyroidism was apparently caused by an autosomal gene causing renal cortical hypoplasia in 41 of 47 affected Cocker Spaniels, Krook.

Paralysis with spinal muscular atrophy (Stockard's syndrome) in crosses between Great Danes, Bloodhounds and St. Bernards is due to at least 3 genetic factors, Stormont, Innes and Saunders.

Spinal dysraphism is an hereditary disease of Weimaraners due to lesions in the caudal spinal cord causing a hopping gait, McGrath.

Hereditary cerebellar ataxia is seen in Smooth Haired Fox Terriers, Bjork et al.. In Basset Hounds a form of ataxia and paralysis was due to deformed cervical vertebrae in males similar to wobbles in horses, Palmer and Wallace.

Progressive cerebellar ataxia starting at 3 months of age has been described in Kerry Blue Terriers, deLahunta and Hutt. There was a neuronal degeneration characterized by involvement of the Purkinje cells of the cerebellum and other nuclei in the brain. It is a possible simple recessive defect.

Other Hereditary Generally Nonlethal Defects in Dogs are:

Proneness to intervetebral disc luxation is inherited in certain long-bodied chondrodystrophoid types of dogs such as Dachshunds, Fox.

Epilepsy is seen in Fox Terriers, Poodles, Boxers and Keeshonds as a single autosomal recessive character, Innes and Saunders.

"Scotch Cramp" or recurrent tetany is a recessive neurosis in Scotch Terriers, Burns and Fraser, Innes and Saunders.

Polydactyly or double dew claws is due to a recessive character in a number of breeds, Fox, Burns and Fraser.

Elbow dysplasia with osteoarthritis with or without an ununited aconeal process is seen especially in German Shepherd Dogs, and also Pekinese, Poodles, Cocker Spaniels, Bassett Hounds, Great Danes, Newfoundlands,

Labradors and others, Fox, Ljunggren et al.. It is probably due to the presence of 3 dominant genes. Corley et al..

Proneness to vaginal prolapse is possibly inherited in Boxers and Bulldogs, Schutte.

Patellar luxation is a tibiofemoral deformity in toy-breeds and Poodles, Fox, Hodgman.

Hip dysplasia is inherited in a polygenic manner, Hutt (1967) and is seen in German Shepherd dogs, Labrador Retrievers, Newfoundlands, Alsatians, and many others, Fox.

Perthes Disease of the hip joint is seen in Fox Terriers, Alsatians and Cairn Terriers, Young.

Malocclusion or brachygnathism of the mandible is observed in Dachshunds and Cocker Spaniels and **prognathism of the mandible** in Bulldogs, Fox, Young, Burns and Fraser.

Shortened spine, "baboon" dogs of S. Africa is characterized by a humped back, very short neck and short tail, Hutt.

Hydrocephalus may be hereditary in Chihuahuas, Boston Terriers and others.

Achondroplasia and other related skeletal abnormalities in Scotch Terriers, Bulldogs, Sealyhams, Bassets, and Beagles, Fox.

Prolongation of soft palate and laryngeal collapse is seen in brachycephalic dogs as Boxers and Bulldogs, Fox.

Crooked tails is inherited in Fox Terriers, Young.

Taillessness or anury or brachyury is inherited in Cocker Spaniels and other breeds, Fox.

Inguinal hernia is seen most commonly in female Cocker Spaniels and Dachshunds, Young.

Umbilical hernia has a complex polygenic inheritance and is seen in Pekinese, Cocker Spaniels, Collies, Bull Terriers and others, Stormont, Fox, Young.

Diaphragmatic hernia may possibly be inherited as an autosomal recessive character, Feldman et al..

Cystinurea, causing soft, yellow urinary calculi in Dachshunds and other breeds, is apparently an autosomal recessive character and possibly sex-limited as it has been seen only in males, Patterson.

High uric acid excretion in Dalmatians is inherited as a simple recessive autosomal character, Hutt.

Epitheliogenesis imperfecta, ichthyosis, alopecia, acanthosis nigrans are congenital, possibly hereditary, defects of the skin in dogs, Kral and Schwartzman.

Hairlessness. The hairless breeds, such as the Mexican Hairless dogs, are heterozygous for this defect. In the homozygous state the fetuses are expelled dead or have an occlusion of the esophagus, Kral and Schwartzman, Stormont.

Merle or harlequin coloring is seen in heterozygotes, while in homozygotes the animals are white, show deafness and eye defects, such as microphthalmia. It is seen in Collies, Great Danes, and Bull Terriers, Stormont, Roberts, Cello.

Nasal solar dermatitis or "Collie nose" is seen in Collies and Shetland sheep dogs.

Proneness to dermatitis and skin diseases such as demodectic mange occurs in Dachshunds and Great Danes; alopecia in Chows and Boxers; and eczemas in Chows, Fox.

Dermoid sinuses on the back are seen in Rhodesian Ridgebacks, Fox, Stratton.

Trichiasis and distichia are seen in Poodles, Spaniels, Pekinese and Toy breeds, Fox, Hodgman.

Ectropion and entropion is genetic in a number of breeds such as: Spaniels, Bloodhounds, St. Bernards, and Chows, Fox, Hodgman.

Ocular fundus anomaly, ectasia syndrome or chorioretinal dysplasia is seen in nearly one-third of Collies and is a simple autosomal recessive character with variable expressivity, Fox, Yakely et al., Donovan and Wyman, and Roberts.

Cataract is a dominant defect in Beagles and Alsatians, Fox, Anderson and Schultz.

Microphthalmia is seen in homozygous "merles" or "harlequins," Fox, Cello. In Australian Sheperd dogs this is an autosomal recessive character, Gelatt and Veith.

Retinal detachment is a recessive character in Bedlington Terriers, Fox, Rubin.

Persistent pupillary membrane is possibly inherited as an autosomal, non-sex-linked type of inheritance with variable expression in Basenjii, Roberts and Bistner.

Progressive retinal degeneration and atrophy in Irish Setters, Gordon Setters, Laborador Retrievers, Norwegian Elkhounds, Minature and Toy Poodles and others usually progressing to blindness at adulthood or middle age, is usually an autosomal recessive character but other modes of inheritance are possible, Stormont, Patterson, Barnett.

Luxation of the lens and secondary glaucoma is seen in many breeds especially Wirehaired Fox Terriers, Hodgman; and in Norwegian Elkhounds and Sealyhams, Bistner.

Hemeralopia is reported in Alaskan Malamutes and Poodles as a simple autosomal recessive, Rubin, Bourns and Lord.

Dermoid cysts of the cornea are seen in St. Bernard and Newfoundlands and the mode of inheritance is not known, Fox.

Proneness to disease of the ear canal is seen in breeds such as Poodles, Bedlingtons, Sealyhams and

Wirehaired Fox Terriers with an excessive hair growth in the external ear canal, Young.

Deafness is seen in Bull Terriers, Dalmatians and Sealyhams and is often linked with the white coat color, Fox, Hodgman.

Cryptorchidism is seen commonly in brachycephalic breeds and has an irregular mode of inheritance, probably a modified recessive mode, Young. In Cocker Spaniels it is apparently a sex-linked autosomal recessive character, Fox, Ashdown.

Hydrocephalus is seen in Bulldogs and Beagles and is due to recessive genes, Fox.

Abnormal maternal behavior is seen most commonly in toy breeds, Fox.

Aggressive behavior is seen in German Shepherd Dogs and others, Fox.

Proneness to neoplasia such as: mastocytoma in Boxers, and pituitary tumors in Boston Terriers is observed, Fox, Burns and Fraser.

Inherited Semilethal or Nonlethal Defects in Cats are:

Porphyria is due to a simple autosomal dominant character, Tobias, Glenn et al..

Taillessness is noted in true Manx cats. It may be associated with a rabbity or hopping gait.

Strabismus or crosseyedness is seen in Siamese cats, Hyde.

Polydactyly is a dominant, autosomal character with a variable expression. All four feet or just the front feet, but never just the hind feet, may be affected. The extra toe may hang loosely from the skin or be attached with normal bones, Hutt (1964), Holzworth.

Hydrocephalus is a simple recessive gene in Siamese cats, Silson and Robinson. (See Figure 35)

Deafness is associated with white or albino color in cats, as in dogs. It is associated with agenesis of the organ of Corti, the spiral ganglion and the cochlear nuclei. A further study of the genetics of this condition is indicated, Innes and Saunders.

Retinal atrophy was reported occasionally in Siamese and Persian cats and might be hereditary as in dogs, Barnett.

"Cerebellar hypoplasia" has been described by Innes and Saunders and others as a possible genetic lesion since it is familial in nature. However, Kilham, Margoulis and Colby have reported that congenital infection of feline fetuses with panleucopenia virus produced cerebellar hypoplasia.

"Osteogenesis imperfecta" is **not** a genetic defect although it has been described as one in cats and dogs for many years because litter mates were often affected. Riser and Krook et al. have shown this to be a nutritional disease caused by all meat diets high in phosphorus and low in calcium.

It should be recognized that domestic animals probably carry many harmful genes in a recessive manner. For example Mead et al. found on breeding tests that six dairy bulls selected at random carried two lethal genes, four semilethal defects and two characters causing female sterility. According to Stormont probably few lethals ever reach frequencies higher than 0.10 in the general population and in most cases are at a level of 0.05 or less. In certain herds or kennels the incidence can become much higher. When a heterzygous male is bred to his daughters a 7:1 ratio of normals to abnormals should be found.

The actual frequency of lethals or the genetic load is not known for genetic defects. To get this information would require careful postmortem and diagnostic examination of all dead or defective newborn animals and those developing possible genetic diseases later in life. When the defective gene frequency of 0.50 is reached as in achondroplastic Dexter cattle all or 100 per cent of the animals are heteroygous for the lethal gene and 25 per cent of their progeny, a 3 to 1 ratio, are affected, or a ratio of 2 carriers to 1 lethal.

In a study of about 5,000 calves sired artificially, Herschler and coworkers reported that a high figure of 6.26 per cent were abnormal at birth but of these nearly half were expelled dead at term but appeared normal. The remaining calves had a variety of abnormalities. Of 1276 calves sired by 9 bulls 7.7 per cent were abnormal with a range of 3.8 to 15.7 per cent between bulls. Gilmore reported that losses due to inherited lethals might be as high as 5 to 6 per cent and in certain herds might be higher. The incidence of fetal anormalies in sheep is very low. Ercanbrack reported on over 54,000 lambs over a 15 year period in which bilateral cryptorchidism occurred in .0005 per cent, wry neck in .0007 per cent and crooked legs, unilateral cryptorchidism and "undershot" or "overshot" jaws in .001 per cent of the lambs. "Stillbirths" occurred in 4.4 per cent of the parturitions. Inbred groups of ewes had the highest number of defects. A careful recording system for defects found in the purebred cattle breeds is highly desirable to detect carrier bulls used in artificial insemination to prevent deleterious genes from becoming widely disseminated. This is particularly necessary when bulls used in artificial insemination are not progeny tested.

Most lethal and semilethal characters in animals cannot be detected in the heterozygous or carrier state. One of the best but costly way to test for carriers is test mating or progeny tests. According to Stormont and Hutt the minimum number of progeny needed to prove with 95 per cent assurance that a male is not a heterozygous carrier of a lethal trait is:

5 normal progeny if the sire is mated to homozygous carrier females.

11 normal progeny if the sire is mated to heterozygous carrier females.

23 normal progeny if the sire is mated to his daughters.

23 normal progeny if the sire is mated to his sibs with one parent heterozygous.

17 normal progeny if the sire is mated to his sibs with two parents heterozygous.

23 normal progeny if the sire is mated to his half sibs.

Since carriers are often difficult to locate, limited progeny testing may be carried out by inbreeding a sire to his daughters. With a defective gene frequency of .10 in a breed or herd, random mating would produce an incidence of 1 per cent defective animals. With a defective gene frequency of .01, random mating would produce an incidence of 0.1 per cent defective animals. But if a carrier or heterozygous sire was used at random in these latter two populations the incidence of defective animals would rise to 5 and 0.5 per cent, respectively. This is why it is highly desirable to mate a prospective AI stud to 200 to 600 random cows during his testing period. Adequate, prompt and complete reporting of defective calves from these matings is essential, Van Vleck.

Certain harmful traits may be spread widely if they are associated with desirable traits. This is called **pleiotropism,** Young. For example, the simple autosomal recessive defect with incomplete penetrance of gonadal hypoplasia in Swedish Highland cattle was greatly increased by selection for the white color. In 1936 it was present in 17.3 per cent of the cattle of the breed. By careful inspection and pedigree controls the condition was reduced to 9.4 per cent in 1948 and to 4.2 per cent in 1964, Bane. It will take many decades of careful control measures to reduce the incidence to below 1 per cent of the cattle. Thus early detection and control of defective traits is imperative. To eliminate a lethal or semilethal trait in a herd it is much easier to outcross with unrelated animals. For example to reduce hermaphroditism in polled goats rapidly, a horned buck should be used. This hides the undesirable character in the hetrozygotes produced.

Environmental conditions may play an important role in the expression of many lethal or semilethal defects. Some animals have a recessive character but won't exhibit it unless the environment is proper. For example porphyria in cattle requires a white skin and sunlight to produce the characteristic dermal lesion. It is not unusual for a defect of one gene to produce a chain reaction in the early embryo resulting in a variety or syndrome of signs and lesions in the newborn. In reviewing the lists of lethal or semilethal characters it is obvious that similar defects or homologies appear in a number of species including man. A study of these defects in animals may thus be of benefit to the understanding of human medicine and genetics. There is no doubt but that genetics or inheritance plays an important role in the resistance or susceptibility of certain animals to bacterial, viral or parasitic diseases, tumors, metabolic and endocrine diseases. The inheritance of these characters is probably polygenic. If management, drugs, nutrition or surgery are not adequate to control the disease, selection for disease resistance has proven of definite value and probably should be used more in animals than it is at present. For further excellent discussions of the control of defective characters see Hutt and Young.

Neither destroying nor ignoring defective animals is effective in eliminating a genetic problem appearing in a herd or kennel. The veterinarian should provide genetic counseling for his clients after he has mastered an understanding of genetic principles and is knowledgeable concerning the known hereditary animal diseases. According to the American Veterinary Medical Association's code of ethics, the performance of surgical procedures to conceal or correct genetic defects in animals to be shown, bred or sold is unethical.

"One principle is clear; it is as much the duty of the veterinarian to the community and to the state to use whatever influence and power he possesses to prevent the production of defective animals as it is to prevent the spread of infectious diseases. Each leads eventually to the same port.", Fincher and Williams.

Nongenetic or Congenital Defects or Anomalies in Domestic Animals

The non-genetic anomalies, or monsters, may be of innumerable types and degrees. If the malformation involves only an organ or part of the body it is called an **anomaly;** if the deformity is extensive the animal is spoken of as a **monster.** If a similar defect appears quite frequently in related individuals or those tracing back to a common ancestor, a genetic cause should be suspected. But some of these defects appearing in families or related animals in a herd may be due to environmental causes that would be impossible of differentiation without a carefully controlled experiment. Many nongenetic anomalies are similar to genetic anomalies and are called **phenocopies.** The nongenetic anomalies or monsters are caused by a variety of environmental factors or agents called **teratogens.** In recent years much basic research has been done on identifying the many factors that can effect genes or their function and produce anomalies, Kalter and Warkany, Wilson and Warkany, Nishimura, Willis, Wolstenholme and O'Connor, and Langman.

The period of high susceptibility to teratogenesis is the period of early differentiation in the embryo or about the time germ layers and organs are rapidly developing. The zygote is not as susceptible to teratogens during the period of the ovum or blastula or the period of the fetus as it is during the period of the embryo and organogenesis, especially the first half of that period.

The teratogenic agents or factors include the following:

Nutritional deficiencies in the dam including: Vitamin A and E, riboflavin, folic acid, pantothenic acid, niacin and other vitamin deficiencies, minerals such as iodine and possibly manganese, and amino acids such as tryptophane may cause congenital defects. Hypervitaminoses A and D will also cause anomalies in animals.

Endocrine disturbances of the dam as in: diabetes, thyroid malfunction, and large exogenous doses of glucocorticoids, ACTH, insulin, androgens, progestagens, estrogens, thyroxine and thiouracil will cause defects of the embryo. Large doses of glucocorticoids in pregnant animals at the proper stage of gestation may cause cheilo- or palatoschisis, Evans et al.. Progestagens given during pregnancy may cause masculinization of the genitalia of female fetuses, Curtis and Grant.

Physical factors such as: reduced atmospheric pressures, hypothermia, hyperthermia and anoxia cause anomalies.

Radiation by X-ray or radioactive substances induces congenital defects, McFee et al..

Drugs or chemicals as: thalidomide, quinine, sulphonamides, tetracycline, streptomycin, salvarsan, lead, mercury, nicotine, malathion, carbon tetrachloride, apholate, selenium, fluorine, cytotoxic agents including aminopterin in sheep, James and Keeler, nitrogen mustard, actinomycin D, 6 mercaptopurine, azoserine, azo dye, trypan blue and other dyes, salicylates, histamines, ergot, "Diamox," reserpine, phenylmercuric acid, galactose, E.D.T.A. and certain plant compounds as in **Veratrum californicum** and locoweeds possibly containing lathyrogens, Keeler et al. have all produced fetal anomalies in animals under certain conditions.

Infections such as the viruses of: blue tongue in sheep, Griner et al., hog cholera in swine, Emerson and Delez and Harding et al., feline panleucopenia in cats, Kilham et al., bovine virus diarrhea—mucosal disease virus, Ward and Roberts, and rubella or measles in women, Mullins et al., and toxoplasma can cause anomalies in the embryo.

Ageing of ova by delaying ovulation 24 to 48 hours was characterized by a three-fold increase in chromosomal anomalies with a higher incidence of embryonic death in rats, Butcher and Fugo. Similarly ageing of rabbit spermatozoa before permitting them to fertilize eggs resulted in normal fertilization but greater embryonic death losses, Tesh and Glover. Pregnancy in older women resulted in greater numbers of mongoloid newborn, while achondroplasia was much higher in children from older fathers, Lenz. Thus age affects the genes and chromosomes as does other agents, Potter.

Other agents not mentioned have also been shown to be teratogens. These above agents behave very similar to genes by acting at certain critical stages of development on specific tissues. Some teratogens, as x-rays, have an acute or sudden effect on the early embryo and others exert a chronic effect such as in vitamin deficiencies. Environmental factors that effect teratogenesis include the age of the embryo at time of the insult, genetic predisposition of the species, the drug or agent present, the dose, the mode of administration, rate of excretion and the presence or absence of protective factors. In humans Assali reported that 30 per cent of congenital anomalies were genetic, 10 per cent due to viral infections of early pregnancy and 60 per cent due to other environmental factors. Gilmore and Fechheimer reported that of 8627 calves sired by 532 bulls the incidence of congenital abnormalities was 5.49 per cent with 1.77 per cent being small weak newborn, 1.05 per cent having defects of bone, joints or cartilage, 2.66 per cent "stillbirths," 0.16 per cent nerve and eye defects, and 0.19 per cent epithelial and genital abnormalities. The two greatest periods of death losses were during the first trimester of pregnancy and at the time of parturition.

The noninherited teratologic defects of development may be divided into two general classes, Potter and Runnells:

1. Those malformations due to alterations in tissue differentiation that have arisen from a single area in the embryonic disc. Most of these are due to the local arrest in the normal process of tissue development and produce:

Defects due to excessive division—for example, polydactylia, polythelia, polydontia.

Defects due to failure of structures to fuse normally—for example, palatoschisis, cheiloschisis, cranioschisis, spina bifida, and schistosomus.

Defects due to arrest in division—for example, cyclopia; ren arcuatus or horseshoe kidney; and syndactyly.

Defects due to complete local failure of tissue growth; for example amelia or lack of limbs; ectrodactyly or absence of phalanges; vertebral or costal abnormalities; epitheliogenesis imperfecta; acrania; agnathia; and anophthalmia.

Defects due to arrest in assumption of final form or position—for example, ectopia cordis, hypognathia, and dextro-position of the aorta.

Defects in the persistence and disappearance of contiguous structures that normally follow a certain pattern—for example, the aortic arches, foramen ovale, urachus, ductus arteriosus and persistence of the median wall of the paramesonephric or Mullerian duct.

Defects due to overdevelopment of local tissues—for example, polycystic kidneys; tumors such as sarcomas, hemagiomas and teratomas.

Defects due to displacement of tissue such as teratomas and dermoid cysts.

Defects due to fusion of sexual characters—such as, true hermaphrodites, false hermaphrodites, and freemartins.

Defects due to miscellaneous causes—for example, ichthyosis, chondrodystrophies, osteogenesis imperfecta, and porphyrinuria.

2. Anomalies or teratologic defects may be grouped for naming by the organs or tissues involved, Potter and Runnells.

Anomalies of the heart and blood vessels are relatively common in animals. Lilleengen reported on 159 cases of cardiac anomalies in animals, of which 37 were observed by that author. Of these, 91 cases were in cattle, 28 in horses, 17 in dogs, 8 in pigs, and 5 in cats. Olafson has described 15 cases in animals, most of which were in cattle. The author has recorded 37 cases of cardiac anomalies in cattle in which about one-third were associated with other teratologic defects. In many animals with cardiac defects death occurred soon after birth. A few animals survived a long period due to compensatory factors. For example subaortic septal defects in some cyanotic calves cause early death, while other calves similarly affected may live for years. In cervical ectopia cordis most calves die soon after birth while others survive; the author knew of one such cow that lived for 13 years.

In cattle a subaortic septal defect was found by the author in 18 of 37 cattle with cardiac aberrations. This defect was commonly associated with anopthalmus or micropthalmus and a twisted shortened tail and was seen mainly in Guernseys. Clinically the affected animals showed shortness of breath on exercise, rapid pulse rate, increased cardiac area, cyanosis, and a marked systolic bruit especially over the right side of the thorax where a thrill was often palpable. Another very common defect, observed in 12 out of 37 cases in cattle, was the transposition of the aorta into the dextroposition or Eisenmenger complex, where it arose from the right ventricle or over the right ventricle and interventricular septum. In these cases and those cited by Sass and Albert the left ventricle was usually very small or nonfunctional and a persistence of a foramen ovale or a subaortic septal defect or both were necessary so that blood from the left atrium could get into the right ventricle. Not infrequently the ductus arteriosus was persistent. In these cases, especially with the latter defect, similar symptoms were shown but the systolic bruit was more pronounced on the left side of the thorax and a thrill was not palpable.

Other cardiac anomalies include atresia of the aorta with persistence of the ductus arteriosus; cor triloculare biatrium; teratology of Fallot; ectopia cordis, either cervical, pectoral or abdominal, Kurtz and Ellery; (See Figure 52) persistence of the right aortic arch with absence of the left causing stenosis of the esophagus; and various types of acardiac monsters.

In dogs congenital heart anomalies are quite common with an incidence of about 1 percent. Since many neonatal pups die without a postmortem examination some deaths could be due to cardiac defects. Some of these are genetic. The most common congenital heart defects in dogs are: pulmonic stenosis, aortic stenosis, patent ductus arteriosus, interventricular septal defect, tetratology of Fallot, persistent right aortic arch with a left ductus arteriosus resulting in compression of the esophagus and pericardial defects, Patterson, Wysong.

Cardiovascular anomalies in the **cat and sheep** are uncommon and have been reviewed by Will and Dennis and Leipold. The latter reported that of 4,417 lambs necropsied, 401 had congenital defects and 51 or 12.7 percent had cardiac defects, most commonly septal defects. **In horses** congenital valvular defects are most common, Lilleengen. Bartels and Vaughn described a foal with a persistent right aortic arch with a left ductus arteriosus. Dennis reported 45 newborn lambs with ventricular septal defects. Excellent medical discussions of various human cardiac anomalies are provided by Abbott and Langman.

Other anomalies of the thorax and lungs are not common in domestic animals. Occasionally congenital diaphragmatic hernias have been described in the dog and cat, Frye and Taylor, and in cattle, Troutt et al. **Anomalies of the lungs** are rare in animals. Thomson described 2 calves with accessory lungs and one with bronchial hypoplasia. He also reviewed the lung anomalies described in animals.

Anomalies of the digestive or alimentary tract. The brachycephalic breeds of dogs quite commonly are affected with cleft palate and hare-lip or cheiloschisis. The condition results in difficulty in nursing or drinking and milk may return through the nostrils. This condition is occasionally seen in cattle and horses. A ranula or retention cyst of the sublingual or submaxillary salivary gland is observed occasionally in dogs and other animals and is usually due to injury to the salivary ducts. True branchial cysts are less frequently seen but are lined with epithelium, not granulation tissue as are salivary cysts, Karbe. These cysts are probably due to an anomaly in the development or regression of branchial duct II, pharyngobranchial duct II and the cervical vesicle. Severe anomalies of the face and head and thorax, obstruction of the esophagus or high intestinal obstructions in monster fetuses are often associated with hydramnios. According to Potter no meconium is normally evaculated during intrauterine life except when the oxygen supply is reduced. With anoxia the fetus becomes distressed and the anal sphincter relaxes. Atresia ani is seen in all domestic animals but most commonly in swine. It may be a genetic defect. In females the anus is imperforate but often a union with the urinary and genital structures has occurred, resulting in a common cloaca, Dennis.

Abdominal hernias such as umbilical hernias are due to failure of the normal closure of the abdominal ring and may also be genetic in nature. Failure of the abdominal wall to close may be due to large retention cysts or overgrowth of certain abdominal organs. The liver is seldom affected by anomalies except for cysts and other abnormalities in cases of bovine **Schistosomus reflexus.** Congenital diaphragmatic and peritoneopericardial diaphragmatic hernias have been reported, Feldman et al. and Bolton et al..

Anomalies of the urinary system are not uncommon. Polycystic kidneys are seen in almost all domestic animals, especially swine. Fusion of the caudal poles of the kidneys, ren arcuatus, to form a single horseshoe-shaped kidney is occasionally observed especially in monster fetuses. Occasionally marked hypoplasia of one or both kidneys may occur, or in rare cases one or both kidneys may be absent: unilateral or bilateral agenesis, Murti. Stenosis due to local muscle hypertrophy of the ureter at the bladder, or atresia of the ureters, will cause cystic dilation, hydroureter and hydronephrosis. Cauley and Archibald reported on two dogs with ectopic ureters opening into the vagina resulting in constant dribbling of urine from the vulva. Sager noted a similar condition in a mare. Carrig et al. reported on an ectopic ureter in a heifer that opened into the urethra and caused incontinence. Osborne and Perman reported on a rare ectopic ureter in a male dog that terminated in the urethra. They also reviewed the congenital anomalies of the urinary system in the dog and cat. In occasional instances the urachus fails to close at birth, resulting in a persistent dribbling of urine from the navel. This is seen most commonly in foals.

Anomalies of the sexual organs and gonads will be discussed in future chapters on infertility in female and male animals.

Mammary gland anomalies include fused teats and supernumerary glands and teats. Some of the supernumerary teats, polythelia, may be fused to the normal teat. The mammary glands in virgin animals may enlarge and secrete a small amount of milk during gestation due to the effect of hormones from the placenta or from the ovary, or from granulosa cell tumors. Congenital atresia, or stenosis of one or more teats or glands, may occur but this is difficult to differentiate from pathological processes that may have occurred prior to or after parturition. A rare case of total mammary gland aplasia was reported in a fertile cow, Gaunya and coworkers.

Hermaphrodism or intersexuality occurs most commonly in goats and pigs and less commonly in horses and dogs. It is occasionally present in sheep and cattle and is rare in the cat. **Intersexes** are individuals in which the diagnosis of the sex is confused because of congenital anatomical variations. Conditions in intersexes include hermaphroditism, abnormalities of the accessory genital organs, gonadal dysgenesis, and freemartinism, Biggers and McFeeley, McFeeley et al.. These latter two conditions will be discussed later. Eaton reported that pseudohermaphrodites occurred in 11.1 percent of Saanen and 6 percent of Toggenburg goats. According to Asdell this figure may be as high as 14.9 percent of pseudohermaphrodites in certain herds, with a sex ratio of 55.1 percent males, 30 percent females and 14.9 percent pseudohermaphrodites. Thus these caprine pseudohermaphrodites, even though they have testes, are females according to the sex ratio, sex chromatin studies and chromosome analyses. In goats this condition is a simple recessive sex-limited character associated with hornlessness or the polled condition. Horned hermaphrodites are extremely rare. A similar recessive type of hermaphroditism in swine was described by Gerneke. Pond et al.. reported on an inbred swine herd where of 106 pigs from 11 litters sired by a single boar there were 68 males, 22 females and 16 intersexes. Some hermaphrodites may be congenetic.

Intersexes may be separated into males or females based on (1) their genetic sex, either chromosomal or nuclear sex, (2) their gonadal sex or presence of ovaries or testes, (3) their phenotypic sex or the morphology of their accessory genital organs, and (4) possibly their hormonal or behavioral sex, Hafez. Hermaphrodites are usually classified on the basis of gonadal sex with **true hermaphrodites** having both testes and ovaries or ovotestes and **pseudohermaphrodites** having gonads of only one sex. **Male pseudohermaphrodites** phenotypically resemble females but have testes and **female pseudoherma-**

phrodites resemble males but have ovaries. Some workers such as Crew and others prefer to consider the terms true hermaphroditism and pseudohermaphroditism as misnomers indicating they should be regarded as degrees of intersexuality.

The true hermaphrodite is rare and has internal genitalia resembling both sexes and external genitalia of an intermediate type that may tend either toward the male or female. True hermaphrodites are reported most frequently in swine. In most cases the genetic sex is female (XX) but it is likely that on further study many of these cases may prove to be mosaics or chimeras produced by nondisjunction and/or other mitotic errors during mitosis early in embryogenesis or dispermic fertilization of an ovum by an X-bearing sperm and a nonextruded polar body by a Y-bearing sperm resulting in tissues with variable sex chromosome complements such as: XX/XY, XXY, XXYY or XXXY and etc., Dunn et al. and Dunn. Two such cases of true hermpahrodites in cattle were described by these authors as occurring in single born animals; one had XX/XY and the other XX/XXY cell types especially noted in the kidneys and gonads. Both cattle appeared to be males with a penis but no testes in the scrotum. On internal examination one had an ovary and an ovotestis; the other had a normal ovary and a very undeveloped gonad consisting of primitive medullary tissue. Both had a fairly well developed uterus.

The female pseudohermaphrodite is also rare in animals. Intersexes with female gonads and external genitalia resembling the male may be produced by exposure to androgens during embryonic life. This might be caused by a lesion of the adrenal gland or a biochemical lesion of steroidogenesis. Female or true hermaphrodites with fairly normal external and internal female structures may rarely be fertile since ovulation may occur, Hulland.

The male pseudohermaphrodite is very common with testes in the abdominal cavity or beneath the skin in the scrotal region. (See Figures 35, 36, 37) The scrotum seldom develops in these animals, due to the anomalous growth of the external genital organs which usually

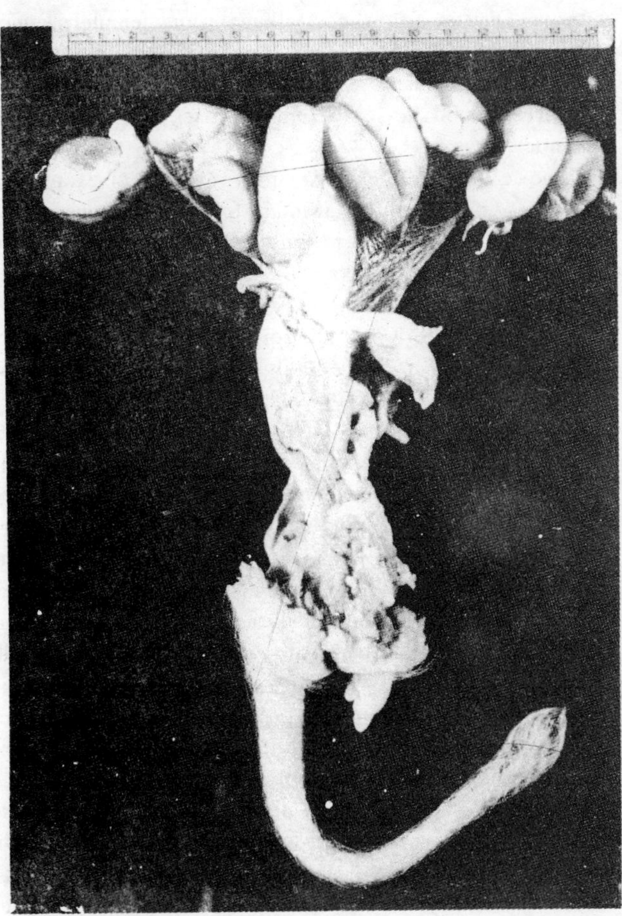

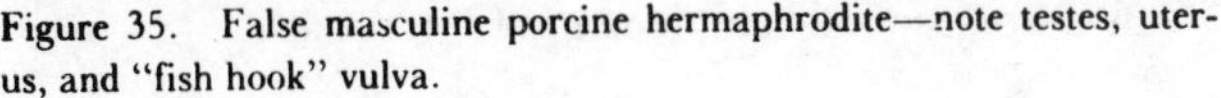

Figure 35. False masculine porcine hermaphrodite—note testes, uterus, and "fish hook" vulva.

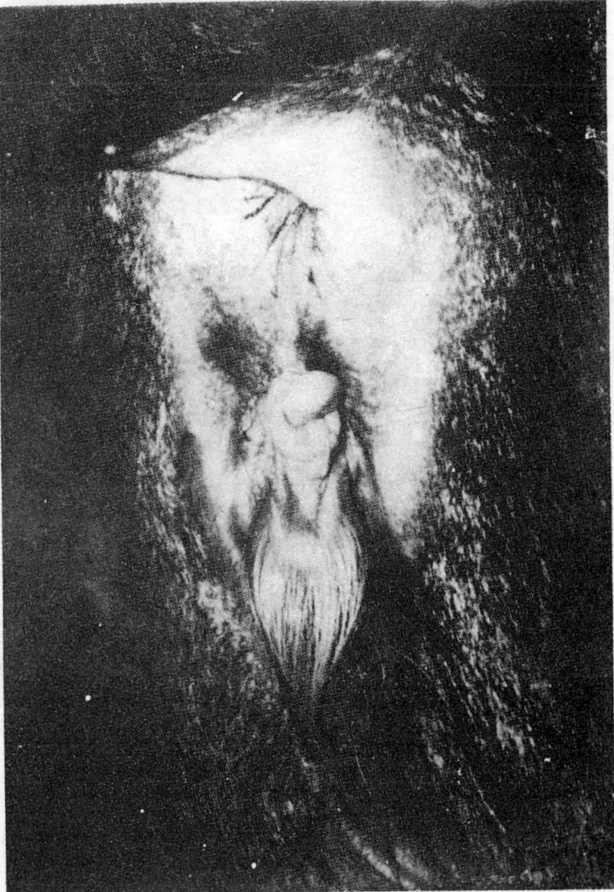

Figure 36. False masculine bovine hermaphrodite—The testes were beneath the skin in the inguinal region.

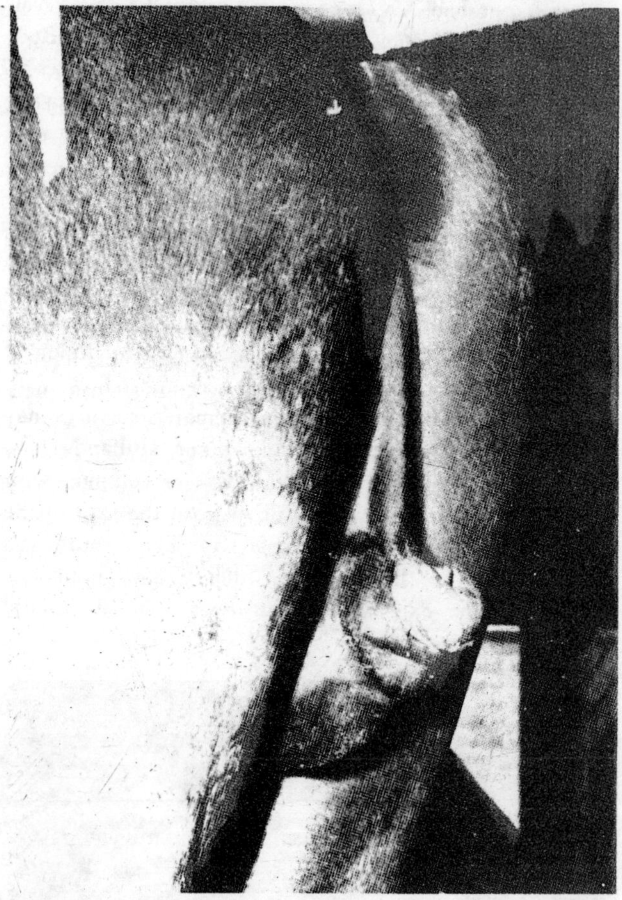

Figure 37. False masculine equine hermaphrodite—This horse behaved like a stallion.

Figure 38. Diphallus or double penis in a bull.

resemble the female. Often a greatly enlarged clitoris is present, which with the vulvar configuration, called "fish-hook" vulva in swine, often causes these animals, when urinating, to direct the stream in a greater dorsal arc than does the normal female. The location of the urethral opening may be anywhere from that of the normal female to one in a penis-like structure with hypospadias in the scrotal or abdominal region. If animals possessing these abnormal characters resemble the female sufficiently to deceive the owners, they may be detected by their failure to show signs of estrum, and by their body appearance of a male castrate. Hermaphrodites commonly resemble cryptorchid males or nymphomaniacs in their male actions and attitudes. In the male pseudohermaphrodite the internal genitalia resemble both sexes and a uterus-like structure is nearly always present. Hermpahrodites are invariably sterile, especially males with intraabdóminal or subcutaneously located testes. A male pseudohermaphritic dog developed pyometra in its large bicornuate uterus, Frey et al.. Almost all male and female pseudohermaphrodites are genetic or chromosomal females (XX) and are positive on nuclear sexing as indicated by the presence of the sex chromatin mass or Barr body in the nucleus.

The technic of nuclear sexing consisting of examining certain somatic cells of animals for the presence of the inactive X chromosome in the nucleus has been described by Ashley, Moore, and Sohval. Cells from various tissues that are most satisfactory to examine will differ from species to species but buccal epithelium, nerve cells and polymorphonuclear neutrophils are most commonly utilized. The Feulgen staining method is highly satisfactory after the cells are fixed. The cells are examined for a dark-staining, small, about 0.8 by 1.2 micron, planoconvex mass or body against the inside of the nuclear membrane. In neutrophils this body is observed as a similar-sized small projecting mass, a sessile body or "drumstick," attached by a small stalk to the nucleus. These sex chromatin masses or Barr bodies, named after the person who first described them, are observed in most female cells examined and are absent in the cells of males. Thus females are sex chromatin positive and males are sex chromatin negative. In female or male cells with abnormal numbers of sex chromosomes, XXX, XXXY, and etc., the number of Barr bodies observed is always one less than the number of X chromosomes. Although nuclear sexing is a very helpful and simple technique, examination of the chromosomes by karyotyping is more accurate and informative especially for the determination of the true chromosomal complement of intersexes.

When gonadal tissue in the embryo remains undifferentiated, undeveloped, is absent, or is removed early in embryonic life, the internal and external genitalia become female in character. The Y chromosome is apparently necessary to initiate the development of the testis and the testicular secretions produce the external genital organs characteristic of the male animal. An individual with XXY or XXXY chromosome make-up will have a male phenotype but he is sterile. In humans in which extensive cytogenetic studies have been conducted in these XXY individuals with Kleinfelter's syndrome there are certain characteristic distinguishing features in their anatomical appearance and they may also be mentally deficient. In another common chromosomal deficiency in humans called Turner's syndrome the Y chromosome is missing. The individual which has an XO chromosomal complement is a short, stocky female often with a webbed neck, mentally deficient and with undifferentiated rudimentary gonads or gonadal dysgenesis, Sohval, Armstrong and Marshall and Crew and others. Gerneke has reported, however, that in male pseudohermaphroditic swine, and probably the same would be true in goats where this condition is also genetic, that cells have only an XX chromosome complement. Hypoplastic testicular development with modification of the external genital tract occurs in the absence of the Y chromosome. Gerneke discussed how autosomal modifiers in this sex-limited recessive condition might cause the development of the testes. Injections of male sex hormones into the dam during gestation will cause modification of the external genitals of a female fetus in the male direction, Curtis and Grant. Thus hormones or substances from the embryonic testis after differentiation are responsible for the development of the external male genital organs.

Hybrids are an extreme outcross, such as a cross of the ass on the mare to produce the mule or the sheep on the goat, the dog on the coyote, and the bison on the cow. Workers in the field of cytogenetics have been making interesting conclusions from the study of hybrids, Benirschke. The ass with a diploid chromosome number of 62 when mated with the horse with a diploid chromosome number of 64 produces a mule with the chromosome number of 63. The female mule has an undisturbed ovarian hormonal function producing normal follicles and corpora lutea, exhibiting estrum and occasionally showing mammary development with the production of milk. The female and male mules are sterile, probably due to a failure of gametogenesis caused by asynapsis during the first meiotic division. A number of alleged fertile female mules examined by Benirscke were found to be donkeys rather than mules when chromosome studies of their body cells were made.

Berry reported that 45 percent of female goats bred to rams conceived, however they all aborted before 145 days. The diploid chromosome number of sheep is 54, goats, 60 and their embryonic hybrids was 57. Both the dog and coyote have similar karyotypes with 78 chromosomes each and although many believe these hybrids may produce fertile offspring further experimentation is needed. Williams reported that the dystocia occurring at the birth of a hybrid produced by mating a bison bull with possibly 60 chromosomes and a domestic cow having 60 chromosomes was due to the severe amnioallantoic dropsy regularly present. Further study is also needed with this hybrid to determine the mechanisms involved in this abnormality.

Anomalies of the head and central nervous system may include:

Microcephalus is characterized by a small cranial cavity and brain.

Cyclopia or cebocephalus is characterized by a single orbit in which global tissue is absent or rudimentary or in which the eyeballs vary from a single apparently normal eye through all degrees of doubling to one consisting of two complete but small adjacent globes (See Figures 41 and 42). Eyelids are rudimentary or absent and the nose is usually absent or in the form of a tubular appendage placed above the centrally located eye. This rudimentary nose does not communicate with the pharynx. The **skull** is usually small and the lower jaw, being longer than the defective upper jaw, is curved dorsally at its cranial end. Cyclopia is seen most commonly in the pig and sheep but may be present in all species.

Binn and coworkers (1959) studied a congenital malformation of sheep that affected 1 to 8 percent of the newborn lambs in flocks in southwestern Idaho characterized by cyclopia or a "monkey-faced" condition, harelip, cleft palate, hydrocephalus, short upper jaw, prolonged gestation of 200 days or more with fetal weights up to 20 lbs., associated with involution of the mammary gland, a small dark vulva, and occasionally rupture of the prepubic tendon due to the large size of the fetus or fetuses. They determined this condition was not due to a genetic character. Head defects were severe in the overtime fetuses. The pituitary gland or hypophysis was absent or grossly defective, Binns et al. (1960). Subsequent work by Binns et al. (1963) showed the cause of this condition to be the ingestion of **Veratrum californicum** between 8 and 17 days and later the critical day was found to be the 14th day of gestation. If the feeding of this plant was continued after the 15th day, embryonic death apparently occurred in a high percentage of ewes. If they were on range the incidence of "dry" ewes at lambing was 10 to 15 percent rather than the normal 1 percent. The teratogenesis of this condition was described by Evans et al..

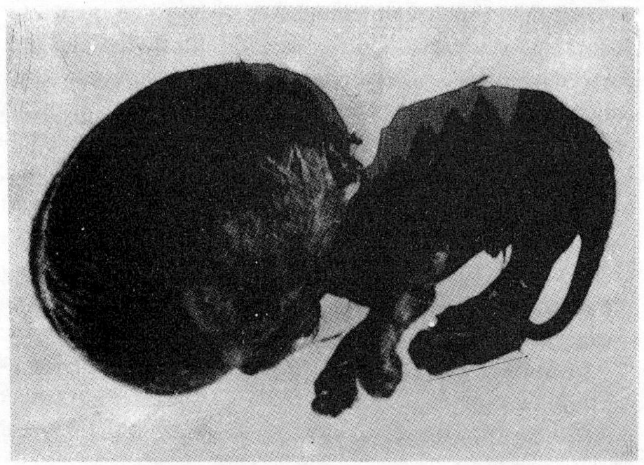

Figure 39. Hydrocephalus in a Siamese cat fetus.

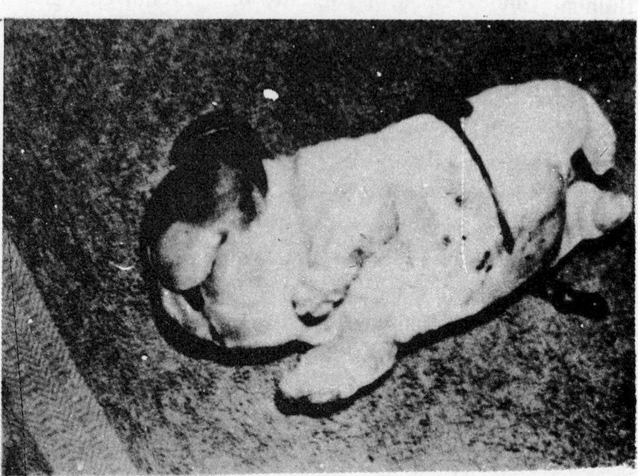

Figure 40. Anasarca or edema of a Beagle fetus.

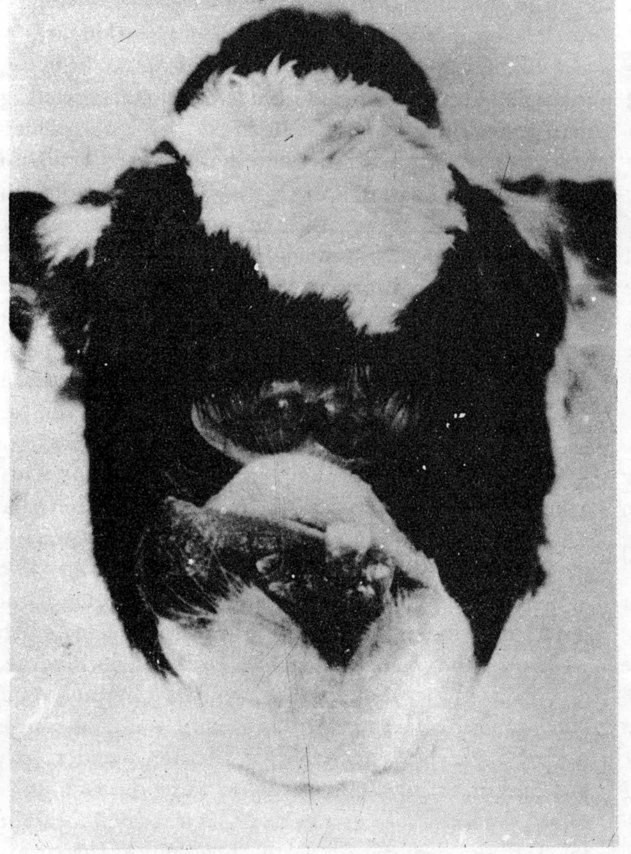

Figure 41. Cyclopia or cebocephalus of a Holstein calf.

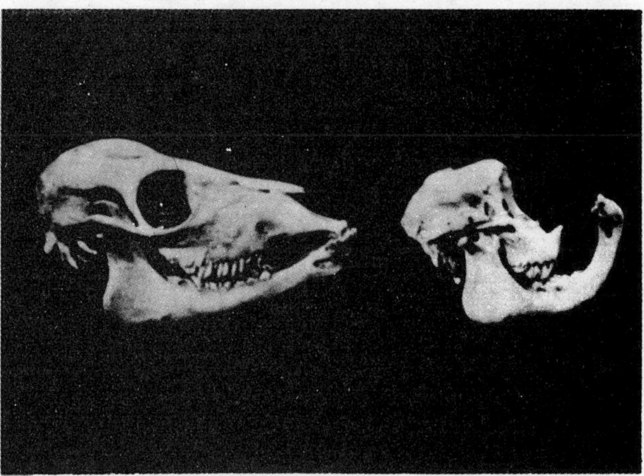

Figure 42. Skulls of normal and cebocephalic calves.

Hydrocephalus is due to an abnormal accumulation of fluid in the cranial cavity. Internal hydrocephalus is due to excessive fluid in the ventricular system. External hydrocephalus is rare and due to excessive fluid between the brain and dura mater. Internal and external hydrocephalus may be combined. About 99 percent of human cases are caused by an obstruction to the passage of the cerebral spinal fluid into the arachnoid spaces usually due to an associated spina bifida in the fetus. Potter. In marked cases the dorsal portion of the brain is encompassed only by the skin, the subcutaneous tissues, and the brain coverings. (See Figure 39)

Cranioschisis or crania bifida are defects of the skull that may result in meningocele or meningoencephalocele. In the later instance the skull defect is large, so that parts of the brain and the meninges are extruded.

Anomalies of the head—Facial fissures include palatoschisis, cheiloschisis, macrostomia, and schistoprosopus or divided face. Lack of cranial or facial structures include acephalia, or absence of a head; acrania; hemicrania; astomia; microstomia, arhinencephalia or absence of a nose, agnathis, hypognathia, anophthalmus, microphthalmia, aprosopia or partial or complete absence of a face, anotia or absence of ears, polyotia and polydontia or anodontia, Elzay and Hughes. Congenital defects of the head and ears of ovine fetuses are common. (See Figure 53) Anophthalmus and microphthalmia may possibly be related to a severe vitamin A deficiency, Palludan.

Cerebellar hypoplasia and allied defects have been described as a possible genetic or congenital abnormality in all domestic animals. **Cerebellar hypoplasia** or **aplasia** can be produced in newborn kittens by infecting the pregnant dam with feline panleucopenia virus, Kilham et al.. It can be produced in newborn calves by infecting the pregnant dam around the fifth month of gestation with BVD-MD virus. Eye lesions, especially cataracts, were also present, Ward and Kahrs, Scott and deLahunta. Hog cholera virus introduced into a pregnant sow may cause lesions of the fetal brain resulting in myoclonia congenita or "shivering" pigs, Harding et al.. Blue tongue virus will cause central nervous system anomalies in ovine fetuses if it infects them around 40 to 50 days of gestation, Griner et al.. All of these lesions are due to the effect of the virus on the developing fetal nervous tissues. Koch and Rubin have described **nonhereditary congenital cataracts** in dogs as possibly due to some intrauterine virus infection of the fetuses. Congenital cataracts are also observed in foals, Gelatt et al.. **Optic nerve hypoplasia** with blindness has been observed in horses, Gelatt et al. and in cattle where it may be associated with a vitamin A deficiency. **Entropion** is common in newborn lambs, certain breeds of dogs and occasionally is seen in foals. Some of these cases are probably congenital but a genetic cause is likely in most animals.

Hydranencephaly and **arthrogryposis** or muscle contractures in newborn calves of various breeds have been described as due to non-hereditary causes in Australia by Whittem. Blindness was also a part of this syndrome in some calves. The agent causing the anomalies was believed to have been active between 2 and 6 months of gestation.

Crooked calf disease characterized by arthrogryposis, torticollis, scoliosis and occasionally cleft palate has been described in northwestern United States and Alaska and resembles the Australian disease clinically except for the hydranencephaly and blindness in the latter, King, Shupe and coworkers. The latter have shown the cause of crooked calf disease to be the feeding of lupines between the 40th and 70th day of gestation. Lupine toxicosis was due to the high alkaloid content of the grazed plant. An incidence of up to 2 to 3 percent of affected calves was reported in certain breeds. Certain species of locoweeds, **Astragalus** and **Oxytropis,** were toxic for sheep and cattle when ingested causing abortion and deformed limbs in fetuses. These plants accumulate selenium but feeding selenium experimentally did not produce the congenital defects. Feeding the plants from the 1st through 100th day of gestation produced contracted tendons, anterior flexure and hypermobility of hock joints and flexure of the carpus, James et al.. Manganese deficiency in cattle produced newborn calves with contracted tendons of the fore and hind limbs, Rojas, Dyer and Cassatt. Rooney reported on the commonly observed condition of contracted foals and indicated that no genetic cause was suspected for this congenital defect. Mild cases could be associated with intrauterine crowding. In most cases the characteristic anatomical changes were hypoplasia of the intervertebral articulations, hypoplasia and twisting of the long metacarpal and metatarsal bones and asymmetry of the cranial skeleton. The cause was unknown. Pritchard and Voss have reported on 4 males grazing Sudan pasture early in gestation, about 20 to 50 or more days, that delivered dead foals with ankylosed extremities at term. Evidence of a toxic reaction to Sudan pasture with cystitis and ataxia have been reported in adult horses.

These anomalies of the central nervous system are often characterized externally by ankylosed joints, deformed fetlocks or "club feet" and other defects including hydramnios in some severely affected fetuses. As with other markedly defective fetuses their size is usually smaller than normal.

Anomalies of the skeleton. These are observed quite frequently in domestic animals and include:

Achondroplasia, chondrodystrophy or dwarfism—There are apparently several types and degrees of this defect and most, or all, are hereditary. In achondroplastic fetuses the long bones are abnormally short. The trunk is of normal length and the abdomen is large. The head is moderately enlarged and flattened. "Bulldog" head and brachygnathism of the maxilla, "undershot," or prognathism of the mandible, "overshot," are common. In Herefords, the recessive gene for dwarfism is found commonly in the heterozygous "comprest" animal. Most dwarfs are the result of a complex mode of inheritance. (See genetic bovine defects)

Spina bifida or rachischisis is the absence of the dorsal portions of the vertebrae or vertebral arches often in the lumbar or sacral region with defective rear limbs and tail and paralysis of the rear parts. It is seen in Angus, Holsteins, Bull terriers and other animals. This anomaly may resemble the **Perosomus elumbis** monster.

Tailessness, anury or Perosomus acaudatus is seen as a common defect in dairy and beef cattle characterized by a lack of coccygeal vertebrae and deformed sacral vertebrae with a sunken perineal region and in some cases a characteristic hopping gait. The condition could not be proven to be genetic in nature by Gilmore and Fechheimer and Huston and Wearden.

Hemivertebrae have been seen most commonly in English bulldogs and Boston terriers resulting in failure of the centers of ossification to unite. Scoliosis, kinked tails and a shortened spine are present if many vertebrae are involved, Archibald.

Anomalies of the trunk—Schistosomus reflexus is seen most commonly in cattle but in rare cases may be observed in sheep, goats, Dennis, and Meyer and Bedford, and swine. It is characterized by a marked ventral curvature of the spine so the occiput of the head lies near the sacrum. The body and chest walls are bent laterally and the thoracic and abdominal viscera are exposed. The pelvis is deformed. The liver is abnormal in shape and cystic. The rumen is occasionally distended with fluid. The limbs are usually ankylosed and rigid. In rare cases the limbs and head may be enclosed in a complete sac of skin. (See Figure 43) **Campylorrachis scoliosa** is a fetal monster, rarely seen in cattle and swine, characterized by a lateral curvature of the spine. The limbs are usually deformed and ankylosed. **Persomus elumbis** is seen occasionally in cattle and swine and is characterized by a lack of vertebrae and spinal cord caudal to the thoracic region. The monster has a small, flattened, deformed pelvis with strongly ankylosed and flexed hind limbs and atrophy of the muscles of the real quarters (See Figure 44) **Perosomus horridus** is a bovine fetal monster with general ankylosis and muscle contractures. It is characterized on external examination by a short spine. This is due to a marked double S-shaped lateral twisting of the vertebrae. (See Figure 45) Fetal monsters may be present with a normal, probably dizygotic twin.

Anomalies of the limbs include amelia, missing or "amputated" extremities; (See Figure 54) micromelia; hemimelia, or absence of the distal half of the limb; sirenomelus, or fusion of the hind limbs with varying amounts of hypoplasia and deformity of the pelvis and pelvic organs; hypoplasia of the extremities; polydactyly, or the increased number of digits or claws in cats, dogs, cattle, horses and swine; syndactyly or the union of digits or claws, especially in cattle and swine; and ectrodactyly or absence of phalanges, Leipold et al.. Amelia or hemimelia were characteristic congenital defects in thalidomide toxicity in humans in the early 1960's. Ectopia of the patella has been reported in cattle, dogs and horses, Finocchio and Guffy.

Miscellaneous anomalies due to displacement of tissues include teratomas, dermoids, and dentigerous cysts. The last condition, characterized by a displaced dental follicle containing fluid and teeth, is seen most commonly in the horse. These dentigerous cysts may be located beneath the ear and are called an "ear tooth." Dermoids are seen occasionally on the cornea, third eyelid or on the neck in cattle and other species. In horses dermoid tumors may rarely involve the ovary or testis, especially the retained testis. Teratomas are occasionally seen in all species

Embryonic duplications are malformations due to abnormal duplication of the germinal area giving rise to fetuses whose body structures are partially but not completely duplicated. According to Potter, embryonic duplications include:

A. Free monozygotic or dizygotic twins or triplets
   1. Symmetrical twins are either monozygotic or identical, or dizygotic or fraternal.
   2. Asymmetrical twins consist of a normal and an acardiac or monster individual. These may include three types:

      Hemicardius is a very imperfect individual but parts are recognizable and a rudimentary heart is present.

      Holocardius acephalus—The cranial part of very imperfect individual is lacking. No heart is present. (See Figure 50)

      Holocardius amorphus or **Amorphus globosus**—The general body form is unrecognizable. It may occasionally be seen, most commonly in the cow, but also in the mare, ewe

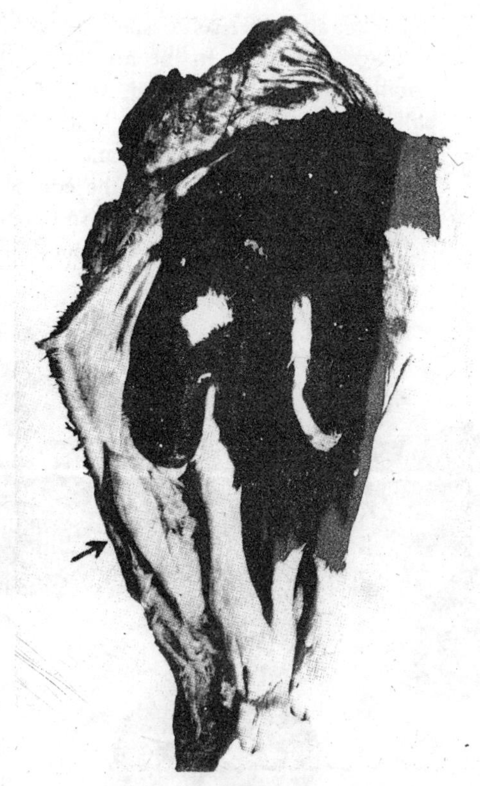

Figure 43. A bovine **Schistosomus reflexus** monster. This is an unusual type in which a sac of skin encloses the entire fetus. Note accessory limb attached to skin.

Figure 44. **Perosomus elumbis,** note lack of development of the caudal part of body and functionally ankylosed rear limbs.

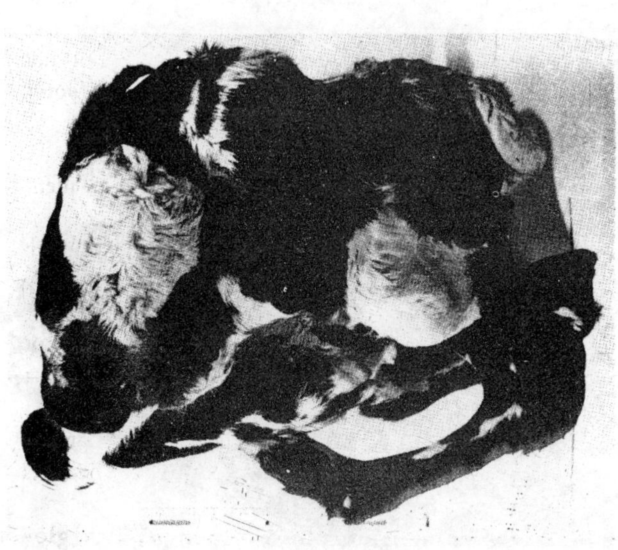

Figure 45. **Perosomus horridus.** The spine has many lateral bends and all joints are functionally ankylosed.

Figure 46. Porcine double monster, monocephalus tetrapus tetrabrachius.

and goat, attached to the placenta of the normal monozygotic or dizygotic twin. These very imperfect zygotes are parasitic upon the placenta of the normal twin and are never observed in single births. The bovine **Amorphus globosus** usually appears as a round or oval, edematous structure weighing 1/2 to 7 lbs. covered with skin and hair and containing connective tissue, fat and other soft tissues and occasionally cartilage and bone. In the mare this structure usually consists of a round, thin, fenestrated ball of cartilage 3 to 5 inches in diameter. It is covered with mucous membrane (See Figures 47, 48, 49). The interior of the equine amorphus monster is jelly-like tissue. In humans this is observed in the chorion in about 1 in every

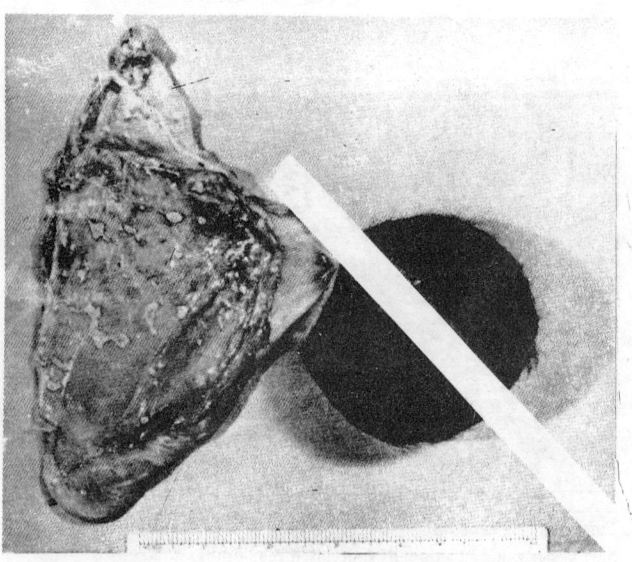

Figure 47. **Amorphus globosus** attached to the bovine fetal membranes.

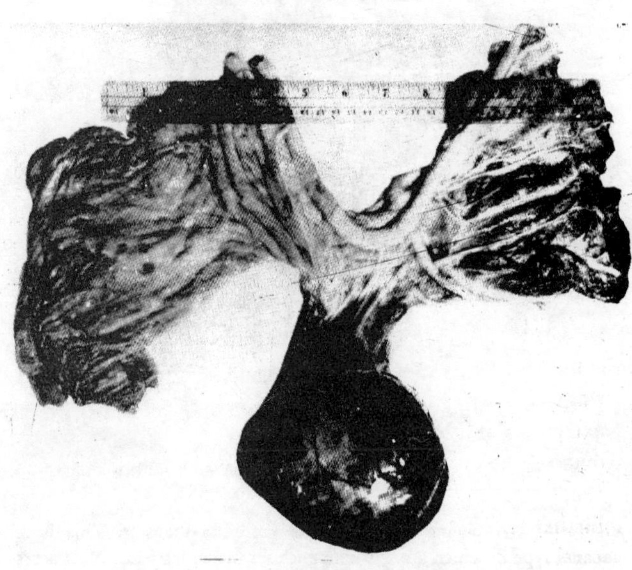

Figure 48. **Amorphus globosus** on a mare's placenta. A thin cartilagenous shell surrounds a gelatinous mass.

Figure 49. A bovine **Amorphus globosus** attached by a stalk containing blood vessels to the placenta of a normal fetus.

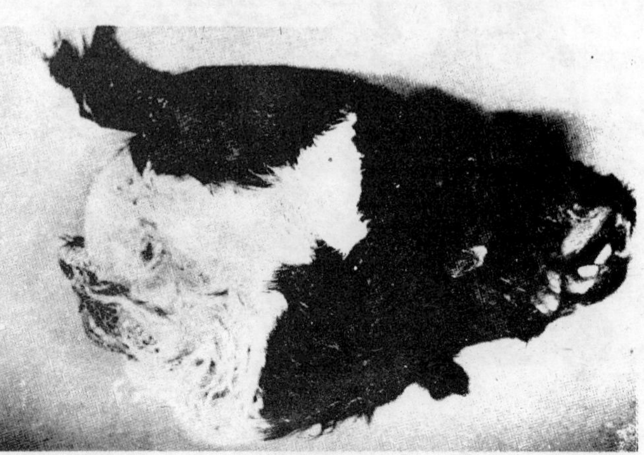

Figure 50. A holocardius bovine monster without a heart. Note the imperfect face, muzzle, teeth and a tail.

100 single births, Kappelman. Based on karyotypic studies of chromosomes, human acardiac monsters were found to be the same sex as their normal twin supporting the theory of their monozygotic origin. However, in cattle Dunn et al. demonstrated in a similar manner that one acardiac monster was female and its normal cotwin was male. This confirmed Williams theory that the **Amorphus globosus** was an imperfect zygote of dizygotic twins. It was demonstrated that the leucocytes of the normal male calf only contained the XY or male chromosome complement and no blood cell chimerism occurred. The monster composed mainly of stomach and intestinal tissues was enclosed in its own amnion. Neal and Wilcox described a case where two acardiac monsters were attached to the placenta of a normal bovine calf. The author has observed a placenta of a normal calf containing six teratomatous growths.

B. **Conjoined twins** in which the components or component parts are symmetrical are called **Diplopagus** monsters or "Siamese" twins. **Triplopagus** is extremely rare. Conjoined twins arise from a single ovum and are monozygotic. Hancock and Arthur reported they occurred about once in 100,000 bovine births. They are most common in cattle but are seen rarely in sheep, pigs, dogs and cats and are exceedingly rare in horses.

1. Those conjoined twins in which each component is complete or nearly so include:

   Thoracopagus, sternopagus, or **ziphopagus** twins are joined at or near the sternal region. The internal organs are usually duplicated. The components are face to face.

   Pygopagus monsters are connected at the sacrum and the components are back to back.

   Craniopagus twins are united at the heads. Components may be facing in the same or in the opposite direction.

   Ischiopagus fetuses are joined at the lower pelvic region and the bodies extend in a straight line and the heads in the opposite directions.

2. The two components equal one another in this group but each is less than an entire individual. This is usually associated with lateral fusion. These may vary from single normal individuals to those of two normal but superficially joined individuals. Duplication may lead to doubling of the cranial end of body while the caudal end remains single; or the caudal part may be doubled and the cranial part single. Duplication can occur at both cranial and caudal ends with the middle area of the monster remaining single. Duplication of the cranial part of the fetus is more common than that of the caudal portion.

   a. Duplication in the cranial region. (See Figure 46)

      (1) **Monocephalus** includes those monsters with partial duplication of the frontal region, nose and mouth called Diprosopus or double face. Either face may be complete or one eye of each may be fused into a common medial orbit. **Di-, tri-** or **tetraophathalmus** and **di-, tri-** or **tetraotus** may be present.

      (2) **Dicephalus** or two heads, with **distomus** or **monostomus** occasionally is seen. Tricephalus is very rare. A **Dicephalus dipus dibrachius** monster has two forelimbs and two hind limbs with partial duplication of the spine and one or two tails, **dicaudatus. Dicephalus dipus tribrachius** has 3 forelimbs; **Dicephalus dipus tetrabrachius** has 4 forelimbs.

   b. Duplication in the caudal region is designated as **Dipygus.** Tripygus is very rare.

      (1) **Monocephalus tripus dibrachius** has 3 rear limbs.

      (2) **Monocephalus tetrapus dibrachius** has 4 rear limbs.

      (3) **Cephalothoracopagus** has a single neck and more or less complete fusion of the heads to form an almost single face. **Syncephalus** has one face, four ears, and a single or partially doubled cerebrum. **Janiceps** is a monster with two faces on opposite sides of the head.

   c. Duplication of both cranial and caudal regions is **Dicephalus dipygus.**

      (1) **Dicephalus tripus tribrachius, Dicephalus tetrapus tetrabrachius, Dicephalus tripus tetrabrachius,** or **Dicephalus tetrapus tribrachius** have been described.

C. **Unequal and asymmetrical conjoined twins** are composed of one very imperfect and incomplete twin, called the **parasite,** dependent on the other twin, the **autosite.** This is called a **heteropagus monster.** The autosite is nearly normal and the parasite is attached to it as a dependent growth. (See Figure 51)

1. The parasite may be attached to the visible surface of the autosite. Common junction sites are the

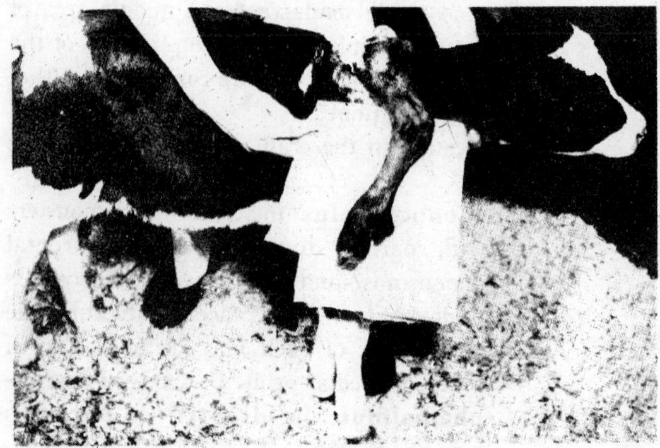

Figure 51. A parasitic limb attached to a calf.

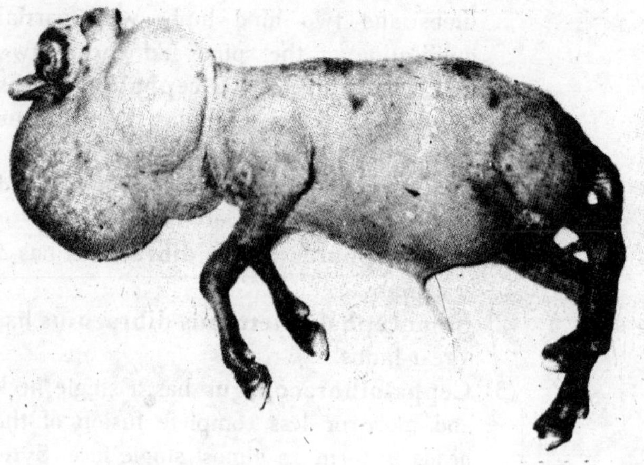

Figure 53. An ovine monster twin to a normal lamb—A cystic esophagus, agnathia, cyclopia and microcephalus were present.

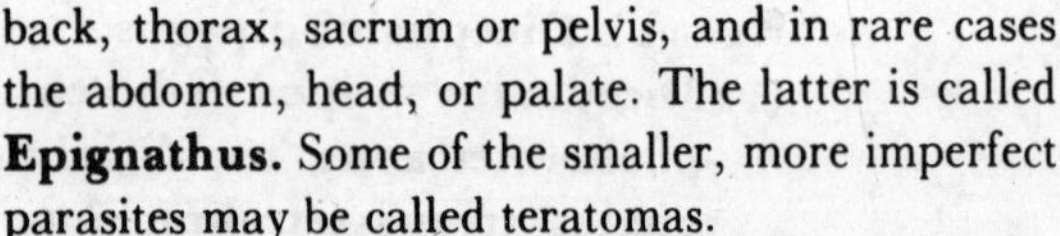

back, thorax, sacrum or pelvis, and in rare cases the abdomen, head, or palate. The latter is called **Epignathus.** Some of the smaller, more imperfect parasites may be called teratomas.

2. A parasite can rarely develop within the autosite usually in the abdominal, thoracic, pelvic or cranial cavity, or in the spinal canal or scrotum. Teratomas in the abdominal cavity and between the mandibles were described in two calves by Hibbs et al..

Figure 52. **Ectopia cordis** in a calf, with the heart beneath the skin ventral to the neck and cranial to the thoracic inlet.

Figure 54. Amelia in a Jersey calf—A portion of the humerus and the distal portion of the left forelimb was missing at birth.

General References

Blood, D. C. and Henderson, J. A. (1963) Veterinary Medicine, 2nd Ed. The Williams Wilkins Co., Baltimore, Md.

Catcott, E. J. and Smithcors, J. F. (1967) Progress in Canine Practice. I Part 3, Amer. Vet. Public. Inc., Wheaton, Ill.

Fechheimer, N. S. (1968) Genetic Aspects of Calf Losses, in Prenatal and Postnatal Mortality in Cattle," Nat. Acad. of Sci., Publ. 1685, Washington, D.C.

Gilmore, L. O. (1952) Dairy Cattle Breeding, J. B. Lippincott Co., N.Y.C.

Gotink, W. M., DeGroot T. and Stegenga, T. (1955) Hereditary Defects in Cattle in the Netherlands, Tijdschr. vor Diergeneesk **80,** 1.

Hutt, F. B. (1946) Some Hereditary Abnormalities of Domestic Animals, Cor. Vet. **36,** 2, 180.

Hutt, F. B. (1964) Animal Genetics, Ronald Press Co., N Y.C.

Innes, J. R. M. and Saunders, L. Z. (1962) Comparative Neuropathology, Academic Press, N.Y.C.

Johansson, I. (1961) Genetic Aspects of Dairy Cattle Breeding, Univ. of Ill. Press, Urbana, Ill.

Johansson, J. and Rendel, J. (1968) Genetics and Animal Breeding, W. H. Freeman and Co., San Francisco, Cal.

Jubb, K. V. F. and Kennedy, P. C. (1970) Pathology of Domestic Animals, Academic Press, N.Y.C. Volumes I and II. 2nd Ed.

Koch, P., Fischer, H., and Schumann, H. (1957) Erbpathologie der Landwirtschaftlichen Haustiere, Paul Parey, Berlin, Germany.

Lauvergne, J. J. (1968) Bibliography of the Hereditary Anomalies of Cattle, Tech. Bull I, Dept. of Animal Genetics, National Institute for Research in Agronomy, 149 rue deGrenelle, 75 Paris, France.

Lerner, I. M. (1944) Lethal and Sublethal Characters in Farm Animals, J. of Hered. **35,** 6, 219.

Potter, E. L. (1961) Pathology of the Fetus and Infant, 2nd Ed., Yearbook Med. Publisher, Chicago, Ill.

Searle, A. G. (1969) Comparative Genetics of Coat Colour in Mammals, Logos Press Ltd. (distributed by Academic Press Inc., N.Y.C.)

Stormont, C. (1958) Genetics and Disease, Advances in Vet. Sci., Vol. 4, 137. Academic Press Inc., N.Y.C.

Wiesner, E. (1960) Die Erbschaden der Landwirtschaftlichen Nutztiere, (Hereditary Defects in Farm Animals) Gustav Fischer, Jena.

Willis, R. O. (1962) The Borderland of Embryology and Pathology, 2nd Ed. Butterworth Publ. Co., Washington, D.C.

Young, G. B. (1967) Hereditary Diseases in Livestock, Vet. Rec **81,** 24.

Specific References

Abbott, M. E. (1936) Atlas of Congenital Cardiac Disease, The American Heart Assoc., New York.

Albright, J. L. (1960) Multiple Lipomatosis in Dairy Cattle, J. Hered. **51,** 231.

Ament, D. F. and O'Mary, C. C. (1963) Albinism and Related Blood Disorders in Herefords, J. An. Sci. **22,** 3, 1815.

Anderson, A. C. and Schultz, F. T. (1958) Inherited (Congenital) Cataract in the Dog, Amer. J. Path. **34,** 965.

Anderson, D. E. (1959) Genetic Aspects of Bovine Ocular Carcinoma in **Genetics and Cancer,** Univ. of Texas Press, Austin, Texas.

Anderson, D. E. (1960) Studies on Bovine Ocular Squamous Carcinoma ("Cancer Eye")—Nutritional Effects, J. An. Sci. **19,** 3, 790.

Archibald, J. and Cawley, A. J. (1959) Congenital Deformities of the Locomotor System, in **Canine Medicine,** Amer. Vet. Public. Inc., Santa Barbara, Calif.

Armstrong, C. N. and Marshall, A. J. (1964) Intersexuality in Vertebrates Including Man, Academic Press, N.Y.C.

Arthur, G. H. (1956) Conjoined and Identical Twins, Vet. Rec. **68,** 389.

Asdell, S. A. (1964) Patterns of Mammalian Reproduction, 2nd Ed. Cornell Univ. Press, Ithaca, N.Y.

Ashdown, R. R. (1963) The Diagnosis of Cryptorchidism in Young Dogs; A Review of the Problem, J. Small An. Pract. **4,** 261.

Ashley, D. J. B. (1959) The Technic of Nuclear Sexing, Amer. J. of Clin. Path. **31,** 3, 230.

Assali, N. S. (1968) Biology of Gestation, Vol. 2, in **The Fetus and Neonate,** N.Y. Academic Press.

Baker, M. L., Payne, L. C. and Baker, G. N. (1961) The Inheritance of Hydrocephalus in Cattle, J. Hered. **52,** 135.

Bane, A. (1968) Personal Communication.

Barnett, K. C. (1965) Retinal Atrophy, Vet. Rec. **77,** 1543.

Barnett, K. C. (1969) Primary Retinal Dystrophies in the Dog, J.A.V.M.A. **154,** 7, 804.

Bartels, J. E. and Vaughn, J. T. (1969) Persistent Right Aortic Arch in the Horse, J.A.V.M.A., **154,** 4, 406.

Bearn, A. G. and German, J. L. III (1961) Chromosomes and Disease, Scient. Amer. **205,** 5, 66.

Becker, R. B., Simpson, C. F. and Wilcox, C. J. (1963) Hairless Guernsey Cattle; Hypotrichosis a Nonlethal Character, Jour. of Hered. **54,** 3.

Becker, R. B., Wilcox, C. J., Simpson, C. F., Gilmore, L. O. and Fechheimer, N. S. (1964) Genetic Aspects of Actinomycosis and Actinobacillosis in Cattle, Univ. of Fla., Agr. Exp. Stat. Tech. Bull. 670.

Bedford, P. G. C. (1967) Schistosoma Reflexus in a Goat: A Case Report, Vet. Rec., **80,** 326.

Belling, T. H., Jr. (1962) Genetic Effect of Cardiac Ventricular Septal Defect in Hereford Cattle, Vet. Med. **57,** 11, 965.

Belling, T. H., Jr. and Holland, L. A. (1962) Variations of Internal Hydrocephalus, Vet. Med. **57,** 5, 405.

Benirschke, K. (1967) Sterility and Fertility in Mammalian Hybrids, in **Comparative Aspects of Reproductive Failure,** Springer Verlag New York, Inc., 218.

Benirschke, K. (1968) Personal Communication.

Berry, O. (1938) Comparative Studies on the Chromosome Numbers in Sheep, Goat and Sheep-Goat Hybrids, J. Hered. **29,** 343.

Biggers, J. D. and McFeely, R. A. (1966) Intersexuality in Domestic Animals, in **Advances in Reproductive Physiology,** Academic Press, N.Y.C., Vol. I, 29.

Binns, W., Thacker, E. J., James, L. F. and Huffman, W. T. (1959) A Congenital Cyclopian-Type Malformation of Lambs, J.A.V.M.A. **134,** 4, 180.

Binns, W., Anderson, W. A. and Sullivan, D. J. (1960) Further Observations on a Congenital Cyclopian-Type Malformation in Lambs, J.A.V.M.A. **137,** 9, 515.

Binns, W., James, L. F., Shupe, J. L. and Everett, G. (1963) A Congenital Cyclopian-Type Malformation in Lambs Induced by Maternal Ingestion of a Range Plant, **Veratrum californicum,** Am. J. Vet. Res. **24,** 103, 1164.

Bjork, G., Dyrendahl, S. and Olsson, S. E. (1957) Hereditary Ataxia in Smooth-Haired Fox Terriers, Vet. Rec. **69,** 871.

Bolton, G. R., Ettinger, S. and Roush, J. C. (1969) Congenital Peritoneopericardial Diaphragmatic Hernia in a Dog, J.A.V.M.A. **155,** 5, 723.

Butcher, R. L. and Fugo, N. W. (1967) Overripeness and the Mammalian Ova II Delayed Ovulation and Chromosome Abnormalities, Fert. and Steril, **18,** 3, 297.

Butcher, R. L., Blue, J. D. and Fugo, N. W. (1969) Overripeness and Mammalian Ova III, Fert. and Steril., **20,** 2, 223.

Burns, M. and Fraser, M. M. (1966) Genetics of the Dog—in **The Basis of Successful Breeding,** 2nd Ed. J. B. Lippincott Co., Philadelphia.

Carnahan, D. L., Guffy, M. M., Hibbs, C. M., Leipold, H. W. and Huston, K. (1968) Hip Dysplasia in Hereford Cattle, J.A.V.M.A. **152,** 8, 1150.

Carrig, C. B., Grandage, J., Ruth, G. R. and Seawright, A. A. (1969) Etopic Ureter; Ureteral Stricture and Hemivertebra in a Heifer, J.A.V.M.A. **155,** 2, 143.

Carter, A. H. (1960) An Inherited Blindness (Cataract) In Cattle, Proc. N. Z. Soc. of An. Prod. **20,** 108.

Cawley, A. J. and Archibald, J. (1960) Etopic Ureter, A Report of Two Cases, Vet. Med. **55,** 11, 48.

Cello, R. M. (1969) Comments on Collie Eye Anomaly, J.A.V.M.A., **155,** 6, 870.

Corley, E. A., Sutherland, T. M. and Carlson, W. D. (1968) Genetic Aspects of Canine Elbow-Dysplasia, J.A.V.M.A. **153,** 5, 543.

Cornelius, C. E. and Cromwall, R. R. (1968) Congenital Photosensitivity and Hyperbilirubinemia in Southdown Sheep in the United States, Amer. J. Vet. Res. **29,** 2, 291.

Craft, W. A. and Blizzard, W. L. (1934) Semihairless Gene in Cattle, J. Hered. **25,** 384.

Crawley, J. P. and McGloughlin, P. (1963) Hereditary Entropion in Lambs, Vet. Rec. **75,** 43, 1604.

Crew, F. A. E. (1965) Sex Determination, Methuen Co. Ltd., London.

Crew, F. A. E. and Buchanan-Smith, A. D., Genetics of the Horse, Bibliographia Genetica, VI, (1930), 124.

Christensen, E. and Christensen, N. O. (1952) Congenital Hereditary Paralysis in Calves, Nord. Vet. Med. **4,** 861.

Curtis, E. M. and Grant, R. P. (1964) Masculinization of Female Pups by Progestagens, J.A.V.M.A. **144,** 4, 395.

Dale, D. E. and Moxely, J. E. (1952) Prenatal Tendon Contractures in a Herd of Milking Shorthorns, Canad, J. Comp. Med. **16,** 11, 399.

Deas, D. W. (1959) A Note on Hereditary Opacity of the Cornea in British Friesian Cattle, Vet. Rec. **71,** 619.

deLahunta, A. and Hutt, F. B. (1969) Personal communication.

DeMoor, A., Bouckaert, J. and Tol, W. (1964) Surgical Handling of Spastic Paresis By Denervation of the Gastrocnemius Muscle, Vlaams Diergeneesk. Tijdschr. **33,** 1.

Dennis, S. M. (1969) Patent Urachus in a Neonatal Lamb, Cor. Vet. **59,** 4, 581.

Dennis, S. M. (1970) Cardiovascular Conditions in Newborn Lambs, Cor. Vet. **60,** 1, 9

Dennis, S. M. and Meyer, E. P. (1965) Schistosomus Reflexus in a Sheep. Vet. Rec. **77,** 1386.

Denniston, J. C., Shive, R. J., Friedli, U. and Boucher, W. B. (1968) Spastic Paresis in Calves, J.A.V.M.A. **152,** 8, 1138.

Detweiler, D. K. (1962) Advances in Canine Cardiology, Sm. An. Clinician **2,** 6, 315.

Dev, V. G. and Lasley, J. F. (1969) Growth Hormone Level in the Blood of Dwarf and Normal Hereford Cattle, J. An. Sci. **29,** 3, 384.

Dimock, W. W. (1950) "Wobbles"—An Hereditary Disease of Horses, J. of Hered. **41,** 319.

Dinkel, C. A. and Gregory, K. E. (1965) Evaluation of the Profilometer for the Detection of Hereford Bulls Heterozygous for the Snorter Dwarf Gene, J. An. Sci. **24,** 2, 438.

Donald, H P. (1949) Inheritance of a Tail Abnormality Associated with Urogenital Disorders in Pigs, J. Agric. Sci. **39,** 164.

Donald, H. P., Deas, D. W. and Wilson, L. A. (1952) Genetical Analysis of the Incidence of Dropsical Calves in Herds of Ayrshire Cattle, Brit. Vet. Jour. **108,** 227.

Done, J. T., Loosmore, R. M. and Saunders, C. N. (1967) Dermatosis Vegetans in Pigs, Vet. Rec. **80,** 9, 292.

Donovan, E. F. and Wyman, M. (1965) Ocular Anomaly in the Collie, J.A.V.M.A. **147,** 1465.

Dunn, H. O. (1969) Personal communication.

Dunn, H. O., Lein, D. H. and Kenney, R. M. (1967) The Cytological Sex of a Bovine Anidian (Amorphous) Twin Monster, Cytogenetics **6,** 412.

Eaton, O. N. (1943) An Anatomical Study of Hermaphroditism in Goats, Am. J. Vet. Res. **4,** 13, 333.

Eldridge, F. E., Smith W. H. and McLeod, W. M. (1951) Syndactylism in Holstein Friesian Cattle: Its Inheritance, Description and Occurrence, J. Hered. 42, 241.

Eldridge, F. E. and Atkeson, F. W. (1953) Streaked Hairlessness in Holstein Friesian Cattle, a Sex-Linked Lethal Character, J. Hered. **44,** 265.

Elzay, R. P. and Hughes, R. D. (1969) Anodontia in a Cat, J.A.V.M.A. **154,** 6, 667.

Emerson, J. L. and Delez, A. L. (1965) Cerebellar Hypoplasia, Hypomyelinogenesis and Congenital Tremors of Pigs, Associated with Prenatal Hog Cholera Vaccination of Sows, J.A.V.M.A. **147,** 47.

Ercanbrack, S. K. (1968) Frequencies of Various Birth Defects of Sheep, J. An. Sci. **27,** 4, 1126.

Eriksson, K. (1955) Hereditary Aniridia with Secondary Cataract in Horses, Nord. Vet. Med. **7,** 9, 773.

Evans, H. E., Ingalls, T. H. and Binns, W. (1966) Teratogenesis of Craniofacial Malformations in Animals, Archiv of Envir. Health **13,** 706.

Ewing, G. O. (1969) Familial Nonsperocytic Hemolytic Anemia of Basenji Dogs, J.A.V.M.A. **154,** 503.

Feldman, D. B., Bree, M. M. and Cohen, B. J. (1968) Congenital Diaphragmatic Hernia in Neonatal Dogs, J.A.V.M.A. **153,** 7, 942.

Fincher, M. G. and Williams, W. L. (1926) Arrested Development of the Muellerian Ducts Associated with Inbreeding, Cor. Vet. **16,** 1.

Finocchio, E. J. and Guffy, M. M. (1970) Congenital Patellar Ectopia in a Foal, J.A.V.M.A. **156,** 2, 222.

Fox, M. W. (1964) The Otocephalic Syndrome in the Dog, Cor. Vet. **54,** 2, 250.

Fox, M. W. (1965) Diseases of Possible Hereditary Origin in the Dog, A Bibliographic Review, J. Hered. **56,** 169.

Fox, M. W. (1966) Congenital and Inherited Abnormalities in **Canine Pediatrics,** C. C. Thomas Co., Springfield, Ill.

Freeman, A. E. (1958) Curved Limbs—A Lethal in Dairy Cattle, J. Hered. **49,** 229.

Frey, D. C., Tyler, D. E. and Ramsey, F. K. (1965) Pyometra Associated With Bilateral Cryptorchidism and Sertoli's Cell Tumor in a Male Pseudohermaphrodite Dog, J.A.V.M.A. **146,** 7, 723.

Frye, F. L. and Taylor, D. O. M. (1968) Pericardial and Diaphragmatic Defects in a Cat, J.A.V.M.A. **152,** 10, 1507.

Gaunya, W. S., Daniels, W. H., and Hirth, R. S. (1968) Mammary Aplasia in a Fertile Cow, J. Dairy Sci. **51,** 5, 809.

Gelatt, K. N., Leipold, H. W. and Coffman, J. R. (1969) Bilateral Optic Nerve Hypoplasia in a Colt, J.A.V.M.A. **155,** 4, 627.

Gelatt, K. N. and Veith, L. A. (1970) Hereditary Multiple Ocular Anomalies in Australian Sheperd Dogs, Vet. Med. **65,** 39.

Gerneke, W. H. (1967) Cytogenetic Investigations on Normal and Malformed Animals with Special Reference to Intersexes, Onderstep. J. Vet. Res. **34,** 1, 219.

Gilman, J. P. W. (1956) Congenital Hydrocephalus and Brain Hernia in Domestic Animals, Cor. Vet. **46,** 4, 487.

Gilman, J. P. W. and Stringham, E. W. (1953) Hereditary Umbilical Hernia in Holstein Cattle, J. Hered. **44,** 113.

Gilmore, L. O., Fechheimer, N. S. and Herschler, M. S. (1962) Evidence for Inherited Susceptibility to Lumpy Jaw, J. An. Sci. **21,** 4, 972.

Gilmore, L. O. and Fechheimer, N. S. (1969) Congenital Abnormalities in Cattle and Their General Etiologic Factors, J. Dairy Sci. **52,** 11, 1831.

Glenn, B. L., Glenn, H. G. and Omtveldt, I. T. (1968) Congenital Porphyria in the Domestic Cat **(Felis catus):** Preliminary Investigations on Inheritance Pattern, Amer. J. Vet. Res. **29,** 8, 1653.

Grant, H. T. (1956) Underdeveloped Mandible in a Herd of Dairy Shorthorn Cattle, J. of Hered. **47,** 165.

Gregory, K. E., Kock, R. M. and Swiger, L. O. (1962) Malocclusion: A Hereditary Defect in Cattle, Jour. of Hered. **53,** 168.

Gregory, P. W. (1959) Inguinal Hernias in Female Hermaphrodite Pigs, J.A.V.M.A. **135,** 12, 624.

Gregory, P. W., Tyler, W. S. and Julian, Q. M. (1966) Dwarfism Complex in Cattle, Growth, **30,** 393.

Griner, L. A., McCrory, B. R., Foster, N. M. and Meyer, H. (1964) Bluetongue Associated with Abnormalities in Newborn Lambs, J.A.V.M.A. **145,** 10, 1013.

Hafez, E. S. E. (1968) Reproduction in Farm Animals, 2nd Ed., Lea and Febiger, Philadelphia.

Hancock, J. (1954) Monozygotic Twins in Cattle, in **Advances in Genetics 6,** 141, Academic Press, Inc., N.Y.C.

Harding, J. D. J., Done, J. T. and Darbyshire, J. H. (1966) Congenital Tremors in Piglets and Their Relation to Swine Fever, Vet. Rec. **79,** 14, 388.

Henderson, J. A. (1955) Personal Communication.

Herrick, J. H. (1958) Personal Communication.

Herrick, J. H. and Eldridge, F. E. (1955) Hereditary Edema in Ayrshire Cattle, J. Dairy Sci.**38,** 4, 440.

Herschler, M. S., Fechheimer, N. S. and Gilmore, L. O. (1962) Congenital Abnormalities in Cattle: Their Association with Hereditary and Environmental Factors, J. Dairy Sci. **45,** 12, 1493.

Hibbs, C. M., Schoneweis, D. and Leipold, H. W. (1968) Teratomas in Two Calves, Amer. J. Vet. Res. **29,** 9, 1891.

High, J. W., Kincaid, C. M. and Smith, H. J. (1958) Doddler Cattle: An Inherited Congenital Nervous Disorder of Hereford Cattle, J. Hered. **49,** 250.

Hodgman, S. F. J. (1963) Abnormalities and Defects in Pedigree Dogs, J. Sm. An. Pract. **4,** 447.

Holmes, J. R. and Young, G B. (1954) Symetrical Alopecia in Cattle, Vet. Rec. **66,** 704.

Holzworth, J. (1968) Personal Communication.

Hsu, T. C. and Benirschke, K. (1967) An Atlas of Mammalian Chromosomes, Vol. I, Springer Verlag New York, Inc.

Hulland, T. (1964) Pregnancy in a Hermaphrodite Sow, Canad. Vet. J. **5,** 2, 39.

Huston, K., Eldridge, F. E. and Oberst, F. H. (1961) Congenital Hydrocephalus in Ayrshires, J. An. Sci. **20,** 4, 908.

Huston, K., Leipold, W. H. and MacFadden, D. L. (1969) Smooth Tongue in Brown Swiss Cattle, J. of Hered. **59,** 1, 65.

Huston, K. and Wearden, S. (1958) Congenital Taillessness in Cattle, J. Dairy Sci. **41,** 10, 1359.

Hutchins, D. R., Lepherd, E. E. and Crook, I. G. (1967) A Case of Equine Hemophilia, Austral. Vet. J. **43,** 83.

Hutt, F. B. (1961) Identification nd Elimination of Defects in Animals, Germ Plasm Resources, Amer. Soc. for Adv. of Sci., Wash., D.C.

Hutt, F. B. (1967) Genetic Selection to Reduce the Incidence of Hip Dysplasia in Dogs, J.A.V.M.A. **151,** 8, 1041.

Hutt, F. B., and Saunders, L. Z. (1953) Variable Genetic Hypotrichosis in Guernsey Cattle, J. Hered. 44, 3, 97.

Hyde, J. E. (1962) Cross Eyedness: A Study in Siamese Cats, Amer. J. Ophthal. **53,** 70.

James, L. F., Shupe, J. L., Binns, W. and Keeler, R. F. (1967) Abortive and Teratogenic Effects of Locoweed on Sheep and Cattle, Amer. J. Vet. Res. **28,** 126, 1379.

James, L. F. and Keeler, R. F. (1968) Teratogenic Effects of Aminopterin in Sheep, Teratology, **1,** 4, 407.

Johnston, W. G. and Young, G. B. (1958) A Congenital Muscle Contracture and Chondroplasia Syndrome in Cattle, Vet. Rec. **70,** 1219.

Jorgensen, S. K. (1959) Congenital Porphyria in Pigs, Brit. Vet. J. **115,** 160.

Jorgensen, S. K. (1961) Studies on Congenital Porphyria in Cattle in Denmark, Brit. Vet. Jour. **117,** 1, 61.

Julian, L. M., Tyler, W. S. and Gregory, P. W. (1959) The Current Status of Bovine Dwarfism, J.A.V.M.A. **135**, 2, 104.

Kahrs, R. F., Scott, F. W. and deLahunta, A. (1970) Epidemiological Observations on Virus Induced Cerebellar Hypoplasia and Cataracts in Calves, Teratol. **3**, 2, 181.

Kahrs, R. F., Scott, F. W. and deLahunta, A. (1970) Congenital Cerebellar Hypoplasia and Ocular Defects in Calves Following Bovine Viral Diarrhea-Mucasal Disease Infection in Pregnant Cattle, J.A.V.M.A. **156**, 7, 851.

Kalter, H. and Warkany, J. (1959) Experimental Production of Congenital Malformation by Metabolic Procedure, Physiol. Rev. **39**, 69.

Karbe, E. (1965) Lateral Neck Cysts in the Dog, Am. J. Vet. Res. **26**, 112, 717.

Keeler, R. F., James, L. F. Binns, W. and Shupe, J. L. (1967) An Apparent Relationship Between Locoism and Lathyrism, Canad. J. Comp. Med. and Vet. Sci., **31**, 12, 334.

Kendrick, J. W. and Sittman, K. (1966) Inherited Osteoarthritis of Dairy Cattle, J.A.V.M.A. **149**, 1, 17.

Kilham, L., Margolis, G. and Colby, E. D. (1967) Congenital Infections of Cats and Ferrets by Feline Leucopenia Virus Manifested by Cerebellar Hypoplasia, Laborat. Invest. **17**, 465.

King, J. A. (1965) Malformed Calf Syndrome on Kodiak Island, Alaska, J.A.V.M.A. **147**, 3, 239.

King, J. (1960) Personal Communication.

Koch, S. A. and Rubin, L. F. (1967) Probable Nonhereditary Congenital Cataracts in Dogs, J.A.V.M.A. **150**, 11, 1375.

Koger, M. and Crockett, J. R. (1964) Intermating Carriers and Bovine Dwarfs of Various Forms, J. An. Sci. **23**, 3, 850.

Koger, M., Dollahon, J. C., Warnick, A. C., Kirk, W. G., Hentges, J. F. and Palmer, A. Z. (1955) Forms of Dwarfism in English and Brahman Breeds of Beef Cattle, J. An. Sci. **14**, 4, 1186.

Kral, F. and Schwartzman, R. M. (1964) Veterinary and Comparative Dermatology, J. B. Lippincott Co., Philadelphia, 406.

Krook, L. (1957) Spontaneous Hyperparathyroidism in the Dog, Acta. Path. et Microbiol. Scand. **41**, Suppl. 122, 7.

Krook, L., Barrett, R. B., Usui, K. and Wolke, R. E. (1963) Nutritional Secondary Hyperparathyroidism in the Cat, Cor. Vet. **53**, 2, 224.

Kurtz, H. J. and Ellery, J. C. (1969) Ectopia Cordis in a Bovine Fetus, Am. J. Vet. Res. **30**, 3, 471.

Langman, J. (1963) Medical Embryology, The Williams and Wilkins Comp., Baltimore, Md.

Leipold, H. W. and Huston, K. (1967) Dominant Heterochromia Irides and Albinism in a Hereford Herd, J. Dairy Sci. **50**, 6, 988.

Leipold, H. W. and Huston, K. (1967) Dominant Incomplete Albinism in Cattle, J. Dairy Sci. **50**, 6, 988.

Leipold, H. W., Adrian, R. W., Huston, K., Trotter, D. M., Dennis, S. M. and Guffy, M. M. (1969) Anatomy of Hereditary Bovine Syndactylism: I-IV, J. Dairy Sci., **52**, 9, 1422–1444.

Leipold, H. W. and Huston, K. (1968) Incomplete Albinism and Heterochromia Irides in Herefords, J. of Hered. **59**, 3.

Leipold, H. W. and Huston, K. (1969) Dominant Incomplete Albinism of Cattle, J. of Hered. **59**, 4, 223.

Leipold, H. W., Huston, K., Dennis, S. M. and Farmer, E. L. (1969) Hyperthermia in Syndactylous Holstein Friesian Cattle, J. Dairy Sci. **52**, 6, 923.

Leipold, H. W., Huston, K., Guffy, M. M. and Dennis, S. M. (1969) Syndactyly in an Aberdeen Angus Calf; Ectrodactyly inTwo Beef Calves, Amer. J. Vet. Res. **30**, 9, 1685 and 1689.

Leipold, H. W., Huston, K., Guffy, M. M. and Noordsy, J. L. (1967) Spastic Paresis in Beef Shorthorn Cattle, J.A.V.M.A. **151**, 5, 598.

Lennox, B. (1961) Chromosomes for Beginners, The Lancet, May 31st, 1046.

Lenz, W. (1965) Epidemiology of Congenital Malformations, Ann. of N.Y. Acad. of Sci. **123**, 228.

Littlejohn, A. I. (1954) Entropion in Newborn Lambs, Vet. Rec. **66**, 211.

Ljunggren, G., Cawley, A. J. and Archibald, J. (1966) The Elbow Dysplasias in the Dog, J.A.V.M.A. **148**, 8, 887.

MacKellar, J. C. (1960) The Occurrence of Muscular Hypertrophy in South Devon Cattle, Vet. Rec. **72**, 26, 507.

Marlowe, T. J. (1964) Evidence of Selection for the Snorter Dwarf Gene in Cattle, J. An. Sci. **23**, 2, 474.

Mason, I. L. (1963) Symptoms of Muscular Hypertrophy on Heterozygous Steers, Animal Prod. **5**, 57.

Mason, I. L. (1964) Genetical Aspects of Breeding Cattle for Beef, Vet. Rec. **76**, 28, 765.

McFee, Q. F., Murphree, R. L. and Reynolds, R. L. (1965) Skeletal Defects in Prenatally Irradiated Sheep, Cattle and Swine, J. An. Sci. **24**, 4, 1131.

McFeely, R. A., Hare, W. C. D. and Biggers, J. D. (1967) Chromosome Studies in 14 Cases of Intersex in Domestic Mammals, Cytogenetics, **6**, 242.

McGrath, J. E. (1965) Spinal Dysraphism in the Dog, Path. Vet., Suppl. 2, 1.

Mead, S. W., Gregory, P. W. and Regan, W. M. (1942) Proportionate Dwarfism in Jersey Cows, J. Hered. **33**, 411.

Mead, S. W., Gregory, P. W. and Regan, W. M. (1946) Deleterious Recessive Genes in Dairy Bulls Selected at Random, Genetics, **41**, 574.

Merritt, A. M. and Riser, W. H (1968) Laminitis of Possible Hereditary Origin in Jersey Cattle, J.A.V.M.A. **153**, 8, 1074.

Moore, K. L. (1966) The Sex Chromatin, W. B. Saunders Co., Philadelphia.

Morgan, J. P., Carlson, W. D. and Adams, O. R. (1962) Hereditary Multiple Exostoses in the Horse, J.A.V.M.A. **140**, 12, 1320.

Mullins, J. H., Ferris, J. A. and Atkinson, J. C. (1960) Fetal Damage from Rubella During Pregnancy, J. Obst. and Gynec **15**, 320.

Murti, G. S. (1965) Agenesis and Dysgenesis of the Canine Kidneys, J.A.V.M.A. **146**, 10, 1120.

Neal, F. C. and Wilcox, C. J. (1967) Double Acardius Amorphus Case in a Brown Swiss Cow, J. Dairy Sci. **50**, 2, 236.

Nes, N. (1953) Hereditary Muscle Contracture in Dole Cattle, Nord Vet. Med. **5,** 869.

Nes, N. (1958) Hereditary Abnormal Tongues, Cleft Palates and Harelips in Pigs, Nord. Vet. Med. **10,** 625.

Nestel, B. L. (1958) Bovine Congenital Porphyria (Pink Tooth) with a Note on Five Cases Observed in Jamaica, Cor. Vet. **48,** 4, 430.

Nihleen, B. and Ericksson, K. (1958) Fetal Dystocia due to an Hereditary Defect, Nord. Vet. Med. **10,** 113.

Nishimura, H. (1965) Chemistry and Prevention of Congenital Anomalies, C. C. Thomas Co., Springfield, Ill.

Nordlund, S. (1961) Lethal Defects and Their Combating in Swedish Friesian Cattle, Proc IV Internat. Congr. on An. Reprod., The Hague, Vol IV, 765.

Nuss, J. I., McCarl, R. L., Mulay, I. L. and Mulay, L. N. (1967) Copper and Free Radical Accumulation in Liver of Calves with Inherited Hydrocephalus, Amer. J. Vet. Res. **28,** 127, 1909.

Osborne, C. A., Clifford, D. H. and Jensen, C. (1967) Hereditary Esophageal Achalasia in Dogs, J.A.V.M.A. **151,** 5, 572.

Osborne, C. A. and Perman, V. (1969) Ectopic Ureter in a Male Dog, J.A.V.M.A. **154,** 3, 273.

Osborne, J. C. and Legates, J. E. (1963) Six Cases of Bovine Intestinal Anomaly, J.A.V.M.A. **142,** 10, 1104.

Padgett, G. A., Leader, R. W., Gorham, J. R. and O'Mary, C. C. (1964) The Familial Occurrence of the Chediak—Higashi Syndrome in Mink and Cattle, Genetics, **49,** 505.

Pakes, S. P. and Griesemer, R. A. (1965) Current Status of Chromosome Analysis in Veterinary Medicine, J.A.V.M.A. **146,** 2, 138.

Palludan, B. (1961) The Teratogenic Effects of Vitamin A. Deficiency in Pigs, Acta Vet. Scand. **2,** 32.

Palmer, A. C. and Wallace, M. E. (1967) Deformation of Cervical Vertebrae in Basset Hounds, Vet. Rec. **80,** 430.

Patterson, D. F. (1967) Hereditary Lymphedema in the Dog, J. Med. Genet. **4,** 145.

Patterson, D. F. (1963) Clinical and Epidemiologic Studies of Congenital Heart Disease in the Dog, Proc. A.V.M.A. N.Y.C., 128.

Patterson, D. F. and Detweiler, D. K. (1967) Hereditary Transmission of Patent Ductus Arteriosus in the Dog, Amer. Heart Jour. **74,** 289.

Patterson, D. F. and Flickinger, G. L. (1964) Congenital Subaortic Stenosis in the Dog, J.A.V.M.A. **145,** 4, 376.

Patterson, D. F. and Medway, W. (1966) Hereditary Diseases of the Dog, J.A.V.M.A. **149,** 12, 1741.

Pond, W. C., Roberts, S. J. and Simmons, K. R. (1961) True and Pseudohermaphroditism in a Swine Herd, Cor. Vet. **51,** 3, 394.

Pritchard, J. T. and Voss, J. L. (1967) Fetal Ankylosis in Horses Associated with Hybrid Sudan Pasture, J.A.V.M.A. **150,** 8, 871.

Quinlan, J. and Morton, D. D. (1957) Paralysis of the Nervus Vagus—N. Recurrens,—N. Pharyngeus and N Laryngens cranialis—as an Etiological Factor in Whistling and Roaring in Horses, J. South Afr. Vet. Med. Assoc. **28,** 1, 63.

Rae, A. L. (1956) The Genetics of the Sheep, in **Advances in Genetics,** Academic Press Inc., N.Y.C., **8,** 190.

Regan, W. M., Gregory, P. W. and Mead, S. W. (1944) Hereditary Strabismus in Jersey Cattle, J. of Hered. **35,** 233.

Riser, W. H. (1961) Juvenile Osteoporosis (Osteoporosis Imperfecta) —A Calcium Deficiency, J.A.V.M.A. **139,** 1, 117.

Roberts, E. (1921) Polydactylism in Cattle, J. Hered. **12,** 84.

Roberts, S. J. (1965) Hereditary Spastic Diseases Affecting Cattle in New York State, Cor. Vet. **55,** 4, 637.

Roberts, S. R. and Bistner, S. I. (1968) Persistent Pupillary Membrane in Basenji Dogs, J.A.V.M.A. **153,** 5, 523.

Roberts, S. R. (1967) Hereditary Diseases of the Eye in Dogs: The Collie Ectasia Syndrome, Vet. Scope. I, 1, 2, and Amer. J. Ophthal. **50,** 451 (1960).

Roberts, S. R. (1969) The Collie Eye Anomaly, J.A.V.M.A. **155,** 6, 859.

Roberts, S. R., Dellaporta, A. and Winter, F. C. (1968) The Collie Ectasia Syndrome, Pathology of Eyes of Young and Adult Dogs, Am. J. of Ophthal., **62,** 728.

Rojas, M. A., Dyer, I. A. and Cassatt, W. A. (1965) Manganese Deficiency in the Bovine, J. An. Sci. **24,** 3, 664.

Rollins, W. C., Genetic Improvement in Horses, in **Introduction to Livestock Production,** Edit. by H. H. Cole, (1966), 2nd Ed., W. H. Freeman Co., San Francisco.

Rooney, J. R. (1966) Contracted Foals, Cor. Vet. **56,** 2, 172.

Rubin, L. F. (1968) Hereditary Retinal Dysplasia in Bedlington Terriers, J.A.V.M.A. **152,** 3, 260.

Rubin, L. F., Bourns, T. K. R. and Lord, L. H. (1967) Hemeralopia in Dogs: Heredity of Hemeralopia in Alaskan Malamutes, Am. J. Vet. Res. **28,** 128, 355.

Sager, R.. (1962) Personal Communication.

Sanger, V. L., Mairs, R. E. and Trapp, A. L. (1964) Hemophilia in a Foal, J.A.V.M.A. **144,** 3, 259.

Sass, B. and Albert, T. F. (1970) A Case of Eisenmenger Complex in a Calf, Cor. Vet. **60,** 1, 61.

Saunders, L. Q., Sweet, J. D., Martin, S. M., Fox, F. H. and Fincher, M. G. (1952) Hereditary Congenital Ataxia in Jersey Calves, Cor. Vet. **42,** 4, 559.

Schutte, A. P. (1967) Vaginal Prolapse in the Btich, J. So. Afr. Vet. Med. Assoc. **38,** 2, 197.

Shelton, M. and Menzies J. W. (1970) Repeatability and Heritability of Components of Reproductive Efficiency in Fine-Wool Sheep, J. An. Sci. **30,** 1, 1.

Shupe, J. L., James, L. F. and Binns, W. (1967) Observations on Crooked Calf Disease, J.A.V.M.A. **151,** 2, 198.

Shupe, J. L., James, L. F., Binns, W. and Keeler, R. F. (1967) A Probable Hereditary Skeletal Deformity in Hereford Cattle, J. Hered. **58,** 311.

Silson, M. and Robinson, R. (1969) Hereditary Hydrocephalus in the Cat, Vet. Rec. **84,** 477.

Smith, S. T., Huston, K.; Eldridge, F. E. and Mudge, J. W. (1961)

Studies on Brachygnathia in Dairy Cattle, J. An. Sci. **20,** 4, 911.

Sohval, A. R. (1963) Sex Chromatin, Chromosomes and Male Infertility, Fert. and Steril. **14,** 2, 180.

Sohval, A. R. (1963) Chromosomes and Sex Chromatin in Normal and Anomalous Sexual Development, Physiol. Reviews **43,** 2, 306

Sponseller, M. L. (1967) Equine Cerebellar Hypoplasia and Degeneration, 13th Ann. Meeting Am. Assoc. Eq. Pract., New Orleans, 123.

Stratton, J. (1964) Dermoid Sinuses Reduced by Selective Breeding, Vet. Rec. **76,** 846.

Tasker, J. B., Severin, G. A., Young, S. and Gillette, E. L. (1969) Familial Anemia in the Basenji Dog, J.A.V.M.A. **154,** 2, 158.

Tennant, B., Asburg, A. C., Laben, R. C., Richards, W. P. C., Kaneko, J. J. and Cupps, P. T. (1967) Familial Polycythemia in Cattle, J.A.V.M.A. **150,** 12, 1493.

Ternan, P. R., Kidwell, J. F. and Walker, L. (1957) Evidence of a New Lethal in Cattle, J. Hered. **48,** 81.

Tesh, J. M. and Glover, T. D. (1966) The Influence of Ageing of Rabbit Spermatozoa on Fertilization and Prenatal Development, J. Reprod. and Fertil. **12,** 414.

Thompson, N. R., Cranek, L. J. Sr. and Ralston, N. P. (1957) Genetic and Environmental Factors in the Development of the American Red Danish Cattle, J. Dairy Sci. **40,** 1, 56.

Thomsen, R. G. (1966) Congenital Bronchial Hypoplasia in Calves, Path. Vet. **3,** 89.

Thomson, R. G. (1966) Failure of Bone Resorption in a Calf, Path. Vet. **3,** 234.

Thurley, D. C., Gilbert, F. R. and Dove, J. T. (1967) Congenital Splayleg of Piglets, Myofibrillar Hypoplasia, Vet. Rec. **30,** 9, 302.

Tobias, G. (1964) Congenital Porphyria in a Cat, J.A.V.M.A. **145,** 5, 462.

Troutt, H. F., Fessler, J. F., Page, E. H. and Amstutz, H. E. (1967) Diaphragmatic Defects in Cattle, J.A.V.M.A. **151,** 11. 1421.

Urman, H. K., and Grace, O. D. (1964) Hereditary Encephalomyopathy: A Hydrocephalus Syndrome in Newborn Calves, Cor. Vet. **54,** 229.

VanVleck, L. D. (1969) How to Detect Carriers of Abnormal Traits, Dairy Herd Manag., May, 29.

Voss, J. L., Eppling, G. P. and Faulkner, L. C. (1960) A Bovine Fetal Monster (Holocardius entericus) Twin to a Normal Fetus, J.A.V.M.A. **136,** 7, 323.

Ward, G. M. (1968) Bovine Cerebellar Hypoplasia Apparently Caused by BVD-MD Virus, Cor. Vet. **59,** 4, 570.

Warren, T. R. and Atkeson, F. W. (1931) Inheritance of Hernia in a Family of Holstein Friesian Cattle, J. Hered. **22,** 345.

Wass, W. M. and Hoyt, H. H. (1965) Bovine Congenital Porphyria: Studies in Heredity, Am. J. Vet. Res. **26,** 112, (and Vet. Scope 8, 3, 113 (1963)).

Wheat, J. D. (1960) Harelip in Shorthorn Cattle, J. Hered. **51,** 99.

Whittem, J. H. (1957) Congenital Abnormalities in Calves: Arthrogryposis and Hydranencephaly, J. Path. and Bact. **73,** 2, 375.

Williams, W. L. (1943) Veterinary Obstetrics, 4th Ed. Miss Louella Williams, Upland Rd., Ithaca, N.Y.

Wilson, J. G. and Warkany, J. (1964) Teratology: Principles and Techniques, Univ. of Chicago Press, Chicago, Ill.

Wipperсht, C. and Horlacher, W. R. (1935) A Lethal Gene in Jersey Cattle, J. Hered. **26,** 363.

Wolstenholme, G. E. W. and O'Connor, C. M. (1961) Congenital Malformations, Little, Brown and Comp, Boston, Mass.

Wysong, R. L. (1969) Embryology of Persistent Right Aortic Arch, Vet. Med., **64,** 3, 203.

Yakely, W. L., Wyman, M., Donovan, E. F. and Fechheimer, N. S. (1968) Genetic Transmission of Ocular Fundus Anomaly in Collies, J.A.V.M.A. **152,** 5, 457.

Young, G. B. (1955) Inherited Defects in Dogs, Vet. Rec. **67,** 1, 15.

Young, G. B. (1967) Hereditary Abnormalities in Cattle, 85th Ann. Congr. Brit. Vet. Assoc.

Young, S. (1962) Hypomyelinogenesis Congenita (Cerebellar Ataxia) in Angus-Shorthorn Calves, Cor. Vet. **52,** 1, 78.

Zwiep, I. N. (1958) Congenital Blindness in Lambs, Tijdschr. vor Diergeneesk. **83,** 1220.

Chapter IV

PHYSIOLOGY OF THE GESTATION PERIOD

In this chapter the estrous cycle, estrum, ovulation, and fertilization are purposely omitted inasmuch as they will be discussed later in Chapter XII on Physiology of Reproduction.

Shape and Location of the Pregnant Uterus

In all domestic animals the uterus with its contents is drawn forward and downward in the abdominal cavity as pregnancy progresses. In the cow and mare the uterus rests on the abdominal floor beneath the intestines after the fourth or fifth month of gestation. In the ruminant the uterus is usually located on the right side of the abdomen because the left side contains the rumen. In advanced pregnancy in the cow and mare the length of the fetus may exceed the distance from the diaphragm to the pelvis. In the mare this often results in the uterus and fetus assuming a diagonal position in the abdominal cavity. In the cow, in the last month of gestation, the nose and the forefeet of the fetus, together with the enveloping uterine wall and fetal membranes, may enter the pelvic cavity and extend caudally over the cervix.

The mesometrium, or broad ligament, attaching the lesser curvature of the uterus of the cow to the caudal lateral flank and pelvic regions, is stretched and pulled forward by the weight of the gravid uterus. However the ovary is never further than 8 to 12 inches, 20 to 25 cm, from the pelvic brim. The uterus of the cow is cornuate in shape and conical, with its greatest diameter from the cervix through the middle of the horn containing the fetus. The distal third of this horn narrows rapidly toward the apex. The opposite horn in both the cow and mare remains relatively small even though fetal membranes extend into it. These characteristics of the uterus in the cow facilitate torsion of the uterus.

In the mare the mesometrium is attached to the dorsolateral aspect of the uterus and dorsally to the sublumbar and dorsal pelvic regions. As the uterine weight increases the ovary is pulled ventrally, but seldom more than 12 inches, 25 cm, from the lumbar vertebrae; the ovary can frequently be felt per rectum for much of the gestation period. The apices of the horns are directed dorsally by the traction of the broad ligament. The body and the horn containing the fetus are tubular and about the same diameter from the cervix to near the apex of the horn.

In the ewe the shape and location of the pregnant uterus is similar to that of the cow. The frequent incidence of bicornual twin pregnancy and the relatively smaller abdominal cavity in the ewe may be a factor in preventing uterine torsion.

In multiparous animals, as the dog, cat and sow, the gravid horn is tubular and about the same diameter its entire length. The fetuses are usually nearly equally distributed between each horn. The horns become very long in the sow. Each pregnant horn may be 1.8 meters or 6 feet in length. They rest on the floor of the abdominal cavity in a folded manner, similar to intestines.

In the cow twinning usually results in bicornual twins, one fetus developing in each horn. In about 10 percent of twin pregnancies, both twins develop the same horn, unicornual twins. In these cases the horn containing both fetuses is very long and is bent at an 180° angle at the diaphragm, with one fetus lying parallel to the other. The fetus in the apex of the horn may be delayed in its expulsion at parturition or be overlooked.

Rectal examination of the cow during gestation often reveals a rotation of the uterus of from 20 to 90 degrees. This amount of rotation is apparently corrected spontaneously before or at the time of parturition. It seems probable that some of the 180° torsions of the uterus causing dystocia at the time of parturition may have their onset at some earlier period of gestation. If circulatory embarrassment of the uterus does not develop, no symptoms of torsion will be observed until the onset of parturition when the fetus cannot be expelled due to the narrow, twisted birth canal.

In 1 in 1,000 equine pregnancies, according to Vandeplassche, a single fetus may develop in both horns, bicornual pregnancy, instead of the body and one horn. With this unusual type of development, the uterus and fetus must lie diagonally in the abdominal cavity, since the length of the fetus is longer than the transverse diameter of the cavity. Bicornual pregnancy in other species of domestic animals rarely occurs because of the acute angle at which the horns leave the body of the uterus. In the mare a bicornual pregnancy may in rare cases become rotated ventrally so that the two horns and the fetus come to rest under the body of the uterus. At the time of parturition this condition produces a long birth passage and severe, often fatal, dystocia.

Position of the Fetus in the Uterus

In domestic animals the tubular uterus that lies more or less parallel to the long axis of the dam requires the developing fetus the last third of gestation to assume a longitudinal position in relation to the long axis of the dam. During the first half of gestation the small fetus could lie in any direction. The length of the bovine and equine fetus after 5 months of gestation is greater than the diameter of the gravid horn. The umbilicus of the fetus, in the cow and ewe opposes the lesser curvature of the uterus with the dorsum of the fetus lying against the greater curvature or dorsal surface of the uterus. This relationship of the dorsum of the fetus to the unattached portion of the horn occurs in the cow and ewe but not the horse, sow, dog, and cat. Most authors, including Benesch, but excepting Williams, agree that in advanced pregnancy in the mare, sow, dog, and cat, the fetus rests with its dorsum or dorso-lateral side against the abdominal wall and ventral portion of the uterine horn in a dorso-pubic or dorso-ilial position. This is said to account for the rolling tactics of the mare at the time of parturition. At birth the fetus of the mare, sow, cat, and dog normally passes through the birth canal with its dorsum against the sacrum of the dam. This is brought about by a rotation of the fetus. In the mare the lack of space for fetal development in bicornual pregnancy often results in flexion of the fetal head and neck alongside the body, and because movement is thereby limited wry neck often results. Arthur reported that in the cow 95 percent of the fetuses were in anterior presentation, with the cranial extremities toward the pelvis, by the sixth month of gestation. However, Vandeplassche reported that at 7 months of gestation in the mare only about 60 percent of the fetuses were in anterior presentation but by the 9th month 99 percent were in anterior presentation. Arthur indicated these late rotations of the equine fetus probably are made possible by a rotation of the amnion and fetus within the allantoic cavity.

In late gestation in the cow 95 percent of the fetuses are in anterior presentation with their cephalic poles facing the cervix, Williams and others. In 5 percent of the fetuses the caudal poles face the cervix in the posterior presentation. During the early months of gestation the incidence of anterior and posterior presentations is about 50 percent each. In the ewe about 95 percent of the fetuses are in anterior presentation at parturition. Benesch and Arthur stated that in swine 54 percent were anterior, and that in dogs 70 percent were anterior presentations. Jones and Dzuik and Harmon reported that 75.7 and 64 percent respectively of swine fetuses at birth were in anterior presentation. In twins, particularly unicornual twins, in uniparous animals it is not unusual to find one fetus in anterior and the other in posterior presentation. Woodward and Clark reported a high incidence of posterior presentations over a 2-year period in an inbred line of Hereford cattle bred to one bull and suggested an hereditary factor might condition such a malpresentation. The reason for the very high incidence of anterior presentations late in gestation and at birth in the cow and mare is not known.

Williams indicated that since in the cow and mare the percentage of anterior presentations is so much higher than that of posterior presentations and the incidence of dystocia or difficult birth is so much higher in posterior presentations than in anterior, posterior presentation in these two species is pathological. He cited other authors who reported that 14 to 32 percent of the dystocias in mares and up to 50 percent of the dystocias in cows occurred with the fetus in posterior presentation. Other authors indicated that since birth can and often does proceed without incident in posterior presentation in the cow and mare, posterior presentations in uniparous animals may be normal. The evidence, however, tends to support Williams. Benesch and Arthur proposed further reasoning to indicate that posterior presentation is abnormal. In posterior presentation, compression of the fetal abdomen as it enters the pelvis expands the ribs and costal arch; while in anterior presentation the fetus is wedge-shaped thus tending to dilate the birth canal during parturition. In dog fetuses the occiput, often the broadest bony structure of the fetus, makes a sudden engagement in the pelvis in posterior presentation. The passage of the fetus in posterior presentation is against the direction of its hair creating more friction and resistance. Lastly, more space is required in uniparous animals to extend flexed hind limbs in the posterior presentation.

Number of Fetuses in the Uterus

Domestic animals may be divided into two groups with respect to the number of ova normally released at the time of ovulation and therefore the number of fetuses in the uterus.

Unipara, or monotocous animals such as the cow and mare, normally have one ovum released at ovulation and one fetus develop in the uterus. Occasionally twins or in exceptional instances triplets or greater numbers of fetuses may be present. This uniparous group of animals is characterized by the presence of a well-developed cervix. The placenta of the single fetus fills both horns and the body of the uterus. The weight of the fetus at the time of parturition is about 10 percent the weight of the postpartum dam, Benesch. In unipara the large size of the fetus and their long extremities, make dystocia due to wedging of twins in the pelvis quite common. Sheep are usually classified as unipara but the incidence of twins is so common that the term "bipara" has been suggested for this species.

Multipara or polytocous animals such as the dog, cat and sow, normally have 3 to 15 or more ova released at each ovulatory period and although an embryonic mortality of 20 to 40 percent commonly may occur during early gestation in these species, usually more than two fetuses are present in the uterus. In unusual cases multipara may have only one viable fetus. In general multipara have a poorly developed cervix. The placenta of each fetus is limited to a portion of the horn. The fetuses are nearly equally distributed between the horns. The fetal membranes of one fetus rarely extend through the body and into the opposite horn. The weight of each fetus at the time of parturition is only 1 to 3 percent of the postpartum weight of the dam. The small size of the fetus and its short extremities make it more bullet-shaped. Dystocia due to wedging of the fetuses in the pelvis at parturition is rare. The average numbers of fetuses usually present in the uterus of multipara are as follows: sow 6 to 12; dog, variable between breeds, large dogs 6 to 10, medium-sized dogs 4 to 7, and small dogs 2 to 4; and cats 3 to 5.

Females that have never conceived or carried young are called **nullipara.** Those that have conceived and have had only one gestation period are called **primipara.** Females that have conceived two or more times and had two or more gestation periods are called **pluripara.**

Twinning and Multiple Births in Unipara

When an uniparous animal aborts or gives birth to two or more fetuses or young they are called twins, triplets, quadruplets, quintuplets, or sextuplets.

In the mare the incidence of twin births is about 0.5 to 1.5 percent. Asdell reported that only 0.5 percent of equine births were twin. He cited other reports of twinning in mares as 1.1, 1.23, 1.5 and 1.6 percent but these reports included aborted twin fetuses. Arthur and Osborne reported that double ovulation occurred in 18 to 20 percent of the estrous periods of mares. Doll and Rooney reported that although nearly all twin equine pregnancies are of the fraternal or dizgotic type that rarely an identical or monozygotic twin pregnancy is observed with a single allantois chorion, two separate amnions and with both fetuses of the same sex and markings. The incidence of triplets in mares is reported as about 1 to 300,000 single births. Herman and Bouters reported that in 95 percent of mares with twin ovulation one or both ova were lost during the early embryonic period. The surviving twin embryos were usually bicornual. They stated that between 7 and 9 months of twin pregnancy, death of both fetuses and abortion is common. Occasionally one embryo or fetus may die, be resorbed or macerated, mummify or rarely be aborted and the other twin develop normally. In 38 twin parturitions they had 33 surviving foals. Some of the fetuses expelled at term with normal foals were mummified. Benesch stated that 78 percent of twin equine fetuses were expelled dead. Williams cited Richter as stating that of 59 mares with twin pregnancies 51 aborted, 7 gave birth to one viable twin and one gave birth to two viable twins—or a mortality rate of 92 percent. Blakeslee and Hudson cited 403 parturitions in 102 draft mares in which 13 twin pregnancies were recorded. Nine of these twin pregnancies resulted in abortion or death of the fetuses. In two twin births both twins survived and in the other two only one twin survived. The high death rate of twins in mares is reported by Williams and Errington to be due to a competition between the twin fetuses for placental area. Although the chorions may fuse anastomosis of the blood vessels does not occur. One chorion invaginates into the other, and in time the smaller fetus dies due to a lack of nutrients and mummifies or both fetuses die and are prematurely expelled.

In sheep, deer and goats the incidence of twinning is greatly influenced by the nutritional status of the animal at the time of ovulation as well as the hereditary background of twins in the breed. Johansson and Hanson reported on nearly 60,000 sheep in Sweden of different breeds in which 45 percent of ewes had twins; 2.3 percent, or 1 in 50 had triplets, 0.1 percent, or 1 in 1,000 had quadruplets and 0.009 percent, or 1 in about 10,000 had quintuplets. Benesch indicated that under favorable conditions 60 to 70 percent of sheep may have twins, 25 to 30 percent triplets, and 2 percent quadruplets. As low as 2 percent twins are reported as occurring in certain breeds and under less favorable environmental conditions. Primiparous ewes bear twins and triplets much less often than do pluriparous ewes. Finnish Landrace sheep normally produce 2 to 4 lambs per pregnancy and larger numbers are not uncommon. These have been imported into the U.S. for crossbreeding experiments.

In goats, according to Richter, about 63.3 percent of births are of twins. In a report from the New York State Conservation Department (1949), the northern mountainous wooded Adriondack region of the state had a deer herd producing 4 young per 100 female fawns and 93 young per 100 does. In the southern part of the State, where much more feed was available, the deer herd produced 38 young per 100 fawns and 161 young per 100 does. This clearly illustrated the effect of environmental conditions on the rate of reproduction of deer in the same State. Asdell and Stansfield reported that monozygotic twins in sheep were uncommon.

In cattle multiple births have been the subject of much study, Gilmore, Johansson, and Hancock. Dairy cattle records indicate that the incidence of twinning in dairy cattle is about the same as for humans but that triplets and higher multiples occur with slightly lower frequency than in humans. Gilmore cited records on over two million births in dairy and beef cattle and reported that the incidence of twinning is 1.04 percent or 1:96 single births in dairy cattle. The incidence of twins is 1:87 in humans, and about 0.5 percent or 1:227 single births in beef cattle. Arthur reported an incidence of twinning of about 2 percent for dairy cattle and 1 percent for beef cattle. Hancock reported an incidence of twinning of 1.2 to 4.6 percent in 9 breeds of cattle. Despite inadequate reporting the frequency of multiple births in dairy cattle may be estimated according to Gilmore as follows:

Twins	1 to 96 single births
Triplets	1 to about 7,500 single births
Quadruplets	1 to about 700,000 single births
Quintuplets	1 to about 60 million single births

Thus in the U.S. about 200,000 twin calves, 2,000 triplets and 30 sets of quadruplets are born each year. From data on nearly 750,000 beef cattle the ratio of triplets was 1:106,979 and quadruplets 1:748,855 births.

Twinning is to some extent a breed characteristic, Johansson. With the frequency of twinning being 3.3 percent in Holsteins, 2.7 percent in Brown Swiss and about 1 percent for Jerseys. Meadows and Lush reported the incidence of twinning in about 33,000 dairy cows in the U.S. to be 2.58 percent with 8.85 percent for Brown Swiss, 3.08 percent for Holsteins, 2.8 percent for Ayrshires and 1.95 percent for Guernseys. The twinning rate for Holstein heifers of 1.3 percent was lower than at the second calving when it was 4.4 percent. It rose thereafter to 7 percent at 10 years of age, Erb and Morrison.

Kidder, Barrett, Casida reported a high incidence of infertility associated with double ovulation in cows. In a total of over 600 ovulations 13.1 percent had double ovulations but the incidence of twinning was only 1.92 percent. Many multiple conceptions terminate early in the gestation period in embryonic death and absorption, and later in abortion or premature birth. Erdheim reported that 90 percent of bovine twin pregnancies were bicornural and 10 percent were unicornual. This is probably a reflection of a higher embryonic death rate in unicornual pregnancy after double ovulation on the same ovary.

According to Gilmore, Hancock, Johansson and Bonnier the incidence of monozygotic or identical bovine twins and dizygotic or fraternal twins to all twins was 4 to 6 percent and 93 to 95 percent, respectively. The incidence of monozygotic bovine twins to all like-sexed twins was 8 to 12 percent or about 10 percent. The incidence of monozygous twins to all cattle births was 0.05 to 0.3 percent. The incidence of monozygotic twins to all twins varied from 0.7 to 18 percent. Monozygotic twins arise from one fertilized ovum that divides into two zygotes in the oviduct. Dizygotic twins usually arise from the rupture of two follicles, often one in each ovary, or rarely the rupture of a single follicle containing two ova, Arthur. Monozygotic twins may occur as members of triplet or greater multiple births. According to Gilmore, the higher the order of multiple births, the more likely the occurrence of monozygotic pairs. Monozygotic twins are of value in many types of nutritional, physiological and behavior experiments in which animals with the same hereditary genes are desired for the evaluation of different environmental factors. Monozygotic twins have similar characters in respect to color, color pattern, number of teats, topline, tail, hair whorls, muzzle pattern, etc. They are always of the same sex and have the same blood type. Skin or organ grafts survive for an indefinite period when exchanges are performed between monozygotic twins.

Dizygotic or fraternal twins bear no greater resemblance to each other than do full siblings. Dizygotic twins have different blood types that frequently show blood chimerism due to early anastomosis of the placental vessels of the two twins and the exchange of primitive erythrocytic cells that become established in both embryos, Stormont and Stormont et al.. From information based on a study of freemartinism by Williams et al. approximately 90 to 92 percent of all bovine twins develop placental anastomoses. In 21 cases studied all 9 unicornual twins developed placental anastomoses. Hemoglobin and transferrin characters in blood also showed chimerism. Thus the study of immunogenetics is of value in the diagnosis of freemartins.

Immunogenetics is the branch of genetics concerned with the inheritance of antigenic and other characters, especially blood factors, relating to the immune response. Rapid advances in this science have been made in recent years. In animals the most study and progress has been made in cattle where blood typing using 70 different reagents, about 50 routinely, has contributed significantly to the artificial insemination industry. Blood typing can usually solve problems of questionable parentage in over 90 percent of cattle by eliminating animals that are not the sire or dam of a particular individual. Rendel and coworkers reported on the basis of 1347 parentage tests that 20 percent of cows bred artificially to two different sires at 1 to 11 day intervals became pregnant on the first service while 6 percent of cows conceived on the first service when bred twice at 15 to 24 day intervals. Thus blood typing for determining parentage should be performed when a cow is bred to two different sires at an interval of 16 days or less or when the gestation length is 8 to 10 days shorter than expected on the basis of the date of the last service.

Immunogenetics has proven useful in the study and identification of monozygous twins and nonchimeric or chimeric dyzygotic twins and freemartins by means of blood factors. It has even aided in the discovery of chimeric animals born as a single fetus where the other "twin" was lost, aborted, or mummified. In recent years electrophoretic studies of serum proteins and transferrin types in blood and the use of tissue transplants or grafts have expanded the scope of this field. Studies have been made to see if certain blood characters are related to other desirable or undesirable traits in cattle to aid in early selection or elimination of animals. At present there appears to be little hope of progress in this area, Stormont, Stone et al..

In horses and dogs a limited amount of progress has been made in immunogenetics and blood typing, Stormont and Suzuki, and Swisher and Young. Blood typing in horses is practical and with the present number of only 16 reagents parentage determination was satisfactory in 65 percent of the cases. An excellent review of blood groups in the domestic animals was compiled in 1962 in cattle by Stormont, in horses by Franks, in sheep by Rasmussen, and in pigs by Saison and Ingram. With further work and the development of more reagents greater accuracy in parentage determination will be possible. In dogs the study of blood groups has indicated that most cases of hemolytic disease in newborn pups is associated with type A positive pups and A negative dams immunized against type A blood. More immunogenetic studies in these and other species of animals will undoubtedly be made in the future.

A freemartin is an infertile female with a modified genital tract born cotwin, or in greater multiples, with a bull with which it has exchanged whole blood, Biggers and McFeely. In a summary of reports on 348 unlike-sexed twins Gilmore found that 91.4 percent of the female twins were sterile and the other 8.6 percent were fertile. Thus out of 10 to 12 females cotwin to bulls only one is fertile. This infertility is of importance and interest from both the economic as well as the scientific standpoint. The freemartin is one of two dizygotic individuals that are of different sexes and do not resemble each other. Two corpora lutea are invariably present in the ovaries. Judging from statistics on sex ratios the freemartin should be a female. There is rarely any sex intergrading between the fremartin and the male. Freemartins have recently been proven to be genetic females as they are positive for sex chromatin bodies and their tissue cells have a female, XX, karyotype, Moore et al., and Herschler et al..

Gilmore and Biggers and McFeely further described the development of the freemartin condition by indicating that the blastodermic vesicles from each developing zygote meet in the uterus by about the 18th to 20th day of gestation. The allantois soon meet and by the time the embryo is 28 days old the allantois chorion and blood streams of the two placentas have united. This occurs well before sex differentiation, which takes place about the 30-mm. stage or about 40 to 50 days of gestation.

Lillie (1916) proposed that the genital structures, especially the interstitial cells of the testes, of the male developed earlier than the female ovaries. It was believed that some chemical substance secreted by the male reached the female embryo by way of the anastomosing blood vessels in the placenta. This chemical substance, apparently not an androgen as originally believed by Lillie, inhibited the development of the cortex of the undeveloped female gonad and the genital tract.

Lillie's **humoral or "hormonal" theory** is presently questioned. Most bovine twins are blood cell chimeras because of early placental vessel anastomosis. Stone et al. reported that of 74 pairs of heterosexual twins 89.2 percent had erythrocyte chimerism including 12 freemartins and their bull cotwins. None of 8 females born cotwin with bulls and not having erythrocyte chimerism were freemartins. Billingham and coworkers showed that the percentage of heterozygous twins that would tolerate reciprocal skin grafts was the same as the incidence of freemartins indicating that the early transfer of blood elements between the fetuses caused the development of tolerance. Fechheimer et al. and Dunn have shown that about 90 percent of unlike-sexed twins have XX/XY white blood cell chimerism (See Figure 57). The percentage of XX to XY white cells in the blood of freemartins and cotwin bulls is highly variable. Stone et al. recently showed that tolerance to skin grafts by bovine heterozygotes with placental anastomoses of vessels was not as great as in monozygotous twins.

Muramoto et al. demonstrated XX/XY chimerism in the mesodermal and endodermal tissue cells of freemartins and their cotwin. Since anastomosis of the placental vessels precedes migration of the primordial sex cells from the wall of the yolk sac to the genital ridge, there is the possibility, requiring further confirmation, that migratory primordial germ cells could pass from the male fetus to the female fetus in early pregnancy causing the freemartin condition by the presence of the XY cells in the gonadal ridge. This is called the **cellular theory** of freemartinism proposed by Fechheimer et al. and Ohno et al..

Much more experimental work is necessary before the "humoral" or "cellular" hypothesis is proven correct. Both Short et al. and Dunn et al. indicated the former is probably most likely correct with an inductor substance such as "medullarin" passing from the male to the female fetus causing the retention of the medullary cords in the female genital ridge, Witschi, resulting in atresia of the XX germ cells before birth.

In freemartins the ovaries usually fail to develop and remain small, about the size of a flattened barley grain, and undifferentiated. In rare cases some differentiation toward the female or male gonad may occur. The genital tract, especially the portion arising from the paramesonephric duct, is markedly arrested in development. Often in the region of the cervix two tubular structures or remnants of the mesonephric duct resembling seminal vesicles are present. (See Figures 55 and 56). The vagina is undeveloped but the vulva is fairly normal except for the occasional presence of a prominent clitoris and a large tuft of vulvar hair. In the yearling animal, no estrous cycles develop; the udder and teats remain very small and the external characteristics resemble a steer.

For a definite diagnosis Fincher advised that a 3/8- to 1/2-inch test tube or glass speculum be inserted with lubrication into the vulva of the "heifer" in question. (See Figure 56) If the animal is a freemartin the tube will go no farther than the hymen, or the caudal portion of the vagina or about 7.5 to 10 cm, 3 to 4 inches, in a young calf, as there is no normal vagina. If the female is normal some resistance may be encountered when the test tube passes through the vulvovaginal region but it then will pass 12 to 18 cm, 5 to 7 inches into a freely dilatable vagina. The use of a light will reveal a normal small cervix. In the freemartin the vaginal opening cannot be found anterior to the urethral opening on the floor of the vulva. The only chance for error in this technique is in heifers with an imperforate hymen. After the freemartin becomes 8 to 14 months of age, a rectal examination is possible. This reveals the marked arrest in the development of the vagina, cervix, uterus, and gonads. Usually these structures cannot be found on rectal examination or they are very minute.

Although the male cotwins to freemartins are usually considered to be fertile, Dunn et al. reported on 4 chimeric bulls. Two had testicular degeneration with sterility, one had testicular degeneration and oligospermia, one had reduced fertility with a sex ratio of 29 males to 71 females. Short et al. also questioned the reproductive normality of the male twin. If the cellular theory of freemartinism is valid then XX germ cells should be in the male twin's testis. Although a few possible XX cells have been reported in young calves by a few authors, Ohno et al., no one has reported XX germ cells in mature males.

Freemartinism is rare in other domestic species of animals but it has been reported in sheep, pigs and possibly goats, Alexander and Williams, Gerneke, Hughes and McFeely. The chorions of twins or greater multiples in these species will often fuse but anastomosis of blood vessels is rare.

The Undesirable Nature of Twinning in Horses and Cows

Multiple births or twinning in uniparous animals is undesirable and in most cases is pathological and often disastrous to the dam as well as to the fetuses. According to Williams and others, twinning represents an economic waste or loss and is a reflection of genital disease rather than of health. The abortion rate of twin fetuses in horses is exceedingly high, about 90 percent. After twin birth in mares usually less than half of the foals survive and these frequently require careful nursing care. There is little data on the subsequent performance of these viable twin foals. In cows the abortion rate for twins after 3 months of gestation is much greater than for single fetuses. It is estimated that 30 to 40 percent of twin pregnancies terminate in abortion, Gilmore and Erb and Morrison; Williams stated that this percentage may be as high as 50 percent. In normal single pregnancies only 3 to 5 percent end in observable abortions. Kidder et al. reported a 13.1 percent incidence of double ovulations in a herd but only a 1.92 percent incidence of twin births. This was an 85 percent loss of twin zygotes. Labhsetwar et al. reported a 5.4 percent incidence of double ovulations in another herd. The conception rate after double ovulations was one half that following single ovulations. Erdheim's report of a ratio of 10 percent unicornual twins and 90 percent bicornual bovine twins; together with the report of a 35 to 41 percent death loss of embryos in ewes with double ovulation on one ovary, a 31 percent loss with an ovulation on each ovary and only a 22 to 26 percent loss with a single ovulation, Casida et al., underscore the high embryonic losses associated with multiple ovulations in

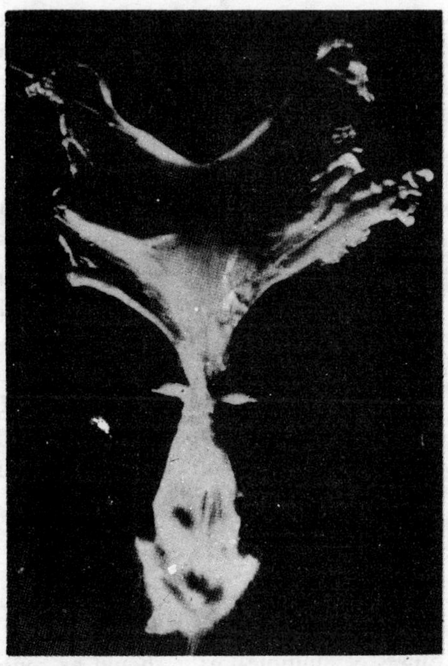

Figure 55. Freemartin genital tract. Note rudimentary uterine horns, grain-sized gonads, lack of a cervix and remnants of seminal vesicles (mesonephric duct structures).

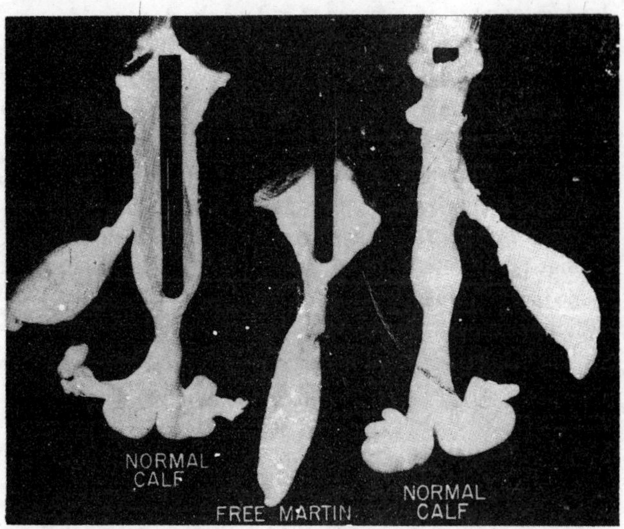

Figure 56. Clinical diagnosis of a freemartin. Note a normal vagina is lacking. (Courtesy M. G. Fincher)

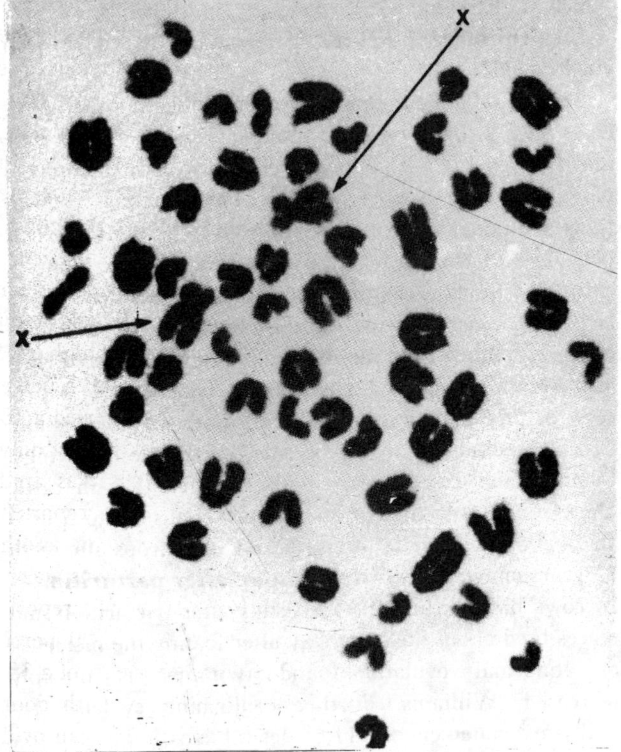

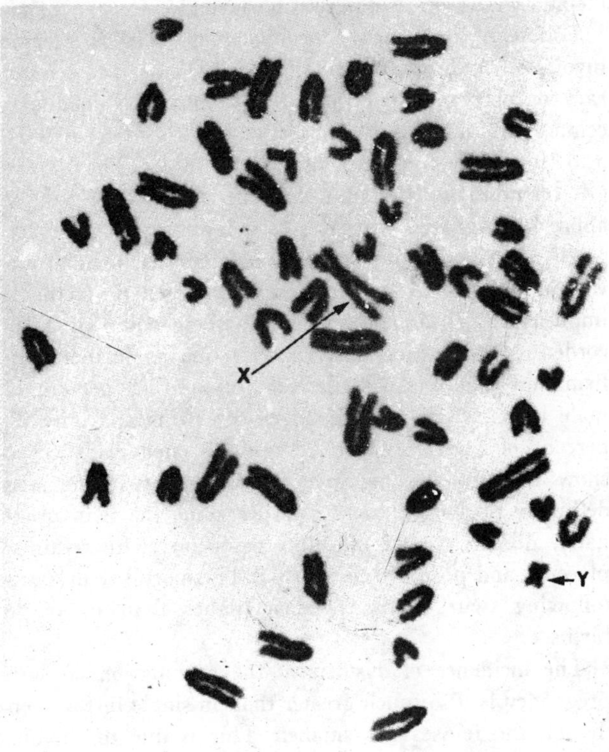

Figure 57. XX and XY white blood cells from a chimeric bull, cotwin to a freemartin. The chromosomes are in metaphase. (Courtesy of H.O. Dunn)

uniparous animals, especially in double ovulations from the same ovary.

Many twin pregnancies terminate prematurely. Gilmore cited records indicating that the gestation period for bovine twins is an average of 5 days shorter than for single calves. Male twins were carried 1 to 2 days longer than twins of both sexes, and 3 to 5 days longer than female twins. The incidence of abortion and premature birth is even higher in triplets and greater multiples. Erb and Morrison reported fewer fertile female progeny are associated with twinning in cattle than with single births.

Viable twins are of smaller size and vigor than single young. Gilmore stated that single bovine males weigh 25 to 45 percent more than twin males, and single females weigh 40 to 50 percent more than twin females. This reduced weight of the individual twin is possibly due to a reduced placenta area or a reduced amount of available nutrients for each fetus, and to the shortened gestation period. The combined weight of both twins is usually 35 to 50 percent greater than that of a single calf. A much higher percentage of dead twin fetuses are expelled at term than is the case in single pregnancies. Gilmore cited Johansson, who stated that 4.5 percent of twins are expelled dead at term, as compared with 0.9 percent for single calves. In addition about three times as many twins die at a young age as do calves born singly.

Following twin births or abortions, delayed uterine involution, retained placenta, septic metritis, and temporary or permanent sterility are common. Retained placenta occurs in about 50 percent or more of twin calvings, 5 to 10 times as frequently as in single births. The placental retention is probably due in most cases to the abbreviated gestation period, to a lowering of the resistance to infection by the overloaded uterus, to poor involution of the uterus and possibly a genetic factor is implicated, Erb and Morrison. Comberg and Velten recorded an interesting observation requiring further confirmation that retained placenta followed 75 percent of male twins, 42 percent of mixed-sex twins and only 20 percent of female twins. All authors cited evidence to show that the calving interval following twinning was definitely prolonged over those preceding the twin pregnancy due to greater infertility associated with retained placenta and postpartum metritis. The mortality in dams following twin births is much higher than in single births.

The incidence of dystocia at the termination of twin pregnancy is also much greater than in single births even though the fetuses are smaller. This is due to various causes including: the atonicity of the distended uterus; the frequent presence of a dead, flaccid fetus; the wedging of the extremities of bicornual twins in the pelvis; and the frequent occurrence of posterior presentation in one of the twin fetuses with the hind limbs extended beneath the body.

In dairy cows decreased milk production, probably associated with the postpartum metritis, usually follows a twin pregnancy. Twins are uneconomical for herd replacements since half the pairs consist of male and female and 91 percent of these females are sterile. The male calf may be normal or have reduced fertility, but in most herds these are sold for veal. In beef herds this latter factor is not as important. The incidence of fetal monsters is increased in twin pregnancy in which anastomosis of placental vessels makes possible the nutrition of acardiac or amorphus monsters. Incomplete separation of monozygotic twins results in double monsters, constituting a severe obstetrical problem.

Causes of Twinning

The causes of multiple births should be considered so that possible suggestions may be obtained for the prevention of this undesirable and often disastrous occurrence. The causes of twinning in uniparous animals may be divided between those which are environmental and those which are hereditary.

Environmental causes of twinning that have been cited include:

Season—Gilmore cited references indicating that dairy cows have a slightly greater number of twins during June and July calvings, while beef breeds have greater numbers of twins during August calvings. The respective conceptions had taken place in September, October, and November. **Age of the dam**—It is well known that in sheep, cattle and humans the incidence of twinning in the young is low and increases with age until senile changes commence, at which time the incidence again is lowered. Erb and Morrison reported a twinning frequency of 1.3 percent for first calvings, 4.4 percent for second calvings and then a gradual rise to 7.1 percent for the tenth calvings. Gilmore and Labhsetwar et al. reported that in cattle there is a consistent rise in multiple births up to 5 or 6 years of age. This rise levels off and then drops after 8 to 12 years of age. **Breeding too soon after parturition**—In cows bred within 30 to 40 days after parturition and mares bred about the ninth day after foaling the incidence of abnormal ovulations and twinning is possibly increased, Williams. Further confirming evidence for Williams' statement would be desirable as Labhsetwar et al. noted no correlation between the length of interval after calving up to 90 days and the incidence of multiple ovulations in the cow. **Sires**—The immediate influence of sires on the production of twins is limited to monozygotic twins, a relatively small percent of the total number of twins. **Hormone injections of F.S.H.**—A number of experiments have been reported in which multiple births were induced in beef-type cattle by the intramuscular injection of 800 I.V. to 2000 I.V. of P.M.S. on the 16th or 17th day of the estrous cycle or at the time of manual removal of the corpus luteum. Superovulation was not induced if the cow exhibited estrum within 3 days after the injection of P.M.S. Conception rates at 60 days where 2, 3, 4 and 5 to 6 ova were released were 55.3, 48.7, 29.2 and 25.0 percent, respectively. Low conception rates were frequently observed when superovulation was confined to a single ovary. Superovulation and conception results were unpredictable and in general not highly satisfactory usually only about 25 to 30 percent of treated cattle had twin or triplet pregnancies, Milk Marketing Board, Hammond, Turman et al. Gordon, Williams and Edwards, and Hafez et al..

The hereditary basis for twinning has been reviewed by Gilmore and Erb and coworkers and has been established by records of breed differences, differences between herds, sires, and families within a breed, the repetition of multiple births in the same cow, and the effect of inbreeding on the incidence of twinning. **Breed differences**—The incidence of twinning in beef cattle is low which may be an indication that twinning in dairy cattle is related to the high production of milk and to the pituitary deficiencies associated with abnormalities of ovulation, such as cystic ovaries. In the dairy breeds the incidence of twinning is reported by Gilmore and Johansson to be highest in Holsteins and Brown Swiss, with Guernseys intermediate, and Ayrshires and Jerseys the lowest. He cited an example illustrating this inherited tendency for twinning. In one college herd the incidence of twinning in Holsteins was 8.8 percent as compared to less than 2 percent for the three other dairy breeds on the same farm. **Differences between dams, sires and families**—In the case just cited as well as others recorded by Gilmore, the herd incidence of twinning may reach 20 percent as against the overall average of 1.04 percent or slightly more. It has been noted that dizygotic twinning is affected more by inheritance than is monozygotic twinning. Gilmore cited an instance in which 2.65 percent of a bull's 377 offspring were twins; but in his daughters that produced 360 calves sired by other bulls, twins occurred 9.17 percent of the time. Thus the hereditary tendency for twinning was passed by the sire to his daughters. In a large herd of Holsteins Erb and coworkers reported 313 multiple births or 4.2 percent of 7387 calvings. Fourteen percent of 1905 cows produced twins at one or more calvings. Daughters of twinning cows had twins significantly more frequently than daughters of nontwinning cows, 17.4 percent and 13.0 percent respectively. It was also demonstrated that the sire contributed to the twinning tendency of his daughters, Erb et al.. The frequency of twinning in certain cow families has been observed by many veterinarians, farmers, and research workers. In another herd, 10 of 21 families comprising 90 percent of the dairy had no twins. The other 11 families had an incidence of twinning ranging from 2.6 to 18 percent, Gilmore. **The repetition of multiple births in the same cow** is principally a tendency for multiple ovulation. After the first multiple birth the frequency of succeeding multiple births was from 8 to 12 percent. **Cystic ovaries**—This pathological condition, occurring usually in high-producing cows during their peak of lactation, has been associated by many workers with twinning. Although cystic ovaries are associated with high production and heavy feeding in cattle, no reports or studies have been made on the effect of a high versus a low plane of nutrition on the incidence of double ovulation in cattle. Clapp, Williams, and others have stated that conceptions occurring soon after recovery from cystic ovaries resulted in a high percentage of twins At that time recovery was spontaneously aided by repeated removal of the cysts by manual pressure. Labhsetwar et al. noted an incidence of 12.9 percent multiple ovulations in cystic parities as compared to 4.2 percent in noncystic parities. Erb et al. reported that 15 percent of cows that conceived within 75 days after treatment for cystic ovaries had twins compared to 4.9 percent of the cows conceiving 75 or more days after therapy for cystic ovaries. It has been observed by the author that cows treated with luteninizing hormones and bred the following heat period did not have the high incidence of twinning noted by Clapp although an increased incidence of twinning should be expected in individuals with a tendency toward ovarian cysts. Garm, Palsson and others have reported that the condition of cystic ovaries is hereditary and bulls may transmit this tendency to their daughters.

In herds where selection for twinning was followed, the incidence rose to 29 percent. These facts show that twinning is definitely influenced by heredity. Labhsetwar et al. reported more multiple ovulations in outbred cattle than inbred cattle. Erb et al. stated that it would even be possible to postulate that twinning was caused by a simple recessive character with modifying genes and environmental factors that could influence its expression. With the increase of artificial insemination in dairy cattle and the rise in production of milk per cow, that has been shown to be closely associated with an increased incidence of cystic ovaries, the problems arising from twinning will probably become greater. This is further complicated by the generally successful treatment of cystic ovaries with gonadotropic hormones that allow cows with this inherited tendency to produce many daughters who are also affected. There is need for further research to see to what extent the hereditary tendency toward cystic ovaries is related to the hereditary tendency toward twinning. If twinning is a serious problem in a herd, involving 25 percent or more of the cows, an older sire with a low percentage of his daughters producing twins or a son from this bull from a family free of twins should be selected as a herd sire. There is no evidence on the heritability of twinning in horses. Rendel has reported that the heritability of multiple birth in sheep is rather low. However Shelton and Menzies stated that the repeatability of twinning in ewes was high and amenable to selection for improving reproductive efficiency.

Sex Parity

Sex parity or the sex ratio is usually expressed as the percent of male births; in older references the complete ratio of males to females was given. From a theoretical genetic basis the union of a haploid, X, ovum with either an X or Y haploid sperm cell should produce 50 percent males. From records of large numbers of animals this theoretical percentage is closely approximated. According to Altman and Dittmer the sex ratio expressed as percentage of males at birth is:

Table 6. Sex Ratios in Domestic Animals (per cent males)

Animal	% males	Animal	% males
Horse	49.9	Ass	48.6
Cow (Bos taurus)	48.6 - 51.5	Goat	50.1 - 51.3
(Bos indicus)	50.5 - 51.1	Man	50.5 - 51.3
Guernseys	44.4	Dog	50.4 - 55.9
Sheep (All)	48.3 - 51.0	Hybrids - Jack X Mare	44.4
Merino	46.8	Bison Bull X Cow	15.7
Pigs	48.5 - 51.9	Bull X Bison Cow	31.0

Spector provided essentially the same figures on the sex ratio of animals. On a basis of 197,936 births cited by different workers on cattle, Gilmore stated that the sex ratio of calves averaged 51.12 percent males with variations from 42.6 to 53.7 percent because of the low numbers of cattle in some reports. Brands et al. reported on about 200,000 bovine births in the Netherlands with 50.6 percent male calves. Fifty-six percent of abortions were male calves and at parturition 7.9 percent of males and 4.8 percent of females were stillborn. Williams reported on a healthy beef herd of high fertility which at branding time had 94,436 calves, with a sex ratio of 51.1 percent males. The variations from approximately 50 percent are highly interesting but not explainable at present. Gilmore summarized a number of theories for this. The age of the dam or the sire and the season of the year had no effect on this ratio. Most workers agreed that there is a higher percentage of males at conception than at birth. On the basis of sex chromatin studies of human fetuses obtained at lawful abortions Hnevkosky et al. reported sex ratios at 6, 10 and 14 weeks of gestation to be 89, 68 and 58 percent males, respectively. Chapman, Casida and Cote found the sex ratio of fetal calves, of 5 to 10 cm crown-rump length, 11 to 20 cm and 81 to 90 cm were 66, 56 and 50 percent males, respectively. A higher percentage of males than females are absorbed, aborted, expelled dead at term, or present in dystocia, Williams. Clark et al. reported that of 11,527 calvings in range cattle 397 fetuses were expelled dead, 59.5 percent of these were males. This is further illustrated by sex ratios in multiple births, in which there apparently is an increased intrauterine mortality of males, possibly due to a lowered resistance. According to Gilmore the ratio on cattle for single births is 51.1 percent males, for twins 49.1 percent, for triplets 47.6 percent and for quadruplets and quintuplets about 45 percent. The sex ratio for premature twin births in cattle was 52.7 to 53.7 percent males.

Occasionally claims are made that certain specific and intentional procedures will influence the sex ratio. One of these early claims which received wide publicity was the altering of the pH of the vagina. These claims are usually premature and false. With the widespread use of artificial insemination further experiments have been conducted in efforts to separate the Y-bearing spermatozoa from the X-bearing spermatozoa by electrophoresis, centrifugation and sedimentation. These experiments have not been successful. There is no basis for beliefs such as prolonged storage of semen, breeding at certain times during estrum, using young or old males and others having any effect on the sex ratio. The number of animals used in an experiment should be considered; this number should be very large for the substantiation of any claim.

The Bacterial Flora of the Pregnant Uterus

Although the literature reveals an apparent controversy on this subject, practically all workers, including Miller and Williams, agreed that from 20 to 80 percent of pregnant bovine uteri have some bacteria between portions of the maternal and fetal placentas, in the uterine cavity or in the organs of the fetus. Many pregnant uteri are bacteriologically negative. Although this may be ideal, it apparently is not essential for a healthy gestation and parturition. A careful examination of almost all placentas will show a few areas where some pathology or disease process, either acute and active or chronic and inactive, is present. The organisms most commonly found are streptococci, staphylococci, and coliform bacilli. Many other bacteria, molds, and viruses have been reported. These organisms gain access to the uterine cavity and placenta by way of the cervix and the caudal portions of the genital tract at the time of estrum and service, are still present from the time of a previous parturition, or they may come from the blood stream of the dam and localize in the uterus. During most of the gestation period in domestic animals, the uterus and uterine endometrium is under the influence of progresterone from the corpus luteum or placenta. Rowson and Black and their coworkers have shown that during the estrual cycle the uterus of the cow is resistant to infections at the time of estrum when under the influence of estrogens, and more susceptible to infection during the rest of the cycle when the uterus and endometrium is under the influence of progesterone. It is possible that the favorable environment produced by progesterone may favor the establishment of infections in the gravid uterus.

The above findings may indicate to some that the presence of bacteria is of itself dangerous or harmful to the pregnancy. This is not necessarily true. One might liken the condition to an internal parasitism where a few parasites, particularly nonpathogenic parasites have no effect on the individual. It is only when the individual's resistance is overcome or an excessive number of "parasites" are present that the condition reaches disease proportions with definite symptoms and extensive pathology. It is difficult to delineate between health and disease. Slight to definite infection and evidence of disease of the placenta may be present in an apparently physiological birth. In the more severe infections greater damage to the placenta and endometrium may produce maceration of the fetus, abortions, premature births, dystocia, retained placentas, septic metritis, and subsequent sterility. These latter diseases may be associated with the lowering or lack of resistance of the dam or the fetus; previously undiagnosed damage to the endometrium; and the type, pathogenicity, virulence and numbers of organisms present during the various stages of gestation.

Although healthy, gravid uteri frequently have some bacteria present, the healthy, nongravid uteri does not have a bacterial flora. Most workers, according to Miller, find healthy nongravid bovine uteri free of bacteria. Judging from extensive work based on cervical and uterine cultures made during estrum, this is true in the normal healthy mare. A number of other workers, including Miller and Brus, have reported that infertile cows, or cows that have an obvious genital disease and have failed to conceive often may have infection and endometritis of a sufficient degree to prevent conception.

Many factors influence the duration of gestation. The length of the gestation period differs between the breeds and certain hybrids. In cattle and horses male fetuses are carried one to two days longer than female fetuses. Male fetuses in cattle also weigh 2 to 10 lbs. more than female fetuses. Young cows in their first and second gestation carry fetuses one to two days less than older cows. It appears that calves born during the winter or spring have slightly longer gestation periods. Foals born from January through April have gestation periods about 10 days longer than foals born from May through September, Howell and Rollins, Matthews et al.. Sager and others have reported that mares will occasionally have gestation periods up to 375 days in length, and rarely even up to 400 days with a live foal being produced. Most studies indicated that the sire has an influence on gestation length in cattle, horse hybrids and pigs, Holm, Banerjee-Schotsman, Andersen and Plum, and DeFries et al.. The latter observed that the length of gestation is primarily a characteristic of the fetus and that by selection of male and female calves having a short gestation period the mean length of gestation could probably be decreased 10 days within three generations.

Short gestation periods are often associated with abortions and premature births. The gestation period of twin fetuses in cattle is an average of 3 to 6 days shorter than gestation periods of single fetuses; in sheep and goats this is only 0.6 days shorter, Holm. Turman et al. reported that in beef cows with multiple pregnancies following the administration of P.M.S. the duration of pregnancy for single fetuses, twins, triplets, quadruplets and quintuplets was 280.8, 277.4, 269.2, 262.5 and 258.0 days, respectively. Adverse disease factors influencing the health of the endometrium and placenta or infecting the

Table 7. Duration of Pregnancy in Animals* (In Days)

Animal	Days	Animal	Days
Cow - 273 to 296			
Aberdeen Angus	273 to 282		
Ayrshire	277 to 278		
Jersey	277 to 280		
Holstein	278 to 282		
Shorthorn	281 to 282		
Guernsey	282 to 285		
Hereford	283 to 286		
Brown Swiss	288 to 291		
Brahman	292 (Range 271 - 310) (Plasse et al.)		
Afrikaner	293 to 296		
Horse - 327 to 357			
Light breeds	340 to 342 (Average), Rossdale, Estes and Worth		
Draft breeds	330 to 340 (Average)		
Stallion X Ass	350 (Hinny), Holm		
Jack X Mare	355 (Mule), Holm		
Ass	365 to 375		
Sheep - 140 to 155, Smith			
Coarse or Medium Wool Breeds	140 - 148		
Southdown	143 to 145		
Dorset	144		
Hampshire	145		
Shropshire	146		
Corriedale	149		
Fine Wool Breeds			
Rambouillet	150		
Merino	150 (147 - 155)		
Swine	111 to 116	**Squirrel**	28 to 40
Dog	60 to 63	**Coyote**	60 to 68
Cat	56 to 65	**Deer**	200 to 210
Siamese cat	63 to 69	**Elephant, Indian**	615 to 650
Goat	148 to 156	**Fox**	51 to 52
Chinchilla	111 to 128	**Kangaroo**	38 to 40
Guinea pig	63 to 70	**Lion**	105 to 112
Hamster	16 to 19	**Woodchuck**	28 to 32
Mouse	10 to 20	**Mink**	42 to 53
Rabbit	30 to 32	**Opossum**	7 to 13
Rat	22 to 23	**Raccoon**	63
Bear	208 to 240	**Rhinoceros**	530 to 548
Bison	270 to 276	**Tiger**	105 to 113
Egyptian buffalo	316 to 318	**Wolf**	63
Camel, Bactrian	333 to 430		
Dromedary	315 to 350		

*The above are data from various sources, including Dukes, Kenneth, Altman and Dittmer, Andersen and Plum, and Asdell.

fetus may cause abortion or short gestation periods. Besides infections these adverse influences may also include malnutrition, chronic debilitating diseases, deficiency diseases, starvation, severe stress or other conditions favoring or causing abortion. Van Rensburg (see abortion in sheep and goats) has reported on a genetic involution of the corpus luteum of pregnancy associated with hyperplastic adrenal cortices resulting in abortion in inbred Angora goats.

Prolonged gestation periods are observed, according to Holm in a variety of conditions in animals including:

(1) Iodine deficiency in sows, or the administration of thiouracil to produce hypothyroidism, caused gestation periods 4 to 10 days longer than normal with poorly viable, goiterous, hairless pigs.

(2) Delayed parturition in sows, dogs, sheep and cows has been produced with large continued injections of progesterone or progestins. Most fetuses died in the month following a normal length of gestation and became macerated or mummified, Bengtsson and Schofield, Kiesel, and Autrey.

(3) Ewes consuming **Veratrum californicum** about the 14th day of gestation, causing severe deformities of the face and head with hypoplasia or aplasia of the .hypophysis, had greatly prolonged gestation periods of up to 230 days with fetal giantism and even rupture of the prepubic tendon. Prolonged gestation in Karakul sheep in South Africa associated with giant fetuses has been described but the cause, possibly genetic in nature, is unknown, DeLange.

(4) Vitamin A deficiency resulted in prolonging the gestation period 1 to 4 weeks.

(5) Holm, cited Nalbandov, in reporting an inbred line of sows that carried their fetuses 3 to 4 weeks overtime.

(6) Decapitation of ovine fetuses resulted in overtime small, weak edematous lambs with adrenals one-fourth to one-fifth normal size, Lanman and Schaffer.

(7) Liggins destroyed the pituitary glands of ovine fetuses by electrocautery at 90 to 142 days of gestation and produced prolonged gestations..

(8) In a number of cattle breeds three types of prolonged gestations have been observed:

 (a) Prolonged gestation was seen associated with postmature, long-haired fetal giants in Holsteins and Ayrshires, Wilson and Young, and in other breeds in which a homozygous recessive autosomal gene was involved. These postmature fetuses had long hooves; their incisor teeth were erupted and dehydration was evident. These calves had hypoplastic adrenals, Drost, Holm. In this condition the gestation was prolonged for 20 to 90 or more days and the fetuses weighed from 130 to 200 lbs. Vaginal delivery was impossible and severe dystocia resulted unless a cesarean operation was performed early. Affected calves had hypoglycemia and died shortly after delivery with an Addisonian-like syndrome characterized by marked adrenal insufficiency and possible anterior pituitary gland abnormalities. Following birth by caesarean section a continuous regimen of corticosteroids was necessary to maintain the life of the calf.

 (b) Prolonged gestation is also seen associated with cretin-like, immature fetuses with cranial and central nervous system anomalies, including hydrocephalus, anencephaly, or cyclopia and short, deformed loose-jointed legs with an aplasia of the anterior pituitary gland and a degree of hairlessness. The adrenal glands may be very hypoplastic or absent. These defective fetuses may be carried 20 to over 230 days overtime, average 120 days, and they are relatively small in size. Hydramnios is frequently present. If parturition commences dystocia may occur but is not a serious problem. It is seen most frequently in Guernseys, Swedish Red and White Cattle and possibly Ayrshires. This anomaly is due to an autosomal recessive mode of inheritance, Kennedy et al.. (See Figure 33)

 (c) The author has observed 4 Holstein calves with cerebral hernia, "catlin mark," a sloping forehead, a greatly reduced cranial cavity and abnormal brain, long hooves and hair, dystocia due to its excessive size after a prolonged gestation, 20 to 60 days overtime, and death before or soon after birth. (See Figure 29) In one of these calves that was autopsied the adrenals were markedly hypoplastic. Callahan et al. reported on a similar case in which the cerebellum was absent, the cerebrum was small and the pituitary gland was absent on gross examination. The calf weighed 130 pounds and was delivered by caesarean section on the 329th day of gestation.

In these last three conditions no prepartum or partum changes are observed at the time of expected parturition and the udder is undeveloped until after the fetus has been removed. Parturition does not occur unless the fetus dies **in utero.** As pointed out by Holm no bonafide prolonged gestation in a cow has ever produced a morphological or metabolically normal calf.

In a recent report Drost and Holm performed bilateral adrenalectomies on ovine fetuses at 110 to 120 days of gestation. This resulted in prolonged gestations of 157 to 180 days. When only one of a pair of twin fetuses was operated on the normal intact fetus died **in utero** while the adrenalectomized fetus survived the prolonged gestation period but died at or soon after birth. Thus there is a good correlation between prolonged gestation in cows and ewes and abnormal anterior pituitary glands and adrenal cortices. Aplastic, hypoplastic or damaged pituitary glands of the fetus result in prolonged gestation. Hyperplasia of the adrenal gland results in abbreviated gestations in goats. Aplasia or severe hypoplasia of the adrenal gland, secondary to a pituitary deficiency, results in prolonged gestation in cattle. The control the fetus exerts through its pituitary-adrenal axis over the duration of gestation is obvious. This control is probably triggered by the release of ACTH from the fetal pituitary gland, Liggins.

Premature birth of viable young can occur in the cow from about 240 to 270 days and in the mare from 310 to 320 days. Delayed births in cows are usually considered as gestation periods over 295 days except for Brown Swiss and Brahman cattle and in mares over 350 days. These figures are relative but are given because viable, apparently normal young may be produced, the parturitions be uneventful and the dams survive over a wide range of gestation lengths.

The birth weight of newborn animals is closely associated with gestation length and other factors acting during the gestation period. In this area studies in cattle have predominated. The average birth weight of calves for the various breeds are as follows: Sindhi, 45 lbs; Jersey, 55 lbs; Aberdeen Angus, 60 lbs; Guernsey, 68 lbs; Africander, 71 lbs; Hereford, 72 lbs; Shorthorn, 72 lbs; Ayrshire, 73 lbs; Holstein, 92 lbs; South Devon, 100 lbs; Brown Swiss, 101 lbs. and Charolais, 105 lbs., Anderson and Plum. Calves born to mature cows are heavier than calves from heifers. There is a positive correlation between the weight of the dam and sire and the calf. Season of the year at birth had little influence on the weight. Bull calves were generally 2 to 9 lbs. heavier than female calves. Most authors indicated the sire had a significant effect on the calf's birthweight. In general the longer a fetus was carried the greater the birth weight. Birth weight, as gestation length, is influenced by heredity and is influenced more by the calf than the dam that carries the calf except where breeds of great disparity in size are crossed. Newborn single lambs weighed 7.5 percent of the average weight of both parents. Individual twin lambs weighed 16 percent less than single lambs but their combined weight was 67 percent more than singles. The sire had little effect on the birthweight of lambs, Stark et al.. Boar pigs weighed 5 percent more than gilts at birth, Craig et al..

Hormonal Control of Gestation

The placenta connecting the fetus and mother provides best for the needs of viviparity, Amoroso. Because it is able to provide this protection, the mammal relies less on large numbers of eggs released and more on the survival of a few young in order to perpetuate the species. During evolution the placenta has developed endocrine functions that allow a longer gestation period with the birth of young which are more mature and thus better able to cope with the external environment. In marsupials the gestation period is equal to the length of the estrous cycle, and removal of the ovary any time during pregnancy terminates the pregnancy. In the higher mammals such as the horse and primates the placenta tends to assume some of the endocrine control of pregnancy. Nervous control of the uterus is not essential during gestation in man and other animals. Conception, gestation, and possibly normal parturition can occur with complete paralysis and lack of nerves in the lower portion of the body. Gestation and the onset of parturition are entirely under hormonal control.

In the cow, sheep, and pig, and probably the mare, about 12 to 16 days after estrum and fertile coitus, the trophoblast of the embryo grows very rapidly and its presence causes a persistence of the corpus luteum and a cessation of the estrous cycle. This is accomplished by the effect of the trophoblast acting on the endometrium (1) to cause a continuing release of pituitray luteotrophin by means of a neuro-humoral mechanism acting on the hypothalamus and anterior pituitary gland, and (2) to prevent the release or formation of uterine luteolysin and thus block the transport of this substance by the local utero-ovarian pathway to the corpus luteum, Ginther, Nalbandov, Hafez. When ovariectomy was performed 5 to 7 days after fertile coitus injecting 25 mg of progesterone in oil together with 6.25 micrograms of estrone in oil daily per 100 lbs. of body weight subcutaneously resulted in 5 of 6 cows having a viable normal fetus at 50 to 62 days of gestation, Hawk et al..

In dogs and cats this early provision for promoting the attachment of the developing embryos is pseudopregnancy. In dogs which ovulate spontaneously, the corpora lutea that develop after every estrous period last for about 60 days or the duration of gestation. In the cat, which requires mating or a similar stimulus to produce ovulation, the cause of pseudopregnancy is also ovulation and corpora lutea formation. The length of pseudopregnancy in the cat is about 30 to 40 days, Nalbandov.

During pregnancy the progesterone from the corpus luteum or the fetal placenta is essential for endometrial gland growth and secretion of uterine milk, for endometrial growth and attachment of the placenta for the later nourishment of the fetus, and for inhibiting uterine motility to aid in placental attachment. A certain amount of ovarian or placental estrogen appears necessary to enhance the effect of progesterone and in later pregnancy to produce udder development, relaxation of the pelvic ligaments, initial uterine tonus and cervical relaxation and to sensitize the uterus to oxytocin. Other hormones essential in maintaining pregnancy are the gonadotropic or luteotropic hormones from the anterior pituitary gland necessary for the persistence of the corpus luteum and its active secretion of progesterone. In the mare these gonadotropins can be produced by the endometrial cups and in woman by the chorion of the fetal placenta. It is also becoming increasingly obvious, as noted in the previous section on prolonged gestation, that the endocrine glands of the fetus, thyroid, adrenals, gonads, anterior pituitary gland and possibly others besides the fetal placenta, play important roles in maintaining and terminating pregnancy. Further study is necessary to determine the exact interplay between maternal and fetal hormones in maintaining pregnancy in the various species of animals.

In the cow, goat and probably the bitch the corpus luteum of pregnancy is required throughout gestation to maintain a normal gestation period and permit a normal parturition, Gomes and Erb, Estergreen et al.. Staples et al. reported that normal corpora lutea in cows contained about 270 micrograms of progesterone. Levels below 100 micrograms were not conducive to embryo survival. The average weight of single corpora lutea throughout pregnancy was 6.4 gms (5.5 to 8.5 gms) and of twin corpora lutea was 3.9 gms., Wickersham and Tanabe. In sows, ovaries are essential for the maintenance of pregnancy throughout most of the gestation period, deMesnil du Buisson and Dauzier. The ovaries or corpora lutea may be removed in the latter half of gestation in the ewe, mare, woman and possibly the cat without interrupting or interfering with pregnancy or parturition. In the latter animals the placenta assumes the necessary production of the steroid hormones, progesterone and estrogen. Erb et al. have recently reported the estrogen excretion in the urine of pregnant cows was 322 micrograms (10^6) per hour at 10 to 123 days of gestation, 604 for 165 to 175 days, 640 for 200 to 212 days, 767 for 226 to 237 days, 2,165 for 250 to 254 days and 3,641 micrograms per hour from 271 to 285 days of gestation. The progesterone levels in peripheral blood plasma averaged 30 millimicrograms (10^9) per ml. from 16 to 284 days of pregnancy in the cow. Their data suggested an extraovarian source of progesterone, possibly the adrenal gland, during late pregnancy. The relatively short life of progesterone was demonstrated by Imori using labelled progesterone. He found the estimated half-life of progesterone during pregnancy was 10 to 15 minutes indicating that secretion of progesterone by the corpus luteum was rapid in the cow even though the blood level was low. Pregnancy may be maintained in most ovariectomized cows by the injection of 100 mg of progesterone daily, 500 to 1000 mgm of Repositol progesterone every 7 to 10 days, Cates, Wickersham and Tanabe or feeding 4 mgm MGA (melengestrol acetate) daily. A small amount of progesterone is probably produced in the placenta in the cow, Gomes and Erb. Neher and Zorrow reported that in sheep the placenta was the major source of progesterone the last 100 days of gestation since removal of ovaries from ewes after 66 days of gestation did not cause abortion or a drop in the blood serum level of progestin.

In the mare, follicles develop on the ovaries about 17 days after a fertile coitus. At 40 days of gestation the gonadotropin, largely follicle-stimulating in character, from the endometrial cups causes continued follicle formation until about 100 to 120 days of gestation. During this period most large follicles become atretic but some ovulate and the progesterone produced by the corpus luteum of pregnancy is supplemented by that from the accessory corpora lutea forming after 6 weeks of gestation besides the progesterone being formed in the placenta. From the 4th to 5th months of gestation the FSH from the endometrial cups declines as does the follicular activity of the mare's ovaries. The accessory corpora lutea involute, the ovaries atrophy and the placenta assumes the total responsibility of secreting progesterone and estrogen. After about the 170th day of gestation the mare may be ovariectomized without causing abortion, Short. He reported that the estrogen level in the mare's serum rises rapidly from the 4th month to a peak at about the 8th to 10th month of gestation but serum progesterone levels are low. Recent work has shown that at term large amounts of progesterone are in the placenta and fetal blood but little or none of this is passing from the placenta into the dam's circulation. Short explained that in the mare with a diffuse placenta the progesterone needed to maintain pregnancy is diffused from the placenta into the endometrium and myometrium where it exerts its action and is metabolized. It wasn't necessary as in other animals to have a high level of progesterone in the maternal blood to produce the needed effects. There has been speculation on the possible cause and endocrine role of the greatly enlarged gonads in equine fetuses occurring from the 4th or 5th to 9th month of gestation. An increase in interstitial cells results in gonads 5–7 cm long, 4 cm in diameter and weighing 150 gms which are as large or larger than in adult horses. The fetal gonads reduce markedly in size the last several months of pregnancy in the mare. There is evidence that the placenta is permeable to the sex steroid hormones but that the fetal endocrines do not affect the dam, Deansley.

The hormonal and other factors initiating the onset of parturition at the prescribed time for the various species of animals is less well understood but undoubtedly is caused by a fairly rapid series of hormonal changes involving progesterone, estrogen, oxytocin, cortisol and possibly other hormones and will be discussed later.

Duration of Reproductive Ability

The duration of reproductive ability in domestic animals depends basically on two factors. **First,** the breeding or reproductive life of an animal ceases when at any age physical decrepitude occurs. This may be caused by disease or by defective nutrition secondary to a loss of teeth resulting in senility and emaciation. **Second,** reproduction ceases when the reproductive organs are injured severely or their function destroyed by disease factors. In the female those diseases limiting reproduction affect mainly the endometrium and epithelium lining the tubular genital organs and less often the ovaries. In the male, pathological changes in the seminiferous tubules of the testes caused by diseases, trauma, or senile changes, are the most common causes for loss of reproductive ability. Occasionally sires may develop arthritic joints or spinal lesions that make copulation impossible and thus their natural reproductive life is terminated.

The average duration of reproductive life in the dairy cow is about 8 to 10 years of age, with the production of about four to six viable calves. In beef cattle this average duration of reproductive life may be slightly longer, 10 to 12 years. Exceptions to these averages are numerous. Williams, Altman and Dittmer, Wolstenholme and O'Connor and other authors recorded cows that had calves regularly to 16 to 18 years of age and in rare cases to 25 or more years of age. Bulls usually can breed until 10 to 14 years of age and in exceptional cases up to 18 years of age.

The average duration of reproductive life in the mare is approximately 18 to 22 years. The number of mares that become pregnant and carry a foal after 24 years of age is low although a few mares were reported to have had foals from 25 to 33 years of age. In ewes the average duration of reproductive life is about 6 to 10 years of age but ewes have been known to reproduce until 16 to 20 years of age, Parkes. The sow is capable of reproducing until 6 to 8 years of age and occasionally to 10 or even 15 years of age. In sows the size of the litter tends to decrease after 4 to 5 years of age. Beyond this time, although the female may be capable of reproduction, the litters produced are so small that it is uneconomical to continue breeding the sow. In dogs and cats the average duration of reproductive life is about 8 to 12 years of age. However, dogs and cats have been known to produce young from 14 to 17 years of age.

Animals prevented from breeding after puberty have increased difficulty to conceive the longer the non-pregnant state is maintained. Mares that do not have foals before 10 to 12 years of age experience difficulty in conceiving after that time even though their physical condition may be excellent. DeLange reported that cattle not bred until 4 to 5 years of age are also difficult to impregnate and frequently develop cystic ovaries and endometrial abnormalities. Bitches that are not bred by 4 to 6 years of age frequently develop cystic endometrial hyperplasia associated with infertility and often endometritis and pyometra. Possibly in our other domestic animals, and also in humans, delaying conception for a long period after puberty appears to have a depressing effect on reproductive ability by the adverse effects on the endometrium.

In women changes resulting in the menopause take place at an average age of 49 years, Dukes. In animals, this condition characterized by a complete loss of oocytes from the ovaries and cessation of the estrous cycle, has not been observed. Domestic animals usually die or are disposed of for other reasons before this stage of life. Observations of animals tend to indicate that cessation of reproduction in females with little or no genital disease is a more gradual process than it is in humans. It is rather closely linked with the lack of nutrition caused by the wearing out of the teeth and the resulting senile changes produced. It has been proven in practice that if genital and mammary disease could be controlled many cows could have 2 or 3 or more additional years of reproductive life. This would be of great economic value to the farmer.

Rate of Reproduction in Animals

The rate of reproduction depends basically on three factors: the length of duration of reproductive life, the number of young produced at each parturition, and the frequency of parturition.

The first factor has been discussed. The second factor is

largely a characteristic of the species of animals concerned, whether unipara or multipara. However, the number of young produced at each parturition in any species may be increased or decreased to a limited extent by hereditary factors and selective breeding. Environmental factors apparently play a minor role in most animals, but in sheep and deer a high level of nutrition during the breeding season favors a greatly increased incidence of twins and triplets over single births. In multiparous animals such as the sow the size of the litter tends to increase slightly up to maturity and then decrease in size with advancing age. A high level of nutrition prior to breeding and a lower level thereafter increases the number of porcine ova ovulated and reduces the embryonic death rate in swine, respectively.

The third factor in the rate of reproduction, namely the frequency of parturition, is of great concern to the farmer as well as to the veterinarian, since any delay in getting farm animals to conceive is of economic importance. Once conception has occurred the duration of gestation is definitely established for each species. In an ideal breeding program most cattle or horse breeders strive for a calf or foal every 12 months. Although this can be attained with certain individual animals, it is a difficult goal to reach on a herd basis. Many adverse management, hereditary, and disease factors are present to prevent the achievement of this goal. It requires the close cooperation and active interest of both the farmer and the veterinarian, especially in dairy cattle and Thoroughbred horses, if these adverse factors are to be kept at a minimum. Williams stated that the greatest departure from the ideal breeding performance is seen in those breeds most artificially maintained, that is, the dairy cow, the race horse, and the breeds of pet dogs. The adverse management, hereditary, and disease factors that tend to produce infertility, cause abortion, or result in dystocia and postpartum disease, are being studied intensively by veterinarians and animal husbandrymen in an effort to curb or control the economic waste they produce.

Abnormalities of Fertilization and the Gestation Period

Wandering of the ovum—When in a uniparous animal such as the cow the corpus luteum of pregnancy is found in one ovary and the embryo or fetus is located in the opposite horn, one of five possibilities may have occurred. These were discussed under pregnancy diagnosis in the cow. The incidence of this occurrence in the cow is less than 1 percent, Perkins and coworkers, Arthur and others. Transuterine migration of the zygote the second week of gestation is common in the mare, ewe, sow and dog but uncommon in the cow. Transperitoneal migration of the ovum has not been described in the domestic animals. In sows Dzuik et al. reported that when fertile ova were surgically implanted in the apices of both horns that 34 percent of the zygotes migrated to the opposite horn from the 10th to 13th day of gestation. Casida and coworkers reported in sheep that 7 to 10 percent of single zygotes migrated when double ovulation occurred on one ovary. Embryonic death loss was much greater where both zygotes remained in the same horn after double ovulation from that ovary. This is apparently also true in cattle because twin fetuses in one horn are seen in only 10 percent of cattle twins while bicornual twin fetuses are seen in 90 percent of cattle twins, Erdheim. The mechanism of the intrauterine migration or spacing of zygotes in multipara is not well understood but probably involves the muscular activity of the uterine wall, the lubrication provided by the uterine secretions and the attainment of a certain size of blastodermic vesicle.

Superfecundation is produced by a female ovulating two or more ova during one estrum and copulating with two or more males during that estrum with ova being fertilized by spermatozoa from each male. This condition may be suspected by the breeding history. After parturition it may be obvious because of offspring resembling each sire. Superfecundation is observed more commonly in multipara, especially dogs and cats, because multipara regularly ovulate two or more ova, have long heat periods, and opportunities for services by different males are greater than in unipara. Superfecundation in unipara has occasionally been reported, for example, the birth of twin horse and mule foals and twin Holstein and Hereford calves.

Telegony is a superstitious belief prevalent especially among dog breeders that offspring from one sire may derive characteristics from a sire to which the same dam has previously borne offspring. This belief is most commonly recalled when by accident a purebred female is bred by a mongrel and has offspring from this mating. It is then falsely believed that the dam is "tainted" and that even though she may be bred later to a purebred sire the offspring from this purebred mating will have certain mongrel characteristics. There is no scientific basis for this erroneous belief.

Superfetation is produced when a pregnant female, carrying one or more live fetuses comes in estrum, is bred again, and a second conception occurs in a uterus already containing at least one live fetus. This condition is seemingly authentically reported more often in multipara and only rarely in unipara. It appears unlikely that in uniparous animals, even if ovulation occurred, the spermatozoa could pass through a cervix closed by an adhesive cervical seal and through the pregnant uterus to the oviduct. If the ovum was fertilized and reached the uterus, the endometrial area of both horns would in most instances already be utilized by the first embryo or fetus. If by chance the second zygote should develop in the horn opposite to the one containing the embryo, when the earlier fetus was expelled the later fetus would probably be expelled at the same time. These viscissitudes cause many authors to doubt the occurrence of superfetation in uniparous animals.

Although the literature includes many reports of alleged cases of superfetation, most are unauthentic and lack essential details. Twin foals are usually of different sizes, one large and one small. The expulsion of unequal size twins, even though the mare has been bred twice, does not constitute a claim for superfetation. In cases in which one cow in a herd gave birth to twins on pasture with one of the twins being adopted and suckled by a second cow in advanced pregnancy, superfetation is often claimed when this second cow, especially if it had been bred twice at the proper intervals, gives birth later to her own calf. A third condition may possibly occur wherein a cow or mare carrying bicornual twins in separate membranes gives birth to one twin a number of weeks or months before the second twin, Hagyard. The first twin is always smaller at birth than the twin born several weeks or more later. Arthur reported on several ewes that aborted one of twin fetuses at 105 days of gestation. The retained placentas were expelled after putrefying. The ewes delivered normal lambs at term over a month later. This phenomena, although rare, has been reported in cattle, swine, sheep and humans as double parturition. It seems a more logical explanation for the birth of young at different periods following service than does superfetation, Williams.

In multiparous animals with a poorly defined cervix and cervical seal, superfetation is more likely to occur, Kawata and Tiba, Markee and Hinsey. Hoogewey and Folkers reported delivering 2 normal feline fetuses from one uterine horn by cesarean section. A small 5 week-old fetus, 33 mm CR length, was found in the opposite horn of the uterus. They cited references to indicate that pregnant cats will develop mature follicles and ovulate as late as 6 weeks after conception. All the fetuses of one service might develop in one horn and then subsequently an estrum occur with ova fertilized from the second service developing in the opposite horn. Parturitions could occur at different times from each horn. Vanderplassche believes this unlikely; as in double parturition in swine, fetuses are expelled from both horns at each farrowing period. This possibility might occur in cows with a true uterus didelphys or double uterus with a separate cervix for each horn. In the apparently authentic bovine case cited by Dalrymple and Jenkins, and several others reported to the author, a double uterus was not present.

Although superfetation may occur very uncommonly in multipara and rarely in unipara, it would appear highly improbable in most reported instances. Many reports on superfetation are obviously incorrectly diagnosed without proper information and sufficient detail on which to base a claim. A few rare reports, however, appear sufficiently authentic to make one unwilling to state positively that superfetation does not occur in domestic animals, especially swine and cattle.

Pseudopregnancy in the dog and cat—False pregnancy or pseudocyesis is common in the bitch because the metestrus, luteal, or postestrus phase of the cycle is about 8 to 9 weeks long, or approximately the same duration as pregnancy, Nalbandov. During this metestrus period in the bitch the endometrium resembles that in pregnant dogs. The corpora lutea are large and active during postestrus but gradually reduce in size and become inactive at 8 to 9 weeks after estrum or sterile coitus. At this time many bitches exhibit mammary development and will lactate if nursed. The mammary development is not as great as in pregnant bitches. Toward the end of pseudopregnancy, false pregnancy or pseudocyesis certain dogs may be nervous, aggressive, excitable, restless or withdrawn and may even exhibit "phantom whelping" by making a "nest" and mothering and protecting some inanimate object. Often certain bitches in pseudopregnancy will put on weight and their abdomen will increase in size. Most dogs do not exhibit these signs. If the symptoms at the termination of this period are objectionable to the owner about 5 mg. of stilbestrol or 2 to 10 mgs. of testosterone daily may possibly aid in hastening the return to normal. The use of tranquilizers in the affected bitch may reduce the objectional behavior patterns during this transient period. In the cat pseudopregnancy or metestrum lasts about 30 to 40 days but without noticeable signs. In most affected bitches these symptoms tend to recur following each estrum so ovariectomy may be indicated unless the bitch is to be bred.

The Mammary Gland and Lactation

Although the mammary gland is a highly modified and specialized sebaceous cutaneous gland, it is normally considered as an accessory gland of the reproductive system because of its intimate association with reporductive functions and hormones. In domestic animals the mammary secretion provides early passive immunity to the newborn as well as supplying its nutritive needs. In the cow most of the immune globulins transferred from the blood to the udder secretion or colostrum takes place a short time before, during and after parturition whether the cow has been premilked or not. If the cow has been premilked the amount of globulin present per unit of lacteal secretion is reduced because of dilution, Rook, Larson. In the mare, cow, ewe, and goat, the mammary gland is located in the inguinal region. In the mare, ewe, and goat the gland is divided into two halves with a single lactiferous sinus in each half opening into the two teats. In the cow the udder is divided into four quarters, each with its own lactiferous sinus and teat. Supernumerary teats and glands are common in the cow. There is no communication between the halves or quarters of the mammary gland. In the sow, bitch, and cat the paired mammary glands are located on the ventral surface of the body in the pectoral, abdominal and inguinal regions. There are from 4 to 9 pairs of glands. The lactiferous ducts or streak canals at the ends of the teats are closed by a sphincter muscle. There is a single streak canal in the teats of cows and ewes but two streak canals in mares and sows. Dogs have 7 to 16 duct openings in the teat. The blood supply of the inguinal mammae is the external pudic artiers, of the pectoral mammae the branches of the internal thoracic arteries, and of the abdominal mammae from both sources. In the cow the main veins of the udder are the external pudic and the subcutaneous abdominal or "milk" vein. The latter empties into the internal thoracic veins. A well-developed lymphatic system is also present in mammary tissue, Smith. The nerve supply is the inguinal nerve from the ventral branches of the second through fourth lumbar nerves and the mammary branch of the internal pudendal nerve supplies the caudal part of the bovine udder. The motor nerve supply to the udder is entirely autonomic or sympathetic; the cell bodies of these nerves are located in the lateral horns of the spinal cord. Superficial innervation and blood supply of the skin of the udder comes from the subcutaneous vessels and nerves in the skin regions surrounding the udder.

Relatively little mammary development occurs before puberty. In the newborn, slight mammary and teat development is noted along with a slight amount of serous secretion. This is probably due to the placental transmission of some of the circulating maternal steroidal hormones. In rare cases this may be marked in dairy calves. There have been a few instances of dairy heifers 5 to 12 months of age or older that developed marked mammary development with milk secretion. The cause is usually not known. Granulosa cell tumors of the ovary may rarely be the cause. Suckling by other heifers causes udder growth and an increase in the amount of milk secretion. After isolation, usually the mammary development of the heifer will recede spontaneously within four to six weeks. With the onset of estrual periods after puberty there is a slight mammary development. In animals exhibiting pseudopregnancy such as the dog, mammary development may be quite marked and be nearly equal to the development in the pregnant bitch, and milk secretion will occur.

During the first half of gestation in the cow cellular proliferation of the mammary ducts and alveoli occurs under the influence of the steroid hormones, progesterone and estrogen, from the ovaries and the placenta. By the fifth month growth of the secretory tissue is nearly complete. During the latter half of gestation cellular hypertrophy and limited secretion is noted. Abortion after the middle of gestation followed by regular milking of a cow or heifer results in lactation. The nearer to the calving date the abortion occurs the greater the production of milk. Rice and Andrews attributed the failure of animals to reach high levels of production after an abortion to insufficient hormonal stimulation for secretion rather than to incomplete development of the mammary gland. In the normal high-producing heifer or young cow excessive edema or engorgement of the mammary gland and the adjacent skin and tissues dorsal to the udder and forward on the abdominal floor to the xiphoid region may occur. This is apparently a circulatory phenomena caused by a greater blood supply to the gland than the venous system can accommodate. Excessive edema of the abdominal floor is sometimes confused with rupture of the prepubic tendon, umbilical hernia, a hematoma, or an abscess. Occasionally the greatly enlarged and edematous mammary gland may result in pain and discomfort, necrosis of the skin, failure to let down milk and stretching or even rupture of its supporting ligaments. Massage, the use of mild counterirritants, premilking, udder supports, cold and hot applications, and exercise may be used to prevent or treat excessive udder edema. (See Figure 58)

In recent years the oral or intramuscular administration of diuretics, specifically the carbonic anhydrase inhibitors with or without corticosteroids, for udder edema before or after parturition has been particularly helpful especially in young cows. The carbonic anhydrase inhibitors include: acetolamide (Diamox),[1] chlorothiazide (**Diuril**)[2]—2 gms once or twice a day orally, hydrochlorothiazide (**Vetidrex**)[3]—0.5 to 1 gm orally to 125 to 250 mg. parenterally twice a day) or trichlormethiazide and dexamethazone (**Naquasone**)[4]—200 mg and 5 mg, respectively, orally as a bolus once daily. **Lasix**[5] or furosemide may be given orally, 50 mg/25 lb or parenterally

(1) American Cyanamid Co., (2) Merck and Co. (3) Merck and Co. and Ciba Pharm. Co., (4) Schering Corp. (5) National Laboratories.

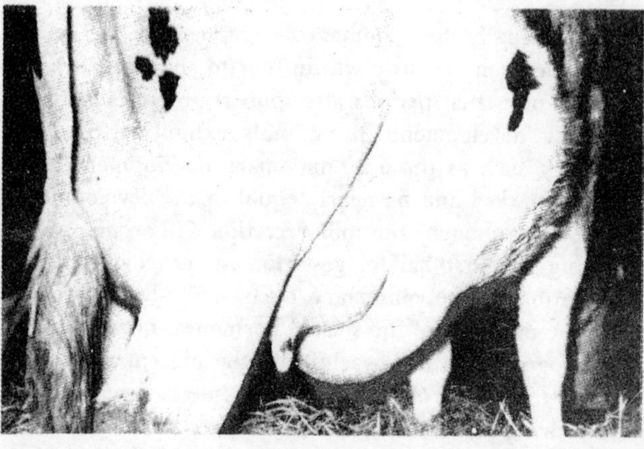

Figure 58. Udder and subcutaneous edema in a parturient heifer. (courtesy D. Morrow)

0.25 to 0.50 ml/10 lb. to dogs or parenterally to horses, 5 to 10 ml/1000 lb once or twice daily. This latter drug is not approved for food-producing animals. These treatments are usually given for one to 3 days, Morrow and Schmidt. Large doses or prolonged intake of lower doses of the glucocorticoids late in gestation may cause premature parturition often associated with retention of the placenta in cattle. The level of grain feeding, before parturition, whether high or low, had no influence on the degree of udder edema that developed according to Schmidt and Schultz, Huffman and others. However, Emery et al. indicated high prepartum grain feeding increased slightly the udder edema in heifers but not in cows.

Mammary growth and lactation is mainly under the control of hormones. Nerves in the teats and skin of the udder may play an indirect part in milk secretion by stimulating the pituitary gland to release prolactin and possibly other hormones necessary to initiate and maintain lactation and oxytocin necessary for milk-ejection or "let-down." This latter term by signifying the ability of the animal to control her milk flow at will is incorrect, Folley and Knaggs. Vasomotor nerves probably play an indirect role in milk secretion by regulating the blood supply to the gland. Inguinal nerves have been cut without producing any change in milk production. Estrogens and progesterone produced in the ovaries and in the placenta work together in animals to produce mammary development. The estrogen causes the initial budding and the growth of the duct system. Progesterone causes further duct growth and alveolar development. In certain species, such as goats, estrogen alone induces complete udder growth and lactation but some of the female's other endocrine secretions might play a role. Either one of these hormones or testosterone given in large doses to the intact or spayed heifer will produce mammary growth and development.

The onset of lactation at the time parturition coincides with the drop in progesterone and especially estrogen levels in the blood that have provided for mammary growth, and with a marked rise in the levels of prolactin or lactogenic hormone from the pituitary gland necessary for the initiation of secretion and maintenance of lactation. High prolactin levels are favored by the mammary stimulation of suckling and removal of colostrum and milk from the alveoli of the mammary gland except in sheep and goats, Hafez and Reece. Prolactin is responsible for broodiness in hens and possibly the parental instinct in higher mammals. Nalbandov indicated that growth or somatotropic hormone might be the hormone that initiated lactation in cattle. Smith and Cowie and Tindal cited references to indicate that oxytocin released by suckling might be closely associated or cause the release of prolactin and growth hormone or STH from the anterior pituitary gland. Low levels of administered estrogens aid in the release of prolactin and stimulate milk production, Turner. This may account for the drop in milk production in high-producing cows following treatment for cystic ovaries.

Lactation requires the interaction of a variety of hormones. Anterior pituitary gland hormones essential for lactation are prolactin or the lactogenic hormone and growth or somatotropic hormone. ACTH is indirectly needed to maintain the adrenal glands. Desoxycorticosterone acetate and cortisone are necessary to maintain lactation in adrenalectomized goats. ACTH and thiouracil have a depressing effect on lactation. Thyroid stimulating hormone, TSH, has a galactopoietic effect. Thyroxine or other similar substances such as iodinated casein also have a galactopoietic effect on lactation. Parathyroidectomy results in a marked decrease in milk production due to the effect on calcium metabolism. Insulin from the pancreas is also concerned with lactation. Because of the enormous amount of work performed by the lactating udder in a high-producing cow, 450 volumes of blood are required to produce one volume of milk, it is obvious that all of the endocrine secretions necessary to control lactation must be in adequate and balanced supply.

The daily feeding of iodinated casein or thyroprotein with a 3 percent throxine potency at a level of about 1 gram per 100 lbs. of body weight to lactating cows has caused increases in milk production and butter fat of 5 to 25 percent depending upon the cow's genetic constitution and the level of feed intake, Hindery and Turner. Increased intake of T.D.N. or energy is essential in most treated cows. Since not all cows respond equally, individual supervision of cows is necessary. Milk records of cows on thyroprotein are not officially recognized by the Dairy Herd Improvement Assoc. If thyroprotein is removed suddenly from the ration a marked drop in milk flow usually occurs. Although a few well-managed dairy herds have had good results by the properly supervised use of this product, many herds have experienced poor results. In properly-conducted experimental long-term trials the use of thyroprotein has not appeared promising. Some dairymen are using this product selectively to boost production in cows the latter half of lactation when the cow's production declines below 40 pounds per day to prevent a prolonged dry period.

The artificial or hormonal induction of lactation in cattle and to a lesser degree in sheep, goats, and laboratory animals has been the subject of much experimental work over the past 20 years. Nulliparous cattle have given a much more uniform and satisfactory response than have sterile pluriparous cattle. The general technique consists of administering by injection or implants estrogen, estrogen and testosterone, or preferredly estrogen and progesterone into animals to maintain fairly high daily levels for a period of two to four months to promote mammary duct and alveolar growth. After proper mammary growth has been achieved the injections are stopped or the implants are removed and regular frequent milking is started. The quantity of milk secreted is extremely variable between animals and ranged from 250 to 500 ml. daily to amounts normal for cattle after a gestation period. The response of nulliparous animals is more consistent than multiparous animals but in general this procedure is not satisfactory enough for practical use.

Two complications may be observed in this procedure: The cattle may develop cystic ovaries with symptoms of nymphomania. Fractures of the pelvis and limbs have been reported due to excessive mounting and a marked relaxation of the pelvic ligaments. If cystic ovaries do not occur the ovaries become small and inactive. The suppression of the gonadotropic hormones and ovarian activity is released when the estrogens are withdrawn. If lactating cows are injected with estrogens lactation promptly declines. If cows are pregnant they usually abort due to the long-continued estrogen stimulation. Fluoroprednisolone acetate (**Predef**) given daily at doses of 10 to 15 mg. for 15 days caused the induction of lactation during gestation in heifers, Tucker and Meites.

The diverse effect of estrogens on lactation requires further explanation. In therapy for humans, estrogens are widely used in low doses to relieve swollen, engorged breasts or in larger doses to suppress and stop lactation. This effect is evident when stilbestrol is used toward the end of pseudopregnancy in bitches with mammary enlargement. Estrogenic ointments or injections have been used only to a limited extent in dairy cattle to relieve congested udders after parturition. Most veterinarians are fearful of causing a decline in milk production and almost all such cases generally respond to less heroic therapy. In the preceding paragraph the use of an estrogen was described to promote mammary growth and lactation. In the nonlactating cow estrogen at low, prolonged levels promotes mammary growth and development. While this is occurring, secretion is slight. The high blood levels of estrogen must drop so that the full secretion of milk may begin, since maximal growth and secretion cannot occur simultaneously. Prolonged high estrogen levels may suppress or hold in check the pituitary secretion of prolactin and growth or somatotropic hormone or more likely effect the mammary tissue so it can't respond to the stimulus of the anterior pituitary hormones necessary for lactation. When this estrogenic check is removed the pituitary hormones are released and lactation results. In lactating animals the administration of estrogens in large doses possibly suppresses the secretion of pituitary hormones necessary for lactation or more likely causes mammary growth effects and markedly reduces milk secretion. At the time of estrum a slight drop in milk production often results due to the increased restlessness and nervousness of the cow at this period as well as to the increased estrogen production from the follicle. In most pregnant dairy cows the gradual increase in estrogens produced by the placenta from the fifth month to term together with the increased nutritive needs of the fetus, tend to result in a regular decline in milk production. Sterile high-producing cows may lactate at a high level for two or more years. There is no evidence or proof that ovariectomy of lactating cows has any influence on prolonging lactation or increasing production, Asdell. Some cows and mares may be difficult to "dry off" because of the high production of milk 10 or 12 months and 5 or 6 months, respectively, after parturition.

The ejection or "let-down" of milk which is closely associated with the reproductive organs and their hormones, is caused by stimuli, such as suckling, milking or massage of the udder and teats and conditioned stimuli developed by routine premilking barn procedures that effect a release of oxytocin and vasopressin from the posterior pituitary gland by means of neural stimuli acting on the hypothalamus. These hormones are carried to the udder by the blood stream and cause contraction of the myoepithelial cells around the alveoli and ducts. Vasopressin exhibits about 20 percent of the milk-ejection activity of oxytocin, Folley and Knaggs. This results in an increase in intracistern pressures from 15 to 20 mm. up to 30 to 45 mm. of mercury with distention of the teat and gland cisterns with milk, Cleverly. Cleverly and Knaggs reported that oxytocin was released transiently and at low levels, about one-twentieth to one-tenth of a unit, to cause milk let-down in a cow within about 40 to 50 seconds. The elevated intramammary pressure was maintained for about one hour unless the cow was milked. The half-life of oxytocin in animals is quite short, only one to two minutes. The posterior pituitary glands of goats and cows contain about 10 to 15 and 30 to 50 units of oxytocin, respectively, Knaggs. The effectiveness of the expulsion reflex is transitory and prompt removal of the milk is desirable for effective proper milking. This neurohormonal reflex mechanism is suppressed by excitement, noise and fright which cause the secretion of adrenalin or epinephrine. Cross reported that this failure of milk let-down was probably due to a central block of the release of oxytocin from the hypothalamus and pituitary gland rather than to an inhibitory effect exerted by adrenal stimulation. Hafez and Reece reported that adrenalin caused vasoconstriction and reduced the blood supply and the amount of oxytocin to the myoepithelial cells in the udder. The release of oxytocin does not occur at milking time in goats and is not essential for the complete milking of the goat udder, Folley and Knaggs. The understanding of this mechanism is helpful in cows in developing a proper, relaxed, quiet, regular procedure of milking that results in good milk ejection and rapid and prompt evacuation of the mammary gland. Prolonged milking caused by improper milking procedures results in loss of time, loss of milk, greater rate of involution of the mammary gland, and decline of milk production, besides favoring mastitis in chronically-infected glands. In certain heifers with greatly engorged and painful udders after calving, ejection does not occur, due to the pain and irritation of the swollen edematous udder. These cases benefit greatly from the intravenous or intramuscular injection of 5 to 15 units of pituitrin or oxytocin, and the prompt removal of the milk as the injected hormone rapidly induces milk let-down. These low recommended doses of hormone are massive when compared to the physiologic amounts released by posterior pituitary gland. In cows given an intravenous dose, this let-down occurs within one to two minutes; in intramuscular doses it occurs within four to six minutes. The ejection of milk can frequently be stimulated by massage of the uterus, vagina or intrapelvic structures per rectum. It may be noted at the time of removal of a retained placenta, or in performing an infertility or pregnancy examination. It is also observed on vaginal or vulvar examination or stimulation in cows and mares. Mares may exhibit milk ejection and leaking of milk just prior to, during or after coitus with a stallion.

Milk is produced by a true secretory process. The initial portion of bovine milk at a milking has a low fat content of about one percent while the "strippings" have a ten percent fat content. Most of the milk given at a single milking is present in the udder at the time of milking. In highproducing cows this causes a stretching of the udder tissues, and an intramammary pressure develops which suppresses further secretion. In high-producing cows more frequent milking yields greater amounts of milk per day. Cessation of milk secretion or "drying off" is accomplished by allowing the intramammary pressure of milk to increase and remain high for four to five days. A six to eight week dry period between lactation periods is essential in cows for maximum milk yield. In most cows a shorter dry period is accompanied by a 20 to 30 percent decline in milk production the following lactation period, Schmidt and Swanson and Claycomb.

The average composition of milk in domestic animals is given in Table 8.

Table 8. Composition of Milk in Percent in the Domestic Animals*

	Water	Fat	Protein	Lactose	Ash
Cow	86.2	4.4	3.8	4.9	.7
Ewe	82.9	6.2	5.4	4.3	.9
Goat	87.1	4.1	3.7	4.2	.8
Sow	83.0	7.0	6.0	4.0	.9
Cat	82.0	5.0	7.0	5.0	.6
Dog	79.0	8.5	7.5	3.7	1.2
Horse	89.0	1.6	2.7	6.1	.5
Man	87.4	3.8	1.6	7.0	.2

*According to Espe and Smith and others.

The amount of milk produced by domestic animals varies greatly between species, breeds, individual animals, the level of energy intake, the quality and amount of protein and the amount of minerals, salt and water intake. Environmental, management and disease factors play an important role in determining the amounts of milk produced. In general, cows produce 25 to over 100 pounds daily, mares 20 to 50 pounds, goats 3 to 15 pounds, ewes 2 to 10 pounds and sows 5 to 20 pounds daily.

General References

Asdell, S. A. (1964) Patterns of Mammalian Reproduction, 2nd Ed. Cornell Univ. Press, Ithaca, N.Y.

Arthur, G. H. (1964) Wright's Veterinary Obstetrics, 3rd Ed., Williams and Wilkins, Co., Baltimore, Md.

Benesch, J. (1952) Lehrbuch der tierarztlichen Geburtshilfe und Gynecologie, Urban and Schrwarzenberg, Wien-Innsbruck, Austria.

Gilmore, L. O. (1952) Dairy Cattle Breeding, F. B. Lippincott Co., N.Y.C.

Hafez, E. S. E. (1968) Reproduction in Farm Animals, 2nd Ed. Lea and Febiger, Philadelphia.

Johansson, I. (1961) Genetic Aspects of Dairy Cattle Breeding, Univ. of Ill. Press, Urbana, Ill.

Johansson, I. and Rendel, J. (1968) Genetics and Animal Breeding, W. H. Freeman Co., San Francisco, Cal.

Nalbandov, A. V. (1964) Reproductive Physiology, 2nd Ed. W. H. Freeman and Co., San Francisco, Cal.

Rendel, J.—see Johansson, I.

Richter, J. and Gotze, R. (1960) Tiergeburtshilfe, 2nd Ed. Paul Parey, Berlin and Hamburg, Germany.

Williams, W. L. (1943) Diseases of the Gential Organs of Domestic Animals, 3rd Ed., Louella Williams, Upland Rd., Ithaca, N.Y.

Special References

Form and Shape of the Uterus and Position of the Fetus

Dzuik, P. J. and Harmon, B. G. (1968) The Succession of Fetuses at Parturition in the Pig, Amer. J. Vet. Res. **30,** 3, 419.

Jones, J. E. T. (1966) Observations in Parturition in the Sow, Brit. Vet. J. **122,** 471.

Vandeplassche, M. (1957) The Normal and Abnormal Presentation, Position and Pasture of the Foal-Fetus During Gestation and at Parturition. Publication of the Veterinary School of the State Univ., Ghent, Belgium and Vlaams Diergeneesk. Tijd. **1,** 4, 3a.

Woodward, R. R. and Clark, R. T. (1959) A Study of Stillbirths in a Herd of Range Cattle, J. An. Sci. **18,** 1, 85.

Twinning and Freemartinism

Alexander, G. and Williams, D. (1964) Ovine Freemartins, Nature, **201,** 4926, 1296.

Biggers, J. D. and McFeely, R. A. (1966) Intersexuality in Domestic Mammals, in **Advances in Reproductive Physiology,** Academic Press Inc., N.Y.C. **1,** 29.

Billingham, R. E. and Lampkin, G. H. (1957) Further Studies in Tissue Homotransplantation in Cattle, J. Embryol. Exp. Morph. **5,** 351.

Blakeslee, L. H. and Hudson, R. S. (1942) Twinning in Horses, J. An. Sci. **1,** 2, 155.

Bonnier, H. (1946) Studies on Monozygous Cattle Twins, II Frequency of Monozygous Twins, Acta Agr. Suecana **1,** 2, 147.

Casida, L. E., Woody, C. O., and Pope A. L. (1966) Inequality in Function of the Right and Left Ovaries and Uterine Horns of the Ewe, J. An. Sci. **25,** 4, 1169.

Clapp, H. (1934) Cystic Ovaries and Twinning in Holsteins, Cor. Vet. **24,** 309.

Comberg, G. and Velten, U. (1962) The Effect of Twin Births on Fertility and Health in Black Pied Cattle, Zuchtungskunde **34,** 49.

Craig, J. V., Norton, H. W. and Terrill, S. W. (1956) A Genetic Study of Weight at Five Ages in Hampshire Swine, J. An. Sci. **15,** 242.

Doll, E. R. and Rooney, J. R. (1964) Superfetation or Twin Pregnancy, J.A.V.M.A. **144,** 8, 832.

Dunn, H. O., Kenney, R. M. and Lein, D. H. (1968) XX/XY Chimerism In a Bovine True Hermaphrodite: an Insight into the Understanding of Freemartinism, Cytogenetics I, 390.

Dunn, H. O., Kenney, R. M.,, Stone, W. H. and Bendel, S. (1968) Cytogenetic and Reproductive Studies of XX/XY Chimeric Twin Bulls, 6th Congr. Internat. Reprod. Anim. Insem. Artif., Paris, Vol. II, 877.

Erb, R. W., Anderson, W. R., Hinze, P. M. and Gildow, E. M. (1960) Inheritance of Twinning in a Herd of Holstein Friesian Cattle, J. Dairy Sci. **43,** 3, 512.

Erdheim, M. (1942) The Incidence of Right and Left Horn Pregnancies in Dairy and Beef Cattle, J.A.V.M.A. **100,** 781, 343.

Errington, B. J. (1942) Equine Twin Placentation, Cor. Vet. **32,** 4, 367.

Fechheimer, N S., Herschler, M. S. and Gilmore, L. O. (1963) Sex Chromosome Mosaicism in Unlike Cattle Twins, in **Genetics Today** edit. by S. J. Geerts, MacMillan Co., N.Y.C.

Fincher, M. G. (1946) Methods of Increasing Fertility In Domestic Animals, Trans. Amer. Soc. for Study of Steril. 1.

Garm, Otto (1949) A Study of Bovine Nymphomania with Special Reference to Etiology and Pathogenesis, Acta Endocrinol. Vol. II, Suppl. 3.

Gerneke, W. H. (1965) Chromosomal Evidence of the Freemartin Condition in Sheep, **Ovis aries,** J. South Afr. Vet. Med. Assoc. **36,** 1, 99.

Gordon, I., Williams, G. and Edwards J. (1962) The Use of Serum Gonadotrophin (P.M.S.) in the Induction of Twin Pregnancy in the Cow, J. Agric. Sci. **59,** 143.

Hafez, E. S. E., Rajakoski, E., Anderson, P. B., Frost, O. L. and Smith, A. G. (1964) Problems of Gonadotropin-Induced Multiple Pregnancy in Beef Cattle, Amer. J. Vet. Res. **25,** 107, 1074.

Hammond, J. (1959) Twinning in Cattle for Beef Production, Vet. Rec. **71,** 168.

Hancock, J. (1954) Monozygotic Twins in Cattle, in **Advances in Genetics,** Academic Press Inc., N.Y.C., **6,** 141.

Herman, J. and Bouters, R. (1965) Die Zwillingstrachtigeit bei der Stute (Twinning in the Horse), Deutsche Tierarztl. Wochenschr. **72,** 23, 541.

Herschler, M. S., Fechheimer, N. S. and Gilmore, L. O. (1966) Identification of Freemartins by Chromosomal Analysis, J. Dairy Sci. **49,** 1, 113.

Hughes, W. (1929) A Freemartin Condition in Swine, Anat. Rec. **41,** 213.

Johansson, I. and Hansson, A. (1943) Multiple Births in Sheep, Annals of the Agric. Col. of Sweden Vol. 11.

Kidder, H. E., Barrett, G. R. and Casida, L. E. (1952) A Study of Ovulations in Six Families of Holstein Friesians, J. Dairy Sci. **35,** 5, 436.

Labhsetwar, A. P., Tyler, W. J. and Casida, L. E. (1963) Analysis of

Variation in Some Factors Affecting Multiple Ovulations in Holstein Cattle, J. Dairy Sci. **46,** 8, 840.

Lillie, F. R. (1917) The Freemartin: A Study of the Actions of Sex Hormones in the Fetal Life of Cattle, J. of Exp. Zool. **23,** 371.

McFeely, R. A. (1968) Chromosomes and Infertility, J.A.V.M.A. **153,** 12, 1672.

Meadows, C. E. and Lush, J. L. (1957) Twinning in Dairy Cattle and Its Relation to Production, J. Dairy Sci. **40,** 11, 1930.

Milk Marketing Board, Report of Production Division (1959/60) Twinning in Beef Cattle, Thames Ditton, Surrey, England, 101.

Moore, K. L., Graham, M. A. and Barr, M. L. (1957) Sex Chromatin in the Freemartin, Anat. Rec. **118,** 402.

Muramoto, J., Ishikawa, T. and Kanagawa, H. (1965) XX/XY Cell Chimerism in Heterosexual Bovine Twins, The Nucleus, **8,** 1, 25.

Ohno, S. and Gropp, A. (1965) Embryological Basis for Germ Cell Chimerism in Mammals, Cytogenics, **4,** 251.

Osborne, V. E. (1966) An Analysis of the Pattern of Ovulation as it Occurs in the Annual Reproductive Cycle of the Mare in Australia, Austral. Vet. Jour. **42,** 149.

Palsson, E. (1961) Investigations of the Incidence of Cystic Ovarian Degeneration in Swedish Lowland Cattle and the Effect of Individual Bulls on its Occurrence, Proc. 4th Internal. Congr. on An. Reprod., the Hague. Vol LV, 768.

Rendel, J. (1956) Heritability of Multiple Birth in Sheep, J. An. Sci. **15,** 1, 193.

Short, R. V., Smith, J. Mann, T., Evans, E. P., Dickson, J., Fryer, A. and Hamerton, J. L. (1969) Cytogenetic and Endocrine Studies of a Freemartin Heifer and Its Bull Cotwin, Cytogenetics **8,** 369.

Stansfield, W. E. (1968) A Serological Estimate of Monozygous Twinning in Sheep, J. of Hered. **59,** 3, 211.

Stone, W. H., Cragle, R. G., Swanson, E. W. and Brown, D. G. (1965) Skin Grafts: Delayed Rejection Between Pairs of Cattle Twins Showing Erythrocyte Chimerism, Science, **148,** 1335.

Stormont, C. (1966) What Blood Typing Tells Us., Hoards Dairyman, Oct. 10, 1151.

Stormont, C., Morris, B. G. and Suzuki, Y. (1964) Mosaic Hemoglobin Types in a Pair of Cattle Twins, Science **145,** 600.

Turman, E. J., Renbarger, R. E. and Stephens D. F. (1968) Multiple Births in Beef Cows Treated with P.M.S., J. An. Sci. **27,** 4, 1198.

Williams, G., Gordon, I. and Edwards, J. (1963) Observations on the Frequency of Fused Fetal Circulations in Twin Bearing Cattle, Brit. Vet. Jour. **119,** 467

Witschi, E. (1965) Hormones and Embryonic Induction, Arch. Anat. Microsc. Morph. Exp. **54,** 601.

Immunogenetics

Kiddy, C. A. (1964) Inherited Differences in Specific Blood and Milk Proteins in Cattle: A Review, J. Dairy Sci. **47,** 5, 510.

Rendel, J., Bouw, J. and Schmid, D. O. (1962) The Frequency of Cows Served Twice Which Remain Pregnant to First Service: A Study of Results from Parentage Tests, An. Prod. **4,** 359.

Stone, W. H., Cragle, R. G., Swanson, E. W. and Brown, D. G. (1965) Skin Grafts: Delayed Rejection between Pairs of Cattle Twins Showing Erthrocyte Chimerism, Science **148,** 1335.

Stormont, C. (1966) What Blood Typing Tells Us, Hoard's Dairyman, Oct. 10, 1151.

Stormont, C. (1967) Contribution of Blood Typing to Dairy Science Progress, J. Dairy Sci. **50,** 2, 253.

Stormont, C., Franks, D., Rasmussen, B., Saison Rand Ingram, D. G. (1962) Blood Groups in Infrahuman Species, Ann. New York Acad. Sci. **97,** Art. 1, 1-328.

Stormont, C., Morris, B. G. and Suzuki, Y. (1964) Mosaic Hemoglobin Types in a Pair of Cattle Twins, Science **145,** 600.

Stormont, C. and Suzuki, Y. (1965) Paternity Tests in Horses, Cor. Vet. **55,** 365.

Swisher, S. N. and Young, L. E. (1961) The Blood Grouping Systems of Dogs, Physiol. Rev. **41,** 495.

Sex Parity and the Bacterial Flora of the Pregnant Uterus

Altman, P. L. and Dittmer, D. S. (1962) Growth Including Reproduction and Morphological Development, Biological Handbook, Feder. Amer. Soc. for Exper. Biol., Washington, D.C.

Black, W. G., Ulberg, L. C., Kidder, H. E., Simon, J., McNutt, S. H. and Casida, L. E. (1953) Inflammatory Response of the Bovine Endometrium, Amer. J. Vet. Res. **14,** 51, 179.

Brands, A. F. A., Banerjee-Schotsman, J. VanDieten, S. W. J. and VanLoen, A. (1965) Sex Ratio at Birth in Cattle, Tijdschr. vor Diergeneesk **90,** 13, 909.

Brus, D. H. J. (1954) Biopsia Uteri, Thesis, Univ. of Utrecht, Utrecht, Netherlands.

Chapman, A. B., Casida, L. E. and Cote, A. (1938) Sex Ratio of Fetal Calves, Proc. Amer. Soc. of An. Prod., 303.

Clark, R. T., O'Mary, C. C., Brinks, J. S. and Kieffer, N. M. (1963) Sex Ratios in Hereford Range Cattle, J. An. Sci. **22,** 3, 817.

Hnevkosky, O., Petrikova, E. and Cerny, M. (1964) Prenatal Sex Ratio in Man, Acta. Univ. Carolinae Med. **18,** Suppl. 105.

Miller, J. G. (1950) A Method of Endometrial Biopsy in the Bovine and the Stud of Biopsy Specimens in Cases of Infertility, Thesis, N.Y.S. Vet. Col., Ithaca, N.Y.

Rowson, L. E. A., Lamming, G., and Frye, R. M. (1953) The Relationship between Ovarian Hormones and Uterine Infection, Vet. Rec. **65,** 335.

Spector, W. S. (1956) Handbook of Biological Data, W. B. Saunders Co., Philadelphia, Penna.

Duration and Hormonal Control of Pregnancy including Birth Weights.

Amoroso, E. C. and Marshall, F. H. A. (1952) in **Marshall's Physiology of Reproduction,** A. S. Parkes Ed., Vol II, Longmans Green and Co., London, N.Y.C.

Altman, P. L. and Dittmer, D. S. (1962) (See Sex Parity)

Andersen, H. and Plum, Mogens (1965) Gestation Length and Birthweight in Cattle and Buffaloes: A Review, J. Dairy Sci. **48,** 9, 1224.

Banerjee-Schotsman, O. (1965) A Study Concerning the Gestation Period in Cattle—A Biochemical Contribution, Tijdschr. vor Diergeneesk. **90,** 14, 971.

Bengtsson, L. P. and Scofield, B. M. (1963) Progesterone and the Accomplishment of Parturition in the Sheep, J. of Reprod. and Fertil. **5,** 423.

Callahan, C. J., Fessler, J. F., Erb, R. E., Plotka, E. D. and Randel, R. D. (1969) Prolonged Gestation in a Holstein Friesian Cow, Clinical and Reproductive Steroid Studies, Cor. Vet. **59,** 3, 370.

Cates, W. F. (1965) Progesterone Requirement During the Preimplantation and Implantation Stages of the Gestation Period in the Cow, School of Vet. Med., Univ. of Minn., St. Paul, Minn., PhD Thesis.

Deanesly, R. (1961) Fetal Endocrinology in Fetal and Neonatal Physiology, Brit. Medical Bull **17,** 2.

DeFries, J. C., Touchberry, R. W. and Hays, R. L. (1959) Heritability of the Length of the Gestation Period in Dairy Cattle, J. Dairy Sci. **42,** 4, 598.

DeLange, M. (1961) Prolonged Gestation in Karakul Ewes in Southwest Africa, Proc. 4th Internat. Congr. on An. Reprod., The Hague Vol. III, 590.

Drost, M. (1969) Fetal Effects on the Initiation of Labor, J.A.V.M.A. (Proc. A.V.M.A. Meeting, Minneapolis), in press.

Drost, M. and Holm, L. W. (1968) Prolonged Gestation in Ewes after Fetal Adrenalectomy, J. Endocrin. **40,** 263.

du Mesnil du Buisson, F. and Dauzier, L. (1957) Influence de l'ovarectomie Chez la Truia pendant la Gestation, Compt. Rend. Soc. Biol. **151,** 311.

Erb, R. E., Randel, R. D. and Estergreen, V. L. Jr. (1967) Urinary Estrogen Excretion and Levels of Progesterone in Blood Plasma of the Cow During Pregnancy, J. Dairy Sci. **50,** 6, 1001.

Estergreen, V. L. Jr., Frost, O. L., Gomes, W. R., Erb, R. E. and Bullard, J. G. (1967) Effect of Ovariectomy on Pregnancy Maintenance and Parturition in Dairy Cows, J. Dairy Sci. **50,** 8, 1293.

Estes, J. A. and Worth, W. B. (1943) The Gestation Period of Thoroughbreds, Blood Horse **40,** 26, 838.

Ginther, O. J. (1966) The Influence of the Uterus on the Life-Span of the Corpus Luteum, Vet. Med. (Dec. 1966), 1199.

Ginther, O. J. (1968) Utero-ovarian Relationships in Cattle—Part I —Physiological Aspects, J.A.V.M.A. **153,** 12, 1665.

Gomes, W. R. and Erb, R. E. (1965) Progesterone in Bovine Reproduction: A Review, J. Dairy Sci. **48,** 3, 314.

Hawk, H. W., Turner, G. D., Brinsfield, T. H., Whitmore, G. E., Norcross, N. A. and Sykes, J. F. (1960) Maintenance of Pregnancy during Early Gestation in Ovariectomized Dairy Cattle, J. An. Sci. **19,** 4, 1325.

Holm, J. W. (1967) Prolonged Pregnancy, in **Advances in Veterinary Science** Vol. **11,** Academic Press Inc., N.Y.C. 159.

Howell, C. E. and Rollins, W. C. (1951) Environmental Sources of Variation in the Gestation Length of the Horse, J. An. Sci. **10,** 4, 789.

Imori, T. (1967) The Biological Half Life of Progesterone in the Peripheral Blood of Cows, Jap. Jour. of Vet. Sci. **29,** 4, 201.

Kennedy, P. C., Kendrick, J. W. and Stormont, C. (1957) Adenohypophyseal Aplasia, an Inherited Defect Associated with Abnormal Gestation in Guernsey Cattle, Cor. Vet. **47,** 1, 160.

Kiesel, G. K. and Autrey, K. M. (1961) Relationship of Progesterone to Prolonged Gestation in Cattle, J.A.V.M.A. **138,** 10, 557.

Lanman, J. T. and Schaffer, A. (1968) Gestational Effects of Fetal Decapitation in Sheep, Fert. and Steril. **19,** 4, 598.

Liggins, G. C. (1968) Premature Parturition after Infusion of Corticotrophin or Cortisol into Fetal Lambs, J. of Endocrin. **42,** 323.

Matthews, R. G., Butterfield, R. M., Moss, F. P. and McFadden, W. J. (1969) The Duration of Pregnancy in Thoroughbred Mares, Vet. Rec. **84,** 552.

Mead, S. W., Gregory, P. W. and Regan, W. M. (1949) Prolonged Gestation of Genetic Origin in Cattle, Jour. Dairy Sci. **32,** 705. (1945).

Neher, G. M. and Zarrow, M. X. (1954) Concentration of Progestin in the Serum of the Nonpregnant, Pregnant and Postpartum Ewe, J. of Endocrin. **11,** 323.

Plasse, D., Warnick, A. C. and Koger, M. (1968) Reproductive Behavior of **Bos Indicus** Females in a Subtropical Environment, J. An. Sci. **27,** 1, 94.

Rossdale, P. D. (1967) Clinical Studies in the Newborn Thoroughbred Foal, Brit. Vet. Jour. **123,** 470.

Sager, F. (1970) Long Equine Gestation Periods, Chronicle of the Horse, Jan, 30, p. 12.

Short, R. V. (1965) Recent Advances in Equine Reproductive Physiology, 4th Ann. Congr. of the Brit. Equine Vet. Assoc.

Smith, E. D (1967) Breed Differences in the Duration of Gestation in Sheep, Austral. Vet. Jour. **43,** 2, 63.

Staples, R. E., McEntee, K. and Hansel, W. (1961) Luteal Function as Related to Pituitary and Ovarian Cytology and Embryo Development in the Bovine, J. Dairy Sci. **44,** 11, 2049.

Starke, J. S., Smith, J. B. and Joubert, D. M. (1959) The Birthweight of Lambs, An. Breeding Abstr. **27,** 63.

Turman, E. J., Renbarger, R. E. and Stephens, D. F. (1968) Multiple Births in Beef Cows Treated with P.M.S., J. An. Sci. **27,** 4, 1198.

Wickersham, E. W. and Tanabe, T. Y. (1967) Functional Status of Bovine Corpora Lutea of Pregnancy, 62nd Ann. Meeting Amer. Dairy Sci. Assoc., Cornell Univ., Ithaca, N.Y.

Wilson, A. L. and Young, G. B. (1958) Prolonged Gestation in an Ayrshire Herd, Vet. Rec. **70,** 73.

Zimbelman, R. G. and Smith, L. W. (1966) Maintenance of Pregnancy in Ovariectomized Heifers with Melengestrol Acetate, J. An. Sci. **25,** 1, 207.

Duration and Rate of Reproduction and Abnormalities of the Gestation Period

Altman, P. L. and Dittmer, D. S. (1962) Growth Including Reproduction and Morphological Development, Biological Handbook, Fed. of Amer. Soc. for Exper. Biol., Washington, D.C.

Arthur, G. H. (1964) Wright's Veterinary Obstetrics, 3rd Ed., Williams and Wilkins Co., Baltimore, Md., 344.

Casida, L. E., Woody, C. O. and Pope, A. L. (1966) Inequality in Function of the Right and Left Ovaries and Uterine Horns of the Ewe, J. An. Sci. **25,** 4, 1169.

Dalrymple, B. H. and Jenkins, D. (1951) A Probable Case of Superfetation in the Bovine, Cor. Vet. **41,** 4, 340.

Dukes, H. H. (1947) The Physiology of Domestic Animals, 6th Ed. Comstock Publ. Co., Ithaca, N.Y.

Dzuik, P. J., Polge, C. and Rowson, L. E. A. (1964) Intrauterine Migration and Mixing of Embryos in Swine Following Egg Transfer, J. An. Sci. **23,** 1, 37.

Hagyard, C. E. (1956) Personal Communication.

Hoogeweg, J. H. and Folkers, E. R. (1970) Superfetation in the Cat, J.A.V.M.A. **156,** 1, 73.

Kawata, K. and Tiba, T. (1961) A Rare Case of Schistosomus Reflexus (and Superfetation) in the Cat., Jap. Jour. Vet. Res. **9,** 4, 179.

Markee, J. E. and Hinsey, J. C. (1935) A Case of Probable Superfetation in a Cat, Anat. Rec. **61,** 241.

Perkins, J. R., Olds, D. and Seath, D. M. (1954) A Study of 1000 Bovine Genitalia, J. Dairy Sci. **37,** 10, 1158.

Vandeplassche, M. (1952) Bijdrage Tot Juistere Kennis en Begrip van Superfetatio en Van Dubbel Partus, Uit de Verhandelingen van de Koninklijke Vlaamse Academie voor Geneeskunde van Belgie **14,** 4, 327.

Wolstenholme, G. E. W. and O'Conner, M. (1959) The Life Span of Animals, Ciba Foundation Symposium, Vol. 5, Little, Brown and Co., Boston.

Lactation

Asdell, S. A. (1957) Personal Communication.

Cowie, A. T. and Tindal, J. S. (1964) Some Aspects of the Neuroendocrine Control of Lactation, Proc. 2nd Internat. Congr. of Endocrinol, London; 646.

Cleverly, J. D. (1968) The Detection of Oxytocin Release in Response to Conditioned Stimuli Associated with Machine Milking in the Cow, Jour. of Endocrinol. **40,** 2.

Cross, B. A. (1955) Neurohormonal Mechanisms in Emotional Inhibition of Milk Ejection, J. of Endocrinol., **12,** 29.

Emery, R. S., Hafs, H. D., Armstrong, D. and Snyder, W. W. (1969) Prepartum Grain Feeding Effects on Milk Production, Mammary Edema and Incidence of Diseases, J. Dairy Sci. **52,** 3, 345.

Espe, D. L. and Smith, V. R. (1952) Secretion of Milk, 4th Ed., Iowa State College Press, Ames, Iowa.

Folley, S. J. (1961) Recent Advances in the Physiology and Biochemistry of Lactation, Dairy Science Abstr. **23,** 11, 511.

Folley, S. J. and Knaggs, G. S. (1965) Oxytocin Levels in the Blood of Ruminants with Special Reference to the Milking Stimulus, from **Advances in Oxytocin Research,** Pergamon Press, N.Y.C., London.

Folley, S. J. and Knaggs, G. S. (1966) Milk-Ejection Activity (Oxytocin) in the External Jugular Vein Blood of the Cow, Goat and Sow in Relation to the Stimulus of Milking or Suckling, J. Endocrinol. **34,** 197.

Hindery, G. A. and Turner, C. W. (1965) Effect of Administration of L Thyroxine 25 and 50 percent Above Secretion Rate on Lactating Cows, J. Dairy Sci. **48,** 5, 596.

Huffman, C. F. (1961) High Level Grain Feeding For Dairy Cattle, J. Dairy Sci. **44,** 11, 2113.

Knaggs, G. S. (1969) Personal Communication.

Larson, B. L. (1958) Transfer of Specific Blood Serum Proteins to Lacteal Secretion near Parturition, J. Dairy Sci., **41,** 1033.

Morrow, D. A. and Schmidt, G. H. (1964) Udder Edema, Ciba Veterinary Monograph Series/one, Ciba Pharm. Co., Summit, N. J.

Rook, J. A. F. (1961) Variations in the Chemical Composition of the Milk of the Cow, Part II, Dairy Sci. Abstr. **23,** 7, 303.

Schmidt, G. H. (1969) Personal Communication.

Schmidt, G. H. and Schultz, L. H. (1959) Effect of Three Levels of Grain Feeding During the Dry Period on the Incidence of Ketosis, Severity of Udder Edema and Subsequent Milk Production of Dairy Cows, J. Dairy Sci. **42,** 1, 170.

Smith, V. R. (1959) Physiology of Lactation, 5th Ed., Iowa State College Press, Ames, Iowa.

Swanson, E. W. and Claycomb, J. E. (1969) Oxytocin in Dry Period Inhibits Lactation, J. Dairy Sci. **52,** 7, 1116.

Rice, V. A. and Andrews, F. N. (1951) Breeding and Improvement of Farm Animals 4th Ed., McGraw Hill Book Co., N.Y.C.

Tucker, H. A. and Meites, J. (1965) Induction of Lactation in Pregnant Heifers with 9 Fluoroprednisolone Acetate (Predef), J. Dairy Sci. **48,** 3, 405.

Turner, C. W. (1958) Estrogen Content of Colostrum and Milk of Dairy Cattle, J. Dairy Sci. **41,** 5, 630.

Chapter V

DISEASES AND ACCIDENTS OF THE GESTATION PERIOD

ABORTION

Abortion is the expulsion from the uterus of a living fetus before it reaches a viable age, or more commonly the expulsion of a dead fetus of recognizable size at any stage of gestation. Many fertilized ova, embryos, or early fetuses may be aborted without being seen. This is especially true in beef cattle, sheep and other animals not closely observed. Early death and unseen expulsion of the ova, embryos, or fetuses is usually classified as infertility. Early deaths of the fertilized ova may be associated with regular estrual cycles. Irregular or prolonged periods without estrum may be caused by the death and unobserved expulsion or absorption of older embryos or fetuses. (See Figures 59 and 60) Thus through common usage the term abortion has come to mean the expulsion of nonviable or dead fetuses of recognizable size. In the cow and mare, pregnancy usually progresses for 1-1/2 to 3 months before the expelled fetus is large enough to be recognized. The animal usually fails to show estrum for a period long enough for the owner to believe that conception had occurred. Any abnormal discharge from the vulva should be investigated and the animal observed for subsequent periods of estrum. In the cow, abortions occurring before the fifth month of gestation are seldom followed by retention of the placenta, but those occurring after the fourth month of pregnancy are frequently characterized by retention.

The nature of the causative agent of the abortion may determine the degree of damage to the fetal membranes and endometrium and the frequency of retained afterbirths and sterility that follows the abortion. Abortions are usually caused by agents affecting the fetus or its placental membranes or both. Because of the intimate contact between the fetal and maternal placentae, disease of the former is closely reflected in the latter. Agents causing a severe stress reaction in the dam may also cause abortion. Many single factors or combinations of factors may cause abortion in the various animals. Economically, abortions are of great concern to the farmer, because the fetus is lost; a prolonged period of uterine disease and sterility may follow; the unproductive female must be maintained for a long period or sold, and if the cause of the abortion is infectious, it threatens the rest of the herd.

Diseases of the fetus and pregnant uterus do not always result in fetal death. The fetus may be expelled prematurely or at term and live or it may be weak and diseased and die shortly after birth. In most abortions the fetus dies in the uterus and is expelled with 24 to 72 hours by which time varying degrees of postmortem decomposition or autolysis has developed. Sterile autolytic changes of the fetus after its death and before expulsion have been described in humans and sheep are probably the same in all species, Dillman. At 12 hours after death the fetal corneas are cloudy and grey; at 24 hours the kidneys are soft and the abomasal contents are cloudy, mucoid and yellowish. From 36 to 96 hours after fetal death, color changes occur in the skin, the subcutis is gelatinous and blood tinged, the liver is soft and the abomasal contents are cloudy, mucoid and reddish. As a sequel to some cases of intrauterine fetal death, especially of one or more of a number of fetuses in multiparous animals, failure of expulsion may occur and fetal mummification or fetal maceration may result.

The various agents causing abortion may be classified into groups that include: physical causes, genetic or chromosomal causes, nutritional causes, chemical, drug, or toxic causes, hormonal causes, miscellaneous causes and infectious causes. The latter are most important and include bacterial, viral, fungal and protozoal agents. Since the causes of abortion in animals are numerous only those that cause serious losses will be discussed in some detail. The others will be briefly enumerated. The various causes of abortion will be discussed by species.

Abortion in Cattle

In cattle herds an incidence of abortion of more than 2 to 5 percent should be viewed seriously and efforts made to determine its cause so that proper methods of control may be instituted. Unfortunately at the present time, in areas where the incidence of brucellosis is very low, only 20 to 25 percent of the aborted bovine fetuses and membranes submitted to a competent diagnostic laboratory yield a definitive diagnosis of the causative agent. In some instances serological testing of the aborting cow at the time of abortion and two to three weeks later may be helpful by the presence of a rise in titer for a certain infectious agent between the first and second samplings. A single serologic test is often of questionable value as the time of the infection in most instances is not known. One of the main reasons for the failure of cultural or histologic tests on promptly-submitted, well-protected, chilled or frozen fetuses and membranes is the degree of autolysis undergone by the fetus and membranes after intrauterine death and before expulsion. The use of fluorescent antibody techniques developed in recent years has been of definite assistance in the diagnosis of certain infectious causes of abortions.

Infectious Bacterial Abortions in Cattle

Brucellosis (Contagious or Infectious Abortion, Bang's Disease) is caused by a small gram-negative rod, **Brucella abortus,** that grows intracellularly. It was first described in Denmark by Bang in 1897. It is the most important worldwide cause of abortion in cattle except in countries such as the U.S. where the widespread use of strain 19 vaccination has been incorporated into a control and eradication program to greatly reduce the incidence of the disease. The incidence of bovine brucellosis in cattle in the U.S. was 11.5 percent in 1935 and at present (1970) it is less than 0.5 percent with more than 15 states being certified as brucellosis-free areas.

Br. abortus causes abortion in cattle the last trimester of pregnancy and a subsequent period of infertility is

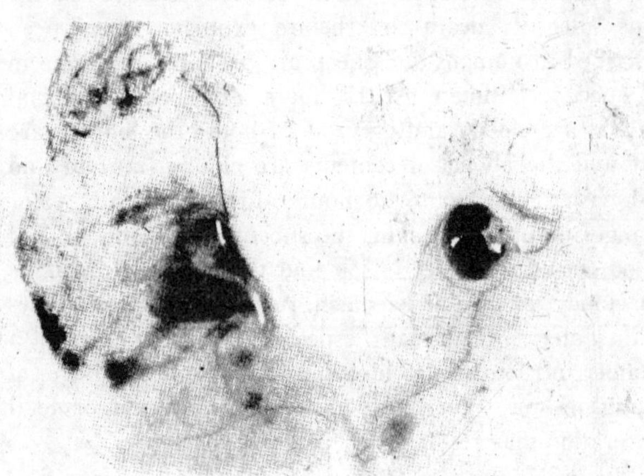

Figure 59. Embryonic death of one of twin 35-day bovine zygotes.

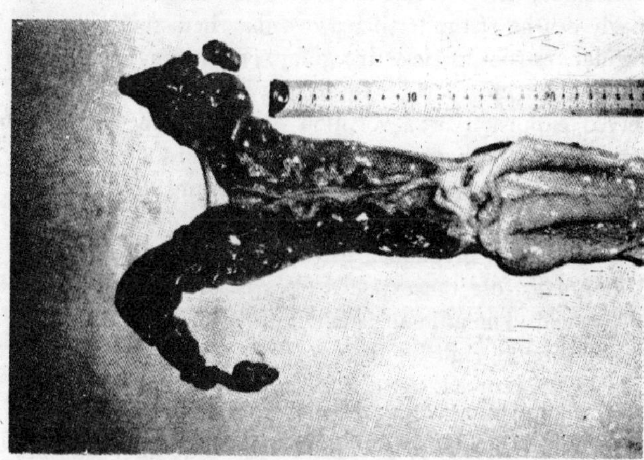

Figure 60. Bovine fetal resorption 60 days post-conception.

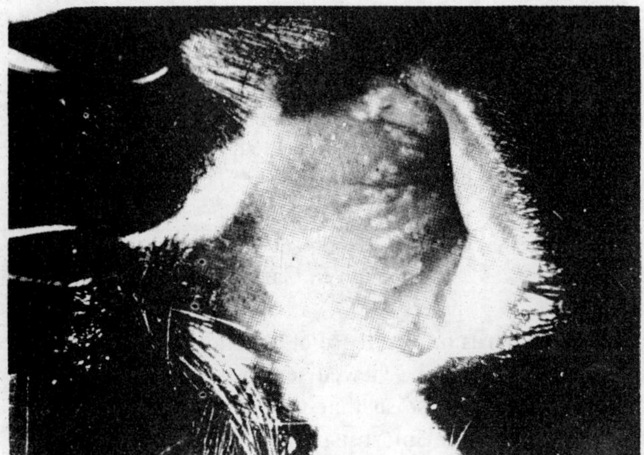

Figure 61. Pustular vulvovaginitis in a heifer due to IBR-IPV virus.

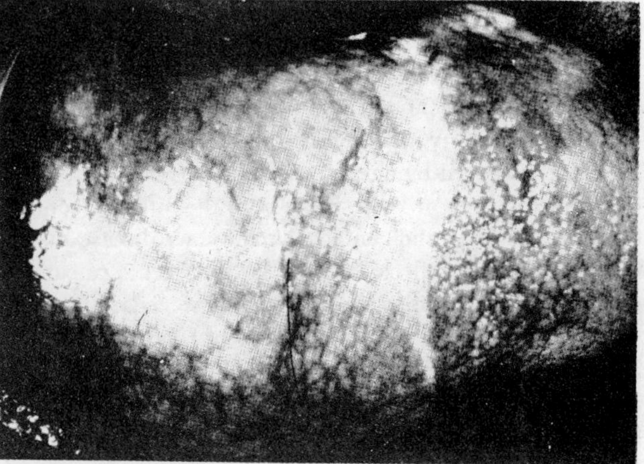

Figure 62. Nodular chronic lesions of the fetal liver in epizootic bovine abortion

Table 9. Summary of Causes of Abortion in Cattle

Infectious Causes

Bacterial—Brucellosis (Br. abortus), Leptospirosis (Leptospira pomona and others), Listeriosis (L. monocytogenes), Tuberculosis (Mycobacterium bovis) and Vibriosis (V. fetus venerealis).

Miscellaneous Bacterial—Streptococci, diplococci, staphylococci, E. Coli, Alcaligenes fecalis, Pseudomonas aeruginosa, Corynebacterium pyogenes, Erysipelothrix insidiosa, Hemophilus, Vibrio fetus intestinalis, Mycobacterium avium, Pasteurella multocida, Salmonella paratyphi B, S. cholera-suis and S. dublin, B. anthracis, Nocardia asteroides, and Mycoplasma.

Viral—Infectious bovine rhinotrachitis (IBR-IPV), Epizootic bovine abortion (E.B.A. or Chlamydia).

Miscellaneous Viral—Foreign diseases such as: foot and mouth disease, rinderpest, Rift Valley fever, bovine infectious petechial fever and tick borne fever; Native diseases as bovine virus diarrhea—mucosal disease (BVD-MD), Myxovirus parainfluenza—3, malignant catarrhal fever and pseudorabies.

Mycotic or Fungal—Aspergillus spp., Mucorales Spp. (including Absidia, Mucor, Rhizopus), and yeasts.

Protozoal—trichomoniasis, toxoplasmosis, besnoitis or globidiosis, trypanosomiasis, anaplasmosis, babesiasis or piroplasmosis.

Noninfectious Causes

Chemical, Drug and Poisonous plants—nitrates, chlorinated napthalenes, arsenic, locoweeds, perennial broomweed, pine needles.

Hormonal—estrogens, glucocorticoids, progesterone deficiency.

Nutritional—starvation, malnutrition, vitamin A deficiency, iodine deficiency.

Physical—douching, infusing or insemination of the pregnant uterus, rupture of the amniotic vesicle and/or trauma to embryo, removal of the corpus luteum, torsion of the uterus or umbilical cord, marked stress due to severe fatigue due to transport, work, severe systemic diseases, or major operations.

Genetic or chromosomal—certain defects of the embryo or fetus.

Miscellaneous—twinning, allergies and anaphyactic reactions, tumors and etc.

usually experienced. The disease is also important because **Br. abortus** causes undulant fever or brucellosis in man from drinking raw or unpasturized infected milk or from exposure to infected discharges or tissues by farmers, packing house workers, veterinarians and others. McCullough has described briefly the medical procedures to follow after the accidental injection of **Br. abortus** strain 19 into a man. The disease is well-described by Bruner and Gillespie, Blood and Henderson and Jubb and Kennedy.

Br. abortus is mainly infective for cattle but occasionally other species of animals such as sheep, swine, dogs and horses may be infected. In sheep rare abortions are recorded and in horses **Br. abortus** together with **Actinomyces bovis** is commonly present in poll evil and fistulous withers. A high incidence of brucellosis has been reported in herds of bison and elk but the incidence in white-tailed deer and other wild ruminants is low, Meyer.

The organism is rather easily destroyed by disinfectants, sunlight, drying, putrefaction, and pasteurization. It may survive for several months in a moist, cold environment. The **Br. abortus** organism is found in the chorion of the placenta where it produces severe pathologic changes including necrosis and edema and in the digestive tract and lungs of the fetus. It also is found as a persistent infection in the udder and the supermammary, retropharyngeal and internal and external iliac lymph nodes of adult cows and in the testes, epididymides, vasa deferentia and seminal vesicles of bulls. After abortion the organism does not persist in the uterus and disappears in one to five months, Lambert et al., as apparently it grows well only in the fetal placenta. Persistently infected udders appear clinically normal. Occasionally Brucella organisms persist in joints or bursae. Infections and blood titers in calves or immature cattle seldom persist as they do in the sexually mature animal. Infection may be introduced into susceptible herds by the purchase of an infected cow. Infective material may occasionally be carried by dogs or persons from one farm to another or contact of infected and susceptible animals across a line fence may occur. Infection may be transmitted in contaminated trucks or at fairs or shows.

Infection of cattle with **Br. abortus** occurs most frequently by the ingestion of infected genital discharges of aborting animals that contaminate the feed and water. Transmission may also occur through the mucous membranes of the eye and by intrauterine artificial insemination of infected semen. Bartlett cited Danish workers who reported on one infected bull used artificially. He infected 71 percent of the cows in which his semen was used and brucellosis appeared in 41 previously brucella-free herds. There is little evidence to show that brucellosis is spread from an infected bull to susceptible cattle by natural service, Manthei. Calves nursing infected cows may spread the disease by fecal contamination of food ingested by susceptible animals. Occasionally **Br. abortus** may be spread by discharges from fistulous lesions of horses or possibly by quarter to quarter spread of organisms as occurs in mastitis, Kerr and Rankin. Once infection is established in sexually mature animals it tends to persist indefinitely.

Abortions due to **Br. abortus** usually occur from the 6th through 9th month of gestation and premonitory signs of udder enlargement and vulvar edema often are present. The incidence of abortion will vary from 5 to 90 percent in a herd depending upon the number of susceptible pregnant animals, the rate of transmission, the virulence of the organism and other factors.

The fetal membranes are edematous, hemorrhagic, leathery and necrotic and often there is a brownish-yellow pasty exudate in the uterochorionic space. Retained placenta and metritis with a following period of genital discharge and infertility are common sequelae. After recovery most cows carry their subsequent calves normally but a few cows may abort two or three times. Occasional fetuses may be born alive but most are weak and premature and die within a few hours. The dead fetus may exhibit some autolytic changes of edema and hemorrhages of the tissues and body cavities and may be stained with meconium.

A diagnosis of brucellosis requires laboratory tests that include:

(1) Isolation of the organism from the fetal lungs, stomach or placenta. In adult animals organisms may be recovered from the milk or semen, or from lymph nodes after slaughter. The organism is usually isolated in culture media or guinea pigs.

(2) Serologic tests for agglutinins in the blood, which are usually present at the time of abortion and often rise thereafter, include: the tube and plate agglutination tests, heat inactivation test, acidified plate antigen (APA) test, the acridine compound (Rivanol) precipitation test, the complement fixation (CF) test and the 2-mercaptolethanol (ME) test. The efficacy of these tests in identifying infected cattle in problem herds from which **Br. abortus** was recovered was 52 to 61, 66, 98, 95, 96, 98 and 97 percent, respectively, Nicoletti. The tube test was the most efficient test in classifying cows that were noninfected. The tube, and in some states, the rapid plate agglutination, test nevertheless is the routine official test performed and has been highly successful in identifying infected cattle except in a few problem herds. A 1:50 reaction in a nonvaccinated cow is a suspicious reaction and 1:100 is positive. In an officially calf-hood vaccinated cow 1:100 is suspicious and 1:200 is positive, Bruner and Gillespie. Cattle with suspicious reactions should be retested in two to four weeks. There is no practical method at present to distinguish between a serological titer for brucellosis due to vaccination with Strain 19 and infection with a field strain of the organism. The other supplemental specialized serological laboratory tests for brucellosis diagnosis described above and by Anderson and coworkers and recently by Nicoletti (1969) are very helpful in locating in problem herds infected animals that fail to show a reaction to the regular tube or rapid plate agglutination test. It is important to note that 82 percent of the cattle from problem herds from which Nicoletti isolated **Br. abortus** were cattle vaccinated with Strain 19. In recent years the Card test, a rapid, sensitive accurate test for field screening of a herd especially in range areas, has been developed. This test was superior to the tube agglutination test in classifying infected animals. It appeared best suited as a field screening procedure in areas with a low incidence of infection and for detecting infected animals earlier than the tube test, Nicoletti (1967). Although blood samples in cattle may easily be drawn from the jugular or external abdominal veins, especially in dairy cattle, bleeding from the tail is also simple and rapid and is favored by many in collecting blood samples from beef cattle, bulls and even dairy cattle, Brown and Carrow. In blood testing cattle one should use proper hygenic precautions so that if anaplasmosis or other disease of the blood is present in the herd the spread of the disease is not favored. Occasionally immunization or infection with **Pasteurella multocida** and **Vibrio fetus,** but not **L. pomona,** will produce nonspecific agglutinations in a cow resulting in a moderate rise in the brucella titer of her serum, Downey and Morter. Cross-reactions between brucella and pasteurella antibodies were not observed in a trial conducted by Nicoletti and Holmes.

(3) Agglutination tests on milk include the milk ring test (M.R.T., or the Brucellosis Ring Test, B.R.T.) and the whey agglutination test. In infected cattle in problem herds the efficacy of these tests for the detection of reactor cattle was 92 and 73 percent, Nicoletti. As a herd screening procedure on bulk milk the M.R.T. is highly effective in indicating herds containing one or more brucella-infected cows. Such detection is followed by blood testing of the individual animals in the herd. The testing of all dairy herds in an area two or more times a year with the M.R.T. has proven highly effective in the diagnosis and elimination of reactor cows, Janney et al.. After testing over 36,000 cows in 645 dairy herds Nicoletti and Burch concluded that periodic blood tests on cattle negative to the milk ring test (M.R.T.) were unnecessary. This procedure is not applicable to beef herds.

(4) Agglutination tests may be conducted on seminal plasma from bulls in which it is highly effective in detect-

ing an increased local antibody level and on vaginal mucus from cows when a virulent infection is present in the uterus, Kerr.

The herd history may be useful in the diagnosis of the cause for abortion. Differential diagnosis between the causes of abortion may be very difficult and often impossible without good laboratory assistance. The placental lesions in brucellosis, vibriosis and mold or fungal infections in cattle appear similar.

The control of brucellosis in cattle is based on hygiene or sanitation, vaccination of calves with Strain 19 and the testing and disposal or elimination of reactors. Treatments for brucellosis, including a variety of antiseptics and antibiotics, have been attempted in cattle but with no success. Hygienic measures are essential to a control program within a herd. Infected animals should be sold for slaughter or should be kept carefully isolated especially if abortion is impending and at the time of parturition and for a few weeks thereafter when the greatest spread of Brucella organisms may occur. Aborted fetuses and placentas should be buried or burned and contaminated areas should be disinfected with a 4 percent compound solution of cresol or a similar disinfectant. All cattle, horses and pigs coming onto the farm should be tested and isolated for four weeks and retested before placing with the herd unless they came from a brucella-free herd. These hygienic procedures are necessary even in vaccinated herds where the field strain of the organism may infect and spread to the udder and lymph tissues in the cattle. In vaccinated herds abortions usually will not occur.

Vaccination of calves from 3 to 7 months of age with 5 ml of freeze-dryed, refrigerated, stabilized, low virulent strain 19 Brucella vaccine subcutaneously immediately after reconstitution produces a rapid rise in serum antibody titer that recedes in over 90 percent of young cattle before thirty months of age. Because of persisting titers in older calves increased emphasis is now placed on vaccinating calves at 3 to 6 months of age. The titers produced in these younger calves usually disappears by 18 months of age, Redman et al.. The immunity in cattle vaccinated at 3 to 6 months of age is equal to that in calves vaccinated at 6 to 8 months of age and lasts in most cattle through their fifth gestation, Manthei. Lyophilized, dated, refrigerated vaccine should be used to be certain of good liveability and antigenicity of the organisms. Care should be used in vaccinating calves as Strain 19 can produce brucellosis or undulant fever in man. Vaccination of cattle over 8 months of age tends to cause persistent blood titers and in pregnant cows may occasionally cause abortion but the immunity produced is no greater than that achieved by calfhood vaccination. In a heavily infected area, some veterinarians will vaccinate a susceptible adult herd of cows in which an abortion epizootic is imminent to prevent severe economic losses by the farmer. This should not be done in an area where control and eradication procedures are being carried out or are being contemplated within the next 5 years.

Occasionally calves or cows show generalized reactions for up to 7 days after vaccination with Strain 19 including, elevated temperatures, rapid respiration, dullness and anorexia. In rare instances deaths of calves due to anaphylaxis or brucella septicemia may occur within a few hours or several days, Roberts et al.. Bull calves should not be vaccinated as Strain 19 rarely localizes in their genital tract or a persistent serum titer may occasionally develop. No useful purpose is achieved by the vaccination of male cattle. To avoid systemic reactions seen most commonly in cattle of the Channel Island breeds some workers have advocated intradermic vaccination with 0.2 to 1.0 ml. of Strain 19 vaccine. Gilman and Hughes demonstrated that the intradermal injection did not produce as good a level of immunity as the larger subcutaneous injection of vaccine. Veterinarians should use great care that syringes used for vaccinating calves with Strain 19 are not used for other injections as infection and serum titers can be produced in other cattle in this manner, Beck et al.. After vaccination of large numbers of calves in an area has continued for 4 to 8 years, various test and eradication programs can be instituted until the area is free of brucellosis resulting in minimal losses to the farmer. At this time the need for vaccination of calves declines and ultimately it can be eliminated in many areas freed of the disease.

In the final control and eradication program for brucellosis the use of the M.R.T. as a herd screening test in dairy areas together with blood testing of M.R.T. positive herds, small family dairies and beef herds has proven highly successful. In the few remaining problem brucellosis herds under quarentine, using the M.R.T., and the supplemental serological tests at frequent intervals on each animal and culturing of the milk has given excellent results in eliminating hard to detect reactor and/or carrier and spreader animals, Nicoletti. These problem herds are characterized by a continual spread of infection, the periodic Ring tests are positive but there are no reactors to the serum agglutination test and/or low grade serum agglutination reactions occur with a negative Ring test. In beef, and some dairy, areas the Market Cattle Testing "back tag" program to identify the herd of origin of cattle going to auction sales and abattoirs where a blood sample is taken for serologic testing, locates herds in which brucellosis is present. These herds can then be quarantined, blood tested and made brucella-free. Such programs are rapidly eliminating, in a practical economical manner, brucellosis in cattle in the U.S. It appears hopeful that the goal set by the U.S. Dept. of Agriculture of a brucellosis-free cattle population can be achieved by the target date of 1975.

Leptospirosis in cattle is due to a small, filamentous spirochete with about 40 serotypes, the most common of which are **Leptospira pomona, L. hardjo, L. grippotyphosa** and **L. canicola.** In the U.S. **L. pomona** is the most common and serious of the five as a cause of disease and abortion in cattle, Galton, Stoenner. Michna and Campbell cited an outbreak of leptospirosis in cattle characterized by abortion, stillbirth and weak calves. **L. sejroe** was isolated from the kidneys of aborting cows and serologic evidence of the infection was confirmatory. Another outbreak of abortion in Israel due to the **hebdomadis** group of **Leptospira** of which **L. sejroe** is one of the strains has been described, Van der Hoeden. Leptospirosis is not amenable to eradication because of the widespread occurrence of several serotypes in many species of wild and domestic animals and because of the difficulties in detecting carrier animals. Leptospira are found in all species of domestic animals including dogs and cats but are most widespread in swine and cattle. Swine may shed organisms in the urine after infection for six months to a year or more and might well be the primary host of **L. pomona.** Some of the wild animals found to shed leptospira in the urine include: skunks, raccoons, opossums, foxes, wild cats, beavers, nutria, rabbits, woodchucks, moles, shrews, mice, rats, deer and others. The first three animals have the highest incidence of infection and the skunk, like the pig, can shed organisms for a year or longer. Man can become infected with various leptospira but more than half of the human cases in the U.S. due to **L. pomona** has been due to swimming in contaminated water or has occurred in abattoir or dairy workers, Galton. These organisms are readily destroyed by heat, sunlight, drying, acid, and chemical disinfectants. They can survive for days or weeks in a moist environment at moderate temperatures as in stagnant ponds, streams or wet soil.

Leptospirosis was first described in cattle in the U.S. in 1944 by Jungherr, and the agent was recovered by Baker and Little in 1948. Subsequent work has shown the disease to be widespread in cattle in the U.S. as it is in most other countries of the world. Outbreaks of the disease in cattle herds may be rather sporadic. The incidence of herd epizootics varies from year to year and may be more common in certain geographical areas. Leptospira enter the cow by penetration of the abraded skin of the feet and legs when wading and by passage through the mucous membranes of the mouth and pharynx, nose and eyes by contact with contaminated water and feed or urine. The incubation period is 3 to 7 days or longer when an elevation of body temperature to 103 to 107° F occurs together with a leptospiremia that lasts for 2 to 6 days. The signs of the acute disease may vary from mild or inapparent signs in about 70 percent or more of affected cows, to moderate signs with anorexia, a drop in milk flow with a slack udder containing slightly thick "gargety" milk in about 25 to 30 percent of the cases in dairy cattle, to severe signs in a few cattle with a marked drop in milk with a thick, slightly bloody secretion, a flaccid udder, severe loss of appetite and loss of condition, anemia, hemoglobinuria, dyspnea, icterus and often death in one to three days. The severe cases are seen more frequently in young cattle up to 8 months of age. In rare cases neurologic manifestations due to leptospiral meningitis in young cattle have been reported, Blood and Henderson. Following recovery from the acute period of illness the leptospira tend to localize in the tubules of the bovine kidney and organisms are shed in the urine in variable numbers for 2 to 3 months and in a few cases slightly longer. Leptospira may also be shed in the milk during the acute stage of illness. A serologic response can usually be elicited within one week after exposure to leptospira and the serum titer usually reaches a peak in about 4 to 6 weeks and then declines to more moderate levels but persists in most cattle for years, Roberts. After intravenous inoculations of heifers pregnant 6 to 7 months with **L. pomona** organisms, abortions occurred 18 to 19 days later. In 5 heifers dead fetuses were present in heifers 17 days after inoculation. No **L. pomona** organisms were present in the blood after the 6th day and antibody titers of 1/100 to 1/1,000 were present on the tenth day. No organisms were recovered from the fetuses due to autolytic changes, Murphy et al..

In all forms of the disease abortions, especially in cows in the last half of gestation, may occur from 1 to 3 weeks after recovery from the acute febrile stage. The incidence of abortion may vary from 5 to 40 percent of the herd depending upon the number of susceptible cattle in the last third of gestation, the numbers and virulence of the infective organisms and the opportunity for the spread of the infection. Not all susceptible infected cows in advanced pregnancy will abort. Occasionally an infected cow will give birth to a live, weak calf that dies within a few days. Retained placenta and its sequelae of metritis and infertility are common. Recovered animals are immune to the leptospiral serotype causing the illness and abortion but are still susceptible to infection with other serotypes, Stoenner. Abortion outbreaks are seen most often in susceptible cattle during the summer and early fall months while on pasture. The disease can be introduced into a herd by purchasing an infected cow, from cows infected at fairs or shows, from swine running with cattle or from contact with infected wildlife. In range herds serious outbreaks have followed the concentration of stock for winter feeding, blood testing, vaccination, dipping, worming or pregnancy examinations, or other situations where the spread of the infection is favored.

Sleight and Williams demonstrated that bulls infected with **L. pomona** shed the organisms in their semen for a month or more and could infect susceptible cows by natural service. Bryan and Boley reported that **L. pomona** could survive for 7 days at 5° C in standard bovine semen extender containing 500 units of penicillin and 500 micrograms of streptomycin per ml. It was later shown that the addition of penicillin (1000 units) and streptomycin (1000 micrograms) per ml. of extended semen prevented the transmission of **L. pomona** in extended frozen semen because of the combined effects of dilution, antibiotic action and chilling on the organism. However, in artificial insemination studs only bulls free from leptospirosis should be used, Sleight, Bartlett.

Although a number of theories to explain the mechanism of the intrauterine death of the fetus have been proposed, Fennestad and Borg-Petersen have demonstrated rather conclusively that death is the consequence of fetal infection. Organisms can be demonstrated on silver-impregnated stained sections of fetal livers and kidneys. Organisms are seldom isolated from aborted fetuses because they fail to survive the 12 to 48 hours between the death of the fetus and abortion and the autolysis that occurs in the decomposing fetal tissues. The time of 2 to 5 weeks from the initial infection of the cow and abortion is the time required for the two consecutive infections in the dam and fetus to complete their courses. Autolytic lesions characteristic of abortions due to a variety of causes in the cow may be observed in the fetus and fetal membranes but gross diagnostic lesions are not present.

The diagnosis of abortions due to leptospira in cattle is more difficult than those due to brucellosis. Clinical symptoms as described above, together with necropsy findings of widespread petechia indicative of a severe septicemia are very helpful. Culture of the fetus or membranes for leptospira in laboratory animals or media is seldom successful in cattle. Silver staining of liver and kidney sections may be helpful if autolysis is not severe. In recent years the use of the fluorescent antibody technique on tissue homogenates of lung, liver or kidney of aborted fetuses have proven quite accurate even when autolysis was severe, Smith and coworkers. However, the F.A. conjugate used was only genus specific and thus would stain a number of leptospiral serotypes. The fluorescent antibody technique may also be used to stain leptospires in infected urine from aborting cows; culturing of urine at this time may also be successful.

Serologic tests for the diagnosis of leptospiral abortion have a number of shortcomings. Two serum samples taken about 2 to 3 weeks apart are needed to show a strongly rising leptospiral titer for diagnostic purposes. These samples should preferredly be taken at the time of the acute illness and then at the time of or shortly after abortion. Samples taken at the time of abortion and then several weeks later may not be as satisfactory. Stoenner recommended taking at least 10 blood samples from the herd in which leptospiral abortion is suspected including some from cows that have aborted which should show a high titer and from nonaborting cows. Cautious interpretation of the results of such a serologic test might be an aid in diagnosis. If recently aborting cows have a high titer and nonaborting cows generally have negative titers a diagnosis may be warranted; but if some of the cows that recently aborted are positive only in a low titer a diagnosis of leptospirosis is not justified.

A variety of serologic tests have been recommended and are used by various diagnostic laboratories. Galton recommended the rapid macroscopic plate agglutination test using about 12 different formalin-killed leptospiral antigens. She also used the microscopic agglutination test with live antigens. The agglutination-lysis test is an excellent test but is cumbersome and requires careful laboratory control. Stoenner's plate test has been widely used but is not as sensitive as some of the other tests. Stoenner's capillary tube test has not been generally accepted. The complement-fixation test is not practical and the hemolytic test requires further study and evaluation. A milk agglutination test has also been used in the diagnosis of bovine leptospirosis. Because of the variety of serologic tests, the differences between diagnostic laboratories and their control procedures, and the number of serologic leptospiral antigens employed, the interpretation of test results by veterinarians in the field may be difficult without guidelines from the laboratory.

Since eradication of leptospirosis is not possible, control and treatment of bovine leptospirosis may be accomplished by hygiene and sanitation, vaccination and antibiotic therapy. Water supplies should be protected from contamination, wet areas should be drained or fenced off, ingestion of contaminated feed should be prevented and exposure to infected urine and semen should be avoided. Newly purchased animals should be serologically tested, isolated and retested in two or three weeks. Since cattle recovering from leptospirosis are immune from reinfection with that serotype, various vaccines have been developed and evaluated. Living avirulent or attenuated vaccines have proven satisfacotry experimentally but so far have not been approved for commercial use, Stalheim. Living vaccines produced a high serum titer while bacterins produced a low serum titer that couldn't be confused with a natural infection. Bacterins are widely used and provide an excellent immunity for a relatively short period of time, 6 to 12 months. For this reason many cattle are vaccinated twice yearly. If breeding is limited to a short period or infection usually occurs only during certain seasons of the year, once a year vaccination may be satisfactory. Vaccination will provide protection against the clinical forms of the disease but it does not provide protection against infection and the urinary shedder state. In the face of a herd outbreak of abortion due to leptospirosis, all cattle, especially pregnant cows should be promptly vaccinated. It may be advisable to give aborting, or exposed cows, 25 mg of dihydrostreptomycin per kg. of body weight intramuscularly to eliminate the carrier or shedder state and reduce the spread of the infection in the herd, Stalheim. Abortions may continue for several weeks until an immunity from the bacterin is produced. Vaccination of cows in advanced pregnancy provides a degree of colostral immunity for calves that lasts until they are 4 to 6 months of age when vaccination is indicated in areas or on farms with a high incidence of the disease. Vaccination of calves having a passive colostral immunity at one to two months of age is of no value. At present only the monovalent **L. pomona** bacterin is available in the U.S. Anaphylactic reactions were quite common on second, third or subsequent vaccinations with the early leptospiral bacterins containing rabbit serum. These reactions were occasionally accompanied by abortions. With the advent of more highly concentrated purified bacterins the incidence of cases of anaphylaxis at vaccination has declined markedly but a few cases are still reported due to the anaphylactic nature of the leptospiral antigen itself. Anaphylactic reactions should be watched for following herd vaccination and any cattle showing typical signs of pulmonary distress should be given adrenaline or antihistamines promptly.

The treatment of the acute stages of leptospirosis includes the parenteral administration of large doses of antibiotics including penicillin, 3 million units, and streptomycin, 5 gms, twice daily, or the tetracyclines, 2.5 to 5 gms, daily, per 1,000 lb. animal for 5 days. Early treatment is essential to possibly prevent death or abortion. Treatment to eliminate the carrier state is similar. Stalheim reported that a single intramuscular injection of dihydrostreptomycin at the dose level of 25 mg per kg, about 8 to 15 gms of a commercial preparation of dihydrostreptomycin for a 500 to 1,000 pound bovine or porcine animal, would eliminate the renal carrier state. In cases of hemoglobinuria and anemia, blood transfusions and supportive therapy may also be indicated but the prognosis in severe cases is poor, Galton, Blood and Henderson.

Vibriosis due to **Vibrio fetus venerealis** is an occasional cause for abortion with a 2 to 10 percent incidence in susceptible herds. Vibriosis is a venereal disease that can be transmitted at coitus. Older bulls may be chronically infected. The organism may be present and infective in improperly treated semen. With widespread artificial insemination using antibiotic-treated semen, abortions due to **V. fetus** are presently uncommon in dairy areas. Occasional sporadic abortions due to **V. fetus intestinalis** occur in cattle. Because vibriosis in cattle is more closely associated with infertility and early embryonic deaths this disease will be discussed in Chapter XIII on Infertility in Cattle.

Listeriosis is caused by **Listeria monocytogenes** which is usually a gram-positive slightly motile rod or coccoid organism with a wide host range among mammals and birds throughout the world. Although infection with Listeria is frequent, the occurrence of clinical disease is uncommon. Numerous antigenic serotypes are recognized. **L. monocytogenes** is widespread in nature and is resistant to adverse environmental factors as it can be found in moist or dry soil, bedding, fecal material and secretions and tissues of normal and diseased animals. It has been found in silage and actually propagates in poor quality silage with a high pH, Gray, Blenden et al.. The organisms can penetrate the intact mucous membrane of the respiratory or alimentary tracts producing a transient rise in body temperature due to a bacteremia. A latent infection in various organs may then be established although clinical signs are uncommon and these carrier animals may spread the organism for a long period in their nasal secretions and feces. Sudden changes in management or feeding practices inducing stress and lowered resistance are often associated with outbreaks of clinical cases of listeriosis. A close relationship between silage feeding and the incidence of this disease is frequently observed.

Three clinical forms of listeriosis are observed: **the septicemic form** affecting young perinatal animals and humans and characterized by the early death of the newborn with hepatic lesions, gastroenteritis and meningitis, Gray et al.; **the encephalitic form** affecting relatively mature animals, especially ruminants and swine with a meningoencephalitis; and **the reproductive** form, especially in ruminants and humans, characterized by abortion the last trimester of gestation without clinical illness. The above forms usually occur independently but rarely the forms may be observed together in the same outbreak. Young reported that in cattle aborting from the 7th to 9th month of gestation the fetus was well-preserved with few if any lesions in the fetal organs. Retained placenta, metritis and dystocia were commonly observed. If fetal death occurred before the 7th month the fetus was often retained **in utero** for up to 5 days before expulsion, autolysis of the fetus was advanced and retained placenta and metritis were not uncommon. In women infection due to Listeria apparently persists and may result in habitual abortion, Seeliger, and Banner et al.. Osebold et al. has reported recurrent bovine abortions each year on some farms and even in the same animal.

Sporadic bovine abortions due to Listeria are seen most frequently but occasionally herd outbreaks may occur with a 5 to 15 percent, and rarely higher, incidence, Young, Osebold et al., and Young and Firehammer. Fetuses are usually expelled dead but a few calves may be weak at birth and die shortly thereafter. A history of the introduction of carrier animals from affected herds, or a recent change to silage feeding, or some severe stress may be associated with an outbreak. Dennis cited Dijkstra in reporting that Listeria were isolated from the feces in 25 percent and from the milk in 16 percent of the cattle aborting due to listeriosis. The healthy carrier animal may be a latent and important reservoir of infection. Listeria infection may pass between different species. There are no suggestive or pathognomonic lesions of listeriosis in aborted fetuses and membranes. The diagnosis is based on the isolation and identification of the organism which may be difficult.

Fetuses should be collected, chilled and cultured promptly. Young and Osebold et al. recommended taking a large volume of tissue from the fetus, preferredly the liver and thoroughly macerating and emulsifying it in a nutrient broth. After inoculating bacteriologic media, the emulsion should be stored at 4° C. and recultured repeatedly especially if listeriosis is suspected. This latter procedure is important for the recovery of **Listeria monocytogenes.** In most of their cases the organism was recovered on reculture within 20 days of storage but sometimes recovery occurred only after 6 months of storage. A rapid method for the isolation of Listeria by inoculating 20 day old mice intracerebrally with suspect material was described by March. Osebold et al. recovered listeria occasionally from the exudate in the genital tract taken shortly after abortion, the placentomes, the spleen, the brain, the stomach and the kidneys of aborted fetuses. In fetuses that have undergone little autolysis small pin-point yellow foci of necrosis may be observed in the liver and spleen, Jubb and Kennedy and Osebold et al. In experimental aborting cattle, Listeria were recovered from the genital tract for about 10 days after abortion, and from body tissues at slaughter 25 to 36 days after abortion, Osebold et al.. The immunofluorescent methods for the detection of Listeria in fetal and maternal tissues as described for sheep may be of diagnostic value in cattle, Smith et al..

Osebold et al. also reported a rise in the agglutinin titer in affected animals based on the somatic agglutination tests conducted on blood samples taken at the time of abortion and 60 to 90 days later, and on the basis of the antigen-fixation test. They showed this infection to be widespread in animals in affected herds. In the experimental cattle the antibody titers reached a peak at the time of abortion and dropped rapidly within the next 30 days. Further work is necessary to develop serologic tests to the stage where they are precise enough for routine diagnostic application.

Therapy or treatment of herds with abortions due to Listeria would include the cessation of silage feeding if this was occurring and controlling other factors that might lower the resistance of the cattle. Hygiene and sanitation practices consisting of segregation of aborting cattle and destruction of aborted fetuses and membranes should be followed. Antibiotic therapy with large doses of the tetracyclines or penicillin and streptomycin for four to five days might be attempted in valuable animals. In herds where the disease tends to recur the use of an autogenous bacterin might prove of value, Eveleth et al.. No commercial bacterin is available.

Tuberculosis caused by **Mycobacterium bovis** is present worldwide in cattle and is of major importance in dairy cattle that are closely housed or pastured in limited areas. In the past 30 years tuberculosis in cattle has been reduced to a very low level in the U.S. and outbreaks of tuberculosis, particularly advanced cases in which the genital organs may be involved are extremely rare. In other countries where tuberculosis is still common it may be a fairly common cause of metritis, salpingitis, infertility and recurring abortion. Tuberculosis due to **M. bovis** may also occur in man, goats, pigs, deer and occasionally other wild animals. The infected animal may spread the disease organisms in excreted air, sputum, feces, milk, urine, semen and genital tract discharges. Susceptible animals either ingest or inhale the infective organisms. Moisture favors the survival of the organism for long periods outside the body. Occasionally cows may become infected at coitus with a bull with lesions of the prepuce and penis, accessory glands or testes, Williams, or by intrauterine insemination of infective semen, Bartlett, Roumy. The bull may on occasions be only a carrier or contact spreader between an infected cow with a tubercular genital discharge and a susceptible cow. Uterine tuberculosis however is uncommon but may result from, coitus with an infected bull, intrauterine insemination with infective semen, by continuity from peritoneal tuberculosis, or probably most often by hematogenous spread. In tuberculous metritis infertility is frequent and recurrent abortion or the birth of a tubercular calf that dies a short while later may occur. Retained placenta and lesions in the placenta similar to those of brucellosis may occur and a chronic "curdled milk" type of uterine exudate that persists is often observed in this form of tuberculosis, Blood and Henderson. The bilateral granulomatous uterine lesions, salpingitis and adhesions may be palpated per rectum in the nonpregnant cow or cow in early pregnancy.

Infected animals should be eliminated and the disease eradicated in the herd and geographical area if possible. The intradermal tuberculin test applied regularly with the removal and salughter of reactors has been used quite successfully in the U.S. to greatly reduce the incidence of the disease. False positive reactions to this test may occur due to other mycobacteria. In cases of uterine tuberculosis the disease may be so advanced that no reaction will be elicited on the intradermal tuberculin test, Williams. In isolated cases of uterine infections, culture of the fetus, the fetal membranes and the genital discharges usually reveal the organism. If cases of this type are present in a herd usually other cases of generalized pulmonary or intestinal types are present also.

Miscellaneous bacterial infections associated with sporadic bovine abortions include the so-called "wound" infection organisms that are probably carried to the pregnant uterus by the blood stream, Roberts. These organisms probably originate in infectious processes such as: traumatic gastritis, liver abscesses, ulcers of the stomach or intestine, abscesses in the lung, foot rot, acute mastitis, and pneumonia. These organisms include: streptococci; diplococci, Van Ulsen; staphylococci; **E. coli; Alcaligenes fecalis; Pseudomonas aeruginosa; Corynebactium pyogenes, Erysipelothrix insidiosa; Hemophilus, Firehammer; and Spherophorus necrophorus, Van Ulsen. Vibrio fetus intestinalis,** a common cause of abortion in sheep, only occasionally causes sporadic abortion in cattle, Jubb and Kennedy. This ovine strain of vibrio is not very pathogenic when introduced into the genital tract of susceptible nonpregnant heifers. The infection was transitory, Wagner et al.. **Mycobacterium avium** has been reported by Plum and Burgisser and Schneider as a cause of sporadic abortions in cattle that are housed with infected chickens. In this latter disease small granulomatous lesions develop in the endometrium and placenta and recurrent abortions may occur as with **M. bovis.**

Sporadic abortions are infrequently associated with febrile septemic bovine diseases such as pasteurellosis due to **Pastuerella multocida,** salmonellosis due to **Salmonella paratyphi B, S. dublin,** Van Ulsen, actinomycetes (**Nocardia asteroides**) and anthrax. O'Berry and coworkers, Al-Aubaidi and Fabricant and Carmichael have reported recovering mycoplasma or PPLO from aborted bovine fetuses. Kundsin has reported finding mycoplasma in the fetal membranes of spontaneous abortions in women. To illustrate the ability of a variety of organisms to cause abortion in cattle by the hematogenous route, the author observed a pregnant cow given **Streptococcus agalactiae,** an organism not considered pathogenic outside the bovine udder, intravenously to produce a high level of immunity. Ten days later the cow aborted and a pure culture of the organism was recovered from the fetal organs. If mixed cultures of organisms are obtained from the aborted fetus the possibility of contamination of the fetus following death is likely.

Braude, and Osborne reported on the ability of the potent endotoxin of gram negative organisms to cause abortions in cows, ewes, sows and goats. Dennis concurred in this observation and believed that endotoxins were the cause of some abortions in animals rather than the elevated body temperatures that frequently accompany septicemic infections with gram-negative organisms. Dennis indicated that endotoxin was abortifacient due to its vasomotor and thrombotic effects especially in the latter half of gestation. The vasomotor effects were probably due to the release of serotonin and the production of a Schwartzman reaction. Endotoxin abortion probably occurs in brucellosis, salmonella, vibrio and coliform infections. On some instances it may be associated only with an enteritis and without uterine infection.

Viral Causes of Abortion in Cattle

Infectious bovine rhinotracheitis ("red nose") and infectious pustular vulvovaginitis (I.B.R.-I.P.V.) virus is a common cause of abortion in cattle in the U.S. and in other countries. This is a Herpes virus and has many features similar to rhinopneumonitis virus, a Herpes virus in horses, and **Herpes simplex** in humans. This disease of cattle has received much study over the past 10 years. Other domestic animals are not susceptible to this virus but it has been reported in mule deer, Chow and Davis. I.B.R.-I.P.V. virus is widely distributed over the world and in the U.S. The clinical morbidity may vary from 10 to 100 percent in a herd. The mortality is generally under 10 percent with only occasional deaths in adult animals in uncomplicated outbreaks. Deaths in prenatal fetuses and neonatal calves may be high. Although a generalized viremia develops in nearly all I.B.R.-I.P.V. infections, localized manifestations of the disease occur that confuse the diagnosis.

The varied clinical forms of this disease include: (1) The **upper respiratory form** or "red nose" which is most commonly seen in cattle feed lots and dairy herds in the Fall and Winter months and is characterized by fever of 104°–107° F., anorexia, depression, reddened nasal mucous membranes and nasal discharge, pustules and ulcers in the mucosa of the nose, pharynx and trachea, infrequent coughing, and a drop in milk production lasting 2 to 7 days except in severe cases in which secondary tracheitis and pneumonia may occur. (2) The **conjunctival form** which exhibits marked lacrimation changing to a mucopurulent profuse discharge from the eye along with the septicemic signs exhibited in (1). The conjunctiva is reddened and swollen and contains necrotic pustules and ulcers, Albinanti and Plumer. (3) The **neonatal digestive form** in young calves from birth to 2 to 3 weeks of age is associated with a high mortality and is characterized by severe signs of septicemia resembling that associated with **E. coli** but exhibiting necrotic lesions in the mouth, pharynx, larynx, esophagus and forestomachs with diarrhea and death within 1 to 3 days, Van Kruiningen and Bartholomew. (4) The **meningo-encephalitic form** is seen occasionally in young cattle 4 to 10 months of age and is characterized by dullness, incoordination, tremors, amaurosis, opisthotonus, coma and death within 3 to 4 days, French. (5) The **vulvovaginal form** is characterized as in the others by signs of a generalized septicemia but also pustules and ulcers of the vaginal and vulvar mucosa especially in the region of the lymphoid follicles with swelling and a purulent discharge, Kendrick et al.. (See Figure 61) This form of the disease was previously called coital vesicular exanthema or Blaschenausschlag. Occasionally in this form small abscesses beneath the mucous membrane are observed, McEntee. The respiratory form of the disease is rarely observed in outbreaks of this genital form, Kahrs and Smith. (6) The **preputial form** in bulls is characterized by pustules and ulceration of the penis and prepuce, Studdert et al. IBR in bulls usually causes severe degenerative changes of the seminiferous epithelium and a period of infertility or sterility lasting up to 3 to 4 months. (7) The **prenatal or abortive** form of the disease is characterized by infection and intrauterine death of the fetus and abortion 2 to 5 or more days later, Kendrick and Straub. Abortions may occur in all three trimesters of gestation according to Owen et al. but are most common from midgestation to term. The incidence of abortion in a herd will vary from 5 to over 60 percent with an average of 5 to 20 percent depending on the virulence of the organism and the numbers of susceptible cows in advanced pregnancy, Pierson and Vair. Abortions are most common following the respiratory and conjuctival forms and rarely occur in cases of infectious pustular vulvovaginitis. Retention of the placenta occurs in about 50 percent of the abortions. (8) The **intrauterine form** of the disease caused a necrotizing endometritis when I.B.R.-I.P.V. virus was present in semen at the time of artificial insemination. This resulted in an erect, edematous uterus and a short estrous cycle of 9 to 15 days in length. Conception did not occur in 11 of 12 heifers inseminated with semen containing virus but did occur at the next estrus when noninfected semen was used, Kendrick and McEntee. Guss reported a herd outbreak of I.B.R.-I.P.V. where strong evidence indicated the infection was introduced by frozen semen shipped from another state. Spradbrow recovered I.B.R.-I.P.V. virus from three ampules of frozen semen from a single collection of one bull. Frozen semen ampules from 39 other bulls from 3 AI centers were negative for this virus. The author has received a number of reports from veterinarians that a period of infertility lasting about 3 to 4 weeks followed the vaccination of heifers with I.B.R. vaccine.

As noted above all forms are characterized by a viremic and septicemic phase with an elevated temperature, depression, and anorexia lasting from 2 to 10 days but in many animals these signs may be subclinical. In general if one form appears on a farm the other forms are seldom observed but conjunctivitis is seen occasionally, and meningo-encephalitis on rare occasions terminally, with the upper respiratory form. The author has observed a few outbreaks of the upper respiratory form with concurrent vulvovaginal lesions.

Abortions may occur from 2 weeks to 2 to 3 months after any form of the disease in pregnant animals but is only rarely observed in the vulvovaginal form. Although septicemic signs are seen with the I.P.V. form of the disease, viremia may not occur as with the respiratory or conjunctival forms of the disease, therefore abortions do not follow, Mc Kercher.

Since abortion is not associated with genital form of the disease in cattle and since in humans the oral and genital forms of Herpes viruses are serologically distinct, some have speculated that the genital and respiratory forms might also be different in cattle. However, Bowling et al. could find no serological or other differences between viruses recovered from the two sites in cattle.

McKercher and Wada and Gratzek et al. have reported that the virus is carried in the blood on the leucocytes and abortions occurred 18 to 64 days after inoculation of the virus. I.B.R.-I.P.V. virus may cause infection following intranasal, conjunctival, intravaginal, preputial, oral, intrauterine, and intramammary as well as subcutaneous, intramuscular or intravenous inoculation. The site of inoculation determines the form of the disease produced especially in the first four modes of administration. The incubation period for viremia and the acute manifestations of the disease is 1 to 5 days experimentally and may range from 3 to 10 or 20 days naturally. Kendrick and Straub have shown that the I.B.R.-I.P.V. virus from the dam's blood stream during viremia, 2 to 10 days postinoculation, entered the cotyleden but produced no local inflammatory reaction or spread of virus. The viremia terminated with the development of antibodies detectable in the blood. After a week to 2 months the virus, protected from the maternal antibody by its location in the cotyledon, infected the fetus and caused its death within about 24 hours.

Signs of impending abortion are usually not observed. Aborted fetuses are invariably expelled dead with a degree of autolysis. Premature births or living infected fetuses or calves at term have not been reported. Calves normal at birth may become infected and die in 24 to 48 hours with I.B.R.-I.P.V. viral infection. The lesions described in aborted fetuses may be of diagnostic value. There is no evidence of uterine disease. The placenta shows autolytic nondistinctive lesions characterized by edema and the presence of a yellow, brown amniotic fluid. Autolysis of the fetus is always present to a varying degree with reddish-brown subcutaneous edema and dark red watery fluid in the body cavities. Hemorrhages and petechiae are often widespread in the fetus.

Microscopically characteristic lesions of focal necrosis in the liver, lymph glands, kidneys, other organs and placenta are usually observed. The most striking gross changes occur in the kidneys which are usually surrounded by a marked hemorrhagic edema. A severe hemorrhagic necrosis is confined largely to the cortex and is often so severe that the medulla and part of the cortex are floating in dark red fluid. Pin-point necrotic, white foci may be observed in the adrenal glands, McEntee. Intranuclear inclusion bodies are seen infrequently in these autolysed fetuses, Kendrick and Straub and Kennedy and Richards. During the acute state of illness in cattle virus may be recovered from the nasal cavity, the vagina, the conjunctiva and the prepuce in the upper respiratory, the vulvovaginal, the conjunctival and the preputial forms, respectively. Usually within 10 to 26 days after the acute illness the virus disappears.

Culture of the fetal organs and fluids and especially the fetal cotyledon may recover the I.B.R.-I.P.V. virus, Owen and coworkers (1968). In many cases the virus cannot be recovered because of the advanced autolysis of tissues in the fetus. However as Kendrick and Straub have pointed out the fetal cotyledon may contain a high level of virus and because of its close proximity to the maternal circulation, autolysis of the fetal placenta and chorion are delayed. Both the above authors and Snowden have reported recovering I.B.R.-I.P.V. virus from a cotyledon following the birth of a normal calf. Snowden and Saxegaard have shown that in bulls the disease may be highly subclinical and require a number of passages for recovery and the infection may persist for over 360 days. The former worker recovered I.B.R.-I.P.V. virus intermittently from the vagina and from the nasal cavity of infected heifers for 578 and 510 days, respectively. This prolonged intermittent appearance of the virus even though antibody titers were present in the blood of the animal is characteristic of Herpes virus infections and may explain the frequent reoccurrence of the clinical disease in the field.

Serological testing using the serum-neutralization test is best conducted on double serum samples taken at the time of the acute illness, when most samples are negative, and again 2 to 6 weeks later. In cases of abortion the serum titers are usually elevated in the dam at the time of the abortion but a second sample taken two or three weeks after abortion may reveal a rising titer. In a herd outbreak of I.B.R.-I.P.V., samples might be taken of representative cattle that are normal, recovered, aborting or acutely ill. Samples should be taken in as near sterile a manner as possible in sterile vacuum vials so the serum-neutralization test, utilizing tissue cultures will be satisfactory. From reports by McKercher and Wada, Snowden, Kendrick and Staub, Saxegaard, and Kahrs and Baker antibody response following the various forms of the disease, experimental intravenous or intramuscular inoculations and vaccination is variable. It appears the greatest and most rapid antibody response occurs after abortion and the intravenous and intramuscular administration of virulent I.B.R.-I.P.V. virus. The antibody response is the slowest and poorest after the vulvovaginal and the preputial forms of the disease when the rise in titer may be slow and extend in the latter over 8 months. After vaccination with a number of commercial vaccines some titers did not develop until 4 to 30 months after vaccination. In 9 vaccinated calves, 22 percent showed titers at 3 weeks, 44 percent at 6 weeks and 56 percent at 36 weeks after inoculation. There was evidence that once serum titers developed that fluctuations occurred due to anamnestic responses following recrudescence of virus multiplication but titers remained for at least 2 to 3 years or more. Thus it was evident from serologic studies that I.B.R.-I.P V. virus acts like **Herpes simplex** in humans and rhinopheumomitis virus in horses where clinical lesions with multiplication of the virus may develop even when antibodies are present in the blood stream. Factors of stress that lower resistance appear favorable for the reappearance of the I.B.R.-I.P.V. virus in body secretions. Obviously more work and study is necessary to further clarify the pathogenesis of this disease.

Gratzek et al. and Peter et al. have reported that the I.B.R.-I.P.V. virus tends to localize in lymphoid tissue. Vulvar scrapings from cattle affected with the vulvovaginal form of I.B.R.-I.P.V. can be examined by means of the fluorescent antibody technique for the presence of virus. Kendrick and coworkers reported that this virus could be demonstrated in the placentome of infected cows 3 days after the death of the fetus with the fluorescent antibody technique. This technique could also be used to diagnose the presence of virus in other infected tissues of the adult or fetal animal.

Control and treatment of I.B.R.-I.P.V., as with other infectious viral diseases, can be assisted by blood testing and isolation of new arrivals into the herd with a second sample taken one to two months later. Any animal with a positive titer should be considered as a potential carrier of the virus. In an outbreak, contact between animals should be kept at a minimum depending upon the facilities available on the farm. In cases involving the vulvovaginal or preputial form of the disease, breeding should be stopped for 3 to 4 weeks. Local oily antibiotic preparations might be applied to the ulcerated mucous membranes of the genital tract in severe cases. In valuable cattle suffering from the respiratory form of the disease, antibiotics are often administered to prevent pneumonia or secondary respiratory complications. In abortions due to I.B.R.-I.P.V. the fetus and its membranes should be destroyed and the cow isolated from other pregnant susceptible cattle for 3 to 4 weeks. If calves on a farm are infected and ill, pregnant cows should be kept from contact with them. If virus-free semen is desired, then I.B.R.-I.P.V. infection of donor bulls must be prevented, Spradbrow.

I.B.R.-I.P.V. vaccines are available either alone or in combination with B.V.D.-M.D. (Bovine virus diarrhea-mucosal disease) virus or parainfluenza virus. These vaccines should be handled carefully and kept refrigerated so as to maintain their potency. **Pregnant cows at any stage of gestation should not be vaccinated with I.B.R.-I.P.V. vaccine.** The incidence of abortion following I.B.R.-I.P.V. vaccination has varied from 0 to 25 percent, in most instances it is under 10 percent. These abortions have occurred at any period of gestation but most commonly the last half of gestation. They usually occur 2 to 10 weeks after vaccination. Abortions may occasionally occur up to 3-1/2 months after vaccination, McFeeley et al.. Gratzek et al. indicated that severe signs of disease with diarrhea often was associated with natural combined I.B.R.-I.P.V. and B.V.D.-M.D. viral infections. It has appeared possible that more severe clinical reactions in adult cattle following vaccination have occurred with the combined vaccines and where other diseases such as salmonellosis or B.V.D. are present and active at the same time as I.B.R.-I.P.V. vaccination. To provide protection against I.B.R.-I.P.V. virus, vaccination is best carried out in heifers at 6 to 8 months of age when a good immunity will develop that will last 3 or more years, Kahrs and Baker. Vaccination if done earlier may be ineffectual because of maternal colostral antibodies present in calves getting colostrum from immune dams. In order to evaluate the effectiveness of a vaccine the titer of blood samples taken at the time of vaccination should be compared with the titers of samples taken 8 to 10 or more weeks later. From the above reports the evidence to support the yearly vaccination of cattle against I.B.R.-I.P.V. infection requires more evaluation. Kahrs and Baker, and Chow reported little if any spread of attenuated I.B.R.-I.P.V. virus from vaccinated to nonvaccinated susceptible cattle.

Epizootic Bovine Abortion (E.B.A.) is caused by an agent of the psittacosis lymphogranuloma, **Chlamydia** or **Migawanella** group of organisms, Storz et al. (1960). Although the organisms in this group are considered viruses they differ from most viruses in that they are susceptible to antibiotics, they grow well in the yolk sac of chick embryos, and they have developmental cycles during which large elementary bodies are formed. Howarth and coworkers in 1956 called this disease, that had been observed in California since 1923, epizootic bovine abortion (E.B.A.) because it occurred mostly in first calf heifers or newly introduced cattle during the months of July through October because of breeding practices in beef herds in the foothills adjacent to the Sacramento and San Joaquin valleys. Fetuses were expelled during the 6th to 8th months of gestation. The incidence of abortion would reach 30 to 40 percent in some herds with occasionally up to 75 percent or more of susceptible females aborting. In a susceptible herd animals of all ages would abort but thereafter abortion was largely limited to heifers. In recent years Storz et al. has reported the disease in the Intermountain region in both the epizootic and sporadic forms and as occurring in February and March in beef herds and throughout the year in dairy herds. McEntee and coworkers in New York State have tentatively diagnosed rare sporadic cases of this type of abortion in dairy cattle from its characteristic lesions although the causative agent has not been isolated. The disease has been described in central and southern Europe, Schoop and Kauker. Storz and McKercher et al. have reported on the great similarity between E.B.A. and enzootic abortion of ewes or E.A.E. which is due to the same, or very similar, agent.

Calves infected P.L. organisms recovered from ovine polyarthritis, ovine abortion and cases of sporadic bovine encephalomyelitis (SBE) had similar lesions, Harshfield. This agent has also been isolated from bulls affected with the seminal vesiculitis syndrome. Thus the present name of the disease may be a misnomer because it is not limited to epizootic outbreaks and it may cause abortion and possibly other diseases in both cattle and sheep.

Outbreaks of E.B.A. occur suddenly without premonitory signs of illness or impending abortion. The disease primarily affects the fetus as there is no clinical evidence of infection in the cow. Intravenous inoculation of the agent causes abortion 3 to 6 weeks later, intramuscular inoculation 3 months later and subcutaneous inoculation 4 to 4-1/2 months later. Abortions occur from the fourth month of gestation to term but most commonly the 7th, 8th, and 9th months. Some fetuses were expelled dead at term or calves were born alive and weak and succumbed later. About 50 percent of aborting cows had retained placentae and the subsequent fertility of the cows was impaired at least for a number of months, Storz, McKercher. Once a cow aborted an immunity was apparently produced and only occasionally did cows abort a second time due to this P.L. agent. Aborted fetuses were clean, fresh and pale or anemic and death had apparently occurred during delivery or shortly thereafter, Kennedy et al.. Since fresh fetuses with no autolysis are seen in relatively few forms of abortion in animals for example E.B.A. in cattle and equine herpesvirus 1 in horses, the author would hesitantly speculate that the adrenals of these fetuses might be hyperplastic thus causing the onset of parturition or abortion prior to the death of the fetus. (See section on hormonal causes of abortion).

Aborted fetuses exhibited characteristic lesions of anemia and extensive petechial hemorrhages of the conjunctival and oral mucosa and skin. The subcutaneous tissues were edematous especially those of the head. Straw-colored fluid was usually present in the body cavities. The most striking lesion seen in 50 to 60 percent of E.B.A. abortions is the swollen coarsely nodular yellow-colored liver that develops secondary to chronic vascular lesions and chronic passive congestion. (See Figure 62) Petechial hemorrhages were present in most organs and tissues. Nearly all the lymph glands were enlarged and edematous. The basic histological change of this disease was a granulomatous inflammatory process or a diffuse or focal reticulo-endothelial hyperplasia that irregularly involved all organs. Storz reported that fetuses aborted before the 7th month usually do not have the above typical lesions. The fetal membranes in cases of E.B.A. abortion are usually edematous but are not of diagnostic value unless the entire placenta was expelled in the later stages of gestation when the intercotyledonary tissue of the apices of the placenta was often tough, leathery and reddish-white in color and the edges of the cotyledons contained small round focal areas of necrosis, Storz.

The recovery of the P.L. viral agent from aborted bovine fetuses is more difficult than from aborted ovine fetuses probably because of fewer organisms present due to the chronic disease process in the bovine fetus together with the generalized reaction present indicative of an active defense response. Cultures into the yolk sacs of chicken embryos should be made from any or all organs and the placenta and even then many fetuses yield negative results. If the fetus is positive the organism is usually recovered from only one or two organs. The E.B.A. and E.A.E. agents have similar biological and pathogenic properties and share common specific antigens. Pregnant cows aborted after being inoculated with E.A.E. agent and pregnant sheep aborted after inoculation with the E.B.A. agent, Storz.

The modes of transmission, the reservoirs of the agents or other epidemiological aspects of E.B.A., and E.A.E., have not been clarified. The two diseases occur independently and an interchange of infection between cattle and sheep is probably of minor importance. In sheep the present evidence incriminates the infected ewe as the source of infection. Some have indicated that in cattle an arthropod vector may carry the infection but this is doubtful. Although the ram does not seem to play a role in the transmission of the P.L. agent in sheep, Storz et al. (1968) reported orchitis in two rams given a P.L. agent isolated from polyarthritic lambs. They noted that McKercher and coworkers recovered a P.L. agent from rams with epididymitis. Venereal transmission may possibly play a role in cattle since the above workers have recovered a P.L. agent, similar to that of E.B.A., from the semen and epididymis of young bulls with the seminal vesiculitis syndrome. It has not been proven that the disease can be transmitted at coitus, McKercher. Oral or nasal exposure to the viral agent has not produced disease. The relation of E.B.A. to other common P.L. agents in the intestinal tract has not been investigated. Lincoln et al. produced E.B.A. in 23 heifers by inoculating the P.L. agent intravenously. Abortions occurred in 12 heifers from 5 to 49 days after the inoculation. All heifers had C.F. antibodies in their blood serum before inoculation probably due to P.L. agents in the intestine. The inoculated agent persisted only in the pregnant uterus.

The complement fixation test may be of diagnostic value on paired serum samples taken at the time of abortion and 2 to 3 weeks later if a rising titer is observed. This may be used as a test on an animal being introduced into a herd to see if it has been exposed to a P.L. agent. If there is no titer it does not mean the animal is free from P.L. infection and high reactions are found frequently in many herds, Storz.

At present there is little that can be done to control the disease. Since abortion produces an immunity to future natural infection in most animals but not a good immunity to a challenge infection, various vaccines have been tried without success. The apparent success of the oil-adjuvant vaccine used in England for E.A.E. offers a possible hope that a satisfactory vaccine for this cattle disease may be developed. However, recent work by McKercher et al. with various types of vaccines for E.B.A. has been discouraging since the vaccines produced good antibody levels in blood but immunized animals were more susceptible to a challenge infection and had a higher abortion rate than the controls. More study is needed on the epidemiologic factors in the transmission of this disease. At this time hygiene, sanitation and isolation procedures are indicated but their scientific application is not at hand. A recent report by McKercher (1969) offered a highly promising method for the possible control of this type of abortion. Seventeen pregnant heifers were fed 2.5 to 5 gms chlortetracycline in 2 pounds of pelletted alfalfa daily and challenged with the E.B.A. organism. Two of the treated heifers that did not consume the pellets and 4 of 5 untreated challenged heifers aborted. The remaining 15 treated heifers did not abort. Thus feeding "high risk" cattle 2 gms of chlortetracycline daily may prove a satisfactory way to control this disease.

Miscellaneous Viral or Rickettsial Infections associated with bovine abortions have been reported. Those viral diseases not present in the U.S. include **foot and mouth disease, rinderpest, Rift Valley fever** and **bovine infections petechial fever,** U.S. Livestock Sanitary Assoc..

Bovine virus diarrhea-mucosal disease (B.V.D.-M.D.) virus was reported as a cause of abortion in over 20 percent of the cows from 2 to 9 months of gestation in 5 herds with severely affected cattle, Olafson et al. (1946), Kahrs and Ward. Since 1946 few outbreaks have been recorded in N.Y. State and the clinical disease has been largely limited to a few young unbred heifers, 6 to 18 months of age, where the outcome is uniformly fatal. Within the past year Kahrs and coworkers have studied two herds having an epizootic disease characterized by fever, depression, some anorexia and diarrhea in older lactating cattle. In one herd good circumstantial evidence indicated the disease was due to virus diarrhea and in the other herd serologic evidence confirmed the cause to be B.V.D.-M.D. virus. In the first herd 39 pregnancies terminated with 24 normal parturitions, 11 or 28% abortions, 2 early neonatal deaths and 2 live ataxic calves with cerebellar hypoplasia. In the second herd, 5 or 20%, abortions occurred in 25 pregnant cows, 1 calf was "stillborn" and 2 calves had cerebellar hypoplasia. Abortions occurred 1 to 5 months or more after the initial epizootic and in the latter half of gestation. A few fetuses showed evidence of death and delayed expulsion from the uterus. Six months after the time of infection in the first herd, 97 percent of the animals had B.V.D.-M.D. antibody in their serums. Dual I.B.R.-I.P.V. and B.V.D.-M.D. infections exhibit severe signs of disease, Gratzek et al.. Gillespie et al. reported on the recovery of B.V.D.-M.D. virus from 2 aborted bovine fetuses 7 and 8 months of age. They cited the experimental evidence that incriminated B.V.D.-M.D. virus as a probable cause of sporadic abortions. Ward et al. infected 11 susceptible heifers at 5 to 7 months of gestation with this virus recovered from an aborted fetus. One heifer calved prematurely, 3 calves had mild ulcerative mucosal lesions at birth referrable to an intrauterine infection including one calf with cerebellar hypoplasia. Thus fetal lesions may resemble lesions seen in the mouth and digestive tract in older animals with the acute form of the disease, Jubb and Kennedy. All calves in the above experiment had active B.V.D.-M.D. titers in their serum at birth and before colostrum ingestion. These titers persisted for over 6 months. Serological surveys using serum neutralization tests to determine the incidence of antibody titers for the B.V.D.-M.D. agent in the cattle population have revealed an incidence of 50 to 70 percent B.V.D.-M.D. reactors in the U.S. and 20 to 50 percent in Europe, Kahrs et al. and Mills and Luginbuhl. Thus cattle are the main reservoir of infection and most infections are inapparent as the clinical form of the disease is seldom observed. It is obvious, because of the widespread presence of this virus and serologic reactions in cattle, that a rise in titer or a titer going from negative to positive as determined by paired samples is necessary for a possible or probable diagnosis of B.V.D.-M.D. abortion. Langer and Hillman reported that of 47 paired blood samples taken from cows at the time of abortion and two to three weeks later 15 percent showed a rise in titer of B.V.D.-M.D. antibodies. According to Kahrs et al. abortions were most common when susceptible cows were infected the first half of pregnancy. Occasional mummified fetuses were observed. After a natural infection a lifelong solid immunity developed.

Commercial vaccines are available that induce a permanent immunity if administered to calves at 9 to 10 months of age. Vaccination at an earlier age may be ineffective because of a passive immunity induced by the maternal colostral antibodies, Kahrs and Baker. Vaccination during pregnancy should be avoided. Dual I.B.R.-I.P.V. and B.V.D.-M.D. vaccines tend to produce moderate to marked postvaccination reactions especially in lactating cows.

Myxovirus parainfluenza 3 was recovered from an aborted bovine fetus and produced abortion in a pregnant cow 9 days after intrafetal inoculation, Satter et al.. Signs of fetal septicemia with petechial hemorrhages were observed. Abortions have not been produced by virus inoculated by natural means. This virus is apparently widespread in cattle as serological studies have revealed it to be present in 48 percent of the cows in N.Y. State, Kahrs et al.. Viruses such as B.V.D.-M.D. and bovine parainfluenza 3 are present so commonly in cattle that occasional isolations from fetuses might be accidental or in association with another agent that caused the abortion.

Wilson et al. have reported on a bovine strain of **tick-borne fever** due to a Rickettsia-like organism seen in leukocytes that caused abortion in cattle in Ireland and Scotland. **Pseudorabies** virus may occasionally cause abortion in cattle as will the virus of **malignant catarrhal fever. Bluetongue** virus has also been reported as a cause of abortion in cattle, Bowne et al.. Bluetongue is fairly widespread in the United States. Outbreaks of so-called "mycotic stomatitis" observed in recent years in the midwest and east may be epizootics of bluetongue in cattle, Olafson. White-tailed deer are highly susceptible to the bluetongue virus and may be a natural host, Thomas and Trainer. Further work is needed on this disease in cattle.

Mycotic or Fungal Causes of Abortion

Almost all mycotic bovine abortions are caused by two groups of fungi. About 60 to 80 percent are caused by **Aspergillus** spp. and most of these are **Aspergillus fumigatus.** The **Mucorales** order of fungi are responsible for most of the remainder of mycotic abortions. The three most common genera of this latter order causing abortion are **Absidia, Mucor** and **Rhizopus** in descending order of frequency. The few remaining are due to other types of fungus and rarely yeasts, Winter, Austwick and Venn, Bendixen and Plum, Hillman. The incidence of bovine mycotic abortion varied from 0.5 to 16 percent of all bovine abortions. The higher incidence is noted in areas where brucellosis and vibriosis have been controlled. Most mycotic abortions are sporadic but the author has observed a number of herds having 3 to 5 abortions, up to 5 to 10 percent of the herd, in a winter season.

Aspergillus and mucor molds are ubiguitous in nature and are usually saprophytic. Occasionally they may localize in the body producing serious systemic diseases. The above authors as well as Hugh-Jones and Austwick and others have reported the highest incidence of mycotic abortion in the winter months often following a wet summer season when the hay and straw was baled while damp and mold developed. Molds apparently are taken into the body by inhalation into the lungs or by ingestion. The mold spores are then carried to the placenta in the bloodstream from lesions in the respiratory tract or ulcers, mycotic rumenitis or other lesions of the digestive tract. This results in a slowly developing fungal placentitis and interference with the nutrition of the fetus and fetal death and abortion after a period of a number of weeks or months. Abortion occurred about 35 days after the intravenous inoculation of spores of **Aspergillus fumigatus,** Hillman. Most mycotic abortions occur about the 5th through the 7th month of gestation but may occur from the fourth month to term. The fetus is usually expelled dead with a degree of autolysis present but in some cases premature or full term calves are alive but weak at birth and die shortly thereafter. Mycotic infections could not be established by the intrauterine infusion of **Aspergillus fumigatus** spores at the time of insemination at estrus. The nongravid uterus appeared quite resistant to mycotic infection, Hillman.

Mycotic abortion is usually characterized by marked changes in the fetal membranes resembling, but much more pronounced than, those due to **Br. abortus, V. fetus** and the P.L. agent. The chorion is thick, edematous, leathery, and necrotic. The primary lesions are in the placentomes. Both the maternal caruncle and fetal cotyledon are very large, swollen, edematous, and necrotic. The enlarged cotyledons may be firmly incarcerated and resist detachment for 8 to 10 days or more after abortion. The placentomes may then become completely detached due to severe necrosis involving the cotyledons, caruncles, and the caruncular stalks. In a few instances these necrotic structures remain in the uterus for several months after abortion or normal birth and retained placenta, and resemble a macerating fetus. The cow must often be sold as sterile.

The necrotic cotyledons show a dull grey center surrounded by areas of hemorrhage and are firmly attached to the leathery chorion. In the utero-chorionic space is usually some reddish fluid with large flakes of pus. The fungus spreads by extension through the fetal membranes to the fetal fluids. The fetus may be normal in appearance or in about 30 percent of the cases, mold may grow on the skin in patches or plaques that resemble congenital ichthyosis or ringworm, Hillman. (See Figure 63) Straw-colored serous fluid may be present in the fetal tissues or body cavities. In rare instances the liver is enlarged and swollen. The mold can often be recovered from the stomach contents or from the diseased chorion or cotyledons of the placenta. In a few fetuses the lungs are involved with a mycotic bronchopneumonia. The endometrium is as severely involved as is the chorion but even with this severe uterine infection, generalized symptoms of septic metritis are seldom exhibited. Recovery in severe cases may be slow and prolonged or permanent sterility may follow.

The diagnosis is confirmed by microscopic observation of the mold from the placenta or fetus, from histologic examination of the placental or fetal tissues and by culture of the mold on artificial media. In submitting specimens to the laboratory for diagnosis it is imperative to include placental tissues as frequently the placenta is severely affected by mold but the fetus is not infected.

Infectious Protozoal Causes for Bovine Abortion

Trichomoniasis due to **Trichomonas fetus** is a venereal disease characterized as is vibriosis by infertility and early embryonic death. Abortions due to trichomoniasis usually occur during the first trimester or through the fourth month of pregnancy. Abortions after the fifth month of pregnancy are rare. For this reason retained placenta is uncommon in trichomonad abortion. Observed trichomonad abortions are uncommon. The disease is

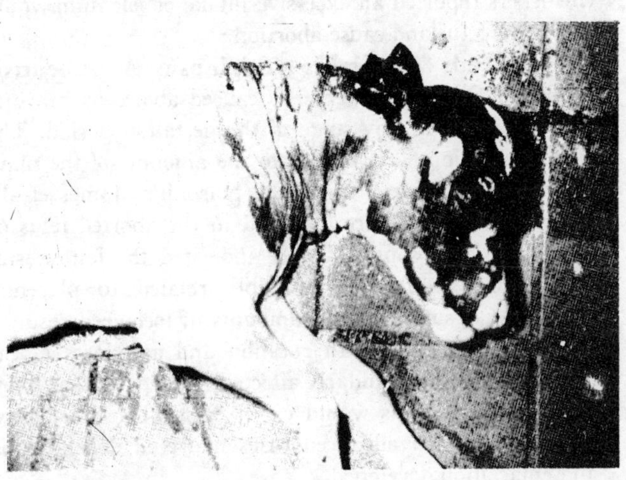

Figure 63. **Aspergillus fumigatus** or mold infection of the skin of an aborted 7-month bovine fetus.

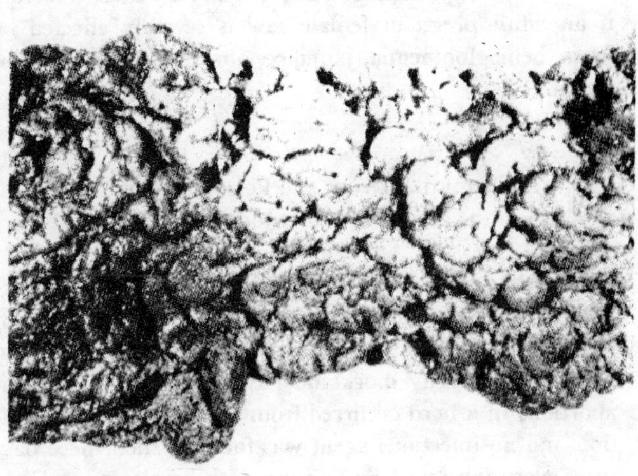

Figure 64. **Aspergillus fumigatus** or mold infection of the equine fetal placenta (courtesy K. McEntee)

Figure 65. Chronic ergot poisoning of a Jersey cow carrying a normal 6-month fetus.

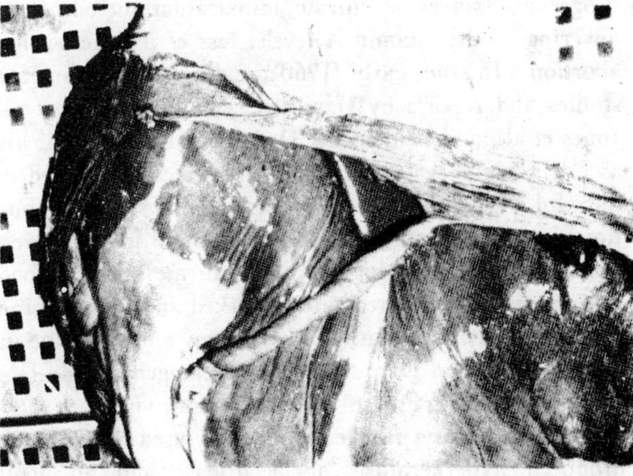

Figure 66. Torsion of the umbilical cord of a 6-month bovine fetal cadaver undergoing early mummification.

fully discussed in Chapter XIII on Infertility in Cattle.

Abortions in cattle due to other protozoal diseases are uncommon but have been described in toxoplasmosis due to **Toxoplasma gondii,** Bruner and Gillespie. Abortion due to toxoplasmosis is common in sheep and humans, Eckerling and coworkers. Dikmans and coworkers recovered **Trypanosoma theileri** from the stomach of an aborted bovine fetus. Rare abortions associated with anaplasmosis due to **Anaplasma marginale** has been reported by Hafez and Gibbons and Boynton. **Globidiosis** or **besnoitiosis** due to **Besnoitia besnoiti** causes a chronic severe dermatitis, loss of condition and abortion in cattle in Africa, Bruner and Gillespie. Blood and Henderson reported that **babesiosis** or piroplasmosis due to **Babesia bigemina** and **argentina** may cause abortion if an adult pregnant female cow is severely affected by fever, hemoglobinemia, jaundice, anemia and loss of condition.

Chemicals, Drugs and Poisonous Plants as Causes for Abortions in Cattle

Nitrate poisoning ("lowland or marshland abortion") was originally described by Simon et al. (1958) (1959) in Wisconsin as occurring in cattle pastured on unimproved weedy muckland pasture. Up to 80 percent abortions in a herd occurred from 3 to 9 months of gestation and no infectious agent was found. When these pastures were improved by treating with herbicides and fertilizer to promote the growth of grasses abortions no longer occurred. It was considered that nitrate concentrated in certain plants was possibly the cause of the abortions. Workers in Missouri published extensively on the progressive stages of nitrate intoxication including the lowering of the vitamin A levels, loss of production and abortion. In the early 1960's extensive experimental studies and reports by Davidson et al., Crawford et al., Jones et al., and Winter and Dodd demonstrated that low to fairly high levels of nitrates in the feed produced no harmful effects on cattle or caused abortions. A few abortions in experimental cattle were produced but they were associated with very high levels of nitrate ingestion producing severe toxic reactions, marked methemoglobinemia and occasional death. It would now seem that the ingestion of certain plants or some other agent would be a more likely cause of these "lowland" abortions.

Chlorinated napthalenes formerly used in lubricants produced hyperkeratosis or X disease and an acute vitamin A deficiency characterized by dry, thick, wrinkled skin, metaplasia of the epithelium of many internal structures and glands, metritis, abortion, dystocia and retained placenta, Hansel and McEntee. The occurrence of this disease in recent years has been rare.

Chronic arsenic poisoning has been reported to be a cause of abortion by Udall. Although **lead** poisoning has been associated with abortions in humans it has not been reported in animals. Sodium iodide given in large doses intravenously has occasionally been reported as causing abortion in pregnant cows. Sodium iodide injected in large doses often causes a rise in body temperature, depression, and anorexia. However, the author has on numerous occasions administered sodium iodide to pregnant cows without abortion resulting. Other chemicals or drugs such as sodium chlorate have occasionally been claimed to cause abortions but proof is lacking. Beath and coworkers reported an excessive intake of selenium would injure the fetus and cause abortion.

Locoweeds (Astragalus lentiginosus, A. pubentisimus and **Oxytropis sericea**) caused abortions in cattle when ingested at any stage of the gestation period. The rate of abortions was related to the amounts of the plant ingested and the severity of the poisoning, James et al.. No typical lesions were observed in the aborted fetus or membranes but some evidence indicated the fetuses suffered from malnutrition possibly related to placental changes. Consuming lesser amounts of locoweed resulted in deformed fetuses with rotation and ankyloses of the limbs. Sheep were similarly affected. This plant was habituating and animals would eat it even when good grass was available. In advanced cases neuronal degeneration and emaciation developed.

Perennial Broomweed (**Gutierrezia microcephala**) when ingested caused 10 to 60 percent of the fetuses in affected herds to be expelled prematurely either dead or weak at birth. Calves were small, 8 to 50 lbs., and retained placentas were common. A variation in the toxicity of the plant grown in different types of soil was noted. Abortions were due to a saponin in the plant, Dollahite et al..

Sweet Clover Hay or Silage may cause fatal fetal hemorrhage due to the action of dicoumarol. None of 14 calves born to dams fed sweet clover hay survived for more than a few hours. The cows were not affected. Elimination of sweet clover hay from the ration resulted in a cessation of losses, Bracken.

Pine needle (**Pinus ponderosa**) ingestion causes abortion in cattle from 21 to 142 days after beginning the ingestion of the pine needles. Abortions may occur from 6 to 9 months of gestation. Many affected calves are born premature, small and weak and die soon after birth. Retained placentas are common. The toxic agent, which is believed to be an anti-estrogenic substance, is heat labile. Vitamin A levels in aborting cattle are normal,

Tucker and Bracken and Faulkner.

Ergot poisoning due to the consumption by cattle of **Claviceps purpurea,** a fungus that grows on rye, wheat, barley and many grasses, has been reported to cause outbreaks of abortion. These reports in most cases were in error as abortion is seldom a feature of ergot poisoning in cattle, Ainsworth and Austwick. The abortions were probably due to some other agent. In cattle and humans large continued doses of ergot usually resulted in gangrene of the extremities and central nervous disturbances, Goodman and Gilman, Woods et al.. The author has observed, as did the latter authors, cows with gangrene of the extremities still maintaining a normal pregnancy. (See Figure 65) There are 6 or more toxic principles, mostly alkaloids, produced by ergot. Ergonovine, which is one of these, produces an oxytocic effect on uterine muscle that lasts a number of hours following a single dose. In recent years tall fescue grass, **Festica arundinacea,** containing alkaloids similar to ergot, Kingsbury, when consumed by cattle caused a similar necrosis of the extremities. No abortions have been reported in these cattle, Jensen et al.. Ergotism was produced in pregnant sows by feeding them barley containing 1 percent ergot. No abortions occurred in the sows but the pigs were weak and small and the sows had a lack of udder development and agalactia. Agalactia has been reported in other species of animals that have consumed ergot, Nordskog and Clark.

Hormonal causes of abortion in cattle

Estrogenic compounds if given in large doses over a period of time will cause abortion in cattle. Hill and Pierson administered 100 mgm of **Repositol** diethylstilbestrol intramuscularly to pregnant heifers up to 4 months of gestation and 25 mgm more for each additional month of gestation and produced abortions in 3 to 12 days after the injection in 79 percent of 761 heifers. Those that failed to abort were retreated with slightly larger doses and 50 percent of those aborted after the second treatment. Retained placentas occurred in some cows aborted in late gestation. Ayalon et al. caused abortions in 19 heifers pregnant 2 to 6 months with 80 mgm of stilbestrol in oil given twice at 3 day intervals. Similar results can be expected with similar high doses, or repeated doses, of estradiol cyclopentylate (E.C.P.), aqueous suspensions of estrogens, pellet implants of estrogen or even high levels of orally ingested estrogens. Rankin reported on abortions in heifers fed silage sealed with manure from hexestrol-fed steers. Griel and coworkers reported on abortions in 13 of 33 cattle from 105 to 204 days of gestation after consuming poultry litter from birds being fed grain containing dienestrol. Much estrous activity was exhibited by the herd during this same period. When feeding of the poultry litter stopped, abortions and the estrous activity ceased. Single moderate doses of estrogen such as 20 to 40 mgm of stilbestrol or 2 to 4 mgm of estradiol have not produced abortions on experimental injections into pregnant cattle. If larger doses are administered to cattle to overcome anestrus, the uterus should be carefully palpated per rectum to make certain that a pregnancy is not present. Abortion under these circumstances can be highly embarrassing for a veterinarian even though the owner did not know the animal was pregnant and reported her to be anestrous.

The **glucocorticoids or hydrocortisone** may cause abortion in cattle. Van Rensburg has reviewed the close relationships between the adrenal cortex and the maintenance of pregnancy. The gonads and adrenals have a common embryological origin and produce steroids that are chemically similar and closely related. The adrenal gland can readily convert progesterone and androgens into cortisone and cortisol. Transportation stress in ewes and swine induces follicular growth and ovulation. Lactational stress may induce increased A.C.T.H. and F.S.H. release and a decreased release of L.H. resulting in ovarian cysts. Prolonged gestation in Holsteins and Guernseys, as discussed previously, are caused by inherited fetal defects including hypoplastic adrenal glands and adeno-hypophyseal hypoplasia or aplasia. Veratrum poisoning in sheep causes defects of the fetal head and brain and if severe enough the pituitary gland fails to form normally which in turn causes hypoplasia of the adrenal gland of the fetus resulting in prolonged gestation. Hyperadrenalism in humans causing Cushing's disease often results in abortion in affected women. In spontaneous or habitual abortions in Angora goats due to a spontaneous involution of the corpus luteum, all affected does had adrenal hyperplasia. (see abortion in sheep and goats) Selection for fleece quality favored goats with adrenal hyperplasia. Continuous administration of A.C.T.H. to single fetal lambs at 88 to 129 days of gestation resulted in parturition in 4 to 7 days. At birth these very premature lambs had adrenal glands that weighed as much as adrenal glands from normal fetuses at the end of gestation, Liggins. Sheep given large doses of cortisone have an increased F.S.H. synthesis and release. Cortisone administered daily in large doses to sheep in the last trimester of gestation caused fetal death while similar doses given earlier in gestation had no effect. After 140 days of gestation a small dose of cortisone, 25 mg. caused premature birth, Van Rensburg. McEntee and coworkers gave 5 heifers, pregnant 193 to 222 days, recommended amounts of glucocorticoids for 4 to 8 days; 4 heifers were injected with 5 mg daily of flumethasone and 1 heifer received 2 boluses orally daily of dexamethasone, 5 mg per bolus. All heifers aborted between the 4th and 13th day after the start of the experiment; one fetus was undergoing beginning maceration. The evidence indicated that abortion was precipitated by endocrine effects rather than by the cortisone producing a metritis from its effect on the organisms present in nearly all pregnant uteri. Adams injected 20 mgms of dexamethasone intramuscularly into 22 cows, 235 to 280 days pregnant and 19 calved or aborted within 22 to 56 hours or an average of 45 hours. Three of 5 cows under 260 days of gestation failed to calve or abort. Smaller doses of dexamethasone would probably produce the same effects. All but one of the cows produced live calves but only 2 of the 22 treated animals dropped their afterbirths normally. Within 24 hours after the injection the vulva was swollen and relaxed and the udder had filled with milk. Estrogens and especially glucocorticoids might well be indicated to produce abortion in occasional cows with a prolonged gestation. It is interesting to speculate on the role of stress and increased cortisone production on abortions or premature births that occur following severe systemic diseases, malnutrition or starvation, severe prolonged physical work or long distance transportation to shows or fairs of cows late in gestation.

Progesterone deficiency appears to be a cause of early abortion in cattle but confirmed cases have not been described. Maintaining pregnancy by the supplementation of existing progesterone levels during pregnancy by the parenteral injection of 500 mgm of **Repositol** progesterone every 7 to 14 days starting 20 to 30 days before the expected abortion until 200 to 230 days of gestation in habitually aborting cows provided circumstantial evidence that a lack of progesterone may be the cause of the abortion, Morrow and Woelffer. Tanabe reported that 1100 mgm of **Repositol** progesterone every 10 days was required to maintain pregnancy from 30 to about 100 days of gestation and 550 mgm after 100 days when the corpora lutea were removed from cattle. Risley has reported success in using an oral progestin ("Repromix"), 200 mgm daily, to maintain early pregnancy in cattle prone to abortions possibly due to a progesterone deficiency. Another practice that might prove helpful in these cases is to administer a large dose, 5000 to 10,000 I.V., of chorionic gonadotropin to the cow about 4 days after service to promote the growth of a larger than normal corpus luteum that could produce more progesterone, Hansel. Abortions due to progesterone deficiency occurred at 45 to 180 days, especially at 40 to 45 days, 60 to 65 days and 120 to 180 days, but most often, 83 percent, prior to 100 days of gestation, Morrow. The same cow tended to have repeated early abortions. At these times a large follicle may develop possibly resulting in a high estrogen level and involution of the corpus luteum and abortion. These cows appear to have an unstable endocrine constitution. Possibly improved techniques now available will permit more careful monitoring of the progesterone level in the serum during pregnancy in these animals and thus aid in determining whether an actual progesterone deficiency does occur in cattle. Osburn et al. reported that reduced levels of plasma progesterone were noted at fetal death and prior to abortion caused by experimental inoculation of **V. fetus** into pregnant cows the last half of gestation.

Pituitrin or oxytocin given during gestation will not cause abortion in animals. In humans the latter hormone has been used by the slow intravenous drip method to induce labor once certain preparturition changes have occurred including the suitable relaxation of the cervix. This technique shows promise in horses but has not been the subject of careful experimental study in animals.

Nutritional Deficiences as a Cause of Abortions in Cattle.

Nutritional deficiencies may occasionally be a cause for abortion. The response of both wild and domestic animals to their food supply is markedly reflected in their reproductive processes. If food supply is low or very short, reproduction either is greatly reduced or ceases under these adverse conditions. Prolonged malnutrition results in a cessation of the estrous cycle and failure of conception. Acute severe starvation may result in abortion in pregnant cattle. Reid stated that it is very difficult to assess the more specific effects of nutrition on reproduction because only a few nutrients exert a direct effect on reproduction. In many cases animals are suffering from multiple deficiencies and thus present a confusing picture. Much of the data is not based on carefully controlled experiments, or is based on too limited a number of animals.

Multiple deficiencies brought on by starvation during the severe drought in the Midwest in the 1930's caused many cattle to become extremely emaciated and cachetic, resulting in a high incidence of abortion and birth of dead, weak, or premature calves. Animals on a very low plane of nutrition abort as a protective mechanism to conserve their own body reserves. Hyperplasia of the adrenals may be present.

Vitamin A deficiency adversely affects reproduction in all species. Pregnancy usually terminates in abortion late in pregnancy, or in the birth of weak or dead young, Thomas. As mentioned previously severe vitamin A deficiency may cause birth defects especially involving the eyes. According to Reid, the female animal requires more vitamin A than does the male, and the pregnant female apparently requires more vitamin A than does the non-pregnant female. Vitamin A deficiency causes keratinization of the vaginal epithelium and degeneration of the placenta leading to abortion. If pregnancy goes to term, birth may be difficult and infection and retained placenta follow. Reid indicated the likelihood that under range conditions protein, phosphorus, and carbohydrates, as well as vitamin A, are also deficient.

An iodine deficiency and the associated hypothyroidism in cattle has been reported by Allcroft et al. to cause weak or dead calves at term and abortion in cattle. **A possible selenium deficiency** was described in northeastern California characterized by the birth of dead, weak or premature calves, as has been described in sheep, and a high incidence of retained placenta that appeared to respond to the injection of a therapeutic dose of selenium, Mace et al.. There is no evidence that other vitamin, mineral, protein or other nutritional deficiencies will cause abortion in cattle.

Physical causes for abortion in cattle

Douching the uterus by invading the cervix with a pipette or catheter and introducing 50 to 100 ml. of a weak, Lugols' solution (1 to 2 ml per 100 ml of water), 200 ppm chlorine solution or a mild potassium permanganate solution or other aqueous or oily antiseptic solutions from 7 to 60 days of gestation will usually induce abortion in the cow without producing a severe metritis. If this practice is followed the third or succeeding months of gestation complications may arise including metritis or fetal maceration. Intrauterine insemination or douching should never be performed if the cow is pregnant as this act often results in abortion. All cows inseminated for the second or subsequent times should have the semen deposited in the mid-cervical region.

Manual rupture of the amniotic vesicle or rupture of the fetal heart or large vessels by manual pressure on the amniotic vesicle in early pregnancy, 30 to 60 days of pregnancy and division the fetus after rupture of the amniotic vesicle at 60 to 70 days will terminate pregnancy, Ball and Carroll. In some cases the fetal membranes persisted and even grew for 2 to 3 weeks before resorption or expulsion. The latter was rarely observed. Thus estrus may not occur for a month or longer after the death of the embryo. The dangers of abortion by failure to handle the amniotic vesicle gently when it is easily traumatized during pregnancy diagnosis at 35 to 45 days of gestation, requires emphasis. Palpation of the amniotic vesicle as a diagnostic aid in early pregnancy examinations should be avoided by all but skilled examiners. After 45 to 50 days of gestation it is much more difficult to damage the amniotic vesicle by routine pregnancy examinations. To prevent twinning Philipsen reported rupturing the amniotic vesicle of one of the embryos at 33 to 45 days of gestation. In two experiments about 50 to 70 percent of the pregnancies terminated with estrus recurring in 4 to 8 weeks even though only one amniotic vesicle was crushed.

Removal of the corpus luteum of pregnancy in the cow invariably results in abortion. Removal of the corpus luteum to bring a cow into estrum should never be performed without a careful examination of the entire uterus to detect a possible pregnancy. Probably waiting until the fourth week after service to be sure the cow has conceived is indicated before the corpus luteum is removed by manual manipulation of the ovary through the rectal wall where abortion is desired. This technique should be employed before the fifth or sixth month of pregnancy since by this time removal is difficult or impossible because the ovary is pulled forward and downward out of reach. After the sixth month, abortion may not occur and dystocia may result, particularly in heifers. It is advisable to watch the cow for symptoms of estrum and abortion after removal of the corpus luteum, to make sure that abortion has occurred. In exceptional instances abortion may not result because all of the corpus luteum might not have been removed, or another corpus luteum may be present in the opposite ovary.

Other miscellaneous physical causes for fetal death and abortion in cattle include **severe torsion of the uterus,** more than 180° and **rare displacements of the umbilical cord** over the head and neck of the fetus or **torsion of the umbilical cord** causing fetal death by interference with the circulation of fetal blood. (See Figure 66)

Occasionally abortions in cattle are observed following severe transportation fatique, severe systemic diseases and major operations such as for traumatic gastritis late in gestation. Excess production of glucocorticoids from the adrenal may be implicated in these abortions. Violence and trauma are explanations often relied upon by laymen and veterinarians as an easy way to explain certain abortions where the cause cannot readily be ascertained. Jetter stated, "It is a popular misconception among lay people that gymnastics, severe exercises, external trauma to the lower abdomen, hot baths, and so forth can induce abortion. Successful abortion after these procedures is fortuitous. In the vast majority of cases abortion is spontaneous and caused by a pre-existing abnormality of fetal or maternal tissues. Unless trauma is so severe as to produce serious injury of the mother none of these measures are successful."

Genetic or chromosomal causes of abortion.

Inbreeding has resulted in increased embryonic deaths, abortions and stillbirths because of a greater concentration of lethal genes per zygote than in crossbreeding. Abortion at term or "stillbirths" were increased with inbreeding in cattle and were associated with posterior presentation, dystocia, malposture of the fetus, twinning and fetal abnormalities, Woodward and Clark. Sixty-two percent of the "stillbirths" were males. The incidence in first calf heifers was 6.7 percent compared to 2.4 percent of the rest of the cattle. They cited Craft as reporting that an increase in "stillborn" pigs also occurred with inbreeding. Certain genetic defects of the bovine fetus may result in intrauterine death and abortion such as, fetal anasarea in Ayrshires and severe achondroplasia in Dexters (See teratology).

Carr, and Thiede and Metcalfe have reported an incidence of 20 and 45 percent, respectively, of chromosomal anomalies in over 300 spontaneous abortions in humans. About half of these abnormal embryos had an extra chromosome, trisomy; others were monosomic or polyploid. Stenchever et al. studied nearly 40 human couples in which the female partner had a history of habitual abortion. On the basis of somatic cell chromosomal analyses it was shown that most of these men and women did not have demonstrable genetic chromosomal abnormalities and this was not a cause of the recurring abortions. However, one female heterologous translocation carrier was discovered that was traced through three generations. Impairment of fertility occurred in 3 of the 4 female carriers of this chromosomal defect. Gustavsson reported on abnormal diploid chromosome numbers in the Swedish Red and White breed. In 1173 animals examined 14 percent were heterozygous with a chromosome number of 59 and 0.34 percent were homozygous with 58. This was caused by a translocation between the largest and smallest chromosome pairs. This resulted in a 2 to 3 percent lower conception rate in heterozygous bulls and cows due to an increased incidence of early embryonic deaths. Few reports of similar cases in animals of early embryonic deaths and aborted embryos and fetuses are available. It is probable that a certain percentage of abortions in cattle are due to chromosomal abnormalities. McFeely (1969) reported that 10 to 12 percent of the blastocysts from normal sows had detectable chromosome defects and thus may account for about 30 percent of the total pregnancy wastage which in sows is about 30 to 40 percent of the fertilized ova. Polyploidy was the most common chromosomal abnormality in these defective zygotes. He also reported (1968) on finding tetraploid cells in a bovine blastocyst. Polyspermy associated with delayed insemination of sows may be a factor in causing polyploid embryos. In one Holstein herd abortions and fetal mummification occurred commonly at 120 to 180 days of gestation in daughters of two popular sires when they were mated to the other sire. It was postulated these abortions and mummified fetuses were caused by an autosomal recessive gene carried by the heterozygous sires and dams. When the owner ceased to use these two bulls on each other's daughters the losses stopped, Stevens and King. The genetic aspects of fetal and newborn calf losses has been carefully reviewed by Fechheimer.

Miscellaneous causes of abortion

Twinning in cattle, as discussed previously, is associated with a higher rate of premature births, abortions, dystocias and expulsions of dead or weak fetuses at term than occurs with single fetuses. Retained placenta is also common after the birth or abortion of twins. This may be associated with a lack of placental area and nutrition for the fetuses, a lack of sufficient progesterone to maintain pregnancy to term, uterine inertia or "wedging" of the fetus from each horn into the pelvis at the time of expulsion or possibly other causes. Also as previously indicated abortions and fetal loss is more common with unicornual than bicornual twin pregnancies in cattle.

Allergies and anaphylactic reactions may cause abortion in cattle. Abortions that followed within 2 to 3 days the anaphylactic reactions observed after using leptospiral bacterin containing rabbit serum were described previously. Kemen reported on 4 cows aborting within two or three days following an allergic reaction due to the intravenous administration of tuberculin. Uticaria associated with milk allergies in cattle, especially Jerseys and Guernseys, occurring at the time of "drying off" have resulted in abortions, Mullins and others. Wright reviewed attempts to produce abortions in cattle as a sequel to an incompatible blood transfusion and concluded these probably did not occur despite the report by Laing and Blakemore. However, he demonstrated that organisms such as **Alcaligenes fecalis,** Pseudomonas and others or their products present in contaminated sodium citrate solution if added to blood at the time of blood collection would produce a severe anaphylactoid reaction resembling either an incompatible transfusion reaction, or most likely an endotoxin reaction, described under bacterial causes, in transfused cows resulting in abortion several days later. He recommended making up the sodium citrate solution fresh, just before use, with pyrogen-free sterile water to prevent these untoward apparently incompatible transfusion reactions in cattle.

Other miscellaneous abortions have been associated with lymphocytoma where the uterine wall was extensively involved, in **C. pyogenes** abscesses of the uterine wall, in extensive adhesions of the uterus to the body wall or other viscera limiting uterine enlargement, and in cattle where there is a congenital or acquired lack of most of the uterine caruncles and endometrial glands. Shemanchuk et al. reported on abortion in anemic cattle severely infested with the sucking louse.

Fetal mummification due to the intrauterine death of the fetus and failure of its expulsion or abortion is due to many of the factors described above as causing bovine abortions. These will be discussed later in this chapter.

Aids in the Diagnosis of Abortion Causes

In order to improve the possibility of making a diagnosis of the actual cause or causes of abortion in cattle the attending veterinarian should secure a very careful, detailed history of the herd and cows involved over the past 6 to 9 months including breeding dates, sires used, whether natural or A.I. service, previous breeding history of the cow or herd, herd health history especially noting any illness in the herd over the past few months, new arrivals into the herd or possible contacts between the herd and other herds should be noted. The health and reproductive history of the herd of origin of purchased cattle or the contact herd is desirable. The number of abortions and the time in gestation they occurred should be recorded. The freshly expelled fetus and its membranes including the cotyledons and amniotic fluid, if available, should be taken as cleanly as possible and placed in a waterproof plastic bag or clean can and refrigerated and delivered immediately to the diagnostic laboratory. If the fetus is large, a careful necropsy should be performed and specimens of the stomach, tied off at each end, lungs, liver, spleen and kidneys should be saved for culture and gross and histologic examination. These also should be carefully refrigerated and taken immediately to the laboratory along with representative portions of the fetal placenta. Freezing of tissues while good for recovery of most organisms and viruses may interfere with the diagnosis of certain protozoal causes of abortion and with tissue sections and their examination. In an outbreak of abortion it may be necessary to examine 3 or 4 fetuses to find one that may yield clues to the cause of the outbreak. Blood samples from the aborting cows should be taken in a near sterile manner at the time of abortion and then again 2 to 3 weeks later. Samples from other cows in the herd, those acutely ill, representative cows or recently introduced cattle might also be collected for blood testing. The serum from these samples should be removed and saved, even by freezing, if necessary, for serologic determinations. Sending whole blood samples into the laboratory during the hot summer months may result in hemolyzed samples if they become overheated or in the winter if they become frozen. It should be recognized at the present time that because of the multiplicity of causes for bovine abortion, the as yet unknown causes, and the great frequency of partially autolyzed fetuses by the time they are expelled that only about one in four bovine fetuses can be accurately diagnosed with respect to the causative agent.

General References

Arthur, G. H. (1964) Wright's Veterinary Obstetrics, 3rd Ed., Williams and Wilkins Co., Baltimore, Md.

Bartlett, D. E. (1968) The A.V.M.A.-N.A.A.B. Code and the U.S.L.S.A. Recommended Regulations, Proc. of 2nd Tech. Conf. on Art. Insem. and Reprod., Feb. 1968, Chicago, Ill.

Blood, D. C. and Henderson, J. A. (1963) Veterinary Medicine, 2nd Ed., Williams and Wilkins Co., Baltimore, Md.

Bruner, D. W. and Gillespie, J. H. (1966) Hagan's Infectious Diseases of Domestic Animals, 5th Ed., Cornell Univ. Press, Ithaca, N.Y.

Dennis, S. M. (1968) Comparative Aspects of Infectious Abortion Diseases Common to Animals and Man, Internat. J. of Fertil. **13,** 3, 191.

Dennis, S. M. (1969) Diagnosis of Infectious Abortion in Cattle, Vet. Med. **64,** 5, 423.

Dillman, R. C. (1968) Sequential Sterile Autolysis in the Ovine Fetus, Proc. 72nd Meeting U.S. Livestock Sanit. Assoc., 478.

Hafez, E. S. E. (1968) Reproduction in Farm Animals, 2nd Ed., Lea and Febiger, Philadelphia, Pa.

Jubb, K. V. F. and Kennedy, P. C. (1970) Pathology of Domestic Animals, 2nd Ed., Academic Press, Inc., N.Y.C.

Lawson, J. R. (1962) Bacterial and Mycotic Agents Associated with Abortion and Stillbirth in Domestic Animals, Livestock Infertility, Monograph #5 FAO, Rome.

Specific References

Infectious Bacterial Causes

Brucellosis

Anderson, R. K., Pietz, D. E., Nelson, C. J., Kimberling, C. V. and Werring, D. F. (1962) Epidemiologic Studies of Bovine Brucellosis in Problem Herds in Minnesota, Proc. 66th Ann. Meeting U.S. Livestock Sanit. Assoc., 109.

Beck, C. C., Ellis, D. J., Fichtner, G. J., Laiho, E. R. and Whitehead, G. L. (1964) Brucella Tube-Agglutination Titers Resulting from the Use of Syringes Containing Viable Strain 19 Vaccine, J.A.V.M.A. **144,** 6, 620.

Brown, R. and Carrow, R. (1963) Vascular Anatomy of the Bovine Tail, J.A.V.M.A. **143,** 11, 1214.

Downey, W. L. and Morter, R. L. (1963) Serological Relationship Between **Brucello abortus** and **Leptospira pomona,** Proc. 67th Ann. Meeting U.S. Livestock Sanit. Assoc. 193.

FAO-WHO Joint Expert Committee Report on Brucellosis, (1964) Fourth Report, FAO Agric. Studies 66, Tech. Report Series 289, Rome.

Gilman, H. L. and Hughes, D. E. (1957) The Relative Immunity to Brucellosis of Calves Vaccinated Intradermally Compared to Those Vaccinated Subcutaneously, Cor. Vet. **47,** 2, 291.

Janney, G. C., Berman, D. T. and Erdmann, A. A. (1958) The Relative Efficiency of the Milk Ring Test and Area Blood Tests for Bovine Brucellosis, J.A.V.M.A. **133,** 12, 586.

Kerr, W. R. (1955) Vaginal and Uterine Antibodies in Cattle With Particular Reference to **Br. abortus,** Brit. Vet. Jour. **III,** 169.

Kerr, W. R. and Rankin, J. E. F. (1959) The Spread of Brucellosis within Herds—The Milk Problem, Vet. Rec. **71,** 178.

Lambert, G., Amerault, T. E., Manthei, C. A. and Goode, E. R. (1960) Further Studies on the Persistence of **Brucella abortus** Infection in Cattle, Proc. 64th Ann. Meeting U.S. Livestock Sanit. Assoc. 109.

Manthei, C. A. (1968) Brucellosis as a Cause of Abortion Today, in **Abortion Diseases in Livestock,** edit. by L. C. Faulkner, C. C. Thomas Co., Springfield, Ill.

Manthei, C. A. (1967) Brucella Vaccine Immunizes Young Calves, 18th World Vet. Congr. Vol I, 355.

McCullough, N. B. (1963) Medical Care Following Accidental Injection of **Brucella abortus,** Strain 19, in Man, J.A.V.M.A. **143,** 6, 617.

Meyer, M. E. (1966) Host-Parasite Relationship in Brucellosis I Reservoirs of Infection and Interhost Transmissibility of the Parasite, Proc. 70th Ann. Meeting, U.S.L.S.A., 129.

Nicoletti, P. (1967) Utilization of the Card Test in Brucellosis Eradication, J.A.V.M.A. **151,** 12, 1778.

Nicoletti, P. And Burch, G. E. (1969) A Comparison of the Tube Agglutination, Supplemental and Brucellosis Ring Tests in Selected Dairy Herds in New York, Cor. Vet. **59,** 3, 349.

Nicoletti, P. (1969) Further Evaluations of Serologic Test Procedures Used to Diagnose Brucellosis, Amer. J. Vet. Res. **30,** 10, 1811.

Nicoletti, P. and Holmes, J. (1968) Attempts to Produce Cross Reactions for **Brucella** in Cattle Treated with Hemorrhagic Septicemia Bacterins, Cor. Vet. **58,** 3, 421.

Nicoletti, P. and Muraschi, T. F. (1966) Bacteriologic Evaluation of Serologic Test Procedures for the Diagnosis of Brucellosis in Problem Cattle Herds, Amer. J. Vet. Res. **27,** 118, 689.

Redman, D. R., Deyoe, B. L. and King, N. B. (1967) Resistance of Cattle to **Brucella abortus** Following Vaccination at Two and Three Months of Age, J.A.V.M.A. **150,** 4, 403.

Roberts, S. J., Squire, R. A. and Gilman, H. L. (1962) Deaths in Two Calves Following Vaccination with **Brucella abortus** Strain 19 Vaccine, Cor. Vet. **52,** 4, 592.

Leptospirosis

Baker, J. A. and Little, R. B. (1948) Leptospirosis in Cattle, J. Exp. Med. **88,** 295.

Bryan, H. S. and Boley, L. E. (1955) Studies on Leptospirosis in Domestic Animals, IV Survival of **Leptospira pomona** in Bovine Semen Extender. Mich. State Vet., Fall **16,** 1.

Fennestad, K. L. (1963) Experimental Leptospirosis in Calves, Thesis, Royal Vet. and Agr. College, Copenhagen, Denmark.

Fennestad, K. L. and Borg-Petersen, C. (1958) Fetal Leptospirosis and Abortion in Cattle, J. of Infect. Dis. **102,** 227.

Galton, M. M. (1963) Recent Advances and Needs for Future Emphasis in Research on Leptospirosis, Proc. 67th Ann. Meeting U.S. Livestock Sanit. Assoc., 201.

Hanson, L. E. (1960) Bovine Leptospirosis: A Review, J. Dairy Sci. **43,** 4, 453.

Hanson, L. E., Mansfield, M. E. and Andrews, R. O. (1964) Epizootiology of Enzootic Leptospirosis in a Cattle Herd, Proc. 68th Ann. Meeting U.S. Livestock Sanit. Assoc. 136.

Jungherr, E. (1944) Bovine Leptospirosis, J.A.V.M.A., **105,** 812, 276.

Michna, S. W. and Campbell, R. S. F. (1969) The Isolation of **Leptospira Sejroe** from Kidneys of Aborting Cattle, Vet. Rec. **84,** 83.

Morse, E. V. and McNutt, S. H. (1956) Experimental Leptospirosis—I. The Course of **Leptospira pomona** Infection in Pregnant Heifers, J.A.V.M.A. **128,** 5, 225.

Murphy, J. C. and Jensen, R. (1969) Experimental Pathogenesis of Leptospiral Abortion in Cattle, Amer. J. Vet. Res. **30,** 5, 703.

Roberts, S. J. (1958) A Study of Leptospirosis in a Large Insemination Stud, Cor. Vet. **48,** 4, 363.

Sleight, S. D. (1965) The Role of Penicillin and Streptomycin in the Prevention of Transmission of Bovine Leptospirosis by Artificial Insemination, Amer. J. Vet. Res. **26,** 111, 365.

Sleight, S. D. and Williams, J. A. (1961) Transmission of Bovine Leptospirosis by Coition and Artificial Insemination (A Preliminary Report), J.A.V.M.A. **138,** 3, 151.

Smith, R. E., Reynolds, I. M. and Clark, G. W. (1967) Immunofluorescence in the Diagnosis of Fetal Leptospirosis, Cor. Vet. **57,** 4, 517.

Stalheim, O. H. V. (1968) Vaccination of Hamsters, Swine and Cattle with Viable, Avirulent **Leptospira pomona,** Amer. J. Vet. Res. **29,** 7, 1463.

Stalheim, O. H. V. (1969) Chemotherapy of Renal Leptospirosis in Cattle, Amer. J. Vet. Res. **30,** 8, 1317.

Stoenner, H. G (1966) Bovine Leptospiral Abortion, Symposium on Abortion Diseases in Livestock, Colo. State Univ., Ft. Collins, Colo.

Stoenner, H. G., Crews, F. W., Crouse, A. E., Taschner, L. E., Johnson, C. E. and Wohleb, J. Jr (1956) The Epizootiology of Bovine Leptospirosis in Washington, J.A.V.M.A. **129,** 6, 251.

Stoenner, H. G., and Davis, E. (1967) Further Observations on Leptospiral Plate Antigens, Amer. J. Vet. Res. **28,** 259.

Van der Hoeden, J. (1964) An Outbreak of Leptospirosis in a Herd of Dairy Cattle, Refuah Vet. **21,** 107.

Listeriosis

Banner, E. A., Johnson, T. R., Onstad, G. R., Weed, L. A. and Sayre, G. P. (1964) **Listeria Monocytogenes** in Pregnancy, Mayo Clinic Proc. **39,** 12, 919.

Blenden, D. C., Gates, G. A. and Khan, M. S. (1968) Growth of **Listeria Monocytogenes** in a Corn Silage Extract Medium, Amer. J. Vet. Res. **29,** 11, 2237.

Eveleth, D. F., Goldsby, A. I., Bolin, F. M., Holm, G. C. and Turn, J. (1953) Field Trials and Laboratory Tests with Listeria Bacterins, Proc. Ann. Meeting A.V.M.A., 154.

Gray, M. L. (1960) Isolation of **Listeria Monocytogenes** from Oat Silage, Science **132,** 1767.

Gray, M. L., Lassiter, C. A., Webster, H. D., Huffman, C. F. and Thorp, F. (1956) Isolation of **Listeria Monocytogenes** from the Liver of Calves and a Discussion of Intrauterine Infection, Vet. Med. **51,** 7, 316.

Jones, S. M. and Woodbine, M. (1961) Microbiological Aspects of **Listeria Monocytogenes** with Special Reference to Listeriosis in Animals, Vet. Rev. and Annot. I, 2, 39.

March, R. W. (1956) A Rapid Method for the Isolation of **Listeria Monocytogenes** from Bovine Brain, Cor. Vet. 46, 274.

Osebold, J. W., Kendrick, J. W. and Njoku-Obi, A. (1960) Abortion in Cattle Experimentally Infected with **Listeria Monocytogenes,** J.A.V.M.A. **137,** 4, 227.

Osebold, J. W., Kendrick, J. W. and Njoku-Obi, A. (1960) Cattle Abortion Associated with Natural **Listeria Monocytogenes** Infections, J.A.V.M.A. **137,** 4, 221.

Seeliger, H. P. R. (1961) Listeriosis, Hafner Publ. Co., Inc., N.Y.C.

Young, S. (1968) Listeriosis in Cattle and Sheep, in **Abortion Diseases in Livestock,** edit. by L. C. Faulkner, C. C. Thomas Co., Springfield, Ill.

Young, S. and Firehammer, B. D. (1958) Abortion Attributed to **Listeria Monocytogenes** Infection in a Range Herd of Beef Cattle, J.A.V.M.A. **132,** 10, 434.

Miscellaneous Bacterial Causes for Abortion Including Tuberculosis

Al-Aubaidi, J. M. (1969) Bovine Mycoplasma: Purification, Characterization, Classification and Pathogenicity, PhD. Thesis Cornell Univ., Ithaca, N.Y.

Al-Aubaidi, J. M. and Fabricant, J. (1968) Technics for the Isolation of Mycoplasma from Cattle, Cor. Vet. **58,** 4, 555.

Braude, A. I. (1964) Bacterial Endotoxins, Scient. Amer. **210,** 3, 36.

Burgisser, H. and Schneider, P. A. (1957) Abortion in Cows Following Infection with Tubercle Bacilli of Avian Origin. Schweiz. Arch. Tierheilk. **99,** 257.

Carmichael, L. E., Fincher, M. G. and McEntee, K. (1964) P.P.L.O. (Mycoplasma) Causing Abortion in Cattle, Ann. Meeting on Cattle Disease Res. Progress, Vet. Virus Res. Instit., Cornell Univ., Ithaca, N.Y.

Dennis, S. M. (1966) The Effect of Bacterial Endotoxin on Pregnancy, Vet. Bull. **36,** 123.

Firehammer, B. D. (1959) Bovine Abortion due to Hemophilus Species, J.A.V.M.A. **135,** 8, 421.

Kundsin, R. B. (1969) Mycoplasma and Infertility, Ob.-Gyn. Observer, **8,** 5, 5.

O'Berry, P. A., Bryner, J. H. and Frank, A. H. (1966) Isolation of Mycoplasma From an Aborted Bovine Fetus and Vaginal Mucus, Amer. J. Vet. Res. **27,** 118, 677.

Osborne, C. J. (1965) Pathologic Responses in Animals after **Vibrio fetus** Toxin Shock, Amer. J. Vet. Res. **26,** 114, 1056.

Plum, N. (1937) Tuberculosis Abortion in Cattle, Acta Pathol. et Microbiol. Scand. Suppl. **37,** 438.

Roberts, S. J. (1956) Veterinary Obstetrics and Genital Diseases, 1st ed., Edwards Bros., Inc., Ann Arbor, Mich.

Roumy, B. (1966) An Enzootic of Bovine T. B. Transmitted by Artificial Insemination, Rec. Med. Vet. **142,** 729.

Van Ulsen, F. W. (1955) Schimmel Abortus bij Runderen, Tijdschr. vor Diergeneesk. **80,** 20, 1081.

Wagner, W. C., McEntee, K. and Gilman, H. L. (1961) The Experimental Inoculation of Heifers with **Vibrio fetus** of Ovine Origin, Cor. Vet. **51,** 3, 441.

Williams, W. L. (1943) Diseases of the Genital Organs of Domestic Animals, 3rd Ed., Miss Louella Williams, Upland Rd., Ithaca, N.Y.

Infectious Viral Causes

I.B.R.-I.P.V. Virus

Abinanti, F. R. and Plumer, G. J. (1961) The Isolation of Infectious Bovine Rhinotracheitis Virus from Cattle Affected with Conjunctivitis, Amer. J. Vet. Res. **22,** 13.

Bowling, C. P., Goodheart, C. R. and Plumer, G. (1969) Oral and Genital Bovine Herpesviruses, J. Virol. **3,** 1, 95.

Chow, T. L. (1968) Infectious Bovine Rhinotracheitis, in **Abortion Diseases of Livestock,** edit. by L. C. Faulkner, C. C. Thomas Co., Springfield, Ill.

Chow, T. L., Mollelo, J. A. and Owen, N. V. (1964) Abortion Experimentally Induced in Cattle by Infectious Bovine Rhinotracheitis Virus, J.A.V.M.A. **144,** 105.

Chow, T. L. and Davis, R. W. (1964) The Susceptibility of Mule Deer to Infectious Rhinotracheitis, Amer. J. Vet. Res. **25,** 105, 518.

French, E. L. (1962) Relationship between Infectious Bovine Rhinotracheitis (I.B.R.) Virus and a Virus Isolated from Calves with Encephalitis, Austral. Vet. Jour. 38, 555.

Gratzek, J. B., Peter, C. P., and Ramsey, F. K. (1965) Pathogenesis Studies of Infectious Bovine Rhinotracheitis by Fluorescent Antibody Tracing, Proc. 69th Ann. Meeting U.S. Livestock Sanit. Assoc. 190.

Guss, S. B. (1967) Personal Communication.

Kahrs, R. F. and Baker, J. A. (1965) Combined Vaccines for Dairy Cattle, Proc. 69th Ann. Meeting U.S. Livestock Sanit. Assoc., 177.

Kahrs, R. F. and Smith, R. S. (1965) Infectious Bovine Rhinotracheitis, Infectious Pustular Vulvovaginitis and Abortion in a New York Dairy Herd, J.A.V.M.A. **146,** 3, 217.

Kendrick, J. W. (1970) Personal communication.

Kendrick, J. W., Gillespie, J. H., McEntee, K. (1958) Infectious Pustular Vulvovaginitis of Cattle, Cor. Vet. **48,** 458.

Kendrick, J. W. and McEntee, K. (1967) The Effect of Artificial Insemination with Semen Contaminated with I.P.V. Virus, Cor. Vet. **57,** 1, 3.

Kendrick, J. W. and Straub, O. C. (1967) Infectious Bovine Rhinotracheitis-Infectious Pustular Vulvogaginitis Virus Infection in Pregnant Cows, Amer. J. Vet. Res. **28,** 126, 1269.

Kennedy, P. C. and Richards, W. P. C. (1964) The Pathology of Abortion Caused by the Virus of Infectious Bovine Rhinotracheitis, Path. Vet. **1,** 7.

Lukas, G. N., Weidenbach, S. J., Palmer, K. G., Dickie, C. W., Duncan, R. F. and Barrera, J. (1963) A Bovine Fetal Viral Isolate Neutralized by Immune Serum as a Cause of Abortion in Cattle, Proc. 67th Ann. Meeting U.S. Livestock Sanit. Assoc., 108.

McEntee, K. (1968) (1970) Personal Communication.

McFeely, R. A., Merritt, A. M. and Stearly, E. L. (1968) Abortion in a Dairy Herd Vaccinated for Infectious Bovine Rhinotracheitis, J.A.V.M.A. **153,** 6, 657.

McKercher, D. G. (1966) Viral Abortion in Cattle, Proc. Intermountain Vet. Meeting, Las Vegas, Nev.

McKercher, D. G. (1969) Relationship of Viruses to Reproductive Problems, J.A.V.M.A. **154,** 10, 1184.

McKercher, D. G. and Wada, E. M. (1964) The Virus of Infectious Bovine Rhinotracheitis as a Cause of Abortion in Cattle, J.A.V.M.A. **144,** 2, 136.

Owen, N. V., Chow, T. L. and Molello, J. A. (1964) Bovine Fetal Lesions Experimentally Produced by Infectious Bovine Rhinotracheitis Virus, Amer. J. Vet. Res. **25,** 109, 1617.

Owen, N. V., Chow, T. L. and Molello, J. A. (1968) Infectious Bovine Rhinotracheitis: Correlation of Fetal and Placental Lesions with Viral Isolations, Amer. J. Vet. Res. **29,** 10, 1959.

Peter, C. P., Gratzek, J. B. and Ramsey, F. K. (1966) Isolation and Characterization of a Strain of Infectious Bovine Rhinotracheitis Virus Associated with Enteritis in Cattle: Pathogenesis Studies by Fluorescent Antibody Tracing, Amer. J. Vet. Res. **27,** 121.

Pierson, R. E. and Vair, C. (1965) The Economic Loss Associated with Infectious Bovine Rhinotracheitis in a Dairy Herd, J.A.V.M.A. **147,** 4, 350.

Saxegaard, F. (1966) Problems Connected with the Diagnosis of Subclinical Infection with Infectious Pustular Vulvovaginitis Virus (I.P.V. Virus) in Bulls, Nord. Vet. Med. **18,** 10.

Saxegaard, F. (1968) Serological Investigations of Bulls Subclinically Infected with Infectious Pustular Vulvovaginitis (I.P.V. Virus), Nord. Vet. Med. **20,** 28.

Snowden, W. A. (1964) Infectious Bovine Rhinotracheitis and Infectious Pustular Vulvovaginitis in Australian Cattle, Austral. Vet. Jour. **40,** 8, 277.

Snowden, W. A. (1965) The I.B.R.-I.P.V. Virus: Reaction to Infection and Intermittent Recovery of Virus from Experimentally Infected Cattle, Austral. Vet. Jour. **41,** 5, 135.

Spradbrow, P. B. (1968) The Isolation of Infectious Bovine Rhinotracheitis Virus from Bovine Semen, Austral. Vet. Jour. **44,** 410.

Studdert, M. J., Barker, C. A. V., and Savan, M. (1964) Infectious Pustular Vulvovaginitis Virus Infection of Bulls, Amer. J. Vet. Res. **25,** 303.

Van Kruiningen, H. J. and Bartholomew, R. C. (1964) Infectious Bovine Rhinotracheitis Diagnosed by Lesions in a Calf, J.A.V.M.A. **144,** 9, 1008.

Epizootic Bovine Abortion (P.L. agent or Chlamydia).

Bassan, Y. (1966) A Virus of the Psittacosis—Lymphogranuloma-venereum (Bedsonia) Group as a Cause of Abortions in a Dairy Herd, Refuah Vet. **23,** 2, 127.

Harshfield, G. S. (1970) Sporadic Bovine Encephalomyelitis, J.A.V.M.A. **156,** 4, 466.

Howarth, J. A., Moulton, J. E. and Frazer, L. M. (1956) Epizootic Bovine Abortion Characterized by Fetal Hepatopathy, J.A.V.M.A. **128,** 9, 441.

Kennedy, P. C., Olander, H. J. and Howarth, J. A. (1960) Pathology of Epizootic Bovine Abortion, Cor. Vet. **50,** 4, 417.

Lincoln, S., Kwapein, R. P., Reed, D. E., Whiteman, C. E. and Chow, T. L. (1969) Epizootic Bovine Abortion: Clinical and Serologic Responses and Pathologic Changes in Extragenital Organs of Pregnant Heifers, Amer. J. Vet. Res. **30,** 12, 2105.

McEntee, K. (1967) Personal Communication.

McKercher, D. G. (1969) Cause and Prevention of Epizootic Bovine Abortion, J.A.V.M.A. **154,** 10, 1192.

McKercher, D. G., Robinson, E. A., Wada, E. M., Saito, J. K. and Franti, C. E. (1969) Vaccination of Cattle Against Epizootic Bovine Abortion, Cor. Vet. **59,** 2, 211.

McKercher, D. G., Wada, E. M., Robinson, E. A. and Howarth, J. A. (1966) Epizootiologic and Immunologic Studies of Epizootic Bovine Abortion, Cor. Vet. **56,** 3, 433.

Schoop, G. and Kauker, E. (1956) Infection in a Herd of Cattle with a Virus of the Psittacosis-lympho-granuloma Group, Accompanied by Numerous Abortions, Dtsch. Tierarztl. Wschr. **63,** 233.

Storz, J. (1968) Comparative Studies on E.B.A. and E.A.E., Abortion Diseases of Cattle and Sheep Resulting from Infection with Psittacosis Agents, in **Abortion Diseases of Livestock,** edit. by L. C. Faulkner, C. C. Thomas Co., Springfield, Ill.

Storz, J., Call, J. W., Jones, R. W. and Miner, M. L. (1967) Epizootic Bovine Abortion in the Intermountain Region, Some Recent Clinical Epidemiologic and Pathologic Findings, Cor. Vet. **57,** 1, 21.

Storz, J., McKercher, D. G., Howarth, J. A. and Straub, O. C. (1960) The Isolation of a Viral Agent from Epizootic Bovine Abortion, J.A.V.M.A. **137,** 9, 509.

Miscellaneous Virus Abortions

Bowne, J. G., Luedke, A. J., Jochim, M. M. and Metcalf, H. E. (1968) Bluetongue Disease in Cattle, J.A.V.M.A. **153,** 6, 662.

Gillespie, J. H., Bartholomew, R. T., Thomson, R. G., McEntee, K. (1967) The Isolation of Noncytopathic Virus Diarrhea Virus from Two Aborted Bovine Fetuses, Cor. Vet. **57,** 4, 564.

Gratzek, J. B., Peters, C. P. and Ramsey, F. K. (1966) Isolation and Characterization of a Strain of Infectious Bovine Rhinotracheitis Virus Associated with Enteritis in Cattle: Isolation, Serologic Characterization and Induction of the Experimental Disease, Amer. J. Vet. Res. **27,** 121, 1567.

Kahrs, R. F. (1969) Personal Communication.

Kahrs, R. F., Atkinson, G., Baker, J. A., Carmichael, L., Coggins, L., Gillespie, J., Langer, P., Marshall, V., Robson, D. and Sheffy, B. (1964) Serologic Studies on the Incidence of Bovine Virus Diarrhea, Infectious Bovine Rhinotracheitis, **Bovine Myxovirus Influenza-3** and **Leptospira pomona** in New York State, Cor. Vet. **54,** 3, 360.

Kahrs, R. F., Bartholomew, R., House, J. A. and Ward, G. M. (1970) Epidemiological Investigation of Bovine Virus Diarrhea-Mucosal Disease in an Unvaccinated Dairy Herd. A Case Report, Cor. Vet. **60,** 1, 16.

Kahrs, R. F., Lein, D. F., Fuller, H. K., deLahunta, A., Braun, R. K., Brown, T. T., Duncan, R., Kenney, R. M., McEntee, K., McKenzie, B., Parsonson, I. M., Scott, F. W., Wilkie, B. N. and DeRock, O. (1969) An Epizootiologic Investigation into Bovine Viral Diarrhea-Mucosal Disease as a Suspected Etiologic Agent of a Series of Abortions, Stillbirths, Early Neonatal Deaths and Congenital Cerebellar Disease in a New York Dairy Herd, Paper No. 1 Epizootiology Series, N.Y. State Veterinary College, Ithaca, N.Y.

Kahrs, R. F., Scott, F. W. and deLahunta, A. (1970) Bovine Viral Diarrhea-Mucosal Disease, Abortion and Congenital Cerebellar Hypoplasia in a Dairy Herd, J.A.V.M.A. **156,** 7, 851.

Kahrs, R. F. and Ward, G. M. (1967) Bovine Virus Diarrhea Abortion, 71st Ann. Meeting U.S. Livestock Sanitary Assoc., 493.

Kahrs, R. F. and Baker, J. A. (1965) Combined Vaccines for Dairy Cattle, Proc. 69th Ann. Meeting U.S. Livestock Sanit. Assoc., 177.

Langer, P. and Hillman, R. (1962) Personal Communication.

McKercher, D. G. (1966) Viral Abortion in Cattle, Proc. Intermountain Vet. Meeting, Las Vegas, Nev.

Mills, J. H. L. and Luginbuhl, R. E. (1965) Incidence of Bovine Mucosal Disease in Connecticut, Cor. Vet. **55,** 4, 583.

Olafson, P. (1970) Personal Communication.

Olafson, P., MacCallum, A. D. and Fox, F. H. (1946) An Apparently New Transmissable Disease in Cattle, Cor. Vet. **36,** 3, 205.

Sattar, S. A., Bohl, E. H., Trapp, A. L. and Hamdy, A. H. (1967) **In Utero** Infection of Bovine Fetuses with **Myxovirus parainfluenza-3,** Amer. J. Vet. Res. **28,** 122, 45.

Thomas, F. C. and Trainer, D. O. (1970) Bluetongue Virus in White-Tailed Deer, Amer. J. Vet. Res. **31,** 2, 271.

U.S. Livestock Sanit. Assoc. (1954) Foreign Animal Diseases, Trenton, N.J.

Ward, G. M., Roberts, S. J., McEntee, K. and Gillespie, H. (1969) A Study of Experimentally Induced Bovine Virus Diarrhea-Mucosal Disease in Pregnant Cows and Their Progeny, Cor. Vet. **59,** 4, 525.

Wilson, J. C., Foggie, A. and Carmichael, M. A. (1964) Tickborne Fever as a Cause of Abortion and Stillbirths in Cattle, Vet. Rec. **76,** 1081.

Mycotic or Fungal Abortion

Ainsworth, G. C. and Austwick, P. K. C. (1959) Fungal Diseases of Animals, Commonwealth Agric. Bureau Review Series # 6, 108.

Austwick, P. K. C. and Venn, J. A. J. (1961) Mycotic Abortion in England and Wales, Proc. 4th Internat. Congr. On An. Reprod., Hague, Vol. 3, 562.

Bendixen, H. C. and Plum, N. (1929) **Aspergillus fumigatus** and **Absidia ramosa** als Abortusursache beim Rind, Acta Pathol. et Microbiol. Scand. **6,** 3, 252.

Hillman, R. B. (1969) Bovine Mycotic Placentitis in New York State, Cor. Vet. **59,** 2, 269.

Hillman, R. B. and McEntee, K. (1969) Experimental Studies on Bovine Mycotic Placentitis, Cor. Vet. **59,** 2, 289.

Hugh-Jones, M. E. and Austwick, P. K. C. (1967) Epidemiological Studies in Bovine Mycotic Abortion I The Effect of Climate on Incidence, Vet. Rec. **81,** 12, 273.

McEntee, K. (1966) Causes of Abortion in Cattle, The Victorian Vet. Proc. 1965–1966, Australia.

Weikl, A. (1965) Mycotic Abortion in Cattle, Vet. Med. Review **2,** 71.

Winter, A. J. (1968) Mycotic Abortion, in **Abortion Diseases in Livestock,** edit. by L. C. Faulkner, C. C. Thomas Co., Springfield, Ill.

Infections Protozoal Causes for Abortion

Boynton, W. H. (1932) Further Observations on Anaplasmosis, Cor. Vet. **22,** 10.

Dikmans, G., Manthei, C. A. and Frank, A. H. (1957) Demonstration of **Trypanosoma theileri** in the Stomach of an Aborted Fetus, Cor. Vet. **47,** 344.

Eckerling, B., Neri, A., and Eylan, E. (1968) Toxoplasmosis, A Cause of Infertility, Fertil. and Steril. **19,** 6, 883.

Abortions due to Chemicals, Drugs and Poisonous Plants

Beath, O. A., Gilbert, C. S., Eppson, H. F. and Rosenfeld, I. (1953) Poisonous Plants and Livestock Poisoning, Wyo. Agr. Exp. Stat. Bull. 324.

Bracken, F. K. (1968) Losses due to Disease in Prenatal and Postnatal Mortality in Cattle, Nat. Acad. of Sci. Publication 1685, Washington, D.C.

Crawford, R. F., Kennedy, W. K. and Davidson, K. L. (1966) Factors Influencing the Toxicity of Forages that Contain Nitrate When Fed to Cattle, Cor. Vet. **56,** 3.

Davidson, K. L., Hansel, W. M., Krook, L., McEntee, K. and Wright, M. J. (1964) Nitrate Toxicity in Dairy Heifers I Effects on Reproduction, Growth, Lactation and Vitamin A Nutrition, J. Dairy Sci. **47,** 10, 1065.

Dodd, D. C. (1966) Nitrate-Nitrite Poisoning of Cattle, Proc. 70th Ann. Meeting U.S. Livestock Sanit. Assoc., 581.

Dollahite, J. W. and Anthony, W. V. (1957) Poisoning of Cattle with **Guitierrezia microcephala,** a Perennial Broomweed, J.A.V.M.A. **130,** 12, 525.

Dollahite, J. W., Shaver, T. and Camp, B. J. (1962) Injected Saponins as Abortifacients, Amer. J. Vet. Res. **23,** 97, 1261.

Faulkner, L. A. (1968) Pine Needle Abortion, in **Abortion Diseases of Livestock,** edit. by L. C. Faulkner, C. C. Thomas Co., Springfield, Ill.

Garner, G. B. (1958) Learn to Live with Nitrate, Missouri Agr. Exp. Stat. Bull. 708.

Goodman, L. S. and Gilman, A. (1965) The Pharmacological Basis of Therapeutics, 3rd Ed., McMillan Co., N.Y.C.

Hansel, Wm. and McEntee, K. (1955) Bovine Hyperkeratosis (X-Disease) A Review, J. Dairy Sci. **38,** 8, 875.

James, L. F., Shupe, J. L., Binns, W. and Keeler, R. F. (1967) Abortive and Teratogenic Effects of Locoweed on Sheep and Cattle, Amer. J. Vet. Res. **28,** 126, 1379.

James, L. F., Von Kampen, K. R. and Staker, G. R. (1969) Locoweed (**Astragulus lentiginosus**) Poisoning of Cattle and Horses, J.A.V.M.A. **155,** 3, 525.

Jensen, R., Deem, A. W. and Knaus, D. (1956) Fescue Lameness in Cattle I Experimental Production of the Disease, Amer. J. Vet. Res. **17,** 196.

Jones, E. R., Wesig, P. H., Bone, J. F., Peters, M. A. and Alpan, S. O. (1966) Effect of High-Nitrate Consumption on Lactation and Vitamin A Nutrition of Dairy Cows, J. Dairy Sci. **49,** 4, 491.

Kingsbury, J. M. (1964) Poisonous Plants of the United States and Canada, Prentice-Hall Inc., Englewood Cliffs, N.J.

Nordskog, A. W. and Clark, R. R. (1945) Ergotism in Pregnant Sows, Female Rats and Guinea Pigs, Amer. J. Vet. Res. **6,** 19, 107.

Rosenfeld, J. and Beath, O. A. (1950) Toxic Effects of Crude Ergot, J.A.V.M.A. **116,** 308.

Simon, J., Sund, J. M., Wright, M. J., Winter, A. and Douglass, F. O (1958) Pathological Changes Associated with Lowland Abortion Syndrome in Wisconsin, J.A.V.M.A. **132,** 4, 164.

Simon, J., Sund, J. M., Wright, M. J. and Douglas, F. O. (1959) Prevention of Noninfectious Abortion in Cattle by Weed Control and Fertilization Practices on Lowland Pastures, J.A.V.M.A. **135,** 6, 315.

Stewart, G. A. and Merilan, C. P. (1958) Effect of Potassium Nitrate Intake on Lactating Dairy Cows, Missouri Agr. Exp. Stat. Res. Bull. 650.

Tucker, J. S. (1961) Pine Needle Abortion, Proc. Amer. Coll. of Toxicologists, 35.

Udall, D. H. (1954) Practice of Veterinary Medicine, 6th Ed., Publ. by D. H. Udall, Ithaca, N.Y.

Winter, A. J. (1968) Nitrate Toxicosis as a Cause of Abortion, in **Abortion Diseases of Livestock,** edit. by L. C. Faulkner, C. C. Thomas Co., Springfield, Ill.

Woods, A. J., Jones, J. B. and Mantle, P. G. (1966) An Outbreak of Gangrenous Ergotism in Cattle, Vet. Rec. **78,** 742.

Hormonal Causes of Abortion

Adams, W. M. Jr. (1968) The Elective Induction of Labor and Parturition in the Bovine, J.A.V.M.A. **154,** 3, 261.

Adams, W. M. (1970) Personal Communication.

Adams, W. M. and Wagner, W. C. (1970) Role of Corticoids in Parturition, Biol. of Reprod. In press.

Ayalon, N., Harari, H. and Mindel, Y. (1961) Induced Abortions in Friesian Heifers, Refuah Vet. **18,** 3, 155.

Griel, L. C. Jr., Kradel, D. C. and Wickersham, E. W. (1969) Abortion in Cattle Associated with the Feeding of Poultry Litter. Cor. Vet. **59,** 2, 226.

Hill, H. J. and Pierson, R. D. (1958) Repositol Diethylstilbestrol as an Abortifacient in Feedlot Heifers, J.A.V.M.A. **132,** 12, 507.

Liggins, G. C. (1968) Premature Parturition after Infusion of Corticotrophin or Cortisol into Fetal Lambs, J. of Endocrinol, **42,** 323.

McEntee, K. (1968) Personal Communication.

Morrow, D. A. (1968) The Role of Progesterone in the Prevention of Some Early Bovine Abortions, Vet. Med. **63,** 8, 790.

Osburn, B. I., Stabenfeldt, G. H. and Ewing, L. L. (1969) Relation of Plasma Progesterone to Mid and Late Term Bovine Abortions due to **Vibrio fetus** Infection, J. Reprod. Fert. **20,** 77.

Rankin, J. E. F. (1959) Abortions in Heifers Which Had Been Fed Silage Containing Hexestrol, Vet. Rec. **71,** 924.

Risely, H. B. (1968) Personal Communication.

Tanabe, T. Y. (1966) Margin of Safety of Ovarian Progesterone in Maintenance of Single and Twin Pregnancies in Dairy Cattle, J. An. Sci. **25,** 3, 931.

Van Rensburg, S. J. (1965) Adrenal Function and Fertility, J. S. Afr. Vet. Med. Assoc. **36,** 4, 491.

Van Rensburg, S. J. (1967) Gestation in Sheep after Fetal Adrenalectomy and Cortisol Acetate Administration, J. of Endocrin. **38,** 83.

Woelffer, E. A. (1953) Use of Progesterone to Control Habitual Abortion in Cattle, J.A.V.M.A. **122,** 505.

Nutritional Causes of Abortion

Allcroft, R., Scarnell, J. and Hignett, S. L. (1954) A Preliminary

Report on Hypothyroidism in Cattle and Its Possible Relationship with Reproductive Disorders, Vet. Rec. **66,** 367.

Mace, D. L., Tucker, J. A., Bills, C. B. and Ferreira, C. J. (1963) Selenium Deficiency and Abortion in Cattle, Dept. of Agr., State of Calif. Bull. 1, **52,** 21.

Reid, J. T. (1956) Nutrition and Feeding of Dairy Cattle, J. Dairy Sci. **39,** 6, 735.

Thomas, D. O. (1968) Nutritional Aspects of Calf Losses, in Prenatal and Postnatal Mortality in Cattle, Nat. Acad. of Sci., Publ. 1685, Washington, D.C.

Physical Causes of Abortion

Ball, L. and Carroll, E. J. (1963) Induction of Fetal Death in Cattle by Manual Rupture of the Amniotic Vesicle, J.A.V.M.A. **142,** 373.

Philipsen, H. (1956) Continued Investigations on Twin Pregnancy Among Cattle and Two Methods to Prevent Twin-Birth, Proc. 3rd Internat. Congr. on An. Reprod., Cambridge.

Genetic and Chromosomal Cause of Abortion

Carr, D. H. (1967) Chromosome Anomalies as a Cause of Spontaneous Abortions, Amer. J. Obst. and Gynec. **97,** 3, 283.

Carr, D. H. (1967) Cytogenetics of Abortions in "Comparative Aspects of Reproductive Failure," Springer Verlag New York, Inc., N.Y.C.

Fechheimer, N. S. (1968) Genetic Aspects of Calf Losses, in Prenatal and Postnatal Mortality in Cattle, Nat. Acad. of Sci., Publ. 1685, Washington, D.C.

Gustavsson, I. (1969) Cytogenetics, Distribution and Phenotypic Effects of a Translocation in Swedish Cattle, Hereditas **63,** 68.

Stenchever, M. A., Jarvis, J. A. and MacIntyre, M. N. (1968) Cytogenetics of Habitual Abortion, Obst. and Gynec. **32,** 4, 548.

Stevens, R. W. C. and King, G. J. (1969) Genetic Evidence for a Lethal Mutation in Holstein Friesian Cattle, J. of Hered. **59,** 6, 366.

Thiede, H. A. and Metcalfe, S. (1966) Chromosomes and Human Pregnancy Wastage, Amer. J. Obst. and Gynec. 96, 8, 1132.

Miscellaneous Causes of Abortion

Kemen, M. J. (1964) Personal Communication.

Laing, J. A. and Blakemore, J. (1951) Erythrocyte Antibodies as a Cause of Abortion in Cattle Nature **168,** 656.

Mullins, J. (1960) Milk Allergy, N.Z. Vet. Jour. **8,** 68.

Shemanchuk, J. A., Haufe, W. O. and Thompson, C. O. M. (1960) Anemia in Range Cattle Heavily Infected with the Short Nosed Sucking Louse, **Hematopinus eurysternus,** Canad. J. Comp. Med. and Vet. Sci. **24,** 158.

Woodward, R. R. and Clark, R. T. (1959) A Study of Stillbirths in a Herd of Range Cattle, J. An. Sci. **18,** 1, 85.

Wright, J. N. (1962) Some Incompatabilities in the Blood of Cattle, Cor. Vet. 52, 3, 327.

ABORTION IN MARES

The incidence of equine abortion is higher than that experienced by cattle and is given as about 5 to 15 percent by Nishikawa and others. Many of these abortions are apparently not associated with infectious agents. A good diagnostic laboratory supplied with fresh, properly-handled, chilled equine fetuses and membranes can usually determine the cause of abortion in more than 60 percent of the cases. This is particularly true if there is an enzootic outbreak of abortion on a farm and a number of specimens are examined. This is in sharp contrast to our present knowledge of abortion in cattle. Most observed abortions in mares occur after the 4th month of gestation. The diagnosis of the cause of early unseen embryonic deaths in mares is still very difficult. As in other species of animals, equine abortions may be due to bacterial; viral; fungal; protozoan; chemical or hormonal; nutritional, physical, genetic or chromosomal, and miscellaneous causes

Infectious Bacterial Abortions in Mares

Streptococcus genitalium or **zooepidemicus** is the most common bacteria found in genital infections in horses. This organism is a hemolytic streptococcus, Lancefield's Group C, found ubiquitously on the external genital organs of all mares and stallions. It may be cultured from the genital tract for a few days after foaling in about 90 percent or more of mares. It is usually found as a contaminant from the prepuce in the semen of stallions. It is the most common organism associated with metritis, cervicities, and vaginitis secondary to pneumovagina or "windsucking." Streptococcal abortions are most common on poorly managed farms. By proper management procedures, routine genital examinations and cultures, antibiotic therapy, vulva-suturing, sexual rest, and regulated, supervised breeding, almost all mares infected with this organism can be cured and the infection prevented. This results in a very low incidence of "strep-infected" mares on a well-managed farm. Mares with a lowered resistance, trauma, or disease of the genital tract, mares bred on the ninth day after foaling, mares with lesions of the genital tract and pneumovagina, and old mares with localized areas of dilation of the uterine wall and cystic degeneration of the endometrium are most prone to the establishment of this common infection in the genital tract. The healthy genital tract of normal mares is resistant to infection including **Str. zooepidemicus** commonly introduced at parturition and breeding.

Streptococcus zooepidemicus may cause 10 to 20

Table 10. **Summary of Causes of Abortion in Mares**

Infectious causes

Bacterial—Streptococcus zooepidemicus (genitalium), Salmonella abortus equi and leptospirosis (Leptospira pomona and possibly other leptospira)

Miscellaneous Bacterial—anaerobic, motile (Lancefield Group D) and other streptococci, E. coli, Pseudomonas aeruginosa, Corynebacterium equi, Actinobacillus (Shigella) equi, Streptococcus equi, staphylococci, Klebsiella pneumoniae var genitalium, Brucella abortus, mycoplasma, diptheroids, sarcina

Viral—rhinopneumonitis or Equine Herpes I virus, arteritis virus

Miscellaneous viral—equine infectious anemia virus

Mycotic or fungal—Aspergillus fumigatus, Mucorales, and Allescheria boydii

Protozoan—Trypanosome equiperdum (dourine) and Babesia equi and caballi (piroplasmosis)

Noninfectious causes

Chemicals, drugs and poisonous plants (No material or substance confirmed as a cause for equine abortion) (Phenothiazine?)

Hormonal--estrogen, oxytocin (?), progesterone deficiency (?) and cortisone excess (?)

Nutritional—reduced energy intake

Physical—manual dilation of the cervix and douching of the uterus, natural service during pregnancy (?), trauma or injury to the very young blastodermic vesicle, torsion and strangulation of the umbilical cord and torsion of the uterus or strangulation of the uterus by a lipoma

Genetic or chromosomal—fetal anomalies, early embryonic deaths

Miscellaneous causes—twinning, early embryonic deaths

percent of abortions especially on poorly managed farms and has been reported in up to 40 percent of the aborted fetuses infected with bacteria. Since this infection is limited to the genital tract and is not spread by ingestion or other means, abortions occur in chronically-infected mares in a sporadic manner. Streptococcic abortions may occur at any stage of gestation. This organism also is a common cause of infertility and early abortion from 2 to 6 months of gestation and infection in newborn and postnatal foals. Following streptococcic abortions in the last third to one-half of gestation, retained placentas are frequent and infections of the uterus tend to persist after abortions. Some abortions are preceded by a mucopurulent vaginal discharge.

Aborted fetuses show autolytic changes that vary from slight changes to complete maceration of the fetus. **Streptococcus genitalium** may be recovered from the fetus, the fetal membranes and the genital discharges. There is no serologic test for streptococcal antibodies.

Prevention of abortion due to **Streptococcus genitalium** relies on proper management and the breeding of only normal healthy mares. Barren mares should be cultured in the fall of the year and if infected should be given suitable antibiotic and surgical treatment so the infection is overcome before breeding. Proper hygiene in the breeding shed and avoiding frequent copulations may be helpful. Certain older pluriparous mares with a lowered resistance to infection may require local antibiotic therapy after service. Chapter XIV on Infertility in Mares discusses in detail the diagnosis, therapy and preventive procedures for **Streptococcus genitalium** infection of the mare's genital tract.

Salmonella abortus equi causing contagious equine abortion was first mentioned by Kilborne in 1893 and studied and described in Kentucky in 1911 where outbreaks were common. This cause of abortion in mares has been reported in a number of states in the U.S., several European countries, Canada, South Africa, South America, and Japan. Salmonella abortion in mares has not been described in the United States since 1932 except for two isolated outbreaks in Illinois and Washington, Benner and Rhoades, Bruner, Bryans. The reason for the near disappearance of this disease is not known. **Salmonella abortus equi** may be carried in the intestinal tract of apparently normal horses. Other Salmonella serotypes have not been described as a cause of abortion in mares.

Salmonella abortus equi is spread by ingestion of feed and water contaminated by feces or genital discharges from aborting mares, especially when horses are on pasture. The incubation period is from 10 to 28 days and just before abortion occurs the mare may exhibit a general reaction, depression, anorexia and fever. If the mare is not observed closely these signs are missed and abortion results without apparent premonitory signs. Retention of the placenta may occasionally follow abortion. Most abortions occur between the 6th and 9th month of gestation but some may occur as early as the 4th month to as late as the 11th month. Infected foals born at term are weak and usually die within several days. In a susceptible band of mares the incidence of abortion may reach 50 to 90 percent. The abortion usually has no effect on the future fertility of the mare unless lacerations or infections cause subsequent chronic infection of the mare's genital tract.

The allantois chorion of the placenta often shows nonspecific edema, necrosis, and hemorrhage. The fetus exhibits the usual autolytic lesions of edema and the presence of reddish serous fluid in the body cavities. The organism may be cultured readily from the fetal organs and tissues, the fetal membranes, and the uterine exudate. Organisms in the uterine discharge disappear rapidly within a few days after abortion. Further diagnostic confirmation can be obtained by the agglutination test on the serum of the aborting mare. Infected animals at the time of abortion usually have a titer of 1:500 to 1:5000; while noninfected animals have a titer of 1:300 or less.

The use of bacterins has been highly successful in the yearly immunizing of mares against Salmonella infection contracted by ingestion. Mares are vaccinated subcutaneously at 4 months of gestation at 3 weekly intervals with 1 ml, 2 ml, and 2 ml (double strength) bacterin. This procedure is repeated 3 to 4 months later. Isolation, quarantine, and sanitation procedures are very helpful in limiting or preventing severe outbreaks of abortion. For the past 15 years vaccination of mares has not been performed in the U.S.

In an outbreak, or preferably before, the mares should be kept in small units or bands isolated from each other. Aborting mares should be isolated from the normal mares. All fetuses and membranes should be removed and destroyed and the area disinfected. The bacterin is usually used in an outbreak but some mares may abort before immunity has developed.

Leptospirosis due to **L. pomona,** and possibly other leptospiral serotypes, has occasionally been reported as a cause for abortion in mares from the seventh through eleventh month of gestation, Crane, Jackson et al., Hults and Murray, Little et al., and Roberts. The mares may show a mild systemic reaction with a moderately elevated temperature of 102 to 103° F, slight icterus, anorexia, and depression that lasts for 3 to 4 days. One to 3 weeks later abortions may occur. The aborted fetus may be slightly icteric and show some autolysis. The mare will often exhibit a high leptospiral titer of the blood at the time of abortion. The blood testing of normal, acutely ill, aborting and recovering mares in an outbreak may aid in diagnosis. A rising titer associated with abortion is highly significant. Recovery of the organism from autolysed, aborted equine fetuses, as in cattle, is difficult. Special staining of fetal organ sections and the fluorescent antibody technique may prove of diagnostic value in leptospiral abortion in mares. Morter et al. reported that following experimental infection, horses can shed **Leptospira pomona** in the urine for 70 to over 94 days, but less than 120 days. Periodic opthalmia occurred in these horses 12 to 14 months later. Treatment of leptospirosis in horses is similar to the treatment in cattle and swine. Yearly vaccination of horses with a bacterin the first trimester of gestation may prevent abortion as well as periodic ophthalmia due to **L. pomona.** If the early mild signs of acute illness due to leptospirosis are observed including: moderately elevated body temperature, depression, inappetance and slight icterus, the affected animal should be placed on therapeutic levels of streptomycin and penicillin or a tetracycline for 4 to 5 days. This therapy may prevent abortion as well as periodic opthalmia caused by **L. pomona.**

Miscellaneous bacterial infections associated with sporadic abortions in horses may cause from 5 to 10 percent of the total abortions due to bacterial agents. These include: anaerobic **Streptococci viridans,** motile **Streptococci** (Lancefield Group D), **Streptococcus equi, Escherichia coli,** staphylococci, **Actinobacillus (Shigella) equuli, Corynebacterium equi, Klebsiella pneumoniae var genitalium, Pseudomonas aeruginosa,** Dimock et al., diptheroids, sarcina, **Brucella abortus,** McNutt and Murray, McCaughey and Kerr, and mycoplasma, Aubaidi. Pure cultures of organisms from the organs of aborted fetuses is the usual means of diagnosing these sporadic bacterial causes of abortion. Many bacterial agents causing abortion may be present in the uterus at conception and persist for a varying period while others, such as leptospira and salmonella, gain access to the uterus hematogenously during pregnancy. It is probably uncommon for organisms to enter the uterus through the normal closed and sealed cervix during pregnancy.

Viral Causes of Abortion in Mares

Abortion in mares is known to be caused by the rhinopneumonitis or equine Herpes I and arteritis viruses. Rarely abortions are reported associated with equine infectious anemia and other viral diseases.

Abortion due to the equine Herpes virus I or rhinopneumonitis virus.

Abortion in mares is commonly due to equine Herpes virus I. This virus belongs to the Herpes-group of viruses and it has many similarities in common with the IBR-IPV virus in cattle, McKercher et al.. However, the IBR viral vaccine did not produce antibodies or heterotypic immunity to equine herpes virus in horses. Other herpes viruses have been isolated from horses with respiratory diseases and coital exanthema or genital horse pox however there is no evidence that they can cause abortion, Bryans (1968).

Virus abortion was prevalent in Kentucky at least as early as 1922. It was shown to be caused by a virus in 1936, Doll (1954). In 1941 Manninger and Csontos indicated that in mares virus abortion was secondary to influenza. In 1954 Doll and Kintner demonstrated that the virus of equine virus abortion and equine "influenza" virus were the same. Since then two true influenza viruses, Prague, A_1 and Miami, A_2, have been isolated, so the name rhinopneumonitis and then equine Herpes virus I was given to this herpes virus causing an upper respiratory disease in horses and abortion in mares.

Rhinopneumonitis and abortion due to equine Herpes virus I have been commonly diagnosed in Europe, Japan, Canada, Corner et al., and the U.S.. The disease may be introduced to a farm by infected foals or horses and by infective material carried there by persons, dogs, foxes, or carrion birds. This virus is quite resistant and may survive 7 to 42 days or more in dry stable surroundings, Doll et al. (1959). Following a natural infection or vaccination with live virus vaccine, the horse may spread the virus for 3 to 4 weeks. It is highly possible that this virus, as other herpes viruses, may persist in the organs and tissues of certain "carrier" animals for long periods of time. Stress may play a role in releasing this virus or causing an exacerbation of the disease. The equine Herpes Virus I is only naturally pathogenic for horses, but it can cause abortion when inoculated into guinea pig fetuses. It can be adapted and grown in suckling hamsters and in cultures of kidney tissue cells from a number of animal species, McCollum et al..

The clinical signs of rhinopneumonitis are those of a mild, febrile respiratory disease usually observed in young horses 4 to 8 months of age in the fall and early winter months. The incubation period is 2 to 3 days. The body temperature is elevated to 102 to 104° F. A serous rhinitis with congestion of the nasal mucosa and conjunctiva occurs often associated with coughing, inappetence, and depression. A leucopenia usually is present. In about 7 to 10 days, the febrile period ends and a mucopurulent rhinitis, "the snots," develops which, along with a cough, lasts for several weeks or longer. The disease can occur in any age of horse at any time of the year. The virus is highly infectious and contagious and is spread mainly by inhalation or droplet infection or occasionally by ingestion. In older animals this disease may frequently be so mild as to be unrecognized.

The incubation period for abortion in natural infections due to rhinopneumonitis virus or equine Herpes virus I is 20 to 30 days with a range of 18 to 90 days. Since evidence indicates that fetuses die soon after they are infected with Herpes virus I and are aborted, the long incubation period of this disease is intriguing. Bryans has shown that a viremia with the virus in the leucocytes may last for about 21 days. Kendrick has hypothesized that the virus may reside in the chorion of the placenta for a time, as is possible with IBR virus in cattle, before infecting and killing the fetus. Thus abortions in mares on breeding farms often follow the outbreak of the respiratory disease in foals by several months, Doll and Bryans. If the mare exhibits typical respiratory signs of the disease, abortions follow apparent recovery by several weeks or months. In many affected mares respiratory disease due to this virus may be undiagnosed. Fetal deaths and abortions seldom occur before 5 months of gestation and over 90 percent of the abortions occur from 8 to 11 months of gestation. Often infected foals may be born alive but die within a few minutes to 4 days postpartum. Thus breeding practices largely determine the season or time when abortions occur; in Kentucky 90 percent of the abortions occurred from December through April.

The degree of immunity in a band of mares and the number of pregnant mares in a band at the time of the outbreak determine the abortion rate which may vary from 1 to 90 percent of a band of mares. Keeping the pregnant mares on a farm separated into small units well-isolated from other mares, horses, and young stock does much to reduce the spread and incidence of abortion in an outbreak. In Kentucky 85 percent of the farms had 3 or fewer cases of virus abortion with an average abortion rate per farm per year of 2.5 percent, with a range of 1.6 to 6 percent. Abortions on a farm will occur over a period of 2 weeks to 3 months with 88 percent of the abortions occurring within 60 days of the first abortion. Data from Kentucky indicated that this virus was present in 52 percent of aborted, infected fetuses and caused 26 percent of the total abortions in mares, Doll and Bryans.

The equine Herpes virus I causes the death of the fetus and no signs of impending abortion are observed. Retention of the placenta is uncommon. The mare is not traumatized unless a large fetus causes tearing of the tissues in the vulva or perineal region. Following viral abortions, mares usually conceive readily the next breeding period unless secondary infections have occurred.

Examination of the aborted fetus and membranes in this disease usually reveals an edematous amnion, yellow amniotic fluid, a slightly yellow or icteric color of the fetal body tissues, straw-colored fluid in the thoracic cavity, edema and small hemorrhages in the lung, petechial and ecchymotic hemorrhages in the epicardium, and small whitish-yellow, pinhead-sized foci of necrosis in the liver. On microscopic examination of stained liver, bile duct, lymph node, thymus, and bronchial cells, intranuclear inclusion bodies are frequently found. These latter signs in the fetus are of great diagnostic value. (See Figures 67 and 68)

Signs of paresis in both females and males have been associated with a few outbreaks of rhinopneumonitis and abortion that have been reported, Bruner, Jennings, Saxegaard. The first symptom noted is a dragging of the toes of the rear hoofs. This progresses into ataxia, paresis, prostration, and death in up to 60 percent of the horses. These nervous signs are apparently due to the neurotropic form of the equine Herpes virus I (rhinopneumonitis virus) that can cause myelitis and encephalitis. Saxegaard recovered the virus from the central nervous tissue. This condition may be the same as the Landry-Guillain-Barre syndrome described in humans and characterized by a segmental demyelination of nerve fibers in the spinal nerves and cord, Haymaker and Kernohan, Asbury, Arnason and Adams, and Martens, Stewart and Eichholtz. Other diseases may also cause posterior paresis, see "Wobblers," and must be differentiated from this condition.

There is no permanent immunity to viral rhinopneumonitis or abortion. Many aborting mares apparently develop a fairly long immunity of one to two years. The respiratory form of the disease apparently does not provide as long nor as good as an immunity as occurs follow-

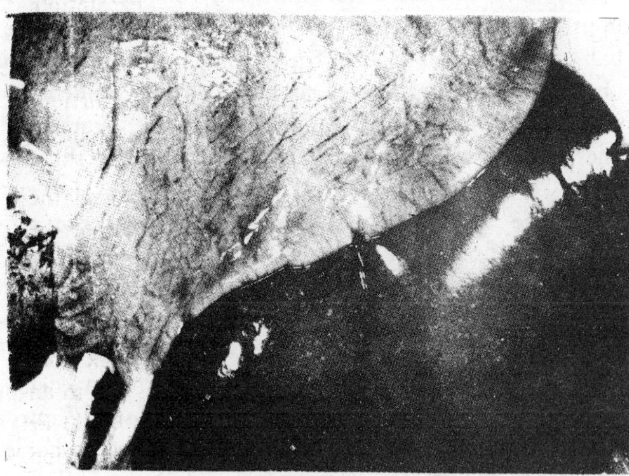

Figure 67. Liver and lung of an aborted 10-month equine fetus. Fetal death was due to equine Herpes virus I. Note small necrotic foci in the liver and edema of the lung. (Courtesy K. McEntee).

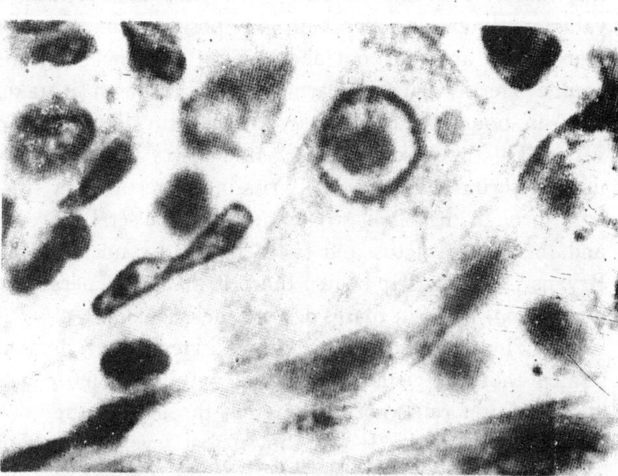

Figure 68. Intranuclear inclusion body in a liver cell of an equine fetus following Herpesvirus abortion. (Courtesy K. McEntee).

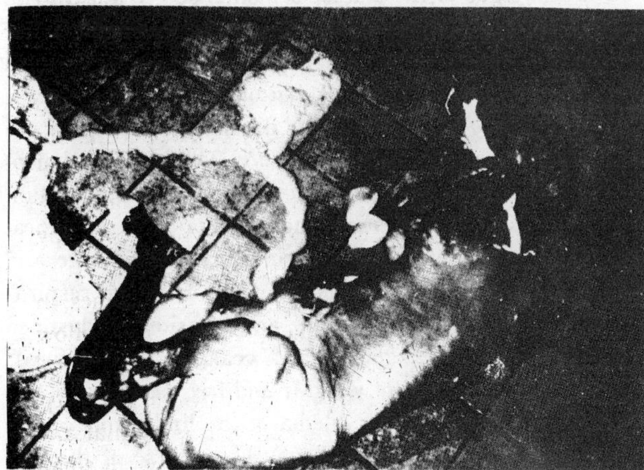

Figure 69. Torsion of the umbilical cord of a 7-month equine fetus resulting in abortion.

Figure 70. **Toxoplasma gondii** abortion in a ewe. Note the white toxoplasma bodies in the maternal caruncles.

ing an abortion. Some horses may lose their immunity within 3 to 6 months after infection or vaccination but the disease is so common that most horses are frequently exposed and thus maintain a satisfactory immunity. Repeated frequent exposures to diseased horses or repeated vaccinations with a living vaccine increases the level of resistance. Strict isolation of mares on breeding farms without vaccination is therefore likely to increase their susceptibility.

The complement fixation (CF) test or serum neutralization test can be used to determine antibody levels in the serum of horses following this viral respiratory disease or abortion but it is not diagnostic. Antibodies persist for only a month or two up to one year even in aborting mares, Doll and Bryans. This test is also of limited value in diagnosis since both CF positive and negative mares may abort or not abort when challenged by the equine Herpesvirus I. Carmichael has shown it takes over an hour for immune serum to neutralize virus **in vitro.** This may explain why some mares with antibody in their serum may have the virus in the respiratory tract pass through the blood stream and into the fetal placenta and then to the fetus and cause its death and abortion. Bryans (1969) has indicated there is a viremia persisting for up to 3 weeks in mares despite the coexistence of virus neutralizing antibody in the blood. He further demonstrated that the virus was carried within the leucocytes and the latter cells carried the virus throughout the body and to the placenta. It was shown that several "grades" of immunity existed depending upon the amount of antibody present at the site of infection in the nasopharynx. This immunity was a reflection of the level of virus neutralizing antibody in the blood. Culture of the liver or lungs of freshly aborted fetuses on tissue culture medium may result in the recovery of the virus.

Viral abortion may be effectively controlled on a breeding farm by the routine use of a live vaccine prepared from hamsters, Doll and Bryans. The earlier killed vaccine prepared from equine fetal tissues and hamster tissues did not produce a satisfactory immunity. The use of the former often produced isoantibodies in the mare resulting in neonatal isoerythrolysis in the foal, Doll et al.. Hamster tissues have produced higher levels of virus than have tissue cultures of the virus. The live vaccine is administered intranasally in a 3 ml. dose with a flexible plastic catheter, late in June or early in July and again in October for those farms with a breeding season extending from February 15 to June 15, Doll. This program is not satisfactory for those farms breeding throughout the year or through the summer and early fall months as there is too great a variation in stages of gestation among mares on these farms. The intranasal inoculation of horses recently wormed by means of a stomach tube should be avoided. This vaccine should not be used in sick animals or those under stress. It should not be used simultaneously with other viral vaccines. Vaccination of mares after the fifth month or late in gestation is contraindicated. All horses on the farm including foals should be vaccinated. Vaccination may cause mild clinical respiratory infections in susceptible horses. Vaccinated horses should not be taken off the farm for a month or more as they may spread the virus for a period of 3 to 4 weeks and thus produce the disease in susceptible horses.

This "controlled infection," vaccination procedure has prevented severe outbreaks of virus abortion in mares, Doll, Doll and Bryans. In 6,680 properly vaccinated horses there was an incidence of only 0.8 percent abortions due to this virus, one-half due to field virus and one-half due to vaccine virus. In a comparable number of unvaccinated mares there was a 15 percent incidence of virus abortion. Properly applied isolation, quarantine, and sanitary measures may also aid in limiting this disease.

Equine arteritis or epizootic cellulitis-pinkeye syndrome is caused by the arteritis virus that produces signs of severe general respiratory disease including abortion. These signs are closely related to the constant and characteristic necrotic lesions of the media of the small arteries produced by the arteritis virus and resulting in edema, hemorrhages, and infarcts. The disease is usually introduced on a farm by an infected or convalescent horse. Outbreaks are presently very infrequent in the U.S. The disease has been described in Europe by Burki and Gerber. The virus is spread by droplet or aerosol infection and contracted by inhalation. Thus close contact between horses is necessary for the spread of this disease.

Clinical signs of the disease are often severe and should not be confused with the milder "shipping fever" type diseases of influenza or rhinopneumonitis. Horses of all ages may be affected. The incubation period of the disease is 3 to 9 days. The signs of the disease often include: an elevation of the body temperature to 103 to 106° F; leucopenia with panlymphopenia; conjunctivitis, lacrimation and occasionally keratitis, photophobia and palpebral edema; severe depression; a serious nasal discharge and congested nasal mucous membranes; an increased respiratory rate of 30 to 50 per minute, and occasionally dyspnea with a "heave line"; generalized weakness and stiffness; anorexia; a rapid loss of weight; and frequently colic and diarrhea. In a few horses edema of the limbs and/or the ventral abdominal wall develops. The course of the disease is 2 to 15 days. Deaths in natural outbreaks are not common but experimentally infected old horses, pregnant mares, and weanlings may develop a severe illness with a

30 to 50 percent mortality due to pulmonary edema, pleural effusion, and secondary cardiac disturbances. However, some natural cases of the disease may be so mild the signs of illness may pass unnoticed.

Abortions are closely associated with the febrile and early convalescent period of the disease and occur 1 to 14 days after the onset of signs of illness. The mare fails to show signs of impending abortion. Abortion may occur in up to 50 percent of the pregnant susceptible mares exposed to the virus. Some mares abort without obvious signs of clinical illness and some mares with definite signs of illness will not abort. Most abortions occur in mares from the fifth through tenth month of gestation. Retention of the placenta is uncommon in aborting mares. Some fetuses apparently die 2 to 4 days before abortion because autolytic changes are common. Postmortem fetal lesions include petechial hemorrhages on the peritoneal and pleural surfaces, epicardium and endocardium, and pleural effusions. No inclusion bodies are found with this disease but the virus can be recovered from many fetal tissues including the liver and lungs, Wilson et al.. The virus can be grown on tissue cultures of horse and hamster kidney cells. There is evidence that a serum neutralization test could be developed to detect antibodies.

Following recovery a prolonged immunity to the arteritis virus is probable. An attenuated virus vaccine has been prepared that shows promise as an effective preventative, McCollum. This has not yet become available commercially, probably because of the limited occurrence of the disease. Proper segregation, isolation, and quarantine along with other sanitary procedures would be helpful in preventing the spread of this infection on a farm.

Equine infectious anemia is occasionally characterized by abortion in infected pregnant mares, Ishii, Bruner and Gillespie, Medearis. The pathogenesis of abortion due to equine infectious anemia virus has not been established and more study is indicated.

Mycotic or fungal agents of the species **Aspergillus fumigatus,** the order **Mucorales** and **Allescheria boydii,** may cause sporadic abortions in mares. Rooney reported that mycotic agents may cause 5 to 10 percent of all abortions in mares in central Kentucky; it has also been reported in Germany and England. The cause of the abortion is apparently a severely diseased necrotic, thickened allantois chorion which interferes with fetal nutrition and causes fetal death. (See Figure 64) Mold may be cultured from the placenta, and occasionally the fetal organs such as liver, stomach, lungs and the fetal skin. It is likely that the mold is carried to the placenta in the blood stream from lesions in the wall of the intestine or lungs. It may also be associated, as in cattle, with the ingestion or inhalation of mold spores from moldy hay or straw during pregnancy. Because of the excellent equine uterine defense mechanism, it is unlikely that mold introduced into the uterus at the time of copulation would remain viable for months and then infect the placenta. Mold abortions usually occur from the 4th to 8th month of gestation. Following abortion the mold infection does not persist in the uterus but service on the foal estrum should be avoided.

Protozoan organisms including **Trypanosome equiperdum** causing dourine, Gibbons, and **Babesia equi** and **caballi** causing piroplasmosis may occasionally or rarely produce abortion in mares. Dourine is transmitted almost entirely by sexual contact. It was first recognized in the U.S. in Illinois in 1885 by Dr. W. L. Williams in horses bred to a stallion shipped from France. By the use of the complement-fixation test and destroying all reactors the disease has probably been eradicated from the last infected area in southwest U.S. This disease is discussed in more detail in a later chapter.

Babesiasis or **piroplasmosis** may result in abortion in severely affected horses. This disease has been reported in South Africa; at present in the U.S. it is limited mainly to Florida. Signs of the disease closely resemble those of equine infectious anemia except icterus and hemoglobinuria may also be present. The parasite is spread by bloodsucking ticks and may be found, for diagnostic purposes, within the erythrocytes by proper staining techniques. In infected, aborted, premature or term fetuses or foals, icterus and anemia is present requiring differentiation from equine infectious anemia, rhinopneumonitis virus abortion, neonatal isoerythrolysis, and leptospirosis. The fluorescent antibody technique may be helpful in detecting the parasite in the red blood cells of the fetus or foal. The complement-fixation test on horse serum is highly specific for **B. caballi** infection and persists for 1 to 5 years, Frerichs et al..

Noninfectious Causes for Equine Abortion

Chemicals, drugs and poisonous plants including: phenothiazine; thiabendazole; "Lentin"; purgatives, such as arecoline, aloes; sudan or sorghum pastures, Romane et al. and Van Kampen, organic phosphate insecticides and anthelmintics; ergot and others have been reported as possibly causing abortions if given to or ingested by mares in advanced pregnancy. Such causes of sporadic abortions are often proposed but the scientific basis for these reports has not been adequately substantiated. If abortion should follow the administration or ingestion of these or other possibly toxic materials the attending veterinarian should obtain a careful history and have the fetus(es) necropsied and examined carefully for the more common, known causes of abortion in horses.

Hormonal causes of abortion in horses may be similar to those described for cattle but little or no experimental or controlled studies have been performed on mares.

Estrogens in large doses over a long period regularly produces abortion in other species of animals. Wohanka reported that 50 to 150 mg of estrogen caused abortion in one of 3 mares.

Oxytocin or pituitrin administered to pregnant mares has not been proven to cause abortion but may induce parturition in mares after 345 days of gestation.

A deficiency of progesterone has been reported as a common cause of abortion in mares from 1-1/2 to 8 months of gestation. The initial corpus luteum of pregnancy in the mare should provide the necessary progesterone for the maintenance of pregnancy from a few days after fertilization of the ovum to about 40 days of gestation when the endometrial cups begin producing FSH to cause continued follicle growth, ovulation and the formation of many accessory corpora lutea. These accessory corpora lutea produce the necessary progesterone until the fourth to fifth month of gestation when the endometrial cups disappear and the mare's ovaries, along with the accessory corpora lutea, atrophy and the equine placenta, which has been producing fairly large amounts of progesterone since 90 days of gestation, maintains pregnancy to term, Short, Ryan and Ainsworth.

Osborne reported that normal mares' ovaries are packed with accessory corpora lutea about the third month of gestation. In some mares she autopsied soon after an early abortion, as determined by the presence of endometrial cups in the uterus, very few if any accessory corpora lutea were present and in a few cases only the original corpus luteum following the last estrus was present.

In recent years a number of commercial horse farms have been established in New York State and Canada to provide pregnant mare's urine as a source of estrogen for medical purposes. Many of these farms have experienced a large number of abortions between 100 and 150 days of gestation in the Fall of the year which were not due to bacterial, viral or mycotic agents. Mitchell reported on 51 outbreaks of abortion on 42 farms from 1962 to 1966. Seventy percent or 35 of these outbreaks were in the Fall of the year. Of 1870 mares at risk on these 35 farms, 224 mares aborted for an incidence of 12 percent. Lein reported on one farm where 22 of 50 mares aborted from 3 to 5 months of gestation. Mitchell further reported that 214 of the 224 aborting mares aborted during October and November and abortions suddenly ceased by mid-December. One hundred and fifty-seven mares or 65 percent aborted from 1 to 14 days and 89 percent aborted from 1 to 28 days after removing the pregnant mares from pasture and stabling them. In 237 abortions 87.3 percent occurred from 91 to 150 days of gestation. In 19 herds where the management and husbandry was poor the incidence of abortions was 19.3 percent compared to 8.6 percent in 16 herds with adequate or good management. Mitchell indicated that the 100 to 150 day period was a critical stage of gestation and the "stresses" associated with stabling including: a lowered plane of nutrition, trucking and rough handling, restriction of water intake to concentrate the urinary estrogens, the application of the urine-collection harness and any debilitating condition such as pediculosis, excessive humidity and close confinement would precipitate abortion. If these factors were ameliorated by gradual confinement and improved husbandry and management including better nutrition, abortions could largely be prevented. Progesterone therapy at the time of stabling has been suggested. After a limited trial using repositol progesterone Mitchell was doubtful that a progesterone deficiency was the primary problem. Further studies are indicated.

The author observed and studied 5 abortions at 4 to 5 months of gestation in 6 two-year old pregnant mares shipped by rail from New Mexico to New York. The trip required 7 days and all 5 mares aborted 3 to 7 days after arrival. No infectious cause was found on careful autopsy and cultural studies. The author suggests in light of the discussion on the abortifacient properties of the glucocorticoids reported in the section on abortion in cattle that stress resulting in hypersecretion of glucocorticoids by the adrenals might be the factor precipitating the abortions on the horse farms cited above. Van Niekerk reported on a close correlation between early embryonic deaths in mares and malnutrition. Obviously further studies are needed. It is an open question whether a progesterone deficiency or a glucocorticoid excess is a factor in these outbreaks. Possibly with the restriction of water intake, an increased production and release of vasopressin or antidiuretic hormone from the posterior pituitary gland might effect the uterine masculature producing abortion.

The current use of progesterone to prevent abortions in mares with a previous history of one or more abortions due to an unknown or undiagnosed cause is empirical. The indications for, the value of, and the daily amount of progesterone needed to prevent abortion in mares is not known. Present doses of progesterone recommended by different equine practitioners vary from 100 mg in pellet form given once intramuscularly at 42 days of gestation to 500 to 1000 mg of "Repositol" progesterone given intramuscularly every 7 to 10 days from 42 days of gestation to near term. A recent report by Loy and Swan showed that 100 mg of progesterone in oil daily would block estrus and ovulation in mares; but neither aqueous suspensions of 500 mg of crystalline progesterone nor synthetic progestogens, 400 to 1700 mg. of MAP or 10 to 20 mg. of MGA, fed orally, had any effect on blocking estrus and ovulation in mares. It would thus appear likely that progesterone pellets or **Repositol** progesterone and progestagens would be of questionable or no value in mares as replacement therapy for a progesterone deficiency. Short has reported that after midgestation the progesterone levels in the peripheral blood of mares is very low or nondetectable but a large amount of progesterone is present in the placenta and probably maintains pregnancy by a local effect on the uterus. Whether parenteral injections of progesterone will produce the desired effects in late gestation will require further study. In the early stages of gestation in some mares it might be advisable to inject FSH followed by LH to produce additional accessory corpora lutea. Nishikawa recommended the injection of 2 to 10 mg. of stilbestrol every 2 to 4 days for a period of about 60 days around the 4th to 5th month of gestation to prolong the functional life of the corpus luteum to prevent abortion due to hormonal causes. Five hundred and seventy-six mares, of which 56.8 percent had experienced 1 to 5 previous abortions, treated in the above manner, or by the oral administration of stilbestrol, only 3.3 percent aborted compared to 12.7 percent abortions in untreated mares.

Ryan and Ainsworth reported that in humans the fetal adrenal glands, possibly the fetal gonads, and the maternal adrenals produce steroid precursors for the placental production of steroid hormones to help maintain pregnancy the latter half of gestation. They also reported that abortions in humans due to a lack of progesterone are commonly diagnosed but are difficult to prove. Ryan stated that at present, despite the widespread use of progesterone for the prevention of human abortions, there is no critical evidence proving its value. Many interesting and careful endocrine studies remain to be performed during gestation in mares to determine the actual incidence of equine abortion due to a progesterone deficiency and to develop proven methods of therapy.

Nutritional deficiencies as a cause for abortion in mares has been reported by Van Niekerk and Mitchell. The former reported early embryonic deaths 7 to 10 days after the mares were placed on poor pasture at 18 days of gestation. The latter reported a high incidence of abortion at 3 to 5 months of gestation in mares 1 to 14 days after confinement in barns and the feeding of a poor ration together with a reduced water intake. These early embryonic and fetal deaths although associated with a lowered level of nutrition may have been due to other hormonal or physiological factors previously discussed. There are no authoritative reports on abortions due to vitamin or mineral deficiences in horses. Further nutritional studies in pregnant mares are needed.

Physical causes for abortion in mares

The manual dilation of the cervix and the introduction of several hundred milliliters of physiological saline, dilute Lugol's solution or iodized oil readily produces abortion within 3 to 10 days in most mares. Occasionally a second treatment may be necessary, Wohanka, Richter. Purposely aborting mares the last 3 months of gestation is not recommended because complications may arise due to the large size of the fetus.

Natural service during pregnancy, especially the first 3 months of gestation, is not uncommon due to increased ovarian follicular activity during this period. Abortions following natural matings during pregnancy are rare.

Trauma or injury has been reported as a cause of abortion in mares. These reports are not well-documented. Rough manipulation of the blastodermic vesicle from 20 to 50 days of gestation should be avoided. Wohanka reported on 27 mares that were frequently examined between 20 to 82 days of gestation with no abortions resulting. Only 2 of 6 mares aborted after 145 days of gestation when exposed to severe rectal and vaginal mechanical and thermal irritation. Thus a normal pregnant mare is relatively resistant to abortion produced by physical means. In twin pregnancy diagnosed prior to 30 days of gestation, Garbers has reported the successful crushing of one blastodermic vesicle permitting the other to develop normally. Severe stress produced by prolonged difficult shipping, hard sustained work, difficult and complicated operations, vigorous struggling and trauma during casting may cause abortion in mares as discussed previously.

Torsion or strangulation of the umbilical cord is responsible for about 1 percent of the fetal deaths and abortions the latter half of gestation, Dimock et al.. The normal long umbilical cord in the foal has from 1 to 3 rotations. In occasional fetuses the cord becomes excessively twisted, swollen and edematous (See Figure 69) or rarely becomes wrapped tightly around a fetal extremity closing the lumen of the blood vessels between the placenta and the fetus. This appears to be accidental. Strangulation of a uterus by a lipoma or torsion of the uterus may rarely cause fetal death in the mare.

Genetic or chromosomal causes of abortion

Fetal anomalies as a possible cause for equine abortion have been reported in about 1.3 percent of aborted equine fetuses, Dimock et al.. Chromosomal defects of the equine zygote as in other animals (See abortion in cattle) may cause early embryonic death. These defects are favored by aging of the spermatozoa or ovum prior to fertilization which is highly possible in mares due to their long estrous period, Lanman.

Miscellaneous causes of abortion

Twinning is a very common cause of equine abortion. Asdell reported that 3.8 percent of ovulations in mares were double ovulations; Osborne and Arthur reported much higher figures of 14.5 and 18.5 percent respectively. However, only 0.5 to 1 percent of mares give birth to twins. Certain mares, as cows, apparently produce twins more frequently than other mares; one mare observed by the author aborted twins in 4 of 9 gestation periods. About 80 to 90 percent of twin fetuses that live through the fourth month of gestation are aborted from 5 months to term. Jennings and Dimock et al. reported that 9 and 12 percent respectively of the total incidence of equine abortion was due to twins. This figure would undoubtedly be higher if unobserved abortions early in gestation were noted. A failure of the placental vessels of the allantois chorion of one twin to anastomose with the other, possibly because of the physical distance between the two blastocysts together with a lack of sufficient placental area for adequate nutrition of one of the fetuses results in the death of that fetus and the abortion of both fetuses, Errington. Occasionally mummification or maceration of the dead fetus will occur with its subsequent expulsion at a later date when the other fetus is aborted or born at term. This unequal size of the placental areas available for nutritional exchange probably accounts for the unequal size of most equine twin fetuses. This is often incorrectly diagnosed as superfetation. Since it is probable that in the latter half of gestation in the mare progesterone necessary to maintain pregnancy is produced in the allantois chorion, it may be possible that abortion is due to a sudden drop in progesterone levels caused by the death of one fetus and its membranes. Evans has reported that removing too many canine fetuses and their membranes in late gestation in the bitch results in the abortion of the remainder unless supplemental progesterone is injected parenterally.

Early embryonic deaths in horses have received little experimental study. There is no evidence for venereal diseases causing early embryonic deaths in horses, such as vibriosis and trichomoniasis in cattle. Most recognized abortions in mares occur after 4 months of pregnancy. However, many unrecognized and unseen expulsions or abortions of embryos and fetuses may occur from 1 to 4 months of gestation. In the first few months of gestation maceration and partial or complete absorption of the dead conceptus may occur as described by VanNiekerk. Probably most of these macerating embryos are expelled after a variable period except in cases involving the death of only one of twin embryos with the other embryo remaining viable. This has been observed by Arthur, the author and others.

Many cases of early embryonic death, especially from 20 to 60 days of pregnancy, are erroneously diagnosed as failure of conception, "missed" or "silent" estrous periods, or "spurious" conceptions. A mare with a "spurious" conception has been serviced by a stallion, apparently conceived, and failed to exhibit estrus thereafter, even with a good "teasing" program. She exhibits normal vaginal signs of pregnancy but is not pregnant when examined rectally 30 to 50 days after service. On well-managed farms with veterinary supervision of the mares, a 2 to 10 percent and occasionally up to 20 percent loss of embryos and fetuses is experienced between routine pregnancy diagnoses at 40 and again at 110 days of gestation, Britton, Jennings, Knudson, Patterson and Sager. Merkt reported an incidence of 21 percent early embryonic death loss the second month of pregnancy in 573 foaling mares compared to only 2 percent loss in barren mares. The incidence was highest in the mares conceiving on the foal estrum. The possible relationship between these early embryonic deaths and lactation was considered. Van Niekerk reported embryonic deaths from 25 to 31 days of gestation associated with malnutrition. On the basis of studies in other species, some of these losses in mares may be presumed to be due to genetic or chromosomal defects resulting in improper development of the embryo or fetus. Britton reported that one infertile stallion produced conceptions with twice the early embryonic death loss of other stallions. Others may result from an abnormal uterine environment in mares infected with **Streptococcus genitalium** or other bacteria. Bacterial infections are often associated with breeding at the foal estrus, improper closure of the genital tract due to poor conformation, lacerations and chronic scarring of the vulva resulting in pneumovagina, severe chronic lacerations or scarring of the cervix, and cystic degeneration of the endometrium in older mares. Some mares may lack sufficient progesterone to maintain early pregnancy.

References on Equine Abortion

General

Bain, A. M. (1963) Common Bacterial Infections of Fetuses and Foals, Austral. Vet. Jour **39,** 413.

Blood, D. C. and J. Henderson (1963) Veterinary Medicine, 2nd Ed., Williams and Wilkins Co., Baltimore, Maryland.

Bruner, D. W., and J. H. Gillespie (1966) Hagan's Infectious Diseases of Domestic Animals, 5th Ed., Comstock Publishing Co., Ithaca, N.Y.

Dimock, W. W., P. R. Edwards, and D. W. Bruner (1947) Infections Observed in Equine Fetuses and Foals, Cor. Vet. **37,** 2, 89.

Jennings, W. E. (1950) Twelve Years of Horse Breeding in the Army, J.A.V.M.A. **116,** 11, 874.

Roberts, S. J. (1956) Veterinary Obstetrics and Genital Diseases, 1st Ed., Distributed by Edwards Bros., Inc., Ann Arbor, Mich.

Specific References

Bacterial Infections

Aubaidi, J. (1969) Personal Communication.

Benner, Ernest R., and Rhoades, H. E. (1966) Charlestown, W. Va. and Univ. of Illinois, Urbana, Ill. Personal Communication.

Bruner, D. W. (1965) Personal Communication.

Bryans, J. T. (1967) Personal Communication.

Bryans, J. T. (1968) Equine Salmonellosis, Animal Health News, March 3.

Crane, C. S. (1956) A Report on Leptospirosis in a Herd of Shetland Ponies, J.A.V.M.A. **129,** 260.

Dimock, W. W., Edwards, P. R. and Bruner, D. W. (1947) Infections Observed in Equine Fetuses and Foals, Cor. Vet. **37,** 2, 89.

Hults, C., and Murray, R. W. (1966) Rutland, Vermont. Personal communication.

Jackson, R. S., Jones, E. E. and Clark, D. S. (1957) Abortion in Mares Associated with Leptospirosis, J.A.V.M.A. **131,** 12, 564.

Little, R. B., Beck, J. D. and McCahon, J. V. (1950) An Outbreak of Bovine Leptospirosis in Pennsylvania, Vet. Med. **45,** 3, 104.

McCaughey, W. J. and Kerr, W. R. (1967) Abortion due to Brucellosis in a Thoroughbred Mare, Vet. Rec. **80,** 186.

McNutt, S. H. and Murray, C. (1927) **Bacterium abortum** Isolated from the Fetus of an Aborting Mare, J.A.V.M.A. **65,** 2, 215.

Morter, R. L., Herschler, R. C., Fessler, J. F. and Lavignette, A. (1964) Experimental Equine Leptospirosis (**L. pomona**), Proc. 68th Annual Meeting U.S.L.S.A., 147.

Roberts, S. J. (1952) An Outbreak of Leptospirosis in Horses on a Small Farm, J.A.V.M.A. **121,** 907, 237.

Viral Infections

Rhinopneumonitis

Anonymous, (1961) Virus Research, Blood Horse, Dec. 9, 1451.

Asbury, A. K., Arnason, B. G. and Adams, R. D. (1969) The Inflammatory Lesion in Idiopathic Polyneuritis. Its Role in Pathogenesis, Medicine, **48,** 173.

Bryans, J. T. (1968) The Herpesvirus in Disease of the Horse, Proc. 14th Ann. Meeting A.A.E.P., Phila., 119.

Bryans, J. T. (1969) On Immunity to Disease Caused by Equine Herpesvirus I, Symposium on Immunity to Selected Equine Diseases, Lexington, Ky., J.A.V M.A. **155,** 2, Part 2, 295.

Bruner, D. W. (1958) Personal Communication.

Carmichael, L. E. (1962) Personal Communication.

Corner, A. H., Mitchell, D., Meads, E. B., and Girard, A., Greig, A. S. and Mitchell, D. (1963) Equine Virus Abortion in Canada, Cor. Vet. **53,** 1, pp 78 and 88.

Dimock, W. W. (1940) The Diagnosis of Virus Abortion in Mares, J.A.V.M.A. **96,** 665.

Dimock, W. W., Edwards, P. R., and Bruner, D. W. (1942) Equine Virus Abortion, Kentucky Agr. Exp. Stat. Bulletin 426.

Doll, E. R. (1954) History of Research on Equine Virus Abortion, Dept. of Animal Path., Kentucky Agr. Exp. Stat., Lexington, Ky.

Doll, E. R. (1960) A Catheter for Nasal Inoculation of Large Animals, Amer. J. Vet. Res., **21,** 82, 518.

Doll, E. R. (1961) Immunization against Viral Rhinopneumonitis of Horses with Live Virus Propagated in Hamsters, J.A.V.M.A., **139,** 12, 1324.

Doll, E. R. (1963) Respiratory Diseases, Dept. of Animal Path., Univ. of Kentucky, Stud Managers Short Course.

Doll, E. R. (1963) Viral Respiratory Diseases of Horses, Proc. Amer. Assoc. of Eq. Pract.

Doll, E. R. and Bryans, J. T. (1962) Incubation Periods for Abortion in Equine Viral Rhinopneumonitis, J.A.V.M.A., **141,** 3, 351.

Doll, E. R. and Bryans, J. T. (1962) Development of Complement-Fixing and Virus Neutralizing Antibodies in Viral Rhinopneumonitis of Horses, Amer. J. of Vet. Res. **23,** 95, 843.

Doll, E. R. and Bryans, J. T. (1963) Immunization of Young Horses Against Viral Rhinopneumonitis, Cor. Vet. **53,** 1, 24.

Doll, E. R. and Bryans, J. T. (1963) A Planned Infection Program for Immunizing Mares Against Viral Rhinopneumonitis, Cor. Vet. 53, 2, 249.

Doll, E. R. and Bryans, J. T. (1963) Epizootiology of Equine Viral Rhinopneumonitis, J.A.V M.A. **142,** 1, 31.

Doll, E. R. and J. H. Kintner, (1954) A Comparative Study of Equine Abortion and Equine Influenza Viruses, Cor. Vet. **44,** 3, 355.

Doll, E. R., McCollum, W. H. Bryans, J. T., and Crowe, M. E. W. (1959) Effect of Physical and Chemical Environment on the Viability of Equine Rhinopneumonitis Virus Propagated in Hamsters, Cor. Vet. **49,** 1, 75.

Doll, E. R., Richards, M. G., Wallace, M. E. and Bryans, J. T. (1952) The Influence of an Equine Fetal Tissue Vaccine Upon Hemagglutination Activity of Mare Serums: Its Relation to Hemolytic Icterus of Newborn Foals, Cor. Vet. **42,** 495.

Haymaker, W. and Kernohan, J. W. (1949) The Landry-Guillain-Barre Syndrome, Medicine, **28,** 59.

Kendrick, J. W. (1969) Comments on Equine Herpesvirus Infection (Equine Rhinopneumonitis) and Bovine Herpesvirus Infection (Infectious Bovine Rhinotracheitis), J.A.V.M.A. **155,** 2 (Part 2), 306.

Martens, R., Stewart, J. and Eichholtz, D. (1970) Chronic Neuritis of the Cauda Equina and Cranial Nerves, J.A.V.M.A. **156,** 4, 478.

McCollum, W. H., Doll, E. R., Wilson, J. C. and Johnson, C. B. (1962) Plaque Formation by Equine Rhinopneumonitis Virus on Monolayer Cell Cultures of Equine, Ovine and Porcine Kidneys, Cor. Vet. **52,** 4, 534.

McKercher, D. G., Saito, J. K. and Mathis, R. M. (1969) Comparative Aspects of Immunity Against Bovine and Equine Herpesviruses, J.A.V.M.A. **155,** 2 (Part 2), 300.

Miller, W. C., Mahaffey, L. W., Dove, J. T., Harding, J. T. J. and Dudgeon, J. A. (1966) Virus Infections Affecting the Fetus in Animals and Man, Proc. Royal Soc. of Med. **59,** 1080.

Plummer, G., and Waterson, A. P. (1963) Equine Herpes Virus, Virology **19,** 3, 412.

Saxegaard, F. (1966) Isolation and Identification of Equine Rhinopneumonitis Virus from Cases of Abortion and Paralysis, Nord. Vet. Med. **18,** 504.

Arteritis Virus

Bryans, J. T., Doll, E. R., Crowe, M. E. W., and McCollum, W. H. (1957) The Blood Picture and Thermal Reaction in Experimental Viral Arteritis of Horses, Cor. Vet. **47,** 1, 42.

Burki, F. and Gerber, H. A. (1966) Virologically Certified Large Scale Outbreak of Equine Arteritis, Berl. and Munich. Tierartzl. Wochschr. **79,** 20, 391.

Doll, E. R., Bryans, J. T., McCollum, W. H., and Crowe, M. E. W. (1957) Isolation of a Filterable Agent Causing Arteritis of Horses and Abortion of Mares, Its Differentiation from the Equine Abortion (Influenza) Virus, Cor. Vet. **47,** 1, 3.

Jones, T. C., Doll, E. R., and Bryans, J. T. (1957) The Lesions of Equine Viral Arteritis, Cor. Vet. **47,** 1, 52.

Jones, T. C. (1969) Clinical and Pathologic Features of Equine Viral Arteritis, J.A.V.M.A. **155,** 2 (Part 2), 315.

Knappenberger, R. E., and Bryans, J. T. (1957) An Outbreak of Abortion Caused by the Equine Arteritis Virus, Cor. Vet. **47,** 1, 69.

McCollum, W. H., Doll, E. R., Wilson, J. C. and Johnson, C. B. (1961) Propagation of Equine Arteritis Virus in Monolayer Cultures of Equine Kidney, Amer. J. Vet. Res. **22,** 89, 731.

McCollum, W. H., Doll, E. R. and Wilson, J. C. (1962) The Recovery of Virus from Horses with Experimental Cases of Equine Arteritis Using Monolayer Cell Culture of Equine Kidney, Amer. J. Vet. Res. **94,** 23, 465.

McCollum, W. H. (1969) Development of a Modified Virus Strain and Vaccine for Equine Virus Arteritis, Symp. on Immunity to Selected Equine Diseases, Lexington, Ky., J.A.V.M.A. **155,** 2 (Part 2), 318.

Other Viruses

Ishii, S. (1963) Equine Infectious Anemia or Swamp Fever, Adv. in Vet. Sci. **8,** 263.

Medearis, D. N. (1967) Comparative Aspects of Reproductive Failure Induced in Mammals by Viruses, in **Comparative Aspects of Reproductive Failure,** Edit. by K. Benirschke, Springer-Verlag, Inc., New York.

Mycotic or Fungal Infections

Hensel, L., Bisping, W. and Schimmel-Pennig, A. (1961) Aspergillus-abort beim Pferde, Berl. Munch. Tierartzl. Wchnschr. **74,** 290.

Mahaffey, L. and Adam, N. (1964) Abortions Associated with Mycotic Lesions of the Placenta of Mares, J.A.V.M.A. **144,** 1, 24.

Mahaffey, L. and Rossdale, P. O. (1965) An Abortion Due to **Allescheria boydii** and General Observations Concerning Mycotic Abortions of Mares, Vet. Rec. **77,** 19, 541.

Rooney, J. (1964) Cleanliness is the Best Safeguard Against Mycotic Placentitis, The Blood-Horse **87,** 15, 772.

Protozoan Infections

Duplessis, J. L. and Basson, P. A. (1966) Babesiosis in Aborted Equine Fetuses, J. South Afric. V. M. A. **37,** 267.

Gibbons, W. J. (1968) Reproduction in Farm Animals, Edit. by E. S. E. Hafez, 2nd Ed., Lea and Febiger, Philadelphia, 399.

Frerichs, W. M., Holbrook, A. A. and Johnson, A. J. (1969) Equine Piroplasmosis; Complement Fixation Titers of Horses Infected with **Babesia caballi,** Amer. J. Vet. Res. **30,** 5, 697.

Madden, P. A. and Holbrook, A. A. (1968) Equine Piroplasmosis: Indirect Fluorescent Antibody Test for **B. caballi,** Amer. J. Vet. Res. **29,** 1, 117.

Meynard, J. A. (1951) Congenital Piroplasmosis in the Horse, Rec. Med. Vet. **127,** 340.

Neitz, W. O. (1956) Babesiasis: Some Protozoan Diseases of Man and Animals, Art. 2, Ann. N.Y. Acad. Sci. **64,** 56.

Sippel, W. L., Cooperrider, D. E., Gainer, J. H., Allen, R. W., Mouw, J. E. B. and Tiegland, M. B. (1962) Equine Piroplasmosis in the United States, J.A.V.M.A. **141,** 6, 694.

Noninfectious Causes of Equine Abortion

Asdell, S. A. (1964) Patterns of Mammalian Reproduction, 2nd Ed. Comstock Publishing Co., Ithaca, N.Y.

Arthur, G. H. (1958) An Analysis of the Reproductive Function of Mares Based on Post-mortem Examination, Vet. Rec. **70,** 682.

Arthur, G. H. (1964) Wright's Veterinary Obstetrics, 3rd Ed., Williams and Wilkins Co., Baltimore.

Britton, J. W. (1947) Clinical Studies of Early Equine Abortion, Cor. Vet. **37,** 1, 14.

Errington, B. J. (1942) Equine Twin Placentation, Cor. Vet. **32,** 4, 367.

Evans, H. E. (1966) Personal Communications.

Garbers, G. (1967) Personal Communication.

Knudson, Odd (1964) Endometrial Cytology as a Diagnostic Aid in Mares, Cor. Vet. **54,** 3, 415.

Lanman, J. T. (1968) Delays During Reproduction and their Effects on the Embryo and Fetus, New Engl. J. of Med. **278,** 993, 1047, 1092.

Lein, D. (1967) Personal Communicaion.

Loy, R. G. and Swan, S. M. (1966) Effects of Exogenous Progestogens on Reproductive Phenomena in Mares, J. An. Sci. **25,** 3, 821.

Merkt, H. (1966) Foal Heat and Fetal Resorption, Zuchthyg, **1,** 102.

Mitchell, D. (1967) (1969) Personal Communication.

Nishikawa, Y. (1959) Studies on Reproduction in Horses, Japan Racing Assoc. Tokyo, Japan, p. 152.

Osborne, V. E. (1960, 1965) Personal Communication.

Osborne, V. E. (1966) An Analysis of the Pattern of Ovulation As it Occurs in the Annual Reproductive Cycle of the Mare in Australia, Austral. Vet. Jour. **42,** 149.

Patterson, A. W. (1962) Personal Communication.

Richter, W. (1963) Investigations into the Interruption of Pregnancy in Mares, Zuchthyg. Fortpfl. und Besam. der Haust. **7,** 2, 81.

Romane, W. M., Adams, L. G., Bullard, T. L. and Dollahite, J. W. (1966) Cystitis Syndrome of the Equine, Southwestern Vet. **19,** 2, 95.

Ryan, K. J. and Ainsworth, L. (1967) Comparative Aspects of Steroid Hormones in Reproduction in **Comparative Aspects of Reproductive Failure,** edit by K. Benirschke, Springer Verlag New York Inc.

Sager, F. (1962) Personal Communication.

Short, R. V. (1965) Recent Advances in Equine Reproductive Physiology, 4th Ann. Congr. of Brit. Eq. Vet. Assoc.

VanKampen, K. R. (1970) Sudan Grass and Sorghum Poisoning of Horses: A Possible Lathyrogenic Disease, J.A.V.M.A. **156,** 5, 629.

Van Niekerk, C. H. (1965) Early Embryonic Resorption in Mares, J. S. Afr. Vet. Med. Assoc. **36,** 1, 61.

Wohanka, K. (1961) Untersuchungen Der Ursachen Der Verfohlens, Proc. 4th Internat. Congr. on An. Reproduction, The Hague, **III,** 622.

Abortion in Swine

Abortions in swine, as in other species, are comprised of early embryonic deaths and abortions or absorptions, fetal deaths and either abortion of the entire litter or mummification and stillbirths of a variable portion of the litter. The latter two categories in contrast to uniparous animals are common in swine. In a herd relatively free of infectious bacterial and viral diseases Pond et al. reported an incidence of 3 to 8 percent stillbirths and 1 to 5 percent fetal mummification in 551 litters of over 5000 pigs in a ten year period. Abortions were very rare. Lawson cited references on over 58,000 pigs having an incidence of 5 to 14 percent stillbirths. Stillbirths comprise those fetal deaths occurring within the last 20 to 30 days of gestation which terminate in abortion at term; mummification comprise those deaths occurring from 35 to approximately 85 days of gestation, Pond et al. and Dunne. The incidence of swine abortion is variable, possibly about 5 percent, and abortions usually occur from 75 to 95 days of gestation, Saunders, Dunne. Stillbirths and mummification will be discussed later in more detail but are an integral part of the porcine prenatal death loss.

Table 11. Summary of Causes of Abortion in Swine

Infectious causes:
- Bacterial—Leptospirosis (L. pomona, L. grippotyphosa, L. hardjo and L. canicola), Brucellosis (Br. suis)
- Miscellaneous bacterial—streptococci, Staphylococcus aureus, E. coli, Salmonella enteriditis, avian tuberculosis, Listeria monocytogenes (?), B. anthracis, C. pyogenes and Erysipelothrix rhusiopathiae
- Viral—Hog cholera, pseudorabies (Aujesky's disease), picorna (S.M.E.D.I.) (?) viruses
- Miscellaneous viral causes—foot and mouth disease, Japanese B. encephalitis, hemagglutination virus, influenza, African swine fever
- Mycotic or fungal—Aspergillus fumigatus and other molds
- Protozoan—Toxoplasma gondi (?), eperythrozoonosis (?)

Noninfectious Causes:
- Chemical, Drug and Plant—dicoumarin, aflatoxin B (moldy corn), pentochlorophenols and creosote
- Hormonal—estrogen, glucocorticoids (?)
- Nutritional—deficiencies of iodine, vitamin A, iron, and calcium
- Physical—stress and exhaustion coincident to transportation, fighting and injury
- Genetic or chromosomal—anomalies, early embryonic deaths
- Miscellaneous—poor management, increased stillbirths associated with large or small litters and in older sows

About 25 to 50 percent of the causes of abortions in swine are diagnosed when investigated by competent veterinary laboratories. This level of diagnosis is only slightly better than in cattle and lower than in sheep and horses.

Infectious Causes of Swine Abortion

Bacterial Causes

Leptospirosis is the most common cause of swine abortion in the U.S. now that brucellosis is on the decline due to regulatory activities. The causative agent is usually **L. pomona** although **L. grippotyphosa, L. hardjo, L. canicola, L. hyos** and **L. sejroe** have also been reported as causing abortion, stillbirths or weak pigs that die shortly after birth, Dunne, McErlean, Bohl, Fennestad and Borg-Petersen, and Hanson. Leptospirosis in swine is widespread in the U.S., Europe and other countries throughout the world. The incidence of leptospirosis in swine in the U.S. varies from 3 to 25 percent, Morse et al..

L. pomona organisms usually enter the body of the susceptible pig through breaks in the skin or through the mucous membrane of the nasal, conjunctival, digestive or reproductive tracts. A leptospiremia and general infection develops and lasts for 5 to 10 days after which serum antibodies can be detected. The highest serum antibody titers are observed about 3 to 4 weeks after exposure and persist for a year or more. The organisms usually localize in the kidney tubules and are discharged in the urine for 1-1/2 to 6 months. In a few pigs the renal carrier state or leptospiruria may persist for 12 months. The greatest number of organisms are shed 20 to 30 days after exposure, Morse et al., and Bohl. Leptospiral organisms may be spread directly by the urine or indirectly by contaminated feed and water to susceptible pigs. As reported previously under abortions in cattle, leptospira can survive in a moist environment outside the body for a period of over a week, Ryley. Infected boars might infect susceptible sows at coitus and have been shown to introduce the infection into a susceptible sow herd. It is possible that leptospirosis might be spread from infected boars by artificial insemination. Infection, but not abortion, was produced by infecting sows intravaginally after coitus, Ferguson and Powers. Abortions occurred only in sows infected late in the second month, during the third month or early in the fourth month of gestation. **L. pomona** can also be spread from cattle to swine or swine to cattle by infected urine. As in leptospirosis in cattle, wild animals may be a source of infection for swine.

Only rarely do swine infected with **L. pomona** demonstrate acute or obvious clinical signs of illness such as hemoglobinuria. In experimental animals inappetence, a mild fever and slight depression may be seen for several days during the leptospiremic stage of the disease but under farm conditions these signs are not observed. Thus nearly all leptospiral infections of swine are inapparent except for abortions that occur in pregnant females. Following leptospirosis in swine small widespread greyish foci are found scattered throughout the kidneys and liver, Morse et al. and Ryley. Some degeneration and necrosis of kidney tubules may also be present.

Abortions in susceptible sows infected with **L. pomona** occur 1 to 4 weeks prior to term. Kemenes and Szemeredi reported that of 800 aborting sows the earliest abortions were 72 to 78 days of gestation. Infections occurring between 55 and 88 days of gestation in sows most commonly produce abortions, Ryley. Abortions usually occur 3 to 4 weeks after the initial infection of the sow. Some or all of the fetuses may be infected and deaths are due to a leptospiral septicemia. Stillbirths or deaths of fetuses late in gestation, and the birth of infected weak, "squealer" pigs that die within several days after birth are common in leptospiral epizootics in swine herds. The incidence of abortion in sows in a herd or of dead fetuses or dying newborn pigs may vary from 20 to 100 percent depending on the numbers of susceptible sows in late gestation and the rate of spread and virulence of the organism, Powers et al..

Leptospirosis may be diagnosed by leptospiral serum titers of 1:800 to 1:3200 or higher in the aborting sows as determined by the agglutination-lysis test. Other serologic tests may be used. Low titers might indicate a prior infection with **L. pomona** and abortion due to another cause. A rising titer is highly diagnostic in blood samples taken at abortion and several weeks later. **L. pomona** can often be isolated on culture or animal inoculation from the liver, kidneys, peritoneal or pericardial cavities of aborted fetuses, stillbirths, or weak, ill newborn piglets. Histopathological examination of silver-stained kidney sections from fetuses may reveal the organism. Leptospira often cannot be isolated from the urine of acutely infected aborting sows but several weeks following abortion leptosira can frequently be cultured from the sow's urine. Direct dark field examination of the pericardial or peritoneal fluid or kidney scrapings may reveal the small, fine, filamentous, motile leptospiral organisms, Bohl, and Dunne. The fluorescent antibody technique for the diagnosis of leptospirosis may also be used, Nakamura, Dunne. Following abortion caused by leptospira the sows are immune and resistant to reinfection for at least 11 to 14 months, Morter et al..

Leptospirosis in swine may be controlled by sanitation, vaccination and antibiotic therapy. Maintaining a herd free of leptospirosis is possible but may be difficult due to reservoirs of infection in cattle, other domestic animals and in wild animals, such as skunks and rats. A sanitary environment free of water holes, swampy areas and mud puddles may aid in preventing the spread of the disease. Covered feeding and watering troughs not easily contaminated by infective urine are also desirable. Cattle and swine should not be housed together as leptospirosis may be transmitted between the species. By proper sanitation and management, frequent blood testing, segregation and isolation or measures used to produce a specific pathogen-free herd, a leptospirosis-free herd may be attained. If the swine herd is free of leptospirosis, purchased swine should be negative to the blood test, isolated away from the herd for a month and retested before being placed in the herd.

Since in chronically-infected swine herds the acute disease is inapparent, most commercial swine owners routinely vaccinate their sows and gilts before the breeding season, early in pregnancy or every six months with a killed **L. pomona** bacterin that provides a good but relatively short-lived immunity against abortion. Polyvalent bacterins or bacterins of other strains of leptosira causing swine abortions are not available at present. The bacterin may also be used early in an outbreak but abortions may continue for 3 to 4 weeks in infected sows. Vaccination of swine two weeks before going to fairs or shows is recommended. Leptospiruria may develop in exposed vaccinated sows but abortions do not occur, Bohl. Vaccination with the bacterin produces low A.L. serum tirers, 1:10 to 1:500, Burnstein et al..

In recently infected susceptible herds, antibiotics have been used effectively to treat the carrier state as well as the acute infection to reduce the incidence of abortion for a period of several weeks until immunity develops to vaccination. According to Bohl and Dunne the following regimens have been recommended: for pregnant animals in an infected herd 400 to 500 gms of chlortetracycline (**aureomycin**) or oxytetracycline (**Terramycin**) per ton of feed for 10 to 14 days should be provided. For treating the chronic carrier or shedder state in pigs of all ages, chlortetracycline or oxytetracyline at levels of 400 to 500 up to 1000 gms per ton of feed should be fed for 7 to 10 days. Individual treatment of swine may also be used with 5 daily intramuscular injections of tetracycline (**Polyotic**) at a dose level of 3 mg. per pound of body weight or a single injection of 25 mg per kg. of body weight of dihydrostreptomycin, Stalheim.

Brucellosis in swine, due to **Brucella suis,** is a much more insidious disease than brucellosis in cattle. The disease has been widespread especially in the hog-raising areas of the Midwest. Corson reported in 1966 the incidence of animal infection in the U.S. to be 1.2 percent and lot infection to be 2.9 percent. An aggressive eradication program is continuing in the U.S. to increase the numbers of validated herds, counties and states. Blood testing of adult sows and boars at slaughter to locate infected herds has proven highly effective in eradicating this disease. Swine brucellosis exists in all swine producing countries and occurs in wild pigs. **Br. suis** may also occur naturally in horses, cattle, dogs, fowl and the European hare. **Br. abortus** may cause brucellosis in swine but clinical signs are rare, Lawson, Dunne. Brucellosis due to **Br. suis** is the most common type found in humans in swine-raising areas.

Clinically the disease is endemic on certain farms. According to Dunne and Manthei about 30 percent of adult swine are naturally resistant to **Br. suis** infection. This level of resistance is much higher in young pigs nursing infected dams. Clinical signs of the disease usually occur after sexual maturity. New infections in a herd are often traced to a recently introduced boar. The organism, **Br. suis,** enters the body through the mouth by ingestion of feed and water contaminated by uterine discharges, urine, or feces of infected animals. A main cause of infection in the sow is mating with an infected boar. A persistent bacteremia develops that lasts for 3 to 8 weeks in animals that recover. Most infected swine develop brucellosis with clinical signs and an intermittent bacteremia that lasts for about 8 months and may, in a few animals, last for nearly 3 years. A diagnostic level of serum antibody develops 10 to 21 days after exposure. Antibody levels are higher and persist longer in adult than in immature swine.

The main clinical signs of brucellosis in swine are abortion, birth of stillborn or weak pigs, infertility due to early embryonic deaths, and less commonly orchitis and posterior paralysis and lameness due to vertebral lesions. Vandeplassche and coworkers reported that nearly all brucella-infected boars had lesions in the epididymis and seminal vesicles and produced normal appearing but infected semen. Pus in the semen was uncommon and fertilization was normal. Following service to infected boars abortions may occur as early as 22 days of gestation and are usually not observed under field conditions as no vaginal discharge is present. Sows or gilts infected at coitus frequently return to estrum in 30 to 45 days. Infections acquired by the sow after 30 or 40 days of gestation result in abortions from 46 to 105 days, average 65 to 80 days, Thomsen, and Dunne and Manthei. Genital infection may persist from 1 to 30 months in females and for 3 years or more in boars. The period of infertility in sows is related to the duration of the genital infection and the degree of pathology present. Many sows lose the genital infection within one to two months and then have good conception rates thereafter. **Br. suis** may persist in granulomatous lesions and in mucosal cysts of the endometrium and catarrhal endometritis may occur. Vandeplassche stated that 75 percent of susceptible gilts bred to an infected boar became pregnant and 80 percent of these had a normal gestation period but when an infected sow was bred to a clean boar only a 35 percent conception occurred due to chronic endometrial lesions causing early embryonic deaths and prolonged periods between estrums. Nodular or granulomatous lesions containing **Br. suis** may also be found in lymph glands, spleen, liver, kidneys, testes, ovaries, and accessory male reproductive glands.

The disease may be diagnosed by recovering the organism by cultural methods from organs of the infected sow or boar, from the stomach contents of aborted fetuses or from the chorion of the placenta. The tube or plate agglutination tests may be performed on blood serum from suspected or infected swine. This test is not as reliable as the blood test in cattle. Certain swine harboring and spreading the organism may have low serum titers or be negative to the agglutination test. Most swine with localized infections and those with clinical signs of brucellosis will have a titer of 1:100 or higher at some stage of the disease, Dunne and Manthei. Nonspecific antibodies producing titers of up to 1:50 are common in swine. The blood titer in swine drops more rapidly than in cattle. Testing the herd and eliminating the reactors is not a practical method of eradicating the disease. The agglutination test is of value, however, as a herd test for indicating the presence of infection. Hoerlein and coworkers reported that the presence of any reactors in the adult swine herd with a titer of 1:100 or a higher indicates that the herd is infected. A herd with no animals with titers over 1:50 on repeated tests and no clinical signs of brucellosis is considered negative. Supplemental tests such as the acidified plate antigen test, the heat inactivation test, the rivanol test, the complement fixation test and the Card test may be helpful in the diagnosis of carriers of **Br. suis,** Nicoletti and Dunne and Manthei. A single negative blood test on one individual is of no diagnostic value. The prognosis is guarded in this insidious disease, since sterility may follow abortion and the sow may spread the disease for several months or more. In respect to the herd situation, rather drastic steps need to be taken to eradicate the disease.

The methods of eradicating the disease in commercial herds consist of: (1) selling all the stock for slaughter, cleaning and disinfecting the premises or moving to clean quarters and then restocking from known noninfected or validated herds. (2) In valuable purebred herds in which it is desired that breeding lines be maintained, the pigs may be raised on infected sows until eight weeks old, weaned, and moved from the infected herd, isolated, and raised on clean ground. These pigs are tested individually by the agglutination test at intervals of 1 to 2 months. Any reactors are sold for slaughter. Methods of blood collection from the anterior vena cava and the tail of swine are described by Hoerlein et al. and Getty and Goshal, respectively. When the gilts are of breeding age they are bred to noninfected boars. After farrowing in isolation the gilts are retested and if they are negative their litters, when weaned at 8 weeks, are the basis of a new, clean herd. The original herd is disposed of as soon as practical. (3) Repeated blood testing at 30-day intervals together with the slaughter of reactors may occasionally be advisable and successful. In most herds this is not as satisfactory and efficient as the two previous methods, Hoerlein and coworkers, Hubbard and McNutt. Chemotherapy is of no value in this disease. Manthei and the above workers reported that **Br. abortus** strain 19 vaccine does not immunize swine. Natural resistance or immunity to **Br. suis** is present in about 30 percent of swine, Dunne and Manthei. No vaccine of value for combatting brucellosis in swine has been introduced. Animals purchased from herds of unknown brucellosis status should not be placed in a brucellosis-free herd on the basis of a single negative blood test. Herd replacements should only come from a brucellosis-free herd.

Miscellaneous bacterial causes of abortion in swine have been described in sporadic cases or rare outbreaks. The following organisms have been recovered in pure culture from freshly aborted porcine fetuses: **Staphylococcus aureus** Fennestad et al., Thorne and Nilsson; **Mycobacterium avium,** Plum; **Listeria monocytogenes,** Ray; **Salmonella enteriditis, E. coli,** streptococci and **Coryn. pyogenes,** Lawson. Other organisms isolated from aborting sows include: **Erysipelothnix rhusiopathiae; Pseudomonas** spp., **B. anthracis** and **Pasteurella,** Dunne. Davis and Thomas described an outbreak of abortions stillbirths and moribund neonatal pigs apparently due to streptococci and **E. coli.** The former organism was resistant to 4 antibiotics that had been used in the herd in past years as a feed additive. The use of effective oral antibiotics, determined by sensitivity testing, for the last 30 days of gestation greatly increased the numbers of live pigs per litter at birth, 10 and 6, and the number of weaned pigs per litter over the untreated controls, 8.5 and 3.8, respectively.

Viral Causes for Porcine Prenatal Losses

The major viral causes for prenatal loss in swine are hog cholera, pseudorabies or Aujesky's disease and various picorna or SMEDI viruses. It is important to recognize that in swine these and other viruses may affect the developing embryos or fetuses and result in: (1) infertility or sterility related to early embryonic deaths that are aborted unseen or absorbed, (2) fetal mummification, (3) defective or anomalous fetuses (4) stillbirths (5) birth of live but poorly viable pigs and (6) birth of live normal pigs that may be carriers of the virus. Abortions of entire litters late in gestation are rare.

Hog cholera virus strains may differ markedly in virulence, Sorensen et al.. **In utero** transmission of hog cholera did not occur in immune sows given virulent hog cholera virus, Stewart. Field strains of low virulence or attenuated or modified strains used as vaccines if inoculated into pregnant susceptible sows the first 10 to 20 days of gestation resulted in absorbtion of the embryos and fetal malformations, Young et al., Cowart and Morehouse, Dunne and Clark. If the virus gained entrance to the sow's body from 30 to 90 or more days of gestation, mummification of fetuses, stillbirths and weak pigs were common. Pregnant sows vaccinated with attenuated or modified hog cholera virus apparently did not spread the virus to susceptible contact pigs. Furthermore only about 30 percent of the pigs in litters in which the virus was intrauterine were infected, Cowart and Morehouse. Vaccination of pregnant sows with an attenuated vaccine or natural exposure to hog cholera virus of low virulence can cause cerebellar hypoplasia, hypomyelinogenesis and congenital tremors or myoclonia congenita in newborn pigs, Emerson and Delez. Stillborn pigs often exhibited edema of the subcutaneous tissues. This probably is an autolytic change.

The hog cholera virus in infected fetuses, stillbirths or live newborn pigs may be cultured on tissue culture media or demonstrated by the fluorescent antibody technique, Aiken et al., Dunne. Cowart and Morehouse further indicated that pigs in infected **in utero** may survive and after birth become immune and tolerant carriers of this virus. Under stress these carrier pigs may become ill and die of cholera weeks or months after birth. These are some of the reasons for the active campaign to control hog cholera in the U.S. and prohibition of live attenuated vaccines. BVD-MD vaccine prepared for cattle has been used in swine for the heterotypic immunity provided against hog cholera, Baker et al.. Because of the hog cholera eradication program presently underway in the U.S. based on test and slaughter methods the use of this product is controversial.

Pseudorabies or Aujezsky's disease, due to a herpes virus, is apparently widespread in swine in the U.S. with most outbreaks reported in the midwest. The virus apparently persists in recovered swine and may be present in most domestic animals and some wild animals, Trainer and Karstad. Akkermans has shown the disease can result in a high mortality in young pigs from birth to 30 days in age. In older pigs and adults signs of dullness, anorexia, constipation and occasionally posterior paresis are observed but the mortality is low. In pregnant sows the pseudorabies virus invades the uterus and causes fetal deaths, mummification, stillbirths and the birth of poorly viable pigs, Gordon and Luke. Saunders et al. reported on a swine herd where 50 percent of 112 sows aborted. Csontos et al. examined 46 porcine fetuses from sows aborting or delivering stillbirths due to pseudorabies and found pinpoint to poppyseed-sized necrotic foci in the liver of 41 percent of them. They also have isolated the virus from the vagina of sows and the prepuce of boars. If this Herpes virus is like others in domestic animals it is unlikely the boar transmits the virus at coitus except at irregular intervals.

Diagnosis is based on the history, the recovery and identification of the virus from stillborn or weak, dying pigs and finding serum neutralizing antibodies in the serum of the sow, Saunders and Gustafson. These latter authors cited work done in eastern Europe on a possible vaccine. Globulin concentrates from immune swine are effective for passive immunization.

Picornaviruses, enteroviruses or SMEDI (Stillbirth, Mummification, Embryonic Death and Infertility) **viruses,** Dunne et al., have been shown to cause occasional abortions but mainly the aforementioned effects on intrauterine embryos or fetuses in sows. (See Figure 74) In a tentative classification of over 40 porcine picornavirus strains isolated in North America, Japan, England and Czechoslovakia, 17 groups were determined serologically. The 5 strains of SMEDI viruses isolated in Pennsylvania fell into Groups 1, 6, 7 and 13, Wang and Dunne. These 5 strains of picornaviruses (SMEDI) when inoculated into cholera-immune or cholera-susceptable pregnant swine cause a similar syndrome to that caused by hog cholera, pseudorabies or other viruses that will be mentioned. Susceptible pregnant gilts inoculated with SMEDI viruses at 25 days of gestation had embryonic deaths within 5 days of the inoculation; death of fetuses and mummification occurred 15 to 40 or more days after inoculation; and thereafter stillbirths and weak pigs dying within 6 hours after birth were observed. Fetuses in the same sow may become infected and die at different stages of gestation. If embryos die before 30 days of gestation when no skeletal development has occurred, absorbtion results; if fetuses die at later stages of gestation after skeletal development occurs mummification or stillbirths result. The position of the fetus in the uterus was not related to the time of fetal deaths. In some sows where early embryonic deaths occurred the sow returned to estrum at a varying interval following the initial service. In other cases where fetal deaths occurred at 30 to 60 days of gestation and mummification resulted, "parturition" did not take place at the end of gestation and the sow exhibited prolonged anestrus, Dunne et al. (1965). These signs are usually limited to one breeding season in a herd. Recovered immune sows have normal gestations during the next breeding season.

The virus is apparently spread through the susceptible animals in the breeding herd after its introduction by an infected animal or from contact with infected pigs. The boar may also be a temporary carrier of the virus. The virus may be isolated in suspected outbreaks from cultures of the internal organs of stillborn fetuses or weak, poorly viable, newborn pigs. Sows infected before breeding are apparently immune as are sows at the next breeding period following an episode or outbreak of stillbirths, mummified fetuses, abortions, embryonic deaths and apparent infertility.

Miscellaneous viral causes for porcine deaths, fetal mummification and abortions include: **Japanese** B encephalitis and Japanese hemagglutinating viruses which produce signs similar to the pseudorabies and SMEDI viruses; influenza virus and transmissible gastroenteritis virus are also suspected of producing similar effects, Dunne (1965); swine abortions have also been described as accompanying acute cases of vesicular stomatitis, foot and mouth disease and African swine fever. These latter viral abortions usually occur late in gestation and may be caused by the marked systemic effects, fever or stress. The Japanese viruses and the latter two virus diseases are not present in the U.S. Vesicular stomatitis is rare in this country.

Dunne stressed the importance of controlling viral diseases in swine, since vaccines are not available, by bringing the breeding herd together a month or more before breeding and then maintaining a closed herd until after farrowing. The boar may have through-the-fence contact with sows prior to breeding. Visitors to the lots should be prohibited.

Mycotic or fungal procine abortions due to **Aspergillus fumigatus** or **Nocardia asteroides** have been described on rare occasions, Dawson, Dunne (1968).

The Protozoan causes of abortion in swine possibly include the agents of **Toxoplasma gondi** (?) and **Eperythrozoon suis** (?) Congenital toxoplasmosis has been described in humans as a cause for abortions, congenital malformations, and diseased newborn infants, Neri and Eylan. Toxoplasmosis causes abortion in sheep but has not been reported as causing abortion in swine. However newborn pigs occasionally show illness, incoordination and tremors due to central nervous system lesions. Thus toxoplasmosis of the newborn should be differentiated from viral diseases, Koestner and Cole, Sanger and Cole. The evidence that eperythrozoonosis may cause abortion is not conclusive.

Noninfectious Causes of Porcine Abortion

Chemical, drug or plant poisonings are rather seldom causes for abortion in swine. **Dicoumarol** poisoning has been cited by Dunne. Schipper reported that wood preservatives such as the **pentachlorophenols** and **creosote** were toxic for prenatal and postnatal pigs. Wood so treated should be thoroughly dryed before placing sows or pigs in contact with it. **Moldy corn toxicosis** probably due to aflatoxin B associated with penicillin, aspergillus and rhizopus molds, caused bloody diarrhea, anorexia, depression, ataxia and abortion, Blevins et al.. **Ergot** was not shown to be a cause of abortion in swine even when ergotism produced necrosis of the extremities, Ainsworth and Austwick. Early embryonic deaths and mummification followed the consumption of a tropical shrub legume, **Leucaena leucocephala** by sows, Wayman et al..

Hormonal causes for porcine abortions are also rare. Feed additives containing estrogens may accidentally be added to rations for pregnant sows or spoiled moldy corn or barley caused by **Gibberella zea** that produces an estrogen, Stob et al. and McErlean, can cause signs of estrus and a swollen vulva, especially in young gilts, and might cause abortion. Glucocorticoids have not been reported to cause abortion in swine but severe stress conditions have been associated with porcine abortions.

Nutritional causes of swine abortion, stillbirths and anomalous fetuses include deficiencies of iodine, vitamin A, iron and calcium, Dunne, Reid, Pullar, Moore et al., and Palludan. **Iodine deficiency** is characterized by hairlessness, goiter, edema of the fetus and a slightly prolonged gestation. This condition is rare at present because iodine is commonly added to salt in most rations. **Vitamin A deficiency** usually related to a lack of pasture, alfalfa hay and the feeding of 2 or more-year-old corn may result in weak, moribund newborn pigs or stillbirths with edema, ascites, cleft palate, anophthalmia, microphthalmia, hydrocephalus and cardiac defects. **Iron deficiency** may cause stillbirths or weak newborn pigs suffering from a severe anemia. **Chronic calcium deficiency** due to exclusive grain feeding, a lack of roughage or pasture or no mineral or tankage supplementation results a progressive increase in the number of mummified fetuses and stillbirths with each litter produced.

Physical causes of porcine abortion as reported by Dunne and Hokanson, and Dunne and Saunders include stress and exhaustion due to transportation, fighting between sows, and injury inflicted by boars.

Genetic or chromosomal causes for stillbirths or moribund pigs include the congenital or genetic lethal defects described previously. About 10 to 12 percent of the blastocysts from normal sows had chromosome defects, mainly polyploidy, which may account for about 30 percent of the total pregnancy wastage in swine, McFeely. These defective zygotes that die early in gestation may comprise a significant number of the ova released and fertilized that fail to result in pigs produced at parturition. This loss may be determined by counting the corpora lutea in the ovaries at farrowing.

Miscellaneous abortions or loss of neonatal pigs may be due to **poor management** at the time of farrowing resulting in smothering, crushing or chilling of newborn pigs. These are often called "stillbirths." Attendance of a caretaker at farrowing is desirable. At parturition sows should be neither too fat nor too thin. Farrowing crates or guarded stalls and heat lamps or heated floors are very helpful in preventing neonatal losses. Asdell and Willman reported that the larger the litter or the smaller the litter, above 12 or below 4, the greater the percentage of stillbirths. The number of stillbirths increased as the age of the sow increased. Most of the dead pigs were born late in the act of parturition. In large litters deaths might have been due to delays in birth associated with exhaustion of the sow or uterine inertia. In small litters the larger-sized fetuses presented may have resulted in slower expulsion. Administration of pituitrin to hasten farrowing did not reduce the mortality.

General References

Bennett, P. C. (1960) Differential Diagnosis of Swine Abortions, Proc. 64th Ann. Meeting U.S.L.S.A.

Dunne, H. W. (1964) Diseases of Swine (2nd Ed.), Iowa State Univ. Press, Ames, Iowa.

Dunne, H. W. (1968) Abortion and Stillbirth in Swine, from **Abortion Diseases of Livestock** edit. by L. C. Faulkner, Charles C. Thomas, Springfield, Ill., 139.

Lawson, J. R. (1963) Bacterial and Mycotic Agents Associated with Abortion and Stillbirth in the Domestic Animals, from **Infertility of Livestock**, Animal Health Branch monograph No. 5, F.A.O., Rome.

Pond, W. G., Roberts, S. J., Dunn, J. A., and Willman, J. P. (1960) Late Embryonic Mortality and Stillbirths in Three Breeds of Swine, J. An. Sci. **19,** 881.

Saunders, C. N. (1958) Abortion and Stillbirths in Pigs, An Analysis of 67 Outbreaks, Vet. Rec. **70:** 48, 965.

Infectious Causes

Bacterial Causes

Leptospirosis

Burnstein, T., Bramel, R. C. and Jensen, J. (1957) Vaccination of Swine with a **Leptospira pomona** Bacterin, Vet. Med. **52,** 2, 58.

Bohl, E. H. (1961) Leptospirosis in Swine—Review and Comments, Proc. 65th Ann. Meeting, U.S.L.S.A., 133.

Fennestad, K. L. and Borg-Petersen, C. (1968) Experimental Leptospirosis in Pregnant Sows, J. of Infect. Dis. **116,** 57.

Ferguson, L. C. and Powers, T. E. (1956) Experimental Leptospirosis in Pregnant Swine, Amer. J. Vet. Res. **17,** 471.

Hanson, Lyle (1969) Personal Communication.

Kemenes, F. and Szemeredi, G. (1961) Effect of Leptospirosis in Sows, Acta Veterinaria (Budapest), 11, 1 (Abstr. Vet. Med. **56,** 9, 398.)

McErlean, B. A. (1964) Abortion and Infertility in Sows in Ireland Apparently Due to Infection by **Leptospira canicola,** Vet. Rec. **76,** 9, 248.

Morse, E. V., Bauer, D. C., Langham, R. F., Lang, R. W. and Ullrey, D. E. (1958) Experimental Leptospirosis, IV Pathogenesis of procine **Leptospira pomona** Infections, Amer. J. Vet. Res. **19,** 71, 388.

Morter, R. L., Morse, E. V. and Langham, R. F. (1960) Experimental Leptospirosis VII Reexposure of Pregnant Sows with **Leptospira pomona,** Amer. J. Vet. Res. **21,** 80, 95.

Nakamura, R. M. (1964) The Fluorescent Antibody Technique. Its Use in Diagnosis of Disease of Animals, Proc. 65th Ann. Meeting, U.S.L.S.A., 427.

Powers, T. E., Bohl, E. H. and Ferguson, L. C. (1956) Clinical Studies on Leptospirosis as a Cause of Abortion in Swine, J.A.V.M.A. **129,** 12, 568.

Ryley, J. W. (1956) Leptospirosis in Swine, Austral. Vet. J. **32,** 1, 4.

Stalheim, O. H. V. (1967) Chemotherapy of Renal Leptospirosis in Swine, Amer. J. Vet. Res. **28,** 122, 161.

Brucellosis

Corson, O. D. (1967) The Cooperative State-Federal Brucellosis Eradication Program, A Progress Report, Proceedings of National Brucellosis Committee, Agr. Res. Service, U.S. Dept. of Agr.

Getty, R. and Ghoshal, N G. (1967) Applied Anatomy of the Sacrococcygeal Region of the Pig as Related to Tail-Bleeding, Vet. Med. **62,** 4, 361.

Hoerlein, A. B., Hubbard, E. D., Lieth, T. S. and Biester, H. E. (1954) Swine Brucellosis, Vet. Med. Res. Inst., Iowa State Coll., Ames, Iowa.

Hubbard, E. D. and McNutt, S. H. (1961) Swine Brucellosis Eradication, Proc. 65th Meeting, U.S.L.S.A., 120.

Manthei, C. A. (1968) Brucellosis as a Cause of Abortion Today, in **Abortion Diseases of Livestock** edit. by L. C. Faulkner, Charles C. Thomas Co., Springfield, Ill.

Nicoletti, P. (1964) Personal Communication.

Nicoletti, P. (1967) Utilization of the Card Test in Brucellosis Eradication, J.A.V.M.A. **151,** 12, 1778.

Thomsen, A. (1934) Brucella Infection in Swine, Acta Pathol. et. Microbiol. Scand. Suppl. 21.

Vandeplassche, M. (1969) **Brucella suis** Infection and Infertility in Swine, Medel. der. Veeartsenijsch. van de Rijkuniv. Gent., **11,** 37, (Abstr. J.A.V.M.A. 154, 9, 1050).

Miscellaneous Bacterial Causes

Davis, J. W. and Thomas, H. R. (1966) The Use of Gallimycin Injectable, Erythromycin and Furacin Water Mix in a Problem Herd of S.P.F. Sows, Vet. Med. **61,** 1, 62.

Fennestad, K. L., Pedersen, P. S. and Moeller, T. (1955) **Staphylococcus aureus** as a Cause of Reproductive Failure and So-Called Actinomycosis in Swine, Nord. Vet. Med., **7,** 929.

Plum, N. (1937) Tuberculous Abortion in Cattle, Acta Pathol. et Microbiol. Scand. Suppl. **37,** 438.

Ray, J. D. (1952) Abortion in Swine, N. A. Vet. **33,** 626.

Thorne, H. and Nilsson, P. O. (1961) **Staphylococcus aureus** as the Cause of Abortion in Swine, Acta Vet. Scand. **2,** 311.

Viral Causes

Hog Cholera

Aiken, J. M., Hoopes, K. H. and Stair, E. L. (1964) Rapid Diagnosis of Hog Cholera. A Direct Fluorescent Antibody Technique, Proc. Book, J.A.V.M.A., 282.

Baker, J. A., Coggins, L., Robson, D. and Sheffy, B. (1963) Possibility of Hog Cholera Eradication with BVD Vaccine, Proc. U.S.L.S.A. **67,** 366.

Baker, J. A., Coggins, L., Robson, D., Sheffy, B. and Volenec, F. J. (1969) A Possibility of Reducing the Cost of Hog Cholera Eradication with Use of a Heterotypic BVD vaccine, Proc. A.V.M.A. Convention, Minneapolis, Minn., J.A.V.M.A., **155,** 12, 1866.

Cowart, W. O. and Morehouse, L. G. (1967) Effects of Attenuated Hog Cholera Virus in Pregnant Swine at Various Stages of Gestation, J.A.V.M.A. **151,** 12, 1788.

Dunne, H. W. and Clark, C. D. (1968) Embryonic Death, Fetal Mummification, Stillbirth and Neonatal Death in Pigs of Gilts Vaccinated with Attenuated Live Virus Hog Cholera Vaccine, Amer. J. Vet. Res. **29,** 4, 787.

Emerson, J. L. and Delez, A. L. (1965) Cerebellar Hypoplasia, Hypomyelogenesis, and Congenital Tremors in Pigs Associated with Prenatal Hog Cholera Vaccination of Sows, J.A.V.M.A. **147,** 47.

Sorensen, D. K., Martinsons E., and Perman, V. (1961) Clinical and Hematological Manifestations of Hog Cholera, Proc. Sympos. on Hog Cholera, Coll. of Vet. Med., Univ. of Minn.

Stewart, W. C. (1968) **In Utero** Transmission of Hog Cholera Virus in Pregnant Sows, Sympos. on Factors Producing Embryonic and Fetal Abnormalities, Death and Abortion in Swine, Chicago, Ill. Sponsored by Nat. Acad. of Sci, U.S.L.S.A. and the A.R.S. of the U.S. Dept. of Agr.

Young, G. A. Kitchell, R. L., Leudke, A. J. and Sautter, J. H. (1955). The Effect of Viral and Other Infections of the Dam on Fetal Development in Swine I Modified Live Hog Cholera Viruses—Immunological, Virological and Gross Pathological Studies, J.A.V.M.A. **126,** 165.

Pseudorabies, Aujeskey's Disease

Akkermans, J. P. W. M. (1963) Aujesky's Disease in Swine in the Netherlands, Abstr. J.A.V.M.A. **143,** 8, 860.

Csontos, L., Hejj, L., and Szabo, I. (1962) A Contribution to the Etiology of Aujesky's Disease in the Pig. Fetal Damage and Abortions Due to the Virus, Acta. Vet. Acad. Sci. (Hungary) **12,** 17.

Gordon, W. A. M. and Luke, D. (1955) An Outbreak of Aujesky's Disease in Swine with Heavy Mortality in Piglets, Illness in Sows and Deaths **in Utero,** Vet. Rec. **67,** 591.

Saunders, J. R. and Gustafson, D. P. (1964) Serological and Experimental Studies of Pseudorabies in Swine, Proc. 68th Ann. Meeting U.S.L.S.A., 256.

Saunders, J. R., Gustafson, D. P., Olander, H. J. and Jones, R. K. (1963). An Unusual Outbreak of Aujesky's Disease in Swine, Proc. 67th Ann. Meeting, U.S.L.S.A., 331.

Trainer, D. O. and Karstad, I. (1965) Pseudorabies, A Disease of Wild and Domestic Animals, Zoonoses Res. **2,** 146 (Abstr. J.A.V.M.A. **146,** 10, 1058.)

Picornaviruses (Enteroviruses or SMEDI viruses)

Dunne, H. W. 1964 and 1968—See General References

Dunne, H. W., Gobble, J. L., Hokanson, J. F., Kradel, D. C. and Bubash, G. R. (1965) Porcine Reproductive Failure Associated with a Newly Identified "SMEDI" Group of Picorma Viruses, Amer. J. Vet. Res., **26,** 115, 1284.

Wang, J. T. and Dunne, H. W. (1969) Comparison of Porcine Picornaviruses Isolated in North America and Their Identification with SMEDI Viruses, Amer. J. Vet. Res. **30,** 9, 1677.

Protozoan Infections

Koestner, A. and Cole, C. R. (1960) Neuropathology of Porcine Toxoplasmosis, Cor. Vet. **50,** 4, 362.

Neri, A. and Eylan, E. (1968) Toxoplasmosis as a Cause of Infertility, Fert. and Steril. **19,** 6, 883.

Sanger, V. L. and Cole, C. R. (1955) Toxoplasmosis VI Isolation of Toxoplasma from Milk, Placenta and Newborn Pigs of Asymptomatic Carrier Sows, Amer. J. Vet. Res. **16,** 536.

Noninfectious Causes of Abortion

Ainsworth, G. C. and Austwick, P. K. C. (1958) Fungal Diseases of Animals, Commonwealth Agric. Bureau, Farmham Royal, Bucks, England

Asdell, S. A. and Willman, J. P. (1941) The Causes of Stillbirth in Swine and an Attempt to Control it, J. Agr. Res. **63,** 6, 345.

Blevins, D. I., Glenn, M. W., Hamdy, A. H., Brodasky, F. F. and Evans, R. A. (1969) Mycotoxicosis Associated with Hemorrhagic Enterocolitis and Abortion in Swine, J.A.V.M.A. **154,** 9, 1043.

Dunne, H. W. and Hokanson, J. F. (1963) A Modern Approach to Abortion and Stillbirth Problems in Swine, Proc. A.V.M.A. Nat. Meeting, N.Y.C., 54.

McErlean, B. A. (1952) Vulvovaginitis of Swine, Vet. Rec. **64,** 37, 539.

McFeely, R. A. (1967) Chromosome Abnormalities in Early Embryos of the Pig, J. Reprod. and Fert. **13,** 579.

Moore, R. W., Redmond, H. E. and Livingston, C. W. (1965) Iron Deficiency Anemia as a Cause of Stillbirths in Swine, J.A.V.M.A. **147,** 746.

Palludan, B. (1961) The Teratogenic Effect of Vitamin A Deficiency in Pigs, Austral. Vet. J. **26,** 1, 4.

Pullar, E. M. (1950) Nutritional Abortion and Stillbirth in Victorian Pigs, Austral. Vet. J. **26,** 1, 4.

Reid, J. T. (1949) Relationship of Nutrition to Fertility in Animals J.A.V.M.A. **114,** 158 and 242.

Schipper, I. A. (1961) Toxicity of Wood Preservatives for Swine, Amer. J. Vet. Res. **22,** 88, 401.

Stob, J., Baldwin, R. S. Tuite, J., Andrews, F. N. and Gillette, K. G. (1962) The Isolation of An Anabolic Uterotrophic Compound from Corn Infected with **Gibberella zea,** Nature (London), **169,** 4861.

Wayman, O., Iwanaga, I. and Hugh, W. I. (1970) Fetal Resorption in Swine Caused by **Leucaena Leucocephala** (Lam) DeWit in the Diet, J. An. Sci. **30,** 4, 583.

ABORTION IN SHEEP AND GOATS

Abortions in sheep and goats, as in other larger domestic animals, are due to a wide variety of infectious and noninfectious agents. Because of the methods of breeding and management of sheep in flocks, many animals are at the same stage of pregnancy at the same time and prompt exposure of pregnant ewes to introduced infectious diseases is favored. When an abortion outbreak does occur in a flock it is usually possible to secure 2 to 5 or more fresh fetuses and their placentas for examination and laboratory diagnosis. For this reason, the percentage of confirmed or accurate diagnoses for abortions in ewes is higher than in cattle, about 40 to 60 percent. In most flocks an incidence of 1 to 5 percent abortion and stillbirth is considered "average" or acceptable, Watson. Higher rates of abortion or stillbirth should be carefully investigated. For this purpose fresh fetuses and placentas from aborting ewes should be collected in a clean container, chilled and promptly transported to a well-equipped diagnostic laboratory.

Infectious Causes of Ovine and Caprine Abortion
Bacterial Causes

Vibrionic abortion or vibriosis due to **Vibrio fetus** var **intestinalis** is the most common cause for epizootic

Table 12. Summary of the Causes of Ovine and Caprine Abortion

Infectious causes

- Bacterial causes—Vibrio fetus var. intestinalis; Listeria monocytogenes; Brucella melitensis, abortus, and ovis; Salmonella abortus ovis, dublin, typhimurium and others; Leptospira pomona and others; Corynebacterium pyogenes, pseudotuberculosis and others; and Pasteurella tularensis, pseudotuberculosis and others.
- Miscellaneous bacterial causes—E. coli and other coliforms, streptococci staphylococci, Clostridium feseri and Bacteroides fragilis.
- Viral and rickettsial causes—Enzootic abortion in ewes (EAE) due to Chlamydia.
- Miscellaneous viral and rickettsial causes—Tick-borne fever, Wesselbron virus, Rift Valley fever, Nairobi sheep disease, rinderpest, foot and mouth disease, bluetongue and Coxiella (Rickettsia) burneti (?)
- Mycotic causes—Aspergillus fumigatus
- Protozoan causes—Toxoplasma gondi

Noninfectious Causes for Ovine Abortion

- Drugs, chemical and plant poisonings—phenothiazine, carbon tetrachloride, lead, nitrate, locoweeds, lupines, sweet clover, Veratrum and onion grass.
- Hormonal—estrogens, progesterone deficiency, cortisol and ACTH excess.
- Miscellaneous—Chromosomal or genetic lethals. severe physical stress, dystocia due to malpresentation and small birth canal, possibly twinning.

ovine abortion in the United States. It is a cause of serious economic losses in bands of sheep in the Rocky Mountain states and elsewhere in the U.S. It is widespread, occurring in nearly all the sheep-raising areas of the world, Dennis. The **V. fetus intestinalis** organism in sheep is similar to **V. fetus venerealis** in cattle in various bacteriologic and morphologic characteristics. The former organism in sheep seldom spreads to or infects cows under natural conditions.

V. fetus intestinalis is catalase positive and H_2S positive; while **V. fetus venerealis** is catalase positive and H_2S negative. The former will grow in 1% glycine while the latter will not. These organisms may be confused with nonpathogenic vibrios, **V. bubulus,** which is catalase negative and **V. fecalis** which is catalase positive but resembles **V. bubulus,** Bruner and Gillespie, and Firehammer. In affected flocks the incidence of abortion varies from 5 to 70 percent, with an average of 10 to 20 percent, Dennis. These authors reported that the disease was observed uncommonly in flocks kept on range the year around, but that it was more commonly seen in sheep kept in feed lots on cut feed for a part of the winter especially if sanitation was poor. The disease has been transmitted orally by feeding infective material from aborting ewes as well as by intravenous injection of cultures of **V. fetus intestinalis.** Following oral exposure of susceptible ewes, a period of bacteremia follows as in brucellosis, Miller et al.. Under natural conditions infection is probably introduced into clean flocks by carrier sheep that may carry the organisms in their intestines or gall bladder and shed them in their feces for weeks or months. Carrion birds such as magpies and crows may also carry the organism in their gut from one herd to another, Smibert, Waldhalm et al., and Watson et al.. **V. fetus** is rather easily destroyed by sunlight, heat, or drying, but may remain viable for some time at low temperatures in moist surroundings. This may partly account for the higher incidence during the winter months.

Vibriosis in sheep in contrast to vibriosis in cattle is not a venereal disease. The ram is not a factor in the transmission of the disease except as he may be an intestinal carrier of the infection, Jensen et al., Firehammer et al.. Infertility due to embryonic deaths is not present in ewes mated to experimentally infected rams. The disease is transmitted from infected or aborting sheep to susceptible pregnant ewes the third through the fifth month of gestation. Pregnant ewes infected prior to the third month of gestation do not abort, Dennis. There is an incubation period of 7 to 25 days. During the bacteremic period the vibrio enter the maternal placenta where inflammatory changes occur with extension of the infection to the fetal placenta and chorion. The organisms are then carried to the fetus by the placental circulation causing fetal bacteremia, Jensen et al. (1961). Abortions may continue in a flock for 6 to 12 weeks. In vibrionic abortion there are often no premonitory symptoms. Occasionally the vulva will swell and a slight reddish discharge may be present. The fetuses are usually expelled the last 4 to 6 weeks of pregnancy. Abortions occurred 1 to 3 days after the death of the fetus, Miller. In some cases lambs may be expelled prematurely or at term but die soon after birth. At the time of abortion the fetuses are fairly fresh and only seldom are they decomposed or mummified. The aborted fetuses may have subcutaneous edema and reddish serum in the body cavities due to autolytic changes. The fetal membranes, especially the cotyledons, show inflammatory changes characterized by edema and necrosis. About 5 percent of aborting ewes may die due to uterine sepsis, Dennis. About 20 to 60 percent of the fetuses have characteristic necrotic areas or infarcts 1/4 to 1-1/2 inches in diameter in the liver. These contain large numbers of vibrios. The cotyledons may be necrotic and organisms may be recovered from these placental structures. **V. fetus** may be recovered from the fetal stomach and lungs. The agglutination test on the blood has been of very limited value in the diagnosis of the disease. Fluorescent antibody technique may be of value in the rapid diagnosis of the disease, Dennis. Vaginal mucus agglutination tests may also be useful.

Most workers agree that sheep aborting one year are usually immune the second year and carry their lambs normally, but immunity is probably not permanent, Miller, and Meinershager et al.. In some flocks the disease may appear two years in a row but usually the incidence is much lower the second year. Aborting ewes should immediately be removed from the rest of the flock and isolated for 2 to 4 weeks until genital discharges cease. The fetus and membranes should be buried or destroyed. Disinfection of the infected pen or area after an abortion is desirable.

Other precautionary sanitary measures to prevent the contamination of feed and water by infective material is indicated. Injection of 300,000 units of penicillin and 1 gm. of dihydrostreptomycin intramuscularly for 2 daily doses or the daily feeding of 80 mg of chloretetracycline in grain until lambing if done in the early stages of an outbreak of vibriosis will reduce the incidence of abortion about 10 percent, Hulet et al., and Ryff and Breen. Miller indicated that feeding of antibiotics was not highly effective unless started prior to an outbreak. Although additional injections of antibiotics might be indicated, it is probably not practical.

Work by Miller has shown that **V. fetus intestinalis** serotypes I and V are the most common causes of ovine vibriosis and cross immunity between these two types does not occur. Two injections 15 to 30 days apart of a commercial bivalent alum adjuvant, killed bacterin before breeding or during the first half of pregnancy provided an excellent immunity if done at yearly intervals, Storz et al.. Recent work has shown that an oil adjuvant bacterin produced an immunity that lasted for 3 years, Miller. All replacement ewes to an infected flock should be vaccinated, Storz et al.. Vaccination has been recommended in outbreaks of ovine vibriosis. Since 10 to 14 days are required for immunity to develop, early and prompt diagnosis and administration of the vaccine is indicated for even fair results to be obtained. Frank et al.. The combination of bacterin and antibiotic injections are frequently used.

Listeriosis caused by **Listeria monocytogenes** is a worldwide disease affecting a variety of species including man with the septicemic, the encephalitic or the reproductive or abortifacient forms of the disease, Jones and Woodbine, Young. It is uncommon to see more than one of these forms in a group of animals at one time. The septicemic form occurs most commonly in newborn or very young ruminants even though the dam may appear normal. The encephalitic form is most common in sheep and cattle. The reproductive form occurs naturally as an epizootic outbreak in occasional flocks of pregnant ewes and does. Listeria is a cause of habitual abortion in women. Humans can contract this disease from animals.

Listeriosis in sheep due to **Listeria monocytogenes** is a much less common cause of abortion than **V. fetus.** Eveleth and his coworkers, Watson and Diplock, reported that in abortion outbreaks due to **L. monocytogenes** on 44 farms there was always a history of a purchase of sheep within a year prior to the outbreak. In 30 of these 44 flocks, sheep were purchased from flocks where listeriosis had previously been demonstrated. Apparently the disease can be carried by clinically normal sheep. The disease may spread from cattle to sheep on the same farm. They reported that in nearly all cases of ovine abortions due to listeria some radical change in management had proceded the outbreak such as withholding food and water, feeding silage in which Listeria organisms may multiply, Marsh, Gray, or heavy feeding to condition ewes for show. The incidence of abortions due to listeriosis varied from 1 to 25 percent which is lower in general than in vibrionic abortion. Abortions usually occur late in gestation and may take place over a period of several months. Some fetuses may be aborted at any stage of pregnancy. Sheep showing the encephalitic form of listeriosis may rarely also be observed in the flock. The mode of spread is not known but experimental abortions were produced by oral administration of the organisms, Gray et al., and Smith et al.. Intravenous injections of **L. monocytogenes** regularly produced abortions in 7 to 12 days, Paterson. The fetuses had usually been dead for several days before expulsion. Thus autolysis and decomposition of the fetus and membranes were often present. Retained placentas were common and associated with metritis, Lawson. Placental lesions and fetal lesions were not distinctive, Molello and Jensen.

Postmorten examination of the fetuses revealed evenly distributed foci of necrosis in the liver and edema and congestion of the meninges. Some lambs near term may be born alive but die within several days with keratitis and liver necrosis. Listeria may be recovered by culture from the placenta, brain, abomasum, meconium, Dennis, and most organs of the fetus. The genital tract of infected ewes sheds organisms in the uterine discharge for several days after the abortion. Isolation of the organism may be difficult and require repeated cultures of large amounts of refrigerated material (See listerial abortion in cattle). The uterus is usually free of organisms 2 to 3 weeks after abortion. It is assumed that after one abortion the ewe is immune inasmuch as second abortions or consecutive yearly flock outbreaks due to this cause have not been reported. Smith and coworkers have reported on the fluorescent antibody technique as an aid in diagnosis. Serological tests have been tried with only limited success, Watson, Njoku-Obi.

Treatment would logically call for division of the flock into small units, isolation of aborting or convalescent ewes, and proper sanitation and disinfection of premises. Silage feeding should be discontinued. Environmental stresses should be eliminated. Purchase of ewes should be confined to flocks free of listeriosis. Eveleth and his coworkers and Osebold et al. described preliminary studies on vaccines. The value of antibiotics in an epizootic outbreak has not been determined.

Brucellosis due to **Brucella melitensis, Brucella abortus** or **Brucella ovis** is uncommon in the United States as a cause for abortion in sheep and goats. In certain areas in and around the Mediterranean region of Europe and Africa, in Russia and possibly Central and South America brucellosis due to **Br. melitensis** is an enzootic and common cause for abortion, especially in goats. Ovine abortion due to **Brucella melitensis** has not been reported in the United States. An outbreak of ovine abortion due to **Br. abortus** in Minnesota apparently contracted from infected cattle was reported by Luchsinger and Anderson. This was apparently a rare occurrence as sheep are quite resistant to **Br. abortus,** Marsh, Watson. The third form of brucellosis, due to **Brucella ovis** (ram epididymitis organism) has been reported in Australia and New Zealand, Central Europe,

S. Africa and the United States where its principal pathologic effect has been in rams causing infertility. In California the incidence of infected rams was 20 to 25 percent, Marsh. Abortion in ewes due to **Br. ovis** is of little importance and is seldom reported except in New Zealand where an incidence of 7 to 10 percent was noted in some flocks by Hartley et al..

In brucellosis in goats due to **Br. melitensis** the incidence of abortion may reach 40 to 60 percent. Abortions occur the last third of gestation and weak moribund lambs may be born at term or prematurely. Like brucellosis in cattle the disease is contracted by pregnant sheep or goats by ingestion of food and water contaminated with organisms from aborting fetuses and their membranes or genital discharges. After intravenous inoculation of **Br. melitensis** abortions may occur from 10 to 21 days. A placentitis involving the placentomes with necrosis of the chorioallantois occurs in advanced cases. The fetus is also infected with inflammatory and necrotic foci in the liver and other organs, Collier and Molello, Molello et al.. Diagnosis of the disease is based on cultures of aborted fetuses or stillbirths and serologic tests, the most useful of which is the agglutination test. Following abortions or infection some ewes or does may carry the infection for months or years in various organs, especially the udder, Mayer. Control of the infection is patterned after the control of brucellosis in cattle and swine. Sanitation, blood testing, isolation or quarentine and slaughter are necessary. Vaccines have been tried in the control of **Br. melitensis. Br. abortus** strain 19 vaccine is of questionable value. Two other vaccines have been more effective; one is an oil and water adjuvant killed vaccine of **Br. melitensis** that produces a severe local reaction and persistent titers and the other is an avirulent living **Br. melitensis** vaccine (Rev 1) recommended for use in sheep and goats at 3 to 8 months of age, Jones, FAO-WHO Expert Committee.

In brucellosis due to **Br. abortus** in sheep and goats the signs, lesions and diagnosis are similar to those with **Br. melitensis.** The disease may rarely spread from infected cattle to pregnant sheep or goats and cause abortions the last third of gestation. The occurrence of this form is rare. It should be controlled promptly in a manner similar to brucellosis in cattle, except for vaccination. Isolation, quarentine and slaughter procedures are recommended.

Brucellosis due to **Br. ovis** in ewes is lower in pathogenecity than **Br. melitensis** or **Br. abortus.** Ewes abort only if infected during pregnancy especially the first or second month of pregnancy since it requires 1-1/3 to 3 months or more to produce severe enough lesions of edema and coalescing areas of necrosis in the placentome and intercotelodonary placenta to interfere with fetal nutrition and result in the death of the fetus and abortion or the birth of weak diseased lambs, McGowan et al., Lawrence, Molello et al.. Apparently ewes are difficult to infect with **Br. ovis** unless they are pregnant. Breeding ewes with infected rams seldom causes the disease in ewes. Ewe to ewe passage of infection is rare. Ram to ram infection occurs most commonly by a susceptible ram breeding a ewe recently bred by an infected ram and contaminating his prepuce with the **Br. ovis** organism. Oral infection from pasture, feed, or water contaminated with material from aborted fetuses, membranes or genital discharges can occur but is of little importance. The disease can be produced in pregnant ewes by the inoculation of the conjunctional, nasal or rectal mucous membranes or by parenteral injection, Keogh et al., and Lawrence. Since intravaginal deposition of infected semen, as in cattle, seldom produces the disease it has been suggested that intrarectal ejaculation of infected semen, sodomy, may be a means of spread of this form of ovine brucellosis from ram to ewe or ram to ram, Keogh et al. and others.

The incidence of abortion due to **Br. ovis** is low. Hartley et al. who reported the highest incidence, indicated that in 40 naturally-infected flocks the incidence was 7 to 10 percent. Abortions usually occur the last trimister of pregnancy. Chronic placental lesions of necrotic plaque-like thickening and edema of the intercotyledonary areas of the placenta is characteristic of **Br. ovis** infection, Molello et al., Lawrence. Smears of these areas often reveal the organism. The organism may be cultured from the fetus, the membranes and the uterine discharges for a week after abortion or premature lambing. The complement fixation (CF) test is a highly satisfactory serological test for determining the presence of **Br. ovis** in a flock or individual, Marsh. The fluorescent antibody technique may also be used to detect **Br. ovis** in contaminated material in the placenta or semen, Van Drimmelen et al.. Infection in ewes persists from one breeding season to the next in only a few ewes, Keogh et al.. However, rams may be chronically infected for 3 or more years. There is no evidence that lambs born from infected ewes retain infection. There is little evidence **Br. ovis** causes infertility in ewes. Infertility in rams is the major cause for losses from this disease. Since the effects of **Br. ovis** infection in the ewe are limited and the infection is transient, most control efforts are aimed at the rams. Palpation of the testes for the presence of lesions, especially in the region of the cauda epididymis will clinically diagnose most individual infected rams. The use of the C.F. test on all rams will detect clinical and nonclinical infected males. Repeated clinical and serological testing and the elimination of infected rams will rapidly reduce the infection rate and eliminate the infection in a flock. Replacement rams should be raised or purchased from disease-free flocks and tested prior to and after a 2 to 3 months isolation period. An effective vaccination procedure for young rams combining the simultaneous use of **Brucella abortus** Strain 19 and a formalin-killed oil adjuvant **Br. ovis** vaccine has been used widely in Australia and New Zealand, Buddle. A vaccination procedure consisting of injecting an alum-precipitated **Br. ovis** bacterin subcutaneously in 2 doses 30 to 60 days apart and followed by a single injection each year has been used in California, Crenshaw and McGowan. Because of the nature of the disease it is probably unnecessary to vaccinate ewes, Lawrence. Antibiotic therapy, especially in chronic cases, is of doubtful value, Bruner and Gillespie.

Paratyphoid abortion, a form of salmonellosis, in sheep is principally caused by **Salmonella abortus ovis.** This type of infection has been described in England and Europe, especially Germany, but not in the U.S. The incidence of abortion varied from 8 to 33 percent, Watson, Marsh. Other Salmonella organisms have been reported to cause ovine abortions: **Salmonella dublin,** Watson 1960 and Shearer in England. **Salmonella typhimurium,** Vickers et al. in the U.S., **Salmonella meleagridis,** Rae and Wall in Australia and possibly **Salmonella menston,** Watson (1962). The infection is contracted orally by contamination of feed and water with aborted material or organisms from other common animal sources. Italian investigators have reported that rams may transmit the Salmonella organisms to ewes at coitus, Watson (1962). An outside animal added to the flock may introduce the disease. In a few cases diarrhea or other evidence of infection of the ewe has been noted but in most cases no signs other than abortions in the last third of gestation or stillbirths at term are observed, Vickers et al..

The organisms are readily isolated from the internal organs of the fetus, the placenta, and the uterine discharges for a few days after abortion. An agglutination test can demonstrate antibodies in the blood serum of infected ewes or rams. Aborting ewes should be isolated and aborted fetuses and placentas should be destroyed. Contamination of feed and water must be prevented. Although autogenous bacterins have been used in reducing the incidence of abortion, their use has not been scientifically evaluated, Marsh, and Watson.

Leptospirosis due to **L. pomona** is seen much less frequently in sheep and goats then in cattle and swine as they appear more resistant to infection. The disease is more common in young lambs than in older ewes, Marsh, Hartley. Beamer and coworkers described outbreaks of leptospirosis in older pregnant ewes that caused abortion in up to 20 percent of the flock. Other symptoms included icterus, hemoglobinuria and death of the ewes. Alston and Brown cited Van der Hoeden in reporting an outbreak of abortion in goats due to **L. grippotyphosa** in Israel. Based on experimental infections, sheep may have a leptospiruria for up to 40 to 100 days. Lindquist et al.. No fetal infections were observed before 21 days after intraarterial inoculation of **L. pomona,** Smith et al.. Leptospira may be cultured from fresh fetal or placental material or seen by histologic techniques. In autolyzed fetal or placental tissues cultural methods are unsuccessful but fluorescent antibody procedures were highly successful, Smith et al.. As in cattle and swine, serologic tests may be of value in the diagnosis of the disease. Treatment of the disease should be conducted along lines similar to those employed in cattle. Vaccination with a bacterin does produce immunity, Brightenback and coworkers.

Pasteurella tularensis and **P. pseudotuberculosis** are causes of abortion in ewes the latter part of the gestation period, Marsh, Bruner and Gillespie, Jellison et al., and Watson. The latter organism was reported by Watson to produce white necrotic foci in the liver of fetuses. Tularemia is common in western United States where it causes enzootic outbreaks of disease in wild rodents and can be transmitted to sheep by the common wood tick, **Dermacentor andersoni** and other ticks. Man is also susceptible to infection. The disease has been described in Europe and Japan. Affected sheep show depression, anorexia, elevated temperature, increased pulse and respiratory rates, coughing, premature births, stillbirths and abortions. Tick paralysis may be a complicating sign. Death losses may be high. One attack confers a long-lasting immunity with a persisting antibody titer. The agglutination test on the serum is useful for diagnostic purposes but may cross react with Brucella organisms. Injections of streptomycin or oxytetracycline produced a prompt clinical response and reduced losses. Controlling tick infestation of sheep by dipping or by keeping sheep from infected ranges is indicated.

Corynebacterium pyogenes, C. pseudotuberculosis and even **C. renale** and **C. equi** have been recovered from aborted ovine fetuses. **C. pyogenes** is the most common strain, Sorum, and Dennis and Bamford. This organism may also cause deaths in newborn lambs.

Other miscellaneous bacteria causing abortion in ewes include: **E. coli** and other coliform organisms, streptococci and staphylococci, Watson, Lawson. Blackleg of the fetus due to **Clostridium feseri** infection following shearing wounds resulted in death of the fetus and distension of its tissues and the uterus and abortion, Butler and Marsh, and Blood and Henderson. **Bacteroides fragilis** was described as a cause of abortion in ewes by Lindquist, and Watson, as was an organism resembling **Bacillus cereus,** Smith and Frost.

Viral Causes of Abortion in Ewes

Enzootic abortion of ewes (EAE) or ovine virus abortion is caused by a viral agent of the psittacosis—lymphogranuloma (PL) or Chlamydia group. There is good evidence that the agent causing epizootic bovine abortion, EBA, and EAE are the same, Storz, McKercher. Enzootic abortion in ewes has been described in Scotland and England, Europe and in western United States, McKercher et al.. PL or chlamydia viruses have also been described as causing pneumonia and polyarthritis in sheep, Page. Latent persistent PL infections of the ovine intestinal tract is common, Storz, Shupe and Storz. Further study is necessary to determine the relationship of these PL agents to each other and to abortion in ewes as evidence indicated that all these PL agents caused abortion in experimental ewes. Ewes with a latent intestinal PL infection showed no increased resistance to superinfection and often aborted when challenged, Storz.

Ovine virus abortion is characterized by abortions from 100 days of gestation to term but most commonly the last month of pregnancy. Occasionally macerated or mummified fetuses are observed. The birth of dead fetuses or weak, moribund lambs is not uncommon. One fetus of twin lambs may be affected. The incidence of abortions in a flock is usually 1 to 5 percent but in susceptible flocks the incidence may reach 30 percent. Most abortions occur in two- and three-year-old ewes in chronically infected flocks. Retained placenta is common and associated with a brownish genital discharge. Occasionally ewes may die from metritis and other complications after abortion. Most ewes bred satisfactorily following abortion as an immunity was developed, Marsh, Watson, Storz, Tunicliff. The disease may be difficult to differentiate from vibriosis, in fact occasionally both infections may occur concurrently in a flock, Frank. This Chlamydia agent causing abortion in sheep and cattle also causes abortion in goats, McCauley and Ticken, and Shefki.

Enzootic abortion of ewes can be produced by oral feeding of the PL agent to susceptible ewes. The incubation period is about 7 weeks. Infection is probably most commonly due to ingestion of feed or water contaminated with infective material from aborting ewes. Although rams may become infected as determined by the C.F. test on serum there is no indication they are implicated in the spread of this disease. Ewe lambs born in infected flocks may later show evidence of disease during pregnancy. Susceptible ewes contracting the infection at one lambing period may abort during their next pregnancy. The disease is not tick-born.

The fetal membranes are similar grossly to the fetal membranes present in bovine abortions due to **Br. abortus.** The chorionic membranes and cotyledons are thickened, edematous, necrotic and leathery. The aborted fetuses usually show signs of autolytic changes that are not distinctive. Staining of placental smears and examination with the microscope may demonstrate the elementary coccoid virus. The virus may be cultured in chick embryos and mice from the fetal membranes. Virus is seldom found in the fetus. Most ewes show a complement fixation titer in the serum from two weeks to 4 months after abortion. This C.F. test is not highly accurate because some infected ewes may show no titers. Other nonaborting ewes may carry a titer due to natural infection or due to the latent PL agent commonly found in the digestive tract, Marsh, Watson, Storz, Parker and Younger, Parker et al..

Workers in Scotland produced a formolized killed adjuvant vaccine that proved highly effective as an immunizing agent for EAE. The immunity lasted for 2 to 3 years after a single injection. A granuloma usually developed at the site of the injection. Experimentally this vaccine proved of value in the United States but it is not commercially available because of a lack of demand for it, Frank et al.. Experimentally chlortetracycline fed to exposed or inoculated ewes largely prevented abortions. However this treatment is not practical and once the infection was established in the placenta some abortions could still occur, Hawkins, Watson.

Miscellaneous virus diseases of sheep causing abortion are as follows:

Tickborne fever is due to **Rickettsia phagocytophilia.** It has been reported in Scotland and Scandinavia, Watson. After inoculation of infected blood, fever developed in 4 to 8 days and lasted for 10 days. During this period abortions occurred. When susceptible pregnant ewes are moved from tick-free to tick-infested pastures late in gestation abortions may occur in up to 50 percent of the ewes and deaths in aborting ewes may occasionally reach 20 percent. The causative agent may be found with difficulty by microscopic examination of the blood of aborting ewes. The inclusion bodies of this organism are seen in the cytoplasm of neutrophiles and large monocytes. Ewes reared on tick-infected pastures are apparently immune, Stamp and coworkers.

Wesselsbron virus is a cause of abortion in sheep and death in newborn lambs in South Africa, Watson. A few affected ewes may die. The virus is transmitted by mosquitoes. Antibodies to the virus are present in the serum of sheep after recovery. The virus apparently affects and kills the fetus **in utero** and may be cultured from the aborted fetus. Weiss et al. and McKercher and coworkers indicated a possibility that a vaccine could be produced.

Rift Valley Fever virus or enzootic hepatitis; was a major cause of abortion in Kenya and South Africa until a vaccine was developed and used extensively. Signs of abortion and deaths in newborn lambs resembled disease due to Wesselsbron virus. Occasional deaths occurred in older ewes. This disease is also transmitted by insects. As with Wesselsbron virus the disease may affect man causing an influenza-like syndrome.

Nairobi sheep disease virus in Africa, Watson, or **rinderpest** and **foot and mouth disease,** U.S.L.S.A. and Hutyra, Marek and Manninger although not present in the United States cause abortions in sheep in countries where these diseases are prevalent.

Bluetongue virus vaccine, a live viral preparation, if used on pregnant ewes between the fourth and eighth week of gestation caused fetal losses characterized by stillborn or spastic lambs and lambs with a variety of defects, Schultz and DeLay. Losses associated with the natural disease have not been described. Bluetongue has been reported in most states west of the Mississippi river and in many other countries. It is spread between animals during warm weather by insect vectors, especially the culicoides fly, Marsh. The viremic stage may last for four months in sheep even though neutralizing antibodies are in the blood. Cattle may also harbor the virus and be a factor in the spread of the disease to sheep, Leudke et al..

Coxiella or Rickettsia burneti or Q fever virus has been recovered from the placenta of ewes and goats. In several flocks abortions occurred and antibodies were also found in the blood of ewes. Both Watson and Tamarin et al. concluded however, that this virus was not highly pathogenic for sheep and probably seldom was a cause for abortion.

Bovine virus diarrhea—mucosal disease virus when experimentally inoculated into ewes 22 to 105 days after breeding caused abortions, mummified, autolyzed and stillborn fetuses and one fetus with cerebellar hypoplasia and hydrocephalus and one fetus with hydrocephalus, Ward.

Aspergillus fumigatus, a fungus, has rarely been described as a cause for abortion in ewes and goats.

Toxoplasma gondii, a protozoa, may infect all domestic animals but only in sheep is it a common and serious cause of abortion. Toxoplasmosis occurs widespread throughout the world, in the United States and Canada. The incidence and mode of transmission of acquired infections is not known. A recent report indicated that the infective form of **Toxoplasma gondii** is found as an oocyst in cat feces resembling that of the coccidia, **Isospora,** Sheffield and Melton, and Frenkel, Dubey and Miller. Experimental infections have been produced by inoculating infective material, Hartley. Heavy rainfall favors the spread of the disease. Stress may cause latent toxoplasmosis to become active. Occasional cases of congenital or intrauterine infections of the newborn have been described in most species of domestic animals. If antibodies are present in the dam no transmission of the infection to the fetus occurs, Siim et al., Eckerling et al.. The importance of toxoplasmosis as a cause of early fetal resorbtion, mummification, abortion and neonatal deaths varies in different countries. In New Zealand 50 to 60 percent of abortions and neonatal deaths were due to this disease; in Yorkshire, England about 15 percent and in the U.S. only sporadic outbreaks have been reported. The incidence of abortion in a flock may vary from 3 to 30 percent. Ewes infected prior to breeding do not abort. Those infected from 30 to 90 days postbreeding usually have fetal resorbtion or mummification. Most observed abortions occur the last trimester of gestation, 2 to 3 weeks before term. One normal twin and one dead twin may be born at term. Ewes aborting due to toxoplosmosis often have a retained placenta. Affected ewes bred back and produced normal lambs the next season. Stillbirths, living defective lambs and normal lambs, as well as aborted fetuses may carry **Toxoplasma gondii.** This organism produces a characteristic placentitis with multiple small, 1 to 3 mm., soft white nodules amongst the fetal villi in the dark red caruncle or cotyledon. (See Figure 70) The organism is readily identified either free or in cysts. The intercotyledonary placenta is often edematous. Fetuses or stillbirths show no gross lesions but organisms may be recovered from the liver, lungs, or brain.

The Sabin-Feldman dye test of ewe's blood detects antibody usually present at the time of abortion and the titer usually continues to rise for several weeks. C.F. tests and skin sensitivity tests have also been used but are of less value in the diagnosis of toxoplasmosis, Siim et al., Watson, and Marsh. Occasionally vibriosis or other causes of abortion are found associated with toxoplasmosis. There is no treatment for this disease. Sulfonamides and **Doraprim** have been tried. It should be noted that animal to man transmission of toxoplasmosis can occur.

Noninfectious Causes for Ovine or Caprine Abortion

Drugs, Chemical or Plant Poisonings:

Phenothiazine administered to ewes in late pregnancy may cause abortions within 4 days postworming, Warwick et al.. The author has observed dead emphysematous macerating fetuses causing severe dystocia, metritis and death following this practice.

Carbon tetrachloride, a chemical seldom used currently in parasite control, may cause abortion if administered to pregnant ewes, Watson.

Chronic lead poisoning may cause abortion in pregnant ewes, Allcroft and Blaxter.

Nitrate feeding in doses in excess to that occurring in forage and causing a severe methemoglobinemia may occasionally cause abortion in ewes, Davison et al..

Locoweeds (**Astragalus lentiginosis, A. pubentisimus** and **Oxytropis sericea**) caused abortions in all stages of gestation, and deformed and small weak newborn if fed to pregnant ewes as hay or if grazed upon in pasture, James et al..

Lupine ingestion resulting in chronic lupinosis has been associated with abortions and fetal deaths in ewes, Garner.

Veratrum californicum if consumed by pregnant ewes will cause early embryonic deaths, aborted fetuses and deformed lambs, Van Kampen and coworkers.

Sweet clover hay containing dicoumarol has been reported to cause abortion if fed to pregnant ewes, Stuart.

Onion grass (**Romulea bulbocodium**) when ingested by pregnant ewes may cause abortion, Watson. Although ergot poisoning has been cited by Watson as causing abortion in ewes, it is doubtful if this is correct. (See discussion of ergot poisoning under abortion in cattle).

Hormonal Causes for Abortion in Sheep

Estrogens—Bennetts, Underwood, and Shier reported that the ingestion of excessive estrogens in subterranean clover by sheep in Australia often resulted in uterine inertia, dystocia, and the birth of stillborn lambs. Dystocia and sterility remained at a rather high level even though the sheep were removed from the clover pasture because of permanent uterine damage by the estrogens. Curnow and Bennetts reported that an isoflavone derivative, genistein, was the active estrogen in the clover. It is about equal in estrogenic activity to one-fifth that of estrone. In certain fresh-cut subterranean clovers, such as the dwalganup variety, concentrations of 100 mg. of genistein per 100 gms. of clover was found.

Watson reported that small amounts of hexoestrol in the grain ration the last few weeks of pregnancy caused abortion in 11 of 14 ewes.

Progesterone deficiency, or cortisol or A.C.T.H. excess has been reported as causes of abortion in goats and sheep, Van Heerden reported that many Angora goat farms in South Africa had over 30 percent abortions each year. The condition did not affect other herds of goats and so it was considered to be genetic in nature. Abortions occurred from 2 weeks of gestation to term with over 60 percent occurring from 100 to 120 days of gestation. Fetuses were partially autolyzed when expelled. A higher incidence was present in the older does. Does conceived promptly after aborting. Abortions were caused by regression of the corpus luteum, necessary in the goat to maintain pregnancy. There was evidence of a lack of luteotrophic hormone from the anterior pituitary gland. Stress, such as shearing, seemed to contribute to an increased incidence of abortion. As discussed in cattle abortion the pituitary-adrenal axis largely controls the onset of parturition in sheep and goats. In habitual abortions occurring in Angora goats described by Van Heerden hyperplasia of the adrenals was observed in aborting does and their fetuses, Van Rensburg, 1965. It was considered that selection for fleece quality in Angora goats raised for mohair production favored animals with adrenal hyperplasia.

Van Rensburg and Liggins demonstrated that if ovine fetuses were given ACTH, corticotropin, or cortisol that abortion would occur within 3 to 7 days. If the former hormone was given the fetal adrenals would become as large as those in fetuses at term. Conversely if the fetal pituitary was destroyed or the fetal adrenals removed, prolonged gestation resulted. Injections of cortisol (hydrocortisone) or dexamethasone (**Azium**) in relatively small doses into ewes in late gestation caused the premature induction of parturition, Van Rensburg, and Adams and Wagner. Larger doses of cortisol administered to ewes during early gestation had no effect but after 85 days of gestation they proved lethal to the fetus.

High ambient temperatures and high humidity causing adrenal hyperactivity and hydrocortisone injections shortly after breeding caused increased embryonic deaths, Howarth and Hawk. Stress factors and their effect on the pregnant ewe especially in late pregnancy may play a definite role in inducing abortions as in toxoplasmosis, phenothiazine poisoning, and reduction in energy intake or ketosis.

Nutritional causes of ovine abortion

Lack of TDN or energy has been widely reported in England and elsewhere as a cause of abortion. A high incidence of up to 80 percent abortions and/or maternal deaths have been associated with pregnancy toxemia or ketosis in ewes, especially those having 2 or more fetuses, and on a restricted energy intake and lack of exercise in late pregnancy. Watson reported on ewes fed only roots during pregnancy in which the reduced energy intake resulted in a high abortion rate.

Copper deficiency was reported by Watson to be associated with stillbirths in ewes. **Colbalt deficiency** has been reported associated with a high death rate in neonatal lambs, Reid.

Vitamin A deficiency of long standing caused a high incidence of stillbirths or poorly viable newborn lambs, Watson.

Iodine deficiency has also resulted in congenital goiter and abortion or stillbirths in sheep, Watson.

Selenium deficiency in ewes in New Zealand has been reported to cause abortion or neonatal deaths of lambs with congenital white muscle disease affecting the heart. It has been associated with farms having a large number of barren ewes and reduced lambing percentage, Hartley, and Grant et al.. Experimental diets high in sulfur caused fetal deaths and abortion with evidence of white muscle disease despite the administration of selenium and vitamin E to the pregnant ewes, Boyazoglu et al.. Possibly the administration of sulfur interfered with the absorbtion or utilization of selenium. Hartley recommended the administration of 5 mg of sodium selenate or selenite monthly for 3 doses before breeding and again one month before lambing. Stamp has described a muscular dystrophy in sheep with early neonatal deaths not associated with selenium deficiency.

Chromosomal, physical and miscellaneous causes

Lethal genetic defects causing fetal deaths, abortions and stillbirths have been described previously. Severe physical stress, fright and exhaustion, such as caused by dogs chasing a flock of ewes in advanced pregnancy, has occasionally been reported as a cause of abortions or premature births. Young ewes have a higher incidence of stillbirths than older ewes, Watson. He also reported that ewes carrying twins, especially if on a low protein level were more apt to abort or have stillbirths than those carrying single fetuses. **Malpresentation** of fetuses at birth with dystocia is a common cause of stillbirths.

References on Ovine Abortion

General References

Blood, D. C. and Henderson, J. A. (1963) Veterinary Medicine, 2nd Ed., Williams Wilkins Co., Baltimore, Md.

Dennis, S. M. (1968) Comparative Aspects of Infectious Abortion Diseases Common to Animals and Man, Internat. J. of Fert. **13,** 3. 191.

Dillman, R. C. (1968) Sequential Sterile Autolysis in the Ovine Fetus, Proc. 72 Ann. Meeting, U.S.L.S.A., 478.

Faulkner, L. C. (Editor) (1968) Abortion Diseases of Livestock, Charles C. Thomas Company, Springfield, Ill.

Hawkins, W. W. Jr. (1968) Diseases Affecting the Reproductive Capacity of the Ewe, Symposium on Sheep Diseases and Health, Univ. of Calif., Davis, Calif.

Lawson, J. R. (1962) Bacterial and Mycotic Agents Associated with Abortion and Stillbirth in Domestic Animals, Livestock Infertility, Animal Health Branch Monograph No. 5, FAO, Rome.

Marsh, Hadleigh (1965) Newsom's Sheep Diseases, 3rd Ed., Williams Wilkins Co., Baltimore, Md.

Watson, W. A. (1962) Abortion and Stillbirth in Sheep, Vet. Bull. **32,** 5, 259.

Watson, W. A. (1962) Ovine Abortion, Vet. Rec. **74,** 49, 1403.

Stuart, J. E. (Chm.) (1962) Report of the Committee on Transmissible Diseases of Sheep and Goats, Proc. 66th Ann. Meeting U.S.L.S.A., 282.

Bacterial infections

Vibriosis

Bruner, D. W. and Gillespie, J. H. (1966) Hagan's Infectious Diseases of Domestic Animals, 5th Ed. Cornell Univ. Press, Ithaca, N.Y.

Dennis, S. M. (1961) **Vibrio fetus** Infection in Sheep, Vet. Reviews and Annot., **7,** Part 2, 69.

Firehammer, B. D. (1965) The Isolation of Vibrios from Ovine Feces, Cor. Vet. **55,** 482.

Firehammer, B. D., Marsh, H. and Tunnicliff, E. A. (1956) The Role of the Ram in Vibriosis of Sheep, Amer. J. Vet. Res. **17,** 65, 573.

Frank, F. W., Waldhalm, D. C., Meinershagen, W. A. and Schrivner, L. H. (1965) Newer Knowledge of Ovine Vibriosis, J.A.V.M.A. **147,** 12, 1313.

Hulet, C. V., Ercanbrack, S. K., Price, D. A., Humphrey, R. D., Frank, F. W. and Meinershagen, W. A. (1960) Effects of Certain Antibiotics in the Treatment of Vibriosis in Sheep, Amer. J. Vet. Res. **21,** 82, 441.

Jensen, R., Miller, V. A., Hammarlund, M. A. and Graham, W. R. (1957) Vibrionic Abortion in Sheep—Transmission and Immunity, Amer. J. Vet. Res., **18,** 67, 326.

Jensen, R., Miller, V. A. and Molello, J. A. (1961) Placental Pathology of Sheep with Vibriosis, Amer. J. Vet. Res. **22,** 87, 169.

Meinershagen, W. A., Frank, F. W., Hulet, C. V. and Price, D. A. (1969) Immunity in Ewes Resulting From Natural Exposure to **Vibrio fetus,** Amer. J. Vet. Res., **30,** 2, 203.

Miller, V. A. (1968) Ovine Genital Vibriosis, in **Abortion Diseases of Livestock** edit. by L. C. Faulkner, C. C. Thomas Co., Springfield, Ill., 128.

Miller, V. A., Jensen, R. and Gilroy, J. J. (1959) Bacteremia in Pregnant Sheep Following Oral Administration of **Vibrio Fetus,** Amer. J. Vet. Res. **20,** 77, 677.

Ryff, J. F. and Breen, H. (1961) Experimental Treatment of Ovine Vibriosis, J.A.V.M.A. **139,** 6, 665.

Smibert, R. M. (1965) **Vibrio fetus** var **intestinalis** Isolated From Fecal and Intestinal Contents of Clinically Normal Sheep, Amer. J. Vet. Res. **26,** 111, 315.

Storz, J., Miner, M. L., Marriott, M. E. and Olson, A. E. (1966) Prevention of Ovine Vibriosis by Vaccination; Duration of Protective Immunity, Amer. J. Vet. Res. **27,** 116, 110.

Storz, J., Miner, M. L., Olson, A. E., Marriott, M. E. and Elsner, Y. Y. (1966) Prevention of Ovine Vibriosis by Vaccination; Effect of Yearly Vaccination of Replacement Ewes, Amer. J. Vet. Res., **27,** 116, 115.

Waldhalm, O. G., Mason, D. R., Meinershagen, W. A. and Schrivner L. H. (1964) Magpies as Carriers of Ovine **Vibrio fetus,** J.A.V.M.A. **144,** 5, 497.

Watson, W. A., Hunter, D. and Bellhouse, R. (1967) Studies on Vibrionic Infection of Sheep and Carrion Crows, Vet. Rec. **81,** 10, 220.

Listeriosis

Diplock, P. T. (1957) Ovine Listerial Abortion, Austral. Vet. Jour. **33,** 68.

Eveleth, D. F. Goldsby, A. I., Bolin, F. M., Holm, G. C. and Turn, J. (1953) Epizoology of Vibriosis and Listeriosis of Sheep and Cattle, Vet. Med. **48,** 8, 321.

Gray, M. L. (1960) A Possible Link in the Relationship Between Silage Feeding and Listeriosis, J.A.V.M.A. **136,** 205.

Gray, M. L. (1963) Listeric Infection in Animals in the U.S., 2nd Symp. on Listeric Infections, Montana State College, Bozeman, Mont.

Gray, M. L., Singh, C. and Thorp, F., Jr. (1956) Abortion and Pre- or Postnatal Death of Young Due to **Listeria monocytogenes,** Amer. J. Vet. Res. **17,** 64, 510.

Molello, J. A. and Jensen, R. (1964) Placental Pathology IV Placental Lesions of Sheep Experimentally Infected with **Listeria monocytogenes,** Amer. J. Vet. Res. **26,** 105, 441.

Njoku-obi, A. N. (1962) The Antigen-Fixation Test for the Sero-Diagnosis of **Listeria monocytogenes** Infection, Cor. Vet. **52,** 3, 415.

Osebold, J. W., Njoku-obi, A. N. and Abare, J. M. (1959) Acquired Resistance of Sheep to **Listeria monocytogenes** and Pilot Studies on Vaccination, Amer. J. Vet. Res. **20,** 79, 966.

Paterson, J. S. (1940) Studies on the Organisms of the Genus Listerella IV An Outbreak of Abortion Associated with the Recovery of Listerella from Aborted Fetuses, Vet. Jour. **96,** 8, 327.

Smith, R. E., Reynolds, I. M. and Clark, G. W. (1968) Experimental Ovine Listeriosis I Inoculation of Pregnant Ewes, Cor. Vet. **58,** 2, 169.

Smith, R. E. Reynolds, I. M. and Harris, J. C. (1968) Experimental Ovine Listeriosis. Immunofluorescent Methods Applied to Maternal and Fetal Tissues, Cor. Vet. **58,** 3, 389.

Young, Stuart (1968) Listeriosis in Cattle and Sheep, in **Abortion Diseases of Livestock,** edit. by L. C. Faulkner, C. C. Thomas Co., Springfield, Ill.

Brucellosis

Buddle, M. D. (1958) Vaccination in the Control of **Brucella Ovis** Infection in Sheep, New Zealand Vet. J. **6,** 41.

Collier, J. R. and Molello, J. A. (1964) Comparative Distribution of **Brucella abortus, Brucella melitensis** and **Brucella ovis** in Experimentally Infected Pregnant Sheep, Amer. J. Vet. Res., **25,** 107, 930.

Crenshaw, G. L. and McGowan, B. (1966) Ram Epididymitis Vaccination, Proc. 70th Ann. Meeting U.S.L.S.A., 476.

FAO-WHO Joint Expert Committee (1964) Brucellosis, 4th Report FAO Agric. Studies 66, Tech. Report Series 289, Rome.

Hartley, W. J. Jebson, J. L. and McFarlane, D. (1954) New Zealand Type II Abortion in Ewes, Austral. Vet. J. **30,** 216.

Jones, L. M. (1962) A Review of Experiments on Vaccination of Goats and Sheep Against **Brucella melitensis** Infection, Refuah. Vet. **19,** 2, 101.

Keogh, J., Doolette, J. B. and Clapp, K. N. (1958) The Epidemiology of Ovine Brucellosis in South Australia, Austral. Vet. J. **34,** 412.

Lawrence, W E. (1961) Ovine Brucellosis: A Review of the Disease in Sheep Manifested by Epididymitis and Abortion, Brit. Vet. Jour., **117,** 435.

Lucksinger, D. W. and Anderson, R. K. (1967) Epizootiology of Brucellosis in a Flock of Sheep, J.A.V.M.A. **150,** 9, 1017.

Mayer, H. (1958) Experimental Studies on Brucellosis in Sheep, Monatsch f. Tierheilk. **10,** 21, 43.

McGowan, B., Biberstein, E. L., Harrold, D. R. and Robinson, E. A. (1961) Epididymitis in Rams: The Effect of the Ram Epididymitis Organism (R.E.O.) on the Pregnant Ewe, Proc. 65th Ann. Meeting U.S.L.S.A., 291.

Molello, J. A., Flint, J. C., Collier, J. R. and Jensen R. (1963) Placental Pathology II Placental Lesions of Sheep Experimentally Infected with **Brucella melitensis,** Amer. J. Vet. Res. **24,** 102, 905.

Molello, J. A., Jensen, R., Flint, J. C. and Collier, J. R. (1963) Placental Pathology I Placental Lesions of Sheep Experimentally Infected with **Brucella ovis,** Amer. J. Vet. Res., **24,** 102, 897.

Van Drimmelen, G. C., Botes, H. J., Claassen, N., Ross, F. W. and Viljoen, C. C. (1963) The Use of Fluorescent Antibody in the Diagnosis of **Brucella ovigenitalium** Infection in Sheep Semen Smears, J. S. Afr. Vet. Med. Assoc. **34,** 265.

Paratyphoid Abortion

Rac, M. and Wall, M. (1952) A Case of Uterine Infection with **Salmonella meleagridis** in a Sheep, Austral. Vet. J., **28,** 173.

Shearer, G. C. (1957) An Outbreak of Abortion in Ewes due to **Salmonella dublin,** Vet. Rec., **69,** 693.

Vickers, C. L., Bierer, B. W., Atkinson, R. E., Mudge, C. and Baker, D. E. (1958) Paratyphoid Dysentery and Paratyphoid Abortion in a Flock of Bred Yearling Ewes, J.A.V.M.A. **132,** 1, 22.

Watson, W. A. (1960) **Salmonella dublin** Infection in a Lambing Flock, Vet. Rec. **72,** 62.

Leptospirosis

Alston, J.M. and Brown, J. C. (1958) Leptospirosis in Man and Animals, E. and S. Livingstone Ltd., London.

Beamer, P. D., Hardenbrook, H. Jr. and Morrill, C. C. (1953) Studies in Leptospirosis in Domestic Animals I Leptospirosis in Sheep, Vet. Med. **48,** 365.

Brightenback, G. E., Scheidy, S. F. and Jensen, J. H. (1960) **L. pomona** Vaccination Studies in Sheep, Vet. Med. **55,** 4, 63.

Hartley, W. J. (1952) Ovine Leptospirosis, Austral. Vet. J. **28,** 169.

Lindquist, K. J., Morse, E. V. and Lundberg, A. M. (1958) Experimental **Leptospira pomona** Infection in Pregnant Ewes, Cor. Vet. **48,** 3, 277.

Smith, R. E., Hench, E. C. and Reynolds, I. M. (1966) Experimental Leptospirosis in Pregnant Ewes, VI, Cor. Vet. **56,** 4, 640.

Smith, R. E., Reynolds, I. M. and Clark, G. W. (1966) Experimental Leptospirosis in Pregnant Ewes, V, Cor. Vet. **56,** 3, 418.

Smith, R. E., Reynolds, I. M. and Clark, G. W. (1970) Pathogenesis of Fetal Infection and Mechanism of Abortion in Experimental Leptospirosis in Ewes, Cor. Vet **60,** 1, 40.

Corynebacterium, Pasteurella and Miscellaneous Bacteria

Butler, H. C. and Marsh, H (1956) Blackleg of the Fetus in Ewes, J.A.V.M.A. **128,** 8, 401

Dennis, S. M. and Bamford, V. W. (1966) The Role of Corynebacteria in Perinatal Lamb Mortality, Vet. Rec. **79,** 4, 105.

Jellison, W., Jacobson, H. and Flora, S. (1964) Tick-borne Tularemia and Tick Paralysis in Cattle and Sheep, Proc. 68th Ann. Meeting U.S.L.S.A., 60.

Lindquist, K. (1956) A Case of **Bacteroides fragilis** Abortion in a Ewe, Nord. Vet. Med. **5,** 995.

Smith, I. D. and Frost, A. J. (1968) The Pathogenicity to Pregnant Ewes of an Organism of the Genus **Bacillus,** Austral. Vet. Jour. **44,** 17.

Enzootic Abortion of Ewes

Frank, F. W. (1963) A Comparison of Some Aspects of Viral Abortion and Vibriosis of Sheep. Proc. 67th Ann. Meeting U.S.L.S.A., 308.

Frank, F. W., Schrivner, L. H., Thomas, L. and Waldham, D. G. (1968) Artificially Induced Immunity to Enzootic Abortion in Ewes, Amer. J. Vet. Res. **29,** 7, 1441.

McCauley, E. H. and Ticken, E. L. (1968) Psittacosis-Lympho-granuloma Venereum Agent Isolated During an Abortion Epizootic in Goats, J.A.V.M.A. **152,** 12, 1758.

McKercher, D. G., McGowan, B., Wada, E. M., Harrold, D. R. and Studdert, M. J. (1964) Isolation of the Virus of Enzootic Abortion of Ewes from California and Oregon Sheep, J.A.V.M.A. **145,** 6, 564.

Page, L. A. (1966) Interspecies Transfer of Psittacosis—L.G.V.-Trachoma Agents. Pathogenicity of Two Avian and Two Mammalian Strains for Eight Species of Birds and Mammals, Amer. J. Vet. Res. **27,** 117, 397.

Parker, H. O., Hawkins, W. W. Jr. and Brenner, E. (1966) Epizootiologic Studies of Ovine Virus Abortion, Amer. J. Vet. Res. **27,** 119, 869.

Shefki, M. D. (1963) Enzootic Abortion in Goats, Brit. Vet. Jour. **119,** 430.

Shupe, J. L. and Storz, J. (1964) Pathologic Study of Psittacosis-Lymphogranuloma Polyarthritis of Lambs, Amer. J. Vet. Res. **25,** 107, 943.

Storz, J. (1963) Superinfection of Pregnant Ewes Latently Infected with a Psittacosis-Lymphogranuloma Agent, Cor. Vet. **53,** 4, 469.

Storz, J. (1968) Comparative Studies on EBA and EAE Abortion Diseases of Cattle and Sheep Resulting from Infection with Psittacosis Agents, in **Abortion Diseases of Livestock,** edit. by L. Faulkner, C. C. Thomas, Springfield, Ill., 108.

Storz, J. Shupe, J. L., James, L. F. and Smart, R. A. (1963) Polyarthritis of Sheep in the Intermountain Region Caused by a Psittacosis-Lymphogranuloma Agent, Amer. J. Vet. Res. **24,** 103, 1201.

Tunicliff, E. A. (1960) Ovine Virus Abortion, J.A.V.M.A. **136,** 3, 132.

Miscellaneous Viral and Rickettsial Infections

Hutyra, F., Marek, J. and Manninger, R. (1938) Pathology and Therapeutics of the Diseases of Domestic Animals Vol. I, 415.

Luedke, A. J., Jockim, M. M. and Jones, R. H. (1969) Bluetongue in Cattle: Viremia, Amer. J. Vet. Res. **30,** 4, 511.

McKercher, D. G., Biberstein, E. L. and Wada, E. M. (1959) A Review of Recent Findings in Infectious Diseases of Sheep: I Virus Diseases, J.A.V.M.A. **134,** 12, 459.

Schultz, G. and DeLay, P. (1955) Losses in Newborn Lambs Associated with Bluetongue Vaccination of Pregnant Ewes, J.A.V.M.A., **127,** 224.

Stamp, J. T., Watt, J. A. and Jamieson, S. (1950) Tick-borne Fever as a Cause of Abortion in Sheep, Vet. Rec. **62,** 32, 465.

Tamarin, R., Rosenfeld, S. and Landau, M. (1964) Experimental Infection of Pregnant Sheep with **Coxiella burneti,** Refuah Vet. 21, 180.

U.S. Livestock Sanitary Assoc. (1954) Foreign Animal Diseases, Report of Comm., Secr. Treas., Trenton, N.J.

Ward, G. M. (1970) Experimental Infection of Pregnant Sheep with Bovine Viral Diarrhea-Mucosal Disease Virus, N.Y.S. Dept. of Health, Albany, N.Y. Unpublished data.

Weiss, K. E., Haig, D. A. and Alexander, R. A. (1956) Wesselbron

Virus—A Virus not Previously Described Associated with Abortion in Animals, Onderst. J. of Vet. Res. **27**, (2), 183.

Fungal Causes of Abortion

Cysewski, S. J., Pier, A. C. and Richard, J. L. (1968) Mycotic Abortion in Ewes Produced by **Aspergillus fumigatus,** Amer. J. Vet. Res. **29,** 6, 1135.

Toxoplasmosis

Eckerling, B., Neri, A. and Eylan, E. (1968) Toxoplasmosis as a Cause of Infertility, Fert. and Steril. **19,** 6, 883.

Frenkel, J. K., Dubey, J. P. and Miller, N. L. (1970) **Toxoplasma gondii** in Cats: Fecal Stages Identified as Coccidian Oocysts, Science **167,** 893.

Hartley, W. J. (1961) Experimental Transmission of Toxoplasmosis in Sheep, New Zeal. Vet. Jour. **9,** 1.

Sheffield, H. G. and Melton, M. L. (1970) **Toxoplasma gondii:** The Oocyst, Sporozoite, and Infection of Cultured Cells, Science **167,** 892.

Siim, J. C., Biering-Sorensen, U. and Moller, T. (1963) Toxoplasmosis in Domestic Animals, in **Advances in Veterinary Science,** Vol. 8 Edit. by C. A. Brandly and E. L. Janghers, Academic Press Inc., N.Y.C., 335.

Smith, I. D. (1961) Toxoplasmosis as a Cause of Ovine Reproductive Failure, 4th Internat. Congr. on An. Reprod., The Hague, Vol. III, 607.

Noninfectious Causes of Abortions in Ewes and Goats

Adams, W. M. (1970) Personal Communication.

Adams, W. M. and Wagner, W. C. (1969) The Elective Induction of Parturition in Cattle, Sheep and Rabbits, J.A.V.M.A. Proceedings Research Section, 106th Nat. Meeting, Minneapolis, Minn. and (1970) Role of Corticoids in Parturition, Biol. of Reprod., In Press.

Allcroft, R. and Blaxter, K. L. (1950) Lead as a Nutritional Hazard to Farm Livestock, J. Comp. Path. **60,** 209.

Bennetts, H. W., Underwood, E. J. and Shier, F. L. (1946) A Specific Breeding Problem of Sheep on Subterranean Clover Pastures in Western Australia, Austral. Vet. J. **22,** 1, 2.

Boyazoglu, P. A., Jordan, R. M. and Meade, R. J. (1967) Sulfur-Selenium—Vitamin E. Interrelations in Ovine Nutrition, J. An. Sci. **26,** 1390.

Curnow, D. H. and Bennetts, H. W. (1952) Estrogenic Hormones in Plants in Relation to Animal Physiology, Proc. 6th Grasslands Congress, Penn. State College.

Davison, K. L., McEntee, K. and Wright, M. J. (1965) Responses in Pregnant Ewes Fed Forages Containing Various Levels of Nitrate, J. Dairy Sci. **48,** 7, 968.

Garner, R. J. (1967) Veterinary Toxicology, Bailliere, Tindall and Cox, London.

Grant, A. B., Hartley, W. J. and Drake, C. (1960) Further Observation on White Muscle Disease in Lambs, N.Z. Vet. Jour. **8,** 1.

Hartley, W. J. (1961) Personal Communication.

Howarth, B. Jr. and Hawk, H. W. (1968) Effect of Hydrocortisone on Embryonic Survival in Sheep, J. An. Sci. **27,** 1, 117.

James, L. F., Shupe, J. F., Binns, W. and Keeler, R. F. (1967) Abortive and Teratogenic Effects of Locoweed on Sheep and Cattle, Amer. J. Vet. Res. **28,** 126, 1379.

Liggins, G. C. (1968) Premature Parturition after Infection of Corticotrophin or Cortisol into Fetal Lambs, J. Endocrin. **42,** 323.

Reid, J. T. (1949) Relationship of Nutrition to Fertility in Animals, J.A.V.M.A. **114,** 864 and 865, 158 and 242.

Stamp, J. T. (1960) Muscular Dystrophy in Sheep and Neonatal Mortality, J. Comp. Path. **70,** 296.

Van Heerden, K. M. (1963) Investigations into the Cause of Abortions in Angora Goats in South Africa, Onderst. J. Vet. Res. **30** (1), 23.

Van Kampen, K. R., Binns, W., James, L. F. and Balls, L. D. (1969) Early Embryonic Deaths in Ewes Given **Veratrum californicum,** Amer. J. Vet. Res. **30,** 4, 517.

Van Rensburg, S. J. (1965) Adrenal Function and Fertility, Jour. S. Afr. Vet. Med. Assoc. **36,** 4, 491.

Van Rensburg, S. J. (1967) Gestation in Sheep after Fetal Adrenalectomy and Cortisol Acetate Administration, J. Endocrin. **38** (1), 83.

Warwick, B. L., Turk, R. D. and Berry, R. O. (1946) Abortion in Sheep Following the Administration of Phenothiazine, J.A.V.M.A. **108,** 826, 41.

ABORTION IN DOGS AND CATS

Abortions in dogs and cats are much less common than in the larger domestic animals. Most canine and feline abortions are sporadic except for enzootic or epizootic outbreaks in kennels due to **Br. canis.** Very little experimental work has been done on other causes of abortions in small animals.

Infections Causes of Canine and Feline Abortions

Bacterial Causes

Brucella canis is the most common cause of abortion in dogs and can be a serious cause for losses in breeding kennels. This highly contagious disease is widespread in the United States and is most commonly observed in Beagles although it is present in other breeds of dogs including Pointers, Greyhounds, Foxhounds, Weinaraners, Old English Sheepdogs, mongrels and others. The disease in dogs resembles brucellosis in swine, but is relatively mild. Canine brucellosis is characterized by abor-

Table 13. **Summary of the Causes of Canine and Feline Abortion**

Infectious causes:
Bacterial causes—Br. canis.
Miscellaneous bacterial causes—Br. abortus (?), staphylococci, streptococci and coliform organisms, paratyphoid, leptospirosis (?).
Viral Causes—Distemper viruses, infectious canine hepatitis virus (?), feline coryza and panleukopenia viruses (?)
Other infections—Toxoplasma gondi in dogs and cats.

Noninfectious Causes:
Drugs, chemical, poisons—O-diazoacetyl-L-serine, N-desacetyl chiocolchicine, malucidin.
Hormonal—progesterone deficiency.
Physical—severe trauma.
Miscellaneous—anemia and pregnancy toxemia (?) in cats, hyperactivity of sympathetic nervous system (?) and others.

tion occurring between gestation days 30 and 57 with about 85 percent of the observed abortions occurring between days 45 and 55. Apparent failure of conception was also commonly observed and this was due to early unrecognized embryonic deaths between gestation days 10 to 35, Carmichael and Kenney, Moore and Bennett, and Moore. Early abortions were largely unobserved because the affected bitches would ingest the expelled membranes and embryos. Two or more consecutive abortions or conception failures were common. Occasionally a bitch would abort, have a normal pregnancy and then abort again. The incidence of abortion in a susceptible kennel of dogs may reach 80 percent. Retained placentas were not observed. However, prolonged vaginal discharges were commonly seen lasting from 1 to 6 weeks after an abortion. Aborted fetuses were both alive and dead. The living pups often died and some fetuses had degrees of autolytic changes. The few surviving pups were infected and bacteremic although they appeared healthy. In adult male dogs orchitis was a consistent sign and the scrotum was hyperemic and swollen. The epididymides were enlarged and firm and testicular degeneration and atrophy were often observed.

Transmission of the disease can occur by inoculations of infective organisms but probably occurs naturally by oral ingestion of infective material or contaminated food or water. Aborting bitches discharge large numbers of infective organisms. Of lesser importance is the infected male which can transmit brucellosis to the bitch at coitus by infected semen. Organisms from the epididymis, testes and prostate are in semen. The male dog might rarely spread infection in his urine. Spread of infection by fecal contamination does not readily occur. Following exposure to **Br. canis** a bacteremia develops within 1 to 3 weeks. A generalized lymphadenitis and splenitis occurs and antibodies become detectable by the serum agglutination test. The brucella organisms persist for many months or indefinitely in nearly all organs of the body. After one year blood cultures may become negative in some dogs but a few dogs may have a bacteremia lasting for 26 to 33 months or more.

The organisms can be readily cultured from organs of aborted fetuses, placental tissues and vaginal discharges. Blood cultures are often positive. Agglutinating antibody titers a month or more after the initial exposure varies from 1:100 to 1:1600 and persists for long periods. Serums from dogs with high titers to **Br. canis** antigen do not cross react with **Br. abortus** antigen. Low level cross reactions, 1:25, may occur with other gram negative bacteria.

Efforts to develop a bacterin have been unsuccessful, Carmichael and Kenney. Although **Br. canis** is susceptible **in vitro** to a combination of tetracyclines, dihydrostreptomycin and sulfonamides, therapy with these drugs has been unsatisfactory as only a temporary cessation of the bacteremia resulted. One recovery was reported using heroic and sustained therapy for up to 3 weeks. Prevention and control in kennels is based on eradication by repeated monthly serologic tests of all dogs, young, old, male and female, segregation and destruction of infected animals, and concommitant sanitary measures, Moore et al.. All dogs to be introduced into kennels should be isolated for 3 to 4 weeks and blood tested. Human cases of brucellosis due to **Br. canis** have been reported, Nat. Comm. Dis Center. Cats are resistant to natural infectious with Brucella spp., McEntee.

Miscellaneous bacterial causes of canine and feline abortion include:

Brucella abortus, suis and **melitensis** can cause occasional sporadic abortions in pregnant bitches when they ingest infected material. These cases may be diagnosed on culture of aborted, infected fetuses or membranes and by the serum agglutination test, Morse, Kimberling et al. and Nicoletti et al.. As with **Br. canis,** dogs infected with these other species of Brucella may infect humans.

Nonspecific organisms such as **coliforms, staphylococci, streptococci** and **paratyphoid** are frequently associated with sporadic abortions especially in older bitches and queens and often accompanied by cystic endometritis, Bloom, Kirk, Sheppard, Freak, Mantovani et al.. These abortions are usually associated with infertility, a persistent vulvar discharge, chronic metritis, and repeated abortions. Few bacteriological studies have been reported in dogs or cats to indicate the more common or even the occasional bacterial causes of abortion. Spaulding, Sheppard, and Holzworth reported that abortion in cats is more common than in dogs and was seldom observed before 4 to 5 weeks of gestation. Holzworth reported an apparent greater incidence of abortion in short-haired cats.

By the administration of large doses of penicillin and streptomycin or other antibiotics for 7 to 14 days or longer, some veterinarians have reported apparent success in preventing abortion in cats and dogs showing early symptoms of impending abortion or especially during the first two weeks following breeding in the postestrous period in those having a history of repeated abortions or metritis. If impending abortion is due to a susceptible organism this therapy might be of value in a few cases but it seems likely that extensive damage to the placentas and fetus has already been produced before therapy is instituted. Although a few reports have linked **Leptospira pomona** with abortion in dogs and cats, evidence indicates that they do not abort from this cause. Dogs and cats can become urinary shedders of leptospira, Fessler and Morter, Kirk.

Viral causes of abortion—In contrast to the larger species of domestic animals, dogs and cats relatively seldom abort due to viral infections of the fetuses. Abortions in dogs have been described following an acute attack of distemper, Kessler, Holzworth and Engstrom. Because most bitches at puberty are immune to distemper, abortion due to this virus is rare. Holzworth reported abortion in two cats, one during an attack of infectious coryza and the other during an illness suggestive of panleucopenia. Although Freak reported aborting and neonatal deaths and stillbirths due to infectious canine hepatitis virus, this was questioned, Gillespie.

Fungal causes of abortion have not been reported in dogs or cats.

Protozoal causes of abortion in dogs and cats are uncommon. **Toxoplasma gondi** may cause abortions, birth of premature, dead or moribund pups or kittens or living pups or kittens with congenital toxoplasmosis, Petrok and Carpenter, Siim et al., Cole et al.. Toxoplasmosis may clinically resemble other infectious diseases of dogs and cats. As with sheep and other domestic animals the organism may be recovered from fetal organs, especially the brain or be observed in histologic sections. The Sabin-Feldman dye test may also be used on the blood of the dam. The complement-fixation test is useful, Bruner and Gillespie. If infected dogs or cats are pets in a household, especially with a pregnant woman, they should be removed as the disease may pass to humans and the fetus.

Noninfectious Causes for Canine or Feline Abortion

A number of drugs have been described that when administered to pregnant bitches caused fetal death and abortion. These drugs include: N-deacetylthiocolchicine, Thiersch; O-diazoacetyl-L-serine (azoserine), Friedman; and malucidin, a yeast extract, Whitney. This latter drug also caused resorbtion of fetuses and abortion when administered to pregnant cats. These drugs have been suggested for mismatings but have not been generally accepted for this purpose.

Progesterone deficiency—Bloom reported that abortion in bitches and cats due to hypoluteoidism may occur the sixth to seventh week of gestation because of premature regression of the corpus luteum, or it may occur the second to fifth week of gestation due to faulty development of the corpus luteum. He advised 5 to 25 mg. doses of progesterone in oil 2 to 3 times a week until the eighth week of pregnancy, or the "repositol" form could be used less often. Much more work needs to be done to assess the incidence of abortions due to endocrine deficiencies.

Nutritional causes of abortion in dogs and cats have not been reported. It is rather significant that in our motorized society that only a few abortions in dogs and cats following severe trauma have been described, Holzworth. This author has reported a few abortions in cats associated with severe anemia and pregnancy toxemia. The latter was characterized by subnormal temperatures malaise, "running fits" and tremors. Autonomic sympathetic hyperactivity apparently caused vasoconstriction of the subplacental decidual vessels of the uterus in early pregnancy causing fetal deaths and abortion, Toth et al.. Genetic defects of the developing embryo or fetus may result in fetal death. Dystocia due to achondroplasia in certain breeds of dogs and lack of proper growth in young animals may cause dystocia and stillbirths.

References

Abortion in The Dog and Cat

Bloom, F. (1954) Pathology of the Dog and Cat, Amer. Vet. Public. Inc., Evanston, Ill.

Bloom, F. (1968) Canine Medicine, Edit by E. J. Catcott Amer. Vet. Public. Inc., Wheaton, Ill., 445.

Bruner, D. W. and Gillespie, J. H. (1966) Hagan's Infectious Diseases of Domestic Animals, 5th Ed., Cornell Univ. Press, Ithaca, N.Y.

Carmichael, L. E. and Kenney, R. M. (1968) Canine Abortion Caused by **Brucella canis,** J.A.V.M.A. **152,** 6, 605.

Cole, C. R., Sanger, V. L., Farrell, R. L. and Kornder, J. D. (1954) The Present Status of Toxoplasmosis in Veterinary Medicine, N. A. Vet. **35,** 265.

Engstrom, D. S. (1964) Canine Distemper—Student-Faculty Seminar, Cornell Univ., Ithaca, N.Y.

Fessler, J. F. and Morter, R. L. (1964) Experimental Feline Leptospirosis, Cor. Vet. **54,** 2, 176.

Freak, M. J. (1962) Abnormal Conditions Associated with Pregnancy and Parturition in the Bitch, Vet. Rec. **74** 1323.

Friedman, M. H. (1957) The Effect of O-Diazoacetyl-L-Serine (Azoserine) on the Pregnancy of the Dog, J.A.V.M.A. **130,** 4, 159.

Gillespie, J. H. (1962) Personal communication.

Holzworth, J. (1964) Personal Communication.

Jetter, W. W. (1950) Criminal Abortion, New Engl. J. of Med. **242,** 9, 344.

Kessler, S. M. (1949) Spontaneous Abortion in a Bitch, J.A.V.M.A. **114,** 865, 210.

Kimberling, C. V., Lucksinger, D. W. and Anderson, R. K. (1966) Three Cases of Canine Brucellosis, J.A.V.M.A. **148,** 8, 900.

Kirk, R. W. (1954, 1965) Personal Communication.

Mantovani, A., Restani, R., Sciarra, D. and Simonella, P. (1962) Streptococcus Infection in the Dog, J. Small Anim. Pract. **2,** 185.

McEntee, K. (1970) Pathology of Domestic Animals, 2nd Edit. by Jubb, K. and Kennedy, P., Academic Press, Inc., N.Y.C.

Moore, J. A. (1969) **Brucella canis** Infection in Dogs, J.A.V.M.A. **155,** 12, 2034.

Moore, J. A. and Bennett, M. (1967) A Previously Undescribed Organism Associated with Canine Abortion, Vet. Rec. **80,** 604.

Morse, E. V. (1951) Canine Brucellosis—A Review of the Literature, J.A.V.M.A. **119,** 304.

National Communicable Disease Center (1969) **Brucella canis** Infection in Man, General Brucellosis Summary, Zoonoses Surveillance.

Nicoletti, P. L., Quinn, B. R. and Minor, P. W. (1967) Canine to Human Transmission of Brucellosis, N.Y. State Jour. of Med. **67,** 21, 2886.

Petrak, M. and Carpenter, J. (1965) Feline Toxoplasmosis, J.A.V.M.A. **146,** 7, 728.

Sheppard, M. (1951) Some Observations on Cat Practice, Vet. Rec. **63,** 44, 685.

Spaulding, R. H. (1923) Reproductive Diseases of Cats, Cor. Vet. **13,** 4, 312.

Siim, J. C., Biering-Sorensen, U. and Moller, T. (1963) Toxoplasmosis in Domestic Animals, in **Advances in Veterinary Science,** Vol. 8, Edit. by C. A. Brandley and E. L. Junghess, Academic Press Inc. N.Y.C.

Thiersch, J. B. (1967) Abortion in the Bitch with N-Desacetyl-Thiocolchicine, J.A.V.M.A. **151,** 11, 1470.

Toth, A., McEwen, R. and Shabanah, E. H. (1964) Role of the Autonomic Nervous System in the Nutrition of the Products of Conception, Fert. and Steril. **15,** 3, 263.

Whitney, L. F. (1960) Further Studies on the Effect of **Malucidin** on Pregnancy, Vet. Med. **55,** 12, 57.

GENERAL OBSERVATIONS ON ABORTION

In the past 20 years many new causes of abortions of animals have been discovered, particularly the virus diseases. The affinity of fetal and placental tissues for viral multiplication and growth in susceptible, rapidly growing tissues is evident. Although many advances in our knowledge concerning abortions has been made it is noteworthy that confirmed diagnosis of the etiologic agent, even with the necessary aid of a highly competent laboratory with trained microbiologists and pathologists, are made in 50 percent or less of the submitted specimens. This fact emphasizes the importance of obtaining an excellent history, securing aborted fetuses and membranes promptly, refrigerating or possibly freezing them and taking them to the laboratory in good shape and in sufficient numbers, if possible, so a diagnosis may be made on one or more of them. Paired serologic samples obtained from aborting animals before or at the time of abortion and 2 to 3 weeks later may be helpful in those diseases that produce antibodies. The low level of laboratory diagnoses of the causative agent is caused in many cases to the intrauterine death of the fetus and autolytic changes due to delayed expulsion of the fetus that makes recovery of the infective agent difficult or impossible. Furthermore it should be noted that if a pathogenic agent is recovered from a fetus or its membranes that this is not positive proof that this agent caused the abortion.

The endocrine and chromosomal aspects of embryonic deaths, premature birth and abortion are very interesting but require further study to ascertain their definitive role. Death of the bovine fetus caused by **V. fetus** resulted in a decline in plasma progesterone levels several days before abortion. If living fetuses were aborted prior to term, the progesterone levels also declined prior to abortion, but the decline was more gradual. Death or disease of the fetal placenta may reduce placental production of progesterone in the cow, Osburn et al.. It is highly possible that death of the fetal placenta releases the uterine luteolytic factor that results in involution of the corpus luteum and marked reduction in progesterone secretion and abortion.

Violence and trauma are explanations often relied upon

by laymen and veterinarians as an easy way to explain certain abortions where the cause cannot readily be ascertained. Jetter stated, "It is a popular misconception among lay people that gymnastics, severe exercise external trauma to the lower abdomen, hot baths and so forth can induce abortion. Successful abortions after these procedures is fortuitous. In the vast majority of cases abortion is spontaneous and caused by a preexisting abnormality of fetal or maternal tissues." Certain traumatic acts such as removal of the bovine corpus luteum of pregnancy or dilation of the cervix of the pregnant mare usually results in abortion. Severe prolonged trauma or stress may cause abortion possibly due to the excess production of glucocorticoids. Certain animals that abort repeatedly or in which abortion is easily produced by estrogens or glucocorticoids may have a weak endocrine constitution.

Mummification of the Fetus

Fetal death in domestic animals occurring the middle or last third of gestation that does not result in involution of the corpus luteum and abortion of the fetus within the next week or 10 days or decomposition or maceration of the fetus within the next several months, is followed by autolytic changes in the fetus, absorbtion of placental and fetal fluids, involution of the maternal placenta, and mummification of the fetus. Conditions necessary for the occurrance of fetal mummification include the maintenance of the dead fetus within the uterus by the presence of a normal viable fetus or fetuses or the persistence of the corpus luteum of pregnancy associated with a single, or rarely twin, bovine mummified fetuses. One or more mummified fetuses present in the uterus with one or more normal viable fetuses is observed frequently in swine, occasionally in dogs, and cats and uncommonly in sheep, goats, cattle and horses. Fetal mummification associated with a persistent corpus luteum is observed mainly in cattle and rarely in goats. The maintenance of pregnancy in these latter two species is due to progesterone produced by the corpus luteum. In the other species progesterone is produced by the fetal placenta or chorion after midgestation and the corpora lutea involute. Fetal mummification apparently does not occur the first trimester of gestation because embryonic or fetal death prior to the development of the fetal bones usually is followed by absorbtion or resorbtion of the fetal and placental tissues. Fetal death the last month or six weeks of gestation with beginning fetal mummification may be undiagnosed at parturition and called a stillbirth, especially in multiparous animals. Williams described some of these fetuses in cattle as "static fetal cadavers." Fetal mummification may occur and subsequently bacteria may invade or gain entrance to the uterus and cause secondary maceration of the uterine contents.

Two types of fetal mummification have been described in animals, the hematic type in cattle and the papyraceous type in the other species. The process by which these two types form are basically similar. In cattle as the maternal placenta or caruncle undergoes involution a variable amount of hemorrhage occurs between the endometrium and fetal membranes which after the plasma has been absorbed leaves a reddish-brown, gummy, tenacious mass of autolyzed red cells, clots and mucus. This imparts a reddish-brown color to the fetal membranes and fetus. A similar discharge of blood from the caruncles is noted in normal parturient cows 10 to 14 days after calving and is characterized by a bloody genital discharge. The similarity between the tenacious sticky reddish mucus around the membranes of the bovine mummified fetus and that found in the rectum following intussusception of the intestine in cattle is striking. In the other species mummification is not characterized by placental hemorrhage and the fetus is usually a brownish color and the fetal membranes are not covered with this reddish-brown tenacious material. In both types of mummification the longer the condition exists the greater the loss of fluids from the placenta, the membranes and the fetus.

Mummification of the bovine fetus occurs in cattle of all ages. It is observed most often in Guernsey cattle although other breeds are commonly affected. The condition usually affects single fetuses but may occasionally involve one or both fetuses in twin pregnancies. Bovine fetal mummification occurs the third to eighth month of gestation but most commonly the fourth, fifth and sixth months. (See Figures 71, 72, 73) If the condition is undiagnosed the mummified fetus will remain in the uterus for months beyond a normal gestation period. Spontaneous abortions before or near the expected end of gestation are not uncommon. In one study of 32 mummified fetuses in one herd the range of the "gestation," period from conception to spontaneous abortion, was 131 to 342 days with an average of 215 days, Erb and Morrison. The sex of mummified fetuses are nearly equally divided between males and females, Roberts. No premonitory signs are observed before the abortion of a mummified fetus except occasionally those of estrus.

The causes of fetal death and mummification in cattle are often the same as causes for fetal death and abortion. The cause of fetal mummification is often impossible to determine because the time of fetal death is not known and autolysis and mummification of the fetus and mem-

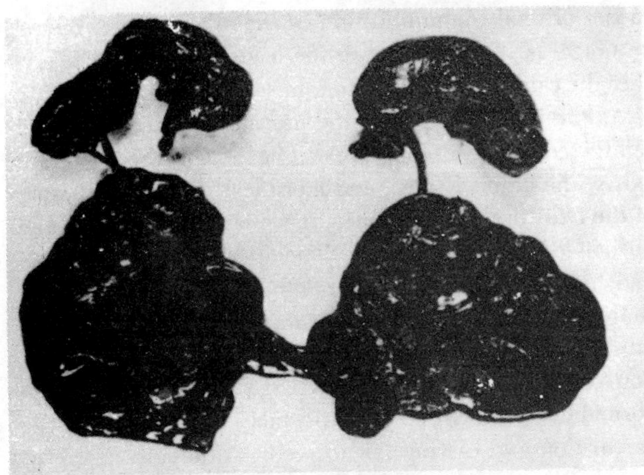

Figure 71. Mummification of twin, bovine, 3-month-old fetuses. These were spontaneously aborted at four months of gestation.

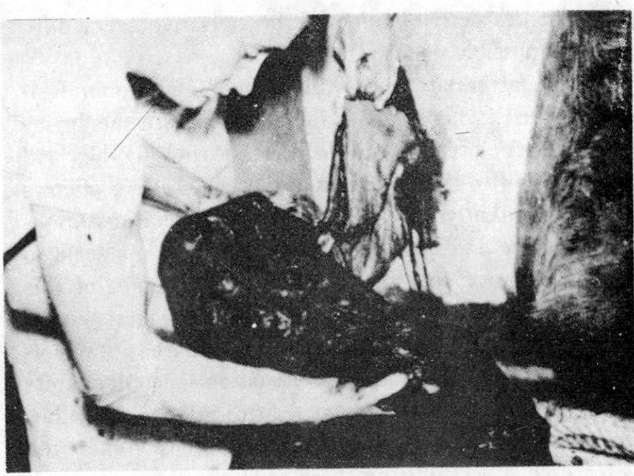

Figure 72. Removal by caesarean section of a bovine mummified fetus that died at 7 months of age.

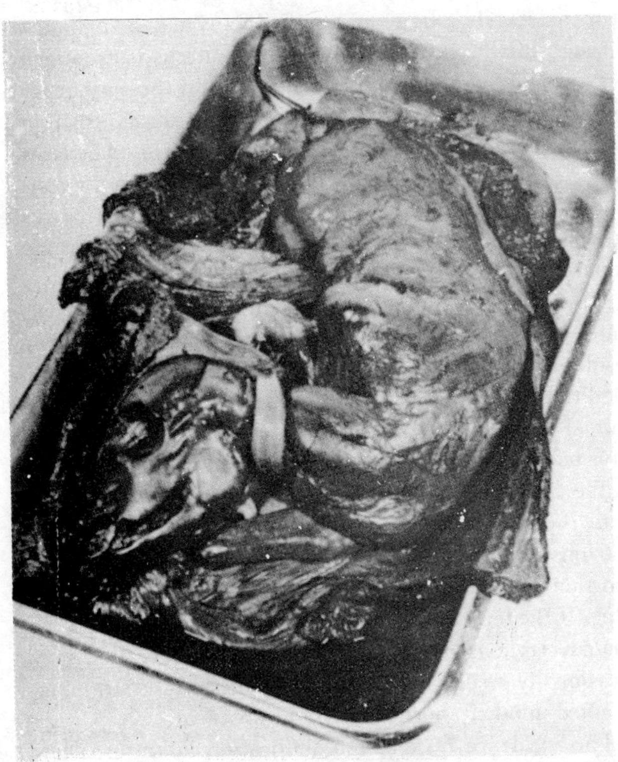

Figure 73. Death and mummification of a bovine fetus due to the displacement of the umbilical cord around the neck of the fetus.

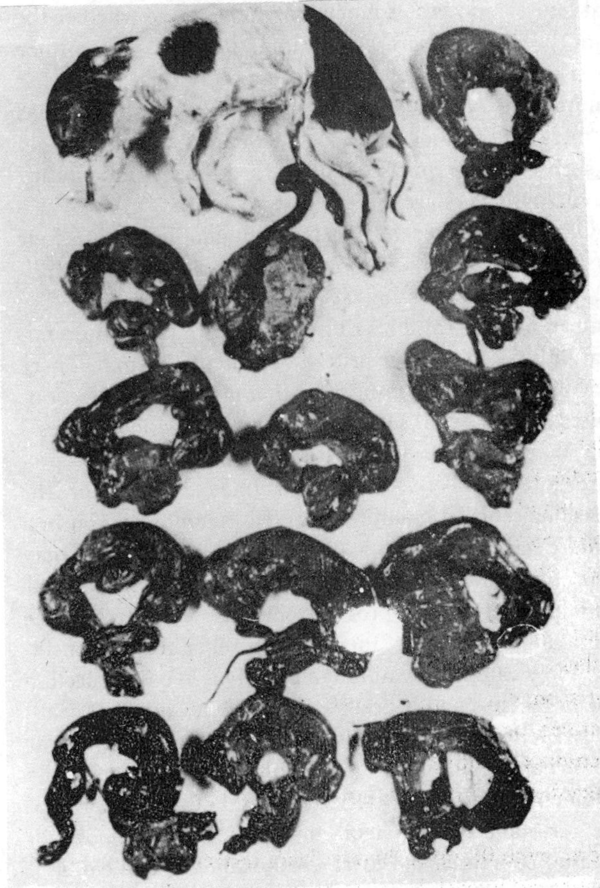

Figure 74. Porcine fetal death and mummification different times in gestation and a stillbirth, with abortion of the uterine contents near term. This might possibly have been due to a SMEDI virus.

branes makes determination of the causative agent difficult or impossible.

Genetic factors are involved in bovine fetal mummification, Roberts. There is a greater incidence in the Jersey and Guernsey breeds of cattle. Certain cow families will have mummified fetuses in two to four generations of cows bred to apparently unrelated males by artificial insemination. In these and other studies the male did not seem to play a causative role in the genetic inheritance of this condition. However, Stevens and King suggested that abortions and fetal mummification experienced in a Holstein herd at 120 to 180 days of gestation when daughters of two popular sires were mated artificially to the other sire were due to autosomal recessive genes. When the owner used other bulls on these cows the losses stopped. Further evidence that this condition may be due to an inherited endocrine or other defect of certain cows is the fact that as many as 20 to 50 percent, average 30 percent, of subsequent conceptions in cows that have had mummified fetuses may result in fetal mummification whether the same or different sires were used, Roberts. The author observed one Guernsey cow that had 5 normal calves and 5 mummified calves within a period of 9 years. Abortions at midgestation not associated with fetal mummification in such cows are quite common. Rare cases of mummified anomalous calves are recorded.

Other causes for bovine fetal mummification include torsion of the umbilical cord or compression of the umbilical cord by its passing around a fetal extremity. (See Figures 66 and 73) This causes fetal death. Fetal mummification may then occur instead of prompt abortion. There is evidence that fetal mummification may follow infectious causes of fetal death such as **V. fetus,** molds, leptospirosis and B.V.D.-M.D. virus, Roberts, and Kahrs. Leptospirosis and B.V.D.-M.D. virus may account for the occasional epizootic outbreaks of fetal mummification in a herd. Fetal death and a degree of mummification may occur in animals in which the duration of gestation has been prolonged by progesterone or progesterone-like compounds. Torsion of uterus and trauma are not considered to be causes of fetal mummification. Wound infection type organisms and brucella organisms causing fetal death are not followed by fetal mummification. It would appear that organisms causing an inflammatory response in the endometrium are characterized by fetal death and prompt abortion and not by fetal mummification. Almost all mummified fetuses and uteri when examined and cultured are sterile and free of organisms and the endometrium is involuted and normal. This is further substantiated by the observations that cows usually conceive the first or second estrum after the expulsion of the mummified fetus. The causes of fetal mummification in the other species should be noted as these might provide leads for explaining further the causes of the condition in cattle.

As the fetus mummifies the uterine walls contract and tightly enclose the conceptus. The longer the condition exists, the dryer, firmer, and more leather-like the tissues of the fetus become. The uterine walls are fairly thick and no cotyledons are palpable. The uterine artery is small and has no fremitus. Fetal mummification in the cow is characterized by failure of estrum with a persistent corpus luteum. It is usually not suspected until late in gestation or until after the normal length of gestation, when normal development of the fetus, body changes incident to parturition and calving fail to occur. Although the uterus may be drawn forward by the weight of the mummified fetus and a normal cervical seal may be present, a careful rectal examination will readily reveal the nature of the disease. If the uterus is dropped downward out of reach it may be pulled up to the pelvic cavity manually by grasping the cervix or intercornual ligament, by placing Knowles cervical forceps on the cervix and drawing the uterus back, or by having two men raise the caudal abdominal viscera by means of a pipe or bar held by each of them. Rarely a large mummified fetus may be ballotted through the flank. In cases where the uterus is examined very early after the death of the fetus and the occurrence of the interplacental hemorrhage, it feels distended by a doughy mass, which is the large, soft blood clot. The fetus is not easily palpated in this doughy mass within the contracting uterus. Within a few weeks the typical changes associated with fetal mummification in the cow become apparent.

The bovine fetal mummy remains in this semi-moist state without odor or pus until spontaneous abortion results in from 1 to 2 months to 1 to 2 years, or until the condition is diagnosed, treated, and corrected, or the animal is slaughtered. If spontaneous abortion occurs, the fetus may be expelled into the vaginal cavity and a portion of the dark brownish-red stained fetal membrane hangs from the vulva until noticed by the caretaker or owner. Estrum usually occurs about the time of the spontaneous abortion and the cow will come into estrum 16 to 24 days later. If the fetus should be large and passage through the dilated cervix is not possible then fetal maceration may occasionally result. In large fetuses tenesmus or straining, as noted in other abortions, may be observed.

The incidence of fetal mummification in cattle is low and sporadic. In three large herds the incidence was 0.43 to 1.8 percent of the pregnancies, Roberts. In some herds the incidence may be higher and in a few instances apparent epizootics of mummified fetuses may occur.

To expel the mummified fetus in the cow the simplest treatment is to administer 50 to 80 mgs. of stilbestrol or 5 to 8 mg. of estradiol intramuscularly. The injected estrogen causes contraction of the uterine muscles, relaxation of the cervix, involution of the corpus luteum and results in the expulsion of the fetus. In about 80 percent or more of the cases this single injection of an estrogen is all that is required and the fetus is expelled within 37 to 72 hours. If the fetus has not been expelled within this time, a similar dose of estrogen may be administered a second time. In unusual instances 3 or more doses at 48-hour intervals may be needed. Some veterinarians use repositol diethylstelbestrol, 100 to 150 mg., intramuscularly. Occasionally examination of a cow either after treatment or before will reveal the fetus entering into or wedged in the cervical canal, with the cervix not yet dilated sufficiently to allow passage. Administration of a single large dose of estrogen at this time usually results in successful dilation of the cervix and the expulsion of the fetus within 24 to 36 hours. When the fetus is large, or mummification occurs at 6 to 8 months of gestation, or the cow is small or immature, the genital tract should always be examined within 48 to 72 hours after the injection to make sure dystocia does not occur with secondary infection of the uterus and maceration of the fetus. Occasionally a second dose of estrogen, much lubrication, gradual traction with a snare or Knowles cervical forceps by one hand and pushing on the fetus with the other hand in the rectum, may be needed to help remove the fetus. The use of large doses of potent glucocorticoids to cause the expulsion of mummified fetuses has not been reported, Adams.

Removal of the persistent corpus luteum of pregnancy will usually result in estrum and the evacuation of the uterus. There is the added danger of trauma and damage to the ovary by the forceful or surgical removal of the deeply imbedded corpus luteum of pregnancy. It has been found that massage of the uterus daily for several days frequently provides enough stimulus to cause evacuation of the uterus. In exceptional cases in which the affected animal is a small heifer, or the fetal cadaver is very large, or previous treatment has been unsuccessful, a cesarean operation through either the right or left flank is usually successful in correcting the condition. Manual dilation of the cervix is not indicated. It has been reported that filling and distending the vagina with cotton will cause the expulsion of a mummified fetus. The author has had no experience with this method of treatment.

Following treatment and expulsion of the mummified fetus, most cattle recover promptly since no infection is present to delay recovery. Conception usually occurs within 1 to 3 months. Any cow with a history of having one mummified calf may have another one at any gestation period; hence the prognosis should always be guarded.

Fetal mummification in horses occurs seldom and has only been reported in one of twin fetuses that has died during pregnancy possibly due to a lack of placental area. The equine mummified fetus remains in the uterus only as long as pregnancy is maintained by the viable twin. Since spontaneous abortion of twin fetuses is common in mares the discrepancy between the size and development of the partially mummified fetus and recently dead fetus often leads to the improper diagnosis of superfetation.

Fetal mummification in sheep is occasionally observed as affecting single ovine fetuses or one or both twin fetuses. It has been associated with and probably caused by infections in sheep causing fetal deaths and abortions. These include: toxoplasmosis, EAE (Enzootic Virus Abortion), **Listeria monocytogenes,** possibly **L. pomona** and unknown causes associated with prolonged gestation, Roberts.

Fetal mummification in swine is an important cause of prenatal losses. Fetuses dying in utero from 40 to 90 days of gestation usually mummify and are expelled at parturition along with the normal fetuses. In a herd relatively free of disease, single mummified fetuses in a litter were more common than two or more, Pond et al.. In three breeds of pigs in this herd, Berkshire, Chester White and Yorkshire, the percentages of mummified pigs were 4.97 and 1.95 and 1.08 respectively. The high incidence of mummified fetuses in Berkshires in this herd accounted in part for the smaller litter size in this breed. Single mummified fetuses were more common in large litters. The presence of occasional mummified fetuses were not related to the incidence of stillbirths. The cause of these occasional mummified fetuses in certain litters is not known. Epizootic herd outbreaks of abortions, early embryonic deaths, mummified fetuses and stillbirths have been described in swine. (See Figure 74) A high incidence of mummified porcine fetuses has been reported in five viral diseases of swine: Aujezsky's disease or pseudorabies, Japanese encephalitis B. virus, Japanese hemagglutination virus, modified hog cholera virus, and a number of picorma, entero- or SMEDI viruses, Dunne et al. and Dunne and Hokanson (See abortion in swine). In this latter viral disease mummification occasionally resulted in a prolonged gestation period, Dunne et al. (1965). Following outbreaks of the above viral diseases, affected sows usually conceive promptly and produce normal litters. A natural immunity is apparently produced.

Fetal mummification in dogs and cats is uncommon

and sporadic in nature but apparently similar to that seen commonly in swine where one to three mummified fetuses are expelled with normal pups at the time of whelping.

Fetal Maceration

Maceration may occur at any stage of gestation and has been observed in all species. It is described most often in the cow. (See Figures 75 and 76) When the fertilized ovum or embryo succumbs to bacterial or viral infection or other disease or abnormality early in gestation it is usually absorbed in the uterus or a slight and often insignificant purulent uterine or vaginal discharge may be evident. The embryo is seldom observed. The interval between estrual periods may be prolonged if the embryo did not succumb until 20 to 50 days after conception. Early embryonic death and maceration are probably caused by a variety of miscellaneous organisms that may be found in the uterus, and are of common occurrence in cows affected with trichomoniasis or vibriosis. In occasional cases of pyometra seen in trichomoniasis, fetal shreds and placental remnants are often found floating in the pus. In cases of early fetal maceration the cervix may be tightly sealed or some discharge of pus may be evident in the vagina or from the vulva. These cases usually are diagnosed and treated as pyometra or endometritis. In the former, estrum is not present; in the latter estrum may occur. In multipara, maceration of early embryos and fetuses usually ends in their being absorbed. The other fetuses develop normally or occasionally some become macerated in turn by the extension of the infection. Rarely in cattle, sheep and horses one fetus may die the first half of gestation and macerate and be expelled with the placenta and the normal twin at parturition.

In the cow fetal maceration that occurs after the third month of gestation, by which time fetal bones are fairly well developed, may be caused by similar wound-infection bacterial agents. Septic metritis of pregnancy, resulting in the death, emphysema, and maceration of the fetus in a closed uterus, is uncommon. It may be characterized in the cow by abortion and/or dystocia usually occurring from the middle of gestation to near term. The symptoms of septic metritis of pregnancy are similar to septic metritis after parturition. The condition may be more serious and fatal due to the presence of the decomposing fetus(es), failure of the cervix and genital canal to dilate normally, and a uterine inertia.

More commonly fetal emphysema and maceration follow fetal death and beginning abortion in the cow in which the cervix dilated but the fetus was not expelled due to a failure of the genital tract to dilate sufficiently or contract normally or because the fetus was dead and in an abnormal position and posture. In rare instances fetal emphysema and maceration may be associated with uterine torsion during gestation. The two factors of an open cervix and a dead fetus at body temperature cause a rapid bacterial invasion of the fetus and membranes of organisms already present in the uterus or from the more caudal portions of the reproductive tract. Fetal emphysema and maceration follow. If the bovine fetus is beyond the third month of pregnancy and if the usual expulsive

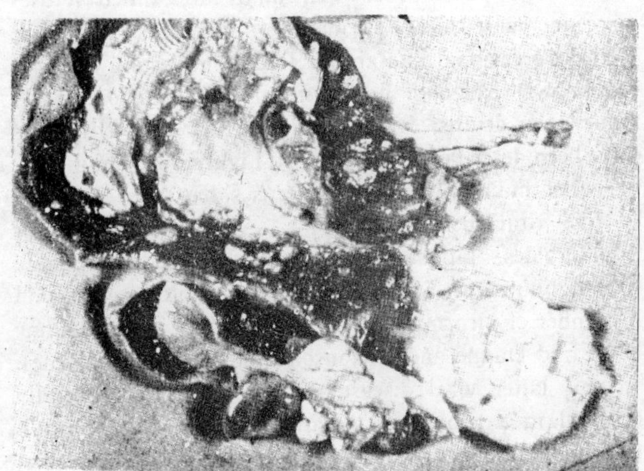

Figure 75. Maceration of a 4-month-old bovine fetus.

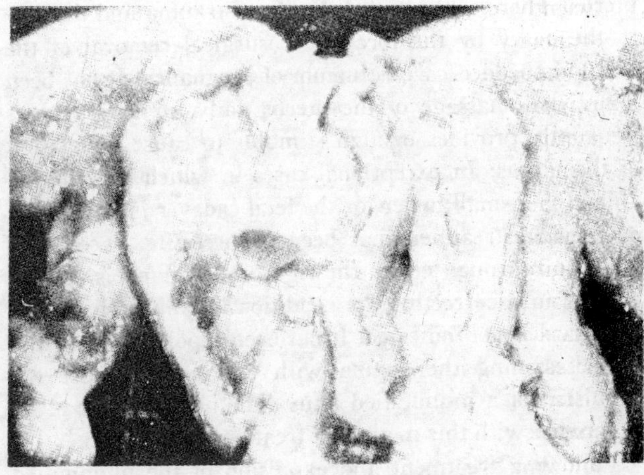

Figure 76. Bones of a 6-months-old macerated bovine fetus in the uterus. Note the thickened uterine wall and degenerated fibrotic endometrium (Courtesy K. McEntee).

efforts are not observed or are unsuccessful, the fetus develops emphysema in 24 to 48 hours and in 3 to 4 days maceration begins. If fetal emphysema and maceration develop in a fetus late in gestation, the handling or treatment of the case is the same as similar cases occurring as a sequelae to an ordinary dystocia at term and will be described later under the handling of dystocia.

Because of the relatively smaller size of the fetus, those cases of fetal emphysema and maceration accompanying an abortion during the middle period of gestation are treated differently. Usually these cases have a history of intermittent straining for several days accompanied by a foul, fetid, reddish-grey vulvar discharge. The temperature and pulse are often elevated. Anorexia and drop in milk production are usually present. Occasionally diarrhea is present. Palpation per vaginum or rectum of a distended, swollen fetus with gas crepitating in the tissues is diagnostic of fetal emphysema. In bovine abortion from the fourth to seventh month with fetal emphysema, the fetus usually may be removed by careful and gradual traction if the cervix is sufficiently dilated and lubrication is used. In the mare the cervix may be carefully dilated manually prior to removal of the decomposing fetus. After removal the uterus should be reexamined to make certain another fetus is not present and to remove the placenta if possible. Aftercare is similar to that described for septic metritis and retained placenta. In those few cases in cattle in which the cervix is contracted and the fetus cannot be removed, heroic treatment is not indicated. Supportive treatment consisting of antibiotics and sulfanomides parenterally along with large doses of estrogens, 50 to 100 mg. of stilbestrol or 5 to 10 mg. of estradiol daily or every other day for perhaps 4 to 7 days, is administered until the cervix is relaxed enough or the fetus is macerated sufficiently to effect its removal in its entirety or in pieces without injury to the cow. With this treatment the danger of excessive traction or embryotomy causing lacerations or rupture of the cervix and uterus is avoided. Because the uterus and its contents are relatively small the development of a septic metritis and a severe toxemia is prevented by the supportive therapy. Cesarean section should be considered as a last resort in the cow but is seldom required. The cow should not be rebred for at least three to four months and the outlook for her reproductive life is guarded. Aftercare and treatment of the infected uterus is necessary.

In long-standing fetal maceration the acute emphysematous stage has passed, straining is seldom observed, and the cervix is usually quite contracted. Generalized symptoms of elevated temperature and pulse and anorexia are usually not present. There is often a history of a chronic, fetid, mucopurulent discharge from the vulva over a period of several weeks or months. Only rarely is the cervix sealed. There may be a history of a gradual drop in milk flow and a loss of weight. The presence of diarrhea is variable. Diagnosis in the dog and cat is aided by abdominal palpation and radiographs besides observing the other symptoms. In most cases no external symptoms of illness are noted except possibly a uterine discharge appearing occasionally at the vulva. On rectal examination in the cow or mare, fetal bones may be palpated in the uterus either floating in pus or crepitating against each other with little pus around them. The uterine wall is thick and heavy and the cervix is usually large and hard. Severe degenerative and sclerotic changes have occurred in the endometrium.

The prognosis is poor. Treatment in the cow is difficult. If much pus is present, treatment as for pyometra is indicated and possibly the bones may be passed through the cervix with the pus. More often the amount of pus is slight and the condition has existed long enough so that the bones are deeply imbedded in the endometrium and uterine wall. The cervix is hard and indurated and not dilatable even with estrogens. Laparohysterotomy is difficult because of the small size of the uterus and its infected contents. It is seldom indicated and then only as a last resort in a valuable cow, since the future breeding life of these cattle is very questionable. The longer the condition has existed the greater the damage to the endometrium and the poorer the prognosis. In most cases in cattle, slaughter is recommended. In multiparous animals hysterectomy or hysterotomy may be performed, depending upon the circumstances.

In rare instances fetal emphysema and maceration may cause a local perimetritis or even rupture of the uterus, with the macerating fetus being walled off in the abdominal cavity where it may remain indefinitely; or the mass may slough through the abdominal floor, into the rumen or into the rectum. In rare cases, torsion of the uterus may cause a similar condition in the cow and multipara.

Prevention on Conception after Mismating and Induced or Artificial Abortion in Domestic Animals.

Induced or artificial abortion or preventing of conception is occasionally desirable in veterinary medicine from an economic or therapeutic standpoint. For example if a purebred female is bred by accident to a scrub male or a male of another breed, or if a female is bred at too young an age, induced abortion is often indicated. The earlier this abortion is brought about, the less time is lost in the female's reproductive life. Abortions are often desirable in meat-producing animals upon entering the feed lots. If the owner of an animal requests an abortion there are no legal complications to consider as in human medicine. Induced abortion and prevention of conception following accidental breeding may logically be discussed together.

The most conservative methods of preventing conception or producing abortion should be used. Heroic measures while often effective may adversely affect the animal's health or its future potential as a breeding animal.

Prevention of conception following an accidental or unwanted service is best accomplished in animals by the injection of an estrogen within 24 to 48 hours after the undesired service. In the cow or heifer 40 to 80 mg. of stilbestrol or 4 to 8 mg. of estradiol intramuscularly usually prevents conception. In the bitch 0.5 to 1.0 mg. of diethylstibestrol/lb. of body weight may be given intramuscularly, followed by 0.5 to 1.0 mg. daily for 5 to 7 days orally, or 1 mgm. of "repositol" diethylstilbestrol per pound of body weight may be injected intramuscularly. Soon after estrum or before attachment of the ovum or embryo in the uterus, pregnancy can be prevented in the cat by 6 daily injections of 1000 R. U. of an estrogen according to Asdell citing Gros. In cows estrum may be prolonged 2 to 3 days. In the bitch estrum is usually prolonged 7 to 10 days. Conception fails to occur after estrogen therapy due either to the locking or slowing of the passage of the fertilized ovum through the oviducts, its too rapid passage through the oviducts and uterus, or else to the production of an uterine environment inimicable to the fertilized ovum.

The practice of douching female animals with mild antiseptics immediately after service often fails to prevent conception because in the cow, sperm cells reach the pavilion of the oviducts in less than 4-1/2 minutes and in other species it is apparently only a matter of minutes for some of the spermatozoa to reach the oviducts and hence out of reach of the antiseptic douche fluid. There is no need or reason for a veterinarian to attempt to "separate" copulating dogs even when this is desired by the owners of the bitch. This is difficult, dangerous and often highly embarrassing. By the time the dogs are separated sperm cells have advanced into the cranial portions of the uterus.

The use of agents such as progesterone or progestins or ICI or "Match" or "Aimax" to suppress the release of the gonadotropins and stop the estrous cycle preventing follicle formation, ovulation and corpus luteum formation have been used experimentally to synchronize estrus. They are used in a manner similar to the steroidal compounds of progestins, estrogens and androgens used in humans to prevent conception. These however must be given over a long period of time; they are quite expensive and very few have yet been approved by the Food and Drug Administration for use in meat-producing animals. Progesterone-like agents used for prolonged periods in dogs have produced cystic degeneration of the endometrium and secondary endometritis and pyometra. They are of no value in preventing conception after coitus, in fact some of these agents actually promote conception and maintenance of pregnancy if given at this time.

Experimentally in cattle the injection of oxytocin, 100 to 200 I.U. daily from day 2 to day 7 after estrus causes an inhibition of the growth and development of the corpus luteum and its secretion of progesterone necessary to maintain pregnancy. Usually cattle treated in such a manner return to estrus in 8 to 10 days. Thus this treatment should also prevent conception in bovine animals bred accidentally.

In areas such as India where bulls and cows are not confined and the amount of feed available is limited, Roy and Rowson have demonstrated the value of a small stainless steel spring similar to a "bobby pin." This pin may be readily inserted into the cervix of a heifer or cow and will remain indefinitely. Although under these conditions estrous cycles, coitus and conception may occur, abortion results due to the failure of the cervix to be able to seal itself properly. This technique was an early application of the presently widely accepted intrauterine devices (I.U.D.) now used in women to prevent conception. Depending upon the species of animals the I.U.D.'s prevent fertilization, prevent implantation or interfere with normal corpus luteum development. Ovariectomy effectively suppresses the estrous cycle and prevents conception in all domestic animals.

The induction of abortion in domestic animals following conception can be accomplished in a variety of ways depending on the species of animal, the duration of pregnancy and the desires of the owner.

Douching the uterus by means of a catheter or pipette with antiseptics such as 1 to 2 percent Lugol's solution, 200 ppm. chlorine solution, dilute acetic acid or potassium permanganate solution 7 to 20 days or longer after service in the cow or mare, is often successful in destroying the developing ovum or embryo. Injecting of irritating solutions such as dilute Lugol's solution around the third to sixth day after service in the cow may result in similar changes as produced by the injection of oxytocin with a shortened time between estrous periods. In mares abortion may be produced readily up to 8 months of gestation by manual dilation of the cervix in a sterile manner and injecting several hundred ml. of dilute Lugol's solution or other suitable antiseptic. Trum reported that he had aborted over 100 mares by injecting 500 cc. of sterile iodized oil or physiological saline into the gravid uterus. Possibly manual dilation alone would be sufficient in the mare. Aborting mares with fetuses over 8 months of age may cause injury or result in infection or dystocia in the mare. Douching the uterus and dilating the cervix is not practical or possible in the ewe, bitch, sow or cat.

Injection of estrogens in large and/or repeated doses will invariably abort animals in any stage of gestation. In cattle these include: stilbestrol, 500 to 1000 mg. every 4 days or 50 to 150 mg. daily; estradiol, 10 to 20 mg. every 2 to 4 days; stilbestrol pellets, 1 to 2 gms. implanted subcutaneously; and "Repositol" diethylstilbestrol, 100 to 150 mg. every 7 days.

The estrogen should be administered until abortion occurs. There are marked variations between cattle in the amount of estrogen required to cause abortion. These high prolonged doses of estrogen cause an involution of the corpus luteum of pregnancy. The cervix also relaxes. Invariably the fetus dies prior to abortion. Occasionally cystic ovaries follow this therapy. In fetuses aborted the middle and third trimesters of pregnancy retained placenta and metritis are common sequelae. Occasionally in abortions after the fifth month of gestation dystocia may develop requiring veterinary assistance. In pregnant beef heifers weighing about 500 to 600 lbs. entering feed lots, a single dose of 100 to 125 mgm of repositol diethylstilbestrol will abort about 80 percent of them; Hill and Pierson. In most cases abortions occurred 3 to 6 days and occasionally up to 12 days after the initial large dose of estrogen. One dose of 50 to 100 mg. of stillbestrol in oil seldom produces bovine abortion but a single dose of 8 to 10 mg. of estradiol will occasionally cause abortion. In other species continued comparable large doses of estrogen might also produce abortion but this treatment has seldom been reported in those species.

Manual removal of the corpus luteum of pregnancy in the cow invariably results in abortion in about 3 to 5 days. Waiting until the fourth week after service to be certain the cow has conceived is indicated before the corpus luteum is removed by manual manipulation of the ovary through the rectal wall. This technique must be employed before the fifth or sixth month of pregnancy and preferably before the third month as after this time the ovary is drawn forward out of reach of the hand introduced into the rectum. It is advisable to watch the cow after removal of the corpus luteum to observe abortion and the presence of estrum that usually occurs in 3 to 6 days. Rarely following this therapy abortion does not occur due to failure to remove all of the luteal tissue or the presence of another corpus luteum or the rapid development of luteal tissue at another ovarian site. There is some danger of hemorrhage and uterine adhesions after manual removal of the corpus luteum so the induction of abortion in cattle with estrogens is preferred. Removal of the corpus luteum during early pregnancy in the mare or other domestic animals is not possible except by laparatomy and ovarotomy or ovariectomy.

Manual rupture of the amnionic vesicle in the cow and the chorionic vesicle in the mare with destruction of the embryo is possible by digital pressure through the rectal wall from 30 to 50 days of pregnancy in the cow and 17 to 30 days in the mare. After pregnancy has progressed to 60 days in cattle and 50 days in mares this technique is impossible to carry out because of the strength of the fetal membranes. This has been attempted in mares and cows to eliminate one of twin embryos; the latter being undesirable in uniparous species. Although Garbers has reported some success with this technique in mares further work is needed. In cattle Steere reported this to be generally unsuccessful since both embryos succumbed when one was damaged. It was interesting to note that in single pregnancies when the embryo was destroyed that "pregnancy" continued and the membranes grew for 2 to 3 weeks following the rupture of the amnionic vesicle, Ball and Carroll. Estrus seldom occurred until 30 or more days after inducing embryonic death.

The administration of moderate to large doses of glucocorticoids will usually produce abortion in cattle. More experimental work is needed to determine the endocrine mechanisms involved and the dosages needed. It appears that cortisone affects the production of gonadotropins and thus may interfere with the production of progesterone necessary for the maintenance of pregnancy (See discussion under Abortion in Cattle). Producing abortion with glucocorticoids is more difficult the first two trimesters of pregnancy than the last portion of the third trimester. This may be related to the increased estrogen levels in the body at this time. Stress and possibly cortisone injections might more easily induce equine abortion around the fourth and fifth months of gestation when the corpora lutea are involuting and the placental production of progesterone is increasing. In cattle 6 to 7-1/2 months pregnant 5 mg. flumethasone daily intramuscularly and 10 mgm. of dexamethasone orally for 4 to 8 days caused abortion in 5 heifers, McEntee. Siegrist reported that 20 mg. of flumethasone given as a single dose would regularly cause abortion in feedlot heifers. Adams produced abortion in 19 of 22 cows 235 to 280 days pregnant within 22 to 56 hours after a single dose of 20 mg. of dexamethasone intramuscularly. Retained placentas and metritis were common in these animals. Adams reported later (1970) that 180 cows, 80 percent, of 202 cows given 20 mg of dexamethasone intramuscularly the last two weeks of pregnancy, average gestation age of 271 [illegible] calved with a live calf within 72 hours of the single injection. Twelve sheep 140 days pregnant were given 10 mg dexamethasone subcutaneously twice at a twenty-four hour interval and all ewes lambed from 42 to 66 hours, average 50 hours, from the first injection. Van Rensburg and Adams and Wagner regularly caused abortion in sheep in late pregnancy by a small dose of 25 mg. of hydrocortisone. Further study is obviously needed on the abortifacient effects of the glucorticoids in cattle and other domestic animals. The combination of estrogens and glucocorticoids appear to be more efficient in producing abortions around mid-gestation in cattle. Settergren and Wright in preliminary studies caused rapid involution of the corpus luteum of pregnancy and cervical relaxation and dilation in the cow from 3 to 8 months of gestation with 10 to 20 mg. flumethasone and 25 mg. of stilbestrol in oil given intramuscularly. They suggested that more prompt abortion at about 50 to 60 hours after the injections might occur if oxytocin were administered at 48 hours after the injections when the cervix was dilated. The fetuses were expelled alive or in a fresh state. Adams also reported (1970) that a severely affected cyclopian ovine fetus was promptly expelled by the administration of dexamethasone at 140 days of gestation. He felt certain this condition would have caused a prolonged gestation if it had not been treated.

Injection of 20 to 30 I.U. of oxytocin in mares late in gestation may induce parturition within 1 to 3 hours. These results are regularly observed in mares over 340 days in gestation. (See Parturition) Similar results have been reported in sows with milk present in their udders and close to farrowing.

Ovariohysterectomy, laporohysterotomy or caesarean section effectively terminates an unwanted pregnancy, Noordsy. In the former procedure, done mainly in dogs and cats, future conceptions are prevented. These operations are progressively more difficult and risky the later in gestation they are undertaken. It may be advisable to allow natural birth and destroy the offspring and perform the ovariohysterectomy several months later. Curettage, as commonly performed in humans in producing early abortion, is not applicable to animals except possibly the mare.

References

Fetal Mummification

Adams, W. M. (1969) The Elective Induction of Labor and Parturition in Cattle, J.A.V.M.A. **154,** 3, 261.

Dunne, H. W., Gobble, J. L., Hokanson, J. F., Kradel, D. C. and Bubash, G. R. (1965) Procine Reproductive Failures Associated with a Newly Identified "SMEDI" Group of Picorn Viruses, Amer. J. Vet. Res. **26,** 115, 1284.

Dunne, H. W. and Hokanson, J. F. (1963) A Modern Approach to Abortion and Stillbirth Problems in Swine, Proc. Book AVMA, 54.

Erb, R. E. and Morrison, R. A. (1957) Effect of Mummified Fetuses on the Prolificacy of Holsteins, J. Dairy Sci. **40,** 1030.

Pond, W. G., Roberts, S. J., Dunn, J. A. and Willman, J. P. (1960) Late Embryonic Mortality and Stillbirths in Three Breeds of Swine, J. An. Sci. **19,** 3, 881.

Roberts, S. J. (1962) The Enigma of Fetal Mummification, J.A.V.M.A. **140,** 7, 691.

Stevens, R. W. C. and King, G. J. (1969) Genetic Evidence for a Lethal Mutation in Holstein Friesian Cattle, J. Hered. **59,** 6, 366.

Williams, W. L. (1943) Diseases of the Genital Organs of Domestic Animals, 3rd Ed. Miss Louella Williams, Upland Rd., Ithaca, N.Y.

Prevention of Conception and Induced Abortion

Adams, W. M. (1970) Personal Communication.

Adams, W. M. (1969) The Elective Induction of Labor and Parturition in Cattle, J.A.V.M.A. **154,** 3, 261.

Adams, W. M. and Wagner, W. C. (1970) Role of Corticoids in Parturition, Biol. of Reprod. In press.

Ball, L. and Carroll, E. J. (1963) Induction of Fetal Death in Cattle by Manual Rupture of the Amniotic Vesicle, J.A.V.M.A. **142,** 373.

Ball, L. and Carroll E. J. (1968) Rupture of the Amniotic Vesicle, in **Abortion Diseases of Livestock,** edit. by L. Faulkner, C. C. Thomas Inc., Springfield, Ill.

Garbers, G. (1967) Personal Communication.

Hill, H. J. and Pierson, R. E. (1958) Repositol Diethyl-stilbestrol as an Abortifacient in Feedlot Heifers, J.A.V.M.A. **132,** 12, 507.

McEntee, K. (1968) Personal Communication.

Noordsy, J. L., Huston, K., Oberst, F. H. and Smith, S. T. (1964) Successive Preterminal Gestation Cesarean Sections in the Cow: Surgical Studies, Amer. J. Vet. Res. **25,** 107, 1027.

Roy, A. and Rowson, L. E. A. (1955) A Method of Inducing Sterility in the Cow, Vet. Rec. **67,** 10, 177.

Settergren, I. and Wright, J. (1970) Personal communication and unpublished data.

Steere, J. H. (1959) Bovine Gynecology in Denmark, Mod. Vet. Prac. **40,** 32.

Siegrist, J. (1969) Personal Communication.

Trum, B. (1950) Personal Communication.

Van Rensberg, S. J. (1967) Gestation in Sheep after Fetal Adrenalectomy and Cortisol Acetate Administration, J. of Endocrin. **38,** 83.

Whitney, G. D. (1968) Prevention of Pregnancy, in **Current Veterinary Therapy,** 3rd Edit., edit. by R. W. Kirk, W. B. Saunders Co., Philadelphia, Pa., 679.

Extrauterine Pregnancies and Fetuses

True Extrauterine Pregnancy is characterized by a fertilized ovum, embryo, or fetus that has established nutritive relations with organs or tissues other than the endometrium and has undergone in this location a degree of embryological development. In humans ovarian and tubal pregnancies may occur, the latter being fairly common. True abdominal pregnancies, with the fetal placenta attaching to the mesentery and omentum, have been described as rarely occurring in humans. In ovarian, tubal, and abdominal pregnancies the embryonic development proceeds only a short time and then the fetus succumbs. In human tubal pregnancy the oviduct ruptures, usually accompanied by severe hemorrhage. No authentic cases of true extrauterine pregnancies have been described in domestic animals. This difference is apparently related to the manner in which the developing zygote establishes nutritive relationships with the dam. In humans and rodents the developing zygote erodes the mucosa and buries itself in the maternal tissues while in domestic animals the villi of the trophoblast attach themselves in the maternal crypts formed in the endometrium.

False or Secondary Extrauterine Pregnancy is seen occasionally in all domestic animals and very rarely in the mare. In this condition the fertilized ovum, embryo, or fetus develops normal placental relationships with the endometrium and the fetus reaches recognizable size. It then escapes from the uterine cavity either into the abdominal cavity or the vagina. This condition usually occurs the last two-thirds of the gestation period. Almost all secondary extrauterine fetuses are dead by the time the condition is diagnosed. In so-called "vaginal pregnancies" it is obvious on examination that the fetus came through the cervix from the uterine cavity. The cause for uterine rupture, allowing the escape of the fetus into the abdominal cavity, is frequently unknown. The condition is seen in uterine torsion, fetal emphysema, chronic perimetritis and following dystocia and oxytocin administration especially in the bitch, Krichel, Lederer and Fisher. It may occur spontaneously or possibly associated with violence in advanced pregnancy. In multipara, uterine torsion may involve a part of one horn or the entire horn with the enclosed fetuses being separated from the rest of the uterus. The adhesions that take place may cause the condition to be diagnosed as an extrauterine pregnancy or fetus. In many cases in domestic animals in which a sterile fetus is released into the abdominal cavity little or no external symptoms may be evident. The fetus dies and with its membranes becomes walled off as a sterile foreign body in the ventral portion of the abdominal cavity and remains there as an inert mass for months, Spanabel. Often extensive adhesions between it and other abdominal viscera develop. The site of the rupture may only be a small or invisible scar after the uterus involutes. Since most of these fetuses are well-walled off, no external symptoms are usually seen. Occasionally mild digestive disturbances may be evident. In rare cases a large extrauterine fetus may be diagnosed on rectal examination in the cow if the fetus was near term when it escaped from the uterus. A differential diagnosis must be made, considering mummification of the fetus, tumors, and fat necrosis. Diagnosis of most cases in the larger domestic animals is made at the time of slaughter. In the dog and cat abdominal palpation, radiographs and exploratory laparotomy may aid in revealing the extrauterine fetus(es) especially in an ailing animal soon after parturition. These fetuses may be or become infected, macerate, cause peritonitis and the death of the dam or rarely be walled-off and be expelled into the alimentary tract or through the abdominal wall, Keyser, Williams.

If extrauterine fetuses are diagnosed in large animals the prognosis is guarded and the animal is usually slaughtered. A laparatomy operation to remove the extrauterine fetus would be difficult and many adhesions would remain. In the dog and cat an operation might be considered in cases of chronic, walled-off extrauterine fetuses.

In animals with uterine rupture late in pregnancy or at the time of parturition, secondary to trauma, torsion, fetal emphysema or possibly spontaneous rupture, the fetus and uterine contents escape into the abdominal cavity. If the fetus is emphysematous or grossly infected, fatal peritonitis and shock frequently follow. In rare cases the fetus may still be found alive and the dam and possibly the young can be saved by an immediate laparotomy to remove the dead or live fetuses and repair the ruptured uterus.

In the mare a rotated or compound bicornual pregnancy may be confused with an extrauterine abdominal fetus. In this condition the birth passageway is very long and the fetus may be palpated beneath the stretched vagina and uterine body and simulate an extrauterine fetus. In humans some long-existing extrauterine fetuses become quite firm and encapsulated with calcium laid down in the capsule, causing them to be spoken of as lithopedions. These well-encapsulated extrauterine fetuses in animals may occasionally be referred as extrauterine fetal mummies.

Dropsy of the Fetal Membranes and Fetus

These pathologic conditions in pregnant domestic animals may include hydramnios, hydrallantois, edema of the allantois chorion, fetal anasarca, or fetal edema with ascites and hydrothorax. These conditions are usually found singly but on rare occasions may be associated. In hydramnios and hydrallantois in uniparous animals the abdomen is usually distended as if twins or triplets are present. All cows in which twins are suspected should be examined promptly for these possible dropsical conditions. Of these conditions hydramnios and hydrallantois are most common with the latter occurring 10 to 15 times more frequently than the former. In 7 percent of cases both hydramnios and hydrallantois were present together, Vandeplassche et al..

Hydramnios or hydrops of the amnion is characterized by a gradual enlargement or filling of the amniotic cavity that is associated with a genetic or congenitally defective fetus. The condition is seen most commonly in cattle, occasionally in sheep, rarely in pigs and carnivores, and it has not been reported in horses, Arthur (1969). It may affect one of twin fetuses. Arthur (1957), (1965) has observed that at midgestation the amniotic fluid is watery and slightly yellow and in normal bovine conceptuses only increases in amount very slowly until the last month of pregnancy when it nearly doubles in amount. In normal sheep there is a sudden increase around the 100th day of pregnancy. From midgestation onward the amniotic fluid becomes more viscid and glairy because the early watery fluid is swallowed or possibly inhaled into the large bronchi and absorbed and a large volume of saliva is continually produced. In defective fetuses swallowing is impaired and the amounts of amniotic fluid increase gradually to 5 to 30 gallons. During the last few months of gestation, when hydroamnios becomes apparent, the amount of amniotic fluid is 1 to 2 gallons in normal cows.

Genetic or hereditary conditions resulting in defective fetuses often associated with hydramnios are 1) Dexter cattle pregnant with "bull dog" calves. In these animals the disease is apparent at 3 to 4 months of pregnancy, Crewe. 2) Angus cattle pregnant with small brachygnathic, defective calves that lack of a marrow cavity in the bone. These exhibit increased abdominal enlargement the last month of gestation. 3) A muscle contracture monster associated with hydrops of the amnion has been described in Red-Danish cattle, Loje. 4) Prolonged gestation in Guernsey cattle characterized by an immature defective fetus with pituitary hypoplasia or aplasia may be associated with hydramnios. 5) A lethal muscle contracture monster in sheep accompanied by dropsy of the amnion has been described by Roberts. Hydramnios was commonly observed with hydrocephalic fetuses in Hereford cattle, Baker et al.. All of the above defective fetuses have been caused by recessive autosomal genes (See chapter on Anomalies of the Fetus). Hydramnios is also seen in cattle with congenitally anomalous fetuses such as conjoined twin monsters, **Schistosomus reflexus,** and fetuses with certain anomalies of the cranial portions of the body. Hybrids produced by mating of an American bison bull with a domestic cow resulted in hydrops of the amnion, Williams. Anencephaly is frequently the cause of hydramnios in humans, Cassady and Cailliteau.

Hydramnios develops slowly over several months during the latter half of pregnancy. If the condition causes obvious abdominal enlargement it is usually the last month or six weeks of the gestation period. Often the condition is not recognized until parturition when large quantities of syrupy, viscid amniotic fluid, occasionally continuing meconium, is released. The differential diagnosis between hydramnios and hydrallantois will be described under the latter. The prognosis for the future breeding life of the dam is fair to good in hydramnios but the fetus is invariably defective and dies. Retention of the placenta and metritis are not serious problems as with hydrallantois. Abortions and premature parturitions are frequent in cases of hydramnios. Because of the enlarged uterus, uterine inertia, and defective fetuses, dystocia at parturition is not uncommon. It is usually easily handled because of the small size of the fetus. In hydramnios associated with prolonged gestation and fetuses with defective or missing pituitary glands injections of large doses of glucocorticoids and estrogens might be indicated to produce abortion or parturition. Cesarean section, as described under hydrallantois, can also be used to terminate a pregnancy with hydramnios. The genetic implications in salvaging an affected dam should be considered. If the defective fetus and hydramnios is due to a recessive character then the dam and sire are carriers. Such animals should be eliminated from the herd and any inbreeding in the herd should be discouraged.

Hydrallantois, dropsy or hydrops of the allantois, is the single factor present in 85 to 90 percent of the dropsical conditions affecting the bovine fetus and its membranes. This condition is seen sporadically in dairy and beef cattle. It is usually associated with a diseased uterus in which most of the caruncles in one harn are not functional and the rest of the placentomes are greatly enlarged and possibly diseased. Adventitious placentae are commonly observed. Portions of the placenta may be necrotic and edematous. Hydrallantois is seen quite commonly in cattle carrying twin fetuses. Hydrallantois apparently is caused by structural or functional changes in the allantois chorion including its vessels with transudation and collection of fluid, differing from normal allantoic fluid but resembling plasma, Skydsgaard. One may remove many gallons of this transudate from the allantoic cavity with a trocar but within 2 to 4 days it has been restored. This would tend to indicate that the fetal kidneys probably seldom play a role in causing this disease. Neal and others have indicated that the presence of cystic kidneys, hydronephrosis, or dysfunction of the fetal renal tubules resulting in polyuria might be concerned in the pathogenesis of hydrallantois. The author has seldom observed such abnormalities in the fetal kidneys of fetuses from affected cows and further suggests these changes are probably secondary to the hydrallantois. Torsion of the uterus and torsion of the umbilical cord are not associated with this condition. The navel cord in the cow is short and seldom ever twisted. In the mare torsion of the umbilical cord may occur and be severe enough to cause the death of the fetus but dropsy of the fetal membranes and fetus does not occur. Williams and Lynd noted that this condition appeared to be more prevalent in seasons when forage has been damaged, with a possible loss of vitamin A resulting in a lowered resistance of the endometrium to disease. In cases of hydrallantois associated with a reduced number of placentomes and uterine disease the fetuses are usually slightly smaller than normal and show some edema and ascites. Hydrallantois usually affects cows 3 or more years of age although rarely the condition may be seen in heifers in which possibly a congenital lack of caruncles was present. In older cows this lack of caruncles characteristic of hydrallantois may be due to prior uterine infection or even tuberculous metritis, Arthur, 1969.

The signs of dropsy of the allantois vary depending on the degree of the involvement and the stage of pregnancy. In mild cases, where the amount of fluids is moderate, 10 to 20 gallons, the condition may not be diagnosed until parturition. At this time an excessive amount of clear, watery, amber fluid with the characteristics of a transudate is expelled. The fetal membranes may be tough and rupture with difficulty. The uterus is greatly enlarged and atonic and the small fetus may exhibit some edema and ascites. Dystocia may result at the time of abortion or parturition due to uterine inertia. The fetus is usually dead at birth or dies shortly thereafter. Retention of the fetal membranes and septic metritis are common sequelae to this dropsical condition. In severe cases, symptoms of hydrops of allantois may occur as early as the fifth month of pregnancy. Hydrallantois usually develops rapidly within 5 to 20 days and is characterized a distended uterus and enlarged abdomen. (See Figure 77) Spontaneous abortion at 6 to 9 months may frequently be observed, Vandeplassche et al.. In the more severe cases the amounts of fluid may reach 20 to 50 gallons. The fetal membranes may be heavy and edematous and the cow frequently has ascitic fluid in her abdominal cavity. Thus the weights of the dropsical fluids, membranes, and uterus frequently total 350 to 550 lbs. This excessive volume of fluid distending the abdomen causes the owner to believe his records of breeding dates are wrong or else the cow is going to have triplets. Later, digestive symptoms with anorexia, lack of ruminations, and constipation are noted. The condition is frequently misdiagnosed as indigestion, bloat, or traumatic gastritis. The cow may drink excessive amounts of water. The temperature is normal. The pulse is elevated to 90 to 140 per minute and is weak and wiry. The cow may exhibit anxiety, restlessness, and an expiratory grunt. Because of the excessive volume of fluid, the fetus can seldom be ballotted or felt per rectum. On rectal examination the uterus is greatly distended and tense. Placentomes can seldom be felt, due to the tense uterine wall, but the uterine arteries are "whirring" indicative of a live fetus. The uterus appears to fill the abdominal cavity. As the condition progresses—and it may progress quite rapidly at any time during pregnancy—the abdomen becomes more distended. The gait is stiff, slow, and cautious. The cow loses body condition, and eventually is unable to rise. Dislocation of the hips or backward extension of the rear limbs may occur and the cow lies on her sternum looking like a "bloated bull frog." (See Figure 77) Rarely rupture of the prepubic tendon or ventral hernia may occur due to the excessive weight of the uterus. Rupture of the uterine wall has also been described, Vandeplassche et al. and Oehme. For a differential diagnosis between hydrallantois and hydramnios see Table 14. Other dropsical conditions affecting the uterus are much less common.

Edema of the allantois chorion characterized by extensive and severe edema distending these tissues to a thickness of 4 to 6 inches has been associated with **Brucella abortus** infection causing placental disease in cattle and therefore is rarely seen at present in the United States. Hydrallantois is rarely associated with **Brucella abortus** infection.

Fetal ascites severe enough to cause dystocia may also rarely be due to **Br. abortus** infection. Slight fetal ascites and edema as well as mild placental edema is frequent'y associated with intrauterine fetal death and sterile autolytic changes.

Fetal anasarca or excessive edema of fetus is seen most commonly in cattle but may affect sheep. It may develop in a single fetus or one of twins. It is also rarely observed in one or two of a litter in swine or carnivores. Rarely mild hydrops of the amnion and/or allantois and edema of the placenta may accompany fetal anasarca. Abortions of affected fetuses are fairly common from 4 to 8 months in uniparous animals. The condition has been described by Donald et al. and others affecting Ayrshire cattle. This is caused by a recessive autosomal character.

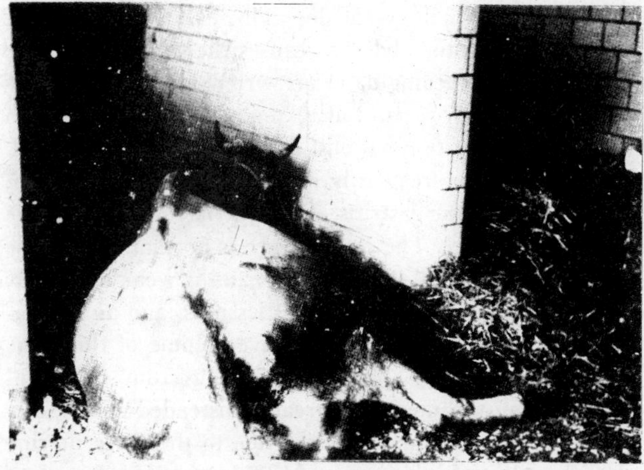

Figure 77. Jersey cow about 7 to 8 months pregnant affected with hydrops and a transverse rupture of the abdominal muscles 8 inches cranial to the pubis. The cow was unable to stand.

Figure 78. Same Jersey cow with marked ventral hernia with signs of rupture of the prepubic tendon two weeks after a cesarean section.

Table 14. The Differential Diagnosis Between Hydrallantois and Hydramnios in Cattle

Hydrallantois	Hydramnios
Occurs in 85 to 90% of cases of uterine dropsy.	Occurs in 5 to 10% of cases of uterine dropsy.
Abdominal enlargement develops rapidly within 5 to 20 days.	Abdominal enlargement develops slowly over weeks and months.
Abdominal wall is round, distended and tense.	Abdominal wall is pear-shaped and less tense.
Distended horns of uterus easily palpated per rectum and fill the abdominal cavity.	Uterine horns hard to palpate, not very tense and don't fill the upper and caudal abdominal cavity area.
Fetus and placentomes are not able to be palpated or ballotted per rectum or through the abdominal wall.	Placentomes and often the fetus may be palpated per rectum and the latter may occasionally be ballotted through the abdominal wall.
Sporadic in incidence.	Usually sporadic but in an inbred herd may have a number of cases.
Allantoic fluid is watery, clear and amber, with characteristics of a transudate.	Amniotic fluid usually syrupy and viscid, and often contains meconium.
Fetuses are normal but small twins are occasionally present.	Associated with a defective, anomalous fetus.
Placenta, especially the allantois chorion, is usually diseased and abnormal with a reduced number of greatly hypertrophied placentomes.	Placenta, allantois chorion and placentomes normal.
After removing much fluid by caesarean section or by allantocentesis, the allantoic cavity rapidly fills again.	After removing much fluid by caesarean section or by amniocentesis, the amnion does not refill in the former and only slowly in the latter.
Retained placenta and severe metritis usually occurs.	Retained placenta may occasionally occur and metritis is much less common or severe.
Sequelae such as uterine rupture, abdominal hernias and dislocation of the hips are common in severe cases.	Adverse sequelae are rare due to gradual onset and the nature of the disease.
Prognosis—guarded to poor for life and fertility.	Prognosis—fair to good for life and fertility.

Most anasarcous fetuses were expelled dead. In all of these latter conditions with the possible exception of edema of the allantois chorion, enlargement of the abdomen is not noted.

The prognosis for hydramnios is fair to good for the dam unless she is a carrier of a recessive gene responsible for the defective fetus producing the condition. Salvage of the defective fetus is usually impossible. In many of these cases following induced abortions or caesarean section the placenta is often expelled or if it is retained, metritis associated with uterine inertia is not as severe as that following hydrallantois. The prognosis in cases of hydrallantois is poor. In advanced cases in which the cow is unable to rise, the prognosis is often hopeless. Even if the fetus can be removed, the mortality in cows is high, because the uterus is very atonic, the membranes diseased, and shock or severe septic metritis usually follows the expulsion or removal of the fetus. If the cow should survive, its future reproductive life is questionable. In almost all cases, except the occasional mild one that goes to term, the fetus dies **in utero** or soon after birth. Milk production in dairy cows for the next lactation after either hydramnios or hydrallantois is usually poor. Dropsy of the allantois at term is often associated with dystocia due to a dead edematous fetus in an abnormal position or posture, uterine inertia, and a cervix that may fail to dilate completely. If the dystocia is not handled promptly emphysema of the fetus soon develops. The prognosis in rare cases of edema of the allantois chorion is similar to hydrops allantois. In both severe fetal ascites and fetal anasarca, dystocia usually results at the time the overly large fetus enters the birth canal, whether the fetus is aborted or expelled at term.

The treatment or handling of cases of hydramnios and hydrallantois varies with the duration and severity of the condition. In mild cases undiagnosed until the time of abortion, premature birth or at normal parturition, excessive volumes of fluids are observed accompanied by the presence of a poorly viable, small or defective fetus, dystocia related to the diseased or dead fetus, and uterine inertia secondary to the uterine distention. Mutation and forced extraction of these fetuses is usually easily effected. In cases of fetal anasarca or ascites greater amounts of traction and lubrication may be needed. In a few cases embryotomy might have to be resorted to in order to mutilate the fetus to allow the excess fluid to escape. Retained placenta and a secondary severe metritis frequently follows hydrallantois and edema of the allantois chorion but is less frequently observed and is less severe in hydramnios. Early treatment for these conditions with parenteral and local antibiotics and ecbolics such as oxytocin, stilbestrol and ergonovine are indicated.

In severe cases of hydramnios and hydrallantois occurring during the gestation period with a closed cervix, the prompt termination of the abnormal pregnancy is usually desired. In some slowly developing cases late in gestation it may be expedient to observe the cow and wait for parturition. In other severe cases an early decision to slaughter the cow while she is still in good physical condition is often the best method of handling these cases when all factors are considered. Daily administration of large doses of stilbestrol, 50 to 120 mgm., or estradiol, 8 to 10 mgm. for 4 to 7 days alone or together with injections of glucocorticoids and antibiotics may frequently result in cervical dilation and abortion, Milne, Vandeplassche et al.. Precipitating abortion is more successful with hydramnios than hydrallantois. Because the uterus is atonic and distended and the cervix usually dilates poorly, the cow should be watched carefully. The abortion should be aided when necessary. Pituitrin or oxytocin may be given but its effect may be negligible because of the atonic, stretched, and diseased uterine wall. Cesarean section has been attempted in many cases with success but in some the cow succumbs. Various authors including Gibbons and Neal recommended the use of a trocar or plastic tube inserted through the abdominal and uterine walls to draw the fluid off gradually over a period of 24 hours before the Cesarean is performed. This helped to avoid possible shock from removing too much fluid too rapidly. Since most severely affected cows are very dehydrated with marked electrolyte imbalances, appropriate fluid therapy in large volumes is indicated before, during and after the operation. Once the cow is down and unable to rise due to the weight of the fluid, any treatment is usually unsuccessful because of complications such as abdominal hernia or dislocated hips. Following the relief of these dropsical conditions severe metritis usually associated with the retained placenta almost invariably follows. The severity of this metritis varies with the severity of the condition and is a common cause for the high mortality. In all hydrops cases the treatment for septic metritis should begin before or at the time the condition is relieved. Since treatment of this condition is not very successful, most of the more severe cases are sent to slaughter as soon as they are diagnosed. This is especially true if the cow is of only moderate value. If more than 1 or 2 cases of hydramnios occur in a herd the hereditary nature of this disease should be suspected and investigated, and further inbreeding prevented.

An interesting observation made by Milne, the author and others is that after terminating hydrops of the allantois by cesarean section the uterus may continue to fill with transudative fluid for about 48 hours and require further draining.

Abdominal Hernias Resulting in Hysterocele

The pregnant uterus may drop into, or be present in, umbilical, inguinal, perineal, diaphragmatic, or ventral hernias. In cases of rupture of the prepubic tendon, the pregnant uterus will drop into the sac formed by the skin and cutaneous muscles. This may cause dystocia or death of the fetuses or dam or both.

Umbilical and inguinal hernias may, if large enough, contain a portion of the uterine horn and developing fetus. **Umbilical hernias** have been described as hereditary in all species of animals. In cattle most of them are small. Such animals should not be used as breeding animals, inasmuch as Gilmore indicated that umbilical hernia in cattle, especially Holsteins, is an autosomal dominant with low penetrance. Most female animals with large umbilical hernias are not bred. In males an umbilical hernia may prevent copulation. **Inguinal hernias** are hereditary or acquired and are described as common in the bitch, and rare in the cat, sow and mare. They have not been described in the cow or ewe. Bitches over 5 years of age are most commonly affected, Wright. Riser reported that spayed bitches given large amounts of estrogen developed inguinal hernias within 90 days. One bitch with an inguinal hernia was spayed through a midline incision and the hernia was left intact. One year later the hernia had spontaneously disappeared. These observations indicate a close relationship between estrogen production by the ovary and the development of inguinal hernia in bitches. Inguinal hernias may be bilateral or unilateral, usually the latter, and are characterized by a swelling in the inguinal region. This becomes larger as pregnancy progresses if a portion of the pregnant uterine horn is present in the hernial sac. In the bitch one to three fetuses may develop in the hernial sac. If pregnancy is allowed to progress it results in the death of the fetuses or in dystocia at the time of parturition. In the bitch this condition should be differentiated from a mammary neoplasm and a local abscess. **Diaphragmatic hernia** is usually secondary to trauma in the dog and in rare cases a pregnant uterine horn may be present in the thoracic cavity, Snow citing Riser. A **perineal hernia** containing a portion of the fetus has been dsscribed in the goat by Benesch and is possible but probably rare in the dog. Small **ventral hernias** are usually traumatic in origin and may occur in all species. If they are large a portion of the uterine horn and fetus may develop therein. If ventral hernias in large animals are extensive they are difficult if not impossible to repair. Fortunately, in large animals the uterus in early pregnancy does not drop far enough downward or forward to drop into most hernial sacs and in later pregnancy the uterus is too large to enter them.

In the bitch, an inguinal hernia containing a portion of a pregnant horn can be handled surgically early in pregnancy by reducing and repairing the hernia, if necessary by enlarging the ring and/or using a synthetic mesh for a lasting support. From mid pregnancy to near term, hysterotomy can be performed and the fetus or fetuses removed, the uterus replaced in the abdominal cavity, and the hernial ring sutured. Occasionally the portion of the herniated uterine horn containing fetuses may be removed by a partial hysterectomy. In other cases ovariohysterectomy may be indicated. The rare cases of umbilical or ventral, diaphragmatic or perineal hernias encountered containing a portion of the pregnant uterus could be handled in a manner similar to the repair of inguinal hernias.

Extensive unilateral ventral hernias in large animals occur occasionally in advanced pregnancy in cows, sheep, and goats, but rarely in mares. These hernias are usually due to trauma. The greatly increased weight of the gravid uterus and fetus, and possibly other changes, weaken the abdominal floor. These extensive hernias are seen most commonly in ruminants on the right side of the abdominal floor. According to Benesch and Wright they are observed most often on the left side in the mare. In rare instances they may be associated with twins or with hydrops of the amnion and allantois. Large unilateral ventral hernias are characterized by a unilateral ventral sagging of the abdominal floor, 6 to 8 inches or more below that of the normal side. Calving or foaling may be difficult because of the inability of the abdominal muscles to contract equally and strongly and force the fetus toward and through the birth canal. Following calving, the abdominal floor of the affected side may retract in some cattle and the abdominal contour become nearly normal. This may occasionally remain normal during subsequent pregnancies. However, it usually recurs during the latter stages of each gestation period. The involvement is so great that treatment or operations other than those outlined under rupture of the prepubic tendon are not indicated.

Rupture of the prepubic tendon or prepubic desmorrhexis of pregnancy is seen most commonly in the mare, and rarely in the cow and ewe. This condition is seen most frequently in the draft mare that is idle and well-fed, and infrequently in light mares. According to Emmerson it is rather rare in cattle because the subpubic tendon, a structure that does not exist in horses, gives added support to the prepubic tendon. (See Figures 78, 79, 80) Rupture of the prepubic tendon occurs during the last 2 months of gestation. In the mare and occasionally the cow it is often preceded by a marked tense, painful edema, 3 to 5 inches thick, on the abdominal floor, start-

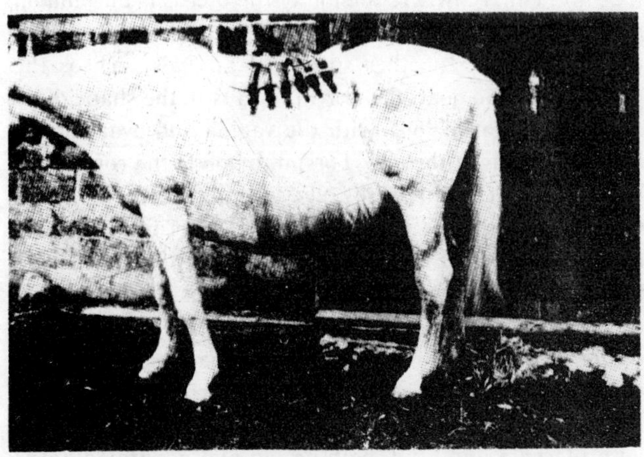

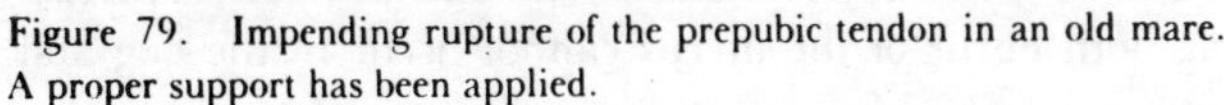

Figure 79. Impending rupture of the prepubic tendon in an old mare. A proper support has been applied.

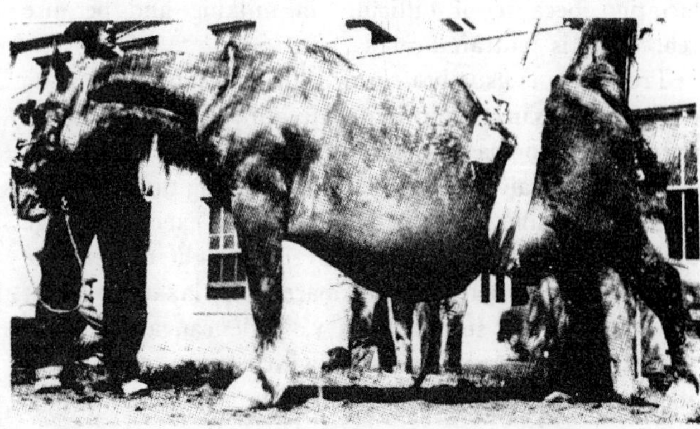

Figure 80. Acute rupture of the prepubic tendon in a mare.

Figure 81. A massive hematoma cranial and dorsal to the mammary gland of a pregnant cow resembling a rupture of the prepubic tendon.

ing at the udder and extending to the ziphoid region. Severe edema of the abdominal floor in the mare in advanced pregnancy should always be viewed seriously. Physiological edema of the abdominal floor in the cow is common and does not indicate a possible weakness or rupture of the abdominal floor as in the mare. Rarely massive hematomas in the region of the bovine udder may be mistaken for rupture of the prepubic tendon, Hughes et al.. (See Figure 81)

The rupture is predisposed by the increased weight of the gravid uterus on the abdominal floor and possible degenerative changes due to the edema and the weight. Occasionally, due to violence or trauma, the condition occurs suddenly without the development of edema. Twins, hydrops of the fetal membranes, fetal giants in prolonged gestation, as in **Veratrum** poisoning in ewes, favor rupture. In this condition there is a transverse rupture of the prepubic tendon, the ventral abdominal muscles, abdominal tunic, and peritoneum letting the viscera and gravid uterus drop downward into a sac formed by the skin and cutaneous muscles. Only very rarely does complete eventration occur. In rupture that occurs suddenly due to violence, besides the sudden enlargement in the ventral abdominal region and the sinking of the flanks, there usually occurs intense pain and colic together with a cold sweat, fast respirations, rapid weak pulse, and a tendency toward collapse due to shock, and possible hemorrhage (see Figure 80). Occasionally a mare and her intrauterine fetus will perish at this time despite supportive treatment of blood, saline, stimulants, and support for the abdominal wall. In most cases the onset is more gradual, with a preceding painful edema of the abdominal floor, a stiff, careful, cautious gait, and refusal to lie down. After rupture has occurred the udder and teats are stretched forward and downward on the abdominal floor. The attitude is a typical sawhorse one, with an elevation of the tail head and the ischial tuberosities and a lordosis. The pelvis is tilted backward because the prepubic tendon is not intact to maintain the pelvis in its proper relationship to the spinal column.

The prognosis in rupture of the prepubic tendon is always poor, as most mares and foals succumb before foaling occurs. If foaling should terminate successfully the mare's condition will improve, and she might do light work; but usually the mare is so unsightly that she is destroyed. Rebreeding these mares is definitely not indicated. Affected cows are usually sold after calving and lactation because of difficulty in milking and because rebreeding is contraindicated.

Treatment is usually unsatisfactory, once rupture of the tendon has occurred. Preventive treatment of mares showing marked edema of the ventral abdominal floor and a stiff cautious gait should consist of confining the mare in a large confortable box stall and restricting exercise. Large bulky feeds should be withheld and a light concentrate ration should be fed. In some mares mild laxatives might be indicated. A suitable heavy, wide canvas webbing should be tightened securely with straps around the abdomen, to transfer the weight of the abdominal viscera to the spine. Padding over the back usually is necessary to prevent pressure necrosis. (See Figure 79) The mare should be watched closely for the beginning of parturition so that aid may be given at once and the fetus withdrawn by traction. This aid is necessary since abdominal contractions are very weak and parturition cannot take place without aid and direction. In most cases uterine contractions and cervical dilation may take place but since the fetus does not engage or enter into the pelvic cavity, abdominal contractions, or labor do not begin. Periodic vaginal examinations may be necessary. In some cases the wide band in a horse sling to support the abdominal viscera may be useful and the mare can be kept standing. Possibly parturition should be induced in late pregnancy by the injection of 30 to 40 units of oxytocin. Williams suggested inducing premature labor in the mare by manual dilation of the cervix, followed by withdrawing the fetus. Another possibility in these mares is cesarean section which, though often successful permits the fetus to be saved, although the affected mare is usually destroyed. This latter procedure is indicated in sudden rupture, with impending collapse and death of the mare. In the cow abdominal support or slings are not tolerated. By confinement and careful observation, the fetus may be promptly withdrawn by traction. In the cow cesarean section is more successful than in the mare and may possibly be indicated in this condition. In relieving dystocia due to rupture of the prepubic tendon, rolling the cow or mare on its side or back will aid in bringing the fetus to the pelvic inlet for removal. If the mare is in a standing position, horse slings may be applied and tightened to bring the fetus near the pelvic inlet.

TORSION OF THE UTERUS

Torsion of the uterus may occur in all species of animals. Uterine torsion is usually defined as the revolution or twisting of the uterus on its long axis. This might be true in the mare, where torsion of the uterus is uncommon due to the dorsally attached broad ligaments that tend to prevent torsion. In other species of animals such as the cow, sheep, and goat, the gravid horn is in the shape of an arc or a U-shaped loop with the vagina and ovary at the respective ends of the arc. Torsion involves the rotation of this arc on its transverse axis, similar to an intestinal volvulus. This same type of torsion occurs in multipara, as illustrated by Benesch, when one horn rotates at its base. A modification of this same volvulus type of torsion occurs in multipara when only a portion of one horn, containing usually only one fetus, may be twisted or rotated. In unipara, because of the strong intercornual ligament and the distention of the uterine horns and body with placenta and fluid, both gravid and nongravid horns are involved in torsion. Bloom stated that torsion involving both horns of the uterus cannot occur in the dog and cat.

Torsion of the uterus is most commonly observed in dairy cattle, and is occasionally seen in beef cattle, dogs, cats, sheep, goats and mares and rarely seen in the sow, Wenswoort, Nijhof. These authors reported two rare cases of torsion of both uterine horns in swine. The incidence of uterine torsion in dairy cattle was 7.3 percent in 1555 dystocia cases treated over a 10-year period in the Ambulatory Clinic of the New York State Veterinary College. The possible causes for torsion of the uterus in the cow are many. The lesser curvature of the uterus in advanced pregnancy is supported dorsal laterally by the broad ligament. The greater curvature lies free in the abdominal cavity resting on the abdominal floor and supported by the rumen, the viscera, and the abdominal walls. The ovarian end of the gravid horn of the bovine uterus is a relatively small or narrow base upon which the uterus rests. If the nongravid horn is small or nonfunctional the instability of the uterus is increased. This anatomical arrangement, together with the manner in which the cow lies down, with the fore quarters going down first, and rises, by elevating the rear quarters first, so that each time the cow lies down or rises the gravid uterus is suspended in the abdominal cavity, means that a sudden slip or fall in either lying down or rising could cause torsion. Other factors aiding torsion of the uterus in advanced pregnancy are lack of fetal fluids, and violence such as sudden falls or rolling. In dogs and cats this latter factor is probably important. Confinement in stables for long periods favors torsion in the cow. Williams cited Tapken, who stated that the incidence of torsion as a cause of dystocia in pastured cattle was 2.7 percent and in stabled cattle 8.6 percent. In the experience of many veterinarians in New York State most of the cases of uterine torsion occur during the early spring months after cows have been stabled for 4 to 6 months. Torsion is observed more commonly in pluriparous than in primiparous animals. A lack of tone of the pregnant uterus—a condition composed of a lack of fluids, flaccid uterine walls, a small nongravid horn, a long flaccid mesometrium—favors uterine torsion. A deep capacious abdomen predisposes to uterine torsion. Twins in ruminants tend to prevent torsion by making a broader base for the uterus to rest upon and by filling the abdominal cavity. In a few cases strong movements of the fetus probably can cause uterine torsion.

Uterine torsion is observed most commonly in advanced pregnancy. However, cases of uterine torsion in the cow have been observed from 70 days of gestation to term. Torsions occurring before the seventh month of pregnancy in the cow are unusual. Williams recorded several cases in which uterine torsion occurred in nonpregnant uteri containing pus. Arthur stated that most torsions occurred during the early part of the second stage of labor or the latter part of the first stage. This conclusion was based on observations that the cervix is found to be dilated immediately after the torsion is relieved in most of the dystocia cases due to torsion of the uterus. In only occasional cases is there a severe edema due to venous congestion or other circulatory disturbance in the uterus or its contents. In cases diagnosed early the fetus may still be alive. Uterine torsion at this time may be favored by unequal contractions of the uterus or by active movements of the fetus. These movements are greatest during the first stage and early second stage of parturition. Settergren observed a mare that developed uterine torsion immediately after a period of intense fetal activity. Probably other factors may be involved in the torsion, as it appears difficult for either uterine contractions or fetal activity alone to produce torsion.

Williams stated that uterine torsions of cattle of 180° may be present for days or weeks without clinical symptoms until labor begins and dystocia results. In these cases cited by Williams and the occasional similar cases observed by the author no evidence of circulatory interference was present. If circulatory interference of the blood supply to the uterus was present, acute clinical symptoms and death of the fetus would probably occur. During pregnancy 45° to 90° torsions or rotations of the uterus are rather frequently found on rectal examination. These often appear to correct themselves before or at parturition.

For the above reasons this writer believes that many cases of bovine uterine torsion of 90 to 180° occur during the last few months of gestation, persist for weeks or months and only become evident at the time of parturition. In unusual instances torsion of the uterus may involve a 180° to 360° rotation of the uterus. Williams cited a case involving two complete turns. In these torsions of greater than 180° the birth canal at parturition is usually tightly closed, so that the cervix and the fetus are not palpable per vaginum. These severe torsions cause obstruction to the blood supply of the uterus, with resulting congestion, edema, shock, death of the fetus, and even gangrene of the uterus. In neglected cases transverse rupture of the uterus or vagina, emphysema and maceration of the fetus, shock, collapse, and death may occur. In rare cases one of the large uterine vessels may rupture, followed by severe hemorrhage into the abdominal cavity. In the dog transverse rupture of the twisted segment of the uterus often occurs at parturition when the uterus contracts and the dead fetuses are released into the abdominal cavity. Rarely uterine torsion may be associated with mummification of the fetus late in gestation, instead of emphysema and maceration. This probably occurs in the absence of infection, hemorrhage, and air in the uterine cavity. Mummification of extrauterine fetuses in the abdominal cavity has been reported.

In torsion in cows, mares and ewes the cephalic portion of the vagina is usually twisted. Occasionally in a uterus lacking fluid or tone the torsion may occur cephalad to the cervix and in severe torsions at the time of parturition the twist may actually involve the cervix. In multiparous animals, since there is no intercornual ligament, usually one entire horn rotates at the point of its junction with the body and the other horn. Occasionally only a portion of the horn is involved; the twisted portion may occur anywhere throughout the horn. In rare cases in multipara in which both uterine horns are involved in the torsion, the cranial portion of the vagina is twisted. There are a number of reports in the literature on multipara in which the twisted portion of the horn or the entire horn with its fetuses separated completely from the body of the uterus during pregnancy. The fetuses may rupture from this blind sac into the abdominal cavity at the time of parturition, or this separated portion of the horn may be walled off as a passive body in which the fetus or fetuses may macerate or mummify.

Torsions in uniparous animals are either torsions to the right (clockwise) or to the left (counter-clockwise). Most authors agree that right torsion occurs more often than left. Others state that if the right horn is gravid the torsion is to the right and if the left horn is gravid the torsion is to the left. This latter statement is not always true. If it were, it might explain why right torsion is more common, since right horn pregnancies are more common than left. Probably the rumen occupying the left side of the abdominal cavity tends to prevent left torsions.

The signs, prognosis, and handling of torsions causing dystocia at the time of parturition will be discussed later.

These next paragraphs will deal with the symptoms and prognosis of severe torsions during the gestation period that may be recognized prior to parturition. Although treatment of these antenatal torsions will be mentioned at this time they are similar for torsions resulting in dystocia and so will be discussed in detail in Chapter 10.

The symptoms of torsions of the uterus in the cow prior to parturition may be completely lacking if the torsion is of a mild degree, 45° to 90° or even 180°. When the torsion is 180 degrees or more, definite signs of abdominal pain usually may be noted, such as anorexia, constipation, lack of ruminations, weak and slow rumen contractions, rapid pulse rate, restlessness or colicy symptoms, treading, and tail switching. These symptoms may be confused with traumatic gastritis, indigestion, pyelonephritis, or intestinal intussusception. Uterine torsion during pregnancy in the ewe is characterized by a stiff, stilted gait and a stretched, "sawhorse" attitude resembling signs of peritonitis and intussusception or volvulus, Pugh. Whenever any cow over six months pregnant shows these suggestive symptoms, a rectal examination should always be made to determine if torsion of the uterus is present. In right torsion the right broad ligament is pulled strongly downward and under the twisted uterine body or vagina, and the left broad ligament is pulled tightly across over the top of the cervix, the body of the uterus, and the vagina, toward the right side. In counter-clockwise, or left torsion the location and direction of the two broad ligaments is reversed, with the right broad ligament crossing over the top of the twisted portion of the birth canal (See Chapter X). The middle uterine arteries on both sides are tightly stretched. The amount of tension on the broad ligaments and arteries will indicate the severity of the torsion. The fetus is often difficult to palpate but the position of the fetus in the uterus in advanced pregnancy may help indicate the degree of torsion. A dorso-pubic position of the fetus usually occurs when the torsion is 180°. A rectal examination is preferred over a vaginal examination because occasionally the twisted portion of the genital tract may lie cephalad to the cervix in the region of the body of the uterus and not extend back into the vagina. In most cases of torsion of the uterus in cows or mares the cephalic portion of the vagina is involved, the vaginal walls are spirally twisted and a stenosis of the vagina is present. Starting from the dorsum of the vagina, if the folds spiral forward and downward to the left, or counter-clockwise left torsions is present; and if the folds spiral downward and forward to the right or clockwise it is a right torsion of the uterus. Rarely torsion may be suspected on external examination of the vulva by the dorsal commissure being pulled forward to the left or right. This is more noticeable in advanced pregnancy when the vulva is relaxed and edematous. In severe cases of torsion occurring in late pregnancy the blood supply to and from the uterus is severely restricted or cut off. In these cases marked symptoms of complete anorexia and constipation, fetid diarrhea, complete lack of ruminations and rumen activity, very rapid and weak pulse, rapid respirations, expiratory grunt, normal to subnormal body temperature, cold extremities, shock, collapse, and death may occur within 24 to 72 hours. In other cases the fetus may die, become emphysematous and macerate or become mummified and the cow develop only slight or mild symptoms. A rectal examination may reveal chronic adhesions, perimetritis, or even an extrauterine fetus if the uterus has ruptured. This latter condition usually occurs at the time of parturition. In sheep symptoms are similar to those in cattle. In multipara, symptoms of abdominal involvement in advanced pregnancy should always cause suspicion of torsion of the uterus. An exploratory laparotomy in sheep and multipara is often indicated.

The prognosis in torsion of the uterus prior to parturition depends upon the degree of torsion, the severeity of symptoms, and the length of time it has existed. In mild cases without symptoms—found by accident on rectal examination—in which the torsion is occasionally 180° but usually 90° or less, the prognosis is good, since the torsion seldom worsens, and treatment is often not necessary. In 180° to 270° torsions causing definite symptoms that are diagnosed and treated early, the immediate prognosis is usually good for the dam and fetus, but the torsion may occasionally recur prior to parturition. In advanced, severe, and neglected cases the prognosis is poor for the life and reproductive life of the dam and usually the fetus is dead.

Depending upon the circumstances the two treatments most apt to be successful in antenatal cases of 180° to 270° torsions in which the condition is diagnosed promptly are: rolling of the cow, Schaffer's method described by Arthur, or correcting the torsion manually by means of a laparotomy. This latter technique was highly satisfactory by a flank approach in either the recumbent or standing mare, Skjerven, Vandeplassche et al., and Van der Kaay and de Bois. The latter authors reported that 5 of 10 mares in which torsion of the uterus was corrected by rolling died; this technique was more dangerous than a laparotomy. Attempts at correcting torsion by manipulation through the rectum or vagina or both in cows in which the cervix is sealed are usually not successful. Hoisting the rear parts of the cow to effect reduction of the torsion is crude and unnecessary. In rare cases cesarean section may be indicated when pregnancy is near term. Extrauterine fetuses, fetal maceration, or mummification associated with torsion are handled as described previously. In advanced severe cases in which gangrene of the uterus is present, laparohysterectomy is indicated in the bitch and cat but is usually unsuccessful in the cow. Further detailed description of the handling of uterine torsions is discussed in Chapter 10 under handling of torsions causing dystocia.

Vagino-cervical Prolapse

Prolapse of the vagina usually involves a prolapse of the floor, the lateral walls and a portion of the roof of the vagina through the vulva with the cervix and uterus moving caudad. Not infrequently the entire vagina and cervix are prolapsed through the vulva. Vagino-cervical prolapse is seen in all species of domestic animals but most commonly in the cow, especially Herefords, and the ewe. Jones reported the incidence of ovine vaginal prolapse to be about 0.5 percent but in some flocks this may reach 20 percent. In cattle it is observed most often in Herefords and the larger dairy breeds such as Holstein and Brown Swiss. In young, brachycephalic dogs prolapse of the vagina at the time of estrum is fairly common. It is practically unknown in cats, Bloom.

The causes of prolapse of the vagina and cervix are probably multiple. It is observed in the cow most commonly the last 2 to 3 months of gestation when a large amount of estrogenic hormone is being secreted by the placenta. This causes a relaxation of the pelvic ligaments and adjacent structures and an edema and relaxation of the vulva and vulvar sphincter muscles. When the cow lies down the intra-abdominal pressure especially in late pregnancy is transmitted to the flaccid pelvic structures tending to force the relaxed and loosely attached vaginal floor and walls through the vulva. Farquharson stated that the vesico-genital pouch is the least restraining part of the pelvic structures and when subjected to increased abdominal pressure the bladder and other viscera are forced against the most yielding part—the floor of the vagina. Why this condition affects certain cows and not others is not known but it can be theorized that certain cows produce more estrogens and develop a greater relaxation of the pelvic structures earlier in pregnancy. Conformation may favor prolapse. Williams rather vaguely attributed the cause to atony of the reproductive tract and general weakness of the patient. Prolapse of the vagina may be influenced or due to hereditary or genetic factors in Hereford cattle and sheep and Boxer and Bull dogs, Bloom, Woodward and Quesenberry, Jones, and Schutte. Since prolapse of the vagina is observed more commonly in pluripara than primipara, injuries or stretching of the birth passage at the first or subsequent parturitions may predispose to prolapse during following gestation periods. This is probably a very common predisposing cause in older cattle especially if they were immature or poorly grown heifers and required great traction to relieve dystocia occurring at the first parturition. The condition is favored by close confinement especially in stanchions in which the cow's rear parts project over the gutter and in sheep, especially those confined on lush pastures and carrying twins, Arthur. It is seen less commonly in pastured cattle. Over-distention of the abdomen or excessive amounts of loose pelvic fat favor the condition by increasing the intrapelvic pressure. These factors are not important unless the pelvic and vulva structures are relaxed enough to allow the vaginal wall to prolapse. Edgar reported from New Zealand that in ewes there is a possible hereditary predisposition for prolapse of the vagina in 1 to 8 percent. He cited several references in which this condition is also indicated to be hereditary in cattle. This cause is suspected occasionally in cattle if a dam and her daughter both develop vaginal prolapse. The high incidence of this condition in Hereford cattle may indicate a possible hereditary factor in this breed.

This condition is occasionally observed in cattle following parturition. At this time it is often associated with cystic ovaries, another condition characterized by excessive estrogen production.

In dogs, especially noted in Boxers and the larger breeds, most cases of vaginal prolapse occur during proestrus and estrus and regress during metestrus, only to recur again at the next estrus. Protrusion of the hypertrophied vaginal mucosa or prolapse may occur. The latter is usually due to heredity, excessive estrogens and their relaxing effect on pelvic and perineal structures, tenesmus, forcible separation of the male before the end of coitus and disproportion in size between the two sexes. In a few instances the ration may play a role in the cause of this condition. In swine and occasionally cattle the feeding of moldy corn or barley may cause edema of the vulva, relaxation of pelvic ligaments, tenesmus, and prolapse of the vagina and even the rectum. Young swine and cattle are more often affected. Even barrows showed an enlargement of the prepuce and mammary glands, Koen and Smith, Libke. This condition has been called vulvovaginitis and is generally considered to be due to a high estrogen content in the moldy feed, McErlean. Certain types of legumes such as subterranean clover in Australia may contain a high level of estrogens and produce permanent sterility in ewes due to cystic degeneration of the endometrium, marked mammary growth and development, great enlargement of the bulbo-urethral glands in wethers, uterine inertia and dystocia, as well as a high incidence, 10 to 12 percent, of prolapse of the vagina in nonpregnant ewes, Bennetts and coworkers. The development of vaginal prolapse ceased after removing the ewes from the subterranean clover pastures, Schinkel. Proper fertilization and rotation of pastures to maintain a certain percentage of grasses largely prevented this condition in sheep pastured on this type of clover, Carne. The use of stilbestrol or estrogens in fattening lambs in the United States may produce vaginal prolapse, Clegg and coworkers.

Once prolapse of the vagina or cervix has occurred the exposed mucous membranes as well as the vulvar and vestibular mucosa become very edematous, inflamed, irritated, infected, and occasionally necrotic. The bladder may prolapse through the vulva within the vaginal floor and continue to fill with urine. These factors tend to prevent the return of the prolapsed structures when the cow rises, and favor tenesmus, or straining, that may lead to prolapse of the cervix and the rectum and to exhaustion. In most cases occurring during the late gestation period, after parturition has occurred the symptoms usually cease. There is no relationship between prolapse of the vagina and cervix prior to parturition and prolapse of the uterus after parturition. Prolapse of the uterus is no more likely to occur when prolapse of the vagina has preceded parturition than in cows not affected. Prolapse of the vagina and cervix will invariably recur and become more severe during subsequent pregnancies.

The symptoms of vagino-cervical prolapse are obvious

Figure 82. Prolapse of the vagina in a heifer.

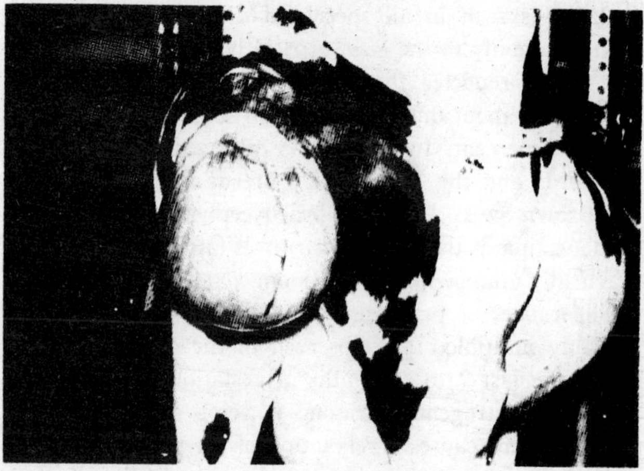

Figure 83. Prolapse of the vagina, including the bladder, in a cow.

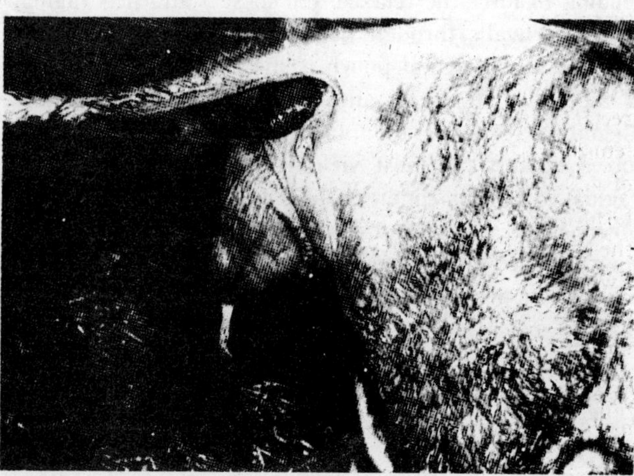

Figure 84. Prolapse of the vagina and cervix with a secondary prolapse of the rectum in a cow.

and the condition is often spoken of by the farmer as "casting of the wethers." In the cow this condition is usually observed the last 2 to 3 months of gestation with an increasing incidence as parturition is approached. Occasionally it is seen as early as 4 to 5 months of gestation. In a few cases it is observed after parturition in the cow. In the ewe and other species of domestic animals it seldom occurs other than a few weeks prior to parturition except in the dog. Prolapse of the vagina in the bitch is seen most commonly at the time of estrum. The symptoms may vary from a mild protrusion of the vaginal mucous membrane through the vulvar lips when the cow lies down, to a severe necrotic vagino-cervical prolapse containing a greatly distended bladder and complicated by a prolapse of the rectum due to the constant tenesmus (see Figures 82, 83, 84). In mild cases the prolapsed vaginal wall returns to its proper position when the cow rises. The degree of vulvitis, vaginitis, and cervicitis will vary depending upon the length of time the condition has existed and the type of mechanical, thermal, or infectious agents acting upon the prolapsed mucous membranes. The symptom of straining or tenesmus may be absent, intermittent and mild, or severe and nearly constant, depending upon the degree of the prolapse, the degree of inflammation, edema and irritation involving the genital canal, and the degree of distention of the bladder. Edema of the prolapsed vagina and cervix occurs because of the irritation and trauma to the exposed mucous membrane, and because this portion drops over the ischial arch thereby causing a passive venous congestion. This edema tends to accumulate in the submucosa and cause a separation of the mucousa from the underlying thin muscular vaginal wall. The cervical seal usually remains intact; although if the cervix is prolapsed and inflamed, the external portion of the seal may be absent. Occasionally the cervix relaxes, the cervical seal is lost and abortion or premature parturition occurs within 24 to 72 hours. A rectal or vaginal examination should be made to see if the fetus is still alive and to determine the approximate stage of gestation, if breeding records are not available. These factors are important in the prognosis and treatment. If the fetus is alive, the uterine artery has its characteristic "whirr," or fremitus, and the fetus moves when its foot or eyeballs are pinched or its leg or jaw is pulled. In some recently purchased cows vulvar scars may be found indicating previous treatments for vaginal prolapse during other pregnancies. In neglected, severe cases the exposed mucous membrane may be necrotic resulting in a toxemia and septicemia. This together with exhaustion caused by the constant straining may cause a fast, weak pulse, anorexia, rapid loss of weight, general body weakness, death of the fetus, possible uterine infection and death. Necrosis or gangrene may even involve the cervix and the caudal portion of the uterus secondary to severe vascular insult and thrombosis. If prolapse of the vagina occurs postpartum, the ovaries should always be examined for the presence of cysts and if no cysts are present the vulva should be examined for injuries. In the ewe suffering from prolapse of the vagina or cervix, death and maceration of the fetus followed by the death of the dam is not uncommon. Severe infections of the birth canal associated with prolapse of the vagina may result in uterine infections or retained afterbirth following parturition or abortion. Differential diagnosis should rather easily distinguish between prolapse of the vagina and cervix, and cystic Bartholin's glands, hematomas of the vulva, tumors of the vagina or vulva, prolapse or eversion of the bladder, rupture of the vagina and prolapse of perivaginal fat, and thick heavy fetal membranes. Cows will usually calve without assistance in nearly all uncomplicated cases. After parturition the prolapse is usually immediately relieved.

The prognosis in prolapse of the vagina and cervix depends upon the severity of the condition and the length of time it has existed. Except in extreme or severe cases, the prognosis is generally fair to good for the life of the animal and the fetus if treatment is prompt and aftercare is good. The condition will recur again at subsequent gestation periods unless suitable procedures are followed to prevent it. In the more extreme conditions complicated by prolapse of the rectum, death of the fetus, impending abortion, septic metritis, severe necrosis of the prolapsed organs, exhaustion, septicemia and toxemia, marked debility of the patient, or constant and violent straining, the prognosis is guarded to poor. Slaughter should be considered after parturition or weaning of the newborn because of the tendency for this condition to recur and the possible hereditary nature of the condition. In sheep the prognosis is more guarded, since 20 to 30 percent of pregnant ewes may die or expel dead fetuses.

The method of treatment selected for handling prolapse of the vagina and cervix will vary with the species and breed of animal, the severity of the condition, the stage of pregnancy and the ability of the owner to care for and observe the animal until after parturition. Early prompt treatment often permits the use of simple conservative methods and obviates the necessity of using more heroic techniques. Many methods of handling prolapse of the vagina are available. These will be discussed in order from the conservative to the more heroic methods used in cattle and then the handling of prolapse in the other species will be mentioned. The operator should select the most conservative method possible under the circumstances and caution the owner that as pregnancy progresses other methods may need to be used to control the condition. Combinations of methods may be used.

(1) In mild cases in cattle in which only a slight prolapse occurs when the cows lie down, the cow should be removed from the stanchion and placed in a box stall. In slightly more advanced cases (2) one may elevate the rear parts of the cow in a stanchion by means of an inclined platform that raises the rear quarters 2 to 6 inches higher than the front quarters. In a stall this may be done by building up the bedding under the rear quarters or digging out the soil under the front quarters. This practice has been frequently followed in many of the mild cases of prolapse without any untoward effects with the exception that the rear quarters of the dairy cow have been difficult to keep clean. This simple procedure has prevented many mild cases from becoming more severe and has circumvented the use of trusses or vulvar sutures. It is most practical in dairy cattle.

(3) The use of 50 to 100 mgm. of progesterone intramuscularly daily or 500 mgm. of "respositol" progesterone once every 10 days has been advocated for prolapse of the vagina in the cow. The rationale for such therapy is not clear, as it would have no value in reducing straining and no value in antagonizing or neutralizing the excess estrogens. If doses are continued through late gestation, parturition could be delayed by progesterone therapy. Therapy should be discontinued after 275 to 280 days of pregnancy. (4) Unilateral pudendal neurectomy was advocated for the relief of difficult cases of vaginal prolapse, Watts, Ebert and Bierschwal. Although a few cases have benefited from progesterone therapy and pudendal neurectomy, in the author's experience these methods are generally unsatisfactory.

In replacing the prolapsed bovine vagina and cervix epidural anesthesia using 5 to 10 cc. of 2 percent procaine or xylocaine solution is very helpful and usually necessary particularly in the more severe cases where tenesmus is present. Blocking the internal pudendal nerves in cows, in the manner described by Larson for bulls, anesthetizes the vulva and vestibular structures without affecting any motor nerves which is often observed in epidural anesthesia. It is advisable to have the animal standing, preferredly with the rear parts elevated to facilitate replacement of the prolapsed organs. In smaller animals the lifting or even suspending of the rear parts off the ground is easily accomplished and greatly aids replacement. The prolapsed portions should be washed free of dirt and debris with a mild, nonirritating antiseptic solution or physiological saline. If irritation, infection, or straining is present a bland antiseptic oil, such as 1 oz. of bismuth formic iodide in a pint of mineral oil; or sulfonamides or antibiotics in oil or ointment, might be of value when applied to the prolapsed vagina before replacing, and injected into the vagina once or twice daily for several days or more after replacement. If difficulty is encountered in replacement of the prolapsed vagina with the distended bladder inside it, the prolapsed portion may be raised dorsally to reduce the sharp kink in the urethra, thus permitting the urine to escape. In exceptional cases it may be necessary to trocarize the bladder through the prolapsed vagina wall with a large-gauge needle. Once the vaginal floor and walls are replaced the normal circulation is restored and the edema in the vaginal walls and mucous membrane is rapidly reduced. If the vagina is badly infected the animal may have an elevated body temperature. In these cases or those in which the cervix is relaxed and dilated and abortion appears likely, a course of antibiotic or sulfonamide therapy is indicated to control infection and septicemia, and if abortion does occur to prevent septic metritis.

(5) The vulvar truss is of practical value in controlling prolapse of the vagina in dairy cattle confined in stanchions or box stalls where the owner is able to check and adjust the truss as needed. These trusses may be made of rope, leather, or metal. An aluminum rod truss introduced by Payton and held in place with ropes is easily molded to fit the individual cow. These trusses are held in place by ropes or leather straps securely fastened to a surcingle around the cow's chest and neck. The truss, as it fits over the vulva, may be padded with toweling or burlap to prevent abrasions or necrosis where it lies against the ischial arch. When the cow arches her back to urinate or calve the truss will loosen. Cows have been reported to have calved with the truss in place. Many dairy farmers prefer these simpler, less drastic methods, 1 through 5, for handling vaginal prolapse. Most cases are mild and when treated early the results are satisfactory. The above techniques are not usually satisfactory when tenesmus is severe or vagino-cervical prolapse is marked.

(6) Pessaries which are popular in Europe consist of a long narrow wine bottle or similar blunt round object inserted into the vagina after replacement. Pessaries are held in place by a narrow piece of wood or metal placed into the bottle with a ring or loop on the end projecting out of the vulva. A rope is fastened through this ring similar to ropes that hold a metal or leather truss in place. Jones described a light metal rod pessary shaped like a hairpin with long lateral arms containing eyes so it could be fastened to the wool of ewes. Pessaries have not been popular in the United States because there is an impression that an object placed in the vagina tends to cause straining.

(7) Vulvar sutures that do not pass through the vulvar lips are often a satisfactory method of treating vaginal prolapse for a limited period especially the last 2 to 3

weeks of gestation. The sutures should be located at least 2 to 3 inches lateral to the vulvar lips in the hair line. This affords a much tougher and thicker skin for the suture, which does not tear out as readily nor cause as much irritation as one in the vulvar lips. It is desirable to use a type of suture that can be untied or released, so that if a cow appears to be near or in the first stage of parturition the vulvar sutures can be unfastened, so that calving can occur. If the calving time has been misjudged and prolapse again results, the prolapsed vagina may be washed and replaced. If prolapse does not occur, the sutures can be retied. This is not possible with the simple horizontal figure-eight or horizontal mattress sutures that do not pass through the vulvar lips or deep horizontal mattress sutures, usually of double thickness one-eighth to one-quarter-inch thick umbilical tape, that have been passed through each lateral wall of the vulvar vestibule and including the vulvar lips. Another advantage of the type of suture that can be untied is that if there is some possibility of postpartum prolapse of the vagina, or even the uterus, the sutures can be retied after parturition and left for several more days. Although some suppuration occurs around these stitches they may be left in place for as long as 6 to 8 weeks. The vulva-suturing technique preferred by the author is one described by Frank employing 4 to 5 small separate loops of doubled 1/4-3/8 inch umbilical tape on either side of the vulva in the hair line from the level of the anus to about opposite the lower commissure of the vulva. About 2 feet of 1-1/2-inch to 3-inch gauze bandage, doubled, is used to lace up the loops in a manner similar to lacing a shoe. This gauze may be removed or replaced as desired. A similar but crude technique is the use of hog rings instead of umbilical tape loops. These tend to tear out or work out of the skin much more rapidly than does the tape. Benesch advocated a metal skewer type of needle with large wooden buttons to hold the vulvar lips together. Other metallic clamp-like devices have been advocated by other European veterinarians. Some veterinarians prefer quill, button, or deep horizontal mattress sutures of umbilical tape through the vulvar skin, muscle, and mucous membrane.

8) A buried or "hidden" purse-string type of suture, Buhner's method, for the vulva following replacement of a prolapsed vagina has been described by Pierson, Arthur (1966) and Woelffer. This technique may be used in chronic postpartum prolapse as well as prepartum prolapse. Under epidural anesthesia and with a near-sterile procedure, two one-half inch incisions are made one to two inches above the upper commissure and below the lower commissure of the vulva, respectively. With a long eye-point needle similar to a seton needle, an 18-inch piece of one-eighth inch thick nylon cord or heavy "Vetafil" is passed within the tissues from one incision to the other lateral to one vulvar lip. The needle is withdrawn and reinserted in the opposite direction lateral to the opposite vulvar lip to the lower incision site and again withdrawn. The purse-string suture around the vulva is tightened sufficiently to allow 4 fingers in the vulva, and the knot is tied and buried beneath the skin of the upper incision by suturing the skin over the heavy purse-string suture leaving it buried within the vulvar tissues until parturition when it is removed.

(9) A vulva-closing technique modified from the Caslick operation in mares has been of great assistance in the treatment of chronic prolapse of the vagina 2 months or more before parturition or in postpartum prolapse. It has also proved very valuable in controlling tenesmus associated with "windsucking" and a highly inflamed vaginal and vulvar mucous membrane. The drawing of air into and forcing it out of a highly inflamed vagina appears to stimulate and produce violent straining. This operation is performed under epidural anesthesia. After replacement of the prolapsed structures, the caudal 3/4 inch of mucous membrane of both vulvar lips from and including the superior commissure to about 1-1/2 inches above the ventral commissure is removed with scissors. These raw areas of both vulvar lips are sewn together with interrupted vertical mattress sutures of fine catgut, nylon, silk, or stainless steel suture closely spaced. One or two deep horizontal mattress vulvar sutures of umbilical tape are placed through the skin 2 or 3 inches lateral to the vulva and through the vulvar muscles and mucous membrane to prevent the vaginal wall being forced against the fine sutures in the vulvar lips and thus tearing them out if tenesmus occurs (see Figure 85). After 10 days all sutures may be removed. The vulvar opening is then so small that the vaginal wall cannot prolapse and air cannot gain admittance to the vaginal lumen. Just before or at the time of calving it is necessary to slit this adhesion between the vulvar lips to prevent its tearing out. Because of the tendency to repeated prolapse at each gestation period, resuturing is advised immediately after calving if artificial insemination is employed or after breeding if natural service is used.

(10) Minchev's method for controlling prolapse of the vagina by surgically fastening the cranial portion vaginal wall through the lesser sciatic foramen to the dorso-lateral wall of the sacroscatic ligament, muscles and skin of the croup was slightly modified by Bouckaert et al. to place the stay sutures cranial to the lesser sciatic foramen Habel, Norton, Hentschl. After replacement of the prolapsed vagina under epidural anesthesia the anterior portion of the vagina is fastened to either side of the pelvic cavity preventing a prolapse by means of anchoring

devices including guage rolls, heavy plastic buttons, large overcoat buttons or 3/16th inch thick pads of industrial belting. In securing the vaginal walls to the pelvic walls with these anchors inside the vagina and outside on the skin of the croup, heavy suture material such as 1/4 or 3/8 inch umbilical tape doubled or heavy Vetafil or nylon cord so that if straining does occur the vaginal wall will not be lacerated freeing it from its attachment to the pelvic wall. The sutures fastening the vaginal and skin buttons together may be inserted under local anesthesia by making small incisions in the skin of the croup over the sacrosciatic ligament and inserting to the vaginal cavity a small rumen trocar or a crochet-type hook to guide or carry the suture material fastened to the vaginal button to the outside button on the skin. One may also do this by carrying a 4 to 6 inch needle threaded on the suture material attached to the vaginal button into the vagina and forcing the needle dorsolaterally through the skin. In inserting the needle or trocar care should be taken to avoid the rectum, the pudendal nerve and vessels and the sciatic nerve that can be palpated medial to the sacrosciatic ligament. The authors originally describing this technique recommended that the sutures be removed in 10 to 14 days at which time the vaginal wall was firmly adhered to the pelvic wall. Firm attachment frequently does not occur by this time and prolapse of the vagina may again recur. For this reason many veterinarians leave the buttons and sutures in place until after calving.

(11) Another recently introduced technique for handling prolapse of the vagina is fixation of the cervix to the prepubic tendon, Winkler. This procedure minimized tenesmus, required no aftercare during gestation or at parturition, prevented recurrent prolapse at subsequent pregnancies and could be used in all types of cases. Under epidural anesthesia the prolapsed vagina is carefully cleaned and replaced. A 3 or 4-inch half circle cutting edge suture needle is bent into a U-shape and threaded with 36 to 48 inches of heavy nylon or "Vetafil," noncapillary suture material. Material such as umbilical tape should not be used. The needle and suture material is carried into the vagina. The bladder is pushed laterally away from the midline. The needle is passed through the floor of the vagina beneath the external os of the cervix into the prepubic tendon in a lateral to medial direction just cranial to the pubic symphysis and then back up through the vaginal floor. This suture should include 1-1/2 to 2 inches of vaginal floor and 3/4 to 1 inch of prepubic tendon. The needle is then passed through the ventral half of the cervix at least one-half inch cranial to the external os. The suture is tied outside vulva and the knot

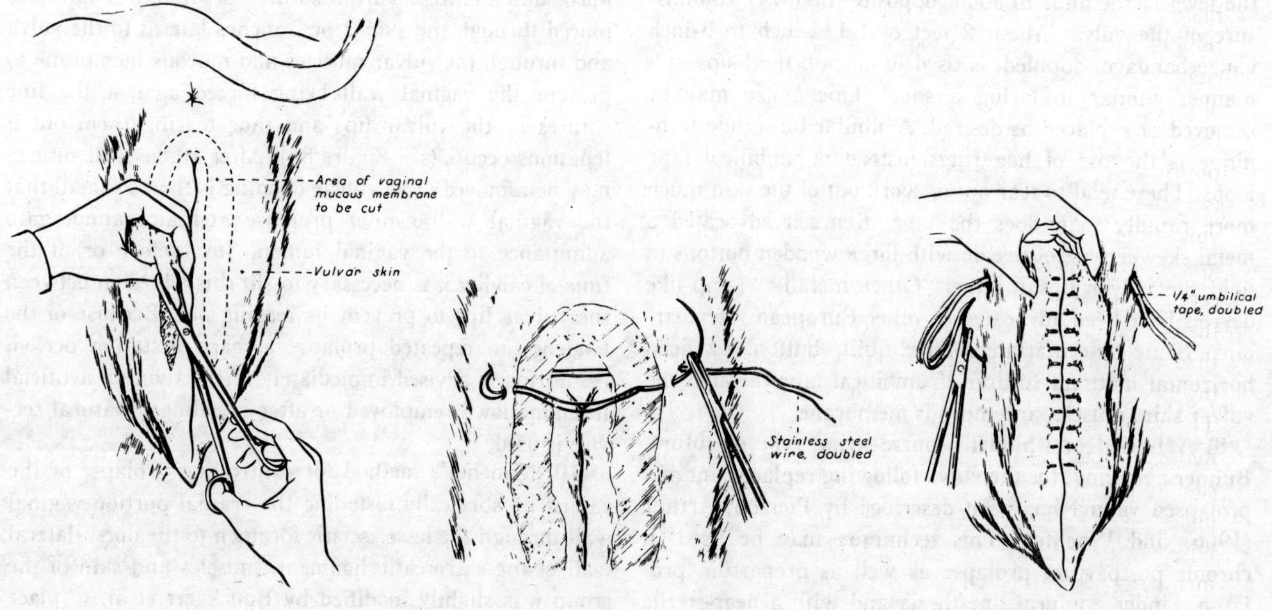

Figure 85. A technique for the control of chronic prolapse of the vagina. (Left) Under epidural or local anesthesia a three-quarter inch strip of mucosa is removed from just inside the vulvar lips. (Center) An interrupted vertical mattress suture is used to draw the wound edges gently together. (Right) If the animal is straining a deep mattress suture is placed through both vulvar lips cranial to the suture line.

carried forward so the cervix is fastened closely to, but not necessarily tightly against, the floor of the pelvis. It may be desirable to pass a catheter into the bladder to make certain it was not included in the suture. These latter two operations (10 and 11) avoid placing sutures in the region of the vulva which is richly supplied with sensory nerves and thus tenesmus is minimized.

(12) Farquharson has described another surgical technique for correction of chronic vagino-cervical prolapse, particularly adapted to selected cases in beef cattle.This consists of a submucous resection of the edematous, devitalized mucous membrane from the prolapsed portion of the vagina. If the prolapsed portion of the vagina is large due to the presence of a distended bladder this should not be reduced before the operation as it will make surgery more difficult. Surgery can be performed under epidural anesthesia. Adrenaline injected or applied locally may aid in reducing hemorrhage during the peeling-off of the diseased, often necrotic, edematous mucous membrane. The sleeve of vaginal mucous membrane that is peeled off is narrow at the dorsum and wide ventrally, as more of the floor of the vagina is usually involved in the prolapse. Incisions on the prolapsed vagina are made in the normal mucous membrane near the cervix caudally and near the urethral orifice or hymen cranially. As the diseased mucous membrane is peeled off, mostly by blunt dissection, No. 3 or 4 chromic catgut suture is used to approximate the two cut edges of normal mucous membrane. As the operation progresses, this is done to control hemorrhage, which is usually quite severe but of a capillary oozing type, and to get most of the incision sewed before the prolapsed vagina begins to drop back into its proper position. In most operations traction applied to the cervix is necessary to keep the vagina retracted and outside the vulva until the suturing is completed. The vagina is greatly shortened by this reefing operation so that the cervix is nearer the vulva. Since the excess vaginal wall is thereby eliminated, the prolapse will not recur during that particular gestation though in rare cases it may during subsequent ones. Tenesmus ceases after the operation. The muscular coat of the vaginal wall is drawn up in folds under the suture line that joins the cephalic and caudal edges of normal vaginal mucous membrane. In operating on cows in which most of the vagina is prolapsed, care should be exercised in removing the mucous membrane on the dorsal surface of the vagina not to cut too deeply and enter the recto-genital pouch of peritoneum, that extends about 5 inches caudad on the dorsal surface of the vagina. Care should also be used to prevent incising the urethral opening or urethra. Obviously this operation should not be performed if the cow is due to calve within 3 to 4 weeks or if abortion appears likely. This is not an operation to select as a last resort in a neglected case, with the patient exhibiting symptoms of toxemia and exhaustion. The type of case indicated for this operation should be selected carefully. The prolapse should have occurred relatively early in the gestation period or be a chronic postpartum prolapse. The cow should be in good condition for the operation. It is particularly indicated in that type of cow, usually beef, in which regular observation and care of the cow is not possible.

(13) Guard and Frank have described techniques for the removal of large amounts of perivaginal fat that favored the production of the prolapse. Guard advised incising the dorsal wall of the vagina to remove the fat. Frank, according to Oberst, recommended a modification of Farquharson's technique, in which the incisions are extended through the vaginal wall and excess fat is removed before the vaginal walls are brought into apposition.

In the bitch, no treatment of mild cases of vaginal hyperplasia and prolapse is indicated, as the condition corrects itself after estrum. In breeding dogs the removal of the prolapsed mucous membranes by a technique similar to Farquharson's in the cow gives good results. This is described by Merrillat as Whipple's operation for the treatment of prolapse of the vagina in the bitch. Episiotomy in the dorsal position may be necessary as an aid in resection of the mucous membrane in the dog. (14) In nonbreeding dogs ovariectomy results in a permanent cure.

(15) In chronic prolapse in postpartum cows treatment with a gonadotropic hormone rich in the luteinizing factor is indicated, if cystic ovaries are present. (16) In unusual cases other methods of handling might be indicated such as a cesarean section late in gestation.

If prolapse of the rectum occurs along with prolapse of the vagina the prognosis is more grave and either a purse-string suture to retain the rectum, a reefing operation, or amputation of the rectum might be indicated, along with feeding or administering mild laxatives or large amounts of fluids to prevent constipation. Prompt slaughter of many animals affected with severe prolapse of both vagina and rectum is advisable as persistent tenesumus is common in these animals.

If constant tenesmus after replacement is a problem, repeated use of local epidural anesthesia at one to two hour intervals may be helpful if accompanied by intravaginal infusions of bland, protective antiseptics in oil. In certain beef cattle some veterinarians have injected epidurally 3 to 8 ml. of benzyl, ethyl or isopropyl alcohol that destroys the nerve tissue resulting in anesthesia to the perineum and paralysis of the tail lasting from 2 to 6 months. This technique is not desirable for dairy cattle for sanitary reasons. The old technique of a tracheotomy operation to prevent straining is rarely, if ever, necessary or recommended. Recently some of the local anesthetics such as benzocaine, nupercaine, and cyclaine have been incorporated into ointment bases. The application of these ointments to the vaginal and vulvar mucous membranes have been recommended to control local surface irritation and the resulting tenesmus. However, the author has not found these local anesthetic ointments very effective.

Espersen and Svendson have reported about 70 to 80 percent success in controlling tenesmus or straining in cattle and sheep due to inflammatory or traumatic lesions of the vulva, vagina, uterus or rectum or straining due to unknown causes by artificial pneumoperitoneum. A sterile 4 inch hypodermic needle attached to a sterile udder inflation pump is inserted in an aseptic manner into the right paralumbar fossa. Air is pumped intra-peritoneally until the flanks are distended above the rib cage by about 25 to 40 liters of air. In nearly 200 cases so treated no serious complications were experienced. About 17 cases had subcutaneous emphysema. Animals so treated usually cannot be slaughtered for 2 months. This treatment will prevent tenesmus for several days to a week or more. It should not be used without close observation in animals with prepartum prolapse of the vagina close to parturition or if abortion is eminent. Otherwise fetal death and emphysema may ensue without external signs of labor. This procedure is effective because it forces the diaphragm forward so taking a deep breath and closing the glottis necessary for straining cannot be done without producing a sensation of suffocation in the animal. The use of tranquilizers have also proven helpful to reduce tenesmus especially in animals where straining is not severe.

Paraplegia of Pregnancy

There are numerous causes for paraplegia, or paresis, during pregnancy. Most of these conditions occur in or are aggravated by advanced pregnancy, during which period there is very rapid growth of the fetus and an increase in weight of the gravid uterus as well as a progressive relaxation of the pelvic ligaments and an increase in the size and development of the udder. The factors, and several may operate together, that may cause a cow to exhibit paresis in advanced pregnancy are:

Nutritional deficiencies and starvation—A lack of various minerals such as phosphorus and calcium may result in debility, pica, bone and joint lesions, and even an increase in incidence of fractures. A lack of trace minerals, principally copper, cobalt, and iron, has been reported as resulting in anemia and debility, which if extreme may cause weakness and inability to rise. In certain areas in Florida with high molybdenum levels in the soil and forage, chronic diarrhea coupled with a lack of copper, iron, and cobalt favor debility. Lack of vitamin A in the ration may lower resistance and favor uterine infections. Most nutritional deficiencies are multiple, including a lack of minerals, proteins, carbohydrates, and fats. The classic symptoms of severe underfeeding or starvation are debility, cachexia, weakness, and finally inability to rise; and in advanced cases, death of the fetus, and abortion. In certain areas of the country specific deficiency diseases occur commonly and are known by the local veterinarians. In the high-producing dairy cow it is usually desirable to supply additional minerals to the ration as well as offering them free-choice to compensate for the loss of minerals in the milk.

Ketosis—Pregnancy disease in ewes due to a lack of carbohydrates is a common cause for debility and paraplegia in ewes in advanced pregnancy. Twin pregnancy is a frequent complication. Usually the fetus dies and the ewe often succumbs. If the fetus is aborted promptly the ewe may recover; or treatment administered early in the disease may bring about recovery. Therapy for ketosis consists of glucose intravenously, propylene glycol or glycerol orally and glucocorticoids in small doses parenterally. Large doses of glucocorticoids may favor abortion. In advanced cases in a valuable ewe cesarean section may be indicated. The carbohydrate intake of the rest of the pregnant ewes in the flock should be increased by feeding grain or molasses. Provision for increased exercise may be helpful. This condition may rarely be observed in the cow prior to parturition, Kingrey et al..

Grass tetany is seen in pregnant cattle on lush pasture, such as wheat pastures, particularly in the fall or early spring. It is apparently due to a lack of calcium causing hypoclacemia and/or magnesium causing hypomagnesemia. Some believe it is associated with the high potassium or high vitamin A levels of the lush, green immature forage. Mineral feed or feeding of good-quality alfalfa or clover hay rich in calcium and phosphorus tends to prevent the condition. It is probably best to remove the stock from the lush pasture for a time. The paretic cases usually respond to calcium therapy, or if paresis and marked nervous symptoms are present both calcium and magnesium therapy are indicated.

Milk fever or parturient paresis may occur just prior to parturition in the high-producing dairy cow, at which time it is called preparturient milk fever or paresis. Most preparturient cases occur during the first stage of parturition, when milk letdown is favored by the action of the oxytocin released at that time. Following treatment, active labor and calving will often follow within 4 to 6 hours. In a few cases preparturient milk fever due to a sudden drop in blood calcium may be observed 24 to 72 hours before parturition.

Puerperal tetany, or eclampsia in dogs and rarely cats associated with a hypocalcemia characterized by nervousness, restlessness, whining, and then staggering, stiffness of the legs, and finally collapse with clonic spasms, labored respirations, salivation, and elevation of temperature, may be seen occasionally prior to parturition although it is far more commonly observed the first 2 weeks after parturition.

Dropsy of the fetal membranes and fetus—This may occur from 5 months to term and is associated with a great increase in abdominal weight and size and the inability to rise. The increased abdominal weight may lead to injury such as dislocation of the hips.

Joint and tendon injuries especially to the rear limbs may render the animal unable to rise. Dislocation of the hip is common in the cow in advanced pregnancy. Dislocation or subluxation of the stifle are occasionally observed. Separation of the ligaments of the ilio-sacral articulation is infrequently observed. Sometimes painful lesions of the joints, due to chronic arthritis of the stifle or hip or suppurative lesions of the hock or coffin joint, may cause reluctance to rise; in time, stiffness and weakness may result, followed by inability to rise. Sudden rupture of the prepubic tendon in the mare or rupture of the gastrocnemius tendon, usually secondary to Zenker's muscle degeneration, in the cow may occasionally be causes in these animals of their being unable to rise or rising with difficulty.

Fractures of the rear limbs or spine—Fractures of the femur and pelvis are the most common of those occurring in advanced pregnancy. They may occur when a cow in advanced pregnancy is mounted by another cow. Osteomalacia due to a prolonged mineral deficiency favors fracture. Excessive relaxation of joints and ligaments due to estrogens present in advanced pregnancy may also lead to fractures. Spinal injuries or fractures in the lumbar region with severe posterior paresis, may occasionally occur. If a cow or bull mounts the pregnant animal, the impact of the sternum on the coccygeal and sacral vertebrae may cause a subluxation, dislocation, or fracture of these vertebrae and subsequent posterior weakness and paralysis of the tail.

Septic or infectious processes associated with advanced pregnancy may cause paresis. They may be any of the following: septic metritis of pregnancy with death and maceration of the fetus; rupture of the uterus with severe peritonitis secondary to an emphysematous fetus; traumatic gastritis with diffuse peritonitis; severe torsion of the uterus with gangrene and shock, or death of the fetus and rupture of the uterus; severe pyelonephritis aggravated by advanced pregnancy; or septic mastitis.

Other conditions that may cause paresis or paraplegia in animals at any time may affect the pregnant animal. These are as follows: rupture of a large uterine vessel with hemorrhage, toxic indigestion, diseases of the central nervous system, such as rabies and listeriosis; severe prolonged illness resulting in debility such as: Johnes disease, severe mange, advanced actinomycosis of the jaw, and senility; tumors especially of the brain and spinal cord, such a lymphocytoma; severe septicemic diseases such as: anthrax, blackleg, pasteurellosis, leptospirosis and anaplasmosis; and severe foot lesions.

If an animal is down, struggles to rise, but remains down for a period of time particularly on a hard concrete floor, decubital injuries, contusions, abrasions, joint, muscle and tendon injuries, and exhaustion are common. These cause progressive soreness, stiffness, awkwardness, and even greater difficulty in rising. Many so-called malingerers probably have arthritis, myositis or tendonitis painful enough so that they refuse to rise even though they are probably able to do so. These animals would benefit from good nursing, a dirt floor or heavily bedded box stall, and slings to get them up periodically so as to restore movement and circulation to the legs. The further handling of these animals in advanced pregnancy depends upon their value for food, their sentimental value, the value of the offspring, the nature and severity of their diseases or injuries, and the owner's ability, means, and interest in nursing these paraplegic, paretic or "downer" animals.

Miscellaneous Accidents of Pregnancy

Hemorrhages of pregnancy—The most common hemorrhage of pregnancy is that associated with hematic mummification of the bovine fetus. This occurs in the utero-chorionic space of a sealed uterus. Slight hemorrhages occur between the maternal and fetal placenta that may be noted on examination of the placenta after parturition. In the cow "uterine sand," occasionally found in the utero-chorionic space, is dryed or inspissated granules of serum about 1/64 to 1/16 inch in diameter. Occasionally due to trauma or violence causing rupture of the larger vessels, hemorrhage or large blood clots sufficient to cause death may be found around the vagina or in the broad ligament in the cow or mare in late pregnancy. Mares should not be transported or subject to violent exercise in late pregnancy for this reason. Hemorrhage or bleeding from the genital tract appearing at the vulva during pregnancy is rare in domestic animals. It may be noted in pyelonephritis, in a traumatic injury to the vagina, vulva or bladder, in tumors of the vulva or vagina that bleed readily, or by recurrent slight bleeding from a ruptured varicose or surface vein in the vagina or hymenal region. The latter is not serious; it may heal spontaneously or be corrected by cautery or by ligating the lesion. A reddish-brown vulvar exudate containing free blood may be associated with beginning abortion and a dead fetus or a septic metritis of pregnancy with an open cervix. Hemoglobinuria due to leptospirosis and other acute hemolytic diseases may be confused in the pregnant animal with bleeding from the genital tract.

Rupture of the gravid uterus—This may occur either spontaneously due to unknown causes, or secondary to abortion, dystocia, emphysematous fetuses, chronic peritonitis with uterine adhesions, torsion of the uterus, dropsy of the fetal membranes and fetus, and extreme violence and trauma in advanced pregnancy.

Strangulation of the large colon by the gravid uterus—Williams described a mare with unexplainable symptoms of digestive distress which on postmortem examination proved to have been caused by displacement of the large colon beneath the gravid uterus.

Strangulation of the pregnant uterus by a pedunculated lipoma—Benesch cited and illustrated a case of a 4-month pregnancy in a cow in which a lipoma wrapped around the uterus.

References

Extrauterine Fetuses

Keyser, D. D. (1964) Displacement of an Ovine Fetus, Vet. Med. **59,** 5, 465.

Krichel, J. H., Jr. (1969) A Report of Six Cases of Uterine Ulceration in the Dog, Vet. Med. **64,** 10, 872.

Lederer, H. A. and Fisher, L. E. (1960) Ectopic Pregnancy in a Dog, J.A.V.M.A. **137,** 1, 61.

Spanabel, J. J. (1957) Extrauterine Mummified Fetus in a Bitch, N. A. Vet. **38,** 8, 239.

Williams, W. L. (1943) Veterinary Obstetrics, 4th Ed., Luella Williams, Ithaca, N. Y. 151.

Dropsy of the Fetal Membranes and Fetus

Arthur, G. H. (1957) Some Notes on the Quantities of Fetal Fluids in Ruminants with Special Reference to Hydrops Amnii, Brit Vet. Jour. **113,** 17.

Arthur, G. H. (1965) Further Observations on the Fetal Fluids of Cattle, Vet. Rec. **77,** 623.

Arthur, G. H. (1969) The Fetal Fluids of Domestic Animals, J. Reprod. and Fertil., Suppl. 9, 45.

Baker, M. L., Payne, L. C. and Baker, G. N. (1961) The Inheritance of Hydrocephalus in Cattle, Jour. Hered. **52,** 135.

Cassidy, G. and Cailliteau, J. (1967) Amniotic Fluid in Anencephaly, Amer. J. of Obst. and Gynec. **97,** 3, 395.

Crew, F. A. E. (1924) The Bulldog Calf; a Contribution to the Study of Achondroplasia, Vet. Rec. **4,** 785.

Donald, H. P., Deas, D. W. and Wilson, L. A. (1952) Genetical Analysis of the Incidence of Dropsical Calves in Herds of Ayrshire Cattle, Brit. Vet. Jour. **108,** 227.

Gibbons, W. J. (1957) Dropsy of the Fetal Membranes, N. A. Vet. **38,** 8, 233.

Jakobsen, K. J. and Simesen, M. G. (1959) Hydrops Amnii in Cows, Nord. Vet. Med. **11,** 81.

Loje, K. (1930) Letalegenuer hos Husdyrene Specielt hos Kvaeg af Rod Dansk Malkrease, Tidskr. f. Landokonomi, **10,** 517.

Lynd, F. I. (1956) Amnioallantoic Dropsy in Cows, Southwest. Vet. 9, 2, 137.

Milne, F. J. (1953) Treatment of Hydrops Amnii with E.C.P., J.A.V.M.A. **123,** 520.

Neal, P. A. (1956) Bovine Hydramnios and Hydrallantois, Vet. Rec. **68,** 5, 89.

Oehme, F. W. (1964) Hydrops Allantois Associated with Twin Pregnancy and Uterine Rupture in a Cow, J.A.V.M.A. **145,** 7, 688.

Roberts, J. A. F. (1929) The Inheritance of Lethal Muscle Contracture in the Sheep, Jour. Genet. **21,** 57.

Skydsgaard, J. M. (1965) The Pathogenesis of Hydrallantois Bovis, Acta. Vet. Scand. **6,** 193.

Vandeplassche, M., Oyaert, W., Bouters, R. Vandenhende, C., Spincemaille, J. and Herman, J. (1965) Uber die Eihautwassersucht beim Rind, Wiener Tierarztl. Monatsschr. **5,** 52, 461.

Williams, W. L. (1943) Veterinary Obstetrics, 4th Ed., Miss Louella Williams, Ithaca, N.Y., 179.

Abdominal Hernias Associated with Hysterocele

Benesch, F (1952) Lehrbuch der Tierarztlichen Geburtshilfe und Gynakologie, Urban and Schwarzenberg, Wien-Innsbruck, Austria.

Benesch, F. and Wright, J. G. (1951) Veterinary Obstetrics, Williams and Wilkins Co., Baltimore, Md.

Emmerson, M. A. (1944) Rupture of the Prepubian and Subpubian Tendons in the Cow, Univ. of Penn. Vet. Ext. Quart. **94,** 3.

Hughes, D., Moore, R. A. and Fincher, M. G. (1958) Massive Hematomas, Mod. Vet. Pract. **39,** 7, 56.

Riser, W. H. (1963) Inguinal Hernia Containing a Portion of the Uterine Horn and a Fetus, J.A.V.M.A. **143,** 1, 64.

Snow, R. (1956) Inguinal Metrocele (Gravid) in a Bitch, J.A.V.M.A. **129,** 8, 359.

Wright, J. C. (1964) Inguinal Hernia in the Bitch, Abstr. J.A.V.M.A. **144,** 5, 500.

Torsion of the Uterus during Pregnancy

Arthur, G. H. (1964) Wright's Veterinary Obstetrics, 3rd Ed. Williams Wilkins Co., Baltimore, Md.

Arthur, G. H. (1966) Recent Advances in Bovine Obstetrics, Vet. Rec. **79,** 22, 630.

Benesch, F. (see above)

Bloom, F. (1954) Pathology of the Dog and Cat, Amer. Vet. Public, Inc., Evanston, Ill.

Nijhof, W. J. (1959) Torsion of the Uterus in a Sow, Tijdschr. v. Diergeneesk. **84,** 774.

Pugh, D. M. (1963) Uterine and Abomasal Torsion in the Ewe, Vet. Rec., **75,** 40, 1028.

Settergren, I. (1969) Personal communication.

Skjerven, O. (1965) Correction of Uterine Torsion in the Mare by Laparotomy, Nord. Vet. Med., **17,** 377.

Vandeplassche, M., Pardis, F. and Bouters, R. (1961) Surgical Correction of Uterine Torsion in the Mare, Vlaams Diergeneesk. Tijdschr. **30,** 10.

Van der Kaay, F. C. and de Bois, C. H. W. (1958) Torsion of the Uterus in the Mare, Berl. und Munch. Tierartzl. Wchnschr. **71,** 112.

Wensvoort, P. (1956) Two Cases of Torsion of the Uterus in the Sow, Tijdschr. v. Diergeneesk. **15,** 71.

Williams, W. L. (1943) Veterinary Obstetrics 4th Ed., (see above), 295.

Prolapse of the Vagina

Arthur, G. H. (1964) Wright's Veterinary Obstetrics, 3rd Ed. Williams, Wilkins Co., Baltimore, Maryland.

Arthur, G. H. (1966) Recent Advances in Bovine Obstetrics, Vet. Rec. **79,** 22, 630.

Bennetts, H. W., Underwood, E. J. and Shier, F. L. (1946) A Specific Breeding Problem of Sheep on Subterranean Clover Pastures in Western Australia, Austral. Vet. J. **22,** 1, 2.

Bloom, F. (1968) Canine Medicine, 1st Catcott Ed., Amer. Vet. Public. Inc., Wheaton, Ill.

Bouckaert, J. H., Oyaert, W., Wijverkens, H. and Meirhaeghe, E. (1956) Prolapse of the Vagina in the Cow, Vlaams Diergeneesk. Tijdschr. **25,** 119.

Carne, H. (1955) Personal communication.

Clegg, M. T., Albaugh, R., Lucas, J. and Weir, W. C. (1955) A Comparison of the Effect of Stilbestrol on the Growth Response of Lambs of Different Age and Sex, J. An. Sci. **14,** 1, 178.

Ebert, E. F. and Bierschwal, C. J. (1956) Pudendal Neurectomy, Winter Veterinary Scope, Upjohn Comp.

Espersen, G. (1962) Artificial Pneumoperitoneum for Tenesmus in Cattle, Wien. Tierartzl. Mschr. **49,** 825.

Farquharson, J. (1949) Vaginal Prolapse in the Bovine, Rept. of the 14th Internat. Vet. Congr., London, England, **3,** 264.

Frank, E. R. (1953) Veterinary Surgery Notes, Burgess Publ. Co., Minneapolis, Minn.

Guard, W. F. (1953) Surgical Principles and Technics, 2274 Yorkshire Rd., Columbus, 12, Ohio.

Habel, R. E. (1957) Prevention of Vaginal Prolapse in the Cow, Transl. J.A.V.M.A. **130,** 8, 344.

Hentschl, A. F. (1961) The Button Technique for Correction of Prolapse of the Vagina in Cattle, J.A.V.M.A. **139,** 12, 1319.

Jones, B. V. (1958) Control of Vaginal Prolapse in Ewes, Vet. Rec. **70,** 17, 362.

Koen, J. S. and Smith, H. C. (1945) An Unusual Case of Genital Involvement in Swine Associated with Eating Moldy Corn, Vet. Med. 40, 4, 131.

Larson, L. L. (1953) The Internal Pudendal (Pudic) Nerve Block for Anesthesia of the Penis and Relaxation of the Retractor Penis Muscle, J.A.V.M.A., **123,** 916, 18.

Libke, K. G. (1960) Personal communication.

McErlean, B. A. (1952) Vulvovaginitis of Swine, Vet. Rec., **64,** 37, 539.

Merrillat, L. A. (1943) Whipple's Operation for Prolapse of the Vagina in Bitches, J.A.V.M.A., **103,** 800, 286.

Minchev, P. (1956) The Use of a New Surgical Method in Eversion and Prolapse of the Vagina in Animals, Veterinariya, **33,** (see Habel).

Norton, E. S. (1969) External Fixation of the Bovine Vagina after Reduction of a Prolapse, J.A.V.M.A. **154,** 10, 1179.

Payton, J. (1951) The Payton Uterus and Vaginal Prolapse Preventer, J.A.V.M.A., **119,** 897, 434.

Pierson, R. E. (1961) A Review of Surgical Procedures for Correction of Vaginal Prolapses in Cattle, J.A.V.M.A. **139,** 3, 352.

Schinkel, P. G. (1948) Infertility in Ewes Grazing Subterranean Clover Pastures, Austr. Vet. J., **24,** 289.

Schulte, A. P. (1967) Vaginal Prolapse in the Bitch, Jour. S. Afr. Vet. Med. Assoc. **38,** 2, 197.

Svendsen, P. (1967) Artificial Pneumoperitoneum, Nord. Vet. Med. **19,** 163 (also **18,** 226).

Watts, R. E. (1954) Preparturient Prolapse of the Vaginal Wall, Proc. A.V.M.A., 91st Ann. Meeting, 382.

Williams, W. L. (1943) Diseases of the Genital Organs of Domestic Animals, 3rd Ed., Miss Louella Williams, Upland Rd., Ithaca, N.Y.

Williams, W. L. (1943) Veterinary Obstetrics, 4th Ed., Miss Louella Williams, Upland Rd., Ithaca, N.Y.

Winkler, J. K. (1966) Repair of Bovine Vaginal Prolapse by Cervical Fixation, J.A.V.M.A., **149,** 6, 768.

Woelffer, E. A. (1953) Use of Progesterone to Control Habitual Abortion in Cattle, J.A.V.M.A., **123,** 921, 505.

Woodward, R. R. and Quesenberry, J. R. (1956) A Study of (Postpartum) Vaginal and Uterine Prolapse in Hereford Cattle, J. An. Sci. **15,** 1, 119.

Paraplegia of Pregnancy and Miscellaneous Accidents

Benesch, F. (1952) Lebrbuch der Tierartzlichen Geburtshilfe and Gynakologie, Urban and Schwarzenberg, Wien-Innsbruck, Austria.

Kingrey, B. W., Ludwig, V. D., Monlux, W. S. and Ramsey, F. K. (1957) Pregnancy Disease in Cows, N. A. Vet. **38,** 11, 321.

Williams, W. L. (see above).

Chapter VI

PARTURITION

Parturition encompasses the various physiological processes involved in the birth of young. Prior to parturition the dam should have been fed a properly balanced ration in amounts sufficient to provide the necessary carbohydrates, protein, fat, vitamins, minerals, and water so that at the time of parturition she is neither fat nor thin. Most livestock men prefer to feed their animals approaching parturition a light, slightly laxative feed. Under most systems of management the pregnant animal is provided adequate opportunity for exercise. For the last 2 to 3 weeks prior to parturition violence and excessive exercise or work should be avoided. The animals should be segregated from the rest of the herd in clean, sanitary, comfortable, quiet surroundings.

One of the best locations possible for parturition of farm animals is a small pasture free of woods, steep slopes, or wet brush areas. This location is clean and the newborn are not exposed to the common barn or barnyard diseases. The principal disadvantage of such a location is that frequently close observation or supervision of parturition cannot be followed. During periods of adverse cold and wet weather, a dry, relatively warm building or shed supplied with heat lamps is necessary for parturition for all domestic animals. A satisfactory place often used for parturition of the large domestic animals is a clean, well-bedded, roomy, disinfected box stall. Facilities for sanitation and isolation at the time of parturition or abortion are of prime importance in herds affected with reproductive diseases.

In swine in which heavy death losses of 20 to 30 per cent of the newborn are frequently experienced during parturition and the following 48 to 72 hours, many life-saving innovations have been introduced. The farrowing pen should have guard rails. The bedding should not be too deep. Farrowing crates are highly desirable. Constant watch should be kept on farrowing sows to prevent them from lying on the newborn pigs. In many cases the newborn pig is removed immediately after birth. After farrowing is completed, the pigs are returned to the sow. To prevent the newborn pigs from becoming chilled, farrowing houses are built singly and small, or larger farrowing houses are artificially heated. The use of heat-lamp-type brooders placed in the corner of the pens not only prevents chilling but provides a safe place for pigs when they are not nursing. In some farrowing houses heating cable is placed in the concrete floor to provide heat for the pigs. The optimum environmental temperature for newborn pigs is 85° to 95° F. For dogs, the owner should set aside a whelping place or box about two to three feet square with six to eight inch sides for medium-sized dogs. If possible the bitch should be kept in this familiar environment for at least a month before whelping.

It is important that veterinarians be familiar with normal parturition as it occurs in the various domestic animals so that there may be immediate recognition of any pathological symptoms. Assistance or interference with the birth process, occasionally necessary to save the fetus or dam, must be performed at the proper time. The time of parturition is one of the most critical stages in the life of any animal. It is one of the periods of highest death rate in animals. It can be a period in which not only the fetus, but also the dam, may be severely damaged or injured and thus affect its future reproductive and productive efficiency. This period, therefore, is of vital concern to the farmer who has a large economic investment in his animals.

Symptoms of Approaching Parturition

The signs of approaching parturition in domestic animals are somewhat similar but vary in certain important respects. The symptoms are inconstant between individual animals and between consecutive parturitions. These symptoms therefore do not permit an accurate prediction as to the exact time of parturition in a certain animal but they are useful indications as to the approximate time parturition may be expected. The practicing veterinarian is frequently asked to examine and predict the time of parturition of an animal in advanced pregnancy. Although the following discussion will be helpful in this respect, he should refrain from making too positive or definite a statement concerning the exact time of parturition, as subsequent events will more often than not prove him wrong.

The breeding date, if known, is helpful in predicting the approximate time of parturition. Breeding records are necessary on the well-managed farm. Just prior to parturition most animals tend to segregate themselves from the others. The sow, dog, and cat attempt to make a suitable bed. Changes in the pelvis, genital organs, and mammary glands take place.

In the cow the pelvic ligaments, especially the sacro-sciatic, become progressively more relaxed, causing a sinking of the croup ligaments and muscles. The caudal border of the sacro-sciatic ligament between the coccygeal vertebrae and ischial tuberosity becomes less cord-like and tight, and more relaxed and flaccid. Relaxation of the pelvic ligaments, cervix and possibly the structures around the perineum is due to edema and changes in the collagen fibers in connective tissue probably caused by an increase in estrogen from the placenta and possibly other endocrine glands like the adrenals. Relaxin may also play a role. In most cows the presence of very relaxed ligaments indicates that parturition will probably occur in 24 to 48 hours. This relaxation of the ligaments is also noted by the elevation of the tail head. The vulva becomes progressively edematous and more flaccid until it is 2 to 6 times its normal size. The udder becomes enlarged and edematous. In heifers this udder enlargement begins about the fourth month of gestation. In older, pluriparous cows it may not be noticeable until 2 to 4 weeks before parturition. In high-producing, especially younger cows, the amount of edema in the udder may be extensive and cause difficulty in walking. Edema may extend forward on the abdominal floor to the xiphoid region and be 2 to 6 inches deep. In the region of the navel it may resemble an umbilical hernia. It may extend caudally above the udder and involve the region of the escutcheon and even the vulva. This edema may be severe enough to interfere with circulation in the skin between the udder and legs or in the region between the fore quarters of the udder, resulting in areas of necrosis at these sites. Just prior to parturition the udder secretion changes from a honey-like dry secretion to a yellow, turbid, opaque cellular secretion called colostrum. At this period the udder and teats are so distended with colostrum that in "easy milkers" it may leak out. The cow usually exhibits a tenacious, whitish, stringy type of mucus coming from the cranial part of the vagina, starting at about 7 months of pregnancy. This mucus becomes more profuse as parturition approaches. Just prior to parturition the amount of mucous increases markedly and the cervical seal liquefies. During the last few hours before calving the cow may exhibit anorexia and restlessness. Heifers may show signs of abdominal pain as kicking at the abdomen, treading, switching their tails and lying down and rising.

In the mare somewhat similar symptoms of approaching parturition are present. The sinking of the sacrosciatic ligaments is not so pronounced, due to the heavy croup muscles. The vulva does not become as edematous as in the cow but edema and flaccidity are noted the last few weeks of gestation. No discharge of vaginal mucus prior to foaling is noted in the mare. The udder starts to develop noticeably about 3 to 6 weeks before foaling. In most mares the udder becomes filled and distended with colostrum about 2 days before foaling, and oozing of this colostrum from the teats, called "waxing," is usually observed in 95 percent of mares 6 to 48 hours before foaling, Rossdale. In a few cases no waxing is observed before foaling and in other cases it may occur a week or so before parturition. Within 4 hours of parturition slight sweating in the flank region and behind the elbows is frequently noticed. Anorexia occurs only within 1 to 2 hours of foaling. As the first stage of labor advances the mare becomes restless, shows slight colicy symptoms, switches her tail and lies down and gets up frequently. These symptoms become progressively more marked until the allantois chorion ruptures and the second stage of actual labor begins.

The mare greatly prefers solitude and quiet at parturition and seems more able than other animals to control or suppress parturition until the night hours, when stable activities are at a minimum. Trum reported that of 567 foals, 59.8 percent were born from 6:00 p.m. to midnight, 23.4 percent from midnight to 6:00 a.m. and only 16.8 percent from 6:00 a.m. to 6:00 p.m. Thus about 83 percent of the foals were born during the night. Asdell reported that 73 percent of farrowings occurred between 2:00 p.m. and 4:00 a.m.

In the ewe and goat the conditions are similar to the cow with the exception that udder development is not so great. **In the sow and cat** the symptoms are somewhat similar to those in the bitch. As pregnancy progresses, **the bitch** becomes quieter and as parturition approaches the vulva becomes flaccid, enlarged, and edematous. The mammary glands also become enlarged and edematous and milk may be present in the udder several days before parturition. The bitch becomes restless and shows anorexia for a few days before parturition. This becomes more noticeable 12 to 24 hours before whelping. During the first stage of labor, the bitch may pant or exhibit an increased respiration rate. During the latter stages of pregnancy in the ewe, sow, and bitch a mucoid vulvar discharge is usually evident. Environmental disturbances, especially those caused by other dogs, will delay or interrupt the birth process in bitches, Bleicher.

The Initiation of Parturition

The exact mechanism concerned with the onset of parturition after a rather regular and definite length of gestation for each species of animals is not well understood. Probably hormonal factors are of prime importance, as parturition can take place without innervation of the uterus.

Within a week or two of conception the blastocyst that is present in the uterus affects the endometrium so that a luteolytic substance normally released and essential for regulating the estrous cycle by causing the involution of the corpus luteum fails to be released and the corpus luteum persists. Its secretion of progesterone maintains pregnancy by its effect on the uterine musculature and the endometrium which secretes uterine "milk" the first third of gestation period until placental attachments have become functional. Progesterone also inhibits the production of F.S.H. so follicles and estrous periods are suppressed. A neuro-hormonal stimulus from the pregnant uterus causes the continued secretion of LH to maintain the corpus luteum throughout pregnancy in the cow, pig and goat. In the mare gonadotropic hormones secreted by the endometrial cups from 40 to 120 days of gestation causes the development of follicles, ovulation and many accessory corpora lutea. Pregnancy is maintained by progesterone produced mainly in the chorioallantois or placenta, or possibly the adrenal gland, in the mare, the sheep, and the dog and cat from 150 to 200 days, 55 days, 30 days and 50 days of pregnancy, respectively, to term, Catchpole, Cates, Gomes and Erb. In the mare Short has reported high levels of progesterone in the placenta after midgestation but none was evident in the serum. Gillette has reported that even the cow's placenta may produce progesterone that has a local effect on the uterus by diffusion. In the mare and ewe the corpora lutea are not necessary during the latter half of pregnancy and they involute. Progesterone or certain progestins administered late in gestation may prolong gestation, McDonald, Kiesel and others. (See prolonged gestation).

The onset of parturition, although not completely understood, is apparently brought about by a gradually increasing level of estrogens from the placenta that occurs late in gestation, Mellin et al. and Hunter et al.. In the cow the estrogen level increased 2 to 3-1/2 times from day 245 to calving; while the progesterone content of the blood plasma declined from 19 to 6 ng/ml the last month before calving and then to a very low level of 0.5 to 3.0 ng/ml at calving, Pope and Gupta. Relaxin which is also released in large amounts late in gestation in the cow and sow also aids in relaxing pelvic structures and the cervix, McDonald, and Egger and Dracy. The increased levels of estrogens sensitize the uterine musculature to oxytocin that plays an important role in parturition especially during the first and second stages of labor. However, parturition can take place in the absence of the hypophysis.

In humans and mares induction of labor once the cervix is properly relaxed can readily be produced by intravenous infusions of small amounts of oxytocin. Administering epidural anesthesia had no effect on parturition, Henry et al.. The intramuscular injection of oxytocin initiated parturition with 3.5 hours in 84 percent of sows with milk in the udder and within 24 hours of farrowing according to the breeding records, Muhrer et al.. Settergren reported that oxytocin given to about 25 mares near foaling, after 340 days of gestation, induced parturition within one to three hours and obviated the necessity of observing them during the night hours. Treated mares should be kept in a quiet place for foaling and observed during parturition.

It is likely however that parturition is triggered by a mechanism causing a decline in the LH and progesterone levels, Labhsetwar et al. Hunter et al. and Saiduddin et al.. This may occur in some species by aging of the placenta with a decline in progesterone production. In cattle, goats and probably pigs (see prolonged gestation) the fetal pituitary-adrenal axis by controlling the output of corticoids from the fetal adrenal may trigger parturition. As the fetus becomes increasingly stressed due to its decreasing supply of nutrition, cortisone should be produced that together with the high level of estrogen results in a decline in LH, involution of the corpus luteum and a rapid decline in progesterone levels. Large doses of either estrogen or hydrocortisone have the ability to involute the corpus luteum and cause abortion in cattle. This probably occurs due to the suppression of LH from the pituitary necessary to maintain the corpus luteum of pregnancy. Prolonged gestation in cattle occurs as an hereditary condition in Guernseys with aplasia of the anterior pituitary gland. Thus the fetus regulates its own length of intrauterine existence. It is very possible the steroid hormone levels, elevated estrogen and cortisone and lowered progesterone, control the initial and developing stages leading to parturition and that oxytocin release regulates the occurrence of actual labor. The release of oxytocin is subject to environmental influences thus accounting for the delay of parturition until the night hours in mares and other species. Further studies which are presently being conducted will undoubtedly greatly add to our knowledge concerning the initiation of parturition, McDonald, Arthur, Adams, Schofield. In advanced pregnancy in humans the removal of amniotic fluid or the introduction of hypertonic saline into the amniotic cavity precipitates parturition. It has been suggested that the injection of hypertonic saline suppressed placental function including the production of progesterone. In cattle such procedures had no effect, Adams. The hormonal mechanisms involved in pregnancy and parturition are well discussed by Catchpole, Hunter et al.. Moberg reported that during parturition there was a marked rise in the total white blood cell count due to an increase in the circulating neutrophiles. An eosinopenia accompanied these changes.

The Stages of Parturition

Although the act of parturition is continuous, for purposes of definition it is usually divided into three stages or phases.

First Stage—This stage is characterized by the active contractions of both the longitudinal and circular muscle fibers of the uterine wall, and the dilation of the cervix. Gillette and Holm reported that bovine uterine muscle contractions were due to the removal of the progesterone block and the increased conduction excitability and synchronous action caused by higher levels of estrogens. Oxytocin is seldom released from the hypo hysis prior to the second stage of labor so is not essential ı the induction of parturition or labor, McDonald, VanDongen and Hayes and Folley and Knaggs. Uterine peristalsis starting in the apices of the uterine horns was initiated by circular muscle contractions synchronized by propagation of the action impulse through the longitudinal muscles. Uterine contractions performed 90 percent of the work of the parturition and these contractions were directly proportional to fetal resistance. There is a greatly increased activity of the uterine musculature the last 1 to 2 hours before birth. The average prepartum amplitude of uterine muscle contraction was 80 cm. of H_2O. Uterine contractions force the fetal membranes and their fluids against and into the relaxed cervix. Arthur (1966) cited Abusineina who reported that the external os of the bovine cervix relaxed sufficiently a week or so before calving to accomodate 2 to 4 fingers. The cervix of heifers remained tightly closed until the day before parturition. In the first stage of parturition the cervix was not dilated by the allantois chorion but was pulled open by the contraction of the longitudinal uterine muscles. For most of the first stage the cervix easily contained the allantois chorion that projected into it. True dilation of the internal os started 2 to 4 hours after the external os had reached a diameter of 3 to 6 inches and by 6 to 12 hours the whole cervix was 6 to 7 inches wide and the cervix and vagina were a continuous canal filled with the distended allantois-chorion.

During this first stage in the cow, uterine contractions occur about every 10 to 15 minutes and last 15 to 30 seconds. As the stage advances they increase in frequency, strength, and duration until contractions occur about every 3 to 5 minutes, Benesch and Wright, Gillette and Holm. In uniparous animals the contractions start at the apex of the cornua while the caudal part does not contract but rather dilates from the pressure of the fetus and fluids forced caudally. In this stage in the mare and probably the bitch the fetus is rotating from its dorso-pubic or dorso-lateral position into the dorso-sacral position. As it passes through the cervix into the birth canal the legs and head are extended. In the bovine and ovine fetus no rotation is necessary, as it is already in a dorso-sacral position. By the end of this stage the cervix is completely dilated.

According to Benesch and Wright and Arthur the multiparous animals have a more complex mechanism of uterine contractions. The contractions of the uterus occur just cephalad to the most caudad fetus forcing it through the cervix into the birth canal, while the rest of the uterus remains quiescent. Then the same process is repeated for the most caudad fetus in the other horn, or the fetus immediately cranial to the one just expelled. This may help explain why in the second stage two fetuses may be born nearly simultaneously. The longitudinal fibers of the parts of the horn just emptied contract, but the circular fibers remain relaxed, so that the next fetus may pass through. This shortens the uterus as parturition progresses, so that each fetus in turn is brought back nearly to the cervix. This is important in multipara so that the fetuses at the apex of the uterine horn do not have to traverse a long uterine horn after the placenta has been detached or the navel cord ruptured. The normal and abnormal behavioral patterns, or ethology, of the various species of animals before, during and after parturition has been well described by Fox and Fraser.

During this first stage of parturition which lasts about 1 to 4 hours, straining or labor is not exhibited in the mare. The symptoms of restlessness, anorexia, colicy pains, slight sweating behind the elbows and around the flanks, lying down and getting up, tail switching, elevating of the tail, repeated periodic sudden complete arrest in motion even chewing, repeated stretching as if to urinate, frequent small bowel evacuations, and looking at the flank are characteristic of abdominal discomfort in the mare during the latter part of this period. Usually the pulse and repiratory rates are accelerated. During the latter part of the first stage just prior to labor the mare may roll back and forth in an apparent effort to rotate the fetus into a dorso-sacral position or crouch, go down on her knees, rise again and be highly restless. The body temperature may become slightly lower than normal during this period, Arthur.

In the cow and ewe the symptoms of abdominal pain or discomfort may not be evident especially in pluriparous animals. In heifers, colicy symptoms and restlessness usually are observed and may last for 1 to 24 hours. The cow and ewe will show anorexia, stand with an arched back and raised tail, strain occasionally, and ruminate irregularly. The cow may lie down and get up frequently. Pulse and respiratory rates increase but lowering of the body temperature is inconstant.

In the bitch, sow, and cat nervousness, anorexia, and an increase in pulse and respiratory rates usually occur. In dogs this may result in panting. The signs of various stages of parturition in the bitch were well described by Freak. Occasionally vomiting is observed. This stage usually lasts for about 2 to 12 hours. In the dog there is usually a sudden drop of 1 to 2° F. in body temperature to below 100° F. just before or during this phase of parturition.

Ewbank, and Wrenn et al. and others have reported a drop in body temperature of 1 to 1.5°, 24 to 48 hours before parturition in cattle and sheep. This decline in temperature was related to the decline in progesterone levels as noted in variations of body temperature in women and cattle during the menstrual or estrous cycles. However because of its variability this fall in body temperature was of little practical value in predicting the onset of parturition in the cow or ewe. It was suggested that a healthy cow late in gestation is unlikely to calve the following 12 hours if its rectal temperature is 102° F. or above. Although there is some evidence this same temperature pattern at parturition exists in mares and sows as in cows, its practical value in predicting the time of parturition is questionable. In all animals in which a drop in body temperature occurs during this first stage, the temperature afterwards rises and reaches a peak during and shortly after parturition due to exertion.

This first stage is apparent for longer periods in primiparous than pluriparous animals. During this stage in some animals of all species, milk or colostrum may leak or run from the udder. Usually toward the end of this first stage the allantois chorion ruptures as it is forced through the dilated cervix into the vagina. After the allantois chorion ruptures, the amnion pushes into and through the cervix, and the fetus—because of the shortening and contracting of the uterus and dilation of the cervix—passes into the cervix and vagina. Once a portion of the fetus enters the pelvis, reflex stimuli result in straining or labor. This is produced by contractions of the abdominal muscles and diaphragm together with a closing of the glottis; and the second stage of parturition begins.

Presentation, Position and Posture of the Fetus—It is essential for the sake of accuracy to describe the various presentations, positions, and postures a fetus may assume at the time of its entrance into the birth canal or pelvis. These definitions were established by Williams and are commonly used in the description of both normal and abnormal births.

The **presentation** includes: (1) The relation of the spinal axis of the fetus to that of the dam. Presentations are either longitudinal or transverse. (2) The portion of the fetus that is approaching or entering the pelvic cavity or birth canal. This portion of the fetus is anterior or posterior in the longitudinal presentation, or dorsal or ventral in the transverse presentation.

The **position** includes: (1) The relation of the dorsum of the fetus in longitudinal presentation, or the head in transverse presentation, to the quadrants of the maternal pelvis. These are the sacrum, the right ilium, the left ilium, and the pubis.

The **posture** signifies the relation of the extremities, or the head, neck, and limbs, to the body of the fetus. The extremities may be flexed or extended or retained beneath, on the right or left side, or above the fetus.

In outline form the presentation and position include all possible variations of the manner in which the fetus may enter the birth canal at parturition.

Presentations	Positions
Anterior, longitudinal	Dorso-sacral
	Right dorso-ilial
Posterior, longitudinal	Left dorso-ilial
	Dorso-pubic
Transverse ventral	Right cephalo-ilial
Transverse dorsal	Left cephalo-ilial

The normal presentation in uniparous animals is the anterior longitudinal presentation, dorso-sacral position with the head resting on the metacarpal bones and knees of the extended fore legs. Birth can take place without assistance if the fetus is in the posterior longitudinal presentation, dorso-sacral position. Unless the fetus is small, other positions result in dystocia. The transverse presentation is seen only rarely in ruminants and multipara. It can occur in the mare, in which the fetus develops in both horns, rather than in the body and one horn. Dystocia invariably results. The posterior longitudinal presentation, dorso sacral position, with the hind limbs retained or extended beneath the body, is commonly spoken of as **breech presentation.** Two old terms, only rarely used, are "sterno-abdominal" presentation, which is a transverse ventral presentation in the mare, and "poll" presentation which is an anterior longitudinal presentation, dorso-sacral position, with the head flexed beneath the neck. The position of the fetus in the uterus was discussed in Chapter 4. Thirty to 40 percent of the fetuses of multipara are presented posteriorly and this is considered normal or physiological. Because of the short neck of swine fetuses, the head and neck are seldom deviated. Since the limbs in multipara are small, short and flexible, their posture is of no importance. They may be extended beneath or in front of the body or flexed without resulting in dystocia. Arthur citing Wallace reported that in ewes 69.5 percent of fetuses were in normal anterior presentation with the extremities extended and 17.8 percent of the fetuses were normal except for one retained or flexed leg. In sheep, fetuses may be expelled without assistance in anterior presentation with one fore limb extended beneath or alongside the body. When both fore limbs are retained beneath the body dystocia usually results, Whitlock.

The Second Stage—This stage is characterized by the entrance of the fetus or fetuses into the dilated birth canal; rupture of the allantoic sac; abdominal contractions, or labor; and the expulsion of the fetus through the vulva. Gillette and Holm reported that in the cow abdominal contractions occurred only after the feet of the fetus were in the cervix or vagina. Breaking of the allantoic sac caused a sudden increase in abdominal contractions that were superimposed on the crest of each uterine wave with amplitudes of 80 to 320 cm H_2O, average 180 cm H_2O. In the cow following the rupture of the allantoic sac, the amnion is pushed through the cervix and may appear at the vulva as a translucent distended membrane. During this second stage of labor, uterine contractions occurred in the cow about 4 to 8 times every 10 minutes and lasted 80 to 100 seconds, according to Van der Kaay, as cited by Benesch and Wright, Gillette and Holm. Intermittent tenesmus or straining continues and the feet of the fetus appear at the vulva. As the feet pass through the vulva the amniotic sac usually ruptures. Point pressure rather than diffuse pressure such as that exerted by the allantoic sac is the stimulus to abdominal contractions. Passage of the head, shoulders and hips of the fetus through the pelvis caused an increase in abdominal contractions. The fetal head starts through the vulva and at this point the greatest and strongest abdominal straining in the birth process usually occurs. In the larger uniparous animals as the head is being forced into the vulva, the chest is entering the pelvic canal. Often after the head passes the vulva the dam will rest for a few minutes before beginning straining again with strong abdominal efforts as the chest passes through the birth canal and vulva. The hips usually follow through the birth canal fairly rapidly but occasionally the hind limbs may remain in the vagina until the fetus or dam moves. Folley and Knaggs and Van Dongen and Hayes have shown in goats and cows that during the passage of the fetus through the birth canal and when the vagina was dilated there was a great increase in the levels of oxytocin in the jugular blood over that present during the first and early second stages of labor when in general it was similar to the very low blood levels present during pregnancy. The release of oxytocin during most of the second stage of labor was continual in contrasts to spurts in the release of oxytocin during the milking act. The levels of oxytocin in the blood plasma of goats, sheep and cows during the second stage of labor was 77 to 381, 3000, and 400 to 1000 microunits per ml., respectively. The half life of oxytocin in the blood is one to one and one-half minutes. In the goat the posterior pituitary gland contains about 9 to 13 units of oxytocin and about one-tenth that amount is released during parturition.

Almost all animals, as soon as straining commences, lie down. Occasionally the foal or calf may be born with the dam standing. According to Rossdale this occurred in only 1.5 percent of mares. The mare and the sow usually lie out flat with the legs extended, whereas the cow, bitch, and ewe are more likely to lie on their sternum. In the mare straining is usually characterized by several, 2 to 5, strong expulsive efforts followed by 2 to 3 minutes of rest. This procedure is repeated at fairly regular intervals. Arthur stated that in the mare one fore leg of the fetus precedes the other by 6 inches as the fetus passes through the birth canal. This indicates that one elbow and shoulder enters the birth canal before the other. The foal's cheek is usually lying on the limbs with its muzzle midway between the knee and fetlock joints. Although parturition is quite rapid in the mare it is accompanied by such great expulsive efforts that the mare is usually exhausted and will lie on her side for 15 to 30 minutes before rising, Rossdale. Since the umbilical cord in the mare is long it often does not rupture as the fetus passes through the birth canal. It will remain attached to the fetus for an average of 8 to occasionally 30 minutes until the mare or foal moves, when it breaks at a point about 2 inches from the foal's body.

Pulsations can usually be felt in the umbilical artery for one to 9 minutes. If the umbilical cord is separated immediately 400 to 1,500 ml of blood is lost to the fetus, Rossdale. In the cow the straining is not as forceful or as frequent as in the mare. During the early part of labor the cow may remain standing. Its body temperature may increase to a high normal level and the pulse and respiration rate will rise due to the exertion, as is observed in other animals. In the ewe the second stage of birth is similar to that in the cow. According to Whitlock once the second stage in sheep begins the abdominal contractions develop with gradually increasing frequency and intensity until birth has occurred. If these contractions become reduced in number or intensity usually assistance will be necessary to deliver a live fetus, as this condition does not occur in normal deliveries. Once the feet have passed through the vulva they should stay there and not appear and disappear at each abdominal contraction. This same pattern is followed by other domestic animals.

In the bitch the amnion as it appears at the vulva before the first pup is usually broken by the bitch as she licks the vulva. In the bitch the delivery of the head through the vulva requires the greatest expulsive efforts. The umbilical cord, which is still intact at birth, is usually broken by the bitch. After the birth of each pup the bitch rests, licks the pup and her vulva. When the fetal membranes are expelled—in about 10 minutes after the birth of the pup—they are eaten by the bitch. It is probably best to let the bitch eat only 2 or 3 placentas and then remove the rest, as consumption of too many placentas may cause vomiting and diarrhea. The greenish-black fluid that is discharged following the fetal membranes is normal and is due to the breakdown of blood resulting in the presence of bile-like pigments, uteroverdin, around the edges of the placental zone of attachment. Straining begins again after 0.5 to 1 hour or more and another pup is expelled. Although it may take about 1 hour of labor for the first pup to be born, the periods of straining for the second and third pups are usually progressively shorter. The rate of expulsion of the fetuses is very irregular. Some bitches may not expel the second fetus for several hours after the first. Then the next 2 or 3 may be expelled rapidly, followed by another delay. Rarely are the pups expelled rapidly, in a short time. They may also be expelled at somewhat regular intervals. The sow and cat have a second stage of birth similar to that in the bitch. The period of time between the expulsion of pigs varied from 3 to 45 minutes or rarely longer. The longest intervals were observed between the first and second pig and before the last pig, Jones. About three-quarters of the pigs were born with the umbilical cords intact and it took 2 to 6 minutes average time before rupture. After farrowing the sow usually urinates copiously.

In multipara the fetuses are expelled in an irregular manner from each horn, that is, one fetus may be expelled from one horn and then 2 or 3 from the other and then 2 from the first and one from the second, and so forth. Dzuik and Harmon reported that about half of the pigs born came from the same horn as its predecessor and the other half from the opposite horn. In some sows most of one horn would empty and then all of the other and the remainder of the first horn and etc. In general pig fetuses came randomly. They did not pass each other within the horn. The presence of a dead fetus may delay the emptying of that horn. Occasionally in the mare, bitch, and cat, and only rarely in the other domestic animals, the fetus may be born with the amnion or a portion of it wrapped around its head. In the mare this may cause suffocation of the foal if not promptly removed. In carnivora, death is not likely from this cause since in the bitch and cat the dam promptly licks and eats the amnion if it is around the fetal head.

During this stage the contracting and shortening uterine walls force and direct the fetus into the birth canal and pelvis and abdominal contractions, or labor, drives the fetus through the birth canal. The intra-uterine pressure in the cow, according to Benesch citing DeBruin, was 66 mm. of Hg between uterine contractions during the second stage of labor. The pressure reached about 170 mm. of Hg at the time of abdominal contraction. Thus the total pressure at the opening of the pelvic inlet is about 150 to 170 lbs., or about what one man could apply by traction on the fetus. The intra-abdominal pressure, caused by contraction of the abdominal muscles and diaphragm and closure of the glottis, is equal in all directions. The uterus is necessary to direct the fetus into the path of least resistance—the pelvic canal. If a large hernia is present abdominal contractions could force the uterus into the hernia. Not uncommonly traumatic gastritis or displacement of the abomasum may occur as a sequelae to parturition, due to the abdominal pressure. A healthy fetus, intact abdominal walls and a healthy uterus are necessary for normal birth.

In uniparous animals the large fetuses pass through an arc from the abdominal cavity upward into and through the pelvis and then downward again as they pass through the vulva. In the cow the fetus must pass over the high ischial tuberosities. This arc-like direction of the fetus as it passes through the pelvis causes stretching of its dorsal and pelvic muscles and a relaxation of the linea alba and abdominal muscles. The latter is important because it allows the pelvis to be extended backward on the fetal sacrum, thus reducing the sacro-pubic diameter of the fetal pelvis. The downward direction of the cranial portion of the fetus as it passes the vulva tends to push the fetal pelvis high in the maternal pelvis, where the bisiliac diameter is greater. This helps prevent a hiplock condition frequently encountered when traction is incorrectly applied. In hiplock the greater trochanters fail to pass between the shafts of the ilia.

The time for this second stage of birth in the cow is

from 0.5 to 3 or 4 hours. In pluriparous cows this second stage usually requires 0.5 to 1 hour. Primipara may take longer, up to 3 hours or more. In ewes and goats the second stage of labor is completed in about 1 hour, range 0.5 to 2 hours, or slightly longer if twins or triplets are present. In mares this second stage is normally completed in 5 to 40 minutes with an average of 20 minutes, Rossdale. In rare cases it may extend slightly longer, possibly up to 70 minutes, Arthur. In multiparous animals the length of the second stage of birth is variable, often depending upon the number of fetuses in the uterus. In the bitch the expulsion of the first pup may take up to 1 hour and a variable time for each fetus thereafter. The average total time for the second stage of parturition in a bitch is 3 to 6 hours. Twelve hours would certainly be a maximum. In the sow the second stage is usually completed within 1 to 5 hours but occasionally may last up to 8 hours normally, Jones. In the cat the time is similar to that in the dog.

When the umbilical cord ruptures, the two umbilical arteries together with the urachus retract into the abdominal cavity of the fetus. By the contraction of the arteries into the body tissues provision is made for the prevention of bleeding from the navel. The umbilical vein collapses, the blood drains from it and the fluids in the umbilical cord drain out, often aided by the licking of the cord by the dam. The umbilical cord becomes necrotic, dries up and drops away in 7 to 21 days.

The Third Stage—The third and last stage of parturition is the expulsion of the fetal membranes and the involution of the uterus. These two conditions are discussed separately because the expulsion of the fetal membranes is normally completed within a few hours after the expulsion of the fetus, whereas involution of the uterus to its normal nonpregnant state may take more than a month in some species.

Expulsion of the Fetal Membranes—With the birth of the fetus, the vessels in the fetal placenta collapse and the villi become small and shrunken. After the expulsion of the fetus the uterus still contracts strongly for 48 hours and less vigorously, but more frequently, thereafter, Gillette and Holm, Jordan. This is necessary to prevent hemorrhage and to aid in the expulsion of the fetal membranes. These peristaltic and contraction waves besides reducing the size of the uterus and aiding in forcing the placenta and membranes into the birth canal probably markedly reduce the amount of blood circulating in the endometrium. This causes a dilation or relaxation of the maternal crypts. The shrinking of the villi and the dilation of the maternal caruncular crypts probably play a major role in the separation of the fetal trophoblast and cryptal epithelium of the maternal placenta. No maternal tissue is shed in the afterbirth of cattle. However a few fetal villi may be caught and left in the maternal crypts, Bjorkman. The middle uterine artery immediately contracts following parturition. The artery becomes thick-walled and the characteristic thrill or "whirring" is absent although it may be several weeks or more before it involutes to near its normal size. In exceptional cases an aneurism of this artery may occur and a thrill or "whirr" may be palpated over a portion of the artery for several weeks or longer following parturition. The uterine contractions during this third stage produce movement of the uterine wall and caruncles that may aid in freeing or separating the fetal placenta. There is no muscular tissue in the caruncles. The weight of the amnion and the portion of the allantois in the birth canal tends to help remove the afterbirth from the uterus. Vinattieri, Hayward, and Artioli showed that the incidence of retained afterbirth was much higher in buffalo in which the young were not allowed to suckle, 22.7 percent, than when the young were allowed to suckle, 4.9 percent. It is well-known that suckling stimulates the release of oxytocin from the pituitary. McDonald and his co-workers showed that a lack of progesterone during the last month or so of pregnancy resulted in the occurrence of parturitions 10 to 20 days earlier than normal together with a high incidence of retention of the placenta. Early parturition, twin pregnancy or a shortened gestation period have frequently been observed associated with retained placenta. In these instances infection may play a pathogenic role. This will be discussed further under retention of the fetal membranes. Normal expulsion of the fetal membranes can be said to be a complex process involving both mechanical and hormonal factors, although the exact mechanism is still not completely understood.

In dogs and cats the fetal membranes are usually expelled irregularly between the fetuses; or one fetus may be expelled with its own placenta and that of a fetus expelled earlier. In rare instances expulsion of a few placentae may be delayed for 12 hours or more. In the sow, since a number of the allantois chorions may be fused, the fetal membranes may be expelled at only 2 to 3 intervals during parturition. Jones reported that most porcine afterbirths were expelled from 20 minutes to 12 hours, average 4 hours, after the birth of the last pig. Occasionally placentas were retained with no observed ill effects. The fetal membranes of the last fetuses in the bitch are usually expelled shortly after the birth of the last pup. This third period of labor is characterized by relatively short, infrequent, and mild periods of straining usually at the time the larger mass of membranes are expelled or when much of the placenta is hanging from the vulva especially in uniparous animals. In most unipara the amnion and umbilical cord start through the birth canal first and as the allantois chorion separates from the endometrium at the apex of the horn due to peristaltic waves starting there, the chorion or fetal placenta is inverted and the allantoic surface is outside as the membranes are expelled from the uterus, Jordan. If placental expulsion is delayed for a longer period of time than normal the chorion or fetal placenta may be exposed when it falls from the vulva. Occasionally when fetal expulsion is delayed the fetal placenta may separate, and later both the dead fetus and the fetal membranes are expelled or withdrawn together. Unlike the mare, placental separation in the cow is slower than in most other species of animals, so that the second stage of labor can be prolonged without the danger to the fetus. The umbilical cord in the bovine fetus is ruptured as the fetus passes through the birth canal. In the cow the length of time required for the expulsion of the fetal membranes is normally 1/2 to 8 hours. The ewe is similar to the cow. The mare normally expels its fetal membranes within 0.5 to 3 hours after the birth of the foal. Generally, the healthier the animal the more prompt is the expulsion of the fetal membranes. Domestic animals, with the exception of the mare, will usually eat the expelled fetal membranes. Instances of cow's choking and suffocating while eating their placentas have been reported by Williams and Ulrich. Ruminants will not eat their fetal membranes if the membranes are decomposed. Multipara usually eat the fetal membranes as well as any fetal cadavers. The act of eating the fetal membranes is not known to be beneficial in any way. In ruminants the placenta may lie in the rumen and slowly macerate or decompose over a period of several weeks or more and is occasionally suspected of causing indigestion. This is questionable, since nearly all cattle eat their fetal membranes and symptoms of indigestion or toxemia rarely occur. Occasionally the cow may begin eating her fetal membranes before they have dropped away from the uterus. After the expulsion of the fetal membranes in a normal birth, the cervix secretes a rather thick tenacious mucus that tends to seal the cervix and thus prevents infection gaining entrance to the uterus.

Involution or regression of the uterus in domestic animals, with the exception of the cow and the ewe, has not been extensively studied. In multiparous animals and the ewe, rebreeding the female within the next 2 to 6 months is seldom practiced. In the dog, sow, and cat estrum usually does not occur until after the young are weaned. In the sow an estrum may be exhibited about 3 days postpartum but if copulation is allowed the conception rate is extremely low. In the mare, commonly bred 9 to 30 days after foaling, relatively few studies have been made on the involution of the uterus. Andrews and McKenzie reported that regression of the mare's uterus proceeds at a rapid rate. The endometrium, however, had seldom completely involuted by the onset of the foal heat. In many mares the endometrium must be largely restored by the third to fifth day of foal heat, or 9 to 12 days postpartum as conception often occurs from service at this estrum. By 13 to 25 days after parturition the endometrium was fully restored in all normal foaling mares. At the time of onset of foal heat they reported that the subepithelial areas of glandular epithelium were highly disorganized and contained large number of leukocytes. This would indicate the uterus was not yet in a completely involuted and normal state. The mare may discharge a slight amount of lochia for about one week postpartum. Involution appears more rapid in primaparous mares than in pluriparous mares. Exercise appears to hasten involution. The rapid involution of the endometrium in the mare and sow is probably related to the simple diffuse placental attachments. Bruner reported that the genital tract of all mares became infected, usually with streptococci, at the time of foaling or within one to three days. In normal mares this infection was overcome soon after the onset of foal heat or about the sixth to tenth day after parturition.

In cows the involution of the uterus has been studied by Rasbech, Benesch, Casida and Venske, Buch and coworkers, Marion and Gier, Morrow and others. Following the expulsion of the fetal membranes in the cow the uterine contractions and peristalsis continue as strong rhythmical waves that gradually diminish through the fourth day. In the cow the uterine muscle cells shortened from 750 microns after parturition to 400 microns one day later. From the fourth to eighth days there are only irregular undulations of the horn, Benesch.

According to Rasbech, Gier and Marion, and Marion and Gier, the maternal placenta involuted by the necrosis of the caruncular stalk due to vasoconstriction, leucocytic infiltration and by the dissolution of the uterine caruncle by fatty infiltration, solution, sloughing and detachment of the entire superficial layer of the caruncle that became part of the uterine lochia. The caruncle and its stalk were necrotic by the fifth day after parturition. The dissolution and sloughing of the caruncle was generally completed by the twelfth day leaving a raw surface with protruding blood vessels where the stalk was attached. The caruncles had returned to nearly their original size by the second or third week. This delayed loss of maternal placental tissue through necrosis would lead to the observation that cattle and sheep are not true nondeciduate species of animals. By about 25 to 30 days postpartum, epithelium covered the caruncles and repair was complete. Thus a 70 gm. caruncle by 48 hours after birth reduced in size and weight to 26 gms. and was quite small 5 days later. Even when the caruncles are nearly normal in size at 30 days postpartum a large vascular bed of vessels remains. These feel rather fibrous and are present for a long period even if the animal does not become pregnant, Marion. Marion and Gier reported that the intercaruncular epithelium may be eroded by bacterial lysis but is normally repaired by 20 days postpartum.

The lochia in the bovine uterus the first 48 hours after parturition was greatest in amount of any period, about 1400 to 1600 ml. By the eighth day postpartum the amount had decreased to 500 ml. and by 14 to 18 days there were only a few ml. of lochia. The amount of lochia discharged from the vulva was variable. Most primipara discharged about 50 ml.. Some primipara discharged almost no lochia but absorbed it from the uterus. Some pluripara discharged from 800 to 2000 ml. of lochia. Usually this discharge of uterine lochia, consisting of mucus, tissue, detritus, and blood, commenced about 3 to 4 days postpartum and increased until the ninth day. The detritus was light yellow-brown to red in color. After the ninth to tenth day postpartum, there was an increased amount of blood mixed with the lochia. This apparently originated from the surface of the caruncles. This bloody lochia usually ceased about the twelfth day. Hyperleukocytosis was found only the first 2 to 3 days postpartum. The process of normal involution took the course of an aseptic process. However, in the examination of apparently normal cows, Rasbech indicated that cattle often contracted a spontaneous puerperal infection causing a massive bacterial growth in the uterine lochia. Elliott et al. reported that 93 percent of bovine uteri were infected from parturition to 15 days postpartum, 78 percent between 16 and 30 days, 50 percent between 31 and 45 days and 9 percent between 45 and 60 days. Lymphocytes were extremely numerous in the endometrium of infected uteri and only moderate in most bacteriologically sterile uteri, Gier et al. (1962). In puerperal cows infections due to **C. pyogenes, E. coli,** staphylococcus, **Pseudomonas aeruginosa,** streptococci, or mixed infections were most commonly cultured. These infections in cows resulted in the lochia assuming a white, yellow-white or grey mucopurulent character toward the latter part of the puerperal period. Tennant et al. reported vaginal exudates of 5 to 200 ml volumes in 30 to 35 percent of all cows examined 10 to 20 days postpartum but only 2 to 5 percent had this volume at 30 to 50 days. These latter cases were probably those with persisting infections.

The involution of the uterus and cervix based on rectal palpation during the postpartum period was reviewed and reported upon by Morrow et al.. The size of the bovine uterus decreased slowly between the fourth and ninth days postpartum. By the tenth day the involuting uterus could be completely defined by rectal examination. A marked decrease in uterine size and an increase in uterine tone occurred from days 10 to 14 coinciding with the onset of the first estrus in normal cows and the voluminous discharge of the uterine lochia. Fluid or lochia could be detected in the uterus by palpation on days 7 to 12 postpartum in many cows. During this period of 10 to 14 days postpartum the size of the postgravid uterine horn declined from 12 cm to 7 cm in diameter. The rate of uterine regression was quite rapid from 14 to 25 days postpartum. There was a decreased rate of involution between days 26 and 39. Between days 40 and 50 there was little change noted. Prior to day 20 postpartum the diameter of the cervix, 4 to 7 or more cm, was smaller than the horn and after days 22 to 25 the cervical diameter, 3 to 4 cm, was greater than the horn diameter, Tennant et al. and Morrow et al.. Marion reported the following postpartum regression in the weight of cows' uteri: 10 Kg at parturition, 5 Kg at 6 days, 2 Kg at 12 days, 1 Kg at 25 days and 0.7 Kg at 50 days. Within 24 to 36 hours after a normal parturition the hand could not be passed through the cervix and by the fourth day postpartum only two fingers could be introduced. If retained placenta was present the rate of closure of the cervix was delayed and the hand could still be inserted at 48 hours and often at 72 hours postpartum. In general the major gross palpable or physical involution of the uterus occurred by 25 to 30 days postpartum. Changes after 30 days were much less marked and more gradual. Morrow summarized nine reports on uterine involution as determined by palpation in which the time for involution varied from 26 to 56 days postpartum with a majority of authors reporting complete regression between 42 and 47 days.

Riesen et al. and Graves et al. demonstrated that during involution the muscle layers decreased in mass both by a decrease in cell size and a loss of cells. Involution was more rapid for suckled animals than for nonsuckled animals from day 1 to day 30 postpartum. Marion et al. showed that ovariectomy and estradiol injections had no effect on uterine involution; while progesterone injections slightly delayed uterine involution. Primparous cows' uteri involuted slightly more rapidly than pluriparous cows'. During the spring and summer months cows' uteri involuted more rapidly than cows calving during the fall or winter months. Cows suffering from periparturient diseases such as retention of the afterbirth had a slightly slower rate of uterine involution. These authors citing Singh reported that the normally regressing uterus did not become histologically normal until 50 to 60 days postpartum or about 20 days after the uterus had returned to a clinically normal or involuted state. Following a retained placenta leucocytic infiltrations occurred in large numbers and remained for 20 to 30 days beyond the normal histologic involution in normal parturition or until about 70 to 90 days postpartum. Corpora albicantia replacing the corpora lutea of pregnancy usually are larger, containing more connective tissue, than are corpora albicantia replacing corpora lutea that were active for only a short period of time. In some cows these may persist for a number of years. In nearly 20 percent of the cattle, resorption of the corpora albicantia occurred after the fourth pregnancy, Dawson.

In the bitch the uterine horns are back to nearly normal size in 4 to 5 weeks. But as late as 3 months after parturition, when the uterus is the size and appearance of the normal diestrous uterus, slight pigmented ring-shaped stripes may be observed in the endometrium indicating the former placentation sites. The bitch discharges much dark, mucoid, green lochia after parturition. According to Flexner and his associates this green pigment is uteroverdin and comes from the "green border" of the placenta. This color is produced by the breakdown of hemoglobin. This decomposition product is the same as bilirubin and biliverdin. In the cat the placental border is brown. The first week the lochia is amber to red in color and by the second week it should be normal, clear mucus. The walls of the gravid horn remain slightly thickened. In primipara and other young animals the uterus never returns to its pregravid size.

The rate of involution in the other animals is not as well known but Benesch indicated that in sows a lochial discharge may be observed for about a week and involution of the uterus was fairly rapid. Uren reported that the uterine mucosa of the ewe was completely involuted by 30 days after parturition and he described the process in detail. McEntee reported the uterine weight of postpartum ovine uteri as 700 gms at 3 days, 200 to 250 gms at 7 days, 60 gms at 21 days, and 30 gms at 35 days.

Artificial Interference in Normal Parturition

If parturition is a normal one there is no need or necessity for outside aid by attendants. Such aid is ill-advised. In the artificial environment under which many domestic animals are kept certain sanitary and preventive precautions may be necessary. Valuable animals should be observed during the act of parturition so that injury to the newborn is not caused by the dam or the surroundings, such as a mare or cow trying to give birth with its rear quarters wedged into a corner of a box stall. The afterbirth of ruminants should be removed after its expulsion so that the dam will not eat it or choke on it. If the dam becomes excited after parturition, or for some other reason attacks the newborn, they should be separated from the dam. This condition is seen occasionally in the sow and in rare cases in the dog, in which the dam kills and even eats her young. The young cow may rarely attack her newborn offspring. Upon arising and feeling the placenta against her hocks, the mare may become excited, kick, and possibly injure the foal. Occasionally in young mares, heifers, gilts, and ewes the udder may be so sensitive, edematous, and sore that they will not allow the newborn to nurse. In these cases the dam must be restrained or given a sedative or tranquilizer to allow the newborn to suckle. If the cow or mare gave birth in a box stall, the wet, contaminated straw should be removed and replaced with clean, dry straw. If parturition took place in an unsanitary environment the navel requires disinfection. It is desirable to have a comfortable, quiet, isolated, sanitary place in which the animal can give birth. The dam and the newborn should be left alone unless the course of parturition is definitely abnormal. Close observation and knowledge of the normal course of parturition is necessary. If the first stage of parturition in the cow and ewe is over 6 to 12 hours, in the mare over 4 hours, in the bitch and sow over 6 to 12 hours; or if the second stage of parturition in the cow or ewe is over 2 to 3 hours, in the mare over 20 to 30 minutes, in the cow and bitch is over 6 to 12 hours, outside help is indicated. If at anytime the normal progression of the fetus(es) into and through the birth canal fails, assistance is usually needed. This should be obtained at once if severe injury to the dam or death of the fetuses is to be prevented. This aid to the dam is indicated if the frequency or intensity of abdominal contractions declines before the birth of the young or if the feet of the fetus in unipara appear and disappear with each labor contraction without progress in the passage of the fetus. In posterior presentation in primiparous dams, outside traction may be desirable to avoid asphyxiation of the newborn. The help or assistance provided at parturition should be competent and experienced.

During the act of parturition it is not desirable or necessary to rupture the fetal membranes, either the amnion or allantois. It is not desirable to apply traction in physiological birth when the fetus first appears at the vulva.Such traction is likely to result in laceration and trauma of the dorsal commissure of the vulva or the perineum. Traction if applied too early before the cervix, vagina, or vulva is fully dilated, pulls these structures caudally and makes the lumen or diameter of the birth canal smaller, requiring trauma or rupture of the structures if birth is to be accomplished with traction. Williams stated, "In an experience exceeding 60 years I do not recall vulvar or perineal laceration in physiological birth in a domestic animal when not tampered with by attendants." There is no indication for or advantage to the administration of pituitrin before or after normal parturition. The umbilical cord should be allowed to break of its own accord in the mare. In the cat and bitch the dam usually bites it off or it breaks off naturally by traction. Ligation of the umbilical cord in animals is usually unnecessary and frequently predisposes to umbilical infection.

Care of the Newborn and the Dam

At the time of the birth of the young especially in the mare, an attendant should be present to remove the amnion that may be wrapped around the muzzle and nose and cause asphyxiation. The onset of fetal respiration may begin before the fetus is completely expelled in some parturitions, especially those that are delayed. In normal parturitions respiratory movements in the fetus are initiated by several deep inspirations about 10 to 60 seconds after expulsion. In the foal this will often occur before the umbilical cord has ruptured. It is believed that either a rise in the CO_2 levels in the fetal blood, Barcroft, an increased hydrostatic pressure in the fetal vessels when the cord ruptures or when the fetus lies below the level of the dam, removal of the amnion from over the nostrils, or a combination of these factors initiates breathing in the newborn. If respiration in the newborn is delayed various procedures should be used to stimulate this activity. The mucus should be removed from the nose and mouth. The newborn should be laid on its side on straw, not loose chaff or shavings that might be inhaled, with the head and fore quarters slightly lower than the hind quarters. Vigorous rubbing of the newborn with a burlap bag, or shaking its head, or tickling its nostrils, will help bring about respiratory activity. The use of an oxygen tank and an attached short rubber tube has proven useful in saving some weak newborn. The tube is passed into the pharynx and the nostrils and mouth are closed tightly. Oxygen under moderate pressure distends the lungs. Opening the nostrils and pressure on the chest collapses the lungs and the process is repeated as often as necessary. A warm oxygen tent or chamber may help save some weak pups or kittens. In recent years several simple resuscitators with attachments for an oxygen tank are commercially available. These actively remove excess mucus from the lungs and provide oxygen. Other practices, such as artificial respiration, aromatic spirits applied to the nostrils or mouth, injections of adrenaline or cardiac and respiratory stimulants such as "Coramine," "Metrazol," and "Picrotoxin" into the heart, since intravenous administration is difficult and slow, have not proved very satisfactory or saved many weak newborn animals. Electrocardiographic studies showed a rapid rise in the heart rate occurred at birth, from 54 to 60 to 108 to 216 beats per minute in the equine newborn and from 72 to 108 to 96 to 120 per minute in the newborn calf, Too et al.. Some veterinarians advocate dipping the pup or kitten in cold then hot water to stimulate respiration. Other workers advise holding the young up by their hind legs to aid cleaning mucus from the larger bronchi, throat, and nose. If this is done in the newborn calf a copious flow of mucus is often passed from the nose and mouth. Most of this mucus obviously must come from the stomach. It has been observed by the author that in the handling of nearly all newborn which at expulsion are so weak that respirations do not begin normally within 1 to 2 minutes, any treatment of a drastic nature is often unsuccessful, although such efforts are usually indicated and are appreciated by the owner.

Umbilical disinfection is not necessary if births occur on clean pasture. The licking of the navel and the absence of barn or barnyard infections usually ensure the rapid and normal healing of the newborn's umbilicus. If parturitions take place in a barn or barnyard, particularly if navel infections are prevalent on the farm, careful disinfection of the navel may help prevent the disease. It is doubtful if a hasty, careless application of a disinfectant or antiseptic to the navel would be of any value. To be effective an antiseptic should be carefully applied 1 to 3 times daily for the first 2 to 3 days following birth. Tincture of iodine, 1:1000 solution of alcoholic sublimate, 5 percent tannic and 5 percent salicylic acid in 70 percent alcohol, 10,000 ppm neutral iodophor solution, 40,000 to 50,000 ppm sodium hypochlorite solution with a very low hydroxide content, or any similar antiseptic, may be applied by carefully soaking the navel stump and squeezing it with cotton soaked in the antiseptic. Some prefer to use a powdered astringent such as alum or tannic acid and an antiseptic. This is carefully dusted on the navel stump to hasten dessication. In foals it is often advisable to administer a prophylactic dose of tetanus antitoxin. O'Dea reported on two foals that developed tetanus even though the dam received a booster injection of tetanus toxoid during pregnancy. A contributing factor may have been that both mares leaked milk for a week before parturition. In a valuable newborn, antibiotics such as penicillin, streptomycin, terramycin or aureomycin may be administered for several days to prevent navel infection or septicemia. Clean, sanitary, well-bedded stalls for the calf and parturient cow help greatly in preventing navel infections. On farms or ranches where large numbers of females give birth in a confined area sanitation practices and facilities are highly important to prevent navel infections, infectious diseases of the newborn as well as retained placenta, metritis and mastitis in the dam. If young calves are placed together they may lick the umbilical stumps and cause navel infection. In areas or countries with the screw worm, **Cochlyomyia americana,** infestation during the warm seasons, it may be necessary to treat the navels of newborn animals with Smear 62 or a similar product to prevent screwworm infestation of the navel stump.

The newborn should nurse and thus get the colostrum within 1 or 2 hours after birth. From birth to suckling averaged 111 minutes, range 35 to 420, in the foal and an average of 10 to 35 minutes, range 3 to 153, in the pig, Rossdale, and Jones. In the sow this may be slightly delayed if the pigs are removed as they are born—to prevent their injury by the sow—and returned after parturition is completed. Fructose is the principal sugar in fetal blood and placental fluids of certain species such as sheep and swine. Apparently the placenta converts glucose to fructose. There is little evidence that fructose is used for the early energy needs of newborn pigs as it is largely excreted in the urine within two days after birth, Aherne et al.. The great importance of globulins in the colostrum, which are only absorbed from the gut 12 to 36 hours after birth by the newborn animal, has been discussed under placental transfer of immunity. This does not occur in domestic animals except to a slight degree in the dog and cat, Harding et al.. Under highly unsanitary or infected environmental conditions, it is desirable to get colostrum into the newborn promptly, within 15 to 30 minutes after birth. If necessary this may be given by stomach tube. The amount of colostral antibodies absorbed and available to the newborn is in direct proportion to their levels in the colostrum and the amount of colostrum consumed within a few hours after parturition. Premilking in cows, sometimes practiced to avoid severe edema of the udder, may reduce the immune globulins available to the newborn calf because of their dilution in large quantities of milk stimulated by this practice. Larson has shown that the transfer of globulins from the blood to the milk starts about one month before calving but reaches a peak just before parturition. Besides the important immune bodies absorbed from the colostrum by the intestines during the first 24 to 36 hours of life there are laxative properties in the colostrum. In the cow the colostrum is about five times as high in protein, two times as high in fat and minerals, ten times as high in iron as ordinary milk. In the newborn lamb this first feeding of colostrum is essential to getting it on its feet, and making it strong and active. Clipping of the udder in heavily fleeced ewes may aid the lambs to find the teats and nurse promptly. If for some reason colostrum is not available, another source may be indicated. Colostrum may be frozen and stored for such emergencies. The amount of immunoglobulins absorbed from the colostrum is directly related to the susceptibility of the newborn to the neonatal diseases of scours, septicemia and pneumonia. House has shown that in 300 baby calves purchased at auctions that deaths occurred in 16 percent of calves with 1 to 6 percent of the serum protein formed by gamma globulins while only 1 percent deaths occurred in calves with 19 to 46 percent gamma globulins in their total serum protein fraction. House has devised a simple field test where 10 ml. of 22.5 percent ammonium sulphate solution is added to 0.5 ml. of calf serum. The degree of turbidity developing in one-half hour as measured against barium sulphate standards indicates the level of gamma globulins present in the calf's blood. If colostrum is not available a transfusion of dam's blood or blood from an animal of the same species is indicated to provide the necessary antibodies. Dam's blood should not be used in newborn where hemolytic diseases are suspected. In large animals 200 to 500 ml. of blood or serum is usually administered subcutaneously, as large amounts of fluids are difficult to inject intravenously and the process frequently causes violent struggling in the newborn. In the smaller animals 20 to 100 ml. of blood or serum may be given.

The use of the antibiotics, such as penicillin, streptomucin, aureomycin or terramycin parenterally and orally, have been of further help in bringing these animals lacking immune bodies through the first critical week or so of postnatal life. The newborn of animals except dairy cows and goats suckle the dam until weaned. In the sow each pig selects its own teat, the stronger often getting the better mammary gland, so that in a week or two there are only as many functioning glands as there are pigs. This teat preference occurs in kittens but not in pups, Fox. The other glands, that are not being suckled, involute. In uniparous animals the young suck all teats. There are many methods of managing the newborn calf to prevent digestive upsets or diarrhea, after he has suckled the dam for the first 12 to 24 hours.

The Problem of Handling and Feeding of Orphan Animals is occasionally presented to the veterinarian when the dam dies at parturition or fails to give sufficient milk. It is well known that the young of a species thrives best on milk of its own kind. Therefore having the orphan adopted by another postparturient female of the same species is indicated. This is fairly easy and can often be done in all domestic animals when such an animal is available. Occasionally it is necessary in the sow to make the young smell like the foster dam's offspring by rubbing her fetal membranes or genital discharges over the orphan, or sprinkling the entire litter of orphans and sow with a material having a similar strong odor such as a weak cresol solution or an aerosol deodorant. In sheep it is a common practice to cover the orphan with the hide of the dead offspring or the wool of the ewe that is to be its foster mother. In the large animals, as in cows, the foster mother usually adopts the orphan fairly promptly but occasionally she may have to be restrained for a number of times to permit feeding. In the dog most postparturient bitches will readily adopt the newborn of another. The problem is more difficult when a foster mother is not available. All domestic animals can be raised with proper care and attention by artificial nursing and feeding.

In calves the problem is simple, since cow's milk is nearly universally available. In the other animals the problem can be solved to a great extent by referring to Table 8 on the composition of the milk from the various animals. From this table it is noted that milk of the ewe, goat, and cow are nearly similar in composition. The milk of the sow is richer in fat. Mare's milk is similar in composition to human milk and foals therefore thrive on formulas for human babies. After foals are several months of age, cow's milk might be satisfactory; but younger foals may develop a stubborn diarrhea when fed cow's milk, Rice and Andrews. Pigs, pups and possibly kittens may be raised on rich cow's milk, evaporated milk, or prepared formulas. Presently there are fortified powdered milk products for foals, "Foal-lac,"* for pups, "Esbilac,"* and for pigs, "SPF-Lac."* These are mixed with the proper amounts of warm water and fed as are the synthetic or formulated starters for calves. The milk should be warm and fresh. The newborn animal should be fed every 1 to 3 hours for the first week or so and then every 4 or 12 hours thereafter. The amount of milk fed daily to the young of cattle, horses, sheep, goats, and swine should be about 10 percent of the body weight, divided into the aforementioned number of feedings. In dogs and cats the feeding of orphan young is discussed in Chapter 9 following cesarean section in the bitch. All animals can be fed by nipple bottle with either calf, lamb, human, or doll nipples. At an early age most animals except lambs usually may be taught to drink milk from a shallow pan or bucket. This makes raising them easier. If symptoms of diarrhea develop, the amount of milk should be reduced markedly for 24 to 48 hours and oral and parenteral antibiotic therapy should be instituted. In some cases one may increase the amount of milk gradually to more than 10 percent of the body weight after the first week or so of age. It is hard to starve a young animal, but easy to overfeed it. Orphan pigs may be reared on special commercial pig starters or formulas containing antibiotics.

The orphan young should be encouraged to eat solid food as early as possible so that the amount and frequency of milk feeding can be reduced. In general for the first 1 to 2 months of life the orphan young will not appear as well nourished as animals that are not orphans, and will more often have digestive disturbances. Care and nursing are of utmost importance in the proper rearing of orphan young on artificial diets; otherwise artificial feeding is not particularly difficult. If diarrheas develop they can be controlled by reducing the feed intake and by the administration of streptomycin, neomycin, tetracycline derivatives or other antibiotics orally. In some cases the addition of vitamins, especially A and D, may be necessary or advisable. In pigs, iron may be provided by injections of an iron dextran product intramuscularly, or clean soil supplied to prevent anemia.

A Persistent Urachus is invariable seen with infection of the navel either as a cause or a result of an open urachus. This condition is seen most commonly in the newborn foal and rarely in cattle. Since it is often followed by pyemia, septicemia, and navel or joint ill, the condition should be viewed seriously. Penicillin and streptomycin, terramycin, aureomycin or tetracycline administered over a period of about a week or 10 days is indicated together with local treatment of the navel with antibiotics or sulfonamides. If, after several days, the urine continues to flow through the urachus keeping the navel and the surrounding skin moist, the lower 4 to 5 inches of the urachus should be cauterized with a small swab containing Lugols' solution or the instillation of about 2 to 5 ml. of 5 to 10 percent formalin solution. This or similar treatments will swell and close the urachus.

Retained Meconium—In the newborn foal the meconium in the rectum may be found in hard pellets from 1/2 to 2-1/2 inches in diameter that within 24 or 36 hours after birth become impacted just cranial to the bony pelvis. The condition is seen more often in colts than in fillies. The diameter of the bony pelvis is very small in the newborn foal. The affected foal usually nurses normally but within 24 to 48 hours after birth exhibits symptoms of colic and persistent to intermittent straining, frequently getting up and lying down, elevating the tail and assuming a straddled attitude similar to that assumed during defecation. Colicy symptoms may become more severe, and anorexia occur. Impaction may be confirmed by inserting a lubricated finger into the rectum and palpating the mass of hard pellets of meconium. This disease is rather common in foals, and for that reason many veterinarians recommend that all newborn foals be given an enema soon after birth. This enema may be of physiological saline, mineral oil, olive oil, caster oil, mild soap and water, or several ounces of glycerin in a pint of soapy

*Borden Milk Co., 350 Madison Avenue, N.Y.C.

water; the author has found the commercial obstetrical lubricants like "Lubrivet" very satisfactory and non-irritating. About 4 to 8 ounces are introduced at a time through a soft rubber horse catheter. This may be repeated as often as necessary. In cases of impaction of meconium with colicy symptoms this may have to be repeated frequently at intervals of 10 to 30 minutes until the condition is relieved. Oral administration of laxatives such as castor oil, or the injection of "Lentin," is not usually indicated as the fecal material in the rectum and small colon behind the hard meconial pellets is soft. Gentle, persistent treatment usually results in recovery. Heroic or drastic treatment with a looped wire or forceps is seldom necessary.

Rupture of the Bladder may occur in rare instances in the newborn foal. This probably occurs due to a full bladder especially in male foals at parturition or when the navel cord is ruptured. According to McGee and DuPlessis the foal appears normal for 12 to 24 hours; but by the second to fourth day the foal is depressed, pulse and respirations are increased, and the abdomen is slightly to markedly distended. Tapping the abdominal cavity with a needle in a sterile manner will release the urine and confirm the diagnosis. Laparotomy on the midline, and suturing of the ruptured bladder is indicated. Supportive and antibiotic therapy with good nursing often results in a successful termination.

Many Congenital or Heredity Conditions such as atresia ani, cleft palate, edema, undershot jaw, contracted tendons, blindness, cerebellar hypoplasia, and others may affect newborn animals. (See Chapter III). Some of these defects such as umbilical and scrotal hernias and cryptorchidism noted at birth may spontaneously recover within a few weeks to months. The observation and study of anomalies in the newborn is interesting. It may be of value to the owner, if the condition has occurred several times in a herd, to check carefully for inbreeding and a hereditary recessive factor causing the condition. If the veterinarian is acquainted with the reported hereditary defects or anomalies in the newborn he may be able to advise his client properly even though only one defective individual has been produced. If the defects or anomalies are recognized early, treatment is possible in some; but in others slaughter must be recommended. Many anomalies or defects are observable at birth or cause noticeable symptoms to develop within several days after birth. Others may not be diagnosed for months or years.

Infections of the Newborn Contracted in Utero are rather uncommon compared to the infections contracted after parturition due to contact with virulent organisms in the outside environment. Many diseases of the newborn such as various septicemias, enteritis, pneumonia, and others may develop shortly after birth. Williams indicated that a few of these diseases may be contracted **in utero** or in the birth canal at parturition. Probably most of them are contracted after birth from infected surroundings either through the raw umbilical or navel area, by ingestion or by inhalation. Many diseases of the newborn are favored by improper nutrition, management and housing facilities. The numerous infectious, managerial and nutritional problems affecting the newborn will not be discussed in this text inasmuch as they are not directly associated with parturition or gestation.

Relatively few of the organisms known to cause placental and fetal disease with abortion commonly cause septicemia of the newborn. Many of the organisms mentioned under causes for abortion may be present occasionally in fetuses born at term and cause their early or delayed death.

In cattle these include **Brucella abortus, Leptospira spp., Listeria monocytogenes, E. coli, Streptococci, Toxoplasma gondii, Aspergillus spp.,** and **Salmonella spp.** Antibody titers for brucella, leptospira and BVD-MD virus in the serum of newborn calves that have never suekled have been reported. This indicates a prenatal exposure and response by the fetus to these organisms whether the organisms can or cannot be recovered from the fetus after birth. There is evidence, reviewed by Kopecky et al. that **Mycobacterium paratuberculosis** may be transferred **in utero** from an infected cow to its fetus and be carried into the postnatal period.

In horses the fetal infections contracted **in utero** causing abortion, as well as early neonatal deaths after premature or term births, include: **Streptococcus zooepidemicus** or **genitalium, E. coli, Actinobacillus** or **Shigella equuli, Leptospira** spp, **Salmonella abortus equi,** and rhinopneumonitis or Herpes I virus. It may be difficult to determine in some infections, such as the first two, whether the fetus was infected before birth, during birth or whether the foal became infected soon after birth. If the newborn animals are visibly ill at the time birth or within a few hours then the infection was probably prenatal especially if retained placenta or metritis develops in the mare. Only 7 of 3,346 aborted fetuses yielded **Actinobacillus equuli** on culture but if postnatal death occurred within 24 hours of birth the **Actinobacillus** infection probably occurred prenatally, Rooney, Bain. Intrauterine infection of fetuses with equine infectious anemia virus has been suggested but not proven, Dreguss and Lombard.

In swine prenatal infections that may cause neonatal infections or death include: **Leptospira spp, E. coli,** hog cholera virus, Emerson and Delez, Carbrey et al., **Toxoplasma gondii** Sanger and Cole, and **Eperythrozoon**

suis (?), Berrier and Gouge. Newborn pigs may become chronic carriers of the last three organisms. Tweihaus was unable to demonstrate that **Eperythrozoon suis** was transmitted to porcine fetuses from infected sows.

In sheep and goats intrauterine infections that may be present in newborn lambs include: **Vibrio fetus** var **intestinalis, Brucella melitensis, Salmonella** spp., **E. coli,** enzootic abortion virus or **Chlamydia, Toxoplasma gondii** and **Mycobacterium johnei.** Tamarin and Landau. The latter organism is not a cause for abortion in sheep.

In dogs and cats neonatal infections of pups and kittens that may be contracted **in utero** include: **Streptococci** spp., **Staphylococci** spp., **E. coli, Pseudomonas aeruginosa,** Kirk and Mosier et al., canine herpes virus infection or "fading pup syndrome," Carmichael et al. and Cornwell and Wright, feline panleukopenia virus, Kilham et al., distemper virus and **Toxoplasma gondii.** The latter protozoal infection of prenatal fetuses has been reviewed in dogs and cats as well as in swine, sheep and cattle by Sanger and Cole, Siim and Biering—Sorensen and Eckerling et al..

Parasites Transmitted in utero from the Dam to the Fetus include:

In horses—**Strongylus vulgaris larvae,** Bruner. This is very rare as Rooney had never seen a case. A verminous aneurysm in a 2 day-old fetus was infected with **Actinobacillus equuli. Babesia caballi,** Tsur and Krieger. Lyons et al. have reported that **Strongyloides westeri** larvae may be transmitted to the foal in the dam's milk as early as 5 days after parturition. As noted below strongyloides in swine and hookworm and ascarid larvae in dogs may be transmitted to the newborn in the colostrum.

In cattle—**Neoascaris vitulorum,** Refuerzo and Jimenez; **Theileria annulata,** Tsur and Krieger, **Anaplasma marginali** (?), Tsur and Krieger; and **Cysticercus bovis,** McManus.

In swine—**Strongyloides ransomi** and **Stephanurus dentatus** or swine kidney worm, Batte et al., Stewart et al.. Although a few reports indicated that **Ascaris suis** infection of fetuses may occur, several studies including that of Olson and Gaafar proved that this does not occur.

In dogs—**Toxocara canis,** Koutz et al., Douglas and Baker; **Ancylostoma caninum,** Adler and Clark; and **Dirofilaria immitis,** Mantovani and Jackson. **Demodex canis** infection of pups probably occurs the first few hours of life as there was no evidence it was acquired **in utero,** Greve and Gaafar. Griesemer and Gibson have described a difficult therapeutic regimen used to obtain ascarid-free pups. This regimen included rearing pups without colostrum and in isolation and treating the pups daily or 2 to 3 times a week with diethylcarbamazine citrate for up to 19 months. There is presently no treatment to prevent **Toxocara** larvae from migrating from the dam to the fetus during pregnancy.

Neonatal Isoerythrolysis, or Hemolytic Icterus of the Newborn, has been described in the horse, pig, and dog. In 1948 Bruner, Hull, Edwards and Doll described this condition in foals. Since then they and their co-workers have done much to clarify the causative factors and describe methods of diagnosis and treatment. Cronin also has presented an excellent report on this disease. He reported an incidence of 1 percent affected mares in the New Market area in England. Neonatal isoerythrolysis of foals occurs when mares become isoimmunized to certain types of erythrocytes either through (1) placental breakdown and absorption of the antigens from placental tissue or fetal blood at previous gestation periods or (2) by transfusions of blood or (3) injection of fetal tissue vaccines. When these mares are bred to stallions which transmit to the fetus the type of erythrocyte to which the mare was previously immunized the disease develops. The icteric condition occurs when the apparently normal foal suckles and receives in the dam's colostrum large amounts of antibodies composed of hemagglutinins and hemolysins. Hemolytic icterus has very rarely been observed in foals from primiparous mares. It is usually not observed in foals until the mare's third or fourth parturition. Although most mares apparently become sensitized from the placenta of their foals, Doll and his co-workers showed that equine-fetal-tissue vaccine such as was used for vaccination against virus abortion may cause certain mares to be immunized to the erythrocytes in the vaccine. Since vaccines prepared from equine tissues are not now used the incidence of neonatal isoerythrolysis has declined. Neonatal isoerythrolysis in foals is apparently not due to an Rh-like factor as in humans but is probably caused by an isoimmunization of pregnancy due to intraspecies blood group factors.

The symptoms, which may resemble foal septicemia, usually develop rapidly after the foal begins nursing, with mild to severe clinical symptoms occurring from 12 to 96 hours after birth. These include: somnolence; anorexia due to weakness; usually no rise in body temperature; increased pulse and respiration rate; slight to marked jaundice and anemia; and in severe cases prostration and hemoglobinuria. Cronin reported that foals which die rapidly have little icterus but an acute anemia. Foals that die of this disease after several days of illness usually show icterus and have severe liver and kidney damage. Icterus is also seen in foals that do not show illness until several days after birth. Hemoglobinuria and hemoglobinemia are unusual symptoms. The red blood cell count drops from a normal of 10 to 12 million, down to as low as 2 to 3 million in the most severe cases. In severe cases the death of the foal may result in 24 hours or less. In slight or mild cases where the amount of antibody from the ingested colostrum is minimal, recovery may occur without treatment. The condition should be carefully differentiated from septicemia of the newborn usually characterized by elevation of temperature, injection and congestion of the conjunctiva with icterus being absent or slight. Cases of septicemia, if treated fairly early, usually respond to treatment with penicillin and streptomycin or terramycin, aureomycin or tetracycline given parenterally or intravenously, while cases of neonatal icterus do not respond to antibiotic therapy. The red blood cell count does not fall below 5 to 6 million in septicemia of the newborn.

The laboratory diagnosis was described by Bruner. The technique of testing the blood of mares and their foals, and stallions to which the mare was to be bred is relatively simple with proper equipment such as a centrifuge and microscope. In agglutination tests, using the serum of mares and a 50 percent suspension of carefully washed red cells of the foal or his sire, if the serum titer of the mare is no higher than 1:2 and the colostrum titer no higher than 1:4, the foal may safely nurse its dam. If the serum titer of the mare is 1:4 or the colostrum titer 1:8 the foal is likely to develop icterus and may or may not recover without treatment. If the serum titer in the mare is higher than 1:4 or the colostrum titer is 1:16 or higher it would be dangerous for the foal to nurse its dam. The development of an hemolysin titer of 1:10 or more is apparently necessary to produce marked symptoms of the disease. The serum of sensitized mares may be tested against the red blood cells of a stallion and if a titer of 1:2 or less occurs the mare may safely be mated with that stallion. The prognosis in hemolytic icterus depends upon how early the condition is diagnosed and the promptness with which treatment is instituted. Advanced severe cases often die.

The treatment of clinical cases consists of promptly removing the foal from the mare or muzzling it. If symptoms are mild and the condition was not noted until the third to fifth day following foaling, treatment is unnecessary. In severe cases several blood donors should be obtained and the blood of the dam and foal tested against various donors' blood. If they are compatible, a large blood transfusion of 1500 to 2000 cc. of blood or more should be given the affected foal by injecting the blood into one jugular vein and removing an equal amount from the other by means of a 14-gauge needle. Occasionally another 500 to 1500 cc. of blood may be given the next day. In less severe cases 500 ml of blood may be transfused once or twice daily to carry the foal through the critical period of the disease which usually lasts only one to three days. Cronin stated that transfusions are usually necessary when the symptoms of the disease are exhibited within 24 hours of birth; when the foal is weak and unable to stand; and when the red blood cell number drops below 4,000,000 per cmm. or 8 gm. of hemoglobin per 100 cc. of blood. Cronin recommended that 7000 cc. of blood be transfused in a large exchange transfusion in severe or critical cases. If this was done the average foal would then have only 15 percent of its original blood and 6 percent of its original erythrocytes. In practice this is often not possible and usually only about 50 percent of the foal's original blood is removed. Cronin reported the blood volume of horses and foals to be 8.11 to 9.7 percent of the body weight or in the average foal about 4000 to 6000 cc. He advised the administration of antibiotics and confinement to prevent excessive exercise. The foal's dam should never be used as a blood donor.

The dam should be milked out frequently by hand or by allowing another older foal to nurse her. Bruner, Doll Hull and Kincaid reported that the newborn foal could absorb antibodies from its digestive tract for only about 36 hours after birth. It had been shown in earlier work that the first colostrum had the highest titer and that this titer dropped rapidly in 12 to 18 hours with frequent milking even though slight amounts were secreted for several weeks postpartum. Most authors reported that after 48 hours postpartum it is safe to allow the foal to nurse if the mare has been milked out frequently.

This disease in foals can usually be prevented if the sensitized mare is recognized because of having previously produced an icteric foal, or by testing the mare's serum against the red cells of the stallion to which it is to be bred. A positive test indicates that the disease will probably occur. A negative test is not significant as the mare may have become sensitized during pregnancy to the stallion's red cells. A better procedure, recommended by Cronin, is to test the mare's serum against the stallion's red cells the last month, or preferredly the last week, of pregnancy. Even if the stallion's blood is compatible with the mare's serum when tested before breeding, the foals of sensitized or isoimmunized mares should not be allowed to nurse until its red blood cells are tested with the mare's colostrum or serum. This is the most practical test. This may be done by immediately muzzling the newborn foal until the test is completed. If the foal's erythrocytes agglutinate in a 1:4 dilution or higher with the dam's serum or 1:8 or higher with the dam's colostrum, the foal should be fed either "Foal-lac," a human baby milk formula, low-fat cow's milk to which some sugar syrup and possibly lime water have been added or the foal may be placed on another mare for several days. On the larger farms banks of frozen colostrum permit the foal to be provided needed colostrum after first crossmatching the red blood cells of the foal and the milk. These foals should be given prophylactic treatment with penicillin and streptomycin or the other antibiotics for 4 to 6 days. The dam should be milked out thoroughly at frequent intervals by hand or by an older foal. After 48 hours the dam's foal may be unmuzzled and allowed to suckle. Some veterinarians prefer to give the foal 500 cc. of compatible donor's serum to replace the antibodies lost to the foal by not nursing its dam the first 48 hours after birth. In the convalescent period injections of iron dextran intramuscularly may aid recovery. Once a mare produces a foal affected with neonatal isoerythrolysis, subsequent foals are apt to be affected especially if the mare is bred to the same stallion. Recent further reviews on hemolytic icterus in foals have been published by Doll (1963), Roberts and Archer (1966) and Jeffcott (1969).

A similar condition has been described in dogs previously immunized by blood transfusions, Swisher and Young, Wright, and Fluharty. Natural isoimmunization of the bitch during pregnancy is apparently rare. Although there are 7 blood types, A through G in the dog, only A is of significance in regard to incompatibility. In blood transfusions especially in breeding females, only A negative donors should be used to avoid producing hemolytic disease in the pups after nursing. Leakage of blood from affected pups during parturition and subsequent uterine absorbtion may be one way of sensitizing the bitch, Fluharty. The signs of hemolytic anemia in affected pups are similar to those in foals. Most severely affected pups die within 72 hours of birth. Not all pups in a litter are usually affected, only those with type A positive blood. Treatment involves withdrawing 10 to 15 ml of blood from the jugular vein of affected pups and replacing it with a similar amount of A negative blood. In affected bitches the pups should be fed formula and not be allowed to nurse the bitch for 36 hours after birth. After this period their gut will not absorb the antibodies present in the colostrum and they may be returned to their dam for nursing, Kirk, Sheffy.

Neonatal isoerythrolysis also occurs in pigs from 1 to 7 days after farrowing. Bruner and co-workers first reported on this condition in swine. Similar signs to that in foals and pups of weakness, depression, paleness of mucous membranes, anemia, icterus, prostration and occasionally hemoglobinuria are noted in some pigs, but not all, in a litter. As in dogs this condition may only rarely occur naturally. Most porcine cases have been due to vaccination of sows with crystal violet or swine tissue vaccines against hog cholera. In a few cases mildly affected pigs recover without treatment. Andresen et al. reported on producing this disease by the injection of the anti-Ba blood group and indicated that in swine probably several blood group antibodies can cause the condition. Other excellent reports on this disease in swine have been published by Buxton et al. and Meyer et al.. Hemolytic disease of the newborn has not been described in cattle, sheep and cats.

An excellent review of blood groups in the larger domestic animals and their relationship to hemolytic disease of the newborn were published in 1962 by Stormont et al..

Nutritional deficiencies causing disease in the newborn animals include: (1) copper deficiency causing enzootic ataxia, swayback of demyelinating encephalopathy in lambs in Colorado, Peru, Australia, New Zealand and Great Britain. This is characterized by a progressive locomotor incoordination and partial or complete paralysis. Feeding additional, minute amounts of copper sulphate to the pregnant ewes prevents this condition, Jensen et al..

(2) Iodine deficiency or excess causing enlargement of the thyroid glands or goiter is most frequently observed in foals. This may be prevented by feeding iodized salt and by avoiding the excessive feeding of iodides especially in the form of seaweed, Baker and Lindsey.

(3) Selenium deficiency causes congenital white muscle disease or myopathy in newborn lambs in New Zealand and other countries, Hartley and Grant, Hartley and Dodd. This condition has also been described in dogs, Manktelow, and calves, Kradel. Myocardial degeneration and degeneration of skeletal muscles, especially of the neck, are causes for weakness, inability to nurse and early death.

(4) Vitamin A deficiency causes increased susceptibility for infectious diseases. This may occur rarely in newborn animals whose dams have been on a vitamin A deficient diet for many months. The teratogenic effects of vitamin A deficiency on fetal development have been described previously.

Neoplasms of newborn animals are rare and have been summarized by Misdorp. Tumors of the skin included papillomas of horse fetuses, and subcutaneous melanomas, a subcutaneous mixed tumor and a subcutaneous lymphangioma in bovine fetuses. Abdominal tumors included mesotheliomas of the peritoneum, a sublumbar lipoma and a retroperitoneal chondrosarcoma in bovine fetuses. As in adult animals, mesotheliomas of the abdominal cavity produced ascites and resulted in dystocia that was relieved by caesarian section. Neoplasms of the gonads included adenomas of the testicles and granulosa cell tumors of the ovary of bovine fetuses, Kanagawa et al.. Congenital lymphoid leucosis often with skin involvement has been reported most often in bovine fetuses and newborn calves, and occasionally in a newborn piglet and a feline fetus, Tanzer. Other tumors included reticulosarcomatosis, carcinomatosis originating in the liver, nephroblastomas, a fibrosarcoma, Cowie, and teratomas. It is interesting to note the relatively high incidence of congenital leucosis reported in fetuses in cattle and cats in light of recent findings indicating these may be caused by a virus passed "vertically" from the dam to the fetus, Rickard. In most cases the dams of affected fetuses were normal. The actual mechanism of this vertical transfer of the disease may be a virus, an incomplete virus, or genetic information on the formation of viruses. Cat lymphocytic tumor viruses may be transmitted readily if inoculated into one to three-day-old kittens.

Miscellaneous diseases or causes of death of newborn animals include:

Persistent bleeding from the navel stump. This occurred more often when the cord was cut with a sharp instrument instead of being broken by traction. If ligation of the cord is necessary to prevent excessive bleeding then the newborn should be placed on parenteral antibiotics for 3 to 7 days and the ligature removed in 24 to 48 hours. Repeated disinfection is indicated. Fraser and Nelson have reported a hemorrhagic disease of calves where the dams were normal but had been fed sweet clover hay during the gestation period. Four newborn male and female calves from one dam bled severely from the navel after birth. Three of the calves died but one survived after repeated transfusions. These calves suffered from a multiple coagulation defect of their blood. A possible hereditary nonsex-linked character might have been present, Bentink-Smith et al.. Hemophilia in foals and pups have been previously described as affecting the male newborn in these species.

Fibroelastosis of the heart valves due to an unknown cause has been described in pups and kittens and rarely in calves causing enlarged hearts and deaths of the newborn within 2 to 3 months after birth, Eliot et al..

Respiratory distress syndrome and convulsions in Thoroughbred newborn foals have been described in England and the continent. These foals have been called "barkers," "dummies," and "wanderers" depending upon the signs exhibited, Mahaffey and Rossdale (1957). It is possible several different etiological factors or diseases were present in foals reported in this initial report. Recently Rossdale, Pattle and Mahaffey (1967) reported on the respiratory distress syndrome indicating the foals affected were normal for 24 hours. Respiratory distress began on the second day and became more severe. The respiratory rate went from 25 to 85 per minute. Inability to stand developed and extensor spasms occurred by the third day with death of the foals by the end of the third day or early on the fourth day. The lungs were atelectic and edematous with an absence of the surface-active lung lining or hyaline membrane. Thus this disease in foals resembled the respiratory distress syndrome in human babies. Further study of this syndrome is indicated.

Management and environmental conditions may cause or predipose to the death or disease of the newborn animal. Based on extensive and careful records VanDieten reported that 6 percent of calves die at parturition or within 25 hours of birth, 3 percent in multipara and 14 percent in primipara. There was a higher mortality rate in male calves and more abnormal parturitions associated with male calves. Calf mortality was eight times higher in moderately to severe abnormal parturitions or dystocia than at normal parturitions. The incidence of abnormal parturitions was twice as high for male calves than for female calves. Certain sires produced calves having a higher mortality rate at parturition in primipara, 18 to 19 percent, than other sires, 8 to 10 percent. These sires should not be used on heifers. Cupps and Laben also reported in a study of inbred matings that calves from certain sires had a much higher postnatal mortality rate than calves from other inbred sires. DeRouen et al. noted a higher than normal mortality rate within several days after birth in Brahman cattle and cows calving on range during cold wet weather. Anderson and Bellows also reported that a greater number of male beef calves were lost at parturition; these losses were greatest in primiparous cattle 9.5% and least in pluriparous cows, 2.4%

Pups, pigs and lambs, in fact all newborn animals, have a poikilothermic nature and are often unable to respond to cold by increasing their metabolic rate until 3 to 7 days of age. This is most noticeable in thin, underweight, malnourished, "runt" newborn animals where nutritional reserves are not present. Many of these neonates appear immature. Curtis et al. reported that as high as 30 percent of baby pig losses after birth were due to chilling. Fox (1963) stressed the importance of chilling in pups as a cause of death. Alexander reported on high death losses in newborn lambs when the weather was cold and especially when the lambs were small and undernourished prenatally. Lambs weighing 4 pounds or less at birth suffered 65 percent or greater death losses compared to 5 to 8 percent losses in lambs weighing 10 to 14 pounds, Shelton, Hoversland et al.. High environmental temperatures during gestation and underfeeding caused the birth of smaller lambs. The mortality in twin lambs with lower birth weights is 30 to 40 percent higher than in single births, Purser and Young. Other causes for mortality in the newborn is lack of vigor due to inbreeding, prematurity, or lack of nutrition for the dam during the gestation period, Stamp, and a failure of the dam to own or accept her newborn, resulting in starvation. Rarely certain Hereford cows may have such large teats that a small weak calf is unable to obtain colostrum. Occasionally postpartum dams suffer from agalactia due to disease, such as mastitis or endocrine causes and the newborn must be raised as an orphan in order to save its life. Disease factors in mortality in lambs was carefully reviewed by Beck et al.. Subcutaneous edema associated with low serum protein levels was commonly present in all pigs the first two days after birth. This edema disappeared after the ingestion of colostrum raised the serum protein levels of the pigs, Edwards. Supplying artificial heat to the newborn and seeing that colostrum is ingested early to supply both energy and antibodies will save many weak neonatal animals.

Injuries to the fetus during normal parturition are rare, but in dystocia forced extraction may result in fractures of the fore or hind limbs, especially in cattle. Fractures most often occur in the metacarpal or metatarsal bone in the region of the "break joint" or epiphysis, due to applying the chain or rope above the fetlock and placing a severe strain on the leg by twisting, jerking, or excessive traction. If the fetus is dead this is of no consequence but if the fetus is alive the fracture may be highly embarrassing for the veterinarian. By bandaging the leg and padding it well after correction of the displaced ends of the bone, and applying a light wood splint and covering and hardening the bandage with waterglass, a firm but light cast is made that allows the calf or young animal to walk. In 5 to 6 weeks this may be removed, and complete healing usually results. A light-weight plastic cast may be desirable. If a compound fracture occurs the prognosis is more guarded and antibiotics locally and parenterally are indicated.

Fracture of the jaw may result from excessive traction or twisting. Occasionally the snare or chain may slip forward and fracture the bony plate holding the incisor teeth, thereby causing them to point forward. In cattle these fractures are difficult to hold in place after correction. Frequently slaughter may be advised if both halves of the mandible are broken through the body, although surgery and wiring or pinning may be successful in selected cases. If only the incisor teeth are involved in the fracture, the animal will usually nurse satisfactorily or will drink from a pail, and healing occurs promptly even though the teeth may be at a more acute angle than normal.

Fractures of the ribs occur in foals due to injury of the fetus in its expulsion through the birth canal or due to the dam accidently stepping on the foal. Dyspnea often develops within a day or two with a jerky painful respiration and an audible grunt on expiration. The foals move slowly and stiffly. Death usually results. Occasionally taping the chest snugly with wide adhesive tape may be helpful if the lungs are not damaged.

Dennis reported 174 hepatic ruptures and 1 splenic rupture in 4,417 lambs necropsied. Similar ruptures might occur in other species but they are rarely reported.

Dislocation of the hip joint is very rare in the newborn of the larger domestic animals. If excessive traction or twisting is applied to the rear legs in posterior presentation dislocation is possible in the dog; also in anterior presentation of the fetus when the head protrudes through the vulva and the fetal body is wedged in the birth canal, twisting or excessive traction on the head may cause dislocation of the occipital joint and the death of the canine or feline fetus.

Edema of the tongue is common in calves in anterior presentation, in which the normal passage of the fetus is delayed and the head is retained for several hours in the birth canal or protruding through the vulva. This edema of the tongue and often of the entire head is due to passive congestion caused by the intrapelvic pressure exerted on the calf's neck interfering with or blocking venous circulation from the head. Edema of the forelimbs is observed frequently in prolonged dystocia when the forelimbs are extended so the fetlocks are outside the vulva. If the young is still alive the edema disappears within 3 to 24 hours after birth and the fetus can then suckle in a normal manner.

Injury or death of the newborn caused by the dam—Occasionally the dam, usually a primiparous female, may become excited, belligerent, or vicious, and injure or destroy the young soon after birth. This is a further reason for having a quiet environment to which the animal is accustomed, and an attendent present during parturition. It occurs rarely in the cow or mare but is seen occasionally in swine and dogs. When the cow attacks, butts or kicks its calf, the calf should be removed or the cow restrained or tranquilized until it becomes reconciled to and accepts the calf. In a few mares colic associated with uterine involution and expulsion of the fetal membranes may be quite severe. A sedative or tranquilizer is indicated and in some instances the foal should be removed from the stall for several hours to prevent accidental injury by the dam. Occasionally a mare will refuse to allow a colt to nurse and kicks him away from her flank. This calls for restraint of the mare at regular intervals even to an attendant employing a twitch to allow the foal to nurse. Between nursings the foal should be confined in a partitioned part of the box stall. The dam usually accepts the foal after 1 to 2 days when the congestion and soreness has left her udder.

In swine this viciousness may be marked and the primiparous or young sow will attack and kill her offspring. According to Kingrey, 1.1 percent of the pigs farrowed in Iowa, Illinois, and Indiana are eaten by sows. The sow may kill her pigs as they are farrowed or farrowing may be normal and then the sow kills the entire litter at one time. Some pigs are eaten but most are merely killed thus this condition is not a true "cannabalism." This condition rarely occurs after 24 hours after farrowing. The "berserk" sow may even attack the owner. Obviously it is necessary to have this type of sow farrow in a farrowing crate or for the attendant to remove the pigs immediately after birth. Nutrition as a cause of this condition is doubtful since usually only one sow in a drove fed the same ration is affected. It may be due to an inherited or congenital excitability, psychosis, or viciousness. Gilts from affected or related sows may also develop a similar aggressive attitude after farrowing. The hereditary or genetic nature of this condition has not been proved but seems more likely than the nutritional theory as the cause of this condition. Quiet sows and gilts should be selected for breeding.

In order to attempt to induce this type of sow to accept her pigs the surroundings should be quiet. Some owners and veterinarians truss the sow up and allow the pigs to nurse at regular intervals. Spontaneous recovery may occur at any time. Often the sow is given a sedative or narcotic dose of chloral hydrate or pentobarbital before the pigs are placed on her. Kingrey recommended 1 cc. or 1 grain of pentobartital for each 30 to 40 pounds of body weight intravenously or 5 to 10 cc. intramuscularly deep into each ham. The effects of intramuscular injection occur in 10 to 15 minutes and last 6 to 18 hours. No harmful effects were observed. Intravenous sedation was much shorter in duration and for that reason was not as satisfactory. Along with this, some veterinarians advise the injection of 2 to 5 cc., or 20 to 50 units, of posterior pituitary hormone, but its value is questionable. The sow and her pigs should be closely watched, since as soon as they regain consciousness some sows will again attack their pigs. If this viciousness is pronounced and the sow refuses to accept her pigs in 1 to 2 days they should be placed on other dams or hand fed. Treatment frequently fails. This undesirable inherent disposition was aggravated by parturition. This type of sow is usually sent to slaughter.

The same condition is also observed in dogs, especially Cocker Spaniels and rarely in cats after parturition. Their surviving offspring usually have to be reared as orphans, Leonard, Fox. Hayes and Perryman described a bitch who killed all pups in 3 successive litters but reared the last litter when she was tranquilized for 45 days postpartum. Animals should not be reared from such unstable psychotic dams for fear of perpetuating such individuals.

Care of the Postpartum Dam—Following parturition the dam should be allowed to lick and nurse her young. All undue excitement, noise, or unusual happenings should be eliminated or prevented. Rest and quiet following parturition is imperative. The roughage fed to large animals should be of good quality. The grain ration should be rather laxative and light, such as bran, oats, and a little linseed meal. In most animals the amount of grain should be increased gradually during the first three weeks after parturition. In the dairy cow it may have to be increased more rapidly, to prevent acetonemia or ketosis. In the sow the light grain feed should be continued for a week and then gradually increased. If it is increased too rapidly the pigs may get too much milk, and diarrhea may develop. In the mare a bran mash or two following foaling may be of value if the mare is constipated. Some veterinarians routinely administer one gallon of mineral oil to mares soon after foaling to help prevent constipatior due to the pain occasioned by the act of defecation the first few days after foaling. The cow should be watched carefully for several days after calving for symptoms of milk fever. Excess edema of the udder should be controlled by massage, frequent milking, or preferredly diuretics such as the carbonic anhydrase inhibitors with or without the glucocorticoids as described under lactation. Udder suspensories may be indicated in some cows to help support the edematous udder. Although urticaria due to the absorbtion of milk proteins into a sensitized animal occurs most commonly at the time of drying off, especially in Guernsey and Jerseys, it may occasionally develop after parturition if milking is limited in order to prevent the occurrence of milk fever. In most animals it takes about 10 to 14 days to return the dam to full feed. Moderate and light daily exercise is advisable in animals after parturition. Mares should be turned out for about one hour a day for the first week and then for longer periods thereafter. Draft or saddle mares can begin light work in two weeks.

In domestic animals retention of the fetal membranes occasionally occurs. The membranes are considered as being retained if they are not expelled within 8 to 12 hours in the cow, 3 to 6 hours in the mare, and 8 to 12 hours in the ewe. VanDieten reported that retained placenta occurred twice as frequently in cattle when the calf died at birth than in normal parturitions and these cows had a lower conception rate. In multipara, membranes usually cannot be observed hanging from the vulva and they frequently go unnoticed until they are expelled in 1 to 2 days or decompose and a mucopurulent discharge is noted in 4 to 10 days. It is desirable, especially in the cow and mare—in which species retained placenta occurs most commonly—to have this condition treated by a veterinarian. Veterinarians prefer to treat retained placenta in the cow within 1 to 3 days after parturition. Mares should be treated earlier, within 12 to 24 hours, to avoid septicemia, toxemia, and possible parturient laminitis.

If genital discharges persist beyond 14 to 20 days postpartum or if they are abnormal in amount or purulent in nature, the genital tract of the animal should be examined and treated as described under uterine infections. It is desirable especially in valuable cows to examine the genital tract about 30 days postpartum even when the calving and the postpartum period were apparently normal. In mares an examination and culture should be made about 6 days postpartum if breeding is to be at the foal estrum, or early in the second estrum if the mare is to be bred at that estrum. Early treatment of uterine infections or pathology or repair of vulvar lacerations after parturition is essential if the animal is to conceive promptly.

Occasionally animals develop an acute septicemia from uterine or mammary infections within 24 to 48 hours postpartum. The symptoms may be severe and death result. The dam may be so severely affected that lactation is greatly suppressed and the young may perish or must be raised as orphans. Any illness occurring immediately after parturition should be treated promptly.

Agalactia, or a lack of milk after parturition, may be due to the failure of milk let-down or failure of milk production. In the former condition adrenalin, due to stimuli such as pain and fright, is thought to be secreted. This hormone antagonizes or prevents the let-down of milk by the posterior pituitary hormone, oxytocin. This condition is noticed occasionally in heifers with a greatly congested, edematous, painful udder; injections of pituitrin or oxytocin intravenously or intramuscularly cause rapid and complete milk let-down. Sometimes repeated injections at each milking are required. The failure of milk production, if not caused by diseases such as: acute metritis, acute or chronic mastitis, traumatic gastritis, indigestion and others, is due to a hormonal deficiency or to defective development of the mammary gland with a lack of secretory tissue. Prolactin from the anterior pituitary apparently is important in initiating lactation, while the growth or somatotropic hormone is responsible for the maintenance of proper and high secretory levels. Injections of crude anterior pituitary extract have been used by veterinarians with questionable succes as a possible aid in stimulating lactation. With the commercial production of the separate hormones of the anterior pituitary gland, such as prolactin and growth hormone, the therapy of these animals with low production of milk after parturition, may be improved in the future. Marked agalactia in sows was associated with the feeding of ergot the last few weeks of pregnancy. Mortality in piglets due to starvation was heavy, Shone et al.. At present the treatment or correction of severe agalactia is unsatisfactory and usually the newborn must be reared as orphans. In most cases with no obvious cause, rebreeding is questionable and affected food-producing animals should be slaughtered.

Occasionally it may be desirable to hasten mammary involution in animals that have lost their newborn young, or in bitches in pseudopregnancy. Cessation of milking; application of mild liniments, such as camphorated oil, to the udder; withholding or drastically reducing water and TDN intake, and injections of estrogens, 5 to 10 mgm. of stilbestrol in dogs and 30 to 50 mgm. in larger animals at repeated intervals if necessary, are valuable in reducing udder size and suppressing milk secretion.

References

Parturition and Involution

Adams, W. M. (1969) The Elective Induction of Labor and Parturition in Cattle, J.A.V.M.A. **154**, 3, 261.

Adams, W. M. (1970) Personal Communication.

Adams, W. M. and Wagner, W. C. (1970) Role of Corticoids in Parturition, Biol. of Reprod. In press.

Andrews, F. N. and McKenzie, F. F. (1941) Estrus, Ovulation and Related Phenomena in the Mare, Univ. of Missouri, Agr. Exp. Stat. Bull. 329.

Arthur, G. H. (1966) Recent Advances in Bovine Obsterics, Vet. Rec. **79**, 22, 630.

Arthur, G. H. (1964) Wright's Veterinary Obstetrics, 3rd Ed. Williams and Wilkins Comp., Baltimore, Md.

Asdell, S. A. (1946) Patterns of Mammalian Reproduction, Comstock Publishing Co., Inc., Ithaca, N.Y.

Benesch, F. (1952) Lehrbuch der Tierartzlichen Geburtshilfe and Gynakologie, Urban and Schwartzenberg, Wien-Innsbruck, Austria.

Benesch, F. and Wright, J. G. (1951) Veterinary Obstetrics, Williams and Wilkins Co., Baltimore, Md.

Ben David, B. (1960) Obstetrical Problems in the Israeli Friesian Cow-Observations on Normal Parturition, Refuah Vet. **17**, 3, 149.

Bjorkman, N. and Sollen, P. (1960) Morphology of the Bovine Placenta at Normal Delivery, Acta Vet. Scand. **1**, 347.

Bleicher, N. (1962) Behavior of the Bitch During Parturition, J.A.V.M.A. **140**, 10, 1076.

Bruner, D. W. (1954) Personal Communication.

Buch, N. C., Tyler, W. J. and Casida, L. E. (1955) Postpartum Estrus and Involution of the Uterus in an Experimental Herd of Holstein-Friesian Cows, J. of Dairy Sci., **38,** 1, 73.

Casida, L. E. and Venzke, W. G. (1936) Observation on Reproductive Processes in Dairy Cattle and Their Relation to Breeding Efficiency, Proc. Amer. Soc. of An. Prod., 221.

Catchpole, H. R. (1969) Hormonal Mechanisms in Pregnancy and Parturition, in **Reproduction in Domestic Animals,** 2nd Ed., edit. by H. H. Cole and P. T. Cupps, Academic Press, N.Y.C.

Cates, W. F. (1965) Progesterone Requirement During the Pre-implantation and Implantation Stages of Gestation in the Cow, Thesis, Univ. of Minn., School of Vet. Med., St. Paul, Minn.

Dawson, F. L. M. (1958) Observations on the Corpora Albicantia in the Ovaries of Normal and Infertile Dairy Cows, J. Agric. Sci. **50,** 3, 322.

Dukes, H. H. (1947) The Physiology of Domestic Animals, 6th Ed., Comstock Publishing Co., Ithaca, N.Y.

Dzuik, P. J. and Harmon, B. G. (1969) Succession of Fetuses at Parturition in the Pig, Amer. J. Vet. Res. **30,** 3, 419.

Egger, C. J. and Dracy, A. E. (1966) Histological Study of the Effects of Relaxin on the Bovine Cervix, J. Dairy Sci. **49,** 9, 1053.

Elliott, K., McMahon, K. J., Gier, H. T. and Marion, G. B. (1968) Uterus of the Cow after Parturition; Bacterial Content, Amer. J. Vet. Res. 29, 1, 77.

Ewbank, R. (1963) Predicting the Time of Parturition in the Normal Cow, Vet. Res. **75,** 14, 367.

Ewbank, R. (1969) The Fall in Rectal Temperature Seen Before Parturition in Sheep, J. Reprod. and Fert. **19,** 569.

Flexner, L. B. (1954) Gestation, Trans. of 1st Conf. on Gest., Corlies, Macy and Co., Inc., N.Y.C.

Folley, S. H. and Knaggs, G. S. (1964) Oxytocin Levels in the Blood of Ruminants with Special Reference to Milking Stimulus, **Advances in Oxytocin Research,** Pergamon Press, N.Y.C.

Folley, S. J. and Knaggs, G. S. (1965) Levels of Oxytocin in the Jugular Vein Blood of Goats During Parturition, J. Endocrinol. **33,** 301.

Fox, M. W. (1968) Abnormal Behavior in Animals, W. B. Saunders Co., Philadelphia, Pa.

Fraser, A. F. (1968) Reproductive Behavior in Ungulates, Academic Press, N.Y.C., London.

Freak, M. J. (1962) Abnormal Conditions Associated with Pregnancy and Parturition in the Bitch, Vet. Res. **74,** 1323.

Gier, H. T. and Marion, G. B. (1968) Uterus of the Cow after Parturition: Involutional Changes, Amer. J. Vet. Res. **29,** 1, 83.

Gier, H. T., Singh, N. P. and Marion, G. B. (1962) Histopathology of the Postpartum Bovine Uterus, J. An. Sci. **21,** 4, 1023.

Gillette, D. D. (1966) Placental Influence on Uterine Activity in the Cow, Amer. J. Physiol., **211,** 5, 1095.

Gillette, D. D. and Holm, L. (1963) Prepartum to Postpartum Uterine and Abdominal Contractions in Cows, Amer. J. Physiol. **204,** 1115.

Gomes, W. R. and Erb, R. E. (1965) Progesterone in Bovine Reproduction: A Review, J. Dairy Sci. **48,** 3, 314.

Henry, J. S., Jr., Kingston, M. B. and Maughan, G. B. (1967) The Effect of Epidural Anesthesia on Oxytocin—Induced Labor, Amer. J. Obst. and Gynec. **97,** 3, 350.

Hunter, D. L., Erb, R. E., Randel, R. D., Garverick, H. A., Callahan, C. J. and Harrington, R. B. (1969) Changes in Reproductive Steroids During Late Gestation, J. Dairy Sci. **52,** 6, 904.

Hunter, D. L., Erb, R. E., Randel, R. D. Garverick, H. A., Callahan, C. J. and Harrington, R. B. (1970) Reproductive Steroids in the Bovine. I Relationships During Late Gestation, J. An. Sci. **30,** 1, 47.

Jones, J. E. T. (1966) Observations on Parturition in the Sow II Parturient and Postparturient Phases, Brit. Vet. Jour. **122,** 471.

Jordan, W. J. (1952) The Puerperium of the Cow—A Study of Uterine Motility, J. Comp Path. and Therap. **62,** 54.

Kiesel, G. K. (1961) Personal Communication.

Labhsetwar, A P., Collins, W. E., Tyler, W. J. and Casida, L. E. (1964) Some Pituitary-Ovarian Relationships in the Periparturient Cow, J. Reprod. Fert. **8,** 85.

Marion, G. B. (1963) Personal Communication.

Marion, G. B. and Gier, H. T. (1959) Postpartum Regression of Bovine Caruncles, J. Dairy Sci. **42,** 5, 941.

Marion, G. B. and Gier, H. T. (1959) Histological and Cytological Changes in the Bovine Uterine Epithelium, J. An. Sci. **18,** 4, 1552.

Marion, G. B., Norwood, J. S. and Gier, H. T. (1968) Uterus of the Cow after Parturition: Factors Affecting Regression, Amer. J. Vet. Res. **29,** 1, 71.

McDonald, L. E. (1969) Veterinary Endocrinology and Reproduction, Lea and Febiger, Philadelphia.

McDonald, L. E., McNutt, S. H. and Nichols, L. E. (1953) On the Essentiality of the Bovine Corpus Luteum of Pregnancy, Amer. J. Vet. Res. **14,** 53, 539.

McEntee, K. (1964) Personal Communication.

Mellin, T. N., Estergreen, V. L. Jr., and Erb, R. E. (1964) Bovine Urinary Estrogen Excretion Before and After Normal and Induced Parturition, J. An. Sci. **23,** 3, 910.

Moberg, R. (1955) The White Blood Picture in Sexually Mature Female Cattle with Special Reference to Sexual Conditions, Dept. of Obstetrics and Gynecology, Royal Vet. College, Stockholm, Sweden.

Morrow, D. A., Roberts, S. J. and McEntee, K. (1969) A Review of Postpartum Ovarian Activity and Involution of the Uterus and Cervix of Cattle Cor. Vet. **59,** 1, 134.

Morrow, D. A., Roberts, S. J. and McEntee, K. (1969) Postpartum Ovarian Activity and Involution of the Cervix in Dairy Cattle II Involution of the Uterus and Cervix, Cor. Vet. **59,** 2, 190.

Muhrer, M. E., Shippen, O. P. and Lasley, J. F. (1955) The Use of Oxytocin for Initiating Parturition and Reduction of Farrowing Time in Sows, J. An. Sci. **14,** 4, 1250.

Pope, G. S. and Gupta, S. K. (1967) Levels of Progesterone in the Systemic Plasma of the Cow, Ann. Rept. Nat. Inst. for Res. in Dairying, Reading England, 58.

Rasbech, N. O. (1950) The Normal Involution of the Uterus of the Cow, Nord. Vet. Med., **2,** 8, 655.

Riesen, J. W., Saiduddin, S., Tyler, W. J. and Casida, L. E. (1968) Studies on the Postpartum Cow, Res. Bull, 270, Univ. of Wisconsin, 27.

Rooney, J. (1962) Personal Communication.

Rossdale, P. D. (1967) Clinical Studies in the Newborn Thoroughbred Foal, Brit. Vet. J. **123,** 470.

Saiduddin, S., Riesen, J. W., Graves, W. E., Tyler, W. J. and Casida, L. E. (1966) Pituitary Luteinizing Hormone Activity in the Postpartum Cow, J. An. Sci. **25,** 930.

Schofield, B. M. (1968) Parturition, in **Advances in Reproductive Physiology,** Vol. 3, Edit. by A. McLaren, Academic Press, N.Y.C.

Settergren, I. (1969) Personal Communication.

Short, R. V. (1965) Recent Advances in Equine Reproductive Physiology, Brit. Eq. Vet. Assoc. 4th Ann. Congr.

Tennant, B., Kendrick, J. W. and Petticord, R. G. (1967) Uterine Involution and Ovarian Function in the Postpartum Cow: A Retrospective Analysis of 2338 Genital Organ Examinations, Cor. Vet. **57,** 4, 543.

Trum, B. F. (1947) What Time Will a Mare Foal, Blood Horse, **27,** 2, 106.

Ulrich, Carl (1969) Personal Communication.

Uren, A. W. (1935) Involution of the Uterine Mucosa in the Ewe, Mich. State Col. Agr. Exp. Stat., Tech. Bull. 144.

VanDongen, C. G. and Hayes, R. L. (1966) Oxytoric Activity in Unextracted Blood Plasma During Calving, J. Reprod. and Fert. **11,** 317.

Vinattieri, E., Hayward, A. H. S. and Artioli, D. (1945) Retention of Placenta in the Buffalo, with Associated Sequelae, Vet. Rec., **57,** 46, 509.

Whitlock, J. H. (1955) Personal Communication.

Williams, W. L. (1943) Veterinary Obstetrics, 4th Ed., Miss Louella Williams, Upland Rd., Ithaca, N.Y.

Wrenn, T. R., Bitman, J. and Sykes, J. F. (1958) Body Temperature Variations in Dairy Cattle During the Estrous Cycle and Pregnancy, J. Dairy Sci. **41,** 8, 1071.

Care and Diseases of the Newborn Animal, Aftercare of the Dam

Adler, S. and Clark, E. J. (1962) Intrauterine Infection with **Ancylostoma caninum** in Dogs, Ann. of Trop. Med. and Parasit., **15,** 354.

Aherne, F. X., Hays, V. W., Ewan, R. C. and Speer, V. C. (1969) Glucose and Fructose in the Fetal and Newborn Pig, J. An. Sci. **29,** 6, 906.

Alexander, G. (1961) Energy, Expenditure and Mortality in Newborn Lambs, Proc. 4th Internat. Congr. on An. Reprod., the Hague.

Anderson, D. C. and Bellows, R. A. (1967) Some Causes of Neonatal Calf Losses, J. An. Sci. **26,** 4, 241.

Andresen, E., Preston, K. S., Ramsey, F. K., and Baker, L. N. (1965) Further Studies on Hemolytic Disease in Pigs Caused by Anti Ba, Amer. J. Vet. Res. **26,** 111, 303.

Bain, A. (1963) Common Bacterial Infections of Foetuses and Foals and Association of the Infection with the Dam, Austral. Vet. J. **39,** 11, 413.

Baker, H. J. and Lindsey, J. R. (1968) Equine Goiter Due to Excess Dietary Iodide, J.A.V.M.A. **153,** 12, 1618.

Barcroft, J. (1952) Fetal Respiration and Circulation, in **Marshall's Physiology of Reproduction,** Vol. II, Longmans Green and Co., London, 398.

Batte, E. G., Moncol, D. J. and Barber, C. W. (1966) Prenatal Infection with the Swine Kidney Worm (**Stephanurus dentatus**) and Associated Lesions, J.A.V M.A. **149,** 6, 758.

Beck, C. C., Bronson, G. M. and Henneman, H. A. (1968) Factors in Disease and Mortality of Lambs, in **Proc. of Sympos. on Sheep Disease and Health,** Univ. of Calif, Davis, Cal.

Bentinck-Smith, J., Roberts, S. J. and Katz, E. M. (1960) A Bleeding Disease of Newborn Calves, Cor. Vet. **50,** 1, 15.

Berrier, H. H. and Gouge, R. E. (1954) Eperythrozoonosis Transmitted **in Utero** from Carrier Sows to their Pigs, J.A.V.M.A. **124,** 923, 98.

Bruner, D. W. (1950) Laboratory Diagnosis of Hemolytic Icterus in Foals, Cor. Vet., **40,** 1, 11.

Bruner, D. W. (1954) and (1962) Personal Communication.

Bruner, D. W., Brown, R. G., Hull, F. E. and Kincaid, A. S. (1949) Blood Factors and Baby Pig Anemia, J.A.V.M.A., **115,** 868, 94.

Bruner, D. W., Doll, E. R., Hull, F. E. and Kincaid, A. S. (1950) Further Studies on Hemolytic Icterus in Foals, Amer. J. Vet. Res. **11,** 38, 22.

Bruner, D. W., Hull, F. E. and Doll, E. R. (1948) The Relation of Blood Factors to Icterus in Foals, Amer. J. Vet. Res., **9,** 32, 237

Buxton, J. C., Brooksbank, N. H. and Combs, R. R. A. (1955) Hemolytic Disease of Newborn Pigs Caused by Maternal Isoimmunization, Brit. Vet. J. **111,** 463.

Carbrey, E. A., Stewart, W. C., Young, S. H. and Richardson, G. C. (1966) Transmission of Hog Cholera by Pregnant Sows, J.A.V.M.A. **149,** 1, 23.

Carmichael, W. E., Squire, R. A. and Krook, L. (1965) Clinical and Pathologic Features of a Fatal Viral Disease of Newborn Pups, Amer. J. Vet. Res. **26,** 113, 803.

Cornwell, H. J. C. and Wright, N. G. (1969) Neonatal Canine Herpes Virus Infection, Vet. Rec. **84,** 2.

Cronin, M. T. I. (1955) Haemolytic Disease of Newborn Foals, Vet. Rec., 67, 26, 479.

Cowie, R. S. (1964) Cancer in the Newborn Calf, Vet. Rec. 76, 20, 566.

Cupps, P. T. and Laben, R. C. (1965) Physiological Changes Accompanying Decreased Vigor in a Group of Inbred Calves, J. Dairy Sci. **98,** 6, 792.

Curtis, S. E., Heidenreich, C. J. and Harrington, R. B. (1967) Age Dependent Changes of Thermostability in Neonatal Pigs, Amer. J. Vet. Res. **28,** 127, 1887.

Dennis, S. M. (1970) Splenic Rupture in a Newborn Lamb, Amer. J. Vet. Res. **31,** 1, 205.

DeRouen, T. M., Reynolds, W. L. and Meyerhoeffer, D. C. (1967) Mortality in Beef Calves in the Gulf Coast Area, J. An. Sci. **26,** 1, 202.

Dimock, W. W., Edwards, P. R. and Bruner, D. W. (1947) Infections Observed in Equine Fetuses and Foals, Cor. Vet., **37,** 2, 89.

Doll, E. R. and Brown, R. G. (1954) Isohemolytic Disease of Newborn Pigs, Cor. Vet., **44,** 1, 86.

Doll, E. R. and Hull, F. E. (1951) Observations on Hemolytic Icterus of Newborn Foals, Cor. Vet., **41,** 1, 14.

Doll, E. R., Richards, M. G., Wallace, M. E. and Bryans, J. T. (1952) The Influence of an Equine Fetal Tissue Vaccine upon Hemagglutination Activity of Mare Serums: Its Relation to Hemolytic Icterus of Newborn Foals, Cor. Vet., **42,** 4, 495.

Doll, E. R. (1963) Neonatal Isoerythrolysis, in **Equine Medicine and Surgery,** 1st Ed., Amer. Vet. Public Inc. Wheaten, Ill., 517.

Douglas, J. R. and Baker, N. F. (1959) The Chronology of Experimental Intrauterine Infections with **Toxocara canis** in the Dog, J. of Parasitol., **45,** 4, Sect. 2, 43.

Dreguss, M. N. and Lombard, L. S. (1954) Experimental Studies in Equine Infections Anemia, Univ. of Penn. Press, Philadelphia, Pa.

DuPlessis, J. L. (1958) Repair of Ruptured Bladder in Foals, J. South Afr. Vet. Med. Assoc. **29,** 261.

Edwards, B. L. (1961) Oedema in Newborn Pigs, Vet. Rec. **73,** 22, 540.

Eliot, T. S., Jr., Eliot, F. P., Lushbaugh, C. C. and Slager, U. T. (1958) First Report of the Occurrence of Neonatal Endocardial Fibroelastosis in Cats and Dogs, J.A.V.M.A. **133,** 5, 271.

Emerson, J. L. and Delez, A. L. (1965) Prenatal Hog Cholera Infection; A Potential Source of Hog Cholera, Proc 102nd Meeting A.V.M.A., 1346.

Fluharty, D. M. (1965) Some Incompatible Reactions of Canine Blood Group A, J.A.V.M.A. **147,** 12, 1656.

Fox, M. W. (1963) Neonatal Mortality in the Dog, J.A.V.M.A. **143,** 11, 1219.

Fox, M. W. (1966) Canine Pediatrics, C. C. Thomas Co., Springfield, Ill.

Fräser, C. M. and Nelson, J. (1959) Sweet Clover Poisoning in Newborn Calves, J.A.V.M.A. **135,** 5, 283.

Greve, J. H. and Gaafar, S. M. (1966) Natural Transmission of **Demodex canis** in Dogs, **148,** 9, 1043.

Griesemer, R. A. and Gibson, J. P. (1963) The Establishment of an Ascarid-Free Beagle Colony, J.A.V.M.A. **143,** 9, 965.

Harding, S. K., Bruner, D. W. and Bryant, I. W. (1961) The Transfer of Antibodies from the Mother Cat to her Newborn Kittens, Cor. Vet. **51,** 4, 535.

Hartley, W. J. and Dodd, D. C. (1957) Muscular Dystrophy in New Zealand Livestock, New Zeal. Vet. J. **5,** 61.

Hayes, F. A. and Perryman, B. S. (1958) Temporary Alleviation of Cannibalism in a Staffordshire Terrier Bitch, N. A. Vet. **39,** 1, 54.

House, J. (1968) Personal Communication (N.Y.S. Veterinary College).

Hoversland, A. S., Safford, J. and Van Horn, J. L. (1963) Some Characteristics of Newborn Lambs Associated with Mortality, J. An. Sci. **22,** 3, 856.

Jeffcott, L. B. (1969) Haemolytic Disease of the Newborn Foal, Eq. Vet. J. **1,** 4, 165.

Jensen, R., Maag, D. D. and Flint, J. C. (1958) Enzootic Ataxia from Copper Deficiency in Sheep in Colorado, J.A.V.M.A. **133,** 6, 336.

Jones, J. E. T. (see preceding section).

Kanagawa, H., Kawata, K., Nakao, N. and Sung, W. K. (1964) A Case of Granulosa Cell Tumor of the Ovary in a Newborn Calf, Jap. J. Vet. Res. **12,** 1, 7.

Kilham, L., Margoulis, G., and Colby, E. D. (1967) Congenital Infections of Cats and Ferrets by Feline Leucopenia Virus Manifested by Cerebellar Hypoplasia, Laborat. Invest. **17,** 465.

Kingrey, B. W. (1955) Hysteria in the Parturient Sow, Iowa State Col. Vet. **17,** 2, 83.

Kirk, R. W. (1958) Canine Pediatrics, Mod. Vet. Pract. **39,** 5, 45.

Kirk, R. W. (1965) Canine Pediatrics, J.A.V.M.A. **147,** 12, 1475.

Kirk, R. W. (1968) Pediatrics, in **Canine Medicine,** 1st Catcott Ed., Amer. Vet. Public Inc., Wheaton, Ill. 805.

Kopecky, K. E., Larsen, A. B. and Merkal, R. S. (1967) Uterine Infection in Bovine Paratuberculosis, Amer. J. Vet. Res. **28,** 125, 1043.

Koutz, F. R., Groves, H. F. and Scothorn, M. W. (1966) The Prenatal Migration of **Toxocara canis** Larvae and their Relationship to Infection in Pregnant Bitches and in Pups, Amer. J. Vet. Res. **27,** 118, 789.

Kradel, D. C. (1963) Developing Concepts of Nutritional Muscular Degenerations in Livestock, Proc. A.V.M.A. N.Y. City, 63.

Larson, B. L. (1958) Transfer of Specific Blood Serum Proteins to Lacteal Secretions Near Parturition, J. Dairy Sci. **41,** 8, 1033.

Leonard, E. P. (1954) Personal Communication.

Lyons, E. T., Drudge, J. H. and Tolliver, S. (1969) Parasites from Mare's Milk, Blood Horse, **95,** 29, 2271.

Mahaffey, L. W. and Rossdale, P. D. (1957) Convulsive and Allied Syndromes in Newborn Foals, Vet. Rec. **69,** 1277.

Manktelow, B. W. (1963) Myopathy of Dogs Resembling White Muscle Disease of Sheep, New Zeal. Vet. J. **11,** 52.

Mantovani, A. and Jackson, R. F. (1966) Transplacental Transmission ot Microfilaria of **Dirofilaria immitis** in the Dog, J. of Parasitol. **52,** 116.

McGee, W. R. (1954) Disease Problems in Foals, Vet. Med., **49,** 8, 311.

McManus, D. (1960) Prenatal Infection of Calves with **Cysticercus bovis,** Vet. Rec. **72,** 41, 847.

Meyer, R. C., Rasmussen, B. A. and Simon, J. (1969) A Hemolytic Neonatal Disease in Swine Associated with Blood Group Incompatibility, J.A.V.M.A. **154,** 5, 531.

Misdorp, W. (1965) Tumors of Newborn Animals, Path. Vet. **2,** 328.

Mosier, J. E., Twiehaus, M. J. and Cowan, J. H. (1956) Septicemia in Puppies, Univ. of Penn. Bull. Vet. Ext. Quart. **143,** 111.

O'Dea, J. (1961, 1966) Personal Communication.

Olson, L. D. and Gaafar, S. M. (1963) Absence of prenatal Infection with **Ascaris lumbricoides** in Swine, J.A.V.M.A. **143,** 11, 1217.

Refuerzo, P. G. and Albis-Jimenez, F. S. (1954) Studies on **Neoascaris vitulorum,** Amer. J. Vet. Res., **15,** 57, 532.

Rice, V. A. and Andrews, F. N. (1951) Breeding and Improvement of Farm Animals, 4th Ed., McGraw Hill Book Co., Inc., N.Y.C.

Rickard, C. (1970) Seminar, N.Y. State Veterinary College, Personal Communication.

Roberts, E. J. and Archer, R. K. (1966) Current Methods for the Diagnosis and Treatment of Haemolytic Disease in the Foal, Vet. Rec. **79,** 61.

Rooney, J. R. (1962) Personal Communication.

Rooney, J. R. (1962) Joint Ill. J.A.V.M.A. **141,** Part II, 10, 1259.

Rossdale, P. D., Pattle, R. E. and Mahaffey, L. W. (1967) Respiratory Distress in a Newborn Foal with Failure to Form Lung Lining Film, Nature **215,** 1498.

Sanger, V. L. and Cole, C. R. (1955) Toxoplasmosis VI Isolation of Toxoplasma from Milk, Placentas and Newborn Pigs of Asymptomatic Carrier Sows, Amer. J. Vet. Res. **16,** 61, 536.

Sheffy, B. E. (1965–1966) Factors Affecting Colostral Absorbtion (Dog) Rept. N.Y.S. Vet. Col., 53.

Shelton, M. (1964) Relation of Birth Weight to Death Losses and to Certain Productive Characters of Fall-Born Lambs, J. An. Sci. **23,** 2, 355.

Shone, D. K., Philips, J. R. and Christie, G. J. (1959) Agalactia in Sows Caused by Fielding the Ergot of the Bulrush Millet, **Pennisetum typhoides,** Vet. Rec. **71,** 7, 129.

Siim, J. C. and Biering-Sorensen, U. (1963) Toxoplasmosis in Domestic Animals, in **Advances in Vet. Sci.,** Vol. 8, Ed. by Brandley, C. A. and Jungherr, E. L., Academic Press, N.Y.C.

Stamp, J. T. (1967) Perinatal Loss in Lambs with Particular Reference to Diagnosis, Vet. Rec. **81,** 21, 530.

Stewart, T. B., Smith, W. N., Jones, D. J. (1963) Prenatal Infection of Pigs with the Intestinal Threadworm; **S. ransomi,** J. Parasitol. **49,** Suppl. 15.

Stormont, C., Rasmussen, B. Saison, R. and Ingram, P. G. (1962) Blood Groups in Infrahuman Species. Ann. N.Y. Acad. Sci. **97,** Art. 1., 1–328.

Swisher, S. N. and Young, L. E. (1961) The Blood Grouping Systems of Dogs, Physiol. Rev. **41,** 495.

Tamarin, R. and Landau, M. (1961) Congenital and Uterine Infection with **Mycobacterium johnei** in Sheep, Refuah Vet. **18,** 44.

Tanzer, H. (1965) Personal Communication.

Too, K., Kanagawa, H. and Kawata, K. (1967) Fetal Electrocardiograms in the Mare and Cow at Parturition, Jap. J. Vet. Res. **15,** 1, 5 and 21

Tsur, I. and Krieger, A. (1960) Congenital **Theileria annulata** in a Calf, Refuah. Vet. **17,** 3, 147.

Twiehaus, M. J. (1965) Personal Communication.

Van Dieten, S. W. J. (1963) Stillbirth in Bovine Cattle, Thesis, Univ. of Utrecht, Utrecht, Netherlands.

Wright, J. N. (1962) Blood Incompatibilities in the Dog, Cor. Vet. **52,** 4, 523.

Young, L. E., O'Brien, W. A., Swisher, S. N., Miller, G. and Yuile, C. L. (1952) Blood Groups in Dogs—Their Significance to the Veterinarian, Amer. J. Vet. Res., **8,** 47, 207.

Chapter VII

DYSTOCIA—ITS CAUSES

When the first, or especially the second, stages of parturition is markedly prolonged, becomes difficult or impossible for the dam without artificial aid, the condition is termed **dystocia.** The term dystocia comes from the Greek and means difficult birth. **Eutocia** is safe, easy, natural, or physiological parturition. There is no clear line between normal parturition and dystocia. Dystocia is one of the most important obstetrical conditions with which the veterinarian must cope. The incidence of dystocia in the various species is not satisfactorily recorded. Williams indicated that the incidence in cattle was about 3.3 percent. It is apparently higher in dairy than beef cattle. The incidence of dystocia appears higher in the larger breeds, such as the Holstein, Brown Swiss, and Hereford. In horses the incidence was about 1.1 percent on a large well-managed farm, Williams; it might be greater if horses under all conditions were considered. The incidence in sheep and swine is not known. In dogs it is highest in the Boston, Scotch Terrier, Pekinese, Sealyham, and other small brachycephalic breeds. It is lowest in the more natural breeds such as the hounds and in mongrels. In cats the incidence of dystocia is probably lower than in dogs. It is obvious that the incidence of dystocia is highest in the more specialized breeds and those kept under greatest confinement in the most artificial manner. Dystocia is much more common in primipara than in pluripara. The incidence of dystocia is greater in pregnancies that terminate early due to uterine disease, fetal death, and twinning, or that terminate after a prolonged gestation period due to excessive size of the fetus.

The causes of dystocia may be divided into the basic and the immediate causes. The basic causes should be studied for the purpose of obtaining knowledge that will help prevent the occurrence of dystocia. If basic causes are known and recognized, dystocia may largely be avoided; or if unavoidable the veterinarian and owner will know in advance that dystocia is highly probable. The latter circumstance requires certain preparations and precautions so that if dystocia should occur, prompt handling may prevent injury or death of either or both the dam and fetus.

The Basic Causes of Dystocia

The basic causes of dystocia may be divided into the following categories: hereditary, nutritional and management, infectious, traumatic, miscellaneous, or combined causes. Many cases of dystocia may have two or more basic causes.

Hereditary Causes—The hereditary causes for dystocia may be divided into those that have produced defects in the dam which predispose to dystocia, or those hidden or recessive genes in the dam and sire which may produce a defective fetus.

Those hereditary defects in the dam predisposing to dystocia are inguinal hernia; persistence of the median wall of the Mullerian duct with a large band in, or caudal to, the external os of the cervix; double uterus or uterus didelphys; hypoplasia of the vagina, vulva or uterus; uterus unicornus; twinning; and inherited breed characteristics. Inguinal hernia as a cause of dystocia especially in the dog has been discussed previously. Persistence of the median wall of the Mullerian or paramesonephric duct may cause dystocia by obstructing the passage of the fetus if one leg should pass on one side and the other leg on the other side of this strong band. In a true double uterus in the cow the placental area is limited to only one horn. A severe dystocia may result from overlooking a twin in the other horn. Hypoplasia of hereditary origin is only rarely a cause for dystocia, as the hypoplasia often affects the uterus and ovaries, and conception does not occur. Twinning in uniparous animals is usually associated with double ovulation. Monozygous twins are uncommon. The release of two or more ova at one estrum is usually predisposed by the dam's hereditary constitution or may be associated with cystic ovaries. Twinning may be influenced to a lesser degree by the season and the age of the dam. Twin bicornual pregnancy in cattle commonly results in dystocia because the long extremities frequently cause wedging of the fetuses in the pelvis. In twinning, uterine inertia associated with unicornual twins, posterior presentation of one fetus, death of one or both fetuses, and premature twin birth or abortion also favor dystocia. Certain breeds of cattle, such as Brown Swiss, with a long gestation period and large fetuses; and certain brachycephalic or dwarf breeds of dogs, such as Bulldogs, and other breeds with a large, broad head and a relatively small pelvis and underdeveloped or weak reproductive systems, are more prone to dystocia. Scotch Terrier fetuses have a tendency toward premature hardening of the skull bones that may lead to dystocia. Most of the hereditary defects of the dam resulting in or predisposing to dystocia, with the possible exception of the inherited breed characteristics, are favored by inbreeding or close breeding practices.

The hidden and usually recessive genes in both male and female animals may produce a variety of pathological conditions affecting the fetus or fetal membranes, thus causing dystocia. Most of these are lethal genes, as they usually result in the death of the fetus. The known genetic lethals for cattle and the other domestic animals have been outlined in Chapter III. Dropsy of the fetal membranes and fetus may be caused by mating hybrids such as the bison with the domestic cow or zebu. Inbreeding in Dexter and Tux-Zillertaler cattle and others has resulted in **achondroplastic calves** and occasionally hydramnios. Certain types of muscle contracture monsters may be associated with hydrops of the amnion. If this condition of the fetal membranes should go to term it usually is associated with uterine inertia and a weak or dead fetus. Both of these conditions favor fetal emphysema and dystocia. Achondroplastic and "ankylosed" calves have been produced without dropsy of the fetal membranes by inbreeding animals with the recessive gene for those conditions. Dystocia often results at parturition due to the increased size of the fetus or certain of its parts. Hereditary lethals causing amputated limbs of fetuses, **Acroteriasis congenita, hydrocephalus,** and stillborn fetuses frequently may cause dystocia at the end of gestation. Hydrocephalus in cattle is frequently associated with deformed limbs. The early death of these fetuses at the time of parturition, and abnormal postures more common in defective fetuses, increase the incidence of dystocia. An hereditary condition called congenital dropsy resulting in large, anasarcous fetuses or calves occasionally causes dystocia in Ayrshire or Swedish Lowland cattle when carried 200 days or longer. An autosomal recessive gene causing a **prolonged gestation** of 300 to 370 days in Holstein cattle and terminating in severe dystocia due to the oversized, giant calves has been described. In this case the fetuses were already dead, died at birth, or were killed during the difficult delivery. The dam's life was greatly imperiled and a number of the dams died as a result of the dystocia. Mummified fetuses in cattle occasionally may be hereditary. Dystocia may result at the time the mummified fetus is expelled, especially in cases of fetuses that mummify after the fifth month of gestation. Muscular hypertrophy or "double muscling" in cattle is an hereditary condition that when present in fetuses, especially in primipara, often causes severe dystocia. Muscular hypertrophy has been described in Charolais, Holstein, South Devon, Hereford, Angus and Piedmont cattle. Vandenbussche et al. reported that 50 percent of oversized fetuses in Belgium causing dystocia were double-muscled. More of these lethal conditions causing dystocia affect bone development than any other tissue. The so-called muscle contracture monsters are usually produced by general functional ankylosis with an abnormal development of muscles and tendons, causing an immobility and extreme rigidity of the affected limbs. In sheep inherited lethals of general ankylosis and amputation and in swine general ankylosis have been described. There are many other inherited lethal genes such as cerebral hernia, epitheliogenesis imperfecta, and short spine that might contribute to dystocia because the fetus is weak and usually dies at the time of parturition. This factor of a dead or weak fetus at parturition favors abnormal postures of the fetus even though its size may be small, and its shape normal or nearly normal. A recessive hereditary condition should be suspected when several similar abnormal fetuses or dystocias are seen in related animals, especially over a period of several years.

Nutritional and Management Causes—The nutrition of a pregnant animal and its management at parturition are closely associated and may be the basic causes of many dystocias. Dystocia due to the small size of the dam is frequently observed in primipara. Bellows measured the area of the pelvic opening in 3-year-old heifers. As the pelvic opening increased in size from 200 sq. cm. to over 279 sq. cm. the incidence of heifers without dystocia rose from 44 to 100 percent. Almost all severe dystocias were in heifers with pelvic areas of 200 to 240 sq. cm. Improper nutrition of the growing heifers was the most important factor in retarding body and pelvic growth. Rice and Wiltbank reported that the average pelvic area for 90 two-year-old Hereford heifers three months before calving was 218 sq. cm. Heifers with pelvic areas less than 200 sq. cm. and more than 200 sq. cm. had dystocia rates of 68.7 and 28 percent. In 93 Angus heifers measured at breeding, 6 to 7 months of gestation and one week prepartum had pelvic areas that averaged 147 sq. cm., 184 sq. cm. and 227 sq. cm. respectively. This condition may be caused by breeding the female at too young an age or by breeding a poorly grown, under-fed female that may be old enough to breed but the body growth has been greatly retarded due to poor nutrition, parasitisms, or diseases. Most domestic animals reach puberty before their body growth is great enough for a normal gestation and parturition. Dairy calves may show estrum at 3 to 12 months of age. Range calves still nursing their dams may occasionally come into estrum and be bred by a bull that is running with the herd. Many cases of severe dystocia have been reported in cattle 13 to 18 months of age. Stonaker reported that 26 percent of 2 year-old range heifers had dystocia as compared to 4 percent of the older cows. It did not appear that the size of the heifer or the calf were important factors in calving difficulties in these heifers.

Well-grown, well-nourished heifers are usually not bred before 12 to 20 months of age, horses 3 years of age, swine 6 to 8 months of age, sheep 1 to 1.5 years of age, and dogs 1 year of age. Bratton and coworkers reported that dairy heifers should be bred by size or weight rather than by age. Holstein or Brown Swiss heifers should be bred when they weigh 750 pounds; Ayrshire and Guernsey heifers when they weigh 600 pounds and Jerseys when they weigh 500 pounds. Depending on the levels of energy intake these weights may be reached from 10 to 19 months of age. The optimum feeding levels produce heifers of these weights from 13 to 17 months of age. During the gestation period animals should be fed sufficiently well to maintain their rate of growth so that at calving Holstein and Brown Swiss heifers weigh about 950 to 1000 pounds, Guernseys and Ayrshires 700 to 725 pounds and Jerseys 670 to 690 pounds. Restricting growth by underfeeding frequently results in dystocia and other parturition difficulties. The breeding of animals that are immature or otherwise unfitted for a normal parturition is usually the result of an accident or gross carelessness in management. If discovered soon enough steps may be taken to prevent or terminate pregnancy.

Animals that are stunted frequently develop dystocia at parturition. This delayed development may be due to a low nutritive plane or to chronic diseases such as enteritis, pneumonia, severe pediculosis, mange or internal parasites or both. A low level of energy intake is the most common cause and frequently is an important factor in the development of chronic parasitic diseases. Stunting of a young female animal's growth is not permanent unless underfeeding is continued for a long period of time. In many young animals the stunting effects of a low plane of nutrition may be overcome by a high plane of nutrition for 6 months or more. Many farmers in dairy sections stunt the growth of their young stock by feeding milk substitutes improperly and by limited grain feeding, by feeding poor hay, pasturing the young stock on poor pastures, and by housing the young stock under unfavorable environmental conditions. Thus at the time of parturition the heifers are thin, small and weak. Dystocia is invited by the small pelvis and underdeveloped, juvenile genital tract, the lowered resistance to disease, and the lack of strength to expel the fetus in a normal manner. Growth and development in young animals should proceed normally from birth to puberty, from puberty to conception, and during the gestation period, if parturition is to be physiological. A proper nutritive level and efficient management are necessary to secure this goal.

High feeding levels may favor dystocia, especially in heifers, by excessive deposition of fat in the pelvic region, predisposing to difficult parturition. Hammond has shown the influence of over-and underfeeding of pregnant animals and its effect on increasing or decreasing the weight of the newborn. Many owners try to compensate for low levels of feeding and poor growth in their young stock by high feeding levels during the last third of pregnancy. This is particularly true in dairy cattle, in which lactation is of major importance. This practice is of questionable value and may even be harmful, as it is during this last third of pregnancy that the fetus grows very rapidly and the high feeding levels favor the development of a larger fetus while increase in body size and growth of the immature dam occurs much more slowly. The balance between fetal size and pelvic or genital tract diameters is thus upset and dystocia is favored. Overly fat, underexercised sows and dogs often develop dystocia possibly due to uterine inertia.

Malformation of the pelvis, such as pelvic rickets in humans due to improper mineral balance or lack of vitamin D is rarely seen in animals. Although animals may develop other symptoms resembling rickets in humans, they seldom develop pelvic deformities of sufficient degree to cause dystocia. Severe vitamin A deficiency and other deficiencies may predispose to uterine infections and death of the fetus and thus be a factor in producing abortions and dystocia.

Failure to keep animals approaching or beginning parturition under close observation may not actually be a cause of dystocia but this neglect may cause a relatively early and simple dystocia to become more severe, with danger to the life of the fetus and the dam. During parturition all animals should be watched closely, if possible, so that prompt aid may be given if parturition is not normal. This aid may prevent secondary uterine inertia, death of the fetus, rupture of the uterus or birth canal, fetal emphysema, septic metritis, retained placenta, and injuries, such as obturator paralysis, to the dam. Vaccination of pregnant sows with attenuated hog cholera virus, pregnant sheep with bluetongue virus, pregnant cattle with IBR virus, and these and other pregnant animals with living viruses that may affect their fetuses is to be avoided. Feeding or grazing pregnant animals on plants that may damage the fetus such as ewes on Veratrum, should be prevented in an effort to control fetal losses and dystocia that may accompany such losses.

Breeding too soon following parturition may occasionally favor sterility, abortion, and dystocia in mares and cows. As a general rule it is best to withhold breeding in the mare until the second estrum, or about 30 days after parturition, and in cows until after 50 to 60 days. In animals in which parturition was abnormal, breeding should be withheld for a longer period. Breeding too soon after parturition does not afford the uterus an opportunity to involute completely, and resistance to infection and its sequelae, sterility and abortion, is lowered. Most of the bicornual or transverse pregnancies observed in mares by the author were preceded by a history of dystocia or retained placenta the previous year. Following a severe dystocia in the mare, rebreeding that same year should be regarded with caution.

Pregnant animals which are not exercised and are kept in close confinement are more prone to difficulties such as torsion of the uterus and uterine inertia than those kept under more natural conditions, as on pasture. Exercise increases body tone, strength, and resistance and results in stronger labor contractions, less fatigue, shorter duration of parturition, less uterine inertia, and prompter recovery. Pregnant animals closely confined for long periods are more prone to abnormalities in the function of smooth muscle including prolapse of the vagina and uterus, intussusception, torsion of the cecum and displacement of the abomasum. Arthur citing Abusineina stated that in the first stage of labor the limbs of uniparous animals are flexed while during the second stage of labor they are extended. He hypothesized that the strong contractions of the myometrium initiated active fetal movements and righting reflexes resulting in extension of the limbs. Thus uterine disease as reported by Williams, as well as fetal disease, may greatly influence the incidence of dystocia.

Infectious Causes—Any infection or disease affecting the pregnant uterus and its contents may cause abortion, uterine inertia, fetal death, and occasionally septic metritis of pregnancy. In any severe infection of the uterus the uterine wall may lose its tone or ability to contract—a condition resulting in incomplete dilation of the cervix and uterine inertia. In the latter instance the second stage of labor may be abnormally delayed. Death of the fetus prior to parturition or premature birth renders the fetal extremities prone to postural abnormalities, and may result in a dorso-pubic position of the fetus in the mare. The relation of uterine disease and pathology to hydrops of the allantois and edema of the fetus has been cited and may be a cause for uterine inertia and dystocia. Infections may be the immediate cause of conditions that predispose to dystocia, or they may be responsible for chronic uterine damage such as loss of caruncles, or a nonfunctional uterine horn, either of which may result in abortion, uterine inertia, hydrops, torsion, rare transverse pregnancies, and other abnormalities at subsequent pregnancies. To help control infections that predispose to uterine disease and fetal death both the sire and dam should be free of infection at the time of service. A proper interval between parturition and service should be observed. All practices of hygiene and cleanliness at the time of service, especially in the horse, should be followed. All known infectious diseases such as brucellosis, leptospirosis, vibriosis, salmonella, viral, and other septicemic or infectious diseases should be controlled according to our best knowledge at the present time so that late abortions or premature births, in which dystocia is common, will be kept at a minimum. These infections were discussed under abortions.

Traumatic Causes—Traumatic causes for dystocia are not common. Ventral hernia and rupture of the prepubic tendon late in gestation may occur from traumatic causes. These injuries predispose to dystocia by rendering the abdominal wall incapable of strong contractions, with a resulting inability of the dam to force the fetus through the birth canal. Torsion of the uterus may be caused by sudden slipping, falling, or rolling in advanced pregnancy. This is not the only factor but it is an important one in the etiology of torsion. The resulting twisting of the birth passage is a common cause of dystocia in the dairy cow and a less common cause in the other species. Fractures of the pelvis with secondary deformity and exostoses is seen most commonly in small animals struck by motor vehicles. These may result in a stenosis of the birth passage, resulting in a severe dystocia at parturition.

Miscellaneous Causes—The causes of certain minor abnormalities in posture, such as a flexed knee or lateral deviation of the head and neck, resulting in dystocia with a live fetus and an apparently normal uterus, are difficult to explain except as an accidental catching of the nose or foot on the brim of the pelvis or in the soft structures of the birth canal during the early stages of parturition. A degree of uterine inertia or disease of the fetus may also be important factors. As the second stage progresses and more of the fetus enters the birth canal the deflection of the extremity is further increased. The causes of posterior presentation of the fetus, a relatively common cause for dystocia in uniparous animals, have not been satisfactorily explained. The exact causes or even satisfactory theories are not given to explain transverse pregnancies in domestic animals. Williams stated, and it also has been noted by the author, that previous uterine disease in mares may predispose to transverse pregnancy and dystocia. Vandeplassche disagreed and reported that in 11 cases of bicornual pregnancy in mares there was no previous history of uterine disease. In multipara a single fetus may be located transversely in the uterine body, with the two ends of its body in separate horns. This might be due to the intrinsic ability of the uterus in polytocous animals to distribute or balance the burden of pregnancy between the two horns. The factors causing only 1 to 3 fetuses to develop in multipara, that normally have 6 to 12 fetuses, have not been completely explained. It is not known whether this is a hormonal problem, a problem of early death of the embryos, or due to other causes. In multipara with only about one-third the normal-sized litter the fetuses are often larger than normal due to increased nutrition and uterine room available. This may result in dystocia at parturition. Hammond stated that in swine the most important factor determining the birth weight of pigs was the number of pigs in a litter, the larger the litter the smaller the pigs. Improper hormone balance of estrogens, progesterone or relaxin, or failure of the uterine muscle to react to oxytocin, or a failure of the normal release of oxytocin may result in delay of the first stage or second stage of parturition, and in uterine inertia.

Uterine Inertia is defined as the lack of normal physiologic uterine contractions during or after parturition. Two types of uterine inertia are recognized, primary and secondary. Primary uterine inertia is seen most often in the dog, occasionally in the cow and sow and rarely in the mare or ewe. The following conditions may be factors causing primary inertia or lack of uterine tone and feeble contractions at the time of parturition. It is observed more often in animals that are closely confined and hence lack exercise. It is more common in dairy than beef cattle. Excessive fat may be a possible factor in dogs and other species. Certain brachycephalic breeds of dogs tend to develop uterine inertia despite the size of the litter, Fox, Freak. Overstretching or overloading of the uterus in hydrops and twin pregnancy in cows, and a large number of fetuses in small dogs and sows favor uterine inertia. It is observed more often in older dairy cows and dogs. It is frequently associated with debility or debilitating diseases. It may be possibly associated with disease or degeneration of the uterine wall due to uterine infections or secondary to peritonitis as in traumatic peritonitis. It may be associated with an improper stimulus being applied to the posterior pituitary gland, a deficiency of that gland, or an inability of the uterine musculature to respond to the stimulation of oxytocin. Since the hormonal mechanisms of parturition are not completely understood other hormonal imbalances may play a part in the production of primary uterine inertia. Benesch and Wright described a primary uterine inertia in dogs associated with a small number of fetuses where symptoms of parturition are absent and the fetuses die. They indicated this is probably due to a hormonal disfunction. A combination of the above factors may be present.

Secondary uterine inertia, which is seen in all species, is the result of or follows dystocia and is due to exhaustion of the uterine muscle. In multiparous animals it may follow dystocia with one fetus; the remaining fetuses not be expelled when the fetus causing the dystocia has been removed. Certain "sensitive" dams will refrain from vigorous labor because of pain, and secondary inertia may ensue. In other multiparous animals lacking body condition or strength several young may be born and then the dam and also the myometrium appears exhausted. After several hours rest the birth process will again occur or may fail and outside aid will be necessary. Secondary inertia is frequently followed by uterine infection, septic metritis, retained placenta, and a failure of the normal involution of the uterus. In prolonged dystocia in unipara and possibly multipara, the uterine muscle may become fatigued and produce contraction or retraction rings, also called Bandl's rings, that contract tightly around the fetus or caudal to it. This may further complicate the relief of the dystocia or if not recognized it may result in rupture of the uterus if forced extraction is applied to the fetus. A condition in dogs—especially Scotch terriers and toy Dachshunds—is described by Benesch and Wright that is intermediate in character between primary and secondary uterine inertia. In these cases the bitch may have 1 or 2 fetuses and then labor ceases with a number of fetuses still in the uterus. There is no visible cause for the dystocia. Many cases of secondary uterine inertia may be avoided by careful observation of the female during parturition so that proper help can be given as soon as difficulty arises.

Fetal monsters other than those described under hereditary causes for dystocia are considered accidental occurrences at the present time. Many of these are double monsters, with doubling of parts or nearly all of the fetus. These double monsters apparently arise from incomplete development or separation of monozygotic twins very early in the stage of the ovum. These could be the result of an imperfect ovum or sperm or both or the result of some environmental influence on the fertilized ovum at that early stage. Since these more extreme monsters occur sporadically as a cause for dystocia and since their origin is so early in the gestation period little is known of their basic causes.

There is a common erroneous belief among laymen, that excess size of the sire over the dam results in dystocia. The size of the dam generally regulates the size of the fetus. The weight of newborn animals in unipara is between 6 and 10 percent of the dam's weight. This is seldom exceeded by more than 1 to 2 percent. Experiments by Walton and Hammond using artificial insemination by which Shire horses and Shetland ponies were mated to each other—Shire stallions on Shetland mares and Shetland stallions on Shire mares—proved that foals by a Shire stallion out of Shetland mares were not appreciably larger than pure Shetland foals. Foals by Shetland stallions out of Shire mares were three times as large as pure Shetland foals but not quite as large as pure Shire foals. This difference was not as marked in cattle and sheep. Hilder and Fohrman reported little difference between the size of calves produced by crossing Holstein bulls on Jersey cows or Jersey bulls on Holstein cows. Joubert and Hammond, however, reported a greater difference when the small Dexter cattle and the large South Devon cattle were crossed. The results of their experiment were as follows:

	S. Devon Dams & Dexter Sires	Dexter Dams & S. Devon Sires
Wt.* of dams (postpartum)	1031.7	535.3
Wt. of crossbred calves at birth**	72.0	57.5
Wt. of placenta	10.6	3.2
Wt. lost at birth	127.0	78.7

* Weight—pounds.
** Purebred South Devon calves average 94.5 pounds and purebred Dexter calves average 52.3 pounds.

Hammond reported that this difference was greater in horses and less in the other species because the length of gestation in horses was longer and thus the influence of the maternal environment was greater. Of farm animals the foal is born in the most advanced state of physiological development, while the pig is by far the most immature. At birth the foal weighs 9 percent and the pig less than 1 percent of their mature weight. The breeding of a small Jersey or Angus bull to a Holstein cow or heifer would result in a calf only slightly smaller than a purebred Holstein calf. Heifers of the larger breeds of cattle often experience difficulty in calving, usually due to having been bred at too young an age, having been raised under unfavorable conditions, or having been grown poorly during the gestation period. A sire of a small breed such as Jersey, Ayrshire or Angus is often used on heifers to help avoid dystocia by producing slightly smaller crossbred calves. Arthur, citing Donald, reported that Holstein and Hereford bulls when mated to heifers sired larger calves than bulls of the smaller breeds. He and Edwards reported that Charolais sires mated to dairy breed dams quadrupled the incidence of dystocia, from 2 to 9 percent. When Charolais bulls were mated with Jersey and Guernsey dams only a slight increase in dystocia was noted, Hanson, Mason. Apparently this was due to the relatively large pelvis in these latter breeds. The dystocias associated with crossbreeding with Charolais bulls were usually caused by male calves. Similar results may also be noted with certain Holstein sires mated to heifers. Thus the breed of the sire has a greater influence on the incidence of dystocia than does the breed of the heifer. Conversely Jamison et al. found little difference in size or body measurements of offspring of 7 breeds of rams mated to grade native black-faced ewes in northwestern United States. A slight increase in the size of the heads of lambs sired by Hampshire rams was noted. Fetuses from primipara are usually smaller and lighter than those in subsequent births. Hammond reported that heifers calving for the first time had calves that were an average of 10 pounds lighter than calves from older cows. Gilts also produced smaller offspring than sows. This condition probably arises because the nutritive needs of the growing body of the dam are competing with the fetal needs. Males at birth are larger and heavier than females in all animals except the horse. This may account in part for the higher incidence of dystocia in the birth of males. VanDieten. He has also demonstrated that dystocia is influenced by the sire but the large size of the fetus was only one of the influencing factors. Benesch and Wright cited an instance in which rams of a breed with large heads, possibly Hampshires, if bred to females of a smaller breed produced an increased incidence of dystocia due to the large fetal heads. Hammond cited Hunter as reporting that when large Border Leicester sheep and the small Welsh sheep were crossed, a slight maternal effect was found. The large ram had a greater influence on the size of the lamb from the small dam than from the large dam. When Angus, Charolais and Hereford bulls and cows were crossbred over a 3-year period, it was noted that Charolais and Hereford bulls on Angus cows produced 30 and 29 percent dystocia, respectively, while crosses of males on other females produced no dystocia problem, Sagebiel et al.: Boyd and Hafs demonstrated that Holstein bulls bred to Holstein cows produced calves averaging 93 pounds in weight, 30.8 inches in heart girth and 5.1 inches in head width; Angus bulls bred to Holstein cows produced calves averaging 79 pounds, 29.3 inches and 5.0 inches, respectively. Two of 10 Holstein bulls sired significantly larger calves than the other 8 Holstein bulls and 1 of the 4 Angus bulls sired significantly smaller calves. The incidence of dystocia in the purebred births were 4.7 percent and the crossbred births 1.5 percent. Sires used in artificial insemination should be ranked for size of calves.

The basic causes for dystocia are multiple, but by properly applying our knowledge its incidence may be kept at a minimum. In general all elements that lower resistance or otherwise unfavorably affect the general health and vigor of the dam or fetus increase the possibility of dystocia.

The Immediate Causes of Dystocia

Attendant upon dystocia are many forms of interference with physiological birth. The veterinarian handling dystocia is largely concerned with correcting or relieving the immediate interferences to birth, which may be divided for convenience into maternal and fetal types of dystocia; some overlapping may occur in certain conditions. In 95 cases of dystocia in cattle reported by Wright 25 percent were due to maternal causes and 75 percent due to fetal causes.

The Maternal Causes of dystocia are largely those factors that produce a narrowing or stenosis of the birth passage or prevent the normal entrance of the fetus into the birth canal. These include: fractures and exostoses of the pelvis; small size of the pelvis due to breeding at too young an age, or due to improper rearing with resultant stunting of body growth; hereditary or congenital hypoplasia of the birth canal or vulva; compression or stenosis of the cervix, vagina, or vulva by indurations caused by scars and connective tissue usually from injuries at previous parturitions; intrapelvic hemorrhage; perivaginal fat; impaction of the colon or distension of the bladder in dogs; tumors such as chondrosarcoma of the pelvic bones, fibromas, lipomas or leiomyomas of the uterus, cervix or vagina, or lymphomas of the large pelvic lymph glands; torsion of the uterus; persistence of the medial wall of the Mullerian duct; failure of the cervix to dilate or "ringwomb" in ewes; uterine inertia; hydrops of the fetal membranes, inguinal or ventral hernias; rupture of the prepubic tendon; transverse presentations; uterine infections resulting in uterine inertia, death, abortion, or emphysema of the fetus; and twinning. In uniparous animals twinning is considered a maternal cause for dystocia since it is usually due to double ovulation.

The Fetal Causes of dystocia are more numerous and are due in general to abnormal presentation, position and posture and to excessive size of the fetus. (See Figure 86) These include: certain posterior longitudinal presentations in uniparous animals and all transverse ventral and dorsal presentations; dorso-ilial or dorso-pubic positions; flexion of the limbs beneath the body in uniparous and large multiparous fetuses; ventral, lateral or dorsal flexing of the head and neck; fetal anasarca, ascites, large fetal tumors, distention of any hollow organ such as the brain, stomach, cutaneous sac in **Schistosomus reflexus,** kidneys and ureters; fetal giantism in prolonged gestation; and fetal abnormalities or monsters such as mummified fetus, general ankylosis, double monsters, achondroplastic fetuses, and others.

The incidence of dystocia in posterior presentations of the fetus in unipara is high. In 800 births in Holsteins reported by Ben-David, 4.5 percent were posterior presentations but 47.2 percent of these were accompanied by dystocia. Woodward and Clark reported that one Hereford sire used on an inbred line of cattle produced a high incidence of posterior presentations suggestive of an hereditary factor conditioning such a malpresentation. Up to 30 percent of the fetuses in multipara are commonly expelled in posterior presentation without dystocia occurring. Williams pointed out that in rare cases transverse pregnancies in mares may correct themselves and become anterior or posterior longitudinal presentations. This may be suspected by the discovery that the fetus has a wry neck, caused by a lack of room for movement in transverse pregnancy and proven by examination of the fetal membranes. Some equine fetuses in longitudinal presentations may also develop a wry neck, Vandeplassche. If the fetus is presented in a dorso-ilial or dorso-pubic position, torsion of the uterus may be present. Many of the abnormal postures resulting in dystocia undoubtedly arise during the first and second stages of labor, with the fetal extremities catching on the pelvic brim or soft structures in the birth canal. These abnormal postures may often be predisposed by a weak or dead fetus. Benesch and Wright stated that lateral deviation of the head is seen in all species. Since this is seen more often in fetuses located in the terminal or apical portions of the horns, it may rarely be caused in multipara by a lack of space. In posterior presentation lateral deviation of the head is corrected by passage of the fetus through the birth canal and hence it is not observed unless a wry neck is present.

The Common Forms of Dystocia in Domestic Animals

In the Mare dystocia is most often caused by an abnormal presentation, position, or posture. The long extremities of the fetus tend to predispose the mare to dystocia. Abnormal posture of the head and neck is one of the most common causes of dystocia in mares. Hammond has cited Issachsen to show that at birth the foreleg from the fetlock to the elbow is 73 percent of its adult length. Dystocia due to monsters or to disproportion between fetal size and pelvic diameters is rare. Transverse ventral

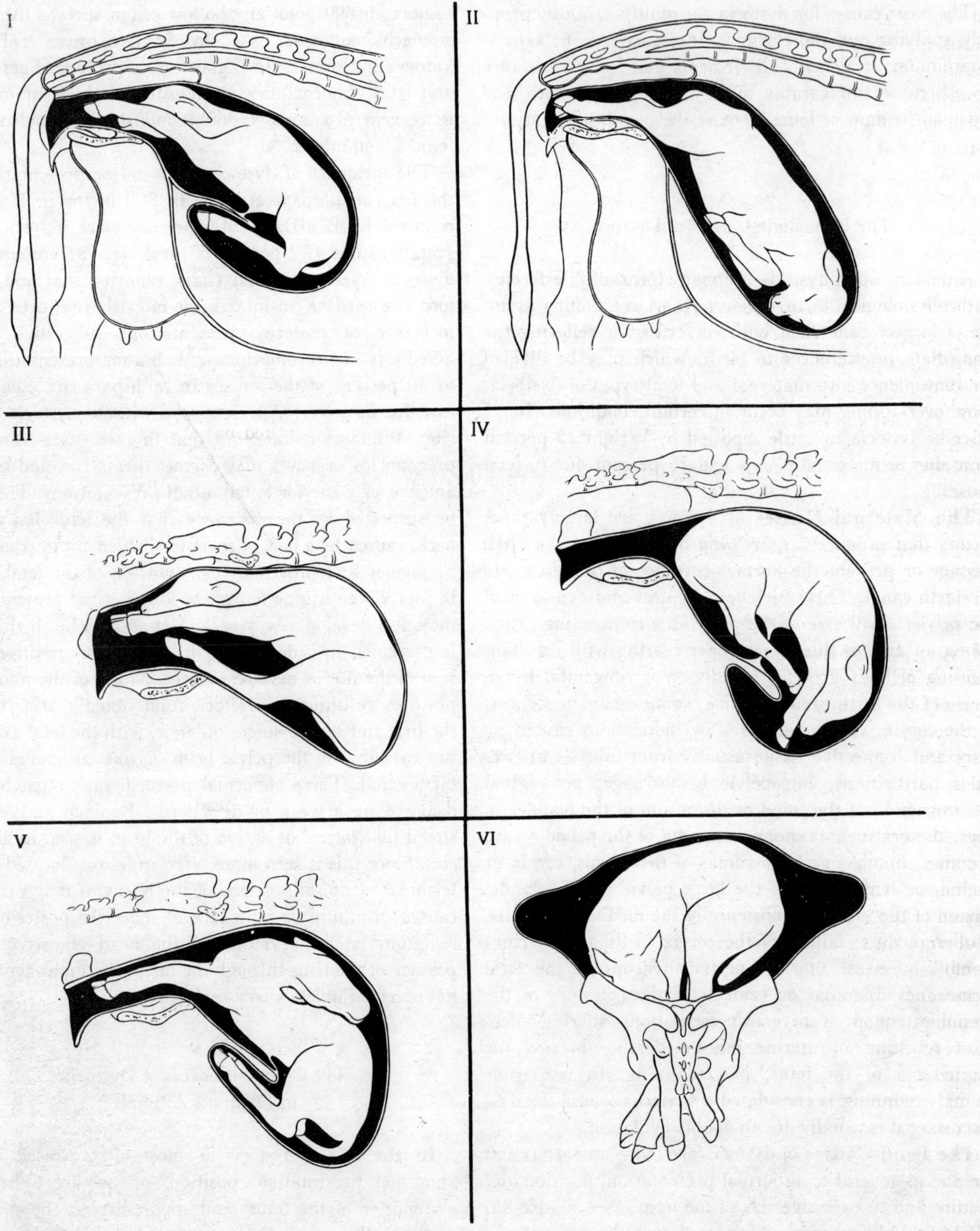

Figure 86. Normal and abnormal presentations, positions and posture in bovine and equine births. I Normal anterior presentation, II Posterior presentation, III Anterior presentation with the rear legs extended beneath the fetus ("dogsitting" posture), IV Posterior presentation with the rear limbs extended beneath the fetus (breech presentation), V Anterior presentation with the head and neck extended over the fetus, VI Transverse ventral presentation of a foal. (as adapted from Diseases of Cattle U.S.D.A., 1942, Harm's Textbook of Veterinary Obstetrics, and Veterinary Obstetrics, 2nd Ed., G. H. Arthur).

presentation is not uncommon, whereas transverse dorsal and rotated bicornual or transverse pregnancies are very unusual (See Figure 86) The ratio of transverse to longitudinal presentations in mares at foaling was 1:1000, Vandeplassche. Dorso-ilial or dorso-pubic positions are occasionally found in the mare due to the fetus failing to rotate to the normal dorso-sacral position early in parturition. All forms of abnormal posture may occur in the mare. One or both of the long forelimbs may even become lodged over the neck of the fetus. Wry neck is seen most commonly in the equine fetus in which it may or may not be associated with transverse pregnancy. Wry neck is characterized by an ankylosis and atrophy and contraction of the neck muscles, thus causing the head and neck to be fixed in a lateral direction alongside the body, similar to a severe, long-standing case of torticollis. It cannot be straightened even after the fetus is delivered. The abnormal positions and postures, together with violent labor contractions, frequently result in impaction of the fetus in the pelvis or in laceration of the vagina, rectum or vulva.

In the Cow disproportion between the fetal size and pelvic diameters are common, especially in primipara. Fetal giantism, hydrops of the fetal membranes and fetus, and fetal emphysema are not uncommon. The incidence of monsters such as achondroplastic fetuses, **Schistosomus reflexus, Perosomus elumbis,** double monsters and fetuses with general ankyloses is higher than in other species. Transverse pregnancy is rare. Uterine inertia and failure of the cervix to dilate are occasionally noted. Twin dystocia and dystocia due to uterine torsion are common. Breech presentation, lateral deviation of the head and neck, and postural abnormalities of the limbs are often observed.

In the Ewe and Goat postural abnormalities and twin or triplet dystocias are common. Marked disproportion between fetal size and pelvic diameters are uncommon. However Stamp cited Moule who reported that about 70 percent of Romney ewes delivering lambs weighing over 10 pounds had dystocia. Fetal anasarca or emphysema are occasionally seen. Relative oversize of the head is seen as a cause for dystocia in certain crosses in sheep. Wyssmann reported that in 50 cases of dystocia in goats 7 were triplet and 21 were twin births; 3.5 percent were in transverse presentation, 15.3 percent in posterior and 81.2 percent in anterior presentation. In the anterior presentation 31.5 percent had a deviated head and neck. In posterior presentations 80 percent of the single births had one or both hind limbs flexed. Ellis and Grommers reported that in 1200 dystocias in ewes 65 percent of the fetuses were in anterior presentation, many with a lateral deviation of the head or with one or both forelegs flexed; 27 percent were in posterior presentation and two-thirds of these were in breech presentation; and 8 percent were in a transverse dorsal presentation. Failure of the cervix to dilate occurred in 15 percent of the cases.

In the Sow the incidence of uterine inertia is fairly high. Small litter size tends to cause larger fetuses that may predispose to dystocia. Dystocia in immature or poorly grown gilts is occasionally observed in certain sections of the country. Abnormal fetuses such as cyclops and hermaphrodites are not unusual but they seldom cause dystocia. Double monsters are rare. (See Figure 46)

In the Bitch disproportion between fetal size and pelvic diameters is common in toy and achondroplastic breeds. In the latter the large size of tne head is the principal cause of the dystocia. Oversized fetuses are occasionally seen when there are only one or two fetuses. Uterine inertia, either primary or secondary, is a frequent cause of dystocia. Nervous voluntary inhibition of parturition may occur due to excitement, a strange environment or pain, Freak. A prolonged first stage of birth may occur in posterior presentation of the first fetus because of failure of the head to engage in the pelvis and stimulate uterine and abdominal contractions, Fox. Poll presentation and lateral deviation of the head and neck are quite frequent causes of dystocia. Postural abnormalities of the limbs are of little importance. Dorso-ilial and especially dorso-pubic positions are seen as a cause of dystocia. Monsters are rare except for occasional cases of hydrocephalus, Freak. Transverse presentation is rare and usually occurs only with bicornual pregnancy with a single fetus.

In the Cat dystocia may be due to postural abnormalities of the head and neck and to breech presentation. Only rarely are two fetuses wedged in the pelvis.

References

Arthur, G. H. (1964) Wright's Veterinary Obstetrics, 3rd Ed., Williams and Wilkins Co., Baltimore, Md.

Arthur, G. H. (1966) Recent Advances in Bovine Obstetrics, Vet. Rec., **79,** 22, 630.

Bellows, R. A. (1966) Improving Reproductive Efficiency in Beef Cattle, Veterinary Scope, Upjohn Co., Kalamazoo, Mich. **11,** 3.

BenDavid, B. (1961) Obstetrical Problems in the Israeli Friesian Cow II Observations on Abnormal Parturition, Refuah Vet. **18,** 152.

Benesch, F. and Wright, J. G. (1951) Veterinary Obstetrics, Williams and Wilkins Co., Baltimore, Md.

Boyd, L. J. and Hafs, H. D. (1965) Body Size of Calves from Holstein Dams and Sired by Holstein and Angus Bulls, J. Dairy Sci. **48,** 9, 1236.

Bratton, R. W. (1957) Breeding Difficulties in Dairy Cattle, Cornell Univ. Agr. Exp. Stat. Bull. 924, Ithaca, N.Y.

Edwards, J. et al. (1966) The Charolais Report, Milk Marketing Board, Thames, Ditton, Surrey, England.

Ellis, T. H. (1958) Observations on Some Aspects of Obstetrics in the Ewe, Vet. Rec. **70,** 952.

Fox, M. W. (1966) Canine Pediatrics, C. C. Thomas Co., Springfield, Ill.

Freak, M. J. (1962) Abnormal Conditions Associated with Pregnancy and Parturition in the Bitch, Vet. Rec. **74,** 1323.

Grommers, F. J. (1967) A Preliminary Study on the Actual and Potential Perinatal Lamb Mortality in Texel Sheep, Tijdschr. v. Diergeneesk. **92,** 222.

Hammond, J. (1955) Progress in the Physiology of Farm Animals, Vol. 2, Butterworths Scientific Publications, London, England.

Hansen, L. H. (1966) Incidence of Dystocia and Postparturient Disorders in Jersey Cattle after Crossbreeding with Charolais Bulls, Brit. Vet. Jour. **122,** 273.

Hilder, R. A. and Fohrman, M. H. (1949) Growth of First Generation Crossbred Dairy Calves, J. Agr. Res., **78,** 11, 457.

Jamison, H. J., Carter, R. C., Gaines, J. A. and Kincaid, C. M. (1961) The Effect of Breed of Sire on Body Size of Lambs at Birth, J. An. Sci. **20,** 154.

Joubert, D. M. and Hammond, J. (1954) Maternal Affect on Birth Weight in South Devon and Dexter Cattle Crosses, Nature **174,** 4431, 647.

Mason, I. L. (1964) Genetical Aspects of Breeding Cattle for Beef (Muscle Hypertrophy), Vet. Rec. **76,** 28, 765.

Rice, L. E. and Wiltbank, J. N. (1970) Dystocia in Beef Heifers, J. An. Sci. **30,** 6, 1043.

Sagebiel, J. A., Krause, G. F., Sibbit, W. R., Langford, L., Comfort, E. Dyer, A. J. and Lasley, J. F. (1968) Dystocia in Reciprocally Crossing Angus, Charolais and Herefords, J. An. Sci. **27,** 4, 1128.

Stamp, J. T. (1967) Perinatal Loss in Lambs with Particular Reference to Diagnosis, Vet. Rec. **81,** 21, 530.

Stonaker, H. H. (1958) Breeding for Beef, Colo. State Univ. Exp. Stat. Bulletin 501-5, Ft. Collins, Colo.

VandenBussche, O., VandenBussche, P. and Vandeplassche, M. (1964) Dystocia in the Red Cattle of West Vlaanderen, Vlaams Diergeneesk Tijdschr, **33,** 5, 205.

Vandeplassche, M. (1958) The Normal and Abnormal Presentation, Position and Posture of the Foal-Fetus during Gestation and Parturition, Dept. of An. Obst. and Reprod., State Univ., Ghent, Belgium.

VanDieten, S. W. J. (1963) Stillbirth in Bovine Cattle, Thesis, Univ. of Utrecht, Utrecht, Holland.

Walton, A. and Hammond, J. (1938) The Maternal Effects on Growth and Conformation in the Shire Horse-Shetland Pony Crosses, Proc. Royal Soc. B., **125,** 311.

Williams, W. L. (1943) Veterinary Obstetrics, 4th Ed., Miss Louella Williams, Upland Rd., Ithaca, N.Y.

Woodward, R. R. and Clark, R. T. (1959) A Study of Stillbirths in a Herd of Range Cattle, J. An. Sci. **18,** 1, 85.

Wright, J. G. (1958) Bovine Dystocia, Vet. Rec. **70,** 17, 347.

Wyssmann, E. (1945) Statistics on Dystocia in Goats (Trans.) Schweitz. Archiv. fur Tierheilk., **87,** 57.

Chapter VIII

PROCEDURES PRELIMINARY TO THE HANDLING OF DYSTOCIA

Dystocia cases are handled promptly as emergency calls but it is essential to a successful outcome that the animal be given a routine careful examination to establish the correct diagnosis so that a sound course of action can be outlined.

The History of the Case

As the preliminary examinations and preparations for handling the dystocia are being made, the history of the case as well as certain other information should be obtained from the owner or by observation. This information should include: the duration of gestation; the previous breeding history; whether dystocia or any other abnormal condition was present at previous parturitions; whether the animal had exhibited any illness or unusual symptoms during the two months to the last few hours prior to parturition; the length of time the animal has been acting uneasy and shown anorexia or restlessness, or the length of time the animal has been in active labor. What is the nature of the straining—strong or weak, intermittent or regular, increasing or decreasing in frequency? Has the allantoic sac ruptured, the amnionic sac appeared at the vulva, or has any portion of the fetus appeared? In multipara have any fetuses been expelled and if so were they living or dead? Has any assistance such as traction been used by the owner, his neighbors, or even other veterinarians? Is the animal primiparous or pluriparous? Has the animal been able to get up if recumbent? This information is useful and necessary for the intelligent examination and handling of a dystocia case. The answers to some of these questions may have been obtained at the time the veterinarian was called or can be gotten along with the general examination of the patient.

The General Examination

The general examination of the patient with dystocia should include its physical condition, whether it is thin and emaciated, too fat, or in good condition. If the animal is recumbent the veterinarian should determine the following: Is it able to rise or is it exhausted? If it is a heifer is it affected with obturator paralysis usually seen in hiplock conditions. In older dairy cows parturient paresis or other conditions causing paraplegia of pregnancy may be present. It is much better to diagnose the presence of such conditions as obturator paralysis and inform the owner before the operation. Afterwards, if this has not been done, the owner often will blame the veterinarian for having produced the paralysis during the relief of the dystocia. The pulse and temperature should be noted. In most dystocia cases the pulse is moderately elevated and the temperature may be slightly higher than normal due to the efforts at parturition. The degree of abdominal enlargement should be noted. Dystocia in dogs is often characterized by depression and futile laboring during which the bitch's mouth is open and its head is repeatedly thrown back. In exhausted prostrate animals the color of the mucous membranes should be noted for evidence of internal hemorrhage or shock due to rupture of the uterine vessels or rupture of the uterus. The general appearance and attitude of the animal should be observed, since some cattle affected with rabies frequently show tenesmus that might be confused with labor. Particular attention should be paid to the vulva. The nature of the vulvar discharge, whether it is watery, mucoid, bloody, or fetid will often indicate the condition of the fetus. If much fresh blood is present, injury to the birth canal has probably occurred due to the intervention of the owner or someone else. The character of the fetal membranes if hanging from the vulva are of further assistance in determining the condition of the fetus and the length of time the dystocia has existed. If a portion of the fetus protrudes from the vulva its condition and position and posture should be observed. The vulva itself should be noted to gain information on the amount of edema or trauma present as an indication of the length of time the dystocia has existed and whether someone has already been trying to deliver the fetus.

The Specific Examination and Restraint

The specific examination consisting of the detailed examination of the genital tract and fetus should be undertaken only after the animal has been properly confined and restrained, as the obstetrical operations usually follow immediately after this examination.

If the animal is on pasture it is usually advisable, especially at night, in rough country, or during inclement weather to advise the owner, at the time he calls, to take the animal to a box stall in the barn, or to a shed near the dwelling house. This will usually insure light, easy access to hot water, and fairly comfortable working conditions. These are definitely desirable if a clean, careful obstetrical procedure is to be followed. It may avoid chilling and exposure of the operator as well as the patient. Aftercare and proper nursing are easier if the animal is near the owner's residence. A clean pasture lot or even a well-bedded stanchion stall are better locations in which to work than is a dirty, dark, cramped or too-small box stall. These suggestions are only common-sense practices and precautions but often if the veterinarian does not suggest or insist upon them the owner will neglect to provide satisfactory surroundings for the patient and operator. Working in the hot summer sun, on "the northside of a barbed wire fence" in winter, knee-deep in water or filth, or in a dusty, dark, low ceilinged swine house is not conducive to proper surgical cleanliness or technique. If a good supply of hot water is not available the veterinarian should take it with him.

If possible the animal should be standing at the time of the examination. A satisfactory examination and the handling of dystocia are much more difficult in the recumbent patient, with the viscera and fetus forced into the pelvic cavity. Most animals rise promptly when urged. Others may be fatigued or may not wish to stand, and more vigorous methods, such as prodding them over the loins and rump with a sharp object, rolling the tail, sudden thumping of the ribs over the chest with the operator's knees, the use of the electric prod, or the intravenous injection of central nervous stimulants such as **Amfetasul, Coramine** or **Pyribenzamine.** Occasionally a cow which has refused to rise will do so after a small dose of anesthetic epidurally has relieved the pain. If the animal fails to get up, its rear parts should be raised above the front by lowering the front parts; or the rear parts may be placed on bags of straw, or elevated on a door or a plank resting on blocks and the animal held in place by a breast-harness. The rear parts may be hoisted by means of a figure-of-eight knot of rope around the hocks, which places the animal on its back, or by passing loops of rope around each leg up to the crotch and hoisting the animal's rear parts. If this latter method is used, the animal often falls sideways if it struggles. In recent years the judicious use of commercially available hip slings is highly advantageous in these cases. In nearly all cases of dystocia a standing position or the elevation of the rear parts is necessary in order that the veterinarian may work with relative ease and effect a prompt correction of the dystocia. It is therefore desirable that the animal be placed in this position prior to the examination.

The animals should be properly restrained so that they do not injure the operator at the time of the examination or operation. In mares a twitch usually should be applied to the lip and one foreleg held up. In range cattle a well-constructed chute is desirable, or cows might be fastened securely with a rope halter in a corner of a large box stall. If they kick, a nose lead will often divert their attention. In sheep the forelimbs should be tied together and the rear parts elevated by an assistant straddling the ewe. This position minimizes straining, aids repulsion and the introduction of a lubricant, Ellis. Sows can be fastened securely by a strong rope with a loop around the upper jaw and behind the canine teeth. The sows may be secured or placed in a farrowing crate. Restless sows may be restrained by a short obstetrical chain around the metacarpus of the left foreleg and above the hock on the left rear leg and laying the sow on her left side, Railsback. Dogs should be muzzled or have their jaws tied together and cats should be held firmly by an assistant. The use of epidural anesthesia, tranquilizers or slight or deep narcosis may be necessary to properly restrain some animals.

In doing obstetrical work on large animals, the most satisfactory dress is: rubber boots, the type that slip on over the shoes; a pair of rubber pants or overalls; in warm weather a sleeveless cotton shirt or jacket and in cold weather a rubber jacket with no sleeves and the armholes cut or adjusted with elastic to fit tightly over the upper arm. Rubber gloves and sleeves can be worn, when indicated, to prevent infection and odors from contaminating the arms of the operator. These rubber gloves and sleeves are often damaged by instruments if fetotomy is employed. The long obstetrical gown is generally undesirable because it is extremely hot in the summer and does not provide proper protection to the lower portion of the operator's body when he has to kneel to work on the recumbent animal.

The animal's external genitalia and the surrounding structures should be washed thoroughly with warm water and soap. In sheep and long-haired dogs it is necessary to clip the wool and hair in the perineal area. The tail should be held to one side by an assistant or tied with a tail rope over the back to the opposite elbow. In the mare the tail should be bandaged. Adding a sanitizing detergent like the quaternary ammonium compounds and a wetting agent to the water used in washing the rear parts of the dam will aid in thoroughly cleansing the area. In cattle epidural anesthesia is helpful in preventing frequent defecation of loose feces that would contaminate the area as well as the operator's arm. In some cases, however, epidural anesthesia might not be desirable, as it would cause a cessation of straining or labor. This straining may be helpful in the withdrawal of a normally-presented fetus. During the examination and obstetrical operation the perineal area should be kept washed and clean at all times. The operator should wash and lubricate his arms with water and soap before making an examination of the birth canal and fetus. In the cat and bitch, after giving an enema and catheterizing the bladder, the rear parts may be cleansed and covered with a sterile drape; the veterinarian should wear sterile rubber gloves.

If the history of the case leads the veterinarian to know or suspect that others have been examining and attempting to relieve the dystocia, it is extremely important that the birth passages and caudal portions of the uterus be examined very carefully for evidence of trauma. In the middle of an obstetrical operation it is highly embarrassing to find a tear in the vagina or uterus which was present or had been produced before the operation was begun. If this injury causes the death of the animal, the owner might accuse the veterinarian of having injured the animal. The veterinarian would not be able to prove his innocence. The birth canal should be examined to see if it is dilated, twisted, moist or slippery, inflamed, swollen, dry, necrotic, contains pathological bands, stenotic areas or tumors, or contains gummy mucus indicating that parturition has not yet begun or is in the early stages. The degree of dilation or relaxation of the cervix should be noted as well as whether there is any evidence of torsion. The size of the pelvic inlet, vulva, and vagina in relation to the size of the fetus should be checked. Any other abnormalities of the birth canal should be noted.

The fetus should be examined to see if it is dead or alive as this will alter the prognosis and make a difference in the manner in which the case is handled. If the fetus is alive, grasping the foot and pulling or pinching it will cause movement of the limb. Pinching the eyeballs will cause the live fetus to shake its head. Placing the fingers in the mouth of the fetus may cause sucking or movements of the tongue and jaw. Putting fingers in the anus in breech presentation will cause contraction of the anal sphincter. If the fetus is dead the degree of decomposition should be accurately assessed by the amount of subcutaneous edema or emphysema, whether or not the hair is sloughing and whether or not a putrid fetid odor is present. When fetal emphysema and sloughing of the hair is present the fetus has been dead for 24 to 48 hours or more depending on the degree of changes noted. After a dead fetus has been removed from the uterus, if no emphysema is present, the length of time death has existed may be approximately determined by the degree of cloudiness, turbidity or greying of the cornea. After the fetus has been dead 6 to 12 hours the corneas are grey and opaque.

The fetus should be carefully examined to determine any abnormality of presentation, position, and posture, or any teratologic defects. In a breech presentation the tail is often observed hanging from the vulva or lying in the birth canal. If the head is not in the birth canal in anterior presentation its location can be determined by finding the neck, the mane of the equine fetus, or the ears and head, by swinging the arm and hand around the cephalic part of the body. If the feet are lying in the birth canal it should be determined whether they are front or hind feet. Inexperienced students frequently confuse the front and hind legs by mistaking the hock for the elbow or the elbow for the hock. Front limbs have two joints, fetlock and knee, between the hoof and elbow, while hind limbs have only one joint, the fetlock, between the hoof and hock.

If the feet are protruding through the vulva with the soles ventral then the fetus is in either anterior longitudinal dorso-sacral position or posterior longitudinal dorso-pubic position. The latter rarely occurs. If the soles of the feet are dorsal then the fetus is in either posterior longitudinal presentation, dorso-sacral position; or anterior longitudinal presentation, dorso-pubic position. This latter condition is only rarely observed. In fetal monsters the differentiation into the various types may be quite difficult, as ankylosis and marked distortion are frequently present. Most of these abnormal fetuses have severely atrophied muscles of the limbs, making them feel thin, very firm, and rigid. If no part of the fetus is in the vagina of the mare the condition is probably a transverse dorsal or rotated bicornual pregnancy. In the latter condition the birth canal is very long and the fetus can be touched only at arm's length. Occasionally the amnion may not yet be ruptured, in which case if the birth passageway is dilated sufficiently the amnion may be ruptured with the fingers or a knife, so that palpation of the fetus may be facilitated. If more than two limbs are entering or are near the pelvis, the condition should be examined carefully to differentiate between twins that are wedged in the pelvis, a **Schistosomus reflexus**, a double monster, or in the mare a transverse ventral presentation.

It may occasionally be necessary to repel the fetus out of the birth canal and into the uterus in order to diagnose accurately the cause of the dystocia. If the animal is straining severely, epidural anesthesia should be given at once so that the examination can proceed without interruption. Sometimes examination is difficult, especially in a protracted dystocia in heifers, with swollen mucous membranes, a dry, dead fetus, and a uterus contracting tightly around it, making it impossible to repel the fetus. In mares and occasionally other animals, where the owner has applied traction, the fetus may become firmly wedged in the pelvis. A similar examination is made with a finger **per vaginum** in the bitch. Strict cleanliness is necessary, as in other species. If more than one fetus is palpated in the abdominal cavity and the bitch has suffered a prolonged dystocia, inertia has probably developed and cesarean section will in all likelihood be indicated without a vaginal examination. The importance of this complete examination cannot be overstressed, as it is the basis of the prognosis and procedures that follow in the handling of the case. It should be thorough and accurate to be professional, to save time and effort in useless and often harmful procedures, and to determine in severe cases whether or not outside help or consultation is needed.

Prognosis

The prognosis in dystocia varies widely between the different causes and species affected. For this reason the prognosis in the various types of dystocia will be considered as each type is discussed. In general the more prolonged the dystocia, the poorer the prognosis. The greater the trauma, irritation and infection of the birth canal caused by inexperienced laymen attempting to relieve the dystocia, the graver the prognosis. The prognosis in horses is graver than other domestic animals because the fetus usually dies within 30 to 40 minutes after the commencement of labor. The mare's pelvis is longer, and the fetal extremities are longer, making correction of the dystocia more difficult. Labor contractions are violent and powerful, predisposing to impaction of the fetus in the pelvis, lacerations of the birth passages or rupture of the uterine vessels. Lastly, the mare is more susceptible than other animals to trauma, irritation, infection, and inflammation of the birth passage and to peritonitis. It is difficult to save the life of a mare if she has been in labor for more than 24 hours and the fetus is emphysematous. The same is true of other animals but the prognosis is usually better, as other species are more resistant to infection. The fetus in the cow usually dies after 3 to 12 hours of labor and emphysema sets in about 24 to 36 hours after the onset of labor. In the bitch, according to Wright and Benesch, the first fetus usually dies within 6 to 8 hours; after the onset of labor and may become emphysematous in 24 to 36 hours, but some of the other fetuses may still be alive. After 48 hours of labor no living canine fetuses are ever found. In sows the first pig usually dies after 4 to 6 hours of labor. The other pigs may survive for 24 hours. After 24 to 36 hours of labor all fetal pigs are invariably dead. The ewe is similar to the cow.

Williams very aptly described the handling of dystocia as resembling a salvaging operation on a "ship on the rocks." If it is possible, the following should be salvaged:

1. the value of the surviving dam—its future breeding life, its food value for milk or meat, or its value for work.
2. the value of the newborn.
3. the sentimental value of the dam or newborn.

In the prognosis of a case of dystocia these values or credits should be weighed against the:

1. veterinary fees
2. mortality risk of the dam and the newborn
3. cost of labor and feed until the dam has recovered her value for milk, meat, work or breeding.

When these factors are considered and discussed with the owner after a careful examination of the patient, the prognosis and handling of the case will be understood by the owner. In the large farm animals whose value is usually entirely economic and not sentimental, the veterinary fees will then be paid more willingly. If the prognosis is correct these fees should not exceed the salvage or slaughter value. Many young veterinarians have labored diligently and corrected a severe dystocia, visited the animal several times subsequently to provide necessary care and drugs, and then presented the bill only to have the owner exclaim, "That's more than the heifer is worth." This embarrassing position would have been avoided if the above factors had been discussed fully with the owner before the veterinarian undertook the correction of the more severe dystocia cases. Thus the prognosis should take into consideration more than just the life of the dam or fetus unless the sentimental value is of prime importance.

Obstetrical Equipment and Anesthesia

The best guarantee of the proper and satisfactory handling of dystocia is the operator's correctly applied knowledge and experience. Good help and equipment may be available, but if the problem presented in each dystocia case cannot be perceived, the several methods of handling it are not evaluated, a practical and logical approach and procedure are not developed, and the ability to follow the outlined procedure calmly and confidently to a successful termination are lacking, the case will probably end in failure, with a dissatisfied or disgusted owner. The best obstetrical equipment available should be used. Poor or makeshift equipment is not conducive to good surgical procedures. The instruments should be kept clean and sterile. Chrome or other types of plated or stainless steel instruments are desirable. During obstetrical operations surgical procedures of cleanliness should be followed in so far as this is possible. A plentiful supply of hot water and soap are usually necessary. If possible a table should be provided and covered with a sterile sheet upon which the obstetrical instruments may be placed during the operation. Since this is usually lacking a clean pail of water filled with an antiseptic solution can be used in which instruments may be placed or kept to prevent contamination. If the operation must be performed in a barn on a recumbent animal a sterile rubber sheet placed under the rear parts of the cow may help reduce contamination. In practice these sheets are difficult to hold in place. Epidural anesthesia may be necessary to control defecation. If the surroundings are poor the animal should be moved to a more suitable place.

It is not necessary to have all of the following obstetrical equipment for the handling of dystocias. Certain veterinarians become quite adept at using particular instruments while others prefer different ones. The type of practice in the various areas of the country also determines to a large extent the type of equipment that is accepted and used (see Figure 87).

Obstetrical Instruments for Traction on the fetus include:

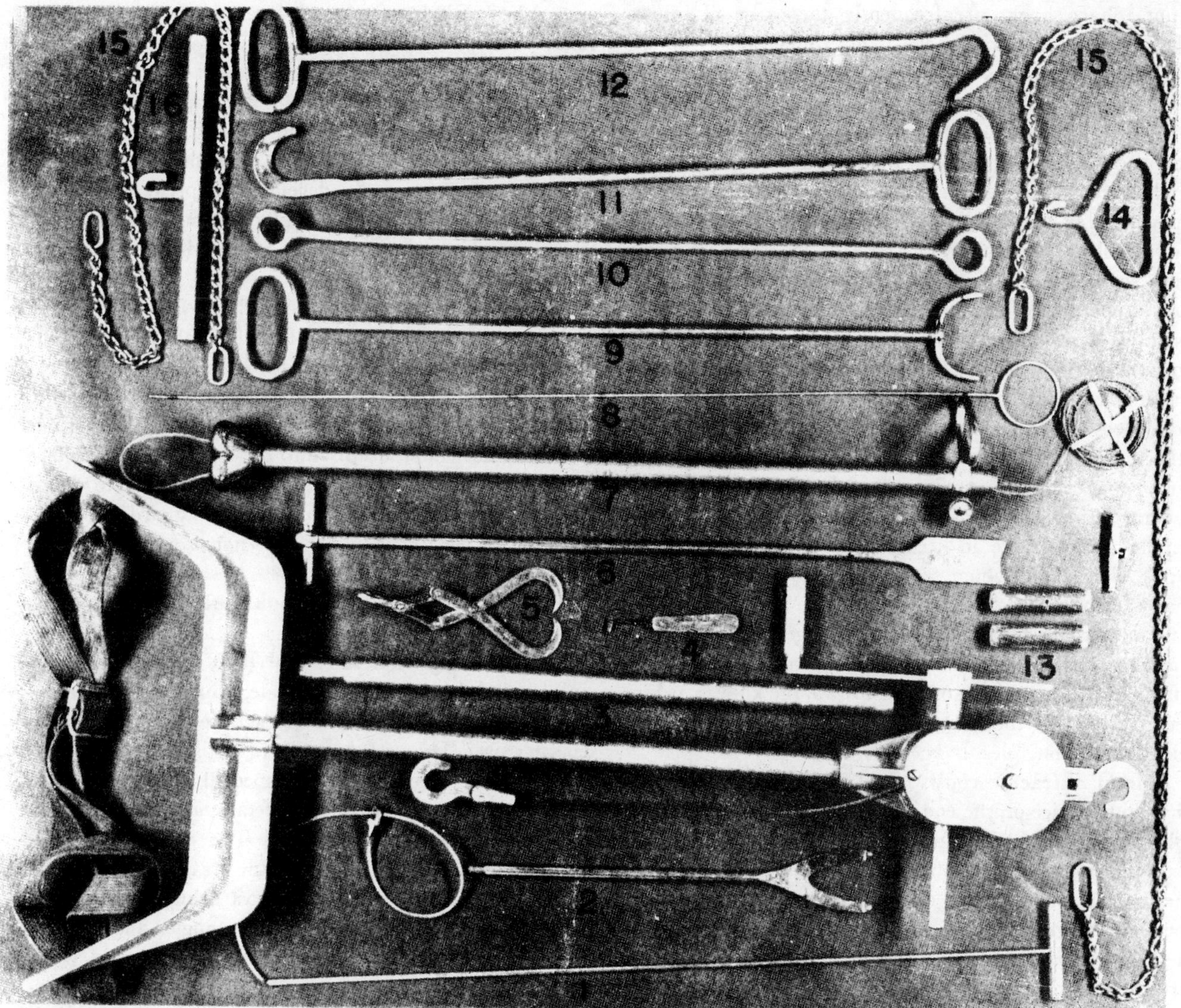

Figure 87. Bovine and Equine Obstetrical Instruments 1. Head snare, 2. Guard's chisel, 3. Fetal extractor, 4. Hoeblade castrating knife, 5. Krey's hook or tongs, Williams' chisel, 7. Fetatome, 8. Threader for fetatome wire, 9. Crutch repeller, 10. Detorsion rod 11. Williams' blunt-pointed cutting hook, 12. Williams' long blunt hook, 13. Handles for wire saw, 14. Muir's chain handle, 15. Moore's obstetrical chains, 16. Gibbons chain handle

Chains and handles: Gibbons' handles, while more bulky than the smaller Muir's handles, are better as they provide a longer, wider hand hold and do not cut into the hands. Obstetrical chains are preferred to sash cord because they may be recleaned and sterilized, provide easier attachment for handles than does sash cord, and do not become stiff. They are more professional in appearance. Obstetrical chains are strong, easily applied, and do not cause injury to the fetus or the genital tract of the dam. They are made in 10-, 21-, 30-, and 60-inch lengths. Lengths of 1- or 2-inch wide sterile gauze may be used for traction in dogs and cats.

Hooks may be long or short but should always be blunt. Sharp hooks are frequently the cause of injury either of the operator or the dam. Blunt hooks can do anything sharp hooks can, but without the added danger. The short hooks have an eye at their base, through which a cord is run. The long hooks have a handle on the end opposite the hook. In general the long hooks are easier to apply because they can be turned or pushed from outside the vulva, but they occupy slightly more room than do the short hooks. The hook should be at a 45° angle from the shaft so that when traction is applied the hook tends to sink deeper into the fetal tissues. Another hook that is useful is Krey's hook or tongs. These may readily be applied to the orbits or other portions of a fetus when traction is desired during fetotomy operations. Krey's hook does not require guarding with the hands, as do other hooks that might pull out of the fetus and injure the birth canal or uterus.

Snares made of thin twisted wire with a long thin handle are valuable in securing the lower jaw or the limbs, since they tighten securely and are much less apt than are chains to slip off and injure the teeth or hooves. The author has found that in an emergency clean hemp cord used for baling hay may be used after disinfection as snares for the lower jaw or limbs. If a large knot is tied in the cord outside the vulva an obstetrical handle may be used for traction.

A **fetal extractor** consisting of a mechanical hoisting or jacking device on the end of a long metal rod fitted into a broad metal breech plate, has proven very useful when used judiciously. When obstetrical chains are fastened to the fetus and to the hoist or jack, traction is applied and the fetus is gradually withdrawn. This instrument has great advantages over the block and tackle and wire stretchers used previously, because it allows traction to be applied upwards, downwards, or to either side. The older block-and-tackle method of traction allowed traction to be applied in only one direction and was much less professional than the fetal extractor.

Forceps of a wide variety are used to relieve dystocia in sheep and swine, dogs and cats. Knowles cervical forceps are very satisfactory in swine as are certain wire forceps or snares. These same forceps and snares work well in many dystocias in sheep. In dogs "clam shell" forceps, sponge forceps, Roberts' snare forceps, or Hobday's type of forceps described by Benesch and Wright are very useful. Leonard preferred the clam-shell type of forcep in which there is a small offset in the handles so that the hinge does not fit tightly and cannot pinch the mucous membrane. Forceps delivery in multipara is necessarily limited to those fetuses that are in the pelvic canal or the body of the uterus just cranial to the pelvic inlet. Great care must be used in applying rigid metal forceps to the extremities of living fetuses as lacerations or injuries are easily produced.

Instruments for section are used in fetotomy or embryotomy to reduce the size of the fetus. These instruments should be kept sharp and in good operating condition. The number and type of instruments are many and each veterinarian usually develops his preferences. Williams stated that there is no place in surgery in which familiarity with an instrument is more important to the operator than in fetotomy.

Knives—A heavy scalpel and a Bard Parker knife are useful in removing a portion of the fetus that may be outside of the body of the cow, as for example, in the operation of decapitation. The hoe or hook-bladed castrating knife is useful within the uterus, particularly the former as it does not cut so deeply into the fetus and is therefore easier to use. These castrating knives are easy to guard with the hand while in the uterus. The guarded Colin's scalpel, ring, or finger knives have not proved as satisfactory.

Williams' long cutting hook with a blunt point is very useful for cutting ribs.

Long cutting chisels are of three types: Williams, with a slightly concave flat blade; Guard's, with a V-shaped head; and the Ames chisel, resembling a nasal septum chisel. The usefulness of chisels is limited.

Fetatomes of many types, especially in Europe, are used to protect and guide the fetatome wire, Benesch, Richter and Gotze, and Arthur. The one most widely used in America is the Benesch Universal fetatome. Fetatomes have the advantage over most chain saws or wire saws in that they can cut at different angles and not just in one caudal direction. The fetatomes use a stiff wire-type threader or guide to place the wire through the fetatome. There are several types of handles for the fetatome wire. The best type is the one in which the fetatome wire is placed between two interlocking rows of "teeth" that firmly secure the crimped wire when the handles are closed. Large forceps are also satisfactory. Several types of heavy metal rings or an obstetrical chain can be used as a guide or leader to carry the fetatome wire around the fetus. The wire should be of the best grade obtainable; it should be kept clean and free from rust, and after having been used for one fetotomy operation should not be used again. Kinking of the wire should be avoided.

In applying and using the fetatome, the fetatome wire should be securely fastened to the guide or an obstetrical chain unless a loop of wire is used. The guide or chain should always be introduced over the top of the fetus, or dorsally and then downwards or ventrally to take advantage of gravity to help carry the weighted guide around the part of the fetus to be removed. If a chain is used a large handful should be coiled in the hand and introduced as far around or over the fetal part as possible before being released. Otherwise the chain may follow the operator's hand and arm as it is pulled back, thus making it impossible to reach when the hand is passed under the fetal structure to pick it up and complete this phase of the operation. This procedure should always be done against the fetal hair, so that fetal membranes will not interfere with nor complicate the prompt placing of the wire. Occasionally the guide or chain will drop into the nongravid horn, making recovery of it impossible when the hand is passed under the fetus or fetal part. If the fetatome wire is already threaded in the fetatome and a loop of this wire is to be slid up and over an extremity, the head of the fetatome should precede and help guide the loop of wire into place. In sectioning the fetus with a fetatome, the head of the fetatome should be held tightly against the fetus, and the handle of the fetatome held or braced with the other hand and arm placed across the chest or hip as the sawing proceeds. The operator performing the sawing should maintain a constant strong tension on the wire with both arms, and use long, smooth strokes. If bone is encountered the wire will become hot and may break; therefore the portion of the wire cutting through the bone should be changed frequently, or sawing should be intermittent in order to allow the wire to cool. Breaking of the wire occurs most often on angular cuts. Care should be used in placing the fetatome, to see that the wires are not crossed between the fetatome and the fetus, as this generally results in immediate breaking of the wire. The fetatome wires should be kept taut at all times to prevent coiling, kinking and breaking. If the progress of the sawing is to be investigated, the assistant who is manipulating the wire should be warned so that the operator's hand or fingers will not be cut.

Wire Saws—There are several wire saws that cost less than the fetatome but they usually cut only in one direction, that is caudally. The pipe used to protect the birth passage from the fetatome wire has no specifically designed head or end of hardened steel. Many other types of wire saws protected by metal spiral tubes or tubular pipes have been designed in Europe. The spiral types may be used to cut in more than one direction, Benesch, Richter and Gotze.

Other more elaborate instruments for section have been devised and used in Europe, Benesch and Wright. The widespread use of the fetatome has made for infrequent use of the long blunt-pointed cutting hook, chisels, and wire saws.

Instruments for Repulsion and Rotation—In repelling the fetus from the pelvic cavity, examining the fetus, or making room for manipulation of the fetus or its extremities, epidural anesthesia and the operator's arm are most commonly used.

Williams' crutch repeller, with or without the removable spike, is very useful when the fetus is firmly impacted in the pelvic inlet. It allows the operator's assistants to provide the strength to repel the fetus, and thus conserves the operator's strength. By use of this crutch the fetus can be repelled downward and forward, upward and forward, or laterally and forward. Kuhn's crutch is strongly advocated by Benesch for the relief of dystocia but it has not become popular in America. Most of the operations performed by this instrument can be performed with greater facility by the operator's hand and arm.

The fetal rotators or uterine detorsion rods are of a number of types and are used to rotate the fetus when it is in longitudinal presentation in an abnormal position. This may be due to torsion of the uterus. As in repulsion the operator's arms or proper direction of traction on the obstetrical chains will correct many torsions of the uterus or dorso-sacral or dorso-pubic positions of the fetus in large uniparous animals. The so-called Cornell detorsion rod is simple and requires only a 60-inch obstetrical chain and handle to make it complete. Other metal rotators, such as Erikson's, resembling a long-handled twitch with snares and chains to fasten the leg to the handle of the instrument have been used. In Europe Cammerer's torsion fork is popular and requires two canvas sleeves, Benesch and Wright.

It is highly desirable that all long-handled instruments, such as the long blunt hook, the blunt-pointed cutting hook, and chisels be solid and rigid, as they often have to be twisted within the uterus or fetus. If they are jointed the instrument can be twisted or rotated in only one direction.

In difficult or prolonged dystocia proper **lubricants** for the genital tract are essential. When the mucous membrane of the vulva and vagina is dry, mild, non-irritating soap, such as Ivory soap flakes, and water or bland liquid soap may suffice in cases needing slight lubrication. In cases requiring much lubrication epidural anesthesia is necessary to prevent the animal straining and throwing out the lubricant, and to cause sufficient relaxation so that the lubricant can flow about and cover the fetus and uterine, cervical, vaginal and vulvar walls. Mineral oil, 1 or 2 quarts, is fairly satisfactory. Older practitioners used linseed infusions or lard. The newer commercial lubricants such as **Lubrivet** and other lubricating jellies in tubes or jars are very good. These solutions or lubricants may be rubbed on the fetus and walls of the birth canal after being pumped in with a stomach pump and tube. In smaller animals the rear parts may be elevated so that the lubricant runs in by gravity. In severe, prolonged operations the lubricant may have to be applied 2 or more times or as frequently as the fetus or birth canal becomes dry. In rotation of the fetus on its long axis lubricants are essential. They help to protect the mucous membranes from irritation, infection, trauma, and even rupture, besides making obstetrical manipulations and operations easier in the prolonged "dry" cases of dystocia associated with a dead or emphysematous fetus.

Other equipment for obstetrical operations should consist of two clean enamel, stainless steel or plastic pails, soap, several types of antiseptics, common surgical instruments including syringes, needles, scalpels, scissors, forceps, suture needles, and various types of sutures, sterile drapes and towels, sponges, razor, cotton, posterior pituitary hormone or oxytocin, anesthetics for local and epidural anesthesia, and general anesthetics such as chloral hydrate for horses, ether, halothane and possibly other intravenous anesthetics for dogs, cats, and swine.

Epidural Anesthesia or Analgesia

Epidural anesthesia in the cow and mare is one of the most useful tools for aiding the operator and relieving pain in the patient suffering from severe dystocia. Prior to this useful tool straining was combatted by a noselead, twitch, sharp object pressed down on the back and even tracheotomy. The former pain-producing techniques are very imperfect or only shortlived. The technique of epidural anesthesia was introduced into the United States by Benesch in 1926. In obstetrical work epidural anesthesia is used frequently because it stops abdominal straining and makes mutation of the fetal extremities, repulsion of the fetus, correction of breech presentation and uterine torsion much easier. It abolishes or reduces all pain and is therefore more humane and should be administered when great power is used as in some forced extractions. It greatly increases the speed, ease, and safety to the operator and patient in fetotomy operations. With proper epidural anesthesia the animal stands quietly without moving about or lying down, which is helpful to the operator. Often the cow that is down and refuses to stand will rise and stand normally following the administration of epidural anesthesia. Defecation is suspended. The animal does not rapidly expel lubricants pumped into the uterus. When used in cesarean section it controls straining and prevents intestinal prolapse through the operative incision. It is used to aid replacement of prolapse of the vagina, cervix, uterus, rectum, or bladder. By controlling straining, it may prevent prolapse of the uterus immediately after a difficult parturition. It alleviates symptoms of straining caused by severe vulvitis or vestibulitis. The use of epidural anesthesia is nearly free of danger and is seldom if ever contraindicated. Normal involution of the uterus is not interferred with and epidural anesthesia does not cause or favor retained placenta. Epidural anesthesia is not required in every dystocia case. In those cases in which a rapid and normal course of parturition is expected or a simple easy manipulation can correct the dystocia, it need not be used.

The technique for administering epidural anesthesia, particularly in the cow, is simple and easily mastered. Most veterinarians use a 16- or 18-guage 1-1/4" to 2" needle. The site for insertion of the needle is determined by elevating and lowering the tail and feeling where the vertebral joints are located by the depression and movement between the vertebrae. The joint between the first and second coccygeal vertebrae is the most moveable in the cow. In proceeding caudally the first vertebrae joint in which movement can usually be felt is between the last sacral and first coccygeal vertebrae. After properly shaving and disinfecting this site, the needle is inserted in the cow between the first and second coccygeal vertebrae or the first coccygeal and last sacral vertebrae. The author prefers the latter site in the cow. The needle is introduced at a 10 degree angle caudally from the perpendicular, and strikes the bottom of the vertebral canal of the last sacral vertebra. This readily determines the depth at which the anesthesia should be injected. Between the first and second coccygeal vertebrae the needle may go entirely through the spinal nerves and joint. Inserting the needle in the mare is more difficult. It is introduced at a slightly greater angle caudally, 30 degrees from the perpendicular, than in the cow, about one inch cranially to the long coarse tail hairs. The veterinarian should be careful to insert the needle directly on the midline. In the cow the needle is inserted about 3/4 to 1-1/2 inches deep, depending on the size, amount of fat and the thickness of the tail. In the mare the needle is usually inserted 1-1/2 to 2-1/2 inches deep. If the needle is inserted carefully one can often feel the point of the needle "pop" through the thick connective tissue sheath covering the nerve. When the needle point has reached the proper location the anesthetic solution flows easily out of the syringe into the epidural space. If the needle is not at the proper site the solution is injected with difficulty. If the anesthetic does not contact the nerve the tail does not become flaccid, and anesthesia of the perineum is not produced. If anesthesia of the motor nerves of the tail is not evident within 3 minutes, this indicates that the anesthetic was not injected properly. Occasionally the needle strikes the artery or vein ventral to the nerve, and blood will flow from the needle. This should be of no concern except that it indicates the needle is at the proper site for injection, or just below the nerve. It should be noted that this epidural injection is a nerve block and not a spinal anesthesia. The injection is outside the dura mater beyond the end of the spinal cord. The spinal cord, containing the spinal fluid, terminates between the second to fourth sacral vertebrae in the cow and the first to third sacral vertebrae in the mare, Arthur.

The amount of anesthetic solution to be injected varies with the type of solution, the weight or size of the animal, the species of animal, and the degree of anesthesia desired. In most obstetrical cases the solution should be injected in repeated small injections, so that the animal remains standing. If too much is given the animal will stagger, and possibly fall and injure itself. The author prefers to use a 2 percent **Xylocaine** or procaine solution in 6 to 10 cc. amounts for 600-pound to 1300-pound cows and mares. **Xylocaine** produces a more rapid and deeper sensory anesthesia than procaine but is more costly. Mixing one part 2 percent **Xylocaine** to two or three parts 2 percent procaine will produce nearly the same excellent effect as **Xylocaine** alone. If 1 percent procaine solution is used the amount of solution injected should be nearly doubled. This anesthesia will last about 1-1/2 to 2 hours. This time may be nearly doubled by adding 0.5 to 1 ml of a 1:1000 solution of epinephrine. Two percent procaine penicillin in 5 to 8 ml. amounts produces satisfactory epidural anesthesia. Many new local anesthetics have been introduced for epidural anesthesia in the cow and mare. Of these, 5 percent **Cyclaine,** 3 to 8 cc. amounts; **Cobefrin** (2 percent novocain with pontocaine and cobefrin); and **Ravocaine** in 4 to 8 cc. amounts are very satisfactory, giving rapid and deep sensory anesthesia lasting over 4 hours with **Cyclaine** and **Cobefrin,** 2 to 3 hours with **Ravocaine,** Roberts. When the animal is recumbent and the operator desires it to remain so, the animal should be placed on its sternum and as much as 20 to 50 cc. of 2 percent procaine or its equivalent may be injected epidurally without any adverse effects and with good sensory and motor anesthesia of the rear quarters. The larger amounts of anesthetic solution are forced cranially to anesthetize the motor nerves to the rear limbs.

Products containing benzyl alcohol, propylene and polythylene glycol when injected into the epidural space produce a prolonged anesthetic effect lasting for 4 to 40 days or more by destroying the nerve fibers. In dairy cattle or horses this is very undesirable; as the animal's rear parts and tail become covered with fecal material because the tail cannot be elevated at the time of defecation and micturition. In rare instances when prolonged destruction of the nerve is desired, 5 to 10 cc. of 70 percent grain alcohol may be injected epidurally. In these instances recovery may be delayed 6 months or more. During the summer months flies and maggots might be a problem.

Epidural anesthesia in sheep and goats is practical but seldom used as the abdominal contractions are not strong enough to interfere greatly with manual manipulations of the fetus. Using an 18-gauge needle 1 to 1-1/2 inches long, the operator may inject 2 to 4 cc. of a local anesthetic solution between the last sacral and first coccygeal vertebrae or between the last two sacral vertebrae.

Epidural anesthesia is seldom used in multipara except for cesarean section because of the number of fetuses and the long period of parturition together with the resulting interruption of labor which would require a prolonged period of observation and assistance for each fetus as it entered the pelvic cavity. Epidural anesthesia or analgesia is obtained in dogs and swine by entering the lumbosacral space with a short-beveled, 2 to 5 inch, 18 to 20 guage, spinal needle with stylet. The space is located on the midline a short distance caudal to a line at right angles to the spinal column and at the level of the crests of the dorso-iliac spines, Klide and Soma, Evers, and Getty. After proper shaving and disinfection of the site, local subcutaneous anesthesia may be administered with a small needle. The spinal needle is passed perpendicularly into the lumbosacral space. When it penetrates the ligamentum flavum or the interarticular spinous ligament a distinct "pop" is felt as the point of the needle enters the epidural space. The stylet should be removed and aspiration applied on the needle to be sure the needle did not penetrate a blood vessel or the subarachnoid space containing the cerebral spinal fluid. This is unlikely as this space is small or not present at this level and is difficult to enter in dogs and swine. The dose of 2 percent **Xylocaine** for epidural anesthesia in the dog is 1 ml per 7.5 to 10 pounds of body weight and for swine is 1 ml per 20 pounds of body weight. If 4 percent procaine is used in swine the dose is 1 ml per 10 pounds of body weight. In dogs 2 percent procaine at a rate of 1 ml per 5 pounds of body weight is recommended, Archibald.

Other Forms of Obstetrical Anesthesia

General anesthesia is often indicated in the mare with severe dystocia when extensive mutation or fetotomy procedures or a cesarean operation must be undertaken. If the fetus is dead, the anesthetic of choice is chloral hydrate in a 6 to 10 percent solution intravenously to effect the desired degree of anesthesia. Most light mares require about 1-1/2 to 2 ounces of chloral hydrate. Many veterinarians use the combination of chloral hydrate 3 parts and magnesium sulphate 2 parts in dilute solution intravenously. Others may add pentobarbital or use the commercial preparation **Equithesin,** containing pentobarbital in combination with chloral hydrate and magnesium sulphate. In the more modern equine clinics inhalation anesthesia of fluothane or a similar agent may be used since these products are safe and relatively nontoxic even when given over a prolonged period of time. If the fetus is alive and saving it is desirable, tranquilizers, epidural or local anesthesia snould be used. On occasion the intravenous or inhalant anesthetics may be used when the fetus is alive, even though the anesthetics cross the placenta, if the fetus is removed immediately after these anesthetics are administered. If the mare is to be given general anesthesia this should be done in a location large enough to work in with ease. With the mare anesthetized, its feet should extend away from the body in a normal manner so that no pressure is placed on the abdominal cavity. The mare may be rolled from one side to the other, to help the operator. For example, if the head and neck of the fetus is retained along the right side of the fetus in anterior presentation the mare should be laid on her right side so the head and neck of the fetus are located above and not beneath its body, where the weight of the fetus would make correction of the deviated head and neck difficult or impossible. Assistants may apply backward pressure to the fetal head through the relaxed upper flank of the mare.

For cesarean section in the cow, tranquilization, epidural, paravertebral, or local anesthesia or combinations of these with chloral hydrate or pentobarbital narcosis or anesthesia may be used. The latter two general anesthetic agents should not be used if a viable fetus is to be delivered. When rolling is used to correct torsion of the uterus in the cow, 1.5 to 2 ounces of chloral hydrate may be given orally in capsules or by stomach tube, or 0.5 to 1 ounce given intravenously to narcotize the animal.

For cesarean section in the sow, ether, chloral hydrate or pentobarbital narcosis with local anesthesia of the operative site is preferred. Spinal anesthesia has been administered to cattle, sows, and dogs, and possibly other animals by injection of procaine into the epidural space of the spinal cord at the lumbo-sacral articulation, but this is more dangerous than the other techniques and is seldom used except in the dog and sow. In the bitch and cat an ether, morphine, and atropine combination is frequently used as a general anesthetic during cesarean operations. In general the long-acting barbituates are not desirable because of their depressing effect on live fetuses.

The proper use of tranquilizers and local and general anesthetics in dystocia and other obstetrical cases is frequently necessary and results in easier, safer, and more rapid handling of birth related problems, to the great benefit of both the animal and the operator.

References

Arthur G. H. (1964) Wright's Veterinary Obstetrics, 3rd Ed., Williams, and Wilkins Co., Baltimore, Md.

Benesch, F. and Udall, D. H. (1926) Contributions from Vienna, Cor. Vet., **16,** 3, 225.

Benesch, F. and Wright, J. G. (1951) Veterinary Obstetrics, Williams, and Wilkins Co., Baltimore, Md.

Ellis, T. H. (1958) Observations on Some Aspects of Obstetrics in the Ewe, Vet. Rec. **70,** 952.

Evers, W. H. (1968) Epidural Anesthesia in the Dog: A Review of 224 Cases with Emphasis on Caesarean Section, Vet. Med. **63,** 12, 1121.

Getty, R. (1963) Epidural Anesthesia in the Hog—Its Technique and Applications, Proc. A.V.M.A., 88.

Klide, A. M. and Soma, L. R. (1968) Epidural Analgesia in the Dog and Cat, JAVMA **153,** 2, 165.

Lacroix, J. V. and Hoskins, H. P. (1952) Canine Surgery, 3rd Ed., Amer. Publicat., Inc., Evanston, Ill.

Leonard, E. P. (1955) Personal Communication.

Richter, J. and Gotze, R. (1960) Tiergeburtshilfe, 2nd Ed., Paul Parey, Berlin, Germany.

Roberts, S. J. (1950) A Comparison of Anesthetics Used in the Bovine Animal, J.A.V.M.A. **116,** 877, 282.

Chapter IX

OBSTETRICAL OPERATIONS

In handling dystocia there are numerous operations or procedures that the veterinarian should be able to perform or use. Following a careful examination, the most conservative procedures should generally be undertaken in the interest of the owner, the veterinarian, the animal, and the fetus. The principal purpose of obstetrical operations is to deliver a viable fetus and to prevent injury to the dam. After a careful assessment of each obstetrical case the procedure selected should best achieve this purpose. Radical and heroic handling of dystocia is seldom necessary and then only when more conservative treatments have failed or when examination indicates the condition is such that ordinary routine methods or a combination of them will not effect relief. In most cases of dystocia one or more combinations of the major obstetrical operations are performed. The plan of operation should be carefully made with alternatives in case one procedure is not successful. If assistance or consultation is needed it should be obtained as soon as possible. In performing obstetrical operations on large animals it is necessary for the veterinarian to conserve his strength by working with both arms and by using lay assistance whenever possible. If the fetal membranes interfere with the obstetrical operations the offending portions of the membranes should be removed manually. The obstetrical operations may be divided into four major classifications: mutation, forced extraction, fetotomy or embryotomy, and cesarean section or laparohysterectomy. For excellent illustrations of various mutation and fetotomy techniques the student is recommended to review those of Benesch and Wright, Benesch, Travernier, Richter and Gotze and Arthur.

Mutation

Mutation is defined as those operations by which a fetus is returned to a normal presentation, position, and posture by repulsion, rotation, version, and adjustment or extension of the extremities. Normal birth will proceed in uniparous animals only with the fetus in anterior or posterior longitudinal presentation, dorso-sacral position, and with the head and neck and limbs extended. Most multipara can have a normal birth with the fetal limbs folded alongside of or beneath the body, since the limbs are small and flexible. In multipara, fetuses may be in a dorso-ilial or dorso-pubic position and be born without difficulty. In unipara only premature or very small fetuses may pass through the pelvis in dorso-ilial or dorso-pubic position or with a flexed limb or limbs. In sheep, the fetus may often be born without assistance in anterior presentation with one forelimb retained beneath the body. After the veterinarian has brought each part of the fetus into its normal posture, the cause of dystocia is usually relieved and the fetus will be expelled normally, or parturition aided or completed by traction.

Repulsion, sometimes called retropulsion, consists of pushing the fetus out of the maternal pelvis or birth canal into the abdominal cavity and uterus, where space is available for the correction of the position or posture of the fetus and its extremities. In nearly all cases in which expulsion is used, epidural anesthesia is indicated since repulsion frequently produces violent straining on the part of the animal. When repulsion is used, the portion of the fetus engaged in the pelvis is pushed cranially. Because the fetus and uterus are in the form of an arc in the cow, the opposite end of the fetus may be pushed somewhat nearer the pelvis. Repulsion is usually necessary because the birth canal or pelvic cavity is so narrow and so confining that it is impossible to correct deviations in position or posture without providing more room in which to manipulate the fetus or its long extremities. Besides its common use for repelling a portion of the fetus out of the pelvis, repulsion may also be used to force a portion of the fetus—usually the proximal portion of an extremity and the part of the body to which it is attached—cranially, dorsally, ventrally, or laterally in the uterine and abdominal cavity so that sufficient room is provided to extend the flexed extremity with facility.

Repulsion may be accomplished by the operator's arm, the arm of an assistant, or by a crutch repeller. If the latter instrument is used it should be guarded by having the operator's hand on the crutch part of the repeller as force is applied, so that slipping of the crutch is avoided. In anterior presentation the crutch or hand of the operator is usually placed on the fetus between the shoulder and chest or across the chest beneath the neck. In posterior presentation it is placed in the perineal region over the ischial arch. Epidural anesthesia is of great value especially in large animals, because the fetus when repelled is not immediately forced back into the pelvis by straining, and therefore it is easier for the operator to correct the abnormal posture or position. If the crutch repeller is used and left in place the person applying the outside force should be properly braced and balanced so if the crutch slips or becomes displaced it will not be forced cranially, possibly through the uterine wall. If it slips it should immediately be withdrawn or replaced. It is somewhat safer to use an assistant and under the operator's direction have him repel the fetus with one arm while the operator's arm corrects the abnormal posture. The only disadvantage to this method is that in heifers with a small birth canal, room for two arms is restricted. In sheep, goats, and swine, repulsion is performed by the arm and hand, or by the finger in bitches and cats.

Having the animal standing, or with its rear parts elevated if it is recumbent, is essential to make room available for repulsion. Repulsion is difficult or impossible in the recumbent animal resting on its sternum, as the abdominal viscera are pushing the fetus back toward the pelvis. If the animal is recumbent it should be laid on its side with its four legs extended. Excessive repulsion may be dangerous, especially in cases in which dystocia has existed for some time, because the uterine wall is often tightly contracted around the fetus. The uterine cavity thus nearly ceases to exist, and hence rupture of the uterus is liable to occur. In cases of neglected dystocia or of emphysema of the fetus, the repulsive force should be carefully controlled. Frequently satisfactory repulsion is impossible and this is the reason why the handling of prolonged dystocia cases is difficult and the prognosis is guarded to poor. In large animals, early diagnosis of minor abnormalities causing dystocia may preclude the need for epidural anesthesia and the fetus can be repelled and its posture or position corrected between abdominal contractions.

Rotation is the turning of the fetus on its long axis to bring the fetus into a dorso-sacral position. This position is necessary in all but very small fetuses in uniparous animals and is the usual presenting position even in multiparous animals. In the latter species an abnormal position of the fetus seldom causes dystocia due to the small size of the fetus compared with the size of the pelvic cavity or inlet. Williams indicated that in the cow the presence of the fetus in a dorso-ilial or dorso-pubic position frequently is accompanied by a 90-to 180-degree torsion of the uterus. In 90-degree torsion of the uterus twisting of the birth canal is often not noticeable. It seems very unlikely that an 180-degree torsion with its accompanying marked twisting of the birth canal would go unnoticed by an experienced veterinarian. In the dorso-pubic positions of the fetus in the cow, a rectal examination and examination of the relation of the broad ligaments and the uterine arteries to the uterus, would reveal whether torsion of the uterus existed and indicate the direction for rotating the fetus in correcting the twisted uterus. **In the mare** and multiparous animals in which the fetus lies in the uterus in a dorso-pubic or dorso-ilial position during pregnancy with the navel cord extending laterally or dorsally toward the uterine attachment of the broad ligament and uterine wall, the fetus must rotate 90 to 180 degrees before entering the pelvic inlet in a dorso-sacral position. If rotation is not complete by the second stage of parturition, dystocia may result. In multiparous animals with the fetus in a dorso-pubic position the nose of the fetus may catch on the pelvic brim in anterior presentation, or the buttocks may catch on the brim of the pelvis in posterior presentation. Leonard indicated that these positions and postures are common causes for dystocia in dogs.

To relieve dystocia in unipara by rotation of the body of the fetus, it should be repelled cranially out of the pelvic cavity. If this cannot be done, due to the contracting uterus, it indicates that the dystocia has existed long enough to also result in a dry mucous membrane of the birth canal. In this case much careful lubrication of the birth canal and fetus is necessary to make rotation of the fetus in the confining structures possible and easier without injuring the uterine or vaginal walls. In dorso-ilial positions repulsion is often not necessary but may be helpful. Lubrication of the fetus and birth canal, caudal and downward traction on the extremities, and rotation of the fetus with the operator's arm in the birth canal, readily corrects this mild abnormal position. After the body of the fetus in anterior presentation, dorso-pubic position,. is repelled out of the pelvis, leaving the fetal limbs in the pelvic cavity, chains are fastened to the fetlocks and cross-traction is applied by two assistants. Depending upon which way the fetus is to be rotated one leg is initially pulled upwards, then horizontally to the left or right and then downwards while the other leg is being pulled underneath the first leg downward and obliquely to the right or left. This type of traction causes a rotation of the body of the fetus that is aided by the operator placing his arm and hand under the withers or body of the fetus and elevating it to the level of the pelvic brim, using the pelvis as a fulcrum, and then pushing the fetus obliquely to either the left or right. In some prolonged cases of dystocia in anterior presentation, the head and neck may be an obstacle to rotation and have to be amputated before rotation can be accomplished. In posterior presentation the fetus is rotated in a like manner, with the operator's hand and arm under the buttocks. This method of cross-traction is superior to placing traction directly backward on one limb and twisting the opposite limb around the fulcrum thus established. This latter technique causes the fetus to become impacted in the maternal pelvis and thus resist rotation, and a great strain is placed on the joints and ligaments of the leg that is twisted around the one to which traction is being applied. In the former technique impaction of the fetus in the pelvis is reduced to a minimum, and elevating the body of the fetus makes correction of the abnormal position rapid and easy. If correction of the position is difficult in one direction, torsion may be present, and the direction of traction may be increasing the degree of torsion. If this is the case, the fetus should be rotated in the opposite direction. In mild cases diagnosed early in parturition or where the fetus is small, the fetlock protruding from the vulva may be flexed and used as a means of exerting a moderate twisting action on the leg to assist rotating the fetus.

In a few cases, rotation may require the use of the detorsion rod or Cammerer's fork as described under torsion of the uterus. In these cases the rod is fastened to the two limbs after lubrication of the fetus and the birth canal and by repulsion and rotation the position is corrected. In sheep and swine the hand and in dogs and cats the finger applied to or alongside the chest or buttocks after lubrication will usually repel and then rotate the fetus into a normal dorso-sacral position. In these smaller animals forceps may also be used with care to rotate the fetus.

Version is the rotation of the fetus on its transverse axis into an anterior or posterior presentation. This is done most often in the mare in transverse ventral presentation and in rare cases in the cow, ewe, and bitch in transverse presentation. Vandeplassche (1957) reported that transverse presentation in the mare occurred about 1 in 1000 pregnancies. Version is usually limited to 90°. By repulsion on the cranial or caudal end of the fetus and traction on the other end, the transverse presentation is changed to a longitudinal presentation. If possible the fetus should be turned into a posterior longitudinal presentation, as that prevents the head and neck from complicating the correction of the abnormal presentation or posture. In the mare partial embryotomy is often indicated before version is attempted in transverse ventral presentation. Often version is only through a relatively small arc if the fetus is lying obliquely rather than in a true transverse presentation. In the tubular type of uteri in domestic animals, version through a 180° arc such as from posterior to anterior presentation is rarely possible and should not be attempted.

Extension and Adjustment of the Extremities is the correction of abnormal postures usually due to flexion of one or more of the extremities causing dystocia. Flexion of the head and neck causes dystocia in all species. Flexion of the limbs usually results in dystocia in uniparous animals but only rarely in multiparous animals. Corrective procedures are difficult and often impossible within the confines of the pelvic cavity. The fetus must usually be repelled out of the pelvis into the larger uterine and abdominal cavities to have sufficient room for the correction of abnormal postures. This is particularly true in the large uniparous animals, in which the fetal extremities are long. Many of these abnormal postures may be caused by the distal portion of the fetal extremity being caught on the pelvic brim, and are aggravated when the body of the fetus passes over this extremity, thereby resulting in greater flexion of the extremity and even its extension beneath the body. The act of repulsion of the fetus cranially into the uterine and abdominal cavities tends to correct the deviated extremity or abnormal posture. Three basic mechanical principles are necessary to effect a prompt, easy correction of a flexed extremity (see Figure 88).

(1) **Repulsion of the Proximal Portion of the Extremity** such as the shoulder or chest is performed in anterior presentation in the correction of a flexed fetlock, carpus, elbow, or shoulder joints with the forelimb extended beneath the body; or the head and neck flexed alongside, beneath or over the body of the fetus. In posterior presentation repulsion is performed on the buttocks, stifle, or tarsus when the hind limbs are flexed at the stifle, tarsus, fetlock, or hip. In the latter condition the legs extend beneath the fetus, a breech presentation.

(2) **Lateral Rotation of the Middle Portion of the Extremity, Carpus, Tarsus, or Neck**—Lateral rotation and repulsion of the flexed tarsus, carpus or neck into the cranial and lateral flank region provides adequate room in most cases for the medial extension of the fetlock or nose into the pelvic cavity. In small equine or bovine fetuses, if the operator firmly grasps the metacarpus or metatarsus, he can with the same motion perform both repulsion and lateral rotation as well as extension of the fetlock into the pelvic cavity. In larger fetuses the operator may require a crutch repeller, or even better an assistant's arm, to force the tarsus or carpus laterally and cranially while the operator brings the fetlock medially and caudally into the pelvic cavity. This latter procedure allows the operator to cup or flex the pastern in his hand so that as the limb is extended the hoof of the fetus will not catch, tear, or lacerate the wall of the birth canal as the foot is drawn into the pelvic cavity.

(3) **Traction on the Distal Portion of the Extremity** such as the pastern, the lower jaw or, until these distal

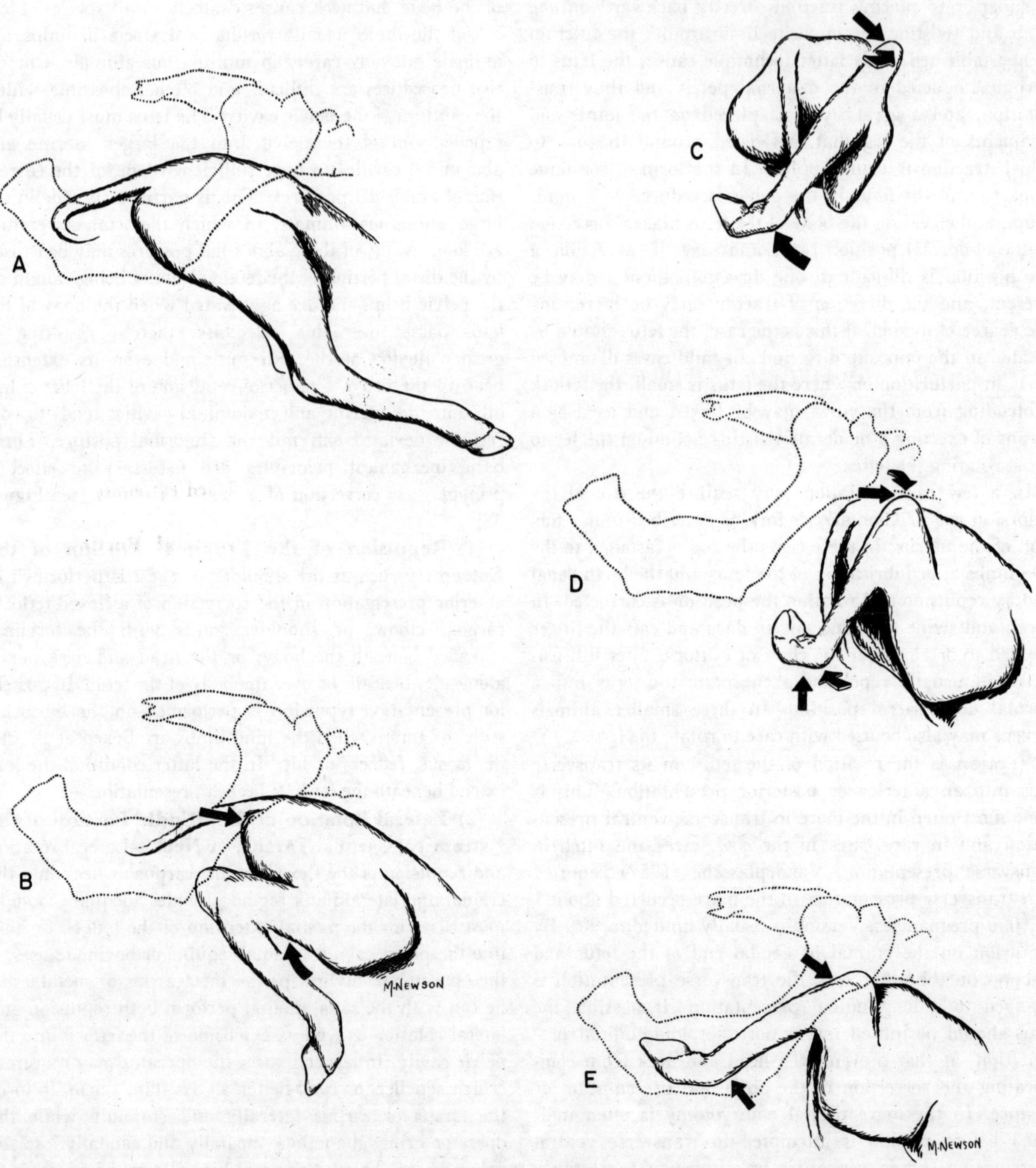

Figure 88 Procedures followed in mutation of deviated fetal extremities: A. Laterial view of a breech presentation of a bovine fetus. B. By repulsion on the buttocks and traction on the tibia the leg is drawn into a hock-flexed posture. C, D and E. caudal and lateral views show how, by upward repulsion and lateral rotation on the hock and medial and caudal traction on the fetlock and pastern, the leg is extended into the pelvis

structures can be reached, the structures between the body and the distal portions of the extremity, is applied to extend the limbs or head and neck. This traction may be applied by the hands and arm, a chain, or a snare. When the fetus is in breech presentation with the legs extended beneath the body, the fetus is repelled cranially out of the pelvic cavity and into the right or left flank. The hand and arm is slid down the tibia on the opposite leg and by traction the leg is pulled into a hock-flexed position and then handled as described. In cases in which the head and neck are deviated alongside the fetal body the fetus is repelled cranially and laterally into the flank of the cow on the side opposite to the head so that as much space as possible is provided in the other flank to allow correction of the deviated head and neck. By traction with the fingers in the orbits, around the lower jaw, in the angle of the mouth, by a snare around the lower jaw or small hooks in the orbits, the head can usually be pulled laterally back to the pelvic inlet without twisting the neck. The head is then returned to its normal posture by manual traction, elevation or rotation of the head, and lateral repulsion on the neck. During these procedures the muzzle of the fetus should be guarded to make sure the lower incisor teeth do not lacerate the uterus, or the lower jaw catch on the pelvic brim of the dam, especially if the type of traction applied causes the mouth to gape. When the dam is recumbent the deviated fetal head should be located in the upper flank before mutation procedures begin. Otherwise the weight of the fetal body resting on the head and neck would make correction nearly impossible.

The combined use of these three mechanical principles will relieve almost all abnormal postures. In rare cases, in order to obtain more room in which to perform these maneuvers when the uterus is contracted tightly around the fetus, a partial embryotomy may be necessary, such as amputation of a forelimb. In multipara, mutation of the fetus is not generally required except in deviation of the head and neck in anterior presentation, impaction of a large fetus in the pelvis in breech presentation or in dorsopubic position when the nose or buttocks of the fetus may catch on the pelvic brim of the dam as the fetus enters the pelvis. By using the finger in the vagina and manipulating the canine or feline fetus through the abdominal wall and floor with the opposite hand these abnormal postures may usually be corrected. Occasionally forceps or snares may be indicated. In a few cases dystocia in cattle is observed due to the impingement of the elevated tail on the dorsal border of the pelvic inlet in posterior presentation. Repulsion of the fetus, holding the tail against the perineum and applying traction to the rear limbs corrects the dystocia. Benesch indicated that Kuhn's crutch was very useful in various mutation operations in the mare and cow. Although the theoretical uses of the instrument are many, it has not proved useful in the author's practice.

Mutation of the fetus must be performed carefully, cautiously, and in a gentle manner in all animals. These manipulations can take place only at the level of or just below the pelvic brim. The earlier the dystocia is diagnosed, the easier is mutation of the fetus accomplished; conversely, the longer aid is withheld or delayed, the more difficult or impossible it is for mutation to be successful. This is true, but to a lesser extent, in the other major obstetrical operations.

Forced Extraction

Forced extraction is defined as the withdrawal of the fetus from the dam through the birth canal by means of the application of outside force or traction.

Manner and Dangers of the Application of Traction Instruments to the Fetus—In anterior presentation obstetrical chains may be applied to the pasterns or above the knee or elbow. If the fetal membranes prevent the prompt application of the chains or snares they should be broken, ripped away, or pushed to one side. The chain should be tightly fastened around the pastern before applying traction or it may slip down over the coronary band of the hoof and when traction is applied the hoof may be pulled off. Applying the chains above the fetlock may be satisfactory in almost all cases but in rare cases excessive traction and tightening of the chain over the epiphysis or "break joint" may fracture the leg. For these reasons many veterinarians place the noose of the obstetrical chain above the fetlock and place a half-hitch around the pastern. This prevents the chain from sliding down over the coronary band and distributes the force over the two sites. Some place the large terminal link in the obstetrical chain ventral to the pastern and pass the chain between the claws of the bovine fetus. This raises and extends the toe and may avoid its catching on the brim of the pelvis.

In anterior presentation a snare may be applied around the lower jaw and tightened firmly so that with traction it will not slip and fracture the dental plate. Obstetrical chains around the lower jaw will not tighten sufficiently, and generally slip off, often damaging the incisor teeth. Excessive traction on the jaw should be avoided, as the jaw bones are not strong and fracture may occur. Moderate traction applied by one man is all that can safely be used on the lower jaw of a bovine fetus. A loop of obstetrical chain around the neck behind the head is used occasionally for traction when the fetus is dead; but the head and muzzle must be directed with the hand so that they will not become deviated. This technique is dangerous to a live fetus as it may cause injury to the spinal cord and vertebrae in the occipital region. A loop of obstetrical chain is more commonly used around the poll, under the ears and through the mouth in the manner of a "war bridle" for applying traction to the head. This causes the mouth to gape when traction is applied; the operator should therefore watch for this and protect himself and the birth canal from injury by the sharp incisor teeth. Wendt has recommended pinching the large link in the end of the obstetrical chain noose in a vise in such a manner that it catches on the chain, thus preventing the chain noose from tightening when traction is applied. A commercial head snare is available that also overcomes gaping of the mouth. By the use of blunt or knobbed Krey's hooks or short obstetrical hooks on a loop or cord in the orbits as described by Benesch, traction may be applied to the head. This technique is safe unless excessive traction causes fracture of the facial bones. Williams described a technique in which an incision is made in the floor of the mouth anterior to the tongue, extending through the skin between the mandibles; a loop of obstetrical chain is then passed over the lower jaw, behind this incision, and the opposite end of the chain is passed through the incision and tightened. This provides a firm, solid hold on the lower jaw that will not slip and by means of which a large amount of traction may be applied. It is used most satisfactorily in dead fetuses, but even in live fetuses the wound heals quite rapidly after birth. The long or short blunt hook placed between the rami of the mandibles is not satisfactory because it frequently slips, or with moderate traction may cause a separation of the symphysis of the mandible. In a dead fetus the long blunt hook may be passed through the mouth into the pharynx, turned dorsally, and then traction may be applied fixing the hook in bones dorsal to the pharynx.

The long blunt hook may be used to advantage in the hiplock condition in anterior presentation. The hook is passed over the top of the fetal croup and turned ventrally to engage the posterior border of the ischium or sacrosciatic ligament. In this position much traction may be applied. By raising the fetal pelvis and pulling the fetal hips at an oblique angle through the maternal pelvis, the veterinarian can often relieve the dystocia.

In sheep and swine the obstetrical chains are too large to be of value. In anterior presentation snares or forceps are applied to the ovine or porcine fetal head, around the neck, or to the forelegs. In small sheep and swine, in which the hand cannot be passed through the pelvis into the uterus, forceps of various types, as well as obstetrical snares, may be used to advantage, Railsback. Whenever forceps are applied, the wall of the genital tract should be examined before traction is applied, to make sure it is not caught in the forceps. In dogs and cats forceps may be applied to the head of the fetus after the head is repelled out of the pelvis into the uterus; but great care should be used to prevent tearing an ear or lacerating the skin, fracturing the mandible, or crushing the skull. Excessive traction or twisting of the head should be avoided, since injury or dislocation of the vertebrae may occur in the occipital region in these small species. Forced extraction in multipara is limited to those fetuses which have entered the uterine body or pelvis. Snares of gauze may be used on the limbs of canine fetuses. Freak described the use of forceps in dystocia in dogs.

In posterior presentation in large animals traction may be applied to the fetal pastern or above the hock by the use of obstetrical chains. The same danger exists as in the anterior presentation whereby excessive traction with chains fastened above the fetlocks or that slide down over the coronary band of the hoof, may cause fracture above the fetlock or removal of the hoof. In sheep and swine, snares may be fastened around the hind legs. In dogs and cats snares or guaze around the hind legs or grasping the hocks with sponge forceps will assist traction. If forceps are used in multipara they should be fastened securely around or across the fetal pelvis, after the fetal hips have been repelled out of the maternal pelvis. In dogs, forceps are generally preferred to applying excessive traction to the hind legs with the accompanying possible danger of dislocating the fetal hips. Excessive twisting of the fetal pelvis by the means of forceps may injure the lumbo sacral articulation; or if the fetus is emphysematous excessive traction may pull it apart. Dislocation of the first cervical joint may occur in posterior presentation in the bitch when the occiput becomes impacted in the pelvis and traction is continued. In this instance abdominal pressure by the operator's hand will raise the chin of the fetus and help force the fetal head through the pelvis.

Technique of Withdrawing Fetus Through the Maternal Birth Canal—In anterior presentation of the fetus in uniparous animals, traction should be applied at three points, the two legs and the head. After the head and legs have passed through the vulva, traction may be applied to the legs only. At the beginning of labor the main portion of the fetus is below the level of the brim of the pelvis. Traction when applied in either anterior or posterior presentation should be dorsally and caudally to lift the fetus up and over the brim of the pelvis into the birth canal. At this stage, with the fetal extremities approaching the vulva, the direction of traction should at first be caudal and slightly dorsal; and as the fetal legs and head engage in the vulva the direction of traction should be obliquely ventral. After the head in anterior presentation or the hips in posterior presentation pass through the vulva, the direction of traction should be more and more ventral until when the back of the fetus is passing through the vulva the direction of traction is perpendicular to the spinal axis of the dam or parallel to her hind legs. Thus the direction of traction and that of the fetus as it passes through the birth canal is in the form of an arc. The ventral structures of the fetus are relaxed and concave, and the dorsal structures of the fetus are stretched and convex. This arc-like application of traction results in the fetus assuming the physiologic curved shape that facilitates its removal through the birth canal; by producing the smallest possible diameters of the fetal body stalling of the fetal pelvis, or the hiplock condition, is prevented. By applying traction to the legs, head, and spine the abdominal wall of the fetus is relaxed and the fetal pelvis is forced backward and upward reducing its sacro-pubic diameter and causing it to pass through the greatest diameter of the maternal pelvis. If traction is applied in a straight caudal direction and not in the form of an arc, both the linea alba as well as the spine are stretched, and the fetal pelvis is pulled ventrally and cranially thus increasing its sacro-pubic diameter and predisposing to hiplock. When the head enters the vulva, if traction is applied dorsally or caudally instead of ventrally the fetal head jams against the dorsal commissure of the vulva and may cause severe stretching or laceration. At this point it is important to place ventral traction on the head.

When the vulva is small, especially in primiparous cattle, ventral traction on the head alone together with insertion of the hands over the top of the head; stretching of the vulva with the wrists, arms or hands; and ventral and caudal traction with the hands over the occiput or with the fingers in the medial canthus of the orbit helps to pass the head through the vulva and prevent lacerations. Often, if this process is prolonged, lubrication of the head and vulva is helpful. Pushing or pulling cranially on the vulva if the vulva is tight will further aid dilation while traction is applied on the fetal head.

When abdominal contractions in the dam occur during parturition the linea alba pulls the pubis forward, increasing the pelvic diameters. When strong traction is applied to the fetus and the pelvic ligaments are relaxed the maternal pubis is pulled caudally and the pelvic diameters are lessened. Williams recommended a rope or breeching around the buttocks of the cow in lateral recumbency fastened securely to the manger so that when traction is applied to the fetus the maternal pubis is pulled forward by this rope or breeching. The metal breech device used in fetal extractors provides this same advantage. Preventing the maternal pubis from extending caudally, and applying ventral traction on the fetus, will usually prevent impaction of the fetal hips in the maternal pelvis. Improper traction such as that produced by a block and tackle pulling directly caudally will in many instances cause severe impaction of the fetus in the maternal pelvis.

When traction is applied the operator should constantly watch, examine, and direct the progress of the fetus by instructing his assistants when to apply traction, when it should cease, and in what direction it should be applied. If the progress of the fetus through the birth canal should cease, traction should be discontinued and the fetus and the birth canal should be carefully examined to determine the cause of the obstruction. This should be overcome or corrected before exerting further traction. The operator should conserve his strength and direct the operation and not join his assistants in applying traction except when necessary. If the patient is straining, traction should be applied principally during expulsive efforts. This both aids the withdrawal of the fetus and to some extent prevents the fetus dragging parts of the uterus and vagina along with it, thereby causing possible rupture or prolapse of the uterus. Traction should be applied in a steady, even manner. Jerky, irregular efforts at traction are ineffectual, painful and dangerous to both the fetus and dam. In most instances traction should not be applied in a hasty manner. To avoid lacerations or ruptures of the soft structures of the birth canal time should be allowed for dilation of the birth canal as the fetus advances. This frequently requires 30 minutes or often longer in heifers. The same general technique of removing fetuses by traction in swine, sheep, dogs, and cats is followed with traction caudally and then downward as the fetus passes through the vulva. In the dog and cat, pressure of the operator's hand upward through the abdominal wall will help the passage of the fetus into the pelvis and through the birth canal.

In uniparous animals traction may be greatly facilitated by lubrication if the fetus and birth canal are dry. Traction on one extremity at a time in an alternate manner is also of great assistance in withdrawing a fetus. This is especially true in posterior presentation, in which traction should be applied to one limb at a time so that the fetal pelvis is pulled through the maternal pelvis in an oblique manner, thus reducing the possibility of hiplock. Even in anterior presentation, after the forelimbs and head have passed through the vulva, pulling the bovine fetus laterally and ventrally around the dam's hips first to one side and then to the other may aid in withdrawal of the fetus and produce an oblique angle to the fetal pelvis, so that one greater trochanter will slip through the maternal pelvic inlet and then the other will follow, preventing or reducing the chances of hiplock or impaction. As traction is applied, twisting of the fetal body from side to side may aid withdrawal of the fetus.

Indications for Forced Extraction of the Fetus Forced extraction is indicated when uterine inertia is present and the fetus does not engage in the birth canal and stimulate straining. It is indicated when epidural anesthesia has been administered and after mutation has corrected the cause for dystocia. Forced extraction is used most often when the fetus is relatively too large to be expelled through the birth canal without assistance and when traction offers greater prospect of success than a fetotomy or cesarean. It is used in many cases in primipara with a small birth canal, as a means of withdrawing the fetus and dilating the canal. It may also be used when the birth canal is compressed by tumors or fat or other pathological conditions. It may be indicated in posterior presentation of the fetus to hasten delivery and prevent the death of the fetus when the umbilical cord is compressed between the fetal abdominal wall and the brim of the pelvis. Within 5 to 10 minutes after the umbilical circulation is cut off the fetus may die if its cranial extremities remain in the uterus and it cannot breathe. Hasty application of forced extraction may occasionally be indicated in mares with dystocia in which the cause for the dystocia has been corrected and the fetus is still alive. Thus it may effect removal of the fetus before separation of the placenta and death of the fetus occurred. Forced extraction may occasionally be used to save time or in order to avoid fetotomy or cesarean section where working conditions are extremely poor. It is indicated in dystocia due to emphysematous fetuses after thoroughly lubricating the birth canal and fetus to avoid fetotomy or a cesarean, which are more hazardous to the dam than is forced extraction under such conditions. In many fetotomy operations, forced extraction is used as an aid.

Forced extraction by forceps or snares in the multiparous animals, sow, dog, and cat, should not be used when one is short of time or patience as it may require a number of hours of intermittent work to complete the delivery of all the fetuses. It is, however, indicated when the owner is not interested in saving the fetuses; when only one or two fetuses are present and secondary uterine inertia has set in; when the fetuses are dead and emphysematous; and when in the opinion of the operator the delivery of one fetus will result in the unaided delivery of the rest of the litter. The veterinarian may even decide to use forceps and forced extraction in cases of primary inertia where the litter is small. Young primiparous bitches may force the fetal head through the pelvis and then rest. This pup becomes cyanotic and must be delivered immediately. Since the vulva is small and tight it is necessary to force the pup's head through by means of outside pressure on the vulvar lips. Then by applying manual traction on the head and placing a finger under the pup's chest, the pup can be eased through the vulva, Leonard. To prevent the fingers slipping, a gauze pad may be used.

Forced extraction should be limited strictly to cases in which the presentation, position and posture of the fetus are normal and in which, in the opinion of the operator, forced extraction is in the best interests of the fetus, the dam and the owner. Forced extraction is contraindicated or should only be undertaken with great care when abnormal presentation, position or postures are present, when the fetus is excessively large or defective, when the birth canal is obviously small, when secondary uterine inertia is present with the uterine walls strongly contracted around the fetus, when the cervix is stenotic or has failed to dilate, when the animal is affected with obturator paralysis and when the birth canal has been severely lacerated.

The Amount of Traction to Apply in Forced Extraction of the Fetus will vary greatly with the species of animal and the condition causing the dystocia. Although forced extraction appears simple and quick it is potentially dangerous to the fetus and to the dam. In the dam, excessive traction or traction in an improper manner or with the fetus in an abnormal presentation, position, and posture may result in trauma, laceration, rupture to the soft structures of the birth canal or wedging of the fetus in the dam's pelvis. It may predispose to prolapse of the uterus, or result in trauma to the obturator or gluteal nerves. However it is remarkable how seldom paralysis occurs even when excessive traction has been applied.

In the mare, abdominal contractions are so violent that if the fetus is in the proper presentation, position and posture, forced extraction is seldom necessary. Aid with obstetrical chains by one or two men may help dilate the birth canal and vulva gradually in old or young primiparous mares. Care should be exercised to avoid lacerating the vulva or the perineal region. If the mare is recumbent and much traction is applied, she will usually get to her feet. If the cow is standing and strong traction is applied to the fetus, the cow will usually fall and may injure itself or the attendants. In the cow, as in the mare, traction under certain circumstances should be moderate and intermittent; for example, if the fetus is alive and the cow already exhibits some obturator paralysis due to a hiplock condition. In normal circumstances the force of 2 to 3 or more men apparently causes no harm and may be indicated. The recent introduction of the fetal extractor with which one can exert great force in the proper manner, if necessary, has been received enthusiastically by many veterinarians because often sufficient manpower is not available and the block and tackle or wire stretchers previously used applied traction in only one direction and in an improper manner, that is, directly caudally. Since excessive power can easily be applied by these fetal extractors judgment, caution, and care must be exercised in its use. Where great amounts of traction are used, epidural analgesia is strongly recommended to avoid excessive pain in the dam. The amount of traction to be applied will vary from case to case and with the judgment of the veterinarian. Traction if properly applied does not result in injury to the fetus or to the genital tract of the mare and cow. However, to quote Williams, "Application of great force in improper position, presentation or posture of the fetus is constantly to be condemned." The use of a tractor or horses to apply traction to the fetus, or tying the fetus to a tree and driving the parturient mare away, are definite examples of malpractice if performed by a veterinarian.

In the ewe and sow the same principles in regard to the degree of traction may be applied. In all cases, however, the force exerted by one man is enough for the relief of dystocia in these species. In the ewe, before applying traction one should make sure the snare is attached to one, not two, fetuses. In dogs and cats traction should be applied carefully and never excessively. Twisting of the fetus should be avoided. Occasionally in emphysematous fetuses traction may pull the fetus apart. In these small species traction should be used with care, especially if secondary uterine inertia has set in, to avoid laceration of the uterus or birth canal at the pelvic brim. This will result in herniation of the viscera through the birth canal or discharge of the fetuses into the abdominal cavity.

Fetotomy or Embryotomy

Fetotomy is defined as those operations performed on the fetus for the purpose of reducing its size by either its division or the removal of certain of its parts. In most cases these operations are performed within the uterus of the dam. Partial embryotomy is most commonly performed. Total embryotomy is performed infrequently. In fetotomy the life of the fetus is sacrificed if it is not already dead as is usually the case. Benesch and Wright indicated that in Germany attention has been paid to humane methods of killing the fetus, before embryotomy is begun. These authors indicate the fetal reflexes and threshold for pain are of a very low order. For this reason incising the carotid artery or rupturing the umbilical cord before fetotomy is not necessary. The injection of a rapid-acting drug to produce euthanasia or an anesthetic state in the fetus has not been investigated but any such agent might well be transferred by the placenta to the dam.

The advantages of fetotomy are: It reduces the size of the fetus. It avoids a cesarean operation. It requires little assistance. It will prevent possible trauma or injury to the dam through the use of excessive traction.

The disadvantages of fetotomy are: It may be dangerous, causing injuries or lacerations to the uterus or birth canal by instruments or sharp edges of bone. It may take a long time, exhausting both the dam and the operator and is conducive to trauma and pressure necrosis of the birth canal. It offers certain dangers to the veterinarian by wounds from instruments, and if the fetus is emphysematous there is a possibility of infection of the operator's arm.

The advantages outweigh the disadvantages, however, and fetotomy in large animals is a practical and successful way of relieving dystocia. It is used, and rightly so, many more times than is cesarean section, which is more costly and time consuming, and requires more help and more aftercare than do most fetotomy operations. Cesarean section is indicated over fetotomy only if the fetus is alive and the owner desires that it be saved; or when total fetotomy under difficult conditions, such as a small narrow birth canal, would probably cause greater trauma to the dam, take longer, and be more fatiguing to both the dam and veterinarian than would cesarean section. If there is little prospect of a successful fetotomy operation and forced extraction is impossible, the owner should be advised to have a cesarean operation performed or to slaughter the dam.

Since cesarean section is more difficult to perform successfully in the mare than in the other domestic animals, fetotomy or forced extraction are methods of choice in this species. Because the genital tract of the mare is more easily traumatized, and with more serious consequences than that of the cow, fetotomy should be performed carefully and gently. For more than a simple embryotomy in the mare, a general anesthesia should probably be administered. The mare should be restrained in a suitable location large enough for the operation to be performed with the mare lying on her side.

Simple fetotomy techniques using the wire saw may be performed in the ewe if the hand can be passed through the pelvis into the uterus. By threading a loop of the obstetrical wire through a pipe of small diameter, portions of the fetus, such as the head and forelimbs, may be removed with safety to the dam. Fetotomies are not performed in the sow, bitch, and cat because cesarean section is easier and safer. In rare cases in the dog the skull of the fetus may be crushed intentionally by means of forceps in order to permit removal by traction.

Vandeplassche and his associates compared the results of 239 embryotomies and 150 cesarean operations in cattle and came to the conclusion that embryotomy was still the more important and practical of the two methods in bovine veterinary practice. In summarizing the data on these 239 cases it was found that in 3 to 5 per cent of them fetotomy was impossible. Six per cent of the cows died, 6 of them from septic metritis, 2 from malignant edema, 3 from necrotic vaginitis, 1 from a ruptured uterus, and 1 from hemorrhage. Thirteen per cent of the cows had retained fetal membranes and 82 per cent conceived within 10 months after the fetotomy operation.

The fetotomy operation may involve any portion of the fetal body and presents many variations and possibilities. It may be performed in any normal or abnormal presentation, position, or posture of the fetus. In many cases it is employed in relieving dystocia due to fetal monsters in which the usual anatomical arrangement of parts may not exist. The operational procedure must be decided upon for each case. Fetotomy operations should be planned and carried out carefully, so that there will be no wasted effort. Generally, by careful planning and by using mutation or forced extraction, only one fetotomy operation, instead of two, may be necessary. It should be borne in mind that the aim of embryotomy operations is to reduce the size of the fetus so it may be removed from the birth canal. The veterinarian therefore should, depending upon the particular conditions and circumstances, plan the operation and procedures using one or more of the standard fetotomy operations or their variations. At the present time the fetatome is standard equipment for the practitioner working with large animals; therefore many of the older techniques described by Williams, using instruments such as the knife, chisel, and blunt-pointed cutting hook are not often used at present. These older techniques, using simple instruments, involved some operations which were difficult to perform, requiring patience, strength, and extreme effort, placing a severe strain on both the operator and the animal. Veterinarians who have become adept through practice may perform many obstetrical operations with the knife, chisel, and hook and seldom use the fetatome. The author has for many years been a staunch advocate of the fetatome primarily because it is easier and safer to use. Except for minor simple obstetrical operations, he prefers it to the older instruments and their accompanying techniques. Some of the simpler older techniques are still practical, however, and will be described.

In dairy practice in New York State 90 per cent of the fetotomy operations performed include: bisecting the pelvis in anterior presentation, (hiplock) or in posterior presentation, (breech presentation), amputation of the head and neck, and decapitation. In some cases evisceration is used prior to bisecting the pelvis in anterior presentation.

Fetotomy Operations in the Anterior Presentation

Decapitation, or Amputation of the Protruding Head is indicated when one or both forelimbs are retained and the head has passed through the vulva and become swollen, edematous, or emphysematous so that it cannot be repelled or can be repelled only with great difficulty. In such cases the fetus is usually dead, and amputation of its head allows the fetus to be repelled, so that the abnormal posture of the forelimbs may readily be corrected by mutation, without the interference of the head.

Decapitation is easily accomplished by fixing a snare on the lower jaw, or eye hooks in the orbits, and exerting traction in any direction desired by the operator. With a scalpel or sharp knife a transverse incision is made behind the jaw through the skin, muscles, pharynx, larynx and esophagus to the cervical vertebra. This incision is continued through the skin ventral to the ears and across the frontal bones. The skin over the head, including the ears, is separated from the underlying muscle and bone to the occipital region, where another transverse incision is made ventrally through the ligamentum nuchae and muscles to the cervical vertebra. The head is grasped firmly and twisted, rupturing the articular ligaments. The remaining soft tissues are cut and the head removed from the neck at the occipital atloid articulation. The flap of skin, including the ears, should be firmly secured by an obstetrical chain or snare which pulls the skin over the exposed cervical vertebra. A small incision in this flap of skin distal to the loop of obstetrical chain and through which the free end of the chain is drawn will secure the chain so it cannot slip off even if strong traction is applied. The fetus is then repelled, and the abnormal posture of the limbs corrected by mutation. Traction on the neck and two front legs usually results in relief of the dystocia. In making the incisions the operator must guard against the knife accidentally slipping and cutting the vulva. The fetatome could also be used in this operation, but the technique just described saves time as well as aftercare of equipment.

Cephalotomy or craniotomy is indicated only rarely when fetal hydrocephalus or other cranial deformity is the cause for dystocia.

Cephalotomy is accomplished by fixing the head with a snare around the lower jaw. In cases of hydrocephalus, sometimes simply incising the distended cranium causes a sufficient reduction in size to permit delivery. In most cases, however, it is necessary to separate the enlarged cranium from the rest of the head by passing the wire of the fetatome around its base. Then the collapsed cranial bones and skin may be removed, and the rest of the fetus can be withdrawn unless this is prevented by ankylosis of the joints, a common characteristic of the hydrocephalic fetus. After the head has been fixed securely, the older technique described by Williams, of breaking the cranial bones with a chisel, might be used.

Amputation of the Head and Neck is indicated when the head and neck are retained alongside, beneath, or above the body of the fetus. Correction of this abnormal posture by mutation may be impossible or extremely difficult or dangerous, due to such conditions as wry neck, a uterus contracted tightly around the fetus, or to a dry, emphysematous fetus. Amputation may possibly be indicated when, due to a juvenile or hypoplastic pelvis or to a large fetal head, there is not room in the birth canal for the simultaneous presence of the head and neck and the two limbs. If this condition is present, one should determine accurately the relative size of the fetus and the birth canal because, if after removal of the head and neck further operations such as a total embryotomy are necessary, cesarean section would probably be preferable.

Amputation of the head and neck may be performed by the wire saw or fetatome. The latter is preferred because if the operation is performed properly the neck is amputated close enough to the body so that traction on the forelimbs will pull the scapulas and shoulder joints over the exposed stump of the neck vertebrae. Occasionally in a large mare it may be necessary to remove the forelimb opposite the side to which the head and neck are flexed, and to apply traction to the fetus in order to enable the operator to reach the neck and pass the fetatome wire around it. With the aid of the fetatome wire guide or obstetrical chain the fetatome wire is threaded over the base of the flexed neck and drawn around it. The head of the fetatome is held forcibly between the shoulder joint and neck of the fetus and the neck is severed as close to the body as possible. The neck and head are then withdrawn by means of the hand, a snare, or Krey's hooks. Traction on the forelegs of the fetus will deliver the fetal body unless further operations must be performed. If the cervical stump is long, it must be guided and guarded with the hand or Krey's tongs to prevent laceration of the birth canal as the fetus is withdrawn.

Amputation of the Forelimb is indicated to provide space so that amputation of the head and neck may be possible or easier. If the foreleg is retained or extended beneath the body and mutation is not possible due to fetal emphysema or contraction of the uterine wall, amputation of the foreleg is necessary. It is indicated in large or emphysematous fetuses to reduce their size and expose the ribs for evisceration. In rare cases it may be indicated in transverse ventral presentation in the mare in which after amputation of the two hind legs at the tarsus, and the underneath foreleg at the humeroradial joint, the upper front leg may be removed in the manner described below and evisceration performed, if necessary, before the fetus is corrected by version into a posterior presentation.

Amputation of the forelimb is initiated by means of constant traction applied to the leg with a snare or obstetrical chain. By making a crescent-shaped incision through the skin of the fetus and its trapezius and rhomboideus muscles dorsal to the scapula with a hoe-bladed castrating knife or other knife, the dorsal end of the scapula is separated from the body. A loop of fetatome wire is placed around the limb and moved up the limb as the head of the fetatome is placed in the pectoral region. The wire loop is then moved upward and placed in the incision under the cartilage of the scapula, and the limb removed. This technique is particularly adapted to the cow; it is more difficult to perform in the mare due to the longer limbs of the equine fetus. Another technique is that of placing the loop of fetatome wire around the limb to be removed while the head of the fetatome is placed just dorsal and caudal to the top of the fetal scapula. The limb is extended tautly by traction and the handle of the fetatome is tied or fastened securely to the metacarpal bone. By means of acute-angled sawing the limb is removed, the wire usually passing through the dorsal part of the scapula. On occasion one forelimb as well as the head and neck can be removed in a like manner by proper placing of the wire to include the head and neck. The removal of the forelimb extended beneath the body is easily performed by passing the fetatome wire behind the elbow and beneath the arm. By placing the head of the fetatome on the withers of the fetus, the entire limb can be removed rapidly.

The above two methods of amputation of the forelimb removes the skin over the chest wall, so that the broken ends of the ribs are not protected if evisceration is performed. The older techniques of **subcutaneous amputation of the forelimb** are relatively simple and rapid, especially when the fetus is emphysematous. The method described by Williams, consists of applying steady traction to the limb by a chain or snare around the fetlock, placing a knife at the top of the scapula, and making an incision through the skin and into the muscle the entire length of the leg to the pastern. The thumb and fingers of the operator separate the skin from the entire length of the underlying limb starting at the fetlock joint. The skin is then separated from the leg at the fetlock by cutting through the fetlock joint so that the pastern bones and hoof remain attached to the skin. Strong traction is applied to the limb by placing the snare or obstetrical chain around the metacarpal bone. The pectoral muscles, nerves, and arteries under the scapula are broken with the fingers or with a knife. Traction will usually separate the muscles at the dorsal end of the scapula, if not, these muscles must be incised. In fetal emphysema the muscles are greatly weakened. In many such amputations the use of the fetal extractor is of aid. A variation of the above method of subcutaneous amputation of the forelimb, described by Guard, consists of making 2 incisions on either side of the metacarpal bone after the leg is extended. Guard's or the Ames' chisel or a metal spatula is introduced into these incisions and forced between the skin and the underlying tissues with the leg strongly extended. One hand of the operator guides the head of the instrument under the skin while the opposite arm forces it back and forth. On the medial side of the leg the chisel is forced through the pectoral muscles. After this procedure the skin is incised from the top of the scapula to the fetlock and the rest of the procedure is the same as described in Williams' technique. By using the chisel some of the more difficult manual work of separating the skin from the underlying structures is accomplished more easily.

Amputation of the Anterior Limb at the Humero-Radial Articulation is indicated only in the removal of the forelimbs in transverse ventral presentation in the mare prior to version of the fetus into a posterior presentation. Amputation of the entire forelimb is difficult or impossible in this presentation. Amputation at the humero-radial articulation is accomplished by exerting traction on the limb. A loop of fetatome wire is placed around the leg and the head of the fetatome is pushed ahead of the wire loop to the pectoral region and held there firmly while the wire loop is passed up the leg and over the olecranon and tightened around the leg. The handle of the fetatome may be fastened or held securely to the extended leg in the metacarpal region, preventing the head of the fetatome from slipping downward as the leg is amputated through the distal end of the humerus. The other limb is removed in a similar manner.

Evisceration in Anterior Presentation is indicated to reduce the size of a large or emphysematous fetus and make it less inflexible, or to release ascitic fluid in fetal ascites. It may be indicated to assist the operator in putting his arm through the birth canal to thread the fetatome wire around the pelvis in hiplock in anterior presentation. It is also helpful in rare cases if the ribs are to be broken down for further reduction of the size of the thoracic or pectoral girdle.

When the fetus is within the birth canal or uterus, evisceration in anterior presentation may be performed by subcutaneous amputation or by amputation of the forelimb with a fetatome which exposes the ribs. The intercostal muscles between the first, second, third, fourth, and fifth ribs are separated by the finger or knife from the spine to the sternum. In order to gain free access to the thoracic and abdominal cavities, the second, third, and sometimes the fourth ribs are removed by cutting the costal cartilage just above the sternum with a knife, chisel, or cutting hook and bending the rib dorsally to break it off next to the spinal column, or with a cutting hook or chisel cutting the rib loose as near the spine as possible. If the cutting hook and chisel are used they should be carefully guided and guarded by one hand of the operator while controlled traction or thrusting motions are provided by the other arm, so that the uterus or birth canal are not injured by slipping of the instrument. The ribs should not be broken in the middle as it is difficult to remove both ends, especially the ventral part, and the broken ends are likely to lacerate the operator's hand or arm. The heart and lungs are removed by manual traction after grasping the heart at its base and clasping the fingers firmly around the large vessels. By grasping the lungs in the region of the bifurcation of the trachea first one and then the other or both lungs can be removed. After the thoracic viscera have been removed the fingers are thrust through the diaphragm in the region of the large vessels and the opening enlarged. The stomach and intestines are easily removed by wrapping them around the hand. The liver, the largest organ to be removed, is pulled loose from the diaphragm and withdrawn, usually in several pieces. The kidneys are small and therefore need not be removed.

On rare occasions, to further reduce the size of the thorax, the remainder of the ribs may be broken down with the cutting hook or the chisel. If the blunt-pointed cutting hook is used, the hook is pushed caudally between the skin and ribs about midway between the spine and the sternum until the end of the hook passes beyond the last rib. The point of the hook is turned medially through the abdominal wall and by short, firm pulls the hook is drawn through one to two ribs at a time until only one rib remains to be broken. To avoid cutting this rib suddenly and having the hook tear out of the fetus and possibly injure the uterus or the operator's hand, this last rib may be broken by twisting the hook instead of applying traction. If necessary the ribs on the other side of the thorax may be broken down by introducing the cutting hook through the body cavity to the last rib turning the point outward through the abdominal muscles and pulling the hook back through the ribs in the manner described above. Since the point of the hook is under the skin and might catch it or cut through a fold of skin, the operator's hand outside the skin should guard and follow the progress of the hook. Another technique is to make a 3- to 4-inch vertical incision through the skin cranial to the opposite shoulder and push the cutting hook along the outside of the ribs beneath the shoulder and skin to the last rib and, turning the point of the hook medially, cut through the ribs as was done on the first side after the foreleg had been removed and the fetus eviscerated. A chisel instead of the blunt cutting hook may be used for breaking the ribs in a fetus fixed in the birth canal by traction.

Detruncation in Anterior Presentation is indicated in rare instances when the fetus is in a "dog sitting" posture with the hind limbs extended alongside or beneath the body and wedged into or against the maternal pelvis. If repulsion and mutation are impossible due to protracted dystocia, or if the head and forelegs are outside the vulva, fetotomy is usually necessary.

Although Williams described a manual technique using only a knife, it is much easier to perform detruncation by means of the fetatome. A loop of fetatome wire is passed around the body of the fetus and the head of the fetatome is inserted into the birth canal over the lumbar region of the fetus. After the wire is manipulated back of the last ribs, detruncation is rapidly accomplished. On occasions two cuts through the trunk of a large fetus may be necessary. Using Krey's tongs on the exposed vertebrae for traction further reduction of the fetal body is facilitated. Evisceration would make this operation safer and easier if the fetus is large or emphysematous, or if the birth canal is swollen, small, or dry. Lubrication to prevent trauma to the birth canal is essential. Following detruncation, chains are applied to the two hind limbs and by traction on the limbs and repulsion on the spine the hind quarters of the fetus are turned to a posterior presentation dorso-pubic position. After the hind quarters have been rotated to a dorso-sacral position they are removed by traction. If the pelvis of the fetus is large, its bisection should be considered.

Bisection of the Pelvis in Anterior Presentation is commonly indicated when the fetal pelvis becomes wedged in the maternal pelvis. In these cases the bisiliac diameter of the maternal pelvis is smaller than the distance between the greater trochanters of the fetal hips thus causing hiplock. When this has existed for a number of hours as a cause of dystocia one should examine the cow carefully, since symptoms of obturator paralysis are present in many such cases. If symptoms of obturator paralysis are present, bisection of the fetal pelvis is indicated in preference to forced extraction to prevent further trauma to the nerve. When the hiplock condition cannot be relieved by traction and lubrication, fetotomy is necessary.

This may be performed with the fetatome or wire saw. In using the fetatome, the wire is passed over the top of the fetal pelvis and as far down as possible behind the ischial arch. By passing the hand under the fetus and fetal pelvis the threader or obstetrical chain which is attached to the wire is pulled between the hind legs. After placing this end of the wire through the fetatome, the head of the fetatome is placed alongside the body of the fetus opposite the ribs. If the loop of the wire is on the right side of the tail the head of the fetatome should be on the left side of the fetus so the fetatome wire passes through the middle of the pelvis and not through the head of the femur. After the pelvis is bisected, the fetus minus one hind leg can be removed; then if the operator grasps the exposed pelvic bones the other hind leg can be withdrawn. This operation is made easier by evisceration, which allows the operator more room in the pelvic cavity for placing the wire and the fetatome in position.

A simple procedure combining forced extraction, evisceration, and bisection of the pelvis is frequently used by the author to relieve dystocia in heifers with a relatively large dead fetus in relation to the size of the birth canal. By means of forced extraction with the fetal extractor, the well-lubricated fetus is pulled through the birth canal until the hips enter the maternal pelvis. In rare instances it may be necessary to amputate the head and neck or the head, neck and one forelimb in order to accomplish this. The forequarters outside the vulva are pulled dorsally, exposing the umbilical region of the fetus. The abdominal wall is cut transversely and evisceration is easily completed through this wide incision. In many cases this incision extends dorsally through the intercostal muscles of one of the last 2 to 4 ribs, but these are short and cause no trouble. If the difference between the size of the maternal and fetal pelvises is not relatively great, traction is once more attempted. The long blunt hook is passed over the top of the pelvis and hooked on the ischial arch or into the caudal border of the sacro-sciatic ligament, providing a firm hold for traction and for elevation of the fetal pelvis. This also causes the fetal pelvis to be turned obliquely, thereby facilitating delivery. Since the abdominal wall has already been cut, and evisceration has greatly reduced resistance in the birth canal and all the traction is on the fetal spine, correction of the dystocia in many such cases can be accomplished without bisecting the pelvis. If the latter is necessary it can easily be done with the fetatome, inasmuch as the fetal trunk does not fill the pelvic cavity.

Fetotomy Operations in the Posterior Presentation

Embryotomy in Normal Posterior Presentation is indicated when the diameter of the fetal pelvis is relatively larger than the diameter of the pelvic inlet and wedging or hiplock occurs. This condition is seen usually in immature or stunted heifers and may be complicated by an emphysematous fetus. Under these conditions cesarean section or slaughter may occasionally be advisable.

Embryotomy consisting of the amputation of one leg, or

preferably one leg and part of the pelvis, may be accomplished by means of the fetatome. A transverse incision just cranial to the external wing of the ilium is made in the fetus through the skin and muscle. A loop of fetatome wire is carried up the hind leg and placed in this incision. The head of the fetatome is placed between the hind legs. One hind leg and a portion of the pelvis are removed. A variation in this technique consists of passing the loop of fetatome wire around both legs and up over the hips to the lumbar region of the fetus. With the head of the fetatome on one hip a cut is made with the wire halfway through the lumbar region just cranial to the fetal pelvis. The head of the fetatome is pulled outside the cow and reinserted to rest between the two legs of the fetus and the rest of the cutting is completed, bisecting the fetal pelvis longitudinally. Another technique, described by Benesch, is that of acute angle sawing with the fetatome. The loop of wire is placed around one leg and the head of the fetatome is placed dorsal to the wings of the ilium or even in the caudal lumbar region. The leg is tautly extended and fastened to the handle of the fetatome outside the dam to insure a portion of the fetal pelvis being included with the amputated limb. Usually, however, the leg is amputated through the hipjoint because it is difficult to hold the head of the fetatome in place.

Bisection of the Pelvis in Breech Presentation is indicated in posterior presentation in uniparous animals with the hind limbs of the fetus extended or retained beneath the body, when dystocia has been present for some time, the uterus is contracted, the fetus emphysematous, and the uterus and birth passages are dry and swollen, so that mutation is difficult or impossible.

The wire saw or fetatome may be used in this operation. The heavy metal guide or obstetrical chain is securely fastened to the fetatome wire and then introduced through the birth canal and over the thigh of the fetus between the leg and abdomen. It is pushed as far as possible ventrally and caudally. The hand is then passed beneath the fetal pelvis and between the legs and the wire is drawn out through the vulva. The threaded fetatome is placed on the hip opposite the leg to be removed; that is, if the wire loop is around the right leg of the fetus the head of the fetatome should be on or just behind the greater trochanter of the left leg to insure a large portion of the pelvis being removed with the leg. If the head of the fetatome is not firmly held in place it will pull directly caudal to the perineal region and the leg will be removed at the hip joint or proximal end of the femur. The inability to bisect the pelvis is the principal disadvantage of the wire saw when compared to the fetatome. After the leg and portion of the pelvis is removed the rest of the fetus can usually be withdrawn by traction on the pelvic bones with the long blunt hook or Krey's hooks, with the opposite leg still extended alongside the body. If this is not possible, the operation may have provided enough room to correct by mutation the posture of the remaining limb. In rare cases evisceration may be performed to assist in the removal of the fetus.

Another method oı reduction of the pelvis in breech presentation is to place a loop of fetatome wire in a fetatome around the presenting buttocks. The head of the fetatome is placed in the region of the lumbar vertebrae and held in place by an obstetrical chain fastened to the handle of the fetatome and by Krey's tongs to the sacrosciatic ligament or sacrum. This removes most of the pelvic bones and tail and permits withdrawal of the fetus with both limbs alongside the body.

Amputation of the Rear Limbs at the Tarsus may be indicated in rare instances in the mare in order to obtain additional room for removal of the forelegs in transverse ventral presentation, in cases in which the metatarsal bone is wedged into or across the pelvis, or when mutation of a hock-flexed posture in a mare is impossible. It may occasionally be necessary in monsters with ankylosed hind limbs, such as **Perosomus elumbis.**

The operation is easily performed by slipping a loop of fetatome wire around the leg. The head of the fetatome is placed on the lower row of tarsal bones or the head of the metatarsal bone, and the leg is cut off in this region. Thus the lower portion of the limb is removed and the os calcis is left attached. The obstetrical chain will find secure lodging above this point when traction is applied.

Evisceration and Breakdown of the Ribs in Posterior Presentation is indicated when further reduction in the size of the trunk is desired in order to effect removal of the fetus.

After removal of one or both of the posterior limbs the opening into the abdominal cavity may be enlarged and the viscera removed as described under evisceration in anterior presentation but in a reverse manner, removing first the abdominal and then the thoracic viscera. The ribs may be broken down in the manner described previously, using the blunt-pointed cutting hook or chisel, but in the reverse order. In certain cases in which it is necessary to break down the thoracic cage after evisceration, the fetatome wire might be passed cranial to the shoulder and between the front legs, thus bisecting the thorax.

Other Fetotomy Operations

There are many other embryotomy operations that may occasionally be used to relieve dystocia. Some are variations of those just described; others are more involved and complicated. Certain complex European instruments and techniques described by Benesch and others have not become popular in this country. In fetal monsters causing dystocia, embryotomy operations must be designed to fit the individual case, using the basic operations and principles as a guide. In these cases embryotomies should be planned carefully and in a manner to reduce the number of cuts to a minimum. Double monsters or those single monsters that are sharply bent, such as **Schistosomus** and **Campylorrhachis,** should be divided as nearly as possible into two equal sections so that removal may be prompt and easy. One should not attempt or start a fetotomy operation without being quite certain that the dystocia can be relieved by the planned operation. In many cases consultation may be advisable. It should be borne in mind that a prolonged, unsuccessful embryotomy will make the prognosis more grave if the operator finally attempts to perform a cesarean section.

Eden and Hird described a technique for splitting of the maternal pelvis at the symphysis pubis in immature or stunted heifers suffering from dystocia due to a small pelvic inlet. It is interesting that a brief notation of this technique was described in a French book in the nineteenth century. After epidural anesthesia has been administered, the area beneath the vulva is washed, shaved, and disinfected. In as aseptic a manner as possible a 2-inch incision is made through the skin and down to the midline of the ischial arch. The incision can be made instead through the ventral floor of the vulva between the clitoris and the urethra. A small, guarded obstetrical chisel is driven into the symphysis, guided by the operator's hand in the vagina, and the pelvis is split. The incision is sutured and traction is applied to the fetus. Because at the time of parturition the ligamentous structures are relaxed, the pelvis spreads 2 to 3 inches and allows the fetus to be withdrawn by manual traction or by the fetal extractor. Aftercare consists of keeping the heifer quiet and confined for several weeks. Although the heifer may show some stiffness and slowness of gait it is able to get up and walk. Hird reported that if symptoms of obturator paralysis are present it is advisable to tie a bowline around each hind fetlock with about 18 to 20 inches of rope between them. This is removed in about 1 to 3 days if the animal can handle itself well. He reported that these heifers need not be confined but could be left on the range. Parenteral antibiotics are given to control possible infection at the operative site. By this technique fetotomy and cesarean section are avoided. Although this practice may be accepted for beef cattle in some of the range sections of the West, eastern dairymen and veterinarians would be reluctant to accept it.

Aftercare and Examination of the Dam after Mutation, Forced Extraction, or Embryotomy

Following a dystocia operation the genital tract should always be examined for the presence of another fetus in the uterus or abdominal cavity. This can readily be determined in the mare, cow, and sheep if the hand and arm can enter the uterus. It can be very embarrassing to a veterinarian to apparently relieve a dystocia only to be called back again in 2 to 4 hours or later for another dystocia in the same cow. Occasionally the second fetus may not be found until 2 to 3 days later when the cow develops anorexia, tenesmus, or attempts are made to remove a retained placenta. In the sow the farrowing of the last fetus is usually followed by the sow's becoming quiet and content, nursing her pigs, urinating, eating, and drinking. If the sow remains restless, uneasy, shows anorexia and intermittent tenesmus, the birth canal should be examined for the presence of another fetus. Similar symptoms are exhibited by the dog and cat. In rare instances, in large breeds of dogs, such as the Great Dane, St. Bernard and Newfoundland, the bitch may exhibit every outward sign of having finished whelping. Several days later the bitch may develop anorexia, depression, elevated body temperature, pulse and respiration, and a green, possibly fetid vaginal discharge due to a decomposing fetus. Careful palpation, or preferredly a radiograph, of the abdomen after whelping would have avoided the leaving of a fetus in the atonic uterus.

After every dystocia operation the genital canal, including the uterus, should be examined for the presence of an invaginated uterine horn, lacerations, or ruptures. Small superficial tears of the cervix, vagina, or vulva are of little importance or significance unless retention of the placenta favors infection. In the region of the vulvo-vaginal border these lacerations may lead to infection and necrosis with secondary swelling, pain, and tenesmus. Parenteral antibiotic therapy and local treatment with healing protective ointments are indicated. Lacerations of the cervix if extensive may lead to cervical induration and chronic cervicitis. Any tears in, or ruptures of, the uterus should be noted, inasmuch as the prognosis in these latter cases is poor. In large tears in the vulva, vagina, cervix, or uterus, suturing might be attempted by working through the birth canal. Pulling the cervix and uterus back to or outside the vulva, if possible, would make suturing easier. A small uterine rupture especially of the dorsal wall of the uterus may heal spontaneously; but the uterus should be stimulated to contract by the use of pituitrin and stilbestrol. Antibiotic therapy and letting the genital tract strictly alone may save a few cases. In extensive ruptures of the uterus, especially where infection exists, slaughter is advised. In less severe cases laparotomy and hysterectomy or suturing of the uterine tear may be indicated.

The placenta and placentomes should be examined in cattle. If the placentomes are firm and hard, retention of the membranes generally follows. If uterine infection is obviously present, preventive steps may be taken to control infection by parenteral antibiotic therapy, local treatment of the uterus with antiseptics or tetracycline or other antibiotic compounds and injections of stilbestrol and possibly pituitrin to stimulate uterine involution and prevent uterine sepsis. In the dog if placentas are still present in the uterus they may be withdrawn by the use of a gauze sponge on a forcep. Twisting the instrument in the uterus may catch and hold the placenta to be withdrawn. If retained placenta is suspected the owner should be instructed about subsequent aftercare of the case.

In most obstetrical cases involving forced extraction or fetotomy a dose of 3 to 5 cc., 30 to 50 units, of pituitrin in large animals; 1 to 3 cc., 10 to 30 units, in sheep and swine; and 1/2 to 1 cc., 5 to 10 units, in dogs and cats is indicated to prevent possible prolapse of the uterus and aid involution of the uterus and dropping away of the fetal membranes.

If the animal is unable to rise, further examination should be made to determine whether obturator paralysis, dislocation of the hips, pelvic, or spinal injuries are present, and if so the degree of severity. Milk fever in the cow may be masked by the dystocia. The cow's udder should be examined to make sure no pathology is present, or that teat wounds and lacerations did not occur during the dystocia.

If the operator has been working with his bare arms in an infected uterus he should wash his arms and hands very carefully and thoroughly with soap and water and apply antiseptic in order to prevent skin infections. If any infectious material has adhered to his clothes they should be changed before he goes to another farm. Boots and equipment should be washed and disinfected.

Cesarean Section

Cesarean section is the delivery of the fetus, usually at parturition, by laparohysterotomy. This operation is performed when mutation, forced extraction, and fetotomy are deemed inadequate or too difficult to be employed to relieve the impending or present dystocia or when it is desired that the fetus be delivered alive. The word cesarean is said to derive either from an edict by Julius Caesar that women about to die in advanced childbirth should have this operation performed to save the child, or from the Latin **caeso matris utera,** cutting of the mother's uterus. It is a misconception that Julius Caesar was born in this fashion, as his mother survived his birth in an era when this was impossible, Johnston.

According to Wright, John Field in 1839 was the first to report this operation in English literature. He operated on two bitches. The next year J. B. Carlisle reported on a cesarean in a sow. Cesareans on cattle, horses, sows, and bitches were reported soon after. Later, with the advent of anesthesia, suturing techniques, aseptic techniques, and antibiotic therapy, this operation became increasingly common. Cesarean section in the domestic animals has been well-described by Arthur and Tillman.

Cesarean section in the Mare may be indicated in pelvic fractures with exostosis, transverse dorsal or transverse rotated bicornual pregnancies, anterior longitudinal presentation with the rear limbs extended beneath the body (dog-sitting posture), torsion of the uterus, fetal monsters such as hydrocephalus, and emphysematous fetuses. In rare dystocia cases in mares where mutation, forced extraction or fetotomy procedures do not offer promise of successful delivery, cesarean section should be considered. In many instances the equine fetus is dead because the severity of the parturient problem is not recognized early enough, preferably before parturition, and the time from the onset of labor to the death of the fetus from placental separation or other causes is only 30 minutes to a few hours. The prognosis for a successful equine cesarean operation is poor if prolonged attempts at forced extraction or fetotomy precede the decision to operate. With modern surgical techniques, asepsis, anesthetics and antibiotics successful terminations of this operation on mares are being reported with increasing frequency. It is no longer necessary to sacrifice the life of the dam to save the fetus. A number of cases have been reported in which the mare conceived following the operation.

Bogedda et al. (1966) reviewed the literature and cited 51 reports of 109 equine cesarean operations. Goldberg in his review added further more recent reports. Other source material used in the following discussion of the cesarean operation in horses was from Milne and Horney, Derivaux and Dewalque, Vandeplassche et al., and Arthur. The first successful equine cesarean operation was performed by Lukacs in Hungary in 1908. Goldberg cited Vandeplassche and his colleagues who have performed 58 cesarean sections in mares since 1947 with 47 or 81 percent recoveries. Of these mares 23 were rebred and 12 became pregnant. Of 63 mares with dystocia relieved by fetotomy, 4, or 6 per cent, died, 10, or 16 per cent, had retained placentas and of 24 mares bred following fetotomy, 11 or 46 per cent conceived.

General anesthesia is indicated when the fetus is dead.

This usually consists of tranquilizers prior to induction by chloral hydrate or chloral hydrate-magnesium sulphate-pentobarbital compounds given intravenously. In modern clinics fluothane inhalation anesthesia may be used. These general anesthetics may have an adverse affect on the fetus if it is living. Tranquilizers and local anesthetics in the form of epidural analgesia and local blocks of the abdominal area, or infiltration of the incision sites have been used when the fetus is alive. Both the barbituates and the tranquilizers cause a great enlargement or distention of the spleen with blood. This may occasionally be a factor in causing shock and death within a few hours after the operation. The mare should be restrained in a recumbent position on the left or right side or back depending on the site of the incision.

Various incision sites have been successfully used in the mare and the site should be determined on the basis of the nature of the dystocia, and the presentation or position of the fetus particularly the location of the head of the fetus. The most popular incision site is the Marcenac approach used by Vandeplassche and others in the left flank starting at the middle of the last rib and extending caudal and ventrally toward the stifle. The incision is usually 12 to 18 inches, 25 to 40 cm, in length. Other reported incision sites have been in the upper left flank or the left paramedian or midline abdominal areas, Goldberg. Herniation is less common with the flank incision sites. Derivaux and Delwalque performed the cesarean operation on 17 Belgian mares of which number 13 recovered. The incision may be paramedian or on the midline of the abdomen. Operations in the right flank area are complicated by the large cecum and its dorsal attachments. When incising the peritoneum care should be taken not to injure the viscera.

The equine uterus is more difficult to bring to the incision than is the uterus in cattle, but if the proper incision site, the Marcenac site in the lower left flank is probably the best, has been selected this can probably be done. Excessive manipulation of the viscera or contents of the abdominal cavity should be avoided as this may precipitate shock symptoms and death. If the uterus is infected great care should be used to avoid contamination of the abdominal cavity. The incision of the uterus should be on its greater curvature over a fetal prominence. Because of the long fetal extremities, mutation, forced extraction and even partial fetotomy may be necessary to remove the fetus. If the placenta comes away easily it should be removed, otherwise the uterus should be promptly sutured. A complication of the equine cesarean operation is the rather diffuse bleeding that occurs from the submucosal area of the uterus after it is incised. To prevent severe intrauterine bleeding Vandeplassche recommended that a continuous "whipstitch" suture of catgut be placed through the endometrium, submucosa and serosa completely around the uterine incision for a depth of 1 cm being careful not to include the placenta. This suture was inverted into the uterine cavity by a double row of Lembert or Cushing sutures used to close the uterus after the fetus had been removed. The peritoneum, muscle and fascial layers of the abdominal wall should be sutured separately with strong #4 chromic catgut. Milne and Horney recommended the modified Mayo or overlapping mattress suture for closure of the wound on the ventral abdomen. The skin incision was closed with a nonabsorbable nylon suture. They also recommended the use of quill sutures. Sherrod preferred the use of a tightfitting canvas support bandage. Severe edema of the incision area with occasional rupture and gaping of the skin wound are not unusual following abdominal surgery in the horse.

Aftercare should include stall confinement, feeding limited amounts of laxative feed, administering tetanus antitoxin, oxytocin and broad range antibiotics both locally and systemically. The latter should be continued for 7 to 10 days. Vandeplassche (1969) reported that retained placenta was a common problem in the 60 or more equine cesarean operations his clinic had performed. They found that if they administered 40 units of oxytocin in 1/2 to 1 liter of saline by a slow intravenous drip method over a period of 1 to 2 hours that more normal physiologic contraction of the uterus apparently occurred, Colic was avoided, and the afterbirth dropped away promptly in about 80 per cent of the cases. Complications occurring in the postoperative period are shock that occurs within a few hours after the operation due to manipulation of the uterus and viscera, peritonitis that may cause illness and death 2 to 5 days later, and fatal colic due to strangulation of the gut that may develop one to three weeks or more after the operation due to fibrinous adhesive peritoneal bands secondary to a non-fatal peritonitis, Juhler. Vandeplassche recommended that 4 to 5 days after the operation a rectal examination be performed to break down any adhesions forming around the involuting uterus. Hysterectomy, as in the cow, is extremely difficult to perform, Milne and Horney.

Cesarean section in the Cow has been performed in increasing numbers by practitioners in the United States since 1940. Prior to that period it was performed only sporadically. Oberst and Frank indicated that since 1942 the clinic at Kansas State College has performed between 50 to 100 cesareans each year. Many more cesareans are performed in the western range states, where immature heifers are bred on pasture, than in the northeastern dairy states, where bulls are closely confined and artificial insemination is widely used.

Indications for cesarean section in the cow are:

In the United States immaturity is by far the most common cause. It is seen particularly in beef cattle when the bull runs on pasture with heifer calves. Some young cattle come into estrum and conceive at 4 to 15 months of age with pregnancy resulting in a severe dystocia due to a very small pelvis and genital tract. In these cases the difference between the size of the fetus and the birth canal is marked. Performing embryotomy operations through such a narrow birth canal is very difficult and the fetus is always lost.

Incomplete dilation or relaxation of the cervix may be associated with secondary uterine inertia with advanced involution of the cervix and uterus secondary to torsion of the uterus, or fetal dystocia and emphysema in which the onset of parturition was not observed, or the cow was neglected for 36 to 48 hours. In other cases it may be observed, without a known predisposing cause, due to a primary uterine inertia, or it may be caused by sclerosis of the cervix. In such cases the fetus may still be alive; pituitrin or oxytocin might be given, and the condition of the cervix observed in 3 to 4 hours or more to make certain that parturition was not in its initial stages.

An abnormally large fetus may be a cause for cesarean section. Apparently normal healthy fetuses may occasionally be too large for birth without total fetotomy or excessive traction. If the forefeet but not the head can enter the pelvic inlet or in posterior presentation if the hips are much too large to enter the pelvis, cesarean section should be considered, as it is frequently easier, safer, and faster than total fetotomy and in many such cases the delivery of a live calf is possible. These large-sized fetuses are most frequently seen in the large breeds, such as Holstein, Brown Swiss, Shorthorn, and Herefords, and they are usually male. The cause of the dystocia may appear to be a large normal fetus; actually, however, the cause may be an abnormal or relatively small pelvis; or both conditions may be present. In breeds of cattle with muscle hypertrophy or double muscling, affected calves frequently require cesarean section for delivery. In other cases the oversized condition of the fetus may be due to emphysema or to anasarca. In rare cases an excessively large fetal giant may be caused by a greatly prolonged gestation period exceeding 300 days. The prognosis in these latter pathologically oversized fetuses is grave because of the overdistention of the uterus, the uterine inertia, and the high incidence of septic metritis and retained afterbirth following the relief of the dystocia. Other causes for oversized fetuses include fetal monsters such as **Schistosomus reflexus,** general ankyloses, and double monsters. At times, certain of these may be more safely and easily removed by cesarean section than by fetotomy.

Other cases where cesarean section is indicated include: a torsion of the uterus that is difficult or impossible to correct by other means; a juvenile hypoplastic genital tract due to poor growth and development; hydrops amnii and allantois when the life of the dam is imperiled by great distention of the uterus and other methods have failed to relieve the condition; marked stenosis of the vagina in prolonged dystocia in heifers due to perivaginal hemorrhage compressing the genital tract; fetal mummification when ordinary treatments fail, or in heifers or young cows with a 6- to 8-month fetal mummy too large to be expelled through the undilated birth canal; when the dam is unable to rise, is exhausted, debilitated, diseased, or near death; and stenosis of the birth canal due to tumors or extensive scar tissue in the pelvic birth canal. In rare cases in cattle with prolonged dystocia the uterine wall contracts tightly around the emphysematous fetus, producing a contraction or retraction ring dystocia. Since forced extraction may cause rupture of the uterus and fetotomy would be difficult, cesarean section may be indicated. Fracture of the maternal pelvis in cattle is rare and therefore cesarean section due to this cause from dystocia is only seldom indicated.

Prognosis—A review of cesarean operations reported by Roberts and Frank of 58 cases, by Wright in 1953 and 1958 of 45 cases and 200 cases, respectively, by Vandeplassche and Paredis of 150 cases, by Arthur of 300 cases, and by Oberst and Frank (1954) on recent cases at Kansas State College of about 50 to 100 cases per year, indicates that in cattle that are good surgical risks, and are operated on within 6 to 18 hours after the onset of labor, in cases where the fetus is still alive or very recently dead and the cow is in good condition physically and has not been damaged by excessive manipulation, injury, or infection of the birth canal or uterus, the mortality rate should be less than 10 per cent, and possibly only 5 per cent. Under field and actual practice conditions the mortality rate might reach 15 per cent.

The mortality rate is about 10 to 30 per cent in cases where the cesarean section is performed from 18 to 36 hours after the onset of the second stage of parturition. The fetuses are generally dead and occasionally slightly emphysematous; the cow is in poorer condition for the operation, and the genital tract is usually injured or traumatized. In cases in which dystocia has existed for 36 hours or more, the fetus is emphysematous, the cow is usually in poor physical condition, and the uterus is atonic and infected, the mortality rate may reach 30 to 50 per cent or more. Vandeplassche et al. (1963) reported on 103 cesarean operations where emphysematous fetuses were removed; the recovery rate was over 80 per cent in their clinic. Debackere et al. reported on 340 cesarean and

80 fetotomy operations; the maternal mortality rate for each series was 5 and 9 per cent, retained placenta was 33 and 20 per cent and conception rates in cows rebred after the operation were 80 and 73 per cent, respectively. Thus the outcome of either cesarean section or fetotomy are similar. The decision therefore as to which procedure to use should be based on the economics of the case.

The more common causes of maternal death are: shock, secondary to exhaustion; toxemia; excessive manipulation of the abdominal viscera as in torsion of the uterus, or when abdominal pressure is released rapidly, as in removal of a large fetus or excessive amounts of fluids as in hydrops; septicemia, pyemia, and toxemia secondary to septic metritis; uterine inertia in prolonged dystocia; retained placenta; peritonitis; or severe necrotic vaginitis due to excessive manipulation and injury prior to the cesarean section. Hemorrhage and ventral hernia are occasional causes of death. In rare cases hemorrhage, especially from the stalk of a torn or lacerated caruncle, may occur in atonic uteri. Ventral hernia may be prevented by proper suturing technique and suture material. Most maternal deaths occur 1 to 8 days after the operation. In recent years improved surgical techniques, asepsis, and antibiotics have greatly improved the possibilities for recovery even in cases offering great surgical risks.

It is generally stated that from 60 to 80 per cent of cows having cesarean section should be fertile and conceive subsequently. Failure of conceive may be due to peritoneal adhesions or to severe endometrial damage secondary to septic metritis. Debackere et al. reported after a series of cesarean operations that of 48 cows without adhesions 81 per cent conceived, while in 47 cows with adhesions only 51 per cent conceived. The incidence of retained placenta following cesarean section is high, between 20 and 35 per cent, and the incidence of metritis may vary from 20 to 50 per cent. Fifty to 80 per cent of recovered cows conceived after the cesarean operation, Vandeplassche, Arthur, Brone et al.. About 80 percent of the cattle operated upon had an abnormal puerperium due to retained placenta, uterine infection and delayed involution of the uterus. Uterine infections should be expected and preventive treatment given. The reason for this high rate of placental retention after cesarean section is not known.

According to the authors named above, the incidence of live calves produced by cesarean section is from 30 to 60 per cent. This varies with the promptness with which dystocia is observed, the veterinarian summoned, and the operation performed. Fetotomy in cattle should be carefully considered before performing cesarean section, since cesarean section requires more trained assistance, is more costly, and results in a higher percentage of subsequent sterility. If it appears that a fetotomy is going to be difficult, prolonged, or dangerous to the dam or operator—such as those requiring total fetotomy involving three or more difficult operations; in cases in which the birth canal is small and the fetus large, or the birth canal is swollen, compressed, or dry—making it difficult to perform a fetotomy; or in cases in which the fetus is emphysematous and the uterus contracted, cesarean section should be considered if it gives promise of being a safer, easier means for relieving the dystocia than do embryotomy or forced extraction. According to Vandeplassche and Paredis fewer than 1 per cent of the dystocias cannot be relieved by cesarean, while 3 to 5 per cent will end in failure if fetotomy is employed.

Selection of the Operative Site, Means of Restraint, and Anesthesia—These will and should vary depending upon the case. The operation has been performed in the upper right flank, with the animal standing. This site makes the operation easier for the veterinarian as he can perform it standing; the incision can be smaller because the muscle tissues can stretch into a circular shape when the fetus is removed; subsequent herniation is less likely, and many veterinarians are experienced in operating in the flank site because of frequently having performed rumenotomies. The right flank approach may be desired when torsion of the uterus is present, as the standing position is of assistance in correcting the torsion. The disadvantages of the right flank incision are that the cow may be more difficult to restrain and control. It is difficult to bring the uterus to the incision, and abdominal contamination with the uterine contents is nearly unavoidable. This is of no consequence when the fetus is alive and little or no infection is present in the uterus; but it is a major disadvantage with a dead fetus and an infected uterus. If during the operation the incision is extended too far ventrally it is difficult to hold the small intestines within the abdomen. If the cow strains, coughs, or struggles an armful of intestines may be expelled through the laparotomy incision and occasionally the cow may put her foot through them.

The operation may be performed in the left flank, at which site intestines usually are not present to offer a problem. The operation can be performed more ventrally on this side if it is desired, but the same advantages and disadvantages apply as for the right flank incision. A large full rumen may make it quite difficult to bring the uterus from the right side of the abdominal cavity to the left. Since these upper flank operations are performed with the cow standing, anesthesia consists of a small dose of epidural anesthesia to control straining; a tranquilizer to quiet the animal; local infiltration or paravertebral nerve block anesthesia of the flank region; and in certain cows a light narcotic dose of chloral hydrate, 1/2 to 3/4 ounce, given intravenously, or 1 to 2 ounces given orally by means of a stomach tube or capsule may be needed.

Some veterinarians prefer to perform the cesarean operation by an oblique abdominal incision in the lower left or right flank region below the fold of skin in the flank and above the attachment of the udder on a line between the stifle and the umbilicus, parallel the ventral borders of the ribs. This site allows easy access to the gravid uterine horn. The muscles in this region stretch easily. It is easier to prevent contamination of the abdominal.cavity by uterine fluids. There is less possibility that hernia will develop than when the incision is on the ventral aspect of the abdomen. The disadvantage of this site on the right side is that it is necessary to control the small intestines during the operation so that they do not prolapse. In most cases intestinal prolapse may be prevented by making the cow lie on her left side, a position necessary for performing the operation. The lower-left flank as a site for the incision requires the cow to be laid on her right side. On the left side the incision is more caudal than on the right side, and the apex of the uterus can be brought to the incision behind the rumen. Control of the intestines is only occasionally necessary when the incision is on the left side. In these lower-flank incisions the cow is restrained or stretched in lateral recumbency by tying the two rear legs together and the two front legs together. A portable simple operating table for large animals that may be manually operated has been used at the clinic in Hannover, Germany, (J.A.V.M.A., **139** (1961) 681). Anesthesia may consist of an epidural of 40 to 60 cc. of 2 per cent procaine or xylocaine solution, which will produce sensory and motor paralysis of the perineum and rear limbs. This will cause the standing animal to stop straining and to go down. If the cow is laying on her side when epidural anesthesia is administered, sensory loss may be incomplete because the uppermost nerves may not be properly blocked. Paravertebral nerve block or local infiltration of the operative site is usually necessary. In some cases a tranquilizer or a light narcotic dose of chloral hydrate or pentobarbital may be desirable.

Other clinicians prefer the ventral approach, with an incision through the abdominal floor. Roberts and Frank and Frank and Oberst recommended the site between the linea alba and the right subcutaneous abdominal vein. Gotze and Vandeplassche and Wright preferred to operate 2 to 4 inches lateral but parallel to the left subcutaneous abdominal vein. In all ventral abdominal incisions, the incision starts at or slightly lateral to the fore udder and extends forward as far as necessary, usually 12 to 14 inches. In this region the apex or ventral portion of the gravid horn can be brought to and outside of the incision, thereby preventing uterine contents being released into the abdominal cavity. This is a great advantage in cases in which the uterus is infected. The abdominal wall is not as thick in this area as in the flank. There is less muscle tissue and fewer blood vessels, especially in heifers, and the abdominal wall is composed mainly of fibrous connective tissue, the abdominal tunic. The presence of the uterus in the abdominal incision usually keeps the intestines within the abdominal cavity. The main disadvantages to this approach is that the abdominal wall at this site is composed of largely fibrous tissue tunics and will not stretch as does muscle tissue. Thus the incision must be longer than in the flank. If the proper suture material and technique are not employed herniation is more common.

The choice of operative site and mode of anesthesia should fit the amount of help available, the nature of the dystocia requiring cesarean section, the type of cow, the nature of surroundings, the location of the fetus and uterus, and the preference of the operator. It is desirable to have one skilled assistant to aid the operator, and two lay assistants to control the cow, especially if the cow is in lateral recumbency.

To perform the operation in lateral recumbency the operator should place the animal down by using the rope squeeze method after heavy tranquilization or should administer a large dose of epidural anesthesia, 40 to 60 cc. of 2 per cent procaine solution. The cow should not be dropped suddenly, as there may be danger of uterine rupture. Local anesthesia may be used on the incision site, or if the incision is lateral to the mammary veins paravertebral anesthesia is satisfactory. Arnold and Kitchell have described the innervation of the abdominal wall in cattle. Wright preferred a moderate general anesthesia of chloral hydrate, 30 to 60 gm. intravenously in a 7- to 10- per cent solution reinforced with pentobarbital as necessary during the operation. Local anesthesia was also used at the operative site. If general anesthesis with chloral hydrate or chloral hydrate, magnesium sulphate and pentobarbitol intravenous solutions is given, it is best to give it after the operative site has been prepared and everything is in readiness for performing the operation. This shortens the length of time from its administration to the removal of the fetus, so that the effect of the anesthetic on the fetus is slight, and no further anesthesia will have to be administered during the operation unless there is some unusual occurrence. In operations on the ventral abdominal floor the hind limbs should be tied together and the front limbs tied together. They should be stretched apart and sufficient help should be available to roll the cow on her back at certain times during the operation. The cow should not be left on her back for a protracted length of time.

The Operation should conform to all other surgical operations on the abdomen with regard to preparation and draping of the operative site. An approach to asepsis should be attempted. All preliminary preparations for the operation should be made prior to giving general anesthesia, if that is used, so the fetus may be removed without delay. Hemorrhage from the incision should be controlled but in the ventral approach hemorrhage, especially in heifers, is slight. The upper flank operation is performed like the laparotomy incision in a rumenotomy, except that the incision is about 12 inches long. The author believes that the ventral paramedian approach recommended by Frank and the oblique lower left flank or ventrolateral abdominal approach recommended by Merkt, Gotze, Aehnalt et al., and Oehme are most satisfactory for the majority of cases. The former technique will be described in detail. After the skin is incised the cow should be rolled on her back and the rest of the incision completed. After incising the abdominal tunic the fascia of the transverse abdominal muscle and peritoneum is opened with a knife and the incision completed with scissors. In about 7 out of 8 cows the omentum is observed covering the uterus and abdominal viscera. This can be incised, but it is better to pull the omentum cranially as it helps to hold the intestines from the incision. One or both arms are inserted into the abdominal cavity and the fetus is grasped through the uterine wall, and the apex of the uterine horn containing the fetus is pulled into or through the abdominal incision as the cow is returned to lateral recumbency. The gravid uterine horn fills the incision and presents the escape of the viscera. The uterine horn and fetal membranes are incised longitudinally over the greater curvature, avoiding the cotyledons. Incising of the caruncular stalk may result in persistent hemorrhaging. Chains are applied to the limbs of the fetus and by exerting traction in a ventral and caudal direction the fetus is removed. If necessary the incision in the abdominal wall and uterus should be enlarged to prevent tearing. If the fetus is in posterior presentation the head should be fastened by a snare and the two forefeet secured before the fetus is withdrawn. In rare cases fetotomy may be required on the fetus to assist removal. If uterine torsion is present the direction of torsion should be accurately ascertained before the cow is forced down. This is not so important when the cow is operated upon standing. The torsion should be corrected, if possible, by grasping the fetus through the uterine wall and rotating the uterus. If this is not easily accomplished, the fetus may be removed before the torsion of the uterus is corrected. In cases in which the uterus is greatly distended due to an emphysematous fetus or hydrops it may be difficult or impossible to draw the apex of the uterus through the incision. If the uterine contents are infected the uterus should be pulled tightly against the abdominal incision and the lips of the incision and the abdominal cavity carefully packed off to avoid contamination when the uterine contents are released. The normal noninfected allantoic and amniotic fluids cause no trouble in the abdominal cavity.

After a live fetus has been removed the fetal membranes are left in the uterus. If the fetus is dead the fetal membranes are removed manually if they drop away readily. Otherwise, they are left within the uterus. Some of the excess fetal membranes may be trimmed away with scissors so that it does not interfere with the suturing of the uterus. Because of the high incidence of uterine infections and retained afterbirths following cesarean section it is advisable to place 1 to 2 grams of oxytetracycline, chlortetracycline, or tetracycline in the uterine cavity whether or not the fetal membranes are removed. The uterine incision is closed with a double row of Lembert or Cushing sutures of No. 1 or 2 chromic catgut. A long straight intestinal needle should be used. The assistant can greatly facilitate the suturing by holding the edges of the uterine incision together. The cow is then rolled on her back, the uterus replaced, and the omentum pulled caudally over the uterus so that when the abdominal incision is sutured the omentum will lie against it. If torsion was not corrected before the fetus was removed it should be corrected after the uterine closure is completed. The uterus should always be examined for the presence of twins, although these are rarely encountered in cesarean sections.

The ventral abdominal incision may be closed in several ways. Oberst and Frank reported good success using a continuous umbilical tape suture through the abdominal tunic, muscle, and peritoneum. Vandeplassche recommended interrupted mattress sutures of No. 4 to 5 chromic catgut doubled with a supplementary continuous suture of doubled catgut along the muscle incision after the peritoneum had been closed. Until this second suture line was used they had occasional cases of herniation; after its use they had no cases of herniation in 48 consecutive cesareans. Wright recommended a continuous suture, tied every 3 inches, of No. 4 or 5 doubled chromic catgut. The use of stainless steel wire or nylon suture has not been satisfactory because they tend to cut tissue when under tension. In the ventral incisions just described, the tough abdominal tunic provides a firm anchorage for the sutures. The superficial muscles and fascia may be pulled together with catgut. Oberst recommended a single continuous suture of umbilical tape that is left in place for closure of the peritoneum and muscle. This prevented possible eventration. Mattress, interrupted, or lock stitches of nylon, silk, linen, or umbilical tape are placed in the skin.

The peritoneal and muscle layers in the upper flank incisions are sewn with catgut or if preferred the stronger figure-eight sutures of umbilical tape through all layers including the skin. The skin sutures are usually removed in 7 to 10 days. This operation generally takes from 30 to 60 minutes to perform if complications are not encountered. Three to 5 ml., 30 to 50 U.S.P. units of posterior pituitary extract or oxytocin is given to stimulate uterine contraction and involution. This should not be given until after the operation, because if given earlier, it may complicate the suturing by contracting the uterus and pulling it away from the abdominal incision.

Postoperative Care—Most cases should receive 3 to 6 million units of penicillin or 1 to 2 grams of the tetracycline compounds parenterally after the operation. This should be repeated daily for 3 to 7 days. Thirty to 50 mg. of stilbestrol or equivalent doses of other estrogens may be given as indicated, to aid involution of the uterus. The cow should be observed closely for the first 24 hours for evidence of shock especially if large amounts of fluid or a large fetus were removed or if there was much manipulation of the uterus or abdominal contents. If shock develops it should be combatted immediately with intravenous injections of blood, saline, and glucose. In rare cases milk fever, and straining due to vulvar irritation or other causes, may occur, requiring prompt attention. If the calf survives it should receive some colostrum soon after birth. If the afterbirth is retained and metritis develops the condition should be handled conservatively by allowing the afterbirth to drop away by itself. It is dangerous to remove the placenta manually, since little can be gained by the attempt, and much lost by injury to the uterus. The cow should be kept quiet and away from contact with other animals after the operation, in order to avoid possible injury to the operative site. The skin sutures may be removed in 7 to 14 days.

Cesarean Section in the Ewe—This operation in the ewe has been performed successfully by many veterinarians in recent years but it requires a careful, aseptic technique oftentimes difficult to achieve under farm conditions. Ellis reported on 69 ovine cesarean operations to relieve dystocia with 77 per cent recovery. Most deaths were due to infection. For this reason the operation is best performed in a veterinary hospital to which the ewe can be transported easily. The operation is indicated in the ewe when the cervix fails to dilate, "ringwomb," or when the ewe is bred too young or is poorly grown and the birth canal is too small to permit the operator to relieve the dystocia by forced extraction. In rare instances monster fetuses, fetal emphysema and other conditions similar to those in the cow may necessitate cesarean section. Prolapse of the vagina is a common cause for the cesarean operation in ewes, DeBois. Another indication for a cesarean is in pregnancy toxemia or ketosis in ewes, in which dead twin fetuses are usually present. Under usual circumstances the severely affected ewe would die before the dead fetuses were aborted despite glucose, A.C.T.H. or cortisone therapy and other supportive treatments. The valuable ewe may be saved by cesarean section. The prognosis should be more guarded than in the cow.

The operation is similar to that in the cow and is performed through the flank, through the ventrolateral abdominal wall, through the ventral abdominal wall between the linea alba and the subcutaneous abdominal vein, or through the midline, Ellis. A satisfactory anesthesia for ewes is chloral hydrate or a combination of chloral hydrate and pentobarbital. Tranquilizers and local or paravertebral anesthesia can be used if the fetus(es) are alive. If bicornual twins are present in the uterus an incision should be made in each horn. No. 4 chromic catgut is satisfactory for suturing the abdominal wall.

Aftercare of the ewe is similar to that of the cow. If pregnancy ketosis is present glucose injections, propylene glycol orally and cortisone or A.C.T.H. may help promote appetite and recovery in the convalescent ewe.

Cesarean Section in the Sow—has been performed successfully for many years. The sow is more resistant to infection and peritonitis than are the ewe and cow. Cesarean is indicated in the sow when because of being bred too young or of being poorly grown, the resulting small pelvis and genital canal prevent normal farrowing. The canal is usually too small to permit the introduction of the hand in order to apply traction. Cesarean may be indicated in primary uterine inertia that fails to respond to oxytocin or in secondary uterine inertia in which the second stage of labor has been prolonged and lay or veterinary assistance failed to correct the dystocia. In this latter type of dystocia the genital tract is usually swollen and may occasionally be severely traumatized. Cesarean may be indicated occasionally due to monster fetuses or to pelvic fractures with exostoses or other abnormalities.

Cesarean section in the sow is 85 to 90 per cent successful when performed soon after the onset of the second stage of parturition, when the fetuses are still alive and the sow or gilt is still strong and vigorous. Mortality in the sow rises when the operation is not performed until 18 to 24 hours after the onset of straining. By this time the pigs are usually dead and the sow is in poorer shape for the operation. If the operation is delayed more than 24 hours the fetuses are usually emphysematous, the uterus infected, and the sow exhausted and toxic. Although some sows may survive surgery at this stage the prognosis is guarded to poor depending upon the condition of the genital tract.

As in the ewe, the operation should be performed in a

veterinary hospital if possible inasmuch as the average hog farm is rather unsanitary and inconvenient for surgery. If it must be performed on the farm the sow's legs and body may be strapped to a panel and the panel placed across two supports, to form a satisfactory operating table set up in a clean, dust-free location. If the fetuses are dead, the type of anesthesia may be general using 0.5 to 1.5 ounces of chloral hydrate and 1/3 to 2/3 ounce of magnesium sulphate in 100 to 200 cc. of water. This is administered intravenously in the ear vein through an 18 guage needle. Pentobarbital may be administered similarly in an approximate dose of 1 cc. or 1 grain per 10 to 15 lbs. of body weight. Fluothane may be used by inhalation. Many veterinarians prefer to use heavy tranquilization or occasionally chloral or pentobarbital in a narcotic dose and to supplement it with local anesthesia along the incision line when the fetuses are alive. Frank and Getty have recommended epidural anesthesia, approximately 1 cc. of 2 to 4 per cent procaine solution or 0.5 cc. of xylocaine for every 10 lbs. of body weight is injected into the epidural space at the lumbo-sacral articulation. The operator should make sure that the sow's foreparts are kept elevated or level, so that the anesthetic solution does not gravitate too far forward. Surgical preparation and procedures similar to those in the cow and ewe should be carried out in preparing the operative area and maintaining near asepsis during the operation on the sow. For this purpose a large sterile rubber or plastic shroud to drape over the sow's body is very helpful.

Frank recommended a vertical incision 7 to 8 inches, 17 to 20 cm., in length in the flank region. Wright and Mather recommended a horizontal flank incision parallel to but 1 to 3 inches above the mammae. The large amount of fat between the peritoneum and the body wall may cause some confusion unless it is recognized. One entire horn may be drawn through the incision to the outside before incising and removing the fetuses; or one fetus can be brought to the outside and removed, then the next fetus brought out and removed through the previously-made incision; and so forth until all the fetuses in the one horn have been removed and the horn is completely outside the abdomen. The fetuses may be pulled from the inside of the horn or forced toward the incision by pressure on the outside of the horn or a combination of both in order to facilitate their rapid removal. The pelvic portion of the canal should be examined to be certain a fetus is not left there. If the fetal membranes are expelled with the fetus they are removed. If not expelled with the fetuses they are left in the uterus to be expelled later—usually within 12 hours. The incision is sutured with a single or double row of Lembert or Cushing sutures of No. 1 chronic catgut and that horn replaced. The same technique is followed on the other horn. In exceptional cases, if the uterus is well-involuted it may be necessary to incise the horn over each fetus. If the uterus is severely infected, introduction of antibiotics—especially the tetracycline derivatives—is indicated prior to closure of the uterine incisions. The peritoneum and muscle layers are sutured separately with chromic catgut by continuous sutures; and the skin with silk, nylon, or umbilical tape.

For aftercare of the sow administration of pituitrin or oxytocin, estrogens, and antibiotics are indicated, as in the cow. The sow should be confined in a clean, quiet place for 8 to 10 days, at which time the skin sutures may be removed. Cesarean section in the sow and ewe has been well-described and illustrated by Tillmann.

Cesarean Section in the Dog and Cat is very common and useful in the correction of dystocia in these species. It is performed most commonly in primary uterine inertia that fails to respond to "feathering," or vaginal stimulation of uterine contractions, or to the injection of pituitrin or pitocin. This condition is seen most commonly in certain toy breeds such as the Dachshund. It is frequently required to relieve dystocia in the brachycephalic breeds of dogs with large heads and small pelves, such as the Boston and other bulldogs, Pekinese, Boxers, Pugs, and even the Scotch Terriers and Sealyhams. There is no doubt but that cesarean section has been a great boon to these breeds of dogs. The discussion that centers around the fact that this operation has been conducive to the perpetuation of such abnormal breeds is a subject of importance, but is not discussed here because it is not appropriate to this text. Cesarean section may be indicated in Cockers, in which for apparently psychotic reasons whelping does not progress normally. It is indicated when pelvic fractures, tumors, rickets, or the rearing of a young dog under unfavorable conditions has resulted in dystocia due to a small pelvic canal. It is indicated in secondary uterine inertia in which more fetuses are still in the uterus and dystocia has been prolonged so that even if 1 or 2 fetuses could be removed by traction, the rest would not be expelled, because of uterine atony and fatigue. It may be indicated with 1 or 2 excessively large fetuses, or when a fetus is transversely located in the uterine body and cannot be removed manually. In rare instances it may be indicated for uterine torsion and for retention of one fetus in the uterus following apparently normal parturition, as is seen occasionally in the large breeds, such as the Great Dane and St. Bernard. The cesarean operation may also be used to remove mummified fetuses from the uterus and in cases of inguinal hernias containing a portion of the pregnant uterus. It may be indicated when general debility and inanition make normal parturition

impossible. When a greenish-black discharge appears at the vulva it is an indication that the placentas are disengaging, and cesarean might be indicated even though probably one pup or more is dead.

The same general indications for this operation apply to the cat. In the cat the most common cause for dystocia is deviation of the fetal head and neck, and if mutation per vaginum is not successful cesarean is indicated.

Many veterinarians perform cesareans when possibly mutation or forced extraction could be used because they are surer of their results with this operation. They are better acquainted with it than with the other techniques in which fetuses might be injured by improper or unskilled use of instruments per vaginum. The operation is frequently employed because it requires much less time and patience of the busy practitioner. Otherwise the veterinarian might have to observe and assist the bitch at intervals for 4 to 6 hours or more. Besides this inconvenience to the veterinarian, it would be more costly to the owner. Lastly, many owners, expecting the bitch to be in dystocia because of its breed or past history, request and expect the veterinarian to perform a cesarean operation.

Prognosis—Cesarean section in the bitch when performed during the first stage of labor or within 12 hours after the onset of the second stage of parturition when the fetuses are still alive, should result in less than a 2 to 3 per cent mortality rate. In many hospitals this may be less than 1 per cent. If the operation is not performed until 12 to 24 hours after the onset of labor some of the fetuses may be dead, but the results nevertheless are usually quite good. If the operation is delayed beyond 24 hours after the onset of labor the maternal mortality rate may be 50 per cent or more due to shock, toxemia, septic metritis, and exhaustion. In these neglected cases the fetuses are usually dead, the uterus diseased and atonic, and hysterectomy may be indicated.

In general, bitches should be examined if they have labored for 3 to 4 hours without delivering a fetus. The cause of the dystocia should be determined and if cesarean is decided upon it should not be delayed too long by efforts to remove fetuses by other means. Fetotomy is rarely possible in the bitch or cat due to the small birth canal. In cases in which dystocia, relievable only by cesarean, is expected on the basis of the previous breeding history or examination, the bitch should be observed closely for signs of beginning parturition. Body temperature readings may be made 2 or 3 times daily and when the temperature drops 1 degree or more below normal or goes below 100° F. the bitch is either in the first stage of labor or beginning the second, and a cesarean operation should be performed immediately. Cesarean section apparently has little effect on the subsequent fertility of the bitch; many bitches have had from 4 to 8 cesareans performed without becoming sterile, even though slight to severe adhesions may form at the operative site. After 3 cesarean operations adhesions are common and the number of pups per litter decrease and operations are more difficult to perform, Archibald and Smith.

The Operation should be performed in a skillful, aseptic manner under hospital or clinic conditions. Complications should be anticipated and prevented or handled. Extra aid should be present for receiving the pups as they are delivered. An incubator that provides warmth, 85 to 90° F, and oxygen may save many pups, Kirk. The anesthetic of choice is usually a small dose, 1/4 to 1/2 gr., of morphine and 1/100 to 1/150 gr. of atropine. About forty minutes later 1/20 to 1/10 gr. of apomorphine is given. After the operative site has been prepared ether, Fluothane or methoxyflurane is administered until the surgical stage of anesthesia is produced. In extremely toxic or debilitated dogs, some practitioners recommend ataractics and local anesthesia in preference to the general anesthetics. Pentobarbital is definitely contraindicated because of its depressant effect on live fetuses. Pentothal or thiobarbiturates such as "Surital" might be used but they are short acting and must be given several times during the operation by means of a syringe and needle taped to the leg with the needle remaining in the vein. These agents and the tranquilizers or ataractics also have a depressing effect on the fetus and make the newborn pup less viable. When fetuses are dead, the barbiturates and ataractics may be used. A single small dose of a thiobarbiturate may be used to intubate a bitch or immediately before removing the fetuses. In the cat, only ether, Fluothane or methoxyflurane is used. Epidural analgesia is the method preferred by some veterinarians, Kilde and Soma.

The incision may be made through the flank at an oblique angle parallel the last ribs. This site reduces the possibility of eventration but may leave a noticeable scar in shorthaired dogs. This approach takes more time, the horns are harder to reach, and an incision must be made in each horn. Benesch and Wright and other veterinarians preferred a left-flank incision 3 to 5 inches long parallel to the spine and beginning 1-1/2 inches behind the costal arch and 1-1/2 inches above the mammary glands. This provided better access to the uterus, and the scar is less noticeable. Many other veterinarians prefer the midline, or linea alba, as an incision site. The greatest disadvantages to this site, which are not serious, are possible eventration or injury to the wound by the pups. It has the advantage of easy access to the uterus. Because the withdrawal of the gravid uterus through the incision might predispose to shock, pressure should be applied to the abdomen after removal of the gravid uterus, and then gradually released. To prevent shock some veterinarians bring the uterus and a fetus to the incision, pack the incision with towels and incise each horn, removing the fetuses by pressure and traction, and keeping the uterus within the abdominal cavity. Because this procedure might result in peritonitis from uterine fluids, it is not desirable unless the fetuses are alive and the uterus not infected. This technique is more time-consuming. Most veterinarians remove one horn of the uterus at a time through the abdominal incision. The horn is incised near the bifurcation. The fetuses may be removed from one or even both horns through the same hysterotomy incision. The uterus is incised longitudinally on the side opposite the attachment of the broad ligament, care being exercised not to incise through a placental area. After the fetus is removed the placenta will come away by pressure on the outside of the uterine horn over the placental area of attachment. This can be aided by tension on the umbilical cord. As the fetuses are removed the umbilical cord is clamped with forceps which should not be allowed to dangle as this might predispose to hernia. The placenta is cut or torn away.

The pups are rubbed with a towel to stimulate respirations. The pup's head is held down, to facilitate drainage of mucus from the nostrils and throat. If respirations are delayed, the pup should be dipped alternately into hot and cold water, or its umbilical vein injected with 0.25 to 0.5 cc. of **Coramine.** When bitches are anesthetized with "Surital," which crosses the placental barrier, the live pups upon delivery should be rubbed vigorously and given 5 to 10 mg. of the anesthetic antagonist "Mikedimide" or possibly doxapram, "Dopram," (Robbins) into the umbilical vein which promptly stimulates respiration and overcomes the sedation effects, Wester. The pups should be kept warm, 80° F. or higher, until placed with the bitch for nursing. Each horn should be carefully checked to be sure all fetuses are removed. If a fetus should be in the birth canal it should be removed by traction through the vagina or drawn cranially through the uterine body incision.

The uterine incision is closed by a single row of Lembert sutures of catgut. The flank incisions are sutured with several rows of catgut, with nylon or silk in the skin. The peritoneum on the midline incision is sutured with continuous catgut, the fascia of the linea alba with interrupted stainless steel, and the skin with interrupted steel or silk sutures. The use of stainless steel wire for suturing the ventral abdominal incision prevents possible eventration. The skin wounds are covered with adhesive if surgery was aseptic. If the wound is likely to be infected it should be left open for daily dressing and bandaging. Gauze or other dressing may be wrapped around the body between the breasts, but not so tightly as to cause discomfort. This is difficult to hold in place. After the operation all pups, especially those of the brachycephalic breeds, should be checked for abnormalities such as cleft palate, hydrocephalus, and so forth, and deformed pups destroyed.

Aftercare of Bitch and Pups—After the bitch has recovered from the anesthesia the pups are placed with her. If she does not encourage their suckling or ignores them she should be restrained or tranquilized while they suckle for the first several days until she "adopts" them. If the bitch should succumb, orphan pups may be raised on rich cow's milk or goat's milk, 1 to 5 parts of evaporated milk and water, or "Esbilac" (Borden's). A formula for feeding pups of 8 ounces of homogenized milk containing 2 egg yolks may also be used. About 1/2 to 3/4 oz. is given every 8 hours for the first week or two and by the third and fourth week about one ounce, 80 to 100 calories per lb. of body weight, is given every 8 hours, Sheffy et al. Pups should be dryed after they are fed. Defecation in the pups will be stimulated after they have eaten by their being rubbed beneath the tail with cotton dipped in olive oil. In a week or so some pablum may be given. Later they can be fed milk from a dish or pan. Ground meat cereal and ordinary cow's milk can be given when they are 3 weeks of age. Pups can be completely weaned at 4 to 5 weeks after birth.

The aftercare of the bitch following cesarean operation is similar to that given the cow, in that a small dose of pituitrin or oxytocin 1/2 to 1 cc., 5 to 20 units, or ergotamine is given to aid contraction of the uterus. The bitch should be placed on parenteral antibiotics for several days or more and observed closely for symptoms of shock, peritonitis or sepsis the first 6 to 48 hours. If this is suspected or occurs, prompt administration of blood and saline is indicated, along with keeping the bitch warm. The abdominal wound should be observed for any evidence of infection or breakdown or evidence that the incision has been licked or chewed. If it has, muzzling of the bitch may be necessary. If the fetuses are dead, the size and congestion of the mammary glands may be reduced by massaging them with camphorated oil, injecting 10 to 15 mg. of stilbestrol, and repeating this injection if necessary. It is advisable to send the bitch home, where she will be in a familiar environment, as soon as possible after the operation. The stitches may be removed about the fifth to seventh day after the operation.

Hysterectomy

Occasionally hysterectomy may be indicated due to prolonged dystocia, in which much trauma, injury, and even rupture of the uterus have been produced by unsuccessful fetotomy, mutation, or forced extraction operations, or the fetus is emphysematous and the uterus is atonic, severely infected and diseased. The dam is usually toxic and exhausted, with a subnormal temperature, anorexia, and a rapid, weak pulse. It may be obvious before the operation or at least at the time of the laparotomy that cesarean section alone, without hysterectomy, will not save the life of the dam. In cases where there is a severely diseased uterus, hysterectomy offers the only hope of saving the dam. The prognosis is always very guarded to poor, since shock and peritonitis generally cause death in these already poor operative risks. In cases such as severe rupture or laceration of the uterus following fetotomy or forced extraction, hysterectomy might occasionally be considered.

In horses, cattle, sheep, and swine hysterectomy is of little value as the economic value of the animal does not generally warrant the expense and effort of surgery and aftercare because the mortality is high. Because of the large size of the uterus and fetus or fetuses it may be necessary to remove the fetuses first in order to remove the uterus. Contamination of the abdominal cavity is difficult to avoid when tying the uterine and ovarian arteries and removing the uterus. After removal of the uterus, eversion of the cervix or uterine or vaginal stump offers further severe difficulties. Shock frequently develops. Successful hysterectomy has been reported only occasionally in cattle and swine and rarely in horses, Milne and Horney.

In dogs and cats hysterectomy is more often successfully employed because working conditions are good and the animals and their uterus and fetuses are relatively small. Hysterectomy is often considered in dogs and cats with a prolonged dystocia of 24 to 36 hours or more, Arthur. In 52 cesareans and 52 hysterectomies the recovery rate was 82 per cent and 67 per cent, respectively. The recovery rate was only 50 per cent when the fetuses were putrid, Nooder. The prognosis in cases in which hysterectomy is necessary in dogs and cats is therefore guarded. Prior to and during surgery, proper attention should be paid to preventing shock and the contamination of the abdominal cavity. A plentiful supply of instruments should be available. Because the animal is a poor surgical risk anesthesia should be selected and used carefully. A relatively small dose of morphine with local anesthesia of the incision site is often used in these cases. A midline incision is favored in a hysterectomy operation. If possible the fetuses should be removed within the intact uterus to avoid contamination of the abdominal cavity or incision. Care must be used in exteriorizing the uterus so that tearing of a vessel and subsequent hemorrhage do not occur. Double ligatures should be fastened securely around the utero-ovarian, uterine and posterior uterine arteries. At times excessive fat complicates the placing of tight ligatures around the large vessels in the broad ligament. Forceps are placed across the body and cervix of the uterus after the broad ligament has been incised and the ovaries and uterus are free. The uterus, fetuses, and ovaries may be removed by incising the body of the uterus between the forceps. The serosa of the stump of the uterus should be inverted by a Parker-Kerr stitch as the forceps are removed. After surgery the bitch should be kept warm and given blood and fluids to prevent the shock that sometimes follc the removal of such a large organ. Antibiotics sho administered to control possible abdominal contami and necrosis of the liver associated with shock. C continuous aftercare and nursing of these cases sho given.

References

General

Archibald, J. (1965) Canine Surgery, American Vet. Publ. Inc., Wheaton, Ill.

Arthur, G. H. (1964) Wright's Veterinary Obstetrics, Williams and Wilkins Co., Baltimore, Md.

Benesch, F. (1952) Lehrbuch der Tierartzlichen Geburtshilfe and Gynakologie, Urban and Schwarzenberg. Wien-Innsbruck, Austria.

Benesch, F. and Wright, J. G. (1951) Veterinary Obstetrics, Williams and Wilkins Co., Baltimore, Md.

Richter, J. and Gotze, R. (1960) Tiergeburtshilfe, 2nd. Ed., Paul Parey, Berlin, Germany.

Tavernier, H. (1955) Guide de Pratique Obstetricale chex les Grandes Femelles Domestiques, Vigot Freres Editeurs, 23 Rue De L Ecole-De-Medicine, Paris, France.

Tillman, H. (1965) Cesarean Section in Veterinary Obstetrics, 2nd Ed., Paul Parey, Berlin, Germany.

Specific

Aehnelt, E., Konerman, H. and Grunert, E. (1962) Vergleichende Untersuchungen uber die Schnittenbindungam Liegenden Rind Ventrolateral Links und am Stehenden Rind in der linken Flanke, Wien. Tierarztl. Monatschr. **49,** 1, 61.

Arnold, J. P. and Kitchell, R. L. (1957) Innervation of the Abdominal Wall of Cattle, Amer. J. Vet. Res. **18,** 229.

Bogedda, G., Lepori, S., Muzzetto, P. and Corta, S. (1966) The Cesarean Operation in Horses, Personal Contribution and Review of the Literature, Veterinaria (Milano) **15,** 1, 6.

Brone, —, Debruyne, —, Boeckx, — and Vandeplassche, M. (1966) Infertility of Cows Following Casarean Section, Vlaams Diergeneesk. Tijdschr. **35,** 2, 87 (Abstr.)

Debackere, M., Vandeplassche, M. and Paredis, F. (1959) Economic Results of a Study on Cesarean Section and Fetotomy in Cattle, Vlaams Diergeneesk. Tijdschr. **28,** 1, 1.

De Bois, C. H. W. (1958) Cesarean Section in Sheep, Tijdschr. v. Diergeneesk. **83,** 7, 248.

Eden, E. L. (1952) Dystocia in Young and Underdeveloped Cattle, Allied Veterinarian, July–Aug. 17.

Derivaux, J. and Dewalque, J. (1963) Notes d'obstetrique Equine, Anneles de Medicine Veterinaire, **107,** 4, 236.

Ellis, T. H. (1958) Observations on Some Aspects of Obstetrics in the Ewe, Vet. Rec. **70,** 47, 952.

Frank, E. R. and Roberts, S. J. (1940) Cesarean Section in the Bovine, N. A. Vet. **21,** 9, 546.

Frank, E. R. (1964) Veterinary Surgery, 7th. Ed., Burgess Publishing Co., Minneapolis, Minn.

Frank, E. R. (1964) Diseases of Swine, Ed. by H. W. Dunne, Iowa State Univ. Press, Ames, Iowa, 779.

Freak, M. J. (1962) Abnormal Conditions Associated with Pregnancy and Parturition in the Bitch, Vet. Rec. **77,** 1323.

Getty, R. (1963) Epidural Anesthesia in the Hog—Its Technique and Applications, Proc. 100th Ann. Meeting A.V.M.A., 88.

Heath, J. S. (1963) Indications and Complications in Cesarean Section in the Bitch, J. Sm. An. Pract. **4,** 289.

Hird, J. J. (1954) Pelvis Splitting as an Aid in Dystocia of Heifers, A.V.M.A., Proc. 91st Ann. Meeting, 384.

Goldberg, M. A. (1970) Cesarean Section in the Mare, A Review of the Literature, Paper for Senior Seminar, N.Y.S. Vet. Col., Ithaca, N.Y.

Johnston, D. R. (1963) History of Human Infertility, Fert. and Steril. **14,** 3, 261.

Juhler, H. (1956) Cesarean Section in Cattle, Nord. Vet. Med. **8,** 165.

Kirk, R. W. (1958) Canine Pediatrics, Mod. Vet. Pract **39,** 3 and 4, 37 and 52.

Klide, A. M. and Soma, L. R. (1968) Epidural Analgesia in the Dog and Cat, J.A.V.M.A. **153,** 2, 165.

Leonard, E. P. (1950) Canine Obstetrics, N. A. Vet., **21,** 9, 590.

Merkt, H. (1957) Die Schnittentbindung beim Rind in der Neuzeitlichen Geburtshilfe, M and H. Schaper, Hannover, Germany.

Mather, E. C. (1966) Lower Flank Incision for Swine Cesarean, Vet. Med. **61,** 9, 890.

Milne, F. J. and Horney, F. D. (1960) Abdominal Surgery in the Horse, Canad. Vet. Jour. **1,** 12, 524.

Nooder, H. J. (1952) De Operatieve Verlossing van Honden, Tijdschr. v. Diergeneesk **77,** 18, 655.

Oberst, F. H. (1954) Personal Communication.

Oberst, F. H. (1962) There is Still a Place for Surgery in Large Animal Practice, Vet. Med. **57,** 3, 219.

Oehme, F. W. (1967) The Ventro-lateral Cesarean Section in the Cow, Vet. Med. **67,** 889.

Railsback, L. T. (1950) Dystocia in the Sow, J.A.V.M.A. **116,** 874, 27.

Rasbech, N. O. (1957) Cesarean Operation in the Cow, Nord. Vet. Med. **9,** 721

Roberts, S. J. and Frank, E. R. (1942) Further Observations on the Cesarean Operation in the Bovine, Cor. Vet., **32,** 4, 395.

Sheffy, B. E., Baker, J. A. and Gillespie, J. H. (1961) A Disease-Free Colony of Dogs, Proc. Animal Care Panel, **11,** 4, 208.

Sherrod, W. W. (1967) Cesarean Section In A Mare, Mod. Vet. Pract. **48,** 13, 60.

Vandeplassche, M. (1957–1958) The Normal and Abnormal Presentation, Position and Posture of the Foal-Fetus during Gestation and at Parturition, Mededelingen der Veeartsenijschool van de Rijksunivsiteit te Gent.

Vandeplassche, M. (1958) Public Lectures on Obstetrics and Gynecology, Cairo Univ. Press, Cairo, Egypt.

Vandeplassche, M. (1969, 1970) Personal Communication.

Vandeplassche, M., Ide, M. Vanheuverswijn, A., Paredis, F. and Sierens, G. (1953) Is Foetotomie bij Dystokie van Runderen nog Aktueel?, Vlaams Diergeneesk Tijdschr., **22,** 7–8, 1.

Vandeplassche, M. and Paredis, F. (1953) Cesarean Section in the Bovine, "Standard Bockhandel" Antwerp-Amsterdam, Netherlands.

Vandeplassche, M. and Paredis, F. (1953) Cesarean Section in the Bovine, "Erasme," Paris and Standard-Bockhandel, Antwerp.

Vandeplassche, M., Paredis, F. and Bouters, R. (1962) Techniques, Results and Indications for Cesarean Section in the Horse, Wien. Tierarztl. Monatschr. **49,** 1, 48.

Vandeplassche, M., Paredis, F., Bouters, R. and Spincemaille, J. (1963) Cesarean Section for Emphysematous Fetuses, Die Blauen Hefte fur den Tierarzt., Heft 3/4.

Vandeplassche, M., Paredis, F. and Debackere, M. (1956) Fertility of Cows After Cesarean Section, Proc. III Internat. Congr. on Animal Reprod., Cambridge.

Wendt, D. O. (1949) Personal Communication.

Wester, R. F. (1961) Respiratory Stimulation of Newborn Pups, J.A.V.M.A. **139,** 4, 448.

Williams, W. L. (1943) Veterinary Obstetrics, 4th Ed., Miss Louella Williams, Upland Rd., Ithaca, N.Y.

Wright, J. G. (1953) Further Observations on Cesarean Section in the Bovine, Jour. Comp. Path. and Therap., **63,** 3, 211.

Wright, J. G. (1958) Bovine Dystocia, Vet. Rec., **70,** 17, 347.

Chapter X

DIAGNOSIS AND TREATMENT OF VARIOUS TYPES OF DYSTOCIA

In previous chapters the causes, equipment, and operations for the handling of dystocia were outlined. In this chapter the various conditions which produce dystocia and the practical handling of these problems will be discussed under the headings of: dystocia due to pathological presentation, position, and posture of the fetus; abnormal size of the fetus; postmortem changes in the fetus; uterine displacements; stenosis of the birth canal; and uterine inertia.

Dystocia Due to Pathological Presentation, Position, and Posture of the Fetus

Pathological presentations, positions, and postures are apparently due to a combination of uterine inertia and a reduced viability and activity in the fetus especially during the first and second stages of parturition. Uterine inertia may be caused by hormonal or disease factors causing a lack of, weak or irregular contractions of the uterine wall. If the fetus is diseased, deformed, lacks vigor, or is dead, its movements and righting reflexes are weak or absent, and postural abnormalities in such cases are common. In the mare, bitch, and sow these factors when combined with a normal dorso-ilial or dorso-pubic position prior to parturition may result in the failure of the fetus to rotate into a normal dorso-sacral position at parturition. As the fetus is forced through the birth canal the catching or impinging of an extremity at the pelvic inlet causes a progressive flexing of that extremity as the remainder of the fetus passes beyond it. Transverse pregnancies caused by uterine disease, abnormal attachment and development of the fetus and its membranes, or in the case of multipara a single fetus developing in both horns transversely across the body, usually result in dystocia. (See Figures 86, 89, 90)

Dystocia in Anterior Presentation may result from the following types of abnormalities:

Dorso-ilial or Dorso-pubic Positions are observed in all species as a cause of dystocia, especially in unipara, particularly when the fetus is of normal or large size. In rare cases small or premature fetuses are expelled in these abnormal positions. In these dystocias the fetus should be rotated into a normal dorso-sacral position before being removed. (See Figure 90) Before doing this, one should carefully observe and examine the uterus and genital canal to make sure that torsion of the uterus is not the cause of the abnormal fetal position. If torsion is present the fetus should be rotated in the direction which will reduce the torsion. Many of the fetuses found in this position are weak or dead. Lubrication of a dry birth canal prior to rotation of the fetus is of great assistance.

Deviations of the Head and Neck are common types of abnormal posture in anterior presentation causing dystocia in all species. In swine, because the neck is so short, this type of dystocia is very rare. The deviation of the head and neck may be in any direction. Lateral deviation of the head is seen most often in unipara. The deviation may be directly lateral, with the head alongside the thorax in the bovine fetus, or alongside the flank of the equine fetus. This lateral deviation may also be obliquely upward or downward, and occasionally the head may be rotated 45 to 90 degrees on the neck. Diagnosis in the cow is easily made by finding the two forelimbs in the birth canal, but not the head. By passing the hand and arm as far alongside the fetal body as possible and then carrying it around the body, the head and neck are found and the direction of the deviation noted. In the mare this may be more difficult because the head is usually out of reach of the hand. By locating the withers and mane or the trachea of the equine fetus these may be followed to the left, right, downward or upward and the direction of the deviation determined. If the bovine fetus is alive and labor has not been in progress more than 4 to 12 hours the deviation may be corrected with the least amount of difficulty by means of mutation. This is best performed under epidural anesthesia with the animal standing. If the animal is down it should be placed in lateral recumbency with the rear parts higher than the foreparts and with the fetal head in the upper flank of the dam, above the fetal body. Repulsion on the fetal chest in an oblique manner is performed. The body of the fetus is pushed away from the fetal head and neck so that room is produced to allow correction by traction on the fetal head. The incisor teeth should be guarded to prevent laceration of the uterus. If the dam is recumbent it is helpful, particularly in the mare under general anesthesia, to have an assistant exert caudal pressure on the fetal head through the mare's flank, helping to force it back toward the operator's hand. If the neck and head are twisted this is corrected in the uterus by grasping the muzzle or the orbits with fingers and rotating the head in the proper direction as traction is applied to the jaw, drawing the head and the forelimbs into the birth canal. In the bitch and cat lateral deviation is corrected by vaginal manipulation with the finger, and pressure applied through the abdominal wall. Forced extraction should never be applied to these cases of deviation of the fetal head and neck without first correcting the abnormal posture. If mutation fails because the fetus is emphysematous or because the uterine wall is contracted tightly around the fetus, fetotomy and amputation of the head and neck with the fetatome or wire saw is indicated. Occasionally it may be necessary to amputate the opposite forelimb at the elbow joint or to remove the entire limb in order to move the fetus nearer the vulva so that the wire can be placed around its neck. In the dog and cat cesarean section or in exceptional cases hysterectomy may be indicated.

Wry-neck is seen in equine but rarely in bovine fetuses. It usually occurs in transverse bicornual pregnancy in the mare in which movement of the fetal head and neck is restricted or prevented during most of the gestation period. It may occur in a longitudinal pregnancy with the fetus in one horn and the body. The outer bones of the face become convex while the facial bones lying against the fetus are concave, due to the pressure applied by the uterine wall. The cervical vertebrae are curved and the articulations and atrophied muscles produce a sharply-bent "muscle contracture" condition of the neck resembling torticollis that cannot be straightened, even outside the dam, without fracturing the cervical vertebrae. A bicornual or transverse pregnancy with a wry-necked fetus may rarely at the time of parturition undergo spontaneous version into an anterior or posterior presentation, Williams. In posterior presentation dystocia seldom if ever occurs. The extreme bend in the neck, the stiff, firm neck, and the fact that the head and neck move with the fetal body and cannot be straightened, aids in confirming the diagnosis. Fetotomy is indicated and amputation of the head and neck is simple and practical with the fetatome or wire saw Removal could also be effected by the removal of the opposite forelimb and evisceration. With forced extraction the fetus could then be withdrawn with the head occupying the space of the removed viscera.

Downward deviation of the head between the forelimbs is occasionally seen in all species except swine. In mild cases, only the nose of the fetus is caught on the brim of the pelvis with the forehead entering the pelvic inlet, "vertex presentation". In more severe flexing of the head and neck the ears and the top of the head are presenting, "poll presentation". This is usually corrected by mutation by repelling the fetus and grasping the muzzle of the fetus and raising it into the pelvic cavity. In the more severe cases the neck extends between the forelimbs, "nape presentation," and the head is against the fetal sternum or abdomen. This latter condition is more difficult to diagnose but by means of careful palpation the operator will notice that the forelimbs do not come together, and that in the mare the mane of the fetus may be felt between the legs, and the head found beneath the fetal body. In cases which are diagnosed early, mutation may correct the deviation. As an aid in relieving this type of dystocia, after the fetus is repelled a forelimb may be flexed alongside the body and the abnormal posture of the head and neck corrected by moving them laterally beneath this leg. The abnormal position of the limb is then corrected and the fetus removed by traction. In the mare, or in bovine cases diagnosed after prolonged dystocia, fetotomy is necessary. Williams recommended removal of one forelimb and then correction of the deviation by mutation. It may be advisable to amputate the head and neck and one forelimb by a single cut with the fetotome when the fetus is emphysematous or the uterus strongly contracted. In some cases cesarean section may be indicated in the dog and cat. Upward deviation of the head is rare in the cow and horse but occasionally it is found as a cause for dystocia in dogs and cats. The handling is the same as in lateral deviation of the head and neck.

Deviations of the Forelimbs are relatively common causes for dystocia in uniparous animals. They are rarely a cause for dystocia in multipara because their forelimbs are short and flexible. In unipara, especially the cow and mare, normal birth cannot occur, unless the fetus is very small or premature, with one forelimb extended or retained alongside the body. Forced extraction should not be attempted. In ewes normal birth can occur with one forelimb retained. If dystocia is present with this posture and the ovine fetus is not too large, dystocia may be relieved by forced extraction without mutation. During birth the shoulder and large shoulder joint are displaced forward alongside the neck when the forelimb is extended in the normal manner. This is made possible by a lack of a clavicle in these species. Pathologically when a portion of the forelimb is caught at the pelvic inlet or in the birth canal the leg is forced backwards toward the body, flexing the shoulder and the elbow joints. Dystocia results from the shoulder being pushed back over the chest, and thereby increasing the pectoral diameter of the fetus. In mild, early dystocia the toe may be caught on the pelvic brim or by a fold in the genital tract, and the fetlock then becomes flexed. The head is present in the birth canal or at the vulva, with one or no forefeet. Mutation by repulsion of the fetus and traction on the retained limb corrects the dystocia. The fetal toe or claw should be cupped in the operator's hand or handled carefully so that a fold of uterus or birth canal is not caught, causing a laceration or rupture of the genital tract. A more severe dystocia is present when the knees are flexed, knee-flexed posture, or the forelimbs are extended beneath the fetal body. In these cases if the fetal head is not extending through the birth canal the condition may be corrected by mutation. The fetus is repelled under epidural anesthesia. The knees are grasped and repelled cranially and laterally into the cow's flank as the feet are extended medially and caudally into the birth canal. If possible the body of the fetus should be repelled into the flank of the dam opposite the side where the abnormal posture of the forelimb is being corrected.

In dystocia cases when the head is outside the vulva repulsion is very difficult or impossible unless the fetus is small, because the head rapidly becomes very edematous. Decapitation should be performed especially if the fetus is dead or emphysematous. Following decapitation the fetus is repelled and the abnormal posture of the forelimbs corrected. If the forelimb is extended beneath the body traction on the forearm and repulsion of the body cranially and dorsally will bring the leg to a knee-flexed posture. In a very few cases it may be necessary when the fetus is emphysematous and the uterine wall closely invests the fetus to remove the forelimb extended beneath the body by a fetotomy operation, with the fetatome or wire saw. Once the legs have been brought into the birth canal they should be extended by traction and the fetus removed by traction on them and on the head or stump of the neck vertebrae if decapitation has been performed. In rare cases to avoid fetotomy a small bovine fetus may be withdrawn with one leg retained, when the head is outside the vulva and the thorax is in the pelvic cavity.

Dystocia due to the one or both forelegs being crossed over the neck is rare except in the mare. This abnormal posture increases the chest diameters as the elbows are forced against the pubis. It may also result in the dorsally-directed hooves engaging the roof of the vagina and causing rupture of the vagina, rectum, or perineum. This condition is readily diagnosed. Traction by the operator's hand or with a snare or chain by an assistant should be placed on the uppermost pastern or foot, if both legs are crossed over the neck, and this leg should be pulled upward and then laterally and downward and medially so the leg is brought beneath the neck and head and fully extended. Elevation of the head helps in placing the legs beneath the head. Repulsion and epidural anesthesia usually are not necessary unless the foot is engaged in the dorsal vaginal wall.

Flexion of the anterior limbs at the elbow is a relatively common cause for dystocia particularly in young cattle. It is caused by the olecranon catching on the brim of the pelvis with the leg not fully extended as the fetus passes into the birth canal. In many instances both elbows are impacted. The elbow and shoulder joints are flexed, greatly increasing the pectoral diameters of the fetus. This condition is diagnosed by the fact that the nose of the fetus is resting on or below the fetlock joints while in the normal extended position the nose rests on the middle of the metacarpal bone. By feeling along the fetal leg the operator finds the olecranon firmly wedged against the pelvic brim. This condition is easily corrected by traction first on one limb and then on the other; or the operator can place his hand under the olecranon and raise it as traction is applied to the limb extending it into its proper posture.

Interlocking of the Maternal and Fetal Pelves or "Hip lock" in Anterior Presentation is commonly observed as a cause for dystocia in heifers. The major trochanters of the fetal femurs are the structures that fail to pass through the bony pelvis of the dam. The tuber coxae in calves are small and rarely if ever are the cause of dystocia. Dystocia due to hip lock may be caused by an improper direction of traction putting tension on the linea alba and increasing the pelvic diameter of the fetus and by traction causing the maternal pelvis to tip caudally and dorsally, thereby reducing the diameter of the pelvic inlet of the dam. In most of the naturally occurring long-standing cases of interlocking of the maternal and fetal pelves, obturator paralysis is observed and always should be looked for before relieving the dystocia. This type of dystocia is easily diagnosed by the fact that the head, forelimbs, and a portion of the thorax extend through the vulva. In dystocia due to fetal ascites, or the hind limbs extending alongside the body or against the pelvis as in the **Perosomus elumbis** monster, the thorax seldom extends through the vulva. There should be a careful examination of the relative sizes of the maternal and fetal pelves. If traction is decided upon, the fetus and birth canal should be well-lubricated. Traction should be applied by assistants or by the fetal extractor, pulling the fetus in an arc-like curve, first backward and then downward. In other cases lateral traction around the dam's hips may aid by pulling the fetal pelvis through the maternal pelvis at an oblique angle. Some veterinarians tie the forelimbs of the dead fetus together and by placing a long handle between them will rotate or twist the fetus as a traction is applied. The use of the long blunt hook placed over the fetal ischial arch or into the caudal border of the sacro-sciatic ligament aids in placing traction on the pelvis, lifts the fetal pelvis in the maternal pelvis, and pulls the fetal plevis in an oblique manner aiding greatly in the relief of the dystocia. If the fetus is dead an extensive transverse incision in the abdomen of the fetus caudal to the xiphoid region followed by evisceration, insures traction being applied not to the linea alba or fetal pubis but only on the spinal column. This produces extension of the fetal pelvis on the spinal column. If judicial traction fails to relieve the dystocia fetotomy should be performed by bisection of the fetal pelvis with a fetatome or wire saw. This is made less difficult by evisceration after transversely incising the abdomen.

Forward Extension of the Hind Limbs beneath the Fetal Body or the "Dog Sitting" Posture is observed uncommonly in the mare and cow. The reason for the dystocia may not at first be obvious. The cranial extremities are usually presented normally and pass into the birth canal before dystocia results. Passing the hand forward along the fetus, the operator can feel the hind feet and limbs entering the pelvic cavity alongside the fetal abdomen. This examination will serve to differentiate the condition from twins, fetal ascites, or a fetal monster such as a **Perosomus elumbis.** Williams theorized that this condition was seen most commonly in the mare because it is probably a vertical form of the transverse ventral presentation in which the anterior portion of the fetus became dislodged and entered the pelvis. The prognosis in the mare should be guarded to poor. Traction by laymen or veterinarians not recognizing this condition may cause severe damage especially if the hind feet are caught beneath the brim of the pelvis instead of extending into the pelvic cavity. Williams stated that in such cases necrosis of the vagina is common. This operation may be handled by mutation only in large mares with a small fetus, or in the cow by repelling the hind limbs into the uterine cavity as the fetus is pulled from the vulva. In a few instances it might be possible to repel the forequarters, apply traction and rotation to the rear quarters to produce a normal posterior presentation. Forced extraction should never be used. Fetotomy is often the method of choice and consists of detruncating the fetus with the fetatome through the posterior thoracic or anterior lumbar region. Sometimes evisceration is helpful if performed before detruncation. Often it is necessary to make two cuts through the trunk in order to remove enough of it so that the rear quarters can be manipulated. Krey's tongs placed into the exposed vertebrae assist greatly in drawing the lumbar portion of the trunk toward the vulva in placing the fetatome wire and in removing more of the trunk of the fetus. After detruncating, chains are placed on the hind pasterns, the rear quarters are repelled into the uterus as the hind feet are drawn into the birth canal and the hind quarters are rotated from a dorso-pubic to a dorso-sacral position and then removed by traction. If necessary the pelvis may be bisected. Williams cited Guard as recommending subcutaneous amputation of the forelimb, evisceration, and breaking the fetal pelvis through each ilial shaft with a chisel. The fetus is then withdrawn with the hind legs extended alongside the collapsed fetal body. In many instances cesarean section may be preferred for the correction of this type of dystocia.

Dystocia in Posterior Presentation is relatively much more common than dystocia in anterior presentation. Posterior presentation is considered pathological in all except the multiparous animals. The frequency of physiological birth in posterior presentation in the mare and cow is quite low. The fetal mortality in posterior presentation is high. Most authorities advise rather prompt removal of the live fetus in posterior presentation to prevent asphyxiation following pressure on or rupture of the umbilical cord. Most fetuses are usually dead at the time of the examination.

Dystocia due to Dorso-ilial or Dorso-pubic Positions in Posterior Presentation is similar in nature to, and handled in the same manner as pathological positions in anterior presentation. They are usually less difficult to correct, because the head and neck are not present to offer obstruction to rotation as in anterior presentation; and, because the rump is more round than the withers, rotation is easier. Occasionally, in the mare in posterior presentation, the hind feet may engage the roof of the vagina and cause lacerations of the vagina, vulva, and rectum. Lifting the fetal buttocks upward and to one side or the other aids rotation of the fetus by opposite traction on the two rear limbs. Prior to correcting the abnormal position, the operator should determine if the birth canal requires lubrication and whether torsion is present.

Deviations of the Hind Limbs in Posterior Presentation are common in uniparous animals. They are rare or of no significance as a cause for dystocia in multiparous animals because of the latter's small, flexible limbs. These are caused by failure of the hind limbs to extend into the pelvic cavity or by the foot or fetlock catching on the birth canal or pelvic brim, causing the hind limb or limbs to become flexed. When one joint becomes flexed all joints in the hind limb flex except when the hind leg is extended beneath the body.

The flexion of the limbs at the tarsus or hock-flexed posture causes the flexing of the rest of the articulations, followed by dystocia. It may be diagnosed by palpation of the perineal region and tail and then below these the point of the flexed hock either in or just below and cranial to the pelvic cavity. This condition should be differentiated from ankylosed rear limbs seen in **Perosomus elumbis.** Correction of this dystocia is easily accomplished by mutation when dystocia has not existed too long. After epidural anesthesia is administered the fetal buttocks are repelled cranially and to one side. The flexed hock is grasped and repelled forward and laterally into the opposite flank while the foot is drawn caudally and medially and extended through the birth canal (see Figure 44). The hoof or claw should be guarded or cupped in the hand as it is brought back over the pelvic brim so that it does not catch and lacerate the soft structures of the uterus or birth canal. If the dam is recumbent the rear parts should be elevated above the fore parts and the flexed fetal limb should be in the upper flank of the dam so that room is available for mutation and so that the weight of the fetus does not rest upon the flexed limb. In cases of a very large or an emphysematous fetus, or a contracted uterus that will not allow repulsion and room for mutation, or in recumbent cases in which mutation is very difficult, fetotomy with amputation of the rear limb at the tarsus may be necessary and is simple to perform with the fetatome or wire saw. Rarely in the mare the flexed rear limb may become wedged in the pelvis with the hock impacted against the sacrum; amputation of the tarsus is the safest procedure to follow as it prevents further laceration or contusion of the birth canal. Occasionally the rear limbs will have the stifles flexed with the tibias impacted against the pelvic brim. Repulsion of the fetus, lifting the femorotibial joint upward with the hand, as traction is exerted on the pastern, will remove this cause for dystocia.

Complete Retention or Extension of the Rear Limbs beneath the Body, or Breech Presentation is observed frequently as a cause for dystocia in animals. This is a more advanced case of retention of the rear limbs than the hock-flexed posture. The rear limbs are usually completely extended beneath the fetus. The buttocks and tail are in the pelvic cavity and occasionally the tip of the tail is hanging from the vulva. Williams believed a few of these breech presentations in the mare might be a sequelae to a transverse or bicornual pregnancy that underwent spontaneous version into a posterior presentation. In many cases no part of the limb can be reached until the fetal buttocks are repelled cranially out of the pelvic inlet. Epidural or general anesthesia is very helpful or necessary. By grasping the cranial aspect of the tibia with the hand or passing a cord around the tibia the operator can pull the fetal leg back into a hock-flexed posture as the fetal hind quarters are repelled forward and upward. If this is possible the procedure is the same as outlined previously (see Figure 88). If, however, the fetus is dead, emphysematous, or large, and the uterine wall has contracted around the fetus so that room for mutation is not available, fetotomy is indicated. Forced extraction is seldom indicated, warranted, or necessary. Bisecting the fetal pelvis in breech presentation in posterior presentation is easily performed with the fetatome by passing the fetatome wire around one hind leg, placing the head of the fetatome on the opposite hip and making a diagonal cut through the fetal pelvis. The wire saw is not as satisfactory since instead of bisecting the pelvis the limb is usually removed through the hip joint. In multipara forceps may be applied across the fetal hips after lubrication and the fetus removed by traction; or the hind limbs may be extended into the birth canal and traction applied by a snare, or manually with guaze wrapped around the rear legs of the fetus. Excessive traction in multipara is to be avoided. In severe or prolonged dystocia in multipara, cesarean section or hysterectomy may be indicated.

Hip Lock in Normal Posterior Presentation is occasionally a cause for dystocia, especially in heifers. In posterior presentations, uterine inertia or delay in the second stage of labor are commonly observed. For this reason, in many cases traction is applied successfully by laymen, or the veterinarian may be called to effect a simple delivery with the fetus in posterior presentation, and its hind limbs lying in the birth canal. This should not be termed, or confused with, true hip lock, where, as in anterior presentation, the width of the fetal pelvis at the level of the greater trochanters is greater than the bisiliac diameter of the maternal pelvis. In hip lock in the posterior presentation, the fetus should be repelled and well lubricated, if necessary. Traction should be applied to only one rear limb at a time. Some veterinarians will tie the two rear limbs together, place a long handle between them and rotate and twist the hips as traction is applied. This causes the fetal pelvis to pass through the maternal pelvis at an oblique ~~angle~~ necessary to effect a correction of the condition. If this fails, because of the large size of the fetus or the small size of the maternal pelvis, or both, then cesarean section or fetotomy should be considered. If the fetal hips can pass through the pelvis, little difficulty will be encountered with the chest and pectoral girdle. In rare cases fetal ascites may cause dystocia in posterior presentation, simulating a hip lock condition. In dystocia due to hip lock, if the fetus is alive and the birth canal small, cesarean section should be given serious consideration. If the birth canal is relatively large and the fetal size not excessive, fetotomy may be the procedure of choice. This is accomplished by amputation of the rear limb at the hip joint with a knife, or preferably by bisecting the pelvis with the fetatome, as previously described under fetotomy.

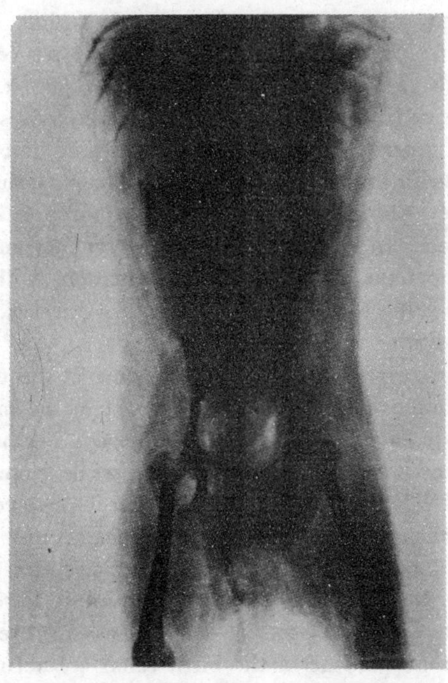

Figure 89. Dystocia due to a transverse presentation of a single fetus in a Pomeranian bitch. This was relieved by a Cesarean operation

Figure 90. Normal dorso-pubic position of an equine fetus late in gestation. The fetus must rotate into a dorso-sacral position during the early stages of parturition or a dystocia will result.

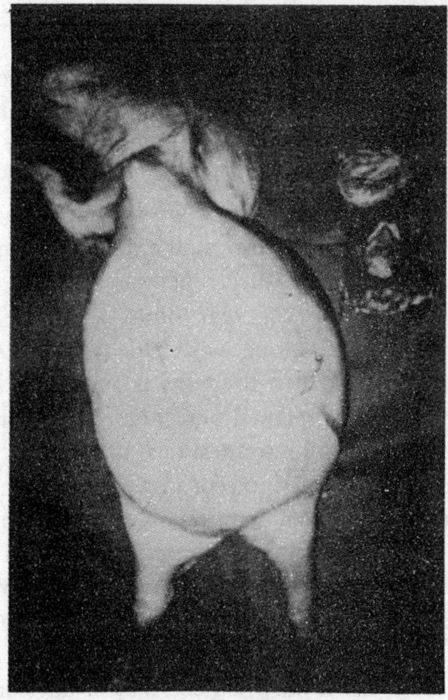

Figure 91. Ascites and mild anasarca of a 6-month bovine fetus that caused dystocia.

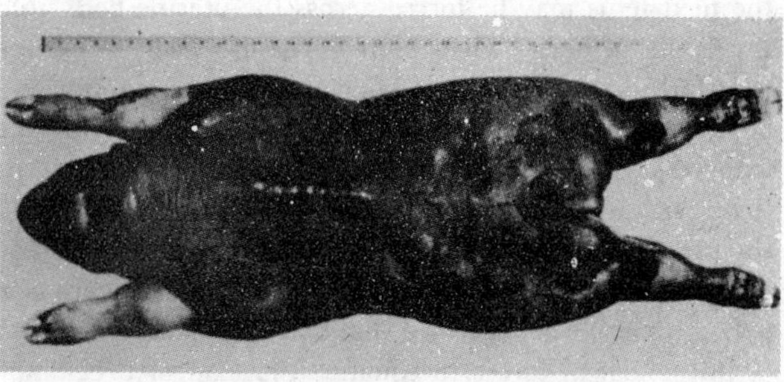

Figure 92. An anasarcous bovine fetus that caused dystocia at the time of abortion.

Lateral Deviation of the Head in Posterior Presentation is only rarely if ever a cause for dystocia in the mare even when the fetus has a wry neck. This should be differentiated from hydrocephalus or fetal ascites. In most cases the wry neck straightens sufficiently to allow the fetus to be removed by moderate traction. If this is not possible one rear limb should be removed by bisecting the pelvic girdle, and then the fetus should be eviscerated. This allows room for the fetus to be removed with the head and neck flexed alongside the body, without resorting to excessive traction.

Dystocia due to Bicornual Pregnancy or Transverse Presentation is rare and is seen most commonly in the mare. In rare instances it may occur in all species except swine, in which it has never been reported. The incidence of this type of pregnancy was reported by Vandeplassche as 1 in 1000 births, this author believes it may be even more rare. Some bicornual pregnancies might possibly undergo spontaneous version at the time of parturition into an anterior or posterior presentation, Williams, but this is questioned. For a transverse presentation to occur it is essential that either a bicornual pregnancy be present or that a fetus in a normal longitudinal pregnancy become deflected at parturition across the pelvic inlet into the opposite horn. The former condition, a primary bicornual pregnancy, has been described most commonly in mares, dogs, and cattle. (See Figures 86 and 89) It is possible for it to occur also in sheep and cats. Secondary bicornual pregnancy may occur occasionally in multiple bicornual pregnancy in sheep and cattle or in dogs and cats. When a fetus is wedged in the birth canal, the next fetus may be forced across the uterine body into the opposite horn; when both horns are large one fetus may fail to enter the birth canal in a proper manner and be forced into the opposite horn. In dogs bicornual or transverse pregnancy is seen most commonly in conceptions with a single fetus that develops across the body of the uterus with the fore quarters in one horn and the rear quarters in the other horn and the dorsum toward the pelvic canal. It is suggested that this is a natural attempt of physiological forces to equalize the load of pregnancy between the two horns. Usually this single canine fetus is large. Transverse pregnancy has not been reported in swine because of the very acute angle at which the horns meet tne body and the short compact body of the swine fetus, making transverse pregnancy a near impossibility. In the cow the transversely developing fetus must assume a U-shape, with portions of the fetus in both horns. It is necessary that the dorsum of the fetus become convex and lies against the cervix. In cattle this condition is extremely rare. In sheep it has been observed occasionally in cases where triplets or quadruplets cause a great distention of the uterine horns, and a transverse presentation of one fetus may develop at the time of parturition. In mares transverse pregnancy occurred in about 4 per cent of the dystocias, according to Williams citing Johnk. In this number are included the exaggerated breech presentations and the anterior presentations with the hind limbs extending beneath the body. This possibly occurs because of the fetus developing transversely in both horns, a bicornual pregnancy. In rare cases a body pregnancy may occur with the fetus in transverse presentation, with only a small portion of the cranial and caudal parts of the fetus in each horn.

Transverse Ventral Presentation is the transverse presentation most commonly observed in the mare. The limbs are extended into the uterine body. The occurrence of wry neck is common in equine fetuses developing transversely. Thus at parturition the four limbs are wedged across each other in the pelvis. The head is usually out of reach alongside the fetal body. Expulsive efforts by the mare or traction by laymen result in failure to relieve the dystocia. Due to the nature of the transverse presentation little or no damage of the birth canal or uterus usually results from these efforts. It is necessary to carefully examine the limbs to differentiate the fore and hind legs, so tightly are they impacted and wedged across each other. In certain cases the feet may protrude from the vulva. The prognosis in transverse ventral dystocia in the mare is fair to good depending upon the condition of the mare and her genital tract. Occasionally the transverse ventral presentation is somewhat oblique in presentation, with no portion of the fetus extending into the pelvis. Possibly these are partially rotated bicornual pregnancies. In these cases it is difficult or almost impossible to relieve the dystocia and save the mare without resorting to cesarean section. To correct the usual transverse ventral pregnancy, mutation alone—by repelling the fore parts and applying traction on the rear limbs as the forelegs are flexed and repelled along with the fore parts—can be accomplished only when the fetus is small and the uterus and birth canal are relaxed and large. Excellent epidural analgesia or general anesthesia is usually necessary. It should not be attempted except under unusual conditions. The generally accepted manner of relieving this type of dystocia is to remove the forelimbs by amputation at the humero-radial joint with the fetatome, or possibly by subcutaneous amputation of one or both of the forelimbs if the fetus is small. In large mares the latter procedure would be difficult. It may be necessary or advisable to amputate the rear limbs at the tarsus in order to provide room for amputating the forelimbs. By applying traction with rotation of the rear limbs and repulsion on the fore quarters or sternum, the fetus is turned by version and rotated into a posterior dorso-sacral position. With the fetus in a posterior presentation the fetal head and neck do not cause difficulty for the operator. Aftercare of these bicornual pregnancies in the mare is important, as metritis and vaginitis are likely to develop.

The Compound or Rotated Bicornual Pregnancy is of rare occurrence in the mare. It is basically a bicornual pregnancy, usually ventral, that during the latter stages of gestation rotates so that the fetus comes to rest beneath the elongated vagina and uterine body. The dorsum of the uterine horns is ventral and the ventral portions of the horns lie dorsal to the fetus, with the legs of the fetus pointing cranially and dorsally. The transverse pregnancy in the mare has not been recognized or diagnosed by rectal examination during late pregnancy. This rotation of the two horns may be nearly a complete 180 degrees. At the time of parturition the birth canal is very long and the elbow may be the only portion of the fetus that can be reached by the operator. The rest of the fetus may be palpated through the long narrow birth canal, below the hand and arm. For this reason it may occasionally be confused with an extrauterine fetus. Occasionally the rotation may not be through 180 degrees, and the fetus may be resting on its back, as the uterine horns have rotated only 90 degrees; but here too the birth canal is long and narrow, offering a serious obstacle to birth. In the author s limited experience on only 6 to 10 of these rotated bicornual pregnancies, the mare in most instances had a history of dystocia or retained placenta the previous year. This tends to bear out Williams' contention that bicornual pregnancy is the result of disease or pathology of the uterus and endometrium and is seen usually in pluriparous mares. Vandeplassche's report did not confirm this association. The symptoms of dystocia in these rotated bicornual transverse presentations are mild, resembling the first stage of labor. Tenesmus or straining is absent or slight because the fetus does not enter the pelvic canal and stimulate labor. In this respect it resembles torsion of the uterus in cattle. By the time the veterinarian is summoned to examine the mare, in many instances 24 to 48 hours after the onset of parturition, the uterus is well-contracted and the fetus is often emphysematous. A cesarean operation offers the only hope for saving the mare with this type of dystocia. The prognosis is usually guarded. In many cases consultation may be desirable whether the mare is destroyed or a cesarean operation performed. As Williams pointed out, if the condition could be diagnosed by rectal palpation in advanced pregnancy, cesarean section might be more successfully employed before the onset of parturition. He also reported that in such cases, placing or rolling the mare on its back brings the fetus within reach for the application of chains to its limbs. In each case, however, when traction was applied the contracted uterus ruptured. Fetotomy is an impossibility because of the narrow, long birth canal.

Transverse Dorsal Presentation is very rarely observed in the mare but usually occurs in the rare transverse pregnancies in ruminants and carnivora because of the sharp angle at which the two horns leave the body. In cases which have had an early diagnosis, mutation may be performed by repelling one end of the fetus—preferably the cephalic portion—and by putting traction on the opposite, or caudal, end of the fetus by means of chains, Kreys hooks, or a blunt hook inserted through an incision in the skin. If version of the fetus into a posterior presentation cannot be brought about then version into an anterior presentation should be attempted. When mutation fails fetotomy is often successful in the large animals and is accomplished by passing a fetatome wire around the fetus in the lumbar region and bisecting the fetus so each half may be removed separately. If this cannot be done with the fetatome then the skin over the lumbar region should be incised transversely, the back bone broken with a chisel, and the fetus eviscerated. The fetatome wire may then be passed around the collapsed body of the fetus and the body divided and removed. In the dog mutation is usually impossible and cesarean section is the method of choice. This may also be decided upon in the cow and mare.

Dystocia Due to the Umbilical Cord and Placenta—Dystocia caused by the cord being wrapped around a portion or extremity of the fetus does not occur in domestic animals. Occasionally the umbilical cord may be found around a leg, especially a rear leg, of the fetus. In this position it will usually rupture before causing dystocia. Thus it may be the cause for the death of the fetus by asphyxia. The belief that amputation of the fetal limbs can be caused by the umbilical cord being looped around them is erroneous. McEntee described a bovine dystocia due to a very thick amnion that required incising to deliver a normal live calf. This appeared to be a vascular lesion involving the entire amnion as little edema was present.

Dystocia Due to Abnormal Size of the Fetus

Dystocia may occur as a result of fetal giantism, excessive volume of parts of the fetus, excessive volume of the fetal fluids (hydrops), fetal monsters, and multiple births in uniparous animals.

Fetal Giantism is observed only in rare instances in

domestic animals. True fetal giantism is seen most commonly in the cow and occurs only as a result of a prolonged gestation period of over 300 to 310 days. True fetal giantism with prolonged gestation has been reported only very rarely in other domestic animals. In mares that carry foals 365 days the foals are not excessively large. In cattle Meade and Jasper have described an inbred herd of Holsteins and Wilson and Young an Ayrshire herd in which fetal giantism was due to a simple recessive hereditary factor. This condition has been described in many other breeds of cattle, Huston and Gier and Holm. The cows carried their fetuses over 310 days. The fetuses were excessively large and the cows showed no signs of pelvic relaxation and little or no mammary development prior to parturition or at the time that normal parturition was expected. All the calves died shortly after birth even when a cesarean had been performed. These calves had possible anterior pituitary gland abnormalities, McEntee, hypoplastic adrenals and an abnormal glucose metabolism. Most fetal giants have long hair, long hoofs, and the incisor teeth are well erupted. In many cases hairballs may be found in the amniotic cavity. Fetal giants are poorly viable and often male. When a bovine fetus weighs over 130 lbs. it may be termed a fetal giant. Prolonged gestation does not necessarily indicate the presence of fetal giantism. In cases of excessively prolonged gestation in Guernsey cattle, Kennedy et al. (See Duration of Gestation and Initiation of Parturition) most fetuses are small, immature and pathological and in some cases mild hydrops of the amnion and allantois may occur. Dystocia in these cases is uncommon and not severe.

Prolonged gestation may also rarely occur in cattle and other species associated with congenital defects of the head such as hydrocephalus, Huston and Gier, in calves with cerebral hernia, or a Catlin mark, with a reduced size of the cranial cavity and in ewes grazing on **Veratrum californicum** resulting in cyclopia of the lambs and often giantism. These animals have an abnormal or hypoplastic pituitary gland, and hypoplastic adrenals. As mentioned previously normal or increased amounts of glucocorticoids are necessary to initiate parturition by involution of the corpus luteum. When this does not occur parturition is prolonged and the fetus continues to grow in size. Oversized lambs weighing more than 20 pounds are occasionally described, Hilton. De Lange described prolonged gestation and oversized lambs in Karakul sheep in Southwest Africa. In these cases of prolonged gestation and fetal giantism in sheep and those in cattle the fetus in many cases dies after a variable period and then a number of days later the dam attempts to expel it. In many cases the pelvic cavity and genital tract is not properly relaxed, there is a lack of fetal fluids, udder development is often lacking and severe dystocia occurs. In a few cases beginning mummification of the large fetus may begin before the fetus is expelled. In cows and ewes the mortality is high due the severe dystocia, uterine inertia, septic metritis, and retained placenta.

The condition of fetal giantism should be carefully differentiated from a large fetus, especially in the large breeds of cattle, causing dystocia at the end of a normal gestation period when the relatively small size of the birth canal makes the large fetus seem a "giant." This condition, resulting in dystocia, may occasionally be handled in a mature cow by forced extraction. Fetotomy is difficult, because total embryotomy must usually be performed. If the birth canal is small and underdeveloped or not relaxed, and the fetus emphysematous, fetotomy is extremely difficult or impossible to perform. Cesarean section should be considered. Under certain conditions slaughter might be recommended.

If fetal giantism is discovered or suspected at 280 to 300 days of gestation, and parturition does not seem imminent, a daily dose of 50 to 100 mgm. of stilbestrol or a large dose of repositol diethylstilbestrol might cause abortion. Twenty mg. of dexamethasone or 20 mg. of flumethasone repeated daily or every third day, respectively and combined with a large dose of estrogen might be indicated to produce an abortion. Verdervelde and coworkers reported that large repeated doses of estrogen, such as 60 to 240 mgm. of stilbestrol every 24 hours, resulted in 13 to 16 cows calving within 2 to 5 days. These were cases of prolonged gestation, where the fetuses had been carried 9-1/2 to 12 months. Lactation was not affected in most of these cattle so treated. (see Artificial Induction of Abortion) When parturition is artificially produced the cow should be observed carefully so that aid may be given if necessary. Cesarean section might be used to terminate the prolonged pregnancy; however, metritis and retained placenta invariably complicate the treatment. Slaughter should be seriously considered in dairy cattle since milk production is greatly reduced.

Dystocia Caused by Excessive Size of Parts of the Fetus may be due to rare instances of hypertrophy of any gland; a tumor such as a melanoma, sarcoma or others (see Tumors of the Newborn); a pathological enlargement or cystic dilation of any hollow or secreting organ or structure due to an anomaly in development causing a stenosis or an obstruction to the release of fluid. Reports show that dystocia may be due to enlarged fetal thyroid, thymus or kidney, cystic dilation of the ureter, hydrocephalus, or distention of the rumen in a **Schistosomus reflexus** monster. If forced extraction is not successful, incision of the abnormal glands or cystic enlargements to allow the escape of the soft parenchyma or fluid will usually relieve dystocia due to these causes. Except in cases of hydrocephalus and ascites further fetotomy is seldom required. In a few unusual cases cesarean section might be indicated.

Dystocia caused by a Disparity between the Size of the Normal Fetus and the Maternal Pelvis. These dystocias occur usually in primipara where the fetus may be slightly larger than normal or the pelvis may be slightly smaller than normal, or both causes may be present. Male calves are carried slightly longer and weigh 5 to 10 pounds more than female calves. Thus male fetuses are frequently present in these dystocias. As discussed under the basic causes for dystocia, crossbreeding of certain breeds and breeding heifers to certain bulls may predispose to dystocia. If primiparous animals are not grown well by proper feeding and management practices the size of the pelvis at parturition may not be adequate.

In these mild to moderate disparities between fetal size and maternal pelvic diameters, application of moderate forced extraction is indicated when the fetus is in a normal presentation position and posture for birth and the genital tract, especially the cervix, has dilated to its fullest extent. Delaying assistance by traction for too long may result in a dead fetus or an exhausted dam. In some cases added lubrication may be desirable. Traction should be in the proper direction. Alternate traction as well as lateral traction should be used. Twisting or rotation of the fetus may be helpful. If excessive traction is to be used epidural anesthesia should be given. If traction is not successful, early consideration of cesarean section should be given in order to save a living fetus. Fetotomy is less commonly indicated in animals with a narrow birth canal and a large fetus.

Dystocia may be caused by Dropsical Conditions, such as Fetal Ascites, Fetal Anasarca, Edema of the Allantois Chorion, and Hydrops of the Amnion or Allantois or both. Fetal ascites is seen as an occasional cause for dystocia in any species but occurs most often in the cow. It is occasionally associated with a dropsical condition of the uterus, mesotheliomas of the fetal abdomen, and has been observed associated with brucellosis. The fetus is usually fairly small but the distended abdomen causes it to become wedged in the pelvic inlet. (See Figure 91) It might be confused, therefore, with the hip lock condition. Close examination of the fetus in the birth canal will readily reveal the cause for the dystocia. To release the fluid from the abdomen the fetus must be sacrificed but this is no great loss as these fetuses are usually dead or weak or would fail to survive if delivered alive. The easiest method is to reach in alongside the fetus and with a castrating knife make a liberal incision through the abdominal wall. In anterior presentation a foreleg could be removed by subcutaneous amputation, and evisceration would release the ascitic fluid; but this operation is more difficult.

The other dropsical conditions of fetal anasarca (see Figure 92), edema of the allantois chorion, hydrops amnii and allantois, and hydrops allantois were discussed in Chapter 5. In removing large anasarcous fetuses, forced extraction is usually successful. If the fetus is too large, fetotomy including amputation of the forelimb and evisceration may occasionally be necessary. This is easily performed because of the soft, friable, edematous fetal tissues. Rarely cesarean section might be indicated. In these dropsical uterine conditions uterine inertia and a weak or dead fetus frequently occur and favor abnormal postures, emphysema and dystocia that can usually be relieved by mutation and forced extraction.

Twinning in Uniparous Animals is a Common Cause of Dystocia. This is produced most commonly by portions of bicornual fetuses becoming wedged in the maternal pelvis. Dystocia is predisposed in unicornual twins because of the inertia of the long, distended uterine horn bent at a 180-degree angle at the diaphragm. Uteri containing multiple fetuses in unipara are prone to develop uterine inertia and uterine disease. The fetuses are less viable. These latter factors usually produce abnormal postures. In many cases one fetus presents anteriorly and the other posteriorly, the latter often in breech presentation. Dystocia due to twins is most common in dairy cows, and less common in beef cattle. Twin dystocia is rare in the mare inasmuch as twins almost always are aborted. Sheep have adapted themselves to two fetuses and twin dystocia is uncommon by comparison with the incidence of twins in that species. Twin dystocia usually may be diagnosed readily on examination of the birth canal by finding three or more limbs attached to two separate fetuses. Diagnosis should differentiate between this condition and double monsters, **Schistosomus reflexus,** campylorrhachis, or dystocia in anterior presentation with the hind limbs extended alongside the body. If twins are wedged in the birth canal usually traction is placed on the twin nearer the vulva. The other fetus is repelled at the same time. Since twin fetuses are small, mutation is invariably successful. Conditions of twin pregnancy and dystocia may be followed by metritis and retained placenta. In cases of unicornual twin dystocia it occasionally happens that one twin is removed and the other overlooked. The same may happen in triplet pregnancies. Thus following all dystocias the uterus should always be examined carefully to be certain no fetus is left in the uterus.

Dystocia due to Fetal Monsters. The relative incidence of fetal monstrosities by species is reported as follows:

Table 15. Relative incidence of fetal monstrosities.

	Craig (citing Gurlt)	Williams	Roberts
Cow	239	15	92
Ewe	179	1	2
Sow	87	1	2
Bitch	78		
Cat	71		
Mare	56		3
Goat	24		2
Total	734	17	101

According to references cited by Craig, out of 2340 foals in one stud, only 9 were monstrosities; in cattle about 0.5 per cent; and in sheep 1 in 768 lambs were anomalous.

Not all anomalous fetuses or monsters cause dystocia. The monsters that are characterized by an increased size of the fetus include: hydrocephalic, anasarcous, or ascitic monsters; monsters with marked skeletal defects such as **Schistosomus reflexus, Campylorrhachis scoliosa, Perosomus elumbis;** monsters due to conjoined twins or double monsters; monsters due to pseudo-ankylosis of the limbs or neck; achondroplastic fetuses with short, broad bodies; and mummified fetuses that died late in gestation. Other anomalous fetuses that are weak or dead at birth may cause dystocia due to abnormal positions and postures because of their lack of movement and muscle tonus. If these latter defective, malformed, nonviable fetuses cause dystocia they can usually be removed by mutation and forced extraction unless emphysema or marked contraction of the uterine wall has resulted.

Among the author's cases the incidence of dystocia in cattle due to excessive size of the fetus was as follows, in order of frequency: **Schistosomus reflexus,** 14 cases; **Persomus horridus** (Gurlt) with ankyloses of the limbs and a short S-curved spine, 13 cases; **Persomus elumbis,** 5 cases, double monsters, 3 cases (two Thoraco abdomino-pagus, one Dicephalus); fetal anasarca, 2 cases; **Achondroplasia,** 2 cases; and **Hydrocephalus,** 2 cases. Hydrocephalus is occasionally seen also in equine, procine, canine and feline fetuses. Most fetal monsters weigh less than normal fetuses, so they are easily handled.

In a dystocia case a careful examination of the fetus should be made for signs of a monster such as: deformed limbs, ankylosed thin limbs with prominent joints, improper placement or location of extremities, atrophied muscles and smaller fetal size. This examination is particularly important in differentiating between twins and double monsters. When traction or repulsion is placed on one end of the fetus and the opposite part also moves, either a double monster or a sharply-bent single monster is present. In other cases of dystocia when proper and normal progress toward the correction of the dystocia ceases the fetus should be carefully reexamined for the possible presence of a monster or an anomalous condition.

In the handling of dystocia due to monsters each case is an individual problem. The operator must rely on a careful examination of the fetus and birth canal and on his own ingenuity and ability to plan a procedure that assures a satisfactory outcome. If the condition is severe and complicated extra assistance and even consultation should be obtained. Double monsters occur most commonly in the cow, sow, dog, and cat, and only very rarely in the mare. Fetotomy, including evisceration, is usually indicated to reduce the size of the monster to the point where the fetatome wire may be placed around conjoined twins at the point of attachment and separate them for removal. A cesarean section to relieve dystocia due to excessive size of the fetus requires a large abdominal incision that may complicate the operation and aftercare.

Hydrocephalus is seen most often in the cow, dog, and mare and when it is severe enough to result in a dystocia that cannot be relieved by mutation and forced extraction the soft portion of the distended cranium should be reduced in size by an incision to release the fluid. An excessive bony enlargement of the cranium may require that a cephalotomy be performed with the fetatome, by placing the wire around the base of the enlarged skull, amputating and withdrawing the collapsed cranial bones and tissues.

An achondroplastic calf generally can be removed by traction with a chain looped around its neck. Lubrication is of vital importance in severe cases. The limbs are quite short and small and cause little trouble. In cases associated with fetal emphysema, removal of the foreleg and evisceration of the fetus may be indicated. This applies also to anasarcous calves (see Figure 92). They are usually aborted prematurely and their tissues are soft and easily mutiliated for the purpose of releasing fluid in order to reduce the size of the fetus. Fetal ascites often is associated with this condition.

Schistosomus reflexus (see Figure 43) is seen in the cow and occasionally the sheep, goat, and pig but never in the other species. It may be presented in the birth canal in a ventral manner, with the viscera easily palpable. When examining these monsters in this presentation, the operator may be startled to feel viscera and even a beating heart. The fetal viscera might be mistaken for the dam's viscera, and a diagnosis of a ruptured uterus may follow. This mistake will be avoided by a careful examination of the fetus The dorsal presentation of the Schistosomus monster consists of the head and the four feet extending into the pelvic cavity. Since many of these monsters are small they may be removed by careful traction especially from adult dairy cows with a large pelvis. In the ventral presentation hooks or Krey's tongs may be used for traction. In dorsal presentation alternate traction on the legs is sometimes successful in relieving dystocia. In many cases, however, fetotomy is indicated. It is desirable to cut the body in half at the point of the greatest ventral curvature of the spine. Every effort should be made to place the fetatome wire around the middle of the fetus and between the front and hind limbs before the actual cutting operation. In some large fetuses after removing the head, forelimbs, and part of the thorax, it may be necessary to bisect the pelvis before the dystocia can be relieved. In rare cases a sac of skin may completely enclose the limbs and must be incised and the enclosed fluid released before starting the embryotomy (see Figure 43). Williams recorded one case of dystocia in this type of monster associated with a greatly distended rumen. **Campylorachis scoliosa** is rarely observed but is handled similarly by cutting the body into two halves with the fetatome. **Perosomus elumbis** if in posterior presentation may be mistaken for a breech presentation. This abnormality is seen most often in cattle and pigs. In anterior presentation the rigid ankylosed hind limbs may obstruct the passage of the caudal portion of the fetus through the maternal pelvis. Since the fetus, especially the rear quarters, are small, atrophied, and loosely attached to the trunk, correction of the dystocia by mutation and careful traction can be accomplished in many instances. Occasionally amputation of the rear limbs at the tarsus or hip with the fetatome may be necessary in order to remove the fetus without endangering the dam. **Perosomus horridus** with genei ankylosis or muscle contractures of the fetus is a commonly-observed anomaly in cattle in New York State. The monster, usually a Holstein, is small and very short due to an S-shaped multiple bending of the spine from the occiput to the sacrum. The vertebrae are definitely abnormal, shortened, and ankylosed. The limbs, neck, and tail are ankylosed and deformed. Due to the small size of the fetus, however, the dystocia is usually relieved by traction.

In any of the above types of dystocia due to monsters with the exception of the achrondroplastic or anasarcous calves, pseudo-ankylosis of one or more joints or limbs is common. If fetotomy does not give promise of success, cesarean section would be indicated; but the abdominal incision will necessarily be large unless fetotomy can be performed on the fetus **in utero** before its removal through the abdominal incision. Most of these animals will conceive on subsequent breeding and produce normal young unless complications following the dystocia cause pathological conditions that delay or prevent conception. In the sow, dog, and cat cesarean section is the method of choice and often is necessary in order to relieve dystocia due to a fetal monster.

Dystocia Due to Uterine Displacements

Dystocia may be caused by uterine displacements such as uterine torsion, displacement of the uterus in inguinal or ventral hernias, rupture of the prepubic tendon, and possibly vagino-cervical prolapse.

Dystocia due to Uterine Torsion is frequently observed in cattle, especially dairy cattle confined for long periods in the stable. It is occasionally observed as a cause for dystocia in sheep, mares, dogs, and cats, and in rare instances in the sow. (See Figure 93) As noted in Chap. 5, in which the etiology, symptoms, and diagnosis of torsion of the uterus in the preparturient animal were discussed, about 90 per cent of torsions of the uterus in cattle are observed at parturition and cause dystocia. Torsion of the uterus as a cause of dystocia was present in 7.3 and 7.0 per cent of 1555 and 998 cases of bovine dystocia observed in the Ambulatory Clinic of the New York State Veterinary College from 1943 to 1953 and 1963 to 1968, respectively. Williams cited records from the same clinic from 1925 to 1945 showing that of 1703 cases of bovine dystocia, 225, or 13.2 per cent, were due to uterine torsion.

The symptoms of uterine torsion of the cow occurring at the time of parturition and resulting in dystocia are frequently so mild that the owner thinks the cow is still in the first stage of labor. The cow is uneasy, restless, may show colic by treading, kicking at its abdomen, and switching its tail. Moderate anorexia is present. Tenesmus, or abdominal straining characteristic of the second stage of labor, is either absent or mild and intermittent because the twisted birth canal prevents the entrance of the fetus into the pelvis—a necessary prerequisite to the initiation of normal abdominal straining. The history given by the owner is usually that the cow has acted as if calving was imminent for the past 8 to 18 hours or more, but true labor or straining has not occurred. This history of a prolonged first stage of parturition is usually observed in uterine torsion causing dystocia and is significant when an owner observes his parturient cows closely.

Examination of the cow reveals increased respirations, and the heart rate is usually elevated to 80 to 100 per minute. In advanced cases with complications of uterine gangrene, uterine rupture, or fetal emphysema, the animal may be toxic, with a very rapid, weak pulse, severe depression, weakness, prostration, low body temperature, cold extremities, and possibly a fetid diarrhea. Hemorrhage from ruptured uterine vessels, occasionally occurs in uterine torsion and causes the cow to exhibit symptoms of anemia, weakness, rapid breathing, rapid pulse rate, and prostration. In some severe 270° to 360° torsions in cattle it may be noticed that the dorsal commissure of the vulva is pulled forward and to the left or right, depending upon which direction the uterus rotated. An accurate diagnosis of uterine torsion may be made by vaginal and rectal examination of the uterus, broad ligaments, vagina, and fetus, as described in Chapter 5 (see Figure 93). Whenever the birth canal is narrow and stenosed in the region of the cephalic portion of the vagina or the cervix at the time of parturition, torsion should be suspected. If the torsion is greater that 180° to 240° it is usually impossible to pass the hand through the twisted portion of the birth canal. This twisted portion usually includes. the cephalic portion of the vagina, the cervix, and occasionally the body of the uterus. Epidural anesthesia is usually necessary, as oftentimes this examination initiates severe straining. The fetus is usually in a dorso-ilial or dorso-pubic position as most torsions in cattle are 180° to 240°. The fetal membranes may have ruptured. The fetus is likely to be dead, and in long-standing neglected cases of dystocia may show evidence of emphysema or maceration. In all cases of dorso-ilial or dorso-pubic positions of fetuses in unipara the birth canal should be carefully examined for the presence of a torsion. The incidence of uterine rupture is fairly high in cases of uterine torsion and therefore an examination for this should be made prior to treatment. The direction of the torsion should be carefully ascertained. Torsions in the mare and cow of 180° or less may recover spontaneously.

The symptoms in the horse and ewe are similar to those in the cow. In the mare the foal is usually dead and often the symptoms are mistaken for colic or indigestion. Torsions of the uterus greater than 180° are fairly common in the mare, Derivaux and Dewalque. In the ewe the

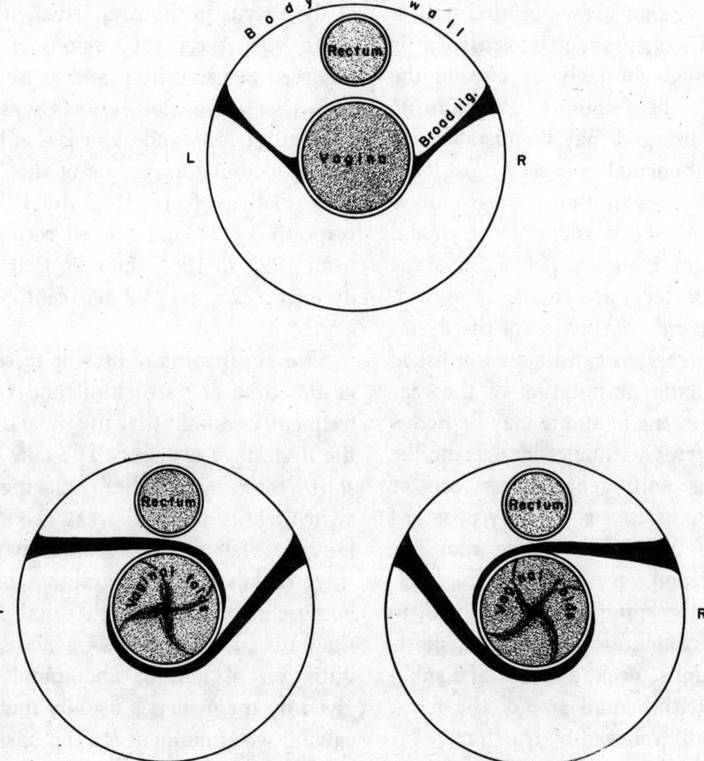

Figure 93. Diagram of a normal and twisted bovine uterus and vagina (Upper center) Normal position of broad ligaments and vagina. (Lower left) 180° right torsion of the uterus. (Lower right) 180° left torsion of the uterus.

fetus cannot be directly palpated, due to the twisted narrow birth canal. In multipara, such as the dog, parturition progresses with the fetuses being expelled from the normal horn and in some cases from the caudal or patent portion of the horn in which torsion may have occurred. Unless the abdomen is palpated fetuses in the twisted or rotated horn or portion of a horn that may be still attached to the rest of the uterus or rarely separated from it will not be noted. Transverse rupture of this uterine segment may release the fetuses into the abdominal cavity. In 24 to 48 hours the bitch will show depression, anorexia, elevated temperature, and rapid pulse, with symptoms of abdominal involvement by a tense, firm abdomen, arched back, and a slow, painful gait and attitude. The extrauterine fetuses may be diagnosed by radiographs or palpated through the abdominal wall. In rare instances, especially in the cat, the twisted segment of the uterus containing one or two fetuses, isolated or separated from the rest of the uterus due to torsion of the uterus, may be walled off in the abdominal cavity by connective tissue causing the fetuses to macerate or mummify.

The prognosis of uterine torsion is usually fair to good when the condition is diagnosed early, before the occurrence of fetal emphysema, secondary contraction of the cervix, uterine rupture and peritonitis. In the 113 cases of bovine uterine torsion occurring in the Ambulatory Clinic from 1943 to 1953 there was an 11 per cent mortality of the dams. In 70 cases of uterine torsion treated from 1963 through 1968 in the same clinic there was only a 4.3 percent mortality. Williams reported on a series of 225 cases of uterine torsion from 1925 to 1945, in which an 18 per cent mortality resulted. In the mare, in 4 cases reported by Williams and 3 observed by the author, one death resulted. Derivaux and Dewalque described 3 cases and cited 11 more cases of uterine torsion in the mare and 8 mares died. The mortality in mares may be equal to or probably greater than that in cattle. The prognosis in the other species is guarded to poor because an early diagnosis is difficult or impossible to make without an exploratory laparotomy operation. The prognosis in respect to the life of the fetus is poor, since in most cases veterinary aid is not summoned until too late and the fetuses, having a reduced oxygen supply, are less viable and die due to asphyxia. In torsion of the uterus with an extensive rupture of the uterus, hemorrhage, or severe uterine edema and gangrene secondary to thrombi in the large uterine vessels, the prognosis is poor, especially when the latter condition is present in large animals. In the dog and cat hysterectomy may be successful if shock and peritonitis can be controlled. Most cases of unrelieved uterine torsion result in the death of the dam. In rare cases the fetus remains in the uterus and macerates, with extensive adhesions developing around the uterus; and the condition may not be diagnosed for several months. Uterine torsion in cattle is likely to be followed by retained placenta, metritis, perimetritis, and delayed conception. Only rarely does torsion recur at the following parturition.

The handling or treatment of dystocia caused by uterine torsion in large animals includes several techniques, such as cesarean section, rolling the dam, and rotation of the fetus and uterus through the birth canal or through a laparotomy incision. These treatments and the modifications thereof are designed to correct the torsion of the uterus and to remove the fetus. The techniques of laparotomy, cesarean, and rolling are indicated when the birth canal is so twisted that the hand cannot be passed through it to grasp the fetus, or when the cervix is not dilated, as may occur in torsion during the gestation period.

Rolling the dam is one of the oldest and simplest of the various methods used to relieve torsion of the uterus. Its principal drawback is that it requires the assistance of 3 to 6 men depending on the size of the cow or mare. If possible, rolling should be done out-of-doors, on a grassy, gentle slope with the cow's head lower than the rear quarters. In the winter months the barn floor, litter alley, or large box stall that are well-bedded or covered deeply with straw or hay may be used. The cow, especially if large and vigorous, should be given a large dose of a tranquilizer intravenously or intramuscularly, or 0.5 to 1.0 ounce of chloral hydrate intravenously or 1.5 to 3.0 ounces orally, as a sedative 20 minutes prior to rolling. After the direction of the torsion has been determined accurately, the cow is laid down in lateral recumbency on the same side as the direction of the torsion. The squeeze method, with half hitches around the thorax and abdomen; or the Alabama technique, with ropes crossed over the back and between the hind legs, is used to force the cow to lie down. The hind leg on the side on which the cow is to be cast is pulled cranially and underneath it by a rope attached to the pastern and passed to the other side at the same time the body ropes are tightened. Occasionally this procedure of dropping the cow suddenly on the same side as the direction of the torsion relieves or partially relieves the condition. The two hind legs of the cow are fastened together and the two front legs are tied together, leaving an 8- to 10-foot end on each rope. The cow's head is held extended by a halter and rope and if necessary a nose lead. The front and hind feet should not be tied together, because this compresses the abdominal cavity and tends to make the gravid uterus rotate with the cow. It is better not to tie the front legs in a flexed position to the body, as the cow will throw her knees apar and brace herself, thus making it difficult to roll her. The object in rolling the cow when relieving torsion is to rotate the body of the cow in the same direction as the torsion of the uterus, rapidly enough to rotate the body around, or faster than, the inert uterus and fetus. The rapidly rotating body of the cow thereby overtakes the more slowly rotating inert gravid uterus. The cow should be rapidly rotated in the same direction as the torsion, by strong coordinated pulling on the ropes attached to the forelegs and hind legs. If because of a lack of assistance, rolling cannot be done rapidly, some other method should be selected to relieve the torsion. After the cow has been rapidly rolled 180 degrees her body must then be either rolled back slowly to the original position or be pushed, usually slowly, over her legs and sternum so that she is once more in lateral recumbency on the same side as the direction of the torsion, ready to be rapidly turned over again. Although some authors advise the operator to keep the hand in the vagina or even to grasp the fetus, in order to hold the gravid uterus in place, this is a very awkward position to assume or maintain as the animal is being rolled, and is unnecessary unless the operator is uncertain as to the direction in which the uterus is rotated. Placing the hand in the cranial portion of the vagina as rolling is performed will reveal at once, by the tightening of the spiral folds in the vagina, if the rolling is in the wrong direction. After each two or three rapid rotations of the cow's body the birth canal should be examined to determine if the torsion is corrected. If so, the spiral folds and stenosis of the birth canal have disappeared and if the cervix is dilated the fetus may be palpated with ease. Occasionally there may be a rush of fetal fluids from the uterus as the torsion is relieved. If the torsion is not relieved, this procedure should be repeated 4 to 5 or more times before failure is admitted and another technique attempted. Rolling mares with torsion of the uterus often results in correction of the torsion as in cattle. Derivaux and Dewalque and Vandeplassche et al. indicated that rolling might result in rupture of the uterus especially of the uterus was edematous.

A modification of this rolling technique, called Schaffer's method has been described by Arthur (1966). This method requires less assistance because the cow with torsion is rolled slowly instead of rapidly. This method has also proven of value for the author. The cow is cast on the same side as the direction of the torsion and tied in a manner similar to that described for the previous rolling technique. A plank 9 to 12 feet long and 8 to 12 inches wide is placed on the cow's abdomen with the lower end of the plank on the ground. An assistant stands on the plank and the cow is slowly rolled in the same direction as the torsion by pulling on the ropes around the front and hind feet. This creates pressure first on the upper abdominal wall, then the floor and finally the opposite side of the abdomen resulting in a correction of the torsion that can be determined by examining the genital tract. If there is any question concerning the direction of the torsion, the operator, by placing his hand in the canal, can readily determine whether the torsion is being relieved or not as the cow is slowly rolled. As in the initial rolling technique if the torsion is not relieved the first time the cow is rolled, the procedure may be repeated several times. In most cases the torsion is corrected on the first rolling. In the Schaffer method the uterus and its contents are held in place by the plank and the weight of the man standing on it while the cow is rotated around them.

Laparotomy for the intra-abdominal correction of torsion is especially valuable during the gestation period or when the cervix is closed. It is usually performed on the standing cow or mare through the left or right paralumbar fossa. This technique has the advantage of requiring less assistance than does rolling. In most cases tranquilizers or a small dose of chloral hydrate, 0.5 to 1.0 ounce intravenously and light epidural anesthesia are given to control tenesmus at the time of the operation. The right flank in the cow is anesthetized by paravertebral or local anesthesia and a 6- to 8-inch vertical laparotomy incision is made. The omentum is pulled cranially if it is over the uterus. If torsion of the uterus is to the right the hand and arm are passed downward between the uterus and abdominal wall until the bottom or ventral surface of the uterus can be felt. A portion of the fetus, usually the leg, is grasped through the uterine wall and by alternately lifting and lowering the uterus it is made to rock up and down in an arc of 10 to 12 inches and finally by strongly lifting the uterus and pushing it toward the midline and downward, correction of the torsion is accomplished. If torsion is to the left the hand and arm are passed over the top of the uterus and down between the rumen and uterus. The same procedure of rocking and then rotating to the right or laterally and downward is carried out to correct the left torsion. A left flank incision is preferred in mares. The laparotomy incision then is closed securely. In rare cases in which laparotomy alone is unsuccessful because of chronic adhesions or a very large distended uterus or rumen, making correction impossible, cesarean section may be indicated. If at the time of parturition the cervix is not dilated sufficiently and the operator does not wish to lose a living fetus by delay, a cesarean may be performed. This may be done by enlarging the laparotomy incision. Although the torsion may be corrected before or after the fetus is removed, it is easier to relieve torsion after cesarean section. If a cesarean section in a cow is decided upon before making the right flank incision, another laparotomy site may be chosen since correction of the torsion is usually easily accomplished, even in the recumbent cow after the fetus has been removed. Torsion in the ewe and goat may be relieved by laparotomy if elevation of the animal by hanging it by the rear legs or by rolling it is not successful. Wensvoort described the relief of uterine torsion in two sows after a laparotomy operation. One sow died due to hemorrhage from a vessel in the broad ligament; the other recovered following correction of the torsion and removal of the pigs.

Rotation of the fetus and uterus through the birth canal is probably the most common way of relieving dystocia due to torsion of the uterus in the cow and may be used in the mare. Since most torsions, about 90 percent, are discovered at the time of parturition when the cervix is relaxed and dilated, and since most torsions are less than 240 degrees, the hand may be passed through the twisted portion of the birth canal and the fetus grasped and rotated. In the mare with a 180° torsion of the uterus the cervix may be dilated and the fetus grasped. It is advisable, and in many cases necessary, to have the cow on its feet or its rear parts elevated, and enough epidural anesthetic injected to prevent straining. If the birth canal is dry, lubrication is necessary. If the fetal membranes have not ruptured and released the fluids this should be done to reduce the size and weight of the uterus. Depending on the position and posture of the fetus and the direction of the torsion, the left or right arm is used for manually rotating the fetus. The leg of the fetus is grasped in the metacarpal or metatarsal region and the knee or hock joint flexed. By repelling the fetus and twisting the leg in rotating manner at regular intervals the fetus and uterus are rocked back and forth through an arc of 10 to 12 inches; and then with a sudden strong twist they are lifted and then pushed downward to the side opposite to the direction of the torsion, thereby in many cases relieving the torsion. Some veterinarians pass the hand alongside the body of the fetus, start it rocking and then lift it upward, over, and downward, in a like manner, opposite to the direction of the torsion. This manual technique is easier in the smaller breeds of cattle with the smaller and lighter calves. It is also easier for the stronger, taller operators.

In the larger breeds of cows when correction of the torsion is not possible by manual rotation of the fetus and uterus the detorsion rod described by DeMott and Roberts, or a similar instrument such as Erickson's detorsion rod or Cammerer's fork is of great value. The DeMott detorsion rod is made of 3/8-inch steel rod, 30 inches long, has an eye at either end with 1-1/4 inch inside diameter. After making an 8- or 9-inch loop in a 60-inch obstetrical chain the end of the loop is passed through one eye of the detorsion rod and the rod and loop of chain are carried into the uterus. The free end of the loop is passed around one leg of the fetus and the rod is pushed up to that leg. The other end of the loop, on the opposite side of the eye of the rod, is passed around the other leg. Both ends of the loop around the legs should be placed around the pasterns or just above fetlocks and the free end of the chain drawn tight. If the loops of chain are passed up the leg to the knees or above the knees of the fetus, the hoofs and feet may be forced into or through the uterine wall as the detorsion rod is rotated unless they are carefully held by the operator. A short piece of broom handle or Gibbon's obstetrical handle is then inserted into the eye of the rod and the tightly drawn chain wrapped several times around the handle.

There is another method of applying this instrument, but it is not as safe inasmuch as it may injure the fetal limbs. If, however, the fetus is dead this aspect is unimportant. A loop is made in the long obstetrical chain. It is carried into the uterus and placed around one or preferably both legs of the fetus. The free end of the chain is placed through one eye of the rod and the rod is pushed into the uterus so that the eye fits tightly on the loop around the leg or legs. The chain is drawn tight and the free end of the chain wrapped around the handle.

Before and during rotation of the fetus and uterus, the hand should be inserted into the vagina and uterus to make certain that no portion of the mucous membrane is being pinched by the chain and that the claws of the feet do not engage or rupture the uterine wall. Vaginal examination during the reduction operation is helpful in making certain that the fetus and uterus are being rotated in the proper direction and in determining when the torsion is corrected. When rotating the fetus, repulsion by means of the rod is definitely helpful. In most cases, rocking the fetus and uterus back and forth a few times before starting reduction of the torsion makes the operation easier. Then the handle is rotated slowly in the direction opposite to that of the torsion, and the torsion is relieved. Rotating a fetus in anterior presentation a quarter of a turn beyond the normal position and then returning the fetus to the normal position will bring the head into the proper posture. If the torsion and stenosis of the birth canal are not severe and both fetal limbs are lying in the vagina, rotation of the fetus and uterus is simplified; but the torsion should not be overlooked.

Other techniques may possibly be used to correct torsion or to assist in the previous procedures. Abdominal ballottment is recommended by Benesch and Wright and may be of use in aiding manual correction of the torsion through the birth canal, or in rolling the cow. In right torsion an assistant on the right side pushes downwards and inwards in the upper right flank while an assistant on the left side pushes upwards and inwards on the lower left flank. In left torsion the upper left flank and the lower right flank are pushed strongly with the fists. These two assistants push alternately, at intervals of about one second. This causes the uterus to roll back and forth, aiding the operator who is working on the fetus and uterus through the birth canal When the cow is on her back during the rolling, alternate pressure through the relaxed abdominal walls may aid in reducing the torsion. If the fetus cannot be palpated per vaginum it is very doubtful that rectal palpation and manipulation would be of much value in aiding correction of the torsion. Benesch and Wright recommended the stimulation of vigorous fetal movement as an aid to correction of early cases of torsion. If the hand can be passed into the uterus, the eyeballs of the fetus should be pressed firmly. This results in strong reflex movements of the fetus that may aid manual correction of the torsion. Richter and Gotze illustrated a technique that may be useful in correction of torsion when manual correction of the torsion is to be accomplished by rotation of the fetus and uterus through the birth canal or through a laparotomy incision. One end of a wide board about 8 feet long is placed on the ground under the abdomen and at a right angle to the body of the standing cow. An assistant pushes upward on the other end of the board into the right flank if right torsion is present or into the left flank if left torsion is present. The operator can lift the twisted gravid uterus and fetus from 4 to 6 inches; the board is pushed into the flank and the uterus rests on the board until the operator can get another hold on the uterus or fetus and lift it higher, where pressure upwards and inward on the board again holds it until the process can be repeated. The gravid uterus is thus "walked up" the board until it is in a position to be pushed over and downward, and the torsion corrected. Another old technique, rather crude and not recommended is that of suspending the cow's body by her hocks. After proper padding and tying of the hocks the rear parts are suspended by a hoist until only the cow's shoulders remain on the ground. The gravid uterus rotates more easily into its normal position when the viscera fall forward. Abdominal ballottement or manual rotation of the fetus through the vagina or rectum, or both, may be necessary to effect correction.

Cesarean section may be indicated in uterine torsion when correction by laparotomy or other means fails; when the cervix is not dilated or only slightly so and it is desired to save the live fetus; when the cervix has undergone a secondary constriction after prolonged dystocia and an emphysematous fetus is present; when uterine rupture has occurred and the fetus is partially in the abdominal cavity; or when torsion of the uterus is suspected in multiparous animals such as the dog, cat, and sow. In these latter species cesarean section should not be delayed. In the ewe, as in the cow, cesarean section may be used whenever ordinary means of handling fail or are not indicated. Before performing cesarean section under these complicated conditions the prognosis should be discussed with the owner, as slaughter may be preferable. In the mare, rolling usually results in correction of this condition. Manual or instrumental rotation of the fetus might be attempted but is more difficult and dangerous than rolling. The rotation of the uterine horns in the mare in rotated bicornual pregnancy has been discussed under transverse presentations. In severe uterine torsion especially in the dog and cat, in which the uterus is severely damaged and necrotic, hysterectomy is indicated and is usually successful if shock or peritonitis do not present severe complications. When hysterectomy is indicated in the cow, the prognosis is very grave. In rare cases in which torsion has become chronic with many adhesions between the involved horn or uterus and the rest of the abdominal viscera, the cow should be slaughtered. In dogs and cats this encapsulated mass containing macerated or mummified fetuses may be removed if necessary.

After the torsion has been corrected by the above methods, with the exception of cesarean section, the fetus may usually be removed by traction after correction has been made of any abnormal posture of its head, neck, or limbs. Before the fetus is removed the uterus should be examined carefully to make certain a rupture, which is usually located transversely in the uterus just cranial to the cervix, has not occurred. In some cases the cervix is not completely dilated. This may be because the stage of parturition has not progressed sufficiently. The treatment indicated in these cases is to administer 20 to 50 units of pituitrin or oxytocin and wait 2 to 4 hours for further dilation or normal parturition to occur. A slow intravenous drip of the same amount of oxytocin over a period of several hours may produce a more physiological dilation of the cervix. In most cases, however, the cervix is only partially dilated due to an atony or inertia of the cervix and uterus caused by the torsion of the uterus and interference with normal circulation. Due to unrelieved dystocia during the period corresponding to the first and second stages of parturition the cervix may partially contract with the fetus still in the uterus. This latter condition is usually observed with a dead fetus and occasionally fetal emphysema is present. The condition of the fetus is an important factor in the decision whether to wait for the cervix to dilate more or to exert moderate, continuous traction with lubrication at once and gradually dilate or, if necessary, even slightly lacerate the cervix in order to remove the fetus. When the cervix is poorly dilated great traction is not indicated, since it may cause severe cervical laceration or rupture of the uterus especially when the fetus is dead, or dry and emphysematous. Under these circumstances cesarean section, using one of the ventral abdominal laparotomy sites, is indicated.

After the fetus has been removed, the uterus, birth canal, and the cow should be carefully inspected. Rupture of the uterus with peritonitis, internal bleeding due to rupture of the large uterine vessels, retained placenta, septic metritis, and perimetritis are common sequelae to torsion of the uterus. There should be proper treatment or preventive treatment of these complications.

Dystocia due to Abdominal Hernias, such as inguinal hernias in the dog and rarely in the cat; large ventral hernias in the mare, cow and ewe; and extensive ventral hernias due to rupture of the prepubic tendon in the mare (see Figure 80) and cow, were described in Chapter 5. Dystocia might be possible but would be of great rarity, due to diaphragmatic, umbilical, or perineal hernias. Inguinal hernias causing dystocia must be relieved by a cesarean section; in some neglected cases hysterectomy might be necessary, Arthur. In rupture of the prepubic tendon in the mare, traction should be provided as soon as the first stage of labor is completed. Cows and ewes may give birth normally even with large ventral hernias but aid should be available if it is needed.

Dystocia due to Vagino-Cervical Prolapse is rarely observed in domestic animals. In most cattle affected with vagino-cervical prolapse that carry their fetuses to term, parturition is usually uneventful. Occasionally abortion with a secondary dystocia may be associated with vagino-cervical prolapse. The vagina or cervix might be severely diseased, atonic, edematous, and traumatized and cause dystocia that might have to be relieved by lubrication and gentle traction. In rare instances vagino-cervical prolapse might be severe enough to indicate cesarean section as an aid to relieving the condition. A cesarean might be necessary if cervical stenosis is present, associated with cervical prolapse (see Chapter 5).

Dystocia Due to Stenosis or Obstruction in the Birth Canal

The immediate causes for dystocia due to stenosis or obstruction of the birth canal may be divided into several groups according to the structures affected—the pelvis, the cervix, the vagina, or the vulva.

Dystocia due to Abnormalities or Injuries of the Pelvic Bones resulting in a stenosis or narrowing of the pelvic inlet is seen commonly in domestic animals. In all animals, especially in the cow and sow, the females may be bred too young and the pelvis at the time of parturition be too small and juvenile to allow passage of the fetus. Primiparous animals, especially the cow and sow, may also commonly have dystocia due to a disparity in the size of the maternal pelvis and the size of the fetus even though bred at the proper age, when they have been grown poorly or stunted, usually due to a lack of the necessary nutrients for normal growth, or have suffered chronic disease processes that prevented or retarded normal growth and development. (See Chapters VII and IX) Dystocia is common in achondroplastic dwarf cattle. In certain breeds of dogs especially the brachycephalic breeds, with a large broad head, dystocia is common due to the relatively small, narrow flattened pelvis. Pelvic fractures and exostoses as a cause for dystocia are uncommon in the large domestic animals but are occasionally seen in dogs and cats that are struck or injured by moving vehicles. Williams cited as a rare cause of dystocia a dislocation of the hip with the head of the femur in the obturator foramen surrounded by a large callus. Fortunately most females with fractures and exostoses of the pelvis are not bred. Occasionally in the cow, rarely in the mare, a large or sharp bony prominence may be found on the cranial portion of the symphysis pubis. This prominence may project into the pelvic canal and cause lacerations or contusions of the vagina or cervix when traction is applied to the fetus. "Rickets" or mineral deficiencies and the resulting bone deformities are rarely if ever observed in animals as a cause for pelvic stenosis and dystocia. It is unlikely that an owner would breed any animal affected severely enough to have pelvic deformities.

Correction of this type of dystocia may be overcome in most cases with steady, moderate traction in the proper direction or directions on a well-lubricated fetus. When there is a bony prominence on the cranial part of the symphysis pubis care should be taken not to rupture or lacerate the vagina, cervix, or uterus. In most cases of severe dystocia due to pelvic stenosis, in which there is a great difference between the size of the fetus and the pelvic diameters cesarean section is indicated. Fetotomy may be indicated in selected cases. If the head of the fetus cannot enter the pelvic cavity at the same time as the forelimbs in anterior presentation, or if the fetal pelvis is much larger than the maternal pelvic inlet in posterior presentation, cesarean section is indicated. Especially if the dystocia is severe, the fetus is alive, and mutation and forced extraction offer little hope of success cesarean section is the method most often selected. If in anterior presentation the fetal extractor can with moderate traction draw the thorax through the birth canal, sometimes after amputation of the head and neck, evisceration through a transverse abdominal incision is performed and the impacted fetal pelvis is bisected with a fetatome. This procedure may be simpler and safer than a cesarean operation. Fetotomy through a narrow birth canal is often difficult, prolonged, and usually must be total rather than partial. The possibility of severe trauma to the birth canal by prolonged fetotomy operations through a small pelvic inlet is great. In severe cases, even those complicated with fetal emphysema, cesarean section may be more desirable and easier for the operator and the cow than a prolonged, difficult fetotomy operation would be. Splitting of the pelvis might rarely be indicated in certain cases in heifers on range areas. In the dog, cat, sow, and probably the ewe, cesarean section should be resorted to immediately as soon as dystocia develops. With the exception of young animals which have been on a low nutritive plane, or been bred at too young an age, or possibly brachycephalic dogs, these females should not be rebred after dystocia.

Dystocia due to Failure of the Cervix to Dilate is seen occasionally in the cow and ewe and very rarely in other domestic animals. In England and Australia this condition is spoken of as "ring-womb", especially in ewes. Failure of cervical dilation is due to a number of causes—cervical induration, primary uterine and cervical inertia, secondary uterine inertia with cervical involution —and in the early stages of normal parturition this condition might be diagnosed erroneously.

The cervix may fail to dilate because of severe fibrous induration or sclerosis of the cervix. This is observed most often in older cows with a history of cervical lacerations and uterine and cervical infections. The incidence of true cervical induration or sclerosis producing dystocia is rare and this diagnosis should only be made after a careful clinical examination.

In other cases the diagnosis of stenosis or atresia of the cervix may be erroneous, because the animal may not yet have entered the first or second stage of labor. If the animal is left alone for a number of hours cervical dilation will often take place physiologically. In these animals the uterine tone is good, the fetus is alive, the uterine artery is very large and has the typical whirring feeling, the tenacious cervical seal is loosening and coming out of the cervix, and the fetal membranes are intact. There have been rare cases in which for some undiagnosed reason the animal began to strain intermittently a day or more prior to parturition. Rabies in cattle, because of the frequent occurrence of tenesmus in this disease, may resemble approaching parturition in a cow in advanced pregnancy.

Stenosis or atresia of the cervix may be associated with dystocia when, in abortion or at term, the cervix does not dilate completely, or relaxation of the cervix fails to take place. This condition is probably caused by hormonal factors that fail to produce a normal relaxation and dilation of the cervix. It is often associated with uterine inertia. This may be due to a failure of the usual or necessary steroid hormones to be secreted or possibly more frequently due to disease of the cervix and uterus that renders the cervical and uterine muscles incapable of responding normally to the hormonal stimulus that relaxes the cervix and produces dilation by contraction of the uterine muscles forcing the fetal membranes and fluids, and the fetus into the cervix. The estrogenic hormone, relaxin, and oxytocin are considered to play important roles in this process but as stated previously the exact mechanism requires further study. Failure of the cervix to dilate properly at the time of parturition is associated with or observed in: uterine inertia, uterine torsion, metritis, placentitis, death of the fetus, septic metritis of pregnancy, diffuse peritonitis due to traumatic gastritis, hydrops of the fetal membranes, a terminal condition in severe septic or toxic diseases, mummified fetus, in certain abortions, preparturient paresis, ketosis in ewes, and twin pregnancies in unipara. The history, evidence of uterine inertia, lack of uterine tone, evidence of a diseased fetal membrane or fetus, possible rupture of the fetal membranes and results of attempted treatment will aid in making a diagnosis.

A further condition resulting in a cervical stenosis is involution of the genital tract. In neglected cases of abortion or dystocia, characterized by a dead and usually emphysematous fetus, ruptured membranes, loss of fluid, and a dry birth canal, a stenosis of the cervix may be observed. It is seen after correction of uterine torsion, a breech presentation or other prolonged type of dystocia, especially one in which no part of the fetus enters the birth canal. As a result there is a contraction or involution of the cervix with the dead fetus still in the uterus. It may be difficult to differentiate this type from failure of the cervix to dilate when uterine disease results in uterine atony and death of the fetus.

The handling of these cases will depend on the cause of the cervical stenosis, the condition of the fetus and uterine contents, and the uterus. In rare cases due to cervical induration and sclerosis the prognosis is guarded and cesarean section is probably indicated if cervical dilation is slight. Dilation of the cervix by mechanical means such as the operator's hands and arms, instruments, a heavy rubber balloon inserted into the cervix and then inflated, or steady, moderate traction on the fetus, will result in success only occasionally and often the cervix is ruptured or severely lacerated in the process. Williams mentioned that incision of the cervix, vaginal hysterotomy might be tried through the dorsal and dorso-lateral portions of the cervix. Such an operation is of questionable value and is dangerous. In cases in which normal parturition is approaching or the animal is in the first stage of labor no treatment is indicated; often, however, veterinarians will give 25 mg. of stilbestrol and 5 cc. of pituitrin or oxytocin and wait for normal birth to occur. As described previously in Chapter VI, parturition in mares may be induced more physiologically by 30 to 50 units of oxytocin in saline given by an intravenous drip technique over a period of several hours.

In the type of case in which the cervix fails to dilate due to uterine inertia, diseased uteri, metabolic diseases, and others, the prognosis is guarded and a careful diagnosis should be made if possible. If sufficient time is available a large dose of stilbestrol, 50 to 100 mg. and/or 20 mg. of dexamethasone, Adams, administered intramuscularly, and repeated every other day if necessary, may aid relaxation of the cervix and initiation of parturition. Injections of oxytocin and calcium gluconate may improve the tonus of the uterus and aid or hasten cervical dilation. Massage of the cervix for one-half to one hour may promote relaxation. The use of drugs, such as atropine, sodium bicarbonate, and others applied to the cervix are probably of questionable or no value. Gradual traction on the fetus along with massage and stretching of the cervix of the cow may relax the partially dilated cervix sufficiently after one-half to one hour to remove the fetus. Strong, forced traction on the fetus is to be avoided, since it pulls the stenosed cervix caudally toward the vulva, narrowing its lumen. Strong traction may cause a transverse rupture of the uterine wall just cranial to the cervix. Occasionally, however, forced extraction, even though it produces a slight to moderate laceration of the cervix, is indicated over fetotomy or cesarean. To avoid a cesarean operation in incomplete cervical dilation in ewes, Perry and Malone recommended the eversion of the vagina and cervix by traction on the cervix. The dorsal wall of the vagina, cervix and portion of the body of the uterus is incised with scissors and the fetus removed. If the placenta is retained the uterus is everted and the placenta is removed. The incised tissues are sutured and the genital tract is replaced. Antibiotics should be given parenterally for several days. No anesthesia is required. The ewe should probably be culled after she has raised her lamb.

Good lubrication is essential. Fetotomy is very difficult because of the small diameter of the cervix. Cesarean section may be indicated especially if the fetus is alive and the uterus free of infection. In cases of parturient paresis occurring during parturition, an intravenous injection of 250 to 750 cc. of a 20 per cent solution of calcium gluconate usually results in parturition within 4 to 6 hours. In ketosis in ewes the fetuses are usually dead and the ewe will die unless the fetuses are aborted or removed promptly; cesarean section therefore may be necessary.

In neglected dystocia cases with cervical stenosis due to involution of the cervix, the prognosis is poor because the fetus is usually emphysematous. The uterus may already be ruptured or may easily be ruptured if forced extraction is applied. Fetotomy, moderate careful forced extraction with much lubrication, or cesarean section, may be attempted depending upon the conditions and the judgment of the operator. Following the correction of the dystocia, the aftercare of the animal is important, as septic metritis, retained placenta, perimetritis, necrotic vaginitis, metritis, and cervicitis are common. In the dog and cat cesarean section or hysterectomy are usually performed in cases where there are conditions associated with uterine inertia.

Dystocia due to Stenosis or Obstruction of the Vagina may be found in all species. It may be due to tumors such as fibromas, lymphomas or leiomyomas. In rare instances in the mare or cow dystocia may be due to compression of the vagina by a massive intrapelvic hematoma. This may develop during forced extraction or a fetotomy operation. In rare cases a pelvic abscess, excessive fat around the vagina, or possibly a perineal hernia may cause dystocia because of compression of the vagina. Williams (1968) reported a high incidence of fat necrosis in beef cattle grazing on heavily fertilized fescue pastures in northern Georgia. In some cattle the fat necrosis was extensive enough to cause a stenosis of the birth canal. In occasional instances a severe necrotic vaginitis may heal and the resulting scar tissue cause a marked stenosis of the vagina and dystocia at the next parturition. A persistent median wall of the Mullerian duct, usually found as a fibrous band from 0.5 to 2 inches in diameter just caudal to the cervix, may cause dystocia if the limbs of the fetus straddle this band. These conditions are seen most commonly in the cow. Some of these conditions may rarely occur in other animals. Either rearing the heifer under unfavorable conditions, or breeding the heifer at too young an age, may cause dystocia due to vaginal infantilism. Occasionally, however, in abortions or premature births in heifers, the normal relaxation of the birth canal does not occur and dystocia results, due in many instances to lack of normal dilation of the cervix and vulva rather than to underdevelopment of the vagina.

The handling of vaginal stenosis will vary with the cause. If a tumor is present it often can be repelled cranial and lateral to the pelvic inlet as the fetus is withdrawn. In dystocia due to a persistent wall of the Mullerian duct, the fibrous band can be located and cut with a knife or scissors as it passes over one of the shoulders or buttocks of the fetus. In mild cases of vaginal stenosis steady moderate traction on the fetus, together with good lubrication, will usually dilate the vagina and allow the fetus to be removed. Occasionally if excessive traction is applied, rupture of the vagina may occur with prolapse of fat or the bladder. In most severe cases of vaginal stenosis, obstruction, or compression, especially in multipara, cesarean section is the method of choice for relief of dystocia. Fetotomy is of very limited value because the small size of the vagina makes manipulations and operations very difficult and conducive to postpartum necrotic vaginitis.

Dystocia due to Stenosis or Constriction of the Vulva and Vestibule is occasionally seen in the heifer or mare and less commonly in the other animals. It is usually observed in heifers with genital hypoplasia due to improper growth of the heifer because of chronic disease or poor nutrition. Dystocia due to a small vulva may be observed sometimes in heifers that abort or calve prematurely before the vulva is properly relaxed. Rice and Wiltbank reported that 54.4 percent of dystocias in two-year-old Angus heifers was due to vulval stenosis. This incidence seems too high unless mild stenosis predominated. In exceptional instances it may be hereditary in nature or be secondary to extensive scarring from lacerations following previous parturitions or dystocias. In anterior presentation the nose and head, and in posterior presentation the thighs or stifles stall at the vulva or vestibule.

The treatment or handling of stenosis of the vulva is best performed by gradual, steady, moderate traction over a period of 1/4 to 2 hours, in order to dilate the vulva slowly. The use of lubrication is essential. Prolonged attempts to dilate the vulva, especially if care and lubrication are not used, may result in an extensive necrosis and cellulitis of the vulvar and vestibular tissues. Stretching the vulva by pulling it over the fetal head and pushing outward on the vulva from the inside with the hands and wrists, helps to dilate it. Moderate traction on the fetal head alone, with the feet released, will help draw the head through the vestibule and aid dilation because of the triangular- or wedge-shape of the fetal head. Patience is essential, since excessive or too-rapid traction will rupture the vulva, vestibule or perineum, causing laceration, severe hemorrhage or contusions. Excessive traction on the fetal jaw may fracture it. Excessive rotation of the fetal head should be avoided. Placing the hand over the poll and pulling the head ventrally and caudally and the vulva cranially and dorsally helps slide the dorsal commissure of the vulva over the top of the fetal head. Severe laceration of the vestibule and vulva rarely occurs, even in the mare, when parturition proceeds unassisted; but if traction is applied, even by one man, laceration may be severe because normal, gradual dilation was not permitted.

If the vulva and vestibule fail to dilate within a reasonable length of time or if haste is imperative, an episiotomy may be performed under epidural anesthesia or local infiltration of the incision sites, Friermuth. Episiotomy should not be performed when the birth canal or fetus is infected. With the vulva under tension an incision should be made on either side of the dorsal commissure in a dorso-lateral direction. This is done to prevent a recto-vaginal laceration or a "gill flirter" in the larger domestic animals, in which the dorsal commissure of the vulva is near the rectum. In multipara the vulva is a greater distance from the rectum and an episiotomy is made in a dorsal direction toward the rectum. After removal of the fetus the episiotomy incisions should be sutured together immediately with interrupted deep vertical mattress sutures of catgut and/or nylon and the animal injected with antibiotics for several days.

Fetotomy is not indicated in these cases for the same reasons as in vaginal or pelvic stenoses. In rare cases cesarean section may be the method of choice particularly in multiparous animals or if the live fetus is to be saved. Williams stated that gradual, moderate traction is the most satisfactory method, inasmuch as dilation of the vulva is necessary or advisable in order that the dam may give birth without assistance at subsequent pregnancies.

In mares in which the vulva has been sutured to prevent pneumovagina, this band of tissue should be cut just before or at parturition in order to prevent uneven or irregular tearing of the scar between the two vulvar lips. This thin band of tissue will not cause dystocia.

Dystocia Due to Uterine Inertia

For convenience in discussing this problem it will be divided into two parts: primary inertia and secondary inertia. Both are characterized by a weakness or absence of uterine contractions during the first or second stage of labor that usually persists into the third and involution stage after parturition.

Dystocia due to Primary Uterine Inertia is observed most frequently in the dog, cow—especially the older dairy cow—and sow. It is rare in the other species. It is produced by a lack of tone or failure of the uterine muscles to contract. The failure of the uterine muscles to contract normally at parturition may be due to a parimary failure of the muscles to respond to hormonal stimuli due to disease of the muscle; or it may be due to an actual lack or failure of release of hormones, such as estrogens and possibly oxytocin, that initiate uterine contractions in normal muscles. In dogs it is observed more frequently in certain small breeds such as the Dachshund.

In a few Cockers it may be associated with psychotic abnormalities and nervous voluntary inhibition of parturition due to pain. Freak reported that primary uterine inertia was common in infertile dogs with 3 or fewer fetuses. Lack of exercise, excessive fatness, debility, and senility are all causes of weakness of uterine contractions at parturition. Overdistension of the uterus in fetal giantism, hydrops of the fetal membranes, fetal anasarca, twins in unipara—especially unicornual twins—and an excessive number of fetuses in small dogs are other conditions conducive to primary uterine inertia. Undoubtedly uterine disease, or pathology associated with uterine infections and placentitis during gestation, also play a role in the production of uterine inertia. Apparent bovine uterine inertia is observed in parturient paresis due to a hypocalcemia. Benesch and Wright have described a type of primary uterine inertia in dogs, especially Chows, Retrievers, Bull Terriers and Spaniels, associated with a small litter, with slight or absent mammary development, and with no signs of parturition at the proper time. The fetuses apparently succumb and by 70 to 80 days after service a dark green viscid fluid escapes from the vulva. They believed this was probably due to a hormone disfunction.

The animals affected with primary uterine inertia are usually and obviously parturient and in the first stages of labor, as shown by relaxation of the soft structures of the pelvis, marked mammary development, and discharge of mucous from the vulva. The animals show no distress and eat and drink nearly normally but the second stage of labor does not occur for 6 to 36 hours or more, if at all. On examination, the cervix is usually relaxed and dilatable but the fetus and fetal membranes are not being forced into the cervix or birth passage. In some cases in cattle the cervix fails to dilate normally due to a lack of hormones or to a failure of the uterus to contract. What may be diagnosed as a failure of the cervix to dilate may in reality be a manifestation of a primary uterine inertia. One or both membranes may have ruptured. There is usually no abnormality in presentation, position, or posture of the fetus. The uterus apparently fails to contract normally, and consequently does not force its contents through the cervix and into the birth canal. Usually in 24 to 48 hours the second stage of labor may set in but in many cases by then the fetus is dead and occasionally infection of the fetal membranes and fetus is apparent. The prognosis is good in most cases that are diagnosed early.

In the cow or ewe this condition is rather easily handled if the cervix is relaxed by rupturing the membranes, correcting any abnormal posture, and removing the fetus by moderate or slight traction. In certain cases in the cow as well as in multiparous animals in which the condition is diagnosed early, intramuscular injections of pituitrin, 2 to 10 cc. (20 to 100 units) for large animals, or 1 to 2 cc. (10 to 20 units) for small animals, or oxytocin at a similar dosage may stimulate uterine contractions and normal birth of the young. Giving this injection in saline by an intravenous drip technique over a period of several hours may be a more physiologic procedure. Some authors have reported that **Lentin** 0.5 to 3 cc. may be a substitute, especially in swine, for posterior pituitary products. Others state that the intravenous injection of calcium gluconate, 500 cc. of a 20 per cent solution in cattle and 10 cc. of a 10 per cent solution in dogs, is of value in these cases, especially if calcium levels of the blood are low or if parturient paresis is present. In the dog, as well as other species, "feathering" the vagina by inserting a finger, and stroking the dorsal wall of the vagina, or in other similar ways stimulating the production of oxytocin by the animal's own pituitary may be helpful. If this treatment does not result in the initiation of normal parturition in 1 to 2 hours the treatment might be repeated. After 3 to 4 hours with no response, cesarean section is indicated and should be performed at once in the multiparous animals. If according to the history primary uterine inertia has existed for 4 to 6 hours before the veterinarian examines the case, cesarean section may be indicated at once rather than the use of the above techniques and waiting for uterine contractions to begin. In the condition described by Benesch and Wright when symptoms of normal parturition failed to occur at the proper time, cesarean section or hysterectomy was indicated. Hysterectomy may be preferred if any evidence of infection is present in the uterus of the dog or cat. Morphine, 1/8 to 1/2 grain, or tranquilizers may quiet nervous, psychotic Cockers sufficiently to permit normal parturition.

Since this inertia extends into the third stage of parturition and beyond, retained placenta, metritis, pyometra, and delayed involution of the uterus are common. Administration of posterior pituitary hormones immediately after removal of the fetuses, several injections of estrogens at 48- to 72-hour intervals, accompanied by intrauterine and parental antibiotic therapy, may help prevent septic metritis and other complications due to delayed involution of the uterus.

Secondary Uterine Inertia usually follows a prolonged dystocia and is characterized by exhaustion of the uterine muscle. This condition is seen in all species and is more common in large animals than is primary uterine inertia. In multiparous animals when prolonged labor or dystocia is relieved by removing the fetus causing the dystocia, it is quite common to find that secondary uterine inertia has occurred and consequently the rest of the fetuses are not expelled. This type of inertia can be prevented by correcting dystocias early. In certain breeds of dogs such as the Scotch Terrier or Dachshund secondary uterine inertia may occur spontaneously early in the second stage of parturition. Usually one or two fetuses are expelled normally and then labor ceases even though more fetuses are present in the uterus.

In cattle examined after prolonged dystocia the uterus is often contracted tightly around the fetus. In some cases this condition closely resembles the condition called retraction, Bandl's, or contraction ring dystocia, described in humans following prolonged dystocia, Pride. In retraction ring dystocia the uterine muscle just cranial to the cervix contracts tightly, so that normal expulsion of the fetus into the birth canal can not take place. A contraction ring may occur any place in the uterus and if it occurs around the fetus it can interfere with birth. These abnormal contractions of the uterine muscle are strong sustained tetanic contractions caused by exhaustion spasms of the muscle which are a fatigue phenomena. Diagnosis of this condition may be based on the history of prolonged dystocia; in multipara on the birth of one or two fetuses with a cessation of labor, or the removal of the fetus causing the dystocia, not followed by the normal resumption of parturition. In large animals intrauterine examination reveals the nature of the condition causing the dystocia—usually an abnormal position, posture, or presentation, and the contraction of the uterine walls upon the fetus. In some uteri in which contraction bands of rings are very strong and broad especially around or caudal to the fetus, this condition will complicate the primary cause for the dystocia. The prognosis in secondary uterine inertia is more guarded than in primary uterine inertia because the fetuses may be weak, dead, or emphysematous, and rupture of the uterus is more common Retained placenta and metritis are usual sequelae.

In the handling or correction of this type of dystocia in large animals the condition causing the original dystocia should be corrected by mutation if possible and the fetus then removed by moderate, careful traction. Lubrication of the fetus and birth canal is usually necessary. Excessive traction should be avoided if strong contraction or retraction rings are present in the uterus and definitely retard removal of the fetus, since transverse rupture of the uterus may occur. This is a highly important reason for examining the uterus carefully in prolonged dystocia cases as occasionally ruptures occur spontaneously or due to previously-applied traction. If contraction rings are not too strong, careful, slow, cautious mutation and traction may be successful in relieving the dystocia. If they are severe and markedly reduce the lumen or diameter of the uterus it may be necessary to resort to fetotomy or cesarean section to relieve the condition. Since infection of the uterus is usually present, the ventral abdominal approach for the cesarean operation is indicated. In humans these contraction or retraction rings may be relaxed by intravenous administration of adrenalin and by general anesthesia; if this fails, a cesarean is necessary. The author in a limited number of bovine cases has had little success using adrenalin. Epidural anesthesia is not effective in relaxing the uterine muscle. In dogs, mild narcosis or anesthesia with morphine may be helpful. This marked contraction of the uterine wall in prolonged gestation is another reason for being very careful not to rupture the uterus by repelling the fetus in an attempt to gain room for mutation operations.

In the sow it is common practice, when several pigs have been expelled before dystocia occurred, to remove by traction the one causing dystocia, lubricate the birth canal, and give 2 to 5 cc. of posterior pituitary hormone, 1 to 2 cc. of oxytocin, or 2 to 3 cc. of **Lentin.** If the rest of the litter is not expelled in 2 to 3 hours, another pig may be removed by traction and the injection repeated; or cesarean section may be decided upon as the method of choice. This decision should not be delayed too long. In dogs the situation is similar to that in sows, in that the handling of the case will depend upon the duration of labor, the number and condition of the fetuses, and the degree of uterine infection. Early cases in dogs may be handled in the same manner as in sows except that **Lentin** should not be used. If the dog appears exhausted but the fetuses are in good condition, 1/4 grain of morphine will relax the bitch and possibly the uterus and after one to two hours rest strong uterine contractions will commence again and whelping continue. In this condition of secondary uterine inertia, helping the bitch with forceps may be indicated if only one or two fetuses remain in the uterus. If, however, there are 3 or more fetuses and dystocia has been prolonged, cesarean section is indicated. If the fetuses are dead and infected, hysterectomy may be desirable. Sheppard reported that cats are quite resistant to infection. Pituitrin usually will reinitiate labor even after dystocia of 48 hours' duration. As in primary inertia, retained placenta, septic metritis, delayed involution, and pyometra are common, following secondary uterine inertia.

Dystocia Due to Postmortem Changes in the Fetus

These dystocias may be caused by mummification of the fetus in cattle, and by fetal emphysema and fetal maceration in all species.

Dystocia due to Fetal Mummification in cattle was described in Chapter 5. In some instances mummified fetuses may macerate. This is probably secondary to a relaxation of the cervix at the time of an unobserved, spontaneous, but incomplete abortion. Organisms entered the previously sterile uterus and start the maceration process. Hematogenous uterine infection may possibly occur.

Dystocia due to Fetal Emphysema is observed in all species and is usually associated with a prolonged dystocia of 24 to 48 hours' duration. The fetus dies and organisms from the vagina invade the uterus and cause rapid emphysema. Fetal emphysema may complicate dystocia in incomplete abortions after the fourth month of pregnancy when the dead fetus is retained in the uterus (see Chapter 5). Although fetal emphysema usually occurs with the cervix open it may occur with a closed cervix in rare conditions such as a septic metritis of pregnancy in which the fetus dies, becomes emphysematous, and may even macerate before the cervix opens Such a condition occurring late in pregnancy especially in a heifer with a small, underdeveloped, or unrelaxed genital tract may result in a serious and often fatal termination Fetal emphysema is also observed in cases of neglected torsion of the uterus in which the fetus dies. It is commonly seen in rotated bicornual pregnancies in mares. In any type of condition causing uterine inertia, fetal death and emphysema may result if treatment is not given promptly. In bovine twin pregnancy one twin may be expelled and the other remain in the uterus and become emphysematous or macerate. This is more commonly seen in unicornual twins. Dystocia due to any condition causing the death of the fetus may result in fetal emphysema if the fetus is not removed promptly. In dogs and sows fetal emphysema may occur in prolonged dystocia in a manner similar to that in other animals. It is also observed in the large breeds of dogs such as Great Danes, Afghans, Boxers, Newfoundlands, and St. Bernards. In these dogs birth proceeds normally until the last fetus, Benesch and Wright. This remains in the uterus and goes undetected for one to two days; by this time the dog shows a fever of 103°, there is a green, black, fetid discharge from the vulva, the dog manifests no interest in the live pups, and exhibits symptoms of depression and toxemia. In these breeds a careful examination should be made for the last pup, if necessary by radiographs of the bitch, since usually this last fetus cannot be palpated through the abdominal wall or felt by forceps through the birth canal.

Fetal emphysema can usually be suspected if dystocia has existed 24 hours or more. The animal is usually depressed, toxic, and shows anorexia. Labor is usually weak and intermittent. The temperature is frequently elevated early but may be normal or subnormal late in the condition or at the time the veterinarian is summoned. This is especially true in the cow. The heart and respiratory rate are elevated. The extremities are cold and the feces may be loose and fetid. Often a fetid, watery, reddish vaginal discharge is observed. The mucous membranes of the genital tract are dry, swollen, and inflamed. In some cases the cervix may be partly involuted or contracted. The uterine walls are contracted closely about the fetus. The fetus is dead and swollen because of gas, that can be felt as it crepitates beneath the skin. In early cases of fetal emphysema only that portion of the fetus nearest the vulva may be emphysematous, but in prolonged dystocia cases the entire fetus is involved. In some cases of twins, the twin nearer the cervix may be emphysematous and the deeper twin may be normal. The fetal hair may be beginning to shed. Fetal meconium is often present on the fetus. The corneas of the eyes are grey; and the teeth usually loose. Rupture of the uterus may be present or be easily produced by traction due to the dry fetus and the tense, contracted uterine walls. Examination is likely to result in violent straining. The prognosis is always guarded to poor as uterine disease, septic metritis, and retained placenta usually follow this condition. The future breeding life of the dam is in doubt. Complications such as rupture of the uterus are likely to arise in the handling of dystocia due to fetal emphysema, making the prognosis guarded to grave.

The least difficult and the best method of correction of fetal emphysema in large animals is forced extraction after mutation, if the latter is necessary. Care should be used in repelling the fetus and in exerting traction of the fetus, so that rupture of the uterus or cervix does not occur. Lubrication of the birth canal and fetus is essential. In dogs forced extraction is probably not indicated unless only the one fetus is present or is wedged in the birth canal so that it would have to be removed by traction before a hysterotomy or hysterectomy is performed. In some cases such a fetus may be pulled apart and a portion may drop back into the uterus and become difficult to remove by forceps because of the danger of injuring the uterus. Occasionally in large animals fetotomy may be necessary. Extensive mutilation of the fetus and its evisceration greatly reduce the size of the fetus by releasing the gases present. The fetal tissues are soft and friable due to the emphysema and operations are performed with greater ease and speed than in normal fetuses. Frequent lubrication is essential to prevent trauma to the birth canal. Necrotic vaginitis or vulvitis or even metritis are likely to follow removal of an emphysematous fetus. In large animals cesarean section is indicated when the birth canal is involuting and is small, swollen, and dry, and when the uterine wall closely invests a greatly swollen and emphysematous fetus. If the cow's life is to be saved a cesarean may be a last resort if fetotomy is not feasible or possible. A total fetotomy on an emphysematous fetus is more exhausting and dangerous for the cow and operator than is a cesarean section. The prognosis should be guarded and the operation performed on the ventral abdominal wall so that contamination of the abdominal cavity can be avoided. In removing emphysematous fetuses in uniparous animals care should be taken not to leave a hoof in the uterus that might remain and act as a chronic foreign body, producing chronic pyometra. In the dog and other multiparous animals cesarean section may be indicated. Many veterinarians prefer to perform a hysterectomy in dogs and cats in order to prevent possible contamination of the abdominal cavity. In these cases care should be taken to prevent shock and to be certain a fetus is not left in the birth canal.

The aftercare of cases of dystocia due to fetal emphysema should consist of antibiotics parenterally and into the uterus, and injections of stilbestrol and ergotamine to stimulate uterine contractions, an increased blood supply to the uterus, and to hasten the overcoming of infection. Other supportive therapy such as blood, saline, and glucose may be given, inasmuch as septic metritis and retained placenta are common sequelae to the removal of an emphysematous fetus.

Fetal Maceration as a Cause of Dystocia in incomplete abortions was discussed in Chapter 5. It may develop in all species during pregnancy, as a sequelae to abortion or mummified fetuses that were not expelled when the cervix dilated. In rare cases this condition may be observed following undiagnosed and untreated torsions of the uterus during pregnancy or at term. In all animals the uterus or a twisted segment of it containing the macerating fetuses may be walled off in the abdominal cavity; or if the uterus ruptures and the fetuses escape into the abdomen, they may become walled off there and macerate. In rare cases some fetuses may slough to the outside or into the alimentary tract. In uniparous animals uterine torsion can cause fetal death and maceration with adhesions between the uterus and the other abdominal viscera. Fetal maceration is often observed in animals at term when a dystocia has been overlooked or neglected for 3 to 10 days.

The symptoms are usually limited to a persistent, fetid, vaginal or vulvar discharge often containing hair, hooves, or bones. The cervix is usually partially dilated and the fetus is in an advanced stage of emphysema, maceration and decomposition and pulls apart when handled. In chronic cases the cervix is only slightly open, and the animal fails to show estrus. On rectal examination fetal bones can be felt to crepitate within the uterus. In some cases a perimetritis may be present. In undiagnosed or untreated dystocias a history of constant but intermittent straining, generally considered by the owner as due to retention of the placenta, is noted, as is also a fetid, purulent discharge. The lack of general symptoms shown in some of these cases is amazing. The author observed a 7-year-old cow with macerating twins in the uterus. The owner believed the cow had calved 7 days before on pasture, although he had found no calf. The cow was eating normally and milking 30 lbs. a day. The fetuses were pulled apart in removal through the cervix, which was about 5 inches in diameter. The uterine wall was about one to two inches thick. Recovery was uneventful. A number of similar cases have been described in mares that subsequently concieved following the removal of the macerating fetus, Milne and Horney. The fact that other veterinarians have similar experiences suggests that in extremely difficult dystocia cases it might be advisable to try only supportive treatment, antibiotics, and estrogens, for 4 to 6 days, until the fetus has macerated sufficiently to be removed easily. During this same period the uterine wall builds up its natural defenses against infection. The only danger might be uterine rupture due to fetal emphysema before the inception of maceration. In multipara fetal maceration is diagnosed by the fetid, green-black discharge from the vulva, symptoms of septicemia, and palpation or radiographic diagnosis of the macerating fetus or fetuses. In certain cases exploratory laparotomy may be advisable. The prognosis in these cases, occurring more than three days to a week following dystocia, is guarded. In the more chronic cases, with the cervix nearly completely closed the prognosis is very poor.

When these cases in large animals occur after dystocia they are handled in a manner similar to that of treating emphysematous fetuses. In the more chronic bovine cases the cervix cannot be dilated manually. Estrogens are usually ineffective in evacuating the uterus, as the bones are more or less imbedded or caught in the endometrium. Laparo-hysterotomy or hysterectomy in the cow is very difficult in chronic cases with only fetal bones and pus in the uterus because the uterus is so small it is difficult to bring to the abdominal incision even if no adhesions were present. The prognosis as far as the future breeding life is concerned is very poor. Since most of these animals are in fair to good health, slaughter is usually advised. In multipara, especially dogs, hysterectomy is advised in most cases.

After handling cases of fetal emphysema or maceration in large animals, especially if fetotomy was performed, the operator should be careful to cleanse and disinfect his arms and instruments carefully, and then boil the instruments. This is done to avoid a severe infection on the arms or the introduction of infection into the next cow through the use of the contaminated instruments. Aftercare of cases of fetal maceration in which the fetuses were removed is similar to that following fetal emphysema.

References

Adams, Wm. M. (1969) The Elective Induction of Labor and Parturition in Cattle, J.A.V.M.A. **154,** 3, 261.

Arthur, G. H. (1964) Wright's Veterinary Obstetrics, 3rd. Ed., Williams and Wilkins Co., Baltimore, Md.

Arthur, G. H. (1966) Recent Advances in Bovine Obstetrics, Vet. Rec. **79,** 22, 630.

Benesch, F. (1952) Lehrbuch der Tierartzlichen Geburtshilfe und Gynakologie, Urban and Schwartzenberg, Wien-Innsbruch, Austria.

Benesch, F. and Wright, J. G. (1951) Veterinary Obstetrics, Williams and Wilkins Co., Baltimore, Md.

Craig, J. G. (1918) Fleming's Veterinary Obstetrics, 3rd Ed., Alex. Eger Co., Chicago, Ill.

DeLange, M. (1961) Prolonged Gestation in Karakul Ewes in South West Africa, 4th Internat. Congr. on An. Reprod., Netherlands, Vol. III, 590.

DeMott, A. R. and Roberts, S. J. (1945) A Simple Instrument for the Relief of Dystocia in the Bovine due to Uterine Torsion, Cor. Vet., **35,** 4, 333.

Derivaux, J. and Dewalque, J. (1963) Notes on Equine Obstetrics, Annales De Medecine Veterinaire, **107,** 4, 236.

Freak, M. J. (1962) Abnormal Conditions Associated with Pregnancy and Parturition in the Bitch, Vet. Rec. **74,** 1323.

Friermuth, G. J. (1948) Episiotomy in Veterinary Obstetrics, J.A.V.M.A. **113,** 231.

Hilton, G. B. (1967) An Oversize Lamb, Vet. Rec. **80,** 10, 336.

Holm, J. W. (1967) Prolonged Pregnancy, Advances in Vet. Sci. Vol II, Academic Press Inc., N.Y.C., 159.

Huston, K. and Gier, H. T. (1958) An Anatomical Description of a Hydrocephalic Calf from Prolonged Gestation and the Possible Relationships of these Conditions, Cor. Vet. **48,** 1, 45.

Jasper, D. E. (1950) Prolonged Gestation in the Bovine, Cor. Vet., **40,** 2, 165.

Kennedy, P. C., Kendrick, J. W. and Stormont, C. (1957) Adenohypophyseal Aplasia, an Inherited Defect Associated with Abnormal Gestation in Guernsey Cattle, Cor. Vet. **47,** 1, 160.

Malone, P. H. (1957) Ovine Obstetrics, New Zealand Vet. J. **5,** 114

McEntee, K. (1969) Personal Communication.

McEntee, K., Roberts, S. J. and Sears, R. M. (1952) Prolonged Gestation in Two Guernsey Cows, Cor. Vet., **42,** 3, 355.

Mead, S. W., Gregory, P. W. and Regan, W. M. (1949) Prolonged Gestation of Genetic Origin in Cattle, J. of Dairy Sci. **32,** 8, 705.

Milne, F. J. and Horney, F. D. (1960) Abdominal Surgery in the Horse, Canad. Vet. Jour. **1,** 12, 524.

Penny, R. H. C. (1958) An Alternative to Cesarean Section in Incomplete Cervical Dilation of Sheep, Vet. Rec. **70,** 431.

Pride, W. T. (1938) Retraction Ring Dystocia—Its Cause and Correction, Surgery, Gynec., and Obstet., **66,** 1047.

Rice, L. E. and Wiltbank, J. N. (1970) Dystocia in Beef Heifers, J. An. Sci. **30,** 6, 1043.

Richter, J. and Gotze, R. (1960) Tiergeburtshilfe, 2nd Ed., Paul Parey, Berlin and Hamburg, Germany.

Roberts, S. J. (1955) Unpublished data.

Sheppard, M. (1951) Some Observations on Cat Practice, Vet. Rec., **63;** 44, 685.

Vandevelde, A., Vandenberghe, J., Vandeplassche, M. and Paredis, F. (1952) Het Gebruik van Stilbestrol bij het Verwekken van Abortus en bij het Inleiden wan de Partus bij Overdracht van Runderen, Vlaams Diergeneesk. Tijdschr., **21,** 5, 93.

Vandeplassche, M. (1957–1958) The Normal and Abnormal Presentation Position and Posture of the Foal-Fetus during Gestation and at Parturition, Dept. of An. Obstet. and Reprod., State Univ., Ghent, Belgium.

Vandeplassche, M., Paredis, F. and Bouters, R. (1962) Technics, Results and Indications For Cesarean Section in the Horse and In Comparison with Fetotomy, Wien. Tierartzliche Monatsschr. **49,** 1, 48.

Williams, J. (1968) Personal Communication.

Wensvoort, P. (1956) Two Cases of Torsion of the Uterus in the Sow, Tijdschr. v. Diergeneesk. **15,** 711.

Williams, W. L. (1931) Studies in Teratology, Cor. Vet., **21,** 1, 25.

Williams, W. L. (1943) Veterinary Obstetrics, 4th Ed., Miss Louella Williams, Upland Rd., Ithaca, N.Y.

Wilson, A. L. and Young, G. B. (1958) Prolonged Gestation in An Ayrshire Herd, Vet. Rec. **70,** 4, 73.

Chapter XI

INJURIES AND DISEASES OF THE PUERPERAL PERIOD

The injuries and diseases of the puerperal period discussed in this chapter include puerperal infections and metabolic diseases as well as hemorrhages, lacerations, contusions, ruptures, and prolapses of various organs, especially the genital organs that may occur during or following parturition. A summary of the causes of postparturient paraplegia is included.

Postpartum Hemorrhages

Hemorrhage or bleeding into the uterus or birth canal may occur postpartum due to trauma, lacerations, or rupture of the genital organs. Hemorrhage into the uterus may be due to bleeding from an incised or torn caruncle or caruncular stalk in the cow or ewe, from the incised or lacerated endometrium in the mare, or from premature removal of the fetal membranes or placenta. This accident may occur at the time of parturition, during a cesarean section or fetotomy, or may take place later due to improper or too early removal of a retained placenta in any uniparous animal. Williams described severe intrauterine hemorrhage in rare cases occurring from several hours to a day or so after calving and dropping of the placenta, that resulted in a massive blood clot filling the gravid horn of the uterus. Rarely death may occur. Slight bleeding may be observed, from the ruptured end of the umbilical cord or from slight lacerations of the uterus, cervix, vagina, or vulva. A hemorrhagic discharge from the vulva in a bitch was due to an invagination of a portion of one horn not visible externally, McMullen et al.. In severe lacerations or rupture—particularly of the cervix, vagina, and in rare instances, the vulva—hemorrhage may be profuse due to a rupture of a large vessel. Blood may flow in a stream from the vulva as soon as the fetus is removed. Most of these lacerations and injuries follow forced extraction. Intraperitoneal or intrapelvic hemorrhage may occur and if severe enough produce acute symptoms of anemia and rarely death, especially in the mare. This is ordinarily seen in cases of dystocia, rupture of the uterus and uterine vessels before, during, or after correction of torsion of the uterus, in prolapse of the uterus, and in trauma especially in fetotomy operations or forced extraction in young heifers. These hemorrhagic conditions would be greatly aggravated in cattle fed sweet clover.

In the treatment or handling of these conditions the usual surgical procedures to control the hemorrhage and supportive treatment are indicated. Most cases of slight bleeding from the genital tract at parturition are not serious and require no treatment. In more severe bleeding from the uterus of large animals posterior pituitary hormone or oxytocin, 20 to 50 units, may help control hemorrhage by contracting the uterus and its vessels. Injecting 500 cc. of saline to which 10 cc. of formalin has been added, or 500 cc. of calcium gluconate may also aid in hastening the clotting of blood, and thus control the hemorrhage. If bleeding occurs from a large vessel through a laceration in the vaginal wall, the vessel may be clamped by forceps. These should be left in place for 24 to 48 hours, or the vessel should be ligated. In severe intrauterine hemorrhage the clot should be left for 24 hours and then may be broken down manually the next 2 or 3 days until entirely removed. According to Williams, douching with saline through a horse catheter is very helpful in washing out the clot. If the clot should not be discovered for several weeks or months the uterus would probably break it down and absorb it, in the same manner as other tissues. Injections of estrogens as in cases of mummification of the fetus may aid the expulsion and absorption of the clotted blood. Intrapelvic or perivaginal bleeding may cause a stenosis of the vagina during or after forced extraction or fetotomy but neither it nor the intrauterine hemorrhage is usually fatal. In 12- to 21-year-old mares rupture of the uterine vessels and sudden death due to hemorrhagic shock may occur before, during or after an apparently normal gestation and parturition. The middle uterine artery was most commonly involved but the iliac or utero-ovarian arteries occasionally were affected. Prepartum rupture occurred most often in the latter vessel, Rooney. Most fatal hemorrhages occur intra-peritoneally due to rupture of the large vessels in the broad ligament caused by degenerative changes in the vessel wall, especially in horses, or by torsion of the uterus or prolapse of the uterus. Definite symptoms of severe hemorrhage may be observed, indicated by weakness, depression, very rapid pulse and respiration rates, and pale mucous membranes. If the operator promptly enters the peritoneal cavity through the abdominal wall in the flank region or through the uterine wall in prolapse, he may be able to control bleeding by ligating the ruptured vessels. The prognosis is very poor in these cases as severe hemorrhage, shock, and death may occur in rapid succession. In mares early signs of colic, sweating, pain, rapid pulse rate and moderate anemia may occur due to rupture of a uterine vessel with relatively slow loss of blood between the two layers of the broad ligament causing a large hematoma. If this ruptures intraperitoneally then severe acute signs of shock, rapid weak pulse, anemia, prostration and death follow. If hemorrhage is severe enough to cause clinical symptoms, blood transfusions of 2000 to 8000 cc. or more in large animals, saline injections, gelatin or other types of solutions designed to maintain blood pressure should be given, and repeated as often as necessary. Excessive fluids should be avoided. The mare should be sedated with a large dose of a tranquilizer and closely confined. In lacerations or ruptures of the genital tract preventive treatments to control infection should be used, such as the administration of sulfonamides, antibiotics, or local mild antiseptics. Thrombosis of the larger uterine arteries and veins is occasionally observed or described in animals, Richter and Gotze. Thrombi are seen most often in the veins following prolapse of the uterus or uterine torsion when circulation has been restricted. Occasionally an aneurism of the middle uterine artery may be palpated on rectal examination after parturition in the cow, or a hematoma in the broad ligament of the mare. Adhesions between the genital tract and ovaries and other pelvic and abdominal organs and tissues may occur following postpartum hemorrhage.

Subinvolution of the placental sites formerly called "persistent decidual reaction" and occasionally mistakenly called uterine chorioepithelioma is observed infrequently especially in younger bitches and is characterized by a persistent discharge of red blood from the vulva for 30 to 60 or more days after whelping, Beck and McEntee. This condition causes localized areas of enlargement of the uterine horn at the former placental sites due to the presence of eosinophilic masses of stromal cells. Subinvolution of the placental sites should be differentiated from cystitis, uterine or ovarian tumors, acute or chronic metritis, and cystic endometrial hyperplasia. Berger reported this condition as occurring in Alaskan Malamutes and in some cases causing a decline in the hematocrit. The bloody discharge was nonfetid and it ceased about two weeks before true estrum. Conception occurred normally. Because of the presence of corpora lutea, Beck and McEntee recommended ovariohysterectomy to avoid possible uterine infection and erosion of the very thin-walled placental sites that might cause secondary, peritonitis. Laparohysterotomy with curettage of the affected endoemtrium was suggested for valuable breeding bitches.

Lacerations and Contusions of the Birth Canal and Adjacent Structures

After each dystocia operation the operator should carefully examine the uterus and genital canal for evidence of contusions and lacerations. Minor lacerations and trauma are common especially to the vulva and cervix in uniparous animals after forced extraction and fetotomy. Since the vagina is freely dilatable it is less often injured. Minor lacerations are of little importance and usually heal promptly without treatment. Although the more severe lacerations of the cervix in cattle seldom result in rupture, a few veterinarians recommend that these be immediately sutured through the vagina to prevent the healed cervix from gaping or being ectropic, and to prevent the formation of excessive connective tissue in the cervix. Mild lacerations of the endometrium heal promptly. These may be aided to heal by the injection of pituitrin or oxytocin and estrogens which hasten involution. Vaginal lacerations generally occur near the vulva-vaginal border. Lacerations of the vulva are usually mild when parturition is physiological. Occasionally the mare, especially if sutured by the Caslick operation, will tear the vulva in a normal parturition. In the mare and cow vulvar lacerations are quite common when strong traction is applied too rapidly to permit normal dilation of the vulva. Mild lacerations need not be sutured. Deep lacerations or episiotomy incisions should be promptly sutured with deep vertical mattress nylon or catgut sutures after parturition to prevent gaping and scarring of the vulva and thereby predisposing to vulvitis and vaginitis. Parenteral antibiotics should be administered. Certain mares and cows with relaxed, flaccid, tipped or horizontal vulvas should have the dorsal half or two-thirds of the commissure sutured as described under the Caslick or vulva-suturing operation. Lacerations, if not sutured, commonly become infected especially if the tissue is traumatized or devitalized or if metritis and retention of the fetal membranes are present. Infected lacerations of the vulva result in pain, swelling, and persistent straining or "wind sucking"—conditions which are particularly undesirable in the postpartum cow or mare. Recommended treatment consists of parenteral antibiotics and local treatment of lacerations by suturing early, or application of protective mild antibiotic dressings. Tetanus antitoxin should be administered in the mare.

Hematomas and Contusions of the Vagina or the Vulva are occasionally noted in all animals but most commonly in the mare and sow. They may be confused with or mistaken for tumors or prolapse of the vagina or bladder. Hematomas involving the vaginal wall are found on examination of the genital tract. In rare instances they may be observed protruding between the vulvar lips. Hematomas of the vulva are readily noted. If left alone they are usually absorbed within 1 to 3 weeks. In some cases they may rupture through the mucous membrane or the owner of the animal may request that they be removed; this can be done by incising, removing the clot and carefully suturing to control further bleeding and to obliterate the area that contained the large blood clot. This should not be performed until after 3 to 4 days following parturition. In occasional cases diagnosed early, ice packs or cold water spray might be indicated. Contusions of the vulva, vagina, and cervix resulting in swelling and edema, occur most frequently due to trauma during fetotomy operations or from external injuries. Occasionally a blow or a kick in the region of the clitoris will result in marked edema of the clitoris and vulva. In most cases these swellings subside fairly promptly and should not be confused with edema from the udder that may extend upward and involve the vulva. If edema is severe, cold and hot applications, massage, and in certain cases small punctures or incisions through the mucous membrane may release the fluid or reduce the swelling of the vulva.

Contusions of the Maternal Pelvic Structures by the fetus or by instruments used during fetotomy may result in intrapelvic hematomas and hemorrhages, or may cause obturator or gluteal paralysis by injury to those nerves at parturition. **Gluteal paralysis** is rare and is described only in the mare; it is brought about by contusions caused by a bony prominence on the fetus pressing on the gluteal nerve as it passes over the bony portion of the lumbo-sacral articulation or ileum. This may be a bilateral or unilateral injury and usually occurs in mares that apparently give birth without difficulty. In this condition the mare will show some difficulty in rising and may require assistance in rising if the injury is bilateral. The gait is characterized by a definite lameness and weakness of the affected limb. After a few days to a week, a marked atrophy of the gluteal muscles on the affected side is very noticeable. After a few weeks the lameness or paralysis of the limb becomes less observable but it may take 6 to 18 months for complete recovery. The prognosis is favorable. Treatment consists of good nursing. The mare should be in a large, well-bedded box stall with good footing. In some cases slings or assistance in rising may be necessary for several days or a week. Affected mares should not be allowed to struggle or exert themselves in rising. External applications, massage, or other treatments are of no value.

Obturator Paralysis may occur in the mare or cow but is most common in the latter. It is much more prevalent in heifers than in cows. Injury to the obturator nerve is observed so often in hip lock in the anterior presentation that before this type of dystocia is relieved obturator paralysis should always be suspected. An examination is done to inform the owner of the paralysis before the obstetrical operation so that later the veterinarian will not be blamed for the injury. The condition may affect one or both rear limbs. If the cow is down and laboring with a hip lock condition, the underneath leg and nerve is the one most commonly and severely affected. This contusion is usually caused by the bony tuberosities of the fetal hips, especially the greater trochanters, rubbing on the obturator nerve as the nerve either passes over the bony prominence of the lumbo-sacral articulation, or much more commonly as it passes down the shaft of the ilium before it enters the obturator foramen. Obturator paralysis in heifers is very common in the hip lock condition that has existed for several hours. Yet when strong forced extraction has to be applied manually or with the fetal extractor to draw a large fetus through a heifer's pelvis, obturator paralysis seldom occurs. Injury to the obturator nerve causes a paralysis of the medial, or adductor, muscles of the thigh, namely, the obturator externus, pectineus, adductor, and gracilis. If the condition is unilateral the cow can stand on the unaffected limb and as it walks the affected limb is moved stiffly forward and is abducted so the foot is placed on the ground 6 to 10 inches lateral from the normal position. The cow is unsteady and is likely to slip and fall. If both obturator nerves are contused and injured, both limbs are stiffly extended and abducted and the cow usually is unable to rise. If assisted to its feet and the hind limbs held together, the animal can stand but when it takes a step the limb is abducted and it falls to the ground.

If paralysis is severe and bilateral the prognosis should be guarded. If the paralysis is mild and the animal can walk, even though with difficulty, the prognosis is good. In most cases the condition improves rapidly and in 2 to 7 days the animal is able to walk quite well. Other cases may take longer for recovery, even up to 4 to 8 weeks. In rare cases the damage to the obturator nerve may be severe and permanent. The chances for recovery after 2 to 3 weeks are poor, and slaughter may be recommended. The only treatments of any value are good nursing and tying the animal's feet together in order to prevent excessive abduction and possible complications of a dislocated hip or fractured pelvis. The use of straps such as hame straps around the pasterns tied with a 14- to 20-inch length of rope or chain aids in preventing abduction of the limbs and helps the animal to rise. Some veterinarians strap or tie the hocks together but it is difficult to fasten straps or ropes above the hocks tightly enough so that they do not slide down, and yet loosely enough to allow movement of the gastrocnemius tendon. In the mare and occasionally in the cow the use of slings may be of value in assisting the animal to rise to its feet and supporting it for a short period. The animal should be kept in a well-bedded large box stall or pen, preferably with a dirt floor. Under such conditions dairy cattle should be milked by rolling the cow first to one side and then to the other.

Peroneal paralysis due to injury or trauma to the peroneal nerve as it passes over the dorsolateral condyle of the tibia and fibula is observed in cattle confined in stanchions with their rear parts over the edge of the gutter. It occurs most often in cows with dystocia and milk fever that struggle to rise. (See Figure 94) Injury to the peroneal or fibular nerve results in anesthesia of the cranial surface of the fetlock and metatarsus and paralysis of the muscles that extend the digit and flex the hock, namely the long and lateral digital extensors, the peroneus tertius and the anterior tibial muscles. This results in knuckling of the fetlock and dropping of the hock and difficulty in rising, standing and walking, Keown. As with injury to the obturator nerve good nursing care and close confinement are essential. A rigid supporting bandage to the lower leg may prevent knuckling of the fetlock. Peroneal paralysis should be differentiated from rupture of the gastrocnemius muscle and posterior paresis due to lesions in the spinal cord. Rarely other paralyses may be observed following dystocia or injury at the time of parturition including brachial or radial nerve paralysis in stanchioned cattle in which the forelimb was caught in the manger and forcefully extended. These miscellaneous nerve paralysis have been well-demonstrated by Worthman.

Rupture of the gastrocnemius muscle is apparently secondary to Zenker's degeneration of the muscle and usually follows considerable struggling or efforts to rise during dystocia or milk fever. (See Figure 95) The author observed one case that followed epidural anesthesia to relieve tenesmus due to a vulvar laceration. Zenker's degeneration may be due to excessive muscular activity especially in cows that have been confined for long periods and provided very limited exercise. Furthermore it is seen more often in states where selenium is known to be deficient, Schnautz. Phillips reported 11 cases of rupture of the gastrocnemius muscle in 3 high-producing herds in one year in his practice area in south-central New York State where selenium is deficient. The condition may be diagnosed by the inability to support weight on the affected leg, the flaccid gastrocnemius tendon and the swelling due to edema and hemorrhage in the region of the gastrocnemius muscle. Mild cases that can stand may recover in several weeks if they are confined and possibly a support such as a metal brace or Thomas splint provided. In most advanced cases slaughter is indicated. Possible prophylactic injections of selenium may be indicated in selenium deficient areas.

Rupture of the Uterus, Cervix, Vagina, and Perineum

Uterine or Vaginal Rupture may occur in any species, Steiner, Allen, O'Neill, Grunert and Geyer, Snoeck, and Vandeplassche, and may be due to prolonged dystocia with fetal emphysema; torsion of the uterus, in which transverse rupture may occur in prolonged cases; to improper manipulations and traction on the fetus; to fatigue of the operator, or to an accident in fetotomy operations in large animals or to forceps removal of a fetus in dogs; to protruding bones of the fetus after fetotomy; or due to inexpert manipulations of the fetus by laymen. For this latter reason and others associated with prolonged dystocia, the uterus and vagina should be carefully examined prior to any obstetrical operation to be certain that a rupture of the uterus, cervix, or vagina is not present. Rupture produced by the operating veterinarian even if due to his fatigue is extremely embarrassing and should be avoided if possible. In the birth of fetuses with long extremities, such as the mare, vaginal rupture may be due to improper presentations, positions, and postures, especially in dorso-pubic positions, anterior longitudinal presentations with the hind limbs extended beneath the body, transverse ventral presentations, and when the forefoot or feet are crossed over the neck. This latter presentation may result in rupture of the vagina, rectum and perineum. (See Figure 96) Rupture of the uterus is common in the mare in rotated bicornual pregnancy if traction is applied. Forced extraction of a bovine fetus in a normal presentation may cause rupture of the uterus, cervix, or vagina by forcing these structures against a sharp bony prominence occasionally found on the cranial portion of the pubic symphysis; or transverse rupture of the uterus may be caused by retraction or contraction rings of the uterine wall; or rupture of the cervix if the cervix is poorly dilated; rupture of the vagina may occur if perivaginal fat is pushed caudally as the fetus is forcibly drawn toward the vulva. In this latter instance the vaginal wall near the hymenal ring or vestibular-vaginal border ruptures to allow the escape of the fat. A similar tear or rupture of the vagina occasionally results

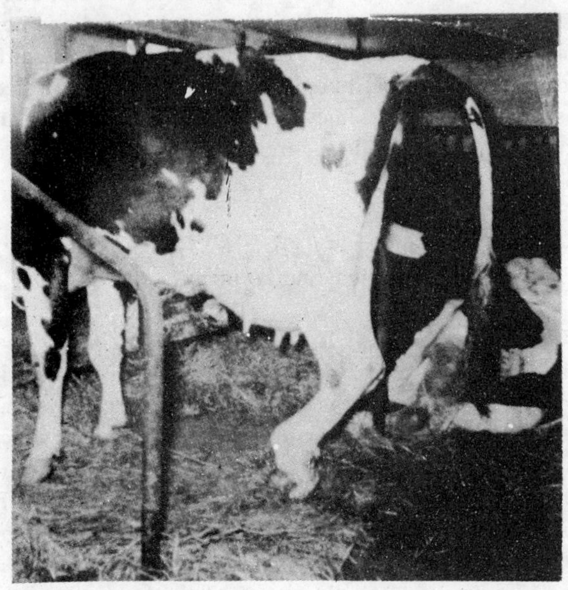

Figure 94. Bilateral peroneal nerve injury and paralysis in a cow.

Figure 95. Unilateral rupture of the gastrocnemius muscle in a cow during postparturient paresis.

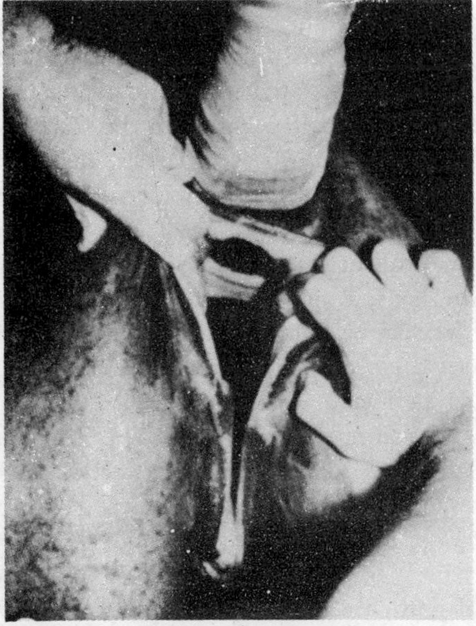

Figure 96. Rupture of the rectum, vagina and perineum of a mare caused by dystocia. This picture was taken 8 weeks after the accident.

Figure 97. Transverse rupture at parturition of the isolated uterine horn containing canine fetuses—this condition apparently followed trauma or torsion of the horn at about midgestation resulting in the separation of the horn from the rest of the uterus, note the scarring.

in a prolapse of the bladder. Forced extraction with the fetus in abnormal posture or position or in torsion of the uterus may cause a portion of the uterine or vaginal wall to be caught by a deviated extremity and folded upon itself to produce a rupture. A dry, emphysematous fetus and a swollen, dry birth canal are conducive to rupture of the vaginal, cervical, or uterine walls when strong traction or repulsion is applied. In one cow rupture of the uterus occurred apparently due to extensive severe adhesions of the uterus to the adjacent viscera. Administration of oxytocin or pituitrin to dogs or other animals with dystocia and/or uterine torsion may cause uterine rupture, Krichel, Smith. (See Figure 97) In a few cases spontaneous uterine rupture may occur due to unknown causes. After each dystocia the veterinarian should carefully examine the uterus and birth canal for the presence of a rupture of the uterus in order that it may be treated promptly or in hopeless cases the cow may be slaughtered and some value thereby salvaged.

The symptoms and prognosis of rupture of the genital tract vary with the animal and the portion of the genital tract involved; the size of the rupture; the character of the rupture, whether regular or irregular, horizonal or vertical; the nature of the uterine contents; the amount of uterine contents that have escaped into the abdominal cavity; and whether or not intestines or bladder have prolapsed through the rent in the wall of the genital tract. In a mare unless the uterine rupture is small and no infection was present in the uterus, a fatal peritonitis usually develops rapidly. In the cow or other domestic animal rupture of the uterus due to an emphysematous fetus rapidly produces a fatal peritonitis. A similar termination can be expected in a uterine rupture in any animal in which the uterine contents are severely infected. In rare cases in cattle, a rupture of the uterus may occur which releases a live or recently dead fetus into the abdominal cavity. Occasionally the symptoms of uterine rupture in the cow may be slight, but usually anorexia, lack of ruminations and rumen contractions, restlessness, rapid pulse and respiration rates, and cold extremities are present. The body temperature is usually normal or subnormal but may occasionally be elevated. If infected fetuses and material are released into the abdominal cavity, acute, severe septicemic symptoms develop rapidly. Shock, prostration, and death usually occur in 1 to 2 days. In less severe cases peritonitis is less marked and the animal may survive with the fetus becoming walled off, or death may occur in 3 to 7 days. The fetus may be removed through a laparotomy incision and the uterus sutured. With proper technique and aftercare some of these cases will survive. In small ruptures of the uterus after parturition or dystocia when no infection is present and the rent is in the dorsal half of the uterus some cattle have survived after repeated doses of oxytocin or prolonged small doses administered by the intravenous drip technique to produce rapid uterine involution, and with parenteral antibiotic therapy. In these cases penicillin (three to six million units), and streptomycin (4 to 5 gms.), or **Aureomycin** or **Terramycin** or tetracycline in 2- to 4- gm. doses or similar antibiotic therapy is given daily to the average 800- to 1000-lb. cow or mare. One to two grams of the latter broad-range antibiotics should be placed in the uterus to control intrauterine infection. The administration of antibiotics and of sodium sulfonamides in concentrations of 5 to 10 per cent, through the abdominal wall into the peritoneal cavity might be indicated in some cases. Occasionally the uterine rupture is large enough to require suturing. This is difficult in cows, but may be performed by working through the birth canal, using continuous or mattress sutures to bring the serous surfaces of the uterus on either side of the rupture into apposition. Some veterinarians have recommended prolapsing the uterus or vagina by pulling it to the outside through the birth canal and then suturing the rent and replacing the organs. A few veterinarians have successfully prolapsed the severely lacerated uterus through the birth canal and amputated it, Carlson. In large animals suturing the uterus through a laparotomy incision may be successful or it may be sutured in this manner with assistance through the birth canal. The presence of a retained placenta, septic metritis, an atonic uterine wall, or prolapsed intestines makes the prognosis poor. In most severe cases of uterine rupture in the cow, sheep, or sow the prognosis is poor and slaughter is usually advised if the animal is in an otherwise satisfactory condition. Even if recovery takes place, the future breeding life of that animal is very questionable, as chronic perimetritis and peritonitis are the probable results. In the dog uterine rupture, as in the larger animals, is usually characterized by anorexia, depression, weakness; in the early stages an elevated and in late stages a depressed body temperature; rapid pulse and respirations; cold extremities; constipation, or fetid diarrhea; pale mucous membranes especially if there is internal hemorrhage or shock; followed by prostration and death in 1 to 3 days. In the dog laparotomy and hysterectomy, if performed early, together with flushing of the abdominal cavity with warm saline solution and antibiotics, and treatment to prevent shock and infection, occasionally results in recovery of the bitch. In all species except the mare extrauterine fetuses may be walled off or encapsulated as described previously. Under no circumstances should fluids be injected into the ruptured uteri nor should manipulations of retained placentas take place. The latter should be allowed to drop from the uterus without assistance. Complete rupture of the cervix in large animals is similar to rupture of the uterus but because proper suturing of this structure is so difficult, the prognosis is poor if the rupture is extensive.

Rupture of the vagina is usually not as serious as uterine rupture and the prognosis is much better unless the rupture extends into the peritoneal cavity. Simple ruptures of the vagina especially of the lateral or dorsal wall need not be sutured unless the operator desires to do so. In most cases there is no need to suture small ruptures even on the floor of the vagina, but some veterinarians prefer to do so in order to prevent a possible perivaginal abscess if a retained placenta or metritis develops. In rare cases these perivaginal abscesses, which may also occur secondary to an infected perivaginal hematoma, become large and finally after 2 to 6 weeks or more break out between the vulvar lips and the tuber ischii. Mild wounds of the vagina heal rapidly. Recto-vaginal fistulas due to rupture of the dorsal wall of the vagina and ventral wall of the rectum are occasionally observed, especially in mares in which parturition is violent. If these are noted promptly they should be sutured immediately, care being taken that the rectal wall is tightly sutured in a transverse manner. Suturing of the vaginal wall is not as essential. If 24 to 48 hours pass before this condition is noticed it usually is impossible to correct at that time and one must wait until the edema, swelling, granulation tissue, and wound edges have completely healed before surgical intervention is undertaken to correct the fistula. In these chronic cases some feces and a mucopurulent discharge are expelled from the vulva.

Due to straining, rupture of the uterus may be followed by prolapse of the intestines into the uterus or birth canal or through the vulva. If rupture of the vagina or cervix extends into the peritoneal cavity it may also result in prolapse of the intestines. The bladder or fat may prolapse through a rupture in the ventral or lateral wall of the vagina. These conditions will be discussed later.

Rupture of the Perineum and Vulva is observed chiefly in the mare but may occasionally be observed in cattle and possibly sheep when excessive traction is applied to rapidly remove the fetus. Thus the vulva and perineal region may rupture before it has time to dilate gradually. This condition has been rarely observed in dairy heifers; hemorrhage may be severe and in some cases fatal, Williams. More often it is observed in the mare in which the fetus' forelegs and even the nose in anterior presentation or in the dorsopubic position the long limbs of the equine fetus may be pushed dorsally into the vaginal roof and rectal floor and this sacculated portion, due to the violence of parturition, is forced into the dilated anus. (See Figure 96) The vagina and rectal floor rupture, the feet protrude from the anus, and as the fetus is expelled the vulva and anus are torn longitudinally. In rare cases the vulva and vestibule remain intact and the fetus is expelled through the ruptured rectum, anus and perineal tissues. The presence of the ruptured perineum or "gill flirter" condition causing the rectum and vestibule to become a continuous cavity or "cloaca" is readily noted. As in recto-vaginal fistula it is advisable to correct and suture the rupture immediately, paying particular attention to suturing the rectal wall and anal sphincter. If the operation is not performed at once it must be postponed about 6 weeks until the swelling and granulation tissue has subsided and the wound has completely healed. If these mares are not operated upon the feces drop into the vagina, the vulva and vaginal mucous membranes are irritated, and the animal sucks air, pneumovagina, and there is a profuse discharge of mucus and feces that soil the rear parts. This condition is seldom observed in the cow but mild vulvo-anal lacerations and ruptures are seen especially in beef heifers and rarely in ewes. Proper use of episiotomy incisions in cattle would prevent this condition. The prognosis for the life of the patient is good if hemorrhage or shock is not immediately fatal. If the condition is not corrected, the future breeding life of the animal is poor. Very rarely "gill-flirter" mares may concieve. The prognosis for this operation is usually guarded. For a discussion of this operation and that of the recto-vaginal fistula the author recommends the standard veterinary surgical texts, the detailed anatomy of the perineal region of the mare by Habel, and a description of the operation by Bemis, Arthur, Straub and Fowler, and Aanes. The author particularly commends the technique of Aanes in which a two-phase operation is recommended for the surgical repair of third degree perineal lacerations and rectal vaginal fistulas. The first operation produces a firm shelf of tissue between the rectum and vagina by suturing the scarified tissues between the rectum and vagina and the vaginal mucus membrane but not placing sutures through the rectal mucosa. In about 2 weeks the second operation is performed that closes and reforms the perineal area, the anus and vulva.

Rupture of the pelvic and abdominal organs other than the genital tract have rarely been described in the cow and mare. D,anelius and Van Kruiningen et al described a rupture of the rectum in cows. Galvan described 4 cases where the free end of the caecum ruptured through the rectal wall. In all these cases the fetus was in posterior presentation. Rupture of the intestine of cattle has been described by Steiner and Stauffer. Rupture of the cecum and ventral colon have been reported during parturition in the mare, Voss and the author. Death always occurred in mares after rupture of the gut and usually occurred in cattle. A few cows operated on immediately after the rupture survived. Rupture of the bladder may occur occasionally. In very rare instances rupture of the diaphragm in a mare may result from violent straining.

Prolapse of the Abdominal or Pelvic Viscera

Prolapse of the Intestines may occur through a rupture or laceration in the uterus, cervix, or cranial portion of the vagina at the time of parturition. The intestines may only enter the uterus or may pass into the vagina and out the vulva. This condition should be differentiated from a **Schistosomus reflexus** or a ruptured umbilical hernia of the fetus. The prognosis is invariably poor, since the dystocia causing the rupture usually is severe, contamination and infection of the intestines and abdominal cavity is probable, and it is difficult to control the intestines to prevent their injury during removal of the fetus. Slaughter of the animal is usually recommended. In occasional cases in which infection or trauma to the intestines is minimal, replacing the intestines, suturing the rupture and removing the fetus might be possible. Closure of the rupture wound in the uterus may be accomplished through the birth canal, or probably a better approach would be through the laparotomy incision after a cesarean operation. If the intestine is traumatized or severely contaminated resection of a portion of it after a laparotomy may be necessary. Perforating lacerations or ruptures of the cervix and anterior vagina are sutured through the birth canal, White and Godkin. Aftercare consists of carefully suturing the rupture, and administering local and parenteral antibiotic treatment to control peritonitis, as recommended for the handling of uterine rupture. Left displacement of the abomasum is a fairly common occurrence before or at parturition in the cow.

Prolapse of the Rectum may occasionally occur in any animal in dystocia due to persistent violent straining and a relaxed anal sphincter. Slight eversion of the rectum at parturition is common, but severe prolapse is rare. In the mare prolapse of 2 to 3 feet of rectum is usually fatal since rupture of the rectum or small colon often occurs secondarily. If prolapse of the rectum begins in the mare if should be controlled by holding the rectum in place forcibly with a towel over the anus until the fetus is expelled or withdrawn. In other species prolapse is neither as serious nor as extensive. It should be prevented if possible or replaced promptly before or after the fetus is removed. A purse-string suture of heavy nylon material around the anus is often indicated after replacement. If unnoticed until trauma and edema are present, surgery, including either the reefing operation or amputation, and retaining sutures may be necessary to replace and maintain it in position.

Prolapse of the Bladder may occur in all species but it is seen most commonly in the larger domestic animals before or after parturition. Prolapse of the bladder usually takes place through a rupture or tear in the floor of the vagina and the bladder is noticed hanging from the vulvar orifice after parturition. Due to the sharp bend in the urethra the prolapsed organ fills with urine. This condition must be differentiated from eversion of the bladder through the urethra, vaginal or vulvar tumors, cysts, a mass of fat protruding through a rupture in the floor of the vagina, or vaginal or vulvar hematomas, Teige. If the bladder is distended with urine it may be replaced and the urine forced out or it may be drained with a needle before replacing. The external surface of the bladder should be carefully cleaned, dusted with a sulfonamide or with an antibiotic solution, and the organ replaced. The rupture in the vaginal floor permitting the prolapse should be sutured.

Eversion of the Bladder has been described mainly in the mare, in which the urethra is large and parturition violent. It has only very rarely been seen in the other animals such as the cow or sow. In rare instances in the mare intestines may prolapse into the everted bladder and prevent reduction, Vandeplassche and Vanheuverswijn. Eversion of the bladder may occur before or during parturition. It seldom if ever obstructs the passage of the fetus but occasionally the everted bladder and urethra may be severely traumatized when the fetus passes through the vestibule. Eversion of the bladder is easily recognized, as this organ is attached to the area of the ventral floor of the vulva where the urethra orifice is normally located. The everted bladder is pear-shaped. The openings of the two ureters drip urine and the mucous lining of the bladder may be noted and felt. If the everted bladder is small it may not become exposed through the vulvar lips until the animal lies down. In handling eversion of the bladder, the bladder should be thoroughly cleansed. If a tear or rupture is present it should be sutured or if a portion is damaged severely that portion might be removed and the edges of the incision sutured. Following the injection of epidural anesthesia, the operator should use both hands to compress the bladder and force it back through the urethra. The bladder should be massaged and pressed through the vagina floor until it is in its proper position. Aftercare consists of irrigating the bladder with saline solution and antibiotics and administering antibiotics parenterally so that the urine will contain a high concentration of the antibiotic for a number of days. It is seldom necessary to place a stitch in the external urinary meatus to prevent another eversion once the fetus has been removed and labor has ceased.

Prolapse of Perivaginal Fat may occur through a small rupture of the caudal portion of the vagina during forced extraction of the fetus especially in fat dairy heifers or beef cattle. These masses of fat should be differentiated from prolapse or eversion of the bladder, as they are likely to resemble those structures. On examination, the vaginal rupture, which is usually quite small, may be found at the base of the prolapsed mass of fat. This fat may be cut off with a knife or scissors, as there will be little bleeding. The vaginal rupture may be sutured or left to heal without suturing. Sulfonamide powder or antibiotics are customarily placed in the wound before suturing. The prognosis is good as a perivaginal abscess seldom develops.

Prolapse or Eversion of the Uterus may be called casting of the "wethers" or casting of the "calf bed." It is observed most commonly in the cow and ewe, occasionally in sows, and rarely in dogs, cats, and mares. It occurs most often immediately after parturition and occasionally up to several hours afterward. In rare cases it may occur 48 to 72 hours after parturition. Benesch and Wright stated that in dogs there may be rare cases of prolapse of one horn while fetuses are still in the other horn. Prolapse of the uterus is predisposed by long mesometrial attachments; violent or strong tenesmus; a relaxed, atonic, flaccid uterus; retention of the placenta especially at the ovarian pole of the gravid horn in cows and of the nongravid horn in mares; and by excessive relaxation of the pelvic and perineal region. In dairy cows it is commonly seen in confined or stabled cattle during the winter months that calve in a stanchion with their rear parts sloping downwards and hanging over the gutter. The use of great force in forced extraction of the fetus predisposes to tenesmus after relief of the dystocia. If the uterus is not contracting it frequently prolapses immediately after relief of the dystocia. In dystocia when the uterus is contracted tightly around a dry fetus, forced extraction is likely to result in prolapse of the uterus. Prolapse of the uterus is seen most commonly in pluriparous dairy cows but is not infrequent in poorly grown, thin, debilitated dairy heifers. In milk fever the atonic uterus may prolapse, possibly due to the increased abdominal pressure of labor. According to Arthur and others prolapse of the uterus was frequently observed in sheep in Australia due to a hyperestrogenism from eating clovers high in estrogenic hormones. Prolapse of the uterus is apparently not hereditary although occasionally it may be seen in dam and daughter. Woodward and Quesenberry stated there was an hereditary basis for prolapse of the uterus and vagina in Hereford cattle. A low plane of nutrition may also be a factor. Prolapse of the uterus very rarely occurs following prolapse of the vagina prior to parturition despite the common belief among owners that if the cow prolapses the vagina prepartum it is apt to suffer prolapse of the uterus postpartum. Prolapse of the uterus rarely recurs at a subsequent parturition.

The symptoms of prolapse of the uterus are obvious. (See Figure 98). The animal is usually recumbent but may be standing, with the uterus hanging to the hocks. Retention of the placenta is likely. The fetal membranes and/or mucous membrane of the uterus is exposed and usually covered with feces, straw, dirt, or blood clots unless of very recent occurrence. The uterus is usually enlarged and edematous especially if the condition has existed for 4 to 6 hours or longer. Benesch and Wright showed excellent illustrations of the condition in various species of animals. In the cow the gravid horn prolapses or everts sufficiently so that the cervix is usually present at the vulva. The nongravid horn is held inside the peritoneal surfaces of the prolapsed gravid horn and does not evert because of the strong intercornual ligament. The opening of the nongravid horn may be observed as an oval or slit-like orifice near the vulva on the ventral or lateral side of the prolapsed gravid horn. Prolapse of the uterus in the ewe is similar to this condition in the cow. In the other species, horses and multipara, usually one horn—or rarely both horns—may be prolapsed or everted. Vandeplassche and Spincemaille stated that 90 per cent of the uterine prolapses in sows were bicornual with the initial invagination occurring in the uterine body. They indicated that in cows the initial invagination also occurred at this site. Prolapse or invagination of the uterine horn should be differentiated from a prolapse of the vagina. In the dog and cat palpation of the abdomen may reveal the thick-

Figure 98. Uterine prolapse in a Hereford cow

ened invaginated uterine horn and abdominal pain, Smith. In the mare the uterine body may compose the major portion of the exposed everted uterus. In most animals prolapse of the uterus results in mild to moderate symptoms of tenesmus, restlessness, pain, anxiety, anorexia, and an increase in pulse and respiration rate. In cases with complicating factors of internal hemorrhage due to rupture of one of the uterine vessels, shock, incarceration and ischemia of intestines present in the peritoneal sac of the prolapsed uterus due to pressure obstructing the circulation of the intestines, or other diseases such as milk fever, may cause the animal to be recumbent. A very rapid, weak pulse, irregular, rapid respiration rates, pale mucous membranes, expiratory grunt, and prostration with severe depression and inability to rise indicate serious complications. When intestines or excessive hemorrhage with a large blood clot appear in the peritoneal sac formed by the prolapsed uterus, the bovine uterus may be 12 to 18 inches or more in diameter. In sheep, intestines frequently are present in the prolapsed uterine horn. In one case death occurred due to rupture of the portal vein at the liver.

The prognosis in uterine prolapse varies greatly. In most cases in which the condition is observed early, the veterinarian called promptly, the cow able to stand and the uterus not severely injured, the prognosis for the life of the cow is good. In 158 cases of prolapse of the uterus in dairy cattle seen from 1943 to 1953 in the Ambulatory Clinic of New York State Veterinary College, the mortality rate was 18 per cent. If cases obviously complicated by other conditions were eliminated the mortality rate in cows in good physical condition at the time of the operation would probably be 5 per cent or lower. The prognosis is poorer in beef cattle on pasture, where the condition may not be observed as early and aid secured promptly, Woodward and Quesenberry. The animals' future breeding history may be good or poor depending upon the severity of the uterine lesions, the promptness of treatment and the rate of involution. In many cases, unless the cow or ewe is valuable, it may be advisable to sell the animal for beef later on and not rebreed, as sterility, abortion, retained placenta, and other such conditions may follow. If the uterus is grossly contaminated, or dried due to exposure to the sun, or if lacerations are present, the prognosis is more guarded due to the possibility of a septic metritis, perimetritis or peritonitis developing, and the prognosis for the future breeding life of the animal is questionable. It is surprising how much trauma, irritation, and contamination the uterus can withstand. Upon replacement of the organ this infection is overcome, the traumatic lesions heal, and the animal recovers. In other cases, with the animal prostrate, unable to rise and conditions complicated by shock, internal hemorrhage, or incarceration of the intestines, the prognosis is usually very poor to hopeless. In the author's experience, mainly with dairy cattle, the percentage of cases of uterine prolapse that terminated fatally due to internal hemorrhage, shock, or incarceration of the intestines was high when the cows were in stanchions and the prolapsed uterus had dropped into the gutter. This is further reason for having box stalls for calving cows or having them calve on pasture. If other diseases are present, such as milk fever or obturator paralysis, the prognosis is based on the severity of those conditions as well. In cattle in which the uterus is so badly damaged or diseased that replacement cannot be considered and amputation of the uterus is the only recourse, the prognosis is poor although some of these cases may survive.

In the ewe the prognosis for prolapse or eversion of the uterus is similar to that of the cow. In the mare the condition is more serious, but if the animals are treated promptly most will survive. Amputation of the uterus in the mare should seldom if every be attempted since it is indicated only when the uterus is severely traumatized and lacerated, and then the prognosis is extremely grave. In the sow the prognosis is poor as extensive prolapse usually results in internal hemorrhages and shock. The author has observed 5 or 6 cases of prolapse of the uterus in the sow and all were either dead on his arrival at the farm or died within 15 to 30 minutes. A few cases of prolapse of the uterus in swine have recovered following prompt treatment. In the dog and cat the prognosis is fair to good even though the condition is rather difficult to handle because of the length of the uterine horns and the inability of the operator to aid replacement with his hand and arm as in the larger domestic animals. Laparotomy and replacement of the uterus in the abdomen may be necessary in the dog, cat and sow. Hysterectomy is more frequently and successfully performed in the dog and cat than in the larger animals. Following proper replacement of the prolapsed uterus very few cases recur in any species.

The treatment or handling of prolapse of the uterus in the cow can be made much easier if the owner is instructed to wrap the cow's uterus in a wet towel or sheet or to place it in a plastic bag to keep it moist and clean until replaced. If the cow is standing the uterus should be raised and supported level with the vulva until assistance arrives. If the cow is recumbent in a stanchion the gutter should be built up to support the uterus and keep it from hanging. This prevents the uterus from becoming edematous and may possibly prevent rupture of the uterine vessels. If possible the cow should be in or near the barn, in a clean paddock or well-bedded stall to make the operation cleaner, more convenient, and less difficult. Good light is essential. Proper restraint of the animal aids in prompt and easy replacement of the everted uterus. Epidural anesthesia should be used routinely in sufficient dosage to provide good anesthesia but at the same time to keep the animal standing. In fact some cows and mares that are down and refuse to stand may get up promptly after epidural anesthesia is given. Epidural anesthesia controls and prevents defecation during replacement of the uterus. Elevation of the rear parts greatly facilitates replacement of the uterus. The ordinary standing posture of the cow usually gives sufficient elevation of the rear parts. If replacement is to be made even easier the fore feet may be lowered or the rear parts elevated by making the animal stand on a slope. If the animal is recumbent and refuses to rise and cannot be stimulated to do so by prodding with a sharp object or an electric prod, by rolling her tail beneath the foot, or the intravenous injection of calcium gluconate, benzidrine stimulants, or 20 to 40 cc. or more of **Pyribenzamine,** or even after being given epidural anesthesia, its hind parts should be elevated mechanically. This is best done by applying hip slings or by tying the hocks and hoisting the rear parts 3 to 4 feet off the ground. It may also be done by placing bags filled with straw under the rear parts, by rolling the cow onto a barn door and raising the end of the door that supports its rear parts; or by placing the animal on a steep slope with the fore quarters lower than the rear quarters. Epidural anesthesia is not necessary in ewes because with the aid of one or two men grasping each hind leg the rear parts can be elevated high enough so that the uterus almost falls into place. In multiparous animals, and possibly the mare, general anesthesia is indicated.

The uterus of the cow should be carefully prepared for replacement. It should be held level with the ischial arch or vulva during these operations. The purpose of this is to relieve pressure on the broad ligament and uterine veins as they pass over the ischial arch, and to restore normal circulation in the prolapsed uterus. This avoids further edema of the uterine wall and aids in absorption and disappearance of the edema already present. This position of the uterus permits the bladder to resume its normal position and if intestines are present in the uterus they return to the abdominal cavity. The danger of possible rupture of the vessels in the broad ligament is greatly reduced and the cow is more comfortable when the uterus is held level with the vulva. This can be done by supporting the uterus in a towel or sheet held by a man on either side of the rear quarters of the cow, or it may be supported on a wooden or metal tray, or held in the arms of the veterinarian if he is suitably attired in a rubber apron, gown, or coveralls. The afterbirth, if present, should be gently removed. Only rarely is the afterbirth attached so securely it cannot be removed. If the removal of the placenta is impossible without severe trauma and hemorrhage resulting, it may be left in place. Following replacement of the uterus, the placenta is handled in the same manner as severe retained placenta in a cow not affected with prolapse of the uterus.

The uterus should be cleansed thoroughly with a warm physiological saline solution, or with water to which a small amount of mild antiseptic such as chlorine or quaternary ammonium compound has been added. To cleanse the uterus thoroughly may require 5 to 10 gallons of water. Usually if the farmer is warned at the time of the call to have plenty of hot water available, it will be ready, but if it is not available, the veterinarian should be equipped to take some with him. In some cases it may be necessary to use cotton to help clean and wipe the uterus. The adjacent vulva and perineal region should be carefully washed and cleansed at the same time, particular attention being given to folds and creases in the skin. If the uterus is lacerated, torn, or perforated, it should be carefully sutured. If hemorrhage from the surface of the uterus is severe the vessel should be ligated. If prolapse of the uterus has been present for some time and edema is severe, the massage of washing the uterus and the holding of the uterus level with the vulva may not be sufficient to readily reduce its size so that it can be replaced. Vigorous massage of the uterus with the palm of the hand, with the fingers extended but held tightly together, may be accomplished by wrapping a towel or piece of sheeting tightly around the uterus and applying pressure through the towel without the danger or possibility of forcing a finger through the uterine wall or edematous mucosa. The author believes that the practice of applying sugar to the edematous uterus on the theory that it removes fluid through the endometrium is crude, unscientific, and not necessary. Probably most of the edematous fluid removed when sugar is massaged into the swollen uterus is forced out through small fissures produced in the endometrium by the sharp granules. It may be well to palpate the bladder before replacing the uterus, since in rare instances it may be distended and require catheterizing so that it will not interfere with the operation.

Some veterinarians advise giving 30 to 50 units of oxytocin or pituitrin to contract the bovine uterus when it is ready for replacement. The author does not advise this, inasmuch as it makes the uterine wall tense, contracted, and difficult to return to its normal position without a portion of the horn remaining invaginated. On several occasions when the prolapse occurred 36 to 72 hours after parturition and pituitrin was administered before replacement, the contracted, tense uterus could not be replaced through the contracted cervix until the uterine walls had relaxed. Many veterinarians advise coating the prolapsed uterus with oil containing a mild antiseptic and protectant such as 1 oz. of bismuth formic iodide to a pint of mineral oil. In replacing the uterus it should be held above the level of the floor of the pelvis; the vulvar lips should be pulled apart, and first the ventral portion and then the dorsum of the prolapsed portion of the uterus should be replaced, starting at the cervical end of the uterus nearest the vulva. Since the uterus is still more or less in the form of an arc, replacing 3 or 4 inches of the ventral or concave portion of the prolapsed horn is accompanied by replacement of 6 to 8 inches of the dorsal or convex portion of the horn. In replacing the uterus, pressure should be exerted with the palm of the hand, with the fingers extended but held tightly together, to avoid perforating the uterus. Finally the ovarian pole of the uterus is pushed by the fist through the vulva, vagina, and cervix, into the uterine cavity. If the cervical rings are contracted, pulling them gently backward with one hand and working the uterus through with the other is helpful. The ovarian pole is pushed through the vagina, cervix, and uterus with the clenched fist and arm by a piston-like or shaking motion on various parts of its perimeter until the horn is completely straightened out and no invagination is present. Williams recommended the replacing of the uterus by starting at the ovarian pole. This is usually much more difficult to accomplish than the technique described. One should use care not to tear or remove a caruncle and thus cause bleeding. If the uterus has been sutured no douching should follow replacement. If complete replacement of the ovarian pole is difficult the introduction of 2 to 3 gallons of very warm water or physiological saline solution into the uterine cavity is often of assistance, since it stimulates uterine contractions and helps to wash out uterine debris. This fluid should be siphoned out. Most cases do not require douching.

After the uterus is replaced properly and completely, 30 to 50 units of oxytocin or pituitrin should be given intramuscularly or intravenously. If it is given by the latter method the uterine wall will contract tightly on the operator's arm within 30 to 60 seconds. Following replacement, most veterinarians use a uterine antiseptic or antibiotic such as those described in treating retained placenta. Probably one to two gms. of **Terramycin, Aureomycin,** tetracycline or furacin is most efficient in controlling infection. In treating valuable cows another dose of pituitrin might be administered in 2 to 4 hours. After the uterus has been replaced properly, epidural anesthesia is usually still present and the pituitrin has contracted the uterus. If the cow is standing and not straining, a recurrence of the prolapse is very rare. Temporary suturing of the vulva with a figure of eight or mattress suture of umbilical tape into the hair line, or some other type of vulvar suture described under vaginal prolapse, or the application of a truss for 1 to 3 days is merely a placebo for the farmer. Very rarely does a prolapse recur if the uterus is properly replaced in a cow. If the owner has the cow under close observation for the next 3 days, as he should, a recurrence of the prolapse can be treated promptly. If the cow is not observed closely vulvar sutures may be necessary to prevent a complete prolapse recurring with possible fatal results. This is much better than having, as the author did in one cow, the prolapse recur into the vagina, and because of the vulvar sutures it went unnoticed for 3 days. It was impossible to replace at that time and the cow was slaughtered. Fincher reported examining a cow that failed to conceive following a prolapse of the uterus and on finding no evidence of the uterus on rectal examination, examined the vagina, where a small involuted uterus was present, protruding through the cervix. If vulvar sutures are used they should be removed in 24 hours. Pessaries are not recommended, as they tend to cause straining. If the cow continues straining following replacement of the uterus it may be due to invagination of the ovarian pole of the uterine horn or an irritation or inflammation of the vulva. The former should be corrected, and oily protectants or anesthetic ointments may be used for the latter condition, together with a long-lasting epidural anesthetic. If the cow is recumbent the rear parts should be kept slightly higher than the fore parts for several days. If the cow can stand this is not necessary. Arthur stated that in uncomplicated cases it is generally found that within 24 hours the cervix is closed tightly enough so that recurrence is unlikely. Parenteral antibiotics are often indicated to help control uterine infection after replacement. In rare cases a severe or even fatal infection with metritis or peritonitis may follow prolapse of the uterus.

In the ewe the same general replacement technique is applied as in the cow but it is less difficult, since the rear quarters can be easily elevated. Recurrence is more frequent and vulvar sutures are also of questionable value. In these cases epidural anesthesia is valuable. Close confinement of the ewe with her rear parts elevated may be indicated. In the mare replacement is similar to the cow except that general anesthesia may be indicated. In the mare the body of the uterus is the only visible portion of the prolapsed organ, Brewer and Kliest, Arthur. Tetanus antitoxin, pituitrin, antibiotics, and other supportive treatments are indicated to prevent secondary tetanus, metritis, and laminitis in the mare. In multiparous animals replacement of the uterus in the manner described in the cow is difficult, but may occasionally be possible if the rear parts of the animal are well-elevated. A laparotomy is usually necessary to accomplish the return of the uterus to its normal position. Some authors advise suturing the apex of the uterine horns to the body wall to prevent a recurrence. Occasionally in the sow and dog one horn of the uterus prolapses and a few fetuses may still be in the other horn. Therefore in most cases in multipara a laparotomy is probably advisable. If the uterus is badly traumatized, amputation of the horn or hysterectomy is indicated in the dog and cat and possibly rarely in the larger animals.

Hysterectomy or amputation of the prolapsed uterus is undertaken only when replacement is impossible or when it is quite certain that replacement of a badly torn, lacerated, necrotic, infected uterus would result in death. In some cases where the cow is unable to rise, chickens or hogs severely mutilate a prolapsed uterus. The prognosis is always guarded to poor because of the severity of the operation and the conditions preceding it. It is contraindicated in the mare, but is often the method of choice in the dog. Although the prognosis is poor there are many recorded cases of successful amputations or hysterectomies. In the cow and ewe amputation of the uterus may be accomplished by making a long longitudinal incision in the prolapsed uterus and cervix on the dorsal and caudal surface between the rows of caruncles starting at the vulvar lips. (See Figures 99 and 100) Through this extensive incision the uterine arteries and veins can be seen in the tense mesometrium. These vessels are carefully ligated in 2 or 3 places and the broad ligament is severed between the ligatures from the uterus. The cranial portion of the vagina anterior to the prolapsed cervix is easily drawn out of the vulva and is carefully ligated with fixation ligatures. The uterus and part or all of the cervix is removed and the stump is replaced in the vaginal cavity. This technique precludes the occurrence of hemorrhage from the uterine vessels, and insures the vagina and peritoneal cavity being closed tightly, Roberts. In the dog and sow a similar technique can be used, but the incision is circular and the uterine stump can be closed by a Cor. '' suture followed by a Lembert stitch. In the dog an episiotomy may be necessary in order to make the operation less difficult. In the cow, Benesch described a technique of laparotomy with ligation and separation of the uterine vessels and mesometrium from their dorsal attachments; a circular incision was made at the base of the prolapsed stump and the ovaries, broad ligaments were pulled out, and the cranial portion of the

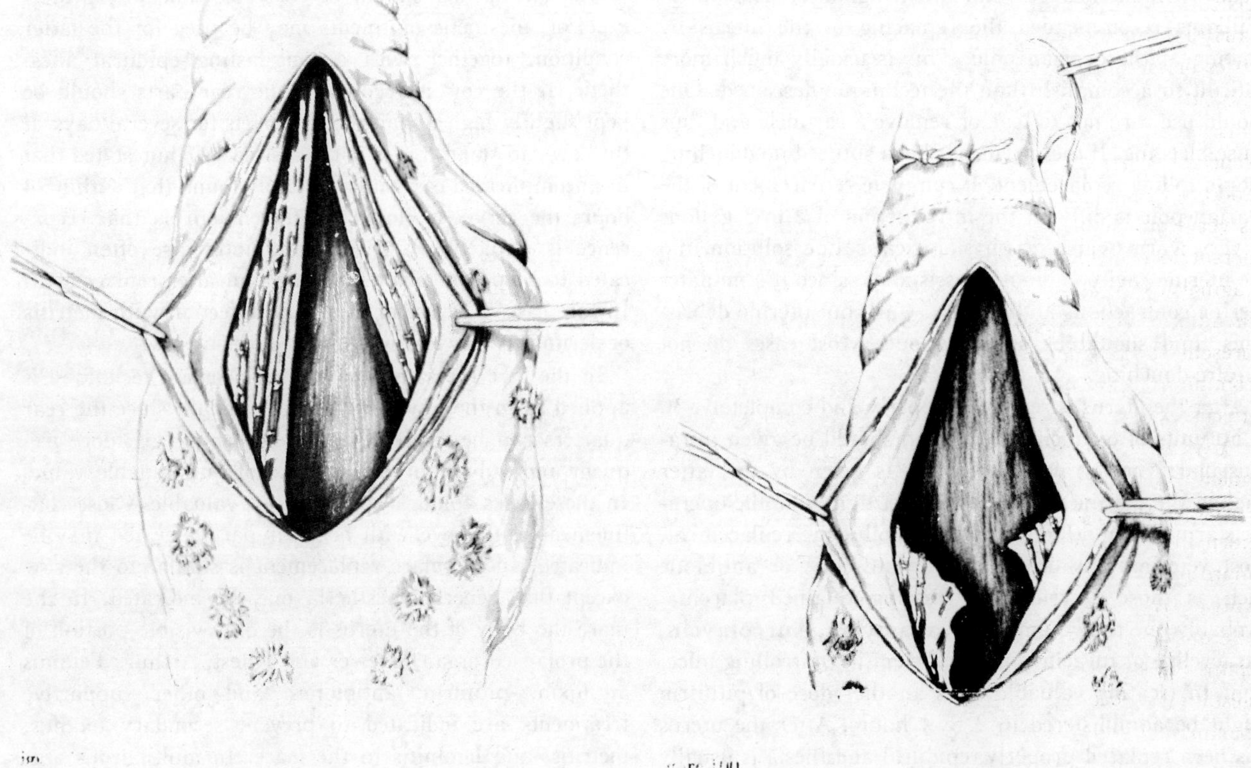

A surgical technique for amputation of a prolapsed uterus in a cow. (Courtesy Cornell Veterinarian).

vagina closed as described above. In the dog, cat and sow a laparotomy can be done, the prolapsed horn returned to the abdominal cavity, and an ovario-hysterectomy performed.

In the cow or ewe the most common technique recommended for amputation of the prolapsed uterus consists of making certain that neither the bladder nor any intestine is present in the prolapsed portion and then ligating that portion close to the vulva, using a strong ligature or preferably a soaped or oiled cord or fine rope tightened by two men pulling on opposite ends of the cord or rope. Three or 4 separate ligatures are firmly tied around the neck of the prolapsed portion of the uterus allowing 15 to 20 minutes to elapse between the application of each ligature. This is necessary as edema is always present in such cases, and the enclosing ligatures must be tight enough so that when the uterus is removed 3 or 4 inches caudal to the ligatures the uterine vessels in the mesovarium will not withdraw and cause fatal hemorrhage into the abdominal cavity. Some veterinarians have successfully used a heavy elastic ligature made of long 2-inch-wide strips of rubber inner tube wrapped a number of times very tightly around the neck of the prolapsed portion in a manner similar to the cord method just described. After a lapse of 20 to 30 minutes to permit the edema to be forced from beneath the ligature, the uterus is amputated, leaving a fairly large stump to be replaced in the vagina. The ligatures or elastic tubing should be held in place by transfixing sutures through the enclosed vaginal wall. Following this operation the cow should be observed closely for evidence of shock, and saline solution, blood, antihistamines, and other stimulants should be administered at once. This is very important if the patient is to survive, as shock or hemorrhage may be fatal. The stump replaced in the vagina will slough in several weeks. It is usually advisable to administer parenteral antibiotics for 3 to 4 days. At present the long elastic ligature is probably used most commonly and successfully for amputation of the bovine uterus.

Invagination of the Uterine Horn is occasionally noted in the cow and mare, but occurs only rarely in other species. In this condition the ovarian pole of the gravid horn in the cow and usually the nongravid horn in the mare is everted but not far enough to be observed at the vulva. Ordinarily the invagination is completely within the uterus and is like an intestinal intussusception. Williams indicated that while it may occur rarely during the gestation period, it is more likely to occur during or after parturition and after replacement of an everted uterus. It may be due to the pull or weight of the attached placenta on the ovarian pole of the uterus. Not infrequently it may be produced by traction on the fetal membranes at the time their removal is attempted. Williams reported that in a few cases the ovarian pole of the uterus may become incarcerated and necrotic with the cow showing symptoms of a septic metritis and peritonitis followed by death. In some mild cases the condition may correct itself spontaneously, while in others the invagination may progress until complete prolapse of the uterus occurs. This is another reason for careful examination of the uterus after relieving a dystocia.

The symptoms of an invaginated horn may be lacking, or there may be evidences of uneasiness, straining, or pain. In an occasional advanced case the invaginated portion of the horn may become necrotic; there may be symptoms of toxemia and septicemia; and a fetid, reddish-black vulvar discharge similar to a septic metritis may appear. On rectal palpation the enlarged uterine mass may feel like a large intussusception, and the mesovarium will be tense and tight. On vaginal examination if the hand can enter the uterus the invaginated horn is recognized as a dome-shaped, tumor-like mass projecting upward into the lumen of the uterus. This is noted most often in removal of an afterbirth in the cow when strong traction is placed on the placenta and the ovarian pole invaginates toward the cervix. In the mare this may also occur and in most cases involves the nongravid horn.

The prognosis is usually good unless the invaginated ovarian pole has been incarcerated by the contracting uterine muscle and becomes necrotic, in which case death usually occurs unless a hysterectomy is performed. The treatment of the condition in large animals consists of kneading the invaginated pole back into place with the fist, with piston-like shaking movements around the edge of the uterine lumen. Douching with 2 to 4 gallons of water may aid in replacing the invaginated pole. If one hand inserted in the rectum puts traction on the cranial portion of the broad ligament and the mesovarium attached to the invaginated pole, and the other hand pushes on the "tumor," this bimanual action may reduce the invagination. Ordinarily when the uterus is contracting strongly this condition cannot be relieved at the time. In cases where the invaginated horn cannot be replaced, when the animal's uterus is examined again in 3 to 6 hours it will be found that the condition often was corrected spontaneously after the uterus relaxed. The attending veterinarian should closely follow and treat such cases of an invaginated uterine horn until the condition is corrected.

Metabolic Diseases of the Puerperal Period

Milk Fever, or Parturient Paresis, is a metabolic disease of dairy cows usually four years of age or older, characterized by an acute disturbance in calcium metabolism with hypocalcemia occurring just before, during, or most often within 72 hours after parturition. Jonsson considered milk fever as an adaptation disease. Predisposing factors include age and both yield and persistency of production. The parathyroid glands and the production of parathyroid hormone is normal and not a factor in this disease, Mayer et al. (1969). Recent studies have suggested that a high total dietary calcium intake together with a high Ca:P ratio in the dry cow may stimulate calcitonin release from the parafollicular cells of the thyroid gland, thus inhibiting bone resorption by parathormone. Thus at the beginning of lactation when there is an increased demand for calcium, the cow is forced into a hypocalcemic state and parturient paresis ensues, Kronfeld and Ramberg, Krook, Nurmio. This theory is further strengthened by the studies of Mayer et al. (1967) and Albright and Blosser who showed that injecting large amounts of calcium intravenously produced a hypercalcemia lasting for several hours in cows with milk fever or in normal parturient cows. This hypercalcemia suppressed parathormone secretion and stimulated the secretion of calcitonin, a substance that lowers blood calcium concentration by inhibiting bone resorption. These effects tend to retard the normal adaptation of the cow toward the loss of calcium at the onset of parturition and lactation and result in a high incidence of relapse of milk fever cases; or as in the report of Albright and Blosser actually produced milk fever in normal parturient cows 36 hours after the calcium injection.

The blood serum calcium level drops from a normal of 8 to 12 mgm. per 100 cc. to 3 to 7 mgm., with symptoms of parturient paresis becoming progressively more pronounced as the calcium level drops. Hypocalcemic paresis is due to a depression of neuromuscular transmission of motor stimuli, Bowen et al.. Mayer et al. (1965) described a practical field test for determining the blood serum calcium levels based on the amount of EDTA needed to prevent the coagulation of blood. This test could also be used for hypocalcemia in grass tetany in cows and lactation tetany in mares, dogs and cats. Hypocalcemia with calcium levels below 8 mg. per 100 ml. of serum may last for 11 to 32 hours in parturient cows without paresis developing. Paralysis was usually associated with calcium levels below 5 mgm. per 100 ml. serum, Mayer et al. (1966). Parturient paresis is observed in all dairy breeds but most commonly in Jerseys. Recurrent attacks of milk fever may occur at subsequent parturitions. The symptoms of parturient paresis are anorexia, cold extremities, lowering of the body temperature, stiff gait, staggering, incoordination, inability to rise, an S-curve in the neck, failure of the pupil to contract on stimulation by light, suppression of urination and defecation, constipation, slight tympany of the rumen, cessation of parturition if it develops during that period, coma, and finally death usually occurring in 6 to 24 hours if treatment is not instituted. Only rarely does spontaneous recovery occur in the paretic cow. With proper care and prompt handling the prognosis is good, and the mortality should be less than 2 to 3 per cent in uncomplicated cases that do not injure themselves in attempting to rise.

Treatment consists of administering 750 to 1500 cc. (depending on the size of the cow) of 20 per cent calcium gluconate, one half of the amount injected intravenously and one half subcutaneously. Only a small amount of milk should be removed from the udder for 2 to 3 days. Complete emptying of the udder should be avoided if possible during this period. Kronfeld and Ramberg recommended giving about one-half the recommended dose of calcium subcutaneously or intravenously early in the disease and repeating it if necessary to avoid suppressing parathormone secretion. Mayer et al. (1967) reported on udder insufflation to raise the plasma calcium concentration by reducing milk secretion and transfering calcium in the udder back into the circulation. This technique did not induce hypercalcemia and was seldom followed by a relapse. They used cotton-filtered compressed air from a cylinder introduced into the barrel of a syringe filled with an antibiotic udder infusion to firmly distend the cow's udder and teats. Following treatment the teats were tied with a tape for several hours to hold in the compressed air. The value of irradiated ergosterol or large amounts of vitamin D to prevent the occurrence or prevent relapses of the disease is questionable, Harshberger and Kendall, Straub and Hughes. Although Poulton et al. and Hibbs and Conrad reported it to be of value. Milk fever or hypocalcemia has been described in the ewe, doe and sow in Europe, but not in the United States. The symptoms are similar to those in cattle.

To prevent the occurrence of parturient paresis which may reach an incidence of 80 per cent or more in the adult cows in certain dairy herds, the total diatary calcium intake late in lactation and during the nonlactating period should be greatly reduced by removing legumes such as clover and alfalfa from the diet as well as common mineral supplements used for lactating cows which are usually high in calcium. Timothy hay, straw and corn silage are low in calcium content and may be fed. If too much of the latter is fed the cows may become overly fat. In certain areas and herds where some or all legume roughage must be fed, the addition of 2.5 to 5 per cent monosodium phosphate to the grain ration, resulting in Ca:P ratio of 1:1 instead of a 3 to 7:1 has greatly reduced the incidence of milk fever, Stott, Boda and Cole.

Ketosis or Acetonemia in Cattle is only rarely observed prior to parturition, Kingrey et al. and the author. It may occur occasionally the first 7 to 10 days after parturition but by far the greatest number of cases occur from 10 to 60 days after parturition. According to Pehrson three types of ketosis in cattle may develop: (1) primary spontaneous ketosis which may have an hereditary predisposition, (2) primary nutritional, which is the most common and (3) secondary ketosis which occurs due to metritis, displacement of the abomasum, traumatic gastritis and other diseases. Kronfeld and Emery have suggested three types of ketosis based mainly on the sites for ketogenesis: (1) alimentary, induced by feeding silage high in butyrates; (2) hepatic, occurring at the peak of lactation from mobilized fat reserves before the peak in feed intake; and (3) mammary, acetoacetate production in the gland. Ketosis is characterized by hypoglycemia, ketonemia and ketonuria. The normal bovine blood levels of 40 to 60 mg. per 100 ml. of glucose drop to 40 to 18 mg. of glucose and the blood ketone levels rise from a norm of 2 to 15 mg. to 15 to 75 mg. per 100 ml. This condition is due basically to a reduced intake of nutrients, especially carbohydrates, in relation to the loss of nutrients through heavy lactation. Secondary conditions such as fatty changes in the liver may occur. There is a marked loss in weight due to the use of body fat, carbohydrates and proteins for milk and energy. A great increase in ketone levels develops in the blood and urine. The condition may develop in dairy cattle at any age.

The symptoms observed are of two types, digestive and nervous. In the common digestive type, the symptoms are anorexia, constipation, gradual drop in milk flow, rapid loss of weight, and occasionally staggering or temporary inability to rise. In the uncommon nervous type the symptoms are more severe, and depression is marked; various nervous symptoms such as trembling, nervousness and licking may be present; paresis is not uncommon, and anorexia and drop in milk flow are also observed. At times it may be difficult to differentiate between acetonemia and metritis following parturition, and both may be present. By testing the urine or milk with Ross reagent, the development of a definite purple color is usually indicative of ketosis. Inasmuch as very few animals die of acetonemia, the prognosis is good; but the loss in milk production and body weight can be of great economic importance to the dairy farmer.

The treatment of ketosis in cattle consists of raising the blood sugar level for a period, thereby restoring the cow's appetite. Following the increased intake of additional nutrients, especially carbohydrates, the cow will recover and a relapse is unlikely. The preparations used to raise blood glucose levels are as follows: glucose solutions of 500 ml. to 1000 ml. of 40 per cent glucose injected intravenously, or continuous, slow intravenous drip of several thousand ml. of 25 per cent glucose; sodium propionate, 1/3 to 3/4 lb. fed daily in small doses or given as a drench or a similar product such as propylene glycol administered orally in 200 to 500 ml. amounts daily to increase the propionic acid in the rumen which is absorbed and used in place of glucose as a source of energy for the cow, thus conserving and raising the blood glucose level; glucocorticoids injected intramuscularly, raise blood glucose levels rapidly and also improve appetite and lower milk production for several days; A.C.T.H., 200 to 600 I.U. injected intramuscularly, stimulates production of the glucocorticoids by the adrenal glands and thus raises the level of blood sugar; and 10 to 30 gms. daily of chloral hydrate in divided doses also raises blood sugar levels. If metritis, mastitis or other infectious process due to bacteria is present the glucocorticoids should not be given or they should be accompanied by parenteral antibiotics. They are contraindicated in viral diseases. Relapses are likely to recur if the level and amounts of nutrients, especially carbohydrates, TDN or energy in the ration are not increased so that the cow will consume 1 lb. of 12- to 14-per cent protein grain to 2-1/2 or 4 lbs. of milk produced, depending upon the quality and quantity of roughage. The level of energy intake must equal the work of milk production so that the cow does not relapse into ketosis.

Ketosis or Pregnancy Disease in Ewes is seen the last 2 to 4 weeks of pregnancy. Usually the dam is carrying twin fetuses. It is caused by a hypoglycemia produced by the rapid growth of the fetuses and insufficient intake of nutrients, especially carbohydrates in the ration. Ketosis is not due to an insufficiency of A.C.T.H. as hydrocortisone levels are elevated, Forbes and Singleton. The affected ewes are usually thin but ketosis may be observed in ewes in good condition. It is also predisposed by a lack of exercise. The liver shows fatty changes and the ketone levels in the blood and urine are greatly elevated. In ewes the symptoms of ketosis are dullness, anorexia, paresis, or inability to rise without assistance, and nervous symptoms of mental derangement such as walking in a circle, pressing the head against some object, drawing the head backward and to one side. Forbes and Singleton indicated that the nervous signs exhibited might be due to inability of nerve cells to utilize sugar. Urine obtained by a small catheter or by stopping respirations by squeezing the nose and mouth firmly shut can be tested by the Ross test, as in cattle, for the presence of ketones. In more advanced cases the fetuses die and if they are aborted promptly the ewe may recover. Ketosis may be differentiated from listeriosis by a lack of paresis of the lips or ears; in listeriosis the limbs are flaccid while in ketosis the limbs will resist flexion if upward pressure is applied to the toe. The course of the disease is 2 to 6 days. The prognosis is usually poor unless cases are diagnosed and treated early or abortion occurs before the ewe is severely affected. Treatment consists of any one or a combination of the following: the injection of 200 ml. of 40 per cent glucose intravenously; administration of glucocorticoids or 50 to 100 I.U. of A.C.T.H. intramuscularly; an increase in the carbohydrate intake of 1/2 to 1 lb. of grain or 1/4 to 1/2 lb. of molasses daily per ewe. Sometimes valuable ewes which are severely affected can be saved by cesarean section; ordinarily in such cases the fetuses are dead. Using stilbestrol or the glucocorticoids to cause or hasten abortion has not been evaluated in ewes with severe ketosis. The disease may usually be prevented in the rest of the flock by increasing the grain ration or by feeding molasses and increasing the amount of exercise. Ketosis in goats is similar to that in ewes but less common.

Grass Tetany, Lactation Tetany, Transport Tetany, "Wheat Poisoning" or Hypocalcemia, or Hypomagnesemia is a metabolic disease of beef and dairy cattle, especially those which are in advanced pregnancy or lactating heavily, grazing on lush, heavily fertilized grass or early wheat pastures or are transported or stressed in the puerperal or early lactation period. This disease complex is well-described by Blood and Henderson. It occurs more commonly on certain types of soils and in certain regions. It is seen most often during the spring or fall months and less often during the summer months. Grass tetany is characterized by a hypocalcemia, occasionally a concurrent hypomagnesemia or hypomagnesemia alone. It is caused by the excessive consumption of young lush grass on well-fertilized pastures. Some veterinarians, Kronfeld and Simensen, believe that the high potassium or trans-aconitate content in grass causes a loss of calcium and magnesium from the body, accentuated in advanced pregnancy or during heavy lactation, when there is an increased drain on body calcium and magnesium. Hypomagnesemia may occur in stabled animals fed rations low in magnesium. The symptoms of grass tetany are similar to those of milk fever when a simple hypocalcemia is present. If, however, a hypomagnesemia is also present, trismus, hyperesthesia, tachycardia, nystagmus, erect ears, tetany of the hind limbs, tremors, twitching of muscles that may progress into general spasms or convulsions, may be exhibited, Kronfeld and Simensen. Paresis is a common symptom. Unknown extrinsic or intrinsic factors apparently play a role in precipitating signs of hypomagnesemia when the serum levels of magnesium are low. Often during the early stages of grass tetany the animal is excitable and may be aggressive. This disease is more gradual in onset than in milk fever. The prognosis is usually good. The treatment consists of injecting 750 to 1500 cc. of 20 per cent calcium gluconate intravenously and subcutaneously in a divided dose, removing the animal from the grass pasture, feeding good alfalfa hay, and supplying a mixture of bone meal or dicalcium phosphate, and a luxury level of magnesium oxide, sulphate or carbonate, up to 60 to 120 gms. daily, free choice or preferably in the grain ration. Magnesium may be combined with the calcium gluconate or 200 to 500 cc. of a 10 to 25 per cent solution of magnesium sulphate may be given subcutaneously. An outbreak of transport tetany or hypocalcemia was described by Asbury in which a flock of ewes kept on stubble field low in calcium was driven 9 miles to a new pasture. The ewes near parturition or in early lactation showed depression, stiff gait, high pulse and respiration rate and excessive salivation. Giving 150 ml. of 20 per cent calcium gluconate subcutaneously resulted in recovery.

Tetany or Eclampsia in the Mare is rare but has been described by Williams and Blood and Henderson. Usually it occurs within several weeks after parturition, in a mare that has a normal foal, is lactating heavily, and is on a good, lush pasture. An attack may be precipitated by unusual handling, transport, or by a change in surroundings. It is probably a hypocalcemia similar to grass tetany in the cow or eclampsia in the bitch. In the early stages, symptoms of restlessness, rapid breathing, staring eyes, twitching, trembling and clonic spasms especially of the diaphragm, are common. In later stages clonic spasms are followed by more tonic spasms, with trismus, marked restlessness, labored breathing, profuse sweating, and injected cyanotic mucous membranes. In advanced cases the animal is unable to stand. Tetany of most muscles is present; the animal becomes prostrate; convulsions are nearly continuous; and death results in 12 to 48 hours. The condition should be differentiated from tetanus. If treated promptly the prognosis should be good but deaths are not uncommon in untreated mares. Spontaneous recoveries have occurred at any time during the course of the disease. The treatment consists of intravenous injections of calcium gluconate and possibly the administration of narcotics such as chloral hydrate, sodium pentobarbital or heavy tranquilization.

Puerperal Tetany or Eclampsia in the bitch and cat is a metabolic disease characterized by a hypocalcemia, Toivola and Mather. It is seen in heavily lactating bitches during the first 3 weeks after parturition, although it may occur prior to, during, or up to 6 weeks after parturition, Bloom, Lawler. The serum calcium level drops from a normal of 9 to 12 mg. per 100 ml. to 5 to 7 mg. It may occur in all breeds but is seen most commonly in the small or medium-sized bitches. The disease is characterized by rapid breathing, a dry mouth and sclera, restlessness, nervousness, and whining, followed by staggering, incoordination, stiffness of limbs, and an elevated body temperature. Later there is the development of symptoms of inability to rise, extended legs, excessive salivation, champing movements, dilated pupils, clonic and tonic spasms and convulsions, congested mucous membranes, labored respirations and a rapid, hard pulse. The prognosis is good if treatment is instituted, but spontaneous recoveries may occur. Treatment consists of administering sodium pentobarbital or 5 to 10 ml. of a 10 per cent calcium gluconate solution intravenously, intraperitoneally or subcutaneously. Giving larger amounts of calcium may favor recurrence of the condition as in cattle with hypocalcemia. Recurrence of the condition is more common following the use of calcium gluconate than of sodium pentobarbital. If the pups are old enough they should be weaned. The bitch and cat should be fed added amounts of calcium lactate or gluconate in the ration. The administration of corticosteroid therapy, 5 mg. prednisolone or 25 mg. hydrocortisme, daily will help prevent a relapse. If given for a week or more the steroid therapy should be withdrawn gradually, Kallfelz. If the bitch has metritis, antibiotics should be given with the corticosteroids. The disease is rare in the cat, but symptoms and treatment are the same as in the dog.

Eclampsia or tetany in the sow has been described in Europe but has apparently not been observed in the United States.

Postparturient hemoglobinuria is an uncommon disease of high-producing, older dairy cows occurring 2 to 4 weeks after calving and characterized by hemoglobinemia, hemoglobinuria, and anemia. It is associated with rations deficient in phosphorus or rations high in rape, turnips, kale, beet pulp or cabbage. The affected cows show anorexia, weakness, dehydration, pale mucous membranes, rapid pulse and respiration, constipation and in the later severe stages, prostration and death after a course of 3 to 5 days. In mild cases or treated cases recovery occurs after several weeks. In severe cases there is a hypophosphatemia as low as 0.5 to 1.5 mg./100 ml. of serum; normal values are 4 to 6 mg./100 ml. Postparturient hemoglobinuria should be differentiated from leptospirosis and pyelonephritis. Treatment consists of blood transfusions to effect; the intravenous injection of phosphorus containing compounds and oral supplementation of the ration with monosodium phosphate or possibly bone meal or dicalcium phosphate especially if cruciferous plants are in the diet, Blood and Henderson.

Puerperal Infections

Uterine Infections and Diseases

Retained Placenta or Retention of the Afterbirth or Fetal Membranes is one of the most common conditions occurring in animals following parturition. It is observed chiefly in the dairy cow and less commonly in the other domestic species.

Retained placenta in the cow. In physiological parturition the afterbirth of the cow falls away within 3 to 8 hours following calving. If the placenta is retained longer than 8 to 12 hours the condition is considered pathological.

Etiology. Retention of the fetal membranes is basically due to failure of the villi of the fetal cotyledon to detach themselves from the maternal crypts of the caruncle. After the fetus is expelled and the umbilical cord ruptures no blood is pumped into the fetal villi and they shrink in size. In the dam, uterine contractions continue and the large amount of blood formerly going to the uterus is markedly reduced. The maternal caruncles become smaller in size, due to a reduced blood supply, and the maternal crypts dilate. Arthur reported that although there is no muscle in the caruncle, during contractions of the uterine wall following parturition the shape of the caruncles may change from oval to round. Detachment of fetal cotyledons from the maternal caruncle was much easier during these contraction waves than between them. Other workers, including Fincher and Shaw, have stated that stimulating uterine contractions by the injection of pituitrin immediately after calving apparently lowered the number of retained placentas, by comparison with control cows not thus injected. Vinattieri, Hayard and Artioli showed that separation of buffalo calves from the dams immediately after birth, so that suckling could not stimulate the release of pitocin from the posterior pituitary lobe, resulted in 22.7 percent retention of the afterbirth in 189 calvings as compared with 4.9 per cent retained placentas in 122 calvings on the same farms when suckling was allowed.

On histologic examination of fetal cotyledons and maternal caruncles taken an average time of 4.75 hours after normal calving, degeneration and necrosis of the fetal villi and necrosis and degeneration of the epithelium of the maternal crypts were present, and the latter were filled with debris, Kennedy. These findings in normal cows were essentially similar to those in cows having a retained placenta. Incomplete data accumulated by Kennedy showed little or no histologic differences between normal cotyledons and caruncles and those in which retained placenta developed. Bjorkman and Sollen reported there were morphologically three types of retained placentas; one type was associated with abortion and premature birth with immature placentomes; the second type was associated with hyperemia and were few in number; and the third and most common type was associated with small portions of necrotic epithelium between the chorionic villi and the cryptal walls. In retained placenta normal separation and loosening of the villi from the maternal crypts is interfered with and adhesions form. In easily removed placentas the loosening process comes about by autolysis of the chorionic villi. After several days leucocytes and bacteria were in the placentomes. Therefore placentitis was a secondary phenomenon. Benesch and Wright indicated that the incidence of retained placenta is high in births occurring several days before the expected date, because the placenta has not undergone the degeneration necessary for normal detachment. Although there is as yet no definite information about the exact manner in which the fetal membranes are expelled or fall away from the caruncles, it is rather apparent that it is a complex process involving a reduction of blood supply followed by shrinking of both maternal and fetal placental structures, degenerative changes, and strong uterine contractions.

There is evidence to show that infections of the uterus during gestation may be a cause for retained placenta. Infectious agents, such as **Brucella abortus,** tuberculosis, **Vibrio fetus** and various mold infections cause a placentitis and cotyledonitis resulting in abortion or pathological parturition with retention of the placenta. Arthur provided sound evidence to minimize the importance of this general cause of retained placenta. This author agrees with Arthur that too much emphasis in the past has been placed on intrauterine infections during gestation as a cause for retained placentas. Fincher reported that about 20 to 25 per cent of 282 cases of retained placenta he studied were infected with **Brucella abortus,** but these were also associated with abortions and premature births. McDonald, Smith and Moore reported the occurrence of many placental retentions in herds affected with **Vibrio fetus.** Benesch and Wright quoted Gotze as stating that 30 per cent of all retained placentas in cattle in Germany were due to **Brucella abortus.** The author has observed many **mold** infections, due to aspergilli or mucor molds, causing a marked cotyledonitis and severe retention of the fetal membranes. Bendixen and Plum reported that examination of 2027 placentas revealed 121 with mold. Of these latter 73 per cent were aspergillus. Many infected placentas were not retained. Other diseases and organisms causing abortion or premature birth might also produce endometritis, placentitis, and retention of the fetal membranes by inflammatory reactions of the cotyledon and caruncle similar to lesions described by Hallman in his article on brucellosis.

Ronning and cow-workers showed that the highest incidence of retained placenta, 69 per cent, occurred in an experimental group of cattle on low levels of carotene intake. The incidence could be correlated with the various feeding levels of carotene. In hyperkeratosis, in which vitamin A levels are very low, the incidence of retained placenta, metritis, and abortion is high. Probably vitamin A is necessary for maintaining the health and resistance of the epithelium of the uterus and placenta. Low vitamin A levels lead to the development of infections. A lack of minerals such as iodine has been reported by Moberg, and Heuken and Vandersall to be a cause of retained placenta, but this requires further substantiation. Dawson has suggested that premature calvings and calves with enlarged thyroid glands together with an increased incidence of retained placentas may occur in iodine deficient herds. Hyperthyroid cattle of the Jersey or Guernsey breeds may also calve early and have retained placentas.

In the cow, many abortions occurring after the fifth month of pregnancy are accompanied by retained placenta. In cattle calving 1 to 2 weeks prematurely, especially in twin pregnancy, retained placenta occurs in 30 to 50 per cent of the animals. Moller et al. reported the ratio of retained placenta to abortions at different times of gestation was 1:7 at 121 to 150 days, 1:6 at 151 to 180 days, 1:3 at 181 to 210 days, 1:2.2 at 211 to 240 days and 1:1.7 at 241 to 250 days of gestation. Practically no retained placentas occurred after abortions prior to 120 days and the incidence dropped to 1.5 per cent of calvings between 271 and 280 days of gestation. McDonald reported on 8 cows in which the corpus luteum was removed between 57 and 68 days of pregnancy, and pregnancy was maintained by daily injections of 75 to 100 mg. of progesterone until between 162 to 237 days of gestation. Most of the calvings occurred from 258 to 273 days, and 7 of the 8 cows retained the fetal membranes. In 2 other cows treated similarly, and 3 cows in which the corpus luteum was removed between 207 and 230 days, progesterone was administered from 248 to 278 days of gestation; all these cows dropped the afterbirth physiologically. Thus, progesterone deficiency may cause the retention of the fetal membranes or indirectly cause it by predisposing to early parturition. It may be possible that some abortions, early calvings, or retained placentas are due to a progesterone deficiency or a cortisol excess late in gestation.

Diseases causing uterine inertia or atony result in a high incidence of retention of the fetal membranes. These are: dropsy of the fetal membranes, uterine torsion, twinning, fetal giantism, primary or secondary uterine inertia, dystocia, and other pathological conditions. DeSutter reported that retained placenta was observed in about 70 per cent of dystocia cases due to uterine torsion and failure of cervical dilation, and in about 25 per cent of dystocia cases due to over-size of a living fetus. Vandeplassche and Martens reported an incidence of 8 per cent retained placenta in normal births but a 55 per cent incidence in abnormal deliveries such as twins, cesareans, fetotomies, dystocias and abortions. Failure of normal uterine involution was frequently associated with retained placenta. The pathological conditions causing these diseases or abnormal conditions resulting in uterine inertia—whether they be infectious, hereditary, nutritional, circulatory, or hormonal—also predispose to retention of the placenta. Erb et al. studied 7,387 calvings in one Holstein herd for a period of 25 years. The incidence of retained placenta averaged 10.5 per cent and affected 38.6 per cent of the 2607 cows. Retained placenta rose from 5.4 per cent in primipara to nearly 25 per cent at the ninth calving. Elimination of brucellosis from the herd did not lower the incidence of retained placentas. Twins and abortions were associated with 37.7 per cent of all retained placentas. Significantly more daughters from dams having retained placentas had retained placentas than daughters from dams not retaining their afterbirth. Retained placentas were more common following the birth of single male calves, 56 per cent vs a 51.6 per cent herd average. Twin births in which two males or one male were present also had a higher rate of retention. They concluded that retained placenta is not entirely caused by previous pathological conditions, a theory strongly supported by Williams. Cohen's report indicating that retained placentas were more common during February through April in the northern hemisphere is also supported by this the data of Erb et al..

Retention of the fetal membranes is less common in beef breeds than in dairy breeds confined in stables for long periods. The incidence of retained placenta varies widely from herd to herd at various times. Boyd and Sellers reported retained placentas in 6.4 per cent of 450 parturitions that included only brucellosis-free cows and births of living, single calves. Palmer recorded 11.7 per cent in 125 cattle free from brucellosis and tuberculosis. Kennedy reported an incidence of 8.3 per cent in 431 calvings in British herds in which brucellosis was either absent or quiescient. Arthur cited Gotze as stating the incidence in Hannover, Germany, as being 4 to 5 per cent. In over 24,000 calvings in Israel, Ben-David reported a 5.08 per cent incidence of retained placenta in single births and a 99 per cent incidence in twin births, for a total over all incidence of 8.4 per cent. In New Zealand the incidence of retained placenta was 1.96 per cent in over 36,000 dairy cattle kept at pasture the year around, Moller et al.. The incidence of retained placenta in herds infected with active brucellosis, in cows producing twins, or in cows aborting due to other causes is high, probably from 30 to 50 per cent or more. Once retention of the afterbirth occurred in a cow, there was about a 20 per cent chance of it recurring again, Erb et al..

It has been repeatedly observed by the author that in a certain year a high incidence of retained placentas 30 to 80 per cent, would develop in a dairy herd that formerly had relatively few cases, 2 to 8 per cent. Once retained placentas started nearly every cow calving thereafter would be affected and/or develop postpartum metritis. These herds were free of the common enzootic infections of reproduction that cause abortion such as brucellosis, vibriosis, leptospirosis, IBR-IPV and mold infections. The affected cows were calving in the same barn and in many instances in the same calving stalls in frequent succession. When there was an hiatus of several months or more when no cows calved or when cows were calving on pasture away from the barn, the incidence of retained placenta and metritis dropped dramatically to the low levels of former years even when calving was again resumed in the barn or calving stalls at a later date. This pattern of retained placentas and postpartum infection closely resembles that seen in calf scours and the metritis-mastitis-agalactia syndrome in sows. In fact the author has observed severe outbreaks of virulent scours in the newborn associated with a high incidence of retained placentas and metritis in the dams in the same herds. From these observations the author hypothesized that these severe enzootic outbreaks of retained placentas and secondary metritis were due to certain highly virulent organisms of **Streptococcus dysgalactiae, E coli, Staphylococcus, Pseudomonas aeruginosa, C. pyogenes** and/or other organisms which developed in these barns or calving stalls infecting the genital tract of the parturient cow at the time of calving and causing an acute metritis, uterine inertia, retained placenta and then secondary placentitis and metritis. As long as cows are calving in frequent succession in such an environment the infection continues from one cow to the next. When a period of several months or more elapses between cows calving in such an environment the infection dies out on the premises. Since it is impossible to thoroughly disinfect a barn or even most calving stalls the only alternative is to remove the parturient cow from this environment to a clean noninfected one for calving. This is difficult on most farms and farmers are reluctant to go to this inconvenience even if suitable noninfected calving stalls or areas can be improvised. On affected farms where the author has secured the cooperation of the farmer to follow this regimen of removing the parturient cow from the infected environment for 5 to 10 days before and after calving whether by placing the cow in a noninfected or noncontaminated separate barn, lot, shed or stall or by putting the cow on pasture, the results have been very gratifying with a marked drop to normal in the incidence of retained placenta and postpartum metritis. Because of the adverse effects on reproduction and milk production the veterinarian should not hesitate to strongly recommend this often troublesome chore upon the farmer. With the increased size of many dairy herds and the trend toward "zero" pasture and the confinement of cows in barnyards and freestall housing, the author forsees the continuation of such serious problems unless management and housing designs develop so that calving stalls can be built isolated from each other and of such construction that lends itself to thorough disinfection as has been necessary for continuous farrowing operations to develop in the swine industry. There is evidence in England, Sweden and the U.S.A. that bedding cows on sawdust is more conducive to coliform mastitis, calf scours and retained placenta and postpartum metritis than bedding the animals on straw. For those of my readers who are reluctant to accept the hypothesis that acute uterine infections resulting in retained placentas and metritis can develop in the few hours between the onset of parturition and the normal time of expulsion of the placenta they should note the very short period needed for the development of acute bovine mastitis, calf septicemia and acute metritis in sows.

The morbid anatomy of retained placenta may vary from slight evidence of disease to severe lesions. According to the location of the inflammatory reactions in the uterus, placentitis may be classified as apical, cervical or diffuse. The nongravid horn may or may not be involved when the placenta in the gravid horn is retained. The degree of placentitis in the nongravid horn is usually not as severe as in the gravid horn since the placentomes are smaller and less complex. The degree of placentitis may vary from a mild peripheral type of necrosis involving only the villi to a severe necrosis involving the entire cotyledon and a part or all of the caruncle.

If the placentitis developed prior to calving or abortion, the allantois chorion may be edematous, necrotic or leathery, or hemorrhagic. Uterine "sand" and old or fresh clotted blood may be present. Often a reddish-brown to yellow exudate is found in the utero-chorionic space. Adventitious placentae may vary from a few small areas to nearly complete involvement of the entire endometrium of one or both horns. In mold infections the cotyledon is usually very large and swollen. Uterine and placental disease may occasionally cause fetal disease or anoxia that results in the presence of fetal meconium in the amniotic fluid, staining the fetus. In most cases of retained placenta the calf appears quite normal.

The symptoms of retained placenta are usually obvious, a portion of the fetal membranes hang from the vulva 12 hours or more following abortion, normal parturition, or dystocia. Occasionally the fetal membranes do not hang from the vulva but are entirely within the vagina or uterus. In the treatment of herds severely affected with genital disease Williams recommended close observation of the cow to observe when the fetal membranes were dropped. Examination of the fetal membranes can be made to be certain they are completely expelled and no portion remains in the uterus. If they are not expelled normally the uterus should be examined manually per vaginum in 24 to 36 hours. After 48 hours it is usually difficult or impossible to insert the hand into the uterus if no fetal membranes are within the cervix. The presence of the membranes lying in the cervix tends to retard contraction of that organ. After a dystocia the placentomes may be felt; if they are very swollen, hard, firm, inflammed, or congested, the placenta will be retained. If the placentomes are soft and pliable the cow will often drop the afterbirth within a few hours.

About 75 to 80 per cent of cattle with retention of the fetal membranes show no marked illness. According to Arthur and Gotze, about 50 to 60 per cent may exhibit slight to moderate illness by a temporary reduction in appetite or milk flow. About 20 to 25 per cent may exhibit moderate to severe symptoms of metritis and septic metritis as shown in some cases by anorexia, depression, elevation of body temperature, increase in pulse rate, decrease in milk flow, and loss of weight. These percentages may differ in certain herds depending upon the severity of the infections causing the secondary metritis. In severely affected animals retained placenta may be associated with or complicated by other diseases such as: mastitis, septic metritis with perimetritis or peritonitis, severe straining, necrotic vaginitis, parturient paresis, and acetonemia. Arthur cited Jordan as stating that the bacteriological picture of the uterus in cases of retained placenta was similar to that of a uterus with delayed involution or atony without retained placenta. First the **Streptococci dysgalactiae** and the staphylococci appear, and later the diptheroids, **Corynebacterium pyogenes,** coliform, and anaerobic bacteria may be found. In retained placenta the white blood cell picture showed a slight to marked shift to the left. In uncomplicated cases a lymphocytosis developed. In more severe cases a definite leucopenia occurred, Moberg. The total number of white blood cells usually do not increase markedly. After 24 hours the placenta begins to macerate and a fetid, putrid odor develops. The afterbirth or secundine may fall away anytime within 24 hours to 14 days, depending upon the severity of the disease and possibly the type of treatment used. In most cows with retained placenta the cervix contracts after 48 to 72 hours, so that it may be difficult to insert the hand through the cervix. This contraction takes place sooner if no fetal membranes are present in the cervix.

Prognosis. Arthur indicated that the mortality rate in retention of the fetal membranes should not exceed 1 to 2 per cent in uncomplicated cases. He cited Gotze as reporting in retained placenta cases a mortality rate of 4 per cent: emaciation, infertility, or unprofitableness in 20 per cent, a short duration of the disease with temporary irregularities of milk production and fertility in 50 to 60 per cent, and a nearly undisturbed puerperium in 15 to 25 per cent. Fincher reported on a substantial number of cases of retained placenta treated by various means in the Ambulatory Clinic of the New York State Veterinary College from 1920 to 1941. During the years 1920 to 1928, 755 cases were treated by early or late removal, and much douching, with a mortality rate of 4.2 per cent. During 1928 to 1934, 1109 cases were treated by removal at 72 hours, with little or no douching, with a mortality rate of 2.8 per cent. From 1934 to 1941, 1680 cases were treated with late removal, 72 hours or more, no douching and liberal use of sulfanilamide, with a mortality rate of 1.1 per cent. In this same clinic, from 1943 to 1953, 3742 cases of retained placenta were treated by late removal, 72 hours or longer, no douching, and the use of sulfonamides and antibiotics, if necessary, with a mortality rate of 1.3 per cent. This latter figure included cases in which septic metritis, mastitis, peritonitis, and other conditions were complications which undoubtedly contributed to or caused the fatalities. Palmer made a very interesting study of 44 cases of retained placenta in 2 herds totaling 125 animals in which no manual removal of the placenta was attempted during a period of 3 years. These herds were free of brucellosis and tuberculosis. No treatment was given to any cows with the exception of 4 that became quite ill. In these 4 cows proflavine and saline solutions were introduced into the uterus but probably had no influence on the course of the disease. Of the 44 cows 81.8 per cent had calved at term, 18.2 per cent had aborted, and 16 per cent had twins. The placentas were retained from 2 to 11 days, an average of 6.8 days before dropping away naturally. During the first two weeks after calving the appetite was good in 31.8 per cent, fair in 54.5 per cent, and poor in 13.6 per cent. Body weight remained normal in 88.6 per cent. Lactation was good in 29.5 per cent, fair in 63.6 per cent and poor in 6.8 per cent. When the 44 cows that had untreated retained placentas were compared with 44 cows in the same herds calving normally without retained placenta there was no significant difference in the numbers of cows in the two groups having to be sold because of sterility, abortion, or delayed conception. In these two herds no cows were bred back until 90 to 150 days after calving.

The effect of retained placentas on subsequent fertility is important to consider, as delayed involution and chronic endometritis following retention of the membranes is common. Apparently after 2 to 3 months and a number of estrous periods most cattle having a retained placenta eliminate the infection and the uterus becomes normal. Buch and coworkers reported that in 71 abnormal calvings the postpartum interval from calving to complete uterine involution averaged 52 days or only 5 days longer than in 252 cows that calved normally. If the owner desired to breed the cow before 90 days after the abnormal calving, these workers recommended examination of the uterus to determine if it was completely involuted. Erb et al. reported that 19.2 per cent of cows having retained placenta had another retention at subsequent parturitions. They showed that young cows having a retained placenta averaged one less calving than cows the same age not affected with retained placenta. Cows not having genital disorders such as chronic metritis following retained placentas were nearly as fertile as normal cows but there was a 30 to 50 per cent greater probability that genital disorders would occur in affected cows. Moller et al. stated in their study that the nonreturn rate to first service before 60 days postpartum was 28.2 per cent in cows with retained placenta and 50.3 per cent for cows without a retained placenta; after 60 days the comparable percentages were 52.2 per cent and 64.0 per cent. When "nonreturn" cows after service were checked to diagnose pregnancy they found 10.6 per cent of 592 cows with retained placenta at their previous calving were not pregnant while only 5.4 per cent of 19,173 cows with no retention were not pregnant. Following retained placenta in some cows, permanent sterility results, due to pyometra, perimetritis, salpingitis, ovaritis, severe damage to the endometrium, or other causes related to the retention. In most of the animals affected with retention of the fetal membranes the major loss is an economic one of a slight to moderate loss of milk and a slight to moderate delay in the involution of the uterus, and subsequent conception.

Treatment. After reviewing the literature on bovine retained placenta and listening to many veterinarians describe their methods of treatment, the author has been amazed and impressed by the infinite number and variety of techniques employed, the drugs and hormones recommended, and the time lapse between parturition and the attempted removal of the placenta. With so many varied techniques and products being used, one is forced to recognize the fact that probably no treatment would be necessary in handling most cases of retention of the fetal membranes. This was demonstrated by Palmer. Arthur indicated that both in England and in Europe there is an increasing volume of opinion in favor of not making any manual attempt to detach the fetal placenta from the maternal caruncles. No matter how carefully the operation is performed some injury to the endometrium may result, and the risk of toxemia and septicemia is thereby increased. A clean, manual examination of the uterus can be made. The operator should wear a surgical rubber glove and long sleeve on one arm and a surgical glove on the other to protect himself from brucellosis or an infection of the arm or hand. Disposable plastic gloves and sleeves of good quality are more sanitary and practical than rubber gloves and sleeves. He should wear rubber coveralls or an apron and boots that may be easily cleaned and disinfected after the operation. The perineal region of the cow should be carefully cleaned and washed with soap, water, and mild antiseptic, and kept clean during the operation. To keep the cow, especially one with loose feces, from either defecating frequently or straining, epidural anesthesia may be used. A plentiful supply of clean water is essential. The cow's tail should be held out of the way by an assistant or tied with a tail rope over the back to one of its fore legs. The free part of the fetal membranes should be drawn through the cervix, thereby reducing the amount of membranes in the uterus and aiding its drainage. If the fetal membranes fall away readily from the caruncles they should be removed. If much fluid is present in the uterus it should be siphoned off by a sterile soft rubber horse catheter or stomach tube held in the fist to keep the fetal membranes from plugging the end of the tube. The siphon may be started by filling the rubber tube with water and holding it pinched off as it is introduced. Douching the uterus is contraindicated when membranes are present as it is difficult to remove the fluid completely. Another method of removing this excess fluid is to use large swabs of absorbent cotton and gently wipe the uterus free of exudate, Fincher. Large amounts of fetid reddish watery fluid in the uterus is usually accompanied by signs of toxemia, depression, and anorexia.

Manual removal of a retained placenta in the cow is practiced by most veterinarians because the diseased, macerating fetal membranes are serving no good purpose and the farmer desires and expects the veterinarian to remove this unsightly fetid mass from the genital tract. In most cases the fetal membranes have not macerated sufficiently for easy removal before 48 hours after parturition. Although in some cases enough autolysis has occurred so the villi separate readily from the crypts and removal may be accomplished easily as early as 12 to 24 hours after calving. Ben-David and Trainer indicated the best time for removal of the placenta was 24 to 48 hours after parturition. In these latter cases the cows would probably have dropped the placenta without aid within another 24 to 48 hours. It has been the practice of the author and many other veterinarians not to examine or treat retained placenta until 72 hours after parturition unless the cow develops anorexia, an elevated temperature or other symptoms of septicemia. At this time the uterus has contracted in most cases so the apex of the horn may be reached. The cervix is usually still sufficiently open to allow passage of the hand and arm without resultant trauma. When removal is attempted at 72 hours after parturition the uterus has by walling it off developed a protective barrier to the infection and there is less chance of a septicemia or toxemia developing than there would be if removal is attempted earlier. At whatever time the placenta is removed this should be done gently and quickly within 5 to 20 minutes, in a clean manner, and with as few withdrawals and reintroductions of the arm as possible. The use of epidural anesthesia controls straining and defecation and makes possible a cleaner, more hygienic, and gentler operation. If the operation cannot be performed in a gentle manner, with as little interference as possible with nature's processes, the fetal membranes should be left alone even though the cervix may contract so that on subsequent visits by the veterinarian the hand cannot be inserted into the uterus. If this happens it is best not to attempt dilation of the cervix, as it is difficult or nearly impossible to do so without severe trauma. The cervix should be left alone, the membranes should be allowed to fall away naturally, or gentle traction on the fetal membranes will remove them after the maternal caruncles and fetal cotyledons have separated from the uterine wall by autolysis. Even if the membranes or a portion of them macerate and are absorbed in the uterus this is better than severely traumatizing the cervix in attempts to dilate it.

It has been observed by the author and others that if the placenta is allowed to drop away of its own accord, or if it is gently withdrawn from the uterus even 10 to 12 days after parturition, involution of the uterus occurs sooner, and cessation of uterine discharge ceases more quickly than when the placenta is removed in a rough manner and portions are left in the uterus. Hammermann showed in a study of 632 cows with retained placenta that a conservative systemic treatment with sulfonamides orally and intravenously resulted in higher subsequent fertility than a more "radical" treatment with manual removal and various local intrauterine treatments. The uterus containing a retained placenta may be compared with a large abscess in which the necrotic core has not separated from the surrounding tissues. The surgical procedures governing the handling of an abscess should also govern the handling of the infected uterus. Conservative treatment is indicated and essential.

The veterinarian should have the courage of his convictions in handling these cases, inasmuch as traumatizing the uterus by attempting to remove the placenta when removal is difficult or impossible results in either immediate septicemia with a marked drop in milk and appetite, elevation of temperature, loss of weight and possible death, or else a prolonged period of convalescence during which time shreds of placenta and exudate are expelled from the uterus, pyometra or chronic metritis develops, or protracted or even permanent infertility may result from uterine abscess, perimetritis, salpingitis or severe endometritis. If in order to avoid traumatizing the uterus or leaving placental shreds and fragments in the uterus a veterinarian refuses to remove a placenta that is not ready to be separated from the maternal caruncles, and explains to the owner his reason for the decision, this may prevent criticism by a client who formerly has been accustomed to having the placenta "taken" on the first and only call in all cases of retained placenta.

Manual removal of the placenta is contraindicated in cows with an elevated body temperature, above 103° F. and in cows or heifers suffering from severe necrotic vaginitis. In the former a septicemia and toxemia are already present and would be aggravated by manual manipulation of the placentomes. Administration of antibiotics parenterally and locally, or sulfonamides orally or intravenously in cows showing toxic symptoms is indicated for a period of several days before removal is attempted. Removal of the placenta particularly in heifers having necrotic vaginitis and vulvitis with a small, dry, swollen genital canal may make the vaginitis and vulvitis worse and may increase straining that is probably already present. Since it has been proved that most cows suffering from retained placenta need no treatment, and the others only parenteral treatment with antibiotics or parenteral and oral treatment with sulfonamides to control septicemia, the removal of the placenta from a cow with an elevated temperature, vaginitis, septic metritis or possibly other diseases, such as acute mastitis and traumatic gastritis, is contraindicated. Removing the placenta in an incomplete, rough, insanitary manner is always inadvisable.

Occasionally when the union between the cotyledons and caruncles is very firm and most of the caruncle becomes necrotic and sloughs, it may be 10 to 15 days before the macerating placenta and cotyledons can be removed. If the fetal membranes are removed prematurely by traction or improper manual removal, thereby leaving the fetal cotyledon on the necrotic maternal caruncle, these necrotic caruncles and cotyledons may become dry and inspissated and remain as a foreign body in the uterus for 3 to 8 weeks or longer. When found several weeks after parturition, they may be removed by injections of estrogens to relax and dilate the cervix and contract the uterus together with gentle massage of the uterus per rectum. A rubber douche tube may be used as a siphon and by suction on the caruncles by the siphon tube they may be coaxed and withdrawn through the cervix. If left in the uterus these may eventually macerate, but recovery is prolonged and chronic metritis, pyometra and sterility usually occur.

In removing the placenta manually the third or fourth days after parturition, or earlier if the placenta can be removed easily, the hand is inserted between the endometrium and chorion in the intercotyledonary space and the individual fetal cotyledon and its caruncle are grasped gently, squeezed, and with the thumb and forefinger the two structures are gently separated by a rolling, pushing, squeezing motion. This may be aided by traction with the other hand on the adjacent portions of the fetal membranes as the separation is completed. The cotyledons in the cervical area of the uterus are removed from the caruncles first and then by traction with the outside hand the placenta is pulled out and tension maintained as the cotyledons in the middle portion of the horn and the nongravid horn are removed. The ovarian pole may be difficult to reach. Sometimes traction on the placenta will pull the apex of the horn nearer the cervix and thus aid removal. As Williams stated, it is highly desirable to remove all of the fetal membranes and not leave remnants in the uterus to act as foci of infection as these must be expelled or macerate before recovery can take place. The blood vessels of the placenta are among the last portions of the placenta to macerate. If the entire placenta cannot be removed, it is better to insert a few capsules, tablets, or a solution of antibiotic and revisit the cow in one to three days, or let the placenta fall away naturally.

The layman's practices of tying a weight on the placenta or of cutting the placenta off close to the vulva are not desirable. First, the weight frequently causes the cow to strain and causes premature and incomplete breaking away of the afterbirth, leaving a part of it still in the uterus. In rare cases this weight may cause invagination of the uterine horn. Removing the placenta close to th vulva in order to prevent the cow from swinging it against the milker is likely to result in the placenta dropping back into the uterus followed by early closure of the cervix. The afterbirth may remain in the uterus long after it has separated from the caruncles, because the weight of the placenta hanging from the vulva is not present to draw it out. If the placenta is dragging on the ground it should be cut off at the level of the hocks to prevent its being stepped on and torn away from the uterus.

Hormones have been widely used in the treatment of retained placenta. The use of pituitrin or oxytocin has been mentioned as being of possible value in preventing retained placenta when given shortly after the expulsion of the fetus or after dystocia operations. In dystocia, besides aiding in the expulsion of the fetal membranes, pituitrin may prevent prolapse of the uterus. It is advisable to inject 3 to 5 cc., 30 to 50 units, immediately after calving. One to 3 further subcutaneous injections of 3 to 5 cc. of pituitrin or 1 to 2 cc., 20 to 40 units, of oxytocin at 1- to 2-hour intervals may be given. Possibly an intravenous drip giving the same dose over a period of several hours would be more physiological and desirable. Pituitrin or oxytocin is of questionable value beyond 24 to 48 hours after calving.

The estrogens have been widely used in the treatment of retained placenta. Stilbestrol or estradiol has little or no effect on the rate of separation of the fetal cotyledons and maternal caruncles. Estrogens do, however, exert a definite action on the uterus by increasing its tone and muscular activity, stimulating the flow of mucus, increasing the circulation, and relaxing the cervix. These facts, together with the reports by Rowson, Lamming and Fry, and Black and coworkers that the uterus is better able to control or overcome infection during estrum or when treated with estrogens, show the logic of using this hormone in the treatment of retained placenta. The author has given 20 to 35 mg. of stilbestrol intramuscularly to hundreds of cows affected with retained placenta. Estradiol in doses of 1 to 4 mg. may also be used. Oftentimes this dose has been repeated 2 to 3 times at 2- to 3-day intervals. No harmful effects have been observed in any of the cattle at the doses recommended. Arthur summarized numerous reports on the use of estrogens for the treatment of retained placenta with inconclusive results. Excessive doses of estrogens should not be given as this may predispose to ovarian adhesions by possible extension of infection through the oviducts (See pyometra). Vandeplassche and Martens reported that the feeding of 30 mg. of stilbestrol daily for the last 9 days, 3 to 20 days, before parturition had no effect on reducing the incidence of retained placenta. Moller et al. stated that in their experiments the parenteral administration of stilbestrol was of no value. Fincher mentioned that some cases of uterine atony associated with retained placenta may greatly benefit from the injection of calcium gluconate especially if a low blood-calcium level is the cause of the uterine atony. If the uterus is severely diseased and atonic the uterine wall may be incapable of responding to the injections of hormones. In recent years many veterinarians have used 1 to 3 mg of ergonovine or a similar product developed from ergot that produce a more prolonged rate of uterine contraction than doses of oxytocin.

A wide range of antiseptics have been used locally to control the bacterial flora in the treatment of retained placenta and the uterus following removal of the retained fetal membranes. These early drugs consisted of such products as charcoal, boric acid, acriflavine, bismith subnitrate, bismuth formic iodide, bismuth thymol iodide, chlorine preparations, iodine in oil, silver oxide, bismuth formic iodide in oil, chlorophyll and bismuth and iodoform in oil (Bipp). This latter product imparted an odor to the milk that prohibited its use in dairy cattle. Various products containing sodium perborate have been advocated to aid in the removal and treatment of retained placenta. On contact with tissue debris these products release much gas and cause foaming similar to that resulting from the use of hydrogen peroxide. These products are slightly irritating and probably should not be used in the uterus if the cervix is contracted. Because of their effect on tissue debris a number of enzyme products containing urea, yeast, pepsin, and papain have been advocated. It is doubtful if these varied preparations greatly alter the course of the disease. Wetherill reported that the proteolytic enzymes and diuretics of the hydrochlorothiazide type are of undetermined effectiveness for the treatment of retained placenta.

Sulfanilimide, sulfathiazole, sulfamerazine, sulfamethazine, and sulfathalidine have been used locally in the uterus and have been approved by some veterinarians, while other veterinarians indicate that these drugs are rather insoluble, tend to settle in the apex of the horn and are of questionable value. Penicillin, streptomycin and tyrothricin have been used widely in the local treatment of retained placenta. The former is usually quickly inactivated by penicillase produced by the infective organisms in the uterus and the latter is rather irritating in large amounts. In recent years 1 to 3 gm. of the broad-range antibiotics such as oxytetracycline (Terramycin), Chlortetracycline (Aureomycin), Tetracycline, Furacin and others have been used locally in cases of retention of the fetal membranes. For immediate response these are used as an infusion in 200 to 500 ml. of saline or warm water. The boluses or powder produce a slightly slower response. These appear to be the first products used locally that definitely alter the course of the infection. The rate of putrefaction and lysis is greatly reduced. The usual fetid odor is largely eliminated. The retained membranes may tend to remain attached to the caruncles in the uterus for a slightly longer period. The use of these products in a case of septic metritis usually eliminates the local infection quite promptly and if used early, 24 to 36 hours after calving or as soon as the temperature becomes elevated or other signs of illness develop they usually bring about a prompt regression of the illness. Beattie and Leaming and Gould et al. reported favorably on the use of **Aureomycin** in the uterus in 612 cows with retained placenta, with only 2 cows developing acute metritis. In 31 cows with retained placenta manual removal was not attempted and 0.5 gm of **Aureomycin** was placed in the uterus every 1 to 2 days until the afterbirth dropped away. This took 2 to 10 days, with an average of 5.2 days. Subsequent conception rates were excellent, Easterbrooks and Plastridge. They recommended that manual removal not be attempted. Moller et al. after treating 508 cows with retained placenta in various ways reported that cows receiving local tetracycline intrauterine medication had a lower conception rate than those cows not receiving medication. If medication was initiated it was better to wait until 36 hours or more postpartum. Whether the retained membranes were removed or allowed to drop away had no effect on subsequent fertility. Banerjee reported that conception rate on first service was higher, 70 percent vs 40 to 50 percent, and days from parturition to conception were lower, 86 vs 91 to 110 days, in cows treated with intrauterine oxytetracycline within 72 hours of calving and the placenta was not removed than in cows receiving no medication. Removal of the placenta definitely lowered the conception rate at first service.

Observations and reports such as that of Kantor and Kamholz, Bierschwal and Uren, and Parr et al. have shown that hormones, sulfonamides, and antibiotics are rapidly absorbed from the uterus into the bloodstream. This systemic effect is further reason for the topical use in the uterus of these easily administered products. If large doses of antibiotics are placed locally in the uterus, the milk from treated cows should not be put in the supply for about 72 hours.

If symptoms of septic metritis develop with retention of the fetal membranes, sulfonamides administered orally, or sulfonamides and/or antibiotics administered parenterally are of great value along with supportive treatment with saline and glucose solutions, possibly blood transfusions intravenously, and estrogens intramuscularly, as described under the treatment of septic metritis. As in horses, laminitis often accompanies septic uterine infections in cattle but is not as obvious. The local treatment of the uterus should be very gentle and manual removal of the placenta should not be attempted. In rare cases a severe anaerobe or necrophorus infection may invade the uterus and these infections are usually fatal. In Europe in areas where anaerobe infections are common antiserum is usually administered after a dystocia. If severe straining is present with retained fetal membranes, epidural anesthesia should be given and the uterus and birth canal carefully and gently examined. In most cases the straining is due to a severe vulvitis or vaginitis, and these should be treated. Rarely it may be due to an invagination of the uterine horn. Tenesmus may also be associated with rabies in endemic areas.

It is recommended that all cows affected with retained placenta be examined 20 to 30 days after removal of the afterbirth to determine if involution of the uterus is proceeding normally and that postpartum metritis or pyometra is not present. If this is not done the cow may fail to show estrum and 90 days or more after parturition the disease condition will be diagnosed too late to prevent a serious delay in conception. Permanent sterility may result. The owner should be advised that many older cows affected with retained placenta should not be bred until 90 to 120 days after parturition. This time interval is usually necessary for proper involution and overcoming of the infection in the diseased uterus. In valuable cows the involution and return of the uterus to normal can be checked by periodic examinations during this period. If the uterus is completely involuted, no genital discharge is present and regular estrous cycles are occurring, cows with a history of retained placenta at the last parturition may be bred at 60 days postpartum with a good conception rate. All cattle having a persistent mucopurulent discharge from the vulva following retained placenta should be reexamined and treated.

Retained Placenta in the Mare is much less common than in the cow. Probably the same factors responsible for retention of the placenta in the cow also are present in the mare. The infection most commonly observed in association with retained placenta in the mare is **Streptococcus genitalium** or **zooepidemicus.** Many genital infections in the mare are related to vulvar defects leading to pneumovagina. In some mares air and infectious organisms may be aspirated through the cervix into the uterus during the act of windsucking. Infection also gains entrance to the uterus following foaling, when the mare gets up promptly and a rush of air fills the dilated genital tract and uterus. If the mare remains recumbent after foaling, until the placenta is about ready to drop away, the uterus is more contracted and less air is aspirated. The rush of contaminated air into the uterus after foaling might play an immediate role in the retention of the afterbirth. Jennings reported that retained placenta more commonly accompanied the large draft foals than the light horse foals. Genital diseases, including retained placenta, occurred more often in mares bred on the ninth day, or foaling heat. These factors, together with a lack of breeding and foaling hygiene might possibly explain why draft mares are more likely to have retained placenta than are Thoroughbred mares. Repeated breedings during one heat period or the breeding of infected mares or infected stallions may cause retained placenta. Jennings reported that placentas weighing over 14 lbs. in light mares were usually associated with infections of the uterus, and that the chorion was characterized by necrotic areas and edema. Retained placenta is probably less common in mares because of the simple, diffuse type of placentation and the strong uterine contractions aiding the separation of the villi from their maternal crypts and expelling the detached membranes. It is interesting that the physiologically expelled placentas of most mares, as in cows, are inverted. This apparently is due to the fact that the allantois chorion first separates from the rapidly contracting apices of the uterine horns and passes into the birth canal before it is separated from the uterine body. Williams reported retained placenta in the mare is likely to occur following abortion and prolonged gestation. Probably the main causes for retention of the afterbirth in the mare are infection, uterine inertia and other factors similar to those affecting cattle.

Symptoms. Physiologically the fetal membranes are expelled within 0.5 to 3 hours after parturition but it is fairly common to have the fetal membranes not drop away until 8 to 12 or more hours later without any observable symptoms of illness. Arthur stated that strong uterine contractions in the mare after foaling and just before expulsion of the placenta are often accompanied by signs of abdominal pain, recumbency, and colic. The mares that retain their afterbirths exhibit no such pains and appear normal, content, eat and drink, and suckle their foals. Slow expulsion of the placenta may be due to uterine inertia or exhaustion following expulsion of the fetus. The onset of delayed expulsion is indicated by the mare's developing colicy pains followed by the dropping away of the membranes in from 10 to 20 minutes. In a few nervous mares it is necessary to tie up or cut off the hanging retained placenta so that it will not frighten the mare into kicking and otherwise possibly injuring the foal. In dystocia the fetal membranes may be detached and wrapped around the fetus. The rapid separation of the fetal membranes probably accounts for the early death of the fetus in many equine dystocias. Retained fetal membranes can usually be observed hanging from the vulva. Occasionally the placenta may partially fall away and the apex or tip of the placenta will remain in the nongravid horn especially if the apex is thickened and edematous, Prickett. The weight of the placenta or the mare stepping on it may rip it away, leaving the tip of the nongravid horn in the uterus. This piece of placenta may act as a focus of infection often resulting in a severe metritis and secondary laminitis the third to seventh day after foaling. The afterbirth of each mare should be carefully examined after it falls away, to make certain no portion of the placenta remains in the uterus. Most cases of laminitis occurring after foaling are due to metritis often associated with a portion of the placenta being retained and floating in a uterus filled with fetid fluid. Uterine invagination or intussusception, usually of the nongravid horn into the uterine body, may accompany retention of the fetal membranes in the mare but it is seldom of a serious nature, Heatley and Fincher. The prognosis of retained placenta in the mare is usually good.

Treatment. It is generally recommended that removal of the placenta in the mare not be attempted for at least 12 hours after foaling. Jennings, Heatley, and Benesch and Wright recommended no treatment until 20 to 24 hours after foaling if the mare continues to eat, has a normal temperature and the pulse rate remains normal. With retained placenta it is common practice to administer 3 to 7 ml. of pituitrin, 30 to 70 units, or 2 to 5 ml. of oxytocin, 40 to 100 units, subcutaneously every 2 to 3 hours starting the fourth to twelfth hour after foaling. Vandeplassche recommended the administration of 40 to 50 units of oxytocin by slow intravenous drip over a period of several hours as a more physiologic way in which to give the hormone. The placenta was often passed during this period. It may be necessary to administer a tranquilizer to control mild colic and pain associated with the uterine contractions produced. Colicy symptoms may be produced by these injections. In most cases the afterbirth drops away within a few hours or before 24 hours have elapsed. Injections of sulfonamides such as sulfamethazine or sulfamerazine, 1 to 1.5 grain per pound of body weight daily, or **Aureomycin,** tetracycline or **Terramycin,** 1 to 3 mgm per pound of body weight daily, intravenously; or the intramuscular injection of 3 to 6 million units of aqueous penicillin daily and 5 gm. of streptomycin twice daily may be indicated to control infection.

After 20 to 24 hours postpartum the veterinarian, in a scrupulously clean manner, should scrub the perineum of the mare with soap and water, and bandage or have the tail held out of the way; then insert his hand and arm enclosed in a sterile rubber or plastic glove and sleeve into the birth canal and grasp the allantois chorion. By means of gentle traction and twisting on the fetal membranes to form a "rope," uniform traction may be applied to the fetal membranes as the hand is gently forced between the endometrium and chorion in the places where it is still attached. The entire placenta, including the tips of the horns, should be carefully removed. If necessary, examine the placenta after removal to be certain that the removal is complete. Sager advised a more conservative and gentle approach, which has much to recommend it, of inserting the hand inside the allantois chorion and gently massaging it away from the endometrium. If removal does not occur promptly supportive treatment should be given and the mare reexamined and treated 4 to 12 hours later. In one mare the author observed retained fetal membranes that remained firmly adherent to the endometrium for 72 hours without any adverse effect on the mare. Five to 10 years ago local treatment consisted of inserting into the uterus a pint of mineral oil and castor oil or an ounce of iodoform and 2 ounces of bismuth subnitrate in a pint of oil. The value of penicillin and of sulfonamides in powdered form in the uterus of mares is questioned by Arthur and the author. It is probable that the more stable but soluble broad-range antibiotics of the tetracycline and furacin groups would be of greater value in the local treatment of the uterus in mares as in cows. Intrauterine therapy is continued daily, usually for 2 to 4 days, until the uterus is well-involuted and the infection is largely overcome. It is highly desirable to administer tetanus antitoxin and probably pituitrin to a mare following removal of a retained placenta. Fincher and others recommended placing temporary clips in the upper two-thirds of the vulvar lips within several hours after foaling if the afterbirth had not been dropped and after removal of a retained placenta in the mare to prevent aspiration of air into the genital tract. At present douching of the uterus after removal of a retained placenta is considered a questionable practice although former workers including Williams advocated the general use of this technique. If the uterus is filled with fetid fluid this should be removed by siphoning through a sterile rubber tube. The danger of laminitis should always be considered. Ice packs should be placed on the feet and sulfonamides and/or antibiotics and antihistamines administered until normal involution of the uterus takes place and the danger of uterine infection subsides. Some advocate the use of stilbestrol, 30 to 60 mg., or estradiol, 3 to 6 mg., and ergonovine, 1 to 3 mg., intramuscularly daily for several injections.

Retained Placenta in the Ewe and Doe is handled in a manner similar to that in the cow except that removal from inside the uterus is seldom possible. If signs of elevated temperature, anorexia, and depression indicative of septic metritis are exhibited, parenteral injections of antibiotics, estrogens, oxytocin and antihistamines are recommended. Manual treatment is limited to occasional gentle traction on the hanging portion of the membranes. Some veterinarians introduce a broad-range antibiotic capsule or tablet 0.5 to 1.0 gm., into the uterus after carefully cleansing the external genitalia. The placenta usually drops away within 2 to 10 days.

Retained Placenta in the Sow is uncommon. It is usually impossible to determine if retention has occurred except by the symptoms of septic metritis, prostration, and a purulent vulvar discharge containing placental shreds. Although Arthur indicated that this condition usually causes a fatal metritis, it has rarely if ever been reported in the United States as being fatal. Since retained placenta is most likely to occur after a dystocia with prolonged labor it would be advisable in these cases to save the expelled fetal membranes, count the unbilical cords, and to give pituitrin, 2 to 3 ml., after relieving the dystocia. When septic metritis does occur because of a retained placenta, administration of stilbestrol, 10 to 20 mg. and the daily injection of intramuscular forms of antibiotics, such as 3,000,000 units of aqueous or oily preparations of penicillin, 1 to 2 gms. of streptomycin or 1 gm of intramuscular **Terramycin,** tetracycline, or **Aureomycin** are indicated. Intrauterine infusions of broad range antibiotics have been used by some veterinarians. A sterile AI catheter or a horse catheter may be used. The value of this type of therapy in the postpartum sow has not been proven. Good nursing is essential.

Retained Placenta in the Bitch and Cat is uncommon. It is seen most often in toy breeds in which dystocia or prolonged labor has occurred. It is occasionally seen during whelping as a temporary condition when the membranes of an expelled fetus may block the expulsion of the following fetuses. If the placenta is not expelled in 12 to 24 hours an acute metritis may result and unless it is treated early or a hysterectomy performed promptly, it usually is fatal in 4 to 5 days due to a necrosis of the uterine wall in the region of the placental attachments. Once toxic symptoms have developed in septic metritis in dogs due to retained placenta, the prognosis should be very guarded. The presence of a dark green vulvar discharge more than 12 hours after parturition is a symptom of retention of fetal membranes. If retained placenta occurs during whelping or is noticed within the first day afterwards, the retained membranes may be gently withdrawn from the birth canal and uterus with the finger. A pair of forceps padded with gauze or cotton may be rotated in the genital tract to wind up the membranes and remove them. Arthur stated that in the small bitch the uterus might be palpated and massaged over the retained membrane to help to force the latter through the cervix. This might be repeated in several hours if unsuccessful initially. In toy bitches after whelping and especially after dystocia a small dose of 1/2 to 1 cc., 10 to 20 units, of pitocin, or 1 to 2 cc., 10 to 20 units, of pituitrin may prevent retained placenta. If the bitch is valuable an attendant could watch her during whelping and save the placentas to make sure all are expelled. If septic metritis is present, with a vulvar discharge, elevated temperature, rapid pulse, and anorexia the prognosis is guarded and treatment with antibiotics parenterally, as well as supportive treatment similar to that in other animals, should be given. Careful injection of a small amount, 30 ml., broad-range antibiotic solution into the uterus might be indicated with a small soft rubber catheter. Injections of pituitrin and estrogens are of value. Supportive therapy with fluids is desirable. Laparo-hysterectomy might be considered but should be performed early.

Septic Metritis Following Parturition may occur with or without retention of the fetal membranes and is observed usually within 1 to 10 days after parturition in all species. The etiology of septic metritis is similar to that of retention of the fetal membranes. It usually is associated with a uterine atony or inertia. The more pathogenic types of organisms are present in the uterus and they or their toxins are absorbed into the circulation, producing severe general symptoms associated with septicemia, toxemia, and pyemia. The organisms most commonly present are coliform organisms, **Coryn. pyogenes,** hemolytic staphylococci, **Ps. aeruginosa,** proteus, hemolytic streptococci, and in rare cases clostridia. These severe infections are characterized by a fetid, red, watery uterine fluid that is very toxic and depressing to the animal. This condition usually follows emphysema of the fetus, severe torsion of the uterus with the presence of a dead and possibly emphysematous fetus, and other conditions associated with a uterine inertia such as dropsy of the fetal membranes, fetal anasarca, fetal giantism, twinning, and peritonitis due to traumatic gastritis. In many cases it may follow rough, improper removal of a retained placenta. Probably every veterinarian in large animal practice can cite several instances in which septic metritis and even death followed the injudicious removal of a retained placenta in a cow when the owner insisted upon its being removed. Septic metritis may follow a prolonged dystocia especially if a difficult fetotomy operation has been performed. It may follow a prolapsed uterus associated with trauma and infection of the endometrium. Occasionally it may result by extension from a necrotic vaginitis. It may occur in all species through the introduction of infection by unsanitary practices during the relief of dystocia or removal of a retained placenta. In dogs and swine it may occur from neglect at the time of parturition or trauma to the uterus with forceps, or accidentally allowing one or more placentas or fetuses to remain in the uterus and macerate.

The symptoms of septic metritis following parturition are very similar in all species of animals. Retention of the fetal membranes is frequently observed; in the cow the placentomes are usually greatly swollen and the fetal cotyledons firmly attached to the maternal caruncles. In the mare a piece of the placenta, often a portion from the nongravid horn, is retained and found in the body or nongravid horn of the uterus. The animals exhibit anorexia and dullness. The pulse is rapid, in the cow from 80 to 120 per minute, and usually weak. The body temperature in the cow may be elevated during the early phase of the disease. In advanced cases the cow's temperature may be either normal or subnormal. The latter condition usually occurs shortly before death of the animal. The cow is less apt to show a prolonged elevation of body temperature than are the other animals. The animal will shiver and its extremities are cold. The respirations are rapid and shallow; the eyes may be sunken; the hair coat is rough; and there is a rapid loss of weight. In severe cases there is a marked atony of the digestive tract. The feces may be hard and firm or may be black, oily, fetid, and liquid in character especially in the cow. A marked drop in milk flow or agalactia occurs in all species and the newborn will exhibit signs of malnutrition or starvation. In sows the agalactia often persists and the pigs must be reared as orphans. There is usually a reddish, watery, fetid discharge from the vulva. The genital passageways are likely to be swollen and inflamed. Straining may be present or absent before the examination but during or after the examination it is generally present. In many cases of septic metritis with enteritis in the cow, a rectal examination, especially if not performed gently, results in straining or tenesmus. The tenesmus may be very persistent and is definitely undesirable and exhausting to the cow. Rectal examinations should usually be confined to cows with no evidence of rectal irritation or enteritis. In some cows having septic metritis without a retained placenta the cervix may be quite contracted. Vaginal examination may reveal a normal vagina and clear, or only slightly cloudy, vaginal mucus, yet the uterine contents may be toxic and fetid, and occasionally toxic enough to cause death. The uterus in nearly all cases is atonic or flaccid. The walls are usually thin and in some cases, especially in dogs and cats, may be very friable or even necrotic. Peritonitis may be present due to extension of the infection through the uterine wall with symptoms of abdominal tenderness or soreness, abdominal distension, slight to moderate tympany of the rumen due to atony of the digestive tract, an arched back, stiff, slow gait, and tense abdominal muscles. The cow may exhibit a characteristic expiratory grunt due to the peritonitis. Perimetritis or peritoneal involvement with the uterine infection may occur naturally or be produced by heroic or too vigorous treatment of a severely infected and inflamed uterus. Rectal examination on these cases in cows may reveal early fibrin deposition and adhesions present between the uterus and the adjacent abdominal viscera. If this is found, the operator should terminate the examination at once, or the peritonitis and adhesions may be made worse, leading to severe peritonitis, abscess involvement of the adjacent structures, marked adhesions around the uterus, broad ligaments, ovaries and oviducts, or even death. Arthritic symptoms, with swelling and stiffness of the joints, particularly the hock, fetlock and knee joints, may occur especially in the cow and sow. Acute laminitis may also be present making the animal reluctant to rise and stand. The animal may be very weak, staggering, or prostrate and show symptoms of paresis and inability to rise. Since under these conditions the extremities are usually cold, this disease in the cow may easily be confused with milk fever. A mild to strong reaction to the Ross test for the presence of ketones may develop on testing the urine of cattle with septic metritis. This may be due to ketosis as a complication of the disease but more often it is caused by the severe anorexia. The blood count usually develops a marked shift to the left, together with a great drop in the total white blood cell level during the early stages of the condition. During the recovery stage the white blood cell count shifts to the right, with a leukocytosis developing. Occasionally secondary complications of pneumonia, and laminitis in the mare, cow, sow and ewe, and in all species pyemia with arthritis, liver, brain, or lung abscesses or endocarditis or myocarditis may develop especially if the condition is prolonged. Rough removal of the placenta, or lacerations of the endometrium encountered in prolapse of the uterus may allow organisms to localize in the uterine wall and cause an abscess.

A careful differentiation should be made between septic metritis and other conditions, such as traumatic gastritis, gastroenteritis, hemorrhagic septicemia pneumonia, parturient paresis, laminitis, and mastitis which may cause paraplegia, reluctance or inability to stand and illness at parturition. The course of septic metritis usually lasts from 2 to 6 days, with recovery or death occurring within that time. In the cow a prolonged course may extend over a period of from 1 to 2 weeks. The prognosis may be guarded to poor in many cases unless treatment is begun early before the uterus is severely damaged, peritonitis develops and the animal becomes extremely toxic. Failure to respond to treatment, persistent straining or complications such as mastitis and pneumonia tend to make the prognosis grave. The prognosis for the future breeding life of the animal may be poor in severe cases as well as in cases of perimetritis, ovaritis or abscesses of the uterine wall.

The treatment of septic metritis should be conservative. Massage and douching of the uterus, attempts to remove the retained fetal membranes should seldom if ever be performed in cases of septic metritis, or the animal's condition may become critical. Septicemia and toxemia should be overcome before these manipulative procedures are used. In early cases pituitrin, 3 to 5 ml. in large animals or 1 to 3 ml. in small animals and/or the estrogens 20 to 40 ml. of stilbestrol or 2 to 4 mg. of estradiol in large animals or 1 to 5 mg. of stilbestrol daily in small animals may be of some value in producing tonus in the atonic uterus. Usually if the condition is severe hormones are of questionable value. If the uterus is filled with a large amount of fetid fluid this should be gently siphoned off. Siphoning the uterus in large animals should be done very carefully with a sterile soft rubber hose or horse catheter since the uterine wall may be very friable and easily ruptured. In the mare and dog, if a portion of the placenta is lying in the uterus it should be removed in as gentle a manner as possible. One to 3 gm. of the broad-range tetracycline derivatives such as **Aureomycin** or **Terramycin** or furacin placed in the bovine or equine uterus in a solution or in a readily soluble form may be of great value in controlling the infection locally and even systemically by absorption from the uterus. Antibiotics and sulfonamide therapy are indicated parenterally. The antibiotics such as procaine penicillin, 3000 to 6000 units per pound of body weight daily and streptomycin, 5 gms. per 1000 pounds twice daily, intramuscularly; **Terramycin,** or tetracycline intravenously; or in large animals except the horse, intramuscularly, at a rate of 1 to 3 mg. per pound of body weight, daily, are of definite value. The sulfonamides such as sulfamethazine or sulfamerazine in daily doses of 1 to 1.5 grains per pound of body weight may be given intravenously, intraperitoneally, or orally. In less severe cases sulfanilamide or sulfathiazole may be given orally in the same amount in 3 to 4 divided doses daily. In valuable cows antibiotics and sulfonamides may be combined. Other supportive therapy such as saline and glucose solutions, and blood may be administered daily. Calcium gluconate seems of value especially in the early cases and may increase the tone of the uterus, but large doses given too rapidly to toxic cattle may cause death. **Pyribenzamine** or other antihistamines may be of value. Forced feeding may be helpful. Good nursing in a suitable stall or other equally comfortable environment is essential. If possible the large animal should be on green pasture each day or provided with fresh-cut green feed and with whole oats or other coarse feeds to tempt and encourage it to eat. If straining is present epidural anesthesia should be used to control it until the cause of the condition is determined and corrected. A drop in pulse rate, an increase in appetite, an improvement in the tone of the uterine wall, a change in the exudate from a watery to a mucoid consistency are all favorable symptoms indicating that the animal is responding to therapy. Treatment should be continued until the animal has safely recovered and septic symptoms have subsided. This should take place before actively treating the uterus and removing the retained fetal membranes in the cow. It may be advisable to let the afterbirth drop away. In the mare septic metritis is likely to cause laminitis, or "colt" founder. The application of ice packs to the feet is indicated as preventive therapy in septic metritis. Laminitis may also follow metritis in the cow, ewe, and sow but is usually less severe and may be unnoticed until months later when deformity of the hooves becomes evident.

Postpuerperal Metritis may be observed from the time of parturition to 2 to 8 weeks or more postpartum in all species. It may persist as a chronic metritis for months or occasionally pyometra with cessation of estrus and persistence of the corpus luteum may occur in the cow. There are no septic or general symptoms of illness accompanying this metritis. In most cases there is a reddish-brown or grey, mucopurulent, occasionally fetid discharge from the vulva. Later a creamy-yellow or grey discharge from the uterus and vulva usually mats the hair on the tail and buttocks. The condition is probably caused by many of the factors producing a retained placenta or septic metritis but either the infection is milder or the animal's resistance and the tone of the uterus are better. It may follow the development of infection in the uterine lochia during involution of the uterus. It may occur following retention of the fetal membranes or a necrotic piece of membrane or caruncle that has remained in the uterus. Occasionally it may be associated with a piece of the fetus, such as a hoof, left in the uterus and which has become a focus of infection. In mares it may follow a vulvar tear or laceration after foaling which causes persistent pneumovagina and chronic metritis. Usually a cervicitis and vaginitis accompany the metritis, as by extension the infection from the uterus involves these structures. Rectal examination in cases of postpuerperal metritis reveals a larger than normal uterus undergoing a delayed involution. Uterine tone is fair but the uterine wall is thick and heavy. There may be from one-half pint to several gallons of mucopurulent material in the uterus of large animals. Vaginal examination may reveal some of this pus lying in the vagina. As late as two weeks after parturition the cervix in the cow with metritis is usually relaxed and dilated enough to admit one finger. The uterine exudate is mucoid in character rather than watery as in septic metritis. Since puerperal metritis usually follows a retained placenta the veterinarian will find it advisable to reexamine valuable cows or mares 2 to 5 weeks after a parturition associated with retention of the placenta and treat the metritis and delayed involution of the uterus if they are present. In valuable cows a routine genital examination is usually performed in 3 to 5 weeks after parturition, even though retained placenta did not occur, to make certain that involution of the uterus is normal and that metritis is not present. There is evidence in mares and cows that probably 100 per cent of parturient animals have infectious organisms invade the uterus for a short period of several days or more after expulsion of the fetus. At the time of the first estrus, at 5 to 12 days in the mare and 12 to 18 days in most cows, these infections are overcome and eliminated. In animals where the first estrus is delayed or in animals failing to eliminate the infection, the infection persists as a mild to moderate metritis. With each subsequent estrous period more of these mild metritis cases recover, Wright and Roberts, Sager.

The prognosis in most of these cases is good. Many animals would recover without treatment but recovery time might be prolonged and conception delayed. Neglected postpuerperal metritis may progress into pyometra, chronic endometritis or cervicitis, and delayed or permanent infertility may result.

Treatment of these cases should start early, and repeated examinations and treatment at 1- to 3-week intervals may be indicated. Douching of the vagina of the cow with a gallon of hot, 120 to 130° F., mild antiseptic solution of chlorine, a soapy antiseptic, dilute **Lysol,** or dilute potassium permanganate 2 to 3 times a week stimulates uterine contractions, and washes the purulent exudate from the vagina. Intrauterine douching should be done gently, using only a soft rubber catheter, so that the endometrium is not traumatized. The exudate is thinned by the introduction of small amounts of a mild antiseptic solution, and then removed by siphoning. If the exudate is very thick, an enzyme like streptococcic dornase or pancreatic trypsin may be used to thin it and thus make it easier to siphon out. The recommendation in most of these cases is to avoid vigorous massage of the uterus or the removal of the corpora lutea in cows, since otherwise adhesions and perimetritis or ovaritis may develop. If the uterus is massaged this should be done gently. Antibiotics, sulfonamides, and other antiseptics, such as 1 to 5 ml. of Lugol's solution in 100 ml. of saline or water, may be introduced into the uterus for local treatment of the infection. The injection of estrogens has been recommended by Moore and others and now is used widely for this condition. In the cow and mare they are usually given in doses of 20 to 40 mg. of stilbestrol or 2 to 4 mg. of estradiol intramuscularly and repeated if necessary in 3 to 4 days or at longer intervals. Estrogens are also effective if introduced into the uterus, where they are readily absorbed. Large or prolonged doses of estrogen should be avoided lest cystic ovaries or the transfer of infection through the oviducts with ovaritis and adhesions result. Breeding of the animal should be delayed until the uterus and cervix are normal and 2 to 3 normal estrous periods have elapsed. Most affected cows should not be bred until 90 days or more after parturition although, as may be determined by rectal examination, some may be normal and be bred at 60 to 80 days. (See Metritis and Endometritis, Chap. XIII). In dogs, cats and swine parenteral treatment of postpuerperal infections with courses of antibiotics and oxytocic agents are indicated to assist recovery. In rare cases laparotomy and hysterotomy with douching and infusing of the uterus with antiseptics and antibiotics may be undertaken, Durfee. The mare may be treated similar to the cow except irritating infusions should not be used. If the mare or cow develops pneumovagina the Caslick operation should be performed. Because of the long period between lambing and breeding most ewes recover from postpuerperal metritis without treatment.

Postparturient Agalactia Syndrome, Agalactia, Toxemia, Metritis-Mastitis-Agalactia (M.M.A.) and "Milk Fever Syndrome" of Sows has become increasingly prevalent with intensive swine production and confinement farrowing. The incidence of this postparturient syndrome varies greatly from farm to farm and it may be seen on both well- and poorly-managed ones. The death loss in affected sows is low, 1 to 2 per cent, but the losses in the young pigs due to starvation, hypoglycemia, overlaying by the sows and from pig scours varies from 20 to 80 per cent.

The principal sign of this syndrome in sows is agalactia that becomes evident between 12 and 36 hours after farrowing. The sows become depressed, lack appetite, show a reluctance to rise and become constipated. The body temperature, as in cows with septic metritis, may be high, 106 to 107° F., or in the moderately elevated to normal range. The udder is usually edematous, hard and swollen with the teats being flaccid and there is a lack of milk in the cistern. The sow often lays on the udder to prevent the pigs from nursing. In a few cases one or more glands have a purulent reddish discharge indicating acute mastitis. In the others the milk that is present, but scanty, may look normal. Metritis may be evident in some cases by the presence of a fetid brownish discharge from the vulva. On vaginal examination occasionally a retained portion of placenta or a dead fetus may be found. Many affected sows tend to be overly fat and often there is a history of a change in the ration a short time before farrowing. This disease tends to affect the sow at the time of her second and third farrowings rather than the first farrowing. Affected sows often have a history of requiring several more hours to farrow than nonaffected sows. On necropsy examination of affected sows the uterus and intestines seem to have a degree of inertia with a lack of tone. There may be necrotic areas and edema observed on section of the mammary gland. Cultures of the uterus and mammary gland reveal a variety of infectious organisms including: streptococci, staphylococci, Klebsiella, and mycoplasma, Moore. Most researchers report that **E. coli** is the predominant organism. Most pigs on affected sows die within 48 to 96 hours unless the sow starts producing milk which in most cases is unlikely, or unless the pigs are put on another nurse sow or fed a synthetic milk product. Intraperitoneal administration of 10 ml. of 5 per cent dextrose containing streptomycin and keeping the pigs warm may prolong the life of the pigs. From the numerous studies it seems apparent that this syndrome is caused by a variety of factors the most important of which is improper management, lack of sanitation and infection but endocrine, nutritional, toxic factors, a lack of exercise and possibly heredity may also play contributing roles, Ringarp, Tharp and Amstutz, Blood, Martin et al., Ross et al. and Vandeplassche et al..

Management plays a highly important role in this syndrome. A balanced but limited ration should be fed at rates of 4 to 6 pounds/day per sow during the gestation period. During this period the sows should be on a legume pasture or fed a ration high in alfalfa meal. Exercise is essential. Sows should be kept fairly thin and not allowed to get fat. When the sow is confined for farrowing half of this ration is replaced with bran for a laxative effect and this is continued for 2 to 3 days after farrowing, Tharp and Amstutz. Feed containing mycotoxins with some estrogenic activity might conceivably play a role in this syndrome and should be avoided, Nelson. Farrowing houses should be thoroughly cleaned and disinfected and let stand idle for one to two months between farrowings. A high-pressure, 200 to 400 lbs/sq. inch, spray rig is very helpful in cleaning and disinfecting the farrowing house and its equipment. The farrowing period should be limited in length to 3 to 4 weeks to avoid "bacteria-build up" in the houses. Sows should be washed before being placed in the farrowing crates.

Some veterinarians recommend feeding high levels of antibiotics in the feed for 7 to 10 days prior to and for a short period after farrowing to prevent infections. Because of a lack of controlled data the value of such a practice is questionable. Others recommend the use of polyvalen autogenous bacterins or serum given during the gestatio period or at farrowing. Conflicting results have been reported, Ringarp and others. The recommended treatment of individual affected sows includes: antibiotics intramuscularly to control infection; oxytocin or pituitrin in small doses 30 to 50 units every few hours to contract the uterus and cause "let down" of milk in the udder, and possibly to stimulate peristalsis. Tharp and Amstutz recommended giving 2 to 3 ml. of **Lentin** intravenously or subcutaneously to stimulate intestinal activity; a laxative given by stomach tube is also used in some cases. Ringarp reported good results using 100 mgm of prednisolone or some other glucocorticoid along with parenteral antibiotic therapy. Local treatment of the uterus by introducing an antibiotic infusion might be of value if done in a clean gentle manner with an insemination catheter.

Postpartum metritis syndrome in cattle described by Herrick in 1963 has been seen with increasing frequency in many dairy herds in the Northeast especially as herd numbers increase and as production rises. It is becoming a serious problem especially in the free-stall herds with over 100 cows and where the cows never are placed on pasture. There are many similarities between this postparturient syndrome in cattle and the postparturient agalactia in swine.

The postparturient metritis syndrome in cattle herds is characterized by a high incidence of retained placenta and subsequent metritis. Even in cows and heifers in which retained placenta does not occur, a postpartum metritis will develop. A few cases of metritis may exhibit septic symptoms but nearly 100 per cent of the cows that calve during the Fall and Winter stabling season will exhibit a chronic metritis with a persistent yellowish discharge of pus that lasts for several months, a delayed involution of the uterus, a lowered conception rate and a calving interval that is increased from about 13 months to 15 to 17 months. Often an abnormally long period of anestrum follows calving. A few cases develop a persistent pyometra. In the early stages of the infection a wide variety of organisms are cultured but after several months **C. pyogenes** is the principal organism found. Economic loss is due mainly to delayed conception and culling because of infertility.

From his studies the author agrees with Herrick that the postparturient metritis syndrome is principally a problem of sanitation in the barn, the free stalls, the exercise yards, and especially the calving stalls. In many instances calvings and postpartum involution of the uterus are normal for a period of a month or more at the start of the calving season. Then after one or two cases of retained placenta and metritis occur nearly every cow that freshens in these barns and calving stalls becomes infected (See Retained Placenta in Cows). In some herds with this problem nearly every calf born in these infected calving stalls will develop scours and die unless prophylactic antibiotic treatment is given as soon as the calf is born. Sometimes the owners in treating the cows prophylactically by placing antibiotics into the uterus may spread the virulent infection that has been established in the barn and calving stalls. Herrick and the author have noted that frequently this may only occur in a herd for one year. When the cows are turned to pasture or when a period of 2 to 3 months passes with no cows calving the infection will disappear. In large herds calving the year around the condition may remain a problem for years. If dry cows and pregnant heifers are removed from the herd and kept separate from the herd, calve at pasture or calve in a clean, noninfected environment and kept there for about 7 to 10 days this metritis syndrome will stop. To solve this problem some farmers have built portable 10 × 10 calving stalls that can be thoroughly disinfected between calvings and can be moved to clean ground after each calving. It is obvious that more study in the field in problem herds is needed to determine the sanitation needs and management practices to control this metritis syndrome in a practical way. Possibly by proper construction, suitable isolation, adequate disinfection and rest after each calving, stalls could be constructed as have farrowing houses, that are adequate for the needs of intensive dairy farming.

Preventive treatment of cows in a herd where postparturient metritis develops in nearly every cow is generally not satisfactory. Autogenous bacterins or commercial polyvalent vaccines have been tried without success. Injections of oxytocin and pituitrin after calving seems to have little or no effect. Parenteral injections or local intrauterine infusions or capsules of broad range antibiotics after calving have limited value and then only in preventing some cases of septic metritis. As an aid to hastening the recovery of the chronic metritis and delayed involution of the uterus, estrogen injections, 20 to 30 mgm of stilbestrol or 2 to 3 mg. of estradiol and intrauterine antibiotics and/or weak Lugol's solution, 2 to 5 ml. of Lugol's solution in 100 ml. of water, infused into the uterus at biweekly or monthly intervals has proven helpful. Although proper management, exercise, and clean, noninfected isolation facilities for the parturient cow are more difficult for the farmer to provide, at present it is the best way to control this economically costly metritis syndrome.

Puerperal Laminitis is most likely to occur in the mare and may be commonly seen in the cow, ewe, and sow. Nilsson stated that 24 per cent of 170 cases of bovine laminitis occurred within 2 to 3 days of calving. It usually occurs secondary to a septic metritis. In the mare the placenta may tear away, leaving the apex of the allantois chorion in the nongravid horn. This placental remnant acts as a focus of infection and the uterus fills with a fetid, watery exudate. Laminitis is apparently caused by the septic uterine contents and results in symptoms similar to those in laminitis of digestive origin. Usually 2 to 4 days after parturition the animal begins to exhibit a foundered gait characterized by the hind legs being placed well forward under the body in order to remove the weight from the even more severely affected forelimbs. The hoofs are hot to the touch and the digital artery has a strong, hard pulse. The animal may lie down continually, standing for only short intervals, or rarely it may refuse to lie down. Weight loss is rapid. The prognosis is fair if treatment is begun early. Any animal with hooves with severe retained placenta or septic uterine infection should be treated early to prevent the possibility of laminitis developing. Treatment consists of the administration of an antihistamine in repeated doses plus the application of ice packs to the feet or having the animal stand in cold water. The placenta of any valuable mare should be examined after expulsion by the veterinarian or, if he is intelligent and informed, by the owner to make certain that none of the placenta has remained in the uterus. If laminitis develops in a mare or other animal several days after foaling the uterus should be treated as for septic metritis by gently removing the exudate and placenta if present. Antibiotics may be used in the uterus and parenterally along with injections of estrogens and possibly pituitrin. The usual treatment of cold packs on the feet and antihistamines should be used as supportive therapy for the laminitis. The uterus should be examined and treated again if necessary in 24 to 48 hours and therapy continued until recovery results.

Puerperal Tetanus may occasionally occur in the mare and cow. It is possible in any species. If it occurs in the mare it usually follows uterine prolapse. In the cow even though of unusual occurrence, puerperal tetanus is the most common form of the disease. It often follows retained placenta and postpartum metritis. Unsanitary handling of a retained placenta when the uterus or birth canal may be traumatized predisposes to tetanus in the cow and mare. The afterbirth drops out a short distance when the cow lies down and becomes contaminated and when the cow rises foreign material on the placenta is drawn into the genital tract. Tetanus is usually observed one to four weeks after parturition. In many cases a postpuerperal metritis is present. If possible the uterine exudate should be removed and the cow or mare treated as for an ordinary case of tetanus resulting from external wounds, that is, by the administration of large doses of tetanus antitoxin, penicillin and tranquilizers. Estrogens hould be injected to evacuate the pus from the uterus. onstant, careful, quiet nursing is essential. The prognosis is poor but there have been rare instances of recovery.

Uterine Abscess may occasionally follow severe septic metritis, dystocia, and necrotic cervicitis or vaginitis that cause an atresia of the birth canal. It is seen in all species, but most commonly in the cow and mare. During the early stages no external symptoms may be evident but after several weeks to a month or more the uterus becomes so greatly distended with pus that it may cause a distention of the abdomen. Usually intermittent straining and frequent urination are present. On rectal and vaginal examination the enlarged fluctuating uterus can be felt protruding into the pelvic cavity and the stenotic or closed portion of the genital canal may be palpated. Adhesions between the vagina and uterus may be present, so that an incision can be safely made through the vaginal wall into the uterus to drain off the pus. In one mare so treated by the author about 15 gallons of pus were removed. Symptoms of shock developed following the removal of this large volume of pus. The uterine abscess may break into the rectum or vagina. The animals occasionally recover, but their breeding life is ended. This condition should be distinguished from an abscess of the uterine wall which is a small, localized lesion.

Infections of the Cervix, Vagina and Vulva

Postpuerperal Cervicitis due to trauma, mild lacerations, infectious material from the uterus passing through the cervix, infection by extension from the vagina, or infection from a retained placenta or material carried into the genital tract on the placenta, is common in animals. It is observed most commonly in the cow and in association with a metritis or vaginitis after calving. The good blood supply, large mucus glands in the cervix, and the folded mucous membrane make severe injury, necrosis, and atresia of the cervix rare except in the mare. If cervicitis is present in the mare the gentle introduction of mild oily antiseptics or antibiotic infusions into the uterus and gentle dilation of the cervix with the gloved fingers may prevent stenosis occurring. This should be repeated until the cervicitis has been cured. As long as a metritis is present local treatment of the cervix is usually ineffective. Once involution of the uterus takes place and the uterus rids itself of infection, the cervix also recovers unless a vaginitis, pneumovagina, or a greatly enlarged chronically infected ectropic cervix persists. Treatment for postpuerperal cervicitis is the same as treatment for metritis or vaginitis. The prognosis is usually good.

Postpuerperal Vaginitis and Vulvitis may occur with or without a concurrent metritis. Following parturition either a severe necrotic vaginitis and vulvitis or a mild catarrhal inflammation of these structures may develop.

Necrotic Vaginitis and Vulvitis is observed most often in dairy and beef heifers having a narrow small birth canal that caused dystocia. The fetus may have been expelled without aid after a difficult, prolonged parturition or traction may have been necessary. These factors, especially the latter, result in trauma, laceration, excessive pressure, and abrasion of the vulvar and vaginal walls. The mucosa of the vagina and vulva may be further irritated by the presence of a retained placenta, a metritis, or a torn or ruptured perineum allowing infection to enter the vulva and vagina. Pressure necrosis of the vulvar and vaginal mucous membranes is often observed following the removal of an emphysematous fetus by traction or after a prolonged fetotomy in a heifer. It may occasionally occur in cows, especially young cows or those of the smaller breeds. In rare cases necrotic vaginitis may be due to douching with too irritating or strong an antiseptic. Occasionally a severe necrophorus infection of the vagina may occur.

The symptoms of necrotic vaginitis are usually observed 1 to 4 days after parturition and last for 1 to 2 weeks or more depending on the severity of the lesions. There is usually an arched back, elevated tail, anorexia, and rapid loss of weight. The animal may exhibit either no straining, straining that is intermittent and mild and only observed at the time of urination or defecation, or nearly continuous straining with air being sucked into the vagina and forcibly expelled. The vulva and vagina may be very swollen, due to a perivulvar and perivaginal phlegmon. A fetid, reddish, watery fluid is present in the vulva. The pulse rate is usually elevated. The body temperature may be moderately elevated. Parting of the vulvar lips reveals a necrotic, diptheritic inflammation of the vulva and vagina, usually most severe at the vulvo-vaginal border. The necrotic portion of the mucous membranes sloughs, and the exposed submucosal tissues granulate and eventually heal with a cicatrix. In an acute case, the passage of the hand through the inflamed vulva and vagina of the cow is likely to cause bleeding. This act is very painful to the animal and because of the swollen dry tissues is usually difficult to perform. Straining is probably due to the vestibular and vulvar inflammation and irritation and possibly the accompanying vaginal swelling or phlegmon, since there are many sensory nerves in the vulva and vestibule but few if any in the vagina. Straining due to vulvitis, vestibulitis and vaginitis should be differentiated from that caused by dystocia, an undiagnosed, retained fetus, rabies, or other conditions which might cause straining.

Some of these cases of vulvitis and vaginitis, no matter how they are handled, develop a marked stenosis or even atresia of the vagina resulting in a distention of the cranial portion of the vagina due to pus or mucus. In advanced chronic cases, even the cervix and the uterus may be distended with 2 to 3 gallons of a mucopurulent material if infection persists, or of mucus alone if no infection is present. The prognosis is fair to good in mild cases treated early. In severe cases that are neglected the prognosis is guarded. If necrosis is extensive, straining constant, and the animal is extremely debilitated, death may result. In cases of severe vaginal atresia—fortunately uncommon—the future breeding life is usually terminated.

The treatment of necrotic vaginitis should be gentle and conservative. Oily bland antiseptics such as 4 to 6 ounces of bismuth formic iodide in oil, together with the broad range antibiotics, may be introduced in a gentle manner into the cranial portion of the vaginia 2 to 3 times a day. As this infusion is expelled it coats the inflamed mucous membranes. If swelling, phlegmon, elevation of the temperature, and rapid pulse rate are present, parenteral administration of antibiotics and/or oral or intravenous administration of sulfonamides are indicated daily for 4 to 6 days or until recovery is evident. Injections of small doses of estrogens, 15 to 25 mg. of stilbestrol every second or third day may stimulate healing of the vaginal mucous membrane. If in the cow, retained fetal membranes are hanging through the vulva they should be removed if this can be done easily and without injury to the vulva and vagina. In most cases the placenta is fastened securely and must be allowed to remain and drop away later. If the membranes are heavy and hang nearly to the floor they should be cut off at the hocks so the added weight does not aggravate the vulvitis and induce straining. If straining is present, the use of one of the longer-lasting epidural anesthetics such as xylocaine or lidocaine to which a small amount of adrenaline solution has been added to retard its rate of absorption, or **Cobefrin** is of value and may be given twice daily or more often if necessary. Pudendal block will also anesthetize the vulva but it is neither practical nor as easily performed as is the administration of epidural anesthesia. The administration of tranquilizers is helpful in controlling pain and tenesmus. Elevation of the rear parts may be helpful. In mild cases of vulvitis and vaginitis with straining, some local anesthetic ointments containing butesin picrate or benzocaine have been used but difficulty has occurred in applying these to a moist mucous membrane and their effect is questionable.

If tenesmus is severe and accompanied by marked sucking and blowing of air into and out of the vagina, the dorsal two-thirds to three-quarters of the vulva should be tightly sutured after administration of epidural anesthesia. This prevents ballooning of the vagina with air and precludes the accompanying irritation and straining. This treatment with other supportive treatments described usually promptly controls the straining. The sutures holding the vulvar lips together may be removed in 4 to 7 days. In rare cases it may be indicated to insufflate the abdominal cavity with air to prevent tenesmus, Svendsen. This increased pressure in the abdominal cavity results in increased pressure in the pleural cavity and relaxation of the abdominal musculature to ease respiration. Control of severe straining is essential to prevent rapid loss of weight, weakness, early exhaustion, and even death. Repeated treating and dilating of a necrotic vagina is not indicated, inasmuch as this procedure prolongs recovery time, increases the inflammatory reaction in the vagina, and produces additional scar tissue. Following healing, breeding may be advised if the stenosis is not severe. At the time of parturition it may be necessary to dilate this stenotic portion of the vagina. In many cases, however, due to the relaxation of the vaginal wall and surrounding tissues, mild stenoses disappear at the time of parturition. If the stenosis is severe and breeding is desired this might be accomplished by artificial insemination and cesarean section at the time of parturition. Most severe cases of stenosis of the vagina are slaughtered. Outbreaks of blackleg have been reported in sheep following lambing where the organism, **C. feseri,** invades the damaged vulvar tissues, Blood and Henderson.

Catarrhal Vaginitis and Vulvitis occurs following or with retained placenta, puerperal metritis, or injuries to the vulva causing pneumovagina. Following parturition this generally is characterized by a persistent mucopurulent discharge from the vulva. The prognosis is good. Dilute, warm vaginal douches, using 200 ppm chlorine, dilute potassium permanganate, dilute **Lysol** or other soapy aromatic antiseptics, or saline or sodium bicarbonate, are indicated. These may be repeated at 1- to 3-day intervals. In the cow, injections of estrogens, 10 to 30 mgm. of stilbestrol or 1 to 3 mgm. of estradiol, may be helpful. If the vulva is torn it should be sutured, to prevent pneumovagina. If puerperal metritis is present the vaginitis may persist in a mild form until the discharge of uterine exudate ceases. In some cases when only a vaginitis is present one to three weeks after parturition, some oily antibiotics or antibiotics in ointment form may be placed in the vagina to aid in overcoming the infection.

Paraplegia of the Parturient Cow, "Downer" Cow Syndrome

The animal that fails to rise after dystocia or the animal that goes down and is unable to rise late in gestation or soon after parturition is likely to cause a perplexing diagnostic problem for the veterinarian. All too often in the case of the cow many of the following conditions are described as "atypical milk fever," without adequate attempts to make an accurate diagnosis. The following great variety of conditions or diseases may cause the parturient animal to be unable to rise. Most of these cases occur following parturition or postparturient milk fever reflecting the possible stresses and injuries developing during this period. It is rather obvious from the following groups of causes of the "downer" cow that the use of the term "atypical milk fever" to include all other conditions than milk fever or combinations of other diseases and milk fever is an indication of ignorance and an unwillingness to study and examine a case thoroughly. Since these cases occur, for the most part, around calving and an early recovery is often imperative and desirable from the standpoint of the animal's future production and even life, a prompt accurate diagnosis is desirable. A complete painstaking physical examination of each system of the animal should be performed, despite the fact that the animal can't "cooperate" and stand for the examination. The use of hip slings may be very helpful in reaching a diagnosis, particularly where traumatic and physical injuries are present.

A check-list of factors and possibilities to consider in the diagnosis of paraplegia before, at and after parturition includes:

Metabolic and/or Nutritional Disturbances

1. Parturient paresis, hypocalcemia, milk fever.
2. Tetany, hypocalcemia and/or hypomagnesemia including grass and transport tetany.
3. Ketosis, usually postparturient.
4. Debility, cachexia, or weakness—due to starvation, senility, acute or chronic wasting diseases including internal or external parasitisms and Johne's Disease.
5. Zenker's degeneration of muscle—due to a lack of selenium, vitamin E, and the presence of other factors including poor quality hay and muscle stress following a lack of exercise or following vigorous attempts to rise in cows with milk fever, nerve paralyses, or cows that are cast.

Traumatic and/or Physical Injuries—These often occur during attempts to rise especially where the footing is slippery or in cows affected with milk fever.

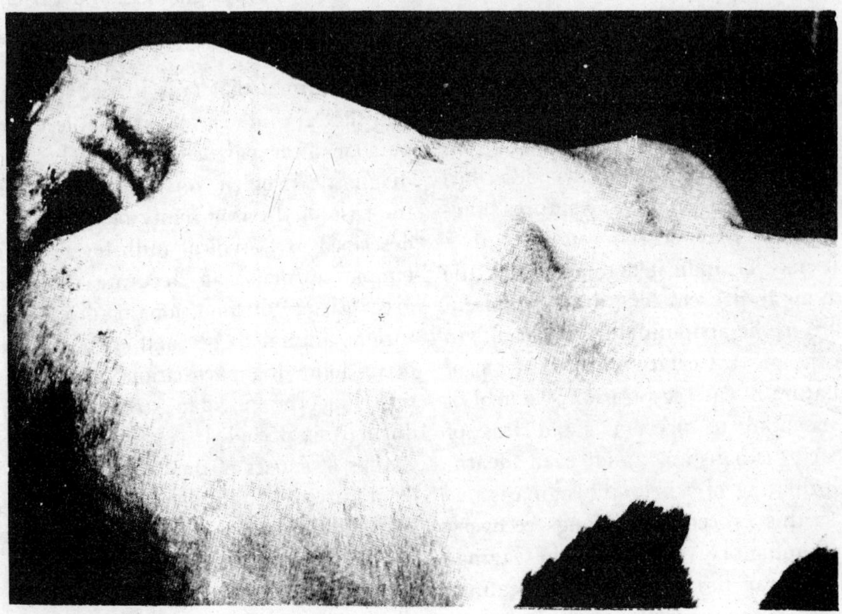

Figure 101. Dislocation of the sacroiliac articulation in a cow. This is occasionally seen in young dairy cattle following a difficult parturition.

1. Paralyses—due to injuries to the obturator, peroneal, gluteal, femoral, and brachial nerves or compression of spinal cord. Besides a severe injury, lymphosarcoma and abscesses may produce spinal compression, Straub et al., Robertson and Shaw.
2. Dislocation of the hip or sacroiliac joints, Adams, Rees (See Figure 101). The latter is seen in young cows, under 5 years of age, often after a dystocia.
3. Fractures of the leg, pelvis, spine, and skull.
4. "Cast" often associated with myositis, Zenker's degeneration, tendinitis, arthritis, muscle asthenia and ischemia, phlebitis and thrombosis, and contusions.
5. Rupture of the gastrocnemius muscle, usually secondary to Zenker's degeneration.
6. Exhaustion from attempts to rise or exertion from dystocia may produce a circulatory crisis, low blood pressure and myocarditis, Sellers et al.. This may be related to a lack of exercise.
7. Hemorrhage, anemia, or shock as in rupture of the uterine or pelvic blood vessels in torsion or prolapse of the uterus, laceration of the genital tract, transportation in advanced pregnancy, violence during foaling in mares, abomasal or duodenal ulcers, coccidiosis, anaplasmosis, leptospirosis and postparturient hemoglobinuria.

Infectious Diseases or Inflammatory Processes

1. Septic metritis, with or without a retained placenta or a vulvar discharge.
2. Septic mastitis.
3. Peritonitis, or pericarditis, secondary to traumatic gastritis, uterine rupture or abomasal ulcers with perforation.
4. Acute laminitis.
5. Septic arthritis—knee, hocks, coffin joint.
6. Miscellaneous diseases—severe pyelonephritis, shipping fever, blackleg, anthrax, necrobacillosis, rabies, listeriosis, meningitis, and brain or cord abscess.

Digestive Disturbances, Diarrheas, Toxemias and Poisonings

1. Enteritis, severe diarrhea secondary to an intestinal stasis associated with hypocalcemia, winter dysentery, salmonellosis, virus diarrhea, etc.
2. Toxic indigestion due to overeating on fruit, grain, or forage.
3. Toxic indigestion of advanced pregnancy has been described by Fox and others as occurring in stabled dairy cows late in the winter confinement period and characterized by partial to complete anorexia, dullness, progressive emaciation and increased pulse rate. Normal activity of the gastro-intestinal tract appears impaired possibly due to large gravid uterus. The recommended treatment consists of exercise, forced if necessary, intravenous fluid therapy, and mild laxatives orally. In a valuable cow cesarean section might be indicated.
4. Poisonings—plant, chemical, etc.

Miscellaneous Causes
1. Hydrops allantois.
2. Lymphocytoma especially involving the spinal cord, heart, and abomasum.
3. "Malingerer."
4. Spastic syndrome ("stretches").
5. Severe albuminuria and uremia secondary to nephritis (rare).

In making a differential diagnosis of the etiology for paraplegia, cows with infectious diseases may have an elevated body temperature and pulse rate. The latter is also elevated in digestive disturbances. Hypocalcemic states usually respond to calcium therapy intravenously or udder inflation although some response to calcium therapy may be observed in digestive disturbances. An expiratory grunt is often exhibited in cases of peritonitis. One or more of the following symptoms would be sufficient reason for questioning the diagnosis of parturient paresis in a cow: a pulse rate of 90 or more per minute, rapid respirations or respirations accompanied by an expiratory grunt, diarrhea, an attitude that is bright and alert, a nearly normal appetite, a body temperature of 102° F. or higher, a hot swollen udder, retained placenta, persistent tenesmus, and failure of expected response to adequate calcium therapy.

Because of his exposure to frequent necropsies on so-called "downer" cows the author is impressed with the frequency of physical and muscular lesions in these cases as well as the variety of the conditions found. A high incidence of muscle damage and tears together with a rising S.G.O.T. level in "downer" cows following parturient paresis was also noted by Bjorsell. The best procedure to follow to prevent "downer" cows is to control, prevent or provide early and prompt treatment of cows with hypocalcemia or parturient paresis, Kronfeld. Although Johnson reported on the value of the careful administration of potassium to the "downer" or alert "creeper" cow following treatment for parturient paresis, his views require further study. In certain herds in selenium deficient areas, the administration of selenium late in gestation might be indicated to assist in preventing Zenker's degeneration of muscle under the stress of struggling at the time of calving or during parturient paresis.

The author is firmly convinced that obesity or excessive condition is highly detrimental and dangerous to the parturient animal especially if it is coupled with a lack of exercise during the latter half of the gestation period. In cases of parturient paresis these two factors combine to greatly lower the cow's resistance to stress, to favor exhaustion and a "malinger-type" of attitude and to result in difficulty in rising with the production of secondary traumatic lesions. A 20 by 20 box stall with a dirt floor for excellent footing is highly desirable for large high-producing parturient dairy cows to avoid injury. Further proof of the possible effect of lack of exercise is the list of diseases of muscular organs that are most commonly observed in cattle in northeastern U.S. in the late winter or early spring months after a long period of confinement namely: displaced abomasum or torsion of the abomasum, prolapse of the vagina, prolapse of the uterus, retained placenta possibly related to uterine inertia, torsion of the cecum, intussusception of the intestine, torsion of the uterus, indigestion of advanced pregnancy and Zenker's degeneration of sketelal muscle. The incidence of these diseases is much lower during the late spring or summer months when cows are on pasture.

References

Injuries, Hemorrhages and Prolapses of the Puerperal Period

Aanes, W. A. (1964) Surgical Repair of Third Degree Perineal Laceration and Rectovaginal Fistula in the Mare, J.A.V.M.A., **144,** 5, 485.

Allen, G. S. (1964) Rupture of the Feline Uterus, Vet. Rec. **76,** 12, 355.

Arthur, G. H. (1964) Wright's Veterinary Obstetrics, 3rd Ed., Williams and Wilkins Co., Baltimore, Md.

Beck, A. and McEntee, K. (1966) Subinvolution of the Placental Sites in a Postpartum Bitch, Cor. Vet. **56,** 2, 269.

Bemis, H. E. (1930) A New Operation for Rectovaginal Fistula, N. A. Vet., **30,** 2, 37.

Benesch, F. (1930) Die Graphische Darstillung der Normalen der Medikamentell Verstarkten und der Abgeschwachten Uterusbewegung an Lebenden Rind im Involutionsstadium, Proc. 11th Internat. Vet. Congr., 351.

Benesch, F. and Wright, J. G. (1951) Veterinary Obstetrics, Williams and Wilkins, Baltimore, Md.

Berger, Charles (1966) Personal Communication.

Brewer, R. L. and Kliest, G. J. (1963) Uterine Prolapse in the Mare, J.A.V.M.A. **142,** 10, 1118.

Carlson, A. (1960) Lacerated Uterus Technique, Haver Glover Messenger, Jan.-Feb.

Danelius, G. (1941) Rupture of the Rectum in Connection with Calving in a Heifer, Cor. Vet., **31,** 4, 393.

Fincher, M. G. (1954) Personal Communication.

Galvan, D. (1938) Rupture de la pointe du Caecum pendant le Velage, Rec. de Med. Vet., **114,** 12, 788.

Godkin, G. T. (1959) Dystocia with Vaginal Rupture, J.A.V.M.A. **135,** 4, 218.

Grunert, E. and Geyer, K. (1964) Beitrag zur Chirurgischen Behandlung von Perforierenden Zervix and Uterusverletzungen beim Rind, Deutsche Tieraztl. Wochenschr. **71,** 9, 241.

Habel, R. E. (1953) The Perineum of the Mare, Cor. Vet., **43,** 2, 249.

Keown, G. H. (1956) Peroneal Nerve Damage, Canad. J. Comp. Med. and Vet. Sci. **20,** 445.

Krichel, J. H., Jr. (1969) A Report of Six Cases of Uterine Rupture in the Dog, Vet. Med. **64,** 10, 872.

McMullen, M. E., Nurse, W. H. and Nurse, H. G. (1964) Telescoping of the Uterus in a Boston Terrier, Vet. Med., **59,** 2, 206.

O'Neill, A. R. (1961) Rupture of the Uterus in the Parturient Ewe, Vet. Rec. **73,** 1041.

Phillips, S. (1965) Personal Communication.

Richter, J. and Gotze, R. (1950) Lehrbuch der Tiergeburtshilfe, H. Laupp Jr., Tubingen, Germany.

Roberts, S. J. (1949) Amputation of the Prolapsed Uterus, Cor. Vet. **39,** 4, 438.

Rooney, J. R. (1964) Internal Hemorrhage Related to Gestation in the Mare, Cor. Vet. **54,** 1, 11.

Schnautz, J. O. (1954) Postparturient Myorrhexis in Cattle, N. A. Vet. **35,** 191.

Snoeck, M. A. (1962) Uterine Rupture in a Pony, Tijdschr. vor Diergeneesk. **87,** 15, 1035.

Stauffer, V. D. (1959) Traumatic Resection of Intestine During Parturition, J.A.V.M.A. **134,** 3, 122.

Steiner, H. (1962) Contribution to Enterectomy after Intestinal Rupture During Parturition in Cattle, Deutsche Tierarztl. Wochenschr. **69,** 13, 362.

Steiner, H. (1962) Spontaneous Rupture of the Uterus in the Sow during Farrowing, Deutsche Tierarztl. Wochenschr. **69,** 10, 283.

Straub, O. C. and Fowler, M. E. (1961) Repair of Perineal Lacerations in the Mare and Cow, J.A.V M.A. **138,** 12, 659.

Teige, J. (1956) Birth Injury of Vesica Urinaria in the Cow, Nord. Vet. Med. **8,** 658.

Vandeplassche, M. (1963) Cesarean Section in Complicated Cases in Cattle, Schweizer Archiv fur Tierhielkunde, **105,** 1, 21.

Vandeplassche, M. and Spincemaille, J. (1963) Comparative Etiology and Pathogenesis of Uterine Prolapse in Domestic Animals, Berl. and Munch. Tierarztl. Wochenschr. **76,** 16, 324.

Vanderplassche, M. and Vanheuverswijn, A. (1953) Behandling van Dystokie door Omegekeerde Blaas met Darmen bij een Merrie, Vlaams Diergeneesk. Tijdschr., **22,** 1, 8.

VanKruiningen, H. J., Fox, F. H. and Weber, W. T. (1961) Rupture of the Rectum, Cor. Vet. **51,** 4, 557.

Voss, J. L. (1969) Rupture of the Cecum and Ventral Colon of Mares During Parturition, J.A.V.M.A. **155,** 5, 745.

White, J. B. (1961) An Unexplained Condition (Vaginal Rupture) in Pregnant Ewes, Vet. Rec. **73,** 281.

Williams, W. L. (1943) Diseases of the Genital Organs of Domestic Animals, 3rd Ed., Miss Louella Williams, Upland Rd., Ithaca, N.Y.

Williams, W. L. (1943) Veterinary Obstetrics, 4th Ed., Miss Louella Williams, Upland Rd., Ithaca, N.Y.

Woodward, R. R. and Quesenberry, J. R. (1956) A Study of (Postpartum) Vaginal and Uterine Prolapse in Hereford Cattle, J. An. Sci. **15,** 1, 119.

Worthman, R. P. (1957) Demonstration of Specific Nerve Paralysis in the Dog, J.A.V.M.A. **131,** 4, 174.

Puerperal Metabolic Diseases

Albright, J. L. and Blosser, T. H. (1957) Blood Levels and Urinary Excretion of Calcium in Normal Cows and Cows with Parturient Paresis After Intravenous Injections with Calcium Borogluconate, J.A.V.M.A. **40,** 5, 477.

Asbury, A. C. (1962) Hypocalcemia in Ewes—A Case Report. J.A.V.M.A. **141,** 6, 703.

Blood, D. C. and Henderson, J. A. (1963) Veterinary Medicine, 2nd Ed., Williams Wilkins Co., Baltimore, Md.

Bloom, F. (1954) Pathology of the Dog and Cat, Amer. Vet. Publicat. Inc., Evanston, Ill.

Boda, J. M. and Cole, H. H. (1956) Calcium Metabolism with Special Reference to Parturient Paresis (Milk Fever) in Dairy Cattle; A Review, J. Dairy Sci. **39,** 7, 1027.

Bowen, J. M., Blackmon, D. M. and Heavner, J. E. (1970) Neuromuscular Transmission and Hypocalcemic Paresis in the Cow, Amer. J. Vet. Res. **31,** 5, 831.

Forbes, T. J. and Singleton, A. G. (1964) Ovine Pregnancy Toxemia: A Review, Brit. Vet. Jour. **120,** 56.

Harshberger, K. E. and Kendall, K. A. (1957) A Test of the Effectiveness of Certain Irradiated Dietary Supplements in Preventing Milk Fever, J. of Dairy Sci. **40,** 6, 615.

Hibbs, J. W. and Conrad, H. R. (1960) Studies in Milk Fever in Dairy Cows—VI Effect of Three Prepartal Dosage Levels of Vitamin D on Milk Fever Incidence, J. Dairy Sci. **43,** 8, 1124.

Jonsson, G. (1960) On the Etiology and Pathogenesis of Parturient Paresis in Dairy Cows, Acta Agric. Scand. Suppl. 8.

Kallfelz, F. A. (1968) Current Veterinary Therapy III, Edit. by R. W. Kirk, W. B. Saunders Co., Philadelphia, 64.

Kingrey, B. W., Ladwig, V. D., Monlux, W. S. and Ramsey, F. K. (1957) Pregnancy Disease of Cows, N. A. Vet. **38,** 321.

Kronfeld, D. S. (1970) The "Downer" Problem, in "Bovine Medicine and Surgery," W. J. Gibbons, E. J. Catcott and J. F. Smithcors Editors, Amer. Vet. Public, Inc. Wheaton, Ill., 394.

Kronfeld, D. S. and Emery, R. S. (1970) Acetonemia in "Bovine Medicine and Surgery," Amer. Vet. Public Inc., Wheaton Ill., 350.

Kronfeld, D. S. and Ramberg, C. F. (1970) Parturient Paresis in "Bovine Medicine and Surgery," Amer. Vet. Publ. Inc., Wheaton, Ill., 382.

Kronfeld, D. S. and Simensen, M. G. (1970) The Hypomagnesemic Tetanies, in "Bovine Medicine and Surgery," Amer. Vet. Public Inc., Wheaton, Ill., 339.

Krook, L. (1969) Personal Communication.

Lawler, D. C. (1963) Lactational Tetany in the Cat and a Review of the Literature, Vet. Rec. **75,** 811.

Mayer, G. P., Raggi, F. and Ramberg, C. F. (1965) A Rapid Semi-quantitative Test for Serum Calcium Suitable for Field Use, J.A.V.M.A. **146,** 8, 839.

Mayer, G. P., Ramberg, C. F. and Kronfeld, D. S. (1966) Hypocalcemia Without Paresis in Cows, J.A.V.M.A. **149,** 4, 402.

Mayer, G. P., Ramberg, C. F. and Kronfeld, D. S. (1967) Udder Insufflation and Its Physiologic Basis for Treatment of Parturient Paresis in Cattle, J.A.V.M.A. **151,** 12, 1673.

Mayer, G. P., Ramberg, C. F., Kronfeld, D. S., Buckle, R. M., Sherwood, L. M., Aurbach, G. D. and Potts, J. T. Jr. (1969) Plasma Parathyroid Hormone Concentration in Hypocalcemic Parturient Cows, Amer. J. Vet. Res. **30,** 9, 1587.

Nurmio, P. (1968) On Plasma Calcium Regulation in Paresis Puerperalis Hypocalcemia in Cattle, Acta Vet. Scand. Suppl. 26.

Pehrson, B. (1966) Ketosis, Acta Vet. Scand. Suppl. 15.

Poulton, B. R., Anderson, M. J. and Dell, J. C. (1962) The Relationships of Various Hereditary and Environmental Factors to the Incidence of Milk Fever (Parturient Paresis) in Dairy Cows, Maine Agric. Exp. Stat. Bull. 604, Univ. of Maine, Orono, Me.

Stott, G. H. (1965) Parturient Paresis Related to Dietary Phosphorus, J.A.V.M.A. **148,** 11, 1485.

Straub, O. C. and Hughes, J. P. (1960) Use of Dihydrotachysterol in the Prophylaxis and Treatment of Hypocalcemia in Dairy Cows, J.A.V.M.A. **137,** 5, 300.

Toivola, B. E. and Mather, G. W. (1968) Puerperal Tetany of the Bitch, Norden News **43,** 1, 16.

Puerperal and Postpartum Infections of the Genital Tract

Arthur, G. H. (1964) Wright's Veterinary Obstetrics, 3rd. Ed., The Williams and Wilkins Comp., Baltimore, Md.

Banerjee, A. K. (1965) A Study of the Action of Terramycin on the Bacterial Flora of the Uterus in Cattle Following Retained Placenta, Tijdschr. v. Diergeneesk. **90,** 8, 531.

Beattie, J. H. and Leaming, J. D. (1952) Prophylactic and Therapeutic Use of Aureomycin in Retained Placenta in Cows, Vet. Med., **47,** 11.

Ben-David, B. (1962) A Survey of the Incidence and Treatment of Retained Placenta in Cattle, Refuah Vet. **19,** 1, 48.

Bendixen, H. C. and Plum, N. (1926) Schimmel-pilze (**Aspergillus fumigatus** and **Absidia ramosa**) Als Abortus Ursache beim Rinde, Acta Pathol et Microbiol. Scand., **6,** 252.

Benesch, F. and Wright, J. G. (1951) Veterinary Obstetrics, Williams and Wilkins Comp., Baltimore, Md.

Bierschwal, C. J. and Uren, A. W. (1956) The Absorption of Chlortetracycline (**Aureomycin**) by the Bovine Uterus, J.A.V.M.A. **129,** 8, 373.

Bjorkman, N. and Sollen, P. (1961) A Morphological Study on Retentio Secundinarum in Cattle, Acta Vet. Scand. **2,** 157.

Black, W. G., Ulberg, L. C., Kidder, H. E., Simon, J., McNutt, S. H. and Casida, L. E. (1953) Inflammatory Response of the Bovine Endometrium, Am. J. Vet. Res., **14,** 51, 179.

Blood, D. C. (1957) Enzootic Metritis of Sows, Austral. Vet. Jour. **33,** 181.

Blood, D. C. and Henderson, J. A. (1963) Veterinary Medicine, 2nd. Ed. Williams and Wilkins Comp., Baltimore, Md.

Boyd, W. L. and Sellers, A. F. (1948) Some Observations on Postparturient Cows in Four Separate Herds as Related to Expulsion of their Fetal Membranes, Cor. Vet. **38,** 3, 263.

Buch, N. C., Tyler, W. J. and Casida, L. E. (1955) Postpartum Estrus and Involution of the Uterus in an Experimental Herd of Holstein Friesian Cows, J. of Dairy Sci., **38,** 1, 73.

Cohen, P. (1956) A Statistical Investigation Covering Retained Afterbirth and Other Factors Associated with Bovine Reproduction, Thesis, Royal Univ. of Utrecht.

Dawson, F. L. M. (1958) Stillbirths in Cattle, Vet. Rec. **70,** Aug 16th.

DeSutter, E. (1954) Puerperale Stoornissen na Keizersnede bij Runderen, Vlaams Diergeneesk Tijdschr., **23,** 11, 273.

Durfee, P. T. (1968) Surgical Treatment of Postparturient Metritis in the Bitch, J.A.V.M.A. **153,** 1, 40.

Easterbrooks, H. L. and Plastridge, W. N. (1955) Aureomycin for Retained Placenta in the Cow, J.A.V.M.A., **126,** 934, 21.

Erb, R. E., Hinze, P. M., Gildow, E. M. and Morrison, R. A. (1958) Retained Fetal Membranes—The Effect on Prolificacy of Dairy Cattle, J.A.V.M.A., **133,** 10, 489.

Fincher, M. G. (1941) Retained Placenta, J.A.V.M.A., **99,** 776, 395.

Fincher, M. G. (1951) Foaling Mares, First Annual Stud. Managers Course, College of Agric., Univ. of Kentucky, Lexington, Ky.

Gould, C. M., Gould, A. C. and Gray, D. F. (1961) The Treatment of Retention of the Placenta in the Bovine Animal, Vet. Rec. **73,** 335.

Hallman, E. T. (1924) Further Studies in the Diseases of the Reproductive Organs of Cattle, Cor. Vet., **14,** 3, 254.

Hammermann, J. (1963) Treatment of Retained Placenta with Special Reference to the Fertility of the Cow, Proc. 9th Nord. Vet. Congr., Copenhagen, 1962, Vol. II, 534.

Heatley, T. G. (1939) A Few Notes on Retention of the Afterbirth in the Mare, Vet. Rec., **48,** 24, 760.

Henken, R. W. and Vandersall, J. H. (1967) Feasibility of an All Silage Forage Program, J. Dairy Sci. **50,** 3, 417.

Herrick, J. B. (1963) A Genital Infection Syndrome in Cattle, Vet. Med. **58,** 4, 329.

Jennings, W. E. (1941) Some Common Problems in Horse Breeding, Cor. Vet., **31,** 2, 197.

Kantor, H. I. and Kamholz, J. H. (1955) Cyclic Endometrial Changes Without Menstruation, Fert. and Steril., **6,** 4, 353.

Kennedy, A. J. (1947) Retention of the Placenta in the Bovine, Vet. Rec., **59,** 38, 519.

Lacroix, J. V. and Hoskins, H. P. (1952) Canine Surgery, 3rd Ed., Amer. Vet. Publicat. Inc., Evanston, Ill.

Madsen, D. E. and Nielsen, H. M. (1939) Parturient Hemoglobinemia of Dairy Cows, J.A.V.M.A., **94,** N.S. 6, 577.

Martin, C. E., Hooper, B. E., Armstrong, C. H. and Amstutz, H. E.

(1967) A Clinical and Pathologic Study of the Mastitis—Metritis—Agalactia Syndrome of Sows, J.A.V.M.A. **151,** 12, 1629.

McDonald, L. E. (1953) Placental Retention in the Cow, Proc. A.V.M.A., 90th Ann. Meeting, 418.

Moberg, R. (1956) The White Blood Picture During Parturition with Special Reference to Retained Fetal Membranes, Proc. III Internat. Congr. on Reprod. at Cambridge, 193.

Moberg, R. (1959) Possible Influences of Iodine—deficiency in Reproductive Performances in Cattle with Special Reference to Retained Placenta, Proc. III World Congr. on Fert. and Steril., Amsterdam.

Moller, K., Newling, P. E., Robson, H. J., Jansen, G. J., Meursinge, J. A. and Cooper, M. G. (1967) Retained Fetal Membranes in Dairy Herds in the Huntley District, N. Z. Vet. Jour. **15,** 7, 111.

Moore, G. R. (1946) Effects of Stilbestrol in Retained Placenta, J.A.V.M.A., **108,** 827, 79.

Moore, G. R. (1946) Effects of Stilbestrol on Pyometra Following Retained Fetal Membranes, J.A.V.M.A., **108,** 828, 153.

Moore, R. W., Redmond, H. E. and Livingston, C. W. Jr. (1966) Mycoplasma as the Etiology of a Metritis—Mastitis Syndrome in Sows, Vet. Med. **61,** 9, 883.

Nelson, G. H. (1969) Mycotoxicosis, Meeting Ill. State Vet. Med. Assoc.

Nilsson, S. A. (1958) About Founder in Cattle and Its Appearance in the Veterinary District at Mellerud, Congr. VII Vet. Nordiscus Helsinki, 313.

Paar, G. E., Cannon, R. Y. and Hawkins, G. E. (1964) Secretion of Sulphonamides in Milk Following Intramammary, Oral and Parenteral Administration, J. Dairy Sci., **47,** 3, 251.

Palmer, C. C. (1932) Clinical Studies on Retained Placenta in the Cow, J.A.V.M.A., **80,** 1, 59.

Ringarp, N (1960) Clinical and Experimental Investigations Into a Postparturient Syndrome with Agalactia in Sows, Acta. Agric. Scand. Suppl. 7.

Roberts, S. J. (1954) Ketosis-Parturient Paresis Complex, J.A.V.M.A., **124,** 926, 368.

Ronning, M., Berousek, E. R., Kuhlman, A. H. and Gallup, D. (1953) The Carotene Requirements for Reproduction in Guernsey Cattle, J. of Dairy Sci., **36,** 1, 52.

Rowson, L. E. A., Lamming, G. E. and Fry, R. M. (1953) The Relationship Between Ovarian Hormones and Uterine Infection, Vet. Rec., **65,** 335.

Ross, R. F., Christian, L. L. and Spear, M. L. (1968) The Role of Certain Bacteria in Mastitis-Metritis Agalactia of Sows, J.A.V.M.A., **154,** 11, 1368.

Sager, F. C. (1949) Examination and Care of the Genital Tract of the Brood Mare, J.A.V.M.A., **115,** 873, 450.

Shaw, R. N. (1938) Pituitary Extract in Cattle Practice, Lederle Veterinary Bulletin, **7,** 1, 9.

Svendsen, P. (1967) Artificial Pneumoperitoneum—The Therapeutic Effect in Tenesmus Rectalis and Rectovaginalis Bovis, Nord. Vet. Med. **19,** 163.

Trainen, D. (1965) Treatment of Retained Placenta in the Cow—A Comparison of Four Methods, Refuah Vet. **22,** 45.

Tharp, V. L. and Amstutz, H. E. (1964) Swine Diseases, 2nd Ed. Edit. by H Dunne, Iowa State Univ. Press, Ames, Iowa, 665.

Udall, D. H. (1953) The Practice of Veterinary Medicine, 6th Ed., D. H. Udall, Ithaca, N.Y.

Vandeplassche, M., Geurden, L., VandenWyngaert, M., Snoeck, G. and DeVos, A. (1960) Puerperal Septicemia and Toxemia in Swine, Deutsche Tierarztl. Wochenschr. **67,** 14, 1375.

Vandeplassche, M. and Martens, C. (1961) The Influence of Oestrogens on Length of Gestation and on Retention of the Placenta in Dairy Cattle, Proc. IV Internat. Congr. on An. Reprod., The Hague Vol. III, 671.

Wetherill, C. D. (1965) Treatment of Cows with Retained Fetal Membranes—A Brief Review, Canad. Vet. J. **6,** 290.

Wright, J. and Roberts, S. J. (1969) Unpublished data.

Paraplegia in the Parturient Cow

Adams, O. R. (1957) Preliminary Report on the Repair of Coxofemoral Luxation and Coxofemoral Subluxation in Cattle, J.A.V.M.A., **130,** 12, 515.

Bjorsell, K. A., Holtineus, P. and Jacobsson, S. O. (1968) Studies on Parturient Paresis with Special Reference to the Downer Cow Syndrome, Acta. Vet. Scand. **10,** 36.

Fox, F. H. (1966) Personal Communication.

Johnson, B. L. (1967) Potassium and Its Role in Parturient Paresis, J.A.V.M.A., **151,** 12, 1681.

Jonsson, G. and Pehrson, B. (1969) Studies on the Downer Syndrome in Dairy Cows, Zent. fur Vetmed. A., **16,** 757.

Kronfeld, D. S. (1970) The "Downer" Problem, in **Bovine Medicine and Surgery,** Amer. Vet. Public. Inc., Wheaton, Ill., 394.

Rees, H. G. (1964) Coxofemoral Dislocation in Dairy Cattle, Vet. Res. **76,** 13, 362.

Robertson, J. M. and Boucher, W. B. (1963) Vertebral Body Abscess in a Heifer, J.A.V.M.A., **143,** 11, 1211.

Sellers, A. F., Pritchard, W. R., Weber, A. F. and Sautter, J. H. (1958) Renal Function Studies on Normal Dairy Cattle and Those with Parturient Albuminurea, Amer. J. Vet. Res., **19,** 580.

Straub, O. C., Olander, H. T. and Theilen, G. H. (1960) A Case Report of Lymphosarcoma in a Cow with Vertebral Involvement. Cor. Vet. **50,** 3, 251.

Part II

INFERTILITY IN DOMESTIC ANIMALS

Although the problem of infertility in domestic animals has been studied for many years there has been a great surge of interest, activity, research, and investigation since 1940 when the widespread use of artificial insemination forcefully brought the problem of bovine infertility to the attention of farmers, veterinarians, animal husbandrymen, physiologists, endocrinologists and others. These basic studies on the problem have rapidly forwarded our knowledge of reproductive physiology in domestic animals. In the past 15 years basic and applied reproductive studies in all species of animals and man has been heavily supported by state and federal governments, as well as private foundations, because of the urgency of thoroughly understanding all areas of reproductive physiology so that effective methods may be devised to control the so-called population explosion. In that time there has also been rapid progress in the field of endocrinology. Nutritional studies have furthered our knowledge of infertility as related to the animal diet.

The losses due to sterility and delayed breeding in dairy cattle have been estimated by Asdell to be about twenty million dollars per year in New York State. While it is possible that the incidence of sterility and delayed breeding is increasing, it is more likely that in recent years, due to more general use of artificial insemination, gradually, increased milk yield, higher value per cow, and increasing feeding problems, farmers have become more conscious of their loss than they were formerly when a cow failed to conceive promptly. The average good cow should provide a farmer a net return of $300 each year over feed costs. Each month delay in conception results in $20 to $30 loss to the farmer.

The studies initiated in the field of artificial insemination on the infertility problems in bulls and cows have done much in recent years to elucidate more clearly the importance of the bull in the overall problem of bovine infertility. These studies in cattle have in turn set the pattern and stimulated studies in other species of animals.

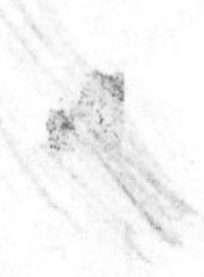

Chapter XII

PHYSIOLOGY OF FEMALE REPRODUCTION

Reproductive Hormones

Reproduction is a luxury function of the body not physiologically necessary for life of the individual and usually not performed until the animal reaches nearly adult size and nutritive supplies are ample for the nutrition of both the dam and fetus. Any adverse influence of environment, nutrition, stress or disease on the individual will, if severe enough, exert its influence on the reproductive system.

Reproduction in mammals is largely controlled by endrocrine glands and the hormones they secrete. These influence all phases of reproduction. At least four temporary reproductive structures or organs elaborate various steroid or protein hormones; these are the ovarian follicle, the corpus luteum, the placenta and the endometrial cups in the mare. The hormonal regulation of reproduction is a complicated and carefully balanced system of checks and controls. The various hormones stimulate or inhibit each other and accordingly their effects on the animal's reproductive organs. The reproductive hormones play a major role in the initiation and regulation of the estrous cycle, ovulation, fertilization, preparing the uterus for the fertilized ovum, protecting, insuring and maintaining pregnancy, initiating parturition, and the development of the mammary gland and lactation. With a complex hormonal system controlling these many phases of reproduction, it is remarkable how seldom reproductive troubles are due to a breakdown of any portion of this mechanism. The nervous system, both central and autonomic, plays a secondary role in reproduction but one that is closely linked to the hormones produced. These nervous mechanisms in reproduction play a definite role in ovulation in those species in which ovulation is not spontaneous; with the period of sexual desire, or estrum and acceptance of the male and in such hormonal disturbances as nymphomania. Thus reproduction is under neuroendocrine or neurohumoral control. In many species of animals all phases of reproduction can take place even with the spinal cord severed in the lumbar region.

The reproductive hormones of each mammal are not species-specific in their effect; that is, the estrogenic hormone from women or mares when injected into a cow produces the same effect as does the estrogenic hormone from the cow. All hormones are highly specific and selective in their action on the genetically-conditioned end, or "target", organ. The "target" organ reacts promptly to a specific hormone to produce the substance or changes for which it has been genetically "programed", Nalbandov. Differences in the amounts of hormone required to produce specific effects occur between species, but the basic effects thus produced are often similar. A wide range of reactions to certain hormones exists.

Another important fact to recognize in the use of reproductive hormones is that hormones produced in a certain organ or gland do not, when injected, affect that organ or gland directly. In other words, endocrine disturbances of the ovary do not respond directly to the ovarian hormones, but if curable usually respond to the pituitary hormones. For example ovarian hormones act in a direct manner on the tubular genitalia and in an inhibitory manner on the anterior pituitary gland through their indirect effect on the central nervous system and hypothalamus. The amount of hormone, the frequency of dosage, and the time of injection in relation to the stage of the estrous cycle have profound influences on the effects produced.

Many external sensory stimuli act upon the central nervous system and hypothalamus and effect reproduction. These include: light, and sight mediated by the eyes, sound, or vocalization, mediated by the ears, smell mediated by the nose, state of nutrition, physical stimuli including cold and heat and the amount of work, stress as mediated by the release of glucocorticoids from the adrenal gland, tactile stimuli as obtained by mounting and intromission and possibly others. The olfactory stimuli have been called "pheromones" by Parkes and Bruce. Certain drugs, as well as hormones, can effect the centers in the central nervous system and produce changes in reproductive physiology. In the central nervous system, spinal cord and hypothalamus are numerous interacting reflex arcs, and centers concerned with reproductive behavior and with production of releasing factors or neurosecretions that result in the release of the tropic hormones from the anterior pituitary gland after they pass to the adenohypophysis through the hypophysial portal system. Such centers, often located in or near the hypothalamus, also control the release of prolactin from the anterior pituitary gland and oxytocin and vasopressin from the neurohypophysis or posterior pituitary gland (see Figure 102). The blood supply to the hypophysis and hypophysial portal system used to carry releasing factors or neurohumors from the hypothalamus to the adenohypophysis has been described by Cummings and Habel. Hansel described the control exerted by the hypothalamus on pituitary function in animals.

The principal or major endocrine gland controlling the reproductive organs and functions is the adenohypophysis. The pituitary gland is composed of two principal parts. The anterior lobe or adenohypophysis is quite vascular. Cells in this lobe produce the gonadotropic hormones and control the activity of the gonads. The posterior lobe or neurohypophysis is divided into the pars nervosa and pars intermedia. The latter structure is small and apparently of limited importance. The pars nervosa, the major portion of the posterior lobe, is attached to the floor of the third ventricle or hypothalamus by a stalk or infundibulum. Thus the anterior and posterior lobes of the pituitary gland are separate and distinct in origin, structure and functions (See Figure 102).

There are 6 major adenohypophyseal hormones that have been isolated and are obtainable in a nearly pure form at the present time:

ACTH—adrenocorticotropic hormone
Prolactin—This hormone is luteotropic in the rat and possibly in the sheep
STH or GH—somatotropic or growth hormone
TSH or TTH—thyroid-stimulating or thyrotropic hormone
FSH—follicle-stimulating hormone
LH—luteinizing and luteotropic hormone
MSH—melanocyte-stimulating hormone—This seventh hormone is of little importance
FSH and LH are the gonadotropic hormones.

All of these hormones are complex proteins in nature and are water-soluble. Jubb and McEntee and McDonald in reviewing the literature on the histology and physiology of the anterior pituitary gland reported that there were three principal cell types composing this endocrine gland; basophilic cells, acidophilic cells and chromophobe cells. FSH, LH, TSH, and probably ACTH are produced by

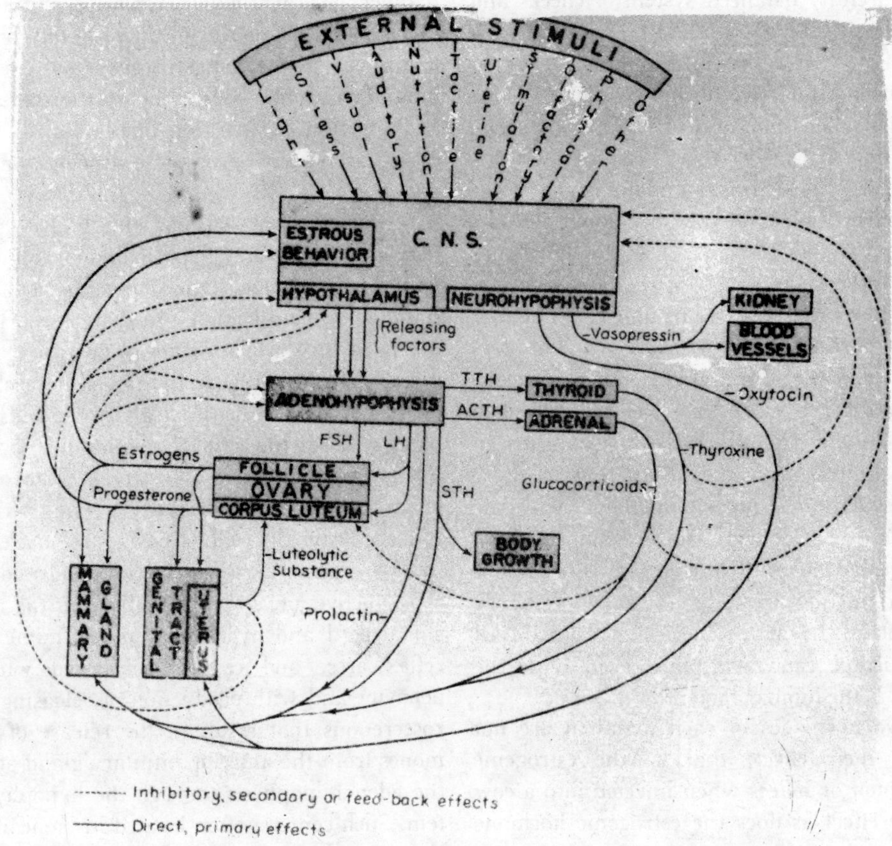

Figure 102. Diagram of the Neuroendocrine Control of Reproduction in Female Animals

certain basophilic cells. Somatotropic or growth hormone and prolactin are produced in the acidophilic cells.

The adrenocorticotropic hormone is essential for the maintenance and functioning of the adrenal cortex. It is sometimes called the "stress" hormone because it stimulates the production of glucocorticoids from the adrenal cortex. Besides its other functions, this latter hormone among other actions raises the blood sugar level and lowers milk production. This explains the value of ACTH and the glucocorticoid hormones in acetonemia or ketosis. **The thyrotropic hormone** is essential for the functioning of the thyroid gland and the regulation of metabolism by its stimulation of thyroxine production. **The somatotropic or growth hormone** is concerned with body growth; moreover, it has been shown to be intimately concerned with udder development and lactation. Somatotropin causes growth of the long bones, affects protein metabolism by increasing nitrogen retention by the body, and markedly influences carbohydrate metabolism. This hormone is probably more concerned with lactation than is prolactin in the cow.

The three anterior pituitary gonadotropic hormones concerned with reproduction are FSH and LH, the gonadotropic hormones, and possibly prolactin in sheep. Probably prolactin should not be listed as a gonadotropic hormone in domestic animals, McDonald. **FSH or follicle-stimulating hormone** is necessary for the growth of the Graffian follicles and the production of estrogens in the ovary. The secretion of this hormone is inhibited by progesterone from the corpus luteum, by testosterone from the interstitial cells of the testes, or by estrogen from the follicular cells and fluid. This is probably a "feedback" effect on the central nervous system and hypothalamus preventing the secretion of the releasing factor for FSH. In castrated animals or postmenopausal women, the levels of circulating FSH and LH are high. **LH, luteinizing or luteotropic hormone** causes ovulation and growth of the corpus luteum from the granulosa cells of the ruptured Graafian follicle. Jubb and McEntee demonstrated that the basophilic delta cells of the anterior pituitary gland produced LH and probably FSH. The continued secretion of LH is necessary to maintain the corpus luteum and the secretion of progesterone to continue pregnancy in the cow, Simmons and Hansel. Although McDonald indicated that LH is probably luteotropic for all domestic animals, Short stated it was luteotropic for cattle and swine but in sheep and rats, prolactin was the luteotropic hormone. Ganong and Kraft reported that LH and probably FSH secretion and release can be stimulated by the drug, clomiphene. The following drugs can inhibit or prevent LH release and ovulation: antiadrenergic agents like dibenamine; anticholinergic agents like atropine; tranquilizers like chlorpromazine; psychic energizers like iproniazid; anticonvulsants; sedatives and anesthetics like barbiturates; and analgesics like morphine. These drugs act in a variety of ways on the cells of the C.N.S. to prevent or inhibit the release of LH. FSH and LH are synergistic in their action on the gonads. **Prolactin** is essential for the maintenance of the corpus luteum and its secretion of progesterone in the rat and possibly to some extent in the sheep, McDonald. Prolactin is primarily involved in the initiation and possibly the maintenance of lactation. It is believed to be intimately connected with maternal instincts in mammals and broodiness in hens.

Because of the many essential hormones produced by the anterior pituitary gland, it has been often called the "master gland" or "motor " of the endocrine system. In the light of recent studies this designation is questionable as it is obvious that the pituitary gland is controlled by the higher reproductive "centers" in the central nervous sytem. Clinical abnormalities of this gland produce many and varied effects. Since the hormones produced by this gland are complex proteins, they cannot be produced synthetically and have no effect when taken orally inasmuch as they are destroyed by the proteolytic enzymes in the digestive tract. DuVigneaud, however, won the Nobel Prize in chemistry in 1954 by synthesizing the neurohypophyseal hormone, oxytocin, which is a complex polypeptid made up of 8 amino acids. Douglas and coworkers showed this synthetic oxytocin to be similar to natural oxytocin. Other workers are busy studying the structure of other pituitary hormones and it is likely a few may be synthesized. Repeated injections of heterologous anterior pituitary hormones into animals may result in the production of antihormones, with the result that the injected hormone is neutralized or no longer effective. This is probably of little importance in most animals and seldom occurs unless repeated injections of these proteinaceous hormones obtained from animal sources are administered, Nakahara et al., Willett et al., Desjardins and Hafs.

The adenohypophyseal content of LH is highest in cattle, sheep and cats and lowest in horses and man, McDonald. Of the domestic animals, the cow and sheep secrete the greatest amount of prolactin. It has been shown that the timing of the release and the amounts of FSH and LH hormone released is very important in the initiation of ovulation and the number of ova released. The blood serum of castrates contains an increased amount of FSH because neither testosterone, estrogen, nor probably progesterone is inhibiting its secretion. Large prolonged injections of these latter steroid hormones suppress pituitary gonadotropic hormones a cause small. atrophic gonads. Smaller doses of estroge or proge[illegible] may cause cystic ovaries. The urine an serum of pregnant women from about 30 to 60 days after the last menstruation and the serum of pregnant mares from about 40 to 120 days of gestation contain large amounts of gonadotropic hormone. In the mare this hormone is not excreted in the urine but is present at a high level in the mare's serum. In humans these gonadotropic hormones are produced in the chorion of the placenta and called chorionic gonadotropins; in the mare they are produced by the endometrial cups of the uterus and are called equine gonadotropins.

The equine gonadotropic hormones from pituitary glands and pregnant mare serum are predominately follicle-stimulating in character although a small amount of LH is present. Sheep and pig pituitary gonadotropic hormones are predominately luteinizing in character although some FSH is present. Chorionic gonadotropic hormone from the urine of pregnant women is almost entirely luteinizing in character, Rowlands.

The biologic sources of the gonadotropic hormones are: human chorionic gonadotropin, HCG, from the urine of pregnant women is sold under many trade names such as "Follutein" (Squibb), and is prepared and packaged in the dry state in a sealed glass vial. This is reconstituted with a saline solution before use. In liquid form it retains its potency for several weeks or months if kept at refrigerator temperature. In rare instances anaphylactic reactions are observed in animals into which this product is injected. These reactions are most common in animals previously treated with this form of gonadotropic hormone. Human menopausal gonadotropin HMG, from urine is also used as a source of gonadotropin high in FSH, Cole. **Anterior pituitary gland** extracts or pituitary gonadotropic hormones, FSH and LH (ICSH), are prepared from the pituitary glands of sheep, horses and pigs. Some of the more common veterinary preparations are "Vetrophin" (Diamond), a sheep pituitary product; "P.L.H." (Armour); and equine pituitary gonadotropin products. These are purified and prepared in sealed vials as a dry powder and reconstituted with a saline solution at the time of use. Anaphylaxis following the use of these products is unusual. **Equine gonadotropic hormone** or pregnant mare serum gonadotropin, PMSG, is prepared from serum that is collected approximately every 10 days, between 50 and 100 days of pregnancy in the mare. The concentration of hormone is about 50 R.U. per ml. A common veterinary preparation is "Gonadin". Repeated doses of this may cause anaphylaxis, especially in the cow. In the mare, rare cases of Theiler's disease or infectious hepatitis have been reported to occur from 50 to 70 days to as long as 120 days after the use of this crude equine serum product. Pituitary FSH (Armour) is a more purified product, sold in the dry state and reconstituted before use. Very few cases of anaphylaxis have been reported after the use of this product.

Cole reported that PMSG in the mare's blood is present at 37 to 42 days of gestation and reaches a peak concentration at 70 days. Shetland ponies have a concentration of 335,000 I.U. per liter of serum between 55 and 76 days of gestation. This is about twice as high as larger horses that have serum concentrations of 50,000 to 100,000 I.U. liter. Mares with twin fetuses have double the serum levels, 240 I.U./ml vs 100 I.U./ml of mares carrying single fetuses. Mares carrying mule foals produce only one-eighth as much PMSG as mares carrying horse foals. The mucoid secretion in the endometrial cups of the mares may contain 5,000 to 210,000 I.U./gm of PMSG. Peak concentrations of HCG in human urine occur at 50 to 70 days of gestation when 20,000 to 450,000 I.U. of HCG per 24 hours of urine is excreted. After this period about 10,000 I.U. HCG is excreted daily to near term.

When the gonadotropic activity of the pituitary glands of man, horse, sheep, pig and ox were compared by assay on rats' ovaries highly sensitive to FSH the comparable percentages were 100, 35, 3, 2, and 1, respectively. When assayed on rabbits' ovaries highly sensitive to LH the comparable percentages were 100, 42, 62, 65, and 42, respectively. In the sheep, pig and cow FSH in the pituitary gland was low but LH was high. In the horse FSH and LH was high and in man FSH and LH were very high.

The principal use of gonadotropic hormones in animals is the administration of LH or luteinizing hormone in the treatment of nymphomania or cystic ovaries in cows to produce active corpora lutea and restore a normal estrous cycle. Other uses include the injection of luteinizing hormone at the time of estrum to hasten ovulation, or about 4 days after ovulation to increase the size of the corpus luteum and the amount of progesterone secretion. Injection of large doses of FSH several days prior to estrus may cause superovulation. The use of FSH to promote estrus in anestrous animals may be of value under certain limited conditions. Generally the results of this therapy for the treatment of anestrus have been poor. The value of gonadotropic hormones to produce descent of testes in cryptorchid animals is questionable. FSH may be of value in producing estrus in sheep during the anestrous period in the spring and summer months and hastening the onset of estrus in lactating sows.

Protein hormones from the pituitary gland are ineffective if given orally because they are digested and broken down in the gut. They are water-soluble and may be given intravenously where they produce a rapid action but are destroyed most rapidly. These hormones given subcutaneously or intramuscularly are absorbed more slowly and provide a more prolonged effect. Protein hormones must be protected from thermal decomposition as they are heat-labile.

Posterior Pituitary Hormones

There are two hormones secreted in the posterior lobe of the pituitary; **oxytocin,** or **pitocin,** which produces its effect by contracting the smooth muscles such as those in the uterus, around the alveoli and lactiferous ducts of the mammary gland, and in the bladder. This fraction of the posterior pituitary lobe is sometimes called "obstetrical pituitrin". **Vasopressin, pitressin,** or "surgical pituitrin" causes contraction of the smooth muscle of the arterioles thus checking postpartum uterine hemorrhage and raising blood pressure, This is also an antidiuretic hormone, ADH. If ADH is deficient diabetes insipidus with symptoms of polyuria and thirst occurs in the dog and cat, McDonald. In this condition vasopressin is not present to regulate the water resorption from the glomerular filtrate in the kidneys.

Oxytocin and vasopressin or ADH are very similar in composition with 6 of the 8 amino acids in these two hormones being similar. Posterior pituitary hormone or extract is a stable extract of the posterior pituitary lobe containing both fractions, oxytocin and vasopressin. A combination of both fractions, rather than one alone, seems to give as good or better results than oxytocin alone for most conditions treated in the veterinary field. These hormones are protein in nature and water-soluble. They are stable and are usually packaged in liquid form with a concentration of 10 or 20 U.S.P. units of each fraction per ml of the solution. Evidence of anaphylaxis following injection of pitocin, vasopressin or posterior pituitary extract is rare in most animals but it has been seen occasionally when the latter crude hormone extract has been injected intravenously in the mare.

At the present time it is generally considered that the posterior lobe hormones are produced by neurons or cells in the hypothalamus. The posterior lobe proper composed of terminal nerve endings only stores and releases the oxytocin and vasopressin, Knaggs indicated that the posterior pituitary gland of a goat contains 10 to 15 units and a cow gland contains 30 to 40 units or more of oxytocin. The half-life of oxytocin or vasopressin in the body is short, only 1 to 2 minutes. However, there are forms of ADH that slowly release small amounts after injection to control diabites insipidus. The posterior lobe cells filled with a fine granular material, release into the blood stream, by means of cell processes extending into the posterior lobe, the hormone represented by this granular material. This is an anatomical means of passing the hormone through the blood-brain barrier. The posterior lobe is not a distinct organ or gland but is a collection of terminal cell processes which store and release the hormone produced by the cells in the hypothalamus, Smith, Palay, McDonald.

The principal use of pituitrin, posterior pituitary extract, or oxytocin, is to hasten the contraction and involution of the uterus after a dystocia or prolapse of the uterus. When used immediately after parturition, it may be of some value in the prevention of retained placenta. If pituitrin or oxytocin is to be used, it is essential that it be administered soon after parturition since by 48 to 72 hours the effects are very slight as compared to the marked contractions produced within 12 hours or so after parturition when the uterus is still sensitized by the estrogens produced by the placenta late in pregnancy. For hastening involution of the uterus, pituitrin is superior to "Lentin" or the other ecbolics with the possible exception of ergonovine which acts more slowly. Pituitrin or oxytocin causes contraction of the smooth muscle or myoepithelial cells in the alveoli of the udder, to produce milk ejection or "let down" in heifers or cows that because of pain or for other reasons refuse to "let down" their milk even after stimulation of the udder by massage. The term "let down" is probably not proper because it infers the cow has voluntary control of milk ejection which she does not have. If 10 units or more are given intravenously the action is very rapid, with prompt "let down" within 30 to 60 seconds. Within this time the intra-cistern pressure increases from 30 to 40 mm to 60 to 70 mm of Hg. Under natural conditions, fright, pain or excitement apparently antagonizes, slows, or prevents the release of pitocin or oxytocin by the posterior pituitary gland by a central nervous sytem block to oxytocin release or possibly by the release of epinephrine which causes a vasoconstriction preventing oxytocin from reaching the myoepethelial cells. In sheep and goats oxytocin release and milk ejection is not necessary for satisfactory milking.

The Ovarian Hormones

The hormones produced by the ovaries are: the estrogens, the progestogens, the androgens and a nonsteroid hormone, relaxin. The first three are steroid hormones that are also produced by testes, adrenal cortices, and the placenta, Turner, Mellin and Erb.

The estrogens are steroid substances with the ability to produce estrum when injected parenterally into female animals, even in the spayed female. **Estradiol** and

estrone are the natural biologic estrogens produced in animals by the cells of the theca interna of the Graafian follicle or the placenta, Asdell. Short has reported that the follicular fluid of a mature bovine Graafian follicle contains about 50 to 90 micrograms per 100 ml of fluid. The amount of fluid averaged 2 to 3 ml per follicle. Estradiol from the Graafian follicle produces the clinical and nervous signs of estrum in the domestic animal. These include growth and keratinization of the vaginal epithelium, especially in dogs and cats, increased vascularity, edema, and growth of the endometrium, uterus and cervix, and increased sensitivity and amplitude of contraction of the uterine muscles. Under its influence the cervix relaxes and goblet cells in the cervix and anterior vagina secrete a large amount of clear viscid mucus in the cow and lesser amounts in the other species. The vulva relaxes and becomes edematous; this is especially noticeable in the dog and sow. Estrogens increase the rate of migration of leucocytes into the uterine lumen and thus increases the bactericidal activity of the uterus during estrum. Thus the genital tract sensitized by the estrogens is in a state of readiness for copulation, which in turn stimulates the release of oxytocin. The greatly increased uterine contractions and characteristic mucus of estrum favor the rapid transfer of spermatozoa to the pavilion of the oviduct, and the viability of the spermatozoa in the female reproductive tract. Certain reproductive tissues can't grow unless stimulated by estrogen. The uterus, vagina and mammary gland are tissues that are hormone dependent. Acting through the central nervous system, estradiol produces the typical clinical signs of estrum, including the female's acceptance of the male. Gonadal hormones not only bring sexual behavior to expression at estrus they also produce a differentiation or organization of neural tissues, before or soon after birth, that establishes the basic femininity, or masculinity of the individual animal, Young et al..

Estradiol is responsible for the secondary sex characteristics of the female. It causes the growth of the duct system of the mammary gland. It has a definite effect on the deposition and distribution of body fat and it hastens the ossification of the epiphyses of the bones. Near the time of ovulation estradiol reaches a high enough level in the body to suppress FSH production and by stimulating the release of LH promotes ovulation, Cole and Cupps. During pregnancy the placenta produces an increasing amount of estrogen, especially the last several weeks. At or near the time of parturition this secretion is at a very high level. At this period estrogen initiates uterine tonus, sensitizes the uterine muscle to oxytocin, relaxes the cervix, vagina and vulva, and the pelvic ligaments. Following parturition the level of estrogens drops rapidly. Estrogens are secreted in increasing amounts in the urine of the mare after 100 to 120 days of gestation as estrone and estriol and other forms. These are recovered as a commercial, biologic source of estrogens. The major urinary estrogen excreted in the cow is estradiol, Mellin et al.. During gestation the action of a low physiologic level of estrogens on the pituitary gland may be necessary to help maintain the corpus luteum by stimulating the release of LH. Asdell suggested that the presence of progesterone during pregnancy probably prevents the occurrence of signs of estrum.

The estrogens being steroid in nature are soluble in oil and therefore are usually administered intramuscularly or subcutaneously. Most steroids are soluble in propylene glycol which can be injected intravenously without harm, Nalbandov. This form of steroid hormone preparation is not available commercially in the U.S.A. Estrogens may be implanted subcutaneously or intramuscularly in the form of a pellet, from which the estrogens are absorbed slowly over a period of several months. To be successful, this procedure requires a nearly sterile technique because if infection is introduced excessive connective tissue is built up around the pellet and absorption might be prevented. Other estrogenic preparations for injection are the aqueous suspension of fine particles of estrogen and the solution of estrogens in an alcoholic base or "Repositol" which precipitates when injected into the body tissues or comes in contact with water. Following intramuscular injections of the aqueous suspension and "Repositol" products the fluid is rapidly absorbed, leaving fine particles of estrogen as a modified type of implant. These preparations are easier to administer but due to the fine size of the estrogenic particle it is absorbed faster than when in pellet form. Consequently injections must be repeated about every 10 days. The esterification of an estrogen will also reduce its rate of absorption and thus prolong its action. For example, the effects of stilbestrol in oil last 24 to 36 hours while the effects of estradiol dipropionate will last 24 to 48 hours and estradiolcyclopentylproprionate in oil, "E.C.P." (Upjohn) and estradiol valerate (Squibb) are effective over a period of 72 to possibly 96 hours or longer. In humans and animals with a simple stomach, such as the dog and cat, the estrogens, like stilbestrol, may also be easily administered orally. Low levels of estrogens, such as 10 mg/day of stilbestrol, added to the ration of feeder cattle and sheep will increase the rate of gain and growth compared to rations not containing this hormone. The naturally-occurring estrogen, estradiol, is more rapidly destroyed than is stilbestrol when given orally, Dukes. All animals can absorb estrogens fed in their ration. Estrogens may be applied by inunctions and absorbed through the skin or from the uterus after intrauterine infusions.

There are two types of estrogens available commercially; the naturally-occurring estrogens such as estradiol, estrone and estriol produced from natural sources such as the urine of pregnant mares and women and from the human placenta and amniotic fluid; and stilbestrol or diethylstilbestrol synthesized from various coal-tar derivatives and other steroids. Presently all types of estrogenic compounds may be synthesized chemically for commercial purposes. In animals both compounds, estradiol and stilbestrol, are equally effective and desirable. While in humans estradiol is preferred because there are fewer undesirable side reactions. Milligram for milligram estradiol is about 10 times as potent as stilbestrol. Therefore a 50 mg. injection of stilbestrol is approximately equivalent to a 5 mg injection of estradiol. Some common trade names for estradiol preparations are "E.C.P." (Upjohn), "Diovocylin" (Ciba), and "Progynon B." (Schering). Stilbestrol, or diethylstilbesterol, is usually marketed under those names in products containing 5 to 25 mg per ml..

The estrogens are probably the most widely-used hormones in veterinary medicine. They are used to evacuate the uterus in cases of a mummified fetus or pyometra in cattle, and to produce therapeutic abortion in all species. By increasing the uterine blood supply, increasing the contraction of the uterine muscles, and stimulating epithelial growth and the flow of mucus they aid in the treatment of such conditions as postpartum metritis and retained placenta. In the normal cow the value of estrogens at this time is questionable. Estrogens have been shown by Rowson et al. and Black et al. to have a definite effect on the uterus and uterine infection by their ability to prevent, reduce, and overcome infection in the uterine cavity by their effect on stimulating the passage of leucocytes and bactericidal substances from the leucocytes into the uterus, Nalbandov, Hawk et al.. When administered soon after an undesirable service, estrogens prevent conception by their effect on the oviduct and uterus and the transport of the fertilized ova. All of these effects on the tubular portion of the genital tract characterize the action of estrogens.

The estrogens have also been used widely to produce signs of estrum in anestrous animals. This action is to be expected since proper doses of estrogens produce estrum or acceptance of the male even in spayed females. This artificial estrum cannot be regarded as physiological since ovulation does not occur unless the estrogen is given at the time in the estrous cycle at which ovulation would normally occur. Large or moderate doses of estrogens given at the time of estrum or ovulation often cause infertility because of their adverse effects on ova transport. Injection of estrogens in large doses over a period of time in virgin heifers or dry cows usually produces varying degrees of mammary development and lactation. The peak of production following the estrogenic initiation of lactation follows a week or two after the estrogen is withdrawn and milking has begun. This phenomena is also observed occasionally in the natural state in newborn heifers and prepubertal heifers due to excessive assimilation of estrogens from the placenta or production of estrogen by the endocrine glands. Large doses of estrogen at the time of parturition inhibit lactation and relieve congestion of the udder. It is also used in bitches at the end of their pseudopregnant period to relieve udder congestion and possibly other symptoms of pseudocyesis. Because of its effect on the muscles and epithelium of the genito-urinary system it is used in bitches affected with urinary incontinence. The estrogens are occasionally used in ointment form for their stimulating effect on epithelial tissues in obscure skin ailments or to produce cornification of the vaginal epithelium in certain types of vaginitis. Stilbesterol and other gonadal steroids have been used in pellet form in young cockerels, lambs and steers and recently incorporated in feed for ruminants to increase rate of gain and deposition of fat. In steers or feeder cattle and lambs about 10 mg and 2 mg, respectively, of diethylstilbestrol fed daily is considered the best feeding level for increased weight gains and improved feed conversion. There was no effect on bovine reproduction by feeding this level, 5 to 15 mg, daily of diethylstilbestrol, Bush and Reuber.

Excessive or prolonged dosing with estrogen will produce cystic ovaries or nymphomania in cattle, abortion, atrophy of the ovaries and cessation of the estrous cycles. In cattle and sheep estrogens will cause the regression of the corpus luteum possibly by suppressing LH secretion or by exhausting the LH levels in the adenohypophysis. In the sow and horse estrogens may prolong the life of the corpus luteum. Large amounts of estrogen produce edema of the vulva, excessive relaxation of the pelvic ligaments and other supporting structures, predisposing to prolapse of the vagina and rectum, and fractures of the pelvic bones. Goetsch reported that in lambs fed or injected with estrogens to increase their rate of growth and efficiency of feed utilization, an enlarged vulva, increased mammary development, and increased size of the bulbo-urethral glands causing swelling in the perineal region developed. Secondary prolapse of the rectum due to straining to urinate was produced by the latter condition. In cattle treated similarly, increased mammary gland growth and teat development occurred in both males and females; heifers developed constant estrum and elevation of the tailhead. Prolapse of the vagina was noted in a few animals, and the ovaries were smaller with fewer follicles and corpora lutea. In the dog excessive or prolonged doses of estrogens can produce a fatal anemia due to their toxic effect on bone marrow.

In domestic animals the level of the gonadotropins in the pituitary, the length of the heat period, and estrogen threshold and excretion during estrum are strikingly parallel. The following order, from high to low, is generally reported: man, horse, hog, sheep, and cow, Asdell.

Progesterone or the corpus luteum hormone, is a steroid hormone produced by the corpus luteum. Progesterone is also produced by the adrenal cortex and the placenta. Following ovulation the corpus luteum develops from the granulosa cells and the theca interna of the Graafian follicle and is maintained by the luteinizing (LH) or luteotrophic hormone of the anterior pituitary gland, Donaldson and Hansel. Under the stimulation of the luteotropic hormone, the lutein cells produce progesterone. The corpus luteum is essential throughout pregnancy in the cow, goat, sow and bitch but for less than full term in mares and ewes. In these latter species the progesterone produced by the placenta maintains pregnancy, Gomes and Erb. In many species the secretion of progesterone by the follicle begins before ovulation occurs, Turner.

Progesterone causes the growth of the glandular system of the endometrium of the uterus and is necessary for the uterine milk from the endometrial glands and the nutrition of the ovum, and the attachment of the embryo. It maintains pregnancy by producing a favorable environment for the survival of the developing embryo and inhibiting the motility of the uterus. By causing an inhibition of the LH and FSH hormones from the pituitary it prevents estrum, ovulation, and the occurrence of the estrous cycle. However enough FSH is released so that follicles form even during the luteal phase of the estrous cycle, and also during early gestation in most domestic animals. Research has indicated that progesterone may act with estrogen to stimulate ovulation by promoting the release of LH, Cole and Cupps. Hansel and Trimberger have reported that small amounts of progesterone injected during early estrum in the cow hasten ovulation. Progesterone probably acts with estrogen in most species to cause signs of estrus and acceptance. If progesterone from a previous corpus luteum is lacking, the first ovulation is usually characterized by a "silent" heat. This is seen in the early part of the breeding season in sheep, in prepubertal heifers, and in the postpartum period in the cow, McDonald. Rowson and coworkers and Black and coworkers have shown that the endometrium and uterus, when under the influence of progesterone during the luteal phase of the cycle, are much more susceptible to infection and provide a favorable environment for its development. Progesterone causes the development of the alveolar system of the udder. It maintains the endometrium and is important for the continuance of pregnancy. Following the first half of the period of pregnancy in humans and in animals such as the horse and sheep, progesterone for the maintenance of pregnancy is produced by the placenta, and the corpus luteum becomes small and inactive. In other species, such as the cow and goat, the corpus luteum is essential during most if not the entire period of pregnancy in order to prevent abortion inasmuch as apparently little progesterone is secreted by the placenta. The half-life of progesterone in the cow is only 20 to 35 minutes. Thus the importance of a continuing constant secretion from the corpus luteum is evident, McDonald, Imori. Because of its ability to inhibit keratinization of the vagina, to prevent sensitization of the uterus, and to prevent estrum, progesterone secreted by the placenta and corpus luteum prevents or possibly counteracts the action of estradiol also produced in large amounts during late pregnancy. In the dog and cat progesterone produces changes characteristic of pseudopregnancy. Excretion products of progesterone metabolism, principally pregnanediol in the woman, horse and sheep, are present in the urine after being broken down in the liver, Nalbandov. In the cow progesterone and its metabolites are excreted mainly in the feces, Williams.

This hormone is usually produced synthetically by the chemical treatment of stigmasterol, a wax obtained from soybeans. Progesterone is prepared in an oily base, in a "Repositol" form, or in finely-divided particles in an aqueous base. The oily preparation is effective for 24 to 48 hours when injected intramuscularly; while the latter preparations are effective for about 10 days since the finely divided particles precipitate in the tissues. The pellet form of progesterone is also available.

Progesterone is used to prevent or control habitual abortion due to a progesterone deficiency. It is also used to promote conception the first 20 days of gestation in the cow. In the ewe, cow, sow, and bitch, it can be injected during diestrum or early proestrum and prevent estrum from occurring by suppressing the release of the gonadotropic hormones, for as long as the injections are continued. Thus it may be used to synchronize estrus in a group of cattle, sheep, or swine. However, the synthetic progestins that may be fed orally, produce better conception rates, are cheaper and cause fewer cystic ovaries. Progesterone has been used experimentally to maintain pregnancy in cows in which the corpora lutea have been removed. If injections are continued beyond the normal length of gestation, prolonged gestation and fetal death may result. It has also been used, but its value is questionable, in the treatment of prolapse of the vagina.

Relaxin is a water-soluble protein hormone apparently

present in the ovaries, probably the corpus luteum, placenta and uterus during the late stages of gestation and is responsible, along with estrogen, for the relaxation of the pelvic ligaments and cervix necessary for parturition. In the pregnant guinea pig and gopher it is able to cause resorption of the pelvic symphysis. This relaxation effect is brought about by a depolymerization of the ground substance or collagen and the increased water content of the connective tissue, Turner.

A luteolytic factor, substance or mechanism apparently present in the endometrium or uterine glands of the cow, ewe and sow is responsible for the regression of the corpus luteum of the estrous cycle. It apparently acts through both the systemic utero-pituitary-ovarian pathway causing a decline in pituitary luteotropin or LH, and probably a local utero-ovarian pathway which may involve the lymphatics, Gunther, Brunner et al.. The existence of this uterine luteolysin has not been demonstrated in the horse, dog and cat. If the cow, sow or ewe conceives, the uterine luteolytic mechanism is inhibited by the embryo or its membranes by the second week of gestation and regression of the corpus luteum is prevented, Moor and Rowson and Cole and Cupps. At the present time this luteolytic substance has not been isolated and identified but research in this area is active.

Other Endocrine Glands

Other endocrine glands that may be connected with reproduction are the thyroid, adrenal, and possibly the pineal gland.

The thyroid gland secretes thyroxine and triiodothyronine, composed of iodinated amino acids, under the regulation of the thyrotropic or thyroid stimulating hormone from the basophilic beta cells in the anterior pituitary gland. Thyroxine and triiodothyronine have been synthesized. The latter is more active and potent, Turner. The thyroid gland contains large amounts of iodine. In humans hypothyroidism is believed by many to be closely associated with sterility, infertility and abortion. Thyroid activity is necessary for normal reproductive functions. In the United States thyroid abnormalities such as goiter are most common in the iodine-deficient areas from around the Great Lakes and the northeastern part of the country to the Pacific coast. Goiter or an enlarged thyroid is produced by excessive stimulation of the thyroid gland by TSH when the gland cannot meet the body's need for thyroxine. Hypothyroidism causes a low metabolic rate that is believed to have an adverse effect on human fertility and pregnancy and often is associated with obesity.

Since thyroxine and triiodothyronine are quite expensive when obtained from animal sources or synthesized, and because there has been little work to show the need of these in various sterility or impotency problems in animals, its use is limited. Reineke and Turner developed an iodinated casein with about a 3-percent thyroxine potency. "Protamone" contained thyroxine and triiodothyronine in concentrations of 0.79 and 0.61 percent, respectively which is equivalent to a 3.28 percent thyroxine potency in the rat, Mischler and Reineke. This has been marketed by the Cerophyll Laboratories in Kansas City, Missouri. In daily doses of 1 gm per 100 lbs. of weight it may be fed to livestock, in which it produces a definite increase in the basal metabolic rate, as shown by an increase of 5 to 20 percent in milk production together with a higher percentage of fat in lactating dairy animals (see section on Lactation). Because of the cost and dangers associated with its feeding to increase milk production, the use of thyroprotein has been limited. It causes a marked loss in weight in fat animals. In fat, sterile heifers it may be of value in reducing obesity, but a reduction in ration and an increase in the amount of exercise will accomplish the same purpose. In males, especially old, fat males, it may increase their activity and reduce their weight. In some few males this may result in some improvement in sexual desire. In this case also, however, the same purpose can usually be accomplished by restricting the rations and increasing exercise. The use of iodinated casein for reproductive diseases in livestock appears limited. Further research is needed, however, on the role of the thyroid gland in reproduction in farm animals. Preliminary clinical studies in cattle suggest thyroprotein or triiodothyronine may be of value in certain types of female infertility such as "silent" estrus, McDonald, or prolonged infertility associated with a steer-like appearance.

The adrenal glands, composed of the medullary and cortical portions, secrete hormones that have limited effects on the reproductive system but have profound effects on other body systems and functions.

The adrenal medulla secretes adrenalin, or epinephrine, which has been synthesized; it is protein in nature and water-soluble. This hormone stimulates the sympathetic nerves, whether the sympathetic nerve of the organ is excitatory or inhibitory. In cows adrenalin may prevent the normal "let down" of milk by preventing pitocin from the posterior pituitary lobe from reaching the mammary gland. It causes a relaxation of the estrogenized uterine muscle in the cow. In other species it may cause contraction of the gravid or nongravid uterus. Epinephrine has been used by some veterinarians to control hemorrhage following the manual removal of the corpus luteum in the cow, but there is no pharmacologic justification for its use in this condition.

The adrenal cortex secretes steroidal hormones, such as corticosterone or cortisol that controls glycogenic activity and protects the individual against various stresses, and desoxycorticosterone or mineralo-corticoids that controls electrolyte and water metabolism. These hormones have no direct effect on the reproductive organs but glucocorticoids in moderate or large doses may cause abortion or premature birth. The adrenal cortex secretes androgens, estrogens and progesterone in small amounts, McDonald. Progesterone is a precursor of cortisol. In rare instances tumors of the adrenal cortex may secrete sufficient androgens to cause masculinization or virilism in a female. In the cow, because of the increased demands of the body for cortical hormones during gestation and the first third of the lactation period, the adrenal cortex is usually larger than normal for that length of time.

The thymus is usually assumed not to be an endocrine gland but it is little understood. It resembles a lymph gland and contains large numbers of lymphocytes. It reaches its greatest size just before puberty. Following puberty it involutes.

The pineal gland or body, attached in most animals by a short stalk to the roof of the third ventricle of the brain, has not been proved to be an endocrine gland. At present there is little evidence to indicate that the pineal gland plays any important role in sexual maturation, Cole and Cupps.

The hormones concerned with reproduction in the male animal are described in Chapter XVIII.

Puberty

Puberty may be defined as the age or time at which the generative organs become functional and reproduction may occur. Puberty does not signify full or normal reproductive capacity, which develops later. In the male, puberty is indicated, along with other secondary sex changes, by the ability to copulate and produce sperm. In the female animal, it is characterized by the appearance of estrum and ovulation. The time of onset of puberty in animals is greatly modified by environmental and genetic factors. A high plane of nutrition hastens the onset of estrum especially in cattle and horses. A low plane of nutrition or deficiencies of various nutrients as well as disease factors will delay puberty. Exposure to stress conditions especially during the cold months of the year delay the onset of puberty. In certain animals such as sheep which have a limited breeding season puberty does not occur until that season, at which time the animal may be fully grown. Inbreeding tends to delay puberty while crossbreeding tends to hasten its occurrence. Brahman and Zebu cattle reach puberty 6 to 12 months later than the European breeds. The larger breeds of cattle and horses tend to have a later onset of puberty than the smaller breeds, Hafez, Foote et al., Zimmerman et al., Wiltbank et al., De Rouen et al., and Menge et al.. The age at puberty was less variable than the weight in gilts on a high and low plane of nutrition, Robinson et al.. Sorenson and coworkers reported that in 3 groups of 21 calves each, fed on the following three levels of nutrition, 140 percent, 100 percent, and 60 percent, as based on Morrison's standards, the heifers on the high level of nutrition reached puberty with the first estrum at an average of 37.4 weeks of age weighing 580 lbs., the heifers on the average level of nutrition reached puberty at 47 weeks of age weighing 597 lbs., and the low level heifers reached puberty at 65 weeks weighing 502 lbs. The attainment of puberty is a slow, gradual process. Graafian follicles must attain a fairly advanced stage of development before the gonadotropins are effective. Puberty depends upon the release of the gonadotropic hormones from the anterior pituitary. Injection of these hormones into prepubertal animals may cause precocious sexual maturity. The gradual nature of the processes leading to puberty is cited by Asdell in the human, in which secondary sex characteristics develop before menstruation occurs, and menstruation takes place for a period of time before ovulation occurs. Morrow reported on 53 Holstein heifers with a mean interval from birth to the first ovulation of 296 days at a mean weight of 609 lbs.. "Silent" estrus was exhibited in 74 percent of the heifers at the time of their first ovulation.

Puberty in most of our domestic animals, especially those reared and fed under the most artificial conditions occurs much earlier than does sexual maturity or full or normal reproductive capacity. As Asdell pointed out, most animals that normally give birth to 2 or more young at a time are less fecund immediately after puberty than they are later. Yearling ewes usually have only one lamb. Primiparous gilts usually have smaller litters than 2- to 4-year-old sows. Fertility denotes the ability to produce young, while fecundity denotes the number of young produced. Fertility is reached at puberty but fecundity increases with age to maturity and then later in life decreases. Early fertility and high initial fecundity usually indicates that an animal will have a good reproductive record in the future.

Because of enviromental influences, frequently estrum occurs at such an early age that if conception occurred parturition would be disastrous due to the small size and lack of development of the dam. Young female animals should not be bred until their body development ensures a normal gestation and parturition. Heifers should probably be bred according to size and weight rather than by their age. It has been recommended that Holstein and Brown Swiss heifers not be bred until they weigh about 750 lbs., Ayrshires about 650 lbs, Guernseys about 550 lbs., and Jerseys about 500 lbs., Olds and Seath. Heifers may reach this size from 10 to 24 months of age depending upon feeding levels and management practices. Rapid pubertal growth in Holstein heifers started during the seventh month after birth. By the tenth month this rapid growth of the genital tract terminated and subsequent growth was much slower, Desjardins and Hafs. By proper feeding and management it may be possible by early breeding of heifers, 10 to 15 months of age, and mares, 2 years of age, to produce one additional calf or foal per female.

The onset of puberty in the domestic animals is as follows:

Horses—10 to 24 months, average 18 months of age.

Cattle—6 to 18 months. Heifers in rare instances may come in estrum as early as 3–4 months of age, or if kept in a cold environment on a low level of nutrition, the first estrum may not occur until 24 months of age.

Sheep—6 to 12 months, usually in the fall.

Swine—5 to 8 months, average 6 months.

Dogs—6 to 12 months, average 7 to 10 months.

Since puberty develops before conception, normal gestation, and parturition can take place, most well-grown dairy heifers are not bred until they are 14 to 18 months of age. Beef and poorly-grown dairy heifers may be bred from 18 to 24 months of age. Fillies should not be bred until 2 or preferably 3 years of age. Gilts, unless well grown, should not be bred before they are 8 to 9 months of age. Ewe lambs under 12 months of age should not be bred. It is generally considered undesirable to breed dogs on their first estrum or dogs or cats before they are a year old. Following breeding of the pubertal animal, the nutritive level during the first gestation should be adequate to continue rapid growth and development so by the time of parturition complications such as dystocia do not occur.

The Estrous Cycle

In all species of domestic animals that have reached puberty there is a definite physiologic functional rhythm of the reproductive system, called the estrous cycle. Although each species has its own peculiarities regarding their estrous cycle pattern, basically all are similar. The estrous cycle is commonly divided into 4 phases or periods that blend one into the other. Some authors prefer to divide the estrous cycle into two periods the **estrogenic** or **follicular** phase comprising proestrum and estrum and the **progestational** or **luteal** phase comprising metestrum and diestrum.

Proestrum is an ill-defined period during which the Graafian follicle is growing under the influence of FSH and producing increasing amounts of estradiol. There are increases in the growth of cells and cilia lining the oviduct, in the vascularity of the uterine mucosa, and in the thickness and vascularity of the vaginal epithelium, with cornification occurring in some species, such as the dog and cat. In the dog, the increased endometrial vascularity is characterized by bleeding. In the bitch and sow the vulva becomes definitely edematous and swollen. There is a gradual relaxation of the cervix and an increased secretion of viscid, slimy mucus from the goblet cells of the

Figure 103. Heifer in Estrum—Standing to be Mounted.

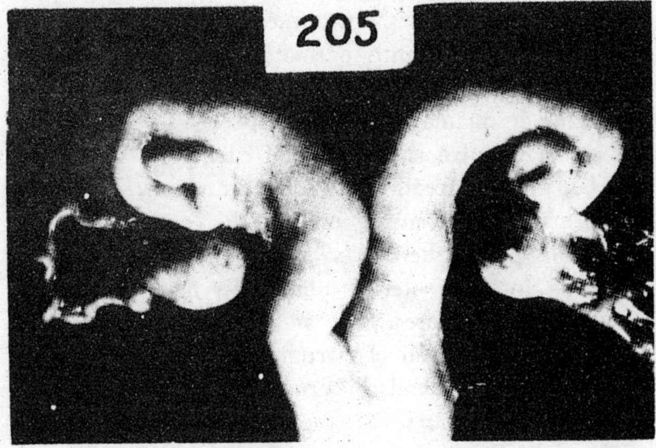

Figure 104. Normal Genital Tract of a Heifer in Estrum—Note maturing follicle in the right ovary and regressing C. L. in the left ovary. (Courtesy K. McEntee)

cervix and anterior vagina and from the uterine glands. In the cow and mare, the sticky, dry mucus of the preceding period changes during proestrum to a milky, viscid mucus, and finally to a clear, transparent, stringy mucus late in the proestrous period. There is an increased excretion of estrogen in the urine and a beginning decrease of progesterone in the blood, Cole and Cupps. The corpus luteum is undergoing rapid vacuolization, degeneration, and decrease in size. The marked increase in growth of the epithelial tissues, of the activity of the musculature of the reproductive tract, of the secretion of mucus, and of the vascularity of the endometrium and vaginal mucosa is spoken of as the building-up period. It is produced by the secretion of increasing amounts of estradiol. Late in this phase of the cycle the female animal usually exhibits interest in the male.

Estrum is the fairly well-defined period characterized by sexual desire and the acceptance of the male by the female domestic animal. (See Figures 103 and 104) This period begins with the time of the first acceptance and ends with the last acceptance of the male. During this period the female will usually seek out and accept the male. The Graafian follicle is large and mature. The ovum undergoes certain maturation changes. Estradiol from the maturing Graafian follicle produces changes in the tubular genital tract that reach their culmination in this period. The oviducts are tonic, the epithelium mature, and the cilia are active; contraction of the oviducts is occurring; and the fimbriated end of the oviduct is assuming a close affinity to the Graafian follicle. Increased amounts of oviduct fluid is being secreted. The uterus is erect, turgid, and in some species, edematous. The blood supply to the uterus is increased; the mucosa is growing rapidly, and mucus is secreted. The vaginal and cervical mucus is greatly increased. The mucosa is pink and congested, due to the increased vascularity. The cervix is relaxed and slightly edematous. The mucosa of the vagina is greatly thickened with many cornified epithelial cells being desquamated in certain species, such as the dog and cat. The vulva is relaxed and edematous in all species, but most noticeably in the bitch and sow. Strings of mucus may hang from the vulva in the cow. Toward the end of this period there may be an increase in leucocytes migrating into the uterine lumen. In most species the rupture of the mature ovisac or ovulation occurs toward the end of this period of estrum, but it is only roughly correlated with the end of estrum. In the cow, ovulation occurs about 12 hours after the end of estrum. In certain species that do not ovulate spontaneously, such as the cat, rabbit, and ferret, ovulation does not occur until coitus and/or mounting takes place; hence in the cat estrum may be prolonged in the absence of a male to 7 to 10 days. The acceptance of the male during estrum is due to the effect of estradiol on the central nervous system, producing the characteristic behavior patterns of receptivity in the various female animals. Hammond has reported that female as well as male sexual behavior patterns are not sex-specific and that under certain conditions each exhibits the behavior patterns of the other.

Metestrum or postestrum is a poorly defined period following estrum during which the corpus luteum grows rapidly from the granulosa cells of the ruptured follicle under the influence of the luteinizing hormone of the anterior pituitary. Metestrum is largely under the influence of progesterone produced by the corpus luteum. The presence of this hormone, by inhibiting the secretion of FSH by the pituitary gland, prevents the development of more Graafian follicles and the immediate development of another estrum. During metestrum in some species the epithelium of the vagina loses most of its new growth through desquamation. In the cow, during the early part of metestrum the epithelium over the caruncles of the uterus is very hyperemic and some capillary hemorrhage occurs. This is called postestrual or metestrual bleeding or "menstruation." This is not similar to true menstruation in primates which occurs at the time of progesterone withdrawal and is associated with a loss of the superficial layers of the endometrium. In cattle postestrual bleeding is associated with estrogen withdrawal. The mucous secretion decreases and the glands of the endometrium grow rapidly. Toward the middle to the end of metestrum the uterus becomes rather soft and pliable, due to a relaxation of the uterine muscle. In dogs, cats, and rabbits this stage includes the pseudopregnant period. In the species having diestrual cycles, including the cow, sheep, sow and mare, the length of metestrum is about equal to the time it takes for the ova to reach the uterus or about 3 to 4 days. In the dog and cat the pseudopregnant period may last about 50 to 60 days and 30 to 40 days, respectively, when the corpora lutea regress and an anestrum of varying length occurs. In the queen that is not bred ovulation and corpus luteum development doesn't occur and the follicles become atretic. Several cycles of this sort may occur in the cat before a period of anestrum sets in. Dogs and cats do not have diestrual periods.

Diestrum is the longest phase or period of the estrous cycle in domestic animals including the cow, sheep, goat, sow and mare. The corpus luteum is mature and the effects of progesterone on the reproductive tract are marked. The endometrium becomes thicker and the glands hypertrophy. The cervix is constricted and the vaginal mucus is scant and sticky. The mucous membrane of the vagina is pale. The uterine muscle is relaxed. Late in this period the corpus luteum begins to show retrogressive changes and gradual vacuolization. The endometrium and its glands atrophy or regress in size. Beginning development of the primary and secondary follicles and finally proestrum occurs. In certain species that are not polyestrous, anestrum may occur.

Anestrum, when referred to in connection with the physiologic estrous cycle, is usually characterized by quiescent, functionless ovaries and reproductive tract. Anestrum is eventually followed by proestrum. Anestrum is observed physiologically in most mares during the winter months and in the ewe during the late spring and summer months. In the bitch and cat a physiologic anestrous period lasting several months may occur two or three times a year. The term anestrum is used, therefore, to differentiate it from diestrum, which lasts only a week or so and is characterized in the cow, sow, and other polyestrous animals by a mature corpus luteum. During anestrum the uterus is small and flaccid and the vaginal mucus is scanty and sticky. The vaginal mucosa is pale and the cervix is pale and tightly closed. Some follicular activity of the ovaries may develop but a mature follicle and ovulation seldom occur during the anestrous period.

The relative lengths of these various periods of the estrous cycle in domestic animals are approximately as follows:

	Estrum	Metestrum
Cow	12 to 24 hours	3 to 5 days
Mare	4 to 7 days	3 to 5 days
Sow	2 to 4 days	3 to 4 days
Ewe	1 to 2 days	3 to 5 days
Bitch	9 days	—

	Diestrum	Proestrum
Cow	13 days	3 days
Mare	6 to 10 days	3 days
Sow	9 to 13 days	3 days
Ewe	7 to 10 days	2 days
Bitch	—	9 days

(See also the Reproductive Tables at the end of this Chapter.)

Animals may be divided into three classes according to their estrous cycles. **Monestrous** animals are those animals having one estrous cycle per year. These are usually wild animals. **Polyestrous** animals are the domestic animals such as the cow, sow, and mare, and that have frequent periodic estrous cycles throughout the year. During the late fall and winter months the mare usually has an anestrous period without estrous cycles. **Seasonal polyestrous** animals are those, like the sheep, that have periodic estrous cycles during only certain seasons of the year. The bitch and cat are more nearly like the monestrous animals. The bitch may have 2 to 4 periods of estrus each year. Three estrous periods per year are not uncommon in small breeds of dogs. The cat may have several heat periods in succession if coitus does not occur. These episodes may occur two or three times a year. This arbitrary classification of animals as monestrous, polyestrous, and seasonally polyestrous must not be taken as entirely accurate.

Excellent nutrition and environment may cause dogs to show estrum at any month in the year, and more frequently than once or twice a year. In horses, these factors may result in successful service during any month in the year. In sheep, recent work reveals a probable subclinical abortive estrual cycle present in most ewes during anestrum, especially the latter part of this phase. Certain breeds of sheep such as the Dorset and Merino regularly have two seasonal polyestrous periods in both the spring and fall. The fall season is more fertile than the spring and summer, and a greater percentage of ewes are cycling, Ortavant et al., Barker and Wiggins. Thus the present classification may be more a clinical than an actual classification. In swine and dogs and in most cats much of the lactation period is usually characterized by a lack of estrum, termed **"lactational anestrum."** This period is prolonged in cows nursing calves, Wagner.

Factors Affecting the Reproductive or Estrous Cycle

Factors influencing the onset of estrous cycles of domestic animals are many and varied and irregularities, especially in the length of the cycle, are frequently observed by veterinarians and farmers. These abnormal estrous cycles may commonly be a cause of infertility. Caslick stated that the failure of mares to have normal estrous cycles was one of the most important causes of infertility in that species. Some of these irregular estrous cycles are due to definite and known causes while others still remain to be completely explained. The causes of irregular estrous cycles include:

Nutritive state—Any severe degree of inanition or starvation caused by a lack of TDN or energy or any nutritive deficiencies, especially those causing a loss of appetite such as phosphorus, cobalt, and possibly iron, copper, iodine, protein and others, may impair or prevent the secretion of gonadotropic hormones by the pituitary gland and result in a failure of the estrous cycle. Meites stated that in humans it is well known that starvation causes a cessation of the estrous cycle and amenorrhea before other body disturbances appear. In rats a 15 percent loss of body weight may stop the estrous cycle. In a nutrition experiment at Cornell, in which sodium chloride was withheld from cows for long periods, the animals became very thin and cachetic, and estrous cycles ceased.

Seasonal Influences and Light: Most animals in the natural or wild state are usually seasonal breeders and parturition generally occurs in the spring and summer when the weather is most favorable for the young and when food is most abundant for the dam. Although domestication has altered this pattern in some animals, the natural tendency remains.

The horse and fur-bearing animals tend to come into estrum and breed during the spring months under the influence of increasing daylight. Even in the cow, which is polyestrous, the best breeding months in the northern hemisphere are May, June, and July and the poorest December, January, and February, Mercier and Salisbury. The reverse condition is seen in sheep and goats in the northern hemisphere; most breeds come into estrum under the influence of decreasing daylight and are fall breeders. This seasonal breeding trait is regulated by the effect of light, through the medium of the eyes, on the hypothalamus and the anterior pituitary gland, Dukes, Andrews, Bissonette, Ortavant et al.. The effect on the animal of the total daily amount of light is important in controlling the onset of the estrous cycle and breeding season of mammals. This is called sexual photoperiodicity. Animals taken from one hemisphere to the other change their breeding seasons in accordance with the amount of daylight. Sheep and goats confined experimentally in a darkened shed for increasing periods of time during the summer months developed estrous cycles earlier than normal. Swine also tend to be seasonal breeders, breeding usually in the spring and fall. Caslick reported that the length of estrum decreased and the length of diestrum increased in horses toward the summer months, or the end of the breeding season. Gradually increasing the total daily hours of light up to 15 hours per day by artificial means will hasten the onset of estrous cycles in mares in the spring of the year by 40 to 60 days (See Chapter XIV, Infertility in the Mare). At the beginning or end of the breeding season, cycle lengths in sheep were more often longer or shorter than the average of 14 to 19 days, Williams et al.. Similarly in mares abnormalities of the estrous cycle are seen most commonly early and late in the breeding season with excessive estrous signs frequently observed early in the season and anestrous or "silent" estrum often observed late in the season. In the seasonal breeders that respond to increasing or decreasing daylight there is a refractory period that occurs at the end of the breeding season, Ortavant et al..

Temperature—the influence of environmental temperature has less direct effect than has the amount of light on reproduction in animals. It has been hypothesized that excessive heat during the summer months, causing decreased thyroid activity, may indirectly reduce reproductive efficiency in swine, possibly cattle and sheep. In the ram "summer sterility" is due largely to the adverse effect of prolonged atmospheric heat on spermatogenesis. Excessive exposure to cold, together with a reduced feed intake during the winter months, may cause failure of the estrous cycle in young growing animals or animals on a borderline of nutritive intake, since this intake must largely be used to maintain the animals' body temperature and necessary activities. By using a temperature-controlled room kept at a temperature of 45–48° F., Dutt stimulated the onset of the estrous cycle in ewes so they came into estrum 20 to 50 days earlier than control ewes subjected to the same amount of light but kept in summer atmospheric temperatures. This was also effective in improving or maintaining the fertility of rams. Estrous periods in dairy cattle in the northern half of the U.S.A. are about 18 hours long, Trimberger and Hansel, while in the Gulf States they are shorter, about 12 hours, Hall et al.. It was also noted that the length of the estrous cycle in cattle under hot conditions increased to 25 days as compared to 20 to 21 day cycles in cooler weather, Gangwar et al..

Age—In cattle and swine, the young female usually has a slightly shorter length of estrum and estrous cycle than has the adult animal. The ewe lamb will not show estrum until the fall hence the sexual cycles in this species depend more upon the season than upon the pubertal age of the young female. Senility accompanied by defective teeth and marked weight loss, often results in a cessation of the estrous cycle or anestrum. Old age itself is relatively seldom a cause for reproductive failure. Senile changes, such as the menopause in women, do not occur in animals. Whereas cessation of reproduction in women is associated with a particular age at which the oocytes in the ovaries are largely depleted, this apparently is rare in animals.

Character of work—Horses that are worked or raced hard and long frequently do not develop regular estrous cycles until the severe work schedule is stopped and they are rested, preferably on pasture for several months. Cows that are very heavy producers of milk may not have estrous cycles for 3 to 4 months or more following parturition due to a negative energy balance.

Transportation stress in ewes, Braden and Moule, and in gilts, Du Mesnil Du Buisson as cited by Cole (1964), induced follicular growth and ovulation in a large number of animals within 4 to 6 days after moving. This phenomena was not reproduced with ACTH injections but severe stress did cause cystic corpora lutea in the ewes. Estrus signs failed to occur in some ewes due to the absence of a regressing corpus luteum and the presence of some progesterone. The author has observed a similar reaction in transported horses and cattle.

Systemic diseases—Severe chronic wasting diseases, such as Johne's disease, tuberculosis, mange, actinomycosis of the jaw, severe parasitisms, and other diseases cause debility and emaciation and cessation of the estrous cycle.

Pathology of the uterus or cervix is a frequent cause for irregularities of the estrous cycle. In cattle such conditions as pyometra, fetal maceration, mummification of the fetus, and rarely mucometra may cause failure of estrum, and a persistence of the corpus luteum, with a cessation of estrual cycles. A similar effect may be produced experimentally by hysterectomizing cattle, swine and sheep, Wiltbank and Casida. Early death of the embryo within 20 to 60 days after conception may cause symptoms of apparent failure of the estrual cycle.

Endocrine disturbances often affect the estrous cycle. Cystic ovaries in cattle are frequently a cause for cessation of the estrous cycle. Nymphomania or cystic ovaries in animals are also characterized by irregularities in the estrous cycle and by frequent or continuous estrum. Following calving, ovulations are often associated with a "silent" estrum. This is also observed in ewes and mares at the outset of the breeding season and in heifers reaching puberty. It is believed that some of these "silent" estrums are due to an imbalance of estrogens and progesterone with the latter often lacking, Melampy et al.. Short estrous cycles in the cow, long or irregular periods of estrum or lack of estrum, or long diestrous periods in the mare, as described by Caslick, are probably of endocrine origin, but the causes for these abnormal estrous cycles are not fully understood. Short estrous cycles of 8 to 14 days in cattle have been produced experimentally by infusing the uterus with bacterial contaminants or viral agents such as IBR-IPV at the time of service, infusing the uterus with irritating iodine compounds about the third to sixth day after estrus, injecting large doses of progesterone IM the first week after estrus, Harmes and Malven, injecting large doses of oxytocin from day 2 to day 7 of the cycle, or surgically implanting a foreign object into the horn corresponding to the ovary containing the corpus luteum about the second or third day of the cycle. It is believed that these treatments affect the luteolytic mechanism especially by their inhibiting effect on the release of L.H. and failure to grow and maintain the corpus luteum, Hansel and Wagner, Nakahara et al.. Large doses of L.H. given during the last week of the estrous cycle may prolong the corpus luteum and the cycle (See chapter XIII, Infertility in Cattle). In rare cases pituitary, ovarian, and adrenal tumors may cause marked changes in the estrous cycle.

Miscellaneous causes for irregularities in the estrous cycle include the individual variations between animals in each species. The individual variations are usually minor. However, Brahman and Zebu cattle may have very short estrous periods of only 3 to 6 hours. Copulation usually occurs at night. Pregnancy causes a prompt physiologic cessation of the estrous cycles. The presence of the ram, stallion, buck or boar hastens the onset of estrum when the male is placed with the females late in the anestrous season. This stimulating effect on the release of gonadotropic hormone is probably mediated by visual, auditory and olfactory stimuli to the CNS, Bruce, Belonje.

Thus it can be seen that although the reproductive cycles of domestic animals are primarily under endocrine control they are greatly influenced by the external environment which acts through the central nervous sytem and the hypothalmus to initiate and regulate the release of tropic hormones from the adenohypophysis, Amoroso, Nalbandov, Cole and Cupps.

Coition or Copulation

Coitus or the act of copulation, includes the insertion of the erect penis into the vagina or intromission, and the subsequent ejaculation of semen. This takes place only during estrum in the domestic animals. An exception to this occurs in certain barren mares early in the breeding season that exhibit a prolonged period of acceptance punctuated occasionally by true estrum and ovulation. During coitus semen is ejaculated into the vagina and onto the external os of the cervix in the cow, ewe, doe and woman. In the sow most of the semen usually is ejaculated into the uterus since the long narrow penis of the boar enters the cervix, Tanabe and coworkers. Laing reported that during coitus in the dog and sow vaginal and uterine contraction waves aid the intrauterine deposition of semen. In the mare the penis may be forced against the relaxed dilated cervix and some semen might be ejaculated into the cervix or uterus. Millar recently demonstrated that at the time of coitus in the mare there is a negative uterine pressure capable of drawing about 80 ml. of fluid into the uterus through the relaxed cervix. This negative uterine pressure has been observed clinically by Benesch and Wright, by the author and others when examining infected, "windsucking" mares especially at the time of estrum. The insertion of the speculum causes a sudden ballooning of the vagina and sometimes the uterus. Bubbles of mucopurulent material have been seen being drawn into the cervix. At the time of intromission the mare can be observed to take a deep inspiration and draw up her abdomen to produce this negative pressure. Often after an equine service at which time 50 to 100 ml or more of semen is ejaculated, only 10 or 15 ml can be recovered from the vagina. Millar stressed the importance of this fact in explaining the cause for infertility in "windsucking" mares and advised against examining the vagina with a speculum or making a rectal examination just before service, as these acts would cause ballooning of the genital tract and prevent the negative pressure normally produced at coitus by the penis sealing the vulva, from drawing the semen into the uterus. More work is necessary on this interesting observation. In the ram the processus urethrae does not enter the external os of the cervix of the ewe during coitus but is responsible for forcibly spraying semen over the cervix and cranial portion of the vagina, Masson.

The duration of coitus in cattle and sheep is only a few seconds. In horses copulation is longer, lasting 10 to 30 seconds. In the swine copulation takes 3 to 8 minutes with an average of about 5 to 7 minutes. In the dog coitus takes 15 to 30 minutes; the bulbus glandis enlarges slowly, until it is large enough to dilate the caudal portion of the vagina. The sphincter muscles of the vestibule and vulva then contract and the male is unable to withdraw the penis until the bulbus glandis is reduced in size. In the cat coitus lasts 2 to 5 minutes. (See Chapter XVIII, Infertility in Male Animals).

It is rather interesting, as pointed out by Hammond and Asdell in citing Slijper, that the structure of the penis is somewhat related to the duration of foreplay and coitus. In ruminants with a fibroelastic type of penis with small vascular sinuses, foreplay and coitus are very brief and the amount of semen ejaculated is small. In animals such as dogs, horses and primates the penis is characterized by extensive vascular sinuses and foreplay and coitus are of moderate to long duration. The exception to this observation is the boar that has a fibroelastic type of penis. The large amount of semen ejaculated in the boar may be a factor causing the prolonged period of coitus in this species. The dog and stallion also have fairly long copulatory periods and they also ejaculate relatively large quantities of semen.

The dangers of coitus to the female animal include the possibility of young, small heifers and fillies or even older females being injured by large or overweight males. These injuries may include fracture of the pelvis, spine, or limbs; dislocation of the hips; muscle or tendon sprains; or injuries to the limbs, udder, or teats. These injuries may be avoided by using smaller males, a breeding rack, or artificial insemination. In both the mare and cow the vagina is shorter than the length of the male's penis, but at the time of coitus the vagina stretches. In spite of this, occasional lacerations and trauma may be produced and cause swelling, hemorrhage, discharge, and straining following coitus. In rare instances the penis of a bull or stallion may actually rupture the vagina of the female and cause a perivaginal inflamination or abscess with signs resembling acute traumatic reticulitis. Fatal peritonitis may rarely be observed especially when heifers are bred on pasture.

Occasional cases of vaginal rupture and penetration of the peritoneal cavity in the heifer and mare may not result in death, especially if the damage is diagnosed promptly and prophylactic injections of a broad range antibiotic are administered parenterally and intraperitoneally and the vulva is closed to prevent aspiration of air, Sager.

When large stallions are bred to small mares a stallion roll, or if this is not available a roll of cotton, may be placed against the stallion's abdomen in front of the sheath to prevent too-deep penetration of the penis. In mares with a small vulva it may be necessary to lubricate the vulva to facilitate insertion of the penis. Vaseline or the ordinary water-soluble, neutral, tragacanth gum lubricating jellies are satisfactory. These lubricants should not contain antiseptics. Occasionally feces and other dirt particles are introduced into the vulva and vagina at the time of service and cause irritation and infection.

In a mare with a tipped or horizontal vulva, occasionally the penis of the stallion may slide over the vulva and enter the rectum, causing a rupture of the rectal mucosa or the rectal wall. This is called "false entry" and may produce a rapidly fatal peritonitis or a pelvic diverticulum that fills with feces and causes severe straining. This is favored in mares with a vulva that has been sutured by the Caslick technique and not opened sufficiently prior to service. A rectal examination immediately prior to service should not be performed as it dilates the sphincter muscles of the anus of the mare permitting the penis to readily enter the rectum. False entry may also occur in the sow, ewe, doe and cow but apparently it causes little harm in these species. In the mare if the diverticulum is in the pelvic region caudal to the peritoneum, gentle, regular enemas of physiologic saline or water should be given to keep the diverticulum free of feces until healing takes place. Antibiotics and tetanus antitoxin parenterally are indicated. False entry can be prevented by proper handling of the stallion at the time of service to make certain by manual direction, that the penis enters the vulva.

Occasionally the withers of the mare may be lacerated by the teeth of a stallion or jack at the time of coitus. This can be prevented by muzzling the stallion or by placing a heavy pad over the withers of the mare. Many horsemen believe the stallion has given a "poor service" when he dismounts and the penis on being withdrawn brings with it an ounce or more of semen. Holding the stallion on the mare a little longer allows the size of the glans penis to be reduced and less semen withdrawn. This condition would be more likely to occur if the genital tract was ballooned with air before service, so that the semen was not drawn into the uterus but remained in the vagina. There is no proof that these occasional so-called "poor services" fail to result in conception.

Rarely a mare or cow may have a stenosis of the vagina due to a previous injury or to a hereditary defect of the vulva or vagina, such as "white heifer disease" with an imperforate hymen. In these animals coitus usually results in vaginal or vulvar lacerations and straining. The author has observed two gilts and a sow that died a few days to a week after natural service with severe peritonitis caused by the boar's penis entering the urethra and bladder and passing into a ureter where it caused a rupture about 2 to 3 inches cranial to the bladder. All of these females had cystitis with signs of straining, bloody urine, a swollen vulva, depression and anorexia shortly after an apparent normal copulation.

Sodomy or carnal intercourse between man and the lower animals is of little importance to the veterinarian, since ordinarily this does not result in injury or disease to the larger animals. In small female animals such perversion may result in injury to the animal's genital canal.

Sadism or sexual perversion in some humans, usually male, may cause them to injure or mutilate, with sharp or solid objects such as broom handles and pointed sticks, the genital organs of animals especially the vagina or rectum of female animals such as mares, cows, goats or sows. Whenever the veterinarian is confronted with a case of injury to the genital organs or rectum of an animal he should attempt to determine the cause, keeping this possibility in mind, especially if several similar injuries are diagnosed. These injuries are most often perpetrated when the animal is in estrum. As Williams pointed out, injuries of this type are rarely produced by coitus or by accident but must be caused by some person, usually of low or abnormal mentality, who has access to the animals when no one else is present.

Ovogenesis or Oogenesis

The ovary, besides secreting the necessary reproductive gonadal hormones, produces ova. Early in the first weeks of embryonal development the primitive large germ cells called primordial germ cells can be identified in the caudal extraembryonal entoblast or yolk sac, Mauleon. These primordial germ cells migrate by ameboid movement from the yolk sac across the dorsal mesentery to the genital ridges, Blandau. This migration occurs in porcine and bovine embryos about 24 and 35 days of gestation, respectively, Erikson (1965). In a few more days the gonadal sex can be distinguished by the formation of the superficial tunica albuginea and the central location of the germinal cells, spermatogonia, in the primitive testes and the peripheral location of the oogonia in the primitive ovary, Mauleon. These oogonia multiply by mitosis after sexual differentiation and enter the prophase of the first meiotic divisions when they are called oocytes. Mauleon suggests that the number of oocytes produced may be determined by the level or amount of FSH in the embryo. Oogenesis is the transformation of oogonia into oocytes. Oogenesis is completed before or shortly after birth in all domestic mammals, Rajakoski, Zuckerman, and others. According to Mauleon sexual differentiation occurs at 30 days of gestation in the feline and porcine embryos, 35 days in the ovine embryo and 45 days in the bovine embryo. The period of oogonial mitoses, the end of which signifies the end of the major portion of the period of oogenesis, are 32 days of gestation to 37 days after birth in cats, 30 days of gestation to 7 days after birth in swine, 35 to 90 days of gestation in sheep and 45 to 110+ days of gestation in cattle. At the end of this period of oogenesis the oocytes enter the first meiotic prophase where they pass through the leptotene and zygotene stage into the pachytene stage. In this stage the ova are surrounded by a single layer of follicular epithelium and these are called primordial follicles.

Thus at birth all female calves and lambs are born with their full complement of oocytes in primordial or older follicles and these are never replenished but only decrease in number during the life of the animal. Bovine oocytes may rest in this pachytene phase for years if the primordial follicle does not grow, Henricson and Rajakoski. In most species this resting stage where the oocyte is in the primordial follicle is the dictyate stage, Rajakoski, Mauleon, Kennelly and Foote, and Kennelly.

In the late dictyate stage as ovulation time approaches follicle growth and maturation occur. The ovum itself will grow and triple in size in order to provide nutrition for early divisions of the fertilized ovum. (See Table 16).

Erickson and others listed three types of follicles present at birth and throughout the life of animals; primordial follicles in which the oocyte is surrounded by a single layer of follicle cells, growing follicles in which the oocyte is surrounded by two or more layers of follicle cells, and vesicular follicles having antrums or fully-formed vesicles. The numbers of germ cells or oocytes in the ovaries of individual cattle is highly variable ranging from 0 (complete sterility) to 700,000. Of 69 cattle from birth to two years of age about 25 percent had 42,000 (0 to

Table 16. Developmental States in the Maturation of the Ovum*

	Chromosome Number			Time Period Prenatal
	2N	Primordial germ cells	Migrate to gonodal area in bovine embryo	from 25-35 days of gestation
Mitosis		Oogonia	Multiplication occurs in bovine embryo	from 45-110+ days of gestation
		Oogonia A Oogonia A (resting)		
		Oogonia B		
		Oocytes, primary		
Meiosis		Prophase I (1st maturation division)		
		Leptotene stage		
		Zygotene stage		
	4N	Pachytene stage - bovine species		Birth to Old age
		Diplotene stage - porcine species	Resting stage	
		Dictyate stage - other species	Primordial follicle	
			Growing follicle	
		(Diakinesis)	Vesicular follicle	
		Metaphase I		
		Anaphase I	Graafian follicle (mature)	Estrum
		Telaphase I		
	2N	Oocytes, secondary - Ova	1st polar body extruded**	
		Prophase II (2nd maturation division)		Ovulation
		Metaphase II		Ova into oviducts
		Anaphase II		
		Telaphase II	2nd polar body extruded	
	1N	Union of male and female pronuclei within ovum***		Ova transport to uterus
	2N	Zygote		Atresia of nonovulating follicles

*After Rajakoski, Henricson and Rajakoski, Kennelly and Foote, Erickson (1965) and Mauleon.
**In dogs and probably horses the 1st polar body is released after ovulation and the 2nd polar body is usually not released unless fertilization occurs. This is probably why the canine ova remain in the oviduct 5 or more days.
***Szollosi has shown that the male and female pronuclei in the rabbit duplicate chromosomes before syngamy thus the fertilized ovum is tetraploid for a very short period until the two-cell stage occurs.

73,000) germ cells, about 60 percent had 137,000 (76,000 to 218,000) germ cells, and about 15 percent of the cattle had 325,000 (223,000 to 724,000) germ cells, Erickson, 1966. The numbers of primordial follicles in cattle remained fairly stable around 140,000 until about 4 to 6 years of age and then declined rapidly thereafter to 25,000 at 10 to 14 years and to near zero at 20 years of age. From 60 days after birth to 10 to 14 years of age the numbers of growing follicles per bovine animal averaged about 150 to 250 and the number of vesicular follicles 25 to 30. In cows over 15 years of age these numbers declined to 70 and 12, respectively. Normal vesicular follicles predominated up to 10 years of age in cows but after that time atretic vesicular follicles were in greater numbers. Two 20-year-old cows that had produced 16 and 17 calves, respectively, were considered to be sterile at slaughter with one cow being anestrous and the other showing irregular cycles. The numbers of primordial follicles in these two cows were 100 and 2000, growing follicles 80 and 50 and vesicular follicles 10 and 7. Thus these old cows were approaching the menopausal state that occurs in women. Hartman and Leathem reported that women had an ovarian oocyte population of 200,000 to 400,000. During the postmenopausal years a complete disappearance of oocytes occur.

Since during the lifetime of a 10-year-old cow producing a calf each year about 30 to 50 ova might be ovulated it is obvious that most oocytes degenerate and die in a process called follicular atresia. Erickson reported in cattle that, although degeneration of oocytes and follicular atresia may occur in the prenatal period, germ cell quality in primordial follicles remains high until 6 to 8 months of age and then it declines rapidly thereafter until at 4 years of age and older most oocytes or primordial follicles are in an obvious degenerative state. The process of bovine follicular atresia and oocyte degeneration is a very protracted process extending over a period of years. Mauleon and others stated that oogonia and oocytes in the first stages of meiotic prophase disappear or degenerate during prenatal and early postnatal periods, only those oocytes in the pachytene through dictyate stages remain into later life.

Erickson presented further evidence that following puberty the average bovine female has only approximately 240 oocytes in growing or vesicular follicles upon which she is dependent for the production of fertile ova throughout the rest of her life. Since the numbers of these growing or vesicular follicles was closely correlated with the total number of primordial follicles there may be a relationship between germ cell numbers and fertility in females. When the ovaries of 6 infertile and 9 fertile 5-year-old cows were compared, the numbers of primordial, growing, and vesicular follicles present were 119,000 and 18,000, 78 and 35, 211, and 54 for the fertile and infertile groups, respectively. Settergren in a study on genetic hypoplasia of the ovaries in Swedish Highland cattle reported normal yearling cattle had an average total of about 50,000 primordial follicles in both ovaries (range 6,000 to 100,000). Heifers with a unilateral partial hypoplasia and unilateral total hypoplasia had 23,000 and 19,000 primordial follicles, respectively, in both ovaries. Of 7 heifers with one ovary completely hypoplasic and the other ovary partially hypoplasic, two heifers had no primordial follicles and five had 100 to 400. In heifers with bilateral total hypoplasia no primordial follicles were present. Animals with less than 500 primordial follicles did not ovulate. Animals with one hypoplasic ovary had definitely fewer Graafian follicles than normal heifers and were more infertile.

Erickson's study also showed the predominance of ovulations from the right ovary by the presence of 18 regressed corpora lutea or corpora albicantia on the right ovaries and 13 on the left ovaries in 32 cows.

Folliculogenesis and Ovulation

Under the influence of the gonadotropic hormones FSH and LH, especially the former, vesicular follicles grow and develop. This development occurs in fetal animals, young animals prior to puberty, and even during the pregnancy period. Follicular growth and development culminating in the mature Graafian follicle and ovulation occurs only in nonpregnant animals after puberty during a reproductive cycle. However horses frequently ovulate during early gestation and cows may very rarely do so. The exact mechanisms governing the follicles that mature and ovulate and those that fail to mature and ovulate but regress and become atretic are not understood. The amount of FSH released has been shown experimentally in studies on superovulation to be closely correlated to the number of follicles that ovulate. Thus gonadotropic control is a major factor in this mechanism.

Without the Graafian follicle signs of estrum would be lacking, ova could not be released and corpora lutea could not form. Growth of the primordial follicles, those where the oocyte is surrounded by a single layer of epithelial cells gives rise to vesicular follicles or those with antrums called Graafian follicles. In Graffian follicles the oocyte has reached the dictyate stage of development in the cow, Rajakoski. By this time the connective tissues around the growing follicle have organized into the theca which consists of an outer zone of stroma cells called the theca externa, and an inner zone of epithelial-like cells called the theca interna which later secretes steroid hormones including estrogens. As growth continues, the antrum forms and enlarges in the epithelial cells around the ovum. The epithelial cells lining this antrum form the membrana granulosa. The fluid in the follicle is called the liquor folliculi. The source of this fluid is not known but is believed to be secreted by the granulosa cells.

In the early stages of the maturation of the ovisac, or follicle, the oocyte is in a mass of epithelial cells, called the discus proligerus, attached to the granulosa layer of cells. The egg and its adjoining granulosa cells are called the cumulus oophorus. Between the cumulus cells and the oocyte proper is the corona radiata, a compact layer of cells surrounding the zona pellucida, which extends cytoplasmic projections through the zona pellucida to the vitelline membrane to provide nutrients to the oocyte for its maintenance and growth, Shettles. The cumulus may be located projecting into the follicular fluid anywhere on the circumference of the membrana granulosa, Rajakoski. As the follicle approaches maturation and ovulation, the cumulus oophorus either separates from the membrana granulosa and floats free in the follicular fluid or more often it is only tenuously attached. The ascent of the follicles to the surface of the ovary coincides with the appearance of the thecal layers. The theca interna develops a wedge-like cone that precedes the follicle through the ovarian stroma to the surface. In all species of domestic animal, except the horse, ovulation can occur over the entire ovarian surface. In the horse ovulation occurs only in the ovulation fossa or concave ventral medial portion of the ovary that is not covered by a dense tunica albuginea and mesovarium, Strassman, Osborne, Prickett, Kupfer.

Ovulation takes place by a thinning process, usually avascularization and rupture, with slight bleeding, of the outer portion of the follicle wall and peritoneum. The ovum with the enclosing cumulus cells are washed out in the gradually-released follicular fluid and are caught by or pass into the fimbriated end of the oviduct, where fertilization takes place. In the cow, mare and other species the outer thin follicular wall that usually feels tense and firm during proestrum and early estrum becomes more flaccid and soft just prior to ovulation. In rare instances the ovum and its cumulus cells may be caught and retained in the collapsing walls of the Graafian follicle at the time of rupture. This may be a rare cause for failure of fertilization.

Blandau reported that in domestic animals a circumscribed avascular area appears on the apex of the follicle that projects above the surface of the ovary. This thins out until a fine transparent membrane bulges above the surface. This is the basement membrane separating the granulosa and thecal layers of the follicle. This breaks and the follicular contents ooze from the follicle. Collapse of the follicle walls doesn't occur until after the cumulus has passed through the small stigma in the surface of the follicle. Ovulation may require a few seconds to several minutes or longer depending on the size of the stigma and the location of the cumulus in the follicle.

Intrafollicular pressure is not the cause for ovulation, Blandau and Rumery. The stigma is small and nearly round or oval. There is no sign of tearing of the follicle wall. As noted above just prior to ovulation the follicle becomes more flaccid and less tonic. Observed ovulations are not violent eruptions. Where the intrafollicular pressures have been measured there has been no increase in pressure prior to ovulation. Recent work presented evidence to indicate that ovulation was probably brought about by the release of LH that releases histamine causing ovarian hyperemia. This hyperemia may stimulate the release of proteolytic enzymes, such as collagenase into the follicular fluid which may be responsible for the separation of the cumulus from the side of the follicle. Thus the proteolyte enzymes weaken the wall of the follicle and the stigma or avascular area develops and ovulation occurs at the superficial projecting area where the wall is not supported by the ovarian stroma, Pool and Lipner, Lipner.

After the follicle ruptures and the ovum is released a slight amount of bleeding may occur into the follicle. This is then called the corpus hemorraghicum in the cow, ewe and sow and other species. In the mare a large blood clot, which can be palpated per rectum fills the large lumen of the follicle. This bleeding occurs through the follicle walls and not at the site of rupture of the follicle. In the cow fibrin "tags" may develop on the ovary or fine adhesions between the ovary and the fimbria may occur following ovulation. This has no effect on fertility. It is possible that the enzyme reaction that weakens the follicle wall to produce ovulation acts for a longer period of time in the mare and therefore a greater amount of bleeding occurs through the follicle wall after ovulation.

Ovulation is largely under endocrine control. Under the stimulus of FSH from the anterior pituitary a number of vesicular follicles begin developing. As these follicles develop, an increasing amount of estradiol is produced by the theca interna and is absorbed into the circulation of the body as well as being present in the follicular fluid. In the body estradiol produces the typical changes in the tubular portion of the reproductive tract seen in proestrum and estrum. It also produces the characteristic symptoms and manifestations of heat by its action on the central nervous system. Except for the follicles that are to mature, usually only one in uniparous animals and a moderate number in the multiparous animals, there is a sudden wave of atresia that strikes all small "second rank" developing follicles a short time, about 12 to 24 hours or possibly more, before ovulation of the mature follicle, Sturgis. Rajakoski reported that atresia of the small Graafian follicles begins in the oocyte while in medium and large Graafian follicles atresia begins with degenerative changes in the granulosa and theca interna with the changes in the oocyte developing slightly later. Obliterative atresia occurs in small and medium-sized follicles but in large follicles cystic atresia occurs in which the antrum and follicle fluid are reduced only after complete degeneration of the follicle wall with fibrotic changes in the theca. Marion et al. agreed with Rajakoski that follicular atresia can occur at any stage of growth, and degeneration of the oocyte may start at any stage of atresia. Cystic atresia may occasionally be associated with a degree of luteinization of the cystic follicle.

The cause for the atresia of the "second rank" smaller follicles and the mechanism controlling the number of follicles allowed to mature and ovulate are not known. Nalbandov explained the process as being based on hormone dilution rather than on the theory of estrogen inhibition of FSH, stating that as the follicles increase in size there is insufficient FSH to maintain all of them and hence most become atretic. This remains to be proved. Sturgis indicated that the transient hypertrophy of the theca interna observed in these atretic follicles in the early degenerative phase may account for the maintenance of the necessary high estrogenic hormone level until ovulation has occured and the new corpus luteum has formed. His theory was that the estrogen produced in the primary and atretic follicles was necessary to stimulate LH release from the pituitary. It is possible that estradiol produced in the follicles depressed FSH production, thus allowing the amount of LH in relation to FSH to rise and produce ovulation. This estrogenic depression of FSH might be a possible factor in the atresia and degeneration of the "second rank" follicles.

Work by Hansel and Trimberger and Hough et al. indicated that progesterone produced in the Graafian follicle before ovulation may play an important role in cattle in the release of LH and ovulation. More work is required in order to elucidate the nature of the exact mechanism of ovulation in animals. Release of LH by the anterior pituitary is necessary for and causes ovulation of the mature Graafian follicle. According to Jubb and McEntee, Hough and coworkers, and Rakha and Robertson, LH is released from the bovine anterior pituitary gland usually within 1 to 5 hours after the onset of estrum.

The corpus luteum which was already developing from the granulosa cells lining the Graafian follicle at the time of ovulation grows very rapidly under the influence of LH following ovulation. The production of progesterone by the corpus luteum then supresses LH and FSH production. If fertilization and pregnancy take place, the corpus luteum is maintained by the secretion of luteotropic hormone or LH from the anterior pituitary gland. If pregnancy does not occur, then the corpus luteum degenerates and, with the decline in the production of progesterone late in the estrous cycle FSH again is produced and a new wave of follicles begins to grow followed by the onset of proestrum. The approximate minimum time required for the development of the follicles and ovulation in domestic animals is 3 to 4 days, as revealed by work on sheep and the manual removal of the corpus luteum in the cow. Rajakoski showed that in the cow that a wave of follicular growth with an accumulation of small Graafian follicles, less than 5 mm in diameter occurred during the third and fourth days of the cycle resulting in a large follicle 9 to 18 mm in diameter at the 13th day. A second-wave of follicular growth occurred between the 12th to 14th day with the production of small follicles 5 to 8 mm in size resulting in a single large follicle, 12 to 16 mm., at 16 days that usually ovulates 4 or 5 days later. A wave of atresia follows each growth wave leaving in most cows only one large follicle. Thus this author indicated it took 7 to 9 days from early follicle growth to ovulation in the cow. Cupps et al. did not agree with Rajakoski and stated that the intermediate-sized follicles in midcycle did not undergo atresia and that the mature Graafian follicle that ovulates comes from the smaller follicles formed about the third and fourth day of the cycle. The author agrees with Rajakoski. This diphasic growth wave of follicles has not been reported in other domestic animals but small follicles are often observed during all phases of the reproductive cycle in most animals.

Even though nearly all the reproductive functions can occur without nervous innervation of the lower portion of the body, there is definite evidence that ovulation, as well as other phases of the reproductive cycle, are influenced by the nervous system in the intact animal. Marion et al. have shown that heifers, when bred by a vasectomized bull, ovulated at an average of 7.7 hours after the end of estrum as compared to 9.9 hours when not bred. Hansel and Trimberger delayed the ovulation of heifers 24 to 66 hours by the administration of massive doses of atropine at the onset of estrum; but when chorionic gonadotropin, or LH was administered shortly after the atropine, ovulation occurred about 10 hours earlier than normal. This indicated that atropine prevented the normal release of LH from the pituitary. Marion and Smith reported that the administration of gonadotropic hormone during early estrum shortened to 1.25 hours the normal time of 10.5 to 12.25 hours from the end of estrum to ovulation. The administration of estrogen, 1000 to 3000 I.U. or epinephrine at the onset of estrum in heifers had no effect on ovulation time, Hansel et al., Hough and coworkers. Progesterone given in 5 to 15 mg doses intramuscularly at the onset of estrum reduced the average length of estrum 3.6 hours, the average time from the end of estrum to ovulation 5.4 hours, and the average time from the onset of estrum to ovulation by 9 hours, Hansel and Trimberger. Hough and coworkers showed that atropine blocked the effect of progesterone and they indicated that this blocking action took place in the hypothalamus. Other workers have shown a neurohumoral mechanism for LH release in the rabbit, rat, and fowl. Thus it appears that the LH release mechanism is stimulated by the action of estrogen and progesterone and other external factors affecting the hypothalamus.

Ovulation is spontaneous in all animals except the rabbit, cat, and ferret. In these latter species one or repeated mountings or intromissions may be required to release the LH from the pituitary and cause ovulation. Ovulation in these three species may be caused by stimuli, such as gently manipulating a glass rod in the vagina simulating coitus or by the injection of luteinizing hormone. Ovulation usually occurs at a fairly constant time following the stimulus of coitus or the injection of LH at estrus. In the rabbit it occurs about 10.5 hours later, and in the cat about 27 hours later. This stimulus in the rabbit is apparently emotional and can be produced by the excitement of being mounted by another doe; it can also be produced by coitus when the vagina and vulva are anesthetized, Asdell.

When 25 I.U. of LH was injected intravenously into isolated mature female rabbits, 50 percent of them ovulated between 10-1/2 and 10-3/4 hours later, Harper. This therapy might be indicated for female cats to terminate estrum. These are other examples of the way in which peripheral and central nervous stimuli affect ovulation.

With the exception of the cow, ovulation usually occurs before the end of estrum in all domestic animals that ovulate spontaneously. The cow, due to its low threshold for estrogen, remains in estrum only a short period and then an "estrous block" of central nervous origin develops and the cow goes out of estrum even though additional amounts of estradiol are being produced, Asdell, DeAlba and Roberts. The approximate time of ovulation for the various domestic animals according to Asdell, Dukes, Hafez is as follows:

Mare—1 to 2 days before the end of estrum, in rare instances 1 to 2 days after estrum.

Cow—12 to 14 hours after the end of estrum, heifers about 3 hours earlier.

Ewe—usually within 12, but occasionally as early as 24, hours before the end of estrum or 12 to 41 hours after the onset of estrum.

Goat—toward the end of estrum

Sow—toward the end of estrum. Most ovulations occur 24 to 40 hours after the onset of estrum.

Dog—near the beginning of estrum, but because the first polar body is not extruded, fertilization and beginning cell division in the oviduct cannot take place until about the fourth day of estrum.

Cat—about 27 hours after coitus.

Superovulation—Discovery of the gonadotropic hormones, and interest and research in transplantation of ova have resulted in experiments on various means of inducing superovulation, or the release of numerous, 10 to 100, ova from the ovaries of uniparous animals. This can be produced during late metestrum, diestrum, and early proestrum by daily subcutaneous injections of FSH for 3 to 6 days, followed by an intravenous injection of LH, or, if timed properly so that the last FSH injection comes just before estrum, the cow may ovulate the numerous artificially produced follicles by means of its own secretion of LH, Willett, Hafez et al. and Hafez. Superovulation can be produced in cattle by injecting 3000 to 5000 I.U. of PMS intramuscularly on the 16th day of the cycle or when the corpus luteum is manually removed. Five days later 2000 I.U. HCG is given intravenously. In sheep and swine 500 to 750 I.U. and 1000 to 1500 I.U. PMS injected on the 12th day and 16th day of the cycle, respectively, will induce superovulation in these species. In cattle about 15 percent of the superovulated ova were morphologically abnormal. Because numerous corpora lutea form following superovulation the bovine ovary may be five to ten times normal size. Thus it is recommended not to inject FSH into animals 4 to 5 days prior to estrum if superovulation is to be avoided. Montfort reported on a cow given P.M.S., "Gonadin" that was bred and conceived 6 days later but aborted septuplets at 6 months of gestation. The above authors have briefly summarized the available data on ova transplantation or inovulation and stated that much more work is required to make this operation practical. After 3 to 4 injections of gonadotropic hormones cows become refractory to them. Since antihormones are produced, repeated injections of the proteinaceous gonadotropic hormones result in fewer ova ovulated. Recovery of the ova without surgery and their subsequent storage will be difficult problems to solve. The fertility and survival ability of superovulated ova, especially those ovulated during the luteal phases of the cycle, are low. Willett reported the successful performance of only 2 inovulations in mammals that did not involve surgery. During the luteal stages when inovulation has to be performed, the increased susceptibility of the uterine cavity to infection renders unsuccessful practical methods such as inovulation through the cervix.

Ova and Spermatozoan Transport and Fertilization

Ova transport—As ovulation approaches there is a marked increase in the tonicity, edema and motility of the fimbriae of the oviducts in domestic animals; the fimbriae nearly clasp the ovary in order to receive the egg. These effects are under the endocrine control of estrogen during the estrous period. Following ovulation, the cumulus oophorus which was liberated from the mature Graafian follicles or ovisacs is transported from the surface of the ovary into the oviduct. This transfer is effected by the direct action of the cilia of the fimbria and infundibulum on the cumulus as well as the currents of fluid created by the beating cilia flowing toward the ostium of the oviduct. Essential to these immediate transport mechanisms are the contractions of the smooth muscle of the mesovarium and regular contractions that change the position of the ovary with respect to the infundibulum and fimbria, Blandau, Hafez, Cole and Cupps.

The rate of transport of the ova through the ampullar portion of the oviduct to the area of the ampullary-isthmic junction is quite rapid and is probably accomplished in a relative few minutes, 8 to 30. This transport is effected by peristaltic and antiperstaltic muscular contractions of the smooth muscle in the ampulla together with ciliary activity under the hormonal control of estrogens. Hafez cited Barrell and associates as reporting that the cilia in the rabbit oviduct beat at a rate of 1500 per minute. The beat of the cilia towards the uterus creates currents in the oviduct fluid and the contractions of the oviduct wall keeps the ovum in constant motion which aids in egg and sperm contact and fertilization. Sperm penetration of the ovum and fertilization which requires several hours occurs in the ampullary-isthmic area of the oviduct. The physiological significance of the oviduct fluid which is secreted in greatest amounts during estrum is not well understood, Hafez and Blandau. Most of this fluid passes into the peritoneal cavity. Adhesions and obstruction or ligation of the distal or fimbriated portions of the bovine oviduct causes hydrosalpinx. Some fluid may pass through the isthmus into the uterus.

The ova or eggs of domestic animals at the time of ovulation are one of the largest cells in the body and vary from 120 to 185 microns or 0.12 to 0.185 mm in diameter not including the zona pellucida, Austin, Hafez. In ungulates the ovum contains very little glycogen but large amounts of lipid material; whereas in rodents the reverse is true. These materials are necessary for energy production to produce protein biosynthesis in the ovum. Certain ova may be defective and have obvious structural abnormalities including: small or giant ova, oval or flattened ova, ova with a ruptured zona pellucida, ova with large polar bodies or vacuoles within the vitellus, ova with an abnormal cytoplasm, abnormal-shaped ova, atypical 2-blastomere ova and etc, Hafez. These abnormal or degenerated eggs may be due to improper maturation of the oocyte, genetic or environmental factors or failure of polar body extrusion. The incidence of abnormal ova varies between the breeds and strains and is greatest in older females, Hafez.

The cumulus and corona cells around the zona pellucida of the ovum in most domestic animals only persist for a few hours or less after ovulation and fall away in the oviduct. In the dog and cat the corona cells may persist for several days. The protoplasmic projections from these cells into the zona pellucida are withdrawn soon after ovulation due to contact with fibrinolytic enzymes in the oviduct fluid. The cumulus and corona cells die and separate from the ovum aided by the ciliary and muscular activity of the oviduct. Inside the zona pellucida is the vitelline membrane or vitellus which is similar to the plasma membrane of somatic cells. The zona pellucida is a homogeneous semipermeable structure surrounding the ovum composed of congugated protein capable of being dissolved by proteolytic enzymes such as trypsin and chymotrypsin, Hafez. After fertilization the vitellus shrinks and a perivitelline space is formed between the zona pellucida and the vitelline membrane into which the polar bodies are extruded.

Most ova of domestic animals have ovulated when the second maturation division has reached metaphase and the first polar body has been extruded. In the dog, probably the horse and rarely in the pig, ova are ovulated as a primary oocyte and maturate in the oviduct, Cole and Cupps. The fertile life of ovulated ova in domestic animals is relatively short, 12 to 24 hours or less except in the dog where they may remain fertile in the oviduct for 4 to 8 days, Cole and Cupps, Hafez. Casida cited Barrett's work to show that in cattle inseminated 2 to 4 hours after ovulation that both the conception rate and the percentage of normal embryos at 35 days were 75 percent. When insemination took place 6 to 12 hours after ovulation the conception rate was 60 to 75 percent but only 30 percent of the embryos were normal at 35 days. Insemination after 12 hours following ovulation resulted in conception rates that were very low, and normal embryos were unusual. Majahan and Menge reported a high rate of fertilization in cows inseminated at 13 hours post-ovulation in cattle but no fertilization at 16 to 22 hours postovulation. The loss of fertility or viability is not rapid or sudden and aging eggs may be fertilized normally but produce embryos that die early in gestation. With further loss of viability of the ovum, fertilization may be abnormal or fail to occur. Under usual conditions of estrus and natural service in situations where a male is running with the females, spermatozoa will reach the site of fertilization in the oviduct before ovulation and the arrival of the ova. Under conditions of artificial insemination this orderly sequence of events may be altered and infertility result. Fertilization of "old" eggs in swine is associated with polyspermy and abnormal development. Aged sperm may also produce embryonic abnormalities, Lanman.

In domestic animals the eggs or ova remain in the oviduct in the ampullary-isthmic area for 3 to 4 days before rapidly passing through the isthmus and the uterotubal junction into the uterus. In the sow the ova may pass into the uterus in 1-1/2 to 3 days possibly due to multiple ovulation, Kelly and Eckstein. Hafez reported that ovine ova remain in the ampullary-isthmic junction for 50 to 60 hours following ovulation due to the strong antiperistaltic contractions in the isthmus. Oxenreider and Day reported that after rapid transfer to the ampullary-isthmic junction, swine eggs remain there for about 30 to 45 hours and enter the uterus 30 to 60 hours after ovulation. In most domestic animals ova require 3 to 5 days to pass through the oviduct into the uterus; but may require 6 to 8 days in the dog, 5 to 9 days in the cat, and 2 to 3 days in the sow, Cole and Cupps, Altman and Dittmer. The normal transport of ova through the oviducts can be severely disturbed by injections of estrogen, progesterone or other drugs and anesthetics. The stage of the estrous cycle, the species of animal and the dose levels of the above agents all produce varying effects on the isthmus and the rate of ova transfer to the uterus, Hafez and Blandau. Depending upon the dose of estrogen and the species injected some ova may be trapped or blocked in the ampullary-isthmic portion of the oviduct, "tubal locking"; while in others the ova are rapidly passed into the uterus and are expelled through the cervix into the vagina, Greenwald. These effects appear to be due to the reaction of the isthmic portion of the oviduct to the injected hormone or drug. Black and Davis have suggested that edema in the isthmic area might play a role in tubal regulation of the time of transport, but muscular effects by the gonadal hormones seem more logical from the evidence. Under ordinary conditions the fertilized ova or developing zygote remains in the oviduct until the corpus luteum is formed and the endometrium is under the influence of progesterone so proper environment and nutrition is available upon entering the uterus. If the egg is not fertilized it fragments into many irregular cytoplasmic segments and disintegrates in the uterus under the influence of phagocytosis, Hafez.

Sperm transport in the female—In the cow, ewe, dog and cat the ejaculate at coitus is forcibly sprayed over the cervix and anterior vagina forming a "seminal pool" in the cranial portion of the vagina. In the dog the large ejaculate, 7 to 20 ml, is carried into the uterus through the relaxed cervix by the muscular activity of the genital tract. In the mare and sow, as described earlier, the semen at coitus is largely placed into the uterus. There is no evidence that seminal fluid passes from the vagina into the uterus in the cow, sheep, cat or man, Noyes et al..

After ejaculation the spermatozoa in the seminal plasma migrate or diffuse from the plasma into the mucus of the female genital tract where they may be protected, nourished and transported. In the cow as much as 150 ml or more of cervical mucus may be obtained at estrum. Bovine cervical mucus contains mucoids (amino acids, sugar and sialic acid), glycogen, protein, enzymes, globulins, salt, urea and very small amounts of glucose. Vaginal and cervical mucus in the other domestic animals under the influence of estrogens also changes from a tough tenacious consistency in diestrus or anestrus to a more liquid, viscid, stringy mucus during proestrum and estrum. This permits and favors sperm cell migration. The velocity of sperm cells in bovine cervical mucus at estrum is 56 microns per second, (3 mm/minute) versus 132 microns per second in saline, Sobrero. The "fern test" of cervical mucus is positive when mucus from the cow or other animals in estrum is smeared on a slide and allowed to dry producing a fern-like aborization due to the high NaCl and water content of the mucus at this stage of the cycle. No specific substance harmful to spermatozoa has been recovered from normal cervical mucus. Leucocytic phagocytosis, bacterial endotoxins, and abnormal pH may play a role in preventing the penetration of sperm cells through cervical mucus. "Hostile" cervical mucus is a catchy term loosely used to describe certain conditions affecting the cervical mucus in women.

The passage or transport of spermatozoa from the vagina through the cervix and uterus and into the oviduct is very rapid, less than 15 minutes, in all domestic animals and man. Asdell reported that sperm cells in the bitch are at the uterine entrance of the oviducts 25 seconds after ejaculation. Spermatozoa have been found throughout the bitch's genital tract within 20 minutes after the onset of copulation. In the mare, Lewis and Wright found spermatozoa in the pavilion of the oviduct within 15 minutes after copulation; Mattner and Braden reported this time as 8 minutes in the ewe. VanDemark and Moeller have demonstrated that in the cow spermatozoa were transported from the cervix to the ovarian ends of the oviducts in less than 2 to 4 minutes. This occurred whether the spermatozoa were living or dead and followed either natural or artificial insemination. Spermatozoa could also gain entrance to the oviducts in cows and sows during the luteal phases of the cycle, First et al..

Movement of the spermatozoa in the uterine lumen is due to strong contractions of the uterine wall augmented by the release of oxytocin at coitus or artificial insemination, VanDemark and Hays. Fright and/or excitement might release epinephrine and interfere or inhibit temporarily the uterine contractions. There is no evidence that epinephrine release at coitus or soon after affects fertility. Prostaglandin, a substance from the seminal vesicles present in sheep, goats, possibly other animals, and human semen is an oxytoxic agent that can stimulate the smooth muscle of the uterus. Since the vaginal mucous membrane is permeable to prostaglandin it may also play a role in spermatozoan transport, Sobero, Bergstrom. Prostaglandin has not been reported in other domestic animals. The spermatozoa are thus transported largely in a fluid medium or mucus by capillary action in the cervix and by contractions of the walls of the genital tract. The sperm cell's contribution to this transport up the female tract is a small one because of the relatively slow rate of movement for the long distance to be traversed. However, this motility of the spermatozoa is probably important at the natural barriers of the cervix, the utero-tubal junction, the isthmus of the oviduct and in the initial penetration of the sperm cell into the cumulus. Motility of the sperm cell is essential to fertility. Since dead sperm cells and inert particles will pass through the uterus, Mattner and Braden, and into the oviduct, the motility may be most essential to traverse the cervix and penetrate the cumulus cells or zona.

Billions of spermatozoa are usually ejaculated into the female genital tract of domestic animals at coitus. In the mare and sow most of these promptly enter the uterus. In the other species only about 10 or 100 million spermatozoa pass through the cervix into the uterus with more sperm cells being in the base of the horns than in the apex of the horns. Several hundred to less than a thousand spermatozoa gain access to the ampulla of the oviduct, and only 10 to less than 100 would be in vicinity of the unfertilized ovum. Apparently the uterotubal junction and the isthmus have some controlling role in the numbers of spermatozoa that gain access to the oviduct. Braden reported that in the rabbit after mating, and just before ovulation, the distribution of spermatozoa in the doe's genital tract were as follows: 20×10^6 sperm cells in the vagina, 12×10^6 in the caudal portions of the uterus, 50×10^4 in the apical portions of the uterus, 4×10^3 in the oviducts but only 500 spermatozoa in the ampulla of the oviduct where the ova were fertilized. Baker et al. demonstrated in sows that the number of spermatozoa in the oviduct is affected by the volume of semen entering the uterus as well as the concentration or numbers of spermatozoa. Lineweaver et al. reported that when 1 ml of fresh or frozen semen containing millions of live spermatozoa was placed in midcervix in heifers, 4 hours later 469 and 191 spermatozoa were in the oviducts, and 1559 and 733 spermatozoa were in the uterus, respectively. After 4 hours after insemination only 3 percent of the inseminated spermatozoa could be recovered.

MacLeod and coworkers, reviewing the literature, reported that in mammals only a small proportion of spermatozoa ejaculated at coitus reach the distal end of the oviduct. A few sperm cells may actually enter the peritoneal cavity, Hafez and Blandau. Apparently natural barriers at the cervix and uterotubal junction limit the number of spermatozoa going to the site of fertilization. Cheng and Casida reported that rabbits inseminated with less than 20,000 to 100,000 spermatozoa per insemination failed to conceive. This number of spermatozoa varied with the extender and the degree of dilution. Willett and Larson reported a 0.6 percent decline in conception rate in cattle with each million decline from 12,000,000 to 4,000,000 spermatozoa inseminated. Below the latter figure the decline in conception rate was very rapid, about 3.6 percent for each million decline in sperm cell numbers to about 1,500,000. Conception rates, when 12 to 14 million, 6 to 8 million, and 1 to 3 million actively motile bovine spermatozoa were inseminated were 67, 64 and 49 to 53 percent, respectively when based on 60 to 90 day nonreturns.

Thus a minimum number of motile spermatozoa is necessary for fertilization and conception. In sows and probably mares and dogs a minimum volume of ejaculate or artificially inseminated semen is also necessary for optimum conception rates.

In most domestic animals sperm cells can only retain their viability and fertility at a high level for about 24 hours in the female genital tract. The longest fertile period for spermatozoa in the female tract is 48 to 72 hours although in the mare and the dog spermatozoa may survive and be fertile for 5 to 6 days, Austin and Doak. As with aging ova, aging spermatozoa may be capable of fertilizing the ovum but this may result in embryonic deaths, Lanman. The most common result of aging spermatozoa whether they age in liquid semen at 5° C or in the female genital tract is failure of fertilization. The loss of fertilizing capacity of frozen semen, especially in liquid nitrogen, is very slow and gradual and extends over a number of years.

The vagina of the sow and ewe is not a favorable site for sperm cell survival and they lose their motility and die in 6 to 12 hours or less. The cervix with its viscid mucus of estrum is the most favorable site for the survival of spermatozoa in the cow and ewe. Sperm cells live in the cervix for 36 to 48 hours or possibly slightly longer and this site appeared to act as a sperm cell reservoir for spermatozoa in the cow, ewe and goat, Mattner, Mattner and Braden. Sperm cells retain their motility in the uterus and oviducts for about 24 hours. The uterus is not a highly favorable site for sperm cell survival because the presence of spermatozoa stimulate the invasion of leucocytes and the phagocytosis of spermatozoa. Lovell and Getty showed in swine that by 30 minutes after service the volume of seminal fluid in the uterus was greatly reduced and leucocytes were entering the lumen. Sperm cell survival in sows appeared to be longest in the mucous folds of the uterotubal junction. Ciliated cells in the apex of the uterine horns of sows were observed. By 8 hours postcoitus the numbers of leucocytes were greater than the spermatozoa and by 27 hours after service only rarely were spermatozoa found in the sow's uterus. Hafez and Blandau stated that the uterotubal junction was a "sperm reservoir" in the sow. The elimination of spermatozoa following their death in the female genital in the other domestic animals is by phagocytosis as in the sow, Mahajan and Merge, Mattner. Possibly a few dead spermatozoa may be expelled through the dilated cervix.

Fertilization of the ovum occurs in the ampulla of the oviduct within one to two hours after ovulation if the spermatozoa are present in the oviduct. Fertilization involves the penetration of the egg by the spermatozoon, the activation of the egg, the formation of the male and female pronuclei and the mingling of the maternal and paternal chromosomes to constitute the genome of the new zygote with a diploid number of chromosomes.

Capacitation of spermatozoa is the process that spermatozoa of rats, rabbits and sheep must undergo in the uterus or oviducts before achieving the capacity to fertilize ova. Capacitation time in sheep is 1-1/2 hours, Austin. If capacitation is required in the other domestic animals the time required must be quite short, Mahajan and Menge. There is evidence that bull, stallion and boar semen has a decapacitation factor. Rabbit spermatozoa can be capacitated in the dog's uterus, Williams et al.. Chang demonstrated in rabbits that spermatozoa placed in the oviducts 2 hours before or after ovulation failed to result in conception. If they were placed in the oviduct 4 hours before, 6 percent of the ova were fertilized, and 6 hours before ovulation, 78 percent of the ova were fertilized. Hunter and Dzuik demonstrated that spermatozoa can penetrate porcine ova within 3 hours of insemination. Capacitation is the enzymic removal of a substance or coating, probably a polysaccharide, on the sperm cell head that is acquired in the seminal plasma, Austin, Dukelow et al.. It can be replaced by mixing capacitated sperm cells with seminal plasma which contains the decapacitation factor. Kirton and Hafs have reported that beta-amylase capacitates rabbit spermatozoa. Capacitation produces a change in the acrosome called the "acrosome reaction" with a release of lytic enzymes such as hyaluronidase. No changes occur in the sperm head proper in the uterus but a functional change in the sperm head may take place when the sperm cell contacts the granulosa cells of the cumulus. Thus capacitation may allow the "acrosomal or vesiculation reaction" to occur to permit the sperm cell to penetrate the granulosa cells and zona pellucida, Redford. This enzyme permits the sperm cell to penetrate the cumulus cell mass around the ovum by depolymerizing the hyaluronic acid-protein matrix of the cumulus. The cumulus cells including the corona radiata in most domestic animals break down and separates from the zona pellucida early. In the dog and cat the corona cells may remain for some period of time. This early breakdown of the cumulus cells is caused by autolytic changes, action of the bicarbonate ions in the oviduct, ciliary and muscular activity of the oviduct and hyduronidase or possibly other enzymes if spermatozoa are present.

According to Bedford and Austin before the sperm cell can penetrate the zona pellucida it loses the acrosome cap and plasma membrane exposing the perforatorium and inner acrosomal membrane which are responsible for the penetration through the zona pellucida. It is reported that a lytic enzyme such as trypsin together with hyaluronidase may permit the sperm cell to dissolve an oblique "tunnel" through the proteinaceous zona into the perivitelline space, Stambaugh and Buckley, Buckley. When the plasma membrane of sperm head and vitelline membrane are in contact, the two structures unite and the entire sperm cell passes into the cytoplasm of the egg. In certain bulls, boars and dogs, the spermatozoa have defective or knobbed acrosomes yet the rest of the sperm cells are normal. These animals are sterile because their spermatozoa cannot penetrate the ovum. Usually when the sperm cell contacts the vitelline membrane in most domestic species, maturation of the ovum by meiosis is resumed with the expulsion of the second polar body. The cause of this "activation" of the ovum is not known but it proceeds to pronucleus formation.

Two factors are apparently responsible for preventing, except on rare occasions, the penetration of more than one sperm cell into the ovum. The first, according to Austin, is the relatively few spermatozoa in the oviduct at the time of fertilization. The second is when the first sperm cell contacts the vitelline membrane a rapid reaction takes place both in the zona pellucida and the vitelline membrane that blocks the further entrance of sperm cells, Austin. It is believed that this reaction is brought about by the release of a substance from the vitelline membrane or the cortical granules just beneath this membrane. It is not uncommon when examining fertilized eggs to see many sperm cells on or in the zona pellucida and in certain species in the perivitelline space.

After the male and female pronuclei form, the chromosomes in each pronuclei unite to form the zygote. This union of the two chromosome groups is called syngamy, at the conclusion of which fertilization is complete. The diploid or tetraploid zygote usually immediately divides into two blastomeres and the cleavage of the ovum progresses rapidly in the next few days to the blastula stage, Szollosi. According to Austin and McLaren the number of days from ovulation to the blastocyst stage of development is 4 to 5 in the horse, 7 to 8 in the cow, 5 to 7 in the sheep, 5 to 6 in the pig and 4 to 5 in the cat. The time of entry of the cleaving fertilized ova into the uterus in domestic animals is about 3 to 4 days after ovulation. This is usually one day shorter in swine and in superovulated cattle, Austin, and two to three or more days longer in dogs and cats. The passage of the ova through the isthmus of the oviduct is rapid. The passage of the fertilized cleaving ovum into the uterus and the control of this passage by the gonadal hormones acting on the muscular isthmus of the oviduct has been described previously. Some interesting time relations in regard to fertilization in domestic animals have been reviewed by Austin. Sperm

Table 17. The Reproductive Cycle of Domestic Animals*

Animal	Onset of Puberty	Average Recommended Age for First Service	Length of Estrous Cycle	Follicle Diameter (mm)	Length of Estrum	Time of Ovulation	Optimum Time for Service	Ovum Transport Time	Advisable Time to Breed After Parturition
Mare	10-24 m. (18 m.)	2-3 yr.	19-23 d. (21 d.)	35-55+	4.5-7.5 d. (5.5 d.)	1-2 d. before the end of estrum	2-4 d. before end of estrum or the 2nd-3rd d. of estrum	4 d.	About 25-35 d. or 2nd estrum; about 9 d. or 1st estrum only if normal in every way
Cow	4-24 m. (6-18 m.)	14-22 m.	18-24 d. (21 d.)	10-20	12-28 h. (18 h.) (Temperate Zone)	10-15 h. after the end of estrum	Just before the middle of estrum to the end of estrum	3-4 d.*	60-90 d.
Ewe	4-12 m. (first fall)	12-18 m.	14-20 d. (16.5 d.)	15-19	24-48 h. (30-36 h.)	12-24 h. before the end of estrum	18-24 h. after the onset of estrum	3-4 d.*	Usually the following fall
Goat	4-12 m. (first fall)	12-18 m.	15-24 d. (20 d.)		30-60 h. (36-48 h.)	About the last day of estrum	24-36 h. after the onset of estrum	3-4 d.*	Usually the following fall
Sow	5-8 m.	8-9 m.	18-24 d. (21 d.)	7-10	1-4 d. (2-3 d.)	30-40 h. after the onset of estrum	12-30 h. after the onset of estrum	2-3 d.	First estrum 4-9 d. after weaning pigs
Dog	6-12 m. (7-10 m.)	12-18 m.	1-4 cycles per year (2 cycles per year)	6-8	4-13 d. (9 d.)	1-2 d. after the onset of true estrum	2-3 d. after onset of true estrum or 10-14 d. after onset of post-estrous bleeding	6-8 d.	Usually the first estrum or 3-4 weeks after weaning pups
Cat	6-15 m. (8-10 m.)	12-18 m.	15-21 d.[1]		9-10 d.[1] 4 d.[2]	24-30 h. after coitus (27 h.)[2]	—[2]	4-8 d.	Usually the 1st estrum or 3-4 weeks after weaning kittens

*Numbers in parenthesis are average figures. From Dukes, Hafez, Asdell, Cole and Cupps, Altman and Dittmer, and Fraser.

[1] The cat has several cycles each breeding period. The latter occur usually 2 or 3 times a year if it is not bred.

[2] The cat does not ovulate spontaneously. If coitus occurs the cat goes out of estrum in about 4 days.

cell penetration of the ovum begins about 3 hours after ovulation in ewes, pronuclei are formed 11 to 39 hours after ovulation in the cow and 3 to 9 hours after ovulation in the ewe. The fertilized egg divides into the two-cell stage about 24 hours after ovulation in the mare and 19 to 24 hours after ovulation in the ewe.

The most common abnormalities of fertilization are polygyny and polyspermy. Polygyny is incomplete maturation of the egg with a failure to expel the second polar body resulting in a triploid zygote. Polyspermy where more than one, usually two, sperm cells enter the egg is also characterized by triploidy or a 3N instead of a normal 2N chromosome complement in the zygote. Aging of the egg increases the incidence of these anomalies. McLaren cited Thibault in reporting that 20 percent or more of swine zygotes were polyspermic or digynic when the sow was bred more than 36 hours after the onset of estrus. Migration of the early zygote from one uterine horn to the other horn is fairly common in sheep, horses, dogs, swine and cats but rare in cows. Migration of the ova across the peritoneal cavity of domestic animals has not been reported.

The formation and development of the corpus luteum under the influence of LH results in the production of progesterone necessary for the preparation of the uterus and probably the rapid passage of the zygote through the isthmus into the uterus. Progesterone is also essential to the maintenance of pregnancy as discussed previously. Because of the effect of the blastocyst on the endometrium, the release of the "luteolytic" substance is inhibited and LH secretion maintains the corpus luteum. Otherwise in nonpregnant animals starting about 16 days in the cow and sow and about 10 to 12 days in the ewe and mare the corpus luteum would involute resulting in another estrous period 4 to 5 days later. Placement of or spacing embryos in the uterus in multiparous animals occurs during this period of the ovum and early embryonic period. The blastocyst elongates rapidly in the cow, ewe, and sow but remains spherical in the mare, dog and cat. The uterine luminal fluid or "uterine milk" is rich in mucopolysaccharides, protein, free amino acids, salts and etc. like an ultrafiltrate of blood plasma supplemented by secretions of the uterine glands. Excess progesterone may produce an adverse uterine environment for the developing embryo. The shedding of the zona pellucida is probably caused by intrinsic factors in the developing blastocyst, Hafez. Normal gestation and zygote passage into the uterus is carefully synchonized. If rat eggs 2-1/2-days-old are transplanted into a uterus 3.5 days postcoitus all eggs die, but if 3.5-day-old eggs are transplanted into uteri 2.5 days after coitus they survive. The early loss of fertilized eggs or embryos is usually not recognizable and is called infertility or sterility.

A thorough knowledge of the various physiologic reproductive phenomena of each domestic species is essential in order for the veterinarian to understand and intelligently treat the various causes of infertility and supervise reproductive health programs. The knowledge in this basic field is being rapidly advanced and as more information is obtained clinical application of this knowledge and treatment will be based increasingly on facts instead of empiricism.

The basic physiologic reproductive knowledge necessary for all veterinarians on the domestic species is given in Table 17. These are average or mean figures. Individual animal variations and differences are common but as a general guide this information is useful. A more complete discussion of the reproductive cycle, endocrine effects on the cycle and the reproductive physiology of the postpartum period and pubertal period will preface each of the following Chapters on infertility in the various female domestic species.

References

General

Altman, P,. H,. and Dittmer, D. S. (1962) Growth Including Reproduction and Morphological Development, Biological Handbook, Federation of Amer. Soc. Exper. Biol., Washington, D.C.

Asdell, S. A. (1964) Patterns of Mammalian Reproduction, 2nd. Ed., Cornell Univ. Press, Ithaca, N.Y.

Benson, G. K. and Cowie, A. T. (1957) Hormones in Reproduction and Lactation (A Review), Jour. Dairy Res. **24,** 2, 252.

Cole, H. H. and Cupps, P. T. (1969) Reproduction in Domestic Animals, 2nd Ed., Academic Press, N.Y.C.

Dukes, H. H. (1947) The Physiology of Domestic Animals, 6th Ed., Comstock Publishing Co., Inc., Ithaca, N.Y.

Fraser, A. F. (1968) Tables of Data on Livestock Reproduction, Edinburgh Univ. Press, Edinburgh.

Hafez, E. S. E. (1968) Reproduction in Farm Animals, 2nd Ed., Lea and Febiger, Philadelphia.

Hartman, C. G. (1963) Mechanisms Concerned with Conception, McMillan Comp., N.Y.C.

McDonald, L. E. (1969) Veterinary Endocrinology and Reproduction, Lea and Febiger, Philadelphia.

Nalbandov, A. V. (1964) Reproductive Physiology, 2nd Ed., W. H. Freeman and Comp., San Francisco.

Parkes, A. S. (1966) Marshall's Physiology of Reproduction, Vol. 3 Little, Brown and Co., Boston.

Teppermen, J. (1962) Metabolic and Endocrine Physiology, Year-Book Medical Publishers, Chicago.

Turner, C. D. (1961) General Endocrinology, 3rd Ed., W. B. Saunders Co., Philadelphia.

Velle, W. (1963) Gonadal Hormones in Domestic Animals, in **Advances in Vet. Sci.,** Vol. 8, Edit. by C. A. Brandley and E. L. Jungherr, Academic Press Inc., N.Y.C.

Von Euler, U. S. and Heller, H. (1963) Comparative Endocrinology, Vol. 1, Academic Press, N.Y.C.

Zuckerman, S. (1962) The Ovary, Vol I and II, Academic Press, N.Y.C.

Reproductive Hormones

Amoroso, E. C. (1955) Hormone Control of the Oestrus Cycle, Vet. Rec. **67,** 1072.

Black, W. G., Ulberg, L. C., Kidder, H. E., Simon, J., McNutt, S. H., and Casida, L. E. (1953) Inflammatory Response of the Bovine Endometrium, Am. J. Vet. Res., **14,** 51, 179.

Brunner, M. A., Donaldson, L, E. and Hansel, W. (1969) Exogenous Hormones and Luteal Function in Hysterectomized and Intact Heifers, J. Dairy Sci. **52,** 11, 1849.

Bush, L. J. and Reuber, H. W. (1963) Effects of Feeding Diethylstilbestrol on Development and Reproductive Performance of Dairy Cattle, J. Dairy Sci. **46,** 7, 740.

Cole, H. H. (1964) Gonadotropins—Their Chemical and Biological Properties and Secretory Control, W. H. Freeman Co., San Francisco, Calif.

Cummings, J. E. and Habel, R. E. (1965) The Blood Supply of the Bovine Hypophysis, Amer. J. of Anat. **116,** 1, 91.

Desjardins, C. and Hafs, H D. (1965) Immunochemical and Electrophoretic Properties of Equine Luteinizing Hormone, J. An. Sci. 24, 2, 347.

Donaldson, L. and Hansel, Wm. (1967) Histological Study of Bovine Corpora Lutea, J. Dairy Sci. **48,** 7, 905.

Douglas, R. G., Bonsnes, R. W., and duVigneaud, V. (1955) Natural and Synthetic Oxytocin, Obstet. and Gynecol, **6,** 3, 254.

duVigneaud, V., Ressler, C., Swan, J. M., Roberts, C. W., and Katsoyannis, P. (1954) The Synthesis of Oxytocin, J. Amer. Chem. Soc. **76,** 3115.

Ganong, W. F. and Kraft, C. L. (1969) The Nervous System and Reproduction, in **Reproduction in Domestic Animals** Edit. by H. H. Cole and P. T. Cupps, 2nd Ed., Academic Press, N.Y.C., 167.

Ginther, O. J. (1966) The Influence of the Uterus on the Life Span of the Corpus Luteum, Vet. Med. **61,** 12, 1199.

Ginther, O. J. (1967) Local Utero-Ovarian Relationships, J. An. Sci. **26,** 3, 578.

Ginther, O. J. (1968) Utero-Ovarian Relationships: Physiologic Aspects and Applied Veterinary Aspects, J.A.V.M.A. **153,** 12, 1656 and 1665.

Goetsch, D. D. (1955) The Effects of Feeding and Implanting Estrogenic Substances in Ruminants, J.A.V.M.A. **127,** 945, 531.

Gomes, W. R. and Erb, R. E. (1965) Progesterone in Bovine Reproduction: A Review, J. Dairy Sci. **48,** 3, 314.

Hansel, W. (1961) The Hypothalamus and Pituitary Function in Mammals, Internat. J. of Fertil. **6,** 3, 241.

Hansel, W. and Trimberger, G. W. (1952) The Effect of Progesterone on Ovulation Time in Dairy Heifers, J. of Dairy Sci., **35,** 1, 65.

Hawk, H. W., Turner, G. D. and Sykes, J. F. (1960) The Effect of the Ovarian Hormones on the Uterine Defense Mechanism During the Early Stages of Induced Infection, Amer. J. Vet. Res. **21,** 83, 644.

Hawk, H. W., Turner, G. D. and Sykes, J. F. (1960) Noncellular Bactericidal Factors in Inflammatory Exudates from Uterine and Pleural Cavities of Estrous and Pseudopregnant Rabbits, Amer. J. Vet. Res. **21,** 83, 657.

Imori, T. (1967) Biological Half Life of Progesterone in the Peripheral Blood of Cows, Jap. Jour. Vet. Sci. **29,** 4, 201.

Knaggs, G. S. (1969) Personal Communication.

Mellin, T. N. and Erb, R. E. (1965) Estrogens in the Bovine—A Review, J. Dairy Sci. **48,** 6, 687.

Mellin, T. N., Erb, R. E. and Estergreen, V. L. (1965) Quantitative Estimation and Identification of Estrogens in Bovine Urine, J. Dairy Sci. **48,** 7, 896.

Mischler, T. W. and Reineke, E. P. (1970) Thyroid Hormone Analysis of Thyroactive Iodinated Casein, J. Dairy Sci., **53,** 2, 233.

Moor, R. M. and Rowson, L. E. A. (1966) The Corpus Luteum of the Sheep: Effect of the Removal of Embryos on Luteal Function, J. Endocrinol. **34,** 497.

Nakahara, T., Yamauchi, M. and Kataoka, T. (1961) Studies on the Antihormone Against Human Chorionic Gonadotropin (Anti-H.C.G.) in Cattle, Jap. J. Animal Reprod. **7,** 1, 27, and **7,** 4, 137.

Parkes, A. S. and Bruce H. M. (1961) Olfactory Stimuli in Mammalian Reproduction, Science, **134,** 3485, 1049.

Rowson, L. E. A., Lamming, G. E. and Fry, R. M. (1953) The Relationship between Ovarian Hormones and Uterine Infection, Vet. Rec., **65,** 335.

Short, R. V. (1962) Steroid Concentrations in Normal Follicular Fluid and Ovarian Cyst Fluid from Cows, J. Reprod. Fertil. **4,** 27.

Short, R. V. (1967) Personal Communication.

Simmons, K. R. and Hansel, W. (1964) Nature of the Luteotrophic Hormone in the Bovine, J. An. Sci. **23,** 1, 136.

Willett, E. L., Buckner, P. J. and McShan, W. H. (1954) Refractoriness of Cows Repeatedly Superovulated with Gonadotropins, J. of Dairy Sci., **36,** 10, 1083.

Williams, W. F. (1962) Excretion of Progesterone and Its Metabolites in Milk, Urine and Feces, J. Dairy Sci. **45,** 1541.

Young, W. C., Goy, R. W. and Phoenix, C. H. (1964) Hormones and Sexual Behavior, Science, **143,** 212.

Puberty

Asdell, S. A. (1948) Sterility and Delayed Breeding in Dairy Cattle, Cornell Extension Bull. 737.

Asdell, S. A. (1955) Cattle Fertility and Sterility: Little, Brown and Co., Boston, Mass.

Desjardins, C. and Hafs, H. D. (1969) Maturation of Bovine Female Genitalia From Birth Through Puberty, J. An. Sci. **28,** 4, 502.

Foote, W. C., Waldorf, D. P., Chapman, A. B., Self, H. L., Grummer,

R. H. and Casida, L. E. (1956) Age at Puberty of Gilts Produced by Different Systems of Mating, J. An. Sci. **15,** 4, 959.

Menge, A. C., Mares, S. E., Tyler, W. J. and Casida, L. E. (1960) Some Factors Affecting Age at Puberty and the First 90 Days of Lactation in Holstein Heifers, J. Dairy Sci. **43,** 8, 1099.

Morrow, D. A. (1968) Estrous Intensity and Ovarian Conditions in Postpuberal Dairy Heifers, J. Dairy Sci. **51,** 6, 949.

Olds, D. and Seath, D. M. (1954) Factors Affecting Reproductive Efficiency in Cattle, Ken Agr. Exp. Stat. Bull. 605.

Ortavant, R., Mauleon, P. and Thibault, C. (1964) Photoperiodic Control of Gonadal and Hypophyseal Activity in Domestic Mammals, Annals N.Y. Acad. of Sci. **117,** Art. 1, 157.

Reynolds, W. L., DeRouen, T. M. and High, J. W. Jr. (1963) The Age and Weight at Puberty of Angus, Brahman and Zebu-Cross Heifers, J. An. Sci. **22,** 1, 243.

Robertson, G. L., Casida, L. E., Grummer, R. H. and Chapman, A. B. (1951) Some Feeding and Management Factors Affecting Age at Puberty and Related Phenomena in Chester White and Poland China Gilts, J. An. Sci. **10,** 4, 841.

Sorensen, A. M., Hansel, W., Hough, W. H., Armstrong, D. T., McEntee, K. and Bratton, R. W. (1959) Causes and Prevention of Reproductive Failures in Dairy Cattle, Influence of Underfeeding and Overfeeding on Growth and Development of Holstein Heifers, Bull. 936, Cornell Univ. Agr. Exp. Stat.

Sorenson, A. M., Jr., Bratton, R. W., Hansel, W., and Hough, W. H. (1954) The Growth and Sexual Development of Young Holstein Heifers as Influenced by Three Levels of Nutrition, J. An. Sci., **13,** 4, 1031.

Wiltbank, J. N., Kasson, C. W. and Ingalls, J. E. (1969) Puberty in Crossbred and Straightbred Beef Heifers on Two Levels of Feed, J An. Sci. **29,** 4, 602.

Zimmerman, D. R., Spies, H. G., Rigor, E. M., Self, H. L. and Casida, L. E. (1960) Effect of Restricted Feeding, Crossbreeding and Season of Birth on Age at Puberty in Swine, J. An. Sci. **19,** 3, 687.

Factors Affecting the Reproductive Cycle

Amoroso, E. C. (1955) Hormone Control of the Oestrus Cycle, Vet. Rec. **67,** 50, 1072.

Andrews, F. N. (1953) The Influence of the Environment on Reproduction in Female Farm Animals, Iowa State Col. J. of Sci., **28,** 1, 9.

Barker, H. B. and Wiggins, E. L. (1959) Estrual Activity in Open Rambouillet Ewes, J. An. Sci. **18,** 4, 1547.

Belonji, C. W. A. (1956) The Operation for Retroversion of the Penis in the Stallion, J. South Afr. Vet. Med. Assoc. **27,** 1, 53.

Bissonette, T. H. (1941) Experimental Modification of Breeding Cycles in Goats, Physiol. Zool, **14,** 379.

Braden, A. W. H. and Moule, G. R. (1964) Effects of Stress on Ovarian Morphology and Oestrous Cycles in Ewes, Austral. J. Agr. Res. **15,** 937.

Bruce, H. M. (1966) Smell as an Exteroceptive Factor, J. An. Sci. **25,** Suppl., 83.

Caslick, E. A. (1937) The Sexual Cycle and Its Relation to Ovulation with Breeding Records of the Thoroughbred Mare, Cor. Vet., **27,** 2, 187.

Cole, H. H. (1964) See reproductive hormones.

Dutt, R. H. and Bush, L. F. (1955) The Effect of Low Environmental Temperature on the Initiation of the Breeding Season and Fertility in Sheep., J. of An. Sci. **14,** 3, 885.

Gangwar, P. C., Branton, C. and Evans, D. L. (1964) Effect of Climatic Stress on Ovarian Activity of Dairy Heifers, J. Dairy Sci. **147,** 3, 348.

Hall, J. G., Branton, C. and Stone, E. J. (1959) Estrus, Estrous Cycles, Ovulation Time, Time of Service and Fertility of Dairy Cattle in Louisiana, J. Dairy Sci. **42,** 6, 1086.

Hammond, J. (1950) Possible Causes for Physiological Sterility in Cattle, Vlaams Diergeneesk. Tijdsch., **19,** 12, 265.

Hammond, J. (1955) Progress in the Physiology of Farm Animals, Vol. 2, Butterworths Scientific Publications, London, England.

Hansel, W. and Wagner, W. C. (1960) Luteal Inhibition in the Bovine as a Result of Oxytocin Injections, Uterine Dilatation and Intrauterine Infusions of Seminal and Preputial Fluids, J. of Dairy Sci. **43,** 6, 798.

Harms, P. G. and Malven, P. V. (1967) Effect of Injected Progesterone on Estrous Cycle Length, J. Dairy Sci. **50,** 6, (Abstr.).

Meites, J. (1953) Relation of Nutrition to Endocrine and Reproductive Functions, Iowa State Col J. of Sci., **28,** 1, 19.

Melampy, R. M. Emmerson, M.A., Rakes, J. M., Hanka, L. J. and Eness, P. G. (1957) The Effect of Progesterone on the Estrous Response of Estrogen—Conditioned Ovariectomized Cows, J. An. Sci. **16,** 967.

Mercier, E. and Salisburg, G. W. (1947) Seasonal Variations in Hours of Daylight under Natural Breeding Conditions, J. of Dairy Sci., **30,** 10, 747.

Nakahara, T., Dormeki, I., Inui, S. and Yamauchi, M. (1967) Effects of Intrauterine Infusion of Iodine Solution on the Estrous Cycle of the Cow, Jap. Jour. of An. Reprod., **13,** 2, 57.

Nalbandov, A. V. (1964) Roles of the Hypothalamus and Hypophysis in the Control of the Estrous Cycle, Proc. of Conf. on Estrous Cycle Control in Domestic Animals, Univ. of Nebr. Miscel. Public. 1005.

Ortavant, R., Mauleon, P. and Thibault, C. (1964) Photoperiodic Control of Gonadal and Hypophyseal Activity in Domestic Animals, Ann. N.Y. Acad. of Sci. **117,** Article I, 157.

Trimberger, G. W. and Hansel, W. (1955) Conception Rate and Ovarian Function Following Estrus Control by Progesterone Injections in Dairy Cattle, J. An. Sci. **14,** 224.

Wagner, W. C. (1966) Remarks, J. An. Sci. **25,** Suppl, 141.

Williams, S. M., Garrigus, U.S., Norton, H. W. and Nalbandov, A. V. (1956) Variations in the Length of Estrous Cycles and the Breeding Season of Ewes, J. An. Sci. **15,** 4, 984.

Wiltbank, J. N. and Casida, L. E. (1956) Alteration of Ovarian Activity by Hysterectomy, J. An. Sci. **15,** 1, 134.

Coition or Copulation

Benesch, F. and Wright, J. G. 1951 Veterinary Obstetrics, Williams and Wilkins Co., Baltimore, Md.

Hammond, J. (See Factors Affecting the Reproductive Cycle, 1955).

Laing, J. A. (1955) Fertility and Infertility in Domestic Animals, Williams and Wilkins Co., Baltimore, 2, Md.

Masson, Jorge (1961) Unpublished data

Millar, R. (1952) Forces Observed During Coitus in Thoroughbreds, Austral. Vet. J., **28,** 5, 127.

Tanabe, T. Y., Warwick, A. C., Casida, L. E. and Grummer, R. H. (1949) The Effects of Gonadotropins Administered to Sows and Gilts During Different Stages of the Estrual Cycle, J. An. Sci., **8,** 4, 550.

Williams, W. L. (1943) Diseases of the Genital Organs of Domestic Animals, 3rd Ed., Miss Louella Williams, Upland Rd., Ithaca, N.Y.

Ovogenesis

Blandau, R., White, B. J. and Rumery, R. E. (1963) Observations on the Movements of Living Primordial Germ Cells in the Mouse, Fert. and Steril. **14,** 5, 482.

Blandau, R. (1965) Biology of Germ Cells in Mammals, Science, **150,** 370 (Abstr.)

Erickson, B. H. (1965) Radiation Effects on Gonadal Development in Farm Animals, J. An. Sci. **24,** 3, 568.

Erickson, B. H. (1966) Development and Senescence of the Postnatal Bovine Ovary, J. An. Sci. **25,** 3, 800.

Hartman, C. G. and Leathem, J. H. (1963) Oogenesis and Ovulation, from Conf. on **Physiol. Mechanisms Concerned with Conception,** Pergamon Press, N.Y.C.

Henricson, B. and Rajakoski, E. (1959) Studies on Oocytogenesis in Cattle, Cor. Vet. **49,** 4, 494.

Kennelly, J. J. and Foote, R. H. (1962) Personal communication.

Kennelly, J. J. and Foote, R. H. (1966) Oocytogenesis in Rabbits, Amer. J. of Anat. **118,** 2, 573.

Mauleon, P. (1969) Oogenesis and Folliculogenesis in **Reproduction in Domestic Animals,** 2nd Ed., by Cole, H. H. and Cupps, P. T., Academic Press, N.Y.C.

Rajakoski, E. (1965) Some Views on Oogenesis in Cattle, Nord. Vet. Med. **17,** 285.

Settergren, I. (1964) The Number of Primordial Follicles in Clinically Normal and Hypoplastic Heifer Ovaries, 5th Internat. Congress on Animal Reprod. and Artificial Insem. Trento, 188.

Settergren, I. (1970) Personal communication.

Szollosi, D. (1966) Time and Duration of DNA Synthesis in Rabbit Eggs after Sperm Penetration, Anat. Rec. **154,** 2.

Zuckerman, S. (1962) The Ovary—Vol. I. Academic Press, N.Y.C.

Folliculogenesis and Ovulation

Asdell, S. A., DeAlba, J. and Roberts, S. J. (1945) The Levels of Ovarian Hormones Required to Induce Heat and Other Reactions in the Ovariectomized Cow, J. of An. Sci., **4,** 3, 277.

Blandau, R. J. (1967) Oogenesis-Ovulation and Egg Transport, in **Comparative Aspects of Reproductive Failure** edit. by K. Benirschke, Springer-Verlag, N.Y.C.

Blandau, R. J. and Rumery, R. E. (1963) Measurements of Intrafollicular Pressure in Ovulatory and Preovulatory Follicles of the Rat, Fert. and Steril. **14,** 3, 330.

Cupps, P. T., Anderson, L. L. and Cole, H. H. (1969) The Estrous Cycle, in **Reproduction in Domestic Animals,** 2nd Ed. Academic Press, N.Y.C., 226.

Hafez, E. S. E. and Sugie, T. (1961) Superovulatory Responses in Beef Cattle and an Experimental Approach for Non Surgical Ova Transfer, 4th Internat. Congr. on An. Reprod., Netherlands.

Hafez, E. S. E. See General References.

Hafez, E. S. E., Sugie, T. and Gordon, I. (1963) Superovulation and Related Phenomena in the Beef Cow, J. Reprod. and Fertil. **5,** 359.

Hansel, W. (1953) Neurogenic Factors in Ovulation, Iowa State Col. J. of Sci., **28,** 1, 1.

Hansel, W. (1958) Neurogenic Factors Affecting Ovulation in Animals, Internat. J. of Fertil. **3,** 1, 42.

Hansel, W. and Trimberger, G. W. (1952) Effect of Progesterone on Ovulation Time in Dairy Heifers, J. Dairy Sci. **35,** 1, 65.

Hansel, W., Trimberger, G. W. and Bearden, H. J. (1952) The Effect of Estradiol on Ovulation Time in Dairy Heifers, J. An. Sci., **11,** 4, 793.

Harper, M. J. K. (1961) The Time of Ovulation in the Rabbit Following Injection of Luteinizing Hormone, J. of Endocrinol. **22,** 147.

Hough, W. H., Bearden, H. J., and Hansel, W. (1955) Further Studies on Factors Affecting Ovulation in the Cow J. of An. Sci., **14,** 3, 739.

Jubb, K. and McEntee, K. (1955) Observations on the Bovine Pituitary Gland, Cor. Vet. **45,** 4, 570.

Jubb, K. and McEntee, K. (1954) Personal Communication.

Kupfer, M. (1928) The Sexual Cycle of Female Domesticated Mammals, 13th and 14th Reports of the Director of Veterinary Education and Research, Part 2, 1211, Union of South Africa, Pretoria.

Lipner, H. (1968) Personal Communication, Cornell University.

Marion, G. B., Gier, H. T. and Chondary, J. B. (1968) Micromorphology of the Bovine Ovarian Follicular System, J. An. Sci. **27,** 2, 451 and 466.

Marion, G. B. and Smith, V. R. (1951) The Effect of Administering an Unfractionated Gonadotropic Pituitary Extract During Estrus on the Time of Ovulation and the Length of the Estrual Period of Dairy Heifers, J. of Dairy Sci., **34,** 6, 496.

Marion, G. B., Smith, V. R., Wiley, T. E. and Barrett, G. R. (1950) The Effect of Sterile Copulation on Time of Ovulation in Dairy Heifers, J. Dairy Sci., **33,** 885.

Montfort, E. L. (1955) Personal Communication.

Osborne, V. (1966) Univ. of Sidney, Personal Communication.

Nalbandov, A. V. (1953) Gonadotrophic Activity of Pituitary Glands and the Induction of Ovulation, Iowa State Col. J. of Sci., **28,** 1, 45.

Pool, W. R. and Lipner, H. (1966) Inhibition of Ovulation by Antibiotics, Endocrinol. **79,** 858.

Prickett, M. E. (1968) Personal Communication.

Rajakoski, E. (1960) The Ovarian Follicular System in Sexually Mature Heifers, Acta Endocrinologica, **34,** Suppl. 52.

Rakha, A. M. and Robertson, H. A. (1965) Changes in Levels of Follicle Stimulating Hormone and Luteinizing Hormone in the Bovine Pituitary Gland at Ovulation, J. Endocrinol. **31,** 245.

Shettles, L. B. (1958) The Living Human Ovum, Amer. J. Obst. and Gynec. **76,** 398.

Strassmann, E. O. (1961) The Theca Cone. The Pathmaker of Growing Human and Mammalian Follicles, Internat. J. of Fert. **4,** 2, 135.

Sturgis, S. H. (1950) The Mechanism and Control of Primate Ovulation, Fert. and Steril., **1,** 1, 40.

Willett, E. L. (1953) Egg Transfer and Superovulation in Farm Animals, Iowa State Col. J. of Sci., **28,** 1, 83.

Ova and Sperm Transport and Fertilization

Austin, C. R. (1962) The Mammalian Egg, C. C. Thomas Publ. Co., Springfield, Ill.

Austin, C. R. (1963) Fertilization and Transport of the Ovum, in "Mechanisms Concerned with Conception" Ed. by C. G. Hartman, McMillan Co., N.Y.C.

Austin, C. R. (1967) Capacitation of Spermatozoa, Internat. J. of Fert. **12,** 1, 25.

Austin, C. R. (1969) Fertilization and Development of the Egg, in **Reproduction in Domestic Animals,** 2nd Ed. Cole and Cupps, Academic Press, N.Y.C.

Baker, R. D., Dzuik, P. J. and Norton, H. W. (1968) Effect of Volume of Semen and Number of Sperm and Drugs on Transport of Sperm in Artificially Inseminated Gilts, J. An. Sci. **27,** 1, 88.

Bedford, J. M. (1967) Experimental Requirement for Capacitation and Observations on Ultra-Structural Changes in Rabbit Spermatozoa during Fertilization, J. Reprod. and Fert. Suppl. 2, 35.

Bedford, J. M. (1968) Ultrastructural Changes in the Sperm Head During Fertilization in the Rabbit, Amer. J. Anat. **123,** 329.

Bergstrom, S. (1967) Prostaglandins—Members of a New Hormonal System, Science **157,** 382.

Black, D. L. and Davis, J. (1962) A Blocking Mechanism in the Cow Oviduct, J. Reprod. and Fert. **4,** 21.

Blandau, R. J. (1967) Oogenesis—Ovulation and Egg Transport, in **Comparative Aspects of Reproductive Failure** edit. by K. Benirschke, Springer-Verlag, N.Y.C.

Braden, A. W. H. (1953) Distribution of Sperm in the Genital Tract of the Female Rabbit after Coitus, Austral. J. Biol. Sci. **6,** 693.

Casida, L. E. (1950) The Repeat-Breeder Cow, Vlaams Diergeneesk. Tijdschr., **19,** 12, 273.

Casida, L. E., Warwick, E. J. and Meyer, R. K. (1944) Survival of Multiple Pregnancies Induced in the Ewe Following Treatment with Pituitary Gonadotropins, J. of An. Sci., **3,** 22.

Chang, M.C. (1951) Fertilizing Capacity of Spermatozoa Deposited into the Fallopian Tubes, Nature, **168,** 697.

Chang, M. C. (1951) Fertility and Sterility as Revealed in the Study of Fertilization and Development of Rabbit Eggs, Fert. and Steril., **2,** 3, 205.

Cheng, P. and Casida, L. E. (1948) Fertility in the Rabbit as Affected by the Dilution of Semen and the Number of Spermatozoa, Proc. Soc. Exptl. Biol. and Med., **69,** 36.

Doak, R. L., Hall, A. and Dale, H. E. (1967) Longevity of Spermatozoa in the Reproductive Tract of the Bitch, J. Reprod. and Fert. **13,** 1, 51.

Dukelow, W. R., Williams, W. L. and Chernoff, H. N. (1965) Biochemical Nature of the Decapacitation Factor in Seminal Plasma, J. Dairy Sci. **48,** 6, 807.

First, N. L., Short, R. E., Peters, J. B. and Stratman, F. W. (1965) Transport of Spermatozoa in Estrual and Luteal Sows, J. An. Sci. 24, 3, 917. (Abstr).

Greenwald, G. S. (1967) Species Differences in Egg Transport in Response to Exogenous Estrogen, Anat. Rec. **157,** 163.

Hafez, E. S. E. (1959) Tuboovarian Mechanisms and Ova Reception in Mammals. A Comparative Study, Cor. Vet. **49,** 4, 459.

Hafez, E. S. E. (1961) Structural and Developmental Anomalies of Rabbit Ova, Internat. J. of Fertil. **6,** 4, 393.

Hafez, E. S. E. (1963) Physiologic Mechanisms of Implantation, Cor. Vet. **53,** 3, 348.

Hafez, E. S. E. (1968) Reproduction in Farm Animals, 2nd Ed., Lea and Febiger, Philadelphia.

Hafez, E. S. E. and Blandau, R. J. (1969) The Mammalian Oviduct, Sympos. at Wash. State Univ., Univ. of Chicago Press, Chicago, Ill.

Hartman, C. G. (1963) Mechanisms Concerned with Conception, McMillan Co., N.Y.C.

Hunter, R. H. F. and Dzuik, P. J. (1966) Fertilization of Pig Eggs Three Hours Postinsemination, J. An. Sci. **25,** 4, 1265.

Kelly, W. A. and Eckstein, P. (1969) Implantation, Development of the Fetus, and Fetal Membranes, in **Reproduction in Domestic Animals,** 2nd Edit. by Cole & Cupps, Academic Press, N.Y.C.

Kirton, K. T. and Hafs, H. D. (1965) Sperm Capacitation by Uterine Fluid or Beta-Amylase **in vitro,** Science, **150,** 618.

Lanman, J. T. (1968) Delays During Reproduction and Their Effects on the Embryo and Fetus, New Engl. J. of Med. **278,** 993, 1047, 1092.

Lineweaver, J. A., Hafez, E. S. E., Ehlers, M. H., Dickson, W. M. and King, J.R. (1970) Sperm Transport in Cattle, Cor. Vet. **60,** 3, 372.

Lovell, J. E. and Getty, R. (1968) Fate of Semen in the Uterus of the Sow, Amer. J. Vet. Res. **29,** 3, 609.

MacLeod, J., Gold, R. Z., and McLane, C. M. (1955) Correlation of the Male and Female Factors in Human Infertility, Fert. and Steril., **6,** 2, 112.

Mahajan, S. C. and Menge, A. C. (1966) Influence of the Uterine Environment on the Fertilizing Capacity of Sperm in Cattle, J. An. Sci. 25, 4, 1083.

Mahajan, S. C. and Menge, A. C. (1967) Influence of Reproductive Phase on the Inflammatory Response and Rate of Sperm Removal in the Uterus and Oviduct of the Cow, Amer. J. Vet. Res. **28,** 125, 1037.

Mattner, P. E. (1968) The Distribution of Spermatozoa and Leucocytes in the Female Genital Tract in Goats and Cattle, J. Reprod. and Fert. **17,** 253.

Mattner, P. E. and Braden, A. W. H. (1963) Spermatozoa in the Genital Tract of the Ewe, Austral. J. Biol. Sci. **16,** 2, 473.

McLaren, A. (1967) Advances in Reproductive Physiology, Academic Press Inc., N.Y.C.

McLaren, A. (1968) Fertilization, Cleavage and Implantation, in **Reproduction in Farm Animals** edit. by E. S. E. Hafez, Lea and Febiger, Philadelphia, Pa.

Noyes, R. W., Adams, C. E. and Walton, A. (1958) Transport of Spermatozoa into the Uterus of the Rabbit, Fert. and Steril. **9,** 4, 288.

Oxenreider, S. L. and Day, B. N. (1965) Transport and Cleavage of Ova in Swine, J. An. Sci. **24,** 413.

Sobrero, A. J. (1963) Sperm Migration in the Female Reproductive Tract, in **Mechanisms Concerned with Conception,** C. G. Hartman, edit., McMillan Co., N.Y.C.

Stambaugh, R. and Buckley, J. (1968) Zona Pellucida Dissolution Enzymes of the Rabbit Sperm Head, Science, **161,** 585.

Starke, N. C. (1949) The Sperm Picture in Rams of Different Breeds as an Indication of their Fertility. II—The Rate of Sperm Travel in the Genital Tract of the Ewe, Onderstep. J. Vet. Sci. and An. Ind., **22,** 2, 415.

Van Demark, N. L. (1958) Spermatozoa in the Female Genital Tract, Internat. J. of Fertil. **3,** 1, 220.

Van Demark, N. L. and Hays, R. L. (1954) Rapid Sperm Transport in the Cow, Fert. and Steril., **5,** 2, 131.

Willett, E. L. and Larson, G. L. (1952) Fertility of Bull Semen as Influenced by Dilution Level, Antibiotics, Spermatozoan Numbers and the Interation of these Factors, J. Dairy Sci. **35,** 11, 899.

Williams, W. L., Abney, T. O. Chernoff, H. N., Dukelow, W. R. and Pinsker, M. C. (1967) Biochemistry and Physiology of the Decapacitation Factor, J. Reprod. and Fert., Suppl. 2, 11.

Chapter XIII

INFERTILITY IN THE COW

It has been estimated by Asdell that sterility and reproductive troubles in dairy cattle in the United States cost $250,000,000 annually. In New York State these losses annually amount to $20,000,000 when figured on the basis of data collected on the causes of culling from Dairy Herd Improvement Association herds. Culling of cows on the basis of sterility has increased from 1.1 percent to 2.5 percent in the last 15 years, Asdell. Much of this rise may be accounted for by better recording. In northeastern United States 12 to 19 percent of dairy cows culled from herds each year were culled because of infertility or sterility, White and Nichols, Thompson and Patterson and O'Bleness and Van Vleck. The great economic importance of cattle infertility on a world wide basis has been considered by Frank. Artificial insemination, increased productivity of cows, higher costs of raising and feeding cows, and better education of the farmer and veterinarian all have served to emphasize the importance of maintaining the fertility and correcting infertility in dairy herds and individual cows.

The control of brucellosis by vaccination and testing, and vibriosis and trichomoniasis by AI, and vibriosis with antibiotic-treated semen and vaccination of cows has largely controlled the severe problem of contagious genital infections but has focused attention on other causes of abortion and infertility. The increased movement of purebred cattle between states and herds has occasionally resulted in the introduction of some infectious venereal disease that will seriously affect the herd's fertility. The widespread use of hormones as aids or cures in treating certain sterility problems has been recognized. With larger herds and greater mechanization of farms, management problems of handling cattle, detecting estrus for artificial insemination, maintenance of records, and nutritional problems are becoming increasingly important. With more veterinarians taking an active interest in this field many farmers are coming to realize the value of the routine preventive health practices of pregnancy and infertility examinations in maintaining good productive and reproductive levels in a herd.

A well-managed dairy herd should have 65 to 70 percent of the cows conceive on first service with an average of 1.3 to 1.7 services per conception There should be less than 10 percent of the cows with reproductive "problems". The calving interval from one calving to the next should be between 12 and 13 months. It has been reported that for every day a cow has failed to conceive beyond 90 to 100 days it is costing the farmer 50 to 75 cents. Thus in a poorly-managed herd of 100 cows with a calving interval of over 13 months for every 30 days reduction in the calving interval the farmer would realize an increase in income of $1,000 to $3,000 per year, Louca and Legates, Speicher and Meadows. Even in high-producing cows it is necessary to maintain this 12 to 13 month calving interval because in the cow's lifetime there would be more peaks of high production and a greater total production of milk. Furthermore with longer calving intervals the cow is more likely to freshen at the time of year when prices for milk are the lowest and there is a greater chance for culling the cow for economic reasons. Since 95 percent of the variation in calving intervals or breeding efficiency is due to nongenetic reasons, the importance of management and veterinary supervision of the reproductive activities in the herd is obvious, Van Vleck and Everett et al..

There is no such thing as a normal infertile cow. Either there is a clinical or nonclinical pathologic cause or the animal has not been properly exposed to fertile semen. In the next section will be a discussion of the reproductive physiology of the bovine animal. This is essential to the understanding of the pathologic causes of infertility and for the devising of management practices that will promote a high level of fecundity.

Bovine Reproductive Physiology

The bovine estrous cycle—The cow is polyestrous and comes in estrum throughout the year. The estrous cycle length in heifers is an average of 20 days with 85 percent of the heifers having cycles of 18 to 22 days. In cows the average length of the estrous cycle is 21 days and 84 percent of the cows have cycles of 18 to 24 days, Asdell. The individuality of the animal may affect the cycle length, but the season has no effect on cycle length. In beef cattle the average length of the estrous cycle is 20 days; 79 percent of the cattle have cycles of 17 to 23 days. According to Asdell, the duration of estrum, or heat, was an average of 13.6 hours. In a later report Asdell stated that 83 percent of the heifers had estrous periods within the range of 10 to 21 hours in length while 93 percent of the cows fell within the range of 13 to 27 hours. Bearden and Hansel and Tanabe and Almquist reported that the average duration of estrum was more nearly 18 than 14 hours. Ovulation is spontaneous and occurs an average of 10.5 to 15.5 hours, average 12 hours, after the end of estrum. This range of time varies from 2 to 26 hours. Heifers tend to ovulate in about 3 hours less time than do cows. About 80 percent of the ovulations occur from 4 P.M. to 4 A.M., Asdell.

In Zebu and crossbred Zebu cattle the length of estrum is short, 4.7 hours and 7.4 hours, respectively, Anderson, Donaldson and Plasse et al.. Zebu cows tend to associate with the bull for a longer period however; with many of the cattle exhibiting estrum during the night and early morning hours, Rollinson. The average duration of estrum in dairy or beef cattle in hot tropical countries and states is shorter, 12 to 13 hours, than in the temperate zone, Hall et al., Gangwar et al. and Donaldson et al.. **Bos indicus,** Zebu or Indian cattle, or their crosses are more heat tolerant, and have a higher fertility in spring, summer and fall months in the countries near the equator, Brody. They tend to be less fertile in the winter months. They seldom come into estrum while nursing their young, possibly for nutritional reasons, Donaldson. They do not moo or bellow but grunt. Zebu or Indian cattle have a great ability to digest crude fiber, Phillips. Their gestation periods vary from 271 to 310 days, average 293 days, Plasse et al.. European cattle, **Bos taurus** or cattle of the temperate zone are less adapted to hot climates.

About 60 percent of the ovulations occur on the right ovary. Neilsen reported that in 5970 pregnancy examinations in cows, 59.2 percent were pregnant in the right horn and 40.8 percent in the left. Of 4290 heifers, 54.4 percent were pregnant in the right horn and 45.6 percent in the left horn. The conceptus, except in rare instances, is located in the horn adjacent to the ovary containing the corpus luteum of pregnancy.

Manual removal of the corpus luteum, which is only possible in cattle, produced estrum in 3 to 5 days, the average time being 4.2 days, Asdell. According to Bonelli, in over 300 Herefords in which the corpus luteum was expressed manually about equal numbers came into estrum on each day from 2 to 7 days. In the author's experience, most cattle show estrum the third day after removal of the corpus luteum and if external symptoms of estrum are not observed, the animal should be inseminated or bred late on the third day or on the fourth day.

The symptoms of estrum in the cow are characterized by a great amount of homosexual behavior. Fraser, Fox, and Hafez have described normal and abnormal behavior patterns in cattle. The objective study of the meaning of animal movements or behavior is called veterinary ethology. According to Asdell, the amount of sexual activity is generally related to the amount of estrogen present but in a few ovariectomized animals large doses of estrogen failed to produce symptoms of estrum possibly due to a lack of progesterone since the latter is synergistic with estrogens in producing signs of estrum, Melampy et al.. There are great differences in individuals in the intensity of estrous symptoms exhibited. Heifers usually exhibit more marked symptoms of estrum than do cows. When artificial insemination is practiced and a bull does not run with the herd, careful observation of cows by the owner or herdsman twice a day or more often is essential for the maintenance of a satisfactory breeding program. Roark and Herman reported that the onset of estrum was gradual over a period of several to 24 hours in 66 percent of the cows and heifers, and abrupt in 34 percent. Animals in the "coming in" stage of estrum were often restless, raised and twitched their tails, discharged some milky-colored mucus from the vulva and often associated with a larger or more aggressive cow. This "coming in" stage was more noticeable in heifers.

The cow in estrum is usually restless and often remains standing rather than lying down. The appetite, ruminations, and milk yield may be slightly decreased. Bellowing is frequent especially if the cow is separated from the herd. The cow in estrum will attempt to mount other cows and will stand to be mounted by other cows. Roark and Herman reported that although the vulva of the cow in estrum was sniffed by other cows, the cow in estrum was never observed to sniff the external genitals of the other cattle. The homosexual behavior of the cow in estrum was always more intense than that of its partners. This latter symptom is of greatest significance. The tail may be raised and there is often a long string of clear mucus hanging from the vulva or present on the tail or buttocks. The vulva is usually somewhat congested, flaccid, edematous, and relaxed. The cow in a stanchion tends to hold her head high and has an alert, interested, even inquisitive, attitude. The cow may urinate frequently. Rahlmans and Meade reviewed the literature and reported that 3 to 6 percent of cows, with occasional reports as high as 14 to 18 percent of cows, Hall et al., and Erb et al., showed signs of estrum after conception. This occurred most often the first trimester of the gestation period over a range 11 to 213 days with a mean of 63 days.

On vaginal examination the vaginal mucosa, especially

the cranial portion, is congested and slightly edematous. The large amount of stringy mucus, 50 to 100 ml., present in the vagina at estrum comes from the vagina and cervical mucous cells under the influence of estradiol, Marinov and Lovell. At the time of estrum the viscosity of the mucus is lowest, and its flow elasticity greatest. When estrous mucus is smeared thinly on a slide and dryed the high salt or NaCl content crystallizes into a fern or arborization pattern. The external os of the cervical canal is usually pink, congested, edematous, and slightly relaxed and open at the time of estrum. The cow in estrum seldom objects to and usually stands well for a vaginal examination. The vaginal speculum slips in easily due to the viscid mucus present in the vagina. Vaginal smears during proestrum and estrum show increased numbers of cornified cells, but variations between cows are so great that the vaginal smear in the cow cannot be regarded as a reliable indication of estrum. Asdell reported a sudden marked increase in the leukocyte content of the mucus about 3 hours after breeding. This is probably due to the presence of semen in the genital tract. During diestrum the vagina is pale and dry and the mucus is scant and rather sticky. The speculum therefore passes with greater difficulty than during estrum.

On rectal examination during estrum and for 1 to 2 days before and afterwards, the uterus is usually erect, turgid, and somewhat edematous due to the estrogenic stimulation of the uterine muscle and tissues. This is most noticeable in heifers. Usually 1 to 5 smaller follicles start development but undergo atresia during estrum and after ovulation. On rectal palpation early in estrum the ovarian follicle is about 0.5 inch in diameter or less, and smooth, convex, tense and slightly fluctuating due to the follicular fluid present. This fluid is amber in color. The maturing Graafian follicle before rupture is 16 to 19 mm, 1.5 to 2 cm, or about 0.6 to 0.8 of an inch in diameter. At the time of ovulation in the cow only a slight amount of bleeding occurs at the rupture site.

The corpus luteum develops rapidly from the granulosa cells of the collapsed follicle under the tropic influence of LH from the pituitary gland. Granulosa cells do not divide but increase in size to 25 to 30 microns in diameter to form the mature corpus luteum, Asdell. By 48 hours after ovulation the corpus luteum is about 1.5 cm. in diameter and slightly crepitant on palpation per rectum. The cells of the theca interna also enlarge and contribute to the corpus luteum. By 7 to 8 days after ovulation the corpus luteum has reached its maximum size of 2 to 2.5 cm or 0.8 to 1 inch in diameter. The corpus luteum in the cow is irregular in shape, usually oval, and with a cone-like projection about 1/2 to 1 cm above the surface of the ovary. The corpus luteum of estrum weighs from 4.1 to 7.4 grams, Benesch and Wright, and is nearly similar in size and weight to the corpus luteum of pregnancy. The corpus luteum of pregnancy decreases in size just before parturition but may be palpable for many months as the corpus albicans, a small fibrous structure, on the ovary. The mature corpus luteum is brownish yellow to yellow orange in color, giving it the common name of "yellow body." Benesch and Wright reported that in about 25 percent of the corpora lutea they examined there is a small cavity about 0.4 cm or 0.166 inch in diameter. They also reported observing in a few cases large cavities 1 cm or more in diameter, filled with an amber fluid that Asdell believed was lymph. These corpora lutea containing large cavities are spoken of as cystic corpora lutea. Cystic corpora lutea have never been observed in a cow in the last third or half of the gestation period, Jubb and McEntee. Graafian follicles that failed to ovulate but became partially luteinized are called luteal cysts. These pathologic luteal cysts have a smooth convex surface due to the thick-walled fluid-filled follicle that failed to ovulate. While the cystic corpora lutea follows a normal ovulation and although it contains a variable amount of fluid in its center, lutein tissue protuding through the site of ovulation produces an irregular, raised area on the surface of the ovary, Benesch and Wright. Normal corpora lutea are irregular in outline and have a liver-like consistency. Cystic corpora lutea are similar to normal corpora lutea on palpation except they are usually larger, more spherical and fluctuate on pressure. The cystic corpora luteum is not considered to be pathological but the luteal cyst is pathological. The corpus luteum maintains its size until about 48 hours before estrum, after which time its size diminishes rapidly. Its color at this time of rapid involution is light orange to yellow. By 48 hours after this estrum its size is about 1 cm and by about 10 days after this estrum 0.5 cm, Benesch and Wright. As it becomes older its color turns to dark orange and then brick red. This eventually becomes a small white fibrous area the size of a large pin head, the corpus albicans. On rectal palpation, when one ovary is definitely larger than the other the difference is usually due to the presence of a corpus luteum in that ovary. Cysts may also cause this discrepancy in size.

Wrenn et al. reported that in cows, body temperatures taken deep in the vagina were lowest just before estrus, high on the day of estrus due to the cow's activity, low at the time of ovulation and high during the luteal phase of the cycle as in women. These authors as well as Bane and Rajakoski, and Howes et al. showed that determining body temperature changes, the glucose content, or the arborization or fern pattern of cervical mucus were not practical tests for indicating estrus or heat and the time to breed cattle. Direct visualization of the ovaries of cattle during the estrous cycle by endoscopic methods has been reported upon by Megale and Baker. The fluids present in the female bovine genital tract during the estrous cycle were reviewed by Olds et al.. Estrogens stimulated the deposition of glycogen in the surface endometrium of the uterus but its release was influenced by progesterone.

About 15 to 36 hours after ovulation, about 24 to 48 hours after estrum, or about 40 to 60 hours after the onset of estrum the discharge of blood and mucus from the vulva may occur in many cows. This metrorrhagia from the edematous endometrium in the caruncular areas occurs due to a breakdown of congested capillaries. Weber, Morgan and McNutt stated that although clinical evidence of bleeding occurred in only 55 of 68 heifers they studied, all showed the presence of red blood cells on examination of vaginal swabbings at this time. Asdell reported that metrorrhagia in cattle was observed in about 75 percent of heifers, and 48 percent of cows. In any particular animal clinical bleeding may not be observed following every estrum.

It is a common belief amongst some farmers and herdsmen that postestrual bleeding following service is an indication that conception did not occur. Trimberger reported that in 100 heifers that were bred, 81 showed clinical postestrual bleeding. Eighty-five percent of those that conceived bled, and of those that did not conceive, 74 percent bled. In another group of 100 cows, 61 bled and 69 percent of those that conceived bled, and of those failing to conceive, 39 percent showed metrorrhagia. This metrorrhagia that occurs in cattle is not similar to menstruation in primates, as it occurs at the end of the estrogenic phase of the cycle or early metestrum, following estrogen withdrawal. While in primates bleeding occurs at the end of the luteal phase of the cycle or the end of diestrum, following progesterone withdrawal, Hansel and Asdell. By using the benzidine test for occult blood in vaginal mucus, Bromberg and Bercovici reported that 94 percent of ovulating women showed intermenstrual bleeding. Weber, Morgan, and McNutt reported the common occurrence of small perimetrial hemorrhages in the subserosa of heifers' uteri observable from estrum to the fourth day postestrum. Hemorrhages of this nature were not observed in pluriparous cows.

Optimal service time—Trimberger and Davis have shown that insemination of cattle between 8 to 24 hours, or especially 7 to 18 hours, before ovulation results in the highest rates of conception. Ovulation should occur in heifers in the temperate zone about 22 to 36 hours after the onset of estrum. Conception rates were still better than 50 percent from service more than 24 hours before ovulation, if the cow was in estrum to within 6 hours of ovulation. Dukes reported similar figures to show that conception rates of 50 percent or better occur from soon after the onset of estrum to about 6 hours after the end of estrum. Conception rates drop rapidly in cows bred after ovulation or after 10 to 18 hours after the end of estrum, Trimberger and Davis, Dukes, and Casida. According to Bearden and Hansel and Trimberger and Davis, conception rates of cows inseminated about 10 hours after the onset of estrum was about 82 percent; at 20 hours after the onset of estrum or soon after going out of estrum 62 percent; by 30 hours after the onset of estrum or at or near the expected ovulation time, the conception rate was about 28 percent. This rate dropped rapidly so that by 50 to 60 hours after the onset of estrum very few cows conceived. However, Larson and Bayley and Autrup and Raspech reported a conception rate of 20 to 30 percent if cattle were inseminated while they were showing metrorrhagia and a bloody mucus discharge. Delayed ovulation reported in 31 percent of 58 cows studied by Hancock may account for some of these conceptions in cows bred 12 to 24 or more hours after estrum. Based on the above data, the best time for insemination is from just before the middle of estrum to 6 hours after estrum.

VanDemark stated that although the possibility of conception may be somewhat less in cows with shorter—or longer-than-normal cycles of 17 to 25 days, many of those cows do settle when they are bred. If this practice is followed, the problem cows could be examined and treated if necessary.

VanDemark concluded from a review of the literature that intravaginal deposition of semen in artificial insemination gives poor conception rates because of the small amounts deposited and he discouraged the use of this site as impractical for artificial insemination. The rectovaginal technique for introducing semen into the cervix was superior to the speculum technique with about a 16 percent better conception rate. He reported, that the deposition of semen in the cervical canal gave equally as good results as semen deposited in the uterine body or horns and that the technique was simpler. Because the endometrium is easily injured, and infection and occasional abortion may result from intrauterine deposition of semen in pregnant cows, and since about 3.5 to 6 percent of pregnant cows show estrum, VanDemark and others have recommended that cervical deposition be used instead of the uterine deposition of semen.

Hormones of the Estrous Cycle—The level of hormones in cattle, with the possible exception of LH, are very low in comparison to other domestic animals. In recent years highly sophisticated assay techniques have been devised that have further delineated the hormonal control of the estrous cycle in cattle. The subject of hormone levels in the reproductive endocrine glands and the blood plasma at different stages of the estrous cycle and during pregnancy was recently reviewed by Hansel and Snook. Hypothalamic luteinizing releasing factor was elevated in the hypothalamus from days 20 through day 7 and depressed days 11 to 18 of the cycle. The period of depression coincided with the period of maximum progesterone secretion. Pituitary FSH declined from a maximum of 450 ug on day 18 to a minimum of 122 ug at estrum. Pituitary LH decreased from 6178 ug on day 20 of the cycle to 684 ug on day 2 of the next cycle, Hackett and Hafs. Fietta et al. reported that the peak LH level in the blood, 20.8 ug/100 ml, occurred 3 to 9 hours after the onset of estrum or 14 to 20 hours prior to ovulation. Serum LH was greatly elevated for about 6 hours from about 8 hours before to 6 hours after the first signs of estrus. Heifers ovulated about 30 hours, 24 to 36 hours, after peak serum LH level or the onset of estrus, Swanson and Hafs.

The level of blood estrogens were highest on days 6 to 8 and 14 to 16 of the cycle and lowest on days 10 to 12. Estradiol secretion in the urine was highest on days 1 to 4 postestrus and estrone secretion was highest on days 6 to 12. The highest total urinary estrogen excretion rate was days 6 to 8 and 18 to 20 days of the cycle, Varman et al.. Estrogen levels in the blood plasma were highest from 2 days before to 1 day after estrus with secondary peaks at days 5 and 6 and 11 to 13 of the bovine estrus cycle, Garverick et al.. Although estrogen apparently stimulates the release of LH in the ewe, it is doubtful that estrogen stimulates release of LH in the cow, Wilkes. Progesterone and estradiol were in highest concentration in bovine follicular fluids of the various progestational and estrogenic compounds found there, Short.

The corpus luteum contains over 90 percent of the progestins present in both ovaries. The total progestins in the corpus luteum increased from 14.2 mg on day 3 to 107.5 mg on day 7 to 267.2 mg on day 15 and then declined rapidly to 33.2 mg on day 17, Mares et al.. This paralleled the blood plasma levels of progesterone and the weight of the corpus luteum which was 0.79 gms on day 3, 3.6 gms on day 7, 6.7 gms on day 15, 4.3 gms on day 16 and 1.8 gms on day 20, Gomes and Erb, Gomes et al. and Plotka et al.. Progesterone in the cow may also be produced in small amounts in the adrenal and placenta. Pope and Gupta reported on the progesterone levels in the plasma from the jugular vein. In the last month of pregnancy levels varied from 2.5 to 7.5 ng/ml, falling to 0.5 to 3.0 ng/ml at calving. During normal estrous cycles progesterone levels reached a peak at midcycle of 7 to 14 ng/ml and were lowest at the 4 to 6 days around estrum and ovulation, 1 to 2 ng/ml. If conception occurred plasma levels of progesterone remained high during pregnancy. Levels in 2 ovariectomized cows were 1.0 ng/ml; this was probably due to the progesterone produced by the adrenals. The half-life of progesterone in the blood in cattle was short, about 10 to 20 minutes, indicating the need during the estrous cycle and pregnancy for a continuous large supply, Imori. Staples and Hansel demonstrated that normal corpora lutea in pregnant heifers at 15 days after insemination contained an average of 270 mg total progesterone and no pregnant heifers had less than 100 mg which was the minimum necessary for embryo survival. It is interesting to note that plasma levels of progesterone decline precipitously between days 16 and 19 of the bovine estrous cycle and within 48 hours of parturition and the corpus luteum greatly decreases in size at the same periods, Hansel and Snook.

Melampy and coworkers reported that in ovariectomized cows conditioned with 0.2 to 0.4 mg of estradiol/1000 lbs that 1 to 4 mg of progesterone would produce maximal synergistic action with the production of typical estrum lasting 6 to 12 hours. Both of these hormones necessary for typical expression of estrus are produced in the ovary during the preovulatory development of the follicle. The CL from the previous cycle contains measurable progesterone for several days after estrus, Gomes and Erb. Large doses of progesterone 30 to 60 mg antagonized or prevented estrous behavior in estrogen-treated ovariectomized cattle.

Puberty and the onset of estrous cycles—As discussed previously placing young heifers on a nutritious diet high in TDN from birth can hasten puberty and the onset of estrous cycles. This can also permit heifers to be bred successfully at a younger age if they are continued to be fed well during the first gestation period. Breeding heifers on the basis of body weight is therefore indicated, so that heifers can calve at about 2 years of age without serious calving problems. Crossbred heifers tend to show estrus a month or so earlier in life than the parent breeds. Depending on the level of nutritional intake, heifers first show estrus from 7 to 18 months or 28 to 72 weeks of age. Morrow reported that in 53 Holstein heifers the time after birth at which first estrus occurred was more variable than the weight which averaged 42 weeks and 610 lbs., respectively. During the prepuberal period most heifers had one or more follicles with a diameter of 0.5 to 2 cm and showed evidence of increased follicular activity about 20 to 40 days before the first ovulation. Variable signs of estrus were observed at these times. At the first estrus 74 percent of the heifers exhibited silent estrus or failed to show signs of estrus. This percentage dropped to 43 percent the second estrus and to 21 percent the third estrus. Thereafter the estrous periods were normal. Ovulation failed to occur in 13 percent of 53 heifers after the first estrus but thereafter failure of ovulation was rare, Morrow. Nearly similar results were reported by Morrow et al. in 37 Holstein heifers in a similar study.

The pituitary levels of FSH and LH from birth to puberty were determined by Desjardins and Hafs. They reported, as occurred in cows, that the level of LH in the pituitary gland dropped markedly at estrus while the level of FSH decreased less markedly but somewhat before that of LH.

The postpartum period and the onset of estrous cycles—Morrow et al. recently reviewed the literature on postpartum ovarian activity and uterine involution and reported the interval from parturition to first observed estrum varied from 30 to 76 days in dairy cattle and 40 to 48 days in beef cattle. The time required for uterine involution based on rectal palpations and clinical observations and measurements varied from 26 to 52 days in dairy cattle and 38 to 56 days in beef cattle. In general the interval from calving to first estrus was greater in cows with higher production, in cows nursing calves or being milked 4 times a day, in cows on a poor or low level of nutritive intake, and in older pluriparous cows with 4 or more parturitions, Saiduddin et al. and Wagner and Hansel. The latter authors also showed that a longer postpartum interval to first estrum occurred in nursed dairy cows, anemic cows and in those being fed thyroprotein.

This relationship of nursing and the delayed onset of estrous cycles after calving was studied by Wiltbank and Cook and they theorized that suckling reduced the supply or the release of gonadotropic hormones. Wagner and Hansel's report indicated that sufficient FSH was present but LH was apparently deficient.

Involution of the uterus was prolonged in pluriparous cows when compared to primiparous cattle and also in abnormal parturitions characterized by dystocia, retained placenta, twinning, metritis and etc. Marion et al. reported that ovariectomy and physiologic doses of estradiol had no effect on uterine involution but progesterone delayed uterine regression. However, Foote and Hunter reported that progesterone and estradiol somewhat shortened the intervals to ovulation and conception. Thus uterine involution proceeds normally even if reproductive cycles and estrus do not occur. Exogenous estrogens or progesterone, ovariectomy, or nursing calves have little or no effect on the rate of uterine involution, Stabenfeldt. Wagner and Hansel confirmed earlier studies reporting the sloughing of caruncular tissue between days 7 and 14 postpartum and the regeneration of surface epithelium over the caruncles which was completed by day 30.

Morrow's review also revealed a high incidence of silent estrous periods associated with ovulation in the postpartum period. In more careful studies, Morrow et al., Wagner and Hansel, and Marion and Gier reported that normal cows usually develop a mature follicle that ovulates and is followed by the formation of a corpus luteum at 13 to 15 days after calving. The duration of the estrous cycle from the first ovulation to the second ovulation was 3 to 4 days shorter than the normal length, 20 to 21 day, cycles that followed thereafter. Silent estrus occurred in 77 percent of the first postpartum ovulations, 54 percent of the second and 36 percent of the third ovulations, and was more common in high-producing cows, Morrow et al.. Cystic corpora lutea and cystic follicles were fairly common and a failure of ovulation occurred occasionally in up to 10 percent of the cycles, Casida. Marion and Gier reported that 90 percent of the first corpora lutea formed within 15 days after calving formed on the ovary opposite to the previously gravid horn; this percentage dropped to 60 percent in cows ovulating 15 to 20 days after parturition. This latter figure agrees with Morrow et al. but is slightly lower than that cited by Saiduddin et al..

During pregnancy there is a decrease in follicular activity due to the inhibition of gonadotropic activity by high levels of progesterone and estrogen. By parturition there appears to be appreciable storage of FSH in the pituitary gland and after parturition and the withdrawal of progesterone and estrogen there is a rapid build-up of LH, Morrow et al., Labhsetwar et al, Saiduddin et al. and Casida. The corpus luteum of pregnancy had regressed at 4 days postpartum to 1 x 1.5 cm in size and was usually not palpable after 14 days postpartum. Thus the corpus luteum of estrus does not persist into the postpartum period as reported by many earlier workers on bovine infertility.

Since Morrow et al., Wagner and Hansel and others have reported that uterine involution in normal cows is largely completed as indicated by the size of the uterus and the condition of the endometrium at about 30 days postpartum and since normal estrous cycles are usually occurring by 30 days after calving, it is logical to ask whether it might not be feasible and practical to commence breeding a month before the generally recommended minimal time of 60 days postpartum. Trimberger (1954) has summarized the previous literature on the subject and in a controlled experiment further demonstrated that breeding cows 60 days or less after parturition was a poor practice and probably should be discouraged. In 50 cows bred 60 days or less after parturition the conception rate on first service was 48 percent as compared to 70 and 76 percent in cows bred 60 to 90 days and over 90 days after parturition, respectively. In cows bred 50 days or less the conception rate was 30.8 percent. It was noted, however, that the cows bred less than 60 days after parturition, but after one normal estrum, had a much higher conception rate than those bred on the first estrum. In three groups of cows, those bred less than 60 days, those bred 61 to 90 days, and those bred over 90 days after parturition the number of services per conception in fertile cows was 2.52, 1.55, and 1.54, respectively. The average number of days from parturition to conception in these three groups was 100.5, 74.5, and 93.8 days, respectively, even though the former group had their first service an average of 40.9 days after parturition. Hofstad observed that cows bred less than 60 days after parturition had a higher incidence of retained placenta, metritis, and abortion than those cows bred after 60 days. Olds (1969) reported that abortions, infertility, or delayed returns were not associated with breeding at 35 days or less post calving. In his study he indicated that on the average for each 10 days that a cow was bred sooner after calving the calving interval was shortened by 8.8 days and this was true even for cows bred less than 40 days. Olds and Cooper recommended that cows be bred starting at 40 instead of 60 days postpartum. Since this would increase the mean number of services only about 0.08 percent, the mean time from breeding to conception would only be increased 5 days and the mean calving intervals could be shortened 15 days. Shannon et al. reported on 70 to 71 cows bred artificially without antibiotics in the semen at different intervals after calving with the following results in fertile cows:

Days after Parturition	Percent Non-returns to 1st Service
1 - 20	20.8
21 - 40	37.7
41 - 50	48.7
51 - 60	52.5
61 - 80	51.2
81 - 100	51.5
101 - 120	54.6
121 - 140	50.7
141 and over	57.8

In small numbers of cows Graves et al. reported that 14 percent conceived between 11 and 20 days after calving, 40 percent from 21 to 50 days and 60 percent from 51 to 90 days. Fertility appeared greater in cows bred after 74 days postpartum. Morrow et al. reported a 40 percent conception rate on first service in normal cows bred 45 to 60 days postpartum. This percentage rose to near 60 percent for the period of 61 to 105 days postpartum and about 65 percent for cows bred 106 to 135 days. The Milk Marketing Board in England reported in 1967 on 7000 cows that were inseminated for the 1st time prior to 31 days postpartum had a nonreturn rate of 40 percent, from 32 to 52 days a 52 percent nonreturn rate, 53 to 73 days a 60 percent nonreturn rate and over this period a 65 to 70 percent nonreturn rate. Boyd and Reed reported similarly on artificial insemination of dairy cattle in which there was a 39.5 percent conception rate on first service in cows bred under 40 days postpartum, 51.2 percent conception for cows bred from 41 to 50 days, a 59.4 percent for cows bred from 51 to 60 days and a 63.7 percent for cows bred 61 to 90 days postpartum.

Thus in cows bred prior to 50 to 60 days postpartum there was a lower conception rate on first service which was associated with a larger number of services per conception and a shorter calving interval. Breeding normal cows prior to 50 to 60 days would increase the cost of artificial insemination because of more repeat services but in selected cases this might be desirable if the farmer recognized that lower conception rates are to be expected. Further study is needed on larger numbers of cows free of genital diseases such as vibriosis and evidence of metritis to evaluate the possible hazards or benefits of early postpartum breeding in cattle.

Erb and Ehlers and Trimberger reported that conception rates for estrous cycles of less than 18 days in length were poor, about 34 percent, in normal cows not bred at the previous estrus. Van Vleck, Belling and others have reported increased calving intervals or infertility in dairy and beef cattle after they reached 5 years of age or after their fourth lactation period.

Physiologic utero-pituitary-ovarian relationships—The corpus luteum, follicle, and the placenta are the only three transitory endocrine glands. The understanding of the mechanisms controlling the formation and involution of the corpus luteum is essential. The corpus luteum is present and active in the fertile cow for about 320 days a year. It only involutes long enough in the normal cow to permit a follicle to mature and ovulate in order to perpetuate the species. The presence of a functioning corpus luteum on the ovary is of much more significance than various stages of follicular development or atresia.

Although more work is required to explain certain aspects of the utero-pituitary-ovarian relationships, Ginther's review (1968) competently outlines the major aspects of this relationship at the present time and in so doing, it encompasses most of the significant advances in physiology and endocrinology in cattle in recent years. (See Stabenfeldt) It is generally accepted that LH which is the principal luteotropic hormone in the cow, Simmons and Hansel, is released from the anterior pituitary gland to produce ovulation; corpus luteum formation from the granulosa and thecal cells; corpus luteum persistence; and secretion of progesterone necessary for suppression of follicle growth, early embryonic growth, development and attachment, and for the maintenance of normal pregnancy. The presence of the embryo with its elongated trophoblast is necessary by about the 14th day of the cycle to prevent the involution of the corpus luteum which starts, in the absence of the embryo, about the 15th to 16th day of the cycle. The process causing the regression or involution of the corpus luteum to permit follicle development is called the **luteolytic mechanism.** This mechanism is rather complicated to explain at the present time, probably because the luteolytic "factor" in the uterine endometrium or endometrial glands which is the "key" to the mechanism has not yet been definitely isolated and defined. The luteolysin theory still requires further proof, Stabenfeldt. (See Hansel in Infertility in the Ewe).

Based on substantial, but indirect evidence Ginther postulated that the uterine luteolytic mechanism or substance exerted its involuting effects on the corpus luteum by 1) a systemic, probably humoral, utero-pituitary-ovarian pathway resulting in a decrease or cessation of LH production and release from the anterior pituitary gland that was probably mediated through the hypothalamus and 2) a local or unilateral utero-ovarian pathway, possibly by means of the lymphatics, from the uterine horn to the ovary on that side. This substance that promotes luteal regression directly by its local action on luteal tissue and indirectly by its effect on the hypothalamus and pituitary gland to reduce the level of circulating LH is produced by the endometrium of the uterus and has been called "uterine luteolysin". Active investigation is progressing in a number of centers to find and isolate this luteolytic substance with promising results, Williams et al.. It apparently is a high molecular weight protein that is related to but distinct from prostaglandin and has the ability to bind both estrogens and progesterone, Hansel. This luteolytic substance acts through both of the above pathways to cause prompt regression of the corpus luteum. The indirect evidence for this theory cited by Ginther and others is as follows:

(1) The corpus luteum persists if an embryo is in the uterus. Removal of embryos before the 12th day of the cycle in sheep results in luteal regression, Moor and Rowson. Later in pregnancy in some species other mechanisms promote pregnancy such as the production of placental luteotropins in humans and placental progesterone in mares and sheep. If the pituitary gland is removed during pregnancy the corpus luteum regresses. Thus pregnancy inhibits the systemic pathway of the uterine luteolytic mechanism by preventing a decrease in circulating LH. In sheep and cattle the embryo can inhibit the local luteolytic mechanism in both uterine horns, probably because of the elongated trophoblast, so that the CL will persist even if the embryo proper is in the opposite horn from the ovary containing the CL.

(2) Hysterectomy greatly prolongs the life of the corpus luteum to about that of the duration of a normal pregnancy or longer. If one-fourth of each uterine horn is left in the cow and three-quarters of the uterus is removed, regression of the CL and normal estrous cycles occur. If the cow is hysterectomized and the CL is removed, estrus and ovulation occur and a new CL is formed that also persists. Thus the uterine luteolytic substance influences the regression not the formation of the CL. If the pituitary gland was removed in hysterectomized sheep the CL involuted but if luteotropic hormones were given after hypophysectomy the CL persisted. Antiserum against bovine LH caused partial regression of the CL in hysterectomized cows. In unilateral hysterectomized cattle the corpus luteum persists resulting in a delayed estrus only when the remaining horn is opposite to the ovary containing the CL. Thus the local as well as the systemic pathways are involved in the luteolytic mechanism.

(3) Exogenous daily subcutaneous injections in heifers of 0.33 units/kg body weight or about 100 units of oxytocin on days 2 through 6 with days 4 and 5 being the most critical, Brunner et al, or 100 mg of progesterone for 10 days, starting on the day after estrus, resulted in a failure of the corpus luteum to develop with an early return to estrum at 10 to 14 days, Woody et al., and Wilkes. It takes two or three times the above dose of oxytocin to produce similar effects in a lactating cow. However in hysterectomized cattle this early regression of the CL did not occur when oxytocin was injected daily for the first week of the cycle. Thus the uterus plays a role in the effect of exogenous oxytocin and progesterone on the CL. Administering LH along with oxytocin resulted in normal CL growth. In fact HCG injections about the 3rd to 4th day of the cycle caused an increased size of the CL with an increased progesterone content over that found in the corpora lutea of normal heifers even though oxytocin was also administered, Donaldson et al.. The lutein cells of the CL come from the granulosa cells and the theca interna. The growth of the cells from the latter structure in response to LH or HCG is responsible for the growth of the CL in cattle after day 4 of the cycle, Donaldson and Hansel. Other work showed that oxytocin injections resulted in a decrease of circulating levels of LH and did not affect LH secretion. The luteolytic effects of exogenous progesterone probably also involve the pituitary gland. In unilaterally hysterectomized cattle the administration of exogenous oxytocin and progesterone caused a short

estrous cycle only when the retained horn was on the same side as the ovary containing the CL, Ginther. When borderline doses of oxytocin, 7 units per 100 lbs. of body weight daily for 14 days after insemination, were given subcutaneously, 18 to 43 heifers conceived and had normal corpora lutea. Ten treated heifers developed cystic corpora lutea and although two were pregnant the levels of progesterone in the cystic corpora lutea were generally low, Staples et al.. Recently Donaldson and Takken showed that doses of 2 units of oxytocin/100 lbs. of body weight daily for 6 days after estrum increased the progesterone content of corpora lutea while 6 and 18 units/100 lbs. inhibited CL function and decreased progesterone levels. Day 5 of the cycle was the critical day through which daily doses of oxytocin were needed to cause luteal inhibition, it was possible to reduce the time of injection to days 2 through 5.

(4) Intrauterine devices (IUD) or agents that act early in the cycle in a similar manner, shorten the estrous cycle to 14 days or less in cows and sheep due to the stimulation of the release of the luteolytic substance in the endometrium. Luteolytic effects with these agents in sows and women does not occur and the estrous cycle is uneffected by their presence. Some of these agents in cattle include: foreign material in the uterus such as rubber tubes or catheters, metal or plastic objects, Ginther et al., waterfilled balloons, and gel-like substances; irritating substances such as an iodine solution, Nakahara et al., IBR-IPV virus in semen, Kendrick and McEntee, and preputial smegma added to semen, Hansel and Wagner. In cattle and sheep the luteolytic effect of an IUD was overcome by the concurrent administration of LH. In cattle and sheep having an IUD in the horn adjacent to the ovary containing the CL, the estrous cycles were shorter than when the IUD was in the opposite horn from the ovary with the CL. Thus both systemic and local pathways were involved in early involution or inhibition of the CL.

(6) Miscellaneous naturally-occurring conditions such as pyometra, mummified or macerated fetuses, mucometra, and a congenital lack of endometrial glands in heifers result in the inhibition of the uterine luteolytic mechanism and the persistence of the CL with anestrus lasting for months. Delayed estrus may occur in cattle with a uterus unicornis if the CL forms in the ovary on the side of the missing horn. Intrauterine injections of escharotic agents or infectious organisms in the middle of the cycle or later apparently inhibit the release of the uterine luteolysin and cause a persistence of the CL. Ginther noted that mild irritation early in the cycle caused the early activation of the luteolytic mechanism and short cycles while a severe or prolonged process or one occurring late in a cycle might interfere with the activation of the luteolytic mechanism or even destroy the mechanism if the endometrium was severly damaged as for example in long-standing pyometra or mucometra.

Other associated endocrine phenomena related to the uterine luteolytic mechanism and uterine-pituitary-ovarian physiology include the following, Ginther. Exogenous estrogens, such as 5 mg estradiol valerate or injections of estradiol having a prolonged effect, given to cattle at midcycle caused early CL regression, Wiltbank et al, Brunner et al.. This is probably due to an interference with LH release since concurrent injections of gonadotropins prevent the regression of the CL. Exogenous estrogen is luteolytic and levels of FSH and LH that promote increased estrogen secretion might also promote luteolysis, Hansel and Snook. Brunner et al. reported that adrenocorticotrapin (ACTH) 100 units daily on days 2 through 8 of the cycle significantly reduced CL weight but was ineffective in hysterectomized cows. The effect of ACTH on the adrenal gland to produce corticosteroids that can cause abortion as well as on the uterine luteolytic mechanism to cause CL involution is noteworthy. An injection of LH in an adjuvant at midcycle or daily injections of HCG starting at day 15 prolonged the life of the CL and increased estrous cycle length in cattle, Wiltbank et al.. Although these injections of HCG caused accessory corpora lutea to develop, it had no effect on embryo survival. Embryos die first before regression of the CL. Ginther gave further evidence to show that the systemic and local pathways of the luteolytic mechanism function simultaneously to produce luteal involution. For example, blocking or removing the local pathway resulted in estrous cycles of longer than normal lengths. Thus, as expressed by Short, the CL can be "murdered" by the local effect of the uterine luteolysin on the CL; it can be "starved to death" by the removal of the tropic stimulus, LH, due to the systemic effect of uterine luteolysin on the hypothalmus and pituitary gland; or the CL can die of "old age" since the CL in each species has a finite life span.

The contraceptive effect of intrauterine devices in the uterus varies with the different species of animals, Hawk, Marston and Kelly. In ewes the IUD even when placed in only one horn interfered with the mechanism that carried spermatozoa to the oviduct and conception did not occur. In cows an IUD was needed in both horns to prevent conception by inhibiting fertilization and ovum survival. When an IUD was in only one horn conception could occur in the opposite horn if ovulation occurred on the ovary adjacent to the untreated horn. In sows the IUD does not prevent conception but interferes with the attachment of the embryos in the treated horn and in sows this is followed by the loss of the embryos in the nontreated horn also. In the water buffalo an IUD interferes with or prevents ovulation. The IUD is being used widely in women to prevent conception apparently by causing either failure of fertilization or too rapid transport of the ovum through the oviduct. The exact mechanism of action is not known.

Ginther reported on evidence linking the uterus to follicular activity as well as luteal activity. An IUD inhibited ovulation in water buffalos and possibly delayed ovulation in cattle, Marston and Kelly. The interval from parturition to the first postpartum ovulation is delayed in cows with poor involution of the uterus associated with metritis. Also the first ovulation after calving tends to occur on the side of the previously nongravid horn. This tendency decreases with longer intervals between calving and ovulation. The high incidence of cystic follicles associated with the postpartum period in cattle, may be due to uterine abnormalities or lesions, Morrow et al.. Intrauterine infusions used in anestrous mares may effect the endometrium and in some way stimulate follicular activity that commonly follows such therapy. There is some evidence that uterine stimulation in the cow may also effect FSH release.

Other endocrine effects—According to Asdell, DeAlba, and Roberts, 0.099 mg of estradiol or .25 mg of stilbestrol daily for 3 days in an ovariectomized heifer or cow will produce typical symptoms of estrum both clinically and on vaginal and rectal examination. Injections of a single dose of 40 mg of stilbestrol or 4 mg of estradiol or more may result in the production of cystic ovaries. Repeated daily injections at a lower level may also cause the same condition. In cattle high levels of estrogen may cause ovarian atrophy if cystic ovaries are not produced. Cystic changes may also be induced in the endometrium. Small or physiologic doses of estrogen stimulate the release of LH and promote ovulation when given just before estrum. The incidence of cystic ovaries may be high if estrogen is injected on the 15th to 16th days of the cycle due to the release of LH prior to its normal time of release at estrum, Cole. Injections of 50 to 100 mg of progesterone daily will suppress estrum but when the injections are stopped an increased incidence of cystic corpora lutea are reported. (See estrous synchronization.)

Thyroidectomized or parathyroidectomized cows were fertile and most could carry fetuses to term and rebreed. Low fertility associated with high environmental temperatures was not associated with depressed thyroxine secretion rates, Williams, and Stott. There was no evidence that feeding iodinated casein caused infertility, even after 2 years of continuous feeding, Wagner and Hansel. The thyroxine secretion rate in dairy cattle was 67 percent higher than in beef cattle, Pipes et al.. Adrenal function in relation to reproduction was reviewed by van Rensburg in relation to ovarian inactivity, cystic ovaries and prolonged or shortened gestations.

Synchronization of Estrous Cycles—Estrous synchronization or regulation of the estrous cycle whereby most of the cattle in a herd or portion of a herd could be brought into estrum at one time, especially in beef herds or in dairy heifers, would be highly desirable from a practical and economic standpoint where artificial insemination of the cattle to proven sires is desired. For such a procedure to be successful a high level of conception should be achieved on the synchronized ovulation.

The principal physiologic basis for estrous synchronization is the fact that progesterone produced by the corpus luteum suppresses LH release from the anterior pituitary gland and thus inhibits the maturation of Graafian follicles. Other methods of ovulation control such as manual removal of the corpus luteum which results in estrum and ovulation in about 3 to 5 days, range 2 to 7 days, daily injections of 100 units of oxytocin from days 2 to 6 of the cycle to shorten the cycle to 8 to 12 days, the use of estrogens with a prolonged effect to involute the corpus luteum and other techniques mentioned previously and cited by Hansel, are presently too cumbersome, impractical or dangerous to use as routine procedures.

Progesterone was first used by Ulberg, Christian, and Casida who reported that if started about 15 days after the end of estrum, 50 mg injections of progesterone in oil daily or 500 mg in "Repositol" form every 10 days would prevent estrus and ovulation in cows. Estrum occurred within 4 to 6 days, with an average of 5.2 days, after the injections were stopped. Trimberger and Hansel reported that in progesterone treatment with 50 to 100 mg daily from the fifteenth to the nineteenth days of the cycle, cows came into estrum an average of 4.6 days after treatment ceased. During the experimental injection period 16 of 30 cows showed early follicular development and some discharged mucus at the expected normal estrum but showed no external symptoms. Only 14 of 25 cows had normal periods of estrum after the injections were stopped; 4 had "silent" estrum; 4 had a long period of estrum, 33 to 52 hours; and 3 had long periods of 56 hours, 65 hours and 8 days between the end of estrum and ovulation. Of 24 cows bred, only 3 or 12.5 percent conceived on this controlled estrum after progesterone injections; at the next estrum 65 percent conceived. After the estrum following the progesterone injections, 15 of the 30 cows had normal corpora lutea, 8 had abnormally large corpora lutea, 4 had very large cystic corpora lutea, one had metestrual bleeding without ovulation followed by smooth ovaries, and 2 cows developed multiple follicles.

Other trials using various forms of injectable progesterone were reviewed by Lamond and Hansel but they were not satisfactory principally because of the low conception rate on the first synchronized estrus and the problems associated with repeated injections and the prolonged period over which the first ovulation occurred.

Oral progestational compounds—MAP, 6-methyl-17-acetoxyprogesterone, (Upjohn Co. "Repromix") was first evaluated in 1960, Hansel and Malven. Cows fed large doses, over 500 mg daily for 20 days, were synchronized but had only a 25 percent conception rate. As with progesterone injections, treated cows would have a normal involution of the corpora lutea but follicle formation and ovulation was suppressed during the treatment period. In 1963 **CAP,** 6-chloro-6-dihydro-17-acetoxyprogesterone, a more potent progestational agent was introduced. The minimal effective dose for MAP is 180 to 200 mg/day per animal fed once daily at the same time each day and for CAP is 10 mg/day per animal. Recently melengestrol acetate, **MGA** has been introduced. It is even more potent and 1 mg/day per animal in limited trials resulted in estrous cycle control, De Bois and Bierschwal, Darwash et al. and Rousel and Beatty. OHPA, dihydroxyprogesterone acetophenide, is another progestagen that can be used to synchronize estrous cycles in cattle, Wiltbank et al.. Only MAP is commercially available in the U.S.A. at this time. The optimal length of the hormone feeding period appears to be 18 days although some workers have suggested shorter periods of 10 to 14 days, Lamming and Amoroso. The conception rate on trials in dairy heifers and beef cattle with these products have resulted in conception rates of 20 to 70 percent on the first synchronized estrus which occurs 2 to 8 days after the end of the treatment period. Following treatment with MAP most cows were in estrus in 3 to 4 days; with CAP and MGA this interval was 2 to 3 days longer. In most cases the conception rates were 10 to 15 percent below those obtained in comparable untreated cattle bred artificially under similar conditions. Conception rates at the next or second estrus period after treatment, which occurs at the interval of about 21 days, are normal. Thus there is no prolonged effect from feeding these progestagens. De Bois and Bierschwal and Astrom and Bane showed that the time of the reproductive cycle, early, middle or late, when the feeding of progestional compounds were started had no effect on conception rates at the first synchronized estrus after treatment. Robinson, Hansel and Smith (1969) reported that the basic cause for lowered conception rates at this estrus was due to failure of fertilization caused by poor sperm-cell transport through the genital tract. Large numbers of spermatozoa placed in the genital tract at this estrus improved conception rates while minimal numbers depressed conception rates. There was no evidence that an estrus-ovulation time relationship was involved in this lowered conception rate. Of less significance was the report of Jainudeen and Hafez that the reduced fertility was due to poor transport of the fertilized ova or early embryonic deaths. Injecting oxytocin at the time of insemination did not improve the conception rates, Hansel.

If larger and older beef cows are to be treated the daily dose of MAP should be raised to 240 mg. In beef and dairy cows this product is incorporated into grain pellets and fed at a rate of about 4 lbs. per day. A common occurrence at the synchronized estrus was ovulation without signs of estrus. In trials reported by Hansel, MAP proved more reliable than CAP in producing synchronization and conception. The intramuscular or subcutanous injection of progestagens are unsatisfactory as they resulted in prolonged periods of anestrus extending in some cases for 6 months to 1 year. Problems administering progestagen pellets to beef cattle and dairy heifers running loose are greater than in stanchioned animals. Adequate bunk space and even distribution of pellets are needed so that each animal gets sufficient drug daily to suppress ovulation for the treatment period. Even missing a day can result in failure. Other management problems of adequate nutritive intake prior to and during the feeding period, careful observation for estrum, adequate facilities for insemination, properly trained inseminators using highly-fertile semen are all of great importance in producing satisfactory conception rates. The use of a progestagen intravaginally in impregnated sponges as in ewes is not satisfactory in cattle because they are often expelled from the vagina before the end of the treatment period, Hansel. Other methods of administration are being investigated.

Nonsteroidal oral drugs—No effective nonsteroid compound for estrus cycle regulation for ruminants has yet been reported. ICI-33828, 1-alpha methylally-thiocarbomayl-2 methylthiocarbamoylyhydrazine or methallibure will control estrous cycles in swine but it is not effective in cattle. Clomiphene or MRL4, an antiestrogen, was tried in cattle and it prevented estrus but synchronization did not follow the withdrawal of the agent. Clomiphene suppressed ovulation and interfered with LH release. Further work with this agent is indicated.

Some workers have investigated the use of estrogens to involute the CL early in a short, 8 to 10 day MAP feeding period, Wiltbank and Kasson. Estrogens have been tried without success following the normal treatment period of MAP to improve the percentage of synchronized animals exhibiting estrus. Graves and Dzuik reported that 500 IU of HCG given intramuscularly to cows 60 hours after the withdrawal of MAP resulted in ovulation about 40 hours later, insemination should be performed about 25 hours after the injection of HCG. Others have tried in limited experiments to utilize FSH at the end of the treatment period and LH several days later followed by a uniform period of about 12 to 24 hours before insemination to try to further improve the degree of synchronization and remove the need for detecting estrus. Results are interesting and promising but require further study and refinement to be practical. Cost factors and problems of multiple ovulation also are significant, Jainudeen and Hafez.

References on Bovine Infertility

Bovine Reproductive Physiology

Anderson, J. (1944) The Periodicity and Duration of Estrus in Zebu and Grade Cattle, J. Agric. Sc., **34,** 57.

Asdell, S. A. (1964) Patterns of Mammalian Reproduction, 2nd Ed., Comstock Publishing Co., Inc., Ithaca, N.Y.

Asdell, S. A. (1948) Sterility and Delayed Breeding in Dairy Cattle, Cornell Extension Bull. 737.

Asdell, S. A. (1955) Cattle Fertility and Sterility: Little, Brown and Co., Boston, Mass.

Asdell, S. A., DeAlba, J. and Roberts, S. J. (1945) The Levels of Ovarian Hormones Required to Induce Heat and Other Reactions in the Ovariectomized Cow, J. of An. Sci., **4,** 3, 277.

Astrom, G. and Bane, A. (1968) Heat Synchronization of Heifers with Norethisterone, Proc. VI Congr. Intern. Reprod. Anim. Insem. Artif. II, 1389.

Autrup, E. and Rasbech, N. O. (1951) Befrugtings Resultater ved Kunstig Inseminering med Tyresperma i den Poststrale Haemorrhagiske Period, Nord. Vet. Med. **3,** 40.

Baker, A. A. (1966) Studies on the Direct Visualization of the Bovine Ovaries Through a Retained Cannula in the Paralumbar Fossa, Univ. of Queensland Papers, Faculty of Vet. Sci. **I.** 4, 137, St. Lucia, Austral.

Bane, A. and Rajakoski, E. (1961) The Bovine Estrous Cycle, Cor. Vet. **51,** 77.

Bearden, J. and Hansel W. (1955) Personal Communication.

Benesch, F. and Wright, J. G. (1951) Veterinary Obstetrics, Williams and Wilkins Co., Baltimore, Md.

Belling, T. H. (1953) Reproduction Efficiency in the Hereford Cow, J.A.V.M.A. **142,** 5, 494.

Bonelli, B. (1947) Personal Communication.

Boyd, H. and Reed, H. C. B. (1961) Investigations into the Incidence and Causes of Infertility in Dairy Cattle—Influence of Some Management Factors affecting Semen and Insemination Conditions, Brit. Vet. Jour. **117,** 74.

Brody, S. (1956) Climatic Physiology of Cattle, J. Dairy Sci. **39,** 6, 715.

Bromberg, Y. M. and Bercovici, B. (1958) Benzidine Test for Detection of Uterine Bleeding at About the Time of Ovulation, Internat. J. of Fert. **3,** 1, 60.

Brunner, M. A., Donaldson, L. E. and Hansel, W. (1969) Exogenous Hormones and Luteal Function in Hysterectomized and Intact Heifers, J. Dairy Sci. **52,** 11, 1849.

Casida, L. E. (1950) The Repeat-Breeder Cow, Vlaams Diergeneesk. Tijdschr., **19,** 12, 273.

Casida, L. E. (1968) Studies on the Postpartum Cow, Res. Bull. 270, Research Division, Univ. of Wisc., 48.

Casida, L. E., Meyer, R. K., McShan, W. H. and Wisnicky, W. (1943) Effects of Pituitary Gonadotrophin on the Ovaries and the Induction of Superfecundity in Cattle, Am. J. Vet. Res., **4,** 10, 76.

Casida, L. E. and Venzke, W. G. (1936) Observations on Reproductive Processes in Dairy Cattle and Their Relationship to Breeding Efficiency, Proc. Amer. Soc. of An. Prod., 221.

Casida, L. E., Warwick, E. J. and Meyer, R. K. (1944) Survival of Multiple Pregnancies Induced in the Ewe Following Treatment with Pituitary Gonadotropins, J. of An. Sci., **3,** 22.

Cole, H. H. (1964) Gonadotropes—Their Clinical and Biological Properties and Secretion Control, W. H. Freeman Co., San Francisco.

Darwash, A. D., Marion, G. B. and Gier, H. T. (1965) Effects of Melengestrol Acetate on Bovine Reproductive Cycles, J. An. Sci. **24,** 3, 915 (Abstr.).

DeBois, C. H. W. and Bierschwal, C. J. Jr. (1970) A 14-Day Medication Period of Melengestrol Acetate to Control the Estrous Cycle of Dairy Cattle, Amer. J. Vet. Res. (In press).

Desjardins, C. and Hafs, H. D. (1968) Levels of Pituitary FSH and LH in Heifers from Birth through Puberty, J. An. Sci. **27,** 2, 472.

Donaldson, L. E. (1962) Some Observations on the Fertility of Beef Cattle in North Queensland, Austral. Vet. Jour. **38,** 447.

Donaldson, L. E. and Hansel, W. (1965) Prolongation of the Life Span of the Bovine Corpus Luteum by Single Injection of Bovine Luteinizing Hormone, J. Dairy Sci **48,** 7, 903.

Donaldson, L. E. and Hansel, W. (1965) Histological Study of Bovine Corpora Lutea, J. Dairy Sci. **48,** 7, 905.

Donaldson, L. E., Hansel, W. and VanVleck, L. D. (1965) Luteotropic Properties of Luteinizing Hormone and Nature of Oxytocin Induced Luteal Inhibition in Cattle, J. Dairy Sci. **48,** 3, 331.

Donaldson, L. E., Little, D. A. and Hansel, W. (1968) Duration of Oestrus and Time of Ovulation in Cattle in Three Breed Types with and without Synchronization of Oestrus with a Progestogen, Austral. Vet. J. **44,** 364.

Donaldson, L. E. and Takken, A. (1968) The Effect of Exogenous Oxytocin on CL Function in the Cow, J. Reprod. and Fert. **17,** 373.

Dukes, H. H. (1947) The Physiology of Domestic Animals, 6th Ed., Comstock Publishing Co., Inc., Ithaca, N.Y.

Erb, R. E. and Ehlers, M. H. (1958) Fertility Rates of Cows Bred Following Estrous Cycles of Different Length, J. Dairy Sci. **41,** 5, 671.

Erb, R. E. and Morrison, R. A. (1958) Estrus after Conception in a Herd of Holstein Friesian Cattle, J. Dairy Sci. **41,** 2, 267.

Everett, R. W., Armstrong, D. V. and Boyd, L. J. (1966) Genetic Relationship Between Production and Breeding Efficiency, J. Dairy Sci. **49,** 7, 879.

Fietta, P. M., Olson, H. H. and Gass, G. H. (1968) Luteinizing Hormone in Cow Plasma During Estrus, J. Dairy Sci. **51, 6,** 949.

Foote, W. D. and Hunter, J. E. (1964) Postpartum Intervals in Beef Cows Treated with Progesterone and Estrogen, J. An. Sci. **23,** 2, 517.

Fox, M. W. (1968) Abnormal Behavior in Animals, W. B. Saunders Co., Philadelphia.

Frank, A. H. (1962) The Economic Importance of Livestock Infertility, Monograph #5, F.A.O., Rome, 3.

Fraser, A. F. (1968) Reproductive Behavior in Ungulates, Academic Press, N.Y.C.

Gangwar, P. C., Branton, C. and Evans, D. L. (1964) Effect of Climate Stress on Ovarian Activity of Dairy Heifers, J. Dairy Sci. **47,** 3, 348 (Abstr).

Garverick, H. A., Erb, R. E. and Callahan, C. J. (1970) Hormone Levels During the Bovine Estrous Cycle, J. An. Sci. **31,** 1, 222.

Ginther, O. J. (1966) The Influence of the Uterus on the Life Span of the Corpus Luteum, Vet. Med., Dec., 1199.

Ginther, O. J. (1968) Utero-Ovarian Relationships in Cattle: Physiologic Aspects, J.A.V.M.A. **153,** 12, 1656.

Ginther, O. J. (1968) Utero-Ovarian Relationships in Cattle: Applied Aspects, J.A.V.M.A. **153,** 12, 1665.

Ginther, O. J., Woody, C. O. Janakiraman, K. and Casida, L. E. (1966) Effect of an Intra-Uterine Plastic Coil on the Oestrus Cycle of the Heifer, J. Reprod. and Fert. **12,** 193.

Gomes, W. R. and Erb, R. E. (1965) Progesterone in Bovine Reproduction: A Review, J. Dairy Sci. **48,** 3, 314.

Gomes, W. R., Estergreen, V. L., Jr., Frost, O. L. and Erb, R. E. (1963) Progestin Levels in Jugular and Ovarian Venous Blood, Corpora Lutea, and Ovaries of the Non Pregnant Bovine, J. Dairy Sci. **46,** 4, 553.

Graves, C. N. and Dzuik, P. J. (1968) Control of Ovulation in Dairy Cattle with Human Chorionic Gonadotropin after Treatment with MAP, J. Reprod. and Fert. **17,** 169.

Graves, W. E. Lauderdale, J. W., Hauser, E. R. and Casida, L. E. (1968) Relation of Postpartum Interval to Pituitary Gonadotropins, Ovarian Follicular Development and Fertility in Beef Cows, Effect of Suckling and Interval to Breeding, Research Bull. #270, Research Div., Univ. of Wisc., 23.

Hackett, A. J. and Hafs, H. O. (1969) Pituitary and Hypothalamic Endocrine Changes during the Bovine Estrous Cycle, J. An. Sci. **28,** 4, 531.

Hafez, E. S. E. (1969) The Behavior of Domestic Animals, 2nd Ed., Williams, Wilkins & Co., Baltimore, Md.

Hall, J. G., Branton, C. and Stone, E. J. (1959) Estrus, Estrous Cycles, Ovulation Time, Time of Service and Fertility of Dairy Cattle in Louisiana, J. Dairy Sci. **42,** 6, 1086.

Hancock, J. L. (1948) The Clinical Analysis of Reproductive Failure in Cattle, Vet. Rec. **60,** 43, 513.

Hansel, W. (1965) Evaluation of Methods for Controlling the Estrous Cycle, Proc. Cong. on Estrous Cycle Control in Domestic Animals, Miscel. Publ. 1005, Univ. of Nebr., Lincoln, Nebr.

Hansel, W. (1967) Control of the Ovarian Cycle in Cattle, in "Reproduction in the Female Mammal" Edit. by G. E. Lamming and E. C. Amoroso, Butterworth, London.

Hansel, W. et al. (1969) Role of the Uterus in Corpus Luteum Involution, Ann. Rept. Coop. Reg. Res. Project NE, 41.

Hansel, W. and Asdell, S. A. (1952) The Causes of Bovine Metestrous Bleeding, J. An. Sci. **11,** 2, 346.

Hansel, W. and Malven, P. V. (1960) Estrous Cycle Regulation in Beef Cattle by Orally Active Progestational Agents, J. An. Sci. **19,** 4, 1324.

Hansel, W. and Snook, R. B. (1970) Pituitary Ovarian Relationships in the Cow, J. Dairy Sci. **53,** 7, 945.

Hansel, W. and Wagner, W. C. (1960) Luteal Inhibition in the Bovine as a Result of Oxytocin Injections, Uterine Dilatation and Intrauterine Infusions of Seminal and Preputial Fluids, J. Dairy Sci. **43,** 6, 798.

Hawk, W. H. (1966) Personal Communication.

Hawk, H. W. (1966) How Do Implanted Spirals Stop Animal Reproduction, Agric. Res. **14,** 7, 4.

Hawk, H. W. (1968) The Effect of Intrauterine Devices on Corpus Luteum Function, J. An. Sci. **27,** Suppl. 1, 119.

Hawk, H. W. (1968) Studies on the Antifertility Effect of Intrauterine Devices in the Cow, Fert. and Steril. **19,** 3, 351.

Hofstad, M. S. (1941) A Study of Breeding Records of One Large Herd of Dairy Cattle, Cor. Vet., **31,** 4, 379.

Howes, J. R., Warnick, A. C. and Hentges, J. F. (1960) Comparison of Different Methods for Detecting Ovulation in Cattle, Fert. and Steril. **11,** 5, 508.

Inıori, T. (1967) The Biological Half Life of Progesterone in the Peripheral Blood of Cows, Jap. Jour. of Vet. Sci. **29,** 4, 201.

Jainudeen, M. R. and Hafez, E. S. E. (1966) Control of Estrus and Ovulation in Cattle with Orally Active Progestin and Gonadotropins, Internat. J. of Fertil. **11,** 1 (Part 1), 47.

Jubb, K. and McEntee, K. (1954) Personal Communication.

Kendrick, J. W. and McEntee, K. (1967) The Effect of Artificial Insemination with Semen Contaminated with IBR-IPV Virus, Cor. Vet. **57,** 1.

Labhsetwar, A. P., Collins, W. E., Tyler, W. J. and Casida, L. E. (1964) Pituitary-Ovarian Relationships in the Periparturient Cow, J. Reprod. and Fertil. **8,** 1, 85.

Lamming, G. E. and Amoroso, E. C. (1967) Reproduction in the Female Mammal, Butterworths, London.

Lamond, D. R. (1964) Synchronization of Ovarian Cycles in Sheep and Cattle, Animal Breeding Abstr. **32,** 3, 269.

Larson, G. L. and Bayley, N. D. (1955) The Fertility of Inseminations Made in Cows Showing Postestrous Hemorrhage, J. of Dairy Sci. **38,** 5, 549.

Lauderdale, J. W., Graves, W. E., Houser, E. R. and Casida, L. E.

(1968) Relation of Postpartum Interval to Corpus Luteum Development, Pituitary Prolactin Activity, and Uterine Involution in Beef Cows (Effect of Suckling and Interval to Breeding), Res. Bull. 270, Res. Div., Univ. of Wisc., Madison, Wisc.

Louca, A. and Legates, J. E. (1968) Production Losses due to Days Open, J. Dairy Sci. **51**, 4, 573.

Mares, S. E., Zimbelman, R. G. and Casida, L. E. (1962) Variation in Progesterone Content of the Bovine Corpus Luteum of the Estrous Cycle, J. An. Sci. **21**, 2, 266.

Marinov, U. and Lovell, J. E. (1967) Secretory and Ciliated Cells of the Bovine Cervix, Amer. J. Vet. Res., **28**, 127, 1763.

Marion, G. B. and H. T. Gier (1968) Factors Affecting Bovine Ovarian Activity After Parturition, J. An. Sci. **27**, 6, 1621.

Marion, G. B., Norwood, J. S. and Gier, H. T. (1968) Uterus of the Cow After Parturition: Factors Affecting Regression, Amer. J. Vet. Res. **29**, 71.

Marston, J. H. and Kelly, W. A. (1966) The Effects and Mode of Action of Intrauterine Devices, Vet. Rec. **79**, 22, 644.

Megale, J. (1967) Endoscopic Photography of Ruminants, Vet. Med. 62, 6, 555.

Melampy, R. M., Emmerson, M. A., Rakes, J. M., Hanka, L. J. and Eness, P. G. (1957) The Effect of Progesterone on the Estrous Response of Estrogen-Conditioned Ovariectomized Cows, J. An. Sci. **16**, 967.

Moor, R. M. and Rowson, L. E. A. (1966) The Corpus Luteum of the Sheep. Effect of the Removal of Embryos on Luteal Function, J. of Endocrin. **34**, 497.

Morrow, D. A. (1969) Estrous Behavior and Ovarian Activity in Prepuberal and Postpuber l Dairy Heifers, J. Dairy Sci. **52**, 2, 224.

Morrow, D. A., Roberts, S. J. and McEntee, K. (1968) Latent Effects of Pregnancy on Postpartum Estrous Cycle Length in Dairy Cattle, J. An. Sci. **27**, 5, 1404.

Morrow, D. A., Roberts, S. J. and McEntee, K. (1969) A Review of Postpartum Ovarian Activity and Involution of the Uterus and Cervix in Cattle, Cor. Vet. **59**, 1, 134.

Morrow, D. A., Roberts, S. J. and McEntee, K. (1969) Postpartum Ovarian Activity and Involution of the Uterus and Cervix of Dairy Cattle, I. Ovarian Activity, II Involution of the Uterus and Cervix, III Days Nongravid and Services per Conception, Cor. Vet. **59**, 2, 173, 190, 199.

Morrow, D. A., Roberts, S. J., McEntee, K. and Gray, H. G. (1966) Postpartum Ovarian Activity and Uterine Involution in Dairy Cattle, J.A.V.M.A. **149**, 12, 1595.

Morrow, D. A., Swanson, L. V. and Hafs, H. D. (1970) Estrous and Ovarian Activity in Puberal Heifers, J. An. Sci. **31**, 1, 232.

Nakahara, T., Domeki, I., Inui, S. and Yamauchi, M. (1967) Effects of Intrauterine Infusion of Iodine Solution on the Estrous Cycle of the Cow, Jap. Jour. of An. Reprod. **13**, 2, 57.

Neilsen, F. (1949) Sterility in Cattle, Especially as a Result of Uterine Infection, Proc. 14th Internat. Vet. Congr., Vol. III, Section 4 (c), 105.

O'Bleness, C. N. and VanVleck, L. D. (1962) Reasons for Disposal of Dairy Cows From New York Herds, J. Dairy Sci. **45**, 9, 1087.

Olds, D. (1969) An Objective Consideration of Dairy Herd Fertility, J.A.V.M.A. **154**, 3, 253.

Olds, D. and Cooper, T. (1970) Effect of Postpartum Rest Period in Dairy Cattle on the Occurrence of Breeding Abnormalities and on Calving Intervals, J.A.V.M.A. **157**, 1, 92.

Olds, D. and VanDemark, N. L. (1957) Physiological Aspects of Fluids in Female Genitalia with Special Reference to Cattle—A Review, Amer. J. Vet. Res. **18**, 68, 587.

Phillips, R. W. (1958) Cattle, Scient. Amer. **198**, 6, 51.

Pipes, G. W., Bauman, T. R., Brooks, J. R., Comfort, J. E. and Turner, C. W. (1963) Effect of Season, Sex, Breed on the Thyroxine Secretion Rate of Beef Cattle and A comparison with Dairy Cattle, J. An. Sci. **22**, 2, 476.

Plasse, D., Warnick, A. C., and Koger, M. (1970) Reproductive Behavior of **Bos Indicus** Females in Subtropical Environment, J. An. Sci. **30**, 1, 63.

Plotka, E. D., Erb, R. E., Callahan, C. J. and Gomes, W. R. (1967) Levels of Progesterone in Peripheral Blood Plasma During the Estrous Cycle of the Bovine, J. Dairy Sci. **50**, 7, 1083.

Pope, G. S. and Gupta, S. K. (1967) Levels of Progesterone in the Systemic Plasma of the Cow, Ann. Rept. N.I.R.D., Reading, England, 58.

Rahlman, D. F. and Mead, S. W. (1958) Occurrence of Post-Conception Estrus in Seven Herds of Jersey Cattle, J. Dairy Sci. **41**, 10, 1484.

Riesen, J. W., Saiduddin, S., Tyler, W. J. and Casida, L. E. (1968) Relation of Postpartum Interval to Corpus Luteum Development Pituitary Prolactin Activity, and Uterine Involution in Dairy Cows, Effect of Suckling, Res. Bull. 270, Research Div., Univ. of Wisc., Madison, Wisc.

Roark, D. B. and Herman, H. A. (1950) Physiological and Histological Phenomena of the Bovine Estrual Cycle with Special Reference to Vaginal Cervical Secretions, Missouri Agr. Exp. Stat. Res. Bull. #455.

Robinson, T. J. (1967) Reproduction in the Female Mammal, Edit. by G. E. Lamming and E. C. Amoroso, Butterworths, London, p. 442.

Rollinson, D. H. L. (1955) Oestrus in Zebu Cattle in Uganda, Nature, **176**, 352.

Roussel, J. D. and Beatty, J. F. (1969) Effect of Melengestrol Acetate on Synchronization of Estrus, Subsequent Fertility and Milk Constituents of Lactating Dairy Cows, J. Dairy Sci. **52**, 12, 2020.

Saiduddin, S. and Foote, W. D. (1964) Pituitary Luteinizing Hormone Activity of the Postpartum Bovine, J. An. Sci. **23**, 2, 592.

Saiduddin, S., Riesen, J. W., Tyler, W. J. and Casida, L. E. (1968) Relation of Postpartum Interval to Pituitary Gonadotropins, Ovarian Follicular Development and Fertility in Dairy Cows, Res. Bull. 270, Res. Div., Univ. of Wisc., Madison, Wisc.

Saiduddin, S., Riesen, J. W., Tyler, W. J. and Casida, L. E. (1967) Some Carry-over Effects of Pregnancy on Postpartum Ovarian Function in the Cow, J. Dairy Sci. **50**, 11, 1846.

Shannon, F. P., Salisbury, G. W. and VanDemark (1952) The Fertility of Cows Inseminated at Various Intervals after Calving, J. An. Sci. **11**, 2, 355.

Short, R. V. (1962) Steroids Present in the Follicular Fluid of the Cow, J. Endocrin. **23,** 401.

Short, R. V. (1967) On Mechanisms Controlling the Corpus Luteum, Seminar, Cornell Univ.

Simmons, K. R. and Hansel, W. (1964) Nature of the Luteotropic Hormone in the Bovine, J. An. Sci. **23,** 1, 136.

Smith, J. F. (1969) Studies on the Physiological and Endocrinological Aspects of the Control of Ovulation and Oestrus in the Ewe, Ph.D. Thesis, Faculty of Agric., Univ. of Sidney, Sidney, Austral.

Speicher, J. A. and Meadows, C. E. (1967) Milk Production and Costs Associated with Length of Calving Interval in Holstein Cows, Paper at 62nd Ann. Meeting Amer. Dairy Sci. Assoc., Cornell Univ., Ithaca, N.Y.

Stabenfeldt, G. H. (1970) Recent Advances in Bovine Reproductive Physiology, Bov. Pract. **5,** 2.

Staples, R. E. and Hansel, W. (1961) Luteal Function and Embryo Survival in the Bovine, J. Dairy Sci. **44,** 11, 2040.

Staples, R. E., McEntee, K. and Hansel, W. (1961) Luteal Function as Related to Pituitary and Ovarian Cytology and Embryo Development in the Bovine, J. Dairy Sci. **44,** 11, 2049.

Swanson, L. V. and Hafs, H. D. (1970) Luteinizing Hormone and Prolactin in Blood Serum Through Estrus in Heifers, J. Dairy Sci. **53,** 5, 652 (Abstr.)

Tanabe, T. Y. and Almquist, J. O. (1960) I Estrus and Estrual Cycles, The Nature of Subfertility in Dairy Heifers, Bull. #672, Penn. State Univ., Univ. Park, Pa.

Thompson, N. R. and Patterson, W. N. (1967) Cow Turnover in Virginia Dairy Herds, J. Dairy Sci. **50,** 4, 610 (Abstr.)

Trimberger, G. W. (1941) Menstruation Frequency and Its Relation to Conception in Dairy Cattle, J. of Dairy Sci., **24,** 9, 819.

Trimberger, G. W. (1948) Breeding Efficiency in Dairy Cattle From Artificial Insemination at Various Intervals Before and After Ovulation, Univ. of Neb. Agric. Exp. Stat. Res. Bull. 153.

Trimberger, G. W. (1954) Conception Rates in Dairy Cattle from Services at Various Intervals After Parturition, J. of Dairy Sci., **37,** 9, 1042.

Trimberger, G. W. (1955) Unpublished data.

Trimberger, G. W. (1956) Ovarian Functions, Intervals Between Estrus, and Conception Rates in Dairy Cattle, J. Dairy Sci. **39,** 4, 448.

Trimberger, G. W. and Davis, G. K. (1943) The Relationship Between Time of Insemination and Breeding Efficiency in Dairy Cattle, Nebr. Agr. Exp. Stat. Res. Bull. 129.

Trimberger, G. W. and Hansel, W. (1955) Conception Rate and Ovarian Function Following Estrus Control by Progesterone Injections in Dairy Cattle, J. of An. Sci., **14,** 1, 224.

Ulberg, L. C., Christian, R. E. and Casida, L. E. (1951) Ovarian Response in Heifers to Progesterone Injections, J. of An. Sci., **10,** 3, 752.

Van Demark, N. L. (1952) Time and Site of Insemination in Cattle, Cor. Vet., **42,** 2, 215.

Van Demark, N. L. and Salisbury, G. W. (1950) The Relation of the Postpartum Breeding Interval to Reproductive Efficiency in the Dairy Cow., J. of An. Sci., **9,** 3, 307.

Van Rensburg, S. J. (1965) Adrenal Function and Fertility, Jour. S. Afr. Vet. Med. Assoc. **36,** 4, 491.

Van Vleck, L. D. (1968) Can You Manage the Calving Interval to Get More Milk, Dairy Herd Management, **5,** 11, 28.

Varman, P. W., Smith, E. P. and Hull, M. W. (1964) Estrogen Secretion and Excretion During Estrus in Dairy Cows, J. Dairy Sci. **47,** 6, 687.

Wagner, J. F., Veenhuizen, E. L., Gregory, R. P. and Tonkinson, L. V. (1968) Fertility in the Beef Heifer Following Treatment with CAP, J. An. Sci. **27,** 6, 1627.

Wagner, W. C. and Hansel, W. (1969) Reproductive Physiology of the Postpartum Cow, J. Reprod. and Fert. **18,** 493.

Weber, A. F., Morgan, B. B. and McNutt, S. H. (1948) Clinical and Post Mortem Observations on Metrorrhagia in the Virgin Heifer, N.A. Vet., **29,** 11, 705.

Weber, A. F., Morgan, B. B. and McNutt, S. H. (1949) Perimetrial Hemorrhage in Virgin Heifers, Cor. Vet., **39,** 3, 261.

White, J. M. and Nichols, J. R. (1965) Reasons For Disposal of Pennsylvania Holstein Cattle, J. Dairy Sci. **48,** 4, 512.

Wilkes, J. (1970) Personal Communication.

Williams, R. J. and Stott, G. H. (1966) Reproduction in Thyroidectomized and Parathyroidectomized Cattle, J. Dairy Sci. **49,** 10, 1262.

Williams, W. F., Johnston, J. O., Lauterback, M. and Fagan, B. (1967) Luteolytic Effect of a Bovine Uterine Powder on the Corpora Lutea, Follicular Development and Progesterone Synthesis of the Pseudopregnant Rabbit Ovary, J. Dairy Sci. **50,** 4, 555.

Wiltbank, J. N. (1965) Discussion, Proc. of Conf. on Estrous Cycle Control in Domestic Animals, Miscel. Publ. 1005, Univ. of Nebr., Lincoln, Nebr., 58, 60 and 62.

Wiltbank, J. N. and Cook, A. C. (1958) The Comparative Reproductive Performance of Nursed Cows and Milked Cows, J. An. Sc. **17,** 3, 640.

Wiltbank, J. N. and Kasson, C. W. (1968) Synchronization of Estrus in Cattle With an Oral Progestational Agent and an Injection of an Estrogen, J. An. Sci. **27,** 1, 113.

Wiltbank, J. N., Rothlisberger, J. A. and Zimmerman, D. R. (1961) The Effect of Human Chronic Gonadotropin on the Maintenance of the Corpus Luteum and Embryonic Survival in the Cow. J. An. Sci. **20,** 4, 827.

Wiltbank, J. N., Shumway, R. P., Parker, W. R. and Zimmerman, D. R. (1967) Duration of Estus, Time of Ovulation and Fertilization Rate in Beef Heifers Synchronized with D.H.P.A., J. An. Sci. **26,** 4, 764.

Woody, C. O., First, N. L. and Pope, A. L. (1965) Effect of Exogenous Progesterone on Estrous Cycle Length, J. An. Sci. **26,** 1, 139.

Wrenn, T. R., Bitman, J. and Sykes, J. F. (1958) Body Temperature Variations in Dairy Cattle During the Estrous Cycle and Pregnancy, J. Dairy Sci. **41,** 1071.

INFECTIOUS DISEASES CAUSING INFERTILITY IN COWS

These infectious diseases may be divided into the systemic diseases such as tuberculosis, which occasionally or rarely may affect the reproductive organs, and the more important venereal diseases which infect the genital tract such as: trichomoniasis, vibriosis, brucellosis and possibly mycoplasmosis. Granular venereal disease, infectious pustular vulvovaginitis due to the IBR-IPV virus and other miscellaneous infections may also affect the reproductive tract. It is significant that in trichomoniasis, vibriosis and brucellosis a local immunity develops in the genital tract and antibodies may be found in the vaginal mucus for variable, but not prolonged, periods. Any combination of these infectious diseases may occur simultaneously in an animal.

Trichomoniasis

Definition—Trichomoniasis is an insidious venereal disease of cattle characterized by sterility, early abortion, and pyometra and is caused by the protozoan, **Trichomonas fetus or Tritrichomonas fetus,** transmitted to cows by the chronically-infected bull.

Etiology—According to Morgan this disease was first described by Kunstler in France in 1888, but Mazzanti of Italy in 1900 is generally credited with the discovery. Because of the widespread interest in the discovery in 1897 of Bang's disease, or contagious abortion, apparently little or no work was done on trichomoniasis until 1924 to 1929 when Drescher, Riedmuller, and Abelein in Germany further described this disease. In 1932 Emmerson discovered trichomoniasis in Pennsylvania and since that time the disease has been found in nearly every state in the United States and has been worked on intensively by many investigators. Trichomoniasis has been reported in many countries throughout the world. In Wisconsin, where trichomoniasis was a problem, Morgan and Wisnicky reported the results of examining 1,577 bovine uteri from a local packing plant for trichomonads. In 997 pregnant uteri only 2 were positive. In 580 nonpregnant uteri there were 100 cases of pyometra and 13 percent were positive for **Trichomonas fetus.** In the 1,577 uteri there was a .95 percent trichomonad infection. Bartlett reported on 9 infected herds involving 800 cattle. It was conservatively estimated that the losses in these 9 herds totaled $200,000 due to loss of potential milk and calves and loss of value of the infected sires. In the United States the disease has been reported in beef as well as dairy breeds. In recent years trichomoniasis has been diagnosed more frequently in beef herds and less frequently in dairy herds probably due to the extensive use of artificial insemination in dairy cattle. Johnson reported on the results of a survey of 828 western range bulls in 34 herd associations for trichomoniasis. Seven and one-half percent of the bulls and 26 percent of the associations were infected. Bartlett cited 10 infected beef and dairy bulls found on examination prior to use in an AI Stud. These bulls were in herds widely scattered over the U.S. Since 1940 over 10 A.I. Studs in the U.S.A. have experienced outbreaks of trichomoniasis in their bulls, Bartlett, and Gabel et al.. Beef herds, dealers' herds, valuable purebred herds, and institution herds that frequently change or purchase bulls and cows, are those in which trichomoniasis is most likely to appear.

The causative agent of this disease, **Trichomonas fetus,** is a flagellated protozoa with a pyriform or pear-like body. Three small flagella are located at the cranial end of the trichomonad. An undulating membrane extends the length of the body and terminates in a single caudal flagellum. Simpson and White have reported on its structure as revealed by the electron microscope. The organism varies from 10 to 25 microns in length and 5 to 10 microns in width. A red blood cell is 5 to 7 microns in diameter. It is about one-third larger than the head of a bovine sperm cell. In fresh preparations the organism is actively motile, exhibiting a jerky, twisting, irregular, spiral, and erratic type of movement. Progressive rapid forward movement is seldom observed. **Trichomonas fetus** is rapidly killed by drying, by the presence of antiseptics, excessive heat and by other adverse conditions or environment. Once dead it quickly loses its shape, so that it is difficult to distinguish from cellular debris. A common type of vaginitis in women is caused by **Trichomonas vaginalis,** an organism distinctly different from **Trichomonas fetus. Trichomonas fetus** may be kept indefinitely in culture media.

Recent studies have shown that it is highly probable that **Trichomonas suis** frequently found in the digestive tract and nasal cavity of swine is similar to **Trichomonas fetus** based on morphology, clinical signs produced by injections of **T. suis** into the genital tract of heifers and on serologic tests, Hammond and Leidl, Hibler et al., Kerr, Robertson, and Fitzgerald et al.. The fact that these two protozoa from different body sites in swine and cattle are apparently identical may well account for the spread of the disease from swine to cattle, especially beef cattle where the two species are often housed or run together.

In cattle, **Trichomonas fetus** is found only in the genital tract, vagina, cervix, uterus, and contents of the uterus of the cow and on the penis and prepuce and possibly a slight distance into the urethra of the bull. In rare and unusual instances retrograde trichomonad infections of the seminal vesicles or epididymides may occur, Bartlett, Bielanski. Hammond and Bartlett demonstrated that the greatest concentration of organisms in the bull was found on the glans penis and adjacent prepuce. They found no organisms in the urethra.

Trichomoniasis is a venereal disease spread from animal to animal at the time of coitus or artificial insemination. Trichomoniasis may be spread from bull to bull in an AI Stud at the time of semen collection or if bulls are allowed to run together and mount each other. Only rarely is it spread by other means such as by grooming animals that have a discharge from the vulva, or by the use of contaminated instruments, speculums or preputial or vaginal douching nozzles, Bartlett.

Garlick in 1939 first reported the transmission of trichomoniasis by artificial insemination. By means of 7 inseminations, Bartlett et al. produced the disease in 6 out of 9 uninfected females, and thus demonstrated that trichomoniasis could be spread by artificial insemination with fresh undiluted semen from an infected bull. Vandeplassche et al. reported on the use of an infected bull for artificial insemination. The semen was diluted 1 to 25 to 1 to 80 times in an egg-yolk-citrate buffer with sulfanilamide. Of 600 cows inseminated by semen from the infected bull 5 showed early abortion and 1 developed pyometra. Joyner and Millar demonstrated that trichomonads were present in 7 out of 28 ejaculates collected from infected bulls and that storage of the liquid infected semen in the usual manner, and the addition of antibiotics and extenders apparently had little or no inhibitory effects on the organisms. In 1953 Bartlett, Moist and Spurrell examined 168 bulls of 5 artificial insemination associations and found that 23 were infected. The rate of transmission of infection by artificial insemination was estimated at less than 1 percent. This would not be serious in artificially inseminated cows and the percentage of conceptions on first service of infected bulls would not be noticeably affected, Kendrick. On the other hand Thorne reported that in some herds bred artificially, the incidence of infection may be as high as 20 percent. The transmission rate might be serious, however, if the infected cows were bred to the herd sire and the disease thereby transmitted. The low incidence of infection from artificial insemination is due to the methods of collection, storing, and dilution of the liquid semen. Only by the recovery of the organism in occasional isolated abortions or pyometra cases can trichomoniasis be traced to infected bulls used in artificial insemination. Ayalon and Tsur-Tschernomoretz reported that in cows bred artificially to a trichomonad-infected bull with the semen diluted only 1 to 10, a much lower dilution rate than commonly used in this country, the conception rate was 52.4 percent in 250 cows but that the calving rate was only 29 percent due to early embryonic and fetal deaths. Vandeplassche and coworkers reported a high infection rate in nonimmune heifers when bred artificially with infected semen even though the semen was extended 1 to 40. They noted, however, a great difference between infected bulls in the ability of their semen to transmit infection when used for artificial insemination. This may be due to the great difference in the number of organisms present in the sheaths of different bulls, Bartlett. Joyner and Bennett restudied and reviewed the previous evidence and confirmed the fact that **T. fetus** could survive in frozen and thawed extended bull semen even though glycerol was toxic to **T. fetus.** In glycerol-egg yolk-citrate extender **T. fetus** did not survive freezing and thawing; while in glycerol-egg-yolk phosphate or glycerol-milk extenders some organisms did survive. Thus bulls used in AI service should be free of trichomoniasis or spread of the disease might occur.

In natural service the transmission rate of the disease is about 80 percent. Bartlett reported that in 24 susceptible females bred to an infected bull, only 28 natural breedings were necessary to produce infection in all the females. After natural service to an infected bull 23 of 26 heifers became infected but the conception rate was 45 percent, Vandeplassche and coworkers. Bulls were also quite susceptible to infection with 4 of 9 bulls becoming infected after the first service to an infected cow. However, 2 of 9 bulls proved highly resistant and could not be infected after 6 services to infected females. Young bulls with less well-developed mucosal crypts and folds in the prepuce are more resistant to experimental infections than are older bulls. Bulls, unlike cows, do not seem to be able to develop immunity, even after 2 or 3 infections. If given sexual rest for a period of time cows will usually develop an immunity and rid themselves of the infection; whereas once a bull becomes infected the infection is permanent and only occasionally does recovery spontaneously occur. Cows may readily be infected experimentally by the introduction of **Trichomonas fetus** into the vagina or uterus. Although bulls are less susceptible to artificial infection of the prepuce, they more readily contract trichomoniasis after natural service to an infected cow. There are possible individual variations, Hammond and Bartlett. Except in sporadic cases due to artificial insemination the disease usually appears in a herd as an insidious venereal enzootic infection.

Signs—Being insidious, trichomoniasis is often well-established in a herd before the symptoms reach proportions sufficiently alarming so that a veterinarian is called.

The breeding records of any herd affected with sterility should be carefully studied. The possibility of the presence of this disease can often be surmised on the basis of good breeding records. Often the original source of the infection can be traced to a certain bull or nonpregnant cow added to the herd. Infertility frequently starts after such additions. Once the disease has been diagnosed, herd records are also of value in planning a control program. After the cows have been exposed by coitus to a trichomonad infected bull the following signs may be observed:

(1) Trichomoniasis will fail to become established in a small number of cows or heifers either because of the small numbers of trichomonads introduced or because of the natural resistance of the female. Conception and a normal gestation period will follow. Approximately 5 to 20 percent of the cows or heifers may fall in this category. According to Morgan and Vandeplassche et al. normal gestation and parturition may result in spite of the infection. Trichomonads have been isolated on rare occasions throughout a gestation period terminating in a normal parturition.

(2) When **Trichomonas fetus** becomes established after coitus there is no reaction nor any clinical lesions or discharge for the first 3 or 4 days. However, by 4 to 9 days the presence of a moderate vulvovaginitis and cervicitis may be observed on clinical examination. Discharges from the genitals are absent or very scanty during most infections unless pyometra occurs and then pus is usually discharged irregularly. Under field conditions these symptoms in most cattle would usually pass unnoticed, Bartlett. The above symptoms are so slight as to be of little significance; since other infections of a nonspecific type may have similar symptoms. In rare instances a more severe and chronic type of vaginitis is observed in the cranial portion of the vagina in cows with trichomoniasis. This is characterized by a rough, rasp-like corrugated vaginal mucosa. Some clinicians indicate that this lesion when observed is nearly pathognomic for the disease. Trichomonads may be found in the vaginal exudate, which is usually watery, clear, or cloudy, often containing whitish-yellow flakes of pus. Beattie reported the presence of trichomonads in a cyst of Gartner's duct 11 weeks after the apparent recovery of the cow from trichomoniasis. In general, clinical symptoms are absent or mild and usually pass unnoticed by the herdsman.

The recently infected bull may develop a mild posthitis and balanitis that is not observable clinically. The chronically-infected bull shows no gross lesions.

(3) The most common symptom of trichomoniasis is infertility, characterized by the necessity for many services per conception and by the frequent occurrence of a prolonged period between estrual periods after breeding. Bartlett cited one herd of 50 cows that during the height of the infection had an average of 5.15 services per conception over a 2-year period. Prior to the development of the disease the conception rate had been a normal 1.82 services per conception. Some cows must be bred 6 to 8 times before conception occurs. **Trichomonas fetus** produces a mild inflammation of the endometrium, cervical and vaginal mucous membranes, and affects the developing embryo and fetus. There is no evidence to show that it may interfere with fertilization of the ova. According to Bartlett nearly 40 percent of infected cows after breeding showed shorter- or longer-than-normal interestrual periods during the time they were infected. The longer interval between estrums were most commonly noted. Most of the trichomonad abortions or resorptions are caused by the early death of the embryo and fetus from 15 to 80 days of gestation rather than the less common and often observable abortions occurring after three months of gestation. In early embryonic deaths the embryos usually macerate and are absorbed in the uterus or are expelled unnoticed. Occasionally pyometra may result from a macerating embryo. If cows are infected at one service to an infected bull and fail to conceive, a subsequent service to a clean bull, either naturally or artificially, will not result in a safe conception until the cow develops an immunity and eliminates the organism. Thus infertility produced by the original infected bull persists even though subsequent breedings are to a noninfected bull. Although trichomoniasis has in the past been characterized chiefly by abortion and pyometra it is actually characterized mainly by infertility and only occasionally by observable abortions and pyometra.

(4) Abortion due to **Trichomonas fetus** usually occurs between 1 and 16 weeks of pregnancy, Morgan. Abortions occurring after 5 months of pregnancy are very rare. If an exposed cow has conceived and carried a normal fetus for 6 months, abortion due to trichomoniasis will probably not occur. Most fetuses aborted before 90 days are not observed. Those aborted the third to fifth month of gestation are usually slightly macerated and autolyzed and are expelled with the fetal membranes around the fetus along with a variable amount of dark, reddish-brown exudate. Occasionally on routine rectal examinations in infected herds these dead fetuses may be diagnosed. Retained placenta is very seldom observed following a trichomonad abortion. The number of observed abortions will vary in an outbreak, depending upon the severity of the infection, the closeness with which the cows are observed, and whether the outbreak is during the summer pasture season or during the winter months when the cows are stabled. Occasionally a mucopurulent reddish-brown discharge may precede an abortion. In a care-

ful study by Bartlett of 50 infected cows, only 2 abortions were recognized; 5 cows developed pyometra. In 5 herds studied in Maryland involving 300 beef and dairy cattle, only 1 abortion and 1 pyometra were observed. In an outbreak involving about 20 cattle which the author was able to study and follow closely, 1 cow aborted a recognizable fetus and 1 had pyometra. Cameron cited an outbreak in New York State in a herd of 75 animals in which 9 observed abortions and 7 unobserved abortions occurred in cows previously diagnosed pregnant. No cases of pyometra were noted. More often the history in an outbreak of trichomoniasis is that the herdsman believed a cow safely pregnant and then 60 to 90 days or more after service, estrum is again exhibited.

(5) Pyometra may be present in 0 to 10 percent of the cows in an outbreak of trichomoniasis. Trichomonad pyometra is postcoital or postservice and not postpartum. When death of the developing embryo occurs and abortion or maceration and absorbtion do not occur, pyometra develops. The corpus luteum in the ovary persists and the cervix may remain tightly closed and sealed with no discharge of pus. More often, however, the cervical seal breaks down and a slight amount of pus escapes into the vagina and is discharged occasionally from the vulva when the cow lies down. Since estrum does not occur with pyometra this condition may pass unnoticed for up to 8 or 9 months unless a vaginal discharge is observed or a diagnosis is made on rectal examination. The amount of pus in the uterus varies from about 60 to 8000 ml with an average of 1500 ml, Morgan and Whitehair. The pus in trichomonad pyometra has a characteristic thin, yellow-grey, watery, flocculent consistency, often containing yellow flakes of pus and shreds of fetal membranes and tissues; in rare cases small fetal bones may be present. The pus has been described as having a potato soup color and consistency. Odor may be absent or rather sweetish, but is not fetid. No evidence of perimetritis or other uterine lesions are present. If on rectal examination a diagnosis of pyometra cannot be made positively, another examination in 1 to 2 months is indicated. Usually trichomonads may be recovered in pure culture from this pus. Morgan and Whitehair in examining 20 cases of trichomonad pyometra found trichomonads in every case in numbers from 320 to 3,520 million per ml, with an average of 1552 million per ml.

Diagnosis—The history of the introduction of a new infected animal into a herd followed by a gradually increasing problem of infertility characterized by failure of conception after frequent services, prolonged periods after service before the next estrual period including cows apparently conceiving but coming into estrum several months later, and the occurrence of occasional early abortions and pyometra are characteristic symptoms of this disease. In recently infected herds all cows and heifers are susceptible. In more chronically infected herds most cows have an acquired immunity, while virgin heifers are susceptible and if exposed exhibit the typical symptoms of the infection. These symptoms are also quite characteristic of vibriosis due to **Vibrio fetus venerealis.** In some bulls both vibriosis and trichomoniasis are present. The positive diagnosis of trichomoniasis requires the finding of the trichomonad organism from one or more infected animals or a diagnosis based on immunologic reactions due to the local immunity developed in the genital tract.

Diagnosis in the bull consists of checking the natural breeding records and finding which bulls are probably infected and checking the preputial smegma of these particular animals carefully, and if necessary repeatedly, by the swab, the pipette, or the douche method. After natural service the numbers of organisms on the penis and sheath are reduced. Following a period of sexual rest for 5 to 10 days to allow the numbers of organisms to increase the bull is confined in a stall, or chute or stanchion. A sideline on the bull is often helpful in restraining the animal in a stall. To avoid fecal or other contamination from the preputial hairs, they are clipped and the preputial orifice is thoroughly washed with soap and water, rinsed, and wiped dry. After its head is fastened and its tail pushed up and forward as restraint, the abdomen is stroked and then the sample is taken from the prepuce.

For direct examination of the preputial smegma for the presence of **T. fetus,** the swab, the pipette or the douche method may be used. In the **swab technique,** a sterile cotton swab or one made with one-half of a 4x4 gauze pad soaked in a physiological saline solution is introduced into the sheath on a 36 to 40 inch wire or long narrow forceps, or wrapped around the bristles of a small brush on the end of a long wire. The sheath is swabbed in a back-and-forth circular motion in the region of the fornix and glans penis where the prepuce and glans penis unite and where most of the trichomonads are located. The swab is then removed and placed in a small amount of physiological saline solution. This may be examined at once on the farm or later in the laboratory. The **pipette technique** described by Bartlett consists of introducing a 24-inch sterile plastic preputial pipette with attached bulb from which the air has been expelled. In the average adult bull which has not been used for service in several days, 1 to 10 cc or more of smegma and fluid may be removed from the sheath by a back-and-forth gentle scraping motion of the end of the pipette in the region of the glans penis. This is flushed into a vial containing 5 ml of physiological saline solution and examined later in the laboratory. The **douche technique** described by Fitzgerald,

Hammond, Miner and Binns consists of introducing 200 to 250 cc of sterile physiological saline into the sheath and closing the external orifice with the fingers to prevent the loss of the saline solution. The solution is vigorously massaged back and forth in the sheath for several minutes and allowed to run back out of the sheath into a broad-mouthed beaker and poured back into a bottle for laboratory examination.

Since **Trichomonas fetus** organisms occur in the infected bull in small numbers they must be located in fresh samples in which the organism is alive and motile. Samples must therefore be handled properly after collection, by avoiding extremes of temperature, contact with harmful chemicals, and evaporation. It is highly desirable to examine samples within a few hours of collection. If an immediate examination is not possible the samples may be kept in a cool place such as a refrigerator or shipped to a laboratory under refrigeration to control bacterial growth, and examined within 24 hours. Ordinary freezing at 32° F. will destroy trichomonads. Pipette samples should be allowed to settle for several hours or centrifuged for 10 minutes at 2000 R.P.M. After most of the supernatant fluid is poured off, the superficial layer and the sediment where the organisms are concentrated are mixed. This material is dropped on a glass slide to make a thin pool that is examined under low power with a reduced amount of light. A cover glass should not be used; 3 slides must be carefully examined before the sample is considered negative. A similar technique is used in examining swabs. In the douche technique the 250 ml of saline solution and preputial washings are centrifuged for 10 minutes at 2000 R.P.M. at the laboratory. After the supernatant fluid is decanted. The remaining material is centrifuged in a like manner in a 15 ml centrifuge tube. The supernatant fluid is poured off and the sediment is mixed with 0.5 to 1 ml of the remaining fluid and examined. Fitzgerald and his coworkers demonstrated that the pipette method was superior to the swab technique, and the douche technique superior to both. In the field where a laboratory was not available the swab and pipette methods were most desirable. Using the pipette technique Bartlett, Moist and Spurrell reported that a positive test was recorded on 42 to 85 percent of the samples from known infected bulls. Two infected bulls were considered atypical inasmuch as only 8.5 to 19.5 percent of the preputial samples from them were positive. They also reported that of 23 infected bulls in 168 bulls examined, 15 were diagnosed on the first sampling, 6 at the second and 2 at the third sample. In rare instances positive bulls may not be found until the fifth sampling with the pipette; for this reason these workers recommended that at least 6 negative samples at weekly intervals be considered as a minimal diagnostic routine under practical conditions. The use of the more cumbersome douche technique might reduce the numbers of preputial samples required. Witherspoon and Walker reported that the direct swabbing or scrubbing of the exposed penis with gauge sponges in saline solution appeared promising in detecting infected bulls when the numbers of trichomonads present were low. The penis was exposed manually after tranquilization of the bull. Semen examinations for trichomonads are not feasible since sperm motility interferes with the examination and bacterial growth will usually kill the trichomonads.

By the use of modified Plastridge medium containing nutrients and antibiotics, including mycostatin, preputial smegma material can be added to culture media and incubated for 3 to 5 days and examined, Gilman, Johnson. This method utilizes the collection techniques outlined above and the modified douche technique of Johnson for obtaining a sample of smegma. Culture techniques save a great deal of time when compared to the direct microscopic examination by a skilled person. It is also a more accurate technique. Todorovic and McNutt described a skimmed milk medium with antibiotics added that was very satisfactory for growing the organisms for as long as two weeks. A fluorescent antibody technique for staining **T. fetus** in preputial mucus samples may be feasible, Dunton.

Diagnosis in the cow may be accomplished by examination of the fetal membranes, the mouth cavity of the fetus, the fetal fluids, the stomach contents of the fetus, or the exudate in the uterus for **T. fetus.** Following abortion the organisms usually disappear within 48 hours. In cows with postcoital pyometra the pus should always be examined for trichomonads. **T. fetus** are often found in such great numbers that dilution is necessary in order to observe them clearly. In cows bred artificially, early abortion and pyometra are about the only conditions in which trichomonads might be found or suspected. The early occurrence of vaginal immunity to the organism is responsible for the disappearance of trichomonads from the vagina. While the organism which is motile and has transversed the cervix into the uterus remains and produces an endometritis that lasts for one to several months. During this time organisms may be found periodically in the vagina. Vaginal samples from suspected females should be examined during the early vaginal phase of the infection, which lasts for about 5 weeks after the coitus that produced the initial infection. Thereafter the presence of vaginal infection may occasionally be observed about 3 to 7 days before estrum, Hammond and Bartlett. This pattern occurs only in previously uninfected animals. Consequently in selecting females to culture it is best to select if possible virgin heifers bred the first time to a supposedly infected or suspect bull and sample the vagina with a 14- to 16-inch-long, plastic pipette in a manner similar to examination of the bull. These samplings should be made 12 to 19 days after the infecting service and then 3 to 7 days prior to each subsequent estrum. Finding the trichomonad organisms in cows cannot be done as regularly nor as easily as in bulls so the cow is seldom employed for diagnostic purposes.

It may be desirable to check certain bulls further and for this purpose 2 or more virgin heifers may be bred naturally and vaginal samples taken regularly from 12 to 19 days later. If no positive recoveries of the organism are made, the bull may tentatively be considered free of the infection. Vaginal exudate, if present, should be taken from any suspected cow and especially from cows exhibiting a rough, rasplike corrugated vagina and examined for **T. fetus.**

The living **Trichomonas fetus** can be readily identified under the microscope by its characteristic size, shape, undulating membrane, and jerky, erratic motion. **Trichomonas fetus** in live culture seldom if ever ceases to move, whereas other protozoa occasionally stop moving. Other protozoa, such as: **T. ruminatum, Entrichomastix ruminatum, Bodo fetus** and others, may also be observed, especially in contaminated samples containing feces, Morgan. Their size and motion however, differs from that of **Trichomonas fetus** and they have no undulating membrane. These other forms of protozoa are more likely to be observed if samples are held for 18 to 48 hours at room temperature before examination or if samples are taken from the cranial portion of the prepuce.

In pregnancies that terminate in abortions at 90 to 150 days or in pyometra, **T. fetus** may survive for 4 to 5 months in the genital tract of a cow. In most cows however the infection may persist for only a few weeks, 4 to 5, in the vagina and for up to about 60 to 90 days, 2 to 3 months, in the uterus before local immunity results in spontaneous recovery. Infected bulls may remain as carriers of **T. fetus** but no lesions or inflammation of the sheath or penis is produced in either acutely or chronically infected males.

A vaginal mucus agglutination test originally reported by Pierce was well-described by Kerr and Robinson, and Kerr. Since agglutination antibodies are developed locally in both the vagina and uterus this has been used as an excellent herd test for **T. fetus** infection. It is not satisfactory for testing individual animals. The antibodies appear as early as 18 to 21 days after infection but reach a high level by 40 days. No systemic antibodies with blood titers were ever observed. In northern Ireland this test was used as herd screening test to locate those herds that were infected. Thus the diagnosis may be based on the herd history and symptoms, finding the organism, or the vaginal mucus agglutination test.

Prognosis—In the herd the prognosis is usually fair to good if the owner follows a carefully planned control program. In the individual cow the prognosis is good because the nonpregnant cow tends to develop an immunity which, although temporary, eliminates the infection in about 3 months. In certain cases of uterine infection in pregnant cows, or of pyometra, the infection may survive in the uterus for much longer periods or until abortion or parturition occurs or the pyometra is corrected. Occasionally secondary invading organisms such as **C. pyogenes** may produce a more severe pyometra and sterility. Cows very rarely, if ever, carry **T. fetus** infection in their uterus through an entire gestation period. In some longstanding cases of infertility due to pyometra or chronic endometritis, conception may fail to occur and the cow is sold for economic reasons. The prognosis for bulls is more guarded. Since older bulls are usually permanently infected and only very rarely recover spontaneously they usually are sold for slaughter unless they are valuable. Bartlett stated that any bull not worth more than 3 times his salvage value should be slaughtered. If the bull is valuable then treatment and posttreatment testing involving a period of 4 to 6 months or more is indicated. Treatment and the many posttreatment test samples required are expensive. Fortunately only a few bulls fail to respond to one or two treatments. Thorne and others estimated that successful treatment is possible in 80 to 90 percent of infected bulls.

Herd treatment—The various possible programs that can be used to eliminate the infection should be carefully explained to the herdsman and the owner. The veterinarian can usually outline a practical plan or procedure to control trichomoniasis in the herd. There is no satisfactory or successful method yet devised to immunize cows artificially against trichomoniasis.

The simplist most practical method to control and eliminate trichomoniasis in a herd is stop all natural service and breed all cows having normal genital tracts by artificial insemination to disease-free bulls for a period of about one to two years before resorting again to natural service by bulls proven free of **T. fetus** or by virgin bulls. Cows with pyometra should be treated and cows that abort or have an embryonic resorption should not be rebred for several months until the uterus involutes to its normal state. This author sees no benefit from requiring that all cows have 3 normal length cycles prior to rebreeding to ensure that most cows will have freed themselves of the infection. This may promote a higher rate of conception on first service but the loss of production by such a delay in service on many cows in the herd that may be nearly recovered or are recovered from **T. fetus** infection would be excessive. However the owner should be warned that an increased number of services will be necessary, especially on cows that had been recently infected and have not developed an immunity. Infected bulls should be sold or, if valuable enough, should be treated. Breeding infected bulls to supposedly immune cows may result in fairly satisfactory conception rates but will continue the infection in the herd. Immunity to trichomoniasis lasts only a short period of months. Even cows that have conceived and had a normal gestation period and parturition should not be bred back by natural service within 90 days of calving, since a few of these cows may rarely carry the infection through the gestation period, Morgan. Infected and noninfected cows may be housed or pastured together with practically no danger of spread of the disease since trichomoniasis is rarely spread except by venereal contact. This above practical artificial insemination procedure will work well for most dairy and some beef herds.

Another control method that is rather difficult to carry out is to divide the herd of female cattle into two groups

(1) the clean nonexposed cows and heifers including virgin unbred heifers, pregnant or open heifers or cows that have never been bred by a known trichomonad-infected bull or a bull suspected of being infected and nonpregnant cows that have recently calved after a normal gestation period and have not had a service by an infected or suspect bull. Any cow or heifer where the breeding history is not definitely known should be placed in the second "infected" group.

(2) The infected or possibly infected cows or heifers include those pregnant or nonpregnant animals that have had coitus with an infected or suspect bull and have not had a normal gestation period following that service.

In Group 1 the noninfected cows and heifers may bred by a noninfected or virgin bull or by artificial insemination. In Group 2 the "infected" or "suspect" nonpregnant females should be given 60 to 90 days, or 3 normal estrous cycles, sexual rest before being rebred to cheap noninfected "sacrifice" bulls which can be slaughtered at the end of the breeding season. All pregnant and nonpregnant cows should be examined at monthly or bimonthly invervals until they are pregnant 6 months or more, or are sold as infertile. Females with pyometra, abortions or metritis should be treated before breeding or sold for slaughter. After calving these cows should not be rebred for a period of 60 to 90 days and then they may be bred naturally to a noninfected bull. This latter method has been employed successfully in a number of beef herds where the "infected" and "noninfected" herds can be kept some distance apart with no danger of contact or mixing of animals between the two herds. In a few beef herds the disease was eradicated by breeding virgin bulls to virgin heifers and keeping these animals together and separate from the infected herd for a number of years until the infected herd could be eliminated or replaced. Accurate breeding records, carefully identified cows and bulls, good fences and intelligent management is necessary to eliminate this disease by methods other than by selling all bulls and going into an artificial breeding program for all the females in the herd.

Individual treatment—The treatment of infected cows is not necessary, inasmuch as these animals if given sexual rest will overcome the infection, except for cases of pyometra and abortion and secondary metritis which must be handled as described later in this chapter. Many veterinarians feel that with treatment recovery may be more rapid and complete and to satisfy the owner that something is being done for these heifers or cows, many of which have been bred repeatedly, treatment is undertaken in many cases. These treatments may include douching of the vagina and possibly the uterus with 2 to 3 ml of Lugol's solution in 100 cc. of water, 4 to 5 percent sodium perborate solution, 1 to 3 percent chlorine solution, or 1 percent acriflavine solution, once or at several intervals a week or 10 days apart. Vandeplassche and coworkers reported that various antiseptic treatments of the genital tract of the infected cow were useless in elimination of the organisms, which can be done only by the development of immunity.

Treatment of bulls has received much much attention in the last 20 years and a number of different techniques and drugs have been used to effect a cure. They are as follows:

(1) The use of "Bovoflavin Ointment" from Farbwerke Hoechst Ag., Frankfurt, (M), Hoechst, Germany, was first described by Abelein in 1938. Swangard (1941) also demonstrated the value of this product and described the technique and the successful results on bulls. Bartlett reported on successful cures in 7 of 8 trichomonad-infected bulls. Vereerbrugghen, Vandeplassche and Paredis have reported on the treatment of 34 bulls, with an 88 percent recovery rate Work by Bartlett has further confirmed the value of "Bovoflavine Ointment" which is composed of trypaflavine, "Surfen" (a protozoacidal agent), and an ointment base. The procedure employed in the use of this product consists of giving the bull an internal pudendal nerve block as described by Larson to produce anesthesia and relaxation of the penis. This is done by restraining the bull. After cleansing, shaving, and disinfecting the site, 5 ml. of 2 percent procaine or xylocaine is injected under the skin in the cranial or deepest portion of the ischio-rectal fossa. An 18-gauge needle 5 to 8 inches, 12.5 to 20.5 cm, long depending on the size of the bull is

passed through the large needle forward and slightly downward, medial to the sacrosciatic ligament. In most bulls anesthesia of the skin of the ischio-rectal fossa is not necessary as a sharp strong thrust will force the 18 gauge needle quickly through the skin if it is held firmly with the cotton about 1 to 2 inches from the point. The long needle is guided by the hand in the rectum to the internal pudendal nerve, which may be easily palpated in dairy bulls about 1.5 to 2 inches dorsal to the lesser sciatic foramen and the pudendal artery that traverses the medial face of the sacrosciatic ligament. Fifteen to 25 ml of procaine or xylocaine is injected around the pudendal nerve and an equal amount to make 30 to 50 ml is injected along the course of the needle as it is withdrawn to block the middle and posterior hemorrhoidal nerves. Since there is an anastomosis between the sciatic nerve and the ventral branch of the internal pudendal nerve, Habel pointed out the importance of blocking the ventral branch of the internal pudendal nerve just medial and caudal to the lesser sciatic foramen as it passes caudally close to the internal pudendal artery and vein. This can be facilitated by manually massaging the injected anesthesia in a ventral manner. In beef, large dairy, or very fat bulls a 7- to 8-inch 18-gauge needle is usually required. The nerves on the opposite side of the pelvic cavity are injected similarly. Anesthesia is usually adequate to permit treatment in 15 to 20 minutes. No impairment of locomotion is noted. This treatment may be supplemented by the injection of a large dose of suitable tranquilizer. In fact some beef and dairy bulls may be treated after tranquilization without administering a pudendal block if the base of the penis is massaged with the hand in the rectum.

This technique is usually much superior to chloral narcosis and epidural anesthesia given slowly to keep the bull standing. It is much safer than general anesthesia or complete epidural anesthesia, producing temporary posterior paralysis since the bull may injure itself when coming out of anesthesia. It is safer than blocking the dorsal nerve of the penis at the sigmoid curve because injection of anesthesia at this site may cause adhesions and render the bull unable to protrude the penis. The injection of the internal pudendal nerve as it passes over the ischial arch is difficult and not uniformly successful.

The relaxed and anesthetized penis is withdrawn from the sheath and the penis and prepuce are thoroughly washed with warm, soapy water, rinsed and dried and 80 to 120 gms. of "Bovoflavin Ointment" thoroughly rubbed into the mucosa of the glans penis and prepuce and all the folds and crevices for a watch-timed period of 15 to 20 minutes. Fifteen to 20 ml of 0.1 percent trypaflavine or acriflavine solution is injected into the urethra with a syringe and the urethral orifice held closed for 5 minutes. Usually the penis will stay in the sheath after treatment but occasionally it may be necessary to tie a light cord around the bull or around the pendant portion of the preputial skin to compress the preputial orifice for an hour or so until the anesthesia disappears. This treatment is repeated in 10 to 14 days, Bartlett. Vereertbrugghen, Vanderplassche and Paredis recommended a careful 10-minute washing of the penis and prepuce with a 0.1 percent trypaflavine solution at body temperature rather than with soap and water. This was followed by the thorough application of "Bovoflavin" ointment" for 10 minutes with smooth rubber gloves, as working with the bare hands caused too much irritation to the penis and prepuce, besides staining the hands. They reported that one treatment was sufficient for a cure by this method except for bulls with granular lesions or lymph follicles on the penis, in which cases 2 treatments are administered 6 to 10 days apart. By this technique they cured 30 of 34 bulls. Vandeplassche and coworkers (1954) reported on the successful cure of 76 out of 85 infected bulls with a single treatment of "Bovoflavin" They did not encounter a bull that could not be cured by the above technique. Most workers do not report such a high percentage of successful treatments in field cases. Judging by the reports by Abelein, Swangard, Bartlett and Vandeplassche and coworkers the treatment with "Bovoflavin ointment" has been used successfully in more bulls than has any other treatment.

(2) Acriflavine ointment, 1 percent, applied to the penis and sheath and 0.5 percent acriflavine solution injected up the urethra in a manner similar to the treatment described for "Bovoflavin ointment" has been advocated by Fincher. The use of this ointment is more irritating than "Bovoflavin" salve. Binns reported on 4 bulls treated with acriflavine ointment that were cured; 1 of these previously had been treated unsuccessfully with "Bovoflavin ointment." Acriflavine is similar to trypaflavin but is more readily obtainable in the United States. Binns and Thorne and Fitzgerald et al. reported that lower concentrations of acriflavine, 0.25 to 0.50 percent in a lanolin base ointment was effective. In many cases the 1.0 percent ointment produced a severe inflammation of the prepuce and penis that might have caused adhesions had not a thin, stainless steel wire, inserted through the thick tunic of the penis about 1 inch behind the glans penis and extending out of the prepuce, been put in place and used to partially withdraw the penis daily for 4 to 5 days to four weeks after treatment. More work needs to be done to evaluate the effectiveness of treatment with acriflavine but from Fitzgerald et al. and other's studies 0.50 percent acriflavine ointment appears quite satisfactory.

(3) The iodide treatment described by Bartlett consisted of intravenous administration to the infected bull of 5 gm of sodium iodide per 100 lbs. of body weight in 500 cc. of sterile distilled water every 48 hours for 5 doses. All animals manifested iodism in varying degrees but there were no permanent harmful effects. The temporary symptoms exhibited were rough, scurfy hair coat in all animals and in others marked symptoms of ptyalism, coughing, nasal discharge, and temporary anorexia. No harmful effects were noted on semen production. In this treatment appreciable amounts of the iodide, a trichomonacidal agent, appeared in the prepuce. This technique has the advantage that no special procedures or drugs are required and it is faster, easier and safer than other forms of therapy. The sodium iodide solution should not be allowed to escape into the tissues around the vein. This technique, according to Bartlett, was used to treat 19 infected bulls with a total of 31 courses of treatment. Ten trichomonad-infected bulls were cured. Kendrick recommended combining the Bovaflavine technique and sodium iodide therapy to produce more cures. Further work should be done on this or similar simple methods of treatment to see if their efficacy could be improved.

(4) Hydrogen peroxide solution infused into the prepuce under pressure was advocated by Hess. Occasional injuries resulting in adhesions and inability to protrude the penis followed some of these treatments. Further work by other investigators should probably be done to determine the efficacy and safety of this apparently radical therapy. This treatment has not been generally accepted in this country.

(5) Bartlett and others have tried douching the sheath with various trichomonacidal agents at frequent intervals, without success. These agents have included sodium perborate, one percent Lugol's solution, sodium hypochlorite, and others.

(6) Recent reports by McLaughlin, Gasparini et al., Brodie, and Cardwell have indicated that metronidazole (Searle, Chicago Ill.) which is widely used for trichomoniasis in humans due to **T. vaginalis,** and dimetridazole (Rhodia Inc., N.Y.C.) show great promise in the treatment of trichomoniasis in bulls. Twenty five bulls were cured by the oral administration of 25 to 50 mg/kg of body weight of dimetridazole daily for 5 days, McLaughlin and Cardwell. One other bull required dosage at the 100 mg/kg level to effect a cure. Intravenous injection of the drug was also successful but slight reactions were observed due to the low pH of the injected solution. Gasparini et al. treated 15 trichomonad-infected bulls with metronidazole either intravenously or topically into the sheath and all recovered. The intravenous dosage which caused some reactions was 75 mg/kg body weight for 3 injections at 12 hour intervals. The topical treatment was applied as a 1 percent ointment similar to "Bovoflavine". Metronidazole can also be injected subcutaneously and/or used in a 1 percent aqueous solution as a douche. These agents are used orally in men and women to eliminate **T. vaginalis** and therefore might be used in infected female cattle to hasten recovery or prevent pyometra or abortion. Fitzgerald et al. reported that infusing 100 to 150 ml of a 1 percent solution of POP-diguanyl-diazoamino-benzene diaceturate "Berenil" ("Ganaseg", Squibb) into the sheath daily for 5 days and massaging it for 15 minutes with the preputial orifice closed cured 12 of 17 bulls; 4 bulls required 2 courses of treatment and one bull remained infected. These and other closely related highly potent trichomonicidal agents need further trials and evaluation; as yet such treatment for bulls has not been approved by F.D.A. for general use.

Treatment of bulls without eradication of **Trichomonas fetus** in the herd is useless, since bulls which have recovered are susceptible to reinfection. Many more controlled trials of treatments for trichomoniasis in bulls should be performed to assess their value accurately and to ascertain their dangers and other shortcomings. Until this has been done, careful observation and repeated checking of the bulls after treatment is necessary. This is the most costly, time consuming and important aspect of the treatment of bulls for trichomoniasis. The failure of careful and repeated examinations after treatment was one of the major shortcomings of the work done by Abelein and Hess. Bartlett reported that for 3 months after treatment negative preputial samples even if collected twice a week have little significance. Furthermore, test matings with susceptible females were not reliable during this period. One bull was negative for 13 weeks after treatment and isolation and then found positive the next week. Preputial samples for culture and direct microscopic examination should be collected weekly during the fourth, fifth and sixth months posttreatment. Coitus with 2 or more virgin heifers should be allowed at intervals during these months and vaginal samples should be examined frequently between 12 and 19 days after coitus. If still negative the bull can be restored to service but careful observations should be made on females bred to him. Preputial samples should be taken from him occasionally for an extended period. Because of the long and costly posttreatment examination period, the actual treatment should be done carefully and thoroughly.

Prevention—Preventing the introduction of trichomoniasis into a herd is of vital interest to an owner and his veterinarian. The precautions should include: knowledge of the reproductive efficiency in the herd of origin of any stock purchased; thorough examination of newly-purchased suspect bulls with a pipette to obtain preputial samples for culture, at least 6 times at weekly intervals; by using the douche technique of Fitzgerald et al. and Johnson, possibly 3 preputial samplings would be adequate since the douche method is more efficient, although more cumbersome; repeated examinations 12 to 19 days after coitus of the vaginal mucus of the first 3 or 4 cows and heifers bred to these bulls; and prohibition of coitus for newly-purchased nonvirgin, nonpregnant heifers and nonpregnant cows that have had coitus since their last calving, to prevent the introduction of trichomoniasis by females. These animals should be bred by artificial insemination. All recently acquired cows that are pregnant should be withheld from coitus for 90 days after calving and allowed to pass at least 2 heat periods before being bred naturally, Bartlett.

In artificial breeding stations the need for a careful examination and history on the bulls before purchase, and proper and frequent examination, 6 negative preputial examinations at weekly intervals, of all service-age bulls as they enter the stud and periodically thereafter is essential to prevent the possible introduction and spread of this infection into many herds. Owners should be careful of their source of semen for artificial insemination in their herds especially if a herd sire is also maintained.

References

Abelein, R. (1938) Behandlung von Bullen mit Trichomonaden, Dtsch. Tierartzl. Wschr., **46,** 46, 721.

Bartlett, D. E. (1946) Experimental Treatment of **Trichomonas Fetus** Infection in Bulls, Am. J. Vet. Res., **7,** 25, 417.

Bartlett, D. E. (1947) **Trichomonas Fetus** Infection and Bovine Reproduction, Am. J. Vet. Res., **8,** 29, 343.

Bartlett, D. E. (1948) Further Observations on Experimental Treatments of **Trichomonas Fetus** Infection in Bulls, Am. J. Vet. Res., **9,** 33, 351.

Bartlett, D. E. (1949) Infectious Disease as a Cause of Infertility: A Review, J. of Dairy Sci., **32,** 1, 36.

Bartlett, D. E. (1949) Procedures for Diagnosing Bovine Venereal Trichomoniasis and Handling Affected Herds, J.A.V.M.A., **114,** 866, 293.

Bartlett, D. E. (1954) (1966) Personal Communication.

Bartlett, D. E. (1968) Bovine Venereal Trichomoniasis and Bovine Abortion in "Abortion Diseases of Livestock" Edit. by L. C. Faulkner, C. C. Thomas Co., Springfield, Ill.

Bartlett, D. E. Moist, K. and Spurrell, F. A. (1953) The **Trichomonas Fetus**—Infected Bull in Artificial Insemination, J.A.V.M.A., **122,** 912, 366.

Bartlett, D. E., Teeter, K. G. and Underwood, P. C. (1947) Artificial Insemination as a Means of Transmission of Bovine Venereal Trichomoniasis, J.A.V.M.A., **111,** 845, 114.

Beattie, H. E. R. (1955) A Bovine "Trichomonad Cyst", Austral. Vet. J. **31,** 6, 146.

Bielanski, W. (1958) Personal Communication.

Binns, W. (1954) Personal Communication.

Binns, W. and Thorne, J. L. (1955) Personal Communication.

Brodie, B. O. (1970) Trichomoniasis, in **Bovine Medicine and Surgery,** Amer. Vet. Public. Inc., Wheaton, Ill., 219.

Cameron, H. S. (1935) Bovine Trichomoniasis, Cor. Vet., **25,** 2, 99.

Cameron, H. S. (1938) Bovine Trichomoniasis, Univ. of Cal., Agr. Exp. Stat., Bulletin 624, Berkeley, Cal.

Cardwell, W. H. (1965) Personal Communication.

Dunton, R. K. (1966) Personal Communication.

Fincher, M. G. (1953) Current Problems in Cattle Practice Including Mastitis, Canad. J. Comp. Med. and Vet. Sci. **17,** 193.

Fincher, M. G. (1954) Personal Communication.

Fitzgerald, P. R., Hammond, D. M., Miner, M. L. and Binns, W. (1952) Relative Efficiency of Various Methods of Obtaining Preputial Samples for Diagnosis of Trichomoniasis in Bulls, Am. J. Vet. Res., **13,** 49, 452.

Fitzgerald, P. R., Johnson, A. E. and Hammond, D. M. (1963) Treatment of Genital Trichomoniasis in Bulls, J.A.V.M.A. **143,** 3, 727.

Fitzgerald, P. R., Johnson, A. E., Thorne, J. L. and Hammond, D. M. (1958) Experimental Infections of the Bovine Genital System with Trichomonads from the Digestive Tract of Swine, Amer. J. Vet. Res. **19,** 73, 775.

Gabel, A. A., Tharp, V. L., Thorne, J. L., Graves, H. F., Koutz, F. R and Amstutz, H. E. (1958) Trichomoniasis in an Artificial Insemination Stud, J.A.V.M.A. **132,** 11, 476.

Garlick, G. (1939) Transmission of Bovine Venereal Trichomoniasis through Artificial Insemination, Vet. Med., **34,** 43.

Gasparini, G., Vaghi, M. and Tardini, A. (1963) Treatment of Bovine Trichomoniasis with Metronidazole, Vet. Rec. **75,** 940.

Gilman, H. (1964) Personal Communication.

Habel, R. E. (1956) A Source of Error in the Pudendal Nerve Block, J.A.V.M.A., **128,** 1, 16.

Hammond, D. M. and Bartlett, D. E. (1943) Establishment of Infection with **Trichomonas Fetus** in Bulls by Experimental Exposure, Am. J. Vet. Res., **4,** 10, 61.

Hammond, D. M. and Bartlett, D. E. (1945) Pattern of Fluctuations in Numbers of **Trichomonas Foetus** Occurring in the Bovine Vagina During Initial Infections, Am. J. Vet. Res., **6,** 19, 84.

Hammond, D. M. and Leidl, W. (1957) Experimental Infections of the Genital Tract of Swine and Goats with **Trichomonas fetus** and Trichomonas Species from the Cecum or Feces of Swine, Amer. J. Vet. Res. **18,** 68, 461.

Hess, E. (1951) Diagnose and Therapie der Trichomonadenseuche beim Zuchtstier, Tierartzl Umschau, **6,** 11 and 12, 191.

Hibler, C. P., Hammond, D. M., Caskey, F. H., Johnson, E. A. and Fitzgerald, P. R. (1960) The Morphology and Incidence of the Trichomonads of Swine, **Tritrichomonas suis** (Greeby and Delafond, **Trichomonas rotunda,** n. sp. and **Tritrichomonas but-**

treyi, n. sp., Jour. of Protozool. **1,** 2, 159.

Johnson, A. E. (1964) Incidence and Diagnosis of Trichomoniasis in Western Beef Bulls, J.A.V.M.A. **145,** 10, 1007.

Johnson, A. E. (1965) The Diagnosis of Trichomoniasis in the Bull, Proc. 69th Ann. Meeting U.S.L.S.A., 183.

Joyner, L. P. (1954) The Elimination of **Trichomonas Fetus** from Infected Semen by Storage in the Presence of Glycerol, Vet. Rec., **66,** 47, 727.

Joyner, L. P. and Bennett, G. H. (1956) Observations on the Viability of **Trichomonas fetus** during the Process of Freezing to -79° C. and Thawing in the Presence of Glycerol, Jour. of Hyg. **54,** 335.

Kendrick, J. W. (1953) An Outbreak of Bovine Trichomoniasis in a Group of Bulls Used for Artificial Insemination, Cor. Vet. **43,** 2, 231.

Kendrick, J. W. (1963) Infectious Causes of Infertility in Bulls, Personal Communication—Seminar.

Kerr, W. R. (1957) Personal Communication.

Kerr, W. R. (1955) Vaginal and Uterine Antibodies in Cattle with Particular Reference to **Br. abortus,** Brit. Vet. Jour. **111,** 4, 169.

Kerr, W. R. (1958) Experiments in Cattle with **Trichomonas suis,** Vet. Rec. **70,** 613.

Kerr, W. R. and Robertson, M. (1953) Active and Passive Sensitization of the Uterus of the Cow **in vivo** against **Trichomonas fetus** Antigen and the Evidence for the Local Production of Antibody in that Site, Jour. of Hyg. **51,** 3, 405.

McLaughlin, D. K. (1968) Dimetridazole Treatment of Bovine Trichomoniasis, J. Parasitol. 54, 1038.

Larson, L. L. (1953) The Internal Pudendal (Pudic) Nerve Block for Anesthesia of the Penis and Relaxation of the Retractor Penis Muscle, J.A.V.M.A. **123,** 916, 18.

Morgan, B. B. (1944) Bovine Trichomoniasis, Burgess Publishing Co., Minneapolis, Minn.

Morgan, B. B. and Whitehair, C. K. (1943) The pH of Bovine Trichomonad Pyometra Fluid, N.A. Vet., **24,** 12, 729.

Robertson, M. (1960) The Antigens of **Trichomonas foetus** Isolated from Cows and Pigs, J. Hyg. Camb. **58,** 207.

Simpson, C. F. and White, F. H. (1964) Structure of **Trichmonas fetus** as Revealed by Electron Microscopy, Amer. J. Vet. Res. **25,** 106, 815.

Swangard, W. M. (1939) Trichomoniasis in Cattle; Biological Studies and a System of Control, J.A.V.M.A., **95,** 749, 146.

Thorne, J. L., Shupe, J. L. and Miner, M. L. (1955) Diagnosis and Treatment of Trichomoniasis in Bulls, Proc. 92 Ann. Meeting, A. V.M.A., 374.

Todorovic, R. and McNutt, S. H. (1967) Diagnosing of **Trichomonas fetus** Infection in Bulls, Amer. J. Vet. Res. **28,** 126, 1581.

Vandeplassche, M., Florent, A., Paredis, F. and Brone, E. (1954) Pathogenese, Diagnose en Behandeling van de Trichomonas-infectie bij Runderen, Competes Rendus De Recherches, No. 13, Dec. 1954.

Vandeplassche, M., Paredis, F. and Doorme, H. (1948) L'Insemination Artificielle Et La Trichomoniase Chez Les Bovine, Zootecnica e Veterinaria-La Fecondazione Artificiale, Numen Speciale in Occasione del I Congress di Fisiopatoligia della riproduzione animale e di Fecondazione Artificiale 23-30, Guigno. 3.

Vereetbrugghen, W., Vandeplassche, M. and Paredis, F. (1952) The Treatment of Trichomoniasis in Bulls, The II Internat. Congr. of Physiol. and Path. of An. Reprod. and of Art. Insem., 132.

Witherspoon, D. M. and Walker, D. F. (1966) New Way to Diagnose Trichomoniasis in Bulls, Mod. Vet. Pract. **47,** 14, 50.

VIBRIOSIS

Definition—Vibriosis is a venereal disease of cattle caused by **Vibrio fetus venerealis** spread at the time of coitus or at the time of artificial insemination with improperly handled and treated semen, and characterized by infertility with an increased number of services necessary per conception. Early embryonic deaths are common and late abortions from 4 months of gestation to term are occasionally observed. The cow develops an immunity to the infection and will have a normal gestation period but may remain a carrier for many months. The older bull remains a chronic carrier.

Etiology—Vibriosis was first described by McFadyean and Stockman in 1910 and 1913 in sheep and cattle. During the period of 1918 to 1923 Theobald Smith made a number of reports on the causative agent, pathogenesis, and other factors associated with this disease. He called the organism **Vibrio fetus.** This organism may appear as motile, or nonmotile, gram-negative, short, comma-shaped rods, or as double spiral-shaped filaments. It grows slowly, scantily, and with difficulty on most laboratory media. All laboratory animals except guinea pigs appear refractory to infection but the organism may be pathogenic for chick embryos. **Vibrio fetus** is pathogenic for man in which it causes an undulating fever, placental infection and abortion, Gilman. There is a close genetic relationship between certain ovine, bovine and human vibrios so human vibriosis might be acquired by contact with animals.

Within the past 15 years the various pathogenic vibrio have been isolated and studied, Florent, Mohanty et al., Bryner et al., Brunner and Gillespie, and Winter (See Table 18). **V. fetus venerealis** is a serologically homogenous strain and both Type I and Subtype 1 (or Type II Mohanty et al.) are similar in antigenicity and pathogenicity, Hoerlein. **V. fetus intestinalis** is also pathogenic in that it is a common cause of abortion in sheep and causes sporadic abortions in cattle. **V. fetus intestinalis** only rarely produces infertility, Florent and DeKeyser. It can survive for a period of time in the gut of animals but does not persist in the genital tract of cows. **V. bubulus** also does not persist in the genital tract of cows. **V. bubulus** is a nonpathogenic vibrio that is commonly found in fecal material and in the cranial portion of the prepuce of bulls. **V. fecalis,** described by Firehammer in sheep was found by Lein et al. and Winter to be a contaminant of the sheath in occasional bulls resulting in some problems when the F.A. test was used to diagnose **V. fetus venerealis** infections in the prepuce of bulls.

V. fetus venerealis is found only in the female genital tract and its contents, fetus and placenta, and in the prepuce and semen of the bull. **V. fetus venerealis** usually invades the uterus about 7 days after natural service to an infected bull. It remains there about to 13 weeks until a local immunity develops and the infection is eliminated. However, the infection may remain in the cervix and vagina for 8 to 18 months or more. Rarely a cow may carry the infection through a normal gestation period, Florent et al., Frank et al, Newsom and Peterson, and Plastridge et al.. Vulvar exposure of susceptible heifers with **V. fetus** failed to produce infection so spread of the disease by contact is unlikely, McEntee et al.. Young bulls under 5 years of age are difficult to infect. They may carry the organism from cow to cow during the breeding season but rapidly become free of infection when isolated from infected cows. In bulls over 5 years of age vibriosis may become a chronic infection in the prepuce and persist for years. The numbers of vibrio organisms in the sheaths of infected bulls varies greatly. Most of the organisms are present in the deeper portions of the sheath around the glans penis and fornix, Samuelson and Winter, Wagner et al, Hoerlein, and Frank. Thus the carrier female as well as the carrier bull are responsible for maintaining the infection in the herd from year to year. Bulls do not develop immunity. The immunity or resistance in cows is not a strong one but is sufficient in most cases to permit conception and a normal gestation even if the organisms survive in the tract for several days or weeks, Hoerlein. **Vibrio fetus venerealis** from the prepuce contaminates the semen as the organism has never been found in the deeper portions of the male reproductive tract. Special media, techniques and experience are required for the laboratory recovery of **V. fetus venerealis** from mucus from the vagina, cervix and uterus of cows and especially the contaminated mucus of the bull's prepuce. The Vibrio organism is highly susceptible to light, drying and other adverse influences. It cannot live in the alimentary tract of the cow, Bryner et al..

Vibriosis is a venereal disease of cattle spread by the chronically-infected bull to susceptible cows by either natural or artificial service. The early work on this disease was done by Stegenga and Terpstra, Terpstra and Eisma, Rasbech, Lawson and McKinnon, and McEntee et al.. **V. fetus venerealis** is probably the most important cause of infertility in beef cattle in the western range states, Hoerlein, Wiltbank et al. and until the advent of the widespread use of artificial insemination with antibiotic-treated semen it was a very common cause of infertility in dairy herds in the U.S.A.

Vibriosis has been reported as widespread in nearly every state in the United States, in Australia, South Africa, Sweden, England, Holland, Canada and other countries in the world. The **V. fetus** organism is found only in the vagina, cervix, uterus and possibly the oviducts of cows and in the prepuce and on the penis of bulls. The presence of **V. fetus** in the semen can be explained in the same manner as the presence of trichomonads in the semen, namely by contamination of the artificial vagina at the time of service. Frank found **V. fetus** infections in 25 of 45 herds investigated in the region of Beltsville, Maryland. Kendrick reported a 38 percent incidence of vibriosis infection in beef herds in California based on the mucus agglutination test. These herds had histories that were suspicious of vibriosis. Boyd reported that 60 percent of

Table 18. Cultural Characteristics of the Common Vibrios

Vibrios	Catalase	H_2S Production	Tolerance to 3.5% NaCl	Tolerance to 1% glycine	Fluorescent Antibody Reaction*
V. fetus venerealis (Type I & Subtype I)	+	-	-	-	+++
V. fetus intestinalis	+	+	-	+	(+)
V. bubulus	-	+++	+	+	-
V. fecalis** (Firehammer)	(+)	+	-	+	+(+)

*Congugate prepared from V. fetus venerealis (Now obtainable from Armour-Baldwin Lab.).
**Appears similar to V. fetus intestinalis but the colony morphology is much different.

the 105 herds in Sweden studied by means of the mucus agglutination test were, or showed evidence of having been, infected with vibriosis. Thus vibriosis is probably much more widespread and common than is trichomoniasis and for this reason is of greater economic importance. Although abortion has been produced in a few animals by the intravenous injection of the organism, introduction of organisms into the animal's body by any means other than the genital tract of the female or the prepuce of the male has not resulted in infection. It is probable that natural infection of the cow except by coitus or artificial insemination is rare. Occasionally the infection might be spread from cow to cow by improperly cleaned instruments or insanitary procedures used in the treatment of the genital tract of cows. Work by McEntee, Hughes and Gilman; and Frank and Bryner; and Lawson and MacKinnon indicated that infection except by coitus or insemination rarely if ever occurs even when infected and noninfected animals run together. In artificial insemination studs there is definite evidence of intrastud spread of infection. In a report by Hughes on 143 bulls in an artificial breeding stud 56 percent were infected; the percentage of infected animals was the same for 39 bulls that had never had a natural service as it was for 104 bulls that had previously been in natural service. It was felt that contact and spread of infection between clean and infected bulls occurred on teaser bulls or steers at the time of semen collection or in pens where a number of bulls run together and mount each other. Rasbech reported that over 20 percent of all bulls used artificially in Denmark were infected with **Vibrio fetus.** The incidence of infection in susceptible cows is high following coitus with infected bulls. For example, of 30 virgin heifers bred with fresh infected semen at a dilution rate of 1 to 4 with extender without antibiotics, 26 heifers developed vibriosis, Hughes, McEntee and Gilman. Rasbech and the author both believe that prior to the addition of antibiotics to semen, artificial insemination was a major factor in the spread of this disease. It is significant that in one large AI organization that conception rates based on 60 to 90 day nonreturns rose from 52 percent in May of 1948 to 74 percent in September of 1949 after the addition of antibiotics to the semen. No other changes or treatments were made in the semen collection, processing, or insemination. Since the advent of the regular and proper addition of antibiotics to semen the incidence of the disease is greater in herds using natural service. As with trichomoniasis the disease is more prevalent in dealer's herds, valuable purebred herds, and institution herds, where there is a higher incidence of purchase and sale of cows and bulls. Virgin heifers and virgin bulls are free of the infection.

Signs—Vibriosis, as trichomoniasis, is insidious in the manner in which it enters a herd. The condition may not be recognized for several months or more, until signs of infertility with failure of conception occur in a large number of cows. Lawson and MacKinnon, Frank and Bryner, and Boyd described the herd infections in the following manner. **The acute** type of infertility problem is seen when the infection is first introduced by an infected bull into a clean or susceptible herd. The drop in conception rate is marked, occasionally to less than 10 percent and the infertility may last for 2 to 6 months or more. Within this time the cows usually develop an immunity or tolerance to the infection and conception will follow breeding to either an infected or noninfected bull. Prior to the development of this immunity, breeding to a noninfected bull or with noninfected semen does not correct the infertility as the **V. fetus** organisms are present in the female from the original infecting service. **The chronic or subacute type** of infertility in a herd may be characterized by a history of an acute fertility problem in the past. Only a vague or intermittent infertility is present in the cows or in newly-purchased cows but a considerable amount of infertility may be present in the heifers after being bred to older infected bulls. This may not occur until the second breeding period if it is a practice to breed the virgin heifers in a herd to a virgin noninfected bull. In some herds the infertility may be limited to the portion of a herd served by a single bull, or it may involve all cows bred naturally, while cows being bred artificially with antibiotic-treated semen conceive normally. Examination of the bull and its semen usually reveals no abnormalities or explanation for the infertility. Abortions may occur in both the acutely or chronically affected herds but are more frequent in the acute outbreaks. Plastridge et al. reported that heifers may also fall into several groups. Some heifers have a natural immunity or develop it promptly and conceive within 2 months. Other conceive promptly but remain carriers of the organism for months. While other remain infected for months, have many services, or abort.

The specific signs of vibriosis in cattle may be listed as follows:

(1) Vibriosis may fail to become established in a susceptible animal after coitus with an infected bull, either due to natural resistance or because the numbers of organisms were too small to cause infection. Conception and normal gestation may occur. Occasionally the infection fails to establish itself rapidly in the uterus and cause the early death of the ovum or embryo. Gestation therefore may continue for a number of months and then terminate in 3 to 8 months in abortion. The number of susceptible animals bred to an infected bull that fail to become infected are small, probably less than 5 to 25 percent. Hughes, McEntee and Gilman cited 30 heifers that were

artificially infected at the time of insemination; 7 conceived on first service and in 24 the infection became established.

(2) **Endometritis** and occasionally salpingitis has been described by Lawson and MacKinnon, Terpstra and Eisma and McEntee, Hughes and Gilman as occurring in **V. fetus** infection of the genital tract of cows and heifers. No vaginitis or cervicitis or other lesions of these organs were noted, Newsom and Peterson, Hoerlein. A slight mucopurulent exudate may be present in the vagina. This may occasionally be noted as a discharge from the vulva and probably comes from the uterus or is due to secondary infections. The infection or inflammation produced by **V. fetus** is mild in its effect on the mucosa. The estrual mucus may be cloudy and increased in amount in recently-infected heifers. The cervix may be reddened and postmortem gross and histologic examination of the uterus may reveal an exudate and a slight to moderate degree of endometritis. Estes et al. indicated that by 30 days after inoculation of the cervix a subacute diffuse muco-purulent endometritis with a periglandular lymphocytic infiltration was present. Dennis has described the pathogenesis of **Vibrio fetus** infection in cattle. As the cow develops immunity and overcomes the infection, the estrual mucus becomes clear before pregnancy is established. In most recently-infected animals these symptoms of endometritis pass unnoticed by the average owner or herdsman or are not detectable clinically. If cows are examined for failure of conception or infertility no specific signs of vibriosis can be observed. Rectal examination of the uterus is of no value in the diagnosis of an endometritis since the inflammation is so mild no obvious uterine changes are produced. No physical symptoms have been observed in the recently-infected bull. Most infertile **V. fetus**-infected cattle conceive before the endometritis and the organisms have completely disappeared, Hoerlein and others.

(3) **Infertility or failure of conception** lasting for a period of 2 to 6 months, and in some herds 12 months, in susceptible cows or heifers bred naturally to an infected bull or bred artificially with fresh or frozen semen to which no antibiotic has been added is the most common symptom of vibriosis. Up to 1950, it was thought that **V. fetus** was characterized principally by abortion; since 1950, however, infertility due apparently to the early death of the ovum or embryo caused by the **V. fetus** organism has been shown to be the cause for the greatest economic loss. This symptom of infertility and failure of conception, as in trichomoniasis, is the most constant and severe condition encountered in connection with vibriosis. This has been demonstrated by field observations by Lawson and MacKinnon, and Frank and Bryner. In experimentally-infected animals McEntee, Hughes and Gilman showed that 19 artificially-infected heifers required from 1 to 16 services, with an average of 5, per recognizable pregnancy. Lawson and MacKinnon in a similar experiment infected 20 heifers, which then required an average of 5.1 services per conception as against 1 to 3 services, or an average of 1.3 to 1.6 services per conception for control heifers bred to uninfected bulls. Frank and Bryner described in detail a herd using 5 bulls, 1 of which was infected with **V. fetus.** The cows bred to the 4 noninfected bulls conceived with an average of 1.1 to 1.8 services per conception with 2.5 to 32 as the average number of days lost from first service to pregnancy. Of 18 cows bred to the infected bull, 5 failed to develop any infection and all 5 conceived on first service while the other 13 became infected and were bred an average of 3 services per conception with an average loss of 89 days from first service to pregnancy. Vibriosis in a beef herd may be suspected when many cows continue to come into estrum in the latter part of the breeding season. The calving season is also prolonged with a fair number of calves produced early followed by a period when relatively few calves are dropped and then late in the calving season more calves are born, Hoerlein, Wiltbank et al..

Pregnancy rates as low as 20 to 70 percent may be seen in some beef herds at the end of the breeding season. In other chronically infected herds the pregnancy rates may be 60 to 85 percent with a poor conception rate in the virgin heifers. If routine vaccination of all breeding stock is practiced the pregnancy rate is usually from 80 to 95 percent, Hoerlein. Willett and coworkers in an extensive field experiment reported that cows inseminated with semen from **V. fetus**-infected bulls had a much greater embryonic mortality rate and much lower nonreturn rate than noninfected semen or semen to which streptomycin had been added. Cows bred with semen from infected bulls to which no antibiotic was added had a 42.7 percent conception rate as compared to a 62.3 percent conception rate from similarly diluted semen from apparently noninfected bulls.

(4) **Long estrous cycles** ranging from 27 to 53 days with an average of 32 days are experienced by many recently-infected cows and heifers, McEntee. Frank and Bryner reported prolonged estrous cycles of 25 to 60 days and even to 100 days as common, following the first service of a susceptible female to an infected bull. This delayed or long interval may occur following any service in infected cows. These irregular, usually prolonged, periods between heats have been described by other authors, Lawson and MacKinnon, Terpstra and Eisma, and Boyd. Long cycles may be explained on the basis that fertilization takes place; the fertilized ovum may survive for 12 to 14 days or longer and is then killed or destroyed

by the **V fetus** organisms; another estrum then follows at a longer interval than the regular estrual cycle. If the fertilized ovum is destroyed prior to 14 days after fertilization then estrum will probably occur at the regular cycle length. From experiments cited by Frank, fertilization is apparently not affected by Vibrio infection.

(5) **Abortion** was formerly considered the principal symptom of the disease. Plastridge and coworkers reported a 4- to 20-percent abortion rate of recognizable fetuses with an average of 12 percent in a herd. Roberts, Gilman and Larsen reported, after reviewing the literature, that 3.4 to 29 percent of aborted fetuses from brucella-free cows were found positive on culture for **V. fetus.** Lawson and MacKinnon reported an incidence of 8.6 percent of 1302 aborted fetuses as positive for the presence of **V. fetus.** In both of these series a fairly large group of fetuses was so contaminated that recovery of pathogenic bacteria such as **V. fetus** was impossible. Of the 112 fetuses found positive in the latter study, 1 aborted embryo was recovered at 38 days, 1 at two months, 1 at two and one-half months, 5 at three months, 8 at four months, 30 at five months, 39 at six months, 15 at seven months, 3 at eight months, and 9 unknown. In a report by Plastridge and his coworkers on 198 aborted fetuses, the number of fetuses and the time of abortion was: 9 from one to two months of gestation, 14 from two to three months, 17 from three to four months, 29 from four to five months, 52 from five to six months, 36 from six to seven months, 26 from seven to eight months, 12 from eight to nine months, and 3 expelled dead at term. This was based on bacteriologic evidence in about 50 percent of the cases and serologic evidence in the rest. Thus the greatest incidence of observed abortion is from 4 to 7 months of gestation. It is highly probable, according to our present knowledge, that abortions prior to 4 months are more common but are not observed and are considered as infertility or failure to conceive. Usually there is some indication of impending abortion after the fourth or fifth month of gestation by the presence of a vulvar discharge and slight edema of the vulva. Some enlargement of the udder may occur. In early abortions the placenta is usually expelled with the fetus. In late abortions retention of the fetal membranes may occur. Pyometra is rarely observed in **V. fetus** infection in cattle. Smith stated that the lesions in abortions at middle or late gestation are mainly in the fetal membranes, the fetus suffering secondarily because of interference with its circulation. The lesions resemble those of **Brucella** abortion, the intercotyledonary spaces being filled with a thick, purulent, viscid material. The cotyledons may be greyish white in color with much cheesy exudate between the maternal caruncle and the fetal cotyledon. The membranes may be thickened and edematous, the amniotic fluid turbid due to fetal diarrhea, and **V. fetus** organisms may be found in the placenta. The aborted fetus usually shows autolytic changes of subcutaneous edema; thin, bloody fluid in the body cavities; and in the stomach a thick, yellow, flocculent, turbid material that usually contains many Vibrio. The stomach contents of normal fetuses are clear, semi-liquid, and mucoid in nature.

Lack of libido in bulls—Infected bulls pasture-bred on susceptible cows copulate frequently. Because of the excessive sexual load occasioned by many of his cows returning to estrus, the bull may lose weight and libido even to the point of refusing to service the cows.

Diagnosis—On the basis of the herd history or symptoms, a careful review of the breeding records, and a careful physical examination of the individual animals in the herd, including the bull, to be certain that no seminal pathology is present, a tentative diagnosis of vibriosis or trichomoniasis might be made. Since in most areas vibriosis is more common than is trichomoniasis as a cause for herd infertility and failure of conception, vibriosis is usually the diagnosis; but trichomoniasis should be suspected until sufficient tests have been made to make certain of the diagnosis.

Pyometra is rare in vibriosis but is occasionally observed in trichomoniasis. Abortions in trichomoniasis usually occur within the first four months and seldom after the fifth month of gestation while in vibriosis abortions in the fifth through eighth months are common. It is possible to find both vibriosis and trichomoniasis in a bull, a cow, or a herd. Herds with infertility due to sterile or infertile bulls with defective semen or infertility due to a lack of energy intake, especially in beef herds, may simulate the signs of vibriosis and a careful differential diagnosis is imperative.

Since vibriosis, similar to trichomoniasis, is not a systemic disease, antibodies are rarely found in the blood serum. Thus blood or serologic tests for diagnosing vibriosis are seldom used at the present time as reliable results cannot be obtained.

Since the infection in the female genital tract produces a local immunity, the agglutination test on vaginal mucus is very useful for diagnosing the presence of vibriosis in a herd. Stegenga and Terpstra first noticed this immunity reaction in the vaginal mucus and it was further described by Terpstra and Eisma. In the United States, Plastridge and his coworkers, McEntee, Hughes and Gilman, and Kendrick have further perfected this test and proved its value. In Sweden, Boyd also showed the value and the reliabilty of this test. The vaginal mucus from a cow or heifer infected with **V. fetus** gives a positive agglutination reaction in approximately 30 to 80 days following the infecting service. This reaction persists in most cows for about 7 months or a range of 4 to 23 months. The mucus should not be taken from cows that have recently calved or for 3 to 4 days after estrum, as these cows may have metestrual blood in the mucus. Samples taken at these times may give false positive reactions. The excessive amounts of mucus from cows in estrum should not be used for this agglutination test as false negative results may be obtained because the antibody level is diluted. In infected heifers only 21 percent of the vaginal mucus samples taken during estrum gave an agglutination reaction while 91 percent of samples taken from about 4 to 5 days after estrum to 1 to 2 days before estrum agglutinated, Lawson and MacKinnon. The agglutination test at the proper time on samples obtained from about 10 heifers which have been bred for the first time at least 2 months but not over 9 months previously should establish or disprove a diagnosis of vibriosis in a herd. The vaginal mucus agglutination test is most useful in dairy herds where the stage of the estrous cycle of open cows is usually known and confinement of cows in stanchions is often possible.

The tampon method of collecting vaginal mucus samples was perfected by Jepson and Vindehilde of Copenhagen and described by Szabo. The technique of collecting vaginal mucus samples consists of holding the cow's tail to one side and washing the vulva and adjacent parts with soap and water. The vulvar lips are held open, and the vulva rinsed with clean water; a plastic 12-inch speculum containing both a tampon made of a gauze pad with a 16 inch string attached and the placement rod is inserted into the vagina. The speculum should be pushed as far forward as possible, and then the rod pushed forward, moving the tampon out of the speculum and into the cranial part of the vagina. To prevent air from entering the vagina and ballooning it, the thumb should be held over the end of the speculum while it is being withdrawn. The free end of the string is tucked between the vulvar lips to prevent its being soiled by feces. The tampon is left in the vagina at least 20 minutes to absorb an adequate sample of mucus. To remove the tampon wash the cow's vulva again, grasp the string and pull out the tampon and place it and the string in a plastic sample bottle. Samples should be kept in a refrigerator until mailed or taken to the laboratory. Inasmuch as no preservatives are added to the samples, they should not be sent through the mail over weekends or holidays to avoid spoilage. The necessary equipment may be supplied by the laboratory or made by the veterinarian. Kendrick has described the use of a human vaginal tampon introduced into the cow's vagina with a plastic insemination pipette and transported in 4 ounce plastic bottles available in supermarkets. The laboratory should be sent an unused tampon and bottle for weighing. This is necessary to ascertain the amount of mucus present in each sample for dilution purposes. Care should be taken that infection is not spread from cow to cow. Separate equipment is necessary for each animal. Boyd pointed out that only certain vibrio antigens were suitable for the vaginal mucus agglutination test. Those that give too many false positive reactions when tested on virgin heifers should be discarded. Hughes, McEntee and Gilman and Kendrick reported that any titer is significant but 1:25 is considered suspicious and 1:50 or more is positive. The number of positives in a representative sampling would vary, but one positive animal is probably sufficient to establish the presence of the infection in a herd.

Cultures of vaginal, cervical or uterine mucus taken at estrum from heifers and cows by a pipette has been described by Terpstra and Eisma. Hoerlein reported that culturing of cervical mucus was the preferred method of diagnosising vibriosis in range beef herds as the animals only needed to be handled once and samples could be taken at any stage of the estrous cycle or even during pregnancy. Hoelein and coworkers adapted artificial insemination pipettes attached to 2-1/2 ml plastic syringes to produce a vacuum to collect cervical mucus samples. The pipettes were passed through a sterile plastic or glass speculum to avoid contamination in the vestibular area. The pipettes were sealed with polybulbs and shipped to the laboratory in dry ice; freezing the pipettes in liquid nitrogen was not satisfactory because of breakage. The efficiency of recovering **V. fetus** from frozen vaginal or cervical mucus samples in the laboratory drops about 20 percent after 2 days in dry ice, Carroll. This technique must be performed carefully and samples taken promptly to a laboratory for culture. In 88 samples of mucus from artificially- or naturally-infected heifers, vibrios were recovered in about 26 percent of the samples, McEntee, Hughes and Gilman. This is a very low recovery rate. Lawson and MacKinnon reported that 83.1 percent of the samples of mucus they recovered from infected heifers at the time of estrum were positive on culture while only 26.5 percent of samples collected at other phases of the cycle were positive. Positive cultures were obtained from vaginal mucus samples taken by Frank and Bryner with a specially-designed instrument, from animals recently bred, repeatedly bred, after calving, and after conception. A total of 420 vaginal mucus samples were collected and 26 percent were positive for **V. fetus.** In Frank and Bryner's cases positive isolations from vaginal mucus were made as early as 11 days and as late as 224 days after conception. Positive cultures were obtained from 8 cows 21 to 196 days after calving. In a total of 114 vaginal mucus samples from 71 known virgin heifers none was positive for **V. fetus.** They regularly examined 42 cows or heifers from which **V. fetus** was recovered from vaginal mucus in 76 percent of the cattle for only 40 days; in 12 percent the organism was found for 2 to 6 months; and in the remaining 12 percent for 7 to 12 months. Hoerlein reported that about 50 percent of heifers were positive one week after exposure to **V. fetus.** From 3 to 9 weeks after breeding large numbers of vibrio were present in the samples. During the first 3 months after exposure nearly all open heifers, 80 to 90 percent, were positive so at this time samples from 6 to 10 open heifers would be adequate. In cattle exposed 6 months previously only 20 percent were positive so 20 samples of mucus should be taken from these open heifers or cows. Samples taken at the time of calving gave poor results. Terpstra and Eisma used a biopsy instrument designed by Nielsen to recover the organism from the uterus of infected cows or heifers.

Culture of V. fetus from semen and preputial smegma—Cultures of **V. fetus** can usually be recovered by a well-equipped laboratory with trained personnel. Hughes reported that in culturing 306 ejaculates taken in as sanitary a manner as possible from 81 infected bulls he recovered vibrio in 20 percent of the samples. In 307 samples Frank and Bryner reported recovering **V. fetus** 20 percent of the time, or once in 5 ejaculates. Shepler et al. and Winters et al. described the culturing of preputial smegma samples taken in the same manner as for recovering trichomonads. They considered this more accurate than the culturing of semen samples. Special techniques were necessary because of other bacterial contaminants in the prepuce. Winters and Mellick et al. developed a **fluorescent antibody screening test** to use on preputial and vaginal mucus samples; a positive test requires confirmatory vibrio cultures.

Another technique used to detect **V. fetus** in bulls is to breed them to 2 or more virgin heifers and obtain vaginal mucus for culture from the fifteenth to the thirtieth day, Frank and Bryner. Sampling as early as 10 or as late as 90 days gave positive results. These workers bred 17 suspected bulls to 82 virgin heifers and 52 percent were positive for **V. fetus** on subsequent culturing of vaginal mucus. Adler reported on inseminating 1 ml of undiluted semen into the cervical canal of 2 or more virgin heifers during estrum. By using Nielsen's biopsy instrument samples were taken from the uterus 4 days after service and once a week thereafter regardless of the phase of the cycle. In 8 heifers bred in this manner to known infected bulls 32 of 35 uterine biopsy samples were positive for **V. fetus,** while only 15 of 35 vaginal mucus samples taken at various times in the estrous cycle were positive on culture. In 31 of 32 positive cultures on uterine biopsy pure cultures of **V. fetus** were obtained. This technique resulted in a positive diagnosis 14 days after breeding the heifer. Later, as a means of diagnosing vibriosis in a bull, Rasbech advocated taking 3 ejaculates from a bull in the same vagina, and douching the prepuce with saline solution. The semen and saline douche fluid were mixed and centrifuged. One ml of sediment was inseminated into the cervix of a heifer in estrum and the heifer was cultured as described previously. Hoerlein and others have infused preputial washings into the cervical canal of several virgin heifers at any stage of the estrous cycle to test for the presence of **V. fetus** in a bull.

Procedures have been developed so veterinary practitioners can collect vaginal mucus, semen or preputial samples in the field in a proper manner and have them reach the laboratory in satisfactory condition for culture. More laboratories are being equipped with facilities and personnel for performing this careful culturing technique. The fluorescent antibody technique may aid greatly in the diagnosis of vibriosis in the future by detecting **V. fetus** in cervical mucus cultures also, Lincoln and Trout.

Aborted fetuses should always be cultured as this is one of the easier methods of diagnosing the presence of **V. fetus** in the herd. Immediately following abortion the fetus and possibly the fetal membranes if clean and not heavily contaminated should be taken to the laboratory for culture. The stomach contents and lungs are the organs in the large fetus from which **V. fetus** may most commonly be cultured. In small fetuses the amniotic fluid may be cultured. Some workers have reported finding the organism on direct smear or by fluorescent antibody techniques of the stomach contents or exudate on the fresh placenta. If the fetus is small and cannot be taken immediately to the laboratory in the fresh state, it may be frozen, packed in dry ice, and sent by special delivery. If the fetus is large, the esophagus, duodenum and trachea may be carefully ligated and the stomach and lungs removed and handled as above. Ten to 30 ml of stomach fluid from the aborted fetus may be removed in an aseptic manner and placed in a sterile vial. This may be frozen and shipped. If the fetus lives for even a short time, usually the stomach contents are contaminated by many bacteria. It is often possible in abortions caused by **V. fetus** to obtain pure cultures of this organism from the stomach contents of the fetus. The finding of the organism is a certain diagnosis that **V. fetus** is present in the herd. A differential diagnosis should be made between **V. fetus venerealis** and **V. fetus intestinalis** in cases of bovine abortion.

Prognosis—In vibriosis the prognosis in cows is usually favorable as the infertility ordinarily is temporary in nature and after a period of 3 to 6 months most infected cows develop immunity to the infection and conceive. The greatest loss is economic and is due to the delay in conception. Most cows if they abort conceive after a suitable period of sexual rest unless a secondary infection produces permanent damage. The old bull remains chronically or permanently infected unless he is isolated and treated. In many young bulls the infection is transient and disappears when he is removed from service.

Treatment—Our present knowledge is adequate to largely control vibriosis in beef herds and to eradicate the disease in dairy herds. Basically, the control methods are the same as in trichomoniasis. Genital contact between infected and noninfected animals should be prevented.

At the present time the best and easiest way to control vibriosis in a dairy herd is to breed only artificially with semen from noninfected bulls; or with semen from infected bulls, that has been diluted or extended at least 1 to 25 with extender to which 500 to 1000 units of penicillin and 500 to 1000 micrograms of streptomycin have been added for each ml of extender. This extended semen should be held at refrigerator temperature for at least 6 hours before use. The semen should be collected, diluted, cooled, and held according to methods outlined in the chapter on artificial insemination, to assure maximum sperm survival. Orthey and Gilman have demonstrated that the handling of infected semen in this manner will, by the time of insemination, destroy any vibrio organisms present. They also demonstrated that 2000 micrograms of streptomycin per ml of extended semen would destroy much-larger concentrations of vibrio than usually found in semen specimens. Clinical experiments by Hughes, McEntee and Gilman, and McEntee, Hughes and Gilman, were conducted to prove this. Vibrio-infected semen diluted 1 to 4 with extender without antibiotics resulted in 26, or 86.6 percent of 30 heifers becoming infected with vibriosis after insemination. When the infected semen was similarly diluted 1 to 25 with an extender without antibiotics and used to inseminate 29 heifers only 4, or 13.8 percent, became infected. This showed the value of dilution in reducing the incidence of infection. In 94 heifers inseminated with infected semen diluted 1 to 25 with extender to which 500 units of penicillin, 500 micrograms of streptomycin and 3 mg of sulfanilamide per ml had been added, then stored for 6 hours, none developed vibriosis. Frank and Bryner reported that **V. fetus** was not isolated from 99 "repeat breeding" cows and heifers and cows from 7 herds that had been artificially inseminated with antibiotic-treated semen from known infected bulls. Willett and coworkers indicated that streptomycin alone was as effective as combinations of streptomycin and penicillin and sulfanilamide in controlling the spread of **V. fetus** in the semen. Their conclusions were based on extensive field trials. They presented evidence to show that storage of vibrio-infected semen at 5° C. caused a reduction in its ability to cause infection even in the absence of antibiotics. The author has never recovered a fetus positive for **V. fetus** from an aborting cow that had been bred only artificially with antibiotic-treated semen. Boyd considered the use of antibiotics in semen an uncertain method of controlling vibriosis. The author knows that on the basis of the above data and his experience this method is effective but agrees that it is only a thin line of defense against the disease. Bulls used for artificial insemination should be free of vibriosis to be certain that they cannot spread the disease in the semen.

The control of **V. fetus** in frozen semen is more difficult than in the extended liquid semen because the glycerol interferes with the effect of the antibiotics on the organism. McEntee et al. (1958) presented evidence to show that frozen semen from vibrio-infected bulls extended with egg-yolk-citrate buffer with penicillin and streptomycin added in the proportions of 500 to 1000 units and 500 to 1000 mg respectively, did not produce vibriosis or infertility when used for the insemination of virgin heifers. They showed that although ampules of frozen semen may contain viable vibrios that the first few weeks of the holding period after freezing apparently resulted in their destruction. This has been confirmed over the past 11 years as very few cases of vibriosis have been reported in cattle bred with properly-treated frozen semen. Morgan et al. reported on 2 heifers infected with frozen semen stored for a year in an antibiotic and glycerol extender. Such occurrences are probably uncommon. Sullivan, Elliott and coworkers have shown that the addition of 500 units of polymyxin B sulphate, 500 units of penicillin and 1000 mg of dihydrostreptomycin per ml of extended frozen semen also was an effective means for the control of vibriosis.

In controlling vibriosis in a herd, artificial breeding to a noninfected bull, or to an infected or suspect bull after proper dilution and treatment of the semen with antibiotics and storage before use, should probably be continued for at least 2 to 3 years, in the light of Frank and Bryner's work indicating that vibrio will survive in the cow for only a short time in 75 percent of the animals, for longer periods of 2 to 12 months or more in another 24 percent of the infected females, and in a few cows for as long as 196 days after the termination of a normal pregnancy initiated by infected semen. Further work is necessary on this aspect of the disease. A total insemination program for most beef herds is impossible to accomplish so other control methods are necessary.

Some veterinarians advocate a period of 3 month's sexual rest for the acutely-infected herd, after which breeding can be resumed with the infected bull or by artificial insemination inasmuch as within this time the cows have probably developed a satisfactory degree of immunity or resistance to the infection. The value of a 3-month rest period is questionable except to conserve the bull, as some females recover more promptly than others and if these were withheld from service the economic loss would be unnecessarily increased. Hoerlein (1968) reported evidence that following natural infection a good immunity to vibriosis is produced that lasts from one to three years. The virgin heifers may be bred to young virgin bulls, which should continue to be used on them for the second pregnancy and thereafter. The infected bulls may be mated to the infected, immune cows and this program continued until the infected herd is eliminated. This procedure is difficult to follow over a period of years without an accident that would allow the infection to spread by venereal contact from the infected cows or bulls to the vibrio-free herd.

In beef herds where artificial insemination is impractical and the maintenance of two herds, a clean one and an infected one, is not possible, vaccination each year with a commercially-available adjuvant bacterin of all animals of breeding age a few months before the breeding season is indicated. Vaccination with a proven highly antigenic bacterin at either one or two intervals provides a good level of immunity even in virgin heifers bred to infected bulls. Although **V. fetus** organisms may be found in the genital tract of vaccinated heifers after service to infected bulls, conception occurs promptly and the organisms disappear in a few weeks in most animals. Thus a vaccinated cow may be a carrier of the infection and infect a susceptible bull that serves her. Conception rates of 90 percent are common in vibrio-positive beef herds following vaccination, Hoerlein, Hoerlein et al., Frank et al. Plastridge et al. and Newhall. Commerical adjuvanted vaccines (**Vibrin,** Norden Lab, **Bo-Vibrio,** Armour-Baldwin Lab. and **Trivib,** Fort Dodge Lab.) with either one to three strains of **V. fetus venerealis** appear equally effective in cattle herds in producing immunity and controlling the disease. Vaccination of bulls is of no value in controlling **V. fetus** infection in the sheath. Vaccination of heifers 6 months or more before the breeding season may result in some loss of immunity by the time of service to an infected bull. Even though a good degree of immunity is present a year or more after vaccination, yearly vaccination is advised in order to maintain a high level of immunity and better conception rates. Hoerlein and Carroll have recently shown that vaccinal immunity and convalescent immunity decreased from 1 to 4 years after vaccination or exposure. They recommended an annual single vaccination of all cows in infected herds 30 to 120 days before breeding. Two injections of an adequately adjuvanted bacterin did not improve the pregnancy rate. Following vaccination circulating antibodies in the blood are low and no antibodies are found in cervical mucus yet protection against the natural disease is afforded. The nature of this immunity is not understood, possibly it is a cellular phenomena, Hoerlein and Kramer. Thus by means of either artificial insemination with properly controlled vibrio-free semen, separation of the herd into vibrio-free and a vibrio-infected groups with proper isolation and control, by yearly vaccination with a bacterin of all breeding females or by a combination of these methods vibriosis as a cause of infertility in a herd can be controlled.

Treatment of individual cows by the intrauterine infusion of about one gram of streptomycin together with penicillin in an aqueous or oily base has proven quite effective in controlled studies in eliminating the vibrio organism from the female genital tract. Elimination is most efficient if given within 24 hours after service to an infected bull, Adler, Te Punga and Boyes, Dozsa and Olson and Melrose et al.. Practitioners evaluating such treatments should realize that within a few weeks after the initial infection and endometritis most cows are developing immunity and recovering from the disease. Treatment of infected cows, unless it closely follows the infective service, is being given to convalescent animals. Thus antibiotic infusions of infected cows are of limited value.

The treatment of bulls for vibriosis—It should be recognized that most young infected bulls have only a transient short-term infection and then spontaneously recover in a few weeks or months if the organism is not reintroduced into the prepuce. Bulls over 5 years of age may remain permanently infected although occasionally even old bulls will spontaneously recover from the disease, Carroll. Bulls do not develop immunity to the infection and if they are cured they may readily be reinfected. There is little value to eliminating infection in a bull if he is to remain in natural service in infected herds. In an AI Stud it is highly desirable to eliminate vibriosis from all bulls even though the addition of antibiotics to the semen has proven quite effective in controlling vibriosis. Swedish and Danish AI studs have eliminated vibriosis and Lein et al. reported on accomplishing this in a large AI stud in the U.S.A. Prior to treatment of the bulls rigid control measures on the movement of bulls and hygienic measures in the collection of semen were instituted. All bulls in the stud were tested semiannually by culturing and immunofluorescence of preputial smegma samples. Each new bull entering the stud was tested similarly during the isolation period of several months. All bulls infected with **V. fetus venerealis** were treated with 5 gm of dihydrostreptomycin sulfate in 10 ml of a 50% aqueous solution infused into the preputial cavity and massaged through the skin for 5 minutes while the orifice was closed. This was repeated daily for 5 treatments. At the time of the first and third treatments two subcutaneous injections of 22 mg/kg of body weight of dihydrostreptomycin was given, Adler and Lindegaarde and Seger et al.. Repeated tests of preputial mucus were conducted at biweekly intervals after treatment. Test breeding of virgin heifers to treated bulls followed by repeated cultures of the cervical mucus of the heifers could be done to determine if the treated bulls had eliminated the infection. This technique is more costly than the direct sampling of the preputial smegma. Treatment produced mild focal reddening and ulcerations of the penile mucosa that healed promptly. Lein, the author and his associates have tried other antibiotics in the treatment of vibriosis in the bull because of fear of producing streptomycin-resistant Vibrio organisms as reported by Vandeplassche, 1969, since streptomycin is also used to control the organism in semen. These antibiotics including tylosin and furacin have not proved as effective as streptomycin in the treatment of infected bulls.

References

Vibriosis

Adler, H. C. (1957) Genital Vibriosis in the Bovine Experimental Investigations with a Special View to Diagnosis, Prophylaxis and Therapy, Nord. Vet. Med., **9,** 474.

Adler, H. C. and Lindegaarde, L. E. (1965) Bovine Genital Vibriosis; Eradication from Danish AI Centers, Nord. Vet. Med. **17,** 237.

Boyd, H. (1955) Bovine Genital Vibriosis, Dept. of Obst. and Gynecol., Royal Veterinary College, Stockholm Sweden. (Thesis)

Bruner, D. W. and Gillespie J. H. (1966) Hagan's Infectious Diseases of Domestic Animals, 5th Ed., Cornell Univ. Press, Ithaca, N.Y., 241.

Bryner, J. H., Frank, A. H. and O'Berry, P. A. (1962) Dissociation Studies of Vibrios from the Bovine Genital Tract, Amer. J. Vet. Res. **23,** 92, 32.

Bryner, J. H., O'Berry, P. A. and Frank, A. H. (1964) Vibrio Infections of the Digestive Organs of Cattle, Amer. J. Vet. Res. **25,** 107, 1048.

Carroll, E. J. (1967) Personal Communication

Dennis, S. M. (1961) Studies on the Pathogensis of **Vibrio fetus** Ph.D. Thesis, Univ. of Sidney, Sidney, Australia.

Dozsa, L. and Olson, N. O. (1964) The Effect of Various Antibiotics on the Uterine Mucosa of **Vibrio fetus**—Infected Cows, Amer. J. Vet. Res. **25,** 104, 108.

Elliott, F. I., Murphy, D. M. and Bartlett, D. E. (1961) The Use of Polymyxin B. Sulphate with Dihydiostreptomycin and Penicillin for the Control of **Vibrio fetus** in a Frozen Semen Process, 4th Internat. Congr. on An. Reprod., III, 539.

Estes, P. C., Bryner, J. H. and O'Berry, P. A. (1966) Histopathology of Bovine Vibriosis and the Effects of **Vibrio fetus** Extracts on the Female Genital Tract, Cor. Vet. **56,** 4, 610.

Florent, A. (1959) Les Deux Vibrioses Genitalles la vibriose due a **V. fetus venerealis** et la vibrios [illegible]rigine intestinale due a **V. fetus intestinalis,** Mededel d. Veea[illegible]yschool v. Gent, **3,** 60.

Florent, A. and DeKeyser, P. (1964) Probelms of Infertility in Livestock in Belgium, Brit. Vet. J. **120,** 407.

Frank, A. H. (1950) Impaired Breeding in Cattle—Field Observations and Results of Treatment, Proc. A.V.M.A. 87th Ann. Meeting, 190.

Frank, A. H. and Bryner, J. H. (1953) Observations on Vibriosis of Cattle in Relation to Impaired Fertility, Proc. U.S. Livestock Sanit. Assoc., 57th Meeting, 165.

Frank, A. H., Bryner, J. H. and O'Berry, P. A. (1964) Reproductive Patterns of Female Cattle Bred for Successive Gestations to **Vibrio fetus**-Infected Bulls, Amer. J. Vet. Res. **25,** 988.

Frank, A. H., Bryner, J. H. and O'Berry, P. A. (1967) The Effect of **Vibrio fetus** Vaccination on the Breeding Efficiency of Cows Bred to **Vibrio fetus**-Infected Bulls, Amer. J. Vet. Res. **28,** 126, 1237.

Gilman, H. L. (1960) **Vibrio fetus** Infection in Man and Animals, Internat. J. of Fert. **5,** 4, 411.

Gilman, H. L. (1962) Personal Communication.

Hoerlein, A. B. (1967) Personal Communication.

Hoerlein, A. B. (1968) Bovine Genital Vibriosis, In "Abortion Diseases of Livestock," Edit. by L. C. Faulkner, C. C. Thomas & Co., Springfield, Ill., 18.

Hoerlein, A. B. (1970) Vibriosis, in **Bovine Medicine and Surgery,** Amer. Vet. Public. Inc., Wheaton, Ill., 91

Hoerlein, A. B. and Carroll, E. J. (1970) Duration of Immunity to Bovine Genital Vibriosis, J.A.V.M.A. **156,** 6, 775.

Hoerlein, A. B., Carroll, E. J., Kramer, T. and Beckenhauer, M. H. (1965) Bovine Vibriosis Immunization, J.A.V.M.A. **146,** 8, 828.

Hoerlein, A. B. and Kramer, T. (1963) Cervical Mucus for the Diagnosis of Vibriosis in Cattle, J.A.V.M.A. **143,** 8, 868.

Hoerlein, A. B. and Kramer, T. (1963) Artificial Stimulation of Resistance to Bovine Vibriosis, Amer. J. Vet. Res. **24,** 102, 951.

Hoerlein, A. B. and Kramer, T. (1964) Artificial Stimulation of Resistance to Bovine Vibriosis; Use of Bacterins, Amer. J. Vet. Res. **25,** 105, 371.

Hoerlein, A. B., Kramer, T., Carroll, E. J., Brown, W. W., Jr., Scott, J. A. and Ball, L. (1964) Vibriosis in Range Cattle, J.A.V.M.A. **144,** 2, 146.

Hughes, D. E. (1953) A Study of the Diagnosis of Bovine Vibriosis with Special Reference to the Detection of Agglutinins in the Vaginal Secretions, Cor. Vet. **43,** 3, 431.

Hughes, D. E., McEntee, K. and Gilman, H. L. (1954) Recent Developments in the Diagnosis and Control of Bovine Vibriosis, Vet. News, **17,** Nov.-Dec., 17.

Kendrick, J. W. (1967) The Vaginal Mucus Agglutination Test for Bovine Vibriosis, J.A.V.M.A. **150,** 5, 495.

Lawson, J. R. and MacKinnon, D. J. (1952) **Vibrio foetus** Infection in Cattle, Vet. Rec., **64,** 763.

Lein, D., Erickson, I., Winter, A. J. and McEntee, K. (1968) Diagnosis, Treatment, and Control of Vibriosis in an Artificial Insemination Center, J.A.V.M.A. **153,** 12, 1574.

Lincoln, G. J. and Trout, K. J. (1967) Evaluation of a New Trivalent Bovine Vibriosis Bacterin Using Fluorescent Antibody Technique, Vet. Med. **62,** 6, 561.

McEntee, K., Gilman, H. L., Hughes, D. E., Wagner, W. C. and Dunn, H. O. (1959) Insemination of Heifers with Penicillin and Dihydrostreptomycin-Treated Frozen Semen from **Vibrio fetus** Carrier Bulls, Cor. Vet. **49,** 2, 175.

McEntee, K., Hughes, D. E. and Gilman, H. L. (1954) Prevention of Vibriosis in Inseminated Heifers by Treating the Semen from Vibrio-infected Bulls with Penicillin, Streptomycin and Sulfanilamide, Cor. Vet. **44,** 3, 395.

McEntee, K., Hughes, D. E. and Gilman, H. L. (1954) Experimentally Produced Vibriosis in Dairy Heifers, Cor. Vet., **44,** 3, 376.

McEntee, K., Hughes, D. E. and Wagner, W. C. (1959) Failure to Produce Vibriosis in Cattle by Vulvar Exposure, Cor. Vet. **49,** 1, 34.

Mellick, P. W., Winter, A. J. and McEntee, K. (1965) Diagnosis of Vibriosis in the Bull by Use of the Fluorescent Antibody Technic, Cor. Vet. **55,** 280.

Melrose, D. R., Morgan, W. J. B. and Stewart, D. L. (1959) The Treatment and Subsequent Reinfection of Heifers Infected with **V. fetus,** Vet. Rec. **71,** 411.

Mohanty, S. B., Plumer, G. J. Faber, J. E. (1962) Biochemical and Colonial Characteristics of Some Bovine Vibrios, Amer. J. Vet. Res. **94,** 23, 554.

Morgan, W. J. B., Melrose, D. R. and Stewart, D. L. (1959) The Effect of Streptomycin on the Survival of **Vibrio fetus** in Semen and Other Diluents Stored at 5° and −79° C., J. Comp. Path. and Therap., **69,** 257.

Newhall, J. H. (1966) Results of Field Trials and Controlled Laboratory Studies on Bovine Vibriosis Bacterins, J.A.V.M.A. **149,** 12, 1643.

Newsom, I. D. B. and Perterson, J. E. (1964) Persistence of **Vibrio fetus** in the Genital Tract of Experimentally Infected Heifers, Brit. Vet. Jour. **120,** 223.

Orthey, A. E. and Gilman, H. L. (1954) The Antibacterial Action of Penicillin, Streptomycin and Sulfanilamide Against Heavy Suspensions of **Vibrio Fetus** Added to Semen Extender, J. of Dairy Sci., **37,** 4, 407.

Orthey, A. E. and Gilman, H. L. (1954) The Antibacterial Action of Penicillin and Streptomycin Against **Vibrio Fetus** Including Concentrations Found in Naturally Infected Semen, J. of Dairy Sci., **37,** 4, 416.

Plastridge, W. N., Easterbrooks, H. L. and Williams, L. F. (1953) The Tampon Method of Collection and the Examinations of Cervicovaginal Mucus for Vibrio Fetus Agglutinins, J.A.V.M.A. **122,** 921, 516.

Plastridge, W. N., Kersting, E. J., and Williams, L. F. (1966) Resistance of Vaccinated Heifers to Vibriosis, Amer. J. Vet. Res. **27,** 116, 186.

Plastridge, W. N., Stula, E. F. and Williams, L. F. (1964) **Vibrio fetus** Infection and Reinfection in Heifers as Determined by Cultural Tests Using Blood Agar Plus Antibiotics, Amer. J. Vet. Res. **25,** 106, 710.

Plastridge, W. N., Williams, L. F., Easterbrooks, H. L., Walker, E. C. and Beccia, R. N. (1952) Vibriosis in Cattle, Univ. of Conn., Storrs Agr. Exp. Stat., Bulletin 281, Storrs, Conn.

Rasbech, N. O. (1951) Study of the Spreading of **V. Fetus** by Bulls Used in Artificial Insemination (Abstr.), Vet. Rec. **63,** 657.

Rasbech, N. O. (1954) La Vibriose Bovine au Danemark, Report of the 22 Session Office International Des Equizooties, R. No. 341.

Roberts, S. J., Gilman, H. L. and Larsen, P. H. (1950) **Vibrio Fetus** Infection in Cattle, Cor. Vet., **40,** 2, 111.

Samuelson, J. D. and Winter, J. A. (1966) Bovine Vibriosis: The Nature of the Carrier State in the Bull, Jour. of Infect. Dis. **116,** 573.

Seger, C. L., Lank, R. B., and Levy, H. E. (1966) Dihydrostreptomycin for Treatment of Genital Vibriosis in the Bull, J.A.V.M.A. **149,** 1634.

Seger, C. L. and Levy, H. E. (1962) Collection of Bovine Cervical Mucus with Insemination Pipettes for the Isolation of **Vibrio fetus,** J.A.V.M.A. **141,** 9, 1064.

Shepler, V. M., Plumer, G. J. and Faber. J. E. (1963) Isolation of **Vibrio fetus** from Bovine Preputial Fluid, Using Millipore Filters and An Antibiotic Medium, Amer. J. Vet. Res. **24,** 101, 749.

Smith, T. (1918) Spirilla Associated with Disease of the Fetal Membranes in Cattle (Infectious Abortion), Jour. Expt. Med. **28,** 701.

Smith, T. (1919) The Bacteriology of Bovine Abortion with Special Reference to Acquired Immunity, Jour. Expt. Med., **30,** 325.

Smith, T., Little, R. B. and Taylor, M. S. (1920) Further Studies on the Etiological Role of **Vibrio Fetus** (Agglutination Tests), Jour. Expt. Med., **32,** 683.

Stegenga, Th. and Terpstra, J. I. (1949) Over **Vibrio fetus**-Infecties bij het rund en "Enzootische Steriliteit," Tijdschr. vor Diergeneesk., **74,** 293.

Sullivan, J. J., Elliott, F. I., Bartlett, D. E., Murphy, D. M. and Kuzdas, C. D. (1966) Further Studies on the Use of Polymyxin B. Sulphate with Dihydrostreptomycin and Penicillin to Control **Vibrio fetus** in a Frozen Semen Process, J. Dairy Sci. **49,** 12, 1569.

Szabo, L. (1951) Infektionspathologiske Problemer i Forbindelsa med Afrugtbarhed hos Kveget, Nord. Vet. Med., **3,** 597.

Te Punga, W. A., and Boyes, B. W. (1959) Vibriosis in Cattle, New Zeal. Vet. Jour., **6,** 147.

Terpstra, J. I., and Eisma, W. A. (1951) **Vibrio Fetus** Infection in Cattle and Enzootic Infertility, Tijdschr. vor Diergeneesk., **76,** 12, 433.

Vandeplassche, M. (1969) Personal Communication.

Wagner, W. C., Dunn, H. O. and VanVleck, L. D. (1965) Incidence of Vibriosis in an AI Stud, Cor. Vet. **55,** 209.

Willett, E. L., Ohms, J. I., Frank, A. H., Bryner, J. H., and Bartlett, D. E. (1955) Nonreturn Rate and Embryonic Mortality From Inseminations by Bulls with **Vibrio Fetus,** J. of Dairy Sci., **38,** 12, 1370.

Wiltbank, J. N., Warwick, E. J., Vernon, E. H. and Priode, B. M. (1961) Factors Affecting Net Calf Crop in Beef Cattle, J. An. Sci. **20,** 3, 409.

Winter, A. J. (1968) Personal Communication.

Winter, A. J., Samuelson, J. D. and Elkana, M. (1967) A Comparison of Immunofluorescence and Cultural Techniques for Demonstration of **Vibrio fetus,** J.A.V.M.A. **150,** 5, 499.

BRUCELLOSIS

Brucella abortus infection has been discussed previously under the section on abortion, as that is the principal characteristic of the disease. However, the evidence indicates that Brucella infection of the uterus plays a definite role in infertility even though Boyd and Reed reported that infertility and endometritis did not occur in the recently infected nonpregnant animal. The role of the bull in the transmission of brucellosis is minor but interesting. According to early field observations, the bull was generally supposed, to be one of the more important factors in the spread of the disease. But the transmission of brucellosis from infected bulls to susceptible cows by natural service has not been demonstrated in controlled experiments. This data has been summarized by Manthei, De Tray and Goode, and Thomsen, who showed that infected bulls when bred naturally to heifers in estrum rarely spread the disease even when the prepuce had been artificially contaminated with Brucella organisms prior to service. However, Bendixen and Blom, Manthei, De Tray and Goode and others have demonstrated that susceptible cows artificially inseminated into the uterus with infected semen from a positive Brucella-infected bull would develop brucellosis. Most infected bulls harboring foci of infection in the genital tract discharge Brucella organisms intermittently in the semen, but a bull studied by Manthei, De Tray and Goode had viable organisms in 80 consecutive ejaculations over a period of 18 months. The uterine infection produced in heifers by intrauterine insemination of infected semen resulted in impaired fertility; only 1 susceptible heifer conceived on the first service out of 12 inseminated; 8 of the 12 susceptible animals became infected; only 2 infected animals conceived, and 1 of these aborted at 104 days of gestation. Each animal was inseminated an average of 3.5 times. The infertility was temporary, lasting 3 to 12 months. These results were interesting when compared with 12 other susceptible heifers bred artificially to the same bull but with the semen being inseminated into the external os of the cervix; 9 of 12 animals conceived on the first service. From these experiments Frank and Bryner indicated that **Brucella abortus** should be included with **V. fetus** and **Trichomonas fetus** as an agent that can and will produce infertility or temporary sterility when introduced into the bovine uterus. Under natural conditions **B. abortus,** not being motile, cannot invade the uterus from its vaginal location as can **V. fetus** and **Trichomonas fetus.** This is a further reason for inseminating cows by placing semen into the cervical canal rather than into the uterus.

Intrauterine insemination may introduce other pathogenic bacteria that may cause failure of conception, endometritis, and temporary sterility especially if insemination is done late in the estrous period or in metestrous when the genital tract is under the influence of progesterone. Following abortion due to **Br. abortus,** a sexual rest period of 90 days or more and possibly several uterine treatments may be necessary to aid involution and recovery of the endometrium necessary for conception. Aborting animals should be isolated, as ingestion of infective material and discharges from the genital tract is the most common means of spreading brucellosis.

Further evidence of the adverse effect of brucella infection of the uterus was a report by Clark that sterility was 4 times more frequent in suspects and 8 times more frequent in Brucella reactors than in negative animals. Miller and Graves reported that Brucella-positive cows averaged 2.8 services per conception following normal calvings and 3.6 services per conception following abortions. Other evidence of this type was cited by Olds. Nielsen emphasized the frequent sporadic infertility in herds chronically infected with brucellosis. Brus reported a more severe endometritis to be present in infertile Brucella-positive cows than in infertile Brucella-negative cows. These many reports serve to emphasize strongly the role of **Brucella abortus** in causing infertility in a herd, and the necessity of controlling this disease to prevent severe economic losses due to reproductive failure and abortion.

Granular Venereal Disease (Nodular Venereal Disease, Granular or Infectious Vaginitis and Vulvitis)

According to Williams this disease was first described in Switzerland by Isepponi in 1887 as a cause for infertility and abortion. Since that time there has been much debate on whether or not the disease is an important cause of infertility. Most workers agree at present that there is no evidence linking this disease with abortion. Bartlett quoted Williams on granular venereal disease as stating: "It may be said to be a lesion without a known cause and regarding the effect of which there is scant knowledge." No disease of the reproductive system of cattle has been so unproductive of results on research as has granular venereal disease. Only in the area of histopathology is there any agreement on the nature of this disease. Merchant reported the cause of this condition to be **Streptococcus vaginitidis,** Crawley; Wills and McGregor reported the cause to be hemophilus-like pleomorphic rod; McDonald expressed the opinion that it was caused by a virus; Hunter et al. carefully reviewed the literature on granular vulvovaginitis and stated that 96 percent of all female cattle over 6 months of age showed signs at one time or another. They isolated many organisms including a virus from the genital tracts of affected cattle.

A small number of spayed heifers developed the infection; hence the disease was apparently not related to the sex hormones. Attempts to raise heifers free of the disease has failed although the onset of symptoms have been delayed. Mycoplasma (PPLO) produced lesions of granular venereal disease in cows on local experimental inoculation, Afshar et al.. Granular vulvitis may also be present in the late stages of the IBR-IPV infection of the genital tract, Van Kruiningen et al.. Bane has reported vulvovaginitis due to **C. pyogenes** and **E. coli** following 1 to 14 days and 1 to 2 days, respectively, after natural service. He reported that PPLO was commonly found in the genital tracts of cows and bulls but were nonpathogenic. Williams stated that clinically granular venereal disease does not behave in the manner usual to a bacterial infection. The size of the lesion in the chronic stage is as large as in the acute stage but the number of the granules is reduced. Although doing so in the face of 50 years of various investigations by other workers the author nevertheless suggests that the lesions and symptoms of granular venereal disease are a reaction of the mucosa and lymphoid follicles of the vulva and vagina, and the prepuce and penis to nonspecific irritants either infectious, mechanical, or chemical. The incidence, lesions, symptoms, and results of treatment of the disease lead him to this observation.

The disease is seen most commonly in heifers during the breeding period for their first and second pregnancies. The condition has been noted occasionally in calves as young as 11 days of age and in heifers prior to puberty. It is less accute and severe in middle-aged and older cows. It is observed most commonly in postpartum heifers and cows especially following natural service and less commonly as pregnancy progresses toward term. It is rarely observed at the time of parturition. Granular venereal disease is seen in practically any herd at any time of year with an incidence varying from 10 to 90 percent of the cows or heifers. The lesions differ greatly in severity between heifers and cows in a herd. In general the disease occurs more commonly and more severely in young cows or heifers being bred naturally by the bull than in those being artificially inseminated. The lesions of this condition may be observed on the penis and prepuce and here again the lesions are present more commonly in bulls serving cows naturally than in bulls in an artificial insemination stud that ejaculate into an artificial vagina. The term granular vaginitis is not the correct name to apply to this disease in the bull. The mode of spread of the disease is not known, but apparently if it is due to an infectious agent, it is spread is rapidly and easily. This is difficult to prove, inasmuch as isolated control heifers can develop the condition.

Troutman reported that Perkins found 28 percent of 1000 cows killed at slaughter affected with granular venereal disease. Patrick and his coworkers found about 10 percent of 2530 cows affected. The fertility of affected animals was 6 percent lower than that of the other 90 percent. Troutman reported on 4616 cows being bred by artificial insemination; 49 percent had no evidence of granular venereal disease; 44 percent, or 2,065 had mild symptoms; and 7 percent, or 289 cows, had severe lesions. The conception rates on first service in each group were 68.9 percent, 65.7 percent, and 58.1 percent, respectively. Therefore the difference in rates was significant. Cows with severe lesions of granular venereal disease had a slightly lower conception rate, 10 percent, on 60-day nonreturns than those with no lesions of the disease. Crawley and coworkers indicated that a temporary sterility is associated with granular venereal disease. It is the author's observation, nevertheless, that this disease—if it is a disease—has little or no effect on fertility; many affected cows even those with severe lesions, conceive if they are permitted to breed.

The incubation period is not known but Crawley and coworkers reported a 2- to 3-week incubation period with an increase in severity and number of granules developing, through the eighth week. The lesions of granular venereal disease consist of small elevated papules or granules found mainly on the vulvar mucosa just inside the vulvar lips most commonly in the region around the clitoris. (See Figure 105) In more severe cases the granules may extend up the lateral walls of the vulva to the dorsal commissure. Only occasionally are these granules found in the vagina and then usually in the caudal portion. A vaginitis and cervicitis may also be present with granular lesions in the vulva, but typical granules cannot be felt on palpation or seen by speculum in the vagina. Therefore this condition more properly should be called a granular vulvitis. Similar granules appear on the penis and prepuce of the bull. In the acute stage in cows these nodules are reddened and highly inflamed, causing a mucopurulent type of discharge that may mat and hang from the vulvar tuft of hairs. If these cattle are bred by a bull, or if a speculum is passed, the granules or nodules are likely to bleed. The cow or heifer in this acute stage exhibits some pain when the vulvar lips are handled and may exhibit irritation and pain when urinating, as well as by not standing quietly to be bred. In these acute severe cases there are many nodules, usually appearing confluent and tending to be in ridges or rows on the top of the folds of mucous membrane. The vulva may be slightly swollen. Bulls with acute severe lesions may occasionally refuse to copulate or will be slow to breed. Coitus tends to aggravate the lesions especially in heifers with a small vulva that are bred to a large bull. In mild cases of granular venereal disease the lesions are few in number and are usually found around the lower half of the vulva and clitoris. The chronic nodules are pale yellow in color and no inflammation of the mucosa is apparent. Following breeding the granules that were pale before breeding ordinarily become congested and reddened. These nodules or granules histologically are lymph follicles, lymphoid accumulations, or hyperplasic lymphoid elements beneath the mucosa and therefore the disease may be a normal response to various insults. It is interesting to note that Bloom has described similar lesions in the dog. In the male dog a follicular balano-posthitis with hypertrophied lymph follicles may occur. In the bitch he described similar lymph follicles in the vulva. These lesions are similar to those observed beneath the third eyelid in follicular conjunctivitis in the dog. Williams stated that these lesions were common in sheep, goats and swine, but in a mild form.

Figure 105. Granular Venereal Disease in a Heifer—Note the concentration of lymphoid follicles around the clitoris.

The prognosis is usually fair to good but in acute cases it may be 2 to 4 weeks or more before the signs subside. As far as completely curing the condition in cows and bulls the prognosis is guarded, as sometimes several months or more are required. Granular venereal disease may remain chronic or acute lesions may recur.

The treatments for granular venereal disease are so many and varied that the author believes this condition fits into the category with other conditions treated with a similar wide variety of therapy in which probably any treatment within reason or no treatment at all would be equally successful. The more commonly-used treatments are antibiotics, including the local application of penicillin, streptomycin, or other antibiotic ointments or sulfonamide powders every 2 to 4 days for several weeks if necessary. The irritant drugs are popular, such as 1 percent acriflavine ointment rubbed into the vulva every 7 to 10 days, or the application of Lugol's solution, or 4 to 5 percent silver nitrate at a similar interval. Various antiseptic washes such as chlorine solutions, or sodium bicarbonate solutions every 2 to 4 days, or dusting the lesions with bismuth formic iodide, silver picrate, or other antiseptic powders by a Shelanski insufflator or manually twice a week have been used. Estrogens have even been advocated by some veterinarians for this condition but

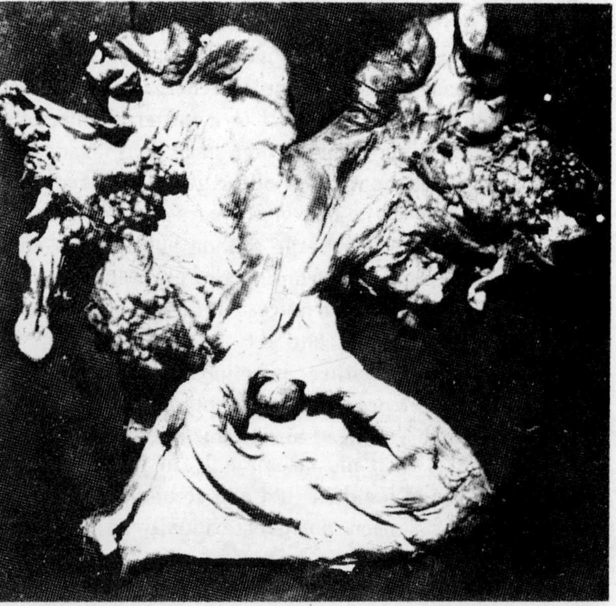

Figure 106. Genital Bovine Tuberculosis—involving the ovaries and mesometrium.

(Courtesy of F. Megale)

there is no basis for their use except that estrogens are used for the treatment of senile vaginitis in women. The two conditions are not, however, similar. In treating the condition in bulls used for artificial insemination the author has employed all the treatments listed above and others not mentioned, such as douching with antiseptics, and antibiotics in oil and in oil-and-water-emulsions, and all other methods ever suggested except cautery, without significantly altering the natural progress of the condition. In long-standing cases in bulls the lymphoid follicles, especially in the prepuce, may become fibrotic.

Since this condition tends to improve with time and since copulation aggravates the condition, breeding is stopped in the severe cases—especially in bulls—for several weeks or longer. The owners are advised to breed their affected cows and heifers artificially if possible. This seems to cause no exacerbation of symptoms. If they cannot be bred artificially, a period of sexual rest for 2 to 4 weeks is advised in the severe cases. More research is needed to determine the etiology of this condition. Therapy can then be more logical and rational.

Infectious Pustular Vulvovaginitis (IBR-IPV) (Vesicular Venereal Disease, Coital Vesicular Exanthema, Genital Cowpox, Vesicular Vaginitis, or Blaschenausschlag)

This viral disease has been described previously as IBR-IPV abortion since the two diseases are caused by the same herpes viral agent, Gillespie et al.. Kendrick and coworkers described infectious pustular vulvovaginitis as a nonvesicular viral disease characterized by papules, pustules, but no vesicles, that rapidly coalesce to form a diptheritic membrane that detaches leaving ulcers in the mucosa of the vulva, vestibule and vagina especially over the areas of the lymphoid follicles. Intranuclear inclusion bodies can be found in affected cells in the mucosa of the genital tract. The cow exhibits an elevated temperature for several days early in the course of the disease. Edema, pain on urination, and a yellowish serous to purulent discharge from the vulva is characteristic of the disease. The disease may spread rapidly through the herd and even affect unbred heifers. The respiratory form of the disease rarely accompanies the genital form. However Kradel et al. reported on one dairy herd that simultaneously had cows affected with the upper respiratory, genital and conjunctival forms of IBR-IPV; no abortions occurred. Furthermore abortions in pregnant cows commonly occur after the respiratory disease but are only rarely observed following the genital form of the disease. The cause for this is not understood but a local immunity may be involved. Natural service by the bull may spread the disease but other means of spread such as by switching tails of cows confined in stanchions or grooming may also spread the disease from one cow's rear parts to the next. The farm dog licking the genital discharges on the vulvas of affected cows and then normal cows may transmit the disease. The IBR-IPV virus may be spread in liquid or frozen semen and cause an endometritis and a temporary shortlived infertility, Spradbrow, and Kendrick and McEntee.

Although the disease is rather common in Europe, it is observed only occasionally in the United States. Even though IBR, the respiratory form of the disease, is common in New York State only 1 to 3 outbreaks of IPV are reported each year. A similar observation was made in California, Studdert et al.. Two outbreaks occurred in the same herd 4 years apart, Roberts. Similar reoccurrences of the disease in the same herds have been reported in Europe.

The onset of the disease is rapid and within 3 to 6 days involves 60 to 90 percent of a herd; the incubation period is short, usually 48 to 72 hours. Similar lesions occur on the penis and prepuce of affected bulls. Affected bulls may refuse coitus. Although infectious pustular vulvovaginitis interferes with breeding until the lesions heal, this form of the disease is not known to result in sterility, infertility, or abortion.

The prognosis is generally favorable, as healing occurs in about 2 to 4 weeks. Occasionally severely affected bulls may develop adhesions between the penis and prepuce, or a stenosis of the prepuce may occur, possibly due to secondary infections. Scarring or adhesions of the vulva or vagina have not been reported.

Treatment is usually unnecessary and oftentimes is difficult to administer because of the problem of restraining the affected cattle due to the painful vulvar lesions. However, some authors recommend douching with mild antiseptics. Regular douching of the sheath of the affected bull with oily preparations might be indicated to distend the sheath and prevent adhesions. Breeding should cease for 3 to 4 weeks or until the affected animals recover. Because of its highly transmissible nature, this disease should be reported to the State Veterinarian. Veterinarians, inseminators, and others working in these herds should be careful not to carry and spread the infection. Vaccination with IBR vaccine is not indicated once the disease has appeared.

Kendrick and McEntee reported that when IBR-IPV virus was present in semen used for intrauterine insemination of heifers it produced a necrotizing endometritis, short estrous cycles of 11 to 15 days in length, many cystic corpora lutea and only 1 of 12 heifers conceived. A number of practitioners have reported that low rates of conception occurred in heifers bred within one month of vaccination with IBR vaccine. (See IPV infection in bulls)

Specific Bovine Venereal Epididymitis and Vaginitis or "Epivag" is a chronic disease of cattle, transmitted by coitus and found only in East, South and Central Africa. The cause is apparently a virus, McIntosh et al.. Vaginitis in cattle in South Africa may also be due to a viral agent similar to the IBR-IPV virus, Mare and Van Rensburg, and Florent. The disease is characterized by a severe mucopurulent vaginal discharge in females, permanent adhesions of the Fallopian tubes, and by a hardening and swelling of the epididymis in the bull. This disease has been carefully described by Hudson, Arthur, and the U. S. Livestock Sanitary Association.

Etiology—European cattle are very susceptible to the infection whereas Zebu cattle are resistant to the disease, at least, clinical symptoms are not exhibited. The disease has been transmitted experimentally by genital swabs from cow to cow or by placing minced infected epididymal tissue in the vagina. The material was bacteriologically sterile and no protozoa were found. The disease in the natural state is transmitted only by coitus. Preliminary attempts to produce the disease by filtrates of the material have failed. The disease is the most important cause of bovine sterility and infertility in Kenya.

In herds having breeding trouble 42 percent had this disease and in these herds 34 percent of the bulls became permanently sterile. The disease may remain latent in a herd for some time, Anderson et al..

Symptoms—The incubation period is 2 to 8 days. During the active stage of the infection there is an odorless, mucoid vaginal exudate, egg-white in consistency but opaque and yellow in color. The discharge from the vulva mats the hair on the tail and buttocks, forming dull, grey, yellow flakes as it dries. Speculum examination reveals diffusely reddened areas in the cranial portion of the vagina but there are no ulcers, vesicles, or granular lesions. A diagnosis of this disease in a herd is easy but in individual animals may be difficult. The acute infective stage may last for 2 weeks to 9 months. Estrous cycles are normal, but service is rarely followed by conception. In grade herds most cows and heifers recover eventually but 15 to 25 percent are permanently sterile due to unilateral or usually bilateral involvement of the oviducts with adhesions, hydrosalpinx, or ovarian and bursal adhesions.

In the bull a balano-posthitis may occur but it is mild and frequently not observed. The characteristic lesion in the bull is an enlargement and hardening of the epididymis that is usually bilateral. Although the entire epididymis is involved, the tail is involved most severely and may resemble a billiard ball in size and hardness. Occasionally an orchitis of a temporary nature may precede this epididymal enlargement and testicular degeneration and atrophy may occur. Bulls can be infected by intraurethral injection. The lesions in bulls take 3 to 6 months to develop and sexual desire remains normal. In advanced cases there are adhesions between the scrotum and the epididymis. On postmortem examination dry adhesive areas of peritonitis or pleuritis may be found. The seminal vesicles of bulls usually become enlarged and firm and changes may take place in the vas deferens, Anderson and coworkers.

Treatment—The disease can easily be controlled by artificial insemination using noninfected bulls. In time it will spontaneously disappear from the females. More work is required on the determination of the etiologic agent, the length of time cows remain infected, and the practical methods of control when artificial insemination is not possible.

Miscellaneous Infections of the Bovine Female Genital Tract

Viral Infections

Contagious Anterior Vagino-Cervicitis in cattle has been described by Van Rensburg in South Africa as resembling the disease just described. However no permanent lesions are produced in the cow and none observed in the bull. The cause is not known.

Van Rensburg and the U.S. Livestock Sanitary Association also described an involvement of the uterus causing sterility as a sequela to lumpy skin disease of cattle in South Africa.

A catarrhal vaginitis and cervicitis clinically similar to "epivag" in cows was described by Kendrick et al. and McKercher in 4 herds. Affected cattle had a profuse nonodorous yellow mucoid discharge from the vulva. The cervix and vagina of the diseased cows was hyperemic and edematous but no pustules were present as in IPV. No other portions of the genital tract were involved. Although the disease appeared to spread following coitus, the bulls showed no clinical signs of the infection. The course of the disease lasted from 7 days to 3 months. Fertility was lowered and conception often was delayed several months. A few cows conceived during the clinical stages of the disease. The cause of this vagino-cervicitis was an enterovirus culturally different from the virus of "epivag." Sterility did not occur in this disease. Antibiotic treatments were of no value and immunity was short-lived.

Viral infertility in cattle has been reported by Millar; it was characterized by a vaginitis, edematous endometritis, a mucopurulent genital discharge, abortions at 2 to 8 months of gestation with edematous fetal membranes, and by a temporary infertility in bulls. The incubation period was 3 to 10 days. The disease could be spread to susceptible cattle by coitus and intravaginal but not intravenous injection of filtered genital mucus from infected cattle. It was reported that the virus—and possibly more than one was present—could be passed through eggs.

Transmissable fibropapillomas due to a virus may occasionally be observed on the vulva and perineal region of heifers and the prepuce and penis of young bulls. The growths may be single or multiple. These tumors might be transmitted at coitus. The tumors in heifers are similar to the common skin wart and usually regress spontaneously in 2 to 6 months. This process may possibly be hastened by the use of wart vaccine. This condition does not cause infertility in heifers. The fibropapillomas may be removed surgically, Gledhill.

Tuberculosis—Tuberculosis of the genital tract of the cow has not been observed the last 40 years in the Ambulatory Clinic of the New York State Veterinary College. With the almost complete eradication of this disease in the United States the opportunities for observing it in this country are rapidly diminishing. However, in other countries where tuberculosis is still prevalent the infection may involve the female genital tract and produce sterility and abortion. Williams and Arthur have described tubercular lesions of the vulva, vagina, cervix, uterus, oviducts, and ovary. (See Figure 106) The disease usually affects the uterus and oviducts producing characteristic nodular swellings, enlargments and adhesions between the uterus, oviduct, ovary, surrounding broad ligaments, rectum, and other organs and tissues. The genital discharge from these lesions is usually non-fetid. In most cases the uterine involvement is bilateral, a fact which may differentiate the condition from other infectious or pathologic lesions of the uterus. Bovine tuberculosis due to **Mycobacterium bovis** is by far the most common type affecting the uterus and causing sterility and abortion. Occasionally the avian type may be found, Plum and Fincher and coworkers; this is characterized by small abscesses about 0.25 inch in diameter, involving the endometrium. The avian type of tuberculosis is not readily diagnosed per rectum because of the lack of enlargement of the uterus or oviducts and the fact that adhesions do not develop. The tuberculin test may fail to detect animals severely affected with bovine tuberculosis. Avian tuberculin may be of assistance in diagnosing the avian form, although it is usually diagnosed on postmortem examination. Culture of the genital discharges together with the presence of characteristic nodular swellings and adhesions aids in the diagnosis of this disease. Severely affected animals are usually hopelessly sterile and should be slaughtered. In milder infections conception may occur, but abortion or retained placenta may result. Infection of the genital tract of the cow may result in the spread of tubercular infection to the penis and prepuce of the bull at coitus. Man may also be infected.

Actinomycosis—Williams described two cases of actinomycosis of the bovine genital tract, characterized by large swellings that proved to be multiple sclerotic abscesses with extensive pelvic adhesions. One of these cases developed following a retained placenta. Actinomycosis is difficult to differentiate from tuberculosis but the swellings in the latter are more nodular Due to the extensive lesions the prognosis was very poor and both cases were cultured and diagnosed after slaughter.

Mycoplasma, a Pleuropneumonia-like organism (Mycoplasma bovigenitalium) was isolated by Edward, Hancock and Hignett from cattle in several herds suffering from infertility and occasional abortions. In some cases ovarian adhesions and cervicitis were present; in others a mucopurulent discharge was noted several days after coitus. The organism was found in semen. Hartman et al. produced varying degrees of endometritis, salpingitis and adhesions between the fimbria and peritoneum in 7 of 8 heifers receiving an intrauterine inoculation of a suspension of mycoplasma recovered from a case of bovine mastitis. The doses used were considered to be excessive. This condition, produced experimentally, has not yet been described as a clinical entity. The common occurrence of mycoplasma in the prepuce of bulls and in the semen has been described under infertility in the male, O'Berry. It is questionable if many of the isolated mycoplasma sp. are pathogenic as heifers inseminated with infected semen samples did not become infertile. Only one group of isolates produced inflammatory changes in the mesovarium. Al-Aubaidi has recently studied many strains of mycoplasma by morphological, cultural and serologic means as an aid to separating pathogenic and saprophytic organisms. Since many mycoplasma cultures are a mixture of several strains, he recovered 166 pure strains by cloning, characterization and serologic techniques and found 13 serotypes not including the bovine T. strains. Serotype B or **Mycoplasma bovigenitalium** caused vulvovaginitis, epididymitis, seminovesiculitis, arthritis and rarely mastitis. Serotype F or **Mycoplasma agalactiae** var **bovis** caused mastitis, endometritis, salpingitis, salpingoperitonitis and abortion. Afshar et al. described this same type of organism as the cause of granular venereal disease. Nielsen reported culturing this type of organism from semen from a bull that when bred to heifers apparently produced conception but the animals came back into estrum in about 4 weeks and thereafter were infertile. Nielsen was unable to express a definite opinion on the importance of the organism as no work had been done to determine whether it was pathogenic or saprophytic in nature. **M. laidlawii** was recovered from the oviducts in 52 or 71 percent of 73 repeat breeders, while only 42 or 24 percent of 179 cows slaughtered for other reasons were infected. Lesions were found in 117 infected oviducts. In some cases these resulted in fibrosis and obstruction of the lumen of the oviduct, Hoare. Many consider this **Mycoplasma** nonpathogenic. Terpstra and Eisma reported finding this pleuropneumonia-like or hemophilus-like organism in cultures in combination with **Vibrio fetus.** Terpstra and Eisma indicated that these pleuropneumonia-like organisms were concerned in the etiology of a vaginitis caused by mating virgin heifers to a certain **V. fetus**-positive bull. It is possible that the early workers in studying this pleuropneumonia-like organism were actually dealing with vibriosis and recovered this rather ubiquitous PPLO organism. Albertsen reported in 1955 that this organism was not related to infertility in cattle and was found as a saprophyte in semen in 94 percent of the bulls. Albertsen reported that they were quite resistant to antibiotics commonly used in semen diluters. Freezing of mycoplasma in semen had no adverse affect on the organisms, Hirth et al. (1967).

Hirth et al. (1966) reported that mycoplasma have been associated with salpingitis, oophoritis and septic metritis in women. In 12 heifers inseminated with semen containing live mycoplasmas, 10 required multiple services and 4 failed to conceive after 5 inseminations. These latter heifers had chronic bilateral suppurative salpingitis and degrees of metritis on necropsy.

Further studies are needed to elucidate the nature and frequency of mycoplasma infection in cattle, to differentiate the pathogenic and saprophytic organisms and to devise suitable diagnostic and therapeutic techniques to enable the disease to be controlled.

Hemophilus spp. was reported to cause an outbreak of vaginitis and cervicitis in a herd of dairy cattle, Ayalon et al., characterized by a copious, purulent, yellowish-white discharge from the vulva and a hyperemia of the vagina and cervix lasting for 2 to 3 months. The disease could be spread by coitus and resembled viral vaginitis described previously. The vulva was not affected. Crawley et al. described a hemophilus-like organism as a cause of granular vulvitis.

Leptospirosis due to **L. pomona** has not been shown to be the cause of infertility or early death of fertilized ova; although abortions, especially the latter half of the gestation period, are common, Lingard and Hanson.

Streptococcic infection characterized by cervicitis was described by Webster in 1932 as a common cause for infertility in cows. This organism was frequently recovered from inflamed genital tracts of cows failing to conceive but it is unlikely that it was responsible for enzootic outbreaks of infertility. The author observed one herd of dairy cattle with much infertility characterized by a mucopurulent discharge from the vulva in some animals and early embryonic deaths with long intervals between services. On culture of the vagina of the cows at necropsy a pure infection of **Streptococcus dysgalactiae** was isolated. Endometritis was present. Sanitary conditions in the herd were marginal; all cows calved in the same calving stall. The bull may have spread the infection at the time of coitus.

Corynebacterium pyogenes has been described by Hignett and McEwen as a cause for failure of conception, for a persistent mucopurulent discharge from the vulva and even occasionally for permanent sterility. Apparently it usually gains entrance to the genital tract at the time of parturition or when a retained placenta occurs. This organism causes a chronic postpuerperal metritis, endometritis, salpingitis, or pyometra with delayed involution of the uterus. This infection may be difficult to cure and the prognosis should be guarded.

C. pyogenes infection of the postpartum genital tract is occurring with increasing frequency as the herds of cattle get larger and close confinement, "zero pasture" and over use of a few calving stalls that are not properly "sterilized" between cows. In affected herds nearly 90 percent or more of cows calving in the infected environment or in those stalls become infected and develop a copious, yellow, mucopurulent discharge that lasts for 2 to 6 months resulting in great delays in conception even though eventually the infection is overcome and the cows conceive. Retained placenta and calf scours are also commonly observed in these same herds due to the unsanitary conditions. Since the infection obviously occurs at or soon after calving, having the cows calve in a different clean environment away from the contaminated facilities or at pasture often results in a prompt and dramatic reduction in clinical cases of vaginitis, cervitis and metritis. Enough properly designed calving stalls that can be thoroughly disinfected or sterilized between calvings and/or moved to a clean location are necessary for large free-stall dairy herds.

Bane has described a vulvovaginitis due to **C. pyogenes** occurring one to four days following coitus. These infections persisted for 7 to 14 days but often recurred at a subsequent breeding to the same bull. Similar **C. pyogenes** organisms were cultured from the vagina of affected cows and the prepuce of the bull. Bane also described an acute vulvovaginitis due to **E. coli** toxins introduced by coitus with an infected bull. Signs developed within 4 to 6 hours of service and lasted for only several days.

Other low grade infections found in the genital tract of sterile or infertile cows or cows exhibiting a mucopurulent exudate include:

*__Micrococci__
*Diptheroids
*__Pseudomonas aeruginosa__
*__E. coli__
Bacilli
Staphylococci, albus and **aureus**
*Enterococci and others

Actinomyces	Yeast
Neisseria	Mycobacteria
Flavobacterium	Salmonella
Sarcina	Alkaligenes
Proteus	Gaffkya
Molds	Chromobacteria

*The organisms most commonly found.

These infections have been described by Lindley and Hatfield, Easley and coworkers, Hignett, Gunter and coworkers and Alford and coworkers as being found in the genital tract and uterus of cows that fail to conceive. Gunter and coworkers reported that these common organisms recovered from the bovine genital tract were mainly saprophytic strains in normal cows but that in infertile cows the strains were primarily pathogenic. Undoubtedly they may gain access to the tract at the time of parturition or breeding and if the conditions are favorable they establish themselves at least temporarily and possibly cause varying degrees of inflammation of the uterus, cervix, vagina, vulva, and oviduct resulting in infertility. Twelve heifers artificially inseminated with semen from bulls with seminovesiculitis due to **Ps. aeruginosa** developed varying degrees of metritis, cervicitis and vaginitis and the organism could be recovered in 4 of 8 heifers 44 days postservice, Getty and Ellis. The discussion of the diagnosis and treatment of these nonspecific infections will be made later in this chapter. Cases of infertility due to these various organisms are usually sporadic and not associated with an enzootic type of infertility. The organisms mentioned above, including streptococci, **C. pyogenes** and pleuropneumonia-like organisms, are ubiquitous and will occur in some cows despite proper management. Their treatment is largely symptomatic. The same organisms are frequently present in bull semen but apparently seldom pass beyond the vagina and cervix to establish themselves in the uterus. Pseudomonas, coliforms, and staphylococci are more common in bulls' semen than in the genital tracts of cows, probably due to contamination of the semen with organisms common in the sheath.

Frank and Bryner reported that a condition similar to an enzootic venereal disease in naturally-bred cattle exists in some artificially inseminated herds, with 15 percent or more of the cattle showing varying degrees of infertility even when neighboring herds of the same breed served by the same technician have less than 5 percent "repeat breeders". This condition may occur after 2 to 3 years of artificial insemination and no **V. fetus** or **Trichomonas fetus** are isolated from the cows. Frank and Bryner have been unable to isolate the causative organism or determine its mode of spread. Boyd and other workers with **V. fetus** have also found similar perplexing problems. In the future, therefore, possibly other organisms may be found as causes of "enzootic" infertility.

Necrotic vulvitis of feedlot heifers has been well-described by Pierson and Hill and Nelson. The cause is unknown. It has been observed in lots where hogs are present and injuries and vulvitis have been blamed on them. It may occur following rectal examinations. Anovulvitis may be observed secondary to a diarrhea where an irritant is apparently present in the fecal material. Body temperatures may be slightly elevated for a few days but healing occurs in two weeks. Infertility in affected heifers has not been reported. It has been suggested that an allergic factor may be involved.

References

Afshar, A., Stuart, P. and Huck, R. A. (1966) Granular Vulvovaginitis of Cattle Associated with **Mycoplasma bovigenitalium,** Vet. Rec. **75,** 15, 512.

Albertsen, B. E. (1955) Pleuropneumonia-Like Organisms in the Semen of Danish Artificial Insemination Bulls, Nord. Vet. Med., **7,** 3, 169.

Alford, J. A., Gunther, J. J. and Edwards, C. D. (1955) Reproductive Tract Infection in a Herd Caused by Group A. Streptococci, Cor. Vet. **45,** 3, 357.

Anderson, J., Plowright, W. and Purchase, H. S. (1951) Pathological and Seminal Changes in Bulls Affected with a Specific Venereal Infection, Jour. of Comp. Path. and Therap., **61,** 3, 219.

Arthur, G. H. (1964) Wright's Veterinary Obstetrics, 3rd Ed. Williams and Wilkins Co., Baltimore, Md.

Al-Aubaidi, J. M. (1969) Bovine Mycoplasma: Purification, Characterization, Classification and Pathogenicity, Ph.D. Thesis, Cornell Univ., Ithaca, N.Y.

Al-Aubaidi, J. M. (1970) Personal Communication.

Ayalon, N., Numan, L., Harrari, H. and Szidon, A. (1960) A Newly Idenitified **Hemophilus spp** Associated with Bovine Vaginitis and Cervicitis, Clinical Observations and Experimental Transmission, Refuah Vet. **17,** 41, 153.

Bane, A. (1964) Fertility and Reproductive Disorders in Swedish Cattle, Brit. Vet. J. **120,** 431.

Bartlett, D. E. (1949) Infectious Disease as a Cause of Infertility: A Review, J. Dairy Sci. **32,** 1, 36.

Bendixen, H. C. and Blom, E. (1947) Investigations on Brucellosis in the Bovine Male, with Special Regard to Spread of the Disease by Artificial Insemination, Vet. Jour., **103,** 337.

Boyd, H. and Reed, H. C. B. (1960) Investigations Into the Incidence and Causes of Infertility in Dairy Cattle, **Brucella abortus** and **Vibrio fetus** Infections, Vet. Rec. **72,** 836, and 870.

Brus, D. H. J. (1954) Biopsia Uteri. Thesis, Univ. of Utrecht, Utrecht, Netherlands.

Clark, C. F. (1931) Correlation of Blood Reactions with the Breeding Records over a Period of Years in an Abortion-Infected Herd of Cattle, J.A.V.M.A., **79,** 290.

Crawley, J. F., Wills, C. G. and MacGregor, K. L. (1950) Bovine Vaginitis, Canad. J. Comp. Med., **14,** 1, 5, 5.

Easley, G. T., Leonard, R. H. and Trotter, D. M. (1951) Bacteriological, Pathological, and Clinical Studies of the Reproductive Tract of the Hereford Cow and a Bacteriologic Study of Hereford Bull Semen, N. A. Vet., **32,** 4, 258.

Edward, D. G., Hancock, J. L. and Hignett, S. L. (1947) Pleuropneumonia-like Organisms from the Bovine Genital Tract, Vet. Rec., **59,** 329.

Fincher, M. G., Evans, W. M. and Saunders, L. Z. (1954) Avian Tuberculosis in a Dairy Cow, Cor. Vet. **44,** 2, 240.

Florent, A. (1962) Viral Infertility in "Livestock Infertility", Animal Health Monograph #5, FAO, Rome, 36.

Frank, A. H. and Bryner, J. H. (1953) Observations on Vibriosis of Cattle in Relation to Impaired Fertility, Proc. U.S. Livestock Sanitary Assoc., 57th Meeting, 165.

Getty, S. and Ellis, D. J. (1967) Experimental Use of Bull Semen Contaminated with **Pesudomonas aeruginosa** Organisms, J.A.V.M.A. **150,** 11, 1300.

Gillespie, J. H., McEntee, K., Kendrick, J. W. and Wagner, W. C. (1959) Comparison of Infectious Pustular Vulvovaginitis Virus with Infectious Bovine Rhinotrachitis Virus, Cor. Vet. **49,** 2, 288.

Gledhill, B. L. (1968) Viral Infertility in Cattle, Cor. Vet. **58,** 3, 466.

Gunter, J., Collins, W. J., Owen, J., Sorenson, A. M., Scales, J. W. and Alford, J. A. (1955) A Survey of the Bacteria in the Reproductive Tract of Dairy Animals and Their Relationship to Infertility, Am. J. Vet. Res., **16,** 59, 282.

Hartman, H. A., Tourtellotte, M. E., Nielsen, S. W. and Plastridge, W. N. (1964) Experimental Bovine Uterine Mycoplasmosis, Res. in Vet. Sci. **5,** 3, 303.

Hignett, S. L. (1940) Bovine Sterility, Vet. Rec., **52,** 19.

Hignett, S. L. (1949) The Complex Nature of Herd Infertility, Proc. 14th Internat. Vet. Congr. Section 4 (c), 128.

Hirth, R. S., Plastridge, W. N. and Tourtellotte, M. E. (1967) Survival of a Mycoplasma in Frozen Bovine Semen, Amer. J. Vet. Res. **28,** 122, 97.

Hirth, R. S., Plastridge, W. N., Tourtellotte, M. E. and Nielsen, S. W. (1966) Genital Mycoplasmosis in Cattle and Man, J.A.V.M.A. **148,** 3, 277.

Hoare, M. (1969) A Survey of the Incidence of Mycoplasma Infection in the Oviducts of Dairy Cows, Vet. Rec. **85,** 351.

Hudson, J. R. (1949 A Specific Venereal Disease of Cattle Characterized by Epididymitis in Bulls and Vaginitis in Cows and Heifers, Proc. 14th Internat. Vet. Congr., II, Section 3 (j), 487.

Hunter, A. G., Henderson, B. W. and Dardiri, A. H. (1958) Infectious Pustular Vulvovaginitis of Cattle, Cor. Vet. **48,** 4, 458.

Hunter, A. G. Henderson, B. W. and Dardiri, A. H. (1958) Granular Vulvovaginitis: A Review, J. Dairy Sci. **41,** 8, 1024.

Kendrick, J. W., Gillespie, J. H., McEntee, K. (1958) Infectious Pustular Vulvovaginitis of Cattle, Cor. Vet. **48,** 4, 458.

Kendrick, J. W. and McEntee, K. (1967) The Effect of Artificial Insemination with Semen Contaminated with IBR-IPV Virus Cor. Vet. **57,** 1, 3.

Kendrick, J. W., McKercher, D. G. and Saito, J. (1956) Preliminary Report of Studies on a Catarrhal Vaginitis of Cattle, J.A.V.M.A. **128,** 7, 357.

Kradel, D. C., Solorzano, R. F., Dunne, H. W. and Michel, R. L. (1961) Infectious Pustular Vulvovaginitis in a Pennsylvania Dairy Herd, Vet. Med. **56,** 8, 333.

Lindley, C. C. and Hatfield, R. C. (1952) Observations on the Bacterial Flora of Infertile Dairy Cows, J.A.V.M.A., **120,** 898, 12.

Lingard, D. R. and Hanson, L. E. (1961) Effect of **Leptospira pomona** on the Reproductive Efficiency of Cattle, J.A.V.M.A. **139,** 4, 449.

Manthei, C. A. and Deyoe, B. L. (1970) Brucellosis, in **Bovine Medicine and Surgery,** Amer. Vet. Public Inc., Wheaton, Ill., 104.

Manthei, C. A., DeTray, D. E. and Goode, E. R. (1950) Brucella Infection in Bulls and the Spread of Brucellosis in Cattle by Artificial Insemination, Proc. A.V.M.A., 87th Ann. Meeting, 177.

Mare, J. and Van Rensburg, S. J. (1961) The Isolation of Viruses Associated with Infertility in Cattle—A Preliminary Report, S. Afr. J. Vet. Med., **32,** 2, 201.

McIntosh, B. M., Haig, D. A., and Alexander, R. A. (1952) Isolation of Viruses Associated with Epididymitis and Vaginitis of Cattle, J. So. Afr. Vet. Med. Assoc., **23,** 3, 165.

McKercher, D. G. (1969) Relationship of Viruses to Reproductive Problems, J.A.V.M.A. **154** 10, 1184.

Millar, P. G. (1955) Viral Infertility in Cattle, Brit. Vet. J., **111,** 7, 309.

Miller, F. W. and Graves, R. R. (1932) Reproduction and Health Records of the Beltsville Herd of the Bureau of Dairy Industry, U.S. Dept. of Agr. Tech. Bull. 321.

Neilsen, F. (1949) Sterility in Cattle, Especially as a Result of Uterine Infection, Proc. 14th Internat. Vet. Congr., Section 4 (c), 105.

Nelson, W. A. (1958) Mass Outbreak of Necrotic Vulvitis, Jen Sal. Jour. **41,** 1, 15.

Olds, D. (1953) Infertility in Cattle—A Review, J.A.V.M.A., **122,** 913, 276.

Pierson, R. E. and Hill, H. J. (1956) Necrotic Vulvitis in Feedlot Heifers, J.A.V.M.A. **128,** 2, 71.

Plum, N. (1926) Tuberculous Abortion Disease in Cattle, Cor. Vet. **16,** 237.

Roberts, S. J. (1949) Vesicular Venereal Disease, Cor. Vet., **39,** 4, 435.

Spradbrow, P. B. (1968) The Isolation of Infectious Bovine Rhinotracheitis Virus from Bovine Semen, Austral. Vet. Jour. **44,** 9, 410.

Studdert, M. J., Wada, E. M., Kortum, K. M. and Graverman, F. A. (1964) Bovine Pustular Vulvovaginitis in Western United States, J.A.V.M.A. **144,** 6, 615.

Thomsen, A. (1943) Does the Bull Spread Infectious Abortion in Cattle? Experimental Studies from 1936 to 1942, Jour. of Comp. Path. and Therap., **53,** 3, 199.

Troutman, E. C. (1954) Granular Vaginitis as a Cause of Infertility ir Dairy Cattle, J.A.V.M.A., **124,** 924, 184.

U.S. Livestock Sanitary Assoc. (1954) Foreign Animal Diseases, Rept. of Committee, Secr. Treas., Trenton, New Jersey.

Van Kruiningen, H. J., Davis, F. H., Pieper, N. W. and Daniels, W. H. (1968) Concomitant Granular Vulvitis, Palate Lesions, and Respiratory Illness in Connecticut Dairy Cattle, J.A.V.M.A. **153,** 12, (1968) 1581.

Van Rensburg, S. W. J. (1953) Bovine Sterility Caused by Infectious Disease in South Africa, Brit. Vet. J., **109,** 226.

Webster, W. M. (1932) Bovine Sterility in New Zealand, Austr. Vet. J., **8,** 6, 199.

Williams, W. L. (1943) Diseases of the Genital Organs of Domestic Animals, 3rd Ed., Miss Louella Williams, Upland Rd., Ithaca, New York.

HORMONAL DISTURBANCES RESULTING IN INFERTILITY

Most hormonal disturbances causing infertility or sterility in cows and other animals are secondary to basic nutritional, hereditary and stress or work factors. Occasionally hormonal disturbances may be due to the ingestion or injection of exogenous steroids or other hormones. Hormonal diseases may include cystic ovaries, failure of estrum and repeat breeders due to failure of ovulation failure of fertilization and early embryonic deaths. The widespread indiscriminate use of many hormones on an emperical basis by veterinarians 15 to 20 years ago has been followed in recent years by a much more selective and knowledgeable employment of the various hormones for their specific action in certain limited and carefully diagnosed infertility conditions.

Cystic Ovaries

Cystic ovaries in dairy cattle is becoming one of the most common conditions causing infertility that the veterinarian is called upon to treat. McKay and Thomsen reported that 12 to 14 percent of all problem breeder cows have cystic ovaries. Cystic ovaries in cattle are character-

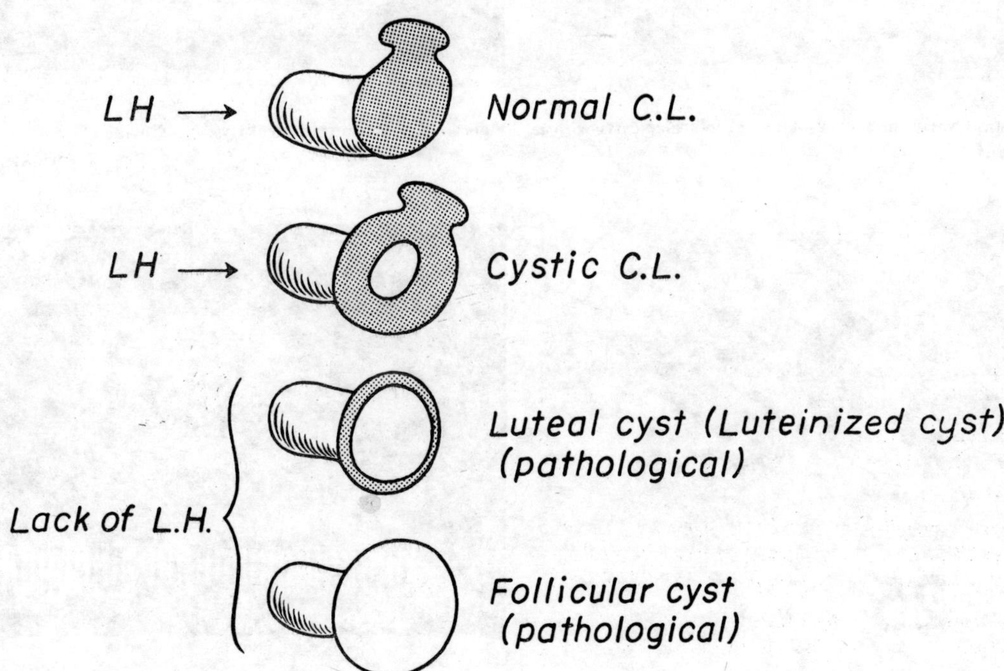

Figure 107 Cysts of the Bovine Ovary.

ized by follicular cysts or cystic degeneration of the Graafian follicle, luteal or luteinized cysts, and cystic corpora lutea. Follicular and luteal cysts are anovulatory cysts while the cystic corpus luteum is an ovulatory cyst. The basic cause for these cystic conditions is a failure of the hypohysis to release sufficient amounts of luteinizing hormone, LH, to produce ovulation and proper development of the corpus luteum. (See Figures 107 through 111)

Follicular cysts are anovulatory follicles that persist on the ovary for 10 days and usually much longer, have a diameter greater than 2.5 cm and are characterized by either nymphomania or continuous or frequent estrus, or by anestrus. Luteal cysts are anovulatory follicles over 2.5 cm. in diameter that are partially luteinized and persist for a prolonged period and are usually characterized by anestrus. Follicular cysts and luteal cysts may be hard to differentiate clinically but the former may be multiple on both ovaries while the latter are more often single. The follicular cyst is thinner-walled and the wall is more tense and distended than the softer thicker-walled luteal cyst. The follicular and luteal cysts have a smooth convex surface since ovulation does not occur. The luteal cyst wall is thicker due to the presence of a thin lining of luteal tissue. The fluid in the luteal cyst is usually more amber or darker yellow or brown in color than the pale yellow clear fluid in the follicular cyst, Stoll. Follicular cysts are much more common than are luteal cysts. Zemjanis reported that 30.5 percent of 1191 cystic ovaries contained luteal cysts. (See Figures 107 through 111).

Cystic corpora lutea follow a normal ovulation but

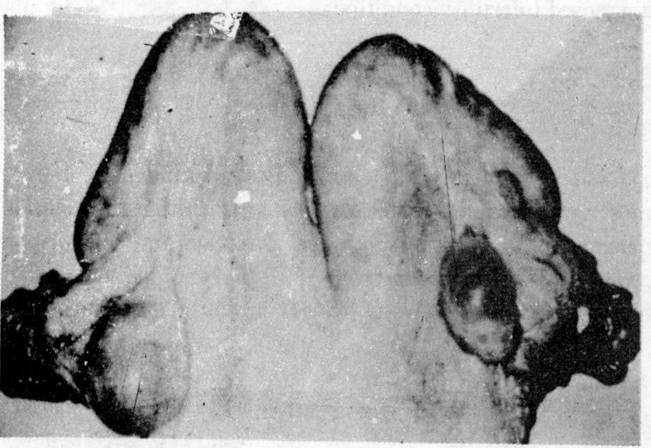

Figure 108 Cystic Ovaries in a Cow—bilateral follicular cysts with a flaccid atonic uterus

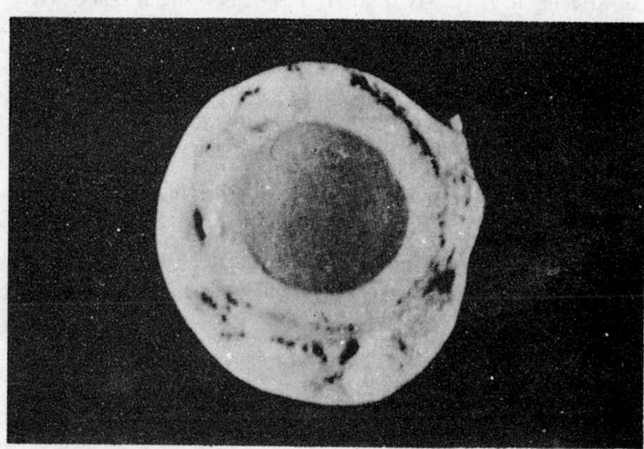

Figure 109 . A Central Luteal Cyst in a Bovine Ovary.

(Courtesy K. McEntee)

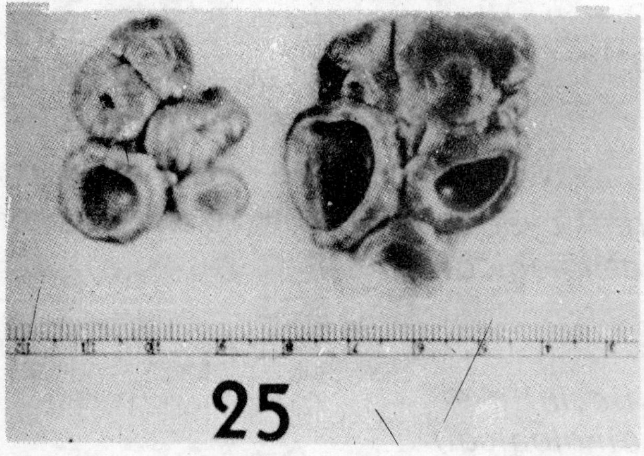

Figure 110 Bovine Luteal Cysts Associated with Superovulation following the Injection of FSH.

(Courtesy M. R. Jainudeen)

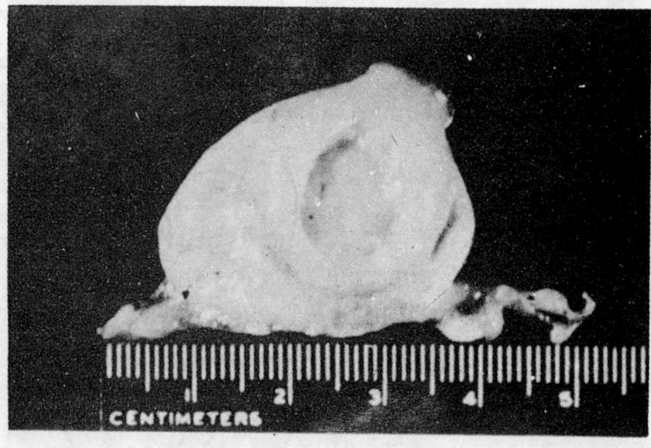

Figure 111 A Bovine Cystic Corpus Luteum.

(Courtesy K. McEntee)

contain a fluid-filled central cavity 7 to 10 mm. or more in diameter. Cystic corpora lutea on rectal palpation feel similar to large, swollen normal corpora lutea as they have a projecting crown of luteal tissue that protrudes through the site of ovulation. Cystic corpora lutea often have a slightly fluctuating, soft consistency. This is the most common of the cystic conditions affecting the bovine ovary with an incidence two and a half times greater than cystic follicles. Thirty seven cystic corpora lutea and 14 follicular cysts were found in 204 nonpregnant cows at slaughter, McEntee. In 357 estrous cycles followed by rectal examinations the incidence of normal corpora lutea, cystic corpora lutea and follicular cysts were 62.4, 25.2 and 12.3 percent, Morrow. The incidence of cystic corpora lutea was 34 to 41 per cent in cycling cows, Donaldson and Hansel, and Hansel. They reported the total progesterone in cystic corpora lutea was about 110 ug at 7 days of the cycle compared to about 180 ug in normal corpora lutea of the same age. About 100 to 150 ug of progesterone is needed in the corpus luteum to permit normal embryo development, Staples and Hansel. By 11 days of the cycle the cystic corpora lutea averaged 223 ug and the normal corpora lutea 295 ug of total progesterone. Hansel reported low levels of estrogen and progesterone in the fluid found in cystic corpora lutea. Possibly this fluid is composed of serum or lymph that has become trapped after ovulation.

Cows with cystic corpora lutea have normal estrous cycles and if conception occurs there is usually sufficient luteal tissue and progesterone to maintain pregnancy, Hansel. Small central cysts less than 7 mm. in apparently normal corpora lutea are common and may be found in up to 30 percent of corpora lutea, Greenstein. These central cysts are lined by a layer of connective tissue, they become smaller late in the estrous cycle as the corpus luteum regresses and are seldom found in pregnant cows' corpora lutea after the fourth or fifth month of gestation, Greenstein, McEntee. For practical purposes most cystic corpora lutea are not pathological as ovulation was normal; they do not influence cycle length, McEntee, Morrow; they may follow a slightly longer than normal estrous period, McEntee, and most cows with cystic C. L. usually maintain the pregnancy to term. However, they may be caused by a mild faulty release of L.H. hormone and thus be caused by the same basic deficiencies producing follicular cysts and luteal cysts, McEntee, Greenstein, and Short. Since cystic corpora lutea have a questionable pathologic significance the term cystic ovaries will be applied only to the common follicular cysts and less common luteal cysts.

Etiology—Cystic ovaries is principally a disease of dairy cows although occasionally beef cattle are affected. While the author has observed the disease most often in Holsteins and Guernsey cattle, it must be pointed out that those are the predominant breeds in New York State. The disease is more common in closely-confined, stabled animals during the winter months of December, January and February, than during the summer and fall months, Henricson, Morrow, and Roberts. The latter authors reported 44 and 48 percent of their cases of cystic ovaries occurring during these three months. Cystic ovaries affects cows of all ages from puberty to senility but is most commonly observed following the second to the fifth parturition, Garm, or from 4-1/2 to 10 years of age, Henricson. In 295 cases studied by the author 41, or 13.9 percent, occurred in cattle from 1 to 3 years of age; and only 3 of these were virgin heifers; 160 or, 54.2 percent, occurred between 4 and 6 years of age; 74, or 25.1 percent, between 7 and 9 years of age; and 20, or 6.8 percent, over 10 years of age. In a study of 64 cystic cows in a herd of 341 head over a period of 10 years Casida and Chapman reported that the number of cows that developed cystic ovaries in any given service period was fairly constant. Certain cows may have repeated attacks of cystic ovaries during a service period or during different service periods. Garm reported that of 433 cows studied by him, 53 suffered repeated attacks. In 341 cows studied by Casida and Chapman 64 cows had cystic ovaries; of these, 12 were affected at 2 service periods, 4 at 3 service periods, and 2 at 4 service periods. Henricson reported that 35 to 45 percent of cows with cystic ovaries had repeated attacks within a service period.

The occurrence of cystic ovaries is closely associated with milk production in that it is seen more commonly in the higher producing cows. Eriksson, Garm and Henricson and Marion and Gier reported that affected cows have a higher quantitative milk yield than do normal cows. In Garm's cases, on the basis of the average milk-yield in the herd, 45 percent of the nymphomaniac cows were excellent producers, 48 percent fair producers and only 7 percent poor producers. In the herd studied by Casida and Chapman similar findings were noted. The occurrence of nymphomania was not associated with the level or percentage of butter fat produced. There were 1280 service periods, 341 of which were in virgin heifers, during which the animals were not milked; 457 records were made during the time the cows were in the milking herd and milked twice daily, and 105 records on animals started on test but returned to the milking herd before conception; and there were 359 service periods of cows on official test being milked 3 or 4 times a day. In these 4 categories the incidence of nymphomania or cystic ovaries was 3.4 percent, 6.8 percent, 8.5 percent and 10.6 percent respectively. The increased incidence of cystic ovaries in the test cows might be explained either on higher production, increased feeding, more frequent daily milking, or all three factors.

Many workers believe that increased feeding especially of rations high in protein stimulate lactation and the development of cystic ovaries. Morrow et al. could not confirm this fact but the evidence was suggestive. The time of onset of cystic ovaries in cattle is usually from 1 to 4 months after calving, with a peak around 15 to 45 days, Morrow, Marion and Gier. This is the time when milk production is usually the highest. This condition may occasionally occur following repeated services as late as 8 and 9 months after calving. Nymphomania or cystic ovaries occurred in heifers that were withheld from service for a number of years in an experiment by DeLange.

In 312 cases of nymphomania or cystic ovaries observed by the author there appeared to be a seasonal incidence of the disease; 151 cases, or 48.4 percent, occurred during the months of December, January and February. During these same months in comparable years the N.Y. State Artificial Breeders Cooperative inseminated only 35.7 percent of over 325,000 cattle bred those years. High feeding levels causing increased milk production, coupled with lack of exercise and sunlight might be contributing factors to the cystic condition during the winter months. Roberts, and Morrow noted a similar seasonal occurrence.

There is evidence to show that nymphomania or cystic ovaries is hereditary. This conclusion has long been held by clinicians. Garm cited Eriksson's conclusion that a hereditary predisposition to nymphomania existed in the Swedish Highland breed. Garm reported that in 331 Swedish Red cattle affected with nymphomania, 26 percent of their dams had nymphomania, 41 percent were normal, and in the remainder this information was not known. In the Frisian breed 102 cows had nymphomania and of these 21 percent of their dams had nymphomania, 45 percent were normal, and in the remainder no information was obtained. Casida and Chapman recorded 245 daughters out of 144 dams. Of these dams 43 had been cystic; they produced 82 daughters, of which 26.8 percent developed nymphomania. The remaining 101 dams had never been cystic; they produced 163 daughters, of which only 9.2 percent developed cystic ovaries. In their data there was no evidence of an hereditability of cystic ovaries from cows staying in the herd for less than 4 service periods. They therefore eliminated those cows and recorded only those that remained in the herd for 4 service periods or more; dams with cystic ovaries had 27 daughters, of which 48.1 percent were cystic, whereas noncystic dams had 46 daughters, of which only 21.7 percent were cystic. Henricson stated that nearly all cows that suffered from a recurrent development of cystic ovaries had a genetic predisposition to the disease. Because of this factual evidence and the many observations by most practicing veterinarians of cystic ovaries in succeeding generations of a cow family, there is every reason to assume the existence of a hereditary predisposition to cystic ovaries and nymphomania. In recent years, with the the increased use of artificial insemination and the increased level of productivity in our purebred and commercial dairy herds, the incidence of this condition is rising abruptly. In a few herds the problem of cystic ovaries became so severe that the owner became discouraged and the herd was dispersed, Haubrich. In the Ambulatory Clinic of the N.Y. State Veterinary College the incidence of cystic ovaries rose from 333 cases between 1948 to 1953, to 1530 cases between 1963 and 1968.—or over a 100 percent increase for each 5 year period in an area where cow numbers declined slightly from 1943 to 1968. Some of this increase may be due to the farmer becoming educated, recognizing the symptoms and calling for treatment; or it may be because treatment is usually successful in maintaining the cow in the herd so that the condition may recur subsequent years; or it may be due to widespread use of bulls by artificial insemination that transmit this inherited predisposition toward cystic ovaries along with high milk production.

Further study should be made of the hereditability of this condition from the male side to ascertain whether, as suggested by Williams, certain males transmit this hereditary predisposition toward nymphomania. Menge et al. noted a significant sire line effect on the incidence of cystic ovaries in a large purebred Holstein herd. Bane reported that in Sweden where AI bulls siring daughters having a higher than normal incidence of cystic ovaries were culled that the frequency of cystic ovaries declined from 10.8 percent in 1954 to 5.1 percent in 1961. Thus Williams' observations have been proven to be correct and AI studs in the United States should heed with concern and action the above known facts. The two abnormalities of ovulation, cystic ovaries and twinning, are closely associated and both are probably hereditary. The relationship was discussed in Chapter IV.

The actual mechanism leading to the development of cystic ovaries is not completely known. The discovery by Casida, McShan and Meyer that injections of gonadotropic substances rich in L. H. had a highly specific and curative effect on this condition, definitely indicated that the disease was probably due to a deficiency of L. H. hormone released prior to or at the time of ovulation. Jubb and McEntee, and McEntee reported that the delta cells of the anterior pituitary that produce gonadotropic hormones degranulate or release their hormone shortly after the onset of estrus in normal cows. In cows that fail to ovulate this degranulation fails to occur, or may occur later, or may not occur as completely as in normal animals. Donaldson and Hansel reported that pituitary gonadotropin potency at estrus and four days after normal estrus and ovulation was 3.0 to 9.1 ug while in cows with follicular cysts, the pituitary glands contained 6.1 to 15.1 ug of gonadotropin at estrus and 4 days later. Thus in cystic ovaries the normal release of L. H. failed. The failure of the release mechanism or an actual deficiency of luteinizing hormone from the anterior pituitary gland prevents normal ovulation and development of the corpus luteum. In the series of cases treated by the author one dose of L. H. was given to each of 5 cows after normal estrum followed by continuous symptoms of nymphomania 2, 5, 5, 6, and 7 days and the presence of cystic ovaries. These cows conceived to the insemination or natural service on the first day of estrum preceding the development of the nymphomaniac symptoms. This probably indicates that enough L. H. was present to cause ovulation but not enough to cause normal luteinization of the follicle and the suppression of further release of F.S.H. with the result that a number of other follicles matured, failed to ovulate and became cystic. The injected luteinizing hormone caused a rapid luteinization soon enough so that normal attachment and development of the fertilized ovum took place. If treatment had not been given, the fertilized ovum would have perished and a well-established case of nymphomania or cystic ovaries would have developed. Others have recorded similar cases treated within 10 days after insemination.

Fincher, the author and others have induced cystic ovaries in cattle by injections of estrogens. Intramuscular injections into cycling cows of doses greater than 4 mg of estradiol or 40 mgs of stilbestrol may result in cystic ovaries. Prolonged or high doses of estrogens have been reported by Dawson and McEntee as causing cystic ovaries. The former author cited evidence to indicate that injected androgens could also cause this disease, Greenstein, and Malven et al. cited reports showing that cystic corpora lutea, possibly a mild nonpathogenic condition related to cystic ovaries, could be induced by daily oxytocin injections early in the estrous cycle, by uterine dilation or by progesterone injections. Thus exogenous injection of steroids and other hormones can interfere with the normal release of L. H. and produce cystic ovaries.

Adler and Trainin (1960) described a hyperestrogenic syndrome in unrelated dairy cattle in Israel characterized by cystic ovaries, udder development in calves, increased incidence of estrus during early pregnancy, estrogenic changes in the genital organs, infertility, and abortions caused by feeding large amounts of alfalfa hay with a high estrogenic content. Adler (1969) suggested estrogens might also be present in higher than normal amounts in red clover, pea ensilage and mold on hay and silage. If a herd experiences more than a 30 percent incidence of cystic ovaries and hereditary factors are not the cause, estrogens in the feed should be suspected. Another source of estrogens might be feed accidentally contaminated with large amounts of synthetic estrogens. The presence of estrogens in plants have been described by Bartlett et al., Bickoff et al. and Kallela. Schoop and Klette reported on an outbreak of sterility in Germany apparently due to a high content of estrogen in the grass.

Garm reported that the pituitary gland and especially the adrenal gland were larger in cows with cystic ovaries than in normal cows. He also reported that certain cows with cystic ovaries exhibited a masculine behavior and appearance and had increased levels of 17-ketosteroids in the urine from the adrenal gland. He called this syndrome "adrenal virilism" Short has reported that the bovine adrenal gland is a poor source of androgens. He questioned Garm's conclusions that "adrenal virilism" actually occurs in cattle. Short has further shown that the bovine ovaries can occasionally produce androgens.

The steroid content of ovarian cysts was studied by Short and the previous literature was reviewed. He concluded that although estradiol-17B was the major steroid in normal ovarian follicles, the concentration of this steroid was significantly lower in follicular cysts, 50 to 75 ug and 20 to 30 ug per 100 ml of fluid, respectively. Histologically the steroid producing cells in the follicular cysts were undergoing atresia. Some cyst fluid samples contained large amounts of progesterone and these cysts on histologic examination showed atretic or luteinizing changes. Other steroids such as estrone and androstenedione were also found in the cyst fluids. The absolute concentrations and relative amounts of various steroids found differed greatly both between animals and within the same animal. There was no correlation between the size of the cyst and the hormone content. Short concluded that the cyst itself was not the primary defect in ovarian disease. Cysts were degenerating structures both histologically and endocrinologically. In normal follicles growth and endocrine activity accompanied each other while in cysts follicular growth continued but endocrine activity declined. Neither the concentrations or the total amount of estradiol indicated the cysts produced increased amounts of estrogen. However, estrogens were produced in cystic ovaries for a longer period of time and more continuously than estrogens in a normal cycling cow.

It was impossible to correlate the behavior exhibited by cystic cows with the steroids present in the cysts. This behavioral pattern was complicated since both progesterone and testosterone can potentiate estrogens in bringing a cow into estrum; progesterone in large doses can inhibit estrus in an estrogen-primed animal; and cows tend to become refractory to even high doses of estrogen and fail to shows signs of estrus. Furthermore the frequency of the development of new follicles and hormonally active cysts will affect the behavior of the cystic cow, Short.

Malven et al. found that nearly all fluids from cystic corpora lutea contained estrogens at a level 2 to 3 times less than normal ovarian follicular fluid. The source of this fluid in cystic corpora lutea is not known. Greenstein also indicated that cystic corpora lutea, although not pathogenic, were a secondary manifestation of a basic hormonal dysfunction. Short and Stein reported that the bilaterally cystic ovarian condition in hirsute women, the Stein-Leventhal syndrome, is dissimilar both histologically and endocrinologically from bovine cystic ovarian disease.

Morrow et al. and others have shown that disease at the time of or shortly after parturition predisposed cows to cystic ovaries. Henricson stated that environmental factors did not contribute in any great degree to an increased frequency of cystic ovaries. Some older authors and veterinarians indicated that cystic ovaries were associated with or even due to uterine infections. Garm examined the uterus histologically and bacteriologically in 62 cows with cystic ovaries and found evidence of an endometritis in only 4 cases. The author agrees with Garm that infection of the uterus is seldom seen in cystic ovaries. Of the author's cases of cystic ovaries or nymphomania, 72 cows conceived promptly within 60 days of treatment without treatment of the uterus. A few cases of infection were encountered. As further evidence that infection is not usually a factor in cystic ovaries Garm reported that parturition prior to the onset of cystic ovaries was normal in 99 percent of his cases and that retained placenta occurred in only 5 percent of them.

Signs—Cystic ovaries develop in nonpregnant cattle most commonly from 15 to 45 days postpartum, Morrow, Marion and Gier, but may occur quite commonly up to 120 days and occasionally thereafter. Behavioral signs are variable for several reasons as discussed under the etiology but for general purposes cows can be divided into two groups, nymphomaniac and anestrous cattle. The cows with nymphomania exhibit frequent, irregular, prolonged, or continuous signs of estrum. These cows are often nervous, restless, and bellow frequently. Only very rarely does a nymphomaniac cow become vicious. These cows may occasionally accept the riding of another cow, or coitus by the bull at any time. Most nymphomaniac cows frequently attempt to ride other cows but often refuse to stand to be ridden. Nymphomaniac cows may be as sexually aggressive as a bull in seeking out and attempting to mount a cow approaching or in estrum. The homosexual characteristics of cattle are aggravated during this disease. The affected cows because of their actions are often spoken of as "bullers." These cows, especially if on pasture are likely to lose weight during the disease because of constantly moving about, attempting to mount, and stirring up the other cows. The cows with cystic ovaries that show anestrum are not observed in estrum for long periods of time, several months or more. In this group of cows the symptoms of estrum, if they are present, are very mild and infrequent. The owner of these cows, if they have been bred, may believe them to be pregnant. Others, about 15 to 20 percent, have had a normal estrum or two and then failed to show estrum thereafter even though they were not bred. Some of these cows may at times act as if they might be in estrum but refuse to stand for the bull or for other cows to mount them. Some cows with cystic ovaries may show anestrum initially and then exhibit nymphomonia later or conversely some nymphomaniac cows may continue to have cystic ovaries but after a varying period of time exhibit anestrum.

The incidence of cows with cystic ovaries exhibiting nymphomania or anestrus varies and is strongly influenced by the postpartum interval at which the condition is diagnosed per rectum. Morrow et al. (1966) and Gier reported more cystic follicles developed from 0 to 30 days than from 31 to 60 days postpartum. According to these authors 82 and 87 percent of the cows, respectively, that developed follicular cysts prior to 60 days exhibited anestrus. Bierschwal in a study of 187 cows with cystic ovaries in which many were examined in the early postpartum period of 30 to 60 days reported a 62.5 percent incidence of anestrus. Roberts in a study of 265 cases of cystic ovaries examined only at the request of owner from about 80 to 150 days after calving reported the incidence of anestrus to be 26.4 percent. Thus as the number of days following calving at which the cystic ovarian condition is diagnosed increase the incidence of nymphomania also increases.

According to Garm the most constant and prominent sign of cystic ovaries is the relaxation of the sacro-sciatic ligament, most noticeable at its caudal border. In cows showing nearly constant estrum 78 percent of the cows had highly-relaxed ligaments, 10 percent moderately relaxed and 6 percent slightly relaxed ligaments. In cows with frequent heats, 50 percent had highly relaxed, 42 percent moderately relaxed and 5 percent slightly relaxed ligaments. In a few cases because of the relaxing effect of estrogens on the pelvic ligaments this constant mounting and being mounted may lead to dislocations of the hips and to pelvic fractures. The pelvic ligaments of anestrous cows were highly relaxed in about 40 percent of the cows, moderately relaxed in 30 percent, slightly relaxed in 12 percent and normal in 18 percent of the cows. The genital organs are usually slightly edematous and atonic. The vulva is often increased in size, and relaxed and swollen. Prolapse of the vagina and symptoms of pneumovagina may occur especially in nymphomaniac cows. An increased amount of mucus may be present and appear as a discharge at the vulva. This mucus is tougher, more tenacious, and more opaque than the mucus of estrum. The mucus is whitish grey in color, giving it the appearance of a mucopurulent discharge. As revealed by the microscope there are usually no leucocytes in the mucus. The external os of the cervix is usually large, dilated, and relaxed.

On rectal examination the relaxation of the pelvic ligaments is very noticeable on palpation. The cervix, especially the external os, is usually large, and the uterus is also enlarged, and its walls are thickened and flaccid. In long-standing cases of cystic ovaries the uterus may be atrophied, small and flaccid. On palpation of the uterus it seldom develops tonicity or becomes erect or turgid as usually occurs in a normal uterus especially at or near estrum. One or 2 to 4 cysts varying in size from 0.75 to 3 inches in diameter are felt on one or both ovaries. These cysts are usually peripheral in location, thin-walled and burst readily with pressure applied by the fingers. At times it may be difficult to differentiate between a cyst and a normal follicle. Repeated examination, a vaginal examination, and the history should be helpful in most cases. Cysts persist for 10 days up to several months or longer. No luteal tissue or corpus luteum is palpable in the ovaries of cows with follicular cysts. Even cystic corpora lutea are not present. Occasionally a thick-walled, rather fluctuating, luteal or luteinized cyst may be found. These are often associated with anestrous cows. Occasionally a large atretic follicle together with a normal corpus luteum may be found in a pregnant cow the first trimester of gestation. This does not affect the pregnancy. Usually the cyst is larger than 0.75 inch in diameter whereas the normal follicle is smaller. The cyst is usually thicker-walled than is the follicle. The uterus of a cow with cystic ovaries is usually flaccid, whereas the uterus during estrum is erect and tonic. The mucus of estrum is much clearer and stringy than that in the cow with cystic ovaries. Occasionally cows 40 to 90 days pregnant may have a good-sized follicle and a normal corpus luteum. A cyst larger than 4 inches in diameter may indicate the presence of a granulosa cell tumor.

The size and number of ovarian cysts were similar for both nymphomaniac and anestrous cows, Garm, Roberts. Garm reported that the incidence of ovarian cysts in 433 cows was as follows: both ovaries cystic 50 percent, right ovary cystic 31 percent, and left ovary cystic 19 percent. The author in a total of 352 cases found the incidence to be 43.8 percent, 33.2 percent, and 23 percent, respectively. Lagerlof and Boyd on post mortem examination of the genital organs of 6286 Swedish Highland cows found an incidence of 14.8 percent cystic ovarian degeneration, 6 percent involved only the right ovary, and 5.5 percent involved both ovaries. Thus in nymphomania, as in the incidence of left- and right-horn pregnancies, the fact that the right ovary of cows is more active or functional than the left is further illustrated.

According to Garm gross examination of cystic ovaries revealed the fact that multiple cysts were more common than were single cysts and the large single cysts frequently showed evidence that they had been formed by the union of several cysts. The lining of the cyst was smooth and basal portions occasionally had a thin circumscribed area of some yellowish lutein tissue. Some lutein tissue has been observed in many ovarian cysts by the author and his associates. The cystic fluid was clear and slightly yellow or amber in color. In large cysts the ovarian tissue was atrophied. On histologic section the granulosa layer of cells and ovum are often missing, but scanty portions of granulosa cells could be found in the basal portions of the cyst and in some cases these appeared luteinized. The theca interna was likely to be flocculent and edematous and show degenerative changes. Some hyaline changes in the theca interna were occasionally observed. The degenerative changes were more marked in the peripheral portions of the cyst.

The gross appearance of the oviduct was normal in most cases, Garm. Sometimes it was thickened and some yellow fluid could be squeezed out after incising the oviduct. Microscopically this was composed of epithelial cells and debris. In cows with cystic ovaries the ovarian bursa or ventricle was larger than normal and the mesometrium was more relaxed. In nymphomaniac cows the uterus and cervix usually were large, edematous, and flaccid. The cervical canal was dilated and relaxed, permitting a finger or pencil to pass through. The endometrium was smooth, moist, semi-transparent, and edematous. In a few cases cystic enlargement of the endometrial glands was noticed as pinhead rounded elevations with transparent capsules. Usually the uterus was empty but the endometrium was covered with thin mucus. Occasionally as much as 100 ml of mucus was found in the uterus. The vagina, clitoris and vulva were swollen. Microscopically the greatest changes are found in the uterine mucosa. These changes, especially in nymphomaniac cows, were characterized by marked hyperplasia of the mucosa and cystic dilation of the endometrial glands. In some cases cystic dilation was so marked that the endometrium developed a typical

Swiss-cheese appearance on histologic section. (See Figure 113) In some of the cases in anestrous cows with a small uterus the mucosa showed slight atrophic changes and hyperplasia and cystic dilation of uterine glands. These hyperplastic and cystic changes in the endometrium are characteristic of changes produced by long-continued action of estrogens from the cystic ovaries. "Adrenal virilism" described by Garm and characterized by a long-standing cystic ovarian disease in which the cow becomes heavy and coarse, develops a thick neck and head and a steer-like appearance (See Figure 115), is considered by the author to be due to the effects of prolonged stimulation by gonadal steroids. The adrenal gland is probably not involved in this condition, Short.

In long-standing cases of nymphomania the relaxation of the pelvic ligaments produces a tipping of the pelvis

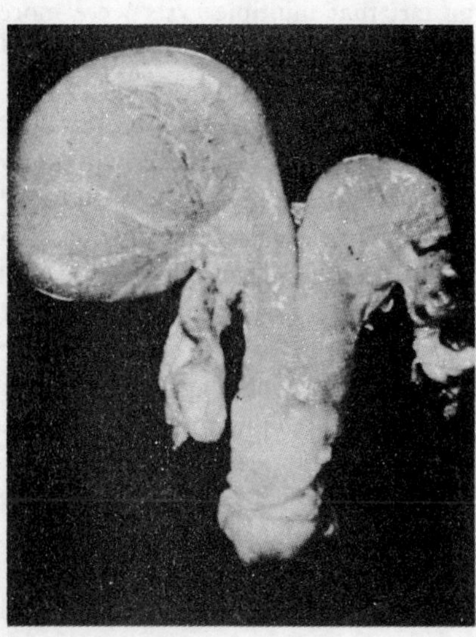

Figure 112. A Chronic Cystic Ovary Associated with a Unilateral Mucometra.
Courtesy K. McEntee

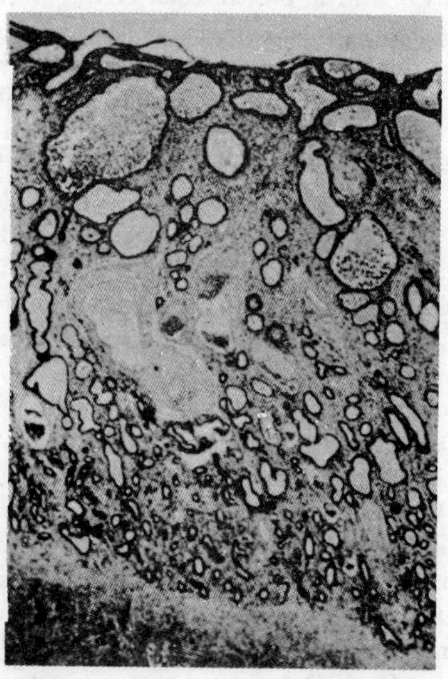

Figure 113. Cystic Endometrial Glands Caused by Cystic Ovaries.
Courtesy K. McEntee

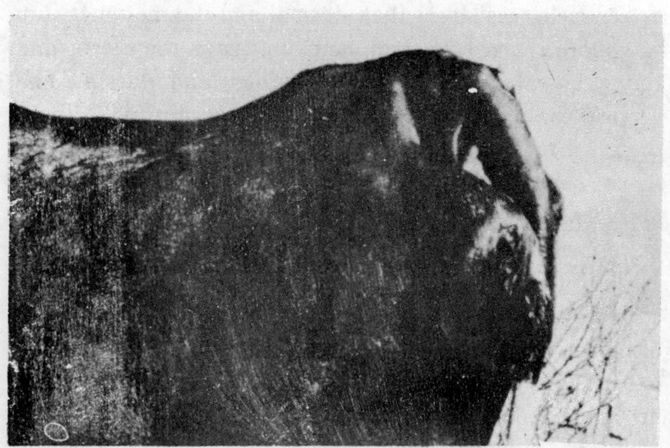

Figure 114. A "Sterility Hump" in a Cow Associated with Chronic Cystic Ovaries and Relaxed Pelvic Ligaments.

Figure 115. A Steer-like Appearence of a Cow with Chronic Cystic Ovaries and Infertility Lasting for Three Years.

and an elevation of the tail head that is made more pronounced by the relaxed sacrosciatic ligaments. This elevated tail head is sometimes called the "sterility hump" because it tends to persist after recovery. (See Figure 114) In many cases the ligaments fail to regain their tone even though recovery and conception occur. Associated with the elevation of the tail head is the elevation of the ischial tuberosities and a ventral dropping of the lumbosacral articulation. This tipping of the pelvis may result in an unsteady gait and a predisposition to injury.

Hydrometra or mucometra may develop following a long-standing condition of cystic ovaries. (See Figure 112) Cows with cystic ovaries observed by the author and his associates were initially treated apparently successfully and bred. The owners believed them to be pregnant but after 6 to 8 months the normal signs of pregnancy did not develop. Rectal examination revealed mucometra and cystic ovaries. A marked atrophy of the uterine wall or myometrium had occurred with severe cystic dilation of the endometrial glands resulting in mucometra with the uteri containing 100 to 1000 cc. of watery mucus. (See Figure 113) On rectal examination in some cases the uterine wall was found to be so thin that it was difficult to palpate. Hydro- or mucometra may affect only one uterine horn or a portion of one horn. The ovaries were usually larger than normal but the cysts were multiple, small (0.5 to 0.75 inch in diameter), and thick-walled. The cysts were extremely difficult or impossible to rupture by manual pressure. DeLange described and illustrated this same condition occurring in 3 heifers that developed chronic cystic ovaries out of 25 heifers that were withheld from breeding for 4 to 5 years. The cervical canal in these cases is usually closed by an accumulation of mucus and debris. In one case in which treatment was instituted by the author to relieve the mucometra by drawing off the mucus, infection was established and pyometra resulted. In another cow with 100 ml of mucus in the uterus, 20,000 I.U. of chorionic gonadotropin was injected intravenously and luteinization of the cysts and evacuation of the mucus from the uterus resulted. Most cases however fail to respond to treatment. The marked similarity of this condition in cattle to cystic degeneration of the uterine wall in horses, and to hyperplasia of the endometrium with cystic dilation of the endometrial glands, hydrometra, and in some cases secondary pyometra in dogs is evident. The endometrial changes are probably produced in the three species by the gonadal steroids, estrogen or progesterone.

In rare cases of chronic cystic ovaries and anestrus the cervix may become greatly enlarged to 5 to 6 inches in diameter and filled with a tenacious mucus, mucocervix. The uterus in these cases is flaccid but not distended with mucus. The cause and prognosis are similar to mucometra.

The effect of cystic ovaries on milk production is variable. Some authors report a drop in milk production in nymphomaniac cows. Others report a good milk production until treatment is given, at which time there is a drop in production. Johnson et al. in a careful study of 74 cows demonstrated that the cystic condition was apparently responsible for increased production. The longer the cows were cystic the greater the production of milk. Cows with anestrus produced more milk than nymphomaniac cows. They indicated that the low levels of estrogen from the cystic ovaries probably stimulated milk production. Others report the rare occurrence of a bitter, salty taste in the milk of these affected cows.

Prognosis—The earlier that cystic ovaries are diagnosed and treated, the better is the prognosis. In a series of 229 cases diagnosed and treated by the author within 6 months of parturition 79 percent conceived after 1 treatment, 10.7 percent had to be retreated, and 10 percent were sold because they were sterile, poor producers, or for other reasons. In 46 cows diagnosed and treated between 6 and 12 months after calving, although 78.3 percent recovered, only 58.7 percent conceived after one treatment and were retained in the herd, 8.7 percent were retreated, and 32.6 percent were sold. Many were sold because it was not economical to maintain them as nonlactating cows for many months in commercial herds. There was no essential difference between the rate of recovery and conception rates between cows showing nymphomaniac symptoms and cows showing anestrus. In 124 cases of nymphomaniac cows treated within 60 days of the onset of symptoms 78.2 percent conceived and 28.9 percent were sold. In anestrous cows, symptoms in many cases were lacking or unnoticed for an undetermined period of time. Of 46 cows, many of which had not been observed in estrum since calving, treated within 120 days of the onset of anestrum, 76.1 percent conceived and 23.8 percent were sold. The size or number of the cysts bore no relation to the symptoms shown or to the rate of recovery. In some cases two or more treatments may be necessary to effect a cure. Recovery is not assured until the affected cows are safely pregnant. About 20 to 30 percent or more of cows with cystic ovaries if they conceive will develop cystic ovaries again at subsequent service periods. Another factor to be considered seriously in the prognosis is the possible furthering of this cystic problem to the future detriment of dairy breeds inasmuch as there is a definite hereditary predisposition to cystic ovaries and twinning. Henricson reported that cows having two or more episodes of cystic ovaries were hereditarily predispositioned toward the disease. He and Bane indicated that bulls with an increased incidence of daughters with cystic ovaries should be slaughtered.

The prognosis in cases of severe cystic degeneration of the endometrium and atrophy of the uterine wall in hydrometra or mucometra is poor. Most cows with mucometra or rare cases of mucocervix should be sold since only a very few cases respond to treatment. Spontaneous recovery from cystic ovaries may occur. Morrow (1969) reported that about 50 percent of the cases of cystic ovaries occurring within 45 days of calving recovered spontaneously before 60 days postpartum. Johnson et al. reported that 13.3 percent of 30 cows with cystic ovaries recovered without treatment. Trimberger reported that in 34 cows treated for nymphomania about 15 percent were sold as sterile and the remainder required about 3 services per conception after treatment; about 40 percent of the cows conceived on first service. A lowered conception rate associated with early embryonic deaths following recovery from cystic ovaries was also noted by Menge et al..

Treatment—Rational treatment should have as its aim the development of a functional normal corpus luteum either by rupture of the cysts, repeatedly if necessary, administration of luteinizing hormone or preventing the continuous release of luteinizing hormone from the pituitary gland by the administration of progestational compounds. As Short has pointed out the bovine corpus luteum is formed mainly from the granulosa cells. Since these cells are the first cells to degenerate in the cystic follicle, treatment to be successful should be undertaken as soon as possible after cyst formation or when newer young cysts are forming on the already cystic ovary containing atretic cystic follicles.

The earliest treatment for cystic ovaries consisted of repeated manual removal or rupture of the cysts at 6- to 10-day intervals until a normal cycle and corpus luteum developed. This frequent manual massage and trauma to the ovary is not desirable if it can be avoided; moreover, repeated visits by a veterinarian for the massage of the cow's ovaries is costly. In a series of 188 cases gleaned by the author from reports of Miller and Graves, Clapp, Williams and Williams, and the N.Y. State Veterinary College Ambulatory Clinic from 1925 to 1935, in which cystic ovaries were treated by manual removal of cysts a recovery rate of 37.2 percent was reported. Vandeplassche reported on this treatment in 54 cows. After one or two treatments, or removal of cysts, a total of 42.5 percent became pregnant within the next one to two months, and of 21 gestation periods that followed, 5 ended in abortion, and 1 cow had twins. According to Clapp, 24 cases of cystic ovaries occurred in a herd of 150 cows and of these 8, or 37.5 percent, conceived twins after treatment. Of 11 animals bred within 35 days after removal of the last cyst 6, or 54.5 percent, conceived twins; only 3, or 23 percent, of 13 animals bred after 35 days following rupture of the last cyst had twins. Because of this high twinning rate Williams recommended that following treatment breeding be deferred until the second normal estrum unless the ovaries were palpated to determine the presence of 1 or 2 ripe follicles, and the cow then bred or not bred accordingly. It might be possible to remove one follicle and allow the other to ovulate. In cows having ovarian cysts centrally located, or thick-walled so that manual rupture was not possible, the treatment required tapping the cyst with a needle or ovarian scalpel through the vaginal wall. Stoll's cyst aspirator works well in these cases. Schjerven reported on 242 cows with cystic ovaries treated by manual rupture of the cysts. Three-quarters of these cases were treated within three months of parturition. Cows with the shortest time interval from parturition to treatment recovered significantly more quickly; 45.7 percent or 107 cases, recovered after one treatment. These results complement Morrow's observation that single ovarian follicular cysts occurring before 45 to 60 days after calving have a 50 percent spontaneous recovery rate and the observations of many veterinarians that manual removal of these early postpartum cysts is often successful in restoring a normal sexual cycle. Many veterinarians may manually remove cysts prior to 50 days but do not treat with LH until 50 to 60 days or more postpartum. Spaying will correct nymphomania but removing only 1 ovary if it is affected with cysts is useless, since the remaining ovary will promptly develop cysts. Affected nymphomaniac cows should be kept isolated from the herd so that they do not annoy or injure themselves or other cattle by mounting.

Although a number of authors had suggested the possible value of LH in treating bovine cystic ovaries and Deubler reported the successful treatment of a few cases with LH ("Antuitrin S") in 1943, it was not until 1944 that Casida, McShan and Meyer reported successful results in the treatment of many cows with cystic ovaries, both follicular and luteal cysts, using unfractionated sheep pituitary extracts intravenously. This demonstrated the value of L.H. in curing the disease. Of 81 cows with nymphomania or cystic ovaries treated, 88 percent recovered and had a normal corpus luteum in 31 days. Of 53 cows bred after a single injection of the pituitary extract, 36 conceived. After retreatment of 16 animals 6 more became pregnant. Thus a total of 68 percent conceived. These workers reported that it was not necessary to rupture cysts prior to treatment. Since then a number of reports on the treatment of cystic ovaries have recorded the successful use of pituitary extracts rich in L.H., or chorionic gonadotropin HCG, Roberts.

Injections of chorionic gonadotropin, 5000 I.U. intravenously and 10,000 I.U. intramuscularly resulted in slightly more conceptions that 2500 I.U. intravenously, 78.4 percent and 81.6 percent as against 73.7 percent conceptions, respectively. Bierschwal reported 68 percent recoveries from cystic ovaries in Guernseys and 78 percent recoveries in Holsteins by the administration of 5000 I.U. chorionic gonadotropin intravenously. Due to the cost of the product it is more economical to treat most cows with 2500 to 5000 I.U. of chorionic gonadotropin intravenously than the 10,000-I.U. dose intravenously or intramuscularly. Intramuscular injections of 1000 to 5000 units of chorionic gonadotropin in 14 cows resulted in a lower conception rate of 64.3 percent, Roberts. No difference was observed from year to year in the efficacy of the pituitary or chorionic gonadotropin products rich in L.H. In a small series of cases treated with 50 Armour units of "P.L.H." preliminary results were similar to those of "Vetrophin," Diamond Laboratories. McKay and Thomsen reported on the treatment of 278 cows with cystic ovaries with the intravenous injection of 10 RU "Vetrophin", 65 cows with 5 R.U. "Vetrophin" intravenously, 41 cows with 2500 to 4000 I.U. HCG intravenously, and 38 cows with 5000 to 10,000 IU HCG intramuscularly. Recovery and conceptions after one treatment were 65.5, 69, 78, and 71 percent, respectively, for these treatments.

Only two cases of anaphylaxis have been observed by the author and both recovered. One severely affected case occurred after the administration of 1500 R. U. of pregnant mare serum even though 5 cc. of adrenalin was administered simultaneously. The other, a moderately-affected case, occurred after the administration of 5000 I.U. of chorionic gonadotropin intravenously. No reaction was observed or reported with the use of the sheep pituitary product, "Vetrophin".

Of 185 cows in which cysts were removed by manual pressure through the rectum at the time of treatment with either pituitary L.H. or chorionic gonadotropin, 156, or 84.3 percent, recovered; 29, or 15.7 percent, did not recover; 133, or 71.9 percent, conceived; 20 or 10.8 percent, were retreated; and 32, or 17.3 percent, were sold. Of 103 cases in which the cysts were not ruptured at the time of treatment with L.H., 87, or 84.5 percent, recovered; 16, or 15.5 percent, did not recover; 79 or 76.7 percent, conceived; 11, or 10.7 percent, were retreated; and 13, or 12.6 percent, were sold. No benefit resulted from removal of cysts at the time of treatment with an L.H.-rich product, Roberts. Since trauma to and adhesions of the ovary may be produced by manual removal of cysts this practice is unnecessary and possibly contraindicated. After injections of L. H. the cysts luteinize and symptoms of nymphomania cease in 3 to 6 days in affected cows that recover. Although most of the unruptured cysts luteinize, the cystic fluid may remain until a few days before the next normal estrum when the luteal tissue and the cystic fluid involute and become absorbed rather rapidly. Yamauchi has reported that occasional cysts in treated cows will spontaneously rupture or ovulate. A normal estrum will occur in most cows from 15 to 30 days after treatment, with most cows exhibiting estrum 20 to 25 days after treatment.

If the cow has calved 50 days or more before the treatment of cystic ovaries and if no definite pathology of the genital tract is present requiring further rest or treatment, the author and others have recommended that the cow be bred the first estrum after the injection of luteinizing hormone. No observable increase in twinning or delayed conception has been caused by this practice. In the large series of cases reported by the author two cows aborted twins, two had viable twin calves, one aborted a single fetus, and one cow had a mummified fetus. Unfortunately not all cases could be followed through parturition. The practice of breeding promptly is indicated because if cows are pregnant cystic ovaries cannot recur! If cows are permitted to have two or three estrous cycles after treatment and before breeding, the condition is likely to recur. The practice of breeding the second normal heat period after treatment was indicated by the work of Williams and Clapp when manual removal of cysts was the only treatment. In the early treatment of certain cases some veterinarians remove cysts manually without injecting L.H. and if there is no response they make a return trip and treat with L.H. In the end this procedure may be more costly to the farmer than if the veterinarian administers L.H. on the initial call.

If a case of cystic ovaries fails to respond to an injection of L.H. and a second call is made a larger dose is indicated. The author also recommends a change of products from pituitary L.H. to chorionic gonadotropin, or vice versa. In 12 cases retreated with the same product 3 to 4 weeks after the first unsuccessful treatment, 5, or 41.7 percent of the animals recovered and conceived. In 31 cases of cystic ovaries in which a different product from a different source was used for the second treatment 26, or 83.9 percent, recovered and 67.7 percent of the cows conceived, Roberts. Since gonadotropic hormones are protein in nature and originate from a species of animal other than the bovine species, antibodies develop in the animal from the first injection, and neutralize some or much of the same hormone when reinjected. Willett and co-workers reported than when repeated injections of gonadotropin were used to superovulate cows the animals rapidly developed a refractoriness or inability to respond to the hormone that persisted for months. Other more recent studies have confirmed the development of antihormones against the injected gonadotropin such as HCG and PMSG, Nakahara et al., Mauer et al., Jainudeen et al. and Greenwald. The more refined the gonadotropin the less antigenic it was in causing antihormones.

Although the LH products have some limitations, they are generally accepted at the present time as the best treatment for the common follicular cysts and the less common luteal cysts.

Roberts, and Vereertbruggen have reported on the injection of small doses, 500 to 2000 I.U. of HCG or 0.5 to 5.0 R.U. "Vetrophin" directly into the ovarian cyst by means of a fine needle inserted through the vaginal wall or ischiorectal fossa while the other hand of the operator in the cow's rectum manipulated the cystic ovary. Although the cost of the hormones used by this technique was less, the results were about the same as other modes of administration of LH. The site of the injection bypassed the body fluids to act directly on the ovarian tissues producing the corpus luteum thus avoiding possible neutralization of the LH by antihormones in repeatedly treated cows. This procedure has not proved to be popular or commonly performed.

The use of FSH or pregnant mare serum (P.M.S.G.) has not resulted in a satisfactory recovery rate in cows with cystic ovaries when compared to the results with L.H. Roberts reported only a 48 percent recovery rate in 27 cows given 1000 to 2000 I.U. subcutaneously. Nishikawa and Sugie recommended large doses of 5000 to 10,000 I.U. PMS for cystic cows that had failed to repsond to HCG. These large doses produced superovulation and greatly enlarged ovaries containing many corpora lutea. These involuted at the next estrus period. This treatment has not been utilized as an acceptable mode of treatment. Furthermore following such a treatment there is a prolonged drop in milk production. Where only atretic degenerated cystic follicles are present, FSH injections might be indicated to produce young active follicles that would react to a dose of LH 3 or 4 days later to produce normal corpora lutea.

Under the influence of estrogens, gonadotropins, particularly LH, are released from the pituitary gland and the supply is depleted. Since progesterone and similar products suppress the release and favor the storage of gonadotropin by the pituitary gland, these products have received attention and use in recent years in the treatment of cystic ovaries, Johnson et al.. Beck and Ellis treated 100 cows that developed cystic ovaries and remained in estrus for a few days after service with 750 to 1500 mg of **Repositol** progesterone intramuscularly. The nymphomaniac signs terminated in most of these cows within 36 to 72 hours and 67 of the cows conceived. Holcomb and Holcomb ruptured the ovarian cysts on 110 cows in Finland and gave 200 to 500 mg. of progesterone capreolate intramuscularly. These cows came into estrum 10 to 14 days later but heats in general were weak. Eighty-five percent of the treated cows recovered but about one-half of the cows that failed to recover developed anestrus and the cystic condition recurred. Johnson et al. gave 98 cows with cystic ovaries 109 treatments of either 50 or 100 mg. of progesterone in oil daily subcutaneously for 14 days. The cysts were not ruptured. Forty-six of the cows exhibited nymphomania and 31 cows were anestrous before treatment. Normal estrous cycles and estrus resulted in 62 percent of the cows; 48.7 percent and 52.5 percent of the cows treated with 50 and 100 mg. of progesterone, respectively, conceived. Of 30 untreated control animals with cystic ovaries only 13.3 percent conceived. The average interval from treatment to conception was about 45 days with about 2+ services per conception.

In preliminary unpublished data by Bartholomew the use of synthetic progestins show promise for the treatment of bovine cystic ovaries. Fifty cows with cystic ovaries an average of 93 days after calving were given 200 mg. of M.A.P. (Repromix, Upjohn) daily for 10 days after manual rupture of the cysts. The average number of days from the start of the treatment to first estrus was 19.3 days and 80 percent of the cows recovered and 58 percent of the cows conceived at this first estrus. Similar early trials with MGA (Upjohn) in the N.Y.S. Ambulatory Clinic have not been as successful. Danieli and Sulman treated a few affectd cows with 250 to 500 mg of the injectable form of M.A.P. intramuscularly but a marked delay in the resumption of estrous cycles occurred. Thus further work is needed on these progestational products in cows with cystic ovaries to make this approach as uniformly successful as the use of luteinizing hormone.

Trainin and Adler, and Spriggs gave 3000 I.U. of H.C.G. and 100 to 125 mg. of progesterone in oil intravenously to 110 and 43 cows, respectively, with cystic ovaries. Eighty-three percent and 67 percent recovery rates, respectively, were reported. The use of progesterone in oil intravenously is questionable and the results compared to other treatments is not outstanding.

In a discussion of the treatment of cystic ovaries in cattle the author would be remiss if he did not again call attention of his readers to the fact that this condition is frequently due to an inherited weak hormonal constitution. The repeated successful treatment of affected cows simply increases the length of time these cows remain in the herd and increases the numbers of their daughters who also have an inherited predisposition for this disease. In many cases the veterinarian would be doing the farmer and the breed a favor by declining to treat certain cows and to recommend their slaughter. Herds with a high incidence of cystic ovaries should be bred to bulls from lines free of cystic ovaries or by bulls shown to have daughters with a very low incidence of the disease.

Failure of ovulation or delayed ovulation due to a failure or delay in LH release from the anterior pituitary gland and not associated with cystic ovaries may occasionally be a cause of infertility in cows and heifers. This is probably a minor cause for infertility since Tanabe and Casida reported failure of ovulation in only 3 out of 104 repeat-breeding cows. Later Casida reported that failure of ovulation occurred in only 3 percent of 247 cows examined. This low incidence of failure of ovulation is further indicated by work by Tanabe and Almquist and Bearden. Morrow reported that ovulation failure occurred in 13 percent of heifers on their first standing estrus and in 2 percent on their second estrus. This present evidence would indicate that failure of ovulation and atresia of the follicle with an absence of cystic follicles is an uncommon cause of infertility in the cow. It appears to be more common in the ewe and mare at the start of the breeding season. Hancock in a careful study of 58 cows reported that 69 percent had ovulated by the day after estrum and 65 percent of those bred conceived. The other 31 percent of cows had ovulated by the second day after estrum and of those that were bred only 36 percent conceived. However in a study of 118 Friesian and 161 Afrikaner cows and heifers over a 4-year period including a total of 536 estrous periods, defective ovulations occurred in 140; 47 cases or 34 percent ended in anovulation and 93 cases or 66 percent had delayed ovulation. 41 of the 47 anovulatory follicles regressed, 4 became follicular and 2 luteal cysts. In delayed ovulation the delay was less than 48 hours in 85 percent of the cases. In 2 cases ovulation occurred 7 and 9 days after the cessation of estrus and both cows conceived to inseminations performed the day before ovulation, Van Rensburg and DeVos. They recommended that if the follicle had not ovulated by 24 hours after service the cow should be inseminated again. In 51 cows reinseminated 24 hours after the first insemination 32 conceived while none of 18 cows that had failed to ovulate within 24 hours of service conceived. They reported that only one of 17 cows inseminated after ovulation conceived and only one of 36 cows conceived when the follicle was manually ruptured at the time of insemination. They indicated that the two main causes for defective ovulation were nutritional defects especially during the winter months and an hereditary predisposition characteristic of certain infertile cow families in both dairy and beef breeds. Because some reports indicated that anovulation or delayed ovulation are rare and other reports indicated they were common, more work is necessary on the incidence and importance of defective ovulation as a cause of lowered fertility. In light of VanRensburg and DeVos' report it should be noted that if cows are bred early in their estrous period, which usually lasts 18 hours, range 6 to 30 hours, ovulation, which usually occurs 8 to 16 hours after the end of estrum, may not have occurred by the end of the 24 hour period after breeding in the normal cow. Thus breeding in the second half of the estrous period is most desirable. Delayed ovulation may result in aging of the sperm and ova and also a lowered rate of fertilization and a higher embryonic death rate. (See repeat breeders)

Suspected failure of ovulation, or delayed ovulation may possibly be diagnosed by the palpation of a mature follicle on the ovary more than 24 to 48 hours after the end of estrum, especially if bloody mucus is in the vagina. For the treatment of delayed ovulation a small dose of a readily-assimilated estrogen ("Dinovex") was advocated by Haubrich on the assumption that this would hasten and promote ovulation by stimulating the release of LH if administerd at the onset of estrum. Spurrell reported that when "Dinovex" and distilled water were used alternately on "repeat breeder" cows that had been bred 3 times without conceiving, the results in both groups were similar. From the work of Spurrell and unpublished data by the author from observations on the actual cases of delayed estrum and the rarity of occurrence of genuine failure of ovulation, this therapy although apparently harmless is probably of no value except as a placebo. There is little evidence that failure of ovulation or delayed ovulation is often repeated at consecutive estrums. If anovulation or delayed ovulation was diagnosed, rebreeding and injections of L.H. be indicated since this hormone hastens and promotes ovulation in the cow. In these cases it might be advisable to rebreed the cow again 24 hours after the first service so fresh viable sperm cells would be available when the ovum was released. More work is needed to assess the importance of delayed ovulation and failure of ovulation without cystic follicles and to improve the diagnosis and treatment of these conditions.

Infertility Associated with Multiple Ovulations in Cattle

Kidder, Barrett and Casida reported on a study of 294 ovulations at which breeding occurred. These included 252 single ovulations and 42 multiple ovulations, as determined by rectal examination. The incidence of multiple ovulations was 14.3 percent. The conception rate in single ovulations was 57.5 percent, and in multiple ovulations 28.6 percent. Of these latter conceptions represented by 12 cows only 3 resulted in twin births. In a previous study in this same herd the incidence of multiple ovulations was 13.1 percent and the incidence of twinning was 1.92 percent. (See Discussion of Twinning in Unipara in Chapter IV, and Superovulation in Chapter XIX). Multiple ovulation is probably due to the release of increased amounts of FSH. Heredity and cystic ovaries may be associated or predisposing factors. Thus multiple ovulations resulted in infertility either due to defective ova incapable of fertilization or growth or because multiple ovulation may be a manifestation of an endocrine disturbance reflected in an abnormal transport of ova or failure of the proper attachment of the ovum. When twin or multiple ovulations occur from one bovine ovary and the fertilized ova develop in the horn corresponding to that ovary, a higher rate of embryonic death results than where twin ova are released from each ovary and each embryo develops in a separate horn, bicornual twins. This low survival rate in multiple ovulations and conceptions is probably a fortunate occurrence, as the harmful effects of twinning in cattle are well known. The work of Kidder, Barrett and Casida may explain the occasional cases in which although on early pregnancy examination two corpora lutea are found, and twinning is therefore suspected, only a single birth occurs.

References

Adler, J. H. (1969) Personal Communication

Adler, J. H. and Trainin, D. (1960) Hypoestrogenic Syndrome in Cattle, Refuah Vet. **17,** 115.

Bane, A. (1964) Fertility and Reproductive Disorders in Swedish Cattle, Brit. Vet. J. **120,** 431.

Bartholomew, R. (1969) Personal Communication, Unpublished data.

Bartlett, S., Folley, S. J., Rowland, S. J., Curnow, D. H. and Simpson S. A. (1948) Estrogens in Grass and Their Possible Effect on Milk Secretion, Nature, **162,** 845.

Bearden, H. J. (1954) Fertilization and Embryonic Mortality Rates for Bulls with Histories of Either Low or High Fertility in Artificial Breeding, Thesis, Cornell Univ., Collvege of Agriculture, Ithaca, N.Y.

Beck, C. C. and Ellis, D. J. (1960) Hormonal Treatment of Bovine Cystic Ovaries, Vet. Med. **55,** 6, 79.

Bickoff, E. M., Booth, A. N., Livingston, A. L. and Hendrickson, A. P. (1961) Estrogenic Activity of Fresh and Dried Red and Subterranean Clovers, J. An. Sci. **20,** 1, 133.

Bierschwal, C. J. (1966) A Clinical Study of Cystic Conditions of the Bovine Ovary, J.A.V.M.A. **149,** 12, 1591.

Casida, L. E. (1953) Fertilization Failure and Embryonic Death in Domestic Animals, Paper No. 448, Dept. of Genetics, Univ. of Wisc., Madison, Wisc., Reprinted from "Pregnancy Wastage" by E. T. Engle, Charles C. Thomas Co., Springfield, Ill.

Casida, L. E. and Chapman, A. B. (1951) Factors Affecting the Incidence of Cystic Ovaries in a Herd of Holstein Cows, J. of Dairy Sci., **34,** 12, 1200.

Casida, L. E. McShan, W. H. and Meyer, R. K. (1944) Effects of an Unfractionated Pituitary Extract Upon Cystic Ovaries and Nymphomania in Cows, J. of An. Sci., **3,** 3, 273.

Clapp, H. (1934) Cystic Ovaries and Twinning in Holsteins, Cor. Vet., **24,** 4, 309.

DeLange, M. (1950) The Influence of Delayed Breeding on the Fertility of Beef Heifers, Onderst. J. Vet. Sci. and An. Ind., **24,** 1 and 2, 125.

Danieli, Y. and Sulman, F. G. (1964) Treatment of Bovine Nymphomania with Medroxyprogesterone Acetate (M.A.P.), Refuah Vet. **21,** 97.

Dawson, F. L. M. (1957) Bovine Cystic Ovarian Disease—A Review of Recent Progress, Brit. Vet. Jour. **113,** 112.

Dawson, F. L. M., (1958) Bovine Cystic Ovarian Disease: An Analysis of 48 Cases, Brit. Vet. Jour. **114,** 96.

Deubler, J. (1943) Personal Communication.

Donaldson, L. E. and Hansel, W. (1968) Cystic Corpora Lutea and Normal and Cystic Graafian Follicles in the Cow, Austral. Vet. Jour. **44,** 304.

Eriksson, K. (1954) Genetic Analyses of Herditary Diseases with Incomplete Phenotypic Manifestation, Royal Swedish Acad. of Agric. Scient. Sect. Rept. No. 6, Uppsala, Almquist and Wiksell.

Fincher, M. G. (1954) Personal Communication, Unpublished data.

Garm, O. (1949) A Study on Bovine Nymphomania, Acta Endocrinologica, Supplementum 3 (III) (Accompanies Vol. II).

Greenstein, J. S. (1960) Experimental Induction of Cystic Corpora Lutea in Dairy Cattle, Internat. J. Fert. **6,** 1, 79.

Greenwald, G. S. (1970) Development of Ovulatory Refractoriness in the Rabbit to Cyclic Injections of Human Chorionic Gonadotropin, Fert. and Steril. **21,** 2, 163.

Hancock, J. L. (1948) The Clinical Analysis of Reproductive Failure in Cattle, Vet. Rec., **60,** 43, 513.

Hansel, Wm. (1964) Sterility Due to Permanent Corpus Luteum and Cystic Degeneration: Some Observations on Bovine Cystic Corpora Lutea, 5th Internat. Congr. on An. Reprod. and Art. Insem., Trento, Italy.

Haubrich, W. (1950) Bovine Infertility, Univ. of Penn. Vet. Ext. Quart., **118,** April, 62.

Haubrich, W. R. (1954) Personal Communication.

Henricson, B. (1956) Genetical and Statistical Investigations into So-Called Cystic Ovaries in Cattle, Acta Agric. Scand. **7,** 1.

Holcombe, R. and Holcombe, R. B. (1961) Treatment of Cystic Ovarian Degeneration in Cattle, Proc. 4th Internat. Congr. on An. Reprod., Hague, **III,** 654.

Jainundeen, M. R., Hafez, E. S. E., Gollnick, D. D. and Moustafa, L. A. (1966) Antigonadotropins in the Serum of Cows Following

Repeated Therapeutic Pregnant Mare Serum Injections, Amer. J. Vet. Res. **27**, 118, 669.

Johnson, A. D., Legates, J. E. and Ulberg, L. C. (1966) Relationship Between Follicular Cysts and Milk Production in Dariy Cattle, J. Dairy Sci. **49**, 7, 865.

Jubb, K. V. and McEntee, K. (1955) Observations on the Bovine Pituitary Gland, I. and II, Cor. Vet., **45**, 4, 570.

Kallela, K. (1962) Investigations on the Occurrence of Plant Estrogens Present in Finnish AIV Silage and Hay with Special Reference to Red Clover, Internat. J. of Fert. **7**, 4, 358.

Kidder, H. E., Barrett, G. R. and Casida, L. E. (1952) A Study of Ovulations in Six Families of Holstein Friesians, J. of Dairy Sci., **35**, 5, 436.

Malven, P. V., Hansel, W., Wagner, W. C. and Roberts, S. J. (1963) Estrogenic Activity in Bovine Luteal Cyst Fluid, J. Dairy Sci. **46**, 9, 995.

Marion, G. B. and Gier, H. T. (1968) Factors Affecting Bovine Ovarian Activity After Parturition, J. An. Sci. **27**, 6, 1621.

Maurer, R. R., Hunt, W. L. and Foote, R. H. (1968) Repeated Superovulation Following Administration of Exogenous Gonadotropins in Dutch Belted Rabbits, J. Reprod. and Fertil. **15**, 93.

McEntee, K. (1958) Cystic Corpora Lutea in Cattle, Internat. J. of Fertil. **3**, 1, 120.

McEntee, K., and Jubb, K. V. (1957) Functional Cytology of the Bovine Adenohypophysis in Relation to Cystic Ovaries, Internat. J. of Fert. **2**, 3, 279.

McKay, G. W. and Thomson, J. D. (1959) Field Observations on the Treatment of Cystic Ovaries in Cattle, Canad. J. Comp. Med. and Vet. Sci. **23**, 175.

Menge, A. C., Mares, S. E., Tyler, W. J. and Casida, L. E. (1962) Variation and Association Among Postpartum Reproduction and Production Characteristics in Holstein Friesian Cattle, J. Dairy Sci. **45**, 2, 233.

Miller, F. W. and Graves, R. R. (1932) Reproduction and Health Records of the Beltsville Herd of the Bureau of Dairy Industry, U.S. Dept. of Agric. Tech. Bull 321.

Morrow, D. A. (1969) Personal Communication.

Morrow, D. A. (1969) Estrous Behavior and Ovarian Activity in Prepuberal and Postpuberal Dairy Heifers, J. Dairy Sci. **52**, 2, 224.

Morrow, D. A., Roberts, S. J. and McEntee, K. (1969) Postpartum Ovarian Activity and Involution of the Uterus and Cervix in Dairy Cattle, Ovarian Activity, Cor. Vet. **59**, 2, 173.

Morrow, D. A., Roberts, S. J., McEntee, K. and Gray, H. G. (1966) Postpartum Ovarian Activity and Uterine Involution in Dairy Cattle, J.A.V.M.A. **149**, 12, 1596.

Morrow, D. A., Tyrrell, H. F. and Trimberger, G. W. (1969) Effects of Liberal Concentrate Feeding on Reproduction in Dairy Cattle, J.A.V.M.A. **155**, 12, 1946.

Nakahara, T., Yamaucki, M., Kataoka, T., Maruyama, Y. and Kaneda, Y. (1961) Studies on the Antihormone Against Human Chorionic Gonadotropin (Anti-HCG in Cattle, Injection of HCG Directly into the Ovarian Cysts, Jap. J. An. Reprod. **7**, 3, 123.

Nakahara, T., Yamauchi, M. Kataoka, T., and Kaneda, Y. (1962) Studies on the Anithormone Against Human Chorionic Gonadotropin in Cattle, Jap. J. of An. Reprod. **7**, 4, 137.

Nakahara, T., Kaneda, Y. and Yamauchi, M. (1964) Studies on the Anithormone Against Human Chorionic Gonadotropin in Cattle, Jap. J. An. Reprod. 10, 1, 9.

Nishikawa, Y. and Sugie, T. (1962) Serum Gonadotropin—New Treatment for Ovarian Cysts in Cows, Amer. J. Vet. Res. 23, 95, 788.

Roberts, S. J. (1955) Clinical Observations on Cystic Ovaries in Dairy Cattle, Cor. Vet., **45**, 4, 497.

Roberts, S. J. (1957) A Preliminary Report on the Treatment of Cystic Ovaries in Dairy Cattle by the Injection of Gonadotropic Hormones Directly into the Follicular Cyst, J.A.V.M.A. **131**, 11, 510.

Schjerven, L. (1965) Treatment of Cystic Ovarian Disease in Dairy Cattle, Nord. Vet. Med. **17**, 382.

Schoop, G. and Klette, H. (1952) Gehaufte Sterilita. durch Oestrogene Stoffe im Weidegras, Rept. of the II Internat. Congr. of Physiol. and Pathol. of An. Reprod. and of Art. Insem., Vol. II, 87.

Short, R. V. (1962) Steroid Concentrations in Normal Follicular Fluid and Ovarian Cyst Fluid From Cows, J. Reprod. and Fertil. **4**, 1, 27.

Spriggs, D. N. (1968) Cystic Ovarian Disease in Dairy Cattle, Vet. Rec. **83**, 231.

Spurrell, F. A. (1954) Personal Communication, Lecture Penn. State Soc. Meeting, Oct. 1954.

Staples, R. E. and Hansel, W. (1961) Luteal Function and Embryo Survival in the Bovine, J. Dairy Sci. **44**, 2040.

Stein, I. F. (1958) Diagnosis and Treatment of Bilateral Polycystic Ovaries in the Stein-Leventhal Syndrome, Internat. J. of Fert. **3**, 1, 20.

Stoll, I. V. (1969) Infertility and Draining Cysts in the Bovine, Mid Atlantic States Vet. Clinic, Baltimore, Md.

Tanabe, T. Y., and Almquist, J. O. (1953) Some Causes of Infertility in Dairy Heifers, J. of Dairy Sci., **36**, 586.

Tanabe, T. Y., and Casida, L. E. (1949) The Nature of Reproductive Failures in Cows of Low Fertility, J. of Dairy Sci., **32**, 3, 237.

Trainen, D. and Adler, J. H. (1962) The Treatment of Ovarian Cysts in Cattle by the Intravenous Injection of Gonadotropin and Progesterone (Report on 110 Cases), Refuah Vet. **19**, 109.

Trimberger, G. W. (1956) Ovarian Functions, Intervals Between Estrus, and Conception Rates in Dairy Cattle, J. Dairy Sci. 39, 4, 448.

VanRensburg, S. W. J. and DeVos, W. H. (1962) Ovulatory Failure in Bovines, Onderst. J. Vet. Res. **29**, 1, 55.

Vereertbruggen, W. (1957) Het Behandelen van Nymphomane Runders door Intrafollicululair Inspuiten van P. U. Hormoon, Vlaams Diergeneesk. Tijdschr. **26**, 1, 19.

Yamauchi, M. (1955) Studies on the Ovarian Cyst in the Cow. IV. The Course of Recovery From Ovarian Follicle Cyst by Chorionic Gonadotropin Therapy, Jap. J. Vet. Sci. **17**, 2, 47.

Zemjanis, R (1970) Diagnostic and Therapeutic Techniques in Animal Reproduction, 2nd Ed. The Williams and Wilkins Co., Baltimore, Md.

FAILURE OF ESTRUM, OR ANESTRUM

Failure of estrum, or anestrum, in cattle is the principal symptom of many conditions that may affect the estrous cycle. (see Physiology of Reproduction) It is the most common single cause for infertility in cattle. In many instances where owners or herdsmen are negligent in observing their cows closely, anestrum is reported to the veterinarians when actually the condition does not exist. Anestrum in cows is observed most commonly either after parturition as postpartum or preservice anestrum, or following service as postservice anestrum, when conception does not occur. In heifers it is frequently observed as a herd problem especially during periods of lowered nutritive intake. Because failure of estrum is due to multiple causes often not directly related to the endocrine system, a complete history should be obtained, a careful clinical examination of the genital tract and ovaries per rectum and vagina by a speculum should be made, and a physical examination of the cow might be necessary so that an accurate differential diagnosis is possible. Unless this is done the veterinarian has permitted the owner or farmer to make the diagnosis, and treatment will be equally unreliable and erroneous. If a hormone is injected on this empirical basis neither the farmer, the animal, or the veterinarian is likely to be benefited. Following this essential examination, the cows or heifers that fail to show estrum may be divided into two classes, Class I cows with a functional corpus luteum, and Class II cows with no functional corpus luteum.

Class I cows are found on rectal examination to **have a normal functional corpus luteum present** in one of the ovaries. Since cystic corpora lutea have a normal function, these are included in this class. In this class are cows or heifers that are pregnant, those with a retained corpus luteum, and those that are ovulating and cycling regularly but are not recognized as exhibiting estrum either because it is "weak" or "silent" or because the owner has failed to observe it. It should be noted that normal cows have a functional corpus luteum in their ovary 85 per cent of the time.

1. **Anestrum due to pregnancy**—All veterinarians performing regular rectal examination on cows have had many cases in which the owner has requested treatment for a heifer or cow that fails to show estrum, only to find on examination that the animal is already pregnant. The history or the owner's records can often be very misleading. This finding has occurred even in well-managed herds where accurate records are kept. This serves to emphasize the importance of a careful rectal examination, including the palpation of both uterine horns to their apices, preceding treatment of any anestrous cow. It is extremely embarrassing to remove a corpus luteum or to inject an estrogen to bring a cow into estrum at the request of an owner, and have the cow abort a 40- to 120-day fetus a few days later. Usually when the veterinarian tells the owner the approximate age of the fetus the owner can recall when or how conception occurred. Only rarely is the owner at a complete loss to know how the conception occurred. If the cow's genital tract feels normal and healthy and there is a possibility of the cow having been serviced within the last 30 days, it is advisable to examine the cow two to six weeks later to determine if conception occurred before any treatment is given. Thus some cases with so-called anestrum may be pregnant and the corpus luteum, if palpable, may be the corpus luteum of pregnancy. One of the most common causes for prolonged anestrum is pregnancy. However, some pregnant cows may exhibit occasional signs of estrum.

2. **Anestrum due to a retained or persistent corpus luteum**—The retained or persistent corpus luteum is usually observed in association with some uterine pathology or distention such as pyometra, fetal maceration, mucometra, mummified fetus and other disease states. **Retained or persistent corpora lutea do not occur in the presence of a normal nonpregnant uterus,** Zemjamis et al. and others. There is no evidence that cystic corpora lutea tend to persist longer than noncystic corpora lutea. The corpus luteum of pregnancy is nearly completely involuted by 7 days postpartum and it never persists, Morrow et al.. The most commonly observed "retained" corpus luteum occurs following breeding and conception and then 10 to 90 days later the embryo or fetus dies, is macerated, and absorbed or expelled, and the cow previously thought to be or even diagnosed as pregnant comes back into estrum or is examined and found not pregnant and is treated. This condition is usually spoken of as early embryonic or fetal death and may be due to infectious, hormonal, genetic, physical or traumatic causes.

(a) **Retained corpus luteum associated with gross uterine pathology.** Retained, imbedded, or persistent corpora lutea are associated with preservice or postservice pyometra, fetal maceration, mummified fetus and rare cases of mucometra, Roberts and Fox. Ginther and others have rarely observed heifers that failed to show estrum and on examination had functional corpora lutea and a normal uterus. When these corpora lutea were removed the heifer came into estrum and another corpus luteum developed. (See Figure 117) This CL also persisted for months and the heifer remained anestrus. The histopathological findings in these heifers after slaughter revealed an absence of endometrial glands and in one heifer a lack of caruncles. In heifers or cows with a uterus unicormis if

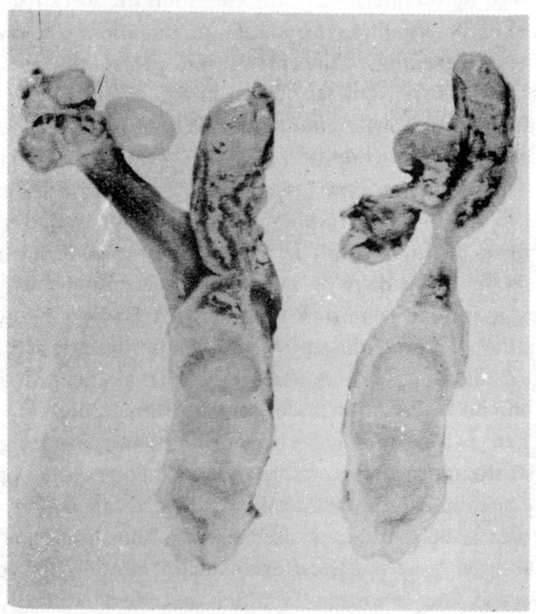

Figure 116. Anestrus Associated with Segmental Aplasia of the Bovine Uterus, Mucometra, Mucocervix and a Retained C. L.

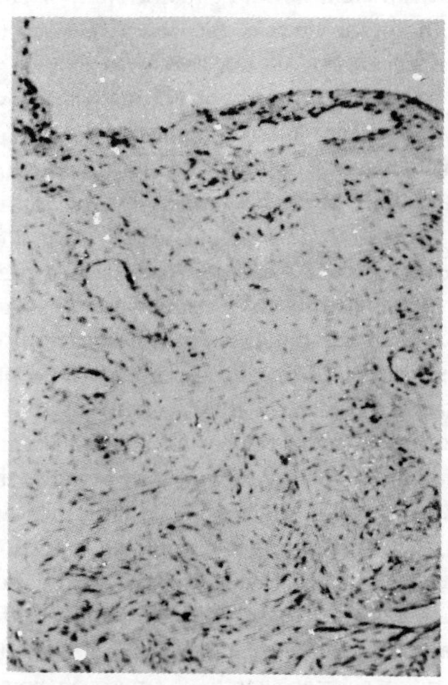

Figure 117. Congenital Absence of Endometrial Glands in a Heifer with Anestrus and a Retained C. L.

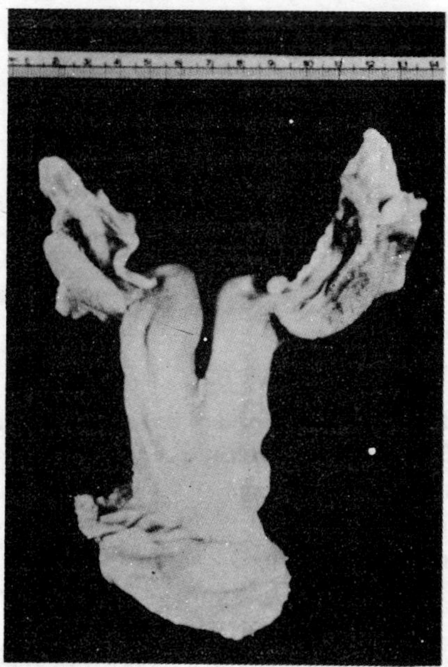

Figure 118. Bilateral Total Hypoplasia of the Ovaries in a 3-year-old Holstein.

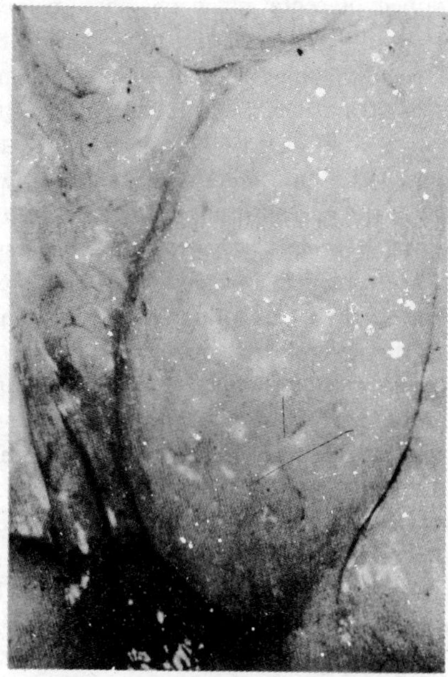

Figure 119. A "Smooth", Inactive Ovary Seen Bilaterally in Debilitated or Thin Heifers and Cows and Causing Anestrus.

the corpus luteum develops on the ovary corresponding to the missing horn, a long period of anestrum may result if there is not sufficient normal endometrium or endometrial glands in the cystic apex of the defective horn to exert a luteolytic effect on the CL on that side. (See Figure 116) This may result in a persistent corpus luteum without a pregnancy occurring. Cases of anestrum associated with uterine pathology and a functional corpus luteum, as well as pregnancy, are probably caused by the failure of the release of the luteolytic substance from the endometrium or endometrial glands, Ginther. As described previously a prolonged persistence of the C.L. can also be produced by hysterectomy. In these pathological cases rectal examination of the uterus will usually reveal the cause of the failure of estrum. In most of these conditions that exist for several months or more the corpus luteum becomes more centrally located in the ovary and may be more difficult to palpate. These conditions have been described already or will be described later under pathologic conditions affecting the uterus. Manual removal of the retained or imbedded corpora lutea in these cases is usually difficult and requires more pressure than do corpora lutea that have been present a shorter length of time. Without a pregnancy diagnosis these conditions are likely not to be diagnosed for 6 to 8 months after breeding because the cow is believed safely pregnant. In most pyometra cases secondary to retained placenta and a postpartum metritis the condition is usually characterized by a vaginal discharge of pus and a failure of estrum following calving. Most cases of mucometra are characterized by chronic follicular or luteal cysts and an absence of a normal corpus luteum and anestrum. When mucometra is associated with anatomic defects of the genital tract, the estrous cycle is regular and normal developing, mature, and regressing corpora lutea are present. Mucometra with a persistent corpus luteum might rarely follow early embryonic death. Occasionally these conditions may recover spontaneously but most would exist for months without estrum unless diagnosed and treated. In diagnosing and treating cases of retained corpora lutea an accurate breeding history is often helpful.

(b) **"Retained" corpus luteum associated with early embryonic or fetal death**—This condition is actually not a true"retained" corpus luteum but is a corpus luteum of a pregnancy that terminated early and was not recognized as an abortion. If because of infection or defective development, the ovum dies early, before the middle of the cycle, then estrum usually occurs at its usual interval; but when the embryo succumbs later, the onset of the next estrum is delayed. In many of these early embryonic deaths under 90 to 120 days, the fetus or embryo is so small it may not be seen when it is aborted, or it may remain and macerate in the uterus and furth. delay the onset of estrum until the trophoblast dies and is resorbed by the uterus. In this condition the so-called "retained or persistent" corpus luteum and anestrum always follow a breeding. Conception and pregnancy are not diagnosed or recognized. The animal usually comes in estrum spontaneously after the embryo or fetus is expelled or resorbed. The condition has been commonly observed in trichomoniasis, vibriosis and trauma to the early embryo by rough manipulation of the uterus. Defective sperm or ova may result in an imperfect zygote that succumbs 15 to 90 days or more after conception and produces a similar condition of a delayed estrum following breeding. This condition of early embryonic deaths has been studied by workers associated with artificial insemination and is described under repeat breeder cows.

There is a marked difference between the percentage of cows actually pregnant and the percentage of cows apparently pregnant on nonreturns at 28 to 35 days after service and at 60 to 90 days after service. This discrepancy is apparently largely due to early death of the embryo or fetus and the condition is often described clinically as "persistence or retention" of the corpus luteum.

Barrett, Casida and Lloyd reported the following comparison between reported nonreturns on 4,286 cows after first insemination and actual pregnancy diagnosis by rectal examination.

Number of Days After First Insemination	Reported Non-Return Percentages	Actual Percentage of Cows Pregnant	Percentage Difference
30 - 60	67.8	52.9	14.9
60 - 90	58.4	52.9	5.5
90 - 120	55.7	52.9	2.8

Thus Barrett and co-workers reported a decline of 23.2 per cent from cows apparently pregnant at 30 to 60 days and cows actually pregnant at 90 to 120 days after the first service. Holt reported that from data on over 29,000 cows bred artificially from 1944 to 1948 there was a decline of 19.2 percent from cows apparently pregnant, as based on nonreturns at 21 days after service, and cows that actually calved. The figures reported by these authors may be a little higher than present figures because antibiotics were not added to the semen and vibriosis was not being controlled before 1949. Foote (1954) reported that on data based on about 44,000 cows the difference between cows apparently pregnant according to 28 to 35 days nonreturns, and actual pregnancies at more than 180 days was about 16 per cent and the difference between cows apparently pregnant at 60 to 90 days, as based on nonreturns, and actual pregnancies at more than 180 days was 6 per cent. Thus the greatest loss of embryos is during the early stages of pregnancy.

Following service many cows fail to conceive; subsequently they come back in estrum after a period usually longer than the normal estrous cycle. In many instances this may be due to early embryonic death and this delayed onset of estrum or period of anestrum may be diagnosed as "persistence" or "retention" of the corpus luteum because the cows are not known to have been pregnant, have not had a history of estrum or abortion, and have a corpus luteum on one ovary. Stewart reported that about 18 per cent of cows bred naturally or artificially returned to service within 28 days while about 25 per cent returned to service after 28 days. On careful clinical examination at weekly intervals on 426 cows in 22 herds he found 332 that failed to come into estrum within 28 days of service; 234 of these were diagnosed pregnant and of these 12 aborted—3 abortions were observed and 9 were not observed. Olds and Seath reported that 48.6 per cent of return services to artificial insemination in Kentucky occurred after a prolonged interval of 25 days or more. In the experiment station herd of cattle, of 1347 cycles following service 44.8 per cent were prolonged; while of 2429 cycles not following service only 26.8 per cent were prolonged. Olds and Seath also reported that breeding cows too soon after calving was not a cause for delayed returns to estrum; on the contrary there was a tendency for the cows to come back into estrum in less than 18 days when bred at 5 weeks or less after parturition. They noted that 11.5 per cent of the cycle lengths were 27 to 33 days for repeat services as compared to 3.3 per cent of the cycles not following service. Thus early embryonic deaths after service are frequently the cause of so-called "retained" corpora lutea.

(3) **Anestrum due to subestrum, "weak" or "silent" estrum,** occurs fairly often, according to many veterinarians on the basis of clinical observations. The cow may not show estrum for 30 to 120 days or longer after calving even though closely observed by a competent herdsman; but on rectal examination during this period the cow shows evidence of having ovulated by the presence of a normal corpus luteum; or occasionally the cow may be in estrum or have just ovulated, as based on the typical changes in the genital tract or ovary and by the presence of estrual mucus or metestrual bleeding. Occasionally after parturition a "silent" estrum or subestrum may follow a normal estrum.

Subestrus, weak estrus, or silent estrus, occurs more frequently between calving and 60 days than it does 60 days or more after parturition. Kidder and co-workers reported on 286 ovulations of which 78 or 27.3 percent were silent. The incidence of silent estrus during the first 60 days after calving was 44.3 per cent of 140 ovulations, but only 11.0 per cent of 146 ovulations were silent during the period of 60 to 308 days. Stewart reported that of cows he examined that had not come into estrus within 28 days of breeding and were not pregnant, 31 or 28.2 percent exhibited silent estrus or subestrum. Casida and Wisnicky reported that ovulation in all cows occurred at an average of 25.4 days earlier than the first postpartum estrum and that 68 per cent of the cows showed at least one "quiet" ovulation or silent estrus before the first clinically apparent estrus. Older cows, over 5 years of age, tended to show longer intervals between parturition and estrum than did the younger cows. A high incidence of silent estrous cycles, when behavioral signs of standing estrus were not observed, were reported during the postpartum period in the cow by Morrow et al. and Marion and Gier. The former authors reported that 77 per cent of the cows at the first estrus after parturition, 55 per cent at the second estrus, and 35 per cent at the third estrus exhibited silent estrus. By 90 days after parturition over 93 per cent of the cows had shown visible signs of estrum. Morrow also reported that 74 per cent of 53 heifers as they reached puberty exhibited silent estrus at the time of their first ovulation, 43 per cent at the time of the second estrus or ovulation and 21 per cent at the time of the third estrus. Trimberger noted that about 10 per cent of the ovulations during the service period were "silent." These periods were observed in 16.5 per cent of the cows. From these reports it is evident that silent estrum is probably a common cause of anestrum and loss of time in rebreeding animals. This condition is clinically characterized by failure of estrum. These animals when turned out twice a day and closely observed for 20 to 30 minutes and teased by a bull will fail to show standing estrum even though they are ovulating. In some cases occasional, mild fleeting signs of estrum might be shown. Trimberger further reported that of 20 cows bred artificially during "silent" estrum 65 per cent conceived. The time of insemination was based on repeated rectal examinations of the ovary and palpation of the maturing follicle. Wiltbank and Cook reported more postpartum silent estrous periods occurred in nursed cows than in cows milked twice a day. The interval from calving to first estrus was 30 days longer in nursed cows than in milked cows; the interval from the formation of the first C.L. to the first estrus was 30 days in nursed cows and 17 days in milked cows. The interval from calving to the first C.L. was 53 days in nursed cows and 36 days in milked cows.

The physiologic basis for the failure of typical symptoms of estrum to accompany ovulation is not known but it may be due to a lack of sufficient secretion of estradiol by the mature and secondary follicles or due to a need for a higher threshold of estrogen in the central nervous system of certain individuals at certain times to produce the nervous symptoms characteristic of estrum and acceptance of the bull. Progesterone can potentiate the action of estrogens in bringing a cow into estrum, Short. Standing estrus may require a regressing C.L. still producing some progesterone to result in good signs of estrus. Lagerlof expressed the opinion that certain breeds of cattle have a herditary predisposition for "weak" estrums whereas other breeds exhibit marked estrous symptoms. In this country the author has observed that the Guernsey breed is more apt to have the predisposition toward "weak" heats than is the Holstein breed. Certain sire lines in a herd of Holstein cows exhibited a significantly higher incidence of silent heats or quiet ovulations than others indicating that a genetic variation affects this condition, Labhsetwar et al.. Cows in advanced age, arthritic cows, cows with footrot or other painful diseases may not show good signs of estrum. They may refuse to mount, or to stand to be mounted, and separate themselves from the rest of the herd.

(4) **Anestrum due to unobserved estrum** is, in most clinical examinations, difficult to differentiate from silent estrum, subestrum, or weak estrum. Estrous periods are usually about 18 hours in length but in some cattle, especially heifers, estrum may be only 8 to 12 hours long. In tropical countries and the southern states the length of the heat periods in the English and dairy breeds is shortened to 12 to 13 hours and in Zebu cattle estrum lasts only 5 to 8 hours. Gangwar et al. showed that when environmental temperatures were maintained at 75 to 95° F that the duration of the estrous period was 11 hours compared to 20 hours in heifers maintained at atmospheric temperatures of 62 to 65 ° F. Under the former stress condition the intensity of estrous signs were also reduced so that the incidence of anestrous was 30 per cent when signs of estrus were watched for twice a day; in the other groups without heat stress the incidence of anestrus was only 7 to 8 per cent (See Bovine Reproductive Physiology) These short periods could be missed especially if the animals were turned out of the stanchions or watched only once a day. This problem and "weak" estrums are difficulties which must be overcome in educating farmers to artificial insemination. If an owner or herdsman does not watch his cows carefully at least 20 to 30 minutes twice a day or more in a yard where the cows are free to move about, a number of heat periods will not be observed. Cows exhibiting weak estrum or subestrum are fertile but often because of poor timing of the insemination, conception rates are lower, Bane. The owner or herdsman should be acquainted with the estrous symptoms of each cow, so that if certain cows show mild or slight symptoms these can be watched for and recognized. In general the larger the herd or the greater the number of cows per man, the greater the incidence of anestrus. Due to laziness, neglect, or carelessness, some farmers cannot use artificial insemination service because they fail to observe and detect estrum in many of their cows. After trying artificial insemination these farmers usually resort to the earlier method of allowing a bull to run with the herd.

Anestrum due to unobserved estrum was reported in 39 per cent of 5848 reproductive cycles in dairy cows, 11 per cent were in preservice cycles and 28 per cent were in postservice cycles, Zemjanis. He termed these cases functional anestrus and indicated that 90 per cent of all anestrous cycles were in this category. Only 10 per cent of the anestrous cycles were due to pathological or organic causes. Twenty per cent of postservice anestrous cows were not pregnant even though the herdsman assumed them to be pregnant. The economic importance and monetary loss due to unobserved estrum was calculated to be 30 and 42 production days for preservice and postservice anestrus, respectively. If this loss was valued at $.50 or $1.00 per day, the annual loss for each dairy herd for the 13 dairies comprising the 2600 cattle in the study was $750 or $1500, respectively. With the advent of larger herds and fewer caretakers per herd the incidence of anestrus due to unobserved estrus continues to rise and has become the greatest single cause for infertility in large dairy herds being bred artificially.

The prognosis in cases of failure of estrum or anestrum in Class I cows found to have a normal functional corpus luteum by a rectal examination depends upon the cause. In anestrum due to a persistent corpus luteum caused by some uterine pathology the prognosis is good in fetal mummification and early embryonic deaths. While in pyometra the prognosis is fair to good and in late fetal maceration, mucometra or a congenital absence of uterine glands in the endometrium the prognosis is guarded to poor. The longer the condition, such as pyometra, has existed the poorer the prognosis for the future breeding life of the cow. Conception following early embryonic deaths may be delayed, especially in diseases such as vibriosis. In weak, silent or unobserved estrum the prognosis is usually fair to good as close observation reduces the incidence of anestrus due to this cause. Often after several silent heats an observable heat will occur.

Treatment of failure of estrum or anestrum in Class I

cows should be based on a careful differential diagnosis, often requiring careful recordings of repeated rectal examinations.

The treatment of retained or persistent corpora lutea due to uterine pathology such as pyometra, mucometra, mummified or macerated fetuses will be described later in this text. These conditions often respond to the injection of 40 to 100 mg. of stilbestrol or 4 to 10 mg. of estradiol, repeated in 2 to 4 days if necessary for several injections to cause an involution of the retained corpus luteum, the evacuation of the uterus, and the reestablishment of the estrous cycle. (See estrogenic therapy for anestrum). In a few cases manual removal of the corpus luteum, as described below, may be indicated but the dangers associated with this treatment, especially in pyometra, greatly limit this mode of therapy.

Treatment of persistence of the corpus luteum due to long-standing pyometra and fetal maceration with the presence of bones in the uterus may occasionally result in the restoration of the estrous cycle but conception usually fails to occur due to the chronic uterine damage caused by the infectious process. In some instances a laparohysterotomy may be necessary to remove the bones from the uterus. In the rare cases of heifers with a congenital lack of endometrial glands causing the persistence of the corpus luteum, no treatment is possible. It might be desirable to take a uterine endometrial biopsy or recover the uterus at slaughter so the diagnosis may be confirmed by histopathological methods.

Treatment of anestrum due to early embryonic death is usually not necessary since once the embryo or fetus and its membranes are expelled, or macerated and resorbed the corpus luteum of that pregnancy involutes and estrous cycles are reestablished. If the latter course is followed it may require two to six weeks following the death of the zygote before estrus occurs. Detection of anestrum due to early or late embryonic deaths, and postservice anestrum due to silent, weak or unobserved estrums requires an early accurate pregnancy diagnosis between 35 to 45 days of pregnancy and possibly a second examination in certain cows or herds with vibriosis, trichomoniasis or a high incidence of fetal mummification at 80 to 150 days or more days of gestation. Because anestrum of pregnancy is expected after service many owners fail to realize the importance of early pregnancy diagnosis to reduce the serious losses incurred due to postservice anestrus in cows failing to concieve or affected with early embryonic deaths, Zemjanis.

Treatment of failure of estrum or anestrum, in the common instances of weak or subestrum, silent estrum or unobserved estrum, often requires careful, frequent and accurately recorded examinations of the genital tract of affected cows, careful assessment of herd management practices, and diplomatic education and instructions for the herdsman and cattlemen. Cows or heifers with a preservice or postparturient anestrus should be examined at 50 to 60 days postpartum or at 15 to 18 months of age, respectively, if they have not exhibited estrus by that time. A variety of treatment regimens, some already suggested under the prior discussion of the etiology of anestrum, have been used. These include:

(a) **Improved management practices**—Owners and herdsmen often need to be trained in how to observe cows for estrum. The signs and degrees of external manifestations of proestrum, estrum and postestrum should be thoroughly understood. Cows to be observed for estrum should be grouped or turned out together and watched carefully for 20 to 60 or more minutes twice or more times per day especially during periods of activity such as before and after milking. Observing cows during the feeding period is not satisfactory. Careful records of these observations on properly identified cows should be made before, during and after the breeding period. The use of heat expectancy charts are very helpful if records of previous estrous periods are accurately recorded. The use of teaser animals will be discussed. Some owners are incapable of properly observing cows for estrum or unwilling to do so. In this instance breeding bull(s) should be run with the herd as an artificial insemination program is impossible to accomplish.

In large, artificially-inseminated dairy or beef herds in which the detection of cows in estrum is difficult, one or more vasectomized young bulls may be allowed to run with the herd. These bulls, if used properly, are very efficient in detecting cows in estrum. Young disease-free bulls can be vasectomized in the standing position under epidural and local anesthesia or they may be cast, tied, and rolled on their backs and vasectomized under local anesthesia. Using careful clean surgical technique the operator makes separate incisions through the skin and the tunics investing each spermatic cord. The hard cord-like vas deferens is separated from the plexus of coiled veins and arteries. Two ligatures are placed on each vas about 2 inches apart and 1 inch of the vas is removed. The skin incisions are closed and antibiotics are administered for 4 to 5 days. Semen should be collected once a week for 3 weeks. By this time practically no spermatozoa are in the ejaculate and those that are present are dead.

Several cases have been reported where apparently properly vasectomized bulls regained their ability to fertilize cows. Schmidt reported in humans that sperm granulomas following vasectomy were common and 5 of 432 vasectomy cases recanalized. He stated that the cut ends of the vas deferens should be fulgurized by electrocautery and the sheath of the vas deferens should be ligated or closed over the cut end of the distal portion of the vas to prevent spontaneous recanalization. It might also be advisable for the operator to place the removed sections of the vasa deferentia into a 10 per cent formalin solution and send them to a laboratory for histological confirmation of the removed tissue to prevent possible errors and lawsuits.

Other methods of preparing teaser bulls have been described. Oehme and Wiltbank recommended epididymectomy by incising the bottom of the scrotum under each testis, separating the tail of the epididymis from the testis, ligating the body of the epididymis and the vas deferens with nylon and removing the tail of the epididymis. This technique is probably better than the injection of a sclerosing agent into the tail of the epididymis, Bierschwal and Ebert, or the crushing of the tail of the epididymis with a Burdizzo emasculatome. These above methods do not prevent normal intromission and the possible spread of venereal diseases such as vibriosis and trichomoniasis. However teaser bulls prepared by the above methods retain a stronger sexual desire and drive than teaser bulls prepared by various operations on the penis and sheath that prevent normal intromission, ejaculation and transmittal of venereal diseases.

Operations on the penis and sheath to prevent conception include: cutting the penis midway between the anus and scrotum and suturing it to the skin, Straub and Kendrick; placing three or four stainless steel or nylon sutures into the dorsal part of the penis cranial to the scrotum and suturing the penis to the abdominal wall, Forgason, Smith; making a small ventral incision in the skin and prepuce two to three inches behind the preputial orifice, suturing the skin and preputial membrane and inserting a 3/8 inch plastic urine drain for five days, followed by the dissecting apart of the skin and preputial membrane at the preputial orifice and suturing the inside membrane and outside skin to make a blind pouch to contain the penis, Smith; and possibly the incising of the skin around the preputial orifice and suturing the orifice so it is directed laterally instead of cranially, so the penis on erection is also protruded laterally. These operations should be performed under good anesthesia and in an aseptic manner for best results. A male pseudohermaphrodite, a nymphomaniac cow or a spayed heifer treated repeatedly with stilbestrol may also be used as a teaser animal if it has sufficient sex drive.

Bulls selected as "teaser" animals should have a strong, vigorous sex drive. If possible it may be desirable to turn these bulls with the herd only for short periods in the morning and evening and then to alternate bulls to maintain their sex drive. A New Zealand company* is marketing a marking device for bulls consisting of a small square stainless steel unit containing an exposed freely rotating steel ball that is fastened securely under the jaw by a special halter. The marker material comes in a variety of colors and is placed in the steel unit where it will store indefinitely. When the bull mounts a cow the marking material is rubbed in streaks down her back as he dismounts. These marks will last for 2 weeks but can be washed off with a detergent. One filling of the steeel container is sufficient to mark 75 to 80 cows. Some ranchers will have a bull in a pen near water, in a corral near salt or feed, or run their cows across a fence from yearling bulls. In these instances cows in estrum will gravitate toward the male animals and be easier to pick up.

Some cattleman have used a cheap, plastic heat detecting device** that is glued to the top of the sacrum. When a cow in estrum is mounted by another cow or teaser bull the normally white plastic device turns red due to release of a dye due to pressure on the device by the brisket of the mounting animal, Boyd and Hignett. These detectors may be helpful to the rancher who is breeding his beef cows by artificial insemination for the first time. Skilled, patient, observant cattlemen by watching range cows in a relatively small pasture for 1 to 2 hours every early morning and evening when it is daylight but cool will more readily detect estrus at these two periods of greater herd activity. In hot weather or climates estrous activity is minimal during the hot midday when most cattle are resting. Taking a cow or two in estrum and slowly working them through a herd may detect 5 or 6 more cows that are in estrum. Proper training of the herdsman, careful 2 or even 3 or 4 times a day observation of the herd will detect more cows showing standing estrum or weak estrus. In stanchion barns it is desirable to turn cows out of the barn twice a day even in the winter months and observe the cows carefully. In a stanchion barn the tails and buttocks of the cows should be carefully observed daily to detect bleeding or a clear mucus discharge. In a dark barn a flashlight might prove helpful in this examination, Phillips. As an aid in stimulating closer observation of cows for estrum some owners offer incentive payments to hired men or herdsmen detecting cows in estrus and concieving to a service at that estrus. The economic importance of a conscientous, observant herdsman or owner cannot be

*Chin-Ball Mating Device, Frank Paviour Ltd., Mahana Rd. TeRapa, Hamilton, New Zealand.

**Heat-mount Detectors by Kamar Inc., Earl D. Smith, Box 26, Steamboat Springs, Colo., 80447.

overestimated in maintaining a good conception rate and a short interval between calvings in a herd. Good breeding records, the careful maintenance of a heat expectancy chart for each cow, and frequent examination of "problem" cows by a veterinarian who can predict the approximate time estrum should occur in many "anestrous" cycling cows, can be helpful in controlling this common infertility problem.

(b) Frequent rectal, and if necessary vaginal, examinations of the genital tract by a veterinarian will determine the proper time to inseminate cycling cows with weak, silent or unobserved estrum. Moberg, and Zemjanis et al. have described the technique for **predicting the time of estrum** which is based on the physiologic and anatomical changes occurring in the genital tract of the cow during the estrous cycle.

During proestrus, days 17 to 20 of the cycle, the second wave of follicular growth is occurring and culminates in the mature Graafian follicle, Rajakoski. The corpus luteum is regressing in size, protrudes less above the surface of the ovary and becomes more firm in consistency. The uterus is developing increased tone, irritability and edema. On vaginal examination the last two days of proestrus the vaginal and cervical mucosa are becoming more pink, congested and edematous. The cervix becomes more relaxed and first a cloudy and then a clear stringy mucus comes from it and collects in the anterior vagina. The cow will be in estrus within 1 to 4 days.

During estrus, day 0 or 1 of the cycle, the cow is receptive to the bull and the changes described as occurring during proestrus are more prominent. The vulva is usually edematous and relaxed. This is the most easily diagnosed stage of the cycle. The cow should be bred. If the cow exhibitis silent estrum rebreeding the following day may be indicated if ovulation has not occurred.

During early postestrum or metestrum, day 1 or 2, the follicle may be soft and fluctuating and easily ruptures on pressure. This should be avoided. In most cases ovulation has occurred and feels like a crater-like depression 1 to 1-1/2 cm. in diameter in one of the ovaries. The uterus is less tonic but more edematous and thick-walled. The corpus luteum of the previous cycle is difficult to detect. Metrorrhagia may be observed by the presence of bloody mucus at the vulvar lips, on the tail or buttocks or by vaginal examination. This discharge may also be observed through day 3 of the cycle. A few atretic follicles may be present

During late postestrus or metestrus, days 3 to 6 of the cycle the soft, small, developing corpus luteum may be palpated. The uterus decreasingly lacks tone and loses its edema.

During diestrus, days 7 through 16, the longest stage of the cycle the corpus luteum is mature, large and liver-like in consistency. The uterus is quiescent but not atonic. During this period the first wave of follicular growth of the cycle occurs and results in one or more fairly large follicles at 10 to 12 days that become atretic and regress by the end of this period. During this period the vaginal and cervical mucosa is rather pale and dry. The cow will return to estrus in one to two weeks.

With practice any veterinarian can develop his skills to predict the occurrence of estrus with a high degree of accuracy. Zemjanis et al. have shown the success of this method to be equal to that of removal of the corpus luteum; 69 per cent of the cows showed estrus within 23 days. The rate of conception on the first estrus was 10 per cent better than removal of the corpus luteum, 55.7 per cent vs 45.7 per cent, respectively. Because of the dangers associated with enucleation of the corpus luteum, estrous predication is the method of choice for handling anestrum due to weak, silent, or unobserved estrus in the cycling cows.

(c) **The removal of the corpus luteum** by manual pressure through the rectal wall is frequently employed in the treatment of anestrus in cattle when a functional corpus luteum is present. This method consists of grasping the ovary in a fold of the rectal wall between the fingers and first knuckle of the thumb and pressing over the proximal end of the corpus luteum and enucleating it from the ovary. Care should be used so as not to rupture the rectal wall. Arthur indicated that the best time to remove the corpus luteum was during the middle of diestrum. Earlier removal of the soft C.L. may result in incomplete removal, and in proestrum the difficulty of removal increases. Some advocate squeezing through the tougher vaginal wall but this is usually not necessary since most corpora lutea are not centrally located and covered by a heavy capsule as occurs in retained corpora lutea.

Although removal of the corpus luteum is a common form of therapy it should seldom be used and then probably as a last resort because of the possible dangers from its practice. Manual removal of the corpus luteum in cows with pyometra or other uterine infections is dangerous due to adhesions and ovaritis that may follow. In a removal of the corpus luteum the cow should not be pregnant or abortion will usually occur. After the corpus luteum is removed it should be dropped into the abdominal cavity and not in the ovarian bursa, where it may cause extensive adhesions. Adhesions of the ovary and, especially the fimbriated portion of the oviduct on the medial free border of the ovarian ventricle frequently follow rough manipulations even though bleeding may not be severe. McEntee, Moberg, and Dawson stated that ovarian adhesions due to rough manipulation of the ovary were a common cause of permanent sterility. After removal of the corpus luteum excessive bleeding may take place from the ovary and cause a large hematoma around the ovary, permanent adhesions, and sterility. Fatal bleeding from the site of an enucleated corpus luteum has occasionally been reported. Teige reported the incidence of fatal hemorrhage as 1:1000 to 1:9000 removals of the corpus luteum. The author has not been so fortunate as in his experience fatalities occurred at a rate of 1 to 300 to 500 enucleations. The method of expression of the corpus luteum had no influence on the fatalities. Moberg cited Heckhausen (1950) who reported that removal of the corpus luteum can result in a loss of as much as 7 liters of blood into the peritoneal cavity. The removal of an imbedded corpus luteum resulted in a loss of one liter of blood. In 22 to 25 cases in which the corpus luteum of estrum was removed, bleeding of one to three liters of blood was reported. In some cases the cow will temporarily develop a rapid pulse, tympany, and anorexia after removal of a corpus luteum. Frank reported that the manual ovarian treatment for anestrum was discontinued in his experiments because the per cent of conceptions showed no improvement over the controls, and furthermore removal of the corpus luteum produced permanent damage in a number of cases. Hofstad reported that hemorrhage and adhesions followed removal of the corpus luteum and he questioned the advisability of the practice. Umbaugh reported experiments on superovulation in which normal corpora lutea were removed. Large amounts of blood were lost from the ovary, causing adhesions that seriously affected the fertility of the cow. Stalfors and others recommended the manual compression of the ovary for at least 5 minutes after removal of a corpus luteum, as a means of controlling bleeding. It is doubtful that epinephrine or other drugs administered parenterally will effectively prevent bleeding and the former drug may be contraindicated. Many workers have reported that removal of the corpus luteum seldom results in any permanent trauma or adhesions; their observations were, however, only clinical. Because of these observations the author does not recommend removal of the corpus luteum in cows except in selected cases or only as a last resort. Properly used estrogenic therapy will result in the involution of the corpus luteum without the dangers present in manual removal. Because manual removal of the corpus luteum is possible only in the cow of our domestic animals, this is not a sufficient reason to employ this mode of

Table 19. Summary of Reports of the Manual Removal of the Corpus Luteum in Nonpregnant Cows

Author	Number of cows	Cows observed in estrum		Days estrum occurred	Conceptions
		No.	Per cent		
Wright	51	36	70	1 to 5	18, or 50% of those in estrum
Hofstad	332	203	61.1	2 to 9	59, or 29.1% of those in estrum
Miller and Graves	64				32, or 50%
Stalfors	105			3 to 10	38, or 35.6% of the total treated
Clark	62	46	70	2 to 9	39, or 85% of those in estrum
Hancock	70	35	50	2 to 7	10, or 28.5% of those in estrum
Bonelli	300			2 to 7	
Lindley	54	27	50		13, or 24.1%
Gibbons	155	98	64.9	1 to 15	51, or 52.1%, on first service
Herrick	36	29	80.6	2 to 7	
Dowling	41	39	95.1	2 to 5	60% (15 of 20 cows bred)
Teige and Jakobsen	2746		62.5	1 to 7	49.7 to 58.7%

treatment in the bovine species. Hurst reported that following 567 parturitions in dairy cattle that 15 per cent did not show estrus by 70 days and 5 per cent by 90 days. In cows in which the CL was removed 24 per cent were in heat in four days, 57 per cent in 15 days and 76 per cent in 30 days. The respective figures for the untreated or control cows was 18, 54 and 85 per cent. In cows of lesser value or in cows in which the production of milk is more important than the value of their offspring, the amount of damage or risk may not be great enough to prohibit the enucleation procedure.

The following reports from the literature summarize the results of manual removal of the corpus luteum. (See Table 19). From this table it appears that removal of the corpus luteum usually results in observable estrum in about 50 to 80 per cent of the cases within 2 to 7 days, with conceptions in 25 to 80 per cent of those cows bred on the induced first estrum. In the author's experience removal of the corpus luteum from normal cows will result in 50 to 60 per cent conceptions at the next service a few days later. Most cows show estrum the third or fourth day after removal of the corpus luteum. A number of workers reported that the induced estrum frequently was "silent", or unobserved, and the animal should be watched closely for signs of estrum. Possibly this condition of "silent" estrum was the reason for the diagnosis and removal of the "retained" corpus luteum. If estrum is not observed the cow may be bred three to four days after the manual removal of the corpus luteum if conception is desired. If the cow shows estrum on the fifth day she should be rebred. Nearly 50 per cent of normal cows thus treated will conceive. If the cow has a normal genital tract and is in anestrum due to silent, or unobserved heat, removal of the corpus luteum should result in a higher rate of conception on the first estrum than if the retained corpus luteum was due to an embryonic death caused by vibriosis or some other infection in which a mild endometritis may be present. These same factors would also influence the conception rate obtained after the use of hormones. Repeated removal of corpora lutea at 10 day intervals in cattle often resulted in the formation of cystic corpora lutea and luteinized and follicular cysts, Purse and Wickersham. These findings may be due to the progressive depletion of pituitary LH reserves by the frequent induced estrous periods.

(d) **Estrogenic therapy for anestrus**—Estrogens have been shown by Wiltbank, Brunner et al. and others to cause regression of the corpus luteum. The effect of estrogens on the corpus luteum is not so marked in hysterectomized heifers as in intact heifers so there is probably an interreaction with the luteolytic mechanism in the endometrium or endometrial glands. Estrogens probably induce regression by decreasing the level of circulating LH also, Brunner et al.. Wiltbank reported that 5 mg. of estradiol valerate given as a single dose intramuscularly on the third or fourth or eighth or ninth day of the estrous cycle caused luteal regression in 17 of 20 heifers with 15 showing estrum before day 17 of the cycle. Seven of 10 heifers injected on days 15 or 16 of the cycle developed large cystic ovaries and many developed signs of nymphomania. Other forms of estrogen caused a similar regression of the corpus luteum. The author has confirmed the effects of 5 to 10 mg. of estradiol valerate in inducing regression of the corpus luteum. He has also produced luteal regression with 40 to 100 mg. of diethylstilbestrol but this tends to require a second or third injection at 48 hour intervals. One or possibly two injections of 3 to 10 mg. of estradiol at three day intervals or estrone, 5 to 15 mg., in a similar manner also will induce luteal regression either during metestrus or diestrus or in cases of retained corpora lutea associated with pyometra, mummified fetus or mucometra. In pyometra high and prolonged doses of estrogens such as 100 mg. of repositol stilbestrol may result in abnormal motility or peristalsis of the oviduct resulting in the introduction of infectious organisms from the uterus to the area of the ovarian bursa or fimbria of the oviduct causing ovaritis and adhesions even in cases where no ovarian manipulations were made. Cystic ovaries may occasionally follow estrogenic therapy. These occur most commonly when estrogens are given late in late diestrum or proestrum. They are rare in cases of retained corpora lutea. Large doses of greater than 4 mg. of estradiol and 40 mg. of stilbestrol are more apt to result in cystic ovaries than are smaller doses of estrogens.

Because the preliminary evidence indicates that the glucocorticoids used to produce abortion cause prompt luteal regression in cows with a fairly high endogenous estrogen level (See abortion), the combination of estrogens and glucocorticoids may prove of value for the treatment of retained corpora lutea in cases of mummified fetuses and mucometra. Because pyometra is a chronic infectious process the use of glucocorticoids might be questionable in this condition. Brunner et al. indicated that ACTH injections caused elevated glucocorticoid levels and reduced corpus luteum weights possibly by decreasing the circulating levels of gonadotropic hormones. The use of estrogens and glucocorticoids should be further investigated to evaluate their effect on the corpus luteum of the estrous cycle and the induction of estrus at a certain regular period following their injection.

Most earlier studies on the use of estrogens for the treatment of anestrus were uncontrolled and empirical. Factors that were not considered in most studies were the cause for the failure of estrum or the type of anestrus; the high rate of spontaneous recoveries and conceptions in cows with normal estrous cycles and genital tracts but having silent, weak or unobserved estrous periods; the time following treatment that estrus and conception occurred and whether normal ovulation occurred at that estrus or whether the signs of estrus that immediately followed the injection were due to the estrogenic hormone. Even spayed cows will exhibit estrus after an injection of an estrogen. Estrogenic hormones do not produce ovulation. The use of low doses of estrogens or estrogens and progesterone a day or two before an expected estrus to improve the external signs of estrus has not proven of value and may lower the conception rate. Although estrogens have been widely used in an empirical and haphazard manner for the treatment of anestrus, recent reports indicate that this type of therapy is of no, or questionable, value and may actually reduce the conception rate compared to heat prediction or removal of the corpus luteum, Belling and El Shafie and Zemjanis et al..

(e) Estrous synchronization by using oral progestagens, such as M.A.P. and M.G.A. or other similar agents for 18 to 20 days to suppress the estrous cycle, may aid in detection of estrum in a similar manner as removal of the corpus luteum. With both M.A.P. and M.G.A. treatment a normal estrous period usually follows withdrawal of the drug in 3 to 5 days or 3 to 8 days, respectively. This knowledge is of value to the farmer or rancher. With estrous synchronization good management is still necessary to detect estrus for proper timing of artificial insemination. Conception rates immediately following estrous synchronization are usually lower than normal.

(f) Other miscellaneous treatments have been used for anestrus when a corpus luteum is on the ovary. Zemjanis et al. and others have used 800 to 1000 I.U. of P.M.S. or F.S.H. to induce estrus by causing follicular growth and the production of endogenous estrogens. The injection of thyroid hormones or feeding iodinated casein has also been used empirically for the treatment of anestrus. Uterine and ovarian massage has been used by some as an empirical treatment for anestrus and infertility. If it is done gently and the CL is not removed probably no harmful effects result and a temporary hyperemia of the organs is produced. There is no confirmed evidence of the value of this treatment. Hays and Carlevaro reported a 43 per cent occurrence of estrus within 7 days following electrical stimulation with the rectal probe of a bull ejaculator in cows that had been anestrous for 50 or more days postpartum. Only 13 per cent of the untreated control cows showed estrus during this same period. Oxenreider reported later that frequent electrical stimulation was ineffective in causing luteal regression in heifers. It is unfortunate the previous authors did not note whether corpora lutea were present or not. Hays and Carlevaro cited Hancock and Laing, who reported the possible release of gonadotropic hormones following uterine irrigation in cows and mares. Recent work indicates that intrauterine treatments at certain stages of the cycle can effect the uterine luteolytic mechanism and the release of gonadotropins, Yamauchi et al., Ginther and others. (See Physiology in the cow)

Since so-called anestrous cows with normal uteri and corpora lutea on the ovaries are probably cycling regularly most or all treated or untreated cows will show an observable normal estrus within 30 days. This probably accounts for the many reports of successful treatments for anestrum in cattle. Probably many or most treatments for anestrum are ineffective and better means of detecting estrum are needed in most herds.

In summarizing the treatment of anestrum in cattle the author feels as stated by Asdell: "It has been a depressing task to bring the literature on the hormonic treatment of sterility together. Very little work is adequately controlled and much of it is anecdotal in character." All work reviewed by the author has failed to distinguish between the various causes of anestrum and has failed to correlate the type of treatment with the various causes. It is recognized that this might be difficult, but nevertheless it should be attempted. At present it appears that most types of anestrum except possibly underfeeding and gross pathology of the uterus, cervix, or ovaries is self-limiting and that recovery is usually spontaneous. This would seriously interfere with the establishment of a valid experiment unless a large number of controls were used. For this reason the author firmly believes that hormone treatment or removal of the corpus luteum for correction of most cases of anestrum is of secondary importance to an accurate diagnosis. During the past 15 to 20 years the author has used little hormone treatment to relieve anestrum unless it was due to uterine pathology or cystic ovaries. More reliance should be placed on an accurate diagnosis than on empirical hormone injections or removal of the corpus luteum.

Class II anestrous cows have small or inactive ovaries with no functional corpus luteum palpable per rectum. Cows in Class II, together with the pregnant cows and cows with retained corpora lutea associated with uterine pathology in Class I, are non-cycling cows. According to Zemjanis et al. these non-cycling dairy cows comprise about 10 per cent of all anestrous cows. In beef cattle herds on range this percentage may be larger due to nutritive deficiencies especially in postpartum heifers. In Class

II are cows that are in estrum, approaching, or recently in estrum with a silent or unobserved heat; cows in anestrum due to a failure of the estrous cycle caused by nutritive deficiencies or debility from other causes; cows with cystic ovaries; and occasionally cows with such miscellaneous conditions as freemartinism, hypoplasia of the ovaries, ovarian tumors, and pituitary disturbances.

(1) **Apparent anestrum, or failure of estrum** in cycling cows as mentioned in cows under Class I, due to silent or subestrum, or due to unobserved estrum, may during the period of one to two days before, during, and one to three days after estrum, have only a small corpus luteum that might lead on a single examination to a diagnosis of anestrum due to failure of ovarian activity or nonfunctional ovaries. Careful examination usually reveals the uterus to be tonic and erect, a condition not seen in true anestrum or failure of the estrous cycle. If the ovaries are examined before ovulation the mature follicle and the regressing firm C.L. may be palpated, or if soon after ovulation the site of ovulation or a slight crepitation characteristic of an early developing corpus luteum may be felt. The corpus luteum of the previous estrous cycle is usually palpable but small. A vaginal examination with a speculum and light is essential since the presence of hyperemia, relaxation of the cervix, and typical vaginal mucus of estrum is indicative of estrum; and the presence of blood in the vaginal mucus indicates that ovulation occurred one to two days previously. It is not unusual in examining a number of normal, well-nourished cows that have a history of failure of estrum to find one or more of these cows approaching, in, or just over estrum. This fact may be missed by a hasty examination especially if a speculum examination of the vagina is omitted. Cows in proestrum, estrum or very early metestrum should be bred. Cows in metestrum after ovulation has occurred should be noted on the heat expectancy chart and watched closely 18 to 20 days later.

(2) **Anestrum will develop secondary to debility or marked loss in weight.** Any severe and chronic adverse conditions that affect the animal's body will produce an effect on the reproductive system, usually by causing a cessation of the estrous cycle and anestrum if the animal is not pregnant; or in more severely debilitating conditions, causing abortion if the animal is pregnant. These adverse debilitating conditions that suppress or stop the estrous cycle and produce anestrum are:

(a) **A low plane of nutrition** due to a lack of sufficient intake of carbohydrates, proteins, and other elements necessary to maintain body weight may cause a failure or delay in the onset of puberty or the onset of the estrous cycle following parturition (See Nutritional Causes for Infertility). This condition is seen most often in heifers maintained on poor hay or on poor pasture or range. Hammond reported that the incidence of "winter sterility" in England characterized by anestrum varied from 5 per cent around Cambridge to 50 per cent in the Yorkshire Mountains, where cattle were kept in cold, dark barns and fed poor hay. Sorenson and co-workers, and Bellows showed that heifers fed on a high level of nutritive intake reached puberty and developed estrum at an average of 9 to 10 months of age, whereas heifers fed on a lower nutritive level did not reach puberty and estrum until 16 months or more of age. These latter heifers were maintained at optimum environmental conditions except for the level of feeding. The various nutritive factors that adversely affect the estrous cycle may also include severe nutritive deficiencies of phosphorus, cobalt, iron, copper and possibly other trace elements. When these substances are lacking, anorexia and debility, with impairment or suppression of the secretion of the gonadotrophic hormones by the pituitary, may develop. It is well known in humans that starvation causes amenorrhea and a cessation of the estrous cycle before other body disturbances appear. In rats a loss of 15 per cent in body weight may stop the estrous cycle. This was illustrated in cows during an experiment on the effects of a sodium chloride deficiency, Aines. When this common element was withheld for long periods the effects became very evident after calving. Lactation caused rapid loss of weight because the appetite was poor. Milk secretion declined and ceased. The cows became cachetic and failed to show estrum. On examination the ovaries were found to be small and inactive; an occasional small 3/8 to 1/2 inch follicle was palpated. Estrum did not return until salt was supplied and the appetite, nutritive state, and body condition improved.

Most practicing veterinarians have observed anestrum on farms where cows and heifers are thin and poorly fed. In a survey of 1533 cows in 28 herds in New York State, carotene, vitamin A, calcium, phosphorus, and iodine deficiencies did not contribute to sterility, Hansel. Inasmuch as reduced hemoglobin, below 9 gm. per 100 ml. of blood, was noted in all anestrous cows, cobalt and copper deficiencies may have been a factor. In heifers or cows that are in a fair state of nutrition but are exhibiting anestrum, the condition may be due to a simple phosphorus deficiency, or a phosphorus and a protein or carbohydrate deficiencies. Morrow described a herd of dairy cattle deficient in phosphorus intake but anestrus was not observed in the deficient cattle in this herd. Blood levels below 3 mgm. per cent usually indicate a phosphorus deficiency, Wagner and McEntee, and Morrow. Failure of estrum with non-functional or "smooth" ovaries is observed most often during the winter months in the northern part of the country in cows on poor and inadequate amounts of feed.

In the southern and western part of the country where the animals are on pasture most of the year the condition is observed most commonly during the dry, late summer pasture season when available feed is greatly reduced. It may also be observed under drouth conditions, Carroll and Hoerlein. Bellows, Wiltbank et al. and ARS, USDA have reported a delay in the occurrence of estrus after parturition especially in range beef heifers on a low level of TDN or energy intake prior to or after parturition. This was also associated with a lower conception rate after estrus occurred. Heavy lactation will often result in the rapid loss in body weight and if this is extreme, cessation of the estrous cycle will occur. If the loss in weight after calving is more gradual, an estrum or two may occur before anestrum develops. In lactating cows showing anestrum of nutritional origin, milk production is usually lowered. Anestrum due to low nutritive intake is usually characterized by the fact that a large number of cows or heifers on a farm show the same symptoms. Examination of 4 or 5 animals that fail to show estrum will usually reveal small, atrophied, inactive ovaries. (See Figure 117) No corpora lutea are palpable. The uterus is usually small, lacks tone, and is doughy and flaccid. On vaginal examination the mucosa of the vagina and cervix is pale and dry. Repeated examinations reveal no change in the reproductive organs. The affected animals are usually thin and have rough hair coats and dry feces.

(b) **Chronic or debilitating diseases,** by causing a decreased appetite, may result in failure of estrum due to a marked reduction of body weight. Examples of these diseases or conditions include severe mange, lymphocytoma, severe chronic acetonemia, displacement of the abomasum, chronic traumatic gastritis, chronic severe pneumonia, Johnes disease, actinomycosis that interferes with eating, either severe external or internal parasitisms, severe suppurative processes such as suppurative arthritis secondary to foot rot with a secondary severe debility, advanced tuberculosis, hyperkeratosis and other similar diseases and conditions. If the cow recovers from the disease or its effects are alleviated and appetite and body condition returns, the estrous cycles will again be reestablished.

(c) **Senility** or old age with loss of teeth and inability to masticate properly, especially in older lactating cows, is a cause of loss of weight, debility, and anestrum or failure of estrum.

(d) **Seasonal influences**—especially environmental temperatures, sunlight, and exercise apparently play a lesser role than does nutrition on the estrous cycle and estrum. Failure of estrum or anestrum in cattle has often been observed in cows and heifers closely confined in dark stables and allowed little or no exercise. A lack of nutritive intake is also usually a factor. Mercier and Salisbury have shown that in the northern part of the country where cows are confined during the winter months, even though the cow is polyestrous the best conception rates occur in May, June, and July whereas the poorest breeding months are December, January, and February. This is undoubtedly a reflection of the amount of sunlight and its effect on the pituitary as well as the feeding levels, amount of exercise, type of feed available and closeness of observation for estrum. During the cold winter months additional nutritive energy is required by animals to maintain body temperature and in heifers an added requirement is necessary for growth. Excessive heat over long periods of time may cause anestrum. Five of 6 two-year-old heifers developed anestrus and cessation of the estrous cycle after being kept for 5 weeks at a temperature of 90° F and 60 per cent humidity, Bond et al..

(3) **Cystic ovaries,** as reported previously, are characterized externally by failure of estrum or anestrum in about 25 to 75 per cent of the cases. On rectal examination one or more follicular or luteal cysts are found. No corpora lutea are present. The uterus is usually doughy and flaccid and may be atrophied. The mucus in the vagina is tenacious, and varying degrees of edema of the vulva and relaxation of the pelvic ligaments occur. Treatment consists of injecting luteinizing hormone. Some cases of mucometra are associated with cystic ovaries and long-standing anestrum. This condition might be confused with pregnancy unless a careful examination is made. Another rare condition the author considers as also associated with prolonged cystic ovaries and anestrum is characterized by a greatly enlarged and dilated cervix filled with copious amounts of tenacious, tough mucus similar to the mucus of a cervical seal of pregnancy. This latter condition may also have mucometra along with the cervical lesion. Cystic corpora lutea are not characterized by anestrum.

(4) **Miscellaneous conditions** characterized by anestrum or failure of normal estrum with no corpus luteum are generally uncommon and sporadic in the United States. These may include occasional cases of:

(a) Non-functional or "smooth" ovaries may occasionally be observed in **apparently** well-nourished older cattle in good condition, the first 2 to 4 months after parturition when the level of lactation is high. Morrow et al. reported that cows stressed at the period of calving by the occurrence of a disease process such as retained placenta, dystocia, milk fever, ketosis, mastitis, twins and other debilitating diseases had a delayed onset of the estrous cycle of an average of 34 days compared to 15 days for cows with a normal parturition. Trimberger reported that 7.5 per cent of the cows and 3.99 per cent of the estrous cycles studied were characterized by a varying period of anestrum with "smooth" or non-functioning ovaries. The uterus is flaccid and lacks tone, Spontaneous recovery usually occurs. This condition is probably due to a reduced level of nutrition associated with a definite loss in weight. When production and energy intake are equalized, the estrous cycle will occur.

(b) Freemartinism may be a rare cause of anestrum in heifers purchased from unknown sources or raised by farmers who did not know that 90 per cent of heifers born cotwin to bulls are sterile. These freemartins are usually steer-like in appearance. They have a small vulva with a coarse tuft of hair and a prominent clitoris. On rectal examination the uterus and ovaries usually cannot be palpated except as thin remnants of the normal structures. Vaginal examination will reveal an undeveloped vagina cranial to the vestibule.

(c) Congenital bilateral hypoplasia of the ovaries is rarely observed in the United States. Fincher described several related cattle with a complete absence of gonads. In rare instances, heifers may have a fairly normal but small infantile genital tract but very hypoplastic, small, flattened, slightly corrugated ovaries the size of a bean or smaller 1/4 to 1 inch long and 1/8 inch in diameter. (See Figure 118) These hypoplastic ovaries may be observed either unilaterally or bilaterally. Heifers unilaterally affected or those with partial hypoplasia of an ovary usually have normal estrous cycles. Small, inactive, immature ovaries 1/4 to 1/2 inches in diameter; especially in heifers, may erroneously be diagnosed as hypoplastic ovaries. Heifers should be in good physical condition with no obvious cause for the small inactive ovaries and be old enough to have estrous cycles before a diagnosis of congenital hypoplasia should be considered. In a few of these congenital or hereditary cases of hypoplasia, the uterus and oviducts on one or both sides may be involved in the hypoplasia. In the United States congenital, or possible hereditary, bilateral total hypoplasia of the ovaries is rare and sporadic. In Sweden, Eriksson and Lagerlof have reported on the widespread hereditary ovarian and testicular hypoplasia present in the Swedish Highland breed of cattle. Inbreeding has been associated with the development of this defect as with other hereditary anomalies of development.

(d) Tumors of the ovary are rarely noted as a cause of anestrum or failure of estrum. In the cow the most common tumor is the granulosa cell tumor that may cause occasional symptoms of either nymphomania or anestrum. The early stages of these tumors usually pass unnoticed and by the time clinical symptoms of pelvic relaxation, edema of the vulva, and others are evident, rectal examination will reveal the nature of the condition by the presence of an abnormally large ovary, 3 inches or 7.5 cm or more in diameter, usually pulled forward and downward in the abdominal cavity. The ovarian artery to the diseased ovary is usually enlarged. Removal of the diseased ovary may be indicated in some cases. Several authors have reported finding granulosa cell tumors in related cattle. Occasionally chronic tumors, abscesses and cysts in the ventral area of the brain affect the pituitary gland by causing pressure atrophy and a lack of FSH and LH, thus producing cessation of the estrous cycle. These lesions are rare in cattle. Other body changes due to the damage to the anterior pituitary gland such as loss of weight and hair, diabetes, and atrophy of the gonads may occur. Large and prolonged doses of the gonadal hormones whether taken orally or by injection will suppress the release of gonadotropic hormones and result in smooth, inactive, nonfunctioning, atrophied ovaries. Anestrus due to this cause is rare except for the purposefull synchronizing of estrus in cattle.

Treatment of anestrum in Class II cows that have no palpable functional corpora lutea will vary with the clinical findings. Anestrous cows with cystic ovaries containing follicular or luteal cysts should be treated by removal of the cysts, injection of a luteinizing hormone, or in other ways described under cystic ovaries. Heifers or cows with freemartin genital tracts, bilateral total ovarian hypoplasia, which should not be confused with infantilism or failure to reach puberty, absence of the gonads, ovarian tumors, or rare lesions of the pituitary gland or the hypothalamus should be slaughtered as treatment is not indicated or successful. Removal of one ovary affected with an ovarian tumor, especially a granulosa cell tumor, may rarely restore fertility to the heifer or the cow. In the case of ovarian hypoplasia the strong possibility that the condition is genetic in nature should be seriously considered. If ovarian atrophy or cystic ovaries are due to exogenous estrogens, or possibly progesterone, testosterone or progestagens, these should be removed from the diet or injections of the same should be stopped. It may take from a week to several months or more before the estrous cycle is reestablished.

Treatment of anestrum due to debility, cachexia or a lack of TDN (energy), protein, or other minerals should follow a careful clinical examination and diagnosis often requiring an analysis of feed. If the cause is due to chronic debilitating diseases these must be corrected or alleviated so the female returns to a good condition with near normal body weight. Additional levels of TDN and other nutrients need to be fed to these animals. Therapy may require a number of months. Stopping lactation in cattle may aid in hastening the return of estrous cycles. In senile animals the prognosis is poor but occasionally pelletted, easily digested feed may be helpful.

Treatment of anestrum due to a low level of nutrition is

obviously corrected by greatly increasing the nutritive levels. Since many farmers refuse to recognize they are underfeeding and mismanaging their stock, particularly heifers, this is a difficult or impossible problem to correct in some herds. Frequently nature corrects it in the spring when the animals are turned out to pasture where the feed is excellent and unlimited; the weather is warmer; the days longer; and exercise is plentiful. Occasionally a farmer or owner can be persuaded to accept your diagnosis and suggested treatment on a trial basis by taking several anestrous heifers with small functionless ovaries and placing them in the barn with the milking cows and feeding them as if they were cows producing 50 lbs of milk a day. In 3 to 6 weeks these heifers usually come into estrum while their less fortunate companions —fed less and on a poor quality feed and usually kept in a colder and less favorable environment—remain anestrous. This same problem may be observed in certain areas of the country and in certain herds where there are deficiencies of either one or more minerals such as phosphorus, cobalt, iodine, copper, salt, iron, and others, or of total digestible nutrients. Often nutritional deficiencies producing cessation of the estrous cycle are multiple. In some heavy-producing old cows that are very thin and poor and are persistent milkers, it may be advisable to stop lactation to enable them to gain enough body reserves so that estrous cycles will begin again. Good pasture is desirable. Estrum will not occur in these debilitated animals until they receive feed over and above the requirements for maintaining life and are in a positive energy balance. In heifers or cows in a fair to good nutritive state but failing to show estrum because of a phosphorus deficiency, steamed bonemeal or dicalcium phosphate should be fed free choice. Complex mineral supplements or specific mineral supplements may be necessary, free choice or incorporated into the salt or feed in anestrous, mineral-deficient cows with a low blood hemoglobin level.

In range beef heifers and cows the delay in the onset of puberty or estrus after calving, especially in nursing two-year-olds and the lowered conception rates have been discussed by Bellows, Sprague and Wiltbank. These authors have demonstrated the importance of feeding proper supplemental levels of nutrients, especially energy and phosphorus to heifers and two-year-old cows after calving. The value of vitamins for anestrus in range cattle is questionable.

There is no value whatsoever in the use of hormones in cases of "deep" anestrum with nonfunctioning ovaries due to a poor physical condition. Some owners insist or demand that their anestrous heifers or cows with no ovarian activity or evidence of any by the presence of a corpus luteum or follicle be given an injection of a hormone. If estrogens, FSH or a similar product is injected to satisfy the owner, he should be urged to increase the feed and improve management practices. Immediate response and conception to hormone injections is rarely observed. Fortunately many of these cases are observed late in the winter or early spring and recovery occurs after these animals are turned out to pasture. In some borderline cases injections of hormones may possibly be of value in initiating, stimulating, or hastening the onset of the estrous cycle. Probably the heifer or cow near the upper border of "nutritional" anestrum is declining in milk production and is about to develop estrous cycles anyway. This may be true if follicular activity is noted. The use of douches of warm saline, an irritant substance such as one to two ml of Lugol's solution in water or uterine massage are of no value in initiating the prompt onset of the estrous cycle unless cycles are about to commence in any event. The effect of various external stimuli on the hypothalmus to cause the production of the gonadotropic releasing factors has been reviewed in the section on bovine reproductive physiology.

Asdell cited 6 references in which different authors reported on using gonadotropes, and 3 which reported on estrogens used empirically for infantile ovaries in heifers with failure of estrum due to underfeeding causing a delayed onset of puberty. The "recovery" rate was 55 per cent and 40 per cent, respectively. In a report on nonfunctional ovaries associated with anestrum Clark cited 15 cows treated by massage alone; 14 conceived. Theoretically to stimulate cows in anestrum with nonfunctional or "smooth" ovaries, F.S.H. is indicated. The usual doses of gonadotropes used empirically to treat anestrum in cattle are 750 to 1500 I.U. P.M.S., "Gonadin" (Cutter) or 40 to 100 A.U. F.S.H. (Armour). Theoretically this F.S.H. treatment might be followed in 3 to 5 days by an injection of L.H. However superovulation is then a possibility. Asdell cited 12 references reporting on a total of 165 cows with "hypoplastic" ovaries treated empirically with gonadotropes, and 9 references on a total of 123 cows with a similar condition treated with estrogens. Estrum and conception occurred after a variable period of a few days to a number of months in about 50 per cent of the cows treated with gonadotropes and about 53 per cent of the cows treated with estrogens. Since in the above types of anestrum no corpus luteum is present, it cannot be manually removed to bring about estrum. There is no physiologic basis for the injection of estrogens in this type of anestrum. By injecting estrogens symptoms of estrum may be produced and thus the owner may be satisfied, but ovulation does not occur. The usual doses used as placebos are 20 to 40 mg. of stilbestrol and 2 to 4 mg. of estradiol. Larger doses may cause cystic ovaries. Zemjanis et al. demonstrated that thyroid therapy was of questionable value in the treatment of bovine anestrum. Its use to increase the metabolic rate is contra-indicated in thin anestrous animals.

Miscellaneous Infertility Conditions Possibly Associated with Hormonal Disturbances

Hormonal therapy for cows that are cycling regularly but fail to conceive has been used empirically in the past by many veterinarians. If the therapy has not been coupled to a careful diagnosis of the etiology of the repeat-breeder cow which is difficult, results are usually unsatisfactory or conception occurs despite the treatment. The use of luteinizing hormone (HCG) to promote ovulation has been described but failure of ovulation or delayed ovulation only occurs occasionally. This hormone may also be used about the third to fourth day after estrum to promote the growth and increase the size and progesterone production of the corpus luteum. Risley has reported favorably on the use of M.A.P. fed as **Repromix** (Upjohn) starting about the fourth day after service in selected cows that appear normal but fail to conceive after repeated services. Other veterinarians have suggested the use of repositol progesterone, 500 mg. every 10 days, in similar cows in which early embryonic deaths apparently occur. The use of small doses of estrogens at the time of estrus to improve the signs of heat or to stimulate the release of L.H. has proven to be of little or no value in infertile cows. As noted under bovine reproductive physiology exogenous estrogens have no effect in either of these conditions. F.S.H. is not indicated in cycling infertile cows. Thyroid therapy in the form of iodinated casein, 1 gm. per 100 lbs. body weight orally daily, 5,000 to 15,000 mg. triiodothyronine (**Cytomel,** Smith Kline and French) in pellet form subcutaneously or 2 to 5 grains of thyroid orally daily has been used for anestrum. It has also been used empirically for infertile cows or heifers, especially those that are obese or have become steer-like in appearance. Thyroid preparations should not be used in thin cattle in which anestrum is due to a lack of T.D.N. or energy intake. Controlled studies in infertile cattle with the above hormones is probably indicated to prove or disprove their value. It is unlikely they will be proven to be of value unless better diagnostic tests are developed so that the use of hormones becomes based on scientific, sound information.

Cupps and coworkers have reported a possible abnormal steroid metabolism in inbred Jersey cattle characterized by delayed puberty, a short estrus, irregular cycles, failure of conception and a decreased secretion rate of sex steroids and cortisol.

References

Aines, P. D. Jr. (1954) An Evaluation of Signs of Sodium Chloride Deficiency in Relation to the Requirement of Dairy Cattle for Salt. Thesis, Cornell Univ., Ithaca, N.Y.

Anonymous (1970) Failure of Vasectomy, J.A.V.M.A. **156,** 8, 954.

Arthur, G. H. (1964) Wright's Veterinary Obstetrics, 3rd. Ed., Williams and Wilkins Co., Baltimore, Md.

ARS-USDA (1965) The Influence of Total Feed and Protein Intake on Reproductive Performance of the Beef Female Through Second Calving, Tech. Bull. 1314.

Asdell, S. A. (1948) Sterility and Delayed Breeding, Cornell Univ., Coll. of Agr. Ext. Bull. 737.

Asdell, S. A. (1949) Nutrition and the Treatment of Sterility in Dairy Cattle: A Review, J. of Dairy Sci., **32,** 1, 60.

Asdell, S. A. (1949) Hormones and the Treatment of Sterility in Dairy Cattle: A Review, J. of Dairy Sci., **32,** 1, 45.

Asdell, S. A., DeAlba, J. and Roberts, S. J. (1945) The Levels of Ovarian Hormones Required to Induce Heat and Other Reactions in the Ovariectomized Cow, J. of An. Sci., **4,** 3, 277.

Bane, A. (1964) Fertility and Reproductive Disorders in Swedish Cattle, Brit. Vet. Jour. **120,** 431.

Barrett, G. R., Casida, L. E., and Lloyd, C. A. (1948) Measuring Breeding Efficiency by Pregnancy Examinations and by Non Returns (Abstr.) J. Dairy Sci., **31,** 682.

Barrett, G. R. Casida, L. E. and Lloyd, C. A. (1950) The Use of Pregnancy Diagnosis with Artificial Breeding, Personal Communication

Belling, T. H. and El Shafie, S. A. (1964) Estrone for Inducing Estrus in Dairy Cows, J.A.V.M.A. **144,** 9, 998.

Bellows, R. A. (1966) Improving Reproductive Efficiency in Beef Cattle, Vet. Scope (Upjohn) **11,** 3, 2.

Bierschwal, C. J. and Ebert, E. F. (1961) Clinical Applications of a Sclerotherapeutic Agent, Vet. Med. **56,** 8, 323.

Bond, J., McDowell, R. E., Curry, W. A. and Warwick, E. J. (1960) Reproductive Performance of Milking Shorthorn Heifers as Affected by Constant Environmental Temperature, J. An. Sci. **19,** 4, 1317.

Bonelli, B. (1947) Personal Communication.

Boyd, H. and Hignett, P. G. (1968) A Device for the Detection of Oestrus in Cattle, Vet. Res. **83,** 2.

Brunner, M. A., Donaldson, L. E. and Hansel, Wm. (1969) Exogenous Hormones and Luteal Function in Hysterectomized and Intact Heifers, J. Dairy Sci. **52,** 11, 1849.

Carroll, E. J. and Hoerlein, A. B. (1966) Reproductive Performance of Beef Cattle Under Drouth Conditions, J.A.V.M.A. **148,** 9, 1030.

Casida, L. E. and Wisnicky, W. (1950) Effects of Diethylstilbestrol Dipropionate upon Postpartum Changes in the Cow, J. of An. Sci., **9,** 2, 238.

Clark, C. F. (1935) The Clinical Treatment of Retained Corpus Luteum in the Cow, Vet. Med., **30,** 536.

Clark, C. F. (1937) Clinical Results in the Treatment of So-Called Functional Sterility of Cows, J.A.V.M.A., **90,** 488.

Cupps, P. T., Laben, R. C. and Huff, R. L. (1970) Steroid Metabolism in an Inbred Strain of Jersey Cattle, J. Dairy Sci., **53,** 1, 79.

Dawson, F. L. M. (1961) Corpus Luteum Enucleation in the Cow: Therapeutic and Traumatic Effects, Vet. Rec. **73,** 27, 661.

Dowling, D. F. (1954) Induction of Ovulation in Cattle, Austral. Vet. J., **30,** 8, 240.

Eriksson, K. (1938) Investigations Respecting the Heredity of Genital Hypoplasia in Cattle, Skand. Vet., **28,** 7, 409.

Fincher, M. G. (1946) Methods of Increasing Fertility in Domestic Animals, Trans. of the Amer. Soc. for Study of Sterility, 1.

Foote, R. H. (1955) Personal Communication. Unpublished Data.

Forgason, J. L. (1963) Winrock Farm Beef Cattle Improvement Program, Vet. Med. **53,** 3, 211.

Gangwar, P. C. Branton, C. and Evans, D. L. (1965) Reproductive and Physiological Responses of Holstein Heifers to Controlled and Natural Climatic Conditions, J. Dairy Sci. **48,** 2, 222.

Gibbons, W. J. (1954) Reproductive Problems in Cattle, Vet. Med., **49,** 8, 323.

Ginther, O. J. (1968) Utero-Ovarian Relationships in Cattle: Physiologic and Applied Veterinary Aspects, J.A.V.M.A. **153,** 12, 1656 and 1665.

Hall, J. B. Branton, C. and Stone, E. J. (1959) Estrus, Estrous Cycles, Ovulation Time, Time of Service, and Fertility of Dairy Cattle in Louisiana, J. Dairy Sci., **42,** 6, 1.

Hammond, J. (1949) Personal Communication. Lecture at Cornell Univ., March 8, 1949.

Hancock, J. L. (1948) The Clinical Analysis of Reproductive Failure in Cattle, Vet. Rec., **60,** 43, 513.

Hansel, W. (1953) Field Observations on the Relation of Nutrition to Sterility in Dairy Cattle, J.A.V.M.A., **122,** 911, 126.

Hays, R. L. and Carlevaro, C. H. (1959) Induction of Estrus by Electrical Stimulation, Am. J. Physiol. **196,** 899.

Herrick, J. B. (1952) Clinical Observations on the Effect of Removing Retained Corpora Lutea in the Cow, N. A. Vet., **33,** 2, 92.

Herrick, J. B. (1953) Progesterone Therapy in Repeat Breeding Heifers, Vet. Med., **48,** 12, 489.

Hofstad, M. S. (1941) A Study of the Breeding Records of One Large Herd of Dairy Cattle, Cor. Vet., **31,** 4, 379.

Hurst, V. (1959) Studies of Anestrum in Dairy Cattle, J.A.V.M.A. **135,** 9, 471.

Kidder, H. E., Barrett, G. R. and Casida, L. E. (1952) A Study of Ovulations in Six Families of Holstein Friesians, J. of Dairy Sci., **35,** 5, 436.

Labhsetwar, A. P., Tyler, W. J. and Casida, L. E. (1963) Genetic and Environmental Factors Affecting Quiet Ovulations in Holstein Cattle, J. Dairy Sci. **46,** 8, 843.

Lagerlof, N. (1950) Personal Communication. Lecture, April 27, 1950.

Lagerlof, N. (1951) Hereditary Forms of Sterility in Swedish Cattle Breeds, Fert. and Steril., **2,** 3, 230.

Laing, J. A. (1955) Fertility and Infertility in Domestic Animals, Williams and Wilkins Co., Baltimore, Md.

Lindley, D. C. (1953) Comparison of Treatments for Anestrum in Dairy Cattle, Vet. Med., **48,** 7, 263.

Marion, G. B. and Gier, H. T. (1968) Factors Affecting Bovine Ovarian Activity After Parturition, J. An. Sci. **27,** 6, 1621.

McEntee, K. (1954), 1968) Personal Communication.

Miller, F. W. and Graves, R. R. (1932) Reproduction and Health Records of the Beltsville Herd of the Bureau of Dairy Industry, U. S. Dept. of Agr. Tech. Bull. 321.

Moberg, R. (1954) Disease Conditions in the Fallopian Tubes and Ovarian Bursae of Cattle, Vet. Rec., **66,** 6, 87.

Moberg, R. (1964) Infertility Due to a Persistent Corpus Luteum, 5th. Internat. Congr. for An. Reprod. and Art. Insem., Trento, Italy.

Morrow, D. A. (1969) Estrous Behavior and Ovarian Activity in Prepuberal and Postpuberal Heifers, J. Dairy Sci. **52,** 2, 224.

Morrow, D. A. (1969) Phosphorus Deficiency and Infertility in Dairy Hiefers, J.A.V.M.A. **154,** 7, 761.

Morrow, D. A., Roberts, S. J., McEntee, K. and Gray, H. G. (1966) Ovarian Activity and Involution of the Uterus and Cervix in Dairy Cattle, 1, Ovarian Activity, Cor. Vet. **59,** 2, 173.

Morrow, D. A., Rboerts, S. J., McEntee, K. and Gray, H. G. (1966) Postpartum Ovarian Activity and Uterine Involution in Dairy Cattle, J.A.V.M.A. **149,** 12, 1596.

Newman, L. (1968) Personal Communication.

Oehme, F. W. (1968) Resection of the Bovine Epididymis, A Procedure for Preparing Teaser Bulls, Vet. Med. **63,** 6, 603.

Olds, D. and Seath, D. M. (1951) Repeatability of the Estrous Cycle Length in Dairy Cows, J. of Dairy Sci., **34,** 626.

Olds, D. and Seath, D. M. (1954) Factors Affecting Reproductive Efficiency of Dairy Cattle, Kentucky Agr. Exp. Stat. Bull. #605.

Oxenreider, S. L. (1968) Ovarian Function in the Cow after Induction of Uterine Motility, J. Reprod. and Fert. **16,** 2, 297.

Phillips, S. (1967) Personal Communication.

Purse, R. M. and Wickersham, E. W. (1969) Effect of Successive Enucleactions of Bovine Corpora Lutea on Formation and Function of Subsequent Luteal Tissue, J. An. Sci. **28,** 6, 767.

Rajakoski, E. (1960) The Ovarian Follicular System in Sexually Mature Heifers, Acta Endocrinol, Suppl. 52, **34,** 7.

Risley, H. B. (1969) Personal Communication.

Roberts, S. J. and Fox, F. H. (1968) An Unusual Case of Bovine Mucometra Associated with a Persistent Corpus Luteum, Cor. Vet. **58,** 1, 116.

Schmidt, S. S. (1966) Technics and Complications of Elective Vasectomy. The Role of Spermatic Granuloma in Spontaneous Recanalization. Fert. and Steril, **17,** 4, 467.

Short, R. V. (1962) Steroid Concentrations in Normal Follicular Fluid and Ovarian Cyst Fluid From Cows, J. Reprod. and Fertil., **4,** 27.

Sorensen, A. M., Hansel, W., Hough, W. H., Armstrong, D. T., McEntee, K. and Bratton, R. W. (1959) Causes and Prevention of Reproductive Failures in Dairy Cattle, Bull. 936, Cornell Agr. Exp. Stat., N. Y. S. College of Agric., Ithaca, N.Y. 14850.

Sprague, J. I. (1963) Range Cattle Nutrition, Coop. Ext. Service, An. Sci. Dept., Colo. State Univ., Ft. Collins Colo.

Smith, L. C. (1963) Surgical Procedures to Make a Bull a Heat Detector, A. I. Digest, **9,** 1.

Stalfors, H. (1930) Some New Observations and Experiments Concerning Sterility in Cattle, Cor. Vet., **20,** 1, 1.

Stewart, D. L. (1952) The Suppression of Oestrus in Dairy Cattle After Mating, Vet. Rec., **64,** 303.

Straub, O. C. and Kendrick, J. W. (1965) Preparation of Teaser Bulls by Penectomy, J.A.V.M.A. **147,** 4, 373.

Teige, J. (1955) Hemorrhage Following Expression of the Corpus Luteum in the Cow (Trans.), Nord. Vet. Med., **7,** 9, 747.

Teige, J. and Jakobsen, K. R. (1956) Investigation on the Effect of Enucleation of Corpus Luteum in Dairy Cattle Proc. Third Internat. Congr. on An. Reprod., Cambridge.

Trimberger, G. W. (1955) Unpublished Data.

Trimberger, G. W. and Davis, H. P. (1943) Conception Rate in Dairy Cattle by Artificial Insemination at Various Stages of Estrus, Univ. of Nebr., Agr. Exp. Stat., Res. Bull. 129.

Wagner, W. C. and McEntee, K. (1960) Herd Approach to Infertility Problems in Cattle, Cor. Vet. **50,** 2, 198.

Wiltbank, J. N. (1961) A Technique for Sterilization of Bulls, The Southwest Vet. **14,** 3, 194.

Wiltbank, J. N. (1966) Modification of Ovarian Activity in the Bovine Following Injection of Oestrogen and Gonadotrophin, J. Reprod. and Fertil. Suppl. 1, 1.

Wiltbank, J. N. and Cook, A. C. (1958) The Comparative Reproductive Performance of Nursed Cows and Milked Cows, J. An. Sci., **17,** 640.

Wilkbank, J. N., Rowden, W. W., Ingalls, J. E. and Zimmerman, D. R. (1964) Influence of Postpartum Energy Level on Reproductive Performance in Hereford Cows Restricted in Energy Intake Prior to Calving, J. An. Sci. **23,** 4, 1049.

Wright, J. G. (1945) Observations on the Clinical Aspects of Reproductive Disorders in Cattle, Vet. Rec.,**57,** 26, 313.

Yamauchi, M., Nakahara, T., Kaneda, Y. and Inui, S. (1967) Effects of Uterine Distension on the Oestrous Cycle of the Cow, J. Reprod. and Fertil. **13,** 379.

Zemjanis, R. (1961) Incidence of Anestrus in Dairy Cattle, J.A.V.M.A. **139,** 11, 1023.

Zemjanis, R., (1970) Animal Reproduction, 2nd. Ed. Williams and Wilkins Co., Baltimore.

Zemjanis, R., Fahning, M. L. and Schultz, R. H. (1969) Anestrus, The Practitioners Dilemma, Vet. Scope (Upjohn) **14,** 1, 14.

Infertility Due to Nutritional Causes

During the past 30 years a great mass of knowledge has accumulated about the effects on animals of various nutrients and their deficiencies. Since much of the early work was done on the rat and on laboratory animals, some nutritional fallacies have developed in so far as they pertain to domestic animals. The effect of nutrition on reproduction, sterility, and infertility has not been discussed but the relation of nutrition or nutritive deficiences to abortion has been reviewed in Chapter VIII. Excellent reviews on this field have been made by Asdell, Reid, Meites, McClure, and Moustguard. Only a few nutrients have a direct effect on fertility. Some infertility conditions blamed on nutrition may in reality be due to other related or nonrelated causes. Most field cases of reduced fertility or of sterility of nutritional origin are usually due to multiple deficiencies. Underfeeding may be accompanied by poor quality of feed and by deficiencies of protein, phosphorus and vitamin A. A protein deficiency is usually accompanied by a phosphorus deficiency, and a vitamin A deficiency by a protein and phosphorus deficiency. Sometimes reduced fertility believed to be of nutritional origin may be caused by the amount of light, environmental temperature, amount or type of work, or some other environmental influence. More work is required in this field as much of our present data is based on poorly controlled experiments and too few observations. It has been found that nutritional data accumulated on one species of animal does not always apply to other species. Symptoms of a certain deficiency in one species may differ from those in another species. Reid noted that at one time or another claims have been made that every known food factor is indispensible for normal reproduction. In so far as reproductive performance is based on the general health of the animal this may be true. Malnutrition leads to lowered vitality and lessened resistance to disease but proof of such effects on the reproductive system are few and all too often not conclusive. If disease is complicating the malnutrition then corrective efforts must be directed at both conditions. Lactation, however, places a heavy drain on an animal already deficient especially in certain minerals and in the general level of feeding. Specific deficiencies seldom cause specific lesions in the reproductive system. Infertility or sterility due to nutritional causes is usually characterized by a failure of estrum or a cessation of the estrous cycle and only under certain conditions is it characterized by a failure of conception or early embryonic death.

Underfeeding, inanition, or starvation has been shown to delay sexual maturity in heifers, Reid et al., McClure, and Moustguard, and to inhibit estrous cycles in mammals of all ages. When dairy heifers were fed various levels of TDN from birth to first calving equivalent to 62, 100 and 146 per cent of the upper level of Morrison's Feeding Standard, the average age at the onset of puberty was 88, 49, and 40 weeks. The body size at the time of puberty was the same for all feeding levels. When the energy intake in the adult animal is low, follicles fail to develop to maturity and follicular atresia results, along with a loss of sexual desire and anestrus. Restricted food intake may have an effect on the early embryo but starvation after this period does not necessarily interupt gestation but may cause stillbirth or birth of small, weak young, Meites. It is nearly impossible to conduct an experiment on a single food deficiency without encountering a partial inanition in animals. Under-feeding or inanition is seen in cattle most commonly during the winter months when they are confined and/or the quality and quantity of the feed is limited or reduced. In older cattle irregular estrous periods and anestrum are manifested as a result of underfeeding. Meites and Moustgaard stated that inanition reduced the secretion of gonadotropic hormones and other hormones by the anterior pituitary although the gonadotropic levels in the pituitary were normal. The fact that the ovaries remain responsive to stimulation by gonadotropes during under-feeding does not mean that normal estrous cycles and pregnancy could be maintained by administration of hormones, since undernutrition probably exerts a direct effect on the reproductive tract although the major effect is on the endocrine glands.

It has been shown in primiparous beef heifers that energy intake levels before and especially after calving and during lactation have a marked effect on the occurrence of postpartum estrus and conception rates, Wiltbank and Faulker. In beef heifers fed high TDN, 9 lbs. and low TDN, 4.5 lbs. daily before calving and then high TDN, 16 lbs., and low TDN, 8 lbs. daily after calving the conception rate for 20 heifers in each group was High-High 95 per cent, High-Low 77 per cent, Low-High 95 per cent and Low-Low 20 per cent. The percentage of cows cycling by 60 days postpartum was 80, 81, 45 and 17 respectively in the four feeding groups. Thus it is more important that cows suckling calves receive more energy than pregnant animals, Wiltbank et al. and Sprague. The birth weight of calves from cows on the low energy ration during pregnancy was 10 lbs. lower on the average than the weight of calves from cows on the high energy ration, 67 lbs. vs 78 lbs.. Wiltbank and Faulkner recommended that beef heifers be fed to gain one pound a day from weaning through the breeding season. The English breeds of cattle should weigh 650 lbs. at the start of the season. Beef cattle should be in good condition at calving and should be fed to gain 0.5 to 0.75 lbs. per day after calving until the end of the breeding season to avoid low reproductive performance. Carroll and Hoerlein reported that in a herd of 327 beef cattle free of infectious causes for infertility the conception rate dropped from 87 per cent to 41 per cent, 28 per cent in lactating and 76 per cent in nonlactating cows, under drouth conditions. Injections of vitamins A, D and E during the breeding season failed to improve the conception rate. Reid et al. reported a higher incidence of dystocia in heifers on a below normal energy intake during the gestation period. Reid (1959) reported, however, that retarded early growth in cattle due to a low plane of nutrition was associated with a prolongation of the life span.

Evidence indicates that animals come into estrum and concieve most readily when their body weight is rising due to an increased plane of nutrition and conversely a low pregnancy rate occurs in cattle losing weight during the breeding season, Dunn et al., McClure, Wiltbank and Faulkner, King, and Kali and Amir. In 179 Ayrshire cows on 3 farms that were weighed every 4 weeks and serviced not less than 56 days postpartum, King reported that 98 cows whose body weight increased had a 77.6 per cent conception rate on first service while 81 cows whose body weight decreased had a 16 per cent conception rate on first service. There was no correlation between conception rate and milk yield. This was also noted by Kali and Amir in Israel who stated that a positive energy balance if achieved fairly promptly after calving resulted in an improved conception rate. They suggested that weighing cows at intervals after calving might be helpful in determining the need for increased energy intake and in determining the time for insemination. McClure described the dairy herd infertility syndrome associated with a negative energy balance and loss of weight to include: (1) low first-service nonreturn rates; these are seldom below 30 per cent, (2) spontaneous recovery but many cows are not pregnant by the third month after the first service, (3) affected cows lose an excessive amount of body weight, 5 to 10 per cent, between calving and first service; such a loss is often not obvious, and (4) low blood glucose, hypoglycemia, is frequently observed in infertile cows at the time of the first service. McClure (1968) further reported that the estrous cycle length was increased from normal to 34 days when cows were given insulin daily from day 17, but not day 18, through day 20 of the cycle. In 11 cows mated 0 to 2 days after the last dose of insulin only 2 or 18 per cent were pregnant at 8 weeks, and of 16 cows given insulin, 400 units protamone zinc, daily the first four days after mating only 6 or 38 per cent were pregnant at 8 weeks. While 15 of 20, or 75 per cent, of the control cows were pregnant. Thus it is possible that a hypoglycemia at estrus and shortly after service may exert a harmful effect on conception. This effect may be brought about by a lowering of the glucose or glycogen levels in the mucosa of the genital tract resulting in a lack of energy for spermatozoa or fertilized ova. Further study of these interesting observations are needed. Dunn et al. found that reproduction in Herefords was more severely affected by low levels of TDN intake after calving than it was in Angus cattle. Bellows reported that weight gain in yearling heifers during the prebreeding period caused by "flushing" or feeding high energy rations was more important in its effect on age at puberty than was the gain during the wintering period. Thus it appears important that feeding practices in dairy and beef herds be such that, despite the stress and energy requirements of lactation, cows to be bred should be in a positive energy balance and gaining weight as soon after calving as is possible to realize the best breeding results.

Obesity due to overfeeding has been considered by many practicing veterinarians to be a cause of infertility in cattle. This is observed particularly in the beef breeds and has often been reported to affect valuable show cattle. Asdell, and Wiltbank et al. (1965) cited early references that in these overly-fat animals the ovaries are small and estrus may fail to occur. Obesity and sterility might arise from the same cause such as hypothyroidism or from a pituitary lesion. Fat deposits in the ovaries and ovarian bursae were suspected of interfering with normal ovulation and transport of ovum to the oviduct. Recent nutritional research has not confirmed the observation that obesity and infertility are associated in cows. Reid stated, "It is as logical to assume that sterility is the cause of high condition as it is to assume the reverse." Olds cited Hansen and Steensberg in reporting that in a rather large controlled experiment animals kept on a high plane of nutrition their entire life had fewer calves and a higher percentage of culling due to infertility than did the animals fed at normal and low levels of nutrition. Swedish data, New Zealand reports, and experiments at Cornell, Reid et al., indicated that heavy feeding hastened the onset of puberty, caused a slight increase in number of services per conception if heifers were withheld from breeding for a number of months after reaching puberty; and resulted in lower milk yields and a shorter life. Reid (1959) reported that cattle reared on a high plane of nutrition had more breeding difficulties later in life and thus had a shorter productive life than cattle reared on a low energy intake. A high level of grain feeding of up to 4790 kg per lactation over a period of years in dairy cows had no significant effect on conception rate, Armstrong et al.. Fat heifers with large deposits of perivaginal fat may have more difficulties at parturition. The problem of the effects of overfeeding on reproduction in cattle is not settled and more controlled experiments are needed and indicated.

Protein deficiencies of either quality or quantity under the usual conditions of management of cattle are not common. Although the quality and quanitity of protein might be important for reproductive functions, deficient amounts are seldom encountered except in severe inanition or underfeeding where vitamin A and phosphorus deficiencies are often complicating factors. The effect of a low level intake of protein on reproduction may be to reduce the total intake of feed, resulting in a delay in estrus, Wiltbank et al. (1965). Knox and Watkins observed that the high content of phosphorus rather than protein may explain why cottonseed meal is a better supplement for beef cattle in the Southwest than is grain during the winter months. Pelleted alfalfa fed at a rate of 2 to 5 lbs. daily per animal is an excellent protein supplement. The level of energy intake is more important for reproduction than is protein.

Vitamin deficiencies in cattle are mainly limited to vitamin A. Deficiencies of the other vitamins are not likely to cause reproductive failure.

Vitamin A deficiency adversely affects reproduction in most species. The effects occur during the latter half of gestation and are characterized by abortion or by the birth of weak or dead calves. It seems remarkable but it is nevertheless true that Vitamin A deficient animals have normal estrous cycles, ovulate and conceive, and early fetal development occurs even though epithelial and other tissue changes have developed. Infertility in cattle and other domestic animals is not associated with Vitamin A deficiency or with a deficiency of the other vitamins.

Vitamin A requirements during pregnancy are higher than in the nonpregnant animal and higher for the female than the male animal. Vitamin A deficiencies are characterized by changes in the epithelial tissues, such as keratinization and degeneration of the placenta. Fetal death, abortion, dystocia, retained placenta, and septic metritis are likely to result. Vitamin A deficiency has been described in cattle grazing dry, bleached pastures and grain fields where possibly protein, phosphorus, and carbohydrate intake were also deficient. When green feed became available, night blindness, lacrimation, anorexia, diarrhea, loss of condition and other general symptoms of vitamina A deficiency, as well as abortions and stillbirths, ceased. The liver has the ability to store considerable amounts of vitamin A for some time; therefore symptoms of vitamin A deficiency take months to develop. Good timothy hay has a much lower content of vitamin A than does alfalfa hay. Under most conditions where roughage is of average quality, vitamin A deficiency is very unlikely to occur and even then the reproductive effects are not those causing infertility in the cow.

Vitamin B or B-complex deficiencies have been demonstrated in animals as producing the same inhibitory effects on reproduction as reduced food intake or starvation. This is not unexpected, as deficiencies of B vitamins are usually accompanied by a reduced appetite. By virtue of ruminal synthesis of these B-complex vitamins, cows are in no danger of suffering from vitamin B deficiencies. One of the B-complex vitamins, vitamin B_{12}, requires cobalt in its synthesis; cattle in cobalt-deficient areas may develop severe inanition due to lack of sufficient intake of feed occasioned by a cobalt and B_{12} deficiency and a lack of appetite.

Vitamin C deficiency does not occur in cattle; only man, monkeys, and guinea pigs manifest symptoms of vitamin C deficiency, or scurvy, and even in these species no reproductive disturbances are produced when severe scurvy is present.

Vitamin D deficiency probably seldom occurs, due to the presence of vitamin D in roughage of almost any quality. If the animal gains access to sunlight or green pasture, adequate amounts are available. Meites stated that an uncomplicated vitamin D deficiency does not interfere with reproduction in mammals.

Vitamin E deficiency, like vitamin A deficiency, does not affect the estrous cycle or ovarian function. In deficient rats pregnancy is interrupted after midterm by resorbtion of the fetuses. In the male rats vitamin E deficiency irreparably damages the seminiferous epithelium giving rise to its early name—the "antisterility" vitamin. In herbivorous animals it is doubtful that a need for vitamin E for reproductive purposes is greater than the quantity liberally present in the natural feed. Cows can reproduce on a vitamin E deficient diet. Gullickson and co-workers found that heifers and bulls receiving vitamin-E-deficient diets were fertile on service. In the past, extravagant claims have been made for the use and value of vitamin E supplementation of rations in the treatment of all types of reproductive disorders in cows and bulls. These claims and reports, largely commercially-developed and exploited, were uncontrolled. The use of wheat germ oil in cases where spontaneous recoveries of infertility are known to be high resulted in a great number of apparent "cures" with this product. Reports on more carefully controlled data and experiments using wheat germ oil or sprouted oats showed no difference in results between the treated and the control groups of cattle. At the present time vitamin E therapy for infertility can not be recommended since it is of no known value.

Mineral deficiencies causing infertility in cattle are limited mainly to phosphorus and occasional trace minerals. Ammerman et al. have reviewed trace minerals in cattle nutrition.

Phosphorus deficiency usually tends to occur when diets low in protein are fed, under range conditions when the grass is dry and dead, in areas where the soil is deficient in phosphorus, and in borderline phosphorus-deficient areas when the cows are lactating and are not fed sufficient protein or mineral supplements to maintain the necessary body levels of phosphorus. Until clinical symptoms of the deficiency, such as inanition, poor hair coat, and depraved and decreased appetite are evident, reproduction usually does not suffer. In some phosphorus-deficient areas cows had calves only every 2 years, and heifers failed to show estrum until over 2 years of age. The condition was most severe in the late winter and spring after a dry summer and fall. Some cows would have one or two periods of estrum after calving and then if they failed to conceive would not show estrum until the end of the lactation period. Silent or irregular estrus periods may occur in heifers. Thus the usual symptoms of phosphorus deficiency are delayed onset of puberty in heifers, and failure of estrum in cows. Morrow reviewed the relationship between phosphorus deficiency and infertility in dairy cattle and reported that with proper phosphorus supplementation the number of services required for conception declined from 3.7 to 1.3 in dairy heifers suffering from a phosphorus deficiency. Hignett reported that the Ca:P ratio, especially excess Ca to P., could influence fertility but this was not confirmed by Littlejohn and Lewis. In some cases the calves may be stillborn or expelled weak, but abortions do not occur with phosphorus deficiency.

According to Asdell the phosphorus requirement for reproduction is about 10 to 12 gm. daily except during lactation when an additional amount is required. Blood levels of phosphorus below 4 mg per 100 ml of blood serum usually indicate a phosphorus deficiency; normal values are 4 to 8 mg per 100 ml. Phosphorus levels are much lower in timothy hay than in legumes. In states where phosphorus deficiency is common, the feeding of mineral supplements or cotton seed meal has resulted in marked improvement or increases in the yearly percentage of calves born. Mineral supplements to supply phosphorus include dicalcium phosphate or bone meal and these should be available free-choice together with trace mineralized salt for all cattle. Adding 1 per cent sodium tripolyphosphate or monosodium phosphate to the grain ration will also increase the phosphorus intake, Morrow. **Calcium deficiency** does not cause reproductive failure in cattle.

Other trace element deficiencies, that may affect reproduction indirectly, are: **Manganese**—In cattle there are few reports of naturally-occuring manganese deficiencies. It appears nearly impossible to devise an otherwise normal ration for cattle that is deficient in manganese, Reid. However, Rogas and Dyer, Wilson, and McClure citing Rasbech and Krolak have reported reduced conception rates and anestrus in cattle deficient in manganese that was corrected by manganese supplementation. **Cobalt** deficiency in certain areas may cause a lack of appetite, depraved appetite, inanition, secondary failure of estrum, and delayed onset of puberty in cattle. Hansel reported low hemoglobin values in many anestrous animals. Cobalt is necessary for normal bacterial growth in the rumen. It is concerned in the production of vitamin B_{12}, which is an important factor in maintaining the appetite. In cobalt-deficient soils, legumes usually contain sufficient cobalt; but timothy hay produced on these soils is deficient in cobalt. **Copper and iron** deficiencies in some areas of the United States result in, or are complicated by, anemia, debility, lack of appetite, and consequently a reduced intake of feed. As with cobalt deficiency a secondary inantition, a failure of estrum, and a delayed onset of puberty may occur. Adams, and Wagner have reported on the apparent association of anemia with hemoglobin values below 10 gms, especially in the range of 8.0 to 8.5 gms, per 100 ml of blood, and anestrus, delayed postpartum breeding and possibly repeat breeding in dairy cattle. In some cases this anemia has been related to low iron or copper levels in the forage. In certain areas such as some in Florida, a high molybdenum content in the feed results in severe scouring and loss of condition when copper is not added as a supplement in the feed. This loss of condition may be reflected in failure of estrum in cows or in the delayed onset of puberty in heifers. Wallace, Alderman, Van Rensburg, and Donaldson et al. reported that copper-deficient cattle in New Zealand, England, South Africa and Australia, respectively, have marked general effects of lowered body health, loss of condition, slow growth and rough hair coat with secondary reproductive symptoms of failure of estrum, delayed conception, and infertility.

Iodine deficiency especially in the northern and northwestern parts of the United States may cause the birth of weak, premature or dead calves affected with goiter. Iodine is not known to affect reproductive processes. However, Meites noted that a lack of iodine can depress thyroid function. Hypo- or hyperthyroidism may reduce the secretion of gonadotropic hormones by the pituitary. Moberg reported an increase in conception rate on first service and reduced irregular breeding intervals in herds in Finland receiving supplementary iodine compared to control herds. In iodine-deficient areas iodine is usually provided in the salt. Severe **salt** deficiency over a long period of time, especially during lactation, will result in severe loss of body weight and anestrus, Smith and Aines. **Zinc** has been shown to be closely associated with reproduction in laboratory animals but deficiencies in the larger domestic animals have not been described.

Treatment of cattle with nutritional deficiencies is essentially one of prevention. In most deficiency areas these deficiencies are known and should be provided for by supplementing the ration. In most areas where cattle raising is profitable, deficiencies are usually uncommon in cattle fed near-normal or balanced rations. Usually general inanition, debility, and other symptoms are evident before reproductive symptoms develop. In most herds expensive mineral supplements are not necessary. Mineral supplements are added to the grain ration at a usual rate of 1 to 1.5 per cent for dairy cattle. In certain mineral-deficient areas and in heavily lactating cows additional amounts or specific mineral supplementation may be necessary. A suitable mineral supplement for dairy areas in the northeast and middlewest consists of 86 lbs. of steamed bone meal or dicalcium phosphate, 12 lbs. of anhydrous ferrous sulfate, and 1.4 lbs of copper sulfate and 1 ounce of cobalt sulphate or cobalt chloride. This can be fed free choice or added in small amounts, 1 ounce daily, to the grain ration, Adams. If rock phosphate is used it should be carefully defluorinated to prevent possible fluorine poisoning. Van Rensburg and de Vos reported that chronic subclinical flourine poisoning induced by feeding 5 to 12 ppm flourine in the drinking water caused anestrum, reduced conception rates and a drop in the pregnancy rate. In some cases subcutaneous injections of 1 to 6 mg of vitamin B_{12}, 10 ml of iron dextran or 300 mg of copper glycinate may be given as needed if feed supplements are difficult to provide, Adams. There are few nutritional factors other than underfeeding that have been shown to have a widespread serious influence on reproductive functions. Bentley and coworkers reported that trace elements had little if any effect on repeat breeding cows. Additional work, adequately planned and controlled, might profitably be applied to this problem of nutrition and fertility.

Miscellaneous nutritive, reproductive problems, especially infertility, may be associated with the consumption of excess estrogens from pasture plants especially during lush growing season. Kallela, Thain, and Green have reported on the high estrogenic content of red clover, Adler and Trainin of alfalfa, Green, and Thain of subterranean clover and Wright of ladino clover. Infertility in cattle consuming such forage has been reported in isolated areas by these authors. Reed, Melrose and Brown, and

Pickard and Crighton have reported that heavy kale feeding caused a reduced conception rate and prolonged intervals between estrous periods after service. No estrogens were found in kale but evidence of a goiterogenic factor was noted. Blood copper and hemoglobin were lower in kale-fed cows, Melrose and Brown.

References

Asdell, S. A. (1949) Nutrition and the Treatment of Sterility in Dairy Cattle: A Review, J. Dairy Sci. **32,** 1, 60.

Adams, R. S. (1969) New Mineral Problems, Cornell Nutrition Conference, January, Mimeographed Material, Penn. State Univ., University Park, Pa.

Alderman, G. (1963) Mineral Nutrition and Reproduction in Cattle, Vet. Rec., **75,** 40, 1015.

Adler, J. H. and Trainin, D. (1960) A Hyperoestrogenic Syndrome in Cattle, Refuah Vet. **17,** 2, 115.

Ammerman, C. B., Thomas, J. W., Miller, W. J., Hogue, D. E. and Hemken, R. W. (1970) Symposium on Trace Minerals—A Review, J. Dairy Sci. **53,** 8, 1097.

Armstrong, D. V., Brown, L. D., Thomas, J. W. and Getty, S. M. (1966) High Level Grain Feeding and Herd Health, J. Dairy Sci. **49,** 6, 730.

Bellows, R. A. (1966) Improving Reproductive Efficiency in Beef Cattle, Vet. Scope **11,** 3, 2.

Bentley, O. G., Quick, V. G., Kastelic, I. and Phillips, P. H. (1951) Certain Trace Elements in the Feeds, Organs and Tissues of a Selected Group of Repeat Breeding Cows in Northeastern Wisconsin, J. of Dairy Sc., **34,** 363.

Carroll, E. J. and Hoerlein, A. B. (1966) Reproductive Performance of Beef Cattle under Drought Conditions, J.A.V.M.A **148,** 9, 1030.

Donaldson, L. E., Harvey, J. M., Beattie, A. W., Alexander, G. I., and Burns, M. A. (1964) Effects of Copper and Cobalt Supplementation on the Growth Rate and Fertility of Shorthorn Heifers in Northern Coastal Queensland, Queensland J. of Agr. Sci. **21,** 167.

Dunn, T. G., Ingalls, J. E., Zimmerman, D. R. and Wiltbank, J. N. (1969) Reproductive Performance of Two-Year-Old Herefords and Angus Heifers as Influenced by Pre- and Post-Calving Energy Intake, J. An. Sci. **29,** 5, 719.

Green, John (1965) Tasmania, Personal Communication.

Gullickson, T. W., Palmer, L. S., Boyd, W. L., Nelson, J. W., Olson, F. C., Caverley, C. E. and Boyer, P. D. (1949) Vitamin E. in the Nutrition of Cattle. Effect of Feeding Vitamin E Poor Rations on Reproduction, Health, Milk Production and Growth, J. of Dairy Sci. **32,** 495.

Hansel, W. (1955) Personal Communication.

Hignett, S. L. (1959) Some Nutritional and Other Interacting Factors Which May Influence the Fertility of Cattle, Vet. Rec. **71,** 247.

Hignett, S. L. (1962) The Influence of Nutrition on the Fertility of Livestock, in **Livestock Infertility,** Animal Health Monograph. #5 F.A.O. Rome, 47.

Kali, J. and Amir, S. (1968) The Relationship between Milk Yield, Level of Nutrition and Body Weight of Cows and their Effect on Conception, Ann. Rept. Oct' 67–Sept '68 "Hasherut" AI Center, Rishon Le Zion, P.O. Box 31, Israel.

Kallela, K. (1965) Finnish Investigations on Plant Oestrogens, Nord. Vet. Med. **17,** 280.

King, J. O. L. (1968) The Relationship Between the Conception Rate and Changes in Body Weight, Yield and S.N F. Content of Milk in Dairy Cows, Vet. Rec. **83,** 492.

Knox, J. H. and Watkins, W. E. (1958) Supplements for Range Cows, N. Mex. Agr. Exp. Stat. Bull. 425, 3.

Littlejohn, S.I. and Lewis, G. (1960) Experimental Studies of the Relationship Between Calcium-Phosphorus Ratio of the Diet and Fertility in Heifers—A Preliminary Report, Vet. Rec. **72,** 1137.

McClure, T. J. (1968) Malnutrition and Infertility in Cattle in Australia and New Zealand, Austral. Vet. J. **44,** 2, 134.

McClure, T. J. (1968) Hypoglycemia, an Apparent Cause of Infertility of Lactating Cows, Brit. Vet. Jour. **124,** 126.

McClure T. J. (1970) A Review of Developments in Nutrition as it is Related to Fertility in Cattle: 1964–1969, New Zeal. Vet. Jour. **18,** 4, 61.

Meites, J. (1953) Relation of Nutrition to Endocrine-Reproductive Functions, Iowa State Col. J. of Sci., **28,** 1, 19.

Melrose, D. E. and Brown, P. B. (1962) Some Observations on the Possible Effect of Kale Feeding on Fertility in Dairy Cattle, J. Reprod. and Fert. **4,** 232.

Moberg, R. (1961) Possible Influences of Supplementary Iodine Administered by Evaporation on Reproductive Performances in Cattle, 4th Intern. Congr. on An. Reprod., The Hague, III, 682.

Morrow, D. A. (1965) The Effect of Energy Intake on Reproduction in Cattle—A Review, Unpublished paper.

Morrow, D. A. (1969) Phosphorus Deficiency and Infertility in Dairy Heifers, J.A.V.M.A. **154,** 7, 761.

Moustgaard, J. (1969) Nutritive Influences Upon Reproduction, in **Reproduction in Domestic Animals,** 2nd Ed. by H.H. Cole and P.T. Cupps, Academic Press, N.Y.C., 489.

Olds, D. (1953) Infertility in Cattle—A Review, J.A.V.M.A., **122,** 913, 276.

Pickard, D.W. and Crighton, D.B. (1967) An Investigation into the Possible Oestrogenic Effect of Kale, Brit. Vet. Jour., **123,** 2, 64.

Reed, H.C. B. (1961) Relationship Between Kale and Fertility in Dairy Cattle, 4th Internat. Congr. on An. Reprod. (Hague) III, 457.

Reid, J. T. (1949) Relationship of Nutrition to Fertility in Animals, J.A.V.M.A. **114,** 864, 158 and 865, 242.

Reid, J. T. (1956) Nutrition and Feeding of Dairy Cattle, J. Dairy Sci. **39,** 6, 735.

Reid, J. T. (1959) Plane of Nutrition and Livestock Performance, Proc. 1959 Cornell Nutrition Conference for Feed Manufacturers, 56.

Reid, J. T., Loosli, J. K., Trimberger, G. W., Turk, K. L., Asdell, S. A. and Smith, S. E. (1964) Causes and Prevention of Reproductive Failures in Dairy Cattle, IV. Effect of Plane of Nutrition During Early Life on Growth, Reproduction, Production, Health and

Longevity of Holstein Cows, Bull. 987, Corn. Univ. Agr. Exp. Stat., Ithaca, N.Y.

Rogas, M. A. and Dyer, I. A. (1964) Manganese Deficiency in the Bovine, J. An. Sci. **23,** 2, 600 (Abstr.).

Smith, S. E. and Aines, P. D. (1959) Salt Requirements of Dairy Cows, Bull. 938, N Y. State College of Agric, Ithaca, N.Y.

Sorensen, A. M., Hansel, W., Hough, W. H., Armstrong, D. T., McEntee, K. and Bratton, R. W. (1959) Causes and Prevention of Reproductive Failures in Dairy Cattle, I Influence of Underfeeding and Overfeeding on Growth and Development of Holstein Heifers, Bull. 936, Cornell Univ. Agr. Exp. Stat. Ithaca, N.Y.

Sprague, J. I. (1963) Range Cattle Nutrition, Coop. Ext. Service and An. Sci. Dept., Colo. State Univ., Ft. Collins, Colo.

Thain, R. I. (1967) Evidence for the Widespread Involvement of Clover Pastures in Bovine Infertility in Tasmania, Austral. Jour. Sci. **29,** 220.

Van Rensburg, S. W. J. (1961) Copper Deficiency Influences Animal Fertility, Farming in S. Afr., March, 50.

Van Rensburg, S. W. J. and de Vos, W. H. (1966) The Influence of Excess Flourine Intake in the Drinking Water on Reproductive Efficiency in Bovines, Onderstepoort J. Vet. Res. **33,** 185.

Wagner, W. C. (1962) Improving Fertility in Dairy Cows, J.A.V.M.A. **140,** 9, 939.

Wallace, L. R. (1949) Nutritional Basis of Fertility, New Zealand Dept. of Agr., Ruakura Animal Research Stat., Hamilton, New Zealand, 3.

Wilson, J. G. (1966) Bovine Functional Infertility in Devon and Cornwall: Response to Manganese Therapy, Vet. Rec. **79,** 20, 562.

Wiltbank, J. N. (1963) Energy Level Important in Reproductive Performance in Beef Cattle, Progress Report, Univ. of Nebr.

Wiltbank, J. N., Bond, J., Warwick, E. J., Davis, R. E., Cook, A. C., Reynolds, W. L. and Hazen, W. M. (1965) Influence of Total Feed and Protein Intake on Reproductive Performance in the Beef Female Through Second Calving, Tech. Bull. 1314, Agr. Res. Service, U.S.D.A., Washington, D.C.

Wiltbank, J. N. and Faulkner, L. C. (1970) The Mangement of Beef Breeding Programs, Bov. Pract. **5,** 23.

Wiltbank, J. N., Rowden, W. W., Ingalls, J. E., Gregory, K. E., and Kock, R. M. (1962) Effect of Energy Level on Reproductive Phenomena of Mature Hereford Cows, J. An. Sci. **21,** 2, 219.

Wright, P. A. (1960) Infertility in Rabbits Induced by Feeding Ladino Clover, Proc. Soc. Exper. Biol. and Med. **105,** 428.

Congenital or Hereditary Causes of Infertility in Cows

Congenital or hereditary causes of sterility or infertility may be divided into those produced by definite anatomical defects of the reproductive organs, and those hereditary forms of infertility that are obscure, possibly due to multiple factors and difficult to assess. Because of the rapid advances in recent years in the control and elimination of many infectious venereal causes of infertility the genetic causes of infertility are assuming greater importance. Excellent reviews of this subject have been made by Young, Gilmore, Rollinson, Foote and Johansson.

Hereditary or Congenital Anatomic Defects of the Reproductive Tract

Hereditary defects are usually due to single gene effects. Certain genes adversely affect both cows and bulls whereas others are sex-limited in their effect. In some females because of the severity of the abnormalities, sterility is manifested at the time of their first service period; while in other cows, in which the defect is less severe, it may not be detected until late in life.

Hypoplasia of the ovaries and testes has been well described by Ericksson, Lagerlof and Settergren, Lagerlot and Boyd, and Settergren. This defect is conditioned by a single recessive autosomal gene with incomplete penetration. This gene affects both cows and bulls in equal proportions. The affected ovary may be partially or totally hypoplastic. Depending on the severity of the hypoplasia and whether the condition is unilateral or bilateral, infertility or sterility will result. (See Figure 118) In the latter instance the affected heifer is anestrous. The origin of this condition in the polled Swedish Highland breed of cattle traced back to two bulls born about 1900. Through extensive use of these bulls and of their offspring, because of the high-butter-fat production of these individuals, the condition was spread widely. In cows with hypoplastic ovaries, 87.1 per cent were left-sided, 4.3 per cent were right-sided and 9.6 per cent involved both ovaries. This condition can be recognized in the affected Swedish Highland heifers by rectal examination as early as 9 months of age. The incidence of partial or transitional hypoplasia occurred in about the same percentage as the total hypoplasia of the ovaries or testes. These intermediate conditions can be evaluated only by repeated rectal examinations of the ovaries over a period of time or at the time of slaughter. The hypoplastic ovary undergoes incomplete development and a part or the whole ovary lacks a normal number or complement of primordial follicles. Settergren (1964) reported that both ovaries of normal heifers contained a total of 50,700 primordial follicles, range 6,800 to 100,000. Both ovaries, in affected heifers in which one ovary was totally or partially hypoplastic averaged 19,000 to 23,000 primordial follicles. In affected heifers with bilateral hypoplasia there was less than 500 primordial follicles in partially affected ovaries and no follicles were present in the heifers with totally hypoplastic ovaries. In heifers the hypoplastic ovary is so small that it may be difficult to locate. It is a thin, narrow, structure of firm consistency, or in severe cases only a cord-like thickening in the cranial border of the ovarian ligament. The ovary has a shriveled or shrunken appearance affecting the entire ovary in total hypoplasia (See Figure 118) or usually the medial half or two-thirds of the ovary in partial hypoplasia. In other cases one-half of the ovary feels slightly raised and firm like a pea. In other cases the ovary of an adult cow may feel like a kidney bean with the surface smooth and stretched. If the surface of the ovary is rough due to luteal scars the ovary can be considered functional. In one-sided hypoplasia the tubular portion of the genital tract develops normally. In bilateral total hypoplasia the genital tract remains very small and infantile; estrum does not occur and there is no development of the secondary sex characteristics due to a lack of estrogens. In bilateral total hypoplasia the heifer is like a steer with long legs, a narrow pelvis, a poorly developed udder with small teats, and a small, firm uterus. In bulls similar hypoplastic changes affect the testes. Settergren reported that Swedish Highland cattle that were totally white or had nearly completely white ears included in their number all cows with hypoplastic ovaries. Those with black or red ears were not affected. Thus the degree of white color was associated with hypoplasia.

Through efforts of the Swedish government, the breed association, owners, and veterinarians, a campaign to control this condition has been established by culling affected animals. The incidence of this condition has dropped from 17.5 per cent of the cattle in the Swedish Highland breed in 1936 to 9.4 per cent in 1948. In 1952 Lagerlof and Boyd on the basis of examination of the genital organs from 6286 Swedish Highland cattle found the incidence of hypoplasia of the left ovary to be 6.6 per cent, right ovary 0.5 per cent, and of both ovaries 0.09 per cent; a partial hypoplasia of the left ovary of 3.3 per cent, of the right ovary 1.1 per cent, and of both ovaries 1.6 per cent; or an incidence of total hypoplasia of 7.2 per cent and partial hypoplasia of 6.0 per cent in the cattle examined. The incidence of this condition was severe enough in certain areas of Sweden that it resulted in a great increase in the incidence of right horn pregnancies which in 1939 was reported by Lagerlof to be about 74 per cent. At the rate of decline in the incidence of the defect observed between 1936 and 1952, it would take more than a century to reduce it to less than 0.5 per cent—a striking demonstration of the insidiousness and seriousness of some hereditary defects! Settergren's recent report showed however that the incidence of gonadal hypoplasia in cattle in Sweden had leveled off and remained about the same from 1954 to 1964.

Hypoplasia of the gonads is not known to occur in any hereditary pattern nor in any particular breed in the United States. Spurrell described the condition in 59 of 2935 cows or heifers. Zemjanis et al. reported an incidence of 1.9 per cent ovarian hypoplasia in over 20,000 cows examined in Minnesota. Gibbons described several cases in closely-related Shorthorn cattle. Many other veterinarians including the author have observed occasional cases of unilateral or bilateral, total, partial or transitional hypoplasia in cows. The rare cattle with bilateral total hypoplastic ovaries are sold as sterile but the danger of breeding the unilaterally or partially affected cattle should be seriously considered, and slaughter probably advised. In hypoplasia treatment with gonadotropes or estrogens is useless. The condition of hypoplasia should be differentiated from nonfunctional or atrophic ovaries in cows and small, inactive ovaries in heifers associated with a delayed onset of puberty due to inanition or marked underfeeding.

A gonadless condition or lack of one or both gonads has been described in cattle by Fincher, and Lagerlof and Boyd. The latter reported one case of a uterus unicornis in which only one ovary was present. In Fincher's report the condition of a complete failure of development of gonads occurred in 3 heifers from the same dam sired by different bulls. The dam was inbred. The cow had 2 normal daughters; one was a twin and the other a full sister of 2 of the gonadless daughters. Gilmore indicated that this was probably an inherited autosomal dominant. These gonadless heifers appeared normal until breeding age, but no estrum occurred and normal udder development was lacking. The genital tracts of these heifers were juvenile and undeveloped. Fincher cited another case of a gonadless heifer, not related to the previous ones, in which a mucometra was present.

Developmental defects in the tubular portions of the bovine reproductive tract—Most of these defects are probably hereditary in origin although some cases may be congenital. **Segmental aplasia of the Mullerian or paramesonephric ducts** and especially an **imperforate hymen** have been called "white heifer disease" because of the association of these genetic defects with white coat color. Ginther and Van Loen in their reviews of these conditions reported that the Mullerian ducts fuse and develop in the bovine embryo when it is 5 to 15 cm. long or is 35 to 120 days of age. The author has grouped these conditions together because the defects as described by Spriggs in England, Boyd in Minnesota, and Fincher and Williams in New York State are very similar. "White-heifer disease" was so named because it occurs most commonly in white heifers of the Shorthorn breed. This condition is considered by Spriggs to be caused by a single, recessive, sex-limited gene with linkage to the gene for white color. Besides occurring commonly in about 10 per cent of white Shorthorns, it has also been described in roan and red Shorthorns, Angus, Holsteins, Jerseys, Guernseys, Ayrshires and other breeds of cattle. Fincher and Williams described the condition they called arrested development of the Mullerian ducts as occurring in a Holstein herd due to inbreeding a valuable sire upon his own daughters. Of 23 female offspring that were raised to breeding age, 12, or 56 per cent, were sterile and 10 were of either low fertility or normal fertility. On the basis of Fincher and Williams' report, Gregory, Regan and Meade stated that the condition was definitely due to a single, autosomal, recessive gene causing a sex-linked sterility due to inbreeding to a sire homozygous for this gene.

No single lesion is descriptive of this condition and a wide variety of anatomical defects may be noted. (See Figures 120–128) For ease of description the author will generally follow Spriggs' classification. Segmental aplasia of oviducts is very rare. Settergren and Galloway reported 2 cases in 2230 organs examined in Sweden. The author has only observed two cases in his entire experience. Rarely a parovarian cyst may obstruct an oviduct.

The most severely affected cattle are sterile due to the bilateral nature of the defects. These may be characterized by a hymenal constriction; absence of either the cranial part of the vagina, the cervix, or the uterine body, including part of the horns; and a cystic dilation of the uterine horns due to a narrow band of aplasia or a defect near the uterine body. (See Figure 128) More commonly just the apices of the uterine horns containing yellow, tan to dark-reddish-brown mucus are present. This cystic apical dilation may vary from the size of an acorn to the approximate size of a 4-months pregnant uterus, containing a few ml to a gallon or more of watery, thick, gummy or inspissated mucus. (See Figures 126, 127) The cystic apices of the uterine horns may be oval, spherical, or nearly the shape of a normal horn, but they are thin-walled and are likely to be sacculated. In rare cases a cystic sacculation of the duct filled with mucus may develop in the region of the cervix (see Figure 120) These cystic dilations may be unilateral and of unequal sizes, depending on the extent of the aplasia. These above conditions as well as alternate constrictions and dilations of the uterine horns are called segmental aplasia of the Mullerian or paramesonephric ducts.

In rare cases 2 small, parallel, firm tubules or cords with a diameter of 0.5 to 0.75 inch are present in the region of the missing vagina, cervix, and uterus for a distance of 4 to 10 inches. They are usually between the cranial portion of the vagina and the uterine horns or vestiges of the uterine horns. These tubules may fuse to form a rudimentary cervix but usually it is imperfectly formed or even absent. The vagina is usually short and narrow, or may have an enlarged or dilated caudal portion containing mucus or occasionally pus, and submucous vaginal channels may be present. These cord-like structures are considered by Fincher, Williams and Boyd, and the author as primitive vestiges of an arrested development of the Mullerian duct. Spriggs indicated that they might be vestiges of the primitive Wolffian ducts. Further embryological studies of this condition may be necessary to establish the correct diagnosis and terminology. In rare instances there is a marked arrest in development, aplasia, or hypoplasia of the vagina and Mullerian duct system, characterized by a lack of a normal vagina, cervix, or uterus (see Figure 121)

Segmental aplasia involving the uterine horns is not uncommon and if only one horn is involved, the condition is called a uterus unicornis. (See Figures 125 and 126) A hymenal constriction may be but usually is not present. These animals may be fertile or infertile, usually the latter with prolonged intervals between estrous periods and repeated services per conception because conception cannot occur if ovulation takes place on the side of the abnormal horn. In a total of 20 cases of uterus unicornis described by Spriggs, Fincher and Williams, Roberts, Lagerlof and Boyd, Woelffer, and Doby, and 2 cases recently observed by the author, there were 14 with a normal left horn and a missing or defective right horn, and 6 had a normal right horn with a defective left horn. Tiege reported on 26 cases of uterus unicornis of which 17 were sterile or probably sterile. He emphasized the hereditary nature of these defects of the tubular portion of the bovine genital tract and the danger of their spread by AI bulls. Hofliger also published a complete literature review of uterus unicornis. The size of the cystic apex of the missing horn varies from 0.5 to 6 or 8 inches in diameter. The rest of the anomalous horn is usually a dense, flat band of tissue. In 2 of these cases of uterus unicornis the cervix was large and thick and filled with masses of dense mucus, like a cervical seal. In 5 cases the mucus in the cystic apex or incomplete, defective horn had become dried and appeared tan to brown in color, putty-like, gummy, or dried like a dense gum eraser into 2 to 7 irregular-shaped, 0.5 to 1 inch solid masses, with fluid mucus like heavy oil around the dried or inspissated masses. These objects were composed of cellular and amorphus material. In most cases the mucus was fluid, watery in consistency and a translucent to opaque, yellow to reddish-brown color. (see Figure 126)

Congenital lack of endometrial glands in the bovine uterus has been observed in a few heifers. (See section on anestrum and report by Ginther). These heifers exhib-

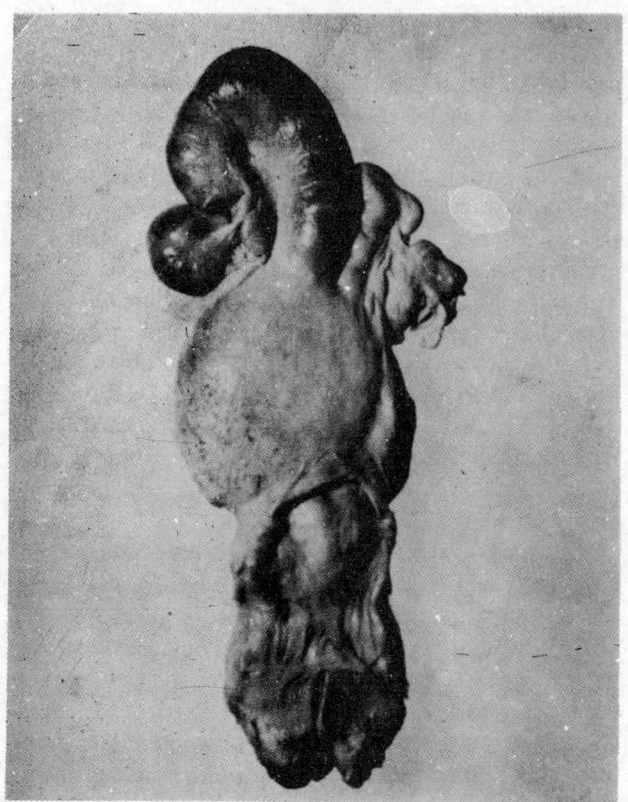

Figure 120. Uterus Didelphys with Unilateral Mucocervix and Mucometra (Note the distention of the left uterine horn simulating a 50-day pregnancy and a CL in the right ovary.)

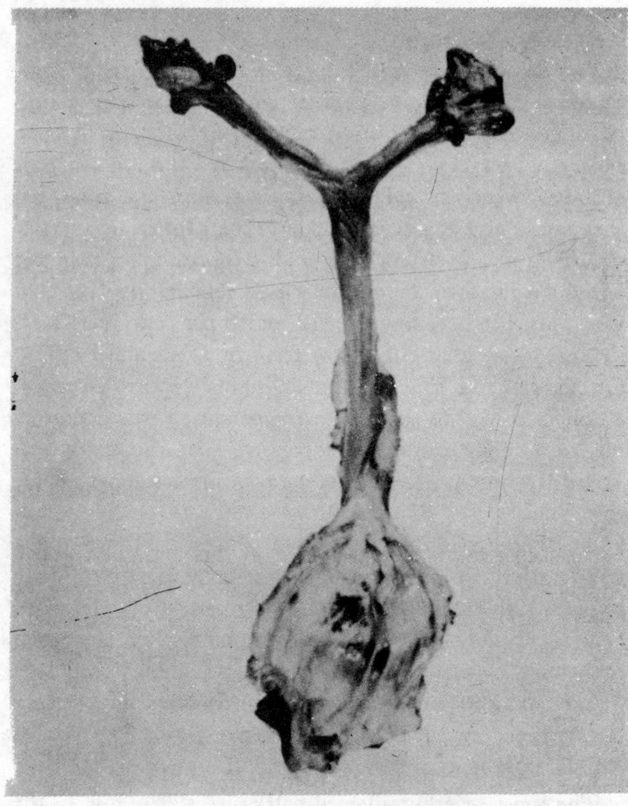

Figure 121. White Heifer Disease With a Marked Aplasia of the Vagina, Cervix and Uterus (Note the normal ovaries, oviducts and vulva).

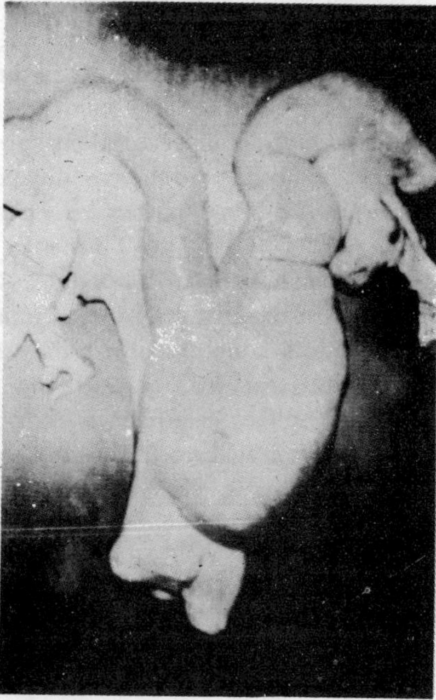

Figure 122. Segmental Aplasia of the Cervix with Secondary Hydrometra in a Heifer. (Note resemblance to a 2-month pregnancy.) (Courtesy K. McEntee).

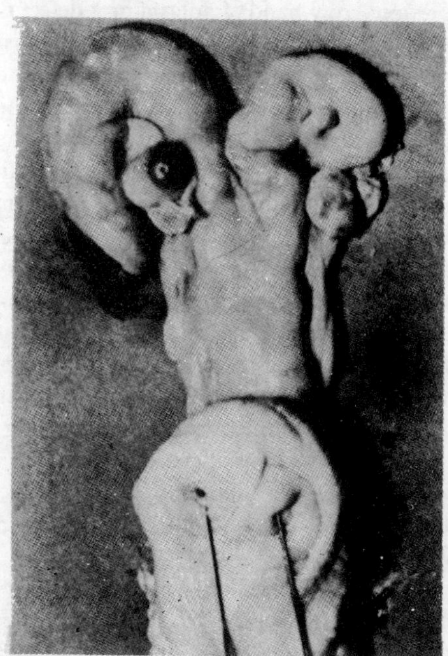

Figure 123. Double External Os of the Cervix Due to the Persistence of the Median Wall of the Paramesonephric Ducts in a Cow. (Courtesy Ohio State Univ.)

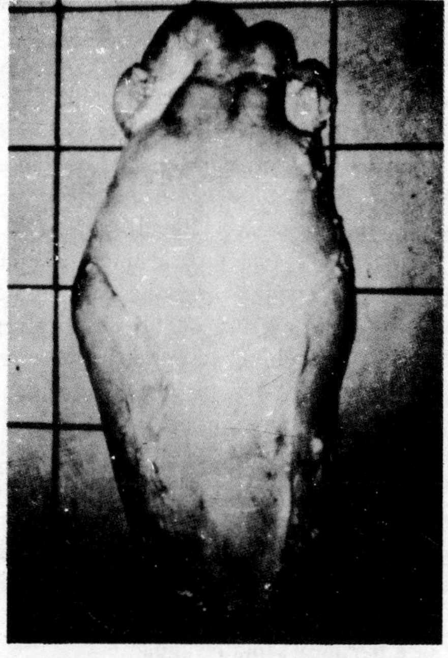

Figure 124. White Heifer Disease with an Imperforate Hymen Causing Mucovagina, Mucocervix and Mucometra.

Figure 125. Uterus Unicornis in a Cow.

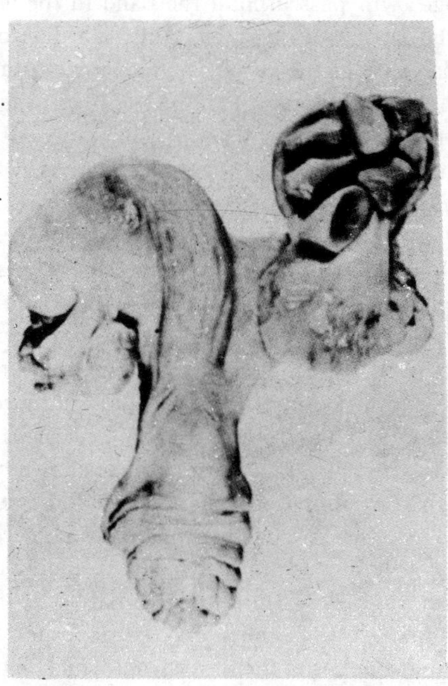

Figure 126. Uterus Unicornis with a Cystic Apex Containing Bodies of Inspissated Mucus.

Figure 127. Segmental Aplasia of the Right Uterine Ho an Accumulation of Inspissated Mucus. (Note the 90 the left horn. The right horn contents resemble a mummi.

ited a failure of estrum and a retained or persistent corpus luteum apparently due to a failure of the endometrium to produce the luteolytic factor necessary for the involution of the corpus luteum. Manual removal of the corpus luteum results in estrum in about 3 to 4 days but the next corpus luteum also persists. The author has observed other sterile heifers that cycled normally but lacked caruncles or caruncular areas in the endometrium. Whether this is genetic or congenital is not known.

Genetic or congenital anomalies of the cervix of cattle is not uncommon. Segmental aplasia may rarely occur resulting in mucometra or a cystic enlargement of the cervix. (See Figure 120 and 128) Petersen et al. described a high incidence of developmental defects of the paramesonephric duct system associated with infertility and sterility in Jersey and Shorthorn heifers in Australia. Besides segmental uterine aplasia infertile heifers had sacculations 1 to 4 cm in diameter, diverticulums 1 to 2 cm deep, and dilations of the cervix due to defects at the third or fourth cervical rings. Similar defects have been observed in Jersey heifers and in other breeds in New York State, McEntee. These defects are invariably filled with thick mucus and most affected heifers fail to conceive. These may often be diagnosed by rectal palpation of the cervix aided by a small metal probe such as a uterine catheter.

Double external os of the cervix in cattle is occasionally observed and is believed to be an instance of failure of the Mullerian ducts to fuse. (see Figure 123) These seldom interfere with conception. Lagerlof and Boyd described the condition as being present in 118 cattle of the Swedish Highland breed, 2 per cent of 5,950, sent to slaughter. Spriggs cited many references of the condition in England and elsewhere and stated that it was present in about 0.2 per cent of the cattle. Settergren and Wright examined 514 genital tracts from dairy cattle, mainly Holstein, in New York State in 1969–70 and found 12 cases or 2.3 per cent of a double cervix; in nearly all cases only the caudal half of the cervix was involved. It is observed in many breeds, such as Shorthorns, British Friesian, Guernseys, Herefords, Holsteins, and Brown Swiss. Murray stated that the condition is normally present in the 7.5-cm.-long bovine fetus but disappears during later fetal life. There is evidence to show that this condition is hereditary and may be transmitted as a recessive gene. Van Loen in an extensive review of the double cervix condition in cattle reported that the incidence varied from 0.1 to 18.2 per cent with an average of 0.3 to 7 per cent. He considered the condition to be due to a dominant gene with incomplete penetrance transmitted by either or both the sire and the dam. Sittman, and Sittman et al. studied this condition in Herefords and stated it was caused by a single autosomal recessive gene with low penetrance and variable expressivity. Most cases are apparently isolated or sporadic and are usually found on clinical examination for sterility or at the time of parturition or slaughter. Engelhardt described 1 bull which sired 18 heifers requiring many services before even 7 became pregnant. Many of the sterile heifers had double cervices and other genital abnormalities.

The lesion often occurs as a band of tissue 0.5 to 2 inches in width and 0.5 to 1 inch in thickness, caudal to the external os of the cervix. On speculum examination it may appear as if there were a double os. In other cases there may be a true double external os of the cervix and the band of tissue separating the 2 openings may extend for a short way into the caudal part of the cervical canal. Rarely a true double cervix or uterus didelphys may occur with a complete septum between the 2 cervical canals, each opening into its respective horn. (See Figure 120) In rare instances in a double cervix the median septum between the 2 cervical canals may extend caudally for 4 to 6 inches, producing a doubling of the cranial portion of the vagina or a partially septate vagina.

Affected cows usually conceive and calve normally. Rarely a portion of the fetus will pass on either side of this band of tissue and result in dystocia that is easily relieved by incising the band. Only slight bleeding will occur. Occasionally the placenta may be caught around this band. On vaginal examination of the nonpregnant cow the finger will pass around the band in the anterior vagina. If the median wall of the Mullerian duct persists in the caudal part of the cervix, a true double cervix or uterus didelphys will appear to be present. Passing metal catheters, probes, or narrow forceps, simultaneuously into each external os will reveal whether there is a caudal band in the cervix or a true double cervix. (See Figure 123) Rectal examination in a case of true double cervix or uterus didelphys reveals the cervix to be characteristically broader and flatter than the normal cervix. On rectal examination of cows with the band caudal to the cervix or the doubling of the external os of the cervix this structure may be felt as a thickening in that region; but more often it is considered as an ectropic or large cervical os, especially in older cows. In many cases diagnosis is not made unless a vaginal examination is performed. Many affected cows undoubtedly never have this condition diagnosed.

In cases of true uterus didelphys with a double cervix, conception may be delayed if the animal is artificially inseminated because the semen may be deposited in the cervix on the side opposite the ovary from which ovulation takes place. The author has observed several "repeat-breeder" cows with this type of uterus. Since only one horn takes part in the placentation of the fetus, abortions, premature births, retained placenta, and infertility are more common in these cows than in animals with a normal uterus and cervix. The cattle with the more extreme aberrations of development should be culled as soon as the condition is diagnosed. The offspring should not be used as breeders without recognizing that the condition is probably hereditary. The lesser abnormalities such as a band caudal to the cervix and possibly a median band in the caudal part of the cervix may be easily removed by surgery. If the band in the cervix is large and extends deep into the cervical canal it should be allowed to remain as it seldom interferes with conception or parturition.

Other anomalies of the bovine cervix may include: a short cervix with one or more transverse rings missing; a lack of development of the cervical rings; and as many as one to three per cent of heifers may have a torturous, a sharply curved cervix or a hypertrophied transverse cervical ring so that an artificial insemination pipette may not be able to be passed, McEntee and Engelhardt. In heifers with a short or underdeveloped cervix, infertility is often due to an endometritis; while the bent, torturous or stenotic cervix often is filled with thick mucus and infertility may be associated with the inability of large numbers of spermatozoa to traverse the cervical canal.

In Brahman or Santa Gertrudis cattle or crossbred Brahman cattle a marked hypertrophy of the cervix, probably genetic in origin, may commonly be noted especially in pluriparous cows. The cervix may be 4 to 6 inches, 10 to 15 cm in diameter and 6 to 8 inches, 15 to 20 cm or more in length. This may be mistaken for a large mummified fetus. Because of its large size and weight the cervix pulls the vagina forward and downward occasionally resulting in pneumovagina and a filling of the vagina with urine, Murray. The cause of this hypertrophy is not known but infertility is often present in affected cattle, especially those bred artificially if intrauterine insemination is not employed. Dystocia does not occur due to this hypertrophied cervix. This infertility may be due to the difficulty of fixing the cervix with the rectal band and passing the insemination pipette through the hypertrophied transverse rings; it may also be due to the lowered number of spermatozoa able to traverse the greatly hypertrophied cervix since these cows are quite fertile if bred naturally. The uterus is normal in size. Further study on this condition is indicated.

Infertile heifers with a double cervix, torturous or kinked cervix or a cervix with a dilation or sacculation probably should be culled because of the possible genetic nature of the defect. However these heifers may concieve on repeated natural or artificial service even though in the latter instance the insemination pipette cannot be passed to the cranial portion of the cervix for the deposition of the semen. Careful expert manipulation of the AI pipette or the use of a metal uterine catheter of small diameter, such as the Luken's, or Woelffer catheters, may enable the operator to deposit the semen properly. These techniques are also indicated in the heifers of small breeds such as the Angus and Jersey with a normal but small, possibly juvenile cervix. Munro reported the incidence of these latter cases with constriction of the cervix to be about 0.1 per cent. He recommended injecting 5 mg dienestrol. Dilation of the cervix occurred in 11 of 15 affected heifers within 5 to 25 hours. Large doses of estrogens at estrus usually interfere with conception. Other veterinarians have injected several doses of estrogens at intervals of several weeks to cause a greater growth or maturity in the genital tract and a larger cervix and cervical canal.

In most cases described above the cervical canal is not completely occluded otherwise mucometra would develop due to the inability of mucus to escape from the uterus. In rare cases when natural service and attempts at artificial insemination fail to result in conception in cattle with cervical defects, diluted or preferably undiluted semen may be injected by means of a long needle through the rectal wall, vaginal wall or ischiorectal fossa into the uterine lumen or into the region of the ovary and fimbria of the oviduct on the side of the ovary with the mature Graafian follicle, Fechheimer et al., McDonald and Sampson, Skjerven, and Kenney. The latter author recommended a small amount of air precede the injection of semen into the uterine lumen to make certain of the location of the tip of the needle. He reported that 4 of 6 heifers that had been bred repeatedly and had a torturous, twisted cervix conceived on first service and calved normally when the semen was injected intraperitoneally adjacent to the ovarian follicle. The prognosis for conception by this procedure to bypass a defective cervix is guarded and is probably seldom indicated or desirable.

Developmental defects of the vagina are largely limited to the partially persistent or imperforate hymen, unusual cases of obliteration of the caudal portion of the vagina, Nordlund, and, as previously described, persistence of the median wall of the paramesomephric duct in the cranial portion of the vagina most commonly seen as a fleshy band just caudal to the external os of the cervix or as a median septum extending 3 to 6 inches caudally resulting in a septate vagina associated with a double cervix. These defects are also probably hereditary in nature although a few may be congenital. (See Figures 121, 123, 124)

Thin fenestrated hymenal membranes or dorsal ventral bands in the region of the vestibular-vaginal border are fairly comm[illegible] in young heifers but are of no significance as they do not obstruct the genital passage and are easily broken at coitus, McEntee. In cases where the hymen is imperforate the condition is also called "white heifer disease". This condition may be associated with segmental defects of the paramesonephric ducts. Rendel reported that in one Shorthorn herd 9 of 23 white hiefers, 4 of 115 roan heifers and 1 of 94 red heifers were affected. He recommended examining all white Shorthorn heifers as calves in a manner similar to that for examining and diagnosing freemartin calves. Spriggs recommended that Shorthorn bulls known to be carriers of the gene for imperforate hymen or segmental aplasia should be bred only to dark roan or red females. The condition of an imperforate hymen may also be seen in Holsteins, Ayrshires, and other breeds of cattle. In these affected cattle the rest of the genital tract is often normal. The animals show regular estrous cycles and symptoms of estrum. The genital tract fills with mucus that is usually amber to dark reddish-brown in color due to metestrual bleeding and may vary in amount from several quarts to 2 or more gallons. Service by artificial insemination is impossible and normal or physiologic coitus by the bull is frequently followed by slight hemorrhage and straining or tenesmus. In rare cases rupture of the vaginal wall may occur with a perivaginal abscess. Rupture of the hymen and a secondary pyometra may develop due to the introduction of infection into the genital tract without proper drainage being possible. If the vaginal distention becomes great, straining may result after service or in heifers even before puberty, and the distended, bulging hymen may show between the vulvar lips with each abdominal contraction or when the heifer lies down. Frequent urination may accompany the tenesmus. In areas in which rabies is endemic this disease may be confused with tenesmus seen in many rabid cattle. In a yearling Holstein heifer observed by the author the greatly distended vagina, containing about 3 to 4 gallons of mucus, caused pressure necrosis of the bladder, rupture of the bladder, and death of the heifer due to peritonitis and uremia. (See Figure 124) Another case was observed in a 7-months-old Shorthorn heifer in which an ulcer and perforation of the distended uterine horn occurred followed by peritonitis and death. In these heifers the cervix is usually somewhat dilated and the uterine horns are distended similar to a pregnancy of 60 days or more. Horns or portions of horns distended with mucus in segmental aplasia of the paramesonephric ducts may also lead to a mistaken diagnosis of pregnancy. If conception does occur with heifers having a nearly complete hymen, in some cases a dystocia may result at the time of parturition that will be relieved only by deep episiotomy incisions of the dorsolateral and lateral walls of the vulva. Bleeding may be severe. The prognosis in cases of imperforate hymen is guarded to poor according to Spriggs. The author operated upon one heifer and the animal calved three times subsequently. Other veterinarians have reported similar results. This operation should be performed early.

In affected heifers following the administration of epidural anesthesia the imperforate hymen may be incised over the point of the greatest bulge allowing the mucus to escape. The incision should then be carefully enlarged at right angles in 4 directions. Some veterinarians advise removing the imperforate hymen by a circular incision completely around the margin of the vulvovaginal border. If the heifer is to be kept for some time before slaughter, or if breeding is to be attempted, the vulvovaginal ring should be dilated with a speculum every 2 to 3 days for 2 weeks. Care and attention should be paid to cleanliness, to prevent the introduction of infection resulting in pyometra or metritis. If the vestibulo-vaginal border is very small and stenosed the prognosis is poor and the animal should not be bred lest severe dystocia result at parturition. Fuller reported on two cases of imperforate hymen that apparently healed following service by a bull and conception occured. At the time of calving dystocia resulted requiring incising of the thickened hymen. The author observed an imperforate hymen in a Guernsey heifer that had been "inseminated" artificially on several occasions by a lay technician. The pipette had apparently been introduced through the urethra and into the bladder causing a severe pyelonephritis.

Nordlund described 12 daughters of one Holstein bull that had various defects of the genital tract causing sterility. In 10 of these heifers the AI pipette could only be inserted 6 or 7 cm or the length of the vestibule and the anterior portion of the vagina was distended up to 8 inches in diameter with mucus. In these cases there was an obliteration of the caudal portion of the vagina, not just an imperforate hymeneal membrane, due to an incomplete recanalization of the vaginal anlage in the embryo. About half of these cases also had a uterus unicornis.

Abnormal Wolffian or Gartner's ducts—Abnormalities of Gartner's ducts which are vestiges of the primitive Wolffian or mesonephric ducts in the embryo are rather common in the cow. (See Figure 129) It is not known whether these defects are hereditary. McEntee and Olafson. reported that in hyperkeratosis due to chlorinated napthalene poisoning the Gartner's ducts become greatly enlarged due to metaplastic changes in the epithelial linings of the ducts. Normally these ducts are located beneath the mucosa of the floor of the vagina. They are 2

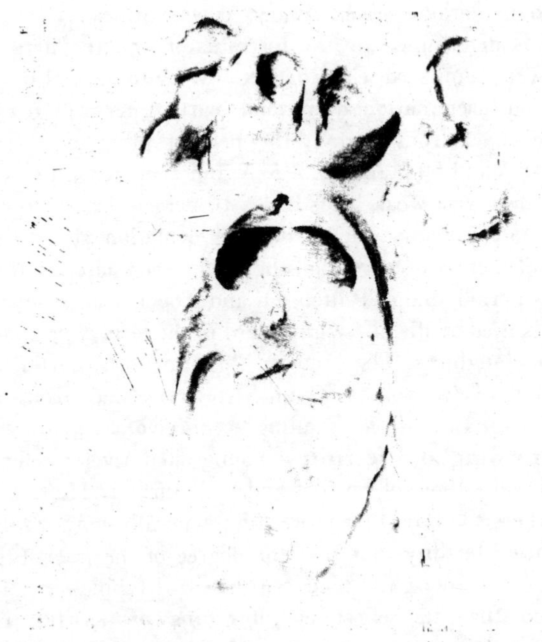
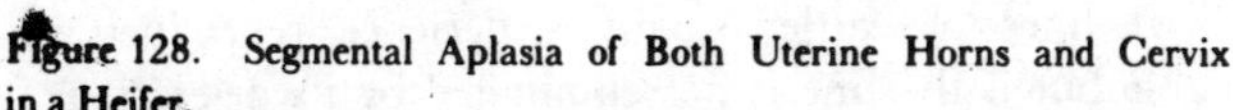

Figure 128. Segmental Aplasia of Both Uterine Horns and Cervix in a Heifer.

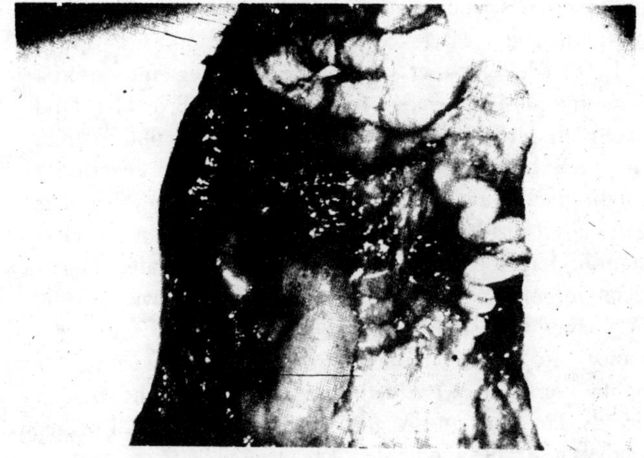

Figure 129. Cystic Gartner's or Mesonephric Ducts in the Floor of the Vagina. (Courtesy K. McEntee)

in number and are usually difficult to detect. The duct may develop multiple cysts along its course toward the cervix or form a long, sometimes rather coiled, cord 0.5 to 1.5 cm. in diameter distended with fluid. In rare instances infection of the duct may occur, with small abscesses forming along its course. In one case Williams found calculi. The ducts may be incised freely, if necessary, to correct these abnormalities but in most cases they are ignored as they do not affect fertility. According to Williams, there may be present in rare cases a cul-de-sac extending forward 2 to 3 inches on either side of the urethral opening. This may be small and admit one finger or less; or it may be large admitting 3 or 4 fingers. This cul-de-sac represents an abnormally large terminus of Gartner's duct and may interfere with coitus.

An infantile, hypoplastic, small vulva was described by Hull and co-workers affecting the daughters of one Jersey bull. In 7 daughters the vulva was so small that at parturition a drastic episotomy operation was required to enlarge it so that the fetus could be removed. In one case cesarean section was necessary. The authors did not report how these heifers were raised, their physical condition, or their size as compared to heifers by other bulls. It is assumed they were probably well grown. These heifers also suffered from a high incidence of albuminuria, nephritis, and urinary calculi.

Miscellaneous Hereditary Forms of Infertility in Cows

Freemartins, or sterile heifers born cotwin to a bull, occur in about 90 percent of the bovine twin births of opposite sexes. Twinning has been discussed and shown previously to be greatly influenced by heredity. This was reviewed by Gilmore and the hereditary aspects of this problem in cattle are fairly well understood.

Intersexes or hermaphrodites are observed occasionally in cattle. There are no reports on cattle that this condition is due to heredity, as in goats, swine and possibly sheep.

Nymphomania or cystic ovaries is influenced by hereditary factors, as indicated previously. This hereditary predisposition toward cystic ovaries is closely associated with high levels of milk production but not to total fat or fat percentage. Garm indicated that the relationship was a physiological-hormonal one and that genetic correlation between high milk yield and cystic ovaries had not been proved. Cystic ovaries are more frequent in daughters of cows having cystic ovaries and in daughters of certain bulls.

Jersey and Holstein female sterility observed in heifers were reported upon by Gregory, Regan and Mead in 1945, by Gregory et al. in 1951, and by Kidwell et al.. Their data indicated that random inbreeding of selected sires and dams showed they carried autosomal recessive genes for female sterility as based on failures of heifers to conceive. The Jerseys showed regular estrum whereas the Holsteins exhibited irregular estrous periods and usually anestrum. It is unfortunate that careful anatomical, histological, and bacteriological examinations of the genital tracts, ovaries, and pituitaries of these sterile heifers were not performed.

In Sweden the per cent of heifers pregnant on first insemination is 6 per cent higher in the SKB or Highland breed, despite the problem of gonadal hypoplasia, than the SRB breed. These breed differences are genetically conditioned, Bane. In the U.S.A. the Guernsey breed is generally considered to have lower fertility than the Holstein or Jersey breeds as based on nonreturn rates to artificial insemination. The pregnancy rate in over 10,000 beef cows was studied over a 5-year period. The pregnancy rate for Zebu purebreds or crosses, Brahman or Santa Gertrudis were definitely lower than the British breeds, Hereford and Angus, 57 vs 72.5 per cent. Further study is desirable and needed, Meade et al..

Sexual behavior in the cow has been shown by Young and others to be affected by heredity. The estrous cycles in an individual cow tend to be of similar length. Variations in cycle length were much more common between cows than within individual cows. When normal cycles of 18 to 24 days are considered there is a great tendency in each cow to maintain a consistent cycle length. Olds and Seath reported that in individual cows there was a definite tendency of the interval between parturition and the first estrum to remain similar after each parturition. Daughters had similar records to their dams, and daughters by the same bull also tended to be similar. Olds and Seath concluded that the heritability for the time at which estrum occurs after calving was about 30 per cent.

Lagerlof noted that "weak" symptoms of estrum were one of the most common or troublesome problems in artificial insemination. These "weak" or nearly "silent" estrous periods were observed most commonly in certain breeds of cattle such as the Swedish Red Cattle, while other breeds such as the Simmenthaler, Telmark, and Swedish Highland catlle exhibited intense symptoms of estrum even in an unfavorable environment. Rollinson also noted the genetic difference in potency and strength of signs of estrus between dairy, beef and other breeds. This difference between breeds has not been as noticeable in the United States. It has been observed by the author as occurring in certain families of Guernsey and Holstein cattle, most commonly in the former breed. Repeat breeding is more common in cows with a weak estrum because of the difficulty of timing artificial insemination in relation to ovulation. When 34,063 cows with weak heat signs, as determined by the inseminator and the herdsman, were compared with 263,906 cows with normal heat signs and inseminations were made early, intermediate or late in the estrous period, the percent pregnant were 39.5, 45.6 and 50.2 and 55.3, 57.9 and 55.1, respectively. Thus cows with weak heats had a 10 percent lower pregnancy rate possibly due to delayed ovulation since the least difference occurred in the cows bred late in the estrous period, Bane. Rottensten and Touchberry studied 29 bulls used artificially with regard to the heat symptoms in their daughters. They showed this trait to be partially hereditary. Cows conceiving on first service had stronger heat signs than those cows failing to conceive.

Inbreeding and fertility—Young cited several references besides those of Fincher and Williams and Hull and co-workers to show that inbreeding generally may result in reduced fertility, but that the degree of the infertility depends on the particular bull used. Krehbiel et al. reported that the effect of inbreeding on fertility is uniquely the property of a particular line or family. Inbred lines of cattle usually experience reproductive trouble but if the line is not eliminated by its deleterious genes, as often happens, then fertility may remain fairly satisfactory. Mares et al. and Conneally et al. showed that inbreeding of the zygote and dam, and homozygosity for blood group factors greatly increased embryonic mortality. Lower conception rates occurred when the potential embryo was inbred rather than outbred and pregnancy loss was greater when the dam was inbred rather than outbred. Heterosis improved fertility.

Production and fertility. Asdell and Phillips as cited by Young have shown on the basis of relatively small numbers that high-producing cows were no more often disposed of as infertile than were low-producing cows. The relationship between high-butter-fat yield and ovarian hypoplasia and high milk yield and cystic ovaries has previously been mentioned. Probably more study on this phase of fertility from the hereditary aspect is indicated but at present there is more data indicating that milk production is not associated with infertility.

The inheritance of normal fertility or lowered fertility may be studied from a number of aspects, including inheritance from bulls to their daughters, from dams to their daughters, from bulls to bulls, and from dams to bulls. Only the first 2 aspects have been studied. It has been noted by Young and Foote that workers in estimating fertility have difficulty in obtaining a standard or means of measuring fertility. This was not a problem when specific genes were involved as in ovarian hypoplasia and segmental aplasia of the Mullerian ducts, but it is a great problem when measuring reduced or subfertility. The conception rate is a good measure but does not take into consideration those animals that fail to show regular estrums. It excludes barren heifers or cows, if figures are obtained from calving dates. If the figures include animals that abort, the results may be biased because some less-valuable animals may be sold as sterile after several breedings while more valuable animals may be retained and eventually conceive. Calving intervals may be used to measure fertility but they include only animals that have calved, and may be biased by a planned extension of calving intervals in cases of persistent or heavy producers. Completely sterile animals may be studied separately but this excludes the large group exhibiting reduced fertility. For these reasons most studies on infertility are not comprehensive. Some investigations using certain indices show that genetic factors are unimportant, but nearly all can be questioned on the basis of bias in the material. Similarly many investigations show genetic factors to be important but these can usually be criticized because they deal with only one breed or herd or family and one particular character. Thus care should be taken to avoid generalizations on the basis of only a few studies. Possibly the problems of inheritance of fertility in cattle cannot be arrived at until the problem of disease has been adequately controlled.

Research on **the relative fertility of the daughters of different bulls** has been summarized by Young, Gilmore, Olds, Deese and Koger, and Rollinson. In these reports and in one by Trimberger and Davis there appeared to be a difference in the fertility of daughters of various bulls. Other studies by Dunbar and Henderson showed that on the basis of nonreturns to first service and calving intervals the difference in fertility between daughters of various sires was small. Tyler et al. reported that the heritability of conception rate from intrasire correlations of paternal half-sib group of cows was about 8.5 per cent. Thus preference in breeding should be given to those sires whose daughters were of high fertility. However, some inbreeding studies and studies in which certain sires transmitted a specific defect must be considered. Sex-linked genes for infertility in daughters of certain bulls was reported by Gregory et al. and Kidwell et al..

The inheritance of fertility from female to female, as shown by many workers cited by Young, Gilmore, Foote, and Rollinson has been studied from the standpoint of the recurrence of any given pattern of breeding ability. Most workers, including Trimberger and Davis, and Olds and Seath have concluded that the condition of "repeat-breeding" is not very permanent. However, there is a slight tendency to repeat the same breeding pattern from one service period to the next. In studying cow families Spielman and Jones cited by Trimberger and Davis and others reported considerable differences in reproductive efficiency as measured by calving intervals and conception rates. Other workers cited by Young reported little difference between cow families and noted that cows in cow families are not as a rule closely related. Thus in respect to cow families the inheritance of infertility based on a number of studies is contradictory and unpredictable. In studying **dam-daughter comparisons** 5 reports cited by Young indicated that the heritability of conception rate is not high and is probably under 10 per cent. **Herd differences in fertility,** according to Trimberger and Davis, Olds and Seath and Young even though genetic composition varied greatly, were affected little or not at all by the genetic differences. Since the genetic composition of a herd does not vary much from year to year and fertility may vary markedly, it is rather obvious that most of the herd differences in fertility are due to environmental rather than to genetic causes.

From the above studies Young concluded that about 80 per cent of the variation in normal fertility in herds is due to environmental causes and that of the remaining 20 per cent about one-half would appear to be due to various additive genetic effects. As Dunbar and Henderson, Foote and Erb et al. have shown, selection for fertility cannot be very effective. Automatic natural selection against infertility is going on constantly. It is possible that epistatic effects are responsible for much of the permanent differences between cows. Young stated that if this is true, cross breeding to produce heterosis is a better genetic method than is selection for improving fertility. In may be true that specific breeds adapted to certain environments would be necessary to obtain maximum fertility. In either case environmental influences would still make genetic progress very slow. Little attention need be paid to selective breeding as an effective means of raising fertility but should be considered constantly when advising farmers on aspects of inbreeding or on definite evidences of a single gene predisposing to or causing sterility. As pointed out by Young there is a great natural prolificacy in the dairy breeds. He showed that in the Dexter breed, despite the death of 25 per cent of the bulldog fetuses, and a ban on breeding another 25 per cent of the Kerry type heifers, the breed can still continue to expand a little. He concluded that although sterility is economically costly it would have to be very severe to cause a reduction in a breed or herd due to lack of replacements.

References

Bane, A. (1964) Fertility and Reproductive Disorders in Swedish Cattle, Brit. Vet. Jour. **120,** 431.

Boyd, W. L. (1944) A Clinical Study of White Heifer Disease, Cor. Vet., **34,** 4, 337.

Conneallv, P. M., Stone, W. H., Tyler, W. J., Casida, L. E. and Morton, N.E. (1963) Genetic Load Expressed as Fetal Death in Cattle, J. Dairy Sci. **46,** 3, 232.

Deese, R. E. and Koger, M. (1967) Heritability of Fertility in Brahman and Crossbred Cattle, J. An. Sci. **26,** 5, 984.

Doby, P. B. (1951) Instances of Reproduction with Uterus Unicornis and Uterus Didelphys, Vet. Med., **46,** 2, 60.

Dunbar, R. S. J. and Henderson, C. R. (1950) Heritability of Fertility in Dairy Cattle, J. of Dairy Sci., **33,** 6, 277.

Engelhardt, B. (1952) Fertility Disorders Due to Malformations of the Female Genitals in Heifers of the Black and White Lowland Breed (Frisian-Holstein) in Sweden, 2nd Internat. Congr. of An. Reprod. Copenhagen, Vol. III, 48.

Erb, R. E., Hinze, P. M. and Gildow, E. M. (1959) Factors Influencing Prolificacy of Cattle II, Tech. Bull. 30, Washington State Univ., Agr. Exp. Stat.

Eriksson, K. (1938) Investigations Respecting the Heredity of Genital Hypoplasia in Cattle, Skand. Vet., **28,** 7.

Eriksson, K. (1954) Genetic Analyses of Hereditary Diseases with Incomplete Phenotypic Manifestation, Royal Swedish Acad. of Agric. Scien. Sect. Rept. No. 6, Uppsala, Almquist and Wilsell.

Fechheimer, N. S., Ludwick, T. M. and Ely, F. (1952) A Method For Intrauterine Insemination for Certain Cows, J. Dairy Sci. **35,** 808.

Fincher, M. G. (1954) Personal Communication.

Fincher, M. G. and Williams, W. L. (1926) Arrested Development of the Mullerian Ducts Associated with Inbreeding, Cor. Vet., **16,** 1, 1.

Foote, R. N. (1970) Inheritance of Fertility—Facts, Opinions and Speculations, J. Dairy Sci. **53,** 7, 936.

Fuller, C. E. (1958) Bovine "Sealed Time Capsule", Med. Vet. Pract. **39,** 18, 44.

Gibbons, W. J. (1953) Some Congenital Conditions Interfering with Fertility in Cattle, Proc. A.V.M.A., 90th Ann. Meeting, 399.

Gilmore, L. O. (1952) Dairy Cattle Breeding, F. B. Lippincott Co., N.Y.C.

Ginther, O. J. (1965) Segmental Aplasia of the Mullerian Ducts (White Heifer Disease) in a White Shorthorn Heifer, J.A.V.M.A. **146,** 2, 133.

Gregory, P. W., Mead, S. W., Regan, W. M. and Róllings, W. C. (1951) Further Studies Concerning Sex-Limited Genetic Infertility in Cattle, J. of Dairy Sci., **34,** 10, 1047.

Gregory, P. W., Regan, W. M., and Mead, S. W. (1945) Evidence of Genes for Female Sterility in Dairy Cows, Genetics, **30,** 506.

Hofliger, H. (1960) Beitrag zur Kenntnis der Uterus Unicornis der Haussauger insebesondere des Rindes, Zuchthy. Fortpfl. Storung. Besamung **4,** 99.

Hull, F. E., Dimock, W. W., Ely, F. and Morrison, H. B. (1940) Reproductive Efficiency in Dairy Cattle, Univ. of Ken., Agr. Exp. Stat., Bulletin 402.

Inskeep, E. K., Tyler, W. J. and Casida, L. E. (1961) Hereditary Variation in Conception Rate of Holstein-Friesian Cattle, J. Dairy Sci. **44,** 10, 1857.

Johansson, I. (1961) Genetic Aspects of Dairy Cattle Breeding, Univ. of Ill. Press, Urbana, Ill.

Kenney, R. (1959) Personal Communication.

Krehbiel, E. V., Carter, R. C., Bovard, K. P., Gaines, J. A. and Priode, B. M. (1969) Effects of Inbreeding and Environment on Fertility of Beef Cattle Matings, J. An. Sci., **29,** 4, 528.

Kidwell, J. F., Walker, L. and McCormick, J. A. (1954) Hereditary Female Sterility in Holstein-Friesian Cattle, J. Hered. **45,** 142.

Lagerlof, N. (1950) Personal Communication. Lecture, April 27, 1950.

Lagerlof, N. (1951) Hereditary Forms of Sterility in Swedish Cattle Breeds, Fert. and Steril., **2,** 3, 230.

Lagerlof, N. (1962) Hereditary Factors in Infertility in Cattle, in **Livestock Infertility,** Animal Health Monograph No. 5, F.A.O. Rome, 63.

Lagerlof, N., and Boyd, H. (1953) Ovarian Hypoplasia and Other Abnormal Conditions in the Sexual Organs of Cattle of the Swedish Highland Breed: Results of Postmortem Examination of over 6,000 Cows, Cor. Vet., **43,** 1, 64.

Lagerlof, N. and Settergren, I. (1953) Results of Seventeen Years' Control of Hereditary Hypoplasia in Cattle of the Swedish Highland Breed, Cor. Vet., **43,** 1, 52.

Lagerlof, N. and Settergren, I. (1961) Gonadal Hypoplasia in the Swedish Mountain Breed of Cattle, Zuchthyg. **5,** 141.

Mares, S. E., Menge, A. C., Tyler, W. J. and Casida, L. E. (1961) Genetic Factors Affecting Conception Rate and Early Pregnancy Loss in Holstein Cattle, J. Dairy Sci. **44,** 1, 96.

McDonald L. E. and Sampson, J. (1957) Intraperitoneal Insemination of a Heifer, Proc. Soc. Exper. Biol. and Med. **95,** 815 (Abstr. J.A.V.M.A. **132,** 4, 163 (1958).

McEntee, K. (1970) Reproduction—The Female Genital System, in **Bovine Medicine and Surgery,** Amer. Vet. Public. Inc., Wheaton, Ill, 641.

McEntee, K. (1970) The Female Genital System, in **Pathology of Domestic Animals,** 2nd ed., by K.V.F. Jubb and P. C. Kennedy, Academic Press, N.Y.C.

McEntee, K. and Olafson, P. (1953) Reproductive Tract Pathology in Hyperkeratosis of Cattle and Sheep, Fert. and Steril. **4,** 2, 128.

Meade, J. H. Jr., Warnick, A. C., Koger, M. and Reynolds, W. L. (1959) Genetic and Environmental Influences on Pregnancy Rate in Beef Cattle, J. An. Sci. **18,** 4, 1549.

Munro, I. B. (1956) Constriction of the Cervix at Oestrus in Cattle and Its Response to Dienestrol, Vet. Rec. **68,** 8, 131.

Murray, J. C. (1939) Cervix Bifida in the Domestic Cow, J. of Comp. Path. and Therap., **52,** 135.

Murray, P. C. (1970) Personal Communication.

Nordlund, S. (1956) A New Type of Genital Malformation in Swedish Friesian Cattle, 3rd Internat. Congr. on An. Reprod., Cambridge, Section II, 80.

Olds, D. and Seath, D. M. (1950) Predictability of Breeding Efficiency in Dairy Cattle, J. of Dairy Sci., **33**, 10, 721.

Olds, D. and Seath, D. M. (1954) Factors Affecting Reproductive Efficiency of Dairy Cattle, Kentucky Agr. Exp. Stat., Bull. #605.

Peterson, J. E., Parsonson, I. M., Newsam, I. D. B. and Clark, B. L. (1966) Infertility in Dairy Heifers with Particular Reference to a High Incidence of Developmental Defects of the Paramesonephric Duct System, Austral. Vet. J. **42**, 430.

Rendel, J. M. (1952) White Heifer Disease in a Herd of Dairy Shorthorns, J. Genet. **51**, 89.

Roberts, S. J. (1950) An Unusual Condition Associated with Uterus Unicornis in Cattle, Cor. Vet., **40**, 4, 357.

Rollinson, D. H. L. (1955) Hereditary Factors Affecting Reproductive Efficiency in Cattle, An. Breeding Abstr. **23**, 3, 215.

Rottensten, K. and Touchberry, R. W. (1957) Observations on the Degree of Expression of Estrus in Cattle, J. Dairy Sci., **40**, 1457.

Settergren, I. (1961) The Relationship Between Body and Ear Color and Ovarian Development in Females of the Swedish Highland Breed, Proc. 4th Intern. Congr. on An. Reprod., Hague, Vol. IV, 752.

Settergren, I. (1964) The Ovarian Morphology in Clinical Bovine Gonadal Hypoplasia with Some Aspects of Its Endocrine Relations, Thesis, Stockholm, Acta Vet. Scand. **5**, Suppl. 1.

Settergren, I. (1964) The Number of Primordial Follicles in Clinically Normal and Hypoplastic Heifer Ovaries, 5th Internat. Congr. on Animal Reprod., Trento, Section IV, 188.

Settergren, I. and Galloway, D. B. (1965) Studies on Genital Malformations in Female Cattle Using Slaughterhouse Material, Nord. Vet. Med. **17**, 9.

Settergren, I. and Wright, J. (1970) Personal Communication.

Sittman, K. (1963) Note on the Double Cervix Condition in Cattle, J. of Hered. **54**, 3.

Sittman, K., Rollins, W. C. and Kendrick, J. W. (1961) A Genetic Analysis of the Double Cervix Condition in Cattle, J. of Hered. **52**, 1, 26.

Skjerven, O. (1955) Conception in a Heifer after Deposition of Semen in the Abdominal Cavity, Fert. and Steril. **6**, 1, 66.

Spriggs, D. N. (1945) Double External Os in Cattle, Vet. Jour., **101**, 6, 142.

Spriggs, D. N. (1945) Some Experiences of a Sterility Officer, Vet. Rec., **57**, 42, 469.

Spriggs, D. N. (1946) White Heifer Disease, Vet. Rec., **58**, 37, 405, and 38, 415.

Spurrell, F. A. (1954) Personal Communication, Lecture Penn. State Soc. Meeting, Oct. 1954.

Teige, J. (1956) Congenital Malformations of Ducti Mulleri and the Urogenital Sinus in Cattle, Nord. Vet. Med. **8**, 289.

Trimberger, G. W. and Davis, H. P. (1945) Predictability of Breeding Efficiency in Dairy Cattle from Their Previous Conception Rate and from their Heredity, J. of Dairy Sci., **28**, 9, 659.

VanLoen, A. (1961) A Contribution to the Knowledge of the Double Cervix Condition in Bovine Cattle, Thesis, Univ. of Utrecht, Scheltema and Holkema, Amsterdam.

Williams, W. L. (1943) Diseases of the Genital Organs of Domestic Animals, 3rd Ed., Miss Louella Williams, Upland Rd., Ithaca, N.Y.

Woelffer, E. (1951) Personal Communication.

Young, G. B. (1953) Genetic Aspects of Fertility and Infertility in Cattle, Vet. Rec., **65**, 18, 271.

Zemjanis, R., Larsen, L. L. and Bhalla, R. P. S. (1961) Clinical Incidence of Genital Abnormalities in the Cow, J.A.V.M.A. **139**, 9, 1015.

Other Pathological Causes for Bovine Infertility

The pathological causes of infertility or sterility due to genetic or congenital defects, hormonal disturbances, and venereal infections have been discussed. Most of the following pathological conditions are the result of trauma or infection or both. They are acquired most commonly at or after parturition, producing lesions that may interfere with the future fertility of the cow. Occasionally tumors of the genital organs may be found. Tanabe and Almquist, Mylrea, Zemjanis et al., Perkins et al., Moberg, Cembrowiz, Lagerlof and Boyd, Lombard et al. and Rowson have surveyed and reviewed the gross abnormalities and pathology of the bovine genital tract by variously studying clinical findings and slaughter house material. These authors attempted to evaluate their findings with regard to infertility, sterility and repeat breeding.

Ovary

Most of the ovarian pathology has been previously considered under the endocrine and hereditary abnormalities of the reproductive tract. However; a few conditions remain to be described.

Ovarian Tumors in the cow have been described fairly often but they are uncommon in occurrence. Williams described two malignant tumors of the ovary of the cow, an angiosarcoma and a carcinoma. Fincher described a fibroma of cow's ovary. Wadsworth cited Stickes as reporting 6 carcinomas of the ovary; Feldman described one. In 6,286 bovine genital tracts examined by Lagerlof and Boyd there were 13 ovarian tumors: 3 were carcinomas, 3 granulosa cell tumors, a sarcoma, a fibrosarcoma, and 5 undiagnosed. In rare cases primary tumors may metastasize to the ovary. Other ovarian tumors include: dysgerminoma, mucinous adenocarcinoma, cystadenoma, arrhenoblastoma, vascular hamartoma, dermoid cyst or teratoma containing hair, and lymphosarcoma,

Studer, Boucher et al., McEntee, Megale, Anderson and Davis, Moulton, and Cotchin. In cases of cystadenomas described by Studer and Boucher et al. the tumor spread by contact to the peritoneum resulting in ascites. The author reported on two granulosa cell tumors, one in a 15-month-old Guernsey heifer, the other in a 14-year-old Angus cow. He cited references in the literature to 7 other reports on granulosa cell tumor of the bovine ovary. (see Figure 130) In 3 cases in which the breeding history was known, the animals showed symptoms of chronic nymphomania with frequent prolonged symptoms of estrum and relaxation of the pelvic ligaments. Two of these cases were heifers in which udder development and lactation occurred. Short et al. reported on a similar case and the cystic fluid in the tumor contained progesterone and estradiol in a ratio of 6:1 parts, respectively, continous estrous was explained on the basis of progesterone potentiating the action of the estrogen. The usual ratio of progesterone to estrogen to produce mammary development is 100 to 1 to 1,000 to 1. In other cases where the history was known either anestrum or no observable symptoms were noted, and the cows were pregnant or had normal estrous cycles. Granulosa cell tumors may be either solid and yellow in color, or filled with multiple cysts 0.5 to 3 inches, or 1 to 7.5 cm in diameter or be composed of a single large cyst. Any cyst larger than a grapefruit, 4 inches, or 10 cm, should be suspected of being a granulosa cell tumor. The weight and size of a a large ovarian tumor tends to drag the ovary downward and forward into the abdominal cavity. The ovarian artery to large tumors is likely to be increased in diameter. Sometimes it is necessary to place forceps on the cervix and pull the uterus and ovary upward and backward in order to palpate the tumor. Granulosa cell tumors may affect cattle of all ages from calves to old cows, Kanagawa et al.. According to McEntee and Zepp 17 of 18 bovine ovarian neoplasms they studied were granulosa cell tumors. Granulosa cell tumors were most commonly observed in Guernsey cows. In 4 cases the tumors were found in related animals. In one cow, with a failure of estrum for 6 months, mucometra developed. Three of the tumors were bilateral and only 1 was malignant. (see Figure 130). The size varied from microscopic growths to tumors weighing over 25 lbs. The granulosa cell tumor is the most common one in cattle. It is rarely malignant and seldom spreads to adjacent peritoneal surfaces; it is usually unilateral. The earlier reported cases of some of the ovarian carcinomas in the cow may have been granulosa cell tumors. Some of these tumors produce estrogen, as shown by the symptoms of nymphomania, relaxation of pelvic ligaments, and lactation in heifers. In rare cases large cysts containing 1 to 2 or more quarts of fluid may be associated with a granulosa cell tumor of the ovary. In the cases observed by the author and his associates these very large cysts contain fluid with no estrogen content on assay or as shown by physical change in the cow. Cows can conceive with unilateral granulosa cell tumors if little or no steroid hormone is elaborated by the tumor. There are very few reports on the successful removal of these tumors, with the cow conceiving following treatment.

Ovaritis, Inflammation or Infection of the Ovary, may occur secondary to trauma, to infection from the uterus that passes through the oviducts, or by extension through the uterine walls causing a peritonitis and perimetritis. Trauma may frequently be produced by rough handling or massage of the ovary. Scars, usually star-shaped or transverse, are common in the ovaries of cows where corpora lutea are enucleated or cysts ruptured by manual manipulation per rectum. Bleeding may occur as previously described and a hematoma form around the ovary; subsequently this hematoma organizes and produces extensive adhesions. (See Figure 131) Inflammation of the ovary or oophoritis will be considered more fully under the discussion of lesions of the oviduct especially the distal, fimbriated end, or pavilion, of the oviduct. Rarely abscessation of the ovary may follow removal of the corpus luteum in cows with pyometra, McEntee. Serosal granulomas may be present on the ovary in peritoneal tuberculosis. Particularly in heifers, tags of fibrin are frequently observed attached to the ovary at the site of a previous ovulation or on the medial attachment of the ovary to the uteroovarian ligament.

Parovarian Cysts are occasionally found in the broad ligament of the cow around the ovary and oviduct. These cysts are vestiges of the Wolffian or mesonephric duct system or the paramesonephric or Mullerian duct system and may be from 0.5 to 2 inches or more in diameter. They are usually round or oval in shape. Most paramesonephric duct cysts are located near or in the fimbria of the oviduct. Germinal inclusion or "serosal" cysts about 0.2 to 0.5 cm in diameter may rarely be noted on the surface of the ovary. Occasionally the corpus luteum is black in color, **corpus nigrum.** This is apparently of no significance, as these corpora lutea apparently function normally. McEntee and Zepp stated that in rare instances the **tubules of the rete ovarii** may be confused with a neoplastic growth. The **rete ovarii,** when found in the cow is a network arrangement of medullary tubules found near the mesovarium. Parovarian cysts are less common in the cow than in the dog, sheep, and horse.

Oviduct

Disease of the oviducts or Fallopian tubes and ovarian bursae of cattle occurs more commonly than is generally assumed or diagnosed. Carpenter, Williams and Gilman reported that pathological changes occurred in the oviduct in 15.3 per cent of 1221 cows. Rowson found that of 296 slaughtered cows pathological changes had occurred in 13 per cent, or 40 cattle; of these 18 were bilateral, 14 right-sided, and 8 left-sided. Spriggs in clinically examining 1250 sterile cows found changes in 50, or 4 per cent, of the cases; of these 17 were bilateral, 23 right-sided, and 10 left-sided. Thygesen examined 1614 cows at slaughter and found 142, or 8.8 per cent, with lesions of the oviduct or bursa. Of these 142 cases, 33 were bilateral, 77 cases right-sided, and 32 cases left-sided. Of 242 pregnant cows that he examined only 2 had lesions. Lombard, Morgan and McNutt described the pathologic lesions of the oviduct in 154 "repeat breeding" cows, and found 5 cases of pyosalpinx, 2 unilateral and 3 bilateral, and 7 cases of mild ovario-bursal adhesions. They reported gross lesions in 13 per cent of their cases, or lesions in 18.8 per cent including the cases of chronic interstitial salpingitis. On clinical examination of 2655 cows Nielsen reported 16.7 per cent had salpingo-ovario-bursal lesions. McEntee on careful postmortem examination of 240 sterile cows found 25, or about 10 per cent of the cases, affected with ovario-bursal adhesions. Moberg in an excellent paper reported that of 1622 cows examined in the slaughter house, 251, 15.5 per cent showed some pathology of the oviducts; whereas on clinical examination of 516 sterile cows only 4.8 per cent had lesions that could be detected. In 276 cows in which lesions were present; 69 cases were bilateral, 118 were right-sided, and 89 were left-sided. Of these 276 cases, 70 were due to malformations and cysts, 212 cases were due to adhesions, and only 11 were due to hydrosalpinx. Cembrowicz reported a lower incidence of pathology of the oviduct. In 1030 cattle examined at two English slaughter houses, pathology of the oviduct was observed in 2 per cent of 300 heifers and 8.9 per cent of 730 cows. In 1.6 per cent of the cases cysts were present in the oviduct; in 3 cases they were bilateral, causing complete sterility. The cysts were inflammatory in origin. Hydrosalpinx occurred in 15 cases, or 0.3 per cent of the heifers and 1.9 per cent of the cows. (See Figure 131 and 132) Adhesions were found in the adnexae in 2.52 per cent of the cattle. In purulent endometritis and pyometra 70 per cent of the affected animals had histologic evidence of involvement of the oviducts. The bacterial flora of the oviduct was mixed and not highly virulent. Tuberculosis affected the genital organs in 2.5 per cent of the cows. Zemjanis et al. reported the incidence of disease of the oviduct was 1.3 per cent based on clinical examination; hydrosalpinx occurred in 0.2 per cent of over 20,000 cows examined. Mylrea reported an incidence of 9.9 per cent of bursitis, mostly slight, and 3.6 per cent of salpingitis, of which only half were bilateral, in 333 cows' genital tracts in Australia. These many workers showed the incidence of disease of the bovine oviduct and ovarian bursae to be about 10 to 15 per cent and of those 25 to 50 per cent may be bilateral lesions and interfere with passage of the spermatozoa, with ovulation, and with passage of the ova to the uterus resulting in infertility or sterility.

The etiological factors causing these lesions are varied. Many lesions are secondary to an ascending infection from the uterus following abortion, retained placenta, septic metritis, and pyometra. Septic metritis with a perimetritis may cause extensive adhesions of the oviducts, ovaries, and uterus to the adjacent structures and organs. Nielsen reported that abortions, retained placenta, and dystocia with forced extraction frequently leads to salpingo-ovarian-bursal changes. In certain countries tuberculosis of the oviduct is not an uncommon cause of lesions.

Anomalies such as segmental aplasia of the paramesonephric duct rarely involve the oviduct. In rare instances periovarian cysts may obstruct the oviduct. (See the previous section on genetic defects of the reproductive tract). McEntee observed one case and Moberg another. Tumors of the oviduct have not been reported.

Diseases of the oviduct are more common in the cow than in the mare, possibly because in the latter the oviduct opens on a muscular papilla in the uterus. In the cow the uterine horns become smaller and blend into the oviduct. A variety of infectious organisms may be found in the oviduct that are similar to those found in the infected uterus; these include streptococci, staphylococci, **E. Coli, C. pyogenes,** and others. Most authors believe that **C. pyogenes** is the most common. It is doubtful that coital infections result in salpingitis except possibly as previously described in "epivag" and mycoplasmosis. Lombard and co-workers found cysts and nodules in the oviduct in 87 cases but these apparently were not significant inasmuch as they failed to prevent the passage of the ovum.

All authors indicated that sterility treatment was a common cause for lesions of the oviduct and bursa. Of these sterility treatments the most common cause of lesions was enucleation of the corpus luteum. The frequency and severity of bleeding due to removal of the corpus luteum has been cited. Moberg stated the majority of the lesions he observed were of the descending type due to hemorrhages occurring at ovulation or manual ovarian treatment with removal of the corpus luteum, and the presence of the corpus luteum and hematomas in the bursa or adherent to some of the pelvic organs. These hematomas organize and produce moderate to extensive adhesions. All serious cases with complete obstruction of the tube resulting in hydrosalpinx were due to extensive hemorrhage. Expressing the corpus luteum at its peak of growth is easily accomplished but bleeding is more likely than in removal of the corpus luteum at a later stage. The latter often requires greater force, and consequently adhesions may be due to the trauma produced. Most authors have noted mild fibrous adhesions between the ovaries and the bursae of heifers or cows that have never been examined or had an infected uterus. These mild adhesions generally follow the slight bleeding occurring at ovulation. Severe trauma caused by manual rupture of thick-walled follicular cysts, luteal cysts or cystic corpora lutea may result in adhesions, although in the former little bleeding occurs. Some authors have reported adhesions following uterine irrigation with or without perforation of the uterus. Adhesions may be more likely to develop if uterine irrigation is performed soon after the time of parturition.

The pathologic lesions may vary from a few slight fibrous threads between the bursa and ovary, partial adhesion of the edge of the bursa to the ovary, roughness of the internal wall of the bursa, shallow or narrow or closed bursa, to extensive ovario-bursal lesions, cysts of the bursa or ventricle, hydrosalpinx, and pyosalpinx. The histologic changes in the oviduct due to chronic salpingitis and other changes have been described by Lombard, Morgan and McNutt, and McEntee. **Hydrosalpinx** has been observed secondary to anaomalies of the reproductive tract, such as segmental aplasia of the paramesonephric duct. It may occur secondary to adhesions of either or both the distal or proximal ends of the oviduct (See Figure 131 and 132). On postmortem examination if the adhesion is near the distal end of the oviduct, the mucus in the oviduct may be pressed into the uterus. The oviduct usually becomes distended to a diameter of 1/4 to 3/8 inch, 0.5 to 1 cm, or more with clear watery mucus and it is elongated, coiled, thin-walled, and fluctuating on palpation. Often a hard fibrous mass may be palpated in the fimbrial area of the oviduct. Hydrosalpinx may be observed in heifers; in these cases anomalies should be suspected. **Pyosalpinx** is less common than hydrosalpinx and usually occurs following severe uterine infections. Pyosalpinx is commonly associated with severe adhesions of the mesosalpinx and mesovarium. In pyosalpinx extensive perimetritis is not unusual. Pyosalpinx may follow the removal of a retained corpus luteum or the injection of large; slowly absorbed doses of repositol stilbestrol for the treatment of pyometra. In rare instances the fimbrial end of the oviduct or pavilion of the oviduct becomes attached around the edges and a large abcess or cyst may form between the bursa or pavilion and the ovary.

Mild cases of salpingitis have been described and found on histologic section but the oviduct is so small and the wall so thick that diagnosis of these minor cases of salpingitis cannot be made antemortem. McEntee, Lombard, Morgan and McNutt and the author have observed **intramucosal cysts,** cysts of the diverticula, in cows with a history of metritis and repeat breeding. (See Figure 133) These may be seen grossly but cannot be palpated per rectum. These minute cysts result from a salpingitis where the epithelium of the free edges of the mucosal folds is denuded and these folds fuse. These cysts apparently do not prevent conception.

Diagnosis—The diagnosis of pathology of the oviduct and ovarian bursa is difficult in most of the mild lesions. In severe, extensive lesions with marked adhesions involving the oviduct, ovary and adjacent structures the diagnosis is usually easily made. In the cow, cases of perimetritis and ovaritis, hydrosalpinx, pyosalpinx, and abscess or cyst in the ovarian bursa may be diagnosed by palpation per rectum. In hydrosalpinx the large, thin-walled, usually coiled and fluctuating oviduct as well as the thickened area of adhesions causing the obstruction, can in most cases be felt by careful palpation. (See Figures 131 and 132) In rare cases adhesions around the ovary may form as in pyosalpinx or a localized peritonitis, and the bursa or pavilion of the oviduct may fill with clear mucus and resemble an abscess secondary to a suppurative pavilionitis with adhesions. When many severe adhesions are present it may be impossible to differentiate pyosalpinx or hydrosalpinx except on the basis of the history of the cow. In most cases adhesions resulting in hydrosalpinx are less pronounced than in pyosalpinx. In the milder cases of ovariobursal adhesions 2 or 3 fingers may be inserted into the ovarian bursa and with the thumb placed on the outside of the bursa, the oviduct and ovarian bursa can be palpated by rolling them betweeen the fingers and thumb. Rectal palpation of the tube may also be performed by carefully palpating the uterine horn to its apex and on to the oviduct to the ovarian bursa. Sometimes, working bimanually, the ovary is grasped with the vaginal hand the oviduct and mesosalpinx are stereteched caudally, making palpation easier. Palpation of the oviduct per rectum requires experience and care. As noted from the references previously cited, only about 1/3 to 1/2 of the pathologic lesions of the oviduct and bursa are felt on palpation as compared to those observed on postmortem examination. The more frequent occurrence of pathology involving the right oviduct and ovary is considered to be due to the fact that the right ovary is functionally more active. A greater number of corpora lutea from the right ovary are removed than from the left and accordingly a greater number of slight adhesions from ovulations would also be found on the right ovary. Peritoneoscopy and visualization of the ovaries and oviducts in the cow as described by Megale and coworkers may be of diagnostic assistance in some cases.

Williams and Moberg citing Hetzel have described the

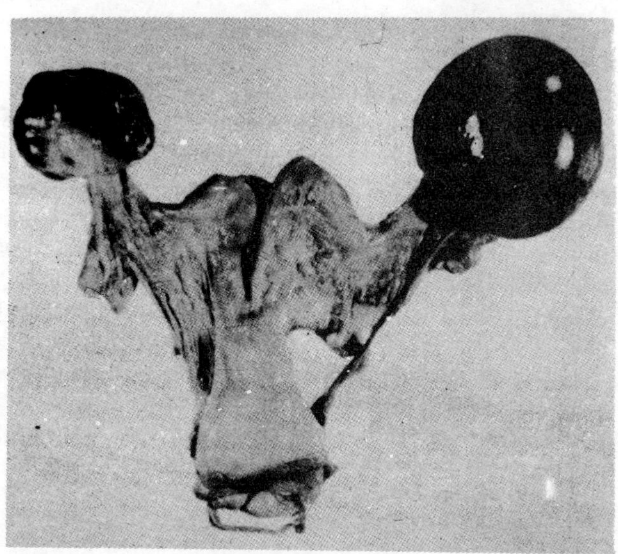

Figure 130. Bilateral Granulosa Cell Tumors of the Ovaries of a Cow. (The tumor on the left ovary is solid and lobulated and on the right the tumor is cystic. The uterine wall is flaccid and atrophied due to prolonged steroid stimulation.)

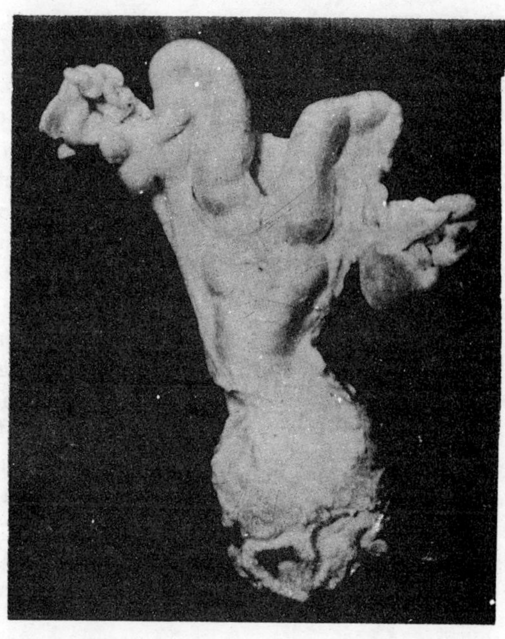

Figure 131. Bilateral Hydrosalpinges with Adhesions Surrounding the Left Ovary of a Sterile Cow.

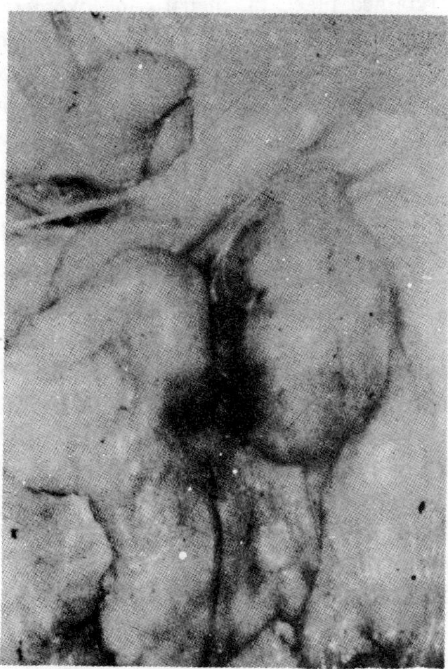

Figure 132. Ovarian Adhesions and Hydrosalpinx in a Cow. (Courtesy K. McEntee)

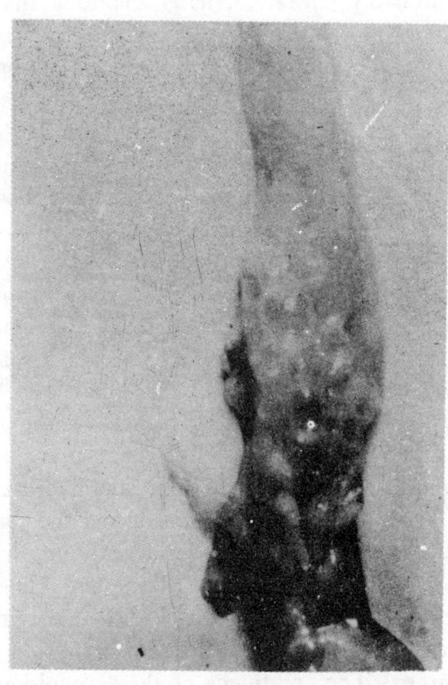

Figure 133. Intramucosal Cysts or Cysts of the Diverticula of the Bovine Oviduct. (Courtesy K. McEntee)

use in cows of the Rubin insufflation apparatus used widely in humans. After the cervix had been sealed, carbon dioxide was passed into the uterus under pressures of 60 to 100 mm. of Hg. If the oviducts were normal and open the pressure gradually fell to 40 to 60 mm. of Hg. This indicated that one or both oviducts were open. The escaping gas could usually be felt on rectal examination at the internal os of the oviduct or heard on auscultation as a gurgling or bubbling sound. The oviducts were distended up to 3 mm. in diameter and were firm. If the pressure failed to drop, this indicated that both tubes were obstructed. If it dropped rapidly this may signify that the air has penetrated the mucous membrane. Moberg cited Fossum who recommended inserting a stethoscope into the rectum in order to hear the escape of the gas. Moberg stated that insufflation is not satisfactory at the time of estrum or immediately following estrum. If this method is used during the diestrous stage of the cycle the danger of causing uterine infection must be considered. The technique has not proven possible or practical in veterinary medicine.

Prognosis. Generally this is considered guarded to poor in most severe cases of pathology of the oviduct or bursa. According to Thygesen, of 142 cases examined and diagnosed, 33 had bilateral lesions; of these, 30 were incurable and 3 eventually curable; of 109 which had unilateral lesions, 62 were curable, 36 eventually curable, and 11 probably curable. Nielsen reported that in 84 cases with diffuse or extensive perimetritis, ovarial parametritis, caudal parametritis, hydrosalpinx, periophoritis, and closed bursae in which only 11 were bilateral, the conception rates were 13 to 40 per cent. In 349 cases in which 72 had bilateral involvement with mild lesions such as a narrow or shallow bursae, slight adhesions of the bursal borders, rough internal wall of the bursa, or thin threads of fibrous connective tissue across the bursa, 63 to 79 per cent of the cows conceived. In Nielsen's cases about 75 to 80 per cent were mild and the lesions noted had only moderate to slight adverse affects on the conception rate. In 69 cases of cysts and nodules described by Moberg only 3 cases had complete obstruction of the tube. He also noted some quite strong adhesions in pregnant cows. The prognosis in bilateral pyosalpinx and hydrosalpinx is hopeless. With conservative treatment and the passage of time, some acute conditions may markedly improve, with absorbtion of many adhesions, fibrin, and blood clots. Depending on the severity of the condition, the prognosis in chronic cases should be guarded to poor.

Treatment. The treatment of these conditions is in general not very satisfactory or specific. Some authors recommend the manual breaking-down of the chronic fine adhesions, while a few condemn this procedure as certain to produce greater adhesions. Treatment of pyometra or endometritis if present may prove helpful along with other stimulative treatments. Vaccine therapy or removal of one oviduct and ovary if the condition is unilateral are questionable procedures.

Most authors including Moberg do not approve of Rubin's insufflation method for the treatment of cows because of the danger of rupturing the uterus and causing peritonitis especially if infection is present. With pressures over 125 mm. of Hg. danger of rupture increases. The gas may escape into the uterine musculature and suspensory and intercornual ligaments. By this technique mucous plugs might be removed but in many cases they would probably be absorbed or expelled without treatment in the next or following estrum. If a strong adhesion was broken down the results probably would not be permanent.

In general, conservative treatment such as mild, gentle massage of the uterus, frequent warm douches of the vagina, possibly mild antibiotic douches or infusions of the uterus might be indicated together with a long period of sexual rest. In the mild salpingitis cases associated with an endometritis the former condition will usually correct itself spontaneously as the uterine endometrium returns to normal. Possibly systemic antibiotic treatment might be indicated in some cases.

The prevention of the pathology of the oviduct, ovarian bursa, and ovary is more important than treatment. In treating retained placenta, metritis, or pyometra the use of large amounts of liquid, high pressures, and strong solutions should be avoided. Removal of the corpora lutea should be performed seldom, and only as a last resort. Repeated enucleations at short intervals should always be avoided. If a corpus luteum is removed the ovary should be pressed between the fingers for 5 minutes to control bleeding. The corpus luteum should not be allowed to lodge in the ovarian bursa. Excessive, rough manipulation of the ovaries and oviducts should always be avoided, because once adhesions are produced they seldom disappear and may result in sterility and in the permanent loss of function of one or both ovaries. In areas where vigorous manipulation of the ovary and removal of cysts or corpora lutea are seldom performed and where conservative treatments of uterine infections is the practice, the incidence of diseases of the oviduct have dropped markedly.

Uterus

Uterine pathology has been reported for many years as a cause of sterility and infertility, Albrechtsen, Williams, Nielsen and others. In recent years more work has been done and data are beginning to accumulate to indicate that the conclusions of these authors, largely based on clinical observations, were correct. These recent findings are substantiated by research into the bacterial causes of uterine infections and histologic sections of diseased uteri. This section of the chapter will consider uterine pathology including: endometritis, pyometra, mucometra, perimetritis, uterine abscess or abscess of the uterine wall, sclerotic metritis and uterine tumors. Previous sections of this text have covered acute or septic metritis, abortions, retained placenta, and postpartum metritis. A significant proportion of failures of conception can be ascribed to varying degrees of chronic metritis or endometritis.

Endometritis due to uterine infection and secondary inflammation has been shown by Albrechtsen, Williams, Nielsen, Miller, Brus, and Kampelmacher to be a common cause for infertility in cattle. An excellent review on endometritis was made by Dawson in 1960. Recent work on vibriosis has provided the incentive and furthered this study.

Etiology. All workers have shown that metritis and endometritis are likely to follow abnormal parturitions such as abortions, retained placenta, premature births, twin births, dystocia, septic metritis, postpartum metritis, pyometra and traumatic lesions or lacerations of the uterus, cervix, vagina or vulva. These factors are generally associated with a delayed involution of the uterus, chronic uterine discharge, slow recovery of the uterine endometrium, and delayed conception often associated with an increased number of services. In cows uterine infections and inflammations interfering with conception are likely to arise during even a normal calving period. As noted in Chapter VI and XI many bovine uteri become infected at the time of parturition and shortly thereafter. In the normal cow this infection is eliminated rapidly most commonly at the first or second estrus or ovulatory period. Severe stretching or trauma to the vulva may occasionally cause windsucking or pneumovagina in cows. This is observed most often in older cows with a sunken anus and a nearly horizontal vulva. (See Figure 135) The vulvar lips are often thin and atrophic. The vagina balloons, and air, feces, and urine may be drawn into the cranial portion of the vagina. In rare cases with chronic cervicitus or during estrum the uterus may become distended with air, causing a persistent endometritis as well as a cervicitis and vaginitis. The condition is similar to pneumovagina in the mare and failure of conception, or "repeat breeding," is a frequent symptom.

Chronic uterine catarrh or endometritis may occur in cows and hiefers following coitus. The importance and severity of trichomoniasis, vibriosis, and brucellosis have been discussed. The penetration of the uterine glands by **V. fetus** organisms has been well described. For successful breeding results it is essential that these diseases be kept under control. The sheath of the bull usually contains many organisms of different types, and even though the introduction of antibiotics into the collected semen has proved helpful in controlling these organisms, it is of vital importance that the semen be collected in a clean manner, to prevent the possible introduction of many organisms into the cervix and uterus at the time of insemination. Insemination should be performed in a clean, sanitary manner and the semen deposited only in the cervix as infection may be introduced and established more readily by the intrauterine deposition of semen. Bulls with acute seminovesiculitis should not be used either naturally or artifically. In cattle the fairly tight, firm cervix, small, erect uterus, and failure of the vagina to balloon and draw the semen into the uterus as is the case in the mare, may have great protective value. Besides the natural defenses against infection at the time of estrum in the cow, these factors help overcome the massive infection often introduced into the vulva and vagina at the time of natural service when little or no breeding hygiene is practiced. Brus and Kampelmacher have indicated that the endometritis accompanying **Br. abortus** and **V. fetus** infections is usually more severe in the former. Both may be primary invaders and the more common streptococci, staphylococci, **C. pyogenes, Ps. aeruginosa, B. coli** and others may be secondary invaders. The severity of the endometritis is related to the type of organisms present. Some organisms, such as **C. pyogenes,** cause severe endometritis whereas others cause a slight endometritis. Hemolytic types are generally more pathogenic than are nonhemolytic types. Since a variety of organisms may be introduced into the uterus or genital tract by various instruments or therapeutic practices, the inseminator and the veterinarian should use care, skill and cleanliness to prevent the possible introduction of infection whenever he inseminates, invades, examines, or treats the genital tract, especially the uterus. It is generally considered that unless much mucopurulent material is in the uterus probably fertilization would not be greatly affected but that normal development and attachment of the fertilized ovum in the uterus might be prevented.

Kampelmacher, Miller and others reported that the normal, nongravid uterus of a cow or a virgin heifer is free of organisms. Miller reported definite evidence of endometritis in 10 of 35 cows examined for infertility by means of endometrial biopsy. Brus reporting on the results of biopsy of the uterine endometrium and submucosa, found 70 per cent of 110 sterile cows showing some degree of endometritis. Of these 110 cows 45, or 41 per cent, had lesions sufficiently severe to probably prevent conception at the time the biopsies were taken. Kampelmacher reported that in 82 sterile cows whose uteri were biopsied and cultured, 38, or 46 per cent, had both infectious organisms and an endometritis present. Most of the earlier clinical workers reported a higher incidence of infection because cultures were from the cervix or external portions of the cervix. Newer instruments and techniques perfected by Nielsen, Frank, and others have enabled workers to obtain samples from the uterus relatively free of cervical contamination. As a result these authors have reported a lower incidence of true uterine infection. As Kampelmacher has shown, mixed cultures from the vagina or external portion of the cervix are common but pure cultures are frequently obtained in uterine cultures.

Signs. According to Brus, the clinical symptoms of an endometritis often cannot be demonstrated by rectal or vaginal examination. In the more severe cases there may be a mucopurulent discharge from the uterus in the vagina. At the time of estrum flakes of pus in the estrual mucus may indicate endometritis. The source of these flakes may be difficult to delineate clinically inasmuch as they may come from the vagina, cervix or uterus. Often the mucus of estrum may be cloudy or milky instead of clear or translucent and contain many leucocytes. Bovine cervical mucus in proestrum may normally be slightly cloudy. In many cases a mild to definite cervicitis may be present with an endometritis or be secondary to it due to contamination from the uterus. In some cases douching of the uterus may wash out flakes of mucopurulent material and then the diagnosis is more certain. The seriousness of endometritis cannot be diagnosed from clinical manifestations except in cases in which purulent material is present or discharged. On rectal examination the uterus may occasionally feel slightly large, heavy, and thick-walled. These changes may be limited to one horn. This evidence of failure of normal, prompt involution of the uterus may accompany chronic endometritis and uterine infection. Diagnosis on the basis of a rectal examination is not reliable. The estrous cycle and periods are usually normal in length but in occasional cases the cycle may be shortened to 8 to 12 days due to acute endometrial inflammation preventing the development of a normal corpus luteum. Because of the abnormal endometrium and infection in the uterus the fertilized ovum may die and the cow again came into estrum. The estrous cycle may vary in length in some cases due to early death and maceration of the embryo as in trichomoniasis, vibriosis, and possibly other infections. Long cycles may follow service and be due to early embryonic deaths. Repeated services and failure of conception are common symptoms of endometritis. Because many or all of the above clinical symptoms are at times variable and frequently absent, with the exception of failure of conception following repeated services performed by a fertile bull, accurate diagnosis in the field is at present usually impossible. Often a careful clinical examination will eliminate other possible causes of infertility and the diagnosis of possible endometritis may be arrived at by a a process of elimination. The most common lesions found in endometritis in cattle, according to Miller, were exudation, a periglandular fibrosis with leukocytic cellular infiltration and subsequent glandular degeneration and dilation.

The use of special equipment for culturing and taking a biopsy of the uterus in the clinical patient as devised by Frank, Nielsen, Miller and Roberts, Brus, Sjkerven, Minocha et al. and Knudsen and Sollen plus certain instruments used in treating humans, have made possible the further study of endometritis. For practical reasons this equipment together with some special equipment used for diagnosing vibriosis and trichomoniasis probably can only be used to a limited extent in the field, but it can be used for special diagnostic and research work on this important phase of sterility or infertility. In the study by Brus on 110 sterile cows, 27, or 87 per cent, of 31 cows that showed some clinically diagnosable abnormalities had an endometritis. In 79 sterile cows without clinically detectable abnormalities 50, or 63 per cent, had endometritis. The endometritis was generally more severe in the first group. It was found that slight cases of endometritis diagnosed by a biopsy did not interfere with conception; therefore if these cows were eliminated from the above groups the percentage in each group having endometritis severe enough to cause sterility or infertility would be 57 and 37, respectively. Brus examined a group of 54 cows that had not been inseminated or served since their last calving; only 11 had been in estrum; 42 showed clinical abnormalities, mainly poor involution of the uterus; and on biopsy 50 of the 54 had evidence of endometritis. The more severe lesions were found in cows that had retained placentas, abnormal parturitions, or brucellosis. The lesions were more severe the nearer the biopsy was taken to the time of calving; and in general, lesions were more severe in cows that had not been in estrum. Brus reported that inflammatory lesions were more likely to be found in the larger horn of the uterus if the horns were unequal in size. On the basis of biopsy examinations Brus was able to predict the approximate time necessary before the inflammatory reaction would subside sufficiently so that conception could be expected. DeBois in an excellent study reported that most abnormalities of the uterus including infection and endometritis recover spontaneously during involution of the uterus, and latent endometritis is not often responsible for reproductive failures in clinically normal cows. Because of the usual prompt natural recovery of endometritis in the involuting uterus, intrauterine infusions of antibiotics according to DeBois was of limited value. Of 99 cows examined at 10 days and 20 days postpartum and at the time of the first insemination, intrauterine infection was present in 49, 25, and 3 per cent respectively. Skjerven reported on endometrial biopsy studies at various stages of the estrous cycle in normal cattle and showed that such a procedure was safe and had no effect on fertility.

Prognosis. The prognosis in most cases of endometritis is fair to good. With each repeated estrous cycle the natural body-defenses and the changes produced within the uterus and the genital tract by the estrogens tend to aid recovery. Thus endometritis is seldom static; nearly all cases recover spontaneously with the passage of a variable period of time and sequential estrous periods. This effect of the estrous period on infection has been described by Rowson, Lamming and Fry, Black and his co-workers, and Hawk et al.. Their work showed, as had Kampelmacher's, that infection introduced into the normal uterus at the time of estrum was rapidly overcome and did not establish itself. When infection was introduced during the progestational phases of the cycle it readily became established and pyometra resulted. Nielsen reported that of 463 cases of cows suffering from a purulent postpartum discharge without pyometra 87 per cent conceived after treatment. In 111 infertile cows bred 2 or more times before taking a biopsy of the endometrium, Brus reported the following results:

Degree of Endometritis	Number of Cows	Percentage Conceiving First Service After Biopsy	Percentage of Total Conceptions	Services per Conception
None	27	74	85	1.57
Slight	31	74	90	1.36
Moderate	25	48	80	1.70
Severe	28	11	60	3.77

Endometritis, as other inflammatory processes in the body, tends to recover spontaneously. The more severe the endometritis the longer the time required for recovery. Slight endometritis may not prevent conception and from a biopsy the approximate length of time for recovery could be estimated, Brus. Williams stated that pregnancy is the supreme burden of reproduction. Any pregnancy is in jeopardy that occurs with an intrauterine infection and endometritis already present.

Treatment—There are many therapeutic agents and procedures used and advocated for the treatment of endometritis. Until controlled experiments are performed using biopsy and cultural methods on large numbers of infertile or "repeat breeding" cows to define the severity of the endometritis (if this is the cause for the signs of failure of conception) and compare the various treatments, it cannot be stated with authority which treatment is superior, or whether the complete omission of treatment may not be best. In vibriosis and trichomoniasis the development of a local immunity will in a few months overcome the intrauterine infection and produce recovery so conception can occur. Most treatments are based on either stimulating the uterus or overcoming the suspected or known intrauterine infection.

The treatments used to stimulate the muscle tone, blood supply, and flow of mucus of the uterus are varied. Regular warm-to-hot, mild antiseptic solutions such as the aromatic soap solutions, mild quaternary ammonium, neutral iodophor, or chlorine solutions, physiological saline, dilute potassium permanganate solutions, sodium bicarbonate solutions, weak "Lysol" solutions, and dilute iodine solutions may be used in 500 to 4000 ml amounts as vaginal douches. Mild, gentle uterine massage per rectum 2 to 3 times a week may possibly be of value in producing similar effects. Either intramuscular injections or intrauterine infusions of estrogens in doses of 20 to 30 mg of stilbestrol or 2 to 3 mg of estradiol at 7 to 10 day intervals might prove of value because of their stimulating effect on the uterus upon absorbtion from their site of deposition. A number of commercial products incorporating an estrogen and antibiotics are now available for infusing into the uterus. Some of the earlier workers advised the repeated removal of the corpus luteum. While this practice might hasten recovery of the endometritis it would certainly result in adhesions around the ovaries in some cattle, and therefore cannot be recommended. Applying 1 per cent acriflavine ointment on the external os of the cervix and cranial portion of the vagina by massage, swabbing the cervix with Lugol's solution or other irritating iodine-base cervicitis mixture may also stimulate circulation, uterine tone and peristalsis, and the secretion of mucus by the endometrium.

Intrauterine infusions or possibly douching the uterus with an irritant antiseptic such as dilute Lugol's solution, 2 to 10 ml in 100 ml of water, will strongly stimulate uterine muscle contraction and tone and greatly increase mucous secretions. In fact, douching the uterus with any fluid including saline, acriflavine solutions, 1:500 to 1:3000 concentrations, chlorine, 200 p.p.m., chlorhexidine, or other antiseptics probably has a mild irritating action on the endometrium, results in the mobilization of leucocytes, stimulates uterine motility, and has an antiseptic and flushing action on any mucopurulent material.

By a combination of rectal manipulation of the cervix and the vaginal introduction of a 2-way-flow catheter of small diameter, the catheter can be passed into the uterus. By means of a funnel and tube, an intravenous outfit, a large syringe or a pressure bulb outfit attached to the end of the catheter, the douche solution is run into the uterus. This is most easily accomplished in heifers and cows at the time of estrum. If a cervicitis is present or an enlarged uterus is hanging down into the abdominal cavity, Knowles' or Hopper's cervical forceps may be applied to the cervix to pull it back toward the vulva. With the uterus and cervix pulled back by the forceps, one hand can grasp the cervix in the vagina and with the aid of a uterine catheter in a rubber horse catheter to provide stiffness, the latter may be inserted into the uterus. After douching the uterus the cervix may be swabbed with gauze soaked in a strong antiseptic and fastened securely on a pair of narrow dressing forceps. Care should be used in passing the catheter through the transverse folds of the cervix and into the uterus so that neither of these organs is injured or ruptured. As an aid to passing the catheter or pipettte, the rectal hand should grasp the cervix and push it forward to obliterate the folds in the vaginal wall. As the catheter is being gently passed through the cervix, the cervix should be manipulated in various directions to help "thread" it over the pipette. During the operation the cow should be well-restrained. Although douching the uterus with a metal catheter or infusing antibiotics or antiseptics into the uterus with a catheter or pipette usually causes no harm, great care should be exercised so that the uterus is not injured or perforated by the catheter and thereby producing more damage than any possible good that could be derived from the infusion. Infusing fluid in excess of 100 ml into the nonpregnant uterus of a heifer or more than 150 ml into a cow's uterus may rupture the uterus or force the fluid into the tissues of the uterus, Smythe. He found it impossible to force fluid through the Fallopian tubes. Rupture of the uterine endometrium occurred and the fluid passed between the peritoneal coverings of the uterus. If more than this amount of fluid is infused some of it should be allowed to flow out through the cervix. Kortum recently reported on a spiralled indwelling plastic uterine infusing instrument that could be passed through the cervix into the uterus and it would remain in place so that repeated twice daily or daily infusions could be given without reinserting a pipette. This instrument if left in place for period of time would act like an I.U.D. resulting in shortened cycles Further study is necessary to ascertain its value and whether or not endometrial damage may result from a prolonged retention in the uterus.

Other treatments have been used for endometritis with the idea that if the infection is overcome the endometritis will heal more promptly and the infertility will be overcome more rapidly. These treatments include the intrauterine infusion of antibiotics such as: penicillin, streptomycin, **Aureomycin, Terramycin,** tetracycline, tyrothricin, neomycin, **Chlormycetin,** tylosin, furacin preparations, polymyxin, and others, alone or in combination, incorporated in saline solution, distilled water, oil, sodium sulfonamide solutions, or oil-in-water emulsions. Many veterinarians will infuse intramammary products with a broad-range of antibiotic activity into the uterus by means of a uterine pipette. Usually 500,000 to 1 million units of penicillin and 0.5 to 1 gm of streptomycin or 0.5 to 1 gm of the broad range antibiotics are infused in 10 to 50 ml of vehicle. Intrauterine infusions of a million units of penicillin and/or a gram of streptomycin did not produce any antibiotic residues in milk, Kendrick and Pier. The treatments using penicillin and streptomycin in saline or distilled water may be given within 3 to 6 hours before service. The other antibiotics or vehicles are usually given within 24 to 48 hours after insemination or breeding as they might have a harmful effect on spermatozoa if administered shortly before service. Some veterinarians advise treatement 3 to 4 days before the expected estrum. Treatment at this time is easier in cows than in heifers. In the latter the cervix may not be sufficiently dilated to allow easy passage of the uterine catheter or pipette. Infusing the uterus during estrum may result in much of the material escaping due to the dilated cervix and contracted uterus. For this reason Bu recommended infusing aqueous easily absorbed solutions during the luteal phase of the cycle. Although Ulberg and co-workers reported more endometrial reaction to infusions during the luteal phase of the cycle; the author and others have reported no definite harmful effects from such a practice.

Both weak Lugol's solutions and tyrothricin solutions are quite irritating to the endometrium. If they are infused about 2 to 4 days after estrum occasionally a short 8 to 12 day cycle may follow due to the failure of a normal corpus luteum to develop. The effectiveness of antibiotic preparations is not known. In vibriosis a few small experiments have been run on the effects of antibiotics, especially dihydrostreptomycin, on vibrio **in vivo** but the results, although not discouraging, leave much to be desired. More work on the value of these preparations will have to be done under controlled conditions to arrive at a true evaluation of the benefits derived. Other preparations used in the uterus to control possible infections have included silver oxide in oil, "Caprokol", or hexylresorcinal in oil, metaphen and mercurochrome solutions, and others.

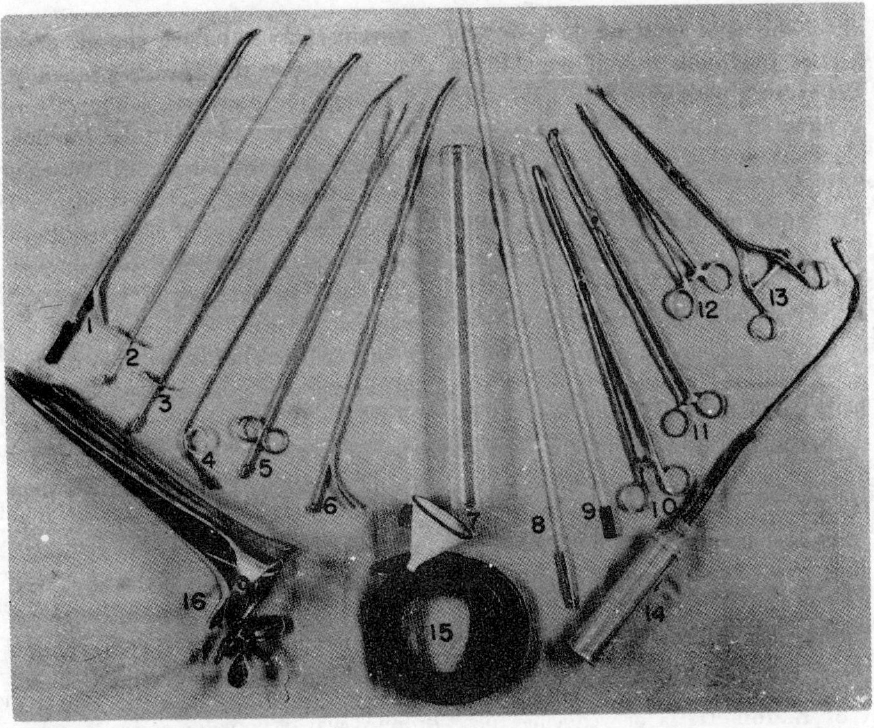

Figure 134. **Some Common Instruments Used in the Treatment of Infertility in the Cow and Mare.** 1. Smith Uterine Catheter with Rubber Adapter. 2. Luken's Intrauterine Infusion Catheter. 3. Chambers' Intrauterine Infusion Catheter. 4. Woelffer's Intrauterine Infusion Catheter. 5. Nielsen's Intrauterine Infusion Catheter. 6. Small Uterine Catheter for Douching. 7. Glass or Plastic Vaginal Speculum. 8. Long Plastic Insemination Pipette with metal adapter for the mare. 9. Insemination pipette with rubber adapter. 10. Knowles' Cervical Forceps. 11. Hopper's Cervical Forceps. 12. Long Dressing Forceps. 13. Palmer's Cervical Dilators. 14. Flexible Extension Flashlight. 15. Rubber Horse Catheter and Funnel. 16. Caslick's Vaginal Speculum for the Mare.

The use of mixed bacterins, the oral feeding of sulfonamides, or iodide preparations are of questionable or no value. Although the author has used most of the aforementioned treatments for possible or probable bovine endometritis, and in some cases the associated repeated failures to conceive, 2 to 5 ml of Lugol's solution in 30 to 100 ml of sterile distilled water as a uterine infusion is presently favored as his treatment of choice. It is usually administered during the estrous period if the cow is not bred, or 12 to 36 hours after service. Treatment 2 to 5 days after estrum should be avoided or a shortened cycle may result. Since the fertilized ovum usually enters the uterus from the oviduct about 3 days after ovulation, infusions of the uterus after 36 to 48 hours after service should be avoided in cows bred the prior estrous period. Eckman et al. have shown that iodine is rapidly absorbed from the uterus. Its beneficial action may be due to its microbiocidal activity, the local irritation, leucocytosis, and hyperemia it produces; and it may correct an iodine deficiency. Moberg and McDonald et al. have reported that empirically providing iodine orally improved fertility.

If a cow is a "windsucker" or has a chronic pneumovagina or pneumo-uterus it is necessary to scarify and suture the vulva in a manner similar to that described for Caslick's operation in the mare. (See Figures 142 and 85) Interrupted vertical mattress sutures should be used, since Michel skin clips are usually rubbed out by the cow's tail. Antibiotics applied locally to the uterus and vagina, and sexual rest are indicated in these cases. After one to 4 normal estrous cycles, artificial insemination is performed. The author has had a high degree of success with this therapy when it was indicated.

In the past many reports on the value of certain infusion products or treatments for failure of conception due presumably to endometritis or uterine infections have appeared in the literature, Roberts (1956). Most of these reports proved nothing more than the fact that most cows respond to whatever treatment was used. Very few of the experiments included control animals and when they did the numbers were not sufficiently large. This is to be expected when work of this type must be done in field practice where controlled conditions usually are difficult to establish. Whenever such a wide variety of treatments is reported as being successful, it indicates that no treatment would probably show similar results. From the figures the author cited in 1956 it was evident that any effective treatment of "repeat breeders" due to a possible endometritis must raise conception rates on the next service to well over 50 per cent. No such treatment has been reported. As DeBois, Brus and others have reported most cases of uterine infection and endometritis recover spontaneously. Sexual rest is indicated for cows with obvious and severe endometritis. In the suspected case of endometritis in the "repeat breeding" cow without any obvious symptoms, conceptions would probably occur sooner if breeding was continued rather than suspended. If the bull is to be conserved, then sexual rest for a month or so in these "repeat breeding" cows may be indicated. There is no evidence that repeated natural service or insemination into the cervix caused any delay in recovery from possible endometritis.

The Prevention of Endometritis or reducing the problem to a minimum requires proper care, sanitation management, and handling of cows at the time of parturition and the early postpartum period to prevent infections of the uterus. (See Chapter VI and XI) If infections occur, prompt and—if necessary—repeated treatments at 1- to 2-week intervals are indicated. Conservative treatment of retained placenta and postpartum uterine infections is usually desirable. If pneumovagina is present prompt closure of the vulva is indicated. Brucellosis, vibriosis, and trichomoniasis should be controlled. If artificial insemination is employed the semen should be free of possible infectious agents and be desposited in clean manner in the cervix and not in the uterine horn. Vaginal examinations and uterine and vaginal treatments should be conducted in a clean, hygienic manner to prevent the introduction of infection. Breeding of cows before 60 days after parturition unless they are known to be healthy, should be done with caution.

Delayed postpartum involution of the uterus is seen most often in older pluriparous cows during the Fall and Winter months and especially in cows with abnormal parturitions including: dystocia, retained placenta, acute metritis, prolapse of the uterus, and cesarean section. Delayed involution was most noticeable the first 30 days postpartum, Morrow et al.. (See Chapters VI and XI) In general cows with abnormal parturitions required about 5 days longer for their uteri to involute than did cows calving normally. Severe uterine infections definitely retarded the rate of involution. An enlarged uterus 30 to 60 days postpartum is often diagnosed clinically by many veterinarians as having chronic endometritis. Morrow et al. stated that the diseases present at parturition and the length of the postpartum interval prior to breeding were of greater importance in determining the conception rate on first service than was the involutionary state of the uterus based on a rectal examination after 30 days postpartum in cows with a grossly normal uterus. Tennant and Petticord examined 1634 cows at 30 to 50 days postpartum. The presence of a mucopurulent exudate in the vagina was considered diagnostic for the presence of a endometritis. They stated that infertility was independent of uterine size, and delayed involution in the absence of disease was unimportant. The presence of endometritis had only a slight influence on uterine size and could not be diagnosed by rectal palpation alone. The average calving interval was 10 days longer, 394 days, for cows with endometritis than it was for the normal cows and conception rate on first service was 12 percent lower. Hinze demonstrated that preventive therapy for postpartum endometritis of 2 gm oxytetracyline or neomycin placed into the uterus immediately after the placenta was dropped was of no value and even delayed conception and reduced fertility in 2 groups of 75 cows each compared to 79 controls. Conception rate after first service, after 3 services and the number of breedings per conception were 49, 40 and 60 percent, 73.3, 72.9 and 85.3 percent and 2.24, 2.56 and 1.67 respectively. Gibbons and Kiesel showed that infusing cows' uteri 20 to 40 days after calving with 100 mg of oxytetracycline as an aid in controlling endometritis did not improve fertility. Olds also reported that it was futile to shorten the interval from calving to conception by attempting to prevent the many conditions causing repeat breeding. DeBois also reported that uterine infusions of antibiotics in the postpartum period were not advantageous.

If delayed involution is obviously accompanied by a chronic metritis or endometritis as noted by a mucopurulent discharge from the uterus or the presence of a variable amount of exudate in the uterus at 30 to 50 days postpartum, treatment as previously outlined in postpartum metritis or pyometra is indicated. The interval between calving and breeding should be extended in affected, diseased cows.

The author has observed that pluriparous cows with a long mesometrium and a deep abdominal cavity permitting the uterus and cervix to be located some distance below the pelvic floor tend to have a larger, heavier, thicker uterus and cervix and be less fertile than cows whose uterus and cervix is located higher in the abdominal cavity on a level, with the pelvic floor. Uterine lochia or infectious material drains out earlier and more completely and possibly the circulation to the uterus is improved resulting in less edema or passive congestion in the latter cows. The author has even considered the possibility of attempting to fasten the cervix in the pelvic cavity in some severely affected cows.

Pyometra in cattle is characterized by the accumulation of pus or mucopurulent matter in the uterus, and by a retained corpus luteum with failure of estrum due to suppression of the endometrial luteolytic factor secondary to the severe endometritis. Uterine distention does not cause anestrus, Hansel. The retained corpus luteum is not the corpus luteum of pregnancy in postpartum pyometra but is the corpus luteum following the first to third ovulation that persists due to the uterine infection. Pyometra usually occurs following an abnormal parturition, a uterine infection, and a tardy involution of the uterus in such conditions as abortion, premature birth, twin birth, dystocia, retained placenta, septic metritis, or postpartum metritis. (See Figure 135) True pyometra seldom recovers spontaneously. Some veterinarians speak of pyometra as the chronic mucopurulent discharge seen for 2 to 3 weeks following calving due to a postpartum metritis. In a narrow sense this may be correct since there is pus in the uterus, but most of these cases come into estrum, cycle regularly, and the pus is expelled within 30 to 60 days after parturition. True pyometra exists for 60 to 90 or more days after parturition with a failure of estrum. It may occasionally follow service and when it does it is usually associated with the early death and maceration of the embryo and its membranes. In these cases trichomoniasis should always be suspected and the pus examined for trichomonads. Other infections due to a variety of organisms, most frequently **C. pyogenes,** may also cause death of the embryo and pyometra, or be a secondary invader. Occasionally pyometra may be produced by the insertion of an inseminating pipette into the uterus of a pregnant cow that may have shown symptoms of estrum. Infection introduced in the semen or by the operation causes the death of the embryo, its maceration, and pyometra. This condition occurs more commonly when the semen contains no antibiotics. In rare instances pyometra may develop secondary to mucometra in a heifer with an imperforate hymen that has been bred by a a bull or artificially and infection is introduced into the genital tract distended with the mucus or it may develop secondary to mucometra caused by chronic cystic ovaries.

Symptoms—Pyometra is characterized by the failure of estrum and the retention of pus or mucopurulent material in the uterus. The amount of this pus may vary from 2 or 3 ounces to 2 to 4 gallons. In most cases of postpartum pyometra the cervix is relaxed so that some of the pus escapes and is observed occasionally when the cow lies down, urinates, or defecates. On examination 3 to 4 ounces of pus are frequently found in the cranial portion of the vagina. The pus is usually thick mucoid and creamy, and yellow, white, or greenish-gray in color. In 67 cases of pyometra recorded by the author in an area where trichomoniasis was not seen, a mucopurulent discharge was observed by the owner in 57, or 86.6 per cent, of the cases on various occasions before the condition was diagnosed and treated. On rectal examination the uterine wall is usually thickened, flaccid, and atonic. The pus that distends the uterus may simulate pregnancy but the consistency of the pus is heavy and not watery like normal placental fluids. Pinching of the uterine wall does not reveal the slipping of the fetal membranes as in pregnancy. The fetus cotyledons, and enlarged whirring uterine artery of a normal pregnancy are not palpable in pyometra. The bovine animal rarely shows any signs of systemic illness even when gallons of pus may be in the uterus. If on the first examination, the diagnosis of pyometra cannot definitely be made, reexamination in 20 to 30 days will reveal a failure of normal developmental changes characteristic of pregnancy. Passing a metal catheter through the cervix will remove some pus, or an injection of about 50 mg of stilbestrol will probably cause the evacuation or release of pus from the uterus. This large single dose of a short-acting estrogen will not interrupt a pregnancy. A white-blood-cell count is of no value in diagnosing pyometra in the cow.

Prognosis—The earlier a case of pyometra is diagnosed and treated, the greater the possibility of its successful correction or cure. In long-standing cases the endometrium is destroyed, the uterine wall undergoes fibrotic changes, and in some cases complete recovery and conception cannot occur. In the cases that have existed for only 60 to 120 days, recovery and conception are more likely than in cases having existed for 120 days or longer. The type of organism and its effect on the endometrium and uterus play an important role. **C. pyogenes** is commonly found in incurable cases. Recovery in cases with over 2 gallons of pus in the uterus seldom occurs because of the degenerative changes in the uterine wall, producing a marked lack of tone. Recovery of cases of pyometra associated with severe perimetritis is hopeless. In a series of 35 cases of pyometra Nielsen reported that 51.4 percent of the cases conceived. The author in a series of 67 cases recorded a conception rate of 46.3 percent.

Treatment—The treatment consists of causing an involution of the retained corpus luteum or removing it so that the estrous cycle is reestablished, the cervix will dilate, the uterus will contract and the pus will be evacuated. The induction of estrum may be brought about by the injection of estrogens or, as a last resort, by the manual removal of the corpus luteum. Douching the uterus with a horse catheter, draining the pus from the uterus, injecting antibiotics, and massaging may in rare cases produce recovery but the other procedures are much more effective in establishing a prompt return to the regular estrous cycle necessary for recovery. Excessive massage of the uterus should be avoided, as perimetritis and adhesions may occur.

The administration of estrogens is preferred over manual removal of the corpus luteum because there is less danger to the cow. Stilbestrol in 50 to 100 mg doses, or estradiol in 5 to 10 mg doses may be administered intramuscularly. Doses of 20 to 40 mg of stilbestrol or 2 to 4 mg of estradiol are too small to be consistently effective. Cystic ovaries are seldom produced by the large doses of estrogen used to treat pyometra. Some cases have responded to 80 to 100 mg of stilbestrol infused into the uterus. More work is necessary on the results of this mode of estrogen administration. In 24 to 72 hours most or all of the pus is usually expelled. If this has not occurred, the corpus luteum has not involuted and the uterus has not become greatly reduced in size, a second and third treatment with lower doses, 20 to 30 mg of stilbestrol or 2 to 3 mg. of estrodiol may be necessary at 2- to 3-day intervals. Some veterinarians have used a single dose of 5 to 10 mg of estradiol valerate with success. The author cautions against the use of repositol stilbestrol because he and other veterinarians have experienced ovaritis and periovaritis due to infection passing through the oviducts even when the ovaries or the uterus were not massaged. Apparently the repositol product causes a marked and prolonged estrogenic response affecting the natural protective mechanisms of the oviduct. Permanent adhesions and sterility often result. Rectal examination 10 to 14 days after successful treatment should reveal a contracted uterus with all of the pus evacuated. Otherwise retreatment may be indicated; the second treatment is often successful. In rare instances the large dose of estrogen used to involute the C.L. and evacuate the pus will produce cystic ovaries that require treatment with luteinizing hormone. If after 2 or 3 treatments with various estrogens at 2 to 4 week intervals recovery does not occur, manual removal of the retained corpus luteum might be considered. Some veterinarians advocate the injection of 5 to 10 ml of pituitrin to aid in the evacuation of pus from the uterus after administration of an estrogen to sensitize the myometrium and dilate or relax the cervical os. Although this has appeared to do no harm the author has not found it to be of value in the treatment of pyometra (See Table 20). The use of estrogens followed by a potent glucocorticoid the next day might result in the involution of the C.L. where estrogens alone have failed. (See Induced Abortion) Parenteral antibiotics should be administered during this treatment. Because the retained or imbedded corpus luteum is removed with difficulty and the presence of pyogenic organisms in the oviduct is likely, severe permanent adhesions frequently follow the enucleation of the corpus luteum. For this reason this operation on valuable cows is recommended only as a last resort even though it may be more effective than is the injection of estrogens in the treatment of pyometra. In some cases that fail to respond the endometrium may be largely destroyed and the uterine wall may be severely fibrosed, atrophied, or thickened. In other cases the internal os of the cervix may be hard and indurated and prevent the prompt and complete evacuation of pus from the uterus.

After treatment and expulsion of the pus from the uterus and the establishment of normal estrous cycles the cows should not be rebred for 3 to 4 normal estrous periods. Before breeding is permitted the uterus should return

Table 20. The Results of Treatment of Pyometra in Cattle

Product or Method	Number of Cases	Recovered No.	Recovered Percent	Conceived No.	Conceived Percent
Stilbestrol (20 to 90 mg)	12	6	60	4	42.9
Estradiol (3 to 10 mg)	23	15		11	
Stilbestrol + Pituitrin	7	4	55.6	2	33.3
Estradiol + Pituitrin	2	1		1	
Stilbestrol + Removal of C.L.	12	9	87	6	56.5
Removal of C.L. only	11	11		7	
Totals	67	46	68.7	31	46.3

to its normal size and consistency and no metritis or cervicitis should be present. The use of antibiotic infusions or other therapy as described under endometritis may be of some value in hastening recovery. The results of the treatment of pyometra obtained by the author are given in Table 20.

A larger number of cases is necessary to give more authority to conclusions drawn from the results in Table 9 but it is rather obvious that pyometra produces severe damage to the endometrium that either prevents conception even though the pus is evacuated, or delays conception so that the owner sells the cow as unprofitable. To prevent pyometra, cows having a postpartum mucopurulent discharge should be treated promptly to hasten involution of the uterus, Moore. Insemination into the uterus and breeding to trichomonad-infected bulls should be avoided.

Perimetritis and Parametritis are observed occasionally in the cow and are characterized by varying amounts of adhesions between the uterus and broad ligaments and the other pelvic and abdominal organs. (See Figure 136) As endometritis and metritis are inflammations of the endometrium and the entire thickness of the uterus, so perimetritis and parametritis involve inflammation of the serosa and uterine ligaments, respectively. Adhesions associated with or secondary to inflammation are usually secondary to one of the following: a severe septic metritis; douching and perforation of the uterus with a catheter releasing irritant material into that area; a nonfatal rupture of the rectum due to carelessness in rectal examination or therapy; a perforation of the vaginal wall by the penis of the bull; an occasional severe hemorrhage, trauma, or rupture of the uterus at the time of calving due to torsion of the uterus, embryotomy, forced extraction, severe cervical or vaginal lacerations; a cesarean section; an extrauterine fetus; excessive bleeding following a manual removal of a corpus luteum; excessive massage or manipulation of an infected uterus such as rough removal of a retained placenta; and occasionally a parametritis due to a diffuse peritonitis secondary to tapping of the rumen or to traumatic gastritis. These conditions may be caused by tuberculosis of the genital organs in countries where tuberculosis in cattle is still common.

The lesions may vary from a few thin fibrous strands of connective tissue to firm adhesions between the uterus, broad ligaments, rumen, omentum, intestines, rectum, bladder, and other organs. The adhesions may be either diffuse or localized. In some cases abscesses may be found in the adhesions around the ovaries or broad ligaments or between the rectum and uterus. These localized abscesses may be either small or large. In rare cases one of these perimetrial abscesses may rupture into the rectum or bladder or may extend through the pelvic cavity to rupture alongside the vulva.

The symptoms of peritonitis in the pelvic region during the acute phase of the disease are the same as for any peritonitis: anorexia; arched back; slow, stiff gait; pain exhibited at the time of urination and defecation or at the time of a rectal examination; decreased rumen activity; and lack of ruminations. The temperature may be elevated for a day or two or may be normal. The pulse is elevated and the respirations increased. A "serous" or expiratory grunt may be heard at the onset of expiration or on percussion of the abdomen. The abdomen may be tense and the rumen slightly tympanitic. A diarrhea may be present. The hair coat may be rough. The drop in milk flow is usually marked. A hemogram may reveal a slight leukocytosis and a shift to the left. A rectal examination in the acute case causes pain, tenesmus, grunting and an anxious expression. Fibrinous adhesions at this acute stage are usually easily broken down manually per rectum. If this condition is found, the rectal examination should be stopped immediately to prevent extension of the inflammatory process. If these acute symptoms are overlooked and the cow survives, the history will often reveal this period of illness. If death does not occur adhesions become chronic, areas of infection are walled off and become encapsulated abscesses that can readily be felt on rectal examination. Sometimes tumors or fat necrosis may be confused with perimetritis and perimetrial abscesses. The prognosis in parametritis or perimetritis varies with the severity of the condition. Slight adhesions may cause no trouble, and sometimes can be broken by the hand in the rectum after the condition has become chronic. In severe, extensive adhesions the prognosis is poor to hopeless, especially if the ovaries and oviducts are involved in the adhesions or if the uterus is adhered to the abdominal organs over an extensive area. Such affected animals are usually sterile. In acute perimetritis conservative treatment with parenteral antibiotic and/or sulphonamide therapy is indicated.

Abscess of the Uterine Wall is occasionally observed in the cow. It is usually round or oval in shape and tense and firm on palpation. It may vary from 0.5 to 4 to 6 inches, 1 to 15 cm, in diameter, changing the normal outline or contour of the uterine horn. (See Figure 137) It frequently occurs as a sequela to a severe metritis, rough or improper removal of a retained placenta, injury to the uterus due to improper or rough use of an inseminating pipette or other instrument and trauma especially to an infected uterus allowing infection to penetrate through the endometrium. Abscess of the uterine wall is easily palpated on rectal examination and should be differentiated from a tumor, cyst, or hematoma. Occasionally some

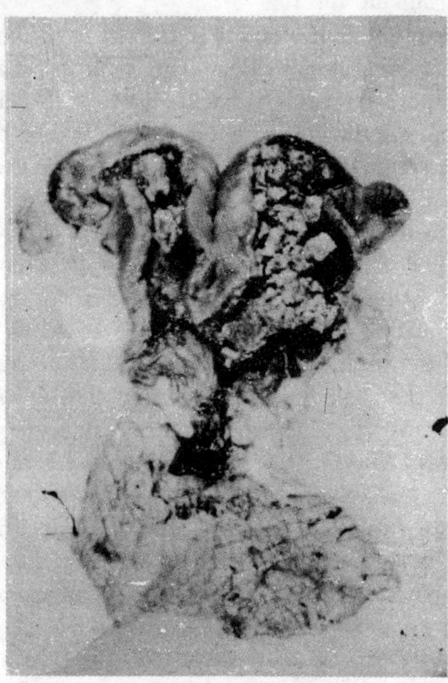

Figure 135. Chronic Postpartum Metritis and Pyometra due to Inspissated Necrotic Cotyledons and Caruncles.

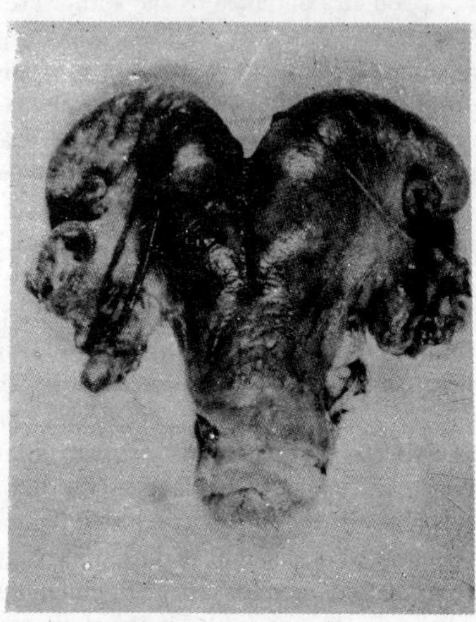

Figure 136. Extensive Perimetritis and Ovaritis with Adhesions Following a Severe Metritis after an 8-month-Abortion.

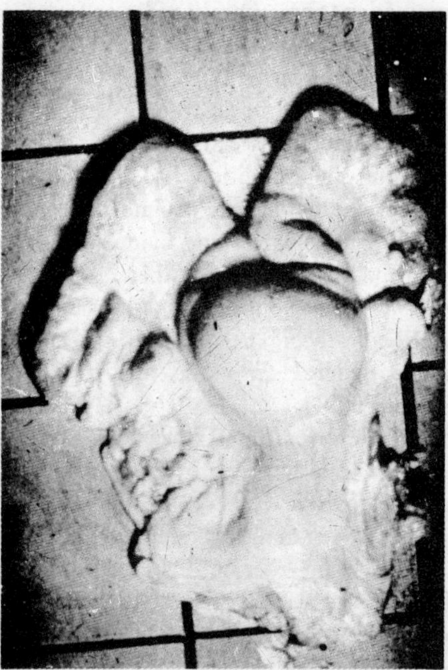

Figure 137. Abscess of the Uterine Wall Caused by the Improper Use of an AI Pipette.

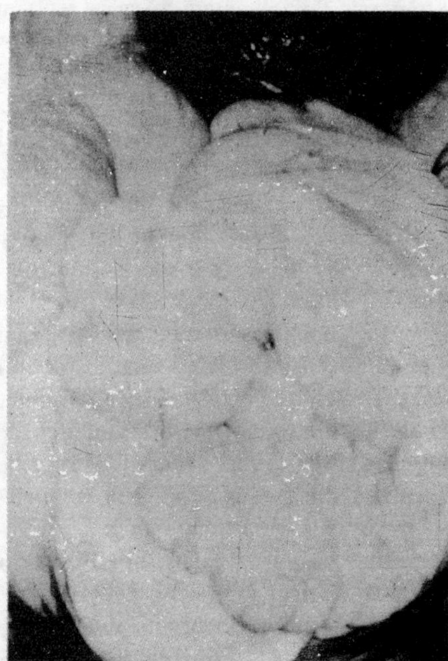

Figure 138. Ectropion of the External Cervical Os (three prolapsed transverse rings can be noted). (Courtesy K. McEntee)

perimetritis or adhesions may be felt around it. There are no general symptoms. In many instances the cow may fail to conceive. In several cases observed by the authoi the affected cows aborted at approximately 4 months of gestation on successive pregnancies and were sold as sterile. In another case the abscess ruptured into the uterus producing a pyometra. Treatment is usually impossible without the danger of causing a severe perimetritis or peritonitis. If the abscess is small the animal may recover but in many cases it is sterile. In rare instances adhesions form and the abscess may rupture into the rectum, bladder, or vagina. Parenteral antibiotic therapy might be indicated in early stages. Rupturing the abscess into the uterine lumen might be attempted as a last resort.

Uterine Abscess, a condition similar to pyometra but characterized by a pathologic scarring or atresia of the cervix or vagina, is usually due to severe trauma and necrosis caused by a dystocia or fetotomy operation. Cervical or vaginal atresia preventing the evacuation of the pus is very rare in the cow. If this condition is diagnosed the prognosis is usually hopeless and the cow is sold for slaughter.

Sclerotic Metritis is caused by a severe chronic metritis that has caused the complete destruction of the endometrium and fibrotic changes in the uterine wall. The endometrium is transformed into a thick, dense layer of connective tissue with foci of infection and purulent exudation into the uterine cavity. The uterus resembles a fistulous tract, McEntee. The condition often involves the cervix. This thickened indurated condition of the uterus usually follows a severe prolonged infection of the uterus such as chronic pyometra or fetal maceration. The uterine caruncles and endometrium are destroyed and the animal is therefore hopelessly sterile. The uterus on rectal examination feels very hard and firm, like cartilage or dense fibrous tissue. It is larger than normal and a chronic exudate may come from the uterus as well as from a thickened indurated cervix. In fetal maceration, bones may still be felt in the uterus. A sclerotic metritis should be carefully differentiated from an adenocarcinoma of the uterus which it may closely resemble. Usually the cow fails to show estrum and the corpus luteum is deeply imbedded or retained. Slaughter is recommended.

Tumors of the Uterus in the cow are uncommon. In 6286 bovine genital tracts examined by Lagerlof and Boyd there were 44 uterine tumors including 15 leiomyomas, 12 fibromyomas, 7 fibromas, 1 scirrhous adenocarcinoma, 1 lymphosarcoma, 1 spindle cell sarcoma, and 7 undiagnosed tumors. In recent years a number of reports have indicated that lymphosarcoma and adenocarcinoma of the uterus are becoming more common, Moulton, Cotchin, Monlux et al., Anderson and Dāvis, McEntee and Lingard and Dickinson. (See Figures 139 and 140) The lymphoid tumor or malignant bovine lymphoma may involve the uterus and result in diffuse plague-like thickenings in the uterine wall. Affected cows may often be pregnant. The tumor is whitish-grey, compact and soft in consistency. Adenocarcinoma of the uterus is less common

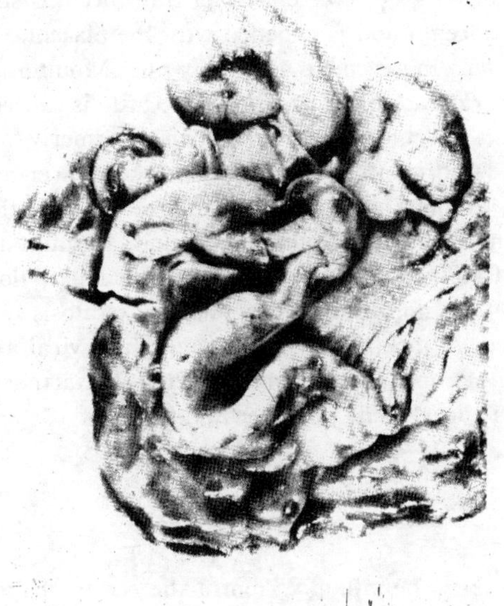

Figure 139. Lymphosarcoma of the Bovine Uterus. (Note the plaque-like thickenings of the uterine wall)

Figure 140. Adenocarcinoma of the Bovine Uterus.

but this tumor may metastasize to other body organs and the peritoneum. In the uterus it feels hard, cartilaginous and umbilicated. It may ulcerate so that a bloody discharge comes from the cervix. Leiomyomas are usually single, firm, round and may resemble abscesses; they are benign. Careful rectal palpation of tumors of the uterus will differentiate them from abscesses, cysts, adhesions, tuberculosis and other uterine diseases.

Mucometra or Hydrometra is seen occasionally in cattle. Both mucometra and hydrometra are similar except for the degree of hydration of the mucin present in the uterus which may vary from a watery fluid to a semisolid mass, McEntee. It has been described previously as a condition secondary to cystic ovaries and cystic endometrial hyperplasia usually associated with an anestrous period of 6 months or more. The ovarian cysts are usually small, 1 to 1.5 cm., two to four are usually present on each ovary. The cysts usually have a thick wall that resists rupture by manual pressure. The condition is further characterized by cystic degeneration of the endometrium and atrophy of the uterine wall, with an ounce to a gallon of thin to viscid mucus in the uterus. (See Figure 112)

Mucometra is also observed in heifers or cows with arrests in the development of the Mullerian duct system or segmental aplasia of the paramesonephric ducts in which part of the vagina, cervix, or uterus may be missing or defective. (See Figures 120, 122, 126, 127) Persistence of the hymen causing mucometra and mucovagina has been previously described. (See Figure 124) These genetic or congenital defects may result in a distention of both horns with watery, viscous, or even rather solid coagulated masses of mucus and cellular debris that may be confused with pregnancy. In these affected cattle the ovaries and endometrium are normal, and estrum therefore usually occurs normally. Rare cases of mucometra may be associated with a retained corpus lutem, Roberts and Fox.

In the cow, as in the dog, mucometra can apparently be produced by prolonged hormonal stimulation by estrogens and/or progesterone. The author has observed one case secondary to trauma and a fine adhesion obstructing the lumen of the cervix at the region of the internal os. In cases of mucometra no infection is usually present unless introduced accidentally by trauma, service, or treatment.

Cases of mucometra may be differentiated from pregnancy on a careful examination of the genital tract. Failure to slip fetal membranes, the presence of anomalies in the uterus, vagina, and cervix; the finding of ovaries that contain a single or multiple small cysts 0.5 to 0.75 inch in diameter; rarely the finding of a persistent corpus luteum on repeated examinations; the lack of enlargement or whirring of the uterine artery; the inability to palpate the fetus or cotyledons, although some cases with firm, gum-like-mucus in one horn or an apex of one horn may simulate a fetus or mummified fetus; the presence of a uterine wall that is usually thin and lacks tone as compared to the normal pregnant uterus; and the absence of regular developmental changes that occur in a normal pregnancy are the clinical findings on rectal examination of cattle affected with mucometra.

Cows with mucometra, or hydrometra due to defects of the genital tract are often sterile unless the case is a uterus unicornis and pregnancy occurs in the normal horn, or a simple imperforate hymen that can be opened. The advisability of using these cattle as breeding animals is questionable from a hereditary standpoint. In cows with mucometra and anestrum due to cystic ovaries, injection of a large dose of L.H. 20,000 IU of H.C.G. or more intravenously may occasionally bring about recovery. In rare cases of mucometra with a persistent corpus luteum injection of estrogens to involute the corpus luteum or manual removal of it may be successful in correcting the condition.

Miscellaneous uterine diseases—McEntee has described a highly unusual **cystic placental mole** that follows embryonic death with the continued life and even growth of the membranes to a size corresponding to a 3 to 4 months' pregnancy together with retention of the corpus luteum. The mole has no lumen but consists of a mass of clear gelatin-like fluid. The "growth" may progress to pyometra or be expelled spontaneously. This condition should not be confused with the hydatidiform mole which appears as a grape-like cluster of translucent cysts or villi of the placenta and is expelled with the placenta. Chorio-epithelioma in the cow is extremely rare, Moulton.

Hyperkeratosis or X disease of cattle is caused by the ingestion of chlorinated napthalenes formerly added to oils and lubricants. It caused a marked lowering of the plasma vitamin A levels, a wrinkled, crusted, thickened skin, anorexia, depression, emaciation, abortion and even death. Retained placenta and metritis usually followed the abortion. In non-pregnant cows hyperkeratosis was characterized by metaplasia of the vaginal, cervical and uterine epithelium. Cystic enlargement of Gartner's ducts regularly developed, McEntee and Olafson.

Cervix

Cervicitis or inflammation of the cervix of the cow is commonly observed associated with metritis and frequently follows abnormal parturitions such as abortions, premature birth, dystocia, especially where forced extraction or fetotomy caused cervical lacerations or trauma, retained placenta, and postpartum metritis. Cervicitis especially of the external os of the cervix may follow injuries to the vulva and vagina allowing "windsucking" and vaginal contamination. Vaginal infections whether viral or bacterial usually produce a cervicitis, especially of the external os of the cervix. Occasionally a cervicitis may occur following trauma or puncture of the cervix by a catheter or insemination pipette. Care, patience, and gentleness should always be used in manipulating a catheter or pipette through the cervix. The cervix appears more resistant to infections than either the uterus or the vagina. The cervical infections are usually miscellaneous in nature and may be due to any of the organisms that infect the uterus or vagina. Certain organisms, such as **C. pyogenes,** are probably more pathogenic than others such as streptococci. It is possible that at coitus there may occur an introduction of infections that might cause some involvement of the external os of the cervix as well as the cranial portions of the vagina. The internal portions of the cervix appear rather resistant to the introduction of miscellaneous infections. Most cases of cervicitis originate at the time of or following parturition and often are associated with a metritis. Prolapse of the external transverse cervical rings or cervical ectropion is a possible factor causing cervicitis in older cows. (See Figure 138) These prolapsed rings are often chronically thickened and fibrosed and circulation to the epithelium may be poor, permitting the establishment of infections. Severe purulent vaginitis or vaginitis associated with pneumovagina due to a lacerated or stretched vulva, atrophy of the perineal body and vulvar lips and horizontal tipping of the vulva may cause a severe cervicitis especially if urine and feces are present in the vagina. A poorly developed short cervix with very small transverse rings as described previously may readily permit an endometritis to develop and a cervicitis may also be present.

Symptoms. Cervicitis can be diagnosed on vaginal examination with a speculum and light. The external os of the affected cervix is usually edematous and swollen, the external folds are often prolapsed, the cervical mucosa is a cherry-red to dark-purple color, and mucopurulent exudate may be seen in and on the cervix. There is little evidence that mild cervicitis without metritis prevents conception or causes sterility. Even when severe forms of cervicitis are present, conception may occur. Many clinicians have observed pregnant cattle with a mucopurulent vaginitis involving the external os of the cervix. Mathews and Buxton reported on the occurrence of certain bacteria in the human cervix such as **E. coli,** streptococci, and others that proved to be spermicidal in vitro. The results of treating these sterility patients with antibiotics were encouraging. In a later report Buxton and co-workers (1954) reported that with the accumulation of adequate controlled material the results in untreated patients were similar to those in treated patients and that treatment with antibiotics had no effect on the pregnancy rates even though both treated and untreated patients had similar bacteria in the cervix. Gibbons et al. demonstrated the presence of a wide variety of bacteria, including streptococci and staphylococci, in the cervical mucus of 40 per cent of postparturient cows. There was no evidence that the presence of these organisms had any effect on fertility. McEntee reported that cervicitis was rather seldom a cause for sterility in the cases he observed at autopsy. Since cervicitis and endometritis are closely associated and the former usually can be observed clinically, cervicitis may often be erroneously blamed for infertility. If a severe cervicitis is present endometritis or metritis is probably also present and should be treated. Occasionally if pregnancy does occur even though a cervicitis is present the gestation may be insecure, with the possibility that abortion, retained placenta, and other uterine pathology may develop. Vigorous manipulation of the cervix will produce a severe hyperemia and congestion of the mucus membrane that should not be confused with infectious cervicitis. On rectal examination the infected cervix may be large and thick or may be normal in size. Hypertrophy of the cervix does not necessarily mean that cervicitis is present. Cervicitis does not occur commonly in the greatly hypertrophied cervices noted especially in Brahman, Zebu and Santa Gertrudis cattle Occasionally in severe chronic cervicitis the cervix may be very thick and sclerotic. The severity of the cervicitis will vary depending on the cause and length of time it has existed. Zemjanis et al. reported the incidence of chronic cervicitis based on clinical examination was 0.6 per cent. It may be difficult to differentiate between cervicitis and metritis. If a metritis is present cervicitis is also invariably present.

Cervical stenosis may follow severe infection or trauma. Cervical atresia or obstruction is very rare in the cow. If it occurs the mucus and exudate remain in the uterus, and the uterus becomes distended. Depending on the nature of the uterine contents a uterine abscess or mucometra develops. Cervical stenosis may occur due to severe cervical inflammation, or an enlarged cervical ring may extend into the cervical canal, making a sharp bend in the lumen so that passage of a catheter is difficult or impossible. These cows frequently conceive promptly when bred naturally or when semen is deposited artificially in the cervix. In rare instances described previously, a severe sclerotic, fibrosed, indurated cervix may result in cervical stenosis at the time of calving causing dystocia. In occasional cases following a dystocia a necrotic cervicitis or a severely lacerated cervix may be present producing a severe scarring of the mucous membrane.

Prognosis—The prognosis in most cases of cervicitis is good and spontaneous recovery usually occurs as the metritis and vaginitis improve. As long as a metritis or severe vaginitis is present, recovery from a cervicitis cannot occur. The cervical infection usually is overcome by the natural body-defense mechanisms particularly if the estrous periods are regular. The more severe forms of cervicitis may take longer to respond. Cervical stenosis or sclerosis frequently fail to respond to treatment, and if the cow conceives these conditions are apt to cause dystocia at the time of the next parturition. Cervical ectropion, or prolapse of the external cervical folds, does not improve. Usually the prolapsed transverse rings become a little more ectropic with each calving.

Treatment—If metritis or vaginitis accompanies the cervicitis then the entire reproductive tract must be treated. The same treatments usually are useful for all 3 conditions. It should be recognized that ordinarily the cow overcomes cervicitis spontaneously, as it does other infections of the genital tract. The following treatments may aid and hasten recovery. Warm or hot mild antiseptic douches of the vagina every 3 to 4 days as described for endometritis are useful in flushing out the mucopurulent exudate and stimulating circulation in the mucosa of the vagina, cervix and uterus. Douching the cervix and uterus may also be useful. Many veterinarians prefer to swab the cervix with one of the following: Lugol's solution; a cervicitis mixture such as (A) phenol 1 part, tincture of iodine 1 part and glycerine 2 parts, or (B) menthol crystals 1 dram, tincture of iodine 4 ounces and glycerine 4 ounces. The cervix is swabbed by pulling it back toward the vulva with cervical forceps and then with gauze wrapped around a long pair of dressing forceps soaked in Lugol's or cervicitis mixture the entire length of the cervix is thoroughly swabbed. Although this treatment probably does not completely eliminate infection it stimulates mucous flow, causes hyperemia, and apparently hastens recovery. The use of stronger preparations such as 10- to 20-per cent silver nitrate solutions are not indicated as they may cause too much damage and may result in cervical adhesions. Some veterinarians inject antibiotic or sulfonamide solutions and preparations into the cervix and uterus and expect that as it is expelled the material will help overcome the infection in the cervix. Some prefer to rub or infuse a sulfonamide or antibiotic ointment or 1 per cent acriflavine ointment into the cervical lumen. If cervicitis is secondary to vaginitis and pneumovagina, a vulva-suturing operation should be performed as described under the treatment of vaginitis.

In certain cases of chronic cervicitis of the external os associated with severely prolapsed cervical rings that fail to respond to treatment, the external cervical rings may be amputated. This may be done readily with large serrated scissors. After the prolapsed rings have been amputated the vaginal mucosa may be sutured to the cervical mucosa to help control hemorrhage and promote rapid healing but this is not necessary. Epidural anesthesia is not required as there are no sensory nerves in the cervix. Trachelorrhaphy is the suturing of cervical lacerations after calving. Partial trachelectomy is the amputation of a portion of the cervix, as described. This operation is probably not necessary since cervical infections of the external os seldom prevent conception and the internal portion of the cervix provides a firm seal even though the external os may be ectropic and inflamed. Usually within 3 to 4 weeks after amputation of the prolapsed cervical rings healing has occurred and breeding can take place. Regular estrous periods have as definite a healing effect on cervicitis as they have on endometritis. If cervicitis is severe, sexual rest is indicated for two or more estrous periods. As with endometritis, the intramuscular injection or topical application of 20 to 40 mg of stilbestrol may have some value if it is repeated every 10 days or so. Frequent removal of the corpus luteum is not desirable. Manual or instrumental dilation of an atretic or stenosed cervical canal is useless. The bovine cervix usually ruptures before a significant dilation occurs.

Cervicitis may be prevented by the same precautions that can be taken to prevent endometritis or vaginitis. Trauma to the cervix should be avoided whenever possible.

Cysts of the Cervix are observed occasionally in the cow. These are sometimes called "Nabothian" cysts or follicles, after the terminology used for this condition in humans. These cysts vary in size from 0.5 to 2 inches, 1 to 5 cm, in diameter. They are apparently retention cysts of the cervical glands; they may be congenital but are usually acquired secondary to trauma or lacerations. Frequently they go unnoticed until they become large and palpable as a fluctuating mass in the cervix on rectal examination. Often a portion of the cyst may be observed in the external os on vaginal examination. These cysts apparently seldom cause infertility but they might be large enough to hold some mucus and debris in the uterus, prevent proper closure of the uterus by the cervical seal during pregnancy or possibly interfere with the passage of spermatozoa. They are easily treated by incising with a needle, teat bistoury, or small knife through the external os of the cervix. Following incision and draining of the mucus from the cyst, the cervix may be swabbed with Lugol's solution or other cervicitis mixture. In some cases a cyst may require differentiation from an abscess; it is usually thin-walled and covered only by mucous membrane whereas the abscess is deeper in the tissues of the cervix and has a thicker, more fibrous wall of connective tissue. Cysts of the cervix should also be differentiated from occasional cystic dilations, sacculations, or diverticulums of the cervical lumen in cattle due to arrests in the development or fusion or developmental defects of the Mullerian ducts. These may be genetic or congenital in nature (See hereditary defects of the cervix), and the prognosis is usually guarded to poor.

Complete Stenosis or Obstruction of the Cervix, except that secondary to trauma or severe inflammation, is probably very rare in the cow. In some heifers with a small or torturous cervical canal an insemination pipette cannot readily be passed. If these animals fail to conceive the stenotic cervix may be considered to be the cause. Olds and Seath reported that in 1711 heifers and 11,112, cows the cervix was impenetrable to an inseminating pipette in 11.7 and 1.1 per cent of the cattle, respectively. When semen was inseminated into the cervix the conception rate in the affected heifers was 54.0 per cent, and in the cows 36.5 per cent, indicating that this condition should not be considered abnormal and a cause of infertility. The author and his associates have observed only one case of cervical atresia in the cow is not associated with an anomalous condition, and this showed evidence of previous trauma. (See Figure 141) If the cervix were actually obstructed the uterus should fill with mucus and other cellular debris similar to that observed in cattle with certain congenital defects of the reproductive tract, such as an imperforate hymen. In heifers with an infantile, abnormal, or stenotic cervix treatment as described under hereditary defects of the cervix should be followed.

Mucocervix—In rare instances the cervix may be greatly enlarged to about 4 to 6 inches in diameter and 6 inches in length with an enormous pathological cervical seal of tough tenacious mucus. This condition is probably a hormonal disturbance due to a deficiency of L.H. It is usually associated with a failure of estrum with chronic cystic ovaries or a retained corpus luteum. The prognosis is usually very poor. The intravenous or intramuscular injection of a very large dose of L.H. may be helpful in the treatment of these cases. An anomaly or defect of the cervix usually fills with mucus.

Tumors of the Bovine Cervix are rare. Wadsworth, Moulton, and Cotchin described fibromas, fibrosarcomas, leiomyomas, and carcinomas affecting the cervix. Most of these tumors were benign. In rare instances adenocarcinomas may be malignant and metastasize to other organs.

Vagina

Vaginitis in the cow is observed as a primary or secondary condition. The secondary condition is often associated with metritis and cervicitis. Vaginitis may occur following trauma, lacerations, and bacterial, viral or protozoal infections produced or introduced at the time of service, abortion, dystocia, fetotomy, retained placenta, prolapse of the vagina, and postpartum metritis. Severe stretching or laceration of the vulva especially of the perineal body, and in older cows sinking of the anus and tipping of the vulva into a horizontal position, with an atrophy of the vulvar lips often results in pneumovagina and severe contamination of the vagina by feces, urine, air, and miscellaneous debris and infection that often cannot be readily expelled because the uterus and cervix have pulled the anterior portion of the vagina forward and downward into the abdominal cavity. (See Figure 142) A vaginitis may occur following coitus but this is usually a mild and transient condition. Occasionally small abscesses may develop in the mucosa or in Gartner's ducts. In rare instances vaginitis may be due to treatment of the vagina with irritant preparations, introduction of infection on instruments, or examination of the vagina in a dirty, unsanitary manner. Most vaginitis is due to non-specific infections such as staphylococci, streptococci, coliform organisms, **C. pyogenes,** and others. The vaginitis due to specific infections such as IBR-IPV, "epivag", and possibly other viral infections, trichomoniasis, vibriosis and granular venereal disease has already been discussed. Necrotic vaginitis and severe vaginal lacerations following calving, dystocia, and fetotomy have been discussed previously in Chapter XI.

Symptoms of Vaginitis—In the cow a mucopurulent, yellow-grey pus is usually discharged from the vulva at irregular intervals and mats the hair of the vulva, tail and buttocks. On vaginal examination the exudate is observed on the floor of the vagina and the vaginal walls are congested, edematous, and inflamed. The more severe the inflammation the more red and inflamed the vagina. In some cases ulceration of the mucosa, lacerations and secondary diptheritic or necrotic lesions occur especially around the vestibulo-vaginal border and in the vestibule and vulva. In severe cases the cow may show tenesmus, irritation, and pain probably due to the concurrent vestibulitis and vulvitis.

If the vulva is stretched, damaged, torn, or deformed, so that pneumovagina results, the vagina may then contain fecal material, urine, and air as well as mucopurulent exudate. (See Figure 142) This may frequently be a cause of failure of conception, particularly in older cows in the large breeds, such as Holsteins, Brown Swiss, Herefords, Santa Gertrudis, possibly Brahmas, and occasionally Guernseys. Under most circumstances an uncomplicated mild vaginitis may not prevent conception. Since vaginitis is often associated with cervicitis and endometritis it is probably the latter condition that in most cases causes the infertility, although a severely diseased vagina and exter-

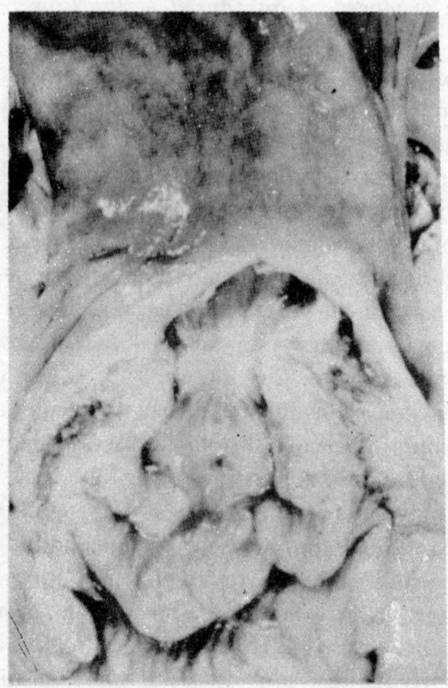

Figure 141. Atresia of the Internal Os of the Cervix Secondary to an Acute Cervicitis. (Mucometra resulted).

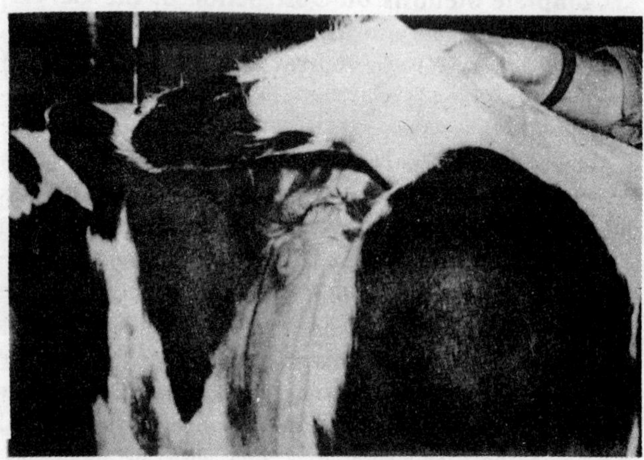

Figure 142. A Horizontally-tipped Abnormal Vulva Causing Pneumovagina in a Cow. (Suturing of the vulvar lips was followed by conception in this cow.)

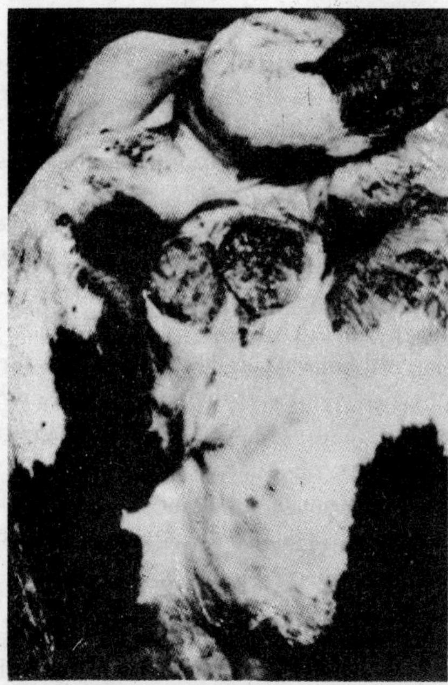

Figure 143. Carcinomas of the Vulva of a Cow.

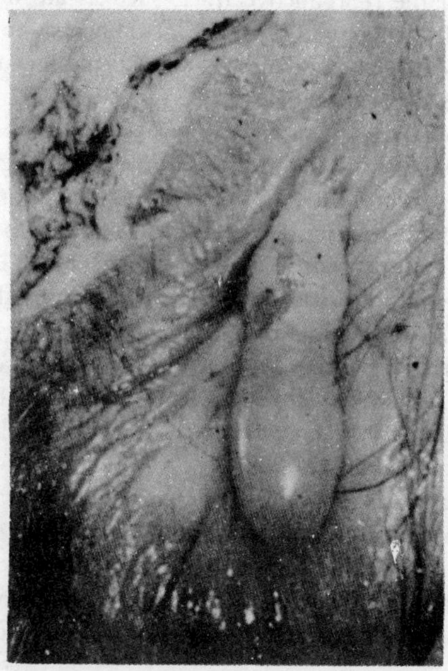

Figure 144. An Anomaly or Wattle, Present on the Vulva of a Heifer. (Courtesy K. McEntee.)

nal os of the cervix filled with pus and debris and having an altered pH may cause rapid destruction of spermatozoa and interfere with fertilization. In pneumovagina in old cows or Indian cattle with a large heavy cervix pulling the vagina forward and downward, an accumulation of material in the vagina, often associated with an atonic uterus hanging low in the abdominal cavity, may cause some infectious material to pass through the infected and relaxed cervix and thereby cause an endometritis. Often in these older cows with the characteristically deformed perineum, the vulvar lips may be parted with the fingers and air will rush into the vagina. In 12 cases of infertility apparently due to pneumovagina treated by the author, the cows had been bred unsuccessfully 2 to 8 times, or an average of 4.5 times. After correcting the condition, 10 (or 83.3 per cent) conceived within 21 to 60 days. Although this is too small a number upon which to base a definite conclusion the fact nevertheless remains that following the closure of the vulva the vaginitis cleared up very rapidly. From what is known concerning the value of the operation in mares the author feels that this procedure has received too little attention in the treatment of sterility in cattle. The external os of the cervix is usually involved in any vaginitis. If metritis or cervicitis is present some of the vaginal discharge may actually come from those sites and the vagina is involved secondarily. Necrotic vaginitis, as described previously following a difficult parturition, may also follow the accidental use of caustic agents as a douche. In rare cases secondary stenosis and even atresia of the vagina may follow a severe vaginitis.

The Prognosis in simple vaginitis due to the causes listed above is good, and most cases will respond spontaneously even without treatment unless pneumovagina is present or unless a severe chronic cervicitis or metritis is also present. The prognosis is poor if stenosis or atresia of the vagina is severe. If the vaginitis is caused by an infectious agent, local antibodies are usually produced that aid in the elimination of infections such as **V. fetus, Tr. fetus** and IBR-IPV.

The Treatment of vaginitis usually consists of mild aqueous douches of 200 ppm chlorine solution, antiseptic aromatic soap solutions, dilute potassium permanganate solutions, 1:1000 to 1:3000 acriflavine solutions, 200 ppm quaternary ammonium compound solutions, sodium bicarbonate solutions, solutions of chlorhexidine, and saline solutions. Irritating douches are unnecessary and should be avoided. Usually 2000 to 4000 ml of a solution are used and introduced either by means of a catheter and funnel, an enema bag and tube, or by holding the extended hand palm upwards in the vestibule pinching down the cow's back, and pouring the solution over the palm of the hand into the vagina. This flushing of the vagina may be repeated several times to wash out mucopurulent material. Retreating may be helpful at daily or at 3- to 4-day intervals. Besides douching, some veterinarians introduce sulfonamides or antibiotics such as: penicillin, streptomycin, neomycin, furacin, tetracyclines or others in an ointment form or in oil-and-water emulsions. Others infuse the vagina with bland antiseptics in oil, such as sulfonamides and bismuth formic iodide, 1 ounce in a pint of oil, or iodine in oil; this may be repeated twice a week. If a cervicitis or metritis is present these should be treated also. Many veterinarians use small doses of 20 to 40 mg of stilbestrol at 7- to 10-day intervals in the treatment of vaginitis.

In cases of pneumovagina the vagina is usually douched thoroughly, an antibiotic solution or preparation is placed in the uterus, cervix, and vagina. Then under epidural or local anesthesia of the vulvar lips, as in the Caslick operation in the mare, the mucosa of the outer 1/2 inch, or 1 to 1.5 cm, of the vulvar lips is scarified from the dorsal commissure to the level of the ischial arch. Often only a 1- to 1-1/2 inch vulvar opening is left after suturing. Sutures should be of chromic catgut, nylon, or stainless steel. Since the cow's tail rests and rubs on her vulva, Michel clips are not satisfactory as they usually are rubbed out. The interrupted sutures should be about 3/8 to 1/2 inch, 1 cm., apart and not put in so tightly that the suture cuts the tissues. The sutures may be removed in 7 to 10 days. (See Figure 85) The vulvar opening after this operation is small and service by artificial insemination usually is necessary. The last week or two of gestation the vulva should be incised along the original suture line so that no tearing of the vulva will occur at parturition. The vulva needs to be resutured after calving.

In former years the acidity or alkalinity of the vagina was considered a cause of infertility in cattle, and sodium bicarbonate douches were often prescribed especially a few hours prior to breeding. There is, however, no basis for this antiquated belief.

Cysts of the Vagina are not uncommon. Cysts of the mesonephric or Gartner's ducts in the floor of the vagina are usually small, 0.5 inch wide and 0.5 to 1 inch long. There may be several cysts along the course of the ducts. (See Figure 129) These cause little harm and usually they are not found except on speculum or manual examination of the vagina. They are seldom treated. Gartner's duct cysts are described under congenital defects since these ducts are remnants of the Wolffian or mesonephric ducts. In rare instances these cysts may become infected. In rare occasions single cysts up to 1 inch, 3 cm in diameter, not of mesonephric duct origin, may be seen in the mucosa of the cranial and dorsal or lateral portion of the vagina.

Tumors of the Bovine Vagina have been described

by Williams, Cotchin, Moulton, and Wadsworth and include: fibromas, fibrosarcomas, leiomyomas, hemangiomas, lymphosarcomas, and carcinomas. Vaginal tumors are unusual in the cow. They seldom cause infertility but may cause dystocia, as do those of the cervix, if they are large enough. Most of the tumors are benign and pedunculated. Occasionally they may protrude through the vulva and surgical removal may be necessary. Excessive bleeding may occur unless steps to control it are taken at the time of the removal of the tumor.

Vestibule and Vulva

Vestibulitis and Vulvitis are similar to and treated in the same manner as vaginitis. Most cases of vulvitis are characterized by granular venereal disease lesions. Severe inflammations of the vulva may cause straining, refusal to copulate, and pain on examination. In severe cases the vulva is usually swollen and a mucopurulent discharge, such as in severe granular venereal disease or IBR-IPV infection, is present. Severe injury and lacerations of the vulva or vestibule caused by tearing of the vulva at the time of parturition, especially in Charolais cattle, or by horn wounds should be sutured at once to prevent pneumovagina. Necrotic vulvitis and vestibulitis may follow severe trauma, ischemia and infections such as **S. necrophorus.** An outbreak of necrotic vulvitis affecting 170 Hereford feedlot heifers was reported by Nelson. This was a localized necrosis of the vulva that varied in size from a small area of sloughing to one involving nearly the entire vulva. The heifers did not become clinically ill and all recovered in 3 to 5 weeks. The cause of the condition was not known but a virulent **S. necrophorus** infection or an allergic type of reaction was suspected. Campbell has reported that edema of the vulva and perineal region in clinical allergies or urticaria is common.

Cystic Vestibular, or Bartholin's, Glands are often observed in the lateral wall of the vestibule. They arise from an atresia of the duct of the gland that usually opens on the lateral wall of the vestibule at the vulvo-vaginal border. This small paired gland secretes a rather clear mucus. Obstruction of the duct opening is usually due to trauma or severe inflammation, such as a local necrotic vaginitis, at the time of calving. This gland may enlarge due to the accumulation of fluid, until it is 1 to 4 inches, 2 to 10 cm, in diameter. When the cystic gland becomes larger than 2 inches or 5 cm in diameter it usually shows between the vulvar lips when the cow is lying down as a round pink mucosa-covered object that is often mistaken for the beginning of a prolapse of the vagina. The cystic vestibular gland is almost invariably unilateral in occurrence and is seen in older cows and only rarely in heifers. It causes no problems at parturition nor does it interfere with conception. Occasionally when it is large it protrudes through the vulvar lips and becomes covered with feces and dirt. When the cow rises and the cyst returns to the pelvic canal contamination of the vestibule, vulva and caudal part of the vagina may occur. These cysts are easily handled by making a liberal incision therein. Painting the opened cyst with Lugol's solution, although commonly done, is probably not necessary.

The Tumors of the Vulva include: fibromas, fibrosarcomas, angiomas, carcinomas and fibropapillomas, Williams, Wadsworth, Moulton, Cotchin, and McEntee. The latter author reported on 28 fibropapillomas from the vulva and vagina of cows and 27 from the penis of bulls and concluded that, because it occurs primarily in young cattle usually in several animals on the same premises, the fibropapilloma is a transmissible tumor of the external genital organs of cattle. This tumor undergoes spontaneous regression in about one to 6 months. McEntee stated that it is similar to or the same as the common wart or papilloma found on the body skin of young cattle and caused by a virus. The prognosis on squamous-cell carcinomas of the vulva are guarded to poor as often the regional lymph nodes may be affected. Slaughter is usually advisable.

References

Albrechtsen, J. (1917) Sterility of Cattle and Methods of Treatment, Cor. Vet., **7,** 2, 57.

Anderson. W.A. and Davis, C. L. (1958) Neoplasms of the Genitalia of the Bovine, Reprod. and Infertil. III Symposium F. X. Gassner Ed., Pergamon Press, N.Y.C.

Black, W. G., Ulberg, L. C., Kidder, H. E., Simon, J., McNutt, S. H. and Casida, L. E. (1953) Inflammatory Response of the Bovine Endometrium, Am. J. Vet. Res., **14,** 51, 179.

Boucher, W. B., Marshak, R. R. and Hubben, K. (1964) Ovarian Adenocarcinoma in a Heifer, J.A.V.M.A. **144,** 10, 1132.

Brus, D. H. J. (1954) Biopsia Uteri, Thesis, Univ. of Utrecht, Utrecht, Netherlands.

Bu, I. (1955) Studies on the Local Treament of the Uterus In the Estrual and Luteal Phase of the Sexual Cycle (Trans), Nord. Vet. Med., **7,** 11, 917.

Buxton, L., Southam, A., Herrmann, W., Girvin, G., and Nadel, H. (1954) Bacteriology of the Cervix in Human Sterility, Fert. and Steril., **5,** 6, 493.

Campbell, S. G. (1970) Clinical Allergies in Cattle, Cor. Vet., **60,** 2, 240.

Cembrowicz, H. J. (1950) Changes in the Fallopian Tubes of the Bovine as a Cause of Sterility, Vet. Rec., **62,** 13, 189.

Cotchin, E. (1956) Neoplasms of the Domestic Mammals (A Review)

Dept. of Path., Royal Vet. Col. London, Review Series #4 Commonwealth Bureau of Animal Health, Farnham Royal, Bucks, England.

Dawson, F. L. M. (1956) The Incidence of Salpingitis and Bursitis Throughout a Series of 200 Permanently Infertile Cows, With Notes on Its Significance and Diagnosis, Proc. 3rd. Internat. Congr. on An. Reprod., Cambridge.

Dawson, F. L. M. (1958) The Diagnosis and Significance of Bovine Endosalpingitis and Ovarian Bursitis, Vet. Rec. **70,** 24, 487.

Dawson, F. L. M. (1960) Bovine Endometritis: A Review, Brit. Vet. Jour. **116,** 12, 448.

Dawson, F. L. M. (1961) The Bovine Uterus-Histopathology, Vet. Reviews and Annot., **7,** 1, 29.

DeBois, C. H. W. (1961) Endometritis and Fertility of the Cow, Thesis, Rijkuniv. Utrecht, Netherlands.

Eckman, L., Holmberg, O., Settergren, I. and Thorell, C. B. (1965) Resorbtion of Iodine in Lugol's Solution and in an Iodophor from the Uterus of Cows, Nord. Vet. Med. **17,** 391.

Feldman, W. H. (1932) Neoplasms of Domestic Animals, W. B. Saunders and Co., Philadelphia, Pa.

Fincher, M. G. (1946) Methods of Increasing Fertility in Domestic Animals, Trans. of the Amer. Soc. for the Study of Sterility.

Frank, A. H. (1950) Impaired Breeding in Cattle—Field Observations and Results of Treatment, Proc. A.V.M.A. 87th Ann. Meeting, 190.

Gibbons, W. J. and Kiesel, G. K. (1964) Antibiotic Uterine Infusion to Aid Fertility, Cor. Vet. **54,** 3, 382.

Gibbons, W. J., Attleberger, M. H., Kiesel, G. K. and Dacres, W. G. (1959) The Bacteriology of the Cervical Mucus of Cattle, Cor. Vet. **49,** 2, 255.

Hansel, W. (1968) Personal Communication.

Hawk, H. W., Brinsfield, T. H., Turner, G. O , Whitmore, G. W. and Norcross, M. A. (1964) Effect of Ovarian Status on Induced Acute Inflammatory Responses in Cattle Uteri, Amer. J. Vet. Res. **25,** 105, 362.

Hinze, P. M. (1959) Diagnosis and Treatment of Nonspecific Infertility in the Dairy Cow, J.A.V.M.A. **134,** 7, 302.

Kanagawa, H., Kawata, K., Nakao, N. and Sung, W. K. (1964) A Case of Granulosa Cell Tumor of the Ovary in a Newborn Calf, Jap. Jour. of Vet. Res. **12,** 1, 7.

Kampelmacher, E. H. (1954) An Examination, Using a Biopsy Apparatus, in Order to Obtain an Opinion of The Microbiology and Histology of the Uterus in Sterile Cattle (Trans.), Thesis. Univ. of Utrecht, Utrecht, Netherlands.

Kendrick, J. W. and Pier, A. C. (1960) Antibiotic Levels in Milk Following Intrauterine Infusion, Calif. Vet. **13,** 5, 27.

Knudsen, O and Sollen, P. (1961) Methods for Taking Samples from the Uterus of Mares and Cows, Nord. Vet. Med. **13,** 449.

Kortum, W. (1969) An Indwelling Uterine Infuser for Cattle and Horses, J.A.V.M.A. **155,** 12, 1942.

Lagerlof, N. and Boyd, H. (1953) Ovarian Hypoplasia and Other Abnormal Conditions in the Sexual Organs of Cattle of the Swedish Highland Breed: Results of Postmortem Examination of over 6000 Cows, Cor. Vet., **43,** 1, 64.

Lingard, D. R and Dickinson, E. O. Jr. (1969) Metastatic Uterine Adenocarcinoma in the Cow, Vet. Med. **64,** 3, 234.

Lombard, L., Morgan, B. B. and McNutt, S. H. (1951) Some Pathologic Alterations of the Bovine Oviduct, Am. J. Vet. Res., **12,** 43, 69.

Marshak, R. (1962) Personal Communication.

Mathews, C. S. and Buxton, C. L. (1951) Bacteriology of the Cervix in Cases of Infertility, Fert. and Steril., **2,** 1, 45.

McEntee, K. (1950) Fibropapillomas of the External Genitalia of Cattle, Cor. Vet., **40,** 3, 304.

McEntee, K. (1954) (1963) Personal Communication.

McEntee, K. (1970) The Female Genital System, in **Pathology of Domestic Animals** ed. by K.V.F. Jubb and P. C. Kennedy, 2nd Ed., Academic Press, N.Y.C.

McEntee, K., and Olafson, P. (1953) Reproductive Tract Pathology in Hyperkeratosis of Cattle and Sheep, Fert. and Steril., **4,** 2, 128.

McEntee, K., and Zepp, C. P. Jr. (1953) Canine and Bovine Ovarian Tumors, Proc. First World Congress on Fert. and Steril., Vol. II, XXIV, 649.

Megale, F. (1963) Personal Communication.

Megale, F., Fincher, M. G. and McEntee, K. (1956) Peritoneoscopy in the Cow-Visualization of the Ovaries, Oviducts and Uterine Horns, Cor. Vet. **46,** 1, 109.

Miller, J. G. (1950) A Method of Endometrial Biopsy in the Bovine and the Study of Biopsy Specimens in Cases of Infertility. Thesis. Cornell Univ., Ithaca, N.Y.

Miller, J. G. (1951) A Technique of Endometrial Biopsy in the Bovine Animal, J.A.V.M.A., **119,** 896, 368.

Minocha, H. C., Marion, G. B., Gier, H. T. and McMahon, K. F. (1964) An Instrument for Obtaining Aseptic Bacteriologic and Histologic Samples from the Bovine Genital Tract, Amer. J. Vet. Res. **25,** 107, 1051.

Moberg, R. (1954) Disease Conditions in the Fallopian Tubes and Ovarian Bursae of Cattle, Vet. Rec., **66,** 6, 87.

Monlux, A. W., Anderson, W. A. and Davis, C. L. (1956) A Survey of Tumors Occurring in Cattle, Sheep, and Swine, Amer. J. Vet. Res. **17,** 65, 646.

Monlux, A. W.., Anderson W. A., Davis C. L. and Monlux, W. S. (1956) Adenocarcinoma of the Uterus of the Cow—Differentiation of Its Pulmonary Metastases from Primary Lung Tumors, Amer. J. Vet. Res. **17,** 62, 45.

Moore, G. R. (1946) Effects of Stilbestrol on Pyometra Following Retained Fetal Membranes, J.A.V.M.A., **108,** 828, 153.

Morrow, D. A., Roberts, S. J. and McEntee, K. (1969) A Review of Postpartum Ovarian Activity and Involution of the Uterus and Cervix in Cattle, Cor. Vet. **59,** 1, 134.

Morrow, D. A., Roberts, S. J. and McEntee, K. (1969) Postpartum Ovarian Activity and Involution of the Uterus and Cervix II, Cor. Vet. **59,** 2, 190.

Morrow, D. A., Roberts, S. J., McEntee. K. and Gray, H. G. (1966)

Postpartum Ovarian Activity and Uterine Involution in Dairy Cattle, J.A.V.M.A. **149,** 12, 1596.

Moulton, J. E. (1961) Tumors of Domestic Animals, Univ. of Calif. Press, Berkeley, Cal.

Mylrea, P. J. (1962) Macroscopic Lesions of the Genital Organs of Cows, Austral. Vet. Jour. **38,** 457.

Neilson, J. (1949) Sterility in Cattle, Especially as a Result of Uterine Infection, Proc. 14th Internat. Vet. Cong., Section 4 (c), 105.

Nelson, W. A. (1958) Mass Outbreak of Necrotic Vulvitis, Jen Sal Jour. **41,** 1, 15.

Olds, D. (1969) An Objective Consideration of Dairy Herd Fertility, J.A.V.M.A. **154,** 253.

Olds, D. and Seath, D. M. (1954) Factors Effecting Reproductive Efficiency of Dairy Cattle, Kentucky Agr. Exp. Stat. Bull. 605.

Perkins, J. R., Olds, D. and Seath, D. M. (1954) A Study of 100 Bovine Genitalia, J. Dairy Sci. **37,** 1158.

Roberts, S. J. (1953) An Ovarian Tumor in a Heifer, Cor. Vet., **43,** 4, 531.

Roberts, S. J. (1956) An Evaluation of Uterine Infusions for the Treatment of Infertility in Cattle, Cor. Vet., **46,** 1, 21.

Roberts, S. J. (1956) Veterinary Obstetrics and Genital Diseases, Edwards Bros. Inc., Ann Arbor., Mich.

Roberts, S. J. and Fox, F. H. (1968) An Unusual Case of Bovine Mucometra Associated with a Persistent Corpus Luteum, Cor. Vet. **58,** 116.

Rowson, L. E. A. (1942) Affections of the Fallopian Tubes of Cattle, Vet. Rec., **54,** 31, 311.

Rowson, L. E. A., Lamming, G. E. and Fry, R. M. (1953) The Relationship between Ovarian Hormones and Uterine Infection, Vet. Rec., **65,** 22, 335.

Short, R. V., Shorter, D. R. and Linzell, J. L. (1963) Granulosa Cell Tumor of the Ovary in a Virgin Heifer, J. of Endocrin. **27,** 327.

Skjerven, O (1956) Endometrial Biopsy Studies in Reproductively Normal Cattle, (Thesis) Acta Endocrinol. Suppl. 26 (with Vol. 22) Vet. Col., Oslo, Norway.

Smythe, R. H. (1942) Notes on Uterine Irrigation on the Cow, Vet. Rec., **54,** 30, 300.

Studer, E. (1967) Mucinous Adenocarcinoma of the Bovine Ovary, J.A.V.M.A. **151,** 4, 438.

Tanabe, T. Y. and Almquist, J. O. (1967) Gross Genital Abnormalities, Bull. 736, Penn. State Univ., Agric. Exp. Stat., University Park, Pa.

Tennant, B. and Peddicord, R. G. (1968) Influence of Delayed Uterine Involution and Endometritis on Bovine Infertility, Cor. Vet. **58,** 2, 185.

Ulbert, L. C., Black, W. G., Kidder, H. E., McDonald, L. E., Casida, L. E., and McNutt, S. H. (1952) The Use of Antibiotics in the Treatment of Low Fertility Cows, J.A.V.M.A., **121,** 909, 436.

Wadsworth, J. R. (1952) The Distribution of Genital Tumors in the Bovine, Univ. of Penn. Bull., Vet. Ext. Quart., **128,** 133.

Williams, W. L. (1943) Diseases of the Genital Organs of Domestic Animals, 3rd Ed. Miss Louella Williams, Upland Rd.. Ithaca, N.Y.

Zemjanis, R., Larson, L. L. and Bhalla, R. P. S. (1961) Clinical Incidence of Genital Abnormalities in the Cow, J.A.V.M.A. **139,** 9, 1015.

THE REPEAT BREEDER COW

The discussion of this important infertility condition has been intentionally left to the end of this chapter because most of the diseases previously described are causes of failure of conception. The repeat breeding cow is one that has normal or nearly normal estrous cycles and estrous periods and has been bred 2 or more times to a fertile bull yet failed to conceive. The clinical examination of the animal may fail to reveal any definite lesion or condition to explain the failure of conception. The major proportions of the problem have been outlined but limited advances have been made in studying some of the various causes and still less on the diagnosis of causes in the individual cow. The greatest advance in this problem of "repeat breeders" has been the demonstration of the role of vibriosis in early embryonic deaths. It is unfortunate that many of the experiments performed before the mid 1950's and cited below did not consider this important cause of infertility.

In recent years Casida, Jainudeen, and Olds have reviewed the problem of repeat breeders and infertility in cattle. Hanley comprehensively reviewed the problem of prenatal mortality in cattle and other domestic animals. Erb and Holtz reported on infertility and breeding efficiency in a large dairy herd over a period of 30 years that included 2607 cows and nearly 10,000 breeding periods. The most common causes for infertility and associated services in which the fetus was carried to term were: short cycles, 24.2 percent; cystic follicles, 11.3 percent; and infection of the genital tract, 15.1 percent. Services carried to term in clinically normal cows was 51.9 percent. The various causes of repeat breeding have been classified differently by investigators. Casida and his coworkers and others in the field of reproductive physiology have divided the causes into two groups: (1) failure of fertilization and (2) early embryonic death. Others, including Zemjanis and the author, prefer a more detailed classification based on pathological and managerial causes namely: 1. congenital or genetic anatomical defects of genital tract, 2. Congenital, genetic or acquired defects of the ova, spermatozoa or early zygote, 3. infectious or traumatic inflammatory processes, 4. endocrine disfunctions, 5. managerial and nutritional deficiencies. Modern herds incorporating large numbers of cattle and employing artificial insemination have many problems in heat detection, timing of service, and in the care and handling of semen in which the herdsmen and inseminators can influence the incidence of infertility and repeat breeding. Because of the multiplicity of causes for repeat breeding that varies from herd to herd, cow to cow, and estrus to estrus, diagnosis and therapy by the veterinarian requires great diagnostic skill and knowledge.

Hewett, in 16,000 cows in 1500 herds, Zemjanis in 5800 cows in 13 herds have surveyed the problem of repeat breeding and have shown the overall incidence to be 10 percent (9.1 to 11.1) and 15.1 percent (6.7 to 20.9), respectively. Over 50 percent of the farms surveyed had this average incidence of affected animals. As the herd size increased so did the incidence of repeat breeders. The highest seasonal incidence of repeat breeders was in the fall and winter months with the lowest incidence in the spring and summer months, 10.2 to 13.7 and 7.1 to 9.4 percent, respectively, Hewett. The incidence of repeat breeders is lowest in heifers that had calved for the first time, 5.2 percent and then in older cattle it rose and in 9-year-old or older cows it was 13.3 percent. There was a marked tendency for cows to revert to spring calving with increasing age. Repeat breeding was also more common in cows with higher milk production. Olds and Seath reported that only 10 percent of the herds or individual cows affected with an infertility or repeat breeding problem one year continued to be affected the following year. The herds with infertility problems remained constant at 6.5 per cent from year to year in Kentucky. Van Dieten of the Netherlands after studying records on 75,000 cows also showed fertility decreased as animals grew older, from 68 to 58 percent in virgin heifers to cows with their tenth calf. As herd size increased there was a decrease in fertility. He found the greatest fertility on farms raising grade cattle.

Olds summarized five of the early classical experiments on repeat breeding cows and heifers. Most were taken from herds artificially inseminated. The animals were examined clinically and those with obvious disease of the reproductive organs and over 10 years of age were eliminated. However, in these early studies **V. fetus** might have been an important cause for infertility. Not more than 2 cows were taken from any one herd. The cows were bred to a fertile bull by artificial insemination on the second estrum after arriving at the central location for the experiment. One-half of these were killed on the third day after breeding and the oviducts were flushed to recover the ova, which were then examined to see if fertilization had taken place. Fertilization was noted by cell division in the ovum. The other half of the animals were scheduled to be killed at 34 days after insemination. If they came back in estrum before this time they were rebred and killed the third day. At the time of slaughter on 34 days the presence or absence of a normal, living embryo was noted. Thus from the findings at these 2 times the percentages of fertilization and of early embryonic deaths were determined. In these five studies 313 ova were recovered with a **fertilization rate** of 65.5 percent.

In two later studies, Bearden et al. and Kidder et al. the fertilization rate of 120 recovered ova in 97 normal virgin heifers was 85.5 percent. Fifty one heifers bred to highly fertile AI bulls (70 to 79 percent conception based on 60 to 90 day nonreturns), had a fertilization rate of 96.1 percent; while 46 heifers bred to AI bulls with low fertility (40 to 60 percent conceptions based on nonreturns at 60 to 90 days), had a fertilization rate of only 76.1 percent. In 299 repeat breeding cattle, as summarized by Olds, 6.4 percent failed to ovulate, 5.4 percent had occluded oviducts and 4.7 percent had abnormal or defective ova which accounts for some definite causes of failure of fertilization. There was no apparent cause for failure of fertilization in over 23 percent of the repeat breeding cows. Low fertility of semen and possibly improper timing of service might have accounted for some of this failure of fertilization due to no apparent cause. The importance of using highly fertile sires for breeding cows, especially repeat breeders, is obvious from the studies of Bearden et al. and Kidder et al..

Olds summarized three studies on 199 repeat breeder cows and reported an incidence of 28.5 percent **early embryonic deaths.** As mentioned before it was unfortunate that the status of these animals with regard to **V. fetus** infection was not ascertained. Bearden et al. artificially inseminated 26 virgin heifers with antibiotic-treated semen from bulls of low fertility and 29 virgin heifers with semen of high fertility; the percent of normal embryos present at 33 days in the two groups were 57.7 and 86.1, respectively, with an estimated embryonic death rate of 19.6 and 10.5 percent respectively. This latter difference was not statistically significant. Kidder et al. reported a slightly higher incidence of embryonic death loss in virgin heifers bred to the bulls with higher fertility than in heifers bred to bulls of lower fertility. The average incidence of embryonic death in virgin heifers was 15 percent as summarized by Olds. The evidence indicated that repeat breeding, when highly fertile bulls were used, was largely due to embryonic deaths; while in repeat breeders bred to bulls of low fertility both failure of fertilization and early embryonic deaths occur. Hawk et al. reported that most embryonic deaths occur soon after 16 days of gestation. Ayalon et al. studied 183 normal and repeat breeding cows in Israel by slaughter at gestation days 3, 11 to 13, 14 to 16, 17 to 19, and 35 to 42, and found the following percentages of viable embryos in the normal and repeat breeder groups, 83 and 71, 89 and 50, 57 and 43 and 69 and 35, respectively. The fertilization rates were about the same in the two groups and most embryonic deaths occurred from 11 to 42 days. Boyd et al. reported that most early embryonic death loss that was going to occur by 26 days had already occurred by 12 days of gestation. They reported a 15 percent failure of fertilization, a 7.5 percent early embryonic death loss by 26 days, and an 8.0 percent further deaths of older embryos and fetuses later in gestation in 112 fertile Ayrshire cows inseminated with fertile semen. Embryonic deaths occurring at 8 to 16 days after breeding usually do not affect the normal cycle length of about 18 to 24 days but embryonic deaths occurring at 16 to 25 days often result in longer periods between service and the next estrus.

In an excellent review of the problem of early embryonic deaths Bishop indicated that a large part was due to genetic causes as evidenced by the unexplained differences in fertility between males and the decline in fertility associated with age. Thus much of the embryonic death rate is unavoidable and should be regarded as a normal way of eliminating unfit genotypes in each generation at a low biological cost. Thus, as illustrated by David, if one accepts the reported conception and pregnancy rate in cattle of 60 percent or 1.6 services per conception, and breeds 100 hypothetically normal cows, 60 will conceive on the first service, 24 of the remaining 40 will concieve on the second service, and 9.6 of the remaining 16 will concieve on the third service. Thus in this hypothetical example using normal cows and bulls 6.4 percent of the cattle will require 4 or more services. Thus a certain percentage of repeat breeders are normal fertile cows.

The possible causes for fertilization failure and early embryonic deaths will be considered in the following classification based on pathological or managerial causes for infertility and repeat breeding.

Pathological Causes for Repeat Breeders

Genetic or congenital anatomical defects of the genital tract—These defects include principally the anomalies or segmental aplasia of: the oviduct, which is rare, the uterus, the cervix, and the vagina as have been described earlier in this chapter. These defects and anomalies largely cause failure of fertilization (F.F.) by preventing the union of the sperm cell and the ovum. Bilateral defects usually result in complete sterility. In some conditions, such as a lack of a normal endometrium, fertilized ova could not survive and form attachments or in underdeveloped cervices proper protection for the uterus is not provided so endometritis and embryonic deaths (E.D.) result. All of these defects are present in heifers at the time of puberty but in the less severe conditions, such as uterus unicornis, repeat breeding may occur but conception and a normal pregnancy may follow and the condition may not be diagnosed until the second or subsequent breeding period. The genetic or congenital anomalies of the genital canal are infrequent causes for repeat breeding and many can be diagnosed by a careful rectal and vaginal examination.

Genetic, Congenital or Acquired Defects of the Ova, Spermatozoa or Early Zygote—A low incidence of about 5 percent of grossly abnormal ova were observed in repeat breeding cows, Olds, and 2 percent in normal heifers, Bearden et al.. The possibility of a greater number of ova with defective chromosomes seems likely from reports cited previously to indicate a higher incidence of infertility in Guernseys and Brahman cattle kept on the same premises and under similar conditions as other more fertile breeds. The lowered fertility of older cows may well be related in part to defective ova, Lanman. He and Olds also cited numerous references to show that postovulatory aging of mammalian ova often resulted in failure of fertilization or polyspermy and early embryonic deaths. This may occur by breeding cows too late following the end of estrus. Mares et al. and Conneally et al. as cited previously, and Casida have shown inbreeding of the zygote and the dam has a deleterious effect on the conception rate and embryonic survival. If intensive inbreeding is followed, certain lines may experience marked infertility, Krehbiel et al.. Inskeep et al. and Fechheimer also cited earlier, have shown that daughters of certain bulls are apparently more fertile than daughters of other bulls. This may partly be a reflection of the chromosomal constitution of the ova. Superior reproductive performance is usually reported in cross-bred cattle, McDowell et al.. Thus heterosis can dilute or render ineffective lethal genes possibly present in purebred or closely bred lines.

Gustavsson reported a chromosome translocation in the Swedish Red and White Breed in which 14 percent were heterozygotes and 0.34 percent were homozygotes for the translocation. Daughters of translocation sires returned to service more often than daughters of normal sires apparently due to an increased embyronic death rate. McFeely reported that about 10 percent of embryos from normal gilts had chromosomal abnormalities, mostly trisomies, that were probably incompatible with life. Stevens and King reported on a probable genetic mutation in cattle that was lethal for the fetus in midgestation. In the future probably more genetic chromosomal anomalies causing infertility will be found.

Lanman has reviewed the literature concerning the deleterious effects of aging of the ova after ovulation and aging of the spermatozoa before and after ejaculation into the female. Gross anatomic genetic defects of the male reproductive tract resulting in oligospermia and aspermia due to anomalies of the mesonephric duct system have been described and result in infertility or sterility in the bull. Many genetic or congenital microscopic defects in spermatozoan morphology and chromosomes that prevent fertilization or result in infertility in bulls have also been described in Chapter XVIII. Some of these affected bulls may have a nearly normal semen picture. Other sperm cell abnormalities such as atypical basic nuclear protein produce degrees of infertility Testicular hypoplasia and degeneration result in abnormal, infertile or sterile semen.

Bishop and others have noted that in bulls used in AI service that there was significant differences in fertility and this difference was generally not related to observed differences in semen characteristics. Bishop suggested that fertility differences were largely due to genetic factors carried by the spermatozoa and not due to the environment in the female reproductive tract. Casida and Bishop discussed the possible incompatability between the sex cells as in hybrids, and in defective embryos from certain males, as well as incompatibility or possible immunological factors between the spermatozoa and zygote and the dam. The former cited Kiddy et al. and Menge et al. who showed in rabbits that sperm treated with low concentrations of sperm antibodies caused fertilization but resulted in an increased. incidence of embryonic deaths. Later Menge et al. showed that immune sera produced against bull semen in cattle caused an antifertility effect, either failure of fertilization or early embryonic death, when used to treat bull semen prior to insemination of heifers. The practical significance of these findings in repeat breeders requires further study to see if such a reaction could occur in the cow's genital tract.

Bishop and Lanman reviewed the relatively slow aging of spermatozoa in the male reproductive tract and cited evidence to indicate that increased embryonic deaths occurred when these aged sperm cells were used for insemination. In contrast aging of spermatozoa in the female reproductive tract occurs in a matter of hours and it appears that the fertilizing capacity of the sperm cell is lost before changes occur in the genetic material, Lanman. Salisbury showed that liquid bull semen stored at 5° C. for five days progressively loses its ability to fertilize ova and the incidence of early embryonic death increases. Fertility rates based on 180 nonreturn rates declined from 60 percent for semen used on day 1 after collection to 47 percent on day 5. The results on aging of spermatozoa in frozen semen were similar in that the decline in fertility went from 66 percent with frozen semen used less than 30 days after collection to 55 percent in semen stored over 6 months. This loss of fertility was probably due to chromosome damage, possibly chromosome leakage.

Thus, genetic, congenital and acquired defects of the ova or spermatozoa may result in failure of fertilization or early embryonic deaths and repeat breeding.

Infectious or Traumatic Inflammatory Processes Affecting the Genital Organs—result in repeat breeding due principally to early embryonic deaths. In a few cases where inflammatory processes have resulted in unilateral or bilateral obstruction of the genital tract as described earlier in this Chapter, failure of fertilization may result. Failure of fertilization may also occur in cows with severe metritis, cervicitis or vaginitis characterized by much inflammatory exudate and large numbers of bacteria that would be toxic to the sperm cells resulting in their loss of motility and death.

The infectious bovine venereal diseases of vibriosis due to **V. fetus,** trichomoniasis due to **Tr. fetus** and probably brucellosis due to **Br. abortus,** IBR-IPV virus and certain pathogenic mycoplasma if introduced into the uterus with semen by artificial insemination can cause infertility and repeat breeding due to early embryonic deaths probably secondary to an endometritis of variable duration. As discussed earlier in this Chapter the above infections, especially the first two, are well-known for their antifertility affects. Other nonspecific infections of a great variety that can produce an endometritis have also been described and can cause a varying period of infertility. **V. fetus** and **Tr. fetus** are harbored for long periods of time or indefinitely in the sheath and on the penis of older bulls and migrate by their own motility through the cervix into the uterus after natural service. Other nonmotile organisms can seldom pass through the cervical barrier following natural service but can be introduced by artificial insemination. Some of these infections such as **C. pyogenes, Ps. aeruginosa,** streptococci, staphylococci, **E. coli** and others may be present in the infected seminal vesicles of bulls and thus be present in large numbers in each ejaculate. Other infections producing endometritis, as mentioned previously in this Chapter, may enter the genital tract at the time of parturition or soon after, in the act of artificial insemination if it is not performed in a clean and sanitary manner, or in miscellaneous conditions such as pneumovagina. As has been discussed previously, only metritis or the severe forms of endometritis characterized by exudate in the uterus can be diagnosed clinically. Refined culture techniques and uterine biopsies are needed to accurately diagnose moderate to mild endometritis in the live cow. Pregnancy, however, can occur in the presence of a mild endometritis, Brus.

It is generally accepted that a young growing zygote seldom can survive in a diseased environment and for optimum fertility an aseptic, sterile uterus free from organisms is desirable or necessary. The genital tract, and especially the uterus, has excellent mechanisms of local antibody production, phagocytosis, mucous flow and uterine contractions that can usually overcome an endometritis at the first estrous period or within the span of 2 to 6 estrous periods. This spontaneous recovery from infection has been well-documented in the postpartum involuting uterus and in vibriosis. Therefore by the time the infertile cow with endometritis is classified as a repeat-breeder she is often well on the way toward recovery or has recovered her fertility. This probably accounts for the divergent reports and observations on this subject as reviewed by Casida, Dawson, Olds, Hawk et al., Simon and McNutt, and Hjerpe. Some authors reported only a very low incidence of pathological or inflammatory changes in the genital tracts of repeat breeder cows as cows with clinical infections were eliminated from the classification. Antibiotic and other infusions to correct possible uterine infections in repeat breeding cows may or may not, usually the latter, reveal significant results over nontreated controls. In many repeat breeding cows at slaughter, cultures of the uterus are negative for bacteria. Nonspecific bacteria are commonly found in the cervix of cows and are always present as contaminants from the prepuce in semen. The presence of antibiotics in the semen used artificially controls or destroys certain infectious organisms such as **V. fetus** but the natural body or uterine defense mechanisms at estrus provide strong protection against infections due to these bacterial or other agents introduced into the genital canal with the semen. This author believes that endometritis due to various infectious agents is a common cause of infertility early in the breeding period but within a variable time a rapid spontaneous complete recovery occurs. Thus if the repeat breeder cow has a normal genital tract on clinical examination, there is no reason for withholding service. The ability to ascertain this state of the genital tract will vary between veterinarians. Increasing the period of sexual rest to improve conception rates on the next service is uneconomical in the clinically normal cow. Neither a natural or artificial service will prolong the time before conception will occur. Rapid spontaneous recoveries followed by conception are common.

Endocrine disfunction as a common cause of repeat breeders is unlikely since the estrous cycle in these animals has been generally reported as normal except for prolonged postservice periods when early or late embryonic deaths occur.

As previously noted, Van Rensburg of South Africa reported a high incidence of abnormal ovulations, 140 or about 25 percent, in 536 estrous periods in 179 Friesian and Afrikaner cattle. These abnormal ovulations included: 99, or 66 percent, delayed ovulations, and 47, or 34 percent, anovulation that terminated in 41 atretic follicles and a few follicular or luteal cysts. The delay in ovulation was less than 48 hours in 85 percent of the cases. Anovulation often tended to recur in the same animal. Abnormal ovulations were most common in Afrikaner heifers and young cows and decreased as the cows got older, while in Holsteins they reached their lowest level in 3-year-olds and then increased with advancing age probably due to the stress of lactation. The abnormalities reached their peak in the winter months associated with nutritional deficiencies. In 4 of 8 cow families there was a definite genetic predisposition toward abnormal ovulations. These were probably due to varying degrees of failure of the release of LH from the anterior pituitary gland. (See cystic ovaries.) Perkins et al. reported that in 17 or 18 percent of 97 estrous periods in repeat breeding heifers, ovulation failed to occur but the length of the estrous cycles were normal. Bane reported cows exhibiting weak heats, which are genetically conditioned, had 10 percent lower conception rates than cows exhibiting normal heats. The evidence indicated that ovulation may be delayed in cows with weak estrous signs. Hancock reported on a study of 58 cows of which 31 percent had delayed ovulations. Conversely previous studies cited by Casida and his coworkers on repeat breeding cows and heifers slaughtered 3 days after service indicated ovulation failure was of little importance and occurred in only 3 to 5 percent of the animals. Ayalon et al. also reported a low incidence of 1.5 percent anovulatory cycles and 4.3 percent delayed ovulations in both normal and repeat breeding cows. Morrow et al. studied 53 pubertal heifers and reported failure of ovulation occurred in 13 percent of the heifers on first estrus but was uncommon thereafter. In his study on 139 cows during the postestrous and service period anovulatory cycles were not observed except in 12.3 percent of the cycles in which cystic follicles developed.

Further study is needed to explain these different reports. As cited in the section on cystic ovaries, infertility is not uncommon in treated and recovered cows, Trimberger. Possibly this infertility was related to anovulatory cycles or delayed ovulation since cystic ovaries are also caused by a failure of the release of LH. Anovulatory cycles result in failure of fertilization; while delayed ovulation may result in failure of fertilization if the sperm cells have become poorly viable as they do in the cow within 24 to 48 hours; or they may fertilize the ova and because of the aged condition of the sperm cell early embryonic death may result. If ovulation has not occurred within 24 hours of the last service, another service should be given, Van Rensburg. If 2 or more ova are released, fertilization usually occurs but embryonic death of one or both zygotes is common, especially if the ova are released from one ovary. (See twinning.)

Although Hawk et al., and Casida have indicated that there is little evidence that repeat breeders are due to an imbalance of ovarian secretion, others including Dawson, Herrick, Johnson et al., Wiltbank et al., Risley and Danieli have noted that progesterone or a progestagen administered 3 to 5 days after service and continued for a variable period of 2 to 3 weeks or longer definitely improves the conception rate in repeat breeder cows over the controls. Doses and products used have been 100 mg progesterone implant, repositol progesterone 400 mg. on days 2, 3, 4, 6 and 9 after breeding, 500 mg. progesterone caproate on day 2 after breeding, 50 or 200 mg. progesterone daily, 500 mg. repositol progesterone at 10 days postservice and every 10 days thereafter, 125 mg progesterone given once 5 to 10 days after breeding, 200 mg. MAP (Provera) fed daily in the grain from day 4 to 18 postservice. Apparently this increased amount of progesterone the first few weeks after fertilization improves the uterine environment for the zygote so a larger number of embryos survive. In repeat breeders most embryonic deaths occur before the corpus luteum regresses. In fact failure of fertilization or the death of the embryo is necessary for repeated cycles to occur in bred cattle. As has been discussed under the physiology of the cow, administering 5000 I.U. of H.C.G. about four days after breeding appears to have a similar effect by increasing the size of the corpus luteum resulting in greater progesterone production. Casida cited experimental evidence to show that repeat breeder cows showed less evidence of an inflammatory response and more prompt destruction of bacteria after the intrauterine inoculation of infection during the luteal phase of the cycle than did normal heifers. Casida indicated these results showed the repeat breeder had a more effective uterine defense mechanism and had a reduced progestational response, possibly due to a lower production of progesterone. Further study of the beneficial effects of progesterone started 3 to 7 days after service is needed. Slack et al. showed that progesterone given postservice at 0 to 2 days and 10 and 14 days produced no beneficial results and treatment at 0 and 2 days postservice was even detrimental to fertility. Schul et al., reported that M.G.A. given orally to normal heifers in doses of 1 to 4 mg daily on day 2, day 4 and day 10 resulted in a low conception rate of 44 percent in heifers when treatment started on day 2 but normal conception rates of 70 to 80 percent for heifers started on M.G.A. on day 4 and 10. Starting treatment with progesterone before day 3 or 4 after service may suppress C.L. growth, hasten ova transport or in some other way lower the fertility of normal and repeat breeder cows.

Hansel et al. treated 36 repeat breeder cows with 20 mg progesterone subcutaneously, 40 repeat breeders with 1000 I.U. chorionic gonadotropin I.V. and 1000 IU. subcutaneously and 28 control repeat breeders were given an injection of saline early in estrus to possibly promote ovulation and improve the conception rate. The percentage of cows conceiving on the service given that same estrous period was 50, 35, and 58, respectively. Thus it was not beneficial to give these hormones unless the cow is known to regularly ovulate late. Chorionic gonadotropin given early in estrus reduced the conception rate in repeat breeders. Wiltbank and Cook reported that 57 percent of nursed cows conceived on the first service compared to 71 percent of milked cows that conceived. Services per conception were 1.84 in nursed cows and 1.54 for milked cows. As noted under the prevention of conception in Chapter V injections of estrogens at the time of estrum or within several days after ovulation will affect the transport of the fertilized ovum in the oviduct resulting in too rapid transport or "tubal locking" of the ova and death of the zygote. Injections of pitocin from day 2 to day 6 after estrum and service causes hypoluteinization of the CL, early embryonic death and shortened estrous cycles. As noted earlier in this chapter under physiology, Staples and Hansel reported that the normal CL at 15 days of gestation contained 270 mg total progesterone while a small hypoluteinized CL with less than 100 mg of progesterone could not maintain the early embryo.

At present the practice of examining repeat breeding cows 24 to 36 hours after service should reveal delayed ovulation or anovulation. Several further daily examinations may be required to determine the time of ovulation and until it occurs the cows should be bred daily. Giving 2000 to 5000 IU. of chorionic gonadotropin I.V. may hasten or promote ovulation in cows ovulating late, after 48 hours after estrus or cows failing to ovulate. If ovulation has occurred by this examination 24 to 36 hours after service then the uterus may be infused with weak Lugol's solution, 1 to 5 ml Lugol's solution in 50 to 100 ml. of saline or distilled water, without interferring with conception. The cow may be placed on several injections of 200 to 500 mg of repositol progesterone I.M. on days 4 or 5 and again on days 10 to 12; or daily injections of 100 mg of progesterone in oil may be given daily or every other day for 2 or 3 weeks starting on day 4; or 200 mg M.A.P. may be fed daily for 18 days starting on day 4 after service; or 5000 I.U. chorionic gonadotropin may be given on day 4 or 5 to promote the growth and development of the corpus luteum and its production of progesterone.

Managerial deficiencies including nutritional deficiencies in the herd are a common cause of lowered fertility and repeat breeding. These must be differentiated from infectious venereal diseases such as vibriosis and trichomoniasis which also are often herd problems. The managerial causes of repeat breeding have become greatly increased with larger herds and the widespread use of artificial insemination. It will probably continue to increase with the trend toward each herd owner or herdsman inseminating his own cows with frozen semen.

It is a significant fact that the larger the herd the greater the infertility or incidence of repeat breeding. Many herdsmen can supervise and watch the cows in small herds but in large herds this is more difficult and more detailed records are necessary. A common cause of repeat breeding is poor observation of the cows at frequent intervals each day for signs of estrus. If this is not done regularly, 2 to 3 times a day, poor timing of insemination in regard to ovulation results and aging of either the ova or spermatozoa or both may occur. (See anestrus.) Fallon reported from a study of 86 herds of cattle that if 1, 2 or 3 cows are presented for service in the same herd at the same time that conception rates were 69.1, 64.5 and 59.2 percent, respectively. The lowered fertility occurring when 2 or more cows were presented for service at the same time was due to the tendency to offer cows in suboptimum breeding condition. Erb and Ehlers summarizing data on fertility in relation to the length of the estrous cycle concluded that there was no practical reason for delaying service because of estrous cycle irregularity if the cow is otherwise normal and the cycle is at least 17 days long. Shorter cycles are indicative of cystic ovaries or acute endometritis. The average length of the bovine estrous period is 10 to 28 hours and ovulation occurs 10 to 15 hours after the end of estrum. Cows should be bred within 10 hours before or after the end of estrum for best fertility. This requires frequent daily heat checks and regulated insemination. Bull spermatozoa have a variable life up to 48 hours in the female but highest fertility rates occur within 12 to 24 hours after service. If estrus and ovulation are normal there is very little increase in conception rates, only about 2 percent, in inseminating cows twice, once late in estrus and again 12 to 20 hours later. Calves resulted from insemination from 14 to 34 hours before ovulation, Aschbacker et al., and Wilcox and Pfau. Trimberger in experimenting with a large group of cattle, demonstrated that cows bred at the beginning of estrum had a conception rate of 44 percent, at midheat 82.5 percent, and at the end of heat 75 percent; 6 hours after the end of estrum 62.5 percent; 12 hours, 32 percent; 18 hours, 28 percent; 24 hours, 12 percent; and 36 hours, 8 percent; 48 hours after the end of estrum no ova became fertilized. This indicated that the ovum probably was unable to survive longer than a few hours after ovulation. There is evidence that spermatozoa might have to be in the genital tract about 6 hours before ovulation for optimum fertilization and conception. It seems likely that the excellent fertilization and conception rate reported by Bearden may have been due largely to careful and frequent observations for estrum, and to artificial insemination at the proper time of estrum.

The effect of nutrition, especially TDN intake and the need for a positive energy balance for high fertility was discussed earlier in this chapter. There is little question but conception rates are better when cows are increasing in body weight. This poses a severe problem for managers of herds with high-producing dairy cows to provide rations and see that cows consume sufficient energy to have a high fertility level. There is no evidence in cattle that increased embryonic deaths occur in overfed animals, Hansel. There is evidence that supplemental iodine, particularly in iodine deficient areas has a beneficial effect on fertility. Moberg reported that when supplemental iodine was provided in a controlled experiment in 190 herds with 1572 cows, that conception rates on first service in treated and untreated herds were 69.1 percent and 62.2 percent, respectively. McDonald et al. used an organic iodine compound fed orally for 8 to 12 days before the next service in 1036 repeat breeding cows and 58 percent conceived on the first service, while in the control cows conception rate was well below 50 percent. It is possible that iodine absorbed from the uterus by uterine infusions of an iodine solution exerts a similar effect.

The Production Division of the Milk Marketing Board in England reported that the conception rate in 125 newly established herds was 60.8 percent as compared to 73.7 percent conception rate in 64 other herds in the same area. The lowered fertility was probably due to a combination of stress placed on the animals by transport and new surroundings, and the difficulty of the new owners in evaluating the heat characteristics and having the cows inseminated at the proper time. Holt also reported that lowered fertility occurred after the stress of transport and in a new environment. Conception rate in 634 cows bred artificially for the first service within 2 months after moving was 54.9 percent; while in over 32,000 first services in cattle born and remaining on a farm the conception rate was 68.6 percent.

Further evidence illustrating the effect of stress on lowered bovine fertility is the reduced fertility associated with high ambient temperatures of over 80° F for long periods in the summer months in the southern portions of the United States. Gangwar et al. demonstrated that under hot climatic conditions the duration of estrus was shorter and the intensity of signs of estrus was reduced. Kelly and Hurst showed that high temperatures depressed feed consumption and milk production and resulted in a 10 percent reduction in pregnancy rate. This decline was even greater than 10 percent when frozen semen collected from bulls during the hot summer months was used. Jerseys and Brown Swiss were more resistant than other dairy breeds to the effects of heat. Stott and Williams in Arizona and Hillin and Rupel in Texas reported lowered conception rates during the summer months due to low fertilization rates and high embryonic death rates. Monthly pregnancy rates in cows bred from June to October ranged from 17.1 to 36.1 percent, while from October through May they ranged from 44.4 to 61.5 percent. More prolonged postservice cycles are observed in the summer months. Ulberg and Bufening in an excellent review on embryonic deaths discussed the stress produced by a rise in temperature affecting the spermatozoa before fertilization or the zygote immediately after fertilization resulting in embryonic deaths at a later date. VanHeerden in reviewing problems of infertility in cattle in a tropical or sub-tropical environment noted that Zebu cattle did not increase their metabolism to the same extent when external temperatures rose above 73° F as did the European cattle. High temperatures affected the latter breeds by supressing estrus and ovulation, causing anestrus and anovulation and causing early death of the embryo.

Thus, during the hot summer months in the southern United States especially in herds using a dairy cattle breed developed in the temperate zones, every effort should be followed to keep the animals cool by providing shaded areas or sheds, especially at higher elevations, that allow the free movement of air, plenty of fresh water and a nutritious diet with a minimal amount of fiber. This would reduce the severity of heat stress, improve feed intake and increase milk production besides resulting in a reduction in repeat breeding cows.

In natural service the bull deposits his semen in the proper site, while in artificial insemination there are many possibilities for man to render infertile the bovine sperm cells. These possibilities include: (1) improper extension, freezing and storing of fertile semen. Warming of frozen semen above -79° is highly detrimental to sperm cell viability and fertilizability; (2) improper thawing of frozen semen. This must be done rapidly in a large volume of luke warm or ice water as slow or erratic thawing rates are harmful to sperm cells; (3) insemination should take place promptly, within several minutes after thawing. Thawing semen and keeping it at 5° C. or 40° F for an hour or more is very detrimental to sperm cells; (4) a proper insemination technique should be followed to place the semen in the middle or anterior portion of the cervix, not into the uterus, in a clean and sanitary manner with little or no trauma to the genital tract.

If liquid extended semen is used, it should be recognized that conception rates decline each day the semen is stored at refrigerator temperatures. Boyd and Reed reported that in 5744 inseminations in 146 Holstein herds, the conception rate declined from 65.4 percent for first day semen to 45.6 percent for over 3-day-old, stored semen. They also showed that for optimum conception rates on first service and a minimal number of repeat breeders that cows should be bred 60 days or later postpartum. The respective conception rates to first service were 39.5 percent for cows bred at less than 40 days postpartum, 51.2 percent for cows bred at 41 to 50 days, 59.4 percent for cows bred at 51 to 60 days, 63.7 percent for cows bred at 61 to 90 days and 65.1 percent for cows bred over 90 days. Similar results were reported in a summary by Salisbury and VanDemark. Warnick reported that in beef cattle a short breeding season was highly desirable. This often required that cows be bred before 60 days postpartum. The percent of cows calving when bred the following number of days postpartum, 11 to 30, 31 to 50, 51 to 70, 71 to 90, 91 to 110 and 111 to 130 was 11.1, 57.7, 77.5, 80.6, 94.14 and 81.8, respectively. The Milk Marketing Board (1968–1969) reported the probability of conception was 40 percent if insemination took place between 11 and 31 days postpartum, 55 percent from 32 to 52 days, 62 percent from 53 to 73 days, 65 percent from 74 to 94 days and 68 percent from 95 to 115 days postpartum. If the service interval is shortened by a single breeding cycle, another 6.4 inseminations per 100 cows are required but the calving interval is shortened by 18 days! These figures were based on hypothetically breeding 100 cows at 84 days post partum. Olds reported that no harmful effects such as delayed conception, evidence of early embryonic deaths or abortions could be attributed to breeding cows at 35 days or less postpartum except that the cows had lower conception rates. He concluded that for each 10 days sooner a cow was bred after calving, the calving interval was shortened 8.8 days. Thus, although there was a slight increase in the number of services required for cows bred less than 50 days, there was no increase in lost days and the economic value to the dairyman of calving intervals of 12 months or even less, was worth the slightly increased number of services per conception.

Palpation of the ovary at the time of insemination should not be done by the lay technician. If an experienced veterinarian or researcher wishes to examine the ovaries to palpate the Graafian follicle and determine the time of ovulation, it should be done in a gentle, skillful manner to prevent manually rupturing the very thin-walled follicle. Aschbacher et al., Vandeplassche, and VanRensburg reported on the accidental manual rupture of the mature follicle at this time and only 1 of 7, 5 of 12 and 1 of 17 cases, respectively, or less than 20 percent conception resulted from service after this accident. Apparently the ova are washed away or possibly caught in the collapsing walls of the unphysiologically "ovulated" follicle.

Conclusions on repeat breeding—The general and broad physiological and pathological causes of repeat breeding in cattle have been outlined. Many excellent studies on various aspects of the problem have been made and advances have been achieved in the past 15 years. However, the treatment or handling of the problem at present is essentially based on the experience, skill, knowledge and thoroughness of the diagnostic procedures employed by the veterinarian to arrive at the cause(s) and contributing cause(s) for this problem. In some instances it may be necessary to permit a degree of repeat breeding if offspring from a relatively infertile or old sire are desired or if it is desired to shorten the calving interval by early postpartum breeding. If artificial insemination is practiced, a painstaking examination of the frozen or liquid semen and the processes employed in storing semen and inseminating the cow must be undertaken. Just because semen is frozen and labeled, its fertility is not assured! If natural service is used then the bulls and their semen and servicing ability must be carefully evaluated. The care the owner or herdsman takes in observing and recording heats and services are important. Some owners are not well acquainted with the behavior of cows and have difficulty recognizing estrum.

If repeat breeding is a herd problem, the semen or bull used, the presence of infectious venereal diseases or the improper observation, recording and breeding of cows is usually at fault. If individual repeat breeding cows are the problem, then a wide variety of causes may be considered. With the many causes for repeat breeding, it is highly possible that in a poorly-managed herd repeat services in a cow could be due to a different cause or combination of causes at each infertile estrous period.

Genetic, congenital or acquired defects or obstructions may be present preventing the union of the spermatozoa and the ovum. Genetic or acquired damage may affect the ova or spermatozoa. In treating repeat breeding cows with normal genital tracts servicing the animals each heat period with spermatozoa from a highly fertile bull is imperative. The few cows that have a history of repeat breeding each year for several years or more should be culled.

Endocrine malfunction in repeat breeder cows is apparently not common except in anovulation or delayed ovulation which requires further study by a number of investigators under a variety of stress conditions and in many herds. Administering progesterone therapy for a variable period starting 3 to 4 days after service shows promise in the treatment of certain cows. Administering progesterone at or within several days after service is not indicated; neither is the administration of estrogens which also affect the transport of the fertilized ova through the oviduct.

Endocrine therapy in most repeat breeders is unsuccessful, especially if used empirically and without an understanding of reproductive endocrine physiology, Roberts (1956). In sporadic infections of the uterus causing repeat breeding, spontaneous recovery in a variable period of time is the rule. Infusions with weak iodine solutions seem to be as good as any other intrauterine therapy and better than many antibiotic preparations.

When one considers the multiplicity of the direct and indirect or predisposing causes for failure of fertilization or early embryonic deaths, the magnitude of the diagnostic problem posed by this problem is challenging. Particularly so in problem herds where careful study will usually indicate the cause and in individual problem cows where the exact cause may be difficult to determine with accuracy. Treatment of these latter cases should never become routine or empirical, but these cases should be studied more carefully and in greater detail and the recommended therapy should be given based on knowledge concerning reproductive physiology, use of highly fertile males, servicing at the proper time of estrum, repeated matings, patience and, if necessary, conservative therapy that will not interfere with or prevent fertilization and early embryonic development.

References

Aschbacher, P. W., Smith, V. R. and Stone, W. H. (1956) Observations on Fertility Following Insemination at Three Stages of the Same Estrus, J. An. Sci. **15,** 4, 952.

Ayalon, N. (1966) Personal Communication.

Ayalon, N., Weiss, Y. and Lewis, I. (1967) The Nature of Fertility Losses in Normal Cows and Repeat Breeders, 1967–1968 Ann. Rpt, "Hasherut" AI Center, Rishon Le Zion, P.O. Box 31, Israel.

Bane, A. (1964) Fertility and Reproductive Disorders in Swedish Cattle, Brit. Vet. J. **120,** 431.

Bearden, H. J. (1954) Fertilization and Embryonic Mortality Rates for Bulls with Histories of Either Low or High Fertility in Artificial Breeding, Thesis, Cornell Univ., College of Agriculture, Ithaca, N.Y.

Bearden, H. J., Hansel, W. and Bratton, R. W. (1956) Fertilization and Embryonic Mortality Rates of Bulls with Histories of Either Low or High Fertility in Artificial Breeding, J. Dairy Sci. **39,** 3, 312.

Bishop, M. W. H. (1964) Paternal Contribution to Embryonic Death—A Review, J. Reprod. and Fert. **7,** 383.

Boyd, H., Bacsich, P., Young, A. and McCracken, J. A. (1969) Fertilization and Embryonic Survival in Dairy Cattle, Brit. Vet. Jour. **125,** 87.

Boyd, H. and Reed, H. C. B. (1961) Investigations Into the Incidence and Causes of Infertility in Dairy Cattle.—Influence of Some Management Factors Affecting the Semen and Insemination Conditions, Brit. Vet. Jour. **117,** 73.

Casida, L. E. (1961) Present Status of the Repeat-Breeder Cow Problem, J. Dairy Sci. **44,** 12, 2323.

Conneally, P. M., Stone, W. H., Tyler, W. J., Casida, L. E. and Morton, N. E. (1963) Genetic Load Expressed as Fetal Death in Cattle, J. Dairy Sci. **46,** 3, 232.

Danieli, Y. (1967) Treatment of "Repeat Breeder" Cows with Progesterone, Refuah Vet. **24,** 1, 38.

David, J. S. E. (1970) Reproductive Expectancy and Management Factors, Internat. Confer. on Cattle Diseases, Philadelphia.

Dawson, F. L. M. (1954) Progesterone in Functional Infertility in Cattle, Vet. Rec. **66,** 324.

Dawson, F. L. M. (1963) Uterine Pathology in Bovine Infertility, J. Reprod. and Fertil. **5,** 397.

Erb, R. E. and Ehlers, M. H. (1958) Fertility Rates of Cows Bred Following Estrous Cycles of Varying Lengths, J. Dairy Sci. **41,** 5, 671.

Erb, R. E. and Holtz, E. W. (1958) Factors Associated with Estimated Fertilization and Service Efficiency of Cows, J. Dairy Sci. **41,** 11, 1541.

Fallon, G. R. (1962) Estrus Detection in Cattle; A Factor in "Management Infertility." Brit. Vet. Jour. **118,** 327.

Fechheimer, N. S. (1968) Genetic Aspects of Calf Losses in **Prenatal and Postnatal Mortality in Cattle,** Nat. Acad. of Sci., Public. 1685, Washington, D.C.

Gangwar, P. C. Branton, C. and Evans, D. L. (1965) Reproductive and Physiological Responses of Holstein Heifers to Controlled and Natural Climatic Conditions, J. Dairy Sci. **48,** 2, 222.

Gomes, W. R. and Erb, R. E. (1965) Progesterone in Bovine Reproduction: A Review, J. Dairy Sci. **48,** 3, 314.

Gustavsson, I. (1969) Cytogenetics, Distribution and Phenotypic Effects of a Translocation in Swedish Cattle, Hereditas **63,** 68.

Hancock, J. L. (1948) The Clincial Analysis of Reproductive Failure in Cattle, Vet. Rec. **60,** 43, 513.

Hanley, S. (1961) Prenatal Mortality in Farm Animals, J. Reprod. and Fert. **2,** 182.

Hansel, W. (1959) Female Infertility in Domestic Animals, Fert. and Steril. **10,** 5, 502.

Hansel, W., McEntee, K. and Wagner, W. C. (1960) Conception Rates of Repeat-Breeder Cows Bred After Progesterone and Chorionic Gonadotropin Treatments During Estrus, Cor. Vet. **50,** 4, 497.

Hansel, W. and Trimberger, G. W. (1952) The Effect of Progesterone on Ovulation Time in Dairy Heifers, J. of Dairy Sci., **35,** 1, 65.

Hawk, H. W., Brinsfield, T. H., Turner, G. D., Whitmore, G. E. and Norcross, M. A. (1963) Embryo Survival In First Service and Repeat Breeder Cattle After Ovariectomy and Hormone Therapy, J. Dairy Sci. **46,** 12, 1397.

Hawk, H. W., Kiddy, C. A., Wilson, J. B., Esposito, M. and Winter, A. J. (1958) Bacteriological Studies of Uteri of Clinically Normal Cows of Low Fertility, J. Dairy Sci. **41,** 1, 120.

Hawk, H. W., Wiltbank, J. N., Kidder, H. E., and Casida, L. E. (1955) Embryonic Mortality Betwen 16 and 34 Days Post Breeding in Cows of Low Fertility, J. Dairy Sci., **38,** 6, 673.

Herrick, J. B. (1953) Progesterone Therapy in Repeat Breeding Heifers, Vet. Med., **48,** 12, 489.

Hewett, C. D. (1968) A Survey of the Incidence of the Repeat Breeder Cow in Sweden with Reference to Herd Size, Season, Age and Milk Yield, Brit. Vet. Jour. **124,** 342.

Hillen, J. M. and Rupel, I. W. (1960) Differential Effect of Season on Conception Rate in Holstein and Jersey Cattle, J. Dairy Sci. **43,** 3, 442.

Hjerpe, C. A. (1961) An Evalutation of Uterine Infusion as a Treatment for Repeat Breeding in Dairy Cattle, J.A.V.M.A. **138,** 11, 590.

Holt, A. F. (1961) Effect of Movement on Fertility in Cattle, Proc. 4th Internat. Congr. on An. Reprod., Hague, Vol. IV, 796.

Inskeep, E. K., Tyler, W. J. and Casida, L. E. (1961) Hereditary Variation in Conception Rate of Holstein-Friesian Cattle, J. of Dairy Sci. **44,** 10, 1857.

Jainudeen, M. R. (1965) Repeat Breeders in Cattle—A Review. Ceylon Vet. J. **13,** 10.

Johnson, K. R., Ross, R. H. and Foust, D. L. (1958) Effect of Progesterone Administration on Reproductive Efficiency, J. An. Sci. **17,** 2, 386.

Kelly, J. W. and Hurst, V. (1963) The Effect of Season on the Fertility of the Dairy Bull and Dairy Cow, J.A.V.M.A. **143,** 1, 40.

Kidder, H. E., Black, W. G., Wiltbank, J. N., Ulberg, L. C. and Casida, L. E. (1954) Fertilization Rates and Embryonic Death Rates in Cows Bred to Bulls of Different Levels of Fertility, J. of Dairy Sci., **37,** 691.

Kiddy, C. A., Stone, W. H., Tyler, W. J. and Casida, L. E. (1957) Effects of Iso-Immunization with Blood and Semen on Fertility in Cattle, J. Dairy Sci., **40,** 6, 629.

Lanman, J. T. (1968) Delays During Reproduction and Their Effects on the Embryo and Fetus, New England J. of Med. **278,** 993, 1047, 1092.

Mares, S. E., Menge, A. C., Tyler, W. J. and Casida, L. E. (1961) Genetic Factors Affecting Conception Rate and Early Pregnancy Loss in Holstein Cattle, J. Diary Sci., **44,** 1, 96.

McDonald, R. J., McKay, G. W. and Thomson, J. D. (1961) The Use of Organic Iodine in the Treatment of Repeat Breeder Cows, Proc. 4th Internat. Congr. on An. Reprod., Hague, Vol. III, 679.

McDowell, R. E., Richardson, G. N , Mackey, B. E. and McDaniel,B. T. (1970) Interbreed Matings in Dairy Cattle V Reproductive Performance, J. Dairy Sci **53,** 6, 757.

McFeely, R. A. (1967) Chromosome Abnormalities in Early Embryos of the Pig, J. Reprod. and Fert. **13,** 579.

McFeely, R. A. (1968) Chromosomes and Infertility, J.A.V.M.A. **153,** 12, 1672.

Menge, A. C., Stone, W. H., Tyler, W. J. and Casida, L. E. (1962)

Fertility of Cattle and Rabbits Inseminated with Semen Treated with Antibodies Produced Against Semen, Spermatozoa and Erythrocytes, J. Reprod. and Fertil. **3,** 331.

Milk Marketing Board, Production Division, (1958–1959 Report and 1968–69 Report) Thames Ditton, Surrey, England, **9,** 87 and **19,** 120.

Moberg, R. (1961) Possible Influences of Supplementary Iodine, Administered by Evaporation, on Reproductive Performances in Cattle, Proc. 4th Intern. Congr. on An. Reprod., Hague, Vol. III, 682.

Morrow, D. A., Roberts, S. J. and McEntee, K., (1969) Postpartum Ovarian Activity and Involution of the Uterus and Cervix in Dairy Cattle, Ovarian Activity, Cor. Vet. **59,** 2, 173.

Morrow, D. A. (1969) Estrous Behavior and Ovarian Activity in Prepuberal and Postpuberal Dairy Heifers, J. Dairy Sci. **52,** 224.

Olds, D. (1969) An Objective Consideration of Dairy Herd Fertility, J.A.V.M.A. **154,** 253.

Olds, D. and Cooper, T. (1970) Effect of Postpartum Rest Period in Dairy Cattle on the Occurrence of Breeding Abnormalities and on Calving Intervals, J.A.V.M.A. **157,** 1, 92.

Olds, D. and Seath, D. M. (1954) Factors Effecting Reproductive Efficiency of Dairy Cattle, Kentucky Agr. Exp. Stat. Bull. #605.

Perkins, J. R., Olds, D. and Seath, D. M. (1959) Observations on Estrous Cycles of Repeat Breeding Dairy Heifers, J. Dairy Sci. **42,** 3, 543.

Risley, H. B. (1968) Progesterone in Cattle Infertility, J.A.V.M.A. **153,** 12, 1607.

Roberts, S. J. (1956) Veterinary Obstetrics and Genital Diseases, Edwards Bros. Inc., Ann Arbor, Mich., 387.

Rowson, L. E. A., Lamming, G. E. and Fry, R. M. (1953) The Relationship between Ovarian Hormones and Uterine Infection, Vet. Rec., **65,** 22, 335.

Salisbury, G. W. (1967) Aging Phenomena in Spermatozoa I, II, III. Fertility and Prenatal Losses with Use of Liquid Semen. Effect of Season and Storage at -79 to -88°C on Fertility and Prenatal Losses. Jour. Dairy Sci. **50,** 1675, 1679, 1683.

Schul, G. A., Smith, L. W., Goyings, L. S. and Zimbelman, R. G. (1970) Effects of Oral Melengestrol Acetate (M.G.A.) on the Pregnant Heifer and Her Resultant Offspring, J. An. Sci. **30,** 3, 433.

Simon, J., and McNutt, S. H (1957) Histopathology of the Bovine Uterus II, Amer. J. Vet. Res. **18,** 241.

Slack N. H., Pfau, K. O., Mixner, J. P., Menge, A. C., Hurst, V. and Rankin, A. D. (1964) Progestagen Treatment in Relation to Time of Insemination and Its Effect on the Breeding Efficiency of Dairy Cows, J. Dairy Sci. **47,** 1, 82.

Stevens, R. W. C. and King, G. J. (1969) Genetic Evidence for a Lethal Mutation in Holstein-Friesian Cattle, J. of Hered. **59,** 6, 366.

Stott, G. H. and Williams, R. J. (1961) Female and Breed Associated with Seasonal Fertility Variation in Dairy Cattle, J. Dairy Sci. **44,** 1698.

Stott, G. H. and Williams, R. J. (1962) Causes of Low Breeding Efficiency in Dairy Cattle Associated with Seasonal High Temperatures, J. Dairy Sci. **45,** 11, 1369.

Tanabe, T. Y., and Almquist, J. O. (1953) Some Causes of Infertility in Dairy Heifers, J. of Dairy Sci., **36,** 568.

Tanabe, T. Y. and Casida, L. E. (1949) The Nature of Reproductive Failures in Cows of Low Fertility, J. of Dairy Sci., **32,** 3. 237.

Trimberger, G. W. (1955) Unpublished Data.

Trimberger, G. W. and Davis, H. P. (1943) Conception Rate in Dairy Cattle by Artificial Insemination at Various Stages of Estrus, Univ. of Nebr., Agr. Exp. Stat., Res. Bull. 129.

Ulberg, L. C. and Burfening, P. J. (1966) Embryo Death Resulting from Adverse Environment on Spermatozoa or Ova, J. An. Sci. **26,** 3, 571.

Salisbury, G. W. and VanDemark, N. L. (1961) Physiology of Reproduction and Artificial Insemination of Cattle, W. H. Freman and Co., San Francisco, Calif.

Vandeplassche, M. (1961) Ovulation and Fertility in Cattle, Rept. of the Dept. of Obstetrics and Sterility of the Veterinary School, Ghent, Vlaams Diergeneesk Tijd. **30,** 2, 65.

Van Dieten, S. W. J. (1968) The Influence of Some Circumstances on the Farm on Bovine Fertility, Tijdschr. v. Diergeneesk, **93,** 19, 1279.

Van Heerden, S. (1963) Aspects of Tropical and Subtropical Infertility in Livestock, in **Livestock Infertility,** Animal Health Monograph, #5, FAO, Rome, 78.

Van Rensburg, S. W. J. (1962) Ovulatory Failure in Bovines, Onderst. Jour. of Vet. Res. **29,** 1, 55.

Warnick, A. C. (1955) Factors Associated with the Interval from Parturition to First Service in Beef Cattle, J. An. Sci. **14,** 4, 1003.

Wilcox, C. J. and Pfau, J. E. (1958) Effect of Two Services During Estrus on the Conception Rate of Dairy Cows, J. Dairy Sci. **41,** 7, 997.

Wiltbank, J. N and Cook, A. C. (1958) The Comparative Reproductive Performance of Nursed Cows and Milked Cows, J. An. Sci, **17,** 640.

Wiltbank, J. N , Hawk, H. W., Kidder, H. E., Black, W. G., Ulberg, L. C., and Casida, L. E. (1956) Effect of Progesterone Therapy or Embryo Survival in Cows of Lowered Fertility, J. Dairy Sci. **39,** 4, 456.

Zemjanis, R. (1963) The Problem of Repeat Breeding in Cattle, Mimeographed Paper presented at New England Vet. Meeting.

Herd Reproductive Health Programs

Foote reviewed the inheritance of fertility and concluded:

"The fertility problem of greatest economic importance in a herd or population is over-all breeding efficiency. As this has been measured by services per conception, per cent nonreturns, first service to conception, calving interval, etc., additive genetic variance has been very small and heritability has been approximately zero Thus, selection for these traits would not be effective and would be at the expense of other traits of economic importance which show a greater response to selection. **Infertility in cows appears to be primarily a management problem."**

Reproductive health programs for both dairy and beef herds are practical and essential for successful herd management. The veterinarian plays a highly important role as a consultant and advisor to the herd manager or owner in setting up the reproductive health program and maintaining its effectiveness to achieve the goal of a calf per cow every 12 to 13 months. In dairy herds fertility can be measured by a number of criteria and realistic herd goals are: a pregnancy rate of 60 percent on first service, an average of 1.5 to 1.7 services per conception, a calving interval of 12 to 13 months per cow or a maximum of an average of 100 days from calving to conception. A calving interval of 12 months produces the highest milk yield and the greatest number of calves. The most common causes of a longer calving interval are long intervals between parturition and first service, long intervals after service if conception has not occurred, or too many services, 5 or more, before conception. Thus the calving interval is more important than services per conception in measuring herd fertility, David. Records should be set up so that periodically they may be reviewed to see if the herd is reaching, maintaining, or failing to reach these criteria necessary for a successful reproductive health program. Records should be maintained in such a fashion that the cause or causes for infertility such as anestrus, silent estrus, repeat breeders, cystic ovaries, semen from certain bulls and etc. can be readily ascertained. In beef herds an achievable goal is a 90 percent calf crop within a 3 month calving period. To reach and maintain these goals requires the close cooperation of the herdsman, manager, owner, inseminator, and veterinarian.

In dairy herds a herd reproductive health program requires a visit by the veterinarian to examine the cows every one to two months or in larger herds, more frequently. Less frequent visits are unsatisfactory. Charges for such regular visits have been made by various veterinarians based on the visit, on an hourly rate, or on a flat rate per cow per visit or year. The former two methods of charging are generally preferred because then the manager or owner of the herd prepares for the visit by getting his records in order, has his cows in and his help organized so the visit goes smoothly and rapidly. Since reproductive health is the core of a general herd health program, the reproductive health program is established first and then other aspects of herd health are added to it as the farmer and veterinarian desire. Education of and cooperation with the farmer and concern for the herd by the veterinarian are essential.

Records must be maintained in a herd reproductive health program. Each cow must be properly and permanently identified. Reproductive herd health forms should be fairly simple and practical for the average dairy farmer to maintain on a daily, monthly and yearly basis. The type of record used should be tailored to the preference of the veterinarian and farmer. Different record forms have been described and used by many veterinarians, Morrow, Plocher, Zemjanis, Fincher, Nickolai and Ulberg, Bates, and Kendrick and Hughes. Records must identify the cow, indicate the time of calving or abortion, heats, services and pregnancy examinations. They should also include all genital examinations noting normal and abnormal findings and the therapy administered.

These records might also be expanded to include the sire and dam, the number and sex of offspring, abnormalities at calving, vaccinations and time administered, the bull used for service of the cow and whether AI or natural service was employed, and the results of blood or other diagnostic tests. These records may further be expanded to include other health records and examinations such as mastitis and other disease problems and even production records. Records of the date of purchase of cows and the name of the previous owner may be desirable.

Any herd reproductive record system should include provisions for daily referral to the records or placing entries in them. In larger herds a herdsman's **daily report form** is helpful to record calvings, breedings, vaccinations and other abnormalities and treatments. **Estrous expectancy charts** are available from feed companies, AI organizations, and extension services and are very helpful to dairymen to note heat dates and service dates so they are reminded in 3 weeks to watch certain cows. More permanent records may be made on forms kept in loose-leaf notebooks, Kardex files, and card files specifically designed for reproductive health programs. These may be made up by the veterinarian or stock forms obtained from one of the above sources. These records should be available in the barn or near it in a clean, dry location free of dust, dirt and excessive moisture.

Several interesting recent innovations to herd reproductive health records have been made. One is the method followed in North Carolina to computerize these records so each month a farmer receives this reproductive record on his cows along with the DHIA record so he knows the calving intervals, breeding dates, when to have the cows checked for pregnancy and etc. This greatly aids him in maintaining the goals of good reproductive health and requires a minimum of record keeping by the farmer, Nickolai and Ulberg, Johnson, Myers and Ulberg. Other states are considering this program. Willard Bates invented a practical breeding control "wheel" now being produced by Agway, Inc. of Syracuse, N.Y. that is an ingenious device that is kept in the dairy barn and records the current reproductive status of every cow which can be determined at a glance. It has proven to be an incentive to herdsmen, by its simplicity, to maintain reproductive health records, watch cows for estrus and breed them at the correct time. Other methods for keeping reproductive records including peg boards, black boards and etc. have been reported. Most good record systems require the veterinarian to assist the farmer in developing and organizing a practical system both can follow and use. Then it requires constant encouragement on the part of the veterinarian to have the farmer maintain the records in a careful, routine, up-to-date manner.

Management practices-In most cattle herds the major cause of infertility and repeat breeding is improper or negligent management practices. Most infertility problems, such as improper heat detection, are herd problems and require a preventive medicine program in which the veterinarian must become an active part of the farm management to be effective.

Young breeding stock should be properly reared by providing nutritious and balanced rations and proper disease and parasite control including vaccinations so that early and planned breeding of virgin heifers can occur at the desired time.

The breeding herd should be fed sufficient balanced rations so that regular estrous cycles occur and the females are in an optimum breeding condition and on a positive energy balance at the time of service. Nutrition should be such that cows at the end of gestation are not too fat nor too thin as both of these conditions predispose to calving and postpartum disease problems that affect the fertility of the herd.

Sanitation and hygienic practices at the time of calving should be followed to prevent postpartum uterine infections and delayed conception. **Diseases affecting the reproductive system** such as brucellosis, vibriosis, trichomoniasis, IBR-BVD, leptospirosis should be controlled by eradication and quarantine methods so as to maintain, as nearly as possible, a disease-free closed herd. If this is not possible a proper and regular vaccination program should be instituted. All purchased stock should be isolated from the herd for 30 days and tested for possible infectious diseases. It is preferable to purchase young animals under 6 months of age as replacement stock to avoid the common venereal diseases. Decisions in regard to the various methods of disease control must be made on the basis of the herd history and management practices, the possible dangers from exposure to disease by neighboring cattle, and the nature of the diseases common in the area. Inbreeding should be avoided and close line-breeding should be carefully monitored so that hereditary defects can be culled from the herd and good fertility can be maintained.

The **detection of estrum** is of great importance especially in a herd being bred by artificial insemination. There is no substitute for frequent careful observation of the nonpregnant cows, recording of the estrus and prompt notification of the inseminator so that future estrous periods may be detected or so that a high conception rate on first or subsequent services can be achieved. Cows should be watched closely for estrum. The herd should be turned out twice daily and the cows closely observed for 15 to 20 minutes morning and evening. Since some cows may be in estrum only 10 to 14 hours this close observation is essential in order that heat periods may not be overlooked. This practice is especially necessary during the winter months when dairy animals may be closely confined in stanchions. Utilizing some form of heat expectancy chart or the regular veterinary examination of the genital tract of open cows to predict the time of estrus are very helpful in breeding cows at the proper time in the postestrous period when a bull is not turned with the herd. Normal cows should be bred at the proper time of each estrous period with highly fertile semen to achieve the best and earliest conception rates.

Highly fertile active bulls with a strong sex drive and free of infectious venereal diseases should be used as sires. If artificial insemination is employed the fertility record of the bull should be noted to be certain of the high fertility of his semen. The semen should be stored, handled, thawed and inseminated in a manner to maintain and promote the high fertility of the spermatozoa. If cows in the herd are handbred naturally to a number of breeding bulls, the records of all cows bred by each bull and the date should be recorded so that if infertility occurs in the cows the bulls' fertility records can be examined for evidence of decreased fertility in a certain or several bulls. Switching cows back and forth between bulls at different natural services is a poor practice as venereal diseases are readily spread in this manner. If a cow fails to conceive to natural service to a certain bull, she should be bred by artificial insemination to other bulls on subsequent services.

All cows in the herd, not already safely pregnant should be examined at each regular monthly, or more frequent, visit of the veterinarian to 1) determine pregnancy if breeding has taken place 35 or more days ago, 2) to determine if normal uterine involution is occurring by an examination between 20 and 40 days postpartum, 3) to determine if any pathological condition such as metritis, adhesions of the oviduct, cystic ovaries and other lesions or diseases, including anestrus, may be present that require treatment, and 4) to determine the physiological state of the normal nonpregnant genital tract and the approximate time to expect estrus and whether service at the next estrus is desirable. If the decision of which cows to examine is left to the farmer or herdsman some infertile, diseased, or nonpregnant cows might be omitted from the examination. It is very helpful for the farmer to prepare a list of all the nonpregnant cows and their previous breeding history prior to the visit by the veterinarian. This requires the farmer to keep his records up-to-date and to have all the cows to be examined confined. It also saves much time for the veterinarian as he examines each cow. This type of complete examination of all nonpregnant cows gives an accurate herd picture of the nature of the fertility or infertility in the herd at the initial visit or at regular intervals throughout the year.

Miscellaneous herd management factors The herdsman, owner or manager who is in daily close continuous contact with the herd is the most important person determining the success of a reproductive health program. He should be a person who is properly educated and motivated or the program is bound to fail.

Beef herds besides some of the aforementioned practices may require some different measures for controlling reproductive diseases than do dairy herds, Carroll, Wiltbank and Faulkner. In beef herds each cow must calve each year to be profitable. The breeding season is shorter than in dairy herds, 45 to 90 days, and conception early in the breeding season is highly desirable requiring proper nutrition of the herd. The best means of expressing reproductive efficiency in the commercial range beef herd is the total pounds of calf weaned divided by the number of cows and heifers exposed to breeding in a calendar year. Calf crop equals the percent of cows bred times the percent of conception times the percent of conceptions weaned. If only 50 percent of the cows are bred or only 50 percent conception results then the calf crop is 50 percent or less. Early prompt conception of heifers and cows is essential because of the short breeding period necessary to produce heavy, large calves. To produce early puberty and to obtain early estrus after calving, heifers should gain 1 lb per day from weaning through breeding and weigh at least 650 lbs at the start of the breeding season, and cows should be in good condition at calving and should gain 0.5 to 0.75 lbs per day until the end of the breeding season. Thus adequate rations and sufficient energy are essential for the onset of the estrous cycle and good conception rates, Wiltbank and Faulkner. Provision for adequate numbers of fertile, active bulls is essential. If young bulls are used more "bull power" is necessary. Cows that fail to conceive should be detected by a pregnancy examination of the herd in the Fall and probably culled. In range cattle where it is nearly impossible to maintain a "closed" herd, vaccination, especially against vibriosis and possibly other diseases, is highly desirable. If the beef herd is to use artificial insemination, the riders, preferably two or more, should bunch the cows at the feed bunks twice a day, usually morning and evening; the cows should be divided and put into small pastures and bred cattle should be kept separate from unbred cattle for easier observation of estrus. Often sorting the fat range cows and thin range cows into separate herds and feeding according is economically advantageous.

Newly assembled herds often exhibit an infertility problem because of a variety of diseases that may be present. It is best to breed these herds by artificial insemination with highly fertile, disease-free semen. If females are brought into a closed herd, they should be bred by artificial insemination for several years. Every effort should be made to avoid the introduction of a venereal infection carried by a bull into the herd. All aborting animals should be carefully and promptly isolated and the fetus and placenta should be examined by a veterinarian and a good laboratory and blood samples taken to detect the possible cause of the abortion. The aborting animal should be treated and maintained in isolation until genital discharges cease. In tropical or subtropical areas heat-tolerant cattle should be raised and/or measures taken to reduce the stress of high ambient temperatures and its effect on fertility in both the bull and cow, Hignett & Rasbech and Phillips et al.. Other diseases especially parasitic diseases should be controlled. Lame cattle lose weight, fail to show signs of estrus and have lowered fertility. Impotency in bulls is frequently due to overgrown, diseased feet that need trimming, and arthritic lesions. There is little evidence that stress or fright in cattle due to restraint at the time of service has any significant effect on the conception rate. Emphasis should be placed on diagnosis rather than treatment in herd reproductive health programs.

Since the veterinarian that specializes in herd health or herd reproductive health programs is often not the "regular" veterinarian that handles sporadic emergency problems and regulatory tests in the herd, it is highly important that he conducts his practice in an ethical manner, consults with the local veterinarian and AI technician, as well as the herd manager or owner and thinks and speaks well of his colleagues. He should practice the "Golden Rule". Often times it is necessary for the local practitioner to carry out recommended treatments and therefore it is important that he understand the reasoning behind the therapy.

Recently Olds and Cooper reviewed the literature on uterine involution after calving and the earlier work on the optimum time to breed cows following calving. They stated that although optimum conception rates on first service occur from 60 to 120 days after calving that breeding cows from 40 to 60 days after calving if no abnormality was present, resulted in about a 50 percent conception rate with no subsequent adverse effects on the pregnancy period. For each 10 days that a cow was bred sooner after calving, a shortening of the calving interval by 8.8 days resulted. Thus if diseases of the postpartum uterus could be avoided or reduced and earlier breeding, down to 40 days postpartum, was practiced, it would be a highly valuable method of reducing the calving interval with only a very slight increase in the number of services per conception.

Ideally only normal, healthy, highly fertile females and males should be mated. It is recognized, however, that both bulls and cows may vary greatly in their level of fertility. As the fertility of the female declines the fertility of the male she is bred to is of greater importance if a good conception rate is to occur. Ramberger illustrated and discussed this in humans. He noted the fertility index of a couple resulted in prompt conception when both partners were relatively quite fertile. Delayed conception occurred when either the male or female was subfertile or below the borderline index of fertility, and conception was unlikely when both male and female partners were subfertile or below the borderline fertility index. Therefore since highly fertile bulls, especially in AI service, are well known, cows of lowered fertility should be bred to them.

Bartlett has proposed an interesting and significant model to explain the importance of the major factors that enter into the determination of the fertility level of any herd. These major factors concerning herd fertility are: 1) the fertility of the cows at the time of service, 2) the fertility of the bull or semen, if AI is used, and 3) the efficiency of the management including heat detection, nutrition, timing of insemination, efficiency of the technician and veterinary consultant and etc.. If theoretical percentages of 90, 90 and 90 were applied to these three factors the percent of calves born would be 73 percent, or 90 × 90 × 90 since these factors are not additive. If the fertility of the bull was only 50 percent then 90 × 50 × 90 would equal 40.5 percent calves born. The pregnancy rate can be no higher than the lowest value of any of the 3 factors. This illustrates the importance of careful veterinary supervision of the reproductive health of the herd to insure that all factors are maximal. The great economic importance of a herd reproductive health program has been illustrated by Morrow and Herschler et al..

In concluding this chapter on infertility in cows the following quotation from Bartlett is concise and applicable: "For some infectious diseases, relatively effective prophylactic and combative procedures have been developed; dairymen and veterinarians need only to take cognizance of the established precepts. However, our present inability to cope rationally with certain other conditions and the meagerness of the knowledge of their total effects and causes must be recognized. Well-directed, well-supported scientific research is the only source from which the necessary facts can be obtained. Such research merits the encouragement, interest and support of the cattle industry and veterinary profession alike. It is obvious that the causes of lowered reproductive efficiency are exceedingly numerous and the problems of achieving optimum reproductive efficiency exceedingly complex and broad in their ramifications. No panaceas must be expected. Precise diagnoses whenever possible, rational corrective actions when indicated, and trained, intellectually honest advisors mark the sound course. There should be no place for the triflers, five-day specialists, self-confident, self-styled, handyman experts and quack remedy peddlers parasitizing and exploiting the field today."

"For the cattleman, consistent observance of sound management and animal hygiene practices is imperative. The keeping of precise, permanent records, together with a system of regular, physical examinations for pregnancy, will reveal any general occurrence of reproductive failures at the onset and by permitting early treatment or disposal of affected animals, will keep to a minimum the economic reverses resulting from infertility."

References

Bartlett, D. E. (1949) Infectious Disease as a Cause of Infertility: A Review, J. of Dairy Sci., **32,** 1, 36.

Bartlett, D. E. (1967) Factors Affecting the Calf Crop, in **Artificial Insemination in Cattle,** edit. by Cunha, T. J.; Warnick, A. C. and Koger, M., Univ. of Florida Press, Gainesville, Fla., 299.

Bates, W. (1968) Personal Communication, Stevensville, Pa. and Agway Inc., Syracuse, N Y.

Carroll, E. J. (1968) Economic Considerations in Beef Cow Management, Mimeographed material, Colo. State Univ., Ft. Collins, Colo.

David, J. S. E. (1970) Reproductive Expectancy and Management Factors, Internat. Confer. on Cattle Diseases, Philadelphia.

Fincher, M. G. (1954) Personal Communication

Foote, R. H. (1970) Inheritance of Fertility in Dairy Cattle, J. Dairy Sci., **53,** 7, 936.

Herschler, R. C., Miracle, C.; Crowl, B.; Dunlap, T. and Judy, J. W. (1964) The Economic Impact of a Fertility Control and Herd Management Program on a Dairy Farm, J.A.V.M.A., **145,** 7, 672.

Hignett, S. L. and Rasbech, N. O. (1962) The Influence of Management on the Fertility of Livestock, in **Livestock Infertility,** Animal Health Monograph #5, FAO, Rome, 57.

Johnson, A. D.; Myers, R. M. and Ulberg, L. C. (1964) A Method for Evaluating the Current Reproductive Status of a Dairy Herd, J.A.V.M.A., **144**, 9, 994.

Johnson, A. D.; Myers, R. M. and Ulberg, L. C. (1964) North Carolina's Evaluation System for Herd Reproductive Status, Animal Science Dept. Series #170, Breeding Section #13, North Carolina State Univ., Raleigh.

Kendrick, J. W.; Theilen, G. H. and Hughes, J. P. (1961) The Maintenance of High Fertility in Cattle, Mimeographed material and forms, School of Veterinary Medicine, Univ. of Calif., Davis, Cal.

Morrow, D. A. (1963) Developing a Dairy Herd Health Program, Vet. Med., **58,** 4 and 8, 308 and 655

Morrow, D. A. (1966) Analysis of Herd Performance and Economic Results of Preventive Dairy Herd Health Programs, Vet. Med., **61,** 5 and 6, 474 and 577.

Morrow, D. A. (1970) Disease Control in Dairy Cattle, in **Bovine Medicine and Surgery,** edited by Gibbons, W. J.; Catcott, E. J. and Smithcors, J. F., Amer. Vet. Public. Inc, Wheaton, Ill., 741.

Nickolai, J. H. Jr. and Ulberg, L. C. (1967) North Carolina's System of Herd Reproductive Status, Proc. 20th Ann. Meeting of the Nat. Assoc. of Animal Breeders, Hershey, Pa.

Olds, D. and Cooper, T. (1970) Effect of Postpartum Rest Period in Dairy Cattle on the Occurrence of Breeding Abnormalities and on Calving Intervals, J.A.V.M.A., **157,** 1, 92.

Phillips, R. W.; McDowell, R. E.; Ulberg, L. C.; Johnston, J. E.; Warwick, W. J.; Bond, T. E.; Kelly, F. C.; Heitman, H. jr and Shrode, R. R. (1958) The Effects of Climate on Animal Performance (A Symposium), J. of Hered., **49,** 2, 47.

Plocher, E. M. (1959) A Dairy Herd Reproduction Program, Vet. Med., **54,** 279.

Ramberger, F. T. Jr. (1965) Classification of Married Couples According to Their Reproductive Capabilities, Fert. and Steril., **16,** 5, 627.

Wagner, W. C. and McEntee, K. (1960) Herd Approach to Infertility Problems in Cattle, Cor. Vet., **50,** 2, 197.

Zemjanis, R. (1956) Personal Communication.

Wiltbank, J. N. and Faulkner, L. C. (1970) The Management of Beef Breeding Programs, Bov. Pract. **5,** 23.

Chapter XIV

INFERTILITY IN THE MARE

The problem of infertility in mares has been the subject of limited study and research. Much more basic research on reproductive physiology and pathology has been carried out in cattle in recent years. (See Chapters XII and XIII.) Caslick has pointed out that the three chief reasons for infertility in mares were (1) the shortness of the breeding season, (2) genital infections, and (3) failure of the mare to have a normal estrous cycle. Caslick indicated that of these three, irregularities of the estrous cycle were most important. Probably the cause of many irregularities of the estrous cycle is the fact that the breeding period for racing breeds does not coincide with the normal or physiological breeding season of horses, Osborne. One can do nothing about the length of breeding season, especially in Thoroughbreds and Standardbreds, whose age is dated from January first of the year they are foaled.

Proper hygiene and preventive procedures, careful examination, and prompt and effective treatment can largely control genital infections in the mare which would cause infertility. Furthermore mares and stallions are generally selected for their racing ability and pedigree not for their fertility. Day has included as other causes of infertility the use of stallions with low fertility, and rare genital abnormalities in the mare, such as stenosis of the cervix that may occur secondary to infections. He estimated that the average fertility in draft mares, usually bred to a stallion that is transported around the country, is about 59 percent; in Thoroughbreds, under somewhat better conditions, about 66 percent; and in wild ponies that run free the year around with the stallion, about 90 percent. Although the average conception rate in mares is usually lower than in other domestic animals, on well-managed farms with good veterinary service the yearly conception rate can reach 80 to 85 percent. The majority of breeding farms have a conception rate of about 60 to 75 percent. Most of the causes of infertility in mares are usually temporary.

All mares should be fed an adequate ration of green roughage with some legume, preferably clover. Legumes contain a higher supply of minerals than does timothy. Good pasture supplies roughage in the best form as well as exercise. Grain intake should be adequate to maintain condition and supply the energy and protein needs of the mare. Fresh water and iodized salt should be available at all times. Most breeding mares are fed and cared for in an adequate manner but if they are not, the same deficiencies and symptoms affect them as affect cattle. If the feed is adequate, trace minerals and vitamins are seldom necessary.

The breeding period for Thoroughbred and Standardbred mares covers only about 4 months, from February 15th through June 15th. A recent ruling of the U. S. Trotting Association extended the breeding season in Standardbreds to December 15. Because of the shortness of the breeding period it is essential that all mares to be bred are normal at the beginning of the season. This requires that barren mares be examined in the fall months and treated if necessary. All apparently pregnant mares should be examined at this time to make certain that an early abortion at 25 to 90 days did not occur. Pregnant mares are usually vaccinated with equine herpes I virus against abortion. Normal but barren mares are put in winter quarters and maintained in a fair to good physical condition but should not be allowed to become too fat. The reproductive physiology of mares has been discussed in Chapter XII but a more detailed presentation of the clinical aspects follows.

Normal and abnormal aspects of equine reproductive physiology.

The Breeding Season—In the northern hemisphere the breeding season of mares normally extends from April to October with the greatest degree of functional activity in June, July and August, Osborne and Arthur. Estrous cycles and ovulation had occurred in June through August in 80 to 90 percent of 6763 equine genital tracts examined at slaughter, Osborne. During the winter months of December through March cycling and ovulation occurred in 18.5 to 26.9 percent of the 6763 mares' genital tracts examined by Osborne and in 16 to 63 percent of the 792 mares' tracts examined by Arthur. Thus some mares if fed adequately and housed will have regular estrous cycles throughout the year but there is a natural and common anestrous period from November to April for most mares, especially those on pasture (See Table 21). Loy has reported three types of mares with regard to the seasonal anestrous period: mares with a clear-cut period of anestrus of 2 to 4 months duration during the winter, mares that may have some cyclic activity of a very irregular nature during the winter season, and mares that have regular cycles the entire year. **Twin ovulations** were highest during the summer months with a yearly incidence of 14.5 and 18.5 percent reported by Osborne and Arthur. Arthur reported 8 cases of triplet ovulations. He cited an incidence of 33.7 to 37.5 percent double ovulations in the summer months and noted the incidence of twin births to be 1 to 1.5 percent indicating a high early embryonic death loss in twin conceptions. Arthur reported 2 cases of twin corpora lutea vera because the embryos were only 2.6 cm long. In both of these cases there was a single normal embryo with evidence of a second degenerating embryo. Hancock also reported that 3 out of 5 twin gestations were lost by 70 days of gestation. This loss might be related to the high FSH level observed in bicornual twin pregnancy, Rowlands. This great loss of early twin embryos may be a more important cause of infertility than is generally recognized. There was no evidence to support Williams' statement that twin pregnancy in mares followed genital disease. Rooney has reported that most twin pregnancies are the result of double ovulation but rarely identical twins are observed in a single allantochorion.

Osborne, Andrews and McKenzie, and Arthur reported that 55.5, 60 and 52.2 percent of the ovulations occurred on the left ovary. As mentioned previously slightly more pregnancies occur in the right uterine horn than in the left uterine horn indicating that transuterine migration of the zygote is probably common.

Failure of ovulation or delayed ovulation in mares has been described by VanRensburg and VanHeerden, Arthur, Day, Hillman, Patterson and others. It is noted by repeated rectal palpation of the ovaries and is seen in mares early or late in the breeding season when cycles are irregular, especially in barren or shy-breeding mares. In failure of ovulation the Graafian follicle will become atretic and regress in 10 or more days and if this occurs in the Fall the mare may go into anestrus. In the spring of the year regression of the first follicle may occur to be followed in several weeks by a normal estrous period, ovulation and the commencement of regular cycles. VanRensburg and Van Heerden reported a high incidence of failure of ovulation or delayed ovulation in 23 of 52 estrous periods in shy-breeding mares.

The estrous cycle in the normal mare is 19 to 23

Table 21. A Frequency Distribution Graph Representing the Monthly Percentage of Ovulation for 5198 Normal Mares in the Years of 1959-1965*

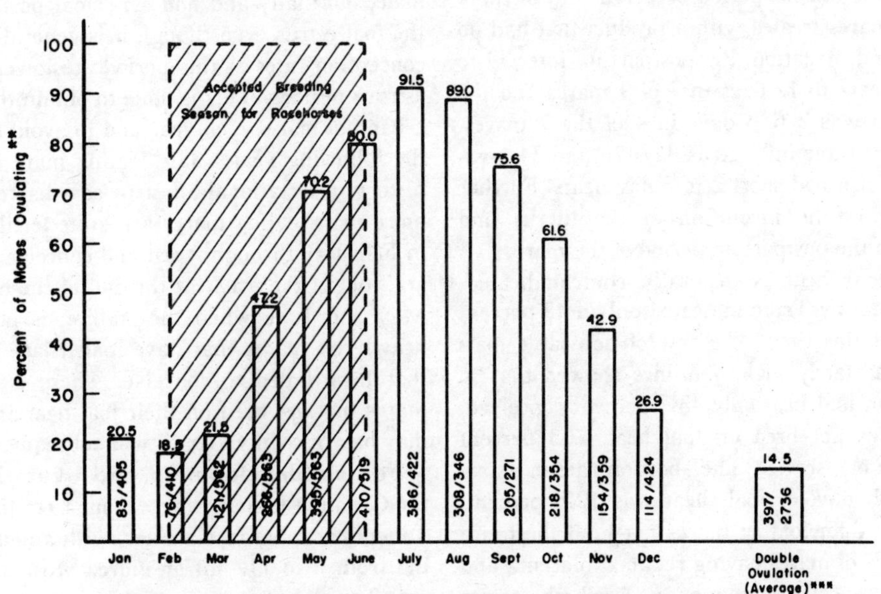

* Adapted to the northern hemisphere from data published by V.E. Osborne, Dept. of Vet. Med., Univ. of Sidney, Australia. Immature and senile mares excluded (Austral. Vet. J. 42, 1966, 149)

** As evidenced by the presence of corpora hemorrhagica or corpora Lutea in the ovaries of mares examined at autopsy. These mares come from an area of eastern Australia between latitudes of 23° 5" and 35° 5" corresponding to Southern N. Car. through the tip of Florida or the northern to southern borders of Texas

*** The range of monthly variation in double ovulation was 7.2 to 21.4 percent.

days in length with an average length of 21 days, Asdell, Andrews and McKenzie. The duration of the period between estrous periods averaged 15 days but the duration of estrum was more variable, 4 to 9 days, with an average of 5.5 days. Breeding has no effect on the length of heat or the time of ovulation. Foaling mares usually come into their first estrum or foaling heat between 4 to 14 days after parturition and stay in estrum until 11 to 20 days, Dukes. In Trum's series of cases 93 percent of the mares showed foal heat between 5 and 18 days and 77 percent showed foal heat between 7 to 10 days after parturition. Most foaling mares have normal or regular estrous cycles. A few may exhibit a prolonged foal estrum and a few more may fail to show estrus and exhibit anestrus for a variable or long period. Often these anestrous foaling mares had a history of this pattern of behavior as a barren mare; this may simulate lactational anestrous in sows, or this may be seen in nervous overly-protective mares that fight the advances of the stallion approaching them and their foals.

Andrews and McKenzie reported the uterine epithelium had not returned to its normal state by 10 days postpartum. But complete recovery did occur between days 13 and 25. Loy and Swan noted that some mares had follicles on the ovaries 1 day postpartum and all mares had palpable follicles by day 5 postpartum. Four mares were in estrum to the teaser on days 6, 6, 7 and 8 postpartum and ovulated on postpartum days 7, 7, 10, and 14, respectively. Thus a short estrous period occurred in 3 of the 4 mares. In other mares treated with a product that had no effect on estrus and ovulation, the postpartum interval to the first estrus was 7 to 12 days in 7 of 9 mares and the duration of estrus was 2 to 3 days in 4 of the 7 mares. The other 2 mares came into estrus days 25 and 34 postpartum and they also had short 2 to 3 day heats. Further study is needed on the involution of the uterus and ovarian activity in the postpartum period of the mare.

Breeding on foal heat is generally contraindicated, inasmuch as reports by Trum indicated only a 43 percent conception rate at this time. The rate of nonviable foals and abortions was fairly high. Jennings showed that in 110 mares bred on foal heat only 43.7 percent conceived, while in 54 mares not bred on foal heat 67.3 percent conceived later on one service. The abortion rate in mares bred on the ninth day, or foal, heat was 12.8 percent, somewhat greater than foaling mares not bred the ninth day. The incidence of mares having retained placenta and of those failing to conceive subsequently were both greater in mares bred on their foal heat than when bred later. All this was true, according to Jennings, even though the 110 mares were selected for ninth-day breeding because they were considered normal and therefore good breeding risks. Andrews and McKenzie reported 50 percent conceptions on foal heat. Caslick reported that 533 mares bred on foal heat had a 36.5 percent conception rate; 304 of these came back in heat and on the second service 56.6 percent conceived. Of 130 mares bred after 21 days following foaling, 58.5 percent conceived on first breeding. Breeding on the foal estrum should be done very cautiously especially in old mares and only in mares that had a normal parturition and foal, with no injuries or inflammation of the genital tract, had a placenta that weighed 14 pounds or less, and are negative on bacteriological culture taken early in estrum.

As noted above, the onset of foal estrus varies widely and this is reflected in the time of ovulation. Mahaffey, and Patterson and others have pointed out that a lowered conception rate on foal estrus may be due to breeding on a fixed date, such as the ninth day postpartum, instead of timing the service based on speculum examination of the vagina and cervix and palpation per rectum of the ovaries for the presence of a mature Graafian follicle.

The above anomalies of gestation following breeding on the foal heat have been reported more commonly in Thoroughbred mares than in the other breeds. In the light of recent studies in cattle with respect to early postpartum breeding, further studies should be undertaken in different breeds of horses, housed and managed under different situations. It is a common practice on many Standardbred and Quarter horse farms to routinely breed all mares that foaled normally and had a normal postpartum period on the foal estrus even though it is generally recognized that conception rates at this period are lower than subsequent estrous periods. This is done to obtain the most foals from a band of mares each year and to avoid holding over until the following year a late foaling mare or a mare with a history of lactational anestrus as a barren mare. Furthermore most foaling mares are quite fertile and if they foal in February through April and conceive on foal heat, they are "out of the way" at the end of the breeding season in May and June when the stallion is being worked very heavily by mares that have foaled late or infertile mares that have failed to conceive. There is no evidence that mares that are bred on their foal heat and fail to conceive may have a reduced fertility at subsequent estrous periods.

Follicle development and ovulation—The size of the Graafian follicle ranges from 1 cm to 7.5 cm or 0.5 to 3 inches or more in diameter, with amounts of fluid ranging from 6 to 112 ml or more. Most follicles are 5 to 6 cm, 2 to 2-1/2 inches, at the time of ovulation. Larger horses tend to have larger follicles. The follicular fluid during estrum contained estradiol-17B and estrone at levels of 48.0 ug and 3.4 ug per 100 ml, as well as a variety of other steroid compounds, Asdell, Short. Almost all

Graafian follicles are tense and firm on rectal palpation the first few days of estrum but within 16 to 24 hours of ovulation many follicles lose their tone and become softer and slightly fluctuating. It is possible they may already be losing some follicular fluid. Short indicated that the follicular fluid is probably a filtrate of blood plasma containing the steroid secretions of the theca interna. Hillman and Loy reported that urinary estrone varied from 15 to 20 mcg per liter one week before ovulation to 60 mcg per liter the day before ovulation. Estrous behavioral signs paralleled the urinary estrogen levels as did the changes in the genital tract associated with estrus. Short reported that a Welsh pony could have amounts up to 0.25 mg per day of estradiol in ovarian vein plasma. They also noted the major steroid secreted by the ovary was androstenedione, a weak androgen. Although the rate of exchange between the steroids in the follicular fluid and the blood were very slow, at the time of ovulation large amounts of estrogen were released. This may be related to the anticoagulant and enzymes in the follicular fluid. Hillman and Loy also reported that injection of 5 mg of estradiol into an ovariectomized mare caused rapid excretion of the estrogen within 3 hours at levels that were 5 to 6 times greater than the peak excretion levels of estrogen at estrus in the normal mare. The size of the follicle is not related to sexual behavior but as the follicle increased in size at estrum, signs of estrus were more intense, Andrews and McKenzie. The equine oviduct secreted 1.5 to 2.5 ml of fluid every 12 hours during estrus; during diestrus the amount dropped to 0.6 to 1.5 ml every 12 hours. The pH of oviduct fluid was 7.2 to 7.4, Engle.

The mature Graafian follicle is somewhat triangular or pear-shaped with the largest portion of the follicle palpable during estrus on the convex curvature of the ovary or at either pole of the ovary. The narrow stalk-like portion of the follicle protrudes toward the concave portion of the ovary called the ovulation fossa where ovulation invariably occurs in close proximity to the rather small fimbriated portion of the equine oviduct. Only rarely does ovulation occur more than 2 cm away from the ovulation fossa, Osborne, Arthur, Bergin, and Prickett. Ovulation usually takes place toward the end of the estrous period, about 24 to 48 hours before signs of estrus cease; only occasionally is ovulation early or delayed so it occurs 48 to 96 hours before the end of estrus or 24 to 48 hours or more after the end of estrus, Asdell, Hancock, Patterson. Although equine follicular fluid has many properties of normal blood plasma it does not clot due to its having a lowered fibrinogen content and also to the presence of an anticoagulant heparinoid substance. This prevents the ovum from becoming trapped in a plasma clot, Stangroom and Weevers. Since the mature follicle is highly vascular and the theca interna layer is hyperemic at ovulation, rupture of some vessels occur and clotting is delayed with the result that hemorrhage occurs into the large cavity of the former follicle producing a soft, pulpy hematoma that can be palpated per rectum as a soft, mushy depression on the greater curvature of the ovary for 24 to 36 hours after ovulation, Day. The mare has by far the largest corpora hemorrhagica of all domestic animals.

The corpus luteum develops rapidly following ovulation and it also is triangular or pear-shaped. It occasionally protrudes as a button-like structure 1 to 2 cm in diameter and 0.5 to 1 cm in heighth beyond the ovarian capsule through the ovulation site into the ovulation fossa where it may be palpated around the second day after ovulation, Andrews and McKenzie. By 72 hours after ovulation the corpus luteum, which is about 3/4 to 1 inch in diameter, definitely smaller than the follicle, cannot be palpated because of the dense tunica albuginea and the central location of the corpus luteum on the mare's ovary. The corpus luteum actively secretes progesterone for 14 to 16 days when it begins to undergo involution or regresssion unless the animal is pregnant. Upon corpus luteum regression, follicle growth occurs under the influence of FSH released from the pituitary gland.

Fossa cysts or cysts of the germinal epithelium are common in the region of the ovulation fossa especially in older infertile or nonbred mares. Osborne, Arthur and others have reported their frequent occurrence and O'Shea reported an incidence of 64 percent in 42 ovaries. These persistent small cysts could be single or multiple; they varied from 1 mm or less up to 0.65 cm and in rare cases could resemble a bunch of small grapes. These large accumulations might rarely interfere with the fimbrial collection of the ovum at the time of ovulation. These cysts most commonly arise after an ovulation from the infolding of the epithelium, which is probably of paramesonephric origin, in the ovulation fossa region. These cysts are lined with ciliated columnar epithelium surrounded by a dense connective tissue layer. Fossa cysts resemble fimbrial cysts except for their location. There is no evidence that the contents of these small cysts have any hormonal activity.

As in other animals two to six or more follicles are stimulated to grow during proestrus and early estrus by the release of FSH which is present in large amounts in the equine anterior pituitary gland. Ovulation occurs in one or occasionally two Graafian follicles under the stimulus of L.H. Ovulation usually occurs from 1 to 24 hours apart in twin ovulations. In some cases two or more days may elapse between ovulations in the same cycle, Day, Patterson. Equine ova are probably ovulated as primary oocytes, like in the dog, and pass through their maturation within a few hours in the oviduct, Cole and Cupps. Removal or loss of the cumulus cells also occurs in the same short period. The fertilized egg undergoes its first cleavage about 24 hours after ovulation and enters the uterus about 4 to 5 days after ovulation. Following ovulation the remaining follicles undergo atresia within 3 to 10 days, Day. Graafian follicles are highly vascular while atretic follicles become avascular and inactive, Prickett.

Since the duration of estrus is quite variable, generally longer in the Spring months and shorter in the Summer months, and variable between mares, determining the time of ovulation which usually occurs 24 to 48 hours before the end of estrus is difficult without repeated rectal palpation of the ovaries. Knowledge concerning the time of ovulation is desirable so that copulation or insemination can be performed within 24 hours of the release of the egg. Day, Loy and Hughes, Nishikawa and others have demonstrated that the administration of a luteinizing gonadotropic hormone early in estrus would usually result in ovulation within 24 to 48 hours. The latter authors recommended the injection of 2000 I.U. HCG intravenously or intramuscularly on the second day of estrus; 32 of 36 mares ovulated 24 to 48 hours later. The length of the estrous period was shortened more than 48 hours. In 15 mares bred the day after treatment 12 conceived. When HCG was given late in a prolonged estrous period, ovulation usually occurred but conception seldom occurred. They recommended treating mares on the second day of estrus when the Graafian follicle was nearly mature and breeding on the third day when it was desired to breed the mare only once during estrus to conserve the stallion. This practice minimized the possibility of trauma or infection in mares with a history of a high susceptibility to infection or, in mares having pneumovagina, or in artificial insemination of mares. Loy reported that 85 percent of treated mares ovulated within 48 hours and the conception rate was 58 percent. Bain reported a conception rate of 65 percent in 164 similarly treated mares. Short suggested that larger doses, up to 10,000 I.U. HCG might be necessary in mares that fail to ovulate after lower doses have been given. Antihormone production to HCG in mares is possible as it is in cattle, but allergic or anaphylactic reactions are rare in mares. Further studies are indicated.

The time of survival of highly fertile equine spermatozoa in the genital tract of mares is up to 6 days, Day Burkhardt, Hafez. The survival time of less fertile semen may be shorter. Whether copulation is performed 24, 48 or 72 hours before ovulation, conception rates are similar, Day. However, most veterinarians prefer to breed mares 12 to 48 hours before ovulation. Day reported that no conceptions occurred in mares bred 2 to 4 hours after ovulation but others have reported conception in mares bred 2 to 14 hours after ovulation, Hughes and Loy (1970), McDonald, Belonje, Asdell. In the mare the sperm capacitation time in the female genital tract is short if indeed capacitation occurs in the horse, Short. Thus if a mare is bred on the second day of the cycle and is still in estrum on the fifth day she probably should be rebred if she has not ovulated. With less fertile stallions more accurate timing of breeding in respect to ovulation will improve the conception rates.

Usually more than one follicle can be palpated on the ovaries during estrum and this is sometimes a cause of an erroneous diagnosis of nymphomania or cystic ovaries, especially if the veterinarian is more accustomed to palpating the smaller follicles of cows' ovaries. In a group of 30 mares examined by Trum, 40 percent ovulated 1 day prior to the end of estrum and 77 percent ovulated during the last 3 days of estrum. Day reported that equally good conception rates were obtained for each of 4 days before ovulation. Trum reported that the second to the fifth day before the end of estrus proved the most fertile time to breed the mare. To conserve stallions Crowhurst recommended that mares should be bred on the second or third day of estrum and teased daily thereafter. If they are still in estrum 4 days later they should be rebred. Of 1187 mares bred, 80 percent had only 1 service per estrum and the overall percentage of pregnancies was 77.7. This method conserved the stallions and by reducing the number of copulations the dangers of introducing infection at the time of service were reduced. Trum in his series of 1543 cases showed that 2 or more services by a stallion during one estrum resulted in only a 3 percent higher conception rate than when there was a single service per estrum. The practice of breeding a mare twice or more in a heat period is called "doubling" a mare. Stocking reported that when mares were bred just once during a heat period and only occasionally more often, there was a 58 percent conception rate on first service. Of 1063 mares bred, 82.6 percent conceived; of the fertile mares, 94.6 percent conceived within 3 services.

Most barren mares show a period of anestrus during the winter months when estrous cycles cease, the ovaries are very firm, hard and inactive and the genital tract is quiescent, pale, and also inactive. Hillman and Loy reported that urinary estrogens were not detectable in winter anestrus in mares but the cervix was atonic and partly dilated. The gradual increasing amount of daylight occurring from January to June, acting through the eyes and the central nervous system results in the production of releasing factors from the hypothalmus that stimulate the production of FSH and the onset of the estrous cycles at various times during the late winter or early spring months depending upon the individual mare, her nutritive state, and the duration of cold dark weather into the spring months. This latter factor will be affected by the latitude at which the horse farm is located. The anestrous period tends to be shorter in the southern states. As in sheep the onset and the end of the breeding season in horses is often characterized by irregularities of the estrous cycle and ovulation. Arthur reported that mares coming into or going out of the breeding season would have follicles without any regressing C.L. Burkhardt noted that towards the end of the breeding season many barren mares would develop a large Graafian follicle that failed to ovulate but would eventually become atretic during the anestrous period. These may be called "autumn" follicles. Cystic follicles similar to those occurring in cattle do not develop in mares, McEntee, Day. Day reported that follicles could be palpated on anestrous mares' ovaries for 14 to 30 days before the first estrus and that failure of ovulation occurred more frequently in the early spring months. Belonji (1952) reported that running a teaser stallion, that was unable to copulate, with a band of mares prior to the onset of the breeding season induced the earlier onset of the estrous cycle and conception. In this respect mares resemble ewes.

Burkhardt, Nishikawa, Loy and others have shown that artificially increasing the amount of exposure to light each day will hasten the onset of the estrous cycles and the shedding of the winter hair coat which are closely associated. By gradually increasing the amount of exposure to light by 30 to 60 minutes per week starting in December, most mares will be cycling and ovulating normally within 40 to 100 days or when the total daily exposure to light reaches 15 to 19 hours in May. Loy reported that by such a regimen: 36 of 89 mares bred and 25 percent were pregnant by the first of March; 76 or 89 mares were bred and 50.5 percent were pregnant by the first of April; 84 of 89 mares were bred and 58.4 percent were pregnant by the first of May and all of the mares were cycling and bred by the first of June. Thus, this technique will induce the earlier attainment of a fertile breeding state. This is advantageous in the racing breeds because it results in earlier foals, better distribution of mares serviced by the stallion and by a greater number of exposures of infertile mares to stallions during the breeding season. This is especially valuable in mares that normally fail to show estrus until late May. During the early breeding season under lights, the same erratic or irregular reproduction periods such as prolonged estrus, irregular estrus, and failure of ovulation may occur as it does at a later period in mares not under lights. Although Burkhardt reported using a 1000 watt light and a reflector in a box stall 2-1/2 feet above the mare's head, Loy demonstrated that 200 watt incandescent light bulbs that provided 7 to 15 foot candles of light, 5-1/2 feet above the floor were satisfactory. Fluorescent or quartz lights up to 600 watts were also satisfactory. It has been suggested by Patterson that the pineal gland because it is influenced by light may be associated with the onset of the seasonal breeding period in the mare. The evidence to support this is tenuous, Cole and Cupps and others do not indicate any relationship. If the mare is normal, artificial lighting should result in the conception of the mare in February, March or April, but if the mare is infertile for a variety of reasons, artificial lighting has no curative properties, Loy.

The transition from the anestrous state into the breeding season whether artificially stimulated by lighting or occurring naturally is a gradual process characterized by certain definite changes especially in the ovaries as detected by palpation. According to Burkhardt the transition from "deep" anestrus, to "shallow" anestrus, to estrus and the estrous cycle is characterized initially by an increase in size of the ovaries a number of days before follicles can be palpated. This is usually associated with a positive energy balance or increasing weight occasioned by spring grass and warmer ambient temperatures, a shedding of the winter hair coat, and an increased vascularity observable in the vagina and cervix. The ovaries feel spongy or rubbery compared to the firm fibrous ovaries of anestrus. In a few cases these mares will show estrus even though follicles cannot be palpated. Probably this is due to small follicles in the ovarian substance that secrete estrogen. Hillman and Loy reported that ovariectomized mares and those in deep anestrus were similar in their reaction to injected estrogen. Signs of estrus were produced in ovariectomized mares with 0.5 mg of estradiol or stilbestrol but mares in shallow anestrus sometimes did not respond to 20 to 250 mg of stilbestrol. Possibly this difference in response may be due to the presence of fairly high levels of progesterone in shallow anestrus. Estrogen assays of blood and urine are indicated and need to be correlated with changes in the genital tract, ovaries and external manifestations of estrus. In "shallow" anestrus, follicles, usually small, 1 to 2 cm in size, are often palpable per rectum and again either signs of estrus or anestrus, usually the latter, may be present. It should be noted that androgens and progesterone in low levels, have been shown in other animals to be synergistic with estradiol or other estrogens in the production of signs of estrus. As reported by Short a variety of estrogens, androgens and progesterone are secreted into the follicles of the mare's ovaries and also are produced in her adrenals. These observations may help to explain the variations or inconsistencies observed in the external manifestations of estrus observed especially in barren or maiden mares early in the breeding season or in mares with granulosa cell tumors or "nymphomania". Thus some mares may exhibit external signs of estrus to a teaser stallion at all stages of the estrous cycle, not only at the time of estrus; signs of estrus may also be seen in mares without follicle formation, or with follicle formation but without ovulation. Conversely a few mares may not exhibit signs of estrus and be experiencing, follicle formation and ovulation.

Caslick, Andrews and McKenzie, and VanRensberg and VanHeerden have shown that barren mares, maiden mares or shy-breeding mares may have irregular estrous cycles. Caslick has divided the irregular estrous cycles as exhibited by these mares into four classes: (1) Long periods of estrum—This class includes 75 percent of these mares. Those in this class usually conceive. Early in the breeding season periods of estrum may last 10 to 20 days or occasionally up to 100 days or more, as shown by external symptoms of the mare toward the teaser. Later in the breeding season, usually by May, these long periods become normal in length. (2) Long periods of diestrum—This class includes about 15 percent of the mares. These mares fail to show estrum at regular normal intervals and have long intervals between estrous periods. These mares are usually poor breeders. (3) Irregular periods of estrum—This class of mares is characterized by an increased number of days in estrum over the days in diestrum. This class may include mares with a "split" estrum. In "split estrum" mares are in estrum 1 or more days, out of estrum for 1 or 2 days, and then back in estrum for 1 or more days. Mares in this class are usually good breeders. (4) No estrum—In this class the teaser is of no value. Ovulation is usually regular, as observed on vaginal and rectal examination, but sexual desire is absent. These mares are usually poor breeders. Most mares with an irregular estrous cycle ovulate regularly and normally. This may be detected by frequent vaginal and rectal examinations at 2- to 4-day intervals. These classes of irregular estrous cycles will be discussed more completely later.

Most mares, especially foaling mares, or mares during the middle portion of the breeding season, June through August, exhibit normal estrous cycles and estrum.

The clinical symptoms of estrum in the mare have been described by Cole and Cupps, Hafez, Andrews and McKenzie, Berliner, Frazer and others as follows: the degree of resistance to the stallion decreases slightly 1 or 2 days before estrum. The greatest estrual response to the stallion occurs 1 or 2 days before the end of estrum or just before ovulation. This is followed by a decrease in sexual desire for the next day or two before estrum ends. Rarely mares will exhibit estrum for 4 or 5 days after ovulation in which case one should suspect a second follicle that ovulates some days after the first, Day. Receptivity or acceptance of the advances of the stallion is usually characterized by the mare seeking out or associating with the stallion, swinging of the rear quarters toward the male, elevation of the tail to one side, squatting and urinating, and "winking" of the clitoris. This is caused by the contractions of the muscles at the base of the clitoris and in the perineum making the clitoris protrude spasmodically between the vulvar lips. The mare will allow the stallion to approach, sniff or nip her and stand firmly to be mounted. Homosexual behavior such as mounting other females rarely occurs. When mares are not in estrum they violently resist the stallion's advances by squealing and kicking at him. Some mares are phlegmatic before and after estrum or in diestrum and show neither much response nor resistance to the stallion. A few mares are always phlegmatic and never show external symptoms of estrum when teased. In these mares showing no receptivity toward the stallion at any time, the estrous cycle is nevertheless usually occurring, as evidenced by typical changes in the vagina, uterus, and ovaries.

For a successful breeding program it is advisable and necessary to tease mares regularly every day or every other day in order to accustom them to the teasing procedure so they will not be frightened by confinement or by the teaser stallion's advances. Changes in their attitude toward the stallion can thus be accurately noted and estrum can be detected early. On some farms a stallion is not available as a teaser and in these cases a gelding may be used. If he is too passive, injections of 250 mg or more of testosterone, "Repositol" form, every 10 days to 3 weeks will usually make the gelding an excellent teaser. The masculine symptoms usually disappear by 4 to 6 weeks after the last injection. Detecting estrum in most mares is nearly impossible without regular teasing. Some may show signs of estrum when groomed about the rear quarters; swelling, relaxation and edema of the vulva is fairly common in mares in estrum. Regular examination of the vagina and external cervical os with a speculum or palpation of the cervix and ovaries per rectum by an experienced veterinarian can replace or substitute for regular teasing of mares, and although these methods are possibly more accurate than teasing in detecting true estrum and the time for service they are also more time consuming and costly under most situations.

The physical symptoms of estrum in the genital tract of mares are characterized by congestion and hyperemia of the mucosa of the vulva, vagina and cervix that increase in intensity from proestrus on to ovulation and then decrease to a pale, quiescent state during late metestrum and diestrum. During estrum the mucosa is very pink, hyperemic, or congested. There is an increased secretion of vaginal mucus that makes the mucosa appear shiny and allows the vaginal speculum to slide or slip with ease over the mucous membrane. Most mares in estrum seldom object to and will stand quietly for the vaginal examination. In the mare the amount of mucus is greatest and its viscosity lowest during estrum. Seldom is mucus observed at the vulva of a mare in estrum as it is in the cow. Also excess mucus is seldom observed on the floor of the vagina unless infection is present. The cervix does not contain tubular mucus glands that secrete copious amounts of mucus, as in the cow. In late metestrum, diestrum, and early proestrum the vaginal speculum on introduction slides over the mucosa with difficulty, since the mucus is scant, sticky, and dry. During gestation this mucus is copious, sticky and gummy. The cervix during proestrum and estrum gradually relaxes, becomes flaccid, edematous, and quite hyperemic until it is very relaxed, hyperemic and edematous at the time of ovulation. Lieux has described and illustrated the clinical appearance of the cervix at different stages of the cycle and pregnancy. At the time of ovulation the cervix is usually relaxed sufficiently to readily admit 2 to 5 fingers of one's hand. The endometrium at the time of estrum in a mare is very edematous and appears as large parallel and scalloped, thickened folds. The old belief that mares require an attendant to insert his arm into the vagina and dilate the cervix with the fingers or "open the mare" before breeding has no basis in fact, and is contraindicated because of the danger of introducing infection. Furthermore if this is done just prior to breeding, pneumovagina may result and this interferes with the normal drawing of the semen into the uterus at coitus. During late metestrum and diestrum the cervix is tightly closed and the external os appears puckered. On rectal palpation during diestrum the cervix is tightly contracted and has a distinct outline. During proestrum, into estrum, and up to ovulation there is a progressive relaxation of the cervix, its tonicity decreases and near ovulation it is difficult to define the cervix because of its thin, relaxed and flaccid walls.

Rectal examination at estrum will reveal follicles present on the ovaries. Asdell stated that 8 to 9 follicles are produced each cycle; normally only one or occasionally two, mature and ovulate and the rest become atretic. The ovaries in young mares 3 to 4 years old are largest. They gradually become smaller with age. Often the ovary containing the Graafian follicle is somewhat sensitive on palpation per rectum. During estrum the uterus is usually noted to be rather flaccid and soft on rectal palpation compared to the pregnant uterus which is usually tonic and tubular.

The vaginal smear in the mare is indefinite and of no value in differentiating the various stages of estrous cycle, Nishikawa, Asdell. The pH of vaginal mucus during estrum in the mare is 7.9 to 8.1. Most normal mares will show these cyclic changes in the genital tract and ovulation during the breeding season even though signs of estrus exhibited on teasing are either lacking, weak, or continuous. Regular, careful vaginal and rectal examinations of mares not showing normal symptoms toward the teaser will in many cases indicate the time of true estrum and ovulation.

Equine gonadotropin present in mare serum during early pregnancy is produced by the endometrial cups in the uterus, Clegg, Boda and Cole, Cole and Cupps, and Asdell. Wynn has observed by electron microscopy that both the endometrial cups and the adjacent chorion have the ultrastructural complexity necessary to produce gonadotropins. At about 35 to 40 days of pregnancy the corpus luteum of pregnancy degenerates, followed by the development of successive follicles some of which ovulate and by accessory corpora lutea that degenerate by 150 days. This provides for the ovarian secretion of progesterone and the maintenance of pregnancy until 90 to 120 days of pregnancy when progesterone production by the placenta is sufficient to maintain pregnancy. The development and regression or ovulation of follicles from about 20 to 90 or more days of pregnancy probably accounts for the frequent observance of signs of estrus in pregnant mares, Bain, Burkhardt and Rowlands. These signs of estrus are usually weak and short-lived because of the presence of accessory corpora lutea and their secretion of progesterone. It is generally believed that service during pregnancy only occasionally results in abortion. After 150 days of gestation the ovaries become small and atrophied, and after about 170 days of pregnancy may be removed without causing abortion, Cole and Cupps, Short.

The ovaries of female fetuses 5 to 9 months of age weigh 120 to 150 grams, compared with 20 grams at birth and 40 to 70 grams in the adult mare, Asdell. Fetal testes also follow this same growth and decline pattern. (See Figure 145) The growth and regression of the interstitial cells of these fetal gonads and their changes in size follow the changes in excretion of estrogen in the dam's urine, which gradually increases up to about 260 days of gestation and then declines, McEntee, Asdell, Nalbandov. Since the fetal gonads do not enlarge until after the fourth month of gestation it is doubtful that PMSG plays a role in this hypertrophy. Although large amounts of progesterone by-products are present in the urine, and progesterone is present in the blood of mares in early pregnancy, it is nearly absent in the blood in middle and late stages of gestation, Short. The blood progesterone levels in early pregnancy are produced by the secretion of progesterone by the corpora lutea. Progesterone is produced in large amounts by the equine placenta as early as 90 days of gestation and can be found in high concentrations in the fetal blood, 3.8 to 6.3 mcg per 100 ml, from 120 to 310 days of gestation. Possibly this may influence the growth of the fetal gonads. Apparently little or none of the placental progesterone gets into the maternal circulation but it must play a vital role by its local effect on the uterus by means of the diffuse type of placenta. The value of progesterone injections in the prevention of early or late abortion in the mare is questionable, Short. The ability of the glucocorticoids to precipitate parturition, especially late in gestation has been noted in cattle. Adams reported that injections of glucocorticoids in pony mares late in gestation did not result in premature parturition. The author wonders from his clinical experience if further experiments might not show that abortions could be produced in mares with glucocorticoids if they were administered throughout gestation when the blood plasma and urinary levels of estrogen were high.

Miscellaneous aspects of equine reproductive physiology. The blood levels of progesterone are very low in the mare, about 0.8 mcg per 100 ml during the luteal phase of the cycle, about 1.2 mcg per 100 ml from 60 to 70 days of gestation and less than 0.4 mcg per 100 ml from 120 to 310 days of pregnancy, Short, Cole and Cupps. Loy and Swan reported that 50 mg of progesterone daily in oil intramuscularly would prevent estrus but not ovulation in the mare if started before the onset of estrus; 100 mg of progesterone in oil daily intramuscularly would block estrus and ovulation. Three of 4 mares treated with 100 mg of progesterone oil daily during the summer months came into estrum 3 to 4 days after the cessation of the injections and ovulated 6 days after the onset of estrum. In 6 mares treated daily with 100 mg of progesterone in oil from 5 days to 12 days postpartum, 5 of these mares ovulated, 3 mares on days 15 and 16 postpartum and two given 2000 I.U. HCG intravenously on days 14 and 16 ovulated on days 16 and 18, respectively. Four of these mares were bred at this time and all conceived. Further study might be given to improving the conception rate on foal estrum by delaying ovulation for about a week by daily injections of 100 mg of progesterone in oil. Intramuscular doses of 500 mg of crystalline (Repositol) progesterone and 500 mg of M.A.P. ("Promone"), and oral doses of 425 to 1782 mg daily of M.A.P. or 10 to 20 mg of M.G.A. daily had no effect on preventing estrus or ovulation in postpartum mares. Thus very high doses or crystalline progesterone and progestagens active in suppressing estrum and ovulation in other species had no effect on the mare.

Loy et al., showed that peak urinary estrogen levels averaging 18.4 mcg per 100 ml; range 8.8 to 23.6 mcg, compared to a peak of 3.6 mcg per 100 ml of urine during diestrus, were present from days 7 through 11 postpartum. Ovulation was associated with the peak of estrogen secretion. Mares given 100 to 200 mg of progesterone in oil daily, days 5 through 14 postpartum showed no estrus and did not ovulate but peak levels of 9 mcg per 100 ml of estrogen were present in the urine. Although follicles developed during this period they did not ovulate, but did so after the end of the treatment. Thus progesterone didn't completely suppress the release of gonadotropins at this time in the mare. Because of the above evidence of the ineffectiveness of crystalline "Repositol" progesterone and the progestagens to suppress estrus, Short, as well as this author, seriously questions the value of progesterone therapy as usually given to prevent abortions in mares.

Day and Rowlands reported that when estrogen implants were given to mares 26 to 41 days after conception that abortions followed in 60 to 90 days after 31 to 91 mg of estrogen had been absorbed from the implant. Nishikawa reported that anestrous mares had a low threshold for exogenous estrogens. Typical signs of estrum were produced by 50 to 100 mg doses of estrone and 2.5 to 5 mg of stilbestrol within 8 to 10 hours that lasted for 3 to 5 days. He also noted as did Hillman and Loy, that much larger doses were necessary to produce signs of estrus during the breeding season in cycling mares due to the progesterone produced by the corpus luteum. Injections of 10 to 15 mg of stilbestrol daily starting 7 to 9 days after ovulation and continued for 13 to 20 days caused the C.L. to persist in mares. A similar effect was noted in sows given 5 mg of stilbestrol daily, while in cows and goats estrogen injections caused a regression of the C.L., Nishikawa. From this work he recommended that 2 to 10 mg of stilbestrol be injected every 2 to 4 days for 9 to 18 doses from 90 to 150 days of gestation for mares that habitually aborted around 4 or 5 months of gestation. This treatment increased the urinary excretion of pregnandiol, a degradation product of progesterone. In about 280 mares that had experienced 1 to 5 midterm abortions, only 3.3 percent aborted during treatment while 12.7 percent of similar untreated mares aborted. Further endocrine studies are needed in mares.

Douching or infusing the uterus of noncycling mares with ovaries containing small immature follicles, mares that are cycling in diestrus but not exhibiting signs of estrus, or anestrous mares that have been bred but are not pregnant at 40 days after service, with 250 to 500 ml of warm physiological saline solution to which antibiotics or a mild antiseptic has been added to control the possible introduction of infection has a definite stimulating effect on the release of gonadotropic hormone resulting in estrum and ovulation within 2 to 8 days, usually within 2 to 4 days. The infusing of the uterus should be done in a thoroughly sanitary manner avoiding any possible contamination of the genital tract. The tail should be bandadged, the perineal region and vulva should be thoroughly washed and rinsed. Sterile plastic gloves and sleeves should be worn and sterile equipment and saline used. Infusion may be accomplished by a rubber horse catheter guided through the cervix after dilation of that organ with two fingers, or the introduction of an insemination pipette attached to an intravenous outfit or pressure flow outfit. The cervix is held closed to prevent the backflow of saline into the vagina. Probably other solutions than saline would be as satisfactory but could be more irritating. The exact mechanism by which the manipulation of the cervix, or the dilation of the uterus brings about estrum is not known but apparently it causes some effect on the hypothalamus to cause the release of F.S.H. from the pituitary gland. Ovulation usually occurs during the induced estrum and many mares, if bred, will conceive on that estrus, Burkhardt, Arthur. The latter reported that estrus with follicle formation was induced in anestrous mares early in the breeding season, but ovulation did not occur and the follicles became atretic. In mares in anestrus in late Fall and Winter, infusions had no effect. The duration of estrum or the time of ovulation was not influenced by the douching of mares during estrum. Thus the results of infusions are predicated on the physiologic state of the mare at the time of the infusions. Repeated infusions at 7- to 14-day intervals may occasionally be indicated, Proctor and others.

Bain reported that about 85 percent of 148 mares given infusions were in estrum within 2 to 12 days and 56 percent conceived on the first service. A few mares in "lactational anestrus" showed no response. Van Niekerk infused 25 mares that showed anestrus 40 days after service and were not pregnant; all responded promptly within 2 to 4 days to the treatment. If they were not infused this anestrous state lasted from 40 to 80 days. Paterson reported a similar response in anestrous mares when he gave 250 mg stilbestrol intramuscularly and bred the mares naturally on the induced estrus 24 hours later. Within 7 to 8 days many mares so handled came into a true standing estrus and ovulated; conception frequently occurred if they were bred in this normal estrus. It is possible that the old empiric technique of "opening up" the mare by the groom manipulating and dilating the cervix was based on the physiological effects and the production of estrus induced by such an act. Uterine "curettage" in the barren or infertile mare by drawing the cervix posteriorly with forceps fastened just lateral to the external cervical os has been accomplished by gently scraping the endometrium of both uterine horns and body with a sterile 28-inch, 70 cm curette. This is supposed to simulate the stimulation effect of douching the uterus with warm saline, Laufenstein-Duffy, Solomon et al., Morrow. The indications for and the value of this empirical technique are questionable. Controlled experiments and studies have not been undertaken.

The anterior pituitary gland of the adult horse contains a high concentration of FSH but is somewhat low in L.H., Asdell. Synchronization of the estrous cycle of large numbers of mares for artificial insemination, as has been done in cattle, sheep and swine, cannot be done at the present time. There is no indication presently of any satisfactory drug or technique to accomplish this. Progestational agents used in the other animals are ineffective in the mare. Bielanski has reported that the estrous cycles and estrous signs, and ovulation were very irregular, but ovulation did occur in female mules. Benirschke and Sullivan reported that in 47 pairs of mule ovaries atretic follicles were found in 12 and corpora lutea were present in 15 of the 94 ovaries. Female mules were infertile and primordial follicles in the ovary were very rare.

Irregularities of the Estrous Cycle as a Cause of Infertility in Mares.

Bain, Day, Andrews and McKenzie, Caslick and others have reported that foaling mares have the highest rate of fertility. Barren or open mares have the next highest rate and maiden or nulliparous mares have the lowest fertility rate.

Caslick stated that irregularities in the estrous cycle were probably the most important cause for infertility in the mare. The failure of veterinarians to recognize and handle these irregularities of the estrous cycle is often based on the lack of regular daily or every-other-day, closely-observed teasing of the mare by a good teaser, and a lack of carefully kept up-to-date breeding, teasing and genital tract examination records. These two practices, regular teasing and the keeping of good records, essential for a high conception rate, are always followed on well-managed, successful breeding farms. As a supplement to these two practices, regular examination of the genital tract and ovaries per rectum and the speculum examination of the vagina and cervix are highly useful and informative.

Teasing of the barren mare should begin 30 days or so before the breeding season or the date of desired breeding. This is done so that the mare will become accustomed to her surroundings, to the teasing stocks and the teaser, and not be frightened, excitable, or nervous when teased during the early part of the breeding season since these latter attitudes make it difficult for the handler, manager, or veterinarian to tell when estrum is present. This practice also acquaints the men observing the mare with its reactions toward the teaser stallion both in estrum and diestrum. This is of great importance in certain mares who do not show marked symptoms of acceptance or rejection of the teaser.

The teasing stocks or bar is usually a solid partition about 4 feet high and 8 feet long often located about 3.5 feet from a solid wall, into which the mare is led and tied. No projecting posts or spaces between the boards should be present as a possible cause of injury to the mare or the teaser. The teaser is led up to the side of the mare and allowed to tease it. The mare's reactions are closely observed for signs of estrum or approaching estrum. There are other techniques for teasing mares, including teasing of mares in their stalls by leading the stallion up to the door and if necessary backing the mare up to him. Mares teased in their stalls should be watched as the stallion enters the barn, as he teases them over the stall door, and after he leaves them. Some mares will "fight" or resist the teaser at their stall but will indicate estrus by relaxing the vulva and urinating after or before they actually see him. A few managers tease their mares by leading the stallion through the pasture and circulating among them to determine their reaction toward the stallion. On other farms a Shetland or small pony stud is run continuously with the mares to detect estrus. Because of his small size he is unable to copulate with them. Belonje has described a surgical technique to direct the penis of a teaser stallion to the rear so that copulation is impossible when he is placed with mares on pasture. A male pseudohermaphodite with defective development of the penis could also serve in a similar capacity. In range areas the stallion is often kept in a large stall or pen where the mares running in the adjacent corral or pasture can go to the fence when they are in estrum.

Teasing a foaling mare should be begun on the third or fourth day after foaling. The foal is usually left in the stall while the mare is led away to be teased, or if the mare objects too much, small box or pen in which to put the foal may be built in front of the teasing rack as shown by Andrews and McKenzie. A few mares fight or resist the teaser at all times even though in estrum. Some of these mares will show estrum promptly when a twitch is applied to their nose, thus distracting their attention so that their true reaction to the teaser is exhibited. In an excellent discussion on teasing mares, Errington stated that certain mares fail to show estrum to certain teasers. Occasionally a mare may show nearly typical heat one day and then not show it again. This symptom is observed most commonly in pregnant mares. Other mares are very phlegmatic and show little resistance to a teaser at any time. The use of a bold, aggressive teaser is very useful with these mares. Occasionally these phlegmatic mares come into estrum so gradually the casual observer might not notice it, but when they pass out of estrum the difference in their reaction to the teaser is usually observable. Then it is too late to breed the mare. Oftentimes a good teaser may recognize estrum and react accordingly although the man observing the mare cannot see signs of it. Excessively fat mares may often be phlegmatic toward the teaser and fail to show estrum. The person who is responsible for the teasing of mares should be a close and careful observer and accurately record his observations. The teaser on a large breeding farm is usually a stallion kept for that purpose or one that is seldom used. On smaller farms where stallions are used sparingly the breeding stallion can act as a teaser. Teasing of mares prior to service increases the volume and total number of spermatozoa in the ejaculate of the teaser stallion as it does in bulls. On farms where a stallion is not available, a gelding may act as a teaser but its teasing ability improves greatly if it is given 250 mg of testosterone, "Repositol" form, every 7 to 14 days or as needed. If a teaser is not available it is very difficult to detect external signs of estrum except in mares showing marked signs of estrum.

Although it is not frequently performed except on well-managed farms with a resident or contract veterinarian, mares that show estrum to the teaser may be examined by speculum, or their ovaries examined per rectum, at least 12 to 24 hours before being bred to make sure they are actually in true estrum and that ovulation is approaching. Speculum examination causes ballooning of the vagina and within an hour or so of coitus may interfere with the proper deposition of the semen. Rectal examination just before a natural cover may dilate the rectum and favor false entry by the stallion. Barren mares and foaling mares should be teased daily or every other day until they are bred the second or third day of estrum, and teasing should continue until the end of estrum. If the mare is still in estrum 2 or 4 days after service she is usually rebred that same estrum. For the next 2 weeks teasing is necessary only every third to fourth day, and then 2 weeks after breeding teasing should begin at daily or every-other-day intervals. If estrum does not recur, teasing every third to fourth day may be continued for several weeks more and then a pregnancy examination should be made. If a pregnancy examination is not performed by a veterinarian about 30 to 40 days after service, regular teasing every third to fourth day should continue during the breeding season, inasmuch as a few barren and foaling mares may show marked irregularities in the estrous cycle or lose an early embryo.

Of the three procedures used for determining the stage of the estrous cycle, the stage of estrum, the time of ovulation and the best time for service, the external manifestations of estrus of the mare in the presence of a teaser or stallion is the most variable and inaccurate but is the only method available for most horse owners. The speculum examination of the vagina and cervix, or "spec exam" , is the next most accurate procedure when performed by a knowledgeable observer. There is danger of introducing infection into the genital tract if this is not done properly. The most accurate procedure is the rectal examination of the ovaries, cervix and uterus by a skilled, experienced veterinarian.

In general, foaling mares have regular estrous cycles of about 21 days **after** the first or foal heat when ovulation may occur from 5 or 6 days to 18 to 20 days postpartum with an average of about 10 to 12 days. Thus the second estrum may occur from 25 to 40 days postpartum. Occasionally, however, mares not bred on the foal heat will develop anestrum and show no estrum for a month or more. This is especially true of mares in poor condition or mares with a phlegmatic, sullen temperment. In reviewing Caslick's work on mares with irregular estrous cycles, these anestrous foaling mares fit into his Group 2 classification. He states these mares ovulate regularly but fail to show heat at every cycle. Crowhurst and Caslick in reviewing the records of Dr. E. A. Caslick, found that of 57 foaling anestrous mares, 42 or 73.6 percent, were bred on the ninth day, or foal, heat. They concluded that there is no basis for the belief that only mares not bred on their foaling heat fail to come back into estrum. In fact their records revealed the opposite! Some of these foaling mares bred on the foal heat and then showing estrum again 45 to 90 days later may have suffered an early abortion. Crowhurst and Caslick cited 17 suspected cases of early abortion of which 10 occurred in foaling mares, 7 of which had been bred on the ninth day after parturition. Britton cited 125 mares bred on the foal heat, of which 81 conceived and 24 showed the characteristic history of early abortion. In another band 56 mares were bred on foal heat, 22 conceived, and 8 of these showed symptoms of early embryonic death. A few mares, especially mares suckling foals, may have a "silent" estrum or fail to show estrum to a teaser, but careful observation of the mare by the attendant, especially when the mare is in the paddock, may reveal restlessness or standing and gazing over the fence, or other changes in attitude indicative of estrum. Sometimes these mares may rarely show estrum to another mare but not to the teaser. Vaginal examination or rectal examination of the ovaries will confirm the suspected estrum. When these mares are bred they usually show little resistance and "breakdown" and accept the stallion. Of 57 foaling mares that showed anestrum, about 80 percent came back into estrum spontaneously without external stimulation in time to be bred before the end of the season, and 23, or 40.4 percent, conceived, Crowhurst and Caslick. Foaling mares, with the possible exception of those having a slightly prolonged foal heat, seldom show the very prolonged periods of estrum exhibited by some barren mares.

The variations in the mare in her external manifestations of estrus toward the stallion, the presence or absence of an estrous cycle and the internal or physiological state of the genital tract and the ovaries, and ovulation are complex and difficult to understand and interpret. As one veterinarian remarked, mares external reactions toward the teaser may not reflect the internal status of the genital organs, or "The mare will lie to you". In order to accurately categorize mares as to their true status in regard to estrum or anestrum, regular every-other-day teasing of mares by a stallion, at least twice weekly examination or speculum examination of the vagina, or both and the maintenance of careful records are necessary.

There are several different ways of describing the irregularities of the estrous periods in mares. The following is a method used by the author. Later the description used by Caslick will be outlined. It is hoped that both descriptions will complement each other and aid the student.

All mares fall into two groups in respect to their reactions toward a teaser or stallion.

I. Mares showing external manifestations of estrum toward the teaser or stallion. These mares are in either:
   A. **Physiologic or true estrum** with typical follicle development on the ovaries and changes indicative of estrum in the genital tract. Signs of estrum may be observed during pregnancy due follicular development, but no changes are noted in the genital tract.
   B. **Psychologic or false estrum** with inactive ovaries or ovaries with no or only slight follicular development and the genital tract is pale, inactive with a closed cervix, no edema and a sticky dry mucosa; the reproductive or estrous cycle is absent. Mares may exhibit psychologic signs of estrus at any stage of the estrous cycle other than estrum.

II. Mares in anestrum and failing to show external signs of estrum toward a teaser or stallion. These mares are in either:
   A. **Seasonal or physiologic anestrum** during the winter months of November through February or March. Some follicular activity of the ovaries may be observed in these mares but the

follicles seldom are large and ovulation does not occur. This follicular activity is more noticeable in the late Fall and early Spring. Most of these mares have small, hard, inactive ovaries and the genital tract is pale, dry and inactive, or—

B. **Pathological anestrum** is noted in diseased or emaciated mares; rare cases of mares with ovarian hypoplasia, pituitary or hypothalamic tumors, or ovariectomized mares. The changes in the genital organs are similar to A, but are more marked, or—

C. **Gestational or post service anestrum** is noted during pregnancy. Before 150 days of gestation occasional fleeting or brief atypical signs of estrus may be observed in some mares due to the great follicular activity occurring in the ovary during early pregnancy. The changes in the genital organs are similar to A but much more sticky adhesive mucus is present in the vagina and on the cervix, or—

D. **Psychological anestrum, or "silent" estrum** is seen especially in certain fat, phlegmatic or lactating mares in which normal physiologic changes in the genital organs characteristic of the estrous cycle including follicle formation, ovulation and regular recurring signs of estrus in the genital tract with hyperemia, edema and increased mucus secretion in the vagina and cervix are occurring, but the mare exhibits no external signs of estrum toward the teaser or stallion. These mares when presented to the stallion for service and restrained with breeding hobbles and a twitch just before ovulation, usually "break down" and show external signs of acceptance of the stallion. In "split" estrum, several days of anestrum or silent estrum occur during a normal estrous period, or—

E. **Lactational anestrum** is due to a variety of causes and is observed in certain foaling mares that may have a **psychological anestrum** and is seen especially in highly nervous mares with marked protective attitude toward their foal, **a pathologic anestrum** due to debility or a **gestational or post service anestrum** in mares bred on the foal or later estrum that conceive but early embryonic death occurs between 20 and 70 days of gestation. True lactational anestrum as occurs in sows and suckled cows does not occur in mares.

Some authors such as Burkhardt, use the terms **"deep" anestrus** to indicate a marked seasonal anestrus or pathologic anestrus and "shallow" anestrus to indicate the transitional periods in the spring and fall when some follicular activity is present but the formation of a normal Graafian follicle, estrus and ovulation does not occur. As in "lactational" anestrus, a number of causes of anestrus may be combined to delay the onset of normal estrous cycles in the spring of the year or at puberty.

Another frequently used classification of irregular equine estrous cycles is described by Caslick. Many barren mares have normal cycles, but irregularities of the cycle in barren mares are common and Caslick has divided these irregularities into 4 types discussed below. He stated of the barren or non-pregnant mare that "The only regularity about her sexual cycle is its irregularity".

(1) **Long periods of estrum**—this type or class includes 75 percent of the barren mares showing symptoms of irregular estrous cycles toward the teaser stallion. In this type of mare, heat periods may last 10 to 20, or rarely, up to 120 days during which time the mare will accept the stallion at any time. This abnormal cycle is usually observed early in the breeding season and as the season progresses the periods of estrum shorten and become normal. Usually breeding is delayed until the cycles become of normal length; most of these mares conceive. This condition is sometimes called "nymphomania." This name is probably incorrect for the condition, because in these mares the condition is temporary, it corrects itself, and pathological lesions such as cystic ovaries are not present as they are in the cow. It should be remembered, however, in checking the ovaries of these or of other normal cycling and ovulating mares, that follicles 1 to 3 inches in diameter are normal and physiological, and that a number of developing follicles 0.5 inch to 2 inches in size may be present in each ovary. According to Caslick, these mares have estrous cycles of normal length and ovulate at regular intervals during these long periods of acceptance of the male. These true heat periods accompanied by ovulations may be determined by speculum examination of the vagina and cervix and by rectal examination, and the mares bred accordingly. The vaginal examination should be made rapidly, since the vagina balloons with air as the speculum is introduced and soon becomes hyperemic or congested, somewhat resembling that of a "windsucking" mare. Examinations should be made probably not more than twice a week or false symptoms due to pneumovagina or irritation may result because of the too frequent examinations, Sager. Regular rectal examination of the ovaries by an experienced veterinarian 3 times a week or more often will assist in determining ovulation time by palpation of the rapid growth of follicles during proestrum and estrum and noting the loss of tenseness and tightness of the mature Graafian follicle just before ovula-

tion, when it softens, becomes thin-walled, and fluctuates. Since this period of long psychological estrum early in the breeding season usually extends only 10 to 30 days, most veterinarians recommend that these mares not be bred until later in the breeding season when the cycles become normal. This abnormal manifestation of estrum was seen more often in thin, maiden mares and preceded the shedding of their winter hair coat. It was less common in well-housed and fed mares, Bain. As foaling mares these animals usually have an excellent sexual rhythm.

(2) **Long periods between estrums or long diestrous periods**—According to Caslick this second group, of about 15 percent of the barren mares shows irregular estrous cycles to the teaser stallion, with estrum occurring infrequently, and with prolonged periods of diestrum or anestrum. When estrum is exhibited it is a true period. Ovulation appears to be as regular in this group as in the preceding one but estrum is not shown at every ovulation. These mares may accept the advances of one stallion but not another. This condition of psychological anestrum appears similar to subestrum or "silent" estrum in cattle. These barren mares do not conceive as readily as do those in Group 1, but as foaling mares about 50 percent have an excellent estrous cycle and the other half maintain the same type of irregular cycle with periods of psychological anestrum as when barren. These mares are bred when they show estrum or bred on the basis of regular speculum and rectal examination at the time of approaching ovulation.

(3) **Irregular periods of estrum**—This third small group of barren mares is characterized by frequent prolonged periods of estrous manifestations toward the teaser in which the days in estrum are more frequent than the days out of estrum, a modification of Group 1. According to Caslick, this type of cycle is seen most often in maiden or nulliparous mares. The mares in Group 3 are difficult to breed properly unless vaginal and rectal examinations are made regularly since much of the manifested heat period is false and not related to ovulation. Occasionally mares of this group may exhibit a "split estrum" by showing estrum for several days, being out of heat a day or two, "silent" estrum, and then back in estrum again for the remainder of the estrous period.

(4) **No estrum**—This very small fourth group of mares fails to show any signs of estrum to the teaser. They act the same to the teaser whether barren or in foal. They are usually very phlegmatic and indifferent. Ovulation is often regular and breeding is based on vaginal and rectal examinations alone. Generally these mares are poor breeders. Some are overly fat due to excessive feeding, lack of exercise, and possibly other reasons.

Mares as a whole are quite true to their behavioral pattern in their manifestation of estrus toward a teaser stallion, either as foaling or barren mares, Caslick. These many irregularities in the estrous cycle and response to the teaser, breeding dates, and findings on rectal or vaginal examinations make the keeping of accurate, complete, up-to date records on all breeding mares imperative for the manager as well as the veterinarian on a breeding farm.

The problem, according to Caslick, appeared to be one of the balance between the various endocrine glands or hormones and the nervous system. The various manifestations of irregular cycles appear to be inherited. Much more work will be required before these various irregularities can be explained either on a basis of overproduction, underproduction, over-release, under-release, or ratios of the various hormones and of their effects on the central nervous system of the mare. This work on the physiology of the reproductive system should also include a study of the estrous cycle throughout the year and the effect of increasing daylight on the pituitary gland. Interesting work on other species of animals such as the sheep and cow is opening new possibilities in the study of the physiology of the estrous cycle and ovulation in the mare. Caslick indicated that mares in Group 4 that fail to show estrum have a sullen temperament and appear to have an antagonistic balance between the nervous and endocrine systems which results in an indifferent individual. Caslick and others have frequently noted that pregnant mares may occasionally show a short estrum of about 24 hours to a teaser. Caslick reported one pregnant mare that was observed to be in heat 5 times one season. Mares exhibiting estrum during the gestation period should be examined before they are bred, to determine if early abortion has occurred and if infection is present. If, on vaginal examination, no signs of estrum are observed and on rectal examination pregnancy may be suspected or diagnosed, the mare should not be bred as coitus might rarely induce abortion.

The Prognosis for conception in cases of irregular estrous cycles, prolonged estrus or anestrus in mares is usually favorable if there is regular, careful teasing of the mare, together with periodic vaginal and rectal examinations, if necessary, to determine when true or physiologic estrus is present and ovulation is imminent. Due to the shortness of the breeding season, these irregularities should be noted early and a proper diagnosis made so that a suitable line of treatment and procedure to follow can be outlined. Certain pathological states causing anestrus may have a poor prognosis.

Treatment of irregular estrous cycles or prolonged estrus or anestrus of apparently normal mares, according ·ick, "appears to lie in a proper understanding of the different variations in the sexual rhythm of the mare and the eternal vigilance of all those associated with breeding". Douching or infusing of the uterus with saline may promote the onset of signs of estrus in mares in Groups 2 and 4 that are not showing regular estrus signs even though they are cycling. In general, hormone therapy to correct irregularities of the estrous cycle in the mare, while usually not doing any permanent harm when not given to excess, have never been of proven value in any condition. Caslick, and Crowhurst and Caslick, and Proctor reported estrogens to be of little value on anestrous mares or mares in Group 2 and 4 as classified by Caslick. Burkhardt reported on the use of estrogens in mares showing anestrum and concluded it to be of no value in mares with "deep" anestrum in which ovaries were small and shrunken. In "shallow" anestrum 10 to 15 mg of stilbestrol was thought to be of value when estrum failed to occur yet follicles were present. He stated that unless follicles were over 1 inch or 2 cm in diameter no results would be obtained with stilbestrol. His description of mares corresponds with Caslick's Group 2 or the transitional stages of seasonal anestrus in the Spring just before the onset of estrous cycles. Since Burkhardt ran no controls, it is likely from the work of others that stilbestrol neither helped nor retarded the natural occurrence of estrum.

During the prolonged periods of estrum exhibited by the Group 1 mares early in the breeding season many veterinarians have empirically tried injecting various gonadotropic hormones, especially those rich in LH, to terminate the prolonged but temporary continuous estrous signs but with no conclusive results. In recent years veterinarians especially at race tracks have used large doses of progesterone in oil, repositol progesterone, MAP or "Promone", and even testosterone. From the work of Loy and Swan daily or every other day doses of 100 to 200 mg of progesterone in oil should be the only agent that would suppress signs of estrus in the mare. With time and without treatment most of these mares go out of continuous estrum and have normal estrous cycles later in the breeding season. In mares with a long estrous period, pneumovagina may become established and require Caslick's operation on the vulva if the breeding life of the mare is to be maintained.

Successful results with any hormone therapy in a certain mare in these various groups can usually be explained on the basis of the normal regular underlying ovulatory cycle and clinical manifestations of estrum described by Caslick. At the present time hormonal therapy in mares is on only an empirical basis and is used all too often as a placebo or substitute for frequent, regular teasing and rectal and vaginal examinations. The use of pregnant mare serum, equine pituitary extracts, thyroid extracts, and chorionic gonadotropin was reported to be of no value in anestrous mares, Burkhardt. A number of veterinarians have indicated that injections of F.S.H., 50 to 100 I.U. were occasionally successful in correcting true anestrum in mares but no controlled or careful work has been reported on this therapy. Injections of pregnant mare serum in horses may in rare instances cause Theiler's disease or infectious hepatitis 50 to 100 days after the injection. More work is obviously necessary on the basic physiology of the estrous cycle and estrum before hormonal therapy in mares will be based on factual knowledge.

Thirty to forty years ago it was a common practice to tap ovarian "cysts" in mares to "cure" infertility due to irregularities in the estrous cycle including prolonged estrus seen in barren mares at the onset of the breeding season and in mares with psychologic anestrus. Workers in those days apparently confused Graafian and atretic follicles which often are 2 to 4 inches, 5 to 10 cm, in diameter with ovarian cysts as seen in cattle. Follicular or luteal cysts associated with nymphomania or anestrum do not occur in mares, McEntee, Arthur, Short. Most atretic follicles persist for only a few days to two weeks after ovulation. Late in the breeding season large follicles may fail to ovulate, become atretic and persist for several weeks or months due to the onset of anestrum. These may be called "autumn" follicles. All atretic follicles eventually recede. They do not prevent the development of new follicles, ovulation and corpus luteum formation. Cystic degeneration of the uterine endometrium is occasionally observed in old mares especially those that have not been used as brood mares, McEntee and Dimock and Edwards. The cause may be the repeated and alternate influence of estrogens and progesterone as reported in cystic degeneration of the endometrium in unbred bitches. Occasionally a parovarian cyst or enlarge epoophoron may erroneously be diagnosed as an ovarian "cyst". Presently the tapping of "cysts" with a needle has been discarded as of no value and being possibly harmful to the mare. Peck and others have indicated it might be of value in unusual cases to tap or rupture manually one of twin follicles approaching ovulation to prevent twin conception in mares that regularly conceive twins.

In seasonal or physiologic anestrum noted by Osborne, Arthur and others, some mares regularly begin to cycle late in the breeding season. (See Table 19) The author has studied some mares that would not go from their seasonal anestrous state into the breeding season or estrous cycle until May despite hormonal treatment with gonadotropes and estrogens, a high plane of nutrition, warm housing and infusing or douching of the uterus. The ovaries remained small and inactive. These mares responded to a regimen of increased daylight beginning in

December as described earlier and advocated by Burkhardt, Patterson, Loy and others. Sometimes mares in seasonal anestrus during the Spring months are approaching the breeding season and some follicular activity is evident by the presence of small follicles, and slightly enlarged, spongy ovaries. These mares in "shallow" anestrus would probably come into reproductive cycling shortly despite any treatment. However, the process might be hastened by douching or infusing the uterus with saline, possibly administering 5 to 15 mg stilbestrol, Burkhardt, or by stressing the mare by placing her in a new environment or by placing a stallion in the next stall or paddock or even the same pasture several weeks before the breeding season, Belonje. These latter factors have been observed as helpful in other seasonal breeders such as sheep and have appeared helpful in the author's practice. Because of the shortness of the breeding season in racing horses, mares of those breeds that only come into estrum late in the breeding season are considered poor breeders, are often barren and for this reason there is a natural selection that tends to eliminate this type of mare.

Pathological, "true" or "deep" anestrum seen in mares that are thin and debilitated due to a lack of TDN and other nutrients or have chronic or acute diseases such as: severe parasitisms, chronic diarrhea, empyema of the sinuses due to a diseased tooth, equine infectious anemia, and others must be differentiated from seasonal or "deep" anestrus seen in the winter months of the year. Senility and defective worn teeth induce this anestrous condition in aged mares. O'Connor has reported that mares with adrenal insufficiency being stressed by exercise will remain indefinitely in "deep", "true" or pathologic anestrum. If these mares are given 6 to 12 months on pasture free of stressing influences, estrous cycles will develop. Anestrum in horses in training may be compounded by a lack of TDN as described by Bengtsson and Knudson in mares being fed a concentrate ration of oats. When these mares were changed to a pelleted feed with more TDN, ovarian activity and cycling developed. Occasionally anestrurn may be due to a prior ovariectomy, ovarian hypoplasia, granulosa cell tumor of one ovary with a very small atrophied opposite ovary or a tumor of the hypothalamus or pituitary gland causing destruction of the latter and a deficiency of gonadotropic hormones. Even though mares are seasonal breeders and are affected by light transmitted through the eyes to the central nervous system, blind mares usually cycle normally and raise foals successfully. Possibly sufficient light reaches the brain to stimulate the onset of the estrous cycle. Treatment of mares with pathologic anestrum characterized by very small, fibrotic ovaries with no follicular activity and no external signs of estrum is unsatisfactory or unsuccessful unless the cause for the suppression of the release of the gonadotiopic hormones can be overcome. Balanced nutritious rations should be fed in proper amounts. Exercise, sunlight and green pasture are helpful. Disease conditions should be corrected or alleviated. Hormone therapy, douching the uterus and other forms of treatment are seldom successful in this type of anestrum. A diagnosis of ovarian hypoplasia should be made with caution in young thin mares.

The possibility of a mare being pregnant as a cause of anestrum should always be considered, especially if a stallion is on the farm or if the mare has been recently purchased and her reproductive history is unknown. All mares should routinely be checked for pregnancy about 40 to 120 days after service. A mare's uterus should never be douched without checking for pregnancy as this act invariably will cause abortion.

Psychological anestrum or "silent estrum" besides being observed in barren mares during the breeding season is also seen in foaling or lactating mares as described previously. These mares are experiencing reproductive cycles but not exhibiting external signs of estrus. Douching or infusing the uterus once or several times 7 to 14 days apart, allowing these animals to be more closely associated with or run with a stallion may assist in getting these animals to exhibit a normal estrum. Those that do not respond should be bred naturally and under proper restrain or bred artificially 6 to 48 hours before ovulation as determined by a rectal examination or vaginal examination or both. Most cycling but psychologic anestrous mares when restrained by hobbles and a twitch will "break down" and show signs of acceptance toward the stallion at the time of service. Mares after service that apparently conceive and pass over the first estrous cycle with no external signs of estrus, may be found nonpregnant at 30 to 40 days after service with a tonic uterus resembling that of pregnancy. This may be called a "spurious" conception. These mares may appear on a speculum examination to be in diestrus, pregnant or anestrous but if there is some follicular activity they usually show a normal estrus and ovulate 2 to 8 days after the uterus is douched or infused. These mares may have conceived to the previous service and had an early death of the embryo.

"Lactational" anestrus in a foaling mare may be a true or pathologic anestrum due to debility or emaciation. More often it is a psychologic anestrum or possibly a "shallow" anestrum similar to that seen in seasonal anestrum. After a careful examination to determine the possible cause or causes treatment should be undertaken as outlined previously. Mares that routinely go into anestrum after foaling may be called "every-other-year" mares since they fail to breed while suckling a foal.

In most of these different types of anestrus it is essential to carefully assess the mare's physical condition, the findings of a careful rectal palpation of the genital tract and ovaries, the speculum examination of the vagina, and the manifestations or signs exhibited on regular teasing of the mare by a suitable stallion. Usually two or more carefully recorded examinations are required to accurately assess the nature of the failure to exhibit estrus to the teaser or the failure to have a normal physiologic estrous cycle synchronized with external heat signs.

Anovulation, Delayed Ovulation and Double Ovulation

Anovulation or delayed ovulation has been commonly described as a cause of infertility in mares by VanRensburg and VanHeerden, Arthur, Patterson, Gadd and others. Anovulation or delayed ovulation can occur during any estrous cycle whether external signs of estrus are exhibited or not. There is no correlation between external signs of estrus and anovulation or delayed ovulation except that in some prolonged estrous periods ovulation is also delayed until just before the end of estrum. Anovulatory cycles were characterized by the development of the Graafian follicle but a failure of this mature follicle to ovulate was noted on repeated rectal examinations. The follicle became atretic and regressed several days to a week or more after the end of estrum. Anovulatory cycles were most common early in the spring at the onset of the breeding season and late in the breeding season in the fall. They have been recorded occasionally at any time in the breeding season and even on the foal heat, Loy and Swan. Anovulatory cycles seem to occur more commonly in certain "shy-breeding" mares. VanRensburg and VanHeerden reported that anovulatory cycles may occur in a normal mare under unfavorable environmental, climatic, or nutritional conditions.

Anovulation or delayed ovulation can only be detected by frequent regular rectal examinations of the ovaries of mares during and after the estrous period and then is subject to error because some follicles that ovulate may be only 1.5 to 3 cm in diameter and be centrally located in the ovary. Short and Patterson have recorded occasional conceptions in mares where ovulation was not detected by careful, frequent rectal examinations. However, many instances are recorded in which estrous mares were bred and conception failed to occur due to anovulation. Most mares with anovulatory cycles or delayed ovulation eventually conceived. In delayed ovulation the estrous period may be prolonged a number of days. If mares have an anovulatory cycle or a delayed ovulation, the conditions cannot be separated unless followed daily by rectal palpation until atresia sets in or ovulation finally occurs. Many veterinarians will give 2000 I.U. or more of H.C.G. intravenously or intramuscularly when a follicle they are following by rectal examination fails to ovulate by the fifth or sixth day of the estrous period. Ovulation usually occurs 24 to 48 hours after treatment. If the mare is bred before ovulation, conception often occurs. Most of the mares with anovulatory cycles recover spontaneously, but VanRensburg and VanHeerden showed the great value of allowing shy breeding mares that exhibited a high incidence of anovulation to run free on pasture with a stallion; 87.5 percent conceived within 2 months.

Delayed ovulation in mares may not prevent conception because equine spermatozoa are capable of fertilizing ova 4 to 6 days after deposition. Only occasionally does ovulation occur more than 24 hours after the end of estrus as exhibited to a teaser or stallion and these mares have conceived, Andrews and McKenzie.

Ovulation may rarely occur 4 to 5 days before the end of behavioral estrus. This may be seen at foal estrum or in twin ovulation when a second follicle ovulates a number of days after the first. As stated previously, douching the uterus during estrus does not affect the duration of estrus or the time of ovulation.

Double ovulation is common and both mature follicles usually ovulate within a few hours of each other. Occasionally the two follicles may ovulate several days or more apart. Twin ovulation might be avoided by tapping one of the follicles with a needle or by rupturing one of the follicles manually if they are discovered in time. The most certain method of preventing twin conception is to refrain from breeding the mare that estrus. One could wait until one follicle ovulated and if the other follicle had not ovulated within 24 hours, H.C.G. could be given and the mare serviced. The unfertilized ovum from the first follicle probably would not survive 24 hours.

Nymphomania

Temporary "nymphomania" or prolonged or irregular estrus that spontaneously recovers within a period of 10 to 150 days has been described previously as psychological estrum and is commonly seen in barren maiden mares early in the Spring at the onset of the breeding season in horses. Caslick has described in his Groups 1 and 3 these barren mares with irregular estrous periods as revealed by signs exhibited toward a teaser or stallion. The prognosis is good and the treatments for this condition have been discussed.

True or chronic nymphomania in mares is dissimilar from nymphomania in cattle as ovarian cysts are not associated with the condition in mares. Arthur has shown that ovaries removed from affected mares reflect all stages of the normal equine estrous cycle and no pathology was evident. Thus the estrous cycle in nymphomaniac mares is normal but the central nervous manifestations shown by these mares are decidedly abnormal. Arthur has described two types of nymphomaniac or psychotic mares. The **mild type,** in which ovariectomy is highly successful, is characterized by an essentially normal mare, except at the time of estrus when her performance is unsatisfactory due to excessive excitability, intractability, stubbornness and refusal to perform.

The **severe type** has a marked abnormal behavior that is constant and of long duration. In the stable the severely affected mare is vicious and may kick, bite, run over, intimidate or jam her handler against the wall. She tends to squeal, kick, squirt urine, and switch her tail if handled about the rear parts. For these reasons many owners think they are in constant estrum and call them nymphomaniacs. These attitudes may be related to the elaboration of estrogens, progesterone and even androgens in the ovary. However, they will not tolerate the approach of another horse, a teaser or stallion; nor will they stand to be covered. They are dangerous to examine per rectum. They are useless as riding or draft animals. Because of the long-standing nervous derangement in these neurotic, unstable individuals, the vicious tendencies are well-ingrained and recovery even after an ovariectomy seldom occurs unless a skilled and knowledgeable horseman will retrain the animal so that it behaves sufficiently well in competent hands to be useful. Relapses to a violent behavior are common. Most of these advanced and long-standing cases of nymphomania or neurotic behavior should be destroyed before they injure a person or another animal. Benesch and Hetzel both reported about a 60 percent recovery rate after ovariectomy. The other 40 percent were long-standing vicious mares and response was not achieved. The value of a clitoridectomy recommended by Benesch is questionable.

Early Embryonic Deaths

Early embryonic deaths are often considered as sterility or infertility because the aborted or resorbed embryo or young fetus is not observed. Early embryonic loss in mares has not received the study that early death of the embryo has received in other domestic animals. On the basis of careful clinical studies, Britton reported on the causes of early abortion between 30 to 90 days after conception in the mare. These findings were made possible on the basis of routine, careful teasing, and the maintenance of accurate records. Abortion at this early period was not accompanied by any observable symptoms unless the mare was seen passing the fetus. No hemorrhage or uterine discharge was observed and in some cases the fetus undoubtedly macerated and was resorbed from the uterus. Britton concluded that the average annual incidence of early death and abortion or resorption of the embryo or fetus varied from 10 to 30 percent with an average of about 18 percent in 40 mares on which careful records were maintained for 5 years. In the same band annual recognizable abortions ranged from 0 to 15 percent, with a 5-year average of 7 percent. These figures are higher than the 5 to 15 percent losses of embryos and fetuses reported by most authors and the 3 to 5 percent losses of embryos and fetuses between 42 and 100 days reported by Sager. (See abortion in mares.) This finding supports Jennings' conclusion that most abortions occur between 45 and 90 days after coitus. It is of interest to note that the year the annual incidence reached 30 percent a mild outbreak of influenza occurred. Andrews and McKenzie reported that an average of 7.5 percent of early embryonic or fetal deaths occurred in mares that they studied. These deaths were detected by pregnancy examinations. Possibly pathologic spermatozoa or ova may be causes for early abortions. Britton cited one relatively infertile stallion that had an early abortion rate twice as high as the combined early abortion rate of 2 fertile stallions. These 3 stallions were used on the same band of mares. In this instance either the stallion transmitted an infection that caused the early death of many embryos or his spermatozoa were defective and the embryos produced had chromosomal defects and died early. Britton reported that 13 out of 15 mares with a hypoplastic, defective vulva aborted, whereas of 10 mares with a normal vulva, only 4 aborted. He recorded 24 mares bred on foal heat, of which only 7 conceived; and of these, 3 showed symptoms of early fetal death. He further cited 125 mares bred on foal heat, of which 81 conceived and 24 had a history of early abortion. In another band 56 were bred on foal heat, 22 conceived, and 8 showed symptoms of early fetal death.

Other causes for embryonic deaths might include aging of the spermatozoa or ova resulting in chromosomal defects in the zygote, infections of the genital tract, twinning, or trauma from rectal examinations. VanNiekerk reported a high incidence of early embryonic deaths from 25 to 31 days of gestation in mares that were malnourished. The lack of TDN did not affect the conception rate or early embryonic growth before 25 days or later embryonic life after 35 days of gestation. Embryos dying between 25 and 31 days resulted in a failure of estrus lasting 40 to 80 days postservice. VanRensburg and Van-Heerden and Osborne have reported the early death of the fetus from 40 to 70 days of age associated with just a single corpus luteum in the ovaries. After 40 days there should be a number of accessory corpora lutea to aid in maintenance of pregnancy. If early abortion occurs late in the breeding season it may be desirable not to breed the mare until the next season. Culturing the cervix is indicated, as infection, especially due to streptococci, frequently may be present. Other treatment such as Caslick's operation on the vulva may be necessary.

Mares that are bred and conceive according to a careful early rectal examination or the blood test for pregnancy and then later show estrum have undoubtedly suffered from early death of the fetus. In other mares with similar histories of coitus in which the mare fails to come back into estrum for a month or more but where pregnancy examinations were not performed the cause may be either early death of the fetus or an irregular cycle characterized by temporary anestrum. This is seen most commonly in foaling mares bred on their foaling heat. Much more study in mares, as has been undertaken in cattle, is necessary on the causes and diagnosis of these early abortions or early embryonic deaths.

Nutrition and Infertility In Mares

There has been little or no research in the past 50 years on nutrients concerned with reproduction in horses, Squibb, Sager and the National Research Council. The pregnant mare should be kept on a maintenance ration in only moderate body condition until the ninth month of gestation when a slight increase in protein and TDN should be provided until foaling. The barren mare should be kept on a maintenance ration also. During the breeding season both barren and foaling, lactating mares should be in a positive energy balance and gaining weight slowly. The lactating mare might need increasing nutritive levels the last few weeks before foaling, and then a rapid increase in TDN intake after foaling to realize the highest conception rates on foal heat. It is highly important that mares to be bred on their foal heat and for a month or more thereafter be placed on a high energy ration. This may cause a problem in some mares that milk heavily by causing scouring in the nursing foal 1 to 2 weeks after birth. The feed intake of the foal may have to be monitored and the mare milked out manually. Thin animals and animals losing weight rapidly, usually fail to cycle and ovulate normally. (See infertility due to nutrition in cattle, McClure and King.)

As cited previously O'Connor, and Bengtsson and Knudson have reported that racing mares in training may remain in true or "deep" anestrus, even in the breeding season, due to stress, overwork, adrenal insufficiency and a probable lack of energy or TDN. In the report of the latter authors changing to a pelleted feed resulted in a resumption of ovarian activity. VanNiekerk showed that a low level of nutritive feed intake had no effect on fertilization. No embryonic resorbtion took place in mares that conceived on a low nutritional plane and thereafter received supplemental feeding before 18 days after ovulation. Eight mares on a low plane of feeding and a low protein intake after 18 days of pregnancy had an early death and resorbtion of the embryo between 25 and 31 days after ovulation as determined by rectal palpation. Mares placed on the poor ration after they were 35 days pregnant maintained normal embryos. Mares having early embryonic deaths usually came back into estrum 40 to 80 days after service. Mares being provided additional hay and grain did not have the early embryonic deaths. Stowe has made the observation that supplementation of the diet with Vitamins A and E appeared to improve the conception rate. A properly balanced ration with sufficient TDN, protein, minerals, vitamins, salt, and water should be provided together with exercise for the foaling and breeding mare.

Overly fat, obese mares on lush pasture often are reported to be poor breeders. Possibly the reason they are fat is that they are poor breeders and do not nurse or carry a foal to use up the excess TDN consumed. Some veterinarians have used 1 gm per 100 lbs. body weight of iodinated casein with a 3 percent thyroxine potency daily in the feed of these obese mares in the form of "Protamone" or "Libidoxin" to cause a loss of weight. These mares should have been reduced in weight sufficiently during the winter months so that in the spring months they could be placed on a slowly rising plane of nutrition to promote the onset of a normal estrous cycle, ovulation and conception.

Genital Infections Causing Infertility in Mares

Etiology and Symptoms. Infectious venereal diseases do not occur in horses in the United States. Genital infections in mares come basically from four conditions. The first and most common is the condition of pneumovagina, "windsucking" or aspiration of air into the genital tract. The normal mare's vulva should be at an angle of about 80° to 90°, or nearly vertical. The lips of the vulva should be full, firm, and evenly closed their entire length. Pneumovagina is predisposed by a conformation that includes a flat croup, elevated tail head, sunken anus, and small, underdeveloped vulvar lips that are pulled nearly horizontal by a sunken anus. (See Figure 146) It is also caused by lacerations, scarring, stretching, or tearing of the vulvar sphincter muscles or the vulva or perineal body at the time of foaling. The perineal body, perineal center, or perineum in the narrow sense, is the complex joining of muscles and fascia between the anus and vulva, Habel. Whether pneumovagina is caused by the conformation of the perineal region or due to injury to the vulva, it results in infection of the vagina, the cervix, and oftentimes of the uterus. The vulvar lips in these "windsucking" mares become atrophic, flaccid, rolled in, gaped, or are sunken just below the dorsal commissure, allowing contamination of the genital tract with feces, air, and pathogenic organisms. Once pneumovagina develops, the habit of aspirating air into the vagina becomes confirmed and it will usually become progressively worse unless treated. This condition is seen more commonly in old and thin mares but may be found even in young thin nulliparous mares. It is more common in Thoroughbred and American Saddle horses with flat croups and a high tailhead than in Standardbred or Quarter horses with more sloping croups and a lower tailhead. (See Figure 146) The peculiar gurgling, sucking sounds and expulsive blowing sounds occurring especially at the time of urination or defecation or at the time the mare is exercised are characteristic in well-developed cases. Caslick and others noted that pneumovagina is more common at the time of estrum. In fact aspiration of air into the vagina may occur in some mares only during estrum. At this time the perineal region and the folds and sphincter between the vestibule and the vagina are more relaxed due to the influence of the estrogens. Pneumovagina may occur in maiden mares in training, especially during the breeding season. According to Caslick, the rare case of the outwardly-tipped vulva in maiden mares may predipose to pneumovagina. Pneumovagina may be a cause or a sequela to infection of the genital tract. In some mares the condition may be mild, infrequent and not suspected unless the mare fails to conceive and speculum examination or culture reveals evidence of a chronic infection of the genital tract. The presence of a small amount of foamy or frothy exudate in the vaginal cavity or a purulent discharge from the vulva about 5 days following coitus are almost pathognomonic symptoms of pneumovagina, Caslick. By introducing air and foreign material this condition may involve not only the vagina but also the cervix and uterus. Many authors such as Dimock, Caslick, and others, have noted that in the mare with definite symptoms of "genital windsucking", air and bubbles of vaginal exudate are sucked through the cervix and results in ballooning and contamination of the uterus. Pneumovagina and pneumouterus are associated with the reflex ballooning of the vagina and the development of a negative pressure in the uterus which occurs in the normal mare at coitus. These ballooned organs may readily be palpated on a rectal examination. According to Millar, air does not usually gain access to the vagina and uterus at coitus when the vagina balloons, since the vulva is effectively closed by the penis. The author has observed a few mares with only pneumovestibule. In these cases air is drawn into and expelled out of the vestibule causing a vestibulitis. The closure of the folds and the sphincter at the cranial or vaginal end of the vestibule apparently has effectively prevented the drawing of air into the vagina. This may be the initial stage of pneumovagina.

The second source of genital infection in the mare is pathological parturition, characterized by dystocia, a dead or diseased foal, retained placenta, or severe trauma to the genital passages. Incomplete or delayed involution of the genital tract and uterine inertia following a pathological parturition was stressed by Day as a common cause of sterility. Bruner reported that the genital tract of all mares becomes infected during or just after parturition. This infection usually enters the genital tract when the mare rises soon after foaling and the vagina and uterus balloon with air. It has been reported that the incidence of infections of the uterus and cervix at the onset of foal estrus can be greatly reduced by carefully washing and disinfecting the perineal region and rear parts of the mare before foaling, wrapping the tail in a sterile or plastic bandage, by allowing the mare to foal on a sterile heavy rubber sheet covering the foaling stall floor, and temporarily closing the vulva with skin clips immediately after foaling, Carricaburu. In normal healthy mares this infection is overcome or eliminated by the ninth or tenth day after parturition or sooner if foal estrus occurs early. Genital infections, injuries and lacerations following a pathological foaling, however, may cause pneumovagina which prevents the normal elimination of the infection

Apparently the same but even more efficient mechanisms that eliminate infection at the time of estrus in cattle, sheep and swine are also operative at estrus in mares. This is an effect due to estrogens causing a massive invasion of leucocytes, the "leucocytic tide", into the endometrium and lumen of the uterus to phagocytize and destroy infective organisms. The increased blood supply, mucus production, and the relaxation of the cervix all combine to rapidly restore the uterus to its nonpregnant, bacteriologically-sterile state in the healthy mare.

Thirdly, some cases of genital infection in mares may be due to infections introduced at the time of copulation from failure to observe proper hygienic procedures. Excessive frequency of breeding during an estrous period, especially in older mares should be avoided as it favors the establishment of a uterine infection. The mare that is to be bred should have her tail bandaged with clean, sterile gauze; the buttocks and perineal region and the wrinkles of the vulvar lips and skin should be thoroughly cleaned and washed with soap and water and wiped dry with pledgets of cotton to make sure that the perineal region is clean and free of dirt and epithelial debris. In a similar manner the stallion's penis and prepuce should be carefully washed with soap and water and rinsed both before and after service. If a mild antiseptic such as quaternary ammonium compound is used on the external genitals of the mare, the washed area should be rinsed with clear water before service. The place in which the mare is to be bred should be clean and free of dust and dirt and protected from wind that would blow dirt or chaff. Occasionally a mare will develop an acute endometritis after service due to **Str. zooepidemicus;** these mares may have a short estrous cycle of 12 days, Sager, Hughes and Loy (1969). These short cycles resemble those seen in cows with acute endometritis. It should be recognized that no matter how frequently or thoroughly the perineal region and vulva of the mare and the penis and prepuce of the stallion are washed and cleansed, a certain number of infectious organisms are going to be carried into the vagina and uterus by the penis. The purpose of breeding hygiene is to minimize the numbers of organisms and the amount of foreign debris that are introduced. Because of the heavy bacterial flora in the sheath and on the vulvar lips, all semen, even that collected in a sterile artificial vagina, is usually fairly heavily seeded with a variety of organisms. If the accessory glands are infected then large numbers of infectious organisms will be in the semen and gain access to the uterus. Fortunately the normal protective mechanisms active at the time of estrus prevent these infectious organisms from becoming established in the mare's uterus and cause an endometritis and sterility.

A group of 97 mares free of genital infection was bred naturally. Careful and thorough breeding hygiene at the time of service was carried out. Twenty four hours later a cervical culture of these mares was made. The incidence of infection in foaling mares, foaling mares bred on foal heat, barren mares and maiden mares was 90, 84, 87, and 81 percent. Six species of infectious bacteria and fungi were recovered. None of the above mares became chronically-infected following this natural service at the time of estrum, Bryans and Sager.

Fourthly, occasional carelessness on the part of the owners or handlers may introduce infection into the mare by means of improperly sterilized instruments such as speculums or douching equipment recently used on infected mares. Artificial insemination or impregnantion if not done in a clean, sanitary manner may also result in the introduction of infection.

Dimock and Edwards (1928) examined and cultured the genital tracts of 1606 barren mares in Kentucky and found 587 or 36.5 percent, of the mares were infected. The types of infections found in these mares were as follows:

Streptococcus zooepidemicus or **Str. genitalium**—390 mares, or 24.3 percent, of the barren mares; or 66.4 percent of the infected barren mares.

Klebsiella pneumoniae var **genitalium**—60 mares, or 3.7 percent, of the barren mares; or 10.2 percent of the infected barren mares.

Miscellaneous infections: **Escherichia coli, Corynebacterium equi, Pseudomonas aeruginosa, micrococci, Salmonella abortivo-equina, Shigella equuli,** chromogenic rods, molds, actinomycetes, staphylococci and streptococci—137 mares, or 8.5 percent, of the barren mares, or 23.3 percent of the infected barren mares.

Bain, and Collins reported nearly similar percentages of uterine infections in barren mares in Australia and Ireland. They noted a larger number of coliform infections. Rasbech in a survey of the literature summarized the bacteriological examination of the genital tract of mares of many authors and of his in Denmark. From 20 to 45 percent of barren mares were infected. According to a report in 1940 by Dimock and his co-workers on cultural examination of 2760 barren mares, 25.7 percent were infected with streptococci and only 2 percent with Klebsiella, 1.9 percent with E. coli, and 4 percent with miscellaneous infections. Moore reported on a rare case of a mare with a gallon of blue-green pus in the uterus from which a pure culture of **Aspergillus fumigatus** mold was recovered.

Streptococcus zooepidemicus is responsible for about 25 percent of the infertility in mares in Kentucky, Dimock. This organism is a beta hemolytic coccus that ferments lactose and sorbitol and belongs to the Lancefield Group C type of streptococcus. Besides being one of the most common causes of abortion and disease in foals it is the most common infection causing infertility. **Streptococcus zooepidemicus** is constantly present as a saprophyte on the external genitals of the mare and stallion and usually does not cause disease until the resistance of the genital mucosa is lowered by parturition, pneumovagina, breeding and other unknown factors which allow the infection to become established. Nearly 100 percent of the mares have **Streptococcus zooepidemicus** as a contaminant of the genital tract for 3 to 6 days following parturition. Normal mares overcome this infection by 9 to 10 days following parturiton, while other mares may not rid themselves of the infection until the second estrum or may remain chronically infected, especially if pneumovagina develops. This infection may not actually prevent conception but pregnancies in infected mares are likely to terminate in early embryonic death, abortion or a diseased foal. Britton and Jennings showed that the incidence of early abortion, from 25 to 150 days, is greatly increased in mares with genital infections, especially streptococci. Most mares that have been sterile for 3 to 4 years usually have a pneumovagina and are infected with streptococci, Day.

The clinical appearance of a mare infected with **Streptococcus zooepidemicus** varies greatly in individuals and with the duration of the infection, Dimock and Edwards. Infected mares are likely to exhibit a discharge from the genital tract. This exudate soils the vulva and perineal region including the buttocks and tail and the hair may become matted. The vulva may gape and the mucous membrane may be visible. Some cases show a marked loss of tone of the muscles and supporting structures of the vulva. The perineal region may be sunken. The vulvar lips are generally thin and atrophic. Examination of the genital tract will reveal a congested, inflamed mucous membrane. The cervix instead of being a pink color is more of a brick red to purple color with the cervical folds being edematous and the os relaxed and open. The mucous membrane is moist and the blood vessels are prominent, distended, and torturous. A thin, slightly cloudy mucopurulent exudate or a thick yellow-white exudate containing flakes of pus may be present in the vagina. Sometimes no exudate is found but in some cases a thin, clear, slightly frothy exudate may be seen coming from the cervix. These evidences of a vaginitis, cervicitis, and endometritis are most noticeable when the examination is made during estrum, since infected mares show a hypersecretion of mucus at that time. If may be difficult to distinguish between an acute and chronic infection, but the breeding history and the fact that old mares are more likely to be chronically infected may assist in the diagnosis. In chronic cases the exudate is mucopurulent and may be quite copious. The cervix may be greatly dilated, enlarged, and indurated. In rare instances adhesions may occur, closing the cervix and causing a pyometra or uterine abscess. In some advanced chronic cases the uterus is dilated. The uterine wall may be atonic, and the mucopurulent exudate that accumulates cannot be readily expelled. In rare cases the uterine endometrium may be destroyed over extensive areas and be replaced by scar tissue. Evidence of pneumovagina is usually apparent.

Mild or recent cases require experience to detect or suspect on vaginal examination, as changes are not pronounced. For this and other reasons, many stallion owners require a health certificate on the mare before service. The certificate requires among other things a cultural examination of the cervix during estrus.

Klebsiella pneumoniae var genitalium, formerly called Friedlander's bacillus or **Encapsulatus genitalium** or viscid rod infection, is observed much less commonly than **Streptococcus zooepidemicus** as a cause for sterility. According to Dimock and Edwards, Klebsiella infection is characterized by a thick, viscid, tenacious, slimy exudate that may contain flocculi. The color of the exudate varies from dull-grey to yellowish-white. On speculum examination the vaginal and cervical mucous membrane is usually a dull reddish-brown color. During estrum exudation is profuse and may soil the vulva and tail and mat the hair of the tail and buttocks. The presence of other infections tends to increase the inflammatory response of the genital tract to the Klebsiella infection. The inflammatory processes affect mainly the cervix and uterus and the principal changes are in the mucous membranes and the underlying structures. Usually several hundred ml of exudate is found in the uterus. On rectal examination the uterine wall feels thickened and the uterus is enlarged. If adhesions occur in the cervix, pyometra results; but these advanced lesions of genital infections are less likely to occur with Klebsiella infection than with the other types of organisms. Depending upon the age of the mare, the length of time infection has been present, the time of the estrous cycle, the number and frequency of services during the breeding season, the symptoms and lesions will vary. In a few cases no clinical signs of the infection were observed, Hunt and Rossdale.

Klebsiella pneumonae var **genitalium** is a gram-negative encapsulated rod. It is readily transmitted from infected to healthy mares by the stallion at the time of service and by the hands or instruments of veterinarians or others who examine and treat mares. This infection is much more difficult to overcome than is the streptococcal infections. The sterility produced in chronic Klebsiella infections tends to be more lasting than in the streptococcic infections. This organism belongs to the Klebsiella-aerogenes group, as do the paracolon bacteria that are so difficult to treat even with antibiotics in cases of bovine mastitis, Hagan and Bruner.

Seventy mares harboring a **Pseudomonas aeruginosa** infection in their genital tract were studied by Hughes et al.. Forty two mares had a slight to definite hyperemia of the cervix and 15 mares had a milky-white exudate containing flocculent material that turned green, watery-grey, or yellowish-green on exposure to light.

The differential diagnosis of these and the other miscellaneous infections should be confirmed by bacteriological examination, as clinical symptoms are not sufficiently distinctive for an accurate determination of the etiologic agent. Routine cultures on suspicious mares should be made to confirm the diagnosis and on obviously-infected mares to determine the etiological agent and its sensitivity to antibiotics, Proctor. Occasionally a mixed infection may be found on culture of the cervix. This is seen more commonly in pneumovagina. The genital tract of the normal mare, with the possible exception of the vulva, vestibule and caudal portion of the vagina, is free of infection or bacteria. A reliable culture may be obtained only by culturing the cervix during estrum since at other times of the cycle infection might be present in the uterus but not appear in the tightly closed cervix. Also, some mares may develop pneumovagina during estrum but it will not be present during the diestrous phase of the cycle.

The usual technique for culturing the cervix of a mare consists of having the mare in favorable surroundings for the examination. The location should be well-lighted, clean, and free from drafts and dust. The tail should be bandaged with sterile gauze and held to one side over the mare's buttocks. The mare should be suitably restrained, a twitch or hobbles being used if necessary. The perineum and vulvar lips should be carefully washed with soap and water to which may be added a mild antiseptic such as quaternary ammonium compound incorporating a wetting agent. The vulvar lips should then be vigorously wiped with a clean, dry cotton swab and if dirt is present on the swab the vulva should be rewashed until clean. A sterile plastic or glass speculum is introduced into the mare's vagina. The vagina usually balloons promptly. The speculum is so placed that the cervix is fixed just above the spoon of the mare speculum, or in the cranial open end of the glass or plastic speculum. A 4-inch heavy platinum needle with a small loop attached to a 20-inch holder is sterilized in the flame of an alcohol lamp. It is passed through the speculum and vagina directly into the cervical canal without touching the vulva or vaginal walls either going to and into or returning from the cervix. In the cervical canal the needle loop is passed back and forth 2 or 3 times. After flaming the mouth of a test tube containing a slant of horse meat infusion agar, the material in the loop is inoculated on the media. The inoculated culture media is placed in an incubator for 24 to 72 hours and read at 24-hour intervals. Streptococci grow readily, whereas other organisms usually grow more slowly. These media tubes can be secured from a number of laboratories. Deubler, and Hughes et al. have recommended using sterile cotton-tipped, 4-inch wooden applicators held by a Knowles forcep. Deubler stated the results were more accurate than with a platinum loop. However, the technique recommended following the return of these swabs to the laboratory is more complicated than direct inoculation of horse meat infusion agar slants by the platinum loop. One should not incubate the organisms in a broth culture before plating out as this technique gives a false impression of the bacterial flora of the cervical canal. A few contaminating organisms can produce results indicating a massive infection. If one does not plate the swab immediately after collection it should be taken to the laboratory in its sterile identified container and plated out within 3 to 4 hours after collection. A second procedure might be to determine the sensitivity of the recovered organisms toward various antibiotics. Besides being of value in diagnosing the presence, type, and antibiotic sensitivity of organisms in the genital tracts of mares suspected of being infected, the cultural examination is of definite value in mares that the owner wishes bred on the first, or foaling, estrum. According to Bruner, cultures taken from mares within the first 5 days after foaling usually show bacterial growth. However, cultures taken on the seventh to ninth day should be negative on culture. If at that time the cultures are positive or if the genital tract has not returned to normal, the mare should not be bred that estrum.

Knudsen and Sollen, Knudsen, Grunert, Tobler, Teigland and Saurino, Rasbech (1964), and Ressang have described endometrial sampling, culturing, and biopsy techniques for determining the status of the mare's uterus. Uterine samples taken by the instruments of Knudsen and Tobler could be cultured bacteriologically and smeared to examine the cytology. A high number of neutrophiles usually were accompanied by a positive bacterial culture and were indicative of an endometritis. Knudsen attempted to correlate certain cell types with the various stages of the estrous cycle. The Teigland swab has proven to be a practical and accurate method of obtaining an intrauterine sample for bacteriological culture. It consists of a rigid plastic outer tube, with an inner flexible tube on which is attached a sterile swab. Both tubes are encased in a thin long plastic bag. After proper cleansing and disinfection of the mare, the telescoped tubes in the plastic bag that has been soaking in a disinfectant is introduced through a speculum, or with the hand encased in a sterile plastic glove and sleeve, into the cervix. The bag is pulled caudally to break it and the plastic pipettes are inserted 4 to 5 inches or 10 to 12 cm beyond the external os of the cervix into the uterine lumen. The flexible tube with the swab on the end is pushed cranially, and the sample taken. The flexible tube and swab are then pulled back into the rigid larger tube and the entire apparatus is pulled from the genital tract. Ressang studied 87 chronically-infertile barren mares that had failed to conceive after treatment. Endometritis was present in 58.6 percent based on endometrial biopsy specimens; 50 percent of these mares were infected with streptococci.

The results of the culture of the mare's cervix or uterus must be properly interpreted. There is an inclination to place too much significance on the finding of a few organisms in the normal appearing cervix of a barren mare. Unless clinical signs of a cervicitis and/or endometritis are present probably several cultures of the cervix should be made at 2 or 3 day intervals or at several estrous periods. Ellsworth indicated an incidence of about 10 percent of positive cultures from clinically healthy mares which if rechecked were usually negative. One positive culture by itself may mean little, so repeated cultures are desirable. He stated that a culture containing coliforms was not significant unless there was clinical evidence of infection. A heavy culture of a variety of organisms might indicate pneumovagina. A very few colonies of several types of organisms may indicate a contaminated sample. Uterine cultures may be superior to cervical cultures but for most purposes the latter is highly satisfactory. Very few normal, healthy mares have any organisms in the cervix or uterus as revealed by samples taken during estrum. The pathology produced in the genital organs of mares by infections have been described by Dimock and Edwards.

Vaginitis due to a variety of infections is commonly observed. The vagina appears to be more resistant to irritation and permanent damage caused by infections than does the cervix and uterus. In severe metritis and cervicitis with a catarrhal exudate the vagina is usually involved. Mares that develop the habit of pneumovagina usually exhibit a vaginitis, often with mucopurulent exudate. Fecal material and urine may occasionally be found in the cranial part of their vaginas. Injuries, trauma, lacerations, or severe infection of the vulva and vagina at parturition may cause chronic vaginitis, pneumovagina, and in rare instances stenosis of the vagina. A rectovaginal fistula causes a severe vaginitis. Occasionally the cloudy, turbid, light-colored urine of the mare may be confused with a vaginal discharge by the owner. In rare instances cystitis in the mare may develop but it is usually secondary to a vaginitis or metritis.

Cervicitis due to a variety of infections is more common and injury to the cervical mucous membrane can occasionally be serious in nature. In cervicitis the mucosa as seen at the external os is usually congested and a dark red to purple color; the os is generally edematous, pendulous, and dilated. In rare cases the cervical glands become cystic; deep suppuration and abscess formation may occur. Fibrosis of the cervix is usually not as pronounced as it may appear clinically, nor as severe as in the cow with advanced cervicitis. The inflammatory process involves mainly the mucosa of the cervix. In rare cases a membranous or solid, thick adhesion may completely obstruct the cervical lumen and since uterine infection is usually present, pyometra is likely to develop. Severe lacerations, scarring, and malformation of the cervix may occasionally occur in the mare at the time of parturition and produce a chronic cervicitis or cause a failure of the normal closure of the cervix by the cervical seal, resulting in repeated early embryonic deaths due to infection and permanent sterility, Proctor.

Metritis due to these same wound-infection type of organisms often results in rather pronounced pathological changes in the uterus. Deep red hemorrhagic areas and intervening areas of whitish-yellow mucosa may be scattered irregularly in the endometrium. In severe cases the endometrium may be denuded at many points and have a dull, red, granular appearance. The character and amount of exudate present may vary. In metritis, as in cervicitis and vaginitis, the changes, depending on the stage of the cycle, the type of organism, and the predisposing causes, vary from a mild superficial involvement of the endometrium readily cured by proper treatment, to severe, advanced, and permanent pathological lesions of the endometrium with small abscesses of the uterine glands and chronic fibrotic, degenerative and proliferative changes in the endometrium and uterine wall. In cases in which the cervix is closed with adhesions the uterus may contain several quarts or gallons of mucopus. In this rare type of pyometra the endometrium may be severely degenerated and eroded. In most cases of pyometra in mares with much mucopurulent exudate, endometrial inflammation is not severe, Prickett. The uterine wall may be thin and atonic and in advanced cases the endometrium is almost completely destroyed. The mucosa in some cases becomes a tough, thick, yellow-white fibrous pyogenic membrane. In the occasional pyometra case due to subinvolution of the uterus with an open or patent cervix, the endometrial pathology is not so severe although edema, degeneration, desquamation and sloughing of small areas of the endometrium may occur. Pyometra in the mare is not associated with a retained or persistent CL and failure of estrum as in the cow. Pyometra in the mare may be associated with a stenotic, indurated cervix that interferes with the expulsion of the mucopurulent exudate in the uterus, McEntee. Perimetritis in the mare was never observed by Dimock and Edwards and is apparently very rare; or else when it does occur the results are fatal due to peritonitis. In some cases of metritis a diptheritic membrane may overlie a portion of the endometrium. In severe chronic metritis, particularly due to Klebsiella infection, a typical chronic productive inflammation results that may produce an atrophy and fibrosis of the uterine wall from mucosa to serosa.

Salpingitis is rare in the mare. Dimock and Edwards never found an enlarged oviduct on rectal examination of the mare. On postmortem examination of 83 mares with a metritis, only 18, or 21.7 percent, showed evidence of salpingitis as determined by gross and microscopic examinations. Not all oviducts that showed inflammatory changes were positive on culture. Salpingitis in the mare is an ascending infection from an infected uterus. Some infected oviducts undergo no pathological changes, while most others exhibit only a slight catarrhal inflammation. In very rare cases, inflammation is severe enough to cause fibrosis of the oviduct and occlusion of the lumen with inflammatory exudates. In no cases were the oviducts thickened and enlarged. Hydrosalpinx has never been described in the mare. The presence of a papilla containing a smooth muscle sphincter through which the oviduct opens into the uterine cavity may furnish a possible explanation of the rarity of salpingitis in the mare.

Ovaritis in the mare is very rare. Senile changes may be characterized by atrophy and fibrosis. No evidence of acute inflammation of the ovary was found by Dimock and Edwards in any of their postmortem cases. They do, however, describe one case of an ovarian abscess in which **Streptococcus zooepidemicus** was found. This might have been secondary to the tapping of an ovarian cyst. Adhesions between the ovary and surrounding tissues has not been described in the mare.

Prognosis of Genital Infections in Mares. Uterine, cervical and vaginal infections in mares due to pneumovagina or infection of the uterus after parturition or abortion usually respond to treatment. The sooner the infection is diagnosed and the proper treatment given, the more favorable the prognosis. In long-standing, severe cases endometrial damage may be severe and permanent and result in sterility. Proctor stated that massive purulent metritis with cicatrization causing a loss of endometrium, and extensive cervical lacerations are two conditions that render a mare hopelessly sterile. Usually it is much more difficult and takes longer, and may occasionally be impossible to correct chronic infections due to **Ps. aeruginosa, E. coli** and Klebsiella than streptococcic infections, as the former organisms are more resistant to antibiotics and other treatments and cause greater tissue damage and change than the latter. In early stages of mild infections proper treatment may result in prompt recovery within 1 to 2 months. In severe or chronic cases treatment and sexual rest for 6 months or more may be necessary in order to effect a cure. When pyometra is due to an obstructive adhesion in the cervix, the prognosis for the future breeding life of the mare is usually poor or hopeless.

Treatment of Genital Infections in Mares. As Bruner, Proctor and Sager (1949) have pointed out, the suturing of the upper part of the vulvar lips, the Caslick operation, sexual rest, and antibiotics enable the veterinarian to give a much more favorable prognosis in cases of uterine infection than was possible 20 or even 10 years ago. Early detection and treatment of genital infections of mares is essential to prevent sterility, early embryonic deaths, and abortions.

Most genital infections in mares can be prevented by proper hygienic handling of the mare and stallion at the time of breeding, by proper attention and hygiene applied to the mare at foaling, by close observation, culturing, and proper sanitary procedures in examining and treating mares, if necessary, prior to breeding. The control of genital infections causing sterility or infertility in mares is mainly a matter of preventative therapy and hygiene. This point cannot be stressed too strongly.

The vulva suturing operation, or Caslick operation, to prevent pneumovagina or the sucking of air and debris into the genital tract has been well described by Delahanty and is performed as follows: the tail is bandaged and the perineal region and vulva carefully cleansed with soap and water. The mare is restrained by means of a twitch being placed on the nose and one foreleg being picked up. If the mare is excitable or vicious, a tranquilizer, or a narcotic dose of chloral hydrate and magnesium sulphate or pentobarbital may be given intravenously for sedation. The mucous membrane of the vulvar lips is anesthetized by infiltration with a local anesthetic solution such as procaine or xylocaine from 1 inch, 2 cm, below the level of the floor of the pelvis or ischial arch to and including the dorsal commissure, to a depth of .5 inch, 1 cm, from edges of the lips of the vulva where the skin and mucous membrane join. In the hypersensitive mare it is desirable to anesthetize a small area of the mucous membrane at the border of the vulvar skin by holding a pledget of cotton that has been soaked in xylocaine or a similar anesthetic that can be applied locally before the 20 to 22 gauge needle is inserted. The mucous membrane elevated by the procaine solution is removed by scissors. The scarified edges of the vulvar lips are brought together by metal wound clips or by catgut or nylon sutures placed about one-fourth to three-eighths inch apart. The sutures are not tightened too firmly inasmuch as they may cut the tissues. Union takes place rapidly; one-half of the clips or nylon sutures usually can be removed the fourth day and the remainder 6 to 10 days after the operation, Caslick. Catgut sutures do not require removal but cause a tissue reaction. If skin clips are left in too long, or over 5 or 6 days, an area of necrosis will develop beneath them. Any soft, antibiotic mastitis or eye ointment may be used to protect the suture line. The administration of tetanus antitoxin is probably not necessary but in valuable mares not protected by tetanus toxoid, it may be a justified precaution. This operation effectively prevents pneumovagina in the barren, infected mare and should be used on any mare if this condition is present or suspected. In mares in which the condition is well-established, the vulva must be kept carefully sutured for the rest of the mare's breeding life since once this operation becomes necessary, seldom does the mare return to normal.

If at the time of breeding of the previously sutured mare, the vulvar opening is enlarged enough to permit entry of the penis, a stay or protective suture of umbilical tape should be placed at the bottom of the adhesion between the vulvar lips or at the top of the vulvar opening. This keeps the thin adhesion between the vulvar lips intact and prevents possible tearing or irregular rupture of the vulvar lips at time time of service. If the vulvar opening is too small, as is usual, the adhesion between the vulvar lips should be incised to make the vulvar opening large enough to admit the penis and then a stay or protective suture is inserted. If the mare is to be bred again in 2 to 3 days, this stay suture may be allowed to remain. The stay suture is usually made of a double thickness of one-fourth- or one-eighth-inch umbilical tape or heavy linen thread inserted into the anesthetized vulvar lips one-half to three-quarter inch, 1 to 2 cm, from the edges, and tied rather loosely. If a nylon or steel suture is used, it may lacerate the penis. A breeding or stallion roll should be used at the time of all natural covers on sutured mares, Sager. Following service in cases in which incision of the vulva was necessary, it should immediately be resutured or clamped again. At the time of parturition, or 7 to 14 days before-hand if a veterinarian is not to be present at the time the mare foals, the vulva is opened by a blunt-pointed bistoury or sharp scissors after local anesthesia has been administered. After foaling the vulva should be resutured within 3 to 6 hours. If the operation is not performed soon after parturition the tissues swell and suturing is not possible for a number of days to a week or longer, by which time pneumovagina may again be well-established and the edges of the incision are granulating or cicatrizing. Resuturing is then difficult and healing prolonged. In the mare the vulva-suturing operation is the single most important procedure in the treatment of pneumovagina and sterility due to infection of the genital tract. Once it is indicated and undertaken it usually must be continued for the breeding life of the mare.

Peck and other veterinarians in this country perform a more complicated operation for correcting this perineal deformity than simple scarification and suturing of the edges of the vulvar lips. Essentially, their operations attempt to reconstruct the defective dorsal portion of the vulva and make the closure of the vulva much firmer and deeper than does the simple Caslick operation. This alternate, more elaborate operation may be indicated in rare cases in which the perineal body is severely injured or lacerated; but in breeding mares it is seldom indicated and more trouble might be expected at the time of a subsequent parturition.

The vulva of normal mares may be temporarily sutured or clamped after foaling, especially if vulvar lacerations or a retained placenta occur, to prevent pneumovagina until the genital tract returns to normal in 1 to 2 weeks. In a few mares windsucking may occur only during estrum or after service when the vulva is relaxed. These mares benefit from temporary closure of the vulva until the vulvar tone returns. When the vulva is temporarily sutured or clamped, scarification is not performed. The vulva lips are simply pulled firmly together, usually by means of clips.

Following the Caslick operation many mares recover and overcome the infection in the genital tract within 2 to 6 months without further treatment, since reinfection due to sucking air and debris into the vagina is not recurring. These mares should not be bred until the infection is overcome and cultures of the cervix are bacteriologically negative. This emphasizes the necessity of checking and treating barren, infected mares during the fall season or a number of months before the breeding season. Although some mares with mild streptococcic infections may conceive, early or late abortion may result, or the foal may be diseased at birth, or the placenta retained at the time of parturition. In recent years the use of antibiotics and sulfonamide solutions parenterally and locally in the genital tract may precede and follow the temporary closure of the vulva or the Caslick operation and result in a greater number of cures in a shorter length of time. Even so, Crowhurst, Caslick and others have shown that the Caslick operation alone, together with a proper period of sexual rest, results in a high rate of recovery. In one winter, of 36 infected mares on which Crowhurst and Caslick performed this operation because of vaginitis and cervicitis and evidence of pneumovagina, 22 or 61 percent became pregnant the next season. No other treatment was used.

The value of sexual rest following the Caslick operation, to allow the natural body defenses to overcome infection, is well proven. It has been observed frequently that apparently normal mares infected on the ninth day, or foaling heat, if not bred will in many cases free themselves of infection by the second estrum, about 25 to 30 days after parturition. Jennings and others recommended that the ninth day breeding, or breeding on foal heat, should not be practiced: if the placenta is retained more than 3 hours; if the placenta weighs over 14 pounds; if the foal is weak, deformed, or dead at birth or dies soon after birth; if the mare needs assistance in foaling; if the mare has abnormal discharges either in color, quantity, or consistency during the first week after parturition; or if the genital tract is not free from any sign of infection, inflammation, or trauma when examined and cultured on the seventh or eighth day after foaling. In some mares even longer periods of sexual rest are required. If a mare foals late in the breeding season and is infected, it may be desirable to hold her over until the next breeding season for service. In mares having difficulties such as retained placenta, dystocia, or severe infection and metritis at parturition, treatment and sexual rest for 2 to 3 months or until the following year is imperative.

Some mares suffering from one or more of these conditions at parturition or after an abortion have a metritis and a delayed involution of the uterus. This can be determined by the breeding history, by the presence of a chronic uterine infection and discharge, and by a rectal examination that reveals a large, thick-walled uterus possibly containing varying amounts of mucopurulent exudate. Frequent douching of the genital tract of the mare with a mild antiseptic solution is seldom practiced because it tends to irritate the mucous membranes rather than to correct mild inflammatory conditions. Kortum developed a plastic indwelling uterine infusing instrument permitting the frequent daily infusing of the uterus with antibiotics or antiseptics. The value of such a cathether is limited and questionable. The author has experienced difficulty in having mares retain the instrument. Nevertheless douching under sanitary procedures at intervals of 2 to 3 days during estrus with a very mild chlorine solution, 50 ppm, a warm physiological saline solution alone, or physiological saline solution to which some penicillin, streptomycin, or broad-range antibiotic, such as a tetracycline, nitrofurazone or furacin, polymyxin B and/or neomycin combinations, has been added, may aid in hastening involution of the uterus and correction of the metritis. If the type of organism(s) causing the infection is known and the sensitivity of these organisms to the various antibiotics has been determined, select the antibiotic that will be most effective. These solutions may be pumped into or run into the uterus by gravity. If a mucopurulent exudate is present in the uterus, this should be douched or siphoned out of the genital tract. Some veterinarians use antibiotics infused or inserted in an oil or tablet form into the uterus and left there to hasten recovery. Stilbestrol in 20- to 30-mg doses intramuscularly may be useful. Some veterinarians have used local infusions of other antiseptic solutions such as chlorhexidine **(Novalsan)** following antibiotic infusions. McGee and Sager indicated this was of value against Klebsiella infections. In some of these cases the Caslick operation may be necessary. Exercise in moderate amounts may have value in improving the tone and hastening the involution of the uterus.

In recent years the use of antibiotics and sulfonamides for uterine infections in mares has become widely practiced, Sager (1968). With the large number of antibiotics and combinations of antibiotics, sulfonamides and estrogens available, each veterinarian treating genital infections of mares uses his favorite intrauterine preparations or combinations. In general, penicillin and the broad-range antibiotics such as **Terramycin** or oxytetracycline, **Aureomycin** or chlortetracycline, and tetracycline are most effective against streptococci, while streptomycin, neomycin, furacin or nitrofurazone, and chloramphenicol are most effective against **E. coli, Ps. aeruginosa,** and other gram-negative organisms. Some veterinarians put these products into oil, others into saline, into mastitis emulsion vehicles, and into dilute sulphonamide solutions. Amounts of 50 to 100 ml are usually used for instillation. Proctor and others prefer to treat the uterus 2 to 3 times at 24 to 48 hour intervals during estrum when the natural uterine defense mechanisms are active.

The author agrees with Sager that antibiotics given parenterally are of little value in chronic uterine infections. Local treatment is indicated. Systemic treatment is indicated in acute or severe uterine infections causing a pyemia or septicemia as may occur after parturition. Autogenous bacterins have been used with some success in genital tracts infected with **Klebsiella** or **Pseudomonas** organisms in mares, Beeman, Bruner. Further controlled studies on the value of autogenous bacterins against specific infectious organisms are needed since spontaneous recoveries after a period of several months or more of sexual rest are not uncommon. It is unlikely that bacterins will eliminate preputial infections in stallions, Beeman. If the Caslick operation is indicated it should be performed, since antibiotic therapy alone cannot permanently correct a genital infection due to pneumovagina. Genital rest will aid recovery, and bacteriological examinations of the cervix will indicate when breeding can be undertaken with an expectancy of conception.

In rare cases of pyometra, or of uterine abscess due to adhesions or obstructions in the cervix it may be necessary to break the adhesions or to make an incision through them to release the pus. Placing a gauze pack in the opening for several weeks will allow establishment of a fistulous opening for drainage into the vagina and prevent the uterus from refilling with pus. Wolff et al., and Milne (See hysterectomy) have successfully removed the uterus and ovaries from mares with severe pyometra or uterine abscess. In one case observed by the author nearly 15 gallons of pus were drained from the uterus of a small mare with cervical and vaginal atresia due to adhesions. The mare had suffered a severe dystocia 6 months previously. Such mares are incurably sterile.

Infections of the genital tract secondary to severe injuries to the perineum or from recto-vaginal fistulas must be repaired in order for subsequent conception to occur. However, the author, Sager, and others have observed mares that have had a recto-vaginal fistula that conceived and delivered a normal foal. Conception in mares with severe injuries involving the recto-vulvar area are not uncommon because of the protection provided the vagina by the vestibular-vaginal sphincter and folds of mucous membrane in that area that prevent pneumovagina.

In 1969 Hughes and Loy and Petersen et al., stated that although bacteria can be recovered from nearly 90 percent of all mares within a few days postpartum and within 24 to 72 hours postcoitus, the normal healthy young mare has an excellent uterine defense mechanism that rapidly and completely eliminates the infective bacteria introduced into the uterus within a few days. This is accomplished by a prompt, intense, acute inflammatory response lasting about 12 to 96 hours, and characterized by hyperemia, edema and relaxation of the cervix and massive invasion of the endometrium and the uterine lumen with leucocytes that phagocytize and destroy the bacteria. This response occurs in both the estrogenic and luteal phases of the cycle resulting in the normal endometrium and cervix becoming bacteriologically sterile.

Barren older mares with a history of recurrent chronic endometritis even though they were free of infection in their genital tract at the time of service or experimental exposure to infectious bacteria such as streptococci or Pseudomonas organisms, showed a greatly reduced uterine and cervical reaction with an increase in polymorphonuclear leucocytes as well as eosinophiles in the endometrium. These older susceptible mares exhibited less mucopurulent exudation and a persistence of the infection and developed a chronic endometritis. There was definite evidence that these chronically infected mares or those that readily become infected had a breakdown or alteration in the non-cellular defense or bactericidal mechanisms in the uterus which set them apart from the normal, healthy, often young mares which exhibit an excellent, prompt, highly effective defense mechanism. There apparently is a delicate balance between the pathogenicity of the infective bacteria and the susceptibility of the mare to infection. Peterson et al. discussed the non-cellular factors possibly involved in this lowered resistance to infection exhibited by some mares.

Hughes and Loy showed that mares with a shortened estrous cycle may have an acute uterine infection as 5 of 7 mares they infected during the luteal phase of the cycle had a shortened interval between ovulations. Prickett reported that an increase in leucocytes or leucocytic tide developed under the endometrium from 6 days before ovulation to a peak in numbers at ovulation and then a gradual disappearance of the leucocytes for 3 days after ovulation. One cannot tell without a good history if a barren mare that is found infected is one that when cured of the infection will be highly susceptible or resistant to reinfection. Mares susceptible to chronic uterine infection and endometritis usually become easily reinfected after foaling or after each service unless preventive therapeutic procedures are taken. Antibiotics in a saline solution infused into the uterus within 24 hours postservice appears to be a promising treatment for preventing the establishment of a chronic infection, endometritis and failure of conception.

Hughes et al. reported that 6 of 10 barren mares and 2 foaling mares exposed to Pseudomonas at the time of service conceived and foaled when they were bred and treated at same estrous cycle; while 19 barren and 12 foaling mares that were treated and then bred on subsequent estrous periods had only 3 and 4 conceptions, respectively, and 2 of the pregnant mares absorbed their embryos. As pointed out by Hughes et al., and Knudsen, postbreeding or postovulation antibiotic treatment using 250 to 500 ml of an antibiotic solution reduced the uterine bacteria present from the natural service or present in the uterus at the time of service and prevented the infection from becoming established in these susceptible mares. Knudsen noted this greater susceptibility to infection and infertility after service in older pluriparous mares that often had a local dilation of the ventral portion of the base of the uterine horns or in the body of the uterus. In these locally dilated areas the mucosal folds were flattened and the endometrium was atrophic and aglandular. The rest of the uterus was normal. Further study is needed to clarify the obvious relationships and observations in these four recent studies, Knudsen, Hughes et al., Peterson et al. and Hughes and Loy.

Prickett has reported that cystic endometrial hyperplasia is focal, is usually located in the base of the uterine horns, and is a permanent senile change commonly associated with atrophic uterine glands. He also noted that chronic endometritis is also focal at the base of the uterine horns and only rarely is it diffuse. It is possible that degeneration of the endometrium and infertility as discussed earlier in cattle associated with delaying service until heifers were 4 or 5 years of age, DeLange, and in unspayed dogs, Dow and others, may be the reason for the decline in fertility in nulliparous mares of middle or older age and be an important factor in endometritis in older mares as it has in older dogs. Possibly in older mares local areas of cystic endometrial degeneration are

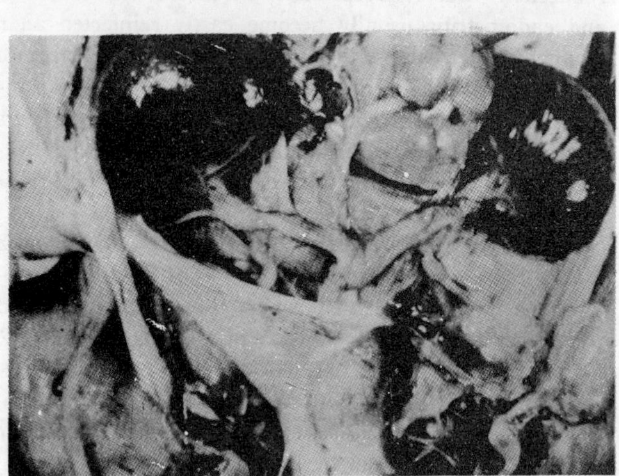

Figure 145. Ovaries in a 5-Month-Old Equine Fetus. (Note their size in relation to that of the fetal kidney located between them).

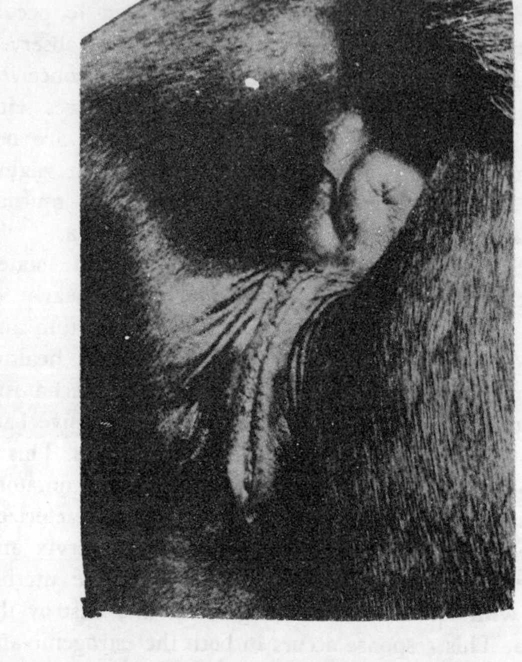

Figure 146. Appearance of the Perineal Region of a Mare with Pneumovagina. (Note the sunken anus, horizontal tipped vulva and the atrophic vulvar lips).

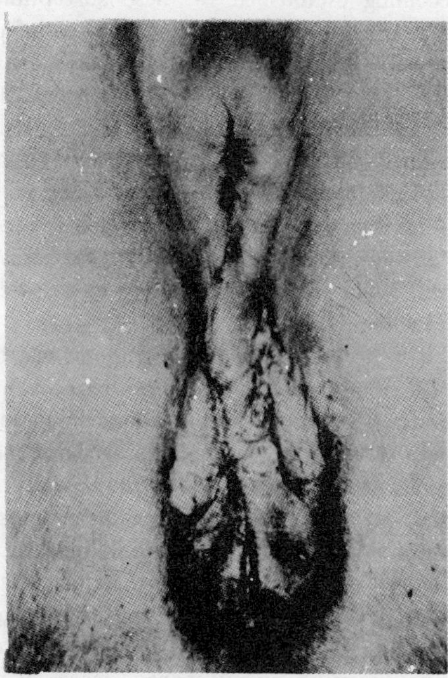

Figure 147. Coital Vesicular Exanthema or Genital Horse Pox in a Mare. (This is due to a herpes virus). (Courtesy T. Clark, Iowa State Univ.)

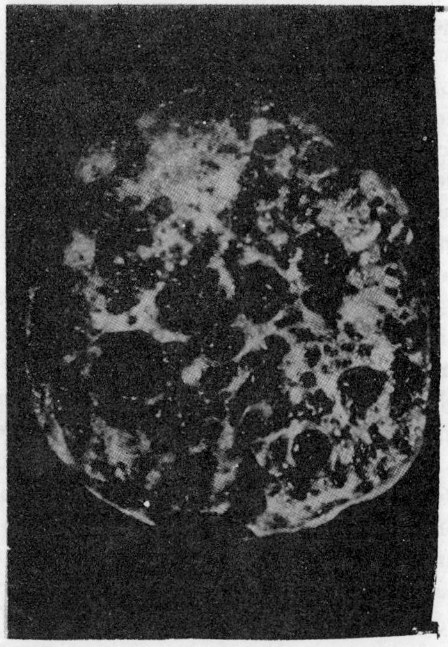

Figure 148. Granulosa Cell Tumor of the Mare's Ovary. (Note the hemorrhages interspersed throughout the tumor). (Courtesy K. McEntee).

present that are highly susceptible to infection because of a lack of normal local defense mechanisms in the affected mucosa resulting in a localized endometritis after the introduction of normal contaminated semen at coitus. This infection apparently prevents normal conception and development of the zygote. Douching the uterus, by eliminating most of the infection, may result in a normal, intrauterine environment in which the zygote can survive.

Knudsen used 200 to 500 ml of a 0.5 percent streptoymcin solution as a postservice intrauterine infusion with excellent results. Hughes et al. added the antibiotic, selected on the basis of the sensitivity of the strain **Pseudomonas** organism, to 250 to 500 ml or normal saline solution or distilled water. Both Hughes et al. and Taylor had quite satisfactory results treating Pseudomonas infections in mares with **Daribiotic** (Schering) containing neomycin and polymyxin B. In this study about 10 percent of 791 mares had **Pseudomonas** organisms in the genital tract. If no clinical signs of inflammation could be observed, the presence of the organisms on culture should not be considered a sign of the disease. In a few cases pyometra and aborted fetuses were associated with the **Pseudomonas** infection. They indicated that frequent or extensive use of intrauterine antibiotics for various organisms lowered the resistance of the mare's uterus allowing the Pseudomonas organism to become established and assume pathogenicity. Maiden mares promptly eliminated **Ps. aeruginosa** or other bacteria introduced at coitus but older mares were more susceptible to the establishment of a chronic infection and endometritis.

Many stallions may harbor Pseudomonas and other organisms in their sheath, Hughes et al., as well as **Streptococcus zooepidemicus,** Spincemaille and Vandeplassche. Even **Klebsiella** may rarely become established in the stallion's sheath, Beeman. Elimination of these infections from stallions is very difficult and usually unsuccessful. Most of these infectious organisms in stallions are not highly pathogenic, but a few stallions may apparently carry and transmit a highly virulent organism that infects a large number of mares bred to him. This fact further accentuates the necessity of careful hygiene in the breeding act. In breeds of horses where artificial insemination is practiced the control of the bacterial flora in the extended semen with antibiotics is indicated especially for the infection-prone mare where the infection has been eliminated, but coitus would probably reestablish the endometritis, Hughes et al.. These authors recommended adding 1000 units of potassium penicillin, 1 mg of dihydrostreptomycin and 200 units of polymyxin B sulphate per ml of skim-milk or cream-gelatin diluter (see Artificial Insemination in horses) and inseminate with 50 ml of the semen extended 1:1 or 1:4.

Other Infectious Diseases of the Genital Organs of Mares

Coital vesicular exanthema, genital horse pox or equine venereal vulvitis or balantitis, is a viral disease of horses described in the U.S., Canada, Australia and the European countries. The causative agent is a Herpes virus, Bryans, Girard et al., and Pascoe et al.. It is a different virus from equine herpesvirus 1 or equine rhinopneumonitis virus as it does not cause abortion. It may cause a mild upper respiratory infection if inoculated intranasally. The disease is rather uncommon in the United States. It is generally believed to be transmitted by coitus but the virus apparently may be readily transmitted by other means as it spreads very rapidly through a band of mares. In rare cases even young foals may be affected, Udall. Williams stated that coital vesicular exanthema is highly contagious and may be spread by grooming. The incubation period is short, 6 to 8 days. No fever, anorexia, or other signs of a systemic reaction are present. In the United States the disease appears suddenly, and often the source of infection is unknown. The disease is characterized by the early appearance of many papules 1 to 3 mm in diameter that may become confluent. These exude serum that dries and forms crusts. (See Figure 147) When these crusts are rubbed off, a punched-out, irregular ulcer or erosion is observed. These erosions enlarge and coalesce and become filled with exudate and dried scabs. Intranuclear inclusion bodies may be seen in the cells obtained from scraping the vulvar lesions. A purulent discharge may be present in the vulva. The vulva is reddened, swollen, and very painful. Urination may be frequent and painful and tenesmus may occasionally be noted. Lesions often appear on the skin of the vulva which on healing leave small nonpigmented spots that may last for several weeks. In stallions coital exanthema develops on the penis, glans and prepuce and some stallions may be reluctant or refuse to cover a mare due to pain until the lesions heal. Occasionally secondary bacterial infection may occur. Neutralizing antibodies in the blood are also produced. Some veterinarians will use mild astringent protective preparations such as calamine lotion or other similar products on the lesions. Healing is usually rather rapid within 10 to 14 days even without treatment. Breeding activities should be suspended for 3 to 4 weeks or more until the infection has subsided and the lesions have healed. The disease does not affect fertility or cause abortion. One attack does not confer permanent immunity. Affected animals should be quarantined for 60 days.

Dourine is a disease of horses due to **Trypanosoma equiperdum,** and is transmitted almost entirely by coitus. This is the only trypanosome disease of importance in domestic animals in the United States. Dourine has long been known in Europe. It was first recognized in the United States in 1885 by W. L. Williams in Illinois, where it was believed to have been spread by a Percheron stallion imported from France. By the use of the complement fixation test and the destruction of all reacting animals, the disease was apparently eradicated from the states west of the Mississippi to which it had spread. In 1939 and 1940 another outbreak occurred in Nevada, California, Colorado, Arizona, New Mexico and apparently Mexico, affecting mainly the wild horses and horses of Indians living in rather isolated areas. Vigorous efforts at eradication were again undertaken and it is believed at present that dourine is probably eradicated from the United States, Barner, Hagan and Bruner. Dourine is widespread throughout the world in temperate as well as tropical countries.

Dourine is transmitted at coitus and can also, but apparently not commonly, be spread by bloodsucking flies, because some geldings have been found affected. Members of the horse family are the only animals that contract the infection and therefore no other reservoirs of infection exist.

Except in the tropics the disease is chronic and the onset is slow. Udall stated the incubation period is 1 to 8 weeks, or that occasionally it may be much longer. The disease may exist in the animal for months or years with the affected animal alternately improving and relapsing. In the terminal stages emaciation and nervous symptoms develop, rendering the animal worthless and it is usually destroyed.

The early symptoms of the disease are characterized by swelling of the vulva and vagina of the mare, and a mucous discharge containing trypanosomes. The affected stallion's penis, prepuce, and scrotum become swollen and reddened. The swelling may vary in size. On palpation the area is nearly free from heat and pain. In mares genital irritation caused by this organism is evidenced by frequent urination and tail switching. After the acute genital symptoms subside, peculiar raised plaques appear in the skin over the body. These are often called "dollar" plaques because of their similarity in size to a silver dollar, though some may be much larger. They appear suddenly and disappear within a few hours or days and are replaced by others. These plaques are said to be pathognomonic of the disease. Occasionally abortion may occur, Williams. Depigmentation of the mucosa and skin of the vulva, penis, and prepuce may occur. There are irregular periods of fever in the late stages of the disease and symptoms of paralysis, involving the facial muscles, the limbs, and the penis gradually develop. Emaciation progresses until death occurs. Mortality is estimated at 50 to 75 percent, Udall. Treatment is expensive and impractical as results are poor, Barner.

The trypanosome may be found in the mucoid genital discharge of the mare and from the urethra of stallions, in the edematous fluids in the plaques under the skin but only rarely in the blood stream. A positive, accurate diagnosis can be made on the basis of the complement-fixation test.

Miscellaneous Factors in Infertility in Mares

Tumors of the Genital Tract in mares are uncommon. On examination of over 2,000 mares Dimock and Edwards reported only 6 true tumors. Of these 6, 3 were in the ovary. Cystadenomas and cystadenocarcinomas have been described as rare tumors in horses that may spread to the adjacent peritoneal surfaces and cause ascites, Moulton, Fujimoto and Sakar. Granulosa cell tumors are the most common ovarian tumor in the mare. (See Figure 148) In older mares the author has observed 3 cases in which the tumor weighed over 30 pounds and caused the death of the mare by slow hemorrhaging into the tumor or into the peritoneal cavity. In young mares the affected ovary may be 5 to 8 inches in diameter and the opposite ovary and may be very small and atrophied possibly due to the steroid hormones secreted by the tumor. The granulosa cell tumor is not uncommon in young mares 3 to 5 years of age. Some affected mares will have an enlarged clitoris and their actions and attitudes resemble a stallion with excitement on the approach of another horse, aggressiveness, roaring like a stallion, and rearing, Moulton, Finocchio and Johnson, Day, Peck, Arthur, Cotchin, Cordes and Howard. These actions and attitudes may be due to estrogens, progesterone or even androgens elaborated by the tumor. Most granulosa cell tumors are unilateral and rarely metastasize. Some granulosa cell tumors may be solid and others contain cysts. It is important that they be differentiated from large ovaries due to several large follicles. Normal ovaries fluctuate in size during the year while the granulosa cell tumor will gradually increase in size. Granulosa cell tumors may be removed through a flank incision and possibly conception might occur subsequently from ova released from the opposite ovary. These mares usually become quieter and more manageable for the rider and stablehands. Other rare tumors of the ovary include: epithelioma, Dimock and Edwards, melanomas and teratomas or dermoids, Fujimoto and Sakar, Williams, and Megale.

Backstrom, Day, and the author have each observed mares with a pronounced hirsutism. The hair is 3 to 4 inches long and fine and thick resulting in sweating, poly-

Figure 149. Squamous Cell Carcinoma of the Vulva of the Mare.

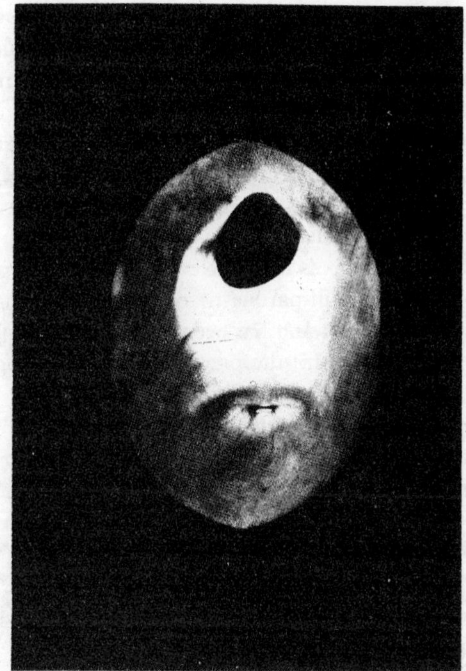

Figure 150. Persistent Hymen in a Filly (Note the urethral orifice caudoventral to the hymen).

dipsia and incoordination associated with an adenoma of the pituitary gland.

Uterine tumors include leiomyomas, which are usually small and 1 to 2 inches in diameter or they may be multiple or rarely large, fibromas, and carcinomas which are rare, Moulton, Grant, McEntee, Cotchin and Dimock. These tumors may also be found in the cervix and vagina. Squamous-cell carcinomas, melanomas that frequently metastasize in white horses, and papillomas are the most common tumors of the vulva of mares, Feldman, Pires, Cotchin and Moulton. (See Figure 149)

Parovarian cysts are common in the mare and only rarely cause infertility, Osborne. They may arise from several primitive structures during embryonic development. The **epoophoron** is grossly observable in all equine ovaries. It is located in the dorso-antero-medial aspect or pole of the ovary in the ovarian capsule. It usually consists of 6 to 8 small, 0.5 to 2.0 cm, thick-walled or rarely larger, persistent cysts. It arises from remnants of the mesonephros and is the counterpart of the head of the epididymis and efferent tubules in the male. Other cysts include the **paroophoron** in the mesosalpinx ventral, posterior and medial to the ovaries, and the **mesonephric duct cysts** in the uterine horn. **Hydatids of Morgagni or fimbrial cysts** arising from the paramesonephric duct remnants are very common and seen in nearly all mares. These cysts may be from 2 mm to 2 or 3 cm in diameter and are very thin-walled. **Rete ovarii cysts** may rarely be present near or in the hilus of the ovary. Rarely blind ends or remnants of the primitive Mullerian or **paramesonephric duct cysts** will be found in the region of the ovary and uterus in later life, McEntee, Anderson, O'Shea, Prickett and Osborne. **Germinal or epithelial inclusion cysts** lined with peritoneum as described earlier are commonly seen in older mares in the region of the ovulation fossa. In rare cases they may feel like a tight bunch of small grapes. They may rarely interfere with conception if there are many of them. Williams has described parovarian cysts in the mare that became large and were attached by a long pedicle that caused strangulation of the rectum. If diagnosed this pedunculated cyst might be removed from the animal by surgery before it could cause a fatal strangulation of the gut.

In a few older mares strands of fibrous tissue may extend from the ovulation fossa to the fimbria and probably arise from bleeding that occurs at the time of ovulation. In mares strongyles may cause fibrin tags on the ovaries. Thrombosis, large varices and hematomas may involve the superficial vessels on the equine ovary. Accessory adrenal tissue about 1.5 cm in diameter may be noted in up to 20 percent of the mares on the greater curvature or convex side of the ovary, Osborne, McEntee. Drudge et al. have described the presence of a bot, **G. intestinalis,** in a 3-inch cyst of the ovary.

Ovarian hypoplasia is rarely observed in mares and is usually unilateral. Osborne (1964) described 2 cases that were bilateral and 5 that were unilateral in over 5000 equine genital tracts. Day also described 2 cases. Ovarian hypoplasia is often erroneously diagnosed in young, anestrous nulliparous mares. Until the mare is older and well-grown and has been examined a number of times, especially during the breeding season, a diagnosis of hypoplasia should not be made.

Lesions of the oviduct in the mare are rare. Pyosalpinx has not been described in mares. Hydrosalpinx is also very rare although Arthur (1958) described two cases; both were unilateral. The author is unaware of any reported genetic defects or arrests in development of the equine oviduct. Osborne has reported rare cases of small under-developed fimbriae that might have difficulty in picking up ova.

Uterine cysts, Anomalies and Lesions, except those associated with uterine infections and senile degenerative changes in the endometrium, are rare. Occasionally large single cysts 2 to 4 inches, 5 to 10 cm, in diameter in the endometrium are observed in older mares, Rooney, Arthur. These large cysts might be a cause for an incorrect pregnancy diagnosis. Segmental aplasia of the uterus has been described by one or two authors but apparently is very rare, Milne.

Mucometra is occasionally observed in older mares. The mucus present in mucometra is usually a milky-white color. It is often associated with a pendulous type of uterus at the time of estrum when the uterus is quite flaccid or is seen in anestrous mares. It probably is associated in many cases with cystic and degenerative changes of the endometrium which may be due to estrogen or progesterone stimulation, McEntee, Zebracki, Thain. Edema of the uterine wall with mucometra at estrus has been described by Arthur. Cystic degeneration of the uterine wall has been described by Dimock and Edwards and Proctor as a rare condition that renders the mare hopelessly sterile. The condition is observed in both infected and normal mares. It is characterized by numerous submucous cysts that vary in size from 1 to 5 cm in diameter. The cyst contents are clear amber in color and bulge into the lumen of the uterus. A few uteri have been described that contained innumerable numbers of small, upright, finger-like cysts just beneath the endometrium. The endometrium had a moist, shiny, glistening appearance. The uterine wall was thick, soft, and spongy and when jarred had the appearance of a gelatinous mass. This condition may be diagnosed by the finding of a characteristic spongy, thick uterine wall on rectal examination. The cause for this condition is unknown. Knudsen described 24 mares with lymph stasis of the endometrium in which lymphocytes predominated in the endometrial biopsy smears. Most of these mares had poor fertility; in 2 cases pregnancy terminated in early fetal death. These mares cycled normally and appeared normal on speculum examination. On rectal examination the uterus was large and edematous. Only 3 of 24 mares were positive on bacteriological culture of the uterus. On postmortem examination the endometrium was very edematous. Knudsen indicated that rarely these mares recovered without therapy, and conceived after being barren for one to two years. There is no treatment for lymph stasis.

Lesions of the Cervix and Vagina are rare in the mare. The most common lesion is an acquired occlusion of the cervix with adhesions due to severe irritation of the cervix at the time of foaling, from a severe infectious cervicitis, or from the use of irritating procedures and drugs that produce a severe cervicitis. Mild obstructions may be broken down, a pessary introduced and left in place for 2 to 4 weeks until healing has occurred, McGee, Lieux. A recurrence of the adhesion across the cervical lumen is not uncommon. VanLoen has described a double cervix and vagina and a band in an incomplete double cervix in 2 mares. Schlotthauer and Zollman described a segmental aplasia of the paramesonephric duct resulting in a missing cervix and a small uterine horn. In this case the ureter entered the antero-lateral wall of the vagina. Also rarely seen in the cervix of the mare are ampullary diverticula or cysts, homologues of glands of the male ampulla. Cysts of Gartner's duct or remnants of the mesonephric or Wolffian duct in the floor of the vagina are rarely observed, Osborne and Anderson. Previously mentioned was the severely lacerated and scarred cervix that cannot close properly; affected mares are infertile or sterile.

Persistence of a Portion of the Hymen is not unusual in maiden mares and it is usually ruptured at the time of service. (See Figure 150) Some veterinarians advise rupturing it with a vaginal speculum 1 to 2 months before service so it is healed before a natural service, Harris, Proctor, Hagyard. In rare cases an imperforate hymen is noted in a maiden mare and requires incising to release the mucus and epithelial debris trapped in the vagina and uterus. Occasional tenesmus may be exhibited in these mares, with a slight protrusion of the distended hymen between the vulvar lips. Occasionally a severe vaginitis or vestibulitis may result in a stenosis of the vulvovaginal border, Gibbons. It is not uncommon to note on speculum examination **varicose veins in the**

hymenal folds. Occasionally one of these may break and a chronic slow dripping of blood may be observed from the vulva. This is most commonly seen late in gestation.

Congenital Defects, Developmental Arrests, and other Anomalies of the reproductive system of the mare are rare. Hermaphroditism has occasionally been described and is usually characterized by a large, protruding clitoris and irregular sexual symptoms. (See Figure 37) McEntee cited Levens (1911) who described 15 cases of male pseudohermaphroditism in stallions descended from the same sire.

There is some evidence to show that certain Thoroughbred female lines, as in cattle, are characterized by infertility of a hereditary nature resulting in a particular mare's female descendants being "shy breeders". The relative importance of this factor requires more scientific appraisal. Payne et al. described a sterile mare that had 63 instead of 64 chromosomes in a karyotype of her leucocytes. Normal chromosomes were not present.

Breeding Farm or Stud Management

Management practices on breeding farms are basically similar to those described for cattle. The veterinarian and stud manager and/or owner must work closely together in a program designed for the farm to secure the highest number of mares pregnant at the end of the breeding season and then these pregnant mares should be handled so that they will produce normal, live, strong foals. A goal of over 80 percent conception in the band of mares is considered a satisfactory goal on most farms raising racing stock where the breeding season is short and some of the stallions and mares being used as sires and dams are not highly fertile. Conceptions below 60 to 70 percent are definitely unsatisfactory and require remedial measures.

In a study of reproductive efficiency on 14 horse farms encompassing 6 breeds and a total of 1876 mare-years, conception, foaling and weaning efficiency averaged 80.1, 73.8 and 70.8 percent. It was significant that on 2 farms using pasture breeding, conception rates were 94 and 100 percent. The conception rates were very low in February, 27.8 percent and rose to a peak in May through July of 57 to 59 percent and declined thereafter. Conception efficiency in young mares fluctuated until age 7, reached a peak at age 9 of 89.6 percent, remained on a plateau above 70 percent until age 15 and declined thereafter. Conception rates on 5 Thoroughbred farms ranged from 53 to 80 percent and on 5 Quarterhorse farms from 72 to 92 percent, Hutton and Meachem.

Every effort should be made in the Fall to examine, treat, if necessary, and outline a plan of breeding for the coming season of all barren mares. Infected mares should be treated and cured or eliminated well before the breeding season. Infertile mares, and especially maiden mares, should be booked to the most fertile stallions. Barren mares that have failed to conceive in a number of years should be culled. If a stallion's conception rate is low his semen should be examined carefully on a number of occasions during the breeding season or preferably before the season. If a stallion is of low fertility, his book should probably be reduced and close attention should be paid to having the mare bred within 24 hours of ovulation. The time of breeding may be determined by careful rectal palpation. Foaling mares should be properly cared for during foaling, given exercise and examined critically before being permitted to breed on the foal estrum. Teasing all barren, foaling or recently bred mares on a regular every other day basis before and during the breeding season is essential. If this is not done regularly a veterinarian should examine the mare's ovaries for the presence of a mature Graffian follicle and impending ovulation on the same schedule. Frequent speculum examinations or services should be avoided especially on the infection-prone mare.

Breeding shed hygiene and restraint should be thorough and on a routine basis. The external genitals should be carefully washed and disinfected. Care should be taken not to have disinfectant on the stallion's penis at the time of service. Mares with Caslick operations should be carefully supervised and the number of services should be reduced to the bare minimum consonant with good conception rates. The stallion's semen should be examined at each cover to determine if ejaculation occurred and to observe the quality of the semen. If artificial insemination is employed this should be carefully supervised, monitored and performed in a clean, sanitary manner.

Careful, continuous and complete daily and even lifetime records on all aspects of the breeding program must be kept up-to-date, accurately and in an easily accessible form. These records should be analyzed for each stallion and for the mares during and at the end of the breeding season. All treatments, services, teasing, pregnancy and genital tract examinations must be recorded. A variety of breeding record forms have been devised and used by veterinarians and managers of stud farms. Daily record and permanent record forms are essential. Satisfactory record forms may be purchased from The Lifetime Horse Records Company, 6060 South Broadway, Littleton, Colorado. Records used by Andrews and McKenzie and Beeman were excellent.

The mares and stallions must be on a balanced ration and maintained in good condition being neither too fat nor too thin. Mares at the time of breeding should be in a positive energy balance on a rising plane of nutrition. Daily exercise is essential for all breeding stock. It has proven to be a helpful practice if it is possible, to allow a fertile stallion to run at pasture with barren or infertile mares if infection or other countra-indications are not present.

As in cattle careful and constant attention to many and all details by the veterinarian and the farm manager are essential to a successful reproductive program. Vaccination, worming and other measures are essential for a good foaling rate and the limiting of losses of newborn animals.

It is unfortunate that the breeding season of racing mares does not extend from April 15 to August 15, instead of the present February 15 to June 15. The conception rates on many farms would probably rise 10 to 20 percent by this accomodation to the physiologic breeding season of the mare. Dr. V. Osborne found in studying the records of the English Jockey Club, "The Jockey Club and Its Founders" and "Ponds Racing Calendar" of 1751 that the age of a horse originally was dated from the first of May. In 1833 this was changed to the first of January to accomodate the stewards at the race course and it has remained the same for over 135 years. It was unfortunate for the veterinarians and breeding farms that the early traditional birthdate of May 1 for racing horses was changed.

The publications from the Stud Manager's Short Courses held at the University of Kentucky in the past 15 years provided excellent source material on knowledgable practices, management and feeding on equine breeding farms and The **Veterinary Notebook** by W. R. McGee can also be strongly recommended to laymen.

References

Adams, Wm. (1970) Personal Communication.

Amoroso, E. C. (1955) Hormone Control of the Oestrus Cycle, Vet. Rec. **67,** 1072.

Anderson, W. A. D. (1953) Parovarian Cysts in **Pathology** 2nd Ed, C. U. Mosby Co., St. Louis, Mo., 1063.

Andrews, F. W. and McKenzie, F. F. (1941) Estrus, Ovulation and Related Phenomena in the Mare, Res. Bull. 329, Agric. Exp. Stat., Univ. of Mo., Columbia, Mo.

Arthur, G. H. (1958) An Analysis of the Reproductive Function of Mares Based on Postmortem Examination, Vet. Rec. **70,** 682.

Arthur, G. H. (1963) Equine Ovariectomy, Vet. Rec. **75,** 18, 465.

Arthur, G. H. (1964) Wright's Veterinary Obstetrics, 3rd Ed. The Williams and Wilkins Co., Baltimore, Md.

Arthur, G. H. (1968) The Effects on Equine Reproductive Function of Uterine Infusion of Saline, 5th Internat. Congr. on An. Reprod. and Art. Insem., Paris, Vol. II, 1551.

Arthur, G. H. (1968) The Ovary of the Mare in Health and Disease, Eq. Vet. Jour. **1,** 4, 1.

Asdell, S. A. (1964) Patterns of Mammalian Reproduction, 2nd Ed. Comstock Publishing Co., Inc., Ithaca, N.Y.

Backstrom, G. (1963) Hirsutism Associated with Pituitary Tumors in Horses, Nord. Vet. Med. **15,** 778.

Bain, A. M. (1957) Estrus and Infertility of the Thoroughbred Mare in Australasia, J.A.V.M.A. **131,** 4, 179.

Bain, A. M. (1963) Common Bacterial Infections of Foetuses and Foals and Association of the Infection with the Dam, Austral. Vet. Jour. **39,** 413.

Bain, A. M. (1967) The Ovaries of the Mare During Early Pregnancy, Vet. Rec. **80,** 229.

Barner, R. O. (1963) Dourine, in **Equine Medicine and Surgery,** Amer. Vet. Public. Inc., Wheaton, Ill.

Beeman, G. M. (1965) Brood Mare Problem Panel, 10th A.A.E.P. Meeting (Abstr. J.A.V.M.A. **146,** 3, 268).

Beeman, G. M. (1969) Brood Mare Records and Examination of the Mare, Proc. of Conference on Reprod. Problems in Animals, Univ. of Georgia, Nov., 42.

Belonje, C. W. A. (1949) Observations on Reproduction in the Thoroughbred Mare, J. South Afr. Vet. Med. Assoc. **20,** 1, 21.

Belonje, C. W. A. (1951) Some Diseases Associated with the Breeding of Horses, Part I, J. South Afr. Vet. Med. Assoc. **22,** 4, 203.

Belonje, C. W. A. (1956) The Operation for Retroversion of the Penis in the Stallion, J. South Afr. Vet. Med. Assoc. **27,** 1, 53.

Belonje, C. W. A. (1956) The Influence of Running a Stallion with Non-pregnant Thoroughbred Mares, J. South Afr. Vet. Med. Assoc. **27,** 1, 57.

Belonje, C. W. A. (1960) The Physiology of Reproduction in the Mare with Special Reference to the Thoroughbred, J. South Afr. Vet. Med. Assoc. **31,** 1, 115.

Benesch, F. (1955) Over de Aetiologie en Therapie der Nymphomanie bis Rund en Paard, Vlaams Diergeneesk. Tijdschr., **24,** 5, 120.

Benesch, F. and Wright, J. G. (1951) Veterinary Obstetrics, The Williams and Wilkins Comp., Baltimore, Md.

Bengtsson, G. and Knudsen, O. (1963) Feed and Ovarian Activity of Trotting Mares in Training, Cor. Vet. **53,** 3, 404.

Benirschke, K. and Sullivan, M. M. (1966) Corpora Lutea in Proven Mules, Fert. and Steril. **17,** 1, 24.

Bergin, W. C. and Shipley, W. D. (1968) Genital Health in the Mare, Vet. Med. **63,** 4, 362.

Berliner, V. R. (1963) The Physiology of Reproduction in the Mare, Chapt. 23, in **Equine Medicine and Surgery,** Amer. Vet. Public. Inc., Wheaton, Ill.

Bielanski, W. (1955) Observations on Ovulation Processes in She-Mules, Bull. De L'Acad. Polon. des Sci. **3,** 7, 243.

Britton, J. W. (1947) Clinical Studies on Early Equine Abortion, Cor. Vet., **37,** 1, 14.

Britton, J. W. and Howell, C. E. (1945) Observations on Sterility, Vet. Med., **40,** 8, 264.

Bruner, D W. (1951) Notes on Genital Infection in the Mare, Cor. Vet., **41,** 3, 247.

Bruner, D. W. (1954) (1963) Personal Communication.

Bruner, D. W. and Gillespie, J. H. (1966) Hagan's Infectious Diseases of Domestic Animals, 5th Ed., Comstock Press, Ithaca, N.Y.

Bryans, J. T. (1968) The Herpesviruses in Disease of the Horse, Proc. 14th Ann. Conv. A.A.E.P., Philadelphia, 119.

Bryans, J. T. and Sager, F. (1962) Research on Bacterial Disease of Horses, Lectures Stud Managers' Short Course, Lexington, Ky. (Abstr. Cor. Vet. **57,** 1, (1967), 66).

Burkhardt, J. (1947) Anestrus in the Mare and Its Treatment with Estrogens, Vet. Rec., **59,** 26, 341.

Burkhardt, J. (1947) Transition from Anoestrus in the Mare and the Effects of Artificial Lighting, J. Agric. Sci. **37,** 64.

Burkhardt, J. (1948) Some Clinical Problems of Horse Breeding, Vet. Rec. **60,** 243.

Burkhardt, J. (1949) Sperm Survival in the Genital Tract of the Mare, J. Agric. Sci. **39,** 201.

Burkhardt, J. (1954) Treatment of Anestrus in the Mare by Uterine Irrigation, Vet. Rec. **66,** 375.

Carricaburu, J. B. (1968) Improved Techniques on the Brood Farm, Proc. 12th Ann. Conv. A.A.E.P., Los Angeles (Abstr. J.A.V.M.A. **150,** 3, (1967), 344).

Caslick, E. A. (1937) The Vulva and the Vulvo-Vaginal Orifice and Its Relation to Genital Health of the Thoroughbred Mares, Cor. Vet., **27,** 2, 178.

Caslick, E. A. (1937) The Sexual Cycle and Its Relation to Ovulation with Breeding Records of the Thoroughbred Mare, Cor. Vet., **27,** 2, 187.

Clegg, M. T., Boda, J. M. and Cole, H. H. (1954) The Endometrial Cups and Allantochorionic Pouches in the Mare with Emphasis on the Source of Equine Gonadotrophin, Endocrin. **54,** 448.

Cole, H. H. and Cupps, P. T. (1969) Reproduction in Domestic Animals, 2nd Ed., Academic Press, N.Y.C.

Collins, S. M. (1964) A Study of the Incidence of Cervical and Uterine Infection in Thoroughbred Mares in Ireland, Vet. Rec. **76,** 673.

Cordes, D. O. (1969) Equine Granulosa Tumors, Vet. Rec. **85,** 186.

Cotchin, E. (1956) Neoplasms of the Domesticated Animals; A Review, Commonwealth Bureau of Animal Health. Review Series #4, Royal Vet. Coll., London, Eng.

Crowhurst, R. C. and Caslick, Wm. (1946) Some Observations on Equine Practice and Its Relation to the Breeding of Thoroughbred Mares, N.A. Vet., **27,** 12, 761.

Danks, A. G. (1955) Personal Communication.

Day, F. T. (1939) Sterility in the Mare Associated with Irregularities of the Oestrous Cycle, Vet. Rec., **51,** 36, 1113.

Day, F. T. (1939) Ovulation and Descent of Ovum in the Fallopian Tube of Mare After Treatment with Gonadotrophic Hormones, J. Agric. Sci. 29, 458.

Day, F. T. (1940) Clinical and Experimental Observations on Reproduction in the Mare, J. Agric. Sci. **30,** 244.

Day, F. T. (1942) Survival of Spermatozoa in the Genital Tract of the Mare, J. Agric. Sci. **32,** 108.

Day, F. T. (1957) The Veterinary Clinician's Approach to Breeding Problems in Mares, Vet. Rec. **67,** 1258.

Day, F. T. and Rowlands, I. W. (1946) Serum Gonadotropin in Welsh and Shetland Ponies, Jour. of Endocrin. **5,** 1.

Delahanty, D. D. (1968) Surgical Correction of Contributory Causes of Uterine Disease in the Mare, J.A.V.M.A. **153,** 12, 1563.

Deubler, M. J. (1952) Observations of the Routine Use of Cervical Cultures in Mares, Vet. Med., **47,** 5, 182.

Dimock, W. W. (1939) Equine Breeding Hygiene, J.A.V.M.A., **94,** 5, 469.

Dimock, W. W. and Bruner, D. W. (1949) Notes on Procedure for Handling the Barren Mare, N.A. Vet., **30,** 7, 435.

Dimock, W. W. and Bruner, D. W. (1949) Barren Broodmares, Ken. Agr. Exp. Stat., Univ. of Kentucky, Circ. 63, Lexington, Ky.

Dimock, W. W. and Edwards, P. R. (1928) The Pathology and Bacteriology of the Reproductive Organs of Mares in Relation to Sterility, Ken. Agr. Exp. Stat., Res. Bull. 286.

Drudge, J. H., Leland, S. E. and Behlow, R. F. (1945) A Bot in an Equine Ovary, J.A.V.M.A. **128,** 7, 72.

Ellsworth, K. (1966) Significance and Interpretation of Cervical Cultures in the Mare, Proc. 12th Ann. Conv. A.A.E.P., 129.

Engle, C. C. (1969) Some Biological and Physiological Aspects of Equine Reproduction, Proc. of Conf. on Reprod. Problems in Animals, Univ. of Georgia, Nov., 27.

Errington, D. J. (1951) Barren Mares, Lectures to the First Annual Stud Managers Course, Univ. of Ken., Lexington, Ky.

Feldman, Wm. H. (1932) Neoplasms of Domestic Animals, W. B. Saunders Co., Phila., Pa.

Fincher, M. G. (1950) Prevention of Breeding Failures in Mares, Lecture given at Saratoga Springs, N.Y.

Finocchio, E. J. and Johnson, J. H. (1969) Granulosa Cell Tumor in a Mare, Vet. Med./An. Clin. **64,** 4, 322.

Fraser, A. F. (1968) Tables of Data on Livestock Reproduction, Edinburgh Univ. Press, Edinburgh.

Fujimoto, Y. and Sakai, T. (1955) On a Case of An Ovarian Cystadenoma Associated with a Teratoma (Dermoid) in a Horse, Jap. J. Vet. Res. **3,** 1, 8.

Gadd, J. (1961) Follicle Examaination Related to Optimum Breeding Time, Proc. 7th Ann. Conv. A.A.E.P.

Gibbons, W. J. (1967) Equine Mucometra.—Case Report—Mod. Vet. Pract. **48,** 7, 64.

Girard, A., Grieg, A. S. and Mitchell, D. (1968) A Virus Associated with Vulvitis and Balanitis in the Horse.—A Preliminary Report, Canad. J. Comp. Med. **32,** 603.

Gotze, R. (1938) Dammrissnaht Vulva u Scheiden vor hof Plastik bei Stuten u Kuhen, Dtsch. Tierartz. Wschr. **46,** 11, 163.

Grant, D. L. (1964) Uterine Tumor in a Mare—Leiomyoma, Vet. Rec. **76,** 17, 474.

Grunert, E. (1955) Die Biopsie der Uterus Schleimhaut der Stute, Arch f Expt Vet., **9**, 3, 265.

Habel, R. E. (1953) The Perineum of the Mare, Cor. Vet., **43**, 2, 249.

Hafez, E. S. E. (1969) The Behavior of Domestic Animals, 2nd Ed. Williams and Wilkins Co., Baltimore, Md.

Hafez, E. S. E. (1968) Reproduction in Farm Animals, 2nd Ed. Lea and Febiger, Philadelphia.

Hagan, W. A. and Bruner, D. W. (1951) The Infectious Diseases of Domestic Animals, 2nd Ed., Comstock Publishing Co., Inc., Ithaca, N.Y.

Hagyard, C. E. (1956) Reproductive Diseases of Mares, Cor. Vet. **46**, 3, 329.

Hancock, J. L. (1948) Notes on Estrus, Ovulation and Pregnancy in the Mare, Vet. Rec. **60**, 679.

Harris, A. S. (1956) Persistent Hymen in a Mare, Abstr. J.A.V.M.A. **129**, 11, 508.

Hetzel, H. (1938) Die Nymphomanie der Stuten, Tierarztl. Rundsch., **44**, 42 and 43, 681 and 697.

Hillman, R. B. and Loy, R. G. (1969) Estrogen Excretion in Mares in Relation to Various Reproductive States, Proc. 15th Ann. Conv. A.A.E.P., Houston, Ill.

Howard, F. A. (1949) Granulosa Cell Tumor of the Equine Ovary, J.A.V.M.A. **114**, 864, 134.

Hughes, J. P., Asbury, A. C., Loy, R. G. and Burd, H. E. (1967) The Occurrence of **Pseudomonas** in the Genital Tract of Stallions and Its Effect on Fertility, Cor. Vet. **57**, 1, 53.

Hughes, J. P. and Loy, R. G. (1969) Investigations on the Effect of Intrauterine Inoculations of **Streptococcus zooepidemicus** in the Mare, Proc. 15th Ann. Conv. A.A.E.P., Houston, 289.

Hughes, J.P. and Loy, R. G. (1970) Artificial Insemination in the Equine. A Comparison of Natural Breeding and Artificial Insemination of Mares Using Semen from Six Stallions, Cor. Vet. **60**, 3, 463.

Hughes, J. P., Loy, R. G., Asbury, A. C. and Burd, H. E. (1966) The Occurrence of **Pseudomonas** in the Reproductive Tract of Mares and Its Effect on Fertility, Cor. Vet. **56**, 4, 595.

Hunt, M. and Rossdale, P. D. (1963) Specific Venereal Disease of Thoroughbred Mares (**Klebsiella pneumoniae,** Friedlander's Bacillus), Vet. Rec. **75**, 1092.

Hutton, C. A. and Meacham, T. N. (1968) Reproductive Efficiency on Fourteen Horse Farms, J. An. Sci. **27**, 2, 434.

Jennings, W. E. (1941) Some Common Problems in Horse Breeding, Cor. Vet., **31**, 2, 197.

Knudsen, O. (1964) Endometrial Cytology as a Diagnostic Aid in Mares, Cor. Vet. **54**, 3, 415.

Knudsen, O. (1964) Partial Dilation of the Uterus as a Cause of Sterility in the Mare, Cor. Vet. **54**, 3, 423.

Knudsen, O. and Sollen, P. (1961) Methods for Obtaining Samples from the Uterus in the Cow and Mare, Nord. Vet. Med. **13**, 449.

Kortum, W. (1969) An Indwelling Uterine Infuser for Cattle and Horses, J.A.V.M.A. **155**, 12, 1942.

Laufenstein-Duffy, H. (1968) Indications and Surgical Procedures for Uterine Curettage in the Mare, J.A.V.M.A. **153**, 12, 1570.

Lieux, P. (1963) Reproduction, in **Equine Medicine and Surgery,** Amer. Vet. Publicat. Inc., Wheaton, Ill.

Loy, R. G. (1967) How the Photoperiod Affects Reproductive Activity in Mares, Mod. Vet. Pract. **48**, 5, 47.

Loy, R. G. (1968) Effects of Artificial Lighting Regimes on Reproductive Patterns in Mares, Proc. 14th Ann. Conv. A.A.E.P., Philadelphia, 159.

Loy, R. G. (1966) The Hormonal Control of Reproduction in Farm Animals—Some Current Concepts and Present Status, Calif. Vet., Mar.-April.

Loy, R. G. and Hughes, J. P. (1966) The Effects of Human Chorionic Gonadotropin on Ovulation, Length of Estrus, and Fertility in the Mare, Cor. Vet. **56**, 41.

Loy, R. G., Hughes, J. P., Richards, P. and Swan, S. M. (1967) Effects of Progesterone on Reproductive Functions in Postpartum Mares, J. An. Sci. **26**, 4, 947 (abstr).

Loy, R. G. and Swan, S. M. (1966) Effects of Exogenous Progestogens on Reproductive Phenomena in Mares, J. An. Sci, **25**, 3, 821.

Mahaffey, L. W. (1950) Studies on Fertility in the Thoroughbred Mare, Austral. Vet. Jour. **26**, 295.

McDonald, L. E. (1969) Veterinary Endocrinology and Reproduction, Lea and Febiger, Philadelphia.

McEntee, K. (1965–1970) Personal Communication.

McEntee, K. (1970) The Female Genital System in **Pathology of Domestic Animals,** edit. by K. V. F. Jubb and P. C. Kennedy, 2nd Ed., Academic Press, N.Y.C.

McGee, W. R. (1958) Veterinary Notebook, The Blood Horse, Lexington, Ky.

McGee, W. R. (1962) Some Diseases and Related Conditions Affecting Fertility in Broodmares, Thoroughbred of Calif. **34**, 5.

McGee, W. R. (1969) A Practical Program to Reduce the Incidence of Embryonic and Perinatal Mortality, Proc. 15th Ann. Conv. A.A.E.P., Houston, 141.

McKenzie, F. F. (1940) Recent Reproduction Studies in Equines, Proc. Amer. Soc. of An. Prod., 98.

McKenzie, F. F. and Andrews, F. N. (1937) Estrus and Ovulation in the Mare, Proc. Amer. Soc. of An. Prod., 64.

Millar, R. (1952) Forces Observed During Coitus in Thoroughbreds, Austr. Vet. J., **28**, 5, 127.

Milne, F. (1968) Personal Communication.

Moore, R. (1967) Personal Communication.

Morrow, G. L. (1967) Uterine Curettage in the Mare, J.A.V.M.A. **151**, 12, 1615.

Moulton, J. E. (1961) Tumors of Domestic Animals, Univ. of Calif. Press, Berkley, Calif.

Nalbandov, A. V. (1964) Reproductive Physiology, 2nd Ed. W. H. Freeman and Co., SanFrancisco.

National Research Council (1961) Nutrient Requirements of Horses,

Nat. Acad. of Sci. Publicat. 912, 6, Washington, D.C.

Nishikawa, Y. (1959) Studies on Reproduction in Horses, Japan Racing Assoc., Minatoku, Tokyo, Japan.

O'Connor, J. T. jr. (1969) Avoiding and Treating the Untoward Effects of the Corticosteroids, Proc. 15th Ann. Conv. A.A.E.P., Houston, 75

Osborne, V. E. (1961, 1964, 1968) Personal Communication.

Osborne, V. E. (1966) An Analysis of the Pattern of Ovulation as It Occurs in the Annual Reproductive Cycle of the Mare in Australia, Austral. Vet. Jour. **42,** 149.

O'Shea, J. D. (1968) A Histological Study of Non-Follicular Cysts in the Ovulation Fossa Region of the Equine Ovary, J. Morphol. **124,** 3, 313.

Pascoe, R. R., Spradbrow, P. B. and Bagust, T. J. (1969) An Equine Genital Infection Resembling Coital Exanthema Associated with a Virus, Austral. Vet. Jour. **45,** 166.

Patterson, A. W. (1960–1967) Personal Communication.

Patterson, A. W. (1964) The Pineal Body, Maryland Vet., Aug. and Norden News, Oct.

Payne, H. W., Ellsworth, K. and DeGroot, A. (1968) Aneuploidy in an Infertile Mare, J.A.V.M.A. **153,** 1293.

Peck, G. K. (1952) Infertility in Mares, Vet. Med., **47,** 9, 359.

Peterson, F. B., McFeely, R. A. and David J. S. E. (1969) Studies on the Pathogenesis of Endometritis in the Mare, Proc. 15th Ann. Conv. A.A.E.P., Houston, 279.

Pires, A. (1950) Clinical Aspects of Tumors in the Horse, Rev. de Med. Vet., enero 1.

Prickett, M. E. (1966) Pathology of the Equine Ovary, Proc. 12th Ann. Conv. A.A.E.P. 145.

Prickett, M. E. (1968, 1969) Personal Communication, Discussion, Proc. 15th Ann. Conv. A.A.E.P., Houston, 113.

Proctor, D. L. Jr., (1953) Sterility in Mares, Proc. A.V.M.A., 90th Annual Meeting, 409.

Proctor, D. L. Jr., (1962) Personal Communication.

Rasbech, N. O. (1964) Fertility and Reproductive Disorders of Various Species of Farm Livestock in Denmark, Brit. Vet. J. **120,** 415.

Rasbech, N. O. (1965) Effect of Equine Genital Infections on Reproduction, Nord. Vet. Med. **17,** 305.

Ressang, A. (1954) Sterility in Mares, A Clinical, Bacteriological and Histopathological Investigation, Thesis, Univ. of Utrecht, G. Van Dijk, Breukelen.

Rooney, J. R. (1966) Personal Communication.

Rooney, J. R. and Doll, E. R. (1964) Superfetation or Twin Pregnancy, J.A.V.M.A. **144,** 832.

Rowlands, I. W. (1950) Serum Gonadotrophin and Ovarian Activity in the Pregnant Mare, Jour. Endocrinol. **6,** 184.

Sager, F. C. (1949) Examination and Care of the Genital Tract of the Brood Mare, J.A.V.M.A., **115,** 873, 450.

Sager, F. C. (1951) Practical Feeding, 1st Ann. Stud Managers' Course, Univ. of Kn., Lexington, Ky.

Sager, F. C. (1962) Personal Communication.

Sager, F. C. (1966) Care of the Reproductive Tract of the Mare, J.A.V.M.A. **149,** 12, 1541.

Sager, F. C. (1968) Management and Medical Treatment of Uterine Disease, J.A.V.M.A. **153,** 12, 1567.

Schlotthauer, C. F. and Zollman, P. E. (1956) The Occurrence of So-Called "White Heifer Disease" in a White Shetland Pony Mare, J.A.V.M.A. **129,** 7, 309.

Short, R. V. (1959) Progesterone in Blood IV Progesterone in the Blood of Mares, J. of Endocrinol. **19,** 207.

Short, R. V. (1960) Steroids Present in the Follicular Fluid of the Mare, J. of Endocrinol. **20,** 147.

Short, R. V. (1965) Recent Advances in Equine Reproductive Physiology, 4th Ann. Congr. Brit. Eq. Vet. Assoc.

Solomon, W. J., Raber, C. W., McFeeley, R. A. and Peterson, F. B. (1970) Effects of Uterine Curettage in the Mare, J.A.V.M.A. **156,** 3, 333.

Spincemaille, J. and Vandeplassche, M. (1964) **Streptococcus zooepidemicus:** A Venereal Disease in Horses?, 5th Internat. Congr. on An. Reprod. and Art. Insem., Trento.

Squibb, R. L. (1958) Fifty Years of Research in America on the Nutrition in the Horse, J. An. Sci. **17,** 4, 1007.

Stangroom, J. E. and Weevers, R. de G. (1962) Anticoagulant Activity of Equine Follicular Fluid, J. Reprod. and Fertil. **3,** 269.

Stud Managers' Course, Annual Lectures 1951 to the present time, P.O. Box 1520, Lexington, Ky. (Univ. of Ken., Dept of An. Path.)

Stowe, H. D. (1967) Reproductive Performance of Barren Mares Following Vitamins A and E Supplementation, Proc. 13th Ann. Conv. A.A.E.P., New Orleans, 81.

Taylor, E. L. (1967) Practice Tips, Proc. 13th Ann. Conv. A.A.E.P., New Orleans, 16.

Teigland, M. B. and Saurino, V. R. (1960) Sterile Disposable Swabs for Bacteriological Diagnosis, J.A.V.M.A. **136,** 3, 104.

Thain, R. I. (1968) Cystic Endometrium in Mares, Abstr. A.A.E.P. Newsletter, #2, June.

Tobler, E. E. (1966) Collection of Uterine Fluid and Uterine Biopsy, Vet. Med/Sm. An. Clin., **61,** 8, 779.

Trum, B. F. (1950) Personal Communication to M. G. Fincher.

Udall, D. H. (1954) The Practice of Veterinary Medicine, 6th Ed., Published by the author, Ithaca, N.Y.

VanLoen, A. (1961) A Contribution to the Knowledge of the Double Cervix Condition in Bovine Cattle, Thesis, Univ. of Utrecht, Scheltema and Holkema, Amsterdam.

VanNiekerk, C. H. (1964) Early Embryonic Resorption in Mares, Jour. South Afr. Vet. Med. Assoc. **36,** 1, 61.

VanRensburg, S. W. J. and VanHeerden, J. S. (1953) Infertility in Mares Caused by Ovarian Dysfunction, Onderstep. J. of Vet. Res. **26,** 2, 285.

Williams, W. L. (1943) Diseases of the Genital Organs of Domestic Animals, 3rd, Ed., Miss Louella Williams, Upland Rd., Ithaca, N.Y.

Wolff, A., Dunderman, T. A. and Dunderman, B. J. (1963) Surgical Correction of Pyometra in a Mare, J.A.V.M.A. **143,** 9, 1004.

Wynn, R. (1967) Cellular Biology of the Uterus, Meredith Publ. Co., N.Y.C.

Zafrakas, A. (1964) Treatment of Anestrus Mares by Intrauterine Irrigation with Saline Solution, Bull. Soc. Vet. Hell. **14,** 75.

Zebracki, A. (1962) Cystic Hyperplasia of the Endometrium of the Horse Diagnosed by Uterine Biopsy, Wien Tierartzl. Monatschr., **49,** 1, 135.

Zemjanis, R. (1970) Animal Reproduction, 2nd Ed. Williams and Wilkins Co., Baltimore, Md.

Chapter XV

INFERTILITY IN FEMALE SWINE

The incidence of sterility in sows may approach that seen in cattle. Because of their lower value and the difficulties of diagnosis and treatment, sterility in sows has not been studied as much as has infertility in cattle or horses. Phillips and Zeller reported the incidence of sterility in a herd where brucellosis was present as 21.9 percent in 382 sows over 1354 breeding seasons. This varied from 13.9 to 36.9 percent in various breeds. Nalbandov (1950) reported that 5 percent of sows and gilts were sterile, another 5 percent were hard to settle, and another 10 to 15 percent showed some impairment of fertility by a small litter size due to high intrauterine death rate of the embryos or fetuses. Goethals found on postmortem examination only 1.4 percent of 1000 sows and gilts completely sterile and another 2.2 percent with lowered fertility. Hutchings noted that because swine are multiparous, complete sterility in swine is lower in incidence than in cattle but that reduced fertility is fairly common. Phillips reported that in 250 sows, 42, or 16.8 percent, failed to conceive or farrow. Of the rest, 84 percent conceived on 1 service, 12 percent after 2, 2.5 percent after 3, and 1.5 percent after 4 services. Hutchings cited several references to show that litter size rose to a peak at the fifth to sixth litter and then decreased. Warnick et al. reported that 20.8 percent of sows failed to conceive and that 29.7 percent of the matings were infertile. Nalbandov (1952) reported that 10 percent of female swine were sterile. The most common causes of sterility were hydrosalpinges and cystic ovaries; these two accounted for about one-half of the failures to conceive.

Hutchings classed stillborn pigs as a form of infertility. McPhee and Zeller reported that stillbirths occurred in 259, or 23.1 percent, of 1121 litters. Litters of over 12 pigs had an incidence of 11.7 percent stillbirths, while medium-sized litters had an incidence of only 3.9 percent. The birth weight of stillborn pigs was higher than that of normal pigs. Asdell and Willman reported an incidence of 6 percent stillborn pigs, occurring usually in large litters, old sows, and in spring farrowings. Stillborn pigs were more common in the latter half of the litters as they were born or in those fetuses nearer the apex of the horn. Attempts to hasten parturition with pituitrin gave inconclusive results. These authors reported that according to the literature the incidence of stillborn pigs is 8 to 9 percent. The mortality in the two sexes was about equal.

Physiology of Porcine Reproduction

Puberty occurs in gilts at 6 to 7 months of age with a range of 4 to 8 months. It may be delayed slightly by inbreeding or severely restricting the TDN intake to one-half recommended amounts. It may be hastened slightly by crossbreeding and by allowing the boar to contact the gilts, Zimmermann. The greater the number of estrums after puberty and before service in gilts, the greater is the ovulation rate, Day.

The Estrous Cycle—The sow is polyestrous the entire year. Estrum usually does not occur during lactation. After 6 to 10 years of age senility may affect the estrous cycle. The estrous cycle averages 21 days in length and may vary from 18 to 23 days, Dukes, Day, Ito et al., Atkins and Morrissette, Cole and Cupps. The estrogenic phase of the cycle is 6 to 7 days and the luteal phase is 14 days with C.L. regression beginning on day 16. The duration of estrum is 1 to 4 days, with an average of 2 to 3 days, or 60 hours. Ovulation usually occurs between 24 to 42 hours, or an average of 36 hours, after the onset of estrum. Nearly all sows examined had ovulated by 40 hours. Older sows have a slightly longer estrous period and cycle than gilts. Failure of ovulation results in a longer estrous period, and premature ovulation will shorten the period. Ovulation is spontaneous in sows. It takes about 4 to 6 hours from the rupture of the first follicle to the rupture of the last follicle. The rate of ovulation is 10 to 15 ova and 12 to 20 ova for the gilts and sows, respectively. A slightly higher ovulation rate occurs in crossbred gilts and in young sows from 2 to 4 years of age. Younger gilts and older sows have a lower ovulation rate. Markedly restricting the energy intake will decrease the ovulation rate but this can readily be restored by feeding a high level of energy, or "flushing", for several weeks. High rates of ovulation result in larger litter size at 25 days of gestation, but at farrowing the litter size is not increased by increased ovulation rates, Day. It is generally recommended that gilts be bred late on the first day and/or early during the second day of estrum and that sows be bred late during the second day. Ovulations are slightly more frequent, 51 to 55 percent on the left than on the right ovary. The size of the follicles at ovulation is 0.7 to 1 cm in diameter, Asdell.

Small follicles are present in the porcine ovary during diestrum, but during proestrum and estrum although approximately 15 to 40 follicles approach maturity only about 10 to 20 ovulate. The mature Graafian follicle is about 8 to 10 mm in diameter. From 7 to 16 days after ovulation the corpora lutea are at their maximum size, about 1 cm in diameter, Asdell. The weight of the ovary during diestrum may reach 8 to 10 gm. Degeneration of the corpora lutea is rapid just before and during the next estrum and a few days before and after parturition.

The symptoms of estrum in the sow are definite and usually marked, Dukes, Hafez, Signoret and Du Mesnil Du Buisson, Fox, Fraser, Cole and Cupps. The sow has a reduced appetite and is restless and nervous, often pacing back and forth by the fence. Salivation, champing of the jaws, and frequent grunting may be pronounced. The sow, if suckling, may ignore her pigs; may try to escape, or if free will seek out the boar and stand for service. During estrum the vulvar lips become swollen and congested and the mucous membrane is pinkish-red in color. Some mucus may be present at the vulva. The most noticeable feature of estrum in the sow is her grunting and standing motionless for long periods in a position for service. This peculiar, immobilizing reflex or stance can be produced in over half of the estrous sows by the pressure of the hands on the sow's back or by straddling the sow. In the presence of the boar with his characteristic odor, his grunts or acoustic signals, and his pushing and lifting of the rear parts of the sow by placing his snout between her rear legs, this sawhorse-like immobile stance and acceptance of the boar will be induced in nearly 100 percent of estrous sows. In late estrum or early metestrum, a whitish mucous discharge composed of mucus, cellular debris and leucocytes may be seen on the vulva, Dukes. The vaginal smear or the body temperature do not produce an accurate indication of the stage of the estrous cycle, Ito et al.. The vaginal epithelium in the sow undergoes cyclic thickening during estrus when it has 8 to 15 cell layers. During diestrus this will decrease to 4 to 5 layers and during pregnancy to 2 to 3 layers in the vagina. This permits vaginal biopsies to be utilized for the diagnosis of pregnancy in swine, Day. The musculature of the uterus and oviduct is most active during estrum. The endometrium and especially the region where the oviduct enters the uterus is quite edematous, requiring 50 to 155 mm of mercury to force fluid from the uterus into the oviduct but only 25 mm of Hg to force fluid from the oviduct into the uterus, Asdell.

Based on the gonadotropic hormone content of the anterior pituitary gland, LH is lowest during and shortly after estrus and highest just before estrus. FSH is low during estrus and it then rises so it is at a high level from 10 to 18 days of the estrus cycle and then declines the last 3 days of the cycle. Plasma progesterone levels rise rapidly a few days after estrus to reach a peak at 8 to 10 days of the cycle of 25.2 ng per ml. After days 14 to 16 progesterone levels decline to a low level during estrus of 7.5 ng per ml, Tillson et al., Day, Cole and Cupps. Blood removed from the ovarian vein of cycling sows showed levels of progesterone of 0.03, 1.07. and 0.04 mcg per ml of plasma on days 1, 10 to 12, and 19 to 21, respectively, Gomes et al.. Estrogen levels in the plasma and urine are at their peak during estrus and are low at other stages of the cycle. Raeside reported that the principal urinary estrogen in sows was estrone. The peak in urinary estrone excretion occurred just before estrus. Ovulation usually occurs about 30 to 36 hours after the onset of estrus when the follicles are about 8 to 11 mm in size. If 500 I.U. of HCG is injected intravenously or intramuscularly late in proestrus on days 19 or 20 of the cycle, ovulation occurs 40 to 42 hours later, Hunter. In the normal sow, LH is probably released from the pituitary gland early in estrus or late in proestrus.

Estrous signs can be induced by estrogen injection in ovariectomized sows or in sows without functional corpora lutea. However, if estrogens are injected into sows with mature corpora lutea during the luteal phase of the cycle, estrus does not occur. In fact, even a single injection of estrogen into sows at this period will prolong the life of the corpus luteum causing anestrus that may persist for a number of weeks. Thus, indiscriminate use of stilbestrol or estradiol in sows to promote estrus is to be avoided, Day, Gardner et al..

There is enough FSH and LH in the pituitary gland of gilts for several weeks before puberty to cause the onset of the estrous cycle. If prepubertal gilts are stressed by transport or a marked change in environment, estrus will often occur within 4 to 7 days after the stress indicating the release of FSH. This same period of time is required to produce estrus in prepubertal gilts after the injection of PMS. Recurrent estrus may not follow this early induction of estrus and ovulation in gilts. In general, increased amounts of PMS injected to induce follicle formation and estrus and HCG to induce ovulation results in a greater number of ova released at the induced ovulation. However, there is a great inconsistency in the number of ova released by exogenous gonadotropins injected into different sows in various seasons, herds, and years, Day, Cole and Cupps.

About 60 to 90 percent of sows will exhibit signs of estrus 2 to 3 days, range 1 to 5 days, after farrowing and will accept the boar, Cole and Cupps. If sows are bred at this estrus they do not conceive because ovulation rarely occurs, Warnick et al., and Baker et al.. Furthermore if a few ova are shed and fertilized they do not develop. McDonald speculated that this estrus could be due to estrogens from the ingestion of the placentae at parturition. The uterus of the sow is completely involuted in 21 to 28 days after parturition. The uterine weight decreased from 2.8 kg on the day after farrowing to 0.2 or 0.3 kg at 21 to 28 days, Palmer et al.. Sows that are suckled go into a lactational anestrus that lasts for 6 weeks or longer or until the pigs are weaned. Self and Grummer reported that sows weaned of their pigs 10, 21, and 56 days after farrowing came into estrum an average of 9.4, 6.2 and 4.0 days later, respectively. Ovulation and fertilization rates were normal.

Synchronization of Estrus—During lactation, estrum does not occur. But after the pigs are weaned estrum usually develops in about 4 to 9 days or an average of 5 to 7 days, Ito et al., Day. Under some circumstances, when it is desirable to bunch or synchronize the breeding and farrowing dates, estrum may be produced in a lactating sow by removing her pigs each night for 4 to 5 nights and allowing the pigs to nurse during the day, Robeson, or by weaning the pigs at 3 to 5 weeks of age. Lactation may be suppressed by the former practice. Some sows, if fed well and with a boar nearby come into estrum 5 to 7 weeks after farrowing even with pigs still suckling, Willman. Grummer and Self reported on the reproductive effects of early weaning on sows. Sows whose litters were weaned at 10 days after parturition came into estrum more than 9.4 days later, 2 sows developed cystic ovaries, and only 12.8 ova were released at the first estrum. Sows whose litters were weaned at 21 days came into estrum at an average of 6.2 days later, and ovulated an average of 15.2 ova. Sows whose litters were weaned at an average time of 56 days, came into estrum an average of 4 days later and ovulated an average of 16.6 ova. Heitman and Cole showed that estrus was induced with 1100 to 3000 I.U. PMS given intramuscularly in 76 percent of sows between 20 and 39 days of lactation and 86 percent of sows between 42 and 50 days of lactation. Conception and farrowing rates in these two groups were 44 and 66 percent, respectively. Estrus occurred an average of 4.8 days, range 3 to 7 days, after the injection of PMS. Only in 3 of 101 injected sows was estrus delayed beyond 7 days. They also cited good evidence to show that mating on the second day of estrus was the best time to breed sows. In six sows bred on the first and second day of estrus by boars of different breeds, 45 of 56 pigs farrowed were sired by the boar used on the second day. In sows given 1200 I.U. PMS on the day the pigs were weaned, estrus and superovulation resulted with 20 to 30 ova released within 7 days, and 75 percent of the sows conceived, Longnecker et al.. Superovulation can also be induced by the same dose of P.M.S. given on cycle day 16 or 17. Although litter size is increased at day 25 of gestation by this injection, there is no increased litter size at farrowing. Superovulation can even be induced during the luteal phase of the estrous cycle by an injection of P.M.S. followed in 4 days by 500 I.U. of HCG also injected intramuscularly. Estrus doesn't occur and sows inseminated artificially fail to conceive, Day. Estrus could be induced in ovariectomized gilts by 0.2 to 2.0 mg. of estradiol benzoate per 100 lbs. of body weight, but when 50 to 200 mg of progesterone per 100 lbs. was also injected, no estrum was induced, Day et al.. Casida has reviewed the low fertility rates in eggs produced by the injection of gonadotropins soon after parturition in sows and those produced during the luteal phase of the cycle and indicated that making eggs available for fertilization without the occurrence of estrus has not led to appreciable fertility.

Much research has recently been conducted on estrous synchronization in swine because of intensified management and breeding and the value of artificial insemination with semen from progeny-tested boars. Besides the various methods of synchronization of estrus by weaning at different times after farrowing, by the injection of PMS or FSH during lactational anestrus and by the application of stress to prepuberal gilts, much work has been done with progesterone, progestins and other compounds to synchronize cycling gilts or sows.

Day, Baker et al., and others have reported that exogenous progesterone in oil, 25 to 100 mg daily, would prevent estrus and ovulation and synchronize estrus but low conception rates and a high incidence of cystic ovaries occurred at the first estrus after the termination of the injections.

Nellor et al., and Dzuik demonstrated that 6-methyl-17-acetoxyprogesterone or M.A.P. if fed at levels of 0.4 to 1.6 mg per lb. of body weight daily in 3 to 4 lbs. of ration divided into two feedings would prevent estrus and ovulation during the treatment period and result in estrus and ovulation in 50 to 90 percent of the females 4 to 5 days after the cessation of the drug. However, conception rates were low at this first estrus and the incidence of cystic ovaries was increased apparently due to either an inadequate or excessive intake of progestins. These cysts varied from thin-walled small or large follicular cysts with no luteinization to large luteal cysts, Nellor et al., First et al.. Conception rates at subsequent estrous periods were normal. Attempts to improve results of the basic progestin treatment with estrogens and gonadotropes have not been sufficiently successful to make the progestin methods of estrous synchronization satisfactory and practical, Day et al., Day.

Another method for estrous synchronization in swine is the administration of 1200 to 3000 I.U. of PMS intramuscularly and then injecting 500 to 1000 I.U. chorionic gonadotropin or HCG 3 to 4 days later to induce ovulation and corpora lutea formation. About 18 to 24 days or an average of 21 days after the injection of HCG, a fertile estrus is exhibited. By producing new C.L. this regimen will prevent estrus, even in sows in the luteal phase of the cycle, until the induced C.L. involute, Day et al., and Day. This procedure did not decrease conception rates or lower subsequent reproductive performance. Day reported that no adverse effects such as the possible production of antihormones or refractoriness were observed in sows so treated at 3 consecutive breeding periods. More work is needed on this procedure.

Estrus and ovulation can also be prevented by feeding 100 mg of ICI 33828 **(Aimax, Match, Methallibure)** a dithio-thiocarbamoyl-hydrazine compound that suppresses the release of the pituitary gonadotropins, daily in 1.8 kg of feed to each sow singly or in small groups. This compound is fed for 18 to 20 days to cycling swine. Most sows and gilts will exhibit normal estrus in 5 to 6 days after the cessation of the treatment, Gerrits et al.. Normal conception rates occur at this first estrus. Cystic ovaries do not occur as they do with progesterone and progestin treatments. Recent studies by Weber et al., and Christensen et al., have indicated that if 1500 I.U. PMS is given intramuscularly on the last day of treatment with ICI 33828 and 500 to 800 I.U. of HCG is given 96 hours later, ovulation would occur 40 to 42 hours after the injection of HCG. This treatment resulted in about 90 percent of the females in estrus in a two day period either on the day or one day after the day of the HCG injection. Thus artificial insemination could be performed 12 to 24 hours after the injection of the HCG and 80 to 90 percent conception occur. Further study on this method of estrous synchronization under farm conditions is indicated. King demonstrated that 100 mg of ICI 33828 fed daily to sows between 29 and 49 days of gestation produced teratogenic defects in pigs characterized by cranial deformities and contracted tendons. In late 1970 ICI 33828 had not yet been approved for general use by the Food and Drug Administration.

Ovulation, Fertilization and Ova Transport—The best time to breed or inseminate sows or gilts is the second day of estrus. Hancock and Hovell reported that sows bred the day before heat, the first day of heat, the second day of heat and the third day of heat had 9.8, 68.8, 98.2 and 15.2 percent fertilized ova, respectively. The average number of fertilized ova in sows mated at the proper time was 95.5 percent. Sperm cells were present in the oviducts of sows within 15 minutes of breeding. Thirty minutes after breeding, although billions of spermatozoa were in the uterus, only about 90 spermatozoa were in the oviducts, First et al.. Seminal plasma and spermatozoa were rapidly lost from the uterus and phagocytosis of sperm cells began 6 to 7 hours after mating. Although both live and dead cells may enter the oviduct, the live sperm cells remain motile in the oviduct for 24 hours while those in the uterus showed a greatly reduced motility after 2 hours. A mass of sperm cells accumulate at the uterotubal junction in the apices of the uterine horns for 24 hours and then decline during the next 24 hours. Ito et al. stated that the fertilizing ability of swine spermatozoa lasts only 25 to 30 hours in the sow. The best time to breed sows was 10 to 25 hours after the onset of estrus. If the sow is bred the first day of estrus she should be rebred the second if she is still in standing estrus.

When ovulation time was controlled by an injection of HCG during proestrus and gilts were inseminated 2 hours before ovulation, 2, 6, 10 and 14 hours after ovulation, the proportion of CL represented by normal embryos at 25 days of gestation were 73, 61, 53, 28 and 32 percent, respectively. In control gilts bred 6 hours before ovulation, 88 percent of the CL were represented by normal embryos at 25 days of gestation, Hunter. When sows were bred with extended semen 6 and 54 hours old, the fertilization rate was 61 and 39.3 percent, the sows pregnant at 25 days were 68.8 and 29.2 percent, respectively. Thus, aging of ova and spermatozoa significantly affected the number of surviving embryos at 25 days, First et al. (1963). Bomsel-Helmreich reported that 26 percent of sows bred 44 hours after the onset of estrus had heteroploid embryos 17 days later probably due to polyspermy. Four percent of heteroploid embryos were observed. They concluded that fertilization of female swine must take place before 60 hours after the onset of estrus to become pregnant and before 50 hours to produce cytologically normal embryos. The block in the ova to polyspermy is highly effective when the sow is mated the first half of estrus, Day.

Thus, it would appear from the above data that capacitation of spermatozoa may have to occur before fertilization. Fertilization can occur within 2 to 3 hours after insemination. The corpus luteum develops steadily requiring a full week for development, McDonald. Fertilized ova in swine pass through the first half of the oviduct very rapidly and remain near the ampullary-isthmic junction until 24 to 39 hours after ovulation or 60 to 75 hours after the onset of estrum. The fertilized ova at the 4-cell stage of development pass into the uterus about 30 to 54 hours after ovulation or 66 to 90 hours after the onset of estrus, Oxenreider and Day. Thus swine ova enter the uterus sooner than in the other domestic animals. The morula stage develops and the zona pellucida is shed in the apices of the uterine horns 6 to 8 days after the onset of estrus, Day. The blastocyst grows very rapidly from 4 mm in diameter on the 9th day of gestation to 110 cm in length on the 16th day, Perry and Rowlands.

Intrauterine migration of fertilized zygotes occurs in sows and has been confirmed by comparing the number of C.L. in each ovary with the number of embryos in the corresponding horn. Although 55 percent of the C.L. were on the left ovary, each horn contained 50 percent of the fetuses, Lasley et al.. In sows that are unilaterally ovariectomized before mating or sows in which one oviduct is ligated, equal numbers of embryos implant in each horn, Waite and Day. It has been estimated that 40 percent of the zygotes migrate from one horn to the other. This migration of embryos from one horn to the other was also shown by Dzuik et al. by ova transplantation. This migration of zygotes occurs about 11 days after fertilization just before the great elongation of the blastodermic vesicle, Waite and Day. This is apparently accomplished by the motility and activity of the uterine musculature.

Hormones During Pregnancy—Progesterone concentration in the blood plasma increases during early gestation to a peak of 3.0 ug per 100 ml at midgestation and then declines to a very low level just before parturition, Cole and Cupps. Urinary estrogens probably arising from the placentas reaches a peak from 20 to 30 days of gestation, declines to a low level until about 70 or 80 days of gestation and then high levels occur until just after parturition, Cole and Cupps. Ovariectomy causes abortion if performed before 90 days of gestation. Pregnancy can be maintained after ovariectomy early in gestation by daily injections of progesterone or progesterone and estrogen, Day, Spies et al.. The ratio of progesterone to estrogen is about 2000:1 to 4000:1. The amount of progesterone and estrogen injected varied from 0.03 mg to 1.2 mg and 0.075 mcg to 0.5 mcg, respectively, daily per lb. of body weight.

Litter Size—Much study has been conducted on causes of reduced litter size. The prenatal mortality in swine has been estimated to be about 45 percent, Spies et al.. Most of these losses of zygotes occur during the first 25 days of gestation. About 6 percent of these losses occur in late gestation and at parturition resulting in stillbirths. The average sow produces 17 eggs, 16.2 embryos start to develop and only 9.4 live pigs are farrowed and 7.2 pigs are weaned, Self. Gilts bred the first, second and third estrum after puberty have 6.9, 8.0 and 9.4 pigs per litter, respectively. There is an increase in prenatal mortality with increased age of the sow and parity because the increased ovulation rate in sows is not associated with a similar increase in litter size. The peak in litter size occurs about the 5th to 7th litter, Day, McDonald. The decline in litter size in older sows is due to an increase in embryonic death rate.

Heritability of litter size is low, 10 to 15 percent, Day, Boylan et al.; also the size of the first litter, which is usually small, is not indicative of future litter size. Litter size will differ between breeds by an average of 3 to 4 pigs per litter. This difference in litter size between breeds may be associated with an increased ovulation rate in certain breeds, England and Chapman. Inbreeding of the dam causes a decrease in litter size and crossbreeding an increase in litter size due to heterotropic effects, Bereskin et al., and Day. Embryonic mortality may also be a characteristic of the individual sow. The sire of the sow is also an influencing factor, Perry. Shelby and Singleton mated each of 9 boars with 10 gilts and found that boars exerted a significant effect on conception rate ranging from 40 to 100 percent, and the number of live embryos at 30 days of gestation ranging from 3 to 17, but the average litter size by each boar at parturition was similar, 9 to 11.8 pigs. However, Boender reported that if a boar had a conception rate below 65 percent that this could be an important cause of reduced litter size.

Litter size is usually larger in spring farrowings than in fall farrowings. One disadvantage to multiple farrowing in sows is the lowered fertility in the summer months. Teague noted that failure of conception and repeat breeding was 10 percent higher in the summer months of June through August. With heat stress, body temperature is elevated and rapid respirations are common in an attempt to expel excess body heat. Sows stressed by exposure to 85 to 100° F. heat from days 1 to 5 or 15 of gestation caused an increase in embryonic death rates, Edwards et al., and Tompkins et al.. If the sows were stressed by heat before breeding or from 15 to 30 days of gestation, there was no effect on embryonic death rates. Thus, cooling sows with sprinklers on hot days may only be needed the first week or two after breeding. Severe cold stress did not affect litter size, Swierstra. Stress due to transportation or change of environment has not been reported to effect fetal mortality.

Although 14 percent greater conceptions occurred in sows with double matings on days 1 and 2 of estrum compared to single matings on either day, there was no significant difference in litter size in sows serviced once on either day, or serviced on both days, Craig et al.. Swierstra reported that sows bred once during an estrum had 68 percent conception rate and sows bred twice had a 78 percent conception rate. Two services produced 0.5 to 0.7 more pigs per litter than one service. Self also demonstrated that there was no significant difference in the number of ovulations and litter size in sows bred the first or second heat after weaning their pigs.

Fenton et al., showed that the quantity of uterus affected the uterine capacity to maintain fetuses. When they removed one horn and ovary from 59 gilts the litter size at 25 days of gestation was similar to the intact control gilts, but at 105 days of gestation the treated gilts had 5.5 fetuses in the single horn compared to 9.4 fetuses in the intact gilts. Pope et al. transferred either 12 or 24 fertilized ova into the oviducts of recipient gilts 24 to 36 hours after ovulation and found that at 26 to 29 days of gestation the smaller number of transplanted ova resulted in an average litter size of 6.8 compared to 16.3 in the sows receiving twice as many fertilized ova. In contrast to the above reports, Dzuik demonstrated in a variety of ways in a large number of gilts that intrauterine crowding was not important in early embryo survival and only when a gilt had 14 or more embryos did it appear likely that uterine crowding was a possible limiting factor in embryonic survival. Similarly Bazer et al. transferred either 16, 22 or 28 fertilized ova to the uteri of 3 groups of gilts and the average litter size of these groups were 8.8, 8.5 and 9.9, respectively. The size of these litters was similar to the control gilts. Thus, uterine capacity is an effective factor in limiting litter size. This effect apparently occurs prior to day 25 of gestation. Possibly more work is needed in this area.

A high level of nutrition or energy intake in gilts and sows for several weeks prior to breeding and during the breeding period results in higher ovulation rates. This increased energy intake apparently released greater amounts of gonadotropic hormones, FSH and LH, Kirkpatrick et al.. After a 4 to 8 week lactation period, Longnecker and Day gave 1200 I.U. P.M.S. on the day the sow's pigs were weaned. At 25 days of gestation the treated sows had 25 C.L. and 15.3 living embryos and had 11.3 pigs per litter compared to 13 C.L., 10.1 living embryos and 9.3 pigs farrowed in the control or untreated sows. This was significant. The level of feeding has no effect on fertilization but a high level of energy intake for four weeks after conception results in a variable but greater embryonic mortality depending upon the amount of energy given. This may possibly be related to heat or other stresses. Limited feeding of female swine is indicated following breeding, Hansel. The number of pigs born is not affected by the plane of nutrition as long as it is adequate during the latter two-thirds of gestation, Tassell, O'Bannon et al., Self and Reid. The level or quantity of protein is not as critical as energy in its effect on reproduction, Holden et al.. Most swine nutritionists recommend 5 to 10 percent alfalfa in the ration during gestation to promote normal farrowing of healthy well-grown pigs, Seerley and Wahlstrom. Sows should be kept in lean or moderate condition during gestation for economic reasons and to avoid dystocia or farrowing problems common in fat sows or gilts.

Although both progesterone and estrogen are needed to produce a proper intrauterine environment for the growing embryo, there has been no evidence that implants or daily injections of progesterone and estrogen at a ratio of 2000:1, or single injections of either hormone have any beneficial effect on embryonic mortality, Day et al.. Daily injections of 50 to 400 mg of progesterone for 4 to 26 days starting with the day after service had no beneficial effect, in fact, doses of 150 to 400 mg caused a higher embryonic mortality and regression of the C.L., Sammelwitz et al., and Day et al..

It has been suggested that uterine infections during the breeding period and shortly after conception may account for a reduction in litter size. The evidence supporting such a factor limiting litter size is present but not conclusive, Davis and Thomas, and Messersmith et al.. These authors reported on the use of injectable gallimycin, erythromycin and furacin during gestation and chlortetracycline orally for 3 weeks during the breeding season, respectively. Sewell and Carmen and Dean and Tribble fed chlortetracycline and tetracycline continually and only during the breeding period, respectively. In the former report there was no significant beneficial effect on reproduction and in the latter the number of pigs farrowed were slightly larger in the treated than in the control sows. The author questions the beneficial effect of antibiotics fed at the time of breeding on reproduction, but recognizes that in a herd acutely infected with leptospirosis or a similar bacterial infection, antibiotic treatment during the gestation period may be beneficial in reducing fetal mortality and stillbirths. Increased numbers of stillbirths, mummies and weak pigs at farrowing may be due to leptospira, brucella and miscellaneous bacterial infections, such as streptococci and staphylococci, as well as viral infections including hog cholera, Aujeszkys's disease, SMEDI picorna viruses and others. (See Chapter 5.)

The 30 to 45 percent deaths of fertilized ova or early embryos characteristic of pregnancy in swine and the other species may well be nature's way of eliminating unfit or abnormal genotypes at a low biologic cost. The incidence of genetic or congential abnormalities in the newborn is low because most are eliminated early in pregnancy. McFeely reported that 10 percent of the 10-day old blastocysts collected from normal healthy gilts had grossly detectable chromosome defects. In addition, 2.3 percent of the blastocysts recovered were already degenerating possibly due to lethal chromosome combinations. McFeely's study indicated that chromosome abnormalities account for about 33 percent of the early embryonic mortality in sows. Further studies are indicated to assess this apparently very important cause of early embryonic death and reduced litter size in swine.

The utero-ovarian relationship in swine is generally similar to cattle and sheep. Hysterectomies performed in sows the first half of the estrous cycle caused prolonged anestrus and the maintenance of corpora lutea for the approximate duration of gestation, about 110 days. If the operation is performed late in the cycle, ovulation occurs and the subsequent corpora lutea produced persist for a similar period. If nearly all of the uterus is removed from nonpregnant sows leaving only a portion that is less than one-fourth the length of the horn, then the C.L. will regress only on the side of the retained small portion of the horn; the C.L. on the opposite side will persist. If the portion of the uterine horn left in place is one-fourth the length of the uterine horn or longer then the C.L. will regress on both sides because sufficient amount of the luteolytic substance is released from the endometrium to cause involution or regression of the corpora lutea. Thus in swine if there is a blind horn due to a localized segmental aplasia involving only a portion of the horn so that zygotes are present only in one horn, then the luteolytic substance released in the nonpregnant horn or segment of that horn will cause C.L. regression and prevent implantation and pregnancy. Destruction of the porcine endometrium by a variety of agents prevents the production of the luteolytic substance resulting in a persistance of the corpora lutea. If one horn is ligated near its base, and the sow is bred at estrum, the developing zygotes will not be present in that horn and the luteolytic substance will be released resulting in a regression of the C.L. and the onset of estrum terminating the early, unicornual, pregnant state. If one horn **and** ovary are completely removed then pregnancy can occur in the remaining horn. Thus an intact, but nonpregnant horn will cause C.L. regression on both ovaries in swine but not in cattle, Ginther, McLaren, Anderson, Dhindsa and Dzuik.

Embryos can move throughout the uterus and implant up to day 11 or 12 of gestation but not at day 13 or later. Once pregnancy is established with zygotes throughout the uterus the luteolytic factor is suppressed and cycling ceases and corpora lutea persist, Polge and Dzuik. Polge et al. showed that 4 embryos or more are necessary in gilts to suppress the luteolytic substance and maintain luteal function during early pregnancy. Dhindsa and Dzuik (1968) and Niswender et al., also showed that when all the fetuses or embryos in one horn were killed between 4 and 50 days of pregnancy, that pregnancy was maintained in gilts so treated between 12 and 50 days, but was not maintained in gilts so treated from 4 to 10 days of gestation. In these latter gilts the C.L. regressed on both ovaries. Thus after day 12, pregnancy will continue even if all of the fetuses in one horn die or become mummified. The author has observed a sow with all of the fetuses mummified except one and pregnancy was maintained. (See Figure 74).

Anatomical, Congenital, and Possibly Genetic Abnormalities of the genital tracts of female swine are a fairly common cause of failure of conception which can be explained by the close utero-ovarian relationship previously described that results in early regression of the C.L. induced by the release of the luteolytic substance before day 12 of gestation in the uterine horns not containing developing embryos. Warnick, Grummer and Casida reported on 19 "repeat breeding" sows and 44 "repeat breeding" gilts. In those 63 animals 5, or 11.4 percent, of the gilts had a unilateral missing segment of the uterine horn, or uterus unicornis. Nineteen, or 43.2 percent, of the gilts and 2, or 10.5 percent, of the sows had bilateral tubal abnormalities; 2, or 4.5 percent, of the gilts had bilateral missing segments such as a missing vagina, cervix, or body of the uterus. Animals with bilateral tubal abnormalities were included with those having hydrosalpinx, "pyosalpinx", and bursitis. Present in the broad ligaments of some of the gilts were structures that appeared to be rudimentary ducts or remnants of the mesonephric or Wolffian duct system. With so many abnormalities affecting gilts, the logical conclusion was that they were developmental defects or arrests. Wilson, Nalbandov and Krider studied 79 female swine that had been bred an average of 2.8 services without conception. A unilateral missing segment was found in 1 gilt and 1 sow, or 2 percent and 3.6 percent, respectively. A unilateral blind segment was present in 4, or 7.8 percent of the gilts, and 1, or 3.6 percent, of the sows. A blind uterine body was found in 1, or 2.0 percent, of the gilts. In many cases the blind horn was distended with mucus. One gilt had a missing cervix. Another 354 day-old gilt had infantile reproductive organs with a complete lack of estrual periods. In several cases one uterine horn, oviduct and ovary were missing. In cases in which one horn, usually the left horn, and the adjacent ovary were missing, pregnancy occurred normally in the other horn but the litter size was reduced by about one-half. Dhindsa and Dzuik reported that they observed a partial doubling of the uterine horns in 5 of 500 gilts. Some of these became pregnant and farrowed. This might be genetic in nature. Goethals, in Belgium, reported that 2.2 percent of 1000 female swine examined had missing segments of the uterine horn; 3 percent of the gilts had hydrometra; there were 4 cases of a uterus didelphys (double cervix); and 1 had a missing uterine body. Morris also reported a case of uterus didelphys in swine. Teige and VanLoen reported on other cases of a double cervix and median septums of varying lengths in the vagina located most commonly near the hymen and extending cranially. Wiggins, Casida and Grummer, after examining 2967 gilts and 1288 sows, reported the following incidence in slaughter house material missing and double parts of the genital tract:

	Percent
Missing uterine horn	**0.3**
Missing segment of uterine horn	**0.3**
Missing vagina, cervix, and uterine horns (with male ducts in broad ligaments)	**0.02**
Missing cervix	**0.02**
All reproductive organs missing except vulva	**0.04**
Double cervix	**0.04**
Double uterine horn	**0.02**
Total	**0.74**

There were 1.8 percent of the open gilts, 0.6 percent of the pregnant gilts, and 1.2 percent of the open sows—or a total of 1.5 percent of 5088 sows and gilts—with tubal abnormalities. None of these abnormalities, except possibly a missing vagina or cervix, could be diagnosed in the living animal by practical methods. Thus it was emphasized by the above figures that anatomic arrests in development were common. Of these, hydrosalpinx was the cause of by far the greatest amount of sterility. Nalbandov reported anatomic defects in 21.5 percent of the sterile female swine examined by himself and Wilson and co-workers. Warnick and co-workers reported 33.3 percent of "repeat breeding" swine having bilateral tubal abnormalities. The incidence of defects in gilts in these 2 reports was 31.3 percent and 43.2 percent, respectively, in sows the incidence was much lower, only 3.6 percent and 10.5 percent, respectively, since they had previously farrowed pigs. Tubal abnormalities reported by Wiggins and co-workers were present in 1.4 percent of female swine. Teige reported on 142 or 3.3 percent genital tract anomalies in 9250 gilts and 9 or 1.8 percent anomalies of the genital tract in 476 sows; about one half of the anomalies were either segmental or total aplasia of the paramesonephric ducts. Thus in swine, especially gilts, anomalies of the genital tract are not uncommon. The incidence is definitely higher than in other species of farm animals. Hermaphrodism in swine is seen occasionally and the affected animals are usually male pseudohermaphrodites, (See Chapter III).

Tubal abnormalities are common in swine in the U.S., but uncommon in Europe, Nalbandov, Teige. They are usually bilateral and probably genetic in origin and result in hydrosalpinx or "pyosalpinx". In sterile female swine, usually gilts, 35 percent had obstruction of the oviducts, Nalbandov. In hydrosalpinx, which was by far the most common lesion, there appeared to be an obstruction in the lumen of the oviduct about two-thirds of the distance from the ovary to the horn, causing an accumulation of fluid, Wilson and co-workers, and Warnick and co-workers. They reported that bursitis, or adhesions between the oviduct and ovary, occur commonly in cases of hydrosalpinx. Becker reported that these adhesions were probably secondary to mycoplasmosis, polyserositis, peritonitis or intraperitoneal injection of an irritating substance in piglets. Goethals reported that 20, or 2 percent, of the 1000 female swine he examined had bursal adhesions. These apparently are not so common or serious as the hydrosalpinx that may be associated with them. Occasionally "cysts" of the bursa developed secondary to severe adhesions. Wilson and co-workers reported that in hydrosalpinx, which was very common, 97 percent of the cases were bilateral and usually the uterine third of the oviduct was involved or obstructed. In some cases the oviduct was patent and a light yellow bacteriologically-negative material was flushed with some force from the lumen. This would effectively prevent the passage of ova. In most cases of hydrosalpinx or "pyosalpinx", adhesions of the fimbriae to the ovaries were present. Nalbandov also reported there was some evidence that these hydrosalpinges and "pyosalpinges" might have been caused by the obstruction of the oviduct by embryonal rests of the Wolffian duct system. He reported that the condition was invariably bilateral and showed some tendency to be inherited. It appeared almost entirely in nulliparous gilts. Attempts were unsuccessful to reproduce this condition experimentally in normal females by inoculating their oviducts with contents from affected oviducts. Whether hydrosalpinx and adhesions are due to disease, to congenital lesions, or to some other factors is not definitely known. More work is needed on this aspect of the problem.

Pathological Lesions or Diseases of the Reproductive System in swine, besides those just mentioned, are cystic ovaries and inflammations of the genital tract. The former will be discussed later under hormonal causes of sterility. Nonspecific postpartum or postservice metritis is not considered as common in the sow as in the cow and mare; retained placenta is of less frequent occurrence; delayed involution of the uterus with endometritis, a common cause of postpartum sterility in cattle, is not common in sows. Normal nonpregnant or pregnant swine uteri are bacteriologically sterile. Goethals, and Wilson and co-workers each described only one case of pyometra. Wiggins and co-workers, on examination of 5088 sows and gilts, reported no gross uterine infections.

In Chapter XI the mastitis, metritis, agalactia (MMA) syndrome or "milk fever" in sows was discussed. This acute condition occurs soon after parturition and has been the subject of much recent intensive research. According to Armstrong and Ringarp the disease MMA has largely been described as a clinical entity characterized by a degree of lactational failure or agalactia also associated with signs of anorexia, stiffness, fever, swollen mammary glands and a vaginal discharge. Infertility has not been described following this MMA syndrome. The postpartum vaginal discharge is often not associated with a uterine infection. **Mycoplasma hyogenitalium** cannot be incriminated nor is it reproducible as a cause of MMA. A variety of infections may be found in the mammary glands. Thurman and Simon, Ross et al., and Martin have recently reported on this syndrome. **E. coli** and actinobacillus were recovered from the glands more frequently than streptococci or staphylococci. Acute endometritis and mastitis were noted histologically. Martin noted that sows often recovered after intrauterine and parenteral antibiotic injections. Martin in his review suggested the possibility of an **E. coli** toxemia as MMA often is associated with digestive signs and constipation. Bran and/or molasses has been suggested to be fed in large amounts before and after farrowing. He also suggested it might be an "adaptation" disease. The syndrome is not reproducible experimentally. More study of the MMA syndrome is indicated.

Specific Infections of the Genital Tract causing sterility in swine include brucellosis caused by **Brucella suis.** The uterine lesions of brucellosis in swine are well described by Thomsen. Hutchings reported that often the only recognized symptom of brucellosis in swine is an increased incidence of sterility. He reported that in one brucella-infected herd 37 of the first 100 sows bred failed to conceive. Eight naturally-infected sows studied over a 2-year period farrowed only 14 litters, even though bred for 2 litters a year. Of the 129 pigs born in these 14 litters, 44 were stillborn and 17 were weak and died within 2 days of birth, a loss of nearly 50 percent. In another herd, having 80 percent reactors to the brucellosis test and much sterility, 3 gilts were slaughtered; all had a purulent cervicitis and metritis from which **Br. suis** was recovered. Warnick and co-workers reported that in "repeat breeding", brucella-positive, female swine the incidence of embryonic death was 87.5 percent as compared with an incidence of 46.5 percent in brucella-negative females. Vandeplassche reported that when sows infected with Brucella were serviced by a fertile boar the pregnancy rate was only 35 percent compared to 90 percent in uninfected gilts. This infertility was due to macroscopic and microscopic lesions of the endometrium causing early embryonic deaths with prolonged periods between heats. When sterility is a problem in a herd of swine, the brucellosis status of the herd should be determined.

Fennestad and co-workers reported on a boar with **Staph. aureus** infection of the seminal vesicles that bred 18 females and only 4 conceived, 3 conceived subsequently to another boar, 3 were sold as sterile, and the remaining 8 sows developed an acute metritis with a vaginal discharge. Two of these 8 sows were rebred later and aborted. On postmorten all showed a chronic metritis resembling that due to brucellosis. There is no evidence that leptospirosis causes sterility in swine, even though there is much evidence that it may cause abortions. Young and Dunne reported on the high incidence of defective pigs and early embryos and mummified fetuses, in nonimmune sows vaccinated against hog cholera with the modified virus vaccines 10 to 16 days after conception. Other viruses described under mummified fetuses in Chapter III including SMEDI or picorna viruses, Ajueszky's disease (Herpes) virus, and several other viruses described in Japan will cause prenatal mortality, Dunne, and Dunne et al..

Hutyra, Marek, and Manninger, as well as Williams, stated that coital vesicular exanthema, or vesicular venereal disease, may in rare cases affect the caudal portion of the genital tract of sows and gilts. This has not been described, and if present is probably rare, in the United States.

Wilson and co-workers reported on several cases of a ruptured cul-de-sac of the cranial and lateral portion of the vulva. These lesions were apparently caused by penetration of the vulvar mucosa by the penis. They were inflamed bulb-like structures containing coagulated blood. Intromission was apparently painful and was resented. In many instances the affected females, even though in estrum, would often refuse to accept the boar. Sometimes the female would have a normal service followed by evidence of pain at subsequent services. These lesions did not cause permanent sterility and did not affect the more cranial portions of the genital tract.

Vulvovaginitis, characterized by swelling of the vulva with a mucus discharge, enlarged mammary glands and occasional prolapse of the rectum has been described in a previous chapter. This condition is due to the feeding of moldy corn or barley in which estrogenic compounds were apparently present. Griel et al. reported swollen, reddened vulvas in pigs consuming a poultry feed containing dienestrol. These animals exhibited estrous behavior. Stob et al. and Kurtz et al. reported on the isolation of a mycotoxin from **F. graminearum (Gibberella zea)** that caused vulvovaginitis, vaginal prolapse, perineal relaxation and ovarian atrophy in young gilts. Squamous metaplasia of the mucosa of the vagina and cervix was observed histologically. The action of the mycotoxin was identical to estradiol.

Hormonal or Endocrine Disturbances are described by Nalbandov as being responsible for about 4 percent of the infertility in female swine or 20 to 50 percent of infertile sows. This is the second most common cause of infertility in swine. Perry and Pomeroy reported a 24 percent incidence of cystic ovaries in 821 sows and 83 or 10 percent of these sows were sterile. Nalbandov reported that occasional ovarian cysts were found in all stages of pregnancy, as well as in nonpregnant sows and gilts. In pregnant sows, cysts apparently developed after conception inasmuch as ovulation in nonpregnant, cystic females rarely, if ever, occurred. The presence of these cysts in pregnant sows was not related to litter size and did not interfere with gestation Estrus and service may occur during pregnancy in sows possibly associated with the development of follicles. Cystic ovaries in pregnant female swine could invariably be produced by a single injection of 200 to 400 I.U. of PMS. Perry and Pomeroy did not observe cysts on ovaries in pregnant sows. They noted about twice as many cysts, 35 percent, during the spring months as in the fall months, 15 percent.

Wiggins and co-workers reported the incidence of cystic follicles in ovaries with corpora lutea at 1.1 percent and cystic follicles alone at 0.6 percent of 5088 female swine. Goethals reported that 8, or 1.4 percent, of 578 cases of complete sterility in female swine were due to ovarian cysts or tubal abnormalities. Wilson and co-workers reported cystic ovaries with corpora lutea in 7.6 percent and with no corpora lutea in 2.5 percent of 79 infertile or sterile sows. Warnick and co-workers reported 6.4 percent cystic ovaries with corpora lutea and 3.2 percent cystic ovaries with no corpora lutea in 63 "repeat breeding" sows.

Cystic ovaries in nonpregnant swine were of 3 types—single cysts, multiple, large cysts, and multiple, small cysts, Nalbandov. **Single cysts** were found in 2 percent of 1751 pairs of ovaries. In these cases only 1 or 2 cysts were present on the ovary. They were 2 to 3 cm in diameter, whereas a normal follicle is only .7 to .9 cm in diameter. The reproductive tract and behavior of these female swine were normal. These single cysts were found during the luteal phase of the cycle with normal corpora lutea present. Nalbandov reported that these were probably atretic follicles that failed to rupture when ovulation occurred and were not associated with sterility.

Multiple cysts were always associated with permanent or temporary sterility. Three to 4 percent of nonpregnant females were affected. Usually both ovaries were affected. It is usually impossible to differentiate clinically between sows with large or small multiple cysts as estrous cycles in both are irregular and characterized by anestrous periods of varying lengths.

Large multiple luteal cysts were most common. These measured 2 to 10 cm in diameter and an average of 5.6 cysts were present on each ovary. Thus the number of these cysts was nearly the same as the normal number of follicles. The walls of these large cysts were either heavily luteinized or contained lutein patches. The uterine endometrium in these cases showed progestational changes. The external symptoms manifested by these sows were extreme irregularity of the estrual cycle with intervals of 2 to 90 days between estrous periods. The heats were of greater intensity but of the same duration as those in normal noncystic females. In 60 percent of the affected female swine the clitoris was larger and longer up to 1 to 2 cm in length, than the clitoris of normal females that is 1 to 2 mm in length. The amount of estrogen present in these large cysts was less than in normal ovarian follicles. Androgens were not present. Although progesterone was present, the amount could not be measured. It was believed that progesterone, or progesterone converted into androgens, was the probable cause of the enlarged clitoris. There was no significant difference between the gonadotropic activity of the hypophysis in cystic and noncystic sows. There was a small but significant rise in the thyrotropic hormone content of the pituitary. Further work must be done to prove whether or not this condition of multiple cysts is associated with hyperthyroidism. In sows with large cysts given injections of L.H., neither ovulation or further luteinization of the cysts resulted. This does not mean that L.H. deficiency might not be the cause of the condition, as the animals treated had been affected for a long period, Nalbandov. Perry and Pomeroy also observed a few cystic C.L. that developed after ovulation.

Small multiple follicular cysts were observed only occasionally. They resembled a cluster of grapes and were always present in numbers exceeding the number of follicles found normally. These cysts were about 1 cm in diameter. An average of 22.5 small cysts per ovary was reported by Nalbandov. The walls of these small cysts were lined by normal granulosa cells. The uterus showed an estrogenic type of endometrium and the clitoris was not enlarged. These animals showed marked irregularities in the length of the estrual cycle. Symptoms of estrum were intense, similar to the symptoms produced by the larger cysts. In neither large nor small multiple cysts was nymphomania, or continuous estrum, observed. These small cysts were found to be as rich in estrogen per unit weight as the normal follicles, but because of the large number of small cysts the total concentration of estrogen was 4 to 5 times that of the normal ovary just before ovulation and several hundred times that of sows affected with large luteal cysts. The pituitary assays showed no increase in gonadotropic hormones over that seen in normal sows but the thyrotropic hormone was slightly increased over that occurring in sows with large cysts. A single injection of 250 to 400 of P.M.S. always produced cystic ovaries in nonpregnant swine but the cysts never reached the size of large luteal cysts.

Thus it appeared that multiple cysts may be due to lack of luteinizing hormone necessary to cause ovulation and corpus luteum formation. It is doubtful that sows once they develop cystic ovaries recover spontaneously, Perry and Pomeroy. Whether there is a genetic basis or cause for cysts in sows as in cows is not known. Further work is required to determine the actual cause and possible therapy of cystic ovaries in swine.

Porcine ovarian abnormalities other than cysts include: ovotestes in hermaphrodites, ovarian abscesses, rare parovarian cysts, and aplastic or missing ovaries, Perry and Pomeroy.

Anestrum and the Production and Synchronization of Estrum in Female Swine. The production and synchronization of estrum in swine have been discussed earlier in this chapter and in chapters XII and XIX. Anestrus in swine is usually due to postweaning anestrus in sows or delayed puberty in gilts. Rasbech reported on treating 1655 female swine with gonadotropes and estrogens to produce estrum. The best results in inducing estrum and normal conceptions were with pregnant mare serum and HCG. Poorer results were obtained with chorionic gonadotropin and estradiol. The poorest results were obtained with stilbestrol alone, especially with the higher doses of 15 to 30 mg. Even 5- to 15-mg doses produced undesired effects. The injection of stilbestrol produced estrum at frequent irregular intervals in 30.3 percent of female swine and caused symptoms of estrum associated with normal cycles to disappear in 27.4 percent of the animals. These poor results with estrogens, diethylstilbestrol and estradiol, in the treatment of anestrum were also reported by First and Day. These adverse effects were due to prolonging the life of corpora lutea by the estrogens resulting in some cases in an actual delay in the onset of estrum. Estrogens are contraindicated for anestrus in female swine. The use of HCG, or LH, or PMS, or FSH, may produce varying results depending upon the dosage and the phase of the cycle at the time they are administered. The results of using 500 to 1500 I.U. of P.M.S. intramuscularly were most satisfactory for the treatment of anestrus. Rasbech reported that 8 to 9 percent of female swine were treated for anestrus in Denmark with LH and FSH. Dzuik and Dhindsa reported on 126 gilts that had failed to show estrum by 9 months of age and were given 500 I.U. of P.M.S. Ninety-five or 75 percent, of the gilts were in estrum 4 to 5 days after the injection and 67 percent conceived. Paredis studied 63 anestrous gilts over 7 months of age and 28 sows that failed to show estrum within 5 weeks of weaning. On laparotomy less than 10 percent of the gilts and more than 40 percent of the sows had corpora lutea indicating the presence of an estrous cycle. After the stress of transporting the gilts to the study center and changing their environment 68 percent of the gilts and 25 percent of the sows came into estrum within 10 days. Daughters of late maturing gilts were also late maturing so a genetic factor was involved in this type of anestrus that might be susceptible to improvement by selection for early puberty. Kudlac reported on the highly successful treatment of anestrus in sows using PMS. He indicated that the longer the period of anestrus the poorer were the results of treatment. Wilson et al. and others have reported on rare cases of infantile or hypoplastic ovaries and genital tracts in well-grown gilts. Besides a careful physical examination, Adams suggested obtaining a good history and examining several anestrous sows from a herd at slaughter as an aid in diagnosis.

Repeat Breeders in Female Swine, as in other animals, are also caused by high embryonic death rates and low fertilization rates. These are also causes for reduced litter size. Baker et al. reported that embryonic death was of more importance than was the ovulation rate in controlling litter size in swine. Wiggins and co-workers, Nalbandov, and others reported between 10 to 25 percent of sows and gilts fail to conceive. In these sterile swine, gross abnormalities of the reproductive tract were the cause of sterility in 25 to 50 percent of the gilts and 25 percent of the sows. In the rest of the sterile females there was no apparent cause for the failure of fertilization or early embryonic deaths. Failure of reproduction due to embryonic deaths appeared less common in gilts than in sows.

Warnick and co-workers, in an experiment modeled after those made on "repeat breeding" cattle, assembled 63 "repeat breeding" female swine. These had previously been bred 2 to 4 times without conceiving. They represented 5 breeds and included both gilts and sows. Part of the 63 were killed 4 days after service to a fertile boar and the rest were killed at 25 days. Those that came in estrum again before 25 days were rebred and killed 4 days later. Gross abnormalities were found in 63.7 percent of the gilts and 31.6 percent of the sows. Some of these were unilateral and permitted conception. In the percentage of reactors to the blood test for brucellosis there was no significant difference between either the gilts and the sows, or between those with gross abnormalities and those with no gross abnormalities. The difference in percentage of fertilized ova between brucella-positive and brucella-negative animals was not significant but the incidence of embryonic death was 87.5 percent in the positive animals, and 46.5 percent in the negative animals. This experiment showed the importance of brucellosis in sterility in swine. These workers concluded that "repeat breeding" was due to failure of fertilization in 53.4 percent of the gilts and 32.6 percent of the sows. Gross abnormalities accounted for failure of fertilization in 50 percent of the gilts and 15.8 percent of the sows. Thus unaccountable failures of fertilization occurred in 3.4 percent of the gilts and 16.8 percent of the sows. Embryonic death caused "repeat breeding" in 23.9 percent of the gilts and 67.4 percent of the sows. "Repeat breeding" swine with normal embryos 25 days after the one additional breeding included 22.7 percent of the gilts and none of the sows. Therefore, the major cause of "repeat breeding" in gilts was genital abnormalities causing failure of fertilization. In sows the major cause of "repeat breeding" was embryonic deaths.

Wilson and co-workers assembled 79 "repeat breeding" sows and gilts that had been bred 3 to 10 times previously. After having been bred to a fertile boar on the first estrum, 53.2 percent conceived. They considered that this high conception rate in infertile females may have been due to breeding an average of 3.9 times per estrum as compared to only 1.4 times per estrum previously. There was some indication that these animals might have ovulated early. In a later publication, Nalbandov indicated that failure of conception in this group of female swine might have been due to delayed ovulation with faulty synchronization between estrum and ovulation. Wilson and co-workers concluded that only 5 to 10 percent of their animals could be considered to have experienced embryonic deaths. This is in marked contrast to the 20- to 70-percent rate of embryonic deaths reported by Warnick and co-workers. This is interesting in light of the fact that Wilson and his co-workers eliminated all brucella-positive females from their experiment. Nalbandov, in commenting later on Wilson and his co-workers' experiment, noted that the 5 to 10 percent of the animals exhibiting extreme embryonic mortality were apparently fertile but that a reduction in litter size had occurred soon after implantation. Some of these losses were probably due to segmental aplasia and defects of the uterine horns and genital tract resulting in early and complete loss of embryos.

Paredis showed that repeat breeders could also be due to poor management and infertile boars. Of 75 female "repeat breeding" swine brought to the study center and bred the next heat to a fertile boar, 49 females conceived on that service. The conception rate experienced by "travelling" boars on first service was 62 percent for gilts and 56 percent for sows; in herds using their own breeding boars the respective percentages were 82 and 77. The lower conception rate in "travelling" boars may have been due to overuse, the presence of genital infections, or poor timing of services.

Tumors of the genital tract in female swine are rare, possibly because most swine are slaughtered at a relatively young age. Feldman has described leiomyomas and a fibroma of the uterus in sows and one case in which a lymphoblastoma involved one ovary. The author has observed a 5 × 3 × 2 inch hamartoma on the ovary of a sow. Moulton described a rare teratoma of the porcine ovary. Cotchin reported a rare carcinoma and a lymphoid tumor of the mammary gland. Monlux et al. reported on embryonal nephromas and sarcomas of the vagina and cervix. Nelson et al. found 2 hemangiomas, a papillary cystadenoma and a granulosa cell tumor of swine ovaries. They also cited other reports on ovarian cystadenomas, sarcomas, teratomas and a fibroma.

Nutrition may have a definite effect on fertility in female swine. Except for a few important differences, the same general principles apply to swine as to the other farm animals. As in all animals, inanition due to a low plane of nutrition in swine results in a delay in the onset of puberty, and failure of estrum, or irregular estrum after weaning. The detrimental effects on embryonic survival of overfeeding and a high energy intake immediately after breeding have been discussed. The beneficial effects of a temporary high plane of nutrition to promote early puberty and a high ovulation rate have also been described. Gilts on a protein-free diet failed to cycle normally or conceive, Adams et al.. Davidson reported that a protein deficiency acute enough to cause severe retardation of growth in sows did not affect the incidence of fetal atrophy.

Hale, Bendixen, and Bauer reported the presence in newborn swine of embryonic defects and abnormalities caused by a vitamin-A deficiency in sows during early pregnancy. These anomalies included eye defects or the absence of eyes. Reid cited evidence to indicate that deficiencies of vitamin E, C, B complex, and D are seldom, if ever, the cause of infertility in the sow or other farm animals. He failed to report any evidence to show that phosphorus-deficiency occurred in swine or was a cause of reproductive disturbances. Unless the plane of nutrition is very low, in which case disturbances of reproduction may develop, most sows are fed enough grain and protein to provide sufficient phosphorus.

Apparently swine are the only farm animals in which a deficiency of calcium may affect reproduction. Davidson reported that sows developing a severe calcium deficiency had a tendency toward an increase in fetal atrophy and stillbirths. This, however, became severe in deficient sows only in succeeding litters. Other nutritive deficiencies may have been present also, Reid. Estrum and conception occurred in calcium-deficient sows even when severe "rickets" and temporary paralysis were present. Plumlee et al. reported that pigs fed 0.5 ppm manganese in an experimental ration developed irregular estrous cycles, absence of estrus in some pigs and resorption of fetuses. Trapp et al. noted that some swine herds with a deficiency of Vitamin E and selenium had problems with infertility and spraddle-legged newborn pigs. These conditions improved greatly when supplements were fed.

References

General

Asdell, S. A. (1964) Patterns of Mammalian Reproduction, 2nd Ed., Cornell Univ. Press, Ithaca, N.Y.

Cole, H. H. and Cupps, P. T. (1969) Reproduction in Domestic Animals, 2nd Ed., Academic Press, N.Y.C.

Dukes, H. H. (1947) The Physiology of Domestic Animals, 6th Ed., Comstock Publishing Co., Inc., Ithaca, N. Y.

Dunne, H. W. (1964) Disease of Swine, Iowa State Univ. Press, Ames, Iowa.

Hafez, E. S. E. (1968) Reproduction in Farm Animals, Lea and Febiger, Philadelphia, Pa.

McDonald, L. E. (1969) Veterinary Endocrinology and Reproduction, Lea and Febiger, Philadelphia, Pa.

Nalbandov, A. V. (1964) Reproductive Physiology, 2nd Ed., W. H. Freeman and Co., San Francisco, Calif.

Williams, W. L. (1943) Diseases of the Genital Organs of Domestic Animals, 3rd Ed., Miss Louella Williams, Upland Rd., Ithaca,

Specific—

Adams, C. R., Becker, D. E., Terrill, S. W., Norton, H. W. and Jensen, A. H. (1960) Rate of Ovulation and Implantation in Swine as Affected by Dietary Protein, J. An. Sci. **19,** 4, 1245.

Adams, W. W. (1970) Hormonal and Anatomical Causes of Infertility, Colloquium on **Effect of Diseases and Stress on Reproductive Efficiency on Swine,** Iowa State Univ., June.

Akins, E. L. and Morrissette. M. C. (1968) Gross Ovarian Changes During the Estrous Cycle of Swine, Amer. J. Vet. Res. **29,** 10, 1953.

Anderson, L. L. (1966) Pituitary-Ovarian Relationships in Pigs, J. Reprod. and Fert. Suppl. I, 21.

Armstrong, C. H. (1970) Bacterial Flora of the Porcine Uterus, Colloquium on **Effect of Diseases and Stress on Reproductive Efficiency on Swine,** Iowa State Univ., June

Asdell, S. A. and Willman, J. P. (1941) The Causes of Stillbirth in Swine and an Attempt to Control It, J. Agr. Res., **63,** 345.

Baker, L. N., Ulberg, L. C., Grummer, R. H. and Casida, L. E. (1954) Inhibition of Heat by Progesterone and Its Effect on Subsequent Fertility in Gilts, J. of An. Sci., **13,** 3. 648.

Baker, L. N., Woehling, H. L., Casida, L. E. and Grummer, R. H. (1953) Occurrence of Estrus in Sows Following Parturition, J. of An. Sci., **12,** 1, 33.

Bauer, H. R. (1950) Piglet Mortality and Blind-Born Piglets Due to Avitaminosis of Vitamin A (Trans.), Tierarztl. Umschau., **5,** 366.

Bazer, F. W., Robison, O. W., Clawson, A. J. and Ulberg, L. C. (1969) Uterine Capacity at Two Stages of Gestation in Gilts Following Embryo Superinduction, J. An. Sci. **29.** 1, 30.

Becker, Neil (1970) Field Problems in Fertility in Swine, in Colloquium on **Effect of Diseases and Stress on Reproductive Efficiency on Swine.** Iowa State Univ., June.

Bendixen, H. C. (1944) Littery Occurrence of Anophthalmia or Microophthalmia together with other Malformations in Swine —Presumably Due to Vitamin A Deficiency of the Maternal Diet in the First Stage of Pregnancy and the Preceding Period, Acta. Pathol. et Microbiol. Scand. Suppl. No. **54,** 161.

Bereskin, B., Shelby, C. E., Rowe, K. E., Kempel, W. E., Dettmers, A. E. and Norton, H. W. (1970) Inbreeding and Swine Productivity in Minnesota Experimental Herds, J. An. Sci. **31,** 2, 278.

Boender, J. (1966) The Development of AI in Pigs in the Netherlands and the Storage of Boar Semen, World Review of An. Prod. II, 29 (Special Issue).

Bomsel-Helmreich, O. (1961) Experimental Heteroploidy in Sows, Proc. IV Internat. Congr. on An. Reprod., The Hague, Vol. III, 579.

Boyland, W. J., Rempel, W. E. and Comstock, R. E. (1961) Heritability of Litter Size in Swine, J. An. Sci. **20,** 3, 566.

Casida, L. E. (1953) Prenatal Death as a Factor in the Fertility of Farm Animals, Iowa State Col. J. of Sci., **28,** 1, 119.

Casida, L. E. (1964) Some Side-Effects and After-Effects of Experimental Endocrine Treatments Used to Modify the Natural Estrual Rhythm, Proc. of Conference on Estrous Cycle Control in Domestic Animals, Univ. of Nebraska, Lincoln, Nebr., July.

Christian, R. E. and Nofziger, J. C. (1952) Puberty and other Reproductive Phenomena in Gilts as Affected by the Plane of Nutrition, J. of An. Sci., **11,** 789.

Cole, H. H. and Hughes, E. H. (1946) Induction of Estrus in Lactating Sows with Equine Gonadotropin, J. of An. Sci., **5,** 1, 25.

Christensen, R. K., Pope, C. E., Zimmerman, A. and Day, B. N (1970) Synchronization of Ovulation in Superovulated Gilts, J. An. Sci. **31,** 1, 219.

Cotchin, E. (1956) Neoplasms of the Domesticated Mammals (A Review), Review Series No. 4, Commonwealth Bureau of An. Health, Bucks, England.

Craig, J. V., Norton, H. W., Rio P. R. and Lasley, J. P. (1955) The Effect of Day and Frequency of Mating on Conception Rate and Litter Size in Swine, J. An. Sci. **14,** 4, 1178.

David, J. S. E. (1970) Reproductive Expectancy and Management Factors, Proc. Internat. Conference on Cattle Diseases, Philadelphia, Pa.

Davidson, H. R. (1930) Reproductive Disturbances Caused by Feeding Protein-Deficient and Calcium-Deficient Rations to Breeding Pigs, J. Agr. Sci., **20,** 233.

Davis, J. W. and Thomas, H R. (1966) The Use of Gallimycin Injectable, Erythromycin and Furacin Water Mix in a Problem Herd of S.P.F. Sows, Vet. Med. **61,** 1, 58.

Day, B. N. (1966) Control of Estrus and Ovulation in Swine, Mimeographed Material, Univ. of Ill. Veterinarians' Workshop.

Day, B. N. (1967) Artificial Insemination and Ovulation Control in Swine, Notes, Proc. Amer. Vet. Soc. for Study of Breeding Soundness, Univ. of Mo., Columbia, Mo.

Day, B. N. (1968) Reproduction in Swine, in **Reproduction in Farm Animals,** 2nd Ed. by E. S E. Hafez, Lea and Febiger, Philadelphia, Pa.

Day, B. N., Anderson, L. L., Emmerson, M. A., Hazel, L. N. and Melampy, R. M. (1959) Effect of Estrogen and Progesterone on Early Embryonic Mortality in Ovariectomized Gilts, J. An. Sci. **18,** 2, 607.

Day, B. N., Anderson, L. L., Hazel, L. N. and Melampy, R. M. (1959) Synchronization of Estrus and Ovulation in Swine, J. An. Sci. **18,** 3, 909.

Day, B. N., Neill, J. D., Oxenreider, S. L., Waite, A. B. and Lasley, J. F. (1965) Use of Gonadotropins to Synchronize Estrous Cycles in Swine, J. An. Sci. **24,** 4, 1075.

Day, B. N., Romack, F. E. and Lasley, J. F. (1963) Influence of Progesterone-Estrogen Implants on Early Embryonic Mortality in Swine, J. An. Sci. **22,** 3, 637.

Dean, B. T. and Tribble, L. F. (1962) Effect of Feeding a Therapeutic Level of Antibiotic at Breeding on Reproductive Performance in Swine, J. An. Sci. **21,** 2, 207.

Dhindsa, D. S. and Dzuik, P. J. (1967) Partial Doubling of the Uterine Horns in the Gilt, Vet. Med. **62,** 9, 900.

Dhindsa, D. S. and Dzuik, P. J. (1968) Effect on Pregnancy in the Pig After Killing Embryos or Fetuses in One Uterine Horn in Early Gestation, J. An. Sci. **27,** 1, 122.

Dhindsa, D. S. and Dzuik, P. J. (1968) Influence of Varying the Proportion of Uterus Occupied by Embryos on the Maintenance of Pregnancy in the Pig, J. An. Sci. **27,** 3, 668.

Dunne, H. W., Gobble, J. L., Hokanson, J. F., Kradel, D. C. and Bubash, G. R. (1965) Porcine Reproductive Failure Associated with a Newly Identified "SMEDI" Group of Picorna Viruses, Amer. J. Vet. Res. **26,** 115, 1284.

Dzuik, P. J. (1960) Influence of Orally Administered Progestins on Estrus and Ovulation in Swine, J. An. Sci. **19,** 4, 1319.

Dzuik, P. J. (1968) Effect of Number of Embryos and Uterine Space on Embryo Survival in the Pig, J. An. Sci. **27,** 3, 673.

Dzuik, P. J. and Dhindsa, D. S. (1969) Induction of Heat, Ovulation and Fertility in Gilts with Delayed Puberty, J. An. Sci. **29,** 1, 39.

Dzuik, P. J., Polge, C. and Rowson, L. E. (1964) Intrauterine Migration and Mixing of Embryos in Swine Following Egg Transfer, J. An. Sci. **23,** 1, 37.

Edwards, R. L., Omtvedt, I. T., Turman, E. J., Stephens, D. F. and Mahoney, G. W. A. (1968) Reproductive Performance of Gilts Following Heat Stress Prior to Breeding and in Early Gestation, J. An. Sci. **27,** 6, 1634.

England, D. C. and Chapman, V M. (1962) Relationship of Ovulation Rate and Embryo Survival to Litter Size in Swine, J. An. Sci. **21,** 3, 671.

Erb, R. E., Nofziger, J. C., Stormshak, F. and Johnson, J. B. (1962) Progesterone in Corpora Lutea, Ovaries and Adrenals of Pregnant Sows and Its Relationship to Number of Implants, J. An. Sci. **21,** 3, 562.

Feldman, Wm. H. (1932) Neoplasms of Domestic Animals, W. B. Saunders, Co., Phila, Pa.

Fennestad, K. L., Pedersen, P. S. and Moller, T. (1955) **Staphylococcus Aureus** as a Cause of Reproductive Failure and so-called Actinomycosis in Swine, Nord. Vet. Med., **7,** 11, 929.

Fenton, F. R., Bazer, F. W., Robison, O. W. and Ulberg, L. C. (1970) Effect of Quantity of Uterus on Uterine Capacity in Gilts, J. An. Sci. **31,** 1, 104.

First, N. L. (1970) Factors Affecting Sperm Survival and Fertility, Colloquium, **Effect of Diseases and Stress on Reproductive Efficiency on Swine,** Iowa State Univ., June.

First, N. L., Short, R. E., Peters, J. B. and Stratman, F. W. (1968) Transport of Boar Spermatozoa in Estrual or Luteal Sows, J. An. Sci. **27,** 4, 1032.

First, N. L., Short, R. E., Peters, J. B. and Stratman, F. W. (1968) Transport and Loss of Boar Spermatozoa in the Reproductive Tract of the Sow, J. An. Sci. **27,** 4, 1037.

First, N. L., Stratman, F. W. and Casida, L. E. (1963) Effect of Sperm Age on Embryo Survival in Swine, J. An. Sci. **22,** 1, 135.

First, N. L., Stratman, F. W., Rigor, E. M. and Casida, L. E. (1963) Factors Affecting Ovulation and Follicular Cyst Formation in Sows and Gilts Fed 6-Methyl-17 Acetoxyprogesterone (Provera), J. An. Sci. **22,** 1, 66.

Fox, M. W. (1968) Abnormal Behavior in Animals, W. B. Saunders, Co., Philadelphia, Pa.

Fraser, A. F. (1968) Reproductive Behavior in Ungulates, Academic Press, N.Y.C.

Gardner, M. L., First, N. L. and Casida, L. E. (1963) Effect of Exogenous Estrogen on Corpus Luteum Maintenance in Gilts, J. An. Sci. **22,** 1, 132.

Gerrits, R. J., Krehbill, E. V. and Kincaid, C. M. (1966) Synchronization of Estrus and Reproductive Performance of Gilts Fed ICI 33828, J. An. Sci. **25,** 3, 923.

Ginther, O. J. (1968) Utero-Ovarian Relationships in Cattle: Applied Veterinary Aspects, J.A.V.M.A. **153,** 12, 1665.

Goethals, P. (1951) Studies on the Sexual Organs of Sows with Reference to Sterility and Reduced Fertility (Trans.), Vlaams Diergeneesk Tijdschr., **20,** 155.

Gomes, W. R., Herschler, R. C. and Erb, R. E. (1965) Progesterone Levels in Ovarian Venous Effluent of the Nonpregnant Sow, J. An. Sci. **24,** 3, 722.

Griel, L. C. Jr., Kradel, D. C. and Wickersham, E. Q. (1969) Abortion in Cattle Associated with the Feeding of Poultry Litter, Cor. Vet. **59,** 2, 226.

Grummer, R. H. and Self, H. L. (1955) Pig Nutrition and Sow Reproductive Phenomena Associated with Early Weaning, J. An. Sci. **14,** 4, 1245.

Hafez, E. S. E. (1969) The Behavior of Domestic Animals, 2nd Ed., Williams and Wilkins Co., Baltimore, Md.

Haines, C. E., Warnick, A. C. and Wallace, H. D. (1955) The Effect of Two Levels of Energy Intake in Gilts on Puberty, Ovulation, Fertilization, Embryonic Survival and Pigs Born, J. of An. Sci., **14,** 4, 1246.

Hale, (1935) The Relation of Vitamin A to Anophthalmos in Pigs, Am. J. Opthal., **18,** 1087.

Hammond, J. (1921) Further Observations on the Factors Controlling Fertility and Fetal Atrophy, J. Agr. Sci., **11,** 337.

Hancock, J. L. and Hovell, G. J. R. (1962) Insemination Before and After the Onset of Heat in Sows, An. Prod. **4,** 91.

Hansel, W. (1959) Female Infertility in Domestic Animals, Fert. and Steril. **10,** 5, 502.

Heitman, H. and Cole, H. H. (1956) Further Studies on the Induction of Estrus in Lactating Sows with Equine Gonadotropin, J. An. Sci. **15,** 4, 952.

Holden, P., Lucas, E., Speer, V. C., Hayes, V. W. and Ewan, R. C. (1967) Long Term Effects of Protein Level on Swine Reproduction, J. An. Sci. **26,** 1478.

Hunter, R. H. F. (1967) Effect of Aging Eggs on Embryonic Survival in Pigs, J. An. Sci. **26,** 4, 945.

Hunter, R. H. F. (1967) Porcine Ovulation after Injection of Human Chorionic Gonadotropin, Vet. Rec. **81,** 1, 21.

Hutchings, L. M. (1948) Sterility in Swine, J.A.V M.A., **112,** 851, 114.

Hutyra, F. Marek, J. and Manninger, R. (1946) Special Pathology and Therapeutics of the Diseases of Domestic Animals, Vol. I., Alex. Eger, Inc., Chicago, Ill.

Ito, S., Kudo, A. and Niwa, T. (1959) Studies on the Normal Oestrus in Swine with Special Reference to Proper Time for Service, Biol. Abstr. **35,** (9), #24424.

King, G. J. (1969) Deformities in Piglets Following Administration of **Methallibure** During Specific Stages of Gestation, J. Reprod. and Fert., **20,** 551.

Kirkpatrick, R. L., Howland, B. E., First, N. L. and Casida, L. E. (1967) Some Characteristics Associated with Feed and Breed Differences in Ovulation Rate in the Gilt, J. An. Sci., **26,** 1, 188.

Kirkpatrick, R. L., Howland, B. E., First, N. L. and Casida, L. E. (1967) Ovarian and Pituitary Gland Changes in Gilts on Two Nutrient Energy Levels, J. An. Sci., **26,** 2, 358.

Kurtz, H. J., Nairn, M. E., Nelson, G. H., Christensen, C. M. and Minocha, C. J. (1969) Histologic Changes in the Genital Tracts of Swine Fed Estrogenic Mycotoxin, Amer. J. Vet. Res. **30,** 4, 551.

Kudlac, E. (1961) Erhohung Der Fruchtbarkeit von Sauen Durch Das Serum Trachtiger Stuten (PMS), Proc. IV Internat. Congr. on Animal Reproduction, The Hague, 662.

Lasley, J. R., Day, B. N. and Mayer, D. T. (1963) Intrauterine Migration and Embryonic Death in Swine, J. An. Sci. **22,** 2, 422.

Longnecker, D. E. and Day, B. N. (1968) Fertility Level of Sows Superovulated at Post-Weaning Estrus, J. An. Sci. **27,** 3, 709.

Longnecker, D. E., Lasley, J. F. and Day, B. N. (1965) Fecundity in Gilts and Sows Administered PMS, J. An. Sci., **24,** 3, 924.

Martin, C. E. (1969) Lactation Failure (MMA) in the Sow, Proc. of Conference on Reprod. Problems in Animals, Univ. of Georgia, Nov., 56.

Martin, J. E. (1964) Physiology, in **Diseases of Swine,** 2nd Ed. H. W. Dunne., Iowa State Univ. Press, Ames, Iowa.

McFeely, R. A. (1966) Chromosome Abnormalities in Early Embryos of the Pig, J. Reprod. and Fert. **13,** 579.

McFeely, R. A. (1968) Chromosomes and Infertility, J.A.V.M.A. **153,** 12, 1672.

McLaren, A. (1966) Advances in Reproductive Physiology. Vol. I., Academic Press, N.Y.C.

McPhee, H. C. and Zeller, J. H. (1934) The Still Born Pig, J.A.V.M.A. **85,** 224.

Messersmith, R. E., Johnson, D. D., Elliott, R. F. and Drain, J. J. (1966) Value of Chlortetracycline in Breeding Rations for Sows, J. An. Sci., **25,** 3, 752.

Monlux, A. W., Anderson, W. A. and Davis, C. L. (1956) A Survey of Tumors Occurring in Cattle, Sheep and Swine, Amer. J. Vet. Res. **17,** 65, 646.

Morris, P. G. D. (1954) An Unusual Case in Swine of Uterus Didelphys, Brit. Vet. J., **110,** 205.

Moulton, J. E. (1961) Tumors of Domestic Animals, Univ. of Calif. Press, Berkeley, Cal.

Nalbandov, A. V. (1950) Problems in Swine Reproduction, Vet. Med., **45,** 12, 477.

Nalbandov, A. V. (1952) Anatomic or Endocrine Causes of Sterility in Female Swine, Fert. and Steril., **3,** 2, 100.

Nalbandov, A. V. (1953) Gonadotrophic Activity of Pituitary Glands and the Induction of Ovulation, Iowa State Col. J. of Sci., **28,** 1, 45.

Nalbandov, A. V. (1969) Tubal Abnormalities, in **The Mammalian Oviduct; Comparative Biology and Methodology** by E. S. E. Hafez and R. J. Blandau, Univ. of Chicago Press, Chicago, Ill.

Nellor, J. E., Ahrenhold, J. E., First, N. L. and Hoefer, J. A. (1960) Estrus, Ovulation and Fertility in Gilts Subsequent to the Oral Administration of 6-Methyl-17 Acetoxyprogesterone, J. An. Sci., **19,** 4, 133.

Nellor, J. E., Ahrenhold, J. E., First, N. L. and Hoefer, J. A. (1961) Estrus, Ovulation and Fertility in Gilts Subsequent to the Oral

Administration of 6-Methyl-17-Acetoxyprogesterone, J. An. Sci., **20,** 1, 22.

Nelson, L. W., Todd, G. C. and Migaki, G. (1967) Ovarian Neoplasms in Swine, J.A.V.M.A. **151,** 10, 1331.

Niswender, G. D., Dzuik, P. J., Kaltenbach, C. C. and Norton, H. W. (1970) Local Effects of Embryos and the Uterus on Corpora Lutea in Gilts, J. An. Sci. **30,** 2, 225.

O'Bannon, R. H., Wallace, H. D., Warnick, A. C. and Combs, G. E. (1966) Influence of Energy Intake on Reproductive Performance of Gilts, J. An. Sci., **25,** 3, 706.

Oxenreider, S. L. and Day, B. N. (1965) Transport and Cleavage of Ova in Swine, J. An. Sci., **24,** 2, 413.

Palmer, W. M., Teague, H. S. and Venzke, W. G. (1965) Macroscopic Observations on the Reproductive Tract of the Sow During Lactation and Early Postweaning, J. An. Sci., **24,** 2, 541.

Paredis, F. (1962) Fertility and Artificial Insemination in Pigs, Internat. J. of Fert. **7,** 3, 223.

Perry, J. S. (1960) Incidence of Embryonic Mortality as a Characteristic of the Individual Sow, J. Reprod. and Fertil., **1,** 71.

Perry, J. S. and Pomeroy, R. W. (1956) Abnormalities of the Reproductive Tract of the Sow, J. Agric. Sci. **47,** 2, 238.

Perry, J. S. and Rowlands, I. W. (1962) Early Pregnancy in the Pig, J. Reprod. and Fertil., **4,** 2, 175.

Phillips, R. W. (1939) Reproductive Failures in Livestock, Yearbook, U.S.D.A., 476.

Phillips, R. W. and Zeller, J. H. (1941) Some Factors Affecting Fertility in Swine, Am. J. Vet. Res., **2,** 5, 439.

Plumlee, M. P., Thrasher, D. M., Beeson, W. M., Andrews, F. N. and Parker, H. E. (1956) The Effects of a Manganese Deficiency Upon the Growth, Development and Reproduction of Swine, J. An. Sci. **15,** 2, 352.

Polge, C. and Dzuik, P. J. (1970) The Time of Cessation of Intrauterine Migration of Pig Embryos, J. An. Sci., **31,** 3, 565.

Polge, C., Moor, R. M., Day, B. N., Booth, D. W. and Rowson, L. E. A. (1967) Embryo Numbers and Luteal Maintenance During Early Pregnancy in Swine, J. An. Sci., **26,** 6, 1499.

Pomeroy, R. W. (1955) Ovulation and the Passage of the Ova Through the Fallopian Tubes in the Pig., J. Agric. Sci., **45,** 327.

Pope, C. E., Christensen, R. K., Zimmerman, V. A. and Day, B. N. (1970) Effect of Number of Embryo on Embryonic Survival in Recipient Gilts, J. An. Sci., **31,** 1, 227.

Raeside, J. J. (1961) A Chemical Estimation of Urinary Estrogens During the Oestrus Cycle in the Pig, Proc. IV Internat. Congress on Animal Reprod., The Hague.

Rasbech, N. O. (1953) Investigations on the Use of Anaphrodisiacs in Gilts and Sows; Estrus Promoting Effect and the Size of Litter in 1,655 Animals, Nord. Vet. Med., **5,** 131.

Rasbech, N. O. (1964) Fertility and Reproductive Disorders of Various Species of Farm Livestock in Denmark, Brit. Vet. Jour. **120,** 415.

Reid, J. T. (1949) Relationship of Nutrition to Fertility in Farm Animals, J.A.V.M.A., **114,** 864, 158, and 865, 242.

Reid, J. T. (1960) Effect of Energy Intake Upon Reproduction in Farm Animals, Suppl. to J. Dairy Sci., **43,** 103.

Ringarp, N (1960) Clinical Investigations into a Postparturient Syndrome with Agalactia in Sows, Acta Agric. Scand. Suppl. 7.

Robeson, W. L. (1918) Mating Sows Before Their Litters are Weaned, Monthly Bulletin, Ohio Exp. Stat., **3,** 5.

Robertson, G. L., Casida, L. E., Grummer, R. H. and Chapman, A. B. (1951) Some Feeding and Management Factors Affecting Age at Puberty and Related Phenomena in Chester White and Poland China Gilts, J. of An. Sci., **10,** 841.

Ross, R. F., Christian, L. L. and Spear, M. L. (1969) Role of Certain Bacteria in Mastitis-Metritis-Agalactia of Sows, J.A.V.M.A. **155,** 12, 1844.

Sammelwitz, P. H., Dzuik, P. J. and Nalbandov, A. V. (1956) Effects of Progesterone on Embryonal Mortality of Rats and Swine, J. An. Sci., **15,** 4, 1211.

Seerley, R. W. and Wahlstrom, R. C. (1965) Dehydrated Alfalfa Meal in Rations for Brood Sows, J. An. Sci. **24,** 2, 448.

Self, H. L. (1955) A Comparison of Reproductive Efficiency of Sows at the First and Second Post-Lactation Heats, J. An. Sci. **14,** 4, 1254.

Self, H. L. (1962) More Pigs Per Litter Through Better Management, Mod. Vet. Pract., **43,** 11, 28.

Self, H. L. and Grummer, R. H. (1958) Rate and Economy of Pig Gains and the Reproductive Behavior of Sows When Litters are Weaned at 10 Days, 21 Days, or 56 Days, J. An. Sci., **17,** 3, 862.

Sewell, R. F. and Carmen, J. L. (1958) Reproductive Performance of Swine Fed Chlortetracycline over Several Generations, J. An. Sci., **17,** 3, 752.

Shelby, D. R. and Singleton, W. L. (1968) Effect of Boars on Conception Rate and Litter Size, J. An. Sci., **27,** 6, 1789.

Signoret, J. P. and DuMesnil DuBuisson, F. (1961) Study of the Behavior of Sows in Estrus, Proc. IV Internat. Congress on An. Reprod., The Hague, Vol. II, 171.

Spies, H. G., Zimmerman, D. R., Self, H. L. and Casida, L. E. (1960) Maintenance of Early Pregnancy in Ovariectomized Gilts Treated with Gonadal Hormones, J. An. Sci., **19,** 1, 114.

Squiers, C. D., Dickerson, G. E., and Mayer, D. T. (1952) Influence of Inbreeding, Age, and Growth Rate of Sows on Sexual Maturity, Rate of Ovulation, Fertilization, and Embryonic Survival, Missouri Agr. Exp. State. Res. Bull. 494.

Stob, M., Baldwin, R. S., Tuite, J., Andrews, F. N. and Gillette, K. G. (1962) Isolation of an Anabolic Uterotrophic Compound From Corn Infected with **Gibberella Zeae,** Nature, **196,** 1318.

Swierstra, E. E. (1970) Effect of Environmental Temperatures on Semen Composition and Conception Rates Colloquium on **Effect of Diseases and Stress on Reproductive Efficiency on Swine,** Iowa State College, June.

Tanabe, T. Y., Warnick. A. C., Casida, L. E. and Grummer, R. H. (1949) The Effects of Gonadotrophins Administered to Sows and Gilts During Different Stages of the Estrual Cycle, J. of An. Sci., **8,** 4, 550.

Tassell, R. (1967) The Effects of Diet on Reproduction in Pigs, Sheep and Cattle, I Plane of Nutrition in Pigs, Brit. Vet. Jour. **123,** 2, 76.

Teige, J. (1957) Congenital Malformations of the Mullerian Ducts and

Sinus Urogenitalis, Nord. Vet. Med., **9,** 609.

Thomsen, A. (1934) Brucella Infection in Swine, Acta Pathol. et Microbiol. Scand., Suppl 21.

Thurman, J. C. and Simon, J. (1970) A Field Study of 12 Sows Affected with the MMA Syndrome, Vet. Med., **65,** 3, 263.

Tillson, S. A., Erb, R. E. and Niswender, G. D. (1970) Comparison of Luteinizing Hormone and Progesterone in Blood and Metabolites of Progesterone in Urine of Domestic Sows During the Estrous Cycle and Early Pregnancy, J. An. Sci., **30,** 5, 195.

Tomkins, E. C., Heidenreich, C. J. and Stob, M. (1967) Effect of Post-Breeding Thermal Stress on Embryonic Mortality in Swine, J. An. Sci., **26,** 2, 377.

Trapp, A. L., Keahy, K. K., Whitenack, D. L. and Whitehair, C. K. (1970) Vitamin E—Selenium Deficiency in Swine: Differential Diagnosis and Nature of Field Problem, J.A.V.M.A. **157,** 3, 289.

Ulberg, L. C., Grummer, R. H. and Casida, L. E. (1951) The Effects of Progesterone Upon Ovarian Function in Gilts, J. of An. Sci., **10,** 3, 665.

Vandeplassche, M. et al., (1967) Effect of Brucellosis on Fertility in Swine, Vet. Col, State Univ., Ghent, Belgium **2,** 37, (Abstr. J.A.V.M.A. **154,** 5, 502 (1969).

VanLoen, A. (1961) A Contribution to the Knowledge of the Double Cervix Condition in Bovine Cattle, Thesis, Univ. of Utrecht, Scheltema and Holkema, Amsterdam, Netherlands.

Waite, A. B. and Day, B. N. (1967) Intrauterine Migration Following Unilateral Fertilization in Gilts, J. An. Sci., **26,** 4, 790.

Warnick, A. C., Casida, L. E. and Grummer, R. H. (1950) The Occurrence of Estrus and Ovulation in Post Partum Sows, J. of An. Sci., **9,** 66.

Warnick, A. C., Grummer, R. H. and Casida, L. E. (1947) Some Genital Conditions Associated with Lowered Fertility in Sows, J. of An. Sci., **6,** 4, 502.

Warnick, A. C., Grummer, R. H. and Casida, L. E. (1949) The Nature of Reproductive Failures in Repeat-Breeder Sows, J. of An. Sci., **8,** 4, 569.

Webel, S. K., Peters, J. B. and Anderson, L. L. (1970) Control of Estrus and Ovulation in the Pig by ICI 33828 and Gonadotropins, J. An. Sci., **30,** 5, 791.

Wiggens, E. L., Casida, L. E. and Grummer, R. H. (1950) The Incidence of Female Genital Abnormalities of Swine, J. of An. Sci., **9,** 3, 269.

Willman, J. P. (1954) Personal Communication.

Wilson, R. F., Nalbandov, A.V. and Krider, J. L. (1949) Impaired Fertility in Female Swine, J. of An. Sci., **8,** 4, 558.

Young, G. A. (1954) Personal Communication.

Zimmermann, W. (1970) Discussion in Colloquium on **Effect of Diseases and Stresss on Reproductive Efficiency in Swine,** Iowa State Univ., Ames, Iowa, June.

Chapter XVI

INFERTILITY IN EWES AND DOES

Infertility or sterility in ewes and does is uncommon when compared with the incidence of these conditions in other domestic animals. This is probably true for two reasons: first, there has been little or no study of the infertility or sterility occurring in these animals; and, second, the incidence of disease or infertility apparently is much lower in these species. In examining the genital tracts of 90 ewes, Dutt found no structural defects or other abnormalities that would be a barrier to fertilization. The structure and functions of the various portions of the genital tracts of ewes and does are similar to that of the cow, and treatment of pathologic conditions is similar to that used in the cow except for the fact that the smaller size of sheep and doe renders impossible the use of certain procedures and types of therapy employed in the cow.

Reproductive Physiology

There are many similarities between the genital tracts, the ovaries, the reproductive hormones and other facets of reproduction between ewes and does and cows.

Puberty occurred in spring lambs at a mean age of 249 to 293 days, 8 to 9 months; Rambouillet or crossbred lambs born in the fall had their first estrus at 316 days range 199 to 577 days, Foote et al., Wiggins et al.. About 90 percent of the lambs had ovulated before the first standing estrus, as noted by laparotomy and the presence of a corpus luteum. In lambs that were not bred, it was noted that over 53 percent ovulated after the last standing estrus of the breeding season. Many lambs only exhibit one or a few estrous periods their first breeding season. Sexual maturity varies with the breed and rate of growth. Merino sheep mature more slowly than the Hampshire or Suffolk breeds. Crossbred lambs generally mature earlier than purebred lambs. A high plane of nutrition may hasten the onset of puberty and a low plane of nutrition will delay it as in cattle, Terrill. Most ewes are bred at the first breeding season after they reach one year of age. Under good conditions of feeding and management 60 percent or more of spring lambs of the early-maturing breeds will become pregnant if placed with males in the fall. Wiggins et al. reported that virgin ewes were still fertile after reaching 4 years of age; this is different from 4 to 5 year-old virgin cattle. (See DeLange).

The estrous cycle—The common coarse-wool breeds are seasonally polyestrous. The fine-wool breeds like the Merinos, Rambouillet and the coarse-wool horned Dorset and crossbreds of these breeds may be polyestrous the year around, depending upon climatic and feed conditions. The coarse-wool breeds in the northern hemisphere usually come into estrum about September 1. If they are not bred or do not conceive they continue to come into estrum until about January 1 or slightly later. Rambouillets tend to come into estrum the earliest in the breeding season; followed by the Hampshires, Southdowns, and Shropshires, Asdell. Similarly to the coarse wool breeds of sheep, goats are polyestrous during the breeding season of August through January; few conceptions occur at other months of the year.

About 12 to 48 hours after parturition about 10 percent of ewes exhibited estrus whether or not they ate their placenta, Wiggins and Barber, and Gardner et al.. After this brief estrous period, lactational anestrum lasting 5 to 7 weeks usually develops. After this period some ewes suckling lambs will exhibit estrus but most heats are not observed until about 2 weeks after the lambs are weaned. As determined by the fern pattern of cervical mucus, lactating ewes have one or more quiet or silent ovulations before the first estrus after lambing. It is very difficult to induce estrus unless an involuting corpus luteum is present or exogenous progesterone is given, Miller and Wiggins, Foote et al.. In sheep as in cattle progesterone apparently is necessary to potentiate the effect of estrogen to produce signs of estrus.

In fall-lambing Rambouillet ewes the average interval from lambing to the start of regular estrous cycles was 72 days, range 12 to 212 days; this varied from 46 days for ewes lambing in August to 98 days for ewes lambing in January, Barker and Wiggins. The onset of estrous cycles is hastened by early weaning of lambs. Wagner noted that the interval from lambing to breeding had a significant effect on conception but had no effect on the induction of estrus. Apparently, as in cattle, a 40 to 60 day interval postpartum was necessary for an optimal conception rate. Foote et al. reported that uterine involution is largely completed by 24 days postpartum. Thus, with the Dorset, Rambouillet, or Merino breeds or their crosses, it is possible, but very difficult on a flock basis, to obtain two lamb crops or a 200 percent lamb crop each year. By alternating breeding in the spring and fall, it would be possible to get 3 lamb crops in two years, Hogue. Shelton and Morrow studied 539 Rambouillet ewes over a two-year-period when they were mated for six weeks begining the 21st of March, the 21st of June, the 21st of September and the 21st of December. The incidence of estrus in open ewes for the four mating periods was 84.5, 96.4, 97.2 and 99.1 percent, respectively; the ovulation rates were 105.6, 140.8; 175.4 and 151.9, respectively, and the lambing rates were 83.9, 96.5, 126.8 and 135.2, respectively. The higher ovulation rates in June and September were not reflected in higher lambing rates because the higher environmental temperatures during the breeding season had a detrimental or modifying effect on embryonic survival.

Hulet and Foote reviewed the factors limiting the achievement of the goal of two lamb crops or a 200 percent lambing rate per year in the coarse-wool breeds. They concluded that the manipulation of light and temperature was not practical because of the long latency period required to induce results. Although ovulation rates could be increased by: (1) breeding during the middle of the breeding season instead of late in the season, (2) "flushing" the ewes by increasing the TDN or energy intake for several weeks prior to breeding, or (3) by the injection of PMS combined with a progestin 3 or 4 days before the next estrus, or on days 12 or 13 of the cycle, only 20 percent of the ewes with 3 CL were carrying 3 fetuses while 75 percent of the ewes with 2 CL were carrying two fetuses. Thus although a combination of breeding management and hormonal therapy makes 2 lamb crops per year feasible, much more research is needed to make it practical and a routine procedure for most breeds of sheep.

The presence of a ram stimulates the breeding activity or the onset of estrum in ewes in the transitional period between the anestrous period and the breeding season, Smith et al., Hulet, and Wishart. As noted previously the first ovulation thus induced is often silent and the next period associated with a regressing corpus luteum that provides some progesterone is manifested by signs of estrus. This technique can be used to obtain a degree of synchronization of estrus in a flock. Smith et al. reported that when rams were introduced from July 1 to August 8th, the maximum conception period occurred from 17 to 32 days later. When rams were introduced after August 8th conception rates for the first and second 16-day periods of the breeding season were similar. Wishart showed that if a vaginal pessary containing a progestagen was placed in the vagina of the ewes for 12 days during this transitional period before the breeding season and then removed the day the ram was placed with the flock, over 90 percent of the ewes were in estrus within 4 days and 62.5 percent lambed to first service. Thus combining a progestational agent and the introduction of a ram resulted in a high level of synchronization. Shelton reported a similar stimulating effect on does by the introduction of the buck at the beginning of the breeding season. He reported that 66 percent of does kidded between the 8th and 12th day of the kidding season and this corresponded with observations that most does came into estrum about 10 days after the introduction of the bucks into the flocks. This is a factor to consider since the heavy breeding load at this period might have a harmful effect on the fertility of certain males or require the presence of additional bucks. As with boars, Shelton and Hulet demonstrated that in the presence of a buck the senses of smell, sight and contact all combine to produce the stimulation of the onset of the estrous cycle and ovulation in the doe and ewe. This effect was not produced when the ram ran continuously with the ewes, Hulet.

Photoperiodism is a characteristic of the reproductive cycle or the sexual activity in sheep and goats, as in horses, Hafez, Thibault et al., Godley et al., and Means et al.. The onset of the estrous cycle and the breeding season in most breeds of sheep is principally influenced by the reduction in the length of daylight in the late summer and fall in the northern hemisphere. A reduction in daylight to about 10 or 11 hours, whether it occurs naturally or whether it is induced artificially by penning the ewes in a darkened area during part of the day, will induce the onset of the estrous cycle in anestrous ewes. The seasonal nature of the breeding season permits the birth of lambs at the most favorable time or in the late spring months when feed supply and ambient temperatures are nearly optimal. Hafez also noted that the breeding season of sheep tends to become shorter at latitudes near the poles. Near the equator ewes tend to have estrous cycles throughout the year and not exhibit a restricted breeding season. In the northern latitudes there are year to year variations in the onset of the breeding season as in horses. Dutt and Bush, and Godley et al. have shown that a reduction in ambient temperature occurring naturally or induced artificially also has an effect on promoting the onset of the reproductive cycle and the breeding season.

There is a wide breed difference in the number of estrous periods per year from 2 to 3 periods in a short breeding season in some breeds to estrous periods in other breeds occurring all the year around, Hafez. The ram and buck, similar to the stallion, do not show a restricted breeding season as does the female but there are seasonal variations in semen production and characteristics, Hafez. (See Male Infertility.) Bucks and rams are sexually more active and produce better quality semen during the breeding season. Reid reported that the onset of the breeding season could be somewhat advanced by a high energy intake before the season.

Most breeds of sheep have an average estrous cycle length of 16.5 days, with a range of 14 to 19 days, Asdell. Most of the breeds are in estrum for a period of 24 to 48 hours, with an average of about 28 to 36 hours. DeBois cited Brand as reporting the Texel ewe has two follicular growth waves. The first wave began on days 1 and 2 and ended on days 11 to 12 but atretic changes were evident beginning on days 5 to 6. The second growth wave began on days 9 and 10 and resulted in mature follicles at the next estrum. Thus these changes were similar to those reported by Rajakoski in bovine ovaries during the estrous cycle. The follicle size varied from 0.5 to 1.0 cm and the corpora lutea were about 1 cm in diameter. "Silent" heat or ovulation without estrum occurs frequently at the beginning and after the end of the breeding season. The estrual cycles tend to be longer or shorter in duration than the average at the beginning or end of the breeding season. Short cycles are more frequent in older ewes. Cycle length does not affect fertility, Williams and co-workers. There was no tendency for individual ewes to have an early or late onset of the breeding season, so selection on this basis is not possible.

The goat has an average estrous cycle length of 20 days, range 15 to 24 days, The duration of estrus in goats is about 40 hours, range 24 to 96 hours.

Sexual behavior in ewes and does has been described by Hafez, Cole and Cupps, and Hulet. Sexual activity and signs in ewes and does, as in the mare, are nearly lacking in the absence of the male. Proestrus is rather indefinite and the onset of estrum is abrupt. Cessation of estrum is gradual. The symptoms of estrus in the ewe include restlessness, seeking out the ram, frequent switching of the tail as if the vulva itched, teasing the ram and standing to be mounted and bred. In estrum the Dorset has a characteristic stance. During an average heat period a ewe was teased 18 times, mounted 25 times and mated 6 times, Hulet et al.. The goat frequently shows a peculiar, continuous bleating and the milk yield may drop. Anorexia and swelling of the vulva are usual symptoms of estrum in the goat as well as in the ewe. Most owners allow the ram to run with the ewes during the breeding season. Painting the brisket of the rams or having them wear a harness containing a marking device, in which various colors can be placed, is a common practice. Thus by observation of the rumps of the ewes service can be noted and recorded. After 17 to 20 days a different color may be used to determine which ewes return to estrum. If many return, the fertility of the ram is questionable. Vasectomized rams can be used as teasers and "heat detectors" for ewes that are to be bred artificially. The ewe secretes mucus from the cervical glands but not in large amounts like the cow. Smearing the estrous mucus on a slide and allowing it to dry results in a fern or arborization pattern, similar to that in the cow, due to the high salt content in the mucus of estrum, Daniel et al.. The vaginal smear in the ewe is of limited diagnostic value in determining the stages of the estrous cycle, Hafez. As in the cow, increased activity of the uterine muscle and edema of the endometrium occur during proestrum and estrum. The endometrium in some ewes may be black due to the presence of melanoblastic pigment. This is not associated with stages of the cycle. The cervix is somewhat dilated and relaxed during estrum. Asdell indicated that often ewes may attract rams by the odor of the vaginal mucus before the ewe is ready to accept coitus. Ewes may occasionally show estrum during pregnancy. Williams and co-workers reported that 11 of 50 pregnant ewes had 1 to 3 "heats" during pregnancy.

According to Asdell, the time of mating or artificial insemination during estrum in sheep is not as important as in other animals. The optimum time to breed is about 12 to 18 hours after the onset of estrum. Ovulation is spontaneous and usually occurs from 18 to 24 hours after the onset of estrum or from 12 to 24 hours before the end of estrum. In rare cases ovulation may occur after the end of estrum. In twin ovulation several hours or more may separate the time of ovulation of each follicle. Usually 1 to 3 ovulations take place and the rest of the follicles become atretic.

Ovulation Rate—Placing ewes on a high plane of nutrition or flushing for 2 weeks before mating increased the lamb crop by about 20 percent and flushing ewes for 3 to 5 weeks increased the rate of twinning to 40 percent or higher, compared to a 4 to 6 percent twinning rate in control, non-flushed ewes. Increasing the length of time of flushing beyond 4 to 5 weeks did not give a further ovulatory response, Reid, and El-Sheikh et al.. Foote et al. showed that breeding ewes fed a high plane of nutrition for 6 to 8 months before flushing had a higher rate of twin ovulation than ewes fed a low plane of nutrition before flushing. Hart and Miller were able to increase the lamb crop of range ewes from 80 to 135 percent for a 6-year period, by continuously feeding on a high plane of nutrition. There is no evidence that high condition predisposes the ewe to sterility. El-Sheikh and co-workers reported that ewes on a high nutritional level had a higher ovulation rate, possibly a higher fertilization rate, and a slightly lower embryonic survival rate than ewes on a low nutritional level. A high energy ration of 2 lbs. of grain per ewe and hay were fed daily for several months of the early breeding season and resulted in greater pituitary gland weights, Howland et al., Memon et al.. It was suggested that higher feeding levels caused an elevated plasma glucose, greater hypothalamic stimulation and release of larger amounts of gonadotropin causing greater ovarian activity and twin ovulations. The evidence that a high plane of energy intake was detrimental to embryo survival in the weeks following conception was not observed in sheep as in swine, Foote et al., and Reid. In flushing ewes a high energy or TDN intake is needed, an increased intake of protein is not necessary, Memon et al.. Ewes fed a low level of energy during the gestation period, especially the latter third, experience a much higher neonatal loss of lambs than ewes on a high plane of energy, Reid. The lambs, especially twins, of the ewes on a high plane of nutrition, were heavier, larger and stronger.

Other factors also influence the ovulation rate and the subsequent lamb crop. Ewe lambs, yearlings and young ewes as well as old ewes produce fewer twins and have lower lamb liveability. The peak percent of lambs weaned was in 4-year-old ewes, range 3 to 6 years. However, a higher percentage of single lambs are viable at birth and are weaned than are twins or triplets, Hafez, and Sidwell et al.. Crossbred ewes produced a 9 to 23 percent larger lamb crop than purebred ewes when bred as ewe lambs, and as older ewes produced 10 to 16 percent larger lamb crops, McArthur and Shelton. Ovulation rates are higher in the early to middle portions of the breeding season and decline later in the season, Hafez, and Nalbandov. Shelton reported that in Angora does the second and third ovulations were more fertile and more ova were released than at the first estrum. Certain ewes tend to have higher ovulation rates than other ewes. Thus selection of ewes born as twins or greater multiples from young mothers, large sheep of certain breeds, and those with open faces, free of wool, can be used to increase the lambing rate to 150 percent or greater in a flock, Hafez. The mature ewes of the Finnish Landrace and Romanov breeds or their crosses frequently produce triplet or greater numbers of lambs.

Ovulations were slightly more frequent on the right ovary of ewes than on the left, 53 to 55 percent and 44 to 47 percent, respectively, Hulet et al., and Casida et al.. In single ovulations 62 percent were on the right ovary. Casida et al. reported that 26 to 32 percent of embryos migrated from one horn to the other when twin ovulations occurred on one ovary; while only 0 to 10 percent migration occurred when a single ovulation occurred from one ovary. As in cattle, an increased embryonic loss occurred, in twin ovulations especially with twin ovulations from one ovary.

Roberts and Rakha reported that both FSH and LH were necessary for ovulation in ewes. The FSH content of the anterior pituitary decreased beginning 8 hours before the onset of estrum and continued to decline for 6 hours after the onset of estrum. The LH content of the anterior pituitary gland started to be discharged at the onset of estrum and was completed 6 hours later when 52 percent of the LH in the pituitary gland had been released. Stabenfeldt reported that the production surge in estradiol stimulated by FSH coincided with or preceded LH release. Small amounts of estrogen injected into sheep stimulated LH release. Asdell, and Kammlade et al. noted that gonadotropin levels in the anterior pituitary gland were high and constant during the nonbreeding season as were the presence of follicles on the ovaries. Thus the onset of the estrous cycle in the late summer months associated with declining daylight may be triggered by a greater release of FSH and/or LH associated with an increased estrogen production. The ewe's pituitary gland is about 10 times as potent as the cow's in LH content and 5 times as potent in FSH content, Asdell.

Cole and Cupps cited Robinson in reporting that in the ewe progesterone is needed as well as estrogen to produce psychic estrus. In fact a fairly long course of about several weeks of progesterone activity appears necessary in ewes before a full response to estrogen can be obtained. This accounts for some silent heats accompanying ovulations at the outset of the breeding season. Asdell reported that 64 ug of estradiol was necessary to induce psychic estrus in ovariectomized ewes; if the injection was preceded by progesterone administration only 20 to 25 ug of estradiol was needed to produce psychic estrus. During the estrous cycle 10 to 15 mg of progesterone in oil daily inhibited estrus. After ovulation, progesterone levels in blood plasma increased from 22.2 ng per ml to 37.6 ng by 9 or 10 days of the cycle and then decreased to 21.8 ng per ml about 13 to 15 days after estrus or 2 to 3 days before the next estrus, Plotka and Erb. The concentration and content of progesterone in the corpus luteum in sheep increased from estrus to 9 to 11 days of the cycle, when the C.L. weighed 0.5 gm, and then declined. The highest rate of estrogen excretion in the urine occurred at estrus with the lowest rate of excretion two days after estrus. No estrogens were found in the urine in sheep in the anestrous season. The principal estrogen excreted was estrone but some estradiol was also present in the urine, Plotka and Erb (1969). If conception occurred the level of progesterone in the peripheral plasma generally rose from 0.2 to 0.4 ug the first few weeks of gestation to 0.3 to 0.8 ug per 100 ml the last few weeks of gestation, Cole and Cupps.

Ovariectomy after 55 days of gestation in the ewe is not generally followed by abortion because progesterone is produced in the placenta. During pregnancy in sheep and pigs luteal function is maintained by the constant secretion of a pituitary gonadotropin, Whitten. This luteotropic hormone in the ewe is probably prolactin, Short. From 10 to 20 ug per kg of progestational agents including progesterone were present in the placenta of the ewe, Asdell. He further reported that when fertilized ova were transferred to ewes ovariectomized at the time of transfer that pregnancy could proceed normally to term by administering 10 to 20 mg of progesterone daily through the first 60 days of pregnancy. In the goat the corpus luteum is necessary the entire gestation period to maintain pregnancy. The secretion of oviduct fluid is under the control of the gonadal steroid hormones. From 1.0 to 1.5 ml of fluid is secreted daily by each oviduct of the ewe at peak production during the estrogenic phase of the cycle of 1 day before to 3 days after the onset of estrus. About 0.5 to 0.75 ml per day is secreted from each oviduct during the rest of the cycle. About one-third to one-half of this fluid flows through the utero-tubal junction, especially at estrus and the remainder flows out the ovarian end of the oviduct into the peritoneal cavity, Murray et al., and Perkins and Goode. The latter authors analyzed the fluid and found it contained high levels of protein, lactic acid and alkaline phosphatase.

Following copulation and ejaculation of sperm into the vagina of the ewe, sperm cell transport is very rapid with spermatozoa appearing in the oviduct within 15 minutes. Dead spermatozoa were also transported at a similar rate. Although about 800 million spermatozoa are in an ejaculate of a ram, some hours after copulation less than 100,000 sperm cells were in the uterus and several thousand or less were in the oviduct. Spermatozoa retain viability and fertility for about 24 hours in the genital tract of the ewe, Cole and Cupps. They indicated that the capacitation time for spermatozoa in ewes was 1.5 hours. Fertilization occurs in the oviduct with sperm penetration of the ovum beginning about 3 hours after ovulation, pronuclei formed about 3 to 9 hours after ovulation, and the first cleavage of the ovum occurred about 20 to 30 hours after ovulation in the ewe and doe, Cole and Cupps. The fertilized ovum enters the ovine uterus 3 to 4 days after ovulation, Hulet and Foote. The low rate, 9 to 10 percent, of embryo migration from one horn to the other after single ovulations and the high rate, up to 60 percent or greater, after double ovulations has been discussed previously, Cloud and Casida.

As in cows, estrogens injected into sheep cause a regression of the corpus luteum. Ginther gave 0.5 mg of estradiol daily on cycle days 8 to 11 and the estrous cycle length decreased to 12.4 days, compared to 17.0 days in control ewes. Bolt and Hawk reported that 1 mg of estradiol given once on cycle day 10 caused the regression of the corpora lutea in 9 of 11 ewes by day 14. In only 2 of 8 ewes did the corpus luteum regress when both estradiol and 750 I.U. of HCG or LH, were given. Thus exogenous gonadotropins protected the C.L. of the ewe from regressing after an injection of exogenous estradiol. Ginther, and Stormshak et al. further reported that when estradiol was given on cycle days 8 to 11 the C.L. regressed, but the length of the next cycle was prolonged to 20 days. When estradiol was given on day 4 it caused the release of LH from the pituitary with new ovulations. Ginther also reported that follicles play a role in the regression of the C.L. in ewes. Corpora lutea in sheep were caused to regress by the injection of antibovine LH, Fuller and Hansel (1970). They also demonstrated that LH is a major luteotropic factor in the ewe and is also necessary for follicular development and estrogen production. Because ewes experience about 20 percent early embryonic deaths especially those mated early in the breeding season, 0.4 mg per lb. of body weight of progesterone in oil was given daily subcutaneously to ewes for varying periods after breeding. This had no beneficial or harmful effects on fertility or embryonic deaths. Injections day 1 through 5 did tend to cause smaller C.L. weighing 231 to 430 mg compared to the C.L. of controls that weighed 642 to 756 mg, but all ewes carried normal embryos, Zimbelman et al.. Giving gonadotropins to cause follicle formation, ovulation and new C.L. between heat periods or in diestrum did not effect the estrous cycle length as it does in swine and all C.L. involuted at the regular time. Murphree and co-workers showed that ovulation could be induced experimentally in both the luteal and follicular stages of the estrous cycle of ewes but that ova produced during the luteal phase had a very low incidence of fertilization. When natural C.L. were removed by laparotomy on day 5, 9 or 13, ewes came into estrum at 2 to 3.5 days after removal, Inskeep et al..

Van Rensburg reported that transportation stress induced follicular growth and ovulation in anestrous ewes but since no declining C.L. were present no estrum was exhibited. He also cited evidence to show that adrenal secretions, probably androgens, in hyperadrenocorticism were responsible for the formation of cystic corpora lutea by inhibiting L.H. When hydrocortisone acetate was given to ovariectomized sheep, a marked increase in FSH occurred. In intact goats hydrocortisone stimulated the growth of luteal phase follicles and reduced the size and progesterone concentration of corpora lutea. The effect of hydrocortisone on inducing parturition in late pregnancy in ewes, cows and rabbits has been discussed previously. Adams and Wagner induced parturitions in sheep late in gestation within 48 hours by the injection of 10 to 20 mg of dexamethasone.

Utero-ovarian relationships in the ewe are similar to those observed in cows. Hysterectomy from early to mid-cycle in the ewe results in the maintenance or persistance of the C.L. for about 150 days or for the approximate length of gestation, Short, Inskeep and Butcher. They also showed, as did Moor and Rowson, that unilateral ovariectomy alone had no effect on the estrous cycle. Unilateral hysterectomy regularly prolonged the life span of the C.L. on the adjacent or ipselateral ovary about 17 days, but had no effect on the opposite or contralateral ovary. In one ewe with a C.L. on each ovary, unilateral hysterectomy prolonged the life of the ipselateral C.L., while normal regression of the C.L. on the opposite ovary occurred. As in the cow the regression of the C.L. in a nonpregnant intact ewe is caused by a luteolytic substance released from the endometrium after the middle of the estrous cycle. The presence of an embryo with an elongated blastocyst in the uterus at 13 days of the cycle prevents the normal involution of the C.L. and the initiation of another estrous cycle by an "antiluteolytic" effect or by inhibiting of the release or formation of the luteolytic substance and pregnancy is allowed to proceed, Short. Moor and Rowson showed that a single embryo in one horn can maintain a C.L. in both ovaries in intact ewes because the blastocyst extends into both horns. Short further demonstrated that removal of the hypophysis of the pregnant ewe on day 30 of gestation caused abortion due to luteal regression because of the removal of the source of luteotrophin or prolactin. If the hypophysis is removed from a pregnant ewe after day 60 of gestation, no abortion occurs because progesterone and possibly a luteotrophin are secreted by the placenta.

The presence of intrauterine plastic spirals or coils or an intrauterine device or I.U.D. causes a variety of effects in ewes that are somewhat similar to cows. Intrauterine foreign bodies have no effect in the pig, Whitten. A plastic coil in one horn of the ovine uterus inhibits sperm cell transport into the oviduct and fertilization on both sides of the reproductive tract, and promotes spermacidal conditions in the uterine lumen, Hawk (1966). Treatment of ewes with an I.U.D with a variety of drugs known to affect uterine muscle activity, had no effect on promoting sperm cell transport and fertilization, Warren and Hawk. Mann demonstrated that the presence of an I.U.D. in the ewe's uterus caused more than 75 percent of the contractions to be propagated toward the cervix; while in control ewes over 60 percent of contractions were propagated toward the oviduct.

Warren and Hawk and Ginther showed that an I.U.D. introduced into a ewe's uterus within the first 3 days after estrus would prevent the normal development of the C.L. and hasten its regression and shorten the estrous cycle. If the plastic coil (I.U.D.) and the C.L. were on the same side, the cycle would be about 7 days and if the C.L. was on the opposite side from the I.U.D. the cycle length would be about 8 to 9 days. If the I.U.D. was inserted on the 8th day of the cycle, the cycle length was normal or slightly prolonged, Whitten, Ginther. In I.U.D.-treated ewes about 25 percent of the ovulations were quiet or silent apparently due to a lack of enough progesterone from the regressing C.L. to cause the normal manifestations of estrus, Ginther. If an I.U.D. was in the horn adjacent to the C.L. the cycle length was 12 days, but if it was in the opposite horn from the I.U.D. the estrous cycle length was normal, or 17.8 days, Ginther et al.. When a uterine infection was produced by injecting **E. coli** into a ligated horn with adjacent C.L. on day 3, C.L. growth was suppressed and early regression of the C.L. and a shortened cycle occurred; infection at day 11 of the cycle caused a prolonged cycle. Thus infection acted in a manner similar to an I.U.D., Brinsfield et al.. Tubal obstruction or salpingectomy did not alter the estrous cycle lengths in the normal ewe or in ewes with an I.U.D., Conley and Hawk. The mechanism of how the luteolytic substance from the endometrium reaches the ovary and C.L. to cause luteolysis apparently does not involve nervous pathways or the lumen of the genital tract. Hansel (1970) stated that recent unpublished work has indicated that the luteolytic substance may be a prostaglandin, since prostaglandin F2 alpha when injected into the ovarian vein of a ewe caused luteal regression. This latter effect may be due to vasoconstriction of the ovarian vessels or a pharmacologic effect on the C.L., probably the latter. Evidence indicated that the luteolytic substance in the endometrium after midcycle is carried to the ovary by the lymphatics which are plentiful in the mesometrium and mesovarium or by uterine veins that communicate with the ovarian vessels. Further work on the luteolytic mechanism is indicated.

Synchronization of estrus in ewes has received much study in recent years.

In cycling ewes during the fall breeding season 96 percent, or 43 of 45 ewes exhibited estrus within a two day period after being fed 60 mg of MAP (6-methyl-17-acetoxy-progesterone) in 0.2 lb. of grain daily for 20 days and the conception rate was 62 percent in the bred ewes. Of 19 cycling Dorset ewes treated similarly in the spring, 15 came into a synchronized estrus within 3 days after the last day of feeding MAP and 11 or 73 percent conceived. The conception rate on the second estrus of 64 ewes synchronized with MAP was 83 percent, Brunner et al.. Cycling ewes injected with 10 or 12.5 mg of progesterone in oil daily or 20 mg every 2 days, for 16 or 17 days also failed to ovulate or come into estrum during the injection period, Foote and Waite, Lamond, and Cullen et al.. Synchronized estrus occurred 2 to 4 days after the last injection but only 28 percent of the ewes bred on the first service conceived compared to 68 percent conceiving on the second estrus and 67 percent of the controls conceiving, Foote and Waite. If progesterone injections were used to synchronize ewes they recommended breeding on the second or third estrus. Robinson, and Wishart reported that 20 to 40 mg of SC-9880, (**Cronolone** or **Synchromate,** Searle) which is about 25 times as potent as progesterone could be impregnated in a polyurethrane foam sponge or pessary and inserted into the anterior portion of the ewe's vagina and left for 16 or 17 days. The sponge is placed in the anterior portion of the vagina by inserting a plastic speculum or tube into the vagina, pushing the sponge through the tube and then withdrawing the tube. The progestagen was absorbed from the inserted pessary and prevented follicle formation and ovulation. Vaginal infections are a possible troublesome problem but they are only serious in 1 to 500 to 1,000 ewes, Robinson. At the end of this period the pessary was removed by the attached string and 95 percent of treated ewes came into estrus within 5 days. Of 631 ewes bred on the first estrus 58 percent conceived while 80 percent of 242 ewes bred on the second service, 12 to 20 days after removal of the pessary conceived, Wishart. Giving 750 units of PMS had no effect on the fertility at the first estrus after treatment. Dzuik et al. placed implants of MGA in silicone subcutaneously in 361 cycling ewes and 95 percent of the cycles were inhibited with 75 percent of the ewes showing estrus 36 to 54 hours after the implants were removed. About 50 percent conception occurred in 121 ewes bred on the first estrus. Roberts and Hafez used vaginal sponges impregnated with 60 mg MAP and covered with a bacteriocidal ointment to reduce vaginal infections in 330 cyclic ewes. They found that if 500 to 1500 I.U. of PMS was injected on the 11th day of treatment and the sponges were removed on the 13th day that a 58 percent conception rate occurred on the first estrus which was superior to PMS treatments at 9 and 13 days. About 80 to 90 percent of the ewes were in estrus within 3 days after the removal of the sponge. When the doses of PMS were 500 I.U., 1000 I.U. and 1500 I.U. the number of ovulations and corpora lutea produced were 2.7, 3.6 and 5.2, respectively. Embryonic deaths were high in ewes with 4 or more embryos. Hulet and Foote reported that when an injection of PMS was combined with progestagen treatment that only 20 percent of subsequently pregnant ewes that had 3 corpora lutea were carrying 3 fetuses while 75 percent of ewes with 2 corpora lutea were carrying 2 fetuses.

Robinson, Foote and Waite, and Cullen et al., reported that the lower conception rate on first service following a course of progesterone or progestagen in either cycling or anestrous ewes was due to altered sperm transport resulting in a failure of fertilization. Fifty five percent of control ewes had more than 6,400 sperm cells in the oviduct compared with only 5 percent of the treated ewes. While only 10 percent of the control or untreated ewes had less than 200 sperm cells in the oviduct, 28 percent of the treated ewes had less than 200 spermatozoa.

Robinson discussed the frequent occurrence of low conception rates reported in the various trials on synchronizing estrus in both cycling ewes and anestrous ewes approaching the breeding season. He and Hulet and Foote cited a number of authors to show that a 20 to 24 percent loss of fertilized eggs is normal in the ewe. Robinson reported that there was a wide variation between rams in their fertility and much infertility could be overcome by providing sufficiently large numbers of viable spermatozoa by insemination with fresh semen or using an excess of rams in natural service. Dilution of spermatozoa even at rates as low as 1:1 to 1:1.5 in artificial insemination or by overuse of rams by synchronizing many ewes at the same time also contributes to a lower fertilization rate.

In anestrous ewes, or noncycling ewes, the use of progesterone or progestagen for about 5 or more days together with the injection of 500 to 1000 I.U. of PMS will cause a single and fairly fertile estrus in ewes in the middle of their anestrous period. If ewes are near the breeding season in late July or early August in the northern hemisphere, this treatment regimen will often result in the initiation of the estrous cycles, especially if rams are placed in the flock, Lamond, Robinson. In late anestrus PMS injections may not be necessary to induce synchronous estrus following progestagen treatment. The progesterone or progestagen exerts a priming effect on the late anestrous ewe that results in an estrous response when PMS induces the formation of follicles containing estrogen. If silent or quiet heats are commencing at the outset of the breeding season then PMS may not be necessary to induce follicle formation. Dutt (1953) found that by giving anestrous ewes five 30 mg doses of progesterone at 3 day intervals, followed by a 500 mg dose of PMS 3 days later, 9 out of 9 ewes ovulated normally and had a normal length estrum 1 to 2 days after the injection of PMS. The fertilization rate was 50 to 60 percent. Lamond reported that attempts at bringing lactating ewes into estrus with progesterone and PMS have been successful but fertility has been poor. Probably at least one ovulatory cycle is needed before reasonable fertility can be expected. Brunner et al. reported that when 750 I.U. PMS was injected on day 1 in 17 anestrous ewes near the breeding season and then 60 mg MAP was fed daily for days 7 through 14 and 750 I.U. of PMS was given on day 15, that 100 percent of the ewes were in estrus within 6 days and 82 percent conceived. Brannon reported that this procedure resulted in over 90 percent of the treated ewes exhibiting synchronized estrus and slightly over 50 percent conceptions from service on the first estrus with 50 to 60 percent multiple births. Ray et al. induced estrus in anestrous ewes by feeding 1 mg CAP daily in their ration for 10 to 16 days followed by 750 to 1000 I.U. PMS and 0.5 to 5.0 mg estradiol after the PMS in some ewes. Normal post-treatment estrus occurred in 70 percent of the ewes. Estradiol did not improve the percentage of ewes exhibiting estrus and may have adversely affected the fertility rate in ewes receiving the higher doses of estradiol. Fertility rates at the induced estrous periods were lower than fertility rates during the regular breeding season.

Roberts and Edgar used intravaginal sponges containing 400 mg progesterone or 40 mg MAP for 13 days in anestrous ewes in early summer. At the time the sponges were removed the ewes were injected with 1000 I.U. PMS. A high degree of fertile synchronized estrous periods resulted. Uchovsky reported that 15 mg of progesterone in oil was given daily for 5 days in ewes approaching the breeding season. On the sixth day 400 to 1000 I.U. of PMS caused good estrous synchronization and a fairly high incidence of twins and triplets. Robinson cited work by Moore and Holst that showed that about 65 percent of eggs recovered from mated ewes were fertile and 50 percent of the ewes lambed when PMS was given 0 to 24 hours after progestagen therapy, but only 38 percent of the eggs were fertilized and only 17 percent of the ewes lambed when PMS was given 48 hours after stopping progestagen treatment. These above methods of a combined progesterone or progestagen and PMS therapy are superior to the two injections of PMS at 16 day intervals discussed by Roberts (1956) that gave very erratic and unpredictable results.

Further observations by Lamond have important implications on stimulating the estrous cycle in Merino crossbred ewes experiencing "shallow" anestrus during the anestrous spring and early summer season. He reported that a course of progesterone early in the anestrous period would result in estrus and ovulation with good fertility. Phillips and co-workers and Venzke have reviewed the numerous reports on the uniformly poor results accompanying the use of estrogens to produce conceptions in ewes during the anestrous period. Venzke reported that in 77 ewes given 2 to 8 mg of estradiol (E.C.P.) during the anestrous period 90.0 percent came into estrum but only 1 ewe lambed. The introduction and removal of rams from the flock for periods of 14 to 18 days and 12 to 14 days, respectively, resulted in 92 percent of over 3000 ewes coming into estrus in the late winter and early spring months and two-thirds of them lambed. Lamond cited further studies to indicate that the use of HCG after synchronization of estrus by progesterone or progesterone and PMS would result in ovulation 20 to 30 hours after injection. Thus although progesterone would induce estrus, HCG at the onset of estrus might prove a fairly good way to control the precise time of ovulation in regard to insemination. Dzuik et al. used silicone rubber implants impregnated with progesterone placed subcutaneously for 14 days in 180 ewes late in the anestrous period. At the time of removal of the implant 500 I.U. of PMS was given; 29 hours later 250 I.U. of HCG was administered, and the ewes were mated or bred 12 hours later. Sixty seven percent of the 60 control ewes lambed, 44 percent of the 60 ewes inseminated with fresh semen lambed but only 13 percent of the remaining 60 ewes inseminated with frozen semen lambed. Thus even with timed breeding, results with artificial insemination with frozen semen were poor. This is one of the major limiting factors for further use of estrous synchronization in ewes and does. If natural service is used in synchronized ewes, one would need 6 rams or more per 100 ewes compared to 3 rams per 100 ewes without synchronization. The somewhat lowered conception rate on first estrus in synchronized ewes must also be considered. For these reasons and also the added cost of the treatments, synchronization of estrus in ewe flocks has not been a practical and accepted procedure.

Although progesterone, progestagens and PMS have not been used extensively in does, there is definite evidence that the effects would be similar to those in ewes. Pigon et al., and Hulet and Foote have shown that antigonadotropins or antihormones can develop in sheep injected with repeated doses of PMS, a foreign protein, Twice a week injections of PMS resulted in a cessation of the estrous cycle in ewes. The refractoriness that developed in ewes following PMS injections would dissipate in one year or so. Based on the ovulatory response to PMS it was found that 2 injections per year during anestrus for 3 consecutive years gave a satisfactory response in the ewes each year.

Pathological Changes in the Reproductive System of the Ewe

Anatomic defects of the genital tract of female sheep and goats are rare except for a high incidence of intersexes, or pseudohermaphrodites, in goats. This was discussed in Chapter III. Hermaphrodism was noted most commonly in polled and Saanen goats, Asdell, Eaton. In one Saanen herd the incidence of pseudohermaphodites, was as high as 11 percent; in a Toggenburg herd the incidence reached 6 percent. The intersexes are usually male pseudohermaphrodites. The condition appears to be inherited as a simple recessive character associated with hornlessness. Horned hermaphrodites are extremely rare, if they occur at all. Eaton stated that to eliminate hermaphrodism in a flock, the polled goats that were normal should be mated to horned goats. Intersexes may occasionally be observed in sheep. Freemartins, such as occur in twin births in cattle, are rare in sheep and goats. Since other anatomic defects or arrests in development such as uterus unicornis, uterus didelphys, persistence of the median wall of the Mullerian duct with a fleshy pillar caudal to the cervix, other arrests in development of the Mullerian duct, and persistence of the hymen occur in other species, they probably occur in sheep and goats but are rarely recorded. Undoubtedly they are highly unusual.

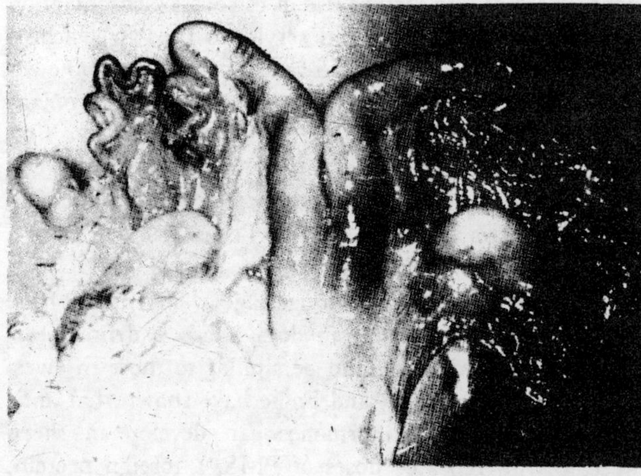

Figure 151 Parovarian Cysts Adjacent to the Left Ovary in a Ewe. (Courtesy K. McEntee)

Dutt reported on one ewe with a bifurcation of the cranial part of the vagina.

Pathological lesions or diseases of the reproductive system in sheep and goats are similar in most respects to those in cattle. Vulvitis, vaginitis, cervicitis, metritis, pyometra, perimetritis, and salpingitis may occur in sheep and goats usually as sequelae to dystocia, embryotomy, difficult parturition, retained placenta, and delayed involution of the uterus. These acute or chronic infections in the ewe and doe are handled in a manner similar to the treatment for these infections in cattle. In retained placenta, which is much less common in ewes and does than cattle, the uterus may be treated locally, preferably with a broad-range antibiotic, and the placenta is allowed to drop away. For a valuable ewe a better treatment is to give parenteral antibiotics for 3 to 5 days and not to place any drug in the uterus or to attempt to remove the afterbirth. Manual removal of a retained placenta is not indicated due to the small size of the genital tract.

In the 1954 Annual Report of the Department of Agriculture of New Zealand a group of 25 ewes that had failed to breed for two consecutive seasons were mated a third season. Eleven ewes lambed after only one service. Five ewes were bred and apparently conceived, but on postmortem examination showed evidence of interruption of pregnancy before term, and 8 ewes were bred at several estrous periods but failed to conceive. On postmortem examination 6 of these sterile ewes were found to have occluded or cystic Fallopian tubes and one ewe had a mummified fetus. Newsom reported that these lesions apparently account for only a small percentage of the infertility in ewes. McEntee and Olafson have reported that extensive and severe changes could be produced in the genital tract in the ewe by feeding chlorinated napthalenes. These changes were characterized by an enlarged uterine horn and cervix due to marked squamous metaplasia with profuse keratinization of the endometrial glands as well as keratinization and ulceration of the vulva. Naturally-occurring cases of hyperkeratosis or X disease are not seen in sheep.

Tumors of the ovaries and genital tract of the ewe are rare. Feldman recorded several leiomyomas affecting the uterus of sheep. He stressed the point that genital tumors in goats were extremely rare. Moulton and Cotchin reported on rare granulosa cell tumors of the ovaries and leiomyomas of the uterus of sheep. The latter author reported on an adenoma of the pituitary gland of a ewe. Monlux et al. described rare cases of lymphosarcoma or reticulum-cell sarcoma, myeloma and squamous cell carcinoma of the vulva of ewes.

Infections of the genital tract other than postpartum infections apparently are seldom a cause for infertility in ewes and goats. This may be explained in part by the long period between breeding seasons, in which recovery can take place. Vibriosis and brucellosis, the latter usually due to **Br. melitensis,** are characterized by abortion. Infertility in ewes and goats associated with vibriosis and brucellosis is not described. Dutt has shown that the incidence of embryonic deaths in ewes bred early in the breeding season was about 20 percent. There was no indication of an infection associated with the condition. Gunn and co-workers and Wiggins and co-workers, in observing and examining rams with various degrees of infertility, have not reported an enzootic venereal type of infertility spread by the ram to the ewe, as is observed in cattle. The infectious causes of abortion, such as listeria, rickettsial agents, and others have not been associated with infertility.

Ulcerative dermatosis, lip and leg ulceration or ulcerative venereal disease described by Marsh, and Tunnicliff and due to a virus can be spread by an infected ram or buck to a susceptible ewe or doe through breaks in the skin, causing a necrotic, swollen, bleeding lesion on the cutaneous and mucous surfaces of the vulvar lips. The lesion usually starts at the inferior commissure of the vulva and spreads upward. Only rarely is the vagina involved. The lesion is an ulcer covered by a scab. Removal of the scab revealed a shallow, bleeding crater containing a small amount of creamy pus. The disease is usually spread to the ewe at the time of coitus by an infected ram that has similar lesions on its penis and sheath. Newsom reported that occasionally the disease would spread to wethers and to ewes that have not been bred. This venereal disease of the external genitals should not be confused with contagious ecthyma which is due to a different virus and the lesions are proliferative. In a recent report Trueblood indicated that the viral agents causing these two diseases might be related since there was cross neutralization between the two viruses in serologic studies. The symptoms of ulcerative dermatosis usually subside within a week or 10 days. No successful specific treatment is available. Five percent copper sulphate has been advised for use in treating these lesions but should only be applied externally. No vaccine is available. Rams with lesions on the prepuce causing posthitis should not be purchased or placed with ewes during the breeding season.

Williams and Hutyra, Marek and Manninger reported that vesicular venereal disease or coital vesicular exanthema may occasionally spread through flocks of sheep and goats, with symptoms similar to those observed in cattle and horses. This condition has not been reported in the United States. These latter two diseases, although a cause for cessation of breeding until lesions are healed, are not characterized by infertility. In the acute phase, however, the ewe may refuse to copulate due to the irritation and pain present.

Moule, and Young have reported on Mules' operation for the prevention of blowfly strike caused by folds of skin on either side and below the vulva becoming moist with urine or soft fecal material resulting in an inflammation, bacterial growth, and an odor that attracts the blow flies to lay their eggs in the site. The moist fleece provides the hatching maggots with food, warmth and protection. Since clipping the wool in the area or applying insecticides to prevent blowfly strike are short-lived practices, Mules' operation has been used extensively in Australia to increase the area of smooth skin around the vulva and anus in Merino or other heavily-fleeced breeds. Also, the tail should be docked short so that no long wool lies against the vulva. Mules' operation is performed on recently clipped sheep during the cold season in the spring when there are no flies. The folds of skin ventral and lateral to the vulva are removed and healing is allowed to occur without suturing, Young. The resulting healing and scarring eliminates the skin folds and long wool lateral and ventral to the vulva and prevents blowfly strike.

Southcott and Moule in Australia have described a vulvitis that occurred in ewes on clover pasture similar to the noncontagious posthitis that was seen in wethers on lush clover pasture. There was no evidence that estrogens in the clover were a factor in this disease. The ulceration, scabbing and scarring of the ventral commissure of the vulva in this disease led to its disfigurment or loss with a resulting soiling of the rear parts with urine predisposing to flystrike even in ewes on which Mules' operation had been performed.

Short has reported on an unusual condition in goats, in which the doe is mated and passes through an apparently normal gestation period. At term, or about 150 days after service, gallons of fluid are expelled but no membranes or fetus. This has been termed a "cloudburst" condition in goats. A CL is in an ovary, the cervix is moderately closed and a hydrometra or mucometra is present.

Nutritional deficiencies in sheep and their effect on fertility have been extensively studied. The same general nutritive deficiencies affecting reproduction and fertility in cattle also affect sheep. Most deficiency diseases affecting reproduction in ewes on range are multiple and involve a lack of minerals, especially phosphorus and cobalt, a lack of protein, and a lack of vitamin A. The effects of inanition on fertility are more pronounced in immature than in adult animals and they are characterized by failure of estrum. A low plane of nutrition in ewes resulted in subestrus with undetected estrus, with cycles 26 to 42 days in length, Hunter.

Miller and co-workers reported that a low protein diet is to be avoided if a high percentage of lambs is to be produced. The symptoms of vitamin A deficiency are similar in the ewe and cow, Reid, and Hignett. Pregnancy in vitamin A deficient ewes usually terminates in abortion or the birth of dead or weak young. The female is more susceptible to vitamin A deficiency than is the male. Reid reported that the estrous cycle, ovulation, and early fetal development are not noticeably affected in sheep even when partial night blindness due to Vitamin A deficiency is exhibited. In drouth years feed low in vitamin A is often also low in energy, protein, and phosphorus. Vitamins E, C, B complex, and D are not necessary for reproduction in the ewe or goat. It is possible, however, that a lack of cobalt, an essential part of vitamin B_{12}, would cause a deficiency of rumen bacteria, and anorexia with secondary inanition. Severe deficiencies of cobalt may result in debility, failure of estrum, and the birth of weak lambs. Bowstead and co-workers reported that estrum in ewes was regular on a cobalt-deficient diet but that only 48 percent of the lambs born to cobalt-deficient ewes were strong, as compared to 92 percent of the lambs from ewes fed a cobalt supplement. Postnatal losses of lambs from ewes fed low levels of cobalt were 58 percent as compared to 17 percent for the lambs nursing the ewes receiving cobalt in their diet. Copper deficiency in sheep characterized by infertility and irregular estrous periods has been reported in certain areas of South Africa.

Reproduction is not affected by a low phosphorus diet until the usual symptoms of phosphorus deficiency develop, Reid. Symptoms of phosphorus deficiency in sheep are the same as in cattle. Hart and Miller showed that a low protein diet was not as severe as one low in both protein and phosphorus. The reproductive symptoms of a phosphorus deficiency, which is usually complicated by a low protein and viatmin A level, are: delay in onset of puberty and estrum, irregular estrous periods, and a tendency to produce only one lamb every two years. Abortions are uncommon but weak or dead young may be expelled at term. Phosphorus deficiency is usually due to a lack of the mineral in the hay or pasture. Impaired fertility is unlikely when the ewe or doe is receiving protein supplements or minerals containing phosphorus. Other trace mineral elements such as iron and iodine may also be lacking. In severe mineral and protein deficiencies, ewes may pull and eat the wool of other ewes in the flock.

Hartley and Grant, Drake et al., and Buchanan-Smith et al. have reported that ewes but not rams, require Vitamin E and selenium to have satisfactory reproduction. The first two groups of authors reported that not only could selenium deficiency in ewes in New Zealand cause neonatal death losses due to severe myocardial lesions but in selenium deficient areas, farms would experience an incidence of 10 to 30 percent barren or open ewes after service and apparent conception. Giving ewes 5 mg of selenium monthly during pregnancy or 25 mg in one dose after mating reduced the number of barren or open ewes to 2 to 4 percent compared to 30 percent open ewes in the control or untreated ewes. Although evidence would indicate that a selenium deficiency occurred in New Zealand, it should be noted that Hartley and Grant referred to the diseases corrected by selenium therapy as "selenium responsive" diseases. It is possible that some other factor(s) may cause the primary or basic disease.

Williams et al. reported that ewes fed kale had a short duration of estrus of about 22 hours and a slight increase in embryonic deaths. Kale feeding also resulted in anemia and a goiterogenic effect.

In Australia a specific type of infertility in sheep due to pasturing on subterranean clover rich in estrogens is observed. In this condition, according to Bennett and co-workers, and Shier, the incidence of sterility in ewes may be 30 percent or even greater. Dystocia due to uterine inertia may have accounted for 30 to 40 percent of the fetuses being expelled or removed dead and for the death of 15 to 20 percent of the ewes. Prolapse of the vagina was seen in approximately 10 to 12 percent of the ewes. The sterile ewes failed to conceive on repeated services and on postmortem examination of the genital tract a cystic degeneration of the endometrium was observed that varied from microscopic to gross lesions. The estrous cycles were normal and cystic ovaries did not occur. Schinckel, and Underwood and Shier reported that the infertility persisted and was irreversible even when the affected ewes were changed to pastures free of the subterranean clover. Ovulation occurred regularly but fertilization or implantation were prevented by the pathologic "Swiss cheese" type of endometrium. Curnow and Bennetts, and East reported that the "toxic" principle in the Dwalganup strain of subterranean clover was an isoflavone derivative, genistein or 5:7:4 trihydroxyisoflavone, that was one-fifth as potent as estrone in estrogenic activity. Genistein may be found in amounts of 100 mg per 100 gm of fresh subterranean clover. Reducing the amount of subterranean clover in a pasture by increasing the amount of grasses would control the disease. Possibly since the pasture season coincides with the anestrous season in sheep, when the ewe is not cycling and progesterone is not produced, the ingested estrogens may cause more severe lesions and disease in sheep than in cattle which are generally not affected by the level of estrogen in the clover pastures, Underwood. Barrett et al. reported that ewes in Australia, grazing red clover pastures were similarly affected as ewes on subterranean clover pastures.

Estrogens have also been found but in lower quantities in other legumes such as ladino clover and birdsfoot trefoil, Pope, Sanger and Bell, and Bickoff et al.. Underwood et al. injected 0.03 to 0.09 mg of stilbestrol per ewe 3 days a week for 6 months to 2 years and caused a high incidence of sterility, persistent and permanent cystic change in the endometrium, and a few ewes with cystic endometritis developed pyometra in a manner resembling that seen in dogs. The estrous cycle remained normal. Cystic ovaries have not been described in ewes and goats.

Prenatal or Embryonic Death Rates and Fertilization Rates in Ewes. Hammond (1921) reported that in 80 pregnant ewes there were normal fetuses equal to only 87 percent of the corpora lutea present. The numbers of atrophic fetuses and missing eggs were about equal. Henning (1939) estimated the incidence of fetal death in a similar manner and reported that 16 percent of the corpora lutea were not accounted for by live fetuses but he noted that early embryonic death with complete resorption could not be detected. He called attention to the increased fetal deaths with the increase in number of ova released, 8 percent with 1 ovum, 26 percent with 2, and 43 percent with 3 ova. As Casida pointed out, this fetal mortality may be more apparent than actual when these figures are interpreted to indicate that with a large number of eggs more embryos must die before the pregnancy is terminated. Citing the unpublished data of Voigtlander and Hulet on fertilization rates and embryonic death rates in Western ewes bred throughout the breeding season, Casida reported that the overall embryonic death rate on the basis of 18-day nonreturns was 20 percent but that on the basis of the lambing rate the embryonic death rate was nearly 30 percent. Hulet and Foote, as noted previously, reported a much higher embryonic death loss in ewes with 3 CL compared to ewes with 1 or 2 CL. These authors as well as Robinson reported that a 20 to 24 percent loss of fertilized eggs is normal in the ewe. Morley reported a prenatal death loss in Merino sheep in Australia of about 25 to 30 percent from 3 weeks after conception to term. Dutt reported that 180 northwestern ewes bred once early in the breeding season, August and September, showed an embryonic death rate of 20 percent and a failure of fertilization in 38.9 percent of the ewes. Failure of fertilization was the most important factor accounting for the low lambing rate. Fifty-four of these ewes bred artificially with semen having a 20 to 50 percent spermatozoan motility rate had about a 31 percent conception rate, while 100 ewes bred with semen having a 60 percent or better motility rate had a 62 percent conception rate. The embryonic death rate in both groups was about equal.

Hulet et al. reported that ewes bred early, August 1 to September 15, had a fertilization failure of 64.3 percent, 16.7 percent due to defective ova and 47.6 percent due to poor sperm, with a conception rate of 25.5 percent. In ewes bred from September 16 to October 25, the respective figures were 34.3 percent, 29 and 31.4 percent, and a conception rate of 59.2 percent. The deaths of the ovum and embryo were high early and late in the breeding season, Averill. In asynchronous heats and ovulation, the eggs failed to fertilize. He reported the high figure of 40 percent early embryonic deaths by 24 days of gestation in 65 ewes.

High ambient temperatures, especially during and shortly after estrus, have an adverse effect on fertilization and the survival of the zygote. Dutt et al. reported that ewes exposed to an ambient temperature of 90° F on the 12th day of the cycle through estrus had a fertilization rate of 51.9 percent, as determined 3 days after breeding, compared to a 92.6 percent rate for control ewes kept in a cool environment. Only 3.7 percent of ova from the controlled ewes were grossly abnormal compared to 44.2 percent of the ova from the ewes kept at 90° F. Embryo loss based on fertilized ova that died was 91.7 percent compared to 4 percent loss in control ewes at 24 days after breeding. In sheared ewes there were 32 percent abnormal ova and the rise in body temperature was 1.8° F. In unsheared ewes there were 55.6 percent abnormal ova and the rise in average body temperature was 2.6° F. Dutt later showed that ewes kept at an ambient temperature of 90° F for 24 hours during estrum had only a 10 percent lamb crop from service at that estrum. If the 90° F temperature was maintained for 24 hours at 3 or 5 days of gestation the lamb crop in each group of ewes was 35 and 40 percent. The control ewes produced an 85 percent lamb crop. Thus the ovum in the oviduct during the initial stage of cleavage is most sensitive to heat. This effect on the early zygote in ewes is similar to the effect of high ambient temperatures on cattle shortly after service, Stott and Williams. (See Infertility in Cows) Rams exposed to high ambient temperatures, especially with much wool on the scrotum also have a greatly lowered sperm quality due to degeneration of the seminiferous tubules. Alliston et al. further confirmed the above effects of high ambient temperatures on the early ova by ova transfer. Thus 90° F ambient temperatures are harmful to fertilization and early embryo survival and may be a cause of early season infertility in ewes. Ewes to be bred early in the season should be kept sheared and cool. Possibly early breeding in the summer months should be avoided. Shelton and Huston reported that ewes that were heat-stressed during the last two-thirds of the gestation period when compared to ewes kept cool, had fewer lambs, 81 vs 100 percent, the lambs were lighter and smaller and fewer lambs survived, 57 vs 81 percent. A high plane of feeding had no effect on embryonic or fetal death rates. Ewes giving birth in the hot environment had a significantly shorter gestation period. This is interesting in the light of the influence of the glucocorticoids and stress on the initiation of parturition.

References

General.

Asdell, S. A. (1964) Patterns of Mammalian Reproduction, 2nd Ed., Cornell Univ. Press, Ithaca, N.Y.

Cole, H. H. and Cupps, P. T. (1969) Reproduction in Domestic Animals, Academic Press, N.Y.C.

Hafez, E. S. E. (1968) Reproduction in Farm Animals, Lea and Febiger, Philadelphia, Pa.

Marsh, H. (1965) Newsom's Sheep Diseases, 3rd Ed., Williams and Wilkins Co., Baltimore, Md.

McDonald, L. E. (1969) Veterinary Endocrinology and Reproduction, Lea and Febiger, Philadelphia, Pa.

Nalbandov, A. V. (1964) Reproductive Physiology, W. H. Freeman and Co., San Francisco, Cal.

Specific.

Adams, W. M. and Wagner, W. C. (1969) Elective Induction of Parturition in Cattle, Sheep and Rabbits, presented at the Nat. A.V.M.A. Convention, Minneapolis, Minn., Unpublished data.

Alliston, C. W., Egle, G. E. and Ulberg, L. C. (1961) Loss of Potential Young in the Ewe Due to High Ambient Temperature, J. Appl. Physiol. **16,** 2, 253.

Alliston, C. W. and Ulberg, L. C. (1960) Early Pregnancy Loss in Sheep at Ambient Temperatures, of 70° and 90° F., J. An. Sci. **19,** 4, 1316.

Asdell, S. A. (1944) The Genetic Sex of Intersexual Goats and a Probable Linkage with the Gene for Hornlessness, Science, **99,** 124.

Asdell, S. A. (1962) Personal Communication.

Averill, R. L. W. (1955) Fertility of the Ewe, Studies on Fertil. **7,** 139. (Edit. by R. G. Harrison, Blackwell Scient. Publ., Oxford, England.)

Barker, H. B. and Wiggins, E. L. (1958) Estrual Activity in Fall-Lambing Rambouillet Ewes, J. An. Sci. **17,** 4, 1231.

Barker, H. B. and Wiggins, E. L. (1964) Estrual Activity in Lactating Ewes, J. An. Sci. **23,** 4, 973.

Barrett, J. F., Moule, G. R., Braden, A. W. H. and Harris, A. N A. (1961) Cystic Glandular Hypoplasia of the Endometrium in Ewes in New South Wales and Queensland, Austral. Vet. Jour. **37,** 1, 14.

Bennetts, H. W., Underwood, E. J. and Shier, F. L (1964) A Specific Breeding Problem of Sheep on Subterranean Clover Pastures in Western Australia, Austr. Vet. J., **22,** 2.

Bickoff, E. M., Booth, A. N., Lyman, R. L., Livingston, A. L., Thompson, A. R. and DeEds, F. (1957) Coumestrol, A New Estrogen Isolation from Forage Crops, Science, **126,** 969.

Bolt, D. J. and Hawk, H. W. (1970) Reduction in the Luteolytic Effect of Estradiol by Gonadotropin Injection in Ewes. J. An. Sci. **31,** 1, 218.

Bowstead, J. E., Sackville, J. P. and Sinclair, R. D. (1942) The Development of Cobalt Deficiency in Sheep, Scientif. Agric., **22,** 314.

Brannon, W. F. (1966) Personal Communication.

Brinsfield, T. H., Higginbotham, D. K. and Hawk, H W. (1969) Influence of Induced Uterine Infection at Various Stages of the Estrous Cycle on the Corpus Luteum of the Ewe, J. An. Sci. **29,** 9, 616.

Brunner, M. A., Hansel, W. and Hogue, D. E. (1964) Use of 6-Methyl-17 Acetoxyprogesterone and Pregnant Mare Serum to Induce and Synchronize Estrus in Ewes, J. An. Sci. **23,** 1, 32.

Buchanan-Smith, J. G., Nelson, E. C., Osburn, B. I., Wells, M. E. and Tillman, A. D. (1966) Effects of Vitamin E and Selenium Deficiencies in Sheep Fed a Purified Diet During Growth and Reproduction, J. An. Sci. **29,** 5, 808.

Casida, L. E. (1953) Prenatal Death as a Factor in the Fertility of Farm Animals, Iowa State Col. J. of Sci., **28,** 1, 119.

Casida, L. E., Warwick, E. J. and Meyer, R. K. (1944) Survival of Multiple Pregnancies Induced in the Ewe Following Treatment with Pituitary Gonadotropins, J. of An. Sci., **3,** 22.

Casida, L. E., Woody, C. O. and Pope, A. L. (1966) Inequality in Function of the Right and Left Ovaries and Uterine Horns of the Ewe, J. An. Sci. **25,** 4, 1169.

Cloud, J. G. and Casida, L. E. (1969) Local Effect of Early Sheep Embryo Upon Uterine Motility, J. An. Sci. **29,** 1, 48.

Conley, H. H. and Haw, H. W. (1970) Effect of Tubal Obstruction, Salpingectomy or Uterine Devices on Estrous Cycle Lengths and Mating Behavior of the Ewe, Internat. J. of Fert. **15,** 2, 115.

Cotchin, E. (1956) Neoplasms of the Domesticated Mammals. (A Review.) Review Series #4, Commonwealth Bureau of An. Health, Bucks, England.

Cullen, R., Hovell, G. J. R. and Shearer, G. C. (1968) The Control of Estrus and the Effect on Fertilization Following Progesterone Treatment in Ewes, Vet. Rec. **83,** 10.

Curnow, D. H. and Bennetts, H. W. (1952) Estrogenic Hormones in Plants in Relation to Animal Physiology, Proc. 6th Internat. Grasslands Congress, Penn. State College.

Daniel, D. L., Bell, D. S. and Sanger, V. L. (1960) Crystalization Patterns of Cervicovaginal Mucus of Sheep. J. An. Sci. **19,** 4, 1319.

Dhindsa, D. S., Hoversland, A. S. and Smith, E. P. (1966) Estrous Synchronization and Lambing Rate in Ewes Treated with MAP, Vet. Med. **61,** 11, 1094.

DeBois, C. H. W. (1969) Estrous Synchronization During the Normal Breeding Season and Synchronized Estrous Induction During the Anestrous Season in the Ewe and Related Phenomena, Mimeographed paper from the Univ. of Utrecht, courtesy C. Bierschwal.

Drake, C., Grant, A. B. and Hartley, W. J. (1960) Further Observations on White Muscle Disease in Lambs, New Zeal. Vet. Jour. **8,** 1.

Dutt, R. H (1953) Induction of Estrus and Ovulation in Anestrual Ewes by Use of Progesterone and Pregnant Mare Serum, J. of An. Sci., **12,** 2, 515.

Dutt, R. H. (1953) The Effect of Low Environmental Temperatures on the Initiation of the Breeding Season and Fertility in Sheep, J. of An. Sci., **12,** 4, 945.

Dutt, R. H. (1963) Critical Period for Early Embryo Mortality in Ewes Exposed to High Ambient Temperature, J. An. Sci. **22,** 3, 713.

Dutt, R. H. and Bush, L. F. (1955) The Effect of Low Environmental Temperatures on the Initiation of the Breeding Season and Fertility in Sheep., J. of An. Sci. **14,** 3, 885.

Dutt, R. H. and Casida, L. E. (1948) Alteration of the Estrual Cycle in Sheep by Use of Progesterone and Its Effect Upon Subsequent Ovulation and Fertility, Endocrin., **43,** 4, 208.

Dutt. R. H., Ellington, E. F. and Carlton, W. W. (1959) Fertilization Rate and Early Embryo Survival in Sheared and Unsheared Ewes Following Exposure to Air Temperature, J. An. Sci. **18,** 4, 1398.

Dzuik, P. J., Cook, B., Niswender, G. D., Kaltenback, C. C. and Doane, B. B. (1968) Inhibition and Control of Estrus and Ovulation in Ewes with a Subcutaneous Implant of Silicone Rubber Impregnated with a Progestagen, Amer. J. Vet. Res. **29,** 12, 2415.

Dzuik, P. J., Lewis, J. M. and Graham, E. F. (1970) Insemination of Ewes with Fresh or Frozen Sperm, J. An. Sci. **31,** 1, 221.

East, J. (1954) The Oestrogenic Activity of Some Leguminous Plants, J. of Endocrin. (Proc. of Soc. of Endocrin.), **10,** March, viii.

Eaton, O. N. (1943) An Anatomical Study of Hermaphrodism in Goats, Am. J. of Vet. Res., **4,** 333.

Eaton, O. N. (1945) The Relation Between Polled and Hermaphroditic Characters in Dairy Goats, Genetics, **30,** 51.

Eaton, O. N. and Simmons, V. L. (1953) Inducing Extra-seasonal Breeding in Goats and Sheep by Controlled Lighting, U.S.D.A., Circular 933, Washington, D.C.

El-Sheikh, A. S., Hulet, C. V., Pope, A. L. and Casida, L. E. (1955) The Effect of Level of Feeding on the Reproductive Capacity of the Ewe, J. of An. Sci., **14,** 4, 919.

Feldman, Wm. H. (1932) Neoplasms of Domestic Animals, W. B. Saunders Comp., Philadelphia, Pa.

Foote, W. C., Call, J. W. and Hulet, C. V. (1967) Effects of Lactation and Hormone Treatment on Ovulation, Estrus and Uterine Involution in the Ewe, J. An. Sci. **26,** 4, 943.

Foote, W. C., Pope, A. L., Chapman, A. B. and Casida, L. E. (1959) Reproduction in the Yearling Ewe as Affected by Breed and Sequence of Feeding Levels. I Effect on Ovulation Rate and Embryo Survival, J. An. Sci. **18,** 1, 453.

Foote, W. C., Sefidbakht, N. and Madsen, M. A. (1970) Puberal Estrus and Ovulation and Subsequent Estrous Cycle Patterns in the Ewe, J. An. Sci. **30,** 1, 86.

Foote, W. C. and Waite, A. B. (1965) Some Effects of Progesterone on Estrous Behavior and Fertility in the Ewe, J. An. Sci. **24,** 1, 151.

Fox, C. W., Eller, R., MacArthur, J. A. B. and Shelton, M. (1964) Reproduction Performance from Purebred and Crossbred Ewe Lambs, J. An. Sci. **23,** 2, 591.

Fraser, A. F. (1968) Reproductive Behaviour in Ungulates, Academic Press, N.Y.C.

Fuller, G. B. and Hansel, W. (1970) Regression of Sheep Corpora Lutea after Treatment with Antibovine Luteinizing Hormone, J. An. Sci. **31,** 1, 99.

Gardner, A. W., Bell, T. D. and Smith, W. H. (1955) A Study of Breeding Behavior in a Group of Western Ewes, J. An. Sci. **14,** 4, 1182.

Ginther, O. J. (1968) Influence of an Intrauterine Device on Ovarian Activity in the Ewe, J. An. Sci. **27,** 6, 1611.

Ginther, O. J. (1970) Effect of Destruction of Follicles on the Corpus Luteum, J. An. Sci. **31,** 1, 233.

Ginther, O. J. (1970) Length of Estrous Cycle in Sheep Treated with Estradiol, Amer. J. Vet. Res. **31,** 6, 973.

Ginther, O. J., Pope, A. L., and Casida, L. E. (1966) Local Effect of an Intrauterine Plastic Coil on the Corpus Luteum of the Ewe, J. An. Sci. **25,** 2, 472.

Godley, W. C., Wilson, R. L. and Hurst, V. (1965) Effect of Controlled Environment on the Reproductive Performance of Ewes, J. An. Sci. **25,** 1, 212.

Hafez, E. S. E. (1969) The Behaviour of Domestic Animals, Williams and Wilkins Co., Baltimore, Md.

Hansel, W. (1970) Personal Communication.

Hartley W. J. and Grant, A. B. (1961) A Review of Selenium Responsive Diseases of New Zealand Livestock, Fed. Proc. **20,** 679.

Hawk, H. W. (1966) Some Effects of Plastic Spirals in Sheep Uteri, J. An. Sci. **25,** 3, 924.

Hawk, H. W. (1969) Some Effects of Intrauterine Devices on Reproductive Function in the Ewe, Fert. and Steril. **20,** 1, 1.

Hignett, S. L. (1963) The Influence of Nutrition on the Fertility of Livestock, in **Infertility in Livestock** Animal Health Branch Monograph #5, FAO, Rome, 47.

Hogue, D. (1965) Personal Communication.

Howland, B. E., Kirkpatrick, R. L., Pope, A. L. and Casida, L. E., Pituitary and Ovarian Function in Ewes Fed on Two Nutritional Levels, J. An. Sci. **25,** 3, 716.

Hulet, C. V. (1966) Behavioral, Social and Psychological Factors Affecting Mating Time and Breeding Efficiency in Sheep. J. An. Sci. **25,** (Suppl.), 5.

Hulet, C. V., Blackwell, R. L., Ercanbrack, S. K., Price, D. A. and Wilson, L. O. (1962) Mating Behavior of the Ewe, J. An. Sci. **21,** 870.

Hulet, C. V. and Foote, W. C. (1962) Observations in the Ewe on the Effect of Ovum Age on Percent Recovery and Recovery Site and Age of Embryo on Crown Rump Length, J. An. Sci. **21,** 3, 600.

Hulet, C. V. and Foote, W. C. (1967) Physiology Factors Affecting Frequency and Rate of Lambing, J. An. Sci. **26,** 3, 553.

Hulet, C. V. and Foote, W. C. (1969) Ovulatory Response of the Ewe to Repeated Injections of PMS, J. An. Sci. **29,** 3, 457.

Hulet, C. V., Foote, W. C. and Price, D. A. (1969) Ovulation Rate and Subsequent Lamb Production in the Nulliparous and Primiparous Ewe, J. An. Sci. **28,** 4, 512.

Hulet, C. V., Voigtlander, H. P., Jr., Pope, A. L. and Casida, L. E. (1956) The Nature of Early-Season Infertility in Sheep, J. An. Sci. **15,** 3, 607.

Hunter, G. L. (1961) Some Effects of Plane of Nutrition on the Occurrence of Oestrus in Merino Ewes, Proc. IV Intern. Congress on An. Reprod., Hague, Vol. II, 197.

Hutyra, F., Marek, J. and Manninger, R. (1946) Special Pathology and Therapeutics of the Diseases of Domestic Animals, Vol. I., Alex. Eger. Inc., Chicago, Ill.

Inskeep, E. K. and Butcher, R. L. (1966) Local Component of Utero-Ovarian Relationship in the Ewe, J. An. Sci. **25,** 4, 1164.

Inskeep, E. K., Oloufa, M. M., Pope, A. L. and Casida, L. E. (1963) Functional Capabilities of Experimentally Induced Corpora Lutea in Ewes, J. An. Sci. **22,** 1, 159.

Kammlade, W. G., Welch, J. A., Nalbandov, A. and Norton, H. W., (1952) Pituitary Activity of Sheep in Relation to the Breeding Season, J. of An. Sci., **11,** 4, 646.

Lamond, D. R. (1964) Synchronization of Ovarian Cycles in Sheep and Cattle, Animal Breeding Abstr. **32,** 3, 269.

Mann, L. I. (1969) Effect of the ICUD on Uterine Motility in the Ewe, Fert. and Steril. **20,** 6, 951.

McEntee, K. and Olafson, P. (1953) Reproductive Tract Pathology in Hyperkeratosis of Cattle and Sheep, Fert. and Steril., **4,** 2, 128.

McLaren, A. (1966) Advances in Reproductive Physiology, Vol. I Academic Press, N.Y.C. (Chapt. on Uterus and Control of Ovarian Function).

Means, T. M., Andrews, F. N. and Fountaine, W. E. (1959) Environmental Factors in the Induction of Estrus in Sheep, J. An. Sci. **18,** 4, 1388.

Means, T. M., Andrews, F. W., Bullard, T. F. and Fountaine, W. E. (1960) The Effects of Light and Temperature on Ovarian Activity in Sheep, Amer. J. Vet. Res. **21,** 80, 81.

Memon, G. N., Antoniewicz, R. J., Benevenga, N J., Pope, A. L. and Casida, L. E. (1969) Some Effects of Differences in Dietary Energy and Protein Levels on the Ovary and the Anterior Pituitary Gland of the Ewe, J. An. Sci. **28,** 1, 57.

Miller, R. F., Hart, G. H., and Cole, H. H. (1942) Fertility in Sheep as Affected by Nutrition During the Breeding Season and Pregnancy, Calif. Exp. Stat. Bull. 672.

Miller, W. W., III and Wiggins, E. L. (1964) Ovarian Activity and Fertility in Lactating Ewes, J. An. Sci. **23,** 4, 981.

Monlux, A. W., Anderson, W. A. and Davis, C. L. (1956) A Survey of Tumors Occurring in Cattle, Sheep and Swine, Amer. J. Vet. Res. **17,** 65, 646.

Moor, R. M. and Rowson, L. E. A. (1966) Local Maintenance of the Corpus Luteum in Sheep with Embryos Transferred to Various Isolated Portions of the Uterus, J. Reprod. and Fert. **12,** 539.

Moule, G. R. (1955) The Case for the Mules Operation, Queensland (Austral.) Agric. Jour., April (Reprint).

Moulton, J. E. (1961) Tumors of Domestic Animals, Univ. of Calif. Press, Berkeley, Cal.

Murphree, R. L., Warwick, E. J., Casida, L. E., and McShan, W. H. (1944) Potential Fertility of Ova from Ewes Treated with Gonadotrophins, J. of An. Sci., **1,** 12.

Murray, F. A., Goode, L. and Linnerud, A. C. (1969) Effects of Season, Mating and Pregnancy on the Volume and Protein Content of Ewe Oviduct Fluid, J. An. Sci. **29,** 5, 727.

Newsom, I. E. (1953) Sheep Diseases, The Williams and Wilkins Comp., Baltimore, Md.

New Zealand, Dept. of Agr. (1954) Annual Report, 37-41.

Niswender, G. D., Dzuik, P. J., Graber, J. and Kaltenbach, C. C. (1970), Function of the Corpus Luteum in the Ewe Following Relocation of the Uterus or Embryo, J. An. Sci. **30,** 6, 935.

Perkins, J. L. and Goode, L. (1966) Effects of Stage of Estrous Cycle and Exogenous Hormones Upon the Volume and Composition of Oviduct Fluid in Ewes, J. An. Sci. **25,** 2, 465.

Phillips, R. W., Frapp, R. M. and Frank, A. H. (1945) Hormonal Stimulation of Estrus and Ovulation in Sheep and Goats (A Review), Am. J. Vet. Res. **6,** 165.

Pigon, H., Clegg, M. T. and Cole, H. H. (1960) The Formation of Antigonadotrophin in Sheep and Its Effect on the Endocrines and Reproductive System, Acta Endocrinol. **35,** 253.

Plotka, E. D. and Erb, R. E. (1967) Levels of Progesterone in Peripheral Blood Plasma during the Estrous Cycle of the Ewe, J. An. Sci. **26,** 6, 1363.

Plotka, E. D. and Erb, R. E. (1969) Identification and Excretion of Estrogen in Urine During the Estrous Cycle in the Ewe, J. An. Sci. **29,** 6, 934.

Plotka, E. D., Erb, R. E. and Harrington, R. B. (1970) Female Sex Steroid Relationships During the Estrous Cycle of the Ewe, J. An. Sci. **30,** 3, 412.

Pope, G. S. (1954) The Importance of Pasture Plant Estrogens in the Reproduction and Lactation of Grazing Animals, Dairy Sci. Abstr. **16,** 334.

Ray, D. E., Bush, L. F. and Wagner, J. F. (1966) Induction of Estrus and Fertility in Anestrous Ewes, Tech. Bull. 28, S. Dakota Agr. Exp. Stat.

Reid, J. T. (1949) Relationship of Nutrition to Fertility in Animals, J.A.V.M.A., **114,** 864, 158, and 865, 242.

Reid, J. T. (1960) Effect of Energy Intake Upon Reproduction in Farm Animals, Suppl. to J. of Dairy Science **43,** 103.

Roberts, E. M. and Edgar, D. G. (1966) The Stimulation of Fertile Oestrus in Anestrous Romney Ewes I and II, J. Reprod. and Fert. **12,** 561 and 565.

Roberts, E. M. and Hafez, E. S. E. (1969) Synchronization of Estrus in Cyclic Merino Ewes with Vaginal Sponges and Pregnant Mare Serum, Amer. J. Vet. Res. **30,** 2, 207.

Roberts, S. J. (1956) Veterinary Obstetrics and Genital Diseases, Edwards Bros., Ann Arbor, Mich.

Robertson, H. A. and Rakha, A. M. (1966) The Sequence, Time and Duration of the FSH and LH in Relation to Estrus and to Ovulation in Sheep, J. of Endocrin. **35,** 177.

Robinson, T. J. (1966) Control of the Ovarian Cycle in the Sheep, in **Reproduction in the Female Mammal** edit. by G. E. Lamming and E. C. Amoroso., Butterworths, London.

Sanger, V. L. and Bell, D. S. (1959) Estrogenic Activity in Green Forage Crops and Its Effect on Breeding Ewes, J.A.V.M.A. **134,** 5, 237.

Schinckel, P. G. (1948) Infertility in Ewes Grazing Subterranean Clover Pastures, Austr. Vet. Jour., **24,** 289.

Shelton, M. (1960) Influence of the Presence of a Male Goat on Initiation of Estrous Cycling and Ovulation of Angora Does, J. An. Sci. **19,** 2, 368.

Shelton, M. (1960) A Comparison of the Ovulation Rate at First Three Heat Periods of Angora Goats, J. An. Sci. **19,** 4, 1227.

Shelton, M. and Huston, J. E. (1967) High Temperature Stress During Gestation and Reproduction in the Ewe, J. An. Sci. **26,** 1, 230.

Shelton, M. and Morrow, J. T. (1965) Effect of Season on Reproduction of Rambouillet Ewes, J. An. Sci. **24,** 3, 795.

Shelton, M. and Morrow, J. T. (1966) Influence of Certain Exteroceptive Factors on the Initiation of Estrus in Angora Does, J. An. Sci. **25,** 1, 252.

Short, R. V. (1967) Comparative Endocrinology of Early Gestation, in **Fetal Homeostasis,** Vol. II, Edit. by R. Wynn, N.Y. Acad. of Sciences, N.Y.C., 224.

Sidwell, G. M., Everson, D. O. and Terrill, C. E. (1962) Fertility, Prolificacy and Lamb Livability of Some Purebred Breeds and Their Crosses, J. An. Sci. **21,** 4, 875.

Southcott, W. H. and Moule, G. R. (1961) Vulvitis in Merino Ewes, Austral. Vet. J. **37,** 8, 291.

Smith, H. J., McLaren, J. B., Odom, J. A. and Miller, H. (1958) Influence of the Use of Sterile Teaser Rams Prior to Breeding on Subsequent Fertility of Ewes, J. An. Sci. **17,** 4, 1231.

Stabenfeldt, G. H. (1970) Recent Advances in Bovine Reproductive Physiology, Bov. Pract. **5,** 2.

Starke, N. C. (1949) The Sperm Picture in Rams of Different Breeds as an Indication of their Fertility. II—The Rate of Sperm Travel in the Genital Tract of the Ewe, Onderstep. J. Vet. Sci. and An. Ind., **22,** 2, 415.

Stormshak, F., Kelley, H. E. and Hawk, H. W. (1969) Suppression of Ovine Luteal Function by 17B-Estradiol, J. An. Sci. **29,** 3, 476.

Thibault, C., Courot, M., Martinet, L., Mauleon, P., DuMesnil DuBuisson, F., Ortavant, R., Pelletier, J. and Signoret, J. P. (1966) Regulation of Breeding Season and Estrous Cycles by Light and External Stimuli in Some Mammals, J. An. Sci. **25,** (Suppl.) 119.

Terrill, C. E. (1968) Reproduction in Sheep, in **Reproduction in Farm Animals,** edit. by Hafez, E. S. E., 2nd Ed. Lea and Febiger, Philadelphia, pa.

Trueblood, M. S. (1966) Relationship of Ovine Contagious Ecthyma and Ulcerative Dermatosis, Cor. Vet. **56,** 4, 521.

Tunnicliff, E. A. (1949) Ulcerative Dermatosis of Sheep, Am. J. Vet. Res., **10,** 240.

Tunnicliff, E. A. (1960) Report of Committee on Diseases of Sheep and Goats, 64th Ann. Meeting U.S.L.S.A., 38.

Uchovsky, D. (1970) Personal Communication.

Underwood, E. J. (1957) Personal Communication.

Underwood, E. J., and Shier, F. L. (1951) The Permanence of the Oestrogenic Effects of Subterranean Clover Grazing on the Ewe, Austral. Vet. J., **27,** 63.

Underwood, E. J., Shier, F. L., Davenport, N. and Bennetts, H W. (1959) Further Studies of the Effects of Prolonged Injections of Stilbestrol on the Ewe, Austral. Vet. J. **35,** 84.

VanRensburg, S. J. (1965) Adrenal Function and Fertility, Jour. S. Afr. Vet. Med. Assoc. **36,** 4, 491.

Venzke, W. G. (1953) Efficacy of Estradiol Cyclopentylpropionate (E.C.P.) in Anestrous Ewes, Am. J. of Vet. Res., **14,** 52, 411.

Wagner, J. F. (1964) Hormonal Control of Reproductive Activity in the Ewe, Proc. Conference on Estrous Cycle Control in Domestic Animals, A. R. S., U.S.D.A., Misc. Public. 1005, 28 (Lincoln, Nebr.)

Warren, J. E., Jr., and Hawk, H. W. (1968) Attempts to Overcome the Antifertility Effect of Intrauterine Plastic Spirals in the Ewe, J. An. Sci. **27,** 1, 131.

Whitten, W. K. (See McLaren).

Wiggins, E. L. and Barker, H. B. (1958) Occurrence of Post-Partum Estrus in Ewes, J. An. Sci. **17,** 4, 1230.

Wiggins, E. L., Barker, H. B. and Miller, W. W. III (1970) Estrual Activity in Open Rambouillet Ewes, J. An. Sci. **30,** 3, 405.

Wiggins, E. L. Miller, W. W., III, Barker, H. B. (1970) Age of Puberty in Fall Born Ewe Lambs, J. An. Sci. **30,** 6, 975.

Wiggins, E. W., Terrill, C. E. and Emik, L. O. (1954) The Effect of Year, Breed, Age, and Number of Ewes Bred on Fertility in Range Rams, J. of An. Sci., **13,** 2, 455.

Williams, H. L., Hill, R., Alderman, G. (1965) Effects of Feeding Kale to Breeding Cows, Brit. Vet. Jour. **121,** 2.

Williams, S. M., Garrigus, U. S., Norton, H. W. and Nalbandov, A. (1956) Variations in the Length of Estrous Cycles and the Breeding Season in Ewes, J. An. Sci. **15,** 4, 984.

Williams, W. L. (1943) Disease of the Genital Organs of Domestic Animals, 3rd Ed., Miss Louella Williams, Upland Rd., Ithaca, N.Y.

Wishart, D. F. (1966) The Induction of Earlier Breeding Activity in Sheep. A Comparison Between the Use of Vasectomized Rams the the Use of Intravaginal Pessaries Impregnated with a New Progestin, Vet. Rec. **79,** 13, 356.

Wishart, D. F. (1967) Synchronization of Oestrus in Sheep, The Use of Pessaries, Vet. Rec. **81,** 12, 276.

Young, R. B. (1960) 10 Points on Mulesing, Leaflet #266 Queensland Dept. of Agr. and Stock., Australia.

Zimbelman, R. G., Pope, A. L. and Casida, L. E. (1959) Effect of Exogenous Progesterone on the Corpus Luteum of the Bred Ewe, J. An. Sci. **18,** 4, 1327.

Chapter XVII

INFERTILITY IN BITCHES AND QUEENS

Infertility in the female dog and cat has not been studied either as carefully or as extensively as in the other domestic animals. Most of the reports are clinical in nature, as limited experimental work has been performed. Much of this probably stems from the fact that most, or nearly all, dog and cat owners are often more interested and concerned in preventing conception in their females than in promoting it. The use of hormone products to influence the estrual cycle or the reproductive organs in dogs and cats is largely empirical and the effects of hormone therapy and the doses required are uncertain.

Infections of the uterus are common in the intact female dog and cat, especially at middle and older ages. Tumors of the reproductive organs are also fairly common in older bitches.

Reproductive Physiology

Dogs or bitches—The onset of puberty in the bitch occurs about 8 to 12 months of age but may occasionally occur as early as 6 months of age or rarely as late as 22 months of age. The plane of nutrition and other tress or disease factors may influence the onset of puberty as in other species. The breed of dog also greatly influences the onset of puberty, being earlier in the small breeds and later in the larger breeds. Confined dogs exhibit their first estrus later than free-roaming dogs, McDonald, Harrop. If the bitch is well-grown there is no reason for not breeding on the first estrum, Hancock. Asdell cited Schotterer in reporting that the ovaries of female pups at birth contain 700,000 oocytes; at puberty there are 355,000, at 5 years of age there are nearly 40,000 and at 10 years of age only about 500 follicles remain in the bitch's ovaries. The ova, including the zona pellucida, at ovulation are about 100 microns in diameter.

The dog is usually considered a monestrous animal and has two estrous cycles a year, although some small breeds may have 3 or 4 and large breeds only 1, Asdell. Anderson et al. reported that in Beagles estrus occurred every 7 months, ±2 months, so twice a year whelping could not be achieved. Greyhounds and other large breeds may only have one estrous period a year, Burns and Fraser. There is evidence that the frequency of estrus is genetically conditioned. In older bitches the periods between estrums become longer and more irregular. Burns and Fraser quoted Frost in reporting that in nearly 500 bitches, 338 had an estrous interval of 5 to 7 months, over 100 had an interval of over 7 months and only 16 had an interval of less than 5 months. Evans reported that the same bitch seldom came into estrum at the same time each year. Papanicoloau and Blau have demonstrated the possibility that the dog is polyestrous, with most of the estrous cycles less accentuated than those which are clinically obvious. They reported that successive or rhythmical changes about every 15 to 16 days were exhibited by means of vaginal smears during anestrum. By using FSH an "abortive estrus" during the anestrous period could be accentuated and converted into a normal observable estrum. There is a marked similarity between this period in the dog and the anestrous period in sheep. More work should be done on this interesting observation.

The periods of estrum usually occur in the late spring and fall, but may occur at any time. Most females of the Basenji breed exhibit estrus in the autumn, Burns and Fraser, but other breeds tend to show estrus at any time of the year with the greatest frequency in late winter and early spring.

The dog is monestrous with only one estrous cycle occurring during the breeding season. The onset of estrum is gradual, with a long proestrous period of 3 to 12 days with an average length of 7 to 10 days, Harrop. During this period the vulva is swollen, firm, and edematous and a bloody discharge from the uterus is observed at the vulva. This is due to the effect of estradiol from the follicles on the uterus. This is not similar to menstruation in primates, as it is seen in proestrus and is caused by edema and escape of erythrocytes from the endometrium by diapedesis, Asdell. During this period the discharge from the vulva attracts males. Estrum, true heat or the period when the bitch will accept the male, lasts from 3 to 21 days, with an average of 4 to 12 days. Proestrum blends gradually into estrum. Blood in the vaginal discharge may continue for one or two or more days into estrum. Bloom reported that the swollen firm vulva seen in proestrus remains large, but softens. A yellowish to slightly pink discharge is present inasmuch as during estrum the edema of the endometrium remains but marked bleeding ceases. During proestrum and estrum the horns of the uterus become enlarged, erect, and round.

Ovulation usually occurs 1 to 3 days after the onset of true estrum, taking 12 to 72 hours for the follicles to rupture, McDonald. The released oocytes, that promptly pass to the ampullary region of the oviducts, do not mature into ova for a day or more at which time the first polar body is extruded. For this reason the immature ova shed by the dog and fox remain viable for several days after ovulation before the male and female pronuclei join and cell division begins. Thus in canine ova, sperm penetration occurs while the egg is still a primary oocyte but the sperm head remains quiescent in the vitellus until the second polar body is emitted. The ova of the bitch differs from those of other domestic animals in not requiring prompt fertilization within 8 to 12 hours; the fertile life of ova in the dog may exceed 4 days, McDonald, Cole and Cupps. The number of follicles that mature and rupture may vary from 4 or fewer in small breeds to 20 or more in the larger breeds. As the bitch gets over 4 to 5 years of age the number of ova released and the number of pups produced declines. Bloom has reported that follicles containing several ova are commonly present in the dog. The follicle size at ovulation is about 0.6 to 1 cm. The turgid fimbriae effectively close the ovarian bursa at ovulation to prevent the loss of ova. It takes from 6 to possibly 10 days for the fertilized ova to reach the uterus after ovulation. This is a longer time than is required in most animals. This longer period may be necessary to allow the extrusion of the first and second polar bodies and the necessary cell divisions so that the ovum is mature enough to survive in the uterus. Following ovulation there is a redistension of the follicle with fluid that is soon replaced by the growing corpus luteum.

In the bitch the corpora lutea are mature by 10 days after ovulation and are about 0.6 to 1.0 cm in diameter. As in the pig, migration of the zygote within the uterine horns before implantation is common. In pregnant bitches the CL remain large until parturition and then regress rapidly. After 30 days of pseudopregnancy, the corpus luteum may begin to slowly atrophy or regress, Arthur. Vestiges of these corpora lutea may still be seen at the next estrum. This progestational, or pseudopregnant period of 30 to 90 days in the nonpregnant bitch is characterized by proliferative changes in the uterus and mammary glands. Endometrial hypertrophy is greatest about 20 to 30 days postestrum. As the corpus luteum regresses at about 60 days after estrum, bitches may lactate, make a nest, and often act like bitches that are about to whelp or have recently whelped. The regression of the corpus luteum in the nonpregnant bitch is not under the influence of luteolysin as in the cow, ewe, or sow. For this reason this period is often called pseudocyesis or false or pseudopregnancy. The endometrium and udder gradually regress.

The anestrous stage is not reached until about 85 to 90 days after estrum. Anestrus lasts for about 3 months with a range of 2 to 8 months, Harrop. During this period the reproductive system is relatively inactive. There are great normal variations between dogs in the intensity, duration, and seasonal occurrence of each phase of the estrous cycle, caused by the age, breed of the dog, and environmental and individual differences. After whelping, bitches do not have estrum while nursing their young but usually come into estrum 2 to 3 months after parturition.

During estrus the bitch does not exhibit very marked psychological or external signs and in this regard is similar to the mare. However the male actively seeks out the bitch in proestrum and estrum by the sexual odor of the vaginal secretions given off during these periods. Bruce reported that urine from estrous bitches was attractive for males. The source of the attractive odor was the vestibule of the bitch under estrogen stimulation. The vagina, uterus and anal glands were not the source of the sexual odor. Thus the cycling bitch is attractive to male dogs for two to four weeks. During the period of estrum or acceptance the bitch encourages the male by holding her tail to one side and standing to be mounted. This attitude of acceptance usually nearly coincides with the cessation of the hemorrhagic vulvar discharge and increases in intensity the first third or half of estrum and decreases the latter two-thirds or one-half of the estrous period. Asdell reported that daily doses of 200 I.U. of estrogen into a ovariectomized bitch caused typical signs of proestrum and estrum including bleeding. Leathem reported that 20 to 50 micrograms of estradiol daily would produce all the normal signs of estrum in anestrous bitches. In early postestrum or metestrum the vulva becomes flaccid and shrinks due to the decline of estrogens, Hafez, Harrop, McDonald. Females to be bred should be taken to the male dog as the male's libido is more affected by a strange environment. The presence of a stranger at a copulation will often prevent the mating of two dogs, Hafez. Toward the end of estrum, a marked influx of leucocytes appears in the vaginal discharge, The vaginal smear is very useful in determining the stages of proestrus and estrus in the bitch and the queen. The vaginal smear is of little or no value in the other larger domestic animals.

The vaginal smear—In the bitch the vaginal smear accurately reveals the stages of the estrous cycle. It is very useful in bitches in which artificial insemination has to be employed because they are timid or frightened and refuse to accept the male, or in bitches that have to be transported some distance to the stud, to be certain the stage of estrum is proper for service. The vaginal smear may be made by inserting a bulb pipette or a glass rod into the vagina and smearing or rolling the mucus secretion on a clean glass slide and staining with Wright's, Leishman's, or Giemsa's stain. According to Evans and Cole, Harrop, Schutte, Gier, Simmons, and Venzke during **anestrus** leukocytes, mostly neutrophiles, are present but scanty. No red blood cells are present. Noncornified, round or oval epithelial cells, whose nuclei and cytoplasm stain uniformly are the principal cell type. The vagina is dry with little or no mucus present. During **proestrum** the vaginal smear contains many red blood cells and a gradual increase in the appearance of large, flat, cornified epithelial cells with an increased staining capacity. These latter cells and red blood cells predominate the last 3 days of proestrus. Leukocytes and noncornified epithelial cells disappear before the end of proestrus. During early **estrum** there are no leukocytes, a variable number of red blood cells early in the period and many large, flat, cornified epithelial cells. About 0.5 to 2.0 ml of fluid may be removed from the vagina with the bulb pipette. Late in estrum the cornified cells become wrinkled and ragged. During the last day or two of estrum beginning 24 to 36 hours after ovulation and especially the first 3 days of **metestrum,** large numbers of polymorphonuclear leukocytes are observed. These slowly disappear and are absent by the tenth to twentieth day of metestrum. In metestrum small epithelial cells whose cytoplasm may be vacuolated are observed. Several smears at daily or every-other-day intervals through proestrum and estrum are of definite diagnostic value. Gier and Simmons reported that large numbers or masses of leucocytes during anestrus, proestrus, estrus and late metestrus are indicative of endometritis or uterine infection. Thus the vaginal smear may be useful to detect pathological conditions as well as determine the stage of the estrous cycle.

Gier reported that ovulation time in the bitch was about 36 hours before the first appearance of leucocytes and about 72 hours before the last acceptance of the male. Conception rates were good for as long as 3 days before ovulation and 2-1/2 days after ovulation due to the long life of the canine ova and spermatozoa in the female genital tract. Doak et al. reported that canine sperm remained motile and viable in the female genital tract for 5 or 6 days and even up to 11 days. Disappearance of spermatozoa coincided with the onset of metestrus. Since ovulation occurs about 24 to 48 hours after the onset of true estrum and the ova mature within several days and are fertile for at least 4 days or longer after ovulation, breeding is usually advised about the third to fifth day of estrum, Asdell. Breeding twice at a 2 to 3-day interval during estrum has been recommended. Evans reported that one service on the first or second day of true estrum or after acceptance of the male resulted in a high rate of conception. Breeding late in estrum when many leukocytes are present in vaginal smears probably is not advisable and would result in a lower conception rate. Hancock and Rowlands reported a high rate of conception on the first to fourth day of true estrum or acceptance with a slight decline on the fifth and sixth days. Griffiths and Amoroso reported that no fertile matings took place later than the sixth day of estrus. The former authors stated that dogs should be bred in relation to estrum or acceptance rather than to the onset of proestrus or bleeding.

Following conception the blastocysts do not attach in the canine uterus until 18 to 20 days or later, McDonald, Evans. Prior to this time the zygotes migrate and rather evenly space themselves between and within the two horns of the uterus. As in other domestic animals, Evans and others have reported a 10 per cent or greater loss of fertilized ova in the bitch. Most fetal resorptions occurred at about 30 days of gestation. Ovariectomy during the first half of pregnancy is followed by resorption of the embryos or abortion. Evans reported that in removing embryos for study after midgestation that removal of only one or two would not cause abortion of the remainder but if more were removed then the rest would probably be aborted unless supplemental progesterone, 25 mg every 48 hours, was administered. This would suggest that the canine placenta might secrete progesterone after midgestation. Curtis and Grant reported that progestogens administered daily to a bitch from 28 to 58 days of gestation caused a masculinization of the female pups. Cole and Cupps reported that estrogens alone had no stimulating effect on the canine mammary gland but progesterone alone would cause complete mammary development. The pubic portion of the pelvic symphysis in Beagles is resorbed and replaced with cartilage by 40 days of gestation but the ischial portion of the symphysis remains ossified, Evans.

Little or no work has been done on determining the blood levels or urine excretion levels of estrogen or progesterone during the various stages of the canine or feline estrous cycle or pregnancy. Neither has there been work done on the gonadotropic blood levels or pituitary levels during the canine estrous cycle. Eik-Nes has reported on limited studies on the effects of gonadotropins on steroid secretion in dogs. Hall and Dale, and Schutte reported that various gonadotropes, FSH and/or LH, given during proestrus had no effect on ovulation or on the length of the estrous period. Leathem, Asdell, Gier and others have reported that gonadotropic hormones, especially FSH injected during anestrum and early proestrum will produce estrus and ovulation. Large doses of estrogens given to dogs are toxic and will, after prolonged therapy, cause atrophy of the skin and alopecia, Dow, or anemia due to hemorrhages into the digestive and urinary tracts or aplastic anemia, Baisset et al., Kirk, Blye. The latter author reported deaths in dogs due to thrombocytopenia and hemorrhages caused by injections of 5 mg. doses of estrogens for 30 to 50 days. Steinberg and others reported aplastic anemia and death after two injections of a slowly-absorbed estradiol compound. Doses of estrogens should be kept small and if given over a prolonged period, frequent regular blood examinations should be performed. Obviously more work is needed on all phases of endocrinology in canine reproduction. The effect of exogenous progesterone or progestagens on the canine endometrium is marked and will be discussed later under cystic endometritis and pyometra.

Cats or Queens—Puberty in cats usually occurs between 7 and 12 months of age depending upon the kittens' nutritive state and genetic background. Females may have their first estrus as early as 5 months of age and weighing about 2.5 kg.. Males usually reach puberty slightly later at a weight of 3.5 kg., U.F.A.W. Handbook, Asdell, Gilman, Joshua, McDonald, Cole and Cupps and Catcott.

The queen is seasonally polyestrous, closely resembling the mare. In the temperate zone nonpregnant females usually exhibit estrous cycles from January or February until the following September and the female is usually in anestrus from late September until late January. Thus increasing hours of day-light may stimulate the onset of the breeding season in the cat, Scott and Lloyd-Jacob, McDonald, and Asdell. Aronson and Cooper have demonstrated that there is a latent sexual season or cycle in male cats that corresponds to that of the queen. The estrous cycles are 13 to 15 days in length with a range of 10 to 22 days. In the presence of a male estrus lasts 3 to 6 days or an average of 4 days, but if coitus does not occur then estrus lasts 5 to 10 days. Mating usually occurs several times a day for 3 to 4 days, Scott and Lloyd-Jacob. Ovulation is not spontaneous in the cat. Coitus is necessary to cause ovulation which occurs 24 to 30 hours, or an average of 27 hours, later. If copulation doesn't occur the follicles become atretic and regress. Ovulation can be induced in queens in estrus by stimulation of the cervix with a glass rod, Asdell, or by injecting 25 to 50 I.U. of HCG. Ovulation occurred 26 to 27 hours after the stimulus or the injection. The fertilization rates were nearly 100 per cent for a natural service from the time of treatment through 27 hours. Fertilization rates declined to 35 to 80 per cent from 30 hours to 49 hours after treatment and no conceptions occurred 52 or more hours after treatment indicating the fertile life of the feline ovum after ovulation was about 24 hours, Sojka et al..

Most queens will have two litters of 2 to 6 kittens with an average of 4 each per year; some will produce 3 litters per year. Mating is observed most frequently in February, May or June and occasionally in September. Most queens will exhibit a lactational anestrus for 4 to 6 weeks while nursing and come back into estrum about 2 weeks after weaning their litter. Rarely a queen will have an estrum and fertile copulation 7 to 10 days postpartum; and conception at 4 weeks of lactation is not uncommon. Early weaning will hasten the onset of estrum, Livingstone. Arthur reported that if the kittens are removed from the queen at birth she will come into estrum in 3 to 4 weeks postpartum. Sperm cells enter the ova 1 or 2 days after ovulation and the dividing zygote enters the uterus 5 to 7 days after ovulation. Corpora lutea reach their maximum size about 17 days after ovulation when they are about 0.3 cm. in diameter. In pregnancy the CL remain at this size until 30 days of gestation and from this point on they regress and are small at parturition but are still able to be observed several weeks or more after parturition. Implantation occurs about the second or third week after internal migration and spacing of the zygotes has occurred. Early embryonic deaths and resorbtions are also common in the queen; they occur most commonly in the body of the uterus and the apices of the horns, Evans, Livingstone. If the cat is ovariectomized before 50 days of gestation, abortion occurs, Cole and Cupps. Sterile copulation is followed by pseudopregnancy or pseudocyesis which lasts for 30 to 40 days, with the corpus luteum regressing after the fourth week following the sterile copulation. Pseudopregnancy is usually absent in unmated females since ovulation and the formation of corpora lutea do not occur. Abnormal behavior patterns do not accompany pseudopregnancy in the cat as they do in occasional dogs.

According to Todd, Hafez, Scott and Lloyd-Jacob, and Fox queens in estrum exhibit a behavior pattern of crouching, extension of the pelvis, treading and lateral deflection of the tail. The queen gives a "heat" cry to indicate she is in estrum and then in the presence of the male an "appeasement" cry to stimulate the male to mount. These vocalizations and posturings are more important than odor in attracting and stimulating the tom, Todd. The queen, especially at her first estrus, may "call" or cry and roll and tread on frequent occasions for the duration of estrum. Many owners will call their veterinarian at this time thinking their female is in agony or pain, Joshua, Holzworth. Young has further carefully described the behavior of the queen in estrus as follows. During proestrum the cat exhibits courtship activities and seeks out the male but will not accept his advances. Estrum is characterized in the female cat by playful rolling, excessive rubbing, a curious low call, and a characteristic crouching or lowering of the forepart of the body accompanied by treading with the hind feet. Grasping of the skin of the neck during estrum may produce this crouching of the forepart of the body and the elevated rear parts. Acceptance of the male and coitus is performed in this position. The male grasps the skin of the neck in his teeth. Withdrawal of the penis is usually accompanied by the female's loud cry or growl, possibly due to pain caused by the penile spines. Sojka et al. reported that cats yowled and immediately attempted to lick their perineal region when the insemination pipette or a glass rod touched the cervix inducing the stimulus for ovulation. This latter observation is probably the correct one to explain the yowl of the female at coitus. Following coitus the female cat has a characteristic reaction of rolling with her fore and hind limbs completely extended and with claws exposed—sliding, rubbing, squirming, and licking. The female will not accept the male again until this period is past. Michael stimulated mating behavior in ovariectomized cats by the introduction of small implants of diethylstilbestrol into the hypothalamus. Certain neurons near these implants had a selective affinity for the hormone.

The vaginal smear in cats is of value to determine the stage of the estrous cycle, Scott and Lloyd-Jacob, Asdell, Livingstone. It is similar at the different stages of the cycle to that in the dog except that bleeding from the uterus with the presence of red blood cells in the smear in proestrum and early estrum is not observed. During diestrum the stained vaginal smear contains a few round or oval nucleated epithelial cells. In proestrum many nucleated epithelial cells are present. With the onset of estrum great numbers of large cornified epithelial cells appear. In metestrum degenerating cornified cells and many leucocytes are noted.

Asdell and McDonald discussed the induction of estrus in anestrous cats in late summer or fall by injection of FSH and LH. Results were variable and not reliable. Further work is indicated. Pregnancy can be easily terminated prior to the second week of pregnancy by injections of estrogens; later larger doses of 1000 R.U. over a 6 day period are needed, Asdell. The mammary glands of the queen require stimulation of both estrogens and progesterone to grow and mature, Cole and Cupps.

Anatomic or congenital defects or abnormalities of the reproductive system in female dogs and cats are unusual. Leonard et al., McFeely and Biggers, Smith, and Lee and Allam reported that hermaphrodism, usually characterized by male pseudohermaphrodism, may occasionally be observed in the dog. Lee and Allam, and McQuown have described cases of true hermaphrodism in the dog and cat. In dogs this condition may be characterized by an abnormally large clitoris that may have to be removed surgically for esthetic reasons. These animals may show abnormal manifestations of sexual desire and activity until castrated.

In approximately 2000 spays, Sweet and Martin observed 3 cases of uterus unicornis in unrelated dogs. According to Stephenson and Leonard, this condition was rare. It occurred in their experience only once in about every 5,000 to 10,000 dogs. Stephenson observed uterus unicornis in only 3 cats. Sheppard reported 21 cases of uterus unicornis in cats, or an incidence of 1 in 1,000. These cats had only 1 to 2 kittens in a litter. She reported observing one feline hermaphrodite. Robinson reported on one feline case and cited two others in which a uterus unicornis was associated with renal agenesis on the same side. Bloom, Smith, and McEntee stated that partial fusion and unequal length of the horns may occur in dogs. A persistent, and nearly imperforate, hymen is rarely seen in dogs. Binder, and Lavignette have each described a case. Hematocolpos or hematometra may occur secondary to congenital atresia of the vagina, Bloom. Higgins and Thomas reported dogs with but a single horn and ovary. The opposite horn and ovary were both missing. McEnte reported that agenesis of one or both ovaries is occasionally observed in the bitch and if bilateral, the tubular genital tract may be infantile or absent. Leonard and coworkers, and Bloom have reported that small, cystic remnants of the Wolffian ducts between the ovary and uterine horn are frequently seen in the dog but are rare in the cat. These remnants may be parametrial, occasionally parovarian, rarely myometrial, or in the fimbriated end of the oviduct, where they are called hydatids of Morgagni. Hypoplastic as well as missing ovaries have rarely been reported.

Bloom stated that cysts of Gartner's ducts in the dog and cat and Bartholin's gland in the cat were rare. Smith has described hypoplasia of the vagina and a septum in the vagina. Beck noted two related Cairn bitches with hypoplasia of the vulva. McEntee has described cystic rete tubules on the ovaries of the bitch that may resemble cystic follicles. Tortoise-shell, or black-and-yellow, cats are almost invariably females. (See Chapter III).

Nutritional causes for infertility in dogs or cats have not been described. As in other animals, severe emaciation or inanition will cause delayed puberty or failure of estrum. Obese, aged female dogs or cats are likely to be sterile but in these animals either an endocrine disturbance or chronic uterine changes may be the cause for irregularities in the estrous cycle and for sterility. The relation of nutrition to reproduction is probably not

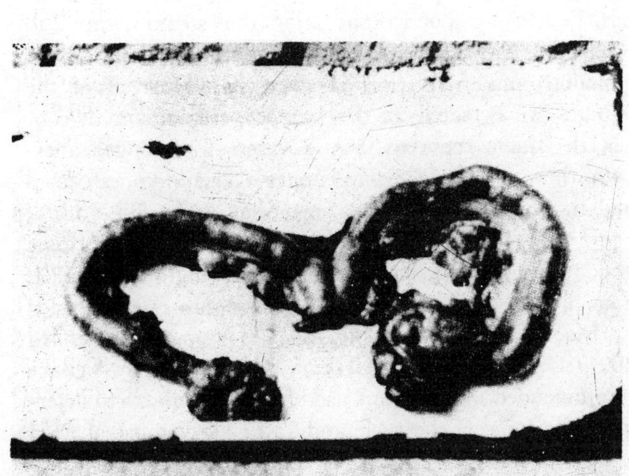

Figure 152 Pyometra in a Bitch (Pseudomonas organisms were recovered from the uterus of the ill 8-year-old female)

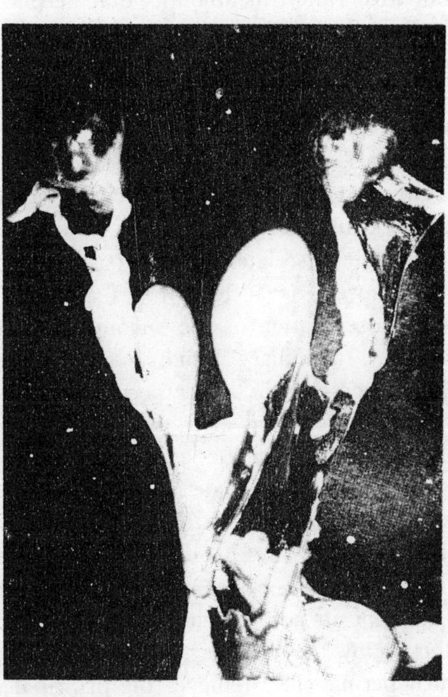

Figure 153 Segmental Aplasia of the Uterine Horns with Mucometra in a Bitch. (Courtesy K. McEntee)

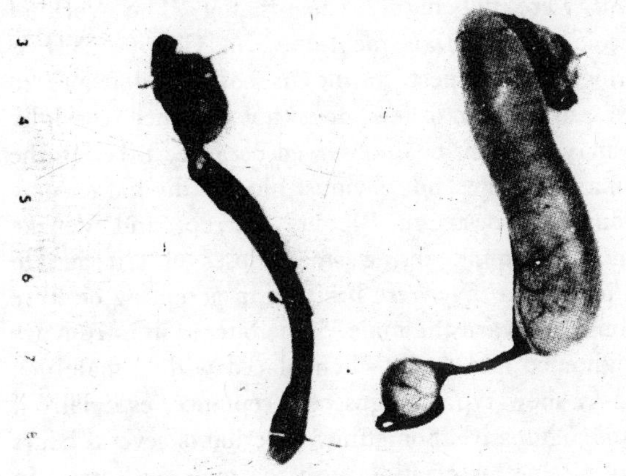

Figure 154 Segmental Aplasia of the Right Uterine Horn with Mucometra in a Queen (Courtesy K. McEntee)

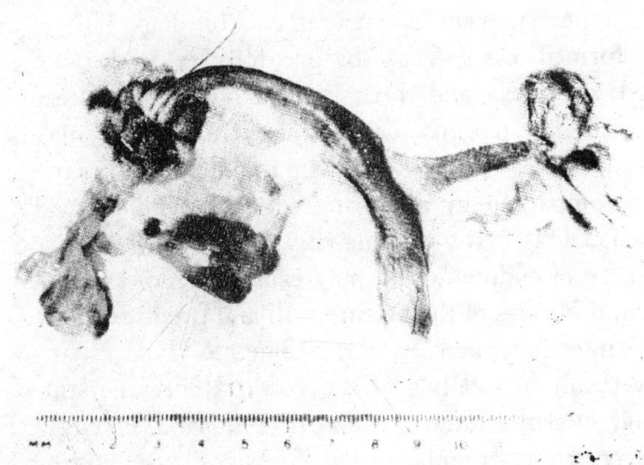

Figure 155 Uterus Unicornis in a Bitch (Courtesy J. D. Sweet)

important in dogs, McCay, Morris. Leathem reported that in protein deprivation in the dog there was a reduction in the blood levels of gonadotropic hormones causing reproductive malfunction. Brood bitches should be fed a balanced nutritive ration in amounts that keep them in good physical condition.

Hormonal disturbances influencing or causing infertility appear to be common in the dog, but less common in the cat. It is well known that in most old male dogs an increased secretion of testosterone frequently causes an enlarged prostate and associated symptoms, while in females an increased secretion of progesterone and estrogen, often associated with persistent C.L. and cystic ovaries causes, or at least plays a role in producing, cystic degeneration of the endometrium, hydrometra, pyometra, mammary tumors, inguinal hernias, and even hairlessness of the lower portions of the body. It is interesting to note that after the reproductive ability reaches its peak at middle age, an increased production of estradiol in the female and testosterone in the male under the influence of F.S.H. causes many disease problems in old dogs. These conditions can be relieved either by injecting the sex hormone, estrogen or androgen, from the opposite sex, which temporarily suppresses FSH production by the pituitary, or by removal of the gonads which permanently removes the principal source of the offending hormone. The ovarian cysts commonly observed in dogs and cats increase in incidence with age. According to Bloom nearly 90 per cent of older female dogs have ovarian cysts. Cysts 0.5 to 6 cm in diameter may be present. In dogs having old cysts formed by atretic follicles, hyperestrinism is uncommon. In dogs having recently formed cysts from mature follicles with well developed granulosa and theca interna layers, the cystic fluid is rich in estrogens. Cysts and corpora lutea may coexist as in the sow. Hyperestrinism in older dogs invariably is accompanied by a varying degree of endometrial hyperplasia. This cystic endometritis, or so called "Swiss cheese" type of endometrium, may cause hydrometra and atrophy and fibrosis of the uterine wall and predispose the uterus to infection, metritis, and pyometra. Hyperestrinism may result in swelling of the vulva, alopecia, mammary and uterine tumors, abnormal uterine bleeding during proestrum, irregularities of the estrus cycle, sterility, and possibly abortion. The important role of hormones, especially progesterone, in the production of metritis and pyometra in the dog and cat will be discussed later under pathology of the uterus.

Anestrum in the bitch may be observed in young females 1-1/2 to 2 years of age that never had an estrum but are healthy, normal and in good physical condition. In these dogs the ovaries are small, hypoplastic, and juvenile, Benesch and Wright. Treatment of these young dogs is usually unsuccessful. If anestrum or delayed puberty is due to a nutritive deficiency, proper feeding usually corrects the condition after several months. In young or middle-aged bitches that fail to exhibit estrum for periods of 10 to 24 months after having normal cycles previously, the condition is probably due to a lack of gonadotropic hormones from the pituitary. (See Discussion in Physiology of Reproduction in the Bitch) Scorgie reported on 18 cases of dogs with abnormally prolonged anestrous periods. Fourteen responded and came into estrum within 2 to 6 days after the administration of relatively small doses of gonadotropins rich in FSH and LH. Thirteen of the females were mated at the induced estrum and 9 conceived. Bloom reported that in cases of prolonged anestrum there might also be a primary ovarian hypoestrinism and for this reason, besides injecting 200 to 800 I.U. of equine gonadotropin and 200 to 500 I.U. of chorionic gonadotropin, stilbestrol in small doses might be of value. The high doses of gonadotropic hormones recommended by Bloom are probably excessive. Harrop recommended 200 I.U. of FSH and LH at 3-day intervals. Venzke recommended the frequent use of vaginal smears to determine the stage of the cycle and 250 I.U. or more of FSH (PMS) at 9 day intervals. If the bitch comes into proestrum, LH should be given later in proestrum or early in estrum. Although estrogen will produce signs of estrum in anestrous bitches, ovulation and fertile service rarely occurs. Hancock and Rowlands reported that the results in their use of P.M.S. and stilbestrol on dogs exhibiting anestrum were not highly encouraging. The work of Papanicoloau and Blau mentioned in Chapter XII is interesting with respect to the use of gonadotropes to produce estrum. In a few dogs not watched carefully estrum may be silent or unobserved because, although the vulva may enlarge, no obvious bloody discharge may occur during proestrum. Bloom, Harrop, and Venzke recommended administering small doses of estrogen to bitches in estrum that were hesitant in accepting or were unresponsive toward the male. Some bitches in estrum are very frightened and timid when placed with a male dog and fail to show typical signs of acceptance, especially if he is quite aggressive. Sometimes a period of several hours to a day of close association with the male will result in acceptance of service or the bitch may be forcibly restrained to permit the male to mount and copulate, or another alternative is artificial insemination. In dogs with cystic ovaries the estrous cycle may be quite irregular although long periods between estrums are less common than are short periods.

Nymphomania in the bitch is characterized by excessive sexual desire which may be indicated by mounting

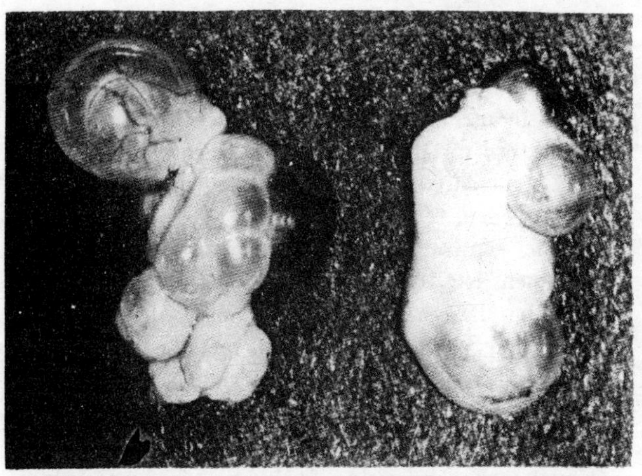

Figure 156. Cystic Ovaries from a Bitch
(Courtesy K. McEntee)

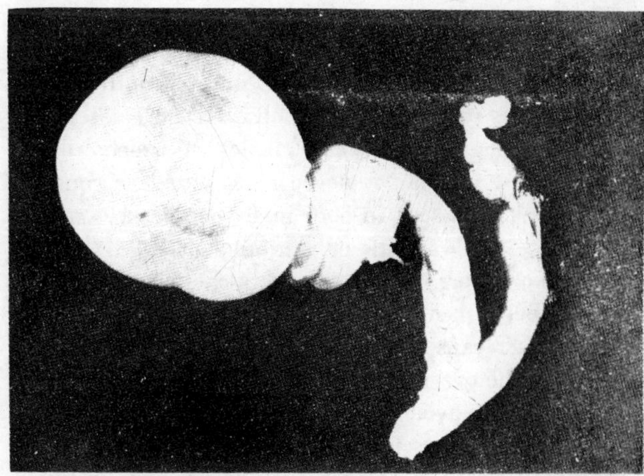

Figure 157 Cystadenoma of a Feline Ovary
(Courtesy K. McEntee)

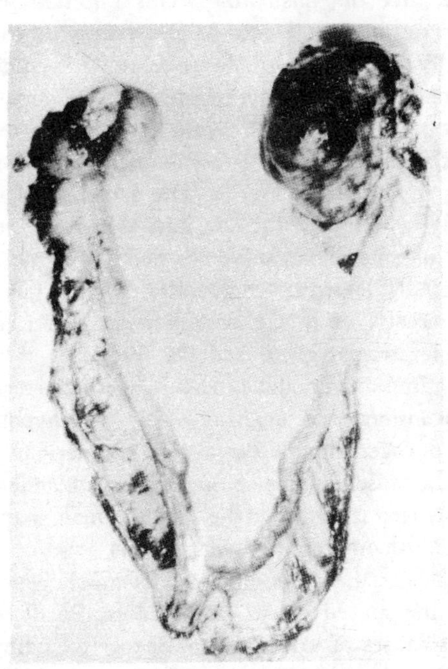

Figure 158 Granulosa Cell Tumor of a Canine Ovary
(Courtesy K. McEntee)

and riding males. Usually copulations will not be permitted. Such bitches are often very nervous, ill-tempered, or possibly psychotic, Harrop. Ordinarily the vulva is swollen and edematous and a bloody discharge from the vulva may be observed. These females are usually sterile. This condition is due to multiple follicular cysts of the ovary that are usually thin-walled and less than 1 inch in diameter. These cysts apparently produce estrogens. The uterine endometrium is hyperplastic and cystic due to the prolonged estrogenic stimulation, Leonard and co-workers, and Bloom. McEntee and Dow reported that follicular and luteal cysts occur commonly in older dogs and cats. The cysts may be multiple or single and the latter were probably not significant. The pathogenesis of these cysts in the dog is not known but is probably similar to that in the cow. Follicular cysts besides causing nymphomania may cause a vulvar swelling, cystic endometrial hyperplasia, cystic mammary hyperplasia, and genital fibroleiomyomas or fibroids. Functional luteal cysts may predispose the endometrium to endometrial hyperplasia and metritis or pyometra. The above cysts should be differentiated from cystic rete tubules, germinal inclusion cysts, parovarian cysts, and cystadenomas.

Spaulding reported that severe nymphomania with nearly 100-per-cent sterility was observed in cats with cystic ovaries. These cats were often nervous, very timid, occasionally exhibited skin trouble, and often had fits. In some cats the enlarged cystic ovaries could be palpated through the abdominal wall behind the kidneys. In dogs an exploratory laparotomy will reveal cystic ovaries but in many cases rupture of the cysts failed to cure the condition. Leonard and Bloom recommended the injection of chorionic gonadotropin in doses of 100 to 500 I.U. or more to luteinize these ovarian cysts and reestablish a regular estrual cycle, but they reported that the results of this treatment were uncertain. This treatment seems more logical than does the administration of progesterone or testosterone recommended by some veterinarians. Both workers concluded that ovariectomy was the most satisfactory treatment for nymphomania.

Certain female dogs, although they are sexually attractive to males for long periods of time, will not accept the male because they are not in true estrum. This condition is called by some veterinarians "constant or perpetual estrum." This condition may be observed in females with cystic ovaries and in spayed females in which all the ovarian tissue was not removed. "Perpetual or constant estrum" has been seen in both intact or properly spayed females due to a vaginitis or vestibulitis, Bruce. Metritis and uterine tumors, even in spayed bitches if hysterectomy was not performed, and possibly infected anal glands, may be other causes for "constant" estrum. When dogs are spayed the ovaries, uterus, and cervix should be carefully removed to avoid the above conditions. If a vestibulitis or vaginitis is present in an intact or spayed female, the vagina may be irrigated with a dilute antiseptic solution and antibiotic ointments injected. In some cases, removal of the anal glands may possibly be helpful.

In cats a diagnosis of cystic ovaries and nymphomania should be made with caution as certain cats, especially Siamese, make a great fuss during estrum. In these cats estrum will last 9 to 10 days in the absence of the male and recur in 15 to 21 days, Asdell. In cats that are not bred, 3 to 4 or more estrous periods are exhibited each breeding season usually during the early spring and summer. In the presence of the male, estrum usually lasts only 4 days, as ovulation is induced by coitus. In cats, injections of chorionic gonadotropin early in estrum would produce ovulation, as it does in the rabbit, and thus shorten the estrous period, Sojka et al.. The use of luteinizing hormone together with progesterone might be useful in the bitch with prolonged proestrous bleeding or a prolonged estrous period, Harrop, Venzke.

According to Bloom, **sterility due to insufficient secretion of progesterone** causes the loss of early embryos or fetuses in bitches. He advised intramuscular doses of progesterone from the end of estrum until the eighth week of gestation.

Pseudopregnancy or pseudocyesis in bred or unbred bitches produces the typical symptoms of mammary development, abdominal enlargement, impending parturition and development of maternal instincts at the approximate time of normal parturition. These signs, which may be slight or severe were discussed previously as manifestations of the metestrous or luteal phase of the cycle, at which time the genital tract is under the effect of progesterone secreted by the corpora lutea. The corpora lutea begin to cease functioning and undergo involution in the dog between 30 and 90 days after estrum. The injection of estrogens, 0.1 to 1.0 mg. daily of diethylstilbestrol, or 10 to 50 mg. of testosterone has been recommended by Bloom for the treatment of pseudocyesis or false pregnancy that usually occurs around the end of the second month of the metestrual period. Whitney (1967) reported that many bitches with signs of false pregnancy during metestrus had endometrial hyperplasia and placenta-like zones in the uterus. Twenty of 155 bitches with pyometra had a history of false pregnancy. Ovariectomy will prevent its occurrence. The value of estrogens or testosterone in the treatment of pseudopregnancy has not been determined in a controlled experiment. Most bitches recover if no treatment is given since this is a normal physiological process that has more noticeable and recurrent psychic manifestations in some bitches than in others. Large doses of estrogens over a period of time should be avoided as they might cause endometrial changes or anemia. Tranquilizers have proven helpful.

Preventing conception in bitches bred accidentally can, as discussed previously in Chapter V, be accomplished in nearly all cases by the injection of 0.1 to 1 mg per pound of body weight of diethylstilbestrol within 24 to 48 hours after the mismating. This injection probably should be repeated in 3 days or small daily doses can be given orally for 3 or 4 more days, Whitney. Cystic ovaries and prolonged estrum may be produced in dogs by this treatment but these dangers should not prevent its use.

Incontinence of urine is common in spayed bitches, especially in the larger breeds. The dribbling of urine is apparently involuntary due to a lack of estrogen resulting in a lack of tone in the sphincter muscles of the urinary tract. Diethylstilbestrol, 1 mg orally daily, is given these affected bitches until the condition is corrected. The amount of estrogen given and the frequency is reduced until the minimum amount needed to prevent a recurrence of the incontinence is determined. It was hypothesized that the estrogen affects the autonomic nervous system and smooth muscle in the sphincter of the bladder. If the dose of estrogen is too large the spayed female may attract male dogs. Bloom reported that if this practice did not result in a cure, the cause might be adhesions between the stump of the spayed uterus and bladder. Small reported that other causes of urinary incontinence including pathologic lesions in the central nervous system could occur. DeVita reported highly favorably on the use of estrogens in incontinence in spayed females.

Dystrophia adiposogenitalis or Frohlich's syndrome is occasionally observed in dogs of either sex and is caused by tumors of the pituitary gland or hypothalamus. The condition usually develops in older dogs and is characterized by localized obesity of the trunk and neck; genital atrophy; a scanty, soft haircoat; a thin, delicate skin; occasional cutaneous ulcers of the extremities; and diabetes insipidus with polyuria, polydipsia and polyphagia. Bloom recommended x-ray therapy or possibly the surgical removal of the pituitary along with a restriction of diet, the administration of thyroid, 5 to 20 grains, and chorionic gonadotropin. Diabetes insipidus can be controlled by injections of posterior pituitary hormones, specifically vasopressin or ADH. The prognosis is poor.

Endocrine dysfunction involving the gonads, thyroid and possibly the adrenal glands are occasionally observed in 6- to 9-year-old bitches and is often characterized by symetrical, bilateral alopecia, especially of the trunk, with an absence of inflammation or pruritus, Schwartzman, Schwartzman and Kral, Goyings et al., Dow, Muller and Kirk.

Hypoestrogenism is usually observed in spayed bitches and is characterized by alopecia of the perineum, the posterior part of the abdomen, and the thighs. No pruritis is present. The condition is most common in bitches spayed before the occurrence of the first estrous cycle. Treatment with 1 mg of diethylstilbestrol daily for 2 to 3 weeks and repeating the treatment if necessary after 1 to 2 months usually corrects this condition in dogs. Doses of 0.25 to 0.5 mg daily are used for cats. Testosterone may also be used.

Hyperestrogenism due to multiple follicular cysts or prolonged administration of large doses of estrogens cause atrophy of the epidermis and thinning of the hair over the abdomen, thighs and perineal region and finally alopecia, as well as cystic endometrial hyperplasia, Dow.

Disorders of the pituitary-thyroid axis, especially in Dachshunds, may result in acanthosis nigricans. This is a lichenification and pigmentation of the groin, and later the axilla and ventral neck, forearm, and ears. Often the hair coat is dull and a dry seborrhea is present. Affected animals may have ovarian disease, abnormal estrous cycles, infertility, and pseudocyesis. Ovariectomy is indicated in old bitches. In dogs spayed early in life estrogens should be administered along with thyroxine or TSH. **Hypothyroidism** is characterized by a dry, dull, scaly hair coat, thinning of the coat and alopecia of the top of the neck or the rump. Affected animals are often obese and lethargic. The condition is often observed in Bulldogs and Dachshunds. Hypothyroidism can be confirmed by a number of tests such as the protein-bound iodine test, radioactive iodine test, or the serum cholesterol test. In the latter test, values of over 400 mg per 100 ml of serum indicate hypothyroidism. Affected animals usually exhibit irregular estrous cycles, infertility, or anestrus, Goyings et al.. Treatment with 1 to 2 mg thyroprotein or 4 to 10 mg of thyroid per kg of body weight daily was fairly satisfactory. Schwartzman and Kral reported good success by treatment with 5 to 25 mg of triiodothyronine (**Cytomel,** Smith, Kline and French Lab.) daily for 4 weeks. Treatment was repeated after 2 to 4 weeks rest.

Skin disorders may also be observed rarely in the bitch secondary to pituitary tumors (See dystrophia adiposogenitalis) or adrenal lesions of hyperadrenocorticism. The latter unusual condition is seen mainly in male dogs and is corrected by castration or removal of the pathologic adrenal gland. Hypo- or hyperestrogenism with alopecia is also observed in cats.

Pathology of the Genital Tract

In the dog and cat this is due mainly to two principal conditions, neoplasms and infections or inflammations.

Neoplasms or tumors of the genital tract are common in the dog but rare in the cat. Ovarian neoplasms in the dog have been ably described by McEntee and Zepp. Granulosa cell tumors were the most common neoplasms of the dog's ovary with 8 of the 19 tumors reported by them being thus classified. Most of the bitches affected with this tumor had a cystic hyperplasia of the endometrium with varying amounts of uterine mucus and lesions of advanced metritis and pyometra. The largest tumor measured 11 x 9 x 5 cm and weighed 213 grams. The tumor growths were irregular in shape, encapsulated, and grayish-white to yellow in color. Some were solid while others were composed largely of cysts. Bloom reported similar pathological changes associated with these tumors. The affected dogs were 2 to 8 years of age. One case was bilateral and 3 had metastisized to other organs. Metastasis of granulosa cell tumors is uncommon, Dow.

McEntee and Zepp described 6 papillary cystadenocarcinomas. Marked ascites was present in two of these cases. Cystic endometrial hyperplasia with a blood-tinged vaginal discharge, and irregular estrous cycles, were commonly observed. These 6 tumors occurred in bitches 6 to 15 years of age. Bilateral involvement of the ovaries was present in 3 cases. Papillary tumors in bitches have been induced by prolonged administration of diethylstilbestrol, McEntee, and Jabara. The tumors were fairly small, the largest being 7 x 6 x 4 cm. The gonads were largely replaced by shaggy, spongy masses of tumor tissue. Peritoneal implants occurred in 5 of the 6 cases and lung involvement occurred in 2 cases. This type of malignant tumor is seen only in the dog.

Other canine ovarian tumors described were luteomas, theca-cell tumors, cystadenomas, dysgerminomas, and a fibroadenoma. Other canine ovarian tumors mentioned by Bloom, Mulligan, McEntee, Cotchin, Moulton, Dow, and Feldman were carcinomas, cystomas, myxosarcomas, teratomas, fibromas, adenomas, sarcomas, cystadenomas, cystadenocarcinoma, and secondary lymphoid tumors. Feldman mentioned a carcinoma and McEntee cystadenomas involving the ovary of cats. Bloom reported that in the cat cystadenomas were rare and granulosa cell tumors had not been observed. McEntee, and Baker indicated that granulosa cell tumors were rarely observed in cats. Mammary carcinomas in the bitch may metastasize to the ovary. These mammary carcinomas in the dog can be produced by prolonged estrogenic stimulation.

In old dogs, uterine neoplasms, especially leiomyomas, which may be single or multiple, are quite common. Bloom suggested that hyperestrinism may be of etiologic importance in these tumors. Feldman, Cotchin, Moulton, McEntee, Brodey and Roszel, and Bloom described fibromyomas, leiomyosarcomas, secondary lymphoid tumors, lipomas, fibroadenomas, rare adenocarcinomas, fibromas, adenomyosis, carcinomas, lipomas, angiomas and sarcomas of the canine uterus. McEntee reported that the uterine fibroleiomyoma or fibroid in the bitch is common and may be associated with bleeding from the genital tract. Endometrial hyperplasia especially with a superimposed infection may result in bleeding also. Both lesions are endocrine dependent. They are not malignant. Small benign tumors cause no trouble, but large uterine tumors may cause hydrometra, pyometra, digestive or urinary disturbances, abdominal enlargement, uterine bleeding, dullness, and emesis. A leiomyoma, cystic fibromyoma and a metastasis of a lymphoblastoma to the uterus has been described in cats by Feldman. Meier described two cases of carcinoma of the uterus in cats. Whitehead described adenocarcinomas of the uterus of the cat and he, Schmidt and Langham and Wolke described leiomyomas and leiosarcomas of the feline genital tract.

Tumors of the canine cervix, vagina, and vulva include leiomyomas, fibromas, neurofibromas, fibroleiomyomas, and lipomas, Bloom, Cotchin, Moulton, McEntee, and Brodey and Roszel. Many leiomyomas were found in the canine vestibule, Brodey and Roszel. Malignant tumors were rare. Feldman, Bloom and others described carcinomas, fibrosarcomas and sarcomas of the canine vagina and vulva. Cotchin, Moulton, and Riser described rare chorioepitheliomas of the placenta of the bitch and a hydatiform mole in a cat. The former is characterized by a bloody discharge after parturition and should be differentiated from the more common condition of subinvolution of the placental sites.

Infectious or transmissible venereal tumor, lymphosarcoma or histiocytoma in the dog has been well-described by Feldman, Jackson, Bloom and coworkers, Mulligan, McEntee, Moulton, and others. It is the only naturally transplantible tumor, Barron et al.. It commonly affects the vagina of the female and the penis and prepuce of the male Moulton cited an infected male that transmitted the disease to 11 of 12 females at mating. Licking of the genitals may also transmit the tumor cells. It is usually spread at coitus. About 5 to 8 per cent of canine neoplasms were of this type, according to Feldman and Mulligan. McEntee, Higgins, and Moulton reported the incidence to be high in the tropics and the Caribbean area. In the United States the incidence was formerly high around New York City and Chicago but the incidence is now low. This tumor can implant in any epithelial tissue. Mulligan, Higgins, and McEntee reported that in a few cases the tumor may implant on the head, ears, and forequarters. Transmission is due to cellular implants. On a mucous surface the tumor appears as a glistening, nodular, cauliflower-like elevation that becomes larger and in many cases reseeds itself; it may spread to the surrounding tissues and lymph glands. In advanced cases a bloody, purulent, fetid discharge usually comes from the vagina of affected dogs. The tumor may protrude through the vulvar lips. Feldman reported Sticker's findings that 16 per cent of all transplanted tumors spontaneously disappeared and that recovered animals were immune. Moulton reported that the tumors grow to maximum size in 5 to 7 weeks and spontaneously regress in about 6 months. Occasionally the tumors may be pedunculated, nodular, or papillary. They are often ulcerated and inflamed on the surface. Prier and Johnson reported that older dogs were susceptible and young dogs were refractory to experimental infection. Regression of the tumor can be induced by partial surgical removal with cautery or by single or divided doses of 2,000 roentgens of X-irradiation. Prier and Johnson and others have also reported the common occurrence of marked chromosomal anomalies in the transmissible venereal tumor cells. Moulton and others reported that metastasis, other than the secondary extension into the regional lymph nodes, is rare with only 5 metastatic cases in 564 diseased dogs in an experimental series. Regression of the tumor due to development of immunity is the rule and recovered dogs remain immune for a long period, McKenna and Prier. For this reason the success of various treatments used in the therapy of transmissible venereal tumor in dogs should be viewed with skepticism. Ladds et al. have reported that malignant lymphoma may clinically resemble the transmissible venereal tumor. Sapp and Adams have observed C-type virus particles in both of these types of tumors.

Mammary neoplasms in the dog and cat are common. The incidence increases with age, especially in nonparous, intact females and usually more than one gland is involved. There is a close relationship betwee mammary tumors and estrogen-secreting cystic ovaries the dog and cat, McEntee. Malignancy and degenerative changes in these tumors are common. These mixed tumors usually contain fibrous tissue, cartilage and bone. Some mammary tumors are benign while others are carcinomatous. Moulton reported that 65 per cent of mammary tumors were benign mixed tumors and 25 per cent were adenocarcinomas with the remainder being a variety of benign or malignant tumors. The adenocarcinoma was most common in the cat; while adenomas and mixed tumors were uncommon in this species. Cotchin described 424 mammary tumors from bitches; 249 were benign and 187 were malignant. Metastases were present in only 41 bitches. Bloom noted that the mammary tumor was apt to grow rapidly during proestrum, estrum and metestrum and tended to become smaller and firmer with a retardation in growth during anestrus and after ovariectomy. However Brodey et al. and Fidler et al. reported that the incidence of dogs with mammary tumors and normal dogs were similar with regard to normal and irregular estrous cycles, signs of pseudopregnancy, and pregnancy; suggesting that oophorectomy at the time of mastectomy was of questionable value. Mammary tumors should not be confused with inguinal hernias in the bitch.

Tumors or neoplasms of the pituitary gland that affect the estrous cycle in dogs and cats are rare. These are usually adenomas or adenocarcinomas. Tumors of the chromophobe or acidophile cells of the anterior pituitary gland are most common. As mentioned previously these tumors frequently result in diabetes insipidus and adiposogenitalis or Frohlich's syndrome, Moulton, and Hottendorf et al.. Ovarian and uterine tumors usually can successfully be removed by a laparotomy and an ovariohysterectomy. Mastectomy is indicated for mammary neoplasms. If metastasis has occurred, the prognosis is guarded to poor. Many of these malignant tumors metastasize into the lung. In cases in which accompanying diseases such as pyometra are present, the prognosis is guarded. Many vaginal and vulvar tumors are pedunculated and can be removed easily after ligating the pedicle. When the base of the tumor is broad, a dorsal episiotomy may be indicated in order to obtain a good exposure of the vagina and the tumor so that complete excision can be accomplished.

Specific infections of the genital tract of the dog and cat causing infertility or sterility in the female have not been reported. Bloom stated that tuberculosis of the uterus of the dog and cat is rare. Canine abortion due to **Brucella canis,** described in Chapter V, may be characterized in some bitches by early embryonic deaths and resorption of embryos at 10 to 20 days postservice and thus appear to be a failure of conception, Carmichael and Kenney.

Infection and inflammations of the canine and feline genital tract are common.

Ovaritis is rare in the dog and cat. Bloom reported that an abscess of a corpus luteum may rarely be observed associated with pyometra.

Lesions of the oviduct are rare in the dog and cat, Bloom. Pyosalpinx when it does occur is usually secondary to pyometra.

Acute metritis and vaginitis may follow difficult parturition, dystocia, careless instrumentation, emphysematous fetuses, contusions and lacerations of the birth canal and uterus, retained placenta, abortion, and delayed uterine involution from other causes. These conditions are usually characterized by an elevated body temperature, anorexia, a drop in milk flow, vomiting, diarrhea, depression, a fetid, bloody vulvar discharge, and other symptoms associated with an acute, septic metritis. Sheppard reported that acute metritis may develop in cats after several abortions. The diagnosis, prognosis and symptoms are discussed in Chapter XI. In dogs there is a danger of uterine rupture and peritonitus. Oxytocin, antibiotics parenterally and locally, and supportive therapy with saline and whole blood are indicated.

Chronic vaginitis may occasionally be observed in the spayed or intact female of any age. Carpenter has described a prepubertal primary vaginitis with a grey to yellow-green exudate that usually recovers spontaneously at the first estrus. The causes are similar to those of vaginitis and vulvitis in other animals, that is, trauma or infection. The infectious organisms include coliforms, streptococci, staphylococci, fungus infections, and others. In the dog, debilitating diseases predispose to vaginitis, Bloom. In rare instances a vaginitis in a spayed bitch may be secondary to a fistula from the ligature around the stump of the vagina or cervix, especially if a nonabsorbable suture was used. Vaginitis may be secondary to tumors and foreign bodies. Bloom, and Carpenter have reported the normal presence of lymph follicles in the vulvar and vaginal mucosa of the dog. Clinical signs of a vaginitis include a vulvar discharge, licking of the vulva, and occassionally a perivulvar dermatitis and an attraction of male dogs The vulvar discharge of pus is characteristic of both vaginitis and metritis. Treatment of vaginitis and vulvitis consists of mild antiseptic douches and the introduction of antibiotics. If a ligature is causing a fistula and vaginitis in a spayed bitch it should be removed. Parenteral antibiotics and the judicious use of estrogens may be indicated in some cases of vaginitis.

Vulvitis may occur rather commonly with or without a vaginitis. The vulva is usually hyperemic and edematous. The bitch may be uneasy and lick the vulva after urination. Knoop, and Smith reported that obesity causing folds of fat alongside the vulva may secondarily result in dermatitis, eczema, and severe irritation. Vulvitis may be treated topically with antibiotics and/or nonirritating antiseptic preparations. The Mules operation, as described for strike in sheep in Chapter XVI, should be performed to remove the folds of irritated skin with dermatitis in affected obese dogs and produce a smooth, flat skin surface.

Cystic Hyperplasia, Endometritis, Metritis and Pyometra Complex in the Dog and Cat

Chronic or subacute metritis or endometritis is common and may be seen in intact bitches and cats of all ages, but is most frequently seen in animals over 6 years of age. It is commonly associated with diffuse endometrial hyperplasia due to prolonged hormonal stimulation. In the bitch and cat progesterone plays the major role in producing endometrial hyperplasia as the condition can be produced most promptly by the alternate administration of the gonadal hormones, progesterone and estrogen. But the injection of estrogen alone does not produce the marked hyperplasia and endometritis observed in the naturally-occurring disease, Dow, McEntee. These gonadal hormones come from Graafian follicles or follicular cysts, and corpora lutea or luteal cysts. It is possible but unlikely that any considerable amount of progesterone or estrogen comes from the adrenal cortex. This differs from the cow and ewe in that cystic hyperplasia of the endometrium in the latter species is due to and can be produced by estrogens. DeLange reported on the close relationship between cystic ovaries, cystic endometrial hyperplasia and mucometra in 4 to 5-year-old nulliparous cattle. In contrast to dogs and cats, endometritis and pyometra seldom accompany cystic endometrial hyperplasia in cattle and sheep. In all species cystic hyperplastic endometrial changes may lead to mucometra and atrophy of the myometrium.

Dow (1959) reported 4 subdivisions or gradations of the cystic hyperplasia-pyometra complex in the dog. **Type I** was characterized by uncomplicated cystic hyperplasia of the endometrium with a mucoid discharge during metestrus. Twenty-three of the 100 bitches in the study were in this group. **Type II** was characterized by diffuse plasma cell infiltration of the endometrium superimposed on cystic hyperplasia. There were 17 of the 100 bitches in this group and in 14 animals **E. coli** was cultured from the uterus. A mucus discharge from the vagina persisted for several weeks in the metestrus period and a mild leucocytosis was present with 12,000 to 15,000 W.B.C. per cmm. **Type III** was characterized by an acute endometritis, metritis or pyometra superimposed on cystic endometrial hyperplasia. The distention of the uterus was dependent on the patency of the cervix. Forty-nine of the 100 bitches were of this type. **E. coli** was cultured from 40 bitches, staphylococci from 6 and streptococci from 5 bitches. Most of these cases were presented 5 to 80 days or an average of 30 days after estrus. Illness of 4 to 10 days duration had been present with 32 dogs experiencing increased thirst, and 21 had vomited. Thirty-eight of the 49 bitches had a vulvar discharge; 40 had a distended abdomen and 8 had an elevated temperature. A leucocytosis with white cell counts of 19,000 to 145,000 per cmm, mainly neutrophiles, was present. Counts over 50,000 per cmm were indicative of pyometra. **Type IV** was characterized by a chronic endometritis, often with squamous metaplasia of the endometrium. The chronic endometritis was either mild or severe with corresponding degrees of leucocytosis, abdominal distention and illness. These dogs were usually 10 to 13 years of age. There were 11 cases in this group.

It was significant that corpora lutea were present in the ovaries of 96 of the 100 bitches in the study. Ovarian cysts were present in 19 and granulósa cell tumors in 8. Most of the bitches had shown irregular estrous cycles. A history of previous attacks of postestrual endometritis, especially in Type IV cases, was common. Nearly all were nulliparous or had had litters 3 to 11 years previously. A few had histories of phantom or false pregnancies.

Dow (1962) also reported rather similar groups of cases in cats affected with the cystic hyperplasia-pyometra complex. **Group I** consisted of 16 of the 100 unselected intact nulliparous female cats that had cystic glandular endometrial hyperplasia without any superimposed inflammatory changes. Most of these cats were over 3 years of age. Four of these cats exhibited vulval hemorrhage, from which one cat died, and the others had a chronic discharge of blood and were severely anemic. This bleeding was due to torsion of endometrial polypi that ranged from 1 to 6 cm in length and were attached by narrow pedicles. **Group II** consisted of 39 cats, 3 to 11 years of age. Most were nulliparous and nearly half had been in estrus within 2 months. These queens had an acute endometritis and pyometra with an illness that had been present for 3 to 14 or more days. The inflammatory reaction was superimposed on a cystic hyperplasia of the endometrium. All cats in this group were dull, depressed and anorexic. Vomiting was a fairly common sign. The vulval discharge was green, brownish or blood-stained in two-thirds of the cats; abdominal distension also was present in about 60 percent of the affected cats in this group. Total blood leucocyte counts ranged from 23,000 to 74,000 cells per cmm. Thirty four of these 39 cats were treated successfully by ovariohysterectomy. Many uteri contained variable amounts of pus up to 2 liters; the pus was yellow-green in color unless bleeding had occurred into the uterus. Thirty-two of 37 cases were positive on culture for **E. coli** and six yielded streptococci. Corpora lutea were present in 33 of the 39 queens; a few follicles or follicular cysts were present in the remainder.

Group III consisted of 10 of the 100 cases. These cats had a subacute inflammatory reaction superimposed on cystic endometrial hyperplasia. Cats in this Group were 4 to 11 years old, and 7 were nulliparous. Illness was less marked but of a longer duration, of 2 months or more, than Group II. Total white cell counts ranged from 21,000 to 32,000 per cmm. A chronic vulval discharge was present. Most of these cats were thin. The uterine horns were slightly enlarged containing about 10 to 15 ml of greenish-grey mucopus. **E. coli** was recovered from all uteri. Luteal tissue was present in 9 of the 10 cases. **Group IV** contained 22 queens with chronic endometritis and cystic endometrial hyperplasia. Their ages ranged from 5 to 14 years, and 14 of them were nulliparous. Fourteen of these cases had shown an intermittent vulvar discharge for 3 to 10 months; all 14 recovered after ovariohysterectomy. The remaining 8 cats were ill, some near collapse, with the history of a chronic low-grade endometritis with a discharge and an acute illness occurring within the last 7 to 10 days. In all of these 8 cases the abdomen had recently become greatly enlarged and anorexia was present; 4 of these cats had severe attacks of vomiting. W.B.C. counts ranged from 24,000 to 64,000 per cmm. In these cases the cervix was patent and the uterus was only moderately enlarged. **E. coli** was isolated from 18 and hemolytic streptococci from 6 of these queens. Corpora lutea were present in 18 cats; 2 cases had normal follicles and 2 cases had follicular cysts. There was a degree of cervical fibrosis in all cases. In the distended uteri; all layers of the uterine wall were atrophied. Atrophy and squamous metaplasia of the endometrium were present in most cases.

In these 4 groups of cats over 75 percent were over 6 years of age. No cats under 3 years of age had cystic endometrial hyperplasia. The similarities between this complex in the bitch and queen are striking. There is also a similarity between these older affected bitches and queens and the "infection prone" older and often nulliparous mare. Over 77 percent of affected cats were nulliparous and had C.L. in their ovaries. Dow speculated on this high incidence of corpora lutea present in older nulliparous cats, a species that is considered to ovulate only after the stimulus of coitus. He indicated that possibly petting and stroking of the cat by the owner might be sufficient to induce ovulation. This disease in cats seldom appeared during the anestrous season of October through January. In the cat, as in the bitch, pyometra often becomes clinically evident in the metestrous or pseudopregnant period. Joshua and Spaulding have reported that in breeding queens early signs of cystic endometrial hyperplasia and a low grade endometritis were characterized by a succession of normal pregnancies, followed in order by stillbirths, a decreased number of fetuses in a litter, abortions at 42 to 52 days, and finally endometritis and sterility.

Dow (1959) showed experimentally that cystic hyperplasia-pyometra complex in the cat and dog were basically similar. In the latter species the cystic endometrial hyperplasia could be produced by cyclic treatment with the estrogens and progesterone. The inflammatory reaction of endometritis and pyometra is progesterone-dependent. Progesterone greatly increases the susceptibility of the uterus to infection, maintains the functional closure of the cervix and causes a relaxation of the myometrium, McEntee. The ease with which pyometra may be produced during the luteal phase of the cycle in the cow and rabbit has been cited previously, Black and co-workers, and Rowson and co-workers. (See Infertility in Cattle.)

Further evidence of the hormonal basis for this syndrome is the numerous reports in the mid-sixties describing cystic glandular hyperplasia, mucometra, and pyometra in bitches injected with progestational compounds, such as medroxyprogesterone acetate given intramuscularly or subcutaneously to prevent estrus. These long-lasting injections would effectively suppress estrus and ovulation for 6 to 24 months or more. Not all bitches or queens would develop endometritis and pyometra but a sufficiently large enough number, over 10 percent, were affected that these products were withdrawn from the market and presently are contraindicated, especially for a female that is expected to be bred at a later date, Anderson et al., Brodey and Fidler, Harris and Wolchuk, and Sokolowski et al..

In dogs severely affected with pyometra, acute metritis, a high W.B.C. count and severe illness, ulceration of the endometrium with bleeding into the lumen may occur; rarely an ulcer may perforate and result in a fatal peritonitis. Severe intoxication in the bitch and cat due to the bacteremia and toxemia associated with acute metritis and pyometra also results in a depression of the bone marrow and anemia, glomerulonephrosis of the kidneys with a secondarily high B.U.N. level and occasionally hemorrhage and necrosis of the adrenal cortex and death associated with signs of shock. The high W.B.C. numbers are predominately neutrophiles or polymorphonuclear cells.

Occasionally polyuria, polydipsia and diabetes insipidus and mellitus may complicate the illness due to the acute endometritis and pyometra. Cystic hyperplasia of the endometrium may involve all or part of both horns or all or part of one horn. McEntee stated that endometrial hyperplasia is a precancerous lesion in women but this is not the case in animals since carcinoma of the canine uterus is rare. In the bitch with cystic endometrial hyperplasia, adenomyosis, or the presence of endometrial glands in the uterine muscle is common. Pyometra following parturition or abortion in the bitch is seldom observed. If the bitch is frequently pregnant, pyometra does not occur. Erickson, Benesch and Wright, Teunissen, DeVita, Dow, McEntee, and others reported that pyometra developed most commonly during the metestrous or pseudopregnant period of the estrous cycle. Ericksen reported canine pyometra developed with only corpora lutea in the ovaries or with both corpora lutea and cystic follicles in the ovaries.

Other uterine lesions noted in cystic hyperplasia and secondary endometritis are: edema, hemorrhage, diffuse leukocytic infiltration of the endometrium, fibrosis of uterine wall, and occasionally ulceration, abscessation, necrosis, and thrombosis. The cystic endometritis tends to be latent or quiescent at all stages of the cycle except metestrum, at which stage most cases exacerbate under the influence of progesterone with clinical signs of varying degrees of severity. In pyometra there is a cystic hyperplasia of the endometrial glands and severe leukocytic infiltration of the endometrium. The cystic glands may or may not be filled with exudate. Certain portions or most of one horn may be more severely affected than other portions of the same horn or the opposite horn. Necrosis of the endometrium may be present in advanced cases. The myometrium may show some evidence of fibrosis and invasion by endometrial glands or adenomyosis. If pyometra and stenosis or functional closure of the cervix results in distension of the uterus, all layers of the uterine wall are markedly stretched and atrophied.

Symptoms of the cystic endometrial hyperplasia-endometritis-pyometra syndrome in the dog and cat are as follows:

In cystic endometrial hyperplasia seen in intact animals over 3 years of age no clinical signs of illness are present, as no infection is present in the uterus. The vulva may be hypertrophied and swollen the first half or throughout the metestrous period. There may be an excessive mucus discharge from the vulva that contains no bacteria, red blood cells and few or no leucocytes. Atresia or functional closure of the cervix may produce mucometra or hydrometra with one or usually both horns distended by a clear, watery or yellowish-grey, nonodorus fluid with a secondary distension of the abdomen in a few cases.

In cystic hyperplasia associated with endometritis and metritis, clinical signs and illness usually appear in the metestrous period 10 to 90 days after estrum. Breeding may or may not have occurred. Some veterinarians report that affected bitches often have a history of breeding failures, irregular estrous cycles, pseudopregnancy, and are nulliparous. Fidler et al., and Brodey studied 68 affected bitches and 248 intact control bitches of the same age, average 7.7 years. They reported there was no correlation between estrous cycle irregularities, abnormal estrus, pregnancies, and cystic endometritis and pyometra. Pseudopregnancy characterized by lactation, and abnormal signs exhibited by the bitch about 60 days postestrum was observed less frequently in dogs that developed an infected diseased uterus than in the control dogs. The injection of progestagens causing a prolonged progesterone-like effect on the genital tract and an artificial anestrous may cause this syndrome in young, one to two-year-old bitches. If suppression of estrus is desired for a limited period 1 to 1.5 mg per pound of body weight of **Repositol** progesterone might be given for several injections at 10-day intervals, Murray and Eden and Candlin. Any prolonged use of progesterone in older intact bitches is contraindicated. It may even stimulate mammary gland neoplasia, Brodey.

Dogs and cats with secondary endometritis and metritis may or may not show signs of illness with an elevated temperature and heart rate, anorexia, dullness, debility, and a rough, dull haircoat. The blood leucocyte levels are often somewhat elevated to 20,000 to 30,000 per cmm. Most of these animals will have a fetid mucopurulent discharge from the vulva that will persist for several weeks or more and must be differentiated from a discharge caused by a vaginitis or cystitis. After a number of weeks the signs spontaneously regress only to reappear following the next estrous period often in a more severe form. Chronic endometritis may be associated with stillbirths, abortion, embryonic deaths, small litters and infertility in dogs and especially cats.

In pyometra there is usually a nearly complete closure of the cervix preventing the escape of the mucopurulent, odorous exudate from the uterus with a distension of the uterine horns and definite to marked signs of illness usually occurring during the metestrous period. The general condition and hair coat may be good or poor, depending upon the acuteness of the onset of the condition. Pyometra may develop rapidly within a week or may take several months. The body temperature in acute cases may be elevated, in chronic cases normal, or in severe toxic cases it may be subnormal. Anorexia, thirst, polyuria, dehydration, and occasionally vomiting may occur. Ascheim reported that polydipsia was common in pyometra due to renal damage caused by a possible toxin that resulted in a failure of the concentrating ability of the kidney tubules. In toxic cases, nephritis with an elevated B.U.N. may be noted occasionally, Brodey. The white blood cell count in pyometra is usually elevated to over 50,000 cells per cmm, most of the leucocytes are neutrophiles. The discharge from the vagina may be absent, scanty, or occasionally profuse. The discharge varies in color from yellowish-gray to reddish-brown and usually has a characteristic stinking odor. The degree of toxicity or dullness will depend upon the severity of the condition. Usually those cases with a closed cervix are more toxic than those in which a discharge is present. The pulse is usually elevated and rapid. The mucus membranes may be pale and in some chronic cases anemia is present. The abdomen in some cases may be distended and pear-shaped. The palpation of the abdomen may reveal the distended uterus.

The course of pyometra is variable. Some cases become acute and severe within a week or 2 and require immediate and early attention to save the patient's life. In other cases, especially those with an open cervix from which pus is draining, the disease may run a course of a month or more. Frost reported on a strangulated inguinal pyometrocele in a bitch. Bloom has reported on 2 cases of pyometra with unicornual uterine torsion. He reported that in the cat a purulent peritonitis may occur secondary to pyometra, while in the dog a perimetritis, a parametritis or a peritonitis may occasionally develop. Remissions in the condition may be frequent in middle or late metestrum or early anestrum. Remissions would not occur in animals in which the cervix was obstructed by a tumor. Krook et al. reported on the possible genetic relationship of obesity, diabetes mellitus and pyometra in certain breeds of dogs such as the Rottweiler and St. Bernard.

Other aids used in diagnosing this syndrome have included rectal examination of the distended uterus with the index finger with the dog's foreparts raised. Radiography, either with or without pneumoperitoneum and preferably with the animal in lateral recumbency so that both horns are superimposed on each other and a better outline is thereby obtained, is a good diagnostic aid. Cobb and Archibald reported that injecting contrast media into the uterus with a metal urethral catheter with the bitch under general anesthesia was of diagnostic value in the cystic endometritis syndrome. As a supplement to blood studies, bone marrow biopsies will often indicate the true severity of the condition, Bloom.

The prognosis in cystic endometrial hyperplasia, endometritis, and pyometra is guarded to poor as complete recovery never occurs, the condition is progressive, and relapses are frequent. The breeding life of the queen or bitch can only rarely be restored and then only in cases diagnosed early. Pyometra is one of the more common causes for death in older female dogs. Kidney damage with nephritis is often associated with pyometra. Ovariohysterectomy is indicated in most affected animals. If the aged females are ill and toxic they are poor surgical risks.

Treatment—All authorities agree that ovariohysterectomy is the procedure of choice for the treatment of pyometra, Brodey, Kirk, Bloom, Engle, Lacroix, and Nooder. Other palliative measures such as the injection of estrogens or pituitrin along with antibiotics and sulphonamides parenterally may be of temporary value, especially in cases with an endometritis or mild metritis with a patent cervix. If early embryonic deaths, abortions and stillbirths are due to a chronic endometritis secondary to cystic endometrial hyperplasia, the parenteral, or even local administration of large doses of broad range antibiotics during proestrum, estrum and early metestrum may be indicated, but the prognosis should be guarded. Relapses invariably occur and the most satisfactory treatment is to remove the uterus and ovaries inasmuch as the reproductive life of these animals is terminated in any event.

All reports stressed the importance of preparing the patient for surgery, if good results are to be achieved. Lacroix stated that 65 percent of the cases presented to him were unfit for surgery. If the patient's condition is good, the operation is performed at once. Delayed surgical intervention is often associated with severe damage to the parenchymatous organs, a prolonged recovery period or death. In toxic patients in poor condition with a history of vomiting, severe depression, a high B.U.N. and incipient shock, several hours or possibly a day of preparation may be necessary before the operation. Blood, saline solution, dextrose solution, or plasma transfusions and antibiotic therapy are given as needed. In toxic cases "marsupialization" of the uterus may be performed under local anesthesia through the ventral abdominal wall. A small laparotomy incision is made and the uterus is sutured to the wound edges. A stab wound through the uterine wall establishes drainage. After the animal has been properly prepared by supportive treatment, the ovariohysterectomy may be performed. The anesthetic of choice according to Engle, Brodey and others, is atropine and a short acting thiobarbiturate, reinforced by a light plane of ether, methoxyflurane or halothane anesthesia. Venoclysis with a 16 or 19 gauge needle should be instituted before and during the operation, so if shock signs develop, fluids can be given rapidly. A liberal incision is made from the s num to near the pubis so that the uterus can be gently slowly removed from the abdominal cavity without trauma to avoid shock or possible rupture of the uterus. The incision should be packed with sponges. The ovarian vessels should be carefully ligated and incised. The uterine vessels should be ligated close to the cervix with individual ligatures, and the broad ligament separated. Pile clamps may be placed across the entire genital canal in the region of the middle of the cervix and the uterus is then removed by cutting between the clamps. The other clamp is removed after a Parker-Kerr stitch is in place, and the cervix is then inverted. A portion of the omentum should be sutured over the stump. Some veterinarians prefer to ligate the cervix, remove the uterus, cauterize the stump with phenol and neutralize the phenol with alcohol. The abdominal incision should be closed carefully, since wound healing in debilitated dogs is likely to be slow or delayed. Hysterectomy for pyometra in the bitch and cat was well-described by Arthur. Aftercare is important and should consist of physiological saline-and-dextrose solution and plasma or blood given intravenously if needed and close observation to prevent shock and death. Antibiotic therapy is usually continued.

Miscellaneous diseases of the genital tract in dogs and cats include endometrial polyps which are rare in dogs and uncommon in cats. These polyps may cause bleeding from the vulva as mentioned previously in cystic endometrial hyperplasia in cats; polyps may favor prolapse of the affected horn resulting in the polyp protruding from the vagina, McEntee. Cysts of the endometrium may be secondary to obstruction of the endometrial glands in cystic endometrial hyperplasia in the dog and cat. Large serosal cysts may occur in old dogs in which they may be secondary to adenomyosis, McEntee.

Subinvolution of the placental sites described previously under involution of the uterus is characterized by a persistent discharge of blood from the vulva following parturition. This discharge may last for months and result in anemia in the bitch. Corpora lutea were found in the ovaries of affected dogs and secondary infection is a possibility. This condition may be mistaken for a postpartum endometritis, a rare chorioepithelioma, endometrial hyperplasia and/or uterine neoplasms. In the placental areas of endometrial subinvolution or decidual reaction, the myometrium and serosa may be eroded and weakened and result in peritonitis. Hysterolaparotomy and gentle curettage of the affected endometrium might be considered in selected valuable brood bitches, but in most cases, ovariohysterectomy is the treatment of choice. Blood transfusions may be indicated prior to surgery in anemic animals, Beck and McEntee, and Kirk et al.. Possibly the injection of oxytocin after whelping might prevent the development of subinvolution of the placental sites.

References

General

Archibald, J. (Editor) (1965) Canine Surgery, Amer. Vet. Public. Inc., Wheaton, Ill.

Asdell, S. A. (1964) Patterns of Mammalian Reproduction, 2nd Ed. Cornell Univ. Press, Ithaca, N.Y.

Burns, M. and Fraser, M. M. (1966) Genetics of the Dog—The Basis of Successful Breeding, 2nd Edition, J. B. Lippincott Co., Philadelphia, Pa.

Catcott, E. J. (Editor) (1964) Feline Medicine, Amer. Vet. Public. Inc., Wheaton, Ill.

Catcott, E. J. (Editor) (1968) Canine Medicine, Amer. Vet. Public. Inc., Wheaton, Ill.

Cole, H. H. and Cupps, P. T. (1969) Reproduction in Domestic Animals, 2nd Edition, Academic Press, N.Y.C.

Harrop, A. E. (1960) Reproduction in the Dog, Williams and Wilkins Co., Baltimore, Md.

McDonald, L. E. (1969) Veterinary Endocrinology and Reproduction, Lea and Febiger, Philadelphia, Pa.

Jubb, K. V. F. and Kennedy, P. C. (1970) Pathology of Domestic Animals, 2nd Edition, Academic Press Inc., N.Y.C.

Kirk, R. W. (Editor) (1968) Current Veterinary Therapy III, Small Animal Practice, W. B. Saunders Co., Philadelphia, Pa.

Specific

Anderson, A. C., McKelvie, D. H. and Phemister, R. (1962) Reproductive Fitness of the Female Beagle, J.A.V M.A. **141,** 12, 1451.

Anderson, R. K., Gilmore, C. E. and Schnelle, G. (1965) Utero-Ovarian Disorders Associated with the Use of Medroxyprogesterone in Dogs, J.A.V.M.A. **146,** 1311.

Aronson, L. and Cooper, M. (1966) Seasonal Changes in the Mating Behavior in Cats after Desensitization of the Glans Penis, Science **152,** 3719, 266.

Arthur, G. H. (1964) Wright's Veterinary Obstetrics, 3rd Ed., Williams and Wilkins Co., Baltimore, Md.

Ascheim, A. (1965) Pathogenesis of Renal Damage and Polydipsia in Dogs with Pyometra, J.A.V.M.A. **147,** 7, 736.

Baisset, A., Bessou, P., Montastruc, P. and Planet, H. (1957) Hemorrhage Produced by Large Doses of Estrogen in Dogs, Vet. Bull. Item 628, 98 (Abstr.)

Baker, E. (1956) Malignant Granulosa Cell Tumor in a Cat. J.A.V.M.A. **129,** 7, 322.

Banks, W. C. (1954) Roentgen Ray Therapy in Venereal Granuloma, N.A. Vet., **35,** 10, 769.

Barron, C. N., Saunders, L. Z., Seibold, H. R. and Heath, M. K. (1963) Intraocular Tumors in Animals.—V. Transmissible Venereal Tumor of Dogs, Amer. J. Vet. Res. **24,** 103, 1263.

Beck, A. (1965) Personal Communication.

Beck, A. M. and McEntee, K. (1966) Subinvolution of Placental Sites in a Postpartum Bitch. A Case Report, Cor. Vet. **56,** 2, 269.

Benesch, F. and Wright, J. G. (1951) Veterinary Obstetrics, The Williams and Wilkins Company, Baltimore, Md.

Binder, R. (1957) Case of Vulvo-Vaginal Stricture in a Beagle Bitch, Vet. Med. **52,** 2, 88.

Bloom, F. (1953) Canine Medicine (Edited by H P. Hoskins, J. V. Lacroix and K. Mayer) Chapter 9, 244 and Chapter 24, 547, Amer. Veterinary Publicat. Inc., Evanston, Ill.

Bloom, F. (1954) Pathology of the Dog and Cat, Amer. Vet. Publicat. Inc., Evanston, Ill.

Bloom, F. (1968) Diseases of Endocrine Glands, Geriatrics, in **Canine Medicine,** edited by E. J. Catcott, Amer. Vet. Public. Inc., Wheaton, Ill., 419, 826.

Bloom, F. Pfaff, G. H. and Noback, C. R. (1951) The Transmissible Venereal Tumor of the Dog, An. J. Path. **27,** 119.

Blye, R. P. (1967) Toxicity and Steroid Hormones in Dogs, 22nd Ann. Conference of the Bureau of Biol. Res., **Reproductive Physiology and the Dog,** Rutgers Univ. New Brunswick, N.J.

Brodey, R. S. (1968) Pyometra, in **Current Veterinary Therapy III** edited by R. W. Kirk, W. B. Saunders Co., Philadelphia, Pa.

Brodey, R. S. and Fidler, I. J. (1966) Clinical and Pathological Findings in Bitches Treated with Progestational Compounds, J.A.V.M.A. **149,** 11, 1406.

Brodey, R. S., Fidler, I. J. and Howson, A. E. (1966) The Relationship of Estrous Irregularity, Pseudopregnancy and Pregnancy to the Development of Canine Mammary Neoplasms, J.A.V.M.A. **149,** 8, 1047.

Brodey, R. S. and Roszel, J. F. (1967) Neoplasms of the Canine Uterus, Vagina and Vulva: A Clinicopathologic Survey of 90 Cases, J.A.V.M.A. **151,** 10, 1295.

Bruce, H. M. (1966) Smell as an Exteroceptive Factor, J. An. Sci., **25,** Suppl., 83.

Candlin, F. T. (1955) Suppression of Estrum in Bitches, N. A. Vet., **36,** 3, 213.

Carmichael, L. E. (1968) Contagious Abortions in Dogs, in **Current Veterinary Therapy III** edited by R. W. Kirk, W. B. Saunders Co., Philadelphia, Pa., 602.

Carmichael, L. E. and Kenney, R. M. (1968) Canine Abortion caused by **Brucella canis,** J.AV.M.A., **152,** 6, Part I, 605.

Carpenter, J. L. (1968) Vaginitis, in **Current Veterinary Therapy III,** edited by R. W. Kirk, W. B. Saunders Co., Philadelphia, Pa., 674.

Cobb, L. M. and Archibald, J. (1959) The Radiographic Appearance of Certain Pathological Conditions of the Canine Uterus, J.A.V.M.A., **134,** 9, 393.

Cotchin, E. (1954) Neoplasia in the Dog, Vet. Rec., **66,** 879.

Cotchin, E. (1956) Neoplasms of the Domesticated Mammals, A Review, Review Series #4, Commonwealth Bureau of Animal Health, Bucks, England.

Cotchin, E. (1958) Mammary Neoplasms of the Bitch, J. of Comp. Path., **68,** 1.

Curtis, E. M. and Grant, R. P. (1964) Masculinization of Female Pups by Progestogens, J.A.V.M.A., **144,** 4, 395.

DeLange, M. (1950) The Influence of Delayed Breeding on the Fertility of Beef Heifers, Onderstep. J. of Vet. Sci. and An. Ind., **24,** 1 and 2, 125.

DeVita, J. (1939) Hyperplastic Endometritis or so called Pyometra of the Bitch, Preliminary Report, J.A.V.M.A., **95,** 448, 50.

Doak, R. L., Hall, A. and Dale, H. E. (1967) Longevity of Spermatozoa in the Reproductive Tract of the Bitch, J. Reprod. and Fertil. **13,** 51.

Dow, C. (1957) The Cystic Hyperplasia-Pyometra Complex in the Bitch, Vet. Rec., **69,** 1409.

Dow, C. (1958) The Cystic Hyperplasia-Pyometra Complex in the Bitch, Vet. Rec., **70,** 49, 1102.

Dow, C. (1959) The Cystic Hyperplasia-Pyometra Complex in the Bitch, J. of Comp. Path. & Ther., **69,** 3, 237.

Dow, C. (1959) Experimental Reproduction of the Cystic Hyperplasia-Pyometra Complex in the Bitch, J. of Path. & Bact., **78,** 1, 267.

Dow, C. (1960) Estrogen Induced Atrophy of the Skin of Dogs. J. of Path. & Bact., **80,** 2, 434.

Dow, C. (1960) Ovarian Abnormalities in the Bitch, J. Comp. Pathol. and Therap., **70,** 1, 59.

Dow, C. (1962) The Cystic Hyperplasia-Pyometra Complex in the Cat, Vet. Rec., **74,** 5, 141.

Eik-Nes, K. (1967) Secretion of Steroids by the Dog Ovary and Testis, in Reproductive Physiology and the Dog, 22nd Ann. Conference of the Bureau of Biol. Res., Rutgers Univ., New Brunswick, N. J.

Engle, J. B. (1940) Pyometra, N. A. Vet., **21,** 6, 358.

Ericksen, S. (1952) Follicular Cysts, Hypoestrogenism, and Pathogenesis of Pyometra, Nord. Vet. Med., **4,** 1078.

Evans, H. E. (1954, 1963) Personal Communication.

Evans, H. E. (1956) Breeding and Prenatal Development in the Dog, Mimeographed Notes for Cornell Conference for Veterinarians.

Evans, H. M. and Cole, H. H. (1931) An Introduction to the Study of the Oestrus Cycle in the Dog, Mem. Univ. of Calif., 9, 2, 66, Univ. of Calif. Press, Berkley, Cal.

Feldman, W. H. (1932) Neoplasms of Domestic Animals, W. B. Saunders Comp., Phila., Pa.

Fidler, I. J., Abt, D. A. and Brodey, R. S. (1967) The Biological Behavior of Canine Mammary Neoplasms, J.A.V.M.A., **151,** 10, 1311.

Fidler, I. J., Brodey, R. S., Howson, A. E. and Cohen, D. (1966) Relationship of Estrous Irregularity, Pseudopregnancy and Pregnancy to Canine Pyometra, J.A.V.M.A., **149,** 8, 1043.

Frost, C. (1958) Strangulated Inguinal Pyometrocele in the Bitch, Vet. Rec., **70,** 573.

Gier, H. T. (1960) Estrous Cycle in the Bitch: Vaginal Fluids, Vet. Scope, **5,** 2, 2.

Gilman, J. P. W. (1957) Reproductive Cycle of the Cat, Personal Communication.

Goyings, L. S., Reineke, E. P. and Schirmer, R. G. (1962) Clinical

Diagnosis and Therapy of Hypothyroidism in Dogs, J.A.V.M.A., **141,** 3, 341.

Griffiths, W. E. B. and Amoroso, E. C. (1939) Prooestrus, Oestrus, Ovulation and Mating in the Greyhound Bitch, Vet. Rec., **51,** 1279.

Hafez, E. S. E. (1969) The Behavior of Domestic Animals, Williams and Wilkins Inc., Baltimore, Md.

Hall, A. and Dale, H. E. (1964) The Effect of Gonadotropic Hormones and Progesterone on the Estrous Cycle of the Female Dog, Vet. Med., **59,** 8, 852.

Hancock, J. L. and Rowlands, I. W. (1949) The Physiology of Reproduction in the Dog, Vet. Rec., **61,** 47, 771.

Hancock, R. C. G. (1967) Early Breeding of Bitches, Vet. Rec., **80,** 10, 336.

Harris, T. W. and Wolchuk, N. (1963) The Suppression of Estrus in the Dog and Cat with Long Term Administration of Synthetic Progestational Steroids, Amer. J. Vet. Res., **24,** 1003.

Higgins, C. C. (1942) Anatomical Abnormality in the Bitch, N. A. Vet., **23,** 11, 46.

Higgins, D. A. (1966) Observations on the Canine Transmissible Venereal Tumor as Seen in the Bahamas, Vet. Rec., **79,** 3, 67.

Hogg, A. H. and Holroyd, H. (1955) A Case of Unilateral Pyometritis in the Bitch, Vet. Rec., **67,** 2, 41.

Holzworth, H. (1969) Personal Communication.

Hottendorf, G. H., Nielsen, S. W. and Lieberman, L. L. (1966) Acidophil Adenoma of the Pituitary Gland and Other Neoplasms of the Boxer, J.A.V.M.A., **148,** 9, 1046.

Huggins, C. and Moulder, P. V. (1944) Studies on Mammary Tumors of Dogs, Lactation and the Influence of Ovariectomy and Supradrenalectomy Thereon, Jour. Expt. Med., **80,** 441.

Jabara, A. G. (1962) Induction of Canine Ovarian Tumors by Diethylstilbestrol and Progesterone, Austral. J. of Exp. Bio. and Med. Sci., **40,** 139

Jackson, C. (1944) The Cytology of the Contagious (Venereal) Tumor of the Dog, Onderstep. J. Vet. Sci. and An. Ind., **20,** 97.

Joshua, J. (1964) Feline Geriatrics, Jour. Small An. Pract., **5,** 525.

Kirk, R. W. (1962) Personal Communication.

Kirk, R. W., McEntee, K. and Bentinck-Smith, J. (1968) Diseases of the Urogenital System, in **Canine Medicine,** edited by E. J. Catcott, Amer. Vet. Public. Inc., Wheaton, Ill., 387.

Knoop, K. W. (1969) Surgical Aid in Treatment of Vulvar Dermatitis in the Obese Dog, Vet. Med., **64,** 3, 212.

Kral, F. and Schwartzman, R. M. (1964) Veterinary and Comparative Dermatology, J. B. Lippincott Co., Philadelphia, Pa., 61, 142.

Krook, L., Larson, S. and Rooney, J. R. (1960) The Interrelationship of Diabetes Mellitus, Obesity and Pyometra in the Dog, Amer. J. Vet. Res., **21,** 80, 120.

Ladds, P. W., Strafuss, A. C. and Clifford, J. R. (1969) Malignant Lymphoma in a Young Dog, J.A.V.M.A., **155,** 8, 1343.

Lacroix, J. V. (1947) The Management of Pseudocyesis and Pyometra, N. A. Vet., **28,** 5, 301.

Lacroix, J. V. and DeVita, J. (1952) Canine Surgery (Edited by J. V. Lacroix and H. P. Hoskins) Chapter 25, 424, Amer. Vet. Publicat. Inc., Evanston, Ill.

Lavignette, A. (1964) Personal Communication.

Leathem, J. H. (1959) Reproductive Physiology and Protein Nutrition in the Dog, Rutgers Univ. Press, New Brunswick, N.J.

Leathem, J. W. (1938) Experimental Induction of Estrus in the Dog, Endocrinology, **22,** 559.

Lee, D. G. and Allam, M. W. (1952) True Unilateral Hermaphroditism in a Dog, Univ. of Penn., Vet. Ext. Quart. No. 128, 142.

Leighton, R. L. (1959) Common Cat Diseases, Vet. Scope, **4,** 2, 3.

Leonard, E. P., Rickard, C. G., and McEntee, K. (1953) Canine Medicine (Edited by H. P. Hoskins, J. V. Lacroix and K. Mayer) Chapter 6, 140, American Vet. Publicat. Inc., Evanston, Ill.

McCay, C. M. (1949) Nutrition of the Dog, 2nd Ed., Comstock Publishing Co., Inc., Ithaca, N.Y.

McEntee, K. (1962) Personal Communication.

McEntee, K. (1970) The Female Genital System, in **Pathology of Domestic Animals,** 2nd Ed., K. V. F. Jubb and P. C. Kennedy, Academic Press Inc., N.Y.C., Vol. I.

McEntee, K. and Zepp, C. P. Jr. (1953) Canine and Bovine Ovarian Tumors, Proc. of 1st World Congress on Fert. and Steril., Vol II, xxiv, 649.

McFeely, R. A. and Biggers, J. D. (1965) A Rare Case of Female Pseudohermaphroditism in the Dog, Vet. Rec., **77,** 696.

McKenna, J. M. and Prier, J. E. (1966) Some Immunologic Aspects of Canine Neoplasms, Cancer Res., **26,** 137.

McQuown, J. B. (1940) An Unusual Case of Sexual Excitement in a Kitten, J.A.V.M.A., **97,** 762, 266.

Meier, H. (1956) Carcinoma of the Uterus in the Cat—Two Cases, Cor. Vet., **46,** 2, 188.

Michael, R. P. (1962) Estrogen-Sensitive Neurons and Sexual Behavior in Female Cats, Science, **136,** 322.

Morris, M. L. (1960) Nutrition and Diet in Small Animal Medicine, Mark Morris Associates, Denver, Colo., 138.

Moulton, J. E. (1961) Tumors of Domestic Animals, Univ. of Calif. Press, Berkeley, Calif.

Muller, G. H. and Kirk, R. W. (1969) Small Animal Dermatology, W. B. Saunders Co., Philadelphia, Pa.

Mulligan, R. M. (1949) Neoplasms of the Dog, The Williams and Wilkins Co., Baltimore, Md.

Murray, G. H. and Eden, E. L. (1952) Progesterone to Delay Estrum in Bitches, Vet. Med., **47,** 11.

Nooder, H. J. (1954) Chronische Endometritis bij Honden en Haar Chirurgische Behandeling, Tijdschr. vor Diergeneesk, **79,** 22.

Papanicolaou, G. N. and Blau, N. F. (1927) Existance of a Sexual Rhythm and Experimental Induction of Heat in the Dog During Anestrus, Anat. Rec., **35,** 47.

Prier, J. E. and Johnson, J. H. (1964) Malignancy in a Canine Transmissible Venereal Tumor, J.A.V.M.A., **145,** 11, 1092.

Rehfeld, C. E. (1954) Clinical Laboratory Diagnosis of Pyometra in the Bitch, Vet. Med., **49,** 12, 531.

Riser, W. H. (1940) Chorioepithelioma of the Uterus of a Dog, J.A.V.M.A., **96,** 755, 271.

Robinson, G. W. (1965) Uterus Unicornis and Unilateral Renal Agenesis in a Cat, J.A.V.M.A., **147,** 5, 516.

Rowlands, I. W. (1950) Some Observations on the Breeding of Dogs, Proc. of the Soc. for the Study of Fertility, **2,** 40.

Sapp, W. J. and Adams, E. W. (1970) C-Type Viral Particles in Canine Venereal Tumor Cell Cultures, Amer. J. Vet. Res. **31,** 7, 1321.

Schmidt, R. E. and Langham, R. F. (1967) A Survey of Feline Neoplasms, J.A.V.M.A., **151,** 10, 1325.

Schutte, A. P. (1967) Canine Vaginal Cytology, Small An. Pract., **8,** 301.

Schwartzman, R. M. (1968) Nonparasitic Dermatoses in **Canine Medicine,** edit. by E. J. Catcott, Amer. Vet. Public. Inc., Wheaton, Ill.

Scorgie, N. J. (1939) The Treatment of Sterility in the Bitch by the Use of Gonadotropic Hormones, Vet. Rec., **51,** 9, 265.

Scott, P. P. and Lloyd-Jacobs, M. A. (1955) Some Interesting Features in the Reproductive Cycle of the Cat, in Studies in Fertility I, 123. (Proc. Soc. for Study of Fertility), Edit. by R. G. Harrison, Blackwell Scient. Public., Oxford, England.

Sheppard, M. (1951) Some Observations on Cat Practice, Vet. Rec., **63,** 44, 685.

Small, E. (1968) Urinary Incontinence and Atony of the Bladder, in **Current Veterinary Therapy III** edit. by R. W. Kirk, W. B. Saunders Co., Philadelphia, Pa., 647.

Simmons, J. (1970) The Vaginal Smear and Its Practical Application, Vet. Med. (S.A.C.) **65,** 4, 369.

Smith, K. W. (1965) The Female Genital Tract, in **Canine Surgery,** Archibald, J. Edit., Amer. Vet. Public. Inc., Wheaton, Ill.

Sojka, N. J., Jennings, L. L. and Hamner, C. E. (1970) Artificial Insemination in the Cat (Felis catus L.), Laboratory Animal Care, **20,** 2 (Part I), 198.

Sokolowski, J. H., Medernach, R. W. and Helper, L. C. (1968) Exogenous Hormone Therapy to Control the Estrous Cycle of the Bitch, J.A.V.M.A., **153,** 4, 425.

Steinberg, S. (1970) Aplastic Anemia in a Dog, J.A.V.M.A. **157,** 7, 966.

Stephenson, H. C. and Leonard, E. P. (1954) Personal communication.

Sweet, J. D. and Martin, S. M. (1955) Personal Communication.

Thomas, L. (1955) Absence of One Ovary and Horn in a Dog, N. A. Vet. **36,** 7, 538.

Teunissen, G. H. B. (1952) The Development of Endometritis in the Dog and the Effect of Oestradiol and Progesterone on the Uterus, Acta Endocrinologica, **9,** 407.

Todd, N. B. (1963) Behavior and Genetics of the Domestic Cat, Cor. Vet., **53,** 1, 99.

U.F.A.W. Handbook on the Care and Management of Laboratory Animals (1967), 3rd Ed., Edit. by U.F.A.W. Staff, E. S. Livingstone Ltd., Edinburgh and London, 512.

Venzke, W. G. and Donovan, E. F. (1966) Canine Reproductive Problems, Veterinary Scope, **11,** 2, 10.

Whitney, G. D. (1968) Prevention of Pregnancy, in **Current Veterinary Therapy III** edit. by R. W. Kirk, W. B. Saunders Co., Philadelphia, Pa., 679.

Whitney, J. C. (1967) The Pathology of the Canine Genital Tract in False Pregnancy, J. Small An. Pract. **8,** 247.

Wolke, R. E. (1963) Vaginal Leiomyoma as a Cause of Chronic Constipation in the Cat, J.A.V.M.A., **143,** 10, 1103.

Chapter XVIII

INFERTILITY IN MALE ANIMALS

It is probable that infertility or sterility is as common in the male as in the female. Because of the greater hazards presented by parturition and pregnancy, acquired infertility or sterility is much more frequent in the female. The degree of fertility in males may vary greatly but is more easily evaluated because of the large numbers of females bred by each male, especially by those males used in artificial insemination. Becker and Roman reported that 36 to 48 per cent of bulls used in artificial insemination are slaughtered for low breeding efficiency. Probably many of these might have given further satisfactory natural service. Only 28 per cent of nearly 9,000 dairy sires used artificially were useful at 10 years of age and older. A report of the Jockey Club showed a great range in fertility in Thoroughbred stallions with an average conception rate of 57 per cent for all stallions. This survey considered the fertility of both the stallion and his mares. Laing cited further data on the incidence of infertility or sterility in the male.

Because the male genital organs can be readily examined and semen examination by means of the artificial vagina, or by electroejaculation in nearly all domestic animals is easily accomplished, many aspects of male infertility have been studied. With the rapid advances made in artificial insemination in recent years has come a greatly increased knowledge concerning male infertility. Whenever a serious infertility problem with a marked drop in conception rate occurs in a group of females, the male or the semen is always to be suspected until proven otherwise. The selection of males for sires should be done very carefully from the genetic standpoint since the male is responsible for 50 percent of the genes present in his daughters; after 3 generations the sires used in a herd are responsible for 88 per cent of the genes in the females.

When any genital organ becomes severely impaired by disease, it usually cannot be restored to its ideal physiological state. For this reason one must look with extreme skepticism on cures claiming a high rate of recovery. The prognosis in treating sterility or infertility in males should always be guarded. There is increasing evidence that the genetic make-up of a sire largely determines his fertility and potency. Only severe diseases, nutritive deficiencies, aging effects or injuries have important or lasting effects on male fertility. There is usually little that treatment or therapy can do to significantly improve the level of fertility in a congenitally infertile male.

References

Becker, R. B. and Dix Arnold P. T. (1953) Tenure and Turnover of Desirable Dairy Bulls in Artificial Studs, J. of Dairy Sci., **26,** 6, 483.

Becker, R. B. and Dix Arnold P. T. (1958) Density of "Sampler" Bulls J. of Dairy Sci., **41,** 5, 736.

Jockey Club Data (1954) Stallion Fertility, Blood Horse, **68,** 18, 1016.

Laing, J. A. (1955) Fertility and Infertility in Domestic Animals, Williams and Wilkins Co., Baltimore, Maryland.

Roman, J., Wilcox, C. J., Becker, R. B., and Koger, M. (1967). Life Span and Reasons for Disposal of AI Beef Sires. J. An. Sci., **26,** 1, 136.

Roman, J., Wilcox, C. J., Becker, R. B., and Koger, M. (1969). Tenure and Reasons for Disposal of Artificial Insemination Dairy Sires, J. Dairy Sci., **52,** 7, 1063.

The Anatomy of the Testes and the Male Genital Tract

The **scrotum** is present in all the domestic animals and encloses the testes. The scrotum of the domestic animals with the exception of the boar and cat is located between the thighs. In the boar and cat the scrotum is located caudal to the thighs and caudal and ventral to the ischiatic arch. It is composed externally of skin that is relatively free of hair except in cats, sheep, and goats. Beneath the skin is the dartos consisting of fibro-elastic tissue and unstriped muscle. The dartos is connected closely with the tunica vaginalis and the remnant of the gubernaculum forming the scrotal ligament. Blom and Christensen reported that there was no scrotal ligament in the bull. The testis and epididymis are fixed in the scrotum by means of the scrotal ligament attached near the tail of the epididymis, and the mesorchium. The latter is a fold of peritoneum from the tunics along a line running proximally from the scrotal ligament between the body of the epididymis and the vas deferens. The scrotum has a medial septum formed by the dartos dividing the scrotum into two halves. The spermatic or scrotal fascia is fastened by loose areolar tissue to the dartos and this fascia is lined by the tunica vaginalis communis, a fibro-serous sac continuous with the parietal peritoneum. The tunica vaginalis communis is thin above, but thicker in the scrotum. The scrotum and cremaster muscles, as well as the pampiniform plexus, regulate testicular temperature, keeping it lower than body temperature. The marked contractibility of the scrotum, causing wrinkling in cold weather, is due to the dartos and cremaster muscles.

The principal blood supply to the scrotum is the external pudendal artery and also the internal pudendal artery in the boar and cat. Innervation of the scrotum is by means of the genital nerve, a branch of the genitofemoral nerve arising from the second to fourth lumbar nerves and the perineal nerve. The smooth muscle of the scrotum is supplied by the spermatic plexus from the pelvic plexus of nerves.

The testis is supported in one of the two scrotal pouches where it is held by its tunics and by the spermatic cord, the latter is composed of the following: the spermatic artery tortuously coiled just dorsal to the testes; the spermatic veins, which form a plexus of veins, the pampiniform plexus, around the spermatic artery; the internal cremaster muscle; lymphatic vessels and the autonomic nerves from the renal and posterior mesenteric plexuses which form the spermatic plexus around the vessels in the cord; the vas deferens; and the tunica vaginalis propria. The distal end of the testis is attached to the scrotum by the scrotal ligament.

The testis proper is closely covered by a thin serous membrane, the tunica vaginalis propria. Beneath this structure is a dense, thick connective tissue capsule, the tunica albuginea, from which, except in the horse, septa radiate to the mediastinum testis to form the lobules of the testis. Within these lobules are the seminiferous tubules, which are lined by germinal epithelium that produces spermatozoa. The length of these seminiferous tubules has been estimated by Bascom to be: for the boar 6,000 meters, the bull 5,000 meters, the ram 4,000 meters, the dog 150 meters, and the cat 25 meters. Between the seminiferous tubules are islands of interstitial or Leydig cells. The seminiferous tubules converge at the apex of the lobule at the receptacle (Marin-Padilla) to join the tubuli recti, or straight tubules that enter the rete testis, a structure of anastomosing spaces located in the mediastinum testis. There is no mediastinum testis in the stallion as is present in the other animals and the collecting tubules join the efferent tubules. From the rete testis the sperm passes to the head of the epididymis through 6 to 24 efferent tubules or ducts. The spermatic artery enters the testis from the spermatic cord and passes to the distal end of the testis before sending branches through the tunica albuginea and the substance of the testis. The veins, small at the distal end, tend to enlarge as they unite at the proximal or spermatic cord end of the testis. On examination of the testes the torturous configuration of blood vessels is most readily noted in the tunica albuginea in the bull. This is a further provision assisting the heat regulatory mechanism of the testis. The consistency of the testis is usually turgid. The parenchyma is yellow to reddish brown in color and bulges on section.

The **epididymis** is composed of a single, torturous, coiled tubule that is essential for the transportation, nutrition, storage, and maturation of the spermatozoa. It has a smooth muscle coat that moves the sperm along in peristaltic waves toward the vas deferens. Much absorbtive and secretory activity occurs in the epididymis. The length of the epididymal tube is about 30 meters, 100 feet, in the bull, 50 meters, 155 feet, in the boar and 20 meters, 65 feet, in the horse, Foote. The proximal or spermatic cord end of the epididymis is more or less flat, broad and U-shaped; and is called the head of the epididymis. The intermediate narrow part is called the body, and the distal enlarged end, which acts as a storage site for spermatozoa, is called the tail of the epididymis. This is continuous with the vas deferens. The epididymis is closely attached by fibrous tissue to the surface of the testis proper.

The testicle of the **bull** is oval in shape, about 10 to 15 cm, 4 to 6 inches, long and 5 to 8.5 cm, 2 to 3-1/2 inches, in diameter and weighs about 200 to 500 gm. The long axis of the testis is vertical and the body of the epididymis lies caudal and medial to the testis. The head of the epididymis is dorsal and the tail ventral to the testis. The vas deferens lies parallel to the body of the epididymis and medial and cranial to it.

The testicle of the **stallion** is oval in shape but slightly compressed from side to side, about 7.5 to 12.5 cm, 3 to 5 inches long, 4 to 7 cm, 2 to 3 inches, dorsal-ventrally and about 5 cm, 2 inches, thick. It weighs about 200 to 300 gm. The long axis of the testis is nearly horizontal. When the testis of the stallion is retracted it becomes nearly vertical. The tail of the epididymis is caudal and loosely attached to the testis. The body lies dorsal to the testis with the head of the epididymis cranial. The vas deferens lies dorso-medial to the body of the epididymis and testis. The horizontal plane of the testis makes torsion of the testis possible in the stallion, although it occurs only rarely. The appendix testis is nearly always present as a small protruding structure on the cranial pole of the equine testis. It is a remnant of the paramesonephric duct. It is also present occasionally on the testis of rams.

The testicles in the **ram** and buck are oval in shape 7.5 to 11.5 cm, 3 to 4.5 inches, long and 3.8 to 6.8 cm, 1.5 to

2.5 inches, in diameter and weighs 200 to 400 gm. The plane of the testis is similar to the bull.

The testicles in the **boar** are oval in shape, 10 to 15 cm, 4 to 6 inches, long and 5 to 9 cm, 2 to 3.5 inches, in diameter. Holst reported that the testis of boars weigh between 500 to 800 gm, with an average of 600 gm. McKenzie, Miller and Bauguess reported the weight of the testes of one to one and one-half year old boars as 200 to 500 gm. Their long axis is almost vertical. The free border of the testis is caudal. The tail of the epidiymis is dorsal, the body cranial and the head of the epididymis ventral. The tail of the epidiymis is quite large. The vas deferens lies cranial and medial to the testis. The spermatic cord is long.

The testicles of the **dog** are similar in location to those of the stallion, but lie slightly more obliquely. The tail of the epididymis is caudal and the head cranial. The testis of the dog is small, about 2 to 4 cm, 0.75 to 1.5 inches, in length and 1.2 to 2.5 cm, 0.5 to 1 inch, in diameter. The dog testis weighs about 7 to 15 gm.

The testicles of the **cat** are similar in location to those of the boar. They are small, 1.2 to 2 cm, 0.5 to 0.75 inches, in length and 0.7 to 1.5 cm in diameter.

The inguinal canals of domestic animals are well described by Ashdown. There are marked species differences. The dog and ox are similar to the pig with large internal inguinal rings and short inguinal canals, while the horse has a small internal inguinal ring and a long inguinal canal. The canal is a slit-like space between the internal abdominal oblique muscle forming the internal inguinal ring and the external inguinal ring formed by the tendons of the external abdominal oblique muscle.

The **vas deferens** or **ductus deferens** extends from the tail of the epididymis to the colliculus seminalis of the pelvic urethra. The wall of the vas is thick and the lumen quite small. It passes parallel to the testis, into the spermatic cord through the inguinal canal in a fold of the vaginal tunic and dorso-medially to the neck of the bladder in the medial edge of the genital fold. From its origin to the dorsal surface of the bladder the vas deferens is of a

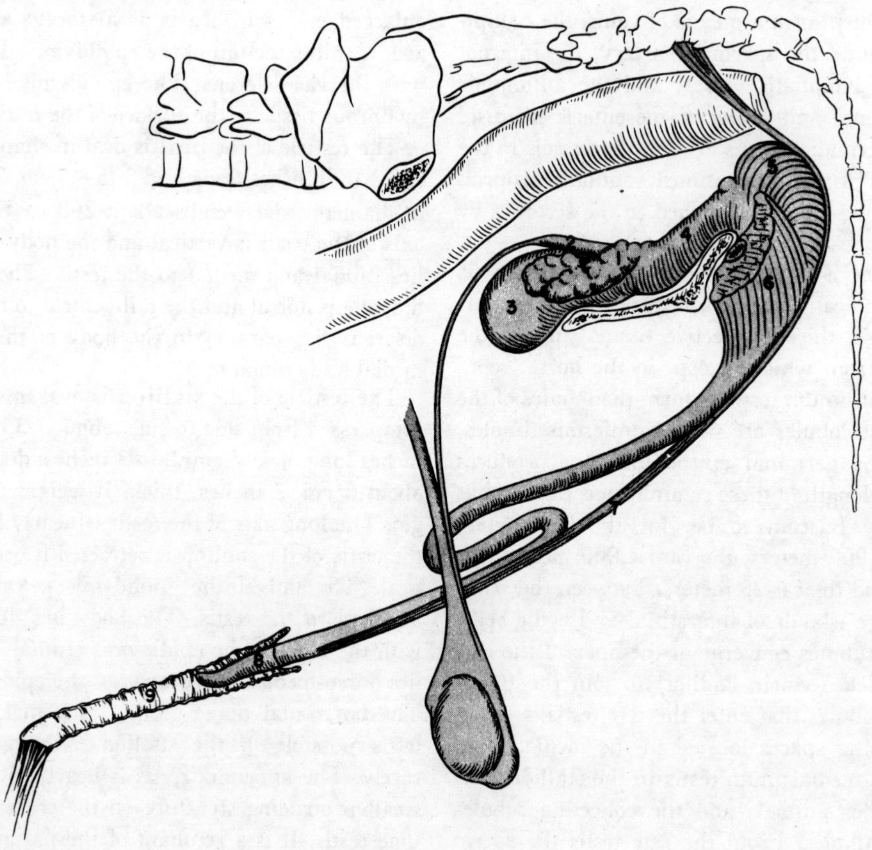

Figure 159. The Genital Organs of the Bull
1. Seminal Vesicle 2. Ampulla of the Vas Deferens 3. Bladder. 4. Urethral Muscle Surrounding the Pelvic Urethra 5. Bulbocavernosus Muscle 6. Ischiocavernosus Muscle 7. Retractor Penis Muscle 8. Glans Penis 9. Preputial Membrane and Cavity.

uniform thickness of about 3 and 6 mm in diameter in the bull and stallion, respectively. The fusiform enlarged terminal glandular portion of the vas is called the **ampulla** of the vas deferens. In the bull it is 10 to 12 cm, 4 to 5 inches, long and about 1 to 1.5 cm in diameter, and in the stallion 15 to 20 cm, 6 to 8 inches, long and about 2 to 2.5 cm in diameter. There is no ampullae in the dog and cat and they are small in the boar. The ampullae in the bull lie dorsal to the neck of the bladder parallel to each other and in close apposition. Caudally the ampullae narrow and pass under the body of the prostate and open through a rounded prominence, the colliculus seminalis, into the cranial portion of the pelvic urethra. Blom and Christensen and others reported that one or both ampullae may be entirely dorsal, entirely ventral, or intermediate in position to the seminal vesicles in the bull. The blood supply of the vas deferens is the spermatic artery and internal pudic artery. The nerve supply is from the pelvic plexus. The accessory male genital glands include the seminal vesicles, the prostate and the bulbourethral glands.

The **seminal vesicles, glandulae vesiculares,** are paired accessory genital glands of the male located on the floor of the pelvis, cranial and lateral to the ampullae and neck of the bladder. The lobes of the vesicular glands have small central dilatations in ruminants and the boar but a large central dilatation in the horse. The recently approved name for the seminal vesicles in domestic animals, except the horse, is the vesicular gland because of its gland-like nature in most animals. In the horse, because this structure is more bladder-like with the glands in the walls, it is still called the seminal vesicle, Sack. These glands secrete a clear fluid that adds volume, nutrients, and buffers to the semen. They open into the pelvic urethra in close proximity to the openings of the vasa deferentia. They do **not** store spermatozoa. The seminal vesicles are absent in the dog and cat.

In the **bull** the vesicular glands are lobulated, 10 to 15 cm, 4 to 6 inches, long, and 2 to 4 cm, 0.75 to 1.75 inches, in diameter.

In the **stallion** the seminal vesicles are smooth, 15 to 20 cm, 6 to 8 inches, long and about 2.5 to 5 cm, 1 to 2 inches, in diameter.

In the **boar** the vesicular glands are proportionately very large, 12 to 15 cm, 5 to 6 inches, long, 5 to 8, 2 to 3 inches, wide and 5 to 8 cm, 1.5 to 2 inches, thick. They cover the caudal portion of the bladder and extend into the abdominal cavity.

A portion or much of the seminal vesicle is covered with peritoneum in the bull and stallion and the boar, respectively. The seminal vesicles of the ram resemble those of the bull.

The **prostate** gland has variable forms in the domestic animals but is located on the floor of the pelvis, caudal to the bladder and on or around the neck of the bladder or cranial portion of the pelvic urethra. It adds its secretions to the semen at the time of ejaculation by means of many ducts opening into the pelvic urethra lateral to the colliculus seminalis. In the dog there are only two excretory ducts.

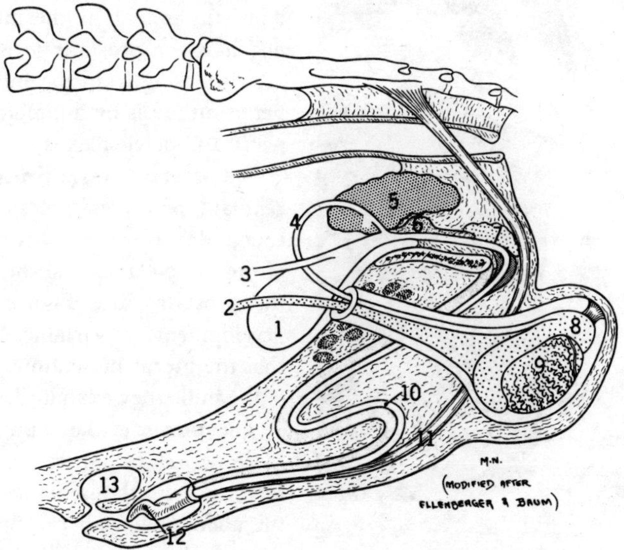

Figure 160. The Urogenital System of the Boar.
1. Urinary Bladder 2. Spermatic Vessels and Nerves 3. Ureter 4. Ductus Deferens 5. Seminal Vesicle 6. Prostate 7. Bulbourethral Gland 8. Tail of the Epididymis 9. Testis 10. Urethra 11. Retractor Penis Muscle 12. Glans Penis 13. Preputial Diverticulum

In the **bull** the body of the prostate gland is 2.5 to 4 cm, 1 to 1.5 inches, wide and 1 to 1.5 cm, 0.5 inch, thick. It can be felt per rectum as a distinct transverse oval protuberance on the cranial end of the pelvic urethra. The pars disseminata of the prostate gland surrounds the pelvic urethra. Dorsally it is about 1 to 1.5 cm thick and 10 to 12 cm, 4 to 5 inches, long and is covered by the urethral muscle.

In the **ram** the prostate gland has no body and is diffused over a large portion of the pelvic urethra.

In the **stallion** the prostate gland is situated over the neck of the bladder and cranial portion of the urethra. It consists of two lateral lobes connected by an isthmus. It is about 5 cm, 2 inches, long and 2.5 cm, 1 inch, wide.

In the **boar** the body of the prostate gland is located dorsal to the bladder and is covered by the seminal vesicles. As in the bull and ram the disseminate prostate gland around the pelvic urethra is quite extensive.

In the **dog** the prostate gland is relatively large and lies at the cranial border of the pubis. It surrounds the neck of the bladder and urethra at their junction and is thin dorsally. The excretory ducts are two in number. The size of the gland varies greatly and may be quite enlarged in older dogs. In a 2 to 5-year-old, 25-pound dog it may vary from 1.7 x 2.6 x 0.8 cm to a near perfect spheroid 2 cm in diameter weighing about 7 gms, Miller. A few disseminate lobules of the prostate gland are present in the wall of the urethra.

Figure 161. The Uterus Masculinus in a Bull (It is usually located between the ampullae and dorsal to the bladder)

The **bulbourethral glands,** or **Cowper's glands,** are paired glands lying on either side of the pelvic urethra, near the ischiatic arch. They are generally ovoid in shape. In the horse they are about 2.5 to 5 cm, 1 to 2 inches, in diameter. In the bull they are slightly smaller than in the stallion. In the ram Cowper's glands are relatively large, 0.5 to 1 cm. In the boar the bulbourethral glands are large, dense, and cylindrical in shape. They are about 12 cm, 5 inches long and 2.5 to 3 cm, 1 to 1.5 inches, in diameter. They are absent in the dog. In the cat the bulbourethral glands are nearly as large as the prostate. These glands have 6 to 8 excretory ducts each, opening into the urethra in the stallion. But only a single duct from each gland is present in the bull and boar. In the castrated male the accessory glands and the penis are small and undeveloped.

Urethral glands, although prominent and numerous in man, are not present in the bull, horse, dog, and cat. The pelvic urethra in the bull, ram, and boar contains many glands similar to those in the prostate gland and this diffuse layer of glands is correctly called the disseminate part of the prostate gland and should not be called "urethral glands", Sack, Kainer.

The blood supply to the accessory glands in the larger domestic animals is the internal pudendal artery. In the dog it is the prostatic artery, a branch of the urogenital artery arising from the internal iliac artery, Miller. The nerve supply is by autonomic nerves from the hypogastric nerve and pelvic plexus.

The **uterus masculinus** is a rudimentary structure, a remnant of the paramesonephric ducts, situated on the caudal dorsal surface of the bladder between the ampullae of the vas deferens and the seminal vesicles and cranial to the prostate. (See Figure 161) Its presence, size, and development are variable. Blom and Christensen reported that the uterus masculinus was found in 50 to 70 per cent of the bulls they examined.

The **penis** is the copulatory organ of the male. It is more or less cylindrical in form in all species. It extends forward from the ischiatic arch to the umbilical region on the abdominal wall except in the cat. It is supported by the penile fascia and skin. Prescrotally it is situated in the prepuce or sheath. The terminal portion of the penis is called the glans and this lies free in the sheath. The body of the penis is composed of the large corpus cavernosum penis which is enclosed by a thick fibrous capsule, the tunica albuginea. Ventral to this is the corpus cavernosum urethrae, a smaller structure surrounding the urethra. These two corpora are spongy in character and divided into many spaces that can be regarded as greatly enlarged capillaries. They are continuous with the veins of the penis. Erection of the penis is caused by a distention of these spaces with blood. The root of the penis is formed by two crura that fasten the penis to either side of the ischiatic arch. The ischio-cavernosus or erector penis muscle is a short paired muscle arising from the tuber ischii and sacrosciatic ligament and is inserted on the crura and body of the penis. It causes erection by its compressing and pumping action on the bulbous portion of the corpus cavernosum penis underlying the muscle. The retractor penis muscle is a smooth muscle which arises on the first and second coccygeal vertebrae, divides and meets again under the anus. This paired muscle passes along the ventral caudal surface of the penis and attaches to the tunica albuginea of the penis. Its action is to draw the penis back into the sheath after erection.

The muscles of the pelvic urethra include the urethral muscle, which is a circular muscle consisting of dorsal and ventral layers of transverse fibers. By its forcible contraction it aids ejaculation and micturition. The bulbocavernosus muscle extending from the ischiatic arch to the glans penis is a continuation of the urethral muscle on the extrapelvic urethra. It is thickest at the root of the penis. It empties the extrapelvic urethra. The blood supply of the penis is the internal pudendal artery to the root, the obturator artery to the body of the penis, and external pudendal artery that gives rise to the dorsal artery of the penis after passing through the inguinal canal. The nerves to the penis are the autonomic nerves of the pelvic plexus and the pudendal and hemorrhoidal nerves. These latter nerves are the motor nerves for the retractor penis muscle. The sensory fibers to the glans penis come from the dorsal nerve of the penis, a branch of the pudendal. The glans penis is plentifully supplied with nerves and nerve endings.

The penis of the **bull** is characterized by an S-shaped curve, or sigmoid flexure, caudal and dorsal to the scrotum. The penis in the adult bull is approximately 36 inches long from the root to the tip of the glans. The erectile tissue is small in amount as compared to that of the stallion. The penis of the bull in the erect state is seldom over 4 to 5 cm, 1.5 to 2 inches, in diameter. The glans penis is about 7.5 to 12.5 cm, 3 to 5 inches, long and is rather pointed. During erection the S-curve is obliterated. The well-developed retractor penis muscle attaches to the penis at the cranial or distal end of the sigmoid flexure with fibers extending dorsally on the penis to near the glans to unite with the fibrous tunic surrounding the distal 7.5 cm, 3 inches, of the corpus cavernosum. The thickened dorsal portion of this fibrous sheath is known as the dorsal apical ligament of the penis, Ashdown et al.. At the time of erection and service the penis is protruded 10 to 24 inches out of the sheath.

The penis of the **stallion** has a large amount of erectile tissue. It is about 50 cm, 20 inches, long and 2.5 to 6 cm, 1 to 2.5 inches in diameter; 15 to 20 cm, 6 to 8 inches lies free in the prepuce. At the time of erection the penis will double its length and thickness, with the glans penis enlarged three or more times its normal size. Dorsal to the urethral process of the glans penis is the urethral sinus, or diverticulum, which is sometimes filled with smegma which is called the "bean." The retractor penis muscle is not as strong as in the bull. No sigmoid flexure is present.

The penis of the **ram** is characterized by a urethral process extending 4 to 5 cm, 1.5 to 2 inches, beyond the glans penis. The glans penis is 5 to 7.5 cm, 2 to 3 inches long. The diameter of the penis in the ram is relatively small, 1.5 to 2 cm, as in the bull. The ram's penis is about 30 cm, 12 inches, long with a well-developed sigmoid flexure.

The penis of the **boar** is similar to the bull but the sigmoid flexure is prescrotal. The cranial portion of the penis has no glans but is spirally twisted counterclockwise. The penis is 45 to 55 cm, 18 to 20 inches, in length and at the time of copulation about 20 to 35 cm, 8 to 14 inches may protrude beyond the preputial opening.

The penis of the **dog** has in its caudal part two distinct corpora cavernosa separated by a median septum. The length of the non-erect penis in the dog is 6.5 to 24 cm, 2.5 to 9.5 inches. In the cranial free portion there is a bone, the os penis, which varies from 5 to 10 cm, 2 to 4 inches in length depending on the size of the dog. Ventrally this bone is grooved for the urethra. A penile bone is also present in foxes, seals, raccoons, and hedgehogs. The glans penis consists of two parts, the pars longa glandis, the distal or cranial two-third of the glans, averaging 5.3 cm in length, and the bulbus glandis, the proximal one-third of the glans, averaging 2.4 cm in length and about 2 cm in diameter. The bulbus glandis expands greatly at the time of erection and prevents withdrawal during ejaculation.

The penis of the **cat** is short and is directed caudally and downward. The urethra is located dorsally. The os penis is often lacking but when present is short, 3 to 4 mm long. There is no glans penis, but merely a terminal cap about 1 cm long that contains numerous, about 120, papillae or spines pointing toward the base of the penis. These may cause the female to cry out on intromission, Aronson and Cooper. In the cat the bulbus glandis is absent.

The **prepuce,** or sheath, is a double invagination of skin which contains and covers the free portion of the penis when not erect and covers the body of the penis behind the glans when the penis is erect. The external opening of the prepuce is called the preputial orifice. The body skin covers the prepuce ventrally. The lining of the prepuce is a freely movable membrane or modified skin that is attached firmly only at the glans penis and the preputial orifice. The blood supply of the prepuce is branches of the external pudendal artery and the innervation is from the pudic, ilio-hypogastric, and ilio-inguinal nerves.

The prepuce in the **bull** is long and narrow, 35 to 40 cm, 15 inches, in length and 4 cm, 1.5 inches, in diameter. The preputial orifice is about 5 to 7 cm, 2 inches, behind the umbilicus and is small, 2 to 4 cm, 1 to 1.5 inches, in diameter, and surrounded by a tuft of long preputial hairs. There are usually two pairs of cranial and caudal preputial muscles, protractors and retractors, that draw the preputial opening either forward or backward. The fornix of the sheath in the bull is the point at which the prepuce reflects upon the penis just caudal to the glans.

The prepuce in the **stallion** has a preputial cavity 15 to 20 cm, 6 to 8 inches, deep and then a second reflection of prepuce to form the prepuce proper of the penis. The opening between these two cavities is called the preputial ring. The engaging and disengaging of the glans penis in the preputial ring causes the sucking noise frequently heard when the gelding or stallion trots. The secretion of the preputial glands and epithelial debris causes the formation of smegma in the sheath of the horse and males of other species.

The prepuce of the **ram** is similar to the prepuce of the bull but is relatively not as long.

The prepuce of the **boar** has a small orifice. The caudal part of the prepuce is narrow and the cranial part wide. In the dorsal wall of the wide part is an opening that leads into the preputial diverticulum. This, when filled with urine, semen and smegma, can resemble an umbilical hernia.

The prepuce in the **dog** has no outstanding characteristics.

Swine and ruminants tend to urinate inside the prepuce, whereas horses, dogs and cats extend the penis beyond the sheath. In ruminants and swine castrated before puberty, the prepuce remains firmly attached to the glans penis, as it is in the prepubertal state.

References

Aronson, L. R. and Cooper, M. L. (1967) Penile Spines in the Domestic Cat: The Endocrine Behavior Relations, Anat. Rec., **157,** 1, 71.

Ashdown, R. R. (1963) The Anatomy of the Inguinal Canal in the Domestic Mammals, Vet. Rec., **75,** 50, 1345.

Ashdown, R. R., Ricketts, S. W. and Wardley, R. C. (1968) The Fibrous Architecture of the Integumentary Coverings of the Bovine Penis, J. of Anat. **103,** 3, 567.

Bascom, K. F. and Osterud, H. L. (1925) Quantitative Studies of the Testicle: II Pattern and Total Tubule Length in the Testicles of Certain Common Mammals, Anat. Rec., **31,** 2, 159.

Benesch, F. (1952) Lehrenbuch Der Tierarzlichen Geburtshilfe and Gynakologie. Urban and Schwarzenberg, Wien-Innsbruck, Austria.

Blom, E. and Christensen, N. O. (1947) Studies on Pathological Conditions in the Testis, Epididymis and Accessory Sex Glands in the Bull, Skand. Vet., **37,** 1.

Bloom, F. (1954) Pathology of the Dog and Cat, American Veterinary Publications Inc., Evanston, Ill.

Dukes, H. H. (1947) The Physiology of Domestic Animals, 6th Ed., Comstock Publishing Co., Ithaca, N.Y.

Foote, Robert (1967) Personal Communications.

Harrop, A. E. (1955) Some Observations on Canine Semen, Vet. Rec., **67,** 26, 494.

Julian, L. M. and Tyler, W. S. (1959) Chapter 2. Anatomy of the Male Reproductive Organs, in **Reproduction in Domestic Animals,** edited by H. H. Cole and P. T. Cupps. Academic Press, N.Y.C. and London, Vol. I, 29.

Kainer, R. A., Faulkner, L. C. and Abdel-Raouf, M. (1969) Glands Associated with the Urethra of the Bull, Amer. J. Vet. Res. **30,** 6, 963.

Marin-Padilla, M. (1964) The Mesonephric-testicular Connection in Man and Some Mammals, Anat. Rec. **148,** 1.

McKenzie, F. F., Miller, J. C. and Bauguess, L. C. (1938) The Reproductive Organs and Semen of the Boar, Univ. of Mo., Agric. Exp. Stat. Research Bull. 279.

Miller, M. E. (1964) Anatomy of the Dog. W. A. Saunders Co., Phila, London.

Sack, W. (1968) Personal Communication.

Schmaltz, R. (1937) Male Urogenital Apparatus of the Cat, Vet. Med., **32,** 11, 500.

Sisson, S. and Grossman, J. D. (1953) The Anatomy of the Domestic Animals, 4th Ed. Revised, W. B. Saunders, Co., Philadelphia, Pa.

St. Clair, L. E. (1958) Chapter on Anatomy, in **Diseases of Swine,** edited by H. W. Dunne, Iowa State College Press, Ames, Iowa, 3.

Williams, W. L. (1943) Veterinary Obstetrics, 4th Ed., Miss Louella Williams, Upland Rd., Ithaca, N.Y.

The Embryology of the Male Reproductive Tract

The urogenital system is formed mainly from mesodermal tissue that in early embryonic life forms the nephric and genital regions. In the cranial portion of the nephric region segmental tubules initially form the pronephros each with a pronephric duct that runs to the primitive cloaca. Later other segmental tubules form caudal to the pronephros and unite with the pronephric ducts to form another temporary excretory organ, the mesonephros and mesonephric ducts or Wolffian body and ducts, and the pronephros degenerates. Later a third and more permanent excretory organ forms more caudally from an outgrowth of the mesonephric duct to become the metanephros or true kidney with its ureter and bladder. The mesonephros then degenerates but its duct system is utilized in the male to transport spermatozoa from the testes to the pelvic urethra. The development of the paramesonephric or Mullerian duct has been described in the section on the embryology of the female genital tract. Remnants of the paramesonephric or mesonephric ducts may persist in the adult male as the appendix testis and the uterus masculinus. In the fetus most of the urine from the fetal kidneys passes into the bladder and through the urachus into the allantoic cavity.

The testes form initially as undifferentiated gonads late in the embryonic period in the genital region or gonadal or genital ridge between the dorsal mesentery and the mesonephros. Although the sex of the embryo is determined at the time of fertilization, sexual differentiation doesn't occur until the early fetal period after the primordial germ cells have migrated to the gonadal ridge from the wall of the yolk sac in the region of the hind gut and structural changes occur in the gonad. Testis cords, rete testis cords and the tunica albuginea form early in the fetal period. Primary medullary cords are characteristic of the early male gonad. These testis cords of primitive germ cells and supporting Sertoli cells remain solid until just before puberty when the seminiferous tubules are formed and join the rete testis by means of the tubuli recti. The rete testis in turn enters the efferent tubules, epididymis and ductus deferens that are formed from the mesonephric tubules and duct. Certain tubules of the mesonephros that do not form the testicular duct system may remain as small remnants called the ductuli aberrantes and appendix testis near the head and the paradidymis near the body or tail of the epididymis. During the middle trimester of gestation the interstitial or Leydig cells are numerous especially in the equine fetus.

In the very early fetal period the external genitalia in the cloacal region are also in the indifferent stage characterized by a genital tubercle which elongates to form the phallus or penis with two genital folds that form the urethra and the two genital swellings that form the scrotum. Development of the external genitalia in males is hormonally controlled by androgens presumably from the fetal gonad. (See Table 2)

During fetal development, the testicle covered by the visceral peritoneum moves caudally from its location near the caudal pole of the kidney guided by the gubernaculum testis, Blockhouse and Butler, and Wensing. At the same time the vaginal process forms as an invagination of the body cavity with its parietal peritoneum into the genital swelling and gubernaculum. Only in the bitch is this female vaginal process still visible in the adult animal. As the testis approaches the internal vaginal ring of the inguinal canal, the caudal part of the gubernaculum increases enormously in size dilating the inguinal canal and scrotum. It may be mistaken in some fetuses for the descended testis. As the enlarged jelly-like mass of the gubernaculum decreases in size and shrinks, the testis sinks through the inguinal canal and into the scrotum where the gubernaculum forms the ligamentum testis and scrotal ligament. It is possible that the scrotal fascia and the external cremaster muscle are also derivatives of the gubernaculum, Ashdown. Thus the testis always remains outside the peritoneal cavity but the vaginal cavity formed between the tunica vaginalis communis, the parietal layer of peritoneum, and the tunica vaginalis propria, the visceral layer, is continuous with the abdominal cavity throughout life. If the internal inguinal ring is large, an inguinal hernia may develop in this cavity.

Testicular descent and enlargement of the gubernaculum is probably hormonally controlled by androgens from the testes or adrenals. Failure of normal testicular descent appears in most cases to be genetic in nature and results in cryptorchidism seen most commonly in pigs, horses and dogs and least commonly in cattle, sheep and cats. An abnormal development of the gubernaculum could account for the cryptorchid condition, Wensing. According to Arthur testicular descent into the scrotum occurs in the domestic animals at the following periods: horse, 9 to 11 months of gestation; cattle, 3-1/2 to 4 months of gestation; sheep, 2-2/3 months of gestation; pig, 3 months of gestation, and dog, about 5 days after birth.

References

Arey, L.B. (1954) Developmental Anatomy, 6th Ed., W. B. Saunders, Co., Philadelphia.

Arthur, G. H. (1964) Wright's Veterinary Obstetrics, Williams and Wilkins Co., Baltimore, Md., p. 475.

Ashdown, R. R. (1963) The Anatomy of the Inguinal Canal in the Domestic Mammals, Vet. Rec. **75,** 50, 1345.

Blockhouse, K. M. and Butler, H. (1960) The Gubernaculum Testis of the Pig, Jour. of Anat. **94,** 1, 107.

Langman, J. (1963) Medical Embryology, Williams and Wilkins, Co., Baltimore, Md.

Miller, M. E. (1964) Anatomy of the Dog, W. B. Saunders, Co., Philadelphia and London.

Patten, B. M. (1948) Embryology of the Pig, 3rd. Ed., The Blakiston Co., Philadelphia, Pa.

Wensing, C. J. G. (1968) Testicular Descent in Some Domestic Mammals, Koninkl. Nederl. Akademie Van Wetenschappen—Amsterdam—Reprint from Proc. Series C 71, 4, 423.

Physiology of Male Reproduction

Hormones—In the developing male embryo soon after the primordial germ cells have migrated to the gonads, differentiation into a testis with recognizable medullary cords occurs sooner than in the female where cortical cords develop more slowly. The primitive testis apparently secretes or produces an "androgen" or androgen-like substance that is responsible for the development of the mesonephric duct system and the formation of male external genitalia and at the same time causes a degeneration or atrophy of the paramesonephric ducts. A lack of this substance or "androgen" as occurs when the testes are removed experimentally early in the fetal period results in differentiation into female genital organs. Excessive and prolonged doses of androgens given to animals in early pregnancy may cause a degree of masculinization of the external genital organs of their female fetuses.

Prior to the onset of puberty, releasing substances secreted by the sex centers in the hypothalamus, pass through the hypophyseal portal system to the anterior pituitary gland to cause the release of the protein, water-soluble gonadotropic hormones from the basophilic delta cells. The gonadotropic hormones are the same as in the female and consist of two closely associated fractions FSH and LH or ICSH (interstitial cell stimulating hormone). FSH has been considered responsible for spermatogenesis from the initial division of spermatogonia through the formation of the secondary spermatocytes. Thereafter testosterone is thought responsible for sperm cell development. Steinberger and Duckett reported that hormones may not be required for the progression from a spermatongonia to the late stages of primary spermatocytes. Testosterone is required for the reduction division of primary spermatocytes and possible early spermatid formation. ICSH stimulates the growth of the interstitial

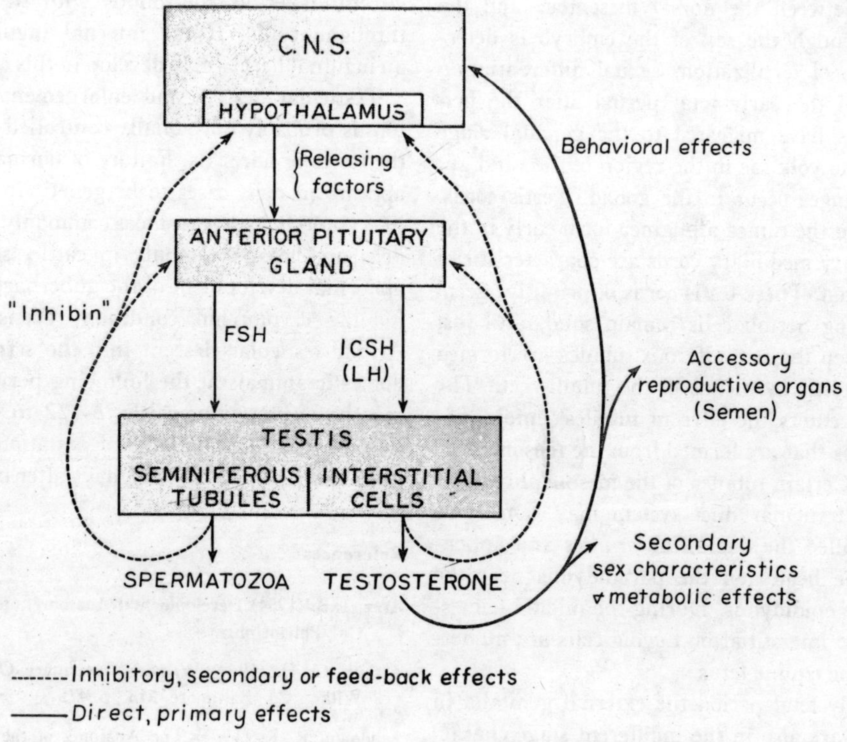

Figure 162. Diagram of the Neuroendoerine Control of Reproduction in Male Animals

or Leydig cells located between the seminiferous tubules in the testes and the secretion of testosterone and other androgens from these cells. All gonadotropins are prepared from biologic sources as they are complex high-molecular weight proteins. Chorionic gonadotropin (H. C.G.) from the urine of women in early pregnancy and sheep pituitary and purified pituitary products from other animals with a high LH (ICSH) content are commercially available. Equine gonadotropin either from the endometrial cups (pregnant mare serum) or equine or other purified animal pituitary products high in FSH activity are also available for use. Levels of gonadotropic hormone, especially FSH, are high in castrated mature animals and postmenopausal women. (See Figure 162)

Hypophysectomy is followed by involution of the seminiferous epithelium and a lack of libido; injections of FSH and ICSH (LH) can restore spermatogenesis, libido and ejaculation of normal motile spermatozoa, Macleod et al.. The amounts of FSH and ICSH produced and secreted are controlled by feedback mechanisms whereby high levels of testosterone and other gonadal steroids or "inhibin" from the seminiferous epithelium, Tepperman, act on the hypothalamus and/or anterior pituitary gland to decrease the production of gonadotropic hormones. High continuous levels of testosterone or other gonadal steroids such as progesterone, progestins, or estrogen, maintained by either parenteral injection, feeding, or from steroid-producing tumors of the testes or adrenal gland will cause degeneration and atrophy of the seminiferous epithelium and the interstitial cells. This process can be reversed by withdrawal of the exogenous source of steroids, resulting in the "rebound phenomena". The high level of estrogens found normally in stallion urine is probably due to estrogen production by the interstitial and/or Sertoli cells of the testis. Sertoli cell tumors of the canine testis are not uncommon and produce high estrogen levels with signs of feminization and testicular atrophy.

Testosterone, a steroid hormone, is soluble in oil or alcohol but not in water. In the interstitial cells the biosynthesis of testosterone is as follows: acetate → cholesterol → progesterone → androstenedione → testosterone. Testosterone is the major androgen elaborated by the testis in the bull, dog and human. In the bull testosterone is 16 times more active than androstenedione but the latter is the major androgen in the stallion testis, Savard et al.. These authors reported an average androgen titer of 3.0 micrograms per ml in the peripheral plasma of 3 to 4-year-old bulls. In 3 of 4 bulls injected daily with large doses of H.C.G., a marked increase in the androgen level was produced. Based on studies of prostatic fluid, 2.5 mg per kg of body weight daily of testosterone was needed to maintain prostatic function in male canine castrates, Rosenkrantz and Ilievski. Androgens are excreted in the urine as androsterones.

Testosterone or androgens from the testis are necessary for: (1) the sexual differentiation of the external male genitalia, Curtis and Grant, and the descent of the testis into the scrotum in fetuses or neonates; (2) the keratinization of the preputial epithelium, the separation of the glans penis from the prepuce, and the growth of the penis and prepuce at puberty; (3) the growth and maintenance of the accessory genital glands so they can contribute their secretions to the semen at the time of ejaculation; (4) sexual desire or libido and the ability for normal erection and copulation; (5) secondary sex characteristics of hair and horn growth, male attitudes, timbre of the voice, increased bone thickness, increased muscle tissue with a different distribution of fat from the female due to protein anabolic effects; and (6) the maintenance of secretory and absorptive activities and structures of the efferent ducts, epididymis and ducti deferentia including the ampullae. Spermiogenesis or development and maturation of the spermatids and spermatozoa in the testicular and mesonephric ducts are largely maintained by testosterone produced by the interstitial cells which in turn are stimulated by ICSH. Testosterone can restore sexual desire and copulatory ability when injected into the castrated male animal.

In older dogs and men excessive amounts of testosterone may be produced by overstimulation of the interstitial cells by the pituitary gonadotropic hormones causing hypertrophy and hyperplasia of the prostate gland. In dogs this may result in compression of the rectum, signs of constipation with tenesmus and may lead to perineal hernia.

Castration, if performed before puberty, prevents the development and function of those organs and activities requiring testosterone and if performed after puberty results in the atrophy of organs and of activities that are testosterone dependent. There are no interstitial cells in the epididymis so the early belief and practice of "cutting a horse proud" by leaving a portion of the epididymis at the time of castration is fallacious, Bemis and Emmerson. There is no antagonism between estrogens and androgens per se. Their apparent antagonism is due to their similar effects on the hypothalamus and the anterior pituitary gland in preventing the release of the gonadotropic hormones. Taylor et al. reported marked abnormal antler growth in deer with severe hypogonadism. Asdell reported that in the bull interstitial cells were active by 3.5 months of age and the androgen content of the testis increased through 5 years of age and from then on tended to decrease.

Occasionally male, or female, reproductive steroid hormones are produced by the adrenal cells or tumors.

Presently all commercial veterinary sources of androgens are synthesized from cholesterol-like compounds and are sold in solution in oil or alcohol ("Repositol"), in suspension in aqueous preparations, or in pellets for implantation. Testosterone may be administered orally especially to dogs and cats because of their simple stomachs.

Oxytocin administered intramuscularly prior to ejaculation in a limited number of bulls has resulted in a larger volume and greater numbers of spermatozoa in the ejaculate. Fjellstrom et al. indicated that contractile mechanisms involved in sperm transport in the male are in part regulated by oxytocin. (See erection and ejaculation) Although they are essential for normal body function other pituitary hormones such as ACTH, somatotropic hormone, prolactin, thyrotropic hormone, and oxytocin and vasopressin, as well as thyroxine from the thyroid gland, the glucocorticoids and adrenaline from the adrenal gland and others have only moderate secondary effects of limited importance on reproduction in the male domestic animal.

Puberty—The onset of puberty in male domestic animals occurs at approximately the same time after birth as puberty in females of the same species. It is brought about by the release of gonadotropic hormones from the anterior pituitary gland resulting in the secretion of steroid hormones from the gonads that cause growth of the genital organs and secondary sex characteristics. Injections of gonadotropic hormones into prepuberal animals results in precocious sexual maturity. In the male the onset of puberty is characterized by secondary sex signs, sexual desire, ability to copulate and the presence of viable spermatozoa in the ejaculate. The onset of puberty is a gradual process and is variable in time since it may be influenced within a species by the plane of nutrition, breed of animal, crossbreeding, Bellows et al., methods of management, presence of chronic disease processes, and individual differences.

The development of puberty in bulls has been carefully studied by Abdel-Raouf, McMillan and Hafs, and others. Primary spermatocytes appear in the seminiferous tubules by 4 to 6 months of age, spermatids by 6 to 7 months, and spermatozoa by 7 to 9 months of age in bulls. Seminal secretion from the accessory glands appears by 5 to 6 months. Separation of the penis from the sheath in bulls proceeds caudally beginning at 1 month and ending with complete separation by 8 months of age. The period from 6 to 10 months of age in bulls is characterized by the accelerated growth rate of the genital system, increases in LH releasing factor in the hypothalamus and in plasma LH, external manifestations of puberty and the rapid onset of spermatogenesis. Abdel-Raouf considered puberty was reached at 10 months of age, 40 weeks, in well-fed, healthy Swedish Red and White bulls and by 12 months, 48 weeks, when fed on a lower plane of nutrition. However Bichan and Hunter and others have reported that fertile semen with conception has been produced by well-reared bulls at 6 months of age. McMillan and Hafs stated that puberty probably commences at 2 months and is qualitatively completed by 10 months of age in Holstein bulls.

The attainment of puberty does not signify full reproductive capacity. Almquist and Cunningham, Abdel-Raouf, Christian, and others reported highly significant increases in ejaculate volume, output of motile spermatozoa, and concentration of spermatozoa in bulls for 6 to 9 months after the onset of puberty. Abdel-Raouf noted a marked reduction between 9 and 12 months in the number of proximal protoplasmic droplets on bovine spermatozoa. Lagerlof and Carlquist noted the same reduction in protoplasmic droplets and abnormal spermatozoa in ejaculated boar semen between 150 and 200 days of age. Niwa et al. reported a rapid growth of the testis and epididymis from 4 to 8 months of age in the boar. Detachment of the sheath from the penis occurred at 4 to 6 months and sexual maturity in the boar was reached at 7 to 8 months of age. Hauer et al. noted that 16 to 17-month-old stallions produced only 16.4 ml of gel-free sperm per ejaculate with 22 percent progressive motility and 48 percent abnormal sperm cells. Because of the above indications of a lack of maturity after the onset of puberty and because of individual differences in libido, spermatozoan reserves, and the ability to produce large numbers of normal spermatozoa, immature male animals should be used sparingly for breeding purposes for one-half to one year or more after reaching puberty.

The time of puberty in male animals is:

Horses—18 months (range 12 to 24 months)
Cattle—9 to 12 months (range 6 to 18 months)
Sheep—7 to 8 months (range 4 to 12 months)
Swine—5 to 7 months (range 4 to 8 months)
Dogs—7 to 10 months (range 5 to 12 months)
Cats—8 to 10 months (range 6 to 15 months)

The Scrotum and Heat Regulation of the Testes—The testicles in all domestic animals are located normally in the scrotum. In certain wild species of rodents the testes are retained in the abdominal cavity except during the breeding season when they descend into the scrotum. The whale, elephant, rhinoceros and seal have no scrotum and the testes are intra-abdominal. In the domestic animals the scrotum performs a vital temperature-regulating function for the testes. If the testes are maintained at body temperature, as occurs in bilateral cryptorchidism, spermatogenesis does not occur. High, prolonged fevers, insulation of the scrotum or prolonged exposure to high atmospheric temperature and humidity can also seriously impair spermatogenesis. However, testosterone production by the interstitial cells or Leydig cells is not affected by temperature.

Phillips and MacKenzie and others have shown that the dartos muscle, by contracting in cold weather to hold the testes against the body and relaxing in warm weather is the principal thermoregulator of the testis. The external cremaster muscle, by raising the testis, may also play a role.

According to Ferguson and coworkers, scrotal temperature in three dairy bulls varied from 93.2° F (34.1° C) to 100.4° F (37.9° C) while rectal temperature varied from 100.4° F (37 9° C) to 102.2° F (38.9° C) during the same 8-hour period. Scrotal temperature can rise rapidly when bulls recline. Fluctuations of 18° F (10° C) in environmental temperature had little effect on scrotal temperature. The testicular temperature of the ram may vary from about 85° F (28° C) to about 104° F (40° C).

Waites and Moule reported in rams that blood in the spermatic artery winding through the pampiniform plexus of spermatic veins cools 9.4° F (5.2° C) when the testicular temperature is about 93.2° F (34° C). Thus the arrangement of the spermatic artery and vein in the region of the pampiniform plexus provides an efficient heat exchange mechanism that, although it is not regulatory, rapidly transfers any benefit of scrotal thermoregulation to all parts of the testis. In this regard in the bull the extensive network of superficial veins in the tunica albuginea plays an important role in lowering the temperature of the venous blood before it passes through the torturous spermatic vein.

The Testicles and Spermatogenesis—The testicles perform a dual function in producing testosterone from the interstitial cells and spermatozoa from the seminiferous tubules. The male domestic animal is capable of fertile copulation at any time. However, in certain wild animals such as deer, camels and elephants there is a certain definite seasonal period of sexual excitement or "rut" and spermatogenesis occurs only during this period. In some domestic animals such as the ram and stallion there may be some seasonal variations in spermatogenesis and semen quality due to environmental, nutritional or other conditions.

Spermatogenesis is a highly synchronized process whereby spermatozoa are formed from the precursor diploid cells, type A spermatogonia. **Spermatogenesis** includes both **spermatocytogenesis** (spermiocytogenesis) or formation of primary and secondary spermatocytes from type A spermatogonia and **spermiogenesis** or the formation of mature fertile spermatozoa from the immature spermatids. Spermatocytogenesis is under the regulation of F.S.H. from the anterior pituitary gland and conditions favorable for spermiogenesis are under the control of LH and testosterone. Under normal conditions spermatogenesis is a very orderly continuous process. In any single small area of the seminiferous epithelium various stages of the well-organized extremely regularly occurring cycle of the seminiferous epithelium may be observed.

The duration of spermatogenesis is comprised of 4 cycles of the seminiferous epithelium starting with type A spermatogonia (4.68 cycles if spermatogenesis is started with a dormant type A spermatogonia). At each cycle of the seminiferous epithelium the spermatogonia renew themselves by producing new stem cells and cells that will produce spermatocytes. Each cycle length in the bull is 13.5 days, in the boar 8.6 days and in the ram about 12.2 days. In the boar, bull and ram a succession of 8 highly characteristic cellular associations or stages occur in each cycle which takes place in the form of a spiral along a portion of the seminiferous tubule as well as at one transverse area. In each stage there are several distinct groups of cells present on cross-section of the seminiferous tubule. At stage 8, for example, nearly mature spermatozoa line the lumen of the tubule. Spermatids at a certain stage in development, or a generation of germ cells, are always associated with the same types or other generations of spermatogonia and spermatocytes. The distance between two similar cellular associations or stages in the seminiferous tubule is called a spermatogenic wave, Ortavant, Foote. (See Table 22) Any agent that damages spermatogonia could lead to permanent damage of the testis; but if only differentiating cells are damaged, repair is possible.

Spermiogenesis begins as soon as the spermatid is formed. At this stage the spermatid has a spherical nucleus surrounded by cytoplasm containing many mitochondria and in which a Golgi complex or zone soon forms. The acrosome and head cap arise from the Golgi complex. The cytoplasm and centrioles move to the opposite side of the nucleus. The centrioles give rise to the flagellum or axial filament and later the body and tail of the spermatozoa. The mitochondria later become arranged like a collar around the upper region of the flagellum as the mitochondrial helix to form the middle piece. At the end of spermiogenesis when the spermatozoa are in the head of the epididimis, unused cytoplasm and Golgi material, now called the protoplasmic or cytoplasmic droplet, is located in the neck region of the sperm cell in the testis, and is cast off as the spermatozoa pass through the epididymis, Bloom and Nicander.

During part of its transformation to a spermatozoon the spermatid is closely associated with "nurse" or Sertoli cells in the seminiferous tubules. After it leaves the Sertoli cell and is "free-living" in the lumen of the seminiferous

Table 22. Outline of Spermatogenesis in the Bull, Boar and Ram

Stage	Process	Chromosome Complement	No. of** cells	Time in Days* Bull	Boar	Ram
Type A Spermatogonia (dormant)		2N (diploid)	1			
Type A Spermatogonia		2N	2			
Intermediate Type Spermatogonia		2N	4			
Type B Spermatogonia		2N	8		about 10-20	
Primary (Preleptotene) Spermatocytes (active DNA synthesis)		4N (tetraploid)	16			
Leptotene stage						
Zygotene stage	Meiotic					
Pachytene stage	Prophase I (long, 16 days in ram)					
Diplotene stage						
Diakinesis						
Metaphase I					25-26	
Anaphase I	1st Meiotic (maturation)			40-42		36-37
Telophase I	Division					
Secondary Spermatocytes		2N	32			
Diakinesis	Meiotic Prophase II (very short, hours)					
Metaphase II						
Anaphase II	2nd Meiotic (maturation) Division					
Telophase II						
Spermatids	Spermiogenesis	1N (haploid)	64			
Spermatozoa	(long, 15 days, ram)	1N	64			

*** It takes approximately 10 days in the bull and 13-15 days in the ram and boar for spermatozoa to traverse the epididymis. Thus from type A spermatogonium to ejaculated spermatozoa is about 60 to 70 days in the ram and bull and 50 to 60 days in the boar.**

**** Theoretically in the bull and ram 16 primary spermatocytes and 64 spermatozoa develop from one type A spermatogonium; boars and rats have 24 primary spermatocytes and 96 spermatozoa from one spermatogonium. However a certain loss in cells, about 25%, is experienced during meiosis and is characterized by the presence of pycnotic nuclei.**

tubules it is moved into the rete testis and efferent tubules by a large volume of secreted fluid. There is little evidence of any contractile tissue and no cilia in the seminiferous tubules, straight tubules or rete testis. Spermatozoa do not develop any significant degree of motility until ejaculation. The testicular capsule apparently contains smooth muscle that contracts and relaxes and this alternate activity exerts a pumping action on the seminiferous tubules forcing the nonmotile sperm cells and plasma out of the testis and into the epididymis.

Almquist and Amann, Foote and Ortavant have estimated that normal bulls produce 12 to 17 million and rams 12 million spermatozoa per gram of testicular tissue daily. Boars produce 25 to 30 million sperm cells per gram of testis daily because of the shorter duration of spermatogenesis and the larger number of spermatozoa produced from one type A spermatogonium, Kennelly and Foote. Thus daily sperm production for a bull with testes weighing 400 gms each, a ram with testes weighing 250 gms each, and a boar with testes weighing 300 gms each would be 12 billion, 7 billion and 15 billion spermatozoa, respectively. Sperm numbers in the testis are highly correlated with testis weight, and testis diameter and size. Voglmayr and Mattner and others have reported that by four months after unilateral castration in the ram the weight of the remaining testis increased by 76 per cent and sperm cell production was nearly double that of a normal testis. As in rabbits and dogs after hemicastration the diameter of the seminiferous tubules increased greatly to produce a compensatory hypertrophy of the single testis. Further study of this interesting observation is needed in these and other species.

The Morphology of Spermatozoa—In recent years electron microscopy has done much to elucidate the fine structure of spermatozoa. Although the size and shape of spermatozoa differ between the domestic species of animals the basic morphological structure is similar. The head length and width is about 8 to 10 microns by 4 to 4.5 microns in bull, ram and boar spermatozoa and smaller, 5.5 to 7 microns in length and 2.7 to 4.0 microns in width, in stallion, dog and cat spermatozoa. The head thickness is about 0.5 to 1.5 microns or less in all species. The spermatozoan body or middle piece is about one and one-half to two times as long as the head, 10 to 15 microns, and about 1.0 micron in diameter in all species. The tails of spermatozoa are 35 to 45 microns long and 0.4 to 0.8 microns in diameter. The total length of spermatozoa of domestic animals is thus about 50 to 70 microns or 1/300 of an inch, Blom and Birch-Anderson and Altman and Dittmer.

The head of the spermatozoa is elongated and ovoid in shape, broad and flat in one plane and narrow in the other with the thickest portion at the base and tapering to a fairly thin apex. The head is entirely filled with a nearly homogenous nuclear material containing the genetic material, DNA or deoxyribonucleic acid, surrounded by the nuclear membranes. (See Figure 163). DNA is the amazingly concentrated coded genetic material. Each spermatozoon contains about 2.5 billion bits of information necessary to form a fetus yet it takes 300 billion spermatozoa to make 1 gram of DNA, Foote. The anterior part of the nuclear membrane or the inner membrane of the acrosome, is modified to form the perforatorium which is poorly developed in spermatozoa of domestic animals when compared to sperm cells of the rat, Hancock. The anterior 60 per cent of the nucleus and its modified membrane, the perforatorium, is covered by the acrosome cap or head cap which is a double-walled pouch-like structure about 0.1 microns thick enclosing the acrosomal substance and the denser acrosomal corpuscle, Kojima, or vacuole, Blom and Birch-Anderson. The equatorial zone or segment is the posterior part of the acrosome or head cap around the middle portion of the sperm head corresponding to the area where the acrosomal substance is most scanty. The posterior 40 per cent of

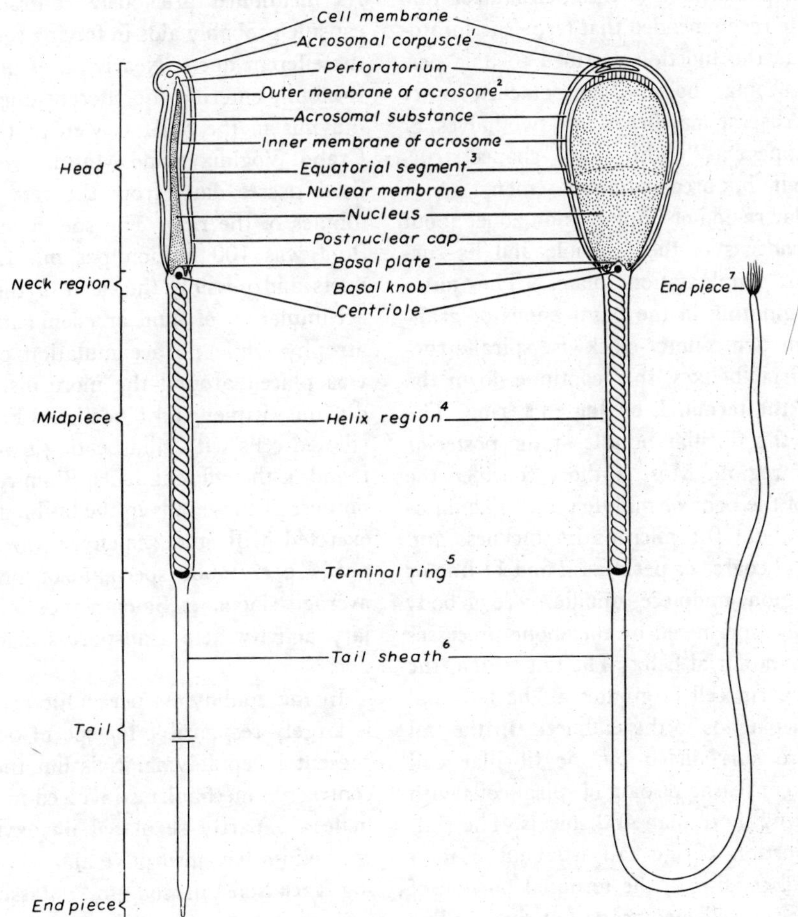

Figure 163. Diagram of the Ultrastructure of the Sperm Cell. (Blom, Birch-Anderson and Kojima)
Synonyms: 1. Acrosomal Vacuole or Apical Body 2. Galea Capitis or Sperm Cap 3. Equatorial zone 4. Mitochondrial Helix 5. Jensen's Ring 6. Cytoplasmic or Fibrillar Sheath 7. Terminal Filament

the nucleus and nuclear membranes from the equatorial zone to the base of the cell are covered by the postnuclear cap or nuclear sheath. The differences between the acrosome cap and postnuclear cap explain the differences in affinity for stains observed in these two regions. The cell membrane composed of several layers completely encloses the head, body, and tail of the spermatozoon. The membrane is closely applied to the cell at the anterior portion of the acrosome cap, the postnuclear cap, and at Jensen's ring. The outer membrane of the acrosome cap is identical with the galea capitis, described in the earlier literature, that is detached either spontaneously in the tail of the epididymis by long, sexual abstinence, artificially in vitro, or during fertilization, probably as a step in sperm capacitation. Detachment occurs by rupture of the cell membrane and the outer membrane of the acrosome cap in the equatorial zone which exposes enzymes such as hyaluronidase in the acrosome cap that are necessary along with the perforatorium for penetration of the spermatozoa into the ovum, Hadek. He recommended that term "perforatorium" be dropped as the function ascribed to it is performed by the acrosomal body. The detached outer membranes of the acrosome may break into two halves, or remain joined and appear as "bathing-cap"-shaped structures in stained or India ink preparations of semen.

The neck, centriolar region or implantation zone, about 1.5 microns long, consists of the centriole and its surrounding radixes or implantation plates. The mitochondrial sheath originating in the basal knobs or granules of the head form two counter-clockwise spiral structures, the mitochondrial helixes, that continue down the body or midpiece to the terminal, or Jensen's, ring. The radixes change into the fibrillar bundle at the posterior portion of the neck region. Most authors consider the neck region as part of the body or middle piece. The mitochondrial sheath is about 0.1 microns in thickness and surrounds the fibrils, 9 coarse or peripheral and 11 fine or central. The helix region, midpiece, middle piece or body supplies energy for the sperm cell by metabolic processes occurring in the mitochondrial helix. The tail region, the longest part of the sperm cell originates at the terminal ring of the body and extends to the endpiece. In the tail region the fibrils are surrounded by the fibrillar coil sheath or tail sheath consisting of pair of spiral coils with each of the coils making more than 400 spirals. The endpiece or terminal portion of the tail is about 3 to 4 microns in length and consists of the terminal portion of the fibrils covered by the cell membrane but the fibrillar coil sheath of the tail is absent, Kojima. The wave-like or whip-like action of the tail originates in the neck region of the body and generates contractile force as it proceeds distally. Helical oscillations of the tail of the spermatozoon are very rapid and provide the force necessary for sperm cell motility which under optimum conditions of temperature, and medium is about 100 microns per second, range 10 to 352, in bull spermatozoa, White, Lustig and Lindahl, Moeller and VanDemark, Janick and MacLeod, and Bishop, or about 4.23 mm per minute, Baker et al.. The motility rates for equine, ovine and human spermatozoa were 80 to 100, 200 to 250 and 30 to 75 microns per second.

Spermatozoan Transport, Maturation and Storage and Accessory Gland Secretion—Spermatozoa are carried in a large amount of secreted fluid from the seminiferous epithelium and rete testis into the torturous efferent ducts or ductuli efferentes, usually about 13 to 15 in number, located adjacent to the head of the epididymis and opening into the epididymal duct. These structures since they arise from the mesonephros have kidney-like functions in respect to absorbtive and secretory activities. As mentioned previously contractions of the testicular capsule probably aids in forcing semen from the testes into the efferent ducts. Nearly all of the fluid, 200 ml daily in the bull, entering the efferent ducts and head of the epididymis in the bull, as well as the boar, was absorbed, Crabo. Voglmayr and Mattner reported that 30.2 ml of fluid passes daily from the rete testis into the efferent tubules of the ram. The sperm cell concentration in this fluid was 100 million per ml. Ligation of the efferent ducts and possibly the head of the epididymis caused an accumulation of fluid or edema in the testes followed by atrophy while no accumulation occurred if the ligature was placed around the more distal portions of the epididymis, Ripley and Igboeli and Foote. Both secretory and ciliated cells with cilia beating toward the epididymis are found in the efferent ducts. Blom reported that the ciliated borders of these cells in the bull may become detached and excreted with the semen at the rate of one "medusa head" per 10,000 spermatozoa or about 500,000 in the average ejaculate. Smooth muscle activity as well as ciliary activity help transport sperm through the efferent ducts.

In the epididymis peristaltic activity of smooth muscle is largely responsible for sperm transport. Microvilli are present in epididymal cells but they are nonmotile. The contractile mechanisms involved in sperm transport in the male are partly regulated by oxytocin. The epididymal epithelium has absorptive and secretory functions producing variations in sodium, potassium, calcium, chlorine and phosphorus ion concentrations and in concentrations of proteins, enzymes and glycerylphosphorylcholine in the luminal contents in different portions of the epididymis, Gustafsson. The composition of epididymal plasma is closely related to testicular function, the passage of sperm cells and the hormonal and physical testicular environment. Plasma volume in bulls was doubled by secretions in the caput and halved by absorption in the cauda; while in boars the epididymal content underwent continuous dilution from the caput to the cauda epididymis. The time required in the domestic animals for spermatozoan transport through the epididymis is about 7 to 15 days. Sexual rest slows the passage and frequent ejaculations hasten the passage of spermatozoa.

Although physiologic mechanisms of the epididymis are largely under the hormonal control of testosterone they are not well understood. It is generally considered that the sperm cell matures in its passage through the epididymis as indicated by the passage of the cytoplasmic droplet from the neck region, down the middle piece and tail from which it is lost before ejaculation. This is most commonly described in ungulates. Amann and Almquist reported proximal protoplasmic droplets in 44% of the spermatozoa in the caput and only 2% in the cauda epididymis of bulls. The percent of proximal protoplasmic droplets in the caput of swine is higher. Spermatozoa removed from the tail of the epididymis were 2 to 10 times more fertile than spermatozoa from the caput apparently due to abnormalities in locomotion of the sperm cells taken from the head of the epididymis, Blandau and Rumery, Paufler and Foote. Igboeli and Foote reported that the percentage of motile bovine sperm cells in the caput and cauda epididymis were 0 and 41 respectively. Staining with an eosin or vital stain revealed equal numbers of live, unstained cells and morphologically normal spermatozoa in both sites. Spermatozoa removed from the cauda epididymis exhibited normal fertility.

The seminal fluid in bulls is concentrated as it passes through the epididymis, especially in the head region, so sperm cell concentration in the tail of the epididymis in bulls is 4,000,000 or more per cmm. In the epididymis sperm cells exhibit a very low rate of motility and are resistant to cold shock, Bialy and Smith. In the tail of the epididymis storage conditions are optimal. Spermatozoa can remain viable and fertile for up to 60 days in the ligated epididymis of the bull, Blom. After long periods of sexual rest, however, many spermatozoa in first ejaculates may be dead or infertile. Almquist and Amann have reported that bulls have about 70 billion spermatozoa outside the testis proper, extragonadal sperm reserves (ESR), with 19 billion (29%) in the head, 5 billion (7%) in the body, 37 billion (53%) in the tail of the epididymides, 2 billion (3%) in the ducti deferentia and 6 billion (8%) in the ampullae. Thus the major storage site for spermatozoa is the tail of the epididymis. Depletion trials in the bull, consisting of 20 or more ejaculates taken within several hours, removed about 53 percent of the extragonadal sperm reserves. In the ram depletion trials reportedly removed only 31 percent of the extragonadal sperm reserves. In the bull these depleted extragonadal sperm reserves are completely replenished within about 7 days and a significant replenishment of spermatozoan numbers in the tail of the epididymis occurred within 60 to 90 minutes after the last ejaculate. During depletion trials no increase in proximal protoplasmic droplets or abnormal spermatozoa were noted.

Unejaculated spermatozoa or spermatozoa confined to the epididymis by resection or ligation of the ductus deferens or vasectomy have been reported to be removed from the epididymis by selective phagocytosis by macrophages or resorbed, Amann and Almquist; Roussel, Stallcup and Austin; Lambiase and Amann, and Phadke. In normal bulls, rabbits, monkeys and men, histologic examination has failed to show extensive degeneration or phagocytosis of sperm cells in the epididymis. Early workers reported in rats, dogs and man that spermatozoa were voided in the urine and recently Bielanski and Wierzbowski and Lino, Braden and Turnbull have reported that resorption of spermatozoa in the epididymis is not important in the disposal of surplus spermatozoa in rams. The number of sperm cells voided daily in the urine of sexually-rested rams was about the same as the total daily sperm cell production. Long term vasectomy in the bull did not abolish spermatogenesis and testis size was unaffected even after 5 years, Igboeli and Rakha. Thus a mechanism must exist for the removal of sperm cells from the epididymis. Further work is needed to elucidate the fate of unejaculated sperm cells. Masturbation in domestic animals may cause some depletion of sperm cell reserves from the tail of the epididymis. Thus there are apparently several routes for eliminating excess, dead, or abnormal spermatozoa from the epididymis.

The ductus or vas deferens is a firm muscular duct, about 2 mm in outside diameter in the bull, that transports spermatozoa by peristalsis especially at the time of precoital stimulation and ejaculation to the ampullae and the pelvic urethra. The ampulla of the ductus deferens, present in the bull, stallion and ram, is a thickening of the ductus abundantly supplied with glands that are similar to the vesicular glands. The ampullae have a limited role in the storage of spermatozoa. They are very small in the dog and cat and absent in the boar.

The accessory glands including the seminal vesicles or vesicular glands; the prostate; and Cowper's or bulbourethral glands are under the control of testosterone from the interstitial cells of the testis and secrete the major portion of the seminal plasma into the urethra at the time of ejaculation. The seminal plasma acts primarily as a carrier for spermatozoa and secondarily stimulates spermatozoan activity by providing fructose, a readily available energy source, and buffers. While seminal plasma is capable of influencing the fertilizing ability of spermatozoa there is no evidence it is essential for it.

In 7 vesiculectomized bulls the volume of the ejaculate decreased as did the motility of the spermatozoa while the concentration of sperm cells increased. Five of these bulls were mated with heifers and had acceptable fertility. King and Macpherson reported that seminal vesiculectomy in bulls nearly eliminated fructose in semen and reduced the protein level and ejaculate volume. There was a greater loss in sperm cells after freezing in the treated bulls but the libido was not affected. The seminal vesicular secretion is not essential as the metabolic needs of the sperm cells are provided by the secretions in the female genital tract. In the bull the vesicular glands contribute slightly to the presperm semen fraction but mainly to the sperm cell rich fraction of the ejaculate, Faulkner et al.. The seminal vesicular glands secrete fructose, citric acid, potassium, proteins, enzymes and other substances. Certain fatty acids called prostaglandins have been recently reported to be present in the seminal plasma of man, guinea pigs and rams. These have a strong pharmacodynamic effect on the smooth muscle of the genital tract of females facilitating sperm migration, Ventura et al.. In certain Holstein, Hereford and Guernsey bulls, and possibly in other breeds, the semen may have a definite yellow color due to riboflavin secreted in the seminal vesicles. This may be inherited as a dominant character. Upon standing in sunlight for several hours the yellow color will fade, White and Lincoln. In the boar, secretions from the seminal vesicle and Cowper's glands when mixed form a gelatinous, waxy, tapioca-like material. Certain horses, especially grade animals and only occasionally Thoroughbreds, produce a thick, glairy, "egg white", sticky secretion probably from the seminal vesicles, Day, Berliner. This is of interest in light of the production of a vaginal plug or coagulum in the rat and guinea pig when Cowper's gland and the secretions from the coagulating gland, a portion of the prostate, combine with secretions from the seminal vesicles, Hart. This promotes fertility in these species by sealing the vagina and preventing the escape of semen. No useful function of this viscous portion of the ejaculate is evident in swine or horses.

About 50 per cent of the volume of semen in the bull and 20 per cent in the boar come from the seminal vesicles, Hess and coworkers. The prostate gland in the dog and cat provides most of the volume of the ejaculate as in these species the seminal vesicles are absent and Cowper's glands in the cat are fairly small. Even in the boar the prostate gland is relatively small weighing about 20 gms, compared to the other large accessory glands.

A number of references appear in the literature referring to urethral glands in domestic animals. As indicated previously urethral glands are not present in domestic animals; it is likely that some authors are extrapolating from the human or mistake the disseminate or diffuse portion of the prostate glands around the pelvic urethra for urethral glands. Cowper's or the bulbourethral glands are relatively small in all species except swine where they provide about 20 per cent of the volume of the ejaculate. The clear secretions dribbling from the sheath or penis during sexual stimulation in bulls, stallions, and rams are considered to originate from the Cowper's and possibly the prostate and vesicular glands, Blom, Faulkner et al. and Nalbandov, and may assist in clearing or flushing the urethra before ejaculation.

Erection and Ejaculation

The penis has a twofold function—the expulsion of urine, and the deposition of semen in the genital tract of the female. Before the latter process can occur the penis must become erect. This is provided for by the erectile structures, the 2 large corpora cavernosa penis and the small corpus cavernosum urethrae. Stimulation of the nervi erigentes composed of parasympathetic fibers from the pelvic and sacral nerves results in erection. Erection is accomplished by dilation of the internal and external pudendal arteries to the penis. The cavernous blood sinuses dilate with blood, the outflow of which is retarded by the increased venous pressure caused by contractions of the smooth muscles of the corpora cavernosa and the extrinsic, ischiocavernosus muscles at the base of the penis, Miller.

Lewis and coworkers, Watson, and Goldston in preliminary reports on erection in the bull stated that the dilation and filling of the bulbous areas of the penile crura under the ischiocavernosus muscle together with 4 or 5 contractions of this muscle "pumps" blood into the corpus cavernosum causing rapid erection with the resulting blood pressure in the corpus being over 1,700 mm of Hg or 33.0 pounds per square inch. Normal systolic blood pressure is 175 mm of Hg, or 3 to 4 psi. The mechanisms causing this exceedingly high pressure and the means by which the blood is prevented from returning to the systemic circulation has not been determined. Since Goldston has shown that the high blood pressure in the corpus cavernosum is maintained for only a short period of time, it is suggestive that full erection only persists as long as the ischiocavernosus muscle is contracted and forcing and holding the blood in the penis. Beckett reported that the blood pressure in the corpus cavernosum penis at the time of erection in the buck goat was similar to that of the bull, about 1,800 mm of Hg.. Miller gave an excellent description of the mechanism of erection in the dog which is aided by the contraction of the vulvar sphincter muscles after intromission. A similar pumping action to that in the bull and buck is noted in the dog and ram, Watson. He also explained how this "pumping" action of the pelvic urethral muscle and the bulbocavernosus muscle causes an intermittent increased blood pressure in the corpus cavernosum urethrae to compress the urethra to expel the semen.

The anatomic structure of the male penis influences the precoital sexual behavior of the animal, Hammond. The vascular penis in the stallion and dog is slow to erect and foreplay before copulation is essential. The fibro-elastic penis of the bull, ram, and boar, containing much less vascular erectile tissue, erects rapidly and there is less foreplay in these species. According to Dukes the acts of erection and ejaculation are reflex, with the centers being located in the lumbar region of the spinal cord. Normally the nervous paths responsible for erection and ejaculation also involve the cerebral cortex of the brain. Erection can take place, however, even if the spinal cord is divided in the thoracic region. Reflex stimulation from the testicles, urethra, prostate, or penis, especially the glans penis, causes erection. Sectioning of the sensory pudendal or dorsal nerve of the penis prevents ejaculation when the glans penis is stimulated. Hafez stated that erection is predominantly under the influence of the parasympathetic system and ejaculation is controlled by the sympathetic system.

Animals such as the horse, dog, and boar, which ejaculate large amounts of semen have a prolonged period of coitus. The bull and ram ejaculate small amounts of semen and their period of coitus is short.

Although copulation initiates ejaculation by sensory stimuli from the glans penis, certain stimuli are more important than others in the various species, Hammond. In the bull and ram the warmth of the vagina is most important and pressure and friction less important as stimuli for ejaculation. In stallions, boars, and dogs, pressure on the penis is relatively more important than temperature.

In the bull Seidel and Foote reported penile extension from the sheath was about 55 cm or 22 inches. The interval of time from contact of the glans penis with the vulva to ejaculation averaged 1.0 second. Semen emission time averaged 0.29 seconds. During more than half of the ejaculations by 8 Holstein bulls a twisting of the glans penis was observed ranging from a slight bending to a 360° counterclockwise coil 6 cm in outside diameter. In the ram the urethral or vermiform process engorges with blood, the urethral dilatation in the base of the process fills with semen and the semen is forced through the narrow orifice at the end of the urethra under considerable pressure producing a back and forth spraying or "fire hose" effect at the time of ejaculation, Masson. In the boar the corkscrew glans engages in the thick-walled, spiral, transverse ridges of the sow's anterior vagina and cervix that are erect and edematous at estrus. The porcine penis becomes "locked" in the cervix by further erection and dilation of the corpus cavernosum before ejaculation commences.

The process of ejaculation probably starts in the epididymis and travels along the ductus deferens at the same time the walls of the accessory glands contract and force their contents into the urethra. Sexual stimulation in the male may involve oxytocin release as Fjellstrom et al. reported an increased volume and total number of spermatozoa of the ejaculate following oxytocin injection. It would seem logical that oxytocin is involved in the transport of semen in the epididymis and the ductus deferens. The urethra is emptied by the rhythmic contractions of the urethral, ischiocavernosus, and bulbocavernosus muscles, Dukes. The stallion, for example, requires about 10 seconds for complete ejaculation, and about 10 pulsations of the urethra occur approximately a second apart.

The sheath or prepuce is a modified skin membrane and not a true mucous membrane. It is rich in glands producing sebum and smegma. The preputial glands, which are under the influence of testosterone, are located in the dorsal lateral region of the preputial orifice of boars. They are modified sebaceous glands that are responsible along with the preputial diverticulum, that fills with smegma, urine and semen from masturbation, for the typical boar odor. These preputial glands that secrete a muscone type of material may be surgically removed along with the preputial diverticulum to eliminate the odor characteristic in boar tissues, Dutt and coworkers. The highly odoriferous musk-like odor characteristic of adult intact male goats may be similar but further studies are necessary in this animal. In goats these glands are located in the skin around the base of the horn. By removing this area of skin, about 24 x 14 x 5.5 mm, at the time of dehorning prepubertal male goats, the odor characteristic of mature male goats is eliminated, Habel and Biberstein, Ford, Weibe and Roberts.

Semen and the Ejaculate

Semen or sperm is the entire seminal discharge of the male during normal ejaculation. It consists of cellular elements, the spermatozoa produced in the seminiferous tubules, seminal plasma or the liquid portion of the semen produced by secretions of the seminiferous tubules, epididymis, ducti deferentia and ampullae, seminal vesicles, prostate, and bulbo-urethral glands. Sperm cells constitute about 10 per cent of bull semen by volume. Two to 5 per cent of boar semen is made up of spermatozoa and epididymal secretions. The amount of semen and concentration of spermatozoa varies greatly between species and individuals. (See Table 23) By "teasing" males before service the amount of semen and concentration of spermatozoa are increased. Some bulls producing a small volume of semen with a low total number of sperm cells on either collection with the artificial vagina or electroejaculation will often produce larger ejaculates with much greater sperm cell numbers if given 50 to 100 units of oxytocin intramuscularly 5 to 10 minutes before collection.

Frequent, continuous service reduces the amount of semen and the concentration of spermatozoa and if carried to extremes, as in depletion or exhaustion trials, marked reductions may occur. Almquist and Hale reported on 44 depletion trials in 21 adult bulls where 20 consecutive ejaculations were collected in an artificial vagina from each bull within 1-1/2 to 7 hours. The average volume of semen declined from 4.2 ml to 2.1 ml between the first and twentieth ejaculate. The concentration of spermatozoa decreased from 1.35 billions per ml to 0.3 billions per ml and the total average number of spermatozoa per ejaculate decreased from 5.8 billion to 0.65 billion. Except for a slight reduction in semen volume, semen characteristics including concentration of sperm cells had returned to normal within 7 days. Weekly output of spermatozoa was increased 112 per cent in 10 bulls by collecting six ejaculates per week instead of two. Hafs, Hoyt and Bratton reported that bovine semen collected daily showed no difference in ability to store or freeze, fertility, abnormalities

Table 23. Semen Characteristics in Domestic Animals

Semen Constituent	Bull	Stallion	Ram (Goat)	Boar	Dog	Cat
Volume (ml)	4* (1-15)**	70 (30-250)	1 (0.7-3.0)	250 (125-500)	10 (1.0-25.0)	0.04 (0.01-0.12)
Spermatozoan Concentration (millions/ml)	1200 (300-2500)	120 (30-600)	3000 (1000-6000)	150 (25-1000)	125 (20-540)	1730 (96-3740)
pH	6.8 (6.2-7.5)	7.4 (7.0-7.8)	6.8 (6.2-7.0)	7.4 (7.0-7.8)	6.7 (6.0-6.8)	7.4
Total Spermatozoa per Ejaculum (billions) (Approx.)	4.8	8.4	3.0	37.5	1.25	0.057
Fructose (mg/100 ml)	530 (150-900)	2 (0-6)	250	13 (3-50)	0	—
Glycerylphosphorylcholine (mg/100 ml)	350 (100-500)	(40-120)	1650 (1100-2100)	(110-240)	180 (110-240)	—
Potassium (mg/100 ml)	140 (80-210)	60	90 (50-140)	240 (80-380)	—	
Sodium (mg/100 ml)	230 (140-280)	70	190 (120-250)	650 (290-850)	90 (50-124)	—
Phosphorus (Total in mg)	80	17	375	66	13	—
Citric Acid (mg/100 ml)	700 (300-1100)	25 (8-60)	140 (110-260)	80 (60-100)	Trace	—
Inositol (mg/100 ml)	35 (25-46)	30 (20-47)	12 (7-14)	530 (380-630)	—	—
Sorbitol (mg/100 ml)	(10-140)	40 (20-60)	92 (76-120)	12 (6-18)	0	
Ergothionine	0	(40-110)	0	(6-23)	—	—

Other substances found in seminal plasma include calcium, magnesium, chloride, carbon dioxide, proteins (1-7 gms/100 ml), amino acids (cattle and sheep), lipids, urea, uric acid, lactic acid, ascorbic acid, phosphatase, mucoproteins, fatty acids, vitamins (riboflavin), peptides, other enzymes, hormones, and water (85-98%) (White, I. G. and Mann, T., and other references including Roberts) * = average ** ( ) = Range.

of spermatozoa, motility, or pH from semen of bulls collected only once weekly. The volume of semen, concentration of spermatozoa, per cent motility and total spermatozoa per ejaculate for bulls collected one time per week vs bulls collected 6 times per week were 9.5 vs 6.2 ml., 1.9 vs 0.8 billion/ml, 63 vs 69 per cent and 17.8 billion vs 4.8 billion per ejaculate, respectively. Deficiencies in the quality of semen of abnormal bulls may be revealed by a high frequency of collection but are not caused by a high frequency of collection, Almquist. Semen characteristics were most severely affected by a high frequency of ejaculation in young immature bulls and they took longer to return to normal with sexual rest, VanDemark and Manger.

Elliott reported that a study of 350 beef bulls and 870 dairy bulls from 1958 to 1966 indicated that beef bulls comprised a different "population" than dairy bulls. Beef bulls had lower sperm cell production, lower post-freeze motility and higher numbers of abnormal sperm cells (50 per cent of beef bulls had above 10 per cent abnormal cells). Beef bulls reached puberty one to three months later, and their libido was generally lower than dairy bulls. The period of recovery after ejaculation was not evident in beef bulls as in dairy bulls. Once a beef bull was sexually stimulated 4 or 5 successive ejaculates could be collected in nearly the same time as required to obtain the first ejaculate. Sexual preparation did not significantly increase sperm cell output in the following ejaculate in beef bulls, Fasten, Almquist and Martig.

MacLeod and McGee reported that a stallion performed 12 normal services or covers within 72 hours. Two days previously he had ejaculated 50 ml. of semen containing 8 billion spermatozoa. On the twelfth ejaculate 90 ml of semen containing 4 billion spermatozoa were delivered. In depletion trials with stallions an average of 20.8 billion spermatozoa were obtained in each trial. After one day of sexual rest 11.8 billion of spermatozoa were obtained in a second depletion trial. With 5 days of sexual rest after the first depletion trial 25.7 billion spermatozoa were collected. Only 2 to 4 collections could be made in each depletion trial with stallions due to a lack of libido, Bielanski and Wierzbowski. Stallions ejaculated daily during the breeding season produce about 5 billion spermatozoa per day.

Rice and Andrews cited Anderson, who reported that in an exhaustion test a ram ejaculated 42 times in 9 hours and still delivered a total of 100 million spermatozoa in the last ejaculate.

In dogs libido remained high with one to two ejaculations per day. The total sperm cell count per ejaculate dropped from 580 and 548 million in dogs collected 2 and 3 times per week to 286 million and 147 million in dogs collected daily or twice daily, respectively. The total number of spermatozoa per ejaculate returned to normal after 2 to 3 days of sexual rest, Boucher, Foote and Kirk.

In boars collected once every 4 days and once a day for 20 days the average ejaculate volume dropped from 286 to 193 ml, the sperm cell concentration from 275 to 143 million per ml and total average daily sperm cell numbers from 55 to 24 billion. No changes were noted in per cent motility, per cent abnormalities, or pH in the same boars on the two frequencies of ejaculation, Gerritus, Graham and Cole. There may be a great variation between males in the same species in respect to their ability to copulate frequently and produce a satisfactory ejaculate. (See Table 23)

In the pig, horse and dog the seminal plasma is in contact with the spermatozoa for a fairly long period of time in the uterine lumen while in man, cattle and sheep the sperm cells are in contact with the seminal plasma in the vagina after ejaculation only a relatively short period of time before the cells migrate into the cervical canal. In all animals however the seminal plasma is not necessary for sperm cell metabolism or prolonged survival in the female genital tract.

Fructose is the normal sugar providing a source of energy for spermatozoa in the semen of the bull, ram and goat, but is low in the boar, very low in the stallion and absent in the dog. It is produced mainly by the seminal vesicles. The rate of fructolysis in semen is generally correlated with the concentration of spermatozoa. It is also related to the availability of oxygen and the buffering capacity of the seminal fluid. Spermatozoa can utilize glucose for energy was well as or better than fructose. Sorbitol is a sugar alcohol that can be oxidized to fructose and provide a source of energy. Lactic acid in semen increases as fructose is broken down and may reach levels in the bull and ram where it immobilizes the spermatozoa. The metabolism of sperm cells is characterized by appreciable respiratory activity. Glycerol when added to semen protects spermatozoa during the freezing process but is not readily oxidized by the cells. Of the amino acids in seminal fluid, glycine has been shown to improve sperm cell survival. Glycerylphosphorylcholine is present in high levels in epididymal secretions. By means of a compartmental analysis model, Seidel and Foote reported that in bulls the mean volume contributions to the ejaculate were 32 to 38 percent (1.5 to 2.0 ml) from the seminal vesicles, 31 to 36 percent (1.7 ml) from the epidiymides, and 31 to 32 percent (1.5 to 1.7 ml) from the prostate and bulbourethral glands.

Inositol from the seminal vesicle occurs in a high concentration in boar semen where it may act as an osmotic pressure regulator. Ergothionine, a sulphydryl-containing compound from the seminal vesicle, occurs in appreciable amounts in boar and stallion semen. High sulphydryl levels were claimed by Haag and Werthhessen to be associated with infertility in stallions but this has been refuted by Mann, Shor, Walton, Archer and Miller. An antiagglutinin that prevents the head to head agglutination of spermatozoa is also found in the seminal plasma. Dog semen contained 7 times as much copper and 20 times as much zinc as corresponding blood samples, Bartlett. Catalase has been found at low levels in bull and ram semen, 0.3 to 1.1 units per ml, and its addition to bull semen prolonged sperm cell survival by preventing the formation of hydrogen peroxide, Foote, Voigt and Schales.

The sticky, gelatinous, tapioca-like material secreted from the bulbourethral glands in the boar makes up about 20 to 30 per cent of the total porcine ejaculate, Swierstra and Rahnefeld, and may act to help seal the cervix to prevent a backflow of semen during or after ejaculation. In stallions this heavy, glairy, gelatinous substance is uncommon in light Thoroughbred horses but may be present in certain individuals or certain ejaculates in amounts of 30 to 50 percent or more of the total ejaculate.

Ram and bull semen which have a high concentration of spermatozoa are opaque white in color with a creamy consistency. The boar, stallion and dog semen which have a much lower concentration of sperm cells have a pearly white to grey translucent color with a more watery consistency. The difference between species in the volume of semen is largely due to the amount of secretion from the accessory glands.

Coitus and ejaculation are long in the boar and dog, 5 to 25 minutes, moderately long in the horse about 10 to 30 seconds and very short in the bull, ram, goat and cat, 1 to 3 seconds. In the boar and the dog most of the "sperm-rich" fraction of the semen is ejaculated the first 3 to 6 minutes of coitus. In boars there may be several episodes during the long ejaculation characterized by the passage of a "sperm-rich" fluid in between the longer periods where gelatinous and "sperm-poor" fractions are emitted. Apparently the ejaculate of all domestic animals can be divided roughly into 3 portions. The first is a sperm-free, clear, watery secretion probably from the diffuse portion of the prostate or possibly the bulbourethral glands or seminal vesicles that may often be observed in some animals in the precopulatory period of sexual arousal, Sack. This is followed by the relatively short period of the emptying of the ampullae ducti deferentia and the urethra characterized by the sperm-rich fraction. The third phase or portion of ejaculation is much longer and composed mainly of sperm-poor seminal plasma from the accessory glands. This latter portion in the boar and stallion contains the gelatinous material. In the horse the last part of this third portion of the ejaculate is spoken of as the "tail end" or "dismount" sample. It is not representative of the entire ejaculate in the horse or in other species. This last phase of ejaculation comprises about 40 to 60 per cent or more of the entire volume of the ejaculate. In the bull the presperm fraction is low in fructose and the sperm-rich and post-sperm fractions have a high fructose content indicating admixture with the secretions of the seminal vesicles, Faulkner, Masken and Hopwood.

Frequency of Service—Since spermatozoan production is a continuous process not affected by frequency of ejaculation, theoretically there should be no limit to the number of services. There are, however, limitations in all males to the number of services possible within a given time. (See Table 24) As noted previously, frequent repeated ejaculations over a relatively short period of time tend to cause a reduction in sexual desire, semen volume, and number of spermatozoa per ejaculate. Young or immature males should be used conservatively inasmuch as the decline in semen quality is probably more easily produced, and undesirable habits associated with decreased sexual desire might be developed.

Each male should be handled, observed, and bred as an individual. In young males a certain degree of size must be attained before coitus can be performed with physical safety. Rice and Andrews emphasized the importance of establishing proper breeding habits in male animals and of not permitting these habits to develop in a haphazard fashion. The frustration of small, immature males following unsuccessful attempts to copulate with females that are too large, are improperly restrained, or in an unsuitable location; conditions which may result in slipping and falling, or in head injuries because of a low ceiling; may produce both physical and psychological injury. The latter may have a prolonged effect on a sire's attitude toward service. Some males develop sexual desire slowly. Proper development of breeding habits in a male is just as important as training a heifer to milk or a horse to ride.

In male animals offered frequent opportunities for copulation, libido usually declines before the quality of the ejaculate is lowered to a degree that would affect fertility. Sumner and coworkers reported on 16 bulls and 8 rams under natural mating conditions. The bulls bred each estrous female an average of 1.73 times with the greatest number of services in a day being 10; in rams these respective figures were 4.03 and 29. After several matings with one female, libido declined in bulls and rams but finding another female in estrus rapidly restored their sexual drive.

Foote reported on the average optimum weekly frequency of semen collection to maintain libido and to secure the greatest number of spermatozoa; these were as

Table 24. Approximate Guide to the Frequency of Service and the Number of Females Allotted to Male Domestic Animals*

	Immature Males Hand Breeding		Adult Males Hand Breeding	
Species	No. of Services/week	No. of Females per Season (year)	No. of Services/week	No. of Females per Season (year)
Stallion	2-5	15-40	3-12	30-120
Bull	2-4	20-60	4-12	80-120
Boar	2-4	10-40	4-10	30-60
Dog	1-2	(20-40)	2-6	30-80
Ram	6-12	(30-40)	6-24	40-80

	Pasture Breeding (No. of Females) per season (year)	Pasture Breeding (No. of Females) per season (year)
Bull	10-15	10-25**
Boar	10-20	20-40
Ram	20-30	40-80***

*** This guide will vary greatly for individual males according to their fertility, sperm producing capacity, degree of libido, age and physical condition. It will also be influenced by systems of management, size of pasture or range and nutrition of the sire and dam. Frequent short periods of sexual rest are desirable.**
**** This figure is for range cattle with a limited breeding season. For dairy cattle on improved pasture with a year-long breeding season this figure could be increased 3 or 4 times.**
***** Vigorous yearling to adult rams may breed up to 30 to 40 ewes per month.**

follows: for the bull 4 ejaculations and 30 billion spermatozoa, for the stallion 3 to 4 and 30 billion, for the ram 20 and 25 billion, for the boar 3 and 110 billion, and for the dog 3 and 2 billion.

Coital Injuries of Male Animals

Balanitis and Posthitis of a severe nature frequently leading to adhesions and inability to protrude the penis are occasionally observed in bulls, especially young bulls with great sexual desire the first few weeks on pasture with cows or heifers. Trauma and infection incurred by frequent service and contamination of the sheath or by exposure to the IBR-IPV virus in the cows' genital tract may result in severe necrotic and pyogenic infections of the penis and prepuce. Young rams may be similarly affected. This type of infection involving the penis and prepuce will be discussed later in this chapter.

Injury or Trauma to the Penis. In rare instances in the stallion this may be due to the mare kicking at the stallion and striking the erect penis at the time of service. This may cause a hematoma, paraphimosis, laceration, or rupture of the penis. It is easily avoided by the proper supervision of breeding and by being certain that the mare is definitely in estrum. If necessary breeding hobbles should be used in nervous, excitable mares. In the bull, occasionally the penis catches on the vulvar lips, in a hymenal remnant, beneath the vulva, or if the bull thrusts and the penis is bent sharply at right angles by the cow suddenly collapsing, a rupture of corpus cavernosum and tunica albuginea, usually on the dorsal surface of the penis occurs. A hematoma is thus produced. This is often spoken of as a "fractured", ruptured, or broken penis. This condition is rare in handbred dairy bulls but is not uncommon in beef bulls on pasture.

Hemorrhage from the Prepuce and Penis following service may be due to tumors of the penis or to lacerations of the penis or prepuce. In rare instances bleeding from the urethra may be observed in stallions and bulls; it is usually of unknown origin, Williams. Adams has observed several affected boars that had a small vascular outgrowth or polyp in the urethra that caused blood to be mixed with semen at ejaculation. In several bulls observed by the author irregular-shaped calculi have lodged in the urethra and caused bleeding at the time of service but for a while only slight or moderate symptoms of difficult urination were observed. In young bulls there may occasionally be a small fistula in the glans penis extending into the corpus cavernosum. On erection a fine stream of blood comes through the fistula. Some veterinarians have described the presence on the glans penis of blue-red raised areas or ulcers that rupture and bleed. In artificial breeding, rubber bands from the artificial vagina may slip over the penis at the time the bull thrusts. These usually cause deep lacerations or even amputation of all or part of the glans penis if they are not removed promptly. Such an occurrence may be prevented by not using rubber bands on the artificial vagina, or by tying them with cord so they cannot slip off. Occasionally persons trimming preputial hairs on bulls will snip off the tip of the penis if care is not taken to hold the penis caudal to the preputial orifice. Bloom reported that bleeding from the urethra in dogs is frequently a symptom of fracture of the os penis.

Tumors should be removed. Sexual rest should be given most animals with hemorrhage from the prepuce and penis. In cases of urinary calculi the prognosis is often hopeless for future breeding. When bleeding occurs from the corpus through a fine fistula, sexual rest or surgery to close the defect are indicated. In young bulls observed by the author which bled from a fine fistula or ulcer on the glans penis the fertility of the bulls when bred naturally did not appear affected. Adams has successfully incised the urethra of a few boars and removed the vascular tissue causing the bleeding.

Miscellaneous Injuries at the time of coitus in the stallion may include kick injuries resulting in a ventral hernia, fracture of the hind limbs, or severe orchitis. Breeding hobbles, tying up a front leg and a twitch applied to the mare may be indicated to prevent kicking. In all breeds of animals, especially the larger ones, the footing of the male should be good and the female restrained properly to prevent the male's slipping and falling, possibly causing gonitis, seen most commonly in the bull; dislocation of the hip; fractures of the limb or pelvis; fractures of the spine; muscle or tendon strains or ruptures; as well as the harmful psychological effect on the male from falling or injuring himself during coitus. Large females should not be bred naturally to small males unless restrained with their rear limbs or all four limbs in a hole or pit. Occasionally inguinal hernia with strangulation of the intestine may follow service in stallions and cause severe colic within 1 to 3 hours. The author observed 2 improperly-handled young bulls that had fractured the humerus by dismounting from a cow sideways, with the affected front leg having been caught across the cow's back.

Vices of Male Animals

Vices are much more common in male animals, especially in the larger species, than in female animals because many males are improperly handled or abused, closely housed or confined in dark, poor quarters, lack exercise, sunlight, normal surroundings, and associations provided other female or castrated animals. Intact mature males are more aggressive than castrated males or females. Behavioral disorders in male animals are often related to or effect the sex act and may reduce copulatory efficiency, Fraser. Marvin reported that androgens acting during the early period of differentiation organize neural tissue which mediates later sexual behavior in the male. The time this period occurs in the larger animals is not known but in rats it occurs within 5 or 6 days after birth.

Masturbation or Onanism is observed in male animals of all species. There is little or no evidence that it has any significant effect on fertility or even on libido or desire to copulate. If males are being used regularly and frequently for service the frequency of masturbation declines. In stallions being raced it is considered to have a detrimental effect on training. Some persons consider accumulations of smegma in the sheath to cause irritation and masturbation in stallions and therefore advise regular cleansing of the sheath with soap and water. Regular exercise under harness or saddle, in a large outside paddock away from nonpregnant females or by providing "company" in the form of pregnant mares will help control masturbation. Owners or veterinarians may also use a stallion (Man-of-War) shield or wire brush suspended just in front of the preputial opening, a metal ("birdcage") device over the glans or a plastic or adhesive tape ring applied just behind the glans penis to prevent erection and masturbation. These latter ring-like appliances must be removed and penis cleaned once a week or irritation may occur. It is the author's observation that erection is common in the confined stallion but masturbation with ejaculation is uncommon.

In other animals regular exercise in a large outside paddock helps greatly to avoid masturbation. In bulls, rams, bucks or dogs a suture of stainless steel wire tied loosely through and across the preputial orifice may be of value. In the pet dog not used for breeding, castration can be performed. Boars may masturbate by inserting their penis into the preputial diverticulum and ejaculating there, resulting in a condition called "balling up." Once this vice has developed it can only be corrected by the surgical removal of the diverticulum, Adams. Turkheimer et al. recommended that young boars in artificial insemination studs should be kept isolated in separate pens to prevent **ped-**

erasty or rectal "copulation" which is common in this species. In may occur occasionally in young bulls or rams running together.

Viciousness in Males is often a result of confinement and ill treatment. Dairy bulls are usually confined and are much more apt to be dangerous than are beef bulls, that have freedom to run with the herd. Proper, intelligent handling of male animals from a young age, together with regular daily handling, firm training, and exercise makes most males fairly tractable and easily controlled. Since the larger intact male animals are usually closely confined and caretakers are often afraid of them they are very apt to be teased, irritated and handled indecisively which tends to encourage viciousness. Once a male of a large animal species has become vicious and difficult to manage and this vice is well-developed, it is a very difficult, dangerous, and often an impossible task to correct these habits without elaborate facilities and intelligent, trained help. Not infrequently following castration a formerly vicious stallion will retain his same disposition unless he is retrained. In this respect the vicious stallion is similar to the vicious "nymphomaniac" mare.

Slowness in Breeding is often an acquired vice in male domestic animals that is favored by improper training, rough or ill treatment or painful accidents that have occurred at the time of copulation. This is discussed much more fully later in the section on impotency under forms of infertility in the male. Many male animals develop interesting idiosyncrasies exhibited at the time of mating that usually have their origin in various restraint practices employed by owners prior to permitting service by the male.

Other vices seen commonly in stallions as a result of close, unnatural confinement are stall-walking, weaving, cribbing and self-biting or mutilation. Stall walking may possibly be controlled by regular exercise, closing the stall tightly, hobbling, or tying the animal, by placing bales of straw around the stall or by putting the stallion in a large outside paddock or pasture. Cribbing should be controlled by a cribbing strap or by radical surgery. Weaving is difficult to correct, but proper exercise, a large and well-lighted box stall, or an outside paddock may be helpful. Using a cradle may be indicated in self-biting stallions if proper exercise and management can't control it.

References

Physiology of Male Reproduction Hormones

Asdell, S. A. (1964) Patterns of Mammalian Reproduction, 2nd. Ed., Comstock Publishing Co., Ithaca, N.Y.

Bemis, H. E. and Emmerson, M. A. (1926) Observations on the Various Methods of Surgical Sterilization of Swine, Veterinary Pract. Bull., Iowa State College. **8,** 1, 258.

Dukes, H. H. (1947) The Physiology of Domestic Animals, 6th Ed., Comstock Publishing Co. Inc., Ithaca, N.Y.

Erickson, R. J. and Dutt, R. H. (1963) Progesterone and 6 Methyl-17 Acetoxy-Progesterone as Inhibitors of Spermiogenesis in the Ram, J. An. Sci. **22,** 3, 856.

Macleod, J., Pazianos, A., and Ray, B. (1966). The Restoration of Human Spermatogenesis and the Reproductive Tract with Urinary Gonadotropins Following Hypophysectomy, Fert. and Steril. **17,** 1, 7.

Matsuyama, S., Richkind, M. and Cupps, P. T. (1967) Effects of Supplemental Progesterone on Semen from Bulls, J. Dairy Sci. **50,** 3, 375.

Matsuyama, S., Richkind, M. and Cupps, P. T. (1967) Effects of High Levels of Exogenous Testosterone Proprionate on Bovine Semen, J. Dairy Sci. **50,** 3, 378.

Meineke, C. F. and McDonald, L. E. (1961) The Effects of Exogenous Testosterone on Spermiogenesis of Bulls, Amer. J. Vet. Res. **22,** 87, 209.

Rosenkrantz, H., and Ilievski, V. (1964) Estimated Testosterone Requirements of the Castrated Male Dog, Amer. J. Vet. Res. **25,** 104, 47.

Savard, K., Mason, N. R., Ingram, J. T. and Gassner, R. X. (1961) The Androgens of Bovine Spermatic Venous Blood, Endocrin. **69,** 2, 324.

Steinberger, E., and Duckett, G. E. (1967) Hormonal Control of Spermatogenesis, Reprod. and Fertil., Suppl. 2, 75.

Taylor, D. O. N., Thomas, J. W. and Marburger, R. G. (1964) Abnormal Antler Growth Associated with Hypogonadism in White-Tailed Deer in Texas, Amer. J. Vet. Res. **25,** 104, 179.

Tepperman, J. (1962) Metabolic and Endocrine Physiology, Yearbook Medical Publishers. Chicago.

Turner, C. D. (1961) General Endocrinology, 3rd. Ed. W. B. Saunders Co., Philadelphia.

Zarrow, M. X. (1968) Reproduction in Farm Animals Edit. by E. S. E. Hafez, Lea & Febiger, Philadelphia, 2nd Edit. 3.

Puberty

Abdel-Raouf, M. (1960) The Postnatal Development of the Reproductive Organs in Bulls with Special Reference to Puberty, Acta Endocrin, **34,** Suppl. 49.

Abdel-Raouf, M. (1965) Sexual Behavior and Semen Picture of Bulls of the Swedish Red and White Breed Between the Ages of 9 and 15 Months, Nord. Vet. Med. **17,** 318.

Almquist, J. O. and Cunningham, D. C. (1967) Reproductive Capacity of Beef Bulls I. Postpuberal Changes in Semen Production at Different Ejaculation Frequencies, J. of An. Sci. **26,** 1, 174.

Altman, P. L. and Dittmer, D. S. (1962) Growth Including Reproduction and Morphological Development, Biological Handbook, Federation of Amer. Soc. Exper. Biol., Washington, D.C. p. 188.

Ashdown, R. R. (1962) Adherence Between Penis and Sheath in Beef Calves at the Time of Castration, J. Agric. Sci. **58,** 71.

Bellows, R. A., Riley, T. M., Kieffer, N. M., Urick, J. J., Brinks, J. S. and Clark, R. T. (1964) Preliminary Studies of Sperm Production and Breeding Ability in Young, Straight and Crossbred Bulls, J. An. Sci. **23,** 2, 593.

Bichan, P. E. and Hunter, W. K. (1961) A Study of the Sexual Development of a Stud of Performance-Tested Bulls, Proc. of IV Intern. Cong. on An. Reprod. (Hague), IV, 793.

Christian, R. E. and Wolf, F. R. (1963) Electroejaculation in the Young Beef Bull, J. of An. Sci. **22,** 3, 855.

Hauer, E. P., Kellgren, H. C., McCraine, S. E. and Vincent, C. K. (1970) Puberal Characteristics of Quarter Horse Stallions, J. An. Sci. **30,** 2, 321.

Lagerlof, N. and Carlquist, H. (1961) The Semen of Boars of the Yorkshire Breed Between the Ages of Five and Nine Months, Proc. IV Intern. Cong. on An. Reprod. (Hague) IV, 818.

McMillan, K. L. and Hafs, H. D. (1968) Pituitary and Hypothalamic Endocrine Changes Associated with Reproductive Development of Holstein Bulls, J. An. Sci. **27,** 6, 1614.

McMillan, K. L. and Hafs, H. D. (1969) Reproductive Tract of Holstein Bulls from Birth Through Puberty, J. An. Sci. **28,** 2, 233.

Niwa, T., Mizuko, A. and Ito, S. (1959) Studies on the Age of Sexual Maturity in the Boar, Biol. Abstr. **35,** 9, 1959.

Scrotum and Heat Regulation of the Testes

Ferguson, M. B., Miller, O. C. and Graves, C. N. (1967) Internal Scrotal Temperatures of Dairy Bulls, J. An. Sci. **26,** 6, 1498.

Phillips, R. W. and McKenzie, F. F. (1934) The Thermoregulatory Function and Mechanism of the Scrotum, Missouri Exp. Stat. Bull. 217.

Waites, G. M. H. and Moule, G. R. (1961) Relation of Vascular Heat Exchange to Temperature Regulation in the Testis of the Ram, J. Reprod. and Fertil. **2,** 213.

The Testicles and Spermatogenesis

Almquist, J. O. and Amann, R. P. (1961) Reproductive Capacity of Dairy Bulls. II. Gonadal and Extragonadal Sperm Reserves as Determined by Direct Counts and Depletion Trials; Dimensions and Weight of Genitalia, J. of Dairy Sci. **44,** 9, 1968.

Bloom, G. and Nicander, L. (1962) Electron Microscopical Study of the Protoplasmic Droplet of Mammalian Spermatozoa, Internat. J. of Fert. **7,** 4, 355.

Clermont, Y. (1966) Spermatogenesis in Man—Study of the Spermatogonial Population, Fert. and Steril. **17,** 6, 705.

Foote, R. H. (1966) Bovine Male Anatomy and Spermatogenesis, Proc. First Tech. Conf. Nat. Assoc. Art. Breeders.

Foote, R. H. (1968) Personal Communication.

Kennelly, J. J. and Foote, R. H. (1964) Sampling Boar Testes to Study Spermatogenesis Quantitatively and to Predict Sperm Production, J. An. Sci. **23,** 1, 160.

Knudsen, D. and Bryne, N. (1960) The Spermiocytogenesis of the Bull, Acta, Vet. Scand., **1,** 140.

Langman, J. (1963) Medical Embryology, Williams and Wilkins Co., Baltimore.

Leblonde, C. P., Steinburger, E. and Roosen-Runge, E. C. (1963) Spermatogenesis, in **Mechanisms Concerned with Conception,** C. G. Hartman Ed., Pergamon Press, McMillan Co., N.Y. City.

Orbegin, M. C. (1961) Experimental Determination of the Rate of Transit of Spermatozoa in the Bull, Proc. IV Internat. Congr. on An. Reprod. Hague. Vol. II, 232.

Ortavant, R., Courot, M. and Hochereau, M. T. (1969) Spermatogenesis and Morphology of the Spermatozoon, in **Reproduction in Domestic Animals,** by H. H. Cole and P. T. Cupps, Academic Press, N.Y.C. and London, 2nd Ed.

Swierstra, E. E. (1947) Duration of Spermatogenesis in the Boar, J. of An. Sci. **26,** 4, 952.

Voglmayr, J. K. and Mattner, P. E. (1968) Compensatory Hypertrophy in the Remaining Testis Following Unilateral Orchidectomy in the Adult Ram, J. Reprod. and Fert. **17,** 179.

Morphology of Spermatozoa

Altman, P. L. and Dittmer, D. S. (1962). Growth Including Reproduction and Morphological Development, Federation of Amer. Soc. Exper. Biol. Biological Handbook, Washington, D.C.

Baker, M., Cragle, R. G., Salisbury, G. W. and Van Demark, N. L. (1957) Spermatozoan Velocities in Vitro, Fert. and Steril. **8,** 2, 149.

Bishop, D. W., (1962) Spermatozoan Motility, Amer. Assoc. for the Adv. of Science, Washington, D.C. 322.

Blom, E. and Birch-Andersen, A. (1960) The Ultrastructure of Bull Sperm I. The Middle Piece, Nord. Vet. Med. **12,** 261.

Blom, E. and Birch-Andersen, A. (1965) The Ultrastructure of Bull Sperm II. The Sperm Head, Nord. Vet. Med. **17,** 193.

Foote, R. H. (1966) Bovine Male Anatomy and Spermatogenesis, Proc. 1st Tech. Confer. Nat. Assoc. Art. Breeders.

Hadek, R. (1969) Mammalian Fertilization, Academic Press, N.Y.C.

Hancock, J. L. (1966) The Ultrastructure of Mammalian Spermatozoa, in **Advances in Reproductive Physiology,** A. McLaren, Ed., Vol. I, Academic Press, N.Y.C.

Janick, J. and MacLeod, J. (1970) Measurement of Human Spermatozoan Motility, Fert. and Steril. **21,** 2, 140.

Kojima, J. (1966) Electron Microscopic Study of the Bull Spermatozoon, Jap. Jour. Vet. Res. **14,** no's 1 and 2.

Lustig, G. and Lindahl, P. E. (1970) Activation of Motility in Bull and Rabbit Spermatozoa by Ultrasonic Treatment Recorded by a Photographic Method, Internat. J. of Fert. **15,** 3, 135.

Moeller, A. N. and Van Demark, N. L. (1955) **In vitro** Speed of Bovine Spermatozoa, Fert. and Steril. **6,** 6, 506.

White, I. G. (1968) Mammalian Semen, **Reproduction in Farm Animals,** E. S. E. Hafez Ed. 2nd Ed., Lea and Febiger. Philadelphia 39.

Wu, A. S. H. and Newstad, J. D. (1966) Electron Microscope Study of Bovine Epididymal Spermatozoa, J. An. Sci. **25,** 4, 1186.

Sperm Transport, Maturation and Storage, and Accessory Gland Secretion

Almquist, J. O., Amann, R. P. and O'Dell, W. T. (1958) Sperm Reserves of Dairy Bulls as Determined by Depletion Trials and Post Slaughter Sperm Counts, J. Dairy Sci. **41,** 5, 733.

Almquist, J. O. and Amann, R. P. (1961) Reproductive Capacity of Dairy Bulls II Gonadal and Extragonadal Sperm Reserves as Determined by Direct Counts and Depletion Trials; Dimensions and Weight of Genitalia, J. Dairy Sci. **44,** 9, 1668.

Almquist, J. O. and Amann, R. P. (1962) Reproductive Capacity of Dairy Bulls VI. Effect of Unilateral Vasectomy and Ejaculation Frequency on Sperm Reserves; Aspects of Epididymal Physiology, Jour. Reprod. and Fertil. **3,** 260.

Amann, R. P. and Almquist, J. O. (1962) Reproductive Capacity of Dairy Bulls VII Morphology of Epididymal Sperm, J. Dairy Sci. **45,** 2, 1516.

Asdell, S. A. (1964) Patterns of Mammalian Reproduction, 2nd. Ed., Comstock Publishing Associates, Ithaca, N.Y.

Berliner, V. (1963) Equine Medicine and Surgery, Amer. Vet. Publ. Inc., Wheaton, Ill. p. 635.

Bialy, G. and Smith, V. R. (1959) Cold Shock of Bovine Epididymal Sperm, J. Dairy Sci. **42,** 12, 2002.

Blandau, R. J. and Rumery, R. E. (1964) The Relationship of Swimming Movements of Epididymal Spermatozoa to their Fertilizing Capacity, Fert. and Steril. **15,** 6, 571.

Blom, E. (1968) Reproduction in Farm Animals, 2nd Ed., Edited by E. S. E. Hafez, Lea and Febiger, Philadelphia, Pa.

Crabo, B. (1965) Studies on the Composition of Epididymal Content in Bulls and Boars, Acta Vet. Scand. **6,** Suppl. 5.

Day, F. T. (1940) The Stallion and Fertility, Vet. Rec. **52,** 34, 597.

Dukes, H. H. (1955) The Physiology of Domestic Animals, 7th Ed., Comstock Publishing Assoc., Ithaca, N.Y.

Faulkner, L. C., Hopwood, M. L. and Wiltbank, J. N. (1968) Seminal Vesiculectomy in Bulls, J. Reprod. and Fertil. **16,** 2, 179.

Gustafsson, B. (1966) Luminal Contents of the Bovine Epididymis Under Conditions of Reduced Spermatogenesis, Luminal Blockage and Certain Sperm Abnormalities, Thesis, Dept. of Obst. & Gynec., Royal Vet. Col. Stockholm, Sweden.

Hart, R. G. (1968) The Mechanism of Action of Cowper's Secretion in Coagulating Rat Semen, J. Reprod. and Fertil. **17,** 223.

Igboeli, G. and Foote, R. H. (1968) Maturation Changes in Bull Epididymal Spermatozoa, J. Dairy Sci. **51,** 10, 1703.

Igboeli, G. and Foote, R. H. (1969) Maturation and Aging Changes in Rabbit Spermatozoa Isolated by Ligatures at Different Levels of the Epididymis, Fert. and Steril. **20,** 3, 506.

Igboeli, G. and Rakha, A. M. (1970) Bull Testicular and Epididymal Functions after Long Term Vasectomy, J. An. Sci. **31,** 1, 72.

King, G. J. and Macpherson, J. W. (1969) Influence of Seminal Vesiculectomy on Bovine Semen, J. Dairy Sci. **52,** 11, 1837.

Lambiase, J. T. Jr. and Amann, R. P. (1969) The Male Rabbit V Changes in the Sperm Reserves and Resorbtion Rate Induced by Ejaculation and Sexual Rest, J. of An. Sci. **28,** 4, 542.

Lino, B. F., Braden, A. W. and Turnbull, K. E. (1967) Fate of Unejaculated Spermatozoa, Nature, **213,** 5076, 594.

Mann, T. (1964) The Biochemistry of Semen, John Wiley and Sons, N.Y.C.

Nalbandov, A. V. (1964) Reproductive Physiology, 2nd Ed., W. H. Freeman and Co., San Francisco and London.

Paufler, S. K. and Foote, R. H. (1968) Morphology, Motility and Fertility of Spermatozoa Recovered from Different Areas of Ligated Rabbit Epididymides, J. Reprod. and Fert. **17,** 125.

Phadke, A. M. (1964) Fate of Spermatozoa in Cases of Obstructive Azoospermia and After Ligation of Vas Deferens in Man, J. Reprod. and Fertil. **7,** 1.

Ripley, P. L. (1963) Physiology of the Male Accessory Organs, in **Mechanisms Concerned with Conception.** C. G. Hartman, Editor, Pergamon Press, McMillan Co., N.Y.C.

Roussel, J. D., Stallcup, O. T. and Austin, C. R. (1967) Selective Phagocytosis of Spermatozoa in the Epididymis of Bulls, Rabbits and Monkeys, J. of Fert. and Steril, **18,** 4, 509.

Ventura, W. P., Freund, M. and Knapp, F. (1968) Motility of the Vagina, Uterine Body and Horns of the Guinea Pig. Effects of Semen and Male Accessory Gland Secretions, Fert. and Steril. **19,** 3, 462.

Voglmayr, J. K. and Mattner, P. E. (1968) See The Testicles and Spermatogenesis.

White, D. G. and Lincoln, G. J. (1958) Riboflavin in Yellow Semen, Nature, **182,** 667.

Erection and Ejaculation

Beckett, S. D. (1968) Personal Communication.

Dukes, H. H. (1955) The Physiology of Domestic Animals, 7th Ed., Comstock Publishing Associates, Ithaca, N.Y.

Dutt, R. H., Simpson, E. C., Christian, J. C. and Barnhart, C. E. (1959) Identification of the Preputial Glands as the Site of Production of Sexual Odor in the Boar, J. An. Sci. **18,** 4, 1557.

Fjellstrom, D., Kihlstrom, J. E. and Melin, P. (1968) The Effect of Synthetic Oxytocin upon Seminal Characteristics and Sexual Behavior in Male Rabbits, J. Reprod. and Fert. **17,** 207.

Ford, R. S. (1968) Buck Deodorizing Possible Now with New Researched Method, Dairy Goat Jour., Nov., 3.

Goldston, R. T (1969) The Bovine Penile Hematoma, Proc. of Conference on Reproductive Problems in Animals, Univ. of Georgia, Nov., p. 63.

Habel, R. E. and Biberstein, E. (1952) Fundamentals of the Histology of Domestic Animals, edited by Troutmann and Febiger (English Translation), Comstock Publ. Co., Ithaca, N.Y. p. 356.

Hafez, E. S. E. (1968) Reproduction in Farm Animals, 2nd Ed., Lea and Febiger, Philadelphia.

Lewis, J. E., Walker, D. F., Beckett, S. D. and Vachon, R. I. (1968) Blood Pressure Within the Corpus Cavernosum of the Bovine Penis, Jour. Reprod. and Fert. **17,** 155.

Masson, Jorge (1961) Personal Communication, Unpublished data.

Miller, M. E. (1964) Anatomy of the Dog, W. B. Saunders, Co., Philadelphia, London.

Seidel, G. E. Jr. and Foote, R. H. (1967) Motion Picture Analysis of Bovine Ejaculation, J. Dairy Sci. **50,** 6, 970.

Seidel, G. E. Jr. and Foote, R. H. (1969) Motion Picture Analysis of Ejaculation in the Bull, J. of Reprod. and Fert. **20,** 313.

Watson, J. W. (1964) Mechanism of Erection and Ejaculation in the Bull and Ram, Nature, **204,** 95.

Weibe, E. and Roberts, S. J. (1969) Unpublished studies.

Semen and the Ejaculate

Adams, Wm (1970) Personal Communication.

Aitken, R. N. C. (1960) A Histochemical Study of the Accessory Genital Glands of the Boar, J. Anat. **94,** (1) 130.

Almquist, J. O. and Hale, E. B. (1956) An Approach to the Measurement of Sexual Behavior and Semen Production of Dairy Bulls, III Internat. Congr. on An. Reprod., Cambridge.

Almquist, J. O., Amann, R. P. and O'Dell, W. T. (1958) Sperm Reserves of Dairy Bulls as Determined by Depletion Trials and Post Slaughter Sperm Counts, J. Dairy Sci. **41,** 5, 733.

Altman, P. L. and Dittmer, D. S. (1962) Growth Including Reproduction and Morphological Development, Federation of Amer. Soc. Exper. Biol. Biological Handbook, Washington, D.C.

Bartlett, D. J. (1962) Studies on Dog Semen, I and II, J. Reprod. and Fertil. **3,** 173 and 190.

Bielanski, W. and Wierzbowski, S. (1961) Depletion Test in Stallions, Proc. IV Intern. Cong. on An. Reprod., Hague, Vol II, 279.

Boucher, J. H , Foote, R. H. and Kirk, R. W. (1958) The Evaluation of Semen Quality in the Dog and the Effect of Frequent Ejaculation on Semen Quality, Libido and Depletion of Sperm Reserves in the Dog, Cor. Vet. **48,** 1, 67.

Dukes, H. H. (1955) The Physiology of Domestic Animals, 7th Ed., Comstock Publishing Associates, Ithaca, N.Y.

Elliot, I. (1969) Symposium on the Management of Beef Cattle for Reproductive Efficiency, Ft. Collins, Colo.

Fasten, J., Almquist, J. O. and Martig, R. C. (1970) Reproductive Capacity of Beef Bulls. IV Changes in Sexual Behavior and Semen Characteristics among Successive Ejaculations, J. An. Sci. **30,** 2, 245.

Faulkner, L. C., Masken, J. F. and Hopwood, M. L. (1964) Fractionation of the Bovine Ejaculate, J. Dairy Sci. **47,** 7, 823.

Foote, R. H., Voigt, V. J. and Schales, N. (1960) Catalase Content of Rabbit, Ram and Bull Semen, J. An. Sci. **19,** 4, 1218.

Foote, R. H. (1969) Physiological Aspects of Artificial Insemination, in **Reproduction in Domestic Animals** by Cole and Cupps, 2nd Ed., Academic Press, N.Y.C.

Gerritus, R. J., Graham, E. F. and Cole, C. L. (1962) Effect of Collection Interval on the Characteristics of the Ejaculate of the Boar, J. An. Sci. **21,** 4, 1022.

Haag, F. M. and Werthhessen, N. T. (1956) Relationship Between Fertility and the Nonprotein Sulfhydryl Concentration of Seminal Fluids in the Thoroughbred Stallion, Fert. & Steril. **7,** 516.

Hafs, H. D., Hoyt, R. S. and Bratton, R. W. (1958) Effects of Daily Ejaculation on Sperm Output, Fertility and Libido of Dairy Bulls, J. Dairy Sci. **41,** 5, 734.

Hafs, H. D., Hoyt, R. S. and Bratton, R. W. (1959) Libido, Sperm Characteristics Sperm Output and Fertility of Mature Dairy Bulls Ejaculated Daily or Weekly for Thirty-Two Weeks, J. Dairy Sci. **42,** 4, 626.

McLeod, J. and McGee, W. R. (1950) The Semen of the Thoroughbred, Cor. Vet. **40,** 3, 233.

Mann, T., Minotakis, C. S. and Polge, C. (1963) Semen Composition and Metabolism in the Stallion and Jackass, J. Reprod. and Fertil. **5,** 109.

Mann, T. (1964) The Biochemistry of Semen and the Male Reproductive Tract, 2nd Ed., John Wiley and Sons, Inc., N.Y.C.

Maule, J. P. (1962) The Semen of Animals and Artificial Insemination, Technical Communication No. 15, Commonwealth Agricultural Bureau, Farmham Royal, Bucks, England.

Nalbandov, A. V. (1964) Reproductive Physiology, 2nd Ed., W. H. Freeman and Co., San Francisco and London.

Sack, W. (1968) Personal Communication.

Seidel, G. E. Jr. and Foote, R. H. (1970) Compartmental Analysis of Sources of the Bovine Ejaculate, Biol. of Reprod. **2,** 189.

Sojka, N. J., Jennings, L. L. and Hamner, C. E. (1970) Artificial Insemination in the Cat. (Felis Catus L.), Lab. An. Care. **20,** 2, 198.

Sumner, S. L., Ancalmo, R. and Warnick, A. C. (1968) Behavior of Bulls and Rams During the Breeding Season, J. An. Sci. **27,** 4, 1197.

Swierstra, E. E. and Rahnefeld, G. W. (1967) Semen and Testis Characteristics in Young Yorkshire and Lacombe Boars, J. An. Sci. **26,** 1, 149.

Roberts, S. J. (1956) Veterinary Obstetrics and Genital Diseases, 1st Ed., Edwards Bros, Ann Arbor, Mich.

Rosenkrantz, H., Langille, J. and Mason, M. M. (1961) The Chemical Analysis of Normal Canine Prostatic Fluid, Amer. J. Vet. Res. **22,** 91, 1057.

Rice, V. A. and Andrews, F. N. (1951) Breeding and Improvement of Farm Animals, 4th Ed., McGraw Hill Book Comp. Inc., N.Y.C.

White, I. G. and MacLeod, J. (1963) Composition and Physiology of Semen, in **Mechanisms Concerned with Conception,** C. G. Hartman, Editor, Pergamon Press, McMillan Co., N.Y.C.

White, I. G. (1968) Mammalian Semen, in **Reproduction in Farm Animals,** E. S. E. Hafez, Editor, 2nd Ed., Lea and Febiger, Philadelphia.

VanDemark, N. L. and Mauger, R. E. (1958) Factors Affecting Replenishment of Sperm Numbers in Bulls Frequently Ejaculated, J. An. Sci. **17,** 4, 1215.

Vices of Male Animals

Adams, W. (1967) Personal Communication.

Bloom, F. (1954) Pathology of the Dog and Cat, Amer. Vet. Public. Inc., Evanston, Ill.

Fraser, A. F. (1968) Abnormal Behavior in Animals, Edit. by M. W. Fox, W. B. Saunders, Co., Phila., 179.

Marvin, C. (1968) Abnormal Behavior in Animals, Edit. by M. W. Fox, W. B. Saunders, Co., Phila. 208.

Turkheimer, A. R., Young, D. C. and Foote, R. H. (1958) Technique for Semen Collection; Semen Production in Young Boars, Cor. Vet. **48,** 3, 291.

Williams, W. L. (1943) Diseases of the Genital Organs of Domestic Animals, 3rd. Ed. Louella Williams, Upland Rd., Ithaca, N.Y.

Nutrition and Infertility in the Male

The nutritional requirements of males are in general similar to those of females. On the basis of our present knowledge, the qualitative and quantitative requirements for reproduction in the male do not exceed those for the growth of young animals or for the maintenance of older animals in a state of good health. Reid reported that in bulls, rams, and boars rations that are satisfactory for normal growth to 3 years of age are normal for reproduction. The requirements for pregnant, and especially lactating, animals are higher than for the male. In large animals the ration should include a good quality of roughage. The value of a good pasture cannot be over-emphasized. The ration should be properly balanced in carbohydrates, protein, and minerals and supply the vitamins known to be essential for good reproduction. Although numerous attempts have been made to formulate rations that will increase spermatozoan production and semen quality, it still appears that there are no specific nutrients concerned only with fertility, Rice and Andrews. Reid stated that in few fields are there more opinions with less supporting evidence than in the field of infertility. A definite deficiency of any single nutrient is seldom found. Natural-occurring deficiencies are usually multiple. The breeding male should be kept in good physical condition and should not be permitted to become overweight.

A low plane of nutrition is frequently encountered in practice. As physical deterioration progresses into inanition in the male there occurs an atrophy of the testes, a decrease in the number of spermatozoa per ejaculate, and a progressive loss of sexual desire. Delayed puberty will occur when there is a low plane of nutrition in the young male animal, Bratton and coworkers and Flipse and Almquist. Underfeeding during the growth period had a limiting effect on sperm cell production at maturity in bulls, Van Demark and coworkers. Thus a low plane of nutrition may adversely affect reproductive functions in the male but severe effects on reproduction are not observed unless emaciation and inanition is marked.

A high plane of nutrition is frequently cited as a cause of infertility, especially in fat, overfed, obese, show animals. There is no experimental evidence that a high level of feeding and body condition has any effect on semen production. McKenzie and Berliner reported that fertile rams fitted for show continued to be fertile even though in a very high state of nutrition. These workers found that overweight did not increase rectal or scrotal temperatures or cause any degenerative changes in the testes. Some authors have suggested that certain male animals develop excessive fatness because of an endocrine disturbance such as hypothyroidism, that predisposes the male to infertility. This is possible but it has not been proven. Phlegmatic, lazy bulls tend to put on excessive weight. Rearing intensity did not affect a bull's mating behavior, Bane.

High body condition may result in slowness, difficulty or inability to copulate because of paunchiness, laziness, weaknesses in legs and feet, Flipse and Almquist, and a lack of sexual desire in some males but this is not associated with defective spermatogenesis. Deakin and others indicated that excessively fat bulls may have enough fat around the testes in the scrotum, especially the dorsal part, to insulate the testes and possibly affect spermatogenesis but this has not been proven. Some very fat beef bulls are highly fertile. In some bulls excessive fat in and above the scrotum may be confused with an inguinal hernia. When the obesity in these males is corrected by underfeeding and exercise the inguinal fat is slow to disappear. Therefore high energy intakes are not desirable for bulls past the stage of rapid growth but moderately heavy early feeding may promote early semen production.

Feed Constituents. Under the usual conditions of management the possibility of a deficiency in either the quality or quantity of **protein** fed to males seems remote. When the protein in the ration was below 2 percent, low feed intakes, loss of weight, weakness and reduced libido and sperm cell production occurred in rams and bulls, Warnick et al., and Meacham et al.. Urea was satisfactory as source of protein in ruminant male animals. Although some veterinarians have recommended feeding animal protein such as skim milk, fish meal, turkey mash, or other high-quality protein pellets, there is no evidence that it is necessary, providing adequate grain and good roughage are fed.

Vitamin deficiencies are seldom observed as a cause of

infertility in the larger male domestic animals if the roughage in the ration is near normal in quality or quantity. Vitamin A deficiency, if severe and characterized by night blindness and stiffness, may cause cessation of spermatogenesis and atrophy of the seminiferous epithelium and a decline in semen quality as well as a decrease in sexual desire. In young bulls vitamin A deficiency may result in cystic pituitary glands, Ghannam et al. and Erb and coworkers. Reid reported that 35 to 100 micrograms of vitamin A per kilogram of body weight daily is ample for reproduction in bulls. There is little evidence that deficiencies of vitamins B, C, D or E are even occasional causes of infertility. Although vitamin E is essential for reproduction in the rat there is no proof or indication that it is necessary for reproduction in domestic animals, Salisbury.

Mineral deficiencies affecting reproduction in male animals are rare. Deficiencies of calcium, manganese, zinc, iodine, potassium have not been proven to be causes of male infertility. Deficiencies of cobalt, iron and copper may cause anemia, lack of appetite and loss of weight, and thus have an adverse influence, usually mild in nature, on male reproduction. A lack of phosphorus, often associated with a lack of protein and low levels of vitamin A under natural conditions may cause reduced appetite, a loss in condition and reduced reproductive function. Krook et al. have theorized that osteopetrosis with accompanying spondylitis and arthritis in the bull may result from ultimobranchial body hyperplasia or neoplasia which may be caused by excessive dietary calcium. Arthritis and spondylitis may cause hesitancy or inability to copulate. High dietary calcium levels may be caused by feeding alfalfa or clover hay and dairy grain rations fortified with minerals needed by lactating cows but not by bulls.

Most reproductive disturbances related to nutrition are caused by underfeeding. If the male is fed a normal balanced ration that will produce normal growth or maintain normal health, reproduction will not suffer because of nutritional deficiencies. In some areas owners feed special fortified rations to breeding males. These special fortified rations have added amounts of various types of protein, vitamins, especially vitamin A, manganese, cobalt, phosphorus and other minerals that when fed to bulls amply supply their supposed needs for a high level of reproduction. The value of these feeds is highly questionable.

Along with proper nutrition and adequate water and salt, factors such as exercise, sunlight, pasture, and other environmental influences play an important role in maintaining the health and activity of the breeding male and in prolonging his usefulness.

References

Bane, A. (1954) Sexual Functions of Bulls in Relation to Heredity, Rearing Intensity and Somatic Conditions, Acta Agric. Scad. **4,** 2, 97.

Bratton, R. W., Musgrave, S. D., Dunn, H. O., Foote, R. H. and Henderson, C. R. (1956) Semen Production and Fertility of Young Bulls Raised on Three Different Levels of Feed Intake, J. An. Sci. **15,** 4, 1296.

Erb, R. E., Andrews, F. N., Hauge, S. M. and King, W. A. (1947) Observations on Vitamin A Deficiency in Young Dairy Bulls, J. Dairy Sci. **30,** 9, 687.

Flipse, R. J. and Almquist, J. O. (1961) Effect of Total Digestable Nutrient Intake from Birth to Four Years of Age on Growth and Reproductive Development and Performance of Dairy Bulls, J. Dairy Sci. **44,** 5, 905.

Ghannam, S., Alaliley, H. and Deeb, S. (1966) The Effect of Different Levels of Vitamin A on the Reproductive Organs of Young Bulls, Internat. Jour. of Fertil. **11,** 3, 306.

Krook, L., Lutwak, L., and McEntee, K. (1969) Dietary Calcium, Ultimobranchial Tumors and Osteopetrosis in the Bull; Syndrome of Calcitonin Excess, Amer. J. of Clin. Nutr. **22,** 2, 115.

McKenzie, F. F. and Berliner, V. R. (1937) The Reproductive Capacity of Rams, Mo. Agr. Exp. Stat. Res. Bull. 265.

Meacham, T. N , Cunha, T. J., Warnick, A. C., Hentges, J. F., Jr. and Hargrave, D. D. (1963) Influence of Low Protein Rations on Growth and Semen Characteristics of Young Beef Bulls, J. An. Sci. **22,** 1, 115.

Reid, J. T. (1949) Relationship of Nutrition to Fertility in Animals, J.A.V.M.A. **114,** 864 and 865, 158 and 242.

Rice, V. A. and Andrews, F. N (1951) Breeding and Improvement of Farm Animals, 4th Ed., McGraw Hill Book Co. Inc. N.Y.C.

Salisbury, G. W. (1944) A Controlled Experiment in Feeding Wheat Germ Oil as a Supplement to the Normal Ration of Bulls Used for Artificial Insemination, J. Dairy Sci. **27,** 551.

Stevermer, E. J., Kovacs, M. F., Jr., Hoekstra, W. G. and Self, H. L. (1961) Effect of Feed Intake on Semen Characteristics and Reproductive Performance ~~of Mature~~ Boars, J. An. Sci. **20,** 4, 858.

Van Demark, N. L. and Mauger, R. E. (1964) Effect of Energy Intake on Reproductive Performance of Dairy Bulls, J. Dairy Sci. **47,** 7, 798.

Warnick, A. C., Meacham, T. N., Cunha, T. J., Roggins, P. E., Hentges, J. F., Jr., and Shirley, R. L. (1961) Effect of Source and Level of Nitrogen on Semen Production and Libido in Rams, Proc. IV. Internat. Congr. on An. Reprod., Hague, Vol. II, 202.

Hormonal Causes of Infertility in Males

In male animals there is no infertility condition due to a hormonal cause that uniformly responds to endocrine therapy. Therefore hormonal treatments for lowered fertility or impotency are disappointing and of questionable value.

A lack of sexual desire or libido and reduced spermatogenesis with testicular atrophy may be caused by a failure of ICSH and FSH to be released from the anterior pituitary gland by factors originating in the hypothalamus. There are many "stress" factors, the most important one being inanition due to a low plane of nutrition, that may cause this failure. In rare cases, especially in dogs, tumors in the pituitary area may cause atrophy of the pituitary gland and failure of gonadotropin production. More satisfactory response to treatment will follow a correct diagnosis of the cause or causes of a lack of libido or reduced spermatogenesis than the use of gonadotropic hormones in an empirical manner. Because of their protein constitution animals become refractory to repeated doses of gonadotropic hormones. Successful results following their use is usually fortuitous and can usually be explained by other therapeutic or management practices.

If the pituitary gland is functioning normally and releasing ICSH, failure of libido is seldom caused by a lack of testosterone produced in the interstitial cells of the testes. Occasionally in young males, testosterone injections may hasten sexual maturity and improve sex drive. Only in severely hypoplastic testes with a lack of interstitial cells would there be a deficiency of testosterone in the intact male. Rarely Sertoli cell tumors may produce sufficient estrogen to suppress the release of ICSH and cause impotency. Testosterone may be used empirically in bulls with abnormalities of spermiogenesis or evidence of an abnormal environment of the storage of sperm cells in the epididymis. As with gonadotropins; testosterone is seldom successful alone in the treatment of a lack of sex drive in adult males.

Peterson and coworkers reported that thyroidectomy in a bull resulted in impotency. Hypothyroidism may be present in some obese, lethargic males. Hypothyroidism in male animals has not been proven but a few fat males fed or injected with thyroid hormone or iodinated casein have lost some weight and become more alert with an improvement in libido. Thyroxine therapy has little or no effect on spermatogenesis and is not uniformly or highly successful in males lacking sexual desire.

Cupps and coworkers have reported that some bulls with low fertility have fascicular cortical nodules in the adrenal that apparently convert progesterone into large amounts of cortisol. This results in a high concentration of spermatozoa and a low fructose concentration in the semen.

Cryptorchidism is considered to be an inherited defect and the male is castrated or slaughtered. In humans cryptorchidism has been treated before puberty by gonadotropins or testosterone with limited success, Hurxthal and Musulin. Most attempts in animals to use hormones to induce descent of the testis have failed.

Prostatic hyperplasia in old male dogs is usually due to the excessive production of testosterone by the testes and can be alleviated to some extent by injections of estrogens. A more satisfactory method is castration, which removes the source of the testosterone in the body. Prostatectomy is difficult and seldom used. Estrogenic therapy is often temporarily successful because it inhibits secretion of the gonadotropic hormone from the pituitary gland necessary for androgen production from the interstitial cells in the testes. No function has been ascribed to oxytocin in the male but it is most likely concerned with sperm transport and ejaculation. The oxytocin levels in the plasma of men and women are similar, Rorie and Newton.

Endocrine therapy for infertility in males is seldom indicated. It is usually used as a secondary or supportive line of therapy. It is improper and illogical to administer only hormones such as testosterone, thyroid products, or gonadotropic hormones in impotency, or gonadotropic hormones or thyroid products in cases of low fertility, and then expect satisfactory results. A good history and careful clinical evaluation of the male should be made to determine, if possible; the etiology of the impotency or infertility, so that intelligent recommendations and treatments can be made. If hormones are used for therapy in male animals their limitations should be recognized.

References

Cupps, P. T., Briggs, J. R., Garm, O. and Onstad, O. (1964) Metabolism of Progesterone by Adrenal Gland Homogenates from Bulls, J. of Dairy sci. **47,** 7, 803.

Hurxthal, L. M. and Musulin, N. (1953) Clinical Endrocrinology, Vol. II, J. B. Lippincott Co., Philadelphia, Pa.

Peterson, W. E., Spielman, A., Pomeroy, B. S. and Boyd, W. L. (1941) Effect of Thyroidectomy Upon the Sexual Behavior of the Male Bovine, Proc. of the Soc. Exper. Biol. and Med. **46,** 16.

Rorie, D. K. and Newton, M. (1964) Oxytoxic Factors in the Plasma of the Human Male, Fert. and Steril. **15,** 2, 135.

FORMS OF INFERTILITY IN THE MALE

According to Lagerlof these may be divided into three general categories:

I. Reduced to Complete Lack of Sexual Desire and Ability to Copulate (Impotentia coeundi).
II. Inability or Reduced Ability to Fertilize due to Path-

ology of the Testes, Mesonephric Duct and the Accessory Glands (Impotentia generandi).

III. Miscellaneous Diseases Affecting the Reproductive Organs.

These conditions are present in males of all species. The degree of each condition present in males varies considerably between species, breeds, families, and individuals. There are many degrees, from mild to severe, in each category of the various forms of infertility; a fact which demonstrates strikingly that in males there is a wide range of reproductive ability. Sometimes reduced sexual desire and ability to copulate may be associated with reduced fertility and poor quality semen but in most cases of infertility in males the two conditions are not related. In male animals semen collection is usually possible so that direct measurements of sperm quality and other tests may be applied. In examining males for infertility or sterility, accurate breeding and health records on the male and the herd should be obtained and examined. Secondly, there should be a careful, painstaking physical examination of the male including the observation of his mating behavior. Thirdly, one or more thorough semen examinations by a trained veterinarian or qualified laboratory are necessary. To evaluate the nature of a male's infertility and sterility so that proper recommendations for therapy, treatment, or disposal of the animal may be made, all three of the above examinations are essential. The prognosis in nearly all forms of infertility or sterility in male animals should be guarded.

REDUCED TO COMPLETE LACK OF SEXUAL DESIRE AND ABILITY TO COPULATE (IMPOTENTIA COEUNDI)

Potency is the physical capability of the entire body to coordinate and perform the male's normal role at coitus including erection, mounting, intromission and ejaculation. A lack of potency is observed in certain males in all species and is characterized by symptoms ranging from a complete lack of sexual interest and inability to copulate to a slight slowness or delay in the exhibition of libido, mounting and copulating. Mating and copulatory behavior of males has been reviewed by Hafez and Hammond and Fox in various species, by Hale and Fraser in bulls, by Wierzbowski and Hafez in stallions, and by Hulet and coworkers in rams. In the female animal reproductive behavior is relatively simple requiring only a willingness to stand to be mounted, or an attitude of acceptance. This attitude is primarily under the control or influence of estrogen which may be enhanced by progesterone. In the male animal reproductive behavior is more complex requiring identification, seeking out, teasing and then the performance of the complicated act of copulation. This is under the control or influence of testosterone and other central nervous system mechanisms. The components of the act of copulation consist of sexual excitement, courtship, erection, mounting, intromission, ejaculation, dismounting and refractoriness. There is a great variation in the duration of these components between species and individual males within a species. Mating behavior depends to a varying degree on visual, olfactory, auditory, and tactile cues. In all species visual and tactile cues are probably most important in the actual act of copulation but even blind males may copulate if experienced. Height, width, and color of the female, attitudes of acceptance, such as her stance as the male approaches, reaction of the female to pressure of the bulls head on her rump or back, pressure of the shoulder on the mare's rump or biting of the skin of the mare's rear parts by the stallion and by the boar's snout lifting of the sow's rear quarters, odor of the rear parts in horses and sheep, and vocalization by the stallion and boar are all factors in the precopulatory and copulatory acts in domestic animals.

It is the opinion of Lagerlof, Bane, Young, Walton and others that sex drive, libido, or sexual desire of the male is largely determined genetically but that environmental influences play an important role in modifying it. It is well known that males differ widely in their ability to copulate frequently. In male guinea pigs Grunt and Young demonstrated that those with strong sex drive before castration returned to a strong sex drive when treated with increasing amounts of testosterone after castration whereas animals with a weak sex drive returned to a weak sex drive. They postulated that the differences between animals were due to the reactivity of their tissues, such as the brain, rather than to the differences in the amount of hormone secreted or present in the body. Thus variations in endocrine function may be linked with changed reactivity in the target organs, especially the central nervous system, as well as with the hormone-producing organ. Many of the complex components of copulatory behavior are determined by hormone action during various stages of development and may persist after castration, Goy. Bane's studies on identical twin bulls showed many similarities in copulatory behavior between brothers but large differences between pairs. Hultnas reported a significant relationship between the degree of libido in father and son groups of Swedish Red and White bulls. Young cited Smith as stating that Herefords and North Devons are genetically slow breeders. It is extremely difficult to evaluate the libido and mounting ability of Brahman, Zebu or Santa Gerturdis bulls since these breeds copulate mainly at night and rapidly so the copulatory act can only rarely be observed, Murray. It may be necessary in these breeds to place a bull with nonpregnant cycling cattle and then check them for pregnancy in 40 to 80 days or to use the chin-ball mating device (Frank Paviour Ltd, Hamilton, New Zealand) to determine if the bull in question mounted cows in estrus. This latter device marks a cow's back as the bull's chin rubs over it during copulation. But European breeds, especially the dairy breeds, will actively mount confined cows in any stage of the estrous cycle and also bulls. Sexual activity in boars and bulls may also be reduced in hot climates, Fraser.

Innate virility is reflected in the number and frequency of copulations that occur in a period of time and these vary widely between males. Almquist and Hale reported on two bulls one of which ejaculated over 40 times in 4 hours and another bull under similar conditions that ejaculated only 10 times. With a new stimulus animal or mount the first bull produced over 30 more ejaculates within the next hour. Hulet and coworkers reported that some rams copulated an average of 20 times a day over a 7-day period whereas rams with low libido averaged only 4 copulations per day.

In over 2000 rams the incidence of sexually-inhibited rams when they were first placed with ewes was about 30 percent. Within a few days 80 percent of this inhibited group of rams developed normal libido and sex drive. In about 2000 stallions examined each year for 3 years Bielanski and coworkers reported a low incidence of 0.34 to 1.07 percent of stallions with a lack of sexual desire or libido. Impotency is not uncommon in stallions in the U.S. and is frequently characterized by normal intromission and failure of ejaculation.

Roman and coworkers reported that about 16.7% of 625 beef sires of English breeds selected by artificial insemination studs were disposed of because of problems in the collection of semen, mainly refusal to serve an artificial vagina. Very few Brahman or Zebu bulls will mount and ejaculate into an artificial vagina. Lagerlof noted that selection of bulls for their feminity, docility and gentleness tended to favor the selection of bulls with reduced desire.

Although sex drive, mating behavior or libido is largely genetic in nature it is subject to great modification by many environmental or physical factors. Males with a stong sex drive require more severe and prolonged environmental and physical insults to significantly affect their mating behavior than do males with a weak sex drive.

Environmental Factors Affecting Sex Desire and Copulatory Ability: Nutrition—Thin, emaciated, semistarved males or those suffering from deficiencies of TDN., vitamin A, protein, and certain minerals such as phosphorus and cobalt may have a definitely reduced sex drive. If inanition is severe enough, a complete lack of libido results. As indicated previously a low level of energy intake in growing males retards puberty and the onset of libido.

Overfed males tend to become obese and lazy and often suffer from joint and foot troubles related to their overweight condition. Excessive roughage fed to bulls and rams may cause great enlargement of the rumen and abdomen interfering with normal, easy copulation and contributing to a lack of sexual desire.

Male animals should be fed a properly balanced nutritive ration in adequate amounts to maintain a fair to good body condition.

Systemic diseases—Any chronic or acute, severe, debilitating disease resulting in rapid or prolonged marked loss of weight, or in anorexia, depression, and weakness will cause a varying degree of loss of sexual desire. These diseases may include: pneumonia, enteritis, tuberculosis, paratuberculosis, severe mange and pediculosis, actinomycosis; lymphocytoma, progressive fat necrosis, severe internal parasitosis, advanced metastic tumors, alveolar periostitis, traumatic gastritis, severe chronic peritonitis, and others. All bulls, especially in an A.I. stud, should be given magnets orally at about one year of age to prevent traumatic gastritis or pericarditis, Dunn et al.. Early and prompt diagnosis and treatment of all diseases of male animals is indicated to prevent loss of reproductive ability.

Age—Very young males or old males frequently exhibit a reduced-to-complete lack of sexual desire. In older animals this may be due to a decline in testosterone levels, to senility, to a loss of condition, to overuse or to arthritis. Bane in his experiments with identical twins showed that the time of onset of the lack of sexual desire in older bulls seemed to be largely determined genetically.

There is a great deal of variation in young bulls in the onset of sexual desire and puberty. That this may be modified significantly by the nutritive level has been well demonstrated. High feeding levels hasten the onset of puberty and sexual desire whereas low or subnormal feeding levels greatly retard the time at which the young male shows sexual desire and will mount females. Inexperience in young males may also be confused with a lack of libido.

Management practices—Libido will vary within animals depending upon their inherent sex drive and the way they are trained, handled and managed. Young males which are isolated apart from others of their species are frequently frightened by the presence and activity of females and other males and are slow to mount and copulate because of their inexperience and timidity. This is not uncommon especially in bulls, rams and dogs. Young males should be carefully, patiently and quietly trained and handled, especially if they are to have their semen collected in an artificial vagina. If a male associates "sex" with pain or punishment, he may decide to give up "sex". Males with a lack of libido or naturally "slow breeders" can be easily discouraged and made slower by the insertion of a nose ring in a bull, harsh or abusive handling of the male by attendants, improper restraint of the mount animal, improper footing, mount animals that are not in estrum or are too tall or wide, use of an artificial vagina that is too cold or hot, improper preparation of the male for mounting, breeding large males in a confined area with a low ceiling, unskilled persons using an artificial vagina, and excessive use of a male. Males lacking libido if continually used on the same female for semen collection frequently develop sexual indifference or satiation. Frequent changing of the stimulus or mount animal and the collection or breeding site are indicated in bulls inclined to show a lack of libido. The presence of other males near the mount animal or in sight of the breeding male provides further stimulus. Hale and Almquist, Hafs and coworkers and others have shown that proper sexual preparation of dairy bulls by prolonging the period of sexual stimulation beyond that adequate for mounting and ejaculation will produce higher quality semen with 36 to 250 percent more spermatozoa. This is accomplished by a longer period of restraint before permitting copulation, frequent changing of the mount animals, allowing several "false" mounts where copulation is not allowed, and moving the male to several different sites for "teasing" or "stewing". Olfactory stimulation has not been demonstrated to play a role in the sexual behavior in bulls, Hale. Some stallions and jacks with low desire will fail to copulate with mares that are well-scrubbed and their tails bandaged. Others will so vigorously bite the withers and neck of the mare after mounting that erection is lost. Muzzling of these males is indicated. Other stallions will perform intromission and make thrusting movements but fail to ejaculate. This is common in stallions with reduced libido that are being used too frequently for their reproductive capacity, Vandeplassche. This failure to ejaculate can be noted by careful observation of the male at copulation by the absence of the usual "flagging" of the tail, the absence of pulsations of the penile urethra, the failure of the stallion on dismounting to be "content" and "relaxed", and also the lack of spermatozoa in the "tail-end" sample of the ejaculate collected from the penis as the stallion dismounts.

Psychic factors interfering with normal coitus have been observed in males of all species. Males with a genetically lowered sexual desire are much more apt to develop this apparent psychic refusal to breed. Usually there is no obvious clinical reason for this failure but if a good history is available it often reveals a traumatic painful experience at the last attempt at copulation, Kendrick. Some bulls with apparent psychic impotency as described by Fraser may actually be afflicted with lesions of the spinal column as described by Bane and Hansen in the next section. These bulls would apparently have good sexual desire, mount rapidly, have lordosis in the lumbar region and the penis would be directed at the escutcheon well below the vulva. Rapid pelvic thrusts and "seeking" motions would occur but penile exposure was greatly reduced. A prolonged period of sexual rest, a change in the site of copulation and careful preparation may be necessary to encourage the male to again start to breed. Shy or slow breeding boars may also be observed.

Males should be properly handled and exercised to maintain optimum condition. They should be observed and managed so as to prevent their being bred excessively and losing their sexual desire. The frequency of breeding or the individual capacity of each male should be determined. If the male is bred excessively over a short period, this should be followed by a period of sexual rest. These above management factors should encourage the timid, slow breeding male and control and conserve the vigorous active male.

Hypothyroidism, hypogonadism, or a pituitary deficiency causing a diminished secretion of thyroxine, testosterone, or gonadotropin has not been described or proved by experimental tests in normal whole male animals to be a cause for a lack of sexual desire. It is possible that moderate deficiencies of these hormones might exist without clinical symptoms other than reduced sexual desire. It is the opinion of the author, based on results of hormone therapy, that a lack of hormones is not a common cause for a lack of sexual desire in male animals.

Prognosis for the reduced sexual desire exhibited in association with the aforementioned conditions is guarded to poor depending upon the cause and the degree of the inherited or acquired lack of libido. The environmental factors causing or promoting the lack of sex drive can be overcome or moderated so that libido and breeding ability can reach their maxium expression for the individual male. For bulls affected with a lack of libido it often requires 3 to 6 months of proper handling for sexual desire to noticeably improve after adverse environmental influences have been corrected.

Treatment should only be instituted after a careful study of the male's breeding history, after a thorough physical examination of the male, and after careful and repeated observations of the male during coitus. Proper amounts of good quality grain and roughage should be provided to reduce obesity, if present, or to increase body condition if the male is too thin. Sufficient exercise should be provided. Chronic disease states, especially parasitisms in young males, should be corrected or alleviated if possible. The virility and service potential of the male should be assessed and the frequency of service should be reduced, if necessary, to the male's inherent capacity. Often a period of several months of sexual rest is desirable in males that have been excessively overused. If necessary, changes should be made in the location where service occurs to assure good footing and adequate room. Proper restraint of the female, and care, consideration and patience in the handling of the "slow breeding" male may improve his sexual behavior. If the male is collected with the artificial vagina then a skilled operator should be used. The artificial vagina should be neither too warm nor too cold and adequate pressure should be applied to the penis. Some bulls prefer a coarse; heavy rubber liner to a light, smooth, thin one. A bull that is a "slow breeder" at an artificial insemination stud may benefit from a long period of sexual rest or transferring to another stud with a different group of handlers and different practices. Frequent changes of mounts and a longer period of "teasing" or stimulation is often helpful. In some instances libido may be restored by allowing the male to run loose with one or more quiet non-pregnant females in a pasture or enclosure. As a last resort when the condition fails to respond, bulls, rams and boars may be collected by electroejaculation and dogs may be collected by manual manipulation.

Drug and hormone treatments are of questionable value in most males lacking sex desire. Testosterone in oil or in the "Repositol" form may be used in intramusucular doses of 100 to 500 mg in bulls and stallions, 50 to 100 mg in boars and rams and 10 to 50 mg in dogs and repeated every 5 to 10 days for several injections. Prolonged high level androgen therapy should be avoided because of the possibility of producing testicular degeneration and atrophy caused by the suppression of the gonadotropic hormones. One or more injections of chorionic gonadotropin at 4 to 7-day intervals in doses of 5000 to 10,000 I.U. for large animals and 100 to 500 I.U. for dogs may help stimulate testosterone production by the interstitial cells. Other forms of ICSH or LH may also be used. Males that are obese and lazy, possibly due to a hypothyroid condition, may benefit from feeding iodinated casein with a 3 percent thyroxine potency at a rate of 1 gm per 100 lbs of body weight daily. Thyroxine may also be used. This helps increase the metabolic rate, hastens the loss of weight and occasionally improves the libido. Benzidrine and other stimulants as well as the glucocorticoids have been used with questionable success one-half to 24 hours before breeding the impotent male. Injections of vitamins and feeding of trace minerals, protein and iodine have little value in most slow breeding males.

Other factors such as structural lesions of the limbs and diseases of the penis and sheath may cause a reduction in libido in some males but in others can actually interfere with or prevent normal copulation. Initially males that develop an inability to mount and ejaculate may exhibit good libido, but with repeated failures, or due to painful lesions, sexual desire may become greatly reduced or lost.

Joint, Muscle, Nerve, Bone and Tendon Injuries and Pathology. Lesions affecting these structures particularly if they involve the rear quarters may cause a reduction or even cessation of mating behavior and copulation especially in males with genetically reduced virility or sex drive. **Coxitis** is seen most commonly in dogs and boars, and less frequently in bulls and stallions. It is characterized by a short stride and adduction of the limb. Rupture of the round ligament may be observed in bulls with degenerative coxitis. Occasionally bulls or other males may have one or both hips dislocated resulting in inability to copulate. (See Figure 174) **Gonitis** is common in bulls and is characterized by a short, stiff gait and distention and enlargement of the capsule of the stifle joint. Rupture of the anterior cruciate ligament of the stifle occurs rarely in bulls but is common in the smaller breeds of dogs. This condition in the adult bull usually prohibits mounting. Excessively straight rear limbs, resembling the Elso-heel condition described in cattle by Gotze, predispose bulls and stallions to injury of the stifle joint and tarsus. Tarsitis or degenerative joint lesions in the fetlock or phalangeal joints, or ringbone, may result in pain and reluctance or refusal to mount and copulate.

Other conditions causing similar signs of reduced libido include over-grown claws or hooves, suppurative pododermatitis, quittors or interdigital granulomas, especially in beef cattle, foot rot or interdigital necrosis, tendonitis, suppurative arthritis of the coffin joint, traumatic injury to the peroneal nerve resulting in a "dropped" hock and "cocked" fetlock joints, myositis or muscle rupture especially involving the gastrocnemius or large gluteal or croup muscles and other traumatic lesions of the lower portions of the rear limbs. A progressive lameness resembling laminitis eventually resulting in refusal to stand, was described in related Hereford bulls and was probably caused by a recessive character, Brown and coworkers. Polyarthritis may occur in swine due to swine erysipelas, mycoplasma or other organisms. Occasionally polyarthritis may occur in bulls secondary to a primary site of infection. Fractures of the pelvis are rare in males.

In bulls and dogs symptoms of impotency may be related to spinal disease and characterized by stiffness and soreness in gait, spinal rigidity, and pain over the vertebrae. If the spinal cord is compressed then a slight to marked paresis may be present with a swaying, unsteady gait, a slightly flaccid tail and a dragging of the rear limbs. Thomson, Bane and Hansen and others reported that vertebral osteophytes were very common in dairy and beef bulls over six years of age with the possible exception of Brown Swiss bulls and resulted in ankylosis and spondylosis of the thoracic and lumbar vertebrae with occasionally a secondary fracture of the spine. Synostosis of the sacroiliac joint begins at 2 to 4 years of age in the bull and is complete at 6 to 10 years of age. This is physiologic and no inflammatory signs are observed. Bulls with spondylarthroses especially of the lumbosacral joint, would mount too far caudally on the cow, exhibited lordosis and the penis was extended only a short distance and directed too far ventrally but sexual desire was good, Bane and Hansen. Bulls with spondylosis, often involving most intervertebral spaces and discs, exhibited kyphosis, a stiff back, short stiff hind leg movements or "goose stepping", and loss of liveliness and mobility. In some bulls mounting was aided by the jaw and neck of the bull pressing on the back of the cow. Spondylarthrosis affected bulls at an average age of 5 years and spondylosis was most common in older bulls, about 10 years of age. Although Bane and Hansen indicated that common dysplastic lesions in bulls might be genetically conditioned, the possibility that these conditions and arthritis might be nutritional due to excessive calcium intake was postulated by Krook et al..

In dogs, especially those of the brachycephalic breeds, such as the Dachshund, prolapse of the intervertebral discs causing compression of the spinal cord results in similar symptoms associated with an inability to copulate. Rarely tumors, such as lymphocytoma may invade the spinal canal producing compression of the spinal cord and chronic progressive paresis. Depending on the severity of the spinal cord compression, stallions with the wobbler syndrome may or may not be able to mount and copulate. Einarson cited evidence to show that Swedish Landrace boars, especially certain sire lines, had difficulty in copulating due to bone and joint lesions or arthrosis deformans.

In spastic syndrome, crampiness or "stretches" in bulls, severe acute attacks may interfere with or prevent copulation due to the prolonged spasms of the skeletal muscles of the rear limbs and back. (See Figure 175) Spastic syndrome has been observed in all breeds of cattle but most commonly in the Holstein Friesian and Guernsey breeds. It is probably inherited as a single recessive factor with incomplete penetrance, Becker and coworkers and Roberts. It is seen most often in bulls over 3 years of age and is often associated with arthritis or painful lesions of the rear limbs. Spastic signs are not observed when the bull is lying down but become evident on standing. In most bulls the signs are mild and persist for the lifetime of the bull with occasional periods of exacerbation.

The **prognosis** for future breeding in males with joint, muscle, tendon, bone, or nerve lesions depends upon the nature and severity of the condition and the species, age and value of the animal.

The **treatment** in most cases will consist of sexual rest and restriction of activity enforced by confinement in a box stall or small paddock with good footing. In fractures of the spine, dislocation of the hips and compression of the spinal cord due to arthritic lesions and tumors in large animals, the prognosis is poor to hopeless. In arthritic lesions, the prognosis is also poor but often two to eight months or more of rest may permit limited use of the male. Improved or recovered males should be handbred where the footing is good and where the rear parts or the entire female animal are placed in a pit so the male can easily copulate or breed an artificial vagina. In bulls or rams judicious use of an electroejaculator might permit the collection of semen from males that are unable to copulate or that might further injure themselves if allowed to mount naturally. Some males can be trained to ejaculate into an artificial vagina with all four feet on the ground. In dogs with disc lesions surgery may be indicated. In suppurative arthritis of the coffin joint prolonged conservative therapy, not amputation of the claw, is indicated so ankylosis of the joint will occur and even if the joint is left deformed it will help the remaining normal claw support the animal's weight. Quittors or interdigital granulomas should be removed surgically followed by stall rest and possibly wiring the toes together. In bulls with acute attacks of spastic syndrome where treatment is necessary, "Tolserol" (Squibb) or "Mephinesin" (Abott) in 8 to 10 gm doses orally three times a day (24 to 30 gms daily) for 2 to 3 days may be administered. Tranquilizers will also help these affected bulls but the bulls should then be observed closely for the duration of the treatment to prevent injury to themselves upon rising. Glucocorticoids or butazolidin for several days may also be of supportive value for the alleviation of arthritic signs. Regular hoof trimming is desirable for all large male animals. Lesser infectious or traumatic lesions should receive appropriate and prompt treatment.

Diseases of the penis and prepuce are common causes for inability or difficulty in copulating and frequently result in a marked reduction in sexual desire.

Inability to normally protrude the penis may be due to: (1) a congenital anomaly in the development of the penis and prepuce, with or without hypospadias, or male pseudohermaphroditism. This may be observed in all species but is seen most commonly in Boston Terriers in which the penis is very short and opens through a defective prepuce just anterior to the scrotum, Crowshaw and

Brodey. Copulation is not possible. The author has observed one case of a double penis, diphallus, in a bull that prevented normal copulation because of its forked configuration. The urethra was present in only one of the two glans of the penis. (See Figure 164) A congenital urethral opening ventral to the anus associated with two separate scrotums each containing a testis has been described in a ram, Noice and Schipper. (2) a congenitally short penis in bulls, bucks, boars and horses. Carroll and the author suspect this condition may be hereditary since the former observed it in 20 sons of a Hereford bull and the latter observed it in two closely-related Guernsey bulls. The retractor penis muscle in these bulls was normal. No adhesions or lesions were present in the prepuce or around the penis preventing normal extension of the penis. As young bulls these affected males may breed heifers naturally even though only 3 to 6 inches of the erect penis protrudes from the sheath. As the bulls get older, their abdomen gets deeper and they become less agile, copulation is impossible as the penis cannot reach the vulva of the cow. In one Guernsey bull the penis was 10 inches shorter from the tip of the glans to the ischial arch than a penis from a similar-sized bull of the same age. These males can still be collected by an artificial vagina but their use as sires should be discouraged. The author has observed one 12-year-old stallion with a short penis the glans of which failed to "bell" when copulation occurred. This stallion had a normal breeding history from 5 to 10 years of age but then an inability to ejaculate on intromission developed. In bulls with a short penis the sigmoid flexure does not form a sharp S-curve in the resting state. A similar defect in bucks was described by Richter and in boars by Holst, and Adams. In the latter the pendulous, infantile, incompletely erect penis would only extend one to two inches beyond the preputial orifice. (3) a congenital short retractor penis muscle. This was described as a probable recessive character in Friesians in Holland and symptoms were similar to those exhibited by bulls with a short penis, DeGroot and Numans. Myectomy of this paired muscle under epidural or local anesthesia midway between the anus and the base of the scrotum, or removing a 4 cm section of muscle, resulted in improvement in the ability to protrude the penis at erection in some of the affected young bulls. This operation was forbidden in Holland because of the hereditary nature of this defect, VanderSluis. It is possible that some of the affected young bulls failing to respond to the operation had a short penis. Ten of 38 affected bulls mated normally as young bulls and the other 28 cases were diagnosed at a young age. Of interest in regard to the above condition is the observation by McEntee that old bulls may have the retractor penis muscle nearly completely calcified yet copulation may be normal with a fully extended penis. Hofmeyr reported that if myectomy of the retractor was performed it should be done just below the ischial arch to prevent adhesions which occurred if the operation was performed just above the sigmoid flexure of the penis. Passive stretching of the retractor penis muscle was of value in some cases. (4) other conditions that cause an inability to normally protrude the penis are psychic impotency, Kendrick and Fraser, injury or lesions of the lumbar or sacral region, Haq and Bane and Hansen, phimosis due to adhesions in the sigmoid flexure area of the penis or of the prepuce, stenosis of the preputial opening from congenital, traumatic or infectious causes, and tumors of the penis and sheath. Rare instances of eunuchoidism have been described by Williams and Bloom in bulls and dogs characterized by a complete lack of sexual desire and marked hypoplasia of the genital organs and penis. This might be a congenital condition in young males or due to Sertoli cell, pituitary, or hypothalamic tumors. In the three psychic infertility cases described by Kendrick the affected adult bulls would protrude their penis normally but then on mounting the cow the penis would be retracted before coitus. Sexual rest and use of an artificial vagina on one bull and resection of the retractor muscle on the other two bulls restored their ability for natural service. Bane and Hansen reported sexual rest helpful in some of their cases.

If a bull is unable to protrude his penis normally a careful physical examination of the penis and prepuce should be made. The use of tranquilizers, pudendal nerve blocks or an electroejaculator may be helpful in arriving at an accurate diagnosis. A good history and careful observation at several attempts at natural service are very informative. The penis should be drawn from the prepuce and the penis, the retractor penis muscle and the prepuce should be carefully examined. Occasionally young poorly-grown males may be slow to reach puberty and the inability to protrude the penis may be due to the normal prepuberal adhesions between the prepuce and the penis. Bulls with a short penis should be slaughtered and not used for breeding purposes because of the possible hereditary nature of the defect.

Deviation of the penis or phallocampsis is a common cause for difficulty or inability to copulate and a loss of libido. These deviations are observed most commonly in the polled, English beef breeds including the Angus, Shorthorn and Hereford, Milne, Herrick and Carroll, and are seldom observed in the Charolais, Brahman and dairy breeds that have a generally larger thicker penis. Deviations of the penis may also be due to congenital persistence of the ventral frenulum in many breeds of bulls and rarely in dogs. Congenital curvature of the penile bone in the dog is rare, Johnston.

The spiral or corkscrew type of deviation of the penis is most commonly seen in young bulls, 2-1/2 to 5 years of age. (See Figure 165) Many affected bulls have successfully bred cows for a year or more before the deviation is noted as a cause of infertility, Walker, Carroll. There is evidence to indicate that this condition may be inherited as many cases have been noted in sons or closely related descendants of an affected bull. The author agrees with Walker and others that in most cases of a spiral deviation, the corpus cavernosum appears longer than the supporting structures of the penis including the fibrous tunics. The anatomical basis for the spiralling of the bovine penis is well-described by Ashdown et al. (1968) (1969). When complete erection occurs the corpus cavernosum in the free end of the penis rolls inside the fibrous tunic and the penis slips and pushes laterally under the dorsal apical ligamant through the less dense portion of the fibrous tunic and the glans penis spirals counterclockwise, ventrally and to the right around the line of the penile raphe. This may be favored by the early maturation of the supporting structures of the penis and the later maturation and growth of the penis under the continued influence of testosterone especially in the English beef breeds that have a narrow, thin penis. "Cork-screwing" of the penis occurs at the peak of erection when the integument covering the free end of the penis is stretched. If erection is only partial it does not occur. This may account for the fact that some bulls will only "cork-screw" occasionally. The author observed an affected Angus bull that was collected several times in rapid succession in an artificial vagina. On the fourth collection "corkscrewing" of the penis didn't occur until after the penis entered the artificial vagina. Thus the report of Seidel and Foote who photographed the penis through a transparent artificial vagina at the moment of ejaculation and noted a transient twisting of the penis during more than half of the ejaculations in normal Holstein bulls is significant. Scott, and Ashdown and Combs reported that up to 30 percent of Hereford bulls have a normal straight penis on intromission but have a curled or twisted penis on dismounting. Ashdown and Smith suggested that spiralling of the penis after intromission in normal bulls may increase the tactile stimulus and promote ejaculation. In affected bulls premature full erection occurs prior to intromission resulting in "corkscrewing" that prevents the completion of coitus. Ashdown and Combs also suggest that contraction of the retractor muscles of the sheath during erection might be a causative factor in spiralling of the penis. Spiralling of the glans penis is also observed in bulls being collected by the electroejaculator. Some bulls that show a spiral deviation during electroejaculation, especially if the penis is manually manipulated, may breed cows naturally without a deviation being evident.

Other much less common types of deviations of the penis are the ventral or "rainbow" and the mild S-shaped curvatures. The latter is of little importance and some affected bulls breed successfully. The former definitely prevents normal copulation as the more erect the penis becomes the greater the ventral curvature. A persistence of the frenulum or a short retractor penis muscle are not present. Rarely trauma and scarring of the penis and/or prepuce may cause a penile deviation.

A persistent frenulum is a band of tissue that extends from near the ventral tip of the glans penis to the prepuce. It is seen occasionally as a cause for a sharp ventral bending or deviation of the glans penis in bulls, Ashdown. It has been reported in dogs where it caused discomfort and pain at puberty, Joshua, McEntee, and also in boars, Adams. At birth the epithelial surfaces of bovine penis and sheath are fused and ventrally the penis and prepuce are united by a band of connective tissue called the frenulum. Epithelial separation and rupture of the frenulum occur normally at puberty. When a persistence of the frenulum occurs there is usually a blood vessel present in the center of the tissue band comprising the frenulum. There is some evidence that this is hereditary in nature as Carroll and coworkers noted it more commonly in Angus with a 1 percent incidence, and Shorthorns than in other beef breeds. In some herds the incidence reached 4 to 5 percent. The use of these bulls after treatment is questionable for genetic reasons.

Treatment of the ventral curvature and the S-curvature of the penis is not satisfactory and surgical attempts at correction have only been occasionally successful. Cutting of the connective tissue band, with or without ligation, is a simple procedure and is uniformly successful for the correction of a persistent frenulum. Walker has described surgical techniques to correct a spiral or "corkscrew" curvature by preventing the rotation of the corpus cavernosa within the fibrous tunic. This was accomplished by producing adhesions between the two structures by either a closed or open technique.

The penis was withdrawn from the prepuce by manual traction, the use of the electroejaculator, the use of tranquilizers, or blocking of the pudendal nerves. The open technique was most successful after producing nerve block or local anesthesia; a 17 cm, 7 inch, incision was made through the mucosa and connective tissue on the dorsum of the penis from within one-half inch of the tip end of the glans to 2 inches caudal to the attachment of the prepuce exposing the fibrous tunic and the thickened portion of it, the dorsal apical ligament. Two 1/8 inch-wide strips from the midportion of this dorsal ligament the length of the

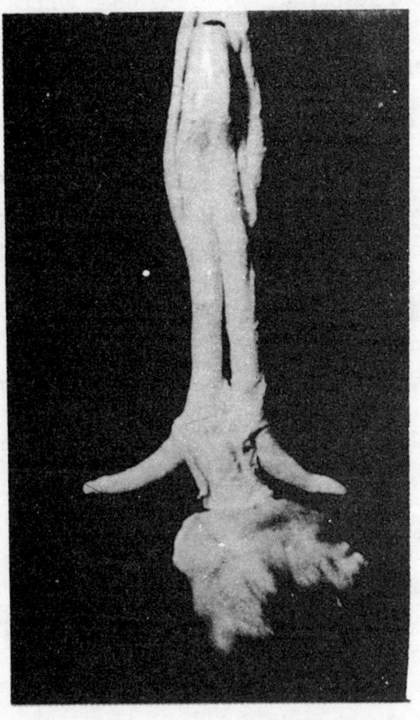

Figure 164. Diphallus in a Bull

Figure 165. A Spiral or Corkscrew Deviation of the Penis of an Angus Bull.

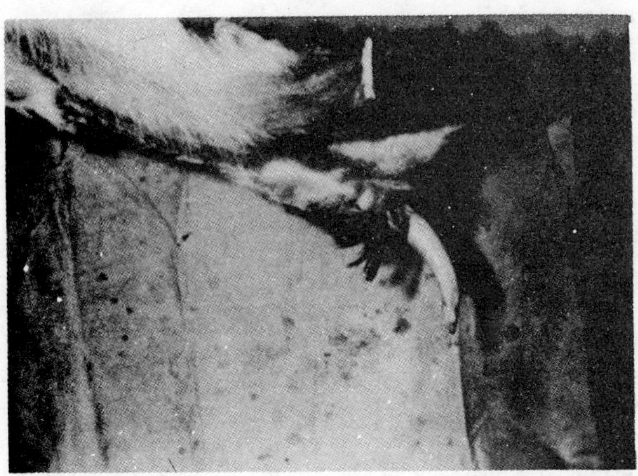

Figure 166. Ventral or "Rainbow" Deviation of the Penis of a Hereford Bull.

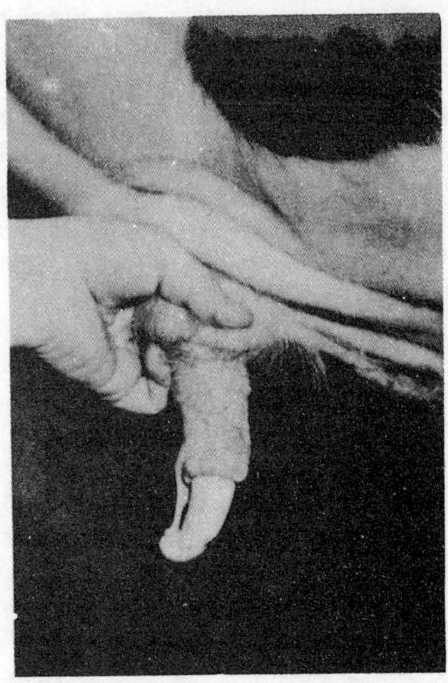

Figure 167. A Persistent Frenulum, a Cause of Deviation of the Bovine Penis.

incision were isolated and cut free at the distal end. The ligament was sutured together. The two ligamentous strips were sutured in a "shoelace" pattern through the dorsal ligament and into the tunica albuginea for a distance of about 8 to 10 cm, 3 to 4 inches, cranially from the firm caudal attachment of the dorsal ligament. They were securely fastened to the elastic tunic, and the mucous membrane was closed by catgut sutures. Antibiotics were given both locally into the sheath and systemically for three days and the bulls were isolated for two weeks. The closed technique consisted of placing six nonabsorbable sutures through the mucous membrane, dorsal apical ligament of the fibrous tunic and into the tunica albuginea, 3 at the base of the glans near the preputial junction, 2 one inch cranial to these and 1 an inch cranial to the latter two sutures. All were placed in the dorsum of the glans and left in place for 10 days and then removed. The bull was placed in isolation for one week after removal. The open technique was most successful, even correcting one case of ventral curvature of the penis. In 12 bulls treated with the closed technique 3 recovered, 6 recovered temporarily but recurred after 90 days, and 3 were unsuccessful. One or a series of V-shaped spiral incisions through the mucosa and into the tunica albuginea, formerly used to correct bovine penile deviations, were less satisfactory. Since deviations, especially "corkscrewing" of the penis, are probably genetic defects, it would probably be best to cull such an animal rather than operate upon it.

Adhesions of the Penis and Prepuce, Tumors, Phimosis and Paraphimosis—Decreased libido and inability to copulate may be associated with phimosis of the penis due to adhesions of the sigmoid flexure of the penis or the deeper portions of the prepuce, tumors of the penis and prepuce, stenosis of the preputial orifice, paraphimosis or paralysis of the penis secondary to edema and congestion due to nerve damage, a stenosed preputial ring or tumors of the penis and sheath.

1. **Adhesions of the penis in the region of the sigmoid flexure** in bulls and rams may be due to trauma from horn injuries or in bulls from injections of local anesthetics to block the dorsal nerve of the penis as was earlier performed to produce anesthesia of the penis to aid withdrawal from the sheath. These connective tissue adhesions prevent obliteration of the S-curve and protrusion that normally occurs at the time of erection. Treatment to relieve these adhesions often results in more severe adhesions.

Adhesions of the deeper or caudal portions of the freely-moveable prepuce in the region of the fornix to the abdominal wall or to the skin produces a more severe phimosis than adhesions of the cranial portion of the prepuce. These adhesions may be secondary to lacerations of the prepuce especially in young bulls where the prepuce has not yet completely separated from the glans, or in older vigorous bulls, especially those used in artificial breeding studs and collected with artificial vagina, in which a vigorous thrust may tear the prepuce away from its attachment to the glans for one-third to the entire circumference of the penis. Infection that follows this injury may produce abscesses and/or adhesions to the surrounding structures preventing the free movement of the prepuce and penis at erection. (See Figures 168 and 169) Prompt antibiotic therapy both locally in an oily base and parenterally for 7 to 14 days is recommended together with sexual rest for 6 to 12 weeks. Suturing of the prepuce to the mucous membrane of the glans and the underlying connective tissue appears indicated but permitting healing by second intention without suturing has proven more satisfactory for the author.

A ruptured, "fractured," or "broken" penis with a secondary hematoma is usually observed in the bull but in rare instances may occur in the stallion due to the mare's kicking the erect penis as the stallion mounts. In the dog, fracture of the penile bone may be caused by a traumatic injury and may require amputation of the penis or resection or removal of the penile bone, Johnston. Similar traumatic injuries in the other species are uncommon. In the bull, the condition of a "fractured", "broken," or "ruptured" penis occurs most commonly in active bulls with a strong sex drive breeding cows on pasture. It is rarely observed in dairy bulls that are hand bred. The injury apparently occurs at coitus either when the cow or heifer suddenly goes down under the weight of the bull, or due to a sudden ventral bending of the erect penis against the escutcheon of the cow at the moment the bull thrusts, causing a dorsal rupture of the tunica albuginea usually near the distal portion of the sigmoid flexure and opposite the initial attachment of the retractor penis muscle. Penile hematomas are apparently due to a sudden angulation or bending of the erect penis at service and they are not only due to a high blood pressure in the corpus cavernosum. Pressures of 78.8 lbs per square inch have been experimentally induced in the corpus cavernosum without causing a rupture or hematoma of the penis, Goldston. It usually occurs in 2- to 4-year-old bulls and is seen most commonly in Herefords. The symptoms of the injury include a shortening of the stride, stiffness, pain and a slight arching of the back that are generally mild and may not immediately prevent subsequent copulations which produce a larger hematoma. A swelling rapidly develops just cranial to the scrotum that varies in size depending upon the amount of hemorrhage from the ruptured penis. Hemorrhage is profuse and in a "hand grenade" effect because of the exceedingly high blood pressure present in the erect corpus cavernosum penis. Prolapse of the prepuce may occur secondary to the edema that develops. There is usually no difficulty in urination. At first the swelling is soft and fluctuating; later it becomes firm and hard as the hematoma clots and organizes. Pain may be evident but heat is slight. Systemic symptoms are usually lacking. The bull shows definite reluctance and inability to copulate. If treatment is not undertaken the clot organizes. It may become infected producing an abcess. (See Figure 169) Adhesions may occur between the prepuce, penis, abdominal wall and skin rendering the bull useless for future service. A differential diagnosis from other conditions such as tumors, chronic fibrous adhesions, and rupture of the urethra should be considered.

The prognosis in these cases should be guarded even when an operation is performed. If a nearly aseptic surgical operation cannot be performed an operation should not be attempted. In this situation the bull should be given large doses of parenteral antibiotics and possibly a proteolytic enzyme for one to two weeks to prevent abscessation. Some bulls may recover spontaneously with time and sexual rest, Walker. Hematomas that become infected seldom respond to treatment and surgery. Hofmeyr indicated the size of the lesion rather than its location was of greatest importance in the prognosis. Walker reported that some affected bulls damage the dorsal nerve of the penis at the time of the "rupture" so they lose sensation in the glans. Therefore upon recovery these bulls can't find the vulva and achieve intromission and ejaculation. Before surgery the penis should be withdrawn from the sheath. If the penis can be extended completely or up to 6 to 8 inches and sensation is present in the glans the prognosis is good. If the penis can only be extended 2 to 4 inches the prognosis is guarded and if the penis can't be withdrawn from the prepuce and/or the glans lacks sensory innervation the prognosis is poor, Noordsy. Pattridge, indicated that nearly 50 percent of the hematomas not operated upon became infected by the second week after the injury. If abscesses are present, they should be drained and allowed to heal before surgery is performed. Conditions requiring surgery to remove extensive adhesions, abscesses, and scar tissue usually have a poor prognosis.

The operation commonly undertaken to correct this condition of a ruptured penis and hematoma should not be performed until after the blood in the hematoma has clotted firmly and before organization of the clot occurs. This is usually between the fourth and tenth days after the rupture has occurred. From the time of the occurrence of the hematoma until the time of the operation the bull should be given parenteral antibiotics. About the tenth day after the injury prior to surgery, Walker recommended the electroejaculator be used to determine if normal engorgement of the penis occurs and if sensation is present in the glans penis. If normal engorgement of the penis does not occur it is probably due to an intrapenile hematoma preventing normal distention of the distal portions of the corpus cavernosum. If either of these two conditions is present the prognosis is poor.

To perform this operation the bull should be restrained in lateral recumbency after the administration of a general anesthetic such as chloral hydrate or after a large dose of epidural anesthesia (40 to 60 cc of a 2-per-cent procaine or xylocaine solution) together with a narcotic dose of chloral hydrate, if necessary. This latter method of anesthesia is supplemented by local anesthesia under the skin at the operative site. The operation should be conducted under favorable conditions with as close an approach to aseptic surgery as possible, since second-intention healing produces many adhesions. After shaving and disinfecting the operative site, an incision 6 to 10 inches long is made through the skin over the swelling. All bleeding must be controlled. The clotted blood in the hematoma is carefully removed and the penis brought to the incision. The fibrin is removed. The break in the tunica albuginea is thoroughly exposed, coagulated blood in the corpus cavernosum is expressed, and the rent, which is usually 1 to 3 inches long, spiral, oblique, or longitudinal in direction, is sutured with No. 2 chronic catgut. Most ruptures are in the dorsal or dorso-lateral portion of the penis just cranial to the terminal curve of the sigmoid flexure. Following complete control of hemorrhage, the cavity may be flushed with an antibiotic solution. The subcutaneous tissues are approximated with catgut and the skin closed with nylon sutures. The wound should heal by primary intention. Following the operation, parenteral antibiotic therapy is continued. Noordsy reported that the clot in the corpus cavernosum cannot be removed and suturing the tunica albuginea is unnecessary and of questionable value.

Copulation should not be permitted for at least 2 weeks and preferably longer, 4 to 8 weeks, Wheat, Noordsy. Farquharson and Milne reported success in preventing the development of firm adhesions around the penis by keeping the bull sexually stimulated. Housing it next to a heifer or cow in estrum or teasing the bull daily was recommended. Noordsy recommended extending the penis several times a week under tranquilization; he did not recommend using the electroejaculator until healing had taken place. Gibbons recommended placing long steel wire sutures through the tip of the glans that extended through the preputial orifice so they could be grasped and traction exerted several times a day to extend the penis. Pattridge, however, recommended coitus 48 hours after the operation, daily coitus for the next 5 days, and then service every other day for 10 more days. Hofmeyr recommended daily massage of the affected area for 10 to 20 minutes to break down adhesions and prevent new ones. This should be continued for 2 to 3 months. Conservative treatment resulted in recovery in 37 of 47 cases.

Chronic abscesses secondary to hematomas or perforating injuries to the prepuce should be drained into the prepuce if possible to prevent adhesions between the prepuce and skin that occur when abscesses are drained through skin incisions. (See Figure 169) If the abscess heals but adhesions are left preventing normal function of the penis and prepuce then the bull may be operated on as described above to separate the adhesions of the prepuce and penis from the skin or abdominal wall. The prognosis is guarded to poor.

2. **Tumors of the penis and prepuce** in bulls, stallions and dogs may cause phimosis or paraphimosis or prevent normal intromission. In bulls the only significant tumor is the transmissible fibropapilloma, McEntee. (See Figure 170) There is definite evidence that this tumor and cutaneous papillomas, or warts, in cattle are similar and caused by the same agent. It is probably infectious in nature and the etiologic agent is considered to be a virus. The fibropapillomas are similar to those observed on the vulva of heifers. They are single or multiple, firm, cauliflower-like growths. Young bulls, 9 to 18 months of age, are most commonly affected with cutaneous papillomas. Young bulls housed together frequently mount each other and may injure the prepuce, affording an invasion site for the tumor virus. Injury to the penis is also predisposed by breeding the young bull before the prepuce and glans penis are fully separated. For these reasons young beef bulls are most commonly affected. Hemorrhage from the sheath after service and hesitancy or refusal to copulate are frequently noted in bulls with penile tumors.

In stallions tumors of the penis are uncommon and when present are usually squamous cell carcinomas of low malignancy. (See Figure 171) In rare instances papillomas, angiomas and melanomas may occur in or on the sheath and penis of horses, Feldman. Carcinomas often ulcerate and usually bleed at the time of service and produce a fetid preputial discharge. They should be differentiated from granulomas caused by Habronema larvae.

The transmissable venereal tumor is the most common one seen on the penis and prepuce of dogs. It is usually spread by coitus. In rare instances the disease may be spread by licking of the vulvar or preputial discharges of affected dogs. Intact cells must be transplanted to transmit the tumor; it is not transmissable by filtrates. The incubation period is from 5 to 6 weeks. All breeds of dogs are susceptible. It is characterized by a discharge of a bloody, fetid exudate from the vagina of the female and from the prepuce of the male. When the penis is exposed, greyish-red nodular growths are observed on the penis and the prepuce. The tumor masses are friable and bleed when handled. In advanced cases the tumor may also be observed involving the inguinal lymph glands. The tumor ulcerates easily. It may be found in other cutaneous sites but internal involvement is rare, Higgins. The transmissible venereal tumor has been reported widespread throughout the world but most commonly in tropical countries. The disease may be common in an area and then in the next decade or two disappear or be rarely observed. Papillomas, squamous cell carcinomas, sarcomas, and other tumors may occur in the sheath or on the penis of dogs, Bloom.

In the **treatment** of penile tumors in the bull it should be noted that spontaneous recovery from infectious fibropapillomas usually occurred in an average time of less than 4 months, range 1 to 15 months, Bagdonas and Olson, Olson et al., and McEntee. Formston reported that the nearer the bull was to 2 years of age the better the prognosis. If the tumors are multiple on the penis, treatment may be difficult and some veterinarians have empirically recommended the use of wart vaccine. Bagdonas and Olson indicated that the tissue vaccine was more effective in producing an immunity than was the egg-yolk vaccine. Olson et al. reported that formalin-killed vaccine given intradermally to calves at 2 weeks to 6 months of age provided good protection. The vaccine was of questionable value in affected bulls. They recommended that semen from affected bulls not be used or frozen because of the danger of transmitting the virus to cows. Pearson and coworkers reported disappearance of penile tumors in 4 out of 5 young bulls after the administration of an autogenous vaccine. However, Olson, Segre, and Skidmore found the vaccine induced no appreciable regression in experimentally induced warts. The value of wart vaccine in the treatment of cutaneous papillomatosis is questionable on the basis of their work, which indicated fairly rapid spontaneous recoveries. VanderSluis and the author have removed fibropapillomas from the penis of bulls when they had a narrow base or were pedunculated, by grasping and pulling them off as the bull mounts a cow. Some bleeding occurred, but it was not excessive. By means of a pudendal block or tranquilizers and local anesthesia the penis can be withdrawn from the sheath and the tumors removed with scissors or by cautery and the mucous membrane of the penis or prepuce sutured with fine catgut. The prognosis is good whatever treatment is used.

In the stallion the occasional squamous cell carcinoma can be removed by a liberal incision or if necessary by amputation of the penis. Castration should be performed

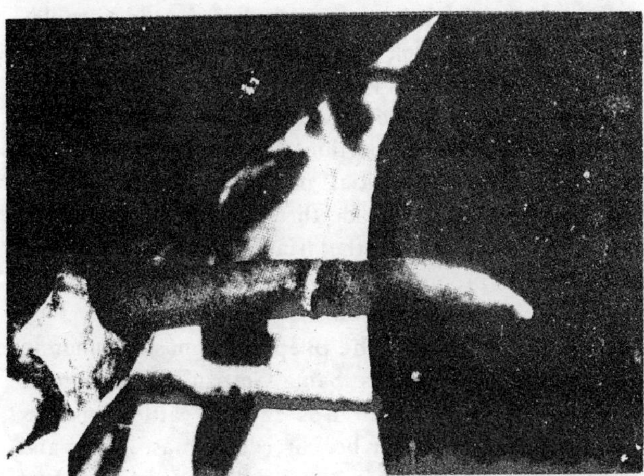

Figure 168. Tearing of the Prepuce from its Attachment to the Glans Penis in a Bull.

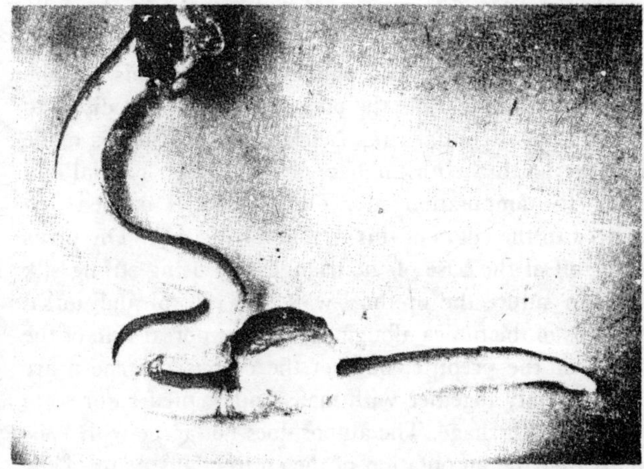

Figure 169. A Chronic Abscess Causing a Severe Phimosis in a Bull. (This abscess was probably secondary to a laceration of the prepuce or a small hematoma or "fracture" of the penis)

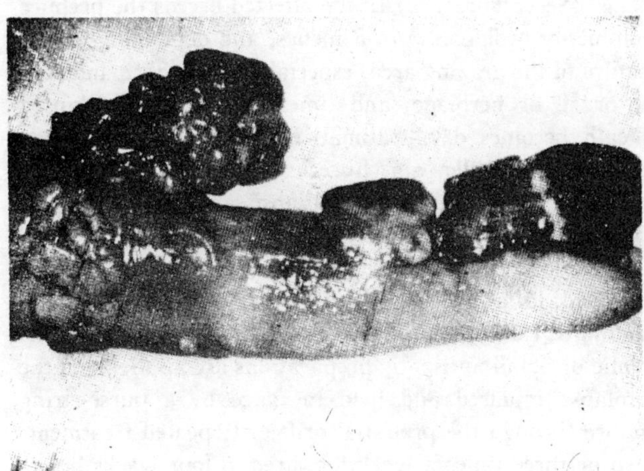

Figure 170. Transmissable Fibropapilloma of the Penis in a Young Bull. (Courtesy K. McEntee)

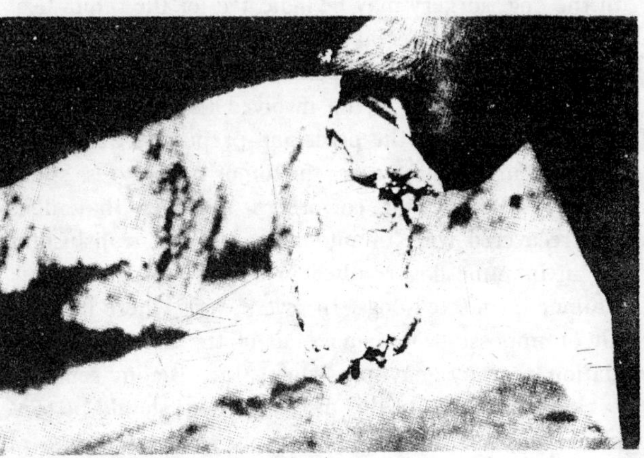

Figure 171. Squamous Cell Carcinoma of the Penis and Sheath in a Stallion.

prior to amputation of the penis, since both operations performed simultaneously might cause too much tissue reaction and swelling. The operation for amputation of the penis is a standard one described by Williams and other authors. After restraining the animal in lateral recumbency and giving general or local anesthesia, the penis is withdrawn and thoroughly washed and prepared for surgery. A catheter is introduced into the urethra. To control hemorrhage, an elastic ligature is placed tightly around the proximal end of the extended penis. In the prolapsed equine penis the operative site is just distal to the internal preputial ring. A triangular incision is made over the urethra with the base of the triangle cranial and under the amputation site. The urethra is opened and sutured to the edges of this triangular incision. The penis is cut off at the base of the triangle. By using strong silk or linen suture the urethral wall, the ventral and dorsal portions of the tunica albuginea, and the dorsal skin of the penis, or the prepuce, but not the corpus cavernosa are drawn firmly together with many interrupted sutures, to control hemorrhage. The author does not agree with Williams that the amputation of the entire glans penis of the bull and stallion does not interfere materially with breeding, as it has been observed that if the glans penis is removed the male will not be able to locate the vulva and ejaculate.

In the dog, surgery may be indicated for the removal of the transmissible venereal tumor. The earlier surgery is undertaken, the better the likelihood of a successful operation. Liberal excision of the involved tissue is desirable. Complete removal of the penis and prepuce is questionable as even in advanced cases the tumor may regress spontaneously. Bloom and coworkers reported that dogs which recovered were immune. Whole-blood transfusions from an immune dog resulted in a cure or regression of the tumor in infected dogs. In severe cases where it is difficult or impossible to remove all of the involved tissue, radiation therapy may prove of value. Bloom reported that claims for cures of this disease in dogs should be considered with caution because of the high incidence of spontaneous regression usually occurring in less than six months. Spaying of females and elimination of stray dogs is very helpful in controlling the disease, Higgins.

3. **Phimosis or stenosis of the preputial orifice** preventing normal protrusion of the penis is a cause of inability to copulate. It may occasionally be congenital in young dogs, cats and horses. Stenosis of the preputial orifice is usually acquired due to injuries, wounds and infections. In cattle with pendulous sheaths, the preputial orifice may be stepped on causing severe contusion and swelling. In beef bulls chronic prolapse of the prepuce is a very common cause of posthitis and phimosis. (See Figure 172)

Congenital stenosis in dogs may be successfully corrected by a dorsal incision of the external preputial orifice. Christian reported incising a stenotic internal preputial ring in a stallion to permit normal erection and protrusion of the penis. Kirk reported on removal of the preputial ring in a young cat with dysuria and paraphimosis. In the bull, dog or ram the usual procedure to correct a simple stenosis of the preputial orifice caused by cicatricial tissue is to remove from the ventral portion of the sheath a triangular portion of skin. The base of the triangle is at the preputial orifice. After the skin is removed an incision is made through the midline of the prepuce to the apex of the triangle and after careful hemostasis the preputial membrane is sutured to the skin by interrupted catgut sutures.

Chronic prolapse of the prepuce is most common in **Bos indicus** cattle such as: Santa Gertrudis, Brahman or Zebu, or their crosses; in **Bos taurus** cattle it is less common but is seen in the beef breeds such as: Angus and Polled Hereford cattle. It is occasionally seen in other beef breeds and is rare in dairy cattle. It probably is an inherited trait associated with a pendulous sheath, a large preputial orifice and a relaxed preputial membrane and penis. (See Figure 172) In the affected breeds the prepuce commonly prolapses 3 to 8 inches, and depending on the nature of the grazing area, especially the heighth and type of brush or herbiage, and time of year, the prolapsed sheath becomes dry, traumatized, lacerated, frost-bitten edematous, swollen and fibrotic. Screwworm infestation may also occur resulting in phimosis and rarely paraphimosis.

In mild cases diagnosed early the affected bull may be confined in a well-bedded stall. The prolapsed organ should be carefully washed, cleansed and dried. Oily antibiotic or bland antiseptic preparations are applied and the prolapse replaced and held in place by a purse-string suture through the preputial orifice. Repeated treatments two or three times a week for three to four weeks before allowing breeding are indicated, Megale. In more severe cases where replacement is not possible circumcision or even amputation of the affected portion of the prepuce is necessary.

Before surgery in severe cases Walker has suggested that the sheath and penis be cleaned with hydrogen peroxide and furacin solution, and oily antiseptics or antibiotics and lanolin be applied for about a week to the prolapsed structures under a stockinette held in place by a rubber band. The pendulous sheath and prolapsed membranes should be supported for this period to possibly control or

Figure 172. Chronic Prolapse and Stenosis of the Preputial Orifice of a Santa Gertrudis Bull.

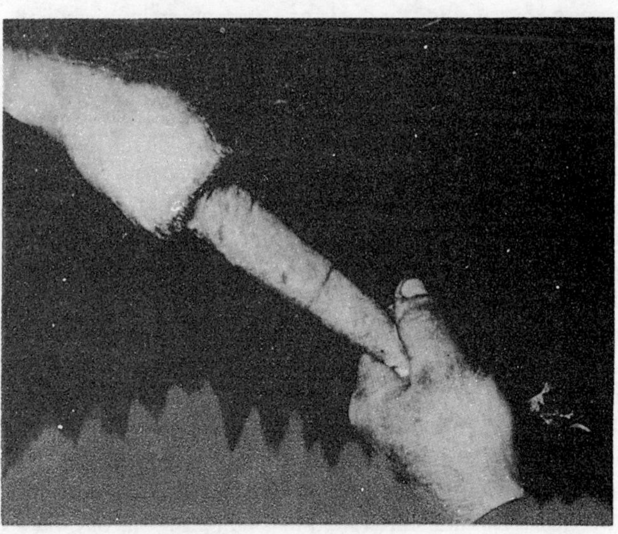

Figure 173. Chronic Granular Venereal Disease Lesions of the Bovine Penis and Sheath.

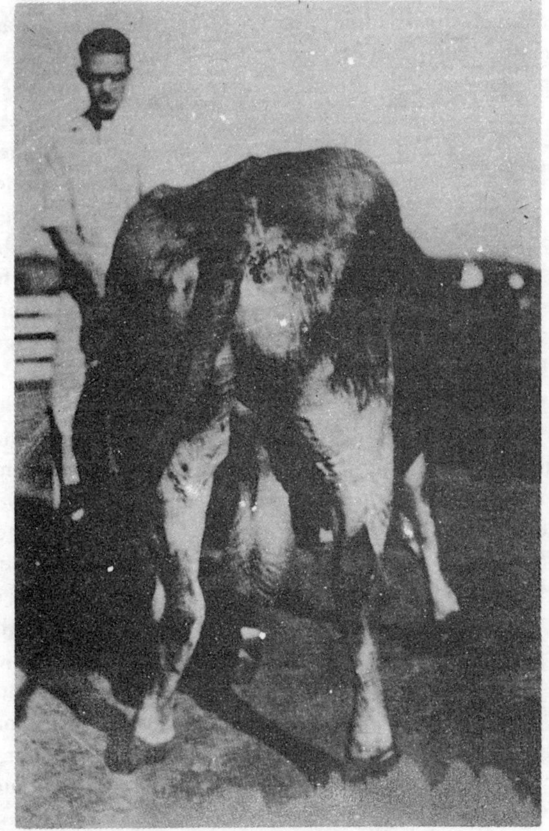

Figure 174. Dislocated Hip in a Jersey Bull.

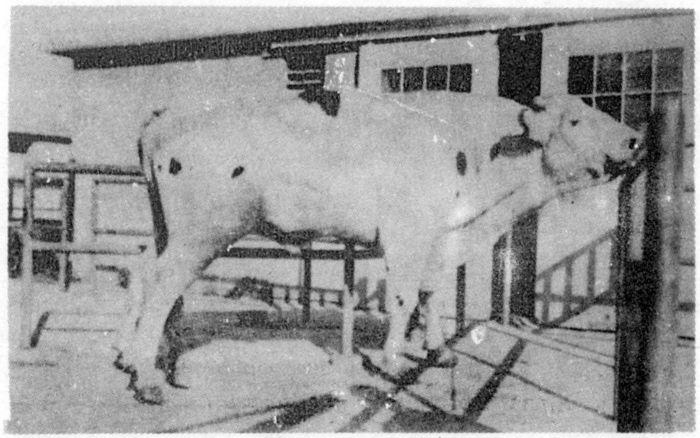

Figure 175. Spastic Syndrome or Stretches in an 8-year-old Holstein Bull.

reduce the swelling and edema. Systemic administration of antibiotics and diuretics may be indicated. Other authors suggested that immediate circumcision was more practical and economical, Donaldson and Aubrey, Cardwell. In any surgical procedure as much of the prepuce should be conserved as possible. Removal of large portions of the prepuce may result in inability to protrude the penis the necessary length for natural service. In all severe preputial lesions requiring surgery or extensive treatment a long recovery period of 30 to 120 days is required for complete healing before service should be permitted.

Circumcision is most commonly employed and about 90 percent of over 200 bulls returned to service within 30 to 45 days, Romane. Following tranquilization and restraint in lateral recumbency the area is washed, cleansed and anesthetized. General anesthesia may be used. An inverted triangular incision, 5 to 7 cm, 2 to 3 inches, on a side is made on the ventral, posterior aspect of the sheath through the skin only. The base of the triangle is at the preputial orifice. After removal of the skin an incision is made through the ventral caudal midline of the prepuce to the apex of the triangle. Careful hemostasis is highly essential before placing interrupted nonabsorbable nylon sutures to secure the internal preputial membrane to the skin. This later prevents the possibility of scarring and stenosis of the preputial orifice. Then the diseased prolapsed portion of the prepuce is removed after placing interrupted nylon sutures around its circumference firmly securing the internal preputial membrane to the external membrane at the preputial orifice. These sutures are usually about 4 cm apart on the outside and 1.5 cm apart on the inside. They should be drawn tightly and overlap to completely control hemorrhage then the prolapsed portion of the prepuce is removed about 1 cm distal to the suture line. Following the operation the sheath should be supported against the body wall for two weeks. The sutures can be removed in about 6 to 8 days. Parenteral antibiotics should be given for 7 to 10 days.

Amputation of the prepuce is indicated where the prepuce is more extensively involved. Although some veterinarians have described an amputation technique where the entire prolapsed part is removed by through and through overlapping sutures over a perforated plastic ring securely fastened by interlocking sutures into the preputial orifice, this may result in too great a loss of normal preputial membrane. A "reefing" type of operation is more desirable. An incision is made at the skin line of the preputial orifice and at the distal end of the prolapse where the "inner" preputial membrane is normal. A longitudinal incision is made between these two initial transverse incisions and the diseased "outer" preputial membrane and underlying edematous, fibrous or abscessed tissue is removed. Hemorrhage must be carefully controlled. Electrocautery is a useful adjunct to ligatures. The normal preputial membrane and underlying tissue is sutured carefully by many interrupted catgut sutures to the skin and subcutaneous tissues at the preputial orifice, Donaldson and Aubrey, Cardwell, Walker. Antibiotics should be administered locally and systemically for the next 7 to 10 days. Walker recommended using a large Penrose drain fastened into the sheath and around the penis to prevent irritation of the suture line by urine and a purse-string suture in the skin at the orifice to invert the suture line. This purse-string is removed after one week. If following this treatment constriction of the preputial orifice occurs then a second operation consisting of a triangular-shaped incision on the ventral-caudal aspect of the preputial orifice is performed as previously described. As a preventive measure in bulls affected with chronic prolapse of the prepuce, Berry has suggested removing a large-V-shaped wedge of skin from the suspensory skin flap of the sheath to reduce its pendulous attachment.

Bulls with a lack of libido and sex drive may fail to breed satisfactorily after these treatments because of pain associated with erection and coitus. Chronic prolapse of the prepuce may be prevented or controlled by the selection of bulls with smaller preputial orifices and with less tendency to prolapse their preputial membrane. It is questionable and probably undesirable to operate on affected bulls since this condition is genetically predisposed. These bulls should be culled to decrease the frequency of this trait in the population. Males should be selected for lighter, less pendulous sheaths with smaller preputial orifices and stronger retractor penis muscles, Murray, Lagos and Fitzhugh.

4. **Paraphimosis,** the inability to withdraw the penis into the prepuce, results in edema, swelling, and balanoposthitis. It may occur following erection of the penis through a stenotic preputial ring or orifice caused by a congenital or acquired stricture or by tumors as noted above under phimosis. Paralysis of the penis and paraphimosis may be due to spinal disease or trauma. Paralysis of the penis is seen in bulls with rabies and in horses in the late stages of dourine. It is possible that the posterior paresis reported in a few cases of rhinopneumonitis, due to equine herpes virus I, might be the cause of occasional unexplained cases of penile paralysis in stallions. Paraphimosis secondary to the edema and swelling that occurs postoperatively may follow castration of stallions. Resection of the retractor penis muscle in bulls with pendulant sheaths may cause paraphimosis. It is not observed in the dairy breeds with a sheath that is closely attached to the abdominal wall. In recent years, the author has observed and had reported to him at least 15 cases of paralysis of

the penis with paraphimosis in geldings and stallions following the use of tranquilizers. This has not been reported in bulls.

The prognosis in paraphimosis in males is guarded and depends upon the promptness of treatment and the degree of trauma or necrosis present. Support of the prolapsed penis and sheath is essential to minimize gravitational edema, Milne. Cases of paraphimosis in horses following castration and the use of tranquilizers should have the penis supported or held within the sheath within an hour or two of its occurrence to prevent a chronic prolapse of the organ often necessitating amputation. Cold packs and pressure may reduce the swollen penis and allow replacement. In many cases in dogs and occasionally in bulls, enlargement of the preputial opening is necessary in order to replace the penis and prevent a recurrence of the condition. For necrosis of the penis secondary to acute paraphimosis and for chronic paralysis and prolapse of the penis in dogs, amputation is recommended, Allam.

In bulls Wheat recommended the cleaning of the penis, the removal of necrotic tissue, and the liberal application of ointment. Gauze should be wrapped around the penis to protect it. The penis with its gauze dressing should be placed inside the sheath as soon as possible. Petroleum jelly should be packed into the sheath to prevent adhesions. Frequent withdrawal of the penis and applications of ointment are indicated.

Balanoposthitis due to infectious or noninfectious causes may produce a stenosis of the preputial orifice, adhesions of the penis and prepuce to each other or to the surrounding tissues or produce sufficient pain and discomfort that copulation is impossible or not attempted. **Balanitis** is an inflammation of the glans penis, and **posthitis** is an inflammation of the prepuce. They are often both involved in an inflammatory reaction because of their close apposition. Balanoposthitis is common in the bull, ram and dog and uncommon in the boar and cat. It is observed occasionally in the stallion.

The preputial cavity in the bull may normally contain a wide variety of bacteria, molds, protozoa and viruses including: vibrios, **E. coli,** streptococci, staphlococci, **B. pyocyaneus, Pseudomonas aeruginosa, C. pyogenes, proteus, Actinomycetes necrophorus,** actinobacilli, molds **(Aspergillus, Mucor, Absidia),** mycoplasma, Bakos et al., **Trichomonas fetus,** IBR-IPV virus, and other pathogenic and saprophytic organisms.

Other male animals have a similar variety of infectious agents as inhabitants of the prepuce. It is often difficult to recover specific slow growing pathogens from the prepuce of bulls and other males because rapid growing contaminants overgrow the cultures. Granular venereal "disease" lesions or hypertrophy of lymphoid nodules on the penis and prepuce of bulls and dogs are common, but are not associated with any specific organism and have little significance. (See Figure 173) Sexual rest and protective antibiotic solutions in oil infused into the sheath usually alleviate acute signs of granular venereal disease. No obvious balanoposthitis generally accompanies the presence of the above organisms in the preputial cavity with the possible exception of **M. tuberculosis** and the acute form of IBR-IPV virus infections.

Williams has described tuberculosis of the sheath, penis, prepuce, and penile lymph glands of bulls. This avenue of invasion in the bull is invited by tuberculosis of the female genital tract. Tuberculosis of the sheath and penis may be characterized by enlarged, granulomatous bleeding lesions of the glans penis, adhesions of the penis, prepuce, and sigmoid flexure with secondary phimosis. The penile lymph glands are enlarged and are likely to be abscessed. In suspicious cases either culture of the lesions or a tuberculin test will probably establish the diagnosis. This type of tuberculosis is at present extremely rare in the United States. Williams also described several rare cases of actinomycosis affecting the sheath and glans penis of bulls. The lesions resembled those of tuberculosis.

Trauma, abrasions, lacerations of the prepuce or glans penis usually result in the introduction of the above wound-infection organisms into the deeper tissues with resulting swelling, inflammation, pain and discharge. This is observed most commonly in young bulls especially those in which the glans penis is not completely separated from the sheath. In artificial insemination studs injuries from the artificial vagina may occur including the loss of a rubber band from the vagina onto the glans penis. This may cause a deep laceration or amputation of the glans. Young bulls running together in the early spring months may, by their homosexual behavior and frequent mounting, draw hair into their prepuce where it forms a stenosing ring at the base of the glans with an associated balanoposthitis. In rare cases this ring of hair may result in the sloughing or amputation of the glans penis, Scott. Rollinson and Haq reported on a bull that had preputial catarrh. Both the preputial washings of the bull and the cervical mucus of 1 of 2 cows bred to him that aborted at 7 to 8 months showed a profuse growth of Absidia mold. This was probably a coincidence. The preputial catarrh was largely overcome by treatment but the mold persisted. Mild balanitis and posthitis have been observed in virgin bulls or in young bulls after they have bred older cows. Bane has reported that **C. pyogenes** and **E. coli,** but not mycoplasma, present in the prepuce of certain bulls may cause a temporary vulvovaginitis in females after coitus. Although many miscellaneous organisms may be introduced into the prepuce, recovery is usually spontaneous.

The herpesviru- of cattle, IBR-IPV, can produce an acute inflammation and ulceration of the penis and prepuce accompanied by a short period of elevated body temperature when introduced into the preputial cavity of susceptible bulls, Bouters and coworkers, Studdert and coworkers. This disease was formerly called vesicular venereal disease in the U.S.· or blaschenausschlag in Germany. The initial area of involvement is the epithelium over the lymphoid follicles that becomes necrotic and sloughs. The ulcers on the glans and prepuce caused by the virus are secondarily infected by the bacterial flora of the sheath resulting in a severe pustular balanoposthitis. Abrasions of the penis and sheath that occur at copulation make the lesions in the acute stage more marked. The virus can usually be recovered from the acutely affected bull's prepuce and penis for about 10 to 14 days. Bulls may spread this disease during this period to cows by copulation producing pustular vulvo-vaginitis. Some cases of balanoposthitis may be so mild that infection may go undetected. Snowden has reported the recovery of this virus from the prepuce of a bull for a period of up to 361 days. These are often refractory or immune animals. Serum antibodies are developed but the titers are low 1:10 to 1:100, on the serum neutralization test, Saxegaard. On histologic section of affected tissues eosinophilic nuclear inclusion bodies may be found in many cells. Epizootic outbreaks of balanoposthitis in range bulls could be due to this agent, Delahanty. A few outbreaks have been reported in artificial breeding studs where there is a great danger of this virus being disseminated in liquid or frozen semen as antibiotics commonly placed in semen extenders have no effect on this virus, Saxegaard. Straub reported that coital exanthema due to the IPV virus was common in dairy herds and was occasionally seen in AI Centers in Germany. He demonstrated by electrophoresis that the IPV virus differed from the IBR virus even though by serological methods they were similar. He prepared a highly attenuated vaccine that would protect the cows and bulls if instilled intranasally and intravaginally or into the prepuce of bulls yet would not produce signs of the disease even if semen from recently vaccinated bulls was used for artificial insemination. The field strain of IPV virus if present in the the semen would reduce conception rates by about 7 percent and produce signs of the disease. This highly attenuated vaccine was administered as noted above twice at 6-week intervals and then once yearly thereafter. No abortions were produced by the vaccine given to pregnant cows and challenged cattle showed no evidence of disease. The local immunity produced by this vaccine was better than the immunity produced by an intramuscular injection of a vaccine.

In severe cases acute swelling, pain and later local scarring may cause difficuity or slowness in copulation. True adhesions were not observed by Bouters and Studdert although in range bulls with great libido repeated abrasion of infected and inflamed tissues might occasionally produce them. For treatment sexual rest is recommended together with local antibiotic therapy of the sheath. Most bulls recover within one to two weeks but it may take up to a month before normal copulation will occur. Because of the infectious nature of this disease bulls should not be used for service until after 6 to 8 weeks from the onset of the attack. Since herpes viruses tend to persist in the body, recurrent dissemination of virus may occasionally be possible, Saxegaard, Snowdon. A virulent IBR-IPV vaccine is available in the U.S.A. but careful consideration should be given to the contraindications for the use of this living viral vaccine in adult cattle. It is not recommended for use in artificial insemination studs. Packard and Poste from Oklahoma and England, respectively, were cited by Carmichael as recovering a new herpesvirus from the sheath of dogs. The significance of this finding is not known.

Balanoposthitis in rams, "pizzle rot" or "sheath rot" may be infectious or noninfectious. The most common infectious form of balanoposthitis is due the virus that causes ulcerative dermatosis, lip and leg ulceration or necrotic venereal disease. This disease has been described in the U.S., England, France and Germany, Marsh. The lesions on the preputial orifice, prepuce and glans penis are ulcerative and covered by a scab. Removal of the scab reveals a shallow, raw, bleeding crater containing a creamy odorless pus. The preputial lesions may cause phimosis or paraphimosis, and an extensive penile lesion may render the ram useless as a breeder. Lesions may also be present on the lip, nostril, feet, or vulva. The disease should be distinguished from contagious ecthyma and common non-specific lesions occasionally seen on the preputial orifice of rams. Ulcerative dermatosis is spread by venereal contact and other means. The disease in rams may persist for weeks or months. Affected rams should not be used for breeding. There is no vaccine available nor is there any specific treatment for the lesions.

Noninfectious balanoposthitis has been described in Australia by Beveridge and Johnstone, Watson and Murname, and McEntee. Two degrees are recognized, an ulceration of the prepuce near the preputial orifice and a stenosis of the orifice with a secondary chronic ulceration of the deeper portions of the prepuce accompanied by the accumulation of pus and necrotic material. This occurs in wethers or rams 2 to 4 years of age. It is often associated with a wet spring and pasturing sheep on lush grass, rye, clover or lucerne that are high in protein. Changing of the diet to dry feed with a lower protein intake, or fasting, results in an improvement in the balanoposthitis. Young rams housed together may develop similar lesions possibly due to trauma and contamination. In severe cases the sheath may have to be surgically opened ventrally to permit urination and the saving the life of the animal. Extending the preputial incision too far caudally may render a ram useless for service. Superficial external lesions may be treated by proper local therapy.

Balanoposthitis in the horse may occur in geldings or stallions. A thick, fibrous, fatty or edematous sheath is often diagnosed erroneously as due to a balanoposthitis when no inflammatory lesions are present. Balanoposthitis due to bacterial agents are uncommon in stallions even though various infectious agents may be carried from mare to mare on the penis and prepuce. Early symptoms of **dourine,** a reportable venereal disease of horses transmitted by coitus, are swelling, edema and reddening of the penis and prepuce. This disease, not seen in the U.S., is caused by **Trypanosma equiperdum.** Later in the disease depigmentation of the skin of the genital organs may occur, Hagan and Bruner.

Girard and coworkers and Bryans described an **equine venereal balanitis** and **vulvitis,** formerly called **genital horse pox** or **coital exanthema,** caused by a herpesvirus. (See Figure 147) After an incubation period of 6 to 8 days circular, confluent, poxlike lesions occurred on the skin of the penis. These leions healed in 10 to 14 days if secondary infections did not occur. Depigmentation of affected areas was common. There was no effect on fertility but affected stallions refused or were hesitant to copulate. With-holding affected stallions from service to prevent the spread of infection to susceptible mares and local conservative treatment of the lesions are indicated. One attack doesn't confer a permanent immunity, Kral and Schwartzman. This virus is not the rhinopneumonitis virus. The disease is occasionally seen in the U.S. especially on breeding farms where it may spread rapidly by coitus or grooming.

Cutaneous habronemiasis, summer sores or genital bursatti may affect the equine penis and prepuce. The Habronema larvae may produce fungoid granulomatous growths 1 to 3 cm in diameter that may contain firm necrotic irregular-shaped masses or "kunkurs". These lesions bleed readily on manipulation, Kral and Schwartzman. The lesions are not seen on the genitals of mares. These lesions may produce intense pruritis. In some cases their presence near the urethral process results in difficult urination similar to that produced when the urethral diverticulum is distended with smegma causing compression of the urethra. In the colder northern states these lesions subside and usually disappear during the winter months. Wheat recommended local treatment with camphophenique in scarlet oil daily and a systemic organic phosphate insecticide ("Ronnel") at a dose of 45 gms per 1000 pounds orally repeated in two weeks. In countries where the screwworm or Cochliomyia fly is present, severe infestations of the sheath and glans penis of geldings or stallions may occur resulting in pain, bleeding and swelling. Good restraint, often requiring general anesthesia, is necessary to get adequate exposure for local treatment of lesions with Smear 62 or camphophenique Further infestation should be prevented by confining the animal in a barn and treating the external preputial opening with fly repellant. Osborne and Bain reported on multiple, small ulcerous lesions on the penis and prepuce of a horse associated with spirochetes. The lesions healed in about three weeks and the spirochetes disappeared. In some horses excessive accumulations of smegma within the prepuce may be associated with a keratin-like coating of the penis and prepuce. Manual cleansing of the equine sheath with soap or oily antiseptic solutions is accomplished by restraint and the liberal use of cotton swabs. Wearing plastic or rubber gloves is advisable because of the odor of the smegma.

Balanoposthitis seldom occurs in the boar. The preputial diverticulum in the boar often fills with foul-smelling urine and smegma and externally may resemble an umbilical hernia. (See Figure 160) This can readily be differentiated from a hernia on clinical examination by squeezing the enlarged diverticulum and expressing its contents. Hutchings stated that in boars concretions and preputial calculi occasionally were present, causing difficult urination and inability to protrude the penis. Extirpation of the preputial diverticulum of boars will markedly reduce the bacteria in semen collected for artificial insemination and also greatly reduce the boar odor, Aamdal et al.. The boar's sheath may become infested with screwworms. In pigs with hog cholera, Dunne has reported ulcers of the prepuce as a result of infarction. Ulcerations of the porcine penis due to other causes may be observed. These conditions in boars are usually easily diagnosed and treated.

In the dog, balanoposthitis is occasionally observed but seldom, if ever, is a cause of failure of copulation. It is characterized by a discharge of pus from the prepuce and it usually responds well to mild antiseptic douches followed by bland antibiotic ointments or solutions. Balanoposthitis in the dog should be differentiated from the prostatitis as both are characterized by pus appearing at the preputial opening. Bloom reported that suppurative, ulcerative and follicular balanoposthitis or preputial catarrh is common in the dog. It is interesting to note that follicular lesions occur in the prepuce of the dog and are similar in nature to the enlarged lymph follicles or to the granular venereal disease lesions seen in the prepuce of the bull. (See Figure 173) As noted under IBR-IPV infection of the prepuce and penis in bulls, Carmichael reported the isolation of a herpesvirus from the sheath of dogs. Balanoposthitis in the dog, as in other animals, is due to mixed infections, trauma, foreign bodies, other general diseases, and debility. The malicious or ill-considered placement of a rubber band around a dog's penis causes great discomfort, severe balanoposthitis and even necrosis of the penis. In the dog acquired phimosis is less frequent than is congenital phimosis, Bloom.

The prognosis in balanoposthitis depends upon the severity of the trauma or the infection. In mild cases the prognosis is good. In severe chronic cases with adhesions between the penis and prepuce or between the prepuce and adjacent tissues, the prognosis is guarded to poor. In cases of prolapse of the prepuce requiring amputation, the prognosis is usually fair to good if the amount of prepuce removed is not excessive. Some males may be slow to regain their libido following a painful balanoposthitis.

Treatment of mild cases of balanoposthitis may consist of douching the prepuce with aqueous or oily antiseptics or antibiotic preparations such as saline, 50 to 200 ppm. of chlorine solution, 1:2,000 acriflavine or potassium permanganate solutions, 1 percent hydrogen peroxide solution, one ounce of bismuth formic iodide in a 500 ml of mineral oil, 1 gm iodine in one gallon of mineral oil, infusions of aqueous furacin and other antibiotics in oil in about 25 to 100 ml volumes. Caustic or irritating antiseptics should be avoided. Treatments may be repeated at daily to weekly intervals. In cases of severe balanoposthitis with extensive necrosis of the prepuce and penis adhesions may result if much oily antiseptics or antibiotic ointments and systemic antibiotics are not employed. Regular gentle protrusion of the penis may be desirable to prevent possible adhesions. Tranquilizers, anesthetics, pudenal nerve block and adequate restraint are helpful in applying treatment for balanoposthitis. Sexual rest is essential during and for sometime after the treatment of acute balanoposthitis to promote recovery and to prevent a loss of libido associated with the painful condition.

Miscellaneous Causes for Loss of Libido or Inability to Copulate include: (1) hernias (2) premature erection (3) loss of sensory innervation of the glans penis (4) urinary calculi and (5) other causes.

(1) Umbilical and ventral hernias as well as a deep pendulous abdomen may interfere or prevent normal copulation by affecting the entry of the penis into the vagina at a natural mating. Umbilical and small ventral hernias may respond to surgery but since umbilical hernia may be hereditary the affected male should not be used as a sire. Murray reported that about 1 percent of Santa Gertrudis bulls and Holsteins in Australia have umbilical hernias. These affected animals should be culled and not operated upon. Extensive unilateral hernias or a deep "paunchy" abdomen usually observed in older bulls or rams may interfere with normal intromission and thrusting especially if arthritic lesions are also present. Marked reduction of roughage and bulky feeds is indicated in these males but the prognosis is usually guarded to poor.

(2) Premature erection may occur in the dog, stallion and certain bulls and interfere with normal intromission. Leonard and coworkers described premature erection in the dog as an obstacle to coitus and a cause of impotency. Complete erection does not take place until the canine penis is in the vagina. He recommended artificial insemination as the quickest and easiest solution for this problem. In stallions the glans penis occasionally becomes too large to readily enter the vulva of a small mare or a mare whose vulva has been sutured to prevent pneumovagina. This cause of inability to copulate can usually be overcome by helping to direct the penis into the vulva before it becomes fully erect, by lubricating the vulva, or by incising the sutured vulvar lips dorsally. The mare may be artifically inseminated or may be bred to a stallion of more suitable size. As described previously certain beef bulls with a strong sex drive and with a narrow penis develop a "corkscrewing" or coiling of the free end of the penis at premature full erection that prevents intromission. (See Figure 165)

(3) Loss of sensory innervation of the glans penis prevents natural intromission and the "thrust" reflex necessary for ejaculation and leads to a pronounced decline in sex drive. Lack of sensation of the glans penis may be caused by injury to the dorsal nerve of the penis secondary to rupture and hemorrhage of the corpus cavernosum penis, by the improper technique of injecting local anesthesia on the dorsal nerve at the sigmoid flexure of the penis, rarely by an operation to correct the spiralling of the bovine penis or by a rubber band from an artificial vagina or other source that is placed around the penis and not removed for several days. Lack of sensation of the glans penis may also be due to severe necrosis of the mucosa of the glans due to severe balanitis of an infectious etiology or due to trauma resulting in severe scarring. Amputation of the glans penis due to a rubber band or following extensive surgery for a tumor produces the same effect. Males that have had experience breeding before the loss of sensation in the glans penis remain sexually active but suffer from a definite loss of libido. Immature males with a similar loss seldom show much sexual desire as demonstrated by mounting and actively seeking the vulva with their penis An excellent experimental study of the results of desensitization of the glans penis in the cat was

reported by Aronson and Cooper. Damage to the nerve supply of the ischiocavernosus muscle may cause its atrophy and result in the inability of the penis to become erect.

(4) Urinary calculi lodging in the urethra may occasionally be a cause of acute pain, obstruction and rupture of the urethra in male domestic animals and cause reluctance to copulate and inability to ejaculate. Urinary calculi were described by VanderSluis in a bull with inability to copulate and exhibiting impotentia coeundi. The author has observed several bulls with urethral calculi, that refused to copulate and one that copulated and bled from the urethra. In cases of urinary or urethral calculi the prognosis for the future breeding life of the male is grave. Although an operation can be performed and the calculi removed, suturing of the urethra often results in a stricture. When the urethral and skin incisions in the bull are left open to heal by second intention, in order to save the animal for future breeding, an urethral fistula or strictures often form. Other calculi may lodge in the same area; or adhesions form in the region of the sigmoid flexure and the ability to protrude the penis is lost. Leaving the skin and urethra open to heal by second intention is however occasionally successful in the dog and has been reported in the bull. Depending on the location of the urethral fistula the male may be unable to properly place the semen in the vagina. Oehme has described a urethral calculi retriever (Haver-Lockhart Lab., Shawnee, Ks.) modified after a human retriever for ureteral calculi that has proven successful in cases where tranquilizers and muscle relaxants when administered early failed to result in the passage of the calculi from the usual site of lodgement at the sigmoid flexure. The bull is placed in lateral recumbency under tranquilization. Pudendal nerve block may also be used. The penis is fully extended and the retriever with proper lubrication is passed beyond the calculi and then withdrawn removing the obstruction. Stricture formation was reported not to be a serious problem.

In the ram calculi may lodge in the sigmoid flexure area as in bulls but are more commonly found in the urethral process. Amputation of the urethral process just proximal to the calculi is usually performed. If most of the urethral process is removed conception rates may be markedly reduced due to poor distribution of semen in the vagina at the time of ejaculation, Masson.

Calculi are common in the male cat and uncommon in the dog. In order to preserve the breeding potential of these animals conservative therapy such as massage and flushing in the removal of the urethral calculi and in the aftercare is indicated, surgery should be used only as a last resort. Crago has described the use of a loop of no. 26 twisted steel wire to remove urethral calculi and mucous plugs in the anesthetized cat. Rich has indicated that up to 10 percent of male cats may develop calculi and recurrence is common. He recommended using a 3″ nasal lacrimal duct needle rather than a tom cat catheter and small amounts of 50 percent vinegar in water to remove urethral calculi from anesthetized cats. There was experimental evidence that an infectious viral agent, a picornavirus, was an important etiologic factor, Fabricant et al.. Antibiotics such as chloromycetin, reduction of minerals in the diet, lowering the pH of the urine, and increasing the water intake may be helpful in controlling urolithiasis in these animals. In the dog calculi tend to lodge at the caudal end of the os penis since the urethra passes along the ventral groove in the penile bone, Kirk and coworkers, and Whitehead. Udall and Jensen and Marsh reported urinary calculi, ruptured urethrae and bladders, greatly enlarged bulbourethral glands, and seminal vesicles in feedlot lambs or wethers given 12 to 15 mg implants of stilbestrol or 2 to 5 mg of stilbestrol daily in the feed. This occurred as early as 10 to 14 days after the administration of the stilbestrol.

(5) Pain caused by infection of the genital organs or peritoneum may be a cause of impotency or refusal to copulate. Williams described a stallion with infection of the ampullae and seminal vesicles that refused to copulate. The author has observed several bulls with severe acute semino-vesiculitis that were slow or refused to mount. Hutchings and Andrews reported on two boars with brucellar orchitis that refused to copulate and two more that had a markedly reduced libido. Acute prostatitis in dogs might similarly affect copulation. Necrobacillosis and traumatic gastritis with acute peritonitis may be associated with failure or refusal to copulate in bulls. Severe congenital or acquired cardiac diseases often result in dyspnea and inability to perform coitus by male animals.

Reduced to Complete Lack of Sexual Desire and Ability to Copulate

Almquist, J. O. and Hale, E. B. (1956) An Approach to the Measurement of Sexual Behavior and Semen Production of Dairy Bulls, Proc. III Internat. Congress on An. Reprod., Cambridge.

Bane, A. (1954) Studies on Monozygous Cattle Twins XV Sexual Functions of Bulls in Relation to Heredity, Rearing Intensity and Somatic Conditions, Acta Agric. Scand. **4,** 95.

Barton, A. (1960) Instinct and Sexuality in the Dog, Vet. Med. **55,** 5, 49.

Bielanski, W., Wierzbowski, S. and Zakrzewska, G. (1957) The Results of Mass-wise Evaluations of the Semen and Sexual Reflexes of Stallions, Zesz. Nauk. Wyzs. Roln. W. Krakowie, Zootechnica **21,** 4, 97.

Dunn, H. O., Roberts, S. J., McEntee, K. and Wagner, W. C. (1965)

Prevention of Traumatic Gastritis in Bulls by Use of Magnets, Cor. Vet **55,** 2, 204.

Fox, M. W. (1968) Abnormal Behavior in Animals, W. B. Saunders, Co., Philadelphia.

Fraser, A. F. (1957) Intromission Phobia in the Bull, Vet. Rec. **69,** 621.

Fraser, A.F. (1968) Reproductive Behavior in Ungulates, Academic Press, N.Y.C.

Goy, R. W. (1966) Role of Androgens in the Establishment and Regulation of Behavioral Sex Differences in Mammals, J. An. Sci. (suppl) **25,** 21.

Hafez, E. S. E. (1960) Analysis of the Ejaculatory Reflexes and Sex Drive in the Bull, Cor. Vet. **50,** 4, 384.

Hafez, E. S. E. (1968) Reproduction in Farm Animals, 2nd Ed. Lea and Febiger, Philadelphia.

Hafez, E. S. E. (1969) The Behavior of Domestic Animals, Williams and Wilkins Comp., Baltimore, Md.

Hale, E. B. (1966) Visual Stimuli and Reproductive Behavior in Bulls, J. An. Sci. **25,** Suppl, 36.

Hale, E. B. and Almquist, J. O. (1960) Relation of Sexual Behavior to Sperm Cell Output in Farm Animals, J. Dairy Sci. **43,** 145.

Hafs, H. D., Knisely, R. C. and Desjardins, C. (1962) Sperm Output of Dairy Bulls with Varying Degrees of Sexual Preparation, J. Dairy Sci. **45,** 6, 788.

Hulet, C. V. (1966) Behavioral, Social and Psychological Factors Affecting Mating Time and Breeding Efficiency in Sheep, J. An. Sci. Suppl. **25,** 5.

Hulet, C. V., Blackwell, R. L. and Ercanbrack, S. K. (1964) Observations on Sexually Inhibited Rams, J. An. Sci. **23,** 4, 1095.

Hulet, C. V., Ercanbrack, S. K. Blackwell, R. L. Price, D. A. and Wilson, L. O. (1962) Mating Behavior of the Ram in the One-Sire Pen, J. An. Sci. **21,** 4, 857.

Hulet, C. V., Ercanbrack, S. K., Blackwell, R. L., Price, D. A. and Wilson, L. O. (1962) Mating Behavior of the Ram in the Multi-Sire Pen, J. An. Sci. **21,** 4, 865.

Hultnas, C. A. (1959) Studies on Variation in Mating Behavior and Semen Picture in Young Bulls of Swedish Red and White Breed and on Causes of this Variation, Acta. Agric. Scand. Suppl. 6.

Kendrick, J. W. (1954) Psychic Impotence in Bulls, Cor. Vet. **44,** 3, 289.

Lagerlof, N. (1938) Infertility in Male Domestic Animals, Proc 13th Internat. Vet. Congr. Vol I, 214.

Murray, G. R. (1970) Personal Communication.

Roman, J., Wilcox, C. J., Becker, R. B. and Koger, M. (1967) Life Span and Reasons for Disposal of A.I. Beef Sires, J. An. Sci. **26,** 1, 136.

Vandeplassche, M. (1955) Ejakulationsstorugen beim Hengst, Fortpfl. Zuckthyg. and Haustier **5,** 11, 134.

Wierzbowski, S. and Hafez, E. S. E. (1961) Analysis of Copulatory Reflexes in the Stallion, Proc of IVth Internat. Congr. on An. Reprod., The Hague.

Joint, Muscle, Nerve, Bone and Tendon Injuries and Pathology

Bane, A. and Hansen, H. J. (1962) Spinal Changes in Bulls and Their Significance in Serving Ability, Cor. Vet. **52,** 362.

Becker, R. B., Wilcox, C. J. and Pritchard, W. R. (1966) "Crampy" Progressive Posterior Paralysis in Mature Cattle, Bull 639. Univ. of Florida, Agr. Exp. Stat. Gainesville, Fla.

Brown, C. J., Roussel, J. D. and Stallcup, O. T. (1967) Genetic and Other Aspects of a Hoof Anomaly of Hereford Bulls, J. Dairy Sci. **26,** 1, 201.

Einarsson, S. (1968) Fertility and Serving Ability of Swedish Landrace and Swedish Yorkshire Boars, Nord. Vet. Med. **20,** 616.

Krook, L., Lutwak, L. and McEntee, K. (1969) Dietary Calcium, Ultimo-branchial Tumors and Osteopetrosis in the Bull, Amer. J. Clin. Nutr. **22,** 2, 115.

Roberts, S. J. (1965) Hereditary Spastic Diseases Affecting Cattle in New York State, Cor. Vet. **55,** 4, 637.

Thompson, R. G. (1965) A Study of Vertebral Body Osteophytes in Bulls, Thesis, Cornell Univ., Ithaca, New York.

Diseases of the Penis and Prepuce and Congenital Defects

Adams, W. M. (1970) Hormonal and Anatomical Causes of Infertility, Colloquium on **Effect of Diseases and Stress on Reproductive Efficiency in Swine,** Iowa State Univ., Ames, Iowa.

Bloom, F. (1953) Endocrine Glands, Canine Medicine. Amer. Vet. Public. Inc. Evanston, Ill.

Carroll, E. J. (1967) Personal Communication.

Crowshaw, E. J. and Brodey, R. S. (1960) Failure of Preputial Closure in a Dog, J.A.V.M.A. **136,** 9, 450.

DeGroot, T. and Numans, S. R. (1946) Over de Erfelijkheid der Impotentia Coeundi bij Steiren, Tijd. v. Diergeneesk **71,** 372.

Haq, I. (1949) Causes of Sterility in Bulls on Southern England, Brit. Vet. Jour. **105,** 71, 114, 200.

Hofmeyr, C. F. B. (1967) Surgery of Impotentia Coeundi, J. So. Afr. Vet. Med. Assoc., **38,** 3 & 4, 275, 395, 399.

Holst, S. J. (1949) The Semen of Sterile Boars, Proc. 14th Internat. Vet. Congr. Vol. III. Sect. 4(c), 118.

Kendrick, J. W. (1954) Psychic Impotence in Bulls, Cor. Vet. **44,** 3, 289.

McEntee, K. (1969) Pathology of Domestic Animals, 2nd Ed. Vol I by Jubb, K. V. and Kennedy, P. C., Academic Press, N.Y.C., London.

Noice, F. and Schipper, I. A. (1958) Abnormal Urogenital Tract of a Ram, J.A.V.M.A. **132,** 2, 75.

Richter, J. (1919) Die Unfruchtbarkeit den Zeigenbocke, R. Schoetz, Berlin.

Williams, W. L. (1943) Diseases of the Genital Organs of Domestic Animals, 3rd Ed., Louella Williams, Upland Rd., Ithaca, N.Y.

Deviations of the Penis

Ashdown, R. R. (1962) Persistence of the Penile Frenulum in Young Bulls, Vet. Rec. **74,** 50, 1464.

Ashdown, R. R. and Combs, M. A. (1967) Spiral Deviation of the Bovine Penis, Vet. Rec. **80,** 738.

Ashdown, R. R., Rickets, S. W. and Wardley, R. C. (1968) The Fibrous Architecture of the Integumentary Coverings of the Bovine Penis, J. of Anat. **103,** 3, 567.

Ashdown, R. R. and Smith, J. A. (1969) The Anatomy of the Corpus Cavernosum Penis of the Bull and its Relationship to Spiral Deviation of the Penis, J. Anat. **104,** 1, 153.

Carroll, E. J., Aanes, W. A. and Ball, L. (1964) Persistent Penile Frenulum in Bulls. J.A.V.M.A. **144,** 7, 747.

Herrick, J. (1958) Personal Communication.

Johnston, D. E. (1965) Repairing Lesions of the Canine Penis and Prepuce, Mod. Vet. Pract. **46,** 1, 39.

Joshua, J. O. (1962) Persistence of the Penile Frenulum in a Dog, Vet. Rec. **74,** 52, 1550.

McEntee, K. (1969) Pathology of Domestic Animals, Vol I, 2nd Ed., Jubb, K. V. and Kennedy, P. C., Academic Press, N.Y.C.

Milne, F. J. (1954) Penile and Preputial Problems in the Bull, J.A.V.M.A. **129,** 922, 6.

Scott, J. A. (1962) Personal Communication.

Seidel, G. E. and Foote, R. H (1967) Motion Picture Analysis of Bovine Ejaculation, J. Dairy Sci. **50,** 6, 970.

Seidel, G. E. Jr. and Foote, R. H. (1969) Motion Picture Analysis of Ejaculation in the Bull, J. of Reprod. and Fert. **20,** 313.

Walker, D. F. (1964) Deviations of the Bovine Penis, J.A.V.M.A. **145,** 7, 677.

Adhesions and Tumors of the Penis and Prepuce

Bagdonas, V. and Olson, C. Jr. (1953) Observations on the Epizootiology of Cutaneous Papillomatosis (Warts) of Cattle, J.A.V M.A. **122,** 914, 393.

Bloom, F. (1954) Pathology of the Dog and Cat, Amer. Vet. Public. Inc., Evanston, Ill.

Farquharson, J. (1952) Fracture of the Penis in the Bull, Vet. Med. **47,** 5, 175.

Feldman, W. H. (1932) Neoplasms of Domestic Animals, W. B. Saunders Co., Philadelphia, Pa.

Formston, C. (1953) Fibropapillomatosis in Cattle with Special Reference to the External Genitalia of the Bull, Brit. Vet. Jour. **109,** 244.

Gibbons, W. I. (1956) Genital Diseases of Bulls 1. Diseases of the Penis and Sheath. N. Amer. Vet. **37,** 650.

Goldston, R. T. (1969) The Bovine Penile Hematoma, Proc. of Conference on Reprod. Problems in Animals, Univ. of Georgia, Nov., p. 63.

Higgins, D. A. (1966) Observations on the Canine Transmissible Venereal Tumor as Seen in the Bahamas, Vet. Rec. **79,** 3, 67.

Hofmeyr, C. F. B. (1967) See Diseases of Penis and Prepuce.

McEntee, K. (1969) Pathology of Domestic Animals, 2nd Ed., Vol. I. Jubb, K. V. and Kennedy, P. C. Academic Press, N.Y., London.

Milne, F. J. (1954) Penile and Preputial Problems in the Bull, J.A.V.M.A. **124,** 922, 6.

Noordsy, T. L. (1970) Personal Communication.

Olson, C., Robl, M. G. and Larson, L. L. (1968) Cutaneous and Penile Fibropapillomatosis and its Control, J.A.V.M.A. **153,** 9, 1189.

Olson, C. Jr., Segre, D. and Skidmore, L. V. (1960) Further Observations on Immunity to Bovine Cutaneous Papillomatosis, Am. J. Vet. Res. **21,** 81, 233.

Pattridge, P. D. (1953) Surgical Repair of the Fractured Penis in the Bull, Southwest Vet. **7,** 1, 31.

Pearson, J. K. L., Kerr, W. R., McCartney W. D. J. and Steele, T. H. J. (1959) Tissue Vaccines in the Treatment of Bovine Papillomas, Vet. Rec. **70,** 48, 971.

Walker, D. F. (1967) Personal Communication.

Wheat, J. D. (1951) Diseases of the Penis and Prepuce of the Bull Requiring Surgery, J.A.V.M.A. **118,** 890, 295.

Williams, W. L. (1943) Diseases of the Genital Organs of Domestic Animals, 3rd Ed., Louella Williams, Upland Rd., Ithaca, N.Y.

Phimosis or Stenosis of the Preputial Orifice

Berry, D. M. (1958) Jamaica Letter, Mod. Vet. Pract., **39,** 9, 31.

Cardwell, W. H. (1961) The Surgical Correction of the Preputial and Penile Disorders of the Bull, Southwestern Vet., **14,** 4, 270.

Christian, A. B. (1955) Personal Communication.

Donaldson, L. E and Aubrey, J. N. (1960) Posthitis and Prolapse of the Prepuce in Cattle, Austral. Vet. Jour., **36,** 380.

Kirk, H. (1931) Phimosis and Paraphimosis in the Cat, Vet. Rec., **11,** 832.

Lagos, F. and Fitzhugh, H. A. Jr. (1970) Factors Influencing Preputial Prolapse in Yearling Bulls, J. An. Sci. **30,** 60, 949.

Lenert, A. A. (1956) Surgical Conditions Affecting the Reproductive Tract of the Bull, J.A.V.M.A., **129,** 11, 506.

Megale, F. (1963) Personal Communication.

Milne, F. J. (1954) Penile and Preputial Problems in the Bull, J.A.V.M.A., **124,** 922, 6.

Murray, G. R. (1970) Personal Communication.

Romane, Wm. M. (1960) Circumcision of the Bull, Personal Communication.

Walker, D. F. (1967) Diseases of the Penis and Prepuce of the Bull Requiring Surgery, J.A.V.M.A., **118,** 890, 295.

Paraphimosis (See Phimosis)

Allam, M. (1953) Canine Surgery, 3rd Ed. Ed. by J. V. Lacroix and H. P. Hoskins, Amer. Vet. Public., Evanston, Illinois.

Greene, J. E. (1957) Amputation of the Penis (Dog), N. A. Vet., **38,** 6, 187.

Johnston, D. E. (1965) Repairing Lesions of the Canine Penis and Prepuce, Mod. Vet. Pract., **46,** 1, 39.

Milne, F. J. (1956) Personal Communication.

Wheat, J. D. (1951) Diseases of the Penis and Prepuce of the Bull Requiring Surgery, J.A.V.M.A., **118,** 890, 295.

Balanoposthitis

Aamdal, J., Hogset, I. and Filseth, O. (1958) Extirpation of the Preputial Diverticulum of Boars Used for Artificial Insemination, J.A.V.M.A. **132,** 522.

Bakos, K., Bane, A. and Thal, E. (1962) Mycoplasma (PPLO) in Relation to Fertility in the Bull, Zentralbl. f. Veterinar. Med. **9,** 4, 397.

Bane, A. (1964) Fertility and Reproductive Disorders in Swedish Cattle, Brit. Vet. Jour. **120,** 431.

Beveridge, W. I. B. and Johnstone, I. L. (1953) Sheath Rot, Non-contagious Posthitis or Chronic Ulceration of the Prepuce of Sheep, Austral. Vet. Jour., **29,** and **30,** 326 and 1.

Bloom, F. (1954) Pathology of the Dog and Cat, Amer. Vet. Public., Inc., Wheaton, Illinois.

Bouters, R., Vandeplassche, M., Florent, A. and Devos, A. (1960). Ulcerative Balanoposthitis in Bulls, Vlaams Diergeneesk. Tijdschr., **29,** 171.

Bruner, D. W. and Gillespie, J. H. (1966) Hagan's Infectious Diseases of Domestic Animals, 5th Ed., Comstock Publishing Assoc., Cornell Univ. Press, Ithaca, New York.

Bryans, J. T. (1968) The Herpesviruses in Disease of the Horse, Proc. of 14th Annual Meeting AAEP, Philadelphia, 119.

Carmichael, L. E. (1970) Personal Communication.

Delahanty, D. D. (1955) Personal Communication.

Dunne, H. W. (1961) The Pathogenesis and Pathologic Anatomy of Hog Cholera, Proc. Symp. on Hog Cholera, Univ. of Minn., St. Paul, Minn., 45.

Girard, A., Greig, A. S. and Mitchell, D. (1968) A Virus Associated with Vulvitis and Balanitis in the Horse—A Preliminary Report, Canad. J. of Comp. Med. **32,** 603.

Hutchings, L. M. (1948) Sterility in Swine, J.A.V.M.A., **112,** 851, 114.

Kral, F. and Schwartzman, R. M. (1964) Veterinary Comparative Dermatology, J. B. Lippincott Co., Philadelphia, Pa.

Marsh, H. (1965) Newsom's Sheep Diseases, 3rd Ed., Williams and Wilkins Co., Baltimore, Md.

McEntee, K. (1969) Pathology of Domestic Animals, 2nd Ed. by Jubb, K. V. and Kennedy, P. C., Academic Press, N.Y.C.

Osborne, V. E. and Bain, R. V. S. (1961) Genital Infection of a Horse with Spirochetes, Austral. Vet. Jour., **37,** 190.

Rollinson, D. H. L. and Haq, I. (1948) Mycotic Infection of the Prepuce of the Bull, Vet. Rec., **60,** 68.

Saxegaard, F. (1968) Serological Investigations of Bulls Subclinically Infected with Infectious Pustular Vulvovaginitis, Nord. Vet. Med., **20,** 28.

Scott, J. A. (1962) Personal Communication.

Snowden, W. A. (1965) The IBR-IPV Virus Reaction to Infection and Intermittent Recovery of Virus from Experimentally Infected Cattle, Austral. Vet. Jour., **41,** 135.

Southcott, W. H. (1962) The Etiology of Ovine Posthitis: Transmission of the Disease, Austral. Vet. Jour., **38,** 441.

Straub, O. C. (1970) Personal Communication.

Straub, O. C. (1970) Vaccination Against Coital Exanthema (IPV) Internat. Conf. on Cattle Diseases, Philadelphia.

Studdert, M. H., Barker, C. A. V. and Savan, M. (1964) Infectious Pustular Vulvovaginitis (I.P.V.) Virus Infection of Bulls, Am. J. Vet. res., **25,** 105, 303.

Watson, R. H. and Murname, D. (1958) Noncontagious Ovine Posthitis (Sheath Rot): Some Aspects of its Course and Etiology, Austral. Vet. Jour., **34,** 125.

Wheat, J. D. (1961) Habronemiasis of the Equine Prepuce, Vet. Med., **56,** 11, 477.

Williams, W. L. (1943) Diseases of the Genital Organs of Domestic Animals, 3rd Ed. Louella Williams, Upland Rd., Ithaca, New York.

Miscellaneous Causes in Loss of Libido and Inability to Copulate

Aronson, L. R. and Cooper, M. L. (1966) Seasonal Variation in Mating Behavior in Cats after Desensitization of the Glans Penis, Science **152,** 226.

Crago, W. H. (1969) A Simple Method for Removing Urethral Calculi in Male Cats, J.A.V.M.A. 154, 11, 1386.

Fabricant, C. G., Rich, L. J. and Gillespie, J. H. (1969) Feline Viruses XI Isolation of a Virus Similar to a Myxovirus from Cats in Which Urolithiasis was Experimentally Induced, Cor. Vet., **59,** 4, 667.

Hutchings, L. M. and Andrews, F. N. (1946). Studies on Brucellosis in Swine; Brucella Infection in the Boar, Amer. J. Vet. Res., **7,** 25, 379, 385, 388.

Kirk, R. W., McEntee, K., and Bentinck-Smith, J. (1968) Canine Medicine, Edited by E. J. Catcott, Amer. Vet. Public., Inc., Wheaton, Illinois.

Leonard, E. P., Rickard, C. G. and McEntee, K. (1953) Impotence, Canine Medicine, Amer. Vet. Publ., Inc., Evanston, Illinois, 165.

Marsh, H. (1961) Urethral Occlusion in Lambs on Feed Containing Stilbestrol, J.A.V.M.A. **139,** 9, 1019.

Masson, J. (1963) Personal Communication.

Murray, G. R. (1970) Personal Communication.

Oehme, F. W. (1968) A Urinary Calculi Retriever for Nonsurgical Treatment of Urolithiasis in Bulls, Vet. Med., **63,** 1, 53.

Rich, L. J. (1969) Feline Urethral Obstruction, Etiologic Factors and Pathogenesis, Thesis, N.Y.S. Veterinary College, Cornell University.

Rich, L. J. and Fabricant, C. G. (1969) Urethral Obstruction in Male Cats, Transmission Studies, Canad. J. Comp. Med. **33,** 2, 164.

Udall, R. H. and Jensen, R. (1958) Studies on Urolithiasis II The Occurrence in Feedlot Lambs Following Implantations of Diesthylstilbestrol, J.A.V.M.A. **133,** 10, 514.

VanderSluis, L. (1953) Experiences with Examination into Herd Infertility, Proc. First World Congr. on Fert. and Steril., Vol. II, 25, 703.

Whitehead, J. E. (1964) Feline Medicine and Surgery, Edited by E. J. Catcott Amer. Vet. Public., Inc., Wheaton, Illinois.

Williams, W. L. (1943) Diseases of the Genital Organs of Domestic Animals, 3rd Ed., Louella Williams, Upland Rd., Ithaca, New York.

Incapacity or Reduced Capacity to Fertilize in Males (Impotentia Generandi)

Fertility is the normal functioning of the testes, accessory glands and ducts to deliver sperm of normal quanity and quality. Fertility and potency are not correlated or related and may be divergent in the same male animal. Infertility or sterility in males is usually characterized by normal sexual desire and the ability to copulate and ejaculate, but a complete or abnormally high percentage of failure of fertilization or conception, or delayed returns to estrum indicating early embryonic death in the females. This incapacity or reduced capacity to fertilize may be characterized by either of two findings following a careful semen examination. In one the semen is essentially normal on examination, and in the other, the semen is abnormal in morphology, concentration, motility, or other qualities. The former condition is often difficult to explain satisfactorily with our present knowledge; however, recent findings have indicated several promising leads.

Impotentia Generandi Associated with Apparently Normal Semen Production in cattle has been reviewed in Chapter XIII in the discussion of herd infertility, "repeat breeders," or failure of conception in females due to service by bulls infected with brucellosis, vibriosis, trichomoniasis, and possibly IBR-IPV virus, mycoplasma or other organisms. Active brucellosis in a herd of cattle is associated with symptoms of infertility; and the intrauterine insemination of brucella-infected semen usually results in infertility. Boars infected with **Br. suis** may carry and transmit the organisms to the female at coitus resulting in early embryonic death and signs of infertility as well as abortions. VanderSluis, after examining 828 bulls for infertility, reported 374, or 45.2 per cent, affected with vibriosis or trichomoniasis. In his series of cases, however, only 15 of the 374 bulls had trichomoniasis. Boyd reported that 60 per cent of 105 herds in all parts of Sweden were or had been infected with vibriosis. The incidence of vibriosis in naturally-bred herds in the United States is probably equally high.

Frank and Bryner investigated a number of herds with infertility resembling vibriosis, but without finding the cause. VanderSluis reported on herd infertility problems arising in 47 herds in which no diagnosis could be made because no pathological conditions were found in the bulls or cows to explain the sterility. Errors or deficiencies in management, as discussed in Chapter XIII may be the cause of widespread infertility in some herds.

Abnormal acrosomes, knobbed spermatozoa, **related** to defective spermiogenesis involving the Golgi apparatus has been described in bulls, boars and dogs as a cause of infertility in semen with normal motility and concentration of spermatozoa. Certain of the stains or techniques used for preparing spermatozoa for morphological examination do not reveal this defect; while others such nigrosin eosin, India ink or Giemsa show a refractile unstained or lightly stained area in the anterior pole or acrosome of the head of the spermatozoa. Wells and Awa have reported on an eosin B. and fast green stain for the acrosome of spermatozoa that permit examination by a light microscope. Bane reported that certain sterile Swedish Landrace boars had as many as 80 to 90 per cent of their spermatozoa with an acrosomal, knobbed defect. He cited Madden as reporting that boars having 50 per cent of their spermatozoa with acrosomal defects had low fertility. Phase contrast microscopy revealed these defective acrosomes. Sometimes the anterior border of the porcine spermatozoa was flattened due to a protrusion and bending over of the acrosome, Bane. Nearly all of the spermatozoa in some bulls were affected. The defective acrosome rendered the sperm cell incapable of penetrating and fertilizing the ovum, Buttle and Hancock. Blom and Birch-Anderson and Bane have illustrated the nature of this defect in bulls as seen under the electron microscope. This defect in spermiogenesis is apparently due to an autosomal recessive sex-linked defect in Friesian cattle, Donald and Hancock. McEntee has reported this defect in a sterile Boxer dog and Charolais and Holstein bulls in the U.S. (See Figure 178) Saacke and coworkers reported this defect in two subfertile bulls, a Holstein and a Jersey. On artificial insemination they had nonreturn rates of 40 and 59 per cent, respectively. Three of four sons of the Holstein bull were similarly affected. In the latter Holstein bull 0.3 to 6.2 percent of the spermatozoa had knobbed acrosomes, 1.7 to 9.1 percent had ruffled acrosomes and 2.1 to 21.9 percent had an incomplete or missing portion of the acrosome. This was a defect in spermiogenesis and could be seen in the spermatids.

Aamdal reported on two nearly sterile bulls that had semen with normal motility and concentration of spermatozoa. After staining with opal blue and examining the stained cells with a phase-contrast microscope, **eversion of the galea capitis and crater-shaped depressions in the nucleus** were found. Bane and Nicander described apparently similar invaginations of the nuclear envelope in the bull and the boar that were associated with a severe disturbance of spermiogenesis with many other abnormalities of the sperm cell. Feulgen stain and phase-contrast microscopy revealed these invaginations to be located near the anterior border of the postnuclear cap in the equatorial segment of the sperm head. A sterile Ayrshire bull produced sperm cells with normal motility and concentration but with up to 20 per cent abaxial tails and 17 per cent swollen midpieces, Aughey and Renton. Even though the concentration and motility of sperm cells in the ejaculate is normal, careful staining and examination of cells from infertile males is indicated.

Recent studies in cytogenetics have shown that gene or chromosome defects may occur at the time of meiosis and result in infertility. An apparently normal semen picture may accompany these defects. Knudsen reported on certain bulls with excellent appearing semen in which genital infections were excluded but a low fertility was present due to intrachromosomal aberrations. The spermiogenic epithelium showed a cytologic picture indicative of structural changes in the chromosomes including translocations and inversions. Although affected spermatozoa may fertilize the ovum, the zygote will often lack a balanced gene complement and death often results at an early stage of gestation or this defective chromosome complement may be carried into the next generation where usually about 50 per cent of the male individuals are affected with infertility. Some offspring from affected bulls may be completely normal. Generally the greater the number of genes involved in translocation or inversion the greater the sterility. If only a few genes are involved in small intrachromosomal aberrations fertility may be only slightly lowered. In affected bulls diagnosis at present can only be made with an electron microscopic study of the germinal epithelium. By this technique acquired disturbances in spermatogenesis can be distinguished from the congenital or constitutional disturbances. Knudsen indicated that these forms of sterility represented only a small number of all those that actually occurred. Gustavsson reported on a translocation defect of the chromosomes in the Swedish Red and White breed of cattle. About 14 percent of the cattle were heterozygotes and 0.34 percent were homozygotes for the translocation. Daughters of translocation sires exhibited a greater infertility rate, apparently due to early embryonic deaths, than daughters of normal sires.

Henricson and Backstrom analyzed the metaphase and anaphase figures from the meiotic divisions of the spermatocytes in the seminiferous epithelium in 4 boars and 7 bulls with normal semen pictures that were relatively or completely sterile. Two boars had acrosomal defects of their spermatozoa. They concluded that even though some chromosome changes were apparent, the primary or principal cause of defective spermatzoa was to be found in the nonchromosomal structures, namely the divisional apparatus.

Leuchtenberger and coworkers reported that the variation in the mean amount of DNA or deoxyribonucleic acid in the spermatozoa of infertile bulls was greater than in fertile bulls. Many infertile bulls had lower DNA values of the spermatozoan nucleus than fertile bulls. Salisbury and coworkers, using essentially the same measuring techniques based on Feulgen staining of spermatozoa, showed that a marked decrease in DNA content of bovine spermatozoa occurs during storage in semen extenders. They associated the loss of DNA in stored semen with an increase in delayed returns caused by embryonic mortality. Recently Gledhill using different methods demonstrated there was no difference in the mean amount of DNA between fertile and infertile bulls. He reported that the infertility present in the 8 bulls in his studies that had essentially normal semen pictures except for a slightly lowered average motility might be due to an altered, immature or atypical basic nuclear protein due to a defect in the sperm cell chromatin occurring during spermiogenesis that possibly interfered with normal penetration of the sperm cell into ova and/or activation of ova. The DNA was not primarily involved in this defect. The difference in the staining properties of the altered nuclear protein to Feulgen stain in infertile bulls may account for the difference between the DNA content of spermatozoa in infertile and fertile bulls as reported by Leuchtenberger et al. and Salisbury et al..

MacLeod reported on a group of stallions with impaired fertility but which had semen of normal quality. He indicated the deficiency in these stallions might be related to some inherent enzymatic disturbance that resulted in the early death of the sperm cell in the female genital tract.

These above preliminary studies on infertile males with essentially normal semen and spermatozoa have indicated that defects in genes and chromosomes especially during meiosis, and developmental defects of the sperm cell during spermiogenesis may occur. Future studies in the fields of cytogenetics, cellular biology and electron microscopy will undoubtedly further elucidate the mechanisms of male infertility occasionally associated with an apparently normal or nearly normal semen picture.

Impotentia generandi associated with abnormal semen production is due to pathology of the testes, the epididymis, the vas deferens, the accessory glands and the urethra whereby sufficient numbers of healthy fertile sperm cells are not deposited properly at the time of coitus to cause the fertilization of the ovum and the normal development of the embryo. Abnormal semen may be due to congenital or hereditary causes or to acquired causes. The latter are the most common. The former is highly important in the selection of sires because of the genetic implications. Occasionally both groups of causes are involved in an infertile male.

Pathology of the Testes

Prior to the work of Lagerlof in 1934, studies on the pathology of the testis were incomplete and generally limited to the more obvious and severe clinical lesions such as orchitis and fibrosis. Since then a great amount of work has been done on correlating semen abnormalities with testicular pathology. The two are closely related and semen examinations reflect fairly accurately the conditions present in the seminiferous tubules of the testes. However, it is necessary to consider that it requires about 60 days from the first stages of spermatogenesis to the ejaculation of spermatozoa.

Lagerlof divided the pathological conditions affecting the testis proper into testicular hypoplasia, testicular degeneration, testicular fibrosis, and testicular inflammations. The author believes that since testicular fibrosis usually follows testicular degeneration and testicular inflammation, and since testicular inflammation usually produces an acute, severe testicular degeneration, the testicular fibrosis and testicular inflammations should be considered under testicular degeneration. If this classification is accepted then the two most common changes occurring in the testes causing disturbed spermatogenesis are hypoplasia, which is congenital or hereditary, and degeneration of the seminiferous tubules, which is usually acquired but may be predisposed by genetic defects, weaknesses, or inherent constitution.

Testicular pathology due to congenital or hereditary causes includes hypoplasia, certain defects in the seminiferous tubules and sperm cells including cytogenetic and chromosomal defects, cryptorchidism and inguinal hernias. In the latter two conditions interference with the normal thermal regulation of the testes is the immediate cause of the sterility or infertility.

Hypoplasia of the testes is observed as a unilateral or bilateral condition at the time of puberty or later in all of our domestic animals but is noted most commonly in bulls, rams, boars and stallions. Lagerlof described testicular hypoplasia as a cause of 23 per cent of the testicular pathology in Swedish bulls; he did not include in this total the cases of inherited testicular hypoplasia of the Swedish Highland breed. This is a slightly higher than the 12 to 17 per cent given by other workers, Blom and Christensen, Haq, and VanderSluis. Lagerlof reported on the hereditary type of hypoplasia affecting as many as 25 to 30 per cent of the male and female animals of the Swedish Highland breed, a polled breed. Settergren also showed that gonadal hypoplasia in this breed was largely limited to those cattle that were nearly all, 90 per cent or more, white. Cattle with black ears were not affected. In these cattle hypoplasia of the left testis occurred in about 25 per cent of all the bulls, in the right testis in 1 per cent, and in both testes in 4 to 5 per cent. This condition in cattle is due to a single recessive autosomal gene with incomplete penetrance, Eriksson. A similar widespread condition affecting the gonads of both males and females of a breed has not been described outside of Sweden. Most workers agree that testicular hypoplasia is congenital and possibly hereditary in origin and is caused by a marked lack of or reduction in spermatogonia in the gonads during fetal life. Hypoplasia may be partial or total due to a failure of germinal cells to develop in the yolk sac, failure to migrate to the gonad, failure to multiply in the gonad or extensive degeneration of early germinal cells after they have entered the gonad. Unilateral or bilateral hypoplasia in bulls of both beef and dairy breeds and in other species have been observed occasionally in the United States but the incidence is generally low and the condition is sporadic. (See Figure 177 and 178) In a few instances a familial trend was noted. It has been reported that dwarfs or beef cattle with a dwarf tendency are likely to show evidence of testicular hypoplasia. Carroll and Scott have reported that some valuable beef bulls with unilateral testicular hypoplasia have been used as breeders and may produce as many as 20 per cent of offspring with hypoplasia and poor quality semen.

The symptoms of testicular hypoplasia in bulls vary greatly. In most cases sexual desire is excellent and coitus is prompt. Because of this the owners may not suspect the sterility for some time. The degree of either unilateral or bilateral testicular hypoplasia varies from nearly complete hypoplasia and sterility to only slight and often unsuspected hypoplasia. Lowered conception rates are often evident in bilaterally affected males.

Severe testicular hypoplasia is usually observed in young bulls one to two years of age. In sterile bulls with bilateral hypoplastic testes the semen is usually clear and watery with few or no spermatozoa. If the ejaculate is centrifuged and the sediment stained, giant cells and oftentimes medusa cells or ciliated cells from the efferent tubules may be observed. Giant cells or multinuclear cells with 6 to 8 nuclei apparently result from incomplete maturation divisions of the primary spermatocytes. The nuclei divide but the cytoplasmic divisions are not completed, Cupps and Laben. These cells are seen in testicular hypoplasia and severe degeneration. The sexual organs develop normally except for the affected testes. Histologically the seminiferous tubules are very underdeveloped, with usually only the basal layer of cells being present.

Males which are severely affected are nearly sterile, but an occasional conception may occur in females bred to them. The semen picture shows a low concentration of spermatozoa, usually less than 75,000 per cmm, low motility, many abnormal spermatozoa, and the possible presence of a few giant cells. The affected testes are one-third to two-thirds normal size, but are usually firmer, or occasionally softer, than normal. Histologic section reveals that one-half to two-thirds of the seminiferous tubules are undeveloped. Varying degrees of spermatogenesis may be present from spermatogonia, spermiocytes, spermatids, to abnormal and normal mature spermatozoa. Carroll and Ball reported on three types of testicular hypoplasia in 3 inbred lines of Hereford cattle. The first type was characterized by seminiferous tubles lined only with Sertoli cells. These bulls were sterile and the line became extinct. In the second line of bulls about 30 to 40 percent of the tubules were normal but only a few tubules were stage 8 with sperm cells lining the lumen. Reduced spermatogenesis was present. In the third line the bulls had reduced spermatogenesis, conglutination of spermatids and many giant cells. In another line of cattle the bulls had large firm testes but reduced sperm cell output due to blockage of the tubules before they entered the rete resulting in sperm stasis and atrophy of the seminiferous epithelium.

In some bulls with a moderate to slight amount of testicular hypoplasia the conception rate is low, about 20 to 40 per cent. The testicles may appear nearly normal in size and consistency. The spermatozoan concentration is from 100,000 to 500,000 per cmm, the motility is usually low, and the number of pathological or abnormal spermatozoa is high, 30 per cent or greater.

Depending upon the degree of hypoplasia, affected bulls will have a small firm epididymis especially in the tail region indicating reduced spermatogenesis and low gonadal sperm reserves. This will also be revealed by rapidly decreasing concentrations of spermatozoa in successive ejaculates, Haq. Slight or mild cases of hypoplasia with reduced spermatozoan concentration and motility predispose the bull to testicular degeneration. In some bulls sterility due to mild testicular hypoplasia may not be observed or become apparent until the bulls reach 3 to 4 years of age.

The spermatic cords of hypoplastic testicles are shorter as the testes are less heavy and the scrotum smaller than in normal males. In obese bulls with much fat in the inguinal region the thermal insulation so provided these hypoplastic testes may contribute to the infertility.

Testicular hypoplasia may be erroneously diagnosed in young immature males that are underdeveloped or are retarded in growth at the generally accepted time of puberty for the species. The fertility and the percentage of normal spermatozoa produced increased from puberty to two years of age in beef bulls, Martig and Almquist. The diagnosis of testicular hypoplasia should not be made before two years of age in the bull and horse or before one year of age in the boar, ram, dog or cat, unless the hypoplasia is marked and the male is well-grown. Adams and Swierstra reported infertility in young 6- to 8-month boars when placed with gilts or sows. This may be due to immaturity, timidity, inexperience or possibly overuse. To correct the former causes a period of conditioning of young boars by allowing them to be "across the fence" from the sow herd for a period of time is essential. Young boars may only ejaculate 2 to 3 billion spermatozoa when they are bred 2 to 3 times a week. If they are bred more often, the number of spermatozoa ejaculated may drop below 2 billion and infertility result. At 10 to 12 months of age most boars have matured sufficiently so that large numbers of spermatozoa are produced and infertility due to oligospermia is not a problem.

Gunn and coworkers reported that testicular hypoplasia and atrophy were observed in about 3.4 per cent of 9,000 rams examined in Australia. The condition was usually unilateral and of a permanent nature. The spermatic cord was usually short and the affected testis was drawn up toward the inguinal canal. The consistency of the testis was either soft and flabby, or hard, indurated and fibrotic. The testes were decreased in size. The semen was always abnormal, with an increased number of abnormal spermatozoa and small, round, non-nucleated, germinal epithelial cells. An association between this type of testicular hypoplasia and unilateral cryptorchidism was suggested. The fibrotic small testes in some of the rams described above might have been due to trauma or other causes, producing secondary atrophy.

Holst reported that sterility in boars is relatively uncommon. In 30 boars with testicular pathology, 8 or 26.6 per cent had hypoplasia. These were young boars that were sterile or of very low fertility. In the limited number of cases reported, Holst indicated that a genetic or hereditary factor was probably present in hypoplasia in boars. In cases in which semen examination was possible, spermatozoa were either absent or present in low concentrations of 20,000 to 70,000 per cmm. The number of pathologic spermatozoa was not high but there was a large percentage of unripe sperm cells with a protoplasmic droplet on the middle piece. The motility was usually poor. The average weight of the hypoplastic testes was 226 to 240 gm, while normal testes weighed 594 to 632 gm. Histologic examination showed hypoplasia varying from only a single layer of germinal cells to widespread changes in the seminal epithelium.

MacLeod cited one young stallion with a very low spermatozoan concentration, poor motility, and a low conception rate; but the clinical examination of the testes was not reported.

Bloom and Williams reported that eunuchoidism, complete lack of sexual desire, may rarely occur in dogs and bulls with testes in the normal position or in unilateral or bilateral cryptorchidism. The testes are small and atrophic. The interstitial cells are hypoplastic or fail to secrete androgen. Testosterone given parenterally will produce secondary sex characteristics but the male relapses to the eunuchoid state if injections are discontinued. Taylor and coworkers reported on hypoplasia associated with a decrease in interstitial cell activity and a failure of normal antler growth in white-tailed deer in southwestern U.S. Testicular hypoplasia in the dog and cat is seldom described. Cheville described gonadal hypoplasia in a strain of grey collies that also had abnormalities of the blood, eyes and digestive tract.

In the diagnosis of testicular hypoplasia, especially where it may be associated with a lack of sexual drive, the stage of development of the male and whether or not puberty has occurred must be considered, since testicular hypoplasia may be diagnosed erroneously in young, poorly-fed, slow-maturing males.

The prognosis in testicular hypoplasia is poor. Affected animals should not be used for breeding because the condition may be hereditary. Severely affected animals are sterile or highly infertile. Mildly or moderately affected animals may have only a lowered fertility but are more prone to early testicular degeneration. The numbers of motile normal spermatozoa per ejaculate or insemination largely determine the fertility of the animal in question not the percentages of the dead, poorly viable, immotile and abnormal spermatozoa.

The treatment of testicular hypoplasia in animals has been unsuccessful. The germinal epithelium of these affected animals apparently cannot respond to gonadotropic therapy because spermatogonia are reduced in numbers or lacking.

Hereditary or Congenital Sperm Cell Defects, Male Intersexes and Cryptorchidism

Sperm Cell Defects, possibly heritable, have been described in male domestic animals in which large numbers of spermatozoa produced by a male are similarly affected.

Returned tails and narrow heads were reported by Blake to be hereditary in certain bovine families of the Jersey breed exhibiting much sterility. Swanson and Boyd also reported on infertile Jersey bulls with coiled or returned tails with a lowered motility rate. With repeated frequent ejaculations the numbers of abnormal sperm cells was greatly reduced. The defect in these bulls was apparently genetic.

Dag-defect—Blom described 2 full brothers in the Danish Jersey breed that had a low initial spermatozoan motility of 10 to 15 per cent and very poor fertility. These bulls had about 40 per cent of their spermatozoa with strongly coiled, folded or split tails, the Dag-defect. The fibers in the axial filament were normal in the testis but abnormal when the cells reached the cauda epididymis. Coubrough and Barker also reported a midpiece abnormality in 3 unrelated bulls somewhat similar to the "Dag defect". These bulls were sterile. Settergren also studied an infertile Holstein bull with a normal volume and concentration of semen but only 10 to 20 percent motility. About 25 percent of the spermatozoa had tail abnormalities somewhat resembling the Dag defect with an aberrant, defective arrangement of the fibrils. There was no evident abnormality of the seminiferous epithelium.

Corkscrew sperm defect—Blom also described a nongenetic defect seen in the Red Danish, Jersey, Friesian and Abderdeen Angus breeds due to an irregular distribution of the mitochondrial sheath together with a high incidence of persistent proximal droplets in affected sperm cells.

Pseudo-droplet defect—A third defect Blom described was the "pseudo-droplet defect" seen in 5 related Friesian bulls. From 7 to 26 per cent of spermatozoa in affected bulls had rounded or elongated, thickened areas on the midpiece. Reduced motility and infertility increased as the bulls became older.

Lack of intact sperm cells was described by Hancock and Rollinson and Jones in Guernsey bulls with a history of complete sterility. The ejaculates of these bulls contained practically no intact spermatozoa, but only free heads and tails. Motility was low. Intact spermatozoa were fewer than 5 per cent of the total. All heads showed a deep indentation marking the point of separation from the tails. The middle piece was thickened and varying

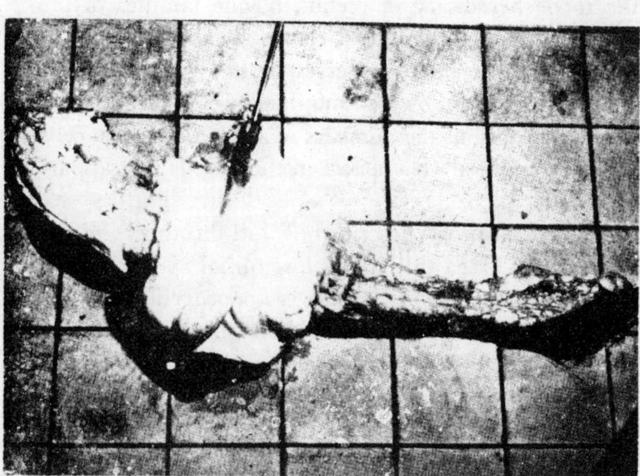

Figure 176. Bilateral Testicular Hypoplasia in a Fat 3-Year-Old Angus Bull.

Figure 177. Bilateral Testicular Hypoplasia in a 2-year-old Holstein Bull.

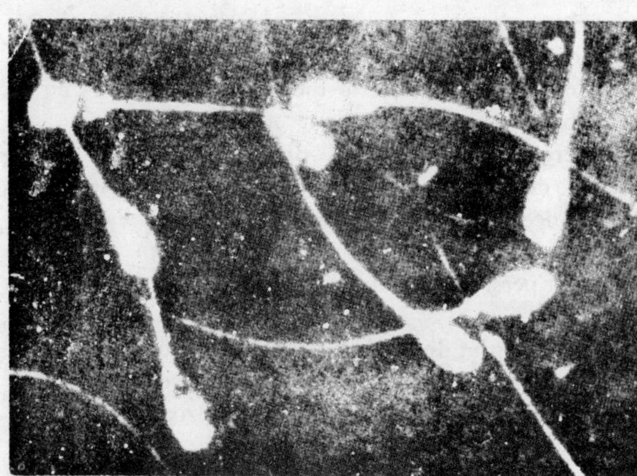

Figure 178. Abnormal Acrosomes or Knobbed Spermatozoa in a Sterile Bull. (Courtesy K. McEntee)

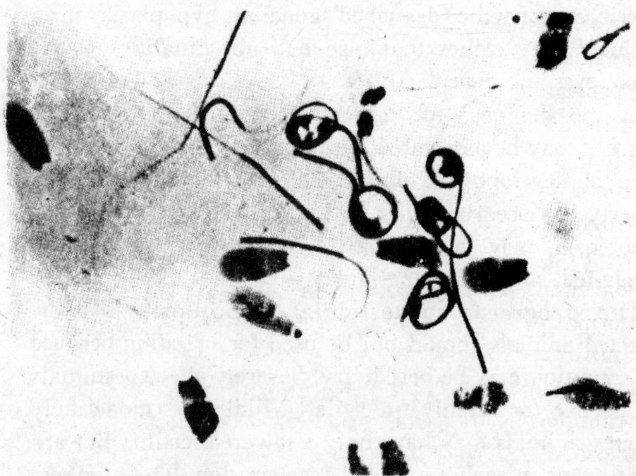

Figure 179. Lack of Intact Sperm Cells and Coiled Tails in a Sterile Guernsey Bull. (Spermatozoan motility was nearly absent)

degrees of coiling of the middle piece and tail occurred. Hancock reported that this disintegration or separation of the heads and tails of spermatozoa in the sterile Guernsey bulls was associated with the migration of the protoplasmic droplet from the proximal to the distal end of the middle piece. This occurred in the head of the epididymis. While there was no conclusive evidence that the defect was inherited, the evidence was very suggestive. Williams reported on eight Hereford bulls with low fertility that had a high percentage of tailless heads.

Acrosomal defects or knobbed spermatozoa have been described in bulls, boars and dogs. This defect has been reported as due to an autosomal recessive gene in Holstein Friesian bulls. As described previously, certain stains and techniques are very helpful in diagnosing this defect in what often appears to be a normal semen sample associated with complete sterility or infertility, Bane, Blom and Birch-Anderson, Donald and Hancock, and McEntee.

Deficiency in tail development and lack of motility was reported by MacLeod and McGee in stallions of one Thoroughbred blood line in which the condition might have been genetic in nature. The author has studied two stallions with congenitally lowered fertility with 50 to 75 per cent of their spermatozoa having a single abnormality; in one stallion, a Standardbred, a grossly defective midpiece and the other, a Thoroughbred, an abaxial attachment of the midpiece to the head. In stallions abaxial attachment of the midpiece to the head of the spermatozoa is commonly observed and this usually is not associated with infertility in the stallion and boar as it often is in the other species of animals, Settergren, Bierschwal and Hendrikse. (See Semen Evalution) Aughey and Renton reported on a sterile Ayrshire bull with up to 20 per cent abaxial tails and 17 percent swollen midpieces; sperm cell concentration and motility was normal.

Inbreeding generally results in reduced fertility accompanied by an increase in the number of abnormal seminiferous tubules, lowered semen quality, and hypoplasia, McNitt and coworkers, and Carroll. There were wide differences in fertility between inbred lines of cattle from a few with excellent fertility to those in which the line died out because of infertility. The response to inbreeding with respect to fertility is variable with each line or family. Inbred lines usually undergo a period of infertility or sterility and if the line does not become lost due to deleterious genes, the fertility of the remaining animals in the line is often fairly satisfactory, Krehbill et al.. Gregory, Mead, Regan, and Rollins reported that 5 inbred, related bulls showed a low sperm cell concentration and a large number of pathological spermatozoa with a reduced motility. They considered that the infertility in these bulls might be due to an autosomal recessive gene. In identical twin bulls Bane has reported on the great similarity of the semen and spermatozoa, duration of motility, and frequency of abnormal sperm heads. He concluded that the great difference between identical twin pairs of bulls and the similarity of each bull of a twin pair indicated that the differences between the twin pairs as well as the similarities within the pairs, were genetic, since all were reared under similar conditions. Young reported that Hereford, Angus, Holstein and Shorthorn bulls had the best conception rate in England. In the United States Guernsey bulls generally have a lower conception rate than other breeds.

Cytogenetic disturbances in spermatogenesis caused two abnormalities in the primary spermatocytes including (1) "stickness" of chromosomes in which they failed to separate at anaphase, and (2) a pyknotic nucleus and multiple spindle formation due to a dysfunction of the nechanism of cell division due to extra centrosome divisions resulting in the formation of giant cells with a number of nuclei, Knudsen. In both conditions the semen was thin and watery. In the former the semen centrifugate was made up almost entirely of pyknotic nuclei and was characteristic for this condition seen most often in the Swedish Lowland Holstein Friesian breed, where intensive inbreeding had occurred. The latter condition occurred in only a few bulls. The semen centrifugate was composed of giant cells and pyknotic nuclei and these affected bulls belonged to the same family so a recessive gene might have been involved. As mentioned previously Gustavsson described a chromosomal translocation occurring in Swedish cattle that resulted in a degree of infertility characterized by early embryonic deaths. Probably many other primary cytogenetic disturbances of spermatogenesis occur and will be described in the future.

The male tortoise-shell cat is uncommon and theoretically can't exist because the gene for yellow color is carried on the female, X chromosome. However, the rare male tortoise-shell cats may have an abnormal sex chromosome constitution of XXY resembling the more common Klinefelter's syndrome in man. These male cats have small testes and are sterile due to failure of the seminiferous tubules to develop. Loughman et al. reported on 3 male tricolor cats with an XY/XXY bone marrow mosaicism. All had small testes and one affected cat had no spermatogonia in the seminiferous epithelium. The possible incidence of male to female tricolored cats was 1:200. They cited Thuline and Norby as reporting on 5 other types of chromosome combinations in tricolored male cats: XXY, XX/XY, XX/XX/XXY, XX/XXY and XX/XXY.

Very rare fertile male tortoise-shell cats have been described and they are believed to be XX/XY chimeras, Biggers and McFeely. A true feline hermaphrodite with one blue and one yellow eye had a cryptorchid testis and a normal ovary. This cat was shown by Thuline to have both XX and XY cells.

Infertility in hybrids usually occurs when there are major differences in the chromosomes of the parents. Minor gene differences may be overcome so fertility is possible. The failure of gametogenesis in some hybrids is apparently due to asynapsis during the first meiotic division of the primary spermatocyte. Sterility is more common in the male hybrids. Even in some intraspecies crosses where the chromosomes are nearly similar, hybrid fertility, particularly of males, may not result, Benirschke. A common example of the above hybrid infertility in domestic animals is the horse and ass cross producing the hybrid mule, with chromosome numbers of 64, 62 and 63, respectively. Hancock has attempted hybridization of goat and sheep and obtained conception but all the embryos died.

Gilmore and Deaken reported that in the bison x domestic cattle cross, as well as the yak x domestic cattle, and yak x zebu crosses, the bulls are likely to be sterile. This was believed due to the inheritance of the small, thick scrotum from the bison or yak causing an elevated scrotal temperature that adversely affected the large testes inherited in these hybrids from the domestic cattle or zebu that required a lower testicular temperature for the normal functioning of the seminiferous tubules. Recent cytogenetic studies indicate that chromosomal incompatabilities are more likely a cause for the infertility of these hybrid males, Young.

In bovine twins of unlike sex the female twin or freemartin is sterile due to the vascular anastomosis with the male twin which is usually considered to be normal. Dunn and coworkers studied chimeric bulls cotwin to freemartins that were raised and used in AI studs. They found 2 of the bulls were sterile and 2 were infertile. These bulls had noninflammatory degenerative changes in their testes. One of the infertile bulls had a skewed sex ratio of 29 males to 71 females suggestive for germ cell chimerism. Further study on bulls cotwin to freemartins is indicated.

Male intersexes are invariably sterile. According to Biggers and McFeely intersexuality may arise from aberrations of genetic or chromosomal origin, aberrations of gonadogenesis, and reversal of sex involving the accessory or external genital structures. Male pseudohermaphroditism is found in the caprine, porcine and occasionally the bovine, equine and other species. True hermaphroditism is uncommon. In the Saanen and Toggenburg breeds of goats the incidence of intersexes vary from 5.8 to 14.9 per cent. They have a wide range of abnormality from phenotypically nearly normal males to nearly normal females. This condition is caused by a single recessive gene linked to the dominant gene for polledness. No case of a horned pseudohermaphrodite has been described. Most affected goats have testes, often intra-abdominal, and external genitalia of an intermediate type. They are genetic females (XX) with positive sex chromatin. Soller et al. reported on a high incidence of infertility in polled Saanen goats in which the recessive character caused pseudohermaphroditism in female goats and hypoplasia, sperm granulomas of the epididymis and a high percentage of sperm cell abnormalities in some male goats. The infertility problem in Saanen goats could be largely avoided by raising for breeding purposes only those goats with one horned parent.

Intersexes in pigs are common but not as common as in goats. They also are of the male pseudohermaphrodite type. The cause is probably a recessive gene. The affected animals are genetic females, the testes are invariably intra-abdominal and externally a characteristic "fish hook" vulva with a prominent "clitoris" or phallus is present. Male pseudohermaphrodites are also occasionally observed in cattle, horses and dogs. Gilmore cited Yapp's report of 3 affected sons of a Brown Swiss bull.

Cryptorchidism in animals, if bilateral, results in sterility. In horses cryptorchids may be spoken of as "ridglings," "rigs" or "originals." Unilateral cryptorchidism is more common and usually results in near normal fertility because of normal sperm production from the testis located in the scrotum. The term "monorchidism" is incorrect. Cryptorchidism or incomplete descent of the testis or retention of the testis occurs in all domestic species but is seen most commonly in stallions, boars, dogs, less commonly in rams and bucks, uncommonly in cattle, and rarely in cats. The undescended testis may be located anywhere from just caudal to the kidney to within the inguinal canal. Many abdominal testes are located close to the internal inguinal ring. Often the loosely attached epididymis in the horse may have descended into the inguinal canal.

Occasionally testes not in the abdominal cavity, inguinal canal or scrotum may be located ectopically under the skin of the ventral caudal abdomen, alongside the penis, or rarely in the femoral canal or in the perineal region. This is more commonly the case in male pseudo hermaphrodites where no scrotum is present.

In some cases where the testis is retained in the inguinal canal it will descend spontaneously into the scrotum in a few months to a year after birth. In a few cases in colts, testes may be descended into the scrotum at birth and later become cryptorchid and located in the inguinal canal. All retained or cryptorchid testes are small, soft and flaccid weighing in the horse 25 to 131 gms; normal descended testes usually weigh 170 to 325 gm., Bishop and coworkers. No spermatozoa are produced by the retained testis but well-developed or degenerate seminiferous tubules may be present, McEntee. Spermatogenesis is completely inhibited by the elevation of the temperature of the affected testis. The interstitial or Leydig cells are not affected so sexual activity is normal or even exaggerated in bilateral cryptorchids. Cryptorchid animals should never be used for breeding.

The Technical Development Committee in England reported that cryptorchidism in the horse is inherited in a dominant manner while in the other species it is a recessive trait. Unilateral cryptorchidism more often affects the right testes especially in dogs, possibly because the right testis develops in the embryo a greater distance from the scrotum, Brodey and Martin. In the horse Lowe and Higginbotham reported on 417 cryptorchid animals, 388 were unilaterally and 29, 7 percent, were bilaterally affected. Testes were located abdominally in 251, 60.2 percent, of the horses, inguinally in 163, 39.1 percent and in both sites in 3, 0.7 percent. These figures may be somewhat biased as many cases were referred by other veterinarians. Bishop and coworkers in 78 cryptorchid horses reported, 61 percent inguinal and 49 percent abdominal sites for the retained testes. In the report by Lowe and Higginbotham abdominal testes were found on the left side in 178 cases, 65 percent and on the right side in 93 cases, 30 percent. In Bishop's report 29 abdominal testes were on the left side, 59 percent, and 20, 41 percent, on the right. Sixteen of these cases were bilaterally affected. Bishop and coworkers also reported that 3 of the cryptorchid testes contained teratomas or cysts, two of these were abdominal. They reported on 15 castrates with attitudes of an intact male from which they removed long spermatic cords and signs of maleness ceased. No testicular tissue was left attached to the cords but possibly Leydig, accessory or heterotropic testicular or adrenal tissue rests that produced testosterone may have been present in the cord. Removal of cryptorchid equine testes has been well-described by Arthur, Adams, and Lowe and Higginbotham; the latter described a paramedian laparotomy approach for abdominal testes.

In dogs cryptorchidism is seen most commonly in the brachycephalic breeds including: Boxers, Pomeranians, Dachshunds, Sealyhams, Cairn Terriers, and also in Whippets, Chows, Cocker Spaniels, Poodles, and others. The incidence of cryptorchid testes in dogs in England was reported to be between .05 to 0.1 per cent. In most dogs the testes are in the inguinal canal at birth and descend into the scrotum during the first week after birth. In some dogs the testes don't descend till near puberty, Ashdown. Possibly because dogs are maintained intact for many years, retained testes are predisposed to neoplasms. Sertoli cell tumors and seminomas in undescended testes tend to be more malignant, McEntee, Brodey and Martin, Brodey and Reif, and Reif and Brodey. The latter reported a highly significant association of cryptorchidism and testicular tumors; 58, 53 percent of 108 Sertoli-cell tumors and 23, 33.8 percent of 68 seminomas were in retained testes. These tumors affected the retained or abdominal right testes more frequently than the retained left testes. Reif and Brodey reported that dogs with scrotal testicular tumors were older than dogs developing cryptorchid testicular tumors. Signs of feminization were present in 16.7 percent, 50 percent, and 70 percent of the dogs with Sertoli cell tumors in the scrotum, inguinal canal and abdominal cavity, respectively. This may be due to the earlier detection and removal of affected testes in the external sites. Charny and Wolgin reported that tumors of undescended testes in man occurred 50 times more often than tumors of scrotal testes. Early removal of undescended testes is recommended.

McPhee and Buckley stated that cryptorchidism in swine is a monogenic sex-limited recessive. To eliminate this condition in swine or other species all parents of cryptorchid animals should be discarded as breeders. The incidence in swine may reach 1 to 2 per cent in some herds. If affected pigs are fattened rapidly and sold at or before six months of age very little or no boar odor will develop in the carcass.

Warwick has described the rapid progress possible in the elimination of this defect in flocks of Angora goats by rigid culling of parents and even close relatives of affected animals. Mann has compiled an excellent bibliography on cryptorchidism in dogs and other animals. Wheat has reported on a few cases of left-sided cryptorchidism in Hereford cattle in which the condition appeared to be due to a dominant gene with variable expressivity. Cryptorchidism is common in male fetal monsters and other defective individuals.

Treatment of cryptorchid animals, especially those where breeding is to be considered, should be discouraged. In humans where treatment is more frequently undertaken Charney and Wolgin reported that only those testes that would ultimately descend spontaneously would descend after gonadotropin therapy. Orchiopexy has proven to be a failure in producing satisfactory spermatogenesis.

Torsion or rotation of the descended testis on a horizontal axis is observed most commonly in the stallion, especially trotting Standardbreds. The testis is freely moveable within the scrotum. Often the tail of the epididymis is lateral instead of caudal. On assuming a fast trotting gait pain is evident by abduction or "hiking" of the leg on the side of the affected testis. Some affected stallions appear unable to draw the testis out of the scrotum and into the inguinal canal. Suspensories are of limited value and unilateral or bilateral castration is indicated. Because of their loose attachment, torsion of the retained abdominal or inguinal testis may rarely occur. This is usually accompanied by severe pain, swelling and congestion of the involved organ; it is reported most commonly in the dog and stallion and rarely in the pig.

Imperfect descent of the testes in cattle not associated with cryptorchidism has resulted in testes located horizontally and fairly high in the scrotum. This may be due to the attachment of the cremaster muscle to the caudal aspect of the testis, fixation of the distal end of the scrotum to the perineal region, VanderSluis, or lower than normal attachment of the gubernaculum. (See Figure 180) This imperfect descent of the testes may result in impaired fertility with degeneration and atrophy due to difficulty of the thermoregulatory mechanism of the testes to operate properly. Carl reported that this condition might be genetic. Stallions that carry the testes high in the external inguinal ring may have low fertility for the same reason.

Multiple heterotropic nodules of testicular tissue scattered over the peritoneum have been described in a few pigs, Todd et al.. These may be confused with a malignant neoplasm

Scrotal or inguinal hernias, if large, may seriously depress fertility by markedly interfering with the normal thermoregulatory function of the scrotum and testes. (see testicular degeneration). If the inguinal ring and hernia is small there is a greater chance for strangulation of the intestine. Inguinal hernia is considered a common hereditary defect in horses and pigs; it is less common in bulls, dogs and rams, and rare in the cat. Warwick reported that the incidence in swine was greatly increased from 7.5 to 43.2 percent in two generations by selective inbreeding. It was most common in the left side of the scrotum. Hernias usually appeared from birth to 30 days of age. It was considered to be a double recessive character. In cattle Noordsy, Milne and Kingrey reported left-sided scrotal hernias were most common especially in the Hereford or Polled Hereford breeds. (See Figure 181) In an inbred strain of Basenjii about 75 per cent of the pups had inguinal hernias, Fox. Animals with inguinal hernias should be castrated and not used for breeding. Reduction of the hernia and closure of the hernial ring can be performed through the inguinal canal, through an incision in the abdominal wall just cranial and medial to the ring or by a flank incision above the ring.

References

Impotentia Generandi, Failure to Fertilize with Apparently Normal Semen

Aamdal, J. (1951) Changes in the Chromatin Substance of the Sperms and Galea Capitis as a Cause of Sterility in Bulls, Nord Vet. Med. **3**, 102.

Aughey, E. and Renton, J. P. (1968) Abnormal Spermatozoa in An Ayrshire Bull, Vet. Rec. **82**, 129.

Bane, A. (1961) Acrosomal Abnormality Associated with Sterilty in

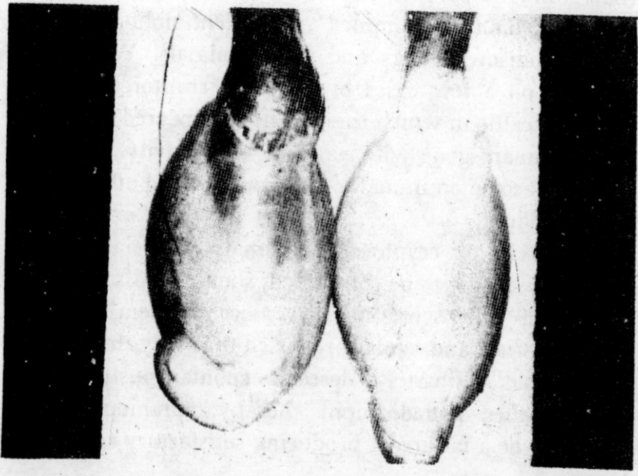

Figure 180. Abnormal Attachment of the Cremaster Muscle to the Left Testis Causing a Nearly Horizontal Position of the Testis High in the Scrotum (The right testis of the bull was normal)

Figure 181. Left Inguinal Hernia in a Hereford Bull.

Boars, Proc IV Internat. Congr. on An. Reprod (Hague) Vol IV, 810.

Bane, A. (1968) Personal Communication.

Bane, A. and Nicander, L. (1965) Pouch Formations by Invaginations of the Nuclear Envelope of Bovine and Porcine Sperm as a Sign of Disturbed Spermiogenesis, Nord. Vet. Med. **17,** 149.

Blom, E. and Birch-Andersen, A. (1965) The Ultrastructure of the Bull Sperm II The Sperm Head, Nord. Vet. Med. **17,** 4, 193.

Boyd, H. (1955) Bovine Genital Vibriosis, Thesis, Royal Vet. Col, Stockholm, Sweden.

Buttle, H. R. L. and Hancock, J. L. (1965) Sterile Boars with Knobbed Spermatozoa, J. Agric. Sci. **65,** 255.

Donald, H. P. and Hancock, J. L. (1953) Evidence of a Gene-Controlled Sterility in Bulls, J. Agric. Sci. **43,** 178.

Frank, A. H. and Bryner, J. H. (1953) Observations on Vibriosis of Cattle in Relation to Impaired Fertility, Proc. U.S. Livestock Sanit. Assoc. 57th. Meeting, 165.

Gledhill, B. L. (1966) Studies on the D.N.A. Content, Dry Mass and Optical Area of Ejaculated Spermatozoal Heads from Bulls with Normal and Lowered Fertility, Acta Vet. Scand. **7,** 166.

Gledhill, B. L. (1970) Enigma of Spermatozoal Deoxyribonucleic Acid and Male Infertility: A Review, Amer. J. Vet. Res. **31,** 3, 39.

Gledhill, B. L., Gledhill, M. P., Rigler, R. Jr., and Ringertz, N. R. (1966) Atypical Changes of Deoxyribonucleoprotein During Spermiogenesis Associated with a Case of Infertility in the Bull, J. Reprod. Fert. **12,** 575.

Gustavsson, I. (1969) Cytogenetics, Distribution and Phenotypic Effects of a Translocation in Swedish Cattle, Hereditas **63,** 68.

Henricson, B. and Backstrom, L. (1964) A Systematic Study of Meiotic Divisions in Normal and Subfertile or Sterile Boars and Bulls, Jour. Reprod. Fertil. **7,** 53.

Knudsen, O. (1954) Cytomorphological Investigations into the Spermiocytogenesis of Bulls with Normal Fertility and Bulls with Acquired Disturbances in Spermiogenesis, Acta Path. et Microbiol. Scand. Suppl. C 1.

Knudsen, O. (1958) Studies on Spermiocytogenesis in the Bull, Internat. Jour. of Fert. **3,** 389.

Leuchtenberger, C., Murmanis, I., Murmanis, L., Ito, S. and Weir, D. R. (1956) Interferometric Dry Mass and Microspectrophotometric Arginine Determinations on Bull Sperm Nuclei with Normal and Abnormal DNA Content, Chromosoma (Berl.) **8,** 73.

MacLeod, J. (1951) Fertility in Thoroughbred Stallions, Lecture, 1st Annual Stud Managers Course, College of Agr., Univ. of Kentucky, Lexington, Ky., 102.

McEntee, K. (1954) (1968) Personal Communication.

Saacke, R. G. and Amann, R. P. (1966) Inherited Abnormal Acrosomal Caps of Bull Spermatozoa, J. An. Sci. **25,** 3, 929.

Saacke, R. G., Amann, R. P. and Marshall, C. E. (1968) Acrosomal Cap Abnormalities of Sperm from Subfertile Bulls, J. An. Sci. **27,** 5, 1391.

Salisbury, G. W., Birge, W. J., DeLeTorre, L. and Lodge, J. R. (1961) Decrease in Nuclear Feulgen Positive Material (DNA) Upon Aging **in vitro** Storage of Bovine Spermatozoa, J. Biophys. Biochem. Cytol. **10,** 353.

Salisbury, G. W. and Flerchinger, F. H. (1967) Aging Phenomena in Spermatozoa, I, II, III, J. Dairy Sci. **50,** 10, 1675, 1679, 1683.

VanderSluis, L. (1953) Experiences with the Examination into Herd Infertility, Proc. First World Congr. on Fert. and Steril. II, 25, 703.

Wells, M. E. and Awa, O. A. (1970) New Technique for Assessing Acrosomal Characteristics of Spermatozoa, J. Dairy Sci. **53,** 2, 227

Wells, M. E. and Awa, O. A. (1970) Distribution of Acrosomal Abnormalities Among Types of Spermatozoa, J. Dairy Sci. **53,** 3, 382 (Abstr.).

Abnormal Semen Production, Hypoplasia

Adams, W. M. (1970) Hormonal and Anatomical Causes of Infertility, Colloquium on **Effect of Diseases and Stress on Reproductive Efficiency on Swine,** Iowa State Univ., Ames, Iowa.

Blom, E. and Christensen, N. O. (1951) Congenital Absence of the Epididymis, Ductus Deferens, or Glandula Vesicularis (Aplasia Segmentalis Ductus Wolfii) in the Bull, Yearbook Royal Vet and Agr. Coll., Copenhagen Denmark 1.

Bloom, F. (1954) Pathology of the Dog and Cat, Amer. Vet. Public. Inc., Evanston, Ill.

Carroll, E. J. and Ball, L. E. (1969) See Inbreeding.

Cheville, N. F. (1968) The Gray Collie Syndrome, J.A.V.M.A. **152,** 6 (Part 1), 620.

Cupps, P. T. and Laben, R. C. (1960) Spermatogenesis in Relation to Spermatozoa Concentration in Bovine Semen, J. Dairy Sci. **43,** 6, 782.

Eriksson, K. (1950) Hereditability of Reproductive Disturbances in Bulls of Swedish Red and White Cattle, Nord. Vet. Med. **2,** 943.

Gunn, R. M. C., Sanders, R. N. and Granger, W. (1942) Studies in Fertility in Sheep, Commonwealth of Austral, Council for Sci. and Ind. Res. Bull 148.

Haq, I. (1949) Causes of Sterility in Bulls in Southern England, Brit, Vet. Jour. **105,** 3, 4, 5 and 6; 71, 114, 143, 200.

Holst, S. J. (1949) Sterility in Boars, Nord. Vet. Med. **1,** 2, 87.

Johansson, I. (1961) Genetic Aspects of Dairy Cattle Breeding, Univ. of Ill. Press. Urbana, Ill.

Lagerlof, N. (1934) Morphologische Untersuchungen uber Veranderungen in Spermabild und in den Hoden bie Bullen mit vesminderter oder aufgehabener Fertilitat, Acta Path. et Microbiol. Scand. Suppl. XIX.

Lagerlof, N. (1938) Infertility in Male Domestic Animals, Proc 13th Intern. Vet. Congr. **1,** 214.

MacLeod, J. (1951) Fertility in Thoroughbred Stallions, 1st Annual Stud Managers Course, College of Agr. Univ. of Ken. Lexington, Ky., 102.

Martig, R. C. and Almquist, J. O. (1969) Reproductive Capacity of Beef Bulls III, J. An. Sci., **28,** 3, 375.

McEntee, K. (1969) Pathology of Domestic Animals, 2nd Ed., Vol I, edited by Jubb, K. V. and Kennedy, P. C., Academic Press, N.Y.C. and London.

Settergren, I. (1961) The Relationship Between Body and Ear Colour and Ovarian Development in Females of the Swedish Highland Breed, Proc. 4th Internat. Congr. on Animal Reprod. (The Hague) 752.

Swierstra, E. E. (1970) Personal Communication.

Taylor, D. O. N., Thomas, J. W. and Marburger, R. G. (1964) Abnormal Antler Growth Associated with Hypogonadism in White-Tailed Deer in Texas, Amer. J. Vet. Res. **25**, 104, 179.

Sperm Cell Defects

Aughey, E. and Renton, J. P. (1968) Abnormal Spermatozoa in an Ayrshire Bull, Vet. Rec. **82**, 129.

Blake, T. A. (1945) Inheritance of Morphological Characters in the Sperms of Cattle, Nature. **155**,631.

Blom, E. (1959) A Rare Sperm Abnormality "Corkscrew-sperms", Associated with Sterility in Bulls, Nature **183**, 1280.

Blom, E. (1966) A New Sterilizing and Hereditary Defect (the "Dag Defect") Located in the Bull Sperm Tail, Nature, **209**, 739.

Blom, E. (1968) A New Sperm Defect "Pseudo droplets" in the Middle Piece of the Bull Sperm, Nord. Vet. Med. **20**, 279.

Blom, E. and Birch-Andersen, A. (1966) The Ultrastructure of a Sterilizing Tail Defect (the "Dag Defect") in the Bull Sperm, State Veterinary Lab., Copenhagen, Denmark.

Coubrough, R. I. and Barker, C. A. V. (1964) Spermatozoa: An Unusual Midpiece Abnormality Associated with Sterility in Bulls, Proc 5th Internat. Congr. on An. Reprod., Trento, Vol 5, 219.

Hancock, J. L. and Rollinson, D. H. L. (1949) A Seminal Defect Associated with Sterility in Guernsey Bulls, Vet. Rec. **61**, 742.

Jones, W. A. (1962) Abnormal Morphology of the Spermatozoa in Guernsey Bulls, Brit. Vet. Jour, **118**, 257.

MacLeod, J. and McGee, W. R. (1950) The Semen of the Thoroughbred, Cor. Vet. **40**, 3, 233.

Settergren, I. (1970) Unpublished data and personal communication.

Swanson, E. W. and Boyd, L. J. (1962) Factors Affecting Coiled Tail Spermatozoa in the Bull, Amer. J. Vet. Res. **23**, 93, 300.

Williams, G. (1965) An Abnormality of the Spermatozoa of Some Hereford Bulls, Vet. Rec. **77**, 41, 1204.

Inbreeding, Hybrids and Chromosoma Abberations

Benirschke, K. (1967) Sterility and Fertility of Interspecific Mammalian Hybrids, in **Comparative Aspects of Reproductive Failure,** Springer-Verlag. New York Inc. p. 218.

Carroll, E. J. (1968) Testicular Pathology in Young Beef Bulls with Special Reference to Inbreeding, Thesis, Cornell Univ., Ithaca, N.Y.

Carroll, E. J. and Ball, L. E. (1970) Effects of Mating Systems on Reproductive Functions in Beef Bulls, Amer. J. of Vet. Res. **31**, 2, 241.

Deaken, A. (1943) Field Fertility Tests and Causes of Sterility in Bulls, Dept. of Agr., Central Exper. Farm, Ottawa, Can.

Dunn, H. O., Kenney, R. M., Stone, W. H. and Bendel, S. (1968) Cytogenetic and Reproductive Studies of XX/XY Chimeric Twin Bulls, 6th Internat. Congr. on Anim. Reprod. and Art. Insem., Paris Vol II, 877.

Gilmore, L. O. (1949) The Inheritance of Functional Causes of Reproductive Inefficiency, A Review, J. of Dairy Sci. **32**, 71.

Gregory, P. W., Mead, S. W., Regan, W. M. and Rollins, W. C. (1951) Further Studies Concerning Sex-limited Genetic Infertility in Cattle, J. Dairy Sci. **34**, 1047.

Gustavsson, I. (1969) Cytogenetics, Distribution and Phenotypic Effects of a Translocation in Swedish Cattle, Hereditas **63**, 68.

Hancock, J. L. (1964) Attempted Hybridization of Sheep and Goats, 5th Internat. Congr. on Animal. Reprod. and Art. Insem., Trento, Italy **3**, 445.

Knudson, O. (1958) Studies on Spermiocytogenesis in the Bull, Internat. J. of Fertil. **3**, 3 and 4, 390.

Krehbiel, E. V., Carter, R. C., Bovard, K. P., Gaines, J. A. and Priode, B. M. (1969) Effects of Inbreeding and Environment on Fertility of Beef Cattle Matings, J. An. Sci. **29**, 4, 528.

McNitt, J. E., Stonaker, H. H. and Carroll, E. J. (1966) Breeding Soundness in Beef Bulls, Proc. Western Sect. Amer. Soc. Animal Science, **17**, 25.

Young, G. B. (1953) Genetic Aspects of Fertility and Infertility in Cattle, Vet. Rec. **65**, 271.

Male Intersexes, Hermaphrodites

Biggers, J. D. and McFeely, R. A. (1966) Intersexuality in Domestic Animals, Advances in Reproductive Physiology Vol I Edit. by A. McLaren, Academic Press, N.Y.C.

Gilmore, L. O. (1949) The Inheritance of Functional Causes of Reproductive Ineffeciency. A Review, J. Dairy Sci. **32**, 71.

Loughman, W. D., Frye, F. L. and Congdon, T. B. (1970) XY/XXY Bone Marrow Mosaicism in Three Male Tricolor Cats, Amer. Jour. Vet. Res. **31**, 2, 307.

Soller, M., Laor, M., Barnea, R., Weiss, Y., and Ayalon, N (1964) Polledness and Infertility in Male Saanen Goats, J. of Hered. **54**, 237.

Thuline, H. C. (1964) Personal Communication.

Cryptorchidism

Adams, O. R. (1964) An Improved Method of Diagnosis and Castration of Cryptorchid Horses, J.A.V.M.A. **145**, 5, 439.

Arthur, G. H. (1961) The Surgery of the Equine Cryptorchid, Vet. Rec. **73**, 16, 385.

Ashdown, R. R. (1963) The Diagnosis of Cryptorchidism in Young Dogs: A Review of the Problem, J. Sm. An. Pract. **4**, 261.

Bishop, M. W. H., David, J. S. E. and Messervy, A. (1966) Cryptorchidism in the Stallion, Proc Royal Soc. of Med. **59**, 769.

Brodey, R. S. and Martin, J. E. (1958) Sertoli Cell Neoplasms in the Dog. The Clinicopathological and Endocrinological Findings in Thirty-seven Dogs; J.A.V.M.A. **133,** 249.

Brodey, R. S. and Reif, J. S. (1969) The Relationship Between Canine Testicular Neoplasia and Cryptorchidism (Abstr.) J.A.V.M.A. **154,** 11. 1385.

Carl, J. (1943) An Inherited Defect in Bulls, (Horizontal Testes), Berl. Munch. Tierarztl. Wschr., p. 8.

Charney, C. W. and Wolgin, W. (1957) Cryptorchidism, Hoeber-Harper Inc. N.Y.C.

Fox, M. W. (1963) Inherited Inguinal Hernia and Midline Defects in the Dog. J.A.V.M.A., **143,** 6, 602.

Kingrey, B. W. (1961) Personal Communication.

Lowe, J. E. and Higginbotham, R. (1969) Castration of Abdominal Cryptorchid Horses by a Paramedian Laparotomy Approach, Cor. Vet. **59,** 1, 121.

Mann, P. H. (1956) A Case of Unilateral Cryptorchidism in a Mongrel Dog, Cor. Vet., **46,** 1, 6.

McEntee, K. (1969) Pathology of Domestic Animals, 2nd Ed. Edited by Jubb, K. V. and Kennedy, P. C. Academic Press, N.Y.C. and London.

McGee, W. R. (1967) Personal Communication.

McPhee, H. C. and Buckley, S. S. (1934) Inheritance of Cryptorchidism in Swine, Jour. of Hered. **25,** 295.

Milne, F. (1958) Personal Communication.

Noordsy, J. L. (1966) Inguinal Herniorraphy in the Bovine Male, Vet. Med., **61,** 2, 147.

Reif, J. S. and Brodey, R. S. (1969) The Relationship Between Cryptorchidism and Canine Testicular Neoplasia, J.A.V.M.A. **155,** 12, 2005.

Technical Development Committee. (1954) Cryptorchidism with Special Reference to the Condition in the Dog, Vet. Rec. **66,** 482.

Todd, G. C., Nelson, L. W. and Migaki, G. (1968) Multiple Heterotropic Testicular Tissue in the Pig—A Report of 7 Cases, Cor. Vet. **58,** 4, 614.

Warwick, B. L. (1926) A Study of Hernia in Swine, Wisc. Agr. Exper. Stat. Bull 69.

Warwick, B. L. (1961) Selection Against Cryptorchidism in Angora Goats, J. An. Sci., **20,** 1, 10.

Wheat, J. D. (1961) Cryptorchidism in Hereford Cattle, J. Hered., **52,** 244.

VanderSluis, L. (1953) Experiences with Examination into Herd Infertility, Proc. First World Congr. on Fert. and Steril. II, XXV, 703.

Acquired Testicular Pathology

Testicular Pathology Due to Acquired Causes is much more common than congenital or hereditary causes and includes testicular degeneration, orchitis, fibrosis and calcification. (See Figures 180 through 190) Lagerlof and others estimated that 75 to 80 percent of testicular pathology is related to testicular degeneration including fibrosis and orchitis. The epithelium of the seminiferous tubules is highly sensitive to any adverse influences with resulting marked effects on spermatogenesis. Testicular degeneration may be mild or severe and is usually bilateral as it is most commonly due to generalized disease processes. Unilateral degeneration can occur secondary to local testicular lesions such as tumors. Testicular degeneration may develop very rapidly within a few days or hours; while testicular regeneration proceeds slowly over weeks and months. If the basal layers of the germinal epithelium including the spermatogonia and Sertoli cells are destroyed regeneration of the germinal epithelium is nc possible and the animals is sterile. The pattern and signs of testicular degeneration are about the same despite the species or the etiologic factor(s) involved. In all cases degenerative changes in the mechanism of cell division or centrosomes are present in the primary spermatocytes and are responsible for reduced motility and increased numbers of pathologic spermatozoa with an abnormal morphology. Sperm cell numbers and concentration are decreased depending on the degree of degeneration of the seminiferous tubules. In severe disturbances of spermatogenesis, spermatocytes with restitution nuclei with double the normal number of chromosomes as well as pyknotic nuclei are present in the ejaculate, Knudsen. Testes with degeneration of the seminiferous tubules are usually atrophic and softer and smaller than normal testes. In chronic cases the testicle may be firm due to fibrosis; even calcium may be deposited especially in the areas just peripheral to the rete testis. Histologically it may be difficult to distinguish between slight degrees of testicular degeneration and hypoplasia. Hypoplastic testes have a predisposition to degeneration.

Causes of Testicular Degeneration include:

Thermal influences associated with elevation of the testicular temperature such as: cryptorchid and ectopic testes; inguinal hernias; (See Figure 180 and 181) scrotal dermatitis due to, irritants, choriopic mange (See Figure 182), myiasis in sheep, and localized skin infections or wounds; contusions and hematomas of the scrotum and testes; prolonged elevated body temperature as in certain infectious diseases and in prolonged high environmental temperatures, particularly associated with high humidity. Testicular degeneration is most common in tropical climates and involving breeds originating in the temperate zones, Donaldson. "Summer" infertility in bulls in the temperate zone is usually an individual bull problem.

Direct heating of the scrotum may also be involved, Maule and Waites. Bulls were exposed to heat stress for 8 hours a day for 7 days; this resulted in a deleterious effect on semen quality reaching its peak at 2 to 3 weeks after the stress with recovery by 9 weeks, Johnston and coworkers. Gunn and coworkers and Dutt and Hamm have shown that rams maintained at ambient temperatures of 90° F. or above develop a marked drop in semen quality with about 10 per cent motility and 70 per cent abnormal sperm cells within a few weeks. Recovery was not complete until 2 to 3 months after normal temperatures were restored. Shearing rams monthly during the summer months greatly improved conception rate and embryo survival, Hulet and coworkers. High ambient temperatures will also cause lowered fertility due to testicular degeneration in boars. Heat primarily affects the spermatids, the spermatozoa and the spermatocytes but usually does not affect the spermatogonia, Steinberger and Dixon. Heat has no effect on the Leydig cells. Many earlier experiments by Lagerlof and others on the effects of scrotal insulation and the production of testicular degeneration have been reproduced. Austin and coworkers have shown that even 24 hours insulation of the scrotum with a plastic bag that raised the skin temperature from 93.1 to 96.9° F. had a definite depressing effect on semen quality. Lagerlof carried out early classical experiments demonstrating that overheating or insulation of the scrotum of bulls caused rapid testicular degeneration and when normal scrotal temperature was restored, recovery was slow. Males that lie down for long periods of time such as bulls with bovine spastic syndrome, or males that are unable to rise, often develop testicular degeneration and atrophy due to the prolonged elevation of testicular temperature from the testes being held close to the body. Gerona and Sikes reported that when the scrotal temperature of bulls was raised to 38.4° C or 0.3° C below body temperature, the motility and percent of live spermatozoa in the semen decreased to zero by the second week. After normal scrotal temperature was restored 11 weeks elapsed before motile cells were observed and 18 weeks were required for the recovery of normal semen quality.

Faulkner and coworkers have reported on the damage to spermatogenic function induced in range beef bulls by low temperatures down to -25° F. associated with winds of 60 miles per hour causing frostbite, necrosis of skin, scrotal dermatitis, heat, swelling, testicular degeneration and adhesions. Older bulls with the most pendulous scrotums were most seriously affected. The severity of the after effects were related to the amount of adhesions produced. Bulls provided proper wind shelter and dry bedding were not affected by such temperatures and wind. The presence of excessive fat in the inguinal region probably has little effect on the thermoregulatory mechanisms of the scrotum and testes unless short spermatic cords or other defects in the testes are present. The author has observed several bovine cases of scrotal hydrocele of unknown etiology where semen quality was not significantly affected.

Vascular lesions of the testes—Interference with the circulation and infarction of the testis can be produced by manual torsion of the testis or by the emasculatome used for castration of lambs or calves. Congestion and pain of the scrotal testis due to naturally-occurring torsion or contusion has been reported in racing stallions, particularly Standard-bred trotters. With vigorous exercise these animals would start to spraddle their rear legs, become lame and then change from a trotting to a pacing gait. Affected Thoroughbred stallions would race normally for nearly one-half mile and develop an altered "hopping" gait. The testes would be swollen, congested and painful for the next 3 to 4 days. Dogs with inguinal or abdominal cryptorchid testes may occasionally develop torsion of the testis with a sudden onset of pain and associated symptoms. The author has observed one case in a cryptorchid pig. Hemorrhagic infarction of the testis may follow torsion. Tumors of the abdominal testes may also predispose to torsion.

Testicular biopsies, particularly in bulls, often result in focal areas of testicular necrosis because of vessel damage when a desirable size of testicular material is obtained, Roberts. For this reason Knudsen recommended a technique of aspiration biopsy in bulls for cytologic but not for histologic studies. Testicular biopsies are more easily and safely done in the horse, Clark, and other animals, including man.

Inflammation of the testicular artery in the horse may be caused by strongyle larvae, the equine arteritis virus and other unknown agents. This may produce areas of testicular degeneration, McEntee. Strongyle larvae can produce adhesions between the testis and its tunics. McEntee also reported on age-associated vascular lesions such as hyaline degeneration in older bulls, rams and dogs causing degenerative changes in the seminiferous tubules. Suspensories of any type whether solid or mesh should not be used in shipping male animals. They have not proven necessary. The solid type might result in over-heating of the testes and both types might become maladjusted and cause pressure on the spermatic cord and affect testicular circulation, Fincher and coworkers. Varicocele is seen occasionally in the spermatic vein of rams and stallions. (See Figure 183) As in man the adverse effects on semen quality especially motility are probably slight to moderate, Jensen and coworkers, Dubin and Hotchkiss, MacLeod. Varicocele may effect both the circulation of blood and the

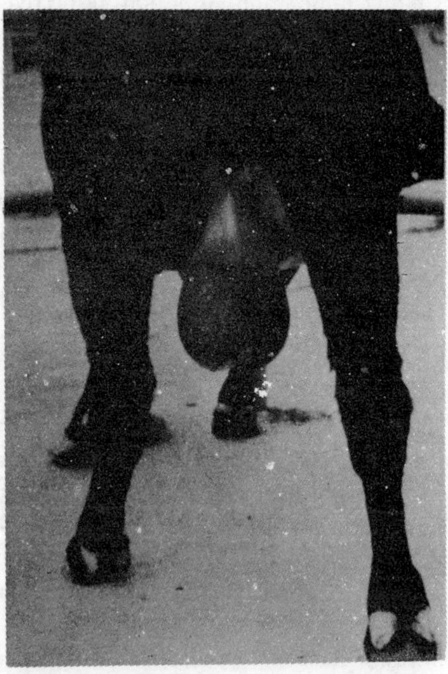

Figure 182. Scrotal Dermatitis and Edema in a Bull Secondary to Chorioptic Mange. (Temporary testicular degeneration and infertility resulted that lasted for 2 to 3 months)

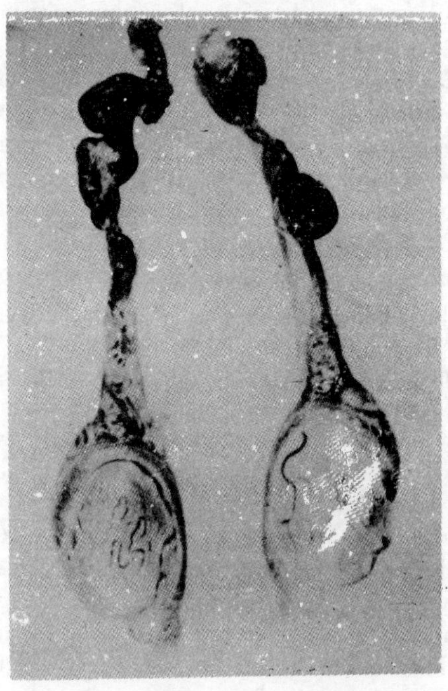

Figure 183. Varicoceles or Thrombosis of the Spermatic Vein in a Ram. (Courtesy K. McEntee)

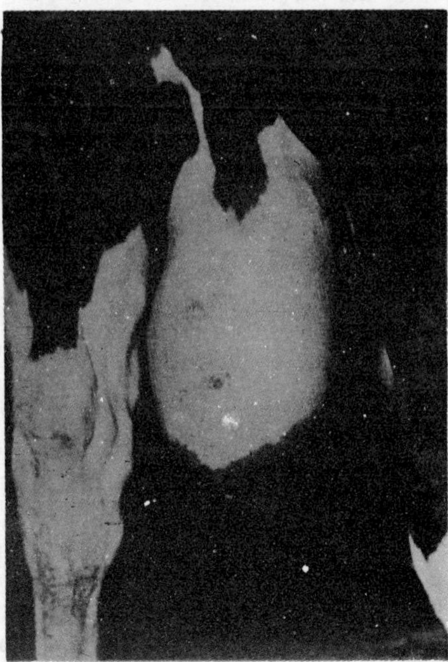

Figure 184. Acute Orchitis of the Right Testis in a Holstein Bull.

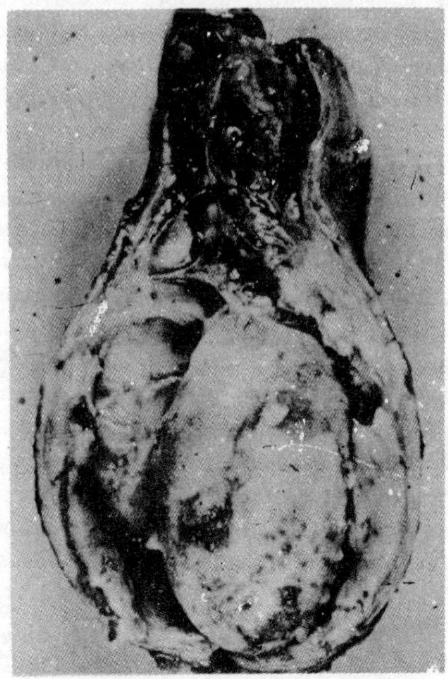

Figure 185. Acute Orchitis and Periorchitis Secondary to a **C. pyogenes** Infection. (After unilateral castration and a 6 to 8 month rest period this bull (Figs. 184 and 185) recovered and was fertile for over 3 years)

heat regulatory mechanism of the pampiniform plexus. Varicoceles may be palpated in rams.

Irradiation, as in other causes of degeneration of the testes, produces interference with spermatogenesis by injuring spermatogonia, spermatocytes and spermatids. The spermatocytes are most sensitive to irradiation while Leydig and Sertoli cells are quite resistant. The amount of irradiation and length of treatment are highly important in the degree of effects produced and the rate of recovery. The first change in the semen noted by Murphree and Parish was abnormal sperm cells about the sixth week after exposure of bulls to 100 to 400 roentgens. A decrease in sperm cell numbers occurred by the eighth week and these did not begin to return to a normal level until 15 weeks. All bulls had reached nearly normal levels by 24 weeks after exposure. Bulls given doses totalling 600 to 1100 roentgens, developed aspermia by 16 weeks, remained aspermic for 10 weeks and fairly good recovery had occurred by 12 to 24 months, Welch and Murphree.

Hormonal causes—Testicular degeneration and atrophy of the testes occurs in the dog and rarely in other animals due to tumors of the anterior pituitary gland or hypothalamus interfering with the production of gonadotropic hormones. This is called dystrophia adiposogenitalis syndrome in dogs. Besides testicular atrophy, obesity and other signs commonly develop. Excessive estrogenic hormone produced by Sertoli cell tumors and testosterone, and rarely estrogens, produced by Leydig cell tumors may suppress F.S.H. production and cause testicular degeneration. For a number of years infertile men with oligospermia were treated with large doses of testosterone for a prolonged period to completely suppress spermatogenesis. Following this treatment a "rebound phenomena" was reported in which higher than normal concentrations and numbers of spermatozoa were produced. In summarizing this data Charney reported that only 7.5 per cent of 840 men treated showed any significant improvement. Prolonged doses of testosterone or estrogens should not be given to male animals, Meineke and McDonald.

Age Effects—McEntee stated, "Permanent and progressive testicular degeneration occurs fairly frequently in all species without any indication of its pathogenesis" Bloom reported that senile atrophy of the testes is common in dogs over 10 years of age and in cats over 12 years of age. Dawson and Collins and coworkers have reported a decline in fertility in bulls as they became older. Vibriosis might have been present as a factor in Dawson's report. Collins et al. reported a decline in fertility in over 150 bulls used in artificial insemination of 0.31 to 0.51 per cent per year as measured by nonreturn rates. Hahn et al. reported that aged bulls, 7 to 13 years old had a lower sperm cell output per ejaculate than young bulls, 2 to 6 years old, 7 billion and 10 billion, respectively. Aged bulls had 10 percent fewer morphologically normal spermatozoa and the motility rate was lower. MacLeod and McGee similarly described degeneration of the testes based on semen examinations in aging stallions. The author has observed that older bulls after they reach 8 to 10 years of age may develop testicular degeneration fairly rapidly at any time. It is an uncommon bull that produces good quality fertile semen up to 15 or more years of age. Many disease, genetic, and management factors influence this age effect.

Subacute or acute trauma, stress, or disease may cause rapid or progressive testicular degeneration in males. Those that have been associated with reduced fertility and a decline in semen quality are: shipping under adverse conditions of heat and cold, severe fatigue, excessive physical work, traumatic gastritis in bulls, Dunn and coworkers, liver or abdominal abscesses, multiple severe contusions with fractured ribs as would occur in a fight between bulls, severe arthritis, severe myiasis or "fly strikes" in rams, severe screw-worm infestations, moderate to severe foot rot in rams, suppurative arthritis and severe quittors in bulls, acute laminitis in rams, horses and possibly other species, buckshot wounds especially of the scrotum and testes, kick wounds and resulting hematomas of the testes and scrotum in stallions, and extensive infected wounds. Good care and management will do much toward avoiding testicular degeneration due to these causes. Although Jackowski and coworkers reported a temporary reduction in fertility for about three months after shipping 29 bulls from Holland to Poland, Willett reported on 60 bulls, used for artificial insemination, moved 300 to 2000 miles in the U.S. without a suspensory in which no reduction in semen quality was noted in the months following shipment.

Acute or chronic, localized or systemic infectious diseases are common causes of testicular degeneration with moderately to severely reduced fertility in males. Infections producing orchitis or epididymitis have a direct effect on the testes due to the inflammatory reaction causing heat, edema, congestion, circulatory interference, ischemia and even infarction due to the thick firm tunica albuginea that restricts normal swelling of the testicular parenchyma. In bacterial diseases localizing in the testes, abscessation may occur. (See Figures 184 and 185) Infectious agents resulting in orchitis are: **Brucella abortus,** both field strains and Strain 19 in bulls, Lambert et al.; **Brucella suis** in boars; miliary or chronic tubercular infections with **Mycobacterium tuberculosis** of the testes in bulls and boars; **Corynebacterium pyogenes,** usually carried to the testes by the blood from primary infection sites in bulls and rams; **Actinomyces bovis** in

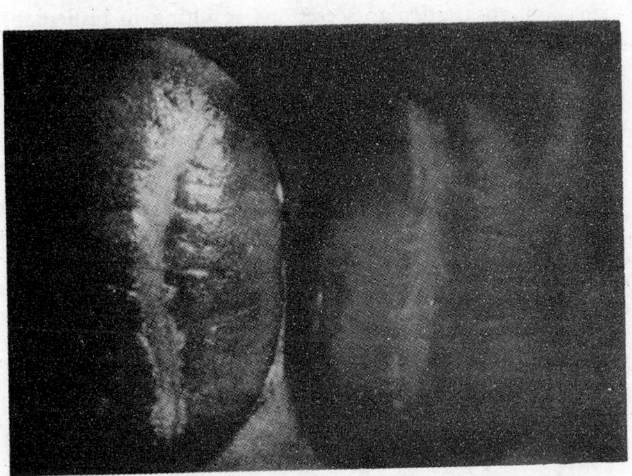

Figure 186. Longitudinal Section of a Normal Bovine Testis (Note the bulging and the uniform color and texture of the parenchyma) (Courtesy K. McEntee)

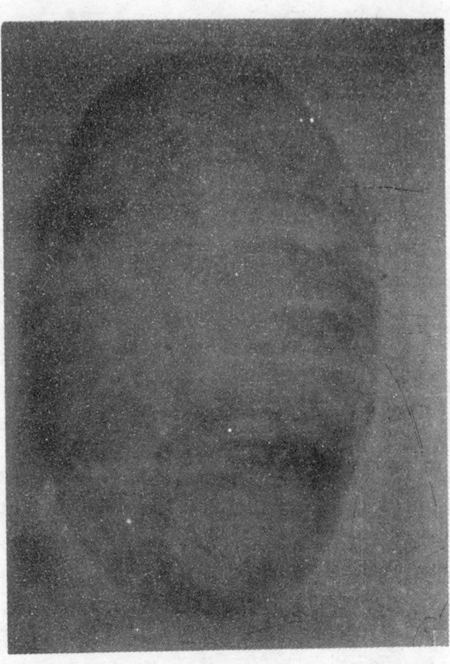

Figure 187. Testis with Advanced Testicular Degeneration, Fibrosis and Calcification (Courtesy K. McEntee)

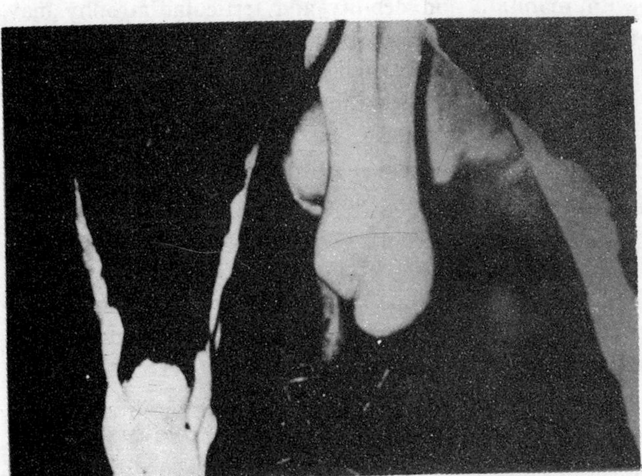

Figure 188. Advanced Testicular Degeneration, Fibrosis and Atrophy, Especially of the Left Testis

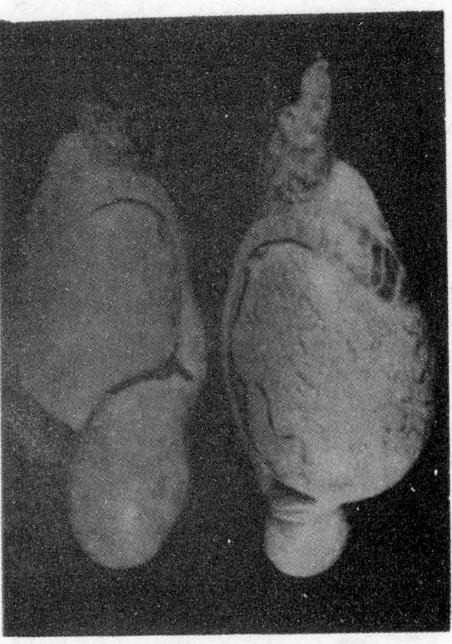

Figure 189. Fibrosis and Sperm Granuloma of the Tail of the Epididymis of the Left Testis in a Ram due to the R.E.O. Agent. (Note the moderate atrophy of the left testis compared to the normal right testis). (Courtesy P. C. Kennedy)

bulls, Kimball and coworkers; **Malleomyces mallei** (glanders organism) in horses; **Salmonella abortus-equi** and "epizootic cellulitis" due to the arteritis and the influenza viruses in horses; **Corynebacterium ovis** and **Pasteurella pseudotuberculosis** in rams; lumpy skin disease in cattle; sheep pox virus in rams, McEntee; an enteric virus, possibly IBR-IPV virus, that markedly affected the spermatocytes and caused arrested spermatogenesis in bulls has been described by Bouters in Belgium; Florent and Bouters and their coworkers (1963) reported on a G-UP virus isolated from the genital organs of bulls that caused infertility and an abnormal sperm picture, degeneration of the seminiferous epithelium, ulcers in the mouth, stiff gait, anorexia and other lesions highly suggestive of foot and mouth disease; a more chronic virus orchitis of bulls has been reported in Checkoslovakia by Mensik and coworkers; and other possible related viruses may cause orchitis in bulls, Gledhill; Vandeplassche, and Sheffy et al. reported that the IBR-IPV virus when injected into susceptible bulls caused a severe and rapid degeneration of the seminiferous epithelium and sterility. Most bulls recovered and were fertile in about 3 months. During the heighth of the degeneration only Sertoli cells and spermatogonia lined the seminiferous tubules. In a few bulls there developed an edema of the scrotum and fibrous adhesions occurred around the testes and spermatic cord. Canine distemper affecting sexually mature dogs may cause a mild orchitis and testicular degeneration as well as an epididymitis, Kirk and McEntee. **Brucella canis** in dogs caused scrotal swelling, epididymitis and unilateral or bilateral testicular degeneration, fibrosis and sterility, Carmichael, Moore and Kakuk. (See abortion and epididymitis due to **Brucella canis**) Any acute or subacute epididymitis would reduce fertility both because of the inflammatory reaction and heat produced as well as by obstructuve lesions in the epididymal tube. (See epididymitis due to **Brucella ovis**). The probable viral disease of specific bovine venereal epididymitis and vaginitis, "epivag", also causes an orchitis with testicular degeneration and atrophy, Bruner and Gillespie. A mycoplasma was isolated from three ovine cases of orchitis, McIlwain and Boline, and **Mycoplasma hyorhinis** infection in swine often results in swelling of the scrotum and adhesions between the testes and the tunics, Switzer. The psittacosis-lymphogranuloma venereum-trachoma, P.L.T., virus may cause orchitis as well as polyarthritis in rams, Norton and Storz. Crenshaw and McGowan reported on two cases of orchitis in rams from which a P.L.T. agent (Chlamydia) was recovered. Storz and coworkers reported on a seminal vesiculitis syndrome in bulls characterized by seminal vesiculitis, epididymitis and orchitis from which they recovered a P.L.T. agent, or Chlamydia. **Nocardia farcinica** in bulls, Bruner and Gillespie, and **Besnoitia besnoiti** have been occasionally reported as a cause for orchitis in bulls, Pols. Severe obstructive lesions such as sperm granulomas affecting the efferent ducts may cause a back pressure from the spermatozoa and the testicular secretions resulting in testicular degeneration. (See Figure 189) The affected testes may be somewhat enlarged, McEntee. Sporadic infections of the testis with staphylococci, streptococci, **E. coli,** proteus and pseudomonas organisms have been reported as a cause of orchitis in dogs and other male domestic animals, Roberts. Gribble reported that erhlichiosis of horses resulted in edema of the legs, sheath and scrotum and also orchitis with secondary testicular atrophy. During the acute disease inclusion bodies were commonly observed in the leucocytes. This disease should be differentiated from equine infectious anemia, piroplasmosis and dourine.

Infectious diseases of a systemic nature that cause testicular degeneration and lower fertility temporarily due to the accompanying high fever include: pneumonia and shipping fever, possibly I.B.R.-I.P.V., equine infectious anemia, actinobacillosis, strangles, blue-tongue virus vaccination, DeBoom, and tick-borne fever infection in rams, Watson. (See Figure 190) Those infectious diseases causing gradual debilitation, loss of weight and testicular degeneration with atrophy include: foot and mouth disease, actinomycosis, Johne's disease, pyelonephritis, chronic peritonitis, and lymphomatosis.

Nutritional factors related to testicular degeneration are usually those caused by underfeeding or starvation. Diets for males sufficient for growth and maintenance are adequate for fertility. **Chronic disease states** associated with inanition and debility and testicular atrophy may include: chronic severe parasitisms, either external or internal such as: lice, mange, ticks, roundworms, flukes, and etc., senile changes due to worn or diseased teeth, chronic arthritis, tumors, fat necrosis around the large intestine in bulls, severe spastic syndrome and other possible diseases interfering with the intake and passage of food through the gut. Malnutrition may complicate these other chronic diseases. Improper care and management of bulls accustomed to special care and feeding may cause a marked loss in weight resulting in impotency and testicular degeneration and atrophy. This has been observed in several instances when a young fertile, but timid, bull was introduced into a new herd and permitted to run with the cows in a small, confined area. The cows would drive the bull away from the feeding racks causing the bull to become emaciated and sterile. Severe vitamin A deficiency characterized by night blindness, lacrimation and opthalmia usually precedes testicular degeneration and poor semen quality. Under range conditions during drouths vitamin A deficiency usually is accompanied by protein and carbohydrate deficiencies. Malnutrition, debility and cachexia produce degeneration and atrophy of the seminiferous epithelium by causing a suppression of the release of gonadotropic hormones from the pituitary.

A high level of feeding and the accompanying obesity has no effect on semen quality in a normal male, but does effect their libido and willingness to breed. The author has observed a number of highly-conditioned beef show bulls producing semen of excellent quality. However, if obesity accompanies testicular hypoplasia, a short spermatic cord and much fat in the inguinal ring it does not follow that the obesity is the primary cause of the resulting infertility.

Poisons or toxins may adversely affect the germinal epithelium. McEntee and Olafson have reported testicular degeneration in bulls and rams with hyperkeratosis caused by the chlorinated napthalenes. Dipping of rams in arsenic solutions causes degeneration of the seminiferous tubules in sheep, Gunn and coworkers. Antimony compounds injected for the treatment of heartworms in dogs have been reported to cause temporary sterility, Bishop. There is no evidence that copper sulphate or phenothiazine used in worming sheep have harmful effects on the testes. There is no evidence that systemic organic phosphate insecticides affect semen quality in bulls, Faulkner and coworkers. Potassium nitrate also had no effect on semen production, Sikes. The author has seen no ill effects from the use of sodium iodide for actinomycosis or actinobacillosis in bulls in artificial insemination studs. McEntee cited a number of chemical, metals and rare earth salts that can produce degeneration of the seminiferous epithelium in a variety of species. These include alkylating agents, cadmium chloride and amphotericin B.

Auto-immunization might play a role in a few cases of testicular degeneration. Degeneration has been produced experimentally in rams, bulls and laboratory animals by the subcutaneous injection of autologous testicular material, together with Freund's adjuvant. Degeneration may occur with or without inflammation. No natural cases of testicular degeneration due to auto-immunization have been reported, McEntee, Losos, Busey and Menge. Faulkner has reported that anti LH serum will induce testicular degeneration and sterility in male animals. This product immobilizes the male's own gonadotropic hormones necessary for spermatogenesis.

Testicular Neoplasms. Testicular tumors are unusual in most domestic animals except the dog and possibly old bulls. Primary testicular tumors are usually of three main types and originate from the interstitial cells, the Sertoli cells and the germinal epithelium. This may be due to a genetic predisposition in dogs and to the maintainance of intact male dogs until they become senile. The incidence of tumors in cryptorchid, or retained testes is high, especially in dogs, for the same reasons. In the larger animals relatively few uncastrated males are kept until they reach an advanced age. Dunn and McEntee have reported that sperm cell production and fertility of bulls with testicular tumors over 1.0 cm. in diameter were significantly lower than in unaffected bulls or bulls with small tumors. Bulls with large interstitial tumors had 30 per cent of their ejaculates discarded as unfit for use for artificial insemination while normal control bulls had only 2 per cent of their ejaculates discarded. (See Figure 191) Thus large tumors result in testicular degeneration probably due to the compressing effect of the tumor on the adjacent seminiferous tubules. McEntee indicated that the degeneration may also be due to the excess steroids produced by the interstitial, or Sertoli cell tumors. (See Figure 192)

In bulls testicular tumors are seldom observed except in old animals. Interstitial cell tumors of a benign type are occasionally observed in bulls over 7 to 10 years of age. These may be multiple and in some cases they are large enough to be palpable as small, round, masses, liver-like in consistency, and causing the testes to feel lumpy on palpation. Dunn and McEntee found interstitial cell tumors in 19 per cent of 52 Guernsey bulls. This was significantly higher than the 6 per cent incidence in 164 bulls of the other breeds. Innes described an interstitial cell tumor in a testis of a 3-month-old calf. This type of tumor is usually a deep ochre or orange-brown color with a homogenous, glassy consistency resembling a corpus luteum, McEntee. (See Figure 191) An adenocarcinoma, seminomas and several Sertoli cell tumors have been described in bulls. (See Figure 192) As pointed out by Innes, the benign interstitial cell tumors in old men, dogs and probably bulls may be related to a hormone imbalance. Small fibropapillomas or melanomas and varicose dilatations of scrotal veins occur in older bulls and are occasionally seen on the scrotal skin. These small varicose lesions on bulls testes may be associated with improper temperature regulation of testes and infertility during the hot summer months.

In stallions testicular tumors have been described only occasionally. Williams and Moulton reported that rare dermoid cysts or teratomas of the testicle of the horse are often found in cryptorchid testes. They often contain cystic structures and occasionally hair or bone. Innes cited Kimura as reporting 49 testicular tumors in 142 neoplasms found in 77,000 slaughtered horses. Knudson and Schantz, Moulton, and Innes described rare seminomas in stallions. The latter described teratomas or dermoids of the equine testis and 2 cases similar to those described by Williams, in which only a clear cystic fluid was found

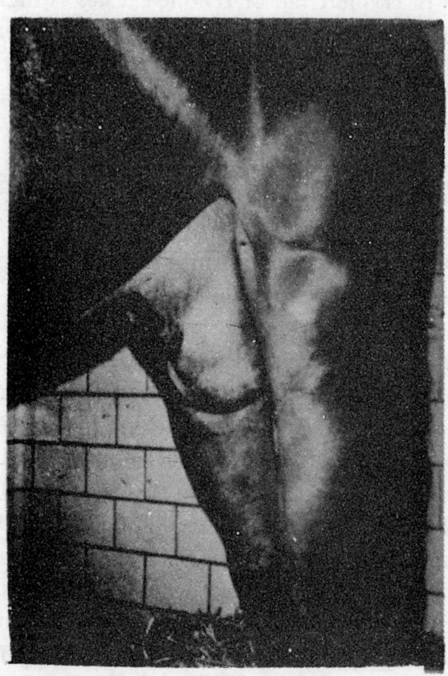

Figure 190. Edema of the Scrotum of A Standardbred Stallion, Associated with Equine Infectious Anemia.

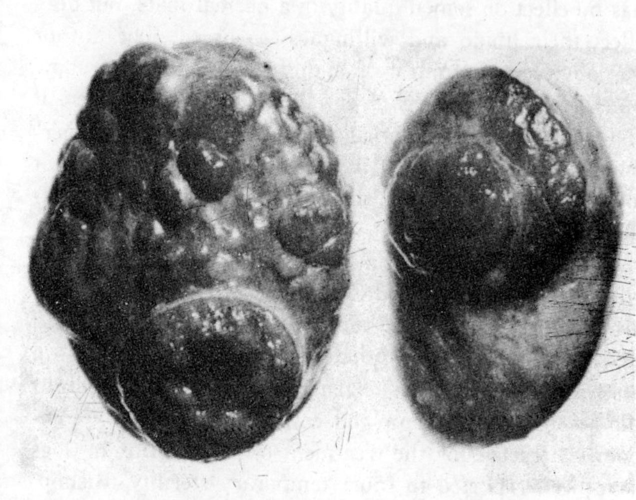

Figure 191. Bilateral Interstitial Cell Tumors of a Testis in an Old Infertile Guernsey Bull. (Courtesy K. McEntee)

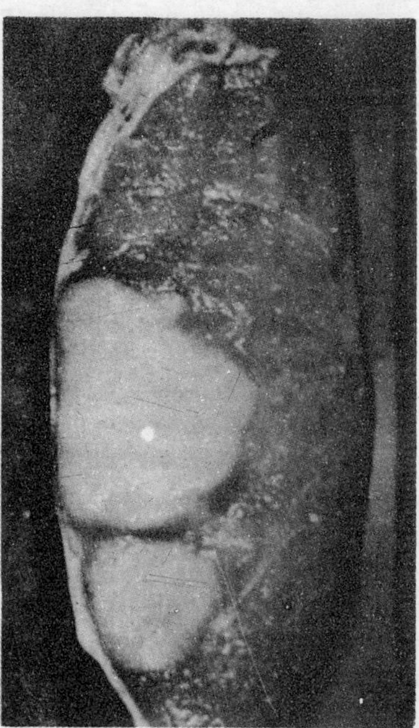

Figure 192. Sertoli Cell Tumor of the Testis of a Bull. (Courtesy K. McEntee)

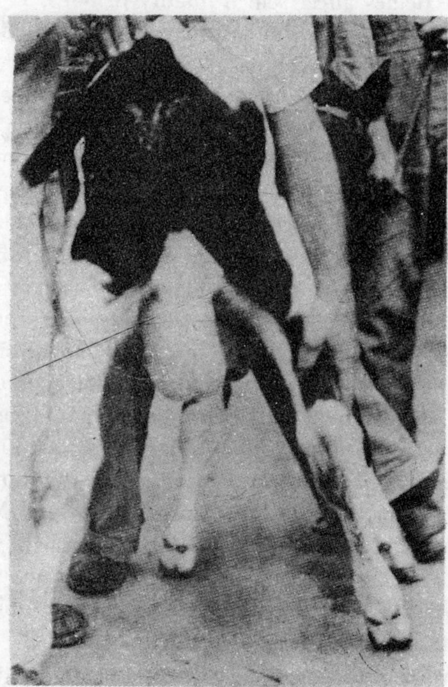

Figure 193. Testicular Abscesses in a 3-Month-Old Calf.

when the enlarged testis was incised. McEntee reported finding only one testicular teratoma in 700 horses castrated at the New York State Veterinary College. Innes, citing Edington and Cappell, described an adenocarcinoma in a retained testicle in a horse with metastasis to the lungs and mediastinum. Smith and McEntee have described occasional interstitial cell tumors of the equine testis. In some of the latter's cases the affected animals were extremely aggressive and vicious but after castration became gentle and quiet. Moulton stated that Sertoli cell or sustenacular cell tumors in horses were rare. A melanoma of the scrotum has been observed in a stallion, Feldman. Lipomas on the surface of the testis are not uncommon, McEntee.

In rams testicular tumors are rare. They were not described by Gunn and coworkers. Innes reported that no large series of testes in old boars, rams, or cats has been examined.

In boars testicular tumors are very unusual. Williams described a malignant tumor of an undescended testis in a boar. Cotchin reported a teratoma in a cryptorchid porcine testis. Holst reported on a seven-year-old boar with a seminoma of a testis that was four times as large as the opposite testis. When the boar was bred, about 250 ml of semen was collected but no spermatozoa were present and on histologic section areas of necrosis were found in the tumor.

In cats testicular tumors apparently are rare. Whitehead and Moulton reported on several Sertoli cell tumors in this species.

In dogs testicular tumors are observed at any age but most commonly in dogs over five years old. Innes reported that there was a higher incidence of testicular tumors in dogs than in humans. Dow reported an incidence of 16 per cent in 580 unselected adult dogs. The three principal testicular tumors in dogs are, seminomas, Sertoli cell tumors (tubular adenomas), and interstitial cell tumors, Moulton. Their comparative incidence is noted in Table 25. Teratomas have not been recorded in canine testes, Cotchin. These canine tumors are usually benign but up to 10 per cent of the Sertoli cell tumors and a few seminomas may be malignant in character, Dow, and Reif and Brodey. Of 177 tumors in 85 dogs described by Scully and Coffin, 55 per cent were multiple, 45 per cent were bilateral and 0.35 per cent of the dogs had two or more types of tumors. Five per cent of all tumors developed in cryptorchid testes. There is a significant correlation of Sertoli cell tumors and seminomas with cryptorchidism in dogs. (See Cryptorchidism). The age of the affected dogs averaged 10 to 11 years but the range was 3 to 20 years. Dogs with affected cryptorchid testes were younger than dogs with affected scrotal testes.

Table 25. Summary of Reports on the Comparative Incidence of Testicular Tumors in Dogs

Tumors	Innes	Dow	Scully & Coffin	Mulligan	Totals No.	Totals Percent
Seminoma	32	45	55	14	146	35.3
Sertoli cell	15	36	33	13	97	23.5
Interstitial cell	14	56	88	12	170	41.1

Seminomas are noted in old dogs, over 7 years of age and arise from the germinal epithelium of the seminiferous tubules, Moulton. Scully and Coffin reported these tumors originate in atrophic seminiferous epithelium and that the tumor is intratubular before becoming diffuse. These tumors grow slowly for months but may develop rapidly at any time. They are rather soft in consistency and hemorrhage or necrosis may be present. On section they appear dull-white or grey in color. Affected dogs may exhibit lameness and pain by crouching and hunching, Leonard, Rickard, and McEntee. Gleiser, and Scully and Coffin reported they were frequently bilateral and occasionally metastasized to the regional lymph nodes. In some cases seminomas and interstitial cell tumors are present together in the testis.

Sertoli cell tumors, or tubular adenomas are the least common of the principal tumors of the canine testis. This tumor arises from the Sertoli or nurse cell of the seminiferous tubules and is usually noted in older dogs. The tumor is often characterized by marked feminization of the male by the estrogens secreted by the tumor cells, Brodey and Martin. Recent studies by Siegel et al. indicated that the estrogenic substances produced by the tumor and causing feminization of the male were not the usual estrogens found in animals. The dog may attract other males. The penile sheath is swollen. There is a definite loss of hair, especially on the abdomen and lower parts of the body, and a loss of sexual desire. Mammary hypertrophy or gynecomastia, and enlargement of the nipples and in some cases development of mammary tumors may occur. Atrophy of the testicular tissues and penis develops. Pigmentation of the abdominal skin and scrotum, and female distribution of body fat are exhibited. The prostate may undergo marked enlargement due to squamous metaplasia and cysts; or it may become markedly involuted due to atrophy of the epithelial elements and collapse of the acini, Scully and Coffin. These tumors are rather large in size, firm, nodular, and fibrous on palpation. On cross section Sertoli-cell tumors are pale-yellow or grey in color and may contain necrotic, cystic, or hemorrhagic foci. If no metastases have occurred recovery from the above dramatic symptoms takes place promptly after the affected testis is removed.

Interstitial-cell tumors or adenomas, or Leydig-cell tumors are the most common tumor in old dogs. Although they are present in many old dogs, they are of little clinical significance. Most of them are found only at autopsy. They are often overlooked because of their small size; 1 mm to 2 cm is their usual size, McEntee. Although 41.1 per cent of testicular tumors cited in Table 25 were of the interstitial cell type, this percentage might well have been higher if all the small interstitial cell tumors had been found and recorded. The careful work of Scully and Coffin showed that 50 per cent of testicular tumors were of the interstitial cell type. Nodular hyperplasia of the interstitial cells is seen commonly in older dogs with senile testicular atrophy. Nodular hyperplasia is probably a preneoplastic change but the division between nodular hyperplasia and interstitial cell tumor is arbitrary, McEntee. These tumors probably produce androgens because the prostate in affected dogs is normal or hypertrophied. In uncommon instances these interstitial cell tumors may produce estrogenic compounds resulting in male feminizing syndrome with alopecia, atrophy of the prepuce and gynecomastia, Muller and Kirk. The tumors consist of single or multiple well-circumscribed nodules, brownish-orange in color and soft in consistency. Large tumors may occasionally by palpated in the testes of old dogs. They are similar in appearance to a corpus luteum and are likely to be bilateral and often contain hemorrhagic and necrotic foci. Innes indicated that this condition probably is nodular hyperplasia of the interstitial cells and that possibly these nodules should not be called true tumors. Although Innes described two cases in which this tumor metastasized, metastasis is rare.

Melanomas and mast cell tumors are not uncommon in the scrotal skin of the dog. The latter are usually malignant, Bloom. Canine tumors should be carefully differentiated from orchitis or epididymitis, traumatic swellings or hydrocele. The latter condition may be either congenital or secondary to orchitis. Canine perianal gland tumors according to Nielsen and Aftosmis are probably androgen dependent tumors that can be arrested by castration; about 85 per cent occur in older male dogs with a definite breed incidence in Cocker Spaniels.

Genetic or hereditary influence on acquired testicular degeneration have been reported in identical twin bulls by Bane. Genetic constitition appeared to influence the onset of generalized arthritis, fat necrosis, traumatic gastritis and associated testicular degeneration in identical twin bulls. McEntee has noted the increased predisposition and earlier occurrence of testicular degeneration in bulls with some testicular hypoplasia. Certain bulls may be more resistant to testicular degeneration than other bulls when affected by similar etiologic agents. Thus the genetic constitution of each male and his seminiferous epithelium and their resistance and ability to withstand adverse influences must be considered in the etiology and signs of testicular degeneration.

The signs of testicular degeneration are similar in all species of animals and range in degree from mild to severe depending upon the cause and duration of the degeneration. As indicated previously the patterns and signs of testicular degeneration are about the same despite the species or the etiologic factor(s) involved.

The fertility of the male may vary from only slightly reduced conception rates, to moderate to severe infertility, to complete sterility.

The age of the male with testicular degeneration may vary from young to old with most cases in the older animals.

The size of the testes is usually reduced from normal to about one-half to two-thirds normal size depending on the duration and degree of atrophy of the seminiferous tubular epithelium. Since 77.1, 72.2 and 49.9 per cent of the testicular volume is comprised of seminiferous tubules in 2.5-year-old, adult and one and one-half-year-old bulls, Amann, the close association of the degree of testicular degeneration and testicular size is apparent. In acute orchitis, inflammatory conditions, obstruction of the efferent ducts, or testicular tumors, an increase in testicular size is usually noted.

The consistency of the testes is soft and flabby in acute moderate to severe testicular degeneration. This is understandable since about 80 per cent of the volume of the testis is composed of seminiferous tubules and their contents. In mild testicular degeneration consistency differs only slightly from an elastic, tonic, slightly tense, fluctuating normal consistency. In these cases comparing the testicular consistency of the bull in question with several normal bulls of the same age may be helpful. The use of a tonometer has proven of value in the objective measurement of testicular consistency, Hahn et al.. In 150 bulls in an A.I. stud, soft, medium and firm consistencies of the testes were found in 14, 30 and 56 per cent, respectively. Bulls with soft testes tended to produce fewer sperm cells. The tonometer test correlated closely with other tests of semen quality.

Acute orchitis is characterized by a tense swelling and enlargement of the testis accompanied by pain and heat. This should be differentiated from hydrocele or hematocele. Chronic degeneration and atrophy of the testes especially in older males whether following severe acute or chronic diseases is characterized by fibrosis of the testes often with calcification. The latter is impossible to palpate but Barker reported about 25 per cent of 158 bovine testes from abattoir material revealed calcification on radiographic examination. Fibrotic testes are hard, firm and often lack tonicity or elasticity. Ultrasonics can be of value in the detection of connective tissue in fibrosis of the testes, Foote and Hahn. Testes containing tumors may be enlarged and have an irregular shape and consistency on palpation.

The libido or sex drive is usually not related or associated with testicular degeneration except in acute orchitis or other painful testicular diseases or in testicular atrophy associated with severe debility or inanition due to a variety of causes. As indicated previously the Leydig-cells are much more resistant to stress factors than the cells of the germinal epithelium.

The semen examination is very helpful in diagnosing testicular degeneration. Semen may be collected by the artificial vagina, by electroejaculation or other methods as will be described later. The former method is preferred. Since it requires about 60 days or more for sperm cells to develop from spermatogonia until they are ejaculated, it may be desirable in diagnosing testicular degeneration to take several samples at weekly or greater intervals. The semen production and quality in young immature bulls continues to improve in motility, concentration and morphology for months after puberty is reached so if an initial semen sample is poor, subsequent samples are indicated. The first semen samples taken after a long period of sexual rest may also be misleading as these are often of poor quality with many dead spermatozoa. In males where testicular degeneration is severe, semen quality is usually poor.

Sperm cell concentration may be reduced to one-third to one-half of normal values or show severe oligospermia or azoospermia. Watery, translucent semen is common in affected bulls and rams.

Sperm cell motility is reduced one-third to one-half or more due to an increase in abnormal cells, dead cells, necrospermia, or poorly viable cells. The duration of motility after ejaculation is shortened.

Sperm cell morphology after staining reveals an increase in dead spermatozoa and abnormal heads, tails, and middle pieces. The degree of change in the morphology of cells may vary from normal semen which usually contains from 5 to 15 per cent abnormal cells, to a 15 to 20 per cent increase in abnormal cells in mild cases of testicular degeneration, to a 20 to 30 per cent increase in moderate testicular degeneration, and to a 35 to 60 per cent or greater increase in severe testicular degeneration. The occurrence of large numbers of primary abnormalities as described by Blom, Lagerlof, and others, that arise during spermatocytogenesis or spermatogenesis and early spermiogenesis are more indicative of a severe testicular degeneration than the presence of secondary abnormalities that occur late in spermiogenesis or during storage of spermatozoa in the epididymis. The appearance of primitive cells such as giant cells and spermatocytes with restitution or pyknotic nuclei together with a marked reduction in sperm cell concentration and motility are signs of severe degeneration of the testes.

Other tests for **viability** and **longevity** may be employed but are more difficult to perform and do not add greatly to the information obtained by the previous tests. The volume of the ejaculate is not related to the degree of testicular degeneration. Testicular biopsies may be of value in certain species such as the dog and horse, Clark, but are impractical for technical reasons in the bull, Roberts. Furthermore the above signs and additional tests of sequential semen samples will accurately reveal the relative degree of testicular degeneration.

Prognosis—The prognosis in testicular degeneration is variable depending upon the causative factors, the duration and degree of the degeneration, and the age and value of the male. Although testicular degeneration can occur rapidly within a few hours, days or a week or more, recovery is very slow usually requiring 3 to 6 months or more in moderate to severe cases. The prognosis in slight or mild cases of testicular degeneration in young or middle-aged bulls due to transient and correctable causes is fair to good. Controlled breeding during the recovery period may result in fair to good fertility in some males.

The prognosis is guarded to fair in young males with only moderate evidence of testicular degeneration; in older males suddenly developing infertility due to a transient disease where advanced testicular changes do not occur; in mild cases of trauma to the testes, scrotal inflammations, toxemia or poisonings, mild exposure to irradiation, chronic but curable systemic diseases causing debility, and inanition due to semi-starvation.

The prognosis is poor in progressive senile testicular degeneration, in acute severe orchitis especially if it is bilateral and associated with abscessation, in advanced fibrosis and atrophy of the testes, in degeneration associated with hypoplasia in young to middle-aged males, and in older males with bilateral tumors of the testes.

Once the testes have been severely damaged regeneration can never be complete. If severe secondary infections or lesions occur in the epididymides, accessory glands, or vasa deferentia the prognosis is also guarded to poor.

The **treatment** of testicular degeneration requires the correction or the alleviation of the causative factor(s). Sexual rest is usually advised, since in most cases fertility is reduced to a point where the use of the male is questionable. Males with mild degrees of degeneration not severely influencing fertility should be used sparingly so as to maintain as large a number as possible of normal, motile spermatozoa in each ejaculate. A balanced ration high in vitamin A and possibly a good quality and variety of protein are indicated. Good-quality roughage or pasture is highly desirable. Some exercise especially on pasture is usually recommended for the larger farm animals, although Snyder and Ralston have shown that forced exercise has no effect on the fertility of the bull. If excessive heat and humidity is the cause of the temporary infertility in bulls, air conditioning or cooling is indicated.

Hormones are of no proven value. Testosterone, various FSH products, and thyroxine have been tried but none have any demonstrated effect in the therapy of testicular degeneration or hypoplasia. Furthermore the gonadotropic hormones to be of any value must be given over a period of a month or more and should be prepared from biologic sources from the same species to prevent antihormones from developing. Howard and coworkers, Weisman, Swyer and others have reported on the uniformily poor results from the hormonal or dietetic therapy of testicular degeneration in men.

In acute orchitis, sexual rest is imperative. Physical rest is usually advisable and can be provided by close confinement of the male. In the early acute stages heavy parenteral broad-range antibiotic therapy is indicated. Glucocorticoid agents along with the antibiotics might be helpful in reducing the inflammatory reaction. Ice packs should be applied to the testes by a suitable sling or bag fixed between the legs and tied over the back. This therapy should be continued until the acute, severe symptoms have subsided. When the orchitis is unilateral, removal of the affected testis may hasten recovery or save the breeding life of a valuable male. The testis should be examined carefully and cultured after removal to detect the responsible agent so that suitable precautions can then be taken for the future use of the sire if his fertility returns. The Brucella-infected bull or boar should not be used either artificially or naturally in a Brucella-free herd. Heat or a mild counter-irritant ointment to the inflamed testis and swollen scrotum should never be used. The preferred treatment for testicular tumors is prompt castration or removal of the affected testis. If metastases have occurred, symptoms caused by the secondary tumors will usually develop within a few months. Cryptorchid testes should be removed while the affected males are still young to prevent the occurrence of tumors so common in these structures in later life.

Acquired Testicular Pathology (Degeneration, Orchitis, Fibrosis)

Thermal effects and vascular lesions

Austin, J. W., Hupp, E. W. and Murphree, R. L. (1961) Effect of Scrotal Insulation on Semen of Hereford Bulls, J. An. Sci., **20,** 2, 307.

Clark, T. L. (1969) Equine Testicular Biopsy (abstr.), J.A.V.M.A., **154,** 11, 1367.

Donaldson, L. E. (1963) Some Observations on the Semen and Testicular Characteristics of Beef Bulls in Northern Queensland, Queensland Jour. of Agric. Sci., **20,** 2, 203.

Dutt, R. H. and Hamm, P. T. (1957) Effect of Exposure to High Environmental Temperature and Shearing on Semen Production of Rams in Winter, J. An. Sci., **16,** 2, 328.

Dubin, L. and Hotchkiss, R. S. (1969) Testis Biopsy in Subfertile Men with Varicocele, Fert. and Steril., **20,** 1, 50.

Faulkner, L. C., Hopwood, M. L., Masken, J. F., Kingman. H. E. and Stoddard, H L., (1967) Scrotal Frostbite in Bulls, J.A.V.M.A., **151,** 5, 602.

Fincher, M. G., Olafson, P. and Ferguson, J. (1942) Sterility in Bulls, Cor. Vet., **32,** 4, 407.

Gerona, G. R. and Sikes, J. O. (1970) Effects of Elevated Scrotum Temperature on Spermatogenesis and Semen Characteristics, J. Dairy Sci. **53,** 5, 659 (Abstr.)

Haq, I.. (1949) Causes of Sterility in Bulls in Southern England, Brit. Vet. Jour., **105;** 3, 4, 5, 6; 71; 144, 143, 200.

Hulet, C. V., El-Sheikh, A. S., Pope, A. L. and Casida, L. E. (1956) The Effects of Shearing and the Level of Feeding on Fertility in Rams, J. An. Sci., **15,** 3, 616.

Jensen, R., Flint, J. C., Brown, W. W. and Collier, J. R. (1962) Arteriosclerosis and Phlebosclerosis in Testes of Sheep, Amer. J. Vet. Res., **23,** 94, 480.

Johnston, J. E., Naelopaa, H., Frye, J. B., Jr. (1963) Physiologic Responses of Holstein, Brown Swiss and Red Sindhi Crossbred Bulls Exposed to High Temperatures and Humidities, J. An. Sci., **22,** 2, 432.

Knudsen, O. (1958) Studies on Spermatocytogenesis in the Bull, Internat. Jour. of Fert., **3,** 3 and 4, 389.

Knudsen, O. (1960) Testicular Biopsy in the Bull, Internat. Jour. of Fert., **5,** 2, 203.

Lagerlof, N. (1934) Morphologische Untersuchungen uber Veranderungen im Spermbild und in den Hoden bie Bullen mit Vesmiderter oder aufgehabener Fertilitat, Acta, Pathol. et Microbiol. Scand. Suppl. XIX.

McEntee, K. (1970) Pathology of Domestic Animals, Ed. 2, Vol. 1, edited by Jubb, K. V. and Kennedy, P. C. Academic Press, N.Y.C. and London.

MacLeod, J. (1969) Further Observations on the Role of Varicocele in Human Male Fertility, Fert. and Steril. **20,** 4, 545.

Moule, G. R. and Waites, G. M. H. (1963) Seminal Degeneration in the Ram and Its Relation to the Temperature of the Scrotum, J. Reprod. and Fertil, **5,** 433.

Roberts, S. J. (1956) Veterinary Obstetrics and Genital Diseases, Edwards, Bros., Inc. Ann Arbor, Michigan, 475.

Steinberger, E. and Dixon, W. H. (1959) Some Observations on the Effect of Heat on the Testicular Germinal Epithelium, Fert. and Steril., **10,** 6, 578.

VanderSluis, L. (1953) Experiences with the Examination into Herd Infertility, Proc. 1st World Congr. on Fert. and Steril, II, XXV, 703.

Irradiation, Hormone, Age and Traumatic Effects

Bloom, F. (1953) Endocrine Glands, Canine Medicine. Amer. Vet. Publ. Inc. Evanston, Ill.

Casarett, G. W. and Hursh, J. B. (1956) Effects of Daily Low Doses of Xrays on Spermatogenesis inDogs, Radiation Res., **5,** 473.

Charny, C. W. (1959) The Use of Androgens for Human Spermatogenesis, Fert. and Steril., **10,** 6, 557.

Collins, W. E., Inskeep, E. K. Dreher, W. H., Tyler, W. J. and Casida, L. E. (1962) Effect of Age on Fertility of Bulls in Artificial Insemination, J. Dairy Sci., **45,** 8, 1015.

Dawson, J. R. (1938) The Breeding Efficiency of Proved Aged Sires, J. Dairy Sci., **21,** 725.

Dunn, H. O., Roberts, S. J., McEntee, K. and Wagner, W. C. (1965) Prevention of Traumatic Gastritis in Bulls by the Use of Magnets, Cor. Vet., **55,** 204.

Hahn, J., Foote, R. H. and Seidel, G. E. Jr. (1969) Quality and Freezability of Semen from Growing and Aged Dairy Bulls, J. of Dairy Sci. **52,** 11, 1843.

Jackowski, L., Walkowdki, L. and Korycki, St. (1961) Studies on the Quality of Semen of Imported Bulls During the Acclimatization Period, Proc. 4th Internat. Congr. on Reprod., Hague, Vol. IV, 801.

MacLeod, J. and McGee, W. R. (1950) The Semen of the Thoroughbred, Cor. Vet., **40,** 3, 233.

McEntee, K. (1970) Pathology of Domestic Animals, 2nd Ed., Vol. 1 edited by Jubb, K. V. and Kennedy, P. C., Academic Press, N.Y.C. and London.

Meineke, C. F. and McDonald, L. E. (1961) The Effects of Exogenous Testosterone on Spermiogenesis of Bulls, Amer. J. Vet. Res., **22,** 87, 209.

Murphree, R. L. and Parish, N. R. (1956) Effects of Whole Body Radiation on Semen Characteristics in Bulls, J. An. Sci., **15,** 4, 1300.

Pace, H. B., Murphree, R. L. and Hupp, E. W. (1959) Effects of Total Body Irradiation on Semen Production of Boars, J. An. Sci., **18,** 4, 1554.

Welch, P. R. and Murphree, R. L. (1965) Sperm Production in Chronically Irradiated Bulls, J. An. Sci. **24,** 4, 1045.

Willett, E. L. (1957) Effect of Transportation upon Fertility of Bulls, J. Dairy Sci., **40,** 10, 1367.

Infectious Causes of Orchitis and Testicular Degeneration

Bouters, R. (1963) Experimentale Onderzoekingen over de Degeneratieve Invloed van een Entero-virus op het Spermaepitheel van Steeren, Thesis, Veterinary College, Ghent, Belgium.

Bouters, R. (1964) A Virus with Enterogenic Properties Causing Degeneration of the Germinal Epithilium in Bulls, Nature **201,** 217.

Bruner, D. W. and Gillespie, J. H. (1965) Hagan's Infectious Diseases of Domestic Animals, 5th Ed. Cornell Univ. Press, Ithaca, N.Y.

Carmichael, L. E. (1968) Personal communication—Cornell Veterinary Virus Research Institute, Ithaca, N.Y.

Carmichael, L. E. and Bruner, D. W. (1968) Characteristics of a Newly-Recognized Species of **Brucella** Responsible for Infectious Canine Abortion, Cor. Vet. **58,** 4, 579.

Carmichael, L. E. and Kenny, R. M. (1968) Canine Abortion caused by **Brucella canis,** J.A.V.M.A. **152,** 6, Part 1, 605.

Crenshaw, G. L. and McGowan, B. (1966) Ram Epididymitis Vaccination, Proc 70th Ann. Meeting U.S.L.S.A., 476.

DeBoom, H. P. A. (. (1962) Personal Communication.

Florent, A. (1963) Viral Infertility, in **Infertility in Livestock,** FAO, Rome, 36.

Gledhill, B. L. (1968) Viral Infertility in Cattle, Cor. Vet., **58,** 466.

Gribble, D. H. (1969) Equine Ehrlichiosis, J.A.V.M.A. **155,** 2, 462.

Kimball, A., Twiehaus, M. J. and Frank, E. R. (1954) **Actinomyces Bovis** Isolated from Six Cases of Bovine Orchitis, Amer. J. Vet. Res. **15,** 57, 551.

Kirk, R. W. (1967) Current Veterinary Therapy, W. B. Saunders, Co., Philadelphia, London, and Toronto.

Lambert, G., Deyoe, B. L. and Painter, G. M. (1964) Postvaccinal Persistance of **Brucella abortus** Strain 19 in Two Bulls, J.A.V.M.A. **145,** 909.

McEntee, K. (1970) Pathology of Domestic Animals, 2nd Ed., Vol. I edited by Jubb K. V. and Kennedy P. C. Academic Press, N.Y.C. and London.

McIlwain, O. D. and Bolin, R. M. (1967) A Mycoplasma Associated with Ovine Orchitis, Amer. Jour. Vet. Res. **28,** 124, 885.

Mensik, J., Bohac, J. and Setka, R. (1961) The Etiology of Infectious Orchitis in Bulls in Czechoslovakia, Vet. Bull. **31,** 323.

Moore, J. A. and Kakuk, T. J. (1969) Male Dogs Naturally Infected with **Brucella Canis**, J.A.V.M.A. 155, 8, 1352.

Norton, W.L. and Storz, J. (1967) Polyarthritis of Sheep, (I) Arthritis and Rheumatism 10, 1, (Abstr. Vet. Med. 170).

Pols, J.W. (1960) Studies on Bovine Besnoitiosis with Special Reference to the Etiology, Onderstepoort, J. Vet. Res 28, 265.

Roberts, S.J. (1956) Veterinary Obstetrics and Genital Diseases. Edwards Bros. Inc., Ann Arbor Mich.

Sheffy, B., Roberts, S. J. and Parsonson, I. (1970) Unpublished data.

Storz, J., Carroll, E. J., Ball, L. and Faulkner, L. C. (1968) Isolation of a Psittacosis Agent (Chlamydia) from Semen and Epididymis of Bulls with Seminal Vesiculitis Syndrome, Amer. J. Vet. Res. **29,** 3, 549.

Switzer, W. P. (1964) Diseases of Swine, 2nd Ed. Edit. by Dunne, H. W., Iowa State Univ. Press, 502.

Vandeplassche, M. (1969) Personal Communication.

Watson, W. A. (1964) Infertility in the Ram Associated with Tick-borne Fever Infection, Vet Rec. **76,** 41, 1131.

Nutritional, Toxic, and Autoimmunizing Causes

Bishop, R. L. (1950) The Effect of Fuadin of the Semen of Dogs, Vet. Med. **45,** 9, 384.

Busey, W. M. (1965) Immunologically Induced Testicular Degeneration in Rams, Dissert. Abstr. **66,** 5379.

Faulkner, L. C. (1970) Personal Communication.

Faulkner, L. C., Carroll, E. J. and Benjamin, M. (1964) Effect of Coumaphos on Bulls, J.A.V.M.A. 145, 5, 456.

Gunn, R. M. C., Sanders, R. N., Granger, W. (1942) Studies in Fertility in Sheep, Commonwealth of Austral. Council for Sci. and Ind. Res. Bull. 148.

Losos, G. J. (1967) Experimental Induction of Testicular Lesions in Bulls by Auto-immunization, Ph.D Thesis., Cornell Univ., Ithaca, N.Y.

Losos, G. J., Winter, A. J. and McEntee, K. (1968) Induction of Testicular Degeneration in Bulls by Isoimmunization, Amer. J. Vet. Res. **29,** 12, 2295.

McEntee, K. (1970) Pathology of Domestic Animals, 2nd Ed., Vol. I edited by Jubb, K. V. and Kennedy, P. C., Academic Press Inc., N.Y.C. and London.

McEntee, K. and Olafson, P. (1953) Reproductive Tract Pathology in Hyperkeratosis of Cattle and Sheep, Fert. and Steril **4,** 2, 128.

Menge, A. C. (1965) Effects of Immunizing Bulls with Semen and Testis, J. An. Sci. **24,** 3, 926.

Sikes, J. D. (1959) Effects of Potassium Nitrate on Bovine Semen Production and Various Spermatozoan Characteristics, J. Dairy Sci. **42,** 5, 930.

Testicular Neoplasms, Genetic and Miscellaneous Causes.

Bane, A. (1954) Sexual Functions of Bulls in Relation to Heredity, Rearing Intensity and Somatic Conditions, Acta. Agric. Scand. **4,** 2, 97.

Bloom, F. (1954) Pathology of the Dog and Cat, Amer. Vet. Public. Inc., Evanston, Ill.

Brodey, R. S. and Martin J. E. (1958) Sertoli Cell Neoplasms in the Dog. The Clinicopathological and Endocrinological Findings in Thirty Seven Dogs, J.A.V.M.A. **133,** 249.

Cotchin, E. (1956) Neoplasms of Domestic Animals; A Review, Commonwealth Bureau of An. Health., #4, Bucks, England.

Dow, C. (1962) Testicular Tumors in the Dog, J. Comp. Path. and Therap. **72,** 3, 247.

Dunn, H. O. and McEntee, K. (1964) Semen Quality and Fertility in Dairy Bulls with Testicular Tumors, Internat. J. of Fert. **9,** 4, 613.

Feldman, W. H. (1932) Neoplasms of Domestic Animals, Philadelphia, Pa.

Holst, S. J. (1949) Sterility in Boars, Nord. Vet. Med. **1,** 2, 87.

Innes, J. R. M. (1942) Neoplastic Diseases of the Testis in Animals, J. of Path. and Bact. **54,** 485.

Knudson, O. and Schantz, B. (1963) Seminoma in the Stallion, A Clinical Cytological and Pathologicoanatomical Investigation, Cor. Vet. **53,** 3, 395.

McEntee, K. (1970) Pathology of Domestic Animals, 2nd Ed., Vol I edited by Jubb, K. V. and Kennedy, P. C., Academic Press Inc. N.Y.C. and London.

Moulton, J. E. (1961) Tumors of Domestic Animals Univ. of California Press, Berkeley, Cal.

Muller, G. H. and Kirk, R. W. (1969) Small Animal Dermatology, W. B. Saunders Co., Philadelphia.

Mulligan, R. M. (1949) Neoplasms in the Dog, Williams & Wilkins Co., Baltimore, Md.

Nielsen, S. W. and Aftosmis, J. (1964) Canine Perianal Gland Tumors, J.A.V.M.A. **144,** 2, 127.

Reif, J. S. and Brodey, R. S. (1969) The Relationship Between Cryptorchidism and Canine Testicular Neoplasia, J.A.V.M.A. **155,** 12, 2005.

Scully, R. E. and Coffin, D. L. (1952) Canine Testicular Tumors, Cancer, **5,** 3, 592.

Siegal, E. T., Forchielli, E., Dorfman, R. I., Brodey, R. S. and Prier, J. E. (1967) An Estrogen Study in the Feminized Dog with Testicular Neoplasia, Endocrin. **80,** 272.

Smith, H. A. (1954) Interstitial Cell Tumor of an Equine Testis, J.A.V.M.A. **124,** 926, 356.

Whitehead, J. E. (1967) Neoplasia in the Cat, Vet. Med. **62,** 1, 44.

Williams, W. L. (1943) Diseases of the Genital Organs of Domestic Animals, 3rd Ed. Louella Williams, Upland Rd., Ithaca, N.Y.

Signs, Diagnosis, Prognosis and Treatment of Testicular Degeneration

Amann, R. P. (1960) Quantitative Testicular Histology and Theoretical Sperm Production of Holstein Bulls, J. Dairy Sci. **43,** 6, 883.

Barker, C. A. V. (1956) Some Observations on Testicular Calcification in Bulls, Cand. J. of Comp. Med. and Vet. Sci. **20,** 2, 37.

Blom, E. (1950) On Methods of Evaluating Bull Semen, Thesis, C. Mortensen, Copenhagen, Denmark.

Foote, R. H. and Hahn, G. (1968) Unpublished data, Ithaca, N.Y.

Hahn, J., Foote, R. H. and Cranch, E. T. (1969) Tonometer for Measuring Testicular Consistency of Bulls to Predict Semen Quality, J. An. Sci. **29,** 3, 483.

Howard, R. P., Simmons, F. A. and Sniffen, R. (1951) Differential Diagnosis in Male Sterility, Fert. and Steril. **2,** 2, 95.

Lagerlof, N. (1938) Infertility In Male Domestic Animals, Proc. .3th Internat. Vet. Congr. Vol. I, 214.

Roberts, S. J. (1956) Veterinary Obstetrics and Genital Diseases, Edwards Bros. Inc., Ann Arbor, Mich., 475.

Snyder, J. W. and Ralston, N. P. (1955) Effect of Forced Exercise on Bull Fertility, J. Dairy Sci., **38,** 2, 125.

Swyer, A. I. M. (1956) Therapeutic Agents in Defective Spermatogenesis, Internat. J. of Fertil. **4,** 360.

Weisman, A. I. (1950) End Results of the Treatment of Male Infertility: A Study of 600 Males, Fert. and Steril. **1,** 3, 216.

Pathological or Functional Disturbances of the Epididymis, Vas Deferens and Accessory Reproductive Glands in the Male Causing Failure of Fertilization or Conception.

Pathology of the Epididymis—Disease of the epididymis includes: infection of the epididymal duct and epididymitis, anomalies often causing sperm granulomas, tumors, and functional or hormonal disturbances.

Epididymitis, or inflammation of the epididymis, is occasionally observed as an acquired lesion in all species of animals and is caused by or may be secondary to the same factors causing orchitis. Infectious causes of epididymitis most commonly involve the duct in the tail of the epididymis but may involve the body and head of the epididymis. These include: **Brucella abortus** in bulls, **Brucella suis** in boars, **Brucella ovis** (ram epididymitis organism, REO) in rams, **Brucella canis** in dogs, Carmichael and Kenney, **Streptococcus zooepidemicus** in a stallion, VanderSchaaf and Hendrikse, **C. pyogenes** and other miscellaneous organisms such as **streptococci, staphylococci, Proteus, E. coli, C. pseudotuberculosis, Actinobacillus seminis,** Livingston and Hardy, and **Pseudomonas aeruginosa.** Infections may be caused by organisms, such as mycoplasma, invading the epididymis through the vas deferens or by way of the blood or lymph vessels. (See seminovesiculitis) Traumatic injuries may also produce an epididymitis, Pulsford and coworkers. Experimental work in dogs has suggested that inflammation of the epididymis may be caused by accidental passage of either normal or infected urine to the epididymis through the vas deferens, Graves and Engel, McEntee. Canine distemper virus in sexually mature dogs causes an epididymitis, Kirk and McEntee, Mensik and coworkers isolated a virus from chronic orchitis and epididymitis that occurred endemically in AI centers in Czechoslovakia. A specific bovine venereal epididymitis and vaginitis or "epivag" has been described in Chapter XIV. This venereal and probably viral disease, found only in East, South, and Central Africa, is usually characterized in the bull by a marked bilateral hardening and swelling of the tail of the epididymis. Pathological fibrotic changes also occur in the vas deferens, testes, and seminal vesicles, Bruner and Gillespie and Mare and VanRensburg. There is no cure for affected males but artificial insemination has been an effective control measure to prevent the spread of this venereal disease. VanRensburg has described other diseases of the testis and epididymis of bulls in South Africa. Besnoitiosis due to **Besnoitia besnoiti** produces elephantiasis of the scrotal skin and cysts in the scrotum, inguinal canal, testes, and epididymis. These cysts may persist and calcify, causing sterility. Storz and coworkers have isolated a psittacoid, Chlamydia or PLT agent from the epididymis of young bulls with epididymitis, orchitis and seminal vesiculitis, that is a possible agent producing the clincial seminal vesiculitis syndrome.

Brucella ovis (ram epididymis organism) is a common cause of ram epididymitis and infertility in Australia, New Zealand, U.S., Central Europe and South America, Lawrence, Keogh. In California in 1956 examination of 1882 rams revealed a 27 per cent incidence of infection. Of 175 ewe lambs bred to clinically clean rams, 75 per cent lambed within a 30 day period while only 47 per cent of 171 ewe lambs bred to clinically-infected rams lambed during the same period, McGowan and Schultz. Ewes bred to infected rams had a greatly increased number of services per conception and fewer lambs per ewe than ewes bred to noninfected control rams, McGowan and Devine. The infective organism is spread mainly by venereal contact to susceptible rams breeding a ewe recently bred by an infected ram, or by rams penned together mounting each other and having rectal copulation or sodomy between rams. Ewes play a minor role in the spread of the infection and are relatively resistant to the infection; but occasional abortions due to **Brucella ovis** are reported. Young rams raised from infected ewes are not infected. Rams are readily infected by the conjunctival or rectal instillation of the organism. Rams may spread the organism for 3 to 4 years while ewes may spread infection for a much shorter period, especially for several days after an occasional abortion. Following infection the antibody levels rise by the third week and persist for more than a year after the bacteremic stage of the disease. The organisms localize in the epididymis, seminal vesicles, ampullae, liver, and kidneys. The organisms cause perivascular lesions with edema and fibrosis in the epididymis resulting in obstruction of the lumen and stasis of the epididymal contents and finally extravasation of semen that because of its high lipid and mycolic acid content results in the formation of a spermatic granuloma resembling tubercular granulomas, Biberstein and coworkers,

McEntee. (See Figure 189) Over 90 per cent of these lesions affect the tail of the epididymis but occasionally the body and head of the epididymis may be involved. If the lesions are unilateral, fertility is normal or only slightly impaired; if they are bilateral, sterility is usually present, Swift and Weyerts. In 29 naturally-infected rams the semen quality, including motility and concentration, was inferior in 50 per cent of the rams and normal in only 25 per cent, McGowan and Devine. It takes 2 to 4 months from the onset of infection to the development of the lesions in the tail of the epididymis that causes it to become 3 to 5 times normal size and fibrotic. Some infected rams fail to develop gross palpable lesions.

Diagnosis is based on clinical palpation of the epididymis to detect induration, spermatic granulomas and enlargements, especially involving the tail of the epididymis. Some affected rams would be difficult to differentiate on clinical examination from those with epididymitis due to other causes such as **C. pseudotuberculosis** or **Actinobacillus seminis.** These latter would be more sporadic, variable in location and resemble abscesses rather than granulomas. Enlargement of the head of the epididymis is more likely due to granulomas secondary to anomalies of the efferent ducts. The combination of clinical palpation of the testes and the complement-fixation test on serum was most effective in locating shedders of **Brucella ovis.** Screening tests were run at 1:10 dilutions, Biberstein and McGowan. Culture of the semen for the presence of organisms is possible but not as accurate nor as practical as the above two diagnostic tests. Matthews and Trueblood have developed a precipitin test for the detection of REO that may prove simpler to run and more accurate than the C.F. test. Fluorescent antibody techniques and the indirect hemagglutination test are also promising diagnostic laboratory techniques.

Controlling ram epididymitis in a flock is highly important to maintaining good fertility in the flock. Before the breeding season all rams that show clinical or serologic evidence of epididymitis should be eliminated. In valuable purebred rams semen examination or actual fertility trials may be used, McGowan and Devine. Various vaccination procedures have been used successfully to protect rams against **Brucella ovis.** In New Zealand they have used a combination of **Brucella ovis** bacterin and strain 19 **Brucella abortus** vaccine, Ris, Buddle. In California Crenshaw and McGowan have developed an alum-precipitated commercial REO bacterin given subcutaneously in two doses 30 to 60 days apart and followed by a single injection repeated each year. This caused a granuloma and some soreness and irritation at the site of the subcutaneous injection behind the elbow, but abscessation was rare. Vaccination caused a serum titer to de elop tha lasted for several years after the combined vaccines were given, Ris. The combination of the vaccine with other control practices was highly effective in infected flocks of sheep. Although **Br. ovis** is reported to be sensitive to some antibiotics, the treatment of chronic lesions is of doubtful value, Bruner and Gillespie.

Canine brucellosis due to **Brucella canis** is apparently widespread in the U.S. among dogs, especially Beagles, Carmichael and Kenney, causing abortion in the females and swelling of the scrotum, firm enlargement of the epididymis, especially in the tail, and degeneration and atrophy of the testis with sterility. The disease is spread by direct contact with aborted fetuses, placental tissues and the infective vaginal discharges of bitches for several weeks after abortion. Venereal transmission to females by the semen from chronically-infected males appears probable. Following exposure a bacteremia develops within one to three weeks with a generalized lymphadenitis. Antibodies develop that can be detected by the agglutination test; 1:100 is considered positive. These antibodies may last indefinitely or as long as a bacteremia persists. The organisms can often be recovered from the lymph glands, spleen, liver, prostate, testes and epididymides. Clinical lesions need not be present. The prognosis is poor in clinically-affected male dogs. Any possible effective antibiotic therapeutic regimen must be heroic and sustained. If the genital organs are seriously damaged or if the lesions are bilateral, recovery is unlikely. Efforts to develop a bacterin have been unsuccessful. Prevention and control of canine brucellosis presently is based on monthly serologic tests of all dogs in the kennel, and those entering, together with segregation and destruction of positive animals. **Brucella canis** has caused human infections.

The prognosis in severe or moderate epididymitis is poor, as obstructions usually occur preventing the discharge of spermatozoa from that testis. There is no practical cure in animals once the epididymis is obstructed. In the occasional case of bilateral epididymitis the prognosis is hopeless. In recent years operations have been devised to bipass the obstructed portion of the epididymis in humans but the percentage of cures is low.

If in a valuable animal the epididymitis is unilateral and the accessory glands and the vas deferens have no lesions or infection caused by the same organisms, unilateral castration may be indicated followed by a long recovery period for the normal testis during which repeated tests and cultures of the semen may be performed to be certain the genital infection has been eliminated.

Anomalies of the Epididymis may be either congenital or hereditary and consist of: (1) a spermiostasis due to distention of aberrant efferent or epididymal tubules with the secondary formation of spermatic granulomas in the region of the head of the epididymis, (2) segmental aplasia of the mesonephric or Wolffian duct, and (3) mesonephric or paramesonephric duct cysts or remnants near the epididymis or vas deferens.

Spermiostasis, resulting in spermatoceles and in time, by the same process as described under infections, spermatic granulomas, resembling tubercular granulomas, may be caused by blind rudimentary mesonephric tubules, ductuli aberrantes. These tubules most often are defective efferent tubules. They may be attached to the rete or epididymis and therefore produce lesions involving the head region, caput, of the epididymis and only rarely other portions of the epididymis. The condition is common in bucks and possibly rams, less common in bulls and rare in the other domestic animals. In rams it has been confused with ram epididymitis which usually causes spermatic granulomas in the tail of the epididymis. In bucks the condition is usually bilateral resulting in complete sterility. The incidence in bucks in Germany was reported to be 20 to 25 per cent and therefore the condition was of great economic importance. In bulls of two Danish breeds the incidence was about 3 per cent, and more than 90 per cent of the cases were unilateral so most bulls remained fertile. Blom and Christensen stated that there was considerable evidence that bovine spermiostasis in the mesonephric ducts is genetically determined by some recessive hereditary factor. The author has observed two related Brown Swiss bulls with spermiostasis and granulomas of the left caput epididymis.. Spermiostasis with spermatocele and spermatic granulomas develop slowly thus young, even bilaterally affected, males may be fertile for a year or more until the fibrous tissue of the granuloma completely obstructs the mesonephric duct. Spermatozoa and fluid are continued to be produced in the seminiferous tubules and absorbed in the efferent ducts and head of the epididymis if the obstruction is located at the distal portion of the head. If the obstruction is located at the proximal portion of the head or in the efferent tubules the back pressure may produce testicular degeneration but the size and consistency of the testicle may remain nearly normal due to the accumulation of testicular secretions, McEntee.

Segmental aplasia of the mesonephric, Wolffian, duct may occur congenitally in all species but has been well-described in bulls by Blom and Christensen. The majority of cases are unilateral and the body, tail, entire epididymis, and even a part or all of the vas deferens may be missing. In unilateral cases the bull is fertile. In the latter instance the seminal vesicle, vesicular gland, on the same side may also be hypoplastic or missing. (See Figures 194 and 195) The incidence of bovine segmental aplasia of the mesonephric duct in Denmark according to Blom and Christensen was 0.59 to 1.18 per cent. VanderSluis recorded a 5 per cent incidence in 828 infertile bulls he examined; while the incidence in 584 "normal" bulls was 1.7 per cent. This condition has been described in dogs, Leonard, Rickard and McEntee. The author has observed a few cases in Holstein, Guernsey and Angus bulls in New York State. Blom and Christensen stated that there was a strong indication that segmental aplasia of the mesonephric duct was hereditary as in 19 male offspring of a unilaterally affected bull there were 4 sons similarly affected. The missing segment was most often lacking on the right side. In older bulls spermatoceles and/or granulomas may develop just proximal to the missing segment.

In unilaterally affected bulls the sperm cell concentration is about one-half normal as is the total number of spermatozoa per ejaculate. Careful clinical palpation of the testes and epididymides, and a rectal examination of the ampullae and seminal vesicles in the larger species will usually detect and delineate the extent of the segmental aplasia. A small epididymis accompanies hypoplasia of the testis. The testis associated with segmental aplasia of the epididymis is usually normal in size or may occasionally be atrophied. Palpation of a very small or missing tail of the epididymis is highly indicative of segmental aplasia. The head of the epididymis, if present, is often enlarged due to distention with sperm. If the segmental aplasia is located in the vas deferens, the tail of the epididymis may be enlarged. In rare cases the missing segment may be located in the vas deferens near the urethra causing distention of the ampulla.

There is no treatment for this condition, other than possible surgery to reunite the unaffected portions of the mesonephric duct. Because of the possible hereditary nature of this anomaly affected males should be discarded.

Mesonephric or Wolffian, or Paramesonephric or Mullerian Duct Cysts or Remnants and miscellaneous anomalies may be found in males and are of little consequence except in cases where they may be large and are confused with defects or diseases of the epididymis on palpation. McEntee reported that ectopic rests of adrenal cortical tissue may be found in the testis, epididymis or spermatic cord, especially in the horse. Carroll reported a rare case of a Holstein bull, twin to a freemartin, that had an area of testicular rete tissue outside of the testis in the region of the head of the epididymis. This is commonly observed in the rat. Paradidymides were seen on the spermatic cord in 25 to 46 per cent of calves and are of no significance, Blom and Christensen. Occasional mesonephric duct cysts may be found in bulls near the head and tail of the epididymis and some may be lined by ciliated cells, "medusa cysts". Paramesonephric cysts or uterus masculinus are seen commonly in 24 to 44 per cent of bulls on the dorsal surface of the urogenital fold between

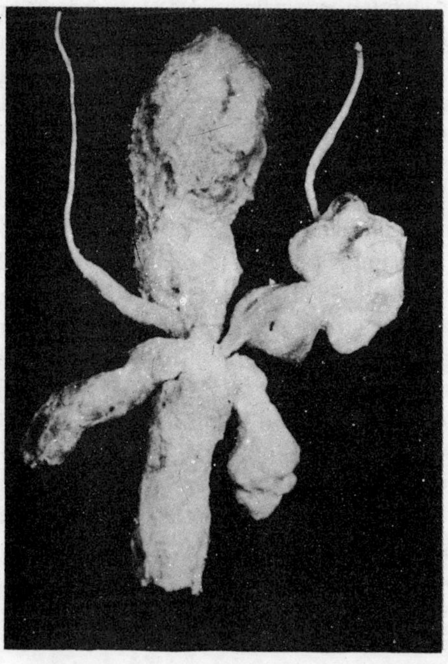

Figure 194. Segmental Aplasia of the Terminal Portion of the Right Ductus Deferens with a Marked Dilation of the Ampulla with Semen in a Bull

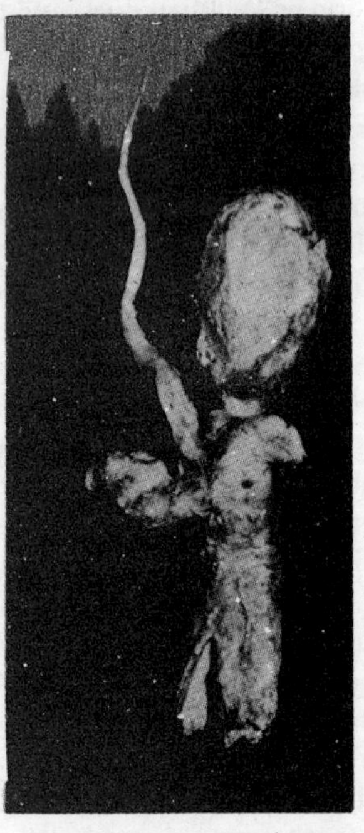

Figure 195. Aplasia of the Right Ampulla and Ductus Deferens and Arrested Development of the Right Seminal Vesicle in a Bull.

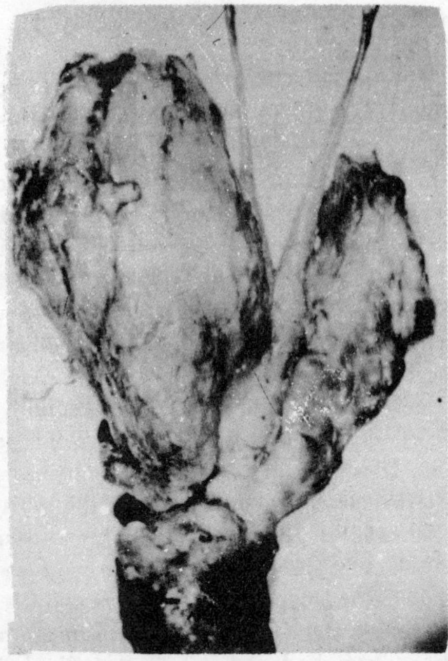

Figure 196. Seminovesiculitis in a Bull.

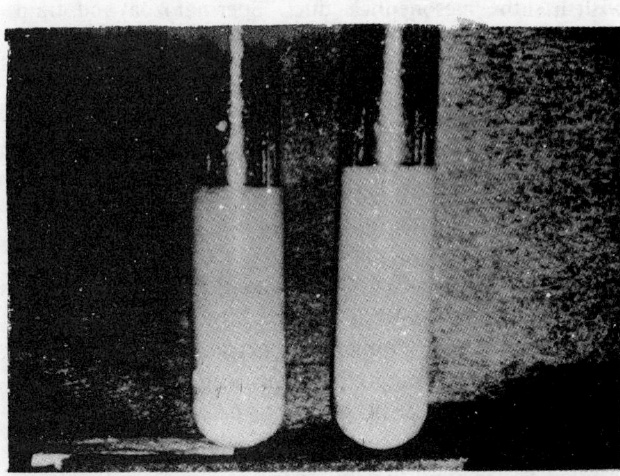

Figure 197. Ejaculates Containing Clots of Pus from a Bull with Seminovesiculitis.

the ampullae and ductus deferens or rarely in or near the epididymis, Blom and Christensen, and Kanagawa and coworkers.

Primary tumors of the epididymis are rare in all animals. Testicular tumors in dogs or other animals may invade the epididymis or spread through the epididymis to the vas deferens and cord. Occasionally metastatic tumors may develop in the epididymis. Bloom reported that primary tumors of the epididymis are nonexistant in the cat and rare in the dog. He described only 2 cases of fibromas of the epididymis in dogs.

Miscellaneous Diseases of the Epididymis—Obstruction and enlargement of the epididymis in bulls resulted from a metaplastic process in hyperkeratosis, McEntee and Olafson. Feeding highly chlorinated napthalenes caused external symptoms of hyperkeratosis and complete sterility. Fertility was gradually regained in about 10 months after withdrawal of the toxic agent. McEntee has described sperm granulomas of the vas deferens and tail of the epididymis secondary to adenomyosis of the duct wall.

There is definite evidence that a change in the environment of spermatozoa, especially in the tail of the epididymis, due to probable changes in the epididymal epithelium may result in a reduction or absence of motility or akinesia or necrospermia associated with bent or looped tails. Testosterone maintains the function of the epididymis. Cupps and Briggs showed that estrogens injected into adult bulls caused an increase in abnormal bent or looped sperm tails. Frequent collection of these treated bulls resulted in a decline of abnormal sperm cells. Cappucci and Cupps reported on three infertile Jersey bulls with many vacuolated basal epithelial cells of the cauda epididymis and with many secretory granules in the lumen of the duct. Later Cupps et al. reported on inbred Jersey bulls with impaired fertility characterized by poor quality semen with bent, looped and coiled tails, tailless heads, abnormal heads and thickened midpieces. This genetic condition was caused by a reduced sex steroid production due to the subnormal formation of its precursor, 17a hydroxyprogesterone. Testicular injury and reduced production of sperm cells, hormonal upsets, as excess estrogen, and insulation of the scrotum produces changes in the epididymal plasma resulting in sperm defects especially reduced motility and tail or midpiece defects. These defects develop in the corpus and tail of the epididymis, Gustafsson. MacLeod indicated that poor sperm cell motility, seen occasionally in stallions, may not be due to an intrinsic defect of the spermatozoa but due to a failure of the epididymis to properly support the cells for their relatively long storage period in that organ. One of the first and most striking effects following hypophysectomy of young human males was the complete loss of motility in sperm cells already present in the epididymis. Exogenous testosterone therapy was suggested. Gustafsson reported on a young bull with spermakinesia associated with a high percentage of bent and coiled tails. When 20 ejaculates were taken within 12 hours the motility increased from 0 to 50 per cent, the live sperm cells increased from 25 to 80 per cent and abnormal tails decreased from 80 to 30 per cent. Thus the increased rate of sperm cell transport through the epididymis improved the semen quality indicating a disturbed function of the epithelium of the cauda epididymis. The sodium and potassium levels in the seminal plasma of the cauda epididymis were very low possibly resulting in a lower than normal osmotic pressure and metabolic disturbance. This may have been due to an imbalance between androgens and estrogens.

Pathology of the Vas Deferens and Ampullitis

Infection and inflammation of the vas deferens is usually associated with an orchitis, epididymitis, or seminal vesiculitis. Infection of the vas deferens apparently occurs less commonly in animals in which the ampullae or dilated proximal portions of the vas deferens are absent. In the stallion and bull, infections with organisms such as **Br. abortus,** streptococci, **C. pyogenes,** tubercle bacillus, **Ps. aeurginosa,** and others including viruses, have been observed. (See infectious causes for orchitis and epididymitis). The infection is usually unilateral but may be bilateral.

As discussed previously, segmental aplasia may occasionally be present in the vas deferens, usually unilaterally and paramesonephric cysts or uterus masculinus, are common in the urogenital fold between the two ampullae, especially in bulls.

Careful rectal examination will usually reveal a thickened, firm and possibly painful enlargement when ampullae are diseased. Semen examination may reveal leukocytes and the infective organisms. In some cases the semen contains clots of pus and the motility of the spermatozoa is poor. If the motility is good immediately after ejaculation, the spermatozoa often lose their motility rapidly on storage. In cases of segmental aplasia where the missing segment is near the urethra, the ampullae may become greatly enlarged and distended with spermatozoa but no inflammatory reaction is present. Often the seminal vesicle on the same side as the missing segment is also hypoplastic or absent. Treatment of infected or diseased ampullae is similar to treatment for seminal vesiculitis.

References

Diseases of the Epididymis and Vas Deferens, Infections of the Epididymis

Biberstein, E. L. and McGowan, B. (1958) Epididymitis in Rams—Studies on Laboratory Diagnosis, Cor. Vet. **48,** 1, 31.

Biberstein, E. L., McGowan, B., Olander, H., and Kennedy, P. C. (1964) Epididymitis in Rams—Studies on the Pathogenesis, Cor. Vet. **54,** 1, 27.

Bruner, D. W. and Gillespie, J. H. (1966) Hagan's Infectious Diseases of Domestic Animals, 5th Ed. Cornell Univ. Press, Ithaca, N.Y.

Buddle, M. B. (1958) Vaccination in the Control of **Br. ovis** Infection in Sheep, New Zealand Vet. J. **6,** 41.

Carmichael, L. E. and Kenney, R. M. (1968) Canine Abortion Caused by **Brucella canis,** J.A.V.M.A. **152,** 6, 605.

Crenshaw, G. L. and McGowan, B. (1966) Ram Epididymitis Vaccination, Proc. 70th Ann. Meeting U.S.L.S.A., 476.

Graves, R. S. and Engel, W. J. (1950) Experimental Production of Epididymitis with Sterile Urine; Clinical Implications, J. Urol. **64,** 4, 601.

Gustafsson, B. (1966) Luminal Contents of the Bovine Epididymis under Conditions of Reduced Spermatogenesis, Luminal Blockage and Certain Sperm Abnormalities, Thesis, Dept. Obstet. and Gynec., Royal Vet. Col., Stockholm.

Keogh, J., Doolette, J. B. and Clapp, K. H. (1958) The Epidemiology of Ovine Brucellosis in South Australia, Austral. Vet. J. **34,** 412.

Lawrence, W. E. (1961) Ovine Brucellosis: A Review of the Disease in Sheep Manifested by Epididymitis and Abortion, Brit. Vet. J. **117,** 435.

Livingston, C. W., Jr. and Hardy, W. T. (1964) Isolation of **Actinobacillus seminis** from Ovine Epididymitis, Amer. J. Vet. Res. **25,** 106, 660.

Mare, J. and VanRensburg, S. J. (1961) The Isolation of Viruses Associated with Infertility in Cattle: A Preliminary Report, J. S. Afr. Vet. M.A. **32,** 201.

Matthews, T. R. and Trueblood, M. S. (1967) Detection of Precipitins Against **Brucella Ovis,** Cor. Vet. **57,** 3, 410.

McEntee, K. (1970) Pathology of Domestic Animals, 2nd Ed., Vol. 1, edited by Jubb, K. V. and Kennedy, P. C. Academic Press, Inc., N.Y.C. and London.

McEntee, K. (1967–1968) Current Veterinary Therapy, 2nd Ed., Edit. by Kirk, R. W. W. B. Saunders, Co., Philadelphia and London.

McGowan, B. and Devine, D. R. (1960) Epididymitis of Rams. The Effect of Naturally Occurring Disease upon Fertility, Cor. Vet. **50,** 2, 102.

McGowan, B. and Schultz, G. (1956) Epididymitis in Rams. Clinical Description and Field Aspects, Cor. Vet. **46,** 2, 277.

Pulsford, M. F., Eastick, B. C., Clapp, K. H. and Roberts, R. (1967) Traumatic Epididymitis of Dorset Horn and Poll Dorset Rams, Austral. Vet. J. **43,** 3, 99.

Ris, D. R. (1967) The Persistence of Antibodies Against **Brucella ovis** and **Brucella Abortus** in Rams Following Vaccination: A Field Study, N.Z. Vet. Jour. **15,** 94.

Storz, J., Carroll, E. J., Ball, L. and Faulkner. L. C. (1968) Isolation of a Psittacosis Agent (Chlamydia) from Semen and Epididymis of Bulls with Seminal Vesiculitis Syndrome, Amer. J. Vet. Res. **29,** 3, 549.

Swift, B. L. and Weyerts, P. R. (1970) Ram Epididymitis: A Study on Infertility, Cor. Vet. **60,** 2, 204.

VanderSchaaf, A. and Hendrikse, J. (1963) Infection of the Internal Genital Organs of a Stallion with **Str. zooepidemicus,** Tijdschr. v. Diergeneesk, **88,** 13, 834.

VanRensburg, S. W. J. (1953) Bovine Sterility Caused by Infectious Diseases in South Africa, Brit. Vet. J. **109,** 226.

Sperm Granulomas and Miscellaneous Diseases of the Epididymis and Vas Deferens

Blom, E. and Christensen, N. O. (1951) Congenital Absence of the Epididymis, Ductus Deferens or Glandular Vesicularis (Aplasia Segmentalis Ductus Wolffii) in the Bull, Yearbook Royal Vet. and Agr. Col. Copenhagen, Denmark, 1–64.

Blom, E. and Christensen, N. O. (1956) Examination of The Genitals of Slaughtered Male Calves as a Means of Elucidating the Frequency of Genital Malformation in the Bovine Male, Proc. 3rd. Internat. Congr. on Animal Reprod., Cambridge.

Blom, E. and Christensen, N. O. (1958) Cysts and Cyst-like Formations (Inter Alia Spermiostasis) in the Genitals of the Bull, Yearbook of the Royal Vet. and Agr. Col., Copenhagen, Denmark, 101–133.

Blom, E. and Christensen, N. O. (1960) The Etiology of Spermiostasis in the Bull, Nord. Vet. Med. **12,** 453.

Carroll, E. J. (1967) Personal Communication.

Kanagawa, H., Ishikawa, T., Kowata, K. and Fujimoto, Y. (1960) Some Observations on Remnants of the Mullerian Duct in Slaughtered Bulls in Hokkaido, Jap. Jour. Vet. Res. **8,** 4, 323.

Leonard, E. P., C. G. Richard, and K. McEntee (1953) Impotence, Canine Medicine, Amer. Vet. Publicat. Inc., Evanston, Ill. 165.

McEntee, K. (1970) The Pathology of Domestic Animals, 2nd Ed. Vol. 1, edit. by Jubb, K. V. and Kennedy, P. C., Academic Press, Inc., N.Y.C. and London.

VanderSluis, L. (1953) Experiences with the Examination into Herd Infertility Proc. 1st World Congr. on Fert. & Steril. II, XXV, 703.

Tumors and Miscellaneous Diseases of the Epididymis

Bloom, F. (1954) Pathology of the Dog and Cat, Amer. Vet. Publicat. Inc., Evanston, Ill.

Cappucci, D. T. and Cupps, P. T. (1966) Lesions of the Epididymides and Testes from Infertile Bulls, J.A.V.M.A. **148,** 11, 1391.

Cupps, P. T. and Briggs, J. R. (1965) Changes in the Epididymis Associated with Morphological Changes in the Spermatozoa, J. Dairy Sci. **48,** 9, 1241.

Cupps, P. T., Laben, R. C. and Huff, R. L. (1970) Steroid Metabolism in an Inbred Strain of Jersey Cattle, J. of Dairy Sci. **53,** 1, 79.

Gustafsson, B. (1965) A Case of Akinesia of Bull Sperm Associated with a Functional Disturbance of the Epididymis, Nord. Vet. Med. **17,** 65.

Gustafsson, B. (1966) The Luminal Contents of the Bovine Epididymis Under Condtions of Reduced Spermatogenesis, Luminal Blockage and Certain Sperm Abnormalities, Acta Vet. Scand. Suppl. 17.

MacLeod, John (1964) Personal Communication.

McEntee, K. (1968) Personal Communication.

McEntee. K. and Olafson, P. (1953) Reproductive Tract Pathology in Hyperkeratosis of Cattle and Sheep, Fert. and Steril. **4,** 2, 128.

Diseases of the Accessory Glands

Diseases of the Seminal Vesicle, Vesicular Gland, Including Seminal Vesiculitis—Although congenital defects, usually unilateral, of the seminal vesicles including hypoplasia, cysts and either absence or doubling of the gland, McEntee, has been reported, often in association with segmental aplasia of the mesonephric duct, seminal vesiculitis is the most common condition found affecting the gland of bulls, stallions and boars. It is rare in bucks and rams. Gross inflammatory lesions are found most commonly in the vesicular gland of all the accessory reproductive glands, and the ampullae. The incidence of seminal vesiculitis in bulls was reported as 0.8 per cent of 2000 bulls examined by Blom and Christensen in Denmark, 4.2 per cent of 828 infertile bulls examined by VanderSluis in Holland, 2.5 per cent of 7359 bulls examined by Carroll and coworkers in Colorado and 4.6 per cent in 343 bulls studied by McEntee in New York State. Ball and coworkers reported on a bovine seminal vesiculitis syndrome seen in midwestern United States that differed from the usual sporadic cases observed elsewhere in that up to 10 per cent, or an average of 5 per cent, of groups of young beef bulls running together and fed heavily and grown rapidly for sale were affected. While breeding bulls grown more slowly on limited rations had an incidence of only 1.3 per cent. Larson reported that in housing arrangements where 10 to 20 young bulls, 10 to 15 months of age, run together, the incidence of seminal vesiculitis may reach 20 to 30 per cent of the bulls. These young affected bulls usually recover without treatment. Seminal vesiculitis in stallions and boars is observed less commonly.

Seminal vesiculitis may be caused by a variety of pathogenic organisms. The most common cause in the United States is **C. pyogenes.** (See Figures 196 and 197) This organism may localize in the seminal vesicle from other primary, pyogenic, infective foci such as rumenitis, liver abscesses, traumatic gastritis, lung abscess or from a navel infection in a young calf, Galloway, McEntee, and others. It may possibly enter as an ascending or descending infection from the prepuce or from an ampullitis, epididymitis or orchitis. Infection may be spread in groups of young bulls by homosexual activities and contact of the penis and prepuce to the rear parts of a bull that another had recently mounted. It is possible that certain organisms as **C. pyogenes** may invade the seminal vesicle secondary to a temporary infection with a virus or other agent.

In countries where brucellosis is still prevelant **Brucella abortus** is the most common cause for seminal vesiculitis. Bendixen and Blom reported on 30 bulls with positive brucella titers in serum and semen plasma. In fifteen or 51.7 per cent of these bulls **Br. abortus** was recovered on culture of guinea pig inoculation of the semen. Twenty six of these bulls were examined and had clinical gross lesions in the genital organs and nineteen had lesions found on autopsy. Seminal vesiculitis was found in 17 bulls, ampullitis in 5 bulls, orchitis in 5 bulls, and epididymitis in 2 bulls; in some a combination of lesions were found. **Brucella suis** commonly localizes in the seminal vesicles in boars, Deyoe. DeKeyser et al. examined 9 boars serologically positive for brucellosis and found **Brucella suis** in the seminal vesicles of 8 boars, in the epididymides of 6, in the prostate of 4 and in the semen of 7. No macroscopic lesions were present. Vandeplassche et al. studied 37 boars infected with **Br. suis** and reported that orchitis was uncommon, occasional macroscopic lesions were observed in the seminal vesicles, while nearly all infected boars had microscopic lesions in the epididymides and seminal vesicles so that 75 per cent of the boars periodically secreted organisms in their semen. Pus and leucocytes were seldom found in infected semen. Infertility in boars is frequently associated with the shedding of **Brucella suis** organisms in apparently normal appearing semen. Vandeplassche and Devos reported the excretion of **Br. abortus** in the semen of a stallion. Other organisms found in infected seminal vesicles included: **streptococci** and **staphylococci** in bulls and boars, Fennestad and coworkers; **Pseudomonas aeruginosa** and **Actinobacillus actinoides,** Jones and coworkers; Proteus, McEntee; **Mycoplasma bovigenitalium,** Blom and Erno, Erno, and Aubaidi et al.; **E. coli** and other coliforms Blom and Dam, and Hoover, and **Mycobacterium tuberculosis.** Virus infections described under orchitis and epididymitis have also been reported to cause seminal vesiculitis including the enteric virus, possible IBR-IPV, of Bouters, the "epivag" virus, Mare and Van-Rensburg, and the P.L.T. agent or Chlamydia described by Storz and coworkers. This latter agent was recovered from the semen or organs of 6 to 10 bulls from two beef herds where the seminal vesiculitis syndrome was commonly observed in young beef bulls. The P.L.T. agent recovered from one of these bulls was indistinguihable from the P.L.T. agent in California responsible for epizootic bovine abortion. The seminal vesiculitis syndrome seen by Ball and coworkers and Storz and coworkers appeared similar to the one described by Mensik and coworkers in Czechoslovakia. Blom and Erno, Erno, Parsonson, and Al Aubaidi et al. reported on naturally occurring cases of seminovesiculitis in bulls due to **Mycoplasma bovigenitalium.** They also conducted experimental studies. In natural cases the semen was stringy and mixed with pus. The seminal vesicles, especially the cranial portions were firm, swollen and nodular. Postmortem examination and culture of all portions of the male genital tract showed the organism had become widely distributed throughout the tract. The organism persisted in the experimental bulls for at least 17 weeks and could be recovered from the semen for 11 weeks. The antibiotics used in extended semen had no effect on **Mycoplasma bovigenitalium.** This organism caused a necrotizing vasculitis in many bulls and was present in the carpal joint of one bull, Parsonson. As noted previously Hartman et al. reported that mycoplasma caused pathologic changes in the genital tract of the cow. This could not be confirmed with **M. bovigenitalium** by Erno and Phillipsen. However these authors showed the organism was pathogenic for the seminal vesicles, udder and joints. Parsonson reported that prior to the inoculation of the seminal vesicles in the experimental bulls, mycoplasma could be recovered from their prepuces and nasal cavities. This could be done also in control bulls but on autopsy no mycoplasma could be recovered from the urethra or internal organs of the control bulls but could be from the experimental inoculated bulls. After inoculation the viability of the spermatozoa decreased markedly in bulls with seminovesiculitis, ampullitis and epididymitis caused by the mycoplasma. Inoculated seminal vesicles became enlarged, swollen and nodular. Many polymorphonuclear leucocytes and eosinophiles were present in the inflamed tissues and exudate.

Seminal vesiculitis affects males of all ages. In bulls it has been reported as early as 10 months to one and one-half years of age. Usually there are no external signs of the disease. Occasionally however some males will show signs of mild peritonitis with an arched back, reduced appetite, pain on defecation or on rectal examination and hesitation in mounting and thrusting. These occasional signs are observed usually in bulls having abscesses of the seminal vesicles caused by **C. pyogenes** infection adjacent to the periotoneum. On rectal examination seminal vesiculitis, especially bovine cases due to the latter infection, are characterized by (1) irregular enlargement of the gland, fibrosis, peritoneal adhesions, loss of lobulations, fluctuation, and abscessation. (See Figures 196 and 197) In rare cases fistulas occur due to rupture of an abscess into the rectum. In other cases (2) a portion or all of the seminal vesicle may become thickened and fibrotic with only slight enlargement and loss of lobulations of the gland and with no adhesions.

According to Galloway the first type of bovine seminal vesiculitis was usually unilateral and due to chronic purulent inflammatory lesions with chronic interstitial changes and was commonly caused by **C. pyogenes.** The second type of seminal vesiculitis was usually bilateral and characterized by degenerative changes in the epithelium and inflammatory changes were variable. Cultures of these latter affected vesicular glands were frequently negative for bacteria. Large amounts of Feulgen positive chromatin masses were found in the lumen of affected glands and in the semen of the latter degenerative type of seminal vesiculitis, but not in the former. In both types varying numbers of polymorphonuclear leucocytes were usually found in the semen. In the former purulent type of seminal vesiculitis large clots or flocculi were commonly observed while in the latter the semen may be viscid or "ropy" Leucocytes in the semen may also come from other portions of the urogenital tract including the prepuce so their presence is not diagnostic of seminal vesiculitis. In some chronic cases few or no leucocytes will be present in the semen of affected bulls. Semen quality will vary between affected bulls, with a lowered motility of the sperm cells, an elevated pH, a high catalase activity, and a lowered fructose content being found rather commonly. Although lowered fertility has been associated with seminal vesiculitis many affected bulls breeding cows naturally have a good conception rate. McEntee reported on one affected bull with good fertility that had been used for at least three years in an artificial insemination stud although periodically a number of ejaculates had to be discarded as being unsatisfactory. He also cited another case where in thirty cows bred to an affected bull 7 or 23 per cent aborted from three months to term. Ball and coworkers reported that in bulls with seminal vesiculitis 40.5 per cent had satisfactory quality semen and 50 per cent had semen of questionable quality, while normal bulls had 83.7 satisfactory and 11.7 per cent questionable quality of semen. The use of a bull for artificial insemination with Brucella infection of the accessory glands or ampullae may spread the disease and cause infertility. Bendixen and Blom reported on one infected bull used artificially that infected 71 per cent of the cows in 41 Brucella-free herds. Carroll et al. reported that in young beef bulls with the seminal vesiculitis syndrome, 8 of 10 affected bulls had substandard quality of semen and leucocytes were consistently found in the ejaculate.

Not infrequently bulls with a seminal vesiculitis will have another focus of infection in the testis, epididymis or ampulla. Ball and coworkers, in reporting on the seminal

vesiculitis syndrome, especially in groups of young beef **bulls,** have observed on histologic examination, focal or diffuse nonsuppurative interstitial inflammatory lesions that were commonly present in the epididymides, testes, ampullae, prostate and less commonly in the bulbourethral glands. This widespread infection of the male reproductive tract was also found in mycoplasmosis, Al-Aubaidi, and Parsonson. The viruses recovered by Mare and VanRensburg from cases of "epivag", Mensik and coworkers from Czechoslovakia, Bouters from Belgium, and Storz and coworkers, also affected a number of the reproductive organs besides the vesicular glands. In the seminal vesiculitis syndrome, however, the principal signs are related to the seminal vesicles, Ball and coworkers.

Diagnosis is based on the clinical signs noted above. Ampullitis and prostatitis are often difficult to diagnose by rectal palpation in the bull and stallion. Culture of the semen is usually an unsatisfactory method for diagnosing the causative bacterial agent because of the contamination from the sheath. A new technique, based on Galloway's procedure, was developed to collect non-contaminated urethral samples from bulls. A tranquilizer was administered to quiet the bull and allow withdrawal of the penis. Rectal massage aided the protrusion of the penis from the sheath. The penis was washed with an antiseptic solution and the urethra was irrigated with sterile saline. A 10 inch or 25 cm sterile silastic tube was inserted up the urethra leaving 1 or 2 inches, about 4 cm, protruding. Rectal massage of the seminal vesicles, prostate and ampullae resulted in the collection of their secretion into sterile vials for cultural purposes, Parsonson et al.. Only 4 of 158 urethral samples were contaminated.

The **prognosis** in seminal vesiculitis is fair to poor depending upon the causative agent, the presence of other foci of infection in the reproductive tract, the duration and severity of the infection and the value of the male. Males with Brucella infections, tuberculosis or mycoplasmosis of the seminal vesicles, or those with secondary lesions of the testes, epididymides, ampullae or prostate should be slaughtered. Many young bulls with the seminal vesiculitis syndrome with catarrhal or degenerative seminal vesiculitis overcome the infection spontaneously in a few months, Carroll et al., and Larson. During this period their use for breeding purposes is questionable. Bulls with active acute lesions of seminal vesiculitis with a discharge of pus in the semen should not be used for artificial insemination as only rarely will the antibiotics used in extended semen destroy the organisms present. Many bulls with seminal vesiculitis caused by organisms other than Brucella or Mycobacterium may be used naturally or even artificially with quite satisfactory conception rates especially if a large amount of mucopurulent material is not present in the ejaculate. Further studies on the possible viral causes of this disease and the duration of the carrier state is definitely needed.

Treatment with high levels of broad range antibiotics, or antibiotics to which the causative agent is sensitive, for two weeks or longer together with mild massage of the vesicular gland to remove its contents may result in recovery or elimination of the infection in some males after 2 to 6 months. In **C. pyogenes** infection the gland is usually left severely indurated and largely destroyed. Acute cases of seminal vesiculitis tend to become chronic and chronic cases, if abscessation does not occur, tend to become fibrotic and indurated similar to the mammary gland following a severe infection. In long-standing chronic cases pus or high leucocyte numbers are seldom observed in the semen. In recent years surgical removal of the affected vesicular glands has been recommended for selected bulls in artificial insemination studs or where conservative treatment has failed or is not deemed advisable, and where the only detectable lesion of the genital tract is in the seminal vesicle and extensive adhesions are not present. In an aseptic manner and under epidural and local anesthesia together with tranquilization, an elliptical incision was made in the ischiorectal fossa after suturing the anus tightly closed, McEntee and Delahanty. By a combination of blunt and sharp dissection the affected gland was isolated and removed close to the urethra after ligation at that point. Some difficulty was experienced if adhesions were present especially in separating the periotoneum from the cranial portion of the gland. Following surgery heavy prolonged antibiotic therapy was recommended. The results were satisfactory in all cases except one bull that developed a degree of paralysis in the sphincter of the bladder with cystitis and urinary complications.

Regular and frequent examination of the genital tract and semen for a year or more should be followed after treatment to be certain the condition doesn't recur at another site due to a resistant or secondary focus of infection.

Pathology of the Prostate—Disease of the prostate gland is uncommon in all animals except the dog in which prostatitis and hyperplasia of the prostate are common. Tumors of the prostate are uncommon. Senile atrophy of the prostate in intact male dogs is rare.

Prostatitis in the dog is often associated with hyperplasia of the gland. It is probably due to an ascending infection through the urethra but may occur secondary to hematogenous infection or even descending infections. A wide variety of organisms have been isolated from infected glands including **Brucella canis, E. coli,** streptococci and **Proteus.** Acute prostatitis in the dog is a diffuse or local suppurative inflammatory reaction with a tendency for abscess formation, McEntee. Bacteria, leukocytes, and blood are frequently found in the urine or observed at the preputial orifice. This should be differentiated from a balanoposthitis. Acute prostatitis may be painful and characterized by constipation, an arched back, elevated temperature and pulse rate, occasionally anorexia and vomiting, and possibly a leucocytosis. Palpation of the infected gland per rectum causes pain and "splinting" of the abdomen. Chronic prostatitis is occasionally observed, McEntee and Bloom.

The treatment of prostatitis is frequently successful. Parenteral injections of broad range antibiotics are indicated over a prolonged period. If the ordinary antibiotics do not control the infection, cultures of the prostatic secretions may be made and the antibiotic sensitivity of the causative organism determined. If prostatitis is due to **Brucella canis** the prognosis is poor. Low doses of X-radiation may be of value in reducing the inflammation in some cases.

Clinical prostatitis in the bull and boar is rare and may be caused by **Brucella abortus** or **suis.** Subclinical infections may be more common and due to a variety of bacteria and viruses as described under seminal vesiculitis.

Prostatic hyperplasia is present in most dogs over 5 years of age that have not been castrated. The condition is probably due to an endocrine imbalance with an excess of testosterone being secreted which causes an enlargement and hyperplasia of the gland. Some speak of this condition as prostatic hypertrophy, but this terminology is not correct. The moderate to greatly enlarged gland may be smooth or nodular and may contain small cysts or occasionally excessively large cysts that extend forward into the abdominal cavity. The cyst walls may be calcified. In rare cases prostatic calculi have been reported, Lumb. When cysts are not present the preputial discharge from an infected hyperplastic prostate is usually purulent; when cysts are present the discharge is watery-grey or bloody. This cystic fluid may be voided with the urine producing albuminuria. Usually dogs with marked prostatic hyperplasia are constipated. Rectal impaction and straining predispose to rectal dilation and the development of a perineal hernia. In uncommon instances the bladder may become strangulated in the perineal hernia resulting in urine retention, hematuria and dribbling of urine. Occasionally cystitis and hydronephrosis may develop. Usually little discomfort is shown by the dog with a hyperplastic prostate unless constipation or bladder strangulation occurs, Kirk and coworkers and Archibald. Obstruction of the urethra does not occur in dogs as in man because of the bilobed nature of the gland in the dog in contrast to the trilobed structure of the gland in man.

Digital examination of the prostate bimanually per rectum and by abdominal palpation may reveal a nodular or smooth, enlarged prostate. It is often helpful to exert pressure through the abdominal wall at the pelvic brim to push the prostate caudally so that it can be palpated. The consistency will vary with the nature of the hyperplasia from firm and fibrous, to soft, or even fluctuating if cysts are present. Normal prostate glands are 2.5 to 3 cm in diameter while hyperplastic glands may be twice as large or even larger if cysts are present. Kirk and coworkers reported a prostatic cyst in a Great Dane containing 15 quarts of sanguineous fluid. Radiography may also be helpful in the diagnosis of prostatic enlargement, Archibald and Bishop. A perineal punch biopsy of the prostate gland as described by Leeds and Leav is conclusive evidence of the nature of the enlargement.

Rectal massage of the gland may give temporary relief by reducing the size of the cysts. Estrogenic therapy, such as injections of 0.5 to 1 mg of stilbestrol per pound of body weight daily and then gradually reducing the dose during the next few weeks, may give relief but continued dosing is required. Estrogens act by suppressing the pituitary gonadotropins and this causes an atrophy of the Leydig cells and suppression of testosterone production. The estrogens do not directly antagonize the androgens. The most satisfactory method of reducing the size of the prostate is castration, as this removes the source of the androgen causing the hyperplasia. Within 2 to 3 weeks after castration the prostate gland begins to noticeably involute and by 6 to 8 weeks it is relatively small in size and atrophied. However castration does not reduce the large cysts or abscesses in infected glands or affect calculi that may rarely be present. In complicated cases, surgery on the gland may be indicated.

Archibald and Cawley and Archibald have described a technique for prostatectomy through a prepubic incision. The urethra is transected and anastomosed into the neck of the bladder and the vasa deferentia are ligated and the proximal portions are removed. An approach to prostatectomy by incision of the pelvic symphysis has been described by Knecht and Schiller, and Howard but the operation is difficult and not without dangers, Pettit.

Preliminary studies have been performed on the therapy of prostatic hyperplasia using a chelating agent, sodium diethyldithio-carbamate, for removing zinc which is in very high concentration in the prostate gland. This causes a probable cessation of much of the glandular enzymal activity and atrophy of the gland but further studies of possible side-effects must be conducted, Kirk and coworkers. Where perineal hernias have developed, perineal herniorrhapy may be indicated, Larsen and Walker.

McEntee reported on the effects of estrogens on the prostate gland. In dogs with Sertoli cell tumors of the testes, estrogens produced by the tumor cause squamous epithelial metaplasia with enlarged cystic prostate glands or atrophy of the glands. These lesions can be produced experimentally by administering estrogens and this is why castration is a more effective therapy than estrogen administration. Furthermore high prolonged dosing with estrogens may cause anemia, leucopenia and aplasia of the bone marrow, Bloom. Estrogen-induced changes in the prostate are apparently irreversible. A squamous metaplasia of the uterus masculinus may also occur.

Similar lesions to those in the dog, but reversible, occurred in wethers grazing on certain clovers such as red clover or subterranean clover that contained high levels of estrogens, Bennetts. The bulbo-urethral glands also became cystic, dilated with urine and debris and greatly enlarged in these castrated sheep. In some cases urinary obstruction, prolapse of the rectum and even death occurred. A similar condition occurred in wethers in feed lots if their ration was supplemented with excessive estrogens or estrogen implants were given to provide growth stimulation, Hale and Cornelius, Bell and Cornelius.

Adenocarcinoma of the prostate in the dog is observed only in rare instances and usually in dogs over 10 years of age, Mulligan, and Bloom. Schlotthauer and Miller reported only 3 cases of carcinoma in over 500 diseased prostate glands. Persistent straining at the time of defecation was characteristic of all 3 advanced cases. Pain was a commonly observed symptom. Adenocarcinoma of the prostate results in a nodular asymmetrical enlargement of the gland. The tumor may vary in consistency from very hard to soft and is slow to metastasize. Castration, estrogen therapy and radiation therapy are of definite value in man in delaying the growth of the tumor even though metastasis has occurred, Huggins. Prostatectomy would be indicated if the carcinoma had not metastasized. However the prognosis is poor. Other tumors of the prostate are rare. More study in dogs is needed on evaluating these therapeutic practices.

Miscellaneous Male Factors Resulting in Failure of Fertilization or Conception and Reduced Fertility.

Failure of proper delivery of semen into the vagina at the time of ejaculation may result in infertility or sterility. This may be secondary to lacerations of the ventral caudal portions of the glans penis with a fistulous opening of the urethra ventrally so semen is deposited in the middle portion of the vagina and not sprayed into the cranial portion or over the cervix at ejaculation. A similar condition may occur in rams following necrosis of most of the urethral process secondary to urinary calculi lodging in the process or due to lacerations or injury to the urethral process, Masson.

The inheritance of normal fertility or subfertility in males is difficult to evaluate because of the wide variation in fertility between males and the difficulty in eliminating environmental factors except in bulls used artificially on many cows. No studies have been made on the transmission of fertility from males and females to their sons, Young. Some bulls used artificially have up to 90 per cent conceptions in some herds and as low as 20 per cent conceptions in others; a fact which leads to the conclusion that environment is probably the most important factor in conception rates of bulls. Young reported that Hereford, Angus, Holstein, and Shorthorn bulls have the best conception rates. In the United States, Guernsey bulls generally have a lower conception rate than that of the other breeds. As stated in the discussion on "repeat breeders," Kidder and coworkers and Bearden demonstrated that low-fertility bulls, when bred artificially to normal heifers, had a lower fertilization rate than that of high-fertility bulls, due to no observable or measurable cause. The routine laboratory examination of semen did not reveal any detectable difference between the semen characteristics of low- and high-fertile bulls but probably cytogenetic differences did exist. In bulls of very low fertility, unsuited for artificial insemination, laboratory tests could probably detect this infertile condition.

In the author's opinion, the character of high fertility may be transmitted genetically; sons of highly fertile artificial sires are usually more fertile in artificial service than are bulls purchased from a variety of sources and selected on the basis of the production of their daughters. More work is needed on this important aspect of infertility to determine accurately to what degree high fertility in males is inheritable. (See Repeat Breeders)

Lanman has summarized the pertinent data in laboratory mammals and domestic animals to show that spermatozoa aged in the epididymis for a number of weeks, aged by storing in liquid semen at 4 to 5° C for a number of days or in the frozen state in bulls for many months caused decreased fertilization rates and increased early embryonic or fetal deaths.

References

Diseases of the Accessory Male Glands
Diseases of the Seminal Vesicle

Al-Aubaidi, J. M. (1970) Bovine Mycoplasma, PhD Thesis, N.Y.S. Vet. Col., Cornell Univ., Ithaca, N.Y.

Al-Aubaidi, J. M., McEntee, K. and Roberts, S. J. (1970) Bovine Seminal Vesiculitis Due to **Mycoplasma Bovigenitalium,** In Press

Ball, L., Griner, L. Q. and Carroll, E. J. (1964) The Bovine Seminal Vesiculitis Syndrome, Amer. J. Vet. Res. **25,** 105, 291.

Ball, L., Young, S. and Carroll, E. J. (1968) Seminal Vesiculitis Syndrome Lesions in Genital Organs of Young Bulls, Amer. J. Vet. Res. **29,** 6, 1173.

Bendixen, H. C. and Blom, E. (1947) Undersogelser over Forekomsten of Brucellose Hos Tyre specielt med Henblik paa Betydmigen velden kunstige Insemation, Maanedsskr. for Dyrl. **59,** 3, 4, 5, 61.

Blom, E. and Christensen, N. O. (1947) Studies on the Pathological Conditions in the Testis, Epididymis and Accessory Sex Glands in the Bull, Skand. Vet. Tijdskr. **37,** 1.

Blom, E. and Christensen, N O. (1965) Seminal Vesiculitis in the Bull Caused by **C. pyogenes,** Nord. Vet. Med. **17,** 435.

Blom, E. and Dam, A. (1964) **Escherichia coli** in Bull Semen and Their Possible Causal Significance for the Etiology of Vesiculitis, Proc. Vth Inter. Congr. on An. Reprod., Trento, V, 253.

Blom, E. and Erno, H. (1967) Mycoplasmosis: Infections of the Genital Organs of Bulls, Acta. Vet. Scand. **8,** 186.

Bouters, R. (1964) A Virus with Enterogenic Properties Causing Degeneration of the Germinal Epithelium in Bulls, Nature, **201,** 217.

Carroll, E. J., Ball, L. and Scott, J. A. (1963) Breeding Soundness in Bulls—a Summary of 10,940 Examinations, J.A.V.M.A. **142,** 1105.

Carroll, E. J., Ball, L. and Young, S. (1968) Seminal Vesiculitis in Young Beef Bulls, J.A.V.M.A. **152,** 12, 1749.

Delahanty, D. D. (1963) Seminal Vesiculitis—One Cause of Infertility in the Bull, Farm Research, Cor. Agr. Exp. State., **29,** 2, 14.

DeKeyser, J., Spincemaille, J. and Brone, E. (1962) **Brucella suis** in Sperm and Genitals of Naturally Infected Boars, Vlaams Diergeneesk. Tijdschr. **31,** 6, 171.

Deyoe, B. L. (1967) Pathogenesis of Three Strains of **Brucella suis** in Swine, Amer. J. Vet. Res. **28,** 125, 951.

Erno, H. (1967) Mycoplasmosis: Demonstration of Pathogenicity of a Danish Strain of Mycoplasma, Acta Vet. Scand **8,** 184.

Erno, H. and Phillipsen, H. (1969) Mycoplasmosis: Cervical and Uterine Infection of Heifers with a Danish Strain of **Mycoplasma Bovigenitalium,** Acta Vet. Scand. **10,** 108.

Fennestad, K. L., Pedersen, P. S. and Moller, T. (1955) **Staphylococcus aureus** as a Cause of Reproductive Failure and so-called Actinomycosis in Swine, Nord. Vet. Med. **7,** 11, 929.

Galloway, D. B. (1964) A Study of Bulls with the Clinical Signs of Seminal Vesiculitis, Acta Vet. Scand. **5,** Suppl. 2.

Hoover, T. R. (1970) Personal Communication.

Jones, T. H., Barrett, K. J., Greenhorn, L. W., Osborne, A. D. and Ashdown, R. R. (1964) Seminal Vesiculitis in Bulls Associated with Infection by **Actinobacillus actinoides,** Vet. Rec. **76,** 24.

Larson, L. L. (1969) Disease Incidence in 1481 Bulls Examined for Use in Artificial Insemination, A.V.M.A. Ann. Meeting, Minneapolis, Mimeographed Notes.

McEntee, K. (1962) Seminal Vesiculitis in the Bull, Proc. U.S.L.S.A (66th Ann. Meeting), 160.

Mare, J. and Van Rensburg, S. W. J. (1961) The Isolation of Viruses Associated with Infertility in Cattle—A Preliminary Report, J. S. Afr. Med. Assoc. **32,** 201.

Mensik, J., Bohac, J. and Setka, R. (1961) The Etiology of Infectious Orchitis in Bulls in Czechoslovakia, Vet. Bull. **31,** 323.

Parsonson, I. M. (1970) **Mycoplasma Bovigenitalium.** Experimental Induction of Genital Disease in Bulls, PhD Thesis, Cornell Univ., Ithaca, N.Y.

Parsonson, I. M., Hall, C. E. and Settergren, I. (1970) A Method for the Collection of Urethral Samples from Bulls for Microbiological Examination, Amer. J. Vet. Res. (In Press).

Storz, J., Carroll, E. J., Ball, L. and Faulkner, L. C. (1968) Isolation of a Psittacosis Agent. (Chlamydia) from Semen and Epididymis of Bulls with Seminal Vesiculitis Syndrome, Am. J. Vet. Res. **29,** 3, 549.

Vandeplassche, M. et. al. (1969) **Brucella Suis** Infection and Infertility in Swine, (abstr) J.A.V.M.A. **154,** 9, 1050.

Vanderplassche, M. and Devos, A. (1960) Excretion of **Brucella abortus** in the Semen of a Stallion, Vlaams Diergeneesk Tijdschr. **29,** 199.

VanderSluis, L. (1953) Experiences with the Examination into Herd Infertility, Proc. 1st World Congr. on Fert. and Steril **II** xxv, 703.

Diseases of the Prostate and Bulbourethral Glands

Archibald, J. (1957) The Surgery and Treatment of the Diseased Canine Prostate Gland, Pfizer Review #18.

Archibald, J. and Bishop, E. J. (1956) Radiographic Visualization of the Canine Prostate Gland, J.A.V.M.A. **128,** 7, 337.

Archibald, J. and Cawley, A. J. (1956) Canine Prostatectomy, J.A.V.M.A. **128,** 4, 173.

Bennetts, H. W. (1947) A Further Note on Metaplasia of the Sex Organs of Castrated Male Sheep on Subterranean Clover, Austral. Vet. J. **23,** 10.

Bloom, F. (1968) Canine Medicine, Edit. by Catcott, E. J., Amer. Vet. Public Inc., Wheaton, Ill.

Hale, W. H., Homeyer, P. C., Culbertson, C. C. and Burroughs, W. (1955) Response of Lambs Fed Varied Levels of Diethylstilbestrol, J. of An. Sci. **14,** 4, 909.

Howard, D. R. (1969) Surgical Approach to the Canine Prostate, J.A.V.M.A. **155,** 12, 2026.

Huggins, C. (1967) Endocrine Induced Regression of Cancers, Science **156,** 1050.

Kirk, R. W., McEntee, K. and Bentinck-Smith, J. (1968) Canine Medicine, Edit. by Catcott, E. J., Amer. Vet. Public, Inc., Wheaton, Ill.

Knecht, C. D. and Schiller, A. G. (1966) Prostatectomy in the Dog by Incision of the Pelvic Symphysis, J.A.V.M.A. **149,** 9, 1186.

Larsen, J. S. (1966) Perineal Herniorrhapy in Dogs. J.A.V.M.A. **149,** 3, 277

Leeds, E. B. and Leav, I. (1969) Perineal Punch Biopsy of the Canine Prostate Gland, J.A.V.M.A. **154,** 8, 925.

Lumb, W. V. (1952) Prostatic Calculi in a Dog, J.A.V.M.A. **121,** 14.

McEntee, K. (1970) Pathology of Domestic Animals, 2nd Ed., Vol. I. edit. by Jubb, K. V. and Kennedy, P. C., Academic Press, Inc., N.Y.C. and London.

Mulligan, R. J. (1949) Neoplasms in the Dog, Williams & Wilkins Co., Baltimore, Md.

Pettit, G. D. (1960) A Clinical Evaluation of Prostatectomy in the Dog, J.A.V.M.A. **128,** 173.

Schlotthauer, C. F. and Miller, J. A. S. (1941) Carcinoma of the Prostate Gland in Dogs, J.A.V.M.A. **99,** 239.

Walker, R. G. (1965) Observations on Perineal Hernia in the Dog, Vet. Rec. **77,** 93.

Miscellaneous Factors Concerned with Reduced Fertility

Bearden, H. J. (1954) Fertilization and Embryonic Mortality Rates for Bulls with Histories of Either Low or High Fertility in Artificial Breeding, Thesis Cornell Univ., Ithaca, N.Y.

Kidder, H. E., Black, W. G., Wiltbank, J. N., Ulberg, L. C. and Casida, L. E. (1954) Fertilization Rates and Embryonic Death Rates in Cows Bred to Bulls of Different Levels of Fertility, Dairy Sci. **37,** 691.

Lanman, J. T. (1968) Delays During Reproduction and Their Effects on the Embryo and Fetus, New England Jour. of Med. **278,** 993, 1047, and 1092.

V[illegible]sson, J. (1961) Personal communication.

Young, G. B. (1953) Genetic Aspects of Fertility and Infertility in Cattle, Vet. Rec. **65,** 271.

DIAGNOSIS OF STERILITY AND INFERTILITY IN THE MALE AND EVALUATION OF BREEDING SOUNDNESS

The diagnosis of any infertility problem in a group of females bred to a certain male requires an examination of the male. A veterinarian is often requested to examine males which the owners suspect are sterile or infertile. A fertility examination is also often desired by the buyer of a sire or by the owner who wishes to sell an animal. Artificial insemination centers have sterile or infertile bulls that require careful examination and diagnosis before a prognosis can be given or treatment undertaken. Carroll, Ball and Scott have reported on their findings on the evaluation of the breeding soundness of 10,940 range bulls. Larson reported on the disease incidence of nearly 1500 bulls examined for use by an A.I. stud. The examination for infertility in any sire should be careful and thorough, following a definite outline of procedure so that no symptom or lesion will be missed. A complete record of this examination should be made as the examination progresses. A careful, complete examination of a male is essential to the assessment of his breeding potential.

History and Records—Breeding records are essential in the diagnosis of fertility. If the male was bred to a sufficient number of normal females, these records accurately indicate the relative fertility of the sire. If possible these records should be reviewed for two time intervals of 1 to 2 years and the past 6 months. This review will indicate the number of services per conception over a period of several years as well as the past few months, which is of value in diagnosing whether a venereal disease or a pathologic lesion affecting the sire is acute or chronic. If records are not available, pregnancy examinations on females recently bred by the male may be necessary. The records of the females bred to this male should also be reviewed to see if there is an increased incidence of abnormal genital discharges, delayed estrums or abortions occurring after breeding, indicating possible vibriosis, trichomoniasis, canine brucellosis or the presence of some other disease causing vaginitis or vulvitis or the early or late death of the embryo or fetus. If two or more males are used for natural breeding in the same herd the breeding records may be necessary to determine if one or more bulls are infertile. The conception rate in a herd is often a good index to the fertility of the bulls in that herd.

If possible a number of the daughters of the bull examined should be observed for conformation and the presence of any inherited defects; also, their conception rates should be noted. In multipara the size, number, and viability of the offspring of the sire and his daughters should be noted. The breeding records of the male's sire and dam should be reviewed if they are available. These animals and/or their relatives should be examined or a record obtained for any evidence of hereditary disease factors. If the male's sire and dam are dead the reasons for their death should be checked. Bulls that have been operated upon for umbilical hernia, deviated penis, or other defects are not desirable, as they may transmit these defects.

The health history of the male should be reviewed. Any illnesses, especially those requiring veterinary treatment, should be investigated. This review should include diseases suffered as a young animal as well as any recent sickness. The records of any and all preventive vaccinations of the male should be secured. Information should be obtained on the ration fed the male, the amount and frequency of feeding and whether any signs of nutritional deficiency occurred or are present.

The Physical Examination of the Male consists of noting the following: its age, according to its registration papers and its teeth; its conformation and the condition of its hoofs, limbs, and joints; any defects either congenital, hereditary, or acquired, and their severity; its general condition, attitude, temperment and hair coat. The body temperature should be taken and a careful examination made of the eyes, circulatory, respiratory, digestive, urinary and lymphatic systems, for evidence of disease that might affect its present or future health. Any unusual symptoms such as coughing, nasal discharge, bloody urine, persistent or intermittent diarrhea, and icterus should be carefully investigated. The teeth, oral cavity, eyes, and face should be examined for actinomycosis, carcinoma or other lesions. A rectal examination of the kidney(s) and bladder, iliac lymph glands, internal inguinal rings and intestines should be performed in large animals. If the conformation of the male is poor or defective, the gait and manner and ease of mounting should be observed carefully. Too straight a rear limb, arthritis and spastic syndrome in bulls are frequently associated. Slightly "sickle-hocked" bulls and bulls with a good heel are preferred over the former. Any signs of posterior weakness or paresis as indicated by a limp flaccid tail and ataxia is very undesirable in breeding males. Examination of the stifle joints for gonitis as evidenced by distention of the joint capsule should be made in bulls with rear limb lameness.

The examination of the male in the presence of the female is desirable and necessary in order to observe the degree of sexual desire or libido, which may vary from no interest in the female to extremely eager mounting. Any abnormalities, hesitancy, or evidence of pain on erection, mounting, copulating, and ejaculating should be noted. At this time the penis and prepuce should be examined for evidence of inflammation, granular venereal disease in bulls, tumors, adhesions, congenital short penis, phimosis, and deviation of the penis. Any history or evidence of vices or bad habits should be watched for before and during the physical examination. In some males it may be desirable to examine the penis further, if necessary under tranquilization, a pudendal nerve block, or general anesthesia. Some owners who sell purebred males take a motion picture of the male copulating with a female before a sale, to prevent having the male being returned with the report that it would not copulate normally. At this time the male's gait and manner of moving, his positioning of himself on the mount, his seeking actions with his penis, his intromission and thrusting action and his dismounting are also noted. Any lameness or abnormal gait should be closely investigated. Spastic syndrome, or "stretches", in bulls may not be noted in the early or mild cases unless the bull is seen as it rises or is backed. Promptness and vigor of intromission and ejaculation, however, are not a guarantee of fertility.

The rest of the reproductive system should be carefully examined. The testes, epididymides, spermatic cord and scrotum may be examined by palpation. This should be done bimanually with the large male properly restrained to prevent injury to the examiner. The size and shape of the scrotum and the position of the testes in the scrotum should be observed. Any wryness or difference in the appearance of the two sides of the scrotum should be a cause for further careful examination. The testes should be palpated for size, shape, consistency, and the presence of adhesions to the scrotum. Any unusual findings should be compared with the other testis or with the testes of a normal male if one is available. The head, body and tail of each epididymis should be carefully palpated for enlargements, missing segments, granulomas and abscesses. Any unusual softness, firmness, swelling, atrophy, heat or pain in the testes, scrotum, or epididymis should be carefully checked. This examination will reveal the possible presence of scrotal hernias, cryptorchidism, testicular hypoplasia, segmental aplasia of the mesonephric duct, testicular degeneration, fibrosis, testicular atrophy, orchitis, possible tumors, and other testicular, epididymal, or scrotal pathology.

Semen production is closely related to testicular size and consistency. Willett and Ohms, Aehnalt and Dittmar, and Hahn et al. have reported a close relationship between scrotal circumference and the volume of water displaced by placing the scrotum and testes in a measuring bucket, and the number of spermatozoa produced in exhaustion trials in bulls. There was no relationship between the scrotal size and body size on the numbers of sperm cells in a single ejaculate. The average scrotal circumference in mature bulls was 40 to 42 cm or a range of 37 to 46 cm. Thus, as mentioned before, the number of spermatozoa produced per gram of normal seminiferous tubules or testes is fairly constant for adult normal bulls since about 75 percent of the testis is composed of seminiferous tubules. For bulls over 6 years of age the scrotal circumference as an indicator of sperm cell production is of limited value because of chronic testicular changes in older bulls.

Hahn, Foote and Cranch developed a tonometer they could use to objectively measure the consistency of the testes. This was highly correlated with semen quality tests and could be used in predicting semen quality; a soft or very firm consistency often was related to poor semen quality.

An examination of the retractor penis muscle, the sigmoid flexure of the penis, and the external palpation of the sheath and penis should follow the examination of the testes and scrotum. Often a short or limited protrusion of the penis in bulls is associated with paunchiness, a "dropped loin" on mounting and inability to copulate successfully. Any swelling, fibrous tissue, abscesses, hematomas, growths or adhesions should be noted and their significance evaluated.

Rectal examination of the accessory reproductive glands as well as other pelvic and abdominal organs is necessary n the physical examination of the male. This can readily »e done with the hand and arm in the bull and stallion, and with the finger in the dog. In the boar and ram ~ mination is difficult or impossible. In the large animals the pelvic urethra is noted as a firm round structure on the floor of the caudal portion of the pelvis. The Cowper's or bulbo-urethral glands are covered with muscle so they cannot be palpated but they are seldom diseased. In the bull and stallion the prostate gland is palpated as a thick transverse fibrous band of tissue around the urethra at the cranial end of the pelvic urethra and just caudal to the neck of the bladder and the ampullae and seminal vesicles. These accessory reproductive glands are carefully palpated for their size, and consistency. Any abnormality is carefully recorded especially if a pathological process, inflammation, induration or abscess is noted by a thickening of the part, atrophy, or swelling of the organ, and if pain is produced on palpation. In severe inflammations extensive adhesions may be present. If one or a portion of one of the accessory glands, ampulla, or vas deferens is missing or dilated a congenital anomaly is usually present. In the dog the size of the prostate can be noted. On palpation through the abdominal wall large prostatic cysts or a distended colon may be palpated if the prostate is hyperplastic. In rare cases in the dog a perineal hernia may be present associated with a hyperplastic prostate, and should be differentiated from a dilation or diverticulum of the rectum. In the bull and stallion the kidneys, intestines, and other pelvic structures may also be examined for evidence of cystitis, nephritis, or possible tumors. Fat necrosis is rarely noted in bulls.

Other Diagnostic Tests and examinations should be performed on valuable sires especially where herd records indicate that a venereal disease might be present. In bulls vibriosis, trichomoniasis, or brucellosis may be present either together or separately. In bulls suspected of having vibriosis repeated cultures of the semen and preputial secretions or the fluorescent antibody test applied to the latter or service to several virgin heifers with repeated cultures and agglutination tests on the vaginal mucus of the heifers might be indicated, as discussed under vibriosis. In trichomoniasis the bull's preputial smegma should be examined and cultured 3 to 6 times at weekly intervals, as described previously. Breeding the bull to several heifers and culturing the vaginal secretions at weekly intervals might also be necessary to determine the presence of trichomoniasis. Blood tests for brucellosis and leptospirosis are desirable in bulls, boars, rams (or bucks) and dogs. In questionable cases semen plasma agglutination tests or other special serologic tests and culture, or inoculation of guinea pigs with semen may be of diagnostic assistance in determining the presence of brucellosis.

Tests for the above diseases and others are usually indicated to prevent introducing infection into a clean herd when purchasing a sire, or in the examination of males for infertility when the semen is apparently normal and the history indicates that possibly a venereal disease is present. A tuberculin test is usually necessary. Tests for Johne's disease, Q fever, anaplasmosis and IBR-IPV infection may be indicated in bulls. In certain bulls on poor feed for a long period, vitamin-A blood levels may occasionally be of value in the diagnosis and treatment of infertility. In regard to these diagnostic tests for certain diseases the history or status of the herd or animals associated with the male should be investigated. It is a sound practice to isolate all newly-acquired males for 4 to 8 weeks to prevent the introduction of these or other diseases into the herd.

SEMEN EXAMINATION

The second part of a careful examination of a male is the semen examination. This is of great diagnostic value in determining the cause, severity and degree of testicular or accessory gland pathology present, as well as being of value in estimating the fertility. There is usually a definite correlation between testicular pathology, disease of the reproductive tract and accessory glands and the semen characteristics and fertility. The techniques and procedures used in the semen examination of bulls, rams and humans are more accurate than in the other animals because more work and detailed observations have been made on these species. More work on the other species of animals is highly desirable and would be useful. From the many reports in humans, bulls, and rams and the less numerous reports in boars, stallions, and dogs the same general principles are applicable in semen examinations of all species. Semen characteristics or quality remain rather constant and within narrow limits for nearly all ejaculates from each male over a period of months and even years. Due to acute, severe, adverse influences, semen quality may decline rather rapidly but improvement is slow and usually requires months for recovery to occur. Since it takes approximately 50 to 70 days for the development of mature sperm cells from spermatogonia until ejaculation it is possible for acute testicular degeneration to be present in the testes yet the semen quality to be fairly satisfactory. The diseased state or infertility may become evident in 2 to 6 weeks. Testicular biopsies are seldom indicated in domestic animals except in aforementioned situations since one or more semen samples usually accurately reflect the condition of the seminiferous tubules of the testes. Males with the highest quality or the lowest quality of semen and fertility on the initial examination usually repeat the same quality when they are re-examined, if no severe systemic disease or stress occurs before the times of collection, Bartlett, MacLeod and Gold, and Williams. Be slow to condemn a male or give a poor prognosis based on a single semen examination revealing poor quality semen; especially if the male is young and immature, if the male has recently been severely stressed or had an acute debilitating disease, if the male is very valuable, if the male has not ejaculated recently, or if his semen has been collected and examined under adverse conditions. The entire ejaculate should be examined and not just a portion of it such as the "tail end" sample taken from a stallion or other male as it dismounts. Usually bulls, rams and men with good to fair semen samples have good to excellent fertility; while males with poor to very poor semen samples are invariably infertile or sterile, Hulet and coworkers, MacLeod, MacLeod and Gold, and Hartman. In stallions, boars and dogs where most of the ejaculate enters the uterus poor to very poor semen samples result in reduced fertility to occasional sterility. Completely sterile stallions are rare. As long as some motile normal sperm cells are present in the ejaculate conception is possible in all species. Occasionally males with apparently normal appearing good quality semen samples may be incapable of producing conception. Therefore the examination of semen samples and the physical examination of the males as a means of evaluating fertility should be performed carefully and the results should be interpreted conservatively. If one criterion used to evaluate semen is poor, the sample should be graded poor or questionable because usually for satisfactory or good fertility all of the criteria must be satisfactory or better. Occasionally one poor criterion of semen quality may be compensated for by a good criterion, for example, good motility and poor concentration often result in fair conception rates.

The Collection of Semen for examination is practical and fairly easy in all species of domestic animals except possibly the boar and cat. Adams and Clark and Sojka et al. have recently described a simple and satisfactory method for semen collection in the latter two species.

The Bull may have semen collected in several ways, but only two are of practical value for semen evaluation. The simplest and earliest method of semen collection was from the vagina, by means of a spoon or syringe with a long nozzle following a natural service. A speculum may be helpful in this method. This technique is unsatisfactory because the relatively small volume of semen is mixed with a large volume of vaginal mucus so this method was not suitable for the evaluation of semen quality. **Rowson** described a technique of surgically producing a fistula in the urethra and inserting a cannula to collect semen. This procedure is impractical and could cause a stricture of the urethra or infection of the urogenital system.

The massage technique in the bull, first described by Case in 1925 as a means of obtaining semen for examination and artificial insemination, has been well-described by Miller and Evans (1934) and Goodwin. This method is employed rather seldom because some skill and experience are necessary to massage the ampullae per rectum; some bulls respond poorly to the procedure; and semen collections are usually not as clean and contain many more bacteria than those produced by other methods because the semen dribbles through the prepuce and drips from the preputial hairs. For this latter reason it is necessary to carefully wash, rinse, and dry with a brush and cotton pledgets or a clean towel the prepuce and the preputial hairs and the region around the preputial opening with warm physiological saline solution or clean warm water. This washing, if combined with stroking of the sheath, may induce urination, which is desirable inasmuch as urine is toxic to spermotozoa and massage of the ampullae is likely to stimulate urination. The prepuce should be carefully douched with 250 to 500 ml of a physiological saline solution to remove epithelial cells, smegma, and dirt. Sexual stimulation of the bull with a cow or another bull is helpful in obtaining a satisfactory semen sample. Goodwin reported that obtaining semen by massage was much easier in young Angus bulls than in older bulls, Herefords or Santa Gertrudis bulls. He reported that 143 of 173 young Angus bull collected by massage of the internal genital organs extended the penis beyond the sheath so that semen free of contamination from the preputial cavity was obtained. The bull should be handled quietly and kept relaxed. The operator, wearing a glove and sleeve, gently inserts his lubricated hand and forearm into the bull's rectum, emptying it of feces. The seminal vesicles are then gently massaged a few times with the fingers by backward and downward strokes toward the urethra and a cloudy fluid containing few if any spermatozoa is expelled. An assistant with a funnel and several test tubes collects the seminal fluid and semen as it drips from the preputial opening or penis. The ampullae are then massaged similarily in a slow, rhythmic manner. With the second finger between the ampullae and the third and fourth fingers on the outside of the ampullae, the ampullae are "stripped" of semen by pressure against the floor of the pelvis and then the pelvic urethra may be massaged. Sometimes the ejaculate is retained in the sigmoid flexure of the penis or in the proximal portion of the prepuce; therefore after massaging the ampullae, the S-curve of the penis should be straightened out. **Miller** and Evans reported about 80 percent successful collections in 100 attempts on 15 bulls. The quantity of fluid from the ampullae and from the seminal vesicles varied from 0.5 to 23 ml and 0.5 to 21 ml, respectively. Debruyn massaged 21 bulls 102 times and collected semen satisfactory for use in artificial insemination with an average volume of 5.9 ml with a slightly reduced concentration. Goodwin also obtained semen that was satisfactory for artificial insemination. He successfully collected 173 of 194 young Angus bulls; 150 were collected on the first massage attempt and 23 by the second or third attempt a week or so later. No injury or bleeding was produced. Fertility was equal to samples collected in the artificial vagina. If massaged regularly by the same operator most bulls usually become accustomed and conditioned to this procedure within 3 to 4 weeks and produce a good semen sample promptly at the time of each collection. The indications for using the massage technique are the same as in the electroejaculation technique, namely, in bulls that are impotent, unwilling, or are unable to copulate. Megale has described a method of gentle manual massage of the glans through the sheath wall to produce erection and ejaculation without restraint in gentle, calm bulls in a quiet isolated environment.

Electroejaculation in bulls has been proved practical by Rowson and Murdock, Marden, Dzuik, Graham and Petersen, and Hill and coworkers. This technique was first described and extensively used in rams by Gunn in 1936. Modifications by the above authors to adopt this technique to bulls have been successful. Marden and Dzuik and coworkers both used a probe that was inserted into the rectum. Marden's and Nicholson's probes are about 3.8 to 5.3 cm, 1-1/2 to 2 inches, and 6.3 to 7.5 cm, 2-1/2 to 3 inches, in diameter and about 32 cm, 13 inches, long and the probe is placed completely within the rectum. In large adult bulls, especially Holsteins and Brahmans the extra large or "jumbo" probe, about 8.9 cm. (3-1/2 inches) in diameter can be used advantageously, Dzuik and coworkers used a probe 60 cm, 24 inches long and about 5 cm, 2 inches in diameter which after being lubricated with "K.Y." jelly or a similar noninsulating lubricant was inserted about 30 to 45 cm, 12 to 18 inches, into the rectum and held from outside the anus on the midline against the ventral floor of the pelvis. The probes may have straight or ring electrodes. Rowson and Murdock and Easley reported on a technique of electroejaculation using a ring or hand electrodes either slipped over the first and third fingers of a rubber glove, or held by the hand over the region of the base of the penis and prostate gland or the posterior portion of the ampullae. This technique is favored over the rectal probe by some veterinarians because the bull reacts more favorably and with less vigorous contractions of the muscles of the rear limbs and back and other undesirable side reactions. Also Easley reported more consistent results including extension of the penis in bulls of all ages, sizes and breeds when the electrodes were carried into the rectum manually.

Hill and coworkers reported that administering a saline enema before inserting the probe was usually not necessary. Dzuik reported that no difference in results were obtained using frequencies of current from 15 to 90 cycles per second. The bulls offer little or no objection to this technique. It is highly desirable to place them in a solid stanchion with a pipe or bar behind their stifles inasmuch as they tend to push forward. The front of the stanchion should be constructed so that the bull's shoulders push against supports and choking cannot occur. The footing should be good to prevent slipping. Injured bulls may require a squeeze chute or a sling to support the bull during semen collection. All bulls stiffen and arch their back or "hunch", the anal sphincter contracts and clear seminal fluid dribbles from the sheath when the current is applied. Some bulls ejaculated with the rectal probe lean to one side or raise and extend one hind leg or rarely even both hind legs. This may be caused by the probe not being located on the midline and stimulating the sciatic or pelvic nerves. It may also be due to using to much power. Some bulls may bellow. Care should be used to not apply the current until the electrodes are through the anus and in the rectum as this is painful to the bull. Occasionally a broken or exposed wire at the base of the probe will cause abnormal reactions especially noticeable on inserting the probe and applying the current. Excessive stimulation at the higher voltage levels may cause a degree of ataxia or the bull may go down. Although the actions of the bull may make this technique appear painful, it apparently is not; repeated electroejaculations do not create fear or resistance to entering the same stall. Hill and coworkers and Scott described the different variations in bulls in response to electroejaculation.

The preputial hairs may be clipped and adjacent area washed, rinsed and dried or the ventral abdomen may be brushed. Teasing or sexually-exciting bulls or a rectal examination of the accessory glands prior to electroejaculation greatly aids the collection of a good sample. To prevent cold shock to the sperm cells, a rubber cone from an artificial vagina with an attached glass or plastic vial is placed in a plastic bag containing warm water at 90 to 100° F. attached to a metal ring about 7.5 cm in diameter with a long handle. The amount and consistency of the ejaculate can thus be observed as it is emitted. An artificial vagina may also be used to collect semen during electroejaculation. The voltage is rhythmically increased and decreased to near zero every 3 to 5 seconds. A resting period of 3 to 5 seconds is allowed between stimulations.

Each bull must be treated as an individual and should be observed as the current is applied to assess his particular response. Only the amount of voltage or power needed to elicit the necessary responses and gently build up stimulation should be used in bulls and rams. About 90 percent of the bulls will erect, protrude their penis and ejaculate a representative semen sample with the rectal probe. As the penis becomes erect and the glans protrudes through the preputial orifice, more power or voltage is applied and nearly full erection occurs. With more power the clear seminal secretion becomes milky and opaque indicating ejaculation is occurring and the semen should be collected. Electroejaculation usually requires about 3 to 5 minutes to accomplish. If a bull fails to protrude his penis with stimulation, change the position of the rectal probe or exert pressure forward on the sigmoid flexure above the scrotum. Occasionally the tip of the glans will catch in the prepuce near the orifice. There may be a variation in effects of electroejaculation between bulls and from time to time in the same bull. In general young bulls respond better to electroejaculation and produce more normal ejaculates than do old bulls. According to Dzuik and coworkers erection and accessory gland secretion begin at about the 5-volt level, but ejaculation usually occurs at the 10- to 15-volt maximum, at which time about 0.5 to 1.0 amperes of current is flowing. The Marden machine produced ejaculation at about the 5.5 volt level. Too many early stimulations at a subejaculatory level will yield much accessory gland fluid but may make it difficult to obtain an ejaculation. Too rapid an increase may lead to resistance on the part of the bull or a preerection ejaculation and to contamination or loss of semen in the prepuce. Neither general nor local anesthesia nor tranquilization prevented normal electroejaculation, Wells and coworkers. Tranquilization may aid in protrusion of the penis. In some bulls excessive seminal fluid may be secreted during electroejaculation resulting in semen with a low concentration of sperm cells. Experienced operators of an electroejaculator can routinely produce ejaculates nearly similar in volume and concentration to ejaculates collected in the artificial vagina; but in general the concentration is somewhat lower, Austin et al., Hill et al., and Carroll et al.. The conception rates of bulls from which ejaculates were collected electrically were the same as when the ejaculates were collected in an artificial vagina.

Electroejaculation has become a useful adjunct to the artificial vagina in artificial insemination stations by allowing routine collections from crippled bulls without mounting. This is useful in utilizing injured bulls; and it can be used in cases of slow-breeding, impotent bulls. However, as pointed out previously impotency may be hereditary and perpetuating this condition may be detrimental to the breed. This technique has proven of great value to veterinarians for obtaining semen from beef bulls, unaccustomed to handling and to the use of the artificial vagina, for evaluating semen of bulls before putting them on range with cows, Hill and coworkers, Carroll and coworkers. It is doubtful if artificial insemination of cows with Brahman, Zebu or Santa Gertrudis semen would be possible without electroejaculation, Murray and others.

Electroejaculators on the market in the U.S. include those manufactured by: Marden Electronics, Box 383 Maxwell Rd., Ft. Collins, Colo.; Nicholson Manufacturing Co., 3990 Ulster St., Denver Colo.; Plectron Corporation, Overton, Nebr.; Production Products, Inc. (Dzuik), 4607 Lyndale Ave., N., Minneapolis, Minn.; and Standard Precision Electric Company, 1138 S. Bannock, St., Denver, Colo. The Nicholson Co. and Standard Precision Company have transistorized electroejaculators that have their own battery or may be attached to a car battery and do not require connection to a power source. Because of the lower power source these battery models eliminate completely any possibility of severely shocking the male or the operator and provide an instrument that can be used in a location without an 110 volt power source. Large old bulls may require more power or voltage to produce ejaculation than younger, immature, smaller bulls. Rowson and Murdock, Bierschwal and Shipley and Williams have described the construction of electroejaculators.

The artificial vagina is the method generally preferred and widely used for the collection of semen from dairy bulls and bulls in artificial insemination studs. By changing the mount, changing the environment, allowing sexual rest, teasing or "stewing", and other means, it will be found that there are relatively few bulls that cannot be kept in artificial service for many years. By the use of the artificial vagina a clean, complete ejaculate can usually be promptly obtained. The early models of the artificial vagina perfected by the Russians consisted of an artificial vagina which fitted inside the vagina of a cow or a dummy. The present widely-used artificial vagina is modeled after the Cambridge type that was developed in England, Perry and Maule. The vagina consists of a heavy rubber cylinder about 7 cm, 2-3/4 inches, in diameter and 35.5 cm, 14 inches, long for young bulls, and 42 cm, 16-1/2 inches, long for older bulls; this is fitted with an inner rubber liner. The longer, winter-type artificial vagina described by Salisbury and Willett is rather awkward and heavy and is seldom used except under farm conditions during the colder winter months. A rough-surfaced thick inner rubber liner apparently is preferred by bulls to a smooth, thin liner. The liner is longer than the heavy rubber cylinder and is turned back over the ends. There is usually a hole or valve in the heavy rubber cylinder for introducing and removing the hot water that is used to warm the vagina. The rubber liner is usually held in place by broad, flat, rubber bands. These should be tied to the vagina so that there is no danger of their slipping off and becoming fastened around the penis of the bull at the thrust of ejaculation and resulting in amputation of the penis if undetected. A short rubber cone containing a glass or plastic collecting tube for semen is fastened to one end of the artificial vagina and is covered with a warmed insulating jacket.

The proper pressure and warmth in the artificial vagina is obtained by filling the water jacket, or the space between the inner liner and the heavy rubber cylinder, about one-half to two-thirds full of water depending on the size of the bull's penis. The water should be 125° to 180° F., 50 to 70° C. The colder the vagina and the outside temperature, the hotter should be the water that is added. At the time of collection the temperature inside the artificial vagina should be between 105° to 125° F. or 40° to 52° C., MacMillan et al.. Only a small amount of lubricant should be applied by means of a sterile glass rod to prevent an excess of lubricant mixing with semen. The lubricant can be sterile white vaseline; a water-soluble tragacanth gum made of 3 gms tragacanth gum, 5 cc glycerine and 50 cc of water, which should be stored in a refrigerator to prevent mold formation; a water-soluble lubricating jelly such as "K.Y." jelly, which is readily obtained commercially; or pure white mineral oil. If the temperature of the artificial vagina is too low, the bull usually fails to thrust and ejaculate; if it is too hot, some spermatozoa may be killed, or it may cause the bull pain and he may develop a temporary fear of this method of collection. The glass tube on the rubber cone may be protected from breakage in the summer by having a piece of flannel or a paper hand towel fastened over it and in the winter a warm flannel of several thicknesses, an old coat-sleeve, or a special, quilted jacket with an impervious covering closed at one end can be slipped over that end of the vagina to keep the rubber cone and the collecting tube warm and protect the latter from accidentally breaking when the sample is collected. If collection is delayed during cold weather, this jacket and tube should be held under the arm or in the coat of the operator to keep the collecting tube warm.

Either a cow or a bull that is trained and quiet may be used for a mount since metal or wooden dummies even though they are heavily padded and covered by a hide, usually are not as satisfactory. If a bull is a slow-breeder, a cow in estrum is desirable, or a mount, either male or female, that is highly attractive to bulls should be used. Bulls or steers are most desirable especially in an A.I. stud in order to prevent the possible spread of disease if the bull were to accidentally breed an infected cow used as a mount.

A few quiet and well-mannered beef and dairy bulls have even been trained to breed an artificial vagina without mounting or even having another animal close. The bull is brushed and stroked along the back and sides, and then along the abdomen, sheath, and testicles. When the penis is extended from the prepuce by this stroking, an artificial vagina is applied and ejaculation occurs.

In artificial breeding studs all dairy bulls are teased before service to increase the total number of spermatozoa ejaculated. In slow breeding bulls this teasing prior to collection also makes mounting and ejaculation more prompt and rapid when the artificial vagina is heated and ready. The animal to be mounted is placed in a breeding rack or confined where the footing should be good to prevent slipping. The underline and preputial hairs of the bull are brushed clean and if necessary washed and dried. Cleanliness and hygienic practices in the collection of semen from bulls is important. The location for semen collection should be clean, dry, and free from dust, dirt, and mud. Douching the preputial cavity with a warm physiological saline solution prior to service is of questionable value in reducing the bacteria present in the semen, Cembrowicz and Osborne.

If the semen collector is right-handed, it is easier for him to work on the right side of the bull. As the bull mounts, the sheath and the erect penis is drawn sidewise toward the collector by the cupped fingers of the left hand, thus deflecting the penis from the vulvar region or escutcheon of the mount animal. The sheath and penis should not be grasped tightly with the thumb and fingers. If the protruded penis is grasped, the bull usually retracts the penis and dismounts, but occasionally immediate ejaculation occurs before the penis can be introduced into the vagina. The tip of the glans penis is introduced into the end of the artificial vagina that is held alongside the buttocks of the cow and tilted downward and backward so that the water collects in the lower or "caudal" end and provides the needed pressure and warmth to stimulate ejaculation on intromission. Swedish workers prefer to hold the vagina against the buttocks or ischial tuberosities of the cow, aiding the direction of the glans penis by the fingers on the prepuce but letting the bull seek, find and thrust into the artificial vagina, Gledhill. The bull should be allowed to thrust its penis into the vagina, since this thrust is necessary for ejaculation. If the operator prematurely pushes the vagina over the erect and extended penis, many bulls will not ejaculate. After ejaculation the vagina should immediately be tipped in the opposite direction so that the semen will run into the collecting tube. If an excess of water has been used, it may be necessary to draw off a portion of the water before all the semen can drain from the artificial vagina into the tube. A possible mishap from using an excess of water is to have the rubber liner burst or the rubber bands forced off at the time the penis is thrust into the vagina. If the latter happens, the rubber bands should be counted and penis should be examined. Some operators make a small nick or hole in the rubber cone to release air at the time of the thrust. For some bulls a heavy rubber band about 1-1/2 inches in diameter is placed around the liner, between it and the heavy rubber casing, at the open end of the vagina to provide more resistance to the entry of the penis and thus promote ejaculation.

Since sperm cells are killed or injured by toxic substances, it is necessary that all new rubber equipment which comes in contact with the semen be carefully cleaned and sterilized before using. New rubber equipment is often coated with a powder to prevent the rubber from sticking together. This powder or coating is often highly toxic to spermatozoa. After each collection the cone and rubber liner should be rinsed immediately in warm water. All glass, metal, and rubber equipment should be washed and brushed with a lukewarm solution of 0.2 to 0.3 per cent sodium hexametaphosphate such as "Calgon," or .3 to .5 percent tetrasodium pyrophosphate, or a good glass cleanser and rinsed thoroughly with warm water. Perry stated that the synthetic organic detergents should not be used in washing and sterilizing artificial insemination equipment. If they are used, very careful rinsing is necessary. After draining, all parts of the equipment are then rinsed in 70 per cent ethyl alcohol and permitted to dry in a dust-free, ventilated storage cabinet. Other types of alcohol such as methyl or denatured should not be used. Some workers use a final rinse of scalding distilled water, followed by a rinse in 70-percent ethyl alcohol. The drying may be aided by replacing the liners on the vagina but a better procedure is to distend the rubber liner with ordinary clothes pins or a special metal rack. If equipment must be used before it has dried, the alcohol should be thoroughly washed away with physiological saline or a sterile citrate- or phosphate-buffer solution. The artificial vagina may be sterilized by boiling or by being placed in an autoclave but this hastens deterioration of the rubber parts.

The artificial vagina method for the collection of bovine semen produces a clean concentrated semen sample with cheap and simple equipment and provides information on sex drive. It has the disadvantages of requiring a relatively trained cooperative bull and a suitable mount. The danger of injury of the operator is greater. While the electroejaculation method of collection gives good results with few specialized facilities and even with untrained bulls, it has the disadvantages of requiring more costly equipment, a greater chance of a contaminated sample with a low concentration of spermatozoa being collected, and no determination of the sex drive or libido of the bull is obtainable.

The stallion may have his semen collected relatively easily by using a condom as described by MacLeod and McGee or by the use of the artificial vagina as described by Lambert and McKenzie, Berliner, Asbury and Hughes, Nishikawa, and Bielanski.

The collection of semen from the vagina or uterus of the mare after natural service is possible and has been described by Frank. However samples collected in this manner are not representative, are diluted and possibly contaminated. This technique requires that the mare be healthy and free of any genital infection and not be in her foal heat. Strict hygienic and sanitary procedures should be followed in the collection of the semen by this method. After service by the stallion the hand encased in a sterile glove and sleeve is introduced into the vagina with a stiff rubber tube 3/16 inch in diameter and about 2 to 2-1/2 feet long. This tube is attached by a bent glass tube in a 2-holer rubber stopper to a 6-ounce sterile bottle and a 12- to 18-inch tube is similarly attached by a glass tube in the other hole of the stopper. By suction applied on the short tube with the mouth, semen is drawn into the bottle from the vagina and if necessary from the uterus. Another but less satisfactory method is to use a vaginal speculum and draw up the semen with a long nozzle attached to a syringe. These techniques are presently seldom used.

Collection of the "dismount" or "tail-end" sample of stallion semen that drips from the glans and urethra after copulation can be easily accomplished by holding a warm enamel cup or large plastic funnel attached to a warmed tube or bottle under the vulva and glans penis as the stallion dismounts. This last portion of the ejaculate has a much lower concentration of spermatozoa, has a different composition than the complete ejaculate, and is usually unsuited for predicting fertility and for inseminating purposes, Mann and coworkers. The amount of semen collected in this manner is small, 10 to 30 ml and it is commonly contaminated with smegma and dirt. Collection and examination of this "tail-end" sample is usually performed to be certain that ejaculation occurred during intromission. Semen collected in this manner is usually filtered through sterile gauze or a coarse-paper filter into a vial before it is used for insemination or "impregnation" following a natural service.

Massage of the ampullae and electroejaculation as described in bulls has been attempted without success by both Day and the author. With the horse completely anesthetized electroejaculation is possible as reported in swine but it is not practical and urine often contaminated the sample, Adams. These above techniques, for obvious reasons, are not as satisfactory as collecting the entire ejaculate in an artificial vagina or a condom.

The condom or breeder's bag was used successfully by MacLeod and McGee on most Thoroughbred stallions. A mare in estrum, a mare that has been given 10 to 20 mg of stilbestrol 24 to 48 hours previously to produce signs of estrus, or a very docile, trained older mare can be used with the usual restraints as a mount. The older type of breeder's bag, made of a heavy gauge rubber was found to be clumsy, of rough construction, and susceptible to tearing. A satisfactory condom for the stallion similar to that used by man was designed. Before use the breeder's bag or condom should be thoroughly cleaned of all rubber preserving powder by thorough washing, rinsing with plain or distilled water and then rinsing with a physiological salt solution. If the condom is to be reused it should be sterilized after washing and rinsing by immersing in ethyl alcohol and dried. Before applying the condom the penis should be carefully washed and rinsed thoroughly several times with plain water and dried to remove dirt and smegma. The condom is fitted to the erect penis, but left loose over the glans with the air squeezed out just prior to service. It is held in place by rubber bands and removed immediately after service. If an excess of fluid collects in the condom before ejaculation empty it out. The ejaculate is poured into a sterile bottle or graduate warmed to about 100 to 102° F. Frank mentioned lubricating the outside of the breeder's bag and vulva, but this is not necessary if the stronger condoms designed by MacLeod and McGee are used.*

The artificial vagina has been widely used in England, Russia, Japan and the United States for the collection of semen from stallions. When this is performed regularly the stallion may be trained in its use. MacLeod and McGee reported less success and more difficulty in Thoroughbred stallions with this method than with the condom. Asbury and Hughes and the author prefer the artificial vagina to the condom because of more satisfactory results and less contaminated samples. The equipment, however, is more expensive. In some countries stallions have been trained to mount dummies or manikins; in the United States a mare in estrum, or one in which estrum has been induced, is usually required. Strict hygienic procedures should be followed, such as: bandaging the mare's tail with a sterile bandage; careful and thorough washing, disinfection and rinsing of her rear parts; and careful washing and rinsing of penis and sheath of the stallion. The usual precautions are taken to restrain the mare and to prevent injury to the stallion.

The method of constructing the Missouri-U.S.D.A. type of vagina has been described by Frank; this artificial vagina is available from Haver-Lockhart Laboratories P.O. Box 390, Shawnee Mission, Kansas. The Mississippi model has been described by Berliner. Lighter more modern artificial vaginas for stallions are also available.*

The diameter of the vagina is about 12.7 to 17.7 cm, 5 to 7 inches, and because of its increased size and weight a handle is provided. A dam is present at the closed end of the Nishikawa vagina that provides a place for contact for the glans penis. A new vagina must be thoroughly washed, rinsed, disinfected with grain alcohol, and dried before it is first used, and following each use thereafter. Mineral oil or preferably the water-soluble lubricating jellies can be used sparingly to lubricate the opening of the vagina. The temperature of the vagina should be between 105 to 120° F., 41 to 50° C. This is provided by introducing hot water at 120° to 130° F., 50 to 65° C., depending on the climatic conditions, between the jacket and the liner of the artificial vagina. Pressure in the artificial vagina simulating that of a mare's vulva may be produced by a 2-inch wide rubber band, 3 inches in diameter, placed between the jacket and the rubber liner near the open end of the vagina. Pumping air into the space occupied by the warm water is helpful but not necessary to make sufficient pressure for ejaculation. Berliner advised manual pressure through the wall of the vagina. Some of the artificial vaginas such as the Japanese type have rigid outside walls. Although the operator may collect semen from either side of the stallion, most prefer the left or near side. The artificial vagina should not be shoved over the stallion's penis as he mounts but rather the stallion should be permitted with help to insert his penis into the vagina. On cold days the bottle receiving the semen should be warmed and protected. The vagina should be held firmly against the flank and buttock of the mare with the open end of the vagina held above the level of the plastic collecting bottle and pressure exerted against the penis equal to that exerted by the stallion. It usually requires about 20 to 30 seconds for ejaculation. If the stallion or

*Condoms for stallions may be purchased from the Pioneer Rubber Co., Willard, Ohio, Youngs Rubber Co., Trenton, N.J., and Dean Rubber Co., East Kansas City, Mo. (Texas Model)

*Artificial Vagina for obtaining stallion semen (Nishikawa Model) Fujihira Industry Co. Ltd., 131 Morikawa-Cho, Bunkujoku, Tokyo, Japan and Goetze's Artificial Vagina for Horses, H. Hauptner, Solingen, Germany. A homemade equine artificial vagina made from a Nalgene pipette washer has been described by B. W. Pickett, Colo. State. Univ.

jack is not properly trained, or lacks desire, a quiet mare or jenny and quiet surroundings are necessary for collection with an artificial vagina. The author has successfully used a bovine artificial vagina for the collection of semen from small ponies. Stallions that require repeated intromissions before ejaculation or are slow to mount and copulate act similarly when semen is collected by the artificial vagina.

The ram and buck may have satisfactory semen samples collected by removing the semen from the vagina of a ewe after coitus, by an artificial vagina or by electroejaculation.

Rams may be mated to restrained diestrual ewes. The vaginas are cleaned prior to use by repeatedly inserting and withdrawing until no more mucus secretion can be removed, a collecting pipette of glass or plexiglass 30 cm, 12 inches, long and 1/4 to 3/8 inch in diameter attached to a rubber bulb for suction. If the ram refuses to breed a diestrual ewe, one in estrum may be used. After coitus semen is removed in a similar fashion. This is a simple method but the semen is usually contaminated. It is faster for collecting from shy, untrained rams than the artificial vagina method and it also detects rams that physically are unable to copulate. Semen evaluation can be performed satisfactorily on such samples, Terrill, Hulet and Ercanbrack.

The artificial vagina for rams is constructed like the artificial vagina for bulls but it is smaller, about 20 cm, 8 inches, long and 5 cm, 2 inches, in diameter. The temperature of the vagina at the time of collection is critical for the ram and should be 45° to 60° C., 113° to 140° F., Bratton. Rams may be readily trained in a suitable environment, with a restrained ewe preferably in estrum. Later any ewe or even a dummy may be used as a mount. As the operator holds the vagina in his hand he should be crouched next to the rear parts of the ewe and be alert as mounting and copulation is very rapid. False mounts without ejaculation are common. The penis should not be touched by the hand but the sheath may be grasped to direct the penis into the artificial vagina. A refractory period of 20 to 30 minutes follows ejaculation in the ram before he will mount again.

Electroejaculation of rams was first described by Gunn in 1936. In recent years improved electroejaculators are available with bipolar rectal probes about 30 cm, 12 inches long and 2 cm, 3/4 inch, in diameter.* The ram responds rapidly to electrical stimulation and often 3 to 5 stimulations of 3 to 5 seconds duration with 3 to 5 seconds rest at 2, 5 and 8-volt peaks result in ejaculation, Dzuik and coworkers, Barker, Hafez and coworkers, and Warren and coworkers. The insertion of the rectal probe to a depth of 15 cm, 6 inches, instead of 20 to 25 cm, 8 to 10 inches, improved the rapidity of response and produced a greater volume of semen. Rams may be electroejaculated in the standing position or restrained on their side with their legs extended. The latter position is more often recommended. The penis should be removed from the sheath and held with gauze so the urethral process is directed into the collection vial or tube to avoid ejaculation into the sheath. Often the penis will protrude from the sheath with electrical stimulation as in the bull. This method results in a great variation in semen volume and concentration. As in the bull the concentration is usually less and the volume greater than in natural service or ejaculation into an artificial vagina. Occasionally urine may contaminate the sample. If the first collection is unsatisfactory it is difficult to get another satisfactory ejaculate until several hours have elapsed. Electroejaculation has the advantages that it may be used on untrained rams and is particularly valuable as a screening test of the semen quality of large numbers of rams, Maule, Ball. Hulet et al. definitely preferred natural ejaculation into a ewe's vagina to electroejaculation when the semen was being examined to assess fertility. Indiscriminate use of electroejaculation without reexaminations could lead to the culling of many potential high-fertility rams as occasional samples of semen obtained by electroejaculation from fertile rams were inferior in quality. Megale has described the induction of erection and ejaculation in rams and bucks by the local massage of the sheath and penis.

The boar may have semen collected by a modified artificial vagina or by electroejaculation.

The artificial vagina may be of various designs to provide the necessary pressure to the spiraled glans penis so that it "locks" at complete erection as it does in the anterior vaginal and cervical folds of the sow. This may be accomplished most simply by a heavy rubber casing 4.5 cm or 1-3/4 inches in diameter and about 12.5 cm or 5 inches long with a rubber liner and small piece of sponge rubber between it and the casing where warm water at 45° to 50° C., 113 to 122° F., is placed to heat the vagina. The sponge rubber causes increased pressure on the penis. A continuous, smooth, thin rubber liner or tubing 40 cm, 16 inches, long and 3 to 3.5 cm, 1-1/4 to 1-3/8 inches, in diameter with a small hole in the upper portion to allow air to escape is passed through the above vagina and fastened to the outer end of the vagina and lubricated. The other end is fastened to a plastic bottle or bag of 500 ml capacity that is in a cup or thermos of warm water at 102° F., 39° C. As the penis passes through the vagina

*Nicholson Manufacturing Co., 3990 Ulster St., Denver, Colo.; Production Products, Inc., (Dzuik Model) 4607 Lyndale Ave. N., Minneapolis, Minn.

pressure is applied to the glans by the hand of the operator through the thin rubber tubing, Bratton, Melrose, Turkheimer et al., Hess and coworkers. After several back and forth motions the penis "locks" in the fingers, continuous moderate pressure is applied, and ejaculation commences and continues for about 15 minutes with much of the sperm-rich fraction being emitted around the third or fourth minute. Frequently there may be a series of sperm-rich fractions interspersed between periods of thin sperm-poor fractions and gelatinous tapioca-like secretions. Perry and Aamdal and coworkers have described a slightly more complex model of artificial vagina the diameter of the artificial vagina for the bull, but only 18 cm, 7 inches, long designed to prevent contamination of semen with preputial secretions. Frank and Hafez, Foote and Trimberger, have described a very simple model consisting of only a 16 inch rubber tubing as described above with a key ring for an orifice that is warmed before use. Other earlier types were similar to the artificial vagina for the bull but with attachments to it so air could be pulsated into the vagina. Niwa cited by Nishikawa and Maule designed a vagina incorporating a heavy spiral ring within the vagina to simulate the folds of the sow's genital tract. Other modified types are described by Rothe. Some workers collect semen from trained boars with only a gloved hand and a wide-mouthed thermos jug containing warm water and lined with a plastic bag to prevent chilling of the semen.

Boars are usually readily trained to mount a dummy composed of a metal or wooden frame covered with burlap or they may be allowed to mount a confined or restrained sow or barrow. The former is preferable. The environment should be quiet and the footing non-slippery, Perry, Maule and Hess and coworkers.

Electroejaculation in boars has been described by Dzuik and coworkers and Adams et al.. The latter reported that the rectal probe used for rams is not as suitable for boars but the larger Dzuik model bull probe is satisfactory if the rectum is evacuated of feces before the probe is inserted. Stimuli must be applied at voltage peaks of 12 to 17 or more volts at 5 to 10 second intervals to obtain ejaculation. The volume of semen obtained is low but the concentration is usually high because of a lack of accessory gland secretions. Boars must be forcibly restrained and collection is a noisy drawn-out affair, often resulting in a heavily contaminated ejaculate. The electroejaculation of boars is not satisfactory as in bulls and rams. Adams preferred to use the electroejaculator on anesthetized boars. One to one and one-half grams of "Surital", sodium thiamylal, Parke-Davis, was given intravenously in the ear vein through a 20 gauge needle producing good anesthesia for 15 to 30 minutes in 300 to 400 pound boars. The genital organs were easily and thoroughly cleansed and the penis was removed from the sheath, held by the hand and directed so the semen would flow into a warmed thermos jug lined with a plastic bag when electroejaculation occurred. Under anesthesia the penis and testes are easily examined. The principal disadvantages of this method besides the slight anesthetic danger is inability to observe the boar's libido and his actions at coitus and the nonphysiologic ejaculate, largely free of accessory gland secretion. But the above method was rapid and quiet and was preferred by Adams for the evaluation of the semen of boars to the use of the artificial vagina which required obtaining sows in estrum or training the boar to mount and use the artificial vagina. Shy, slow, inexperienced, mean, lame or injured boars are difficult to train. Training procedures can't be standardized and are very time consuming. If a live mount is used there may be disease control problems to consider.

In the dog semen may be obtained for examination or artificial insemination by manual manipulation of the penis or by the artificial vagina. Christensen and Dougherty have described a method of electroejaculation of the anesthetized dog modeled after the procedure described by Gunn in rams. This proved useful in a very few males that could not be collected by the former two methods.

Manual manipulation of the base of the penis is the simplest, cheapest, and commonest way to collect semen in the dog. A bitch, preferably in heat, should be presented to the male. When the dog shows sexual interest the preputial skin is pushed caudally, exposing one to two inches of the glans penis. The base of the penis behind the bulbus glandis is grasped through the prepuce and moderate pressure is applied by the fingers. In an impotent male masturbation may aid in producing an erection. Even through no teaser bitch is present some dogs can be trained to ejaculate by manipulation of the base of the penis until erection is induced, but sperm cell concentration is usually low. The semen is collected by means of a warm glass or plastic funnel into a 25 to 30 ml warm tube or vial or the warmed barrel of a 20 ml glass syringe on which a rubber adapter has been placed and doubled over to prevent leakage of semen. The first portion of the ejaculate may be lost due to a brief period of thrusting motions by the male. This is of little importance, as few spermatozoa are present in this portion. When the ejaculation of sperm cells commence thrusting motions cease. The penis should not enter the tube or syringe barrel and in shy or impotent males the tube or syringe barrel should not be allowed to touch the penis. It is important to maintain constant pressure behind the bulbus glandis until sufficient semen has been collected. Leonard and Perry, Maule, Boucher et al., and Kirk. The portion of the ejaculate containing the spermatozoa is a whitish-grey milky fluid. Ejaculatory action can be noted by feeling the pulsations of the urethra in the base of the penis. Ejaculation may last 5 to 15 minutes and the male may even dismount and stand facing away from the bitch.

An artificial vagina for the dog similar in size, 5 cm, 2-1/2 inches, in diameter and 19 cm, 7-1/2 inches , long, and similar in pattern to the artificial vagina for a ram is described by Nooder, Harrop, and Hancock and Rowlands. The latter recommended a firm rubber diaphragm around the open end of the vagina to simulate a bitch's vulva. The temperature of the vagina should be about 40° to 42° C., 104° to 107° F., and no lubricant need be used. The penis is grasped behind the bulbus glandis as described above to produce erection before the vagina is applied. Boucher et al. reported that semen motility was adversely affected by this technique. Possibly this was due to the contact of the sperm cells with the heated walls of the artificial vagina as this finding was not reported by others that used and preferred an artificial vagina for semen collection in the dog.

Sojka et al. have described semen collection from the tom cat. Male cats were selected for their calm temperment and for their strong libido. Teaser queens were either females in estrum or ovariectomized females given 12.5 mg diethylstilbestrol, **Repositol,** every 10 days. It usually required about 2 weeks to train a tom cat for routine semen collection. The artificial vagina was a 2 ml rubber bulb from the end of a bulb pipette or "eye dropper" with the bulb end cut off and fitted over a 3 x 44 mm test tube. This was placed in a 60 ml plastic polyethylene bottle. The bottle was filled with water at 52° C so at the time of collection the temperature would be 44 to 46° C. The open end of the rubber bulb was rolled over the mouth of the bottle and smeared lightly with K.Y. jelly. The artificial vagina was slipped over the penis of the tom as he mounted the teaser queen and developed an erection. The operators other hand was used to steady the tom and teaser queen. Collection took from 1 to 4 minutes. Their study indicated that toms could be collected 3 times a week and daily use for a short period was possible without a great decline in semen quality. Daily collection did not affect the male cats' libido.

Diagnosis of Sterility and Infertility in the Male—History, Physical Examination and Diagnostic Tests

Aehnalt, E. and Dittmar, J. (1961) Arbeitsweise und Ergebnisse der Bullen-Prufstation Nordwestdeutschland, Proc. 4th Intern. Congr. on An. Reprod., The Hague, 1961, II.

Gledhill, B. L. (1967) Swedish Methods for the Evaluation of Breeding Soundness in Bulls, (Mimeographed notes presented at the Amer. Vet. Soc. for the Study of Breeding Soundness, Univ. of Missouri.) FAO/Swedish Internat. Vet. Postgraduate Course on An. Reprod., Royal Vet. College, Stockholm, Sweden.

Hahn, J., Foote, R. H. and Cranch, E. T. (1969) A Tonometer for Measuring Testicular Consistency of Bulls to Predict Semen Quality, J. An. Sci. **29,** 3, 483.

Hahn, J., Foote, R. H. and Seidel, G. E. Jr. (1969) Testicular Growth and Related Sperm Output in Dairy Bulls, J. An. Sci. **29,** 1, 41.

Carroll, E. J., Ball, L. and Scott, J. A. (1963) Breeding Soundness in Bulls—A Summary of 10,490 Examinations, J.A.V.M.A. **142,** 1105.

Larson, L. L. (1967) Health Examination for A.B.S. Bulls, Amer. Breeders Service, Inc., De Forest Wisc.

Roberts, S. J. (1967) Health Examination Forms Used at Eastern Cooperative Breeders, Inc., Ithaca, N.Y.

Willett, E. L. and Ohms, J. I. (1957) Measurement of Testicular Size and its Relation to Production of Spermatozoa by Bulls, J. Dairy Sci. **40,** 12, 1559.

Semen Examination—General

Bartlett, D. E. and Elliott, F. I. (1960) The Constancy of Fertility in "Normal" Bulls as Expressed in Artificial Insemination, Internat. Jour. of Fert. **5,** 3, 307.

Hartman, C. G. (1965) Correlations Among Criteria of Semen Quality, Fert. and Steril. **16,** 5, 632.

Hulet, C. V. and Ercanbrack, S. K. (1962) A Fertility Index for Rams, J. An. Sci. **21,** 489.

Hulet, C. V., Foote, W. C. and Blackwell, R. L. (1965) Relationship of Semen Quality and Fertility in the Ram to Fecundity in the Ewe, J. Reprod. Fertil. **9,** 311.

MacLeod, J. and Gold, R. Z. (1956) The Male Factor in Fertility and Infertility. VIII A Study of Variation in Semen Quality, Fert. and Steril. **7,** 5, 387.

MacLeod, J. and Gold, R. Z. (1958) An Analysis of Human Male Fertility, Internat. J. of Fertil. **3,** 382.

Williams, W. W. (1961) The Enigma of Male Infertility, Internat. J. of Fertil. **6,** 3, 311.

Semen Collection—General References

Foote, R. H. and G. W. Trimberger (1968) Reproduction in Farm Animals, Edit. by Hafez, E. S. E., Lea and Febiger, Philadelphia, Pa.

Frank, A. H. (1950) Artificial Insemination in Livestock Breeding, Circular 567 U.S. Dept. of Agric., Washington D.C.

Maule, J. P. (1962) The Semen of Animals and Artificial Insemination, Commonwealth Agric. Bureaux, Farnham Royal, Bucks, England.

Nishikawa, Y. (1962) Fifty Years of Artificial Insemination of Farm Animals in Japan, Dept. of Animal Science, Kyoto Univ., Japan.

Perry, E. J. (1960) The Artificial Insemination of Farm Animals, 3rd. Ed., Rutgers Univ. Press, New Brunswick, N.Y.

The Bull

Austin, J.W., Hupp, E. W. and Murphree, R. L. (1961) Comparison of Quality of Bull Semen Collected in an Artificial Vagina and by Electroejaculation, J. Dairy Sci. **44,** 12, 2292.

Bierschwal, C. J. and Shipley, G. (1959) Assembling an Electronic Ejaculator, Vet. Med. **54,** 8, 393.

Carroll, E. J., Ball, L. and Scott, J. A. (1963) Breeding Soundness in Bulls—A Summary of 10,940 Examinations, J.A.V.M.A. **142,** 1105.

Case, C. H. (1925) Handling Cases of Sterility in Practice, Cor. Vet. **15,** 1, 37.

Cembrowicz, H. J. and Osborne, A. D. (1961) Effect of Preputial Cavity Treatment on the Number and Types of Bacteria in Semen Samples and Sheath Washings, Proc. 4th Internat. Congr. on An. Reprod. (the Hague) **III,** 468.

Debruyn, R. (1961) The Collection of Semen in Bulls by Massage of the Ampullae Through the Rectum, Proc. 4th Internat. Congr. on An. Reprod., Hague, II, 283.

Dzuik, P. J., Graham, E. F. and Petersen, W. E. (1954) The Technique of Electro-ejaculation and Its Use in Dairy Bulls, J. of Dairy Sci. **37,** 9, 1035.

Easley, G. T. (1970) A Hand Electrode for the Electroejaculation of Bulls, Bov. Pract. **5,** 12.

Gledhill, B. L. (1967) Swedish Methods for Evaluation of Breeding Soundness in Bulls, Ann. Meeting Amer. Vet. Soc. for the Study of Breeding Soundness, Univ. of Missouri, Columbia, Mo., Royal Vet. College, Stockholm, Sweden.

Gunn, R. M. C. (1936) Fertility in Sheep: Artificial Production of Seminal Ejaculation and the Characters of the Spermatozoa Contained Therein, Council of Sci. and Ind. Res. of Austral., Bull #94.

Hill, H. J., Scott, F. S., Homan, N. and Gassner, F. X. (1956) Electroejaculation in the Bull, J.A.V.M.A. **128,** 8, 375.

Larson, L. L. (1969) Disease Incidence in 1481 Bulls Examined for Use in Artificial Insemination, An. Meeting A.V.M.A., Minneapolis, Mimeographed notes.

Marden, W. G. R. (1954) New Advances in Electro-ejaculation of the Bull, J. of Dairy Sci. **37,** 5, 556.

MacMillan, K. L., Hafs, H. D. and Desjardins, C. (1966) Some Semen Characteristics in Dairy Bulls Ejaculated with Artificial Vaginas at Varying Temperatures, J. of Dairy Sci. **49,** 9, 1132.

Megale, J. (1968) Induction of Erection and Ejacultion in the Bull by Local Massage, Cor. Vet. **58,** 1, 88.

Miller, F. W. and Evans, E. I. (1934) Technic for Obtaining Spermatozoa for Physiological Dairy Studies and Artificial Insemination, Jour. Agric. Res. **48,** 10, 941.

Murray, G. R. (1970) Personal Communication.

Rowson, L. E. A. (1947) Collection of Semen by Means of the Urethral Fistula, Vet. Rec. **59,** 289.

Rowson, L. E. A. and Murdock, M. I. (1954) Electrical Ejaculation in the Bull, Vet. Rec. 66, 23, 326.

Scott, J. A. (1966) The Electro-ejaculator: Its Use and Problem Bulls, Proc. 1st. Tech. Conf. on Art. Insem. and Bovine Reprod., N.A.A.B.

Wells, M. E., Philpot, W. N., Musgrave, S. D., Jones, E. W. and Brock, W. E. (1966) Effect on Method of Semen Collection and Tranquilization on Semen Quality and Bull Behavior, J. Dairy Sci. **49,** 5, 500.

Williams, D. J. (1969) Electroejaculation in the Bull, Proc. of Conference on Reproductive Problems in Animals, Univ. of Georgia, Nov., p. 38.

The Stallion

Adams, W. M. Jr., (1968) Personal Communication.

Asbury, A. C. and Hughes, J. P. (1964) Use of the Artificial Vagina for Equine Semen Collection, J.A.V.M.A. **144,** 8, 879.

Berliner, V. (1960) The Artificial Insemination of Farm Animals, 3rd Ed., Edit. by Perry, E. J., Rutgers Univ. Press, New Brunswick, N.Y.

Bielanski, W. (1963) Die Kunstliche Besamung beim Pferd, from **Die Kunstliche Besamung bei den Haustieren,** Schaetz, F. Gustav Fischer Verlag, Jena, Germany.

Day, F. T. (1940) The Stallion and Fertility, Vet. Rec. **52,** 34, 597.

Lambert, W. V. and McKenzie, F. F. (1940) Artificial Insemination in Livestock Breeding, U.S. Dept. Agr. Cir. 567.

MacLeod, J. and McGee, W. R. (1950) The Semen of the Thoroughbred, Cor. Vet. **40,** 3, 233.

The Ram and Buck

Barker, C. A. V. (1958) The Collection of Semen from Bulls, Rams and Bucks, Canad. J. of Comp. Med. **22,** 1, 3.

Bratton, R. (1968) Personal Communication.

Dzuik, P. J., Graham, E. F., Donker, J. D., Marion, G. B. and Petersen, W. E. (1954) Some Observations on Collection of Semen from Bulls, Goats, Boars and Rams by Electrical Stimulation, Vet. Med. **49,** 11, 455.

Hulet, C. V. and Ercanbrack, S. K. (1962) A Fertility Index for Rams, J. An. Sci. **21,** 489.

Hulet, C. V., Foote, W. C. and Blackwell, R. L. (1964) Effects of Natural and Electrical Ejaculation on Predicting Fertility in the Ram, J. An. Sci. **23,** 2, 418.

Megale, F. (1968) Induction of Erection and Ejaculation in the Bull by Local Massage, Cor. Vet. **58,** 1, 88.

Terrill, C. E. (1960) The Artificial Insemination of Farm Animals, 3rd Ed. Edited by Perry, E. J., Rutgers Univ. Press, New Brunswick, N.J.

Warren, E. P., Todd, A. S. and Fakhrnea, B. (1960) Effect of Depth of Probe Insertion and Voltage on Ram Semen Collected by Electroejaculation, J. An. Sci. 19, 4, 1339.

The Boar

Aamdal, J. and Hogset, I. (1957) Artificial Insemination in Swine, J.A.V.M.A. **131,** 1, 59.

Aamdel, J., Hogset, I., Sveberg, O. and Koppang, N. (1958) A New Type Artificial Vagina and a New Collection Technique for Boar Semen, J.A.V.M.A. **132,** 3, 101.

Adams, Wm., Clark, T. L. and Evans, L. E. (1969) Electro-ejaculation of the Anesthetized Boar, An. Meeting, A.V.M.A., Minneapolis, mimeographed notes.

Bratton, R. (1967) Personal Communication, Cornell Univ.

Hess, E. A., Ludwick, T. M. and Teague, H. S. (1960) Artificial Insemination in Swine, Ohio Agric. Exp. Stat, Res. Circ. #90, Wooster, Ohio.

Melrose, D. R. (1963) Artificial Insemination in the Pig. A Review of its Development, Brit. Vet. Jour. **119,** 532 and World Review of Animal Production, 1966, II, 15.

Turkheimer, A. R., Young, D. C. and Foote, R. H. (1958) Techniques for Semen Collection; Semen Production in Young Boars, Cor. Vet. **48,** 3, 291.

Rothe, K. (1963) Die Kunstliche Besamung beim Schwein, Archiv. Fur. Exper. Veterinarmed. Bd. **16,** 957.

The Dog and Cat

Christensen, G. C. and Dougherty, R. W. (1955) A Simplified Apparatus for Obtaining Semen from Dogs by Electrical Stimulation, J.A.V.M.A. **127,** 940, 50.

Boucher, J. H., Foote, R. H. and Kirk, R. W. (1958) The Evaluation of Semen Quality in the Dog and the Effects of Frequency of Ejaculation Upon Semen Quality, Libido and Depletion of Sperm Reserves, Cor. Vet. **48,** 1, 67.

Foote, R. H. (1965) Current Veterinary Therapy, 3rd Ed., R. W. Kirk, Editor W. B. Saunders Co.; Philadelphia and London. p 686.

Hancock, J. L. and Rowlands, I. W. (1949) The Physiology of Reproduction in the Dog, Vet. Rec. **61,** 47, 71.

Harrop, A. E. (1954) A New Type Canine Artificial Vagina, Brit. Vet. Jour. **110,** 194.

Harrop, A. E., (1960) Reproduction in the Dog, Williams and Wilkins Co., Baltimore, Md.

Kirk, R. W. (1959) Artificial Insemination in the Dog, Allied Vet., Mar-April.

Nooder, H. J. (1950) Enkele Mededelingen Omtrent, De K. I. by Teven en het Sperma Van Reuen, Tijdschr v. Diergeneesk. **75,** 3, 81.

Sojka, N. J., Jennings, L. L. and Hamner, C. E. (1970) Artificial Insemination in the Cat **(Felis Catus L.)** Lab. An. Care, **20,** 2, 598.

TESTS FOR SEMEN QUALITY

Examinations for semen quality can only be satisfactorily performed on approximately normal ejaculates within a short period after collection. The ejaculates must be properly protected and handled until examined. Semen evaulation in the laboratory is not a test for fertility. Some factors to consider in the proper handling of semen are: (1) The artificial vagina or the container used for semen in electroejcaultion should be clean and free from contaminants that might injure spermatozoa, such as: alcohol, excessive petrolatum, powder present on new rubber liners, and antiseptics or chemicals of any kind; (2) at the time of collection excessive dirt or debris including preputial smegma and secretions should be kept out of the vagina; water and urine injure spermatozoa by creating a different osmotic pressure; (3) excessive amounts of blood and serum may adversely affect spermatozoa; (4) overheating and too-rapid chilling injure spermatozoa, (5) too much agitation and shaking of the semen damages spermatozoa; and (6) excessive exposure to sunlight should be avoided. It is important that the semen sample be examined as soon as possible after collection.

A good laboratory with the necessary equipment and a well-trained technician, if it is within a few hours drive is the logical place to have the semen examination performed. However, all too often a semen sample is sent to a laboratory at some distance; and the motility and other qualities may be so affected during shipment that the value of such an examination is questionable or limited. In many of these instances only a morphological examination and density estimation of spermatozoa can be performed. Usually a warm "laboratory" at 60 to 80° F. can be set up in an automobile with a good heater. Portable electric incubators that can be connected to a 110 volt circuit are now available for the warming of equipment. For this reason the author firmly believes that by the use of a microscope most trained veterinarians can perform by means of a few simple laboratory procedures on the farm or ranch 3 or 4 semen tests on a male and more accurately determine his probable fertility than can a trained laboratory technician receiving a single ejaculate by mail. The veterinarian also has access to the complete breeding history, information on the male's sexual desire and frequency of service, and other pertinent information, such as his performance during copulation, from a careful physical examination not known to a laboratory. In this testing procedure as in other laboratory techniques the results must be carefully evaluated on the basis of the information obtained and what is known concerning the case; too much reliance should not be placed on the results of the tests on a single ejaculate. The best fertility evaluation test is the conception rate of the females bred to the male. Semen examinations, if carefully done, may provide a ready and reasonably accurate measure of the fertility of the male and be of value in determining the severity and the possible cause of infertility affecting a male. If special staining techniques, electron microscopy or other complicated procedures are necessary for morphological studies on certain semen samples these must be done in specialized laboratoies under the supervision of skilled and knowledgable technicians and scientists.

Semen quality of the first ejaculate after a long period of sexual rest may have a lowered motility and an increased number of dead spermatozoa. Semen quality in many rams and a few bulls may be decreased during the hot summer months. Season of the year had a significant effect on semen quality in stallions with the best quality of semen produced late in the spring or early summer and the poorest quality semen in the winter months, Rajamannan, Pickett et al.. The various common tests on semen are as follows:

Volume—The usual volume of the ejaculate in the various domestic animals has been given previously. Repeated frequent ejaculations may temporarily lower the volume of the ejaculate. However, under the usual breeding conditions the amount of the ejaculate produced remains fairly constant for each species of animal. (See Table 21) Under conditions of artificial insemination, teasing or "stewing" of bulls, horses, dogs and other species is usually practiced to increase the concentration of the spermatozoa and possibly the volume of the ejaculate. Collins, Bratton and Henderson reported that restraining bulls for 2 to 5 minutes or more to induce sexual excitement before allowing ejaculation, was accompanied by increases of about 40 percent in the number of motile spermatozoa per ejaculate over unrestrained bulls. Some males if unrestrained give a very poor first ejaculate with a low spermatozoan concentration. Small volumes of semen may be ejaculated in young males, in males used excessively, in incomplete ejaculation or failure of ejaculation, and in cases of bilateral seminal vesiculitis in bulls and stallions. An increase or decrease in volume of semen ejaculated is usually not correlated with fertility or sterility in a male unless ejaculation fails to occur.

Color—As described previously ram and bull semen is concentrated and the color is milky or creamy white and opaque. (See Table 23 and 26) It is normally like cream in consistency. In the stallion, boar, and dog the spermatozoa are much less concentrated and the color is pearly-white to grey and translucent. Haq reported a creamy consistency of semen in bulls with spermatozoan concentrations of 1,000,000 to 1,200,000 per cmm or higher; a thin milky consistency with spermatozoan concentrations of 500,000 to 600,000 per cmm; and watery, translucent or clear semen with fewer than 300,000 spermatozoa per cmm. Deakin indicated that brownish-colored semen in bulls, probably due to blood pigment, may be observed in cases of orchitis. The light yellow color seen occasionally in the semen of some bulls at the time of collection is due to riboflavin secreted by the accessory glands and it has no significance.

Haq reported that the presence of **Ps. aeruginosa** in bull semen may cause a change from a normal to a yellowish-green color when semen is left standing at room temperature. Clumps, clots or large flakes in semen are due to the presence of pus usually from the accessory glands or ampullae. A dark red to pink color of the semen is due to the presence of varying amounts of blood from the genital tract, urethra or penis. A light brown color may be due to the presence of feces in the semen. When the semen is not a normal color and consistency, further examination should be made of the actual density or concentration of the spermatozoa, since reduced fertility may accompany a reduced or low concentration of spermatozoa or severe contamination with substances or agents harmful to spermatozoa.

Hydrogen Ion Concentration or pH Value of the semen of domestic animals has been given previously. Maule and Swanson and Herman indicated that measurements of the pH of semen at the time of collection is of little practical value in the normal male for predicting fertility. In bulls, rams and dogs the pH of semen is neutral, about 6.7. According to Blom and others a pH of 7.0 or higher in semen was observed in bulls used excessively, in incomplete ejaculates and in pathological or inflammatory conditions affecting the testes, epididymides, ampullae or seminal vesicles. The semen of stallions, boars and cats is normally slightly alkaline in reaction, pH 7.4. Pickett reported that first ejaculates from stallions had an average pH of 7.47 and second ejaculates collected soon after the first were more alkaline, pH from 7.5 to 8.0. The pH of semen may be measured with pH paper, with bromthymol blue or a pH meter. Where an inflammatory condition affecting an accessory genital organ is suspected or present and characterized by an elevation of the pH of the ejaculate, a catalase test is indicated. High catalase activity of semen, a reaction greater than 300 on the tube used for the test, is demonstrable in cases of acute seminal vesiculitis of bulls, Gledhill.

Concentration or Density of Spermatozoa in semen has been given previously for the various domestic animals. (See Table 23) According to Lagerlof the concentration of spermatozoa in ejaculates of fertile bulls varies from 300,000 to 2,000,000 per cmm. with an average of 800,000. Ejaculates collected with the electroejaculator frequently have a lower concentration and a greater volume than those collected with the artificial vagina due to an excess of accessory gland secretion. Haq concluded that spermatozoan density is within normal limits in many bulls with testicular degeneration and therefore other tests are usually necessary for an accurate evaluation of semen quality. He indicated that concentrations of spermatozoa below 600,000 should be looked upon with suspicion. Blom reported that in 24 bulls with serious affections of the testes, 13 had oligospermia, fewer than 200,000 per cmm, and 7 of these had fewer than 10,000 spermatozoa per ml.

Blom, Seidel and Foote, and others noted that some watery translucent ejaculates in bulls were due to incomplete ejaculation. MacLeod reported that in humans low concentrations usually were correlated with infertility but that exceptions were common. In fertile men with low sperm cell counts the motility and morphology of the spermatozoa were good. In general, however, there was a definite correlation between spermatozoan density, motility, and morphology. Gunn and coworkers reported in rams and Holst in boars that testicular degeneration is characterized by a marked decrease in the spermatozoan concentration correlating with the severity of the degeneration. As mentioned previously, spermatozan concentration is usually very low, less than 75,000 per cmm, in testicular hypoplasia of bulls with complete or nearly complete sterility, Lagerlof and Haq. Another characteristic of sperm cell concentration noted by Haq and Rollinson in many infertile or sterile bulls was the rapid decrease in spermatozoan concentration between the first, second, and third successive ejaculates, indicating poor spermatozoan reserves and reduced sperm cell production. Day reported that fertility declined in stallions when there were fewer than 2 billion spermatozoa in the ejaculate. Bielanski reported that the incidence of azoospermia or oligospermia in several thousand stallions he examined was low, 0.04 to 0.14 percent. Fertility usually depends upon the total number of actively motile normal spermatozoa in the ejaculate.

The techniques used for determining concentration of spermatozoa are as follows:

1. The color or macroscopic examination of semen in bulls and rams with concentrated semen is quite satisfactory for an approximation of the density of spermatozoa. (See Table 26) In boars, stallions, and dogs gross examination of semen is not accurate even with the gelatinous portion of the ejaculate of stallions and boars removed. Although as the examiner gains experience this method will give a fair indication of the spermatozoan concentrations in the more concentrated samples in bulls and rams; but in medium to lower ranges the visual estimation of sperm cell concentration is subject to serious errors.

2. The enumeration of spermatozoa may be made with a hemocytometer in a manner similar to that used in making a red blood cell count, Coffin. Salisbury and coworkers' procedure was to fill a red blood-cell pipette to the 0.5 mark with undiluted semen. A 3 per cent chlorazene solution was drawn up to the 1.01-mark in the pipette; this diluted the semen and killed the spermatozoa. This mixture was shaken carefully but vigorously for 2 to 3 minutes. A few drops were released and the shaking was repeated. A few more drops were released and then a drop was placed under the cover slip in a Neubauer blood-cell counting chamber. Sperm cells in 5 large squares were counted in a diagonal direction and the total number of spermatozoa counted were multiplied by 10,000. This procedure rapidly gives an accurate indication of the sperm cell concentration per cmm if the mixing is thorough.

Table 26. Sperm Cell Concentration and Semen Color in Bulls and Rams

Bulls (per cmm)	Rams (per cmm)*	Color of Semen
	2,500,000	Thick, creamy
2,000,000	2,000,000	Creamy
1,000,000	1,000,000	Light creamy
500,000	500,000	Milky
100,000	100,000	Cloudy, watery, translucent
less than 50,000	less than 50,000	Almost clear, transparent, watery

* Gunn and coworkers.

3. The concentration of spermatozoa may be obtained rapidly in a well-equipped laboratory by a photoelectric colorimeter that has previously been properly calibrated by known spermatozoan concentrations, Willett and Buckner. After adding 1 part bovine semen to 40 parts of sodium citrate buffer, the diluted semen is placed in a special tube in the photelometer. By reading the dial on the photelometer and comparing this reading with a chart containing previous readings with known spermatozoan concentrations, the sperm cell concentration of the ejaculate in question can be determined very rapidly. This may be adapted to dogs or other species. In the dog a dilution rate of 1 to 4 to 1 to 16 was recommended by Foote and Boucher. This is used in most bovine artificial breeding laboratories for determining the concentration of spermatozoa. This information is necessary for computing the dilution or extension factor.

4. The comparing chamber described by Blom may be used for a fairly accurate estimation of the concentration

of spermatozoa by comparing the concentration of spermatozoa in a layer of semen 50 microns thick with pictures of known concentrations of 1, 0.5 and 0.2 million spermatozoa per cmm.

5. Other methods not so practical as the above for determining the concentration of spermatozoa include the measuring of packed cell volume, spermatocrit, Foote, and the use of the Coulter electronic counter, Glover and Phipps.

The Motility of spermatozoa at the time of collection is commonly used as a measure of the fertilizing ability of sperm. Care should be taken at the time of collection that the ejaculate is protected from "cold shock" or sudden reduction in temperature that has a marked depressing effect on motility. Excessive heat and chemical or foreign agents also affect sperm cells and reduce motility. The first ejaculate after a long period of sexual inactivity has poor motility and increased numbers of dead spermatozoa. For accurate results this test is best made with an electrically heated microscope stage at body temperature. Motility ratings can be made in the field by gently warming the semen slide by placing it on a flat bottle containing warm water at body temperature. Cooling semen from body temperature down to refrigerator temperature causes a gradual loss of motility of spermatozoa until near-immobility is reached. Therefore, semen should always be examined at body temperature so that accurate and comparative readings can be made. It is desirable to dilute the semen in warm Ringer's saline or 2.9 percent sodium citrate solution to more easily observe the individual spermatozoa so an estimate of the percentage of motile spermatozoa can be made.

Motility is based on the estimated percentage of motile spermatozoa and their degree of motility. Recently Lustig and Lindahl have described a fast, accurate, photographic method of measuring the proportion of moving spermatozoa and their rate of progression. Most investigators, Herman and Swanson, and Haq, described the various degrees of motility of spermatozoa in undiluted semen as follows:

0—spermatozoa are immotile

1—stationary bunting or weak rotary movements are exhibited by spermatozoa

2—oscillatory or rotary movements and fewer than 50 percent of the spermatozoa are in progressive motion, with no waves or eddies

3—progressive rapid movement of spermatozoa, with slowly moving waves and eddies, usually 50 to 80 percent of the spermatozoa must be progressively motile to produce waves and eddies

4—vigorous, progressive movement with rapid and abruptly forming waves and eddies, indicating about 90 percent motile spermatozoa

5—very vigorous forward motion, extremely rapid waves and eddies, indicating about 100 percent actively motile spermatozoa

Blom reported that in the 350 micron thickness of undiluted semen in his comparing chamber at body temperature, 50 to 70 percent living spermatozoa produced rapid whirls and eddies and good to excellent motility; 30 to 50 percent produced sluggish waves and fair motility; and 10 to 30 percent motile spermatozoa produced single propulsions with no waves or whirls and with poor motility. Blom indicated that in normal bovine semen initial motility of 40 to 45 percent or more was essential since lower rates of motility were associated with infertility. Most fertile bulls have 50 to 80 percent of their spermatozoa exhibiting active progressive motility.

Swanson and Herman reported that good initial motility alone is not an accurate indication of fertility in the bull. They cited examples of infertile bull semen with excellent initial spermatozoan motility that rapidly lost its motility when stored or highly motile spermatozoa that were infertile. They reported no difference in conception rates of semen with 50 percent actively motile spermatozoa and higher percentages of motile sperm cells. Motility below 50 percent was often associated with low conception rates or poor fertility.

According to Haq the motility of bovine spermatozoa in testicular hypoplasia was much poorer than in testicular degeneration. Only 10 percent of the bulls with testicular degeneration showed motility above 70 percent and a rate or degree of motility of 3 or higher, which is the average requirement. The number of motile spermatozoa was less than 70 percent in 90 percent of the bulls with testicular degeneration but the degree of motility was below 3 in only 42 percent. Blom reported that 92 percent of 100 normal fertile bulls had satisfactory motility whereas only 32 percent of the "problem" bulls had satisfactory motility. Haq and Rollinson reported that congenitally sterile bulls with a very high percentage of abnormal sperm cells, especially those with defects of the midpiece and tail, had the lowest motility. It is generally assumed that the duration of motility of abnormal spermatozoa is reduced.

MacLeod reported that normal stallion spermatozoa had a degree of motility of 3 to 4, and that 48 to 75 per cent of the spermatozoa in the semen were actively motile about 20 minutes after ejaculation; after the unextended semen had stood 8 hours at room temperature he seldom found any reasonable degree of activity. Bielanski reported the precentage of motile spermatozoa in 54 fertile stallions ranged from 55 to 60 percent. In several thousand stallions examined low motility or asthenospermia occurred in 0.8 to 3.4 percent and necrospermia occurred in 0.09 to 0.3 percent. MacLeod emphasized that even with the minimum of handling, the motility of equine spermatozoa decreased rapidly **in vitro.** This is a possible reflection of the inability of equine spermatozoa to survive in equine seminal plasma that has very low levels of reducible sugar for energy purposes in contrast to the relatively long viability of spermatozoa in seminal plasma of other animals. The addition of isotonic, 5 percent, glucose to horse semen with poor motility of the spermatozoa, may result in marked improvement of the motility, Rajamannan. This is interesting in connection with the work of Day, in which he reported that in the genital tract of the mare equine spermatozoa survived 72 hours or more. In horses it is possible that seminal plasma may have an adverse effect on spermatozoa while the environment of the mare's genital tract is highly favorable for sperm cell survival. Thus some stallions with poor motility in freshly ejaculated sperm may be quite fertile.

Gunn and coworkers in rams, and Holst in boars reported, as did Lagerlof in bulls, a decreased motility of spermatozoa in experimentally-produced testicular degeneration. Fertile boars have semen that usually contain 80 to 95 percent actively motile spermatozoa, while rams have about 60 to 70 percent motile cells. MacLeod and Gold reported that in man 50 to 60 percent active spermatozoan motility was average and 75 percent was good, but that in semen with less than 40 percent actively motile spermatozoa the incidence of sterility rose sharply. MacLeod reported that motility was usually good in fertile men even when the sperm cell count was low.

Sperm cell defects involving the midpiece and tail are often characterized by poor motility. There is an intimate relationship between the epididymis and its secretions on sperm cell motility and tail defects as described under diseases of the epididymis.

Blom and Bentinck-Smith reported that pus and drops of vaseline in the semen reduced spermatozoan motility. Care should be used in lubricating an artificial vagina not to apply an excess of lubricant that might melt and run into the semen-collecting tube or vial.

The importance of the number of actively motile sperm cells in the ejaculate on the fertility of the male has been stressed in different species by many workers. This fact is well-illustrated by a valuable Guernsey bull used in a arge artificial insemination stud that developed senile sticular degeneration associated with a progressive adual decline in motile spermatozoa in the ejaculate om 50 to 10 percent along with a gradual increase from 30 to 60 percent in the number of abnormal spermatozoa. Extending his semen on the basis of the numbers of actively motile spermatozoa present in each ejaculate resulted in satisfactory conception rates even though the extension rates were as low as 1 to 10 in order to provide 6 to 10 million actively motile spermatozoa per ml for each insemination.

Longevity, Viability, or Liveability of Spermatozoa in semen or extended semen at refrigerator, room or incubator temperatures is another measure that can be used for testing or estimating the fertility of semen. A number of studies from 1940 to 1955 were summarized in the first edition of this text and by Maule of work performed on this test for assessing semen quality and fertility. Since that time relatively few experimental studies on these tests have been conducted because they are difficult to run as they extend over a period of hours or days, and thus are not adaptable to semen collected for artificial insemination purposes. MacLeod and McGee indicated that good equine semen maintained reasonably good motility for up to 8 hours after collection at room temperature. Results and correlations with fertility of the male do not provide any greater predictive value than the current simpler tests of semen quality including concentration, motility, including live/dead sperm cell numbers, and morphology.

Differential staining to determine live/dead spermatozoa in an ejaculate was described by Blom, and Swanson and Bearden using a vital stain such as eosin-nigrosin stain. To make the staining solution, weigh out 3 gms of sodium citrate dihydrate and add to 100 ml of sterile double distilled water. To this add 1 gm eosin B and 5 gm nigrosin and mix into solution. The eosin will stain the dead spermatozoa a pink or red color, live spermatozoa remain colorless, and nigrosin provides a blue-black background stain, Blom. This stain will remain stable for one year or more without refrigeration. Place a small drop of stain on a clean warm slide and add a small drop of semen to the stain and mix gently with a round glass rod or a platinum loop. After a few seconds to a minute or more smear out with the glass rod or another glass slide and dry rapidly near a flame. At least 100 to 200 cells, or preferably 500, should be counted by scanning the entire length of the semen smear. Morphologically abnormal cells may be counted at the same time. According to Maule in his review on the assessment of semen quality, most workers found an average of about 20 percent dead cells in most normal bovine semen samples and there was relatively little correlation with fertility. After a prolonged period of sexual rest the percentage of dead spermatozoa may be increased. The live/dead sperm cell count should be evaluated criticially. Poor stain or staining technique may greatly affect the findings. A high-incidence of necrospermia is usually associated with poor motility and low fertility. However, poor motility may be associated with normal levels of live spermatozoa, which depending on the cause of the poor motility, may be characterized by either normal or low fertility

Examination of stained spermatozoa for morphology is of definite value in studying the severity of testicular degeneration or testicular hypoplasia and the congenital or hereditary defects of spermatozoa.

Techniques for preparing and staining sperm cells for morphology examination—Rao and Hart stressed the importance of making smears, and fixing them by air-drying before the semen is cooled to prevent the development of secondary spermatozoan abnormalities. Storing semen a reasonable time had no effect on the primary spermatozoan abnormalities. Extended semen is not satisfactory for morphological examination because of the egg yolk or milk that is present. Blom recommended that semen samples be diluted with a physiological saline solution to a concentration of about 200,000 per cmm before a slide is prepared, so that the stained spermatozoa will not be too concentrated to permit observation of individual cells. All glass slides used in making semen smears should be thoroughly cleaned, soaked in alcohol, and dried. The plasma and gel fraction of horse and boar semen may interfere or make difficult the staining of equine or porcine spermatozoa. Rajamannan recommended the addition of one-half to one part of five percent or isotonic glucose solution to one part of horse semen. This mixture was centifuged at 1500 rpm in a clinical centrifuge for 5 minutes. After pouring off the plasma the sperm cells in the glucose solution are stained in the usual manner.

India ink preparations, described by Blom, are probably the simplest and easiest for the veterinary practitioner to prepare. Five parts or drops of a high-grade India ink, such as Pelican Yellow Label, are gently mixed with 1 part or drop of semen. One should be careful not to contaminate the bottle of India ink with sperm cells or bacteria. A drop of this mixture is placed on the slide and spread by one of the following methods: blowing gently; drawing, not pushing, it out with a spreader as with a blood smear; or gently smearing it out with a 1/8 inch glass rod. The smear is then air-dried or dried slowly over the warm air of a flame. The dried slide is examined under oil immersion or the high dry magnification. All abnormalities of the spermatozoa and semen may be noted. Large round cells, if present, should be recognized as leukocytes or primordial germinal cells.

Eosin-nigrosin stain, as reported by Blom, and Swanson and Bearden is a widely-used simple and effective vital stain. The technique for its use was described previously. It may be used for counting the numbers of live/dead cells as well as the morphologically normal and abnormal cells.

Wright's stain, commonly used for staining blood smears, may also be used for semen examinations. This stain is not as satisfactory as Casarett's stain because it tends to precipitate on the slide, producing artifacts, and it does not stain the spermatozoa as effectively. The semen should be spread gently over a clean slide and fixed by air-drying. The slide should then be immersed in 0.5 or 1 percent chloramine T solution to remove the excess mucus, even though this procedure may cause some breakage of spermatozoa. After being immersed in this chlorine solution for 5 to 7 minutes, the film of semen on the slide is washed gently first with distilled water and then with 95 percent alcohol, and then dried. The semen film on the slide is covered with Wright's stain for 60 seconds. Distilled water is then added until a metallic luster is produced. The stain is left on the slide for 2 to 5 minutes before being rinsed off with distilled water. After the stained slide is air-dried it can be examined under the oil immersion or the high dry power of the microscope. Hematoxylin and eosin and Giemsa's stains are also satisfactory for the examination of semen smears for the presence of cells other than spermatozoa.

Casarett's stain is preferred by McEntee and Bentinck-Smith. Thin films of fresh semen are fixed on glass slides by immersing them for 3 minutes in a mixture of equal parts of ethyl alcohol and ether; the slides are then air-dried. They are stained by immersion for 5 to 7 minutes in a dye solution heated to 40 to 60° C. The dye solution consists of 30 ml, or 2 volumes, of 5 percent watery eosin B. solution and 15 ml, or 1 volume, of 1 percent watery phenol solution. The stained smears are washed with distilled water, air-dried, and mounted in balsam. The spermatozoan structures are very clearly outlined, Casarett. Other good staining techniques include carbolfuchsin and eosin stain and those cited by Shaffer and Almquist, Blom, and Frank.

For long term preservation of spermatozoa Hancock and Gledhill recommended adding a few drops of semen to a small amount of buffered formo-saline made up and used as follows:

Stock buffer soln*	100 ml
Stock NaCl soln.**	150 ml
Commerical formalin (37–40% formaldehyde)	62 5 ml
Aq. dist. ad.	500 ml

***Stock buffer soln.**

soln. A) $Na_2HPO_4.2H_2O$	21.682 gm

	Aq. dist. ad.	500 ml
soln. B)	$K H_2 PO_4$	22.254 gm
	Aq. dist. ad.	500 ml

Take 200 ml of soln. A and mix with 80 ml of soln B Then from the resultant 280 ml, take 100 ml as stock buffer soln.

****Stock NaCl soln.**

NaCl	9.01 gm
Aq. dist. ad.	500 ml

Directions for use:

Add 1 to 2 drops semen to about 5 to 10 ml of buffered formo-saline, gently shake; add 1 to 2 drops of dihydrostreptomycin, incubate for 20 to 30 min. at 37° C. and then refrigerate (about +4° C.); this will preserve sperm cells for up to 18 months.

Wet mounts for phase contrast microscopy are made in a suitable equipped laboratory from preserved samples sent in and are far superior to smeared and stained preparations for estimating the percentage of spermatozoa with proximal protoplasmic droplets and acrosome abnormalities. A phase contrast effect can be partially achieved in a regular light microscope by reducing the amount of light permitted to come through the substage condenser. Following one or more of the several staining procedures 100 to 200 or more up to 500 to 1000 spermatozoa should be examined under oil immersion at 1,200 magnification and classified.

Salisbury and Mercier indicated that an experienced technician could achieve as reliable results counting 100 cells as by counting 500 sperm cells. Spermatozoan abnormalities may be classified as **head, body,** and **tail** defects. Lagerlof and Blom (1950) have classified these three anatomical groups of sperm cell abnormalities in two further groups as **primary** forms that occur due to disorders the seminiferous or germinal epithelium, and as **secondary** forms that occur after they have left the germinal epithelium, during their passage through the mesonephric ducts, during ejaculation, or in manipulations of the ejaculate including excessive agitation, over-heating, too rapid cooling, due to the presence of water, urine or antiseptics in the semen and etc.

Gledhill and the author have serious reservations over using these latter two classifications of spermatozoan abnormalities. If a sperm cell is defective and for that reason can't fertilize an ovum it doesn't matter whether it becomes defective in the seminiferous tubules or mesonephric duct or at ejaculation. If sperm cell artifacts are due to accidents from improper handling of the ejaculate or smearing or staining, a subsequent ejaculate, if handled properly, will usually lack such damaged cells. Furthermore defects occurring in the germinal epithelium may not manifest

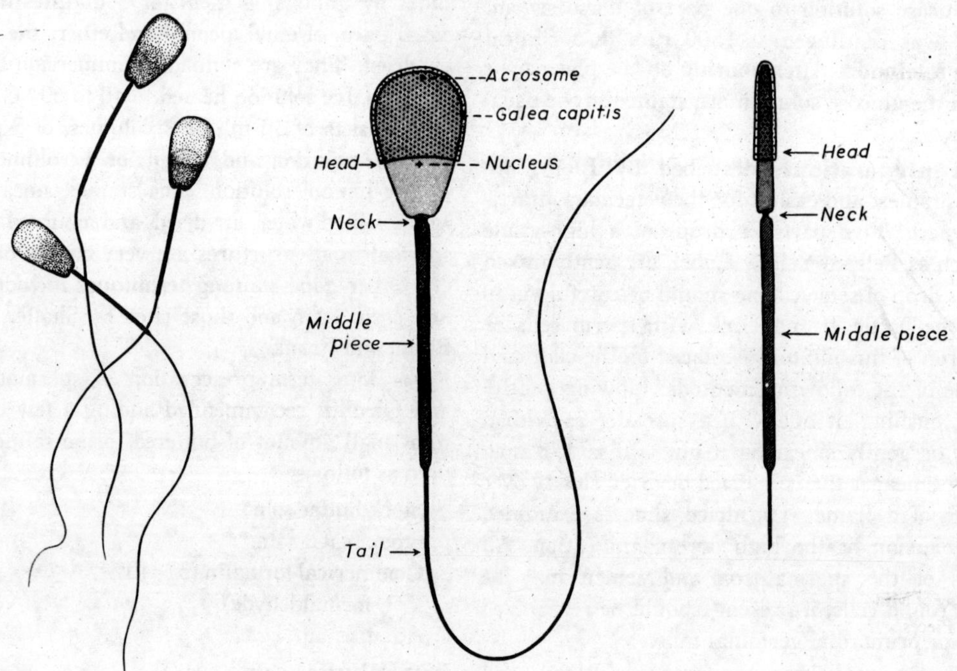

Figure 198. Normal Bovine Spermatozoa (Left) Normal Spermatozoa, (Center) Diagram of Dorsoventral Aspect, (Right) Diagram of Lateral Aspect.

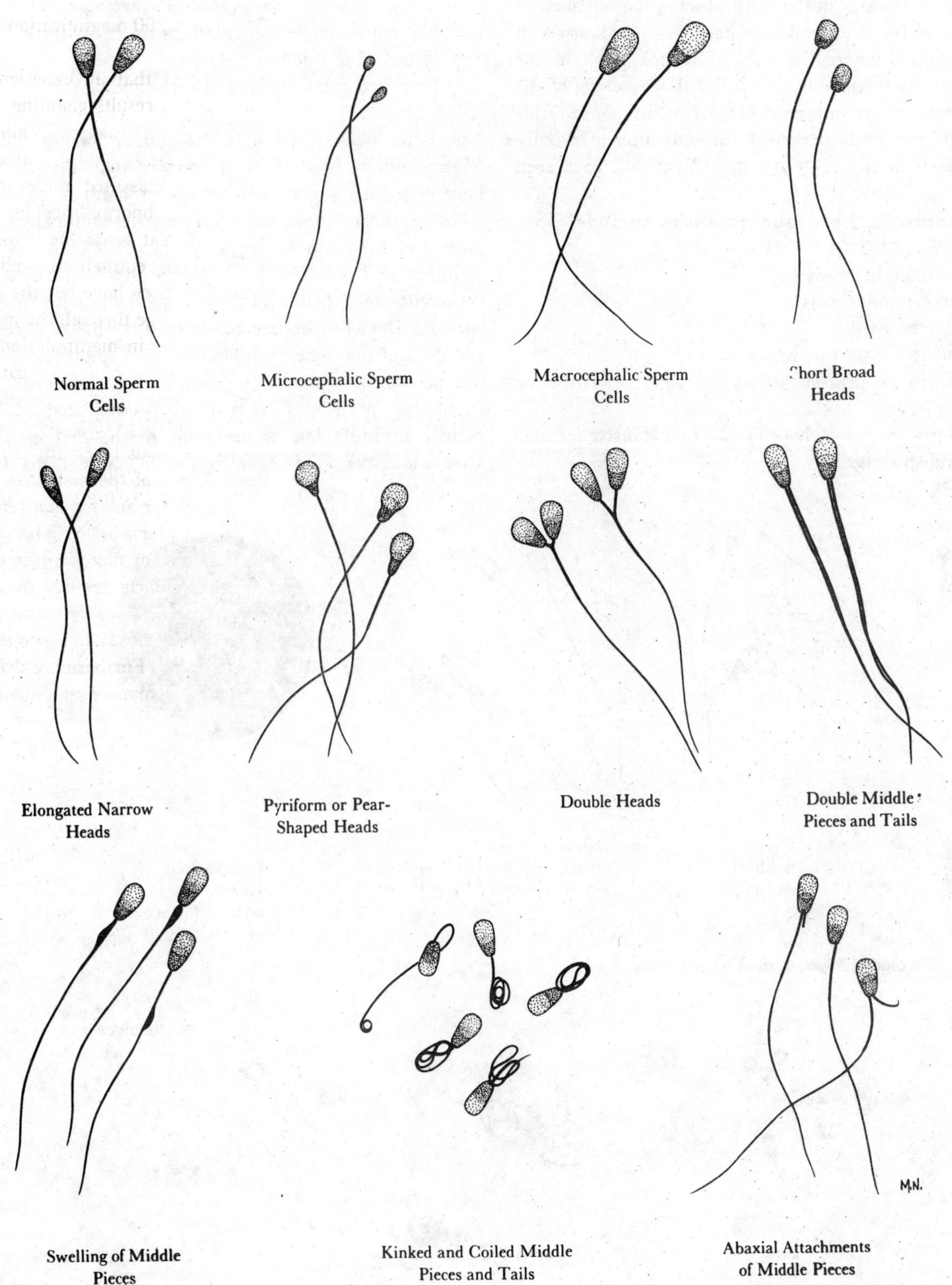

Figure 199. "Primary" Spermatozoan Abnormalities.

themselves until later in the maturation of the cell such as separation of the head and neck described by Hancock in Guernsey bulls where the separation took place in the head of the epididymis at the time of the loosening of the cytoplasmic or protoplasmic droplet which up to this point had apparently prevented the separation. Chromosomal defects in apparently normal sperm cells have been discussed previously.

Spermatozoan head abnormalities include: (See Figures 198, 199, 200)

- Microcephalic heads
- Macrocephalic heads
- Double heads
- Elongated or narrow heads
- Pyriform or pear-shaped heads with a narrow or tapering base
- Twisted, irregular-shaped heads and abortive forms
- Round short heads
- Abnormal acrosomes (knobbed spermatozoa)
- Nuclear envelope invaginations (near equator)
- Detached or free heads (Guernseys)
- Detached galea capitis and acrosome

The latter two are possible "secondary" abnormalities. Macrocephalic heads with a broader than normal base have been shown by various tests to probably be cells with a diploid chromosome content. These were found by Salisbury and Baker in an incidence of 0.104% in a group of inbred or closely line-bred Hereford bulls and as a rare occurrence by Gledhill (1965) in six bulls with lowered fertility. Detached or free heads may be due to excessive agitation of the semen sample or due to improper smearing of the spermatozoa on slides. The detached galea capitis or head cap from dead spermatozoa is seen mainly in India ink preparations in the first ejaculate after a long period of sexual rest or in spermatozoa dying

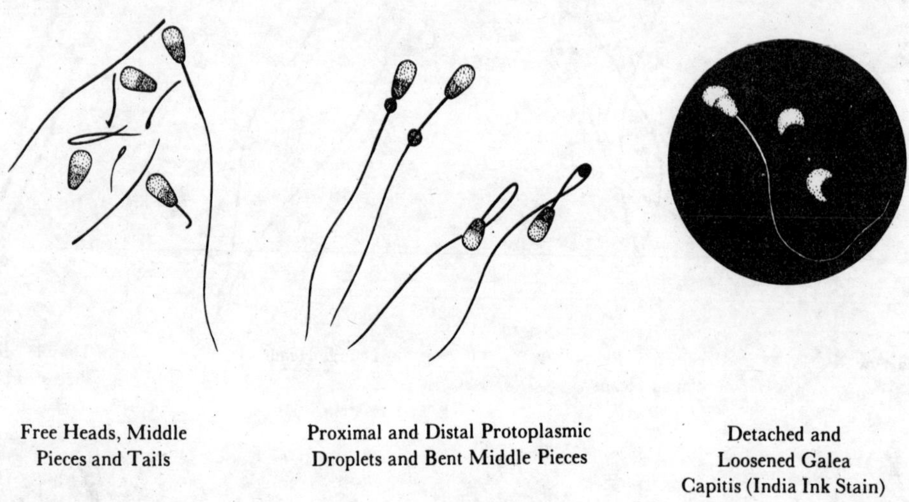

Figure 200. "Secondary" Spermatozoan Abnormalities

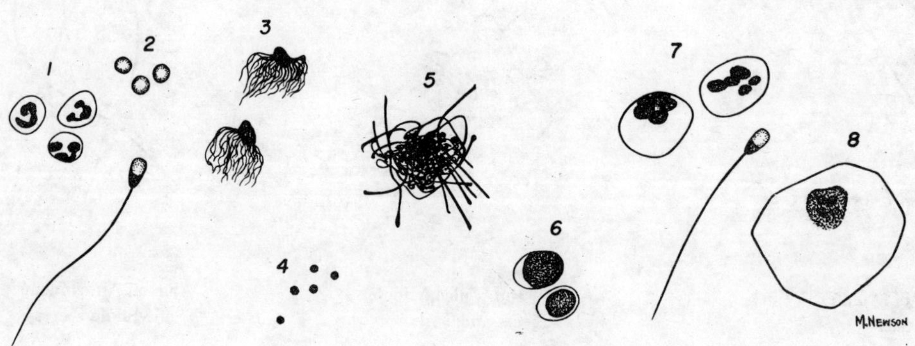

Figure 201. Miscellaneous Cells Found in Semen 1. Leukocytes 2. Erythrocytes 3. Medusa Formations 4. Protoplasmic Droplets 5. Degenerating Sperm Cell Cluster 6. Primordial Spermiogenic Cells 7. Giant or Multinucleated Cells 8. Squamous Epithelial Cells.

after a prolonged storage. They resemble a bathing cap in shape. Using a special stain, Wells et al. found less than 5 percent of acrosomal abnormalities in sperm cells from bulls being collected regularly but an average of 21 percent abnormalities of the acrosome in the first ejaculates of 22 sexually-rested bulls.

Rollinson, Haq, Blom, and others reported that a small proportion of tailless heads was frequently observed but that an increase of tailless heads occurred in the early stages of degeneration in fertile bulls. These authors reported that normal fertile bovine semen contained only 0.5 to 8.6 percent loose heads.

Spermatozoan body or middle piece abnormalities include: (See Figures 199 and 200)

Swollen neck

Kinked neck with coiling of the middle piece and tail about the head

Naked or filiform neck

Abaxial attachment of the neck and middle piece to the head, often with a short vestige of a second body

Swelling of the middle piece, either diffuse, localized, cranial or caudal

Double middle piece

Coiled middle piece

Kinked middle piece with a tightly coiled tail

"Corkscrew" middle piece

Loose or free middle-pieces and tails; these may be weakly motile

Kinked necks

Middle pieces with proximal or distal protoplasmic or cytoplasmic droplets

Bent middle pieces, with or without a protoplasmic drop at the point of the greatest bending.

In counting abnormal sperm cells, loose or free middle pieces and tails should not be recorded if free heads are counted. The presence of a protoplasmic or cytoplasmic droplet on the middle piece has been described by Lagerlof, Blom, Rao and Hart and others and is considered to be normally present on the spermatozoa from the head of the epididymis. As the spermatozoa mature in their passage through the epididymis this protoplasmic drop recedes from the neck down the middle piece and is usually lost before the spermatozoa are ejaculated. Hancock reported that the migration of the protoplasmic droplet from the proximal to the distal portion of the middle piece occurred in the head of the epidiymis. Lagerlof considered these to be immature sperm cells when seen in ejaculated semen. He and Blom stated that no more than 2 to 3 percent of normal spermatozoa should have this protoplasmic drop on the proximal part of the middle piece. Other authors indicated that the presence of a high percentage of middle pieces with protoplasmic droplets may possibly be due to overuse of the male and to too rapid passage of spermatozoa through the epididymis. Holst stated that in boars this condition was associated with testicular degeneration and hypoplasia. A localized swelling of the middle piece should be differentiated from an attached protoplasmic or cytoplasmic droplet. The true developmental abnormality of a swelling of the middle piece is an irregular swelling which stains darkly, in which no differentiation can be seen between the swelling and the central fibril; and the ends of the swelling are tapered, Rollinson. Whereas the protoplasmic droplet stains less intensely and is quite spherical. The corkscrew middle piece is an unusual abnormality described by Blom (1959). Abnormalities of the middle piece and tail interfere with fertility by reducing motility; the swollen and thickened types of mid-piece abnormalities were most serious, Rollinson and Haq. A constant content of 30 to 50 percent of bent middle pieces was usually associated with impaired fertility, Frank. An abnormal environment in the epididymis may result in mid-piece or tail defects An abaxial location of the tail on the head of the spermatozoa is not uncommon in stallions and boars and is less indicative of infertility in those species than in the other domestic animals.

Spermatozoan tail abnormalities include: (See Figures 199 and 200)

Tightly coiled tails

Double tails

Absent or shortened tails, seen most often in stallions

Coiled tails

Bent tails, with or without a protoplasmic drop at the bend

Broken tails

The latter two conditions are possible "secondary" abnormalities. In general abnormalities of the tail are infrequent and of little importance. Tails bent at the junction of the tail and middlepiece; either with or without a protoplasmic droplet, are fairly common. They are usually caused by cold shock or osmotic shock due to the presence of water or urine in the ejaculate.

The presence of 10 percent or more of any single type of the above head; body or tail abnormalities, normally absent from semen of males, is often associated with reduced fertility, Hancock (1959).

Cells other than spermatozoa in semen smears include: (See Figure 201)

Leucocytes are found in cases of inflammation or infection of the reproductive tract; there are very few in normal semen.

Erythrocytes

Squamous epithelial cells—both nucleated and non-

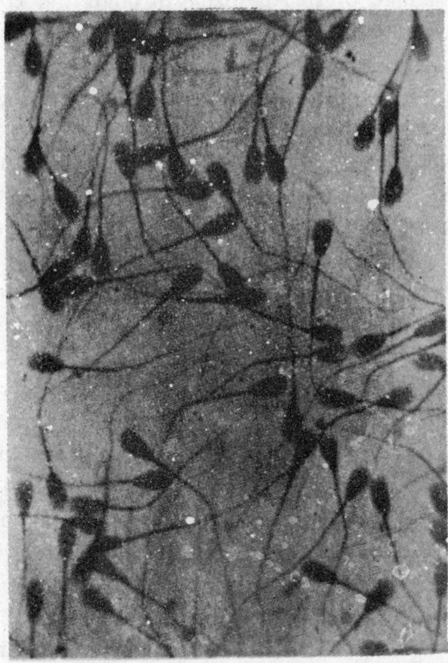

Figure 202. Normal Bovine Spermatozoa

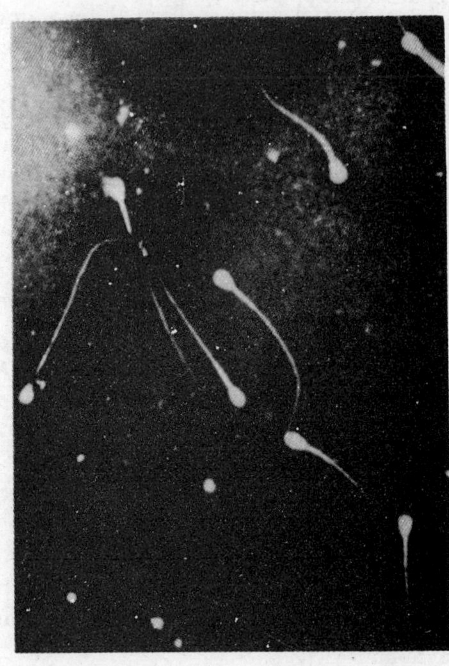

Figure 203. Normal Canine Spermatozoa (India Ink Stain) (Courtesy K. McEntee)

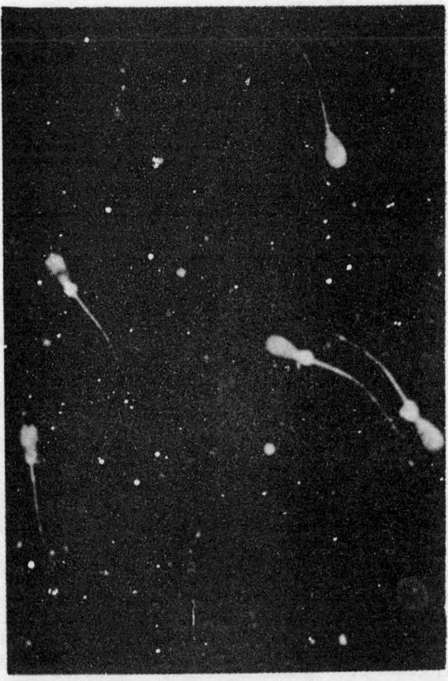

Figure 204. Proximal Protoplasmic Droplets on Bull Spermatozoa (India Ink Stain) (Courtesy K. McEntee)

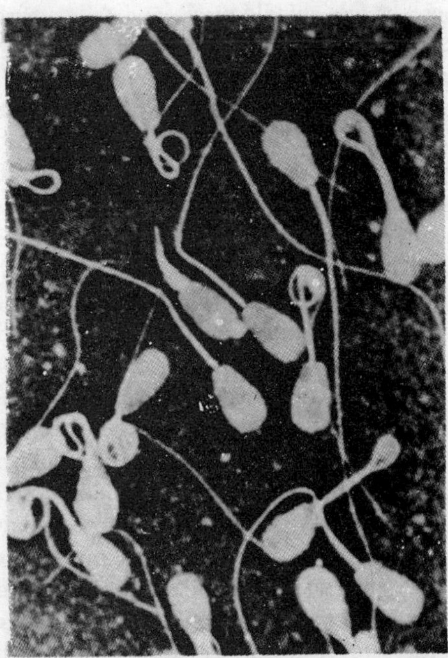

Figure 205. Coiled Tails and Middle Pieces in an Infertile 11-year-old Bull. (The motility rate was between 5 and 10 percent, yet the conception rate was 50 percent with liquid semen extended 1:10 to 20.)

nucleated. These usually come from the epithelium of the prepuce or the urogenital canal.

Boat-shaped spermatogenic cells—These are more common in abnormal than in normal semen and are more likely to be associated with deformed heads than with deformed middle pieces, Haq and Rollinson.

Spermatids—nucleated, non-nucleated, and multinucleated.

Spermatocytes—primary and secondary, often called "spheroids" or primordial spermatogenic cells

Medusa cells or bodies—Blom has described medusa formations, which are portions of ciliated epithelial cells from the efferent ducts of the testis. They are deeply-staining cells about the size of the head of the spermatozoa, with 10 to 30 filiform, or long brush-like, projections or cilia. These cells are seen only in rare instances in the usual sperm cell preparations but may be seen in much greater number in semen preparations from males with severe testicular hypoplasia when the semen is centrifuged and the sediment is placed on a slide and stained. This finding may aid in differentiating between an incomplete ejaculation of a normal bull and a complete ejaculation of a bull with nearly completely suppressed spermatogenesis. These medusa formations are seen at a rate of about 1 to 10,000 spermatozoa in normal bulls. In stallions the incidence is higher.

Protoplasmic or cytoplasmic droplets; floating free in semen, are often observed in fertile semen and are of no significance.

Bacteria, molds, and protozoa are usually contaminants from the prepuce.

Degenerating spermatozoan clusters—were observed by Haq in 19 percent of fertile bulls and 79 percent of bulls with testicular degeneration. Occasionally they were seen in bulls with testicular hypoplasia. These clusters of spermatozoa are apparently produced by a disturbance in spermatogenesis.

Multinucleated giant cells with 6 to 8 nuclei are seen occasionally in males with testicular hypoplasia or degeneration and are due to abnormalities in the divisional mechanism of the primary spermatocytes, Cupps and Laben. The cause of these latter two conditions might be similar.

The determining of the number and type of abnormal sperm cells in an ejaculate should be used along with other examinations conducted immediately after collection such as those for motility, concentration, and live/dead sperm cell numbers. There is a divergence in opinion as to the importance of the presence of varying numbers of abnormal spermatozoa seen on stained semen preparations. Foote and Bratton, Swanson and Herman, and Laing have reported that if the percentage of abnormal spermatozoa is not above 30 to 35 percent it is not correlated with fertility in the relatively fertile **bulls** they studied. Haq reported an average of 31.4 percent abnormal spermatozoa with a range of 15 to 48 percent in 19 bulls with testicular degeneration. He reported an average of 39.1 percent abnormal spermatozoa with a range of 22 to 58 percent in 4 bulls with testicular hypoplasia; whereas normal fertile bulls had an average of 15.1 percent abnormal spermatozoa with a range of 6 to 26 percent. Haq and Rollinson were in near agreement that the semen of normal fertile bulls should not have more than 3 to 4 percent abnormal heads, 4 to 10 percent abnormal middle pieces, 0.5 to 2 percent abnormal tails, and 0.5 to 6 percent, tailless heads. Blom reported similar values in normal fertile bulls of 1.2 to 10.4 percent, with an average of 4.6 percent, primary spermatozoan abnormalities and an average of 2.1 percent, with a maximum of 8.6 percent, loose heads and other secondary abnormalities.

McKenzie and Phillips reported that **rams** having more than 14 percent abnormal spermatozoa in their semen are probably of reduced fertility providing the ejaculate was not taken after a long period of sexual rest. Terrill reported that normal fertile ram semen should not contain more than 5 to 15 percent abnormal spermatozoa. Gunn and coworkers reported that rams having 0.1 percent abnormal spermatozoa in their semen had an approximate fertility of 80 to 100 percent; those with 1 percent abnormal spermatozoa had fertility rates of 60 percent; rams with 10 percent abnormal spermatozoa had fertility rates of 45 percent; those with 30 percent abnormal spermatozoa had a fertility rate of 20 percent; and rams with more than 50 percent abnormal spermatozoa were sterile.

Phillips found no more than 17 percent, with an average range of 6 to 10 percent, abnormal spermatozoa in semen of fertile **boars.** Holst reported no more than 14 percent abnormal spermatozoa in fertile boar semen. In 13 boars with testicular degeneration the abnormal spermatozoa varied from 3 to 36 percent and immature spermatozoa with proximal protoplasmic droplets from 1 to 95 percent. The number of abnormal sperm cell heads was over 20 percent in 5 of the 13 boars and in 5 others the percentage varied from 3 to 8. But the numbers of immature spermatozoa with proximal droplets were high in most cases of porcine testicular degeneration, Holst. Bierschwal and Hendrikse reported that conception rates were 67.7 percent, 57.3 percent and 45.5 percent with boars with 80 to 100 percent, 60 to 79 percent and 40 to 59 percent normal spermatozoa, respectively, including sperm cells with distal protoplasmic droplets. The number of cells with distal and even proximal protoplasmic droplets were extremely variable between boars and between ejaculates. Tightly coiled tails appeared to be a defect in spermatogenesis and doubling of a portion of the cells occurred at a level of 0.3 percent. They stated that a majority of midpiece attachments were slightly abaxial in the boar and that this defect should not be considered as a primary sperm cell defect in the boar as it is in the bull.

Lagerlof and others have reported that it was more difficult to evaluate the spermatozoa of **stallions** than of bulls, rams, boars, and dogs. MacLeod and McGee reported on a sterile stallion with no motile spermatozoa because of a failure of the tails to develop in over half of the spermatozoa, and the remainder of the spermatozoa had only short, stubby tails. They reported on another stallion with semen having excellent motility, concentration and morphology of spermatozoa, but which was practically sterile. Three other nearly-sterile stallions had spermatozoa of normal appearance, but the motility was reduced. They concluded that in the Thoroughbred stallion infertility can exist in the presence of apparently normal semen quality and that the actual fertility of a stallion cannot always be predicted on the basis of a semen examination. Day and Bielanski reported on sterile stallions with semen containing only dead spermatozoa or necrospermia at the time of ejaculation. In other horses of low fertility they found that the concentrations of spermatozoa and the volume of semen were low, 10,000 to 15,000 per cmm and about 10 to 25 ml, respectively. Day described a fertile stallion with 35 to 45 percent of the spermatozoa having a proximal protoplasmic droplet and 4 to 6 percent having double heads; the motility was good. Bielanski reported on 54 stallions with conception rates from less than 25 percent to nearly 100 percent and the primary spermatozoan abnormalities varied from 2.5 to 10 percent and the secondary abnormalities from 22 to 39 percent. The most fertile stallions had less than 3 percent primary abnormalities. The author studied a young Standardbred stallion with 60 to 70 percent grossly abnormal middle pieces and associated poor motility. Under regular handling infertility was evident but by good management, controlled breeding and breeding at the proper time of estrum he achieved a 70 percent conception rate the next four years. Dimock reported that in general the presence of more than 20 percent abnormal spermatozoa in equine semen may be interpreted as indicating low fertility but that there were many exceptions. Some stallions may have apparently normal spermatozoa and low fertility; others are highly fertile even though a rather high percentage of spermatozoa are abnormal. McKenzie reported 5 to 13 percent abnormal spermatozoa in semen of fertile stallions. Berliner reported up to 30 percent abnormal spermatozoa in fertile equine semen. It is obvious that more work must be done on semen examinations of stallions with sterility or low fertility.

Nooder and Harrop reported that not more than 20 percent abnormal spermatozoa were present in **dogs** producing good quality, fertile sperm. Hancock and Rowlands reported only 0 to 10 percent abnormal spermatozoa with an average of 4.8 percent in fertile canine semen. Boucher and coworkers and Bartlett reported 10 to 15 percent abnormal sperm cells in 11 normal dogs they examined. Sojka et al. reported 4 to 10 percent abnormal spermatozoa in ejaculates of 6 fertile male cats. The most common abnormalities were cytoplasmic droplets, double, bent or dubbed tails and enlarged middle pieces.

It is obvious from the above discussion that great care must be used in the interpretation of the morphology of spermatozoa in semen samples. Technicians differ in their classification of sperm cells, some classifying certain cells as abnormal that others would classify as normal. Differences arise due to variations in the technic of handling and preparing slides. There is probably no distinct line of demarcation between animals of good and poor fertility. The morphological examination of semen as an aid in evaluating fertility is apparently of greatest value in the detection of males whose fertility is unsatisfactory in natural matings. It is of limited or questionable value in determining fertility in individual ejaculates from males of fair to good fertility used in artificial insemination.

Bacteriological or virological examination of semen may be indicated under certain circumstances, especially when evidence of genital inflammation or infection is present in females following breeding to a male, a rapid decline in motility of the spermatozoa occurs on storage, or an increase in pH or the presence of leukocytes or frank pus are present in the ejaculate or in the semen smear. Organisms or viral agents in the semen may come from the testes or epididymides, the accessory glands, the vas deferens, the urethra, or the prepuce or penis. Semen examination of bulls by cultural methods or by the injection of semen into test animals may reveal infection with brucellosis, trichomoniasis, and vibriosis. In cattle the fluorescent antibody test has proven useful in the examination of preputial smegma samples for vibriosis. In brucellosis, semen plasma agglutination tests may be indicated if the blood test reveals a positive or suspicious titer. Besides the possible danger to the female by introducing infection at the time of coitus, bacteria and their products may injure the spermatozoa and result in a rapid decline in the motility of stored sperm cells, especially in liquid extended semen. In bulls the organisms that may be found in semen include: diptheroids, **C. renale,** streptococci, **B. pyocyaneus,** Leptospira spp., staphylococci, **E. coli, C.**

pyogenes, Br. abortus, Mycobacterium tuberculosis (bovine and avian types), **Mycobacterium paratuberculosis,** Larsen and Kopecky, **Ps. aeruginosa,** actinomycetes, **Proteus,** micrococci, yeasts, bacilli and molds. Albertsen found mycoplasma in 94 percent of the semen samples from bulls. He stated that this organism was a saprophyte in the prepuce of nearly all bulls. Al-Aubaidi and Fabricant, O'Berry and Jasper readily recovered mycoplasma from the sheaths of 80 percent of 160 bulls, and less commonly from the semen. Whether these mycoplasma are pathogenic remains to be determined. The pathogenic **Mycoplasma bovigenitalium** has been reported from semen from bulls with seminovesiculitis, al-Aubaidi, Blom and Erno, Hirt et al.. Viruses including enteroviruses, genital fibropapilloma virus, foot and mouth disease virus, Gierloff and Jakobsen, and Cottral et al., Chlamydia, epivag, parainfluenza III virus, and IBR-IPV virus have been recovered from the semen or testes of bulls. Freezing semen for the preservation of sperm cells will also preserve most infectious agents including viruses, MacPherson and Fish, Gledhill, Spradbrow, Bartlett. Liquid nitrogen used for the storage of frozen semen may also become contaminated with a variety of organisms and viruses and thus be a source of infection for the cow. Bulls clinically infected with Johnes' disease usually have the organism in the semen, Larsen and Kopecky. Similar types of organisms as well as those responsible for venereal diseases in each species may also be found in other male animals, for example **Br. suis** in swine, **Br. canis** in dogs, **Br. ovis** in sheep, **Trypanosoma equiperdum** (dourine) and possibly influenza and infectious equine anemia viruses and the Herpes virus of coital exanthema in horses. A vaginitis and vulvitis are commonly observed in heifers or cows after natural service, especially to older bulls. Mares may become infected with streptococci by being bred to stallions that have large numbers of these organisms in the sheath or semen. Except for vibriosis, brucellosis, IBR-IPV and trichomoniasis, infections in most cows transmitted to them by natural breeding are not serious and seldom prevent conception or cause subsequent abortion. Many bulls with a seminovesiculitis may have nearly normal conception rates. However; in artificial insemination the author has observed several bulls with **Ps. aeruginosa** or **C. pyogenes** infection of the seminal vesicles that caused a rapid loss of motility of the spermatozoa probably due to the inflammatory products in the ejaculate. Dimock reported that the presence of pus in stallion semen caused a much more rapid decline in motility of the spermatozoa than occurred in normal semen. Hughes and coworkers recovered **Pseudomonas** from semen of 25 of 70 stallions. No lesions were observed in the stallions, no leucocytes were present in the semen and conception rates were comparable to stallions not harboring the organism. However infected stallions could infect mares having a lowered resistance to infection.

In the collection of semen samples for bacteriological or viral studies it is essential that strict sanitary and hygienic practices be observed. Even if the semen is collected in a sterile vagina, some contamination usually occurs. Taking a bacteriologically sterile semen sample in the artificial vagina or by electroejaculation is impossible because of contamination from the urethra, prepuce, penis and air. The method of taking a sample of secretion from the accessory glands for culture as described by Galloway, and Parsonson et al. in the discussion on seminal vesiculitis is most satisfactory. Briefly this consists of exteriorizing the penis and after careful washing and disinfection of the exposed penis, sheath and lower portion of the urethra, a sterile cannula is passed up the urethra and a sample is collected in a sterile vial by massage of the accessory glands. At present this test is seldom used except to determine the causative agent of inflammatory processes of the reproductive tract or accessory glands.

Total solids in the bull semen may be rapidly determined and those samples with less than 4 to 5 percent solids, often indicative of incomplete ejaculation or seminal vesiculitis, should be closely examined, Blom. Foote reported that normal ejaculates from fertile dairy bulls averaged 8.8 to 10.0 g of solids per 100 g of plasma. Semen obtained by electroejaculation averaged 2.0 to 6.7 percent solids and semen in older bulls averaged 8.9 percent solids compared to 10.2 percent solids in young bulls.

Enzyme determinations of semen plasma may prove of value in measuring degrees of damage to sperm cells before ejaculation and during the freezing process. Enzymes such as GOT, LDH, chlolinesterase and alkaline or acid phosphatase and others are intimately related to the sperm cell. When the sperm cell dies these enzymes pass into the plasma. The levels of enzymes are highest in the bull, intermediate in the stallion and lowest in the boar, Graham et al..

Other tests for semen quality and fertility—in particular rapid tests that would be of value in determining the fertility of semen used in artificial insemination —have been developed and tried. These laboratory tests include those that measure the resistance of spermatozoa to temperature shock, hypertonic salt solutions, or to other inimical influences, and tests for measuring the fructolysis or oxidation rate of semen. The methylene-blue reduction test described by Beck and Salisbury and based on the dehydrogenase activity of semen was found to be closely correlated with motility and concentration. Other biochemical tests for semen quality were developed and reported by many workers and reviewed by Maule.

But as stated by Mann in Perry's text, "On the whole, the metabolic processes in semen are more often related to sperm density and motility than they are to the fertilizing power of spermatozoa." Semen evaluation is indicative for, but not a test of, fertility in a male animal.

Conclusions on the Assessment of Semen Quality as it is Related to Fertility. Excellent reviews and summaries of much published data have been presented by Maule, Bishop and Hancock, Buckner et al., and Bratton et al. on the relationship of semen quality to fertility in the relatively fertile males present in artificial insemination bull studs. Many semen quality tests and evaluations have been reported by many workers on known sterile or infertile males from which certain general conclusions can be drawn. Extensive surveys of semen quality in populations of males of known and unknown fertility have been performed in bulls by Lagerlof, Carroll and coworkers, in stallions by Bielanski, MacLeod and McGee, and Day; in rams by Gunn and coworkers, Edgar, and Hulet et al.; in boars by Holst, and Herrick; and in men by MacLeod, MacLeod and Gold, and Freund. But very few studies have been conducted such as those by Hulet and Ercanbrack in rams where semen examinations of males were followed by fertility trials in an evaluation of the factors of semen quality that were related to fertility or infertility in males.

From the above references several generalizations can be made concerning the relationship of semen quality tests and fertility in relatively fertile males used in bovine artificial insemination. The physical activity of semen was more closely related to fertility than was metabolic activity but both were closely related to each other. The value of different measurements as tests of the fertilizing capacity of bull semen is very limited. Presently it is doubtful if more than 20 percent of the differences in fertility can be accounted for by these semen quality tests especially in artificial insemination bulls where the fertility of bulls usually is in a narrow range of 15 percent difference in conception rates from the most fertile to the least fertile bull. For this reason in artificial insemination centers good fertility results are based on providing each cow inseminated a certain number, about 6 to 10 million, of actively motile spermatozoa. Dead, or immotile spermatozoa have no effect on the normal viable spermatozoa. Blom and others indicated that for an ejaculate to be satisfactory for use in bovine artificial insemination it must have a volume of at least 2 ml and be of normal consistency and color, a sperm cell concentration of over 500 million per ml, motility of at least 40 percent with distinct progressive movement of cells, less than 15 percent primary abnormalities and a pH of 7.0 or below.

Only a certain minimum quality for each semen trait is needed for maximum fertility. Once this threshold has been reached the association between fertility and semen quality is nearly random, but below this threshold the correlation between fertility and semen quality is important. The semen quality tests most correlated with fertility in males are the concentration or numbers of spermatozoa, the percent of motile spermatozoa and particularly the rate, degree or vigor of motility, the percent of live normal cells, or conversely the percent of dead, abnormal sperm cells and possibly the pH. Hulet and Ercanbrack demonstrated that rams with satisfactory to very good fertility had 60 to 90 percent motile sperm cells with a moderate to high degree of vigor and progressive movement, 70 to 90 percent live normal spermatozoa, sperm cell concentrations of 1.0 to 1.8 billion/ml and pH values of 6.6 to 7.0. Rams with poor fertility on the basis of actual fertility trials had 15 percent or less motility with no progressive movement and little or no activity of the spermatozoa, 40 percent or less normal live spermatozoa with sperm cell concentrations of 0.1 billion per ml or less and a pH value of 7.4. No male should be permitted to score higher than his poorest semen character.

Carroll and coworkers reported about 6 percent of range bulls had poor fertility and 7 percent had questionable fertility based on essentially the same above criteria for semen quality but also including a careful physical examination. Faulkner reported on Wiltbank's data that 29 bulls with normal or satisfactory semen averaged 60 percent conception, range 14 to 100 percent, to the first service, bulls with questionable semen quality had a 48 percent conception rate, range 31 to 57 percent, on first service; and 11 bulls with poor or unsatisfactory semen had a 30 percent conception rate, range 0 to 69 percent, on first service. If the first semen test reveals poor semen quality, subsequent tests seldom show any improvement except possibly in very young immature males or males recently affected with a severe stress or disease. However in valuable males with poor quality of semen; a number of tests including breeding trials over a period of 6 months to one year may be indicated before the male is pronounced infertile or sterile. If semen collected by means of electroejaculation is of poor quality at least 3 more samples at weekly or greater intervals should be collected and evaluated especially if no physical defect is detected. Even then the ejaculator and the collection technique should be checked carefully. Evaluation of semen of range bulls, rams and possibly range stallions, is desirable before the breeding season because these males may collect and guard a "harem" of females and if they are sterile or infertile the pregnancy rate is greatly reduced even if an adequate ratio of males to females is present.

Only males with azoospermia or necrospermia should be

pronounced sterile. Even if the semen quality is poor, if normal motile spermatozoa are present in sufficient numbers conception can occur. This is especially true in boars, stallions and dogs where the ejaculate is delivered into the uterus at coitus and the few motile cells more readily gain access to the oviducts. In the other species, cattle, sheep, and humans, larger numbers of motile spermatozoa appear to be required as many are lost in the vagina and never traverse the cervix to the uterine cavity. After attempts at semen evaluation in stallions, Worthington reported that stallions with good quality semen had generally satisfactory fertility but a few had low fertility or were nearly sterile. Conversely a few horses with poor semen quality had normal fertility when bred to mares. Pickett et al. collected 2 ejaculates at weekly intervals for one year from 5 young stallions. The volume of gel-free semen and the total spermatozoa per ejaculate were highest during the late spring and summer months and mounting and ejaculation was more prompt. Sperm cell motility was higher in the winter months. Other differences in semen quality were noted between seasons of the year and between stallions.

There is probably no single criterion aside from actual breeding tests that can be used as an accurate overall measure of sperm quality. Lagerlof stated that one should never declare positively on the basis of a semen examination alone that a male is normally fertile, but should only certify in a negative manner that the semen examination showed no changes that have been proved to indicate reduced fertility. All facets of the examination of a male should be considered in the evaluation of his fertility including the physical examination, his sex drive and ability to mount and copulate readily, and the examination of his semen. Other considerations might well include the male's genetic merit and his freedom from disease.

References

Al-Aubaidi, J. M. and Fabricant, J. (1968) Technics for the Isolation of **Mycoplasma** from Cattle, Cor. Vet. **58,** 4, 555.

Albertsen, B. E. (1955) Pleuropneumonia-like Organisms in the Semen of Danish Artificial Insemination Bulls, Nord. Vet. Med. **7,** 3, 169.

Ball, L. (1969) Symposium on Management of Beef Cattle for Reproductive Efficiency, Ft. Collins, Colo., mimeographed notes.

Bartlett, D. E. (1968) The A.V.M.A./N.A.A.B. Code and the U.S. L.S.A. Recommended Regulations, Proc. 2nd Tech. Confer. on Art. Insem. and Reprod., Chicago, 37.

Bartlett, D. J. (1962) Studies on Dog Semen, I Morphological Characteristics, J. Reprod. and Fertil. **3,** 173.

Beck, G. H. and Salisbury, G. W. (1943) Rapid Methods for Estimating the Quality of Bull Semen, J. of Dairy Sci. **26,** 6, 483.

Bentinck-Smith, J. (1955) Personal Communication.

Berliner, V. R. (1946) The Biology of Equine Spermatozoa, in **the Problem of Fertility,** Princeton Univ. Press. Princeton, N.J.

Bielanski, W. (1960) Reproduction in Horses 1. Stallions, Public. #116, Institute of Zootechnics at the Agric. College in Krakow, Poland.

Bielanski, W., Wierzbowski, S., and Zakrewska, I. G. (1957) The Results of Mass-Wise Evaluations of the Semen and Sexual Reflexes of Stallions, Dept. of Animal Hygiene and Zootechnical Institute, Lab. of An. Reproduction, Krakow, Poland., Zootechnica Z. **1,** 3, 97.

Bierschwal, C. J. and Hendrikse, J. (1969) A Preliminary Report of Variations in Morphology of Boar Sperm and its Importance in Evaluation of Fertility of Yorkshire Boars Used in Artificial Insemination, Proc. of Conference on Reproductive Problems in Animals, Univ. of Georgia, Nov., 21.

Bishop, M. W. H and Hancock, J. L. (1955) The Evaluation of Bull Semen, Vet. Rec. **67,** 363.

Blom, E. (1946) Kompartionskammeret, et Hjaelpe Middel tel Forbedret Microscopisk Undersolgelse of Ufortyndel Tyresperma, Skand. Vet. Tidskr. **36,** 613.

Blom, E. (1947) On Medusa Formations (Detached Ciliated Borders) in Bull and Stallion Semen and Their Diagnostic Significance, Skand. Vet. Tidskr. **37,** 257.

Blom, E. (1950) A Simple Rapid Staining Method for the Differentiation Between Live and Dead Sperm Cells by Means of Eosin and Nigrosin, Nord. Vet. Med. 2, 58.

Blom, E. (1950) Interpretation of Spermatic Cytology in Bulls, Fert. and Steril. **1,** 3, 233.

Blom, E. (1950) On the Evaluation of Bull Semen, Thesis, C. Morten sen, Copenhagen, Denmark.

Blom, E. (1959) A Rare Sperm Abnormality "Corkscrew-Sperms" Associated with Sterility in Bulls, Nature, 183, 1280.

Blom, E. (1968) Rapid Refractometric Determination of Total Solids in Bull Seminal Plasma and its Possible Diagnostic Value, Nord. Vet. Med. **20,** 361.

Blom, E. and Erno, H. (1967) Mycoplasmosis: Infections of the Genital Organs of Bulls, Acta Vet. Scand. **8,** 186.

Boucher, J. H , Foote, R. H. and Kirk, R. W. (1958) The Evaluation of Semen Quality in the Dog and the Effects of Frequency of Ejaculation upon Semen Quality, Libido and Depletion of Sperm Reserves, Cor. Vet. **48,** 1, 67.

Bratton, R. W., Foote, R. H., Henderson, C. R., Musgrave, S. G., Dunbar, R. S. Jr., Dunn, H. O. and Beardsley, J. P. (1956) The Relative Usefulness of Combinations of Laboratory Tests for Predicting the Fertility of Bovine Semen, J. Dairy Sci. **39,** 11, 15, 42.

Buckner, P. J., Willett, E. L. and Bayley, N. (1954) Laboratory Tests, Singly and In Combination for Evaluating Fertility of Semen and of Bulls, J. Dairy Sci. **37,** 9, 1050.

Carroll, E. J., Ball, L. and Scott, J. (1963) Breeding Soundness in Bulls: A Summary of 10,940 Examinations, J.A.V.M.A. **142,** 10, 1105.

Coffin, D. L. (1953) Manual of Veterinary Clinical Pathology, 3rd Ed. Comstock Publ. Co. Ithaca, N Y.

Collins, W. J., Bratton, R. W. and Henderson, C. R. (1951) The Relationship of Semen Production to Sexual Excitement of Dairy Bulls, J. Dairy Sci. **34,** 3, 224.

Cottral, G. E., Gailiunis, P. and Cox, B. (1963) Foot and Mouth Disease Transmitted in Bull Semen, J.A.V.M.A. **143,** 784.

Cupps, P. T. and Laben, R. C. (1960) Spermatogenesis in Bulls in Relation to Semen Production, J. Dairy Sci. **43,** 6, 782.

Day, F. T. (1940) The Stallion and Fertility, Vet. Rec. **52,** 34, 597.

Deaken, A. (1943) Field Fertility Tests and Causes of Sterility in Bulls, Dept. of Agr., Div. of An. Husb., Ottawa, Canada.

Dimock, W. W. (1934) Artificial Insemination in Horses, N. A. Vet. **15,** 5, 22.

Edgar, D. G. (1963) The Place of Ram Testing in the Sheep Industry, N. Z. Vet. Jour. **11,** 5, 113.

Faulkner, L. C. (1969) Breeding Soundness in Beef Bulls, Proc. of a Conference on Reproductive Problems in Animals, Univ. of Georgia.

Foote, R. H. (1958) Estimation of Bull Sperm Concentration by Packed Cell Volume, Jour. of Diary Sci., **41,** 8, 1109.

Foote, R. H. (1970) Estimation of Total Solids in Bull Seminal Plasma by Refractometry, J. of An. Sci. **30,** 2, 561.

Foote, R. H. and Boucher, J. H. (1964) A Comparison of Several Photoelectric Procedures for Estimating Sperm Concentration in Dog Semen, Am, J. Vet. Res., **25,** 105, 558.

Freund, M. (1966) Standards for the Rating of Human Sperm Morphology, A Cooperative Study, Internat. J. of Fertil. **11,** 1 (Part 2) 97.

Gierloff, B. Chr. H. and Jakobsen, K. F. (1961) On the Survival of Foot and Mouth Disease Virus in Frozen Semen, Acta Vet. Scand. **2,** 210.

Gledhill, B. L. (1965) Cytophotometry of Presumed Diploid Bull Spermatozoa, Nord. Vet. Med. **17,** 328.

Gledhill, B. L. (1967) Swedish Methods for the Evaluation of Breeding Soundness in Bulls, An. Meeting Amer. Vet. Soc. for Study of Breeding Soundness, Univ. of Missouri, Columbia, Mo. FAO-Swedish Internat. Post-Graduate Course on Animal Reproduction., N. Lagerlof. Mimeographed Notes.

Glover, F. A. and Phipps, L. W. (1962) Preliminary Study of an Electronic Method of Counting and Sizing Bull Spermatozoa, J. Reprod. and Fertil. **4,** 2, 189.

Graham, E., Pace, M. M., and Gibson, C. D. (1969) Some Different Methods for Measurement of Bovine Semen Quality, Proc. Ann. Meeting A.V.M.A., Minneapolis, Lecture Notes.

Gunn, R. M. C., Sanders, R. N. and Granger, W. (1942) Studies in Fertility in Sheep, Commonwealth of Austral. Council for Scien. and Indus. Res. Bull., 148.

Hancock, J. L. (1955) The Disintegration of Bull Spermatozoa, Vet. Rec. **67,** 44, 825.

Hancock, J. L. (1955) The Morphologic Characteristics of Spermatozoa and Fertility, Internat. J. of Fertil. **4,** 4, 347.

Haq, I. (1949) Causes of Sterility in Bulls in Southern England, Brit. Vet. Jour. **105,** (3, 4, 5, 6), 71, 114, 143, 200.

Herman, H. A. and Swanson, E. W. (1941) Variations in Dairy Bull Semen with Respect to its Use in Artificial Insemination, Mo. Agr. Expt. Stat. Res. Bull., 326.

Herrick, J. B. and Self, H. L. (1962) Evaluation of Fertility in the Bull and Boar, Iowa State Univ. Press., Ames, Iowa.

Hirt, R. S., Plastridge, W. N. and Tourtellette, M. C. (1967) Survival of Mycoplasma in Frozen Bovine Semen, Amer. J. Vet. Res. **28,** 97.

Holst, S. J. (1949) The Semen of Sterile Boars, Proc. 14th Internat. Vet. Congr. **III** Sect. 4 (C), 118.

Hughes, J. P., Asbury, A. C., Loy, R. G. and Burd, H. E. (1967) The Occurrence of **Pseudomonas** in the Genital Tract of Stallions and its Effect on Fertility, Cor. Vet. **57,** 1, 53.

Hulet, C. V. and Ercanbrack, S. K. (1962) A Fertility Index for Rams, J. An. Sci., **21,** 3, 418.

Hulet, C. V., Foote, W. C. and Blackwell, R. L. (1964) Effects of Natural and Electrical Ejaculation on Predicting Fertility in the Ram, J. An. Sci., **23,** 2, 418.

Hulet, C. V., Foote, W. C. and Blackwell, R. L. (1965) Relationship of Semen Quality and Fertility in the Ram to Fecundity in the Ewe, J. Reprod. and Fertil. **9,** 311.

Jasper, D. (1969) Personal Communication.

Larsen, A. B. and Kopecky, K. E. (1970) **Mycobacterium paratuberculosis** in Reproductive Organs and Semen of Bulls, Amer. J. Vet. Res. **31,** 2, 255.

Lagerlof, N. (1934) Morphologische Untersuchungen uber Veranderungen im Spermabild und in den Hoden bie Bullen mit vesminderter oder Aufgehabener Fertilitat, Acta Pathol. et Microbiol. Scand. Suppl. XIX.

Larsen, L. L. (1960) Semen Collection and Its Evaluation in the Bull, Southwest Vet. Spring, 187.

Lustig, G. and Lindahl, P. E. (1970) Activation of Motility in Bull and Rabbit Spermatozoa by Ultrasonic Treatment Recorded by a Photographic Method, Internat. J. of Fert. **15,** 3, 135.

MacLeod, J. (1950) Semen Quality in One Thousand Men of Known Fertility and in Eight Hundred Cases of Infertile Marriage, Fert. & Steril. **2,** 115.

MacLeod, J. and Gold, R. Z. (1956) The Male Factor in Fertility and Infertility VIII, A Study of Variation in Semen Quality, Fert. and Steril. **7,** 5, 387.

MacLeod, J. and Gold, R. Z. (1958) An Analysis of Human Male Fertility, Internat. J. of Fertil. **3,** 382.

MacLeod, J. and McGee, W. R. (1950) The Semen of the Thoroughbred, Cor. Vet. **40,** 3, 233.

Mac Pherson, J. W. and Fish, N. A. (1954) The Survival of Pathogenic Bacteria in Bovine Semen Preserved by Freezing, Amer. J. Vet. Res. **15,** 548.

McKenzie, F. F. (1940) Recent Reproduction Studies on Equines, Proc. Amer. Soc. of An. Prod. 98.

McKenzie, F. F. and Phillips, R. W. (1934) Measuring Fertility in the Ram, J.A.V.M.A. **84,** 189.

O'Berry, P. A. (1967) Isolation of Mycoplasma spp. from Bull Semen and Its Role in Infertility, J.A.V.M.A. **150,** 11, 1314.

Phillips, R. W. (1935) The Physiology of Spermatozoa, Proc. Amer. Soc. of An. Prod., 222.

Pickett, B. W. (1969) Personal Communication.

Pickett, B. W., Faulkner, L. C. and Sutherland, T. M. (1969) The Effect of Season on Equine Semen Characteristics, J. An. Sci., **29,** 1, 196.

Pickett, B. W., Faulkner, L. C. and Sutherland, T. M. (1970) Effect of Month and Stallion on Seminal Characteristics and Sexual Behavior, J. An. Sci. **31,** 4, 713.

Rajamannan, A. (1969) Personal Communication.

Rao, C. K. and Hart, G. H. (1948) The Morphology of Bovine Spermatozoa, Amer. J. Vet. Res. **9,** 117.

Rollinson, D. H. L. (1951) Studies on Abnormal Spermatozoa of Bull Semen, Brit. Vet. Jour. **107,** (5, 6, 11); 203, 251, 258.

Salisbury, G. W. and Baker, F. N. (1966) Nuclear Morphology of Spermatozoa from Inbred and Line Cross Hereford Bulls, J. An. Sci., **25,** 2, 476.

Salisbury, G. W., Beck, G. H., Elliot, J. and Willett, E. L. (1943) Rapid Methods of Estimating the Number of Spermatozoa in Bull Semen, J. Dairy Sci. **26,** 1, 69.

Salisbury, G. W. and Mercier, E. (1945) The Reliability of Estimates of the Proportion of Morphologically Abnormal Sperm in Bull Semen, J. An. Sci. **4,** 2, 174.

Seidel, G. E. Jr. and Foote, R. H. (1969) Motion Picture Analysis of Ejaculation in the Bull, J. Reprod. and Fert. **20,** 313.

Sojka, N. J., Jennings, L. L. and Hamner, C. E. (1970) Artific Insemination in the Cat **(Felis Catus L.),** Lab. An. Care **20,** 198.

Spradbrow, P. B. (1968) The Isolation of IBR Virus from Bovi Semen, Austral. Vet. J., **44,** 9, 410.

Swanson, E. W. and Herman, H. A. (1944) The Correlation Between Some Characteristics of Dairy Bull Semen and Conception Rate, J. Dairy Sci. **27,** 4, 297.

Swanson, E. W. and Bearden, H. J. (1951) An Eosin-Nigrosin Stain For Differentiating Live-Dead Bovine Spermatozoa, J. An. Sci. **10,** 4, 981.

Terrill, C. E. (1960) Artificial Insemination of Farm Animals, Edit. by Perry, E. J., Rutgers Univ. Press, New Brunswick, N.J.

Wells, M. E., Awa, O. A. and Wondafrash, J. (1969) Evalution of Acrosomal Morphology with the Wells-Awa Stain, J. Dairy Sci., **52,** 4, 563

Willett, E. L. and Buckner, P. J. (1951) The Determination of Numbers of Spermatozoa in Bull Semen by Measurement of Light Transmission, J. An. Sci. **10,** 1, 219.

Worthington, W. E. (1968) Evalution of Stallion Fertility, 14th Ann. Conf. A.A.E.P., Philadelphia, 133.

Chapter XIX

ARTIFICIAL INSEMINATION

History

The artificial insemination of domestic animals has been practiced for a number of centuries. Williams cited Schmaltz, who reported that in an Arabian book published in the fourteenth century an Arab was reported to have taken semen by means of a pledget of cotton from the vagina of a mare recently bred to a famous stallion; then by inserting this cotton into the vagina of his own mare conception was produced. Leewenhoek and Hamm observed spermatozoa as early as 1677 according to Perry citing Dobell. The first scientific research in artificial insemination of animals was performed on dogs in 1780 by the Italian scientist, Spallanzani. This was confirmed in 1782 by Rossi. Although Spallanzani demonstrated that the fertilizing power of the semen resided in the spermatozoa, few further studies or attempts at artificial insemination were conducted until the latter part of the nineteenth century. Heape reported that a dog breeder, Millais, between 1884 and 1896 artificially inseminated 19 bitches, of which 15 produced young. According to Perry about this time, Pearson at the University of Pennsylvania wrote to Heape and reported the successful insemination of mares. In 1890 Prof. Hoffman of Stuttgart recommended the supplementary artificial insemination of a mare after natural mating. In the early 1900's workers were beginning to realize the possible value of artificial insemination. In 1907 Ivanov reported the successful results of a series of artificial inseminations in mares, cows, and ewes as a means for the widespread improvement of farm animals. As a result a laboratory was established in Russia and several hundred men were trained in the techniques of artificial insemination prior to 1914. After the first World War, activities in this field in Russia increased greatly and by 1938 the number of animals inseminated in that country was reported by Perry as 120,000 mares, 1,200,000 cattle, and 15 million sheep. In 1936 Sorenson and Gylling-Holm organized the first cooperative artificial breeding association in Denmark and by 1952 about 55 percent of the cows in Denmark were bred artificially. Similar activity was occurring in England in the 1930's.

Artificial insemination was first performed on large numbers of cattle in the United States in 1937 and 1938 at the Agricultural Experiment Station in Minnesota. The first cooperative cattle artificial breeding association was organized by E. J. Perry in New Jersey in 1938, with Dr. J. A. Henderson as the first technician.

Artificial insemination in dairy cattle has grown rapidly. In 1956, 21 percent of the dairy cows in the U.S. were bred artificially; in 1969 about 52 percent or 8,000,000 cattle, including 750,000 beef cattle, were bred artificially. In 1969 less than 4 percent of the beef cattle in the U.S. were bred artificially, but this figure may rise sharply in the next few years. During this ten year period the numbers of artificial insemination organizations declined, usually as the result of mergers. A number of countries including Denmark, Japan and Israel breed over 90 percent of their dairy cattle artificially. Artificial insemination in swine has been developed and in the last 10 years has grown rapidly in Europe. In 1969 about 20,000 sows were inseminated in the U.S.. Artificial insemination in horses has recently received widespread attention. The advent of frozen semen in cattle, the development of frozen semen in horses and the newer therapeutic methods for the control of estrus and ovulation all promise the increased use of artificial insemination in the future. In species such as cattle where frozen semen is readily available, semen is currently being shipped by air throughout the world.

Advantages and Disadvantages

The advantages of artificial insemination are well known, and greatly outweigh the disadvantages; if this were not so, the rapid growth of the artificial insemination would not have continued.

1. Artificial insemination greatly increases the utilization of proven sires. The services of outstanding, superior sires are made available to many more owners. Marked increases of about 30 percent in milk production have been achieved in most dairy herds using artificial insemination to proven sires, when compared to herds using

natural service, Van Vleck. This has been of economic benefit to the owner and the country. Many proven bulls have artificially sired between 100,000 and 200,000 calves or more in their lifetime. Stallions may sire over 100 foals in a short breeding season and boars may sire over 1,000 litters of pigs per year. This use of outstanding sires is further increased by the ability to ship frozen semen of some species worldwide.

2. The danger, work, and expense of keeping and handling, what in many cases proved to be, an inferior male is eliminated for the average dairyman. This added saving by the use of artificial insemination can be spent on maintaining an additional cow, which, if profitable, may defray part or all of the yearly cost of breeding a herd artificially. Crossbreeding in herds containing several breeds and having only one bull is eliminated.

3. Bulls used in artificial insemination are more carefully and scientifically selected from outstanding cows and proven sires than is possible in individual dairy herds. About 90 percent of the possible genetic improvement in a commercial herd depends on the genetic improvement in the artificial insemination stud because 88 percent of the genes in any herd came from the males used the last three generations, Magee. Artificial insemination permits earlier and more rapid proving of young bulls on a greater number of cows under varied conditions. This gives a more accurate proof of a male's transmitting ability than can the testing of a bull on only one small group of females under similar conditions of management and feeding. This mode of testing also distributes the risk so that inferior bulls cause little loss to individual owners. In artificial insemination studs it costs at least $8,000 to $10,000 to prove the genetic worth of a young bull even when his initial price may be small. Since only about one of five bulls tested are usually kept as proven sires each of these represents an investment of about $50,000, Van Vleck.

4. If the males are handled carefully, examined closely from a health standpoint to make certain that they are free from disease, if regular semen examinations are made and accurate breeding records maintained, artificial insemination may lessen or eliminate the occurrence of venereal diseases such as vibriosis, trichomoniasis, and brucellosis. Because only highly fertile semen is shipped to farmers, breeding efficiency is improved if the semen is handled properly and the cows are bred at the proper time. Artificial insemination frequently results in improved record keeping, and in heightened interest on the part of the farmer in having cows conceive promptly. This has been helpful in the early diagnosis and treatment of genital abnormalities and has often resulted in an improved breeding efficiency in the herd. In herds affected with vibriosis and trichomoniasis, artificial insemination, may be a valuable means or aid in overcoming the disease. In an emergency, such as an outbreak of foot and mouth disease, previously frozen stored semen can be used safely by an A.I. Stud.

5. With the advent of the widespread use of frozen semen and the classification of the physical characteristics of a proven sire's daughters, careful selection of bulls and line breeding is possible.

6. Miscellaneous advantages of artificial insemination include the following:

a) It makes possible the mating of animals with a great difference in size without injury to either animal.

b) It may extend the usefulness of sires which for some physical reason are unable to copulate normally. It may extend the usefulness of aged or impotent sires.

c) It may be used to increase the usefulness of males of monogamous species such as the fox. It is of value in experiments on hybridization where natural mating cannot take place.

d) Artificial insemination usually stimulates greater interest in livestock breeding and in better management practices.

e) Artificial insemination has proved to be of value for male dogs that are timid or have premature erection, since complete erection of the canine penis does not ordinarily occur until after entry into the female's vagina. In toy breeds of dogs it may be used to prevent exhaustion due to repeated attempts to copulate during hot weather. It may also be of value in relatively impotent male dogs.

f) It may be helpful when used in females who are in true estrum and ovulate but refuse to stand or accept the male.

The disadvantages of artificial insemination should be recognized and carefully considered.

1. Well-trained operators are required to supervise the collection, examination, extending, freezing, shipping, and the insemination of the females in order to ensure that infectious diseases such as brucellosis, vibriosis, trichomoniasis and others are not spread, thereby causing losses in many herds, see Bartlett and Larson in Perry's text. If fertile semen is not collected, extended, and handled properly, poor breeding efficiency results. This also occurs in herds where owners do not watch their cows closely for estrum, and the inseminator does not breed them at the proper time. Careful, complete records must be kept. Inseminators may, if they are not careful, be a means of spreading infectious diseases from one farm to another.

2. There is a great possibility in the widespread use of artificial insemination that the incidence of possible genetic abnormalities, for example in cattle, such as: cystic ovaries, spastic syndrome, poor conformation, espe-

cially of feet and limbs, and lack of libido, may be increased; at present too much emphasis is placed on production and percentage of butter fat. Not enough study and research are being given to the genetic aspects of artificial insemination. It is possible that the great increase in cystic ovaries and spastic syndrome in dairy cattle the past ten years may be due largely to the wide use of certain bulls by means of artificial insemination. Improved feeding practices and successful treatment of cows with cystic ovaries may be added factors in the increased incidence of cystic ovaries.

3. Miscellaneous disadvantages:

a) Artificial insemination is of questionable value in overcoming all infections or abnormalities of the genital tract in females and thereby producing higher conception rates. Only occasionally is artificial insemination indicated as a means of overcoming existing diseases or abnormalities.

b) Intrauterine insemination of a pregnant female may result in abortion.

c) Uncontrolled or unscrupulous operators or owners could substitute sperm of less valuable animals unless blood typing is routinely employed.

d) Artificial insemination cannot be used conveniently on all species or breeds of animals. In some species much more work must be done before artificial insemination becomes practical.

Artificial Insemination in Cattle

Few advances in livestock production have been so rapidly accepted and have had such a profound influence on dairy cattle improvement as has the use of artificial insemination The ability of bull semen to be stored for long periods and the management conditions under which dairy cattle are kept, have made artificial insemination very adaptable to this segment of the livestock industry in the United States and other countries. Artificial insemination has been commonly used on valuable purebred beef cattle, especially on small farms or in foundation herds. Because of the large number of beef cattle scattered over a large area when on range, the principal problem and cost is that of finding cows during estrum and driving them to a central point for insemination. As methods of synchronization of estrus develop, increased numbers of beef cattle will probably be inseminated. At present many owners of larger farms are breeding artificially to their own bulls using frozen semen or purchasing semen from other sources.

The collection of semen from the bull for use in artificial insemination is usually accomplished with the artificial vagina and occasionally where necessary with electroejaculation as described in Chapter XVIII. Austin et al. have reported that semen collected from Hereford bulls by electroejaculation was comparable in quality to that collected by the artificial vagina. The concentration of spermatozoa per ml by electroejaculation was one-half that of semen collected by the artificial vagina; the volume of semen was twice as large and the pH was higher. The motility of the spermatozoa and the total numbers of sperm cells per ejaculate were the same for the two methods of collection. Murray and others have reported that since Brahman and Santa Gertrudis bulls will not ejaculate into the artificial vagina that A.I. is possible in these breeds only with semen collected by electroejaculation. With proper management most mature bulls in artificial insemination studs may be collected one to four times weekly over an extended period of time.

Extended Liquid Bovine Semen

Handling of the semen after collection in the artificial vagina should be done carefully to avoid: cold shock or overheating the semen; contamination by water, urine or chemicals; excessive agitation; or exposure to air or direct sunlight, Foote. If semen is to be used undiluted within two hours, it may be left in a small, closed container in a dark place at room temperature. Undiluted semen from fertile bulls may be used for artificial insemination for 24 to 36 hours after collection. For this purpose the semen should be placed in a small, closed container immediately after collection and any air space may be filled with a high-grade neutral mineral oil. The semen is cooled gradually by placing the vial or tube in a glass of warm water at near body temperature, 80–90° F., and placing the glass in a refrigerator at 3 to 8° C. or 40 to 45° F.. Semen should be maintained at this temperature until used or frozen. Although some motility of bovine spermatozoa may persist for 7 to 14 days under these procedures, conception rates are low if the undiluted bovine semen has been stored 36 hours or more. Less damage due to cold shock occurs if a protective agent or extender is added to the semen before cooling it to 5° C..

Extended Liquid or Frozen Semen rather than fresh, undiluted semen is usually used for artificial insemination for the following reasons: extended semen stores better and maintains its fertility longer, more cows can be bred, the spermatozoa are protected from sudden temperature changes, buffers maintain the proper pH, nutrients are provided, and antibiotics including sulfanilamide added to liquid semen prolong spermatozoan viability, improve fertility, and control vibriosis and bacterial growth. When semen is to be extended, the fresh semen is examined immediately after collection for motility and concentration. If its quality is satisfactory, over 500 million spermatozoa per ml, and 50 percent motility with good forward movement, the fresh semen is mixed with 3 to 4 times its volume of warm, 70 to 90° F., extender and placed in a jar of warm water at the same temperature and both are then placed in a refrigerator to cool slowly so that the semen reaches a temperature of 40° F. or 5° C., in about 1 to 1-1/2 hours. Spermatozoa are more resistant to temperature shock when the extender contains egg yolk or milk.

Only two practical types of extenders with modifications are now in general use although in recent years many have been tried, such as: whole egg, macerated chick embryo, a complex synthetic pabulum, cocoanut milk, carbonated extenders and others, Maule, and MacPherson.

The buffered egg yolk extender was first described by Phillips and Hardy in 1940 who used a phosphate buffer with egg yolk. In 1941 Salisbury et al. described the egg yolk citrate buffer extender which presently is widely used. This extender made possible the rapid advance in artificial insemination. The egg yolk citrate diluter is prepared by adding 2.9 gms of sodium citrate dihydrate ($Na_2C_6H_5O \cdot 2H_2O$) to 100 ml of double distilled water and mixing it at a rate of one part egg yolk to one to five parts of buffer solution. To prepare the egg yolk for the egg yolk buffer extender, fresh eggs should be washed in water and wiped with 70 percent grain alcohol. After allowing the egg to dry, the shell is broken with a sterile knife in a dustfree room. The yolk is separated from the white and placed on a 2-1/2 inch square cardboard with a 1/4 inch hole in the center. The yolk is punctured through the hole and allowed to flow into a sterile graduate, thus eliminating the egg white and the vitelline or yolk membrane. The protective value of the egg yolk is largely due to the lecithin and other substances such as glucose it contains, Maule. The egg yolk citrate buffer is usually prepared fresh each day in an artificial insemination center.

Boiled, pasturized, homogenized milk, and boiled, pasteurized skim milk have been reported to be as satisfactory as the egg yolk buffer diluters as an extender for bull semen, Thacker and Almquist (1953) Almquist (1954). This extender is prepared by placing fresh homogenized or skim milk in the top portion of a Pyrex glass double boiler and heating it to 95° C. or 203° F.. The thermometer is then removed, the lid replaced, and **gentle** boiling is continued for ten minutes. The boiling period should not be excessively prolonged. The boiled milk is cooled to the same temperature as the semen to be diluted. The milk is slowly poured from the boiler leaving the surface scum of albumin on the sides of the boiler. No unboiled or improperly heated milk should be added to the boiled milk, as relatively small amounts of unboiled milk exert a harmful effect on spermatozoa. Copper-lined utensils should not be used. Ordinary fresh pasteurized milk or fortified skim milk has not proved as satisfactory as pasteurized homogenized or skim milk as a semen diluter and their use is not recommended. The milk can be boiled the day before use and stored in a refrigerator. The satisfactory use of 9 percent homogenized sterilized cream was reported by Adler and Rasbech. Skim milk powder, if of a good grade, may be used in preparing a satisfactory extender, Melrose, Maule. The toxic fraction in milk is apparently the lactenin that is destroyed with the removal of the albumin fraction, Maule. The protective fraction is composed of the phospholipids. Skim milk is usually preferred because there are few or no fat globules to interfere with the microscopic examination of the milk, MacPherson.

Controlled fertility trials reported by various workers using egg yolk buffer and milk extenders have been summarized by Maule and the results with both extenders on the same ejaculates of semen were similar.

Antibiotics added to semen extenders have been shown to increase the viability of spermatozoa and to eliminate **V. fetus** organisms in the extended semen. The addition of 300 mg of sulphanilamide per 100 ml of egg yolk citrate diluent resulted in a significant improvement in the viability of bull semen and had no adverse effect on conception rate. At first it was thought that the sulphanilamide prevented bacterial growth but later work by Salisbury and Knodt, and Rasbech showed that its principal effect was on the metabolism of the spermatozoa, causing a pronounced inhibition of fructolysis.

Almquist found that 1000 units of penicillin and 1000 micrograms of streptomycin per ml of extender had no adverse effect on the spermatozoa and effectively controlled bacterial growth in the diluted semen. The addition of antibiotics to semen of low-fertile bulls improved their conception rates 10 to 15 percent. Others confirmed this finding. This definite improvement in conception rates was possibly due to better control of bacterial growth but more likely was due to the control of vibriosis found to be present in the semen in many older bulls (see Chapter XIV), Orthey and Gilman, McEntee et al.. Five hundred units of penicillin and 500 micrograms of streptomycin per ml were found to be as satisfactory as the higher concentrations if semen was extended at least 1:25 times and held for 6 hours before use. At the present time when the egg yolk-buffer or milk extender is prepared 1000 units crystalline penicillin G and 1000 micrograms of dihydrostreptomycin per ml are usually added. Non-contaminated buffer solutions containing antibiotics for the egg yolk extender may be stored for one week at 5° C. For liquid semen extenders sulfanilamide may be added at a concentration of 0.03 gms per ml. Sulfanilamide should not be used for extenders for frozen semen. Excessive levels of antibiotics in semen may be toxic to spermatozoa and amounts above those recommended have no additional beneficial effect.

It should be noted and emphasized that although antibiotics will eliminate a few bacteria in semen such as **V. fetus** and reduce the numbers of certain susceptible bacteria such as streptococci and staphylococci it will not eliminate such organisms as **C. pyogenes, Brucella spp., Trichomonas fetus, Leptospira spp.,** mycoplasma, **Mycobacterium tuberculosis, Pseudomonas, Listeria,** and viruses such as IBR-IPV, Chlamydia, epivag, and others. Freezing of semen to which antibiotics have been added will further preserve nearly all of the above organisms for long periods of time.

Other antibiotics have been tried in semen extenders, Maule, and some are definitely harmful while others were no better than the penicillin and streptomycin combination. The addition of antibiotics to semen cannot be a substitute for the careful, sanitary collection of semen with a low bacterial content from healthy disease-free males.

Modifications of the above egg yolk buffer and milk extenders that have shown possible advantages include the addition of:

Glycerol—Semen is extended to one-half the final desired volume with fresh heated skim milk or homogenized milk containing antibiotics and cooled gradually to 40° F. over a period of about 2 hours. Then an equal volume of cooled milk extender at 40° F. containing a 10 or 20 percent level of glycerol by volume is added stepwise in 20, 30 and 50 percent amounts at 10 minute intervals to the initially extended semen. The final concentration of the glycerol in the extended semen was 5 or 10 percent, Perry, Almquist (1962). This resulted in good fertility for a period of 4 days with milk-glycerol extender, Almquist and Wickersham. Some workers have used glycerol with the yolk-citrate extender.

Glycine at concentrations of 0.5 to 4 percent have been used in yolk citrate buffer and milk extenders with an apparent increase in survival of spermatozoa stored 4 to 6 days but little or no beneficial results on fertility were noted, Maule.

Catalase, at a level of 20 to 100 mg per ml, afforded protection to extended semen, especially in yolk citrate buffers. Catalase prevented the formation of hydrogen peroxide due to the effect of light and agitation on semen, but its effect on fertility was not significant, Foote, Foote and Dunn, and Maule.

Enzymes, with the possible exception of amylase, hormones, tranquilizers, vitamins, glucose, fructose, and other substances have been added to extenders without noticeable success in improving the fertility rate. Kirton and coworkers have reported a 3 percent increase in conception rate in over 17,000 cows by the addition of 1 mg of crude alpha or beta amylase per 100 ml of extender. Although the amylase was initially added for its possible effect on capacitation of spermatozoa, the actual reason for the improved fertility is not known.

In 1957 Van Demark and Sharma, and Van Demark and Bartlett described a modified egg yolk buffer semen extender or the Illini Variable Temperature Diluent, in which carbon dioxide was bubbled through the buffer solution until the pH reached 6.3. The diluted semen was sealed in ampules and stored in the dark at room temperature. Although the results were inconstant some workers reported good conception rates for up to 7 days. For this to be of practical value further studies are indicated.

In 1958 Foote et al. described an improved semen extender called C.U.E. (Cornell University Extender) that contained one part egg yolk to four parts of a special buffer containing sodium bicarbonate, potassium chloride, glucose, glycine, sodium citrate and antibiotics.

The extension rate of bull semen by the various extenders is based on: the need for semen from the bull, the volume of ejaculate, and the concentration of living, actively motile spermatozoa. Minimum standards for semen for use in artificial insemination requires at least 500 million sperm cells per ml of an ejaculate and an initial progressive motility rating of 3 in at least 50 percent of the spermatozoa. Each ml, ampule, or unit of extended semen used for insemination should contain 8 million actively motile spermatozoa. Foote showed in extensive fertility trials that 60 to 90 day non-return rates or conceptions were 75.2 and 76.1 percent for 5 and 10 million motile spermatozoa per insemination, respectively, when extended in C.U.E. extender. Below 5 million motile cells per insemination the fertility dropped rapidly. This standard is generally followed by nearly all insemination associations. The extension of semen is based on the following formula: the percentage of actively motile spermatozoa x the concentration of spermatozoa = the numbers of actively motile spermatozoa in the ejaculate; this latter figure divided by 8,000,000 equals the possible dilution rate. This formula permits dilution rates of 1:150 and 1:200 or more if necessary. Willett reported on dilution rates of semen from 1:100 to 1:300 in highly fertile bulls. Between rates of 1:100 and 1:200 when the numbers of spermatozoa per ml dropped progressively from 10 to 6 million there was a 0.5 percent drop in conception rate per each million decrease. When one unit or one ml of diluted semen contained fewer than 6 million spermatozoa there was a drop of about 2.6 percent for each million decrease. In inseminating cows there was a tendency for higher concentrations of spermatozoa, larger doses, and deeper depositions of the semen to produce the highest fertility rates, Olds and Seath. Since the amount of semen needed is often smaller than the possible extension rate, the dilution rate to control vibriosis should be at least 1:25 and the semen should be in contact with the antibiotics for at least 6 hours. McEntee, Hughes and Gilman.

After the gradual cooling period, the semen is extended by adding a calculated amount of extender, also at refrigerator temperature, 35 to 45° F. or 3 to 8° C., to bring the amount of previously slightly diluted semen to the final quanity of extended semen determined as possible or necessary, whichever amount is smaller. The semen and extender are gently mixed by tilting their container back and forth. In artificial insemination centers the extended semen is poured into various-sized plastic vials which are filled nearly full in order to prevent agitation harmful to spermatozoa. These vials are sealed with a plastic cap that has previously been soaked or washed in distilled water, autoclaved, and dried. These vials are labeled according to the individual bull's semen they contain. In some associations, different colored inert coal-tar dyes are added to the semen extender to help prevent the inseminator from making the mistake of using semen from the wrong breed, Almquist. Some centers use different colored caps instead of adding dye to the semen of different breeds.

Where there is a great demand for services to certain proven sires some associations are still sending out liquid extended semen because this form of semen will permit service of 2 to 3 times as many cows as frozen semen where larger numbers of spermatozoa per ml of extended semen are needed to compensate for the loss of sperm cells in the freezing process. Liquid semen produced the best conception rates 24 and 48 hours after collection. Thereafter the conception rates declined rapidly especially after the fourth day of storage and more early embryonic deaths and delayed returns occurred, Salisbury.

When liquid extended semen is used in small herds from their own bull, collections are usually made at 3 to 4 day intervals and the semen extended and stored. The semen should be extended at least 1:25 times which necessitates throwing away most of the collected semen, since usually only a few cows are bred with each ejaculate. The fresh extender used in these small establishments may be purchased at regular intervals from a large artificial insemination unit. Some veterinarians have reported purchasing a pint of extender at a time, pouring it into small vials, and freezing it until ready for use. Others make their own buffer solution with the antibiotics added and place it in small containers which are then frozen until needed. When they are thawed, an equivalent amount of fresh egg yolk is added, and the semen extended. Hurst has shown that egg yolk citrate extender with antibiotics added can be frozen and stored at 18 to 22° F. for 4-1/2 months and then used successfully to extend semen. Following this practice, normal conception rates occurred. Frozen extender with a 1:4 ratio of egg yolk to buffer was also stored satisfactorily for at least 1 month. In New York State the 1:4 egg yolk to buffer extender is proving to be more satisfactory and is less viscid than the 1:1 mixture following thawing. Hurst reported that the boiled, pasteurized skim milk extender was also satisfactory for storing in the frozen state. No antibiotic levels were determined following frozen storage; however, it was expected that little loss of potency of antibiotic level would occur over the relatively short period of several months, Hurst, Almquist. Because of the ease of making milk extender, many veterinarians use this extender in small herds. Several commercial companies have produced extenders but at present their products have not proved highly successful or been widely used.

Thus on an average farm, a semen sample would be collected, 1 ml of semen would be added to 25 ml of diluter, or 1/2 ml semen to 12-1/2 to 15 ml of diluter. Even if the sperm cell concentration were only 500,000 per cmm., this would still provide over 10 million spermatozoa per ml if only 60 percent were actively motile. Proper antibiotic concentrations may be added to this small amount of prepared extender by making a stock solution of 100,000 units of crystalline penicillin and 100,000 micrograms (100 mg) of dihydrostreptomycin in 10 ml of a citrate buffer solution. To obtain a final concentration of 500 units or micrograms of each antibiotic per ml of egg yolk buffer or milk extender, 0.5, 1.25 or 2.5 ml of the antibiotic stock solution should be added to 10, 25, or 50 ml of extender, respectively. To obtain a final concentration of 1000 units of each antibiotic in the extender the amounts of the added stock solution should be doubled.

Frozen Semen

Within the last 10 years frozen semen has largely supplanted liquid semen for artificial insemination of cattle in the U.S. with over 90 percent of the cows being bred with frozen semen, Herman (1965).

The chief advantages of frozen semen are:

1. More efficient year round use can be made of semen from proven sires or injured or crippled sires.

2. Selected matings can be made at any place at any time to a large number of available proven sires. Custom freezing of semen makes frozen semen available from farmer-owned bulls.

3. Semen can be stored for months to many years at −110° F. (−79° C.) using dry ice and alcohol or at −320° F. (−192° C.) in liquid nitrogen as refrigerants. Apparently a slight decline in fertility occurs after a number of months or years, Salisbury, but many calves have been born with 5- to 10-year-old semen long after the sire has died.

4. Shipping costs are reduced from the bull stud to the technician in the field because semen supplies and liquid nitrogen supplies only need replenishment about once a month. Semen may readily be shipped anywhere in the world.

5. Hahn et al. reported that sperm cell output, percentage of morphologically normal spermatozoa and percentage of motile sperm after freezing was lower in bulls 6 to 12 years of age than in bulls 3 to 6 years of age. Thus semen quality was highest in bulls not yet old enough to complete the progeny test. It might be desirable in certain young bulls with lower quality semen to freeze a supply before he reached an older age and his semen becomes relatively infertile.

The major disadvantages of frozen semen are:

1. Semen from about 10 to 20 percent of bulls will not withstand freezing. These are often bulls with low fertility when their semen was shipped in the liquid form.

2. The ampuling, freezing and storage equipment costs and storing costs at the stud and in the field are high.

3. In the freezing process about 50 percent, range 20 to 80 percent, of the spermatozoa are killed so increased numbers of spermatozoa per insemination ampule are required, Rapatz. When a proven sire is in great demand this reduces the number of cows bred compared to extended liquid semen.

4. If proper bull health is not maintained, frozen semen has great potential for the spread of viral and bacterial diseases.

5. Heavy use of frozen semen will limit the number of sires used, and possibly result in narrowing the genetic base of a breed.

History

In 1949 Polge, Smith, and Parkes reported that spermatozoa of several species, including cattle, could be treated with glycerol and survive at a temperature of −79° C. They showed that the protective action of glycerol, by modifying the type of crystal formed during freezing, resulted in less harm or injury to the cells and thus survival of spermatozoa could be greatly improved by the slow cooling and freezing process which they perfected. In 1951 Stewart reported the birth of the first calf from insemination with frozen semen. In 1952 Polge and Rowson reported on 38 cows artificially inseminated with frozen semen extended 1:40; 79 percent conceived. In May, 1953, the first calf in the United States from artificial insemination with frozen semen was born in Wisconsin. That year Rowson and Polge reported on 208 cows bred artificially with frozen semen diulted 1:4 and stored from 1 to 52 weeks; the average conception rate was 65 percent. There was no evidence of a decline in conception rate with frozen semen stored for longer periods. They reported that semen from some bulls did not store as well as that from others and also that semen frozen in liquid nitrogen at −192° C. was still viable after thawing.

In freezing bull semen the following steps are generally followed, Maule, Perry, Knoop and Hafez:

Freshly collected bull semen is diluted 1:4 with a warm simple egg yolk-buffer extender composed of 1 part egg yolk to 4 parts of citrate buffer and to which 1,000 units per ml of penicillin and 1,000 micrograms of streptomycin, but no sulfanilamide, have been added. Sulfanilamide interferes with the freezing process causing a reduction in spermatozoan survival. Sterilized homogenized milk or sterilized skim milk with penicillin and streptomycin added, described in the early part of this chapter on liquid semen extenders, may also be used. The diluted semen is cooled gradually in the refrigerator to 5° C. or 40° F. within 75 minutes. More of the same extender at refrigerator temperature is added until half the total volume that has previously been determined is reached. The amount of dilution is determined so that after freezing and thawing the total number of actively motile spermatozoa is about 8 to 12 million per ml. This requires knowledge of the original number of actively motile spermatozoa, their concentration and the approximate loss of spermatozoa in the freezing process for each bull. This loss is usually from 20 to 80, average 50, percent but varies from bull to bull in a fairly regular manner, with the semen of some bulls storing better than that of others.

The concentration of actively motile spermatozoa in the extended semen before freezing is usually about 20 to 30 million per ml, Pickett et al.. Boyd and Hafs reported that the number of spermatozoa per ml in extended semen could be reduced from 35 to 12 million per ml in highly fertile bulls before freezing without a decline in fertility. This was not possible in subfertile bulls. The rate of dilution will vary from 1:25 to over 1:100 but usually is about 1:60 to 1:70.

Equilibration time is the period needed before freezing for the sperm cells to become adjusted to the extender so that on freezing excessive loss of sperm cells does not occur. This time varies greatly between species. It is not necessary that bovine sperm cells equilibrate or be in the presence of the glycerol for a period of time before freezing. Recent experiments including fertility trials have indicated that the semen should be in the extender with or without the glycerol for about 4 hours at refrigerator temperature. Because of the adverse effects of glycerol on antibiotics, equilibrating for at least 4 hours in glycerol-free extender is desirable. The second half of the egg yolk citrate buffer extender should contain about 14 percent glycerol by weight making a final dilution rate of 7 percent. If sterilized milk is used as the extender the second half of the extender should contain 20 percent glycerol so the final dilution will be 10 percent. The second half of the diluter is added to the first either in 4 equal amounts at 20-minute intervals or drop-wise so that the entire amount is added over a period of 60 minutes. This should be mixed gently or a mixing or oscillating table in the cold room has been used for this purpose. The diluted semen is then placed in 1 ml amounts in glass ampules that are sealed after being filled. After adding the glycerol portion of the extender to the semen and initial extender, freezing should be accomplished within 4 to 20 hours of collection of the semen, Rajamannan and Foote. Berndtson and Foote reported recently on bull spermatozoa from 10 bulls exposed at 5° C. to extenders containing glycerol for 6 hours, 30 minutes and 10 seconds before freezing. The latter very short equilibration time resulted in a highly significant improvement in sperm motility following freezing and thawing. More study is obviously indicated especially since the Milk Marketing Board in England reported on 6 highly fertile bulls whose semen following freezing had poor conception rates. These bulls' semen responded favorably to a shorter equilibration time.

The glass ampules which are made of a proper type of glass and have rounded bottoms to prevent breaking during freezing should have previously been marked with ink to identify the bull, his registration number, the owner, and the date of collection. The gas burners on the sealing machine should be so adjusted that overheating doesn't occur whether the ampules are tip-sealed or pull-sealed. These sealed vials are then placed in 95 percent ethyl or isoprophyl alcohol or acetone at 5° C. This temperature is reduced at a rate of 0.8° to 1° C. per minute by the controlled addition of fine particles of solid carbon dioxide and the stirring of the alcohol until a temperature of –15° C. is reached in about 25 minutes. Then the temperature is lowered as rapidly as possible to –79° C., or –110° F., by the rapid addition of dry ice, or solid carbon dioxide, to the alcohol. This requires about 10 to 20 minutes.

Some workers recommend cooling at a rate of 5° to 10° C. per minute from –15° C. down to –79° C.; others cool at a rate of 3° to 5° C. from –15° C. down to –50° C. and cool very rapidly to –79° C. while others have recently shown that rapid cooling from 5° C. to –196° C. can be accomplished within 10 minutes, or at a rate of 20° per minute with excellent results, Rajamannan. The ampules of frozen semen are stored in 95 percent alcohol in freezers with the temperature maintained at –79° C. by dry ice, by mechanical equipment, or at –196° C. in liquid nitrogen. Pickett and coworkers and Bean and coworkers have shown that liquid nitrogen storage of spermatozoa at –196° is superior to dry ice storage at –79° C, possibly because slight upward fluctuations in temperature above –79° C. are harmful to sperm cell survival. The Milk Marketing Board in England reported that bull semen can be stored in ampules in liquid nitrogen for at least 2 years without deterioration. Foote reported that the fertility of bovine semen frozen in dry ice declined only 7 percent in 8 years. Herman reported on a long term field trial at the New Jersey Experiment Station using frozen semen from 5 bulls. The percent of conceptions from the use of the frozen semen at 1, 2, 4, 8 and 12 years was 66.2, 66.2, 56.1, 59.2 and 41.7, respectively.

In the past few years most artificial insemination organizations are placing the ampules on metal canes and freezing in a machine at a controlled rate by using liquid nitrogen vapor and after –80° C. is reached the semen is cooled very rapidly to –196° C. This may be done in a less controlled but very satisfactory manner by placing the ampules in the nitrogen vapor one-half to 3 inches above the surface of the liquid nitrogen of a large tank, Forgason et al. and Rajamannan. When the ampules of frozen semen begin to make a crackling or popping noise –80° C. has been reached and the ampules may be placed in the liquid nitrogen. Apparently bull semen must pass rapidly through the critical temperature period of –15° to –30° C. or sperm cell damage may occur, Maule.

Conception rates with extended frozen semen are only slightly below those of extended liquid semen. Bratton, Foote, and Cruthers reported that a 60- to 90-day nonreturn rate for unfrozen liquid semen used as a control was 74.5 percent; the nonreturn rate for the same semen frozen in single-breeding ampules and stored 1 day at –79° C. was 72.7 percent; the nonreturn rate for the same semen frozen in single ampules and stored 103 days at –79° C. was 71 percent; and the same semen frozen to –79° C. in concentrated form, thawed, and then diluted in the usual manner and shipped and used in the liquid form from 24 to 60 hours later had a nonreturn rate of 51.7 percent. This latter procedure is not practical due to the low conception rate.

Other methods of freezing semen—In recent years experiments have been successfully conducted to freeze extended semen in pellets, in plastic pipettes or in polyvinal straws. The extender for the pellets is composed of lactose, 11 percent, or raffinose, 18.5 percent, and 20 percent egg yolk, 5 to 8 percent glycerol, and antibiotics in distilled water. About 3 parts of warm extender are added to semen at 35° C. and cooled to 5° C. in about 1.5 hours. Three or four hours are provided for equilibration. About 0.1 to 0.07 ml of the extended semen containing 12 to 30 million spermatozoa is put directly in depressions made in a block of dry ice for 5 minutes to freeze. Then the pellets are transferred to storage tubes or placed in tin foil and put directly into liquid nitrogen. The pellet is thawed just before use in 1 ml of 3.2 percent sterile sodium citrate solution at 35° C. Milk extenders may also be used. Rarely upon thawing of the frozen pellet of semen, the sperm cells exhibited a reverse motion in a continuous circle, a sperm reversal phenomenon. This was found to be caused by the egg yolk and a change in the source of eggs corrected the problem, Milk Marketing Board 1967–1968.

With the polyvinyl straws and plastic pipettes, extended semen of the proper amount and concentration of sperm cells is drawn in and they are sealed at both ends and frozen rapidly in liquid nitrogen vapor and stored in liquid nitrogen. At the time of use they are placed in a suitable instrument and inserted into the cow's cervix. Thawing takes place rapidly and a plunger forces all of the semen out of the pipette or the straw, L'Aigle.

The advantages of such techniques are: the obvious savings in cost, a simplified technique, and the packaging of smaller amounts, 1/4 and 1/2 ml, of more concentrated semen. The fertility of the semen, even with bulls whose semen freezes poorly in ampules, is as good or better than semen frozen in ampules. At present these methods lack automation and are slightly cumbersome. Sanitation is questionable and contamination in the liquid nitrogen is possible with pellets of semen. Identification methods for the semen are poor. More study and research are required before these techniques for freezing concentrated extended semen in pellet form or in pipettes or straws come into widespread use, Adler, Nogase et al., Graham, Stewart, and the Milk Marketing Board Report.

Antibiotics added to semen to be used in the liquid or frozen form has only very limited value against most pathogenic organisms often present in the semen. As mentioned previously penicillin and streptomycin at levels of 500 to 1000 units and 500 to 1000 micrograms per ml. of liquid semen extended 1:25 or more times and stored for 6 hours before use controls **V. fetus** present in the sheath and semen of bulls. McEntee et al. reported that semen from infected bulls when treated with penicillin and streptomycin, extended, frozen in the usual manner and stored for one week before use was unable to produce infection in susceptible cows. Elliott and coworkers reported later on the addition of polymyxin B sulfate at a level of 500 units per ml of extended semen along with 500 units of penicillin and 2000 micrograms of streptomycin to control **V. fetus** in the semen. The extended semen was incubated at 37° C. for 30 minutes before cooling and freezing. After a review of the literature on **Trichomonas fetus,** Maule concluded that there is little doubt that this cause of venereal disease in cattle can remain viable and infective especially in liquid extended semen and in deep frozen semen containing antibiotics but that the chances of survival of the organism are markedly reduced in semen containing glycerol and experiencing a long equilibration period before freezing. McPherson and Fish and others have shown that organisms such as **Br. abortus, Listeria monocytogenes, C. pyogenes, L. pomona** and other such organisms are not affected by the antibiotics at levels that can be used in either liquid or frozen semen. Of course the viral agents of disease that may be in semen such as IBR-IPV and others are not affected by anitbiotics added to the semen. For this reason and because a human error might occur in adding antibiotics and processing semen, it is imperative that bull studs maintain bulls free of brucellosis, tuberculosis, trichomoniasis, leptospirosis, seminal vesiculitis and ampullitis, and use modern techniques to eliminate vibriosis, Lein et al. and Adler and Lindegaarde, and virus diseases such as IBR-IPV, foot and mouth disease and other viral infections. For the individual owner of purebred bulls, used both naturally and artificially, and employing custom-freezing and for persons using such semen, the problems of disease control are complex and difficult to overcome even with highly competent veterinary and laboratory service.

Freeze drying of bovine spermatozoa, as is employed extensively for the storage of bacteria at room temperature, has been attempted by a number of workers but without reproducible success, Maule, Meryman and Kafig (1959), (1963).

Shipping and Handling Semen

Shipping liquid semen can readily be accomplished for short distances by bus, train, or car and occasionally by air. In artificial insemination centers supplying many inseminators, the vials of liquid semen are wrapped in paper and placed in single or doubled-insulated paper bags along with a one-pound can of solid ice, or a heavy rubber balloon containing this amount of ice which has also been wrapped in paper or placed in a paper bag. The wrapping paper around the vials and ice container absorbs moisture, protects the vials from breaking, and keeps them from assuming too close contact with the ice. The insultated bag containing the ice and semen vials is placed a a well-insulated carton, labeled, and shipped. This package will usually maintain a temperature of about 40° F. for about 36 hours. If the time in transit is to be 2 or 3 days, the semen vial may be placed in a thermos jug containing ice, precautions being taken so that the semen vial is separated from direct contact with the ice and is watertight; and the thermos jug is packed in a refrigerated container such as a small, jacketed, insulated ice cream shipper, Swanson and Herman.

The inseminator should examine the semen to see if the spermatozoa are viable when he receives the shipment especially if the ice has completely melted. The semen should be carefully maintained at about 5° C. or 35° to 40° F., until it is drawn into the pipette for use. This is accomplished by the use of portable thermos jugs or by especially-designed cases with a built-in or insulated compartment for carrying refrigerated semen samples. Semen extended in egg yolk citrate or boiled milk diluters should be used as soon as possible after collection and after a 6-hour storage period necessary for the antibiotics to destroy any vibrio organisms. About 80 to 90 percent of the liquid semen from large artificial insemination centers, is used in 24 to 48 hours after collection. Although most diluted semen maintains satisfactory fertility rates for 3 and possible 4 days, it should not be used after that time even though conceptions may occur up to 6 days. Conception rates will usually be low if 4- to 6-day-old semen is used.

Most fertility problems with frozen semen from well-managed AI studs is due to improper handling of the frozen semen. With frozen semen it is essential that once the ampules have been placed in alcohol in dry ice containers or, as is more commonly done at present, in liquid nitrogen containers, that the temperature be held constant at –79° C. or –196° C., respectively. The level of the liquid nitrogen in the storage tank should not be allowed to get low. Slight fluctuations in temperature particularly in dry ice refrigeration can be harmful to sperm cell survival. Once frozen semen has been thawed it may not be refrozen without losing its fertilizing capacity. When the ampule is removed from the alcohol and dry ice or from the top of the cane stored in liquid nitrogen it should be done promptly and the cane quickly replaced in the liquid nitrogen. The number and length of "exposures" should be kept to a minimum. The ampule should be placed promptly, within 3 to 5 seconds, in about an ounce of ice water to thaw. A few workers reported that thawing in either ice water or 5° C., water at room temperature or 20° C., or at body temperature of 38° to 40° C. gave equally satisfactory fertility results, Maule and Pickett and coworkers. About 8 to 10 minutes should be allowed for thawing of the ampule. No more than a few ampules should be thawed at one time and any ampule thawed for more than 10 to 30 minutes should probably be discarded since the sperm cells are probably infertile. The ampules should not be allowed to freeze together or to a cube of ice. The ampule should be dryed and set upright while withdrawing the semen, Pickett. Insemination should immediately follow the thawing of the ampule.

If it is desired to assess semen quality after thawing, this is done by examination of thin semen smears at body temperature to determine the motility of the spermatozoa. It should be remembered that in most fertile, thawed semen about 50 to 70 percent of the sperm cells will be dead or immotile due to the high "kill rate" caused by the freezing process. Vital staining and determination of the live/dead ratio of spermatozoa is not satisfactory in semen containing glycerol, Maule. MacPherson pointed out that basing fertility on the degree of motility seen in samples after thawing can be quite misleading. As long as the samples reveal living spermatozoa the results of services or familiarity with the appearence of a certain bull's sample are highly important, MacPherson.

In countries or areas where liquid nitrogen is available, several manufacturers* provide excellent insulated tanks at a cost of $300 to $500 to carry 500 or more ampules. Smaller tanks are used for shipping frozen semen. These tanks only require refilling with liquid nitrogen every 2 to 4 weeks depending on their size and frequency of use. Thus semen may be shipped long distances by air or other means of transportation over a period of several days.

Since semen is a living biological product and could carry such diseases as foot and mouth disease and other cattle diseases. Rasbeck and Terpstra, Bartlett and Larsen, health regulations have been established in certain states and in most countries regarding the importation of semen. For those desiring to import or export semen, information and permission should be requested from

*Cryogenic Engineering Comp., 4595 Bannock St., Denver, Colo. (80216), Linde Comp., Division of Union Carbide Comp., 270 Park Ave., N.Y.C. (10017), Minnesota Valley Engineering, Inc., New Prague, Minn. (56071).

either the Animal Inspection and Quarantine Division, Agricultural Research Service, U.S. Department of Agriculture, Washington 25, D.C. or from the Federal or State Veterinarian located in each state. Each semen shipment should be accompanied by the proper official health charts to comply with the regulations of the country or state of its destination. Semen shipped intrastate usually has no restrictions placed on it unless the herd is under quarentine for an infectious disease.

Insemination of the cow should take place during the period from the middle to the end of estrum, about 6 to 24 hours before ovulation, as discussed in Chapter XIV, Bearden and Hansel, Trimberger and Davis. Cows seen in estrum in the morning should be bred that day while those showing estrum later in the day should be bred the next morning. Schindler et al. reported that when no inseminations were provided by technicians on Sundays or holidays, conception rates on the following day was 52 percent compared to the average of all inseminations of 56 percent. About 25 percent of post-holiday inseminations were done later than normal and in this group the conception rate was only 53 percent. Brands et al. have shown that Sunday inseminations may be eliminated if cows are bred through Saturday evening and cows in estrum on Sunday are given priority for Monday morning breeding. No decline in conception rates was observed if semen of good quality was used. Larson and Bayley and Autrup and Rasbech reported conception rates of about 25 percent in cows inseminated 36 to 48 hours after the end of estrus and showing post-estrous bleeding. Some of these cows may have had delayed ovulations. There is no need to inseminate cows twice in an estrous period unless delayed ovulation is a problem. Bovine spermatzoa survive about 30 hours and possibly as long as 56 hours in the cow's genital tract, Maule. Fairly satisfactory conception rates may occur if the cow is bred before 6 hours after the end of estrum, but from then on conception rates drop rapidly. The prompt breeding of cows at the proper time requires the close, twice- or thrice-daily observation of the cows by the farmer or herdsman and prompt notification of the inseminator or AI technician so that insemination can be provided at the proper time.

For reasons of convenience and to improve conception rates, or if technicians aren't available, some large herd owners or herdsmen after receiving proper training maintain a supply of frozen semen on the farm and inseminate their own cows. Semen should be deposited into the cervix. VanDemark cited references to indicate that a 40 percent lower conception rate occurred when semen was placed in the vagina. For producing conceptions, 0.2 ml of semen in the cervix is as effective as placing 4 ml in the vagina. Insemination in the cow is accomplished usually by one or two methods as follows:

The first, and older, method, now generally obsolete, is to use a vaginal speculum after cleansing the external genitals of the cow. With the aid of a light, a long inseminating pipette is introduced and the semen deposited into the external os of the cervix. This is fairly satisfactory but requires the frequent cleaning and disinfection of the speculum or the use of a different speculum on each cow; the latter is preferable for disease control. In some cows it is impossible to introduce the semen into the cervical lumen and it is therefore deposited on the external os of the cervix. According to Gilmore and VanDemark this resulted in a 5- to 10-percent lowering of the conception rate.

At the present time nearly all cows are being inseminated by the operator inserting one hand and arm encased in a rubber or plastic glove and sleeve into the rectum and grasping the cervix. The vulva and vulvar lips are carefully wiped or, if necessary, washed and then wiped dry with cotton or a paper towel, precautions being taken to make certain that no feces are wiped between the vulvar lips. An inseminating pipette is inserted through the vulva and vagina and into the external os of the cervix. If folds of the vaginal wall interfere, the cervix is pulled or pushed forward to straighten the lumen of the vagina. If the external os is hard to locate, the cervix may be held by the fingers and the thumb placed over the external os; the pipette is manipulated to strike the thumb and then into the cervix. By a combination of gently inserting the pipette and working the cervix over the pipette, it is usually readily passed one-half to two-thirds of the distance through the cervix, or into the uterine body on first services, where the semen should be deposited slowly over a period of about 5 seconds.

One ml of diluted semen is usually the standard amount of semen inseminated; more may be used but is not necessary. If the numbers of actively motile spermatozoa are high enough, 1/2 ml or less is satisfactory but these amounts are presently difficult to measure and handle.

The inseminating equipment consists of a disposable 16 inch, 40 cm, plastic pipette with a 6 mm outside diameter and 1 mm inside diameter. Pipettes should be kept cool and not used if above 110° F.. Semen is drawn into this pipette by a disposable small plastic bulb that fits over the end of the pipette. Before the semen is withdrawn in a single column, one or two ml of air should be drawn into the pipette. This aids in the complete expulsion of the semen in the cow.

There has been general acceptance of VanDemark's, Tanabe's, and Maule's conclusions that in cows, cervical deposition of semen is better than intrauterine deposition. MacPherson has recently reported that better conception rates of 73.5 percent and 68.2 percent were obtained by deep cervical or uterine body deposition of semen 8 cm and 12 cm, respectively, from the external cervical os than shallow cervical deposition 4 cm from the external os resulting in a 63.1 percent conception rate. Most technicians tend to inseminate too deeply. Pickett cited a study of 36 experienced technicians where cows to be slaughtered were inseminated with a small amount of dye; only 42 percent of the inseminations were in the anterior cervix or body of the uterus, 42 percent were in the right horn and 4.4, 7, and 3 percent were in the left horn, posterior cervix and anterior vagina, respectively. Although there was no significant difference in the conception rates between the cervical or uterine body deposition of semen, there are several disadvantages to deposition in the latter site. Intrauterine insemination could result in endometritis and a shortened cycle. (Chapter XIV). If insemination occurred during the luteal phase of the cycle it could cause pyometra. Furthermore if non-motile organisms such as **Br. abortus** are placed in the cervix they do not readily become established in the uterus, Manthei et al.. The endometrium of the uterus may be injured by the pipette causing an abscess of the uterine wall. The intrauterine deposition of semen could result in abortion, pyometra, or maceration of the fetus in pregnant cows. About 3 to 6 percent of pregnant cows, especially the first three months of pregnancy, show estrus, Maule. Lastly, intracervical deposition of semen is more easily and quickly accomplished than is intrauterine deposition. If semen is deposited into the uterus on first service it should be placed in the body or in both horns, or the ovaries should be examined to detect the location of the mature follicle and semen placed in the corresponding horn. This latter procedure requires great care not to rupture the follicle manually as this is usually followed by a failure to conceive. Most inseminators require about 2 to 3 months to become adept at inseminating cows. There is a significant difference between technicians and their insemination results. Conception rates may vary from 15 to 20 percent between technicians depending on their attitudes, methods of handling the cow, timeliness of insemination, care of handling semen, their techniques of insemination and the method of record keeping, Pickett.

Traumatization of the cervix is unnecessary and dangerous. If the pipette will not pass readily into the cervix due to its small size in virgin heifers or due to pathologic lesions or defects, the operator should make certain that the animal is in estrum, and, especially if it is a heifer, the semen should be deposited as far into the cervix as the tube can be gently or readily passed. In such instances it is probably desirable to use larger amounts of semen as some may be lost into the vagina. Using a pipette of smaller diameter might be helpful. Maule cited several authors in reporting that it was possible to insert a sharp pipette or needle through the vaginal wall into the uterine lumen or piercing the vaginal wall and depositing egg yolk citrate buffered semen in the region of the ovary containing the maturing follicle and thus bypassing a stenotic cervix. Conception was obtained in a number of heifers by these operations. This is rarely necessary. Complete obstruction of the cervix or uterine horn is characterized by mucometra. Olds and Seath reported that penetration of the cervix with a pipette was not possible in 1.1 percent of 11,112 cows and 11.7 percent of 1,711 heifers but conception on A.I. service occurred in 36.5 percent and 54 percent of these animals, respectively. Munro reported cervical constriction in only 0.1 percent of 16,238 cattle inseminated. After the injection of an estrogen, dilation of a stenotic cervix occurred in 11 of 15 young cattle.

Olds and Seath reported that newly-established local associations hiring an inexperienced inseminator usually had lower 60- to 90-day non-return rates of 49 to 60 percent on first service than established locals hiring experienced inseminators with 65 to 68 percent non-return rates. This lower non-return rate usually lasted 1 to 4 months or until the farmers gained experience in detecting estrum early and the inseminator gained experience and skill in inseminating cows.

In most artificial insemination associations records are kept on computer equipment of all inseminations from each ejaculate of each bull. Conceptions are considered to have resulted from an insemination if no further inseminations are requested for 28 to 35 or 60 to 90 days. These are spoken of as 28 to 35 or 60 to 90 day non-return rates; the latter figure is the most accurate. At present most 60 to 90 day non-return rates in various studs are about 65 to 72 percent. When supposed pregnancies or conceptions are confirmed by careful rectal examination and records of calving these non-return rates at 60 to 90 days are about 5.5 to 6 percent too high. About 1.5 to 2 percent of calves are lost from 90 days to term, Barrett et al. and McSparrin and Patrick. Twenty eight to 35 day non-return rates are about 10 to 15 percent higher than actual pregnancies at 60 to 90 days. Foote cited Andersen that 60 to 90 day non-return rates and conception rates on over 1 million cows were 68 percent and 60 percent, respectively.

For good conception rates in herds bred artificially close cooperation and consultation is necessary between a competent veterinarian, a good herdsman, owner or manager, and the A.I. technician. The herd should be placed on a routine reproductive examination program accompanied by good records that are reviewed periodically. Regular prebreeding or postpartum examinations of cows, pregnancy examinations, twice daily careful heat checks and records, prompt treatment of reproductive abnormalities of the estrous cycle and genital tract, and insemination of cows at the proper time of estrum with highly fertile semen are all important parts of a complete reproductive health program.

Artificial insemination in range beef cattle if it is to be successful requires excellent management and the following of practices of which many ranchers are unaccustomed. Cattle in the herd are usually bred artificially with frozen semen for a period of 24 days, one estrus period, or preferably 45 days, two estrus periods, with semen from a proven beef bull. The technician must be experienced. The cows or heifers to be bred must be placed in a fairly level lush pasture area free of bushes and trees and gullys so cows in estrus can be easily observed. Cows must be well fed. Heifers nursing calves may require added grain or forage so that estrus will occur regularly. At least 3 pens large enough to hold 5 percent of the herd in each pen should be built near the water supply or where cattle are accustomed to feed. Connected to these pens should be a chute to hold 6 to 8 cows with a step-in gate to allow the technician access to the cows. Well-trained and experienced ranch hands who will handle cattle quietly should examine the herd carefully early in the morning when the cows first move about and possibly later after their initial grazing period to detect cows in estrus. One rider can usually observe about 200 cows in a good pasture arrangement. During the middle of the day beef cows are usually rather inactive. The cows are again closely checked in the evening.

Beef cows in estrus are much more quiet than dairy cows and ranch hands should observe that cows in heat tend to group together, may be nervous and walk around, tails may be slightly elevated, and mucus may be present at the vulva which may be edematous. They tend to stand behind other cows. Mounting in beef cows is much less frequent than in dairy cattle so it is harder to note cows standing to be ridden. Often the periods of estrus in the southern states and in Brahman or Zebu cattle are shorter than the estrous periods in the English beef breeds in the more northern states. Cows in estrum should be hazed slowly into the corral and holding pens for breeding. Cows must be identified and records maintained of the dates of service and the bull used. Long hard hours plus careful attention to details are highly important for good conception rates in beef cattle.

The use of "teaser" or vasectomized bulls has not generally been very satisfactory although some ranchers have reported success with them. Some use young 3- to 5-month-old beef bull calves; others use vasectomized bulls; while others use bulls with the penis sutured to the body wall just cranial to the scrotum with stainless steel sutures, Belling; others operate on the preputial orifice to direct the extended penis laterally; while others have surgically removed the tails of the epididymides on both testes as a substitute for vasectomy. These bulls should not be allowed to run continually with the herd but should be turned out in the morning and confined away from the cows in the evening. Some ranchers use commercial "heat detector" patches that may be glued to the sacrum. If the cow is mounted by another cow a dye is released that can be easily observed. After two inseminations about 80 to 85 percent of the cows should be pregnant and one "clean up" bull for every 100 head should be turned in to breed the remaining unbred cows.

Estrus synchronization in range beef cows and heifers and dairy heifers is still rather experimental. It requires excellent management of the herd and ideal facilities to be successful. The only approved product at present is "Repromix" produced by the Upjohn Comp. (This company has another synthetic progesterone compound "M.G.A. 100" that is nearing approval by the federal authorities as are the products of several other companies). A 30-day premedication feeding period is followed by an 18-day period of medication feeding. It has proven a problem to get all cows to eat sufficient of this feed which must have the active ingredient thoroughly mixed into it. After the cessation of the medicated feed the cows come into estrum over a period of 4 to 5 days. Those failing to conceive came into estrus over a period of 5 to 7 days on their second estrus. These long periods cause difficult management and insemination problems. Furthermore there is about a 10 percent reduction in conception on the first estrus after the drug is withdrawn. Further work and improved products may greatly improve estrus synchronization in the future so it can be applied in a practical manner to range cattle to help in concentrating calving dates of a herd, Bartlett.

Artificial insemination organizations. Artificial insemination in cattle is mainly being promoted by two groups in the United States: the purebred breeder and the large central breeding unit which may or may not be a cooperative but maintains and supplies technicians who provide the sales and service for the semen processed in these large central units. Semen is shipped from these centrally located breeding units to the technician, or inseminator, who has been trained at a college or a central unit. This inseminator can usually inseminate 2,000 to

2,500 or more cows a year, depending upon the size of his territory. Most organizations base their charges for services on a per ampule cost or on a per cow inseminated cost. In the latter instance the cost to the farmer includes up to three services per cow should more than one service be needed for conception. These charges vary from $6 to $10 per cow for routine insemination services.

At large bull studs complete, uniform and regular health tests and procedures can be carried out under the supervision of a competent veterinarian. The National Association of Artificial Breeders in the U.S. has adopted a Health Code of Minimum Standards (See References, Bartlett, and Dreher) that requires the following negative tests: tuberculosis, once or twice annually; brucellosis, blood tests and semen plasma tests twice annually; trichomoniasis, twice annually; and leptospirosis, twice annually. All bulls should be tested before coming from the farm to the stud; and should be placed in isolation for 4 to 8 weeks on arrival and retested. If the bull is of breeding age six negative sheath tests for trichomoniasis are requested. For vibriosis control all studs must add the proper amounts of penicillin and dihydrostreptomycin to the extended semen, and vibriosis should be eliminated from the stud since practical methods have been devised, Lein et al.. All AI studs in Sweden and Denmark are free of vibriosis. If a bull develops a blood titer for leptospirosis he should be isolated for 4 months and treated with parenteral dihyrostreptomycin and his blood titer should be stabilized before his semen is used. It is desirable that a progressive health-conscious stud should be free of IBR-IPV on the basis of the serum neutralization test. Morrow and others (See Chapter XVIII) have summarized and reported upon the diseases of bulls that are the concern of AI studs, regulatory officials, cattle farmers, and veterinarians. The purebred breeder is increasing his use of artificial insemination within his own herd to control genital disease and to be able to offer for sale semen from his valuable sires. There is an increasing demand for veterinarians to provide or advise on this type of service.

Further health requirements include general recommendations as to sanitation; investigation into the disease problems of herds of origin of newly purchased males; and investigation and action in elimination of bulls found to harbor genetic recessive defects. As newer knowledge concerning older diseases becomes available and new disease entities that might be spread by semen are reported, steps must be taken by the bull studs to incorporate and use this information to further protect the health of their valuable bulls and at the same time the herds of patrons using their semen. In the U.S. custom freezing and uncontrolled sale of semen from bulls in private small herds provides a potential for wide-spread dissemination of infectious diseases. Such bulls are seldom subject to the rigid, continuing health standards enforced in most of the large AI studs.

The local association, owning a small group of bulls used artificially on cows in a small area, has largely disappeared within the last 10 years. The large central breeding unit has assumed most of the leadership in artificial insemination since more economical use is made of the bulls; a greater number of bulls and more valuable bulls may be purchased and proven; processing and shipping semen, and research on improved and automated methods are greatly facilitated. In the large central unit well-trained men, well-equipped laboratories and other facilities are present that greatly assist in sire selection and in constant improvements in techniques and conception rates, and in the care and training of bulls. Another valuable service of the large central breeding units is the detailed recording of the fertility rates of bulls, and the collecting of data on the proof of production and the type transmitted by the bulls, so that intelligent selection of known proven sires can be made. In the large organization this makes possible the development of proven bulls and rapid improvement of the genetic makeup of cows sired by them, providing the participating members recognize the need and value of this service and cooperate with it. For further information on artificial breeding organizations the reader is referred to Perry.

Blood typing of all bulls used artificially is required by the purebred beef and dairy breed associations. There are about 70 known serum antigens in bovine blood of which about 50 are used routinely for blood typing. The combinations of blood antigens possible are so great that no two animals are similar unless they are identical twins. In questionable-parentage cases the cow's and her calf's blood are typed. Then by a check of the blood types of the two bulls in question, one of the bulls can usually be excluded. It is usually impossible on the basis of this test to state which specific mating resulted in the conception of the calf in question. Based on parentage tests, Rendel et al. reported that 20 percent of cows bred artificially to two different bulls within an eleven day period conceived on the first service, while only 1 percent of cows bred to two different bulls at an 18 to 24 day interval conceived to the first service. They suggested that parentage tests are indicated when cows are bred to different bulls on consecutive heat periods, when the intervals between service dates are less than 16 days or when the gestation length from the last service is shortened 8 to 10 days or more. Blood typing assures the accuracy of pedigrees and the maintenance of the purity of purebreds and has been an important factor in the growth and confidence in artificial insemination in cattle.

Artificial Insemination in the Horse

Although the horse was one of the first animals successfully inseminated by Ivanov on Russian stud farms early in this century, the practice has not become widespread because of difficulties in storing and shipping liquid or frozen stallion sperm as compared to the sperm of bulls; the inability until recently to successfully freeze stallion semen and most importantly the difficulty in detecting and breeding the mare at the proper stage of estrum to obtain a high conception rate. Very few of the purebred equine breed registries recognize artificial insemination, AAEP Newsletter (1968). The Thoroughbred association does not permit or recognize artificial insemination except as it immediately follows a natural service to the same stallion. The Standard Bred Association and American Quarter-Horse Association permit artificial insemination on a farm with fresh, unfrozen semen but do not permit transport of semen. Much work over a number of years will be necessary to develop artificial insemination of horses to the high level of artificial insemination of cattle if indeed it ever reaches that level because of the scattered small horse farms, and the difficulties posed by a long estrous period and in the detection of estrus. Mares do not exhibit homosexual activities during estrus as do cattle. Detection of estrus in mares is best and most easily accomplished by teasing with a stallion. Insemination of considerable numbers of horses has been reported in Russia, China, Japan and Greece. In eastern Europe artificial insemination of horses has been used to control dourine and equine infectious anemia, Maule, Perry. In the immediate future the use of frozen semen would appear most likely to be of greatest value on large commercial horse farms breeding grade horses or possibly on Standardbred or Quarterhorse horse farms where regular teasing and detection of estrum is conducted by professional horsemen. Hughes and Loy indicated that artificial insemination of horses could be used to an advantage when 2 or more mares require servicing the same day by the same stallion. It would also be advantageous in mares with severe physical problems that nearly preclude natural mating, in mares whose resistance to infection is markedly lowered, in mares that fail to exhibit behavioral estrus, and in mares in which the cervix fails to relax and dilate at estrus. Treating semen from stallions whose genital tracts harbor infections pathogenic to mares with antibiotics may also improve conception rates and reduce the chances of infecting mares.

Semen collection from stallions is most satisfactorily accomplished by the artificial vagina or the condom as described in the previous chapter. It is highly important that the penis and prepuce be thoroughly cleansed and rinsed and dryed, especially with the latter collection technique, to avoid severe contamination of the semen with smegma, debrii, bacteria, soap, water or antiseptics.

Handling, extending and storing stallion semen should be done carefully to avoid cold shock. Nishikawa recommended placing warm extender in the artificial vagina so the semen was ejaculated into it. Agitation or shaking of equine semen or extended semen should be prevented. If semen is to be used for insemination within 30 minutes to 1 hour after collection then the semen should be kept in the dark, at near body temperature in a water bath. If a viscid gelatinous material is present in the ejaculate it may be removed with a glass rod after tipping the semen container or by pouring the ejaculate through a couple of thicknesses of cheesecloth or through an inline milk filter with one end sewn to make a pouch, Rajamannan.

Undiluted equine semen kept at room or body temperature usually loses its motility within 8 hours after collection, MacLeod and McGee, Maule. By proper dilution or extension usually at a rate of 1:1 to 1:8, 1:3 or 1:4 was most common, equine semen will remain fertile for 24 to 72 hours and longer if cooled gradually and held at refrigerator temperature. Immediately after collection warm extender should be mixed with semen at a rate of 1:1. Slow cooling should occur in a refrigerator over a period of 90 minutes to 4 to 5° C. or about 40° F., If a greater amount of extender is added it should be added at the same temperature as the cooled semen. The semen should be kept cooled until use. At present insemination is practical with semen stored at 5° C. in the liquid form for up to 96 hours. Hughes and Loy reported that 67.4 percent of 218 mares bred by artificial insemination concieved; while 78.9 percent of 199 mares handled similarly concieved by natural service. If mares that had been barren for several years were eliminated from these figures the conception rates were similar and closely comparable. Twenty-seven or 73 percent of 37 mares concieved when bred artificially with semen extended in a cream-gelatin extender and stored at 0 to 5° C. for 24 to 96 hours.

Equine semen extenders—Horse semen, as noted in the previous chapter, is high in electrolytes and low in sugar; and sperm cells survive only a relatively few hours in the seminal plasma. Most recommended extenders that have proven satisfactory have generally supplied sugar and other protective substances. Some recommended extenders for equine liquid semen include:

(1) Sterilized skim milk or sterilized mare's milk prepared in a manner similar to bovine sterilized skim

milk extender by heating in a double boiler to 96° C. for 5 to 10 minutes, Chacalof, Vlachos.

(2) Distilled water or sterilized skim milk 100 ml, to which 7 gms of glucose and 0.8 gms of egg yolk has been added, Bielanski.

(3) 5 percent reconstituted buttermilk in a 5 percent glucose solution, Berry and Gazder. No fertility trials have been conducted with this extender.

(4) Homogenized sterilized, 9 percent, cream, 400 ml, to which one-half ounce of plain gelatin in 40 ml of water heated to 145° F. was added with gentle stirring while both were warm to prevent the lumping of the gelatin. Penicillin 1000 I.U. and 1000 micrograms of streptomycin per ml were added. This extender could be frozen and stored for several weeks or more, Rasbech.

(5) Dried skim milk and isotonic glucose is satisfactory and easy to prepare if semen is to be used within 4 hours. For storage of semen beyond 4 hours it should be extended in Tris, egg yolk, glucose and glycerol and cooled and held at 5° C., Cranwell et al..

(6) Other diluents or extenders have been recommended or reported upon by Nishikawa (Baken I and II) and by Maule, Hughes and Loy, Cole and Cupps, and Rowson citing Russian workers.

(7) Hughes and Loy used a boiled skim milk diluter (see(1)) for extending semen and inseminating mares up to 24 hours after collection. For storing semen from 24 to 96 hours they used an extender similar to (4) in which half and half cream was heated to 95° C. in a double boiler for 2 to 4 minutes. The scum was removed and the hot cream was added to 1.3 gm of Knox gelatin which had been autoclaved with 10 ml of distilled water, to a final volume of 100 ml. After cooling these two extenders 1000 units of crystalline penicillin, 1 mg of dihydrostreptomycin and 200 units of Polymyxin B sulfate were added per ml. of diluter. These diluters could be made up in advance and stored frozen in a freezer.

Very few comparative fertility studies on extenders for horse semen have been reported.

Freezing of horse semen was first reported by Barker and Gandier who froze epididymal spermatozoa in a sterilized milk, with 10 percent glycerol, extender. One mare, of seven bred, conceived with frozen semen stored for 30 days. In 1963 Buell reported on a technique of layering equine semen over an extender of sterilized skim milk containing glucose, fructose and egg yolk and centrifuging at 1200 rpm for 7 minutes at 30° C. and pouring off the supernatant seminal plasma after 95 percent of the sperm cells had been spun into the extender. Further extender was added and the extended semen was cooled to 40° C. when equal parts of 20 percent glycerol in more extender was added slowly over a period of one hour. The semen was poured into 10 ml. vials, equilibrated for 5 hours and then frozen. Two of 11 mares inseminated with the frozen semen conceived. Polge and Minotakis reported on a similar technique that resulted in about 70 percent recovery of motility after freezing but no fertility trials were conducted. The extender was composed of 4.5 percent glucose, 3.75 percent egg yolk and 7.5 percent glycerol. The semen was centrifuged at 4° C. in a refrigerated centrifuge to concentrate the spermatozoa. In 1966 a private company reported on the successful freezing of horse semen and good conception rates in 37 mares. Details of the freezing process or the fertility trial were not revealed. Promising active work on freezing horse semen and fertility trials with frozen semen was done by Rajamannan at Cornell in 1967 and 1968 and is presently being done there and at Colorado State Universities by Pickett and coworkers, and at American Breeders Service in Wisconsin.

Rajamannan reported that, for horse semen with a low concentration of 30 to 200 million sperm cells per ml, it was necessary to add to the raw semen 20 percent of its volume of 5.6 percent glucose solution and centrifuge for 3 minutes at 3000 R.P.M. in a clincial centrifuge. The supernatant fluid was discarded. If the horse semen was concentrated to 250 to 600 million per ml either on delivery or by fractionation of the ejaculate at the time of collection then centrifuging was not necessary. The semen at body temperature was extended at least 10 times with one of two simple extenders also at body temperature so that 20 million sperm cells were in each ml of extended semen. These two simple extenders were (1) 15 ml of sterilized skim milk, 4.5 gm of glucose, and 4 ml of glycerol, or (2) 10 ml of fresh egg yolk, 4.8 gm of glucose and 4 ml of glycerol both extenders made up to 100 ml with distilled water and containing 500 I.V. of crystalline penicillin G. and 500 micrograms of dihydrostreptomycin per ml. Ten ml glass ampules were filled with extended semen and sealed. The vials of semen were frozen in liquid nitrogen vapor within 15 minutes as described by Rajamannan (Aug. 1966) for freezing bull semen. On rethawing after freezing by placing the ampule in a large amount of warm water at 30° C., about 50 to 75 percent of the sperm cells regained motility. In preliminary fertility trials with semen stored a month or two up to one year a few conceptions have been obtained. He found that semen collected during the winter or non-breeding months would not withstand slow cooling and then freezing as well as semen collected during the late spring or summer months. Bader and Mahler froze 36 equine ejaculates using the pelleting technique and stored the pellets in liquid nitrogen for 1 to 14 months. On thawing these pellets in sterile milk at 40° C. about 50 percent of the spermatozoa were actively motile. Of 21 mares inseminated with this frozen semen 10 conceived, 9 failed to conceive and the result in two mares was unknown. Sullivan and Larson reported that in the first year field trials of artificial insemination in mares with frozen semen by the American Breeders Service Inc., 200 mares with complete records were inseminated during one estrus and of these only 45 were inseminated a second time during a second estrus. Alternate day inseminations were performed on nearly all mares. Forty one foals were born for a foaling rate of 20 percent. These results are quite encouraging and warrant continued trials and studies to improve the results of breeding mares with frozen semen.

Insemination of mares. Berliner, Day, Cole and Cupps and Almquist reported from breeding experiments that each insemination should introduce about one to two billion living spermatozoa into the uterus. The amount of semen or extended semen used at each insemination should be 10 to 50 ml depending upon the size of the mare. At least 10 ml of undiluted semen should be used since smaller amounts such as 5 ml resulted in lower conception rates, Patterson. Apparently the mare is similar to the sow and dog as large amounts of semen or extended semen are required in the uterus for good fertility. Insemination at present is most commonly performed on Standardbred and Quarter horse farms using undiluted semen. This technique provides a means of servicing four or five estrous mares a day to a single stallion thus greatly extending his usefulness. It is helpful, before collecting semen by the artificial vagina or condom, to allow the stallion to tease several mares to increase the volume and concentration of the ejaculate.

The mare should be in estrum before insemination is attempted. Insemination is performed on the second to fourth day, and if the mare is still in estrum on the fifth or sixth day, insemination should be performed again. If the stallion semen is of good quality and fertile, insemination need only be performed every 48 to 72 hours, since spermatozoa retain their fertilizing capacity for up to 4 to 6 days in the mare, Burkhardt. By careful teasing, speculum examination of the cervix or rectal palpation of the follicle on the ovary and the cervix, insemination may often be performed 12 to 24 hours before ovulation. Hughes and Loy summarized reported data that indicated that conception rates increased in mares bred from 48 hours to within 6 hours before ovulation but declined in mares during ovulation and decreased markedly in mares bred 2 to 10 hours after ovulation. A few mares may concieve if bred or inseminated 6 to 14 hours after ovulation. There is less danger of introducing infection if insemination is performed only once, and at the most twice, during an estrum. The administration of 2000 I.U. of chorionic gonadotropin parenterally at the time of the first service usually results in ovulation in the estrous mare within 48 hours thus making a second insemination unnecessary.

The mare should be suitably restrained. After bandaging the mare's tail with sterile gauze or a bandage, the buttocks, perineal region, and external genitalia are thoroughly scrubbed with soap and water, wiped, and rinsed with clear water. Then the semen may be introduced through the cervix in a 1/2- ounce or 1-ounce gelatin capsule. This is done by the hand encased in a sterile plastic disposable glove and sleeve. The upper portion of the arm is lubricated with a water-soluble, non-spermicidal, lubricating jelly. Introduction of the capsule should be done rapidly, to prevent the capsule from softening or dissolving before it is passed through the cervix. If possible, air should be prevented from entering the vagina on withdrawal of the arm.

However, most mares are presently inseminated with a 14 to 16 inch or 35 to 40 cm bovine plastic disposable insemination or uterine infusion pipette attached to a sterile 20 to 40 ml glass or plastic syringe. The tip of the pipette is guided alongside the index finger into and through the cervix of the mare, which is normally relaxed at estrus. The semen or extended semen is deposited into the body of the uterus. A vaginal speculum and a syringe attached to a long catheter or plastic pipette may be used to inseminate mares but occasionally difficulty is encountered in passing the pipette through the cervix. The cervix and uterus may be injured if too much force is used to insert the pipette or if the mare suddenly moves. Since insemination takes place directly into the uterus, great care is essential to insure a clean source of semen and as sanitary a technique of insemination as possible to prevent genital infections.

If cooled liquid extended semen is shipped or transported in an iced container or thermos, the vials of semen should be filled completely to avoid excessive agitation and injury to spermatozoa.

"Impregnation" is a term used by McGee for the placing of fresh semen into the uterus of the mare by means of a capsule or inseminating pipette and syringe after its collection from a stallion as he dismounts from the same mare after a service. This has been a long-established custom, done largely because of the wishes of the owners and also to make certain that the stallion actually ejaculated as determined by microscopic examination of the dismount semen sample for the presence of spermatozoa. There is no evidence that "impregnation" is of any value and there are several good reasons for not performing this operation. MacLeod stated that it is one of the most futile things done in the breeding of horses. The last portion of the ejaculate has relatively few spermatozoa; and there is a great risk of introducing infection. McGee agreed with MacLeod but stated that there might be occasions when "capsuling" or "impregnating" might be indicated, such as a small stallion on a large mare where a "good" cover was not possible, in pneumovagina where the semen lies in the vagina due to a failure of semen to be drawn into the uterus by negative pressure, and in some few mares with vaginal or cervical scars preventing ready passage of semen through the cervix at the time of copulation. McGee concluded that the benefits from routine "impregnation" were negligible.

Artificial Insemination in Swine

Artificial insemination in swine has progressed very rapidly in the last ten years with the development of procedures that have made it practical for field use. In countries such as Russia, Japan, Norway, Holland, France, Germany, Denmark, and Sweden up to 10 to 20 percent of the swine are bred artificially. Conception rates which previously were low, below 50 percent, are now at a level of 60 to 70 percent or higher on first insemination, Melrose. This progress has been accomplished by utilizing better semen extension and storage techniques but more importantly by applying improved management and estrus-detecting procedures. In the United States there are presently only 3 A.I. swine cooperatives located in the midwest, the largest of which has inseminated 11,000 sows in a year, Day. For economic reasons, he doubts that widespread insemination of swine will develop in the U.S., as in the European countries, unless synchronization of estrus becomes practical when many sows could be inseminated within a short period of time.

The advantages and disadvantages of artificial insemination in swine are similar to those in cattle. One boar can be used on 2,000 sows per year resulting in a total of about 20,000 offspring. This stresses the need for progeny-tested proven sires in the A.I. program. If boars in artificial insemination centers are subject to strict health tests and kept in isolation, artificial insemination can be used to safely introduce new blood lines into S.P.F. herds or herds free of such diseases as virus pig pneumonia, brucellosis, tuberculosis, leptospirosis and etc.. Cross breeding in swine is more easily accomplished with artificial insemination. At present the principal disadvantage is the cost because large quantities of liquid extended semen must be carried, 50 to 100 ml per sow, and relatively few sows, about 10 to 25, can be bred per ejaculate. The storage period of extended liquid swine semen is short, 24 to 48 hours. The problem of freezing swine semen has not been solved. When boar sperm cells were stored in seminal plasma without extension the conception rates dropped from 61 percent to 39 percent in semen stored 6 hours and 54 hours, respectively, First. The inefficiencies of insemination include: scattered swine herds of small numbers of sows, the need for individual observation of sows, the inability or inexperience of the herd owner to call the technician or inseminator at the proper time in estrus, and the seasonal nature of swine breeding in the U.S. As a possible means of reducing the costs of insemination in swine some organizations are investigating the feasibility of owners inseminating their own sows when they are located near the A.I. stud, Melrose, Maule and Rowson.

Collection of semen from boars for artificial insemination is done by the use of a simple artificial vagina or by the hand grasping the penis as described in the previous chapter. Young boars are the easiest to train to mount a dummy especially if other boars have mounted the dummy previously and the urine, smegma, semen odor is present on the dummy. Occasionally young boars may require a gilt or sow in estrus for stimulation. Older boars that have been used in natural service are more difficult to train. Collections are made at 3 to 6 day intervals or 2 times per week for best results. Few boars can continue to produce satisfactory ejaculates when collected every 48 hours, Melrose, Maule, Niwa, Perry, Rolfe, Day, and etc..

Depending on his age and the other factors a boar will ejaculate 125 to 500 ml of semen. The presperm fraction, which is usually heavily contaminated with bacteria due to preputial debrii and fluid, should be discarded. Aamdal et al. described the extirpation of the preputial diverticulum to reduce the bacterial contamination of semen at the time of collection. This also reduced the boar odor. Douching of the sheath and preputial diverticulum and washing the skin around the external preputial orifice will help in reducing the large number of bacterial contaminats in boar semen such as **E. coli, Aerobacter sp., Proteus, Corynebacteria, Pseudomonas, Staphylococci,** and **Bordetella.** The gelatinous fraction should be discarded during collection or removed by straining through sterile cheese cloth. Either the sperm-rich fraction or the entire ejaculate minus the presperm and gel fractions should be used for insemination. Using great care to prevent cold shock the semen is examined for concentration, motility and morphology. Hall and First reported that the hemocytometer was more accurate than the photoelectric method for determining porcine sperm cell concentration. Most authors agreed that the numbers of actively motile spermatozoa should be about 65 to 75 percent for best fertility but the relationship between fertility and motility is an inconstant one. Fertile boars, especially those in heavy use, may have up to 20 percent or more proximal protoplasmic droplets. A high percentage of proximal protoplasmic droplets may be associated with infertility. Occasional sterile boars may have a very high percentage, over 80 percent, acrosomal defects. Although this defect is usually considered to be hereditary, Melrose indicated that it might be acquired.

Extension of boar semen is based, as in cattle, on the number of actively motilé spermatozoa required for optimum conception rates. According to a number of authors this varied from 2 to 10 billion actively motile spermatozoa per insemination. Most recommended 5 billion or more but fairly satisfactory conception rates occurred with 2 to 5 billion per insemination. Thus 10 to 20 sows may be inseminated per ejaculate. Conception rates including size of litters are also influenced by the volume of the extended semen inseminated and the length of storage time before insemination. Most authors recommend 50 to 100 ml of extended semen per insemination but a few recommended up to 200 ml for slightly better conception rates. Volumes below 50 ml gave lower conception rates.

Boar semen is usually extended 1 to 1 to 1 to 8 times, depending on the concentration of motile spermatozoa and the volume of the ejaculate, with warm extender at 37° C. or 100° F. immediately after collection. Slow cooling and the addition of phospholipids to the semen protects the sperm cell and aids survival. Dilutions greater than 1 to 5 may adversely affect sperm fertility, First. The extended semen is then cooled gradually to 12 to 20° C., 59° to 68° F., which is the optimum storage temperature for boar semen. Others cool the ejaculate slowly to 12° to 20° C. and then add the extender which is at the same temperature. When boar semen is cooled to 4° to 5° C. within 1 to 2 hours, many sperm cells lose their motility even if extenders have been added, King and MacPherson. In sperm-rich fractionated semen this harmful effect is much less pronounced. Boender reported that the addition of egg yolk or milk to boar semen prevented injury to the sperm cell at 5° C. Temperatures of 35° to 38° C. are definitely unfavorable to porcine sperm cell survival. Problems are presented in maintaining storage temperatures between 15° and 20° C. for a period of time.

Results of many experiments, summarized by Melrose, have shown that frozen boar semen is unsatisfactory even though good motility of spermatozoa may be evident after thawing. A few conceptions have been produced with frozen semen.

A wide variety of extenders are used for the extension of boar semen. Melrose (1963) recommended equal parts egg yolk and 2.9 percent sodium citrate dihydrate in distilled water, or fresh skim milk heated to 92° C. for 10 minutes, or reconstituted skim milk. Madden and Rowson used 30 percent egg yolk and 2 percent glycine in distilled water. Heated homogenized milk was used as an extender by Stratman and Self. Hall and First used an extender composed of 30 percent egg yolk and 70 percent of a solution of 42.6 gm dextrose and 21 gm sodium bicarbonate in a 1,000 ml of distilled water with antibiotics added. Other combinations of egg yolk, milk, and glucose extenders have been used, Maule. Du Buisson and coworkers and Bennett and O'Hagan reported on the use of the modified Illini Variable Temperature (carbon dioxide saturated) diluent used in cattle; it facilitated storage up to 3 days. This permits long distance shipment of boar semen at 15° to 20° C. The use of glycerol in the I.V.T. extender had a markedly inhibiting or adverse affect on conception, Neville et al.. For best results most extended boar semen is presently used within 24 to 36 hours after collection.

Most authors including Park and coworkers and Waltz and coworkers recommended the use of antibiotics to control the large number of bacteria in boar semen stored at near room temperatures. 500 to 1,000 I.U. of crystalline penicillin G. and 500 to 1,000 micrograms of dihydrostreptomycin per ml of extended semen were usually recommended. Neomycin, polymyxin B and sulfadiazine were also of value. Polge and Rowson reported improved conception rate and litter size when antibiotics were added to extended boar semen.

Detection of estrus and timing of insemination are of critical importance in obtaining good conception rates and litter size in artificial insemination of female swine. In this regard the owner's or herdsman's and inseminator's judgement, experience and skills of observation are highly important. Swelling and slight reddening of the vulva in sows and gilts persist for 2 to 3 days of proestrus, 2 to 3 days of estrus and for about 2 days of postestrus with maximum swelling generally seen at the onset of estrus. The degree of swelling of the vulva alone is unreliable. At the proper time for insemination the vulva was less swollen and more wrinkled and a clear or cream-colored flecked mucus was usually present in the lower vulvar commissure. Madden described a method to aid in heat detection consisting of approaching the female quietly, placing the flat of the hands on the loins and exerting moderate downward pressure. If the sow moved away the hands and arms were placed between the hind legs and the rear parts were lifted off the ground, simulating the action of a boar toward a sow in estrum. After a few minutes some sows will stand in a saw-horse attitude on back pressure. If possible the owner, herdsman or technician should mount the female and sit astride the loins and remove the feet from the ground. Clawing the shoulders, digital manipulation of the clitoris or inserting the insemination pipette into the vagina will induce the state of sexual receptivity if the sow is in estrus so she will stand very quietly, in fact nearly insensible to extraneous stimuli. If sows do not show the above signs of estrus, insemination should not be performed as conception rates are apt to be low due to faulty timing in relation to ovulation. Einarsson reported that sows and gilts inseminated during the period of the standing reflex indicating the peak period of estrum had conception rates of 73 and 61 percent compared to 41 and 46 percent in those sows not showing a good standing reflex. Sows and gilts should be bred without restraint. As indicated by Melrose and especially the French workers the presence of a boar is very helpful in heat detection. Both the preputial odor of the boar and his vocalizations evoke external behavioral signs of estrus in the sow that can be confirmed by Madden's procedures. A vasectomized boar may be used as an aid in detection of estrus.

Lactating sows in good physical condition upon weaning their pigs should be watched closely for estrus starting about the third day later, as most come into estrum about four to seven days after their pigs are removed. For best results in insemination of gilts they should not be bred until they have been in heat twice or more, weigh 280 pounds, or are 8 months of age.

According to Niwa and Boender the duration of estrus proper was an average of 55 hours for gilts and 70 hours for the sow. The time of ovulation was 25 to 36 hours after the onset of estrus. Spermatozoa in the sow retained their fertilizing ability up to 25 to 30 hours. The best time for insemination was considered to be 10 to 25 hours after the onset of estrus resulting in about 8 to 10 percent higher conception rates than sows bred later in heat; although about 15 percent greater conception rates were obtained with two inseminations during estrus, Einarsson. This procedure is costly and not necessary if close careful observations and tests for estrus are made.

Maule described three types of insemination catheters and techniques used for inseminating swine. One type was designed to seal the sow's cervix so no semen flows back into the vagina as the semen is infused. This type is made of rubber about 1.0 to 1.5 cm in diameter and 45 to 50 cm long. The anterior end may be tapered, end in a pear-shaped bulb, or have a corkscrew configuration, Melrose and O'Hagan, that is pressed with gentle pressure or rotated or twisted counter-clockwise into the cervix. In the latter case the catheter is not easily dislodged. Aamdal and Hogset have devised a 7 to 8 mm diameter catheter with an inflatable cuff about 4 to 5 cm posterior to the tip. The second type of pipette is designed to penetrate through the cervical canal and into the uterus. The diameter of this plastic or nylon tube with a bent tip is 4 mm. It is rotated with gentle pressure to negotiate the cervical canal. If the plastic is too stiff there is possible danger to the sow. The third type is a combination of the two types, consisting of a double plastic tube. The outer tube is 1 cm in diameter and engages in the cervix while the smaller inner catheter is rotated to the left as it is pressed forward from the larger tube. All types of insemination catheters should be inserted dorsal-cranially through the vulva to avoid entering the urethra.

Presently most containers for holding and transporting extended boar semen are plastic bottles or bags that can be attached to the insemination pipette and the large volume of extended semen squeezed gently over a period of 3 to 5 minutes into the cervix and uterus of the sow. Most workers reported that after a minute or so the semen goes into the sow very rapidly without resistance.

Miscellaneous factors. The results of artificial insemination in swine were more successful in sows than in gilts. Most workers presently report a 50 to 70 percent farrowing rate on first service using fertile semen inseminated correctly at the proper stage of estrus. Conception rates for natural service are 80 to 90 percent.

This difference is probably due to insemination at an improper time in relation to ovulation or failure to place sufficient motile spermatozoa in a large enough volume of extender into the uterus. As noted by Maule and others mentioned previously, increasing numbers of spermatozoa up to 10 billion produced greater conception rates. Self reported where 10, 20 and 50 ml of extended semen with the same numbers of spermatozoa were inseminated, 80 to 90 percent of the ova were fertilized on examination the third day post-service. But on the 25th day only 8 percent of the gilts receiving 10 and 20 ml volumes of semen were pregnant compared to 50 percent of the gilts that were inseminated with the larger volume of semen. Dzuik reported that in two groups of pigs inseminated with fresh semen and semen stored 72 hours that fertilization rates were 88 and 36 percent, respectively and at 35 days of gestation 70 percent of the group inseminated with fresh semen had embryos. Thus the volume of semen and the age of the semen apparently affects the prenatal mortality rate in swine. Boender and others have shown that litter size is largely due to the boar, with a distinct correlation between fertilizing capacity and litter size. Boars with conception rates below 65 percent on first insemination tended to produce smaller litters. Litter size was also slightly reduced when less than 2 billion spermatozoa were inseminated and when semen was stored for more than a few hours, Paredis.

Estrus and ovulation synchronization in swine has been the subject of much research in recent years because of many desirable features in swine management possible if this could be successfully employed. The only natural synchronization observed and practiced in swine is that acheived by weaning pigs from sows. Estrus usually follows weaning in 4 to 7 days. According to Madden (1959) 2 percent of sows were in heat before the fourth day, 12 percent on the fourth day, 35 percent on the fifth day, 16 percent on the sixth day, 16 percent on the seventh day, 6 percent on the eighth day and 13 percent on the ninth to fourteenth days, or 79 percent from 4 to 7 days post-weaning. Day and Paredis further noted that when young pubertal gilts are transported and placed in a new environment, estrus developed in up to 70 percent of the gilts within 5 to 10 days due to the induced stress. Early studies on hormonal control of estrus in gilts and sows with gonadotropes, estrogens and progesterone or progestational agents have not been very satisfactory, often because of the production of cystic ovaries. Within the last few years the use of I.C.I. 33828, a pituitary inhibitor called "Match" or "Aimax" has shown much promise. About 80 to 90 percent of sexually mature gilts fed 4 lbs of feed daily containing 100 mg of I.C.I. for 20 days were in estrus from 5 to 8 days after its withdrawal from the feed and at 21 days after this breeding the fertilization rate based on live embryos was 90 percent, Melrose, Day. Day reported results on preliminary work indicating that a subcutaneous injection of 1,200 I.U. of pregnant mare serum given 24 hours after I.C.I. withdrawal and a 500 I.U. intramuscular injection of human chorionic gonadotropin 3 days later resulted in ovulation about 40 hours after the last injection with good conception rates when gilts were inseminated 24 hours after the H.C.G. injection. With I.C.I., as with progestins, the second estrum is usually also synchronized to a period of about 18 to 24 days after the first. I.C.I. must yet be approved by Federal authorities before it will be commercially available. Further studies are indicated and if synchronization becomes feasible then practical management factors such as: the number of boars available for A.I. or natural service, problems of heat detection if A.I. is to be used, the size of the farrowing house, and other factors must be considered.

Artificial Insemination in Sheep and Goats

In the United States artificial insemination in sheep and goats has not generally passed from the experimental to the practical stage. Artificial insemination with frozen goat semen has been used in a few goat dairies. In Russia sheep have been artificially inseminated on a large scale for many years. In Australia, Argentina, and other countries it has been successfully practiced on large ranches. The advantages and the disadvantages of artificial insemination in sheep are much the same as in cattle. Probably the greatest disadvantages are its high cost when compared to natural service and the difficulties associated with detecting and separating estrous ewes for insemination. Successful freezing of ram semen for wide-scale insemination has not yet been accomplished.

It is very important that rams and bucks used for artificial insemination be highly fertile in order to provide the maximum number of inseminations with a high conception rate. Collection of semen by means of the artificial vagina is the preferred method. Recovery of semen from the dry vagina of the ewe or by electroejaculation does not provide as satisfactory a semen sample. In the latter method a low concentration of spermatozoa, urine contamination, the difficulty of repeated frequent collections in a short period due to refractoriness were fairly common problems. Usually a fertile ram or buck can be collected 2 to 6 times or more daily to provide an adequate number of spermatozoa. As with the bull it is highly important to prevent sudden cooling of the small volume of ejaculated semen. The semen should be immediately placed in a beaker of warm water at body temperature, 37° C. or 100° F.. Nishikawa and others also recommend adding an equal amount of warm egg yolk or milk extender immediately on collection before placing in a beaker of warm water. The latter is then placed in a refrigerator and allowed to cool slowly to about 4° C. or 38° F.. For greatest fertility ram and buck semen should be used within a few hours after cooling whether extended or not. Although fair fertility has been reported by some workers from semen stored over 24 hours after collection, it is best to use the semen within 12 hours after collection, Maule, Emmens and Robinson. They also recommended that although greater extension of ram or buck semen was possible rates of 1:1 to 1:10 were most practical to avoid a severe decline in fertility due to a rapid loss in motility.

Semen extenders for ram and buck semen are enumerated by Maule, Perry, Salamon and Robinson, and Lunca et al.. Heated skim milk; heated homogenized whole milk; egg yolk, one part, to three parts of 2.8 percen sodium citrate dihydrate solution, and egg yolk, 20 percent, anhydrous glucose, 0.8 percent, and sodium citrate dihydrate 2.8 percent in 100 ml of distilled water have all proven satisfactory as ram or buck semen extenders.

Most authors recommended from 50 to 150 million actively motile spermatozoa in a volume of 0.05 ml. to 0.2

ml extended semen introduced one-eighth to one-quarter of an inch into the cervix which is "hooded" and may be difficult for the inexperienced inseminator to locate. Normal undiluted ram semen contains about 150 million spermatozoa in 0.05 ml of semen so 0.1 to 0.05 unextended semen may be inseminated. For intravaginal insemination much larger volumes and numbers of spermatozoa, on the order of 10 times greater, were needed for good fertility. Conception rates on first service varied from 50 to 80 percent possibly due to the variation in fertility of rams. For the shipping of extended cooled liquid ram or buck semen similar procedures were followed as for liquid bull semen giving attention to avoiding excessive exposure to air, sunlight, or agitation.

Although various techniques have been tried for freezing ram semen and although the motility after thawing is usually quite good, fertility is usually low with conception rates of 0 to 30 percent, Maule, Perry and Sevinge and Henneman. Frazer described a technique consisting of extending goat semen 1 to 10 to 1 to 40 in a heated skim milk diluent containing 6 to 9 percent glycerol in a manner similar to the extension of bull semen for freezing. After 1-1/2 to 2 hours equilibration time, the semen was cooled slowly from 4° C. to 0° C. and then at a faster rate and stored at −79° C. According to Herman citing Barker and Frazer, conception rates of about 70 percent were obtained with frozen goat semen.

The most difficult problem to solve in artificial insemination of sheep is the handling of large numbers of ewes under flock conditions while still detecting and sorting for breeding the ewes that come into estrum. Rams with aprons, or vasectomized teaser rams may be turned in with the flock of ewes or led through the flock once or twice daily. Vasectomized rams remaining with the ewes can be painted on the brisket or wear jackets holding different colors of paint or chalk to mark the rump of the ewes that are in estrum. Marked ewes are sorted from the flock daily for insemination. This latter procedure has proven most satisfactory for large flocks. Ewes and does in estrum will often bleat, switch their tails rapidly, have an edematous vulva, seek out the ram or buck and stand to be mounted. Does in estrum may occasionally mount each other. Normally estrum lasts about 30 to 36 hours in the ewe and possibly a little longer in the doe. Ovulation occurs late in estrum.

Insemination should take place the last half of estrum. If insemination is to take place only once in a heat period, this should be about 12 to 18 hours after the onset of estrum. Spermatozoa survive about 30 hours in the ewe's genital tract, Maule. Insemination twice during a heat period is not practical in ewes but might be in does, Fraser. For insemination, the ewe or doe should be placed in a crate that holds her securely and makes examination and insemination easy for the operator. Insemination is accomplished by lubricating and inserting into the ewe's vagina a pyrex glass speculum about 18 cm., 7 inches long, and 2 cm., 7/8 inch, in diameter. By means of a head light, flashlight, or speculum light the cervix is located and a graduated pipette attached to a syringe is introduced into the cervix and the semen deposited. Plans and procedures for the artificial insemination of large numbers of sheep has been outlined by Perry and Maule as management is highly important for savings in labor and for good conception rates. It has been demonstrated that if artificial insemination of sheep and goats is carefully conducted during the natural breeding season the results will compare favorably with those produced by natural mating. Estrous synchronization is possible in sheep and goats as discussed in the chapter on infertility in these species, Hogue et al. and Lyngset et al.. Large numbers of rams are needed however for heat detection and for semen production. The first estrus after withdrawal of the progestational agent is usually accompanied by a reduced conception rate. This procedure reduces the length of the period of heat detection in ewes. After breeding ewes artificially on the first and second synchronized cycles, rams are usually turned into the flock to breed the ewes that failed to conceive.

Artificial Insemination in Dogs

Artificial insemination is performed most commonly in dogs for reasons that prevent or interfere with copulation. These include: shyness or fright on the part of either the male or female in the presence of their partner, lack of libido often associated with sexual inexperience in the male, and for pathological reasons including premature erection preventing intromission, Perry, phimosis due to a small preputial orifice, painful lesions such as arthritis, spinal lesions and acute prostatitis, and exhaustion especially in obese, young or old, inexperienced dogs on hot humid days. It may also be used for the control of infectious diseases such as caused by **Brucella canis,** and following the occasional shipment of liquid extended semen. Freezing of dog semen with resultant conceptions has not yet been accomplished. The American Kennel Club has not encouraged the practice of artificial insemination, but will allow it to be performed under certain restrictions and stipulations, including the issuance of an affidavit by the sire's owner certifying that he witnessed the collection of semen and the insemination by a licensed veterinarian, and another by the veterinarian certifying that he performed the collection and insemination in the presence of the sire's owner. The male and female dogs are identified and the time and place of the insemination is indicated. Relatively little experimental work has been done with artificial insemination in the dog but the techniques of semen collection and insemination are fairly simple and the procedure is often employed by veterinarians.

The favored method of semen collection is by digital manipulation of the penis, with or without the presence of a teaser bitch, to produce ejaculation, Foote, Leonard, and Kirk et al.. Semen may also be collected by means of the artificial vagina, Harrop. The latter designed a special vagina with a closed balloon in the space between the liner and casing attached to a bulb which when squeezed caused a pulsating pressure on the penis simulating the contractions of the vulva of the bitch. This artificial vagina could be used with or without a teaser bitch. In contrast to the good results reported by Harrop, Boucher et al. reported poor motility in the semen collected with the artificial vagina possibly due to overheating of the spermatozoa in the vagina. Digital manipulation is simpler and requires less equipment and produces as good or better semen samples. Dogs may be collected every other day without loss of semen quality. Good quality canine semen should have 70 to 90 percent actively motile sperm cells, less than 10 to 20 percent abnormal cells and a concentration of 90 to 300 million or more spermatozoa per ml.

Semen should be collected in a warm funnel and a 20 ml warm test tube or a 20 to 30 ml warmed syringe from which the barrel has been removed. The semen vial should be placed immediately after collection in warm water at 35° C. or 95° F. in a refrigerator to cool gradually to 5° C. if it is not to be used promptly. Undiluted semen, **in vitro,** usually survives about 20 hours, Maule. Harrop and others have shown that spermatozoa in extended semen remain viable and capable of fertilizing ova for 4 to 5 days if stored at 5° C. or 40° F. Harrop preferred heating pasteurized homogenized milk at 92° C. for 10 minutes. The albuminous scum was removed and 500 micrograms of streptomycin per ml was added. This extender was used at an extension rate of about 1 to 8, with the semen and extender both at either body temperature, room temperature or refrigerator temperature when added together to avoid cold shock. Foote (1964, 1968) reported that the best extender for canine semen was 20 percent egg yolk in a buffer solution composed of 1.45 gm of sodium citrate dihydrate, 0.93 gm of glycine, and 1.25 gm. of glucose per 100 ml of distilled water. The extension rate was 1:10 to 1:20. Each ml of buffered-egg yolk extender contained 1000 units of crystalline penicillin G. and 1 mg of dihydrostreptomycin. This extended liquid semen could be stored at 40° F. or 5° C. for 24 hours before insemination. Good motility was still present after 4 days but no fertility trials were made. Harrop and others have demonstrated that milk extended liquid semen may be shipped over long distances and produce conceptions.

Long term storage of frozen dog semen may be possible but no fertility trials have been conducted. Harrop reported that dog semen placed in 20 percent egg yolk-citrate medium containing 10 percent glycerol and equilibrated for 2 hours before being frozen slowly to −79° C. and stored for 12 months had 45 percent motility after thawing. Foote similarly reported the recovery of good motility of canine spermatozoa frozen for 30 days in liquid nitrogen in an extender containing 20 percent egg yolk, and 11 percent glycerol in a 0.2 M tris-buffered solution. The glycerol was added to the semen in the initial extender. Antibiotics at levels of 1000 U. of crystalline penicillin and 1 mg of dihydrostreptomycin per ml of extender were also added.

Insemination should be performed with undiluted or extended semen 24 to 48 hours after the onset of true estrus, that is when the bitch will accept coitus by the dog. A second insemination may possibly be given one to two days after the first. Usually at this stage the vulva is still swollen, the vulvar discharge is frequently clear instead of hemorrhagic as in proestrum, and vaginal smears reveal many cornified epithelial cells and a few red blood cells. The bitch usually ovulates by the second or third day of estrus but the ova require several days to mature and cast off the polar bodies. Spermatozoa survive 4 to 6 days or more in the female genital tract, Doak and coworkers. Conception is less likely late in estrus or early in postestrus when many leucocytes are present in the vaginal smear. Vaginal smears may be taken with a cotton swab on a six inch applicator stick, placed on a slide and stained with Wright's or some other stain.

A sterile plastic inseminating tube, or pipette, about 20 cm., 8 inches, long and 6 mm. in diameter is fixed to a glass syringe and the semen is drawn into the syringe. A bovine plastic inseminating pipette broken in half makes a good canine inseminating tube. Most bitches in true estrum stand quietly to be inseminated even though previously they may have resisted normal mating. They should be placed on a table of proper height and held by an assistant. The external genitals are washed and dried. Some veterinarians use a lubricated vaginal speculum and light to locate the cervix, and the insemination tube is placed at or into the cervix and 5 to 10 ml or more of undiluted or extended semen containing over 200 million actively motile spermatozoa should be deposited, Foote and Almquist. Most operators insert the insemination tube without a speculum. In this technique the insemination tube is inserted between the vulvar lips and directed in a dorsal direction until it passes into the vagina. It is then directed horizontally and gently pushed to or into the cervix. Frank, Harrop and other suggested that the rear parts of the bitch might be elevated for 3 to 5 minutes during or after insemination to prevent the possible loss of semen. A finger covered with a sterile finger cot may be inserted into the vagina and the dorsal wall gently stroked or "feathered". This appears to promote the passage of the semen into the uterus. Harrop has reported that insemination directly into the dog's uterus is practically impossible. Usually 60 to 80 percent conception rates are realized by artificial insemination with fertile dogs.

Artificial Insemination in Cats

Studies on the reproductive physiology and insemination of cats has been very limited because of their general economic value, and the belief that cats are difficult to handle especially during mating. Sojka et al. recently described successful procedures for the insemination of cats. Donor toms were selected on the basis of their libido and temperment when a "teaser" queen was placed in the tom's cage. Teaser queens were either normal females in estrus or ovariectomized females that had been given 12.5 mg. **Repositol** diethylstilbesterol subcutaneously every 10 days to produce estrus and acceptance. The selected toms required about 2 weeks of training by a technician to get them to ejaculate routinely into an artificial vagina.

The artificial vagina was made by cutting off the bulb end of a 2 ml rubber bulb-pipet and fitting a 3 x 44 mm test tube into the cut end of the bulb to make a water tight system. The artificial vagina is then placed in a 35 x 75 mm (60 ml) polyethylene bottle filled with water at 52° C. to maintain a temperature of 44 to 46° C. at the time of collection. The rolled end of the rubber bulb-pipet is stretched over the rim of the bottle and the opening of the vagina is sparingly lubricated with K-Y jelly. The artificial vagina is slipped over the penis of the tom as he mounts the teaser female and develops an erection. The technicians other hand is used to steady the tom and queen.

The volume of the ejaculate varies from 0.01 to 0.12 ml with an average of 0.04 ml. This may be diluted with 0.1 ml of physiological saline for a sperm cell count with hemocytometer, and a motility rating. The semen is further diluted with saline to give a sperm cell count of 50 x 10^6 spermatozoa per ml for insemination purposes. The sperm cell numbers per ml of ejaculate varied from 100 to 5,100 x 10^6 with an average of 1700 x 10^6. The total sperm numbers per ejaculate varied from 3 to 143 x 10^6 with an average of 57 x 10^6. The motility varied from 35 to 100 percent with an average of about 80 percent. Collection of the semen takes about 1 to 4 minutes with a trained tom. Sojka and coworkers demonstrated that toms could be collected 3 times a week on a regular basis or daily for short periods and maintain good semen quality.

The females to be bred by artificial insemination were checked for estrus daily by stroking them on the neck and down the back to the base of the tail and by gently rubbing the perineal region. A queen in estrus will crouch on its sternum, elevate the pelvis, raise and laterally deflect the tail, extend the hind legs, tread with the hind feet and press up against the hand when it is held over the pelvic region. Estrus was confirmed by vaginal smears which contain only large, cornified cells during the heighth of estrus. Queens in full, natural estrus were stimulated to ovulate by the intramuscular injection of 50 I.U. of HCG. The queen was also inseminated at this time by placing 0.1 ml of the saline-diluted semen containing 50 x 10^6 spermatozoa into the anterior portion of the vagina with a 20 gauge needle, 9 cm long, bulbed at the end with silver solder to make it blunt and attached to a 0.25 ml syringe. A second insemination 24 hours later resulted in a 25 percent increase in conception rate.

These authors found that all queens in estrus would ovulate 26 to 27 hours after the injection of HCG. Successful matings occurred up to 49 hours after HCG injection. The queens would accept toms up to 55 hours after the injection. Greulich and Sojka et al. reported that queens in full estrus could be stimulated to ovulate by probing the cervix with a glass rod. This and the act of artificial insemination would, at the time the rod or pipette contacted the cervix, often result in a characteristic yowl followed immediately by an attempt to lick the perineal region. Thus the spines on the penis are probably not the cause for this postcoital reaction in the female.

Conception did not occur in queens inseminated with less than 1.25 million spermatozoa. Conception rates were 50 percent or better with 5 to 50 million spermatozoa per insemination. In the insemination experiments performed by Sojka and his coworkers the gestation periods ranged from 65 to 72 days which is nearly a week longer than the 56 to 63 day period that follows natural matings. This should receive further study. Thus by artificial insemination outstanding toms could be used to breed 12 to 15 queens per week, or 8 to 10 queens per ejaculate, compared to natural matings conditions where one tom per 15 to 30 females is usually kept.

The same group, Hammer et al., further demonstrated that in the cat no eggs were fertilized by freshly ejaculated semen but spermatozoa became capacitated and capable of fertilizing feline ova after 2 to 24 hours in the uterus of a queen in estrus.

Artificial insemination has also been performed in chickens, turkeys and laboratory and fur-bearing animals, Perry, Frank, Nishikawa.

Transplantation of Fertilized Ova

Transplantation of fertilized ova has been performed on laboratory animals for nearly 70 years, Rice and Andrews. Many experiments and attempts in recent years to apply this knowledge to farm animals have not yet resulted in practical procedures for ova transplantation. However, valuable information on the physiology of reproduction has been gained. Successful experimental transfer of fertilized ova by surgical means has been accomplished in sheep, goats, cattle and swine, Hafez, Hafez and Blandau. Through artificial insemination the desirable genes in males can be widely distributed but no such mechanism has yet been able to be devised to utilize the 100,000 to 300,000 ova present in the ovaries of genetically superior young female animals. If ova transplantation or inovulation could be developed into a practical procedure then superovulated eggs from genetically superior females, fertilized by spermatozoa from genetically superior males, could be transferred to genetically inferior females who would act as foster "embryo incubators". Puberty could be hastened by one year if fertilized eggs could be obtained from superovulated calves, Hafez. International transfer of animals as early zygotes would be possible as described by Adams et al. who transported sheep embryos in the ligated oviduct of a rabbit from England to South Africa where the embryos were transferred successfully back into sheep.

However at present there are a number of serious drawbacks to inovulation or ova transplantation or transfer in animals. There are no reliable methods for superovulation or production of large numbers of fertilized eggs. F.S.H. administered late in the bovine estrous cycle, about 4 days before expected ovulation, followed by L.H. at the time of estrum will usually, but not always, produce superovulation of up to 50 or more ova. Further attempts at superovulation in the same female are usually much less successful because of a refractoriness that apparently is due to production of antihormones, Willett and others. (See therapy of cystic ovaries)

Fertilization rates of large numbers of superovulated ova are lower than realized with a normal number of ova. Fertilization of ova has not been successfully adapted to ova **in vitro,** so **in vivo** fertilization is necessary. Superovulated fertilized eggs may be collected after slaughter of the donor and removal of the genital tract or by means of a laparotomy. The ova in both techniques are flushed from the oviduct before they enter the uterus with physiological saline containing homologous serum. At present there is no simple nearly aseptic non-surgical method for collecting fertilized ova and for transferring them to foster females. The basic reason for this is that ova do not enter the uterus from the oviduct until 2 to 4 days after ovulation. By this time the uterus is under the influence of progesterone and is highly susceptible to infectious processes that makes invasion of the cervix for the transfer of fertilized ova highly unsuccessful. Aseptic surgical techniques of laparotomy and placing the fertilized ova into the uterine cavity are necessary.

A further requirement for ova transplantation is the synchronization of the estrous cycles of donors and recipients. Fertilized ova cannot be routinely stored like spermatozoa although sheep ova have been stored for 48 hours. Freezing of fertilized ova has not been successfully accomplished. After discarding eggs with structural abnormalities, eggs between the 4 and 32-cell stage of division are selected for best transfer results. When the donor is one day further advanced in the estrous cycle than the recipient a better conception rate is generally obtained. For this reason ova recovered from the oviducts of the donor are usually placed immediately into the oviducts of the recipients. Presently there is no evidence that ova transplantation will develop in the near future into more than an interesting experimental procedure.

References

General References on Artificial Insemination

Cole, H. H. and Cupps, P. T. (1959) Reproduction in Domestic Animals, 2nd Edit., Academic Press, N.Y.C.

Emmens, C. W. and Blackshaw, A. W. (1956) Artificial Insemination, Physiol. Reviews **36,** 2, 277.

Foote, R. H. (1969) Physiological Aspects of Artificial Insemination, in **Reproduction in Domestic Animals,** Edit. by H. H. Cole and P.T. Cupps, Academic Press, N.Y.C., 2nd Edit.

Frank, A. H. (1950) Artificial Insemination in Livestock Breeding, U.S. Dept. of Agric. Circ. No. 567, Washington, D. C.

Hafez, E. S. E. (1968) Reproduction in Farm Animals, 2nd Ed., Lea and Febiger, Philadelphia.

Maule, J. P. (1962) The Semen of Animals and Artificial Insemination, Tech. Communic. No. 15, Commonwealth Agricultural Bureau, Farnham Royal, Bucks, England.

Nishikawa, Y. (1962) Fifty Years of Artificial Insemination of Farm Animals in Japan, Dept. of An. Sci., Faculty of Agric., Kyoto Univ., Japan.

Perry, E. J. (1968) The Artificial Insemination of Farm Animals, 4th Ed. Rutgers Univ. Press, New Brunswick, N.J.

Schaetz, F. (1963) Die Kunstliche Besamung bei den Haustieren, G. Fischer, Verlog, Jena, W. Germany.

History and Advantages and Disadvantages of AI.

Herman, H. A. (1965) Artificial Insemination is Used Worldwide, Hoard's Dairyman, Jan. 10th Issue, 32.

Herman, H. A. (1967) Artificial Insemination Services Increased in 1966, Hoard's Dairyman, Sept. 25th Issue, 1115.

Magee, W. T. (1965) How Commercial Herds Change Genetically, Quarterly Bull., Mich. State Univ. Agr. Exp. Stat., **48** 1, 4.

Perry, E. J. (1968) The Artificial Insemination of Farm Animals, 4th Ed., Rutgers Univ. Press, New Brunswick, N.J.

U.S. Dept. of Agr. Reports (1967) Artificial Insemination Rises, An. Health News **1,** 2, 22.

VanVleck, L. D. (1967) Finding the Best of the Best Selected Young Sires by Sampling in Artificial Insemination, Dairy Herd Management. November Issue.

VanVleck, L. D. (1962) The Artificial Insemination Advantage, Farm Research, Cornell Agric. Exp. Station, June issue.

Artificial Insemination in Cattle

Adler, H. C. and Rasbech, N. O. (1956) Skim Milk and Cream as Semen Diluents, Nord. Vet. Med. **8,** 497.

Almquist, J. O. (1951) A Comparison of Penicillin, Streptomycin and Sulphanilamide for Improving the Fertility of Semen from Bulls of Low Fertility, J. Dairy Sci. **34,** 819.

Almquist, J. O. (1954) Diluters for Bovine Semen V, A Comparison of Heated Milk and Egg Yolk-Citrate as Diluters for Semen from Bulls of High and Low Fertility, J. Dairy Sci. **37,** 1308.

Almquist, J. O. (1962) Diluents for Bovine Semen XI Effect of Glycerol on Fertility and Motility of Spermatozoa in Homogenized Milk and Skim Milk, Jour. of Dairy Sci. **45,** 7, 911.

Almquist, J. O. (1964) The Effect of Certain Coal-Tar Dyes Used for Semen Identification on the Livability and Fertility of Bull Spermatozoa, J. Dairy Sci. **29,** 554.

Almquist, J. O. and Wickersham, E. W. (1962) Diluents for Bovine Semen XII, Fertility and Motility of Spermatozoa in Skim Milk with Various Levels of Glycerol and Methods of Glycerolization, J. Dairy Sci. **45,** 6, 782.

Austin, J. W., Hupp, E. W. and Murphree, R. L. (1961) Comparison of Quality of Bull Semen Collected in the Artificial Vagina and by Electroejaculation, J. Dairy Sci. **44,** 12, 2292.

Foote, R. H. (1967) Influence of Light and Agitation on Bovine Spermatozoa Stored with Protective Agents, J. Dairy Sci. **50,** 9, 1468.

Foote, R. H. (1962) Higher Extension Rates of Semen as a Means of Increasing the Usefulness of Sires, J. Dairy Sci. **45,** 5, 689.

Foote, R. H. (1968) Personal Communication.

Foote, R. H. and Dunn, H. O. (1962) Motility and Fertility of Bull Semen Extended at High Rates in Yolk Extender Containing Catalase, J. Dairy Sci. **45,** 10, 1237.

Foote, R. H., Young, D. C. and Dunn, H. O. (1958) Fertility of Bull Semen Stored One and Two days at 5° C. in 20 Percent Yolk Citrate-Glycine-Glucose Extenders, J. Dairy Sci. **41,** 732.

Hurst, V. (1953) Dilution of Bull Semen with Frozen Egg Yolk-Sodium Citrate, J. of Dairy Sci. **36,** 2, 181.

McEntee, K., Hughes, D. E. and Gilman, H. L. (1954) Prevention of Vibriosis in Inseminated Heifers by Treating the Semen from **Vibrio**-infected Bulls with Penicillin, Streptomycin and Sulphanilimide, Cor. Vet. **44,** 3, 395.

Melrose, D. R. (1956) Skim Milk Powder as a Semen Diluent, Proc. 3rd Internat. Congr. on Reprod., Cambridge, Sect. 3, 68.

Murray, G. R. (1970) Personal Communication.

Olds, D. and Seath, D. M. (1954) Factors Affecting Reproductive Efficiency in Dairy Cattle, Ken. Agr. Exp. Stat. Bull 605.

Orthey, A. E. and Gilman, H. L. (1954) The Antibacterial Action of Penicillin and Streptomycin Against **Vibrio fetus** Including Concentrations Found in Naturally Infected Semen, J. Dairy Sci. **37,** 4, 416.

Phillips, P. H. and Lardy, H. O. (1940) A Yolk-Buffer Pabulum for the Preservation of Bull Semen, J. of Dairy Sci. **23,** 399.

Rajamannan, A. H. J. (1966) Vapor Freezing of Bull Semen. A. I. Digest, **14,** 2.

Rajamannan, A. H J. (1966) A New Semen Freezing Technique. A.I. Digest **14,** 8.

Rajamannan, A. H. J. (1968) Personal Communication.

Rasbech, N. O. (1953) Influence of Antibiotics on Fructolysis in Varied Dilutions of Semen, Nord. Vet. Med. **5,** 193.

Salisbury, G. W., Fuller, H. K. and Willett, E. L. (1941) Preservation of Bovine Spermatozoa in Yolk Citrate Diluent and Field Results from its Use, J. Dairy Sci. **24,** 905.

Salisbury, G. W. and Knodt, C. B. (1947) The Effect of Sulphanilamide in the Diluent Upon Fertility of Bull Semen, J. of Dairy Sci. **30,** 6, 361.

Thacker, D. L. and Almquist, J. O. (1953) Diluters for Bovine Semen. Fertility and Motility of Bovine Spermatozoa in Boiled Milk, J. Dairy Sci. **36,** 2, 173.

Van Demark, N. L. and Bartlett, F. D. Jr. (1958) Prolonged Survival of Bull Sperm in the Illini Variable Temperature Diluent, J. Dairy Sci. **41,** 732.

Van Demark, N. L. and Sharma, U. O. (1957) Preliminary Fertility Results from the Preservation of Bovine Semen at Room Temperatures, J. Dairy Sci. **40,** 438.

Willett, E. L. (1950) Fertility and Livability of Bull Semen Diluted at Various Levels to 1:300, J. of Dairy Sci. **33,** 43.

Frozen Semen Processing and Insemination in Cattle

Adler, H C. (1961) Freezing of Bovine Semen with a Cold Gas Generator and Storage in Liquid Air, 4th Internat. Congr. for Am. Reprod. The Hague.

Adler, H. C. and **Lindegaarde, L. E.** (1965) **Bovine Genital Vibriosis, Eradication from Danish A.I. Centers**, Nord. Vet. Med. **17,** 237.

Autrup, E. and **Rasbech, N. O.** (1951) **Conception Results after Artificial Insemination with Bull Semen in the Post-oestrous Hemorrhagic Period**, Nord. Vet. Med. **3,** 40.

Bartlett, D. (1967) Management of Beef Estrus Synchronization, Ann. Meeting Amer. Vet. Sor. for the Study of Breeding Soundness, Univ. of Missouri, Columbia, Mo.

Bartlett, D. (1968) The A.V.M.A./N.A.A.B. Code and the U.S.L.S.A. Recommended Regulations, Proc. 2nd Tech. Conf. on Art. Insem. and Reproduct., Chicago, 37.

Bartlett, D. and Larsen, L. L. (1960) Veterinary Problems in Artificial Insemination, J.A.V.M.A. **137,** 8, 453.

Bartlett, D. and Larson, L. L. (1968) Disease and Artificial Insemination, in **The Artificial Insemination of Farm Animals,** ed. by E.J. Perry, 4th Ed., Rutgers Univ. Press, New Brunswick, New Jersey.

Barrett, G. R., Casida, L. E. and Lloyd, C. A. (1948) Measuring Breeding Efficiency by Pregnancy Examinations and by Non-returns, J. Dairy Sci. **31,** 682.

Bean, B. H , Pickett, R. W. and Martig, R. C. (1962) Some Factors Affecting the Motility and pH of Frozen Bovine Semen, J. Dairy Sci. **45,** 15, 78.

Bearden, J. and Hansel, W. (1955) Personal Communication.

Belling, T. H. Jr. (1961) Preparation of a "Teaser" Bull for Use in a Beef Cattle Artificial Insemination Program, J.A.V.M.A. **138,** 12, 670.

Berndtson, W. E. and Foote, R. H. (1969) The Survival of Frozen Bovine Spermatozoa Following Minimum Exposure to Glycerol, Cryobiology, **5,** 6, 398.

Boyd, L. J. and Hafs, H. D. (1970) Fertility of Frozen Semen Containing, 12, 24 or 35 Million Sperm Extended to 0.5 or 0.9 ml Volume in Yolk Citrate, J. Dairy Sci. **53,** 5, 660.

Brands, A. F. A., Banerjee-Schotsman, J., Van Dieten, S. W. J. and Van Loen, A. (1964) Not Inseminating on Sunday and the Conception Rate, 5th Internat. Congr. on Anim. Reprod. and Artificial Insem., Trento Vol. V, 436.

Bratton, R. W., Foote, R. H. and Cruthers, J. C. (1955) Preliminary Fertility Results with Frozen Bovine Spermatozoa, J. Dairy Sci. **38,** 1, 40.

Dreher, W. H. (1962) The Regulations for Bull Stud Health and Interstate Shipment of Semen, Dept. of Subcommittee on Art. Insem., Proc. 66th Ann. Meeting U.S.L.S.A., 168.

Elliott, F. I., Murphy, D. M., Bartlett, D. E. and Kubista, R. A. (1961) The Use of Polymyxin B. Sulfate with Dihydrostreptomycin and Penicillin for the Control of **Vibrio fetus** in a Frozen Semen Process, Proc. 4th Internat. Congr. on An. Reprod., the Hague.

Forgason, J. L., Berry, W. T. and Goodwin, D. E. (1961) Freezing Bull Semen in Liquid Nitrogen Vapor Without Instrumentation, J. An. Sci. **20,** 4, 970.

Graham, E. F. (1966) Comments on Freezing Spermatozoa, Minn. Agr. Exp. Stat., Sci. Jour. Series Paper No. 5898.

Gilmore, L. O. (1952) Dairy Cattle Breeding, J B. Lippincott Co., N.Y.C.

Hahn, J., Foote, R. H. and Seidel, G. E. Jr. (1969) Quality and Freezability of Semen from Growing or Aged Dairy Bulls, J. Dairy Sci. **52,** 11, 1843.

Health Code of Minimum Standards for Bulls Producing Semen for Artificial Insemination (1962) A.I. Digest Dec., 17.

Herman, H. A. (1960) Frozen Semen, in **Artificial Insemination of Farm Animals** edited by Perry, E. J., 3rd Ed., Rutgers Univ. Press, New Brunswick, N.J., 364.

Herman, H. A. (1965) Frozen Semen, Hoard's Dairyman, July 10 Issue.

Herman, H. A. (1969) How Long Will Frozen Semen Last, Hoard's Dairyman, Dec 10th issue, 1368.

Knoop, C. E. (1966) Production Controls in A.I. Laboratories, Proc. 1st Techn. Conf. on Art. Insem. and An. Reprod., Nat. Assoc. an Breeders. 28.

L'Aigle Artificial Insemination Center (1969), Straw Method of Freezing, L'Aigle France.

Larson, G. L. and Bayley, N. D. (1955) The Fertility of Inseminations Made in Cows Showing Postestrous Hemorrhage, J. Dairy Sci. **38,** 549.

Lein, D., Erickson, I., Winter, A. J. and McEntee, K. (1968) **Diagnosis,** Treatment and Control of Vibriosis in An Artificial Insemination Center, J.A.V.M.A. **153,** 12, 1574.

MacPherson, J. W. and Fish, N. A. (1954) The Survival of Pathogenic Bacteria in Bovine Semen Preserved by Freezing, Am. J. Vet. Res **15,** 548.

MacPherson, J. W. (1966) Extenders and Sperm Metabolism, Proc. 1st Techn. Conf. on Art. Insem. and Bovine Reprod., Nat. Assoc. An. Breeders.

MacPherson, J. W. (1968) Semen Placement Effects on Fertility in Bovines, J. Dairy Sci. **51,** 5, 807.

Manthei, C. A., DeTray, D. E. and Goode, E. R. (1950) **Brucella** Infection in Bulls and the Spread of Brucellosis in Cattle by Artificial Insemination I Intrauterine Injection, J.A.V.M.A. **117,** 106.

McEntee, K., Gilman, H. L., Hughes, D. E., Wagner, W. C. and Dunn. H. O. (1959) Insemination of Heifers with Penicillin and Dihydrostreptomycin-Treated Frozen Semen from **Vibrio Fetus** Carrier Bulls, Cor. Vet. **49,** 2, 175.

McSparrin, B. H. and Patrick, T. E. (1967) Relationships Among 60 to 90 Day Non-returns, Diagnosed Pregnancies and Actual Calvings of Cows Bred Artificially, J. Dairy Sci. **50,** 4, 612.

Meryman, H. T. and Kafig, E. (1959) Survival of Spermatozoa Following Drying, Nature **184,** 470.

Meryman, H. T. and Kafig, E. (1963) Freeze-Drying of Spermatozoa, J. Reprod. and Fertil. **5,** 87.

Milk Marketing Board, (1964–1968) Repts. of Breeding and Production Organ. Thames Ditton, Surrey, England, **15, 16, 17, 18,** 102, 117, 109, 114–134 and 140.

Morrow, D. A. (1970) Bovine Diseases and the AI Industry, Proc. 3rd Tech. Conf. on Artif. Insem. and Reprod., N.A.A.B., February, Columbia, Mo., 79.

Munro, I. B. (1956) Constriction of the Cervix at Oestrus in Cattle and Its Response to Dienestrol, Vet. Rec. **68,** 131.

Nagase, H. and Niwa, T. (1964) Deep Freezing Bull Semen in Concentrated Pellet Form, I, II, III, Proc. 5th Internat. Congr. on An. Reprod. Vol. IV, 410, 498, 503.

Nagase, H. and Graham, E. F. (1964) Pelleted Semen: Comparison of Different Extenders and Processes on Fertility of Bovine Spermatozia, Proc. 5th Intern. Congr. on An. Reprod., Trento, Italy, Vol. IV, 387.

Olds, D. and Seath, D. M. (1954) Factors Affecting Reproductive Efficiency in Dairy Cattle, Ken. Agr. Exp. Stat. Bull 605.

Pickett, R. W. (1969) A Symposium on Management of Beef Cattle for Reproductive Efficiency, Ft. Collins, Colo.

Pickett, R. W., Hall, R. C. Jr., Lucas, J. J. and Gibson, E. W. (1964) Influence of Sperm Numbers on Fertility of Frozen Bovine Semen, J. Dairy Sci. **47,** 8, 916.

Pickett, R. W., Hall, R. C. Jr., Lucas, J. J. and Gibson, E. W. (1965) Investigations on Thawing Frozen Bovine Spermatozoa, Fert. & Steril. **16,** 5, 642.

Pickett, R. W., Martig, R. C. and Cowan, W. A. (1961) Preservation of Bovine Spermatozoa at −79° and −196° C., J. Dairy Sci. **44,** 11, 2089.

Polge, C. and Rowson, L. E. A. (1952) Long Term Storage of Bull Semen Frozen at Very Low Temperatures (−79° C.) Rept. 2nd Internat. Congr. of Physiol. and Path. of An. Reprod. and of Art. Insem. Vol. III, 90.

Polge, C., Smith, A. U., and Parkes, A. S. (1949) Revival of Spermatozoa after Vitrification and Dehydration at Low Temperatures, Nature **164,** 666.

Ramge, J. C. (1963) Artificial Insemination of Beef Cattle, Proc. of A.V.M.A., N.Y.C. 34.

Rapatz, G. L. (1966) What Happens When Semen is Frozen, Proc. 1st Techn. Confer. on Art. Insem. and Bovine Reprod., Nat. Assoc. of Animal Breeders, 45.

Rasbeck, N. O. and Terpstra, J. I. (1962) Artificial Insemination and Deep Frozen Semen; Danger of Dissemination of Infections; Sanitary Measures; Livestock Infertility, Animal Health Monograph #5 F.A.O. 83.

Rendel, J., Bouw, J. and Schmid, D. O. (1962) Frequency of Cows Served Twice Which Remain Pregnant to First Service, An. Prod. **4,** 359.

Salisbury, G. W. (1969) Aging Phenomena in Spermatozoa, I, II, III. Fertility and Prenatal Losses, J. Dairy Sci. **50,** 1675, 1679 and 1683.

Schindler, H., Volcani, R. and Angel, H. (1957) A Note on the Effect of Delayed Insemination on the Conception Rate in Dairy Cows, Ktavim Rec. Agric. Res. Stat. (Rehovot) Engl. Ed.) **5,** 3, 53.

Stewart, D. L. (1951) Storage of Bull Spermatozoa at Low Temperatures, Vet. Rec. **63,** 4, 65.

Stewart, D. L. (1967) Personal Communication.

Swanson, E. W. and Herman, H. A. (1944) A Satisfactory Method of Shipping Dairy Bull Semen Long Distances, J. Dairy Sci. **27,** 2, 143.

Tanabe, T. Y., Heist, C. E. and Almquist, J. O. (1955) Factors Affecting Pregnancy Interrruption in Artificial Insemination in Dairy Cattle, J. Dairy Sci. **38,** 6, 601.

Trimberger, G. W. and Davis, G. K. (1943) The Relationship between Time of Insemination and Breeding Efficiency in Dairy Cattle, Nebr. Agric. Exper. Stat. Res. Bull No. 129.

Van Demark, N. L. (1952) Time and Site of Insemination in Cattle, Cor. Vet. **42,** 2, 215.

Artificial Insemination In Horses

Amer. Assoc. Equine Practitioners (1968) Rules Relative to Registering Foals Produced Artificially, A.A.E.P. Newsletter, 1, 10.

Bader, H. and Mahler, R. (1968) Tiefgefrier-und Besamgungsversuche mit Hengtsperma unter Andwendung des Pellet verfahrens, Zunchthyg. **3,** 1, 6.

Barker, C. A. V. and Gandier, J. C. C. (1957) Pregnancy in a Mare Resulting from Frozen Epididymal Spermatozoa, Canad. J. Comp. Med. **21,** 1, 47.

Berry, R. O. and Gazder, P. J. (1960) The Viability of Stallion Spermatozoa as Influenced by Storage Media and by Antibiotics, Southwest. Vet. **13,** 217.

Bielanski, W. (1963) Die Kunstliche Besamung bei den Haustieren, Ed. by Schaetz, F. G. Fischer, Verlag, Jena, W. Germany.

Buell, R. (1963) A Method of Freezing Stallion Semen and Tests of Its Fertility, Vet. Rec. **75,** 36, 900.

Burkhardt, J. J. (1949) Sperm Survival in the Genital Tract of the Mare, J. of Agric. Sci. **39,** 201.

Chacalof, P. (1961) Personal Communication, Thessaloniki, Greece.

Cranwell, J. E., Roberts, A. D. and Pickett, B. W. (1969) Factors Affecting Survival of Equine Spermatozoa, J. An. Sci. **29,** 1, 186.

Hughes, J. P. and Loy, R. G. (1970) Artificial Insemination in the Equine, A Comparison of National Breeding and Artificial Insemination of Mares Using Semen from Six Stallions, Cor. Vet. **60,** 3, 463.

MacLeod, J. (1951) Fertility in Thoroughbred Stallions, Lectures, 1st Annual Stud Managers' Course, Univ. of Kentucky, Lexington, Ky.

MacLeod, J. and McGee, W. R. (1950) The Semen of the Thoroughbred, Cor. Vet. **40,** 3, 233.

McGee, W. R. (1951) The Mechanics of Breeding, Blood Horse **61,** 17, 808.

Patterson, A. W. (1962) Personal Communication.

Pickett, B. W. (1969) Personal Communication.

Polge, C. and Minotakis, C. (1964) Deep Freezing of Jackass and Stallion Semen, 5th Intern. Congr. on Anim. Reprod. and Art. Insem., Trento, Italy, VII, 545.

Rajamannan, A. H. J. (1966) A New Semen Freezing Technique, A. I. Digest, **14,** 8.

Rajamannan, A. H. J. (1968) Freezing and Fertility Studies with Stallion Semen, Proc. of VIth Internat. Congr. of Animal Reproduction and A.I., Paris, France.

Rajamannan, A. H. J. (1968) Personal Communication.

Rasbech, N. O. (1959) Artificial Insemination in Horse Breeding, Medlemsbl. danske Dyrlaegeforen **4,** 1.

Sullivan, J. J. and Larson, L. L. (1970) Personal Communication from American Breeders Service Inc.

Vlachos, K. (1960) Die Kunstliche Besamung der Stuten in Griechenland durch Versand von Konserviertem and Gekultem Sperma, Berl. Munch. Tierarztl. Wschr. **73,** 424.

Artificial Insemination in Swine

Aamdal, J. and Hogset, I. (1957) Artificial Insemination in Swine, J.A.V.M.A. **131,** 1, 59.

Aamdal, J. Hogset, I., Filseth, O. (1958) Extirpation of the Preputial Diverticulum of Boars Used for Artificial Insemination, J.A.V.M.A. **132,** 522.

Bennett, G. H. and O'Hagan, C. (1964) Factors Influencing the Success of Artificial Insemination of Pigs, Proc. V Internat. Congr. on An. Reprod., Trento, Italy. Vol. IV, 481.

Boender, J. (1966) The Development of A.I. in Pigs in the Netherlands and the Storage of Boar Semen, World Rev. of An. Prod. II Spec. Issue, 29.

Day, B. N. (1967) Artificial Insemination of Swine and Estrus Synchronization. Ann. Meeting Amer. Soc. for Study of Breeding Soundness, Univ. of Mo., Columbia, Mo.

DuBuisson, F. Du Mesnil, Jondet, R. and Locatelli, A. (1961) Utilization of CO_2 in the Insemination of Swine, Internat. Congr. on An. Reprod., The Hague, Vol. IV, 822.

Dzuik, P. J. (1958) Effect of Artificial Insemination of Gilts with Semen Stored for 1/2 Hour vs 72 Hours, J. An. Sci. **17,** 4, 1214.

Einarsson, S. (1968) Factors Affecting Fertility in Artificial Insemination of Swine, Nord. Vet. Med. **20,** 622.

First, N. L. (1970) Factors Effecting Sperm Survival and Fertility, in Colloquium on Effect of Diseases and Stress on Reproductive Efficiency in Swine, Iowa State Univ., Ames, Iowa.

Hall, R. E. and First, N. L. (1964) Swine Artificial Insemination in Wisconsin, Proc. 68th Ann. Meeting U.S.L.S.A., 276.

King, G. J. and MacPherson, J. W. (1966) Boar Semen Studies: I Laboratory Evaluation of Processing Phases, J. Comp. Med. and Vet. Sci. **30,** 12, 322.

Madden, D. H. L. (1959) Progress in the Artificial Insemination of Swine. Some Factors Influencing Fertility Levels in its Field Application, Vet. Rec. **71,** 12, 227.

Madden, D. H. L. (1961) A Method of Obtaining a High Fertility Level with Artificial Insemination of Farm Pigs, Proc. IV Internat. Congr. on An. Reprod., The Hague, Vol. IV, 85.

Melrose, D. R. (1963) Artificial Insemination in the Pig—A Review of its Development, Brit. Vet. Jour. **119,** 532.

Melrose, D. R. (1966) Artificial Insemination of Pigs—A Review of Progress and Possible Development, World Rev. of An. Prod. II, Spec. Issue, 15.

Melrose, D. R. and O'Hagan, C. (1969) Investigations into the Techniques of Insemination in the Pig, Proc. IV Internat. Congr. on An. Reprod., The Hague, Vol. IV, 855.

Neville, W. J., MacPherson, J. W. and King, G. K. (1970) The Contraceptive Action of Glycerol in Gilts, J. An. Sci. **31,** 1, 227.

Niwa, T. (1961) Researches and Practices in the Artificial Insemination of Pigs, Proc. IV Internat. Congr. on An. Reprod. The Hague, Vol. I, 83.

Paredis, F. (1962) Fertility and Artificial Insemination in Pigs, Internat. J. of Fert. **7,** 3, 233.

Paredis, F. and Vandeplassche, M. (1961) Effect of Initial Motility Number and Age of Spermatozoa on Farrowing Rate and Litter Size., Proc. IV Internat. Congr. on An. Reprod., The Hague, Vol. IV, 828.

Park, R. W. A., Melrose, D. R., Stewart D. L. and O'Hagan, C. (1964) The Effect of Various Handling Methods and Antibiotic Additions on the Numbers of Bacteria Present in Diluted Bull and Boar Semen after Storage, Brit. Vet. Jour. **120,** 457.

Polge, C. and Rowson, L. E. A. (1956) The Practical Application of Artificial Insemination in Pig Breeding, Vet. Rec. **68,** 952.

Rolfe, K. (1963) Die Kunstliche Besamung biem Schwein, Archiv for Exper. Veterinarmed. Bd. **16,** 957.

Self, H. L. (1962) A.I. In Swine—Where are We?, Proc. 15th Ann. Conv. of the Nat. Assoc. of An. Breeders; Cedar Rapids, Iowa, 105.

Stratman, F. W. and Self, H. L. (1960) Effect of Semen Volume and Number of Sperm on Fertility and Embryo Survival in Artificially Insemination Gilts, J. An. Sci. 19, 4, 1081.

Stratman, F. W. and Self, H. L. (1961) Comparison of Natural Mating with Artificial Insemination and Influence of Semen Volume and Sperm Numbers on Conception, Embryo Survival and Litter Size in Sows, J. An. Sci. **20,** 4, 708.

Waltz, F. A., Foley, C. W., Herschler, R. C., Tiffany, L. W. and Liska, B. J. (1968) Bacteriological Studies of Boar Semen, J. An. Sci. **27,** 5, 1357.

Artificial Insemination in Sheep and Goats

First, N. L., Sevinge, A. and Henneman, H. A. (1961) Fertility of Frozen and Unfrozen Ram Semen, J. An. Sci. **20,** 1, 79.

Fraser, A. F. (1962) A Technique for Freezing Goat Semen and Results of a Small Breeding Trial, Canad. Vet. Jour. **3,** 5, 133.

Herman, H. A. (1963) Frozen Semen Used for A.I. in Milk Goats, A.I. Digest **9,** 1, 22.

Hogue, D. E., Hansel, W., Bratton, R. W. (1962) Fertility in Ewes Bred Naturally and Artificially after Estrous Cycle Synchronization with an Oral Progestational Agent, J. An. Sci. **21,** 3, 625

Lunca, N., Otel, V., Paraschivescu, M., and Seserman, O. (1961) Progresses Realized by Artificial Insemination in Sheep with Diluted Semen, Proc. 4th Internat. Congr. on An. Reprod., the Hague.

Lyngset, O., Aamdal, J., and Velle, W. (1965) Artificial Insemination in the Goat with Deep Frozen and Liquid Semen After Hormonal Synchronization of Oestrus, Nord. Vet. Med. **17,** 178.

Salamon, S. and Robinson, T. J. (1962) Studies on the Artificial Insemination of Merino Sheep, Austral. J. of Agric. Res. **13,** 1, 52.

Artificial Insemination in Dogs and Cats.

Almquist, J. O. (1959) Reproduction in Domestic Animals, Edit by Cole, H. H. and Cups, P. T. Vol. II, Academic Press, N.Y. and London.

Boucher, J. H., Foote, R. H., and Kirk, R. W. (1958) The Evaluation of Semen Quality in the Dog and the Effects of Frequency of Ejaculation Upon Semen Quality, Libido and Depletion of Sperm Reserves, Cor. Vet. **48,** 67.

Doak, R. L., Hall, A. and Dale, H. E. (1967) Longevity of Spermatozoa in the Reproductive Tract of the Bitch, J. Reprod. and Fertil., **13,** 51.

Foote, R. H. (1964) The Effects of Electrolytes, Sugars, Glycerol and Catalase on Survival of Dog Sperm Stored in Buffered-Yolk Mediums, Amer. J. Vet. Res. **25,** 104, 32.

Foote, R. H. (1964) The Influence of Frequency of Semen Collection, Fractionation of the Ejaculate and Dilution Rate on the Survival of Stored Dog Sperm, Cor. Vet. **54,** 1, 89.

Foote, R. H. (1964) Extenders for Freezing Dog Semen., Amer. J. Vet. Res. **25,** 104, 37.

Foote, R. H. (1968) Current Veterinary Therapy, Edit. by Kirk, R. W., 3rd Ed. W. B. Saunders Co., Philadelphia, London and Toronto.

Foote, R. H. and Leonard, E. P. (1964) The Influence of pH, Osmotic Pressure, Glycine, and Glycerol on the Survival of Dog Sperm in Buffered-Yolk Extenders, Cor. Vet. **54,** 1, 78.

Greulich, W. W. (1934) Artificially Induced Ovulation in the Cat **(Felis domestica),** Anat. Rec. **58,** 217.

Hamner, C. E., Jennings, L. L. and Sojka, N. J. (1970) Cat **(Felis catus L.)** Spermatozoa Require Capacitation, J. Reprod. and Fert., In press.

Harrop, A. E. (1960) Reproduction in the Dog, Williams and Wilkins Co., Baltimore.

Harrop, A. E. (1962) The Semen of Animals and Artificial Insemination, Edit. by Maule, J. P., Commonwealth Agric. Bureaux Farnham Royal, Bucks, England.

Kirk, R. W. (1959) Artificial Insemination in the Dog, Allied Vet. **30,** 2, 38.

Kirk, R. W. (1968) Canine Medicine, Edit. by E. J. Catcott, Amer. Vet. Public, Inc. Wheaton, Ill.

Leonard, E. P. (1968) The Artificial Insemination of Farm Animals, Edit. by Perry, E. J. 4th Ed., Rutgers Univ. Press, New Brunswick, N.J.

Sojka, N. J., Jennings, L. L. and Hammer, C. E. (1970) Artificial Insemination in the Cat **(Felis catus L.),** Lab. Animal Care, 20, 2, 198.

Transplantation of Fertilized Ova

Adams, C. E., Rowson, L. E. A., Hunter, G. L. and Bishop, G. P. (1961) Long Distance Transport of Sheep Ova, Proc. 4th Internat. Congr. on An. Reprod. The Hague. Vol. II, 381.

Hafez, E. S. E. (1961) Procedures and Problems of Manipulation, Selection, Storage and Transfer of Mammalian Ova, Cor. Vet. **51,** 3, 299.

Hafez, E. S. E. (1968) Reproduction in Farm Animals, 2nd Ed. Lea and Febiger, Philadelphia.

Hafez, E. S. E. and Blandau, R. J. (1969) The Mammalian Oviduct, Univ. of Chicago Press, Chicago, Ill.

Hunter, G. L., Bishop, G. P., Adams, C. E. and Rowson, L. E. A. (1962) Successful Long Distance Aerial Transport of Fertilized Sheep Ova, J. Reprod. Fertil. **3,** 33.

Rice, V. A. and Andrews, F. N. (1951) Breeding and Improvement of Farm Animals, 4th Ed. McGraw Hill Book Co., Inc., N.Y.C.

Willett, E. L. (1953) Egg Transfer and Superovulation in Farm Animals, Iowa State College, Jour. of Sci. **28,** 1, 83.

INDEX